The Bill James Handbook 2022

Sports Info Solutions

www.sportsinfosolutions.com

Published by ACTA Sports

A Division of ACTA Publications

ACTA SPORTS

Front Cover Photos by Brian Rothmuller and John Cordes, Icon Sportswire
Back Cover Photo by David J. Griffin, Icon Sportswire

First Edition: November 2021

Published by:
ACTA Sports, a division of ACTA Publications
4848 North Clark Street
Chicago, IL 60640
(800) 397-2282
www.actasports.com www.actapublications.com

ISBN: 978-0-87946-700-5
ISSN: 1940-8668

Printed in the United States of America by McNaughton & Gunn

Dedication

This book is dedicated to my wife April for her support and for putting up with a guy who loves baseball as much as I do. You gave me the greatest gift possible with our son Reid in 2020. I hope he is as selfless, strong, and kind as you are when he grows up.

I also need to dedicate this book to my family in Missouri and my family in Pennsylvania. Your love means everything to me and gives me the conviction to pursue my passion for sports. You have all molded me into the person I am today and I am forever grateful.

Last, thank you to all of the SISers during this past year. It was not an easy year by any means but we've come out of it stronger than ever. I am excited for what the future holds for our company in the coming years.

"People ask me what I do in winter when there's no baseball. I'll tell you what I do. I stare out the window and wait for spring." --Rogers Hornsby

Nathan Phares

Table of Contents

Introduction.. 1
The World's Best Hitter (by Bill James) 3
Shohei Ohtani 11
The Baseball Revolution (by Joe Sheehan)... 17
Projecting Injury Risk.. 21
Hall of Fame Monitor 25
Hall of Fame Value.. 29
In Memoriam 37
Rookie Roundup 43
The World's #1 Starting Pitcher Rankings (by Bill James) 47
Going Broader and Deeper into Baseball in Asia.. 65
Minor League Prospects 67
Team Statistics... 69
Team Efficiency Summary 77
The Fielding Bible Awards.. 79
On Finding the Value of the Monkey Wrench Guy (by Bill James).............. 93
Defensive Runs Saved Leaders 103
Strike Zone Runs Saved (by Bill James)... 107
The Shift Update.. 111
Hits Lost and Gained to the Shift (by Bill James and the SIS R&D Team)..... 115
Four-Outfielder Alignments 123
Home Run Robberies.. 125
Career Register 127
Baserunning (by Bill James).. 395
Stolen Base Attempt Times 409
Pitchers' Repertoires (by Bill James).. 411
Relief Pitching 425
Openers 439
Pitchers Fielding & Holding Runners, and Hitters Pitching......................... 441
Pitchers Hitting 451
Lords of the Flies 455
Hard Hit Balls 459
RBI Percentages... 465
Pinch Hitting.. 469
Manufactured Runs, Productive Outs, & Unproductive Outs (by Bill James). 475
Managers Record.. 483
Ballparks and Park Indices 497
Lefty/Righty Statistics 513
Leaderboards.. 529
Fielding Statistics.. 563
Runs Saved Multi-Year Summary 575
Win Shares... 579
Instant Replay 585
2022 MLB Projections... 587
Career Targets.. 605
The 300-Win Candidates 607
Minor League Abbreviation Key... 609
Baseball Glossary 613
Sports Info Solutions 629
Acknowledgments 631

Introduction

When I was eight years old, I was an avid reader, so avid that my parents thought I was ready for some heavy stuff.

Soon I was talking about what I read in *The 1983 Bill James Baseball Abscart*... except it wasn't an "Abscart." It was an "Abstract."

Cut me some slack! I was only eight and my pronunciations were all over the place.

That was nearly 40 years ago and now I'm here to tell you about this year's edition of *The Bill James Handbook*.

And let me say that this book is more *Baseball Concrete* than *Baseball Abstract*.

Reading this book is to experience informational overload. The numbers come at you in waves.

But take a deep breath. There's goodness everywhere. It can be your own winter version of a Field of Dreams game (minus the corn stalks and the Tim Anderson walk-off home run).

Leaderboards. Projections. Player yearly and career totals. It's all there.

We've got this season covered from run differential to fun differential, both nationally and globally. Shohei Ohtani was his own version of all of that as the 21st century incarnation of Babe Ruth. We felt that he was so important to the season and so important to the future of the sport that we didn't just put him on the cover—we did an entire essay about him, his season, and the sound the ball made off his bat when he hit one of his first home runs.

The book also has a series of short, sometimes witty takes from myself and my colleagues (witty is in the eye of the beholder, but I think you'll enjoy).

We found a player who should be Four-Man Outfield defensed but wasn't, invoked a man who scaled Mount Everest while analyzing if we've reached "Peak Shift," and compared an MLB manager to a oft-victorious game show contestant.

Having baseball around puts us in a good mood, aligned with the 45 million fans able to attend MLB games in the first iteration of a post-pandemic world. And we wanted to put both the present and the future in proper perspective. Joe Sheehan, a writer of similar sensibilities to both Bill and myself, did that for us. The Baseball Revolution is upon us, Joe says. But in the end, no matter what is done to it, the game always prevails.

Given that his name's on the cover, I can assure you that there's plenty of Bill James in here. I saved that for last.

One of my colleagues asked: If we can track The World's No. 1 Starting Pitcher, then why can't we track The World's No. 1 Hitter?

So we asked Bill to show us the way and he devised a system to do just that.

Bill also provided fresh perspective in a couple of other areas. He wrote an essay about positional versatility that changed the way we approached our annual Fielding Bible Awards. He also devised a stat to measure a pitcher's mix of pitches in his repertoire.

And then Bill being Bill, he raised the bar for himself and expanded upon past work, as he's known to do.

As such, there's an essay documenting the history of The World's No. 1 Starting Pitcher back to 1939 (we lament Herb Score and what might have been).

My boss thinks that Bill James book loyalists will like that one. Speaking from nearly 40 years of reading Bill's historical and statistical takes, I agree. And I think new readers will too.

Hope you like the book!

Mark Simon
October 14, 2021
Bethlehem, PA

The World's Best Hitter

Bill James

Q. Who is the best hitter in baseball?

A. It's still Mike Trout.

That was easy. Are we done here?

We here at Sports Info Solutions have maintained a "World's #1 pitcher" list for 10 or 15 years, which is based on Game Scores. The ranking scores are adjusted every day. If a pitcher pitches a good game, he moves up; if he has a poor game, he moves down.

A year ago and some, I developed a system of Game Scores for Batters. Well then, somebody asked, why don't we do a World's Number One Batter system?

I agreed to try it, and here is the first publication of that effort. I modified the system as necessary to make it work for hitters, and I will probably need to tweak it some more in the future. A batter's score is adjusted more cautiously than a pitcher's, since batters play every day rather than every fifth day. A pitcher's score drops after a few days of inactivity, whereas a batter's score does not, since batting ability is much more stable than pitching ability. A batter's score drops between seasons so that the batter has to re-establish his level of ability every season, but it doesn't drop by nearly as much as a pitcher's score drops. The systems are the same, but different.

To be honest, 2021 wasn't a great year to push the Go button on the new system. Mike Trout started the season with a big lead, followed by Mookie Betts and Freddie Freeman:

START OF SEASON

Rank	Player	Score
1	Mike Trout	591
2	Mookie Betts	552
3	Freddie Freeman	551
4	George Springer	550
5	Anthony Rendon	550
6	Juan Soto	547
7	Alex Bregman	547
8	Ronald Acuña Jr.	537
9	Christian Yelich	536
10	Corey Seager	535

Trout came out red hot, even for Mike Trout. Through May 1 he was hitting .429 with an .805 slugging percentage and a 1.332 OPS. He had widened his lead to 47 points, while the list behind him had already churned to a significant extent.

May 1, 2021

Rank	Player	Score
1	Mike Trout	605
2	Ronald Acuña Jr.	558
3	George Springer	553
4	Mookie Betts	553
5	Anthony Rendon	551
6	Freddie Freeman	550
7	Juan Soto	550
8	Alex Bregman	546
9	Nelson Cruz	545
10	Corey Seager	536

Then, however, Trout went into a 6-for-40 slump. By May 18 his score had dropped 16 points:

May 18, 2021

Rank	Player	Score
1	Mike Trout	589
2	Mookie Betts	555
3	Freddie Freeman	552
4	George Springer	551
5	Alex Bregman	549
6	Ronald Acuña Jr.	549
7	Anthony Rendon	548
8	Juan Soto	542
9	Jose Abreu	537
10	Jose Ramirez	535

And then, of course, Trout's season ended. This locked his score in place, but it allowed plenty of time for other hitters to make a run at him. Mookie Betts appeared at that time to be best positioned to make that run, and then Ronald Acuña did.

On May 7 Fernando Tatis was hitting just .218, and had a ranking score of 524, which put him in 20th place. He started blasting homers and having 4-hit games, however, and a 2-homer, 6-RBI game on May 23 lifted him into the top 10. By June 23 Tatis was in third place. On June 25 he hit three home runs. This pushed him ahead of Acuña, making him the #2 man, Trout's top competitor:

June 25, 2021

Rank	Player	Score
1	Mike Trout	589
2	Fernando Tatis Jr.	570
3	Ronald Acuña Jr.	560
4	Jose Altuve	559
5	Mookie Betts	555
6	George Springer	550
7	Freddie Freeman	550
8	Vladimir Guerrero Jr.	546
9	Matt Olson	545
10	Alex Bregman	542

Tatis had gained 46 points in five weeks. He needed only 19 more to claim the position as baseball's best hitter. He homered on June 30, pushing him to 572. He stayed in that range, moved up slowly. By August 15 he was at 579:

August 15, 2021

Rank	Player	Score
1	Mike Trout	589
2	Fernando Tatis Jr.	579
3	Mookie Betts	574
4	George Springer	567
5	Ronald Acuña Jr.	565
6	Freddie Freeman	561
7	Juan Soto	561
8	Max Muncy	558
9	Matt Olson	556
10	Jose Altuve	552

And where, you might ask, is the pitcher dude, Ohtani? Why isn't he on this list? Why isn't he #1 on the list?

Shohei Ohtani ranked #85 on April 12 and dropped to #92 on Apr 20 before he started to rip. He climbed into the top 80 on April 25, and into the top 70 the following day. He was in the top 60 by May 7. He reached the top 50 on May 18, the same day that Trout went out for the year. On June 18 he was in the top 40; on June 20, in the top 30. By June 29 he was in the top 20. By July 18 we had him ranked as the #13 hitter in baseball.

And then he stopped hitting. He didn't COMPLETELY stop hitting, of course, but in June and July he hit .295 with 22 homers, 42 RBI. From August 1 to the end of the season he hit .216 with 9 homers and 18 RBI. He started to slide down the list. By the end of the season he had dropped back to 42nd place.

This is just about *hitting*. Being a hitter/pitcher doesn't help you at all; this is just a hitter's ranking. A similar story is Vladimir Guerrero Jr. He started the season ranked 111th, but he started out a-wallopin'. He moved into the top 90 on April 9, into the top 80 on April 10, into the top 70 on April 15, into the top 60 on April 17. A couple of hot weeks, and he has passed half the list of hitters who were around him, because that is all that it takes when you are in that territory. On April 27 he hit 3 home runs and drove in 7 runs, which put him not only into the Top 50, but into the top 40. He flattened out a little, but he moved into the top 30 on May 19, and into the top 20 on May 25. On June 12 he moved into the #10 spot, then 9, 8, 7, 6, 5. By July 7 he was ranked as the #5 hitter in baseball.

In that time period, I heard several reporters say that Guerrero was probably the best hitter in baseball now. But like Ohtani, that was as high as he got in 2021; he started to slip after that, and wound up the season ranked 12th.

Vladimir may in fact be the best hitter in baseball, or Shohei might, but I want to see them prove it before I put them there. There is always a sensation of the moment, and there are always people who want to say that the sensation of the moment is the brightest star in the firmament. But I look at it this way: that the variations in performance within each player's career are significantly larger than the actual differences in skill levels. That means, when you think about it, that it is rarely true that the player who is playing the best right now, over the last two weeks or the last two months….it is rarely true that the player who is playing the best right now is actually the best player. You need to be skeptical. If one of these men is actually the best hitter in baseball, 2022 will give them another chance to prove it.

But Mike Trout actually did NOT hold the #1 spot until the end of the season. There's this young fella, Juan Soto. Juan Soto did not start out the season in the 90s. He started the season #6. He drifted a little bit after that, dropping as low as the 16th spot on the list on June 28. He was back in the top 10 by early July. By mid-July he was 5th. On August 30th he was 6th.

And then he got hot. He homered and drove in 4 runs on September 2. He homered again on the third. Beginning September 7 he had 29 hits in 16 games. On September 23, he moved ahead of Trout, to be ranked as the #1 hitter in baseball.

September 23, 2021

Rank	Player	Score
1	Juan Soto	592
2	Mike Trout	589
3	Fernando Tatis Jr.	574
4	Bryce Harper	573
5	Freddie Freeman	571
6	Mookie Betts	569
7	Ronald Acuña Jr.	565
8	Vladimir Guerrero Jr.	563
9	Matt Olson	560
10	Jose Altuve	559

And all of a sudden, out of nowhere, he was an MVP candidate. He finished the season in a 3-for-28 slump, which put the static Mr. Trout back in first place;

End of Season

Rank	Player	Score
1	Mike Trout	589
2	Juan Soto	583
3	Bryce Harper	572
4	George Springer	566
5	Mookie Betts	566
6	Ronald Acuña Jr.	565
7	Fernando Tatis Jr.	565
8	Freddie Freeman	565
9	Paul Goldschmidt	561
10	Trea Turner	561

By the end of 2022 any of those men may be the best hitter in baseball, or Ohtani might, or Guerrero might. My money would be on Soto, but Mike Trout is Mike Trout. He's probably got a few hits in him.

Batter Rankings

Player	April 1 Score	April 1 Rank	May 1 Rank	June 1 Rank	July 1 Rank	Aug 1 Rank	Sept 1 Rank	Oct 3 Score	Oct 3 Rank
Trout, Mike	590.7	1	1	1	1	1	1	589.1	1
Soto, Juan	547.3	6	7	8	13	7	4	583.4	2
Harper, Bryce	522.5	18	12	27	30	17	8	572.4	3
Springer, George	550.4	4	3	4	8	8	7	566.4	4
Betts, Mookie	551.8	2	4	5	5	3	3	565.6	5
Acuna Jr., Ronald	536.5	8	2	2	3	4	5	565.3	6
Tatis Jr., Fernando	514.7	21	14	3	2	2	2	565.1	7
Freeman, Freddie	550.6	3	6	7	7	6	6	564.7	8
Goldschmidt, Paul	505.4	30	35	51	55	46	18	561.3	9
Turner, Trea	516.2	19	22	23	24	18	17	560.5	10
Altuve, Jose	525.6	15	16	9	4	5	15	558.2	11
Guerrero Jr., Vladimir	466.1	111	40	17	9	9	14	557.7	12
Olson, Matt	493.2	43	28	21	15	11	12	557.3	13
Semien, Marcus	512.4	25	32	12	6	12	16	556.7	14
Seager, Corey	534.8	10	10	14	18	21	25	555.9	15
Judge, Aaron	506.1	29	23	22	27	27	10	555.9	16
Ramirez, Jose	522.8	17	18	16	16	20	13	555.1	17
Lowe, Brandon	477.7	84	91	109	76	42	21	552.1	18
Muncy, Max	514.5	22	26	10	10	10	9	550.1	19
Hernandez, Teoscar	487.2	56	80	49	50	49	43	548.6	20
Abreu, Jose	527.4	13	17	11	25	22	11	547.1	21
Devers, Rafael	512.5	24	19	15	12	13	19	542.7	22
Alonso, Pete	515.0	20	24	28	38	29	23	542.1	23
Haniger, Mitch	473.1	96	38	29	43	32	53	541.7	24
Bregman, Alex	547.3	7	8	6	14	16	20	541.2	25
Correa, Carlos	490.9	48	46	35	17	30	29	540.7	26
Bichette, Bo	456.9	145	81	59	34	26	50	539.3	27
Machado, Manny	500.0	35	39	55	41	15	30	539.0	28
Riley, Austin	428.9	233	144	86	101	44	28	538.7	29
Perez, Salvador	477.7	86	65	69	77	68	39	537.4	30
Tucker, Kyle	455.1	148	171	64	72	52	59	536.5	31
Anderson, Tim	498.3	38	33	54	67	56	34	536.4	32
Marte, Starling	487.2	57	36	53	46	47	31	536.4	33
Alvarez, Yordan	484.2	63	50	40	31	34	24	535.6	34
Castellanos, Nick	491.0	46	37	25	26	31	32	535.6	35
Cruz, Nelson	530.8	11	9	18	11	24	22	534.3	36
Polanco, Jorge	449.0	172	169	140	94	55	36	533.8	37
Rendon, Anthony	549.8	5	5	13	23	23	26	532.9	38
Schwarber, Kyle	463.2	115	150	99	35	41	41	532.9	39
O'Neill, Tyler	393.3	332	241	130	118	163	124	531.9	40
Stanton, Giancarlo	500.5	34	34	46	45	81	49	531.8	41
Ohtani, Shohei	455.6	146	70	60	21	14	27	531.7	42
Albies, Ozzie	491.6	45	47	45	28	36	40	531.7	43
Votto, Joey	464.2	113	114	152	127	43	48	531.3	44
Hoskins, Rhys	493.2	42	45	36	80	40	33	530.7	45
Grandal, Yasmani	481.5	72	83	88	52	65	38	529.9	46
Arozarena, Randy	476.2	89	76	58	54	57	46	529.1	47
Belt, Brandon	481.7	71	93	103	86	111	82	529.0	48
Reynolds, Bryan	449.0	171	99	79	49	50	56	528.8	49
Winker, Jesse	454.3	149	64	44	37	45	35	528.1	50
Turner, Justin	507.5	28	15	30	32	19	47	527.5	51
Martinez, J.D.	504.1	32	13	20	22	33	45	526.9	52
Bogaerts, Xander	508.9	27	27	26	19	28	44	525.4	53
Lindor, Francisco	479.5	80	133	127	102	72	100	523.2	54
Gurriel, Yuli	473.8	94	49	37	36	35	51	523.1	55
France, Ty	441.8	196	116	157	110	99	57	521.8	56
Meadows, Austin	462.0	120	138	34	44	39	55	520.1	57
Marte, Ketel	498.8	36	41	52	48	58	60	519.9	58
Walsh, Jared	449.6	168	58	68	51	93	85	519.8	59
Baez, Javier	438.0	200	103	73	107	90	98	519.4	60
Smith, Will	473.7	95	85	71	96	82	52	519.4	61
Pollock, A.J.	472.1	99	129	111	145	79	75	518.9	62
Crawford, Brandon	451.6	160	149	90	73	54	77	518.3	63
Buxton, Byron	457.0	144	54	65	74	84	112	518.2	64
Arenado, Nolan	474.4	92	71	57	60	73	73	517.8	65
Robert, Luis	437.0	204	147	182	198	210	111	517.6	66
Renfroe, Hunter	428.3	236	239	142	88	115	68	517.0	67
Ozuna, Marcell	528.2	12	21	32	42	51	63	515.8	68
Yelich, Christian	536.4	9	11	19	20	37	42	515.8	69
Gurriel Jr., Lourdes	482.9	68	106	114	109	130	128	513.5	70
Bell, Josh	478.4	83	94	105	99	102	78	513.1	71

8

Batter Rankings

Player	April 1 Score	April 1 Rank	May 1 Rank	June 1 Rank	July 1 Rank	Aug 1 Rank	Sept 1 Rank	Oct 3 Score	Oct 3 Rank
Nimmo, Brandon	479.9	78	48	62	82	76	86	511.8	72
Conforto, Michael	524.8	16	25	38	65	109	90	511.7	73
Canha, Mark	483.5	65	42	39	39	48	74	511.6	74
Mountcastle, Ryan	430.8	226	281	225	89	112	61	511.6	75
Seager, Kyle	487.3	55	53	63	95	75	66	510.7	76
Donaldson, Josh	486.9	59	75	81	61	77	72	510.7	77
Swanson, Dansby	486.6	60	121	95	135	61	37	510.5	78
Adames, Willy	436.6	206	280	172	121	78	76	510.0	79
LeMahieu, DJ	525.8	14	20	33	33	67	65	509.4	80
Escobar, Eduardo	448.9	173	104	93	104	95	99	509.1	81
India, Jonathan	377.8	403	326	357	157	108	93	509.1	82
Bryant, Kris	479.2	82	30	24	68	60	58	508.7	83
Chapman, Matt	495.3	40	51	101	56	83	62	508.2	84
Cronenworth, Jake	450.9	164	166	110	75	53	71	508.1	85
Moncada, Yoan	479.4	81	61	50	79	92	96	507.9	86
Hernandez, Kike	420.5	257	220	215	153	105	69	507.8	87
Duvall, Adam	460.1	126	162	113	62	87	89	507.7	88
Mullins II, Cedric	402.6	304	151	168	58	64	67	507.5	89
Reyes, Franmil	462.7	116	77	82	98	63	84	507.5	90
McCutchen, Andrew	485.8	61	112	78	63	59	91	507.5	91
Schwindel, Frank	375.0	422			579	625	195	507.0	92
Brantley, Michael	509.4	26	31	42	29	38	64	506.5	93
Crawford, J.P.	459.8	128	145	193	92	147	157	506.1	94
Soler, Jorge	495.9	39	84	177	235	175	116	506.1	95
Gallo, Joey	462.4	117	146	115	40	62	87	506.1	96
Schoop, Jonathan	443.8	186	243	154	70	66	97	506.0	97
Carlson, Dylan	419.2	258	160	149	161	125	120	505.8	98
Sano, Miguel	474.4	91	136	125	132	120	102	505.7	99
Happ, Ian	454.3	150	253	171	252	377	218	504.5	100
Laureano, Ramon	481.2	73	73	43	57	86	95	504.4	101
Garcia, Avisail	443.6	187	167	121	131	100	83	504.4	102
Segura, Jean	459.9	127	141	135	120	103	103	504.3	103
Realmuto, J.T.	495.3	41	55	61	84	70	80	503.9	104
Benintendi, Andrew	438.8	198	120	122	108	150	187	503.8	105
Candelario, Jeimer	457.7	141	154	129	215	126	127	503.7	106
Wong, Kolten	447.8	179	155	118	119	117	106	503.5	107
Cron, C.J.	453.3	153	113	161	196	213	94	503.5	108
Aguilar, Jesus	461.2	121	60	108	126	85	88	503.1	109
Rizzo, Anthony	479.6	79	86	83	100	74	92	503.0	110
Dalbec, Bobby	423.0	252	294	235	166	231	118	502.8	111
Merrifield, Whit	490.4	50	52	70	59	107	79	502.7	112
Taylor, Chris	469.7	102	59	41	53	25	54	502.5	113
Grossman, Robbie	442.8	191	184	94	122	98	104	502.4	114
Franco, Wander					393	261	110	502.4	115
Hays, Austin	433.7	212	159	128	142	170	166	499.5	116
Cooper, Garrett	459.7	129	183	123	116	101	107	497.5	117
Voit, Luke	504.8	31	43	66	83	80	70	497.5	118
Verdugo, Alex	458.8	135	89	97	97	134	113	496.9	119
Yastrzemski, Mike	489.3	52	66	67	64	71	109	495.8	120
Jimenez, Eloy	490.9	47	62	75	91	118	81	495.8	121
Zunino, Mike	375.0	422	252	191	151	192	130	495.7	122
Urias, Luis	375.0	422	254	239	148	172	140	495.5	123
Story, Trevor	482.8	69	69	120	111	140	117	495.2	124
Rosario, Amed	443.0	189	251	206	179	189	101	495.1	125

9

Historical #1 Ranked Batters

Player	Date Took Over	Days on Top
Mike Trout	2021-09-28	Current
Juan Soto	2021-09-23	5
Mike Trout	2019-05-17	860
Christian Yelich	2019-05-16	1
Mike Trout	2019-05-10	6
Christian Yelich	2019-05-08	2
Mike Trout	2016-04-25	1108
Bryce Harper	2016-04-16	9
Mike Trout	2015-08-30	230
Andrew McCutchen	2015-08-29	1
Mike Trout	2014-05-20	466
Miguel Cabrera	2014-05-18	2
Mike Trout	2014-04-02	46
Miguel Cabrera	2014-04-01	1
Mike Trout	2014-03-31	1
Miguel Cabrera	2013-04-28	337
Ryan Braun	2012-05-08	355
Matt Kemp	2012-04-14	24
Ryan Braun	2012-04-13	1
Albert Pujols	2012-04-12	1
Ryan Braun	2012-04-11	1
Albert Pujols	2012-04-10	1
Ryan Braun	2012-04-09	1
Albert Pujols	2011-10-22	170
Ryan Braun	2011-10-20	2
Albert Pujols	2011-10-16	4
Ryan Braun	2011-10-01	15
Albert Pujols	2011-09-28	3
Ryan Braun	2011-09-27	1
Albert Pujols	2011-09-01	26
Jose Bautista	2011-08-31	1
Albert Pujols	2011-08-04	27
Jose Bautista	2011-08-02	2
Albert Pujols	2011-07-30	3
Jose Bautista	2011-07-01	29
Albert Pujols	2011-06-19	12
Jose Bautista	2011-05-15	35
Albert Pujols	2008-09-25	962
Alex Rodriguez	2008-09-24	1
Albert Pujols	2008-09-23	1
Alex Rodriguez	2008-09-14	9
Albert Pujols	2008-09-10	4
Alex Rodriguez	2008-09-09	1
Albert Pujols	2008-09-08	1
Alex Rodriguez	2008-09-02	6
Albert Pujols	2008-08-28	5
Alex Rodriguez	2008-08-27	1
Albert Pujols	2008-08-26	1
Alex Rodriguez	2008-06-08	79
Chipper Jones	2008-06-05	3
Alex Rodriguez	2008-05-30	6
Chipper Jones	2008-05-22	8
Alex Rodriguez	2008-05-20	2
Chipper Jones	2008-05-13	7
Alex Rodriguez	2008-05-10	3
Chipper Jones	2008-05-04	6
Alex Rodriguez	2007-06-13	326
David Ortiz	2007-06-03	10
Travis Hafner	2007-05-31	3
David Ortiz	2007-05-20	11
Travis Hafner	2007-05-19	1
David Ortiz	2007-05-09	10
Travis Hafner	2007-04-24	15
Alex Rodriguez	2007-04-23	1
Travis Hafner	2007-04-20	3
David Ortiz	2007-04-19	1
Albert Pujols	2007-04-18	1
David Ortiz	2007-04-16	2
Albert Pujols	2007-04-15	1
David Ortiz	2007-04-14	1
Albert Pujols	2007-04-13	1
Travis Hafner	2007-04-12	1

Player	Date Took Over	Days on Top
Albert Pujols	2007-04-08	4
Travis Hafner	2007-04-07	1
Albert Pujols	2004-10-13	906

Shohei Ohtani

Mark Simon

I like foreshadowing. Always have, always will.

It's a great literary device. It builds suspense. It keeps you thinking ahead and looking back.

Sometimes in baseball, things happen early in the season that set a tone for the entire year.

And sometimes they don't.

In Shohei Ohtani's case, his first series of the season foreshadowed much of what followed. He lived up to the hype. He was the Babe Ruth of our time.

The Home Run

Ohtani homered in the ninth inning of his second game of the season. I'd categorize it as impressive since it came off White Sox closer Liam Hendriks, but it wasn't necessarily memorable.

His second home run of the season—hit 451 feet off a 97-MPH eye-approaching fastball from Dylan Cease—that one was something else.

You know how sometimes you'll hear a baseball analyst say a player's home runs sound different than everyone else's?

This one did.

"A POWWWW with an echo to it," said Angels broadcaster José Mota, who worked most games at home from field level and got to see and hear much of Ohtani's work close up.

This home run came on ESPN's Sunday Night Baseball, and because ESPN and FOX have better and broader microphone coverage, we got treated to one of the loudest home runs we'll ever hear. It almost sounds like there's a microphone on his bat. Scan the QR code to see and hear it.

Ohtani hit 46 home runs in 2021. We don't know how many of those produced the decibel level of that first one, but we can tell you that Ohtani's 78 barrels (a Statcast measure based on optimal velocity and launch angle…essentially balls hit like that one) were the most in the majors in 2021.

From a technical standpoint, the thing to watch with Ohtani is his hands, said ESPN broadcaster, Eduardo Pérez.

"They're always in the ready position," Pérez said. "No matter what the pitch is."

Ohtani's 46 home runs were one shy of his total in 254 games from 2018 to 2020. They were one shy of Troy Glaus' Angels franchise record set in 2000.

The Triple

One thing that may have slipped under your Ohtani radar this year is that he led the American League and tied for the major league lead in triples.

This wasn't a great year for the three-base hit. For the first time in MLB history, no one had 10 in a full-length season. And Ohtani was only halfway to 10 with 10 days left in the regular season but he snuck in three in his last eight games to win the AL crown.

Ohtani's triple-hitting style is often to slam the ball at a launch angle such that it produces a low line drive or a ground ball into the right field corner. This accounted for five of his eight.

His first one of the season came in the Angels' second game. It was a rocket ground ball that took its first bounce about halfway to José Abreu and then zipped past his glove at about 108 MPH. Abreu had no chance to get in front of the ball. By the time he put his glove down, it was well past him.

"Thank god that ball didn't find José Abreu's chest," Mota said "Oh my gosh, oh my goodness. There's no human being that could have stopped that ball."

Because right fielder Adam Eaton waited to play the pinball carom off the wall in the right field corner, he had no chance to get Ohtani at third base.

The thing about some of Ohtani's triples that is impressive is how he gets to third base so easily after hitting balls so hard. Most players of his size would probably stop at second base and be satisfied with a double. Ohtani likes to 'think three,' and he was fast enough to make it eight times.

"He runs like a track athlete," said Mota.

A little baseball history lesson:

In 1902, a pitcher/utility player, Harry Howell, hit 11 triples for the Baltimore Orioles (not the current ones, the predecessor to the Yankees franchise).

In 1918, pitcher/outfielder Babe Ruth did the same for the Red Sox.

Two Negro League players—Harry Kenyon and Bullet Rogan—hit eight in 1921. Rogan did it for the Kansas City Monarchs and Kenyon for the Indianapolis ABCs. Rogan did it again for the Monarchs in 1925.

It took 96 years for another player to come along who pitched 20 games in a season and hit at least eight triples.

Ohtani was that player.

The Stolen Base

In the fifth inning of the third game of the Angels–White Sox season-opening four-game series, Ohtani stole second base against pitcher Lance Lynn and catcher Zack Collins.

There wasn't anything particularly dramatic about this. The most impressive thing about it, available on an additional camera angle not seen here, was the jump that Ohtani got.

In addition to having incredible power, Ohtani has great speed, which helped him steal 26 bases this season. The speed actually manifests itself better going home-to-first (By Statcast's measures he's fourth fastest in the majors) than trying to steal a base (he got caught 10 times, most in the AL). It seems like this is something he's still trying to figure out.

Ohtani's 46-home run, 26-stolen base combination has been matched by only four other players—Barry Bonds (1993 Giants), Hall-of-Famer Larry Walker (1997 Rockies), Jose Canseco (1998 Blue Jays), and Alfonso Soriano (2006 Nationals).

The Splitter and the Slider

So that first start of the season had foreshadowing, but that requires some specificity not contained within his pitching line. In 4 2/3 innings he allowed three runs and walked five.

But there was something in that start that foretold the future—Ohtani's unhittable splitter and nasty slider.

Ohtani got five outs with his splitter that day, all strikeouts, including ones against the reigning AL MVP, Abreu, and Luis Robert, who hit like an MVP candidate in 2021 when he wasn't injured. He also got three outs with the slider.

Opposing batters went 11-for-128 in at-bats ending with an Ohtani splitter (.086) with two extra-base hits, both doubles. It was one of the best pitches in baseball.

The .233 OPS against the pitch was second-best among the 30 pitchers who threw at least 100 splitters last season. Only Aroldis Chapman, who threw one-third as many splitters as Ohtani, was better (.061...opponents were 1-for-33).

After allowing seven runs and four walks in 2/3 of an inning against the Yankees on June 30, Ohtani's wildness abated.

Ohtani had started throwing his slider more often a few weeks prior to that game, and after that start it really became a difference maker when it was paired with the splitter.

It gave him better options to throw off a fastball that sometimes reached 100 MPH. Ohtani got better as the season went along. He walked 35 batters in his first 60 innings, but only nine in his last 70 1/3 innings.

Opponents hit .171 against the slider from July 6 to the end of the season. And he threw it for a strike 74% of the time, up from 65% prior to that.

"You can hear the buzz behind that pitch," Mota said. "It's hard and late breaking. When teams see it, they're like 'Oh man, he's on.'"

The Total Package

By Baseball-Reference Wins Above Replacement, Ohtani was worth 5 WAR as a position player and 4 WAR as a pitcher.

Babe Ruth never did that.

"He has a hitter's mentality when he pitches and a pitcher's mentality when he hits," Pérez said of Ohtani.

Ohtani was a top-25 hitter AND a top-25 pitcher, but perhaps the best thing about his season was that his best ability was availability.

Yes, the best foreshadowing to come from Ohtani's season-opening series against the White Sox was that he played all four games. He played in 155 out of a possible 162, which meant that we got to see him at his best just about every day of the season.

It was quite a treat.

The Baseball Revolution

Joe Sheehan

It's the first week of October, and I write this against the backdrop of what will likely be the last ten-team playoff field in baseball history. This system, merely a kludge fixing a hole in the previous system, will be ill-remembered if remembered at all. It produced moments, Salvador Perez and Jake Arrieta and Chris Taylor writing their names into baseball history, but it always felt like a transition, a bridge, a temporary structure linking points A and B. MLB had already discussed a 14-team playoff as far back as two years ago. The league and its television partners enjoyed the 16-team field of 2020, and owners pressed hard to gain expanded playoffs in advance of the 2021 season.

The inevitable playoff expansion is just a part of what is happening now. The baseball that was at the end of 2019 is not going to resemble the baseball we have at the start of 2022. We are living through not just a pandemic, but a revolution. We've seen rule changes, such as a three-batter minimum for pitchers, such as expanded rosters. The seven-inning doubleheaders, nominally a pandemic rule, may well go away, but their cousin, the free runner in all extra innings, may well stay in a modified form. I don't need to tell Handbook readers about the growth of data-driven defensive positioning—fine, "shifting." Well, MLB experimented with limiting where teams can play their seven defenders in the minors, and similar rules have many supporters in and outside of the game.

MLB can play with minor-league rules because it now owns the minors. The 2019 season featured champions in the Pacific Coast League, the Eastern League, the California League. No more. The minors were reduced, reorganized, and relabeled for 2021. A process that began in the 1930s and accelerated in the 1950s is finally complete, the minors now defined explicitly as serfs in a player development model. MLB's model.

Maybe you watched 20-game-winner Julio Urías help his own cause, to use the broadcaster's hoary cliché, during the Division Series, the 20-game winner lining an RBI single to right in a 7-2 win over the Giants. That hit is notable because pitchers have been largely reduced to automatic outs, but it is also possibly one of the last we will see. Fifty years after the American League introduced a designated hitter for the pitcher, and more than 100 after the National League first kicked around the idea, we may finally see the two leagues—at this point, more like conferences than league—unified behind the DH rule.

That will be one of the many topics on the table when the players and owners sit down to negotiate the next Collective Bargaining Agreement. We haven't seen a labor hot war in some time, not since 1994-95, but there's been a cold war brewing for some time. There are serious issues getting to the heart of what baseball is—National pastime? Profit center for the .01%? Summer filler for TV networks?—that must be addressed, and each side comes to the table with its own answers, its own plans. The player compensation model was largely set in 1976, and has grown out of date as teams value raw skills more and experience less.

We are once again living through a baseball revolution, the fourth in history.

In 1919, baseball was a rudderless, local entity helmed by squalling businessmen, infected by gamblers all too willing to take advantage of ballplayers ill-treated and poorly compensated by those businessmen. By 1922, it had a national star in Babe Ruth, was forced to confront its gambling problem in the wake of the 1919 World Series, and to do so handed the reins to the game's first commissioner.

At the end of 1946, there had not been a black player in the major leagues since we came to know the leagues as such, an informal color line dating to 1885 keeping not just American blacks but dark-skinned Latin American players out of the game. By the end of 1949, a black man, Jackie Robinson, was voted the Most Valuable Player in the National League. Black players would rewrite the record books, and many would become known not just as great ballplayers, but great leaders, great role models.

As 1975 neared its end, baseball players were tied to their teams in perpetuity by tradition as much as by rule. That winter, Marvin Miller made the case that the "reserve clause," section 10 (a) of the standard player contract, held for one year, not forever, and an arbitrator agreed with him. By the end of 1977, "free agency" had taken on a life of its own. The baseball offseason—baseball itself—would never be the same.

Sometimes it's hard to sense the revolution. The impacts of Arnold Rothstein and Kenesaw Mountain Landis and Babe Ruth would take time to evaluate. For all the grace and grit shown by Jackie Robinson, there were just four integrated teams, of 16, when he accepted his MVP award, and some teams wouldn't welcome a black player until the end of the 1950s. Even free agency came with turbulence, teams learning how to evaluate and compensate players on the fly. Don Gullett and Wayne Garland are as much the story of that era as are Reggie Jackson and Pete Rose.

This one feels different, though. We are living through the revolution and we know it. Two years ago you might have seen a rookie just up from the Pacific Coast League, perhaps as part of September rosters being expanded to 40 men, come into a game, strike out one batter and be relieved, his job done for the day. That whole sentence is fiction now. Come April, you might turn on a Dodgers/Padres game and see Max Muncy, designated hitter, line a ball into short right field for a single as two infielders stand helplessly between second and third base, unable to do anything about it. The baseball itself may change, as the league seeks a solution that allows pitchers to get a grip without, as they have in recent years, applying everything this side of SuperGlue to the horsehide.

The past revolutions happened because something big wasn't working and needed to be fixed. This one is different; there is no one issue, but rather a dozen issues all coming to a head, on-field and off. The game is out of balance, from the dirt to the dugout to the desk of the owner. It will take a revolution to fix these problems.

Revolutions aren't always welcomed, of course. The revamping of the minor leagues was criticized by many, even those within the game who would prefer to see more levels of play for prospects. If we do get a designated hitter in both leagues, many fans who loathe the rule will be alienated. Personally, I think "banning the shift," putting restrictions on where defensive players can stand, is both philosophically wrong and exacerbates the game's biggest problem by rewarding the pull-heavy, swing-and-miss heavy batting style. Recent CBA negotiations have made baseball less competitive by locking in profits for even the worst teams, and there's no guarantee this cycle won't make that problem worse.

When we get to the other side, though, we'll still be here, and if history is our guide, we'll be the better for it. Baseball was better after each of those revolutions, not perfect, not ideal, but better. Less game-fixing. More Black players. More competitiveness. The hope is a year from now we have a game that lets the players show off a broader set of their incredible skills, that treats those players more fairly in the market, that pushes teams to win rather than rebuild.

By 2022, Major League Baseball will look far different than it did in 2019. We are living through the revolution.

The Joe Sheehan Newsletter covers all things baseball, featuring analysis and opinion about the game on and off the field from the perspective of the informed outsider. Joe Sheehan is a founding member of Baseball Prospectus and has been a contributor to Sports Illustrated and Baseball America. He has been writing about baseball for nearly 25 years.

A subscription gets you the newsletter and various related features two to five days a week, year-round. For more information, go to www.joesheehan.com

Projecting Injury Risk

Alex Vigderman

Orioles center fielder Cedric Mullins wildly outperformed expectations in 2021. You might hear more about that in the Bill James Projections recap later in the book, because he hit for an OPS nearly 200 points higher than what we projected him for, going 30-30 when we projected him for fewer than 30 total homers and steals.

Yes, Mullins improved a great deal as a hitter. But the reason Mullins was able to put up an MVP-caliber campaign is that he stayed on the field. He appeared in 159 games, which was more than his career total up to that point. Two other AL MVP candidates through the first month of the season, Mike Trout and Byron Buxton, couldn't say the same.

Mullins led the league in defensive opportunities as an outfielder, saved runs at a representative rate for a center fielder, and did so with one of the lowest rates of dives, slides, and jumps, which look great on highlights but are big factors in injury risk among outfielders.

He (literally) outran his projection of being one of the likeliest position players to suffer an IL-worthy injury in 2021, per last year's Handbook.

The same could not be said for most of his comrades on those lists. We listed 10 pitchers and 10 position players who our model found to be most likely to suffer an injury and miss at least 10 days in 2021, and seven players on each list endured such a fate. That includes Spring Training losses like Mike Clevinger's Tommy John surgery.

How are we going about projecting something as timeless in its unpredictability as physical injuries?

Well, we have collected and aggregated injury data for some years now. It started with just noting when a player suffered some kind of injury event during a game: getting hit by a pitch, pulling up lame while beating out a groundball, or crashing into the wall on a deep fly.

We combine that information with Injured List stints and media reports to create as comprehensive an injury history as anyone outside an MLB organization has. And starting in 2020, we began leveraging that data to investigate injury risk.

If you read last year's edition of this book, you'll recall John Shirley's introduction to the model we built and the different elements involved. In short, we take injury data and combine it with playing time, position, body type, and play style information to create a daily estimate of how likely a player is to suffer an IL stint or miss at least ten days with an injury over the next week, month, two months, and season.

For more info on the model, its inputs, and the kinds of insights we've already gained, scan the QR code below with your phone to check out our presentation from the 2021 SABR Analytics Conference.

So, who are we most concerned about heading into 2022?

As of the end of the 2021 regular season, here's who we have our eye on.

Pitchers with the Highest Predicted Injury Risk Entering 2022

Rank	Player
1	Jose Alvarado
2	Ryne Stanek
3	Max Scherzer
4	Aroldis Chapman
T-5	Pete Fairbanks
T-5	Genesis Cabrera
T-7	Jake Brentz
T-7	Michael Kopech
T-9	Edwin Diaz
T-9	Diego Castillo
T-9	Jonathan Loaisiga

Alvarado, Stanek, Fairbanks, and Castillo were Rays teammates two years ago, and they have eight IL stints between them in the two years since. Perhaps it's not a coincidence that only Fairbanks remains with the team.

Fans of power pitching shouldn't be surprised to see some favorites on this list given the risks associated, but some of the more compelling pitchers to watch over the last few years have warning signs for missed time in 2022. Chapman and Kopech have arguably the fastest fastballs of all time. Scherzer is on the back side of his career (pun intended); he has served time on the IL three times with a back injury over the last three seasons.

Hitters with the Highest Predicted Injury Risk Entering 2022

Rank	Player
1	Alcides Escobar
2	Kolten Wong
3	Miguel Cabrera
T-4	Carlos Santana
T-4	Salvador Perez
6	Raimel Tapia
7	Xander Bogaerts
8	Aledmys Diaz
T-9	Jorge Soler
T-9	Franmil Reyes
T-9	Didi Gregorius
T-9	Jordy Mercer

What you should notice from the hitter list is that three big risk factors for injury are playing an up-the-middle position, being a bulky corner player / DH, and failing to discover the Fountain of Youth.

Alcides Escobar hadn't played in the majors for two years but has already re-signed for a one-year deal with the Nationals, who gave him a bit more than a coffee this season. He doesn't have a dramatic injury history, but his position and age make him something less than a sure bet in '22.

Salvador Perez and Xander Bogaerts would be huge losses to their respective teams if they were to miss time.

Perez missed 2019 to injury and after the short 2020 season was able to start 160 games (120 at catcher) this season. That's not something we expect to continue in 2022.

Bogaerts has played in at least 136 games in every full season of his career, so it'd be a turn for the surprising for him to miss a big chunk of time, but he plays a tough position and his mix of size and just-past-his-prime age make for a cocktail of injury risk.

Hall of Fame Monitor

Mark Simon

You know who has a tough Hall of Fame case?

St. Louis Cardinals first baseman Paul Goldschmidt.

We hold Hall of Fame first basemen to a high standard and rightfully so. It's the position of Lou Gehrig and Albert Pujols, of Jimmie Foxx and Willie McCovey, and a lot of gargantuan offensive numbers.

In last year's book, I was bullish on the Hall of Fame possibility for Freddie Freeman and I still am. But my order may need to include Goldschmidt right beside Freeman. This is appropriate because Freeman is Goldschmidt's most similar player and Goldschmidt is Freeman's most similar player by Bill James Similarity Scores.

Goldschmidt helped his Hall of Fame case considerably with his 2021 season, helping lift the Cardinals from .500-ish to a playoff team with a huge late-season push.

He scored seven points on the Monitor this year for his various offensive accomplishments, with the possibility for more depending on a number of postseason scenarios (like being on a World Series winner or being an MVP, which we won't know when this book goes to press).

Goldschmidt is at 81 Hall of Fame Monitor points, potential additions pending. A score of 100 is not an absolute proclamation of induction, but it tends to be a strong possibility.

As Bill noted, the 100-point threshold from his statistical system (the explanation of which can be found by doing a control-F for "Hall of Fame Monitor" on any Baseball-Reference player page and then clicking the link) is a guide and not an absolute. It's intended to provide a framework for thinking and in this case it gave me reason to think about Goldschmidt's candidacy in a little more detail. Scroll through the Hall of Fame Monitor lists. Perhaps it will do the same for you with someone else.

Hall of Fame Monitor

Player	Age	2021	Career
Ronald Acuna Jr.	**23**	**0**	**21**
Rafael Devers	**24**	**9**	**27**
Ozzie Albies	24	10	24
Julio Urias	24	11	18
Austin Riley	24	10	10
Cody Bellinger	**25**	**0**	**40**
Sandy Alcantara	25	5	10
Carlos Correa	**26**	**6**	**25**
German Marquez	26	2	14
Andrew Benintendi	26	1	13
Lucas Giolito	26	2	11
Francisco Lindor	**27**	**1**	**44**
Edwin Diaz	27	4	32
Alex Bregman	27	0	32
Corey Seager	27	2	28
Josh Hader	27	8	18
Jorge Polanco	27	7	18
Matt Olson	27	9	17
Jose Berrios	27	4	17
Ketel Marte	27	0	15
Joey Gallo	27	3	14
Rougned Odor	27	0	12
Lou Trivino	27	4	11
Lance McCullers Jr.	27	2	11
Mookie Betts	**28**	**2**	**82**
Bryce Harper	28	10	78
Manny Machado	28	5	50
Xander Bogaerts	28	4	49
Jose Ramirez	28	9	45
Javier Baez	28	5	37
Trea Turner	28	14	30
Blake Snell	28	1	28
Trevor Story	28	3	27
Aaron Nola	28	2	23
Josh Bell	28	2	17
Matt Chapman	28	1	17
Tim Anderson	28	5	16
Joe Musgrove	28	3	15
Gary Sanchez	28	1	15
Kyle Freeland	28	0	14
Eduardo Rodriguez	28	2	13
Archie Bradley	28	1	12
Noah Syndergaard	28	0	12
Zach Davies	28	1	11
Scott Barlow	28	4	10
Luis Castillo	28	2	10
Kyle Schwarber	28	1	10
Mike Trout	**29**	**0**	**131**
Christian Yelich	29	0	50
Kris Bryant	29	2	44
Nick Castellanos	29	10	31
Aaron Judge	29	6	30
Robbie Ray	29	14	27
Eugenio Suarez	29	2	22
Carlos Martinez	29	0	21
Willson Contreras	29	1	16
Jonathan Schoop	29	1	15
Jorge Soler	29	1	15
Corey Knebel	29	0	14
Eddie Rosario	29	0	14
Joc Pederson	29	0	14
Michael Wacha	29	0	14
Marco Gonzales	29	1	13
Sean Manaea	29	2	11
Trey Mancini	29	1	11
Alex Claudio	29	0	11

Player	Age	2021	Career
Luke Jackson	29	3	10
Carl Edwards Jr.	29	0	10
Nolan Arenado	**30**	**6**	**103**
Gerrit Cole	30	8	57
Marcell Ozuna	30	0	29
Marcus Semien	30	13	28
Trevor Bauer	30	0	24
Alex Wood	30	1	21
Max Muncy	30	5	19
J.T. Realmuto	30	2	19
Julio Teheran	30	0	19
Hansel Robles	30	3	17
Chris Devenski	30	0	16
Jonathan Villar	30	1	14
Ender Inciarte	30	0	14
Kevin Gausman	30	5	13
Taylor Rogers	30	0	13
Mitch Haniger	30	7	11
Tyler Rogers	30	6	11
Dylan Floro	30	3	11
Chris Taylor	30	1	11
Wil Myers	30	1	11
Avisail Garcia	30	2	10
Marcus Stroman	30	2	10
Emilio Pagan	30	1	10
Jake Lamb	30	0	10
Joe Panik	30	0	10
Jose Altuve	**31**	**7**	**115**
Madison Bumgarner	31	2	73
Freddie Freeman	31	10	72
Giancarlo Stanton	31	4	68
Salvador Perez	31	16	67
Anthony Rizzo	31	1	58
Anthony Rendon	31	0	44
Jeurys Familia	31	1	41
Eric Hosmer	31	1	37
George Springer	31	0	31
Jean Segura	31	1	29
Brad Hand	31	3	28
Raisel Iglesias	31	7	24
Starlin Castro	31	0	24
Kyle Hendricks	31	2	22
Patrick Corbin	31	1	21
Will Smith	31	5	20
Zack Wheeler	31	11	19
Sonny Gray	31	1	18
Andrelton Simmons	31	0	18
Jason Heyward	31	0	18
Matt Barnes	31	3	17
Jackie Bradley Jr.	31	0	14
Andrew Chafin	31	4	13
Nathan Eovaldi	31	2	12
Luis Avilan	31	0	12
Mychal Givens	31	1	11
Jake Odorizzi	31	0	11
Travis Shaw	31	0	11
Richard Rodriguez	31	3	10
Cesar Hernandez	31	2	10
DJ LeMahieu	**32**	**2**	**54**
Chris Sale	32	0	52
Stephen Strasburg	32	0	39
Whit Merrifield	32	6	34
Liam Hendriks	32	14	32
Elvis Andrus	32	1	30
Alex Colome	32	2	29
Starling Marte	32	6	25
Jose Quintana	32	0	23
Mike Moustakas	32	0	20
Hector Neris	32	3	18

Player	Age	2021	Career
Chris Archer	32	0	18
Shane Greene	32	0	16
Corey Dickerson	32	0	15
Ryan Pressly	32	4	14
Eduardo Escobar	32	1	14
Adam Duvall	32	6	13
Hunter Strickland	32	1	13
Matt Harvey	32	1	13
Danny Duffy	32	0	13
Miles Mikolas	32	0	13
Jose Alvarez	32	2	12
Brandon Workman	32	0	12
Yasmani Grandal	32	0	12
Adam Eaton	32	0	11
Marwin Gonzalez	32	0	11
Drew Pomeranz	32	0	10
Drew Smyly	32	0	10
James Paxton	32	0	10
Michael Pineda	32	0	10
Clayton Kershaw	**33**	**0**	**149**
Craig Kimbrel	33	4	107
Kenley Jansen	33	5	82
Paul Goldschmidt	33	7	81
J.D. Martinez	33	6	68
Aroldis Chapman	33	4	60
Jacob deGrom	33	0	53
Dallas Keuchel	33	1	40
Justin Upton	33	0	39
Zack Britton	33	0	39
Khris Davis	33	0	33
Blake Treinen	33	4	28
Neftali Feliz	33	0	27
Bryan Shaw	33	2	23
Mike Minor	33	1	21
Brad Boxberger	33	1	20
Dellin Betances	33	0	20
Trevor Cahill	33	0	20
Kenta Maeda	33	0	18
Kyle Seager	33	4	17
Joe Kelly	33	0	17
Brandon Belt	33	0	16
Aaron Loup	33	4	14
David Peralta	33	1	14
Kyle Gibson	33	1	14
Pedro Baez	33	0	14
Garrett Richards	33	1	13
Brad Peacock	33	0	13
Jhoulys Chacin	33	0	13
Wilson Ramos	33	0	13
Rex Brothers	33	1	12
Tommy Pham	33	1	12
Justin Wilson	33	0	11
A.J. Pollock	33	0	10
Chase Anderson	33	0	10
Buster Posey	**34**	**3**	**84**
Jose Abreu	34	6	60
Andrew McCutchen	34	1	57
Charlie Blackmon	34	1	56
Michael Brantley	34	3	41
Lance Lynn	34	1	41
Brandon Crawford	34	5	36
Jay Bruce	34	0	33
Yu Darvish	34	1	30
Pablo Sandoval	34	0	26
Carlos Carrasco	34	0	24
Derek Holland	34	0	23
AJ Ramos	34	0	22
Alcides Escobar	34	0	22
Jake McGee	34	5	21
Wade Miley	34	3	21
Hyun-Jin Ryu	34	2	18
Daniel Hudson	34	1	17

Player	Age	2021	Career
Tanner Roark	34	0	17
Sean Doolittle	34	1	16
Josh Reddick	34	0	15
Tommy Hunter	34	0	15
Jake Diekman	34	2	11
Alex Avila	34	0	11
Ryan Buchter	34	0	11
Collin McHugh	34	0	10
David Price	**35**	**0**	**89**
Corey Kluber	35	1	83
Josh Donaldson	35	2	55
Johnny Cueto	35	0	51
Greg Holland	35	1	50
Evan Longoria	35	0	50
Jake Arrieta	35	0	44
Wade Davis	35	0	41
Carlos Santana	35	1	35
Matt Carpenter	35	0	34
Jordan Zimmermann	35	0	28
Lorenzo Cain	35	0	28
Steve Cishek	35	1	27
Asdrubal Cabrera	35	0	25
Dexter Fowler	35	0	22
Jonathan Lucroy	35	0	21
Todd Frazier	35	0	17
Adam Ottavino	35	2	16
Brad Brach	35	0	14
Mitch Moreland	35	0	12
Max Scherzer	**36**	**6**	**138**
Mark Melancon	36	9	60
Ian Kennedy	36	2	40
Ryan Zimmerman	36	0	39
Tony Watson	36	1	35
David Robertson	36	0	29
Tyler Clippard	36	0	29
Andrew Miller	36	0	28
Justin Turner	36	3	23
Pedro Strop	36	0	21
Will Harris	36	0	19
Yusmeiro Petit	36	1	16
Brandon Kintzler	36	0	16
Jon Jay	36	0	13
Mike Fiers	36	0	13
Josh Tomlin	36	0	12
Daniel Bard	36	3	11
Blake Parker	36	0	11
Zack Greinke	**37**	**1**	**95**
Joey Votto	37	5	94
Jon Lester	37	1	87
Joakim Soria	37	0	38
Charlie Morton	37	4	25
Yuli Gurriel	37	7	24
Scott Kazmir	37	0	23
Brett Gardner	37	0	21
Joe Smith	37	1	20
Jed Lowrie	37	1	14
Jesse Chavez	37	0	13
Kurt Suzuki	37	0	13
Craig Stammen	37	1	11
Miguel Cabrera	**38**	**1**	**193**
Yadier Molina	38	1	84
Sergio Romo	38	1	44
Ervin Santana	38	0	36
John Axford	38	0	32
J.A. Happ	38	1	26
Darren ODay'	38	0	25
Adam Wainwright	**39**	**5**	**84**
Oliver Perez	39	0	20

Player	Age	2021	Career
Nelson Cruz	40	3	84
Albert Pujols	41	0	243
Rich Hill	41	1	13

Hall of Fame Value

Sarah Thompson

This upcoming Hall of Fame ballot is surely an interesting one. Barry Bonds, Roger Clemens, and Curt Schilling are in their final year of eligibility while some of the early legends of the 21st century, Alex Rodriguez and David Ortiz, will be on the ballot for the first time.

Save for Big Papi, there aren't many slam dunk cases based on Hall of Fame Value, a tool that's helpful in evaluating Hall of Fame candidacy. It's derived by adding a player's career Win Shares and 4 times their WAR. A player with a HOF Value of 500 merits a spot in Cooperstown.

The only players added to the ballot this year that best the 500 mark are A-Rod (961.1) and David Ortiz (537.2). The next-best new candidate behind Ortiz? Jimmy Rollins, obviously.

It's somewhat contradictory to my childhood memories to look back on J-Roll's career and see only five years of above-average offensive production (according to OPS+), only one of which was remarkable (119 OPS+, 2007). What helps Rollins almost reach the 500 mark (493.4) is his consistency throughout his career. He maintained five straight years of 4.5+ WAR and had another 4-WAR season at the age of 35.

We also track Hall of Fame Value for current players. Clayton Kershaw eclipsed the 500 mark this year, settling at 502.6 at the age of 33. The only uncertainty with his candidacy is whether he's a first-ballot selection.

Something else interesting happened this year, too—Bryce Harper eclipsed Mookie Betts as the leader in HOF Value for his age group (28) after an MVP-caliber 2021.

In the tables below, you'll be able to look at current MLB players by age group and their 2021 and career HoF Value stats. Following those tables are the Win Shares, WAR, HOF Value, and HOF Monitor numbers for potentials on the 2022 ballot.

Hall of Fame Values by Age Group

Player	Age	2021 Season			Career		
		Win Shares	WAR	HoF Value	Win Shares	WAR	HoF Value
Soto, Juan	**22**	**31**	**7.0**	**59.2**	**84**	**17.5**	**153.9**
Tatis Jr., Fernando	22	28	6.6	54.5	58	13.6	112.3
Guerrero Jr., Vladimir	22	28	6.8	55.2	44	9.4	81.8
Acuna Jr., Ronald	**23**	**14**	**3.6**	**28.3**	**70**	**14.9**	**129.4**
Bichette, Bo	23	24	6.0	47.9	36	9.4	73.5
Albies, Ozzie	**24**	**25**	**3.5**	**39.1**	**85**	**14.5**	**143.2**
Devers, Rafael	24	25	3.5	39.0	71	10.7	114.0
Torres, Gleyber	24	14	0.8	17.0	64	7.4	93.4
Urias, Julio	24	16	4.7	34.8	34	8.0	66.2
Tucker, Kyle	24	22	5.7	44.8	35	7.6	65.3
Alvarez, Yordan	24	18	3.2	30.6	32	7.0	59.9
Arraez, Luis	24	15	3.4	28.6	36	5.9	59.8
Riley, Austin	24	23	6.1	47.4	33	5.5	55.1
Bellinger, Cody	**25**	**3**	**-1.5**	**-3.2**	**85**	**16.7**	**151.7**
Adames, Willy	25	22	4.2	38.7	54	11.1	98.4
Rosario, Amed	25	20	2.1	28.5	56	5.7	78.9
Flaherty, Jack	25	6	1.0	9.9	34	8.8	69.0
Keller, Brad	25	4	-0.3	3.0	30	8.2	62.8
Verdugo, Alex	25	16	2.2	24.6	33	7.3	62.0
Alcantara, Sandy	25	12	3.9	27.5	28	7.9	59.5
Reyes, Franmil	25	13	1.6	19.3	38	3.7	52.9
Correa, Carlos	**26**	**23**	**7.2**	**51.8**	**124**	**34.1**	**260.3**
Ohtani, Shohei	26	38	9.0	74.2	71	15.1	131.3
Marquez, German	26	13	3.3	26.2	60	17.1	128.2
Benintendi, Andrew	26	16	2.4	25.6	78	12.5	128.0
Moncada, Yoan	26	22	4.0	38.1	70	12.6	120.2
Lowe, Brandon	26	30	4.8	49.1	61	10.9	104.7
Buehler, Walker	26	18	6.7	44.9	43	12.5	93.1
Reynolds, Bryan	26	28	6.0	51.9	50	10.6	92.4
Bieber, Shane	26	8	2.6	18.4	45	11.4	90.7
Margot, Manuel	26	13	2.8	24.3	50	10.1	90.3
Alonso, Pete	26	20	4.3	37.0	49	9.9	88.5
Crawford, J.P.	26	26	3.8	41.1	51	7.9	82.6
Laureano, Ramon	26	11	2.5	21.2	44	9.6	82.3
Giolito, Lucas	26	13	4.4	30.5	38	11.1	82.2
Happ, Ian	26	16	1.6	22.4	56	6.5	82.0
Meadows, Austin	26	22	2.0	30.0	52	6.0	75.9
Smith, Will	26	18	3.5	31.9	35	6.6	73.6
Edman, Tommy	26	20	3.7	34.7	37	8.8	72.3
ONeill, Tyler'	26	22	6.3	47.1	34	8.6	68.4
Mazara, Nomar	26	3	-0.3	1.7	58	1.0	62.0
Kiner-Falefa, Isiah	26	16	4.0	31.8	28	7.5	60.0
France, Ty	26	28	4.2	44.9	40	4.9	59.5
McMahon, Ryan	26	14	3.9	29.5	33	6.4	58.6
Senzatela, Antonio	26	8	1.3	13.3	31	6.3	56.1
Arcia, Orlando	26	2	-0.3	1.0	46	2.2	54.9
Burnes, Corbin	26	16	5.7	38.7	28	6.3	53.2
Biggio, Cavan	26	5	0.4	6.4	29	5.4	50.4
Lindor, Francisco	**27**	**20**	**3.1**	**32.4**	**137**	**31.1**	**261.6**
Bregman, Alex	27	11	2.1	19.4	117	26.1	221.4
Seager, Corey	27	21	3.7	35.8	120	21.3	205.4
Marte, Ketel	27	14	1.8	21.2	86	18.0	158.0
Olson, Matt	27	26	5.8	49.1	83	18.1	155.4
Polanco, Jorge	27	29	4.8	48.2	96	12.4	145.7
Gallo, Joey	27	19	4.6	37.5	67	14.4	124.6
Odor, Rougned	27	9	0.4	10.6	91	6.9	118.5
Buxton, Byron	27	14	4.5	32.1	52	16.2	116.8
DeJong, Paul	27	9	1.6	15.5	64	12.9	115.6
Swanson, Dansby	27	17	2.1	25.4	71	9.0	107.2
Hader, Josh	27	16	3.3	29.4	56	10.4	97.6
Berrios, Jose	27	13	3.2	25.8	52	10.8	95.1
Fletcher, David	27	17	1.9	24.7	50	9.5	87.9
Severino, Luis	27	1	0.3	2.3	40	11.9	87.6
Bader, Harrison	27	15	3.9	30.6	43	10.6	85.4
Fried, Max	27	15	5.4	36.4	35	12.3	84.1
Diaz, Edwin	27	10	1.0	13.9	53	7.5	82.9
McCullers Jr., Lance	27	13	3.5	26.9	41	10.1	81.4

Hall of Fame Values by Age Group

Player	Age	2021 Season			Career		
		Win Shares	WAR	HoF Value	Win Shares	WAR	HoF Value
Candelario, Jeimer	27	22	3.7	36.7	50	6.7	76.8
Winker, Jesse	27	18	2.7	29.0	46	5.4	67.4
Gurriel Jr., Lourdes	27	16	2.8	27.4	42	5.9	65.5
Cronenworth, Jake	27	22	4.8	41.4	29	6.5	55.0
Harper, Bryce	**28**	**31**	**5.9**	**54.5**	**219**	**40.1**	**379.6**
Betts, Mookie	28	18	4.2	34.6	178	50.0	377.9
Machado, Manny	28	27	5.1	47.2	197	45.2	377.8
Ramirez, Jose	28	29	6.7	55.8	148	34.3	285.0
Bogaerts, Xander	28	25	4.9	44.5	148	29.1	264.6
Turner, Trea	28	26	6.5	51.9	117	24.7	216.0
Story, Trevor	28	16	4.2	32.9	97	26.7	204.0
Baez, Javier	28	20	4.5	38.2	98	23.4	191.8
Chapman, Matt	28	14	3.5	28.0	80	23.1	172.5
Nola, Aaron	28	8	2.7	18.8	67	24.3	164.0
Conforto, Michael	28	12	0.9	15.4	95	15.7	157.8
Anderson, Tim	28	23	4.6	41.4	79	16.8	146.0
Sanchez, Gary	28	11	0.7	13.7	63	11.7	131.5
Kepler, Max	28	11	2.1	19.3	69	14.8	128.3
Rodriguez, Eduardo	28	9	1.8	16.2	54	15.4	115.4
Schwarber, Kyle	28	19	3.2	31.6	78	9.0	114.9
Syndergaard, Noah	28	0	-0.1	-0.4	49	15.9	112.4
Sano, Miguel	28	9	0.9	12.7	75	8.4	108.6
Nimmo, Brandon	28	15	3.5	29.2	59	12.1	107.4
Freeland, Kyle	28	8	2.4	17.4	45	15.0	104.9
Hoskins, Rhys	28	13	2.0	21.2	69	8.3	102.4
Castillo, Luis	28	11	4.8	30.2	45	14.2	102.0
Snell, Blake	28	6	1.3	11.1	49	12.5	99.1
Anderson, Brian	28	8	1.3	13.3	62	9.1	98.2
Bell, Josh	28	12	3.1	24.4	72	6.0	96.1
Hernandez, Teoscar	28	22	4.0	37.8	57	8.1	89.4
Rodon, Carlos	28	14	5.0	34.1	41	11.5	87.2
Woodruff, Brandon	28	15	5.7	37.6	37	12.2	86.0
Fulmer, Michael	28	9	1.9	16.6	37	10.7	79.7
Davies, Zach	28	2	-0.9	-1.8	43	8.7	78.0
Sanchez, Aaron	28	2	0.6	4.5	38	9.5	76.1
Franco, Maikel	28	1	-1.5	-4.9	66	1.8	73.3
DeShields, Delino	28	1	0.2	1.7	48	5.1	68.2
Bundy, Dylan	28	1	-0.3	-0.2	33	8.6	67.2
Bradley, Archie	28	5	0.7	7.8	43	6.0	66.8
Walker, Taijuan	28	5	0.4	6.8	36	7.5	66.0
Musgrove, Joe	28	12	3.5	26.0	33	8.0	64.9
Profar, Jurickson	28	5	0.0	5.1	49	3.2	61.6
Means, John	28	10	4.0	26.0	22	9.8	61.3
Alfaro, Jorge	28	5	-0.4	3.4	36	2.2	53.2
Trout, Mike	**29**	**10**	**1.8**	**17.3**	**319**	**76.1**	**623.4**
Yelich, Christian	29	15	1.3	20.2	175	33.5	309.1
Bryant, Kris	29	19	3.3	32.1	148	28.7	263.0
Judge, Aaron	29	31	5.9	54.7	99	26.3	204.0
Schoop, Jonathan	29	19	2.1	27.3	101	20.1	181.3
Castellanos, Nick	29	20	3.3	33.0	124	12.3	173.3
Contreras, Willson	29	15	4.1	31.3	77	16.9	170.9
Suarez, Eugenio	29	8	-0.7	5.2	107	14.1	163.2
Rosario, Eddie	29	11	1.1	15.2	84	12.9	135.8
Hernandez, Kike	29	17	4.8	36.4	71	15.8	134.2
Herrera, Odubel	29	11	1.8	18.2	78	13.2	130.9
Pederson, Joc	29	11	0.0	11.2	83	10.3	124.0
Ray, Robbie	29	17	6.7	43.6	63	15.1	123.5
Martinez, Carlos	29	0	-1.4	-5.7	66	13.3	119.0
Grichuk, Randal	29	10	0.8	13.1	72	10.9	115.7
Frazier, Adam	29	21	4.0	36.8	69	11.4	114.7
Flores, Wilmer	29	12	1.6	18.3	78	6.2	102.7
Narvaez, Omar	29	15	1.5	20.8	53	6.8	95.9
McNeil, Jeff	29	6	1.5	12.0	47	11.3	92.3
Gray, Jon	29	8	1.3	13.3	48	11.1	92.3
Manaea, Sean	29	11	3.4	24.5	41	12.2	89.9
Polanco, Gregory	29	4	-1.3	-1.2	70	3.9	85.7
Mancini, Trey	29	10	0.8	13.1	53	8.1	85.2
Renfroe, Hunter	29	14	2.3	23.4	50	8.1	82.5
Gonzales, Marco	29	9	2.2	17.8	38	9.9	77.5
Taillon, Jameson	29	8	2.2	16.8	35	10.4	76.8
Wacha, Michael	29	2	-0.7	-0.8	47	6.8	74.4
Soler, Jorge	29	10	-0.4	8.4	59	3.5	72.8
Urshela, Gio	29	13	0.5	15.1	46	5.1	66.4

Hall of Fame Values by Age Group

Player	Age	2021 Season			Career		
		Win Shares	WAR	HoF Value	Win Shares	WAR	HoF Value
Lorenzen, Michael	29	3	0.0	2.9	37	6.0	61.2
Owings, Chris	29	3	0.6	5.5	45	2.9	56.4
Knebel, Corey	29	4	0.7	6.8	35	5.0	55.2
Diaz, Yandy	29	17	1.6	23.5	35	4.7	53.8
Claudio, Alex	29	1	-0.1	0.5	30	5.9	53.7
Kemp, Tony	29	18	3.5	31.9	37	3.5	51.1
Arenado, Nolan	**30**	**23**	**4.2**	**39.6**	**176**	**44.3**	**353.1**
Realmuto, J.T.	30	22	3.4	35.6	124	23.2	257.6
Semien, Marcus	30	24	7.1	52.5	140	28.6	254.4
Cole, Gerrit	30	16	5.6	38.6	109	31.6	235.6
Ozuna, Marcell	30	4	-0.2	3.3	131	20.9	214.6
Wong, Kolten	30	18	3.3	31.1	114	19.7	193.0
Bauer, Trevor	30	9	2.8	20.1	84	20.5	166.1
Inciarte, Ender	30	2	-0.1	1.6	88	17.9	159.6
Myers, Wil	30	13	0.8	16.4	110	12.4	159.4
Teheran, Julio	30	1	0.2	1.9	76	19.7	154.7
Taylor, Chris	30	20	2.7	30.8	89	15.2	150.0
Villar, Jonathan	30	12	1.8	19.0	92	13.4	145.5
Stroman, Marcus	30	12	3.6	26.4	66	18.4	139.7
Muncy, Max	30	27	4.9	46.8	78	14.6	136.4
Garcia, Avisail	30	17	2.9	28.6	92	10.9	135.6
Zunino, Mike	30	14	3.7	29.0	68	10.6	132.6
Haniger, Mitch	30	27	2.8	38.4	77	13.8	132.2
Gausman, Kevin	30	16	5.3	37.4	63	16.8	130.3
Barnhart, Tucker	30	11	0.2	11.8	65	7.1	111.4
Wood, Alex	30	8	1.3	13.1	56	12.7	106.8
Piscotty, Stephen	30	4	-0.6	1.4	76	7.2	104.9
Panik, Joe	30	4	-1.5	-2.0	79	5.4	100.6
Duffy, Matt	30	9	1.5	15.2	60	9.2	97.0
Hamilton, Billy	30	1	0.3	2.4	54	10.1	94.3
Marisnick, Jake	30	4	0.2	5.0	42	11.3	87.4
Lamb, Jake	30	2	-0.3	0.9	56	7.4	85.5
Vazquez, Christian	30	9	1.0	13.1	51	4.9	84.1
Garver, Mitch	30	9	2.1	17.2	40	7.2	82.0
Diaz, Aledmys	30	8	1.6	14.3	50	7.5	80.1
Perez, Martin	30	5	0.5	7.0	47	7.2	76.0
Matz, Steven	30	11	2.0	19.0	36	9.3	73.4
Taylor, Michael A.	30	9	2.5	18.9	48	6.1	72.2
Yastrzemski, Mike	30	16	2.6	26.4	40	7.8	71.2
Green, Chad	30	11	2.3	20.4	38	8.0	70.0
Garcia, Leury	30	13	2.0	21.0	45	5.0	65.2
Miller, Shelby	30	0	-0.3	-1.1	35	7.5	65.1
Rogers, Taylor	30	5	0.4	6.7	39	6.1	63.5
Voit, Luke	30	5	0.4	6.4	43	4.9	62.7
Boyd, Matthew	30	4	1.4	9.6	31	7.7	61.6
Graveman, Kendall	30	11	2.1	19.6	32	7.3	61.3
Plawecki, Kevin	30	5	0.2	5.8	32	3.5	54.8
Naquin, Tyler	30	12	0.7	14.7	40	3.4	53.5
Choi, Ji-Man	30	11	1.0	15.1	36	4.1	52.5
Santana, Danny	30	2	-0.3	0.9	42	2.1	50.2
Freeman, Freddie	**31**	**27**	**4.7**	**45.7**	**270**	**43.1**	**442.4**
Altuve, Jose	31	25	4.4	42.6	225	41.4	390.4
Stanton, Giancarlo	31	20	3.1	32.2	195	44.0	371.2
Rizzo, Anthony	31	15	1.7	21.8	207	36.9	354.4
Heyward, Jason	31	4	0.4	5.5	182	39.4	339.4
Perez, Salvador	31	28	5.3	49.1	157	29.6	329.8
Rendon, Anthony	31	4	0.0	4.0	162	32.2	290.7
Bumgarner, Madison	31	5	1.7	11.7	129	38.1	281.4
Simmons, Andrelton	31	7	1.4	12.4	129	37.2	277.8
Segura, Jean	31	20	3.7	35.0	154	26.3	259.4
Springer, George	31	11	2.5	20.8	135	30.3	256.0
Hosmer, Eric	31	13	1.0	16.9	176	18.1	248.4
Castro, Starlin	31	8	1.1	12.4	166	18.2	238.6
Kiermaier, Kevin	31	10	3.4	23.6	88	30.7	210.8
Gregorius, Didi	31	5	-0.8	1.9	116	18.3	189.2
Hendricks, Kyle	31	7	0.9	10.4	82	22.3	171.1
Gray, Sonny	31	8	3.4	21.4	80	22.5	170.1
Hernandez, Cesar	31	16	0.4	17.8	120	12.4	169.7
Bradley Jr., Jackie	31	5	-0.6	2.4	85	17.8	156.0
Wheeler, Zack	31	19	7.8	50.1	61	21.3	146.2
Corbin, Patrick	31	1	-1.0	-3.0	72	17.3	141.2
Iglesias, Jose	31	10	-0.6	7.6	95	10.6	137.5
Galvis, Freddy	31	6	1.0	10.0	94	9.3	131.0

Hall of Fame Values by Age Group

Player	Age	2021 Season			Career		
		Win Shares	WAR	HoF Value	Win Shares	WAR	HoF Value
Cron, C.J.	31	18	3.4	31.5	85	10.8	128.3
Grossman, Robbie	31	22	2.8	33.4	90	9.4	127.6
Hicks, Aaron	31	1	-0.3	-0.2	71	12.3	120.1
Miller, Brad	31	11	0.4	12.5	84	8.0	115.9
Odorizzi, Jake	31	5	0.7	7.7	61	12.9	112.7
Iglesias, Raisel	31	15	2.8	26.2	66	11.4	111.6
McCann, James	31	9	-0.2	8.2	65	7.0	111.3
Ahmed, Nick	31	7	0.7	9.7	61	12.5	110.8
Eovaldi, Nathan	31	14	4.6	32.4	52	14.7	110.8
Shaw, Travis	31	4	-0.6	1.5	72	9.0	108.0
Wendle, Joey	31	14	3.8	29.0	48	11.3	93.2
Hand, Brad	31	7	-0.3	5.9	64	6.7	90.9
Chatwood, Tyler	31	1	-0.4	-0.8	47	10.8	90.2
Familia, Jeurys	31	4	0.0	4.0	58	7.5	87.8
Smith, Will	31	11	1.6	17.6	55	6.5	80.9
DeSclafani, Anthony	31	12	3.9	27.5	39	10.1	79.2
Aguilar, Jesus	31	15	1.3	20.4	59	5.0	79.0
Givens, Mychal	31	7	1.5	12.9	39	8.4	72.8
Lugo, Seth	31	4	0.8	7.1	35	8.5	68.9
Anderson, Tyler	31	7	1.6	13.5	31	8.1	63.4
Chafin, Andrew	31	10	2.9	21.7	32	6.5	58.1
Barnes, Matt	31	10	1.2	14.6	39	4.6	57.4
Stallings, Jacob	31	13	3.0	25.1	24	6.0	57.3
Barnes, Austin	31	4	0.4	5.6	28	4.3	52.5
Sale, Chris	**32**	**4**	**1.0**	**8.1**	**148**	**46.5**	**334.0**
Andrus, Elvis	32	9	0.6	11.4	212	30.4	333.7
Marte, Starling	32	21	4.7	39.9	158	34.8	297.4
LeMahieu, DJ	32	20	1.5	26.1	163	26.6	269.4
Grandal, Yasmani	32	16	3.7	30.9	137	21.7	264.6
Strasburg, Stephen	32	1	0.1	1.4	108	33.2	240.7
Eaton, Adam	32	5	-0.7	2.4	117	18.4	190.6
Quintana, Jose	32	1	-0.7	-1.9	90	23.7	184.6
Merrifield, Whit	32	21	3.5	35.0	102	17.0	170.1
Moustakas, Mike	32	2	-1.0	-2.0	114	13.9	169.5
Escobar, Eduardo	32	17	2.6	27.2	113	11.9	160.8
Duffy, Danny	32	6	2.1	14.5	71	19.8	150.4
Pillar, Kevin	32	8	0.5	10.0	81	16.5	146.9
Dickerson, Corey	32	5	0.3	6.1	88	13.7	142.9
Gonzalez, Marwin	32	4	-0.8	0.8	84	13.5	137.8
Archer, Chris	32	1	-0.1	0.6	63	13.1	115.4
Canha, Mark	32	20	2.5	30.1	75	9.9	114.6
Rojas, Miguel	32	14	2.5	24.0	65	10.3	106.1
Pineda, Michael	32	7	1.4	12.8	54	12.6	104.4
Pomeranz, Drew	32	4	0.7	7.0	54	12.6	104.3
Duvall, Adam	32	19	3.1	31.5	62	10.5	104.0
Paxton, James	32	0	0.0	-0.1	47	12.8	98.1
Lagares, Juan	32	4	-0.3	2.8	48	12.1	96.5
Perez, Roberto	32	3	-0.1	2.5	48	7.5	93.7
Colome, Alex	32	5	-0.7	2.4	64	6.9	91.4
dArnaud, Travis'	32	3	0.2	3.7	58	4.3	89.9
Smyly, Drew	32	6	0.4	7.7	46	10.1	86.6
Pressly, Ryan	32	13	1.9	20.8	50	8.8	85.4
Adams, Matt	32	0	-0.3	-1.0	65	4.9	84.6
Hendriks, Liam	32	16	2.6	26.5	53	7.5	83.0
Neris, Hector	32	8	1.2	12.8	50	7.5	80.0
Harvey, Matt	32	2	-0.7	-0.8	42	9.1	78.2
Bassitt, Chris	32	13	3.9	28.7	37	10.0	76.8
La Stella, Tommy	32	7	0.4	8.5	45	4.5	62.8
Souza Jr., Steven	32	0	-0.2	-0.6	41	5.4	62.7
Casali, Curt	32	6	0.6	8.6	29	5.1	58.9
Leon, Sandy	32	3	-0.8	-0.3	38	1.6	53.0
Moore, Matt	32	0	-0.8	-3.3	36	4.3	53.0
Peralta, Wily	32	6	2.0	14.1	38	3.4	51.5
Kershaw, Clayton	**33**	**8**	**2.3**	**17.4**	**215**	**71.9**	**502.6**
Goldschmidt, Paul	33	28	6.2	52.6	251	50.7	453.7
Seager, Kyle	33	25	2.0	33.2	205	37.0	352.8
Upton, Justin	33	5	-0.7	2.1	211	32.7	341.8
deGrom, Jacob	33	13	5.0	32.9	108	43.4	281.7
Martinez, J.D.	33	19	3.0	30.8	173	26.8	280.3
Belt, Brandon	33	17	2.7	27.6	160	27.2	269.0
Kimbrel, Craig	33	10	2.5	19.9	136	21.9	223.6
Jansen, Kenley	33	14	2.3	23.1	140	18.6	214.3
Ramos, Wilson	33	2	-0.4	0.4	115	15.2	211.0

Hall of Fame Values by Age Group

Player	Age	2021 Season			Career		
		Win Shares	WAR	HoF Value	Win Shares	WAR	HoF Value
Pollock, A.J.	33	18	3.1	30.2	115	22.8	206.0
Chapman, Aroldis	33	10	1.5	16.1	123	19.2	199.9
Gomes, Yan	33	9	2.4	18.8	83	16.9	179.4
Keuchel, Dallas	33	4	0.1	4.2	89	22.2	177.6
Calhoun, Kole	33	1	-0.1	0.6	115	15.6	177.2
Harrison, Josh	33	14	2.0	21.8	105	16.0	169.2
Chacin, Jhoulys	33	6	0.6	8.3	78	20.6	160.2
Peralta, David	33	11	1.0	15.0	98	14.3	155.3
Minor, Mike	33	6	1.0	10.2	72	18.7	146.8
Pham, Tommy	33	9	1.4	14.6	77	16.0	141.2
Britton, Zack	33	0	-0.4	-1.6	85	14.0	141.2
Davis, Khris	33	1	-0.3	-0.4	96	10.7	138.7
Cobb, Alex	33	7	1.7	13.9	59	14.4	116.4
Gibson, Kyle	33	11	3.7	25.6	64	13.0	116.0
Cahill, Trevor	33	0	-0.5	-2.0	68	11.2	112.8
Betances, Dellin	33	0	0.0	-0.1	58	11.2	102.9
Treinen, Blake	33	12	2.3	21.4	59	10.3	100.1
Anderson, Brett	33	3	-0.1	2.5	56	10.3	97.1
Holt, Brock	33	4	0.1	4.3	62	8.2	94.6
Richards, Garrett	33	6	0.3	7.2	51	8.5	85.1
Santiago, Hector	33	2	0.4	3.6	48	9.0	83.9
Feliz, Neftali	33	0	-0.4	-1.5	53	7.3	82.3
Shaw, Bryan	33	6	1.2	10.9	54	5.8	77.1
Anderson, Chase	33	0	-0.5	-1.9	46	7.5	76.2
Wilson, Justin	33	2	0.0	1.9	46	7.3	75.4
Kelly, Joe	33	5	0.7	7.8	48	6.5	74.2
Maeda, Kenta	33	4	0.4	5.6	44	7.4	73.5
Solano, Donovan	33	10	1.1	14.6	56	4.0	72.0
Loup, Aaron	33	9	2.8	20.1	36	7.6	66.6
Boxberger, Brad	33	8	1.1	12.5	39	3.1	51.3
Posey, Buster	**34**	**20**	**3.5**	**34.0**	**243**	**44.9**	**492.4**
McCutchen, Andrew	34	16	1.4	21.5	299	46.0	483.0
Brantley, Michael	34	13	2.5	22.9	180	32.9	311.6
Crawford, Brandon	34	31	6.1	55.3	173	30.1	293.4
Abreu, Jose	34	19	3.0	31.0	166	27.7	276.8
Bruce, Jay	34	0	-0.3	-1.4	168	19.9	247.7
Blackmon, Charlie	34	16	0.9	19.6	169	19.4	246.5
Reddick, Josh	34	3	-0.4	1.3	130	24.7	228.9
Sandoval, Pablo	34	1	-0.2	0.1	149	18.9	225.3
Lynn, Lance	34	15	5.4	36.7	105	29.4	222.7
Avila, Alex	34	2	0.7	4.9	105	17.0	205.9
Darvish, Yu	34	6	1.3	11.2	87	26.4	192.6
Carrasco, Carlos	34	0	-0.9	-3.6	88	20.4	169.8
Escobar, Alcides	34	11	1.5	17.0	125	10.4	166.8
Castro, Jason	34	6	1.0	10.1	85	13.0	164.4
Maybin, Cameron	34	0	-0.3	-1.3	107	13.5	161.0
Parra, Gerardo	34	1	-0.5	-0.8	109	10.8	152.3
Miley, Wade	34	14	6.0	37.9	81	16.6	147.4
Ryu, Hyun-Jin	34	10	1.7	16.6	69	19.4	146.6
Roark, Tanner	34	0	-0.3	-1.1	66	18.6	140.4
Maldonado, Martin	34	8	-0.1	7.8	69	7.2	117.0
Hunter, Tommy	34	2	0.5	3.8	69	11.1	113.3
Doolittle, Sean	34	3	0.7	5.7	65	9.9	104.5
McHugh, Collin	34	8	1.9	15.5	59	10.7	101.8
Mercer, Jordy	34	1	0.2	1.8	73	6.9	100.4
McGee, Jake	34	12	0.9	15.8	65	8.3	98.0
Holland, Derek	34	2	0.1	2.3	62	8.1	94.5
Hudson, Daniel	34	5	0.8	8.0	56	6.6	82.6
Pina, Manny	34	7	1.3	12.2	36	6.5	74.1
Ramos, AJ	34	1	0.2	2.0	45	6.5	71.0
Phelps, David	34	2	0.4	3.7	40	6.2	64.8
Shoemaker, Matt	34	0	-1.8	-7.3	35	6.1	59.4
Vincent, Nick	34	2	0.5	4.1	34	6.0	58.1
Milone, Tommy	34	0	-0.2	-0.7	37	4.5	54.9
Diekman, Jake	34	5	0.4	6.4	37	4.0	52.8
Longoria, Evan	**35**	**9**	**1.8**	**16.1**	**242**	**57.4**	**471.6**
Donaldson, Josh	35	17	3.2	29.7	204	44.4	382.1
Santana, Carlos	35	8	-0.1	7.4	204	31.6	346.0
Cabrera, Asdrubal	35	6	0.4	7.7	212	29.7	330.7
Price, David	35	4	0.7	6.8	148	40.3	309.0
Cain, Lorenzo	35	9	2.2	18.0	154	38.7	308.7
Carpenter, Matt	35	4	-1.0	0.0	188	26.9	295.4
Cueto, Johnny	35	5	0.8	8.2	133	32.9	264.6

Hall of Fame Values by Age Group

Player	Age	2021 Season			Career		
		Win Shares	WAR	HoF Value	Win Shares	WAR	HoF Value
Lucroy, Jonathan	35	1	0.1	1.3	138	17.7	248.7
Kluber, Corey	35	5	1.4	10.6	114	33.6	248.4
Fowler, Dexter	35	0	-0.2	-0.7	170	19.4	247.4
Frazier, Todd	35	0	-0.4	-1.6	125	25.2	225.8
Arrieta, Jake	35	0	-2.6	-10.3	95	23.3	188.2
Zimmermann, Jordan	35	0	-0.1	-0.4	84	21.1	168.3
Moreland, Mitch	35	4	0.0	4.1	103	10.9	146.6
Holland, Greg	35	5	0.1	5.3	91	12.7	141.8
Cishek, Steve	35	5	1.2	9.7	85	13.3	138.2
Davis, Wade	35	0	-0.6	-2.3	94	10.5	136.0
Ottavino, Adam	35	8	0.8	11.3	61	11.5	107.2
Sogard, Eric	35	3	-0.7	0.2	57	6.8	84.3
Brach, Brad	35	0	-0.6	-2.6	47	5.8	70.1
Jones, Nate	35	0	-0.3	-1.3	30	5.8	53.2
Swarzak, Anthony	35	0	-0.3	-1.4	32	4.9	51.5
Scherzer, Max	36	16	5.3	37.2	205	67.2	473.7
Zimmerman, Ryan	36	3	1.2	7.8	211	40.1	371.2
Turner, Justin	36	21	3.7	35.8	175	32.7	305.6
Kennedy, Ian	36	9	1.4	14.6	99	18.1	171.4
Joyce, Matt	36	0	-0.5	-1.9	110	14.6	168.6
Jay, Jon	36	0	0.1	0.2	111	12.7	161.8
Clippard, Tyler	36	2	0.6	4.5	97	16.2	161.6
Melancon, Mark	36	12	2.1	20.3	105	13.9	160.6
Robertson, David	36	0	-0.1	-0.4	96	15.7	158.8
Dyson, Jarrod	36	1	0.1	1.6	70	15.3	131.2
Watson, Tony	36	6	0.8	9.1	76	12.7	126.6
Fiers, Mike	36	0	-0.3	-1.0	61	11.5	107.2
Vogt, Stephen	36	3	0.0	2.8	60	7.7	105.6
Miller, Andrew	36	1	-0.2	0.4	74	7.6	104.3
Strop, Pedro	36	0	0.1	0.4	60	9.0	96.1
Petit, Yusmeiro	36	7	0.8	10.4	56	8.2	88.7
Harris, Will	36	0	-0.2	-0.7	47	7.8	78.2
Kintzler, Brandon	36	0	-0.3	-1.2	47	7.2	76.0
Tomlin, Josh	36	1	-0.7	-1.6	46	5.3	67.0
LeBlanc, Wade	36	2	0.1	2.4	39	5.6	61.6
Bard, Daniel	36	7	-0.2	6.3	34	4.8	53.1
Parker, Blake	36	4	0.9	7.7	32	5.0	51.8
Votto, Joey	37	21	3.3	34.3	333	64.4	590.7
Greinke, Zack	37	9	1.2	13.8	236	73.1	528.4
Gardner, Brett	37	11	1.0	15.0	189	44.3	366.3
Lester, Jon	37	5	-0.3	3.7	182	44.3	359.2
Suzuki, Kurt	37	3	-0.4	1.2	142	19.9	266.1
Lowrie, Jed	37	16	0.1	16.4	147	17.0	214.9
Soria, Joakim	37	2	0.0	2.0	111	18.6	185.5
Kazmir, Scott	37	0	-0.2	-1.0	88	22.4	177.5
Gurriel, Yuli	37	19	3.7	33.9	80	13.8	135.2
Smith, Joe	37	2	0.2	2.9	78	13.6	132.2
Chirinos, Robinson	37	3	0.2	3.6	59	12.7	131.3
Morton, Charlie	37	13	4.0	29.1	81	11.9	128.8
Stammen, Craig	37	7	1.5	13.0	63	9.8	102.3
Rivera, Rene	37	2	-0.1	1.5	46	2.4	66.2
Chavez, Jesse	37	4	1.1	8.4	47	4.3	64.3
Cabrera, Miguel	38	9	-0.5	6.9	420	68.7	695.0
Molina, Yadier	38	16	1.8	23.1	297	42.1	556.6
Santana, Ervin	38	3	0.5	5.1	137	27.1	245.4
Happ, J.A.	38	3	-1.5	-3.0	103	21.3	188.0
ODay, Darren'	38	1	0.3	2.1	74	17.4	143.4
Romo, Sergio	38	3	0.1	3.3	90	10.4	131.8
Axford, John	38	0	-0.1	-0.4	55	4.1	71.4
Mathis, Jeff	38	0	-0.2	-0.9	45	0.4	55.7
Wainwright, Adam	39	16	3.7	30.8	172	44.5	350.1
Perez, Oliver	39	0	0.2	0.6	72	11.3	117.2
Cruz, Nelson	40	16	2.5	26.0	259	42.4	428.6
Pujols, Albert	41	6	-0.6	3.5	494	99.5	892.2
Hill, Rich	41	7	1.3	12.2	74	15.7	136.6

Potential Players on 2022 Hall of Fame Ballot

Player	Win Shares	WAR	HOF Value	HOF Monitor
Bonds, Barry	704	162.8	1355.0	267
Clemens, Roger	437	139.2	993.9	283
Rodriguez, Alex	491	117.5	961.1	283
Ramirez, Manny	408	69.3	685.3	169
Sheffield, Gary	430	60.5	672.2	103
Abreu, Bobby	356	60.2	596.7	76
Rolen, Scott	304	70.1	584.4	82
Schilling, Curt	252	79.5	570.0	122
Helton, Todd	318	61.8	565.1	128
Kent, Jeff	339	55.4	560.7	94
Sosa, Sammy	321	58.6	555.4	134
Ortiz, David	316	55.3	537.2	155
Jones, Andruw	276	62.7	526.8	57
Rollins, Jimmy	303	47.6	493.4	89
Hunter, Torii	277	50.6	479.6	42
Teixeira, Mark	266	50.6	468.5	97
Pettitte, Andy	224	60.2	464.9	104
Vizquel, Omar	282	45.6	464.4	72
Buehrle, Mark	220	59.1	456.3	76
Hudson, Tim	219	57.9	450.5	67
Crawford, Carl	204	39.1	360.4	56
Pierzynski, A.J.	203	23.7	357.6	33
Fielder, Prince	234	23.8	329.3	75
Peavy, Jake	144	39.2	300.9	64
Crisp, Coco	182	28.9	297.5	18
Wagner, Billy	182	27.7	292.8	81
Morneau, Justin	176	26.9	283.8	39
Nathan, Joe	165	26.7	271.8	82
Howard, Ryan	204	14.7	262.8	84
Uribe, Juan	170	22.6	260.6	18
Byrd, Marlon	157	25.8	260.0	16
Papelbon, Jonathan	143	23.3	236.2	59
Bourn, Michael	141	22.8	232.2	24
Pagan, Angel	137	18.0	208.9	15
Infante, Omar	131	16.9	198.6	14
Lohse, Kyle	117	18.9	192.4	32
Butler, Billy	134	11.9	181.7	28
Lincecum, Tim	95	19.6	173.2	73
Francoeur, Jeff	102	6.8	129.0	13
Thornton, Matt	72	13.4	125.8	18
Lewis, Colby	55	9.0	91.1	21
Lopez, Javier	49	8.0	81.1	26
Vogelsong, Ryan	37	1.2	41.9	14

In Memoriam – Hank Aaron

Hank Aaron, one of the greatest legends that baseball has ever had, leaves behind an incredible legacy.

Aaron's baseball career is defined by length and excellence. He played 23 seasons from 1954 to 1976 (21 with the Braves) and was selected to an All-Star team in 21 of them. He ranks second in both home runs and at-bats and third in games played. He's the all-time leader in RBI, extra-base hits, and total bases. He ranked in the top 10 in the former 16 times and in the latter 15 times. He led the NL in total bases in eight different seasons.

Aaron ranks fourth in Bill James' Runs Created stat behind Barry Bonds, Babe Ruth, and Stan Musial. We should also not forget that he was a well-regarded defensive player who won three Gold Glove Awards.

Though Aaron won only one MVP, he received at least one MVP vote in every season from 1955 to 1973 and ranked in the top 10 in voting 13 times. Aaron's MVP came in 1957, the year in which his Braves won the World Series. One of Aaron's most famous home runs was a walk-off shot that clinched the NL pennant that year. He was elected to the Baseball Hall of Fame in 1982.

When Aaron broke Babe Ruth's home run record in 1974, he did so in the face of immense pressure and racism. He regularly received letters with death threats but remained outwardly poised and composed whenever he took the field. On April 8, he homered against Dodgers pitcher Al Downing in Atlanta for No. 715, the record-breaker. He finished his career in 1976 after two seasons with the Brewers, which allowed him to start and finish his career in Milwaukee. After retirement, the record was later broken by Barry Bonds.

Though Aaron would go on to be critical of PED usage in baseball, at the time of Bonds' record-breaking moment, he said that he hoped the achievement would "inspire others to chase their own dreams."

Aaron carried himself in the best way both during and after his baseball career, and his value as an ambassador for the sport is immeasurable.

He was not one to promote himself, but rather to let his actions do the talking. His legacy will be that of humble greatness in every aspect of his life.

Hank Aaron – Career Ranks

		Rank
Games	3,298	3rd
Hits	3,771	3rd
Runs	2,174	4th
HR	755	2nd
RBI	2,297	1st
Total Bases	6,856	1st
Extra-Base Hits	1,477	1st

Hank Aaron died on January 22, 2021 at age 86.

In Memoriam – Phil Niekro

It's one thing to be a great pitcher with an overpowering fastball. It's quite another to be one with a fluttering knuckleball.

Phil Niekro got 24 seasons and 318 wins almost entirely out of one pitch, which earned him the nickname "Knucksie." He then passed the lessons he learned to others who enjoyed success, though not quite to the level that Phil (and his brother Joe) did.

Niekro ranks in the top 5 in games started (716, 5th) and innings pitched (5,404, 4th) and ranks 16th with 318 wins. He also made five All-Star teams and won five Gold Glove Awards.

Niekro threw more than 300 innings four times, peaking in 1979 when he threw 342 and completed 23 of his 44 starts. That was at age 40 for a last-place Braves team, on which he went 21-20.

The lack of arm issues allowed Niekro to pitch longer than most and to chase the 300-win mark. He got to 300 by winning 16 games with the Yankees in consecutive seasons, in 1984 at age 45 and in 1985 at age 46. His 300th win came on the final day of the regular season in a game in which he didn't throw any knuckleballs until the final batter.

Phil's brother, Joe won 221 games in a 22-year career of his own. Their 539 combined wins is an MLB record for MLB siblings.

Niekro was elected to the Baseball Hall of Fame in 1997.

Niekro had a reputation for kindness. He taught the finer points of throwing the knuckleball to almost anyone who would ask. Anyone who throws the pitch in the future will likely do so with lessons passed down from the Hall-of-Famer.

Phil Niekro died on December 27, 2020 at age 81.

In Memoriam – Tommy Lasorda

Back in my ESPN days, I got to meet Tommy Lasorda.

Tommy's first question for the person who introduced me was "Does he love the game?"

There was no doubt that Tommy Lasorda loved baseball, a sport to which he devoted the entirety of his adult life. As it says on his Hall of Fame plaque, he had an "impenetrable passion" for the game.

Though his major league pitching career spanned only 58 1/3 innings, he pitched more than 2,000 innings in the minor leagues. He became a Dodgers scout in 1961, a minor league manager in 1965, a Dodgers coach in 1973, and then Dodgers manager at the end of the 1976 season when Hall-of-Famer Walter Alston retired.

Lasorda's Dodgers won the NL West and LCS in 1977 and 1978 but lost to the Yankees in six games in the World Series in both years. In 1980, the Dodgers overcame a three-game deficit with three games to play but lost to the Astros in a one-game playoff.

Lasorda's 1981 Dodgers won the World Series, though it wasn't easy. The Dodgers overcame a 2-0 deficit to win a best-of-five LDS against the Astros, a 2-1 deficit to win the LCS against the Expos, and a 2-0 hole in the World Series to win four straight and beat the Yankees.

In 1988, the Dodgers faced a powerful Athletics team in the World Series. After Kirk Gibson's dramatic walk-off home run in Game 1, the Dodgers never looked back, winning Lasorda's second title.

Lasorda finished his managerial career in 1996 with 1,599 wins. He was inducted into the Baseball Hall of Fame in 1997.

Tommy Lasorda died on January 7, 2021 at age 93.

In Memoriam – Don Sutton

Don Sutton's career takes on a little bit of a different look when you consider that he made 756 starts over 23 seasons. That ranks third all-time. The active leader in career starts, Zack Greinke, hasn't even reached 500.

Sutton's MLB time was both good and long lasting. He pitched 23 seasons for the Dodgers, Angels, Brewers, Astros, and Athletics, and was more solid than dominant. He ranks in the top 15 in wins (324, 14th), shutouts (58, 10th), strikeouts (3,574, 7th) and innings pitched (5,282 1/3, 7th).

Sutton's second-best season by ERA+ came in 1980 when he was 35 years old. In 1982, he was traded to the Brewers late in the season and helped them win the AL East against the Orioles. Sutton won the clinching game on the final day of the regular season, beating Hall-of-Famer Jim Palmer.

Three years later, Sutton was traded to the Angels, and in 1986, Sutton won his 300th career game and helped them win the AL West.

Sutton led his league in ERA once (with the Dodgers in 1980) but led it in WHIP four times. He ranked in the top five in that stat 10 times and in the top five in strikeout-to-walk ratio 11 times.

It took Sutton a little while to get his career going. In his first five seasons, from 1966 to 1970, he posted a 3.45 ERA. But in 1971, he went 17-12 with a 2.54 ERA, starting a run of success that established him as a premier pitcher. In 1974, Sutton closed a 19-9 season by going 13-1 with a 2.17 ERA in his last 17 starts—his best run as a pitcher.

Sutton had a long post-playing career as a broadcaster, most notably for the Braves from 1990 to 2006. He was elected to the Baseball Hall of Fame in 1998 in his fifth year on the ballot. His plaque refers to him as a "stalwart," an apt description given his consistency and longevity.

Don Sutton died on January 18, 2021 at age 75.

In Memoriam

Other notable people who passed away in 2021 include hard-throwing pitcher **J.R. Richard**, whose promising career was derailed by a stroke in 1980. Richard won at least 18 games four times and struck out 300 in a season twice. **Bill Freehan**, an 11-time All-Star who hit 200 home runs as a catcher for the Tigers from 1961 to 1976; **Mike Marshall**, who set the MLB record with 106 games pitched in 1974 and in retirement became a private pitching instructor who was oft-critical of MLB coaching methods; **Eddie Robinson**, who was in the sport as a player, scout and executive for 65 years and at age 100 was the oldest living major leaguer at the time of his death in October. **Dr. Bobby Brown**, a four-time World Series winning infielder with the Yankees who later became a doctor and then president of the American League from 1984 to 1994; **Rennie Stennett**, a member of the World Series-winning 1971 and 1979 Pirates who in 1975 became the only player in the 20th century to go 7-for-7 in a nine-inning game; **Jim "Mudcat" Grant**, who won 145 games in a career spanning from 1958 to 1971. Grant worked post-retirement to increase the number of black players in the sport. **Dick Tidrow**, who pitched 13 seasons in the major leagues then oversaw a Giants farm system that produced Buster Posey, Tim Lincecum and Madison Bumgarner and won three World Series in a five-year span. **Ray Fosse**, who caught for 13 years and was best known for being run over by Pete Rose in an All-Star Game. Of greater note, he won two World Series titles with the Athletics and a pair of Gold Glove Awards before becoming a beloved A's broadcaster. **Joe Altobelli**, who won a World Series as manager of the 1983 Orioles; Catcher **Del Crandall**, who won four Gold Gloves in a 16-year career and won a World Series with the 1957 Braves; **Grant Jackson**, who pitched 18 seasons in the major leagues and won a World Series with the 1979 Pirates. **Mike Bell**, the bench coach for the Twins and brother of Reds manager David Bell, who also worked in the front office in a number of roles for the Diamondbacks.

--All In Memoriams written by Mark Simon

Rookie Roundup

Mark Simon

They call it the Rookie of the Year Award, but two of the rookies who put up the most impressive numbers would be better qualified for Rookie of the Part-Year.

Baseball's top prospect, **Wander Franco**, lived up to the billing in the 70 regular season games he played for the Rays. He tied the MLB record for consecutive games reaching base by a player aged 20 or younger (43, previously set by Hall-of-Famer Frank Robinson). He ranked in the top 10 among shortstops with six Defensive Runs Saved.

Franco's 3.5 Wins Above Replacement (per Baseball-Reference) was the fourth-highest total by a rookie position player this season. The three players ahead of him (whom we'll get to) all played in more than twice as many games as he did.

The other amazing part-year rookie was 29-year-old **Frank Schwindel**, whom the Cubs claimed off waivers from the Athletics in July as they prepared to do a fire sale of their roster. Schwindel was 4-for-35 as a hitter prior to joining the Cubs, but then channeled his inner Roy Hobbs for a couple months.

In 56 games with the Cubs, Schwindel hit .342/.389/.613 with 13 home runs and 40 RBIs. From July 30 when he made his Cubs debut, he ranked second in MLB in batting average and ninth with a 1.002 OPS. Not bad for a guy who was an 18th-round draft pick in 2013.

As for those guys who were in the big leagues for the whole year, Rays left fielder **Randy Arozarena** picked up where he left off last postseason, hitting .274 with 20 home runs, 20 stolen bases, and a robust .815 OPS. He led all rookies in Baseball-Reference's WAR. It's the second straight year that we've mentioned Arozarena here. Remember, he hit seven home runs in 23 games as a rookie during the 2020 regular season.

Reds second baseman **Jonathan India** was right there with Arozarena. His .376 on-base percentage was second-best among the 40 rookies with the most plate appearances. Like Arozarena, he was a member of the 20-20 club, except his combination was home runs (21) and hit by pitches (23). In fact, he was 20-20-20, if we throw in his 25 Good Fielding Plays, second to Whit Merrifield's 27 at second base.

Adolis García was a fun watch both at the plate and in the field for a Rangers team that led the majors in Defensive Runs Saved but had few other highlights. García hit 31 home runs and was one of seven players to rob a pair of potential homers. He actually led *right fielders* in Defensive Runs Saved even though he played more innings in center field.

Speaking of great defense on a struggling team, Pirates third baseman **Ke'Bryan Hayes** gave us a taste of how good he would be in 2020 but used 2021 to show us his full skill set. Some of his work brought back memories of all-time great Brooks Robinson. Hayes led the hot corner in Defensive Runs Saved. His 16 matched the total recorded by perennial Fielding Bible winners Matt Chapman and Nolan Arenado combined.

Two other exciting rookies to watch were Marlins infielder **Jazz Chisholm** and Tigers outfielder **Akil Baddoo**. Chisholm just missed being a 20-20 player with 18 home runs and 23 stolen bases. Baddoo, a Rule V Draft pick, set the tone for his season by homering in each of his first two games and delivering a walk-off hit in his third. He finished with 13 home runs, 18 stolen bases and 7 triples, getting nosed out for the AL lead in the latter by Shohei Ohtani.

Other notable position player rookies included Cardinals teammates **Dylan Carlson** and **Edmundo Sosa**. Each was a 3-WAR player in 2021, Carlson more for his bat (18 home runs) and Sosa for a good glove at shortstop. Catchers **Tyler Stephenson** of the Reds (.797 OPS) and **Eric Haase** of the Tigers (22 home runs) showed impressive power as did Orioles first baseman **Ryan Mountcastle** (33 home runs), Cubs third baseman **Patrick Wisdom** (28 home runs), and Red Sox infielder **Bobby Dalbec** (25 home runs). Two other solid defensive players were Padres infielder **Ha-seong**

Kim (18 Runs Saved) and Astros outfielder **Chas McCormick** (14 Runs Saved).

Not every rookie can live up to the hype. Mariners outfielder **Jarred Kelenic** significantly struggled for much of 2021 both at the plate and in the field. But there's plenty of reason for hope. Kelenic closed the season with an .854 OPS and seven home runs in his last 29 games.

The most impressive of a host of rookie starting pitchers was **Trevor Rogers** of the Marlins, who pitched to a 2.64 ERA in 133 innings. Armed with an impressive changeup, Rogers provided a much-needed boost to a pitching staff hurt by Sixto Sanchez's season-ending shoulder injury.

The rookie innings leaders were **Luis Garcia** of the Astros (155 1/3) and Tigers teammates **Casey Mize** (150 1/3) and **Tarik Skubal** (149 1/3). Garcia was a mainstay in Houston's rotation all season and led all rookies in strikeouts with 167. Skubal's 164 ranked second.

Mize was less a strikeout pitcher and more finesse. His slider ranked among the best in baseball by FanGraphs pitch run values and he finished second among rookie pitchers in Baseball-Reference's WAR.

Braves pitcher **Ian Anderson** ranked second to Rogers in innings among NL rookies. He pitched to a 3.58 ERA and had moments where he looked like the pitcher who allowed two runs in 18 2/3 innings pitched in the 2020 postseason.

Four of the top AL teams had a prominent rookie starting pitcher. The AL East-winning Rays got 25 starts and a 3.43 ERA out of **Shane McClanahan**, who averaged better than 96 MPH on his fastball and had two dominant breaking pitches.

The Blue Jays went 16-4 in **Alek Manoah**'s 20 starts. He pitched to a 3.22 ERA, with a 1.69 ERA in his last four.

Tanner Houck averaged better than 11 strikeouts per 9 innings and helped the Red Sox make the postseason with five perfect innings in the final weekend against the Nationals.

And **Logan Gilbert** of the Mariners showed signs of being one of the sport's top prospects. Yes, he pitched to a 4.68 ERA, but his ERA was 2.70 in his last 6 starts as Seattle made a playoff push.

The best young power arm was **Emmanuel Clase** of the Indians, who threw more 100-MPH pitches than anyone else, recorded 24 saves, and pitched to a 1.29 ERA.

Pirates rookie **David Bednar** was dominant too. He averaged 11.4 strikeouts per 9 innings and had a 2.23 ERA with a 97 MPH fastball. **Garrett Whitlock**, a Red Sox Rule V pick, similarly impressed (1.96 ERA) in long relief.

Speaking of 97 MPH fastballs, the White Sox had two rookies who threw that hard—**Michael Kopech**, who returned from Tommy John surgery as a long reliever and netted 13.4 strikeouts per 9 innings and **Garrett Crochet**, who pitched to a 2.82 ERA as a lefty setup man. Each had tantalized in previous cameos with the team, then lived up to the billing in 2021.

To bring everything back full circle, I want to pay tribute to a couple more part-year Rookie of the Years. In the AL, that would be **Triston McKenzie** of the Indians and **Yermin Mercedes** of the White Sox. On August 15, 2021, McKenzie retired the first 23 Tigers he faced and finished with eight scoreless innings with one hit and 11 strikeouts. Mercedes went 5-for-5 as a DH in his first game of the season on April 2nd (he hit .271 with 7 home runs in 68 games).

And in the NL, **Tyler Gilbert** of the Diamondbacks went one better against the Padres. The day before McKenzie dominated the Tigers, Gilbert became the fourth pitcher to throw a no-hitter in his first MLB start.

For a few hours, those two got to feel like the Rookies of the Year, MVPs, and Cy Young Award winners, even if they were only Rookies of the Day.

The World's #1 Starting Pitcher Rankings

Bill James

Early last season I got involved in a Twitter tangle disputing the issue of whether Gerrit Cole or Jacob deGrom more deserved to be ranked as the world's #1 starting pitcher. Of course, on Twitter everyone is well-informed about the specific issue, not, and everybody understands exactly what it is that you are actually trying to say, not, and everybody is polite and friendly and cheerful within the debate, not not. A substantial number of Mets fans were quite annoyed that I was "saying" that Gerrit Cole was "better" than Jacob deGrom, and annoyed with me because the best explanation I could give them in twitter-space was "Well, that's what the ranking system says. It's not a personal opinion; it is an outcome of a long series of calculations, updated every time one of them takes the mound or, being a Mets pitcher, fails to take the mound when you were counting on him to do so."

I think the dispute was in late May. Baseball decided to regulate more carefully the amount of ooey-gooey sticky stuff that you could have on your fingers when you pitch, and then Gerrit Cole had two or three rough outings while he was adjusting to the new rules. On June 11 Jacob deGrom did in fact pass Gerrit Cole to be the world's #1 starting pitcher, and then a little after that, deGrom went on the Injured List to hang out with all of his Met Mates. Until that happened, though, I was still hearing regularly from Mets fans who wanted to know whether I was "still insisting" that Gerrit Cole was a greater pitcher than Jacob deGrom, and how the hell could I say such a thing, and didn't I even know what Jacob deGrom's ERA was?

The Pitcher Ranking system represents *a player's current level of ability*, as best we are able to measure that. It doesn't represent how well you have pitched this season. It doesn't represent how well you have pitched in the last month. What it tries to measure is everything relevant to the issue of "How good is this guy at this moment?" You have to prove it over time; you don't jump to the top of the list with a two-month hot streak, unless you were close to the top spot before the two months began. A pitcher enters the system at a low point. When he comes into the league we initially assume that he is only what we might call a 4-A pitcher, and it takes time and consistency to overcome that assumption. Having one great year, even a Cy Young year, doesn't put you at the top of the list; it takes longer than that—but at the same time, a pitcher's most recent start always counts more than any other start. Every good start moves a pitcher up the list; every bad start moves him down, but it takes about 50 starts to overcome the initial assumption of the system, which is that you're just occupying space.

When you are not on the mound, the number by which you are rated sinks slowly, and on August 25 Walker Buehler took over the top spot on the list—or rather, Jacob deGrom surrendered the top spot. A week after that, September 1, Gerrit Cole took it back.

In the past, in presenting the Starting Pitcher Rankings in this book, we would present a big hairy chart listing where everybody was at various points of the season. On July 23, 2020, Dylan Cease ranked as the #158 starting pitcher in baseball, but by August 1, 2020, he had dropped to 195th. By September 1, 2020, he had surged into the top 100, at space #91, but by season's end he had dropped to 96th.

While that kind of stuff is fun to follow in regard to a single pitcher, it occurred to me in the middle of this Cole/deGrom banter that what people really care about is who is #1, and that's about all. That actually is what the system was designed to do: to give a reasonable and objective answer to the question: Who is baseball's #1 starting pitcher?

So I decided to take this year's rankings in a somewhat different direction. The real question here is the history of the #1 spot. What I decided to do, then, was to go way back in history, and make an accounting of who the number one pitcher was over time.

Sports Info Solutions did part of that, the rankings beginning in 2004, and I did some of it, the rankings from 1946 to 2004. For the rankings that I did, I probably didn't EXACTLY match the system that is now used by Sports Info Solutions; it is generally the same system, but some of the details are hard to master without good programming skills. I did the best I could, and I'm sure it would match with the SIS system 90% of the time or more, and also, I would like to say that Dave Pinto does a version of the system on his pages, and, if my account of who was where at some random date in the past is different from Dave's, there is a real good chance that he has it right and I have it wrong. Caveat Emptor.

We're going to start this at the start of the 1946 season, just after the end of World War II, although there is no easy starting point. But I'll start it this way. In late June, 1939, Bob Feller seized the top spot, and held it until he went into the Navy after the 1941 season. To hold the #1 spot for 2½ years is very unusual.

With Feller out of action, Mort Cooper mostly ruled early in the war, and Hal Newhouser for the second half of the war. As the season opened in 1946, then, Hal Newhouser was baseball's #1 starting pitcher. On June 8, 1946, however, Hal Newhouser gave up 5 runs in the first inning to the Boston Red Sox, while Bob Feller beat the Yankees 2-1. This put Feller back in first place. The two men were neck and neck for a month after that. They won 26 games apiece that year. On July 3 both men made outstanding starts, but Newhouser's was more outstanding, so Newhouser moved back ahead. On August 13, 1946, Feller got the upper hand, but held the lead for only two starts, Newhouser moving back into first on August 25.

Newhouser had a 2.00 ERA that September, while Feller, obviously overworked and obviously trying to break the major league record for strikeouts, or what was then believed to be the record…Feller did not pitch well in September, so Newhouser ended the year with a solid grip on the number one spot. So this is the summary from 1946:

Opening Day, 1946	Hal Newhouser
June 8, 1946	Bob Feller took the lead
July 3, 1946	Hal Newhouser
August 13, 1946	Bob Feller
August 25, 1946	Hal Newhouser

Newhouser pitched a shutout on April 15, 1947, the day that Jackie Robinson broke the color line, but then had three straight bad outings, driving his ERA to 4.60 by the end of April. This allowed Feller to move back ahead:

April 26, 1947	Bob Feller
June 25, 1947	Hal Newhouser

July 4, 1947	Ewell Blackwell
August 2, 1947	Bob Feller
August 12, 1947	Ewell Blackwell
September 13, 1947	Bob Feller
June 15, 1948	Hal Newhouser
July 3, 1948	Bob Feller
July 21, 1948	Harry Brecheen
September 3, 1948	Bob Lemon
September 9, 1948	Harry Brecheen

After Bob Lemon temporarily passed him on September 3, Brecheen then won his next five starts, giving up only 3 runs in 43 innings, which put him solidly ahead at the end of the 1948 season, and through April of 1949.   And then:

May 1, 1949	Hal Newhouser
July 19, 1949	Warren Spahn
August 26, 1949	Mel Parnell
August 28, 1949	Bob Lemon
April 21, 1950	Virgil Trucks took the lead
May 4, 1950	Mel Parnell
June 4, 1950	Bob Lemon
June 17, 1950	Don Newcombe
June 19, 1950	Warren Spahn
July 3, 1950	Larry Jansen
July 14, 1950	Bob Lemon
September 6, 1950	Don Newcombe
September 16, 1950	Ewell Blackwell

There weren't any one or two dominant pitchers in 1950, like Feller and Newhouser, so the lead flitted between top starters. Blackwell held the top spot at the start of the 1951 season.   I think I'll start adding notes, summarizing how many times the pitcher has climbed into the #1 spot.

April 23, 1951	Warren Spahn (3)
June 8, 1951	Bob Feller (8) (Including 1939 to 1941)
June 16, 1951	Warren Spahn (4)
July 16, 1951	Bob Feller (9)

July 22, 1951	Allie Reynolds (1)
August 7, 1951	Robin Roberts (1)
September 5, 1951	Early Wynn (1)
September 29, 1951	Warren Spahn (5)
April 29, 1952	Sal Maglie (1)
April 30, 1952	Larry Jansen (2)
May 3, 1952	Sal Maglie (2)
June 2, 1952	Allie Reynolds (2)
July 2, 1952	Robin Roberts (2)
July 12, 1952	Allie Reynolds (3)
July 22, 1952	Bobby Shantz (1)
August 15, 1952	Robin Roberts (3)
August 22, 1952	Bobby Shantz (2)
September 2, 1952	Robin Roberts (4)
September 5, 1952	Billy Pierce (1)
September 6, 1952	Robin Roberts (5)
September 9, 1952	Warren Spahn (6)
September 20, 1952	Robin Roberts (6)

So the number one spot changed hands five times in September, 1952.

It's a *race*, you know. It isn't intended to be a permanent trophy, like winning the Cy Young Award or winning 20 games or making the Hall of Fame. It's a never-ending race. This guy is ahead for a moment, and then this other guy who is just as good has a hot streak, and he's ahead, and then this other guy goes back ahead. There are two-person competitions for the top spot that go on for years. What is more important than gaining the lead repeatedly, of course, is riding time. HOLDING the lead once you have it. If you do that, like Bob Feller did before the War, that means you are clearly better than anybody else, whereas if you claim the lead and give it up and get it back, that just means that you are one of the top guys and you move ahead when you have a little hot streak. Robin Roberts held the lead almost all of 1953, and almost all of 1954:

Start of season, 1953	Robin Roberts
September 4, 1953	Billy Pierce (2)
September 13, 1953	Warren Spahn (7)
April 24, 1954	Robin Roberts (7)

| August 28, 1954 | Warren Spahn (8) |
| September 24, 1954 | Robin Roberts (8) |

May 10, 1955	Johnny Antonelli (1)
May 25, 1955	Robin Roberts (9)
July 1, 1955	Early Wynn (2)
July 19, 1955	Robin Roberts (10)
August 24, 1955	Billy Pierce (3)

Johnny Antonelli's great season was 1954, when Antonelli would have won the Cy Young Award if there had been one. But since Antonelli started the 1954 season as a nobody, it took him until May of 1955 to push into the top spot, just inching ahead of Robin Roberts.

This is going to turn into quite a long article, so I'm going to have to skip a few details and condense the story for some seasons. In 1956 the #1 spot was occupied by three American League left-handers: Whitey Ford, who seized the lead from Billy Pierce on May 6, May 18 and May 28; Billy Pierce, who re-took the lead on May 8, May 25 and June 10, and Herb Score, who blasted past both of them to take the lead on August 6.

Herb Score's famous injury occurred on May 7, 1957, but, like deGrom in 2021, Score was far enough ahead at the moment of his injury that it took a while for anybody to catch him.

June 4, 1957	Billy Pierce (7)
September 15, 1957	Jim Bunning (1)
September 24, 1957	Warren Spahn (9)

You will notice that Spahn often takes the lead near the end of the season. Spahn had a fantastic record late in the season. On April 23, 1958, Herb Score pitched a 3-hit shutout, striking out 13 batters; people thought he was back, and he momentarily regained the top spot. The rest of the season, however, the lead was passed around among Warren Spahn (May 4), Bob Turley (June 15), Whitey Ford (re-took the lead June 17 and July 14), Billy Pierce for a week and Sam Jones, from August 22 to the end of the season. Camilo Pascual took the lead in late 1959 and held it until mid-season, 1960.

April 22, 1959	Whitey Ford (6)
June 13, 1959	Johnny Antonelli (2)
June 20, 1959	Don Drysdale (1)
August 21, 1959	Johnny Antonelli (3)
September 4, 1959	Warren Spahn (11)
September 15, 1959	Camilo Pascual (1)
June 24, 1960	Jim Bunning (2)
July 27, 1960	Don Drysdale (2)
August 2, 1960	Jim Bunning (3)
September 1, 1960	Don Drysdale (3)
June 22, 1961	Whitey Ford (7)
June 29, 1961	Sandy Koufax (1)
June 30, 1961	Whitey Ford (8)
July 29, 1961	Jim Bunning (4)
September 17, 1961	Camilo Pascual (2)
June 18, 1962	Sandy Koufax (2)
July 22, 1962	Bob Gibson (1)
September 10, 1962	Don Drysdale (4)
September 30, 1962	Camilo Pascual (3)

1962 was the third time in four years that Camilo Pascual had wound up the season as the World's #1 starting pitcher. For most of 1963, and at the conclusion of the 1963 season, he was #2. He pitched for non-competitive teams and didn't quite have a Hall of Fame career, so people have mostly forgotten him.

April 19, 1963	Sandy Koufax (3)

Koufax then held the lead for more than three years. He was injured and missed a couple of months in 1964, during which his scores dropped, but he was so far ahead that nobody really came close to catching him, until Marichal finally did:

May 26, 1966	Juan Marichal (1)
May 28, 1966	Sandy Koufax (4)
May 31, 1966	Juan Marichal (2)
June 1, 1966	Sandy Koufax (5)

Koufax retired as #1.

April 10, 1967	Juan Marichal (3)
July 16, 1967	Jim Bunning (5)

In 1968, the year that Bob Gibson had a 1.12 ERA, Luis Tiant and Gibby took turns at the wheel, Tiant gaining the lead or re-gaining it on May 31, June 23, June 29 and July 20, and Gibson ripping it back from him on June 15, June 26, July 12 and July 25, holding it then until the end of the season.

Well, longer than that. Bob Gibson actually held the top spot from mid-season, 1968, all through the 1969 season—one of the few men ever to hold the lead through an entire season—but did not win the Cy Young Award that year. He won in 1968 and 1970 and was great in 1969, but Tom Seaver had a 25-7 won-lost record, which was the biggest thing in the voting at that time. Seaver was great, too, and Seaver finally saw the summit in early 1970:

May 1, 1970	Tom Seaver (1)
September 6, 1970	Bob Gibson (6)
April 10, 1971	Ferguson Jenkins (1)
April 11, 1971	Bob Gibson (7)
April 26, 1971	Ferguson Jenkins (2)
August 21, 1971	Tom Seaver (2)

In 1972 Steve Carlton had an incredible season, causing people to forget that Gaylord Perry did, too; Perry's season is essentially as impressive as Carlton's. Gaylord had three turns in the top spot in 1972, and Tom Seaver, Mickey Lolich and Ferguson Jenkins had one each, but Steve Carlton took over in mid-August and reigned the rest of the year. The guy who controls at the END of the season is often the guy who takes the Cy Young Award:

April 10, 1973	Gaylord Perry (4)
April 27, 1973	Steve Carlton (2)
May 12, 1973	Tom Seaver (4)
July 6, 1973	Don Sutton (1)
July 22, 1973	Tom Seaver (5)

April 5, 1974	Nolan Ryan (1)
April 20, 1974	Bert Blyleven (1)
May 1, 1974	Tom Seaver (6)
May 23, 1974	Gaylord Perry (5)
August 7, 1974	Nolan Ryan (2)
June 25, 1975	Tom Seaver (7)
August 27, 1975	Bert Blyleven (2)
September 1, 1975	Tom Seaver (8)
September 11, 1975	Catfish Hunter (1)

In 1976 there were 12 lead changes, Bert Blyleven taking over early in the season. Catfish Hunter took three turns at the top in 1976, Frank Tanana took three, Tom Seaver two Jim Palmer two, and Andy Messersmith one.

April 29, 1977	Jim Palmer (3)
May 11, 1977	Frank Tanana (4)
September 3, 1977	Nolan Ryan (3)
September 20, 1977	Tom Seaver (11)

To interrupt our narrative for just a moment, can't you just see this becoming a really interesting story line for ESPN and MLB.com to follow, if we could just get it bumped up to that level? *"Nolan Ryan is starting tonight for the Angels. He is currently ranked as the #2 starting pitcher in baseball; he is trying to get past Tom Seaver and move back into the #1 spot for the fourth time in his career."*

Once in a while the top two pitchers in baseball will face off against one another in a duel for the top spot; would happen on average about once a year, I think. Or how about this one: *"Tom Seaver has reclaimed the top spot in the starting pitcher rankings for the 11th time in his career, tying the record set 20 years ago by Warren Spahn!"* Or this one: *"Sandy Koufax has now occupied the top space on the major league starting pitchers list for three years. It is the longest that anyone has ever held that position."* There's potentially a LOT of story lines connected to this, if we could just get a consensus around the method, and get people to stop chirping about little methodological issues that don't really amount to anything. Replace the names of Koufax and Seaver and Spahn with Verlander and Cole and deGrom; we'll get there.

1978 was Ron Guidry's year. The lead went from Nolan Ryan to Jim Palmer to Guidry to Tom Seaver to JR Richard, but Guidry took over in late July and held the #1 spot for almost a calendar year. In 1979:

July 13, 1979	Nolan Ryan (5)
July 21, 1979	Ron Guidry (3)
September 1, 1979	J. R. Richard (2)

JR Richard, assuming the mantle of the best starting pitcher in baseball on September 1, 1979, was still in that position when he suffered a serious health emergency in the middle of a game, akin to a stroke, on July 14, 1980. He never pitched again. Richard thus became the third pitcher to exit the game while ranked as the best pitcher in the world. Bob Feller left to go into the Navy at the start of World War II. Sandy Koufax retired as the #1 pitcher after the 1966 season, and JR Richard was stopped by a medical event in mid-season, 1980.

Steve Carlton	July 17, 1980 (3)

The only lead change of the year, JR Richard to Steve Carlton. Carlton then held the top spot for almost two full years before Steve Rogers nudged past him on June 18, 1982. Rogers was replaced in quick succession by Mario Soto, Soto by Carlton, Carlton by Soto, Soto by Nolan Ryan, Nolan Ryan by Soto, and Soto by Steve Carlton, who reached the top spot for the fifth and final time on September 13, holding the spot until May 16, 1983:

Dave Stieb	May 16, 1983 (1)
Mario Soto	May 27, 1983 (4)
Jack Morris	September 27, 1983 (1)
Mario Soto	September 28, 1983 (5)
Jack Morris	April 12, 1984 (2)
Mario Soto	May 12, 1984 (6)
Jack Morris	May 28, 1984 (3)
Mario Soto	June 6, 1984 (7)
Dave Stieb	July 4, 1984 (2)
Dwight Gooden	April 14, 1985 (1)
Dave Stieb	July 8, 1985 (3)
Dwight Gooden	July 14, 1985 (2)

John Tudor	June 23, 1986 (1)
Dwight Gooden	June 30, 1986 (3)
John Tudor	July 17, 1986 (2)
Mike Scott	July 24, 1986 (1)
Mike Witt	August 26, 1986 (1)
Mike Scott	September 3, 1986 (2)

Mike Scott then stayed at the top of the list for more than a year.

Teddy Higuera	September 16, 1987 (1)
Roger Clemens	September 25, 1987 (1)
Teddy Higuera	August 25, 1988 (2)

Don Drysdale in 1968 threw six consecutive shutouts, and Orel Hershiser in 1988 had a similar streak—but neither man reached the top spot on the list during those streaks. Both came close, but both started the season well down the list, and neither was able to sustain their great runs quite long enough to make the top. In 1989 there were seven lead changes, the spotlight shining on Roger Clemens, Mark Gubicza, Nolan Ryan, Clemens again, Mark Langston, Nolan Ryan again, and Bret Saberhagen, who finished the year on top and won his second Cy Young Award. 1990:

Nolan Ryan	April 26, 1990 (9)
Bret Saberhagen	May 18, 1990 (2)
Roger Clemens	June 13, 1990 (4)
Nolan Ryan	September 14, 1990 (10)
Roger Clemens	September 29, 1990 (5)

Nolan Ryan thus became the second pitcher to top the list in three different decades, the other one being Bob Feller. Roger Clemens, re-taking the lead at the end of the 1990 season, then held the lead through all of the 1991 season, which made him the fourth pitcher to do that, and then through all of the 1992 season, making him only the second pitcher to hold the lead from the beginning to the end of two consecutive seasons. Randy Johnson at that time was still walking the world, but he cut his walk rate sharply in 1993:

Randy Johnson	June 20, 1993 (1)
Roger Clemens	July 21, 1993 (6)

Kevin Appier	July 27, 1993 (1)
Jose Rijo	August 7, 1993 (1)
Greg Maddux	August 15, 1993 (1)
Kevin Appier	September 18, 1993 (2)
Randy Johnson	September 26, 1993 (2)

This began a remarkable three-year period in which two pitchers, one of them a right-hander with phenomenal control and the other a big, scary left-hander who fought his control, traded the number one spot back and forth between them.

Greg Maddux	April 9, 1994 (2)
Randy Johnson	June 25, 1994 (3)
Greg Maddux	July 17, 1994 (3)

Randy Johnson	May 12, 1995 (4)
Greg Maddux	May 28, 1995 (4)
Randy Johnson	October 2, 1995 (5)

Greg Maddux	May 3, 1996 (5)
Randy Johnson	May 12, 1996 (6)
Greg Maddux	May 21, 1996 (6)

Roger Clemens, unhappy in Boston, went to Toronto as a free agent in the winter of 1996-97. He came out in 1997 with his hair on fire, posting a 0.42 ERA in his first three starts, and kept his ERA under 2.00 almost all season.

Roger Clemens	April 2, 1997 (7)
Randy Johnson	June 8, 1997 (7)
Roger Clemens	July 6, 1997 (8)
Randy Johnson	September 13, 1997 (8)
Roger Clemens	September 18, 1997 (9)

Pedro Martinez	April 1, 1998 (1)
Roger Clemens	June 3, 1998 (10)
Curt Schilling	June 17, 1998 (1)
Greg Maddux	June 22, 1998 (7)
Roger Clemens	August 25, 1998 (11)

And then there was Pedro. These were truly great pitchers—Johnson, Maddux, Clemens, Martinez. All four of them were deserving of the #1 spot all the time. In the early 1980s there was a period when somebody had to be #1, but none of them was really at the historic level of a #1 pitcher in baseball. By the late 1990s we were at the opposite pole, with a surfeit of truly great pitchers.

Randy Johnson   April 15, 1999 (9)
Pedro Martinez   May 9, 1999 (2)
Randy Johnson   July 15, 1999 (10)
Pedro Martinez   September 15, 1999 (3)

In the 1999 season Johnson and Martinez both reached rating levels higher than any other pitcher had ever reached—both of them. In 2000, they both surpassed their 1999 levels.

Randy Johnson   April 20, 2000 (11)
Pedro Martinez   May 6, 2000 (3)
Randy Johnson   May 10, 2000 (12)
Pedro Martinez   May 12, 2000 (4)

The highest score for any pitcher ever was for Pedro Martinez on September 26, 2000. Pedro's ERA never went higher than 1.81 at any point of the 2000 season. Pedro ruled until he went on the Disabled List in mid-June, 2001. His extended absence eventually put Johnson back at the top of the list for the 13th time in his career:

Randy Johnson   August 3, 2001 (13)
Pedro Martinez   August 26, 2001 (5)
Randy Johnson   September 17, 2001 (14)

Pedro Martinez   July 14, 2002 (6)
Randy Johnson   September 4, 2002 (15)

Pedro Martinez   April 12, 2003 (7)
Curt Schilling   May 24, 2003 (2)
Pedro Martinez   June 11, 2003 (8)

Pedro then commanded the register for almost another year, before being nudged aside by Jason Schmidt.

Jason Schmidt	May 30, 2004 (1)
Randy Johnson	August 31, 2004 (16)
Pedro Martinez	September 8, 2004 (9)
Randy Johnson	September 10, 2004 (17)
Pedro Martinez	September 14, 2004 (10)
Randy Johnson	September 15, 2004 (18)

Jason Schmidt's ascension to the top spot signals the end of the era of the four super-starters. Pedro Martinez and Randy Johnson in 2004 were still very good pitchers, still the best in baseball I guess, but they were not what they had been from 1999 to 2001. They were still near the top of the list because there weren't any Tom Seavers and Steve Carltons and Jim Palmers to compete with them. Resuming the list:

Pedro Martinez	April 21, 2005 (11)
Randy Johnson	April 24, 2005 (19)
Pedro Martinez	May 22, 2005 (12)
Johan Santana	June 18, 2005 (1)
Pedro Martinez	June 24, 2005 (13)
Roger Clemens	August 3, 2005 (12)
Johan Santana	September 3, 2005 (2)

Roger Clemens thus became the third pitcher to be the #1 starting pitcher in baseball in three different decades.

Pedro Martinez	May 31, 2006 (14)
Johan Santana	June 2, 2006 (3)

And Johan owned it. Johan Santana held the top spot on the list for two years, basically, surrendering it in late May, 2008. Santana held the top spot longer than any other pitcher in the 21st century, although one other pitcher came close.

The years 2008 to 2010 were years of chaos in the rankings, with the lead changing hands a total of 30 times in three seasons. The short version: Brandon Webb and Johan Santana traded the lead back and forth in the first half of 2008, and Santana and CC Sabathia swapped it over the second half. From 2009 until the middle of 2010 it was Sabathia and Tim Lincecum, trading back and forth, and then Sabathia and Roy Halladay. Dan Haren, of all people, had a brief turn at the top there in 2009, and then in September, 2010, Felix Hernandez hit the top for two sessions—the only time in his career he was ever at the top. Sabathia moved to the top of the list ten different times from 2008 to 2010.

Justin Verlander	June 19, 2011 (1)
Roy Halladay	June 21, 2011 (5)
Justin Verlander	June 25, 2011 (2)
Roy Halladay	October 8, 2011 (6)
Justin Verlander	April 11, 2012 (3)
Clayton Kershaw	May 16, 2013 (1)
Max Scherzer	April 28, 2014 (1)
Clayton Kershaw	June 2, 2014 (2)
Max Scherzer	July 2, 2015 (2)
Clayton Kershaw	July 7, 2015 (3)

One can reasonably argue that Clayton Kershaw in his day was the most dominant pitcher since World War II. With two brief interruptions by Max Scherzer, he was the number one pitcher in baseball from May, 2013, until June, 2017. Santana had the longest streak holding the top spot in the 21st century, 720 days, but Kershaw got to 710 days and had two other long streaks totaling another 742 days. No other pitcher in history can match that.

In 2017 and 2018 the lead ping-ponged between Max Scherzer, Clayton Kershaw, Corey Kluber, Chris Sale and Justin Verlander. Scherzer attained and then lost the lead thirteen times in the two seasons, including a record nine times in 2018. In 2019 this continued, the lead going from Verlander to Scherzer to Verlander to Scherzer to Verlander to Scherzer to Verlander to Gerrit Cole. And since then:

Jacob deGrom	September 6, 2020 (1)
Gerrit Cole	September 16, 2020 (2)
Jacob deGrom	June 11, 2021 (2)
Walker Buehler	August 25, 2021 (1)
Gerrit Cole	September 1, 2021 (3)
Max Scherzer	September 12, 2021 (19)

So Max Scherzer has claimed the spot as the #1 starting pitcher in baseball for the 19th time in his career, the first time since August of 2019, and is the current holder of the title of Baseball's #1 starting pitcher. These are the current Top 10 starting pitchers, as of the end of the 2021 regular season:

1. Max Scherzer
2. Walker Buehler
3. Jacob deGrom
4. Gerrit Cole
5. Zack Wheeler
6. Charlie Morton
7. Robbie Ray
8. Max Fried
9. Corbin Burnes
10. Brandon Woodruff.

Thank you for reading.

Starting Pitcher Rankings

Player	April 1 Score	April 1 Rank	May 1 Rank	June 1 Rank	July 1 Rank	Aug 1 Rank	Sept 1 Rank	Oct 3 Score	Oct 3 Rank
Scherzer, Max	400.6	6	7	4	4	5	4	494.7	1
Buehler, Walker	390.0	10	9	10	7	3	2	485.3	2
deGrom, Jacob	423.9	2	2	2	1	1	3	481.6	3
Cole, Gerrit	446.0	1	1	1	2	2	1	481.5	4
Wheeler, Zack	367.4	29	19	11	9	7	7	478.5	5
Morton, Charlie	370.9	26	23	24	17	15	9	472.8	6
Ray, Robbie	339.5	55	72	45	36	19	6	470.7	7
Fried, Max	376.5	17	54	43	40	38	21	464.0	8
Burnes, Corbin	343.2	51	25	25	22	22	13	463.7	9
Woodruff, Brandon	372.6	23	10	5	6	6	5	463.2	10
Giolito, Lucas	400.5	7	12	12	13	11	10	458.6	11
Gausman, Kevin	364.4	33	22	9	10	10	12	456.2	12
Berrios, Jose	371.3	24	21	21	21	14	20	456.2	13
Urias, Julio	348.8	44	35	26	39	23	23	454.7	14
Lynn, Lance	382.0	15	13	13	14	12	14	451.8	15
Bauer, Trevor	420.5	3	3	3	3	4	8	451.0	16
Alcantara, Sandy	354.6	39	34	29	24	27	22	450.4	17
Wainwright, Adam	350.6	42	40	44	27	26	11	450.1	18
Castillo, Luis	373.0	20	28	71	38	25	25	443.0	19
Montas, Frankie	325.0	80	118	92	82	45	33	443.0	20
Kershaw, Clayton	410.1	4	4	7	5	9	15	439.1	21
Nola, Aaron	395.8	8	8	15	20	20	17	436.5	22
Bassitt, Chris	358.8	35	31	22	15	16	18	436.0	23
Musgrove, Joe	339.6	54	27	23	26	29	19	434.3	24
Snell, Blake	386.6	13	14	27	42	59	27	433.6	25
Peralta, Freddy	325.0	80	55	32	19	17	24	432.9	26
McCullers Jr., Lance	336.2	60	49	41	54	42	37	432.5	27
Eovaldi, Nathan	325.0	80	60	55	41	39	35	432.3	28
Darvish, Yu	394.1	9	6	8	8	13	26	432.2	29
Rodon, Carlos	325.0	80	43	33	31	30	30	432.0	30
Marquez, German	374.2	18	18	18	11	8	16	431.9	31
Ohtani, Shohei	325.0	80	122	89	62	46	36	428.1	32
DeSclafani, Anthony	325.0	80	42	69	37	33	43	427.9	33
Mahle, Tyler	328.4	76	48	48	46	41	31	426.8	34
Webb, Logan	325.0	80	116	91	125	92	44	426.3	35
Cease, Dylan	325.0	80	79	77	59	57	34	425.9	36
Bieber, Shane	409.9	5	5	6	12	18	29	423.5	37
Stroman, Marcus	325.0	80	51	46	47	48	39	420.9	38
Gonzales, Marco	367.2	31	29	50	74	90	50	420.6	39
Gray, Sonny	372.6	21	45	34	51	61	40	417.8	40
Manoah, Alek				157	123	87	77	416.8	41
Means, John	349.3	43	20	16	29	36	49	416.1	42
Garcia, Luis	325.0	80	120	61	53	54	42	414.1	43
Ryu, Hyun-Jin	381.5	16	16	17	23	21	32	413.9	44
Greinke, Zack	388.0	12	15	19	18	24	28	413.4	45
Anderson, Ian	346.9	48	32	36	32	43	56	411.9	46
Rogers, Trevor	325.0	80	47	31	25	34	48	411.0	47
Gallen, Zac	367.4	30	33	51	73	85	59	410.9	48
Manaea, Sean	325.0	80	73	82	45	32	66	410.4	49
Hill, Rich	347.1	47	70	28	44	55	60	410.3	50
Valdez, Framber	356.4	37	106	171	86	86	52	410.1	51
Quantrill, Cal	325.0	80	195	181	189	122	76	410.1	52
Gibson, Kyle	325.0	80	44	35	28	40	38	408.4	53
Pivetta, Nick	325.0	80	62	58	58	60	61	407.7	54
Glasnow, Tyler	368.0	28	11	14	16	28	41	406.5	55
Wood, Alex	325.0	80	78	75	78	63	67	406.4	56
Mize, Casey	325.0	80	124	56	52	49	53	406.1	57
Flexen, Chris	325.0	80	94	128	89	77	65	405.5	58
Matz, Steven	325.0	80	84	83	96	103	71	405.0	59
Rodriguez, Eduardo	325.0	80	77	122	110	98	79	404.4	60
Montgomery, Jordan	325.0	80	93	87	65	44	47	403.6	61
McClanahan, Shane			172	120	107	89	78	402.4	62
Lauer, Eric	325.0	80	148	170	135	121	107	402.4	63
Maeda, Kenta	389.2	11	26	37	64	35	46	401.0	64
Houser, Adrian	325.0	80	121	96	98	91	92	400.5	65
Taillon, Jameson	325.0	80	112	110	113	65	70	400.0	66
Skubal, Tarik	325.0	80	173	116	67	78	64	399.7	67
Freeland, Kyle	339.9	53	195	190	152	105	72	399.1	68
Gray, Jon	325.0	80	50	59	63	47	57	399.1	69
Senzatela, Antonio	333.3	66	86	93	71	93	69	398.5	70
Miley, Wade	325.0	80	75	85	55	51	45	397.4	71

Starting Pitcher Rankings

Player	April 1 Score	April 1 Rank	May 1 Rank	June 1 Rank	July 1 Rank	Aug 1 Rank	Sept 1 Rank	Oct 3 Score	Oct 3 Rank
Suarez, Ranger	325.0	80	195	212			143	396.3	72
Minor, Mike	347.6	46	57	39	61	64	74	396.2	73
Hendricks, Kyle	385.1	14	30	30	30	31	51	395.9	74
Bumgarner, Madison	327.2	78	68	70	117	102	75	395.1	75
Flaherty, Jack	369.2	27	17	20	34	50	54	393.1	76
Lopez, Pablo	332.2	69	41	38	33	37	55	392.6	77
Kelly, Merrill	325.0	80	139	97	60	52	62	392.2	78
McKenzie, Triston	325.0	80	143	130	147	140	86	391.5	79
Lyles, Jordan	325.0	80	167	133	112	99	116	390.7	80
Urquidy, Jose	325.0	80	69	67	49	70	95	390.2	81
Walker, Taijuan	332.7	67	71	42	43	76	73	389.7	82
Heaney, Andrew	337.3	58	56	60	79	67	63	389.3	83
Yarbrough, Ryan	345.0	49	59	78	68	68	80	389.2	84
Plesac, Zach	351.9	41	52	40	76	88	83	388.8	85
Kikuchi, Yusei	325.0	80	83	49	35	53	58	388.5	86
Bubic, Kris	325.0	80	195	99	136	117	125	388.2	87
Anderson, Tyler	325.0	80	82	98	88	79	68	387.8	88
Kaprielian, James				132	85	72	88	386.4	89
Gilbert, Logan				160	124	95	112	386.4	90
Gomber, Austin	325.0	80	105	73	48	56	81	383.7	91
Cortes, Nestor	325.0	80	195	212	223	163	131	383.6	92
Ober, Bailey				212	165	132	94	383.5	93
Stripling, Ross	325.0	80	195	121	72	81	82	380.3	94
Irvin, Cole	325.0	80	98	106	69	58	85	380.1	95
Corbin, Patrick	359.0	34	80	94	81	106	121	379.5	96
Civale, Aaron	325.0	80	63	47	50	71	100	379.4	97
Sandoval, Patrick	325.0	80	195	152	119	62	84	378.8	98
Wacha, Michael	325.0	80	90	134	131	115	147	378.1	99
Odorizzi, Jake	325.0	80	149	165	127	118	101	377.6	100
Cobb, Alex	325.0	80	155	119	122	84	105	377.3	101
Peralta, Wily					164	131	127	376.3	102
Suarez, Jose	325.0	80	195	212	171	158	156	375.3	103
Singer, Brady	331.3	71	67	108	93	116	117	373.5	104
Happ, J.A.	354.6	40	36	79	104	146	126	373.4	105
Pineda, Michael	325.0	80	61	88	106	111	123	372.8	106
Ynoa, Huascar	325.0	80	58	86	120	143	120	372.6	107
Gutierrez, Vladimir				168	145	127	90	372.3	108
Houck, Tanner	325.0	80	169	212	223	162	139	371.9	109
Bundy, Dylan	366.9	32	24	54	87	109	91	371.6	110
Rasmussen, Drew					215	200	159	371.5	111
Morgan, Eli				212	184	173	137	371.3	112
Ross, Joe	325.0	80	126	127	66	73	93	371.3	113
Megill, Tylor					181	120	122	370.5	114
Alexander, Tyler	325.0	80	195	185	203	189	161	370.2	115
Dunning, Dane	325.0	80	113	113	102	100	102	369.7	116
Smyly, Drew	325.0	80	178	141	103	97	98	369.3	117
Espino, Paolo	325.0	80	181	212	167	138	149	369.0	118
Kim, Kwang-hyun	325.0	80	133	131	115	75	89	368.7	119
Fedde, Erick	325.0	80	81	102	92	112	113	368.6	120
Keller, Brad	335.3	63	117	104	140	104	97	368.3	121
Keuchel, Dallas	357.6	36	38	53	57	69	96	368.1	122
Gonsolin, Tony	336.6	59	163	212	149	123	142	368.0	123
German, Domingo	325.0	80	115	57	91	74	99	367.8	124
Lester, Jon	328.9	75	152	144	148	148	148	367.1	125

Going Broader and Deeper into Baseball in Asia

Brian Reiff

What more can be said about Shohei Ohtani that hasn't been already? In just his fourth year in MLB, he put up one of the greatest two-way seasons we've ever seen—perhaps the greatest, depending on who you're asking. Going by Baseball-Reference WAR, Ohtani became the first player to be worth 4 Wins Above Replacement as both a position player and as a pitcher…ever. Only one other player had even earned 3 WAR as both before (Bob Caruthers in 1886 and 1887), and only 10 players had ever earned at least 2 (since 1900, just Babe Ruth, Wes Ferrell, Don Newcombe and Don Drysdale).

But we're not here to talk about how great Ohtani's season was—I'm sure it's detailed plentifully in the various other sections of this book. He's worth mentioning, though, as he's one of a group of players who have made their way to MLB in the past few seasons after starting their careers overseas.

SIS began its foray into international baseball a few years back, collecting data for Japanese Nippon Professional Baseball (NPB) back to 2018 and the Korean Baseball Organization (KBO) back to 2019. That means we don't have any of our advanced data for Ohtani's NPB career, but we do for many other recent players such as Kwang Hyun Kim, Ha-seong Kim, Yusei Kikuchi and Yoshi Tsutsugo.

Take Ha-seong Kim as an example. In 2021, he had an average exit velocity of 86.7 MPH, according to Statcast. A natural question one might ask is how that compares to his previous years—did he have a good year, an off year, or was that basically the norm for him? Unfortunately, Statcast data don't exist for NPB (or KBO, for that matter).

SIS, though, calculates something called Synthetic Statcast, a data set that uses advanced modeling techniques to convert the charting data it collects into equivalent Statcast-like metrics, including exit velocity. By that measure, Kim recorded exit velocities of 87.1 and 87.7 in 2019 and 2020, respectively, while playing in the KBO. While an apples-to-apples comparison may not be appropriate given differences in things like pitcher quality, climate and other miscellany, it appears as though Kim's 2021 exit velocity was not too far off from where it had been in the past.

Their seasons are still ongoing at the time of this writing, but here's a look at who leads NPB and the KBO in exit velocity this season.

NPB and KBO Synthetic Statcast Average Exit Velocity Leaders, 2021

NPB		KBO	
Player	**Avg EV (mph)**	**Player**	**Avg EV (mph)**
Hotaka Yamakawa	90.7	Jae-hwan Kim	90.7
Tyler Austin	90.3	Sung-bum Na	90.3
Munetaka Murakami	90.3	Roberto Ramos	89.7
Seiya Suzuki	89.8	Aaron Altherr	89.6
Kazuma Okamoto	89.8	David Freitas	89.3

These numbers align remarkably well with the box score stats. For example, in the KBO, Na is tied for the league lead in home runs and has more total bases than any other player, with Kim and Altherr in the top 10 for both those categories as well. In NPB, Suzuki, Austin and Murakami own the first, second and fourth spots on the OPS leaderboard among qualified hitters.

SIS does more than just estimate Statcast data. Nearly every metric you see in this book has an international counterpart, from hard hit rates to pitcher repertoires to Defensive Runs Saved. For DRS, we measure players against an MLB basis, so that players who record a positive total are actually outperforming an average major league fielder at their position.

The two players who led their respective leagues in DRS this season, shortstop Sosuke Genda in NPB and catcher Jae-hoon Choi in KBO, have both been dominant forces for the past few years; Genda has led NPB shortstops in DRS every year since 2018 and never finished outside the top 10 across all positions, while Choi has led his league twice and never finished outside the top five.

All that is to say, we have a quite a bit of international data at this point, but our goal is always to collect more to create better and more useful insights.

Minor League Prospects

Mark Simon

You may not know this but we chart minor league data too. Our Video Scouts log and categorize plays across all minor league levels. We don't necessarily have every play of every game from 2021 but we're getting closer and we have more than we've ever had before.

Much of that work goes to our team clients and it is proprietary, but we can share some slivers in this space.

We take pride that our Minor League Defensive Runs Saved identified a couple of standouts in their earliest professional days. Players like Matt Chapman and Isiah Kiner-Falefa were defensive stars at Double-A.

It's tough to rack up the Runs Saved in the minors. The basis of comparison we use is the major leagues, so if an inexperienced player muffs a play that a major leaguer often makes, he's taking a big penalty.

As such, when someone like Rome Braves center fielder Michael Harris puts up 14 Runs Saved in a season, we take notice.

"I feel like I can cover a lot of ground," Harris said on *The SIS Baseball Podcast* earlier this season. "I have pretty good instincts out there. I can typically read where a ball is going to land or how hard it's hit by the sound. I know what spot to get to once the ball is hit."

Harris' 14 Runs Saved were the most by any minor league outfielder this season. Only three other infielders/outfielders reached double figures: Jimmy Kerrigan, an outfielder in the Twins organization, Madison Stokes, a first baseman in the Phillies system, and longtime minor leaguer Sean Kazmar, an infielder with the Braves.

Of those, Harris is the most legit prospect. He excelled at High-A this season, hitting .294 with a .362 on-base percentage and 27 stolen bases in 31 attempts. His .798 OPS was 58 points above the league average.

The Braves have a long history of defensive excellence in center field, with players such as Marquis Grissom, Andruw Jones, and Ender Inciarte. It's Inciarte whom Harris measures himself against.

"I looked up to Ender a lot my senior year of high school," Harris said. "That's who I modeled myself after. If I was going to play like one player in the league, I thought I would look a lot like him."

He might get his chance, especially if he plays defense this well.

On the infield, Yankees shortstop Oswald Peraza was the No. 44 prospect on The FanGraphs Top 100 Board and the No. 3 prospect in the Yankees system per MLB.com.

Peraza hit .297 with 18 home runs across three levels in 2021, which certainly merits notice. From a defensive perspective, Peraza may be approaching major league readiness. He ranked second among minor league shortstops with six Runs Saved in 2021.

Six Runs Saved might not sound like much, but relative to other minor leaguers, it's excellent. Remember, Peraza just turned 21 years old.

Another prospect that graded out very well defensively by our metrics was Rays infielder Xavier Edwards.

Eric Longenhagen of FanGraphs described the 21-year-old Edwards as "a callback to infielders of past generations" because of his high-contact, low-power numbers and ranked him No. 63 in his Top 100. Edwards hit .302 with 19 stolen bases at Double-A Montgomery. He saved five runs at second base and four runs in a short stint at third base.

In 2019, Edwards played a little shortstop as well, but with Wander Franco and Taylor Walls in his way there, he seems to be focused on other infield opportunities.

And doing rather well, we must say.

Team Statistics

Lindsay Zeck

There are so many different things to look through in the following pages. I love perusing them to find interesting things that stand out to me. Here are a few of my favorites:

- The Rockies finished the season with a .593 winning percentage at home—the seventh-best record in baseball. Unfortunately for them, they finished with a .325 winning percentage on the road, only ahead of five teams.

  The .268 difference between their home and road winning percentages is the second-biggest in the last decade, if we exclude the 2020 season. The only team to have a bigger differential was the Rockies…again… in 2014 with a .556 home win percentage and a .259 road win percentage.

- The Arizona Diamondbacks relievers saved only 44 percent of their opportunities. This is the lowest percentage in the two decades that Sports Info Solutions has been tracking games (excluding the shortened 2020 season when the Pittsburgh Pirates saved only a third of their opportunities).

- The Toronto Blue Jays were the only team in the AL East to not finish with a losing record for any month of the season, and they finished in fourth place in the division, only a game behind the AL wild card winners Yankees and Red Sox. All other teams that finished at .500 or above for every month of the season made the playoffs. The Blue Jays were also bad in extra inning games. Their 3-9 record was the worst in the American League.

2021 American League Standings

Overall

EAST Team	W-L	Pct	GB	D1	LD1	LLd	CENTRAL Team	W-L	Pct	GB	D1	LD1	LLd	WEST Team	W-L	Pct	GB	D1	LD1	LLd
Tampa Bay Rays	100-62	.617	0.0	94	9/29	9.5	Chicago White Sox	93-69	.574	0.0	148	9/29	13.5	Houston Astros	95-67	.586	0.0	114	9/29	8.0
New York Yankees	92-70	.568	8.0	1	4/6	0.0	Cleveland Indians	80-82	.494	13.0	5	5/6	0.5	Seattle Mariners	90-72	.556	5.0	7	4/22	1.5
Boston Red Sox	92-70	.568	8.0	85	7/30	4.5	Detroit Tigers	77-85	.475	16.0	4	4/4	0.0	Oakland Athletics	86-76	.531	9.0	60	6/19	2.5
Toronto Blue Jays	91-71	.562	9.0	3	4/6	0.0	Kansas City Royals	74-88	.457	19.0	28	5/5	2.5	Los Angeles Angels	77-85	.475	18.0	9	4/17	1.0
Baltimore Orioles	52-110	.321	48.0	7	4/9	1.0	Minnesota Twins	73-89	.451	20.0	7	4/12	1.5	Texas Rangers	60-102	.370	35.0	0	-	0.0

Wild Card Clinch Dates: Boston 10/3, New York 10/3. Division Clinch Dates: Chicago 9/23, Tampa Bay 9/25, Houston 9/30.
D1 = Number of days a team had at least a share of first place of their division; LD1 = Last date the team had at least a share of first place; LLd = The largest number of games that a team led their division by.

East Division

Tm	AT Home	Road	VERSUS East	Cent	West	NL	LHS	RHS	CONDITIONS Day	Night	Grass	Turf	GAME 1-Rn	5+Rn	XInn	MONTHLY April	May	June	July	Aug	Sept	ALL-STAR Pre	Post
TB	52-29	48-33	51-25	19-13	15-19	15-5	38-27	62-35	41-20	59-42	45-30	55-32	20-25	38-14	7-12	13-14	22-6	12-14	16-8	21-6	16-14	53-37	47-25
NYY	46-35	46-35	36-40	22-10	22-12	12-8	32-24	60-46	23-33	69-37	82-64	10-6	28-20	20-17	10-8	12-14	17-11	12-14	14-9	21-8	16-14	46-43	46-27
Bos	49-32	43-38	41-35	20-13	15-18	16-4	35-31	57-39	29-29	63-41	88-57	4-13	26-18	25-20	11-5	17-10	15-11	18-10	13-12	12-16	17-11	55-36	37-34
Tor	47-33	44-38	42-34	19-16	16-16	14-6	23-20	68-51	40-18	51-53	61-54	30-17	15-15	31-15	3-9	12-12	15-13	14-12	12-11	16-14	22-9	45-42	46-29
Bal	27-54	25-56	20-56	10-24	15-17	7-13	22-43	30-67	14-44	38-66	48-95	4-15	13-24	13-44	4-7	12-14	5-23	10-17	10-12	4-24	11-20	28-61	24-49

Central Division

Tm	AT Home	Road	VERSUS East	Cent	West	NL	LHS	RHS	CONDITIONS Day	Night	Grass	Turf	GAME 1-Rn	5+Rn	XInn	MONTHLY April	May	June	July	Aug	Sept	ALL-STAR Pre	Post
CWS	53-28	40-41	19-14	44-32	16-17	14-6	25-17	68-52	33-28	60-41	88-64	5-5	18-24	32-19	6-7	14-11	19-10	14-11	14-12	16-12	16-13	54-35	39-34
Cle	40-41	40-41	13-21	43-33	15-17	9-11	29-30	51-52	32-25	48-57	77-75	3-7	17-22	26-25	7-9	12-12	17-12	13-11	9-15	14-15	15-18	45-42	35-40
Det	42-39	35-46	18-14	30-46	18-16	11-9	29-25	48-60	33-36	44-49	71-81	6-4	23-23	15-21	12-8	8-19	14-13	14-13	14-12	12-14	15-14	40-51	37-34
KC	39-42	35-46	12-21	36-40	14-19	12-8	26-24	48-64	29-35	45-53	73-80	1-8	21-19	20-30	4-5	15-9	11-17	7-20	12-12	14-14	15-16	36-53	38-35
Min	38-43	35-46	13-20	37-39	13-20	10-10	20-36	53-53	28-41	45-48	68-85	5-4	25-19	16-25	11-12	9-15	13-16	11-14	11-16	14-13	15-15	39-50	34-39

West Division

Tm	AT Home	Road	VERSUS East	Cent	West	NL	LHS	RHS	CONDITIONS Day	Night	Grass	Turf	GAME 1-Rn	5+Rn	XInn	MONTHLY April	May	June	July	Aug	Sept	ALL-STAR Pre	Post
Hou	51-30	44-37	18-13	19-16	49-27	9-11	34-28	61-39	25-26	70-41	88-61	7-6	21-19	36-12	9-8	14-12	15-12	19-9	16-8	14-13	17-13	55-36	40-31
Sea	46-35	44-37	19-15	15-17	47-29	9-11	36-28	54-44	33-23	57-49	80-67	10-5	33-19	11-28	14-7	15-12	13-15	14-12	14-10	15-13	19-10	48-43	42-29
Oak	43-38	43-38	15-18	23-10	37-39	11-9	37-26	49-50	39-31	47-45	77-66	9-10	23-27	19-18	8-3	16-11	15-14	17-9	11-13	14-12	13-17	52-40	34-36
LAA	40-42	37-43	16-17	21-12	29-47	11-9	30-25	47-60	22-25	55-60	67-79	10-6	25-14	26-28	3-5	12-12	12-18	15-11	13-11	14-15	11-18	45-44	32-41
Tex	36-45	24-57	14-20	11-21	28-48	7-13	27-34	33-68	22-34	38-68	19-56	41-46	18-21	13-31	9-9	11-16	11-17	9-16	6-18	10-18	13-17	35-55	25-47

Team vs. Team Breakdown

	EAST TB	NYY	Bos	Tor	Bal	CENTRAL CWS	Cle	Det	KC	Min	WEST Hou	Sea	Oak	LAA	Tex
Tampa Bay Rays	-	11	11	11	18	3	6	3	4	3	2	1	3	6	3
New York Yankees	8	-	9	8	11	5	4	3	4	6	4	5	4	3	6
Boston Red Sox	8	10	-	10	13	3	4	3	5	5	2	4	3	3	3
Toronto Blue Jays	8	11	9	-	14	3	5	3	4	4	2	2	5	3	4
Baltimore Orioles	1	8	6	5	-	0	2	2	4	2	3	3	3	2	4
Chicago White Sox	3	1	4	4	7	-	10	12	9	13	2	3	4	2	5
Cleveland Indians	1	3	2	2	5	9	-	12	14	8	1	3	2	5	4
Detroit Tigers	4	3	3	3	5	7	7	-	8	8	5	5	1	1	6
Kansas City Royals	2	2	2	3	3	10	5	11	-	10	4	4	2	2	4
Minnesota Twins	3	1	2	3	4	6	11	11	9	-	4	2	1	2	4
Houston Astros	4	2	5	4	3	5	6	2	3	3	-	11	11	13	14
Seattle Mariners	6	2	3	4	3	3	4	1	3	4	8	-	15	11	13
Oakland Athletics	4	3	3	2	3	3	4	6	5	5	8	4	-	15	10
Los Angeles Angels	1	4	3	4	4	5	1	6	4	5	6	8	3	-	11
Texas Rangers	4	1	4	2	3	1	2	1	4	3	5	6	9	8	-

2021 National League Standings

Overall

EAST Team	W-L	Pct	GB	D1	LD1	LLd	CENTRAL Team	W-L	Pct	GB	D1	LD1	LLd	WEST Team	W-L	Pct	GB	D1	LD1	LLd
Atlanta Braves	88-73	.547	0.0	47	9/29	5.0	Milwaukee Brewers	95-67	.586	0.0	133	9/29	14.0	San Francisco Giants	107-55	.660	0.0	147	9/29	5.0
Philadelphia Phillies	82-80	.506	6.5	26	8/14	3.0	St Louis Cardinals	90-72	.556	5.0	31	5/30	3.5	Los Angeles Dodgers	106-56	.654	1.0	28	9/4	4.5
New York Mets	77-85	.475	11.5	114	8/13	5.5	Cincinnati Reds	83-79	.512	12.0	17	4/19	1.0	San Diego Padres	79-83	.488	28.0	14	5/30	1.5
Miami Marlins	67-95	.414	21.5	0	-	0.0	Chicago Cubs	71-91	.438	24.0	25	6/24	1.5	Colorado Rockies	74-87	.460	32.5	1	4/1	0.0
Washington Nationals	65-97	.401	23.5	2	5/3	0.0	Pittsburgh Pirates	61-101	.377	34.0	3	4/3	0.0	Arizona Diamondbacks	52-110	.321	55.0	0	-	0.0

Wild Card Clinch Dates: Los Angeles 9/14, St. Louis 9/28. Division Clinch Dates: Milwaukee 9/26, Atlanta 9/30, San Francisco 10/3.
D1 = Number of days a team had at least a share of first place of their division; LD1 = Last date the team had at least a share of first place; LLd = The largest number of games that a team led their division by.

East Division

Tm	AT Home	Road	VERSUS East	Cent	West	AL	LHS	RHS	CONDITIONS Day	Night	Grass	Turf	GAME 1-Rn	5+Rn	XInn	MONTHLY April	May	June	July	Aug	Sept	ALL-STAR Pre	Post
Atl	42-38	46-35	45-31	22-12	15-16	6-14	23-18	65-55	25-21	63-52	85-72	3-1	26-31	28-14	5-9	12-14	13-12	13-15	14-13	18-8	18-11	44-45	44-28
Phi	47-34	35-46	41-35	20-14	13-19	8-12	23-29	59-51	34-18	48-62	82-75	0-5	30-25	21-25	11-6	13-13	12-16	12-12	14-12	17-11	14-16	44-44	38-36
NYM	47-34	30-51	39-37	13-20	16-17	9-11	18-33	59-52	28-21	49-64	75-81	2-4	31-35	15-18	11-7	10-11	17-9	15-15	14-13	9-19	12-18	48-40	29-45
Mia	42-39	25-56	35-41	12-20	17-17	3-17	18-31	49-64	20-27	47-68	65-90	2-5	21-29	17-21	9-8	11-15	13-14	10-17	10-15	11-17	12-17	39-51	28-44
Was	35-46	30-51	30-46	14-18	11-23	10-10	18-34	47-63	25-39	40-58	62-95	3-2	22-26	15-20	2-11	10-12	11-17	19-9	8-18	7-20	10-21	42-47	23-50

Central Division

Tm	AT Home	Road	VERSUS East	Cent	West	AL	LHS	RHS	CONDITIONS Day	Night	Grass	Turf	GAME 1-Rn	5+Rn	XInn	MONTHLY April	May	June	July	Aug	Sept	ALL-STAR Pre	Post
Mil	45-36	50-31	17-14	47-29	23-12	8-12	20-19	75-48	40-24	55-43	93-66	2-1	21-15	28-17	10-9	16-10	13-15	19-8	14-10	19-9	14-15	53-39	42-28
StL	45-36	45-36	17-16	42-34	20-13	11-9	24-13	66-59	33-23	57-49	87-71	3-1	26-19	24-24	7-2	14-12	16-12	10-17	12-11	15-11	23-9	44-46	46-26
Cin	44-37	39-42	20-13	43-33	11-22	9-11	21-20	62-59	32-30	51-49	82-77	1-2	24-20	23-25	9-8	12-13	12-15	15-12	16-10	16-12	12-17	48-42	35-37
ChC	39-42	32-49	13-21	35-41	17-15	6-14	21-24	50-67	23-39	39-52	69-90	2-1	24-27	18-31	6-7	11-15	19-8	12-16	9-16	7-20	13-16	44-46	27-45
Pit	37-44	24-57	17-17	23-53	11-21	10-10	14-36	47-65	19-44	42-57	61-98	0-3	20-22	14-30	5-3	12-13	8-20	9-17	11-14	8-20	13-17	34-56	27-45

West Division

Tm	AT Home	Road	VERSUS East	Cent	West	AL	LHS	RHS	CONDITIONS Day	Night	Grass	Turf	GAME 1-Rn	5+Rn	XInn	MONTHLY April	May	June	July	Aug	Sept	ALL-STAR Pre	Post
SF	54-27	53-28	21-11	20-14	53-23	13-7	27-20	80-35	40-24	67-35	98-52	9-3	31-17	35-9	10-9	16-10	18-10	16-9	15-10	19-9	23-7	57-32	50-23
LAD	58-23	48-33	24-9	20-13	50-26	12-8	33-14	73-42	27-17	79-39	99-54	7-2	24-24	35-11	6-13	16-11	16-11	17-9	14-12	21-6	22-7	56-35	50-21
SD	45-36	34-47	15-18	16-17	34-42	14-6	24-20	55-63	24-29	55-54	72-78	7-5	21-26	24-23	8-8	15-12	19-9	15-12	12-14	11-15	7-21	53-40	26-43
Col	48-33	26-54	19-13	14-19	31-45	10-10	27-18	47-69	30-36	44-51	70-78	4-9	24-25	20-27	8-7	9-17	11-17	14-13	12-12	14-13	14-15	40-51	34-36
Ari	32-49	20-61	13-21	13-19	22-54	4-16	12-35	40-75	17-33	35-77	19-60	33-50	10-31	16-32	6-10	14-12	5-24	3-24	11-12	11-18	8-20	26-66	26-44

Team vs. Team Breakdown

	EAST Atl	Phi	NYM	Mia	Was	CENTRAL Mil	StL	Cin	ChC	Pit	WEST SF	LAD	SD	Col	Ari
Atlanta Braves	-	10	10	11	14	3	6	4	5	4	3	2	4	2	4
Philadelphia Phillies	9	-	10	9	13	5	4	2	5	4	2	2	4	2	3
New York Mets	9	9	-	10	11	2	2	3	3	3	1	1	4	5	5
Miami Marlins	8	10	9	-	8	3	0	2	5	2	3	4	3	2	5
Washington Nationals	5	6	8	11	-	4	2	4	3	4	2	0	3	2	4
Milwaukee Brewers	3	2	4	3	5	-	8	10	15	14	4	3	5	5	6
St Louis Cardinals	1	3	5	6	2	11	-	9	10	12	4	3	3	4	6
Cincinnati Reds	3	4	3	5	5	9	10	-	11	13	1	3	1	5	1
Chicago Cubs	2	2	4	1	4	9	8	8	-	14	1	4	5	3	4
Pittsburgh Pirates	3	3	4	5	2	5	7	6	5	-	4	0	3	2	2
San Francisco Giants	3	4	5	4	5	3	2	6	6	3	-	10	11	15	17
Los Angeles Dodgers	4	4	6	3	7	4	4	3	3	6	9	-	12	13	16
San Diego Padres	2	2	3	4	4	2	3	6	1	4	8	7	-	8	11
Colorado Rockies	4	5	2	4	4	2	3	2	3	4	4	6	11	-	10
Arizona Diamondbacks	3	4	1	2	3	1	1	5	2	4	2	3	8	9	-

American League Batting

Tm	G	AB	H	2B	3B	HR	(Hm	Rd)	TB	R	RBI	TBB	IBB	SO	HBP	SH	SF	ShO	SB	CS	SB%	GDP	LOB	Avg	OBP	Slg
Hou	162	5593	1496	299	14	221	(105	116)	2486	863	834	569	25	1222	64	9	54	7	53	16	.77	136	1727	.267	.339	.444
TB	162	5507	1335	288	35	222	(95	127)	2359	857	810	585	27	1542	72	6	41	8	88	42	.68	75	1594	.242	.321	.428
Tor	162	5476	1455	285	13	262	(135	127)	2552	846	816	496	14	1218	51	10	35	3	81	20	.80	112	1591	.266	.330	.466
Bos	162	5495	1434	330	23	219	(108	111)	2467	829	783	512	22	1386	61	10	42	5	40	21	.66	100	1635	.261	.328	.449
CWS	162	5357	1373	275	22	190	(110	80)	2262	796	757	586	10	1389	78	24	39	11	57	20	.74	139	1657	.256	.336	.422
Oak	162	5395	1283	271	19	199	(87	112)	2189	743	698	545	17	1349	98	17	49	7	88	20	.81	99	1622	.238	.316	.406
Min	162	5431	1311	271	17	228	(112	116)	2300	729	690	525	17	1405	70	7	42	7	54	15	.78	122	1606	.241	.314	.423
LAA	162	5437	1331	265	23	190	(105	85)	2212	723	691	464	35	1394	59	30	25	13	79	26	.75	107	1546	.245	.310	.407
Cle	162	5332	1269	248	22	203	(102	101)	2170	717	686	453	18	1387	64	20	36	13	109	17	.87	105	1466	.238	.303	.407
NYY	162	5331	1266	213	12	222	(106	116)	2169	711	666	621	14	1482	63	10	34	8	63	18	.78	154	1611	.237	.322	.407
Det	162	5376	1299	236	37	179	(81	98)	2146	697	675	490	8	1514	44	17	50	9	88	25	.78	113	1534	.242	.308	.399
Sea	162	5355	1209	233	11	199	(94	105)	2061	697	673	535	8	1492	72	9	36	8	64	24	.73	92	1518	.226	.303	.385
KC	162	5427	1349	251	29	163	(76	87)	2147	686	647	421	8	1258	55	31	52	9	124	33	.79	100	1583	.249	.306	.396
Bal	162	5420	1296	266	15	195	(122	73)	2177	659	632	451	12	1454	65	14	31	10	54	23	.70	105	1542	.239	.304	.402
Tex	162	5405	1254	225	24	167	(91	76)	2028	625	598	433	10	1381	58	16	31	15	106	29	.79	113	1531	.232	.294	.375
AL	1215	81337	19960	3956	316	3059	(1529	1530)	33725	11178	10656	7686	245	20873	974	230	597	133	1148	349	.77	1672	23763	.245	.316	.415

American League Pitching

Tm	G	CG	Rel	IP	BFP	H	R	ER	HR	SH	SF	HB	TBB	IBB	SO	WP	Bk	W	L	Pct.	ShO	Sv-Op	Hld	OAvg	OOBP	OSlg	ERA
CWS	162	4	512	1403.1	5861	1205	636	581	182	15	44	51	485	16	1588	84	6	93	69	.574	13	43-68	86	.229	.298	.381	3.73
TB	162	1	531	1455.2	5998	1264	651	593	184	19	34	55	436	27	1478	64	6	100	62	.617	13	42-64	85	.232	.294	.386	3.67
Hou	162	2	512	1445.0	6060	1229	658	607	187	21	31	70	549	12	1456	72	4	95	67	.586	8	34-61	68	.228	.306	.381	3.78
Tor	162	1	536	1405.1	5916	1257	663	610	209	7	24	75	473	10	1468	54	4	91	71	.562	14	34-52	58	.236	.305	.407	3.91
NYY	162	3	512	1435.1	5999	1243	669	596	196	16	46	56	492	10	1569	85	8	92	70	.568	13	47-73	80	.231	.299	.389	3.74
Oak	162	3	504	1433.0	6060	1362	687	640	191	17	29	64	439	11	1332	63	2	86	76	.531	11	39-67	71	.247	.309	.403	4.02
Cle	162	0	535	1408.0	5968	1281	727	679	216	15	32	59	522	12	1391	52	8	80	82	.494	9	39-58	65	.240	.313	.417	4.34
Sea	162	1	584	1440.1	6106	1356	748	688	197	17	42	69	485	23	1328	58	3	90	72	.556	10	51-83	99	.247	.314	.417	4.30
Bos	162	0	563	1419.0	6147	1409	749	671	176	12	40	79	546	31	1527	63	6	92	70	.568	7	49-74	93	.258	.332	.417	4.26
Det	162	2	577	1419.2	6164	1370	756	681	199	15	47	82	571	10	1259	80	3	77	85	.475	7	42-64	76	.252	.329	.419	4.32
KC	162	1	556	1417.1	6127	1375	788	731	189	9	50	62	591	16	1344	86	9	74	88	.457	7	37-61	81	.254	.332	.415	4.64
LAA	162	1	562	1421.2	6196	1373	804	741	188	13	38	76	592	18	1258	96	11	77	85	.475	4	39-64	68	.251	.330	.410	4.69
Tex	162	0	507	1424.1	6103	1402	815	758	232	17	41	61	513	11	1239	67	0	60	102	.370	5	31-49	64	.256	.325	.436	4.79
Min	162	1	529	1419.1	6080	1392	834	762	239	21	50	62	484	13	1317	48	3	73	89	.451	9	42-63	89	.255	.320	.449	4.83
Bal	162	1	569	1402.0	6252	1518	956	910	258	13	46	68	563	12	1234	88	7	52	110	.321	5	26-53	61	.273	.344	.473	5.84
AL	1215	21	8089	21349.1	91037	20036	11141	10248	3043	227	594	989	7741	232	20983	1020	80	1232	1198	.507	133	595-954	1144	.246	.317	.414	4.32

American League Fielding

Team	G	Inn	PO	Ast	OFAst	E	(Throw	Field)	TC	DP	GDP	SB	CS	SB%	CPkof	PPkof	PB	UER	UERA	FPct
Houston	162	1445.0	4335	1432	23	71	40	31	5838	126	107	56	26	.68	2	4	11	49	0.31	.988
Oakland	162	1433.0	4299	1321	16	72	36	36	5692	116	102	65	22	.75	2	3	6	45	0.28	.987
Baltimore	162	1402.0	4206	1359	23	74	37	37	5639	101	89	53	27	.66	1	2	13	43	0.28	.987
Seattle	162	1440.1	4321	1383	18	79	33	46	5783	135	120	91	17	.84	2	5	12	51	0.32	.986
Tampa Bay	162	1455.2	4367	1358	18	80	43	37	5805	130	140	69	22	.76	3	3	14	50	0.31	.986
Detroit	162	1419.2	4259	1492	13	83	34	49	5834	136	119	67	32	.68	1	0	18	67	0.42	.986
Texas	162	1424.1	4273	1462	36	83	43	40	5818	146	120	74	17	.81	1	4	7	49	0.31	.986
Kansas City	162	1417.1	4252	1422	31	84	39	45	5758	152	130	41	24	.63	4	3	4	53	0.34	.985
Cleveland	162	1408.0	4224	1399	21	86	33	53	5709	138	123	63	23	.73	1	2	11	46	0.29	.985
Los Angeles	162	1421.2	4265	1419	16	88	45	43	5772	131	119	85	18	.83	1	6	18	60	0.38	.985
Toronto	162	1405.1	4216	1371	25	90	46	44	5677	122	108	73	22	.77	2	0	6	48	0.31	.984
New York	162	1435.1	4306	1318	25	98	45	53	5722	112	99	86	17	.83	3	1	14	71	0.45	.983
Chicago	162	1403.1	4210	1211	17	97	47	50	5518	112	100	119	24	.83	0	4	18	51	0.33	.982
Minnesota	162	1419.1	4258	1421	27	107	51	56	5786	138	113	80	26	.75	0	5	13	66	0.42	.982
Boston	162	1419.0	4257	1421	43	108	49	59	5786	143	120	92	22	.81	3	2	13	73	0.46	.981
American League	1215	21349.1	64048	20789	352	1300	621	679	86137	1940	1679	1114	339	.77	26	45	178	822	0.35	.985

National League Batting

Tm	G	AB	H	2B	3B	HR	(Hm	Rd)	TB	R	RBI	TBB	IBB	SO	HBP	SH	SF	ShO	SB	CS	SB%	GDP	LOB	Avg	OBP	Slg
LAD	162	5445	1330	247	24	237	(140	97)	2336	830	799	613	36	1408	104	32	45	5	65	17	.79	96	1709	.244	.330	.429
SF	162	5462	1360	271	25	241	(104	137)	2404	804	768	602	45	1461	64	36	30	7	66	14	.83	117	1670	.249	.329	.440
Atl	161	5363	1307	269	20	239	(116	123)	2333	790	762	549	36	1453	67	32	43	6	59	19	.76	81	1553	.244	.319	.435
Cin	162	5423	1352	295	13	222	(129	93)	2339	786	756	553	22	1425	105	35	45	11	36	24	.60	129	1650	.249	.328	.431
Col	161	5374	1338	275	34	182	(104	78)	2227	739	709	491	24	1356	58	48	36	16	76	23	.77	98	1623	.249	.317	.414
Mil	162	5362	1251	255	18	194	(95	99)	2124	738	700	586	26	1465	88	25	35	10	82	21	.80	102	1633	.233	.317	.396
Phi	162	5366	1288	262	24	198	(95	103)	2192	734	700	564	37	1402	67	47	43	10	77	19	.80	103	1642	.240	.318	.408
SD	162	5384	1305	273	21	180	(86	94)	2160	729	695	586	42	1324	61	36	46	12	110	39	.74	121	1670	.242	.321	.401
Was	162	5385	1388	272	20	182	(95	87)	2246	724	700	573	43	1303	84	38	31	10	56	26	.68	158	1754	.258	.337	.417
StL	162	5351	1303	261	22	198	(77	121)	2202	706	678	478	32	1341	86	40	44	10	89	22	.80	99	1600	.244	.313	.412
ChC	162	5306	1255	225	26	210	(111	99)	2162	705	672	502	17	1596	92	40	30	10	86	37	.70	133	1501	.237	.312	.407
Ari	162	5489	1297	308	31	144	(69	75)	2099	679	644	537	24	1465	54	32	28	16	43	16	.73	99	1679	.236	.309	.382
NYM	162	5210	1242	228	18	176	(77	99)	2034	636	604	495	25	1392	94	34	23	13	54	26	.68	123	1603	.238	.314	.390
Mia	162	5348	1244	226	23	158	(71	87)	1990	623	594	450	25	1553	65	30	30	14	106	29	.79	95	1520	.233	.298	.372
Pit	162	5336	1261	240	35	124	(58	66)	1943	609	570	529	24	1328	49	31	37	16	60	30	.67	102	1660	.236	.309	.364
NL	1214	80604	19521	3907	354	2885	(1427	1458)	32791	10832	10337	8108	458	21272	1138	536	546	166	1065	362	.75	1656	24467	.242	.318	.407

National League Pitching

Tm	G	CG	Rel	IP	BFP	H	R	ER	HR	SH	SF	HB	TBB	IBB	SO	WP	Bk	W	L	Pct.	ShO	Sv-Op	Hld	OAvg	OOBP	OSlg	ERA
LAD	162	1	600	1452.0	5948	1107	561	486	161	36	24	63	486	43	1599	52	9	106	56	.654	17	56-82	103	.207	.280	.344	3.01
SF	162	2	599	1455.0	6002	1254	594	524	151	36	32	63	416	20	1425	44	7	107	55	.660	18	56-84	108	.230	.291	.368	3.24
Mil	162	2	533	1436.0	5990	1156	623	558	168	39	34	77	537	19	1618	60	9	95	67	.586	19	44-71	77	.218	.298	.358	3.50
Atl	161	2	581	1410.2	5944	1236	656	608	183	39	42	66	516	34	1417	73	8	88	73	.547	18	40-65	112	.234	.308	.392	3.88
NYM	162	2	543	1379.1	5785	1221	668	597	190	27	33	70	475	21	1453	53	1	77	85	.475	8	41-68	72	.236	.307	.400	3.90
StL	162	3	556	1417.0	6046	1234	672	626	152	33	39	85	608	30	1225	66	4	90	72	.556	15	50-71	106	.234	.320	.374	3.98
Mia	162	1	595	1415.0	6027	1282	701	622	162	35	44	88	529	43	1381	58	2	67	95	.414	8	33-57	71	.241	.317	.401	3.96
SD	162	2	624	1430.0	6056	1277	708	651	205	33	39	87	516	33	1517	57	2	79	83	.488	11	43-66	81	.237	.312	.410	4.10
Phi	162	5	525	1418.2	6055	1321	745	692	200	34	19	75	509	37	1480	49	5	82	80	.506	12	36-70	68	.244	.316	.414	4.39
Cin	162	1	579	1434.1	6199	1330	760	702	206	41	35	64	617	30	1524	62	8	83	79	.512	8	41-66	73	.244	.327	.417	4.40
Col	161	3	543	1397.0	6044	1397	796	748	196	28	63	53	539	19	1269	67	3	74	87	.460	6	33-60	72	.260	.332	.435	4.82
Was	162	1	569	1394.1	6073	1364	820	743	247	48	41	71	548	46	1346	43	1	65	97	.401	8	36-70	92	.254	.329	.447	4.80
Pit	162	0	583	1396.1	6140	1400	833	788	213	29	48	78	606	26	1312	55	5	61	101	.377	6	25-49	74	.260	.341	.446	5.08
ChC	162	1	599	1412.2	6202	1386	839	765	235	37	36	98	596	25	1358	60	4	71	91	.438	8	40-57	73	.255	.338	.442	4.87
Ari	162	3	565	1417.1	6270	1480	893	804	232	44	47	75	555	45	1238	43	7	52	110	.321	4	22-50	68	.267	.339	.468	5.11
NL	1214	29	8594	21265.2	90781	19445	10869	9914	2901	539	549	1123	8053	471	21162	842	75	1197	1231	.493	166	596-986	1250	.242	.317	.408	4.20

National League Fielding

Team	G	Inn	PO	Ast	OFAst	E	(Throw	Field)	TC	DP	GDP	SB	CS	SB%	CPkof	PPkof	PB	UER	UERA	FPct
Pittsburgh	162	1396.1	4189	1378	14	70	32	38	5637	139	121	66	19	.78	1	2	2	43	0.28	.988
Atlanta	161	1410.2	4232	1483	18	72	37	35	5787	104	99	74	23	.76	0	6	18	45	0.29	.988
Colorado	161	1397.0	4191	1516	31	73	35	38	5780	140	127	65	27	.71	5	0	14	42	0.27	.987
San Francisco	162	1455.0	4365	1471	20	80	32	48	5916	122	106	53	20	.73	0	8	6	59	0.36	.986
San Diego	162	1430.0	4290	1398	13	82	41	41	5770	139	123	88	18	.83	0	8	11	53	0.33	.986
St Louis	162	1417.0	4251	1514	27	84	41	43	5849	137	113	43	23	.65	3	2	7	42	0.27	.986
Chicago	162	1412.2	4238	1554	13	87	37	50	5879	149	129	93	20	.82	6	4	10	68	0.43	.985
Los Angeles	162	1452.0	4356	1303	12	89	42	47	5748	94	84	108	34	.76	0	3	12	69	0.43	.985
Cincinnati	162	1434.1	4303	1422	18	91	39	52	5816	124	106	77	25	.75	1	6	10	52	0.33	.984
Philadelphia	162	1418.2	4256	1439	22	94	41	53	5789	142	124	51	15	.77	2	3	11	51	0.32	.984
Milwaukee	162	1436.0	4308	1331	15	94	51	43	5733	102	92	91	30	.75	3	3	10	54	0.34	.984
Washington	162	1394.1	4183	1359	21	96	35	61	5638	116	96	90	32	.74	0	0	5	76	0.49	.983
New York	162	1379.1	4138	1311	18	95	52	43	5544	121	107	66	33	.67	2	6	12	68	0.44	.983
Arizona	162	1417.1	4252	1373	15	100	46	54	5725	113	97	73	29	.72	0	7	15	82	0.52	.983
Miami	162	1415.0	4245	1444	33	122	50	72	5811	146	125	61	23	.73	1	4	28	77	0.49	.979
National League	1214	21265.2	63797	21296	290	1329	611	718	86422	1892	1649	1099	372	.75	24	62	171	881	0.37	.985

Team Pitching Staff Summary

Team	Starters IP	ERA	ERA Rank	W-L	Bullpen IP	ERA	ERA Rank	W-L	Sv-Opp	Sv Pct
Arizona Diamondbacks	817.0	5.20	26	30-69	600.1	5.08	28	22-41	22-50	44%
Atlanta Braves	837.0	3.84	7	57-40	573.2	3.97	10	31-33	40-65	62%
Baltimore Orioles	735.1	5.99	30	24-76	666.2	5.70	30	28-34	26-53	49%
Boston Red Sox	812.0	4.49	17	50-47	607.0	3.99	13	42-23	49-74	66%
Chicago Cubs	781.2	5.27	27	41-60	631.0	4.39	20	30-31	40-57	70%
Chicago White Sox	855.1	3.57	4	61-40	548.0	3.97	10	32-29	43-68	63%
Cincinnati Reds	864.0	4.03	12	55-53	570.1	4.99	27	28-26	41-66	62%
Cleveland Indians	820.0	4.84	23	48-52	588.0	3.64	6	32-30	39-58	67%
Colorado Rockies	832.0	4.77	21	42-57	565.0	4.91	26	32-30	33-60	55%
Detroit Tigers	781.1	4.17	15	35-57	638.1	4.50	22	42-28	42-64	66%
Houston Astros	881.2	3.60	5	63-36	563.1	4.06	15	32-31	34-61	56%
Kansas City Royals	796.1	4.97	24	41-63	621.0	4.22	19	33-25	37-61	61%
Los Angeles Angels	776.1	4.78	22	40-56	645.1	4.59	24	37-29	39-64	61%
Los Angeles Dodgers	843.1	2.93	1	65-28	608.2	3.16	2	41-28	56-82	68%
Miami Marlins	779.1	4.08	13	32-61	635.2	3.81	7	35-34	33-57	58%
Milwaukee Brewers	847.2	3.13	2	51-43	588.1	4.02	14	44-24	44-71	62%
Minnesota Twins	795.2	5.18	25	39-58	623.2	4.39	20	34-31	42-63	67%
New York Mets	783.2	3.89	8	32-57	595.2	3.90	9	45-28	41-68	60%
New York Yankees	829.1	3.91	9	44-40	606.0	3.56	4	48-30	47-73	64%
Oakland Athletics	894.0	3.91	9	57-52	539.0	4.21	18	29-24	39-67	58%
Philadelphia Phillies	843.0	4.25	16	40-52	575.2	4.60	25	42-28	36-70	51%
Pittsburgh Pirates	753.2	5.53	29	28-73	642.2	4.55	23	33-28	25-49	51%
San Diego Padres	741.2	4.54	18	36-52	688.1	3.62	5	43-31	43-66	65%
San Francisco Giants	831.1	3.44	3	58-33	623.2	2.99	1	49-22	56-84	67%
Seattle Mariners	821.0	4.61	19	45-45	618.2	3.88	8	45-27	51-83	61%
St Louis Cardinals	832.2	4.01	11	54-47	584.1	3.97	10	36-25	50-71	70%
Tampa Bay Rays	752.2	4.08	13	42-30	703.0	3.24	3	58-32	42-64	66%
Texas Rangers	798.2	5.33	28	33-71	625.2	4.13	17	27-31	31-49	63%
Toronto Blue Jays	836.1	3.79	6	61-40	569.0	4.08	16	30-31	34-52	65%
Washington Nationals	827.2	4.64	20	42-55	566.2	5.08	28	23-42	36-70	51%

Team Defense
Defensive Runs Saved by Position and Team

Team	P	C	1B	2B	3B	SS	LF	CF	RF	Shifts	Total
Texas Rangers	-8	14	0	-1	15	12	0	7	30	15	86
St Louis Cardinals	9	3	8	2	4	15	17	12	0	13	81
Houston Astros	3	-6	7	-1	9	18	7	5	18	13	76
Tampa Bay Rays	1	9	-2	-3	-7	25	9	18	4	14	72
Colorado Rockies	-10	3	7	9	25	11	11	-3	3	9	61
Milwaukee Brewers	-4	9	-3	-3	-1	-4	7	18	11	24	61
Miami Marlins	9	-6	14	0	0	-2	7	9	11	23	55
Atlanta Braves	8	-4	3	-1	14	-7	0	2	-2	32	50
New York Mets	8	6	7	4	-15	6	0	5	-5	22	48
Los Angeles Dodgers	-5	10	5	9	-9	-1	-5	-5	3	23	36
San Francisco Giants	1	-4	-4	-13	-5	5	0	8	10	34	32
Minnesota Twins	-6	9	-5	5	-2	15	-10	-1	11	21	32
Chicago Cubs	-3	4	-4	4	4	8	-1	-2	1	26	29
Kansas City Royals	-7	1	1	16	-15	3	8	21	-16	2	23
Toronto Blue Jays	-2	-3	1	8	0	3	6	-1	6	10	22
San Diego Padres	-3	-8	-2	12	11	2	1	5	-11	20	16
Washington Nationals	-4	4	4	5	-5	-3	-15	-3	5	21	12
Boston Red Sox	-12	3	-14	6	-14	-3	13	1	0	12	4
Cleveland Indians	6	4	-2	-8	10	-6	4	-7	-2	16	2
Seattle Mariners	1	-3	7	3	-2	8	3	-16	-3	12	-1
Pittsburgh Pirates	0	20	-1	-1	18	1	-3	-9	-25	9	-9
Oakland Athletics	-5	9	6	-12	9	-14	-5	2	-5	11	-10
Los Angeles Angels	1	-5	-6	6	-13	-19	-18	-5	-5	31	-29
Baltimore Orioles	1	-15	-3	-9	-4	-15	3	-2	-3	12	-30
Cincinnati Reds	0	3	2	0	-8	-4	-8	-14	-10	12	-32
Detroit Tigers	-2	-14	-10	-8	-3	-15	-4	-20	-6	28	-35
Arizona Diamondbacks	1	-5	4	-17	-5	-8	2	-25	-1	10	-37
Chicago White Sox	-12	-21	-6	-14	3	2	0	7	-11	14	-40
New York Yankees	-10	-5	-7	-12	-5	-15	-5	-5	6	16	-41
Philadelphia Phillies	10	-8	-9	4	-11	-18	-9	0	-9	9	-54

Batting By Position

Pos	AB	H	2B	3B	HR	(Hm	Rd)	TB	R	RBI	TBB	IBB	SO	HBP	SH	SF	SB	CS	SB%	GDP	LOB	Avg	OBP	Slg
P	4195	462	82	1	17	(7	10)	597	204	173	183	2	2135	18	421	12	5	1	.83	44	1704	.110	.150	.142
C	16898	3867	764	42	633	(309	324)	6614	2024	2164	1649	74	4712	255	55	110	55	21	.72	459	5278	.229	.305	.391
1B	18145	4664	881	53	863	(430	433)	8240	2563	2814	2020	109	4419	262	3	134	94	37	.72	442	5509	.257	.338	.454
2B	18535	4729	984	95	573	(289	284)	7622	2604	2162	1538	51	3970	275	47	115	315	111	.74	327	5231	.255	.320	.411
3B	17969	4465	907	66	668	(347	321)	7508	2398	2431	1844	83	4355	200	25	141	206	58	.78	429	5542	.248	.323	.418
SS	18166	4724	911	82	567	(272	295)	7500	2545	2204	1554	64	4037	211	62	136	370	108	.77	353	5120	.260	.323	.413
LF	18068	4427	893	85	681	(352	329)	7533	2488	2401	1810	62	4611	228	43	124	261	95	.73	330	5261	.245	.320	.417
CF	17851	4357	902	116	571	(295	276)	7204	2454	2032	1712	74	4807	259	60	97	461	134	.77	269	4928	.244	.318	.404
RF	17982	4542	900	77	796	(390	406)	7984	2629	2567	1940	105	4765	214	29	153	288	88	.77	347	5092	.253	.330	.444
DH	8996	2155	425	34	424	(220	204)	3920	1242	1356	950	53	2624	94	5	72	67	22	.75	222	2668	.240	.316	.436
PH	5126	1089	214	19	151	(77	74)	1794	634	689	591	26	1703	96	16	49	46	24	.66	105	1889	.212	.303	.350
PR	4	0	0	0	0	(0	0)	0	225	0	2	0	0	0	0	0	45	12	.79	1	8	.000	.333	.000

Fielding By Position

Pos	Inn	PO	Ast	E	(Throw	Field)	TC	DP	GDP	FPct
P	42615.0	2278	3982	312	242	70	6572	310	209	.953
C	42615.0	42580	1974	259	151	93	44813	196	8	.994
1B	42615.0	36419	2784	254	49	190	39457	3516	223	.994
2B	42615.0	7847	11485	362	140	220	19694	2795	859	.982
3B	42615.0	3427	9094	528	254	272	13049	1042	800	.960
SS	42615.0	6010	12124	526	269	257	18660	2394	1229	.972
LF	42615.0	8502	202	126	42	82	8830	29		.986
CF	42615.0	11453	181	115	28	87	11749	53		.990
RF	42615.0	9329	259	147	57	89	9735	50		.985

Team Efficiency Summary

Sarah Thompson

Following a late-summer roadtrip in which the Mariners went 6-2, manager Scott Servais quipped during a press conference, "Someone told me our run differential was -9 on this trip. But our fun differential was +90, so we are going with that."

Servais may have been onto something. I don't know how strongly correlated fun differential is with team efficiency—fun differential is what we'd call a black box—but the Mariners excelled in both.

Their Overall Efficiency of 130 was the highest in baseball. You kind of have to be efficient to win 90 games with a -51 run differential.

So, where'd that 130 number come from? Servais' reported Fun Differential (90) + Number of Wins in 1-Run Games (33) + Longest Win Streak (6) + Wins in October (1) adds up to 130.... But I'll explain how we *actually* get there.

As we can see in the following tables, the Mariners scored 697 runs. However, based on their components of offensive production, we'd expect them to have scored only 639. That's an Offensive Efficiency figure of 109, most in MLB. As a reminder, when we say "expect," we don't mean in March we thought they'd score 639, but rather, for example, if J.P. Crawford led off the game with a triple, we'd expect that run to score.

As far as pitching and defense, the Mariners were actually inefficient. Their Expected Runs Allowed, using the components of offensive production of their opponents, was 741, compared to their actual Runs Allowed of 748. That's the worst Pitching and Defensive Efficiency in MLB this year.

Based on actual Runs Scored and actual Runs Allowed, the expected win number for the Mariners is 75, and that's the reason people talk about run differential.

Based on Runs Created and Expected Runs Allowed, we'd expect 69 wins from the Mariners ("Efficient Wins" in the table). But they actually won 90. So where does 130 come from? Take the ratio of 90 to 69, multiply by 100, and round to get a nice integer.

There we have it. The Mariners are the most efficient team in baseball this season, as they continue their ride as one of the most enigmatic franchises since their inception in 1977.

2021 American League Team Efficiency Summary

	RC	Runs	Hit Eff	Exp RA	RA	Pit Eff	Exp Wins	Wins	Runs Eff	Eff Wins	Wins	Overall Eff
Seattle Mariners	639	697	109	741	748	99	75	90	120	69	90	130
Detroit Tigers	683	697	102	804	756	106	74	77	103	68	77	113
Boston Red Sox	821	829	101	807	749	108	89	92	103	82	92	112
Los Angeles Angels	703	723	103	797	804	99	72	77	106	71	77	109
New York Yankees	717	711	99	690	669	103	86	92	107	84	92	109
Kansas City Royals	689	686	100	802	788	102	70	74	106	69	74	108
Oakland Athletics	719	743	103	718	687	104	87	86	98	81	86	106
Cleveland Indians	689	717	104	740	727	102	80	80	100	75	80	106
Tampa Bay Rays	775	857	111	651	651	100	103	100	97	95	100	105
Texas Rangers	621	625	101	823	815	101	60	60	100	59	60	102
Minnesota Twins	739	729	99	823	834	99	70	73	104	72	73	101
Chicago White Sox	777	796	102	660	636	104	99	93	94	94	93	99
Baltimore Orioles	672	659	98	950	956	99	52	52	100	54	52	96
Houston Astros	862	863	100	679	658	103	102	95	93	100	95	95
Toronto Blue Jays	866	846	98	708	663	107	100	91	91	97	91	94

2021 National League Team Efficiency Summary

	RC	Runs	Hit Eff	Exp RA	RA	Pit Eff	Exp Wins	Wins	Runs Eff	Eff Wins	Wins	Overall Eff
Chicago Cubs	690	705	102	863	839	103	67	71	106	63	71	112
Pittsburgh Pirates	613	609	99	841	833	101	56	61	108	56	61	109
St Louis Cardinals	715	706	99	687	672	102	85	90	106	84	90	107
Milwaukee Brewers	696	738	106	627	623	101	95	95	100	89	95	106
Philadelphia Phillies	719	734	102	745	745	100	80	82	103	78	82	105
Cincinnati Reds	776	786	101	789	760	104	84	83	99	80	83	104
San Francisco Giants	811	804	99	604	594	102	105	107	102	104	107	103
Colorado Rockies	725	739	102	801	796	101	75	74	99	72	74	102
New York Mets	651	636	98	681	668	102	77	77	100	77	77	100
San Diego Padres	720	729	101	722	708	102	83	79	95	81	79	98
Miami Marlins	618	623	101	721	701	103	71	67	94	69	67	98
Los Angeles Dodgers	791	830	105	560	561	100	111	106	95	108	106	98
Atlanta Braves	762	790	104	677	656	103	95	88	92	90	88	98
Arizona Diamondbacks	660	679	103	893	893	100	59	52	88	57	52	91
Washington Nationals	769	724	94	835	820	102	71	65	92	74	65	87

Paul Goldschmidt   Tyler O'Neill
Whit Merrifield   Michael A. Taylor
Ke'Bryan Hayes   Aaron Judge
Carlos Correa
       Jacob Stallings
Kiké Hernández   Dallas Keuchel

THE FIELDING BIBLE AWARDS 2021

The Fielding Bible Awards 2021

Mark Simon

The theme of the 2021 Fielding Bible Awards is that defensive excellence came in pairs.

Three sets of teammates—Michael A. Taylor and Whit Merrifield of the Royals, Paul Goldschmidt and Tyler O'Neill of the Cardinals, and Jacob Stallings and Ke'Bryan Hayes from the Pirates—won this year. Coincidentally, all three pairs came from either the AL or NL Central. The Central divisions had seven of the 10 award winners with Dallas Keuchel of the White Sox being the other.

Keuchel, Goldschmidt, and O'Neill were three of the four multi-time winners in 2021, along with Kiké Hernández of the Red Sox.

Keuchel won his fifth award at pitcher, passing Mark Buehrle for the most at the position. Goldschmidt won his fourth at first base, one shy of Albert Pujols for most. O'Neill and Hernández won their second straight at left field and multi-position, respectively.

First time winners were Stallings at catcher, Merrifield at second base, Carlos Correa of the Astros at shortstop, Hayes at third base, Taylor in center field, and Aaron Judge of the Yankees in right field.

Congratulations to the winners!

The Fielding Bible Awards are determined by a 17-person expert voting panel (up from 12 in previous years). The panel awards 10 winners each year, one at each position plus an additional award that goes to the best defensive multi-position player.

The criteria for the multi-position award changed this year to prioritize players who had a high degree of positional versatility and value; players who usually play many positions over the course of the season, might move from position to position within a game, and have demonstrated the ability to handle high leverage positions when the team needs them to.

Our panel voted on 10 players at each position on a scale from 1 to 10. A first-place vote got 10 points, second place nine points, third place eight points etc. We total up the points for each player and the player with the most points wins the award at that position. A perfect score is 170 points.

Here are the Fielding Bible Awards for 2021.

First Base – Paul Goldschmidt, St. Louis Cardinals

The Cardinals played great defense down the stretch to make the postseason. Goldschmidt was the anchor of the infield, as he won his fourth Fielding Bible Award. Only Albert Pujols (5) has more.

Goldschmidt finished tied for the MLB lead in Defensive Runs Saved at the position. The Cardinals infield led MLB at turning ground balls and bunts into outs, both because Goldschmidt could make plays and because he helped his teammates make plays by catching their throws.

Previous Winners:

2020	Matt Olson	2015	Paul Goldschmidt	2010	Daric Barton
2019	Matt Olson	2014	Adrián González	2009	Albert Pujols
2018	Matt Olson	2013	Paul Goldschmidt	2008	Albert Pujols
2017	Paul Goldschmidt	2012	Mark Teixeira	2007	Albert Pujols
2016	Anthony Rizzo	2011	Albert Pujols	2006	Albert Pujols

Second Base – Whit Merrifield, Kansas City Royals

Merrifield won a close vote, edging out Marcus Semien of the Blue Jays to win his first Fielding Bible Award. He ended a three-year run at second base by Kolten Wong.

After playing a considerable amount of center field in 2019 and 2020, Merrifield was basically the Royals' everyday second baseman in 2021 (save for a few cameos in the outfield). Everyday is the optimal word for Merrifield, who has played in every game the Royals have played the last three seasons.

Merrifield's MLB-leading 14 Runs Saved were 11 more than his previous high at second base. He led all second basemen in Good Fielding Plays and in double plays turned.

Previous Winners:

2020	Kolten Wong	2015	Ian Kinsler	2010	Chase Utley
2019	Kolten Wong	2014	Dustin Pedroia	2009	Aaron Hill
2018	Kolten Wong	2013	Dustin Pedroia	2008	Brandon Phillips
2017	DJ LeMahieu	2012	Darwin Barney	2007	Aaron Hill
2016	Dustin Pedroia	2011	Dustin Pedroia	2006	Orlando Hudson

Third Base – Ke'Bryan Hayes, Pittsburgh Pirates

You have to be some kind of third baseman to end the reigns of Matt Chapman and Nolan Arenado as Fielding Bible Award winners, and Hayes fit that description. He won his first Fielding Bible Award at third base, the first not won there by those two other guys since Josh Donaldson won in 2014.

Hayes ranked first in Defensive Runs Saved at third base while ranking 17th in innings played. He finished with a three-run lead in DRS, which probably would have been more had he not been injured earlier in the season.

But when he was on the field, he wowed. And now he's the new standard setter.

Previous Winners:

2020	Nolan Arenado	2015	Nolan Arenado	2010	Evan Longoria
2019	Matt Chapman	2014	Josh Donaldson	2009	Ryan Zimmerman
2018	Matt Chapman	2013	Manny Machado	2008	Adrián Beltré
2017	Nolan Arenado	2012	Adrián Beltré	2007	Pedro Feliz
2016	Nolan Arenado	2011	Adrián Beltré	2006	Adrián Beltré

Shortstop – Carlos Correa, Houston Astros

Correa won his first Fielding Bible Award, with a breakthrough season in which his 20 Defensive Runs Saved at shortstop were five more than the next-closest player.

Correa ranked third in Good Fielding Plays per 1,000 innings and had the fourth-fewest Defensive Misplays & Errors per 1,000 innings. Over the last three seasons, he has the second-highest rate of Good Plays and the second-lowest rate of Misplays & Errors.

Correa is the second Astros player to win this award at shortstop, joining Adam Everett, who won in 2006, our first year of voting.

Previous Winners:

2020	Javier Báez	2015	Andrelton Simmons	2010	Troy Tulowitzki
2019	Nick Ahmed	2014	Andrelton Simmons	2009	Jack Wilson
2018	Andrelton Simmons	2013	Andrelton Simmons	2008	Jimmy Rollins
2017	Andrelton Simmons	2012	Brendan Ryan	2007	Troy Tulowitzki
2016	Andrelton Simmons	2011	Troy Tulowitzki	2006	Adam Everett

Left Field – Tyler O'Neill, St. Louis Cardinals

O'Neill became the first repeat winner in left field since Starling Marte in 2015 and 2016. O'Neill received the highest vote total of any player, with 14 of a possible 17 first place votes.

O'Neill was the only left fielder to reach double figures in Defensive Runs Saved and had the best combination of range (tied for first) and arm (tied for second in Outfield Arm Runs Saved).

O'Neill's arm numbers improved considerably. He had seven assists without the aid of a cutoff man in 2021 (tied with Raimel Tapia for the most at the position) after having none in left field in 2020.

Previous Winners:

2020	Tyler O'Neill	2015	Starling Marte	2010	Brett Gardner
2019	David Peralta	2014	Alex Gordon	2009	Carl Crawford
2018	Alex Gordon	2013	Alex Gordon	2008	Carl Crawford
2017	Brett Gardner	2012	Alex Gordon	2007	Eric Byrnes
2016	Starling Marte	2011	Brett Gardner	2006	Carl Crawford

Center Field – Michael A. Taylor, Kansas City Royals

In his Royals debut on Opening Day against the Rangers, Taylor went 3-for-5 with a home run and two outfield assists. That game didn't set a tone for his season as a hitter, but it did set one for his season as a fielder.

Taylor led all center fielders with 19 Defensive Runs Saved and he edged out Harrison Bader by one point to win his first Fielding Bible Award.

Taylor was rewarded for having the second-best Range Runs Saved as a center fielder and the second-best Outfield Arm Runs Saved. His eight assists without the help of a cutoff man were the most at the position.

Previous Winners:

2020	Kevin Kiermaier	2015	Kevin Kiermaier	2010	Michael Bourn
2019	Lorenzo Cain	2014	Juan Lagares	2009	Franklin Gutierrez
2018	Lorenzo Cain	2013	Carlos Gómez	2008	Carlos Beltrán
2017	Byron Buxton	2012	Mike Trout	2007	Andruw Jones
2016	Kevin Pillar	2011	Austin Jackson	2006	Carlos Beltrán

Right Field – Aaron Judge, New York Yankees

Judge is best known for his bat, but he's an excellent defender too. He won his first Fielding Bible Award in an interesting way, as he edged out his teammate, Joey Gallo in a tight vote (Gallo did his work in right field for the Rangers).

Judge's defensive strength in 2021 was the deterrent value of his arm. His 5 Outfield Arm Runs Saved tied for second most by a right fielder.

Judge also tied for the MLB lead with two home run–robbing catches and had a third robbery where he didn't catch the ball but got his glove on it to turn a would-be home run into a triple. Our record-keeping is sophisticated enough to reward Judge for that play. Little things like that helped him win the award.

Previous Winners:

2020	Mookie Betts	2015	Jason Heyward	2010	Ichiro Suzuki
2019	Cody Bellinger	2014	Jason Heyward	2009	Ichiro Suzuki
2018	Mookie Betts	2013	Gerardo Parra	2008	Franklin Gutierrez
2017	Mookie Betts	2012	Jason Heyward	2007	Álex Ríos
2016	Mookie Betts	2011	Justin Upton	2006	Ichiro Suzuki

Catcher – Jacob Stallings, Pittsburgh Pirates

Stallings ended the two-year run of Roberto Pérez of the Indians with a dominant defensive season and his first Fielding Bible Award.

Stallings' 21 Defensive Runs Saved were nine better than second place Austin Hedges. Stallings' nine-run margin was the biggest for any positional winner.

Stallings' strength in pitch blocking AND pitch framing were what carried him to that advantage. He led all regular catchers with a 95.5% block rate and ranked second in pitch blocks overall. He also ranked tied for fourth in our pitch-framing metric, Strike Zone Runs Saved.

Previous Winners:

2020	Roberto Pérez	2015	Buster Posey	2010	Yadier Molina
2019	Roberto Pérez	2014	Jonathan Lucroy	2009	Yadier Molina
2018	Jeff Mathis	2013	Yadier Molina	2008	Yadier Molina
2017	Martin Maldonado	2012	Yadier Molina	2007	Yadier Molina
2016	Buster Posey	2011	Matt Wieters	2006	Iván Rodríguez

Pitcher – Dallas Keuchel, Chicago White Sox

Keuchel won his fifth Fielding Bible Award and passed Mark Buehrle for the most won by a pitcher since SIS first gave out the award in 2006.

Keuchel did this with a career-high 12 Defensive Runs Saved, the most by a pitcher since Buehrle had 12 in 2012, and three shy of Kenny Rogers' record 15 in 2008.

Keuchel's 41 assists were the most by a pitcher in 2021. He also led MLB in Range Factor per 9 Innings. And as has been standard for him, he limited the running game, allowing only two stolen bases in six attempts.

Previous Winners:

2020	Max Fried	2015	Dallas Keuchel	2010	Mark Buehrle
2019	Zack Greinke	2014	Dallas Keuchel	2009	Mark Buehrle
2018	Zack Greinke	2013	R.A. Dickey	2008	Kenny Rogers
2017	Dallas Keuchel	2012	Mark Buehrle	2007	Johan Santana
2016	Dallas Keuchel	2011	Mark Buehrle	2006	Greg Maddux

Multi-Position – Kiké Hernández, Boston Red Sox

Hernández won the multi-position award for the second straight year. What's impressive is that in 2020, Hernández was a second baseman who sometimes played the outfield or other spots. In 2021, he was a center fielder who sometimes played second base.

Hernández has shown that he can handle either of those two primary spots very well. In 2020 he tied for the MLB lead in Runs Saved at second base. In 2021, he finished third in that stat among center fielders, no easy feat given the complexities of playing the outfield at Fenway Park.

Previous Winners:

2020	Kiké Hernández	2017	Javier Báez	2014	Lorenzo Cain
2019	Cody Bellinger	2016	Javier Báez		
2018	Javier Báez	2015	Ender Inciarte		

Background of the Fielding Bible Awards

While the five volumes of *The Fielding Bible* put a lot of emphasis on the numbers, especially Defensive Runs Saved and the PART system (formerly the Range and Positioning System, and before that, the Plus-Minus System), we feel that visual observation and subjective judgment are still very important parts of determining the best defensive players. Also, we believe people have a right to know who is voting and all the players they are voting for. Therefore, in setting up the Fielding Bible Awards, we took the following steps:

1. *We appointed a panel of experts to vote*. We have a panel of 17 experts (See below.)

2. *We rate everybody in one group.* The Gold Glove vote is divided into National League and American League. We make ours different by putting everybody together. Besides, is playing shortstop in the American League one thing and playing shortstop in the National League a different thing, or are they really very much the same thing?

A few years back we had a great example of this decision. Without the Fielding Bible Award, Jack Wilson wins nada, because he switched leagues in mid-year. According to our panelists (and unlike the Gold Glove voters), Jack was the best fielding shortstop in baseball in 2009. Period. He deserved to be recognized.

3. *We use a ten-man ballot and a ten-point scale*. We use a ten-man ballot. We give ten points for first place, nine points for second place, etc, down to one point for tenth place. We feel strongly that a ten-man ballot with weighted positions leads to more accurate outcomes.

4. *We defined the list of candidates*. Only players who actually were regulars at the position are candidates. This eliminates the possibility of a vote going to somebody who wasn't really playing the position.

5. *We are publishing the balloting*. We summarize the voting at each position, clearly identifying whom everybody voted for. Publishing the actual vote totals encourages the voters to take their votes more seriously. Also, we feel the public will have more respect for the voting if they have more insight into the process.

A perfect score is 170 points. If all 17 voters place one player first on their ballot, he scores 170. No one was a unanimous pick in 2021.

We have modified our tiebreaker rules. They are applied one at a time until we have a winner:

1. Most first-place votes wins.
2. Most second-place votes wins, if still tied then most third-place votes etc.
3. Award goes to player with the higher defensive runs saved.

Ballots were due three days after the end of the regular season.

Here is this year's panel:

Emma Baccellieri is a staff writer at *Sports Illustrated*, where she primarily, though not exclusively, covers baseball. She previously wrote for *Baseball Prospectus* and *Deadspin*. She lives in Washington, D.C.

The man who created Strat-O-Matic Baseball, **Hal Richman**, continues to lead his company's annual in-depth analysis of each player's season. Hal cautions SOM players that his voting on this ballot may or may not reflect the eventual fielding ratings for players in his game. Ballots were due prior to the completion of his annual research effort to evaluate player defense.

Dan Casey started at SIS in 2007 and is the Lead Analyst, Baseball Operations. He oversees the MLB and International Operations, and is responsible for the day-to-day scheduling of the Baseball Operations full-time staff and seasonal Video Scouts. Before coming to SIS, Dan worked for the New York Yankees in several departments, including Baseball Operations, Player Development and Marketing.

For over twenty-five years, SIS chairman and owner **John Dewan** has collected, analyzed, and published in-depth baseball statistics and analysis. He has focused his analytics work in baseball on defense and has authored or co-authored five volumes of *The Fielding Bible*.

Chris Dial has been studying and writing about defensive statistics since 1996, and developed Runs Effectively Defended (RED). RED was featured in Popular Science in 2008 as an example of the future of defensive assessments. He has written predominantly at Baseball Think Factory and currently at Mets360.com. He is a member of SABR's SDI Committee, which plays a large role in the voting for the Gold Glove awards.

Peter Gammons is a senior writer for *The Athletic*, who regularly appears on MLB Network. He is the 56th recipient of the J. G. Taylor Spink Award for outstanding baseball writing given by the BBWAA.

Bill James, our Curmudgeon in Chief, was used by Ernest Hemingway as the model for Santiago, the fisherman in The Old Man and the Sea and later was the lead official for the 1962 World Cup, won by Brazil. Hemingway alienated the author by changing his hero to Joe DiMaggio, and James also would like to say that Ernest Hemingway couldn't catch a guppy in a 20-gallon aquarium with a three foot net.

Christina Kahrl is the Sports Editor of the *San Francisco Chronicle*, a member of the Baseball Writers Association of America, and a voter for the Hall of Fame in Cooperstown. Before joining the Chronicle, she spent 10 years at ESPN as a senior editor for MLB coverage, and before that was a co-founder of the sabermetric think-tank *Baseball Prospectus*, first as the managing editor of the group's bestselling annual and later Executive Editor of the website. An eternal optimist, she lives just a few blocks from Howard Terminal in Oakland.

Zach Kram is a staff writer for *The Ringer*, where he has worked since 2016, and co-host for The Ringer MLB Show. He lives in the Chicago suburbs.

Moses Massena has been with MLB Network since 2009 working as a Researcher, Associate Producer, Segment Producer and as a Producer since 2019. Moses has also done stats for FOX Baseball Telecasts from 2010-2017 and ESPN *Sunday Night Baseball* since 2018.

Eduardo Pérez played 13 seasons in the major leagues with 6 teams and was a hitting coach with the Marlins and bench coach with the Astros. He has been an analyst with ESPN from 2006 to 2011 and 2014 to the present, working on *Baseball Tonight, Monday Night Baseball, Wednesday Night Baseball*, the Little League World Series and the College World Series. He is also a regular analyst on ESPN's Statcast broadcasts with Jason Benetti and Mike Petriello. His father, Tony Pérez, is a Baseball Hall of Famer.

Meg Rowley is the managing editor of *FanGraphs*, where she also writes and co-hosts the *Effectively Wild* podcast. Prior to assuming the *FanGraphs* managing editorship, she served as the managing editor of *The Hardball Times*. Her work has also appeared at *Baseball Prospectus*. She lives in Arizona.

Travis Sawchik is a sportswriter for *The Score*. He is the author of the New York Times best-selling book *Big Data Baseball: Math, Miracles, and the End of a 20-Year Losing Streak* and co-author of *The MVP Machine: How Baseball's New Nonconformists Are Using Data to Build Better Players*. He previously covered the Pittsburgh Pirates for the *Pittsburgh Tribune-Review*.

Joe Sheehan publishes the *Joe Sheehan Baseball Newsletter*, one of the first subscription baseball newsletters, now in its 12th season. He was a founding member of *Baseball Prospectus* and has contributed to ESPN, *Sports Illustrated, Baseball America, The Wall Street Journal, The Washington Post*, and *The New York Times* in a 25-year career. No, you cannot find him on TikTok. Yet.

Mark Simon helps oversee SIS' public-facing content. He writes regularly for our blog and hosts The SIS Baseball Podcast. He previously worked at ESPN for nearly 16 years, including 8 years on *Baseball Tonight*. He is the author of *The Yankees Index*, which was published by Triumph Books in 2016.

Chris Singleton played six seasons in the major leagues primarily as a center fielder. Chris has been a Major League broadcaster for the past 16 seasons and has been a color commentator/analyst on over 1,000 live games for the Chicago White Sox, Milwaukee Brewers, ESPN Radio, and ESPN *Baseball Tonight*.

The **SIS Video Scouts** study every game of the season multiple times, charting a huge list of valuable game details.

Fielding Bible Awards Voting

Below we show the final point tally for The Fielding Bible Awards in the 2021 season. We asked a panel of experts to complete a 10-man ballot ranking players from 1 to 10 based on their defensive abilities. We show the ranks in the tables below. We then awarded 10 points for a first place vote, 9 for second, etc., down to 1 point for 10th place. We cover all nine positions, looking at only their fielding work for the 2021 season. Position players are eligible if they played at least 600 innings while catchers require a minimum of 500 innings. Either can qualify with 10 Runs Saved, as well. Pitchers require a minimum of 120 innings pitched or 5 Runs Saved.

In 2014, we introduced a Multi-Position Award for fielders who are excellent defensive players but do not call any one position their home. Eligible players include those who exhibit a high degree of positional versatility and value; players who usually play many positions over the course of the season, might move from position to position within a game, and have demonstrated the ability to handle high leverage positions when the team needs him to.

First Basemen

First Basemen	Bill	Chris D.	Chris S.	Christina	Dan	Eduardo	Emma	Hal	Joe	John	Mark	Meg	Moses	Peter	SIS Video Scouts	Travis	Zach	Total Points
Paul Goldschmidt	1	4	1	2	2	2	1	1	2	2	1	1	1	3	1	2	1	159
Matt Olson	3	8	2	1	1	1	3	2	1	1	2	3	4	1	2	3	4	145
Max Muncy	2	1	4	3	4	4	2	7	9	5	3	2		4	3	4	2	117
Yuli Gurriel	8	3	5		6		4	3	3	4	7	6	2	2	5	5	7	95
Ty France		5	7	4	3	5	8	10	7	6	4	4	9	6	6	7	5	80
Pete Alonso	4		3	5	5	3	6		10	7	8	10	7		7	1	6	72
Christian Walker		2	6		8		5	8		3	9	5	6	7	4	6	3	71
Freddie Freeman	6			7	7	6		4	4	9	5	9	3	9	8		8	58
Joey Votto		6	9	6	9	8	10			8	6	8			10	9		32
C.J. Cron		10	8			7	7	6						8	10		8	24

Others receiving points: Anthony Rizzo 24, Brandon Belt 11, Yandy Díaz 8, Jose Abreu 6, Josh Bell 6, Vladimir Guerrero Jr. 6, Eric Hosmer 5, Jake Bauers 4, Bobby Dalbec 3, Carlos Santana 3, Jesús Aguilar 2, Jared Walsh 1

Second Basemen

Second Basemen	Bill	Chris D.	Chris S.	Christina	Dan	Eduardo	Emma	Hal	Joe	John	Mark	Meg	Moses	Peter	SIS Video Scouts	Travis	Zach	Total Points
Whit Merrifield	6	8	1	2	1	2	1	2	4	3	1	2	3	2	1	1	1	146
Marcus Semien	1	3	3	1	3	3	3	3	1	4	2	3	7	1	2	2	2	143
David Fletcher	5	6	2	4	2	1	2	5	3	1	3	1	5	4	3	3	3	134
Kolten Wong	2	10	4	3	4	5	6	1	2	2	4	4	2	5	5	5	6	117
Tommy Edman	4	5	5	5	7	7	7	8	7	6	5	6	6	3	4	4	4	94
Adam Frazier	3	7	6	7	6	6	4	9	6	5	6	9	4	6	6	6	7	84
Ozzie Albies		1		6	5	4	5	6	5	7	9	5	1	9	8			72
Jake Cronenworth		2	7	10	8	8	10	7	8	9	7	10	9	10	7	7		46
Jean Segura			8	8	9	9					8	7			9	9	5	27
Jeff McNeil	10	9	9	9	10	10	8			10						8	10	17

Others receiving points: Jose Altuve 17, Dylan Moore 13, Jazz Chisholm 12, DJ LeMahieu 7, Jorge Polanco 5, Brendan Rodgers 1

Third Basemen

Third Basemen	Bill	Chris D.	Chris S.	Christina	Dan	Eduardo	Emma	Hal	Joe	John	Mark	Meg	Moses	Peter	SIS Video Scouts	Travis	Zach	Total Points
Ke'Bryan Hayes	3	4	1	1	2	4	1	3	1	2	1	1	7	1	2	1	1	151
Matt Chapman	2	2	4	2	3	2	2	2	2	1	3	5	2	6	1	4	2	142
Nolan Arenado	1	1	7	4	6	3	5	1	3	3	5	8	1	2	3	8	5	121
Ryan McMahon		8	3	7	4	5	3	5	10	5	2	3	6	3	4	3	3	102
Austin Riley	8	9	2	3	1	1	4		6	4	4	2	3	7	6	5		100
José Ramirez	4		5	8	7	6	7	4	5		7	6	9	5	5	2	4	81
Manny Machado	6	5	6	5	10	7	8	6	4	7	8	7	4	9	7	7	7	74
Joshua Fuentes			6	5	8	6	8	9	6	6	4			8	8	6		52
Yoan Moncada	5						9	7			10			4			10	21
Patrick Wisdom		6	9		9	10						10			9	10	6	19

Others receiving points: Joey Wendle 18, Luis Arraez 12, Alex Bregman 11, Gio Urshela 9, Josh Donaldson 6, Justin Turner 6, Charlie Culberson 5, Evan Longoria 4, Kyle Seager 1

Shortstops

Shortstops	Bill	Chris D.	Chris S.	Christina	Dan	Eduardo	Emma	Hal	Joe	John	Mark	Meg	Moses	Peter	SIS Video Scouts	Travis	Zach	Total Points
Carlos Correa	7		1	1	1	1	1	2	2	1	1	1	1	1	1	1	1	152
Andrelton Simmons	2	2	2	2	4	3	2	3	1	4	2	3		9	2	2	2	131
Isiah Kiner-Falefa	10	5	3	4	2	4	3	4	3	2	6	2	3	2	3	3		117
Trevor Story	6	9	4	3	3	2	5	1	4	3	3	4	5	4	4	6		110
Brandon Crawford	1		8	5		5	10	7	7		8	8	8	3	7	5	6	66
J.P. Crawford	3		7	9	8		6	6		9	7	6		6	6	7	10	53
Kevin Newman	5	8	5	8	7	7	8		5			9		10	8	4	7	52
Paul DeJong		1		7	6	10			9	5		7	7					8	39
Edmundo Sosa	4	10	6		9		4			7		9	5		5			9	38
Nick Ahmed	9	7				6		7	5		7				10	9	5	34

Others receiving points: Francisco Lindor 32, Nicky Lopez 30, Tim Anderson 19, Dansby Swanson 15, Miguel Rojas 13, Javier Baez 13, Willy Adames 10, Trea Turner 6, Wander Franco 2

Left Fielders

Left Fielders	Bill	Chris D.	Chris S.	Christina	Dan	Eduardo	Emma	Hal	Joe	John	Mark	Meg	Moses	Peter	SIS Video Scouts	Travis	Zach	Total Points
Tyler O'Neill	1	4	1	1	2	1	1	1	1	1	1	1	2	1	1	1	1	165
Andrew Benintendi	2	6	2	3	1	4	3	2	2	2	3	3	1	2	2	5	3	141
Randy Arozarena	4	2	3	2	4	3	5	4	3	5	4	5		3	4	2	4	119
Raimel Tapia	9	10	6	5	5	5	4	6	4	4	2	6	3	4	3	3	2	106
Alex Verdugo	3		5	6	6	2	2	3	5	3	5	4	8		5	6	5	97
Lourdes Gurriel Jr.	5	5	4	4	3	6		7	6	6	9	2	4	5	6	4		89
Austin Hays	8	8	7	7	7	7	6	8	7	7	6	7	7	6	7	7	6	69
Lewis Brinson			8	8	8	9		5	8	8		8	5		9	10		35
A.J. Pollock	7	7	9	9	10	10	7	10			7	9		7		8	9	34
Michael Brantley	6						8				8	10	6		8	9	10	23

Others receiving points: Christian Yelich 16, Eddie Rosario 15, Ian Happ 8, David Peralta 8, Jurickson Profar 2, Robbie Grossman 2, Trevor Larnach 2, Andrew Vaughn 2, Mark Canha 1, Jesse Winker 1

Center Fielders

Center Fielders	Bill	Chris D.	Chris S.	Christina	Dan	Eduardo	Emma	Hal	Joe	John	Mark	Meg	Moses	Peter	SIS Video Scouts	Travis	Zach	Total Points
Michael A. Taylor	2	2	1	1	1	1	3	2	2	1	1	3		1	1	1	1	152
Harrison Bader	1	1	2	3	3	4	1	1	3	3	4	1	1	2	2	2	2	151
Kevin Kiermaier	4	5	4	5	4	2	2	3	4	2	5	2	3	3	3	4	3	129
Kiké Hernández	5	3	3	2	2	3	5	6	8	5	2	4	2	4	4	3	4	122
Byron Buxton	8	4	5	4	5	5	6	4	1	4	3	5	7	6	5	7	6	102
Jackie Bradley Jr.	3	6	6	6	6	6	4	5	6	6	6	6	6		6	5	7	86
Myles Straw		10	8	7	8	8	8	7		7	7	8	9	5	7	6	5	55
Trent Grisham	10	7	7	10	7	7	7	10	7	8	8	7	8	7	8	8	8	53
Brandon Nimmo	9	9	10	9	9	10			10	9	10	10				10	10	17
Steven Duggar	7		9	8			9					9				9		15

Others receiving points: Cedric Mullins II 12, Ramón Laureano 11, Cody Bellinger 8, Chris Taylor 7, Adolis Garcia 6, Victor Robles 3, Austin Slater 2, Starling Marte 2, Odubel Herrera 1, Bryan Reynolds 1

Right Fielders

Right Fielders	Bill	Chris D.	Chris S.	Christina	Dan	Eduardo	Emma	Hal	Joe	John	Mark	Meg	Moses	Peter	SIS Video Scouts	Travis	Zach	Total Points
Aaron Judge	3	7	1	2	3	1	6	3	2	2	2	3	2	1	3	2	4	140
Joey Gallo	10	2	2	1	1	2	2	5	4	1	1	1	9	3	1	1	2	139
Max Kepler	1	6	5	3	5	4	5	2	5	5	4	5	6		4	4	1	111
Kyle Tucker	6	1	3	5	4	8	4	4	9	4	7	2	3	8	2	3	3	111
Adam Duvall		4	4	4	2		3		3	3	3	7	8		7	6	6	83
Mookie Betts	4	10	9	8		5	7	1	1	9	8	9	1	2	5	9		77
Avisail Garcia	8		6	9	7	6	1	6	6	6	9	4		4	8	10	7	68
Manuel Margot	2	8	7		8		8	9	7	10		6		6	6	5	5	56
Mike Yastrzemski	7	9	8	6	9		9	10			6	8		5	9	8	9	40
Dylan Carlson				7	6	3			8	8	5			4	9			38

Others receiving points: Jason Heyward 28, Hunter Renfroe 18, Juan Soto 12, Michael Conforto 8, Ronald Acuña Jr. 5, Bryce Harper 1

Catchers

Catchers	Bill	Chris D.	Chris S.	Christina	Dan	Eduardo	Emma	Hal	Joe	John	Mark	Meg	Moses	Peter	SIS Video Scouts	Travis	Zach	Total Points
Jacob Stallings	1		1	1	1	1	2	1	2	1	1	6	4	1	1	1	10	141
Austin Hedges	6		2	2	2	7	6	2	1	2	3	4	6	2	2	2	7	120
Sean Murphy	3	9	4	3	4	2	1	3		7	10	1		3	4	3	6	102
Max Stassi			5	5	3	8	3		7	3	2	2		8	3	4	2	88
Yadier Molina	9	5	10	6	9	5		8	4	8	4		3	5	5			62
Mike Zunino	2		9	8	10	4	4	4		6	9	7	9	4	9	9		60
Tomás Nido		6	3	9	5			6	4	5					7	5	8	52
Willson Contreras	4		7	7	3	7	10			5		10	7	9	6	7		50
J.T. Realmuto		4					5						3	1		6	1	46
Jose Trevino			8	8		8		3			6	9		7		10	3	37

Others receiving points: Buster Posey 28, Salvador Perez 26, Elias Diaz 25, Omar Narváez 24, Jonah Heim 19, Christian Vázquez 16, Martín Maldonado 12, Tucker Barnhart 8, Will Smith 5, Curt Casali 4, Reese McGuire 4, Kyle Higashioka 2, Eric Haase 1

Pitchers

Pitchers	Bill	Chris D.	Chris S.	Christina	Dan	Eduardo	Emma	Hal	Joe	John	Mark	Meg	Moses	Peter	SIS Video Scouts	Travis	Zach	Total Points
Dallas Keuchel	1	1	1	1	1	1	1	1	1	1	1	1		3	1	1	1	158
Max Fried	7	8	4	5	4	3	4	2	2	2	2	4	4	2	2	2	3	127
Taijuan Walker		2	2	2	2	5	5	5	5	7	3	2	6	6	3	4	2	115
José Berrios	4		7		7	8	3	4	4	9	6	6	3	1	8	7	7	81
Zach Davies			3	4	5	4	6	8	3	6	7	5			4	3	4	81
Ranger Suárez		4	5	3	3	2	9		7	5	5	3		8	6		5	78
Zack Greinke	2	9	9	8	10	9	8	3	6	3	4	9	8	4	5	5	9	76
Zack Wheeler	5	3	6	7	9		2	9	8	8		8	5	10	7	6	6	66
Marco Gonzales		10	10	6	6	6		6		4		10	9		9	8	10	38
Chris Flexen		7	8	9	8	10		7	10		10		7		5	9	8	34

Others receiving points: Marcus Stroman 24, Adam Wainwright 16, Walker Buehler 9, Wade Miley 7, Corbin Burnes 6, Logan Webb 5, Steven Matz 2, Casey Mize 2, Madison Bumgarner 1, Lance McCullers Jr. 1, Cal Quantrill 1, Tyler Mahle 1, Joe Musgrove 1, Max Scherzer 1

Multi-Position

Multi-Position	Bill	Chris D.	Chris S.	Christina	Dan	Eduardo	Emma	Hal	Joe	John	Mark	Meg	Moses	Peter	SIS Video Scouts	Travis	Zach	Total Points
Kiké Hernández		2	3	1	10	1	9	2	4	3	2	3	3	1	1	2	3	126
Chris Taylor	2	7	5		2	2	2	1	1	2	8	1	1	7	3	3	10	119
Jake Cronenworth		1	1	8	8	3	1	4	2	6	1	7	5	5	2	5	5	112
Kris Bryant	4	6	2	3	5	7	5	9	3	4	9	8	2	2	7			89
Trea Turner	9	8	4	2	9	5	3	3		9	4	2	6		6	1	6	88
Leury García	1	9	7	6	6	4		6	6	1	6		8	4	8	4	9	80
Dylan Moore	6	3	9		4			10	5	5	3	4	7	3	5	9	2	79
Garrett Hampson		4	10	9	3	10		5	8	7	5	9	10	6	4		4	60
Josh Harrison	8	10	6	4		8	10		7	10		6	4		10		8	41
Luis Urias	5		8		7	6	7		9	8	10		9	8		7		37

Others receiving points: Marwin Gonzalez 31, Daulton Varsho 31, Harold Castro 28, Josh Rojas 13

On Finding the Value of the
Monkey Wrench Guy

Bill James

Point 1: The Game Has Changed

In the 1950s, teams had a 25-man roster and no DH, and they usually carried 9 pitchers on the roster, sometimes 8, but mostly 9. So you've got 9 pitchers, 8 men in the field and no DH, you've got an 8-man bench. Now, teams carry 12 or 13 pitchers, occasionally 14, and half of the teams have a DH. 13 pitchers, 8 men in the field and a DH, you've got a 3-man bench. What's that mean?

It means that the three or four players that you have on the bench have to be able to cover you defensively at all eight positions. In the 1950s, teams would have a backup shortstop, a backup second baseman, and three catchers. You would have room for a pinch-hitter/first baseman, and a pinch-hitter/outfielder, and a pinch runner/defensive sub in the outfield. Now, a bench player has to be able to play wherever you need him to play. It's a different game.

In the 1950s, there were bench players who would be on the roster all year and wind up the season with less than 50 at bats. Now, many players who have no fixed position will bat 500, even 600 times in a season. It's a different game.

Point 2: Our Analytical Model is Inappropriate to the modern bench guy

Sabermetrics, as much as I know, relies exclusively on what might be called Direct Benefit Accounting. We try to figure out exactly what benefit accrues to the team from each action that can be directly traced to one player, and what cost was associated with it, just as an accountant does for a retail store. The store purchased these items for $4.17 each, and we sold them for $9.50 each, which would be a profit of $5.33 per item, except that we have to account for overhead—that is, the cost of operating the store—and we attribute $1.88 of overhead to each item. Also, 14% of the stock was stolen, accidentally damaged or unsold and remaindered, and this reduces the profit to an average of $2.12 per item. Figure it out.

That's what we do in baseball, only we use runs and wins rather than dollars and cents, and replacement level rather than overhead. My point is that direct benefit accounting doesn't always catch everything. Take the situation in which a team is losing 12-1 after eight innings, so they ask an outfielder to pitch the 8th and 9th innings. Let's say that he pitches two shutout innings.

In a naïve analysis, the two shutout innings add to the value of the outfielder. But we know that that value is an illusion, because the team had no chance of winning the game anyway, so there was no actual benefit from the two shutout innings.

But we're still missing something. Do you see what it is? There is a value there that our analysis is missing. Why is the outfielder pitching?

The outfielder is pitching that day to save the bullpen. It is irrelevant whether he pitches well or pitches poorly; what matters is that one or two of the team's relievers got the day off. The contribution that he is making is not toward winning *today's* game; it is toward winning tomorrow's game, or the day after tomorrow's.

How do we find that value? We have to learn to think about value in a different way. We have to open up a couple of side doors in our minds. Of course the problem of the outfielder who pitches an inning here and there is a fairly trivial problem, but there is a related problem in finding the value for the versatile extra player who can play anywhere on the field. His value is not in that he is better than replacement level. His value is not that he is +3 runs on defense or -2 runs. His value is in his effect on the rest of the team. In modern baseball we have two or three bench players doing the work that used to be done by seven or eight men. *Their value is in the space that they create on the roster*. That space allows teams to carry deep bullpens, which allows teams to keep a fresh arm on the mound. Relievers come into the game one after another, all of them throwing 95 to 100 miles an hour. They can do that because they're only working one inning at a time. ***It is the modern bench players who make that possible***.

In direct value accounting, you cannot credit the versatile bench player with the value of the five extra relievers that they allow the team to carry. The fact that we cannot do this is a flaw in our analytical systems. Also, the concepts of "Wins Above Replacement" and "Runs Saved above and below average"… those ideas are almost completely irrelevant to understanding the contribution of a Versatile Bench Player.

When you have only a three-man or four-man bench, the "replacement level" can become a chasm. If you're working with a short bench and your center fielder twists an ankle, you can have an unholy mess in the outfield in a big hurry. It is real easy for that to cost you a couple of games, if you have a versatile bench guy who can just *sort of* play center field, as opposed to a bench guy who can *actually* play center field. The replacement level isn't where it usually is, when you have a short bench. It drops, or at least it drops at some positions.

And then we have the same problem with Runs Saved plus or minus, measured from the average. The versatile bench player isn't expected to be an "average" defensive shortstop. If he was an average defensive shortstop, he'd be a regular shortstop. He is expected to hold the fort when the shortstop needs a day off, and not hurt the team too much.

Point 3:   The Post-Season Fielding Awards

This also messes with the Post-Season Awards. The Gold Glove Awards and the Fielding Bible Awards both recognized Defensive Excellence *at a position*, but had no way to deal with defensive excellence for a modern plays-all-over-the-field-but-plays-everyday bench guy. Trying to fill that hole, Tom Tango and myself and I think maybe a couple of other guys, sorry that I don't remember who you were, suggested that we give an award to THAT player, the new TYPE of player, embodied at that time by Ben Zobrist. The Fielding Bible adopted that suggestion.

The Fielding Bible Multi-Position Award was an important first step toward understanding the contribution of those players, but we made some mistakes…well, I made three mistakes. One is, we allowed it to be called the "Multi-Position" Award, which does not at all describe the purpose of the Award. Calling it the "Multi-Position" Award encouraged the people who were voting for the award to think that anybody who split time between two positions and played well at both should be a candidate for the Award. This guy played 90 games at first base and 70 in right field and was good both places; I think he should win the Award. That wasn't at all the purpose of the Award.

My second mistake was, I failed to push back hard enough and consistently enough when the Multi-Position Award started to go off track. The first Award was given to Lorenzo Cain. Lorenzo Cain was a great defensive centerfielder who, in that season, had played about 400 innings in right field, but he wasn't anything even remotely *like* the kind of player who should have won the Award. We should have called it the Cover-Your-Butt Award, because it's an award for the guy who covers the manager's butt when the defense starts to fall apart because a key guy is missing. The Covers-The-Field Award, perhaps, I don't know, or the Monkey Wrench Fielder Award. A Monkey Wrench is an old-style tool that was used to hold difference sizes of pipes or nuts or boards, a one-size-fits-all wrench. I don't know if people still use monkey wrenches; I'm sure we have modern tools that probably do the job better.

There have always been a few guys like that, but now it's different; now you HAVE to have them in order to win. Tony Phillips was maybe the best I ever saw. Junior Gilliam, Zobrist, Gil McDougald, Derrell Thomas…those kind of guys. Phillips was the only player I ever saw who could dominate the game defensively from five different defensive positions. But what is it that defines that type of guy that we are looking for, the Ben Zobrist, Tony Phillips-type player?

I didn't want to say publicly, about our first Award, that we had missed the target, so I didn't say anything. And then ANOTHER guy won who was totally the wrong guy, and another guy. Sometimes we would get the Award in the right player's hands, but sometimes we didn't.

And my third mistake was, I should have written this article years ago. I tried to push back on these awards from within the company, Sports Info Solutions, but I just didn't make any progress. I didn't make any progress because most of the voters didn't understand what the problem was. The problem is that our analytical systems do not work to find the value of this kind of player. We have to think about the problem in a completely different way. I mean, that is what I have done since the 1970s: I try to re-orient how people think about baseball, and sometimes I succeed in doing that, and sometimes I fail. This time, I was failing. Probably I still am.

Point 4: Finding the Value of These Type of Players

In 1967 Carl Yastrzemski won the American League Triple Crown, and was a unanimous MVP selection in the American League, except for one vote. A Minneapolis Sportswriter, Max Nichols, voted for César Tovar. This was quite a brouhaha, back in the day when people used terms like "brouhaha", and a resolution was introduced at the BBWAA meeting that winter to censure Max Nichols for casting this stupid vote for César Tovar when everybody knew that the real MVP was Mike Yastrzemski's grandpa. Writing Max Nichols' biographic summary for the Society for American Baseball Research, Steve West stated as if it was a truth that Nichols "cast the worst vote in MVP history," and my very good friend Joe Posnanski once wrote the same thing.

Everybody knows that Carl Yastrzemski was the MVP, so if you don't agree, you're just wrong. But what if it wasn't Max Nichols who was missing something, but everybody else? What if Max Nichols was simply so far ahead of the discussion that we haven't caught up yet?

Nichols' point was exactly the point that I am now making: that there is great value in a player who can cover the weaknesses that pop up all over the field. César Tovar started the season as the Twins' center fielder, but second baseman Rod Carew was injured in early July, so Tovar went and played second base for much of July and August, while Carew was mending. He played second base as well as Carew did, and the team played their best ball of the season in August, with Tovar playing most of the time at second base. Rich Rollins had been the Twins' third baseman since 1962, but Rollins was having a miserable season, so after Carew came back, Tovar went over and played third base.

For the season, Tovar wound up playing 70 games at third base, 64 in center field, 36 at second base, 10 in left field, 9 at shortstop and 6 in right field. The Twins wound up winning 91 games. The Red Sox won 92. Nichols' point—

perfectly legitimate, it seems to me—was that the Twins' defense would have collapsed without Tovar, and they wouldn't have been within a mile of the pennant race.

Max Nichols, by the way, is the business strategy of every company; maximize the nickels. I don't know that he was right in saying that the Twins would have collapsed without Tovar, but I don't know that he was wrong, either. I'm just suggesting we might consider the thought.

So how do we find the value of that type of guy? To be honest, I don't really know. I have NOT got it all figured out—but I have figured out a little bit of it. I think I can advance the discussion by a step or two, and then perhaps we can figure out how to move on after that.

What we are looking for is two things:

(1) The ability to play a number of *different* defensive positions; that is Positional Versality, and

(2) The ability to play the most *demanding* defensive positions, such as shortstop and center field, to a lesser extent second base, third base and right field. Catcher is, of course, the most demanding defensive position of all, but very few catchers move around the field and also play other positions.

We can measure each of those two things—Positional Versatility, and Positional Value, and we can put them together. It makes the Positional Value and Versatility Score, or PVAVS, which may be the worst Acronym in the history of Acronyms, I don't know. So far we haven't come up with a better name for it.

Point 5: Measuring Positional Versatility

The Positional Versatility Score is ***the square of the sum of the games played at all positions, divided by the square of the games played at each position***. If you play all of your games at one position, you have a Position

Diversity Score of 1.00. If you played an equal number of games at each position, you would have a Position Diversity Score of 8.00, or, I guess, 9.00, if you also played an equal number of games as a pitcher.

César Tovar in 1967 played 70 games as a third baseman, 64 in center field, 36 at second base, 10 in left field, 9 at shortstop and 6 in right field. That's a position versatility score of 3.62:

> 70 squared is 4900
> 64 squared is 4096
> 36 squared is 1296
> 10 squared is 100
> 9 squared is 81
> 6 squared is 36

The sum of those numbers is 10,509. Tovar's total of games played at all positions was 195. 195 squared is 38,025, so Tovar's Positional Versatility Index is 38025 divided by 10509, which is 3.62. It's a high number.

Point 6: The Position Difficulty Rating.

And here I can see that I made a mistake in the formula. This is the formula that I sent to SIS, which they have used to calculate the Positional Difficulty Ratings in this book.

Multiply:

The player's games played at Catcher by 6,
His games played at Shortstop by 5,
His games played in Center Field by 5,
His games played at Second Base by 4,
His games played at Third Base by 3,
His games played in Right Field by 3,
His games played in Left Field by 2, and
His games played at First Base by 1.

Divide the total by the sum of his games played at all eight positions (a number which may be greater than his games played, because players often play two defensive positions in the same game.)

Any catcher who doesn't play at any other position has a Position Difficulty Rating of 6. Any first baseman who doesn't play at any other position has a Position Difficult Rating of 1.

But these are not actually the values that I should have sent. After I constructed this system I sent that to SIS, but I continued to work on the problem. I realized that I needed to create a much wider separation between the top of the chart and the bottom, so the numbers I SHOULD HAVE USED are:

> 12 at catcher
> 10 at shortstop
> 9 in center field
> 8 at second base
> 6 in right field
> 6 at third base
> 2 in left field, and
> 1 at first base.

I apparently forgot to send the updated research to Sports Info Solutions, so we will have somewhat different values next year. My bad.

Anyway, using this year's formula, César Tovar in 1967 would have a Positional Value Index of 3.88—again, a high number, because he played the more difficult positions.

For the sake of clarity and because there surely is some moron reading this who will otherwise yell at us about undervaluing first basemen, we are NOT saying that playing first base is easy or that it is not important. What we are saying is that on a major league roster you will almost always have several players who have the physical ability to play first base. On a major league roster, you are usually going to have one or two players, maybe three, who are quick enough, agile enough and have a strong enough throwing arm to play shortstop. You're usually going to have eight or ten guys who are physically capable of playing first base. They may not know how to do it, and they might be terrible at it if forced to, and the cost of this might be very high. But there is not a shortage of people who have the physical equipment to do it.

Point 7: The Positional Value and Versatility Score

So now we have a score for the player's defensive VERSATILILTY, and a score representing the degree to which he played the most challenging defensive positions. What we have to do now is to put them together into one number, the Positional Value and Versatility Score, or PVAVS, if you like acronyms. We figure the Positional Value and Versatility Score by multiplying:

The Positional Versatility Index, times

The Positional Difficulty Rating, times

His Games Played in the field,

Divided by 100.

On the page that follows are the highest Positional Value and Versatility Scores for 2021. These, I believe, are the legitimate candidates for the Fielding Bible Multi-Position Award in 2021. It may be a little complicated, and it may never gain standing in the immense forest of ratings for major league players. But I believe in what we're trying to do here. We are trying to pry open the lid on the subject, and get you to think about defensive value in a new and different way, which may lead to a better understanding of the value of a player like Leury Garcia or Chris Taylor or Josh Rojas. I ask you to give the method a fair consideration, and we'll see how it goes.

Positional Value and Versatility Score

Player	GP	P	C	1B	2B	3B	SS	LF	CF	RF	Value	Versatility	PVAVS
Chris Taylor	180	0	0	0	46	11	23	30	62	8	4.03	4.28	31.0
Leury Garcia	152	0	0	0	36	11	19	26	26	34	3.66	5.39	30.0
Josh Rojas	166	0	0	0	55	14	42	18	0	37	3.73	4.13	25.6
Kris Bryant	174	0	0	12	0	55	1	48	19	39	2.82	4.12	20.2
Tyler Wade	102	0	0	0	19	27	31	8	10	7	3.91	4.60	18.3
Luis Urias	161	0	0	0	25	68	68	0	0	0	4.00	2.63	16.9
Pavin Smith	169	0	0	54	0	0	0	22	39	54	2.69	3.64	16.5
Harold Castro	111	3	0	15	33	12	43	3	2	0	3.79	3.70	15.6
Daulton Varsho	95	0	41	0	0	0	0	12	30	12	4.80	3.15	14.4
Jorge Mateo	69	0	0	0	18	9	18	6	11	7	4.01	5.09	14.1
Jake Cronenworth	160	1	0	24	94	0	41	0	0	0	3.80	2.31	14.0
Kike Hernandez	148	0	0	0	47	0	8	0	93	0	4.68	2.01	13.9
Jurickson Profar	115	0	0	20	10	0	0	36	20	29	2.77	4.35	13.9
Ian Happ	147	0	0	0	8	2	0	65	56	16	3.37	2.81	13.9
DJ LeMahieu	177	0	0	55	83	39	0	0	0	0	2.85	2.74	13.8
Randal Grichuk	167	0	0	0	0	0	0	0	96	71	4.15	1.96	13.6
Garrett Hampson	145	0	0	0	47	2	5	0	91	0	4.65	2.00	13.5
Mauricio Dubon	80	0	0	0	20	12	21	0	27	0	4.45	3.73	13.3
Austin Slater	139	1	0	0	0	0	0	37	77	24	3.82	2.45	13.0
Adam Duvall	159	0	0	0	0	0	0	51	30	78	3.06	2.64	12.8

Defensive Runs Saved Leaders

Mark Simon

We wish good health to all major league players, but on behalf of these specific pages in the Handbook, we'd really like to wish it to Byron Buxton.

Buxton ranked 5th among center fielders in Defensive Runs Saved despite playing in only 61 games.

That followed a 2020 season in which Buxton led all center fielders with 11 Runs Saved despite playing in only 39 of a possible 60 games. And *that* followed a 2019 season in which Buxton saved 8 runs in 86 games.

Had Buxton not suffered a hip injury and a broken hand and been fully healthy this season, he might have had a chance at a 10-WAR year. He was that good with both the bat (1.005 OPS) and the glove. When Buxton started, he was a high-impact player. The Twins were 29-30 when he did start. When he didn't, they were 44-59.

Turn the page and you'll see that Buxton ranks third among center fielders in Runs Saved over the last three seasons. He's also 15th in innings played. The player who leads in that category, Kevin Kiermaier (outstanding in his own right) has played nearly 800 more innings than Buxton in that time.

Buxton has not been able to avoid injuries no matter how hard he tries. He's played more than 100 games in a season only once. Buxton talked on *The SIS Baseball Podcast* in December 2020 about studying how other outfielders, like Kiermaier and Jackie Bradley Jr., play defense, looking for ways he could still be aggressive without putting his body at risk so it's clearly a point of emphasis.

The good news is that he'll be only 28 next season, so there should still be plenty of time for him to show the best baseball he has to offer.

Infield Runs Saved Leaders

First Basemen 3-Year Leaders

Olson, Matt	21
Gurriel, Yuli	14
Walker, Christian	12
Diaz, Lewin	11
Goldschmidt, Paul	10
Zimmerman, Ryan	10
White, Evan	9
Fuentes, Joshua	9
Adams, Matt	8
2 tied with	6

Second Basemen 3-Year Leaders

Wong, Kolten	28
Hernandez, Kike	21
Fletcher, David	18
Frazier, Adam	18
Merrifield, Whit	15
Edman, Tommy	14
Lux, Gavin	13
Lopez, Nicky	12
Semien, Marcus	11
2 tied with	10

Third Basemen 3-Year Leaders

Arenado, Nolan	42
Chapman, Matt	40
Hayes, Ke'Bryan	20
McMahon, Ryan	20
Machado, Manny	14
Gonzalez, Erik	12
Anderson, Brian	12
Bregman, Alex	11
3 tied with	10

Shortstops 3-Year Leaders

Baez, Javier	40
Story, Trevor	36
Correa, Carlos	36
DeJong, Paul	30
Ahmed, Nick	24
Simmons, Andrelton	21
Lindor, Francisco	16
Crawford, J.P.	14
Kiner-Falefa, Isiah	13
Adames, Willy	11

First Basemen 3-Year Trailers

Voit, Luke	-19
Sano, Miguel	-10
Vogelbach, Daniel	-10
Hoskins, Rhys	-9
Bell, Josh	-8
Nunez, Renato	-8

Second Basemen 3-Year Trailers

Profar, Jurickson	-26
Odor, Rougned	-16
Hiura, Keston	-14
Torres, Gleyber	-13
La Stella, Tommy	-13
3 tied with	-11

Third Basemen 3-Year Trailers

Davis, J.D.	-24
Devers, Rafael	-22
Dozier, Hunter	-21
Bohm, Alec	-19
Moran, Colin	-17
Sano, Miguel	-16

Shortstops 3-Year Trailers

Torres, Gleyber	-22
Andrus, Elvis	-22
Gregorius, Didi	-21
Iglesias, Jose	-19
Bogaerts, Xander	-18
Martin, Richie	-18

First Basemen 2021 Leaders

Diaz, Lewin	9
Goldschmidt, Paul	9
Olson, Matt	6
Muncy, Max	6
Zimmerman, Ryan	5
France, Ty	5
Gurriel, Yuli	5
Alonso, Pete	5
Votto, Joey	4
Walker, Christian	4

Second Basemen 2021 Leaders

Merrifield, Whit	14
Semien, Marcus	11
Fletcher, David	11
McMahon, Ryan	9
Frazier, Adam	7
Wong, Kolten	6
Edman, Tommy	6
6 tied with	5

Third Basemen 2021 Leaders

Hayes, Ke'Bryan	16
Riley, Austin	13
McMahon, Ryan	13
Chapman, Matt	10
Fuentes, Joshua	10
Ramirez, Jose	10
Espinal, Santiago	8
4 tied with	6

Shortstops 2021 Leaders

Correa, Carlos	20
Simmons, Andrelton	15
Walls, Taylor	10
Kiner-Falefa, Isiah	10
Kim, Ha-seong	9
Story, Trevor	9
Sosa, Edmundo	8
Crawford, J.P.	8
Newman, Kevin	7
4 tied with	6

First Basemen 2021 Trailers

Hoskins, Rhys	-7
Dalbec, Bobby	-7
Rizzo, Anthony	-6
Sano, Miguel	-5
10 tied with	-4

Second Basemen 2021 Trailers

Hernandez, Cesar	-11
Lowrie, Jed	-11
Young, Andy	-10
Castro, Willi	-8
3 tied with	-7

Third Basemen 2021 Trailers

Bohm, Alec	-13
Devers, Rafael	-13
Dozier, Hunter	-12
Diaz, Yandy	-9
Panik, Joe	-9
2 tied with	-8

Shortstops 2021 Trailers

Iglesias, Jose	-22
Rojas, Josh	-13
Torres, Gleyber	-10
Andrus, Elvis	-10
Gregorius, Didi	-10
Rosario, Amed	-9

Outfield Runs Saved Leaders

Left Fielders 3-Year Leaders		Center Fielders 3-Year Leaders		Right Fielders 3-Year Leaders	
Verdugo, Alex	21	Kiermaier, Kevin	35	Judge, Aaron	35
O'Neill, Tyler	20	Bader, Harrison	31	Betts, Mookie	34
Tauchman, Mike	18	Buxton, Byron	29	Gallo, Joey	25
Brantley, Michael	17	Cain, Lorenzo	26	Bellinger, Cody	17
Moore, Dylan	11	Robles, Victor	19	Tucker, Kyle	17
Duvall, Adam	10	Taylor, Michael A.	18	Garcia, Avisail	14
Bruce, Jay	9	Hernandez, Kike	17	Kepler, Max	14
Brown, Seth	9	Grisham, Trent	16	Heyward, Jason	13
Arozarena, Randy	8	Bradley Jr., Jackie	14	Garcia, Adolis	13
Hays, Austin	8	4 tied with	12	Yastrzemski, Mike	12

Left Fielders 3-Year Trailers		Center Fielders 3-Year Trailers		Right Fielders 3-Year Trailers	
Upton, Justin	-28	Desmond, Ian	-18	Soler, Jorge	-21
Dickerson, Alex	-15	Jones, JaCoby	-17	Castellanos, Nick	-20
Choo, Shin-Soo	-14	Trout, Mike	-17	Reyes, Franmil	-13
Jimenez, Eloy	-13	Kelenic, Jarred	-16	Dozier, Hunter	-13
Smith Jr., Dwight	-12	Pillar, Kevin	-15	Eaton, Adam	-12
Santana, Domingo	-11	Marte, Starling	-14	3 tied with	-11

Left Fielders 2021 Leaders		Center Fielders 2021 Leaders		Right Fielders 2021 Leaders	
O'Neill, Tyler	11	Taylor, Michael A.	19	Garcia, Adolis	13
Tapia, Raimel	7	Bader, Harrison	15	Gallo, Joey	12
Verdugo, Alex	7	Hernandez, Kike	14	Judge, Aaron	11
Arozarena, Randy	7	Kiermaier, Kevin	13	Tucker, Kyle	11
Benintendi, Andrew	7	Buxton, Byron	10	Hays, Austin	10
Gurriel Jr., Lourdes	6	Bradley Jr., Jackie	9	Kepler, Max	9
Duvall, Adam	6	Grisham, Trent	8	Duvall, Adam	9
McKenna, Ryan	6	Sierra, Magneuris	7	Garcia, Avisail	8
5 tied with	5	Taveras, Leody	6	McCormick, Chas	7
		Cain, Lorenzo	6	Daza, Yonathan	7

Left Fielders 2021 Trailers		Center Fielders 2021 Trailers		Right Fielders 2021 Trailers	
Upton, Justin	-11	Kelenic, Jarred	-16	Soler, Jorge	-11
Canha, Mark	-10	Marte, Ketel	-15	Dozier, Hunter	-9
Hernandez, Yadiel	-9	Smith, Pavin	-10	Myers, Wil	-8
Almonte, Abraham	-8	Verdugo, Alex	-7	Polanco, Gregory	-8
McCutchen, Andrew	-7	Hill, Derek	-7	Castellanos, Nick	-7
2 tied with	-6	Naquin, Tyler	-6	4 tied with	-6

Pitcher/Catcher Runs Saved Leaders

Pitchers 3-Year Leaders		Catchers 3-Year Leaders	
Fried, Max	16	Stallings, Jacob	42
Keuchel, Dallas	15	Perez, Roberto	35
Greinke, Zack	13	Hedges, Austin	32
Suarez, Ranger	9	Pina, Manny	18
Flaherty, Jack	8	Barnes, Austin	16
Davies, Zach	8	Stassi, Max	14
Wheeler, Zack	7	Zunino, Mike	13
Stroman, Marcus	7	Barnhart, Tucker	13
Mikolas, Miles	7	Avila, Alex	12
Walker, Taijuan	7	3 tied with	11

Pitchers 3-Year Trailers		Catchers 3-Year Trailers	
Ottavino, Adam	-10	Suzuki, Kurt	-32
Valdez, Framber	-10	Collins, Zack	-22
6 tied with	-7	Ramos, Wilson	-21
		Severino, Pedro	-20
		Sisco, Chance	-17
		2 tied with	-16

Pitchers 2021 Leaders		Catchers 2021 Leaders	
Keuchel, Dallas	12	Stallings, Jacob	21
Walker, Taijuan	7	Hedges, Austin	12
Davies, Zach	6	Nido, Tomas	10
Suarez, Ranger	6	Murphy, Sean	10
Fried, Max	6	Stassi, Max	10
Flexen, Chris	5	Diaz, Elias	9
Berrios, Jose	5	Contreras, Willson	8
Greinke, Zack	5	Trevino, Jose	8
Wheeler, Zack	5	Zunino, Mike	7
4 tied with	4	Pina, Manny	7

Pitchers 2021 Trailers		Catchers 2021 Trailers	
Cease, Dylan	-7	Collins, Zack	-18
Singer, Brady	-6	Suzuki, Kurt	-12
Valdez, Framber	-5	Sanchez, Gary	-10
Ottavino, Adam	-5	Ramos, Wilson	-9
4 tied with	-4	Severino, Pedro	-9
		Knapp, Andrew	-8

Strike Zone Runs Saved

Bill James

We are dealing here with what is sometimes called "Pitch Framing", although I like to call it Pitch Sneaking. Sneaking pitches into the strike zone before the umpire can realize that their passports were not in order.

It is not in the tradition of a merchant to express doubts about the value of his or her product. I am guessing that you have probably never walked into a bakery to pick up a donut and seen signs reading "Donuts are fattening", "Our products will cause your teeth to rot,", "Have you talked to your doctor recently about diabetes?" or "Does your wife know that you're here?" You have probably never been seated in a restaurant, only to have the waiter come to your table and announce that "Today's crab linguine tastes like kindergarten paste, and there's enough salt in the meatballs to keep a highway from freezing over in a blizzard." This is not the way that business works.

We are purveyors of data, data pimps if you will, but it is still our responsibility to be skeptical of all the data that we look at. Being more skeptical is what made our field what it is. We are the people who taught the baseball world to be more skeptical of Wins and Losses, RBI, Saves and Batting Average. The question I would ask is, are we being as skeptical of our own data as we are of the data we inherited from our grandfathers?

No, we are not, to be blunt. We are often not skeptical enough about newly developed information. You don't look at your own children the way you look at your neighbor's, and you don't look at a statistic that you have developed with the same skepticism that you look at somebody else's.

Speaking for myself, Bill James, and not for anybody else, I have become skeptical of the Strike Zone Runs Saved data. "Skeptical" understates it; I am certain that there is a flaw in their process, and I am certain that I know what it is. This is probably not the place to get into the details of it. It's between me and my friends at Sports Info Solutions.

Their Strike Zone Runs Saved data is not systematically wrong; it's just overconfident. They're probably right 70, 80% of the time, but sometimes they're off. Let's take Salvador Perez. I'm not a Royals fan; I don't care anything about Salvador Perez's defensive reputation. What I care about is getting the things that WE say right.

Perez is generally regarded as a good defensive catcher, and he would rate, based on all the rest of his defensive information, as one of the Top 10 defensive catchers in the major leagues in 2021. However, he is given a score of -11 runs for his poor Pitch Sneaking abilities, which drops him out of the Top 10, out of the Top 15, out of the Top 20, Out of the Top 25, all the way down to a tie for 30th. 35 catchers with enough playing time to rate; he's tied for 30th.

I do not believe that their strike zone analysis supports such a radical re-evaluation of his defensive performance. I acknowledge that SIS has worked very, very, very hard to gather the data relevant to this evaluation and to process it. They go through steps to analyze the data that, unless you are a data analyst, you couldn't possibly understand—and lots of them, lots of different steps. They worked the problem really hard, and they are completely sincere in their efforts to reach valid conclusions.

But that doesn't mean they are right.

Editor's Note from John Dewan: It's the day before we go to press and I just got off the phone with Bill. The first thing I wanted to share with him was to thank him for all the extra effort he put into this year's handbook. Every word that he contributes makes this book better. This year he has gone above and beyond the call of duty—I think we have more words from Bill James in this book than we've ever had in any previous edition! The man is a machine.

We discussed his concerns about Strike Zone Runs Saved and it comes down to the magnitude of the estimates. He said that he could see where the system could produce an estimate for Salvador Perez like -7, but that -11 was too high. We agreed that this will require further research. Having been personally involved with developing the research I believe the techniques developed to estimate how many runs can be attributed to each catcher for "sneaking strikes", as Bill calls it, does a good job. However, it is possible that a systematic process of some sort could be over estimating the magnitude. We will research this further in the coming weeks. Stay tuned! We will share our results in a future Stat of the Week and on our blog.

2021 Catcher Strike Zone Runs Saved Leaders

Catcher	Called Pitches	Called Strikes			Runs Saved	
		Actual	Expected	Extra	Per 1,000 Called Pitches	Total
Stassi, Max	6242	2016	1935	81	1.60	10
Zunino, Mike	6937	2295	2230	65	1.15	8
Smith, Will	8186	2732	2667	65	0.98	8
Murphy, Sean	7559	2436	2390	46	0.66	5
Trevino, Jose	6291	1981	1936	45	0.79	5
Stallings, Jacob	7981	2461	2417	44	0.63	5
Nido, Tomas	3115	1016	974	42	1.61	5
Heim, Jonah	5429	1726	1685	41	0.92	5
Gallagher, Cam	2737	883	847	36	1.46	4
Jeffers, Ryan	5455	1684	1648	36	0.73	4
Narvaez, Omar	7954	2496	2461	35	0.50	4
Alfaro, Jorge	4107	1294	1259	35	0.97	4
Hedges, Austin	6419	1933	1901	32	0.62	4
Higashioka, Kyle	4307	1392	1366	26	0.70	3
Barnes, Austin	3486	1196	1171	25	0.86	3
McGuire, Reese	4636	1476	1452	24	0.65	3
d'Arnaud, Travis	3958	1251	1230	21	0.76	3
Plawecki, Kevin	2813	917	899	18	0.71	2
Mejia, Francisco	4646	1469	1452	17	0.43	2
Raleigh, Cal	2664	850	837	13	0.75	2
Barnhart, Tucker	7934	2445	2432	13	0.25	2
Realmuto, J.T.	8377	2633	2621	12	0.12	1
Stephenson, Tyler	5388	1702	1690	12	0.19	1
Pina, Manny	3899	1197	1186	11	0.26	1
Posey, Buster	7113	2364	2356	8	0.14	1
Nunez, Dom	5402	1672	1664	8	0.19	1
Murphy, Tom	6174	1923	1916	7	0.16	1
Grandal, Yasmani	5371	1609	1604	5	0.19	1
Leon, Sandy	3535	1182	1178	4	0.28	1
Casali, Curt	4017	1352	1350	2	0.00	0
Nola, Austin	3528	1142	1141	1	0.00	0
Vogt, Stephen	4310	1344	1344	0	0.00	0
Garver, Mitch	3836	1229	1230	-1	0.00	0
Vazquez, Christian	9557	3049	3051	-2	0.00	0
McCann, James	6969	2189	2192	-3	0.00	0
Perez, Roberto	3036	937	940	-3	0.00	0
Jackson, Alex	5416	1624	1634	-10	0.00	0
Castro, Jason	3205	969	973	-4	-0.31	-1
Jansen, Danny	4335	1390	1396	-6	-0.23	-1
Rogers, Jake	2715	837	845	-8	-0.37	-1
Sanchez, Gary	7589	2264	2273	-9	-0.13	-1
Perez, Michael	4397	1298	1310	-12	-0.23	-1
Kelly, Carson	6024	1935	1948	-13	-0.33	-2
Molina, Yadier	9003	2821	2835	-14	-0.22	-2
Knapp, Andrew	2751	882	897	-15	-0.73	-2
Kirk, Alejandro	2829	835	851	-16	-0.71	-2
Diaz, Elias	6853	2130	2149	-19	-0.29	-2
Maldonado, Martin	9034	2845	2865	-20	-0.22	-2
Varsho, Daulton	2831	872	895	-23	-1.06	-3
Contreras, Willson	8432	2663	2688	-25	-0.36	-3
Haase, Eric	4812	1462	1491	-29	-0.62	-3
Contreras, William	3497	1071	1100	-29	-0.86	-3
Knizner, Andrew	3611	1036	1069	-33	-1.11	-4
Wynns, Austin	3307	989	1024	-35	-1.21	-4
Caratini, Victor	7091	2304	2341	-37	-0.56	-4
Gomes, Yan	6837	2110	2154	-44	-0.73	-5
Suzuki, Kurt	5131	1555	1606	-51	-1.17	-6
Collins, Zack	4540	1327	1394	-67	-1.76	-8
Severino, Pedro	8078	2456	2526	-70	-0.99	-8
Perez, Salvador	9305	2784	2880	-96	-1.18	-11

Shift Update

Alex Vigderman

Four years ago, Travis Sawchik (a Fielding Bible Awards voter who at the time wrote for FanGraphs) wrote about MLB reaching "peak shift."

At the time, SIS had charted fewer infield shifts on balls in play in 2017 than 2016. The previous five seasons, shifts had increased each time by between 34 and 94 percent year-over-year, so that came as quite a shock to those paying attention.

Clearly that wasn't peak shift. It was more like shifts camping for the night before the next day's hike. I'm sure there's an appropriate mountaineering phrase for this, but this isn't the Sir Edmund Hillary Handbook, after all.

The next three years, infield shifts continued to proliferate. By 2020 there were more shifts than non-shifts on balls in play.

This year, we've reached what might wind up being another camping site. In 2021, there were 59,062 shifts on balls in play, which is a good 5,000 fewer than the prorated total from last year.

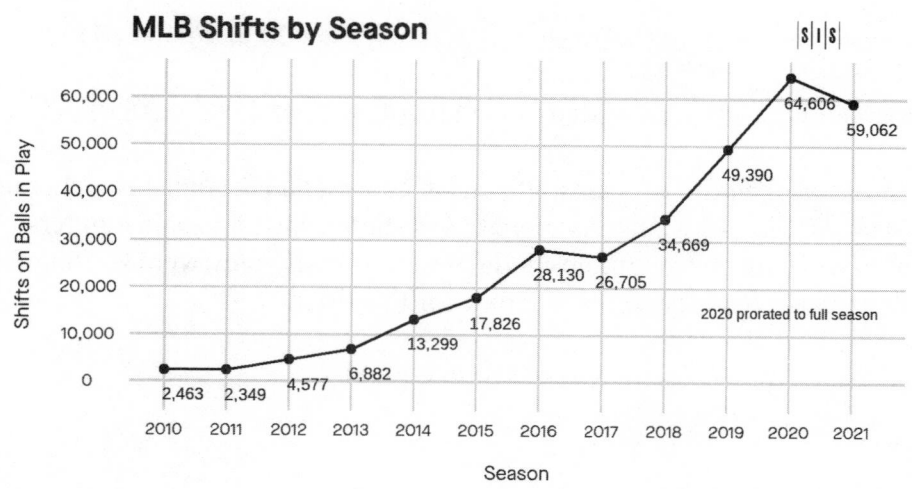

The thing we're really excited about as purveyors of shift analysis is the reason shift usage declined this year. Teams are getting more judicious in who they shift, focusing more on appropriate candidates for shifting.

At SIS we define a candidate for an infield shift as someone who hits way more of their groundballs and short line drives (GSLs) to the pull side. For lefties, that threshold is 75 percent. For righties, 80 percent.

"If shifting really is going to reach an equilibrium, we'll see quite a bit of a decline in shifts as teams identify the situations in which it's not doing them any favors."

Shift candidacy is a huge factor in whether shifting a batter is effective. In 2021, SIS estimates that shifting reduced the GSL batting average of shift candidates by 27 more points relative to non-candidates.

Weighted* Batting Average on Groundballs and Short Line Drives, 2021

SIS Recommendation	No Shift	Shift	Difference
Shift Candidates	.247	.219	Helps by 28 points
Non-Shift Candidate	.256	.255	Helps by 1 point

* The averages are weighted such that players with extreme shift tendencies (high or low) are not over-represented, thus separating the effect of the shift from batter quality.

This year, "candidates" were shifted as much as in 2020 (70% vs 71%).

"Non-candidates" were shifted much less (42% after 48% in 2020).

Over the last handful of seasons, teams in general had become less accurate in their shifting decisions. As more teams started shifting against hitters that weren't the most extreme candidates, eventually they were shifting far too much against players for whom it isn't justified.

The result above shows a reversal of that trend.

Of course, just because the league was more judicious doesn't mean that every team treated shifting the same way. The Mets shifted on nearly twice as many balls in play as their 2020 prorated total, following up eight seasons in which they were in the bottom half of the league in shift usage.

They successfully parlayed that into a few dozen more outs on balls to the infield and a 20-plus run improvement in Shift Runs Saved. That's huge. A big reason that we believe that it's likely that shifts are close to their peak, though, is something that the Mets grappled with this year.

While they did better on GSLs overall after dramatically ramping up their shift usage, there were plenty of times they shifted when that wasn't appropriate. The Mets ended up shifting against the appropriate players often (85 percent), but also shifted against the wrong players way too much (62 percent).

This could all be characterized as growing pains, really. For a game that's a century and a half old, the fact that shift usage has increased by an order of magnitude over the last decade means that there is still time for things to settle at a more optimal place.

By SIS's definition teams shifted erroneously roughly three times as often as they declined to shift in a spot that SIS would recommend them to do so.

If shifting really is going to reach an equilibrium, we'll see quite a bit of a decline in shifts as teams identify the situations in which it's not doing them any favors.

Check out the team shifting results and most-shifted players on the following page. A quick look shows that fans of AL West and NL East teams saw more shifts than anyone. The top six most-shifted players in 2021 were two Braves and four AL West sluggers, and the Braves themselves deployed a shift at the third-highest rate in the majors.

Shifts Employed
American League

Team	2020	2020 Prorated	2021	Change
Minnesota	928	2506	2815	309
Detroit	838	2341	2470	129
Seattle	953	2573	2273	-300
Texas	935	2525	2248	-277
Houston	839	2265	2207	-58
Los Angeles	851	2298	2183	-115
Tampa Bay	787	2125	2171	46
Boston	707	1909	1949	40
Oakland	526	1420	1834	414
Kansas City	813	2195	1811	-384
Toronto	859	2319	1690	-629
Baltimore	854	2306	1568	-738
Cleveland	648	1750	1466	-284
New York	633	1709	1357	-352
Chicago	780	2106	1138	-968
Total	11951	32347	29180	-3167
Average	797	2157	1945	-212

Shifts Employed
National League

Team	2020	2020 Prorated	2021	Change
Los Angeles	1113	3005	2626	-379
Atlanta	1042	2813	2529	-284
New York	513	1385	2499	1114
Washington	868	2344	2189	-155
San Francisco	884	2387	2119	-268
Pittsburgh	949	2562	2095	-467
Cincinnati	788	2128	1997	-131
Miami	761	2055	1954	-101
Arizona	827	2233	1948	-285
Chicago	747	2017	1840	-177
St Louis	604	1687	1826	139
Milwaukee	824	2225	1700	-525
Colorado	671	1812	1603	-208
San Diego	463	1250	1549	299
Philadelphia	872	2354	1408	-946
Total	11926	32257	29882	-2375
Average	795	2151	1992	-159

Top 30 Shifted Batters

Batter	Shifted PA	Shift Percent	Shift GSL BA	No Shift GSL BA
Olson, Matt	580	91.9	.206	.278
Freeman, Freddie	580	90.3	.255	.318
Seager, Kyle	572	90.4	.172	.500
Albies, Ozzie	555	85.0	.227	.308
Alvarez, Yordan	533	93.7	.235	.400
Ohtani, Shohei	509	87.3	.264	.300
Muncy, Max	505	94.0	.151	.222
Santana, Carlos	502	82.8	.220	.250
Rizzo, Anthony	490	89.7	.198	.250
Tucker, Kyle	484	90.8	.246	.429
Lowe, Brandon	480	86.2	.224	.150
Harper, Bryce	480	87.3	.267	.333
Devers, Rafael	471	77.2	.297	.174
Gallo, Joey	469	88.3	.180	.300
Ramirez, Jose	465	79.2	.230	.311
Semien, Marcus	464	69.4	.300	.237
Blackmon, Charlie	463	83.4	.267	.147
Perez, Salvador	457	73.6	.246	.235
Meadows, Austin	456	84.0	.160	.375
Haniger, Mitch	452	70.6	.241	.286
Walsh, Jared	452	83.5	.288	.281
Escobar, Eduardo	448	80.3	.289	.308
Soler, Jorge	447	82.8	.209	.286
Grossman, Robbie	437	71.5	.340	.239
Votto, Joey	435	89.9	.179	.083
Renfroe, Hunter	435	80.7	.211	.258
Carlson, Dylan	434	75.3	.276	.311
Soto, Juan	433	71.0	.278	.294
Kepler, Max	429	92.7	.185	.143
McMahon, Ryan	418	74.5	.301	.204

Hits Gained and Lost to the (Night) Shift

Bill James and the SIS R&D Team

Hi; this is Bill James. I have the honor of writing up the Hits Gained and Lost by Shifts this year because I didn't know any better. I'll explain in a moment what I didn't know better about.

Early last season, a player in a game I was watching beat the shift, hitting the ball through the spot vacated by a shifting infielder. The broadcaster working the game said that that happens sometimes, but the scouts had told him that for every out you lose by shifting, you'll gain ten outs by players hitting into the shift.

Well, that's totally unreasonable, and I knew that that couldn't possibly be true. Although there were periodic examples way back in history of some manager shifting his fielders to try to contain a great hitter, shifting really started in baseball, on an organized and consistent basis, about 130 years after the National League was founded. If the advantage of moving your fielders around to where the batter tends to hit the ball was THAT large—that is, if there was a 1,000% gain by doing so—there is no way that it could have taken baseball men 130 years to figure it out. I mean, we may be dense, but we're not THAT dense.

Responding to the offending announcer on Twitter, I suggested that the ratio of outs gained to outs lost was not 10 to 1; it was more like 26 to 25; in other words, not a 1,000% gain, but a 4% gain. At this point it occurred to me that I didn't really know what I was talking about, either, so I should go do some research.

It turned out that the data I needed was right here in this book; I just didn't know it. It was here last year; it was here the year before. I don't know how long it has been here. There's a LOT of data in this book; nobody actually has mastered all of it.

The actual ratio is about 6 to 5, about a 20% advantage. The advantage last year was 22%; that is, there were 22% more hits taken away by the shift than given away by the shift. Over the 12 years since 2010, the advantage is 29%, which is more like 9 to 7. In 2021 we believe that there were 4,802 hits taken away from batters by defensive shifts, whereas there were 3, 946 hits given away by defenses which were, at the moment, too clever for their own good. 4,802 is 22% more than 3,946. So it's not like 10 to 1, but it's not 26 to 25, either; it's more like 11 to 9.

Now, we're not claiming that 4,802 hits prevented by the shift is precisely the right number; we're not claiming that, or at least I'm not. A ball in play has a lot of variables, and you can't track all of them precisely. But how did we arrive at the number, 4,802?

We have LOTS of data. It's what we do for a living; we count stuff. We've been counting stuff for a long time, so we have millions of plays to look at, and we have computers to sort them with. We know, for example, that when a ground ball is hit 35 feet to the second base side of first base with an exit velocity of 97 MPH, it has a high probability of becoming a hit if the defense is not in a shift. Whether the percentage is 78% or 91% or 96%, I don't personally know, because I don't work with that kind of data, but my point is, somebody here DOES know. Let's say there is a 91% chance of that ball becoming a hit if the defense is not in a shift.

So when that ball is hit INTO a shift and becomes an out, we record two things: the 91% chance that it would have been a hit if the defense was not shifted, and the 1 or 0 indicating that it did become a hit, or that it didn't. I hope that makes sense, because if I try to explain it any better than that I'll get totally confused and have to start over.

So we've resolved that issue; it's a 22% edge. There are, however, many other things we can learn from studying this data. For example, **how much does shifting lower major league batting averages, overall?**

Four points. The major league batting average in 2021 was .244. There were 856 more hits taken away from batters than accidentally given back. If there had been 856 more hits in 856 more at bats, the major league batting average would have been .248. So the shifts lowered the major league batting average by 4 points.

What percentage of all batters are shifted against?

Most of them, anymore. SIS measures shift rates as a percentage of balls in play. There were 115,766 balls in play in the majors in 2021, and 59,062 shifts used on balls in play, so that would be 51%.

How often does the shift work, as a percentage? I mean, if you shift 100 times, how many hits do you prevent?

Eight percent gross, but 1.5% net. There were 59,062 shifts used last year, and 4,802 balls hit into The Shift. That's 8%.

However, as mentioned before, there were also 3,946 outs lost by teams because of the shift, so the net was not 4,802, but 856. So 1.5% of all shifts prevented hits. About one in 70.

What teams gained the most by using the shift?

Depends on how you look at the data. The team which USED the shift...

Maybe this would have more impact if I printed "the shift" in Old English Black Letters, as if it was holy writ or something. The team which used 𝕿𝖍𝖊 𝕾𝖍𝖎𝖋𝖙 most often was the Minnesota Twins, who shifted 2,815 times, taking 219 hits away from the opposition.

219 hits is a lot, but it was not the most in the majors. The Brave Atlanta Braves prevented 221, which led the majors. However, while they prevented 221 hits, they also allowed 163 that they would not have allowed if they were not shifting, so the gain was not 221, but 58.

The 58 was also the largest net gain in the major leagues, so, looked at in one way, the team which gained the most from 𝕿𝖍𝖊 𝕾𝖍𝖎𝖋𝖙 was the Braves. Except they weren't, because we still have looked at only half of the story.

The Brave HITTERS also lost 201 hits to other teams using 𝕿𝖍𝖊 𝕾𝖍𝖎𝖋𝖙, 201 gross and 51 net. So the Braves didn't actually gain 58 hits; they actually gained 7. If the Braves had been the only team using 𝕿𝖍𝖊 𝕾𝖍𝖎𝖋𝖙, they would have come out 58 hits ahead, but since their opposition used it as well, the net-net gain was only 7 hits.

The team which appears to have gained the most by 𝕿𝖍𝖊 𝕾𝖍𝖎𝖋𝖙 was the Colorado Rockies. We think that the Rockies came out 39 hits (or 39 outs) ahead on the deal.

Look, we all know that the Colorado Park/park situation is so unusual that it messes with the data. What I am saying is that we need to be inherently suspicious of conclusions we draw about the Rockies, because any and all of our assumptions about the percentages suffer from a heightened risk of error in that park, simply because the park is so unusual.

However, to the extent that we can rely on the data, this is the data for the Rockies, which can be confirmed by the charts on page 500:

The Rockies shifted 1,603 times in 2021, which is a low number.

They saved 143 hits, but gave up another 95 by having fielders in the wrong places. The net gain was 48 hits.

Colorado hitters, however, had a net loss of only 9 hits, which was the fourth-lowest total in the majors. Thus, the Rockies gained 39 hits (or outs) because of 𝕿𝖍𝖊 𝕾𝖍𝖎𝖋𝖙, making them the Shift Champions of 2021.

Is the Old English annoying you? OK, I'll stop. **What pitcher(s) have benefitted the most from the shift?**

The pitcher who has benefited the most, easily, is Charlie Morton of the Braves. Morton led the majors in hits saved in 2021, 18 net, and he also has the highest career total (41) among active pitchers.

What hitter has been hurt the most?

Anthony Rizzo. Rizzo has lost 95 hits in his career by hitting the ball into the shift.

The hitter who lost the most in 2021, however, was Jeimer Candelario, who lost 20 hits. Candelario would have hit .307 in 2021 were it not for those nasty shifters. Rizzo has lost 19 points off of his career batting average because of the shifts, dropping him from .287 to .268.

The five hitters who have lost the most are Rizzo, Albert Pujols, Carlos Santana, Kyle Seager and Mitch Moreland.

Who is on the opposite end of those charts?

The pitcher who has been most hurt by his team's shifts is Jordan Montgomery of the Yankees. Montgomery has given up 12 more hits in his career than we believe that he would have given up had his team not been shifting, 6 more in 2021.

The two hitters who have most successfully beat the shift, over the years, are both Red Sox: JD Martinez and Xander Bogaerts. JD has gained 18 hits by beating the shift, and Xander has gained 15.

Thank you all for reading. I hope you understand the mathematics of shifting a little better now than you did 20 minutes ago.

Hits Lost and Gained to the Shift for Batters

Player	2021 Season				Career Since 2010			
	Shifts	Lost	Gained	Net	Shifts	Lost	Gained	Net
Candelario, Jeimer	288	33	13	20	688	62	35	27
Muncy, Max	319	29	13	16	931	87	42	45
Votto, Joey	262	29	14	15	1545	135	101	34
Alvarez, Yordan	340	33	18	15	484	52	25	27
Ramirez, Jose	337	35	21	14	1052	83	60	23
Albies, Ozzie	395	34	20	14	987	74	70	4
Conforto, Michael	232	24	10	14	1276	116	81	35
Kepler, Max	290	27	14	13	1190	97	64	33
Suarez, Eugenio	212	21	9	12	855	75	47	28
Grandal, Yasmani	152	20	8	12	1085	104	59	45
Moran, Colin	195	21	10	11	752	74	46	28
Seager, Kyle	369	27	16	11	2368	192	116	76
La Stella, Tommy	157	19	8	11	526	50	29	21
Kelenic, Jarred	171	17	6	11	171	17	6	11
Gallo, Joey	218	19	9	10	860	75	39	36
Freeman, Freddie	420	41	31	10	2302	192	145	47
Kirilloff, Alex	137	18	8	10	137	18	8	10
Lindor, Francisco	172	20	10	10	807	64	50	14
Wade Jr., LaMonte	155	15	5	10	191	16	8	8
Santana, Carlos	356	33	23	10	2326	210	132	78
Olson, Matt	386	35	25	10	1201	101	70	31
Smith, Dominic	268	23	13	10	625	60	32	28
Bellinger, Cody	198	16	6	10	1224	96	94	2
Maldonado, Martin	142	15	5	10	360	37	16	21
Vogelbach, Daniel	143	16	7	9	525	54	23	31
Rizzo, Anthony	344	26	17	9	2624	227	132	95
Tellez, Rowdy	201	21	12	9	503	52	31	21
Moreland, Mitch	152	15	6	9	1758	168	100	68
Winker, Jesse	287	26	17	9	687	60	40	20
Judge, Aaron	221	22	14	8	592	54	49	5
Cronenworth, Jake	282	27	19	8	371	36	21	15
Edman, Tommy	330	27	19	8	528	40	33	7
Heim, Jonah	138	13	5	8	166	15	6	9
McKinney, Billy	152	12	4	8	327	27	11	16
Castro, Willi	117	13	5	8	195	17	13	4
Renfroe, Hunter	297	25	17	8	725	59	40	19
Cabrera, Asdrubal	156	13	5	8	1108	92	56	36
Dickerson, Alex	148	12	4	8	345	28	18	10
Bradley Jr., Jackie	195	18	10	8	1257	125	95	30
Crawford, J.P.	284	22	15	7	577	43	36	7
Goodwin, Brian	143	15	8	7	413	36	24	12
Soto, Juan	269	29	22	7	637	60	54	6
Sheets, Gavin	100	11	4	7	100	11	4	7
Gregorius, Didi	235	18	11	7	846	63	44	19
Hernandez, Yadiel	114	14	7	7	120	15	7	8
Donaldson, Josh	171	15	8	7	752	69	48	21
Meadows, Austin	308	19	12	7	719	42	44	-2
Carpenter, Matt	117	11	4	7	1317	106	57	49
Franco, Maikel	148	14	7	7	723	70	44	26
Narvaez, Omar	263	21	14	7	612	46	34	12
Choi, Ji-Man	138	15	8	7	536	48	39	9
Andrus, Elvis	70	8	1	7	176	18	13	5
Tucker, Kyle	350	26	19	7	537	46	29	17
Reyes, Franmil	133	16	9	7	371	36	32	4
Pollock, A.J.	156	8	15	-7	527	40	42	-2
O'Neill, Tyler	168	9	16	-7	291	16	26	-10
Pillar, Kevin	87	4	11	-7	450	30	39	-9
Lux, Gavin	188	14	22	-8	254	18	26	-8
Turner, Trea	143	10	19	-9	306	20	34	-14

120

Outs Gained and Lost to the Shift for Pitchers

Player	2021 Season				Career Since 2010			
	Shifts	Gained	Lost	Net	Shifts	Gained	Lost	Net
Morton, Charlie	314	33	15	18	1252	122	81	41
Buehler, Walker	364	38	20	18	789	72	48	24
Wainwright, Adam	304	30	14	16	897	79	50	29
Kelly, Merrill	251	29	15	14	567	60	32	28
Marquez, German	214	25	11	14	840	79	57	22
Senzatela, Antonio	249	27	13	14	714	74	49	25
Fried, Max	276	28	15	13	545	53	34	19
Berrios, Jose	339	30	17	13	1114	98	67	31
Espino, Paolo	220	21	8	13	259	26	8	18
Manning, Matt	162	18	6	12	162	18	6	12
Mize, Casey	289	28	17	11	339	33	21	12
Woodruff, Brandon	181	18	7	11	466	38	31	7
Lyles, Jordan	294	21	10	11	886	69	47	22
McCullers Jr., Lance	243	31	20	11	845	90	57	33
Bassitt, Chris	201	20	9	11	462	36	31	5
DeSclafani, Anthony	270	24	13	11	809	68	47	21
Musgrove, Joe	210	21	11	10	922	83	57	26
Greinke, Zack	292	27	17	10	1347	116	82	34
Giolito, Lucas	168	16	6	10	722	71	38	33
Anderson, Ian	244	25	15	10	305	30	21	9
Paddack, Chris	124	15	6	9	321	32	15	17
Hernandez, Elieser	86	11	2	9	302	25	9	16
Civale, Aaron	154	14	5	9	320	29	12	17
Stammen, Craig	145	19	10	9	366	41	26	15
Corbin, Patrick	269	26	17	9	837	88	56	32
Keuchel, Dallas	201	22	13	9	1325	142	108	34
Foltynewicz, Mike	265	22	13	9	652	56	32	24
Davies, Zach	221	22	14	8	1144	108	84	24
Mahle, Tyler	230	23	15	8	571	50	40	10
Ynoa, Huascar	165	18	10	8	218	23	14	9
Plesac, Zach	173	15	8	7	365	30	15	15
Bubic, Kris	160	14	7	7	211	18	12	6
Means, John	129	11	4	7	435	33	18	15
Kinley, Tyler	76	10	3	7	174	19	9	10
Ohtani, Shohei	207	18	11	7	224	21	13	8
Dunning, Dane	198	24	17	7	250	30	20	10
Kittredge, Andrew	134	16	9	7	336	38	25	13
deGrom, Jacob	125	11	4	7	620	55	27	28
Martinez, Carlos	142	15	8	7	489	46	35	11
Gonzales, Marco	215	17	10	7	757	63	47	16
Wacha, Michael	210	22	15	7	675	66	48	18
Chargois, JT	79	9	3	6	142	16	8	8
Taillon, Jameson	157	12	6	6	691	57	46	11
Wheeler, Zack	174	18	12	6	634	56	40	16
Cueto, Johnny	223	17	11	6	798	63	36	27
Anderson, Brett	145	16	10	6	459	56	37	19
Shoemaker, Matt	151	12	6	6	622	58	40	18
Hill, Rich	264	19	13	6	632	48	35	13
Arrieta, Jake	163	13	7	6	775	69	48	21
McKenzie, Triston	130	11	5	6	163	12	7	5
Urquidy, Jose	188	14	8	6	303	24	14	10
Alcantara, Sandy	299	30	24	6	744	65	58	7
Neidert, Nick	54	6	0	6	64	7	0	7
White, Mitch	102	12	6	6	108	12	6	6
Javier, Cristian	144	10	4	6	236	17	8	9
Nola, Aaron	200	17	11	6	786	76	48	28
Crowe, Wil	184	17	11	6	193	17	12	5
Garcia, Luis	257	19	13	6	281	22	15	7
Montgomery, Jordan	165	12	18	-6	340	24	36	-12
McClanahan, Shane	215	13	20	-7	215	13	20	-7
Singer, Brady	169	12	19	-7	273	21	27	-6
Happ, J.A.	242	12	19	-7	951	69	72	-3

Hits Lost and Gained to the Shift by Batting Team

Team	2021 Season				Totals Since 2010			
	Shifts	Lost	Gained	Net	Shifts	Lost	Gained	Net
Seattle Mariners	2307	182	130	52	10369	888	642	246
Atlanta Braves	2453	201	150	51	9349	761	604	157
Minnesota Twins	2158	177	128	49	10328	837	687	150
Milwaukee Brewers	2196	187	139	48	7570	639	487	152
San Francisco Giants	2174	164	118	46	7469	574	444	130
Pittsburgh Pirates	1753	147	103	44	7568	698	513	185
New York Mets	1964	180	138	42	9937	886	593	293
Cincinnati Reds	2098	174	132	42	9019	759	571	188
Oakland Athletics	2125	162	125	37	10714	830	679	151
New York Yankees	1866	147	112	35	10827	951	657	294
Arizona Diamondbacks	2327	189	154	35	7631	651	529	122
Texas Rangers	1613	146	112	34	9849	890	706	184
Cleveland Indians	1759	148	119	29	9696	802	621	181
Los Angeles Dodgers	2252	175	146	29	10063	850	654	196
Houston Astros	2223	179	151	28	9145	768	577	191
Detroit Tigers	1771	142	114	28	7670	622	534	88
Chicago Cubs	1837	152	125	27	10345	902	696	206
Chicago White Sox	1602	140	115	25	6575	578	469	109
Tampa Bay Rays	2013	156	133	23	9616	785	655	130
St Louis Cardinals	1871	141	119	22	7629	583	497	86
Washington Nationals	1822	164	147	17	7746	657	518	139
Los Angeles Angels	1734	151	134	17	9728	892	654	238
Baltimore Orioles	1654	120	103	17	9234	776	626	150
Boston Red Sox	2215	171	154	17	11898	1025	792	233
Kansas City Royals	2001	164	148	16	9043	759	616	143
San Diego Padres	2017	168	154	14	7367	646	521	125
Philadelphia Phillies	1960	157	148	9	8968	815	559	256
Colorado Rockies	1766	153	144	9	7592	623	621	2
Miami Marlins	1498	123	115	8	5622	482	425	57
Toronto Blue Jays	2033	142	136	6	10662	932	634	298

Outs Gained and Lost to the Shift by Defensive Team

Team	2021 Season				Totals Since 2010			
	Shifts	Gained	Lost	Net	Shifts	Gained	Lost	Net
Atlanta Braves	2529	221	163	58	8415	739	573	166
Texas Rangers	2248	196	141	55	8567	736	546	190
Houston Astros	2207	191	138	53	13511	1179	871	308
Colorado Rockies	1603	143	95	48	8715	789	577	212
Minnesota Twins	2815	219	172	47	11011	890	707	183
Chicago Cubs	1840	174	128	46	6010	544	375	169
San Francisco Giants	2119	174	137	37	8273	670	514	156
San Diego Padres	1549	129	95	34	6508	580	421	159
Chicago White Sox	1138	95	61	34	8815	778	578	200
Cleveland Indians	1466	118	84	34	7945	666	439	227
Detroit Tigers	2470	204	172	32	8100	674	546	128
St Louis Cardinals	1826	144	112	32	6759	574	431	143
New York Mets	2499	208	177	31	7356	611	486	125
Pittsburgh Pirates	2095	163	132	31	11817	1004	813	191
Tampa Bay Rays	2171	171	142	29	13727	1179	930	249
Los Angeles Dodgers	2626	218	190	28	9613	845	645	200
Milwaukee Brewers	1700	143	115	28	10810	956	767	189
Washington Nationals	2189	166	140	26	7214	590	484	106
Los Angeles Angels	2183	174	150	24	8509	698	559	139
Cincinnati Reds	1997	166	142	24	8685	717	560	157
Miami Marlins	1954	159	136	23	8316	641	557	84
Seattle Mariners	2273	175	155	20	10407	873	701	172
Philadelphia Phillies	1408	118	98	20	6869	579	480	99
Baltimore Orioles	1568	113	95	18	10667	898	674	224
Oakland Athletics	1834	141	125	16	7409	626	472	154
Toronto Blue Jays	1690	137	121	16	9719	827	607	220
Arizona Diamondbacks	1948	155	143	12	8796	790	576	214
New York Yankees	1357	99	91	8	10303	862	740	122
Kansas City Royals	1811	139	133	6	8266	677	613	64
Boston Red Sox	1949	151	162	-11	8117	671	537	134

Four-Outfielder Alignments

Sarah Thompson

We've seen more four-outfielder alignments in 2021 than in any previous year. And this time, it's not just a Rays Thing™. In 2020, the Rays accounted for 30 four-outfielder alignments on balls in play out of 39 total in MLB.

But this year, the strategy caught on.

The Blue Jays used 38 four-man outfields this year, 10 fewer than the Rays. They used only four in 2019. The players they did it against the most were Austin Meadows and Brandon Lowe.

While the addition of Joey Gallo to the AL East may have had some impact on the Blue Jays' four-outfielder alignment frequency, it's actually Austin Meadows and Brandon Lowe the Jays have strategized for the most, which brings us to the other part of the four-outfielder formula—who is worth sacrificing an infielder for?

You can see which players were defensed with 4 outfielders on the next page. You'll find that most of these batters facing four-man outfields have low groundball to flyball ratios (meaning they hit many more balls in the air than on the ground), or pull the ball a lot, or both. One player not on the list is Adam Duvall, who had the second-lowest groundball/flyball rate in MLB (behind only Meadows) and a 47% pull rate. Perhaps he'll see it in the future.

In the tables on the following page are the total number of four-outfielder alignments that each team has used in each of the last four seasons (and overall) as well as the total number that any batter with two or more such alignments has seen in that same time frame.

Four-Outfielder Alignments Employed
On Balls In Play

Team	2018	2019	2020	2021	Total
Tampa Bay Rays	2	51	30	48	131
Toronto Blue Jays	0	4	1	38	43
Cincinnati Reds	0	36	0	0	36
Minnesota Twins	27	3	0	0	30
Pittsburgh Pirates	0	0	7	0	7
Arizona Diamondbacks	0	5	0	0	5
San Francisco Giants	0	5	0	0	5
Houston Astros	5	0	0	0	5
Detroit Tigers	0	0	0	2	2
Texas Rangers	0	0	0	2	2
Chicago Cubs	2	0	0	0	2
New York Mets	0	0	0	1	1
St Louis Cardinals	0	0	1	0	1
Los Angeles Dodgers	0	1	0	0	1
Seattle Mariners	0	1	0	0	1
Colorado Rockies	1	0	0	0	1
MLB	37	106	39	91	273

Four-Outfielder Alignments By Batter, Career
On Balls In Play (Minimum 2 BIP)

Batter	AB	H	2B	3B	BABIP	SlgBIP
Gallo, Joey	31	12	1	0	.387	.419
Smoak, Justin	25	6	1	0	.240	.280
Biggio, Cavan	23	11	2	0	.478	.565
Olson, Matt	16	5	2	0	.313	.438
Belt, Brandon	12	2	1	0	.167	.250
Duda, Lucas	11	3	0	0	.273	.273
Carpenter, Matt	9	5	0	1	.556	.778
Polanco, Jorge	8	4	0	0	.500	.500
Freeman, Freddie	7	5	0	0	.714	.714
Lowe, Brandon	7	2	0	0	.286	.286
Meadows, Austin	7	1	0	0	.143	.143
Kepler, Max	6	1	0	0	.167	.167
Bellinger, Cody	5	3	2	0	.600	1.000
Grandal, Yasmani	5	3	0	0	.600	.600
Grossman, Robbie	5	0	0	0	.000	.000
Moreland, Mitch	5	0	0	0	.000	.000
Muncy, Max	5	1	0	0	.200	.200
Seager, Corey	5	5	1	0	1.000	1.200
Seager, Kyle	5	1	0	0	.200	.200
Alvarez, Yordan	4	1	0	0	.250	.250
Semien, Marcus	4	0	0	0	.000	.000
Voit, Luke	4	2	0	0	.500	.500
Bruce, Jay	3	0	0	0	.000	.000
Fraley, Jake	3	2	1	0	.667	1.000
Granderson, Curtis	3	0	0	0	.000	.000
Sisco, Chance	3	1	0	0	.333	.333
Albies, Ozzie	2	1	0	0	.500	.500
Collins, Zack	2	1	0	0	.500	.500
Davis, Chris	2	0	0	0	.000	.000
Davis, Khris	2	1	0	0	.500	.500
Encarnacion, Edwin	2	1	0	0	.500	.500
Haase, Eric	2	1	0	0	.500	.500
Higashioka, Kyle	2	0	0	0	.000	.000
Rizzo, Anthony	2	0	0	0	.000	.000
Sanchez, Gary	2	1	0	0	.500	.500
Shaw, Travis	2	0	0	0	.000	.000
Thaiss, Matt	2	0	0	0	.000	.000
Torres, Gleyber	2	2	1	0	1.000	1.500

Home Run Robberies

Lindsay Zeck

In 2021, there were 63 home run robberies. Interestingly, 12 of them came in the last two weeks of the season—that's 19 percent! This is due in large part to something that has never before happened since SIS began tracking home run robberies in 2004. On September 25, there were four home run robberies in one day! Two of those occurred in the Yankees–Red Sox game. The Red Sox's Hunter Renfroe stole a solo shot from Yankees' Rougned Odor in the third inning, and the Yankees' Aaron Judge returned the favor robbing Bobby Dalbec's would-be two-run home run in the fifth.

Two home run robberies in a game has only happened eight times since we started tracking. That's 8 times in 18 seasons. The only time it happened twice in a season was in 2004… until now. Amazingly, not only did the 2021 season have two games with two home run robberies, but they happened on consecutive days! On September 24, the day before the four-home run robbery day, during the Rangers–Orioles game at Oriole Park at Camden Yards, the Rangers' Leody Taveras and DJ Peters stole home runs from Orioles Pedro Severino and Pat Valaika, respectively.

Those two robberies gave the Orioles the most home runs robbed this season with six—five of which were at home. The Orioles robbed two home runs at home, both coincidentally from the Yankees' Gary Sánchez.

Sánchez was one of six batters who had two home runs stolen from him—the highest total in the league. The others were Steven Duggar, Mitch Haniger, Manny Machado, Carlos Santana, and Valaika.

Seven players led the way with two robbed home runs this season: Andrew Benintendi, Adolis García, Kiké Hernández, Aaron Judge, Ramon Laureano, Hunter Renfroe, and Mike Tauchman.

The team that stole the most home runs was the Rangers with six. The Rangers didn't have a single home run stolen from them.

Home Run Robberies

Date	Matchup	Fielder	Pos	Pitcher	Batter	Inn.	Outs	Men On	Score
05/19/2021	Rays@Orioles	Randy Arozarena	7	Ryan Yarbrough	Pat Valaika	6	1	___	3-6
09/25/2021	Royals@Tigers	Akil Baddoo	7	Tarik Skubal	Hunter Dozier	3	0	___	0-0
07/21/2021	Cubs@Cardinals	Harrison Bader	8	Adam Wainwright	Willson Contreras	1	0	1__	0-0
09/20/2021	Nationals@Marlins	Josh Bell	7	Erick Fedde	Lewis Brinson	2	0	___	3-0
08/26/2021	Royals@Mariners	Andrew Benintendi	7	Ervin Santana	Jarred Kelenic	8	0	___	6-4
09/06/2021	Royals@Orioles	Andrew Benintendi	7	Scott Barlow	Anthony Santander	9	0	___	3-2
08/31/2021	Braves@Dodgers	Mookie Betts	9	Walker Buehler	Travis d'Arnaud	2	1	___	0-0
05/15/2021	Braves@Brewers	Jackie Bradley Jr.	8	Angel Perdomo	Ozzie Albies	7	0	___	4-0
06/24/2021	Astros@Tigers	Michael Brantley	7	Luis Garcia	Jonathan Schoop	5	2	_2_	8-1
04/07/2021	Dodgers@Athletics	Seth Brown	7	Jesus Luzardo	Austin Barnes	4	0	___	1-0
04/30/2021	Royals@Twins	Byron Buxton	8	Hansel Robles	Andrew Benintendi	7	2	___	1-5
09/26/2021	Royals@Tigers	Willi Castro	7	Bryan Garcia	Whit Merrifield	9	0	___	2-0
05/14/2021	Rangers@Astros	David Dahl	9	Taylor Hearn	Chas McCormick	7	1	1__	3-10
06/03/2021	Cubs@Giants	Steven Duggar	8	Anthony DeSclafani	Joc Pederson	1	0	___	0-0
04/17/2021	White Sox@Red Sox	Adam Eaton	9	Dylan Cease	Rafael Devers	2	0	1__	2-0
06/06/2021	Tigers@White Sox	Adam Engel	8	Dylan Cease	Niko Goodrum	5	0	___	0-3
06/09/2021	Mariners@Tigers	Jake Fraley	7	Drew Steckenrider	Isaac Paredes	9	1	1__	3-3
07/05/2021	Tigers@Rangers	Joey Gallo	9	Kolby Allard	Akil Baddoo	1	0	___	0-0
09/15/2021	Reds@Pirates	Ben Gamel	7	Mitch Keller	Jonathan India	3	0	___	2-0
05/27/2021	Rangers@Mariners	Adolis Garcia	8	Kolby Allard	Mitch Haniger	1	1	___	0-0
08/19/2021	Mariners@Rangers	Adolis Garcia	9	Joe Barlow	Jake Fraley	11	2	___	9-7
08/25/2021	Reds@Brewers	Avisail Garcia	9	Devin Williams	Max Schrock	8	1	___	0-2
08/26/2021	Dodgers@Padres	Trent Grisham	8	Shaun Anderson	A.J. Pollock	9	0	___	4-0
08/13/2021	Blue Jays@Mariners	Mitch Haniger	9	Chris Flexen	Vladimir Guerrero Jr.	1	2	___	0-0
06/28/2021	Orioles@Astros	Austin Hays	9	Thomas Eshelman	Kyle Tucker	2	1	___	0-0
06/28/2021	Royals@Red Sox	Kike Hernandez	8	Garrett Richards	Carlos Santana	2	2	___	5-1
07/05/2021	Red Sox@Angels	Kike Hernandez	8	Martin Perez	Luis Rengifo	2	2	_2_	2-1
05/26/2021	Phillies@Marlins	Odubel Herrera	8	Aaron Nola	Isan Diaz	6	2	___	2-1
09/14/2021	Angels@White Sox	Eloy Jimenez	7	Lucas Giolito	David Fletcher	3	2	___	1-2
05/19/2021	Tigers@Mariners	JaCoby Jones	8	Jose Cisnero	Jose Marmolejos	7	2	___	5-2
06/17/2021	Yankees@Blue Jays	Aaron Judge	9	Chad Green	Cavan Biggio	6	0	1__	3-4
09/25/2021	Yankees@Red Sox	Aaron Judge	9	Nestor Cortes	Bobby Dalbec	5	0	1__	0-1
08/27/2021	Rays@Orioles	Kevin Kiermaier	8	Shane McClanahan	Ryan Mountcastle	5	1	1__	3-2
07/06/2021	Red Sox@Angels	Juan Lagares	8	Shohei Ohtani	Xander Bogaerts	6	2	1__	2-3
05/21/2021	Athletics@Angels	Ramon Laureano	8	Jake Diekman	Anthony Rendon	7	2	1__	6-4
06/16/2021	Angels@Athletics	Ramon Laureano	8	Cole Irvin	Justin Upton	4	2	___	4-0
09/08/2021	Rays@Red Sox	Manuel Margot	8	Shane McClanahan	J.D. Martinez	3	1	1__	0-0
09/25/2021	Mariners@Angels	Brandon Marsh	8	Jaime Barria	Mitch Haniger	1	2	1__	0-0
06/25/2021	Phillies@Mets	Andrew McCutchen	7	Matt Moore	Albert Almora Jr.	2	2	1__	0-0
05/15/2021	Yankees@Orioles	Ryan McKenna	7	Shawn Armstrong	Gary Sanchez	9	1	12_	8-1
09/15/2021	Yankees@Orioles	Cedric Mullins II	8	John Means	Gary Sanchez	2	2	1__	0-0
09/21/2021	Giants@Padres	Wil Myers	9	Pierce Johnson	Steven Duggar	8	2	1__	5-5
07/10/2021	Pirates@Mets	Brandon Nimmo	8	Marcus Stroman	Bryan Reynolds	1	2	___	0-0
09/15/2021	Cardinals@Mets	Lars Nootbaar	9	T.J. McFarland	Pete Alonso	7	2	1_3	8-4
10/01/2021	Cubs@Cardinals	Rafael Ortega	8	Adbert Alzolay	Paul Goldschmidt	8	0	___	3-3
07/21/2021	Pirates@Diamondbacks	David Peralta	7	Madison Bumgarner	Jacob Stallings	2	0	___	0-0
09/24/2021	Rangers@Orioles	DJ Peters	7	Spencer Howard	Pat Valaika	4	1	___	3-4
08/03/2021	Pirates@Brewers	Gregory Polanco	9	David Bednar	Eduardo Escobar	9	2	___	5-5
08/24/2021	Dodgers@Padres	A.J. Pollock	7	Julio Urias	Manny Machado	4	1	1__	1-0
08/13/2021	Orioles@Red Sox	Hunter Renfroe	9	Nick Pivetta	D.J. Stewart	4	0	___	1-5
09/25/2021	Yankees@Red Sox	Hunter Renfroe	9	Nick Pivetta	Rougned Odor	3	0	___	0-0
08/05/2021	Pirates@Reds	Bryan Reynolds	8	Duane Underwood Jr.	Tyler Naquin	5	0	1__	4-7
04/28/2021	Padres@Diamondbacks	Josh Rojas	9	Yoan Lopez	Fernando Tatis Jr.	8	0	1_3	9-3
05/10/2021	Marlins@Diamondbacks	Pavin Smith	9	Stefan Crichton	Sandy Leon	9	2	___	2-5
08/05/2021	Phillies@Nationals	Juan Soto	9	Joe Ross	Didi Gregorius	7	0	___	2-5
05/28/2021	Giants@Dodgers	Mike Tauchman	7	Tyler Rogers	Albert Pujols	9	2	___	5-5
06/11/2021	Giants@Nationals	Mike Tauchman	7	Anthony DeSclafani	Juan Soto	7	1	___	1-0
09/24/2021	Rangers@Orioles	Leody Taveras	8	Spencer Howard	Pedro Severino	3	1	1__	2-4
09/10/2021	Padres@Dodgers	Chris Taylor	8	Julio Urias	Manny Machado	5	2	1__	0-3
10/02/2021	Athletics@Astros	Kyle Tucker	9	Ryne Stanek	Tony Kemp	6	2	12_	3-6
09/29/2021	Diamondbacks@Giants	Daulton Varsho	7	Tyler Clippard	Steven Duggar	8	2	1_3	0-1
06/18/2021	Reds@Padres	Jesse Winker	7	Ashton Goudeau	Eric Hosmer	5	0	___	2-5
06/07/2021	Royals@Angels	Kean Wong	9	Dylan Bundy	Carlos Santana	1	1	___	0-0

Career Register

Alex Vigderman

Besides the excitement of actually having a full season in 2021, this was a pretty momentous year for baseball fans. Other sections of this book might be better suited for you to explore some of them, but here are a few things to note in the pages that follow.

Shohei Ohtani is, among other things, unique because he has two entries in this section. He did a great many things in 2021 that nobody had done for a long time. If I were to list them all here, we'd probably squeeze out the first few letters of the alphabet in the section that follows. So maybe just check out his once-in-a-lifetime stats when you get to the "O"s.

Diamondbacks pitcher Tyler Gilbert is making his first appearance in this section. He'll probably be remembered for a different first this year, given that he threw a no-hitter in his first MLB start on August 14. That was one of nine no-hitters in total in 2021, a record (and the count bumps up to eleven if you include seven-inning games). His bottom-line numbers of a 3.15 ERA and 2.38 Component ERA (an ERA estimate based on underlying stats) in 40 innings are encouraging.

And speaking of debuts, Major League Baseball experienced two big milestones for those who revere the history of the game. We saw the debut of what might have been the 20,000th Major Leaguer ever, Mariners catcher José Godoy.

However, Godoy's place in history was short-lived, as the long-awaited merging of Negro Leagues into Major League history placed nearly 2,400 players ahead of him in line. The player who takes his place as the 20,000th is himself a notable Mariner, former 2nd overall pick Dustin Ackley. Unfortunately you'll have to travel back in time to the 2017 edition of this book to find Ackley represented in this section.

And if we're continuing this degrees-of-separation exercise, you might recall that Ackley is as well-known for the players selected around him in the 2009 MLB Draft as anything he did in his career. Yes, of course, Stephen Strasburg was selected first and Mike Trout many picks later, but in terms of 2021 performance, the biggest connection here is Phillies surprise ace Zack Wheeler, who was selected sixth by the Giants.

Wheeler had a weird season in 2020, striking out fewer than 20 percent of batters he faced for the first time since his rookie season. This year, he struck out almost 30 percent en route to a Cy-Young-caliber campaign.

A couple things to remember as you walk through this section:

Each Major Leaguer from 2021 appears with his full career statistics. That includes a summary of postseason stats prior to 2021 (this book went to press before the postseason was completed). You won't see every minor leaguer, but you will see the consensus top prospects and their recent stats all the way down to A-ball. And remember, 2020 was a strange one, so don't get spooked by last year's dips in counting stats.

Also, if you want to hear more about Baseball-Reference's effort to incorporate Negro League stats into Major League history, check out this podcast from June.

Fernando Abad

Pitches: L Bats: L Pos: RP-16   ah-BAHD   Ht: 6'2" Wt: 235 Born: 12/17/1985 Age: 36

		HOW MUCH PITCHED					WHAT HE GAVE UP										THE RESULTS							
Year	Team	Lg	G	GS	GF	IP	BFP	H	R	ER	HR	SH	SF	HB	TBB	IBB	SO	WP	W	L	Pct	Sv-Op	Hld	Vel	OPS	ERC	ERA
2021	Norfolk	AAA	26	0	10	25.1	110	30	12	12	5	0	0	0	6	0	27	1	2	1	.667	3- -	-	-	.847	5.15	4.26
2010	Hou	NL	22	0	6	19.0	76	14	6	6	3	0	1	0	5	0	12	0	0	1	.000	0-0	6	90	.636	2.49	2.84
2011	Hou	NL	29	0	1	19.2	99	28	18	16	5	1	2	1	9	0	15	0	1	4	.200	0-2	7	90	.946	8.06	7.32
2012	Hou	NL	37	6	8	46.0	208	57	27	26	6	2	1	3	19	1	38	4	0	6	.000	0-0	3	90	.892	6.13	5.09
2013	Was	NL	39	0	17	37.2	166	42	14	14	3	0	0	1	10	0	32	0	0	3	.000	0-1	2	93	.687	4.05	3.35
2014	Oak	AL	69	0	17	57.1	216	34	11	10	4	1	2	4	15	3	51	0	2	4	.333	0-2	9	92	.499	1.64	1.57
2015	Oak	AL	62	0	17	47.2	205	45	23	22	11	3	3	1	19	3	45	4	2	2	.500	0-3	1	91	.813	4.63	4.15
2016	2 Tms	AL	57	0	15	46.2	198	40	20	19	4	0	1	1	22	2	41	1	1	6	.143	1-5	8	91	.657	3.50	3.66
2017	Bos	AL	48	0	15	43.2	182	40	18	16	4	0	2	1	14	1	37	0	2	1	.667	1-2	6	92	.672	3.32	3.30
2019	SF	NL	21	0	1	13.0	49	9	6	6	2	0	0	0	5	0	9	1	0	2	.000	0-0	8	93	.571	2.26	4.15
2021	Bal	AL	16	0	4	17.2	82	23	12	11	1	0	0	0	7	1	10	0	0	0	-	0-0	2	93	.819	5.31	5.60
16	Min	AL	39	0	8	34.0	138	27	11	10	2	0	1	0	14	2	29	0	1	4	.200	1-2	6	91	.614	2.72	2.65
16	Bos	AL	18	0	7	12.2	60	13	9	9	2	0	0	1	8	0	12	1	0	2	.000	0-3	2	92	.759	5.81	6.39
	Postseason		1	0	0	0.1	1	0	0	0	0	0	0	0	0	0	0	0	0	0	-	0-0	0	95	.000	0.00	0.00
	10 ML YEARS		400	6	101	348.1	1481	332	155	146	43	7	12	12	123	11	290	10	8	29	.216	2-15	48	91	.717	3.88	3.77

Cory Abbott

Pitches: R Bats: R Pos: RP-6; SP-1   Ht: 6'1" Wt: 210 Born: 9/20/1995 Age: 26

		HOW MUCH PITCHED					WHAT HE GAVE UP										THE RESULTS							
Year	Team	Lg	G	GS	GF	IP	BFP	H	R	ER	HR	SH	SF	HB	TBB	IBB	SO	WP	W	L	Pct	Sv-Op	Hld	Vel	OPS	ERC	ERA
2021	Iowa	AAA	19	19	0	96.0	436	97	69	63	20	0	1	5	53	0	130	3	5	6	.455	0- -	-	-	.862	5.76	5.91
2021	ChC	NL	7	1	2	17.1	82	20	15	13	7	1	0	0	11	0	12	2	0	0	-	0-0	0	93	1.026	8.39	6.75

CJ Abrams

Bats: L Throws: R Pos: SS   Ht: 6'2" Wt: 185 Born: 10/3/2000 Age: 21

						BATTING												RUNNING			AVERAGES			
Year	Team	Lg	G	AB	H	2B	3B	HR	(Hm | Rd)	TB	R	RBI	RC	TBB	IBB	SO	HBP	SH	SF	SB	CS	GDP	Avg	OBP	Slg	OPS
2019	2 Tms	Low	34	150	59	13	8	3	(- | -)	97	41	22	41	11	0	14	2	0	2	15	6	3	.393	.436	.647	1.083
2021	SnAnt	AA	42	162	48	14	0	2	(- | -)	68	26	23	-	15	0	36	3	1	2	13	2	3	.296	.363	.420	.782

Albert Abreu

Pitches: R Bats: R Pos: RP-28   Ht: 6'2" Wt: 190 Born: 9/26/1995 Age: 26

		HOW MUCH PITCHED					WHAT HE GAVE UP										THE RESULTS							
Year	Team	Lg	G	GS	GF	IP	BFP	H	R	ER	HR	SH	SF	HB	TBB	IBB	SO	WP	W	L	Pct	Sv-Op	Hld	Vel	OPS	ERC	ERA
2021	S-WB	AAA	10	0	4	16.2	72	10	7	7	0	0	1	1	11	0	31	2	1	0	1.000	2- -	-	-	.509	2.39	3.78
2020	NYY	AL	2	0	1	1.1	11	4	4	3	1	0	0	1	2	0	2	0	0	1	.000	0-0	0	96	1.511	36.34	20.25
2021	NYY	AL	28	0	14	36.2	156	27	21	21	8	0	3	3	19	1	35	3	2	0	1.000	1-1	3	98	.749	4.18	5.15
	2 ML YEARS		30	0	15	38.0	167	31	25	24	9	0	3	4	21	1	37	3	2	1	.667	1-1	3	98	.796	5.00	5.68

Bryan Abreu

Pitches: R Bats: R Pos: RP-31   Ht: 6'1" Wt: 225 Born: 4/22/1997 Age: 25

		HOW MUCH PITCHED					WHAT HE GAVE UP										THE RESULTS							
Year	Team	Lg	G	GS	GF	IP	BFP	H	R	ER	HR	SH	SF	HB	TBB	IBB	SO	WP	W	L	Pct	Sv-Op	Hld	Vel	OPS	ERC	ERA
2021	SgrLnd	AAA	14	0	5	14.1	63	11	3	3	0	0	0	0	11	0	23	0	0	0	-	0- -	-	-	.599	3.48	1.88
2019	Hou	AL	7	0	2	8.2	32	4	1	1	0	0	0	0	3	0	13	0	0	0	-	0-0	0	95	.391	1.05	1.04
2020	Hou	AL	4	0	1	3.1	20	1	2	1	0	0	0	2	7	0	3	0	0	0	-	0-0	0	93	.682	7.75	2.70
2021	Hou	AL	31	0	3	36.0	161	35	26	23	4	0	2	3	18	0	36	4	3	3	.500	1-5	7	96	.754	4.71	5.75
	Postseason		1	0	0	0.2	6	2	2	2	1	0	0	0	2	0	0	0	0	0	-	0-0	0	96	1.917	51.61	27.00
	3 ML YEARS		42	0	6	48.0	213	40	29	25	4	0	2	5	28	0	52	4	3	3	.500	1-5	7	95	.697	4.13	4.69

Jose Abreu

Bats: R Throws: R Pos: 1B-135;DH-18;3B-1   Ht: 6'3" Wt: 235 Born: 1/29/1987 Age: 35

						BATTING												RUNNING			AVERAGES			
Year	Team	Lg	G	AB	H	2B	3B	HR	(Hm | Rd)	TB	R	RBI	RC	TBB	IBB	SO	HBP	SH	SF	SB	CS	GDP	Avg	OBP	Slg	OPS
2014	CWS	AL	145	556	176	35	2	36	(15 | 21)	323	80	107	113	51	15	131	11	0	4	3	1	14	.317	.383	.581	.964
2015	CWS	AL	154	613	178	34	3	30	(16 | 14)	308	88	101	105	39	11	140	15	0	16	0	0	16	.290	.347	.502	.850
2016	CWS	AL	159	624	183	32	1	25	(15 | 10)	292	67	100	92	47	7	125	15	0	9	0	2	21	.293	.353	.468	.820
2017	CWS	AL	156	621	189	43	6	33	(16 | 17)	343	95	102	116	35	6	119	15	0	4	3	0	21	.304	.354	.552	.906
2018	CWS	AL	128	499	132	36	1	22	(11 | 11)	236	68	78	78	37	7	109	11	0	6	2	0	14	.265	.325	.473	.798
2019	CWS	AL	159	634	180	38	1	33	(15 | 18)	319	85	123	103	36	4	152	13	0	10	2	2	24	.284	.330	.503	.834
2020	CWS	AL	60	240	76	15	0	19	(8 | 11)	148	43	60	49	18	1	59	3	0	1	0	0	10	.317	.370	.617	.987
2021	CWS	AL	152	566	148	30	2	30	(18 | 12)	272	86	117	95	61	3	143	22	0	10	1	0	28	.261	.351	.481	.831
	Postseason		3	14	4	1	0	1	(0 | 1)	8	1	2	-	0	0	1	0	0	0	0	0	1	.286	.286	.571	.857
	8 ML YEARS		1113	4353	1262	263	16	228	(114 | 114)	2241	612	788	751	324	54	978	105	0	45	11	5	148	.290	.350	.515	.865

Domingo Acevedo

Pitches: R Bats: R Pos: RP-10   Ht: 6'7" Wt: 240 Born: 3/6/1994 Age: 28

		HOW MUCH PITCHED					WHAT HE GAVE UP										THE RESULTS							
Year	Team	Lg	G	GS	GF	IP	BFP	H	R	ER	HR	SH	SF	HB	TBB	IBB	SO	WP	W	L	Pct	Sv-Op	Hld	Vel	OPS	ERC	ERA
2021	LsVgs	AAA	30	0	21	32.2	126	22	12	9	3	0	1	1	6	0	53	5	2	0	1.000	9- -	-	-	.586	1.71	2.48
2021	Oak	AL	10	0	7	11.0	44	9	4	4	3	0	0	0	4	0	9	0	0	0	-	0-0	0	93	.770	4.18	3.27

Ronald Acuna Jr.

Bats: R Throws: R Pos: RF-80;CF-2;PH-2   Ht: 6'0" Wt: 205 Born: 12/18/1997 Age: 24

Year	Team	Lg	G	AB	H	2B	3B	HR	(Hm	Rd)	TB	R	RBI	RC	TBB	IBB	SO	HBP	SH	SF	SB	CS	GDP	Avg	OBP	Slg	OPS
2018	Atl	NL	111	433	127	26	4	26	(14	12)	239	78	64	83	45	2	123	6	0	3	16	5	4	.293	.366	.552	.917
2019	Atl	NL	156	626	175	22	2	41	(18	23)	324	127	101	122	76	4	188	9	0	1	37	9	8	.280	.365	.518	.883
2020	Atl	NL	46	160	40	11	0	14	(8	6)	93	46	29	37	38	2	60	4	0	0	8	1	3	.250	.406	.581	.987
2021	Atl	NL	82	297	84	19	1	24	(16	8)	177	72	52	63	49	2	85	9	0	5	17	6	0	.283	.394	.596	.990
	Postseason		21	80	21	8	1	3	(3	0)	40	12	9	13	12	0	27	2	0	0	3	2	1	.263	.372	.500	.872
	4 ML YEARS		395	1516	426	78	7	105	(56	49)	833	323	246	305	208	10	456	28	0	9	78	21	15	.281	.376	.549	.925

Jason Adam

Pitches: R Bats: R Pos: RP-12   Ht: 6'3" Wt: 229 Born: 8/4/1991 Age: 30

Year	Team	Lg	G	GS	GF	IP	BFP	H	R	ER	HR	SH	SF	HB	TBB	IBB	SO	WP	W	L	Pct	Sv-Op	Hld	Vel	OPS	ERC	ERA
2021	Iowa	AAA	5	0	3	6.1	24	4	0	0	0	0	0	0	1	0	6	1	1	0	1.000	1--	-	-	.469	1.12	0.00
2018	KC	AL	31	0	14	32.1	142	30	22	22	9	0	2	3	15	1	37	4	0	3	.000	0-2	2	94	.871	5.56	6.12
2019	Tor	AL	23	0	2	21.2	91	15	8	7	1	0	3	3	10	1	18	1	3	0	1.000	0-1	4	94	.601	2.75	2.91
2020	ChC	NL	13	0	5	13.2	58	9	7	5	2	0	0	0	8	0	21	0	2	1	.667	0-0	0	95	.673	3.19	3.29
2021	ChC	NL	12	0	4	10.2	50	10	7	7	1	0	0	3	6	0	19	0	1	0	1.000	0-0	2	94	.795	5.42	5.91
	4 ML YEARS		79	0	25	78.1	341	64	44	41	13	0	5	9	39	2	95	5	6	4	.600	0-3	8	94	.756	4.31	4.71

Willy Adames

Bats: R Throws: R Pos: SS-136;PH-3;DH-2   Ht: 6'0" Wt: 210 Born: 9/2/1995 Age: 26

Year	Team	Lg	G	AB	H	2B	3B	HR	(Hm	Rd)	TB	R	RBI	RC	TBB	IBB	SO	HBP	SH	SF	SB	CS	GDP	Avg	OBP	Slg	OPS
2018	TB	AL	85	288	80	7	0	10	(7	3)	117	43	34	34	31	3	95	1	1	2	6	5	6	.278	.348	.406	.754
2019	TB	AL	152	531	135	25	1	20	(5	15)	222	69	52	60	46	1	153	3	3	1	4	2	9	.254	.317	.418	.735
2020	TB	AL	54	185	48	15	1	8	(1	7)	89	29	23	31	20	0	74	0	0	0	2	1	4	.259	.332	.481	.813
2021	2 Tms		140	497	130	32	1	25	(13	12)	239	77	73	84	57	1	156	0	0	1	5	4	9	.262	.337	.481	.818
21	TB	AL	41	132	26	6	1	5	(3	2)	49	16	15	11	10	0	51	0	0	0	1	2	1	.197	.254	.371	.625
21	Mil	NL	99	365	104	26	0	20	(10	10)	190	61	58	73	47	1	105	0	0	1	4	2	8	.285	.366	.521	.886
	Postseason		26	76	13	5	0	2	(2	0)	24	6	6	7	16	0	30	1	0	0	1	2	1	.171	.323	.316	.638
	4 ML YEARS		431	1501	393	79	3	63	(26	37)	667	218	182	209	154	5	478	4	4	4	17	12	28	.262	.331	.444	.776

Austin L Adams

Pitches: R Bats: R Pos: RP-65   Ht: 6'3" Wt: 220 Born: 5/5/1991 Age: 31

Year	Team	Lg	G	GS	GF	IP	BFP	H	R	ER	HR	SH	SF	HB	TBB	IBB	SO	WP	W	L	Pct	Sv-Op	Hld	Vel	OPS	ERC	ERA
2017	Was	NL	6	0	3	5.0	29	4	4	2	0	0	1	1	8	0	10	1	0	0	-	0-0	0	95	.711	7.11	3.60
2018	Was	NL	2	0	0	1.0	7	1	0	0	0	0	0	0	3	0	0	0	0	0	-	0-0	0	95	.821	13.82	0.00
2019	2 Tms		30	2	3	32.0	130	20	14	14	4	0	1	1	16	0	53	4	2	2	.500	0-2	10	95	.615	2.77	3.94
2020	SD	NL	3	0	1	4.0	17	3	2	2	1	0	0	0	2	0	7	1	0	0	-	0-0	1	93	.694	4.02	4.50
2021	SD	NL	65	0	18	52.2	241	28	28	24	1	3	3	24	35	2	76	4	3	2	.600	0-1	10	94	.610	3.49	4.10
19	Was	NL	1	0	0	1.0	6	0	1	1	0	0	0	1	2	0	2	2	0	0	-	0-0	0	94	.500	7.00	9.00
19	Sea	AL	29	2	3	31.0	124	20	13	13	4	0	1	0	14	0	51	2	2	2	.500	0-2	10	95	.614	2.62	3.77
	Postseason		4	0	0	1.2	9	0	1	1	0	0	0	2	2	0	1	0	1	0	1.000	0-0	0	92	.444	4.82	5.40
	5 ML YEARS		106	2	25	94.2	424	56	48	42	6	3	5	26	64	2	146	10	5	4	.556	0-3	21	95	.629	3.58	3.99

Chance Adams

Pitches: R Bats: R Pos: P   Ht: 6'1" Wt: 215 Born: 8/10/1994 Age: 27

Year	Team	Lg	G	GS	GF	IP	BFP	H	R	ER	HR	SH	SF	HB	TBB	IBB	SO	WP	W	L	Pct	Sv-Op	Hld	Vel	OPS	ERC	ERA
2018	NYY	AL	3	1	1	7.2	34	8	7	6	3	0	0	0	4	0	4	0	0	1	.000	0-0	0	93	.953	7.11	7.04
2019	NYY	AL	13	0	5	25.1	124	39	25	24	7	0	0	2	11	0	23	1	1	1	.500	1-1	0	92	1.068	9.56	8.53
2020	KC	AL	6	0	1	8.2	40	15	9	9	1	0	0	0	0	0	6	2	0	0	-	0-0	0	92	.950	6.92	9.35
	3 ML YEARS		22	1	7	41.2	198	62	41	39	11	0	0	2	15	0	33	3	1	2	.333	1-1	0	92	1.023	8.54	8.42

Matt Adams

Bats: L Throws: R Pos: PH-15;1B-7   Ht: 6'3" Wt: 245 Born: 8/31/1988 Age: 33

Year	Team	Lg	G	AB	H	2B	3B	HR	(Hm	Rd)	TB	R	RBI	RC	TBB	IBB	SO	HBP	SH	SF	SB	CS	GDP	Avg	OBP	Slg	OPS
2012	StL	NL	27	86	21	6	0	2	(1	1)	33	8	13	9	5	0	24	0	0	0	0	0	3	.244	.286	.384	.669
2013	StL	NL	108	296	84	14	0	17	(10	7)	149	46	51	49	23	0	80	0	0	0	0	1	9	.284	.335	.503	.839
2014	StL	NL	142	527	152	34	5	15	(8	7)	241	55	68	65	26	5	114	3	0	7	3	2	5	.288	.321	.457	.779
2015	StL	NL	60	175	42	9	0	5	(1	4)	66	14	24	16	10	1	41	0	0	1	1	0	1	.240	.280	.377	.657
2016	StL	NL	118	297	74	18	0	16	(11	5)	140	37	54	46	25	1	81	2	0	3	0	1	5	.249	.309	.471	.780
2017	2 Tms	NL	131	339	93	22	1	20	(12	8)	177	46	65	55	23	5	88	1	0	4	0	0	5	.274	.319	.522	.841
2018	2 Tms	NL	121	306	73	10	0	21	(12	9)	146	42	57	47	27	3	73	4	0	0	0	0	6	.239	.309	.477	.786
2019	Was	NL	111	310	70	14	0	20	(13	7)	144	42	56	42	20	1	115	2	0	1	0	0	7	.226	.276	.465	.741
2020	Atl	NL	16	49	9	2	0	2	(1	1)	17	4	9	5	2	0	18	0	0	0	0	0	0	.184	.216	.347	.563
2021	Col	NL	22	36	6	1	0	0	(0	0)	7	3	2	1	4	1	9	0	0	0	0	0	0	.167	.250	.194	.444
17	StL	NL	31	48	14	2	0	1	(1	0)	19	4	7	6	4	0	17	0	0	1	0	0	0	.292	.340	.396	.735
17	Atl	NL	100	291	79	20	1	19	(12	7)	158	42	58	49	19	5	71	1	0	3	0	0	5	.271	.315	.543	.858

Year Team	Lg	G	AB	H	2B	3B	HR	(Hm Rd)	TB	R	RBI	RC	TBB	IBB	SO	HBP	SH	SF	SB	CS	GDP	Avg	OBP	Slg	OPS
18 Was	NL	94	249	64	9	0	18	(11 7)	127	37	48	42	24	2	55	1	0	0	4	0	6	.257	.332	.510	.842
18 StL	NL	27	57	9	1	0	3	(1 7)	19	5	9	5	3	1	18	0	0	0	0	0	0	.158	.200	.333	.533
Postseason		30	96	22	3	0	4	(3 1)	37	11	11	13	9	2	25	1	0	0	0	0	2	.229	.302	.385	.687
10 ML YEARS		856	2421	624	130	6	118	(69 49)	1120	297	399	335	165	17	643	12	0	16	4	4	49	.258	.306	.463	.769

Riley Adams

Bats: R Throws: R Pos: C-34;PH-15;PR-2   Ht: 6'4" Wt: 246 Born: 6/26/1996 Age: 26

Year Team	Lg	G	AB	H	2B	3B	HR	(Hm Rd)	TB	R	RBI	RC	TBB	IBB	SO	HBP	SH	SF	SB	CS	GDP	Avg	OBP	Slg	OPS
2021 Buffalo	AAA	35	117	28	6	1	7	(- -)	57	20	17	-	16	0	46	9	0	1	0	0	5	.239	.371	.487	.858
2021 2 Tms		47	99	22	8	1	2	(1 1)	38	13	10	14	15	0	40	6	0	0	0	0	2	.222	.358	.384	.742
21 Tor	AL	12	28	3	2	0	0	(0 0)	5	2	0	0	2	0	12	0	0	0	0	0	1	.107	.167	.179	.345
21 Was	NL	35	71	19	6	1	2	(1 1)	33	11	10	14	13	0	28	6	0	0	0	0	1	.268	.422	.465	.887

Jo Adell

Bats: R Throws: R Pos: LF-25;RF-19   Ht: 6'3" Wt: 215 Born: 4/8/1999 Age: 23

Year Team	Lg	G	AB	H	2B	3B	HR	(Hm Rd)	TB	R	RBI	RC	TBB	IBB	SO	HBP	SH	SF	SB	CS	GDP	Avg	OBP	Slg	OPS
2021 Salt Lk	AAA	73	311	90	17	4	23	(- -)	184	57	69	-	22	0	99	4	0	2	8	2	5	.289	.342	.592	.934
2020 LAA	AL	38	124	20	4	0	3	(3 0)	33	9	7	1	7	0	55	1	0	0	0	1	3	.161	.212	.266	.478
2021 LAA	AL	35	130	32	5	2	4	(2 2)	53	17	26	21	8	0	32	1	1	0	2	1	3	.246	.295	.408	.703
2 ML YEARS		73	254	52	9	2	7	(5 2)	86	26	33	22	15	0	87	2	1	0	2	2	6	.205	.255	.339	.593

Joan Adon

Pitches: R Bats: R Pos: SP-1   Ht: 6'2" Wt: 242 Born: 8/12/1998 Age: 23

		HOW MUCH PITCHED				WHAT HE GAVE UP											THE RESULTS							
Year Team	Lg	G	GS	GF	IP	BFP	H	R	ER	HR	SH	SF	HB	TBB	IBB	SO	WP	W	L	Pct	Sv-Op	Hld	Vel	OPS	ERC	ERA
2021 Wilmg	A+	17	0	0	87.0	373	77	51	48	7	0	0	0	32	0	91	0	6	4	.600	0--	-	-	-	3.10	4.97
2021 Was	NL	1	1	0	5.1	24	6	2	2	1	0	0	1	3	0	9	1	0	0	-	0-0	0	95	.867	7.44	3.38

Ehire Adrianza

eh-EE-ray ah-dree-AHN-zah

Bats: B Throws: R Pos: PH-72;3B-16;RF-14;2B-7;LF-6;SS-5;CF-1;DH-1;PR-1   Ht: 6'1" Wt: 195 Born: 8/21/1989 Age: 32

Year Team	Lg	G	AB	H	2B	3B	HR	(Hm Rd)	TB	R	RBI	RC	TBB	IBB	SO	HBP	SH	SF	SB	CS	GDP	Avg	OBP	Slg	OPS
2013 SF	NL	9	18	4	1	0	1	(0 1)	8	3	3	1	1	0	5	0	1	0	0	0	1	.222	.263	.444	.708
2014 SF	NL	53	97	23	6	0	0	(0 0)	29	10	5	6	5	1	22	1	2	1	1	1	2	.237	.279	.299	.578
2015 SF	NL	52	113	21	7	1	0	(0 0)	30	11	11	12	15	0	20	4	2	0	3	2	2	.186	.303	.265	.569
2016 SF	NL	40	63	16	2	0	2	(1 1)	24	3	7	6	2	0	13	2	4	0	0	1	0	.254	.299	.381	.679
2017 Min	AL	70	162	43	9	2	2	(0 2)	62	30	24	24	16	1	25	1	1	6	8	1	0	.265	.324	.383	.707
2018 Min	AL	114	335	84	23	1	6	(2 4)	127	42	39	38	24	2	82	1	4	2	5	1	4	.251	.301	.379	.680
2019 Min	AL	84	202	55	8	3	5	(3 2)	84	34	22	31	20	1	40	6	2	4	0	2	2	.272	.349	.416	.765
2020 Min	AL	44	89	17	7	0	0	(0 0)	24	10	3	4	11	0	23	1	0	0	1	0	3	.191	.287	.270	.557
2021 Atl	NL	109	182	45	9	2	5	(4 1)	73	32	28	28	21	0	42	2	1	3	0	0	4	.247	.327	.401	.728
Postseason		1	1	0	0	0	0	(0 0)	0	0	0	0	0	0	1	0	0	0	0	0	0	.000	.000	.000	.000
9 ML YEARS		575	1261	308	72	9	21	(10 11)	461	175	142	150	115	5	272	18	17	16	18	8	18	.244	.313	.366	.678

Jesus Aguilar

Bats: R Throws: R Pos: 1B-113;PH-15;DH-4;3B-2   AGG-you-lahr   Ht: 6'3" Wt: 277 Born: 6/30/1990 Age: 32

Year Team	Lg	G	AB	H	2B	3B	HR	(Hm Rd)	TB	R	RBI	RC	TBB	IBB	SO	HBP	SH	SF	SB	CS	GDP	Avg	OBP	Slg	OPS
2014 Cle	AL	19	33	4	0	0	0	(0 0)	4	2	3	0	4	0	13	0	0	1	0	0	1	.121	.211	.121	.332
2015 Cle	AL	7	19	6	1	0	0	(0 0)	7	0	2	4	0	0	7	1	0	0	0	0	0	.316	.350	.368	.718
2016 Cle	AL	9	6	0	0	0	0	(0 0)	0	0	0	0	0	0	1	0	0	0	0	0	0	.000	.000	.000	.000
2017 Mil	NL	133	279	74	15	2	16	(4 12)	141	40	52	47	25	1	94	4	0	3	0	0	8	.265	.331	.505	.837
2018 Mil	NL	149	492	135	25	0	35	(18 17)	265	80	108	82	58	3	143	6	0	10	0	0	19	.274	.352	.539	.890
2019 2 Tms		131	314	74	12	0	12	(5 7)	122	39	50	43	43	0	81	2	0	7	0	0	12	.236	.325	.389	.714
2020 Mia	NL	51	188	52	10	0	8	(1 7)	86	31	34	31	23	0	40	1	0	4	0	1	5	.277	.352	.457	.809
2021 Mia	NL	131	449	117	23	0	22	(5 17)	206	49	93	78	46	4	93	3	0	7	0	0	11	.261	.329	.459	.788
19 Mil	NL	94	222	50	9	0	8	(3 5)	83	26	34	28	31	0	59	2	0	4	0	0	11	.225	.320	.374	.694
19 TB	AL	37	92	24	3	0	4	(2 2)	39	13	16	15	12	0	22	0	0	3	0	0	1	.261	.336	.424	.760
Postseason		15	58	12	4	0	3	(1 2)	25	6	7	4	3	1	22	1	0	0	0	0	2	.207	.258	.431	.689
8 ML YEARS		630	1780	462	86	2	93	(33 60)	831	241	342	285	199	8	472	17	0	32	0	1	56	.260	.334	.467	.801

Miguel Aguilar

Pitches: L Bats: L Pos: RP-9   Ht: 5'8" Wt: 194 Born: 9/26/1991 Age: 30

		HOW MUCH PITCHED				WHAT HE GAVE UP											THE RESULTS							
Year Team	Lg	G	GS	GF	IP	BFP	H	R	ER	HR	SH	SF	HB	TBB	IBB	SO	WP	W	L	Pct	Sv-Op	Hld	Vel	OPS	ERC	ERA
2021 Reno	AAA	43	0	28	40.2	183	48	28	23	7	1	1	0	16	0	45	0	4	4	.500	16--	-	-	.836	5.61	5.09
2021 Ari	NL	9	0	2	7.0	29	6	6	5	0	1	0	0	4	1	3	0	1	1	.500	0-0	2	91	.690	3.16	6.43

Nick Ahmed

Bats: R Throws: R Pos: SS-127;PH-6   Ht: 6'2" Wt: 201 Born: 3/15/1990 Age: 32

Year	Team	Lg	G	AB	H	2B	3B	HR	(Hm	Rd)	TB	R	RBI	RC	TBB	IBB	SO	HBP	SH	SF	SB	CS	GDP	Avg	OBP	Slg	OPS
2014	Ari	NL	25	70	14	2	0	1	(1	0)	19	9	4	3	3	0	10	0	2	0	0	1	2	.200	.233	.271	.504
2015	Ari	NL	134	421	95	17	6	9	(4	5)	151	49	34	38	29	1	81	1	5	3	4	5	4	.226	.275	.359	.634
2016	Ari	NL	90	284	62	9	1	4	(1	3)	85	26	20	18	15	3	58	4	2	3	5	2	9	.218	.265	.299	.564
2017	Ari	NL	53	167	42	8	1	6	(3	3)	70	24	21	18	10	3	39	1	0	0	3	4	6	.251	.298	.419	.717
2018	Ari	NL	153	516	121	33	5	16	(7	9)	212	61	70	62	40	2	109	2	1	5	5	4	15	.234	.290	.411	.700
2019	Ari	NL	158	556	141	33	6	19	(8	11)	243	79	82	73	52	2	113	4	1	12	8	2	15	.254	.316	.437	.753
2020	Ari	NL	57	199	53	10	1	5	(2	3)	80	29	29	32	18	0	46	0	0	0	4	0	3	.266	.327	.402	.729
2021	Ari	NL	129	434	96	30	3	5	(4	1)	147	46	38	41	34	3	104	2	2	1	7	2	9	.221	.280	.339	.619
	8 ML YEARS		799	2647	624	142	23	65	(30	35)	1007	323	298	285	201	14	560	14	13	24	36	20	63	.236	.291	.380	.671

Keegan Akin

Pitches: L Bats: L Pos: SP-17; RP-7   Ht: 5'11" Wt: 235 Born: 4/1/1995 Age: 27

			HOW MUCH PITCHED						WHAT HE GAVE UP											THE RESULTS							
Year	Team	Lg	G	GS	GF	IP	BFP	H	R	ER	HR	SH	SF	HB	TBB	IBB	SO	WP	W	L	Pct	Sv-Op	Hld	Vel	OPS	ERC	ERA
2020	Bal	AL	8	6	0	25.2	116	27	17	13	3	0	2	1	10	0	35	0	1	2	.333	0-0	0	92	.755	4.45	4.56
2021	Bal	AL	24	17	1	95.0	427	110	70	70	17	1	5	2	40	1	82	5	2	10	.167	0-0	0	92	.848	5.76	6.63
	2 ML YEARS		32	23	1	120.2	543	137	87	83	20	1	7	3	50	1	117	5	3	12	.200	0-0	0	92	.828	5.47	6.19

Shogo Akiyama

Bats: L Throws: R Pos: CF-48;PH-37;LF-9;RF-4;PR-4   ah-kee-ah-ma   Ht: 6'0" Wt: 190 Born: 4/16/1988 Age: 34

Year	Team	Lg	G	AB	H	2B	3B	HR	(Hm	Rd)	TB	R	RBI	RC	TBB	IBB	SO	HBP	SH	SF	SB	CS	GDP	Avg	OBP	Slg	OPS
2020	Cin	NL	54	155	38	6	1	0	(0	0)	46	16	9	21	25	0	34	2	0	0	7	3	1	.245	.357	.297	.654
2021	Cin	NL	88	162	33	8	0	0	(0	0)	41	16	12	12	14	1	40	4	1	1	2	3	1	.204	.282	.253	.535
	Postseason		2	5	0	0	0	0	(0	0)	0	0	0	0	0	0	2	0	0	0	0	0	0	.000	.000	.000	.000
	2 ML YEARS		142	317	71	14	1	0	(0	0)	87	32	21	33	39	1	74	6	1	1	9	6	2	.224	.320	.274	.594

R.J. Alaniz

Pitches: R Bats: R Pos: RP-3   Ht: 6'4" Wt: 220 Born: 6/14/1991 Age: 31

			HOW MUCH PITCHED						WHAT HE GAVE UP											THE RESULTS							
Year	Team	Lg	G	GS	GF	IP	BFP	H	R	ER	HR	SH	SF	HB	TBB	IBB	SO	WP	W	L	Pct	Sv-Op	Hld	Vel	OPS	ERC	ERA
2021	Lsvlle	AAA	33	0	5	39.0	167	42	20	15	1	1	1	1	17	2	45	0	1	3	.250	1- -	-		.715	4.27	3.46
2019	2 Tms		12	0	4	15.2	71	19	17	16	3	0	1	0	7	0	13	0	1	0	1.000	0-0	0	94	.890	6.27	9.19
2021	Cin	NL	3	0	0	2.2	13	1	1	1	1	0	0	1	3	0	3	0	0	0	-	0-0	0	93	.829	6.97	3.38
19	Sea	AL	4	0	1	4.0	25	11	10	9	3	0	0	0	3	0	6	0	0	0	-	0-0	0	94	1.605	26.27	20.25
19	Cin	NL	8	0	3	11.2	46	8	7	7	0	0	1	0	4	0	7	0	1	0	1.000	0-0	0	93	.505	1.69	5.40
	2 ML YEARS		15	0	4	18.1	84	20	18	17	4	0	1	1	10	0	16	0	1	0	1.000	0-0	0	93	.883	6.37	8.35

Andrew Albers

Pitches: L Bats: R Pos: SP-3; RP-2   Ht: 6'1" Wt: 200 Born: 10/6/1985 Age: 36

			HOW MUCH PITCHED						WHAT HE GAVE UP											THE RESULTS							
Year	Team	Lg	G	GS	GF	IP	BFP	H	R	ER	HR	SH	SF	HB	TBB	IBB	SO	WP	W	L	Pct	Sv-Op	Hld	Vel	OPS	ERC	ERA
2021	StPaul	AAA	17	16	0	96.0	415	113	50	40	13	1	2	4	11	0	85	4	7	4	.636	0- -	-	-	.765	4.25	3.75
2013	Min	AL	10	10	0	60.0	249	64	34	27	6	2	2	2	7	0	25	0	2	5	.286	0-0	0	86	.698	3.45	4.05
2015	Tor	AL	1	1	0	2.2	11	1	1	1	1	0	0	0	2	0	1	0	0	0	-	0-0	0	86	.717	3.75	3.38
2016	Min	AL	6	2	3	17.0	85	27	16	11	5	0	0	0	6	0	16	1	0	0	-	0-0	0	87	1.034	8.84	5.82
2017	Sea	AL	9	6	2	41.0	178	43	22	16	6	0	1	2	10	0	37	1	5	1	.833	1-1	0	88	.725	4.15	3.51
2021	Min	AL	5	3	2	19.0	89	24	16	16	9	0	0	1	9	1	12	0	1	2	.333	0-0	0	88	1.091	9.18	7.58
	5 ML YEARS		31	21	7	139.2	612	159	89	71	27	2	3	5	34	1	91	2	8	8	.500	1-1	0	87	.808	4.96	4.58

Hanser Alberto

Bats: R Throws: R Pos: 3B-49;2B-31;PH-24;SS-17;DH-9;PR-3   HAHN-zer al-BAIR-tow   Ht: 5'11" Wt: 215 Born: 10/17/1992 Age: 29

Year	Team	Lg	G	AB	H	2B	3B	HR	(Hm	Rd)	TB	R	RBI	RC	TBB	IBB	SO	HBP	SH	SF	SB	CS	GDP	Avg	OBP	Slg	OPS
2015	Tex	AL	41	99	22	2	1	0	(0	0)	26	12	4	3	2	0	17	0	3	0	1	0	2	.222	.238	.263	.500
2016	Tex	AL	35	56	8	1	0	0	(0	0)	9	2	5	1	0	0	17	0	2	0	1	0	1	.143	.143	.161	.304
2018	Tex	AL	13	27	5	2	0	0	(0	0)	7	0	0	0	2	0	4	0	1	0	0	1	0	.185	.241	.259	.501
2019	Bal	AL	139	524	160	21	2	12	(9	3)	221	62	51	64	16	1	50	4	3	3	4	4	9	.305	.329	.422	.751
2020	Bal	AL	54	219	62	15	0	3	(3	0)	86	35	22	23	5	0	30	3	2	2	3	0	6	.283	.306	.393	.698
2021	KC	AL	103	241	65	20	3	2	(1	1)	97	25	24	28	4	0	26	4	4	2	3	1	1	.270	.291	.402	.693
	Postseason		3	10	2	1	0	0	(0	0)	3	0	2	1	0	0	2	0	0	1	0	0	0	.200	.182	.300	.482
	6 ML YEARS		385	1166	322	61	6	17	(13	4)	446	136	106	119	29	1	144	11	15	7	12	6	19	.276	.298	.383	.681

Ozzie Albies

Bats: B Throws: R Pos: 2B-156   Ht: 5'8" Wt: 165 Born: 1/7/1997 Age: 25

Year	Team	Lg	G	AB	H	2B	3B	HR	(Hm	Rd)	TB	R	RBI	RC	TBB	IBB	SO	HBP	SH	SF	SB	CS	GDP	Avg	OBP	Slg	OPS
2017	Atl	NL	57	217	62	9	5	6	(1	5)	99	34	28	36	21	0	36	3	1	2	8	1	3	.286	.354	.456	.810
2018	Atl	NL	158	639	167	40	5	24	(9	15)	289	105	72	82	36	0	116	5	1	3	14	3	9	.261	.305	.452	.757
2019	Atl	NL	160	**640**	**189**	43	8	24	(12	12)	320	102	86	113	54	6	112	4	0	4	15	4	2	.295	.352	.500	.852

Year	Team	Lg	G	AB	H	2B	3B	HR	(Hm	Rd)	TB	R	RBI	RC	TBB	IBB	SO	HBP	SH	SF	SB	CS	GDP	Avg	OBP	Slg	OPS
2020	Atl	NL	29	118	32	5	0	6	(2	4)	55	21	19	20	5	0	30	1	0	0	3	1	0	.271	.306	.466	.773
2021	Atl	NL	156	629	163	40	7	30	(17	13)	307	103	106	107	47	2	128	3	0	7	20	4	0	.259	.310	.488	.799
	Postseason		21	82	21	2	0	3	(0	3)	32	12	7	8	6	0	13	0	0	2	2	0	0	.256	.300	.390	.690
	5 ML YEARS		560	2243	613	137	25	90	(41	49)	1070	365	311	358	163	8	422	16	2	16	60	13	18	.273	.325	.477	.802

Jorge Alcala

Pitches: R **Bats:** R **Pos:** RP-59   **Ht:** 6'3" **Wt:** 205 **Born:** 7/28/1995 **Age:** 26

| | | | HOW MUCH PITCHED | | | | | WHAT HE GAVE UP | | | | | | | | | | | THE RESULTS | | | | | | | | |
Year	Team	Lg	G	GS	GF	IP	BFP	H	R	ER	HR	SH	SF	HB	TBB	IBB	SO	WP	W	L	Pct	Sv-Op	Hld	Vel	OPS	ERC	ERA
2019	Min	AL	2	0	2	1.2	7	1	0	0	0	0	0	0	1	0	1	0	0	0		0-0	0	94	.452	2.03	0.00
2020	Min	AL	16	0	8	24.0	94	21	8	7	3	0	0	0	8	0	27	1	2	1	.667	0-1	0	97	.681	3.52	2.63
2021	Min	AL	59	0	15	59.2	229	45	29	26	10	1	3	2	13	1	61	1	3	6	.333	1-5	11	97	.644	2.70	3.92
	3 ML YEARS		77	0	25	85.1	330	67	37	33	13	1	3	2	22	1	89	2	5	7	.417	1-6	11	97	.651	2.91	3.48

Sandy Alcantara

Pitches: R **Bats:** R **Pos:** SP-33   **Ht:** 6'5" **Wt:** 200 **Born:** 9/7/1995 **Age:** 26

| | | | HOW MUCH PITCHED | | | | | WHAT HE GAVE UP | | | | | | | | | | | THE RESULTS | | | | | | | | |
Year	Team	Lg	G	GS	GF	IP	BFP	H	R	ER	HR	SH	SF	HB	TBB	IBB	SO	WP	W	L	Pct	Sv-Op	Hld	Vel	OPS	ERC	ERA
2017	StL	NL	8	0	3	8.1	39	9	6	4	2	0	0	0	6	0	10	0	0	0	-	0-0	0	98	.869	7.04	4.32
2018	Mia	NL	6	6	0	34.0	146	25	13	13	4	3	2	2	23	0	30	0	2	3	.400	0-0	0	95	.706	3.90	3.44
2019	Mia	NL	32	32	0	197.1	838	179	94	85	23	5	1	8	81	5	151	4	6	14	.300	0-0	0	96	.719	3.86	3.88
2020	Mia	NL	7	7	0	42.0	172	35	22	14	4	1	0	1	15	0	39	1	3	2	.600	0-0	0	97	.653	3.11	3.00
2021	Mia	NL	33	33	0	205.2	837	171	85	73	21	6	3	10	50	2	201	6	9	15	.375	0-0	0	98	.643	2.76	3.19
	Postseason		2	2	0	12.2	55	11	6	6	2	0	0	2	4	0	12	0	1	1	.500	0-0	0	97	.697	3.95	4.26
	5 ML YEARS		86	78	3	487.1	2032	419	220	189	53	14	6	21	175	7	431	11	20	34	.370	0-0	0	97	.684	3.37	3.49

Sergio Alcantara

Bats: B **Throws:** R **Pos:** SS-55;2B-22;PH-12;3B-3;PR-3   **Ht:** 5'9" **Wt:** 151 **Born:** 7/10/1996 **Age:** 25

| | | | BATTING | | | | | | | | | | | | | | | | RUNNING | | | AVERAGES | | | |
Year	Team	Lg	G	AB	H	2B	3B	HR	(Hm	Rd)	TB	R	RBI	RC	TBB	IBB	SO	HBP	SH	SF	SB	CS	GDP	Avg	OBP	Slg	OPS
2021	Iowa	AAA	25	82	25	3	0	3	(-	-)	37	19	9	-	21	1	23	0	0	0	3	0	0	.305	.447	.451	.898
2020	Det	AL	10	21	3	0	1	1	(0	1)	8	2	1	1	2	0	4	0	0	0	0	0	0	.143	.217	.381	.598
2021	ChC	NL	89	220	45	6	3	5	(2	3)	72	30	17	21	30	2	74	2	1	2	3	0	3	.205	.303	.327	.630
	2 ML YEARS		99	241	48	6	4	6	(2	4)	80	32	18	22	32	2	78	2	1	2	3	0	3	.199	.296	.332	.628

Scott Alexander

Pitches: L **Bats:** L **Pos:** RP-18   **Ht:** 6'2" **Wt:** 195 **Born:** 7/10/1989 **Age:** 32

| | | | HOW MUCH PITCHED | | | | | WHAT HE GAVE UP | | | | | | | | | | | THE RESULTS | | | | | | | | |
Year	Team	Lg	G	GS	GF	IP	BFP	H	R	ER	HR	SH	SF	HB	TBB	IBB	SO	WP	W	L	Pct	Sv-Op	Hld	Vel	OPS	ERC	ERA
2021	OkCity	AAA	5	0	0	4.2	17	3	1	1	0	0	1	0	0	0	5	1	0	0	-	0--	-	-	.364	0.86	1.93
2015	KC	AL	4	0	3	6.0	25	5	3	3	0	0	0	1	3	0	3	1	0	0	-	0-0	0	93	.598	3.67	4.50
2016	KC	AL	17	0	4	19.0	84	24	7	7	1	0	1	0	7	0	16	0	0	0	-	0-1	0	91	.790	5.24	3.32
2017	KC	AL	58	0	9	69.0	283	62	23	19	3	1	2	0	28	0	59	3	5	4	.556	4-6	9	93	.645	3.27	2.48
2018	LAD	NL	73	1	8	66.0	268	57	28	27	4	1	0	2	27	2	56	2	2	1	.667	3-6	21	93	.667	3.32	3.68
2019	LAD	NL	28	0	4	17.1	76	17	7	7	2	0	1	0	7	2	9	0	3	2	.600	0-0	6	93	.741	4.09	3.63
2020	LAD	NL	13	0	1	12.1	52	9	6	4	2	1	0	0	9	1	9	0	2	0	1.000	0-2	3	93	.710	4.35	2.92
2021	LAD	NL	18	0	6	15.1	67	15	6	5	2	0	0	1	4	1	8	1	0	2	.000	0-1	2	92	.669	3.62	2.93
	Postseason		4	0	1	2.1	10	1	2	2	0	0	0	0	2	0	2	1	0	0	-	0-0	0	92	.425	2.03	7.71
	7 ML YEARS		211	1	35	205.0	855	189	80	72	14	3	3	5	85	6	160	7	12	9	.571	7-16	41	93	.679	3.63	3.16

Tyler Alexander

Pitches: L **Bats:** R **Pos:** RP-26; SP-15   **Ht:** 6'2" **Wt:** 203 **Born:** 7/14/1994 **Age:** 27

| | | | HOW MUCH PITCHED | | | | | WHAT HE GAVE UP | | | | | | | | | | | THE RESULTS | | | | | | | | |
Year	Team	Lg	G	GS	GF	IP	BFP	H	R	ER	HR	SH	SF	HB	TBB	IBB	SO	WP	W	L	Pct	Sv-Op	Hld	Vel	OPS	ERC	ERA
2019	Det	AL	13	8	1	53.2	235	68	30	29	9	0	1	2	7	0	47	1	1	4	.200	0-0	0	91	.834	5.10	4.86
2020	Det	AL	14	2	0	36.1	152	39	16	16	8	0	1	4	9	0	34	0	2	3	.400	0-0	0	91	.849	5.40	3.96
2021	Det	AL	41	15	7	106.1	451	106	47	45	16	0	4	4	28	0	87	2	2	4	.333	0-0	3	90	.735	3.98	3.81
	3 ML YEARS		68	25	8	196.1	838	213	93	90	33	0	6	10	44	0	168	3	5	11	.313	0-0	3	91	.784	4.53	4.13

A.J. Alexy

Pitches: R **Bats:** R **Pos:** SP-4; RP-1   **Ht:** 6'4" **Wt:** 195 **Born:** 4/21/1998 **Age:** 24

| | | | HOW MUCH PITCHED | | | | | WHAT HE GAVE UP | | | | | | | | | | | THE RESULTS | | | | | | | | |
Year	Team	Lg	G	GS	GF	IP	BFP	H	R	ER	HR	SH	SF	HB	TBB	IBB	SO	WP	W	L	Pct	Sv-Op	Hld	Vel	OPS	ERC	ERA
2021	Frisco	AA	13	7	0	50.1	198	30	9	9	4	0	1	4	21	0	57	1	3	1	.750	0--	-	-	.557	2.29	1.61
2021	Tex	AL	5	4	0	23.0	97	13	12	12	4	0	1	1	17	0	17	0	3	1	.750	0-0	0	93	.666	3.74	4.70

Jorge Alfaro

Bats: R **Throws:** R **Pos:** C-61;LF-21;PH-13;1B-3;PR-1   **Ht:** 6'3" **Wt:** 230 **Born:** 6/11/1993 **Age:** 29

							BATTING													RUNNING			AVERAGES			
Year	Team	Lg	G	AB	H	2B	3B	HR	(Hm | Rd)	TB	R	RBI	RC	TBB	IBB	SO	HBP	SH	SF	SB	CS	GDP	Avg	OBP	Slg	OPS
2016	Phi	NL	6	16	2	0	0	0	(0 | 0)	2	0	0	0	1	1	8	0	0	0	0	0	0	.125	.176	.125	.301
2017	Phi	NL	29	107	34	6	0	5	(3 | 2)	55	12	14	20	3	1	33	4	0	0	0	0	2	.318	.360	.514	.874
2018	Phi	NL	108	344	90	16	2	10	(8 | 2)	140	35	37	44	18	6	138	14	0	1	3	0	2	.262	.324	.407	.731
2019	Mia	NL	130	431	113	14	1	18	(7 | 11)	183	44	57	53	22	1	154	10	0	2	4	4	12	.262	.312	.425	.736
2020	Mia	NL	31	93	21	2	0	3	(2 | 1)	32	12	16	14	4	1	36	3	0	0	2	0	2	.226	.280	.344	.624
2021	Mia	NL	92	295	72	15	1	4	(2 | 2)	101	22	30	31	11	0	99	5	0	0	8	1	8	.244	.283	.342	.625
	Postseason		2	3	0	0	0	0	(0 | 0)	0	0	0	0	0	0	1	0	0	0	0	0	0	.000	.000	.000	.000
	6 ML YEARS		396	1286	332	53	4	40	(22 | 18)	513	125	154	162	59	10	468	36	0	3	17	5	26	.258	.309	.399	.707

Anthony Alford

Bats: R **Throws:** R **Pos:** LF-32;PH-12;CF-6;RF-1   **Ht:** 6'1" **Wt:** 215 **Born:** 7/20/1994 **Age:** 27

							BATTING													RUNNING			AVERAGES			
Year	Team	Lg	G	AB	H	2B	3B	HR	(Hm	Rd)	TB	R	RBI	RC	TBB	IBB	SO	HBP	SH	SF	SB	CS	GDP	Avg	OBP	Slg	OPS
2021	Indy	AAA	56	189	58	12	0	14	(-	-)	112	37	41	-	33	2	78	4	0	0	9	4	1	.307	.420	.593	1.013
2017	Tor	AL	4	8	1	1	0	0	(0	0)	2	0	0	0	0	0	3	0	0	0	0	0	0	.125	.125	.250	.375
2018	Tor	AL	13	19	2	0	0	0	(0	0)	2	3	1	1	2	0	9	0	0	0	1	0	0	.105	.190	.105	.296
2019	Tor	AL	16	28	5	0	0	1	(1	0)	8	3	1	2	1	0	11	1	0	0	2	0	0	.179	.233	.286	.519
2020	2 Tms		18	28	6	0	1	2	(2	0)	14	5	7	3	1	0	8	0	0	0	3	0	0	.214	.241	.500	.741
2021	Pit	NL	49	133	31	6	1	5	(2	3)	54	14	11	10	12	1	58	3	0	0	5	6	4	.233	.311	.406	.717
20	Tor	AL	13	16	3	0	0	1	(1	0)	6	3	3	2	0	0	7	0	0	0	3	0	0	.188	.188	.375	.563
20	Pit	NL	5	12	3	0	1	1	(1	0)	8	2	4	1	1	0	1	0	0	0	0	0	0	.250	.308	.667	.974
	5 ML YEARS		100	216	45	7	2	8	(5	3)	80	25	20	16	16	1	89	4	0	0	11	6	4	.208	.275	.370	.646

Kolby Allard

Pitches: L **Bats:** L **Pos:** SP-17; RP-15   **Ht:** 6'1" **Wt:** 195 **Born:** 8/13/1997 **Age:** 24

			HOW MUCH PITCHED					WHAT HE GAVE UP											THE RESULTS							
Year	Team	Lg	G	GS	GF	IP	BFP	H	R	ER	HR	SH	SF	HB	TBB	IBB	SO	WP	W	L	Pct	Sv-Op	Hld	Vel	OPS	ERC	ERA
2018	Atl	NL	3	1	0	8.0	47	19	12	11	3	1	0	1	4	0	3	0	1	1	.500	0-0	0	89	1.253	17.45	12.38
2019	Tex	AL	9	9	0	45.1	208	52	26	25	3	0	1	2	19	0	33	0	4	2	.667	0-0	0	92	.742	4.82	4.96
2020	Tex	AL	11	8	2	33.2	152	31	29	29	4	0	1	1	20	0	32	1	0	6	.000	0-0	0	92	.734	4.58	7.75
2021	Tex	AL	32	17	3	124.2	534	128	80	75	29	0	3	4	31	0	104	4	3	12	.200	0-0	1	92	.779	4.58	5.41
	4 ML YEARS		55	35	5	211.2	941	230	147	140	39	1	5	8	74	0	172	6	8	21	.276	0-0	1	92	.788	5.05	5.95

Austin Allen

Bats: L **Throws:** R **Pos:** C-2;PH-2   **Ht:** 6'2" **Wt:** 219 **Born:** 1/16/1994 **Age:** 28

							BATTING													RUNNING			AVERAGES			
Year	Team	Lg	G	AB	H	2B	3B	HR	(Hm	Rd)	TB	R	RBI	RC	TBB	IBB	SO	HBP	SH	SF	SB	CS	GDP	Avg	OBP	Slg	OPS
2021	LsVgs	AAA	72	281	89	15	0	20	(-	-)	164	50	53	-	13	0	55	3	0	2	0	0	10	.317	.351	.584	.935
2019	SD	NL	34	65	14	4	0	0	(0	0)	18	4	3	4	6	3	21	0	0	0	0	0	2	.215	.282	.277	.559
2020	Oak	AL	14	31	6	1	0	1	(1	0)	10	1	3	2	1	0	14	0	0	0	0	0	0	.194	.219	.323	.541
2021	Oak	AL	4	8	2	0	0	1	(1	0)	5	2	1	1	0	0	3	0	0	0	0	0	0	.250	.250	.625	.875
	3 ML YEARS		52	104	22	5	0	2	(2	0)	33	7	7	7	7	3	38	0	0	0	0	0	2	.212	.261	.317	.579

Greg Allen

Bats: B **Throws:** R **Pos:** RF-8;LF-5;CF-4;PH-2   **Ht:** 6'0" **Wt:** 185 **Born:** 3/15/1993 **Age:** 29

							BATTING													RUNNING			AVERAGES			
Year	Team	Lg	G	AB	H	2B	3B	HR	(Hm	Rd)	TB	R	RBI	RC	TBB	IBB	SO	HBP	SH	SF	SB	CS	GDP	Avg	OBP	Slg	OPS
2021	S-WB	AAA	69	205	67	13	1	4	(-	-)	94	45	24	-	25	1	45	18	3	0	23	2	1	.327	.444	.459	.902
2017	Cle	AL	25	35	8	1	0	1	(0	1)	12	7	6	4	2	0	8	1	0	1	1	0	0	.229	.282	.343	.625
2018	Cle	AL	91	265	68	11	3	2	(1	1)	91	36	20	26	14	1	58	7	4	1	21	4	5	.257	.310	.343	.654
2019	Cle	AL	89	231	53	9	3	4	(0	4)	80	30	27	24	11	1	53	9	4	1	8	2	3	.229	.290	.346	.636
2020	2 Tms		16	26	4	1	0	1	(1	0)	8	4	4	3	3	0	10	2	0	1	2	0	0	.154	.281	.308	.589
2021	NYY	AL	15	37	10	4	1	0	(1	0)	16	9	2	7	5	0	13	5	0	1	5	0	0	.270	.417	.432	.849
20	Cle	AL	15	25	4	1	0	1	(1	0)	8	3	4	2	1	0	9	1	0	1	1	0	0	.160	.214	.320	.534
20	SD	NL	1	1	0	0	0	0	(0	0)	0	1	0	1	2	0	1	1	0	0	1	0	0	.000	.750	.000	.750
	Postseason		4	1	0	0	0	0	(0	0)	0	0	0	0	0	0	0	0	0	0	0	0	0	.000	.000	.000	.000
	5 ML YEARS		236	594	143	26	7	8	(2	6)	207	86	59	64	35	2	142	24	8	5	37	6	8	.241	.307	.348	.655

Logan Allen

Pitches: L **Bats:** R **Pos:** SP-11; RP-3   **Ht:** 6'3" **Wt:** 200 **Born:** 5/23/1997 **Age:** 25

			HOW MUCH PITCHED					WHAT HE GAVE UP											THE RESULTS							
Year	Team	Lg	G	GS	GF	IP	BFP	H	R	ER	HR	SH	SF	HB	TBB	IBB	SO	WP	W	L	Pct	Sv-Op	Hld	Vel	OPS	ERC	ERA
2021	Clmbs	AAA	12	11	1	48.2	230	61	43	43	9	0	0	4	29	0	52	5	2	3	.400	0-	-	-	.952	7.65	7.95
2019	2 Tms		9	4	3	27.2	127	36	20	19	4	2	1	2	13	0	17	0	2	3	.400	0-0	0	93	.958	7.07	6.18
2020	Cle	AL	3	0	2	10.2	49	12	4	4	1	0	0	1	7	0	7	1	0	0	-	0-0	0	94	.847	6.44	3.38
2021	Cle	AL	14	11	1	50.1	222	58	39	35	12	0	2	4	17	0	37	4	2	7	.222	0-0	0	93	.873	6.18	6.26
19	SD	NL	8	4	2	25.1	118	33	20	19	4	2	1	2	13	0	14	0	2	3	.400	0-0	0	93	.974	7.39	6.75
19	Cle	AL	1	0	1	2.1	9	3	0	0	0	0	0	0	0	0	3	0	0	0	-	0-0	0	94	.778	3.75	0.00
	3 ML YEARS		26	15	6	88.2	398	106	63	58	17	2	3	7	37	0	61	5	4	10	.286	0-0	0	93	.897	6.50	5.89

Nick Allgeyer

Pitches: L Bats: L Pos: RP-1 Ht: 6'3" Wt: 210 Born: 2/3/1996 Age: 26

			HOW MUCH PITCHED					WHAT HE GAVE UP										THE RESULTS							
Year	Team	Lg	G	GS	GF	IP	BFP	H	R	ER	HR	SH	SF	HB	TBB	IBB	SO	WP	W	L	Pct	Sv-Op	Hld	Vel	OPS	ERC	ERA
2021	Buffalo	AAA	21	16	0	84.1	389	89	54	49	12	1	6	3	52	0	74	4	4	5	.444	0- -	-	-	.839	5.74	5.23
2021	Tor	AL	1	0	1	1.0	3	0	0	0	0	0	0	0	0	0	0	0	0	0	-	0-0	0	92	.000	0.00	0.00

Abraham Almonte

Bats: B Throws: R Pos: LF-40;PH-23;RF-4 Ht: 5'10" Wt: 223 Born: 6/27/1989 Age: 33

			BATTING																	RUNNING			AVERAGES			
Year	Team	Lg	G	AB	H	2B	3B	HR	(Hm	Rd)	TB	R	RBI	RC	TBB	IBB	SO	HBP	SH	SF	SB	CS	GDP	Avg	OBP	Slg	OPS
2021	Gwnntt	AAA	19	62	25	4	0	3	(-	-)	38	16	19	-	21	0	14	0	0	0	3	3	0	.403	.554	.613	1.167
2013	Sea	AL	25	72	19	4	0	2	(1	1)	29	10	9	9	6	0	21	0	2	2	1	0	2	.264	.313	.403	.715
2014	2 Tms		59	204	47	10	4	1	(2	1)	68	19	15	18	12	0	60	1	2	4	4	3	5	.230	.275	.333	.609
2015	2 Tms		82	232	58	12	5	5	(4	1)	95	36	24	28	21	0	52	0	3	2	7	1	5	.250	.310	.409	.719
2016	Cle	AL	67	182	48	20	1	1	(1	0)	73	24	22	20	8	1	42	1	0	3	8	0	5	.264	.294	.401	.695
2017	Cle	AL	69	172	40	8	3	3	(2	1)	63	26	14	19	20	0	46	1	1	1	2	1	2	.233	.314	.366	.681
2018	KC	AL	50	134	24	1	2	3	(1	2)	38	15	9	5	15	0	36	0	1	1	2	2	6	.179	.260	.284	.544
2019	Ari	NL	17	31	9	3	1	1	(1	0)	17	11	4	6	7	0	8	0	0	0	0	0	1	.290	.421	.548	.969
2020	SD	NL	7	11	1	0	0	0	(0	0)	1	0	0	0	2	0	4	0	0	0	1	1	0	.091	.231	.091	.322
2021	Atl	NL	64	148	32	12	0	5	(1	4)	59	20	19	18	26	0	38	0	0	1	1	1	2	.216	.331	.399	.730
	14	Sea	AL	27	106	21	5	1	1	(0	1)	31	10	8	10	6	0	40	1	0	3	1	1	.198	.248	.292	.540
	14	SD	NL	32	98	26	5	0	2	(2	0)	37	9	7	8	6	0	20	0	2	1	2	4	.265	.305	.378	.682
	15	SD	NL	31	54	11	3	0	0	(0	0)	14	6	4	3	5	0	19	0	3	0	1	1	.204	.271	.259	.530
	15	Cle	NL	51	178	47	9	5	5	(4	1)	81	30	20	25	16	0	33	0	0	2	6	4	.264	.321	.455	.776
	9 ML YEARS		440	1186	278	70	13	23	(13	10)	443	161	116	123	117	1	307	3	9	11	26	9	28	.234	.302	.374	.676

Yency Almonte

Pitches: R Bats: B Pos: RP-48 Ht: 6'5" Wt: 223 Born: 6/4/1994 Age: 28

			HOW MUCH PITCHED					WHAT HE GAVE UP										THE RESULTS							
Year	Team	Lg	G	GS	GF	IP	BFP	H	R	ER	HR	SH	SF	HB	TBB	IBB	SO	WP	W	L	Pct	Sv-Op	Hld	Vel	OPS	ERC	ERA
2018	Col	NL	14	0	3	14.2	60	15	5	3	1	0	1	0	4	0	14	1	0	0	-	0-0	5	95	.735	3.61	1.84
2019	Col	NL	28	0	6	34.0	157	39	22	21	7	1	1	1	14	0	29	1	0	1	.000	0-1	1	96	.860	5.73	5.56
2020	Col	NL	24	0	4	27.2	113	25	13	9	2	0	1	3	6	0	23	0	3	0	1.000	1-3	4	95	.670	3.14	2.93
2021	Col	NL	48	0	15	47.2	217	47	42	40	9	0	3	4	29	1	47	3	1	3	.250	0-3	3	94	.844	5.87	7.55
	4 ML YEARS		114	0	28	124.0	547	126	82	73	19	1	6	8	53	1	113	5	4	4	.500	1-7	11	95	.800	4.92	5.30

Albert Almora Jr.

Bats: R Throws: R Pos: CF-32;PH-14;PR-7;LF-3;RF-1 Ht: 6'2" Wt: 190 Born: 4/16/1994 Age: 28

			BATTING																	RUNNING			AVERAGES			
Year	Team	Lg	G	AB	H	2B	3B	HR	(Hm	Rd)	TB	R	RBI	RC	TBB	IBB	SO	HBP	SH	SF	SB	CS	GDP	Avg	OBP	Slg	OPS
2021	Syrcse	AAA	41	152	41	6	0	6	(-	-)	65	24	18	-	13	0	18	2	0	2	2	5	2	.270	.331	.428	.759
2016	ChC	NL	47	112	31	9	1	3	(1	2)	51	14	14	16	5	0	20	0	0	0	0	0	5	.277	.308	.455	.763
2017	ChC	NL	132	299	89	18	1	8	(4	4)	133	39	46	44	19	1	53	0	2	3	1	0	8	.298	.338	.445	.782
2018	ChC	NL	152	444	127	24	1	5	(3	2)	168	62	41	51	24	1	83	3	2	6	1	3	12	.286	.323	.378	.701
2019	ChC	NL	130	339	80	11	1	12	(6	6)	129	41	32	25	16	4	62	1	5	2	2	1	8	.236	.271	.381	.651
2020	ChC	NL	28	30	5	1	0	0	(0	0)	6	4	1	1	3	0	9	1	0	0	0	0	0	.167	.250	.200	.465
2021	NYM	NL	47	52	6	3	0	0	(0	0)	9	3	0	0	2	0	17	0	0	0	0	0	1	.115	.148	.173	.321
	Postseason		19	37	7	1	0	1	(0	1)	11	2	3	3	1	0	7	0	2	0	0	0	1	.189	.211	.297	.508
	6 ML YEARS		536	1276	338	66	4	28	(14	14)	496	163	134	137	69	6	244	5	10	10	4	4	34	.265	.303	.389	.692

Pete Alonso

Bats: R Throws: R Pos: 1B-148;DH-3;PH-1 Ht: 6'3" Wt: 245 Born: 12/7/1994 Age: 27

			BATTING																	RUNNING			AVERAGES			
Year	Team	Lg	G	AB	H	2B	3B	HR	(Hm	Rd)	TB	R	RBI	RC	TBB	IBB	SO	HBP	SH	SF	SB	CS	GDP	Avg	OBP	Slg	OPS
2019	NYM	NL	161	597	155	30	2	53	(27	26)	348	103	120	112	72	6	183	21	0	3	1	0	13	.260	.358	.583	.941
2020	NYM	NL	57	208	48	6	0	16	(7	9)	102	31	35	31	24	4	61	6	0	1	1	0	4	.231	.326	.490	.817
2021	NYM	NL	152	561	147	27	3	37	(12	25)	291	81	94	91	60	6	127	12	0	4	3	0	20	.262	.344	.519	.863
	3 ML YEARS		370	1366	350	63	5	106	(46	60)	741	215	249	234	156	16	371	39	0	8	5	0	37	.256	.347	.542	.890

Dan Altavilla

Pitches: R Bats: R Pos: RP-2 all-ta-VILL-ah Ht: 5'11" Wt: 226 Born: 9/8/1992 Age: 29

			HOW MUCH PITCHED					WHAT HE GAVE UP										THE RESULTS							
Year	Team	Lg	G	GS	GF	IP	BFP	H	R	ER	HR	SH	SF	HB	TBB	IBB	SO	WP	W	L	Pct	Sv-Op	Hld	Vel	OPS	ERC	ERA
2016	Sea	AL	15	0	7	12.1	48	11	1	1	0	0	1	1	1	0	10	1	0	0	-	0-1	1	96	.560	2.09	0.73
2017	Sea	AL	41	0	13	46.2	203	43	27	22	9	0	4	1	20	1	52	9	1	1	.500	0-4	3	97	.765	4.38	4.24
2018	Sea	AL	22	0	8	20.2	85	11	7	6	2	0	0	2	15	0	23	4	3	2	.600	0-1	5	96	.609	3.27	2.61
2019	Sea	AL	17	0	3	14.2	64	9	9	9	1	1	0	0	12	1	18	2	2	1	.667	0-2	1	97	.613	3.20	5.52
2020	2 Tms		22	0	7	20.1	89	18	14	13	3	0	0	0	6	0	24	2	2	3	.400	1-1	3	97	.779	4.54	5.75
2021	SD	NL	2	0	1	1.1	5	1	1	1	1	0	0	0	0	0	2	0	0	0	-	0-0	1	96	1.000	4.25	6.75
	20	Sea	AL	13	0	5	11.2	54	12	11	10	3	0	0	0	7	0	14	0	1	2	.333	1-1	1	97	.884	6.13	7.71
	20	SD	NL	9	0	2	8.2	35	6	3	3	0	0	0	0	5	0	10	2	1	1	.500	0-0	2	97	.614	2.54	3.12
	Postseason		2	0	1	2.0	9	2	1	1	0	0	1	0	1	0	2	0	0	0	-	0-0	0	98	.619	3.63	4.50
	6 ML YEARS		119	0	34	116.0	494	93	59	52	16	1	6	4	60	2	129	18	8	7	.533	1-9	12	97	.706	3.82	4.03

Jose Altuve

Bats: R **Throws:** R **Pos:** 2B-144;PH-2;DH-1   al-TOO-vay   **Ht:** 5'6" **Wt:** 166 **Born:** 5/6/1990 **Age:** 32

Year	Team	Lg	G	AB	H	2B	3B	HR	(Hm	Rd)	TB	R	RBI	RC	TBB	IBB	SO	HBP	SH	SF	SB	CS	GDP	Avg	OBP	Slg	OPS
2011	Hou	NL	57	221	61	10	1	2	(2	0)	79	26	12	18	5	0	29	2	5	1	7	3	5	.276	.297	.357	.654
2012	Hou	NL	147	576	167	34	4	7	(4	3)	230	80	37	76	40	0	74	6	4	4	33	11	8	.290	.340	.399	.740
2013	Hou	AL	152	626	177	31	2	5	(4	1)	227	64	52	67	32	5	85	2	4	8	35	13	24	.283	.316	.363	.678
2014	Hou	AL	158	660	225	47	3	7	(4	3)	299	85	59	106	36	7	53	5	1	5	56	9	20	.341	.377	.453	.830
2015	Hou	AL	154	638	200	40	4	15	(9	6)	293	86	66	98	33	8	67	9	3	6	38	13	17	.313	.353	.459	.812
2016	Hou	AL	161	640	216	42	5	24	(15	9)	340	108	96	132	60	11	70	7	3	7	30	10	15	.338	.396	.531	.928
2017	Hou	AL	153	590	204	39	4	24	(9	15)	323	112	81	118	58	3	84	9	1	4	32	6	19	.346	.410	.547	.957
2018	Hou	AL	137	534	169	29	2	13	(7	6)	241	84	61	91	55	4	79	6	3	1	17	4	17	.316	.386	.451	.837
2019	Hou	AL	124	500	149	27	3	31	(18	13)	275	89	74	81	41	0	82	3	1	3	6	5	19	.298	.353	.550	.903
2020	Hou	AL	48	192	42	9	0	5	(1	4)	66	32	18	14	17	0	39	1	0	2	3	2	5	.219	.286	.344	.629
2021	Hou	AL	146	601	167	32	1	31	(19	12)	294	117	83	109	66	3	91	4	1	6	5	3	9	.278	.350	.489	.839
	Postseason		63	255	78	12	0	18	(14	4)	144	49	40	40	29	2	38	1	0	1	5	4	10	.306	.378	.565	.942
	11 ML YEARS		1437	5778	1777	340	29	164	(92	72)	2667	883	639	910	443	41	753	54	26	45	261	80	158	.308	.360	.462	.821

Jose Alvarado

Pitches: L **Bats:** L **Pos:** RP-64   **Ht:** 6'2" **Wt:** 245 **Born:** 5/21/1995 **Age:** 27

			HOW MUCH PITCHED					WHAT HE GAVE UP										THE RESULTS						
Year	Team	Lg	G	GS	GF	IP	BFP	H	R	ER	HR	SH	SF	HB	TBB	IBB	SO	WP	W	L	Pct	Sv-Op	Hld	Vel	OPS	ERC	ERA
2017	TB	AL	35	0	6	29.2	123	24	12	12	1	2	1	0	9	1	29	2	0	3	.000	0-0	7	98	.570	2.19	3.64
2018	TB	AL	70	0	17	64.0	263	42	21	17	1	2	2	1	29	4	80	2	1	6	.143	8-12	32	97	.525	1.90	2.39
2019	TB	AL	35	1	16	30.0	146	29	18	16	2	3	2	0	27	3	39	8	1	6	.143	7-9	8	98	.751	5.28	4.80
2020	TB	AL	9	0	3	9.0	45	9	7	6	2	0	1	2	6	0	13	3	0	0	-	0-0	1	97	.850	6.78	6.00
2021	Phi	NL	64	0	10	55.2	251	42	30	26	5	0	0	7	47	5	68	9	7	1	.875	5-8	16	99	.707	4.79	4.20
	Postseason		2	0	0	1.2	9	1	0	0	0	0	0	0	3	0	4	0	0	0	-	0-0	0	98	.611	6.15	0.00
	5 ML YEARS		213	1	52	188.1	828	146	88	77	11	7	6	10	118	13	229	24	9	16	.360	20-29	64	98	.642	3.46	3.68

Eddy Alvarez

Bats: B **Throws:** R **Pos:** 3B-17;2B-4;PH-3;PR-1   **Ht:** 5'9" **Wt:** 185 **Born:** 1/30/1990 **Age:** 32

Year	Team	Lg	G	AB	H	2B	3B	HR	(Hm	Rd)	TB	R	RBI	RC	TBB	IBB	SO	HBP	SH	SF	SB	CS	GDP	Avg	OBP	Slg	OPS
2021	Jaxnvl	AAA	31	111	32	5	0	4	(-	-)	49	23	16	-	18	1	27	8	1	0	2	5	0	.288	.423	.441	.865
2020	Mia	NL	12	37	7	1	0	0	(0	0)	8	6	2	3	3	0	16	1	0	0	2	0	0	.189	.268	.216	.485
2021	Mia	NL	24	64	12	4	1	1	(0	1)	21	8	6	7	4	1	18	6	0	0	1	0	2	.188	.297	.328	.625
	2 ML YEARS		36	101	19	5	1	1	(0	1)	29	14	8	10	7	1	34	7	0	0	3	0	2	.188	.287	.287	.574

Francisco Alvarez

Bats: R **Throws:** R **Pos:** C   **Ht:** 5'10" **Wt:** 233 **Born:** 11/19/2001 **Age:** 20

Year	Team	Lg	G	AB	H	2B	3B	HR	(Hm	Rd)	TB	R	RBI	RC	TBB	IBB	SO	HBP	SH	SF	SB	CS	GDP	Avg	OBP	Slg	OPS
2021	2 Tms	Low	99	327	89	18	1	24	(-	-)	181	67	70	0	55	0	89	11	0	7	8	5	12	.272	.388	.554	.941

Jose Alvarez

Pitches: L **Bats:** L **Pos:** RP-66; SP-1   **Ht:** 5'11" **Wt:** 195 **Born:** 5/6/1989 **Age:** 33

			HOW MUCH PITCHED					WHAT HE GAVE UP										THE RESULTS						
Year	Team	Lg	G	GS	GF	IP	BFP	H	R	ER	HR	SH	SF	HB	TBB	IBB	SO	WP	W	L	Pct	Sv-Op	Hld	Vel	OPS	ERC	ERA
2013	Det	AL	14	6	0	38.2	172	42	26	25	7	2	2	2	16	1	31	0	1	5	.167	0-0	2	89	.866	5.41	5.82
2014	LAA	AL	2	0	1	0.2	3	1	0	0	0	0	0	0	0	0	1	0	0	0	-	0-0	0	89	.667	4.47	0.00
2015	LAA	AL	64	0	18	67.0	283	58	29	26	5	0	1	5	23	4	59	1	4	3	.571	0-1	7	91	.642	3.13	3.49
2016	LAA	AL	64	0	12	57.1	256	71	29	22	4	1	1	1	15	4	51	2	1	3	.250	0-1	11	91	.745	4.55	3.45
2017	LAA	AL	64	0	12	48.2	203	50	23	21	7	1	0	0	12	5	45	1	0	3	.000	1-3	13	91	.733	3.78	3.88
2018	LAA	AL	76	0	5	63.0	261	51	20	19	3	2	0	2	22	2	59	1	6	4	.600	1-4	14	92	.613	2.59	2.71
2019	Phi	NL	67	1	11	59.0	255	66	25	22	8	1	3	1	18	4	51	3	3	4	.429	1-3	16	91	.766	4.61	3.36
2020	Phi	NL	8	0	1	6.1	27	7	1	1	0	0	0	0	3	0	6	0	0	0	-	0-0	1	92	.745	4.44	1.42
2021	SF	NL	67	1	12	64.2	266	53	23	17	2	1	1	0	19	1	42	1	5	2	.714	0-0	8	91	.551	2.23	2.37
	Postseason		1	0	0	3.0	10	0	0	0	0	0	0	0	1	0	3	0	0	0	-	0-0	0	91	.100	0.13	0.00
	9 ML YEARS		426	8	72	405.1	1726	399	176	153	36	8	8	11	128	21	345	9	20	24	.455	3-12	72	91	.692	3.59	3.40

Yordan Alvarez

Bats: L **Throws:** R **Pos:** DH-98;LF-41;PH-6   **Ht:** 6'5" **Wt:** 225 **Born:** 6/27/1997 **Age:** 25

Year	Team	Lg	G	AB	H	2B	3B	HR	(Hm	Rd)	TB	R	RBI	RC	TBB	IBB	SO	HBP	SH	SF	SB	CS	GDP	Avg	OBP	Slg	OPS
2019	Hou	AL	87	313	98	26	0	27	(14	13)	205	58	78	72	52	4	94	2	0	2	0	0	9	.313	.412	.655	1.067
2020	Hou	AL	2	8	2	0	0	1	(1	0)	5	2	4	2	0	0	1	1	0	0	0	0	1	.250	.333	.625	.958
2021	Hou	AL	144	537	149	35	1	33	(15	18)	285	92	104	96	50	3	145	8	0	3	1	0	16	.277	.346	.531	.877
	Postseason		18	58	14	3	0	1	(0	1)	20	5	3	5	7	1	21	0	0	0	0	0	0	.241	.323	.345	.668
	3 ML YEARS		233	858	249	61	1	61	(30	31)	495	152	186	170	102	7	240	11	0	5	1	0	26	.290	.371	.577	.948

Adbert Alzolay

Pitches: R Bats: R Pos: SP-21; RP-8　　　　Ht: 6'1" Wt: 208 Born: 3/1/1995 Age: 27

			HOW MUCH PITCHED						WHAT HE GAVE UP											THE RESULTS						
Year	Team	Lg	G	GS	GF	IP	BFP	H	R	ER	HR	SH	SF	HB	TBB	IBB	SO	WP	W	L	Pct	Sv-Op	Hld	Vel	OPS	ERC	ERA
2019	ChC	NL	4	2	1	12.1	60	13	10	10	4	0	1	0	9	0	13	0	1	1	.500	0-0	0	94	.923	7.80	7.30
2020	ChC	NL	6	4	0	21.1	87	12	8	7	1	0	2	1	13	0	29	1	1	1	.500	0-0	0	95	.566	2.43	2.95
2021	ChC	NL	29	21	1	125.2	519	112	66	64	25	5	1	5	34	2	128	2	5	13	.278	1-1	0	94	.733	3.75	4.58
	3 ML YEARS		39	27	2	159.1	666	137	84	81	30	5	3	7	56	2	170	3	7	15	.318	1-1	0	94	.729	3.86	4.58

Trey Amburgey

Bats: R Throws: R Pos: RF-2　　　　Ht: 6'2" Wt: 210 Born: 10/24/1994 Age: 27

							BATTING														RUNNING			AVERAGES			
Year	Team	Lg	G	AB	H	2B	3B	HR	(Hm	Rd)	TB	R	RBI	RC	TBB	IBB	SO	HBP	SH	SF	SB	CS	GDP	Avg	OBP	Slg	OPS
2021	S-WB	AAA	69	247	68	22	2	8	(-	-)	118	35	51	-	25	1	78	1	0	5	1	0	7	.275	.338	.478	.816
2021	NYY	AL	2	4	0	0	0	0	(0	0)	0	0	0	0	0	0	2	0	0	0	0	0	0	.000	.000	.000	.000

Brett Anderson

Pitches: L Bats: L Pos: SP-24　　　　Ht: 6'4" Wt: 230 Born: 2/1/1988 Age: 34

			HOW MUCH PITCHED						WHAT HE GAVE UP											THE RESULTS						
Year	Team	Lg	G	GS	GF	IP	BFP	H	R	ER	HR	SH	SF	HB	TBB	IBB	SO	WP	W	L	Pct	Sv-Op	Hld	Vel	OPS	ERC	ERA
2009	Oak	AL	30	30	0	175.1	735	180	94	79	20	4	4	3	45	1	150	0	11	11	.500	0-0	0	93	.711	3.84	4.06
2010	Oak	AL	19	19	0	112.1	470	112	41	35	6	3	2	7	22	2	75	4	7	6	.538	0-0	0	92	.655	3.16	2.80
2011	Oak	AL	13	13	0	83.1	356	86	40	37	8	4	1	7	25	1	61	0	3	6	.333	0-0	0	91	.721	4.20	4.00
2012	Oak	AL	6	6	0	35.0	137	29	11	10	1	0	0	1	7	1	25	1	4	2	.667	0-0	0	92	.565	2.13	2.57
2013	Oak	AL	16	5	4	44.2	200	51	32	30	5	1	0	0	21	1	46	0	1	4	.200	3-3	1	92	.794	5.27	6.04
2014	Col	NL	8	8	0	43.1	180	44	18	14	1	1	1	0	13	3	29	0	1	3	.250	0-0	0	90	.688	3.20	2.91
2015	LAD	NL	31	31	0	180.1	750	194	82	74	18	3	2	2	46	2	116	4	10	9	.526	0-0	0	91	.726	4.05	3.69
2016	LAD	NL	4	3	0	11.1	62	25	15	15	4	1	1	0	4	0	5	2	1	2	.333	0-0	0	91	1.208	14.27	11.91
2017	2 Tms		13	13	0	55.1	251	73	41	39	5	0	3	0	21	0	38	2	4	4	.500	0-0	0	91	.872	5.87	6.34
2018	Oak	AL	17	17	0	80.1	333	90	42	40	10	2	0	2	13	0	47	3	4	5	.444	0-0	0	90	.770	4.15	4.48
2019	Oak	AL	31	31	0	176.0	743	181	80	76	20	4	4	4	49	2	90	4	13	9	.591	0-0	0	91	.724	3.94	3.89
2020	Mil	NL	10	10	0	47.0	202	50	24	22	6	0	3	4	10	0	32	0	4	4	.500	0-0	0	90	.771	4.19	4.21
2021	Mil	NL	24	24	0	96.0	409	102	52	45	11	5	5	2	28	0	58	0	4	9	.308	0-0	0	89	.766	4.21	4.22
17	ChC	NL	6	6	0	22.0	111	34	22	20	2	0	1	0	12	0	16	1	2	2	.500	0-0	0	90	.986	7.85	8.18
17	Tor	AL	7	7	0	33.1	140	39	19	19	3	0	2	0	9	0	22	1	2	2	.500	0-0	0	92	.785	4.62	5.13
	Postseason		3	2	1	9.1	40	10	7	7	1	0	0	0	3	0	10	1	1	1	.500	0-0	0	92	.730	4.23	6.75
	13 ML YEARS		222	210	4	1140.1	4828	1217	572	516	115	28	26	32	304	13	772	20	67	74	.475	3-3	1	91	.735	4.06	4.07

Brian Anderson

Bats: R Throws: R Pos: 3B-65;PH-3;SS-1　　　　Ht: 6'3" Wt: 208 Born: 5/19/1993 Age: 29

							BATTING														RUNNING			AVERAGES			
Year	Team	Lg	G	AB	H	2B	3B	HR	(Hm	Rd)	TB	R	RBI	RC	TBB	IBB	SO	HBP	SH	SF	SB	CS	GDP	Avg	OBP	Slg	OPS
2017	Mia	NL	25	84	22	7	1	0	(0	0)	31	11	8	11	10	0	28	0	0	1	0	0	1	.262	.337	.369	.706
2018	Mia	NL	156	590	161	34	4	11	(7	4)	236	87	65	94	62	2	129	16	0	2	2	4	18	.273	.357	.400	.757
2019	Mia	NL	126	459	120	33	4	20	(10	10)	215	57	66	72	44	1	114	14	0	3	5	1	15	.261	.342	.468	.811
2020	Mia	NL	59	200	51	7	1	11	(4	7)	93	27	38	40	22	1	66	6	0	1	0	0	2	.255	.345	.465	.810
2021	Mia	NL	67	233	58	9	0	7	(4	3)	88	24	28	35	26	2	65	5	0	0	5	0	4	.249	.337	.378	.715
	Postseason		5	19	4	1	0	0	(0	0)	5	1	1	2	1	0	7	1	0	0	0	0	1	.211	.286	.263	.549
	5 ML YEARS		433	1566	412	90	7	49	(25	24)	663	206	205	252	164	6	402	41	0	7	12	5	40	.263	.347	.423	.770

Chase Anderson

Pitches: R Bats: R Pos: SP-9; RP-5　　　　Ht: 6'1" Wt: 210 Born: 11/30/1987 Age: 34

			HOW MUCH PITCHED						WHAT HE GAVE UP											THE RESULTS						
Year	Team	Lg	G	GS	GF	IP	BFP	H	R	ER	HR	SH	SF	HB	TBB	IBB	SO	WP	W	L	Pct	Sv-Op	Hld	Vel	OPS	ERC	ERA
2021	LV	AAA	5	5	0	17.1	76	21	11	11	2	0	0	1	5	0	14	2	1	2	.333	0--	-	-	.798	5.29	5.71
2014	Ari	NL	21	21	0	114.1	486	117	56	51	16	4	4	2	40	2	105	4	9	7	.563	0-0	0	91	.779	4.39	4.01
2015	Ari	NL	27	27	0	152.2	640	158	75	73	18	3	9	7	40	2	111	3	6	6	.500	0-0	0	91	.754	4.08	4.30
2016	Mil	NL	31	30	1	151.2	647	155	83	74	28	4	3	4	53	0	120	4	9	11	.450	0-0	0	91	.819	4.76	4.39
2017	Mil	NL	25	25	0	141.1	569	113	44	43	14	5	2	7	41	1	133	0	12	4	.750	0-0	0	93	.647	2.80	2.74
2018	Mil	NL	30	30	0	158.0	644	131	71	69	30	4	1	7	57	0	128	1	9	8	.529	0-0	0	92	.731	3.85	3.93
2019	Mil	NL	32	27	1	139.0	592	126	67	65	23	6	2	8	50	2	124	1	8	4	.667	0-0	0	93	.763	4.03	4.21
2020	Tor	AL	10	7	0	33.2	154	45	29	27	11	0	0	1	10	0	38	1	1	2	.333	0-0	0	92	.986	7.54	7.22
2021	Phi	NL	14	9	2	48.0	215	51	36	36	10	1	1	3	20	1	35	0	2	4	.333	0-0	0	91	.867	5.49	6.75
	8 ML YEARS		190	176	4	938.2	3947	896	464	438	150	27	22	39	311	8	794	14	56	46	.549	0-0	0	92	.765	4.16	4.20

Drew Anderson

Pitches: R Bats: R Pos: RP-8; SP-1　　　　Ht: 6'3" Wt: 205 Born: 3/22/1994 Age: 28

			HOW MUCH PITCHED						WHAT HE GAVE UP											THE RESULTS						
Year	Team	Lg	G	GS	GF	IP	BFP	H	R	ER	HR	SH	SF	HB	TBB	IBB	SO	WP	W	L	Pct	Sv-Op	Hld	Vel	OPS	ERC	ERA
2021	RdRck	AAA	15	12	0	70.2	288	55	26	24	8	0	0	0	29	0	86	2	4	5	.444	0--	-	-	.655	3.05	3.06
2017	Phi	NL	2	0	1	2.1	14	6	7	6	0	0	1	0	1	0	2	0	0	0	-	0-0	0	94	1.167	13.44	23.14
2018	Phi	NL	5	1	1	12.2	59	17	7	7	0	0	0	2	2	0	11	0	0	1	.000	0-0	0	93	.792	4.81	4.97
2019	Phi	NL	2	1	1	6.0	30	6	5	5	1	0	0	0	6	2	6	0	0	0	-	0-0	0	93	.775	6.27	7.50
2020	CWS	AL	1	0	0	1.1	10	4	6	6	1	0	0	0	2	0	2	1	0	1	.000	0-0	0	92	1.975	41.86	40.50
2021	Tex	AL	9	1	3	22.0	91	20	8	8	1	0	0	1	6	0	9	1	1	1	.500	0-0	0	93	.594	2.92	3.27
	5 ML YEARS		19	2	6	44.1	204	53	33	32	4	0	1	3	17	2	30	2	1	3	.250	0-0	0	93	.779	5.18	6.50

Ian Anderson

Pitches: R Bats: R Pos: SP-24　　　　　　　　　　　　　　　**Ht: 6'3" Wt: 170 Born: 5/2/1998 Age: 24**

Year Team	Lg	G	GS	GF	IP	BFP	H	R	ER	HR	SH	SF	HB	TBB	IBB	SO	WP	W	L	Pct	Sv-Op	Hld	Vel	OPS	ERC	ERA
2017 Rome	A	20	20	0	83.0	355	69	30	29	0	2	1	11	43	0	101	8	4	5	.444	0--	-	-	.617	3.47	3.14
2018 Florida	A+	20	20	0	100.0	414	73	31	28	2	3	1	2	40	0	118	18	2	6	.250	0--	-	-	.530	2.19	2.52
2019 Missi	AA	21	21	0	111.0	462	82	38	33	8	3	4	2	47	1	147	6	7	5	.583	0--	-	-	.581	2.61	2.68
2019 Gwnntt	AAA	5	5	0	24.2	113	23	18	18	5	0	0	0	18	0	25	1	1	2	.333	0--	-	-	.815	5.79	6.57
2020 Atl	NL	6	6	0	32.1	138	21	11	7	1	0	0	2	14	0	41	4	3	2	.600	0-0	0	94	.498	2.04	1.95
2021 Atl	NL	24	24	0	128.1	535	105	51	51	16	5	1	1	53	2	124	7	9	5	.643	0-0	0	95	.671	3.31	3.58
Postseason		4	4	0	18.2	77	11	2	2	0	0	0	0	10	0	24	1	2	0	1.000	0-0	0	95	.467	1.79	0.96
2 ML YEARS		30	30	0	160.2	673	126	62	58	17	5	1	3	67	2	165	11	12	7	.632	0-0	0	95	.635	3.03	3.25

Nick Anderson

Pitches: R Bats: R Pos: RP-6　　　　　　　　　　　　　　　**Ht: 6'4" Wt: 205 Born: 7/5/1990 Age: 31**

Year Team	Lg	G	GS	GF	IP	BFP	H	R	ER	HR	SH	SF	HB	TBB	IBB	SO	WP	W	L	Pct	Sv-Op	Hld	Vel	OPS	ERC	ERA
2021 Drham	AAA	11	0	1	10.2	44	12	7	6	2	1	0	0	1	0	12	0	0	0	-	0--	-	-	.850	4.14	5.06
2019 2 Tms		68	0	3	65.0	264	52	24	24	8	0	1	2	18	4	110	4	5	4	.556	1-5	16	96	.647	2.71	3.32
2020 TB	AL	19	0	9	16.1	58	5	2	1	1	0	0	0	3	0	26	0	2	1	.667	6-6	6	95	.320	0.55	0.55
2021 TB	AL	6	0	6	6.0	24	4	3	3	2	0	1	0	2	0	1	0	0	1	.000	1-1	0	93	.726	3.37	4.50
19 Mia	NL	45	0	3	43.2	186	40	19	19	5	0	1	1	16	3	69	2	2	4	.333	1-2	7	96	.705	3.53	3.92
19 TB	NL	23	0	0	21.1	78	12	5	5	3	0	0	1	2	1	41	2	3	0	1.000	0-3	9	96	.512	1.33	2.11
Postseason		14	0	3	20.1	82	21	10	10	3	0	1	0	4	1	17	2	1	2	.333	1-3	3	96	.733	3.82	4.43
3 ML YEARS		93	0	14	87.1	346	61	29	28	11	0	2	2	23	4	137	4	7	6	.538	8-12	22	96	.597	2.17	2.89

Shaun Anderson

Pitches: R Bats: R Pos: RP-16　　　　　　　　　　　　　　　**Ht: 6'4" Wt: 228 Born: 10/29/1994 Age: 27**

Year Team	Lg	G	GS	GF	IP	BFP	H	R	ER	HR	SH	SF	HB	TBB	IBB	SO	WP	W	L	Pct	Sv-Op	Hld	Vel	OPS	ERC	ERA
2021 StPaul	AAA	5	0	0	6.0	22	2	0	0	0	0	0	0	3	0	5	0	1	0	1.000	0--	-	-	.333	1.00	0.00
2021 ElPaso	AAA	11	0	2	14.1	61	13	7	7	2	0	0	0	6	0	18	3	1	0	1.000	1--	-	-	.730	3.89	4.40
2019 SF	NL	28	16	4	96.0	427	111	61	58	13	4	1	2	38	3	70	6	3	5	.375	2-2	1	93	.818	5.29	5.44
2020 SF	NL	18	0	4	15.1	67	10	6	6	3	0	0	0	12	0	18	2	0	0	-	0-0	2	95	.710	4.30	3.52
2021 3 Tms		16	0	6	23.1	124	36	30	22	4	0	1	2	12	1	19	3	0	0	-	0-0	0	93	.917	8.35	8.49
21 Min	AL	4	0	0	8.2	47	13	12	9	1	0	0	1	5	0	8	0	0	0	-	0-0	0	93	.868	7.97	9.35
21 Bal	AL	7	0	5	10.0	55	17	15	10	3	0	0	1	5	0	7	3	0	0	-	0-0	0	94	1.051	10.61	9.00
21 SD	NL	5	0	1	4.2	22	6	3	3	0	0	1	0	2	1	4	0	0	0	-	0-0	0	94	.679	4.53	5.79
3 ML YEARS		62	16	14	134.2	618	157	97	86	20	4	2	4	62	4	107	11	3	5	.375	2-2	3	93	.827	5.68	5.75

Tanner Anderson

Pitches: R Bats: R Pos: RP-1　　　　　　　　　　　　　　　**Ht: 6'2" Wt: 203 Born: 5/27/1993 Age: 29**

Year Team	Lg	G	GS	GF	IP	BFP	H	R	ER	HR	SH	SF	HB	TBB	IBB	SO	WP	W	L	Pct	Sv-Op	Hld	Vel	OPS	ERC	ERA
2021 LsVgs	AAA	12	0	0	15.0	68	14	6	6	3	0	0	2	12	0	3	2	3	0	1.000	0--	-	-	.875	7.05	3.60
2021 Indy	AAA	17	4	3	36.2	160	36	20	17	2	0	2	5	14	1	25	1	2	4	.333	0--	-	-	.689	4.10	4.17
2018 Pit	NL	6	0	1	11.1	56	15	10	8	1	2	0	1	8	2	6	2	1	0	1.000	0-0	0	93	.911	7.31	6.35
2019 Oak	AL	5	5	0	22.1	105	30	16	15	4	0	0	0	7	1	18	3	0	3	.000	0-0	0	93	.809	6.06	6.04
2021 Pit	NL	1	0	0	5.0	19	5	2	2	0	0	0	0	0	0	1	0	0	0	-	0-0	0	92	.526	2.09	3.60
3 ML YEARS		12	5	1	38.2	180	50	28	25	5	2	0	1	15	3	25	5	1	3	.250	0-0	0	93	.808	5.87	5.82

Tim Anderson

Bats: R Throws: R Pos: SS-122　　　　　　　　　　　　　　　**Ht: 6'1" Wt: 185 Born: 6/23/1993 Age: 29**

Year Team	Lg	G	AB	H	2B	3B	HR	(Hm	Rd)	TB	R	RBI	RC	TBB	IBB	SO	HBP	SH	SF	SB	CS	GDP	Avg	OBP	Slg	OPS
2016 CWS	AL	99	410	116	22	6	9	(5	4)	177	57	30	45	13	0	117	1	6	1	10	2	15	.283	.306	.432	.738
2017 CWS	AL	146	587	151	26	4	17	(7	10)	236	72	56	59	13	0	162	3	2	1	15	1	13	.257	.276	.402	.679
2018 CWS	AL	153	567	136	28	3	20	(10	10)	230	77	64	58	30	2	149	4	2	3	26	8	15	.240	.281	.406	.687
2019 CWS	AL	123	498	167	32	0	18	(9	9)	253	81	56	77	15	0	109	3	0	2	17	5	12	**.335**	.357	.508	.865
2020 CWS	AL	49	208	67	11	1	10	(5	5)	110	**45**	21	31	10	0	50	2	0	1	5	2	4	.322	.357	.529	.886
2021 CWS	AL	123	527	163	29	2	17	(9	8)	247	94	61	82	22	1	119	1	0	1	18	7	5	.309	.338	.469	.806
Postseason		3	14	9	2	0	0	(0	0)	11	2	0	4	0	0	0	0	0	0	0	0	0	.643	.643	.786	1.429
6 ML YEARS		693	2797	800	148	16	91	(45	46)	1253	426	288	352	103	3	706	14	10	9	91	25	64	.286	.314	.448	.762

Tyler Anderson

Pitches: L Bats: L Pos: SP-31　　　　　　　　　　　　　　　**Ht: 6'2" Wt: 220 Born: 12/30/1989 Age: 32**

Year Team	Lg	G	GS	GF	IP	BFP	H	R	ER	HR	SH	SF	HB	TBB	IBB	SO	WP	W	L	Pct	Sv-Op	Hld	Vel	OPS	ERC	ERA
2016 Col	NL	19	19	0	114.1	478	119	50	45	12	6	3	3	28	2	99	4	5	6	.455	0-0	0	91	.742	3.85	3.54
2017 Col	NL	17	15	1	86.0	362	88	48	46	16	5	2	2	26	0	81	6	6	6	.500	0-0	0	92	.820	4.57	4.81
2018 Col	NL	32	32	0	176.0	737	165	94	89	**30**	3	7	3	59	1	164	9	7	9	.438	0-0	0	92	.757	4.04	4.55
2019 Col	NL	5	5	0	20.2	106	33	27	27	8	2	2	0	11	0	23	0	0	3	.000	0-0	0	91	1.159	10.75	11.76
2020 SF	NL	13	11	0	59.2	260	58	32	29	5	1	3	4	25	0	41	1	4	3	.571	0-0	0	90	.746	4.15	4.37
2021 2 Tms		31	31	0	167.0	703	170	87	84	27	9	7	1	38	2	134	1	7	11	.389	0-0	0	90	.753	3.87	4.53

HOW MUCH PITCHED					WHAT HE GAVE UP											THE RESULTS							
Year Team	Lg	G GS GF	IP	BFP	H	R	ER	HR	SH	SF	HB	TBB	IBB	SO	WP	W	L	Pct	Sv-Op	Hld	Vel	OPS	ERC	ERA
21 Pit	NL	18 18 0	103.1	430	99	52	50	16	6	4	1	25	0	86	0	5	8	.385	0-0	0	90	.719	3.60	4.35
21 Sea	AL	13 13 0	63.2	273	71	35	34	11	3	3	0	13	2	48	1	2	3	.400	0-0	0	91	.807	4.33	4.81
Postseason		2 1 0	7.0	28	6	3	3	1	0	0	0	2	0	6	0	0	1	.000	0-0	0	92	.709	3.21	3.86
6 ML YEARS		117 113 1	623.2	2646	633	338	320	98	26	24	13	187	5	542	21	29	38	.433	0-0	0	91	.777	4.24	4.62

John Andreoli

Bats: R **Throws:** R **Pos:** LF-3;CF-2;RF-2;PH-1

Ht: 6'1" **Wt:** 218 **Born:** 6/9/1990 **Age:** 32

BATTING																				RUNNING			AVERAGES			
Year Team	Lg	G	AB	H	2B	3B	HR	(Hm	Rd)	TB	R	RBI	RC	TBB	IBB	SO	HBP	SH	SF	SB	CS	GDP	Avg	OBP	Slg	OPS
2021 ElPaso	AAA	42	133	27	5	3	4	(-	-)	50	22	19	-	29	0	58	1	0	1	6	3	1	.203	.348	.376	.724
2018 2 Tms	AL	26	61	14	2	0	0	(0	0)	16	4	4	5	5	0	19	0	0	1	2	0	1	.230	.284	.262	.546
2021 SD	NL	7	6	1	1	0	0	(0	0)	2	2	0	1	0	0	3	0	0	0	0	0	0	.167	.286	.333	.619
18 Sea	AL	3	5	1	0	0	0	(0	0)	1	0	0	0	1	0	2	0	0	0	0	0	0	.200	.333	.200	.533
18 Bal	AL	23	56	13	2	0	0	(0	0)	15	4	4	5	4	0	17	0	0	1	2	0	1	.232	.279	.268	.547
2 ML YEARS		33	67	15	3	0	0	(0	0)	18	6	4	6	6	0	22	0	0	1	2	0	1	.224	.284	.269	.552

Matt Andriese

Pitches: R **Bats:** R **Pos:** RP-34

ANN-dreese

Ht: 6'2" **Wt:** 215 **Born:** 8/28/1989 **Age:** 32

HOW MUCH PITCHED					WHAT HE GAVE UP											THE RESULTS							
Year Team	Lg	G GS GF	IP	BFP	H	R	ER	HR	SH	SF	HB	TBB	IBB	SO	WP	W	L	Pct	Sv-Op	Hld	Vel	OPS	ERC	ERA
2015 TB	AL	25 8 8	65.2	282	69	32	30	8	1	3	2	18	1	49	2	3	5	.375	2-2	0	91	.728	4.08	4.11
2016 TB	AL	29 19 3	127.2	527	131	64	62	17	0	6	1	25	1	109	3	8	8	.500	1-1	4	92	.720	3.68	4.37
2017 TB	AL	18 17 1	86.0	374	90	48	43	16	0	1	4	28	1	76	3	5	5	.500	1-1	0	92	.795	4.80	4.50
2018 2 Tms		41 5 13	78.2	340	84	51	46	15	1	1	2	25	5	78	3	5	5	.500	1-1	0	92	.819	4.77	5.26
2019 Ari	NL	54 0 13	70.2	310	72	37	37	8	1	3	3	27	4	79	9	5	5	.500	1-4	3	93	.757	4.24	4.71
2020 LAA	AL	16 1 7	32.0	126	21	17	16	5	0	0	1	11	0	33	0	2	4	.333	2-3	3	92	.622	2.56	4.50
2021 2 Tms		34 0 13	48.1	222	65	35	28	7	1	3	4	13	0	50	0	2	3	.400	1-4	3	92	.859	6.26	5.21
18 TB	AL	27 4 6	59.2	251	55	32	27	7	1	1	2	18	3	59	3	3	4	.429	0-0	1	92	.702	3.41	4.07
18 Ari	NL	14 1 7	19.0	89	29	19	19	8	0	0	0	7	2	19	0	0	3	.000	0-0	0	92	1.148	9.93	9.00
21 Bos	AL	26 0 7	37.1	177	55	29	25	7	1	2	3	11	0	38	0	2	3	.400	1-4	3	92	.942	7.56	6.03
21 Sea	AL	8 0 6	11.0	45	10	6	3	0	0	1	1	2	0	12	0	0	0	-	0-0	0	91	.533	2.48	2.45
7 ML YEARS		217 50 54	509.0	2181	532	284	262	76	4	17	17	147	12	474	20	28	37	.431	8-15	15	92	.763	4.32	4.63

Elvis Andrus

Bats: R **Throws:** R **Pos:** SS-143;PR-3;PH-2

AHN-droos

Ht: 6'0" **Wt:** 210 **Born:** 8/26/1988 **Age:** 33

BATTING																				RUNNING			AVERAGES			
Year Team	Lg	G	AB	H	2B	3B	HR	(Hm	Rd)	TB	R	RBI	RC	TBB	IBB	SO	HBP	SH	SF	SB	CS	GDP	Avg	OBP	Slg	OPS
2009 Tex	AL	145	480	128	17	8	6	(3	3)	179	72	40	65	40	0	77	6	12	3	33	6	4	.267	.329	.373	.702
2010 Tex	AL	148	588	156	15	3	0	(0	0)	177	88	35	79	64	0	96	5	17	0	32	15	6	.265	.342	.301	.643
2011 Tex	AL	150	587	164	27	3	5	(2	3)	212	96	60	76	56	0	74	5	16	1	37	12	14	.279	.347	.361	.708
2012 Tex	AL	158	629	180	31	9	3	(1	2)	238	85	62	92	57	0	96	5	17	3	21	10	15	.286	.349	.378	.727
2013 Tex	AL	156	620	168	17	4	4	(1	2)	205	91	67	72	52	1	97	4	16	6	42	8	19	.271	.328	.331	.659
2014 Tex	AL	157	619	163	35	1	2	(1	1)	206	72	41	59	46	0	96	3	9	7	27	15	21	.263	.314	.333	.647
2015 Tex	AL	160	596	154	34	2	7	(4	3)	213	69	62	68	46	1	78	2	8	9	25	9	14	.258	.309	.357	.667
2016 Tex	AL	147	506	153	31	7	8	(3	5)	222	75	69	87	47	2	70	4	4	4	24	8	18	.302	.362	.439	.800
2017 Tex	AL	158	643	191	44	4	20	(7	13)	303	100	88	104	38	0	101	3	1	4	25	10	18	.297	.337	.471	.808
2018 Tex	AL	97	395	101	20	3	6	(4	2)	145	53	33	44	28	0	66	3	0	2	5	3	8	.256	.308	.367	.675
2019 Tex	AL	147	600	165	27	4	12	(4	8)	236	81	72	76	34	1	96	4	1	9	31	8	16	.275	.313	.393	.707
2020 Tex	AL	29	103	20	5	0	3	(2	1)	34	11	7	6	8	0	15	0	0	0	3	1	5	.194	.252	.330	.582
2021 Oak	AL	146	497	121	25	2	3	(1	2)	159	60	37	45	31	2	81	6	3	4	12	2	14	.243	.294	.320	.614
Postseason		42	173	46	4	1	1	(0	1)	55	21	7	15	12	0	24	1	4	1	9	5	6	.266	.316	.318	.633
13 ML YEARS		1798	6863	1864	328	50	79	(34	45)	2529	953	673	873	547	7	1043	50	103	56	317	107	175	.272	.327	.368	.696

Miguel Andujar

Bats: R **Throws:** R **Pos:** LF-37;3B-4;1B-2;PH-2;PR-1

Ht: 6'0" **Wt:** 211 **Born:** 3/2/1995 **Age:** 27

BATTING																				RUNNING			AVERAGES			
Year Team	Lg	G	AB	H	2B	3B	HR	(Hm	Rd)	TB	R	RBI	RC	TBB	IBB	SO	HBP	SH	SF	SB	CS	GDP	Avg	OBP	Slg	OPS
2021 S-WB	AAA	11	36	11	0	0	3	(-	-)	20	6	9	-	3	0	4	0	0	2	0	0	0	.306	.341	.556	.897
2017 NYY	AL	5	7	4	2	0	0	(0	0)	6	0	4	4	1	0	0	0	0	0	1	0	0	.571	.625	.857	1.482
2018 NYY	AL	149	573	170	47	2	27	(16	11)	302	83	92	99	25	2	97	4	0	4	2	1	9	.297	.328	.527	.855
2019 NYY	AL	12	47	6	0	0	0	(0	0)	6	1	1	0	1	0	11	0	0	0	0	0	4	.128	.143	.128	.271
2020 NYY	AL	21	62	15	2	1	1	(0	1)	22	5	5	4	3	0	9	0	0	0	0	0	1	.242	.277	.355	.632
2021 NYY	AL	45	154	39	6	0	6	(4	2)	59	19	12	8	7	0	28	0	0	1	0	1	8	.253	.284	.383	.667
Postseason		4	10	2	0	0	0	(0	0)	2	0	0	1	2	0	2	0	0	0	0	0	1	.200	.333	.200	.533
5 ML YEARS		232	843	234	53	3	34	(20	14)	395	108	114	115	37	2	145	4	0	6	3	2	22	.278	.309	.469	.778

Tejay Antone

Pitches: R **Bats:** R **Pos:** RP-23

Ht: 6'4" **Wt:** 230 **Born:** 12/5/1993 **Age:** 28

HOW MUCH PITCHED					WHAT HE GAVE UP											THE RESULTS							
Year Team	Lg	G GS GF	IP	BFP	H	R	ER	HR	SH	SF	HB	TBB	IBB	SO	WP	W	L	Pct	Sv-Op	Hld	Vel	OPS	ERC	ERA
2021 Lsvlle	AAA	7 0 2	6.2	26	4	2	2	1	0	0	0	3	0	10	1	0	0	-	1--	-	-	.574	2.56	2.70
2020 Cin	NL	13 4 1	35.1	141	20	11	11	4	0	2	2	16	0	45	2	0	3	.000	0-1	8	96	.584	2.34	2.80
2021 Cin	NL	23 0 4	33.2	128	17	8	8	3	0	0	3	13	0	42	1	2	0	1.000	3-7	8	97	.508	1.87	2.14
2 ML YEARS		36 4 5	69.0	269	37	19	19	7	0	2	5	29	0	87	3	2	3	.400	3-8	9	96	.547	2.11	2.48

Aristides Aquino

Bats: R **Throws:** R **Pos:** LF-35;PH-28;RF-27;CF-14;PR-3

Ht: 6'4" **Wt:** 220 **Born:** 4/22/1994 **Age:** 28

							BATTING												RUNNING			AVERAGES			
Year	Team	Lg	G	AB	H	2B	3B	HR	(Hm | Rd)	TB	R	RBI	RC	TBB	IBB	SO	HBP	SH	SF	SB	CS	GDP	Avg	OBP	Slg	OPS
2018 Cin	NL	1	1	0	0	0	0	(0 | 0)	0	0	0	0	0	0	1	0	0	0	0	0	0	.000	.000	.000	.000
2019 Cin	NL	56	205	53	8	0	19	(11 | 8)	118	31	47	39	16	2	60	2	0	2	7	0	5	.259	.316	.576	.891
2020 Cin	NL	23	47	8	1	0	2	(1 | 1)	15	7	8	9	6	0	18	3	0	0	1	0	1	.170	.304	.319	.623
2021 Cin	NL	84	174	33	6	1	10	(6 | 4)	71	25	23	21	27	2	75	1	0	2	2	2	0	.190	.299	.408	.707
Postseason		1	6	2	0	0	0	(0 | 0)	2	0	0	0	0	0	2	0	0	0	0	1	0	.333	.333	.333	.667
4 ML YEARS		164	427	94	15	1	31	(18 | 13)	204	63	78	69	49	4	154	6	0	4	10	2	6	.220	.307	.478	.784

Jonathan Arauz

Bats: B **Throws:** R **Pos:** SS-13;2B-12;PH-4;3B-2;PR-2

Ht: 6'0" **Wt:** 195 **Born:** 8/3/1998 **Age:** 23

							BATTING												RUNNING			AVERAGES			
Year	Team	Lg	G	AB	H	2B	3B	HR	(Hm | Rd)	TB	R	RBI	RC	TBB	IBB	SO	HBP	SH	SF	SB	CS	GDP	Avg	OBP	Slg	OPS
2021 Wrcstr	AAA	63	213	51	5	1	6	(- | -)	76	29	29	-	28	0	43	0	0	4	2	0	6	.239	.322	.357	.679
2020 Bos	AL	25	72	18	2	0	1	(0 | 1)	23	8	9	12	8	0	21	0	0	0	0	0	0	.250	.325	.319	.644
2021 Bos	AL	28	65	12	3	0	3	(2 | 1)	24	9	8	6	8	0	15	0	2	0	0	0	2	.185	.274	.369	.643
2 ML YEARS		53	137	30	5	0	4	(2 | 2)	47	17	17	18	16	0	36	0	2	0	0	0	2	.219	.301	.343	.644

Chris Archer

Pitches: R **Bats:** R **Pos:** SP-5; RP-1

Ht: 6'2" **Wt:** 195 **Born:** 9/26/1988 **Age:** 33

			HOW MUCH PITCHED					WHAT HE GAVE UP										THE RESULTS							
Year	Team	Lg	G	GS	GF	IP	BFP	H	R	ER	HR	SH	SF	HB	TBB	IBB	SO	WP	W	L	Pct	Sv-Op	Hld	Vel	OPS	ERC	ERA
2021 Drham	AAA	5	5	0	14.0	55	9	9	6	3	0	0	1	3	0	16	1	0	1	.000	0- -	-	-	.609	2.42	3.86
2012 TB	AL	6	4	1	29.1	122	23	17	15	3	1	0	1	13	0	36	2	1	3	.250	0-0	0	94	.624	3.24	4.60
2013 TB	AL	23	23	0	128.2	525	107	49	46	15	1	5	8	38	2	101	7	9	7	.563	0-0	0	95	.660	3.13	3.22
2014 TB	AL	32	32	0	194.2	822	177	85	72	12	4	9	8	72	1	173	8	10	9	.526	0-0	0	95	.650	3.36	3.33
2015 TB	AL	34	34	0	212.0	868	175	85	76	19	2	2	3	66	0	252	13	12	13	.480	0-0	0	95	.613	2.79	3.23
2016 TB	AL	33	33	0	201.1	850	183	100	90	30	6	4	3	67	0	233	11	9	19	.321	0-0	0	94	.703	3.66	4.02
2017 TB	AL	34	34	0	201.0	852	193	101	91	27	1	2	5	60	0	249	15	10	12	.455	0-0	0	95	.710	3.75	4.07
2018 2 Tms		27	27	0	148.1	638	155	77	71	19	1	3	6	49	3	162	6	6	8	.429	0-0	0	95	.767	4.41	4.31
2019 Pit	NL	23	23	0	119.2	526	114	73	69	25	6	3	4	55	2	143	6	3	9	.250	0-0	0	94	.793	4.89	5.19
2021 TB	AL	6	5	0	19.1	83	18	11	10	3	0	0	0	8	0	21	1	1	1	.500	0-0	0	92	.727	4.09	4.66
18 TB	AL	17	17	0	96.0	413	102	50	46	11	0	1	4	31	0	102	3	3	5	.375	0-0	0	95	.751	4.43	4.31
18 Pit	NL	10	10	0	52.1	225	53	27	25	8	1	2	2	18	3	60	3	3	3	.500	0-0	0	95	.796	4.36	4.30
Postseason		2	0	0	1.2	6	1	0	0	0	0	1	0	0	0	2	0	0	0	-	0-0	0	96	.367	0.75	0.00
9 ML YEARS		218	215	1	1254.1	5286	1145	598	540	153	22	28	38	428	8	1370	69	61	81	.430	0-0	0	95	.692	3.61	3.87

Orlando Arcia

Bats: R **Throws:** R **Pos:** PH-15;LF-14;SS-5;3B-3;2B-1

ARR-see-ya

Ht: 6'0" **Wt:** 187 **Born:** 8/4/1994 **Age:** 27

							BATTING												RUNNING			AVERAGES			
Year	Team	Lg	G	AB	H	2B	3B	HR	(Hm | Rd)	TB	R	RBI	RC	TBB	IBB	SO	HBP	SH	SF	SB	CS	GDP	Avg	OBP	Slg	OPS
2021 Gwnntt	AAA	74	287	81	16	0	17	(- | -)	148	54	37	-	31	0	38	1	0	3	5	3	3	.282	.351	.516	.867
2016 Mil	NL	55	201	44	10	3	4	(2 | 2)	72	21	17	20	15	0	47	0	0	0	8	0	6	.219	.273	.358	.631
2017 Mil	NL	153	506	140	17	2	15	(8 | 7)	206	56	53	63	36	9	100	1	2	3	14	7	10	.277	.324	.407	.731
2018 Mil	NL	119	348	82	16	0	3	(2 | 1)	107	32	30	26	15	0	87	1	1	1	7	4	9	.236	.268	.307	.576
2019 Mil	NL	152	494	110	16	1	15	(6 | 9)	173	51	59	48	43	5	109	1	2	6	8	5	15	.223	.283	.350	.633
2020 Mil	NL	59	173	45	10	1	5	(3 | 2)	72	22	20	19	14	0	32	1	0	1	2	0	10	.260	.317	.416	.734
2021 2 Tms	NL	36	81	16	3	0	2	(0 | 2)	25	9	14	9	7	1	19	0	0	1	1	0	2	.198	.258	.309	.567
21 Mil	NL	4	11	1	0	0	0	(0 | 0)	1	0	1	0	0	0	3	0	0	0	0	0	0	.091	.091	.091	.182
21 Atl	NL	32	70	15	3	0	2	(0 | 2)	24	9	13	9	7	1	16	0	0	1	1	0	2	.214	.282	.343	.625
Postseason		13	44	13	0	0	4	(1 | 3)	25	8	6	5	1	1	9	0	0	0	0	0	1	.295	.311	.568	.879
6 ML YEARS		574	1803	437	72	7	44	(20 | 24)	655	191	193	185	130	15	394	4	5	12	40	16	52	.242	.293	.363	.656

Nolan Arenado

Bats: R **Throws:** R **Pos:** 3B-155;DH-2

ahr-eh-NOD-oh

Ht: 6'2" **Wt:** 215 **Born:** 4/16/1991 **Age:** 31

							BATTING												RUNNING			AVERAGES			
Year	Team	Lg	G	AB	H	2B	3B	HR	(Hm | Rd)	TB	R	RBI	RC	TBB	IBB	SO	HBP	SH	SF	SB	CS	GDP	Avg	OBP	Slg	OPS
2013 Col	NL	133	486	130	29	4	10	(5 | 5)	197	49	52	48	23	1	72	1	2	2	2	0	16	.267	.301	.405	.706
2014 Col	NL	111	432	124	34	2	18	(16 | 2)	216	58	61	60	25	1	58	4	1	5	2	1	13	.287	.328	.500	.828
2015 Col	NL	157	616	177	43	4	42	(20 | 22)	354	97	130	116	34	13	110	4	0	11	2	5	17	.287	.323	.575	.898
2016 Col	NL	160	618	182	35	6	41	(25 | 16)	352	116	133	128	68	10	103	2	0	8	2	3	17	.294	.362	.570	.932
2017 Col	NL	159	606	187	43	7	37	(19 | 18)	355	100	130	130	62	9	106	4	1	6	3	2	21	.309	.373	.586	.959
2018 Col	NL	156	590	175	38	2	38	(23 | 15)	331	104	110	117	73	10	122	3	1	6	2	2	16	.297	.374	.561	.935
2019 Col	NL	155	588	185	31	2	41	(21 | 20)	343	102	118	123	62	11	93	4	0	8	3	2	14	.315	.379	.583	.962
2020 Col	NL	48	182	46	9	0	8	(7 | 1)	79	23	26	18	15	3	20	0	0	4	0	0	7	.253	.303	.434	.738
2021 StL	NL	157	593	151	34	3	34	(14 | 20)	293	81	105	94	50	8	96	3	0	7	2	0	20	.255	.312	.494	.807
Postseason		5	21	4	0	0	1	(0 | 1)	7	2	3	0	0	0	7	0	0	2	0	0	1	.190	.174	.333	.507
9 ML YEARS		1236	4711	1357	296	30	269	(150 | 119)	2520	730	865	834	412	66	780	25	5	57	18	15	141	.288	.345	.535	.880

Kohei Arihara

Pitches: R **Bats:** R **Pos:** SP-10

Ht: 6'2" **Wt:** 210 **Born:** 8/11/1992 **Age:** 29

			HOW MUCH PITCHED					WHAT HE GAVE UP										THE RESULTS							
Year	Team	Lg	G	GS	GF	IP	BFP	H	R	ER	HR	SH	SF	HB	TBB	IBB	SO	WP	W	L	Pct	Sv-Op	Hld	Vel	OPS	ERC	ERA
2021 Tex	AL	10	10	0	40.2	178	45	31	30	11	0	1	4	13	0	24	1	2	4	.333	0-0	0	91	.948	6.12	6.64

Shawn Armstrong

Pitches: R Bats: R Pos: RP-31   Ht: 6'2" Wt: 225 Born: 9/11/1990 Age: 31

Year	Team	Lg	G	GS	GF	IP	BFP	H	R	ER	HR	SH	SF	HB	TBB	IBB	SO	WP	W	L	Pct	Sv-Op	Hld	Vel	OPS	ERC	ERA
2021	Norfolk	AAA	15	0	1	17.0	79	19	10	6	3	0	1	1	6	0	21	0	1	3	.250	0- -	-	-	.766	5.10	3.18
2021	Drham	AAA	11	0	5	11.0	43	9	4	4	1	1	0	0	2	0	16	0	2	1	.667	0- -	-	-	.587	2.29	3.27
2015	Cle	AL	8	0	5	8.0	30	5	2	2	1	0	0	0	2	0	11	0	0	0	-	0-0	0	94	.590	1.84	2.25
2016	Cle	AL	10	0	2	10.2	44	9	3	3	1	1	0	0	5	2	7	1	0	0	-	0-0	0	92	.668	3.25	2.53
2017	Cle	AL	21	0	14	24.2	108	23	12	12	5	0	0	1	10	0	20	1	1	0	1.000	0-0	0	93	.737	4.50	4.38
2018	Sea	AL	14	0	3	14.2	57	9	2	2	1	0	2	3	3	1	15	0	0	1	.000	1-1	2	94	.569	1.91	1.23
2019	2 Tms	AL	55	0	10	58.0	271	66	38	37	8	1	3	4	29	1	63	4	1	1	.500	4-9	9	93	.815	5.74	5.74
2020	Bal	AL	14	0	2	15.0	57	9	6	3	1	0	0	1	3	0	14	2	2	0	1.000	0-0	3	94	.530	1.51	1.80
2021	2 Tms	AL	31	0	11	36.0	165	39	28	27	10	0	1	2	15	0	44	0	1	0	1.000	0-1	2	94	.870	6.02	6.75
19	Sea	AL	4	0	1	3.2	23	8	6	6	1	1	0	1	3	1	3	0	0	1	.000	0-0	0	93	1.268	16.16	14.73
19	Bal	AL	51	0	9	54.1	248	58	32	31	7	0	3	3	26	0	60	4	1	0	1.000	4-9	9	93	.777	5.14	5.13
21	Bal	AL	20	0	8	20.0	100	28	20	19	5	0	1	1	10	0	22	0	0	0	-	0-1	1	93	.970	8.15	8.55
21	TB	AL	11	0	3	16.0	65	11	8	8	5	0	0	1	5	0	22	0	1	0	1.000	0-0	1	94	.719	3.54	4.50
7 ML YEARS			153	0	47	167.0	732	160	91	86	27	2	6	11	67	4	174	8	5	2	.714	5-11	16	93	.756	4.45	4.63

Randy Arozarena

Bats: R Throws: R Pos: LF-81;RF-53;DH-19;PH-6;CF-1 ah-row-sah-RAY-nah   Ht: 5'11" Wt: 185 Born: 2/28/1995 Age: 27

Year	Team	Lg	G	AB	H	2B	3B	HR	(Hm	Rd)	TB	R	RBI	RC	TBB	IBB	SO	HBP	SH	SF	SB	CS	GDP	Avg	OBP	Slg	OPS
2019	StL	NL	19	20	6	1	0	1	(0	1)	10	4	2	3	2	0	4	1	0	0	2	1	0	.300	.391	.500	.891
2020	TB	AL	23	64	18	2	0	7	(2	5)	41	15	11	15	6	0	22	5	0	1	4	0	2	.281	.382	.641	1.022
2021	TB	AL	141	529	145	32	3	20	(13	7)	243	94	69	91	56	4	170	14	0	5	20	10	9	.274	.356	.459	.815
Postseason			25	81	29	3	1	10	(6	4)	64	19	14	19	8	2	22	2	0	0	1	2	2	.358	.429	.790	1.219
3 ML YEARS			183	613	169	35	3	28	(15	13)	294	113	82	109	64	4	196	20	0	6	26	11	11	.276	.360	.480	.839

Luis Arraez

Bats: L Throws: R Pos: 3B-55;2B-48;LF-27;PH-11;DH-4 ah-RYE-ez   Ht: 5'10" Wt: 175 Born: 4/9/1997 Age: 25

Year	Team	Lg	G	AB	H	2B	3B	HR	(Hm	Rd)	TB	R	RBI	RC	TBB	IBB	SO	HBP	SH	SF	SB	CS	GDP	Avg	OBP	Slg	OPS
2019	Min	AL	92	326	109	20	1	4	(1	3)	143	54	28	59	36	1	29	1	0	3	2	2	2	.334	.399	.439	.838
2020	Min	AL	32	112	36	9	0	0	(0	0)	45	16	13	22	8	0	11	0	0	1	0	0	2	.321	.364	.402	.765
2021	Min	AL	121	428	126	17	6	2	(2	0)	161	58	42	63	43	2	48	2	0	6	2	2	9	.294	.357	.376	.733
Postseason			5	17	5	4	0	0	(0	0)	9	1	1	2	2	0	3	0	0	0	0	0	1	.294	.368	.529	.898
3 ML YEARS			245	866	271	46	7	6	(3	3)	349	128	83	144	87	3	88	3	0	10	4	4	13	.313	.374	.403	.777

Jake Arrieta

Pitches: R Bats: R Pos: SP-24 air-ee-ETT-uh   Ht: 6'4" Wt: 230 Born: 3/6/1986 Age: 36

Year	Team	Lg	G	GS	GF	IP	BFP	H	R	ER	HR	SH	SF	HB	TBB	IBB	SO	WP	W	L	Pct	Sv-Op	Hld	Vel	OPS	ERC	ERA
2010	Bal	AL	18	18	0	100.1	449	106	57	52	9	4	2	4	48	3	52	5	6	6	.500	0-0	0	93	.767	4.74	4.66
2011	Bal	AL	22	22	0	119.1	523	115	70	67	21	3	2	4	59	2	93	0	10	8	.556	0-0	0	92	.791	4.93	5.05
2012	Bal	AL	24	18	1	114.2	496	122	82	79	16	3	4	5	35	3	109	4	3	9	.250	0-0	1	93	.763	4.47	6.20
2013	2 Tms		14	14	0	75.1	324	59	41	40	9	2	3	5	41	1	60	1	5	4	.556	0-0	0	94	.718	3.82	4.78
2014	ChC	NL	25	25	0	156.2	614	114	46	44	5	5	3	3	41	2	167	8	10	5	.667	0-0	0	94	.535	1.85	2.53
2015	ChC	NL	33	33	0	229.0	870	150	52	45	10	4	1	6	48	2	236	6	22	6	.786	0-0	0	94	.507	1.53	1.77
2016	ChC	NL	31	31	0	197.1	795	138	72	68	16	2	1	6	76	1	190	16	18	8	.692	0-0	0	94	.583	2.45	3.10
2017	ChC	NL	30	30	0	168.1	707	150	82	66	23	1	4	10	55	3	163	14	14	10	.583	0-0	0	92	.716	3.64	3.53
2018	Phi	NL	31	31	0	172.2	724	165	93	76	21	1	8	7	57	0	138	11	10	11	.476	0-0	0	93	.724	3.92	3.96
2019	Phi	NL	24	24	0	135.2	594	149	76	70	21	5	4	7	51	3	110	7	8	8	.500	0-0	0	93	.799	5.19	4.64
2020	Phi	NL	9	9	0	44.1	190	51	25	25	6	0	2	1	16	0	32	4	4	4	.500	0-0	0	93	.814	5.34	5.08
2021	2 Tms	NL	24	24	0	98.2	469	131	91	81	24	3	6	6	44	3	83	3	5	14	.263	0-0	1	91	.952	7.58	7.39
13	Bal	AL	5	5	0	23.2	111	25	19	19	2	0	3	2	17	1	23	1	1	2	.333	0-0	0	94	.857	5.91	7.23
13	ChC	NL	9	9	0	51.2	213	34	22	21	7	2	0	3	24	0	37	0	4	2	.667	0-0	0	94	.648	2.94	3.66
21	ChC	NL	20	20	0	86.1	409	113	75	66	21	2	5	4	39	3	74	3	5	11	.313	0-0	1	91	.940	7.39	6.88
21	SD	NL	4	4	0	12.1	60	18	16	15	3	1	1	2	5	0	9	0	0	3	.000	0-0	0	92	1.032	8.97	10.95
Postseason			9	9	0	52.2	218	36	19	18	6	1	1	5	21	1	66	3	5	3	.625	0-0	1	94	.623	2.79	3.08
12 ML YEARS			285	279	1	1612.1	6755	1450	787	713	181	33	40	64	571	23	1433	79	115	93	.553	0-0	1	93	.696	3.58	3.98

Christian Arroyo

Bats: R Throws: R Pos: 2B-51;PH-8;SS-2;DH-2;PR-2;1B-1   Ht: 6'1" Wt: 210 Born: 5/30/1995 Age: 27

Year	Team	Lg	G	AB	H	2B	3B	HR	(Hm	Rd)	TB	R	RBI	RC	TBB	IBB	SO	HBP	SH	SF	SB	CS	GDP	Avg	OBP	Slg	OPS
2021	Wrcstr	AAA	11	33	3	1	0	0	(-	-)	4	4	2	-	2	0	12	2	0	1	1	0	0	.091	.184	.121	.305
2017	SF	NL	34	125	24	5	0	3	(2	1)	38	9	14	7	8	1	32	1	0	1	1	2	4	.192	.244	.304	.548
2018	TB	AL	20	53	14	2	1	1	(1	0)	21	5	6	9	6	0	16	0	0	0	0	0	0	.264	.339	.396	.735
2019	TB	AL	16	50	11	2	0	2	(2	0)	19	8	7	6	5	0	18	1	1	0	0	0	0	.220	.304	.380	.684
2020	2 Tms	AL	15	50	12	1	0	3	(1	2)	22	7	8	10	4	0	11	0	0	0	0	0	2	.240	.296	.440	.736
2021	Bos	AL	57	164	43	10	0	6	(2	4)	73	22	25	26	8	0	44	7	1	0	1	0	1	.262	.324	.445	.769
20	Cle	AL	1	0	0	0	0	0	(0	0)	0	0	0	0	0	0	0	0	0	0	0	0	0	-	-	-	-
20	Bos	AL	14	50	12	1	0	3	(1	2)	22	7	8	10	4	0	11	0	0	0	0	0	2	.240	.296	.440	.736
5 ML YEARS			142	442	104	22	1	15	(8	7)	173	51	60	58	31	1	121	9	2	1	2	2	7	.235	.298	.391	.690

Humberto Arteaga

Bats: R **Throws:** R **Pos:** SS-1
um-BARE-toh ar-teh-AH-gah
Ht: 6'1" **Wt:** 160 **Born:** 1/23/1994 **Age:** 28

						BATTING														RUNNING			AVERAGES			
Year	Team	Lg	G	AB	H	2B	3B	HR	(Hm	Rd)	TB	R	RBI	RC	TBB	IBB	SO	HBP	SH	SF	SB	CS	GDP	Avg	OBP	Slg	OPS
2021	Roch	AAA	61	205	36	4	1	2	(-	-)	48	15	11	-	8	0	56	1	1	0	2	0	5	.176	.210	.234	.444
2019	KC	AL	41	122	24	4	0	0	(0	0)	28	11	4	8	8	0	28	2	3	0	1	1	2	.197	.258	.230	.487
2021	Was	NL	1	3	0	0	0	0	(0	0)	0	0	1	0	0	0	0	0	0	1	0	0	0	.000	.000	.000	.000
	2 ML YEARS		42	125	24	4	0	0	(0	0)	28	11	5	8	8	0	28	2	3	1	1	1	2	.192	.250	.224	.474

Aaron Ashby

Pitches: L **Bats:** R **Pos:** RP-9; SP-4
Ht: 6'2" **Wt:** 181 **Born:** 5/24/1998 **Age:** 24

			HOW MUCH PITCHED					WHAT HE GAVE UP										THE RESULTS							
Year	Team	Lg	G	GS	GF	IP	BFP	H	R	ER	HR	SH	SF	HB	TBB	IBB	SO	WP	W	L	Pct	Sv-Op	Hld	Vel	OPS	ERC	ERA
2018	2 Tms	Low	13	10	1	57.2	242	58	24	23	4	0	0	2	17	0	66	4	2	3	.400	1--	-	-	1.008	3.67	3.59
2019	2 Tms	Low	24	23	0	126.0	530	101	60	49	5	2	6	8	60	0	135	6	5	10	.333	0--	-	-	.581	3.15	3.50
2021	Nashv	AAA	21	12	0	63.1	276	55	35	31	4	0	2	8	32	0	100	6	5	4	.556	0--	-	-	.637	3.58	4.41
2021	Mil	NL	13	4	3	31.2	133	25	20	16	4	0	1	1	12	0	39	1	3	2	.600	1-1	0	97	.613	3.09	4.55

Willians Astudillo

Bats: R **Throws:** R **Pos:** 3B-29;1B-27;C-10;PH-9;2B-4;RF-1
Ht: 5'9" **Wt:** 225 **Born:** 10/14/1991 **Age:** 30

						BATTING														RUNNING			AVERAGES			
Year	Team	Lg	G	AB	H	2B	3B	HR	(Hm	Rd)	TB	R	RBI	RC	TBB	IBB	SO	HBP	SH	SF	SB	CS	GDP	Avg	OBP	Slg	OPS
2021	StPaul	AAA	22	89	25	3	0	2	(-	-)	34	13	8	-	3	1	4	2	0	0	3	0	5	.281	.319	.382	.701
2018	Min	AL	30	93	33	4	1	3	(1	2)	48	9	21	17	2	0	3	1	0	1	0	0	4	.355	.371	.516	.887
2019	Min	AL	58	190	51	9	0	4	(1	3)	72	28	21	19	5	0	8	5	0	4	0	0	6	.268	.299	.379	.678
2020	Min	AL	8	16	4	1	0	1	(1	0)	8	4	3	1	0	0	2	0	0	0	0	0	0	.250	.250	.500	.750
2021	Min	AL	73	208	49	8	0	7	(4	3)	78	17	21	13	3	0	12	4	0	1	0	0	12	.236	.259	.375	.634
	Postseason		1	1	0	0	0	0	(0	0)	0	0	0	0	0	0	0	0	0	0	0	0	1	.000	.000	.000	.000
	4 ML YEARS		169	507	137	22	1	15	(7	8)	206	58	66	50	10	0	25	10	0	6	0	0	22	.270	.295	.406	.701

Alex Avila

Bats: L **Throws:** R **Pos:** C-27;PH-6;2B-1
ah-VEE-lah
Ht: 5'11" **Wt:** 228 **Born:** 1/29/1987 **Age:** 35

						BATTING														RUNNING			AVERAGES			
Year	Team	Lg	G	AB	H	2B	3B	HR	(Hm	Rd)	TB	R	RBI	RC	TBB	IBB	SO	HBP	SH	SF	SB	CS	GDP	Avg	OBP	Slg	OPS
2009	Det	AL	29	61	17	4	0	5	(4	1)	36	9	14	12	10	0	18	0	0	1	0	0	0	.279	.375	.590	.965
2010	Det	AL	104	294	67	12	0	7	(4	3)	100	28	31	26	36	0	71	2	1	0	2	2	12	.228	.316	.340	.656
2011	Det	AL	141	464	137	33	4	19	(10	9)	235	63	82	86	73	9	131	3	3	8	3	1	8	.295	.389	.506	.895
2012	Det	AL	116	367	89	21	2	9	(7	2)	141	42	48	53	61	2	104	2	2	2	2	0	12	.243	.352	.384	.736
2013	Det	AL	102	330	75	14	1	11	(4	7)	124	39	47	37	44	0	112	1	1	3	0	0	10	.227	.317	.376	.693
2014	Det	AL	124	390	85	22	0	11	(3	8)	140	44	47	48	61	1	151	3	1	2	0	3	6	.218	.327	.359	.686
2015	Det	AL	67	178	34	5	0	4	(2	2)	51	21	13	20	40	0	66	0	1	0	1	0	4	.191	.339	.287	.626
2016	CWS	AL	57	169	36	6	0	7	(5	2)	63	19	11	17	38	0	78	1	1	0	0	0	3	.213	.359	.373	.732
2017	2 Tms		112	311	82	13	1	14	(8	6)	139	41	49	55	62	2	120	1	1	1	0	1	10	.264	.387	.447	.834
2018	Ari	NL	80	194	32	6	0	7	(1	6)	59	13	20	17	37	2	90	1	0	2	0	0	4	.165	.299	.304	.603
2019	Ari	NL	63	164	34	8	0	9	(5	4)	69	22	24	23	36	7	68	1	0	1	0	0	8	.207	.353	.421	.774
2020	Min	AL	23	49	9	2	0	1	(1	0)	14	6	2	4	11	0	22	2	0	0	0	0	0	.184	.355	.286	.641
2021	Was	NL	34	89	17	9	1	1	(0	1)	31	5	9	8	19	1	37	2	1	0	0	0	4	.191	.345	.348	.694
17	Det	AL	77	219	60	11	0	11	(6	5)	104	30	32	37	43	2	80	1	0	1	0	1	6	.274	.394	.475	.869
17	ChC	NL	35	92	22	2	1	3	(2	1)	35	11	17	18	19	0	40	0	1	0	0	0	4	.239	.369	.380	.750
	Postseason		36	111	17	2	0	3	(2	1)	28	6	7	5	11	0	43	1	1	0	0	0	1	.153	.236	.252	.488
	13 ML YEARS		1052	3060	714	155	9	105	(57	48)	1202	352	397	406	528	24	1068	19	11	20	8	8	83	.233	.348	.393	.740

Pedro Avila

Pitches: R **Bats:** R **Pos:** SP-1
AH-vee-lah
Ht: 5'11" **Wt:** 210 **Born:** 1/14/1997 **Age:** 25

			HOW MUCH PITCHED					WHAT HE GAVE UP										THE RESULTS							
Year	Team	Lg	G	GS	GF	IP	BFP	H	R	ER	HR	SH	SF	HB	TBB	IBB	SO	WP	W	L	Pct	Sv-Op	Hld	Vel	OPS	ERC	ERA
2021	SnAnt	AA	23	10	7	52.1	226	47	29	27	4	0	2	7	21	0	58	5	1	4	.200	2--	-	-	.704	3.89	4.64
2021	ElPaso	AAA	13	1	1	22.1	101	18	9	8	1	0	1	4	15	0	24	1	1	0	1.000	0--	-	-	.663	4.34	3.22
2019	SD	NL	1	1	0	5.1	23	4	1	1	0	0	0	0	2	0	5	0	0	0	-	0-0	0	94	.504	2.60	1.69
2021	SD	NL	1	1	0	4.0	20	4	2	1	1	0	0	1	3	0	5	0	0	1	.000	0-0	0	93	.762	6.21	2.25
	2 ML YEARS		2	2	0	9.1	43	8	3	2	1	0	0	1	5	0	10	0	0	1	.000	0-0	0	93	.623	4.07	1.93

Luis Avilan

Pitches: L **Bats:** L **Pos:** RP-4
ah-VEE-lan
Ht: 6'2" **Wt:** 220 **Born:** 7/19/1989 **Age:** 32

			HOW MUCH PITCHED					WHAT HE GAVE UP										THE RESULTS							
Year	Team	Lg	G	GS	GF	IP	BFP	H	R	ER	HR	SH	SF	HB	TBB	IBB	SO	WP	W	L	Pct	Sv-Op	Hld	Vel	OPS	ERC	ERA
2012	Atl	NL	31	0	2	36.0	142	27	9	8	1	2	0	1	10	1	33	3	1	0	1.000	0-0	5	92	.547	2.00	2.00
2013	Atl	NL	75	0	7	65.0	256	40	12	11	1	1	1	4	22	3	38	3	5	0	1.000	0-2	27	93	.478	1.62	1.52
2014	Atl	NL	62	0	14	43.1	193	47	22	22	2	3	2	3	21	7	25	5	4	1	.800	0-2	8	93	.764	4.55	4.57
2015	2 Tms	NL	73	0	9	53.1	220	48	24	24	6	1	2	1	15	2	49	2	2	5	.286	0-3	17	94	.665	3.18	4.05
2016	LAD	NL	27	0	5	19.2	82	12	8	7	0	2	0	2	10	4	28	1	3	0	1.000	0-1	5	93	.491	1.84	3.20
2017	LAD	NL	61	0	5	46.0	194	42	16	15	2	0	1	1	22	3	52	1	2	3	.400	0-2	13	93	.703	3.57	2.93
2018	2 Tms	NL	70	0	8	45.1	197	44	22	19	3	1	1	2	18	3	51	2	2	1	.667	2-5	9	91	.692	3.70	3.77
2019	NYM	NL	45	0	8	32.0	141	33	19	18	5	0	3	3	14	0	30	2	4	0	1.000	0-0	5	90	.782	5.28	5.06
2020	NYY	AL	10	0	1	8.1	39	9	4	4	2	0	0	0	5	0	9	0	0	0	-	0-0	0	91	.830	6.32	4.32
2021	Was	NL	4	0	0	5.0	27	7	7	7	1	0	2	1	4	0	9	0	0	1	.000	0-0	0	89	.884	8.61	12.60

Year	Team	Lg	G	GS	GF	IP	BFP	H	R	ER	HR	SH	SF	HB	TBB	IBB	SO	WP	W	L	Pct	Sv-Op	Hld	Vel	OPS	ERC	ERA
15	Atl	NL	50	0	7	37.2	154	35	15	15	4	0	1	0	10	2	31	1	2	4	.333	0-3	11	94	.670	3.16	3.58
15	LAD	NL	23	0	2	15.2	66	13	9	9	2	1	1	1	5	0	18	1	1	1	.000	0-0	6	94	.654	3.21	5.17
18	CWS	AL	58	0	7	39.2	172	40	20	17	2	1	1	2	14	2	46	2	2	1	.667	2-4	9	91	.685	3.68	3.86
18	Phi	NL	12	0	1	5.2	25	4	2	2	1	0	0	0	4	1	5	0	0	0	-	0-1	0	91	.749	3.81	3.18
Postseason			11	0	2	7.2	31	7	0	0	0	0	1	0	2	1	6	1	0	0	-	0-1	2	93	.576	2.30	0.00
10 ML YEARS			458	0	57	354.0	1491	309	142	135	23	11	8	18	140	22	319	19	23	11	.676	2-15	85	92	.653	3.24	3.43

John Axford

Pitches: R Bats: R Pos: RP-1

Ht: 6'5" **Wt:** 234 **Born:** 4/1/1983 **Age:** 39

Year	Team	Lg	G	GS	GF	IP	BFP	H	R	ER	HR	SH	SF	HB	TBB	IBB	SO	WP	W	L	Pct	Sv-Op	Hld	Vel	OPS	ERC	ERA
2021	Buffalo	AAA	9	0	6	10.2	37	2	1	1	0	1	0	0	3	0	14	1	1	0	1.000	2- -			.199	0.33	0.84
2009	Mil	NL	7	0	6	7.2	34	5	3	3	0	0	0	0	6	1	9	1	0	0	-	1-1	0	94	.538	2.62	3.52
2010	Mil	NL	50	0	43	58.0	238	42	17	16	1	2	2	1	27	3	76	4	8	2	.800	24-27	3	95	.588	2.33	2.48
2011	Mil	NL	74	0	63	73.2	305	59	19	16	1	4	1	0	25	1	86	8	2	2	.500	46-48	0	96	.557	2.44	1.95
2012	Mil	NL	75	0	54	69.1	310	61	42	36	10	1	2	2	39	2	93	10	5	8	.385	35-44	3	96	.717	4.33	4.67
2013	2 Tms	NL	75	0	16	65.0	289	73	32	29	10	4	1	2	26	3	65	5	7	7	.500	0-7	19	95	.796	5.25	4.02
2014	2 Tms	NL	62	0	28	54.2	243	43	26	24	6	3	4	2	36	3	63	5	2	4	.333	10-13	2	95	.691	3.96	3.95
2015	Col	NL	60	0	43	55.2	250	56	27	26	4	0	2	0	32	4	62	1	4	5	.444	25-31	2	96	.704	4.45	4.20
2016	Oak	AL	68	0	13	65.2	289	65	30	29	6	4	2	3	30	1	60	4	6	4	.600	3-10	15	96	.711	4.33	3.97
2017	Oak	AL	22	0	8	21.0	109	27	16	15	3	1	2	2	17	0	21	1	0	1	.000	0-1	1	95	.886	8.14	6.43
2018	2 Tms	NL	50	1	12	54.2	233	52	35	32	6	0	2	3	22	1	54	6	4	1	.800	0-0	6	95	.729	4.13	5.27
2021	Mil	NL	1	0	0	0.1	5	2	2	2	0	0	0	1	1	0	0	0	0	0	-	0-0	0	94	1.467	71.88	54.00
13	Mil	NL	62	0	13	54.2	245	62	29	27	10	3	1	1	23	3	54	5	6	7	.462	0-6	19	95	.816	5.53	4.45
13	StL	NL	13	0	3	10.1	44	11	3	2	0	1	0	1	3	0	11	0	1	0	1.000	0-1	0	96	.682	3.75	1.74
14	Cle	AL	49	0	24	43.2	196	34	21	19	6	3	3	1	30	3	51	4	2	3	.400	10-13	2	95	.702	4.11	3.92
14	Pit	NL	13	0	4	11.0	47	9	5	5	0	0	1	1	6	0	12	1	0	1	.000	0-0	0	96	.648	3.33	4.09
18	Tor	AL	45	1	11	51.0	211	44	27	25	6	0	1	2	20	1	50	6	4	1	.800	0-0	6	95	.680	3.61	4.41
18	LAD	NL	5	0	1	3.2	22	8	8	7	0	0	1	1	2	0	4	0	0	0	-	0-0	0	96	1.222	12.47	17.18
Postseason			12	0	8	12.2	51	7	2	2	1	0	0	0	6	0	18	0	1	0	1.000	3-4	0	96	.499	1.91	1.42
11 ML YEARS			544	1	286	525.2	2305	485	249	228	50	14	18	16	261	19	589	45	38	34	.528	144-182	51	96	.695	4.02	3.90

Akil Baddoo

Bats: L Throws: L Pos: CF-66;LF-56;PR-8;RF-5;DH-5;PH-4   uh-KEEL buh-DOO

Ht: 6'1" **Wt:** 214 **Born:** 8/16/1998 **Age:** 23

Year	Team	Lg	G	AB	H	2B	3B	HR	(Hm	Rd)	TB	R	RBI	RC	TBB	IBB	SO	HBP	SH	SF	SB	CS	GDP	Avg	OBP	Slg	OPS
2021	Det	AL	124	413	107	20	7	13	(6	7)	180	60	55	71	45	1	122	0	0	3	18	4	5	.259	.330	.436	.766

Harrison Bader

Bats: R Throws: R Pos: CF-103

Ht: 6'0" **Wt:** 210 **Born:** 6/3/1994 **Age:** 28

Year	Team	Lg	G	AB	H	2B	3B	HR	(Hm	Rd)	TB	R	RBI	RC	TBB	IBB	SO	HBP	SH	SF	SB	CS	GDP	Avg	OBP	Slg	OPS
2017	StL	NL	32	85	20	3	0	3	(0	3)	32	10	10	10	5	1	24	1	0	1	2	1	1	.235	.283	.376	.659
2018	StL	NL	138	379	100	20	2	12	(2	10)	160	61	37	54	31	3	125	11	2	4	15	3	1	.264	.334	.422	.756
2019	StL	NL	128	347	71	14	3	12	(5	7)	127	54	39	41	46	4	117	10	1	2	11	3	3	.205	.314	.366	.680
2020	StL	NL	50	106	24	7	2	4	(4	0)	47	21	11	16	13	0	40	1	0	0	3	1	2	.226	.336	.443	.779
2021	StL	NL	103	367	98	21	1	16	(3	13)	169	45	50	53	27	6	85	5	0	2	9	4	4	.267	.324	.460	.785
Postseason			9	21	3	0	0	0	(0	0)	3	3	3	0	1	0	13	1	0	1	1	1	0	.143	.208	.143	.351
5 ML YEARS			451	1284	313	65	8	47	(14	33)	535	191	147	174	122	14	391	32	3	10	40	12	11	.244	.323	.417	.739

Javier Baez

Bats: R Throws: R Pos: SS-100;2B-35;PH-8   BYE-ezz

Ht: 6'0" **Wt:** 190 **Born:** 12/1/1992 **Age:** 29

Year	Team	Lg	G	AB	H	2B	3B	HR	(Hm	Rd)	TB	R	RBI	RC	TBB	IBB	SO	HBP	SH	SF	SB	CS	GDP	Avg	OBP	Slg	OPS
2014	ChC	NL	52	213	36	6	0	9	(3	6)	69	25	20	12	15	0	95	1	0	1	5	1	5	.169	.227	.324	.551
2015	ChC	NL	28	76	22	6	0	1	(1	0)	31	4	4	5	4	1	24	0	0	0	1	2	0	.289	.325	.408	.733
2016	ChC	NL	142	421	115	19	1	14	(8	6)	178	50	59	53	15	3	108	11	1	2	12	3	8	.273	.314	.423	.737
2017	ChC	NL	145	469	128	24	2	23	(13	10)	225	75	75	69	30	15	144	1	6	2	10	3	10	.273	.317	.480	.796
2018	ChC	NL	160	606	176	40	9	34	(13	21)	336	101	111	96	29	8	167	5	1	4	21	9	10	.290	.326	.554	.881
2019	ChC	NL	138	531	149	38	4	29	(15	14)	282	89	85	82	28	3	156	0	0	2	11	7	16	.281	.316	.531	.847
2020	ChC	NL	59	222	45	9	1	8	(2	6)	80	27	24	15	7	0	75	4	0	2	3	0	3	.203	.238	.360	.599
2021	2 Tms	NL	138	502	133	18	2	31	(19	12)	248	80	87	77	28	2	184	13	0	3	18	5	12	.265	.319	.494	.813
21	ChC	NL	91	335	83	9	2	22	(14	8)	162	48	65	52	15	1	131	7	0	3	13	3	7	.248	.292	.484	.775
21	NYM	NL	47	167	50	9	0	9	(5	4)	86	32	22	25	13	1	53	6	0	0	5	2	5	.299	.371	.515	.886
Postseason			36	122	27	5	0	5	(4	1)	47	12	14	13	5	0	41	0	0	1	7	0	3	.221	.250	.385	.635
8 ML YEARS			862	3040	804	160	19	149	(74	75)	1449	451	465	409	156	32	953	35	8	15	81	30	69	.264	.307	.477	.783

Pedro Baez

Pitches: R Bats: R Pos: RP-4   BYE-ezz

Ht: 6'0" **Wt:** 232 **Born:** 3/11/1988 **Age:** 34

Year	Team	Lg	G	GS	GF	IP	BFP	H	R	ER	HR	SH	SF	HB	TBB	IBB	SO	WP	W	L	Pct	Sv-Op	Hld	Vel	OPS	ERC	ERA
2021	SgrLnd	AAA	9	1	0	9.2	42	13	6	6	1	0	1	0	2	0	7	0	1	1	.500	0- -	-		.896	5.45	5.59
2014	LAD	NL	20	0	8	24.0	92	16	7	7	3	1	0	0	5	1	18	0	0	0	-	0-0	5	95	.537	1.79	2.63
2015	LAD	NL	52	0	8	51.0	208	47	22	19	4	3	1	1	11	1	60	1	4	2	.667	0-3	11	97	.693	2.87	3.35
2016	LAD	NL	73	0	10	74.0	295	52	27	25	11	4	2	2	22	0	83	3	3	2	.600	0-2	23	97	.615	2.52	3.04

Year Team	Lg	G	GS	GF	IP	BFP	H	R	ER	HR	SH	SF	HB	TBB	IBB	SO	WP	W	L	Pct	Sv-Op	Hld	Vel	OPS	ERC	ERA
2017 LAD	NL	66	0	6	64.0	280	56	24	21	9	0	0	2	29	2	64	1	3	6	.333	0-3	23	97	.728	3.84	2.95
2018 LAD	NL	55	0	8	56.1	237	46	19	18	4	2	2	1	23	2	62	0	4	3	.571	0-1	7	96	.652	2.91	2.88
2019 LAD	NL	71	0	9	69.2	276	43	30	24	6	2	0	4	23	1	69	0	7	2	.778	1-7	25	96	.543	1.97	3.10
2020 LAD	NL	18	0	2	17.0	70	10	8	6	2	0	0	0	7	0	13	0	0	0	-	2-2	6	94	.529	2.01	3.18
2021 Hou	AL	4	0	3	4.1	15	2	1	1	1	0	0	0	1	0	5	1	0	0	-	0-0	0	94	.557	1.63	2.08
Postseason		31	0	1	29.1	125	22	17	13	6	1	1	2	16	1	33	0	1	0	1.000	0-1	4	97	.732	4.23	3.99
8 ML YEARS		359	0	54	360.1	1473	272	138	121	40	9	8	10	121	7	374	6	21	15	.583	3-18	100	96	.630	2.66	3.02

Brandon Bailey

Pitches: R Bats: R Pos: P
Ht: 5'10" Wt: 195 Born: 10/19/1994 Age: 27

Year Team	Lg	G	GS	GF	IP	BFP	H	R	ER	HR	SH	SF	HB	TBB	IBB	SO	WP	W	L	Pct	Sv-Op	Hld	Vel	OPS	ERC	ERA
2020 Hou	AL	5	0	1	7.1	30	6	2	2	1	0	0	1	3	0	4	1	0	0	-	0-0	0	92	.756	4.10	2.45

Bryan Baker

Pitches: R Bats: R Pos: RP-1
Ht: 6'6" Wt: 245 Born: 12/2/1994 Age: 27

Year Team	Lg	G	GS	GF	IP	BFP	H	R	ER	HR	SH	SF	HB	TBB	IBB	SO	WP	W	L	Pct	Sv-Op	Hld	Vel	OPS	ERC	ERA
2021 Buffalo	AAA	38	0	31	40.1	163	18	9	6	1	0	2	3	17	0	46	3	6	1	.857	10--	-	-	.403	1.32	1.34
2021 Tor	AL	1	0	0	1.0	4	1	0	0	0	0	0	0	0	0	1	2	0	0	-	0-0	0	95	.500	1.95	0.00

Alberto Baldonado

Pitches: L Bats: L Pos: RP-14
Ht: 6'4" Wt: 250 Born: 2/1/1993 Age: 29

Year Team	Lg	G	GS	GF	IP	BFP	H	R	ER	HR	SH	SF	HB	TBB	IBB	SO	WP	W	L	Pct	Sv-Op	Hld	Vel	OPS	ERC	ERA
2021 Hrsbrg	AA	6	0	1	8.0	28	4	1	1	1	0	0	0	0	0	11	0	3	0	1.000	0--	-	-	.393	0.83	1.13
2021 Roch	AAA	28	0	6	32.2	135	28	13	12	1	0	1	2	9	0	36	3	3	1	.750	0--	-	-	.630	2.61	3.31
2021 Was	NL	14	0	1	10.2	49	10	10	10	3	1	0	0	7	0	12	1	0	1	.000	0-4	3	94	.818	6.00	8.44

Anthony Banda

Pitches: L Bats: L Pos: RP-30
Ht: 6'2" Wt: 230 Born: 8/10/1993 Age: 28

Year Team	Lg	G	GS	GF	IP	BFP	H	R	ER	HR	SH	SF	HB	TBB	IBB	SO	WP	W	L	Pct	Sv-Op	Hld	Vel	OPS	ERC	ERA
2021 Scrmto	AAA	10	5	0	39.1	189	52	38	30	7	3	1	2	18	0	42	4	3	2	.600	0--	-	-	.914	6.97	6.86
2017 Ari	NL	8	4	1	25.2	115	26	17	17	1	0	0	3	10	1	25	2	2	3	.400	0-0	0	94	.771	3.98	5.96
2018 TB	AL	3	1	1	14.2	56	12	6	6	1	1	1	0	3	0	10	0	1	0	1.000	0-0	0	95	.665	2.32	3.68
2019 TB	AL	3	0	1	4.0	18	6	3	3	0	0	0	0	0	0	2	0	0	0	-	0-0	0	93	.889	4.47	6.75
2020 TB	AL	4	0	3	7.0	36	10	9	8	1	0	0	2	5	0	4	0	1	0	1.000	1-1	0	92	1.127	10.08	10.29
2021 2 Tms	NL	30	0	5	33.2	153	39	18	16	6	0	2	2	13	1	32	3	2	2	.500	0-3	4	94	.831	5.67	4.28
21 NYM	NL	5	0	3	7.1	37	14	8	6	2	0	1	0	1	0	7	1	1	0	1.000	0-1	0	94	1.063	9.93	7.36
21 Pit	NL	25	0	2	26.1	116	25	10	10	4	0	1	2	12	1	25	2	1	2	.333	0-2	4	94	.752	4.61	3.42
5 ML YEARS		48	5	11	85.0	378	93	53	50	9	1	3	7	31	2	73	5	6	5	.545	1-4	4	94	.818	4.80	5.29

Caleb Baragar

Pitches: L Bats: R Pos: RP-25
Ht: 6'3" Wt: 215 Born: 4/9/1994 Age: 28

Year Team	Lg	G	GS	GF	IP	BFP	H	R	ER	HR	SH	SF	HB	TBB	IBB	SO	WP	W	L	Pct	Sv-Op	Hld	Vel	OPS	ERC	ERA
2021 Scrmto	AAA	21	1	3	20.1	111	27	22	20	6	0	4	2	20	0	22	4	3	3	.500	0--	-	-	1.100	10.60	8.85
2020 SF	NL	24	1	2	22.1	88	17	10	10	3	0	1	1	5	0	19	1	5	1	.833	0-1	2	94	.656	2.57	4.03
2021 SF	NL	25	0	5	23.0	98	19	7	4	1	0	2	3	12	2	16	0	2	1	.667	2-3	7	93	.693	3.64	1.57
2 ML YEARS		49	1	7	45.1	186	36	17	14	4	0	3	4	17	2	35	1	7	2	.778	2-4	9	93	.677	3.13	2.78

Daniel Bard

Pitches: R Bats: R Pos: RP-67
Ht: 6'4" Wt: 215 Born: 6/25/1985 Age: 37

Year Team	Lg	G	GS	GF	IP	BFP	H	R	ER	HR	SH	SF	HB	TBB	IBB	SO	WP	W	L	Pct	Sv-Op	Hld	Vel	OPS	ERC	ERA
2009 Bos	AL	49	0	12	49.1	212	41	24	20	5	4	3	3	22	3	63	1	2	2	.500	1-4	13	97	.690	3.43	3.65
2010 Bos	AL	73	0	12	74.2	295	45	18	16	6	2	5	2	30	3	76	2	1	2	.333	3-10	32	98	.548	1.99	1.93
2011 Bos	AL	70	0	10	73.0	288	46	29	27	5	5	0	2	24	3	74	2	2	9	.182	1-6	34	97	.546	1.80	3.33
2012 Bos	AL	17	10	2	59.1	277	60	42	41	9	2	3	8	43	1	38	1	5	6	.455	0-0	0	93	.852	6.55	6.22
2013 Bos	AL	2	0	1	1.0	6	1	1	1	0	0	0	0	2	0	1	0	0	0	-	0-0	0	94	.750	9.51	9.00
2020 Col	NL	23	0	10	24.2	106	22	10	10	2	0	0	3	10	2	27	1	4	2	.667	6-6	2	97	.674	3.73	3.65
2021 Col	NL	67	0	44	65.2	304	69	41	38	8	1	0	7	36	1	80	4	7	8	.467	20-28	4	97	.800	5.51	5.21
Postseason		2	0	1	3.0	8	0	0	0	0	0	0	0	0	0	4	0	0	0	-	0-0	1	98	.000	0.00	0.00
7 ML YEARS		301	10	91	347.2	1488	284	165	153	35	14	11	25	167	13	359	11	21	29	.420	31-54	85	97	.682	3.61	3.96

Joe Barlow

Pitches: R Bats: R Pos: RP-31
Ht: 6'2" Wt: 210 Born: 9/28/1995 Age: 26

Year Team	Lg	G	GS	GF	IP	BFP	H	R	ER	HR	SH	SF	HB	TBB	IBB	SO	WP	W	L	Pct	Sv-Op	Hld	Vel	OPS	ERC	ERA
2021 RdRck	AAA	17	0	11	21.0	79	8	6	6	1	0	0	1	8	0	29	1	0	1	.000	7--	-	-	.415	1.14	2.57
2021 Tex	AL	31	0	18	29.0	111	12	9	5	2	0	2	0	12	0	27	1	0	2	.000	11-12	3	94	.433	1.26	1.55

Scott Barlow

Pitches: R Bats: R Pos: RP-71   Ht: 6'3" Wt: 210 Born: 12/18/1992 Age: 29

		HOW MUCH PITCHED			WHAT HE GAVE UP								THE RESULTS							
Year Team	Lg	G GS GF	IP	BFP	H	R	ER	HR SH SF HB	TBB IBB	SO	WP	W	L	Pct	Sv-Op Hld	Vel	OPS	ERC	ERA
2018 KC	AL	6 0 3	15.0	65	16	7	6	2 0 0 6	3 0	15	0	1	1	.500	0-0 0	91	.679	3.73	3.60
2019 KC	AL	61 0 7	70.1	310	64	33	33	6 2 1 3	37 3	92	5	3	3	.500	1-3 14	94	.735	4.03	4.22
2020 KC	AL	32 0 7	30.0	125	27	14	14	4 0 1 2	9 2	39	2	2	1	.667	2-2 7	95	.693	3.54	4.20
2021 KC	AL	71 0 28	74.1	306	61	20	20	4 0 2 2	28 2	91	4	5	3	.625	16-22 14	95	.626	2.81	2.42
4 ML YEARS		170 0 45	189.2	806	168	74	73	16 2 4 7	77 7	237	11	11	8	.579	19-27 35	94	.682	3.44	3.46

Austin Barnes

Bats: R Throws: R Pos: C-52;PH-22;2B-7;DH-1   Ht: 5'10" Wt: 187 Born: 12/28/1989 Age: 32

					BATTING										RUNNING			AVERAGES			
Year Team	Lg	G	AB	H	2B 3B HR (Hm Rd)	TB	R	RBI	RC	TBB IBB	SO	HBP SH SF			SB CS GDP			Avg	OBP	Slg	OPS
2015 LAD	NL	20	29	6	2 0 0 (0 0)	8	4	1	3	6 0	6	1 1 0			0 0 2			.207	.361	.276	.637
2016 LAD	NL	21	32	5	1 0 0 (0 0)	6	3	2	3	5 0	9	0 0 0			0 0 0			.156	.270	.188	.458
2017 LAD	NL	102	218	63	15 2 8 (6 2)	106	35	38	46	39 1	43	5 0 0			4 1 6			.289	.408	.486	.895
2018 LAD	NL	100	200	41	5 0 4 (2 2)	58	32	14	15	31 4	67	6 1 0			4 3 7			.205	.329	.290	.619
2019 LAD	NL	75	212	43	12 1 5 (4 1)	72	28	25	18	23 3	56	5 0 2			3 0 8			.203	.293	.340	.633
2020 LAD	NL	29	86	21	3 0 1 (1 0)	27	14	9	12	13 0	24	2 2 1			3 0 0			.244	.353	.314	.667
2021 LAD	NL	77	200	43	8 0 6 (3 3)	69	28	23	19	20 1	56	4 1 0			1 0 6			.215	.299	.345	.644
Postseason		37	101	20	2 0 2 (0 2)	28	13	10	7	10 0	30	1 1 1			1 1 2			.198	.274	.277	.552
7 ML YEARS		424	977	222	46 3 24 (16 8)	346	144	112	116	137 9	261	23 5 3			16 4 29			.227	.335	.354	.689

Charlie Barnes

Pitches: L Bats: L Pos: SP-8; RP-1   Ht: 6'2" Wt: 190 Born: 10/1/1995 Age: 26

		HOW MUCH PITCHED			WHAT HE GAVE UP								THE RESULTS							
Year Team	Lg	G GS GF	IP	BFP	H	R	ER	HR SH SF HB	TBB IBB	SO	WP	W	L	Pct	Sv-Op Hld	Vel	OPS	ERC	ERA
2021 StPaul	AAA	16 16 0	76.0	324	73	35	32	7 2 1 6	24 0	62	1	6	4	.600	0-- -	-	.698	3.79	3.79
2021 Min	AL	9 8 1	38.0	175	46	27	25	4 2 1 4	16 0	20	0	0	3	.000	0-0 0	90	.835	5.90	5.92

Jacob Barnes

Pitches: R Bats: R Pos: RP-29   Ht: 6'2" Wt: 231 Born: 4/14/1990 Age: 32

		HOW MUCH PITCHED			WHAT HE GAVE UP								THE RESULTS							
Year Team	Lg	G GS GF	IP	BFP	H	R	ER	HR SH SF HB	TBB IBB	SO	WP	W	L	Pct	Sv-Op Hld	Vel	OPS	ERC	ERA
2021 Buffalo	AAA	14 0 8	14.1	53	7	1	1	0 1 0 0	4 0	10	1	1	0	1.000	2-- -		.378	0.98	0.63
2016 Mil	NL	27 0 7	26.2	106	24	9	8	1 1 0 0	6 1	26	2	0	1	.000	1-1 0	95	.612	2.50	2.70
2017 Mil	NL	73 0 8	72.0	304	57	35	32	8 0 3 3	33 4	80	6	3	4	.429	2-7 24	97	.664	3.31	4.00
2018 Mil	NL	49 0 19	48.2	217	51	24	18	4 1 1 0	23 2	47	4	1	0	1.000	2-4 4	95	.723	4.39	3.33
2019 2 Tms		33 1 6	32.2	160	36	30	27	7 0 2 0	22 1	32	3	1	5	.167	0-0 1	94	.840	6.34	7.44
2020 LAA	AL	18 0 5	18.0	78	19	13	11	1 1 2 2	4 0	24	0	0	2	.000	0-0 1	95	.716	3.77	5.50
2021 2 Tms		29 0 7	28.2	128	31	20	20	7 1 0 1	11 0	33	0	1	2	.333	2-2 1	95	.843	5.60	6.28
19 Mil	NL	18 1 3	19.2	95	22	17	15	3 0 1 0	11 1	22	1	1	1	.500	0-0 1	94	.769	5.40	6.86
19 KC	AL	15 0 3	13.0	65	14	13	12	4 0 1 0	11 0	10	2	0	4	.000	0-0 0	94	.951	7.85	8.31
21 NYM	NL	19 0 6	18.2	79	19	13	13	6 1 0 0	5 0	18	0	1	1	.500	2-2 1	94	.856	5.11	6.27
21 Tor	AL	10 0 1	10.0	49	12	7	7	1 0 0 1	6 0	15	0	0	1	.000	0-0 0	95	.816	6.34	6.30
6 ML YEARS		229 1 52	226.2	993	218	131	116	28 4 9 6	99 8	242	15	5	15	.250	7-14 31	95	.727	4.17	4.61

Matt Barnes

Pitches: R Bats: R Pos: RP-60   Ht: 6'4" Wt: 208 Born: 6/17/1990 Age: 32

		HOW MUCH PITCHED			WHAT HE GAVE UP								THE RESULTS							
Year Team	Lg	G GS GF	IP	BFP	H	R	ER	HR SH SF HB	TBB IBB	SO	WP	W	L	Pct	Sv-Op Hld	Vel	OPS	ERC	ERA
2014 Bos	AL	5 0 3	9.0	39	11	4	4	1 0 1 0	2 0	8	0	0	0	-	0-0 0	94	.861	4.72	4.00
2015 Bos	AL	32 2 7	43.0	199	56	28	26	9 2 0 2	15 0	39	4	3	4	.429	0-0 3	95	.887	6.66	5.44
2016 Bos	AL	62 0 13	66.2	287	62	32	30	6 2 1 3	31 1	71	4	4	3	.571	1-2 16	97	.709	4.06	4.05
2017 Bos	AL	70 0 15	69.2	287	57	31	30	7 1 3 1	28 0	83	3	7	3	.700	1-3 21	95	.655	3.20	3.88
2018 Bos	AL	62 0 8	61.2	265	47	25	25	5 0 2 2	31 1	96	8	6	4	.600	0-3 25	97	.624	3.08	3.65
2019 Bos	AL	70 0 14	64.1	285	51	29	27	8 0 1 2	38 2	110	13	5	4	.556	4-12 26	97	.666	3.81	3.78
2020 Bos	AL	24 0 14	23.0	102	18	13	11	4 1 1 2	14 1	31	4	1	3	.250	9-13 4	96	.706	4.43	4.30
2021 Bos	AL	60 0 44	54.2	222	41	25	23	8 0 1 2	20 2	84	3	5	5	.545	24-30 0	96	.641	3.02	3.79
Postseason		11 0 0	10.1	42	6	2	1	1 0 0 0	6 0	10	2	2	0	1.000	0-0 3	96	.536	2.55	0.87
8 ML YEARS		385 2 118	392.0	1686	343	187	176	48 6 10 14	179 7	522	39	32	26	.552	39-63 95	96	.695	3.85	4.04

Tucker Barnhart

Bats: L Throws: R Pos: C-102;PH-13;1B-2   Ht: 5'11" Wt: 192 Born: 1/7/1991 Age: 31

					BATTING										RUNNING			AVERAGES			
Year Team	Lg	G	AB	H	2B 3B HR (Hm Rd)	TB	R	RBI	RC	TBB IBB	SO	HBP SH SF			SB CS GDP			Avg	OBP	Slg	OPS
2014 Cin	NL	21	54	10	0 0 1 (1 0)	13	3	1	2	4 1	10	0 2 0			0 0 0			.185	.241	.241	.482
2015 Cin	NL	81	242	61	9 0 3 (2 1)	79	23	18	22	25 5	45	2 2 3			0 1 10			.252	.324	.326	.650
2016 Cin	NL	115	377	97	23 1 7 (6 1)	143	34	51	51	36 8	72	2 2 3			1 0 12			.257	.323	.379	.702
2017 Cin	NL	121	370	100	24 2 7 (2 5)	149	26	44	50	42 11	68	3 5 3			4 0 12			.270	.347	.403	.750
2018 Cin	NL	138	460	114	21 3 10 (7 3)	171	50	46	48	54 2	96	2 3 3			0 4 13			.248	.328	.372	.699
2019 Cin	NL	114	316	73	14 0 11 (5 6)	120	32	40	40	44 7	83	2 1 1			1 0 5			.231	.328	.380	.708

Year	Team	Lg	G	AB	H	2B	3B	HR	(Hm	Rd)	TB	R	RBI	RC	TBB	IBB	SO	HBP	SH	SF	SB	CS	GDP	Avg	OBP	Slg	OPS
									BATTING												RUNNING			AVERAGES			
2020	Cin	NL	38	98	20	3	0	5	(4	1)	38	10	13	11	12	0	28	0	0	0	0	0	2	.204	.291	.388	.679
2021	Cin	NL	116	348	86	21	0	7	(6	1)	128	41	48	44	29	1	100	8	0	3	0	0	8	.247	.317	.368	.685
	Postseason		2	5	0	0	0	0	(0	0)	0	0	0	0	0	0	3	0	0	0	0	0	0	.000	.000	.000	.000
	8 ML YEARS		744	2265	561	115	6	51	(33	18)	841	219	261	268	246	35	502	19	15	16	6	5	62	.248	.324	.371	.696

Kyle Barraclough

Pitches: R **Bats:** R **Pos:** RP-10   BAIR-ah-claw   **Ht:** 6'3" **Wt:** 229 **Born:** 5/23/1990 **Age:** 32

Year	Team	Lg	G	GS	GF	IP	BFP	H	R	ER	HR	SH	SF	HB	TBB	IBB	SO	WP	W	L	Pct	Sv-Op	Hld	Vel	OPS	ERC	ERA
			HOW MUCH PITCHED					WHAT HE GAVE UP											THE RESULTS								
2021	S-WB	AAA	11	0	1	14.0	55	5	5	5	2	0	0	0	11	0	24	3	4	0	1.000	0--	-	-	.541	2.55	3.21
2021	StPaul	AAA	21	0	7	25.1	100	15	7	7	4	2	0	1	10	0	38	1	4	1	.800	0--	-	-	.610	2.46	2.49
2015	Mia	NL	25	0	5	24.1	98	12	8	7	1	0	2	0	18	2	30	1	2	1	.667	0-1	6	96	.563	2.25	2.59
2016	Mia	NL	75	0	6	72.2	306	45	24	23	1	2	2	2	44	1	113	8	6	3	.667	0-4	29	96	.538	2.31	2.85
2017	Mia	NL	66	0	12	66.0	286	53	25	22	5	3	4	2	38	3	76	6	6	2	.750	1-5	22	95	.638	3.53	3.00
2018	Mia	NL	61	0	25	55.2	245	40	27	26	8	2	1	5	34	3	60	4	1	6	.143	10-17	10	94	.675	3.84	4.20
2019	2 Tms	NL	43	0	9	33.2	164	38	24	21	9	1	1	2	21	2	40	3	1	2	.333	0-3	8	94	.892	7.02	5.61
2021	Min	AL	10	0	2	13.0	60	12	8	8	4	0	1	2	8	0	18	0	2	0	1.000	0-0	1	93	.877	6.74	5.54
19	Was	NL	33	0	6	25.2	124	33	21	19	8	0	1	2	12	2	30	2	1	2	.333	0-2	8	93	.948	7.83	6.66
19	SF	NL	10	0	3	8.0	40	5	3	2	1	1	0	0	9	0	10	1	0	0	-	0-1	0	94	.692	4.59	2.25
	6 ML YEARS		280	0	59	265.1	1159	200	116	107	28	8	11	13	163	11	337	22	18	14	.563	11-30	76	95	.662	3.67	3.63

Manny Barreda

Pitches: R **Bats:** R **Pos:** RP-3   **Ht:** 5'11" **Wt:** 195 **Born:** 10/8/1988 **Age:** 33

Year	Team	Lg	G	GS	GF	IP	BFP	H	R	ER	HR	SH	SF	HB	TBB	IBB	SO	WP	W	L	Pct	Sv-Op	Hld	Vel	OPS	ERC	ERA
			HOW MUCH PITCHED					WHAT HE GAVE UP											THE RESULTS								
2021	Norfolk	AAA	26	2	6	39.0	169	46	21	17	3	0	4	1	11	0	38	5	2	3	.400	1--	-	-	.775	4.62	3.92
2021	Bal	AL	3	0	2	2.2	14	4	4	4	2	0	0	0	2	0	2	0	1	0	1.000	0-0	0	94	1.262	14.59	13.50

Luis Barrera

Bats: L **Throws:** L **Pos:** LF-2;RF-2;CF-1;PH-1;PR-1   **Ht:** 6'0" **Wt:** 195 **Born:** 11/15/1995 **Age:** 26

Year	Team	Lg	G	AB	H	2B	3B	HR	(Hm	Rd)	TB	R	RBI	RC	TBB	IBB	SO	HBP	SH	SF	SB	CS	GDP	Avg	OBP	Slg	OPS
									BATTING												RUNNING			AVERAGES			
2021	LsVgs	AAA	96	341	94	16	6	4	(-	-)	134	53	37	-	39	0	67	1	1	4	10	2	7	.276	.348	.393	.741
2021	Oak	AL	6	8	2	0	0	0	(0	0)	2	1	0	1	0	0	2	0	0	0	0	0	0	.250	.250	.250	.500

Tres Barrera

Bats: R **Throws:** R **Pos:** C-29;PH-1   **Ht:** 6'0" **Wt:** 206 **Born:** 9/15/1994 **Age:** 27

Year	Team	Lg	G	AB	H	2B	3B	HR	(Hm	Rd)	TB	R	RBI	RC	TBB	IBB	SO	HBP	SH	SF	SB	CS	GDP	Avg	OBP	Slg	OPS
									BATTING												RUNNING			AVERAGES			
2021	Roch	AAA	51	162	34	5	0	3	(-	-)	48	14	17	-	22	0	40	2	1	3	0	0	6	.210	.307	.296	.603
2019	Was	NL	2	2	0	0	0	0	(0	0)	0	0	0	0	0	0	0	0	0	0	0	0	0	.000	.000	.000	.000
2021	Was	NL	30	91	24	3	1	2	(1	1)	35	8	10	14	12	2	22	4	0	0	0	0	3	.264	.374	.385	.758
	2 ML YEARS		32	93	24	3	1	2	(1	1)	35	8	10	14	12	2	22	4	0	0	0	0	3	.258	.367	.376	.743

Jose Barrero

Bats: R **Throws:** R **Pos:** SS-9;CF-7;PH-6;2B-2   **Ht:** 6'2" **Wt:** 175 **Born:** 4/5/1998 **Age:** 24

Year	Team	Lg	G	AB	H	2B	3B	HR	(Hm	Rd)	TB	R	RBI	RC	TBB	IBB	SO	HBP	SH	SF	SB	CS	GDP	Avg	OBP	Slg	OPS
									BATTING												RUNNING			AVERAGES			
2018	Dayton	A	125	482	118	22	4	6	(-	-)	166	61	53	51	19	0	112	12	3	1	13	9	11	.245	.290	.344	.634
2019	Dytona	A+	104	404	113	37	1	8	(-	-)	176	58	55	66	25	1	83	17	0	6	15	2	13	.280	.343	.436	.779
2021	Chatt	AA	40	160	48	9	1	6	(-	-)	77	31	28	-	16	0	40	2	0	2	8	1	7	.300	.367	.481	.848
2021	Lsvlle	AAA	45	170	52	10	0	13	(-	-)	101	31	38	-	20	1	44	6	1	3	8	3	6	.306	.392	.594	.986
2020	Cin	NL	24	67	13	0	0	0	(0	0)	13	4	2	0	1	0	26	0	0	0	1	1	1	.194	.206	.194	.400
2021	Cin	NL	21	50	10	4	1	0	(0	0)	16	4	3	5	3	0	17	3	0	0	1	0	2	.200	.286	.320	.606
	Postseason		1	0	0	0	0	0	(0	0)	0	0	0	0	0	0	0	0	0	0	0	0	0	.000	.000	.000	.000
	2 ML YEARS		45	117	23	4	1	0	(0	0)	29	8	5	5	4	0	43	3	0	0	2	1	3	.197	.242	.248	.490

Franklin Barreto

Bats: R **Throws:** R **Pos:** 2B   **Ht:** 5'10" **Wt:** 208 **Born:** 2/27/1996 **Age:** 26

Year	Team	Lg	G	AB	H	2B	3B	HR	(Hm	Rd)	TB	R	RBI	RC	TBB	IBB	SO	HBP	SH	SF	SB	CS	GDP	Avg	OBP	Slg	OPS
									BATTING												RUNNING			AVERAGES			
2017	Oak	AL	25	71	14	1	2	2	(1	1)	25	10	6	5	5	0	33	0	0	0	2	0	1	.197	.250	.352	.602
2018	Oak	AL	32	73	17	4	0	5	(1	4)	36	10	16	11	1	0	29	1	0	0	0	0	3	.233	.253	.493	.746
2019	Oak	AL	23	57	7	2	0	2	(1	1)	15	6	5	1	1	0	23	0	0	0	1	0	0	.123	.138	.263	.401
2020	2 Tms	AL	21	27	2	0	0	0	(0	0)	2	5	2	0	0	0	15	1	0	0	1	0	0	.074	.107	.074	.181
20	Oak	AL	15	10	0	0	0	0	(0	0)	0	5	0	0	0	0	7	0	0	0	0	0	0	.000	.000	.000	.000
20	LAA	AL	6	17	2	0	0	0	(0	0)	2	0	2	0	0	0	8	1	0	0	1	0	0	.118	.167	.118	.284
	4 ML YEARS		101	228	40	7	2	9	(3	6)	78	31	29	17	7	0	100	2	0	0	4	0	4	.175	.207	.342	.549

Jaime Barria

Pitches: R Bats: R Pos: SP-11; RP-2
HIGH-may
Ht: 6'1" Wt: 210 Born: 7/18/1996 Age: 25

Year	Team	Lg	G	GS	GF	IP	BFP	H	R	ER	HR	SH	SF	HB	TBB	IBB	SO	WP	W	L	Pct	Sv-Op	Hld	Vel	OPS	ERC	ERA
2021	Salt Lk	AAA	10	10	0	49.0	210	54	30	24	10	0	1	1	8	0	34	0	3	2	.600	0- --	-	-	.795	4.39	4.41
2018	LAA	AL	26	26	0	129.1	537	117	50	49	17	0	0	6	47	0	98	3	10	9	.526	0-0	0	91	.719	3.89	3.41
2019	LAA	AL	19	13	1	82.2	365	92	61	59	24	0	2	2	27	0	75	1	4	10	.286	0-0	0	92	.903	5.85	6.42
2020	LAA	AL	7	5	2	32.1	132	27	13	13	3	0	1	1	9	1	27	0	1	0	1.000	0-0	0	92	.685	2.76	3.62
2021	LAA	AL	13	11	0	56.2	250	70	29	29	8	0	1	2	19	0	35	0	2	4	.333	0-0	0	93	.838	5.77	4.61
4 ML YEARS			65	55	3	301.0	1284	306	153	150	52	0	4	11	102	1	235	4	17	23	.425	0-0	0	92	.791	4.63	4.49

Joey Bart

Bats: R Throws: R Pos: C-1;PH-1
Ht: 6'2" Wt: 238 Born: 12/15/1996 Age: 25

Year	Team	Lg	G	AB	H	2B	3B	HR	(Hm	Rd)	TB	R	RBI	RC	TBB	IBB	SO	HBP	SH	SF	SB	CS	GDP	Avg	OBP	Slg	OPS
2018	2 Tms	Low	51	204	60	15	3	13	(-	-)	120	38	40	42	13	2	47	10	0	1	2	1	9	.294	.364	.588	.952
2019	SnJos	A+	57	234	62	10	2	12	(-	-)	112	37	37	36	14	0	50	3	0	0	5	2	10	.265	.315	.479	.793
2019	Rchmd	AA	22	79	25	4	1	4	(-	-)	43	9	11	14	7	1	21	0	0	1	0	0	2	.316	.368	.544	.912
2021	Scrmto	AAA	65	249	73	15	0	10	(-	-)	118	37	46	-	21	0	81	5	0	1	0	0	7	.293	.359	.474	.833
2020	SF	NL	33	103	24	5	2	0	(0	0)	33	15	7	8	3	0	41	5	0	0	0	0	1	.233	.288	.320	.609
2021	SF	NL	2	6	2	0	0	0	(0	0)	2	1	1	1	0	0	2	0	0	0	0	0	0	.333	.333	.333	.667
2 ML YEARS			35	109	26	5	2	0	(0	0)	35	16	8	9	3	0	43	5	0	0	0	0	1	.239	.291	.321	.612

Anthony Bass

Pitches: R Bats: R Pos: RP-69; SP-1
Ht: 6'2" Wt: 200 Born: 11/1/1987 Age: 34

Year	Team	Lg	G	GS	GF	IP	BFP	H	R	ER	HR	SH	SF	HB	TBB	IBB	SO	WP	W	L	Pct	Sv-Op	Hld	Vel	OPS	ERC	ERA
2011	SD	NL	27	3	6	48.1	198	41	9	9	3	2	0	1	21	1	24	1	2	0	1.000	0-0	4	93	.655	3.28	1.68
2012	SD	NL	24	15	3	97.0	411	89	59	51	10	2	2	1	39	3	80	5	2	8	.200	1-1	1	92	.719	3.65	4.73
2013	SD	NL	24	0	9	42.0	193	51	26	25	4	1	0	0	20	4	31	5	0	0	-	0-0	0	92	.829	5.41	5.36
2014	Hou	AL	21	0	8	27.0	119	32	20	19	6	0	1	2	7	1	7	2	1	1	.500	2-4	5	94	.840	5.74	6.33
2015	Tex	AL	33	0	9	64.0	272	66	33	32	5	3	3	1	20	1	45	1	0	0	-	0-1	0	93	.756	3.81	4.50
2017	Tex	AL	2	0	1	5.2	31	14	9	9	1	0	1	0	0	0	1	1	0	0	-	0-0	0	92	1.152	12.41	14.29
2018	ChC	NL	16	0	3	15.1	62	18	6	5	1	0	0	0	3	0	14	2	0	0	-	0-0	3	94	.729	4.26	2.93
2019	Sea	AL	44	0	14	48.0	189	30	20	19	5	2	1	1	17	2	43	6	2	4	.333	5-10	6	95	.560	2.04	3.56
2020	Tor	AL	26	0	14	25.2	100	17	13	10	2	1	0	0	9	2	21	0	2	3	.400	7-9	3	95	.563	1.97	3.51
2021	Mia	NL	70	1	12	61.1	260	55	33	26	11	2	3	3	24	6	58	0	3	9	.250	0-4	19	95	.743	4.07	3.82
Postseason			1	0	1	1.0	4	0	0	0	0	0	0	0	2	0	1	0	0	0	-	0-0	0	95	.500	4.48	0.00
10 ML YEARS			287	19	79	434.1	1835	413	228	205	48	13	11	9	160	20	324	23	12	25	.324	15-29	40	93	.724	3.79	4.25

Chris Bassitt

Pitches: R Bats: R Pos: SP-27
Ht: 6'5" Wt: 217 Born: 2/22/1989 Age: 33

Year	Team	Lg	G	GS	GF	IP	BFP	H	R	ER	HR	SH	SF	HB	TBB	IBB	SO	WP	W	L	Pct	Sv-Op	Hld	Vel	OPS	ERC	ERA
2014	CWS	AL	6	5	1	29.2	137	34	13	13	0	0	1	3	13	1	21	0	1	1	.500	0-0	0	92	.721	4.57	3.94
2015	Oak	AL	18	13	3	86.0	361	78	36	34	5	1	1	9	30	0	64	5	1	8	.111	0-0	0	93	.684	3.55	3.56
2016	Oak	AL	5	5	0	28.0	133	35	20	19	5	0	0	0	14	0	23	2	0	2	.000	0-0	0	93	.856	6.44	6.11
2018	Oak	AL	11	7	0	47.2	204	40	21	16	4	0	0	4	19	0	41	2	2	3	.400	0-0	0	92	.624	3.37	3.02
2019	Oak	AL	28	25	2	144.0	612	125	66	61	21	2	5	13	47	0	141	3	10	5	.667	0-0	0	94	.698	3.68	3.81
2020	Oak	AL	11	11	0	63.0	261	56	18	16	6	1	1	2	17	0	55	2	5	2	.714	0-0	0	93	.659	3.05	2.29
2021	Oak	AL	27	27	0	157.1	637	127	55	55	15	0	4	11	39	1	159	5	12	4	.750	0-0	0	93	.626	2.71	3.15
Postseason			2	2	0	11.0	48	15	4	4	2	0	0	0	1	0	9	1	1	0	1.000	0-0	0	93	.780	5.49	3.27
7 ML YEARS			106	93	6	555.2	2345	495	229	214	56	5	12	42	179	2	504	19	31	25	.554	0-0	0	93	.676	3.46	3.47

Brett Baty

Bats: L Throws: R Pos: 3B
Ht: 6'3" Wt: 210 Born: 11/13/1999 Age: 22

Year	Team	Lg	G	AB	H	2B	3B	HR	(Hm	Rd)	TB	R	RBI	RC	TBB	IBB	SO	HBP	SH	SF	SB	CS	GDP	Avg	OBP	Slg	OPS
2021	Bklyn	A+	51	181	56	14	1	7	(-	-)	93	27	34	0	24	0	53	3	0	1	4	3	0	.309	.397	.514	.911
2021	Bnghtn	AA	41	153	41	8	0	5	(-	-)	64	16	22	0	22	0	46	1	0	2	2	0	8	.268	.360	.418	.778

Trevor Bauer

Pitches: R Bats: R Pos: SP-17
Ht: 6'1" Wt: 205 Born: 1/17/1991 Age: 31

Year	Team	Lg	G	GS	GF	IP	BFP	H	R	ER	HR	SH	SF	HB	TBB	IBB	SO	WP	W	L	Pct	Sv-Op	Hld	Vel	OPS	ERC	ERA
2012	Ari	NL	4	4	0	16.1	77	14	13	11	2	1	1	1	13	0	17	2	1	2	.333	0-0	0	92	.795	5.12	6.06
2013	Cle	AL	4	4	0	17.0	81	15	11	10	3	0	1	1	16	0	11	1	1	2	.333	0-0	0	93	.840	6.47	5.29
2014	Cle	AL	26	26	0	153.0	663	151	76	71	16	1	8	11	60	4	143	6	5	8	.385	0-0	0	94	.737	4.27	4.18
2015	Cle	AL	31	30	1	176.0	744	152	90	89	23	4	5	6	79	1	170	7	11	12	.478	0-0	0	93	.713	3.86	4.55
2016	Cle	AL	35	28	3	190.0	811	179	96	90	20	4	7	9	70	1	168	3	12	8	.600	0-0	0	94	.712	3.85	4.26
2017	Cle	AL	32	31	1	176.1	749	181	84	82	25	1	3	5	60	0	196	3	17	9	.654	0-0	0	94	.774	4.46	4.19
2018	Cle	AL	28	27	1	175.1	717	134	51	43	9	2	3	8	57	2	221	12	12	6	.667	1-1	0	95	.582	2.41	2.21
2019	2 Tms		34	34	0	213.0	911	184	118	106	34	5	5	19	82	0	253	10	11	13	.458	0-0	0	95	.743	4.00	4.48
2020	Cin	NL	11	11	0	73.0	278	41	17	14	9	0	0	3	17	1	100	2	5	4	.556	0-0	0	94	.522	**1.59**	**1.73**
2021	LAD	NL	17	17	0	107.2	432	71	36	31	19	2	0	3	37	1	137	3	8	5	.615	0-0	0	94	.632	2.61	2.59

Year Team	Lg	G	GS	GF	IP	BFP	H	R	ER	HR	SH	SF	HB	TBB	IBB	SO	WP	W	L	Pct	Sv-Op	Hld	Vel	OPS	ERC	ERA
19 Cle	AL	24	24	0	156.2	664	127	76	66	22	2	3	14	63	0	185	8	9	8	.529	0-0	0	95	.707	3.65	3.79
19 Cin	NL	10	10	0	56.1	247	57	42	40	12	3	2	5	19	0	68	2	2	5	.286	0-0	0	94	.841	5.02	6.39
Postseason		11	7	1	33.2	143	33	16	11	4	0	1	1	8	1	44	1	1	4	.200	0-1	0	94	.715	3.45	2.94
10 ML YEARS		222	212	6	1297.2	5463	1122	592	547	160	21	29	66	491	10	1416	50	83	69	.546	1-1	0	94	.699	3.60	3.79

Jake Bauers

Bats: L Throws: L Pos: 1B-54;PH-30;RF-23;LF-21;DH-7;PR-1   Ht: 6'1" Wt: 195 Born: 10/6/1995 Age: 26

Year Team	Lg	G	AB	H	2B	3B	HR	(Hm	Rd)	TB	R	RBI	RC	TBB	IBB	SO	HBP	SH	SF	SB	CS	GDP	Avg	OBP	Slg	OPS
2018 TB	AL	96	323	65	22	2	11	(7	4)	124	48	48	45	54	0	104	3	2	6	6	6	3	.201	.316	.384	.700
2019 Cle	AL	117	372	84	16	1	12	(5	7)	138	46	43	44	45	0	115	3	0	3	3	3	3	.226	.312	.371	.683
2021 2 Tms		115	282	59	7	0	4	(1	3)	78	27	19	22	30	1	78	2	0	0	6	1	1	.209	.290	.277	.566
21 Cle	AL	43	100	19	3	0	2	(0	2)	28	7	6	5	12	1	27	0	0	0	0	1	0	.190	.277	.280	.557
21 Sea	AL	72	182	40	4	0	2	(1	1)	50	20	13	17	18	0	51	2	0	0	6	0	1	.220	.297	.275	.572
3 ML YEARS		328	977	208	45	3	27	(13	14)	340	121	110	111	129	1	297	8	2	9	15	10	7	.213	.307	.348	.655

Mike Baumann

Pitches: R Bats: R Pos: RP-4   Ht: 6'4" Wt: 235 Born: 9/10/1995 Age: 26

Year Team	Lg	G	GS	GF	IP	BFP	H	R	ER	HR	SH	SF	HB	TBB	IBB	SO	WP	W	L	Pct	Sv-Op	Hld	Vel	OPS	ERC	ERA
2021 Bowie	AA	10	10	0	38.2	162	29	26	21	6	1	0	1	18	0	39	3	3	2	.600	0- -	-		.671	3.42	4.89
2021 Norfolk	AAA	6	6	0	27.0	108	18	6	6	0	0	2	0	13	0	26	3	1	1	.500	0- -	-		.513	2.06	2.00
2021 Bal	AL	4	0	0	10.0	50	13	12	11	2	0	0	1	6	0	5	0	1	1	.500	0-0	1	94	.958	7.84	9.90

Shane Baz

Pitches: R Bats: R Pos: SP-3   Ht: 6'2" Wt: 190 Born: 6/17/1999 Age: 23

Year Team	Lg	G	GS	GF	IP	BFP	H	R	ER	HR	SH	SF	HB	TBB	IBB	SO	WP	W	L	Pct	Sv-Op	Hld	Vel	OPS	ERC	ERA
2017 Pirates	R	10	10	0	23.2	105	26	12	10	2	0	0	1	14	0	19	5	0	3	.000	0- -	-		.768	5.73	3.80
2018 2 Tms	Low	12	11	0	52.1	244	56	30	26	3	0	1	3	29	0	59	11	4	5	.444	0- -	-		.787	4.89	4.47
2019 BG	A	17	17	0	81.1	342	63	30	27	5	2	6	10	37	0	87	16	3	2	.600	0- -	-		.399	3.32	2.99
2021 Mont	AA	7	7	0	32.2	120	22	9	9	3	0	0	2	2	0	49	1	2	4	.333	0- -	-		.510	1.53	2.48
2021 Drham	AAA	10	10	0	46.0	178	28	10	9	6	1	0	5	11	0	64	2	3	0	1.000	0- -	-		.553	2.09	1.76
2021 TB	AL	3	3	0	13.1	49	6	3	3	3	0	0	0	3	0	18	1	2	0	1.000	0-0	0	97	.531	1.46	2.03

Eduard Bazardo

Pitches: R Bats: R Pos: RP-2   Ht: 6'0" Wt: 165 Born: 9/1/1995 Age: 26

Year Team	Lg	G	GS	GF	IP	BFP	H	R	ER	HR	SH	SF	HB	TBB	IBB	SO	WP	W	L	Pct	Sv-Op	Hld	Vel	OPS	ERC	ERA
2021 Wrcstr	AAA	11	0	4	11.1	57	16	11	11	3	0	1	2	5	0	12	1	1	1	.500	3- -	-		1.097	8.77	8.74
2021 Bos	AL	2	0	1	3.0	12	1	0	0	0	0	0	0	2	0	3	0	0	0	-	0-0	0	94	.450	1.26	0.00

Jeremy Beasley

Pitches: R Bats: R Pos: RP-8   Ht: 6'3" Wt: 235 Born: 11/20/1995 Age: 26

Year Team	Lg	G	GS	GF	IP	BFP	H	R	ER	HR	SH	SF	HB	TBB	IBB	SO	WP	W	L	Pct	Sv-Op	Hld	Vel	OPS	ERC	ERA
2021 Buffalo	AAA	17	2	3	18.2	84	13	7	6	0	1	1	1	15	0	26	1	3	0	1.000	0- -	-		.652	3.35	2.89
2020 Ari	NL	1	0	1	0.1	3	2	0	0	0	0	0	0	0	1	0	0	0	0	-	0-0	0	92	1.667	39.65	0.00
2021 Tor	AL	8	0	6	9.1	47	7	9	8	3	0	1	2	9	2	13	2	0	1	.000	0-0	0	95	.869	6.90	7.71
2 ML YEARS		9	0	7	9.2	50	9	9	8	3	0	1	2	9	2	14	2	0	1	.000	0-0	0	95	.926	7.79	7.45

Matt Beaty

Bats: L Throws: R Pos: PH-62;LF-28;1B-21;RF-20;3B-5;DH-2;PR-2   Ht: 6'0" Wt: 215 Born: 4/28/1993 Age: 29

Year Team	Lg	G	AB	H	2B	3B	HR	(Hm	Rd)	TB	R	RBI	RC	TBB	IBB	SO	HBP	SH	SF	SB	CS	GDP	Avg	OBP	Slg	OPS
2019 LAD	NL	99	249	66	19	1	9	(5	4)	114	36	46	42	17	2	33	2	0	0	5	0	6	.265	.317	.458	.775
2020 LAD	NL	21	50	11	1	0	2	(0	2)	18	8	5	5	2	0	14	2	0	0	0	0	3	.220	.278	.360	.638
2021 LAD	NL	120	204	55	4	1	7	(4	3)	82	35	40	37	20	0	44	10	0	0	2	2	3	.270	.363	.402	.765
Postseason		6	8	3	0	0	0	(0	0)	3	1	0	1	1	0	1	2	0	0	0	0	0	.375	.545	.375	.920
3 ML YEARS		240	503	132	24	2	18	(9	9)	214	79	91	84	39	2	91	14	0	0	7	2	12	.262	.333	.425	.758

David Bednar

Pitches: R Bats: L Pos: RP-61   Ht: 6'1" Wt: 245 Born: 10/10/1994 Age: 27

Year Team	Lg	G	GS	GF	IP	BFP	H	R	ER	HR	SH	SF	HB	TBB	IBB	SO	WP	W	L	Pct	Sv-Op	Hld	Vel	OPS	ERC	ERA
2019 SD	NL	13	0	4	11.0	48	10	8	8	3	2	1	0	5	0	14	0	0	2	.000	0-0	2	95	.876	4.89	6.55
2020 SD	NL	4	0	3	6.1	32	11	6	5	1	0	0	0	2	0	5	0	0	0	-	0-0	0	96	.973	8.59	7.11
2021 Pit	NL	61	0	24	60.2	237	40	15	15	5	0	1	1	19	2	77	1	3	1	.750	3-5	13	97	.577	1.96	2.23
3 ML YEARS		78	0	31	78.0	317	61	29	28	9	2	2	1	26	2	96	1	3	3	.500	3-5	15	96	.660	2.78	3.23

Cam Bedrosian

Pitches: R Bats: R Pos: RP-25; SP-1   beh-DROH-zhee-ann   **Ht:** 6'1" **Wt:** 225 **Born:** 10/2/1991 **Age:** 30

Year	Team	Lg		HOW MUCH PITCHED					WHAT HE GAVE UP											THE RESULTS					
			G	GS	GF	IP	BFP	H	R	ER	HR	SH	SF	HB	TBB	IBB	SO	WP	W	L	Pct	Sv-Op	Hld	Vel	OPS	ERC	ERA
2021	LV	AAA	16	0	7	20.0	84	18	7	5	1	1	0	0	7	0	20	1	2	2	.500	2- -	-	-	.665	2.98	2.25
2014	LAA	AL	17	0	4	19.1	93	23	17	14	2	0	1	0	12	1	20	1	0	1	.000	0-1	1	94	.801	5.88	6.52
2015	LAA	AL	34	0	10	33.1	156	40	21	20	3	1	2	2	19	2	34	2	1	0	1.000	0-0	1	94	.833	6.05	5.40
2016	LAA	AL	45	0	9	40.1	162	30	7	5	1	0	1	2	14	1	51	3	2	0	1.000	1-2	7	95	.532	2.25	1.12
2017	LAA	AL	48	0	13	44.2	190	41	26	22	5	1	1	0	17	1	53	7	6	5	.545	6-11	10	94	.705	3.56	4.43
2018	LAA	AL	71	0	7	64.0	271	63	30	27	7	1	1	2	26	0	57	1	5	4	.556	1-8	10	93	.738	4.31	3.80
2019	LAA	AL	59	7	5	61.1	258	48	30	22	7	0	1	3	22	0	64	9	3	3	.500	1-3	15	93	.619	2.96	3.23
2020	LAA	AL	11	0	3	14.2	58	10	4	4	0	0	1	0	6	0	11	1	0	0	-	0-0	0	92	.531	1.90	2.45
2021	3 Tms		26	1	8	25.0	116	27	14	14	0	0	2	0	17	0	23	0	0	0	-	0-1	1	93	.864	6.86	5.04
21	Cin	NL	6	0	2	5.2	33	10	7	7	2	0	2	0	6	0	7	0	0	0	-	0-0	0	93	1.165	14.39	11.12
21	Oak	AL	9	0	4	9.0	38	9	2	2	2	0	0	0	4	0	8	0	0	0	-	0-0	0	93	.783	5.32	2.00
21	Phi	NL	11	1	2	10.1	45	8	5	5	2	0	0	0	7	0	8	0	0	0	-	0-1	1	93	.728	4.59	4.35
8 ML YEARS			311	8	59	302.2	1304	282	149	128	31	3	10	8	133	5	313	24	17	13	.567	9-26	45	94	.701	3.96	3.81

Tyler Beede

Pitches: R Bats: R Pos: RP-1   **Ht:** 6'2" **Wt:** 216 **Born:** 5/23/1993 **Age:** 29

Year	Team	Lg		HOW MUCH PITCHED					WHAT HE GAVE UP											THE RESULTS					
			G	GS	GF	IP	BFP	H	R	ER	HR	SH	SF	HB	TBB	IBB	SO	WP	W	L	Pct	Sv-Op	Hld	Vel	OPS	ERC	ERA
2021	Scrmto	AAA	16	16	0	48.2	244	50	42	36	7	0	4	6	45	1	50	4	0	6	.000	0- -	-	-	.869	7.17	6.66
2018	SF	NL	2	2	0	7.2	40	9	7	7	0	0	0	0	8	0	9	0	0	1	.000	0-0	0	92	.869	8.41	8.22
2019	SF	NL	24	22	0	117.0	523	127	70	66	22	1	3	5	46	1	113	9	5	10	.333	0-0	0	94	.803	5.29	5.08
2021	SF	NL	1	0	0	1.0	6	2	3	3	0	0	0	1	0	0	2	1	0	0	-	0-0	0	96	1.300	12.01	27.00
3 ML YEARS			27	24	0	125.2	569	138	80	76	22	1	3	7	54	1	124	10	5	11	.313	0-0	0	94	.813	5.49	5.44

Jalen Beeks

Pitches: L Bats: L Pos: P   **Ht:** 5'11" **Wt:** 215 **Born:** 7/10/1993 **Age:** 28

Year	Team	Lg		HOW MUCH PITCHED					WHAT HE GAVE UP											THE RESULTS					
			G	GS	GF	IP	BFP	H	R	ER	HR	SH	SF	HB	TBB	IBB	SO	WP	W	L	Pct	Sv-Op	Hld	Vel	OPS	ERC	ERA
2018	2 Tms	AL	14	1	0	50.2	223	52	31	31	6	1	1	3	24	0	42	0	5	1	.833	0-0	0		.794	4.97	5.51
2019	TB	AL	33	3	5	104.1	464	115	56	50	12	1	5	9	40	1	89	3	6	3	.667	1-1	2	92	.789	5.07	4.31
2020	TB	AL	12	0	3	19.1	78	21	9	7	1	1	0	0	4	0	26	2	1	1	.500	1-1	2	93	.694	3.48	3.26
18	Bos	AL	2	1	0	6.1	34	11	9	9	1	0	0	1	4	0	5	0	0	1	.000	0-0	0	91	1.160	11.16	12.79
18	TB	AL	12	0	0	44.1	189	41	22	22	5	1	1	2	20	0	37	0	5	0	1.000	0-0	0	92	.729	4.20	4.47
3 ML YEARS			59	4	8	174.1	768	188	96	88	19	3	6	12	68	1	157	5	12	5	.706	2-2	4	92	.780	4.86	4.54

Seth Beer

Bats: L Throws: R Pos: DH-3;PH-2;1B-1   **Ht:** 6'3" **Wt:** 213 **Born:** 9/18/1996 **Age:** 25

Year	Team	Lg		BATTING																	RUNNING			AVERAGES			
			G	AB	H	2B	3B	HR	(Hm	Rd)	TB	R	RBI	RC	TBB	IBB	SO	HBP	SH	SF	SB	CS	GDP	Avg	OBP	Slg	OPS
2021	Reno	AAA	100	362	104	33	0	16	(-	-)	185	73	59	-	39	1	76	30	0	4	0	0	7	.287	.398	.511	.909
2021	Ari	NL	5	9	4	1	0	1	(0	1)	8	4	3	4	1	0	3	0	0	0	0	0	0	.444	.500	.889	1.389

Josh Bell

Bats: B Throws: R Pos: 1B-119;PH-17;LF-9;DH-5;RF-1   **Ht:** 6'4" **Wt:** 255 **Born:** 8/14/1992 **Age:** 29

Year	Team	Lg		BATTING																	RUNNING			AVERAGES			
			G	AB	H	2B	3B	HR	(Hm	Rd)	TB	R	RBI	RC	TBB	IBB	SO	HBP	SH	SF	SB	CS	GDP	Avg	OBP	Slg	OPS
2016	Pit	NL	45	128	35	8	0	3	(2	1)	52	18	19	18	21	0	19	0	0	3	0	0	4	.273	.368	.406	.775
2017	Pit	NL	159	549	140	26	6	26	(11	15)	256	75	90	86	66	4	117	1	0	4	2	4	15	.255	.334	.466	.800
2018	Pit	NL	148	501	131	31	4	12	(5	7)	206	74	62	73	77	2	104	0	0	5	2	5	12	.261	.357	.411	.768
2019	Pit	NL	143	527	146	37	3	37	(17	20)	300	94	116	112	74	13	118	5	0	7	0	1	11	.277	.367	.569	.936
2020	Pit	NL	57	195	44	3	0	8	(2	6)	71	22	22	25	22	4	59	2	0	4	0	0	3	.226	.305	.364	.669
2021	Was	NL	144	498	130	24	1	27	(12	15)	237	75	88	69	65	2	101	2	0	3	0	0	22	.261	.347	.476	.823
6 ML YEARS			696	2398	626	129	14	113	(49	64)	1122	358	397	383	325	25	518	10	0	26	4	11	67	.261	.348	.468	.816

Andrew Bellatti

Pitches: R Bats: R Pos: RP-3   bell-LAH-tee   **Ht:** 6'1" **Wt:** 190 **Born:** 8/5/1991 **Age:** 30

Year	Team	Lg		HOW MUCH PITCHED					WHAT HE GAVE UP											THE RESULTS					
			G	GS	GF	IP	BFP	H	R	ER	HR	SH	SF	HB	TBB	IBB	SO	WP	W	L	Pct	Sv-Op	Hld	Vel	OPS	ERC	ERA
2021	Jaxnvl		26	0	18	29.2	115	15	7	5	2	0	1	3	10	1	38	1	1	2	.333	11- -	-	-	.521	1.57	1.52
2015	TB	AL	17	0	6	23.1	95	16	7	6	4	2	1	1	10	0	18	0	3	1	.750	0-0	2	93	.685	3.15	2.31
2021	Mia	NL	3	0	0	3.1	19	6	5	5	0	0	0	0	2	0	4	0	0	0	-	0-0	0	94	.833	8.33	13.50
2 ML YEARS			20	0	6	26.2	114	22	12	11	4	2	1	1	12	0	22	0	3	1	.750	0-0	2	93	.710	3.75	3.71

Cody Bellinger

Bats: L Throws: L Pos: CF-87;RF-7;PH-7;1B-4   **Ht:** 6'4" **Wt:** 203 **Born:** 7/13/1995 **Age:** 26

Year	Team	Lg		BATTING																	RUNNING			AVERAGES			
			G	AB	H	2B	3B	HR	(Hm	Rd)	TB	R	RBI	RC	TBB	IBB	SO	HBP	SH	SF	SB	CS	GDP	Avg	OBP	Slg	OPS
2017	LAD	NL	132	480	128	26	4	39	(19	20)	279	87	97	94	64	13	146	1	0	3	10	3	5	.267	.352	.581	.933
2018	LAD	NL	162	557	145	28	7	25	(11	14)	262	84	76	88	69	9	151	3	0	3	14	1	7	.260	.343	.470	.814
2019	LAD	NL	156	558	170	34	3	47	(27	20)	351	121	115	124	95	21	108	3	0	4	15	5	10	.305	.406	.629	1.035

149

Year Team	Lg	G	AB	H	2B	3B	HR	(Hm	Rd)	TB	R	RBI	RC	TBB	IBB	SO	HBP	SH	SF	SB	CS	GDP	Avg	OBP	Slg	OPS
2020 LAD	NL	56	213	51	10	0	12	(3	9)	97	33	30	34	30	2	42	0	0	0	6	1	4	.239	.333	.455	.789
2021 LAD	NL	95	315	52	9	2	10	(7	3)	95	39	36	23	31	2	94	1	0	2	5	1	2	.165	.240	.302	.542
Postseason		54	201	38	6	3	8	(3	5)	74	24	26	22	20	2	72	0	0	0	9	1	1	.189	.262	.368	.631
5 ML YEARS		601	2123	546	107	16	133	(67	66)	1084	364	354	363	289	47	541	8	0	13	48	11	28	.257	.346	.511	.857

Brandon Belt

Bats: L **Throws:** L **Pos:** 1B-93;PH-11   **Ht:** 6'3" **Wt:** 231 **Born:** 4/20/1988 **Age:** 34

Year Team	Lg	G	AB	H	2B	3B	HR	(Hm	Rd)	TB	R	RBI	RC	TBB	IBB	SO	HBP	SH	SF	SB	CS	GDP	Avg	OBP	Slg	OPS
2011 SF	NL	63	187	42	6	1	9	(2	7)	77	21	18	20	20	1	57	2	0	0	3	2	3	.225	.306	.412	.718
2012 SF	NL	145	411	113	27	6	7	(5	2)	173	47	56	63	54	5	106	3	0	4	12	2	3	.275	.360	.421	.781
2013 SF	NL	150	509	147	39	4	17	(6	11)	245	76	67	82	52	4	125	6	1	3	5	2	4	.289	.360	.481	.841
2014 SF	NL	61	214	52	8	0	12	(2	10)	96	30	27	24	18	2	64	2	0	1	3	1	4	.243	.306	.449	.755
2015 SF	NL	137	492	138	33	5	18	(5	13)	235	73	68	78	56	2	147	4	0	4	9	3	3	.280	.356	.478	.834
2016 SF	NL	156	542	149	41	8	17	(6	11)	257	77	82	105	104	4	148	5	0	4	0	4	7	.275	.394	.474	.868
2017 SF	NL	104	382	92	27	3	18	(8	10)	179	63	51	60	66	2	104	2	0	1	3	2	5	.241	.355	.469	.823
2018 SF	NL	112	399	101	18	2	14	(8	6)	165	50	46	63	49	6	107	6	0	2	4	0	2	.253	.342	.414	.756
2019 SF	NL	156	526	123	32	3	17	(5	12)	212	76	57	72	83	3	127	3	0	4	3	3	6	.234	.339	.403	.742
2020 SF	NL	51	149	46	13	1	9	(7	2)	88	25	30	32	30	1	36	0	0	0	0	0	5	.309	.425	.591	1.015
2021 SF	NL	97	325	89	14	2	29	(13	16)	194	65	59	68	48	3	103	1	0	1	3	2	9	.274	.378	.597	.975
Postseason		37	127	29	2	2	2	(1	1)	41	14	13	16	21	1	40	0	0	3	1	2	0	.228	.331	.323	.654
11 ML YEARS		1232	4136	1092	258	35	167	(67	100)	1921	603	561	667	580	33	1124	40	1	24	46	21	51	.264	.358	.464	.823

Anthony Bemboom

Bats: L **Throws:** R **Pos:** C-7;LF-1   **Ht:** 6'2" **Wt:** 200 **Born:** 1/18/1990 **Age:** 32

Year Team	Lg	G	AB	H	2B	3B	HR	(Hm	Rd)	TB	R	RBI	RC	TBB	IBB	SO	HBP	SH	SF	SB	CS	GDP	Avg	OBP	Slg	OPS
2021 Salt Lk	AAA	40	137	35	6	2	7	(-	-)	66	22	30	-	23	0	33	2	0	3	2	0	6	.255	.364	.482	.845
2021 OkCity	AAA	24	71	14	2	1	1	(-	-)	21	13	7	-	14	0	21	1	0	1	0	0	0	.197	.333	.296	.629
2019 2 Tms	AL	25	54	7	1	0	1	(1	0)	11	2	4	1	1	0	21	0	1	0	0	0	0	.130	.145	.204	.349
2020 LAA	AL	21	48	10	1	0	3	(0	3)	20	9	5	5	7	0	13	2	2	1	0	1	0	.208	.328	.417	.744
2021 LAA	AL	8	27	6	0	0	0	(0	0)	6	2	2	0	1	0	10	0	0	0	0	0	1	.222	.250	.222	.472
19 TB	AL	3	5	2	1	0	0	(0	0)	3	0	1	1	0	0	2	0	0	0	0	0	0	.400	.400	.600	1.000
19 LAA	AL	22	49	5	0	0	1	(1	0)	8	2	3	0	1	0	19	0	1	0	0	0	0	.102	.120	.163	.283
3 ML YEARS		54	129	23	2	0	4	(1	3)	37	13	11	6	9	0	44	2	3	1	0	1	1	.178	.241	.287	.528

Anthony Bender

Pitches: R **Bats:** R **Pos:** RP-59; SP-1   **Ht:** 6'4" **Wt:** 205 **Born:** 2/3/1995 **Age:** 27

		HOW MUCH PITCHED					WHAT HE GAVE UP										THE RESULTS							
Year Team	Lg	G	GS	GF	IP	BFP	H	R	ER	HR	SH	SF	HB	TBB	IBB	SO	WP	W	L	Pct	Sv-Op	Hld	Vel	OPS	ERC	ERA
2021 Mia	NL	60	1	13	61.1	247	45	22	19	5	0	4	6	20	3	71	4	3	2	.600	3-5	12	97	.638	2.62	2.79

Andrew Benintendi

Bats: L **Throws:** L **Pos:** LF-129;PH-5   **Ht:** 5'9" **Wt:** 180 **Born:** 7/6/1994 **Age:** 27

Year Team	Lg	G	AB	H	2B	3B	HR	(Hm	Rd)	TB	R	RBI	RC	TBB	IBB	SO	HBP	SH	SF	SB	CS	GDP	Avg	OBP	Slg	OPS
2016 Bos	AL	34	105	31	11	1	2	(0	2)	50	16	14	20	10	0	25	1	1	1	1	0	0	.295	.359	.476	.835
2017 Bos	AL	151	573	155	26	1	20	(7	13)	243	84	90	96	70	7	112	6	1	8	20	5	16	.271	.352	.424	.776
2018 Bos	AL	148	579	168	41	6	16	(7	9)	269	103	87	105	71	1	106	2	2	7	21	3	9	.290	.366	.465	.830
2019 Bos	AL	138	541	144	40	5	13	(8	5)	233	72	68	88	59	1	140	7	3	5	10	3	6	.266	.343	.431	.774
2020 Bos	AL	14	39	4	1	0	0	(0	0)	5	4	1	1	11	0	17	1	1	2	1	2	1	.103	.314	.128	.442
2021 KC	AL	134	493	136	27	2	17	(5	12)	218	63	73	78	36	0	97	2	1	6	8	9	2	.276	.324	.442	.766
Postseason		21	81	22	5	0	2	(1	1)	33	18	9	13	5	0	17	1	0	0	2	0	2	.272	.322	.407	.729
6 ML YEARS		619	2330	638	146	15	68	(27	41)	1018	342	333	388	257	9	497	19	9	27	61	22	34	.274	.347	.437	.784

Wes Benjamin

Pitches: L **Bats:** R **Pos:** RP-11; SP-2   **Ht:** 6'2" **Wt:** 210 **Born:** 7/26/1993 **Age:** 28

		HOW MUCH PITCHED					WHAT HE GAVE UP										THE RESULTS							
Year Team	Lg	G	GS	GF	IP	BFP	H	R	ER	HR	SH	SF	HB	TBB	IBB	SO	WP	W	L	Pct	Sv-Op	Hld	Vel	OPS	ERC	ERA
2021 RdRck	AAA	14	10	1	45.2	232	70	50	43	6	0	3	0	25	0	42	3	2	5	.286	0--	-	-	.988	8.06	8.47
2020 Tex	AL	8	1	0	22.1	98	24	12	12	4	0	0	0	7	0	21	0	2	1	.667	0-0	0	91	.745	4.60	4.84
2021 Tex	AL	13	2	4	22.2	112	29	23	22	6	0	1	0	17	0	19	1	0	2	.000	0-1	0	91	.953	8.67	8.74
2 ML YEARS		21	3	4	45.0	210	53	35	34	10	0	1	0	24	0	40	1	2	3	.400	0-1	0	91	.853	6.56	6.80

Travis Bergen

Pitches: L **Bats:** L **Pos:** RP-9; SP-1   **Ht:** 6'1" **Wt:** 223 **Born:** 10/8/1993 **Age:** 28

		HOW MUCH PITCHED					WHAT HE GAVE UP										THE RESULTS							
Year Team	Lg	G	GS	GF	IP	BFP	H	R	ER	HR	SH	SF	HB	TBB	IBB	SO	WP	W	L	Pct	Sv-Op	Hld	Vel	OPS	ERC	ERA
2021 Buffalo	AAA	24	0	7	21.2	96	18	8	8	2	1	1	1	15	0	28	0	2	0	1.000	0--	-	-	.717	4.43	3.32
2019 SF	NL	21	0	8	19.2	85	18	12	12	4	0	0	1	9	2	18	1	2	0	1.000	0-0	0	91	.823	4.62	5.49
2020 2 Tms		8	0	2	8.1	36	5	3	3	1	0	0	0	9	0	11	0	1	0	1.000	1-1	0	92	.722	4.93	3.24

Year Team	Lg	G	GS	GF	IP	BFP	H	R	ER	HR	SH	SF	HB	TBB	IBB	SO	WP	W	L	Pct	Sv-Op	Hld	Vel	OPS	ERC	ERA
2021 Tor	AL	10	1	2	10.2	46	5	2	2	1	0	0	2	8	0	6	0	2	0	1.000	0-1	0	92	.576	3.19	1.69
20 Tor	AL	1	0	0	1.2	6	1	0	0	0	0	0	0	1	0	3	0	0	0	-	0-0	0	94	.533	2.46	0.00
20 Ari	NL	7	0	2	6.2	30	4	3	3	1	0	0	0	8	0	8	0	1	0	1.000	1-1	0	92	.764	5.59	4.05
3 ML YEARS		39	1	12	38.2	167	28	17	17	6	0	0	3	26	2	35	1	5	0	1.000	1-2	0	91	.740	4.29	3.96

Jose Berrios

Pitches: R **Bats:** R **Pos:** SP-32

beh-REE-ohs

Ht: 6'0" **Wt:** 205 **Born:** 5/27/1994 **Age:** 28

Year Team	Lg	G	GS	GF	IP	BFP	H	R	ER	HR	SH	SF	HB	TBB	IBB	SO	WP	W	L	Pct	Sv-Op	Hld	Vel	OPS	ERC	ERA
2016 Min	AL	14	14	0	58.1	281	74	56	52	12	2	0	5	35	0	49	1	3	7	.300	0-0	0	93	.932	7.85	8.02
2017 Min	AL	26	25	0	145.2	616	131	71	63	15	3	4	13	48	0	139	7	14	8	.636	0-0	0	93	.693	3.62	3.89
2018 Min	AL	32	32	0	192.1	797	159	83	82	25	2	4	13	61	0	202	0	12	11	.522	0-0	0	93	.665	3.26	3.84
2019 Min	AL	32	32	0	200.1	842	194	94	82	26	2	6	9	51	0	195	8	14	8	.636	0-0	0	93	.707	3.69	3.68
2020 Min	AL	12	12	0	63.0	271	57	28	28	8	0	2	3	26	0	68	5	5	4	.556	0-0	0	94	.701	3.95	4.00
2021 2 Tms	AL	32	32	0	192.0	781	159	83	75	22	2	5	15	45	0	204	3	12	9	.571	0-0	0	94	.661	2.92	3.52
21 Min		20	20	0	121.2	490	95	53	47	14	2	3	8	32	0	126	3	7	5	.583	0-0	0	94	.641	2.76	3.48
21 Tor		12	12	0	70.1	291	64	30	28	8	0	2	7	13	0	78	0	5	4	.556	0-0	0	94	.694	3.22	3.58
Postseason		3	2	0	12.0	52	11	7	5	1	0	0	0	5	0	14	0	0	1	.000	0-0	0	95	.669	3.49	3.75
6 ML YEARS		148	147	0	851.2	3588	774	415	382	108	11	21	58	266	1	857	26	60	47	.561	0-0	0	93	.702	3.67	4.04

Jon Berti

Bats: R **Throws:** R **Pos:** 3B-46;2B-27;PH-16;LF-7;CF-4;SS-2;RF-1

Ht: 5'10" **Wt:** 190 **Born:** 1/22/1990 **Age:** 32

Year Team	Lg	G	AB	H	2B	3B	HR	(Hm	Rd)	TB	R	RBI	RC	TBB	IBB	SO	HBP	SH	SF	SB	CS	GDP	Avg	OBP	Slg	OPS
2018 Tor	AL	4	15	4	1	1	0	(0	0)	7	2	2	2	0	0	4	0	0	0	1	0	0	.267	.267	.467	.733
2019 Mia	NL	73	256	70	14	1	6	(3	3)	104	52	24	37	24	0	73	6	0	1	17	3	2	.273	.348	.406	.755
2020 Mia	NL	39	120	31	5	0	2	(1	1)	42	21	14	22	23	0	37	3	2	1	9	2	1	.258	.388	.350	.738
2021 Mia	NL	85	233	49	10	1	4	(1	3)	73	35	19	22	32	0	61	3	1	2	8	4	7	.210	.311	.313	.624
Postseason		5	17	3	0	0	0	(0	0)	3	1	0	1	2	0	5	2	0	0	2	0	0	.176	.333	.176	.510
4 ML YEARS		201	624	154	30	3	12	(5	7)	226	110	59	83	79	0	175	12	3	4	35	9	10	.247	.341	.362	.703

Dellin Betances

Pitches: R **Bats:** R **Pos:** RP-1

DELL-inn buh-TAN-siss

Ht: 6'8" **Wt:** 265 **Born:** 3/23/1988 **Age:** 34

Year Team	Lg	G	GS	GF	IP	BFP	H	R	ER	HR	SH	SF	HB	TBB	IBB	SO	WP	W	L	Pct	Sv-Op	Hld	Vel	OPS	ERC	ERA
2011 NYY	AL	2	1	0	2.2	16	1	2	2	0	0	1	1	6	0	2	0	0	0	-	0-0	0	93	.625	7.94	6.75
2013 NYY	AL	6	0	3	5.0	26	9	6	6	1	0	0	0	2	0	10	0	0	0	-	0-0	0	96	.965	9.81	10.80
2014 NYY	AL	70	0	8	90.0	341	46	15	14	4	2	3	4	24	1	135	2	5	0	1.000	1-5	22	97	.442	1.24	1.40
2015 NYY	AL	74	0	17	84.0	332	45	17	14	6	1	1	3	40	2	131	9	6	4	.600	9-13	28	97	.510	1.94	1.50
2016 NYY	AL	73	0	20	73.0	299	54	31	25	5	1	1	1	28	0	126	6	3	6	.333	12-17	28	98	.577	2.48	3.08
2017 NYY	AL	66	0	21	59.2	261	29	20	19	3	1	0	11	44	0	100	5	3	6	.333	10-13	19	99	.538	2.86	2.87
2018 NYY	AL	66	0	15	66.2	272	44	22	20	7	3	1	5	26	2	115	4	4	6	.400	4-7	20	98	.578	2.51	2.70
2019 NYY	AL	1	0	0	0.2	2	0	0	0	0	0	0	0	0	0	2	0	0	0	-	0-0	0	94	.000	0.00	0.00
2020 NYM	NL	15	0	2	11.2	59	12	10	10	0	0	0	2	12	0	11	2	0	1	.000	0-0	4	94	.730	6.66	7.71
2021 NYM	NL	1	0	0	1.0	5	0	1	1	0	0	0	1	1	0	1	0	0	0	-	0-0	1	92	.400	3.47	9.00
Postseason		9	0	3	11.0	47	6	4	4	0	0	1	0	7	1	17	1	1	1	.500	0-0	1	98	.482	1.72	3.27
10 ML YEARS		374	1	86	394.1	1613	240	124	111	26	8	7	28	183	5	633	28	21	23	.477	36-55	121	97	.541	2.29	2.53

Alec Bettinger

Pitches: R **Bats:** R **Pos:** RP-3; SP-1

Ht: 6'2" **Wt:** 210 **Born:** 7/13/1995 **Age:** 26

Year Team	Lg	G	GS	GF	IP	BFP	H	R	ER	HR	SH	SF	HB	TBB	IBB	SO	WP	W	L	Pct	Sv-Op	Hld	Vel	OPS	ERC	ERA
2021 Nashv	AAA	20	17	1	92.2	396	100	52	49	15	2	2	2	24	0	94	3	3	6	.333	0--	-		.776	4.47	4.76
2021 Mil	NL	4	1	2	10.0	51	18	15	15	3	1	0	1	3	0	5	1	0	1	.000	0-0	0	92	1.136	10.96	13.50

Mookie Betts

Bats: R **Throws:** R **Pos:** RF-98;CF-30;2B-7;PH-4

Ht: 5'9" **Wt:** 180 **Born:** 10/7/1992 **Age:** 29

Year Team	Lg	G	AB	H	2B	3B	HR	(Hm	Rd)	TB	R	RBI	RC	TBB	IBB	SO	HBP	SH	SF	SB	CS	GDP	Avg	OBP	Slg	OPS
2014 Bos	AL	52	189	55	12	1	5	(1	4)	84	34	18	30	21	0	31	2	1	0	7	3	2	.291	.368	.444	.812
2015 Bos	AL	145	597	174	42	8	18	(9	9)	286	92	77	100	46	2	82	2	3	6	21	6	2	.291	.341	.479	.820
2016 Bos	AL	158	672	214	42	5	31	(17	14)	359	122	113	130	49	1	80	2	0	7	26	4	12	.318	.363	.534	.897
2017 Bos	AL	153	628	166	46	2	24	(8	16)	288	101	102	115	77	9	79	2	0	5	26	3	9	.264	.344	.459	.803
2018 Bos	AL	136	520	180	47	5	32	(13	19)	333	129	80	134	81	8	91	8	0	5	30	6	5	.346	.438	.640	1.078
2019 Bos	AL	150	597	176	40	5	29	(17	12)	313	135	80	118	97	6	101	3	0	9	16	3	11	.295	.391	.524	.915
2020 LAD	NL	55	219	64	9	1	16	(11	5)	123	47	39	52	24	1	38	2	0	1	10	2	1	.292	.366	.562	.927
2021 LAD	NL	122	466	123	29	3	23	(15	8)	227	93	58	80	68	2	86	11	0	5	10	5	5	.264	.367	.487	.854
Postseason		39	159	41	15	0	3	(2	1)	65	31	12	21	20	4	33	1	0	1	8	0	2	.258	.343	.409	.751
8 ML YEARS		971	3888	1152	267	30	178	(91	87)	2013	753	567	759	463	28	588	32	4	38	146	32	48	.296	.373	.518	.890

Joe Biagini

Pitches: R **Bats:** R **Pos:** RP-1

bee-ah-gee-nee

Ht: 6'5" **Wt:** 235 **Born:** 5/29/1990 **Age:** 32

Year	Team	Lg	G	GS	GF	IP	BFP	H	R	ER	HR	SH	SF	HB	TBB	IBB	SO	WP	W	L	Pct	Sv-Op	Hld	Vel	OPS	ERC	ERA
2021	Iowa	AAA	22	19	1	91.2	416	99	57	56	14	1	2	6	43	1	85	5	3	8	.273	0- -	-		.793	5.44	5.50
2016	Tor	AL	60	0	12	67.2	295	69	28	23	3	2	3	5	19	1	62	3	4	3	.571	1-3	8	94	.678	3.52	3.06
2017	Tor	AL	44	18	3	119.2	517	125	78	71	15	0	2	2	42	0	97	6	3	13	.188	1-3	9	94	.752	4.38	5.34
2018	Tor	AL	50	4	7	72.0	328	96	50	48	14	0	1	6	24	0	53	8	4	7	.364	0-0	5	94	.913	7.04	6.00
2019	2 Tms		63	0	15	64.2	281	71	35	33	14	1	0	1	26	3	60	3	3	2	.600	1-3	10	94	.864	5.60	4.59
2020	Hou	AL	4	0	1	4.1	27	10	10	10	1	0	0	4	4	0	4	1	0	0	-	0-0	0	94	1.258	16.51	20.77
2021	ChC	NL	1	0	1	3.0	13	2	0	0	0	1	0	1	1	0	2	0	1	0	1.000	0-0	0	93	.533	2.54	0.00
19	Tor	AL	50	0	11	50.0	212	50	22	21	8	1	0	1	17	3	50	2	3	1	.750	1-3	10	94	.783	4.28	3.78
19	Hou	AL	13	0	4	14.2	69	21	13	12	6	0	0	0	9	0	10	1	0	1	.000	0-0	0	94	1.118	10.95	7.36
	Postseason		6	0	0	7.1	26	3	0	0	0	0	0	0	1	0	6	1	0	0		0-1	0	94	.354	0.55	0.00
	6 ML YEARS		222	22	38	331.1	1461	373	201	185	47	4	6	15	116	4	278	21	15	25	.375	3-9	32	94	.802	5.09	5.03

Bo Bichette

Bats: R **Throws:** R **Pos:** SS-148;DH-11

Ht: 6'0" **Wt:** 185 **Born:** 3/5/1998 **Age:** 24

Year	Team	Lg	G	AB	H	2B	3B	HR	(Hm	Rd)	TB	R	RBI	RC	TBB	IBB	SO	HBP	SH	SF	SB	CS	GDP	Avg	OBP	Slg	OPS
2019	Tor	AL	46	196	61	18	0	11	(3	8)	112	32	21	32	14	0	50	1	0	1	4	4	2	.311	.358	.571	.930
2020	Tor	AL	29	123	37	9	1	5	(3	2)	63	18	23	23	5	1	27	0	0	0	4	1	2	.301	.328	.512	.840
2021	Tor	AL	159	640	191	30	1	29	(15	14)	310	121	102	114	40	0	137	6	0	4	25	1	10	.298	.343	.484	.828
	Postseason		2	6	0	0	0	0	(0 | 0)	0	0	0	1	0	1	0	1	0	0	1	0	0	0	.000	.125	.000	.125
	3 ML YEARS		234	959	289	57	2	45	(21	24)	485	171	146	169	59	1	214	7	0	5	33	6	14	.301	.345	.506	.850

Phil Bickford

Pitches: R **Bats:** R **Pos:** RP-57

Ht: 6'4" **Wt:** 200 **Born:** 7/10/1995 **Age:** 26

Year	Team	Lg	G	GS	GF	IP	BFP	H	R	ER	HR	SH	SF	HB	TBB	IBB	SO	WP	W	L	Pct	Sv-Op	Hld	Vel	OPS	ERC	ERA
2021	OkCity	AAA	5	0	1	5.0	21	5	3	3	0	0	0	0	0	0	12	0	1	0	1.000	0- -	-		.571	1.83	5.40
2020	Mil	NL	1	0	0	1.0	9	4	4	4	0	0	0	2	0	0	2	1	0	0	-	0-0	0	89	1.381	32.97	36.00
2021	2 Tms	NL	57	0	8	51.1	207	36	18	16	7	0	2	3	19	7	59	0	4	2	.667	1-3	9	94	.630	2.67	2.81
21	Mil	NL	1	0	0	1.0	7	2	2	2	1	0	1	1	1	0	0	0	0	0	-	0-0	0	93	1.821	29.25	18.00
21	LAD	NL	56	0	8	50.1	200	34	16	14	6	0	1	2	18	7	59	0	4	2	.667	1-3	9	94	.600	2.33	2.50
	2 ML YEARS		58	0	8	52.1	216	40	22	20	7	0	2	5	19	7	61	1	4	2	.667	1-3	9	94	.659	3.07	3.44

Jesse Biddle

Pitches: L **Bats:** L **Pos:** RP-8

Ht: 6'5" **Wt:** 220 **Born:** 10/22/1991 **Age:** 30

Year	Team	Lg	G	GS	GF	IP	BFP	H	R	ER	HR	SH	SF	HB	TBB	IBB	SO	WP	W	L	Pct	Sv-Op	Hld	Vel	OPS	ERC	ERA
2021	Gwnntt	AAA	31	0	3	31.2	140	28	11	10	3	0	1	4	16	0	51	2	1	1	.500	1- -	-		.671	4.29	2.84
2018	Atl	NL	60	0	14	63.2	266	50	26	22	6	2	1	3	31	5	67	2	6	1	.857	1-4	12	94	.654	3.31	3.11
2019	3 Tms		30	0	3	28.0	152	42	33	26	5	0	2	4	22	1	26	7	0	1	.000	0-1	1	94	.972	9.96	8.36
2020	Cin	NL	1	0	0	0.2	4	1	0	0	0	0	0	0	1	0	1	0	0	0	-	0-0	0	96	.833	10.76	0.00
2021	Atl	NL	8	0	5	10.2	51	10	10	10	1	1	2	2	8	0	11	4	0	0	-	0-0	0	93	.768	5.80	8.44
19	Atl	NL	15	0	1	11.2	64	18	11	7	1	0	0	0	10	1	11	3	0	1	.000	0-0	0	94	.882	8.75	5.40
19	Sea	AL	11	0	1	11.0	60	20	14	12	2	0	2	1	7	0	8	4	0	0	-	0-1	1	94	1.067	11.55	9.82
19	Tex	AL	4	0	1	5.1	28	4	8	7	2	0	0	3	5	0	7	0	0	0	-	0-0	0	93	.979	9.44	11.81
	4 ML YEARS		99	0	22	103.0	473	103	69	58	12	3	5	9	62	6	105	13	6	2	.750	1-5	13	94	.769	5.25	5.07

Shane Bieber

Pitches: R **Bats:** R **Pos:** SP-16

Ht: 6'3" **Wt:** 200 **Born:** 5/31/1995 **Age:** 27

Year	Team	Lg	G	GS	GF	IP	BFP	H	R	ER	HR	SH	SF	HB	TBB	IBB	SO	WP	W	L	Pct	Sv-Op	Hld	Vel	OPS	ERC	ERA
2018	Cle	AL	20	19	0	114.2	485	130	60	58	13	0	4	2	23	0	118	5	11	5	.688	0-0	0	93	.787	4.23	4.55
2019	Cle	AL	34	33	1	214.1	859	186	86	78	31	2	1	6	40	1	259	6	15	8	.652	0-0	0	93	.663	2.94	3.28
2020	Cle	AL	12	12	0	77.1	297	46	15	14	7	0	0	1	21	0	122	1	8	1	.889	0-0	0	94	.494	1.61	1.63
2021	Cle	AL	16	16	0	96.2	405	84	36	34	11	0	1	4	33	0	134	5	7	4	.636	0-0	0	93	.672	3.37	3.17
	Postseason		1	1	0	4.2	25	9	7	7	2	0	0	0	2	0	7	0	0	1	.000	0-0	0	94	1.179	13.07	13.50
	4 ML YEARS		82	80	1	503.0	2046	446	197	184	62	2	6	13	117	1	633	21	41	18	.695	0-0	0	93	.670	3.08	3.29

Brandon Bielak

Pitches: R **Bats:** L **Pos:** RP-26; SP-2

Ht: 6'2" **Wt:** 208 **Born:** 4/2/1996 **Age:** 26

Year	Team	Lg	G	GS	GF	IP	BFP	H	R	ER	HR	SH	SF	HB	TBB	IBB	SO	WP	W	L	Pct	Sv-Op	Hld	Vel	OPS	ERC	ERA
2021	SgrLnd	AAA	6	3	1	17.1	73	16	7	4	0	0	0	1	4	0	22	1	2	0	1.000	0- -	-		.567	2.53	2.08
2020	Hou	AL	12	6	3	32.0	148	39	26	24	9	1	0	2	17	0	26	0	3	3	.500	0-0	0	93	.973	7.84	6.75
2021	Hou	AL	28	2	6	50.0	218	48	29	25	5	2	3	3	21	0	46	4	3	4	.429	1-2	2	94	.714	4.15	4.50
	2 ML YEARS		40	8	9	82.0	366	87	55	49	14	3	3	5	38	0	72	4	6	7	.462	1-2	2	94	.819	5.50	5.38

Cavan Biggio

Bats: L **Throws:** R **Pos:** 3B-52;RF-15;1B-7;2B-7;PR-4;DH-2;PH-2;LF-1
Ht: 6'2" **Wt:** 200 **Born:** 4/11/1995 **Age:** 27

Year	Team	Lg	G	AB	H	2B	3B	HR	(Hm	Rd)	TB	R	RBI	RC	TBB	IBB	SO	HBP	SH	SF	SB	CS	GDP	Avg	OBP	Slg	OPS
2021	Buffalo	AAA	22	77	14	2	0	3	(-	-)	25	15	11	-	11	0	26	1	0	1	0	0	0	.182	.289	.325	.614
2019	Tor	AL	100	354	83	17	2	16	(9	7)	152	66	48	65	71	0	123	2	0	2	14	0	1	.234	.364	.429	.793
2020	Tor	AL	59	220	55	16	0	8	(3	5)	95	41	28	42	41	0	61	3	0	0	6	0	2	.250	.375	.432	.807
2021	Tor	AL	79	250	56	10	1	7	(3	4)	89	27	27	31	37	2	78	1	1	4	3	1	4	.224	.322	.356	.678
	Postseason		2	8	1	1	0	0	(0	0)	2	0	0	0	0	0	6	0	0	0	0	0	0	.125	.125	.250	.375
	3 ML YEARS		238	824	194	43	3	31	(15	16)	336	134	103	138	149	2	262	6	1	6	23	1	6	.235	.354	.408	.762

Braden Bishop

Bats: R **Throws:** R **Pos:** LF-8;PR-1
Ht: 6'1" **Wt:** 178 **Born:** 8/22/1993 **Age:** 28

Year	Team	Lg	G	AB	H	2B	3B	HR	(Hm	Rd)	TB	R	RBI	RC	TBB	IBB	SO	HBP	SH	SF	SB	CS	GDP	Avg	OBP	Slg	OPS
2021	Scrmto	AAA	75	288	94	18	5	12	(-	-)	158	58	43	-	25	0	56	5	0	2	9	3	7	.326	.388	.549	.936
2019	Sea	AL	27	56	6	0	0	0	(0	0)	6	3	4	1	3	0	21	0	1	0	0	0	0	.107	.153	.107	.260
2020	Sea	AL	12	30	5	2	0	0	(0	0)	7	2	4	3	2	0	10	1	1	0	1	0	0	.167	.242	.233	.476
2021	Sea	AL	8	4	1	0	0	0	(0	0)	1	1	0	1	0	0	2	0	1	0	0	0	0	.250	.250	.250	.500
	3 ML YEARS		47	90	12	2	0	0	(0	0)	14	6	8	5	5	0	33	1	3	0	1	0	0	.133	.188	.156	.343

Paul Blackburn

Pitches: R **Bats:** R **Pos:** SP-9
Ht: 6'1" **Wt:** 196 **Born:** 12/4/1993 **Age:** 28

			HOW MUCH PITCHED				WHAT HE GAVE UP										THE RESULTS							
Year	Team	Lg	G	GS	GF	IP	BFP	H	R	ER	HR	SH	SF	HB	TBB	IBB	SO	WP	W	L	Pct	Sv-Op	Hld	Vel	OPS	ERC	ERA
2021	LsVgs	AAA	17	16	0	88.2	400	114	59	49	8	1	3	2	27	0	80	3	4	7	.364	0--	-	-	.803	5.36	4.97
2017	Oak	AL	10	10	0	58.2	238	58	22	21	5	0	0	1	16	0	22	1	3	1	.750	0-0	0	90	.686	3.62	3.22
2018	Oak	AL	6	6	0	27.2	119	33	23	22	2	0	2	2	6	0	19	1	2	3	.400	0-0	0	90	.794	4.62	7.16
2019	Oak	AL	4	1	1	11.0	57	19	14	13	3	1	1	1	4	0	8	1	0	2	.000	0-0	0	91	1.089	10.24	10.64
2020	Oak	AL	1	1	0	2.1	14	5	7	7	0	0	0	0	2	0	2	1	0	1	.000	0-0	0	90	1.083	12.37	27.00
2021	Oak	AL	9	9	0	38.1	175	52	26	25	8	0	0	2	10	0	26	1	1	4	.200	0-0	0	91	.899	6.68	5.87
	5 ML YEARS		30	27	1	138.0	603	167	92	88	18	1	3	6	38	0	77	5	6	11	.353	0-0	0	90	.815	5.26	5.74

Charlie Blackmon

Bats: L **Throws:** L **Pos:** RF-137;PH-15;DH-1
Ht: 6'3" **Wt:** 221 **Born:** 7/1/1986 **Age:** 35

Year	Team	Lg	G	AB	H	2B	3B	HR	(Hm	Rd)	TB	R	RBI	RC	TBB	IBB	SO	HBP	SH	SF	SB	CS	GDP	Avg	OBP	Slg	OPS
2011	Col	NL	27	98	25	1	0	1	(1	0)	29	9	8	10	3	1	8	0	1	0	5	1	2	.255	.277	.296	.573
2012	Col	NL	42	113	32	8	0	2	(1	1)	46	15	9	11	4	0	17	3	1	0	1	2	4	.283	.325	.407	.732
2013	Col	NL	82	246	76	17	2	6	(3	3)	115	35	22	35	7	0	49	3	2	0	7	0	1	.309	.336	.467	.803
2014	Col	NL	154	593	171	27	3	19	(13	6)	261	82	72	87	31	5	96	3	6	5	28	10	3	.288	.335	.440	.775
2015	Col	NL	157	614	176	31	9	17	(7	10)	276	93	58	95	46	2	112	13	5	4	43	13	4	.287	.347	.450	.797
2016	Col	NL	143	578	187	35	5	29	(12	9)	319	111	82	110	43	4	102	13	3	4	17	9	2	.324	.381	.552	.933
2017	Col	NL	159	644	213	35	14	37	(24	13)	387	137	104	151	65	9	135	10	3	3	14	10	4	.331	.399	.601	1.000
2018	Col	NL	156	626	182	31	7	29	(14	15)	314	119	70	110	59	2	134	8	1	2	12	4	10	.291	.358	.502	.860
2019	Col	NL	140	580	182	42	7	32	(22	10)	334	112	86	115	40	1	104	9	0	5	2	5	11	.314	.364	.576	.940
2020	Col	NL	59	221	67	12	1	6	(3	3)	99	31	42	36	19	4	44	2	0	5	2	1	4	.303	.356	.448	.804
2021	Col	NL	150	514	139	25	4	13	(11	2)	211	76	78	86	54	1	91	11	0	3	3	0	8	.270	.351	.411	.761
	Postseason		5	19	2	0	0	0	(0	0)	2	1	2	0	1	0	2	0	1	0	0	0	0	.105	.150	.105	.255
	11 ML YEARS		1269	4827	1450	264	52	191	(111	80)	2391	820	631	846	371	29	892	85	22	31	134	55	53	.300	.359	.495	.854

Alex Blandino

Bats: R **Throws:** R **Pos:** 1B-17;PH-14;3B-9;2B-5;LF-3;SS-1;PR-1
Ht: 6'0" **Wt:** 190 **Born:** 11/6/1992 **Age:** 29

Year	Team	Lg	G	AB	H	2B	3B	HR	(Hm	Rd)	TB	R	RBI	RC	TBB	IBB	SO	HBP	SH	SF	SB	CS	GDP	Avg	OBP	Slg	OPS
2021	Lsvlle	AAA	18	59	6	3	0	0	(-	-)	9	5	3	-	14	0	16	2	0	1	0	0	3	.102	.289	.153	.442
2018	Cin	NL	69	128	30	4	0	1	(1	0)	37	14	8	10	13	1	41	4	2	0	0	0	4	.234	.324	.289	.613
2019	Cin	NL	23	36	9	1	0	1	(1	0)	13	6	3	6	10	0	14	2	0	2	0	0	1	.250	.420	.361	.781
2021	Cin	NL	43	70	14	4	0	0	(0	0)	18	9	5	7	8	0	28	4	0	0	1	0	0	.200	.317	.257	.574
	3 ML YEARS		135	234	53	9	0	2	(1	1)	68	29	16	23	31	1	83	10	2	2	1	0	5	.226	.339	.291	.630

Travis Blankenhorn

Bats: L **Throws:** R **Pos:** PH-16;2B-6;LF-1;RF-1;PR-1
Ht: 6'2" **Wt:** 235 **Born:** 8/3/1996 **Age:** 25

Year	Team	Lg	G	AB	H	2B	3B	HR	(Hm	Rd)	TB	R	RBI	RC	TBB	IBB	SO	HBP	SH	SF	SB	CS	GDP	Avg	OBP	Slg	OPS
2021	Syrcse	AAA	45	151	38	9	0	9	(-	-)	74	22	30	-	27	1	49	2	0	1	3	2	1	.252	.370	.490	.860
2020	Min	AL	1	3	1	0	0	0	(0	0)	2	0	0	1	0	0	0	1	0	0	0	0	0	.333	.500	.667	1.167
2021	2 Tms		24	23	4	2	0	1	(0	1)	9	4	4	2	1	0	8	0	0	0	0	0	0	.174	.208	.391	.600
21	Min	AL	1	0	0	0	0	0	(0	0)	0	1	0	0	0	0	0	0	0	0	0	0	0	-	-	-	-
21	NYM	NL	23	23	4	2	0	1	(0	1)	9	3	4	2	1	0	8	0	0	0	0	0	0	.174	.208	.391	.600
	2 ML YEARS		25	26	5	3	0	1	(0	1)	11	4	4	3	1	0	8	1	0	0	0	0	0	.192	.250	.423	.673

Richard Bleier

Pitches: L **Bats:** L **Pos:** RP-68

BLY-er

Ht: 6'3" **Wt:** 215 **Born:** 4/16/1987 **Age:** 35

Year	Team	Lg	G	GS	GF	IP	BFP	H	R	ER	HR	SH	SF	HB	TBB	IBB	SO	WP	W	L	Pct	Sv-Op	Hld	Vel	OPS	ERC	ERA
						HOW MUCH PITCHED					**WHAT HE GAVE UP**											**THE RESULTS**						
2016	NYY	AL	23	0	8	23.0	92	20	6	5	0	0	1	1	4	0	13	0	0	0	-	0-0	2	89	.586	2.11	1.96
2017	Bal	AL	57	0	14	63.1	265	62	23	14	6	3	4	4	13	3	26	5	2	1	.667	0-0	3	89	.671	3.33	1.99
2018	Bal	AL	31	0	4	32.2	133	36	7	7	0	0	2	1	4	1	15	1	3	0	1.000	0-1	9	88	.673	3.05	1.93
2019	Bal	AL	53	1	13	55.1	235	65	34	33	6	1	2	4	8	2	30	1	3	0	1.000	4-5	5	89	.802	4.39	5.37
2020	2 Tms		21	0	1	16.2	67	14	6	4	0	0	0	1	4	1	11	2	1	1	.500	0-0	6	89	.590	2.18	2.16
2021	Mia	NL	68	0	6	58.0	225	51	20	19	4	1	3	3	6	3	44	1	3	2	.600	0-6	20	90	.603	2.34	2.95
20	Bal	AL	2	0	0	3.0	11	1	0	0	0	0	0	1	0	0	4	1	0	0	-	0-0	0	89	.282	0.69	0.00
20	Mia	NL	19	0	1	13.2	56	13	6	4	0	0	0	0	4	1	7	1	1	1	.500	0-0	6	89	.650	2.68	2.63
	Postseason		3	0	0	2.0	6	0	0	0	0	0	0	0	0	0	0	0	0	0	-	0-0	1	91	.000	0.00	0.00
	6 ML YEARS		253	1	46	249.0	1017	248	96	82	16	5	12	14	39	10	139	10	12	4	.750	4-12	45	89	.673	3.08	2.96

Scott Blewett

Pitches: R **Bats:** R **Pos:** RP-3

BLY-er

Ht: 6'6" **Wt:** 245 **Born:** 4/10/1996 **Age:** 26

Year	Team	Lg	G	GS	GF	IP	BFP	H	R	ER	HR	SH	SF	HB	TBB	IBB	SO	WP	W	L	Pct	Sv-Op	Hld	Vel	OPS	ERC	ERA
						HOW MUCH PITCHED					**WHAT HE GAVE UP**											**THE RESULTS**						
2021	Omha	AAA	20	10	1	65.0	299	73	50	45	18	1	2	3	30	0	63	3	5	3	.625	0- -	-	-	.884	6.51	6.23
2020	KC	AL	2	0	1	3.0	16	6	2	2	0	0	0	0	1	0	4	0	0	0	-	0-0	0	93	1.038	8.97	6.00
2021	KC	AL	3	0	2	5.0	21	3	1	1	0	0	0	0	5	0	4	0	0	0	-	0-0	0	91	.693	3.66	1.80
	2 ML YEARS		5	0	3	8.0	37	9	3	3	0	0	0	0	6	0	8	0	0	0	-	0-0	0	92	.857	5.56	3.38

Xander Bogaerts

Bats: R **Throws:** R **Pos:** SS-138;DH-6;PH-1

ZAN-derr BO-garts

Ht: 6'2" **Wt:** 218 **Born:** 10/1/1992 **Age:** 29

Year	Team	Lg	G	AB	H	2B	3B	HR	(Hm	Rd)	TB	R	RBI	RC	TBB	IBB	SO	HBP	SH	SF	SB	CS	GDP	Avg	OBP	Slg	OPS
								BATTING														**RUNNING**			**AVERAGES**		
2013	Bos	AL	18	44	11	2	0	1	(0	1)	16	7	5	4	5	0	13	0	0	1	1	0	1	.250	.320	.364	.684
2014	Bos	AL	144	538	129	28	1	12	(7	5)	195	60	46	43	39	1	138	8	2	7	2	3	11	.240	.297	.362	.660
2015	Bos	AL	156	613	196	35	3	7	(5	2)	258	84	81	88	32	1	101	3	3	3	10	2	16	.320	.355	.421	.776
2016	Bos	AL	157	652	192	34	1	21	(11	10)	291	115	89	98	58	0	123	6	0	3	13	4	14	.294	.356	.446	.802
2017	Bos	AL	148	571	156	32	6	10	(4	6)	230	94	62	81	56	6	116	6	0	2	15	1	17	.273	.343	.403	.746
2018	Bos	AL	136	513	148	45	3	23	(15	8)	268	72	103	100	55	4	102	6	0	6	8	2	14	.288	.360	.522	.883
2019	Bos	AL	155	614	190	52	0	33	(17	16)	341	110	117	124	76	2	122	2	0	6	4	2	11	.309	.384	.555	.939
2020	Bos	AL	56	203	61	8	0	11	(5	6)	102	36	28	32	21	2	41	0	0	3	8	0	3	.300	.364	.502	.867
2021	Bos	AL	144	529	156	34	1	23	(15	8)	261	90	79	97	62	2	113	5	0	7	5	1	13	.295	.370	.493	.863
	Postseason		33	114	25	5	1	2	(2	0)	38	17	10	11	14	1	25	0	0	2	0	0	4	.219	.300	.333	.633
	9 ML YEARS		1114	4277	1239	270	15	141	(79	62)	1962	668	610	667	404	18	869	36	5	36	66	15	100	.290	.353	.459	.812

Alec Bohm

Bats: R **Throws:** R **Pos:** 3B-103;PH-9;1B-7

Ht: 6'5" **Wt:** 218 **Born:** 8/3/1996 **Age:** 25

Year	Team	Lg	G	AB	H	2B	3B	HR	(Hm	Rd)	TB	R	RBI	RC	TBB	IBB	SO	HBP	SH	SF	SB	CS	GDP	Avg	OBP	Slg	OPS
								BATTING														**RUNNING**			**AVERAGES**		
2021	LV	AAA	15	59	16	5	0	1	(-	-)	24	8	6	-	7	0	15	1	0	1	3	1	0	.271	.353	.407	.760
2020	Phi	NL	44	160	54	11	0	4	(2	2)	77	24	23	33	16	0	36	2	0	2	1	1	4	.338	.400	.481	.881
2021	Phi	NL	115	380	94	15	0	7	(5	2)	130	46	47	42	31	0	111	2	0	4	4	0	12	.247	.305	.342	.647
	2 ML YEARS		159	540	148	26	0	11	(7	4)	207	70	70	75	47	0	147	4	0	6	5	1	16	.274	.333	.383	.717

Ronald Bolanos

Pitches: R **Bats:** R **Pos:** RP-3

boh-LAHN-yos

Ht: 6'2" **Wt:** 230 **Born:** 8/23/1996 **Age:** 25

Year	Team	Lg	G	GS	GF	IP	BFP	H	R	ER	HR	SH	SF	HB	TBB	IBB	SO	WP	W	L	Pct	Sv-Op	Hld	Vel	OPS	ERC	ERA
						HOW MUCH PITCHED					**WHAT HE GAVE UP**											**THE RESULTS**						
2021	Omha	AAA	9	9	0	36.0	161	35	26	25	10	0	1	4	22	0	32	7	0	3	.000	0- -	-	-	.909	6.84	6.25
2019	SD	NL	5	3	0	19.2	88	17	13	13	3	0	1	1	12	0	19	1	0	2	.000	0-0	0	94	.800	4.68	5.95
2020	KC	AL	2	2	0	3.2	21	8	7	5	2	0	0	1	3	0	2	2	0	2	.000	0-0	0	95	1.395	21.97	12.27
2021	KC	AL	3	0	0	6.1	25	4	1	1	0	0	0	0	2	0	10	0	0	0	-	0-0	0	95	.414	1.43	1.42
	3 ML YEARS		10	5	0	29.2	134	29	21	19	5	0	1	2	17	0	31	3	0	4	.000	0-0	0	95	.814	5.44	5.76

Skye Bolt

Bats: B **Throws:** R **Pos:** CF-16;PR-10;LF-6;PH-5;RF-4;DH-3

Ht: 6'2" **Wt:** 180 **Born:** 1/15/1994 **Age:** 28

Year	Team	Lg	G	AB	H	2B	3B	HR	(Hm	Rd)	TB	R	RBI	RC	TBB	IBB	SO	HBP	SH	SF	SB	CS	GDP	Avg	OBP	Slg	OPS
								BATTING														**RUNNING**			**AVERAGES**		
2021	LsVgs	AAA	51	163	63	12	2	9	(-	-)	106	41	29	-	32	1	43	3	0	1	5	0	2	.387	.492	.650	1.143
2019	Oak	AL	5	10	1	1	0	0	(0	0)	2	1	0	0	1	0	3	0	0	0	0	0	0	.100	.182	.200	.382
2021	2 Tms		34	57	5	1	0	1	(1	0)	9	5	4	0	1	0	15	0	2	0	2	0	0	.088	.103	.158	.261
21	SF	NL	2	1	0	0	0	0	(0	0)	0	0	0	0	0	0	1	0	0	0	0	0	0	.000	.000	.000	.000
21	Oak	AL	32	56	5	1	0	1	(1	0)	9	5	4	0	1	0	14	0	2	0	2	0	0	.089	.105	.161	.266
	2 ML YEARS		39	67	6	2	0	1	(1	0)	11	6	4	0	2	0	18	0	2	0	2	0	0	.090	.116	.164	.280

Jorge Bonifacio

Bats: R **Throws:** R **Pos:** CF-3;LF-2;PH-2   **Ht:** 6'1" **Wt:** 220 **Born:** 6/4/1993 **Age:** 29

Year	Team	Lg	G	AB	H	2B	3B	HR	(Hm	Rd)	TB	R	RBI	RC	TBB	IBB	SO	HBP	SH	SF	SB	CS	GDP	Avg	OBP	Slg	OPS
2021	Rdng	AA	49	171	43	13	0	12	(-	-)	92	31	41	-	24	2	41	1	0	2	1	0	1	.251	.343	.538	.881
2021	LV	AAA	40	136	37	12	2	4	(-	-)	65	26	16	-	26	0	33	1	0	4	4	2	3	.272	.390	.478	.868
2017	KC	AL	113	384	98	15	1	17	(8	9)	166	55	40	51	35	0	118	2	0	1	1	1	8	.255	.320	.432	.752
2018	KC	AL	69	236	53	16	2	4	(1	3)	85	31	23	29	29	1	71	2	1	2	0	1	3	.225	.312	.360	.672
2019	KC	AL	5	20	7	3	0	0	(0	0)	10	3	3	5	1	0	7	0	0	0	0	0	0	.350	.381	.500	.881
2020	Det	AL	30	86	19	3	0	2	(0	2)	28	8	17	15	5	0	26	2	0	1	0	0	1	.221	.277	.326	.602
2021	Phi	NL	7	11	1	0	0	0	(0	0)	1	0	2	1	1	0	6	0	0	0	0	0	0	.091	.167	.091	.258
	5 ML YEARS		224	737	178	37	3	23	(9	14)	290	97	85	101	71	1	228	6	1	4	1	2	12	.242	.312	.393	.705

Ryan Borucki

Pitches: L **Bats:** L **Pos:** RP-24   **Ht:** 6'4" **Wt:** 215 **Born:** 3/31/1994 **Age:** 28

Year	Team	Lg	G	GS	GF	IP	BFP	H	R	ER	HR	SH	SF	HB	TBB	IBB	SO	WP	W	L	Pct	Sv-Op	Hld	Vel	OPS	ERC	ERA
2021	Buffalo	AAA	7	0	0	7.1	30	5	3	3	0	0	0	0	5	0	8	2	0	0	-	0-	-	-	.533	2.87	3.68
2018	Tor	AL	17	17	0	97.2	415	96	48	42	7	3	2	2	33	3	67	2	4	6	.400	0-0	0	92	.705	3.58	3.87
2019	Tor	AL	2	2	0	6.2	40	15	10	8	2	0	0	0	6	0	6	0	0	1	.000	0-0	0	92	1.319	17.16	10.80
2020	Tor	AL	21	0	1	16.2	73	12	5	5	1	0	1	0	12	1	21	0	1	1	.500	0-1	3	95	.629	3.35	2.70
2021	Tor	AL	24	0	6	23.2	98	18	14	13	5	1	1	1	11	0	21	2	3	1	.750	0-1	1	95	.738	3.98	4.94
	Postseason		1	0	0	0.2	2	0	0	0	0	0	0	0	0	0	1	0	0	0	-	0-0	0	94	.000	0.00	0.00
	4 ML YEARS		64	19	7	144.2	626	141	77	68	15	4	4	3	62	4	115	4	8	9	.471	0-2	4	93	.740	4.11	4.23

Akeem Bostick

Pitches: R **Bats:** R **Pos:** RP-1   **Ht:** 6'6" **Wt:** 250 **Born:** 5/4/1995 **Age:** 27

Year	Team	Lg	G	GS	GF	IP	BFP	H	R	ER	HR	SH	SF	HB	TBB	IBB	SO	WP	W	L	Pct	Sv-Op	Hld	Vel	OPS	ERC	ERA
2021	Syrcse	AAA	15	8	1	49.1	222	51	31	29	9	1	1	2	30	0	37	5	1	4	.200	1--	-	-	.828	6.05	5.29
2021	NYM	NL	1	0	1	1.0	4	0	0	0	0	0	0	0	1	0	0	0	0	0	-	0-0	0	91	.250	0.95	0.00

David Bote

Bats: R **Throws:** R **Pos:** 2B-61;3B-24;PH-16;DH-3   BOH-tee   **Ht:** 6'1" **Wt:** 205 **Born:** 4/7/1993 **Age:** 29

Year	Team	Lg	G	AB	H	2B	3B	HR	(Hm	Rd)	TB	R	RBI	RC	TBB	IBB	SO	HBP	SH	SF	SB	CS	GDP	Avg	OBP	Slg	OPS
2018	ChC	NL	74	184	44	9	2	6	(5	1)	75	23	33	26	19	1	60	4	0	3	3	4	3	.239	.319	.408	.727
2019	ChC	NL	127	303	78	17	0	11	(3	8)	128	47	41	44	44	4	93	7	0	2	5	1	11	.257	.362	.422	.785
2020	ChC	NL	45	125	25	3	1	7	(1	6)	51	15	29	23	17	0	40	2	0	1	2	0	6	.200	.303	.408	.711
2021	ChC	NL	97	291	58	10	2	8	(6	2)	96	32	35	24	27	0	73	5	1	3	0	1	13	.199	.276	.330	.606
	Postseason		2	6	0	0	0	0	(0	0)	0	0	0	0	0	0	4	0	0	0	0	0	0	.000	.000	.000	.000
	4 ML YEARS		343	903	205	39	5	32	(15	17)	350	117	138	117	107	5	266	18	1	9	10	6	33	.227	.318	.388	.706

Ben Bowden

Pitches: L **Bats:** L **Pos:** RP-39   **Ht:** 6'4" **Wt:** 249 **Born:** 10/21/1994 **Age:** 27

Year	Team	Lg	G	GS	GF	IP	BFP	H	R	ER	HR	SH	SF	HB	TBB	IBB	SO	WP	W	L	Pct	Sv-Op	Hld	Vel	OPS	ERC	ERA
2021	Albq	AAA	12	0	2	11.2	40	2	0	0	0	0	0	0	4	0	17	1	1	0	1.000	2--	-	-	.206	0.39	0.00
2021	Col	NL	39	0	9	35.2	177	44	30	26	6	2	0	1	21	2	42	1	3	2	.600	0-1	1	92	.880	6.50	6.56

Brad Boxberger

Pitches: R **Bats:** R **Pos:** RP-71   **Ht:** 5'10" **Wt:** 211 **Born:** 5/27/1988 **Age:** 34

Year	Team	Lg	G	GS	GF	IP	BFP	H	R	ER	HR	SH	SF	HB	TBB	IBB	SO	WP	W	L	Pct	Sv-Op	Hld	Vel	OPS	ERC	ERA
2012	SD	NL	24	0	4	27.2	120	22	12	8	3	0	1	2	18	1	33	0	0	0	-	0-0	1	92	.734	4.28	2.60
2013	SD	NL	18	0	6	22.0	94	19	9	7	3	3	2	0	13	0	24	0	0	1	.000	1-1	0	92	.760	4.43	2.86
2014	TB	AL	63	0	10	64.2	247	34	17	17	9	2	2	4	20	0	104	3	5	2	.714	2-5	18	93	.538	1.84	2.37
2015	TB	AL	69	0	53	63.0	271	54	29	26	9	2	1	2	32	5	74	5	4	10	.286	41-47	2	93	.703	4.01	3.71
2016	TB	AL	27	0	3	24.1	114	23	13	13	3	0	1	2	19	1	22	0	4	3	.571	0-3	7	92	.734	5.75	4.81
2017	TB	AL	30	0	10	29.1	121	23	11	11	4	1	1	1	11	3	40	1	4	4	.500	0-2	5	92	.665	3.03	3.38
2018	Ari	NL	60	0	45	53.1	235	44	30	26	9	2	1	1	32	4	71	3	3	7	.300	32-40	1	91	.732	4.27	4.39
2019	KC	AL	29	0	9	26.2	122	25	16	16	3	0	1	1	17	0	27	1	1	3	.250	1-4	0	90	.751	4.83	5.40
2020	Mia	NL	23	0	0	18.0	79	17	7	6	3	0	1	0	8	0	18	0	1	0	1.000	0-1	5	93	.749	4.60	3.00
2021	Mil	NL	71	0	12	64.2	266	44	26	24	8	3	2	6	25	1	83	3	5	4	.556	4-9	23	94	.618	2.79	3.34
	Postseason		3	0	0	3.1	12	0	0	0	0	0	0	0	2	0	2	0	1	0	1.000	0-0	0	93	.167	0.38	0.00
	10 ML YEARS		414	0	152	393.2	1669	305	170	154	54	13	13	20	195	15	496	16	27	34	.443	81-112	62	92	.679	3.60	3.52

Matthew Boyd

Pitches: L **Bats:** L **Pos:** SP-15   **Ht:** 6'3" **Wt:** 223 **Born:** 2/2/1991 **Age:** 31

Year	Team	Lg	G	GS	GF	IP	BFP	H	R	ER	HR	SH	SF	HB	TBB	IBB	SO	WP	W	L	Pct	Sv-Op	Hld	Vel	OPS	ERC	ERA
2015	2 Tms	AL	13	12	0	57.1	252	71	50	48	17	1	3	1	20	0	43	4	1	6	.143	0-0	0	91	.979	7.04	7.53
2016	Det	AL	20	18	0	97.1	412	97	51	49	17	0	3	4	29	0	82	1	6	5	.545	0-0	0	91	.765	4.35	4.53
2017	Det	AL	26	25	0	135.0	605	157	84	79	18	3	6	3	53	3	110	2	6	11	.353	0-0	0	92	.826	5.28	5.27
2018	Det	AL	31	31	0	170.1	709	146	87	83	27	2	6	11	51	0	159	6	9	13	.409	0-0	0	90	.704	3.53	4.39

Year	Team	Lg	G	GS	GF	IP	BFP	H	R	ER	HR	SH	SF	HB	TBB	IBB	SO	WP	W	L	Pct	Sv-Op	Hld	Vel	OPS	ERC	ERA
2019	Det	AL	32	32	0	185.1	788	178	101	94	39	4	4	8	50	1	238	6	9	12	.429	0-0	0	92	.766	4.18	4.56
2020	Det	AL	12	12	0	60.1	271	67	46	45	15	1	2	5	22	0	60	5	3	7	.300	0-0	0	92	.900	5.99	6.71
2021	Det	AL	15	15	0	78.2	337	77	37	34	9	1	4	7	23	0	67	4	3	8	.273	0-0	0	92	.716	3.97	3.89
15	Tor	AL	2	2	0	6.2	36	15	11	11	5	0	1	0	1	0	7	2	0	2	.000	0-0	0	91	1.327	17.16	14.85
15	Det	AL	11	10	0	50.2	216	56	39	37	12	1	2	1	19	0	36	2	1	4	.200	0-0	0	91	.918	5.88	6.57
7 ML YEARS			149	145	1	784.1	3374	793	456	432	142	12	28	39	248	4	759	28	37	62	.374	0-0	0	91	.785	4.55	4.96

Brad Brach

Pitches: R Bats: R Pos: RP-35 BROCK **Ht: 6'6" Wt: 215 Born: 4/12/1986 Age: 36**

Year	Team	Lg	G	GS	GF	IP	BFP	H	R	ER	HR	SH	SF	HB	TBB	IBB	SO	WP	W	L	Pct	Sv-Op	Hld	Vel	OPS	ERC	ERA
2021	Lsvlle	AAA	8	0	1	8.2	32	5	1	0	0	1	0	0	1	0	15	1	0	0	-	0- -	-	-	.394	0.90	0.00
2011	SD	NL	9	0	4	7.0	38	9	5	4	0	0	0	1	7	4	11	1	0	2	.000	0-0	0	93	.747	6.51	5.14
2012	SD	NL	67	0	13	66.2	280	50	28	28	11	1	3	2	33	7	75	4	2	4	.333	0-1	15	92	.674	3.47	3.78
2013	SD	NL	33	0	6	31.0	141	36	15	11	3	0	3	0	19	0	31	4	1	0	1.000	0-0	2	92	.819	6.03	3.19
2014	Bal	AL	46	0	8	62.1	254	48	24	22	6	2	4	1	25	1	54	2	7	1	.875	0-0	8	93	.640	2.90	3.18
2015	Bal	AL	62	0	12	79.1	324	57	25	24	7	3	2	0	38	3	89	1	5	3	.625	1-2	14	94	.627	2.78	2.72
2016	Bal	AL	71	0	16	79.0	311	57	23	18	7	0	3	0	25	1	92	4	10	4	.714	2-7	24	94	.578	2.27	2.05
2017	Bal	AL	67	0	36	68.0	275	51	27	24	7	1	3	0	26	1	70	4	4	5	.444	18-24	9	95	.620	2.70	3.18
2018	2 Tms		69	0	32	62.2	289	72	32	25	5	1	1	1	28	2	60	3	2	4	.333	12-16	11	94	.754	4.85	3.59
2019	2 Tms	NL	58	0	6	54.1	242	57	33	33	4	1	4	1	31	2	60	3	5	4	.556	0-3	6	94	.774	4.94	5.47
2020	NYM	NL	14	0	5	12.1	58	8	8	8	2	0	0	1	14	0	14	2	1	0	1.000	0-1	0	90	.745	5.87	5.84
2021	Cin	NL	35	0	5	30.0	139	30	26	21	5	1	1	1	18	2	33	2	1	2	.333	1-3	0	94	.804	5.28	6.30
18	Bal	AL	42	0	24	39.0	185	50	24	21	4	1	0	0	19	1	38	1	1	2	.333	11-13	3	93	.830	5.96	4.85
18	Atl	NL	27	0	8	23.2	104	22	8	4	1	0	1	1	9	1	22	2	1	2	.333	1-3	8	95	.620	3.19	1.52
19	ChC	NL	42	0	6	39.2	181	42	27	27	3	0	4	1	28	1	45	3	4	3	.571	0-2	4	94	.811	5.66	6.13
19	NYM	NL	16	0	0	14.2	61	15	6	6	1	1	0	0	3	1	15	0	1	1	.500	0-1	2	94	.668	3.12	3.68
Postseason			5	0	0	5.0	24	5	1	1	1	0	0	0	5	1	5	0	1	0	1.000	0-1	0	94	.890	7.14	1.80
11 ML YEARS			531	0	143	552.2	2351	475	246	218	57	10	24	8	264	23	589	30	38	29	.567	34-57	99	94	.684	3.63	3.55

Archie Bradley

Pitches: R Bats: R Pos: RP-53 **Ht: 6'4" Wt: 215 Born: 8/10/1992 Age: 29**

Year	Team	Lg	G	GS	GF	IP	BFP	H	R	ER	HR	SH	SF	HB	TBB	IBB	SO	WP	W	L	Pct	Sv-Op	Hld	Vel	OPS	ERC	ERA
2015	Ari	NL	8	8	0	35.2	161	36	23	23	3	1	1	2	22	1	23	0	2	3	.400	0-0	0	92	.768	5.12	5.80
2016	Ari	NL	26	26	0	141.2	638	154	84	79	16	2	7	4	67	8	143	7	8	9	.471	0-0	0	92	.802	4.96	5.02
2017	Ari	NL	63	0	13	73.0	290	55	14	14	4	1	1	1	21	2	79	0	3	3	.500	1-7	25	96	.567	2.14	1.73
2018	Ari	NL	76	0	8	71.2	296	62	30	29	9	1	0	4	20	1	75	2	4	5	.444	3-11	34	96	.672	3.24	3.64
2019	Ari	NL	66	1	32	71.2	317	67	30	28	5	2	2	5	36	2	87	0	4	5	.444	18-21	7	96	.714	4.10	3.52
2020	2 Tms	NL	16	0	10	18.1	73	17	6	6	1	0	0	1	3	0	18	0	2	0	1.000	6-7	2	94	.635	2.78	2.95
2021	Phi	NL	53	0	11	51.0	224	51	24	21	5	0	1	3	22	1	40	1	7	3	.700	2-5	13	94	.743	4.39	3.71
20	Ari	NL	10	0	9	10.2	45	13	5	5	0	0	0	1	3	0	12	0	1	0	1.000	6-7	0	94	.792	4.78	4.22
20	Cin	NL	6	0	1	7.2	28	4	1	1	1	0	0	0	0	0	6	0	1	0	1.000	0-0	2	94	.393	0.87	1.17
Postseason			4	0	1	6.1	31	8	4	3	2	0	0	0	3	0	5	0	1	0	1.000	0-0	1	96	.891	7.26	4.26
7 ML YEARS			308	35	74	463.0	1999	442	211	200	43	7	12	20	191	15	465	10	30	28	.517	30-51	81	94	.718	3.94	3.89

Bobby Bradley

Bats: L Throws: R Pos: 1B-68;DH-5;PH-4 **Ht: 6'1" Wt: 225 Born: 5/29/1996 Age: 26**

Year	Team	Lg	G	AB	H	2B	3B	HR	(Hm	Rd)	TB	R	RBI	RC	TBB	IBB	SO	HBP	SH	SF	SB	CS	GDP	Avg	OBP	Slg	OPS
2021	Clmbs	AAA	26	97	19	1	0	9	(-	-)	47	16	19	-	7	0	35	3	0	2	0	0	0	.196	.266	.485	.751
2019	Cle	AL	15	45	8	5	0	1	(1	0)	16	4	4	1	4	0	20	0	0	2	0	0	2	.178	.245	.356	.600
2021	Cle	AL	74	245	51	10	0	16	(10	6)	109	36	41	36	25	1	99	6	0	3	0	0	3	.208	.294	.445	.739
2 ML YEARS			89	290	59	15	0	17	(11	6)	125	40	45	37	29	1	119	6	0	3	0	0	5	.203	.287	.431	.718

Jackie Bradley Jr.

Bats: L Throws: R Pos: CF-89;PH-20;RF-17;LF-14;PR-2 **Ht: 5'10" Wt: 196 Born: 4/19/1990 Age: 32**

Year	Team	Lg	G	AB	H	2B	3B	HR	(Hm	Rd)	TB	R	RBI	RC	TBB	IBB	SO	HBP	SH	SF	SB	CS	GDP	Avg	OBP	Slg	OPS
2013	Bos	AL	37	95	18	5	0	3	(2	1)	32	18	10	8	10	0	31	2	0	0	2	0	1	.189	.280	.337	.617
2014	Bos	AL	127	384	76	19	2	1	(1	0)	102	45	30	27	31	1	121	4	1	2	8	0	10	.198	.265	.266	.531
2015	Bos	AL	74	221	55	17	4	10	(5	5)	110	43	43	41	27	0	69	3	1	3	3	0	5	.249	.335	.498	.832
2016	Bos	AL	156	558	149	30	7	26	(12	14)	271	94	87	86	63	5	143	10	0	5	9	2	10	.267	.349	.486	.835
2017	Bos	AL	133	482	118	19	3	17	(6	11)	194	58	63	70	48	4	124	9	0	2	8	3	8	.245	.323	.402	.726
2018	Bos	AL	144	474	111	33	4	13	(4	9)	191	76	59	67	46	3	137	11	0	4	17	1	6	.234	.314	.403	.717
2019	Bos	AL	147	494	111	28	3	21	(10	11)	208	69	62	61	56	3	155	12	3	2	8	6	6	.225	.317	.421	.738
2020	Bos	AL	55	191	54	11	0	7	(3	4)	86	32	22	28	23	1	48	2	0	1	5	2	2	.283	.364	.450	.814
2021	Mil	NL	134	387	63	14	3	6	(3	3)	101	39	29	18	28	0	132	10	0	3	7	1	8	.163	.236	.261	.497
Postseason			21	65	12	2	0	4	(1	3)	26	7	15	12	9	0	22	2	0	0	1	2	2	.185	.303	.400	.703
9 ML YEARS			1007	3286	755	176	26	104	(46	58)	1295	474	405	406	332	17	960	64	5	22	67	15	56	.230	.311	.394	.705

Michael Brantley

Bats: L Throws: L Pos: LF-84;DH-30;RF-8;PH-3   Ht: 6'2" Wt: 209 Born: 5/15/1987 Age: 35

Year	Team	Lg	G	AB	H	2B	3B	HR	(Hm	Rd)	TB	R	RBI	RC	TBB	IBB	SO	HBP	SH	SF	SB	CS	GDP	Avg	OBP	Slg	OPS
2009	Cle	AL	28	112	35	4	0	0	(0	0)	39	10	11	16	8	0	19	0	1	0	4	4	3	.313	.358	.348	.707
2010	Cle	AL	72	297	73	9	3	3	(2	1)	97	38	22	32	22	0	38	0	4	2	10	2	6	.246	.296	.327	.623
2011	Cle	AL	114	451	120	24	4	7	(4	3)	173	63	46	56	34	2	76	3	3	5	13	5	11	.266	.318	.384	.702
2012	Cle	AL	149	552	159	37	4	6	(3	3)	222	63	60	76	53	12	56	0	0	4	12	9	7	.288	.348	.402	.750
2013	Cle	AL	151	556	158	26	3	10	(9	1)	220	66	73	86	40	1	67	4	3	8	17	4	11	.284	.332	.396	.728
2014	Cle	AL	156	611	200	45	2	20	(11	9)	309	94	97	114	52	4	56	8	0	5	23	1	16	.327	.385	.506	.890
2015	Cle	AL	137	529	164	45	0	15	(9	6)	254	68	84	94	60	8	51	2	0	5	15	1	14	.310	.379	.480	.859
2016	Cle	AL	11	39	9	2	0	0	(0	0)	11	5	7	5	3	1	6	0	0	1	1	0	1	.231	.279	.282	.561
2017	Cle	AL	90	338	101	20	1	9	(6	3)	150	47	52	51	31	3	50	2	0	4	11	1	8	.299	.357	.444	.801
2018	Cle	AL	143	570	176	36	2	17	(9	8)	267	89	76	86	48	0	60	5	1	6	12	3	15	.309	.364	.468	.832
2019	Hou	AL	148	575	179	40	2	22	(12	10)	289	88	90	103	51	3	66	7	0	4	3	2	21	.311	.372	.503	.875
2020	Hou	AL	46	170	51	15	0	5	(3	2)	81	24	22	35	17	0	28	0	0	0	2	0	3	.300	.364	.476	.840
2021	Hou	AL	121	469	146	29	3	8	(2	6)	205	68	47	71	33	1	53	5	0	1	1	0	11	.311	.362	.437	.799
	Postseason		38	147	42	2	0	4	(4	0)	56	17	16	21	17	2	26	1	0	1	2	0	5	.286	.361	.381	.742
	13 ML YEARS		1366	5269	1571	332	24	122	(70	52)	2317	723	687	825	452	35	626	36	12	45	124	32	127	.298	.355	.440	.795

Rob Brantly

Bats: L Throws: R Pos: C-5;1B-1;PH-1   Ht: 6'0" Wt: 191 Born: 7/14/1989 Age: 32

Year	Team	Lg	G	AB	H	2B	3B	HR	(Hm	Rd)	TB	R	RBI	RC	TBB	IBB	SO	HBP	SH	SF	SB	CS	GDP	Avg	OBP	Slg	OPS
2021	S-WB	AAA	64	213	61	9	1	9	(-	-)	99	35	42	-	19	1	37	14	0	1	1	0	4	.286	.381	.465	.845
2012	Mia	NL	31	100	29	8	0	3	(1	2)	46	14	8	14	13	2	16	0	0	0	1	1	1	.290	.372	.460	.832
2013	Mia	NL	67	223	47	9	0	1	(1	0)	59	11	18	14	15	1	53	2	0	3	0	0	8	.211	.263	.265	.528
2015	CWS	AL	14	33	4	1	0	1	(1	0)	8	3	6	1	2	0	8	0	0	1	0	0	0	.121	.167	.242	.409
2017	CWS	AL	14	31	9	1	0	2	(1	1)	16	4	5	7	3	0	14	2	0	0	0	0	0	.290	.389	.516	.905
2019	Phi	NL	1	1	0	0	0	0	(0	0)	0	0	0	0	0	0	1	0	0	0	0	0	0	.000	.000	.000	.000
2020	SF	NL	1	3	0	0	0	0	(0	0)	0	0	0	0	0	0	0	0	0	0	0	0	0	.000	.000	.000	.000
2021	NYY	AL	6	20	3	1	0	0	(0	0)	4	0	0	0	0	0	4	1	0	0	0	0	0	.150	.190	.200	.390
	7 ML YEARS		134	411	92	20	0	7	(4	3)	133	32	37	36	33	3	96	5	0	4	1	1	10	.224	.287	.324	.611

Ryan Brasier

Pitches: R Bats: R Pos: RP-13   BRAY-zhur   Ht: 6'0" Wt: 227 Born: 8/26/1987 Age: 34

			HOW MUCH PITCHED					WHAT HE GAVE UP										THE RESULTS							
Year	Team	Lg	G	GS	GF	IP	BFP	H	R	ER	HR	SH	SF	HB	TBB	IBB	SO	WP	W	L	Pct	Sv-Op	Hld	Vel	OPS	ERC	ERA
2021	Wrcstr	AAA	5	0	0	4.2	25	9	10	10	1	0	0	0	3	0	3	0	1	0	1.000	0--	-	-	1.116	12.56	19.29
2013	LAA	AL	7	0	7	9.0	35	7	2	2	1	0	1	0	4	0	7	0	0	0	-	0-0	0	94	.648	3.37	2.00
2018	Bos	AL	34	0	5	33.2	124	19	6	6	2	1	5	0	7	0	29	1	2	0	1.000	0-2	10	97	.482	1.26	1.60
2019	Bos	AL	62	0	15	55.2	241	51	33	30	9	0	3	3	21	1	61	3	2	4	.333	7-11	9	96	.722	4.06	4.85
2020	Bos	AL	25	1	1	25.0	110	24	12	11	2	0	1	0	11	1	30	1	1	0	1.000	0-2	10	96	.696	3.71	3.96
2021	Bos	AL	13	0	2	12.0	50	12	5	2	2	0	1	0	4	0	9	0	1	1	.500	0-0	3	95	.742	4.37	1.50
	Postseason		9	0	0	8.2	39	7	1	1	0	0	1	1	5	0	7	1	0	0	-	0-0	5	96	.583	3.31	1.04
	5 ML YEARS		141	1	30	135.1	560	113	58	51	16	1	11	3	47	2	136	5	6	5	.545	7-15	32	96	.661	3.16	3.39

Steven Brault

Pitches: L Bats: L Pos: SP-7   Ht: 6'0" Wt: 195 Born: 4/29/1992 Age: 30

			HOW MUCH PITCHED					WHAT HE GAVE UP										THE RESULTS							
Year	Team	Lg	G	GS	GF	IP	BFP	H	R	ER	HR	SH	SF	HB	TBB	IBB	SO	WP	W	L	Pct	Sv-Op	Hld	Vel	OPS	ERC	ERA
2016	Pit	NL	8	7	0	33.1	166	45	26	18	5	3	0	2	17	1	29	1	0	3	.000	0-0	0	91	.893	6.99	4.86
2017	Pit	NL	11	4	2	34.2	162	41	21	18	3	2	1	2	14	1	23	0	1	0	1.000	1-1	0	92	.790	5.06	4.67
2018	Pit	NL	45	5	6	91.2	413	84	51	47	10	3	1	8	57	4	82	9	6	3	.667	0-0	3	93	.747	4.84	4.61
2019	Pit	NL	25	19	1	113.1	505	117	69	65	15	3	0	7	53	2	100	7	4	6	.400	0-0	0	92	.791	5.00	5.16
2020	Pit	NL	11	10	0	42.2	178	29	17	16	2	0	2	5	22	0	38	3	1	3	.250	0-0	0	92	.563	2.92	3.38
2021	Pit	NL	7	7	0	27.2	127	33	18	18	3	1	0	1	12	2	19	0	0	3	.000	0-0	0	91	.870	5.37	5.86
	6 ML YEARS		107	52	9	343.1	1551	349	202	182	38	12	4	25	175	10	291	20	12	18	.400	1-1	3	92	.771	4.91	4.77

John Brebbia

Pitches: R Bats: L Pos: RP-18   Ht: 6'1" Wt: 200 Born: 5/30/1990 Age: 32

			HOW MUCH PITCHED					WHAT HE GAVE UP										THE RESULTS							
Year	Team	Lg	G	GS	GF	IP	BFP	H	R	ER	HR	SH	SF	HB	TBB	IBB	SO	WP	W	L	Pct	Sv-Op	Hld	Vel	OPS	ERC	ERA
2021	Scrmto	AAA	16	2	0	14.1	58	9	5	5	2	0	1	1	5	0	25	0	3	0	1.000	0--	-	-	.592	2.41	3.14
2017	StL	NL	50	0	13	51.2	209	37	15	14	8	1	0	5	11	3	51	2	0	0	-	0-1	5	94	.640	2.45	2.44
2018	StL	NL	45	0	17	50.2	209	43	18	18	5	1	2	0	16	2	60	1	3	3	.500	2-2	5	95	.647	2.85	3.20
2019	StL	NL	66	0	22	72.2	304	59	31	29	6	0	1	3	27	2	87	0	3	4	.429	0-1	12	93	.626	2.93	3.59
2021	SF	NL	18	0	6	18.1	87	25	13	12	4	1	1	2	4	2	22	0	0	1	.000	0-0	1	93	.917	6.43	5.89
	Postseason		5	0	0	3.0	17	7	2	2	1	0	0	0	1	0	3	0	0	0	-	0-0	0	93	1.408	14.72	6.00
	4 ML YEARS		179	0	58	193.1	809	164	77	73	23	3	4	10	58	9	220	3	6	8	.429	2-4	23	94	.667	3.08	3.40

Alex Bregman

Bats: R Throws: R Pos: 3B-90;PH-1   Ht: 6'0" Wt: 192 Born: 3/30/1994 Age: 28

Year	Team	Lg	G	AB	H	2B	3B	HR	(Hm	Rd)	TB	R	RBI	RC	TBB	IBB	SO	HBP	SH	SF	SB	CS	GDP	Avg	OBP	Slg	OPS
2021	SgrLnd	AAA	11	36	9	3	0	1	(-	-)	15	6	5	-	7	0	2	1	0	0	0	0	0	.250	.386	.417	.803
2016	Hou	AL	49	201	53	13	3	8	(3	5)	96	31	34	37	15	0	52	1	0	0	2	0	1	.264	.313	.478	.791
2017	Hou	AL	155	556	158	39	5	19	(9	10)	264	88	71	87	55	2	97	7	1	7	17	5	15	.284	.352	.475	.827
2018	Hou	AL	157	594	170	51	1	31	(16	15)	316	105	103	135	96	2	85	12	0	3	10	4	15	.286	.394	.532	.926
2019	Hou	AL	156	554	164	37	2	41	(16	25)	328	122	112	126	119	2	83	9	0	8	5	1	9	.296	.423	.592	1.015
2020	Hou	AL	42	153	37	12	1	6	(2	4)	69	19	22	28	24	1	26	2	0	1	0	0	2	.242	.350	.451	.801
2021	Hou	AL	91	348	94	17	0	12	(5	7)	147	54	55	56	44	4	53	4	0	4	1	0	13	.270	.355	.422	.777
	Postseason		57	210	48	9	0	11	(7	4)	90	37	29	25	33	2	33	6	0	1	2	1	6	.229	.348	.429	.777
	6 ML YEARS		650	2406	676	169	12	117	(51	66)	1220	419	397	469	353	11	396	34	1	24	35	10	55	.281	.377	.507	.884

Brandon Brennan

Pitches: R Bats: R Pos: RP-1   Ht: 6'4" Wt: 207 Born: 7/26/1991 Age: 30

			HOW MUCH PITCHED					WHAT HE GAVE UP											THE RESULTS							
Year	Team	Lg	G	GS	GF	IP	BFP	H	R	ER	HR	SH	SF	HB	TBB	IBB	SO	WP	W	L	Pct	Sv-Op	Hld	Vel	OPS	ERC	ERA
2021	Wrcstr	AAA	32	0	6	37.2	173	44	28	25	3	0	3	5	15	0	37	0	1	2	.333	1--	-	-	.783	5.42	5.97
2019	Sea	AL	44	0	7	47.1	196	34	25	24	6	0	3	0	24	4	47	6	3	6	.333	0-2	8	95	.651	3.03	4.56
2020	Sea	AL	5	0	0	7.1	33	7	3	3	2	0	0	0	5	1	7	0	0	0	-	0-0	0	93	.864	6.11	3.68
2021	Bos	AL	1	0	0	3.0	11	3	0	0	0	0	0	0	2	0	1	0	0	0	-	0-0	0	93	.788	5.54	0.00
	3 ML YEARS		50	0	7	57.2	240	44	28	27	8	0	3	0	31	5	55	6	3	6	.333	0-2	8	94	.686	3.50	4.21

Jake Brentz

Pitches: L Bats: L Pos: RP-72   Ht: 6'1" Wt: 205 Born: 9/14/1994 Age: 27

			HOW MUCH PITCHED					WHAT HE GAVE UP											THE RESULTS							
Year	Team	Lg	G	GS	GF	IP	BFP	H	R	ER	HR	SH	SF	HB	TBB	IBB	SO	WP	W	L	Pct	Sv-Op	Hld	Vel	OPS	ERC	ERA
2021	KC	AL	72	0	10	64.0	278	45	32	26	7	2	3	6	37	1	76	8	5	2	.714	2-7	15	97	.665	3.49	3.66

Colten Brewer

Pitches: R Bats: R Pos: RP-1   Ht: 6'4" Wt: 222 Born: 10/29/1992 Age: 29

			HOW MUCH PITCHED					WHAT HE GAVE UP											THE RESULTS							
Year	Team	Lg	G	GS	GF	IP	BFP	H	R	ER	HR	SH	SF	HB	TBB	IBB	SO	WP	W	L	Pct	Sv-Op	Hld	Vel	OPS	ERC	ERA
2021	Wrcstr	AAA	10	0	1	16.0	69	13	7	7	2	0	1	0	9	0	18	2	1	1	.500	0--	-	-	.726	3.82	3.94
2018	SD	NL	11	0	5	9.2	49	15	10	6	0	0	0	0	7	0	10	1	1	0	1.000	0-0	0	93	.878	8.08	5.59
2019	Bos	AL	58	0	8	54.2	253	59	26	25	6	1	3	2	34	1	52	9	1	2	.333	0-1	6	93	.804	5.63	4.12
2020	Bos	AL	11	4	1	25.2	122	31	17	16	6	0	0	1	14	0	25	1	0	3	.000	0-0	0	94	.900	7.07	5.61
2021	Bos	AL	1	0	0	1.0	9	4	4	4	0	0	0	0	3	0	1	0	0	0	-	0-0	0	94	1.444	42.47	36.00
	4 ML YEARS		81	4	14	91.0	433	109	57	51	12	1	3	3	58	1	88	11	2	5	.286	0-1	6	93	.853	6.61	5.04

Austin Brice

Pitches: R Bats: R Pos: RP-13   Ht: 6'4" Wt: 238 Born: 6/19/1992 Age: 30

			HOW MUCH PITCHED					WHAT HE GAVE UP											THE RESULTS							
Year	Team	Lg	G	GS	GF	IP	BFP	H	R	ER	HR	SH	SF	HB	TBB	IBB	SO	WP	W	L	Pct	Sv-Op	Hld	Vel	OPS	ERC	ERA
2021	Wrcstr	AAA	25	2	9	32.0	136	21	9	9	3	0	1	9	14	0	33	1	3	0	1.000	2--	-	-	.663	3.41	2.53
2016	Mia	NL	15	0	2	14.0	59	9	12	11	2	0	0	2	5	1	14	0	0	1	.000	0-0	1	94	.598	2.63	7.07
2017	Cin	NL	22	0	4	32.2	137	33	18	18	6	1	1	3	7	0	26	0	0	0	-	0-0	1	94	.756	4.38	4.96
2018	Cin	NL	33	0	8	37.1	162	39	26	24	9	1	1	3	13	6	32	1	2	3	.400	0-0	3	94	.876	5.26	5.79
2019	Mia	NL	36	0	10	44.2	199	37	21	17	7	0	1	7	18	2	46	2	1	0	1.000	0-1	6	93	.676	3.92	3.43
2020	Mia	NL	21	1	2	19.2	87	17	13	13	3	0	0	2	13	0	25	1	1	0	1.000	0-0	4	94	.826	5.28	5.95
2021	Bos	AL	13	0	4	13.2	64	14	10	10	2	0	0	4	7	0	12	0	0	0	-	0-0	0	93	.843	6.30	6.59
	6 ML YEARS		140	1	30	162.0	708	149	100	93	29	2	3	21	63	9	155	4	4	4	.500	0-1	15	94	.765	4.55	5.17

Lewis Brinson

Bats: R Throws: R Pos: LF-51;CF-33;PH-12;RF-4;PR-3   Ht: 6'5" Wt: 212 Born: 5/8/1994 Age: 28

Year	Team	Lg	G	AB	H	2B	3B	HR	(Hm	Rd)	TB	R	RBI	RC	TBB	IBB	SO	HBP	SH	SF	SB	CS	GDP	Avg	OBP	Slg	OPS
2021	Jaxnvl	AAA	12	46	13	1	1	1	(-	-)	19	3	3	-	2	0	11	0	0	0	2	0	1	.283	.313	.413	.726
2017	Mil	NL	21	47	5	0	1	2	(2	0)	13	2	3	4	7	1	17	1	0	0	1	0	0	.106	.236	.277	.513
2018	Mia	NL	109	382	76	10	5	11	(2	9)	129	31	42	29	17	2	120	4	0	2	2	1	6	.199	.240	.338	.577
2019	Mia	NL	75	226	39	9	1	0	(0	0)	50	15	15	10	13	1	74	6	2	1	1	1	8	.173	.236	.221	.457
2020	Mia	NL	47	106	24	6	0	3	(2	1)	39	14	12	12	6	0	30	0	0	0	4	0	2	.226	.268	.368	.636
2021	Mia	NL	89	274	62	14	0	9	(5	4)	103	24	33	23	13	0	72	1	1	1	1	1	5	.226	.263	.376	.639
	Postseason		5	6	0	0	0	0	(0	0)	0	1	0	0	0	0	2	0	0	0	0	0	0	.000	.000	.000	.000
	5 ML YEARS		341	1035	206	39	7	25	(9	16)	334	86	105	78	56	4	313	12	3	4	9	3	21	.199	.248	.323	.570

Zack Britton

Pitches: L Bats: L Pos: RP-22   Ht: 6'1" Wt: 200 Born: 12/22/1987 Age: 34

			HOW MUCH PITCHED					WHAT HE GAVE UP											THE RESULTS							
Year	Team	Lg	G	GS	GF	IP	BFP	H	R	ER	HR	SH	SF	HB	TBB	IBB	SO	WP	W	L	Pct	Sv-Op	Hld	Vel	OPS	ERC	ERA
2011	Bal	AL	28	28	0	154.1	666	162	93	79	12	8	7	1	62	3	97	7	11	11	.500	0-0	0	92	.735	4.24	4.61
2012	Bal	AL	12	11	0	60.1	270	61	37	34	6	0	1	2	32	3	53	4	5	3	.625	0-0	0	92	.756	4.70	5.07
2013	Bal	AL	8	7	0	40.0	182	52	23	22	4	1	1	1	17	1	18	1	2	3	.400	0-0	0	92	.837	6.14	4.95
2014	Bal	AL	71	0	49	76.1	285	46	17	14	4	0	0	1	23	0	62	0	3	2	.600	37-41	7	95	.500	1.62	1.65

Year	Team	Lg	G	GS	GF	IP	BFP	H	R	ER	HR	SH	SF	HB	TBB	IBB	SO	WP	W	L	Pct	Sv-Op	Hld	Vel	OPS	ERC	ERA
2015	Bal	AL	64	0	58	65.2	253	51	16	14	3	0	0	1	14	1	79	5	4	1	.800	36-40	0	96	.547	2.02	1.92
2016	Bal	AL	69	0	63	67.0	254	38	7	4	1	1	0	0	18	3	74	10	2	1	.667	47-47	0	96	.430	1.18	0.54
2017	Bal	AL	38	0	30	37.1	161	39	12	12	1	1	1	0	18	1	29	4	2	1	.667	15-17	0	96	.690	4.18	2.89
2018	2 Tms	AL	41	0	21	40.2	169	29	16	14	3	0	1	3	21	0	34	7	2	0	1.000	7-10	9	95	.605	3.13	3.10
2019	NYY	AL	66	0	15	61.1	245	38	13	13	3	1	2	1	32	1	53	3	3	1	.750	3-7	29	95	.545	2.32	1.91
2020	NYY	AL	20	0	10	19.0	76	12	6	4	0	0	0	0	7	0	16	4	1	2	.333	8-8	3	95	.482	1.54	1.89
2021	NYY	AL	22	0	4	18.1	82	17	14	12	2	0	1	2	14	0	16	2	0	1	.000	1-4	11	93	.802	5.93	5.89
18	Bal	AL	16	0	11	15.2	63	11	6	6	1	0	1	0	10	0	13	2	1	0	1.000	4-5	1	94	.676	3.63	3.45
18	NYY	AL	25	0	10	25.0	106	18	10	8	2	0	1	2	11	0	21	5	1	0	1.000	3-5	8	95	.564	2.84	2.88
Postseason			21	0	4	23.0	99	13	8	8	3	1	1	0	17	3	22	2	0	0	-	2-2	7	95	.631	2.96	3.13
11 ML YEARS			439	46	250	640.1	2643	545	254	222	39	15	14	12	258	13	531	47	35	26	.574	154-174	59	94	.636	3.12	3.12

Connor Brogdon

Pitches: R **Bats:** R **Pos:** RP-55; SP-1   **Ht:** 6'6" **Wt:** 205 **Born:** 1/29/1995 **Age:** 27

Year	Team	Lg	G	GS	GF	IP	BFP	H	R	ER	HR	SH	SF	HB	TBB	IBB	SO	WP	W	L	Pct	Sv-Op	Hld	Vel	OPS	ERC	ERA
2020	Phi	NL	9	0	3	11.1	44	5	5	5	0	0	0	5	1	17	0	1	0	1.000	0-0	0	95	.612	2.17	3.97
2021	Phi	NL	56	1	8	57.2	235	47	27	22	6	1	2	1	18	2	50	2	5	4	.556	1-5	10	96	.644	2.80	3.43
2 ML YEARS			65	1	11	69.0	279	52	32	27	9	1	2	1	23	3	67	2	6	4	.600	1-5	10	96	.638	2.70	3.52

Mike Brosseau

Bats: R **Throws:** R **Pos:** 2B-27;3B-23;1B-10;PH-10;PR-2;LF-1;RF-1   **Ht:** 5'10" **Wt:** 205 **Born:** 3/15/1994 **Age:** 28

Year	Team	Lg	G	AB	H	2B	3B	HR	(Hm	Rd)	TB	R	RBI	RC	TBB	IBB	SO	HBP	SH	SF	SB	CS	GDP	Avg	OBP	Slg	OPS
2021	Drham	AAA	47	156	31	2	1	7	(-	-)	56	22	20	-	22	1	49	9	0	0	2	0	2	.199	.332	.359	.691
2019	TB	AL	51	132	36	7	0	6	(2	4)	61	17	16	18	7	0	39	2	1	0	1	0	3	.273	.319	.462	.781
2020	TB	AL	37	86	26	5	1	5	(1	4)	48	12	12	16	8	0	31	3	0	1	2	0	1	.302	.378	.558	.936
2021	TB	AL	57	150	28	9	0	5	(3	2)	52	21	18	14	15	0	53	2	0	2	2	0	1	.187	.266	.347	.613
Postseason			15	26	6	0	0	1	(1	0)	9	2	2	3	3	0	12	1	0	0	0	0	1	.231	.333	.346	.679
3 ML YEARS			145	368	90	21	1	16	(6	10)	161	50	46	48	30	0	123	7	1	3	5	0	5	.245	.311	.438	.749

Rex Brothers

Pitches: L **Bats:** L **Pos:** RP-57   **Ht:** 6'0" **Wt:** 205 **Born:** 12/18/1987 **Age:** 34

Year	Team	Lg	G	GS	GF	IP	BFP	H	R	ER	HR	SH	SF	HB	TBB	IBB	SO	WP	W	L	Pct	Sv-Op	Hld	Vel	OPS	ERC	ERA
2011	Col	NL	48	0	6	40.2	172	33	14	13	4	0	0	4	20	2	59	2	1	2	.333	1-3	16	95	.644	3.31	2.88
2012	Col	NL	75	0	10	67.2	295	63	33	29	5	3	3	1	37	7	83	5	8	2	.800	0-5	18	95	.732	3.99	3.86
2013	Col	NL	72	0	40	67.1	281	51	16	13	5	1	0	0	36	2	76	3	2	1	.667	19-21	12	93	.618	3.09	1.74
2014	Col	NL	74	0	15	56.1	273	65	38	35	7	1	4	2	39	0	55	5	4	6	.400	0-6	15	93	.825	6.43	5.59
2015	Col	NL	17	0	1	10.1	46	9	2	2	0	0	1	0	8	0	5	1	1	0	1.000	0-0	0	93	.748	4.12	1.74
2017	Atl	NL	27	0	8	23.2	105	23	19	19	3	0	0	1	12	3	33	2	4	3	.571	0-0	2	95	.767	4.48	7.23
2018	Atl	NL	1	0	0	0.0	2	0	1	1	0	0	0	0	2	0	0	0	0	0	-	0-0	0	96	-	-	-
2020	ChC	NL	3	0	0	3.1	15	2	3	3	2	0	0	0	3	0	8	0	0	0	-	0-0	0	95	1.000	7.36	8.10
2021	ChC	NL	57	0	10	53.0	236	41	31	31	9	0	2	6	35	2	75	5	3	2	.600	1-1	8	95	.746	4.73	5.26
9 ML YEARS			374	0	90	322.1	1425	287	157	146	35	5	10	10	192	16	394	23	23	16	.590	21-36	71	94	.725	4.33	4.08

Seth Brown

Bats: L **Throws:** L **Pos:** RF-75;PH-29;LF-19;DH-8;1B-6;CF-4;PR-2   **Ht:** 6'1" **Wt:** 223 **Born:** 7/13/1992 **Age:** 29

Year	Team	Lg	G	AB	H	2B	3B	HR	(Hm	Rd)	TB	R	RBI	RC	TBB	IBB	SO	HBP	SH	SF	SB	CS	GDP	Avg	OBP	Slg	OPS
2019	Oak	AL	26	75	22	8	2	0	(0	0)	34	11	13	13	7	0	23	1	0	0	1	0	2	.293	.361	.453	.815
2020	Oak	AL	7	5	0	0	0	0	(0	0)	0	0	0	0	0	0	2	0	0	0	0	0	0	.000	.000	.000	.000
2021	Oak	AL	111	281	60	13	1	20	(7	13)	135	43	48	31	23	2	89	1	0	2	4	1	1	.214	.274	.480	.754
Postseason			1	1	0	0	0	0	(0	0)	0	0	0	0	0	0	0	0	0	0	0	0	0	.000	.000	.000	.000
3 ML YEARS			144	361	82	21	3	20	(7	13)	169	54	61	44	30	2	114	2	0	2	5	1	3	.227	.289	.468	.757

JT Brubaker

Pitches: R **Bats:** R **Pos:** SP-24   **Ht:** 6'3" **Wt:** 180 **Born:** 11/17/1993 **Age:** 28

Year	Team	Lg	G	GS	GF	IP	BFP	H	R	ER	HR	SH	SF	HB	TBB	IBB	SO	WP	W	L	Pct	Sv-Op	Hld	Vel	OPS	ERC	ERA
2020	Pit	NL	11	9	0	47.1	205	48	27	26	6	0	2	3	17	0	48	4	1	3	.250	0-0	0	94	.758	4.45	4.94
2021	Pit	NL	24	24	0	124.1	538	123	75	74	28	5	1	9	38	1	129	3	5	13	.278	0-0	0	93	.799	4.74	5.36
2 ML YEARS			35	33	0	171.2	743	171	102	100	34	5	3	12	55	1	177	7	6	16	.273	0-0	1	93	.788	4.66	5.24

Jay Bruce

Bats: L **Throws:** L **Pos:** 1B-10   **Ht:** 6'3" **Wt:** 230 **Born:** 4/3/1987 **Age:** 35

Year	Team	Lg	G	AB	H	2B	3B	HR	(Hm	Rd)	TB	R	RBI	RC	TBB	IBB	SO	HBP	SH	SF	SB	CS	GDP	Avg	OBP	Slg	OPS
2008	Cin	NL	108	413	105	17	1	21	(13	8)	187	63	52	49	33	1	110	0	0	2	4	6	8	.254	.314	.453	.767
2009	Cin	NL	101	345	77	15	2	22	(13	9)	162	47	58	47	38	2	75	2	1	1	3	3	5	.223	.303	.470	.773
2010	Cin	NL	148	509	143	23	5	25	(19	6)	251	80	70	71	58	5	136	1	0	5	5	4	12	.281	.353	.493	.846
2011	Cin	NL	157	585	150	27	2	32	(16	16)	277	84	97	96	71	14	158	5	1	2	8	7	8	.256	.341	.474	.814
2012	Cin	NL	155	560	141	35	5	34	(21	13)	288	89	99	85	62	11	155	4	0	7	9	3	5	.252	.327	.514	.841

BATTING

Year	Team	Lg	G	AB	H	2B	3B	HR	(Hm	Rd)	TB	R	RBI	RC	TBB	IBB	SO	HBP	SH	SF	SB	CS	GDP	Avg	OBP	Slg	OPS
2013	Cin	NL	160	626	164	43	1	30	(16	14)	299	89	109	88	63	13	185	2	0	5	7	3	9	.262	.329	.478	.807
2014	Cin	NL	137	493	107	21	1	18	(10	8)	184	71	66	54	44	5	149	2	1	5	12	3	8	.217	.281	.373	.654
2015	Cin	NL	157	580	131	35	4	26	(13	13)	252	72	87	61	58	8	145	2	0	9	9	5	10	.226	.294	.434	.729
2016	2 Tms	NL	147	539	135	27	6	33	(17	16)	273	74	99	87	44	7	126	3	0	3	4	2	14	.250	.309	.506	.815
2017	2 Tms		146	555	141	29	2	36	(15	21)	282	82	101	94	57	0	139	2	0	3	1	1	11	.254	.324	.508	.832
2018	NYM	NL	94	319	71	18	1	9	(3	6)	118	31	37	44	41	4	75	0	0	1	2	3	3	.223	.310	.370	.680
2019	2 Tms		98	310	67	17	0	26	(8	18)	162	43	59	36	19	0	82	1	0	3	1	0	5	.216	.261	.523	.784
2020	Phi	NL	32	96	19	4	2	6	(4	2)	45	11	14	10	7	1	24	0	0	1	0	0	1	.198	.252	.469	.721
2021	NYY	AL	10	34	4	1	0	1	(1	0)	8	3	3	1	5	0	13	0	0	0	0	0	2	.118	.231	.235	.466
16	Cin	NL	97	370	98	22	6	25	(14	11)	207	60	80	67	27	3	83	2	0	3	4	2	11	.265	.316	.559	.875
16	NYM		50	169	37	5	0	8	(3	5)	66	14	19	20	17	4	43	1	0	0	0	0	3	.219	.294	.391	.685
17	NYM	NL	103	406	104	20	0	29	(11	18)	211	61	75	68	39	0	102	1	0	2	0	1	9	.256	.321	.520	.841
17	Cle	AL	43	149	37	9	2	7	(4	3)	71	21	26	26	18	0	37	1	0	1	1	0	2	.248	.331	.477	.808
19	Sea	AL	47	165	35	11	0	14	(5	9)	88	27	28	19	16	0	53	1	0	2	1	0	1	.212	.283	.533	.816
19	Phi	NL	51	145	32	6	0	12	(3	9)	74	16	31	17	3	0	29	0	0	1	0	0	4	.221	.235	.510	.745
	Postseason		15	52	13	3	0	4	(2	2)	28	8	10	7	6	0	13	1	0	1	0	1	0	.250	.333	.538	.872
	14 ML YEARS		1650	5964	1455	312	32	319	(169	150)	2788	839	951	823	600	71	1572	28	3	46	65	40	101	.244	.314	.467	.781

Justin Bruihl

Pitches: L **Bats:** L **Pos:** RP-19; SP-2   **Ht:** 6'2" **Wt:** 215 **Born:** 6/26/1997 **Age:** 25

			HOW MUCH PITCHED					WHAT HE GAVE UP											THE RESULTS							
Year	Team	Lg	G	GS	GF	IP	BFP	H	R	ER	HR	SH	SF	HB	TBB	IBB	SO	WP	W	L	Pct	Sv-Op	Hld	Vel	OPS	ERC	ERA
2021	Tulsa	AA	8	0	1	15.0	54	7	2	2	1	0	0	1	3	0	20	1	1	0	1.000	0--	-	-	.484	1.15	1.20
2021	OkCity	AAA	18	1	0	22.2	94	22	11	9	2	1	0	1	7	2	30	0	3	0	1.000	0--	-	-	.770	3.60	3.57
2021	LAD	NL	21	2	2	18.2	73	13	7	6	1	1	0	1	7	2	11	3	0	1	.000	0-0	3	90	.542	2.26	2.89

Vidal Brujan

Bats: B **Throws:** R **Pos:** 2B-4;RF-2;PH-2;LF-1;CF-1;DH-1   **Ht:** 5'10" **Wt:** 180 **Born:** 2/9/1998 **Age:** 24

						BATTING														RUNNING			AVERAGES			
Year	Team	Lg	G	AB	H	2B	3B	HR	(Hm	Rd)	TB	R	RBI	RC	TBB	IBB	SO	HBP	SH	SF	SB	CS	GDP	Avg	OBP	Slg	OPS
2017	HudVal	A-	67	261	76	15	6	3	(-	-)	112	52	20	45	34	0	36	5	2	0	17	8	4	.291	.383	.429	.812
2018	2 Tms	Low	67	274	97	14	4	7	(-	-)	140	66	34	60	37	0	36	2	2	1	31	13	2	.354	.433	.511	.944
2019	Mont	AA	55	207	55	9	4	3	(-	-)	81	28	25	30	20	0	35	3	1	2	23	8	2	.266	.336	.391	.728
2019	Charltt	A+	44	176	51	8	3	1	(-	-)	68	28	15	30	17	1	26	2	0	1	24	5	6	.290	.357	.386	.744
2021	Drham	AAA	99	372	98	30	1	11	(-	-)	163	73	54	-	47	1	67	1	1	1	43	6	7	.263	.347	.438	.785
2021	TB	AL	10	26	2	0	0	0	(0	0)	2	3	2	0	0	0	8	0	0	0	1	0	0	.077	.077	.077	.154

Kris Bryant

Bats: R **Throws:** R **Pos:** 3B-55;LF-48;RF-39;CF-19;1B-12;PH-6;SS-1   **Ht:** 6'5" **Wt:** 230 **Born:** 1/4/1992 **Age:** 30

						BATTING														RUNNING			AVERAGES			
Year	Team	Lg	G	AB	H	2B	3B	HR	(Hm	Rd)	TB	R	RBI	RC	TBB	IBB	SO	HBP	SH	SF	SB	CS	GDP	Avg	OBP	Slg	OPS
2015	ChC	NL	151	559	154	31	5	26	(21	5)	273	87	99	104	77	0	199	9	0	5	13	4	7	.275	.369	.488	.858
2016	ChC	NL	155	603	176	35	3	39	(17	22)	334	121	102	120	75	5	154	18	0	3	8	5	3	.292	.385	.554	.939
2017	ChC	NL	151	549	162	38	4	29	(18	11)	295	111	73	110	95	5	128	15	0	6	7	5	8	.295	.409	.537	.946
2018	ChC	NL	102	389	106	28	3	13	(7	6)	179	59	52	65	48	6	107	17	0	3	2	4	5	.272	.374	.460	.834
2019	ChC	NL	147	543	153	35	1	31	(15	16)	283	108	77	107	74	1	145	15	0	2	4	0	10	.282	.382	.521	.903
2020	ChC	NL	34	131	27	5	1	4	(1	3)	46	20	11	15	12	0	40	4	0	0	0	0	1	.206	.293	.351	.644
2021	2 Tms	NL	144	513	136	32	2	25	(11	14)	247	86	73	83	62	4	135	9	0	2	10	2	9	.265	.353	.481	.835
21	ChC	NL	93	326	87	19	2	18	(7	11)	164	58	51	57	39	1	89	8	0	1	4	2	6	.267	.358	.503	.861
21	SF	NL	51	187	49	13	0	7	(4	3)	83	28	22	26	23	3	46	1	0	1	6	0	3	.262	.344	.444	.788
	Postseason		39	153	35	8	1	6	(4	2)	63	17	16	18	13	0	52	1	0	1	1	0	3	.229	.293	.412	.705
	7 ML YEARS		884	3287	914	204	19	167	(90	77)	1657	592	487	607	443	21	908	87	0	21	44	20	43	.278	.376	.504	.880

Kris Bubic

Pitches: L **Bats:** L **Pos:** SP-20; RP-9   **Ht:** 6'3" **Wt:** 225 **Born:** 8/19/1997 **Age:** 24

			HOW MUCH PITCHED					WHAT HE GAVE UP											THE RESULTS							
Year	Team	Lg	G	GS	GF	IP	BFP	H	R	ER	HR	SH	SF	HB	TBB	IBB	SO	WP	W	L	Pct	Sv-Op	Hld	Vel	OPS	ERC	ERA
2020	KC	AL	10	10	0	50.0	222	52	29	24	8	0	0	2	22	1	49	0	1	6	.143	0-0	0	91	.777	5.02	4.32
2021	KC	AL	29	20	3	130.0	556	121	67	64	22	0	3	7	59	0	114	0	6	7	.462	0-0	0	91	.780	4.70	4.43
	2 ML YEARS		39	30	3	180.0	778	173	96	88	30	0	3	9	81	1	163	0	7	13	.350	0-0	0	91	.779	4.79	4.40

Ryan Buchter

Pitches: L **Bats:** L **Pos:** RP-18   BUCK-ter   **Ht:** 6'4" **Wt:** 230 **Born:** 2/13/1987 **Age:** 35

			HOW MUCH PITCHED					WHAT HE GAVE UP											THE RESULTS							
Year	Team	Lg	G	GS	GF	IP	BFP	H	R	ER	HR	SH	SF	HB	TBB	IBB	SO	WP	W	L	Pct	Sv-Op	Hld	Vel	OPS	ERC	ERA
2021	Reno	AAA	16	0	9	16.0	69	13	6	6	1	0	1	1	7	0	20	0	0	0	-	6--	-	-	.654	3.11	3.38
2014	Atl	NL	1	0	0	1.0	3	0	0	0	0	0	0	0	1	0	1	0	1	0	1.000	0-0	0	92	.333	1.26	0.00
2016	SD	NL	67	0	10	63.0	247	34	20	20	4	0	2	2	31	0	78	3	3	0	1.000	1-2	20	92	.559	1.94	2.86
2017	2 Tms		71	0	12	65.1	268	35	25	21	10	0	3	4	26	1	65	0	4	3	.571	1-3	20	93	.642	2.86	2.89
2018	Oak	AL	54	0	4	39.1	163	32	17	12	4	1	1	0	15	1	41	1	6	0	1.000	0-0	16	92	.646	2.96	2.75
2019	Oak	AL	64	0	7	45.1	198	42	16	15	8	3	3	2	23	2	50	1	1	1	.500	0-4	12	93	.799	4.77	2.98
2020	LAA	AL	10	0	1	6.0	29	5	4	3	2	0	0	0	6	0	8	1	2	0	1.000	0-0	0	93	.901	7.31	4.50

Year Team	Lg	G	GS	GF	IP	BFP	H	R	ER	HR	SH	SF	HB	TBB	IBB	SO	WP	W	L	Pct	Sv-Op	Hld	Vel	OPS	ERC	ERA
2021 Ari	NL	18	0	2	16.1	78	16	13	12	6	0	1	2	13	1	16	0	0	2	.000	0-1	0	91	.978	7.75	6.61
17 SD	NL	42	0	5	38.1	161	28	15	13	7	0	1	1	18	0	47	0	3	3	.500	1-3	15	93	.696	3.48	3.05
17 KC	AL	29	0	7	27.0	107	16	10	8	3	0	2	3	8	1	18	0	1	0	1.000	0-0	5	93	.561	2.03	2.67
7 ML YEARS		285	0	36	236.1	986	173	95	83	33	4	10	10	115	8	259	6	17	6	.739	2-10	68	92	.685	3.35	3.16

Walker Buehler

Pitches: R Bats: R Pos: SP-33 Ht: 6'2" Wt: 185 Born: 7/28/1994 Age: 27

Year Team	Lg	G	GS	GF	IP	BFP	H	R	ER	HR	SH	SF	HB	TBB	IBB	SO	WP	W	L	Pct	Sv-Op	Hld	Vel	OPS	ERC	ERA
2017 LAD	NL	8	0	2	9.1	44	11	8	8	2	0	0	0	8	1	12	1	1	0	1.000	0-0	1	98	.932	8.22	7.71
2018 LAD	NL	24	23	0	137.1	541	95	43	40	12	2	3	6	37	1	151	4	8	5	.615	0-1	0	96	.556	2.10	2.62
2019 LAD	NL	30	30	0	182.1	737	153	77	66	20	2	6	7	37	0	215	4	14	4	.778	0-0	0	97	.636	2.66	3.26
2020 LAD	NL	8	8	0	36.2	147	24	18	14	7	0	0	1	11	0	42	4	1	0	1.000	0-0	0	97	.600	2.48	3.44
2021 LAD	NL	33	33	0	207.2	815	149	61	57	19	7	3	6	52	2	212	5	16	4	.800	0-0	0	97	.586	2.13	2.47
Postseason		11	11	0	61.1	242	39	16	16	5	1	0	1	22	1	83	2	3	1	.750	0-0	0	97	.551	2.00	2.35
5 ML YEARS		103	94	2	573.1	2284	432	207	185	60	11	12	20	145	4	632	18	40	13	.755	0-1	1	96	.602	2.39	2.90

J.B. Bukauskas

Pitches: R Bats: R Pos: RP-21 Ht: 6'0" Wt: 208 Born: 10/11/1996 Age: 25

Year Team	Lg	G	GS	GF	IP	BFP	H	R	ER	HR	SH	SF	HB	TBB	IBB	SO	WP	W	L	Pct	Sv-Op	Hld	Vel	OPS	ERC	ERA
2021 Reno	AAA	13	0	3	12.2	51	9	6	6	1	0	0	1	4	0	16	0	0	2	.000	1--	-	-	.622	2.42	4.26
2021 Ari	NL	21	0	4	17.1	81	24	19	15	4	1	1	0	7	1	14	0	2	2	.500	0-1	1	95	.971	7.38	7.79

Madison Bumgarner

Pitches: L Bats: R Pos: SP-26 Ht: 6'4" Wt: 257 Born: 8/1/1989 Age: 32

Year Team	Lg	G	GS	GF	IP	BFP	H	R	ER	HR	SH	SF	HB	TBB	IBB	SO	WP	W	L	Pct	Sv-Op	Hld	Vel	OPS	ERC	ERA
2009 SF	NL	4	1	1	10.0	40	8	2	2	1	1	0	0	3	1	10	0	0	0	-	0-0	0	89	.739	3.14	1.80
2010 SF	NL	18	18	0	111.0	472	119	40	37	11	0	4	5	26	2	86	1	7	6	.538	0-0	0	91	.732	3.98	3.00
2011 SF	NL	33	33	0	204.2	844	202	82	73	12	12	4	5	46	5	191	0	13	13	.500	0-0	0	92	.670	3.14	3.21
2012 SF	NL	32	32	0	208.1	849	183	87	78	23	7	4	7	49	6	191	3	16	11	.593	0-0	0	91	.670	2.95	3.37
2013 SF	NL	31	31	0	201.1	803	146	68	62	15	10	4	6	62	6	199	4	13	9	.591	0-0	0	91	.577	2.23	2.77
2014 SF	NL	33	33	0	217.1	873	194	81	72	21	9	5	6	43	3	219	4	18	10	.643	0-0	0	92	.653	2.83	2.98
2015 SF	NL	32	32	0	218.1	869	181	73	71	21	5	4	7	39	2	234	1	18	9	.667	0-0	0	92	.612	2.43	2.93
2016 SF	NL	34	34	0	226.2	912	179	79	69	26	3	6	8	54	0	251	0	15	9	.625	0-0	0	91	.619	2.57	2.74
2017 SF	NL	17	17	0	111.0	450	101	41	41	17	2	1	3	20	3	101	0	4	9	.308	0-0	0	91	.704	3.14	3.32
2018 SF	NL	21	21	0	129.2	551	118	51	47	14	5	3	5	43	3	109	3	6	7	.462	0-0	0	91	.694	3.44	3.26
2019 SF	NL	34	34	0	207.2	844	191	99	90	30	5	5	10	43	3	203	1	9	9	.500	0-0	0	91	.717	3.38	3.90
2020 Ari	NL	9	9	0	41.2	190	47	31	30	13	0	1	6	13	2	30	0	1	4	.200	0-0	0	88	.924	6.48	6.48
2021 Ari	NL	26	26	0	146.1	613	134	82	76	24	3	7	11	39	2	124	2	7	10	.412	0-0	0	90	.741	3.78	4.67
Postseason		16	14	1	102.1	398	74	25	24	8	6	1	5	18	2	87	0	8	3	.727	1-1	0	92	.544	1.88	2.11
13 ML YEARS		324	321	1	2034.0	8310	1803	816	748	229	62	49	79	480	38	1948	27	127	106	.545	0-0	0	91	.671	3.04	3.31

Aaron Bummer

Pitches: L Bats: L Pos: RP-62 Ht: 6'3" Wt: 215 Born: 9/21/1993 Age: 28

Year Team	Lg	G	GS	GF	IP	BFP	H	R	ER	HR	SH	SF	HB	TBB	IBB	SO	WP	W	L	Pct	Sv-Op	Hld	Vel	OPS	ERC	ERA
2017 CWS	AL	30	0	3	22.0	91	13	11	11	4	1	1	1	15	1	17	1	1	3	.250	0-1	7	93	.692	3.70	4.50
2018 CWS	AL	37	0	9	31.2	144	40	19	15	1	0	0	1	10	0	35	7	0	1	.000	0-1	2	93	.730	4.80	4.26
2019 CWS	AL	58	0	5	67.2	262	43	17	16	4	1	0	3	24	2	60	4	0	0	-	1-3	27	96	.520	1.99	2.13
2020 CWS	AL	9	0	1	9.1	38	5	1	1	0	0	0	0	5	0	14	0	1	0	1.000	0-0	3	96	.415	1.60	0.96
2021 CWS	AL	62	0	6	56.1	242	42	28	22	3	0	1	4	29	3	75	5	5	5	.500	2-8	21	95	.560	2.96	3.51
Postseason		2	0	0	1.1	6	1	0	0	0	0	0	0	1	0	1	0	0	0	-	0-0	1	96	.533	3.21	0.00
5 ML YEARS		196	0	24	187.0	777	143	76	65	12	2	2	9	83	6	201	17	7	9	.438	3-13	60	95	.587	2.89	3.13

Dylan Bundy

Pitches: R Bats: B Pos: SP-19; RP-4 Ht: 6'1" Wt: 225 Born: 11/15/1992 Age: 29

Year Team	Lg	G	GS	GF	IP	BFP	H	R	ER	HR	SH	SF	HB	TBB	IBB	SO	WP	W	L	Pct	Sv-Op	Hld	Vel	OPS	ERC	ERA
2012 Bal	AL	2	0	2	1.2	6	1	0	0	0	0	0	0	1	0	0	0	0	0	-	0-0	0	94	.533	2.46	0.00
2016 Bal	AL	36	14	6	109.2	474	109	52	49	18	1	1	6	42	4	104	0	10	6	.625	0-0	3	94	.766	4.61	4.02
2017 Bal	AL	28	28	0	169.2	698	152	82	80	26	0	7	7	51	0	152	0	13	9	.591	0-0	0	92	.721	3.68	4.24
2018 Bal	AL	31	31	0	171.2	750	188	116	104	41	3	2	6	54	1	184	6	8	16	.333	0-0	0	92	.855	5.39	5.45
2019 Bal	AL	30	30	0	161.2	700	161	95	86	29	1	7	6	58	0	162	7	7	14	.333	0-0	0	91	.784	4.57	4.79
2020 LAA	AL	11	11	0	65.2	267	51	24	21	5	0	4	2	17	1	72	0	6	3	.667	0-0	0	90	.614	2.41	3.29
2021 LAA	AL	23	19	1	90.2	397	89	64	61	20	2	3	6	34	0	84	1	2	9	.182	0-0	0	91	.818	4.94	6.06
7 ML YEARS		161	133	9	770.2	3292	751	436	404	139	7	20	35	257	6	758	16	46	57	.447	0-0	3	92	.774	4.39	4.72

Zack Burdi

Pitches: R **Bats:** R **Pos:** RP-7 **Ht:** 6'3" **Wt:** 210 **Born:** 3/9/1995 **Age:** 27

Year Team	Lg	G	GS	GF	IP	BFP	H	R	ER	HR	SH	SF	HB	TBB	IBB	SO	WP	W	L	Pct	Sv-Op	Hld	Vel	OPS	ERC	ERA
2021 Charllt	AAA	23	0	8	24.2	115	22	23	20	8	0	1	2	15	0	35	5	0	2	.000	2- -	-	-	.834	6.08	7.30
2020 CWS	AL	8	0	0	7.1	37	11	11	9	4	0	0	0	3	0	11	1	0	1	.000	0-1	1	98	1.084	10.46	11.05
2021 2 Tms	AL	7	0	2	10.0	49	13	7	6	3	0	2	2	5	0	7	0	0	0	-	0-0	0	96	.983	8.91	5.40
21 CWS	AL	6	0	1	9.0	45	13	7	6	3	0	2	2	4	0	6	0	0	0	-	0-0	0	96	1.044	10.08	6.00
21 Bal	AL	1	0	1	1.0	4	0	0	0	0	0	0	0	1	0	1	0	0	0	-	0-0	0	97	.250	0.95	0.00
2 ML YEARS		15	0	2	17.1	86	24	18	15	7	0	2	2	8	0	18	1	0	1	.000	0-1	1	97	1.030	9.60	7.79

Jake Burger

Bats: R **Throws:** R **Pos:** 3B-8;DH-5;PH-4 **Ht:** 6'2" **Wt:** 230 **Born:** 4/10/1996 **Age:** 26

Year Team	Lg	G	AB	H	2B	3B	HR	(Hm	Rd)	TB	R	RBI	RC	TBB	IBB	SO	HBP	SH	SF	SB	CS	GDP	Avg	OBP	Slg	OPS
2021 Charllt	AAA	79	300	82	16	2	18	(-	-)	156	46	54	-	21	1	89	4	0	2	0	0	8	.273	.327	.520	.847
2021 CWS	AL	15	38	10	3	1	1	(1	0)	18	5	3	6	4	0	15	0	0	0	0	0	2	.263	.333	.474	.807

Corbin Burnes

Pitches: R **Bats:** R **Pos:** SP-28 **Ht:** 6'3" **Wt:** 225 **Born:** 10/22/1994 **Age:** 27

Year Team	Lg	G	GS	GF	IP	BFP	H	R	ER	HR	SH	SF	HB	TBB	IBB	SO	WP	W	L	Pct	Sv-Op	Hld	Vel	OPS	ERC	ERA
2018 Mil	NL	30	0	6	38.0	152	27	11	11	4	1	1	3	11	2	35	2	1	0	1.000	1-2	3	95	.595	2.42	2.61
2019 Mil	NL	32	4	8	49.0	235	70	52	48	17	3	0	0	20	0	70	2	1	5	.167	1-1	4	95	1.011	8.65	8.82
2020 Mil	NL	12	9	2	59.2	240	37	15	14	2	0	0	3	24	0	88	5	4	1	.800	0-0	0	96	.515	1.91	2.11
2021 Mil	NL	28	28	0	167.0	657	123	47	45	7	1	4	6	34	0	234	5	11	5	.688	0-0	0	97	.521	1.81	2.43
Postseason		6	0	1	9.0	31	4	2	2	0	0	0	1	1	0	11	0	1	0	1.000	0-0	1	96	.400	0.81	2.00
4 ML YEARS		102	41	16	313.2	1284	257	125	118	30	5	5	12	89	2	427	14	23	11	.676	2-3	7	96	.618	2.77	3.39

Andy Burns

Bats: R **Throws:** R **Pos:** PH-5;2B-3;1B-2;3B-2;PR-1 **Ht:** 6'2" **Wt:** 205 **Born:** 8/7/1990 **Age:** 31

Year Team	Lg	G	AB	H	2B	3B	HR	(Hm	Rd)	TB	R	RBI	RC	TBB	IBB	SO	HBP	SH	SF	SB	CS	GDP	Avg	OBP	Slg	OPS
2021 OkCity	AAA	50	166	39	12	1	5	(-	-)	68	35	22	-	33	0	49	1	0	2	10	2	1	.235	.361	.410	.771
2016 Tor	AL	10	6	0	0	0	0	(0	0)	0	2	0	0	0	0	2	1	0	0	0	0	0	.000	.143	.000	.143
2021 LAD	NL	9	11	3	1	0	0	(0	0)	4	2	0	2	3	0	1	1	0	0	0	0	1	.273	.467	.364	.830
2 ML YEARS		19	17	3	1	0	0	(0	0)	4	4	0	2	3	0	3	2	0	0	0	0	1	.176	.364	.235	.599

Ryan Burr

Pitches: R **Bats:** R **Pos:** RP-33; SP-1 **Ht:** 6'4" **Wt:** 220 **Born:** 5/28/1994 **Age:** 28

Year Team	Lg	G	GS	GF	IP	BFP	H	R	ER	HR	SH	SF	HB	TBB	IBB	SO	WP	W	L	Pct	Sv-Op	Hld	Vel	OPS	ERC	ERA
2021 Charllt	AAA	15	0	5	15.2	73	17	11	8	3	0	1	0	7	1	14	1	1	2	.333	3- -	-	-	.760	5.05	4.60
2018 CWS	AL	8	0	1	9.2	44	12	8	8	3	1	0	1	6	1	6	0	0	0	-	0-0	0	95	1.109	9.13	7.45
2019 CWS	AL	16	1	2	19.2	86	17	13	10	3	1	2	0	8	0	20	0	1	1	.500	0-0	0	95	.707	3.54	4.58
2021 CWS	AL	34	1	8	36.2	151	28	11	10	3	2	2	1	21	0	33	5	2	1	.667	0-1	3	95	.656	3.58	2.45
3 ML YEARS		58	2	11	66.0	281	57	32	28	9	4	4	2	35	1	59	5	3	2	.600	0-1	3	95	.742	4.27	3.82

Beau Burrows

Pitches: R **Bats:** R **Pos:** RP-5; SP-1 **Ht:** 6'2" **Wt:** 210 **Born:** 9/18/1996 **Age:** 25

Year Team	Lg	G	GS	GF	IP	BFP	H	R	ER	HR	SH	SF	HB	TBB	IBB	SO	WP	W	L	Pct	Sv-Op	Hld	Vel	OPS	ERC	ERA
2021 Toledo	AAA	9	1	0	17.1	78	21	12	12	4	0	1	0	6	0	17	1	1	1	.500	0- -	-	-	.994	6.02	6.23
2021 StPaul	AAA	12	8	1	43.2	190	35	24	23	9	1	0	4	19	0	44	2	3	4	.429	0- -	-	-	.729	4.09	4.74
2020 Det	AL	5	0	1	6.2	30	8	4	4	3	0	0	1	1	0	3	0	0	0	-	0-0	0	93	.976	7.26	5.40
2021 2 Tms	AL	6	1	2	11.0	58	16	18	17	5	0	4	0	10	0	8	0	0	1	.000	0-0	0	93	1.312	12.53	13.91
21 Det	AL	1	0	0	1.2	9	2	4	4	0	0	0	0	2	0	3	0	0	0	-	0-0	0	95	.873	7.49	21.60
21 Min	AL	5	1	2	9.1	49	14	14	13	5	0	4	0	8	0	5	0	0	1	.000	0-0	0	93	1.395	13.44	12.54
2 ML YEARS		11	1	3	17.2	88	24	22	21	8	0	4	1	11	0	11	0	0	1	.000	0-0	0	93	1.187	10.50	10.70

Matt Bush

Pitches: R **Bats:** R **Pos:** RP-4 **Ht:** 5'9" **Wt:** 180 **Born:** 2/8/1986 **Age:** 36

Year Team	Lg	G	GS	GF	IP	BFP	H	R	ER	HR	SH	SF	HB	TBB	IBB	SO	WP	W	L	Pct	Sv-Op	Hld	Vel	OPS	ERC	ERA
2016 Tex	AL	58	0	15	61.2	243	44	18	17	4	1	3	1	14	0	61	2	7	2	.778	1-4	22	97	.525	1.83	2.48
2017 Tex	AL	57	0	22	52.1	240	57	30	22	7	0	1	4	19	0	58	2	3	4	.429	10-15	10	97	.750	4.81	3.78
2018 Tex	AL	21	0	6	23.0	108	23	13	12	7	0	2	2	14	0	19	1	0	0	-	0-0	3	96	.828	5.37	4.70
2021 Tex	AL	4	0	1	4.0	17	4	3	3	3	0	0	2	1	0	5	0	0	0	-	0-0	2	95	1.107	7.62	6.75
Postseason		2	0	1	3.2	14	1	1	0	0	0	0	0	2	1	6	0	0	1	.000	0-0	0	98	.381	0.66	0.00
4 ML YEARS		140	0	44	141.0	608	128	64	54	17	1	6	7	48	0	143	5	10	6	.625	11-19	37	97	.682	3.58	3.45

Drew Butera

Bats: R Throws: R Pos: C-12   bue-TARE-ah   Ht: 6'1" Wt: 212 Born: 8/9/1983 Age: 38

Year	Team	Lg	G	AB	H	2B	3B	HR	(Hm	Rd)	TB	R	RBI	RC	TBB	IBB	SO	HBP	SH	SF	SB	CS	GDP	Avg	OBP	Slg	OPS
2021	Salt Lk	AAA	49	158	35	7	1	4	(-	-)	56	28	11	-	19	0	50	6	2	0	3	1	5	.222	.328	.354	.682
2021	SgrLnd	AAA	14	44	5	1	0	2	(-	-)	12	8	5	-	8	0	14	2	0	1	0	0	2	.114	.273	.273	.545
2010	Min	AL	49	142	28	6	1	2	(0	2)	42	12	13	7	4	0	25	4	3	2	0	0	5	.197	.237	.296	.533
2011	Min	AL	93	234	39	9	1	2	(1	1)	56	19	23	11	11	0	42	2	6	1	0	0	7	.167	.210	.239	.449
2012	Min	AL	42	111	22	6	0	1	(1	0)	31	7	5	6	9	0	26	2	0	0	0	0	3	.198	.270	.279	.550
2013	2 Tms		6	10	1	0	0	0	(0	0)	1	0	0	0	0	0	5	0	0	0	0	0	0	.100	.100	.100	.200
2014	LAD	NL	61	170	32	6	1	3	(0	3)	49	16	14	10	17	1	41	2	1	2	0	0	0	.188	.267	.288	.555
2015	2 Tms	AL	55	107	21	3	0	1	(0	1)	27	9	5	6	6	0	26	2	5	0	0	1	0	.196	.252	.252	.505
2016	KC	AL	56	123	35	10	1	4	(0	4)	59	18	16	15	8	0	36	0	2	0	0	0	2	.285	.328	.480	.808
2017	KC	AL	75	163	37	4	1	3	(1	2)	52	18	14	18	12	0	41	1	1	0	0	0	0	.227	.284	.319	.603
2018	2 Tms		62	163	31	9	0	3	(2	1)	49	13	21	13	15	0	39	2	0	0	0	0	4	.190	.264	.301	.564
2019	Col	NL	16	43	7	3	0	0	(0	0)	10	6	3	1	4	0	14	0	1	1	0	0	2	.163	.229	.233	.462
2020	Col	NL	29	39	6	2	0	0	(0	0)	8	4	4	0	2	0	11	0	1	1	0	0	3	.154	.190	.205	.396
2021	LAA	AL	12	32	3	1	0	0	(0	0)	4	1	5	0	0	0	16	0	3	1	0	0	0	.094	.091	.125	.216
13	Min	AL	2	3	0	0	0	0	(0	0)	0	0	0	0	0	0	1	0	0	0	0	0	0	.000	.000	.000	.000
13	LAD	NL	4	7	1	0	0	0	(0	0)	1	0	0	0	0	0	4	0	0	0	0	0	0	.143	.143	.143	.286
15	LAA	AL	10	21	4	0	0	0	(0	0)	4	3	0	0	0	0	2	0	0	0	0	1	0	.190	.190	.190	.381
15	KC	AL	45	86	17	3	0	1	(0	1)	23	6	5	6	6	0	24	2	5	0	0	0	0	.198	.266	.267	.533
18	KC	AL	52	149	28	9	0	2	(1	1)	43	11	18	10	13	0	37	2	0	0	0	0	4	.188	.259	.289	.548
18	Col	NL	10	14	3	0	0	1	(1	0)	6	2	3	0	2	0	2	0	0	0	0	0	0	.214	.313	.429	.741
Postseason			4	3	0	0	0	0	(0	0)	0	0	0	0	2	0	0	0	0	0	0	0	0	.000	.400	.000	.400
12 ML YEARS			556	1337	262	59	5	19	(14	14)	388	123	123	87	88	1	322	15	23	10	0	1	27	.196	.252	.290	.542

Byron Buxton

Bats: R Throws: R Pos: CF-60;PH-1   Ht: 6'2" Wt: 190 Born: 12/18/1993 Age: 28

Year	Team	Lg	G	AB	H	2B	3B	HR	(Hm	Rd)	TB	R	RBI	RC	TBB	IBB	SO	HBP	SH	SF	SB	CS	GDP	Avg	OBP	Slg	OPS
2015	Min	AL	46	129	27	7	1	2	(0	2)	42	16	6	10	6	0	44	1	2	0	2	2	1	.209	.250	.326	.576
2016	Min	AL	92	298	67	19	6	10	(6	4)	128	44	38	33	23	0	118	3	4	3	10	2	2	.225	.284	.430	.714
2017	Min	AL	140	462	117	14	6	16	(8	8)	191	69	51	63	38	2	150	4	5	2	29	1	1	.253	.314	.413	.728
2018	Min	AL	28	90	14	4	0	0	(0	0)	18	8	4	3	3	0	28	0	1	0	5	0	1	.156	.183	.200	.383
2019	Min	AL	87	271	71	30	4	10	(4	6)	139	48	46	44	19	1	68	2	2	1	14	3	3	.262	.314	.513	.827
2020	Min	AL	39	130	33	3	0	13	(4	9)	75	19	27	17	2	0	36	1	0	2	2	1	2	.254	.267	.577	.844
2021	Min	AL	61	235	72	23	0	19	(9	10)	152	50	32	50	13	0	62	6	0	0	9	1	0	.306	.358	.647	1.005
Postseason			3	6	1	0	0	0	(0	0)	1	0	1	0	0	0	4	0	0	0	2	1	0	.167	.167	.167	.333
7 ML YEARS			493	1615	401	100	17	70	(31	39)	745	254	204	221	104	3	506	17	14	8	71	10	10	.248	.299	.461	.761

Asdrubal Cabrera

Bats: B Throws: R Pos: 3B-65;PH-35;1B-19;DH-2;SS-1   azz-DRUE-bull   Ht: 6'0" Wt: 235 Born: 11/13/1985 Age: 36

Year	Team	Lg	G	AB	H	2B	3B	HR	(Hm	Rd)	TB	R	RBI	RC	TBB	IBB	SO	HBP	SH	SF	SB	CS	GDP	Avg	OBP	Slg	OPS
2007	Cle	AL	45	159	45	9	2	3	(1	2)	67	30	22	27	17	0	29	2	5	3	0	0	7	.283	.354	.421	.775
2008	Cle	AL	114	352	91	20	0	6	(5	1)	129	48	47	48	46	2	77	4	11	5	4	4	8	.259	.346	.366	.713
2009	Cle	AL	131	523	161	42	4	6	(4	2)	229	81	68	81	44	1	89	1	10	3	17	4	13	.308	.361	.438	.799
2010	Cle	AL	97	381	105	16	1	3	(2	1)	132	39	29	46	25	0	60	5	11	3	6	4	10	.276	.326	.346	.673
2011	Cle	AL	151	604	165	32	3	25	(13	12)	278	87	92	100	44	5	119	11	4	4	17	5	10	.273	.332	.460	.792
2012	Cle	AL	143	555	150	35	1	16	(10	6)	235	70	68	74	52	3	99	6	1	2	9	4	18	.270	.338	.423	.762
2013	Cle	AL	136	508	123	35	2	14	(8	6)	204	66	64	51	35	1	114	8	6	5	9	3	10	.242	.299	.402	.700
2014	2 Tms		146	553	133	31	4	14	(6	8)	214	74	61	57	49	2	108	7	1	6	10	2	15	.241	.307	.387	.694
2015	TB	AL	143	505	134	28	5	15	(7	8)	217	66	58	53	36	4	107	3	1	6	6	3	14	.265	.315	.430	.744
2016	NYM	NL	141	521	146	30	1	23	(18	5)	247	65	62	76	38	3	103	7	0	2	5	1	14	.280	.336	.474	.810
2017	NYM	NL	135	479	134	32	0	14	(5	9)	208	66	59	70	50	1	83	5	1	5	3	2	19	.280	.351	.434	.785
2018	2 Tms	NL	147	546	143	36	1	23	(10	13)	250	68	75	77	41	1	119	3	0	2	0	0	16	.262	.316	.458	.774
2019	2 Tms	NL	131	447	116	25	1	18	(13	5)	197	69	91	79	57	2	103	3	0	7	4	0	9	.260	.342	.441	.783
2020	Was	NL	52	190	46	9	3	8	(2	6)	85	23	31	26	19	0	40	0	0	4	0	0	6	.242	.305	.447	.753
2021	2 Tms	NL	110	309	71	21	0	7	(3	4)	113	34	42	36	36	1	80	3	0	4	1	0	8	.230	.313	.366	.678
14	Cle	AL	97	378	93	22	2	9	(5	4)	146	54	40	36	27	1	79	7	0	4	7	2	11	.246	.305	.386	.692
14	Was	NL	49	175	40	9	2	5	(1	4)	68	20	21	21	22	1	29	0	1	2	3	0	4	.229	.312	.389	.700
18	NYM	NL	98	375	104	23	1	18	(7	11)	183	48	58	57	29	1	81	1	0	2	0	0	12	.277	.329	.488	.817
18	Phi	NL	49	171	39	13	0	5	(3	2)	67	20	17	20	12	0	38	2	0	0	0	0	4	.228	.286	.392	.678
19	Tex	AL	93	323	76	15	0	12	(11	1)	127	45	51	47	38	1	85	3	0	4	4	0	6	.235	.318	.393	.711
19	Was	NL	38	124	40	10	1	6	(2	4)	70	24	40	32	19	1	18	0	0	3	0	0	3	.323	.404	.565	.969
21	Ari	NL	90	283	69	21	0	7	(3	4)	111	34	40	36	33	1	73	2	0	3	1	0	6	.244	.324	.392	.716
21	Cin	NL	20	26	2	0	0	0	(0	0)	2	0	2	0	3	0	7	1	0	1	0	0	2	.077	.194	.077	.270
Postseason			29	98	21	2	0	2	(2	0)	29	8	13	10	4	0	28	0	4	2	0	0	3	.214	.240	.296	.536
15 ML YEARS			1822	6632	1763	401	28	195	(107	88)	2805	886	869	901	589	26	1330	68	51	61	91	32	177	.266	.329	.423	.752

Edward Cabrera

Pitches: R Bats: R Pos: SP-7   Ht: 6'5" Wt: 217 Born: 4/13/1998 Age: 24

	HOW MUCH PITCHED						WHAT HE GAVE UP										THE RESULTS						
Year	Team	Lg	G	GS	GF	IP	BFP	H	R	ER	HR	SH	SF	HB	TBB	IBB	SO	WP	W	L	Pct	Sv-Op	Hld	Vel	OPS	ERC	ERA
2017	Batvia	A-	13	6	1	35.2	165	42	27	21	1	0	3	7	8	0	32	7	1	3	.250	0- -	-	-	.767	4.47	5.30
2018	Grnsbr	A	22	18	0	100.1	440	105	57	47	11	0	0	6	42	0	93	17	4	8	.333	0- -	-	-	.870	4.77	4.22
2019	Jaxnvl	AA	8	8	0	38.2	156	28	12	11	6	0	0	3	13	0	43	11	4	1	.800	0- -	-	-	.653	3.04	2.56

163

Year	Team	Lg	G	GS	GF	IP	BFP	H	R	ER	HR	SH	SF	HB	TBB	IBB	SO	WP	W	L	Pct	Sv-Op	Hld	Vel	OPS	ERC	ERA
2019	Jupiter	A+	11	10	0	58.0	227	37	16	13	1	1	0	5	18	0	73	0	5	3	.625	0--	-	-	.564	1.76	2.02
2021	Pnscla	AA	5	5	0	26.0	97	19	10	8	3	1	0	0	6	0	33	3	2	1	.667	0--	-	-	.605	2.29	2.77
2021	Jaxnvl	AAA	6	6	0	29.1	129	22	13	12	4	0	2	1	19	0	48	5	1	3	.250	0--	-	-	.737	3.99	3.68
2021	Mia	NL	7	7	0	26.1	120	24	20	17	6	0	0	4	19	0	28	3	0	3	.000	0-0	0	97	.897	6.71	5.81

Genesis Cabrera

Pitches: L **Bats:** L **Pos:** RP-71   heh-NEH-sees   **Ht:** 6'2" **Wt:** 180 **Born:** 10/10/1996 **Age:** 25

Year	Team	Lg	G	GS	GF	IP	BFP	H	R	ER	HR	SH	SF	HB	TBB	IBB	SO	WP	W	L	Pct	Sv-Op	Hld	Vel	OPS	ERC	ERA
2019	StL	NL	13	2	5	20.1	99	23	16	11	2	1	1	2	11	0	19	1	0	2	.000	1-1	1	96	.760	5.53	4.87
2020	StL	NL	19	0	1	22.1	96	10	9	6	3	0	0	4	16	0	32	3	4	1	.800	1-1	2	96	.589	3.18	2.42
2021	StL	NL	71	0	5	70.0	296	52	31	29	3	4	2	5	36	2	77	9	4	5	.444	0-3	28	98	.628	2.96	3.73
	Postseason		4	0	1	2.2	13	2	2	2	0	0	1	1	3	0	2	0	0	0	-	0-0	1	98	.712	6.41	6.75
	3 ML YEARS		103	2	11	112.2	491	85	56	46	8	5	3	11	63	2	128	13	8	8	.500	2-5	31	97	.647	3.44	3.67

Miguel Cabrera

Bats: R **Throws:** R **Pos:** DH-83;1B-44;PH-3   **Ht:** 6'4" **Wt:** 267 **Born:** 4/18/1983 **Age:** 39

Year	Team	Lg	G	AB	H	2B	3B	HR	(Hm	Rd)	TB	R	RBI	RC	TBB	IBB	SO	HBP	SH	SF	SB	CS	GDP	Avg	OBP	Slg	OPS
2003	Fla	NL	87	314	84	21	3	12	(7	5)	147	39	62	51	25	3	84	2	4	1	0	2	12	.268	.325	.468	.793
2004	Fla	NL	160	603	177	31	1	33	(14	19)	309	101	112	92	68	5	148	6	0	8	5	2	20	.294	.366	.512	.879
2005	Fla	NL	158	613	198	43	2	33	(11	22)	344	106	116	108	64	12	125	2	0	6	1	0	20	.323	.385	.561	.947
2006	Fla	NL	158	576	195	50	2	26	(15	11)	327	112	114	132	86	27	108	10	0	4	9	6	18	.339	.430	.568	.998
2007	Fla	NL	157	588	188	38	2	34	(19	15)	332	91	119	122	79	23	127	5	1	7	2	1	17	.320	.401	.565	.965
2008	Det	AL	160	616	180	36	2	37	(19	18)	331	85	127	109	56	6	126	3	0	9	1	0	16	.292	.349	.537	.887
2009	Det	AL	160	611	198	34	0	34	(19	15)	334	96	103	114	68	14	107	5	0	1	6	2	22	.324	.396	.547	.942
2010	Det	AL	150	548	180	45	1	38	(17	21)	341	111	126	122	89	32	95	3	0	8	3	3	17	.328	.420	.622	1.042
2011	Det	AL	161	572	197	48	0	30	(15	15)	335	111	105	141	108	22	89	3	0	5	2	1	24	.344	.448	.586	1.033
2012	Det	AL	161	622	205	40	0	44	(28	16)	377	109	139	123	66	17	98	3	0	6	4	1	28	.330	.393	.606	.999
2013	Det	AL	148	555	193	26	1	44	(17	27)	353	103	137	146	90	19	94	5	0	2	3	0	19	.348	.442	.636	1.078
2014	Det	AL	159	611	191	52	1	25	(13	12)	320	101	109	110	60	10	117	3	0	11	1	1	21	.313	.371	.524	.895
2015	Det	AL	119	429	145	28	1	18	(7	11)	229	64	76	93	77	15	82	3	0	2	1	1	19	.338	.440	.534	.974
2016	Det	AL	158	595	188	31	1	38	(20	18)	335	92	108	106	75	15	116	4	0	5	0	0	26	.316	.393	.563	.956
2017	Det	AL	130	469	117	22	0	16	(11	5)	187	50	60	55	54	6	110	3	0	3	0	1	15	.249	.329	.399	.728
2018	Det	AL	38	134	40	11	0	3	(2	1)	60	17	22	23	22	4	27	0	0	1	0	0	6	.299	.395	.448	.843
2019	Det	AL	136	493	139	21	0	12	(5	7)	196	41	59	72	48	4	108	3	0	5	0	0	18	.282	.346	.398	.744
2020	Det	AL	57	204	51	4	0	10	(5	5)	85	28	35	39	24	1	51	1	0	2	1	0	3	.250	.329	.417	.746
2021	Det	AL	130	472	121	16	0	15	(5	10)	182	48	75	58	40	0	118	5	0	9	0	0	21	.256	.316	.386	.701
	Postseason		55	205	57	10	0	13	(4	9)	106	29	38	34	27	7	48	2	1	0	3	0	7	.278	.368	.517	.885
	19 ML YEARS		2587	9625	2987	597	17	502	(249	253)	5124	1505	1804	1816	1199	235	1930	69	5	95	39	21	342	.310	.387	.532	.920

Trevor Cahill

Pitches: R **Bats:** R **Pos:** SP-8; RP-1   KAY-hill   **Ht:** 6'4" **Wt:** 223 **Born:** 3/1/1988 **Age:** 34

Year	Team	Lg	G	GS	GF	IP	BFP	H	R	ER	HR	SH	SF	HB	TBB	IBB	SO	WP	W	L	Pct	Sv-Op	Hld	Vel	OPS	ERC	ERA
2009	Oak	AL	32	32	0	178.2	773	185	99	92	27	4	7	4	72	1	90	5	10	13	.435	0-0	0	90	.810	4.79	4.63
2010	Oak	AL	30	30	0	196.2	783	155	73	65	19	3	6	6	63	1	118	2	18	8	.692	0-0	0	90	.619	2.81	2.97
2011	Oak	AL	34	34	0	207.2	901	214	102	96	19	8	6	8	82	1	147	15	12	14	.462	0-0	0	89	.738	4.34	4.16
2012	Ari	NL	32	32	0	200.0	839	184	93	84	16	12	6	11	74	0	156	10	13	12	.520	0-0	0	89	.706	3.66	3.78
2013	Ari	NL	26	25	1	146.2	636	143	70	65	13	9	9	6	65	2	102	17	8	10	.444	0-0	0	89	.745	4.19	3.99
2014	Ari	NL	32	17	8	110.2	499	123	76	69	9	6	3	4	55	2	105	5	3	12	.200	1-2	0	90	.791	5.11	5.61
2015	2 Tms	NL	26	3	6	43.1	187	44	27	26	4	3	1	2	16	1	36	2	1	3	.250	0-0	2	92	.725	4.15	5.40
2016	ChC	NL	50	1	16	65.2	284	49	22	20	7	0	0	5	35	3	66	3	4	4	.500	0-1	4	92	.621	3.42	2.74
2017	2 Tms	NL	21	14	1	84.0	381	91	50	46	16	2	0	3	45	1	87	16	4	3	.571	0-0	0	91	.850	5.97	4.93
2018	Oak	AL	21	20	0	110.0	450	90	52	46	8	3	3	5	41	0	100	8	7	4	.636	0-0	0	92	.653	3.05	3.76
2019	LAA	AL	37	11	12	102.1	455	111	71	68	25	0	4	6	39	0	81	14	4	9	.308	0-0	2	92	.880	5.78	5.98
2020	SF	NL	11	6	2	25.0	106	16	10	9	3	1	2	2	14	0	31	1	1	2	.333	0-0	1	91	.638	3.15	3.24
2021	Pit	NL	9	8	1	37.0	166	42	29	27	4	1	3	1	14	0	32	2	1	5	.167	0-0	0	90	.767	4.88	6.57
15	Atl	NL	15	3	6	26.1	124	36	23	22	2	2	1	1	11	1	14	1	0	3	.000	0-0	0	91	.843	6.22	7.52
15	ChC	NL	11	0	0	17.0	63	8	4	4	2	1	0	1	5	0	22	1	1	0	1.000	0-0	2	93	.494	1.52	2.12
17	SD	NL	11	11	0	61.0	263	58	29	25	6	1	0	3	24	1	72	14	4	3	.571	0-0	0	91	.712	3.92	3.69
17	KC	NL	10	3	1	23.0	118	33	21	21	10	1	0	0	21	0	15	2	0	0	-	0-0	1	91	1.180	12.52	8.22
	Postseason		6	0	1	5.1	24	7	2	2	0	1	0	0	0	0	8	1	1	1	.500	0-1	2	94	.783	3.29	3.38
	13 ML YEARS		361	233	47	1507.2	6460	1447	774	713	170	52	50	63	615	12	1151	100	86	99	.465	1-3	8	90	.737	4.16	4.26

Lorenzo Cain

Bats: R **Throws:** R **Pos:** CF-70;PH-9   **Ht:** 6'2" **Wt:** 214 **Born:** 4/13/1986 **Age:** 36

Year	Team	Lg	G	AB	H	2B	3B	HR	(Hm	Rd)	TB	R	RBI	RC	TBB	IBB	SO	HBP	SH	SF	SB	CS	GDP	Avg	OBP	Slg	OPS
2010	Mil	NL	43	147	45	11	1	1	(1	0)	61	17	13	23	9	0	28	1	0	1	7	1	1	.306	.348	.415	.763
2011	KC	AL	6	22	6	1	0	0	(0	0)	7	4	1	2	1	0	4	0	0	0	0	0	0	.273	.304	.318	.623
2012	KC	AL	61	222	59	9	2	7	(3	4)	93	27	31	32	15	0	56	3	0	4	10	4	4	.266	.316	.419	.734
2013	KC	AL	115	399	100	21	3	4	(3	1)	139	54	46	46	33	2	90	4	0	6	14	6	10	.251	.310	.348	.658
2014	KC	AL	133	471	142	29	4	5	(3	2)	194	55	53	67	24	2	108	4	0	3	28	5	9	.301	.339	.412	.751
2015	KC	AL	140	551	169	34	6	16	(9	7)	263	101	72	90	37	4	98	12	0	4	28	6	16	.307	.361	.477	.838
2016	KC	AL	103	397	114	19	1	9	(3	6)	162	56	56	53	31	3	84	2	0	4	14	5	15	.287	.339	.408	.747
2017	KC	AL	155	584	175	27	5	15	(3	12)	257	86	49	90	54	1	100	5	0	2	26	2	20	.300	.363	.440	.803

Year Team	Lg	G	AB	H	2B	3B	HR	(Hm	Rd)	TB	R	RBI	RC	TBB	IBB	SO	HBP	SH	SF	SB	CS	GDP	Avg	OBP	Slg	OPS
2018 Mil	NL	141	539	166	25	2	10	(4	6)	225	90	38	94	71	1	94	8	0	2	30	7	10	.308	.395	.417	.813
2019 Mil	NL	148	562	146	30	0	11	(7	4)	209	75	48	61	50	0	106	6	0	4	18	8	14	.260	.325	.372	.697
2020 Mil	NL	5	18	6	1	0	0	(0	0)	7	4	2	5	3	1	2	0	0	0	0	0	1	.333	.429	.389	.817
2021 Mil	NL	78	257	66	13	0	8	(1	7)	103	40	36	37	26	0	48	2	0	1	13	2	5	.257	.329	.401	.729
Postseason		42	171	48	11	0	1	(0	1)	62	28	20	29	19	3	36	1	1	2	8	2	1	.281	.352	.363	.715
12 ML YEARS		1128	4169	1194	220	24	86	(37	49)	1720	609	445	600	354	14	818	47	0	31	188	42	105	.286	.347	.413	.759

Kole Calhoun

Bats: L **Throws:** L **Pos:** RF-39;PH-12;DH-3   **Ht:** 5'10" **Wt:** 205 **Born:** 10/14/1987 **Age:** 34

Year Team	Lg	G	AB	H	2B	3B	HR	(Hm	Rd)	TB	R	RBI	RC	TBB	IBB	SO	HBP	SH	SF	SB	CS	GDP	Avg	OBP	Slg	OPS
2012 LAA	AL	21	23	4	1	0	0	(0	0)	5	2	1	0	2	1	6	0	0	0	1	0	0	.174	.240	.217	.457
2013 LAA	AL	58	195	55	7	2	8	(5	3)	90	29	32	33	21	0	41	1	0	5	2	2	6	.282	.347	.462	.808
2014 LAA	AL	127	493	134	31	3	17	(7	10)	222	90	58	75	38	0	104	2	2	2	5	3	5	.272	.325	.450	.776
2015 LAA	AL	159	630	161	23	2	26	(16	10)	266	78	83	85	45	1	164	5	2	4	4	1	6	.256	.308	.422	.731
2016 LAA	AL	157	594	161	35	5	18	(7	11)	260	91	75	93	67	0	118	6	0	5	2	3	10	.271	.348	.438	.786
2017 LAA	AL	155	569	139	23	2	19	(8	11)	223	77	71	85	71	4	134	1	0	6	5	1	10	.244	.333	.392	.725
2018 LAA	AL	137	491	102	18	2	19	(9	10)	181	71	57	53	53	2	133	1	0	6	6	2	9	.208	.283	.369	.652
2019 LAA	AL	152	552	128	29	1	33	(16	17)	258	92	74	77	70	7	162	7	0	2	4	1	14	.232	.325	.467	.792
2020 Ari	NL	54	190	43	9	0	16	(7	9)	100	35	40	37	28	0	50	6	0	4	1	1	6	.226	.338	.526	.864
2021 Ari	NL	51	166	39	8	0	5	(2	3)	62	17	17	13	15	0	41	0	0	1	1	0	2	.235	.297	.373	.670
Postseason		3	15	5	0	0	0	(0	0)	5	1	0	1	0	0	1	0	0	0	0	0	0	.333	.333	.333	.667
10 ML YEARS		1071	3903	966	184	17	161	(77	84)	1667	582	508	551	410	15	953	36	4	35	31	14	68	.248	.322	.427	.749

Willie Calhoun

Bats: L **Throws:** R **Pos:** LF-41;DH-29;PH-7   **Ht:** 5'8" **Wt:** 200 **Born:** 11/4/1994 **Age:** 27

Year Team	Lg	G	AB	H	2B	3B	HR	(Hm	Rd)	TB	R	RBI	RC	TBB	IBB	SO	HBP	SH	SF	SB	CS	GDP	Avg	OBP	Slg	OPS
2017 Tex	AL	13	34	9	0	0	1	(1	0)	12	3	4	6	2	0	7	1	0	0	0	0	0	.265	.324	.353	.677
2018 Tex	AL	35	99	22	5	0	2	(1	1)	33	8	11	11	6	0	24	1	0	2	0	0	2	.222	.269	.333	.602
2019 Tex	AL	83	309	83	14	1	21	(8	13)	162	51	48	49	23	0	53	3	0	2	0	0	5	.269	.323	.524	.848
2020 Tex	AL	29	100	19	2	1	1	(1	0)	26	3	13	9	5	0	17	1	0	2	0	0	1	.190	.231	.260	.491
2021 Tex	AL	75	260	65	10	3	6	(3	3)	99	26	25	29	21	0	34	2	0	1	0	2	6	.250	.310	.381	.691
5 ML YEARS		235	802	198	31	5	31	(14	17)	332	91	101	104	57	0	135	8	0	7	0	2	14	.247	.301	.414	.715

Daniel Camarena

Pitches: L **Bats:** L **Pos:** RP-6   **Ht:** 6'0" **Wt:** 210 **Born:** 11/9/1992 **Age:** 29

		HOW MUCH PITCHED					WHAT HE GAVE UP									THE RESULTS							
Year Team	Lg	G	GS	GF	IP	BFP	H	R	ER	HR	SH	SF	HB	TBB	IBB	SO	WP	W	L	Pct	Sv-Op	Hld	Vel	OPS	ERC	ERA
2021 ElPaso	AAA	21	18	1	77.1	342	80	50	43	11	2	6	2	29	2	55	7	5	7	.417	1--	-	-	.785	4.44	5.00
2021 SD	NL	6	0	2	9.1	47	16	12	10	2	0	0	0	3	1	7	0	0	1	.000	0-0	0	93	.972	8.75	9.64

Johan Camargo

Bats: B **Throws:** R **Pos:** PH-14;1B-1;2B-1;3B-1   **Ht:** 6'0" **Wt:** 195 **Born:** 12/13/1993 **Age:** 28

Year Team	Lg	G	AB	H	2B	3B	HR	(Hm	Rd)	TB	R	RBI	RC	TBB	IBB	SO	HBP	SH	SF	SB	CS	GDP	Avg	OBP	Slg	OPS
2021 Gwnntt	AAA	99	367	117	22	4	17	(-	-)	198	67	64	-	45	2	70	2	0	1	0	1	6	.319	.395	.540	.935
2017 Atl	NL	82	241	72	21	2	4	(2	2)	109	30	27	32	12	2	51	0	2	1	0	0	5	.299	.331	.452	.783
2018 Atl	NL	134	464	126	27	1	19	(7	12)	212	63	76	72	51	4	108	6	0	3	1	1	13	.272	.349	.457	.806
2019 Atl	NL	98	232	54	12	1	7	(2	5)	89	31	32	27	15	2	43	0	1	0	1	0	5	.233	.279	.384	.663
2020 Atl	NL	35	120	24	8	0	4	(1	3)	44	16	9	7	6	0	35	1	0	0	0	0	1	.200	.244	.367	.611
2021 Atl	NL	15	16	0	0	0	0	(0	0)	0	1	0	0	2	0	6	0	0	0	0	0	0	.000	.111	.000	.111
Postseason		8	23	2	1	0	0	(0	0)	3	1	1	2	3	0	8	0	0	0	0	0	1	.087	.192	.130	.323
5 ML YEARS		364	1073	276	68	4	34	(12	22)	454	141	144	138	86	8	243	7	3	4	2	1	24	.257	.315	.423	.738

Daz Cameron

Bats: R **Throws:** R **Pos:** RF-18;CF-15;PH-3;PR-3;DH-2;LF-1   **Ht:** 6'2" **Wt:** 185 **Born:** 1/15/1997 **Age:** 25

Year Team	Lg	G	AB	H	2B	3B	HR	(Hm	Rd)	TB	R	RBI	RC	TBB	IBB	SO	HBP	SH	SF	SB	CS	GDP	Avg	OBP	Slg	OPS
2021 Toledo	AAA	39	162	48	11	2	6	(-	-)	81	33	23	-	15	0	39	3	0	1	7	3	2	.296	.365	.500	.865
2020 Det	AL	17	57	11	2	1	0	(0	0)	15	4	3	3	2	0	19	0	0	0	1	0	1	.193	.220	.263	.483
2021 Det	AL	35	103	20	5	0	4	(2	2)	37	16	13	11	10	0	38	2	0	0	6	0	2	.194	.278	.359	.637
2 ML YEARS		52	160	31	7	1	4	(2	2)	52	20	16	14	12	0	57	2	0	0	7	0	3	.194	.259	.325	.584

Eric Campbell

Bats: R **Throws:** R **Pos:** 3B-2;1B-1;PH-1   **Ht:** 6'3" **Wt:** 215 **Born:** 4/9/1987 **Age:** 35

Year Team	Lg	G	AB	H	2B	3B	HR	(Hm	Rd)	TB	R	RBI	RC	TBB	IBB	SO	HBP	SH	SF	SB	CS	GDP	Avg	OBP	Slg	OPS
2021 Tacom	AAA	13	50	13	5	0	1	(-	-)	21	8	6	-	4	0	17	1	0	0	0	0	2	.260	.327	.420	.747
2014 NYM	NL	85	190	50	9	0	3	(2	1)	68	16	16	19	17	0	55	1	0	3	3	0	5	.263	.322	.358	.680
2015 NYM	NL	71	173	34	8	0	3	(0	3)	51	28	19	13	26	1	37	4	1	2	5	3	11	.197	.312	.295	.607

Year Team	Lg	G	AB	H	2B	3B	HR	(Hm	Rd)	TB	R	RBI	RC	TBB	IBB	SO	HBP	SH	SF	SB	CS	GDP	Avg	OBP	Slg	OPS
2016 NYM	NL	40	75	13	1	0	1	(0	1)	17	9	9	7	10	1	24	2	0	1	1	0	2	.173	.284	.227	.511
2021 Sea	AL	4	11	3	0	0	0	(0	0)	3	1	0	1	1	0	1	0	0	0	0	0	0	.273	.333	.273	.606
Postseason		1	1	0	0	0	0	(0	0)	0	0	0	0	0	0	1	0	0	0	0	0	0	.000	.000	.000	.000
4 ML YEARS		200	449	100	18	0	7	(2	5)	139	54	44	40	54	2	117	7	1	6	9	3	18	.223	.312	.310	.622

Paul Campbell

Pitches: R **Bats:** L **Pos:** RP-15; SP-1 **Ht:** 6'0" **Wt:** 210 **Born:** 7/26/1995 **Age:** 26

		HOW MUCH PITCHED					WHAT HE GAVE UP										THE RESULTS							
Year Team	Lg	G	GS	GF	IP	BFP	H	R	ER	HR	SH	SF	HB	TBB	IBB	SO	WP	W	L	Pct	Sv-Op	Hld	Vel	OPS	ERC	ERA
2021 Mia	NL	16	1	2	26.2	124	32	24	19	5	1	0	2	10	0	26	2	2	3	.400	0-0	0	93	.844	5.99	6.41

Luis Campusano

Bats: R **Throws:** R **Pos:** C-9;PH-2 **Ht:** 5'11" **Wt:** 232 **Born:** 9/29/1998 **Age:** 23

Year Team	Lg	G	AB	H	2B	3B	HR	(Hm	Rd)	TB	R	RBI	RC	TBB	IBB	SO	HBP	SH	SF	SB	CS	GDP	Avg	OBP	Slg	OPS
2017 2 Tms	Low	37	134	36	4	0	4	(-	-)	52	8	25	19	15	0	25	1	0	1	0	2	4	.269	.344	.388	.732
2018 FtWyn	A	70	260	75	11	0	3	(-	-)	95	26	40	34	19	0	43	4	0	1	0	1	9	.288	.345	.365	.710
2019 Lk Els	A+	110	422	137	31	1	15	(-	-)	215	63	81	87	52	2	57	4	0	9	0	0	15	.325	.396	.509	.906
2021 ElPaso	AAA	81	292	86	21	3	15	(-	-)	158	47	45	-	27	0	66	6	0	1	1	0	9	.295	.365	.541	.906
2020 SD	NL	1	3	1	0	0	1	(0	1)	4	2	1	1	0	0	2	1	0	0	0	0	0	.333	.500	1.333	1.833
2021 SD	NL	11	34	3	0	0	0	(0	0)	3	0	1	0	4	0	11	0	0	0	0	0	2	.088	.184	.088	.272
Postseason		1	1	0	0	0	0	(0	0)	0	0	0	0	0	0	1	0	0	0	0	0	0	.000	.000	.000	.000
2 ML YEARS		12	37	4	0	0	1	(0	1)	7	2	2	1	4	0	13	1	0	0	0	0	2	.108	.214	.189	.403

Jeimer Candelario

Bats: B **Throws:** R **Pos:** 3B-142;DH-7 **Ht:** 6'1" **Wt:** 216 **Born:** 11/24/1993 **Age:** 28

Year Team	Lg	G	AB	H	2B	3B	HR	(Hm	Rd)	TB	R	RBI	RC	TBB	IBB	SO	HBP	SH	SF	SB	CS	GDP	Avg	OBP	Slg	OPS
2016 ChC	NL	5	11	1	0	0	0	(0	0)	1	0	0	0	2	1	5	1	0	0	0	0	0	.091	.286	.091	.377
2017 2 Tms		38	127	36	9	0	3	(2	1)	54	18	16	19	13	0	30	2	0	0	0	0	3	.283	.359	.425	.784
2018 Det	AL	144	539	121	28	3	19	(10	9)	212	78	54	64	66	1	160	9	0	5	3	2	4	.224	.317	.393	.710
2019 Det	AL	94	335	68	17	2	8	(4	4)	113	33	32	35	43	1	99	7	0	1	3	1	3	.203	.306	.337	.643
2020 Det	AL	52	185	55	11	3	7	(3	4)	93	30	29	36	20	0	49	1	0	0	1	1	3	.297	.369	.503	.872
2021 Det	AL	149	557	151	42	3	16	(6	10)	247	75	67	93	65	4	135	4	0	0	0	0	10	.271	.351	.443	.795
17 ChC	NL	11	33	5	2	0	1	(0	1)	10	2	3	1	1	0	12	2	0	0	0	0	1	.152	.222	.303	.525
17 Det	AL	27	94	31	7	0	2	(2	0)	44	16	13	18	12	0	18	0	0	0	0	0	2	.330	.406	.468	.874
6 ML YEARS		482	1754	432	107	11	53	(25	28)	720	234	198	247	209	4	478	24	0	6	7	4	23	.246	.334	.410	.744

Mark Canha

Bats: R **Throws:** R **Pos:** LF-106;RF-27;CF-23;DH-6;1B-2;PH-2 CAN-uh **Ht:** 6'2" **Wt:** 209 **Born:** 2/15/1989 **Age:** 33

Year Team	Lg	G	AB	H	2B	3B	HR	(Hm	Rd)	TB	R	RBI	RC	TBB	IBB	SO	HBP	SH	SF	SB	CS	GDP	Avg	OBP	Slg	OPS
2015 Oak	AL	124	441	112	22	3	16	(8	8)	188	61	70	62	33	0	96	8	0	3	7	2	9	.254	.315	.426	.742
2016 Oak	AL	16	41	5	0	0	3	(1	2)	14	4	6	0	0	0	20	1	1	1	0	1	1	.122	.140	.341	.481
2017 Oak	AL	57	173	36	13	1	5	(3	2)	66	16	14	13	7	0	56	6	0	1	2	0	5	.208	.262	.382	.644
2018 Oak	AL	122	365	91	22	0	17	(8	9)	164	60	52	52	34	3	88	10	0	2	1	2	11	.249	.328	.449	.778
2019 Oak	AL	126	410	112	16	3	26	(15	11)	212	80	58	80	67	1	107	18	0	2	3	2	10	.273	.396	.517	.913
2020 Oak	AL	59	191	47	12	2	5	(3	2)	78	32	33	43	37	1	54	10	0	5	4	0	2	.246	.387	.408	.795
2021 Oak	AL	141	519	120	22	4	17	(7	10)	201	93	61	90	77	0	128	27	0	2	12	2	9	.231	.358	.387	.746
Postseason		9	29	4	0	0	1	(0	1)	7	3	3	0	3	0	10	0	0	1	0	0	0	.138	.212	.241	.454
7 ML YEARS		645	2140	523	107	13	89	(45	44)	923	346	294	340	255	5	549	80	1	16	29	9	47	.244	.344	.431	.776

Griffin Canning

Pitches: R **Bats:** R **Pos:** SP-13; RP-1 **Ht:** 6'2" **Wt:** 180 **Born:** 5/11/1996 **Age:** 26

		HOW MUCH PITCHED					WHAT HE GAVE UP										THE RESULTS							
Year Team	Lg	G	GS	GF	IP	BFP	H	R	ER	HR	SH	SF	HB	TBB	IBB	SO	WP	W	L	Pct	Sv-Op	Hld	Vel	OPS	ERC	ERA
2019 LAA	AL	18	17	1	90.1	384	80	46	46	14	1	4	8	30	0	96	9	5	6	.455	0-0	0	94	.739	3.87	4.58
2020 LAA	AL	11	11	0	56.1	238	54	29	25	8	0	4	1	23	0	56	5	2	3	.400	0-0	0	93	.771	4.33	3.99
2021 LAA	AL	14	13	0	62.2	277	65	41	39	14	0	1	1	28	0	62	3	5	4	.556	0-0	0	94	.841	5.44	5.60
3 ML YEARS		43	41	1	209.1	899	199	116	110	36	1	9	10	81	0	214	17	12	13	.480	0-0	0	94	.779	4.45	4.73

Robinson Cano

Bats: L **Throws:** R **Pos:** 2B kuh-NOE **Ht:** 6'0" **Wt:** 212 **Born:** 10/22/1982 **Age:** 39

Year Team	Lg	G	AB	H	2B	3B	HR	(Hm	Rd)	TB	R	RBI	RC	TBB	IBB	SO	HBP	SH	SF	SB	CS	GDP	Avg	OBP	Slg	OPS
2005 NYY	AL	132	522	155	34	4	14	(5	9)	239	78	62	59	16	3	68	3	7	3	1	3	16	.297	.320	.458	.778
2006 NYY	AL	122	482	165	41	1	15	(9	6)	253	62	78	74	18	3	54	2	1	5	5	2	19	.342	.365	.525	.890
2007 NYY	AL	160	617	189	41	7	19	(10	9)	301	93	97	94	39	5	85	8	1	4	4	5	19	.306	.353	.488	.841
2008 NYY	AL	159	597	162	35	3	14	(7	7)	245	70	72	64	26	3	65	5	1	5	2	4	18	.271	.305	.410	.715
2009 NYY	AL	161	637	204	48	2	25	(14	11)	331	103	85	79	30	2	63	3	0	4	5	7	22	.320	.352	.520	.871
2010 NYY	AL	160	626	200	41	3	29	(16	13)	334	103	109	118	57	14	77	8	0	5	3	2	19	.319	.381	.534	.914
2011 NYY	AL	159	623	188	46	7	28	(16	12)	332	104	118	111	38	11	96	12	0	8	8	2	18	.302	.349	.533	.882
2012 NYY	AL	161	627	196	48	1	33	(22	11)	345	105	94	110	61	10	96	7	0	2	3	2	22	.313	.379	.550	.929

Year	Team	Lg	G	AB	H	2B	3B	HR	(Hm	Rd)	TB	R	RBI	RC	TBB	IBB	SO	HBP	SH	SF	SB	CS	GDP	Avg	OBP	Slg	OPS
2013	NYY	AL	160	605	190	41	0	27	(11	16)	312	81	107	120	65	16	85	6	0	5	7	1	18	.314	.383	.516	.899
2014	Sea	AL	157	595	187	37	2	14	(9	5)	270	77	82	106	61	20	68	6	0	3	10	3	19	.314	.382	.454	.836
2015	Sea	AL	156	624	179	34	1	21	(11	10)	278	82	79	84	43	5	107	3	0	4	2	6	26	.287	.334	.446	.779
2016	Sea	AL	161	655	195	33	2	39	(17	22)	349	107	103	100	47	8	100	8	0	5	0	1	18	.298	.350	.533	.882
2017	Sea	AL	150	592	166	33	0	23	(11	12)	268	79	97	96	49	8	85	4	0	3	1	0	18	.280	.338	.453	.791
2018	Sea	AL	80	310	94	22	0	10	(5	5)	146	44	50	55	32	2	47	4	0	2	0	0	9	.303	.374	.471	.845
2019	NYM	NL	107	390	100	28	0	13	(6	7)	167	46	39	40	25	3	69	5	0	3	0	0	18	.256	.307	.428	.736
2020	NYM	NL	49	171	54	9	0	10	(3	7)	93	23	30	27	9	1	24	1	0	1	0	0	7	.316	.352	.544	.896
	Postseason		51	203	45	10	3	8	(5	3)	85	22	33	23	11	3	28	2	0	1	0	2	7	.222	.267	.419	.686
	16 ML YEARS		2234	8673	2624	571	33	334	(172	162)	4263	1257	1302	1337	616	112	1189	85	10	62	51	38	284	.303	.352	.492	.844

Victor Caratini

Bats: B Throws: R Pos: C-101;PH-16;1B-5;3B-2   **Ht: 6'1" Wt: 215 Born: 8/17/1993 Age: 28**

Year	Team	Lg	G	AB	H	2B	3B	HR	(Hm	Rd)	TB	R	RBI	RC	TBB	IBB	SO	HBP	SH	SF	SB	CS	GDP	Avg	OBP	Slg	OPS
2017	ChC	NL	31	59	15	3	0	1	(0	1)	21	6	2	3	4	1	13	3	0	0	0	0	3	.254	.333	.356	.689
2018	ChC	NL	76	181	42	7	0	2	(1	1)	55	21	21	15	12	0	42	4	2	1	0	0	5	.232	.293	.304	.597
2019	ChC	NL	95	244	65	11	0	11	(4	7)	109	31	34	35	29	0	59	3	0	3	1	0	6	.266	.348	.447	.794
2020	ChC	NL	44	116	28	7	0	1	(0	1)	38	10	16	15	12	1	31	4	0	0	0	1	4	.241	.333	.328	.661
2021	SD	NL	116	313	71	9	0	7	(4	3)	101	33	39	30	35	8	82	4	0	4	2	0	13	.227	.309	.323	.632
	Postseason		3	7	1	0	0	0	(0	0)	1	0	0	0	0	0	1	0	0	0	0	0	0	.143	.143	.143	.286
	5 ML YEARS		362	913	221	37	0	22	(9	13)	324	101	112	98	92	10	227	18	2	8	3	1	31	.242	.321	.355	.676

Dylan Carlson

Bats: B Throws: L Pos: RF-87;CF-60;LF-9;PH-4   **Ht: 6'2" Wt: 205 Born: 10/23/1998 Age: 23**

Year	Team	Lg	G	AB	H	2B	3B	HR	(Hm	Rd)	TB	R	RBI	RC	TBB	IBB	SO	HBP	SH	SF	SB	CS	GDP	Avg	OBP	Slg	OPS
2017	Peoria	A	115	383	92	18	1	7	(-	-)	133	63	42	53	52	1	116	9	4	3	6	6	5	.240	.342	.347	.690
2018	2 Tms	Low	112	423	104	22	3	11	(-	-)	165	68	62	59	62	4	88	7	1	5	8	3	15	.246	.348	.390	.738
2019	Sprgfld	AA	108	417	117	24	6	21	(-	-)	216	81	59	81	52	3	98	7	0	7	18	7	3	.281	.364	.518	.882
2019	Memp	AAA	18	72	26	4	2	5	(-	-)	49	14	9	18	6	0	18	1	0	0	2	1	0	.361	.418	.681	1.098
2020	StL	NL	35	110	22	7	1	3	(2	1)	40	11	16	11	8	0	35	0	0	1	1	1	3	.200	.252	.364	.616
2021	StL	NL	149	542	144	31	4	18	(9	9)	237	79	65	82	57	2	152	11	1	8	2	1	5	.266	.343	.437	.780
	Postseason		3	9	3	1	0	0	(0	0)	4	2	0	3	4	0	3	1	0	0	1	0	0	.333	.571	.444	1.016
	2 ML YEARS		184	652	166	38	5	21	(11	10)	277	90	81	93	65	2	187	11	1	9	3	2	8	.255	.328	.425	.753

Drew Carlton

Pitches: R Bats: R Pos: RP-4   **Ht: 6'1" Wt: 215 Born: 9/8/1995 Age: 26**

			HOW MUCH PITCHED					WHAT HE GAVE UP										THE RESULTS							
Year	Team	Lg	G	GS	GF	IP	BFP	H	R	ER	HR	SH	SF	HB	TBB	IBB	SO	WP	W	L	Pct	Sv-Op	Hld	Vel	OPS	ERC	ERA
2021	Toledo	AAA	31	2	9	51.0	200	44	21	17	5	0	0	0	10	0	49	1	3	3	.500	3- -	-		.670	2.63	3.00
2021	Det	AL	4	0	1	3.2	19	6	2	2	1	0	1	0	4	0	1	0	0	0	-	0-0	0	90	1.312	14.15	4.91

Matt Carpenter

Bats: L Throws: R Pos: PH-77;2B-34;1B-14;3B-6;DH-2   **Ht: 6'4" Wt: 210 Born: 11/26/1985 Age: 36**

Year	Team	Lg	G	AB	H	2B	3B	HR	(Hm	Rd)	TB	R	RBI	RC	TBB	IBB	SO	HBP	SH	SF	SB	CS	GDP	Avg	OBP	Slg	OPS
2011	StL	NL	7	15	1	1	0	0	(0	0)	2	0	0	0	4	0	4	0	0	0	0	0	0	.067	.263	.133	.396
2012	StL	NL	114	296	87	22	5	6	(3	3)	137	44	46	46	34	2	63	3	0	7	1	1	10	.294	.365	.463	.828
2013	StL	NL	157	626	199	55	7	11	(6	5)	301	126	78	119	72	1	98	9	3	7	3	3	4	.318	.392	.481	.873
2014	StL	NL	158	595	162	33	2	8	(4	4)	223	99	59	93	95	2	111	8	2	9	5	3	3	.272	.375	.375	.750
2015	StL	NL	154	574	156	44	3	28	(13	15)	290	101	84	108	81	5	151	6	0	4	4	3	5	.272	.365	.505	.871
2016	StL	NL	129	473	128	36	6	21	(9	12)	239	81	68	87	81	6	108	5	3	4	0	4	4	.271	.380	.505	.885
2017	StL	NL	145	497	120	31	2	23	(9	14)	224	91	69	94	109	4	125	9	2	5	2	1	5	.241	.384	.451	.835
2018	StL	NL	156	564	145	42	0	36	(13	23)	295	111	81	107	102	17	158	6	0	4	4	1	0	.257	.374	.523	.897
2019	StL	NL	129	416	94	20	2	15	(8	7)	163	59	46	61	63	0	129	7	1	5	6	1	3	.226	.334	.392	.726
2020	StL	NL	50	140	26	6	0	4	(1	3)	44	22	24	18	23	1	48	6	0	0	0	0	1	.186	.325	.314	.640
2021	StL	NL	130	207	35	11	1	3	(2	1)	57	18	21	22	35	1	77	6	0	1	2	0	1	.169	.305	.275	.581
	Postseason		50	158	36	9	1	6	(4	2)	65	24	21	23	17	0	49	2	0	4	1	0	1	.228	.304	.411	.715
	11 ML YEARS		1329	4403	1153	301	28	155	(68	87)	1975	752	576	755	699	39	1072	65	11	46	27	17	36	.262	.368	.449	.816

Carlos Carrasco

Pitches: R Bats: R Pos: SP-12   **Ht: 6'4" Wt: 224 Born: 3/21/1987 Age: 35**

			HOW MUCH PITCHED					WHAT HE GAVE UP										THE RESULTS							
Year	Team	Lg	G	GS	GF	IP	BFP	H	R	ER	HR	SH	SF	HB	TBB	IBB	SO	WP	W	L	Pct	Sv-Op	Hld	Vel	OPS	ERC	ERA
2009	Cle	AL	5	5	0	22.1	112	40	23	22	6	0	1	0	11	1	11	0	0	4	.000	0-0	0	92	1.125	11.36	8.87
2010	Cle	AL	7	7	0	44.2	188	47	20	19	6	2	1	1	14	1	38	1	2	2	.500	0-0	0	93	.816	4.42	3.83
2011	Cle	AL	21	21	0	124.2	536	130	66	64	15	3	7	4	40	3	85	3	8	9	.471	0-0	0	92	.754	4.24	4.62
2013	Cle	AL	15	7	5	46.2	218	64	36	35	4	2	3	1	18	2	30	2	1	4	.200	0-0	0	95	.864	6.11	6.75
2014	Cle	AL	40	14	12	134.0	529	103	40	38	7	2	3	3	29	1	140	4	8	7	.533	1-1	1	95	.543	2.00	2.55
2015	Cle	AL	30	30	0	183.2	730	154	75	74	18	1	6	5	43	2	216	5	14	12	.538	0-0	0	95	.646	2.72	3.63
2016	Cle	AL	25	25	0	146.1	599	134	64	54	21	1	3	3	34	2	150	4	11	8	.579	0-0	0	94	.711	3.31	3.32
2017	Cle	AL	32	32	0	200.0	798	173	73	73	21	1	6	10	46	2	226	10	18	6	.750	0-0	0	94	.674	2.99	3.29
2018	Cle	AL	32	30	1	192.0	784	173	78	72	21	4	5	6	43	4	231	9	17	10	.630	0-0	0	93	.669	3.02	3.38
2019	Cle	AL	23	12	3	80.0	341	92	48	47	18	2	2	2	16	1	96	2	6	7	.462	1-2	0	93	.867	5.11	5.29

Year	Team	Lg	G	GS	GF	IP	BFP	H	R	ER	HR	SH	SF	HB	TBB	IBB	SO	WP	W	L	Pct	Sv-Op	Hld	Vel	OPS	ERC	ERA
2020	Cle	AL	12	12	0	68.0	280	55	22	22	8	1	1	2	27	0	82	6	3	4	.429	0-0	0	94	.663	3.30	2.91
2021	NYM	NL	12	12	0	53.2	237	59	39	36	12	0	2	0	18	0	50	1	1	5	.167	0-0	0	93	.827	5.18	6.04
	Postseason		3	3	0	14.0	58	11	6	6	1	1	0	1	7	0	16	0	0	1	.000	0-0	0	94	.660	3.49	3.86
	12 ML YEARS		254	207	21	1296.0	5352	1224	586	556	157	19	40	37	339	19	1355	47	89	78	.533	2-3	0	94	.709	3.49	3.86

Corbin Carroll

Bats: L **Throws:** L **Pos:** CF

Ht: 5'10" **Wt:** 165 **Born:** 8/21/2000 **Age:** 21

							BATTING															RUNNING			AVERAGES			
Year	Team	Lg	G	AB	H	2B	3B	HR	(Hm	Rd)	TB	R	RBI	RC	TBB	IBB	SO	HBP	SH	SF	SB	CS	GDP	Avg	OBP	Slg	OPS
2019	2 Tms	Low	42	154	46	9	7	2	(-	-)	75	36	20	35	29	1	41	1	0	2	18	1	1	.299	.409	.487	.896

Curt Casali

Bats: R **Throws:** R **Pos:** C-64;PH-15;1B-3
cuh-SAL-ee

Ht: 6'2" **Wt:** 220 **Born:** 11/9/1988 **Age:** 33

							BATTING															RUNNING			AVERAGES			
Year	Team	Lg	G	AB	H	2B	3B	HR	(Hm	Rd)	TB	R	RBI	RC	TBB	IBB	SO	HBP	SH	SF	SB	CS	GDP	Avg	OBP	Slg	OPS
2014	TB	AL	30	72	12	3	0	0	(0	0)	15	10	3	3	8	0	23	2	2	0	0	0	2	.167	.268	.208	.477
2015	TB	AL	38	101	24	6	0	10	(7	3)	60	13	18	14	8	0	34	2	1	1	0	0	2	.238	.304	.594	.898
2016	TB	AL	84	226	42	10	0	8	(3	5)	76	23	25	18	25	1	82	2	3	0	0	0	0	.186	.273	.336	.609
2017	TB	AL	9	9	3	0	0	1	(1	0)	6	2	3	2	3	0	3	0	0	1	0	0	0	.333	.462	.667	1.128
2018	Cin	NL	52	140	41	10	0	4	(2	2)	63	15	16	17	12	1	32	2	1	1	0	2	5	.293	.355	.450	.805
2019	Cin	NL	84	207	52	9	0	8	(2	6)	85	24	32	24	25	1	59	1	0	3	0	0	1	.251	.331	.411	.741
2020	Cin	NL	31	76	17	3	0	6	(4	2)	38	10	8	12	14	0	29	3	0	2	2	0	2	.224	.366	.500	.866
2021	SF	NL	77	200	42	11	1	5	(4	1)	70	20	26	23	26	4	66	4	1	0	0	0	3	.210	.313	.350	.663
	Postseason		2	2	0	0	0	0	(0	0)	0	0	0	0	0	0	1	0	0	0	0	0	0	.000	.000	.000	.000
	8 ML YEARS		405	1031	233	52	1	42	(23	19)	413	117	131	113	121	7	328	16	8	6	2	2	17	.226	.315	.401	.716

Triston Casas

Bats: L **Throws:** R **Pos:** 1B

Ht: 6'4" **Wt:** 252 **Born:** 1/15/2000 **Age:** 22

							BATTING															RUNNING			AVERAGES			
Year	Team	Lg	G	AB	H	2B	3B	HR	(Hm	Rd)	TB	R	RBI	RC	TBB	IBB	SO	HBP	SH	SF	SB	CS	GDP	Avg	OBP	Slg	OPS
2019	2 Tms	Low	120	429	110	26	5	20	(-	-)	206	66	81	76	58	3	118	7	0	6	3	2	11	.256	.350	.480	.830
2021	Portlnd	AA	78	277	78	12	2	13	(-	-)	133	57	52	-	49	0	64	3	0	2	6	3	6	.282	.393	.480	.873

Daniel Castano

Pitches: L **Bats:** L **Pos:** SP-4; RP-1

Ht: 6'3" **Wt:** 231 **Born:** 9/17/1994 **Age:** 27

						HOW MUCH PITCHED			WHAT HE GAVE UP										THE RESULTS							
Year	Team	Lg	G	GS	GF	IP	BFP	H	R	ER	HR	SH	SF	HB	TBB	IBB	SO	WP	W	L	Pct	Sv-Op	Hld	Vel	OPS	ERC	ERA
2021	Jaxnvl	AAA	13	13	0	70.1	289	67	35	34	16	1	0	3	16	0	52	0	6	2	.750	0- -	-		.762	4.18	4.35
2020	Mia	NL	7	6	0	29.2	126	30	12	10	3	0	1	0	11	0	12	1	1	2	.333	0-0	0	89	.729	4.08	3.03
2021	Mia	NL	5	4	0	20.1	92	22	12	11	3	1	0	1	8	0	13	0	0	2	.000	0-0	0	90	.792	4.95	4.87
	2 ML YEARS		12	10	0	50.0	218	52	24	21	6	1	1	1	19	0	25	1	1	4	.200	0-0	0	90	.755	4.43	3.78

Ryan Castellani

Pitches: R **Bats:** R **Pos:** SP-1

Ht: 6'4" **Wt:** 218 **Born:** 4/1/1996 **Age:** 26

						HOW MUCH PITCHED			WHAT HE GAVE UP										THE RESULTS							
Year	Team	Lg	G	GS	GF	IP	BFP	H	R	ER	HR	SH	SF	HB	TBB	IBB	SO	WP	W	L	Pct	Sv-Op	Hld	Vel	OPS	ERC	ERA
2021	Albq	AAA	23	22	0	92.0	422	86	69	65	16	1	1	11	70	0	81	11	3	10	.231	0- -	-	-	.857	6.43	6.36
2020	Col	NL	10	9	0	43.1	189	37	30	28	12	0	1	5	26	0	25	1	1	4	.200	0-0	0	92	.882	6.02	5.82
2021	Col	NL	1	1	0	3.1	17	5	2	2	1	0	0	1	4	0	2	0	0	0	-	0-0	0	90	1.422	16.64	5.40
	2 ML YEARS		11	10	0	46.2	206	42	32	30	13	0	1	6	30	0	27	1	1	4	.200	0-0	0	92	.923	6.66	5.79

Humberto Castellanos

Pitches: R **Bats:** R **Pos:** SP-7; RP-7

Ht: 5'11" **Wt:** 222 **Born:** 4/3/1998 **Age:** 24

						HOW MUCH PITCHED			WHAT HE GAVE UP										THE RESULTS							
Year	Team	Lg	G	GS	GF	IP	BFP	H	R	ER	HR	SH	SF	HB	TBB	IBB	SO	WP	W	L	Pct	Sv-Op	Hld	Vel	OPS	ERC	ERA
2021	Reno	AAA	12	12	0	57.2	247	56	32	32	14	0	1	5	14	1	59	1	6	1	.857	0- -	-	-	.793	4.50	4.99
2020	Hou	AL	8	0	4	10.2	51	12	8	8	2	0	0	2	5	0	12	0	0	1	.000	0-1	0	90	.850	6.42	6.75
2021	Ari	NL	14	7	2	45.2	196	48	26	25	7	5	0	2	15	0	29	0	2	2	.500	0-1	1	90	.805	4.68	4.93
	2 ML YEARS		22	7	6	56.1	247	60	34	33	9	5	0	4	20	0	41	0	2	3	.400	0-2	1	90	.814	5.01	5.27

Nick Castellanos

Bats: R **Throws:** R **Pos:** RF-135;DH-1;PH-1
cahs-teh-YAHN-ohs

Ht: 6'4" **Wt:** 203 **Born:** 3/4/1992 **Age:** 30

							BATTING															RUNNING			AVERAGES			
Year	Team	Lg	G	AB	H	2B	3B	HR	(Hm	Rd)	TB	R	RBI	RC	TBB	IBB	SO	HBP	SH	SF	SB	CS	GDP	Avg	OBP	Slg	OPS
2013	Det	AL	11	18	5	0	0	0	(0	0)	5	1	1	1	0	0	1	0	0	0	0	0	0	.278	.278	.278	.556
2014	Det	AL	148	533	138	31	4	11	(6	5)	210	50	66	63	36	3	140	3	0	7	2	2	7	.259	.306	.394	.700
2015	Det	AL	154	549	140	33	6	15	(6	9)	230	42	73	66	39	1	152	1	0	6	0	3	21	.255	.303	.419	.721
2016	Det	AL	110	411	117	25	4	18	(5	13)	204	54	58	67	28	1	111	3	0	5	1	1	4	.285	.331	.496	.827
2017	Det	AL	157	614	167	36	10	26	(14	12)	301	73	101	97	41	0	142	5	0	5	4	5	12	.272	.320	.490	.811
2018	Det	AL	157	620	185	46	5	23	(10	13)	310	88	89	110	49	5	151	6	0	3	2	1	8	.298	.354	.500	.854
2019	2 Tms		151	615	178	58	3	27	(11	16)	323	100	73	94	41	1	143	5	0	2	2	2	12	.289	.337	.525	.863
2020	Cin	NL	60	218	49	11	2	14	(7	7)	106	37	34	29	19	1	69	4	0	1	0	2	5	.225	.298	.486	.784

Year	Team	Lg	G	AB	H	2B	3B	HR	(Hm	Rd)	TB	R	RBI	RC	TBB	IBB	SO	HBP	SH	SF	SB	CS	GDP	Avg	OBP	Slg	OPS
2021	Cin	NL	138	531	164	38	1	34	(23	11)	306	95	100	101	41	5	121	7	0	6	3	1	16	.309	.362	.576	.939
19	Det	AL	100	403	110	37	3	11	(3	8)	186	57	37	54	31	1	96	3	0	2	2	1	7	.273	.328	.462	.790
19	ChC	NL	51	212	68	21	0	16	(8	8)	137	43	36	40	10	0	47	2	0	1	0	1	5	.321	.356	.646	1.002
	Postseason		5	20	4	1	0	1	(0	1)	8	1	1	0	2	1	5	0	0	0	0	0	0	.200	.273	.400	.673
	9 ML YEARS		1086	4109	1143	278	35	168	(82	86)	1995	540	594	628	294	17	1030	34	0	36	14	17	85	.278	.329	.486	.814

Diego Castillo

Pitches: R **Bats:** R **Pos:** RP-61 **Ht:** 6'3" **Wt:** 250 **Born:** 1/18/1994 **Age:** 28

			HOW MUCH PITCHED					WHAT HE GAVE UP									THE RESULTS							
Year	Team	Lg	G	GS	GF	IP	BFP	H	R	ER	HR	SH	SF	HB	TBB	IBB	SO	WP	W	L	Pct	Sv-Op	Hld	Vel	OPS	ERC	ERA
2018	TB	AL	43	11	5	56.2	222	36	21	20	6	0	0	2	18	0	65	5	4	2	.667	0-2	10	98	.554	2.09	3.18
2019	TB	AL	65	6	18	68.2	290	59	32	26	8	1	1	5	26	4	81	5	5	8	.385	8-10	17	98	.685	3.53	3.41
2020	TB	AL	22	0	5	21.2	89	12	4	4	3	0	1	0	11	0	23	0	3	0	1.000	4-5	5	96	.581	2.52	1.66
2021	2 Tms	AL	61	0	32	58.1	233	40	23	18	9	2	3	5	17	2	75	2	5	5	.500	16-22	10	95	.623	2.64	2.78
21	TB	AL	37	0	26	36.1	145	26	14	11	5	2	2	1	10	2	49	1	2	4	.333	14-16	3	95	.613	2.37	2.72
21	Sea	AL	24	0	6	22.0	88	14	9	7	4	0	1	4	7	0	26	1	3	1	.750	2-6	7	94	.639	3.11	2.86
	Postseason		14	1	5	16.2	69	12	3	2	0	1	0	1	9	0	20	0	1	0	1.000	3-3	2	98	.565	2.71	1.08
	4 ML YEARS		191	17	60	205.1	834	147	80	68	26	3	4	13	72	6	244	12	17	15	.531	28-39	42	97	.621	2.76	2.98

Erick Castillo

Bats: R **Throws:** R **Pos:** C-4;PH-1 **Ht:** 5'11" **Wt:** 178 **Born:** 2/25/1993 **Age:** 29

						BATTING														RUNNING			AVERAGES			
Year	Team	Lg	G	AB	H	2B	3B	HR	(Hm	Rd)	TB	R	RBI	RC	TBB	IBB	SO	HBP	SH	SF	SB	CS	GDP	Avg	OBP	Slg	OPS
2021	Tenn	AA	18	57	13	1	0	1	(-	-)	17	6	11	-	7	0	12	3	1	1	0	0	1	.228	.338	.298	.636
2021	Iowa	AAA	39	111	21	4	0	0	(-	-)	25	11	8	-	13	0	22	5	2	2	0	0	2	.189	.298	.225	.523
2021	ChC	NL	4	8	2	0	0	0	(0	0)	2	0	0	1	1	0	1	0	0	0	0	0	0	.250	.333	.250	.583

Ivan Castillo

Bats: B **Throws:** R **Pos:** PH-2;2B-1;3B-1 **Ht:** 5'9" **Wt:** 179 **Born:** 5/30/1995 **Age:** 27

						BATTING														RUNNING			AVERAGES			
Year	Team	Lg	G	AB	H	2B	3B	HR	(Hm	Rd)	TB	R	RBI	RC	TBB	IBB	SO	HBP	SH	SF	SB	CS	GDP	Avg	OBP	Slg	OPS
2021	ElPaso	AAA	109	394	113	15	4	3	(-	-)	145	46	44	-	24	1	73	0	0	5	12	5	9	.287	.324	.368	.692
2021	SD	NL	3	3	1	0	0	0	(-	-)	1	0	1	1	1	0	0	0	0	0	0	0	0	.333	.500	.333	.833

Luis Castillo

Pitches: R **Bats:** R **Pos:** SP-33 **Ht:** 6'2" **Wt:** 200 **Born:** 12/12/1992 **Age:** 29

			HOW MUCH PITCHED					WHAT HE GAVE UP									THE RESULTS							
Year	Team	Lg	G	GS	GF	IP	BFP	H	R	ER	HR	SH	SF	HB	TBB	IBB	SO	WP	W	L	Pct	Sv-Op	Hld	Vel	OPS	ERC	ERA
2017	Cin	NL	15	15	0	89.1	359	64	32	31	11	4	3	3	32	1	98	2	3	7	.300	0-0	0	97	.638	2.70	3.12
2018	Cin	NL	31	31	0	169.2	708	158	89	81	28	3	6	5	49	1	165	4	10	12	.455	0-0	0	96	.732	3.80	4.30
2019	Cin	NL	32	32	0	190.2	781	139	76	72	22	6	1	7	79	1	226	5	15	8	.652	0-0	0	96	.633	2.94	3.40
2020	Cin	NL	12	12	0	70.0	292	62	31	25	5	0	1	6	24	0	89	1	4	6	.400	0-0	0	97	.663	3.10	3.21
2021	Cin	NL	33	33	0	187.2	803	181	94	83	19	8	2	7	75	4	192	1	8	16	.333	0-0	0	97	.733	4.03	3.98
	Postseason		1	1	0	5.1	23	6	1	1	0	0	0	0	1	1	7	0	0	1	.000	0-0	0	98	.623	2.88	1.69
	5 ML YEARS		123	123	0	707.1	2943	604	322	292	85	21	13	23	259	6	770	13	40	49	.449	0-0	0	97	.688	3.41	3.72

Anthony Castro

Pitches: R **Bats:** R **Pos:** RP-25 **Ht:** 6'2" **Wt:** 182 **Born:** 4/13/1995 **Age:** 27

			HOW MUCH PITCHED					WHAT HE GAVE UP									THE RESULTS							
Year	Team	Lg	G	GS	GF	IP	BFP	H	R	ER	HR	SH	SF	HB	TBB	IBB	SO	WP	W	L	Pct	Sv-Op	Hld	Vel	OPS	ERC	ERA
2021	Buffalo	AAA	9	0	4	9.0	32	5	2	2	1	0	0	0	0	0	15	0	0	1	.000	0--	-		.531	0.94	2.00
2020	Det	AL	1	0	1	1.0	5	1	2	2	1	0	0	0	1	0	1	0	0	0	-	0-0	0	92	1.400	14.27	18.00
2021	Tor	AL	25	0	7	24.2	109	23	15	13	4	0	1	3	8	2	32	4	1	2	.333	1-2	1	95	.745	4.05	4.74
	2 ML YEARS		26	0	8	25.2	114	24	17	15	5	0	1	3	9	2	33	4	1	2	.333	1-2	1	95	.771	4.38	5.26

Harold Castro

Bats: L **Throws:** R **Pos:** SS-43;2B-33;1B-15;PH-15;3B-12;LF-3;CF-2;DH-1 **Ht:** 5'10" **Wt:** 195 **Born:** 11/30/1993 **Age:** 28

						BATTING														RUNNING			AVERAGES			
Year	Team	Lg	G	AB	H	2B	3B	HR	(Hm	Rd)	TB	R	RBI	RC	TBB	IBB	SO	HBP	SH	SF	SB	CS	GDP	Avg	OBP	Slg	OPS
2018	Det	AL	6	10	3	0	0	0	(0	0)	3	2	0	1	0	0	2	0	0	0	1	0	0	.300	.300	.300	.600
2019	Det	AL	97	354	103	10	4	5	(2	3)	136	30	38	44	9	0	86	0	2	4	4	2	6	.291	.305	.384	.689
2020	Det	AL	22	49	17	4	0	0	(0	0)	21	6	3	8	5	0	11	0	0	0	0	0	1	.347	.407	.429	.836
2021	Det	AL	106	315	89	13	1	3	(3	0)	113	35	37	36	14	0	72	1	4	5	1	1	7	.283	.310	.359	.669
	4 ML YEARS		231	728	212	27	5	8	(5	3)	273	73	78	89	28	0	171	1	6	9	6	3	14	.291	.315	.375	.690

Jason Castro

Bats: L **Throws:** R **Pos:** C-52;PH-23;DH-2   **Ht:** 6'3" **Wt:** 215 **Born:** 6/18/1987 **Age:** 35

								BATTING											RUNNING			AVERAGES			
Year	Team	Lg	G	AB	H	2B	3B	HR	(Hm | Rd)	TB	R	RBI	RC	TBB	IBB	SO	HBP	SH	SF	SB	CS	GDP	Avg	OBP	Slg	OPS
2010	Hou	NL	67	195	40	8	1	2	(1 | 1)	56	26	8	12	22	2	41	0	0	0	0	0	4	.205	.286	.287	.573
2012	Hou	NL	87	257	66	15	2	6	(3 | 3)	103	29	29	33	31	2	61	1	2	4	0	0	8	.257	.334	.401	.735
2013	Hou	AL	120	435	120	35	1	18	(13 | 5)	211	63	56	76	50	3	130	2	0	4	2	1	4	.276	.350	.485	.835
2014	Hou	AL	126	465	103	21	2	14	(4 | 10)	170	43	56	45	34	1	151	9	1	3	1	0	11	.222	.286	.366	.651
2015	Hou	AL	104	337	71	19	0	11	(8 | 3)	123	38	31	29	33	1	115	2	0	3	0	0	5	.211	.283	.365	.648
2016	Hou	AL	113	329	69	16	3	11	(5 | 6)	124	41	32	34	45	0	123	1	1	0	2	1	9	.210	.307	.377	.684
2017	Min	AL	110	356	86	22	0	10	(6 | 4)	138	49	47	45	45	1	108	4	1	1	0	0	10	.242	.333	.388	.720
2018	Min	AL	19	63	9	3	0	1	(0 | 1)	15	4	3	1	9	0	26	1	0	1	0	0	2	.143	.257	.238	.495
2019	Min	AL	79	237	55	9	0	13	(7 | 6)	103	39	30	31	33	0	88	3	1	1	0	0	0	.232	.332	.435	.767
2020	2 Tms		27	80	15	9	0	2	(1 | 1)	30	8	9	11	12	0	33	0	0	0	0	0	2	.188	.293	.375	.668
2021	Hou	AL	66	149	35	7	0	8	(4 | 4)	66	22	21	23	25	1	54	3	2	0	0	0	0	.235	.356	.443	.799
20	LAA	AL	18	52	10	4	0	2	(1 | 1)	20	5	6	8	10	0	23	0	0	0	0	0	1	.192	.323	.385	.707
20	SD	NL	9	28	5	5	0	0	(0 | 0)	10	3	3	3	2	0	10	0	0	0	0	0	1	.179	.233	.357	.590
	Postseason		8	20	1	0	0	0	(0 | 0)	1	1	2	0	2	0	11	0	0	0	0	0	2	.050	.136	.050	.186
	11 ML YEARS		918	2903	669	164	9	96	(58 | 38)	1139	362	322	340	339	11	930	26	8	17	5	2	59	.230	.315	.392	.707

Kervin Castro

Pitches: R **Bats:** R **Pos:** RP-10   **Ht:** 6'0" **Wt:** 185 **Born:** 2/7/1999 **Age:** 23

			HOW MUCH PITCHED					WHAT HE GAVE UP										THE RESULTS						
Year	Team	Lg	G	GS	GF	IP	BFP	H	R	ER	HR	SH	SF	HB	TBB	IBB	SO	WP	W	L	Pct	Sv-Op	Hld	Vel	OPS	ERC	ERA
2021	Scrmto	AAA	30	0	3	44.0	183	31	14	14	3	0	2	2	22	0	60	3	6	1	.857	1--	-	-	.568	2.85	2.86
2021	SF	NL	10	0	4	13.1	56	13	1	0	0	1	1	0	4	1	13	0	1	1	.500	0-0	0	95	.609	2.76	0.00

Miguel Castro

Pitches: R **Bats:** R **Pos:** RP-67; SP-2   **Ht:** 6'7" **Wt:** 205 **Born:** 12/24/1994 **Age:** 27

			HOW MUCH PITCHED					WHAT HE GAVE UP										THE RESULTS						
Year	Team	Lg	G	GS	GF	IP	BFP	H	R	ER	HR	SH	SF	HB	TBB	IBB	SO	WP	W	L	Pct	Sv-Op	Hld	Vel	OPS	ERC	ERA
2015	2 Tms		18	0	12	17.2	83	21	13	12	4	0	2	0	10	2	18	2	0	3	.000	4-6	1	96	.937	6.61	6.11
2016	Col	NL	19	0	4	14.2	67	18	10	10	3	1	0	1	5	0	12	0	0	0		0-1	7	96	.880	6.21	6.14
2017	Bal	AL	39	1	8	66.1	274	53	29	26	8	3	4	2	28	4	38	2	3	3	.500	0-0	1	96	.682	3.27	3.53
2018	Bal	AL	63	1	16	86.1	376	75	41	38	9	0	3	5	50	7	57	9	2	7	.222	0-2	5	96	.714	4.22	3.96
2019	Bal	AL	65	0	28	73.1	319	63	42	38	10	0	6	0	41	3	71	11	1	3	.250	2-5	9	97	.712	4.08	4.66
2020	2 Tms		26	0	5	24.2	115	28	12	11	4	0	0	1	13	0	38	0	2	2	.500	1-3	5	98	.821	5.95	4.01
2021	NYM	NL	69	2	7	70.1	303	48	30	27	7	0	0	6	43	0	77	8	3	4	.429	0-2	9	98	.619	3.46	3.45
15	Tor	AL	13	0	9	12.1	57	15	7	6	2	0	2	0	6	2	12	2	0	2	.000	4-6	1	96	.858	5.86	4.38
15	Col	NL	5	0	3	5.1	26	6	6	6	2	0	0	0	4	0	6	0	0	1	.000	0-0	0	96	1.112	8.41	10.13
20	Bal	AL	16	0	4	15.2	70	17	7	7	3	0	0	1	5	0	24	0	1	0	1.000	1-3	4	98	.782	5.04	4.02
20	NYM	NL	10	0	1	9.0	45	11	5	4	1	0	0	0	8	0	14	0	1	2	.333	0-0	1	99	.882	7.55	4.00
	7 ML YEARS		299	4	80	353.1	1537	306	177	162	45	4	15	15	190	16	311	32	11	22	.333	7-19	37	97	.717	4.16	4.13

Rodolfo Castro

Bats: B **Throws:** R **Pos:** 2B-20;PH-8;3B-5   **Ht:** 6'0" **Wt:** 205 **Born:** 5/21/1999 **Age:** 23

								BATTING											RUNNING			AVERAGES			
Year	Team	Lg	G	AB	H	2B	3B	HR	(Hm	Rd)	TB	R	RBI	RC	TBB	IBB	SO	HBP	SH	SF	SB	CS	GDP	Avg	OBP	Slg	OPS
2021	Altna	AA	72	285	69	14	1	12	(-	-)	121	43	47	-	19	1	72	4	0	4	7	4	6	.242	.295	.425	.719
2021	Pit	NL	31	86	17	2	0	5	(2	3)	34	9	8	5	6	0	27	1	0	0	0	0	4	.198	.258	.395	.653

Starlin Castro

Bats: R **Throws:** R **Pos:** 3B-85;PH-2;SS-1   STARR-linn   **Ht:** 6'2" **Wt:** 218 **Born:** 3/24/1990 **Age:** 32

								BATTING											RUNNING			AVERAGES			
Year	Team	Lg	G	AB	H	2B	3B	HR	(Hm	Rd)	TB	R	RBI	RC	TBB	IBB	SO	HBP	SH	SF	SB	CS	GDP	Avg	OBP	Slg	OPS
2010	ChC	NL	125	463	139	31	5	3	(1	2)	189	53	41	56	29	7	71	6	4	4	10	8	14	.300	.347	.408	.755
2011	ChC	NL	158	674	207	36	9	10	(4	6)	291	91	66	93	35	2	96	2	0	4	22	9	20	.307	.341	.432	.773
2012	ChC	NL	162	646	183	29	12	14	(7	7)	278	78	78	91	36	5	100	4	0	5	25	13	15	.283	.323	.430	.753
2013	ChC	NL	161	666	163	34	2	10	(9	1)	231	59	44	55	30	0	129	7	1	1	9	6	21	.245	.284	.347	.631
2014	ChC	NL	134	528	154	33	1	14	(3	11)	231	58	65	72	35	4	100	1	0	2	4	4	18	.292	.339	.438	.777
2015	ChC	NL	151	547	145	23	2	11	(3	8)	205	52	69	54	21	6	91	5	1	4	5	5	18	.265	.296	.375	.671
2016	NYY	AL	151	577	156	29	1	21	(15	6)	250	63	70	69	24	1	118	3	1	5	4	0	15	.270	.300	.433	.734
2017	NYY	AL	112	443	133	18	1	16	(10	6)	201	66	63	69	24	4	93	4	0	3	2	0	9	.300	.338	.454	.792
2018	Mia	NL	154	593	165	32	2	12	(7	5)	237	76	54	70	48	3	124	1	0	6	6	4	18	.278	.329	.400	.729
2019	Mia	NL	162	636	172	31	4	22	(11	11)	277	68	86	77	28	2	111	3	0	9	2	2	23	.270	.300	.436	.736
2020	Was	NL	16	60	16	3	1	2	(2	1)	27	9	4	7	3	0	13	0	0	0	0	0	0	.267	.302	.450	.752
2021	Was	NL	87	315	89	20	0	3	(2	1)	118	25	38	39	26	1	62	0	0	4	0	1	6	.283	.333	.375	.708
	Postseason		22	84	17	4	0	1	(1	0)	24	7	3	6	3	1	15	1	0	0	0	0	1	.202	.239	.286	.524
	12 ML YEARS		1573	6148	1722	319	40	138	(73	65)	2535	698	678	752	338	32	1108	38	7	47	89	52	177	.280	.319	.412	.732

Willi Castro

Bats: B **Throws:** R **Pos:** 2B-91;SS-20;LF-10;DH-6;PH-6;PR-4   **Ht:** 6'1" **Wt:** 206 **Born:** 4/24/1997 **Age:** 25

Year	Team	Lg	G	AB	H	2B	3B	HR	(Hm	Rd)	TB	R	RBI	RC	TBB	IBB	SO	HBP	SH	SF	SB	CS	GDP	Avg	OBP	Slg	OPS
2019	Det	AL	30	100	23	6	1	1	(1	0)	34	10	8	9	6	0	34	2	1	1	0	1	4	.230	.284	.340	.624
2020	Det	AL	36	129	45	4	2	6	(3	3)	71	21	24	30	7	0	38	1	1	2	0	1	0	.349	.381	.550	.932
2021	Det	AL	125	413	91	15	6	9	(5	4)	145	56	38	36	23	1	109	8	3	3	9	4	5	.220	.273	.351	.624
	3 ML YEARS		191	642	159	25	9	16	(9	7)	250	87	70	75	36	1	181	11	5	6	9	6	9	.248	.296	.389	.686

Jake Cave

Bats: L **Throws:** L **Pos:** LF-37;CF-29;RF-11;PH-7;PR-6;DH-1   **Ht:** 6'0" **Wt:** 200 **Born:** 12/4/1992 **Age:** 29

Year	Team	Lg	G	AB	H	2B	3B	HR	(Hm	Rd)	TB	R	RBI	RC	TBB	IBB	SO	HBP	SH	SF	SB	CS	GDP	Avg	OBP	Slg	OPS
2018	Min	AL	91	283	75	16	2	13	(6	7)	134	54	45	46	18	2	102	3	2	3	2	1	2	.265	.313	.473	.786
2019	Min	AL	72	198	51	11	2	8	(3	5)	90	28	25	27	21	0	71	8	0	1	0	0	5	.258	.351	.455	.805
2020	Min	AL	42	113	25	3	2	4	(3	1)	44	17	15	15	5	0	44	0	0	2	0	0	0	.221	.285	.389	.674
2021	Min	AL	76	164	31	6	1	3	(1	2)	48	14	13	13	10	0	62	3	1	0	1	1	0	.189	.249	.293	.541
	Postseason		3	5	1	0	0	0	(0	0)	1	0	0	0	0	0	3	0	0	0	0	0	0	.200	.200	.200	.400
	4 ML YEARS		281	758	182	36	7	28	(13	15)	316	113	98	101	54	2	279	19	3	4	3	4	7	.240	.305	.417	.722

Dylan Cease

Pitches: R **Bats:** R **Pos:** SP-32   **Ht:** 6'2" **Wt:** 195 **Born:** 12/28/1995 **Age:** 26

Year	Team	Lg	G	GS	GF	IP	BFP	H	R	ER	HR	SH	SF	HB	TBB	IBB	SO	WP	W	L	Pct	Sv-Op	Hld	Vel	OPS	ERC	ERA
2019	CWS	AL	14	14	0	73.0	326	78	51	47	15	0	1	2	35	1	81	4	4	7	.364	0-0	0	97	.839	5.70	5.79
2020	CWS	AL	12	12	0	58.1	255	50	30	26	12	0	1	5	34	1	44	1	5	4	.556	0-0	0	98	.827	5.17	4.01
2021	CWS	AL	32	32	0	165.2	708	139	77	72	20	1	7	9	68	0	226	13	13	7	.650	0-0	0	97	.670	3.54	3.91
	Postseason		1	0	0	1.0	3	0	0	0	0	0	0	0	0	0	0	0	0	0	-	0-0	0	99	.000	0.00	0.00
	3 ML YEARS		58	58	0	297.0	1289	267	158	145	47	1	9	16	137	2	351	18	22	18	.550	0-0	0	97	.743	4.35	4.39

Gilberto Celestino

Bats: R **Throws:** L **Pos:** CF-22;RF-2;PR-2;LF-1   **Ht:** 6'0" **Wt:** 170 **Born:** 2/13/1999 **Age:** 23

Year	Team	Lg	G	AB	H	2B	3B	HR	(Hm	Rd)	TB	R	RBI	RC	TBB	IBB	SO	HBP	SH	SF	SB	CS	GDP	Avg	OBP	Slg	OPS
2021	Wich	AA	21	84	21	5	0	2	(-	-)	32	10	7	-	11	0	24	1	0	0	0	1	1	.250	.344	.381	.725
2021	StPaul	AAA	44	162	48	11	0	5	(-	-)	74	26	24	-	23	1	38	4	0	0	4	0	4	.296	.397	.457	.854
2021	Min	AL	23	59	8	3	0	2	(0	2)	17	7	3	1	3	0	14	0	0	0	0	0	2	.136	.177	.288	.466

Luis Cessa

Pitches: R **Bats:** R **Pos:** RP-53   SESS-uh   **Ht:** 6'0" **Wt:** 208 **Born:** 4/25/1992 **Age:** 30

Year	Team	Lg	G	GS	GF	IP	BFP	H	R	ER	HR	SH	SF	HB	TBB	IBB	SO	WP	W	L	Pct	Sv-Op	Hld	Vel	OPS	ERC	ERA
2016	NYY	AL	17	9	5	70.1	285	64	36	34	16	1	1	3	14	0	46	2	4	4	.500	0-0	0	95	.744	3.81	4.35
2017	NYY	AL	10	5	2	36.0	160	36	21	19	7	0	0	3	17	0	30	2	0	3	.000	0-0	0	96	.829	5.43	4.75
2018	NYY	AL	16	5	6	44.2	195	51	27	26	5	1	0	0	13	0	39	7	1	4	.200	2-2	0	95	.761	4.50	5.24
2019	NYY	AL	43	0	14	81.0	343	75	42	37	14	0	4	3	31	1	75	1	2	1	.667	1-1	0	94	.751	4.26	4.11
2020	NYY	AL	16	0	6	21.2	93	20	10	8	2	0	0	5	7	0	17	1	0	0	-	1-1	1	94	.693	3.20	3.32
2021	2 Tms		53	0	15	64.2	261	55	24	18	5	2	0	0	19	1	54	1	5	2	.714	0-0	4	94	.627	2.74	2.51
21	NYY	AL	29	0	13	38.1	161	31	17	12	2	2	0	0	17	1	31	0	3	1	.750	0-0	1	93	.605	2.83	2.82
21	Cin	NL	24	0	2	26.1	100	24	7	6	3	0	0	0	2	0	23	1	2	1	.667	0-0	3	94	.658	2.57	2.05
	Postseason		5	0	3	8.0	32	5	2	2	0	0	0	1	3	0	7	0	0	0	-	0-0	0	94	.531	1.92	2.25
	6 ML YEARS		155	19	48	318.1	1337	301	160	142	49	4	5	9	101	2	261	14	12	14	.462	4-4	9	95	.732	3.93	4.01

Jhoulys Chacin

Pitches: R **Bats:** R **Pos:** RP-45; SP-1   yoo-LEES cha-SEEN   **Ht:** 6'3" **Wt:** 215 **Born:** 1/7/1988 **Age:** 34

Year	Team	Lg	G	GS	GF	IP	BFP	H	R	ER	HR	SH	SF	HB	TBB	IBB	SO	WP	W	L	Pct	Sv-Op	Hld	Vel	OPS	ERC	ERA
2009	Col	NL	9	1	3	11.0	48	6	6	6	1	0	0	0	11	0	13	2	0	1	.000	0-0	0	91	.667	3.87	4.91
2010	Col	NL	28	21	2	137.1	583	114	64	50	10	6	5	9	61	5	138	4	9	11	.450	0-0	0	91	.650	3.33	3.28
2011	Col	NL	31	31	0	194.0	827	168	87	78	20	5	3	4	87	1	150	7	11	14	.440	0-0	0	91	.707	3.61	3.62
2012	Col	NL	14	14	0	69.0	314	80	35	34	10	1	1	2	32	0	45	3	3	5	.375	0-0	0	90	.821	5.73	4.43
2013	Col	NL	31	31	0	197.1	816	188	82	76	11	3	7	3	61	3	126	5	14	10	.583	0-0	0	90	.685	3.26	3.47
2014	Col	NL	11	11	0	63.1	272	63	38	38	8	2	3	1	28	1	42	6	1	7	.125	0-0	0	88	.790	4.52	5.40
2015	Ari	NL	5	4	0	26.2	111	24	11	10	4	1	0	0	10	0	21	0	2	1	.667	0-0	0	89	.729	3.80	3.38
2016	2 Tms		34	22	5	144.0	632	153	81	77	14	4	6	5	55	4	119	8	6	8	.429	0-0	0	91	.745	4.42	4.81
2017	SD	NL	32	32	0	180.1	765	157	82	78	19	6	6	14	72	5	153	7	13	10	.565	0-0	0	91	.693	3.67	3.89
2018	Mil	NL	35	35	0	192.2	796	153	83	75	18	8	9	11	71	3	156	5	15	8	.652	0-0	0	91	.655	3.01	3.50
2019	2 Tms		25	24	0	103.1	470	115	73	69	25	4	4	5	46	1	101	3	3	12	.200	0-0	0	90	.877	6.13	6.01
2020	Atl	NL	2	0	0	5.0	24	6	4	4	1	0	0	0	3	0	3	1	1	0	1.000	0-0	0	91	.851	6.75	7.20
2021	Col	NL	46	1	3	64.1	269	53	32	31	8	1	1	0	28	0	47	1	3	2	.600	0-2	17	91	.708	3.42	4.34
16	Atl	NL	5	5	0	26.2	117	29	17	16	4	2	1	0	8	0	27	0	1	2	.333	0-0	0	89	.756	4.42	5.40
16	LAA	NL	29	17	5	117.1	515	124	64	61	10	2	5	5	47	4	92	8	5	6	.455	0-0	0	91	.742	4.42	4.68
19	Mil	NL	19	19	0	88.2	403	99	61	57	19	4	4	5	39	1	80	3	3	10	.231	0-0	0	90	.857	5.96	5.79
19	Bos	AL	6	5	0	14.2	67	16	12	12	6	0	0	0	7	0	21	0	0	2	.000	0-0	0	90	.993	7.12	7.36
	Postseason		3	3	0	12.1	51	9	2	2	1	0	0	0	6	1	9	0	2	1	.667	0-0	0	91	.627	2.72	1.46
	13 ML YEARS		303	227	13	1388.1	5927	1280	678	626	149	42	45	54	565	23	1114	49	81	89	.476	0-2	17	91	.718	3.86	4.06

Andrew Chafin

Pitches: L **Bats:** R **Pos:** RP-71   **Ht:** 6'2" **Wt:** 235 **Born:** 6/17/1990 **Age:** 32

Year	Team	Lg	G	GS	GF	IP	BFP	H	R	ER	HR	SH	SF	HB	TBB	IBB	SO	WP	W	L	Pct	Sv-Op	Hld	Vel	OPS	ERC	ERA
2014	Ari	NL	3	3	0	14.0	60	13	6	6	0	2	0	1	8	1	10	2	0	1	.000	0-0	0	91	.685	3.92	3.86
2015	Ari	NL	66	0	6	75.0	306	56	23	23	3	3	2	1	30	6	58	2	5	1	.833	2-2	16	92	.587	2.30	2.76
2016	Ari	NL	32	0	1	22.2	98	22	18	17	1	1	0	1	11	1	28	2	0	1	.000	0-1	6	93	.703	4.01	6.75
2017	Ari	NL	71	0	12	51.1	221	48	21	20	5	2	1	2	21	3	61	1	1	0	1.000	0-0	17	94	.699	3.78	3.51
2018	Ari	NL	77	0	13	49.1	211	41	18	17	0	0	3	2	25	1	53	3	1	6	.143	0-0	17	94	.621	2.99	3.10
2019	Ari	NL	77	0	6	52.2	225	52	23	22	6	3	0	2	18	0	68	2	2	2	.500	0-4	23	94	.691	4.03	3.76
2020	2 Tms	NL	15	0	5	9.2	45	11	7	7	2	0	0	0	5	1	13	0	1	2	.333	1-3	3	94	.856	5.87	6.52
2021	2 Tms	AL	71	0	11	68.2	266	45	14	14	4	0	3	2	19	1	64	3	2	4	.333	5-8	22	92	.521	1.76	1.83
20	Ari	NL	11	0	1	6.2	33	9	6	6	1	0	0	0	4	0	10	0	1	1	.500	0-2	3	94	.877	7.28	8.10
20	ChC	NL	4	0	4	3.0	12	2	1	1	1	0	0	0	1	1	3	0	0	1	.000	1-1	0	94	.795	2.95	3.00
21	ChC	NL	43	0	1	39.1	150	21	9	9	1	0	0	2	12	1	37	2	0	2	.000	0-1	17	93	.461	1.33	2.06
21	Oak	AL	28	0	10	29.1	116	24	5	5	3	0	3	0	7	0	27	1	2	2	.500	5-7	5	91	.597	2.56	1.53
	Postseason		4	0	1	1.0	4	2	1	1	0	0	0	0	0	0	0	0	1	0	1.000	0-0	0	94	1.000	9.49	9.00
	8 ML YEARS		412	3	54	343.1	1432	288	130	126	21	11	9	11	137	14	355	15	12	17	.414	8-18	104	93	.634	3.02	3.30

Yu Chang

Bats: R **Throws:** R **Pos:** 1B-49;3B-21;PH-17;2B-8;SS-7;PR-2   **Ht:** 6'1" **Wt:** 180 **Born:** 8/18/1995 **Age:** 26

Year	Team	Lg	G	AB	H	2B	3B	HR	(Hm	Rd)	TB	R	RBI	RC	TBB	IBB	SO	HBP	SH	SF	SB	CS	GDP	Avg	OBP	Slg	OPS
2021	Clmbs	AAA	15	59	19	5	0	4	(-	-)	36	9	13	-	5	0	19	2	0	0	1	2	1	.322	.394	.610	1.004
2019	Cle	AL	28	73	13	2	1	1	(0	1)	20	8	6	5	11	0	22	0	0	0	0	0	4	.178	.286	.274	.560
2020	Cle	AL	10	11	2	0	0	0	(0	0)	2	1	1	0	2	0	4	0	0	0	0	0	2	.182	.308	.182	.490
2021	Cle	AL	89	237	54	14	3	9	(4	5)	101	32	39	32	11	0	69	2	0	1	1	0	4	.228	.267	.426	.693
	3 ML YEARS		127	321	69	16	4	10	(4	6)	123	41	46	37	24	0	95	2	0	1	1	0	10	.215	.273	.383	.656

Aroldis Chapman

Pitches: L **Bats:** L **Pos:** RP-61   ah-ROLL-diss   **Ht:** 6'4" **Wt:** 218 **Born:** 2/28/1988 **Age:** 34

Year	Team	Lg	G	GS	GF	IP	BFP	H	R	ER	HR	SH	SF	HB	TBB	IBB	SO	WP	W	L	Pct	Sv-Op	Hld	Vel	OPS	ERC	ERA
2010	Cin	NL	15	0	3	13.1	51	9	4	3	0	0	0	0	5	0	19	2	2	2	.500	0-1	4	100	.492	1.82	2.03
2011	Cin	NL	54	0	13	50.0	207	24	21	20	2	1	0	2	41	0	71	4	4	1	.800	1-3	13	98	.534	2.69	3.60
2012	Cin	NL	68	0	52	71.2	276	35	13	12	4	0	1	4	23	0	122	4	5	5	.500	38-43	6	98	.450	1.35	1.51
2013	Cin	NL	68	0	55	63.2	258	37	18	18	7	1	0	3	29	0	112	6	4	5	.444	38-43	6	98	.544	2.33	2.54
2014	Cin	NL	54	0	44	54.0	202	21	12	12	1	1	1	2	24	0	106	4	0	3	.000	36-38	0	100	.406	1.18	2.00
2015	Cin	NL	65	0	54	66.1	278	43	13	12	3	0	2	5	33	1	116	7	4	4	.500	33-36	0	99	.527	2.45	1.63
2016	2 Tms		59	0	52	58.0	222	32	12	10	2	0	1	0	18	0	90	8	4	1	.800	36-39	0	100	.452	1.33	1.55
2017	NYY	AL	52	0	42	50.1	210	37	20	18	3	0	1	3	20	2	69	5	4	3	.571	22-26	1	100	.584	2.53	3.22
2018	NYY	AL	55	0	43	51.1	212	24	15	14	2	0	0	5	30	0	93	9	3	0	1.000	32-34	1	99	.493	1.94	2.45
2019	NYY	AL	60	0	53	57.0	235	38	18	14	3	0	3	1	25	0	85	6	3	2	.600	37-42	0	99	.537	2.21	2.21
2020	NYY	AL	13	0	8	11.2	45	6	4	4	2	0	0	1	4	0	22	0	1	1	.500	3-5	0	98	.619	2.15	3.09
2021	NYY	AL	61	0	46	56.1	243	36	23	21	9	2	2	3	38	2	97	7	6	4	.600	30-34	1	99	.678	3.69	3.36
16	NYY	AL	31	0	29	31.1	120	20	8	7	2	0	0	0	8	0	44	2	3	0	1.000	20-21	0	100	.519	1.59	2.01
16	ChC	NL	28	0	23	26.2	102	12	4	3	0	0	1	0	10	0	46	6	1	1	.500	16-18	0	101	.370	1.04	1.01
	Postseason		35	0	27	41.1	168	28	14	11	3	1	1	2	16	1	62	2	3	4	.429	10-14	0	100	.566	2.31	2.40
	12 ML YEARS		624	0	465	603.2	2439	342	173	158	38	5	11	29	290	5	1002	62	40	31	.563	306-344	26	99	.523	2.07	2.36

Matt Chapman

Bats: R **Throws:** R **Pos:** 3B-150;SS-3;PH-1   **Ht:** 6'0" **Wt:** 215 **Born:** 4/28/1993 **Age:** 29

Year	Team	Lg	G	AB	H	2B	3B	HR	(Hm	Rd)	TB	R	RBI	RC	TBB	IBB	SO	HBP	SH	SF	SB	CS	GDP	Avg	OBP	Slg	OPS
2017	Oak	AL	84	290	68	23	2	14	(8	6)	137	39	40	42	32	0	92	2	0	2	0	3	2	.234	.313	.472	.785
2018	Oak	AL	145	547	152	42	6	24	(8	16)	278	100	68	94	58	0	146	9	0	2	1	2	18	.278	.356	.508	.864
2019	Oak	AL	156	583	145	36	3	36	(21	15)	295	102	91	109	73	0	147	1	1	3	1	1	12	.249	.342	.506	.848
2020	Oak	AL	37	142	33	9	2	10	(7	3)	76	22	25	20	8	0	54	1	0	1	0	0	2	.232	.276	.535	.812
2021	Oak	AL	151	529	111	15	3	27	(10	17)	213	75	72	68	80	0	202	4	0	9	3	2	6	.210	.314	.403	.716
	Postseason		2	8	2	0	0	0	(0	0)	2	0	0	0	1	0	0	0	0	0	0	0	0	.250	.333	.250	.583
	5 ML YEARS		573	2091	509	125	16	111	(54	57)	999	338	296	333	251	0	641	27	0	17	5	8	40	.243	.330	.478	.808

JT Chargois

Pitches: R **Bats:** B **Pos:** RP-56   SHAHG-wah   **Ht:** 6'3" **Wt:** 200 **Born:** 12/3/1990 **Age:** 31

Year	Team	Lg	G	GS	GF	IP	BFP	H	R	ER	HR	SH	SF	HB	TBB	IBB	SO	WP	W	L	Pct	Sv-Op	Hld	Vel	OPS	ERC	ERA
2016	Min	AL	25	0	10	23.0	100	25	12	12	0	1	0	0	12	0	17	3	1	1	.500	0-0	6	96	.752	4.67	4.70
2018	LAD	NL	39	0	4	32.1	135	26	13	12	4	1	0	2	15	3	40	3	2	4	.333	0-4	7	95	.697	3.58	3.34
2019	LAD	NL	21	0	9	21.1	88	21	16	15	4	0	4	2	5	2	28	0	1	0	1.000	0-0	6	96	.825	4.28	6.33
2021	2 Tms	AL	56	0	3	53.2	216	38	16	15	5	0	2	6	20	3	53	2	6	1	.857	0-5	15	96	.642	2.80	2.52
21	Sea	AL	31	0	0	30.0	118	23	11	10	2	0	1	5	6	0	29	2	1	0	1.000	0-2	9	96	.618	2.62	3.00
21	TB	AL	25	0	3	23.2	98	15	5	5	3	0	1	1	14	3	24	0	5	1	.833	0-3	6	97	.672	3.03	1.90
	4 ML YEARS		141	0	26	130.1	539	110	57	54	13	1	7	11	52	8	138	8	10	6	.625	0-9	24	96	.706	3.55	3.73

Tyler Chatwood

Pitches: R Bats: R Pos: RP-32

Ht: 5'11" Wt: 200 Born: 12/16/1989 Age: 32

		HOW MUCH PITCHED					WHAT HE GAVE UP										THE RESULTS						
Year	Team	Lg	G	GS	GF	IP	BFP	H	R	ER	HR	SH	SF	HB	TBB	IBB	SO	WP	W	L	Pct	Sv-Op	Hld	Vel	OPS	ERC	ERA
2021	Buffalo	AAA	5	0	0	4.2	25	6	1	1	0	0	0	0	8	0	1	0	1	0	1.000	0- -	-	-	.913	11.52	1.93
2011	LAA	AL	27	25	0	142.0	633	166	81	75	14	6	3	6	71	4	74	3	6	11	.353	0-0	0	93	.830	5.78	4.75
2012	Col	NL	19	12	3	64.2	294	74	43	39	9	4	2	0	33	2	41	4	5	6	.455	1-1	0	94	.836	5.62	5.43
2013	Col	NL	20	20	0	111.1	476	118	44	39	5	2	4	4	41	5	66	10	8	5	.615	0-0	0	93	.711	4.05	3.15
2014	Col	NL	4	4	0	24.0	101	21	13	12	4	0	2	2	8	0	20	2	1	0	1.000	0-0	0	93	.711	3.91	4.50
2016	Col	NL	27	27	0	158.0	669	147	75	68	15	2	3	5	70	2	117	7	12	9	.571	0-0	0	92	.723	4.01	3.87
2017	Col	NL	33	25	3	147.2	631	136	79	77	20	4	3	4	77	2	120	12	8	15	.348	1-1	0	95	.788	4.58	4.69
2018	ChC	NL	24	20	4	103.2	486	92	62	61	9	5	4	7	95	1	85	8	4	6	.400	0-0	0	93	.774	5.72	5.30
2019	ChC	NL	38	5	9	76.2	324	65	33	32	8	1	1	5	37	0	74	8	5	3	.625	2-4	3	96	.685	3.92	3.76
2020	ChC	NL	5	5	0	18.2	86	22	11	11	2	0	1	0	9	0	25	1	2	2	.500	0-0	0	94	.834	5.46	5.30
2021	2 Tms		32	0	5	32.0	145	26	22	20	2	0	0	4	21	0	38	1	1	3	.250	1-2	10	96	.668	4.18	5.63
21	Tor	AL	30	0	3	28.0	125	20	17	17	1	0	0	3	20	0	32	1	1	2	.333	1-2	10	96	.599	3.60	5.46
21	SF	NL	2	0	2	4.0	20	6	5	3	1	0	0	1	1	0	6	0	0	1	1.000	0-0	0	96	1.067	8.68	6.75
10 ML YEARS			229	143	24	878.2	3845	867	463	434	88	24	23	37	462	16	660	56	52	60	.464	5-8	13	94	.762	4.73	4.45

Jesse Chavez

Pitches: R Bats: R Pos: RP-26; SP-4

CHAH-vezz

Ht: 6'1" Wt: 175 Born: 8/21/1983 Age: 38

		HOW MUCH PITCHED					WHAT HE GAVE UP										THE RESULTS						
Year	Team	Lg	G	GS	GF	IP	BFP	H	R	ER	HR	SH	SF	HB	TBB	IBB	SO	WP	W	L	Pct	Sv-Op	Hld	Vel	OPS	ERC	ERA
2021	Gwnntt	AAA	13	0	8	20.0	77	12	6	5	1	1	1	0	8	1	27	0	1	0	1.000	2- -	-	-	.517	1.75	2.25
2008	Pit	NL	15	0	6	15.0	74	20	11	11	2	3	1	0	9	2	16	2	0	1	.000	0-2	0	94	.900	6.76	6.60
2009	Pit	NL	73	0	24	67.1	286	69	33	30	11	1	1	1	22	3	47	5	1	4	.200	0-4	15	94	.783	4.39	4.01
2010	2 Tms		51	0	26	62.2	280	69	44	41	11	5	3	1	23	7	45	2	5	5	.500	0-1	6	95	.834	4.85	5.89
2011	KC	AL	4	0	3	7.2	39	12	9	9	3	0	0	0	5	0	8	0	0	0	-	0-0	0	93	1.112	11.48	10.57
2012	2 Tms		13	2	3	24.2	123	34	29	27	7	0	1	3	11	1	30	1	1	1	.500	0-0	0	93	.983	8.32	9.85
2013	Oak	AL	35	0	16	57.1	248	50	27	25	3	6	2	3	20	4	55	5	2	4	.333	1-2	1	92	.620	2.85	3.92
2014	Oak	AL	32	21	5	146.0	621	142	64	56	17	1	4	5	49	3	136	7	8	8	.500	0-0	4	91	.692	3.89	3.45
2015	Oak	AL	30	26	3	157.0	672	164	78	73	18	4	6	2	48	2	136	3	7	15	.318	1-1	0	91	.730	4.08	4.18
2016	2 Tms		62	0	9	67.0	282	71	36	33	12	0	1	2	18	3	63	1	2	2	.500	0-3	10	93	.779	4.64	4.43
2017	LAA	AL	38	21	6	138.0	586	148	83	82	0	2	2	45	2	119	1	7	11	.389	0-1	1	92	.826	5.06	5.35
2018	2 Tms		62	0	26	95.1	377	84	28	27	13	0	2	0	17	1	92	1	5	2	.714	5-6	7	93	.645	2.84	2.55
2019	Tex	AL	48	9	5	78.0	337	82	48	42	12	1	2	5	22	0	72	1	3	5	.375	1-2	8	91	.787	4.52	4.85
2020	Tex	AL	18	0	5	17.0	77	20	13	13	6	0	3	1	7	0	13	0	0	0	-	0-3	2	91	.985	7.42	6.88
2021	Atl	NL	30	4	6	33.2	133	23	9	8	0	0	2	0	11	1	36	3	3	2	.600	0-1	2	91	.522	1.60	2.14
10	Atl	NL	28	0	16	36.2	162	40	24	24	6	3	2	1	12	3	29	0	3	2	.600	0-0	0	95	.812	4.65	5.89
10	KC	AL	23	0	10	26.0	118	29	20	17	5	2	1	0	11	4	16	2	2	3	.400	0-1	6	94	.864	5.13	5.88
12	Tor	AL	9	2	2	21.1	102	25	22	20	6	0	1	2	10	1	27	0	1	1	.500	0-0	0	93	.925	6.90	8.44
12	Oak	AL	4	0	1	3.1	21	9	7	7	1	0	0	1	1	0	3	1	0	0	-	0-0	0	93	1.261	18.70	18.90
16	Tor	AL	39	0	6	41.1	173	43	22	21	9	0	1	2	10	0	42	1	1	2	.333	0-2	7	93	.799	4.75	4.57
16	LAD	NL	23	0	3	25.2	109	28	14	12	3	0	0	0	8	3	21	0	1	0	1.000	0-1	3	93	.746	4.24	4.21
18	Tex	AL	30	0	15	56.1	234	58	23	22	10	0	1	0	12	1	50	1	3	1	.750	1-1	3	93	.747	4.00	3.51
18	ChC	NL	32	0	11	39.0	143	26	5	5	3	0	1	0	5	0	42	0	2	1	.667	4-5	4	93	.480	1.47	1.15
Postseason			1	0	0	1.0	3	1	0	0	0	0	0	0	0	0	0	0	0	0	-	0-0	0	93	.667	2.79	0.00
14 ML YEARS			511	83	143	966.2	4135	988	512	477	143	21	30	25	307	29	868	32	44	60	.423	8-26	52	92	.754	4.26	4.44

Michael Chavis

Bats: R Throws: R Pos: 2B-29;1B-9;PH-6;3B-4;PR-3;RF-1

Ht: 5'10" Wt: 210 Born: 8/11/1995 Age: 26

			BATTING																RUNNING			AVERAGES			
Year	Team	Lg	G	AB	H	2B	3B	HR	(Hm | Rd)	TB	R	RBI	RC	TBB	IBB	SO	HBP	SH	SF	SB	CS	GDP	Avg	OBP	Slg	OPS
2021	Wrcstr	AAA	24	95	25	2	0	6	(- | -)	45	19	17	-	8	0	20	2	0	2	1	0	1	.263	.327	.474	.801
2021	Indy	AAA	25	97	27	6	0	8	(- | -)	57	19	20	-	6	0	26	7	0	0	1	1	0	.278	.364	.588	.951
2019	Bos	AL	95	347	88	10	1	18	(10 | 8)	154	46	58	47	31	2	127	4	0	0	2	1	11	.254	.322	.444	.766
2020	Bos	AL	42	146	31	5	2	5	(2 | 3)	55	16	19	13	8	0	50	2	0	2	3	0	6	.212	.259	.377	.636
2021	2 Tms		43	121	30	7	1	3	(1 | 2)	48	16	11	8	1	0	42	1	0	1	1	2	4	.248	.258	.397	.655
21	Bos	AL	31	79	15	4	1	2	(0 | 2)	27	12	6	1	1	0	32	1	0	1	1	1	2	.190	.207	.342	.549
21	Pit	NL	12	42	15	3	0	1	(1 | 0)	21	4	5	7	0	0	10	0	0	0	0	1	2	.357	.357	.500	.857
3 ML YEARS			180	614	149	22	4	26	(13 | 13)	257	78	88	68	40	2	219	7	0	3	6	3	21	.243	.295	.419	.714

Robinson Chirinos

Bats: R Throws: R Pos: C-27;PH-20;2B-2;DH-1

chee-REE-nos

Ht: 6'1" Wt: 220 Born: 6/5/1984 Age: 38

			BATTING																RUNNING			AVERAGES			
Year	Team	Lg	G	AB	H	2B	3B	HR	(Hm | Rd)	TB	R	RBI	RC	TBB	IBB	SO	HBP	SH	SF	SB	CS	GDP	Avg	OBP	Slg	OPS
2021	S-WB	AAA	13	36	10	1	0	3	(- | -)	20	6	6	-	9	1	16	0	0	0	0	0	2	.278	.422	.556	.978
2011	TB	AL	20	55	12	2	0	1	(1 | 0)	17	4	7	5	5	0	13	0	0	0	0	0	0	.218	.283	.309	.592
2013	Tex	AL	13	28	5	3	0	0	(0 | 0)	8	3	0	0	2	0	6	0	0	0	0	0	1	.179	.233	.286	.519
2014	Tex	AL	93	306	73	15	0	13	(6 | 7)	127	36	40	38	17	1	71	7	4	4	0	1	4	.239	.290	.415	.705
2015	Tex	AL	78	233	54	16	1	10	(4 | 6)	102	33	34	28	28	0	62	5	5	2	0	0	4	.232	.325	.438	.762
2016	Tex	AL	57	147	33	11	0	9	(1 | 8)	71	21	20	21	15	0	44	5	1	2	0	1	4	.224	.314	.483	.797
2017	Tex	AL	88	263	67	13	1	17	(10 | 7)	133	46	38	44	34	0	79	10	1	1	1	0	5	.255	.360	.506	.866
2018	Tex	AL	113	360	80	15	1	18	(10 | 8)	151	48	65	66	45	0	140	19	0	2	2	0	7	.222	.338	.419	.757
2019	Hou	AL	114	366	87	22	1	17	(10 | 7)	162	57	58	55	51	1	125	13	2	5	1	2	11	.238	.347	.443	.790
2020	2 Tms		26	74	12	3	0	1	(0 | 1)	18	4	7	2	6	0	21	1	0	1	0	0	0	.162	.232	.243	.475
2021	ChC	NL	45	97	22	5	1	5	(3 | 2)	44	13	15	14	9	0	36	5	1	0	0	0	2	.227	.324	.454	.778

173

								BATTING												RUNNING			AVERAGES			
Year	Team	Lg	G	AB	H	2B	3B	HR	(Hm | Rd)	TB	R	RBI	RC	TBB	IBB	SO	HBP	SH	SF	SB	CS	GDP	Avg	OBP	Slg	OPS
20	Tex	AL	14	42	5	1	0	0	(0 | 0)	6	3	2	0	5	0	12	1	0	1	0	0	3	.119	.224	.143	.367
20	NYM	NL	12	32	7	2	0	1	(0 | 1)	12	1	5	2	1	0	9	0	0	0	0	0	2	.219	.242	.375	.617
	Postseason		18	52	9	1	0	4	(0 | 4)	22	5	7	5	4	0	19	1	0	0	0	0	2	.173	.246	.423	.669
	10 ML YEARS		647	1929	445	105	5	91	(45 | 46)	833	265	284	273	212	2	597	65	14	17	4	4	43	.231	.325	.432	.757

Yonny Chirinos

Pitches: R Bats: R Pos: P

chih-REE-nos

Ht: 6'2" Wt: 225 Born: 12/26/1993 Age: 28

			HOW MUCH PITCHED				WHAT HE GAVE UP										THE RESULTS							
Year	Team	Lg	G	GS	GF	IP	BFP	H	R	ER	HR	SH	SF	HB	TBB	IBB	SO	WP	W	L	Pct	Sv-Op	Hld	Vel	OPS	ERC	ERA
2018	TB	AL	18	7	2	89.2	370	84	40	35	7	2	7	5	25	2	75	5	5	5	.500	0-0	0	94	.687	3.36	3.51
2019	TB	AL	26	18	0	133.1	530	112	61	57	23	0	1	3	28	1	114	4	9	5	.643	0-0	0	94	.683	3.05	3.85
2020	TB	AL	3	3	0	11.1	52	14	4	3	2	0	0	2	4	0	10	0	0	0	-	0-0	0	93	.863	6.73	2.38
	3 ML YEARS		47	28	2	234.1	952	210	105	95	32	2	8	10	57	3	199	9	14	10	.583	0-0	0	94	.695	3.34	3.65

Jazz Chisholm Jr.

Bats: L Throws: R Pos: 2B-91;SS-37;PH-3

Ht: 5'11" Wt: 184 Born: 2/1/1998 Age: 24

								BATTING												RUNNING			AVERAGES			
Year	Team	Lg	G	AB	H	2B	3B	HR	(Hm	Rd)	TB	R	RBI	RC	TBB	IBB	SO	HBP	SH	SF	SB	CS	GDP	Avg	OBP	Slg	OPS
2017	Kane	A	29	109	27	5	2	1	(-	-)	39	14	12	14	10	0	39	3	2	1	3	0	1	.248	.325	.358	.683
2018	2 Tms	Low	112	456	124	23	6	25	(-	-)	234	79	70	56	39	0	149	2	0	4	17	4	3	.272	.329	.513	.842
2019	Jacksn	AA	89	315	65	7	5	18	(-	-)	136	51	45	45	41	0	123	6	0	3	13	4	6	.206	.307	.432	.739
2019	Jaxnvl	AA	23	81	23	4	2	3	(-	-)	40	6	10	16	11	0	24	2	0	0	3	0	0	.284	.383	.494	.877
2020	Mia	NL	21	56	9	1	1	2	(0	2)	18	8	6	3	5	0	19	1	0	0	2	2	0	.161	.242	.321	.563
2021	Mia	NL	124	464	115	20	4	18	(11	7)	197	70	53	64	34	0	145	4	2	3	23	8	3	.248	.303	.425	.728
	Postseason		1	3	1	1	0	0	(0	0)	2	0	0	1	1	0	0	0	0	0	0	0	0	.333	.500	.667	1.167
	2 ML YEARS		145	520	124	21	5	20	(11	9)	215	78	59	67	39	0	164	5	2	3	25	10	3	.238	.296	.413	.710

Ji-Man Choi

Bats: L Throws: R Pos: 1B-73;PH-10;DH-4

gee-man choy

Ht: 6'1" Wt: 260 Born: 5/19/1991 Age: 31

								BATTING												RUNNING			AVERAGES			
Year	Team	Lg	G	AB	H	2B	3B	HR	(Hm	Rd)	TB	R	RBI	RC	TBB	IBB	SO	HBP	SH	SF	SB	CS	GDP	Avg	OBP	Slg	OPS
2016	LAA	AL	54	112	19	4	0	5	(3	2)	38	9	12	8	16	1	27	0	0	1	2	4	2	.170	.271	.339	.611
2017	NYY	AL	6	15	4	1	0	2	(2	0)	11	2	5	3	2	0	5	0	0	1	0	0	1	.267	.333	.733	1.067
2018	2 Tms		61	190	50	14	1	10	(5	5)	96	25	32	30	26	1	55	3	0	2	2	0	1	.263	.357	.505	.863
2019	TB	AL	127	410	107	20	2	19	(8	11)	188	54	63	68	64	2	108	6	0	7	2	3	7	.261	.363	.459	.822
2020	TB	AL	42	122	28	13	0	3	(1	2)	50	16	16	17	20	2	36	0	0	3	0	0	0	.230	.331	.410	.741
2021	TB	AL	83	258	59	14	0	11	(4	7)	106	36	45	47	45	0	87	2	0	0	0	0	5	.229	.348	.411	.758
18	Mil	NL	12	30	7	2	0	2	(0	2)	15	4	5	5	2	1	14	0	0	0	0	0	1	.233	.281	.500	.781
18	TB	AL	49	160	43	12	1	8	(5	3)	81	21	27	25	24	0	41	3	0	2	2	0	0	.269	.370	.506	.877
	Postseason		24	56	13	1	0	3	(2	1)	23	10	5	11	17	1	21	1	0	0	0	0	1	.232	.419	.411	.830
	6 ML YEARS		373	1107	267	66	3	50	(23	27)	489	142	173	173	173	6	318	11	0	14	6	7	17	.241	.346	.442	.787

Adam Cimber

Pitches: R Bats: R Pos: RP-72

Ht: 6'3" Wt: 195 Born: 8/15/1990 Age: 31

			HOW MUCH PITCHED				WHAT HE GAVE UP										THE RESULTS							
Year	Team	Lg	G	GS	GF	IP	BFP	H	R	ER	HR	SH	SF	HB	TBB	IBB	SO	WP	W	L	Pct	Sv-Op	Hld	Vel	OPS	ERC	ERA
2018	2 Tms		70	0	16	68.1	284	68	28	26	5	2	2	6	17	9	58	1	3	8	.273	0-1	12	87	.743	3.49	3.42
2019	Cle	AL	68	0	12	56.2	244	56	29	28	6	1	2	4	19	2	41	0	6	3	.667	1-3	19	85	.720	4.01	4.45
2020	Cle	AL	14	0	5	11.1	49	13	5	5	1	0	2	0	2	0	5	0	0	1	.000	0-0	3	86	.751	3.84	3.97
2021	2 Tms		72	0	19	71.2	286	61	24	18	2	0	2	7	16	4	51	1	3	4	.429	1-1	5	87	.604	2.53	2.26
18	SD	NL	42	0	10	48.1	192	42	19	17	2	1	2	2	10	3	51	0	3	5	.375	0-1	5	86	.644	2.42	3.17
18	Cle	AL	28	0	6	20.0	92	26	9	9	3	1	0	4	7	6	7	1	0	3	.000	0-0	7	87	.957	6.53	4.05
21	Mia	NL	33	0	10	34.1	140	30	14	11	0	0	0	5	11	4	21	1	1	2	.333	0-0	0	87	.643	2.90	2.88
21	Tor	AL	39	0	9	37.1	146	31	10	7	2	0	2	2	5	0	30	0	2	2	.500	1-1	5	87	.567	2.17	1.69
	Postseason		3	0	1	2.2	13	4	4	4	0	0	1	0	2	0	0	0	0	0	-	0-0	0	87	.862	8.14	13.50
	4 ML YEARS		224	0	52	208.0	863	198	86	77	14	3	8	17	54	15	155	2	12	16	.429	2-5	39	86	.691	3.31	3.33

Steve Cishek

Pitches: R Bats: R Pos: RP-74

SEE-sheck

Ht: 6'6" Wt: 215 Born: 6/18/1986 Age: 36

			HOW MUCH PITCHED				WHAT HE GAVE UP										THE RESULTS							
Year	Team	Lg	G	GS	GF	IP	BFP	H	R	ER	HR	SH	SF	HB	TBB	IBB	SO	WP	W	L	Pct	Sv-Op	Hld	Vel	OPS	ERC	ERA
2010	Fla	NL	3	0	2	4.1	15	1	0	0	0	0	0	0	1	0	3	0	0	0	-	0-0	0	93	.276	0.35	0.00
2011	Fla	NL	45	0	21	54.2	229	45	18	16	1	3	0	3	19	7	55	5	2	1	.667	3-3	3	93	.591	2.38	2.63
2012	Mia	NL	68	0	36	63.2	275	54	26	19	3	3	2	6	29	6	68	1	5	2	.714	15-19	13	92	.663	3.28	2.69
2013	Mia	NL	69	0	62	69.2	281	53	19	18	3	3	2	2	22	6	74	1	4	6	.400	34-36	1	92	.568	2.15	2.33
2014	Mia	NL	67	0	55	65.1	275	58	26	23	3	5	3	1	21	2	84	1	4	5	.444	39-43	0	92	.643	2.78	3.17
2015	2 Tms	NL	59	0	23	55.1	243	55	26	22	4	1	2	1	27	3	48	1	2	6	.250	4-9	6	91	.720	4.17	3.58
2016	Sea	AL	62	0	40	64.0	258	44	21	20	8	1	0	4	21	2	76	4	4	6	.400	25-32	9	91	.600	2.51	2.81
2017	2 Tms	AL	49	0	11	44.2	174	26	10	10	3	0	1	3	14	1	41	3	3	2	.600	1-4	15	90	.491	1.70	2.01
2018	ChC	NL	80	0	10	70.1	288	45	19	17	5	2	1	9	28	4	78	2	4	3	.571	4-7	25	90	.593	2.39	2.18
2019	ChC	NL	70	0	23	64.0	267	48	22	21	7	0	2	7	29	1	57	0	4	6	.400	7-11	11	91	.642	3.44	2.95
2020	CWS	AL	22	0	8	20.0	93	21	12	12	4	0	2	4	9	0	21	0	0	0	-	0-1	0	90	.853	6.10	5.40
2021	LAA	AL	74	0	9	68.1	308	61	32	26	2	1	4	6	41	5	64	4	0	2	.000	0-4	21	91	.690	3.90	3.42
15	Mia	NL	32	0	15	32.0	144	37	19	16	2	1	2	0	14	3	28	0	2	6	.250	3-7	3	91	.782	4.66	4.50
15	StL	NL	27	0	8	23.1	99	18	7	6	2	0	0	1	13	0	20	1	0	0	-	1-2	3	91	.629	3.53	2.31

Year Team	Lg	G	GS	GF	IP	BFP	H	R	ER	HR	SH	SF	HB	TBB	IBB	SO	WP	W	L	Pct	Sv-Op	Hld	Vel	OPS	ERC	ERA
17 Sea	AL	23	0	8	20.0	80	13	7	7	3	0	1	1	7	1	15	1	1	1	.500	1-4	6	90	.601	2.48	3.15
17 TB	AL	26	0	3	24.2	94	13	3	3	0	0	0	2	7	0	26	2	2	1	.667	0-0	9	91	.399	1.25	1.09
Postseason		1	0	0	0.2	1	0	0	0	0	0	0	0	0	0	0	0	0	0		0-0	0	92	.000	0.00	0.00
12 ML YEARS		668	0	300	644.1	2706	511	231	204	43	19	20	46	261	37	669	26	32	39	.451	132-169	103	91	.628	2.93	2.85

Jose Cisnero

Pitches: R Bats: R Pos: RP-67

siss-NEHR-oh

Ht: 6'3" Wt: 258 Born: 4/11/1989 Age: 33

HOW MUCH PITCHED / WHAT HE GAVE UP / THE RESULTS

Year Team	Lg	G	GS	GF	IP	BFP	H	R	ER	HR	SH	SF	HB	TBB	IBB	SO	WP	W	L	Pct	Sv-Op	Hld	Vel	OPS	ERC	ERA
2013 Hou	AL	28	0	11	43.2	198	49	23	20	5	0	2	1	22	5	41	1	2	2	.500	0-2	5	93	.826	5.21	4.12
2014 Hou	AL	5	0	1	4.2	25	8	5	5	0	0	1	0	4	0	5	0	0	0		0-1	0	94	.930	9.79	9.64
2019 Det	AL	35	0	10	35.1	162	35	21	17	5	2	2	3	19	3	40	1	0	4	.000	0-2	4	96	.805	4.99	4.33
2020 Det	AL	29	0	2	29.2	123	23	10	10	1	0	0	3	10	0	34	0	3	3	.500	0-2	6	96	.584	2.58	3.03
2021 Det	AL	67	0	11	61.2	265	51	34	25	6	2	2	4	31	1	62	4	4	4	.500	4-8	18	97	.672	3.73	3.65
5 ML YEARS		164	0	35	175.0	773	166	93	77	17	4	7	11	86	9	182	6	9	13	.409	4-15	33	95	.733	4.27	3.96

Nick Ciuffo

Bats: L Throws: R Pos: C-2

SHOO-fo

Ht: 6'0" Wt: 205 Born: 3/7/1995 Age: 27

BATTING / RUNNING / AVERAGES

Year Team	Lg	G	AB	H	2B	3B	HR	(Hm	Rd)	TB	R	RBI	RC	TBB	IBB	SO	HBP	SH	SF	SB	CS	GDP	Avg	OBP	Slg	OPS
2021 Norfolk	AAA	17	52	9	1	0	2	(-	-)	16	5	8	-	5	0	22	0	0	1	1	0	2	.173	.241	.308	.549
2018 TB	AL	16	37	7	1	0	1	(1	0)	11	3	5	4	3	0	12	1	2	1	0	0	1	.189	.262	.297	.559
2019 TB	AL	3	6	1	0	0	0	(0	0)	1	0	0	0	0	0	3	0	0	0	0	0	0	.167	.167	.167	.333
2021 Bal	AL	2	5	1	1	0	0	(0	0)	2	0	0	1	1	0	1	0	0	0	0	0	0	.200	.333	.400	.733
3 ML YEARS		21	48	9	2	0	1	(1	0)	14	3	5	5	4	0	16	1	2	1	0	0	1	.188	.259	.292	.551

Aaron Civale

Pitches: R Bats: R Pos: SP-21

Ht: 6'2" Wt: 215 Born: 6/12/1995 Age: 27

HOW MUCH PITCHED / WHAT HE GAVE UP / THE RESULTS

Year Team	Lg	G	GS	GF	IP	BFP	H	R	ER	HR	SH	SF	HB	TBB	IBB	SO	WP	W	L	Pct	Sv-Op	Hld	Vel	OPS	ERC	ERA
2019 Cle	AL	10	10	0	57.2	227	44	18	15	4	1	5	1	16	0	46	2	3	4	.429	0-0	0	93	.638	2.31	2.34
2020 Cle	AL	12	12	0	74.0	312	82	39	39	11	0	2	3	16	0	69	0	4	6	.400	0-0	0	92	.798	4.52	4.74
2021 Cle	AL	21	21	0	124.1	498	108	56	53	23	1	4	4	31	0	99	3	12	5	.706	0-0	0	92	.731	3.52	3.84
3 ML YEARS		43	43	0	256.0	1037	234	113	107	38	2	11	8	63	0	214	5	19	15	.559	0-0	0	92	.731	3.51	3.76

Taylor Clarke

Pitches: R Bats: R Pos: RP-43

Ht: 6'4" Wt: 217 Born: 5/13/1993 Age: 29

HOW MUCH PITCHED / WHAT HE GAVE UP / THE RESULTS

Year Team	Lg	G	GS	GF	IP	BFP	H	R	ER	HR	SH	SF	HB	TBB	IBB	SO	WP	W	L	Pct	Sv-Op	Hld	Vel	OPS	ERC	ERA
2021 Reno	AAA	7	0	1	7.0	27	6	2	0	0	0	1	0	2	0	8	0	1	0	1.000	0-	-		.588	2.42	0.00
2019 Ari	NL	23	15	3	84.2	369	86	55	50	23	1	5	6	30	0	68	3	5	5	.500	1-1	0	94	.882	5.50	5.31
2020 Ari	NL	12	5	2	43.1	183	35	23	21	8	0	1	0	21	2	40	0	3	0	1.000	0-0	0	94	.728	3.84	4.36
2021 Ari	NL	43	0	10	43.1	194	52	28	24	4	0	1	0	14	2	39	2	1	3	.250	0-1	7	96	.776	4.71	4.98
3 ML YEARS		78	20	15	171.1	746	173	106	95	35	1	7	6	65	4	147	5	9	8	.529	1-2	7	94	.816	4.87	4.99

Emmanuel Clase

Pitches: R Bats: R Pos: RP-71

Ht: 6'2" Wt: 206 Born: 3/18/1998 Age: 24

HOW MUCH PITCHED / WHAT HE GAVE UP / THE RESULTS

Year Team	Lg	G	GS	GF	IP	BFP	H	R	ER	HR	SH	SF	HB	TBB	IBB	SO	WP	W	L	Pct	Sv-Op	Hld	Vel	OPS	ERC	ERA
2019 Tex	AL	21	1	7	23.1	94	20	8	6	2	0	0	1	6	0	21	1	2	3	.400	1-1	4	99	.678	2.89	2.31
2021 Cle	AL	71	0	51	69.2	279	51	18	10	2	1	0	0	16	3	74	3	4	5	.444	24-29	6	100	.481	1.61	1.29
2 ML YEARS		92	1	58	93.0	373	71	26	16	4	1	0	1	22	3	95	4	6	8	.429	25-30	10	100	.531	1.89	1.55

Alex Claudio

Pitches: L Bats: L Pos: RP-41

Ht: 6'3" Wt: 188 Born: 1/31/1992 Age: 30

HOW MUCH PITCHED / WHAT HE GAVE UP / THE RESULTS

Year Team	Lg	G	GS	GF	IP	BFP	H	R	ER	HR	SH	SF	HB	TBB	IBB	SO	WP	W	L	Pct	Sv-Op	Hld	Vel	OPS	ERC	ERA
2021 Wrcstr	AAA	8	2	1	11.2	52	15	9	8	0	0	1	0	3	0	13	0	0	0	-	1--	-		.742	4.36	6.17
2014 Tex	AL	15	0	5	12.1	54	14	4	4	0	0	0	0	4	0	14	0	0	0	-	0-0	0	84	.693	3.79	2.92
2015 Tex	AL	18	0	6	15.2	66	12	6	5	4	0	2	1	6	2	13	1	1	1	.500	0-1	3	84	.762	3.74	2.87
2016 Tex	AL	39	0	15	51.2	217	55	19	16	2	4	2	1	10	0	34	0	4	1	.800	0-0	2	85	.662	3.28	2.79
2017 Tex	AL	70	1	38	82.2	323	71	26	23	5	1	3	2	15	4	56	0	4	2	.667	11-15	7	87	.591	2.37	2.50
2018 Tex	AL	66	1	20	68.1	299	91	35	34	4	3	3	3	13	3	41	0	4	2	.667	1-3	14	86	.827	5.03	4.48
2019 Mil	NL	83	0	9	62.0	267	57	29	28	8	1	3	6	24	2	44	1	2	2	.500	0-3	22	86	.751	4.12	4.06
2020 Mil	NL	20	0	7	19.0	81	18	10	9	2	0	1	0	6	0	15	2	0	0	-	1-1	1	86	.687	3.67	4.26
2021 LAA	AL	41	0	11	32.2	148	37	22	20	6	0	0	0	15	1	30	1	1	2	.333	1-1	2	85	.840	5.62	5.51
Postseason		2	0	0	5.0	18	3	0	0	0	0	0	0	3	0	0	0	0	0	-	0-0	0	86	.600	2.46	0.00
8 ML YEARS		352	2	111	344.1	1455	355	151	139	31	5	13	14	93	12	247	5	16	10	.615	14-24	51	86	.721	3.80	3.63

175

Sam Clay

Pitches: L Bats: L Pos: RP-58

Ht: 6'3" Wt: 227 Born: 6/21/1993 Age: 29

			HOW MUCH PITCHED					WHAT HE GAVE UP									THE RESULTS						
Year	Team	Lg	G	GS	GF	IP	BFP	H	R	ER	HR	SH	SF	HB	TBB	IBB	SO	WP	W	L	Pct	Sv-Op	Hld	Vel	OPS	ERC	ERA
2021	Was	NL	58	0	9	45.0	214	55	32	28	4	0	1	5	22	5	34	3	0	5	.000	0-1	11	92	.792	5.84	5.60

Garrett Cleavinger

Pitches: L Bats: R Pos: RP-21; SP-1

Ht: 6'1" Wt: 220 Born: 4/23/1994 Age: 28

			HOW MUCH PITCHED					WHAT HE GAVE UP									THE RESULTS						
Year	Team	Lg	G	GS	GF	IP	BFP	H	R	ER	HR	SH	SF	HB	TBB	IBB	SO	WP	W	L	Pct	Sv-Op	Hld	Vel	OPS	ERC	ERA
2021	OkCity	AAA	9	0	1	9.2	39	7	3	2	0	0	1	0	5	0	20	1	1	0	1.000	0- -	-		.580	2.48	1.86
2020	Phi	NL	1	0	1	0.2	4	2	1	1	0	0	0	0	0	0	1	0				0-0	0	94	1.750	31.01	13.50
2021	LAD	NL	22	1	7	18.0	84	20	11	6	4	1	1	1	12	1	21	0	2	4	.333	0-1	0	96	.890	7.07	3.00
	2 ML YEARS		23	1	8	18.2	88	22	12	7	5	1	1	1	12	1	22	0	2	4	.333	0-1	0	96	.937	7.78	3.38

Ernie Clement

Bats: R Throws: R Pos: 2B-22;3B-16;LF-2;PH-2;SS-1;PR-1

Ht: 6'0" Wt: 170 Born: 3/22/1996 Age: 26

			BATTING																RUNNING			AVERAGES			
Year	Team	Lg	G	AB	H	2B	3B	HR	(Hm | Rd)	TB	R	RBI	RC	TBB	IBB	SO	HBP	SH	SF	SB	CS	GDP	Avg	OBP	Slg	OPS
2021	Clmbs	AAA	30	112	29	12	1	0	(- | -)	43	10	8	-	9	0	22	0	2	2	2	1	2	.259	.309	.384	.693
2021	Cle	AL	40	121	28	4	0	3	(1 | 2)	41	16	9	7	7	0	19	2	3	0	0	1	3	.231	.285	.339	.623

Mike Clevinger

Pitches: R Bats: R Pos: P

Ht: 6'4" Wt: 215 Born: 12/21/1990 Age: 31

			HOW MUCH PITCHED					WHAT HE GAVE UP									THE RESULTS						
Year	Team	Lg	G	GS	GF	IP	BFP	H	R	ER	HR	SH	SF	HB	TBB	IBB	SO	WP	W	L	Pct	Sv-Op	Hld	Vel	OPS	ERC	ERA
2016	Cle	AL	17	10	3	53.0	233	50	31	31	8	0	1	0	29	0	50	2	3	3	.500	0-0	0	93	.768	4.72	5.26
2017	Cle	AL	27	21	1	121.2	502	92	46	42	13	1	0	3	60	0	137	3	12	6	.667	0-0	0	92	.667	3.29	3.11
2018	Cle	AL	32	32	0	200.0	810	164	71	67	21	0	1	4	67	0	207	4	13	8	.619	0-0	0	94	.655	3.02	3.02
2019	Cle	AL	21	21	0	126.0	499	96	38	38	10	0	1	2	37	0	169	0	13	4	.765	0-0	0	95	.602	2.41	2.71
2020	2 Tms		8	8	0	41.2	162	34	14	14	6	0	0	0	14	0	40	2	3	2	.600	0-0	0	95	.713	3.31	3.02
20	Cle	AL	4	4	0	22.2	93	20	8	8	5	0	0	0	11	0	21	0	1	1	.500	0-0	0	95	.818	4.83	3.18
20	SD	NL	4	4	0	19.0	69	14	6	6	1	0	0	0	3	0	19	2	2	1	.667	0-0	0	96	.580	1.75	2.84
	Postseason		8	2	3	13.0	63	8	7	6	3	0	1	1	15	0	16	2	0	0		0-0	0	95	.837	6.09	4.15
	5 ML YEARS		105	92	4	542.1	2206	436	200	192	58	1	3	9	207	2	603	11	44	23	.657	0-0	0	94	.662	3.11	3.19

Tyler Clippard

Pitches: R Bats: R Pos: RP-26

Ht: 6'3" Wt: 200 Born: 2/14/1985 Age: 37

			HOW MUCH PITCHED					WHAT HE GAVE UP									THE RESULTS						
Year	Team	Lg	G	GS	GF	IP	BFP	H	R	ER	HR	SH	SF	HB	TBB	IBB	SO	WP	W	L	Pct	Sv-Op	Hld	Vel	OPS	ERC	ERA
2007	NYY	AL	6	6	0	27.0	124	29	19	19	6	0	0	0	17	1	18	2	3	1	.750	0-0	0	88	.876	6.37	6.33
2008	Was	NL	2	2	0	10.1	48	12	5	5	2	0	0	0	7	1	8	1	1	1	.500	0-0	0	89	.957	6.90	4.35
2009	Was	NL	41	0	8	60.1	246	36	20	18	9	3	1	1	32	1	67	1	4	2	.667	0-1	3	90	.633	2.79	2.69
2010	Was	NL	78	0	18	91.0	378	69	33	31	8	3	7	2	41	4	112	1	11	8	.579	1-11	23	92	.646	2.91	3.07
2011	Was	NL	72	0	8	88.1	329	48	18	18	11	4	3	0	26	2	104	1	3	0	1.000	0-7	38	93	.535	1.61	1.83
2012	Was	NL	74	0	42	72.2	307	55	32	30	7	3	4	2	29	2	84	5	2	6	.250	32-37	13	93	.621	2.73	3.72
2013	Was	NL	72	0	6	71.0	275	37	19	19	9	2	1	4	24	1	73	2	6	3	.667	0-3	33	92	.517	1.79	2.41
2014	Was	NL	75	0	6	70.1	278	47	22	17	5	2	1	4	23	1	82	0	7	4	.636	1-7	40	92	.541	1.98	2.18
2015	2 Tms		69	0	36	71.0	301	49	25	23	8	1	2	4	31	2	64	6	5	4	.556	19-25	8	92	.599	2.72	2.92
2016	2 Tms		69	0	17	63.0	262	54	27	25	10	1	0	1	26	2	72	5	4	6	.400	3-6	25	91	.716	3.80	3.57
2017	3 Tms	AL	67	0	23	60.1	264	47	33	32	10	3	3	2	31	1	72	11	2	8	.200	5-11	9	91	.711	3.73	4.77
2018	Tor	AL	73	1	22	68.2	285	57	29	28	13	3	2	2	23	0	85	7	4	3	.571	7-13	15	91	.719	3.57	3.67
2019	Cle	AL	53	3	7	62.0	241	38	20	20	8	2	1	7	15	0	64	3	1	0	1.000	0-0	8	90	.608	2.13	2.90
2020	Min	AL	26	2	1	26.0	98	19	9	8	2	0	0	0	4	0	26	2	2	1	.667	0-2	7	89	.543	1.74	2.77
2021	Ari	AL	26	0	15	25.1	111	22	12	9	3	1	1	3	11	1	21	1	1	1	.500	6-9	8	89	.727	3.95	3.20
15	Oak	AL	37	0	30	38.2	167	25	12	12	3	0	1	2	21	1	38	1	1	3	.250	17-21	0	91	.567	2.62	2.79
15	NYM	NL	32	0	6	32.1	134	24	13	11	5	1	1	2	10	1	26	5	4	1	.800	2-4	8	92	.637	2.82	3.06
16	Ari	NL	40	0	10	37.2	155	34	18	18	7	1	0	0	15	0	46	1	2	3	.400	1-3	13	91	.764	4.23	4.30
16	NYY	AL	29	0	7	25.1	107	20	9	7	3	0	0	1	11	2	26	4	2	3	.400	2-3	12	92	.646	3.19	2.49
17	NYY	AL	40	0	7	36.1	158	28	21	20	7	3	1	1	19	1	42	5	1	5	.167	1-6	8	91	.735	3.88	4.95
17	CWS	AL	11	0	7	10.0	44	8	2	2	0	0	0	0	5	0	12	3	1	1	.500	2-2	0	91	.585	2.56	1.80
17	Hou	AL	16	0	9	14.0	62	11	10	10	3	0	2	1	7	0	18	3	0	2	.000	2-3	1	90	.740	4.19	6.43
	Postseason		14	0	1	12.2	53	9	6	6	2	1	0	0	5	0	11	1	0	1	.000	0-0	8	92	.673	2.77	4.26
	15 ML YEARS		803	14	209	867.1	3547	619	323	302	111	27	27	29	340	19	952	48	56	48	.538	74-132	225	91	.635	2.79	3.13

Alex Cobb

Pitches: R Bats: R Pos: SP-18

Ht: 6'3" Wt: 205 Born: 10/7/1987 Age: 34

			HOW MUCH PITCHED					WHAT HE GAVE UP									THE RESULTS						
Year	Team	Lg	G	GS	GF	IP	BFP	H	R	ER	HR	SH	SF	HB	TBB	IBB	SO	WP	W	L	Pct	Sv-Op	Hld	Vel	OPS	ERC	ERA
2011	TB	AL	9	9	0	52.2	224	49	21	20	3	0	1	1	21	1	37	2	3	2	.600	0-0	0	91	.655	3.44	3.42
2012	TB	AL	23	23	0	136.1	569	130	67	61	11	3	6	9	40	2	106	4	11	9	.550	0-0	0	90	.690	3.56	4.03
2013	TB	AL	22	22	0	143.1	578	120	46	44	13	1	2	3	45	4	134	5	11	3	.786	0-0	0	91	.644	2.92	2.76
2014	TB	AL	27	27	0	166.1	681	142	56	53	11	4	4	10	47	1	149	8	10	9	.526	0-0	0	92	.619	2.87	2.87
2016	TB	AL	5	5	0	22.0	104	32	22	21	5	1	1	0	7	0	16	0	1	2	.333	0-0	0	90	.968	7.40	8.59
2017	TB	AL	29	29	0	179.1	742	175	78	73	22	2	1	6	44	2	128	8	12	10	.545	0-0	0	92	.709	3.64	3.66
2018	Bal	AL	28	28	0	152.1	661	172	93	83	24	2	6	4	43	5	102	4	5	15	.250	0-0	0	92	.814	4.81	4.90

Year	Team	Lg	G	GS	GF	IP	BFP	H	R	ER	HR	SH	SF	HB	TBB	IBB	SO	WP	W	L	Pct	Sv-Op	Hld	Vel	OPS	ERC	ERA
2019	Bal	AL	3	3	0	12.1	60	21	16	15	9	0	0	0	2	0	8	0	0	2	.000	0-0	0	92	1.297	12.47	10.95
2020	Bal	AL	10	10	0	52.1	226	52	27	25	8	0	0	2	18	0	38	1	2	5	.286	0-0	0	93	.736	4.31	4.30
2021	LAA	AL	18	18	0	93.1	393	85	46	39	5	1	2	3	33	0	98	4	8	3	.727	0-0	0	93	.645	3.22	3.76
	Postseason		2	2	0	11.2	51	13	3	2	0	0	0	1	3	0	10	1	1	0	1.000	0-0	0	92	.695	3.75	1.54
10 ML YEARS			174	174	0	1010.1	4238	978	472	434	111	14	23	38	300	15	816	40	63	60	.512	0-0	0	92	.708	3.71	3.87

Kyle Cody

Pitches: R Bats: R Pos: RP-7

Ht: 6'7" **Wt:** 225 **Born:** 8/9/1994 **Age:** 27

Year	Team	Lg	G	GS	GF	IP	BFP	H	R	ER	HR	SH	SF	HB	TBB	IBB	SO	WP	W	L	Pct	Sv-Op	Hld	Vel	OPS	ERC	ERA
2020	Tex	AL	8	5	3	22.2	92	15	5	4	1	0	0	0	13	0	18	3	1	1	.500	0-0	0	94	.583	2.64	1.59
2021	Tex	AL	7	0	2	11.1	55	16	11	10	3	0	1	3	2	0	14	1	0	2	.000	0-0	0	95	.912	7.93	7.94
2 ML YEARS			15	5	5	34.0	147	31	16	14	4	0	1	3	15	0	32	4	1	3	.250	0-0	0	95	.708	4.25	3.71

A.J. Cole

Pitches: R Bats: R Pos: RP-6

Ht: 6'5" **Wt:** 240 **Born:** 1/5/1992 **Age:** 30

Year	Team	Lg	G	GS	GF	IP	BFP	H	R	ER	HR	SH	SF	HB	TBB	IBB	SO	WP	W	L	Pct	Sv-Op	Hld	Vel	OPS	ERC	ERA
2021	Buffalo	AAA	9	0	1	9.0	35	8	0	0	0	0	0	0	0	0	11	0	1	0	1.000	0--	-	-	.600	1.53	0.00
2015	Was	NL	3	1	1	9.1	44	14	11	6	1	1	1	0	1	1	9	1	0	0		1-1	0	90	.812	5.38	5.79
2016	Was	NL	8	8	0	38.1	168	37	24	22	7	0	3	2	14	1	39	1	0	2	.333	0-0	0	91	.779	4.39	5.17
2017	Was	NL	11	8	0	52.0	229	51	23	22	8	3	1	3	27	0	44	2	3	5	.375	0-0	0	93	.799	5.15	3.81
2018	2 Tms		32	2	14	48.1	221	55	38	33	15	2	1	0	22	1	59	2	4	2	.667	0-1	0	93	.928	6.57	6.14
2019	Cle	AL	25	0	9	26.0	118	31	16	11	4	1	2	0	8	0	30	0	3	1	.750	1-1	0	94	.819	5.03	3.81
2020	Tor	AL	24	0	7	23.1	95	19	9	8	3	1	1	0	9	2	30	3	3	0	1.000	1-4	2	93	.691	3.13	3.09
2021	Tor	AL	6	0	4	8.0	30	6	1	1	1	0	0	0	1	0	7	0	0	0		1-2	1	94	.613	1.99	1.13
18	Was	NL	4	2	1	10.1	53	16	15	15	6	2	0	0	6	0	10	0	1	1	.500	0-0	0	92	1.298	12.42	13.06
18	NYY	AL	28	0	13	38.0	168	39	23	18	9	0	1	0	16	1	49	2	3	1	.750	0-1	0	94	.817	5.17	4.26
	Postseason		1	0	0	0.1	3	1	2	2	1	0	0	0	1	0	1	0	0	0		0-0	0	93	2.667	73.60	54.00
7 ML YEARS			109	19	35	205.1	905	213	122	103	39	8	9	5	82	5	208	9	14	10	.583	4-9	3	93	.813	4.95	4.51

Gerrit Cole

Pitches: R Bats: R Pos: SP-30

Ht: 6'4" **Wt:** 220 **Born:** 9/8/1990 **Age:** 31

Year	Team	Lg	G	GS	GF	IP	BFP	H	R	ER	HR	SH	SF	HB	TBB	IBB	SO	WP	W	L	Pct	Sv-Op	Hld	Vel	OPS	ERC	ERA
2013	Pit	NL	19	19	0	117.1	469	109	43	42	7	5	2	3	28	0	100	4	10	7	.588	0-0	0	96	.638	3.02	3.22
2014	Pit	NL	22	22	0	138.0	571	127	58	56	11	10	0	9	40	1	138	6	11	5	.688	0-0	0	95	.693	3.37	3.65
2015	Pit	NL	32	32	0	208.0	832	183	71	60	11	7	6	10	44	1	202	7	19	8	.704	0-0	0	96	.623	2.66	2.60
2016	Pit	NL	21	21	0	116.0	506	131	57	50	7	4	6	6	36	3	98	5	7	10	.412	0-0	0	95	.754	4.35	3.88
2017	Pit	NL	33	33	0	203.0	849	199	98	96	31	5	1	4	55	1	196	7	12	12	.500	0-0	0	95	.739	3.89	4.26
2018	Hou	AL	32	32	0	200.1	799	143	68	64	19	2	3	7	64	0	276	9	15	5	.750	0-0	0	97	.600	2.40	2.88
2019	Hou	AL	33	33	0	212.1	817	142	66	59	29	1	3	3	48	0	326	4	20	5	.800	0-0	0	97	.579	2.02	**2.50**
2020	NYY	AL	12	12	0	73.0	288	53	27	23	14	0	0	2	17	0	94	2	7	3	.700	0-0	0	98	.655	2.65	2.84
2021	NYY	AL	30	30	0	181.1	726	151	69	65	24	0	6	2	41	0	243	5	**16**	8	.667	0-0	0	98	.639	2.77	3.23
	Postseason		13	13	0	84.0	324	54	26	25	13	0	0	1	20	1	108	1	8	4	.667	0-0	0	97	.568	2.00	2.68
9 ML YEARS			234	234	0	1449.1	5857	1238	557	515	153	34	27	46	373	6	1673	52	117	63	.650	0-0	0	96	.654	2.93	3.20

Dylan Coleman

Pitches: R Bats: R Pos: RP-5

Ht: 6'5" **Wt:** 230 **Born:** 9/16/1996 **Age:** 25

Year	Team	Lg	G	GS	GF	IP	BFP	H	R	ER	HR	SH	SF	HB	TBB	IBB	SO	WP	W	L	Pct	Sv-Op	Hld	Vel	OPS	ERC	ERA
2021	NWArk	AA	18	0	14	24.2	95	19	8	8	2	0	0	0	5	0	37	2	1	1	.500	4--	-	-	.564	2.10	2.92
2021	Omha	AAA	27	0	10	33.0	135	19	16	13	2	1	0	3	17	1	56	6	4	0	1.000	3--	-	-	.537	2.34	3.55
2021	KC	AL	5	0	1	6.1	25	5	1	1	0	0	0	0	1	0	7	1	0	0		0-0	0	98	.532	1.57	1.42

Zack Collins

Bats: L Throws: R Pos: C-73;PH-10;DH-3;1B-1;PR-1

Ht: 6'3" **Wt:** 220 **Born:** 2/6/1995 **Age:** 27

										BATTING										RUNNING			AVERAGES			
Year	Team	Lg	G	AB	H	2B	3B	HR	(Hm | Rd)	TB	R	RBI	RC	TBB	IBB	SO	HBP	SH	SF	SB	CS	GDP	Avg	OBP	Slg	OPS
2019	CWS	AL	27	86	16	3	1	3	(0 | 3)	30	10	12	11	14	1	39	1	0	0			1	.186	.307	.349	.656
2020	CWS	AL	9	16	1	1	0	0	(0 | 0)	2	1	0	0	2	0	5	0	0	0			0	.063	.167	.125	.292
2021	CWS	AL	78	195	41	13	0	4	(2 | 2)	66	25	26	25	34	1	69	1	1	0	1	1	4	.210	.330	.338	.669
	Postseason		1	1	0	0	0	0	(0 | 0)	0	0	0	0	0	0	1	0	0	0	0		0	.000	.000	.000	.000
3 ML YEARS			114	297	58	17	1	7	(2 | 5)	98	36	38	36	50	2	113	2	1	0	1	1	5	.195	.315	.330	.645

Alex Colome

Pitches: R Bats: R Pos: RP-67

COH-loh-may

Ht: 6'1" **Wt:** 225 **Born:** 12/31/1988 **Age:** 33

Year	Team	Lg	G	GS	GF	IP	BFP	H	R	ER	HR	SH	SF	HB	TBB	IBB	SO	WP	W	L	Pct	Sv-Op	Hld	Vel	OPS	ERC	ERA
2013	TB	AL	3	3	0	16.0	71	14	8	4	2	0	0	1	9	0	12	1	1	1	.500	0-0	0	95	.715	4.41	2.25
2014	TB	AL	5	3	1	23.2	97	19	7	7	1	0	1	0	10	0	13	3	2	0	1.000	0-0	0	94	.590	2.77	2.66
2015	TB	AL	43	13	5	109.2	457	112	50	48	9	2	7	4	31	4	88	8	8	5	.615	0-5	8	94	.698	3.78	3.94
2016	TB	AL	57	0	48	56.2	226	43	12	12	6	0	0	2	15	1	71	1	2	4	.333	37-40	1	95	.572	2.46	1.91

			HOW MUCH PITCHED					WHAT HE GAVE UP											THE RESULTS								
Year	Team	Lg	G	GS	GF	IP	BFP	H	R	ER	HR	SH	SF	HB	TBB	IBB	SO	WP	W	L	Pct	Sv-Op	Hld	Vel	OPS	ERC	ERA
2017	TB	AL	65	0	53	66.2	281	57	27	24	4	3	6	3	23	7	58	4	2	3	.400	47-53	1	95	.636	2.79	3.24
2018	2 Tms	AL	70	0	24	68.0	282	59	26	23	7	0	1	3	21	2	72	10	7	5	.583	12-17	30	95	.645	3.15	3.04
2019	CWS	AL	62	0	54	61.0	249	42	28	19	7	2	3	1	23	2	55	4	4	5	.444	30-33	0	94	.617	2.43	2.80
2020	CWS	AL	21	0	18	22.1	90	13	3	2	0	0	0	1	8	0	16	0	2	0	1.000	12-13	0	94	.460	1.45	0.81
2021	Mia	AL	67	0	65	65.0	290	68	41	30	8	1	4	4	23	1	58	2	4	4	.500	17-24	5	94	.740	4.43	4.15
18	TB	AL	23	0	21	21.2	97	24	12	10	1	0	1	0	8	1	23	4	2	5	.286	11-13	0	95	.728	3.99	4.15
18	Sea	AL	47	0	3	46.1	185	35	14	13	6	0	0	3	13	1	49	6	5	0	1.000	1-4	30	95	.601	2.77	2.53
	Postseason		2	0	2	2.0	7	0	0	0	0	0	0	0	1	0	1	0	0	0	-	1-1	0	95	.143	0.27	0.00
	9 ML YEARS		393	19	234	489.0	2043	427	202	169	44	8	22	19	163	17	443	33	32	27	.542	155-185	45	94	.649	3.15	3.11

Michael Conforto

Bats: L **Throws:** R **Pos:** RF-117;PH-11;DH-1 **Ht:** 6'1" **Wt:** 215 **Born:** 3/1/1993 **Age:** 29

			BATTING																		RUNNING			AVERAGES			
Year	Team	Lg	G	AB	H	2B	3B	HR	(Hm	Rd)	TB	R	RBI	RC	TBB	IBB	SO	HBP	SH	SF	SB	CS	GDP	Avg	OBP	Slg	OPS
2015	NYM	NL	56	174	47	14	0	9	(4	5)	88	30	26	29	17	0	39	1	0	2	0	1	4	.270	.335	.506	.841
2016	NYM	NL	109	304	67	21	1	12	(7	5)	126	38	42	35	36	2	89	5	0	3	2	1	6	.220	.310	.414	.725
2017	NYM	NL	109	373	104	20	1	27	(16	11)	207	72	68	77	57	5	113	8	0	2	2	0	3	.279	.384	.555	.939
2018	NYM	NL	153	543	132	25	1	28	(11	17)	243	78	82	87	84	8	159	7	0	4	3	4	10	.243	.350	.448	.797
2019	NYM	NL	151	549	141	29	1	33	(18	15)	271	90	92	97	84	5	149	10	0	5	7	2	11	.257	.363	.494	.856
2020	NYM	NL	54	202	65	12	0	9	(4	5)	104	40	31	39	24	0	57	7	0	0	3	3	6	.322	.412	.515	.927
2021	NYM	NL	125	406	94	20	0	14	(6	8)	156	52	55	58	59	3	104	12	0	2	1	0	14	.232	.344	.384	.729
	Postseason		12	30	6	0	0	3	(2	1)	15	3	6	5	1	0	8	1	0	2	0	0	0	.200	.235	.500	.735
	7 ML YEARS		757	2551	650	141	4	132	(66	66)	1195	400	396	422	361	23	710	50	0	18	18	11	54	.255	.356	.468	.824

Adam Conley

Pitches: L **Bats:** L **Pos:** RP-17 **Ht:** 6'3" **Wt:** 209 **Born:** 5/24/1990 **Age:** 32

			HOW MUCH PITCHED					WHAT HE GAVE UP											THE RESULTS								
Year	Team	Lg	G	GS	GF	IP	BFP	H	R	ER	HR	SH	SF	HB	TBB	IBB	SO	WP	W	L	Pct	Sv-Op	Hld	Vel	OPS	ERC	ERA
2021	Drham	AAA	27	0	9	31.0	128	18	15	15	4	0	1	3	18	0	34	2	2	1	.667	3--	-		.607	3.12	4.35
2015	Mia	NL	15	11	1	67.0	281	65	28	28	7	1	4	3	21	1	59	0	4	1	.800	0-0	0	91	.723	3.80	3.76
2016	Mia	NL	25	25	0	133.1	584	125	59	57	13	7	3	11	62	7	124	9	8	6	.571	0-0	0	91	.738	4.21	3.85
2017	Mia	NL	22	20	1	102.2	463	114	74	70	19	8	2	8	42	4	72	5	8	8	.500	0-0	0	90	.852	5.63	6.14
2018	Mia	NL	52	0	5	50.2	202	37	25	23	5	1	3	1	18	1	50	3	3	4	.429	3-5	16	95	.642	2.57	4.09
2019	Mia	NL	60	0	18	60.2	283	76	45	44	10	2	1	3	29	6	53	2	2	11	.154	2-4	6	95	.908	6.45	6.53
2021	TB	AL	17	0	3	19.2	76	14	5	5	2	0	2	2	6	0	16	0	0	0	-	0-0	0	96	.653	2.75	2.29
	6 ML YEARS		191	56	28	434.0	1889	431	236	227	56	19	15	28	178	19	374	19	25	30	.455	5-9	22	92	.775	4.50	4.71

Roansy Contreras

Pitches: R **Bats:** R **Pos:** SP-1 **Ht:** 6'0" **Wt:** 175 **Born:** 11/7/1999 **Age:** 22

			HOW MUCH PITCHED					WHAT HE GAVE UP											THE RESULTS								
Year	Team	Lg	G	GS	GF	IP	BFP	H	R	ER	HR	SH	SF	HB	TBB	IBB	SO	WP	W	L	Pct	Sv-Op	Hld	Vel	OPS	ERC	ERA
2021	Altna	AA	12	12	0	54.1	218	37	21	16	5	2	1	3	12	0	76	1	3	2	.600	0--	-	-	.536	1.89	2.65
2021	Pit	NL	1	1	0	3.0	12	3	0	0	0	0	0	0	1	0	4	0	0	0	-	0-0	0	96	.697	3.35	0.00

William Contreras

Bats: R **Throws:** R **Pos:** C-49;PH-3 **Ht:** 6'0" **Wt:** 180 **Born:** 12/24/1997 **Age:** 24

			BATTING																		RUNNING			AVERAGES			
Year	Team	Lg	G	AB	H	2B	3B	HR	(Hm	Rd)	TB	R	RBI	RC	TBB	IBB	SO	HBP	SH	SF	SB	CS	GDP	Avg	OBP	Slg	OPS
2021	Gwnntt	AAA	44	155	45	8	0	9	(-	-)	80	26	29	-	13	0	36	3	0	0	0	0	3	.290	.357	.516	.873
2020	Atl	NL	4	10	4	1	0	0	(0	0)	5	0	1	2	0	0	4	0	0	0	0	0	0	.400	.400	.500	.900
2021	Atl	NL	52	163	35	4	1	8	(4	4)	65	19	23	19	19	1	54	2	0	1	0	0	3	.215	.303	.399	.701
	2 ML YEARS		56	173	39	5	1	8	(4	4)	70	19	24	21	19	1	58	2	0	1	0	0	3	.225	.308	.405	.712

Willson Contreras

Bats: R **Throws:** R **Pos:** C-116;PH-13;3B-1;LF-1 **Ht:** 6'1" **Wt:** 225 **Born:** 5/13/1992 **Age:** 30

			BATTING																		RUNNING			AVERAGES			
Year	Team	Lg	G	AB	H	2B	3B	HR	(Hm	Rd)	TB	R	RBI	RC	TBB	IBB	SO	HBP	SH	SF	SB	CS	GDP	Avg	OBP	Slg	OPS
2016	ChC	NL	76	252	71	14	1	12	(8	4)	123	33	35	41	26	0	67	4	0	1	2	2	5	.282	.357	.488	.845
2017	ChC	NL	117	377	104	21	0	21	(10	11)	188	50	74	76	45	2	98	3	1	2	5	4	13	.276	.356	.499	.855
2018	ChC	NL	138	474	118	27	5	10	(6	4)	185	50	54	58	53	2	121	13	2	2	4	1	14	.249	.339	.390	.730
2019	ChC	NL	105	360	98	18	2	24	(15	9)	192	57	64	62	38	2	102	9	0	2	1	2	6	.272	.355	.533	.888
2020	ChC	NL	57	189	46	10	0	7	(3	4)	77	37	26	32	20	1	57	14	0	0	1	2	6	.243	.356	.407	.763
2021	ChC	NL	128	413	98	20	0	21	(14	7)	181	61	57	63	52	1	138	14	0	4	5	4	11	.237	.340	.438	.778
	Postseason		30	78	18	3	0	3	(2	1)	30	9	7	11	13	1	21	0	0	0	0	0	0	.231	.362	.385	.746
	6 ML YEARS		621	2065	535	110	8	95	(56	39)	946	288	310	332	234	8	583	57	3	13	18	15	55	.259	.349	.458	.807

Sam Coonrod

Pitches: R Bats: R Pos: RP-40; SP-2   Ht: 6'1" Wt: 225 Born: 9/22/1992 Age: 29

		HOW MUCH PITCHED					WHAT HE GAVE UP											THE RESULTS							
Year	Team	Lg	G	GS	GF	IP	BFP	H	R	ER	HR	SH	SF	HB	TBB	IBB	SO	WP	W	L	Pct	Sv-Op	Hld	Vel	OPS	ERC	ERA
2021	LV	AAA	5	0	0	5.1	19	2	1	1	1	0	0	0	2	0	4	1	0	0	-	0- -	-	-	.505	1.54	1.69
2019	SF	NL	33	0	9	27.2	114	19	11	11	3	1	0	4	15	1	20	2	5	1	.833	0-1	0	97	.655	3.63	3.58
2020	SF	NL	18	0	5	14.2	71	17	16	16	2	0	1	2	7	0	15	1	0	2	.000	3-5	2	98	.871	5.94	9.82
2021	Phi	NL	42	2	7	42.1	185	41	21	19	5	0	1	3	15	1	48	4	2	2	.500	2-6	8	98	.692	4.02	4.04
	3 ML YEARS		93	2	21	84.2	370	77	48	46	10	1	2	9	37	2	83	7	7	5	.583	5-12	10	98	.715	4.21	4.89

Garrett Cooper

Bats: R Throws: R Pos: RF-41;1B-19;PH-16;DH-2   Ht: 6'5" Wt: 235 Born: 12/25/1990 Age: 31

			BATTING																	RUNNING			AVERAGES			
Year	Team	Lg	G	AB	H	2B	3B	HR	(Hm	Rd)	TB	R	RBI	RC	TBB	IBB	SO	HBP	SH	SF	SB	CS	GDP	Avg	OBP	Slg	OPS
2017	NYY	AL	13	43	14	5	1	0	(0	0)	21	3	6	6	1	0	12	0	0	1	0	0	0	.326	.333	.488	.822
2018	Mia	NL	14	33	7	1	0	0	(0	0)	8	2	2	3	4	0	12	1	0	0	0	0	0	.212	.316	.242	.558
2019	Mia	NL	107	381	107	16	1	15	(6	9)	170	52	50	57	33	0	110	5	0	2	0	0	10	.281	.344	.446	.791
2020	Mia	NL	34	120	34	8	0	6	(3	3)	60	20	20	22	11	0	31	2	0	0	0	0	5	.283	.353	.500	.853
2021	Mia	NL	71	215	61	10	1	9	(6	3)	100	30	33	39	30	0	68	4	0	1	1	1	6	.284	.380	.465	.845
	Postseason		5	18	3	1	0	1	(0	1)	7	2	3	2	3	0	5	0	0	0	0	0	0	.167	.286	.389	.675
	5 ML YEARS		239	792	223	40	3	30	(15	15)	359	107	111	127	79	0	233	12	0	4	1	1	22	.282	.354	.453	.807

Patrick Corbin

Pitches: L Bats: L Pos: SP-31   Ht: 6'4" Wt: 220 Born: 7/19/1989 Age: 32

			HOW MUCH PITCHED					WHAT HE GAVE UP											THE RESULTS							
Year	Team	Lg	G	GS	GF	IP	BFP	H	R	ER	HR	SH	SF	HB	TBB	IBB	SO	WP	W	L	Pct	Sv-Op	Hld	Vel	OPS	ERC	ERA
2012	Ari	NL	22	17	3	107.0	454	117	56	54	14	2	5	4	25	2	86	1	6	8	.429	1-1	0	91	.782	4.31	4.54
2013	Ari	NL	32	32	0	208.1	860	189	81	79	19	8	1	9	54	1	178	13	14	8	.636	0-0	0	92	.671	3.14	3.41
2015	Ari	NL	16	16	0	85.0	357	91	34	34	9	2	1	2	17	0	78	4	6	5	.545	0-0	0	92	.743	3.82	3.60
2016	Ari	NL	36	24	6	155.2	701	177	**109**	89	24	6	5	5	66	2	131	9	5	13	.278	1-1	0	92	.825	5.47	5.15
2017	Ari	NL	33	32	0	189.2	826	208	97	85	26	4	5	3	61	8	178	10	14	13	.519	0-0	0	92	.792	4.55	4.03
2018	Ari	NL	33	33	0	200.0	800	162	70	70	15	3	2	5	48	3	246	8	11	7	.611	0-0	0	91	.607	2.41	3.15
2019	Was	NL	33	33	0	202.0	835	169	81	73	24	8	5	4	70	2	238	4	14	7	.667	0-0	0	92	.668	3.15	3.25
2020	Was	NL	11	11	0	65.2	295	**85**	35	34	10	0	1	0	18	1	60	1	2	7	.222	0-0	0	90	.838	5.61	4.66
2021	Was	NL	31	31	0	171.2	751	192	**114**	111	**37**	10	5	3	60	2	143	0	9	**16**	.360	0-0	0	92	.855	5.47	5.82
	Postseason		8	3	0	23.1	103	21	16	15	2	0	0	1	12	1	36	0	2	3	.400	0-1	2	93	.663	3.90	5.79
	9 ML YEARS		247	229	9	1385.0	5879	1390	677	629	178	43	33	34	419	21	1338	50	81	84	.491	2-2	2	92	.742	3.98	4.09

Franchy Cordero

Bats: L Throws: R Pos: LF-33;1B-11;PH-6;RF-2;PR-2;DH-1   Ht: 6'3" Wt: 226 Born: 9/2/1994 Age: 27

			BATTING																	RUNNING			AVERAGES			
Year	Team	Lg	G	AB	H	2B	3B	HR	(Hm	Rd)	TB	R	RBI	RC	TBB	IBB	SO	HBP	SH	SF	SB	CS	GDP	Avg	OBP	Slg	OPS
2021	Wrcstr	AAA	73	268	79	21	2	12	(-	-)	140	51	47	-	40	2	91	5	0	0	11	1	3	.295	.396	.522	.919
2017	SD	NL	30	92	21	3	3	3	(3	0)	39	15	9	9	6	0	44	0	1	0	1	1	0	.228	.276	.424	.699
2018	SD	NL	40	139	33	5	1	7	(3	4)	61	19	19	19	14	0	55	0	1	0	5	2	1	.237	.307	.439	.746
2019	SD	NL	9	15	5	1	0	0	(0	0)	6	2	1	3	4	0	7	0	0	0	1	0	0	.333	.450	.400	.850
2020	KC	AL	16	38	8	3	0	2	(2	0)	17	7	7	7	4	0	4	0	0	0	1	0	1	.211	.286	.447	.733
2021	Bos	AL	48	127	24	6	0	1	(0	1)	33	12	9	7	8	0	51	0	1	0	1	1	1	.189	.237	.260	.497
	5 ML YEARS		143	411	91	18	4	13	(8	5)	156	55	45	45	36	0	161	0	3	1	9	4	3	.221	.283	.380	.663

Jimmy Cordero

Pitches: R Bats: R Pos: P   Ht: 6'4" Wt: 240 Born: 10/19/1991 Age: 30

			HOW MUCH PITCHED					WHAT HE GAVE UP											THE RESULTS							
Year	Team	Lg	G	GS	GF	IP	BFP	H	R	ER	HR	SH	SF	HB	TBB	IBB	SO	WP	W	L	Pct	Sv-Op	Hld	Vel	OPS	ERC	ERA
2018	Was	NL	22	0	3	19.0	94	23	13	12	2	0	0	2	12	2	12	0	1	2	.333	0-1	0	98	.794	6.39	5.68
2019	2 Tms	AL	31	0	7	37.1	146	26	12	12	4	0	0	3	11	0	31	1	1	1	.500	0-0	4	97	.615	2.52	2.89
2020	CWS	AL	30	0	4	26.2	124	33	21	18	2	1	1	3	9	2	22	3	1	2	.333	0-1	8	97	.784	5.24	6.08
19	Tor	AL	1	0	1	1.1	5	2	1	1	1	0	0	0	0	0	0	0	0	1	.000	0-0	0	97	1.400	12.07	6.75
19	CWS	AL	30	0	6	36.0	141	24	11	11	3	0	0	3	11	0	31	1	1	0	1.000	0-0	4	97	.584	2.27	2.75
	Postseason		2	0	0	3.2	12	1	0	0	0	0	0	0	1	0	2	0	0	0	-	0-0	0	98	.258	0.51	0.00
	3 ML YEARS		83	0	14	83.0	364	82	46	42	8	1	1	8	32	4	65	4	3	5	.375	0-2	12	97	.718	4.21	4.55

Carlos Correa

Bats: R Throws: R Pos: SS-148   coh-RAY-uh   Ht: 6'4" Wt: 220 Born: 9/22/1994 Age: 27

			BATTING																	RUNNING			AVERAGES			
Year	Team	Lg	G	AB	H	2B	3B	HR	(Hm	Rd)	TB	R	RBI	RC	TBB	IBB	SO	HBP	SH	SF	SB	CS	GDP	Avg	OBP	Slg	OPS
2015	Hou	AL	99	387	108	22	1	22	(12	10)	198	52	68	68	40	2	78	1	0	4	14	4	10	.279	.345	.512	.857
2016	Hou	AL	153	577	158	36	3	20	(8	12)	260	76	96	93	75	5	139	5	0	3	13	3	13	.274	.361	.451	.811
2017	Hou	AL	109	422	133	25	1	24	(11	13)	232	82	84	86	53	3	92	2	0	4	2	1	12	.315	.391	.550	.941
2018	Hou	AL	110	402	96	20	1	15	(7	8)	163	60	65	49	53	3	111	2	0	11	3	0	17	.239	.323	.405	.728
2019	Hou	AL	75	280	78	16	1	21	(11	10)	159	42	59	52	35	0	75	2	0	4	1	0	8	.279	.358	.568	.926
2020	Hou	AL	58	201	53	9	0	5	(1	4)	77	22	25	23	16	2	49	3	0	1	0	0	4	.264	.326	.383	.709
2021	Hou	AL	148	555	155	34	1	26	(14	12)	269	104	92	94	75	2	116	4	0	6	0	3	16	.279	.366	.485	.850
	Postseason		63	241	65	12	0	17	(8	9)	128	27	50	43	24	1	66	1	0	1	0	0	6	.270	.338	.531	.869
	7 ML YEARS		752	2824	781	162	8	133	(64	69)	1358	438	489	465	347	19	660	19	0	33	33	8	79	.277	.356	.481	.837

Nestor Cortes

Pitches: L Bats: R Pos: SP-14; RP-8   Ht: 5'11" Wt: 210 Born: 12/10/1994 Age: 27

Year Team	Lg	G	GS	GF	IP	BFP	H	R	ER	HR	SH	SF	HB	TBB	IBB	SO	WP	W	L	Pct	Sv-Op	Hld	Vel	OPS	ERC	ERA
2021 S-WB	AAA	5	1	3	15.0	51	8	2	2	1	0	0	0	1	0	18	0	1	1	.500	1--	-	-	.396	0.95	1.20
2018 Bal	AL	4	0	3	4.2	26	10	4	4	2	0	0	0	4	0	3	0	0	0	-	0-0	0	88	1.357	18.44	7.71
2019 NYY	AL	33	1	7	66.2	298	75	44	42	16	0	2	1	28	1	69	1	5	1	.833	0-1	1	90	.843	5.97	5.67
2020 Sea	AL	5	1	2	7.2	44	12	14	13	6	0	0	2	6	0	8	0	0	1	.000	0-0	0	88	1.379	16.80	15.26
2021 NYY	AL	22	14	0	93.0	374	75	32	30	14	1	1	2	25	0	103	2	2	3	.400	0-0	0	91	.659	2.95	2.90
4 ML YEARS		64	16	15	172.0	742	172	94	89	38	1	3	5	63	1	183	3	7	5	.583	0-1	1	90	.795	4.90	4.66

Jharel Cotton

JUH-rel   Ht: 5'11" Wt: 200 Born: 1/19/1992 Age: 30

Pitches: R Bats: R Pos: RP-23

Year Team	Lg	G	GS	GF	IP	BFP	H	R	ER	HR	SH	SF	HB	TBB	IBB	SO	WP	W	L	Pct	Sv-Op	Hld	Vel	OPS	ERC	ERA
2021 RdRck	AAA	24	2	7	42.0	175	32	19	14	3	0	1	1	17	0	57	0	4	0	1.000	0--	-	-	.587	2.69	3.00
2016 Oak	AL	5	5	0	29.1	112	20	10	7	4	0	0	0	4	0	23	1	2	0	1.000	0-0	0	92	.538	1.70	2.15
2017 Oak	AL	24	24	0	129.0	566	133	91	80	28	4	5	4	53	1	105	9	9	10	.474	0-0	0	93	.833	5.26	5.58
2021 Tex	AL	23	0	5	30.2	137	28	12	12	2	0	2	2	15	0	30	1	2	0	1.000	0-0	3	93	.659	3.84	3.52
3 ML YEARS		52	29	5	189.0	815	181	113	99	34	4	7	6	72	1	158	11	13	10	.565	0-0	3	93	.762	4.41	4.71

Danny Coulombe

KOO-lohm   Ht: 5'10" Wt: 190 Born: 10/26/1989 Age: 32

Pitches: L Bats: L Pos: RP-28; SP-1

Year Team	Lg	G	GS	GF	IP	BFP	H	R	ER	HR	SH	SF	HB	TBB	IBB	SO	WP	W	L	Pct	Sv-Op	Hld	Vel	OPS	ERC	ERA
2021 StPaul	AAA	14	0	7	20.1	79	16	6	4	1	0	0	0	3	0	27	0	1	1	.500	2--	-	-	.530	1.78	1.77
2014 LAD	NL	5	0	0	4.1	22	5	3	2	1	0	0	0	2	0	4	2	0	0	-	0-0	0	91	.768	5.49	4.15
2015 2 Tms		14	0	4	16.0	72	17	10	10	0	0	0	0	9	0	11	2	0	0	-	0-1	2	90	.742	4.32	5.63
2016 Oak	AL	35	0	11	47.2	193	37	24	24	6	2	3	0	17	2	54	3	3	1	.750	0-1	2	90	.634	2.84	4.53
2017 Oak	AL	72	0	10	51.2	219	46	22	20	4	0	1	4	22	1	39	5	2	2	.500	0-1	13	91	.714	3.74	3.48
2018 Oak	AL	27	0	3	23.2	98	24	13	12	5	0	1	0	11	0	26	2	1	1	.500	0-0	0	90	.846	5.58	4.56
2020 Min	AL	2	0	2	2.2	13	2	0	0	0	0	0	0	3	0	3	0	0	0	-	0-0	0	90	.585	4.52	0.00
2021 Min	AL	29	1	13	34.1	139	35	17	14	5	1	0	0	7	1	33	0	3	2	.600	0-1	2	90	.747	3.77	3.67
15 LAD	NL	5	0	3	8.1	40	9	7	7	0	0	0	0	6	0	7	1	0	0	-	0-0	0	90	.816	4.87	7.56
15 Oak	AL	9	0	1	7.2	32	8	3	3	0	0	0	0	3	0	4	1	0	0	-	0-1	0	89	.654	3.72	3.52
7 ML YEARS		184	1	43	180.1	756	166	89	82	21	3	5	4	71	4	170	14	9	6	.600	0-4	17	90	.720	3.84	4.09

Jake Cousins

Pitches: R Bats: R Pos: RP-30   Ht: 6'4" Wt: 185 Born: 7/14/1994 Age: 27

Year Team	Lg	G	GS	GF	IP	BFP	H	R	ER	HR	SH	SF	HB	TBB	IBB	SO	WP	W	L	Pct	Sv-Op	Hld	Vel	OPS	ERC	ERA
2021 Biloxi	AA	8	0	5	9.0	38	6	3	3	1	0	0	2	3	0	14	0	0	1	.000	3--	-	-	.562	2.90	3.00
2021 Nashv	AAA	8	0	2	8.2	35	6	3	2	1	1	0	0	2	0	16	0	1	0	1.000	1--	-	-	.517	1.88	2.08
2021 Mil	NL	30	0	3	30.0	125	16	9	9	3	1	0	4	19	1	44	2	1	0	1.000	0-0	7	96	.582	2.95	2.70

Will Craig

Bats: R Throws: R Pos: 1B-18;PH-2   Ht: 6'3" Wt: 235 Born: 11/16/1994 Age: 27

Year Team	Lg	G	AB	H	2B	3B	HR	(Hm	Rd)	TB	R	RBI	RC	TBB	IBB	SO	HBP	SH	SF	SB	CS	GDP	Avg	OBP	Slg	OPS
2021 Indy	AAA	32	122	35	8	0	8	(-	-)	67	23	23	-	14	2	28	2	0	1	0	0	4	.287	.367	.549	.916
2020 Pit	NL	2	4	0	0	0	0	(0	0)	0	0	0	0	0	0	1	0	0	0	0	0	0	.000	.000	.000	.000
2021 Pit	NL	18	60	13	2	0	1	(1	0)	18	5	3	4	5	1	22	0	0	0	0	0	1	.217	.277	.300	.577
2 ML YEARS		20	64	13	2	0	1	(1	0)	18	5	3	4	5	1	23	0	0	0	0	0	1	.203	.261	.281	.542

Brandon Crawford

Bats: L Throws: R Pos: SS-135;PH-5   Ht: 6'1" Wt: 223 Born: 1/21/1987 Age: 35

Year Team	Lg	G	AB	H	2B	3B	HR	(Hm	Rd)	TB	R	RBI	RC	TBB	IBB	SO	HBP	SH	SF	SB	CS	GDP	Avg	OBP	Slg	OPS
2011 SF	NL	66	196	40	5	2	3	(0	3)	58	22	21	20	23	1	31	0	1	0	1	3	4	.204	.288	.296	.584
2012 SF	NL	143	435	108	26	3	4	(1	3)	152	44	45	40	33	6	95	3	2	3	1	4	4	.248	.304	.349	.653
2013 SF	NL	149	499	124	24	3	9	(2	7)	181	52	43	42	42	6	96	5	1	3	1	2	10	.248	.311	.363	.674
2014 SF	NL	153	491	121	20	10	10	(4	6)	191	54	69	72	59	10	129	2	2	10	5	3	4	.246	.324	.389	.713
2015 SF	NL	143	507	130	33	4	21	(8	13)	234	65	84	69	39	9	119	11	0	4	6	4	18	.256	.321	.462	.782
2016 SF	NL	155	553	152	28	11	12	(4	8)	238	67	84	82	57	10	115	4	0	9	7	0	13	.275	.342	.430	.772
2017 SF	NL	144	518	131	34	1	14	(6	8)	209	58	77	61	42	3	113	1	0	9	3	5	18	.253	.305	.403	.709
2018 SF	NL	151	531	135	28	2	14	(7	7)	209	63	54	60	50	13	122	8	0	5	4	5	12	.254	.325	.394	.719
2019 SF	NL	147	500	114	24	2	11	(2	9)	175	58	59	55	53	5	117	3	0	4	3	2	10	.228	.304	.350	.654
2020 SF	NL	54	172	44	12	0	8	(5	3)	80	26	28	27	15	2	47	4	0	2	1	2	3	.256	.326	.465	.792
2021 SF	NL	138	483	144	30	3	24	(11	13)	252	79	90	100	56	6	105	5	0	5	11	3	8	.298	.373	.522	.895
Postseason		38	127	30	6	1	1	(0	1)	41	13	17	14	15	2	32	0	1	2	2	0	2	.236	.313	.323	.635
11 ML YEARS		1443	4885	1243	264	41	130	(50	80)	1979	588	654	628	469	71	1089	46	6	54	43	33	104	.254	.322	.405	.727

J.P. Crawford

Bats: L Throws: R Pos: SS-160   Ht: 6'2" Wt: 199 Born: 1/11/1995 Age: 27

									BATTING												RUNNING			AVERAGES			
Year	Team	Lg	G	AB	H	2B	3B	HR	(Hm	Rd)	TB	R	RBI	RC	TBB	IBB	SO	HBP	SH	SF	SB	CS	GDP	Avg	OBP	Slg	OPS
2017	Phi	NL	23	70	15	4	1	0	(0	0)	21	8	6	9	16	0	22	0	0	1	1	0	1	.214	.356	.300	.656
2018	Phi	NL	49	117	25	6	3	3	(2	1)	46	17	12	17	13	0	37	5	2	0	2	0	2	.214	.319	.393	.712
2019	Sea	AL	93	345	78	21	4	7	(4	3)	128	43	46	46	43	0	83	2	3	3	5	3	4	.226	.313	.371	.684
2020	Sea	AL	53	204	52	7	2	2	(1	1)	69	33	24	30	23	0	39	3	0	2	6	3	4	.255	.336	.338	.674
2021	Sea	AL	160	619	169	37	0	9	(5	4)	233	89	54	85	58	1	114	5	1	4	3	6	10	.273	.338	.376	.715
	5 ML YEARS		378	1355	339	75	10	21	(12	9)	497	190	142	187	153	1	295	15	6	10	17	12	21	.250	.331	.367	.698

Kutter Crawford

Pitches: R Bats: R Pos: SP-1   Ht: 6'1" Wt: 209 Born: 4/1/1996 Age: 26

			HOW MUCH PITCHED					WHAT HE GAVE UP										THE RESULTS							
Year	Team	Lg	G	GS	GF	IP	BFP	H	R	ER	HR	SH	SF	HB	TBB	IBB	SO	WP	W	L	Pct	Sv-Op	Hld	Vel	OPS	ERC	ERA
2021	Portlnd	AA	10	10	0	46.1	172	33	17	17	7	0	2	0	5	0	64	0	3	2	.600	0--	-	-	.609	1.88	3.30
2021	Wrcstr	AAA	9	8	0	44.2	192	45	26	25	5	0	1	3	13	0	64	1	3	4	.429	0--	-	-	.752	4.01	5.04
2021	Bos	AL	1	1	0	2.0	13	5	5	5	1	0	2	0	2	0	2	0	0	1	.000	0-0	0	94	1.538	21.61	22.50

Stefan Crichton

Pitches: R Bats: R Pos: RP-31
CRY-ton   Ht: 6'3" Wt: 208 Born: 2/29/1992 Age: 30

			HOW MUCH PITCHED					WHAT HE GAVE UP										THE RESULTS							
Year	Team	Lg	G	GS	GF	IP	BFP	H	R	ER	HR	SH	SF	HB	TBB	IBB	SO	WP	W	L	Pct	Sv-Op	Hld	Vel	OPS	ERC	ERA
2021	Reno	AAA	11	0	2	12.0	60	17	12	12	0	0	0	0	7	0	9	0	3	0	1.000	0--	-	-	.909	6.31	9.00
2017	Bal	AL	8	0	1	12.1	62	26	11	11	2	0	1	0	4	0	8	2	0	0	-	0-0	1	94	1.151	12.21	8.03
2019	Ari	NL	28	0	9	30.1	123	23	12	12	3	0	0	2	8	1	33	1	1	0	1.000	0-0	3	93	.578	2.47	3.56
2020	Ari	NL	26	0	8	26.0	109	22	7	7	1	0	0	4	9	4	23	2	2	2	.500	5-7	2	92	.665	3.00	2.42
2021	Ari	NL	31	0	11	23.1	117	33	22	19	3	0	2	4	12	3	17	3	0	4	.000	4-4	5	91	.914	7.75	7.33
	4 ML YEARS		93	0	29	92.0	411	104	52	49	9	0	3	10	33	8	81	8	3	6	.333	9-11	11	92	.782	4.96	4.79

Kyle Crick

Pitches: R Bats: L Pos: RP-27   Ht: 6'4" Wt: 225 Born: 11/30/1992 Age: 29

			HOW MUCH PITCHED					WHAT HE GAVE UP										THE RESULTS							
Year	Team	Lg	G	GS	GF	IP	BFP	H	R	ER	HR	SH	SF	HB	TBB	IBB	SO	WP	W	L	Pct	Sv-Op	Hld	Vel	OPS	ERC	ERA
2021	Charllt	AAA	8	0	3	10.1	36	4	1	1	0	0	0	0	3	0	15	1	2	0	1.000	0--	-	-	.346	0.78	0.87
2017	SF	NL	30	0	14	32.1	134	22	13	11	2	1	0	1	17	1	28	6	0	0	-	0-0	1	96	.596	2.68	3.06
2018	Pit	NL	64	0	13	60.1	255	45	18	16	3	1	1	7	23	3	65	9	3	2	.600	2-3	16	96	.569	2.63	2.39
2019	Pit	NL	52	0	9	49.0	226	41	30	27	10	0	1	7	35	1	61	1	3	7	.300	0-6	13	95	.799	5.73	4.96
2020	Pit	NL	7	0	2	5.2	29	7	6	1	0	0	0	0	4	0	7	0	1	1	.500	0-1	0	91	.699	5.50	1.59
2021	Pit	NL	27	0	6	24.1	107	14	14	12	0	1	2	5	19	0	21	6	1	1	.500	0-1	6	93	.558	3.26	4.44
	5 ML YEARS		180	0	44	171.2	751	129	81	67	15	3	4	20	98	5	182	22	7	11	.389	2-11	36	95	.647	3.65	3.51

Nabil Crismatt

Pitches: R Bats: R Pos: RP-45   Ht: 6'1" Wt: 220 Born: 12/25/1994 Age: 27

			HOW MUCH PITCHED					WHAT HE GAVE UP										THE RESULTS							
Year	Team	Lg	G	GS	GF	IP	BFP	H	R	ER	HR	SH	SF	HB	TBB	IBB	SO	WP	W	L	Pct	Sv-Op	Hld	Vel	OPS	ERC	ERA
2020	StL	NL	6	0	6	8.1	31	6	3	3	2	0	0	0	1	1	8	0	0	0	-	0-0	0	90	.692	2.27	3.24
2021	SD	NL	45	0	14	81.1	351	87	40	34	10	2	0	8	24	2	71	3	3	1	.750	0-0	1	90	.761	4.63	3.76
	2 ML YEARS		51	0	20	89.2	382	93	43	37	12	2	0	8	25	3	79	3	3	1	.750	0-0	1	90	.755	4.41	3.71

Cooper Criswell

Pitches: R Bats: R Pos: SP-1   Ht: 6'6" Wt: 200 Born: 7/24/1996 Age: 25

			HOW MUCH PITCHED					WHAT HE GAVE UP										THE RESULTS							
Year	Team	Lg	G	GS	GF	IP	BFP	H	R	ER	HR	SH	SF	HB	TBB	IBB	SO	WP	W	L	Pct	Sv-Op	Hld	Vel	OPS	ERC	ERA
2021	Rock	AA	13	13	0	72.1	299	70	34	30	10	0	2	5	8	0	87	4	6	4	.600	0--	-	-	.690	3.24	3.73
2021	Salt Lk	AAA	8	8	0	41.0	187	52	32	31	8	0	1	9	11	0	39	1	3	4	.429	0--	-	-	.921	6.95	6.80
2021	LAA	AL	1	1	0	1.1	10	6	3	3	0	0	0	0	0	0	0	0	0	1	.000	0-0	0	87	1.500	26.58	20.25

Garrett Crochet

Pitches: L Bats: L Pos: RP-54
CROH-shay   Ht: 6'6" Wt: 230 Born: 6/21/1999 Age: 23

			HOW MUCH PITCHED					WHAT HE GAVE UP										THE RESULTS							
Year	Team	Lg	G	GS	GF	IP	BFP	H	R	ER	HR	SH	SF	HB	TBB	IBB	SO	WP	W	L	Pct	Sv-Op	Hld	Vel	OPS	ERC	ERA
2020	CWS	AL	5	0	1	6.0	22	3	0	0	0	0	0	1	0	0	8	0	0	0	-	0-0	0	100	.325	0.80	0.00
2021	CWS	AL	54	0	12	54.1	230	42	22	17	2	2	2	1	27	2	65	4	3	5	.375	0-1	12	97	.598	2.79	2.82
	Postseason		1	0	0	0.2	2	0	0	0	0	0	0	0	0	0	0	0	0	0	-	0-0	0	97	.000	0.00	0.00
	2 ML YEARS		59	0	13	60.1	252	45	22	17	2	2	2	2	27	2	73	4	3	5	.375	0-1	12	97	.572	2.52	2.54

C.J. Cron

Bats: R **Throws:** R **Pos:** 1B-130;PH-10;DH-3   CROHN   **Ht:** 6'4" **Wt:** 235 **Born:** 1/5/1990 **Age:** 32

									BATTING										RUNNING			AVERAGES			
Year	Team	Lg	G	AB	H	2B	3B	HR	(Hm | Rd)	TB	R	RBI	RC	TBB	IBB	SO	HBP	SH	SF	SB	CS	GDP	Avg	OBP	Slg	OPS
2014	LAA	AL	79	242	62	12	1	11	(5 | 6)	109	28	37	35	10	0	61	1	0	0	0	0	10	.256	.289	.450	.739
2015	LAA	AL	113	378	99	17	1	16	(11 | 5)	166	37	51	46	17	1	82	5	0	3	3	1	9	.262	.300	.439	.739
2016	LAA	AL	116	407	113	25	2	16	(7 | 9)	190	51	69	66	24	1	75	7	0	5	2	3	9	.278	.325	.467	.792
2017	LAA	AL	100	339	84	14	1	16	(8 | 8)	148	39	56	51	22	0	96	7	0	3	3	2	5	.248	.305	.437	.741
2018	TB	AL	140	501	127	28	1	30	(11 | 19)	247	68	74	65	37	2	145	17	0	5	1	2	11	.253	.323	.493	.816
2019	Min	AL	125	458	116	24	0	25	(10 | 15)	215	51	78	66	29	3	107	10	0	2	0	0	13	.253	.311	.469	.780
2020	Det	AL	13	42	8	3	0	4	(0 | 4)	23	9	8	7	9	0	16	1	0	0	0	0	2	.190	.346	.548	.894
2021	Col	AL	142	470	132	31	1	28	(19 | 9)	249	70	92	95	60	3	117	13	0	4	1	0	11	.281	.375	.530	.905
	Postseason		5	14	2	1	0	0	(0 | 0)	3	1	0		3	0	5	0	0	0	0	0	0	.143	.294	.214	.508
	8 ML YEARS		828	2837	741	154	7	146	(71 | 75)	1347	353	465	431	208	10	699	61	0	22	10	8	70	.261	.323	.475	.798

Jake Cronenworth

Bats: L **Throws:** R **Pos:** 2B-94;SS-41;1B-24;PH-6   **Ht:** 6'0" **Wt:** 187 **Born:** 1/21/1994 **Age:** 28

									BATTING										RUNNING			AVERAGES			
Year	Team	Lg	G	AB	H	2B	3B	HR	(Hm | Rd)	TB	R	RBI	RC	TBB	IBB	SO	HBP	SH	SF	SB	CS	GDP	Avg	OBP	Slg	OPS
2020	SD	NL	54	172	49	15	3	4	(3 | 1)	82	26	20	28	18	0	30	1	0	1	3	1	4	.285	.354	.477	.831
2021	SD	NL	152	567	151	33	7	21	(13 | 8)	261	94	71	88	55	6	90	10	3	3	4	3	8	.266	.340	.460	.800
	Postseason		6	18	7	0	1	1	(1 | 0)	12	5	3		4	0	5	2	0	0	1	0	0	.389	.542	.667	1.208
	2 ML YEARS		206	739	200	48	10	25	(16 | 9)	343	120	91	116	73	6	120	11	3	4	7	4	12	.271	.343	.464	.808

Hans Crouse

Pitches: R **Bats:** L **Pos:** SP-2   **Ht:** 6'4" **Wt:** 180 **Born:** 9/15/1998 **Age:** 23

			HOW MUCH PITCHED				WHAT HE GAVE UP										THE RESULTS						
Year	Team	Lg	G	GS	GF	IP	BFP	H	R	ER	HR	SH	SF	HB	TBB	IBB	SO	WP	W	L	Pct	Sv-Op	Hld	Vel	OPS	ERC	ERA
2021	Frisco	AA	13	13	0	51.0	195	27	20	19	5	0	2	2	19	0	54	2	3	2	.600	0--	-	-	.508	1.79	3.35
2021	Rdng	AA	6	6	0	29.2	122	24	9	9	3	0	0	2	12	0	38	2	2	2	.500	0--	-	-	.691	3.41	2.73
2021	Phi	NL	2	2	0	7.0	32	4	4	4	2	1	0	0	7	0	2	0	0	2	.000	0-0	0	93	.772	5.31	5.14

Wil Crowe

Pitches: R **Bats:** R **Pos:** SP-25; RP-1   **Ht:** 6'2" **Wt:** 235 **Born:** 9/9/1994 **Age:** 27

			HOW MUCH PITCHED				WHAT HE GAVE UP										THE RESULTS						
Year	Team	Lg	G	GS	GF	IP	BFP	H	R	ER	HR	SH	SF	HB	TBB	IBB	SO	WP	W	L	Pct	Sv-Op	Hld	Vel	OPS	ERC	ERA
2020	Was	NL	3	3	0	8.1	46	14	13	11	5	0	1	8	8	0	8	0	0	2	.000	0-0	0	91	1.338	17.20	11.88
2021	Pit	NL	26	25	0	116.2	524	126	75	71	25	3	6	57	1	111	3	4	8	.333	0-0	0	94	.864	6.02	5.48
	2 ML YEARS		29	28	0	125.0	570	140	88	82	30	3	1	7	65	1	119	3	4	10	.286	0-0	0	93	.900	6.65	5.90

Nelson Cruz

Bats: R **Throws:** R **Pos:** DH-133;PH-7;1B-1   **Ht:** 6'2" **Wt:** 230 **Born:** 7/1/1980 **Age:** 41

									BATTING										RUNNING			AVERAGES			
Year	Team	Lg	G	AB	H	2B	3B	HR	(Hm | Rd)	TB	R	RBI	RC	TBB	IBB	SO	HBP	SH	SF	SB	CS	GDP	Avg	OBP	Slg	OPS
2005	Mil	NL	8	5	1	1	0	0	(0 | 0)	2	1	0	1	2	0	0	0	0	0	0	0	0	.200	.429	.400	.829
2006	Tex	AL	41	130	29	3	0	6	(3 | 3)	50	15	22	18	7	0	32	0	0	1	1	0	1	.223	.261	.385	.645
2007	Tex	AL	96	307	72	15	2	9	(4 | 5)	118	35	34	32	21	1	87	2	1	1	2	4	5	.235	.287	.384	.671
2008	Tex	AL	31	115	38	9	1	7	(4 | 3)	70	19	26	30	17	2	28	1	0	0	3	1	1	.330	.421	.609	1.030
2009	Tex	AL	128	462	120	21	1	33	(18 | 15)	242	75	76	72	49	6	118	2	0	2	20	4	9	.260	.332	.524	.856
2010	Tex	AL	108	399	127	31	3	22	(13 | 9)	230	60	78	77	38	5	81	1	1	6	17	4	12	.318	.374	.576	.950
2011	Tex	AL	124	475	125	28	1	29	(19 | 10)	242	64	87	79	33	1	116	2	0	3	9	5	8	.263	.312	.509	.821
2012	Tex	AL	159	585	152	45	0	24	(18 | 6)	269	86	90	80	48	2	140	5	0	4	8	4	7	.260	.319	.460	.779
2013	Tex	AL	109	413	110	18	0	27	(13 | 14)	209	49	76	69	35	2	109	4	0	4	5	1	14	.266	.327	.506	.833
2014	Bal	AL	159	613	166	32	2	**40**	(15 | **25**)	322	87	108	93	55	8	140	5	0	5	4	5	17	.271	.333	.525	.859
2015	Sea	AL	152	590	178	22	1	44	(17 | 27)	334	90	93	108	59	9	164	9	0	1	3	2	6	.302	.369	.566	.936
2016	Sea	AL	155	589	169	27	1	43	(17 | **26**)	327	96	105	101	62	5	159	9	0	7	2	0	15	.287	.360	.555	.915
2017	Sea	AL	155	556	160	28	0	39	(19 | 20)	305	91	**119**	112	70	7	140	12	0	7	1	1	15	.288	.375	.549	.924
2018	Sea	AL	144	519	133	18	1	37	(21 | 16)	264	70	97	90	55	5	122	14	0	3	1	0	15	.256	.342	.509	.850
2019	Min	AL	120	454	141	26	0	41	(**21** | 20)	290	81	108	102	56	8	131	7	0	3	0	1	14	.311	.392	.639	1.031
2020	Min	AL	53	185	56	6	0	16	(6 | 10)	110	33	33	38	25	**5**	58	4	0	0	0	0	8	.303	.397	.595	.992
2021	2 Tms	AL	140	513	136	21	1	32	(12 | 20)	255	79	86	81	51	10	126	7	0	9	3	0	14	.265	.334	.497	.832
21	Min	AL	85	296	87	13	1	19	(9 | 10)	159	44	50	53	35	6	63	5	0	7	3	0	10	.294	.370	.537	.907
21	TB	AL	55	217	49	8	0	13	(3 | 10)	96	35	36	28	16	4	63	2	0	2	0	0	4	.226	.283	.442	.725
	Postseason		46	170	49	12	0	17	(10 | 7)	112	33	37	37	18	2	40	1	0	0	1	1	5	.288	.360	.659	1.019
	17 ML YEARS		1882	6910	1913	351	14	449	(220 | 229)	3639	1031	1238	1183	683	76	1751	80	2	56	79	32	161	.277	.346	.527	.873

Oneil Cruz

Bats: L **Throws:** R **Pos:** SS-2   **Ht:** 6'7" **Wt:** 210 **Born:** 10/4/1998 **Age:** 23

									BATTING										RUNNING			AVERAGES			
Year	Team	Lg	G	AB	H	2B	3B	HR	(Hm | Rd)	TB	R	RBI	RC	TBB	IBB	SO	HBP	SH	SF	SB	CS	GDP	Avg	OBP	Slg	OPS
2017	2 Tms	Low	105	401	94	11	2	10	(- | -)	139	60	44	41	36	1	134	0	0	5	8	7	6	.234	.294	.347	.641
2018	WV	A	103	402	115	25	7	14	(- | -)	196	66	59	68	34	2	100	3	0	4	11	5	6	.286	.343	.488	.831
2019	Altna	AA	35	119	32	8	3	1	(- | -)	49	14	17	18	15	1	35	0	0	2	3	1	1	.269	.346	.412	.757
2019	2 Tms	Low	38	146	47	7	1	7	(- | -)	77	21	17	28	9	1	39	1	0	0	8	0	0	.322	.365	.527	.893
2021	Altna	AA	62	250	73	15	5	12	(- | -)	134	51	40	-	20	0	64	1	0	1	18	3	3	.292	.346	.536	.882
2021	Pit	NL	2	9	3	0	0	1	(1 | 0)	6	2	3	2	0	0	4	0	0	0	0	0	0	.333	.333	.667	1.000

Johnny Cueto

Pitches: R Bats: R Pos: SP-21; RP-1
KWAY-toe
Ht: 5'11" Wt: 229 Born: 2/15/1986 Age: 36

Year Team	Lg	G	GS	GF	IP	BFP	H	R	ER	HR	SH	SF	HB	TBB	IBB	SO	WP	W	L	Pct	Sv-Op	Hld	Vel	OPS	ERC	ERA
2008 Cin	NL	31	31	0	174.0	769	178	101	93	29	6	5	14	68	1	158	6	9	14	.391	0-0	0	93	.803	4.95	4.81
2009 Cin	NL	30	30	0	171.1	740	172	90	84	24	5	3	14	61	0	132	4	11	11	.500	0-0	0	93	.780	4.57	4.14
2010 Cin	NL	31	31	0	185.2	780	181	79	75	19	9	3	9	56	5	138	5	12	7	.632	0-0	0	93	.727	3.75	3.64
2011 Cin	NL	24	24	0	156.0	631	123	51	40	8	10	4	10	47	0	104	5	9	5	.643	0-0	0	93	.593	2.55	2.31
2012 Cin	NL	33	33	0	217.0	888	205	73	67	15	6	6	12	49	5	170	1	19	9	.679	0-0	0	93	.667	3.13	2.78
2013 Cin	NL	11	11	0	60.2	242	46	20	19	7	2	1	1	18	1	51	1	5	2	.714	0-0	0	92	.607	2.57	2.82
2014 Cin	NL	34	34	0	243.2	961	169	69	61	22	7	1	15	65	2	242	1	20	9	.690	0-0	0	93	.574	2.18	2.25
2015 2 Tms		32	32	0	212.0	866	194	87	81	21	5	4	8	46	1	176	0	11	13	.458	0-0	0	92	.675	3.06	3.44
2016 SF	NL	32	32	0	219.2	881	195	71	68	15	7	3	8	45	1	198	3	18	5	.783	0-0	0	91	.633	2.71	2.79
2017 SF	NL	25	25	0	147.1	648	160	77	74	22	7	3	8	53	2	136	4	8	8	.500	0-0	0	91	.814	4.97	4.52
2018 SF	NL	9	9	0	53.0	214	46	19	19	8	3	0	5	13	0	38	2	3	2	.600	0-0	0	89	.702	3.55	3.23
2019 SF	NL	4	4	0	16.0	67	11	9	9	3	2	0	0	9	0	13	1	1	2	.333	0-0	0	91	.754	3.58	5.06
2020 SF	NL	12	12	0	63.1	277	61	41	38	9	2	1	3	26	0	56	1	2	3	.400	0-0	0	91	.748	4.35	5.40
2021 SF	NL	22	21	0	114.2	490	127	57	52	15	10	1	4	30	1	98	0	7	7	.500	0-0	0	92	.801	4.52	4.08
15 Cin	NL	19	19	0	130.2	516	93	42	38	11	4	3	6	29	1	120	0	7	6	.538	0-0	0	93	.577	2.00	2.62
15 KC	AL	13	13	0	81.1	350	101	45	43	10	1	1	2	17	0	56	0	4	7	.364	0-0	0	92	.818	5.05	4.76
Postseason		8	8	0	41.2	170	33	22	21	7	1	1	1	12	0	32	0	2	4	.333	0-0	0	93	.646	3.02	4.54
14 ML YEARS		330	329	0	2034.1	8454	1868	844	780	217	82	36	111	586	19	1710	34	135	97	.582	0-0	0	92	.697	3.46	3.45

Charlie Culberson

Bats: R Throws: R Pos: 3B-68;PH-7;LF-6;1B-4;2B-4;PR-4;SS-3;RF-1;DH-1
Ht: 6'1" Wt: 200 Born: 4/10/1989 Age: 33

Year Team	Lg	G	AB	H	2B	3B	HR	(Hm	Rd)	TB	R	RBI	RC	TBB	IBB	SO	HBP	SH	SF	SB	CS	GDP	Avg	OBP	Slg	OPS
2012 SF	NL	6	22	3	0	0	0	(0	0)	3	0	1	0	0	0	7	0	1	0	0	0	0	.136	.136	.136	.273
2013 Col	NL	47	99	29	5	0	2	(0	2)	40	12	12	13	4	1	23	0	0	1	5	1	5	.293	.317	.404	.721
2014 Col	NL	95	210	41	7	2	3	(2	1)	61	17	24	14	12	2	62	5	4	2	2	2	6	.195	.253	.290	.544
2016 LAD	NL	34	67	20	3	0	1	(1	0)	26	6	7	9	1	0	13	0	0	0	1	0	2	.299	.309	.388	.697
2017 LAD	NL	15	13	2	1	0	0	(0	0)	3	0	1	0	2	0	4	0	0	0	0	0	2	.154	.267	.231	.497
2018 Atl	NL	113	296	80	18	2	12	(5	7)	138	47	45	50	21	5	85	4	0	1	4	2	5	.270	.326	.466	.792
2019 Atl	NL	108	135	35	5	2	5	(3	2)	59	14	20	11	6	0	44	1	1	0	0	1	5	.259	.294	.437	.731
2020 Atl	NL	10	7	1	1	0	0	(0	0)	2	1	2	1	0	0	4	0	0	0	0	0	0	.143	.143	.286	.429
2021 Tex	AL	91	247	60	15	2	5	(1	4)	94	23	22	30	17	1	64	2	4	1	7	1	3	.243	.296	.381	.676
Postseason		21	38	12	2	1	1	(1	0)	19	5	2	5	1	1	10	0	1	1	0	0	3	.316	.325	.500	.825
9 ML YEARS		519	1096	271	55	8	28	(12	16)	426	121	133	128	63	9	306	12	10	6	19	7	28	.247	.294	.389	.683

John Curtiss

Pitches: R Bats: R Pos: RP-39; SP-2
Ht: 6'5" Wt: 220 Born: 4/5/1993 Age: 29

Year Team	Lg	G	GS	GF	IP	BFP	H	R	ER	HR	SH	SF	HB	TBB	IBB	SO	WP	W	L	Pct	Sv-Op	Hld	Vel	OPS	ERC	ERA
2017 Min	AL	9	0	4	8.2	38	9	8	8	2	0	0	1	2	0	10	2	0	0	-	0-0	0	95	.802	4.89	8.31
2018 Min	AL	8	0	2	6.1	30	8	4	4	0	0	0	1	4	1	7	3	0	1	.000	0-0	0	94	.900	5.47	5.68
2019 LAA	AL	1	0	1	2.1	12	2	1	1	0	0	0	0	3	0	1	0	0	0	-	0-0	0	92	.750	5.73	3.86
2020 TB	AL	17	3	7	25.0	99	21	7	5	3	0	0	2	3	0	25	0	3	0	1.000	2-2	0	94	.614	2.62	1.80
2021 2 Tms	NL	41	2	5	44.1	187	42	21	17	6	1	1	1	12	0	44	1	3	1	.750	0-1	4	95	.703	3.45	3.45
21 Mia	NL	35	2	5	40.0	161	34	13	11	4	1	0	1	9	0	40	1	3	1	.750	0-0	1	95	.642	2.72	2.48
21 Mil	NL	6	0	0	4.1	26	8	8	6	2	0	1	0	3	0	4	0	0	0	-	0-1	3	94	1.105	13.06	12.46
Postseason		9	1	3	10.0	48	14	7	7	3	0	0	0	5	0	9	0	1	0	1.000	0-0	2	95	.931	8.62	6.30
5 ML YEARS		76	5	19	86.2	366	82	41	35	11	1	1	4	24	1	87	6	6	2	.750	2-3	4	95	.706	3.61	3.63

David Dahl

Bats: L Throws: R Pos: LF-31;DH-16;RF-12;PH-6;CF-1;PR-1
Ht: 6'2" Wt: 197 Born: 4/1/1994 Age: 28

Year Team	Lg	G	AB	H	2B	3B	HR	(Hm	Rd)	TB	R	RBI	RC	TBB	IBB	SO	HBP	SH	SF	SB	CS	GDP	Avg	OBP	Slg	OPS
2021 Nashv	AAA	27	94	29	9	1	3	(-	-)	49	16	12	-	6	0	14	1	0	1	0	0	1	.309	.353	.521	.874
2016 Col	NL	63	222	70	12	4	7	(3	4)	111	42	24	35	15	0	59	0	0	0	5	0	3	.315	.359	.500	.859
2018 Col	NL	77	249	68	11	3	16	(13	3)	133	31	48	43	19	4	68	1	0	2	5	3	4	.273	.325	.534	.859
2019 Col	NL	100	374	113	28	5	15	(9	6)	196	67	61	70	28	0	110	4	2	5	4	4	3	.302	.353	.524	.877
2020 Col	NL	24	93	17	2	2	0	(0	0)	23	9	9	8	4	0	28	1	0	1	1	0	0	.183	.222	.247	.470
2021 Tex	AL	63	205	43	11	0	4	(1	3)	66	19	18	15	10	0	59	1	1	3	2	1	3	.210	.247	.322	.569
Postseason		3	11	0	0	0	0	(0	0)	0	0	0	0	0	0	3	0	0	0	0	1	0	.000	.000	.000	.000
5 ML YEARS		327	1143	311	64	14	42	(26	16)	529	168	160	171	76	4	324	7	3	11	17	8	13	.272	.319	.463	.781

Bobby Dalbec

Bats: R Throws: R Pos: 1B-123;3B-14;PH-8;SS-2;PR-2;DH-1
Ht: 6'4" Wt: 227 Born: 6/29/1995 Age: 27

Year Team	Lg	G	AB	H	2B	3B	HR	(Hm	Rd)	TB	R	RBI	RC	TBB	IBB	SO	HBP	SH	SF	SB	CS	GDP	Avg	OBP	Slg	OPS
2020 Bos	AL	23	80	21	3	0	8	(4	4)	48	13	16	15	10	0	39	2	0	0	0	0	0	.263	.359	.600	.959
2021 Bos	AL	133	417	100	21	5	25	(14	11)	206	50	78	67	28	1	156	7	0	1	2	0	3	.240	.298	.494	.792
2 ML YEARS		156	497	121	24	5	33	(18	15)	254	63	94	82	38	1	195	9	0	1	2	0	3	.243	.308	.511	.819

Travis d'Arnaud

Bats: R **Throws:** R **Pos:** C-57;PH-3;DH-1 dar-NO **Ht:** 6'2" **Wt:** 210 **Born:** 2/10/1989 **Age:** 33

							BATTING																RUNNING			AVERAGES			
Year	Team	Lg	G	AB	H	2B	3B	HR	(Hm	Rd)	TB	R	RBI	RC	TBB	IBB	SO	HBP	SH	SF	SB	CS	GDP	Avg	OBP	Slg	OPS
2013	NYM	NL	31	99	20	3	0	1	(1	0)	26	4	5	6	12	0	21	0	0	1	0	0	3	.202	.286	.263	.548
2014	NYM	NL	108	385	93	22	3	13	(5	8)	160	48	41	39	32	5	64	2	1	1	1	0	15	.242	.302	.416	.718
2015	NYM	NL	67	239	64	14	1	12	(6	6)	116	31	41	36	23	0	49	4	0	2	0	0	7	.268	.340	.485	.825
2016	NYM	NL	75	251	62	7	0	4	(4	0)	81	27	15	17	19	1	50	3	2	1	0	0	7	.247	.307	.323	.629
2017	NYM	NL	112	348	85	19	1	16	(5	11)	154	39	57	41	23	3	59	2	0	3	0	0	12	.244	.293	.443	.735
2018	NYM	NL	4	15	3	0	0	1	(1	0)	6	1	3	2	1	0	5	0	0	0	0	0	0	.200	.250	.400	.650
2019	3 Tms		103	351	88	16	0	16	(6	10)	152	52	69	59	32	0	85	2	0	6	0	1	4	.251	.312	.433	.745
2020	Atl	NL	44	165	53	8	0	9	(5	4)	88	19	34	31	16	0	50	2	0	1	1	0	8	.321	.386	.533	.919
2021	Atl	NL	60	209	46	14	0	7	(0	7)	81	21	26	21	17	0	53	2	0	1	0	0	7	.220	.284	.388	.671
19	NYM	NL	10	23	2	0	0	0	(0	0)	2	2	2	2	2	0	5	0	0	0	0	0	1	.087	.160	.087	.247
19	LAD	NL	1	1	0	0	0	0	(0	0)	0	0	0	0	0	0	0	0	0	0	0	0	0	.000	.000	.000	.000
19	TB	AL	92	327	86	16	0	16	(6	10)	150	50	67	59	30	0	80	2	0	6	0	1	3	.263	.323	.459	.782
	Postseason		32	116	24	3	0	5	(4	1)	42	10	19	11	8	0	35	3	0	3	0	0	3	.207	.269	.362	.631
	9 ML YEARS		604	2062	514	103	5	79	(33	46)	864	242	291	252	175	9	436	17	3	16	2	1	63	.249	.311	.419	.730

Yu Darvish

Pitches: R **Bats:** R **Pos:** SP-30 YOO DARR-vish **Ht:** 6'5" **Wt:** 220 **Born:** 8/16/1986 **Age:** 35

			HOW MUCH PITCHED					WHAT HE GAVE UP										THE RESULTS							
Year	Team	Lg	G	GS	GF	IP	BFP	H	R	ER	HR	SH	SF	HB	TBB	IBB	SO	WP	W	L	Pct	Sv-Op	Hld	Vel	OPS	ERC	ERA
2012	Tex	AL	29	29	0	191.1	816	156	89	83	14	2	7	10	89	1	221	8	16	9	.640	0-0	0	93	.659	3.31	3.90
2013	Tex	AL	32	32	0	209.2	841	145	68	66	26	0	5	8	80	1	277	7	13	9	.591	0-0	0	93	.611	2.70	2.83
2014	Tex	AL	22	22	0	144.1	605	133	54	49	13	1	2	2	49	1	182	14	10	7	.588	0-0	0	92	.679	3.39	3.06
2016	Tex	AL	17	17	0	100.1	416	81	43	38	12	0	4	3	31	1	132	6	7	5	.583	0-0	0	93	.636	2.87	3.41
2017	2 Tms		31	31	0	186.2	766	159	83	80	27	2	3	6	58	1	209	12	10	12	.455	0-0	0	94	.689	3.35	3.86
2018	ChC	NL	8	8	0	40.0	180	36	24	22	7	1	1	4	21	0	49	2	1	3	.250	0-0	0	94	.766	4.88	4.95
2019	ChC	NL	31	31	0	178.2	731	140	82	79	33	3	4	11	56	1	229	11	6	8	.429	0-0	0	94	.695	3.35	3.98
2020	ChC	NL	12	12	0	76.0	297	59	18	17	5	0	0	2	14	1	93	3	8	3	.727	0-0	0	96	.575	2.03	2.01
2021	SD	NL	30	30	0	166.1	681	138	81	78	28	1	5	8	44	1	199	9	8	11	.421	0-0	0	95	.708	3.23	4.22
17	Tex	AL	22	22	0	137.0	564	115	63	61	20	1	3	5	45	0	148	9	6	9	.400	0-0	0	94	.689	3.39	4.01
17	LAD	NL	9	9	0	49.2	202	44	20	19	7	1	0	1	13	1	61	3	4	3	.571	0-0	0	94	.690	3.27	3.44
	Postseason		7	7	0	33.0	140	32	21	19	9	1	2	4	6	1	31	0	2	5	.286	0-0	0	94	.814	4.58	5.18
	9 ML YEARS		212	212	0	1293.1	5333	1047	542	512	165	10	31	54	442	8	1591	72	79	67	.541	0-0	0	93	.667	3.16	3.56

Tucker Davidson

Pitches: L **Bats:** L **Pos:** SP-4 **Ht:** 6'2" **Wt:** 215 **Born:** 3/25/1996 **Age:** 26

			HOW MUCH PITCHED					WHAT HE GAVE UP										THE RESULTS							
Year	Team	Lg	G	GS	GF	IP	BFP	H	R	ER	HR	SH	SF	HB	TBB	IBB	SO	WP	W	L	Pct	Sv-Op	Hld	Vel	OPS	ERC	ERA
2020	Atl	NL	1	1	0	1.2	13	3	7	2	1	0	0	0	4	0	2	0	0	1	.000	0-0	0	92	1.205	22.80	10.80
2021	Atl	NL	4	4	0	20.0	83	15	8	8	3	1	1	0	8	0	18	0	0	0	-	0-0	0	93	.664	3.00	3.60
	2 ML YEARS		5	5	0	21.2	96	18	15	10	4	1	1	0	12	0	20	0	0	1	.000	0-0	0	93	.730	4.19	4.15

Zach Davies

Pitches: R **Bats:** R **Pos:** SP-32 **Ht:** 6'0" **Wt:** 180 **Born:** 2/7/1993 **Age:** 29

			HOW MUCH PITCHED					WHAT HE GAVE UP										THE RESULTS							
Year	Team	Lg	G	GS	GF	IP	BFP	H	R	ER	HR	SH	SF	HB	TBB	IBB	SO	WP	W	L	Pct	Sv-Op	Hld	Vel	OPS	ERC	ERA
2015	Mil	NL	6	6	0	34.0	139	26	14	14	2	1	0	0	15	0	24	0	3	2	.600	0-0	0	89	.614	2.74	3.71
2016	Mil	NL	28	28	0	163.1	682	166	79	72	20	3	4	6	38	0	135	3	11	7	.611	0-0	0	89	.728	3.83	3.97
2017	Mil	NL	33	33	0	191.1	817	204	90	83	20	7	5	9	55	3	124	2	17	9	.654	0-0	0	90	.755	4.24	3.90
2018	Mil	NL	13	13	0	66.0	280	67	36	35	8	0	5	4	21	3	49	1	2	7	.222	0-0	0	90	.768	4.22	4.77
2019	Mil	NL	31	31	0	159.2	672	155	73	63	20	7	5	2	51	0	102	4	10	7	.588	0-0	0	88	.729	3.83	3.55
2020	SD	NL	12	12	0	69.1	276	55	26	21	9	1	1	0	19	0	63	2	7	4	.636	0-0	0	88	.630	2.71	2.73
2021	ChC	NL	32	32	0	148.0	668	162	99	95	25	8	2	5	75	2	114	0	6	12	.333	0-0	0	88	.852	5.73	5.78
	Postseason		3	2	1	8.0	39	15	8	8	2	0	0	0	1	0	7	0	0	1	.000	0-0	0	89	1.068	9.69	9.00
	7 ML YEARS		155	155	0	831.2	3534	835	417	383	104	27	22	26	274	8	611	12	56	48	.538	0-0	0	89	.748	4.13	4.14

Austin Davis

Pitches: L **Bats:** L **Pos:** RP-29 **Ht:** 6'4" **Wt:** 235 **Born:** 2/3/1993 **Age:** 29

			HOW MUCH PITCHED					WHAT HE GAVE UP										THE RESULTS							
Year	Team	Lg	G	GS	GF	IP	BFP	H	R	ER	HR	SH	SF	HB	TBB	IBB	SO	WP	W	L	Pct	Sv-Op	Hld	Vel	OPS	ERC	ERA
2021	Indy	AAA	11	0	1	14.0	49	6	5	4	0	0	0	0	5	0	18	0	0	1	.000	0- -			.384	1.03	2.57
2018	Phi	NL	32	0	10	34.2	151	35	20	16	4	1	4	2	12	1	38	4	1	2	.333	0-0	2	93	.812	4.17	4.15
2019	Phi	NL	14	0	7	20.2	98	22	15	15	6	0	0	3	14	1	24	0	0	0	-	0-0	0	94	.929	7.79	6.53
2020	2 Tms	NL	9	0	3	6.2	32	11	8	8	1	0	0	0	2	0	5	0	0	0	-	0-0	1	93	.906	8.13	10.80
2021	2 Tms		29	0	7	26.1	117	24	17	15	4	0	2	1	12	2	28	1	1	2	.333	0-3	4	94	.748	4.06	5.13
20	Phi	NL	4	0	1	3.0	20	10	7	7	1	0	0	0	1	0	2	0	0	0	-	0-0	0	94	1.287	22.82	21.00
20	Pit	NL	5	0	2	3.2	12	1	1	1	0	0	0	0	1	0	3	0	0	0	-	0-0	1	93	.258	0.51	2.45
21	Pit	NL	10	0	2	9.2	42	6	7	6	2	0	0	1	5	0	11	0	0	1	.000	0-1	2	94	.702	3.42	5.59
21	Bos	AL	19	0	5	16.2	75	18	10	9	2	0	2	0	7	2	17	1	1	1	.500	0-2	2	94	.773	4.44	4.86
	4 ML YEARS		84	0	27	88.1	398	92	60	54	15	1	6	6	40	4	95	5	2	4	.333	0-3	7	94	.829	5.20	5.50

Brennen Davis

Bats: R **Throws:** R **Pos:** OF
Ht: 6'4" **Wt:** 210 **Born:** 11/2/1999 **Age:** 22

Year	Team	Lg	G	AB	H	2B	3B	HR	(Hm	Rd)	TB	R	RBI	RC	TBB	IBB	SO	HBP	SH	SF	SB	CS	GDP	Avg	OBP	Slg	OPS
2018	Cubs2	R	18	57	17	2	0	0	(-	-)	9	9	3	11	10	0	12	4	0	1	6	1	0	.298	.431	.333	.764
2019	Sbend	A	50	177	54	9	3	8	(-	-)	93	33	30	37	18	0	38	5	2	2	4	1	3	.305	.381	.525	.907
2021	Tenn	AA	77	267	67	20	0	13	(-	-)	126	50	36	-	36	0	97	13	0	1	6	4	5	.251	.366	.472	.838
2021	Iowa	AAA	11	43	14	2	0	4	(-	-)	28	9	9	-	5	0	12	0	0	0	0	0	1	.326	.396	.651	1.047

J.D. Davis

Bats: R **Throws:** R **Pos:** 3B-50;PH-22;DH-1
Ht: 6'3" **Wt:** 218 **Born:** 4/27/1993 **Age:** 29

Year	Team	Lg	G	AB	H	2B	3B	HR	(Hm	Rd)	TB	R	RBI	RC	TBB	IBB	SO	HBP	SH	SF	SB	CS	GDP	Avg	OBP	Slg	OPS
2021	Syrcse		14	38	12	4	0	4	(-	-)	28	8	7	-	10	0	14	1	0	0	0	0	1	.316	.469	.737	1.206
2017	Hou	AL	25	62	14	4	0	4	(2	2)	30	8	7	4	4	0	20	1	0	1	1	1	3	.226	.279	.484	.763
2018	Hou	AL	42	103	18	2	0	1	(0	1)	23	9	5	3	10	0	29	0	0	0	0	0	3	.175	.248	.223	.471
2019	NYM	NL	140	410	126	22	1	22	(16	6)	216	65	57	66	38	2	97	3	0	2	3	0	14	.307	.369	.527	.895
2020	NYM	NL	56	190	47	9	0	6	(2	4)	74	26	19	25	31	1	56	7	0	1	0	0	8	.247	.371	.389	.761
2021	NYM	NL	73	179	51	12	0	5	(1	4)	78	18	23	30	24	1	68	6	0	2	1	0	4	.285	.384	.436	.820
5 ML YEARS			336	944	256	49	1	38	(21	17)	421	126	111	128	107	4	270	17	0	6	5	1	32	.271	.354	.446	.800

Jaylin Davis

Bats: R **Throws:** R **Pos:** PH-3;LF-2;RF-1
Ht: 5'11" **Wt:** 205 **Born:** 7/1/1994 **Age:** 27

Year	Team	Lg	G	AB	H	2B	3B	HR	(Hm	Rd)	TB	R	RBI	RC	TBB	IBB	SO	HBP	SH	SF	SB	CS	GDP	Avg	OBP	Slg	OPS
2021	Scrmto	AAA	43	161	37	7	2	11	(-	-)	81	34	34	-	17	0	59	5	0	3	3	1	3	.230	.317	.503	.820
2019	SF	NL	17	42	7	0	0	1	(1	0)	10	2	3	1	3	0	11	2	0	1	1	2	1	.167	.255	.238	.493
2020	SF	NL	4	12	2	0	0	1	(0	1)	5	2	1	0	0	0	6	0	0	0	0	0	0	.167	.167	.417	.583
2021	SF	NL	5	9	1	1	0	0	(0	0)	2	1	0	0	0	0	1	0	0	0	0	0	1	.111	.111	.222	.333
3 ML YEARS			26	63	10	1	0	2	(1	1)	17	5	4	1	3	0	18	2	0	1	1	2	2	.159	.221	.270	.490

Jonathan Davis

Bats: R **Throws:** R **Pos:** CF-55;PR-11;LF-3;PH-3;DH-2
Ht: 5'8" **Wt:** 190 **Born:** 5/12/1992 **Age:** 30

Year	Team	Lg	G	AB	H	2B	3B	HR	(Hm	Rd)	TB	R	RBI	RC	TBB	IBB	SO	HBP	SH	SF	SB	CS	GDP	Avg	OBP	Slg	OPS
2021	S-WB	AAA	15	52	10	2	1	2	(-	-)	20	12	8	-	7	0	20	5	0	1	3	2	1	.192	.338	.385	.723
2018	Tor	AL	20	25	5	1	0	0	(0	0)	6	3	0	0	1	0	6	1	0	0	3	0	2	.200	.259	.240	.499
2019	Tor	AL	37	83	15	1	0	2	(1	1)	22	8	6	5	5	0	24	5	1	1	3	1	1	.181	.266	.265	.531
2020	Tor	AL	13	27	7	2	0	1	(1	0)	12	4	6	7	3	0	11	2	0	1	1	0	1	.259	.364	.444	.808
2021	2 Tms	AL	64	87	11	1	0	1	(0	1)	15	20	4	5	12	0	26	3	0	1	4	1	1	.126	.252	.172	.425
21	Tor	AL	52	70	10	1	0	1	(0	1)	14	16	4	5	11	0	21	3	0	1	4	1	1	.143	.282	.200	.482
21	NYY	AL	12	17	1	0	0	0	(0	0)	1	4	0	0	1	0	5	0	0	0	0	0	0	.059	.111	.059	.170
4 ML YEARS			134	222	38	5	0	4	(2	2)	55	35	16	17	21	0	67	11	1	3	11	2	5	.171	.272	.248	.520

Khris Davis

Bats: R **Throws:** R **Pos:** DH-31;PH-15;LF-3
Ht: 5'11" **Wt:** 205 **Born:** 12/21/1987 **Age:** 34

Year	Team	Lg	G	AB	H	2B	3B	HR	(Hm	Rd)	TB	R	RBI	RC	TBB	IBB	SO	HBP	SH	SF	SB	CS	GDP	Avg	OBP	Slg	OPS
2021	LsVgs	AAA	16	63	21	3	2	10	(-	-)	58	16	25	-	4	0	13	1	0	0	0	0	1	.333	.382	.921	1.303
2013	Mil	NL	56	136	38	10	0	11	(5	6)	81	27	27	25	11	0	34	5	0	1	3	0	4	.279	.353	.596	.949
2014	Mil	NL	144	501	122	37	2	22	(12	10)	229	70	69	58	32	0	122	10	0	6	4	1	13	.244	.299	.457	.756
2015	Mil	NL	121	392	97	16	2	27	(16	11)	198	54	66	57	44	1	122	1	0	3	6	2	9	.247	.323	.505	.828
2016	Oak	AL	150	555	137	24	2	42	(19	23)	291	85	102	77	42	0	166	8	0	5	1	2	20	.247	.307	.524	.831
2017	Oak	AL	153	566	140	28	1	43	(26	17)	299	91	110	98	73	1	195	6	0	7	4	0	20	.247	.336	.528	.864
2018	Oak	AL	151	576	142	28	1	**48**	(23	25)	316	98	123	104	59	5	175	12	0	7	0	0	16	.247	.326	.549	.874
2019	Oak	AL	133	481	106	11	0	23	(9	14)	186	61	73	60	47	3	146	3	0	2	0	0	11	.220	.293	.387	.679
2020	Oak	AL	30	85	17	5	0	2	(1	1)	28	9	10	4	10	0	26	3	0	1	0	0	5	.200	.303	.329	.632
2021	2 Tms	AL	42	102	21	5	1	3	(0	3)	37	11	10	11	10	0	31	0	0	2	0	0	2	.206	.272	.363	.635
21	Tex	AL	22	51	8	1	1	2	(0	2)	17	8	5	4	8	0	16	0	0	0	0	0	2	.157	.262	.333	.596
21	Oak	AL	20	51	13	4	0	1	(0	1)	20	3	5	7	2	0	15	0	0	2	0	0	0	.255	.283	.392	.675
Postseason			8	32	7	0	0	4	(3	1)	19	4	6	3	0	0	15	1	0	0	0	0	0	.219	.242	.594	.836
9 ML YEARS			980	3394	820	164	9	221	(111	110)	1665	506	590	494	328	10	1017	48	0	34	18	5	99	.242	.314	.491	.805

Taylor Davis

Bats: R **Throws:** R **Pos:** C-2
Ht: 5'10" **Wt:** 200 **Born:** 11/28/1989 **Age:** 32

Year	Team	Lg	G	AB	H	2B	3B	HR	(Hm	Rd)	TB	R	RBI	RC	TBB	IBB	SO	HBP	SH	SF	SB	CS	GDP	Avg	OBP	Slg	OPS
2021	Norfolk	AAA	12	38	11	3	0	0	(-	-)	14	6	5	-	5	0	5	0	0	0	0	0	0	.289	.372	.368	.741
2021	Indy	AAA	39	116	28	3	0	2	(-	-)	37	16	17	-	16	2	16	1	0	0	0	0	6	.241	.338	.319	.657
2017	ChC	NL	8	13	3	1	0	0	(0	0)	4	1	1	2	0	0	4	0	0	0	0	0	0	.231	.231	.308	.538
2018	ChC	NL	5	5	2	0	0	0	(0	0)	2	0	2	0	0	0	1	0	0	0	0	0	0	.400	.333	.400	.733
2019	ChC	NL	7	18	3	0	0	1	(1	0)	6	2	4	2	2	0	4	0	0	0	0	0	0	.167	.250	.333	.583
2021	Pit	NL	2	5	2	0	0	0	(0	0)	2	0	1	0	0	0	1	0	0	0	0	0	0	.400	.500	.400	.900
4 ML YEARS			22	41	10	1	0	1	(1	0)	14	3	7	5	3	0	9	0	0	1	0	0	0	.244	.289	.341	.630

Wade Davis

Pitches: R **Bats:** R **Pos:** RP-40 **Ht:** 6'5" **Wt:** 225 **Born:** 9/7/1985 **Age:** 36

			HOW MUCH PITCHED					WHAT HE GAVE UP										THE RESULTS							
Year Team	Lg	G	GS	GF	IP	BFP	H	R	ER	HR	SH	SF	HB	TBB	IBB	SO	WP	W	L	Pct	Sv-Op Hld	Vel	OPS	ERC	ERA
2009 TB	AL	6	6	0	36.1	150	33	19	15	2	0	0	0	13	1	36	1	2	2	.500	0-0 0	92	.640	3.12	3.72
2010 TB	AL	29	29	0	168.0	722	165	77	76	24	3	6	5	62	2	113	4	12	10	.545	0-0 0	92	.756	4.25	4.07
2011 TB	AL	29	29	0	184.0	795	190	96	91	23	5	7	8	63	1	105	6	11	10	.524	0-0 0	91	.771	4.38	4.45
2012 TB	AL	54	0	15	70.1	284	48	20	19	5	0	1	0	29	2	87	2	3	0	1.000	0-1 6	94	.570	2.25	2.43
2013 KC	AL	31	24	2	135.1	618	169	89	80	15	1	5	4	58	2	114	7	8	11	.421	0-0 0	92	.822	5.88	5.32
2014 KC	AL	71	0	11	72.0	279	38	8	8	0	0	1	3	23	0	109	1	9	2	.818	3-6 **33**	96	.408	1.23	1.00
2015 KC	AL	69	0	24	67.1	251	33	8	7	3	0	2	0	20	1	78	1	8	1	.889	17-18 18	96	.451	1.16	0.94
2016 KC	AL	45	0	40	43.1	176	33	9	9	0	0	0	3	16	0	47	4	2	1	.667	27-30 0	95	.537	2.35	1.87
2017 ChC	NL	59	0	56	58.2	242	39	16	15	6	1	0	3	28	1	79	7	4	2	.667	32-33 0	94	.600	2.77	2.30
2018 Col	NL	69	0	63	65.1	261	43	31	30	8	0	0	2	26	0	78	6	3	6	.333	**43-49** 0	94	.615	2.56	4.13
2019 Col	NL	50	0	32	42.2	206	51	42	41	7	0	0	2	29	0	42	1	1	6	.143	15-18 0	93	.872	7.12	8.65
2020 Col	NL	5	0	2	4.1	25	9	10	10	3	0	0	0	3	1	3	2	0	1	.000	2-3 0	92	1.435	17.88	20.77
2021 KC	AL	40	0	25	42.2	190	44	33	32	8	1	5	2	19	0	38	4	0	3	.000	2-3 2	93	.798	5.25	6.75
Postseason		30	1	14	40.0	160	29	9	8	5	0	0	0	18	0	57	2	4	0	1.000	8-8 3	95	.639	3.05	1.80
13 ML YEARS		557	88	270	990.1	4199	895	458	433	104	11	27	32	389	11	929	46	63	55	.534	141-161 59	93	.695	3.66	3.94

Ronnie Dawson

Bats: L **Throws:** R **Pos:** DH-2;PH-2 **Ht:** 6'2" **Wt:** 217 **Born:** 5/19/1995 **Age:** 27

									BATTING												RUNNING			AVERAGES			
Year Team	Lg	G	AB	H	2B	3B	HR	(Hm	Rd)	TB	R	RBI	RC	TBB	IBB	SO	HBP	SH	SF	SB	CS	GDP	Avg	OBP	Slg	OPS
2021 SgrLnd	AAA	92	345	87	21	1	7	(-	-)	131	58	43	-	46	1	82	4	2	2	15	8	10	.252	.345	.380	.725
2021 Hou	AL	3	5	1	0	0	0	(0	0)	1	2	0	0	1	0	0	0	0	0	0	0	1	.200	.333	.200	.533

Grant Dayton

Pitches: L **Bats:** L **Pos:** RP-13 **Ht:** 6'2" **Wt:** 210 **Born:** 11/25/1987 **Age:** 34

				HOW MUCH PITCHED		WHAT HE GAVE UP											THE RESULTS						
Year Team	Lg	G	GS	GF	IP	BFP	H	R	ER	HR	SH	SF	HB	TBB	IBB	SO	WP	W	L	Pct	Sv-Op Hld	Vel	OPS	ERC	ERA
2016 LAD	NL	25	0	0	26.1	101	14	7	6	4	0	0	1	6	0	39	0	0	1	.000	0-2 6	92	.495	1.56	2.05
2017 LAD	NL	29	0	6	23.2	102	19	13	13	5	1	3	0	12	1	20	0	1	1	.500	0-1 4	91	.749	4.02	4.94
2019 Atl	NL	14	0	4	12.0	51	12	5	4	4	0	0	0	4	0	14	0	0	1	.000	0-1 1	91	.824	5.42	3.00
2020 Atl	NL	18	0	5	27.1	117	22	9	7	4	1	1	1	11	1	32	0	2	1	.667	0-0 0	91	.662	3.32	2.30
2021 Atl	NL	13	0	3	13.0	61	15	10	9	2	0	2	0	6	1	14	0	0	0	-	0-0 1	91	.854	5.27	6.23
Postseason		8	0	1	5.1	34	14	11	11	4	0	0	1	3	0	8	0	0	0	-	0-0 1	92	1.496	24.14	18.56
5 ML YEARS		99	0	18	102.1	432	82	44	39	19	2	6	2	39	3	119	0	3	4	.429	0-4 12	91	.688	3.43	3.43

Yonathan Daza

Bats: R **Throws:** R **Pos:** CF-57;PH-30;RF-22;LF-12;PR-2Y OHN-uh-tuhn DAH-za **Ht:** 6'2" **Wt:** 207 **Born:** 2/28/1994 **Age:** 28

									BATTING												RUNNING			AVERAGES			
Year Team	Lg	G	AB	H	2B	3B	HR	(Hm	Rd)	TB	R	RBI	RC	TBB	IBB	SO	HBP	SH	SF	SB	CS	GDP	Avg	OBP	Slg	OPS
2019 Col	NL	44	97	20	1	1	0	(0	0)	23	7	3	5	7	0	21	0	0	1	1	0	2	.206	.257	.237	.494
2021 Col	NL	107	301	85	12	2	2	(2	0)	107	26	30	36	21	0	60	2	6	1	2	1	9	.282	.332	.355	.688
2 ML YEARS		151	398	105	13	3	2	(2	0)	130	33	33	41	28	0	81	2	6	2	3	1	11	.264	.314	.327	.641

Brett de Geus

Pitches: R **Bats:** R **Pos:** RP-47 duh-GUS **Ht:** 6'2" **Wt:** 190 **Born:** 11/4/1997 **Age:** 24

				HOW MUCH PITCHED		WHAT HE GAVE UP											THE RESULTS						
Year Team	Lg	G	GS	GF	IP	BFP	H	R	ER	HR	SH	SF	HB	TBB	IBB	SO	WP	W	L	Pct	Sv-Op Hld	Vel	OPS	ERC	ERA
2021 2 Tms		47	0	16	50.0	238	62	47	42	6	1	3	8	25	1	41	6	3	2	.600	0-2 3	94	.878	6.76	7.56
21 Tex	AL	19	0	7	26.2	127	31	25	25	3	1	1	6	13	0	26	3	0	0	-	0-0 0	94	.840	6.43	8.44
21 Ari	NL	28	0	9	23.1	111	31	22	17	3	0	2	2	12	1	15	3	3	2	.600	0-2 3	94	.921	7.14	6.56

Alex De Goti

Bats: R **Throws:** R **Pos:** 2B-2 duh-GO-tee **Ht:** 6'0" **Wt:** 192 **Born:** 8/19/1994 **Age:** 27

									BATTING												RUNNING			AVERAGES			
Year Team	Lg	G	AB	H	2B	3B	HR	(Hm	Rd)	TB	R	RBI	RC	TBB	IBB	SO	HBP	SH	SF	SB	CS	GDP	Avg	OBP	Slg	OPS
2021 SgrLnd	AAA	102	375	87	22	5	5	(-	-)	134	53	41	-	44	0	105	4	1	3	7	0	8	.232	.317	.357	.674
2021 Hou	AL	2	6	2	0	0	0	(0	0)	2	2	1	1	1	0	2	0	0	0	0	0	0	.333	.429	.333	.762

Chase De Jong

Pitches: R **Bats:** L **Pos:** SP-9 de-YUNG **Ht:** 6'4" **Wt:** 230 **Born:** 12/29/1993 **Age:** 28

				HOW MUCH PITCHED		WHAT HE GAVE UP											THE RESULTS						
Year Team	Lg	G	GS	GF	IP	BFP	H	R	ER	HR	SH	SF	HB	TBB	IBB	SO	WP	W	L	Pct	Sv-Op Hld	Vel	OPS	ERC	ERA
2017 Sea	AL	7	4	2	28.1	125	31	20	20	5	1	1	0	13	0	13	0	0	3	.000	0-1 0	90	.837	5.49	6.35
2018 Min	AL	4	4	0	17.2	74	18	9	7	3	0	0	0	6	0	13	2	1	1	.500	0-0 0	89	.810	4.53	3.57
2019 Min	AL	1	0	1	1.0	9	3	4	4	1	0	0	0	3	0	0	0	0	0	-	0-0 0	91	1.667	44.28	36.00
2020 Min	AL	3	2	0	7.1	38	12	12	12	2	0	1	1	4	0	9	0	0	1	.000	0-0 0	93	1.010	11.02	14.73
2021 Pit	NL	9	9	0	43.2	196	49	28	28	11	1	0	1	19	2	39	0	1	4	.200	0-0 0	93	.942	6.09	5.77
5 ML YEARS		24	19	3	98.0	442	113	73	71	22	2	2	2	45	2	74	2	2	9	.182	0-1 0	91	.908	6.26	6.52

Bryan De La Cruz

Bats: R **Throws:** R **Pos:** CF-24;RF-23;LF-16;PH-1;PR-1   **Ht:** 6'2" **Wt:** 175 **Born:** 12/16/1996 **Age:** 25

								BATTING												RUNNING			AVERAGES			
Year Team	Lg	G	AB	H	2B	3B	HR	(Hm Rd)	TB	R	RBI	RC	TBB	IBB	SO	HBP	SH	SF	SB	CS	GDP	Avg	OBP	Slg	OPS
2021 SgrLnd	AAA	66	272	88	17	0	12	(- -)	141	48	50	-	17	0	59	1	0	3	2	4	5	.324	.362	.518	.880
2021 Mia	NL	58	199	59	7	2	5	(2 3)	85	17	19	24	18	1	53	1	0	1	1	1	8	.296	.356	.427	.783

Jose De Leon

Pitches: R **Bats:** R **Pos:** RP-7; SP-2   **Ht:** 6'2" **Wt:** 215 **Born:** 8/7/1992 **Age:** 29

		HOW MUCH PITCHED					WHAT HE GAVE UP											THE RESULTS								
Year Team	Lg	G	GS	GF	IP	BFP	H	R	ER	HR	SH	SF	HB	TBB	IBB	SO	WP	W	L	Pct	Sv-Op	Hld	Vel	OPS	ERC	ERA
2021 Lsvlle	AAA	12	0	4	11.2	51	8	7	6	1	2	0	0	7	0	19	0	1	1	.500	1--	-	-	.616	2.91	4.63
2016 LAD	NL	4	4	0	17.0	80	19	17	12	5	3	1	3	7	1	15	0	2	0	1.000	0-0	0	92	.937	6.82	6.35
2017 TB	AL	1	0	0	2.2	15	4	3	3	1	0	0	0	3	0	2	2	1	0	1.000	0-0	0	92	1.133	12.97	10.13
2019 TB	AL	3	0	1	4.0	21	3	2	1	0	0	0	2	3	1	7	1	1	0	1.000	0-0	0	92	.568	4.23	2.25
2020 Cin	NL	5	0	2	6.0	35	6	12	12	1	0	0	0	11	2	10	0	0	0	-	0-0	0	95	.861	9.77	18.00
2021 Cin	NL	9	2	1	18.1	91	22	17	17	4	0	2	2	11	0	33	3	0	1	.000	0-0	0	93	.898	7.30	8.35
5 ML YEARS		22	6	4	48.0	242	54	51	45	11	3	3	7	35	4	67	6	4	1	.800	0-0	0	93	.897	7.51	8.44

Enyel De Los Santos

Pitches: R **Bats:** R **Pos:** RP-33   **Ht:** 6'3" **Wt:** 235 **Born:** 12/25/1995 **Age:** 26

		HOW MUCH PITCHED					WHAT HE GAVE UP											THE RESULTS								
Year Team	Lg	G	GS	GF	IP	BFP	H	R	ER	HR	SH	SF	HB	TBB	IBB	SO	WP	W	L	Pct	Sv-Op	Hld	Vel	OPS	ERC	ERA
2021 LV	AAA	10	0	2	13.1	47	3	4	4	1	0	0	1	5	1	24	0	0	1	.000	0--	-	-	.338	0.83	2.70
2018 Phi	NL	7	2	2	19.0	81	19	10	10	2	1	1	1	8	0	15	1	1	0	1.000	0-0	0	95	.836	4.54	4.74
2019 Phi	NL	5	1	3	11.0	46	13	9	9	4	0	0	0	5	0	9	1	0	1	1.000	0-0	0	93	1.001	8.11	7.36
2021 2 Tms		33	0	13	35.1	173	43	32	25	8	3	0	4	18	4	48	5	2	1	.667	0-2	2	95	.916	6.87	6.37
21 Phi	NL	26	0	10	28.0	137	34	28	21	7	2	0	3	14	3	42	5	1	1	.500	0-2	1	95	.929	6.97	6.75
21 Pit	NL	7	0	3	7.1	36	9	4	4	1	1	0	1	4	1	6	0	1	0	1.000	0-0	1	95	.867	6.47	4.91
3 ML YEARS		45	3	18	65.1	300	75	51	44	14	4	1	5	31	4	72	7	3	2	.600	0-2	2	95	.908	6.37	6.06

Austin Dean

Bats: R **Throws:** R **Pos:** PH-15;LF-6;RF-3   **Ht:** 6'0" **Wt:** 215 **Born:** 10/14/1993 **Age:** 28

								BATTING												RUNNING			AVERAGES			
Year Team	Lg	G	AB	H	2B	3B	HR	(Hm Rd)	TB	R	RBI	RC	TBB	IBB	SO	HBP	SH	SF	SB	CS	GDP	Avg	OBP	Slg	OPS
2021 Memp	AAA	14	47	10	6	0	1	(- -)	19	6	8	-	7	0	19	2	0	0	0	1	2	.213	.339	.404	.744
2018 Mia	NL	34	113	25	4	0	4	(2 2)	41	16	14	12	7	0	22	2	0	1	1	0	1	.221	.279	.363	.642
2019 Mia	NL	64	178	40	14	0	6	(4 2)	72	17	21	16	9	1	47	0	1	1	0	2	5	.225	.261	.404	.665
2020 StL	NL	3	4	1	1	0	0	(0 0)	2	1	0	1	3	0	2	0	0	0	0	0	0	.250	.571	.500	1.071
2021 StL	NL	22	30	7	2	0	1	(1 0)	12	5	7	5	6	0	11	0	0	2	0	0	0	.233	.342	.400	.742
Postseason		1	1	0	0	0	0	(0 0)	0	0	0	0	0	0	1	0	0	0	0	0	0	.000	.000	.000	.000
4 ML YEARS		123	325	73	21	0	11	(7 4)	127	39	42	34	25	1	82	2	1	3	1	2	6	.225	.282	.391	.672

Jacob deGrom

duh-GRAHM

Pitches: R **Bats:** L **Pos:** SP-15   **Ht:** 6'4" **Wt:** 180 **Born:** 6/19/1988 **Age:** 34

		HOW MUCH PITCHED					WHAT HE GAVE UP											THE RESULTS								
Year Team	Lg	G	GS	GF	IP	BFP	H	R	ER	HR	SH	SF	HB	TBB	IBB	SO	WP	W	L	Pct	Sv-Op	Hld	Vel	OPS	ERC	ERA
2014 NYM	NL	22	22	0	140.1	565	117	44	42	7	5	3	1	43	2	144	1	9	6	.600	0-0	0	93	.613	2.57	2.69
2015 NYM	NL	30	30	0	191.0	751	149	59	54	16	10	7	2	38	2	205	6	14	8	.636	0-0	0	95	.574	2.13	2.54
2016 NYM	NL	24	24	0	148.0	604	142	53	50	15	5	3	3	36	0	143	4	7	8	.467	0-0	0	93	.685	3.40	3.04
2017 NYM	NL	31	31	0	201.1	827	180	87	79	28	3	5	2	59	5	239	7	15	10	.600	0-0	0	95	.682	3.36	3.53
2018 NYM	NL	32	32	0	217.0	835	152	48	41	10	3	5	5	46	3	269	2	10	9	.526	0-0	0	96	.521	1.67	1.70
2019 NYM	NL	32	32	0	204.0	804	154	59	55	19	5	3	7	44	1	255	2	11	8	.579	0-0	0	97	.580	2.21	2.43
2020 NYM	NL	12	12	0	68.0	268	47	21	18	7	0	2	0	18	0	104	4	4	2	.667	0-0	0	99	.565	2.00	2.38
2021 NYM	NL	15	15	0	92.0	324	40	14	11	6	0	2	1	11	0	146	1	7	2	.778	0-0	0	99	.402	0.78	1.08
Postseason		4	4	0	25.0	105	21	8	8	2	2	0	0	8	1	29	0	3	1	.750	0-0	0	96	.608	2.65	2.88
8 ML YEARS		198	198	0	1261.2	4978	981	385	350	108	31	30	21	295	13	1505	26	77	53	.592	0-0	0	96	.590	2.28	2.50

Greg Deichmann

DIKE-muhn

Bats: L **Throws:** R **Pos:** RF-7;PH-6;LF-2   **Ht:** 6'2" **Wt:** 205 **Born:** 5/31/1995 **Age:** 27

								BATTING												RUNNING			AVERAGES			
Year Team	Lg	G	AB	H	2B	3B	HR	(Hm Rd)	TB	R	RBI	RC	TBB	IBB	SO	HBP	SH	SF	SB	CS	GDP	Avg	OBP	Slg	OPS
2021 LsVgs	AAA	60	210	63	14	3	4	(- -)	95	48	35	-	50	0	60	0	0	1	7	1	2	.300	.433	.452	.885
2021 Iowa	AAA	34	119	27	8	2	3	(- -)	48	14	13	-	11	0	38	1	0	0	3	2	1	.227	.298	.403	.701
2021 ChC	NL	14	30	4	0	0	0	(0 0)	4	0	1	0	1	0	14	0	0	0	0	0	0	.133	.161	.133	.295

Paul DeJong

de-YUNG

Bats: R **Throws:** R **Pos:** SS-107;PH-6;PR-1   **Ht:** 6'0" **Wt:** 205 **Born:** 8/2/1993 **Age:** 28

								BATTING												RUNNING			AVERAGES			
Year Team	Lg	G	AB	H	2B	3B	HR	(Hm Rd)	TB	R	RBI	RC	TBB	IBB	SO	HBP	SH	SF	SB	CS	GDP	Avg	OBP	Slg	OPS
2017 StL	NL	108	417	119	26	1	25	(11 14)	222	55	65	57	21	1	124	4	0	1	1	0	8	.285	.325	.532	.857
2018 StL	NL	115	436	105	25	1	19	(4 15)	189	68	68	67	36	2	123	12	0	5	1	1	6	.241	.313	.433	.746
2019 StL	NL	159	583	136	31	1	30	(10 20)	259	97	78	76	62	1	149	13	0	6	9	5	15	.233	.318	.444	.762

Year	Team	Lg	G	AB	H	2B	3B	HR	(Hm	Rd)	TB	R	RBI	RC	TBB	IBB	SO	HBP	SH	SF	SB	CS	GDP	Avg	OBP	Slg	OPS
																								BATTING			RUNNING	AVERAGES
2020	StL	NL	45	152	38	6	0	3	(1	2)	53	17	25	23	17	0	50	1	0	4	1	0	4	.250	.322	.349	.671
2021	StL	NL	113	356	70	10	1	19	(5	14)	139	44	45	39	35	0	103	9	0	2	4	1	6	.197	.284	.390	.674
	Postseason		12	40	9	2	0	0	(0	0)	11	5	3	6	6	2	16	1	0	0	0	0	0	.225	.340	.275	.615
	5 ML YEARS		540	1944	468	98	4	96	(31	65)	862	281	281	262	171	4	549	39	0	18	16	7	39	.241	.312	.443	.756

Miguel Del Pozo

Pitches: L **Bats:** L **Pos:** RP-5   **Ht:** 6'1" **Wt:** 205 **Born:** 10/14/1992 **Age:** 29

Year	Team	Lg	G	GS	GF	IP	BFP	H	R	ER	HR	SH	SF	HB	TBB	IBB	SO	WP	W	L	Pct	Sv-Op	Hld	Vel	OPS	ERC	ERA
2021	Toledo	AAA	33	0	16	37.2	150	19	11	11	5	0	1	2	15	0	52	5	1	2	.333	4- --	-	-	.520	1.90	2.63
2019	LAA	AL	17	0	1	9.1	45	10	11	11	3	1	1	0	9	0	11	0	1	1	.500	0-0	0	95	.981	8.30	10.61
2020	Pit	NL	5	0	1	3.2	25	7	7	7	0	0	0	0	8	1	2	1	0	0	-	0-2	0	93	1.129	16.73	17.18
2021	Det	AL	5	0	1	5.1	25	8	2	2	0	0	0	0	2	0	4	0	0	0	-	0-0	0	93	.878	6.23	3.38
	3 ML YEARS		27	0	3	18.1	95	25	20	20	3	1	1	0	18	1	17	1	1	1	.500	0-2	0	94	.991	9.39	9.82

Anthony DeSclafani

Pitches: R **Bats:** R **Pos:** SP-31   DEE-skla-fa-nee   **Ht:** 6'2" **Wt:** 195 **Born:** 4/18/1990 **Age:** 32

Year	Team	Lg	G	GS	GF	IP	BFP	H	R	ER	HR	SH	SF	HB	TBB	IBB	SO	WP	W	L	Pct	Sv-Op	Hld	Vel	OPS	ERC	ERA
2014	Mia	NL	13	5	4	33.0	146	40	23	23	4	4	3	2	5	0	26	2	2	2	.500	0-0	0	93	.801	4.56	6.27
2015	Cin	NL	31	31	0	184.2	785	194	93	83	17	10	5	5	55	5	151	6	9	13	.409	0-0	0	93	.742	4.00	4.05
2016	Cin	NL	20	20	0	123.1	507	120	51	45	16	7	3	4	30	2	105	6	9	5	.643	0-0	0	93	.723	3.67	3.28
2018	Cin	NL	21	21	0	115.0	484	118	68	63	24	5	4	2	30	2	108	4	7	8	.467	0-0	0	94	.792	4.47	4.93
2019	Cin	NL	31	31	0	166.2	696	151	77	72	29	5	3	4	49	5	167	2	9	9	.500	0-0	0	95	.717	3.66	3.89
2020	Cin	NL	9	7	1	33.2	158	41	27	27	7	0	3	3	16	0	25	1	1	2	.333	0-0	0	95	.909	6.91	7.22
2021	SF	NL	31	31	0	167.2	676	141	61	59	19	6	0	2	42	1	152	7	13	7	.650	0-0	0	94	.634	2.79	3.17
	7 ML YEARS		156	146	5	824.0	3452	805	400	372	116	37	21	22	227	15	734	28	50	46	.521	0-0	0	94	.730	3.82	4.06

Delino DeShields

Bats: R **Throws:** R **Pos:** CF-18;PH-5;LF-3;PR-3;DH-1   **Ht:** 5'9" **Wt:** 190 **Born:** 8/16/1992 **Age:** 29

Year	Team	Lg	G	AB	H	2B	3B	HR	(Hm	Rd)	TB	R	RBI	RC	TBB	IBB	SO	HBP	SH	SF	SB	CS	GDP	Avg	OBP	Slg	OPS
2021	RdRck	AAA	66	247	65	9	1	5	(-	-)	91	46	18	-	50	0	62	3	4	1	16	2	1	.263	.392	.368	.760
2021	Wrcstr	AAA	18	62	13	4	1	1	(-	-)	22	10	4	-	13	0	24	1	0	0	5	1	1	.210	.355	.355	.710
2015	Tex	AL	121	425	111	22	10	2	(2	0)	159	83	37	66	53	1	101	3	7	4	25	8	1	.261	.344	.374	.718
2016	Tex	AL	74	182	38	7	0	4	(0	4)	57	36	13	16	15	0	54	2	3	1	8	3	1	.209	.275	.313	.588
2017	Tex	AL	120	376	101	15	2	6	(5	1)	138	75	22	54	44	0	109	3	13	4	29	8	2	.269	.347	.367	.714
2018	Tex	AL	106	334	72	14	1	2	(1	1)	94	52	22	38	43	0	83	3	12	1	20	4	1	.216	.310	.281	.591
2019	Tex	AL	118	357	89	15	4	3	(3	1)	124	42	32	51	38	0	100	3	8	2	24	6	8	.249	.325	.347	.672
2020	Cle	AL	37	107	27	3	2	0	(0	0)	34	10	7	10	9	0	29	0	4	0	3	2	0	.252	.310	.318	.628
2021	Cin	NL	25	47	12	5	0	1	(1	0)	20	4	6	6	9	0	11	0	2	0	2	1	0	.255	.375	.426	.801
	Postseason		7	31	9	3	0	0	(0	0)	12	6	2	5	1	0	4	0	0	0	1	0	0	.290	.313	.387	.700
	7 ML YEARS		601	1828	450	81	19	19	(12	7)	626	302	139	241	211	1	487	14	49	12	111	32	13	.246	.327	.342	.669

Reid Detmers

Pitches: L **Bats:** L **Pos:** SP-5   **Ht:** 6'2" **Wt:** 210 **Born:** 7/8/1999 **Age:** 22

Year	Team	Lg	G	GS	GF	IP	BFP	H	R	ER	HR	SH	SF	HB	TBB	IBB	SO	WP	W	L	Pct	Sv-Op	Hld	Vel	OPS	ERC	ERA
2021	Rock	AA	12	12	0	54.0	225	45	24	21	10	2	2	1	18	0	97	3	2	4	.333	0- --	-	-	.688	3.49	3.50
2021	LAA	AL	5	5	0	20.2	101	26	17	17	5	0	0	2	11	1	19	1	1	3	.250	0-0	0	93	.920	7.51	7.40

Ross Detwiler

Pitches: L **Bats:** R **Pos:** RP-48; SP-5   DETT-why-lerr   **Ht:** 6'5" **Wt:** 210 **Born:** 3/6/1986 **Age:** 36

Year	Team	Lg	G	GS	GF	IP	BFP	H	R	ER	HR	SH	SF	HB	TBB	IBB	SO	WP	W	L	Pct	Sv-Op	Hld	Vel	OPS	ERC	ERA
2007	Was	NL	1	0	1	1.0	4	0	0	0	0	0	0	0	0	0	1	0	0	0	-	0-0	0	93	.000	0.00	0.00
2009	Was	NL	15	14	0	75.2	341	87	43	42	3	4	1	2	33	3	43	4	1	6	.143	0-0	0	91	.767	4.65	5.00
2010	Was	NL	8	5	1	29.2	135	34	22	14	5	2	0	1	14	1	17	1	1	3	.250	0-0	0	90	.826	5.83	4.25
2011	Was	NL	15	10	0	66.0	277	63	26	22	7	7	3	3	20	2	41	2	4	5	.444	0-0	1	92	.704	3.64	3.00
2012	Was	NL	33	27	1	164.1	686	149	75	62	15	8	3	5	52	0	105	4	10	8	.556	0-0	1	93	.681	3.30	3.40
2013	Was	NL	13	13	0	71.1	316	92	37	32	5	4	1	5	14	2	39	0	2	7	.222	0-0	0	92	.811	4.96	4.04
2014	Was	NL	47	0	15	63.0	274	68	34	28	5	4	3	5	21	4	39	3	2	3	.400	1-2	3	93	.734	4.36	4.00
2015	2 Tms		41	7	7	58.1	288	82	51	47	10	1	4	6	36	1	41	3	1	5	.167	0-2	2	92	.984	8.67	7.25
2016	2 Tms	AL	16	7	0	48.2	220	59	34	33	5	0	1	4	19	0	26	3	2	4	.333	0-1	0	92	.806	5.37	6.10
2018	Sea	AL	1	0	0	6.0	23	8	3	3	1	0	1	0	2	0	2	0	0	1	.000	0-0	0	90	.985	7.59	4.50
2019	CWS	AL	18	12	0	69.2	315	86	54	51	20	2	1	3	27	3	46	1	3	5	.375	0-0	1	91	.942	7.05	6.59
2020	CWS	AL	16	0	4	19.2	81	19	8	7	2	0	0	1	5	1	15	1	1	1	.500	0-0	0	92	.695	3.52	3.20
2021	2 Tms	NL	53	5	10	52.1	229	44	28	27	10	0	3	8	20	1	62	2	3	1	.750	0-0	1	92	.764	4.24	4.64
15	Tex	AL	17	7	4	43.0	208	62	37	34	9	1	3	2	20	0	28	3	0	5	.000	0-1	1	91	.991	8.35	7.12
15	Atl	NL	24	0	3	15.1	80	20	14	13	1	0	1	3	16	1	13	0	1	0	1.000	0-1	1	93	.954	9.42	7.63
16	Cle	AL	7	0	0	4.2	21	3	3	3	1	0	1	0	4	0	3	0	0	0	-	0-0	0	91	.833	4.60	5.79
16	Oak	AL	9	7	0	44.0	199	56	31	30	4	0	0	4	15	0	23	3	2	4	.333	0-0	0	92	.804	5.46	6.14

Year Team	Lg	G	GS	GF	IP	BFP	H	R	ER	HR	SH	SF	HB	TBB	IBB	SO	WP	W	L	Pct	Sv-Op	Hld	Vel	OPS	ERC	ERA
21 Mia	NL	46	5	6	45.1	200	41	26	25	8	0	3	7	15	0	56	1	2	1	.667	0-0	1	92	.766	4.30	4.96
21 SD	NL	7	0	4	7.0	29	3	2	2	2	0	0	1	5	1	6	1	1	0	1.000	0-0	0	90	.745	3.84	2.57
Postseason		1	1	0	6.0	25	3	1	0	0	1	1	0	3	1	2	0	0	0	-	0-0	0	92	.400	1.21	0.00
13 ML YEARS		277	100	41	725.2	3189	791	415	368	88	32	21	40	263	18	477	24	30	49	.380	1-5	9	92	.785	4.79	4.56

Chris Devenski

Pitches: R **Bats:** R **Pos:** RP-8 **Ht:** 6'3" **Wt:** 211 **Born:** 11/13/1990 **Age:** 31

Year Team	Lg	G	GS	GF	IP	BFP	H	R	ER	HR	SH	SF	HB	TBB	IBB	SO	WP	W	L	Pct	Sv-Op	Hld	Vel	OPS	ERC	ERA
2016 Hou	AL	48	5	16	108.1	408	79	26	26	4	1	1	3	20	0	104	2	4	4	.500	1-1	5	92	.551	1.74	2.16
2017 Hou	AL	62	0	10	80.2	316	50	26	24	11	0	1	2	26	3	100	2	8	5	.615	4-10	24	94	.588	2.10	2.68
2018 Hou	AL	50	1	8	47.1	196	42	23	22	9	1	1	3	13	1	51	1	2	3	.400	2-5	18	94	.719	3.79	4.18
2019 Hou	AL	61	1	19	69.0	298	69	39	37	13	1	3	3	21	0	72	2	2	3	.400	0-1	7	95	.784	4.42	4.83
2020 Hou	AL	4	0	1	3.2	21	7	6	6	1	0	0	0	3	0	5	0	0	1	.000	0-1	0	93	1.143	13.40	14.73
2021 Ari	NL	8	0	2	7.1	35	11	7	7	2	0	0	1	2	0	5	0	1	0	1.000	1-3	1	91	.994	8.69	8.59
Postseason		13	0	5	11.0	50	12	11	11	3	0	1	1	4	0	11	0	1	0	1.000	0-1	3	95	.954	5.99	9.00
6 ML YEARS		233	7	55	316.1	1274	258	127	122	40	3	6	12	85	4	337	7	17	16	.515	8-21	55	94	.661	2.91	3.47

Jose Devers

Bats: L **Throws:** R **Pos:** 2B-13;PH-7;SS-5;PR-2 **Ht:** 6'0" **Wt:** 174 **Born:** 12/7/1999 **Age:** 22

Year Team	Lg	G	AB	H	2B	3B	HR	(Hm Rd)	TB	R	RBI	RC	TBB	IBB	SO	HBP	SH	SF	SB	CS	GDP	Avg	OBP	Slg	OPS
2021 Jaxnvl	AAA	13	39	9	1	1	0	(- -)	12	4	3	-	1	0	5	0	1	0	0	0	0	.231	.250	.308	.558
2021 Mia	NL	21	41	10	3	0	0	(0 0)	13	7	5	5	3	0	11	1	0	1	0	0	0	.244	.304	.317	.621

Rafael Devers

Bats: L **Throws:** R **Pos:** 3B-151;DH-4;2B-2;PH-1 **Ht:** 6'0" **Wt:** 240 **Born:** 10/24/1996 **Age:** 25

Year Team	Lg	G	AB	H	2B	3B	HR	(Hm Rd)	TB	R	RBI	RC	TBB	IBB	SO	HBP	SH	SF	SB	CS	GDP	Avg	OBP	Slg	OPS
2017 Bos	AL	58	222	63	14	0	10	(6 4)	107	34	30	34	18	3	57	0	0	0	3	1	5	.284	.338	.482	.819
2018 Bos	AL	121	450	108	24	0	21	(9 12)	195	59	66	47	38	6	121	0	0	2	5	2	9	.240	.298	.433	.731
2019 Bos	AL	156	647	201	54	4	32	(13 19)	359	129	115	119	48	7	119	4	1	2	8	8	8	.311	.361	.555	.916
2020 Bos	AL	57	232	61	16	1	11	(5 6)	112	32	43	34	13	0	67	3	0	0	0	0	8	.263	.310	.483	.793
2021 Bos	AL	156	591	165	37	1	38	(16 22)	318	101	113	111	62	7	143	7	0	4	5	5	13	.279	.352	.538	.890
Postseason		15	45	14	0	0	3	(2 1)	23	10	14	10	5	0	17	0	0	1	1	0	1	.311	.373	.511	.884
5 ML YEARS		548	2142	598	145	6	112	(49 63)	1091	355	367	345	179	23	507	14	1	8	21	16	43	.279	.338	.509	.847

Aledmys Diaz

Bats: R **Throws:** R **Pos:** 3B-30;LF-15;2B-13;1B-12;PH-10;SS-9;DH-5;RF-1 ah-LED-mees **Ht:** 6'1" **Wt:** 195 **Born:** 8/1/1990 **Age:** 31

Year Team	Lg	G	AB	H	2B	3B	HR	(Hm Rd)	TB	R	RBI	RC	TBB	IBB	SO	HBP	SH	SF	SB	CS	GDP	Avg	OBP	Slg	OPS
2016 StL	NL	111	404	121	28	3	17	(7 10)	206	71	65	75	41	6	60	7	2	6	4	4	10	.300	.369	.510	.879
2017 StL	NL	79	286	74	17	0	7	(5 2)	112	31	20	27	13	1	42	0	1	1	4	1	9	.259	.290	.392	.682
2018 Tor	AL	130	422	111	26	0	18	(7 11)	191	55	55	50	23	2	62	3	0	4	3	4	9	.263	.303	.453	.756
2019 Hou	AL	69	210	57	12	1	9	(5 4)	98	36	40	36	26	1	28	5	0	6	2	0	10	.271	.356	.467	.823
2020 Hou	AL	17	58	14	5	0	3	(1 2)	28	8	6	5	1	0	12	0	0	0	0	0	1	.241	.254	.483	.737
2021 Hou	AL	84	294	76	19	0	8	(1 7)	119	28	45	42	16	3	62	9	0	0	0	1	7	.259	.317	.405	.721
Postseason		16	26	6	0	0	1	(1 0)	9	3	2	3	2	0	7	0	0	0	0	0	0	.231	.286	.346	.632
6 ML YEARS		490	1674	453	107	4	62	(26 36)	754	229	231	235	120	13	266	24	3	17	13	10	46	.271	.325	.450	.776

Edwin Diaz

Pitches: R **Bats:** R **Pos:** RP-63 **Ht:** 6'3" **Wt:** 165 **Born:** 3/22/1994 **Age:** 28

Year Team	Lg	G	GS	GF	IP	BFP	H	R	ER	HR	SH	SF	HB	TBB	IBB	SO	WP	W	L	Pct	Sv-Op	Hld	Vel	OPS	ERC	ERA
2016 Sea	AL	49	0	23	51.2	217	45	16	16	5	0	0	3	15	2	88	6	0	4	.000	18-21	13	97	.627	3.05	2.79
2017 Sea	AL	66	0	52	66.0	278	44	28	24	10	1	2	3	32	2	89	3	4	6	.400	34-39	2	97	.619	3.01	3.27
2018 Sea	AL	73	0	65	73.1	280	41	17	16	5	0	0	6	17	0	124	3	0	4	.000	57-61	0	97	.470	1.49	1.96
2019 NYM	NL	66	0	48	58.0	254	58	36	36	15	1	2	4	22	3	99	3	2	7	.222	26-33	1	97	.834	5.31	5.59
2020 NYM	NL	26	0	19	25.2	110	18	6	5	2	0	0	2	14	0	50	1	2	1	.667	6-9	2	98	.596	3.12	1.75
2021 NYM	NL	63	0	51	62.2	257	43	27	24	3	3	1	9	23	1	89	5	5	6	.455	32-38	0	99	.580	2.49	3.45
6 ML YEARS		343	0	258	337.1	1396	249	130	121	40	5	5	27	123	8	539	21	13	28	.317	173-201	18	98	.620	2.91	3.23

Elias Diaz

Bats: R **Throws:** R **Pos:** C-98;PH-19 eh-LEE-ahs **Ht:** 6'1" **Wt:** 223 **Born:** 11/17/1990 **Age:** 31

Year Team	Lg	G	AB	H	2B	3B	HR	(Hm Rd)	TB	R	RBI	RC	TBB	IBB	SO	HBP	SH	SF	SB	CS	GDP	Avg	OBP	Slg	OPS
2015 Pit	NL	2	5	0	0	0	0	(0 0)	0	0	0	0	0	0	1	0	0	0	0	0	0	.000	.000	.000	.000
2016 Pit	NL	1	4	0	0	0	0	(0 0)	0	0	1	0	0	0	0	0	0	0	0	0	0	.000	.000	.000	.000
2017 Pit	NL	64	188	42	14	0	1	(0 1)	59	18	19	15	11	0	38	0	0	1	1	0	8	.223	.265	.314	.579
2018 Pit	NL	82	252	72	12	0	10	(3 7)	114	33	34	36	21	1	40	1	0	3	0	1	4	.286	.339	.452	.792

Year Team	Lg	G	AB	H	2B	3B	HR	(Hm Rd)	TB	R	RBI	RC	TBB	IBB	SO	HBP	SH	SF	SB	CS	GDP	Avg	OBP	Slg	OPS
2019 Pit	NL	101	303	73	14	0	2	(2 0)	93	31	28	30	23	0	56	2	1	3	0	0	11	.241	.296	.307	.603
2020 Col	NL	26	68	16	2	0	2	(1 1)	24	4	9	6	5	0	15	0	0	0	0	0	4	.235	.288	.353	.641
2021 Col	NL	106	338	83	18	1	18	(9 9)	157	52	44	32	30	1	60	2	0	1	0	0	15	.246	.310	.464	.774
7 ML YEARS		382	1155	286	60	1	33	(15 18)	447	138	135	119	90	2	211	5	1	8	1	1	42	.248	.303	.387	.690

Isan Diaz

Bats: L **Throws:** R **Pos:** 3B-37;2B-35;PH-23   **Ht:** 5'11" **Wt:** 201 **Born:** 5/27/1996 **Age:** 26

Year Team	Lg	G	AB	H	2B	3B	HR	(Hm Rd)	TB	R	RBI	RC	TBB	IBB	SO	HBP	SH	SF	SB	CS	GDP	Avg	OBP	Slg	OPS
2021 Jaxnvl	AAA	25	87	22	8	0	4	(- -)	42	13	13	-	10	0	26	2	0	0	0	1	1	.253	.343	.483	.826
2019 Mia	NL	49	179	31	5	2	5	(2 3)	55	17	23	19	19	0	59	2	0	1	0	3	2	.173	.259	.307	.566
2020 Mia	NL	7	22	4	0	0	0	(0 0)	4	3	1	0	0	0	7	0	0	0	0	0	0	.182	.182	.182	.364
2021 Mia	NL	89	238	46	9	0	4	(3 1)	67	25	17	17	34	6	73	1	1	3	1	1	2	.193	.293	.282	.575
3 ML YEARS		145	439	81	14	2	9	(5 4)	126	45	41	36	53	6	139	3	1	4	1	4	4	.185	.275	.287	.562

Jhonathan Diaz

Pitches: L **Bats:** L **Pos:** SP-2; RP-1   **Ht:** 6'0" **Wt:** 170 **Born:** 9/13/1996 **Age:** 25

			HOW MUCH PITCHED					WHAT HE GAVE UP										THE RESULTS						
Year Team	Lg	G	GS	GF	IP	BFP	H	R	ER	HR	SH	SF	HB	TBB	IBB	SO	WP	W	L	Pct	Sv-Op Hld	Vel	OPS	ERC	ERA
2021 Rock	AA	13	9	1	61.0	251	50	27	27	5	1	1	13	12	0	78	3	5	3	.625	0- - -	-	.657	3.06	3.98
2021 LAA	AL	3	2	1	13.0	59	11	6	6	1	0	1	1	7	0	9	0	1	0	1.000	0-0 0	89	.682	3.72	4.15

Lewin Diaz

Bats: L **Throws:** L **Pos:** 1B-32;PH-9;PR-1   **Ht:** 6'4" **Wt:** 217 **Born:** 11/19/1996 **Age:** 25

Year Team	Lg	G	AB	H	2B	3B	HR	(Hm Rd)	TB	R	RBI	RC	TBB	IBB	SO	HBP	SH	SF	SB	CS	GDP	Avg	OBP	Slg	OPS
2021 Jaxnvl	AAA	74	278	69	15	0	20	(- -)	144	52	51	-	26	2	60	7	0	1	2	0	7	.248	.327	.518	.845
2020 Mia	NL	14	39	6	2	0	0	(0 0)	8	2	3	2	2	0	12	0	0	0	0	0	1	.154	.195	.205	.400
2021 Mia	NL	40	122	25	4	1	8	(2 6)	55	16	13	9	6	1	33	0	0	0	0	0	1	.205	.242	.451	.693
2 ML YEARS		54	161	31	6	1	8	(2 6)	63	18	16	11	8	1	45	0	0	0	0	0	3	.193	.231	.391	.622

Miguel Diaz

Pitches: R **Bats:** R **Pos:** RP-23; SP-2   **Ht:** 6'0" **Wt:** 224 **Born:** 11/28/1994 **Age:** 27

			HOW MUCH PITCHED					WHAT HE GAVE UP										THE RESULTS						
Year Team	Lg	G	GS	GF	IP	BFP	H	R	ER	HR	SH	SF	HB	TBB	IBB	SO	WP	W	L	Pct	Sv-Op Hld	Vel	OPS	ERC	ERA
2021 ElPaso	AAA	13	2	2	13.2	72	19	12	12	4	0	2	0	13	0	19	0	0	3	.000	0- - -	-	1.111	10.64	7.90
2017 SD	NL	31	3	8	41.2	192	44	35	34	11	2	2	3	25	0	33	5	1	1	.500	0-0 0	96	.929	6.87	7.34
2018 SD	NL	11	0	4	18.2	85	16	11	10	2	0	2	0	12	2	30	1	1	0	1.000	0-0 0	96	.738	3.94	4.82
2019 SD	NL	5	0	2	6.1	29	9	5	5	1	0	0	2	1	0	4	1	0	0	-	0-0 1	95	1.068	7.78	7.11
2021 SD	NL	25	2	10	42.0	172	31	19	17	8	1	0	0	19	0	46	0	3	1	.750	1-1 0	94	.727	3.48	3.64
4 ML YEARS		72	5	24	108.2	478	100	70	66	22	3	4	5	57	2	113	7	5	2	.714	1-1 2	95	.830	5.03	5.47

Yandy Diaz

Bats: R **Throws:** R **Pos:** 1B-81;3B-58;PH-9;DH-5;2B-1   **Ht:** 6'2" **Wt:** 215 **Born:** 8/8/1991 **Age:** 30

Year Team	Lg	G	AB	H	2B	3B	HR	(Hm Rd)	TB	R	RBI	RC	TBB	IBB	SO	HBP	SH	SF	SB	CS	GDP	Avg	OBP	Slg	OPS
2017 Cle	AL	49	156	41	8	1	0	(0 0)	51	25	13	18	21	0	35	1	0	1	2	0	5	.263	.352	.327	.679
2018 Cle	AL	39	109	34	5	2	1	(1 0)	46	15	15	16	11	1	19	0	0	0	0	0	6	.312	.375	.422	.797
2019 TB	AL	79	307	82	20	1	14	(7 7)	146	53	38	38	35	1	61	1	0	4	2	2	9	.267	.340	.476	.816
2020 TB	AL	34	114	35	3	0	2	(1 1)	44	16	11	21	23	1	17	1	0	0	0	0	6	.307	.428	.386	.814
2021 TB	AL	134	465	119	20	1	13	(5 8)	180	62	64	73	69	4	85	3	0	4	1	1	11	.256	.353	.387	.740
Postseason		18	52	11	1	1	2	(0 2)	20	5	3	9	11	0	15	0	0	0	0	0	0	.212	.349	.385	.734
5 ML YEARS		335	1151	311	56	5	30	(14 16)	467	171	141	166	159	7	217	6	0	9	5	3	37	.270	.359	.406	.765

Yennsy Diaz

Pitches: R **Bats:** R **Pos:** RP-20   **Ht:** 6'1" **Wt:** 210 **Born:** 11/15/1996 **Age:** 25

			HOW MUCH PITCHED					WHAT HE GAVE UP										THE RESULTS						
Year Team	Lg	G	GS	GF	IP	BFP	H	R	ER	HR	SH	SF	HB	TBB	IBB	SO	WP	W	L	Pct	Sv-Op Hld	Vel	OPS	ERC	ERA
2021 Syrcse	AAA	14	0	3	16.1	73	14	16	13	5	1	0	0	9	0	18	4	0	3	.000	1- - -	-	.827	5.15	7.16
2019 Tor	AL	1	0	0	0.2	7	1	2	2	0	0	0	0	4	0	0	0	0	0	-	0-0 0	96	1.048	31.81	27.00
2021 NYM	NL	20	0	10	25.0	112	25	16	15	5	0	1	1	12	1	21	0	0	2	.000	0-0 0	95	.788	5.16	5.40
2 ML YEARS		21	0	10	25.2	119	26	18	17	5	0	1	1	16	1	21	0	0	2	.000	0-0 0	95	.807	5.80	5.96

Alex Dickerson

Bats: L **Throws:** L **Pos:** LF-82;PH-35;DH-5   **Ht:** 6'2" **Wt:** 226 **Born:** 5/26/1990 **Age:** 32

Year Team	Lg	G	AB	H	2B	3B	HR	(Hm Rd)	TB	R	RBI	RC	TBB	IBB	SO	HBP	SH	SF	SB	CS	GDP	Avg	OBP	Slg	OPS
2021 Scrmto	AAA	11	38	11	3	0	2	(- -)	20	8	4	-	5	0	8	2	0	0	0	0	1	.289	.400	.526	.926
2015 SD	NL	11	8	2	0	0	0	(0 0)	2	0	0	0	0	0	3	0	0	0	0	0	1	.250	.250	.250	.500
2016 SD	NL	84	253	65	16	2	10	(5 5)	115	39	37	40	26	2	44	4	0	2	5	1	5	.257	.333	.455	.788
2019 2 Tms	NL	68	174	48	13	3	6	(4 2)	85	29	28	27	13	1	42	2	0	1	1	1	5	.276	.332	.489	.820
2020 SF	NL	52	151	45	10	1	10	(5 5)	87	28	27	27	16	2	30	2	0	1	0	0	5	.298	.371	.576	.947

Year	Team	Lg	G	AB	H	2B	3B	HR	(Hm	Rd)	TB	R	RBI	RC	TBB	IBB	SO	HBP	SH	SF	SB	CS	GDP	Avg	OBP	Slg	OPS
2021	SF	NL	111	283	66	10	2	13	(6	7)	119	37	38	40	23	1	76	6	0	0	1	0	7	.233	.304	.420	.725
19	SD	NL	12	19	3	0	0	0	(0	0)	3	1	2	2	0	0	7	0	0	0	0	0	0	.158	.158	.158	.316
19	SF	NL	56	155	45	13	3	6	(4	2)	82	28	26	25	13	1	35	2	0	1	1	1	5	.290	.351	.529	.880
5 ML YEARS			326	869	226	49	8	39	(20	19)	408	133	130	134	78	6	195	14	0	4	7	2	23	.260	.330	.470	.799

Corey Dickerson

Bats: L **Throws:** R **Pos:** LF-77;PH-18;CF-10;DH-6;RF-5   **Ht:** 6'1" **Wt:** 200 **Born:** 5/22/1989 **Age:** 33

Year	Team	Lg	G	AB	H	2B	3B	HR	(Hm	Rd)	TB	R	RBI	RC	TBB	IBB	SO	HBP	SH	SF	SB	CS	GDP	Avg	OBP	Slg	OPS
2013	Col	NL	69	194	51	13	5	5	(4	1)	89	32	17	23	16	0	41	0	1	2	2	2	1	.263	.316	.459	.775
2014	Col	NL	131	436	136	27	6	24	(15	9)	247	74	76	79	37	6	101	1	0	4	8	7	6	.312	.364	.567	.931
2015	Col	NL	65	224	68	18	2	10	(5	5)	120	30	31	39	10	0	56	0	0	0	0	1	3	.304	.333	.536	.869
2016	TB	AL	148	510	125	36	3	24	(7	17)	239	57	70	59	33	6	134	2	0	2	0	2	12	.245	.293	.469	.761
2017	TB	AL	150	588	166	33	4	27	(14	13)	288	84	62	87	35	6	152	3	0	4	4	3	11	.282	.325	.490	.815
2018	Pit	NL	135	504	151	35	7	13	(4	9)	239	65	55	69	21	4	80	4	0	4	8	3	14	.300	.330	.474	.804
2019	2 Tms	NL	78	260	79	28	2	12	(6	6)	147	33	59	50	16	4	56	0	0	3	1	0	4	.304	.341	.565	.906
2020	Mia	NL	52	194	50	5	1	7	(2	5)	78	25	17	20	15	1	35	0	0	1	1	1	5	.258	.311	.402	.713
2021	2 Tms	NL	109	336	91	18	5	6	(2	4)	137	43	29	34	25	1	68	3	0	1	6	5	8	.271	.326	.408	.734
19	Pit	NL	44	127	40	18	0	4	(0	4)	70	20	25	24	13	4	23	0	0	2	1	0	3	.315	.373	.551	.924
19	Phi	NL	34	133	39	10	2	8	(6	2)	77	13	34	26	3	0	33	0	0	1	0	0	1	.293	.307	.579	.886
21	Mia	NL	63	205	54	12	3	2	(0	2)	78	27	14	17	16	0	45	3	0	1	2	4	5	.263	.324	.380	.705
21	Tor	NL	46	131	37	6	2	4	(2	2)	59	16	15	17	9	1	23	0	0	0	4	1	3	.282	.329	.450	.779
Postseason			5	19	4	0	0	1	(0	1)	7	1	3	2	2	0	5	0	0	0	0	0	0	.211	.286	.368	.654
9 ML YEARS			937	3246	917	213	35	128	(59	69)	1584	443	416	460	208	28	723	13	1	18	30	24	64	.283	.327	.488	.815

Brandon Dickson

Pitches: R **Bats:** R **Pos:** RP-2   **Ht:** 6'5" **Wt:** 190 **Born:** 11/3/1984 **Age:** 37

Year	Team	Lg	G	GS	GF	IP	BFP	H	R	ER	HR	SH	SF	HB	TBB	IBB	SO	WP	W	L	Pct	Sv-Op	Hld	Vel	OPS	ERC	ERA
2021	Memp	AAA	12	0	4	11.1	55	20	13	11	4	0	0	0	4	0	7	0	1	0	1.000	0- -	-	-	1.083	11.34	8.74
2011	StL	NL	4	1	0	8.1	34	9	3	3	2	0	0	0	3	0	7	0	0	0		0-0	0	90	.869	5.77	3.24
2012	StL	NL	4	0	2	6.1	32	10	7	5	2	0	0	0	2	0	6	0	0	0		0-0	0	89	1.008	8.59	7.11
2021	StL	NL	2	0	1	2.0	10	5	3	3	1	0	0	0	0	0	1	0	0	0		0-0	0	92	1.500	17.50	13.50
3 ML YEARS			10	1	3	16.2	76	24	13	11	5	0	0	0	5	0	14	0	0	0		0-0	0	90	1.015	8.06	5.94

Jake Diekman

Pitches: L **Bats:** R **Pos:** RP-67   DEEK-man   **Ht:** 6'4" **Wt:** 195 **Born:** 1/21/1987 **Age:** 35

Year	Team	Lg	G	GS	GF	IP	BFP	H	R	ER	HR	SH	SF	HB	TBB	IBB	SO	WP	W	L	Pct	Sv-Op	Hld	Vel	OPS	ERC	ERA
2012	Phi	NL	32	0	7	27.1	131	25	17	12	1	1	0	3	20	3	35	1	1	1	.500	0-1	4	95	.696	4.45	3.95
2013	Phi	NL	45	0	11	38.1	164	34	15	11	1	2	1	0	16	2	41	2	1	4	.200	0-1	11	96	.598	2.89	2.58
2014	Phi	NL	73	0	19	71.0	313	66	36	30	4	2	7	3	35	5	100	7	5	5	.500	0-4	18	97	.692	3.73	3.80
2015	2 Tms		67	0	7	58.1	260	53	28	26	5	0	0	3	31	0	69	2	2	1	.667	0-3	16	96	.689	4.11	4.01
2016	Tex	AL	66	0	14	53.0	221	36	22	20	4	0	2	3	26	1	59	3	4	2	.667	4-5	26	95	.594	2.72	3.40
2017	Tex	AL	11	0	2	10.2	45	4	3	3	1	0	2	0	10	1	13	0	0	0		1-1	5	95	.523	2.58	2.53
2018	2 Tms	AL	71	0	15	53.1	243	49	33	28	4	0	2	6	31	2	66	3	1	2	.333	2-3	17	95	.717	4.46	4.73
2019	2 Tms	AL	76	0	5	62.0	282	49	34	32	3	1	3	11	39	1	84	6	1	7	.125	0-2	31	96	.668	4.00	4.65
2020	Oak	AL	21	0	2	21.1	84	8	2	1	1	1	0	1	12	1	31	2	2	0	1.000	0-1	13	95	.410	1.43	0.42
2021	Oak	AL	67	0	17	60.2	262	47	29	26	10	0	1	4	34	2	83	8	3	3	.500	7-14	14	95	.715	4.11	3.86
15	Phi	NL	41	0	6	36.2	175	40	23	21	3	0	0	2	24	0	49	1	2	1	.667	0-2	6	96	.773	5.60	5.15
15	Tex	AL	26	0	1	21.2	85	13	5	5	2	0	0	1	7	0	20	1	0	0		0-1	10	97	.520	1.89	2.08
18	Tex	AL	47	0	10	39.0	172	31	18	16	2	0	2	3	23	1	48	0	1	1	.500	2-3	14	95	.651	3.53	3.69
18	Ari	NL	24	0	5	14.1	71	18	15	12	2	0	0	3	8	1	18	3	0	1	.000	0-0	3	96	.875	7.29	7.53
19	KC	AL	48	0	4	41.2	188	33	23	22	3	0	1	8	23	0	63	4	0	6	.000	0-2	18	96	.667	3.97	4.75
19	Oak	AL	28	0	1	20.1	94	16	11	10	0	1	2	3	16	1	21	2	1	1	.500	0-0	13	96	.668	4.05	4.43
Postseason			13	0	4	12.0	50	10	6	6	2	0	0	1	4	1	11	0	0	0		1-1	2	96	.700	3.56	4.50
10 ML YEARS			529	0	99	456.0	2005	371	219	189	34	7	18	34	254	18	581	32	20	25	.444	14-35	155	96	.661	3.65	3.73

Wilmer Difo

Bats: B **Throws:** R **Pos:** PH-65;2B-28;3B-18;RF-8;SS-4;CF-4   DEE-fo   **Ht:** 5'11" **Wt:** 200 **Born:** 4/2/1992 **Age:** 30

Year	Team	Lg	G	AB	H	2B	3B	HR	(Hm	Rd)	TB	R	RBI	RC	TBB	IBB	SO	HBP	SH	SF	SB	CS	GDP	Avg	OBP	Slg	OPS
2021	Indy	AAA	12	41	10	2	0	0	(-	-)	12	6	2	-	4	0	10	0	0	1	0	0	1	.244	.304	.293	.597
2015	Was	NL	15	11	2	0	0	0	(0	0)	2	1	0	0	0	0	2	0	0	0	0	0	0	.182	.182	.182	.364
2016	Was	NL	31	58	16	3	0	1	(1	0)	22	14	7	9	8	1	12	0	0	0	3	0	0	.276	.364	.379	.743
2017	Was	NL	124	332	90	10	4	5	(3	2)	123	47	21	34	24	6	74	1	5	3	10	1	7	.271	.319	.370	.690
2018	Was	NL	148	408	94	14	7	7	(5	2)	143	55	42	38	39	5	82	2	3	4	10	3	8	.230	.298	.350	.649
2019	Was	NL	43	131	33	2	0	2	(1	1)	41	15	8	15	12	3	29	0	1	0	1	1	2	.252	.315	.313	.628
2020	Was	NL	12	14	1	0	0	0	(0	0)	1	1	1	0	3	0	4	0	0	0	0	0	0	.071	.222	.071	.294
2021	Pit	NL	116	219	59	7	3	4	(3	1)	84	25	24	29	20	0	54	0	0	2	0	0	2	.269	.329	.384	.713
Postseason			3	3	0	0	0	0	(0	0)	0	0	0	0	0	0	1	0	0	0	0	0	0	.000	.000	.000	.000
7 ML YEARS			489	1173	295	36	14	19	(13	6)	416	158	103	125	106	15	257	3	9	9	24	5	19	.251	.313	.355	.668

Marcos Diplan

Pitches: R Bats: R Pos: RP-23   Ht: 6'0" Wt: 200 Born: 9/18/1996 Age: 25

Year	Team	Lg	G	GS	GF	IP	BFP	H	R	ER	HR	SH	SF	HB	TBB	IBB	SO	WP	W	L	Pct	Sv-Op	Hld	Vel	OPS	ERC	ERA
2021	Norfolk	AAA	17	0	6	19.2	90	23	10	9	1	1	0	0	9	0	26	0	3	1	.750	0--	-	-	.772	4.84	4.12
2021	Bal	AL	23	0	4	30.0	123	22	16	15	6	0	1	0	15	0	24	3	2	0	1.000	0-0	1	94	.712	3.74	4.50

Randy Dobnak

Pitches: R Bats: R Pos: RP-8; SP-6   Ht: 6'1" Wt: 230 Born: 1/17/1995 Age: 27

Year	Team	Lg	G	GS	GF	IP	BFP	H	R	ER	HR	SH	SF	HB	TBB	IBB	SO	WP	W	L	Pct	Sv-Op	Hld	Vel	OPS	ERC	ERA
2019	Min	AL	9	5	4	28.1	118	27	9	5	1	0	0	3	5	0	23	0	2	1	.667	1-1	0	93	.597	2.93	1.59
2020	Min	AL	10	10	0	46.2	200	50	21	21	3	0	1	4	13	0	27	0	6	4	.600	0-0	0	92	.705	4.14	4.05
2021	Min	AL	14	6	3	50.2	228	66	44	43	11	0	1	1	12	0	27	2	1	7	.125	1-1	0	92	.902	6.08	7.64
	Postseason		1	1	0	2.0	13	6	4	4	0	0	0	0	2	0	0	0	0	1	.000	0-0	0	92	1.252	21.10	18.00
	3 ML YEARS		33	21	7	125.2	546	143	74	69	15	0	2	8	30	0	77	2	9	12	.429	2-2	0	92	.765	4.61	4.94

Kyle Dohy

Pitches: L Bats: L Pos: RP-1   Ht: 6'2" Wt: 202 Born: 9/17/1996 Age: 25

Year	Team	Lg	G	GS	GF	IP	BFP	H	R	ER	HR	SH	SF	HB	TBB	IBB	SO	WP	W	L	Pct	Sv-Op	Hld	Vel	OPS	ERC	ERA
2021	LV	AAA	6	0	1	5.1	34	4	5	5	1	0	0	2	12	0	9	3	0	0	-	0--	-	-	.879	12.62	8.44
2021	Rdng	AA	26	0	8	37.1	151	17	9	9	2	1	2	6	16	0	56	7	4	0	1.000	2--	-	-	.458	1.69	2.17
2021	Phi	NL	1	0	1	1.0	5	1	0	0	0	0	0	0	1	0	1	0	0	0	-	0-0	0	90	.650	5.48	0.00

Rafael Dolis

Pitches: R Bats: R Pos: RP-39   DOE-leese   Ht: 6'4" Wt: 235 Born: 1/10/1988 Age: 34

Year	Team	Lg	G	GS	GF	IP	BFP	H	R	ER	HR	SH	SF	HB	TBB	IBB	SO	WP	W	L	Pct	Sv-Op	Hld	Vel	OPS	ERC	ERA
2021	Buffalo	AAA	10	0	0	10.1	47	10	4	2	0	1	0	0	6	1	12	1	1	2	.333	0--	-	-	.698	3.58	1.74
2011	ChC	NL	1	0	0	1.1	4	0	0	0	0	0	0	0	1	0	1	0	0	0	-	0-0	0	95	.250	0.71	0.00
2012	ChC	NL	34	0	15	38.0	173	40	29	27	5	2	1	3	23	1	24	1	2	4	.333	4-6	3	95	.858	5.85	6.39
2013	ChC	NL	5	0	2	5.0	21	3	2	0	0	0	0	0	2	0	0	0	0	0	-	0-0	0	95	.554	1.44	0.00
2020	Tor	AL	24	0	9	24.0	100	16	9	4	1	2	0	1	14	0	31	3	2	2	.500	5-6	7	95	.593	2.78	1.50
2021	Tor	AL	39	0	18	32.0	156	29	21	20	2	0	1	3	27	2	39	4	2	3	.400	3-4	3	95	.730	5.07	5.63
	Postseason		1	0	1	1.0	3	1	0	0	0	0	0	0	0	0	0	0	0	0	-	0-0	0	94	.667	2.79	0.00
	5 ML YEARS		103	0	44	100.1	454	88	61	51	8	4	2	7	67	3	95	8	6	9	.400	12-16	13	95	.737	4.48	4.57

Seranthony Dominguez

Pitches: R Bats: R Pos: RP-1   Ht: 6'1" Wt: 225 Born: 11/25/1994 Age: 27

Year	Team	Lg	G	GS	GF	IP	BFP	H	R	ER	HR	SH	SF	HB	TBB	IBB	SO	WP	W	L	Pct	Sv-Op	Hld	Vel	OPS	ERC	ERA
2021	LV	AAA	11	0	1	11.1	59	13	13	10	1	0	0	3	7	0	15	1	0	1	.000	0--	-	-	.757	6.42	7.94
2018	Phi	NL	53	0	24	58.0	231	32	19	19	4	0	1	4	22	2	74	10	2	5	.286	16-20	14	98	.501	1.74	2.95
2019	Phi	NL	27	0	2	24.2	110	24	13	11	3	1	0	1	12	0	29	1	3	0	1.000	0-2	9	97	.725	4.52	4.01
2021	Phi	NL	1	0	0	1.0	3	0	0	0	0	0	0	0	0	0	1	0	0	0	-	0-0	0	95	.000	0.00	0.00
	3 ML YEARS		81	0	26	83.2	344	56	32	30	7	1	1	5	34	2	104	11	5	5	.500	16-22	23	98	.567	2.42	3.23

Josh Donaldson

Bats: R Throws: R Pos: 3B-92;DH-34;PH-9   Ht: 6'1" Wt: 210 Born: 12/8/1985 Age: 36

Year	Team	Lg	G	AB	H	2B	3B	HR	(Hm	Rd)	TB	R	RBI	RC	TBB	IBB	SO	HBP	SH	SF	SB	CS	GDP	Avg	OBP	Slg	OPS
2010	Oak	AL	14	32	5	1	0	1	(0	1)	9	1	4	3	2	0	12	0	0	0	0	0	0	.156	.206	.281	.487
2012	Oak	AL	75	274	66	16	0	9	(3	6)	109	34	33	33	14	0	61	5	0	1	4	1	6	.241	.289	.398	.687
2013	Oak	AL	158	579	174	37	3	24	(13	11)	289	89	93	112	76	2	110	6	1	6	5	2	15	.301	.384	.499	.883
2014	Oak	AL	158	608	155	31	2	29	(11	18)	277	93	98	105	76	5	130	7	0	4	8	0	16	.255	.342	.456	.798
2015	Tor	AL	158	620	184	41	2	41	(24	17)	352	122	123	131	73	0	133	6	2	10	6	0	16	.297	.371	.568	.939
2016	Tor	AL	155	577	164	32	5	37	(21	16)	317	122	99	121	109	6	119	9	2	3	7	1	16	.284	.404	.549	.953
2017	Tor	AL	113	415	112	21	0	33	(14	19)	232	65	78	98	76	1	111	3	0	2	2	2	5	.270	.385	.559	.944
2018	2 Tms	AL	52	187	46	14	0	8	(4	4)	84	30	23	32	31	2	54	0	0	1	2	0	3	.246	.352	.449	.801
2019	Atl	NL	155	549	142	33	0	37	(22	15)	286	96	94	103	100	2	155	8	0	2	4	2	13	.259	.379	.521	.900
2020	Min	AL	28	81	18	2	0	6	(3	3)	38	14	11	14	18	1	24	2	0	1	0	0	4	.222	.373	.469	.842
2021	Min	AL	135	457	113	26	0	26	(10	16)	217	73	72	77	74	2	114	4	0	8	0	0	22	.247	.352	.475	.827
18	Tor	AL	36	137	32	11	0	5	(2	3)	58	22	16	24	21	2	44	0	0	1	2	0	1	.234	.333	.423	.757
18	Cle	AL	16	50	14	3	0	3	(2	1)	26	8	7	8	10	0	10	0	0	0	0	0	2	.280	.400	.520	.920
	Postseason		39	150	39	11	0	5	(4	1)	65	19	16	22	15	2	39	2	0	0	1	0	2	.260	.335	.433	.769
	11 ML YEARS		1201	4379	1179	254	12	251	(125	126)	2210	739	728	829	649	21	1023	50	5	38	38	8	116	.269	.367	.505	.872

Sean Doolittle

Pitches: L **Bats:** L **Pos:** RP-56   **Ht:** 6'2" **Wt:** 204 **Born:** 9/26/1986 **Age:** 35

Year	Team	Lg	G	GS	GF	IP	BFP	H	R	ER	HR	SH	SF	HB	TBB	IBB	SO	WP	W	L	Pct	Sv-Op	Hld	Vel	OPS	ERC	ERA
2012	Oak	AL	44	0	7	47.1	191	40	18	16	3	2	2	0	11	1	60	0	2	1	.667	1-2	18	94	.611	2.36	3.04
2013	Oak	AL	70	0	11	69.0	266	53	24	24	4	3	0	2	13	1	60	2	5	5	.500	2-7	26	94	.573	2.00	3.13
2014	Oak	AL	61	0	40	62.2	236	38	19	19	5	2	1	0	8	1	89	0	2	4	.333	22-26	5	94	.459	1.23	2.73
2015	Oak	AL	12	0	7	13.2	57	12	6	6	1	0	1	0	5	0	15	0	1	0	1.000	4-5	1	92	.651	3.10	3.95
2016	Oak	AL	44	0	13	39.0	155	33	14	14	6	4	0	0	8	2	45	1	2	3	.400	4-6	10	95	.705	2.79	3.23
2017	2 Tms		53	0	34	51.1	197	34	18	16	5	0	3	0	10	1	62	3	2	0	1.000	24-26	9	95	.517	1.62	2.81
2018	Was	NL	43	0	35	45.0	163	21	8	8	3	0	0	2	6	1	60	1	3	3	.500	25-26	1	93	.391	0.93	1.60
2019	Was	NL	63	0	55	60.0	260	63	27	27	11	1	0	2	15	2	66	0	6	5	.545	29-35	2	93	.772	4.32	4.05
2020	Was	NL	11	0	3	7.2	36	9	6	5	3	1	1	0	4	2	6	0	0	2	.000	0-0	3	91	1.005	7.28	5.87
2021	2 Tms		56	0	13	49.2	223	50	27	25	7	2	2	2	23	3	53	2	3	1	.750	1-5	5	93	.793	4.64	4.53
17	Oak	AL	23	0	6	21.1	79	12	8	8	3	0	1	0	2	0	31	1	1	0	1.000	3-4	8	94	.467	1.23	3.38
17	Was	AL	30	0	28	30.0	118	22	10	8	2	0	2	0	8	1	31	2	1	0	1.000	21-22	1	95	.551	1.99	2.40
21	Cin	NL	45	0	11	38.1	173	40	21	19	6	2	2	1	18	3	41	0	3	1	.750	1-5	4	93	.832	4.91	4.46
21	Sea	AL	11	0	2	11.1	50	10	6	6	1	0	0	1	5	0	12	2	0	0	-	0-0	1	94	.661	3.75	4.76
	Postseason		20	0	8	22.1	87	17	8	6	2	3	1	0	3	0	23	0	0	1	.000	3-6	5	95	.563	1.81	2.42
10 ML YEARS			457	0	218	445.1	1784	353	167	160	48	15	10	8	103	14	516	9	26	24	.520	112-138	80	94	.616	2.41	3.23

Ryan Dorow

Bats: R **Throws:** R **Pos:** 3B-3   **Ht:** 6'0" **Wt:** 195 **Born:** 8/21/1995 **Age:** 26

Year	Team	Lg	G	AB	H	2B	3B	HR	(Hm	Rd)	TB	R	RBI	RC	TBB	IBB	SO	HBP	SH	SF	SB	CS	GDP	Avg	OBP	Slg	OPS
2021	Frisco	AA	24	90	30	9	0	5	(-	-)	54	13	15	-	9	0	20	0	0	0	0	0	1	.333	.394	.600	.994
2021	RdRck	AAA	74	266	61	17	2	9	(-	-)	109	46	31	-	31	0	86	3	0	3	3	1	2	.229	.314	.410	.723
2021	Tex	AL	3	6	0	0	0	0	(0	0)	0	0	0	0	1	0	3	0	0	0	0	0	0	.000	.143	.000	.143

Camilo Doval

Pitches: R **Bats:** R **Pos:** RP-29   **Ht:** 6'2" **Wt:** 185 **Born:** 7/4/1997 **Age:** 24

Year	Team	Lg	G	GS	GF	IP	BFP	H	R	ER	HR	SH	SF	HB	TBB	IBB	SO	WP	W	L	Pct	Sv-Op	Hld	Vel	OPS	ERC	ERA
2021	Scrmto	AAA	28	0	6	30.2	144	28	18	17	3	1	0	3	24	0	44	3	3	0	1.000	1--	-	-	.764	5.46	4.99
2021	SF	NL	29	0	9	27.0	109	19	10	9	4	0	0	1	9	2	37	2	5	1	.833	3-6	5	99	.599	2.59	3.00

Hunter Dozier

Bats: R **Throws:** R **Pos:** RF-60;3B-57;1B-19;LF-14;DH-11;PH-2;PR-2   DOE-zhur   **Ht:** 6'4" **Wt:** 220 **Born:** 8/22/1991 **Age:** 30

Year	Team	Lg	G	AB	H	2B	3B	HR	(Hm	Rd)	TB	R	RBI	RC	TBB	IBB	SO	HBP	SH	SF	SB	CS	GDP	Avg	OBP	Slg	OPS
2016	KC	AL	8	19	4	1	0	0	(0	0)	5	4	1	1	2	0	8	0	0	0	0	0	0	.211	.286	.263	.549
2018	KC	AL	102	362	83	19	4	11	(5	6)	143	36	34	26	24	0	109	1	0	1	2	3	12	.229	.278	.395	.673
2019	KC	AL	139	523	146	29	10	26	(8	18)	273	75	84	91	55	2	148	3	0	5	2	2	9	.279	.348	.522	.870
2020	KC	AL	44	158	36	4	2	6	(4	2)	62	29	12	20	27	0	48	1	0	0	4	0	3	.228	.344	.392	.736
2021	KC	AL	144	487	105	27	6	16	(9	7)	192	55	54	52	43	0	154	7	0	6	5	4	12	.216	.285	.394	.680
5 ML YEARS			437	1549	374	80	22	59	(26	33)	675	199	185	190	151	2	467	12	0	12	13	9	36	.241	.311	.436	.747

Oliver Drake

Pitches: R **Bats:** R **Pos:** P   **Ht:** 6'4" **Wt:** 220 **Born:** 1/13/1987 **Age:** 35

Year	Team	Lg	G	GS	GF	IP	BFP	H	R	ER	HR	SH	SF	HB	TBB	IBB	SO	WP	W	L	Pct	Sv-Op	Hld	Vel	OPS	ERC	ERA
2015	Bal	AL	13	0	5	15.2	72	16	7	5	1	0	2	0	9	0	17	3	0	0	-	0-0	2	91	.708	4.50	2.87
2016	Bal	AL	14	0	5	18.0	74	11	11	8	2	1	0	0	7	0	21	1	1	0	1.000	0-1	0	90	.595	2.01	4.00
2017	2 Tms		64	0	15	56.0	251	63	31	29	6	3	0	0	25	2	62	3	3	5	.375	1-4	5	92	.808	4.96	4.66
2018	5 Tms		44	0	19	47.2	209	52	29	28	4	1	0	1	17	1	51	5	1	1	.500	0-1	1	92	.758	4.33	5.29
2019	TB	AL	50	0	9	56.0	219	36	20	20	9	0	0	1	19	1	70	1	5	2	.714	2-3	10	94	.612	2.43	3.21
2020	TB	AL	11	0	4	11.0	45	7	8	7	2	1	1	0	6	1	7	1	0	2	.000	2-4	1	91	.701	3.10	5.73
17	Bal	AL	3	0	1	3.1	18	6	3	3	0	0	0	0	3	0	3	1	0	0	-	0-0	0	92	1.033	10.76	8.10
17	Mil	NL	61	0	14	52.2	233	57	28	26	6	3	0	0	22	2	59	2	3	5	.375	1-4	5	92	.791	4.63	4.44
18	Mil	NL	11	0	3	12.2	58	14	9	9	0	1	0	0	8	1	15	2	1	0	1.000	0-1	0	91	.794	4.71	6.39
18	Cle	AL	4	0	0	4.1	22	7	6	6	0	0	0	1	1	0	4	0	0	0	-	0-0	0	93	.859	7.03	12.46
18	LAA	AL	8	0	6	8.2	40	15	5	5	2	0	0	0	1	0	8	0	0	1	.000	0-0	0	93	.990	8.66	5.19
18	Tor	AL	2	0	2	1.2	9	4	3	3	0	0	0	0	0	0	2	1	0	0	-	0-0	0	92	1.333	10.16	16.20
18	Min	AL	19	0	8	20.1	80	12	6	5	2	0	0	0	7	0	22	2	0	0	-	0-0	1	92	.511	1.77	2.21
	Postseason		3	0	0	4.0	17	4	2	2	0	0	0	0	1	0	5	0	0	0	-	0-0	0	94	.669	2.77	4.50
6 ML YEARS			196	0	57	204.1	870	185	106	97	24	6	3	2	83	5	228	14	10	10	.500	5-13	19	92	.715	3.68	4.27

Brandon Drury

Bats: R **Throws:** R **Pos:** PH-31;3B-7;LF-6;RF-6;1B-3;2B-2   DROO-ree   **Ht:** 6'2" **Wt:** 230 **Born:** 8/21/1992 **Age:** 29

Year	Team	Lg	G	AB	H	2B	3B	HR	(Hm	Rd)	TB	R	RBI	RC	TBB	IBB	SO	HBP	SH	SF	SB	CS	GDP	Avg	OBP	Slg	OPS
2021	Syrcse	AAA	53	203	51	13	0	9	(-	-)	91	28	32	-	18	0	45	1	0	2	0	0	5	.251	.313	.448	.761
2015	Ari	NL	20	56	12	3	0	2	(0	2)	21	3	8	4	2	0	8	1	0	0	0	0	5	.214	.254	.375	.629
2016	Ari	NL	134	461	130	31	1	16	(12	4)	211	59	53	59	31	2	100	3	0	4	1	1	14	.282	.329	.458	.786
2017	Ari	NL	135	445	119	37	2	13	(7	6)	199	41	63	62	28	1	103	5	0	5	1	1	9	.267	.317	.447	.764
2018	2 Tms	AL	26	77	13	4	0	1	(0	1)	20	5	10	7	7	0	20	2	0	0	0	0	5	.169	.256	.260	.516

Year Team	Lg	G	AB	H	2B	3B	HR	(Hm Rd)	TB	R	RBI	RC	TBB	IBB	SO	HBP	SH	SF	SB	CS	GDP	Avg	OBP	Slg	OPS
2019 Tor	AL	120	418	91	21	1	15	(9 6)	159	43	41	37	25	0	113	1	0	3	0	1	6	.218	.262	.380	.642
2020 Tor	AL	21	46	7	1	0	0	(0 0)	8	3	1	0	2	0	9	0	0	1	0	0	0	.152	.184	.174	.358
2021 NYM	NL	51	84	23	5	0	4	(4 0)	40	7	14	11	3	0	22	1	0	0	0	0	3	.274	.307	.476	.783
18 NYY	AL	18	51	9	2	0	1	(0 1)	14	2	7	5	5	0	12	1	0	0	0	0	4	.176	.263	.275	.538
18 Tor	AL	8	26	4	2	0	0	(0 0)	6	3	3	2	2	0	8	1	0	0	0	0	1	.154	.241	.231	.472
Postseason		3	6	1	0	0	1	(0 1)	4	1	3	1	0	0	2	0	0	0	0	0	2	.167	.167	.667	.833
7 ML YEARS		507	1587	395	102	4	51	(32 19)	658	161	190	180	98	3	375	13	0	10	2	3	42	.249	.296	.415	.711

Mauricio Dubon

Bats: R Throws: R Pos: CF-27;SS-21;2B-20;PH-15;3B-12;PR-5   Ht: 6'0" Wt: 173 Born: 7/19/1994 Age: 27

Year Team	Lg	G	AB	H	2B	3B	HR	(Hm Rd)	TB	R	RBI	RC	TBB	IBB	SO	HBP	SH	SF	SB	CS	GDP	Avg	OBP	Slg	OPS
2021 Scrmto	AAA	58	228	77	13	2	7	(- -)	115	40	29	-	28	0	35	4	0	2	9	3	7	.338	.416	.504	.920
2019 2 Tms	NL	30	106	29	5	0	4	(2 2)	46	12	9	11	5	0	20	0	0	0	3	1	3	.274	.306	.434	.740
2020 SF	NL	54	157	43	4	1	4	(3 1)	61	21	19	22	15	0	36	1	1	2	2	3	4	.274	.337	.389	.726
2021 SF	NL	74	175	42	9	0	5	(1 4)	66	20	22	12	9	2	41	1	0	2	2	1	5	.240	.278	.377	.655
19 Mil	NL	2	2	0	0	0	0	(0 0)	0	0	0	0	0	0	1	0	0	0	0	0	0	.000	.000	.000	.000
19 SF	NL	28	104	29	5	0	4	(2 2)	46	12	9	11	5	0	19	0	0	0	3	1	3	.279	.312	.442	.754
3 ML YEARS		158	438	114	18	1	13	(6 7)	173	53	50	45	29	2	97	2	1	4	7	5	12	.260	.307	.395	.702

Tyler Duffey

Pitches: R Bats: R Pos: RP-64   Ht: 6'3" Wt: 220 Born: 12/27/1990 Age: 31

Year Team	Lg	G	GS	GF	IP	BFP	H	R	ER	HR	SH	SF	HB	TBB	IBB	SO	WP	W	L	Pct	Sv-Op	Hld	Vel	OPS	ERC	ERA
2015 Min	AL	10	10	0	58.0	242	56	20	20	4	3	0	0	20	0	53	1	5	1	.833	0-0	0	90	.702	3.51	3.10
2016 Min	AL	26	26	0	133.0	596	167	103	95	25	2	2	6	32	3	114	9	9	12	.429	0-0	0	90	.876	5.66	6.43
2017 Min	AL	56	0	7	71.0	310	79	41	39	9	1	3	1	18	5	67	4	2	3	.400	1-3	12	92	.721	4.17	4.94
2018 Min	AL	19	1	4	25.0	107	26	22	20	6	2	2	1	4	0	19	2	2	2	.500	0-0	2	93	.830	4.29	7.20
2019 Min	AL	58	0	12	57.2	238	44	23	16	8	1	1	3	14	1	82	3	5	1	.833	0-2	15	94	.595	2.55	2.50
2020 Min	AL	22	0	1	24.0	92	13	6	5	2	0	0	1	6	0	31	0	1	1	.500	0-2	12	93	.488	1.43	1.88
2021 Min	AL	64	0	6	62.1	254	48	25	22	4	1	1	2	28	1	61	5	3	3	.500	3-5	22	93	.619	2.97	3.18
Postseason		4	0	1	3.2	20	6	5	5	1	0	1	1	3	0	6	1	0	0	-	0-1	0	93	1.167	13.41	12.27
7 ML YEARS		255	37	30	431.0	1839	433	240	217	58	8	9	14	122	10	427	24	27	23	.540	4-12	63	92	.734	3.94	4.53

Danny Duffy

Pitches: L Bats: L Pos: SP-12; RP-1   Ht: 6'3" Wt: 205 Born: 12/21/1988 Age: 33

Year Team	Lg	G	GS	GF	IP	BFP	H	R	ER	HR	SH	SF	HB	TBB	IBB	SO	WP	W	L	Pct	Sv-Op	Hld	Vel	OPS	ERC	ERA
2011 KC	AL	20	20	0	105.1	474	119	66	66	17	2	2	5	51	1	87	4	4	8	.333	0-0	0	93	.864	5.76	5.64
2012 KC	AL	6	6	0	27.2	121	26	13	12	2	0	0	0	18	1	28	0	2	2	.500	0-0	0	95	.771	4.58	3.90
2013 KC	AL	5	5	0	24.1	104	19	5	5	0	0	0	1	14	0	22	2	2	0	1.000	0-0	0	94	.608	3.02	1.85
2014 KC	AL	31	25	1	149.1	606	113	52	42	12	3	4	5	53	2	113	5	9	12	.429	0-0	1	93	.605	2.62	2.53
2015 KC	AL	30	24	1	136.2	588	137	64	62	15	3	5	9	53	0	102	11	7	8	.467	1-1	0	94	.746	4.44	4.08
2016 KC	AL	42	26	5	179.2	731	163	71	70	27	4	2	7	42	0	188	4	12	3	.800	0-0	0	95	.710	3.44	3.51
2017 KC	AL	24	24	0	146.1	609	143	67	62	13	6	2	4	41	0	130	2	9	10	.474	0-0	0	93	.709	3.55	3.81
2018 KC	AL	28	28	0	155.0	692	161	86	84	23	2	6	4	70	1	141	14	8	12	.400	0-0	0	93	.767	4.90	4.88
2019 KC	AL	23	23	0	130.2	555	125	69	63	21	0	3	8	46	0	115	4	7	6	.538	0-0	0	92	.760	4.35	4.34
2020 KC	AL	12	11	0	56.1	242	53	33	31	10	1	4	2	22	0	57	3	4	4	.500	0-0	1	92	.756	4.37	4.95
2021 KC	AL	13	12	0	61.0	252	52	19	17	6	0	0	2	22	1	65	3	4	3	.571	0-0	0	94	.650	3.10	2.51
Postseason		9	0	1	10.2	44	10	6	6	2	1	1	0	4	0	14	0	2	0	1.000	0-0	0	95	.878	4.35	5.06
11 ML YEARS		234	204	7	1172.1	4974	1111	545	514	144	21	28	45	432	6	1048	52	68	68	.500	1-1	5	93	.728	3.99	3.95

Matt Duffy

Bats: R Throws: R Pos: 3B-56;PH-25;2B-21;SS-5;LF-3;1B-2   Ht: 6'2" Wt: 190 Born: 1/15/1991 Age: 31

Year Team	Lg	G	AB	H	2B	3B	HR	(Hm Rd)	TB	R	RBI	RC	TBB	IBB	SO	HBP	SH	SF	SB	CS	GDP	Avg	OBP	Slg	OPS
2014 SF	NL	34	60	16	2	0	0	(0 0)	18	5	8	8	1	0	14	2	1	0	0	1	1	.267	.302	.300	.602
2015 SF	NL	149	573	169	28	6	12	(7 5)	245	77	77	84	30	0	96	5	2	2	12	0	22	.295	.334	.428	.762
2016 2 Tms		91	333	86	14	2	5	(1 4)	119	41	28	30	23	0	53	4	2	4	8	5	13	.258	.310	.357	.668
2018 TB	AL	132	503	148	22	1	4	(0 4)	184	59	44	72	47	1	93	7	1	2	12	6	12	.294	.361	.366	.727
2019 TB	AL	46	147	37	8	0	1	(0 1)	48	12	12	19	19	0	29	2	0	1	0	1	4	.252	.343	.327	.670
2021 ChC	NL	97	289	83	12	0	5	(2 3)	110	45	30	40	25	0	63	7	0	1	8	1	16	.287	.357	.381	.738
16 SF	NL	70	257	65	11	2	4	(1 3)	92	32	21	23	20	0	40	4	2	3	8	4	9	.253	.313	.358	.671
16 TB	AL	21	76	21	3	0	1	(0 1)	27	9	7	7	3	0	13	0	0	1	0	1	4	.276	.300	.355	.655
Postseason		11	11	4	0	0	0	(0 0)	4	4	0	0	0	0	2	0	1	0	0	0	0	.364	.364	.364	.727
6 ML YEARS		549	1905	539	86	9	27	(10 17)	724	239	199	253	145	1	348	27	6	10	40	14	68	.283	.341	.380	.721

Steven Duggar

Bats: L Throws: R Pos: CF-93;PH-28;LF-4;PR-4;RF-1   Ht: 6'1" Wt: 187 Born: 11/4/1993 Age: 28

Year Team	Lg	G	AB	H	2B	3B	HR	(Hm Rd)	TB	R	RBI	RC	TBB	IBB	SO	HBP	SH	SF	SB	CS	GDP	Avg	OBP	Slg	OPS
2021 Scrmto	AAA	15	61	17	2	1	1	(- -)	24	13	9	-	9	1	22	0	0	0	8	0	0	.279	.371	.393	.765
2018 SF	NL	41	141	36	11	1	2	(1 1)	55	20	17	19	10	1	44	0	0	1	5	1	0	.255	.303	.390	.693

Year	Team	Lg	G	AB	H	2B	3B	HR	(Hm	Rd)	TB	R	RBI	RC	TBB	IBB	SO	HBP	SH	SF	SB	CS	GDP	Avg	OBP	Slg	OPS
2019	SF	NL	73	261	61	12	2	4	(1	3)	89	26	28	29	16	0	78	1	0	3	1	4	1	.234	.278	.341	.619
2020	SF	NL	21	34	6	2	0	0	(0	0)	8	3	3	1	1	0	11	1	0	0	1	0	1	.176	.222	.235	.458
2021	SF	NL	107	268	69	14	5	8	(5	3)	117	45	35	37	27	3	88	2	0	0	7	0	4	.257	.330	.437	.767
4 ML YEARS			242	704	172	39	8	14	(7	7)	269	94	83	86	54	4	221	4	0	4	14	5	6	.244	.300	.382	.682

Robert Dugger

Pitches: R **Bats:** R **Pos:** RP-8; SP-4   **Ht:** 6'0" **Wt:** 198 **Born:** 7/3/1995 **Age:** 26

			HOW MUCH PITCHED					WHAT HE GAVE UP									THE RESULTS								
Year	Team	Lg	G	GS	GF	IP	BFP	H	R	ER	HR	SH	SF	HB	TBB	IBB	SO	WP	W	L	Pct	Sv-Op	Hld	Vel	OPS	ERC	ERA
2021	Tacom	AAA	14	13	0	63.1	279	71	48	47	12	0	2	1	24	0	58	0	3	5	.375	0--	-	-	.848	5.44	6.68
2019	Mia	NL	7	7	0	34.1	156	33	26	22	6	1	3	5	17	1	25	2	0	4	.000	0-0	0	90	.824	5.29	5.77
2020	Mia	NL	4	1	2	10.2	56	21	16	15	5	0	0	3	3	0	4	1	0	0	-	0-0	0	92	1.315	12.95	12.66
2021	Sea	AL	12	4	5	25.2	121	34	24	21	4	0	2	1	12	0	19	1	0	2	.000	0-0	0	91	.925	6.94	7.36
3 ML YEARS			23	12	7	70.2	333	88	66	58	15	1	5	6	32	1	48	4	0	6	.000	0-0	0	91	.950	6.94	7.39

Justin Dunn

Pitches: R **Bats:** R **Pos:** SP-11   **Ht:** 6'2" **Wt:** 185 **Born:** 9/22/1995 **Age:** 26

			HOW MUCH PITCHED					WHAT HE GAVE UP									THE RESULTS								
Year	Team	Lg	G	GS	GF	IP	BFP	H	R	ER	HR	SH	SF	HB	TBB	IBB	SO	WP	W	L	Pct	Sv-Op	Hld	Vel	OPS	ERC	ERA
2019	Sea	AL	4	4	0	6.2	30	2	2	2	0	2	0	0	9	0	5	0	0	0	-	0-0	0	92	.472	3.04	2.70
2020	Sea	AL	10	10	0	45.2	198	31	23	22	10	0	1	2	31	1	38	0	4	1	.800	0-0	0	91	.732	4.34	4.34
2021	Sea	AL	11	11	0	50.1	218	37	21	21	6	0	1	4	29	0	49	1	1	3	.250	0-0	0	94	.653	3.72	3.75
3 ML YEARS			25	25	0	102.2	446	70	46	45	16	0	4	6	69	1	92	1	5	4	.556	0-0	0	92	.679	3.96	3.94

Dane Dunning

Pitches: R **Bats:** R **Pos:** SP-25; RP-2   **Ht:** 6'4" **Wt:** 225 **Born:** 12/20/1994 **Age:** 27

			HOW MUCH PITCHED					WHAT HE GAVE UP									THE RESULTS								
Year	Team	Lg	G	GS	GF	IP	BFP	H	R	ER	HR	SH	SF	HB	TBB	IBB	SO	WP	W	L	Pct	Sv-Op	Hld	Vel	OPS	ERC	ERA
2020	CWS	AL	7	7	0	34.0	142	25	17	15	4	0	0	2	13	0	35	5	2	0	1.000	0-0	0	92	.597	2.88	3.97
2021	Tex	AL	27	25	0	117.2	511	126	61	59	13	1	1	7	43	0	114	8	5	10	.333	0-0	0	90	.772	4.72	4.51
Postseason			1	1	0	0.2	4	2	0	0	0	0	0	0	0	0	0	0	0	0	-	0-0	0	92	1.000	14.52	0.00
2 ML YEARS			34	32	0	151.2	653	151	78	74	17	1	1	9	56	0	149	13	7	10	.412	0-0	0	91	.734	4.28	4.39

Jon Duplantier

Pitches: R **Bats:** L **Pos:** SP-4   **Ht:** 6'4" **Wt:** 229 **Born:** 7/11/1994 **Age:** 27

			HOW MUCH PITCHED					WHAT HE GAVE UP									THE RESULTS								
Year	Team	Lg	G	GS	GF	IP	BFP	H	R	ER	HR	SH	SF	HB	TBB	IBB	SO	WP	W	L	Pct	Sv-Op	Hld	Vel	OPS	ERC	ERA
2019	Ari	NL	15	3	5	36.2	163	39	18	18	2	1	1	5	18	1	34	2	1	1	.500	1-1	0	92	.774	5.11	4.42
2021	Ari	NL	4	4	0	13.0	70	19	19	19	5	1	0	2	8	0	12	0	0	3	.000	0-0	0	91	1.047	10.64	13.15
2 ML YEARS			19	7	5	49.2	233	58	37	37	7	2	1	7	26	1	46	2	1	4	.200	1-1	0	92	.856	6.50	6.70

Jarren Duran

Bats: L **Throws:** R **Pos:** CF-28;PH-4;LF-1;PR-1   **Ht:** 6'2" **Wt:** 212 **Born:** 9/5/1996 **Age:** 25

			BATTING																	RUNNING			AVERAGES			
Year	Team	Lg	G	AB	H	2B	3B	HR	(Hm	Rd)	TB	R	RBI	RC	TBB	IBB	SO	HBP	SH	SF	SB	CS	GDP	Avg	OBP	Slg	OPS
2021	Wrcstr	AAA	55	222	58	11	1	16	(-	-)	119	42	35	-	27	0	60	6	0	1	15	3	1	.261	.355	.536	.892
2021	Bos	AL	33	107	23	3	2	2	(0	2)	36	17	10	9	4	0	40	0	0	1	2	1	1	.215	.241	.336	.578

Adam Duvall

Bats: R **Throws:** R **Pos:** RF-78;LF-51;CF-30;PH-11   **Ht:** 6'1" **Wt:** 215 **Born:** 9/4/1988 **Age:** 33

			BATTING																	RUNNING			AVERAGES			
Year	Team	Lg	G	AB	H	2B	3B	HR	(Hm	Rd)	TB	R	RBI	RC	TBB	IBB	SO	HBP	SH	SF	SB	CS	GDP	Avg	OBP	Slg	OPS
2014	SF	NL	28	73	14	2	0	3	(2	1)	25	8	5	4	3	0	20	1	0	0	0	0	0	.192	.234	.342	.576
2015	Cin	NL	27	64	14	2	0	5	(3	2)	31	6	9	9	6	1	26	2	0	0	0	0	0	.219	.306	.484	.790
2016	Cin	NL	150	552	133	31	6	33	(16	17)	275	85	103	80	41	1	164	6	0	8	6	5	7	.241	.297	.498	.795
2017	Cin	NL	157	587	146	37	3	31	(12	19)	282	78	99	75	39	1	170	10	0	11	5	3	11	.249	.301	.480	.782
2018	2 Tms	NL	138	384	75	20	0	15	(8	7)	140	48	61	37	37	3	117	5	0	1	2	2	9	.195	.274	.365	.639
2019	Atl	NL	41	120	32	4	1	10	(4	6)	68	17	19	19	7	0	39	2	0	1	0	0	0	.267	.315	.567	.882
2020	Atl	NL	57	190	45	8	0	16	(7	9)	101	34	33	24	15	0	54	3	0	1	0	0	2	.237	.301	.532	.833
2021	2 Tms	NL	146	513	117	17	2	38	(16	22)	252	67	113	89	35	1	174	4	0	3	5	0	7	.228	.281	.491	.772
18	Cin	NL	105	331	68	19	0	15	(8	7)	132	40	61	37	34	3	100	4	0	1	2	2	8	.205	.286	.399	.685
18	Atl	NL	33	53	7	1	0	0	(0	0)	8	8	0	0	3	0	17	1	0	0	0	0	1	.132	.193	.151	.344
21	Mia	NL	91	314	72	10	1	22	(8	14)	150	41	68	54	21	0	105	1	0	3	5	0	4	.229	.277	.478	.755
21	Atl	NL	55	199	45	7	1	16	(8	8)	102	26	45	35	14	1	69	3	0	0	0	0	3	.226	.287	.513	.800
Postseason			11	31	5	1	0	2	(2	0)	12	3	8	3	2	1	16	0	0	0	0	0	0	.161	.212	.387	.599
8 ML YEARS			744	2483	576	121	12	151	(68	83)	1174	343	442	337	183	7	764	33	0	25	18	10	36	.232	.291	.473	.764

Jarrod Dyson

Bats: L **Throws:** R **Pos:** CF-38;RF-34;PR-28;LF-20;DH-5;PH-4   juh-ROD   **Ht:** 5'9" **Wt:** 165 **Born:** 8/15/1984 **Age:** 37

								BATTING													RUNNING			AVERAGES			
Year Team	Lg	G	AB	H	2B	3B	HR	(Hm	Rd)	TB	R	RBI	RC	TBB	IBB	SO	HBP	SH	SF	SB	CS	GDP	Avg	OBP	Slg	OPS
2010 KC	AL	18	57	12	4	2	1	(1	0)	23	11	5	9	6	0	16	0	2	0	9	1	2	.211	.286	.404	.689
2011 KC	AL	26	44	9	1	0	0	(0	0)	10	8	3	7	7	0	14	0	1	1	11	1	0	.205	.308	.227	.535
2012 KC	AL	102	292	76	8	5	0	(0	0)	94	52	9	36	30	1	56	1	4	3	30	5	5	.260	.328	.322	.650
2013 KC	AL	87	213	55	9	4	2	(2	0)	78	30	17	28	21	1	45	1	3	1	34	6	4	.258	.326	.366	.692
2014 KC	AL	120	260	70	4	4	1	(1	0)	85	33	24	32	22	0	52	0	6	2	36	7	5	.269	.324	.327	.651
2015 KC	AL	90	200	50	8	6	2	(2	0)	76	31	18	25	14	0	37	4	6	1	26	3	3	.250	.311	.380	.691
2016 KC	AL	107	299	83	14	8	1	(1	0)	116	46	25	45	26	2	39	3	8	1	30	7	4	.278	.340	.388	.728
2017 Sea	AL	111	346	87	13	3	5	(2	3)	121	56	30	40	28	2	55	10	4	2	28	7	3	.251	.324	.350	.674
2018 Ari	NL	67	206	39	4	2	2	(0	2)	53	29	12	19	27	2	34	0	3	1	16	3	3	.189	.282	.257	.539
2019 Ari	NL	130	400	92	11	2	7	(1	6)	128	65	27	52	47	0	86	2	1	2	30	4	1	.230	.313	.320	.633
2020 2 Tms		32	61	11	0	0	0	(0	0)	11	9	5	4	4	0	11	0	1	0	6	0	0	.180	.231	.180	.411
2021 2 Tms	AL	102	135	28	7	2	0	(0	0)	39	17	10	10	10	0	33	0	3	1	10	5	1	.207	.260	.289	.549
20 Pit	NL	21	51	8	0	0	0	(0	0)	8	6	5	4	4	0	10	0	0	0	4	0	0	.157	.218	.157	.375
20 CWS		11	10	3	0	0	0	(0	0)	3	3	0	1	0	0	1	0	1	0	2	0	0	.300	.300	.300	.600
21 KC	AL	77	122	27	7	2	0	(0	0)	38	13	10	10	6	0	28	0	3	1	8	3	1	.221	.256	.311	.567
21 Tor	AL	25	13	1	0	0	0	(0	0)	1	4	0	0	4	0	5	0	0	0	2	2	0	.077	.294	.077	.371
Postseason		21	21	2	0	0	0	(0	0)	2	3	0	0	2	0	7	0	1	0	4	2	1	.095	.174	.095	.269
12 ML YEARS		992	2513	612	83	38	21	(10	11)	834	387	185	308	242	8	478	21	42	15	266	49	31	.244	.314	.332	.645

Adam Eaton

Bats: L **Throws:** L **Pos:** RF-79;PH-9;LF-2;1B-1;PR-1   **Ht:** 5'9" **Wt:** 180 **Born:** 12/6/1988 **Age:** 33

								BATTING													RUNNING			AVERAGES			
Year Team	Lg	G	AB	H	2B	3B	HR	(Hm	Rd)	TB	R	RBI	RC	TBB	IBB	SO	HBP	SH	SF	SB	CS	GDP	Avg	OBP	Slg	OPS
2012 Ari	NL	22	85	22	3	2	2	(1	1)	35	19	5	13	14	0	15	3	1	0	2	3	0	.259	.382	.412	.794
2013 Ari	NL	66	250	63	10	4	3	(2	1)	90	40	22	27	17	0	44	6	3	1	5	2	4	.252	.314	.360	.674
2014 CWS	AL	123	486	146	26	10	1	(1	0)	195	76	35	77	43	0	83	5	2	2	15	9	4	.300	.362	.401	.763
2015 CWS	AL	153	610	175	28	9	14	(6	8)	263	98	56	96	58	2	131	14	5	2	18	8	5	.287	.361	.431	.792
2016 CWS	AL	157	619	176	29	9	14	(7	7)	265	91	59	92	63	2	115	14	7	3	14	5	6	.284	.362	.428	.790
2017 Was	NL	23	91	27	7	1	2	(1	1)	42	24	13	19	14	0	18	1	0	1	3	1	0	.297	.393	.462	.854
2018 Was	NL	95	319	96	18	1	5	(1	4)	131	55	33	58	38	0	64	11	2	0	9	1	2	.301	.394	.411	.805
2019 Was	NL	151	566	158	25	7	15	(8	7)	242	103	49	88	65	0	106	13	9	3	15	3	8	.279	.365	.428	.792
2020 Was	NL	41	159	36	11	4	0	(4	0)	61	22	17	22	12	1	32	1	4	0	3	0	4	.226	.285	.384	.669
2021 2 Tms	AL	84	254	51	10	2	6	(3	3)	83	38	30	30	22	0	71	7	4	1	3	0	6	.201	.282	.327	.608
21 CWS	AL	58	189	38	8	2	5	(3	2)	65	33	28	29	20	0	55	6	4	0	2	0	5	.201	.298	.344	.642
21 LAA	AL	26	65	13	2	0	1	(0	1)	18	5	2	1	2	0	16	1	0	1	1	0	1	.200	.232	.277	.509
Postseason		17	61	15	2	1	2	(0	2)	25	11	10	12	10	0	9	1	3	0	1	0	1	.246	.361	.410	.771
10 ML YEARS		915	3439	950	167	46	66	(34	32)	1407	566	319	522	346	5	679	75	37	13	87	32	39	.276	.354	.409	.763

Tommy Edman

Bats: B **Throws:** R **Pos:** 2B-130;RF-41;SS-4;PH-4   **Ht:** 5'10" **Wt:** 180 **Born:** 5/9/1995 **Age:** 27

								BATTING													RUNNING			AVERAGES			
Year Team	Lg	G	AB	H	2B	3B	HR	(Hm	Rd)	TB	R	RBI	RC	TBB	IBB	SO	HBP	SH	SF	SB	CS	GDP	Avg	OBP	Slg	OPS
2019 StL	NL	92	326	99	17	7	11	(4	7)	163	59	36	52	16	0	61	7	0	0	15	1	3	.304	.350	.500	.850
2020 StL	NL	55	204	51	7	1	5	(3	2)	75	29	26	26	16	0	48	5	0	2	2	4	5	.250	.317	.368	.685
2021 StL	NL	159	641	168	41	3	11	(2	9)	248	91	56	81	38	1	95	6	2	4	30	5	4	.262	.308	.387	.695
Postseason		12	47	9	3	1	0	(0	0)	14	5	3	4	3	0	10	0	0	0	0	0	1	.191	.240	.298	.538
3 ML YEARS		306	1171	318	65	11	27	(9	18)	486	179	118	159	70	1	204	18	2	6	47	10	12	.272	.321	.415	.736

Carl Edwards Jr.

Pitches: R **Bats:** R **Pos:** RP-7   **Ht:** 6'3" **Wt:** 170 **Born:** 9/3/1991 **Age:** 30

		HOW MUCH PITCHED					WHAT HE GAVE UP											THE RESULTS							
Year Team	Lg	G	GS	GF	IP	BFP	H	R	ER	HR	SH	SF	HB	TBB	IBB	SO	WP	W	L	Pct	Sv-Op	Hld	Vel	OPS	ERC	ERA
2021 Buffalo	AAA	7	0	2	7.0	26	5	3	3	2	0	0	0	8	0	8	0	1	0	1.000	0- -	-	-	.692	2.03	3.86
2021 Charllt	AAA	9	0	6	8.0	30	4	2	2	0	0	0	0	2	0	12	1	0	0		3- -	-	-	.379	0.94	2.25
2015 ChC	NL	5	0	3	4.2	19	3	3	2	0	0	0	0	3	0	4	0	0	0		0-0	0	93	.566	2.50	3.86
2016 ChC	NL	36	0	10	36.0	138	15	15	15	4	0	2	0	14	1	52	5	0	1	.000	2-3	6	95	.456	1.33	3.75
2017 ChC	NL	73	0	8	66.1	262	29	22	22	6	1	1	4	38	2	94	4	5	4	.556	0-4	25	95	.503	1.99	2.98
2018 ChC	NL	58	0	2	52.0	222	36	17	15	2	1	0	0	32	1	67	4	3	2	.600	0-2	23	95	.583	2.75	2.60
2019 2 Tms	NL	22	0	4	17.0	78	12	17	16	3	0	1	1	13	0	19	4	1	1	.500	0-2	4	94	.683	4.48	8.47
2020 Sea	AL	5	0	1	4.2	17	2	1	1	0	0	0	0	1	0	6	0	0	0		1-1	1	93	.489	0.71	1.93
2021 2 Tms		7	0	1	5.2	31	11	7	7	1	0	1	0	3	0	6	2	0	0		0-1	0	94	1.303	14.71	11.12
19 ChC	NL	20	0	3	15.1	64	8	11	10	3	0	1	1	9	0	17	2	1	1	.500	0-2	4	94	.621	3.05	5.87
19 SD	NL	2	0	1	1.2	14	4	6	6	0	0	0	0	4	0	2	2	0	0		0-0	0	94	.971	20.14	32.40
21 Atl	NL	1	0	0	0.1	5	3	3	3	1	0	0	0	1	0	1	1	0	0		0-0	0	93	2.550	136.7	81.00
21 Tor	AL	6	0	1	5.1	26	8	4	4	2	0	1	0	2	0	5	1	0	0		0-1	0	94	1.080	9.14	6.75
Postseason		15	0	0	11.0	48	7	8	8	1	1	0	0	10	0	12	2	1	2	.333	0-1	5	95	.632	4.04	6.55
7 ML YEARS		206	0	29	186.1	767	108	82	78	18	2	5	5	104	4	248	19	9	8	.529	3-13	59	95	.570	2.49	3.77

Scott Effross

Pitches: R **Bats:** R **Pos:** RP-14   **Ht:** 6'2" **Wt:** 202 **Born:** 12/28/1993 **Age:** 28

		HOW MUCH PITCHED					WHAT HE GAVE UP									THE RESULTS						
Year	Team	Lg	G	GS	GF	IP	BFP	H	R	ER	HR	SH	SF	HB	TBB	IBB	SO	WP	W	L	Pct	Sv-Op	Hld	Vel	OPS	ERC	ERA
2021	Tenn	AA	8	0	1	18.2	76	16	9	6	2	0	1	1	5	0	20	0	3	0	1.000	0--	-	-	.652	3.09	2.89
2021	Iowa	AAA	23	2	5	42.0	163	28	18	17	6	1	1	5	10	0	46	0	4	2	.667	2--	-	-	.608	2.51	3.64
2021	ChC	NL	14	0	2	14.2	58	13	6	6	2	0	2	3	1	0	18	1	2	1	.667	0-1	3	91	.716	3.33	3.68

Zach Eflin

Pitches: R **Bats:** R **Pos:** SP-18   **Ht:** 6'6" **Wt:** 220 **Born:** 4/8/1994 **Age:** 28

		HOW MUCH PITCHED					WHAT HE GAVE UP									THE RESULTS						
Year	Team	Lg	G	GS	GF	IP	BFP	H	R	ER	HR	SH	SF	HB	TBB	IBB	SO	WP	W	L	Pct	Sv-Op	Hld	Vel	OPS	ERC	ERA
2016	Phi	NL	11	11	0	63.1	272	67	42	39	12	1	4	1	17	1	31	1	3	5	.375	0-0	0	92	.828	4.49	5.54
2017	Phi	NL	11	11	0	64.1	280	79	45	44	16	2	5	5	12	0	35	2	1	5	.167	0-0	0	93	.896	6.00	6.16
2018	Phi	NL	24	24	0	128.0	548	130	69	62	16	5	4	3	37	4	123	4	11	8	.579	0-0	0	94	.746	3.90	4.36
2019	Phi	NL	32	28	3	163.1	705	172	88	75	28	6	3	6	48	5	129	1	10	13	.435	0-0	0	94	.775	4.53	4.13
2020	Phi	NL	11	10	0	59.0	245	60	28	26	8	1	0	1	15	0	70	1	4	2	.667	0-0	0	94	.759	3.96	3.97
2021	Phi	NL	18	18	0	105.2	442	116	52	49	15	1	1	3	16	2	99	2	4	7	.364	0-0	0	93	.767	4.01	4.17
	6 ML YEARS		107	102	3	583.2	2492	624	324	295	95	16	17	19	145	12	487	11	33	40	.452	0-0	0	93	.785	4.39	4.55

Jerad Eickhoff

EYE-koff

Pitches: R **Bats:** R **Pos:** SP-4; RP-1   **Ht:** 6'4" **Wt:** 246 **Born:** 7/2/1990 **Age:** 31

		HOW MUCH PITCHED					WHAT HE GAVE UP									THE RESULTS						
Year	Team	Lg	G	GS	GF	IP	BFP	H	R	ER	HR	SH	SF	HB	TBB	IBB	SO	WP	W	L	Pct	Sv-Op	Hld	Vel	OPS	ERC	ERA
2021	Syrcse	AAA	16	16	0	79.2	330	80	47	43	17	0	0	2	20	0	79	1	9	2	.818	0--	-	-	.812	4.44	4.86
2015	Phi	NL	8	8	0	51.0	203	40	16	15	5	0	1	0	13	0	49	1	3	3	.500	0-0	0	91	.621	2.40	2.65
2016	Phi	NL	33	33	0	197.1	811	187	88	80	30	6	10	8	42	2	167	6	11	14	.440	0-0	0	91	.740	3.56	3.65
2017	Phi	NL	24	24	0	128.0	576	142	74	67	16	3	9	5	53	4	118	6	4	8	.333	0-0	0	90	.794	5.00	4.71
2018	Phi	NL	3	1	1	5.1	26	10	4	4	1	0	0	0	0	0	11	0	0	1	.000	0-0	0	91	1.038	8.28	6.75
2019	Phi	NL	12	10	1	58.1	245	58	37	37	18	3	0	2	18	0	51	0	3	4	.429	1-1	0	89	.885	5.33	5.71
2021	NYM	NL	5	4	0	19.2	104	30	24	19	9	0	1	3	10	2	13	0	0	2	.000	0-0	0	90	1.136	11.11	8.69
	6 ML YEARS		85	80	2	459.2	1965	467	243	222	79	12	21	18	136	8	409	13	21	32	.396	1-1	0	91	.786	4.37	4.35

Seth Elledge

Pitches: R **Bats:** R **Pos:** RP-11   **Ht:** 6'3" **Wt:** 240 **Born:** 5/20/1996 **Age:** 26

		HOW MUCH PITCHED					WHAT HE GAVE UP									THE RESULTS						
Year	Team	Lg	G	GS	GF	IP	BFP	H	R	ER	HR	SH	SF	HB	TBB	IBB	SO	WP	W	L	Pct	Sv-Op	Hld	Vel	OPS	ERC	ERA
2021	Memp	AAA	30	0	8	35.2	171	44	28	26	3	0	0	2	22	1	46	4	2	2	.500	2--	-	-	.847	6.40	6.56
2020	StL	NL	12	0	5	11.2	52	11	6	6	2	0	0	1	8	0	14	2	1	0	1.000	0-0	0	93	.964	6.03	4.63
2021	StL	NL	11	0	2	11.2	52	13	6	6	1	0	1	1	7	0	11	1	0	0	-	0-0	0	94	.869	6.12	4.63
	2 ML YEARS		23	0	7	23.1	104	24	12	12	3	0	1	2	15	0	25	3	1	0	1.000	0-0	0	94	.916	6.08	4.63

Chris Ellis

Pitches: R **Bats:** L **Pos:** SP-6; RP-1   **Ht:** 6'5" **Wt:** 205 **Born:** 9/22/1992 **Age:** 29

		HOW MUCH PITCHED					WHAT HE GAVE UP									THE RESULTS						
Year	Team	Lg	G	GS	GF	IP	BFP	H	R	ER	HR	SH	SF	HB	TBB	IBB	SO	WP	W	L	Pct	Sv-Op	Hld	Vel	OPS	ERC	ERA
2021	Drham	AAA	15	13	0	57.0	256	61	45	40	14	0	3	1	28	0	58	5	1	5	.167	0--	-	-	.896	6.02	6.32
2019	KC	AL	1	0	1	1.0	5	1	0	0	0	0	0	0	1	0	0	0	0	0	-	0-0	0	93	.650	5.48	0.00
2021	2 Tms	AL	7	6	1	29.1	121	21	7	7	3	0	0	2	14	0	23	3	1	0	1.000	0-0	0	94	.630	3.17	2.15
21	TB	AL	1	0	1	4.0	16	3	0	0	0	0	0	0	1	0	7	1	1	0	1.000	0-0	0	94	.517	1.65	0.00
21	Bal	AL	6	6	0	25.1	105	18	7	7	3	0	0	2	13	0	16	2	0	0	-	0-0	0	94	.648	3.44	2.49
	2 ML YEARS		8	6	2	30.1	126	22	7	7	3	0	0	2	15	0	23	3	1	0	1.000	0-0	0	94	.631	3.24	2.08

Drew Ellis

Bats: R **Throws:** R **Pos:** 3B-17;PH-7;2B-4;PR-1   **Ht:** 6'3" **Wt:** 205 **Born:** 12/1/1995 **Age:** 26

				BATTING																	RUNNING			AVERAGES			
Year	Team	Lg	G	AB	H	2B	3B	HR	(Hm Rd)	TB	R	RBI	RC	TBB	IBB	SO	HBP	SH	SF	SB	CS	GDP	Avg	OBP	Slg	OPS
2021	Reno	AAA	80	291	86	29	2	20	(- -)	179	69	73	-	46	0	84	10	0	6	1	0	4	.296	.402	.615	1.017
2021	Ari	NL	28	69	9	2	0	1	(1 0)	14	10	5	5	10	1	27	4	0	0	0	0	1	.130	.277	.203	.480

Kent Emanuel

Pitches: L **Bats:** L **Pos:** RP-10   **Ht:** 6'4" **Wt:** 225 **Born:** 6/4/1992 **Age:** 30

		HOW MUCH PITCHED					WHAT HE GAVE UP									THE RESULTS						
Year	Team	Lg	G	GS	GF	IP	BFP	H	R	ER	HR	SH	SF	HB	TBB	IBB	SO	WP	W	L	Pct	Sv-Op	Hld	Vel	OPS	ERC	ERA
2021	Hou	AL	10	0	5	17.2	68	12	5	5	4	0	0	1	4	0	13	0	1	0	1.000	0-0	1	92	.631	2.75	2.55

Adam Engel

Bats: R **Throws:** R **Pos:** CF-26;RF-10;LF-4;PH-3;DH-1   **Ht:** 6'2" **Wt:** 215 **Born:** 12/9/1991 **Age:** 30

Year	Team	Lg	G	AB	H	2B	3B	HR	(Hm	Rd)	TB	R	RBI	RC	TBB	IBB	SO	HBP	SH	SF	SB	CS	GDP	Avg	OBP	Slg	OPS
2021	Charllt	AAA	15	54	12	2	0	2	(-	-)	20	7	5	-	3	0	16	2	0	1	5	0	1	.222	.283	.370	.654
2017	CWS	AL	97	301	50	11	3	6	(4	2)	85	34	21	16	19	0	117	8	8	0	8	1	1	.166	.235	.282	.517
2018	CWS	AL	143	429	101	17	4	6	(4	2)	144	49	29	31	18	0	129	8	7	1	16	8	1	.235	.279	.336	.614
2019	CWS	AL	89	227	55	10	2	6	(3	3)	87	26	26	26	14	0	78	6	1	0	3	3	5	.242	.304	.383	.687
2020	CWS	AL	36	88	26	5	1	3	(2	1)	42	11	12	14	3	0	19	2	0	0	1	0	1	.295	.333	.477	.811
2021	CWS	AL	39	123	31	9	0	7	(3	4)	61	21	18	21	11	0	31	5	0	1	7	1	4	.252	.336	.496	.832
	Postseason		3	12	3	1	0	1	(0	1)	7	1	1	0	0	0	5	0	0	0	0	0	0	.250	.250	.583	.833
	5 ML YEARS		404	1168	263	52	10	28	(16	12)	419	141	106	108	65	0	374	29	16	2	35	13	12	.225	.282	.359	.641

Dietrich Enns

Pitches: L **Bats:** L **Pos:** RP-9   **Ht:** 6'1" **Wt:** 210 **Born:** 5/16/1991 **Age:** 31

			HOW MUCH PITCHED					WHAT HE GAVE UP									THE RESULTS							
Year	Team	Lg	G	GS	GF	IP	BFP	H	R	ER	HR	SH	SF	HB	TBB	IBB	SO	WP	W	L	Pct	Sv-Op	Hld	Vel	OPS	ERC	ERA
2021	Drham	AAA	17	11	1	67.2	263	42	20	19	7	0	1	1	18	0	84	3	7	2	.778	0- -	-		.541	1.74	2.53
2017	Min	AL	2	1	0	4.0	21	7	4	3	2	0	0	0	1	0	2	0	0	0	-	0-0	-	90	1.081	10.81	6.75
2021	TB	AL	9	0	3	22.1	88	17	8	7	1	0	0	0	6	0	25	0	2	0	1.000	2-2	0	94	.566	2.05	2.82
	2 ML YEARS		11	1	3	26.1	109	24	12	10	3	0	0	0	7	0	27	0	2	0	1.000	2-2	0	93	.667	3.14	3.42

Nathan Eovaldi

Pitches: R **Bats:** R **Pos:** SP-32   ee-VAUL-dee   **Ht:** 6'2" **Wt:** 217 **Born:** 2/13/1990 **Age:** 32

			HOW MUCH PITCHED					WHAT HE GAVE UP									THE RESULTS							
Year	Team	Lg	G	GS	GF	IP	BFP	H	R	ER	HR	SH	SF	HB	TBB	IBB	SO	WP	W	L	Pct	Sv-Op	Hld	Vel	OPS	ERC	ERA
2011	LAD	NL	10	6	1	34.2	146	28	14	14	2	0	2	2	20	0	23	0	1	2	.333	0-0	1	94	.667	3.75	3.63
2012	2 Tms	NL	22	22	0	119.1	526	133	59	57	10	1	6	3	47	3	78	1	4	13	.235	0-0	0	94	.771	4.67	4.30
2013	Mia	NL	18	18	0	106.1	451	100	44	40	7	6	1	1	40	3	78	3	4	6	.400	0-0	0	96	.681	3.41	3.39
2014	Mia	NL	33	33	0	199.2	854	223	107	97	14	9	5	7	43	5	142	6	6	14	.300	0-0	0	96	.732	3.89	4.37
2015	NYY	AL	27	27	0	154.1	673	175	72	72	10	3	3	3	49	0	121	8	14	3	.824	0-0	0	97	.716	4.34	4.20
2016	NYY	AL	24	21	2	124.2	525	123	66	66	23	1	1	1	40	2	97	5	9	8	.529	0-0	0	97	.778	4.30	4.76
2018	2 Tms	AL	22	21	0	111.0	455	105	55	47	14	1	4	3	20	1	101	4	6	7	.462	0-0	0	97	.685	3.18	3.81
2019	Bos	AL	23	12	2	67.2	302	72	46	45	16	1	2	3	35	0	70	6	2	1	.667	0-1	4	98	.875	6.26	5.99
2020	Bos	AL	9	9	0	48.1	199	51	20	20	8	1	0	4	7	0	52	2	4	2	.667	0-0	0	97	.789	4.24	3.72
2021	Bos	AL	32	32	0	182.1	764	182	81	76	15	1	2	7	35	2	195	6	11	9	.550	0-0	0	97	.696	3.24	3.75
12	LAD	NL	10	10	0	56.1	241	63	27	26	5	0	3	0	20	2	34	1	1	6	.143	0-0	0	94	.771	4.54	4.15
12	Mia	NL	12	12	0	63.0	285	70	32	31	5	1	3	3	27	1	44	0	3	7	.300	0-0	0	94	.770	4.79	4.43
18	TB	AL	10	10	0	57.0	224	48	27	27	11	0	2	1	8	1	53	1	3	4	.429	0-0	0	97	.682	2.85	4.26
18	Bos	AL	12	11	0	54.0	231	57	28	20	3	1	2	2	12	0	48	3	3	3	.500	0-0	0	97	.687	3.48	3.33
	Postseason		6	2	1	22.1	85	15	5	4	1	1	0	0	3	0	16	0	2	1	.667	0-0	2	98	.449	1.34	1.61
	10 ML YEARS		220	201	5	1148.1	4895	1192	564	534	119	26	24	34	336	16	957	41	61	65	.484	0-1	5	96	.733	3.99	4.19

Alcides Escobar

Bats: R **Throws:** R **Pos:** SS-61;2B-17   al-SEE-dess   **Ht:** 6'1" **Wt:** 205 **Born:** 12/16/1986 **Age:** 35

Year	Team	Lg	G	AB	H	2B	3B	HR	(Hm	Rd)	TB	R	RBI	RC	TBB	IBB	SO	HBP	SH	SF	SB	CS	GDP	Avg	OBP	Slg	OPS
2021	Omha	AAA	35	124	34	7	0	5	(-	-)	56	23	16	-	6	0	29	1	1	1	1	0	2	.274	.311	.452	.762
2008	Mil	NL	9	4	2	0	0	0	(0	0)	2	2	0	0	0	0	1	0	0	0	0	0	0	.500	.500	.500	1.000
2009	Mil	NL	38	125	38	3	1	1	(0	1)	46	20	11	16	4	0	18	2	2	1	4	2	0	.304	.333	.368	.701
2010	Mil	NL	145	506	119	14	10	4	(3	1)	165	57	41	51	36	7	70	3	4	3	10	4	8	.235	.288	.326	.614
2011	KC	AL	158	548	139	21	8	4	(0	4)	188	69	46	46	25	1	73	4	18	3	26	9	14	.254	.290	.343	.633
2012	KC	AL	155	605	177	30	7	5	(5	0)	236	68	52	72	27	2	100	8	8	0	35	5	14	.293	.331	.390	.721
2013	KC	AL	158	607	142	20	4	4	(3	1)	182	57	52	51	19	1	84	3	9	4	22	0	12	.234	.259	.300	.559
2014	KC	AL	162	579	165	34	5	3	(2	1)	218	74	50	68	23	1	83	6	8	4	31	6	12	.285	.317	.377	.694
2015	KC	AL	148	612	157	20	5	3	(0	3)	196	76	47	60	26	1	75	8	11	5	17	5	10	.257	.293	.320	.614
2016	KC	AL	162	637	166	24	6	7	(5	2)	223	57	55	66	27	2	96	3	10	4	17	4	16	.261	.292	.350	.642
2017	KC	AL	162	599	150	36	5	6	(2	4)	214	71	54	58	15	1	102	4	7	4	4	7	15	.250	.272	.357	.629
2018	KC	AL	140	485	112	22	3	4	(2	2)	152	54	34	40	29	1	74	5	8	4	14	8	14	.231	.279	.313	.593
2021	Was	NL	75	319	92	21	2	4	(3	1)	129	53	28	49	17	0	56	9	2	2	3	0	2	.288	.340	.404	.744
	Postseason		31	135	42	9	3	2	(1	1)	63	21	14	24	1	0	21	3	6	2	2	1	2	.311	.326	.467	.793
	12 ML YEARS		1512	5626	1459	245	56	45	(23	22)	1951	658	470	577	248	17	832	55	87	35	177	44	112	.259	.295	.347	.642

Eduardo Escobar

Bats: B **Throws:** R **Pos:** 3B-99;2B-42;1B-18;PH-8;SS-1   **Ht:** 5'10" **Wt:** 193 **Born:** 1/5/1989 **Age:** 33

Year	Team	Lg	G	AB	H	2B	3B	HR	(Hm	Rd)	TB	R	RBI	RC	TBB	IBB	SO	HBP	SH	SF	SB	CS	GDP	Avg	OBP	Slg	OPS
2011	CWS	AL	9	7	2	0	0	0	(0	0)	2	0	0	1	0	0	1	0	0	0	0	0	0	.286	.286	.286	.571
2012	2 Tms	AL	50	131	28	4	1	0	(0	0)	34	18	9	12	11	0	31	1	2	0	3	0	0	.214	.278	.260	.537
2013	Min	AL	66	165	39	5	2	3	(2	1)	57	23	10	14	11	0	34	0	2	1	0	2	0	.236	.282	.345	.628
2014	Min	AL	133	433	119	35	2	6	(2	4)	176	52	37	53	24	1	93	4	2	4	1	1	6	.275	.315	.406	.721
2015	Min	AL	127	409	107	31	4	12	(2	10)	182	48	58	55	28	1	86	2	2	5	2	3	7	.262	.309	.445	.754
2016	Min	AL	105	352	83	14	2	6	(3	3)	119	32	37	38	21	1	72	1	2	1	1	3	7	.236	.280	.338	.618
2017	Min	AL	129	457	116	16	5	21	(12	9)	205	62	73	72	33	3	98	5	1	3	5	1	5	.254	.309	.449	.758
2018	2 Tms	AL	151	566	154	48	3	23	(9	14)	277	75	84	93	52	8	126	5	0	8	2	4	12	.272	.334	.489	.824
2019	Ari	NL	158	636	171	29	10	35	(18	17)	325	94	118	108	50	3	130	3	0	10	5	1	8	.269	.320	.511	.831
2020	Ari	NL	54	203	43	7	3	4	(3	1)	68	22	20	19	15	4	41	2	0	2	1	0	5	.212	.270	.335	.605
2021	2 Tms	NL	146	549	139	26	5	28	(15	13)	259	77	90	89	48	1	124	1	0	1	1	0	3	.253	.314	.472	.786

Year	Team	Lg	G	AB	H	2B	3B	HR	(Hm	Rd)	TB	R	RBI	RC	TBB	IBB	SO	HBP	SH	SF	SB	CS	GDP	Avg	OBP	Slg	OPS
12	CWS	AL	36	87	18	4	1	0	(0	0)	24	14	3	7	9	0	23	0	1	0	2	0	0	.207	.281	.276	.557
12	Min	AL	14	44	10	0	0	0	(0	0)	10	4	6	5	2	0	8	1	1	1	0	1	0	.227	.271	.227	.498
18	Min	AL	97	368	101	37	3	15	(7	8)	189	45	63	70	34	6	91	3	0	3	1	3	7	.274	.338	.514	.852
18	Ari	NL	54	198	53	11	0	8	(2	6)	88	30	21	23	18	2	35	2	0	5	1	1	5	.268	.327	.444	.772
21	Ari	NL	98	370	91	14	3	22	(12	10)	177	50	65	60	29	1	85	0	0	1	1	0	1	.246	.300	.478	.778
21	Mil	NL	48	179	48	12	2	6	(3	3)	82	27	25	29	19	0	39	1	0	0	0	0	2	.268	.342	.458	.800
Postseason			1	4	2	0	0	0	(0	0)	2	0	0	0	0	0	0	0	0	0	0	0	0	.500	.500	.500	1.000
11 ML YEARS			1128	3908	1001	215	37	138	(66	72)	1704	503	536	554	293	22	836	22	13	34	21	15	53	.256	.309	.436	.745

Thomas Eshelman

Pitches: R **Bats:** R **Pos:** SP-6; RP-3   **Ht:** 6'2" **Wt:** 225 **Born:** 6/20/1994 **Age:** 28

			HOW MUCH PITCHED					WHAT HE GAVE UP										THE RESULTS							
Year	Team	Lg	G	GS	GF	IP	BFP	H	R	ER	HR	SH	SF	HB	TBB	IBB	SO	WP	W	L	Pct	Sv-Op	Hld	Vel	OPS	ERC	ERA
2021	Norfolk	AAA	15	3	3	30.0	139	42	28	26	6	0	1	5	3	0	18	1	0	4	.000	0- --	-	-	.944	6.57	7.80
2019	Bal	AL	10	4	2	36.0	164	47	31	26	12	0	2	1	11	1	22	0	1	2	.333	0-0	0	86	.953	7.35	6.50
2020	Bal	AL	12	4	3	34.2	143	34	17	15	7	0	2	1	9	0	16	1	3	1	.750	0-1	0	86	.812	4.29	3.89
2021	Bal	AL	9	6	1	27.2	126	34	22	22	6	0	1	1	10	0	11	0	0	3	.000	0-0	0	87	.892	6.27	7.16
3 ML YEARS			31	14	6	98.1	433	115	70	63	25	0	5	3	30	1	49	1	4	6	.400	0-1	0	86	.889	5.93	5.77

Raynel Espinal

Pitches: R **Bats:** R **Pos:** RP-1   **Ht:** 6'3" **Wt:** 215 **Born:** 10/6/1991 **Age:** 30

			HOW MUCH PITCHED					WHAT HE GAVE UP										THE RESULTS							
Year	Team	Lg	G	GS	GF	IP	BFP	H	R	ER	HR	SH	SF	HB	TBB	IBB	SO	WP	W	L	Pct	Sv-Op	Hld	Vel	OPS	ERC	ERA
2021	Wrcstr	AAA	22	20	0	111.2	462	82	49	44	11	1	6	10	41	0	111	5	11	4	.733	0- --	-	-	.633	2.85	3.55
2021	Bos	AL	1	0	1	2.0	8	2	2	2	0	0	0	0	1	0	0	0	0	0	-	0-0	0	93	.804	4.15	9.00

Santiago Espinal

Bats: R **Throws:** R **Pos:** 3B-81;PH-12;PR-7;DH-5   **Ht:** 5'10" **Wt:** 181 **Born:** 11/13/1994 **Age:** 27

			BATTING																		RUNNING			AVERAGES			
Year	Team	Lg	G	AB	H	2B	3B	HR	(Hm	Rd)	TB	R	RBI	RC	TBB	IBB	SO	HBP	SH	SF	SB	CS	GDP	Avg	OBP	Slg	OPS
2020	Tor	AL	27	60	16	4	0	0	(0	0)	20	10	6	6	4	0	16	0	1	1	1	0	1	.267	.308	.333	.641
2021	Tor	AL	92	222	69	13	1	2	(2	0)	90	32	17	29	22	0	30	1	1	0	6	1	4	.311	.376	.405	.781
2 ML YEARS			119	282	85	17	1	2	(2	0)	110	42	23	35	26	0	46	1	2	1	7	1	5	.301	.361	.390	.751

Paolo Espino

Pitches: R **Bats:** R **Pos:** SP-19; RP-16   **Ht:** 5'10" **Wt:** 215 **Born:** 1/10/1987 **Age:** 35

			HOW MUCH PITCHED					WHAT HE GAVE UP										THE RESULTS							
Year	Team	Lg	G	GS	GF	IP	BFP	H	R	ER	HR	SH	SF	HB	TBB	IBB	SO	WP	W	L	Pct	Sv-Op	Hld	Vel	OPS	ERC	ERA
2017	2 Tms		12	2	7	24.0	109	23	17	16	7	1	0	3	10	0	20	0	0	0	-	0-0	1	89	.870	5.64	6.00
2020	Was	NL	2	1	1	6.0	27	8	3	3	1	0	0	0	2	0	7	0	0	0	-	0-0	0	90	.850	6.38	4.50
2021	Was	NL	35	19	11	109.2	455	108	53	52	19	4	3	1	25	2	92	1	5	5	.500	1-1	0	89	.757	3.80	4.27
17	Mil	NL	6	2	3	17.2	82	17	13	12	5	1	0	3	8	0	13	0	0	0	-	0-0	0	88	.860	5.94	6.11
17	Tex	AL	6	0	4	6.1	27	6	4	4	2	0	0	0	2	0	7	0	0	0	-	0-0	1	90	.896	4.79	5.68
3 ML YEARS			49	22	19	139.2	591	139	73	71	27	5	3	4	37	2	119	1	5	5	.500	1-1	1	89	.781	4.21	4.58

Carlos Estevez

Pitches: R **Bats:** R **Pos:** RP-64   **Ht:** 6'6" **Wt:** 277 **Born:** 12/28/1992 **Age:** 29

			HOW MUCH PITCHED					WHAT HE GAVE UP										THE RESULTS							
Year	Team	Lg	G	GS	GF	IP	BFP	H	R	ER	HR	SH	SF	HB	TBB	IBB	SO	WP	W	L	Pct	Sv-Op	Hld	Vel	OPS	ERC	ERA
2016	Col	NL	63	0	26	55.0	246	50	32	32	6	1	4	5	28	4	59	3	3	7	.300	11-18	11	97	.728	4.23	5.24
2017	Col	NL	35	0	9	32.1	149	39	21	20	3	1	0	1	14	2	31	1	5	0	1.000	0-0	6	97	.778	5.31	5.57
2019	Col	NL	71	0	13	72.0	308	70	34	30	12	1	3	1	23	1	81	1	2	2	.500	0-2	11	98	.756	4.03	3.75
2020	Col	NL	26	0	6	24.0	116	33	21	20	6	0	0	3	9	0	27	2	1	3	.250	1-4	6	97	1.003	7.91	7.50
2021	Col	NL	64	0	22	61.2	270	71	32	30	8	1	4	2	21	0	60	5	3	5	.375	11-17	15	97	.804	5.12	4.38
Postseason			1	0	0	0.1	2	1	1	1	0	0	0	0	0	0	1	0	0	0	-	0-0	0	99	1.000	14.52	27.00
5 ML YEARS			259	0	76	245.0	1089	263	140	132	35	4	11	12	95	7	258	12	14	17	.452	23-41	49	97	.792	4.87	4.85

Thairo Estrada

Bats: R **Throws:** R **Pos:** SS-19;PH-17;2B-16;3B-4;LF-4;PR-2;RF-1   **Ht:** 5'10" **Wt:** 185 **Born:** 2/22/1996 **Age:** 26

			BATTING																		RUNNING			AVERAGES			
Year	Team	Lg	G	AB	H	2B	3B	HR	(Hm	Rd)	TB	R	RBI	RC	TBB	IBB	SO	HBP	SH	SF	SB	CS	GDP	Avg	OBP	Slg	OPS
2021	Scrmto	AAA	50	210	70	14	1	9	(-	-)	113	37	40	-	20	0	35	3	0	0	6	4	5	.333	.399	.538	.937
2019	NYY	AL	35	64	16	3	0	3	(1	2)	28	12	12	12	3	0	15	1	1	0	4	0	1	.250	.294	.438	.732
2020	NYY	AL	26	48	8	0	0	1	(1	0)	11	8	3	1	1	0	19	3	0	0	1	0	0	.167	.231	.229	.460
2021	SF	NL	52	121	33	4	0	7	(3	4)	58	19	22	20	9	1	23	2	0	0	1	0	2	.273	.333	.479	.813
3 ML YEARS			113	233	57	7	0	11	(5	6)	97	39	37	33	13	1	57	6	1	0	6	0	3	.245	.302	.416	.718

Demarcus Evans

Pitches: R **Bats:** R **Pos:** RP-25 **Ht:** 6'5" **Wt:** 265 **Born:** 10/22/1996 **Age:** 25

Year	Team	Lg	G	GS	GF	IP	BFP	H	R	ER	HR	SH	SF	HB	TBB	IBB	SO	WP	W	L	Pct	Sv-Op	Hld	Vel	OPS	ERC	ERA
2021	RdRck	AAA	16	0	1	19.2	80	11	7	7	2	0	0	0	9	0	29	2	1	0	1.000	0- -	-	-	.532	1.98	3.20
2020	Tex	AL	4	0	0	4.0	14	3	1	1	1	0	0	1	0	0	4	0	0	0	-	0-0	0	94	.747	3.52	2.25
2021	Tex	AL	25	0	3	26.1	120	24	16	15	4	1	1	1	16	0	33	2	0	2	.000	0-2	2	91	.760	4.82	5.13
	2 ML YEARS		29	0	3	30.1	134	27	17	16	5	1	1	2	16	0	37	2	0	2	.000	0-2	2	91	.759	4.67	4.75

Phillip Evans

Bats: R **Throws:** R **Pos:** 1B-20;PH-20;LF-16;RF-15;3B-14;DH-1;PR-1 **Ht:** 5'10" **Wt:** 210 **Born:** 9/10/1992 **Age:** 29

Year	Team	Lg	G	AB	H	2B	3B	HR	(Hm	Rd)	TB	R	RBI	RC	TBB	IBB	SO	HBP	SH	SF	SB	CS	GDP	Avg	OBP	Slg	OPS
2021	Indy	AAA	36	125	32	10	0	0	(-	-)	42	17	10	-	13	0	29	0	0	1	0	0	5	.256	.324	.336	.660
2017	NYM	NL	19	33	10	2	0	0	(0	0)	12	4	1	5	4	0	8	1	0	0	1	0	0	.303	.395	.364	.758
2018	NYM	NL	15	21	3	0	0	0	(0	0)	3	1	1	1	2	0	8	0	0	0	1	0	1	.143	.217	.143	.360
2020	Pit	NL	11	39	14	2	0	1	(1	0)	19	6	9	12	5	0	7	1	0	0	0	1	1	.359	.444	.487	.932
2021	Pit	NL	76	214	44	5	0	5	(1	4)	64	23	16	18	28	1	53	5	0	0	1	0	3	.206	.312	.299	.611
	4 ML YEARS		121	307	71	9	0	6	(2	4)	98	34	27	36	39	1	76	7	0	0	2	1	5	.231	.331	.319	.651

Pete Fairbanks

Pitches: R **Bats:** R **Pos:** RP-47 **Ht:** 6'6" **Wt:** 225 **Born:** 12/16/1993 **Age:** 28

Year	Team	Lg	G	GS	GF	IP	BFP	H	R	ER	HR	SH	SF	HB	TBB	IBB	SO	WP	W	L	Pct	Sv-Op	Hld	Vel	OPS	ERC	ERA
2019	2 Tms	AL	21	0	3	21.0	99	25	20	16	5	0	0	0	10	0	28	2	2	3	.400	2-2	3	97	.882	6.37	6.86
2020	TB	AL	27	2	2	26.2	117	23	9	8	2	0	0	2	14	0	39	6	6	3	.667	0-2	7	97	.640	3.89	2.70
2021	TB	AL	47	0	17	42.2	189	40	22	17	2	0	1	1	21	1	56	3	3	6	.333	5-7	14	97	.659	3.68	3.59
19	Tex	AL	8	0	0	8.2	41	8	10	9	4	0	0	0	7	0	15	1	0	2	.000	0-0	0	97	.954	8.04	9.35
19	TB	AL	13	0	3	12.1	58	17	10	7	1	0	0	0	3	0	13	1	2	1	.667	2-2	3	98	.836	5.26	5.11
	Postseason		9	0	3	12.1	54	12	5	5	3	0	0	0	6	1	17	3	0	0	-	3-3	3	99	.833	5.16	3.65
	3 ML YEARS		95	2	22	90.1	405	88	51	41	9	0	1	3	45	1	123	11	11	12	.478	7-11	24	97	.709	4.34	4.08

Stuart Fairchild

Bats: R **Throws:** R **Pos:** CF-5;PH-5;LF-2;RF-1;PR-1 **Ht:** 6'0" **Wt:** 205 **Born:** 3/17/1996 **Age:** 26

Year	Team	Lg	G	AB	H	2B	3B	HR	(Hm	Rd)	TB	R	RBI	RC	TBB	IBB	SO	HBP	SH	SF	SB	CS	GDP	Avg	OBP	Slg	OPS
2021	Reno	AAA	43	153	45	7	4	9	(-	-)	87	27	28	-	21	0	38	2	0	2	7	1	5	.294	.382	.569	.951
2021	Ari	NL	12	15	2	1	0	0	(0	0)	3	3	2	1	1	0	3	1	0	0	0	0	1	.133	.235	.200	.435

Bailey Falter

Pitches: L **Bats:** R **Pos:** RP-21; SP-1 **Ht:** 6'4" **Wt:** 175 **Born:** 4/24/1997 **Age:** 25

Year	Team	Lg	G	GS	GF	IP	BFP	H	R	ER	HR	SH	SF	HB	TBB	IBB	SO	WP	W	L	Pct	Sv-Op	Hld	Vel	OPS	ERC	ERA
2021	LV	AAA	8	6	0	30.2	120	23	6	6	3	0	0	0	8	0	44	0	2	0	1.000	0- -	-	-	.580	2.28	1.76
2021	Phi	NL	22	1	6	33.2	139	34	21	21	5	0	1	2	6	0	34	2	2	1	.667	0-0	2	92	.725	3.86	5.61

Jeurys Familia

Pitches: R **Bats:** R **Pos:** RP-65 **jer-ISS fa-MEAL-ya** **Ht:** 6'3" **Wt:** 240 **Born:** 10/10/1989 **Age:** 32

Year	Team	Lg	G	GS	GF	IP	BFP	H	R	ER	HR	SH	SF	HB	TBB	IBB	SO	WP	W	L	Pct	Sv-Op	Hld	Vel	OPS	ERC	ERA
2012	NYM	NL	8	1	4	12.1	52	10	8	8	0	0	0	0	9	0	10	0	0	0	-	0-0	0	96	.644	3.76	5.84
2013	NYM	NL	9	0	3	10.2	52	12	5	5	2	2	0	0	9	1	8	3	0	0	-	1-1	0	95	.908	7.20	4.22
2014	NYM	NL	76	0	16	77.1	322	59	26	19	3	4	2	2	32	5	73	9	2	5	.286	5-10	23	96	.587	2.45	2.21
2015	NYM	NL	76	0	65	78.0	308	59	16	16	6	1	1	2	19	1	86	4	2	2	.500	43-48	1	97	.569	2.19	1.85
2016	NYM	NL	78	0	67	77.2	321	63	25	22	1	2	1	1	31	6	84	3	3	4	.429	51-56	1	96	.574	2.44	2.55
2017	NYM	NL	26	0	15	24.2	111	21	14	12	1	2	2	1	15	3	25	1	2	2	.500	6-7	2	96	.636	3.48	4.38
2018	2 Tms		70	0	36	72.0	302	60	26	25	3	0	1	2	28	1	83	2	8	6	.571	18-24	7	96	.601	2.81	3.13
2019	NYM	NL	66	0	14	60.0	274	62	39	38	7	2	1	3	42	4	63	3	4	2	.667	0-4	14	96	.831	5.84	5.70
2020	NYM	NL	25	0	4	26.2	120	20	11	11	2	0	0	3	19	2	23	1	2	0	1.000	0-1	5	97	.687	3.98	3.71
2021	NYM	NL	65	0	16	59.1	262	57	31	26	10	2	0	2	27	2	72	4	9	4	.692	1-7	11	97	.767	4.58	3.94
18	NYM	NL	40	0	29	40.2	171	36	13	13	1	0	1	2	14	1	43	1	4	4	.500	17-21	1	96	.616	2.88	2.88
18	Oak	AL	30	0	7	31.1	131	24	13	12	2	0	0	0	14	0	40	1	4	2	.667	1-3	6	97	.581	2.73	3.45
	Postseason		14	0	11	16.2	60	7	5	4	2	0	0	0	3	0	11	0	1	0	.000	5-8	0	96	.412	0.97	2.16
	10 ML YEARS		499	1	240	498.2	2124	423	201	182	35	15	8	16	231	25	527	30	32	25	.561	125-158	63	96	.654	3.32	3.28

Johneshwy Fargas

Bats: R **Throws:** R **Pos:** CF-12;PH-6;LF-2;RF-2;PR-2 **Ht:** 6'1" **Wt:** 180 **Born:** 12/15/1994 **Age:** 27

Year	Team	Lg	G	AB	H	2B	3B	HR	(Hm	Rd)	TB	R	RBI	RC	TBB	IBB	SO	HBP	SH	SF	SB	CS	GDP	Avg	OBP	Slg	OPS
2021	Iowa	AAA	22	76	20	4	1	2	(-	-)	32	12	6	-	4	0	26	0	0	0	6	2	0	.263	.300	.421	.721
2021	2 Tms	NL	22	52	13	3	2	0	(0	0)	20	4	5	5	1	0	15	0	1	0	1	2	2	.250	.264	.385	.649
21	NYM	NL	7	21	6	3	1	0	(0	0)	11	1	3	5	0	0	7	0	1	0	0	0	0	.286	.286	.524	.810
21	ChC	NL	15	31	7	0	1	0	(0	0)	9	3	2	0	1	0	8	0	0	0	1	2	2	.226	.250	.290	.540

Jake Faria

Pitches: R Bats: R Pos: RP-20; SP-3 Ht: 6'4" Wt: 230 Born: 7/30/1993 Age: 28

Year	Team	Lg	G	GS	GF	IP	BFP	H	R	ER	HR	SH	SF	HB	TBB	IBB	SO	WP	W	L	Pct	Sv-Op	Hld	Vel	OPS	ERC	ERA
2021	Salt Lk	AAA	7	7	0	36.2	164	41	23	23	7	0	3	0	15	0	46	2	3	2	.600	0--	-	-	.855	5.42	5.65
2017	TB	AL	16	14	1	86.2	357	71	35	33	11	1	4	5	31	0	84	6	5	4	.556	0-0	0	92	.677	3.37	3.43
2018	TB	AL	17	12	1	65.0	281	60	39	39	9	0	3	3	33	1	50	2	4	4	.500	0-0	0	93	.776	4.58	5.40
2019	2 Tms		16	0	4	18.2	95	28	15	14	5	0	1	1	12	0	19	3	0	1	.000	0-0	2	94	1.049	10.00	6.75
2021	Ari	NL	23	3	6	32.2	154	39	21	20	5	1	1	2	13	0	32	3	0	0	-	0-0	0	92	.842	5.64	5.51
19	TB	AL	7	0	1	10.0	47	10	3	3	2	0	0	0	7	0	11	0	0	0	-	0-0	0	95	.837	5.94	2.70
19	Mil	NL	9	0	3	8.2	48	18	12	11	3	0	1	1	5	0	8	3	0	1	.000	0-0	2	93	1.256	15.43	11.42
4 ML YEARS			72	29	12	203.0	887	198	110	106	30	2	9	11	89	1	185	14	9	9	.500	0-0	2	92	.776	4.65	4.70

Buck Farmer

Pitches: R Bats: L Pos: RP-36 Ht: 6'4" Wt: 232 Born: 2/20/1991 Age: 31

Year	Team	Lg	G	GS	GF	IP	BFP	H	R	ER	HR	SH	SF	HB	TBB	IBB	SO	WP	W	L	Pct	Sv-Op	Hld	Vel	OPS	ERC	ERA
2021	Toledo	AAA	9	0	4	11.1	48	11	5	5	0	0	0	1	4	0	7	1	0	2	.000	0--	-	-	.636	3.43	3.97
2021	RdRck	AAA	13	0	11	13.0	53	10	7	5	1	1	0	0	5	0	13	0	2	1	.667	8--	-	-	.565	2.66	3.46
2014	Det	AL	4	2	1	9.1	46	12	12	12	2	0	0	2	5	0	11	0	0	1	.000	0-0	0	93	1.054	8.29	11.57
2015	Det	AL	14	5	0	40.1	186	53	35	33	10	1	1	3	17	2	24	1	0	4	.000	0-0	0	93	.986	7.65	7.36
2016	Det	AL	14	1	7	29.1	131	25	15	15	4	1	1	1	20	1	27	2	0	1	.000	0-0	0	93	.771	4.71	4.60
2017	Det	AL	11	11	0	48.0	219	55	38	36	9	0	2	4	20	0	49	1	5	5	.500	0-0	0	92	.843	5.99	6.75
2018	Det	AL	66	1	12	69.1	308	67	34	32	6	1	2	1	41	1	57	2	3	4	.429	0-0	7	94	.754	4.61	4.15
2019	Det	AL	73	1	8	67.2	288	62	32	28	8	4	4	5	24	2	73	4	6	6	.500	0-3	15	95	.743	3.81	3.72
2020	Det	AL	23	0	9	21.1	89	20	9	9	3	1	1	0	5	0	14	1	1	0	1.000	0-1	7	94	.674	3.29	3.80
2021	Det	AL	36	0	8	35.1	171	40	25	25	9	0	1	5	21	1	37	2	0	0	-	0-1	2	94	.886	7.37	6.37
8 ML YEARS			241	21	45	320.2	1438	334	200	190	51	8	12	21	153	7	292	13	15	21	.417	0-5	31	94	.817	5.30	5.33

Kyle Farmer

Bats: R Throws: R Pos: SS-121;3B-10;2B-9;PH-6;1B-5;LF-2;PR-1 Ht: 6'0" Wt: 205 Born: 8/17/1990 Age: 31

Year	Team	Lg	G	AB	H	2B	3B	HR	(Hm	Rd)	TB	R	RBI	RC	TBB	IBB	SO	HBP	SH	SF	SB	CS	GDP	Avg	OBP	Slg	OPS
2017	LAD	NL	20	20	6	1	0	0	(0	0)	7	1	2	1	0	0	3	0	0	0	0	0	2	.300	.300	.350	.650
2018	LAD	NL	39	68	16	4	1	0	(0	0)	22	1	9	7	5	1	15	3	0	1	0	0	1	.235	.312	.324	.635
2019	Cin	NL	97	183	42	6	0	9	(6	3)	75	22	27	22	10	1	59	3	0	1	4	1	1	.230	.279	.410	.689
2020	Cin	NL	32	64	17	3	0	0	(0	0)	20	4	4	7	5	0	13	1	0	0	1	0	0	.266	.329	.313	.641
2021	Cin	NL	147	483	127	22	2	16	(9	7)	201	60	63	64	22	1	97	18	1	5	2	3	16	.263	.316	.416	.732
Postseason			6	9	0	0	0	0	(0	0)	0	0	1	0	0	0	4	0	0	0	0	0	0	.000	.000	.000	.000
5 ML YEARS			335	818	208	36	3	25	(15	10)	325	88	105	101	42	3	187	25	1	7	7	4	20	.254	.308	.397	.706

Luke Farrell

Pitches: R Bats: L Pos: RP-19; SP-1 Ht: 6'6" Wt: 200 Born: 6/7/1991 Age: 31

Year	Team	Lg	G	GS	GF	IP	BFP	H	R	ER	HR	SH	SF	HB	TBB	IBB	SO	WP	W	L	Pct	Sv-Op	Hld	Vel	OPS	ERC	ERA
2021	StPaul	AAA	7	0	0	9.0	40	5	4	4	0	0	2	2	6	0	16	0	0	1	.000	0--	-	-	.525	2.71	4.00
2017	2 Tms		10	1	3	13.0	61	12	8	8	2	0	0	0	10	0	9	0	0	0	-	0-0	1	91	.753	5.40	5.54
2018	ChC	NL	20	2	8	31.1	141	30	22	18	7	0	1	1	16	2	39	1	3	4	.429	0-1	1	92	.797	5.09	5.17
2019	Tex	AL	9	1	3	13.1	48	6	4	4	3	0	1	0	3	0	12	0	1	0	1.000	0-0	0	92	.574	1.49	2.70
2020	Tex	AL	4	0	1	5.1	27	5	5	5	1	1	0	1	5	0	8	2	0	0	-	0-0	0	91	.923	7.27	8.44
2021	Min	AL	20	1	3	24.2	113	28	13	13	4	0	0	0	13	0	25	0	1	1	.500	0-0	1	91	.843	5.84	4.74
17	KC	AL	1	1	0	2.2	18	7	5	5	1	0	0	0	3	0	2	0	0	0	-	0-0	0	90	1.289	21.83	16.88
17	Cin	NL	9	0	3	10.1	43	5	3	3	1	0	0	0	7	0	7	0	0	0	-	0-0	1	91	.529	2.34	2.61
5 ML YEARS			63	5	18	87.2	390	81	52	48	17	1	2	2	47	2	93	3	5	5	.500	0-1	3	92	.784	4.86	4.93

Erick Fedde

Pitches: R Bats: R Pos: SP-27; RP-2 Ht: 6'4" Wt: 200 Born: 2/25/1993 Age: 29

Year	Team	Lg	G	GS	GF	IP	BFP	H	R	ER	HR	SH	SF	HB	TBB	IBB	SO	WP	W	L	Pct	Sv-Op	Hld	Vel	OPS	ERC	ERA
2017	Was	NL	3	3	0	15.1	76	25	16	16	5	2	0	1	8	2	15	0	1	0	.000	0-0	0	93	1.106	11.01	9.39
2018	Was	NL	11	11	0	50.1	217	55	31	31	8	1	2	0	22	1	46	0	2	4	.333	0-0	0	94	.846	5.32	5.54
2019	Was	NL	21	12	3	78.0	334	81	39	39	11	4	2	2	33	2	41	1	4	2	.667	0-0	0	92	.802	4.88	4.50
2020	Was	NL	11	8	1	50.1	222	47	25	24	10	1	1	3	22	2	28	2	2	4	.333	0-0	0	93	.767	4.65	4.29
2021	Was	NL	29	27	1	133.1	590	144	90	81	23	8	5	4	48	6	128	1	7	9	.438	0-1	0	94	.803	4.88	5.47
5 ML YEARS			75	61	5	327.1	1439	352	201	191	57	16	10	10	133	13	258	4	15	20	.429	0-1	0	93	.819	5.16	5.25

Mario Feliciano

Bats: R Throws: R Pos: PH-1 Ht: 6'1" Wt: 200 Born: 11/20/1998 Age: 23

Year	Team	Lg	G	AB	H	2B	3B	HR	(Hm	Rd)	TB	R	RBI	RC	TBB	IBB	SO	HBP	SH	SF	SB	CS	GDP	Avg	OBP	Slg	OPS
2021	Nashv	AAA	31	102	21	2	0	3	(-	-)	32	12	19	-	4	0	26	2	0	3	0	0	4	.206	.243	.314	.557
2021	Mil	NL	1	0	0	0	0	0	(0	0)	0	1	0	0	1	0	0	0	0	0	0	0	0	-	1.000	-	-

Michael Feliz

Pitches: R **Bats:** R **Pos:** RP-21   **Ht:** 6'4" **Wt:** 250 **Born:** 6/28/1993 **Age:** 29

Year	Team	Lg	G	GS	GF	IP	BFP	H	R	ER	HR	SH	SF	HB	TBB	IBB	SO	WP	W	L	Pct	Sv-Op	Hld	Vel	OPS	ERC	ERA
2021	Lsvlle	AAA	13	0	0	13.2	52	8	3	3	0	0	1	1	1	0	15	0	1	0	1.000	0--	-	-	.396	0.96	1.98
2015	Hou	AL	5	0	5	8.0	38	9	7	7	2	0	0	1	4	0	7	0	0	0	-	0-0	0	94	.884	6.79	7.88
2016	Hou	AL	47	0	17	65.0	270	55	33	32	10	0	2	0	22	0	95	6	8	1	.889	0-3	5	95	.659	3.32	4.43
2017	Hou	AL	46	0	13	48.0	218	53	31	30	8	0	4	0	22	1	70	7	4	2	.667	0-2	2	96	.854	5.28	5.63
2018	Pit	NL	47	0	7	47.2	217	49	33	30	6	0	3	3	23	0	55	3	1	2	.333	0-2	12	95	.776	4.92	5.66
2019	Pit	NL	58	1	5	56.1	239	44	27	25	11	1	1	2	27	1	73	0	4	4	.500	0-1	3	95	.720	3.91	3.99
2020	Pit	NL	3	0	1	1.2	12	4	6	6	1	0	0	1	2	0	2	0	0	0	-	0-0	0	94	1.361	26.50	32.40
2021	4 Tms		21	0	7	20.0	90	26	17	16	4	0	0	0	7	0	22	2	0	0	-	1-1	0	94	.873	6.49	7.20
21	Pit	NL	7	0	2	7.2	31	8	3	2	0	0	0	0	1	0	8	1	0	0	-	0-0	0	93	.690	2.68	2.35
21	Cin	NL	9	0	5	6.2	37	13	12	12	2	0	0	0	4	0	9	1	0	0	-	1-1	0	94	1.035	12.87	16.20
21	Bos	AL	4	0	0	5.1	19	4	2	2	2	0	0	0	1	0	5	0	0	0	-	0-0	0	95	.819	3.84	3.38
21	Oak	AL	1	0	0	0.1	3	1	0	0	0	0	0	0	1	0	0	0	0	0	-	0-0	0	93	1.167	29.63	0.00
	7 ML YEARS		227	1	54	246.2	1084	240	154	146	42	1	10	7	107	2	324	18	17	9	.654	1-9	22	95	.768	4.60	5.33

Neftali Feliz

Pitches: R **Bats:** R **Pos:** RP-5   neff-TAH-lee   **Ht:** 6'3" **Wt:** 235 **Born:** 5/2/1988 **Age:** 34

Year	Team	Lg	G	GS	GF	IP	BFP	H	R	ER	HR	SH	SF	HB	TBB	IBB	SO	WP	W	L	Pct	Sv-Op	Hld	Vel	OPS	ERC	ERA
2021	LV	AAA	15	0	10	14.1	58	8	4	2	1	0	2	0	6	0	23	1	2	1	.667	4--	-	-	.481	1.68	1.26
2021	OkCity	AAA	20	1	1	26.2	112	24	14	13	5	0	3	0	10	0	42	1	2	1	.667	0--	-	-	.748	4.01	4.39
2009	Tex	AL	20	0	3	31.0	117	13	6	6	2	1	0	3	8	0	39	0	1	0	1.000	2-3	9	96	.416	1.14	1.74
2010	Tex	AL	70	0	59	69.1	269	43	21	21	5	1	0	5	18	1	71	5	4	3	.571	40-43	3	96	.516	1.75	2.73
2011	Tex	AL	64	0	56	62.1	252	42	22	19	4	3	2	0	30	1	54	2	2	3	.400	32-38	0	96	.598	2.45	2.74
2012	Tex	AL	8	7	0	42.2	175	28	15	15	5	0	0	2	23	0	37	0	3	1	.750	0-0	0	95	.623	3.11	3.16
2013	Tex	AL	6	0	2	4.2	21	5	0	0	0	0	0	1	2	0	4	0	0	0	-	0-0	0	94	.659	4.78	0.00
2014	Tex	AL	30	0	22	31.2	122	20	7	7	5	1	1	0	11	0	21	1	2	1	.667	13-14	0	93	.586	2.38	1.99
2015	2 Tms	AL	48	0	24	48.0	212	57	34	34	5	1	1	1	18	6	39	4	3	4	.429	10-17	2	95	.821	5.03	6.38
2016	Pit	NL	62	0	6	53.2	218	40	21	21	10	2	1	1	21	1	61	3	4	2	.667	2-4	29	96	.696	3.30	3.52
2017	2 Tms	AL	49	0	31	46.0	196	40	33	28	9	0	1	1	23	2	37	1	2	5	.286	8-9	2	96	.794	4.49	5.48
2021	2 Tms	NL	5	0	1	4.0	19	5	4	4	1	0	0	1	1	0	3	0	0	1	.000	0-1	0	95	.957	7.02	9.00
15	Tex	AL	18	0	12	19.2	91	24	10	10	2	0	0	0	9	3	16	2	1	2	.333	6-9	0	94	.777	5.26	4.58
15	Det	AL	30	0	12	28.1	121	33	24	24	3	1	1	1	9	3	23	2	2	2	.500	4-8	2	95	.854	4.87	7.62
17	Mil	NL	29	0	21	27.0	115	23	22	18	8	0	1	0	15	2	21	0	1	5	.167	8-9	0	96	.866	5.22	6.00
17	KC	NL	20	0	10	19.0	81	17	11	10	1	0	0	1	8	0	16	1	1	0	1.000	0-0	2	96	.646	3.46	4.74
21	Phi	NL	2	0	0	1.0	9	4	4	4	1	0	0	1	1	0	2	0	0	1	.000	0-1	0	96	1.952	47.63	36.00
21	LAD	NL	3	0	1	3.0	10	1	0	0	0	0	0	0	0	0	1	0	0	0	-	0-0	0	94	.200	0.25	0.00
	Postseason		18	0	15	18.2	76	8	4	4	1	1	0	1	13	1	23	1	0	0	-	7-8	0	97	.523	2.04	1.93
	10 ML YEARS		362	7	204	393.1	1601	293	163	155	46	9	6	15	155	11	366	16	21	20	.512	107-129	45	96	.645	2.94	3.55

Ryan Feltner

Pitches: R **Bats:** R **Pos:** SP-2   **Ht:** 6'4" **Wt:** 190 **Born:** 9/2/1996 **Age:** 25

Year	Team	Lg	G	GS	GF	IP	BFP	H	R	ER	HR	SH	SF	HB	TBB	IBB	SO	WP	W	L	Pct	Sv-Op	Hld	Vel	OPS	ERC	ERA
2021	Hrtfrd	AA	13	13	0	72.2	298	68	23	23	7	0	1	1	22	0	80	1	5	2	.714	0--	-	-	.696	3.45	2.85
2021	Spkane	A+	7	0	0	37.1	156	26	9	9	1	0	0	0	18	0	45	0	3	1	.750	0--	-	-	.538	2.27	2.17
2021	Col	NL	2	2	0	6.1	33	9	8	8	3	0	1	1	5	0	6	0	0	1	.000	0-0	0	92	1.185	12.84	11.37

Caleb Ferguson

Pitches: L **Bats:** R **Pos:** P   **Ht:** 6'3" **Wt:** 226 **Born:** 7/2/1996 **Age:** 25

Year	Team	Lg	G	GS	GF	IP	BFP	H	R	ER	HR	SH	SF	HB	TBB	IBB	SO	WP	W	L	Pct	Sv-Op	Hld	Vel	OPS	ERC	ERA
2018	LAD	NL	29	3	7	49.0	202	43	21	19	8	0	0	3	12	1	59	1	7	2	.778	2-3	5	94	.688	3.42	3.49
2019	LAD	NL	46	2	5	44.2	204	39	26	24	7	1	3	6	27	2	54	1	1	2	.333	0-0	4	94	.774	4.99	4.84
2020	LAD	NL	21	1	0	18.2	75	16	7	6	4	0	0	0	3	0	27	0	2	1	.667	0-2	5	95	.670	3.02	2.89
	Postseason		6	0	0	3.0	10	0	0	0	0	0	0	0	1	0	3	0	0	0	-	0-0	1	95	.100	0.13	0.00
	3 ML YEARS		96	6	12	112.1	481	98	54	49	19	1	3	9	42	3	140	2	10	5	.667	2-5	14	94	.721	3.98	3.93

Julian Fernandez

Pitches: R **Bats:** R **Pos:** RP-6   **Ht:** 6'6" **Wt:** 233 **Born:** 12/5/1995 **Age:** 26

Year	Team	Lg	G	GS	GF	IP	BFP	H	R	ER	HR	SH	SF	HB	TBB	IBB	SO	WP	W	L	Pct	Sv-Op	Hld	Vel	OPS	ERC	ERA
2021	Hrtfrd	AA	30	0	11	28.2	123	25	14	11	4	0	2	0	12	1	24	2	2	2	.500	1--	-	-	.695	3.58	3.45
2021	Albq	AAA	14	0	0	14.0	54	10	2	1	0	0	0	0	4	0	18	1	1	0	1.000	0--	-	-	.463	1.68	0.64
2021	Col	NL	6	0	3	6.2	33	9	8	8	2	0	0	0	4	0	4	1	0	0	-	0-0	0	99	.980	8.58	10.80

Junior Fernandez

Pitches: R Bats: R Pos: RP-18   Ht: 6'3" Wt: 215 Born: 3/2/1997 Age: 25

		HOW MUCH PITCHED			WHAT HE GAVE UP									THE RESULTS							
Year Team	Lg	G GS GF	IP	BFP	H	R	ER	HR	SH SF HB	TBB	IBB	SO	WP	W	L	Pct	Sv-Op	Hld	Vel	OPS	ERC	ERA
2021 Memp	AAA	13 0 7	14.1	66	18	11	10	3	0 1 1	5	0	22	0	1	2	.333	1--	-	-	.872	6.47	6.28
2019 StL	NL	13 0 5	11.2	54	9	7	7	2	0 0 4	6	0	16	2	0	1	.000	0-3	0	97	.693	5.01	5.40
2020 StL	NL	3 0 1	3.0	16	6	6	6	1	0 0 0	2	0	2	0	0	0	-	0-0	0	94	1.286	14.84	18.00
2021 StL	NL	18 0 11	20.2	97	25	13	13	2	0 0 0	15	1	15	1	1	0	1.000	0-0	0	98	.864	6.74	5.66
3 ML YEARS		34 0 18	35.1	167	40	26	26	5	0 0 4	23	1	33	3	1	1	.500	0-3	0	97	.851	6.74	6.62

J.P. Feyereisen

Pitches: R Bats: R Pos: RP-55
FIRE-eye-zehn   Ht: 6'2" Wt: 215 Born: 2/7/1993 Age: 29

		HOW MUCH PITCHED			WHAT HE GAVE UP									THE RESULTS							
Year Team	Lg	G GS GF	IP	BFP	H	R	ER	HR	SH SF HB	TBB	IBB	SO	WP	W	L	Pct	Sv-Op	Hld	Vel	OPS	ERC	ERA
2021 Drham	AAA	5 0 0	4.2	19	4	3	3	1	0 0 0	1	0	3	0	0	0	-	0--	-	-	.652	3.23	5.79
2020 Mil	NL	6 0 4	9.1	37	4	6	6	3	0 2 1	5	0	7	0	0	0	-	0-0	0	93	.719	3.39	5.79
2021 2 Tms		55 0 14	56.0	234	36	23	17	5	2 2 0	33	0	53	3	4	4	.500	3-6	15	93	.617	2.80	2.73
21 Mil	NL	21 0 4	19.1	77	10	9	7	2	1 0 0	11	0	20	1	0	2	.000	0-2	9	94	.538	2.26	3.26
21 TB	AL	34 0 10	36.2	157	26	14	10	3	1 2 0	22	0	33	2	4	2	.667	3-4	6	93	.656	3.09	2.45
2 ML YEARS		61 0 18	65.1	271	40	29	23	8	2 4 1	38	0	60	3	4	4	.500	3-6	15	93	.630	2.90	3.17

Mike Fiers

Pitches: R Bats: R Pos: SP-2
FIRES   Ht: 6'2" Wt: 211 Born: 6/15/1985 Age: 37

		HOW MUCH PITCHED			WHAT HE GAVE UP									THE RESULTS							
Year Team	Lg	G GS GF	IP	BFP	H	R	ER	HR	SH SF HB	TBB	IBB	SO	WP	W	L	Pct	Sv-Op	Hld	Vel	OPS	ERC	ERA
2011 Mil	NL	2 0 2	2.0	10	2	0	0	0	0 0 0	3	0	2	0	0	0	-	0-0	0	88	.786	8.25	0.00
2012 Mil	NL	23 22 1	127.2	539	125	56	53	12	4 4 2	36	0	135	4	9	10	.474	0-0	0	88	.694	3.50	3.74
2013 Mil	NL	11 3 4	22.1	103	28	20	18	8	1 2 0	6	0	15	1	1	4	.200	0-0	0	88	.972	6.65	7.25
2014 Mil	NL	14 10 1	71.2	274	46	19	17	7	2 1 0	17	1	76	1	6	5	.545	0-0	0	90	.531	1.68	2.13
2015 2 Tms		31 30 0	180.1	761	162	83	74	24	3 8 6	64	5	180	8	7	10	.412	0-0	0	89	.713	3.64	3.69
2016 Hou	AL	31 30 0	168.2	724	187	89	84	26	3 5 7	42	0	134	17	11	8	.579	0-0	0	90	.801	4.66	4.48
2017 Hou	AL	29 28 0	153.1	671	157	95	89	32	3 1 13	62	0	146	11	8	10	.444	0-0	0	90	.827	5.44	5.22
2018 2 Tms		31 30 0	172.0	714	166	71	68	32	1 2 8	37	1	139	4	12	8	.600	0-0	0	89	.746	3.90	3.56
2019 Oak	AL	33 33 0	184.2	754	166	82	80	30	4 5 9	53	0	126	13	15	4	.789	0-0	0	90	.712	3.76	3.90
2020 Oak	AL	11 11 0	59.0	257	65	31	30	9	0 1 4	16	0	37	1	6	3	.667	0-0	0	88	.767	4.78	4.58
2021 Oak	AL	2 2 0	9.1	45	15	8	8	4	0 0 0	4	0	5	0	2	0	.000	0-0	0	87	1.130	11.15	7.71
15 Mil	NL	21 21 0	118.0	509	117	57	51	14	3 6 5	43	5	121	6	5	9	.357	0-0	0	89	.749	4.11	3.89
15 Hou	AL	10 9 0	62.1	252	45	26	23	10	0 2 1	21	0	59	2	2	1	.667	0-0	0	90	.643	2.78	3.32
18 Det	AL	21 21 0	119.0	502	121	49	46	20	1 1 5	26	1	87	2	7	6	.538	0-0	0	89	.749	4.04	3.48
18 Oak	AL	10 9 0	53.0	212	45	22	22	12	0 1 3	11	0	52	2	5	2	.714	0-0	0	94	.740	3.57	3.74
Postseason		2 1 0	2.2	15	6	2	2	1	1 1 0	1	0	2	0	0	0	-	0-0	0	90	1.500	14.72	6.75
11 ML YEARS		218 199 8	1151.0	4852	1119	554	521	184	21 29 49	340	7	995	60	75	64	.540	0-0	0	89	.747	4.09	4.07

Kyle Finnegan

Pitches: R Bats: R Pos: RP-68   Ht: 6'2" Wt: 200 Born: 9/4/1991 Age: 30

		HOW MUCH PITCHED			WHAT HE GAVE UP									THE RESULTS							
Year Team	Lg	G GS GF	IP	BFP	H	R	ER	HR	SH SF HB	TBB	IBB	SO	WP	W	L	Pct	Sv-Op	Hld	Vel	OPS	ERC	ERA
2020 Was	NL	25 0 4	24.2	107	21	10	8	2	0 0 1	13	4	27	2	1	0	1.000	0-1	4	95	.639	3.49	2.92
2021 Was	NL	68 0 24	66.0	294	64	39	26	9	2 0 2	34	4	68	8	5	9	.357	11-14	13	96	.748	4.61	3.55
2 ML YEARS		93 0 28	90.2	401	85	49	34	11	2 0 3	47	8	95	10	6	9	.400	11-15	17	95	.719	4.30	3.38

Derek Fisher

Bats: L Throws: R Pos: RF-2;LF-1;PH-1   Ht: 6'3" Wt: 215 Born: 8/21/1993 Age: 28

		BATTING																RUNNING			AVERAGES			
Year Team	Lg	G	AB	H	2B	3B	HR	(Hm Rd)	TB	R	RBI	RC	TBB	IBB	SO	HBP	SH	SF	SB	CS	GDP	Avg	OBP	Slg	OPS
2021 Nashv	AAA	25	78	16	5	0	1	(- -)	24	11	8	-	7	0	23	0	0	0	0	0	3	.205	.271	.308	.578
2017 Hou	AL	53	146	31	4	1	5	(3 2)	52	21	17	18	17	1	54	3	0	0	3	3	1	.212	.307	.356	.663
2018 Hou	AL	42	79	13	2	2	4	(2 2)	31	13	11	4	5	0	42	0	0	2	2	0	0	.165	.209	.392	.602
2019 2 Tms	AL	57	146	27	4	1	7	(4 3)	54	23	17	13	21	0	57	0	0	0	5	1	3	.185	.287	.370	.657
2020 Tor	AL	16	31	7	2	1	1	(1 0)	14	5	7	6	7	0	11	0	0	1	0	1	0	.226	.359	.452	.811
2021 Mil	NL	4	8	2	0	1	0	(0 0)	4	1	1	1	0	0	1	0	0	0	0	0	0	.250	.250	.500	.750
19 Hou	AL	17	53	12	2	1	1	(0 1)	19	9	5	7	7	0	14	0	0	0	4	1	0	.226	.317	.358	.675
19 Tor	AL	40	93	15	2	0	6	(4 2)	35	14	12	6	14	0	43	0	0	0	1	0	3	.161	.271	.376	.647
Postseason		5	0	0	0	0	0	(0 0)	0	1	0	-	1	0	0	0	0	0	0	1	0	-	1.000	-	-
5 ML YEARS		172	410	80	12	6	17	(10 7)	155	63	53	42	50	1	165	3	0	3	10	5	4	.195	.285	.378	.663

Jay Flaa

Pitches: R Bats: R Pos: RP-2
FLAW   Ht: 6'3" Wt: 225 Born: 6/10/1992 Age: 30

		HOW MUCH PITCHED			WHAT HE GAVE UP									THE RESULTS							
Year Team	Lg	G GS GF	IP	BFP	H	R	ER	HR	SH SF HB	TBB	IBB	SO	WP	W	L	Pct	Sv-Op	Hld	Vel	OPS	ERC	ERA
2021 Gwnntt	AAA	30 0 8	33.0	156	27	22	19	3	0 0 1	30	1	42	3	1	2	.333	1--	-	-	.692	4.94	5.18
2021 2 Tms		2 0 1	2.2	13	3	4	4	2	0 0 0	3	0	3	0	0	0	-	0-0	0	92	1.362	14.89	13.50
21 Bal	AL	1 0 0	1.1	5	0	0	0	0	0 0 0	2	0	1	0	0	0	-	0-0	0	93	.400	2.46	0.00
21 Atl	NL	1 0 0	1.1	8	3	4	4	2	0 0 0	1	0	2	0	0	0	-	0-0	0	91	1.786	29.13	27.00

Jack Flaherty

Pitches: R **Bats:** R **Pos:** SP-15; RP-2   **Ht:** 6'4" **Wt:** 225 **Born:** 10/15/1995 **Age:** 26

Year Team	Lg	G	GS	GF	IP	BFP	H	R	ER	HR	SH	SF	HB	TBB	IBB	SO	WP	W	L	Pct	Sv-Op	Hld	Vel	OPS	ERC	ERA
2017 StL	NL	6	5	0	21.1	94	23	15	15	4	0	2	1	10	1	20	0	0	2	.000	0-0	0	93	.843	5.71	6.33
2018 StL	NL	28	28	0	151.0	615	108	59	56	20	2	1	11	59	3	182	6	8	9	.471	0-0	0	93	.635	3.01	3.34
2019 StL	NL	33	33	0	196.1	772	135	62	60	25	3	3	7	55	2	231	6	11	8	.579	0-0	0	94	.591	2.31	2.75
2020 StL	NL	9	9	0	40.1	170	33	22	22	6	1	1	3	16	0	49	1	4	3	.571	0-0	0	94	.677	3.68	4.91
2021 StL	NL	17	15	0	78.1	322	57	35	28	12	2	2	6	26	1	85	4	9	2	.818	0-0	0	93	.642	2.94	3.22
Postseason		4	4	0	23.0	98	23	9	9	2	2	0	1	6	0	30	3	1	3	.250	0-0	0	94	.695	3.57	3.52
5 ML YEARS		93	90	0	487.1	1973	356	193	181	67	8	9	28	166	7	567	17	32	24	.571	0-0	0	93	.632	2.87	3.34

Josh Fleming

Pitches: L **Bats:** L **Pos:** RP-15; SP-11   **Ht:** 6'2" **Wt:** 220 **Born:** 5/18/1996 **Age:** 26

Year Team	Lg	G	GS	GF	IP	BFP	H	R	ER	HR	SH	SF	HB	TBB	IBB	SO	WP	W	L	Pct	Sv-Op	Hld	Vel	OPS	ERC	ERA
2021 Drham	AAA	7	0	2	10.0	37	7	1	1	0	0	0	0	1	0	12	0	1	0	1.000	1--	-	-	.411	1.22	0.90
2020 TB	AL	7	5	0	32.1	130	28	10	10	5	0	0	1	7	0	25	0	5	0	1.000	0-0	0	91	.670	3.14	2.78
2021 TB	AL	26	11	1	104.1	448	110	60	59	11	3	1	3	31	5	65	0	10	8	.556	1-1	3	91	.731	4.04	5.09
Postseason		2	0	0	5.2	25	8	4	4	1	0	0	0	2	0	3	0	0	0	-	0-0	0	93	1.009	7.38	6.35
2 ML YEARS		33	16	1	136.2	578	138	70	69	16	3	1	4	38	5	90	0	15	8	.652	1-1	3	91	.717	3.83	4.54

Aaron Fletcher

Pitches: L **Bats:** L **Pos:** RP-4   **Ht:** 6'0" **Wt:** 220 **Born:** 2/25/1996 **Age:** 26

Year Team	Lg	G	GS	GF	IP	BFP	H	R	ER	HR	SH	SF	HB	TBB	IBB	SO	WP	W	L	Pct	Sv-Op	Hld	Vel	OPS	ERC	ERA
2021 Tacom	AAA	37	0	12	47.1	205	53	24	19	6	1	2	4	13	3	43	2	4	0	1.000	2--	-	-	.803	4.74	3.61
2020 Sea	AL	6	0	0	4.1	29	7	6	6	1	0	0	2	7	0	7	0	0	0	-	0-0	1	93	1.102	16.97	12.46
2021 Sea	AL	4	0	2	3.2	20	7	5	5	1	0	0	0	1	0	2	0	0	0	-	0-0	0	92	.979	10.06	12.27
2 ML YEARS		10	0	2	8.0	49	14	11	11	2	0	0	2	8	0	9	0	0	0	-	0-0	1	93	1.054	13.83	12.38

David Fletcher

Bats: R **Throws:** R **Pos:** 2B-142;SS-20;PH-1   **Ht:** 5'9" **Wt:** 185 **Born:** 5/31/1994 **Age:** 28

					BATTING													RUNNING			AVERAGES			
Year Team	Lg	G	AB	H	2B	3B	HR	(Hm | Rd)	TB	R	RBI	RC	TBB	IBB	SO	HBP	SH	SF	SB	CS	GDP	Avg	OBP	Slg	OPS
2018 LAA	AL	80	284	78	18	2	1	(1 | 0)	103	35	25	35	15	0	34	3	3	2	3	0	7	.275	.316	.363	.678
2019 LAA	AL	154	596	173	30	4	6	(3 | 3)	229	83	49	89	55	2	64	0	1	1	8	3	8	.290	.350	.384	.734
2020 LAA	AL	49	207	66	13	0	3	(1 | 2)	88	31	18	38	20	0	25	0	1	2	2	1	4	.319	.376	.425	.801
2021 LAA	AL	157	626	164	27	3	2	(0 | 2)	203	74	47	70	31	1	60	1	6	1	15	3	10	.262	.297	.324	.622
4 ML YEARS		440	1713	481	88	9	12	(5 | 7)	623	223	139	232	121	3	183	4	11	6	28	7	29	.281	.329	.364	.692

Chris Flexen

Pitches: R **Bats:** R **Pos:** SP-31   **Ht:** 6'3" **Wt:** 250 **Born:** 7/1/1994 **Age:** 27

Year Team	Lg	G	GS	GF	IP	BFP	H	R	ER	HR	SH	SF	HB	TBB	IBB	SO	WP	W	L	Pct	Sv-Op	Hld	Vel	OPS	ERC	ERA
2017 NYM	NL	14	9	1	48.0	233	62	44	42	11	1	2	2	35	0	36	1	3	6	.333	0-0	0	92	.981	8.75	7.88
2018 NYM	NL	4	1	2	6.1	40	14	13	9	2	0	0	1	6	1	3	0	0	2	.000	0-0	0	93	1.283	17.26	12.79
2019 NYM	NL	9	1	4	13.2	70	15	12	10	1	0	1	0	13	2	10	1	0	3	.000	0-0	0	94	.829	6.12	6.59
2021 Sea	AL	31	31	0	179.2	741	185	74	72	19	0	7	4	40	0	125	2	14	6	.700	0-0	0	93	.724	3.74	3.61
4 ML YEARS		58	42	7	247.2	1084	276	143	133	33	1	10	7	94	3	174	4	17	17	.500	0-0	0	93	.803	5.05	4.83

Wilmer Flores

Bats: R **Throws:** R **Pos:** 3B-58;PH-39;1B-34;2B-30;DH-4   **Ht:** 6'2" **Wt:** 213 **Born:** 8/6/1991 **Age:** 30

					BATTING													RUNNING			AVERAGES			
Year Team	Lg	G	AB	H	2B	3B	HR	(Hm | Rd)	TB	R	RBI	RC	TBB	IBB	SO	HBP	SH	SF	SB	CS	GDP	Avg	OBP	Slg	OPS
2013 NYM	NL	27	95	20	5	0	1	(0 | 1)	28	8	13	7	5	0	23	0	0	1	0	0	1	.211	.248	.295	.542
2014 NYM	NL	78	259	65	13	1	6	(4 | 2)	98	28	29	25	12	2	31	1	1	1	1	0	6	.251	.286	.378	.664
2015 NYM	NL	137	483	127	22	0	16	(8 | 8)	197	55	59	58	19	2	63	4	2	2	0	1	12	.263	.295	.408	.703
2016 NYM	NL	103	307	82	14	0	16	(12 | 4)	144	38	49	39	23	0	48	2	0	3	1	1	9	.267	.319	.469	.788
2017 NYM	NL	110	336	91	17	1	18	(9 | 9)	164	42	52	39	17	1	54	3	0	6	1	1	14	.271	.307	.488	.795
2018 NYM	NL	126	386	103	25	0	11	(4 | 7)	161	43	51	51	29	1	42	5	0	9	0	0	8	.267	.319	.417	.736
2019 Ari	NL	89	265	84	18	0	9	(6 | 3)	129	31	37	38	15	0	31	4	0	1	0	0	9	.317	.361	.487	.848
2020 SF	NL	55	198	53	11	1	12	(7 | 5)	102	30	32	30	13	1	36	1	0	1	0	0	5	.268	.315	.515	.830
2021 SF	NL	139	389	102	16	1	18	(8 | 10)	174	57	53	56	41	0	56	3	0	3	1	0	11	.262	.335	.447	.782
Postseason		13	41	8	2	1	0	(0 | 0)	12	4	0	5	2	9		1	1	0	1	0	1	.195	.298	.293	.591
9 ML YEARS		864	2718	727	141	4	107	(58 | 49)	1197	332	375	343	174	7	384	23	3	27	5	3	75	.267	.314	.440	.754

Bernardo Flores Jr.

Pitches: L **Bats:** L **Pos:** RP-1   **Ht:** 6'4" **Wt:** 190 **Born:** 8/23/1995 **Age:** 26

Year Team	Lg	G	GS	GF	IP	BFP	H	R	ER	HR	SH	SF	HB	TBB	IBB	SO	WP	W	L	Pct	Sv-Op	Hld	Vel	OPS	ERC	ERA
2021 Memp	AAA	8	5	1	31.1	148	40	24	20	6	2	1	0	18	1	26	0	2	2	.500	0--	-	-	.972	7.19	5.74
2020 CWS	AL	2	0	1	2.0	10	4	2	2	0	0	0	0	2	0	2	0	0	0	-	0-0	0	92	.900	7.48	9.00
2021 StL	NL	1	0	0	0.0	3	1	1	1	0	0	0	0	2	0	0	0	0	0	-	0-0	0	90	2.000		
2 ML YEARS		3	0	1	2.0	13	5	3	3	0	0	0	0	4	0	2	0	0	0	-	0-0	0	92	1.084	15.69	13.50

Estevan Florial

Bats: L Throws: R Pos: CF-11;PH-1;PR-1   Ht: 6'1" Wt: 195 Born: 11/25/1997 Age: 24

						BATTING														RUNNING			AVERAGES			
Year	Team	Lg	G	AB	H	2B	3B	HR	(Hm	Rd)	TB	R	RBI	RC	TBB	IBB	SO	HBP	SH	SF	SB	CS	GDP	Avg	OBP	Slg	OPS
2021	S-WB	AAA	74	296	66	17	1	13	(-	-)	124	64	40	-	41	0	104	3	3	2	13	6	2	.223	.322	.419	.741
2020	NYY	AL	1	3	1	0	0	0	(0	0)	1	0	0	0	0	0	2	0	0	0	0	0	0	.333	.333	.333	.667
2021	NYY	AL	11	20	6	2	0	1	(1	0)	11	3	2	3	5	0	6	0	0	0	1	0	0	.300	.440	.550	.990
	2 ML YEARS		12	23	7	2	0	1	(1	0)	12	3	2	3	5	0	8	0	0	0	1	0	0	.304	.429	.522	.950

Dylan Floro

Pitches: R Bats: L Pos: RP-68   Ht: 6'2" Wt: 203 Born: 12/27/1990 Age: 31

			HOW MUCH PITCHED					WHAT HE GAVE UP											THE RESULTS							
Year	Team	Lg	G	GS	GF	IP	BFP	H	R	ER	HR	SH	SF	HB	TBB	IBB	SO	WP	W	L	Pct	Sv-Op	Hld	Vel	OPS	ERC	ERA
2016	TB	AL	12	0	4	15.0	72	23	8	7	0	0	1	0	5	1	14	2	0	1	.000	0-0	0	93	.813	5.96	4.20
2017	ChC	NL	3	0	2	9.2	45	15	7	7	2	0	1	0	2	0	6	0	0	0	-	0-0	0	91	.971	8.12	6.52
2018	2 Tms	NL	54	0	20	64.0	271	57	17	16	3	3	3	1	23	6	58	1	6	3	.667	0-0	7	93	.634	2.85	2.25
2019	LAD	NL	50	0	4	46.2	201	46	25	22	4	2	1	2	14	5	42	1	5	3	.625	0-3	6	94	.685	3.44	4.24
2020	LAD	NL	25	0	4	24.1	98	23	7	7	1	0	2	0	4	1	19	1	3	0	1.000	0-0	4	93	.623	2.48	2.59
2021	Mia	NL	68	0	32	64.0	270	53	25	20	2	0	1	0	25	3	62	1	6	6	.500	15-21	11	94	.576	2.54	2.81
18	Cin	NL	25	0	13	36.1	159	39	12	11	2	2	3	0	12	3	27	0	3	2	.600	0-0	1	93	.726	3.69	2.72
18	LAD	NL	29	0	7	27.2	112	18	5	5	1	1	0	1	11	3	31	1	3	1	.750	0-0	6	94	.503	1.84	1.63
	Postseason		14	0	3	12.1	51	11	8	6	1	0	0	0	5	2	15	0	0	1	.000	0-0	0	93	.705	3.20	4.38
	6 ML YEARS		212	0	66	223.2	957	217	89	79	12	5	8	4	73	16	201	6	20	13	.606	15-24	28	93	.657	3.22	3.18

Jason Foley

Pitches: R Bats: R Pos: RP-11   Ht: 6'4" Wt: 215 Born: 11/1/1995 Age: 26

			HOW MUCH PITCHED					WHAT HE GAVE UP											THE RESULTS							
Year	Team	Lg	G	GS	GF	IP	BFP	H	R	ER	HR	SH	SF	HB	TBB	IBB	SO	WP	W	L	Pct	Sv-Op	Hld	Vel	OPS	ERC	ERA
2021	Toledo	AAA	32	0	9	34.2	153	34	18	17	5	1	0	4	19	1	36	5	1	1	.500	2--	-	-	.809	5.49	4.41
2021	Det	AL	11	0	1	10.1	45	8	3	3	1	0	0	3	5	0	6	3	0	0	-	0-0	2	96	.761	4.35	2.61

Mike Foltynewicz

Pitches: R Bats: R Pos: SP-24; RP-4   Ht: 6'4" Wt: 195 Born: 10/7/1991 Age: 30

fohl-tuh-neh-vich

			HOW MUCH PITCHED					WHAT HE GAVE UP											THE RESULTS							
Year	Team	Lg	G	GS	GF	IP	BFP	H	R	ER	HR	SH	SF	HB	TBB	IBB	SO	WP	W	L	Pct	Sv-Op	Hld	Vel	OPS	ERC	ERA
2014	Hou	AL	16	0	9	18.2	84	23	11	11	3	0	0	7	0	14	3	0	1	.000	0-0	1	97	.864	5.80	5.30
2015	Atl	NL	18	15	1	86.2	399	112	63	55	17	2	6	4	29	0	77	3	4	6	.400	0-0	1	95	.896	6.43	5.71
2016	Atl	NL	22	22	0	123.1	525	125	61	59	18	5	4	6	35	2	111	13	9	5	.643	0-0	0	95	.761	4.18	4.31
2017	Atl	NL	29	28	0	154.0	692	169	86	82	20	11	2	10	59	2	143	4	10	13	.435	0-0	0	95	.795	4.97	4.79
2018	Atl	NL	31	31	0	183.0	744	130	65	58	17	2	1	6	68	3	202	7	13	10	.565	0-0	0	96	.600	2.49	2.85
2019	Atl	NL	21	21	0	117.0	491	109	65	59	23	5	1	2	37	2	105	5	8	6	.571	0-0	0	95	.764	4.05	4.54
2020	Atl	NL	1	1	0	3.1	16	4	6	6	3	0	0	0	4	0	3	0	0	1	.000	0-0	0	90	1.583	18.39	16.20
2021	Tex	AL	28	24	0	139.0	586	139	86	84	35	3	3	9	36	0	97	2	2	12	.143	0-0	0	94	.843	4.85	5.44
	Postseason		4	4	0	13.1	63	11	12	11	2	2	0	1	10	2	17	0	1	2	.333	0-0	0	95	.761	4.68	7.43
	8 ML YEARS		166	142	10	825.0	3537	811	443	414	136	28	17	37	275	9	752	37	46	54	.460	0-0	2	95	.769	4.32	4.52

Mike Ford

Bats: L Throws: R Pos: 1B-21;PH-2   Ht: 6'0" Wt: 225 Born: 7/4/1992 Age: 29

						BATTING														RUNNING			AVERAGES			
Year	Team	Lg	G	AB	H	2B	3B	HR	(Hm	Rd)	TB	R	RBI	RC	TBB	IBB	SO	HBP	SH	SF	SB	CS	GDP	Avg	OBP	Slg	OPS
2021	Drham	AAA	40	140	34	5	1	11	(-	-)	74	22	31	-	21	0	41	1	0	4	1	0	4	.243	.346	.529	.874
2021	Roch	AAA	25	88	18	3	0	3	(-	-)	30	7	12	-	10	1	24	1	0	0	0	0	1	.205	.293	.341	.634
2019	NYY	AL	50	143	37	7	0	12	(2	10)	80	30	25	27	17	2	28	3	0	0	0	0	0	.259	.350	.559	.909
2020	NYY	AL	29	74	10	4	0	2	(1	1)	20	5	11	3	7	0	16	2	0	1	0	0	4	.135	.226	.270	.496
2021	NYY	AL	22	60	8	0	0	3	(1	2)	17	6	5	3	11	1	23	1	0	0	0	0	1	.133	.278	.283	.561
	Postseason		3	2	0	0	0	0	(0	0)	0	0	0	0	0	0	1	0	0	0	0	0	0	.000	.000	.000	.000
	3 ML YEARS		101	277	55	11	0	17	(4	13)	117	41	41	33	35	3	67	6	0	1	0	0	5	.199	.301	.422	.723

Nick Fortes

Bats: R Throws: R Pos: C-7;PH-6;DH-3;PR-1   Ht: 5'11" Wt: 198 Born: 11/11/1996 Age: 25

						BATTING														RUNNING			AVERAGES			
Year	Team	Lg	G	AB	H	2B	3B	HR	(Hm	Rd)	TB	R	RBI	RC	TBB	IBB	SO	HBP	SH	SF	SB	CS	GDP	Avg	OBP	Slg	OPS
2021	Pnscla	AA	57	195	49	10	1	3	(-	-)	70	21	23	-	22	0	36	5	0	3	6	2	3	.251	.338	.359	.697
2021	Jaxnvl	AAA	38	135	32	7	0	4	(-	-)	51	16	21	-	10	1	18	7	0	0	0	0	11	.237	.322	.378	.700
2021	Mia	NL	14	31	9	0	0	4	(4	0)	21	6	7	8	3	0	8	0	0	0	1	0	1	.290	.353	.677	1.030

Matt Foster

Pitches: R Bats: R Pos: RP-37   Ht: 6'0" Wt: 215 Born: 1/27/1995 Age: 27

			HOW MUCH PITCHED					WHAT HE GAVE UP											THE RESULTS							
Year	Team	Lg	G	GS	GF	IP	BFP	H	R	ER	HR	SH	SF	HB	TBB	IBB	SO	WP	W	L	Pct	Sv-Op	Hld	Vel	OPS	ERC	ERA
2021	Charlt	AAA	14	0	5	14.2	60	14	7	7	2	0	0	2	0	23	2	0	2	.000	0--	-		.732	2.98	4.30
2020	CWS	AL	23	2	4	28.2	109	16	8	7	2	1	0	0	9	0	31	0	6	1	.857	0-1	2	94	.504	1.50	2.20
2021	CWS	AL	37	0	17	39.0	174	43	27	26	9	0	2	2	13	0	40	1	2	1	.667	1-2	2	94	.811	5.47	6.00
	Postseason		1	0	0	0.1	3	0	0	0	0	0	0	0	2	0	0	0	0	0	-	0-0	0	95	.667	19.60	0.00
	2 ML YEARS		60	2	21	67.2	283	59	35	33	11	1	2	2	22	0	71	1	8	2	.800	1-3	4	94	.693	3.58	4.39

Dexter Fowler

Bats: B **Throws:** R **Pos:** RF-7 **Ht:** 6'5" **Wt:** 205 **Born:** 3/22/1986 **Age:** 36

Year	Team	Lg	G	AB	H	2B	3B	HR	(Hm	Rd)	TB	R	RBI	RC	TBB	IBB	SO	HBP	SH	SF	SB	CS	GDP	Avg	OBP	Slg	OPS
2008	Col	NL	13	26	4	0	0	0	(0	0)	4	3	0	0	0	0	5	1	0	0	0	1	0	.154	.185	.154	.339
2009	Col	NL	135	433	115	29	10	4	(2	2)	176	73	34	68	67	1	116	1	14	3	27	10	4	.266	.363	.406	.770
2010	Col	NL	132	439	114	20	14	6	(5	1)	180	73	36	68	57	0	104	2	7	0	13	8	5	.260	.347	.410	.757
2011	Col	NL	125	481	128	35	15	5	(3	2)	208	84	45	79	68	3	130	6	7	1	12	9	6	.266	.363	.432	.796
2012	Col	NL	143	454	136	18	11	13	(10	3)	215	72	53	81	68	1	128	0	6	2	12	5	5	.300	.389	.474	.863
2013	Col	NL	119	415	109	18	3	12	(7	5)	169	71	42	62	65	1	105	6	4	2	19	9	5	.263	.369	.407	.776
2014	Hou	AL	116	434	120	21	4	8	(5	3)	173	61	35	65	66	2	108	3	1	1	11	4	6	.276	.375	.399	.774
2015	ChC	NL	156	596	149	29	8	17	(11	6)	245	102	46	77	84	1	154	5	2	3	20	7	4	.250	.346	.411	.757
2016	ChC	NL	125	456	126	25	7	13	(4	9)	204	84	48	83	79	0	124	11	1	4	13	4	3	.276	.393	.447	.840
2017	StL	NL	118	420	111	22	9	18	(11	7)	205	68	64	74	63	6	101	4	0	4	7	3	10	.264	.363	.488	.851
2018	StL	NL	90	289	52	10	0	8	(4	4)	86	40	31	27	38	0	75	3	0	4	5	2	2	.180	.278	.298	.576
2019	StL	NL	150	487	116	24	1	19	(9	10)	199	69	67	81	74	1	142	8	1	4	8	5	6	.238	.346	.409	.754
2020	StL	NL	31	90	21	2	0	4	(3	1)	35	14	15	11	10	0	28	1	0	1	1	0	2	.233	.317	.389	.706
2021	LAA	AL	7	20	5	0	0	0	(0	0)	5	3	1	2	1	0	6	0	0	0	1	0	0	.250	.286	.250	.536
Postseason			42	169	37	9	0	5	(3	2)	61	23	16	15	9	0	40	1	2	2	2	1	1	.219	.260	.361	.621
14 ML YEARS			1460	5040	1306	253	82	127	(74	53)	2104	817	517	778	740	16	1326	51	43	28	149	68	58	.259	.358	.417	.775

Dustin Fowler

Bats: L **Throws:** L **Pos:** CF-12;PH-6;RF-1 **Ht:** 6'0" **Wt:** 195 **Born:** 12/29/1994 **Age:** 27

Year	Team	Lg	G	AB	H	2B	3B	HR	(Hm	Rd)	TB	R	RBI	RC	TBB	IBB	SO	HBP	SH	SF	SB	CS	GDP	Avg	OBP	Slg	OPS
2021	Indy	AAA	13	37	10	2	1	3	(-	-)	23	8	6	-	9	0	16	1	0	0	2	0	0	.270	.426	.622	1.047
2021	Jaxnvl	AAA	24	88	27	1	1	6	(-	-)	48	13	23	-	2	0	25	1	0	1	0	0	0	.307	.326	.545	.872
2017	NYY	AL	1	0	0	0	0	0	(0	0)	0	0	0	0	0	0	0	0	0	0	0	0	0				
2018	Oak	AL	69	192	43	3	2	6	(2	4)	68	19	23	19	8	0	47	1	0	2	6	4	2	.224	.256	.354	.610
2021	Pit	NL	18	41	7	1	0	0	(0	0)	8	3	2	1	3	0	20	1	0	1	1	0	0	.171	.239	.195	.434
3 ML YEARS			88	233	50	4	2	6	(2	4)	76	22	25	20	11	0	67	2	0	3	7	4	2	.215	.253	.326	.579

Jake Fraley

Bats: L **Throws:** L **Pos:** LF-51;PH-17;CF-16;DH-7;RF-6 **Ht:** 6'0" **Wt:** 195 **Born:** 5/25/1995 **Age:** 27

Year	Team	Lg	G	AB	H	2B	3B	HR	(Hm	Rd)	TB	R	RBI	RC	TBB	IBB	SO	HBP	SH	SF	SB	CS	GDP	Avg	OBP	Slg	OPS
2021	Tacom	AAA	13	40	13	1	0	3	(-	-)	23	8	7	-	9	0	15	1	0	1	3	1	0	.325	.451	.575	1.026
2019	Sea	AL	12	40	6	2	0	0	(0	0)	8	3	1	2	0	0	14	1	0	0	2	0	0	.150	.171	.200	.371
2020	Sea	AL	7	26	4	1	1	0	(0	0)	7	3	0	1	2	0	11	1	0	0	2	1	0	.154	.241	.269	.511
2021	Sea	AL	78	214	45	7	0	9	(3	6)	79	27	36	40	46	1	71	2	1	2	10	2	3	.210	.352	.369	.721
3 ML YEARS			97	280	55	10	1	9	(3	6)	94	33	37	43	48	1	96	4	1	2	12	3	3	.196	.320	.336	.656

Ty France

Bats: R **Throws:** R **Pos:** 1B-106;DH-26;2B-21;3B-5;PH-1 **Ht:** 5'11" **Wt:** 217 **Born:** 7/13/1994 **Age:** 27

Year	Team	Lg	G	AB	H	2B	3B	HR	(Hm	Rd)	TB	R	RBI	RC	TBB	IBB	SO	HBP	SH	SF	SB	CS	GDP	Avg	OBP	Slg	OPS
2019	SD	NL	69	184	43	8	1	7	(4	3)	74	20	24	25	9	0	49	7	0	1	0	2	8	.234	.294	.402	.696
2020	2 Tms		43	141	43	9	1	4	(2	2)	66	19	23	29	11	0	37	3	0	0	0	0	5	.305	.368	.468	.836
2021	Sea	AL	152	571	166	32	1	18	(6	12)	254	85	73	100	46	1	106	27	0	6	0	0	13	.291	.368	.445	.813
20	SD	NL	20	55	17	4	0	2	(2	0)	27	9	10	11	5	0	15	1	0	0	0	0	1	.309	.377	.491	.868
20	Sea	AL	23	86	26	5	1	2	(0	2)	39	10	13	18	6	0	22	2	0	0	0	0	2	.302	.362	.453	.815
3 ML YEARS			264	896	252	49	3	29	(12	17)	394	124	120	154	66	1	192	37	0	7	0	2	24	.281	.353	.440	.793

Maikel Franco

Bats: R **Throws:** R **Pos:** 3B-99;DH-3;1B-2;PH-2;PR-1 MY-kell **Ht:** 6'1" **Wt:** 225 **Born:** 8/26/1992 **Age:** 29

Year	Team	Lg	G	AB	H	2B	3B	HR	(Hm	Rd)	TB	R	RBI	RC	TBB	IBB	SO	HBP	SH	SF	SB	CS	GDP	Avg	OBP	Slg	OPS
2014	Phi	NL	16	56	10	2	0	0	(0	0)	12	5	5	1	1	0	13	0	0	1	0	0	1	.179	.190	.214	.404
2015	Phi	NL	80	304	85	22	1	14	(7	7)	151	45	50	48	26	2	52	4	0	1	1	0	8	.280	.343	.497	.840
2016	Phi	NL	152	581	148	23	1	25	(10	15)	248	67	88	74	40	7	106	5	0	4	1	1	13	.255	.306	.427	.733
2017	Phi	NL	154	575	132	29	1	24	(14	10)	235	66	76	53	41	3	95	2	0	5	0	0	21	.230	.281	.409	.690
2018	Phi	NL	131	433	117	17	1	22	(10	12)	202	48	68	55	29	7	62	0	0	3	0	0	15	.270	.314	.467	.780
2019	Phi	NL	123	389	91	17	0	17	(13	4)	159	48	56	44	36	19	61	0	0	3	0	0	14	.234	.297	.409	.705
2020	KC	AL	60	223	62	16	0	8	(3	5)	102	23	38	36	16	1	38	0	0	4	1	0	4	.278	.321	.457	.778
2021	Bal	AL	104	377	79	22	0	11	(7	4)	134	31	47	30	20	0	67	3	0	3	0	0	12	.210	.253	.355	.609
8 ML YEARS			820	2938	724	148	4	121	(64	57)	1243	333	428	341	209	39	494	14	0	24	4	1	88	.246	.297	.423	.720

Wander Franco

Bats: B **Throws:** R **Pos:** SS-63;3B-8;2B-1 **Ht:** 5'10" **Wt:** 189 **Born:** 3/1/2001 **Age:** 21

Year	Team	Lg	G	AB	H	2B	3B	HR	(Hm	Rd)	TB	R	RBI	RC	TBB	IBB	SO	HBP	SH	SF	SB	CS	GDP	Avg	OBP	Slg	OPS
2018	Prnctn	R+	61	242	85	10	7	11	(-	-)	142	46	57	57	27	1	19	2	0	2	4	3	5	.351	.418	.587	1.004
2019	2 Tms	Low	114	425	139	27	7	9	(-	-)	207	82	53	89	56	3	35	2	0	12	18	14	6	.327	.398	.487	.885
2021	Drham	AAA	40	163	51	11	6	7	(-	-)	95	31	35	-	14	0	21	2	0	1	5	4	1	.313	.372	.583	.955
2021	TB	AL	70	281	81	18	5	7	(2	5)	130	53	39	51	24	0	37	2	0	1	2	1	2	.288	.347	.463	.810

Seth Frankoff

Pitches: R Bats: R Pos: SP-3; RP-1　　　　　　　　　**Ht: 6'5" Wt: 206 Born: 8/27/1988 Age: 33**

Year	Team	Lg	G	GS	GF	IP	BFP	H	R	ER	HR	SH	SF	HB	TBB	IBB	SO	WP	W	L	Pct	Sv-Op	Hld	Vel	OPS	ERC	ERA
2021	Reno	AAA	8	3	0	21.0	102	26	20	19	8	2	0	2	14	0	25	2	2	0	1.000	0--	-	-	1.075	9.60	8.14
2017	ChC	NL	1	0	0	2.0	9	4	2	2	1	0	0	0	0	0	2	0	0	1	.000	0-0	0	92	1.222	13.26	9.00
2020	Sea	AL	2	0	1	2.2	16	6	5	5	0	0	0	0	2	0	0	0	0	0	-	0-0	0	93	1.071	12.64	16.88
2021	Ari	NL	4	3	1	14.2	74	20	15	15	4	3	0	2	9	0	11	3	0	2	.000	0-0	0	91	1.020	9.28	9.20
3 ML YEARS			7	3	2	19.1	99	30	22	22	5	3	0	2	11	0	13	3	0	3	.000	0-0	0	92	1.050	10.16	10.24

Adam Frazier

Bats: L Throws: R Pos: 2B-140;PH-13;LF-12;DH-1;PR-1　　　　　**Ht: 5'10" Wt: 185 Born: 12/14/1991 Age: 30**

Year	Team	Lg	G	AB	H	2B	3B	HR	(Hm	Rd)	TB	R	RBI	RC	TBB	IBB	SO	HBP	SH	SF	SB	CS	GDP	Avg	OBP	Slg	OPS
2016	Pit	NL	66	146	44	8	1	2	(2	0)	60	21	11	23	12	0	26	1	0	1	4	1	0	.301	.356	.411	.767
2017	Pit	NL	121	406	112	20	6	6	(2	4)	162	55	53	61	36	2	57	8	1	3	9	5	9	.276	.344	.399	.743
2018	Pit	NL	113	318	88	23	2	10	(6	4)	145	52	35	49	29	2	53	3	1	1	1	3	3	.277	.342	.456	.798
2019	Pit	NL	152	554	154	33	7	10	(5	5)	231	80	50	72	40	4	75	9	4	1	5	5	6	.278	.336	.417	.753
2020	Pit	NL	58	209	48	7	0	7	(5	2)	76	22	23	23	17	0	35	3	1	0	1	3	3	.230	.297	.364	.661
2021	2 Tms	NL	155	577	176	36	5	5	(4	1)	237	83	43	84	48	2	69	10	3	1	10	5	10	.305	.368	.411	.779
21	Pit	NL	98	386	125	28	4	4	(3	1)	173	58	32	64	35	1	46	6	0	1	5	4	6	.324	.388	.448	.836
21	SD	NL	57	191	51	8	1	1	(1	0)	64	25	11	20	13	1	23	4	3	0	5	1	4	.267	.327	.335	.662
6 ML YEARS			665	2210	622	127	21	40	(24	16)	911	313	215	312	182	10	315	34	10	7	30	22	31	.281	.344	.412	.757

Clint Frazier

Bats: R Throws: R Pos: LF-37;RF-33;PH-9　　　　　　　**Ht: 5'11" Wt: 212 Born: 9/6/1994 Age: 27**

Year	Team	Lg	G	AB	H	2B	3B	HR	(Hm	Rd)	TB	R	RBI	RC	TBB	IBB	SO	HBP	SH	SF	SB	CS	GDP	Avg	OBP	Slg	OPS
2017	NYY	AL	39	134	31	9	4	4	(3	1)	60	16	17	17	7	0	43	0	0	1	1	0	2	.231	.268	.448	.715
2018	NYY	AL	15	34	9	3	0	0	(0	0)	12	9	1	3	5	0	13	2	0	0	0	0	3	.265	.390	.353	.743
2019	NYY	AL	69	225	60	14	0	12	(5	7)	110	31	38	40	16	1	70	2	0	3	1	2	5	.267	.317	.489	.806
2020	NYY	AL	39	131	35	6	1	8	(6	2)	67	24	26	29	25	0	44	3	0	1	3	0	5	.267	.394	.511	.905
2021	NYY	AL	66	183	34	9	0	5	(3	2)	58	20	15	18	32	0	65	3	0	0	2	0	8	.186	.317	.317	.633
Postseason			4	7	2	0	0	1	(0	1)	5	1	1	0	0	0	5	0	0	0	0	0	0	.286	.286	.714	1.000
5 ML YEARS			228	707	169	41	5	29	(17	12)	307	100	97	107	85	1	235	10	0	5	7	2	20	.239	.327	.434	.761

Todd Frazier

Bats: R Throws: R Pos: 1B-4;PH-4;3B-3;DH-3　　　　　　　**Ht: 6'3" Wt: 215 Born: 2/12/1986 Age: 36**

Year	Team	Lg	G	AB	H	2B	3B	HR	(Hm	Rd)	TB	R	RBI	RC	TBB	IBB	SO	HBP	SH	SF	SB	CS	GDP	Avg	OBP	Slg	OPS
2011	Cin	NL	41	112	26	5	0	6	(2	4)	49	17	15	13	7	0	27	2	0	0	1	0	2	.232	.289	.438	.727
2012	Cin	NL	128	422	115	26	6	19	(10	9)	210	55	67	59	36	3	103	3	0	4	3	2	9	.273	.331	.498	.829
2013	Cin	NL	150	531	124	29	3	19	(12	7)	216	63	73	67	50	1	125	14	2	3	6	5	14	.234	.314	.407	.721
2014	Cin	NL	157	597	163	22	1	29	(20	9)	274	88	80	84	52	2	139	7	0	4	20	8	9	.273	.336	.459	.795
2015	Cin	NL	157	619	158	43	1	35	(19	16)	308	82	89	73	44	3	137	7	1	7	13	8	19	.255	.309	.498	.806
2016	CWS	AL	158	590	133	21	0	40	(16	24)	274	89	98	71	64	1	163	4	1	7	15	5	11	.225	.302	.464	.767
2017	2 Tms	AL	147	474	101	19	1	27	(9	18)	203	74	76	69	83	2	125	14	0	5	4	3	10	.213	.344	.428	.772
2018	NYM	NL	115	408	87	18	0	18	(10	8)	159	54	59	48	48	1	112	8	0	8	9	4	10	.213	.303	.390	.693
2019	NYM	NL	133	447	112	19	2	21	(10	11)	198	63	67	70	40	1	106	12	0	0	1	2	9	.251	.329	.443	.772
2020	2 Tms	NL	45	157	37	9	1	4	(3	1)	60	16	12	17	11	0	42	4	0	1	1	1	1	.236	.302	.382	.684
2021	Pit	NL	13	35	3	1	0	0	(0	0)	4	3	4	0	2	0	6	2	0	0	0	0	1	.086	.200	.114	.314
17	CWS	AL	81	280	58	15	0	16	(5	11)	121	41	44	39	48	1	71	4	0	3	4	3	4	.207	.328	.432	.761
17	NYY	AL	66	194	43	4	1	11	(4	7)	82	33	32	30	35	1	54	10	0	2	0	0	6	.222	.365	.423	.788
20	Tex	AL	31	108	26	7	1	2	(1	1)	41	11	7	12	10	0	26	3	0	0	1	1	0	.241	.322	.380	.702
20	NYM	NL	14	49	11	2	0	2	(2	0)	19	5	5	5	1	0	16	1	0	0	0	0	1	.224	.255	.388	.643
Postseason			18	53	10	3	0	1	(1	0)	16	6	6	5	5	0	13	0	0	0	0	1	0	.189	.259	.302	.561
11 ML YEARS			1244	4392	1059	212	15	218	(111	107)	1955	604	640	571	438	12	1085	77	4	38	73	38	95	.241	.318	.445	.763

Kyle Freeland

Pitches: L Bats: L Pos: SP-23　　　　　　　　　**Ht: 6'4" Wt: 204 Born: 5/14/1993 Age: 29**

Year	Team	Lg	G	GS	GF	IP	BFP	H	R	ER	HR	SH	SF	HB	TBB	IBB	SO	WP	W	L	Pct	Sv-Op	Hld	Vel	OPS	ERC	ERA
2017	Col	NL	33	28	0	156.0	688	169	78	71	17	14	7	8	63	4	107	1	11	11	.500	0-0	0	92	.792	4.83	4.10
2018	Col	NL	33	33	0	202.1	844	182	64	64	17	5	6	6	70	2	173	2	17	7	.708	0-0	0	92	.666	3.33	2.85
2019	Col	NL	22	22	0	104.1	473	126	85	78	25	2	4	2	39	3	79	4	3	11	.214	0-0	0	92	.909	6.23	6.73
2020	Col	NL	13	13	0	70.2	304	77	34	34	9	0	1	3	23	0	46	0	2	3	.400	0-0	0	92	.772	4.73	4.33
2021	Col	NL	23	23	0	120.2	515	133	59	58	20	3	1	4	38	1	105	1	7	8	.467	0-0	0	91	.813	5.03	4.33
Postseason			1	1	0	6.2	24	4	0	0	0	0	0	0	1	0	6	0	0	0	-	0-0	0	93	.382	1.06	0.00
5 ML YEARS			124	119	0	654.0	2824	687	320	305	88	24	19	23	233	10	510	8	40	40	.500	0-0	0	92	.776	4.59	4.20

Freddie Freeman

Bats: L Throws: R Pos: 1B-159
Ht: 6'5" Wt: 220 Born: 9/12/1989 Age: 32

Year	Team	Lg	G	AB	H	2B	3B	HR	(Hm	Rd)	TB	R	RBI	RC	TBB	IBB	SO	HBP	SH	SF	SB	CS	GDP	Avg	OBP	Slg	OPS
2010	Atl	NL	20	24	4	1	0	1	(0	1)	8	3	1	0	0	0	8	0	0	0	0	0	1	.167	.167	.333	.500
2011	Atl	NL	157	571	161	32	0	21	(9	12)	256	67	76	79	53	3	142	6	0	5	4	4	15	.282	.346	.448	.795
2012	Atl	NL	147	540	140	33	2	23	(12	11)	246	91	94	82	64	4	129	7	0	9	2	0	10	.259	.340	.456	.796
2013	Atl	NL	147	551	176	27	2	23	(16	7)	276	89	109	124	66	10	121	7	0	5	1	0	10	.319	.396	.501	.897
2014	Atl	NL	162	607	175	43	4	18	(7	11)	280	93	78	101	90	4	145	8	0	3	3	4	18	.288	.386	.461	.847
2015	Atl	NL	118	416	115	27	0	18	(5	13)	196	62	66	77	56	4	98	7	0	2	3	1	6	.276	.370	.471	.841
2016	Atl	NL	158	589	178	43	6	34	(15	19)	335	102	91	119	89	18	171	10	0	5	6	1	12	.302	.400	.569	.968
2017	Atl	NL	117	440	135	35	2	28	(11	17)	258	84	71	93	65	14	95	7	0	2	8	5	9	.307	.403	.586	.989
2018	Atl	NL	162	618	191	44	4	23	(13	10)	312	94	98	115	76	12	132	7	0	6	10	3	11	.295	.388	.505	.893
2019	Atl	NL	158	597	176	34	2	38	(22	16)	328	113	121	126	87	11	127	6	0	2	6	3	17	.295	.389	.549	.938
2020	Atl	NL	60	214	73	23	1	13	(9	4)	137	51	53	68	45	7	37	3	0	0	2	0	6	.341	.462	.640	1.102
2021	Atl	NL	159	600	180	25	2	31	(15	16)	302	120	83	122	85	15	107	8	0	2	8	3	11	.300	.393	.503	.896
	Postseason		26	99	28	6	0	4	(2	2)	46	15	9	15	12	1	20	3	0	0	0	0	1	.283	.377	.465	.842
	12 ML YEARS		1565	5767	1704	367	25	271	(134	137)	2934	969	941	1106	776	102	1312	76	0	41	53	24	126	.295	.384	.509	.893

Mike Freeman

Bats: L Throws: R Pos: SS-12;PH-10;1B-9;3B-7;PR-6;CF-3;2B-2;LF-1;DH-1
Ht: 6'0" Wt: 195 Born: 8/4/1987 Age: 34

Year	Team	Lg	G	AB	H	2B	3B	HR	(Hm	Rd)	TB	R	RBI	RC	TBB	IBB	SO	HBP	SH	SF	SB	CS	GDP	Avg	OBP	Slg	OPS
2021	Lsville	AAA	52	164	41	9	1	6	(-	-)	70	32	23	-	32	1	44	1	0	1	2	0	5	.250	.374	.427	.801
2016	2 Tms		21	22	5	1	0	0	(0	0)	6	1	1	1	2	0	7	0	0	0	0	0	2	.227	.292	.273	.564
2017	3 Tms		35	60	6	2	0	1	(1	0)	11	6	1	2	6	1	19	0	0	0	0	0	1	.100	.182	.183	.365
2018	ChC	NL	1	0	0	0	0	0	(0	0)	0	0	0	0	0	0	0	0	0	1	0	0	0	-	-	-	-
2019	Cle	AL	75	177	49	8	0	4	(3	1)	69	27	24	28	22	0	61	4	6	4	1	2	2	.277	.362	.390	.752
2020	Cle	AL	24	38	9	3	0	0	(0	0)	12	5	3	4	3	0	11	1	0	1	1	0	1	.237	.302	.316	.618
2021	Cin	AL	37	59	11	0	0	0	(0	0)	11	6	3	2	5	1	20	1	0	1	0	0	1	.186	.262	.186	.448
16	Ari	NL	8	9	0	0	0	0	(0	0)	0	0	0	0	2	0	5	0	0	0	0	0	0	.000	.182	.000	.182
16	Sea	AL	13	13	5	1	0	0	(0	0)	6	1	1	1	0	0	2	0	0	0	0	0	0	.385	.385	.462	.846
17	Sea	AL	16	30	2	0	0	1	(1	0)	5	3	1	0	4	1	9	0	0	0	0	0	0	.067	.176	.167	.343
17	LAD	NL	4	5	0	0	0	0	(0	0)	0	0	0	0	0	0	2	0	0	0	0	0	0	.000	.000	.000	.000
17	ChC	NL	15	25	4	2	0	0	(0	0)	6	3	0	2	2	0	8	0	0	0	0	0	0	.160	.222	.240	.462
	6 ML YEARS		193	356	80	14	0	5	(4	1)	109	45	32	37	38	2	118	6	7	5	2	3	6	.225	.304	.306	.612

Luis Frias

Pitches: R Bats: R Pos: RP-3
Ht: 6'3" Wt: 245 Born: 5/23/1998 Age: 24

Year	Team	Lg	G	GS	GF	IP	BFP	H	R	ER	HR	SH	SF	HB	TBB	IBB	SO	WP	W	L	Pct	Sv-Op	Hld	Vel	OPS	ERC	ERA
2021	Amrillo	AA	16	16	0	78.2	330	69	52	46	16	0	1	1	25	0	91	2	5	6	.455	0--	-	-	.714	3.75	5.26
2021	Reno	AAA	5	5	0	21.2	99	21	14	14	1	0	1	0	16	0	20	1	2	1	.667	0--	-	-	.727	4.85	5.82
2021	Ari	NL	3	0	1	3.1	16	2	1	1	0	0	1	0	5	0	3	0	0	0	-	0-0	1	97	.738	5.39	2.70

Max Fried

FREED

Pitches: L Bats: L Pos: SP-28
Ht: 6'4" Wt: 190 Born: 1/18/1994 Age: 28

Year	Team	Lg	G	GS	GF	IP	BFP	H	R	ER	HR	SH	SF	HB	TBB	IBB	SO	WP	W	L	Pct	Sv-Op	Hld	Vel	OPS	ERC	ERA
2017	Atl	NL	9	4	4	26.0	121	30	15	11	3	0	0	4	12	1	22	0	1	1	.500	0-0	0	92	.818	5.92	3.81
2018	Atl	NL	14	5	5	33.2	142	26	12	11	3	2	2	2	20	0	44	2	1	4	.200	0-0	1	93	.688	3.84	2.94
2019	Atl	NL	33	30	1	165.2	702	174	80	74	21	3	2	5	47	3	173	11	17	6	.739	0-0	0	94	.743	4.22	4.02
2020	Atl	NL	11	11	0	56.0	224	42	14	14	2	0	2	4	19	0	50	1	7	0	1.000	0-0	0	93	.622	2.46	2.25
2021	Atl	NL	28	28	0	165.2	667	139	61	56	15	4	3	7	41	0	158	7	14	7	.667	0-0	0	94	.635	2.77	3.04
	Postseason		12	4	2	30.0	129	30	13	13	5	0	0	1	10	0	30	1	0	1	.000	0-0	2	95	.759	4.39	3.90
	5 ML YEARS		95	78	10	447.0	1856	411	182	166	44	9	9	22	139	4	447	21	40	18	.690	0-0	1	94	.691	3.50	3.34

T.J. Friedl

FREE-duhl

Bats: L Throws: L Pos: CF-6;LF-5;PH-4
Ht: 5'10" Wt: 180 Born: 8/14/1995 Age: 26

Year	Team	Lg	G	AB	H	2B	3B	HR	(Hm	Rd)	TB	R	RBI	RC	TBB	IBB	SO	HBP	SH	SF	SB	CS	GDP	Avg	OBP	Slg	OPS
2021	Lsville	AAA	113	386	102	15	5	12	(-	-)	163	59	36	-	44	2	65	13	2	3	13	7	1	.264	.357	.422	.779
2021	Cin	NL	14	31	9	1	0	1	(1	0)	13	9	2	4	4	0	2	0	0	1	0	0	0	.290	.361	.419	.780

Jace Fry

Pitches: L Bats: L Pos: RP-6
Ht: 6'1" Wt: 220 Born: 7/9/1993 Age: 28

Year	Team	Lg	G	GS	GF	IP	BFP	H	R	ER	HR	SH	SF	HB	TBB	IBB	SO	WP	W	L	Pct	Sv-Op	Hld	Vel	OPS	ERC	ERA
2021	Charllt	AAA	33	1	5	39.0	160	21	19	13	3	0	3	4	18	0	59	6	1	4	.200	2--	-	-	.535	2.11	3.00
2017	CWS	AL	11	0	3	6.2	36	12	8	8	1	0	0	0	5	1	3	3	0	0	-	0-0	0	94	1.085	10.97	10.80
2018	CWS	AL	59	1	12	51.1	214	37	28	25	4	2	0	1	20	0	70	5	2	3	.400	4-5	16	93	.567	2.43	4.38
2019	CWS	AL	68	0	6	55.0	251	44	33	29	7	2	1	3	43	3	68	4	3	4	.429	0-2	11	92	.733	4.74	4.75
2020	CWS	AL	18	0	2	19.2	83	16	9	8	3	0	0	0	12	2	24	1	1	0	1.000	0-0	1	90	.732	4.19	3.66
2021	CWS	AL	6	0	2	6.2	31	10	8	8	1	0	0	1	6	0	3	2	0	1	.000	0-0	0	91	1.090	12.42	10.80
	5 ML YEARS		162	1	27	139.1	615	119	86	78	16	4	1	5	86	6	168	15	5	9	.357	4-7	28	92	.712	4.28	5.04

Paul Fry

Pitches: L Bats: L Pos: RP-52
Ht: 6'0" Wt: 205 Born: 7/26/1992 Age: 29

Year	Team	Lg	G	GS	GF	IP	BFP	H	R	ER	HR	SH	SF	HB	TBB	IBB	SO	WP	W	L	Pct	Sv-Op	Hld	Vel	OPS	ERC	ERA
2021	Norfolk	AAA	9	0	0	6.2	35	5	6	6	0	0	1	2	8	0	6	2	0	0	-	0--	-	-	.720	5.91	8.10
2018	Bal	AL	35	0	11	37.2	159	33	20	14	1	0	4	15	0	36	3	1	2	.333	2-4	9	91	.613	3.34	3.35
2019	Bal	AL	66	0	8	57.1	255	54	39	34	7	1	0	6	29	1	55	2	1	9	.100	3-8	11	91	.752	4.72	5.34
2020	Bal	AL	22	0	4	22.0	98	22	7	6	3	0	0	1	9	0	29	3	1	0	1.000	0-0	4	93	.724	4.45	2.45
2021	Bal	AL	52	0	12	47.1	215	37	34	32	3	1	1	4	35	0	60	1	4	5	.444	2-4	11	93	.637	4.18	6.08
4 ML YEARS			175	0	35	164.1	727	146	100	86	14	2	1	15	88	1	180	12	7	16	.304	7-16	35	92	.685	4.21	4.71

Joshua Fuentes

Bats: R Throws: R Pos: 3B-60;1B-32;PH-22;LF-2
Ht: 6'2" Wt: 209 Born: 2/19/1993 Age: 29

Year	Team	Lg	G	AB	H	2B	3B	HR	(Hm	Rd)	TB	R	RBI	RC	TBB	IBB	SO	HBP	SH	SF	SB	CS	GDP	Avg	OBP	Slg	OPS
2021	Albq	AAA	44	175	51	12	2	9	(-	-)	94	27	31	-	10	0	38	4	0	1	1	3	4	.291	.342	.537	.879
2019	Col	NL	24	55	12	1	0	3	(2	1)	22	8	7	4	1	0	20	0	0	0	1	0	0	.218	.232	.400	.632
2020	Col	NL	30	98	30	7	0	2	(1	1)	43	14	17	15	2	0	29	1	0	2	1	0	1	.306	.320	.439	.759
2021	Col	NL	95	271	61	11	1	7	(6	1)	95	30	33	28	12	1	65	0	0	1	0	0	5	.225	.257	.351	.608
3 ML YEARS			149	424	103	19	1	12	(9	3)	160	52	57	47	15	1	114	1	0	3	2	0	6	.243	.269	.377	.646

Carson Fulmer

Pitches: R Bats: R Pos: RP-20
Ht: 6'0" Wt: 210 Born: 12/13/1993 Age: 28

Year	Team	Lg	G	GS	GF	IP	BFP	H	R	ER	HR	SH	SF	HB	TBB	IBB	SO	WP	W	L	Pct	Sv-Op	Hld	Vel	OPS	ERC	ERA
2021	Lsvlle	AAA	36	1	11	38.0	172	35	26	19	2	0	2	2	25	4	48	4	1	4	.200	1--	-	-	.738	4.29	4.50
2016	CWS	AL	8	0	4	11.2	53	12	11	11	2	0	0	2	7	0	10	2	0	2	.000	0-1	0	93	.873	6.57	8.49
2017	CWS	AL	7	5	0	23.1	101	16	10	10	4	1	0	2	13	0	19	0	3	1	.750	0-0	0	93	.639	3.71	3.86
2018	CWS	AL	9	8	1	32.1	164	37	32	29	8	1	2	5	24	0	29	2	2	4	.333	0-0	0	93	.935	8.08	8.07
2019	CWS	AL	20	2	3	27.1	133	26	22	19	5	0	3	3	20	0	25	1	1	2	.333	0-0	1	94	.780	6.01	6.26
2020	2 Tms	AL	10	0	3	10.1	46	8	5	5	1	0	0	2	5	0	11	3	0	0	-	0-0	0	92	.685	3.78	4.35
2021	Cin	NL	20	0	5	25.2	116	26	20	19	3	1	1	3	13	0	24	2	0	0	-	0-0	1	93	.794	5.20	6.66
20	Det	AL	7	0	1	6.2	32	8	5	5	1	0	0	1	3	0	7	1	0	0	-	0-0	0	92	.875	6.33	6.75
20	Bal	AL	3	0	2	3.2	14	0	0	0	0	0	0	1	2	0	4	2	0	0	-	0-0	0	93	.214	0.66	0.00
6 ML YEARS			74	15	16	130.2	613	125	100	93	23	3	6	17	82	0	118	10	6	9	.400	0-1	2	93	.801	5.76	6.41

Michael Fulmer

Pitches: R Bats: R Pos: RP-48; SP-4
Ht: 6'3" Wt: 224 Born: 3/15/1993 Age: 29

Year	Team	Lg	G	GS	GF	IP	BFP	H	R	ER	HR	SH	SF	HB	TBB	IBB	SO	WP	W	L	Pct	Sv-Op	Hld	Vel	OPS	ERC	ERA
2016	Det	AL	26	26	0	159.0	647	136	57	54	16	4	2	9	42	1	132	1	11	7	.611	0-0	0	95	.652	3.02	3.06
2017	Det	AL	25	25	0	164.2	676	150	80	70	13	3	8	8	40	2	114	3	10	12	.455	0-0	0	96	.644	3.04	3.83
2018	Det	AL	24	24	0	132.1	558	128	75	69	19	3	1	8	46	1	110	1	3	12	.200	0-0	0	96	.758	4.18	4.69
2020	Det	AL	10	10	0	27.2	136	45	27	27	8	1	2	1	12	0	20	0	0	2	.000	0-0	0	93	1.046	10.13	8.78
2021	Det	AL	52	4	21	69.2	297	69	27	23	7	0	2	5	20	2	73	2	5	6	.455	14-18	9	96	.694	3.82	2.97
5 ML YEARS			137	89	21	553.1	2314	528	266	243	63	9	16	28	160	6	449	7	29	39	.426	14-18	9	95	.703	3.70	3.95

Kyle Funkhouser

Pitches: R Bats: R Pos: RP-55; SP-2
Ht: 6'3" Wt: 229 Born: 3/16/1994 Age: 28

Year	Team	Lg	G	GS	GF	IP	BFP	H	R	ER	HR	SH	SF	HB	TBB	IBB	SO	WP	W	L	Pct	Sv-Op	Hld	Vel	OPS	ERC	ERA
2020	Det	AL	13	0	4	17.1	81	22	14	14	3	0	1	0	11	0	12	1	1	1	.500	0-0	0	95	.929	7.49	7.27
2021	Det	AL	57	2	7	68.1	298	58	32	26	6	2	2	3	38	0	63	9	7	4	.636	1-5	9	96	.674	3.92	3.42
2 ML YEARS			70	2	11	85.2	379	80	46	40	9	2	3	3	49	0	75	10	8	5	.615	1-5	9	96	.729	4.58	4.20

Cam Gallagher

Bats: R Throws: R Pos: C-46;PH-3
Ht: 6'3" Wt: 230 Born: 12/6/1992 Age: 29

Year	Team	Lg	G	AB	H	2B	3B	HR	(Hm	Rd)	TB	R	RBI	RC	TBB	IBB	SO	HBP	SH	SF	SB	CS	GDP	Avg	OBP	Slg	OPS
2017	KC	AL	13	24	6	1	0	1	(0	1)	10	2	5	4	3	0	4	0	0	0	0	0	1	.250	.333	.417	.750
2018	KC	AL	22	63	13	3	0	1	(1	0)	19	5	7	5	3	0	15	1	1	1	0	0	1	.206	.250	.302	.552
2019	KC	AL	45	126	30	7	0	3	(2	1)	46	14	12	14	11	0	28	3	1	1	0	1	3	.238	.312	.365	.677
2020	KC	AL	25	53	15	5	0	1	(0	1)	23	10	3	6	6	0	11	0	1	0	0	0	0	.283	.356	.434	.790
2021	KC	AL	48	112	28	6	0	1	(0	1)	37	9	7	13	8	0	20	0	2	1	0	0	2	.250	.298	.330	.628
5 ML YEARS			153	378	92	22	0	7	(3	4)	135	40	34	42	31	0	78	4	5	3	0	1	7	.243	.305	.357	.662

Giovanny Gallegos

Pitches: R Bats: R Pos: RP-73
gah-YAY-gohss
Ht: 6'2" Wt: 215 Born: 8/14/1991 Age: 30

Year	Team	Lg	G	GS	GF	IP	BFP	H	R	ER	HR	SH	SF	HB	TBB	IBB	SO	WP	W	L	Pct	Sv-Op	Hld	Vel	OPS	ERC	ERA
2017	NYY	AL	16	0	7	20.1	88	21	12	11	3	1	1	0	5	1	22	1	0	1	.000	0-1	0	94	.740	3.76	4.87
2018	2 Tms		6	0	4	11.1	45	11	5	5	2	1	0	0	3	0	12	0	0	0	-	1-1	0	94	.782	4.10	3.97
2019	StL	NL	66	0	10	74.0	279	44	19	19	9	0	1	3	16	2	93	3	3	2	.600	1-4	19	94	.546	1.66	2.31
2020	StL	NL	16	0	7	15.0	57	9	6	6	1	0	0	4	2	0	21	3	2	2	.500	4-4	1	94	.473	1.51	3.60
2021	StL	NL	73	0	20	80.1	310	51	28	27	6	1	5	6	20	2	95	4	6	5	.545	14-22	24	94	.551	1.81	3.02

Year Team	Lg	G	GS	GF	IP	BFP	H	R	ER	HR	SH	SF	HB	TBB	IBB	SO	WP	W	L	Pct	Sv-Op	Hld	Vel	OPS	ERC	ERA
18 NYY	AL	4	0	2	10.0	40	10	5	5	2	1	0	0	3	0	10	0	0	0	-	1-1	0	94	.833	4.63	4.50
18 StL	NL	2	0	2	1.1	5	1	0	0	0	0	0	0	0	0	2	0	0	0	-	0-0	0	95	.400	1.13	0.00
Postseason		7	0	0	6.1	29	6	3	3	2	0	0	0	4	1	9	0	1	0	1.000	0-1	0	94	.945	5.94	4.26
5 ML YEARS		177	0	48	201.0	779	136	70	68	21	3	7	9	48	5	243	9	11	10	.524	20-32	44	94	.578	2.02	3.04

Zac Gallen

Pitches: R Bats: R Pos: SP-23 **Ht:** 6'2" **Wt:** 189 **Born:** 8/3/1995 **Age:** 26

Year Team	Lg	G	GS	GF	IP	BFP	H	R	ER	HR	SH	SF	HB	TBB	IBB	SO	WP	W	L	Pct	Sv-Op	Hld	Vel	OPS	ERC	ERA
2019 2 Tms	NL	15	15	0	80.0	334	62	26	25	8	0	1	4	36	1	96	3	3	6	.333	0-0	0	93	.660	3.24	2.81
2020 Ari	NL	12	12	0	72.0	291	55	24	22	9	1	0	2	25	0	82	4	3	2	.600	0-0	0	93	.620	2.91	2.75
2021 Ari	NL	23	23	0	121.1	523	108	61	58	19	3	3	5	49	1	139	6	4	10	.286	0-0	0	93	.724	3.96	4.30
19 Mia	NL	7	7	0	36.1	151	25	12	11	3	0	0	2	18	1	43	1	1	3	.250	0-0	0	92	.603	2.83	2.72
19 Ari	NL	8	8	0	43.2	183	37	14	14	5	0	1	2	18	0	53	2	2	3	.400	0-0	0	93	.707	3.60	2.89
3 ML YEARS		50	50	0	273.1	1148	225	111	105	36	4	4	11	110	2	317	13	10	18	.357	0-0	0	93	.679	3.47	3.46

Joey Gallo

Bats: L Throws: R Pos: RF-92;LF-51;DH-14;PH-1 **Ht:** 6'5" **Wt:** 250 **Born:** 11/19/1993 **Age:** 28

							BATTING													RUNNING			AVERAGES			
Year Team	Lg	G	AB	H	2B	3B	HR	(Hm	Rd)	TB	R	RBI	RC	TBB	IBB	SO	HBP	SH	SF	SB	CS	GDP	Avg	OBP	Slg	OPS
2015 Tex	AL	36	108	22	3	1	6	(4	2)	45	16	14	13	15	3	57	0	0	0	3	0	0	.204	.301	.417	.717
2016 Tex	AL	17	25	1	0	0	1	(1	0)	4	2	1	0	5	0	19	0	0	0	1	0	0	.040	.200	.160	.360
2017 Tex	AL	145	449	94	18	3	41	(22	19)	241	85	80	84	75	1	196	8	0	0	7	2	3	.209	.333	.537	.869
2018 Tex	AL	148	500	103	24	1	40	(23	17)	249	82	92	80	74	4	207	3	0	0	3	4	3	.206	.312	.498	.810
2019 Tex	AL	70	241	61	15	1	22	(13	9)	144	54	49	50	52	4	114	2	1	1	4	2	0	.253	.389	.598	.986
2020 Tex	AL	57	193	35	8	0	10	(5	5)	73	23	26	29	29	2	79	4	0	0	2	0	0	.181	.301	.378	.679
2021 2 Tms		153	498	99	13	1	38	(22	16)	228	90	77	84	111	5	213	6	0	1	6	0	6	.199	.351	.458	.808
21 Tex	AL	95	310	69	6	1	25	(15	10)	152	57	55	63	74	4	125	4	0	0	6	0	3	.223	.379	.490	.869
21 NYY	AL	58	188	30	7	0	13	(7	6)	76	33	22	21	37	1	88	2	0	1	0	0	3	.160	.303	.404	.707
7 ML YEARS		626	2014	415	81	7	158	(90	68)	984	352	339	340	361	19	885	23	1	2	26	8	12	.206	.333	.489	.821

Freddy Galvis

Bats: B Throws: R Pos: SS-82;3B-19;PH-5;2B-2;1B-1 GAL-viss **Ht:** 5'10" **Wt:** 190 **Born:** 11/14/1989 **Age:** 32

							BATTING													RUNNING			AVERAGES			
Year Team	Lg	G	AB	H	2B	3B	HR	(Hm	Rd)	TB	R	RBI	RC	TBB	IBB	SO	HBP	SH	SF	SB	CS	GDP	Avg	OBP	Slg	OPS
2012 Phi	NL	58	190	43	15	1	3	(3	0)	69	14	24	14	7	0	29	0	3	0	1	0	6	.226	.254	.363	.617
2013 Phi	NL	70	205	48	5	4	6	(4	2)	79	13	19	20	13	2	45	1	3	0	1	0	5	.234	.283	.385	.668
2014 Phi	NL	43	119	21	3	1	4	(2	2)	38	14	12	9	8	0	30	0	0	1	1	0	0	.176	.227	.319	.546
2015 Phi	NL	151	559	147	14	5	7	(6	1)	192	63	50	64	30	1	103	3	7	4	10	5	11	.263	.302	.343	.645
2016 Phi	NL	158	584	141	26	3	20	(11	9)	233	61	67	59	25	6	136	3	8	4	17	6	16	.241	.274	.399	.673
2017 Phi	NL	162	608	155	29	6	12	(10	2)	232	71	61	77	45	2	111	4	2	4	14	5	12	.255	.309	.382	.690
2018 SD	NL	162	602	149	31	5	13	(8	5)	229	62	67	65	45	2	147	2	1	6	8	6	8	.248	.299	.380	.680
2019 2 Tms		147	557	145	28	1	23	(9	14)	244	67	70	69	28	1	145	1	1	2	4	2	14	.260	.296	.438	.734
2020 Cin	NL	47	141	31	5	0	7	(5	2)	57	18	16	17	13	0	30	5	0	0	1	1	5	.220	.308	.404	.712
2021 2 Tms		104	356	86	15	1	14	(4	10)	145	53	40	39	27	1	77	5	2	3	1	0	6	.242	.302	.407	.709
19 Tor	AL	115	450	120	24	1	18	(7	11)	200	55	54	56	21	1	112	0	1	1	4	1	11	.267	.299	.444	.743
19 Cin	NL	32	107	25	4	0	5	(2	3)	44	12	16	13	7	0	33	1	0	1	0	1	3	.234	.284	.411	.696
21 Bal	AL	72	249	62	12	1	9	(3	6)	103	36	26	27	18	1	58	3	2	1	1	0	5	.249	.306	.414	.720
21 Phi	NL	32	107	24	3	0	5	(1	4)	42	17	14	12	9	0	19	2	0	2	0	0	1	.224	.292	.393	.684
Postseason		2	3	1	0	0	0	(0	0)	1	0	0	0	1	0	1	0	0	0	0	0	0	.333	.500	.333	.833
10 ML YEARS		1102	3921	966	171	27	109	(59	50)	1518	436	426	433	241	15	853	24	27	24	57	21	83	.246	.292	.387	.680

Ben Gamel

Bats: L Throws: L Pos: LF-73;PH-23;CF-20;RF-18;1B-4 **Ht:** 5'11" **Wt:** 177 **Born:** 5/17/1992 **Age:** 30

							BATTING													RUNNING			AVERAGES			
Year Team	Lg	G	AB	H	2B	3B	HR	(Hm	Rd)	TB	R	RBI	RC	TBB	IBB	SO	HBP	SH	SF	SB	CS	GDP	Avg	OBP	Slg	OPS
2016 2 Tms	AL	33	48	9	2	0	1	(0	1)	14	9	5	4	6	0	16	0	3	0	0	0	1	.188	.278	.292	.569
2017 Sea	AL	134	509	140	27	5	11	(5	6)	210	68	59	68	36	1	122	1	1	3	4	1	8	.275	.322	.413	.735
2018 Sea	AL	101	257	70	14	4	1	(1	0)	95	37	19	38	31	1	61	4	0	1	7	3	4	.272	.358	.370	.728
2019 Mil	NL	134	311	77	18	0	7	(4	3)	116	47	33	40	40	2	104	3	0	2	2	2	0	.248	.337	.373	.710
2020 Mil	NL	40	114	27	8	1	3	(1	2)	46	13	10	15	10	0	39	0	0	4	0	2	4	.237	.315	.404	.718
2021 2 Tms		122	340	84	18	3	8	(5	3)	132	43	26	43	51	2	105	3	2	4	3	6	7	.247	.347	.388	.735
16 NYY	AL	6	8	1	0	0	0	(0	0)	1	1	0	0	1	0	1	0	1	0	0	0	1	.125	.222	.125	.347
16 Sea	AL	27	40	8	2	0	1	(0	1)	13	8	5	4	5	0	15	0	2	0	0	0	0	.200	.289	.325	.614
21 Cle	AL	11	14	1	1	0	0	(0	0)	2	1	0	0	3	0	6	0	0	0	0	0	1	.071	.235	.143	.378
21 Pit	NL	111	326	83	17	3	8	(5	3)	130	42	26	43	48	2	99	3	2	4	3	6	6	.255	.352	.399	.750
Postseason		2	2	0	0	0	0	(0	0)	0	0	0	0	0	0	0	0	0	0	0	0	0	.000	.000	.000	.000
6 ML YEARS		564	1579	407	87	13	31	(16	15)	613	217	152	208	177	6	447	11	6	10	16	14	24	.258	.335	.388	.723

John Gant

Pitches: R Bats: R Pos: SP-21; RP-18

Ht: 6'4" Wt: 200 Born: 8/6/1992 Age: 29

Year	Team	Lg	G	GS	GF	IP	BFP	H	R	ER	HR	SH	SF	HB	TBB	IBB	SO	WP	W	L	Pct	Sv-Op	Hld	Vel	OPS	ERC	ERA
2016	Atl	NL	20	7	6	50.0	222	54	32	27	7	3	2	2	21	3	49	4	1	4	.200	0-0	0	92	.831	4.97	4.86
2017	StL	NL	7	2	1	17.1	76	17	9	9	4	0	1	1	10	1	11	0	0	1	.000	0-0	0	93	.884	6.01	4.67
2018	StL	NL	26	19	1	114.0	487	91	54	44	9	2	4	2	57	3	95	5	7	6	.538	0-0	0	93	.646	3.21	3.47
2019	StL	NL	64	0	13	66.1	269	51	29	27	4	0	0	0	34	1	60	1	11	1	.917	3-6	18	96	.639	3.09	3.66
2020	StL	NL	17	0	2	15.0	61	9	6	4	0	0	0	0	7	0	18	1	0	3	.000	0-0	5	94	.447	1.65	2.40
2021	2 Tms		39	21	4	110.0	491	95	56	50	10	3	3	6	71	2	92	3	5	11	.313	0-0	2	92	.720	4.39	4.09
21	StL	NL	25	14	4	76.1	345	64	32	29	6	3	1	5	56	2	56	0	4	6	.400	0-0	1	91	.708	4.53	3.42
21	Min	AL	14	7	0	33.2	146	31	24	21	4	0	2	1	15	0	36	3	1	5	.167	0-0	1	93	.744	4.03	5.61
6 ML YEARS			173	49	27	372.2	1606	317	186	161	34	8	10	11	200	10	325	14	24	26	.480	3-6	25	93	.696	3.80	3.89

Adolis Garcia

Bats: R Throws: R Pos: CF-79;RF-51;DH-13;LF-9;PH-2

Ht: 6'1" Wt: 205 Born: 3/2/1993 Age: 29

Year	Team	Lg	G	AB	H	2B	3B	HR	(Hm	Rd)	TB	R	RBI	RC	TBB	IBB	SO	HBP	SH	SF	SB	CS	GDP	Avg	OBP	Slg	OPS
2018	StL	NL	21	17	2	1	0	0	(0	0)	3	3	1	0	0	0	7	0	0	0	0	0	0	.118	.118	.176	.294
2020	Tex	AL	3	6	0	0	0	0	(0	0)	0	0	0	0	1	0	4	0	0	0	0	0	0	.000	.143	.000	.143
2021	Tex	AL	149	581	141	26	2	31	(19	12)	264	77	90	72	32	0	194	5	0	4	16	5	15	.243	.286	.454	.741
3 ML YEARS			173	604	143	27	2	31	(19	12)	267	80	91	72	33	0	205	5	0	4	16	5	15	.237	.280	.442	.722

Aramis Garcia

Bats: R Throws: R Pos: C-30;DH-1;PH-1

Ht: 6'1" Wt: 228 Born: 1/12/1993 Age: 29

Year	Team	Lg	G	AB	H	2B	3B	HR	(Hm	Rd)	TB	R	RBI	RC	TBB	IBB	SO	HBP	SH	SF	SB	CS	GDP	Avg	OBP	Slg	OPS
2021	LsVgs	AAA	30	112	30	8	0	2	(-	-)	44	15	15	-	9	0	27	1	0	2	0	0	4	.268	.323	.393	.715
2018	SF	NL	19	63	18	1	0	4	(2	2)	31	8	9	8	2	0	31	0	0	2	0	0	1	.286	.308	.492	.800
2019	SF	NL	18	42	6	1	0	2	(2	0)	13	5	5	2	4	1	21	0	0	0	0	0	1	.143	.217	.310	.527
2021	Oak	AL	32	88	18	1	0	3	(1	2)	28	8	7	6	1	0	28	3	2	0	0	0	4	.205	.234	.318	.557
3 ML YEARS			69	193	42	3	0	9	(5	4)	72	21	21	16	7	1	80	3	2	0	0	0	6	.218	.256	.373	.629

Avisail Garcia

Bats: R Throws: R Pos: RF-121;PH-15;CF-1

ah-vee-SAH-eel

Ht: 6'4" Wt: 250 Born: 6/12/1991 Age: 31

Year	Team	Lg	G	AB	H	2B	3B	HR	(Hm	Rd)	TB	R	RBI	RC	TBB	IBB	SO	HBP	SH	SF	SB	CS	GDP	Avg	OBP	Slg	OPS
2012	Det	AL	23	47	15	0	0	0	(0	0)	15	7	3	5	3	1	10	1	0	0	0	2	1	.319	.373	.319	.692
2013	2 Tms	AL	72	244	69	7	3	7	(3	4)	103	31	31	30	9	0	59	1	0	2	3	3	8	.283	.309	.422	.731
2014	CWS	AL	46	172	42	8	0	7	(2	5)	71	19	29	20	14	1	44	2	0	2	4	1	5	.244	.305	.413	.718
2015	CWS	AL	148	553	142	17	2	13	(8	5)	202	66	59	58	36	3	141	8	0	4	7	7	13	.257	.309	.365	.675
2016	CWS	AL	120	413	101	18	2	12	(5	7)	159	59	51	56	34	0	115	4	0	2	4	4	9	.245	.307	.385	.692
2017	CWS	AL	136	518	171	27	5	18	(9	9)	262	75	80	96	33	5	111	9	0	1	5	3	11	.330	.380	.506	.885
2018	CWS	AL	93	356	84	11	2	19	(6	13)	156	47	49	38	20	2	102	4	0	5	3	1	9	.236	.281	.438	.719
2019	TB	AL	125	489	138	25	2	20	(13	7)	227	61	72	70	31	2	125	7	0	3	10	4	15	.282	.332	.464	.796
2020	Mil	NL	53	181	43	10	0	2	(1	1)	59	20	15	21	20	2	49	6	0	0	1	3	2	.238	.333	.326	.659
2021	Mil	NL	135	461	121	18	0	29	(14	15)	226	68	86	79	38	5	121	11	0	5	8	4	12	.262	.330	.490	.820
13	Det	AL	30	83	20	3	1	2	(1	1)	31	12	10	7	4	0	21	0	0	1	0	1	3	.241	.273	.373	.646
13	CWS	AL	42	161	49	4	2	5	(2	3)	72	19	21	23	5	0	38	1	0	1	3	2	5	.304	.327	.447	.775
Postseason			19	51	16	1	0	1	(0	1)	20	4	7	5	2	0	13	0	0	0	1	0	1	.314	.340	.392	.732
10 ML YEARS			951	3434	926	141	16	127	(61	66)	1480	453	475	473	238	21	877	53	0	24	45	32	88	.270	.325	.431	.756

Bryan Garcia

Pitches: R Bats: R Pos: RP-39

Ht: 6'1" Wt: 205 Born: 4/19/1995 Age: 27

Year	Team	Lg	G	GS	GF	IP	BFP	H	R	ER	HR	SH	SF	HB	TBB	IBB	SO	WP	W	L	Pct	Sv-Op	Hld	Vel	OPS	ERC	ERA
2021	Toledo	AAA	19	0	7	23.1	104	25	15	14	3	0	0	2	8	0	19	4	0	1	.000	1--	-	-	.783	4.74	5.40
2019	Det	AL	7	0	1	6.2	33	9	9	9	1	0	0	0	5	1	7	1	0	0	-	0-1	1	94	.924	7.88	12.15
2020	Det	AL	26	0	12	21.2	93	18	6	4	0	0	1	1	10	0	12	1	2	1	.667	4-6	3	94	.559	2.84	1.66
2021	Det	AL	39	0	10	39.1	192	48	38	33	10	2	0	2	25	1	32	7	3	2	.600	2-3	3	94	.947	7.72	7.55
3 ML YEARS			72	0	23	67.2	318	75	53	46	11	2	1	3	40	2	51	9	5	3	.625	6-10	7	94	.829	6.03	6.12

Deivi Garcia

Pitches: R Bats: R Pos: SP-2

Ht: 5'9" Wt: 163 Born: 5/19/1999 Age: 23

Year	Team	Lg	G	GS	GF	IP	BFP	H	R	ER	HR	SH	SF	HB	TBB	IBB	SO	WP	W	L	Pct	Sv-Op	Hld	Vel	OPS	ERC	ERA
2017	2 Tms	Low	10	7	1	44.2	178	32	20	20	6	1	0	3	17	1	67	5	5	1	.833	0--	-	-	.643	3.03	4.03
2018	2 Tms	Low	14	12	0	69.0	279	50	25	21	5	3	1	7	18	0	98	5	4	4	.500	0--	-	-	.617	2.32	2.74
2019	Trntn	AA	11	11	0	53.2	235	43	23	23	2	1	0	6	26	0	87	3	4	4	.500	0--	-	-	.622	3.23	3.86
2019	S-WB	AAA	11	6	0	40.0	178	39	25	24	8	2	3	4	20	0	45	1	1	3	.250	0--	-	-	.848	5.54	5.40
2021	S-WB	AAA	23	22	0	89.2	433	101	72	68	20	0	3	7	68	0	96	7	3	7	.300	0--	-	-	.924	7.75	6.83
2020	NYY	AL	6	6	0	34.1	146	35	20	19	6	1	0	1	6	0	33	0	3	2	.600	0-0	0	92	.710	3.79	4.98
2021	NYY	AL	2	2	0	8.1	38	8	7	6	1	0	1	1	4	0	7	0	0	2	.000	0-0	0	92	.873	6.48	6.48
Postseason			1	1	0	1.0	5	1	1	1	1	0	0	1	0	0	0	0	0	0	-	0-0	0	93	1.400	14.27	9.00
2 ML YEARS			8	8	0	42.2	184	43	27	25	7	1	1	2	10	0	40	0	3	4	.429	0-0	0	92	.742	3.97	5.27

Edgar Garcia

Pitches: R Bats: R Pos: RP-11
Ht: 6'1" Wt: 205 Born: 10/4/1996 Age: 25

Year Team	Lg	G	GS	GF	IP	BFP	H	R	ER	HR	SH	SF	HB	TBB	IBB	SO	WP	W	L	Pct	Sv-Op	Hld	Vel	OPS	ERC	ERA
2021 Lsvlle	AAA	24	0	7	24.0	98	17	9	9	0	0	0	2	13	0	29	5	2	0	1.000	1--	-	-	.604	2.79	3.38
2021 StPaul	AAA	11	0	6	17.0	74	10	4	4	1	0	0	2	12	0	16	4	2	1	.667	1--	-	-	.591	3.12	2.12
2019 Phi	NL	37	0	9	39.0	172	38	25	25	11	1	2	0	26	2	45	4	2	0	1.000	0-0	2	94	.906	6.55	5.77
2020 TB	AL	4	0	1	3.1	16	3	4	4	2	0	0	0	4	0	1	0	0	0	-	1-1	2	93	1.188	11.82	10.80
2021 2 Tms		11	0	2	14.2	72	19	22	20	5	0	0	1	8	0	12	2	0	1	.000	0-1	1	94	1.040	8.62	12.27
21 Cin	NL	5	0	1	4.1	24	10	10	8	2	0	0	0	1	0	4	1	0	1	.000	0-1	0	94	1.328	15.26	16.62
21 Min	AL	6	0	1	10.1	48	9	12	12	3	0	0	1	7	0	8	1	0	0	-	0-0	1	94	.879	6.18	10.45
3 ML YEARS		52	0	12	57.0	260	60	51	49	18	1	2	1	38	2	58	6	2	1	.667	1-2	5	94	.960	7.36	7.74

Jarlin Garcia

Pitches: L Bats: L Pos: RP-58
HAR-lin
Ht: 6'3" Wt: 215 Born: 1/18/1993 Age: 29

Year Team	Lg	G	GS	GF	IP	BFP	H	R	ER	HR	SH	SF	HB	TBB	IBB	SO	WP	W	L	Pct	Sv-Op	Hld	Vel	OPS	ERC	ERA
2017 Mia	NL	68	0	14	53.1	225	47	29	28	6	2	2	4	17	0	42	5	1	2	.333	0-1	15	94	.695	3.46	4.73
2018 Mia	NL	29	7	3	66.0	278	59	37	36	16	1	2	0	28	3	40	1	3	3	.500	0-0	2	92	.792	4.52	4.91
2019 Mia	NL	53	0	11	50.2	206	40	17	17	4	1	2	2	16	2	39	4	4	2	.667	0-1	6	93	.602	2.61	3.02
2020 SF	NL	19	0	5	18.1	73	11	6	1	0	0	3	2	7	1	14	0	2	1	.667	0-0	6	94	.487	1.70	0.49
2021 SF	NL	58	0	13	68.2	269	48	26	20	9	3	1	2	18	3	68	2	6	3	.667	1-3	11	93	.635	2.26	2.62
5 ML YEARS		227	7	46	257.0	1051	205	115	102	35	7	10	10	86	9	203	11	16	11	.593	1-5	40	93	.673	3.08	3.57

Leury Garcia

Bats: B Throws: R Pos: 2B-36;RF-34;LF-26;CF-26;SS-19;3B-11;PH-5
lay-OOH-ree
Ht: 5'8" Wt: 190 Born: 3/18/1991 Age: 31

Year Team	Lg	G	AB	H	2B	3B	HR	(Hm	Rd)	TB	R	RBI	RC	TBB	IBB	SO	HBP	SH	SF	SB	CS	GDP	Avg	OBP	Slg	OPS
2013 2 Tms	AL	45	101	20	1	1	0	(0	0)	23	10	2	4	7	0	34	0	2	1	7	2	0	.198	.248	.228	.475
2014 CWS	AL	74	145	24	3	0	1	(0	1)	30	13	6	0	5	1	48	0	4	1	11	1	6	.166	.192	.207	.399
2015 CWS	AL	18	14	3	0	0	0	(0	0)	3	0	1	2	1	0	7	0	0	0	1	0	0	.214	.267	.214	.481
2016 CWS	AL	18	48	11	1	1	1	(1	0)	17	6	5	5	1	0	13	1	0	0	2	1	0	.229	.260	.354	.614
2017 CWS	AL	87	300	81	15	2	9	(5	4)	127	41	33	39	13	0	69	8	3	2	8	5	4	.270	.316	.423	.739
2018 CWS	AL	82	258	70	7	4	4	(2	2)	97	23	32	38	9	0	69	3	4	1	12	1	2	.271	.303	.376	.679
2019 CWS	AL	140	577	161	27	3	8	(6	2)	218	93	40	60	21	0	139	6	11	3	15	5	6	.279	.310	.378	.688
2020 CWS	AL	16	59	16	1	0	3	(3	0)	26	6	8	9	4	0	20	0	0	0	0	0	0	.271	.317	.441	.758
2021 CWS	AL	126	415	111	22	4	5	(2	3)	156	60	54	60	41	0	97	4	9	5	6	2	12	.267	.335	.376	.711
13 Tex	AL	25	52	10	0	1	0	(0	0)	12	8	1	2	3	0	16	0	2	0	1	0	0	.192	.236	.231	.467
13 Min	AL	20	49	10	1	0	0	(0	0)	11	2	1	2	4	0	18	0	1	0	6	2	0	.204	.259	.224	.484
Postseason		2	6	0	0	0	0	(0	0)	0	0	0	0	0	0	3	0	0	0	0	0	0	.000	.000	.000	.000
9 ML YEARS		606	1917	497	77	15	31	(19	12)	697	252	181	217	102	1	485	22	33	13	62	17	30	.259	.302	.364	.666

Luis Garcia

Pitches: R Bats: R Pos: RP-34
Ht: 6'2" Wt: 240 Born: 1/30/1987 Age: 35

Year Team	Lg	G	GS	GF	IP	BFP	H	R	ER	HR	SH	SF	HB	TBB	IBB	SO	WP	W	L	Pct	Sv-Op	Hld	Vel	OPS	ERC	ERA
2021 S-WB	AAA	18	0	17	17.1	69	16	8	7	2	0	0	0	3	0	19	3	1	2	.333	11--	-	-	94	.654	2.93	3.63
2013 Phi	NL	24	0	6	31.1	138	27	15	13	3	0	0	1	23	0	23	3	1	1	.500	0-0	1	94	.764	4.85	3.73
2014 Phi	NL	13	0	5	14.0	69	14	12	10	2	1	0	0	13	0	12	4	1	0	1.000	0-0	0	95	.815	6.43	6.43
2015 Phi	NL	72	0	14	66.2	304	72	28	26	4	3	2	0	37	8	63	6	4	6	.400	2-4	16	96	.748	4.59	3.51
2016 Phi	NL	17	0	7	15.1	76	21	11	11	2	0	1	1	8	1	14	2	1	1	.500	0-1	1	97	.895	7.04	6.46
2017 Phi	NL	66	0	16	71.1	295	61	22	21	3	1	2	0	26	5	60	9	2	5	.286	2-7	14	97	.593	2.69	2.65
2018 Phi	NL	59	0	7	46.0	204	49	31	31	4	0	1	4	18	1	51	7	3	1	.750	1-4	13	97	.773	4.63	6.07
2019 LAA	AL	64	2	18	62.0	278	61	35	30	13	1	2	5	33	1	57	7	2	1	.667	1-3	6	97	.800	5.68	4.35
2020 Tex	AL	11	2	3	8.1	45	10	9	7	1	0	0	0	9	1	11	2	0	2	.000	0-0	0	97	.839	7.69	7.56
2021 StL	NL	34	0	6	33.1	135	25	12	12	2	0	2	1	8	1	34	3	1	1	.500	2-3	11	98	.550	1.98	3.24
9 ML YEARS		360	4	82	348.1	1544	340	175	161	34	6	10	12	175	18	325	43	15	18	.455	8-22	62	96	.727	4.36	4.16

Luis Garcia

Bats: L Throws: R Pos: 2B-59;SS-8;PH-6;PR-1
Ht: 6'2" Wt: 224 Born: 5/16/2000 Age: 22

Year Team	Lg	G	AB	H	2B	3B	HR	(Hm	Rd)	TB	R	RBI	RC	TBB	IBB	SO	HBP	SH	SF	SB	CS	GDP	Avg	OBP	Slg	OPS
2021 Roch	AAA	37	142	43	3	0	13	(-	-)	85	26	25		15	0	26	1	0	1	1	1	4	.303	.371	.599	.970
2020 Was	NL	40	134	37	6	0	2	(0	2)	49	18	16	16	5	0	29	0	0	0	1	1	3	.276	.302	.366	.668
2021 Was	NL	70	236	57	18	2	6	(3	3)	97	29	22	22	11	1	43	0	0	0	0	2	8	.242	.275	.411	.686
2 ML YEARS		110	370	94	24	2	8	(3	5)	146	47	38	38	16	1	72	0	0	0	1	3	11	.254	.285	.395	.680

Luis Garcia

Pitches: R Bats: R Pos: SP-28; RP-2
Ht: 6'1" Wt: 244 Born: 12/13/1996 Age: 25

Year Team	Lg	G	GS	GF	IP	BFP	H	R	ER	HR	SH	SF	HB	TBB	IBB	SO	WP	W	L	Pct	Sv-Op	Hld	Vel	OPS	ERC	ERA
2020 Hou	AL	5	1	1	12.1	49	7	4	4	1	0	1	1	5	0	9	1	0	1	.000	0-0	0	94	.622	2.08	2.92
2021 Hou	AL	30	28	1	155.1	633	133	62	60	19	2	5	3	50	1	167	9	11	8	.579	0-0	0	93	.687	3.26	3.48
Postseason		1	1	0	2.0	9	0	0	0	0	0	0	0	2	0	1	0	0	0	-	0-0	0	95	.333	1.96	0.00
2 ML YEARS		35	29	2	167.2	682	140	66	64	20	2	6	4	55	1	176	10	11	9	.550	0-0	0	93	.683	3.16	3.44

Robel Garcia

Bats: B **Throws:** R **Pos:** 3B-15;SS-13;PH-10;2B-9;PR-4;1B-1;DH-1   **Ht:** 6'0" **Wt:** 195 **Born:** 3/28/1993 **Age:** 29

Year	Team	Lg	G	AB	H	2B	3B	HR	(Hm	Rd)	TB	R	RBI	RC	TBB	IBB	SO	HBP	SH	SF	SB	CS	GDP	Avg	OBP	Slg	OPS
2021	SgrLnd	AAA	29	106	17	6	0	5	(-	-)	38	12	14	-	17	1	41	1	0	1	0	0	3	.160	.280	.358	.638
2019	ChC	NL	31	72	15	2	2	5	(1	4)	36	8	11	9	7	0	35	0	0	1	0	0	2	.208	.275	.500	.775
2021	Hou	AL	47	106	16	3	0	1	(0	1)	22	8	8	3	8	0	42	1	1	1	0	0	2	.151	.216	.208	.423
	2 ML YEARS		78	178	31	5	2	6	(1	5)	58	16	19	12	15	0	77	1	1	2	0	0	4	.174	.240	.326	.566

Rony Garcia

Pitches: R **Bats:** R **Pos:** RP-2   **Ht:** 6'3" **Wt:** 200 **Born:** 12/19/1997 **Age:** 24

Year	Team	Lg	G	GS	GF	IP	BFP	H	R	ER	HR	SH	SF	HB	TBB	IBB	SO	WP	W	L	Pct	Sv-Op	Hld	Vel	OPS	ERC	ERA
2020	Det	AL	15	2	7	21.0	96	25	20	19	7	0	0	0	9	0	14	1	1	0	1.000	0-0	0	93	.940	7.04	8.14
2021	Det	AL	2	0	0	3.2	12	1	1	1	1	0	0	0	2	0	2	0	0	0	-	0-1	0	92	.650	2.31	2.45
	2 ML YEARS		17	2	7	24.2	108	26	21	20	8	0	0	0	11	0	16	1	1	0	1.000	0-1	0	93	.910	6.28	7.30

Yimi Garcia

yee-mee   **Ht:** 6'2" **Wt:** 228 **Born:** 8/18/1990 **Age:** 31

Pitches: R **Bats:** R **Pos:** RP-62

Year	Team	Lg	G	GS	GF	IP	BFP	H	R	ER	HR	SH	SF	HB	TBB	IBB	SO	WP	W	L	Pct	Sv-Op	Hld	Vel	OPS	ERC	ERA
2014	LAD	NL	8	0	5	10.0	36	6	2	2	2	0	0	0	1	0	9	0	0	0	-	0-0	1	92	.537	1.59	1.80
2015	LAD	NL	59	1	15	56.2	225	44	23	21	8	0	2	2	10	1	68	1	3	5	.375	1-6	11	93	.595	2.40	3.34
2016	LAD	NL	9	0	1	8.1	35	9	3	3	0	2	2	1	1	0	4	0	0	0	-	0-2	1	93	.644	3.23	3.24
2018	LAD	NL	25	0	3	22.1	101	29	18	14	7	0	0	2	4	1	19	0	1	2	.333	0-1	2	94	.957	6.74	5.64
2019	LAD	NL	64	0	22	62.1	247	40	28	25	15	1	1	6	14	2	66	1	1	4	.200	0-3	4	94	.671	2.65	3.61
2020	Mia	NL	14	0	4	15.0	60	9	1	1	0	0	0	0	5	0	19	0	3	0	1.000	1-2	4	94	.452	1.35	0.60
2021	2 Tms		62	0	38	57.2	237	49	33	27	8	2	3	1	18	5	60	0	4	9	.308	15-18	2	96	.698	3.12	4.21
21	Mia	NL	39	0	30	36.1	151	31	18	14	5	1	3	1	13	5	35	0	3	7	.300	15-18	2	96	.729	3.27	3.47
21	Hou	AL	23	0	8	21.1	86	18	15	13	3	1	0	0	5	0	25	0	1	2	.333	0-0	2	96	.646	2.85	5.48
	Postseason		5	0	0	4.1	20	4	3	3	1	0	0	1	2	0	6	0	0	0	-	0-1	1	94	.762	5.68	6.23
	7 ML YEARS		241	1	88	232.1	941	186	108	93	40	5	8	12	53	9	245	2	12	20	.375	17-32	27	94	.670	2.92	3.60

Brett Gardner

Bats: L **Throws:** L **Pos:** CF-105;LF-35;PH-6;PR-3   **Ht:** 5'11" **Wt:** 195 **Born:** 8/24/1983 **Age:** 38

Year	Team	Lg	G	AB	H	2B	3B	HR	(Hm	Rd)	TB	R	RBI	RC	TBB	IBB	SO	HBP	SH	SF	SB	CS	GDP	Avg	OBP	Slg	OPS
2008	NYY	AL	42	127	29	5	2	0	(0	0)	38	18	16	17	8	0	30	2	3	1	13	1	0	.228	.283	.299	.582
2009	NYY	AL	108	248	67	6	6	3	(1	2)	94	48	23	38	26	0	40	3	6	1	26	5	3	.270	.345	.379	.724
2010	NYY	AL	150	477	132	20	7	5	(5	0)	181	97	47	77	79	1	101	5	5	3	47	9	6	.277	.383	.379	.762
2011	NYY	AL	159	510	132	19	8	7	(4	3)	188	87	36	77	60	1	93	8	8	2	49	13	6	.259	.345	.369	.713
2012	NYY	AL	16	31	10	2	0	0	(0	0)	12	7	3	7	5	0	7	1	0	1	2	2	0	.323	.417	.387	.804
2013	NYY	AL	145	539	147	33	10	8	(6	2)	224	81	52	88	52	1	127	8	7	3	24	8	3	.273	.344	.416	.759
2014	NYY	AL	148	555	142	25	8	17	(8	9)	234	87	58	81	56	0	134	6	13	6	21	5	3	.256	.327	.422	.749
2015	NYY	AL	151	571	148	26	3	16	(12	4)	228	94	66	90	68	1	135	6	8	3	20	5	8	.259	.343	.399	.742
2016	NYY	AL	148	547	143	22	6	7	(5	2)	198	80	41	77	70	0	106	8	4	5	16	4	6	.261	.351	.362	.713
2017	NYY	AL	151	594	157	26	4	21	(11	10)	254	96	63	95	72	2	122	8	5	3	23	5	4	.264	.350	.428	.778
2018	NYY	AL	140	530	125	20	7	12	(5	7)	195	95	45	70	65	0	107	5	4	5	16	2	6	.236	.322	.368	.690
2019	NYY	AL	141	491	123	26	7	28	(12	16)	247	86	74	77	52	0	108	4	0	3	10	2	6	.251	.325	.503	.829
2020	NYY	AL	49	130	29	5	1	5	(4	1)	51	20	15	24	26	0	35	1	0	1	3	3	0	.223	.354	.392	.747
2021	NYY	AL	140	387	86	16	4	10	(5	5)	140	47	39	50	60	0	100	5	6	4	4	0	3	.222	.327	.362	.689
	Postseason		67	182	39	4	0	3	(2	1)	52	26	19	18	17	0	58	3	3	3	6	3	2	.214	.288	.286	.574
	14 ML YEARS		1688	5737	1470	251	73	139	(78	61)	2284	943	578	868	699	6	1245	67	69	42	274	64	58	.256	.342	.398	.740

Kyle Garlick

Bats: R **Throws:** R **Pos:** RF-18;LF-12;CF-5;PH-4;PR-2;DH-1   **Ht:** 6'1" **Wt:** 210 **Born:** 1/26/1992 **Age:** 30

Year	Team	Lg	G	AB	H	2B	3B	HR	(Hm	Rd)	TB	R	RBI	RC	TBB	IBB	SO	HBP	SH	SF	SB	CS	GDP	Avg	OBP	Slg	OPS
2019	LAD	NL	30	48	12	4	0	3	(2	1)	25	8	6	7	5	1	19	0	0	0	0	0	0	.250	.321	.521	.842
2020	Phi	NL	12	22	3	1	0	0	(0	0)	4	0	3	0	0	0	7	1	0	0	0	0	0	.136	.174	.182	.356
2021	Min	AL	36	99	23	8	0	5	(1	4)	46	17	10	10	6	0	32	1	0	1	1	0	2	.232	.280	.465	.745
	3 ML YEARS		78	169	38	13	0	8	(3	5)	75	25	19	17	11	1	58	2	0	1	1	0	2	.225	.279	.444	.722

Dustin Garneau

GARR-noh   **Ht:** 6'2" **Wt:** 205 **Born:** 8/13/1987 **Age:** 34

Bats: R **Throws:** R **Pos:** C-20

Year	Team	Lg	G	AB	H	2B	3B	HR	(Hm	Rd)	TB	R	RBI	RC	TBB	IBB	SO	HBP	SH	SF	SB	CS	GDP	Avg	OBP	Slg	OPS
2021	Toledo	AAA	17	51	9	1	0	4	(-	-)	22	8	9	-	7	0	20	1	0	1	0	0	1	.176	.283	.431	.715
2021	Albq	AAA	11	35	8	3	0	1	(-	-)	14	5	6	-	6	0	9	1	0	0	0	0	1	.229	.357	.400	.757
2015	Col	NL	22	70	11	3	0	2	(0	2)	20	6	8	5	6	2	14	0	0	0	0	0	2	.157	.244	.286	.509
2016	Col	NL	24	68	16	6	0	1	(0	1)	25	7	6	6	6	0	22	0	0	1	0	0	0	.235	.293	.368	.661
2017	2 Tms		41	112	21	8	0	2	(1	1)	35	10	9	6	12	0	36	1	1	0	0	0	3	.188	.272	.313	.585
2018	CWS	AL	1	2	1	0	0	0	(0	0)	1	0	1	1	0	0	0	0	0	0	0	0	0	.500	.667	.500	1.167
2019	2 Tms		35	86	21	5	0	3	(1	2)	35	14	14	15	10	0	22	4	0	0	0	0	0	.244	.350	.407	.757
2020	Hou	AL	17	38	6	0	1	1	(1	0)	11	4	4	2	6	0	15	0	2	0	0	0	1	.158	.273	.289	.562
2021	Det	AL	20	62	13	5	0	6	(2	4)	36	9	15	9	3	0	18	1	0	2	0	0	2	.210	.250	.581	.831

Year	Team	Lg	G	AB	H	2B	3B	HR	(Hm	Rd)	TB	R	RBI	RC	TBB	IBB	SO	HBP	SH	SF	SB	CS	GDP	Avg	OBP	Slg	OPS
17	Col	NL	22	68	14	7	0	1	(1	0)	24	5	6	4	4	0	24	1	1	0	0	0	1	.206	.260	.353	.613
17	Oak	AL	19	44	7	1	0	1	(0	1)	11	5	3	2	8	0	12	0	0	0	0	0	2	.159	.288	.250	.538
19	LAA	AL	28	69	16	3	0	2	(1	1)	25	11	7	9	8	0	18	4	0	0	0	0	0	.232	.346	.362	.708
19	Oak	AL	7	17	5	2	0	1	(0	1)	10	3	7	6	2	0	4	0	0	0	0	0	0	.294	.368	.588	.957
	Postseason		2	2	0	0	0	0	(0	0)	0	0	0	0	0	0	2	0	0	0	0	0	0	.000	.000	.000	.000
	7 ML YEARS		160	438	89	27	1	15	(5	10)	163	50	53	40	44	2	127	6	3	3	0	0	10	.203	.283	.372	.655

Amir Garrett

Pitches: L Bats: R Pos: RP-63   Ht: 6'5" Wt: 239 Born: 5/3/1992 Age: 30

			HOW MUCH PITCHED					WHAT HE GAVE UP										THE RESULTS							
Year	Team	Lg	G	GS	GF	IP	BFP	H	R	ER	HR	SH	SF	HB	TBB	IBB	SO	WP	W	L	Pct	Sv-Op	Hld	Vel	OPS	ERC	ERA
2017	Cin	NL	16	14	0	70.2	321	74	60	58	23	1	3	2	40	2	63	1	3	8	.273	0-0	1	92	.937	6.86	7.39
2018	Cin	NL	66	0	7	63.0	264	56	30	30	8	1	1	3	25	3	71	3	1	2	.333	0-2	21	95	.734	3.81	4.29
2019	Cin	NL	69	0	4	56.0	246	44	22	20	7	0	0	4	35	1	78	5	5	3	.625	0-3	22	95	.695	4.19	3.21
2020	Cin	NL	21	0	1	18.1	69	10	5	5	4	0	0	0	7	0	26	0	1	0	1.000	1-2	6	95	.601	2.45	2.45
2021	Cin	NL	63	0	22	47.2	215	46	34	32	9	1	0	0	29	4	61	5	0	4	.000	7-11	7	95	.799	5.19	6.04
	Postseason		1	0	1	0.0	1	1	0	0	0	0	0	0	0	0	0	0	0	0	-	0-0	0	-	2.000	-	-
	5 ML YEARS		235	14	34	255.2	1115	230	151	145	51	3	4	9	136	10	299	14	10	17	.370	8-18	57	94	.788	4.85	5.10

Braxton Garrett

Pitches: L Bats: R Pos: SP-7; RP-1   Ht: 6'2" Wt: 202 Born: 8/5/1997 Age: 24

			HOW MUCH PITCHED					WHAT HE GAVE UP										THE RESULTS							
Year	Team	Lg	G	GS	GF	IP	BFP	H	R	ER	HR	SH	SF	HB	TBB	IBB	SO	WP	W	L	Pct	Sv-Op	Hld	Vel	OPS	ERC	ERA
2021	Jaxnvl	AAA	17	17	0	81.2	339	70	39	35	10	0	4	4	28	0	82	1	5	3	.625	0- -	-		.689	3.44	3.86
2020	Mia	NL	2	2	0	7.2	34	8	6	5	3	0	0	0	5	0	8	1	1	1	.500	0-0	0	90	1.003	8.00	5.87
2021	Mia	NL	8	7	1	34.0	159	42	20	19	3	4	1	2	20	0	32	4	1	2	.333	0-0	0	90	.860	6.53	5.03
	2 ML YEARS		10	9	1	41.2	193	50	26	24	6	4	1	2	25	0	40	5	2	3	.400	0-0	0	90	.886	6.82	5.18

Mitch Garver

Bats: R Throws: R Pos: C-59;PH-11;1B-4;DH-3   Ht: 6'1" Wt: 220 Born: 1/15/1991 Age: 31

			BATTING																	RUNNING			AVERAGES			
Year	Team	Lg	G	AB	H	2B	3B	HR	(Hm	Rd)	TB	R	RBI	RC	TBB	IBB	SO	HBP	SH	SF	SB	CS	GDP	Avg	OBP	Slg	OPS
2017	Min	AL	23	46	9	1	3	0	(0	0)	16	5	3	5	6	0	15	0	0	0	0	0	1	.196	.288	.348	.636
2018	Min	AL	103	302	81	19	2	7	(4	3)	125	38	45	45	29	2	72	2	1	1	0	0	4	.268	.335	.414	.749
2019	Min	AL	93	311	85	16	1	31	(16	15)	196	70	67	71	41	0	87	5	0	2	0	0	5	.273	.365	.630	.995
2020	Min	AL	23	72	12	1	0	2	(2	0)	19	8	5	3	7	0	37	1	0	1	0	0	1	.167	.247	.264	.511
2021	Min	AL	68	207	53	15	0	13	(5	8)	107	29	34	36	31	0	71	3	0	2	1	1	4	.256	.358	.517	.875
	Postseason		4	13	2	0	0	0	(0	0)	2	1	1	1	1	0	6	0	0	0	0	0	0	.154	.214	.154	.368
	5 ML YEARS		310	938	240	52	6	53	(27	26)	463	150	154	160	114	2	282	11	1	6	1	1	19	.256	.341	.494	.835

Justin Garza

Pitches: R Bats: R Pos: RP-21   Ht: 5'10" Wt: 170 Born: 3/20/1994 Age: 28

			HOW MUCH PITCHED					WHAT HE GAVE UP										THE RESULTS							
Year	Team	Lg	G	GS	GF	IP	BFP	H	R	ER	HR	SH	SF	HB	TBB	IBB	SO	WP	W	L	Pct	Sv-Op	Hld	Vel	OPS	ERC	ERA
2021	Clmbs	AAA	14	0	3	22.2	86	8	5	4	2	0	0	0	13	0	31	1	1	1	.500	1- -	-		.463	1.53	1.59
2021	Cle	AL	21	0	6	28.2	128	27	16	15	5	1	1	0	18	0	29	0	2	1	.667	0-1	0	95	.790	5.23	4.71

Ralph Garza

Pitches: R Bats: R Pos: RP-27   Ht: 6'2" Wt: 220 Born: 4/6/1994 Age: 28

			HOW MUCH PITCHED					WHAT HE GAVE UP										THE RESULTS							
Year	Team	Lg	G	GS	GF	IP	BFP	H	R	ER	HR	SH	SF	HB	TBB	IBB	SO	WP	W	L	Pct	Sv-Op	Hld	Vel	OPS	ERC	ERA
2021	SgrLnd	AAA	10	0	3	14.1	58	5	2	2	2	0	1	1	8	0	17	1	2	0	1.000	0- -	-		.471	1.79	1.26
2021	2 Tms	AL	27	0	16	30.1	127	24	15	12	5	0	0	1	14	1	29	1	1	4	.200	1-2	2	91	.718	3.71	3.56
21	Hou	AL	9	0	8	11.0	49	11	6	5	2	0	0	0	7	1	14	1	1	2	.333	0-0	0	92	.867	5.61	4.09
21	Min	AL	18	0	8	19.1	78	13	9	7	3	0	0	1	7	0	15	0	0	2	.000	1-2	2	91	.626	2.74	3.26

Kevin Gausman

Pitches: R Bats: L Pos: SP-33   Gauze-min   Ht: 6'2" Wt: 190 Born: 1/6/1991 Age: 31

			HOW MUCH PITCHED					WHAT HE GAVE UP										THE RESULTS							
Year	Team	Lg	G	GS	GF	IP	BFP	H	R	ER	HR	SH	SF	HB	TBB	IBB	SO	WP	W	L	Pct	Sv-Op	Hld	Vel	OPS	ERC	ERA
2013	Bal	AL	20	5	3	47.2	201	51	30	30	8	2	1	0	13	2	49	4	3	5	.375	0-2	2	96	.792	4.41	5.66
2014	Bal	AL	20	20	0	113.1	476	111	48	45	7	3	7	1	38	0	88	9	7	7	.500	0-0	0	95	.685	3.52	3.57
2015	Bal	AL	25	17	1	112.1	470	109	56	53	17	2	3	2	29	1	103	7	4	7	.364	0-0	1	95	.739	3.74	4.25
2016	Bal	AL	30	30	0	179.2	757	183	76	72	28	4	3	5	47	1	174	8	9	12	.429	0-0	0	95	.742	4.13	3.61
2017	Bal	AL	34	34	0	186.2	816	208	99	97	29	1	3	5	71	0	179	8	11	12	.478	0-0	0	95	.808	5.24	4.68
2018	2 Tms		31	31	0	183.2	776	189	85	80	26	0	4	7	50	1	148	6	10	11	.476	0-0	0	94	.753	4.19	3.92
2019	2 Tms	NL	31	17	6	102.1	451	113	71	65	15	7	6	5	32	3	114	2	3	9	.250	0-0	2	94	.792	4.76	5.72
2020	SF	NL	12	10	1	59.2	245	50	26	24	8	0	2	0	16	0	79	4	3	3	.500	0-0	0	95	.660	2.87	3.62
2021	SF	NL	33	33	0	192.0	775	150	66	60	20	2	4	4	50	1	227	7	14	6	.700	0-0	0	95	.609	2.48	2.81
18	Bal	AL	21	21	0	124.0	534	139	62	61	21	0	2	5	32	0	104	6	5	8	.385	0-0	0	94	.806	4.88	4.43
18	Atl	NL	10	10	0	59.2	242	50	23	19	5	0	2	2	18	1	44	0	5	3	.625	0-0	0	94	.635	2.87	2.87

Year Team	Lg	G	GS	GF	IP	BFP	H	R	ER	HR	SH	SF	HB	TBB	IBB	SO	WP	W	L	Pct	Sv-Op	Hld	Vel	OPS	ERC	ERA
19 Atl	NL	16	16	0	80.0	360	92	60	55	12	6	6	4	27	2	85	2	3	7	.300	0-0	0	94	.814	5.14	6.19
19 Cin	NL	15	1	6	22.1	91	21	11	10	3	1	0	1	5	1	29	0	0	2	.000	0-0	2	95	.705	3.46	4.03
Postseason		4	0	1	10.0	37	6	3	3	1	0	1	0	4	0	11	0	0	0	-	0-0	0	96	.583	2.21	2.70
9 ML YEARS		236	197	11	1177.1	4967	1164	557	526	158	21	33	29	346	9	1161	55	64	72	.471	0-2	5	95	.730	3.92	4.02

Domingo German

Pitches: R Bats: R Pos: SP-18; RP-4

hair-MAHN

Ht: 6'2" Wt: 181 Born: 8/4/1992 Age: 29

Year Team	Lg	G	GS	GF	IP	BFP	H	R	ER	HR	SH	SF	HB	TBB	IBB	SO	WP	W	L	Pct	Sv-Op	Hld	Vel	OPS	ERC	ERA
2017 NYY	AL	7	0	5	14.1	62	11	6	5	1	1	1	0	9	0	18	3	0	1	.000	0-0	0	96	.661	3.44	3.14
2018 NYY	AL	21	14	2	85.2	375	81	55	53	15	0	2	5	30	0	102	7	2	6	.250	0-0	0	95	.774	4.39	5.57
2019 NYY	AL	27	24	0	143.0	594	125	69	64	30	1	1	5	39	0	153	6	18	4	.818	0-0	0	94	.727	3.69	4.03
2021 NYY	AL	22	18	0	98.1	410	89	52	50	17	0	1	2	27	0	98	3	4	5	.444	0-0	0	94	.714	3.58	4.58
4 ML YEARS		77	56	7	341.1	1441	306	182	172	63	2	5	12	108	0	371	18	24	16	.600	0-0	1	94	.733	3.83	4.54

Trent Giambrone

Bats: R Throws: R Pos: 2B-4;PH-2

gym-BROH-nee

Ht: 5'8" Wt: 175 Born: 12/20/1993 Age: 28

Year Team	Lg	G	AB	H	2B	3B	HR	(Hm	Rd)	TB	R	RBI	RC	TBB	IBB	SO	HBP	SH	SF	SB	CS	GDP	Avg	OBP	Slg	OPS
2021 Iowa	AAA	72	235	41	8	1	3	(-	-)	60	27	16	-	31	0	79	2	1	2	5	3	6	.174	.274	.255	.529
2021 ChC	NL	5	13	2	0	0	0	(0	0)	2	0	0	0	0	0	4	0	0	0	0	0	0	.154	.154	.154	.308

Ian Gibaut

Pitches: R Bats: R Pos: RP-3

jih-BOH

Ht: 6'3" Wt: 250 Born: 11/19/1993 Age: 28

Year Team	Lg	G	GS	GF	IP	BFP	H	R	ER	HR	SH	SF	HB	TBB	IBB	SO	WP	W	L	Pct	Sv-Op	Hld	Vel	OPS	ERC	ERA
2021 StPaul	AAA	30	1	10	43.0	199	52	32	32	5	0	1	2	20	0	52	3	1	3	.250	0--	-	-	.821	5.87	6.70
2019 2 Tms	AL	10	0	1	14.1	64	12	9	9	1	0	2	1	10	1	16	1	1	1	.500	0-0	0	95	.732	4.28	5.65
2020 Tex	AL	14	0	1	12.1	59	11	10	9	2	1	0	1	9	0	14	2	0	1	.000	0-1	2	95	.779	5.35	6.57
2021 Min	AL	3	0	0	6.2	28	7	2	2	2	0	0	1	2	0	4	0	0	0	-	0-0	0	95	.917	6.38	2.70
19 TB	AL	1	0	1	2.0	9	1	2	2	0	0	1	0	2	0	2	0	0	0	-	0-0	0	95	.667	2.80	9.00
19 Tex	AL	9	0	0	12.1	55	11	7	7	1	0	1	1	8	1	14	1	1	1	.500	0-0	0	95	.741	4.54	5.11
3 ML YEARS		27	0	2	33.1	151	30	21	20	5	1	2	3	21	1	34	3	1	2	.333	0-1	2	95	.787	5.10	5.40

Kyle Gibson

Pitches: R Bats: R Pos: SP-30; RP-1

Ht: 6'6" Wt: 215 Born: 10/23/1987 Age: 34

Year Team	Lg	G	GS	GF	IP	BFP	H	R	ER	HR	SH	SF	HB	TBB	IBB	SO	WP	W	L	Pct	Sv-Op	Hld	Vel	OPS	ERC	ERA
2013 Min	AL	10	10	0	51.0	238	69	38	37	7	0	2	5	20	0	29	4	2	4	.333	0-0	0	92	.874	6.98	6.53
2014 Min	AL	31	31	0	179.1	757	178	91	89	12	4	3	2	57	0	107	11	13	12	.520	0-0	0	91	.679	3.54	4.47
2015 Min	AL	32	32	0	194.2	821	186	88	83	18	6	6	7	65	6	145	7	11	11	.500	0-0	0	92	.698	3.63	3.84
2016 Min	AL	25	25	0	147.1	653	175	89	83	20	3	4	4	55	3	104	9	6	11	.353	0-0	0	91	.820	5.47	5.07
2017 Min	AL	29	29	0	158.0	693	182	93	89	24	1	2	6	60	0	121	4	12	10	.545	0-0	0	92	.826	5.53	5.07
2018 Min	AL	32	32	0	196.2	826	177	88	79	23	3	7	4	79	2	179	8	10	13	.435	0-0	0	93	.701	3.75	3.62
2019 Min	AL	34	29	0	160.0	706	175	99	86	23	3	2	7	56	0	160	8	13	7	.650	0-1	2	93	.782	4.88	4.84
2020 Tex	AL	12	12	0	67.1	301	73	44	40	12	0	0	6	30	1	58	1	2	6	.250	0-0	0	92	.823	5.75	5.35
2021 2 Tms		31	30	0	182.0	754	158	78	75	17	2	5	8	64	2	155	2	10	9	.526	0-0	0	92	.669	3.32	3.71
21 Tex	AL	19	19	0	113.0	460	92	38	36	9	0	3	5	41	0	94	2	6	3	.667	0-0	0	93	.626	3.04	2.87
21 Phi	NL	12	11	0	69.0	294	66	40	39	8	2	2	3	23	2	61	0	4	6	.400	0-0	0	92	.736	3.80	5.09
Postseason		1	0	0	1.0	7	1	3	3	0	0	0	0	3	0	1	0	0	0	-	0-0	0	94	1.071	13.82	27.00
9 ML YEARS		236	230	0	1336.1	5749	1373	708	661	156	22	31	49	486	14	1058	54	79	83	.488	0-1	2	92	.745	4.37	4.45

Luis Gil

Pitches: R Bats: R Pos: SP-6

HEEL

Ht: 6'2" Wt: 185 Born: 6/3/1998 Age: 24

Year Team	Lg	G	GS	GF	IP	BFP	H	R	ER	HR	SH	SF	HB	TBB	IBB	SO	WP	W	L	Pct	Sv-Op	Hld	Vel	OPS	ERC	ERA
2021 Smrst	AA	7	7	0	30.2	130	24	11	9	2	0	1	0	13	0	50	3	1	1	.500	0--	-	-	.621	2.70	2.64
2021 S-WB	AAA	13	10	1	48.2	212	35	26	26	7	1	3	3	32	0	67	5	4	0	1.000	1--	-	-	.713	4.07	4.81
2021 NYY	AL	6	6	0	29.1	129	20	11	10	4	0	0	1	19	0	38	1	1	1	.500	0-0	0	96	.613	3.56	3.07

Logan Gilbert

Pitches: R Bats: R Pos: SP-24

Ht: 6'6" Wt: 225 Born: 5/5/1997 Age: 25

Year Team	Lg	G	GS	GF	IP	BFP	H	R	ER	HR	SH	SF	HB	TBB	IBB	SO	WP	W	L	Pct	Sv-Op	Hld	Vel	OPS	ERC	ERA
2021 Sea	AL	24	24	0	119.1	503	112	63	62	17	2	3	6	28	2	128	9	6	5	.545	0-0	0	95	.716	3.48	4.68

Tyler Gilbert

Pitches: L Bats: L Pos: SP-6; RP-3

Ht: 6'3" Wt: 223 Born: 12/22/1993 Age: 28

Year Team	Lg	G	GS	GF	IP	BFP	H	R	ER	HR	SH	SF	HB	TBB	IBB	SO	WP	W	L	Pct	Sv-Op	Hld	Vel	OPS	ERC	ERA
2021 Reno	AAA	11	10	0	52.1	219	46	22	20	4	0	1	2	19	0	50	0	5	2	.714	0--	-	-	.661	3.28	3.44
2021 Ari	NL	9	6	0	40.0	157	28	17	14	4	1	2	1	13	0	25	0	2	2	.500	0-0	1	90	.612	2.38	3.15

Lucas Gilbreath

Pitches: L Bats: L Pos: RP-46; SP-1   Ht: 6'1" Wt: 185 Born: 3/5/1996 Age: 26

			HOW MUCH PITCHED					WHAT HE GAVE UP										THE RESULTS						
Year	Team	Lg	G	GS	GF	IP	BFP	H	R	ER	HR	SH	SF	HB	TBB	IBB	SO	WP	W	L	Pct	Sv-Op	Hld	Vel	OPS	ERC	ERA
2021	Col	NL	47	1	9	42.2	185	33	18	16	5	0	2	1	23	0	44	4	3	2	.600	1-1	4	93	.635	3.50	3.38

Ken Giles

Pitches: R Bats: R Pos: P   Ht: 6'3" Wt: 210 Born: 9/20/1990 Age: 31

			HOW MUCH PITCHED					WHAT HE GAVE UP										THE RESULTS						
Year	Team	Lg	G	GS	GF	IP	BFP	H	R	ER	HR	SH	SF	HB	TBB	IBB	SO	WP	W	L	Pct	Sv-Op	Hld	Vel	OPS	ERC	ERA
2014	Phi	NL	44	0	11	45.2	166	25	7	6	1	2	1	0	11	1	64	1	3	1	.750	1-1	13	97	.450	1.15	1.18
2015	Phi	NL	69	0	28	70.0	298	59	23	14	2	1	2	1	25	2	87	1	6	3	.667	15-20	12	97	.569	2.53	1.80
2016	Hou	AL	69	0	24	65.2	286	60	32	30	8	2	1	2	25	1	102	14	2	5	.286	15-20	18	97	.709	3.66	4.11
2017	Hou	AL	63	0	55	62.2	247	44	16	16	4	1	2	1	21	0	83	3	1	3	.250	34-38	2	98	.566	2.17	2.30
2018	2 Tms	AL	55	0	42	50.1	212	54	28	26	6	1	0	1	7	0	53	2	0	3	.000	26-26	1	97	.722	3.59	4.65
2019	Tor	AL	53	0	44	53.0	208	36	11	11	5	0	0	0	17	1	83	2	2	3	.400	23-24	1	97	.574	2.10	1.87
2020	Tor	AL	4	0	1	3.2	19	4	4	4	2	0	0	0	4	0	6	0	0	0	-	1-1	1	94	1.154	11.42	9.82
18	Hou	AL	34	0	24	30.2	129	36	17	17	2	0	0	0	3	0	31	1	0	2	.000	12-12	1	97	.723	3.59	4.99
18	Tor	AL	21	0	18	19.2	83	18	11	9	4	1	0	1	4	0	22	1	0	1	.000	14-14	0	97	.722	3.58	4.12
	Postseason		7	0	4	7.2	40	12	10	10	3	0	0	0	5	1	10	3	0	2	.000	2-3	0	98	1.111	10.90	11.74
7 ML YEARS			357	0	205	351.0	1436	282	121	107	28	7	6	5	110	5	478	23	14	18	.438	115-130	47	97	.613	2.59	2.74

Andres Gimenez

Bats: L Throws: R Pos: SS-42;2B-25;PR-3;PH-2   Ht: 5'11" Wt: 161 Born: 9/4/1998 Age: 23

			BATTING																	RUNNING			AVERAGES			
Year	Team	Lg	G	AB	H	2B	3B	HR	(Hm	Rd)	TB	R	RBI	RC	TBB	IBB	SO	HBP	SH	SF	SB	CS	GDP	Avg	OBP	Slg	OPS
2021	Clmbs	AAA	52	209	60	13	1	10	(-	-)	105	30	31	-	12	1	55	6	5	1	8	4	1	.287	.342	.502	.844
2020	NYM	NL	49	118	31	3	2	3	(2	1)	47	22	12	15	7	0	28	6	0	1	8	1	0	.263	.333	.398	.732
2021	Cle	AL	68	188	41	10	0	5	(3	2)	66	23	16	21	11	0	54	7	1	3	11	0	1	.218	.282	.351	.633
2 ML YEARS			117	306	72	13	2	8	(5	3)	113	45	28	36	18	0	82	13	1	4	19	1	1	.235	.302	.369	.671

Kevin Ginkel

Pitches: R Bats: L Pos: RP-32   Ht: 6'4" Wt: 235 Born: 3/24/1994 Age: 28

			HOW MUCH PITCHED					WHAT HE GAVE UP										THE RESULTS						
Year	Team	Lg	G	GS	GF	IP	BFP	H	R	ER	HR	SH	SF	HB	TBB	IBB	SO	WP	W	L	Pct	Sv-Op	Hld	Vel	OPS	ERC	ERA
2019	Ari	NL	25	0	4	24.1	96	15	7	4	2	0	0	0	9	0	28	2	3	0	1.000	2-2	8	94	.532	1.91	1.48
2020	Ari	NL	19	0	2	16.0	79	21	13	12	3	0	0	0	13	2	18	4	0	2	.000	1-2	0	96	.961	8.38	6.75
2021	Ari	NL	32	0	9	28.1	129	30	24	20	7	1	0	2	14	0	31	3	0	1	.000	0-1	6	95	.904	6.19	6.35
3 ML YEARS			76	0	15	68.2	304	66	44	36	12	1	0	2	36	2	77	9	3	3	.500	3-5	14	95	.799	4.96	4.72

Lucas Giolito

Pitches: R Bats: R Pos: SP-31   jee-oh-LEE-toh   Ht: 6'6" Wt: 245 Born: 7/14/1994 Age: 27

			HOW MUCH PITCHED					WHAT HE GAVE UP										THE RESULTS						
Year	Team	Lg	G	GS	GF	IP	BFP	H	R	ER	HR	SH	SF	HB	TBB	IBB	SO	WP	W	L	Pct	Sv-Op	Hld	Vel	OPS	ERC	ERA
2016	Was	NL	6	4	1	21.1	101	26	18	16	7	0	0	1	12	0	11	1	0	1	.000	0-0	0	93	.988	8.14	6.75
2017	CWS	AL	7	7	0	45.1	179	31	14	12	8	1	0	3	12	0	34	2	3	3	.500	0-0	0	92	.645	2.63	2.38
2018	CWS	AL	32	32	0	173.1	775	166	123	118	27	1	5	15	90	2	125	13	10	13	.435	0-0	0	92	.794	5.05	6.13
2019	CWS	AL	29	29	0	176.2	705	131	69	67	24	1	3	4	57	1	228	6	14	9	.609	0-0	0	94	.646	2.75	3.41
2020	CWS	AL	12	12	0	72.1	288	47	31	28	8	0	3	2	28	0	97	3	4	3	.571	0-0	0	94	.577	2.40	3.48
2021	CWS	AL	31	31	0	178.2	720	145	74	70	27	1	3	2	52	1	201	12	11	9	.550	0-0	0	94	.671	3.03	3.53
	Postseason		1	1	0	7.0	24	2	1	1	0	0	0	0	1	0	8	0	1	0	1.000	0-0	0	95	.212	0.34	1.29
6 ML YEARS			117	115	1	667.2	2768	546	329	311	101	4	14	27	251	4	696	37	42	38	.525	0-0	0	93	.699	3.49	4.19

Chris Gittens

Bats: R Throws: R Pos: 1B-13;PH-6   Ht: 6'4" Wt: 250 Born: 2/4/1994 Age: 28

			BATTING																	RUNNING			AVERAGES			
Year	Team	Lg	G	AB	H	2B	3B	HR	(Hm	Rd)	TB	R	RBI	RC	TBB	IBB	SO	HBP	SH	SF	SB	CS	GDP	Avg	OBP	Slg	OPS
2021	S-WB	AAA	45	146	44	8	0	14	(-	-)	94	37	44	-	36	0	46	1	0	1	0	0	8	.301	.440	.644	1.084
2021	NYY	AL	16	36	4	0	0	1	(0	1)	7	1	5	1	7	0	13	0	0	1	0	0	0	.111	.250	.194	.444

Mychal Givens

Pitches: R Bats: R Pos: RP-54   michael   Ht: 6'0" Wt: 230 Born: 5/13/1990 Age: 32

			HOW MUCH PITCHED					WHAT HE GAVE UP										THE RESULTS						
Year	Team	Lg	G	GS	GF	IP	BFP	H	R	ER	HR	SH	SF	HB	TBB	IBB	SO	WP	W	L	Pct	Sv-Op	Hld	Vel	OPS	ERC	ERA
2015	Bal	AL	22	0	5	30.0	117	20	7	6	1	1	1	1	6	0	38	0	2	0	1.000	0-0	4	94	.538	1.49	1.80
2016	Bal	AL	66	0	8	74.2	313	59	28	26	6	2	1	6	36	2	96	3	8	2	.800	0-1	13	94	.664	3.44	3.13
2017	Bal	AL	69	0	8	78.2	315	57	24	24	10	0	0	5	25	1	88	2	8	1	.889	0-5	21	96	.617	2.74	2.75
2018	Bal	AL	69	0	32	76.2	317	61	37	34	4	1	3	3	30	4	79	4	0	7	.000	9-13	15	95	.622	2.72	3.99
2019	Bal	AL	58	0	33	63.0	260	49	35	32	13	0	2	2	26	1	86	5	2	6	.250	11-19	7	95	.722	3.74	4.57
2020	2 Tms		22	0	5	22.1	93	16	10	9	5	0	1	0	10	0	25	2	1	1	.500	1-3	6	95	.751	3.91	3.63
2021	2 Tms	NL	54	0	22	51.0	216	43	22	19	7	0	3	2	27	4	54	2	4	3	.571	8-11	11	95	.746	4.09	3.35
20	Bal	AL	12	0	3	13.0	51	7	2	2	1	0	1	0	6	0	19	0	1	0	1.000	0-0	5	95	.573	1.84	1.38
20	Col	NL	10	0	2	9.1	42	9	8	7	4	0	0	0	4	0	6	2	1	0	1.000	1-3	1	95	.968	7.42	6.75

	HOW MUCH PITCHED				WHAT HE GAVE UP											THE RESULTS						
Year Team	Lg	G	GS	GF	IP	BFP	H	R	ER	HR	SH	SF	HB	TBB	IBB	SO	WP	W	L	Pct	Sv-Op	Hld	Vel	OPS	ERC	ERA
21 Col	NL	31	0	9	29.2	124	25	11	9	5	0	1	2	14	2	34	2	3	2	.600	0-1	8	94	.751	4.25	2.73
21 Cin	NL	23	0	13	21.1	92	18	11	10	2	0	2	0	13	2	20	0	1	1	.500	8-10	3	95	.740	3.87	4.22
Postseason		1	0	0	2.1	6	0	0	0	0	0	0	0	0	0	3	0	0	0	-	0-0	0	96	.000	0.00	0.00
7 ML YEARS		360	0	113	396.1	1631	305	163	150	46	4	11	21	160	12	466	18	25	20	.556	29-52	77	95	.662	3.15	3.41

Tyler Glasnow

Pitches: R **Bats:** L **Pos:** SP-14

Ht: 6'8" **Wt:** 225 **Born:** 8/23/1993 **Age:** 28

	HOW MUCH PITCHED				WHAT HE GAVE UP											THE RESULTS						
Year Team	Lg	G	GS	GF	IP	BFP	H	R	ER	HR	SH	SF	HB	TBB	IBB	SO	WP	W	L	Pct	Sv-Op	Hld	Vel	OPS	ERC	ERA
2016 Pit	NL	7	4	0	23.1	105	22	13	11	2	1	0	3	13	0	24	2	0	2	.000	0-0	0	94	.774	4.80	4.24
2017 Pit	NL	15	13	0	62.0	305	81	61	53	13	4	1	2	44	2	56	3	2	7	.222	0-0	1	95	.997	8.32	7.69
2018 2 Tms		45	11	9	111.2	468	89	55	53	15	0	1	4	53	3	136	12	2	7	.222	0-0	4	97	.688	3.62	4.27
2019 TB	AL	12	12	0	60.2	230	40	13	12	4	0	1	0	14	0	76	2	6	1	.857	0-0	0	97	.509	1.63	1.78
2020 TB	AL	11	11	0	57.1	238	43	26	26	11	0	1	0	22	0	91	7	5	1	.833	0-0	0	97	.673	3.18	4.08
2021 TB	AL	14	14	0	88.0	340	55	26	26	10	0	0	0	27	0	123	8	5	2	.714	0-0	0	97	.561	1.93	2.66
18 Pit	NL	34	0	9	56.0	243	47	28	27	5	0	0	1	34	2	72	7	1	2	.333	0-0	4	97	.698	3.95	4.34
18 TB	AL	11	11	0	55.2	225	42	27	26	10	0	1	3	19	1	64	5	1	5	.167	0-0	0	97	.676	3.26	4.20
Postseason		8	8	0	35.2	159	35	26	26	10	0	0	0	20	0	48	6	2	5	.286	0-0	0	98	.835	5.96	6.56
6 ML YEARS		104	65	9	403.0	1686	330	194	181	55	5	4	9	173	5	506	34	20	20	.500	0-0	5	96	.693	3.52	4.04

Zack Godley

Pitches: R **Bats:** R **Pos:** SP-1; RP-1

Ht: 6'3" **Wt:** 250 **Born:** 4/21/1990 **Age:** 32

	HOW MUCH PITCHED				WHAT HE GAVE UP											THE RESULTS						
Year Team	Lg	G	GS	GF	IP	BFP	H	R	ER	HR	SH	SF	HB	TBB	IBB	SO	WP	W	L	Pct	Sv-Op	Hld	Vel	OPS	ERC	ERA
2021 Nashv	AAA	6	5	0	30.0	119	21	9	8	4	0	1	0	12	0	34	0	3	2	.600	0- -	-	-	.636	2.76	2.40
2021 Clmbs	AAA	6	6	0	24.0	115	30	19	16	5	0	1	4	11	0	18	3	1	2	.333	0- -	-	-	.906	7.38	6.00
2021 Syrcse	AAA	8	6	2	40.0	170	31	16	16	2	1	2	6	25	0	32	5	3	2	.600	0- -	-	-	.690	4.11	3.60
2015 Ari	NL	9	6	1	36.2	150	29	13	13	4	1	1	3	17	1	34	2	5	1	.833	0-0	0	91	.843	3.67	3.19
2016 Ari	NL	27	9	1	74.2	335	86	54	53	13	7	1	4	25	4	60	5	5	4	.556	0-1	0	91	.844	5.31	6.39
2017 Ari	NL	26	25	1	155.0	627	124	61	58	15	6	2	5	53	2	165	13	8	9	.471	0-0	0	92	.657	2.92	3.37
2018 Ari	NL	33	32	0	178.1	791	177	103	94	16	8	8	12	81	2	185	17	15	11	.577	0-0	0	90	.733	4.40	4.74
2019 2 Tms		33	9	10	92.0	407	96	62	61	14	3	2	5	42	2	70	3	4	5	.444	2-2	0	90	.824	5.17	5.97
2020 Bos	AL	8	7	0	28.2	143	42	26	26	9	0	1	3	14	0	28	3	0	4	.000	0-0	0	90	1.037	9.60	8.16
2021 Mil	NL	2	1	0	3.1	21	4	7	6	2	0	0	1	5	0	5	2	0	1	.000	0-1	0	90	1.214	15.79	16.20
19 Ari	NL	27	9	9	76.0	338	81	55	54	12	3	2	4	35	2	58	3	3	5	.375	2-2	0	90	.834	5.35	6.39
19 Tor	AL	6	0	1	16.0	69	15	7	7	2	0	0	1	7	0	12	0	1	0	1.000	0-0	0	90	.776	4.34	3.94
Postseason		1	0	0	5.0	22	4	3	2	0	1	0	0	2	0	5	1	0	0	-	0-0	0		.496	2.18	3.60
7 ML YEARS		138	89	13	568.2	2474	558	326	311	73	25	15	33	237	11	547	45	37	35	.514	2-4	0	91	.762	4.45	4.92

Jose Godoy

Bats: L **Throws:** R **Pos:** C-14;DH-1;PH-1

Ht: 5'11" **Wt:** 200 **Born:** 10/13/1994 **Age:** 27

	BATTING																		RUNNING			AVERAGES			
Year Team	Lg	G	AB	H	2B	3B	HR	(Hm | Rd)	TB	R	RBI	RC	TBB	IBB	SO	HBP	SH	SF	SB	CS	GDP	Avg	OBP	Slg	OPS
2021 Tacom	AAA	70	286	83	14	1	7	(- | -)	120	44	54	-	19	0	55	3	1	4	1	0	12	.290	.337	.420	.756
2021 Sea	AL	16	37	6	1	0	0	(0 | 0)	7	2	3	2	3	0	14	0	0	0	0	0	2	.162	.225	.189	.414

Paul Goldschmidt

Bats: R **Throws:** R **Pos:** 1B-153;DH-4;PH-1

Ht: 6'3" **Wt:** 220 **Born:** 9/10/1987 **Age:** 34

	BATTING																		RUNNING			AVERAGES			
Year Team	Lg	G	AB	H	2B	3B	HR	(Hm | Rd)	TB	R	RBI	RC	TBB	IBB	SO	HBP	SH	SF	SB	CS	GDP	Avg	OBP	Slg	OPS
2011 Ari	NL	48	156	39	9	1	8	(2 | 6)	74	28	26	26	20	0	53	0	0	1	4	0	4	.250	.333	.474	.808
2012 Ari	NL	145	514	147	43	1	20	(10 | 10)	252	82	82	86	60	4	130	4	0	9	18	3	9	.286	.359	.490	.850
2013 Ari	NL	160	602	182	36	3	36	(17 | 19)	332	103	125	131	99	19	145	3	0	5	15	7	25	.302	.401	.551	.952
2014 Ari	NL	109	406	122	39	1	19	(10 | 9)	220	75	69	83	64	10	110	2	0	3	9	3	10	.300	.396	.542	.938
2015 Ari	NL	159	567	182	38	2	33	(13 | 20)	323	103	110	135	118	29	151	2	0	7	21	5	16	.321	.435	.570	1.005
2016 Ari	NL	158	579	172	33	3	24	(15 | 9)	283	106	95	113	110	15	150	7	0	8	32	5	14	.297	.411	.489	.899
2017 Ari	NL	155	558	166	34	3	36	(20 | 16)	314	117	120	131	94	15	147	8	0	4	18	5	14	.297	.404	.563	.966
2018 Ari	NL	158	593	172	35	5	33	(12 | 21)	316	95	83	118	90	11	173	6	0	0	7	4	7	.290	.389	.533	.922
2019 StL	NL	161	597	155	25	1	34	(17 | 17)	284	97	97	103	78	2	166	2	0	3	3	1	11	.260	.346	.476	.821
2020 StL	NL	58	191	58	13	0	6	(4 | 2)	89	31	21	37	37	0	43	1	0	1	1	0	4	.304	.417	.466	.883
2021 StL	NL	158	603	177	36	2	31	(14 | 17)	310	102	99	107	67	2	136	4	0	5	12	0	13	.294	.365	.514	.879
Postseason		20	82	23	5	0	8	(3 | 5)	52	13	16	16	6	1	22	1	0	1	0	1	0	.280	.337	.634	.971
11 ML YEARS		1469	5366	1572	341	22	280	(134 | 146)	2797	939	927	1071	837	107	1404	39	0	46	140	33	127	.293	.389	.521	.911

Austin Gomber

Pitches: L **Bats:** L **Pos:** SP-23

Ht: 6'5" **Wt:** 220 **Born:** 11/23/1993 **Age:** 28

	HOW MUCH PITCHED				WHAT HE GAVE UP											THE RESULTS						
Year Team	Lg	G	GS	GF	IP	BFP	H	R	ER	HR	SH	SF	HB	TBB	IBB	SO	WP	W	L	Pct	Sv-Op	Hld	Vel	OPS	ERC	ERA
2018 StL	NL	29	11	1	75.0	334	81	40	37	7	4	2	4	32	4	67	3	6	2	.750	0-0	7	92	.786	4.72	4.44
2020 StL	NL	14	4	2	29.0	119	19	6	6	1	0	2	2	15	0	27	1	1	1	.500	0-0	1	93	.563	2.56	1.86
2021 Col	NL	23	23	0	115.1	488	102	64	58	20	2	2	3	41	2	113	1	9	9	.500	0-0	0	92	.721	3.79	4.53
Postseason		1	0	0	1.1	7	2	0	0	0	0	0	0	1	0	2	0	0	0	-	0-0	0	94	.762	7.52	0.00
3 ML YEARS		66	38	3	219.1	941	202	110	101	28	6	6	9	88	6	207	5	16	12	.571	0-0	8	92	.725	3.94	4.14

Yan Gomes

Bats: R **Throws:** R **Pos:** C-92;PH-9;DH-6

YAHN GOHMS

Ht: 6'2" **Wt:** 212 **Born:** 7/19/1987 **Age:** 34

								BATTING												RUNNING			AVERAGES			
Year Team	Lg	G	AB	H	2B	3B	HR	(Hm Rd)	TB	R	RBI	RC	TBB	IBB	SO	HBP	SH	SF	SB	CS	GDP	Avg	OBP	Slg	OPS
2012 Tor	AL	43	98	20	4	0	4	(3 1)	36	9	13	11	6	0	32	3	1	3	0	0	3	.204	.264	.367	.631
2013 Cle	AL	88	293	86	18	2	11	(6 5)	141	45	38	42	18	0	67	7	0	4	2	0	12	.294	.345	.481	.826
2014 Cle	AL	135	485	135	25	3	21	(9 12)	229	61	74	65	24	3	120	3	0	6	0	0	13	.278	.313	.472	.785
2015 Cle	AL	95	363	84	22	0	12	(5 7)	142	38	45	25	13	1	104	7	0	6	0	0	11	.231	.267	.391	.659
2016 Cle	AL	74	251	42	11	1	9	(4 5)	82	22	34	18	9	0	69	2	0	2	0	0	7	.167	.201	.327	.527
2017 Cle	AL	105	341	79	15	0	14	(5 9)	136	43	56	41	31	0	99	8	1	2	0	0	9	.232	.309	.399	.708
2018 Cle	AL	112	403	107	26	0	16	(5 11)	181	52	48	47	21	2	119	8	0	3	0	0	4	.266	.313	.449	.762
2019 Was	NL	97	314	70	16	0	12	(8 4)	122	36	43	39	38	6	84	5	0	1	2	0	7	.223	.316	.389	.704
2020 Was	NL	30	109	31	6	1	4	(4 0)	51	14	13	12	6	0	22	1	0	3	1	0	1	.284	.319	.468	.787
2021 2 Tms		103	349	88	15	1	14	(9 5)	147	49	52	42	19	3	78	6	0	1	0	0	15	.252	.301	.421	.723
21 Was	NL	63	218	59	11	1	9	(6 3)	99	30	35	30	13	3	47	4	0	0	0	0	12	.271	.323	.454	.778
21 Oak	AL	40	131	29	4	0	5	(3 2)	48	19	17	12	6	0	31	2	0	1	0	0	3	.221	.264	.366	.631
Postseason		22	51	13	4	0	0	(0 0)	17	6	4	6	5	2	17	0	0	0	0	0	1	.255	.321	.333	.655
10 ML YEARS		882	3006	742	158	8	117	(58 59)	1267	369	416	342	185	15	794	50	2	31	5	0	82	.247	.299	.421	.720

Stephen Gonsalves

Pitches: L **Bats:** L **Pos:** RP-3

Ht: 6'5" **Wt:** 218 **Born:** 7/8/1994 **Age:** 27

		HOW MUCH PITCHED					WHAT HE GAVE UP										THE RESULTS							
Year Team	Lg	G	GS	GF	IP	BFP	H	R	ER	HR	SH	SF	HB	TBB	IBB	SO	WP	W	L	Pct	Sv-Op	Hld	Vel	OPS	ERC	ERA
2021 Wrcstr	AAA	20	10	1	71.0	321	63	41	38	13	2	0	6	51	0	100	3	5	4	.556	0--	-	-	.788	5.79	4.82
2018 Min	AL	7	4	0	24.2	122	28	22	18	2	0	0	1	22	0	16	2	2	2	.500	0-0	0	90	.822	6.92	6.57
2021 Bos	AL	3	0	1	4.1	18	2	2	2	0	0	0	1	2	0	4	2	0	0	-	0-0	0	93	.478	1.70	4.15
2 ML YEARS		10	4	1	29.0	140	30	24	20	2	0	0	2	24	0	20	4	2	2	.500	0-0	0	90	.777	6.01	6.21

Tony Gonsolin

Pitches: R **Bats:** R **Pos:** SP-13; RP-2

Ht: 6'3" **Wt:** 205 **Born:** 5/14/1994 **Age:** 28

		HOW MUCH PITCHED					WHAT HE GAVE UP										THE RESULTS							
Year Team	Lg	G	GS	GF	IP	BFP	H	R	ER	HR	SH	SF	HB	TBB	IBB	SO	WP	W	L	Pct	Sv-Op	Hld	Vel	OPS	ERC	ERA
2019 LAD	NL	11	6	1	40.0	163	26	15	13	4	0	1	1	15	0	37	2	4	2	.667	1-1	0	94	.580	2.21	2.93
2020 LAD	NL	9	8	1	46.2	176	32	13	12	2	1	1	1	7	0	46	3	2	2	.500	0-0	0	95	.518	1.48	2.31
2021 LAD	NL	15	13	0	55.2	239	41	20	20	8	2	0	0	34	0	65	4	4	1	.800	0-0	0	94	.686	3.72	3.23
Postseason		4	3	0	9.1	46	9	9	9	4	0	0	0	9	0	13	0	0	2	.000	0-0	0	95	1.013	8.82	8.68
3 ML YEARS		35	27	2	142.1	578	99	48	45	14	3	2	2	56	0	148	9	10	5	.667	1-1	0	94	.603	2.48	2.85

Marco Gonzales

Pitches: L **Bats:** L **Pos:** SP-25

Ht: 6'1" **Wt:** 197 **Born:** 2/16/1992 **Age:** 30

		HOW MUCH PITCHED					WHAT HE GAVE UP										THE RESULTS							
Year Team	Lg	G	GS	GF	IP	BFP	H	R	ER	HR	SH	SF	HB	TBB	IBB	SO	WP	W	L	Pct	Sv-Op	Hld	Vel	OPS	ERC	ERA
2014 StL	NL	10	5	0	34.2	156	32	16	16	4	0	1	1	21	1	31	0	4	2	.667	0-0	1	90	.737	4.59	4.15
2015 StL	NL	1	1	0	2.2	16	7	4	4	1	0	1	0	1	0	1	0	0	0	-	0-0	0	89	1.286	17.70	13.50
2017 2 Tms		11	8	1	40.0	185	59	27	27	8	0	1	1	11	0	32	2	1	1	.500	0-0	0	92	.924	7.40	6.08
2018 Sea	AL	29	29	0	166.2	686	172	76	74	17	1	4	6	32	0	145	2	13	9	.591	0-0	0	90	.720	3.65	4.00
2019 Sea	AL	34	34	0	203.0	866	210	106	90	23	1	9	6	56	1	147	2	16	13	.552	0-0	0	89	.736	3.96	3.99
2020 Sea	AL	11	11	0	69.2	277	59	27	24	8	0	0	4	7	0	64	0	7	2	.778	0-0	0	88	.614	2.43	3.10
2021 Sea	AL	25	25	0	143.1	585	125	64	63	29	1	2	5	42	3	108	1	10	6	.625	0-0	0	88	.760	3.78	3.96
17 StL	NL	1	1	0	3.1	16	6	5	5	0	0	0	0	0	0	2	0	0	0	-	0-0	0	91	1.500	13.65	13.50
17 Sea	AL	10	7	1	36.2	169	53	22	22	5	0	1	1	11	0	30	2	1	1	.500	0-0	0	91	.865	6.82	5.40
Postseason		6	0	0	6.0	24	4	3	3	0	1	0	0	2	0	4	0	2	1	.667	0-1	0	91	.451	1.57	4.50
7 ML YEARS		121	113	1	660.0	2771	664	320	298	90	3	18	23	170	5	528	7	51	33	.607	0-0	1	89	.741	3.94	4.06

Chi Chi Gonzalez

Pitches: R **Bats:** R **Pos:** SP-18; RP-6

Ht: 6'3" **Wt:** 210 **Born:** 1/15/1992 **Age:** 30

		HOW MUCH PITCHED					WHAT HE GAVE UP										THE RESULTS							
Year Team	Lg	G	GS	GF	IP	BFP	H	R	ER	HR	SH	SF	HB	TBB	IBB	SO	WP	W	L	Pct	Sv-Op	Hld	Vel	OPS	ERC	ERA
2015 Tex	AL	14	10	1	67.0	280	49	33	29	6	1	2	3	32	1	30	2	4	6	.400	0-0	0	91	.632	3.00	3.90
2016 Tex	AL	3	3	0	10.1	62	21	13	10	1	0	1	0	9	0	7	0	0	2	.000	0-0	0	91	.984	12.48	8.71
2019 Col	NL	14	12	0	63.0	278	59	39	37	11	3	1	1	33	0	46	1	2	6	.250	0-0	0	92	.784	4.78	5.29
2020 Col	NL	6	4	0	19.2	91	22	16	15	3	1	1	3	10	0	16	2	0	2	.000	0-0	0	92	.889	6.34	6.86
2021 Col	NL	24	18	1	101.2	448	127	74	73	18	3	2	6	28	0	56	2	3	7	.300	0-0	0	92	.900	5.96	6.46
Postseason		1	0	0	1.2	8	2	1	1	1	0	0	0	2	0	0	0	0	0	-	0-0	0	93	1.333	15.09	5.40
5 ML YEARS		61	47	2	261.2	1159	278	175	164	39	8	7	13	112	1	155	7	9	23	.281	0-0	0	92	.812	5.12	5.64

Erik Gonzalez

Bats: R **Throws:** R **Pos:** 3B-38;SS-17;1B-13;PH-13

Ht: 6'3" **Wt:** 205 **Born:** 8/31/1991 **Age:** 30

								BATTING												RUNNING			AVERAGES			
Year Team	Lg	G	AB	H	2B	3B	HR	(Hm Rd)	TB	R	RBI	RC	TBB	IBB	SO	HBP	SH	SF	SB	CS	GDP	Avg	OBP	Slg	OPS
2021 Indy	AAA	14	43	6	2	1	0	(- -)	10	6	4	-	4	0	10	2	0	1	0	0	1	.140	.240	.233	.473
2016 Cle	AL	21	16	5	0	0	0	(0 0)	5	2	0	1	1	0	8	0	0	0	0	1	0	.313	.353	.313	.665
2017 Cle	AL	60	110	28	6	0	4	(1 3)	46	18	11	9	3	0	37	0	1	1	1	2	1	.255	.272	.418	.690
2018 Cle	AL	81	136	36	10	1	1	(0 1)	51	17	16	14	5	0	34	2	0	0	3	0	0	.265	.301	.375	.676
2019 Pit	NL	53	142	36	4	1	1	(1 0)	45	15	6	7	9	3	37	1	3	1	4	1	5	.254	.301	.317	.618

Year	Team	Lg	G	AB	H	2B	3B	HR	(Hm	Rd)	TB	R	RBI	RC	TBB	IBB	SO	HBP	SH	SF	SB	CS	GDP	Avg	OBP	Slg	OPS
2020 Pit	NL	50	181	41	13	1	3	(1	2)	65	14	20	21	8	0	51	0	1	3	2	3	5	.227	.255	.359	.614
2021 Pit	NL	71	220	51	7	1	2	(1	1)	66	17	21	18	8	0	40	0	0	1	2	2	4	.232	.258	.300	.558
Postseason		2	2	0	0	0	0	(0	0)	0	0	0	0	0	0	0	0	0	0	0	0	0	.000	.000	.000	.000
6 ML YEARS		336	805	197	40	4	11	(4	7)	278	83	74	70	34	3	207	3	5	6	12	9	15	.245	.276	.345	.621

Luis Gonzalez

Bats: L Throws: L Pos: RF-3;LF-2;PH-2   Ht: 6'1" Wt: 185 Born: 9/10/1995 Age: 26

Year	Team	Lg	G	AB	H	2B	3B	HR	(Hm	Rd)	TB	R	RBI	RC	TBB	IBB	SO	HBP	SH	SF	SB	CS	GDP	Avg	OBP	Slg	OPS
2021 Charllt	AAA	40	137	33	4	0	7	(-	-)	58	24	20	-	22	0	41	2	1	1	9	2	1	.241	.352	.423	.775
2020 CWS	AL	3	1	0	0	0	0	(0	0)	0	1	0	0	1	0	1	1	0	0	0	0	0	.000	.500	.500	.500
2021 CWS	AL	6	8	2	2	0	0	(0	0)	4	2	0	1	3	0	2	0	0	0	0	0	0	.250	.455	.500	.955
2 ML YEARS		9	9	2	2	0	0	(0	0)	4	3	0	1	3	0	3	1	0	0	0	0	1	.222	.462	.444	.906

Marwin Gonzalez

MARR-win

Bats: B Throws: R Pos: 2B-39;1B-17;SS-12;LF-12;3B-11;PH-10;RF-2;DH-2;PR-1   Ht: 6'1" Wt: 205 Born: 3/14/1989 Age: 33

Year	Team	Lg	G	AB	H	2B	3B	HR	(Hm	Rd)	TB	R	RBI	RC	TBB	IBB	SO	HBP	SH	SF	SB	CS	GDP	Avg	OBP	Slg	OPS
2012 Hou	NL	80	205	48	13	0	2	(1	1)	67	21	12	12	13	0	29	0	1	0	3	3	9	.234	.280	.327	.607
2013 Hou	AL	72	204	45	8	0	4	(2	2)	65	22	14	10	9	0	37	0	8	1	6	2	5	.221	.252	.319	.571
2014 Hou	AL	103	285	79	15	1	6	(3	3)	114	33	23	26	17	0	58	4	4	0	2	4	6	.277	.327	.400	.727
2015 Hou	AL	120	344	96	18	1	12	(6	6)	152	44	34	39	16	0	74	3	7	0	4	5	9	.279	.317	.442	.759
2016 Hou	AL	141	484	123	26	3	13	(8	5)	194	55	51	47	22	1	118	6	1	6	12	6	16	.254	.293	.401	.694
2017 Hou	AL	134	455	138	34	0	23	(15	8)	241	67	90	93	49	4	99	6	3	2	8	3	8	.303	.377	.530	.907
2018 Hou	AL	145	489	121	25	3	16	(5	11)	200	61	68	61	53	3	126	3	5	2	2	3	14	.247	.324	.409	.733
2019 Min	AL	114	425	112	19	0	15	(10	5)	176	52	55	58	31	2	98	6	0	1	1	0	7	.264	.322	.414	.736
2020 Min	AL	53	175	37	4	0	5	(3	2)	56	15	22	21	17	0	41	3	0	4	0	0	1	.211	.286	.320	.606
2021 2 Tms	AL	91	276	55	14	0	5	(2	3)	84	30	28	22	20	0	78	9	1	1	3	2	8	.199	.275	.304	.579
21 Bos	AL	77	242	49	14	0	2	(1	1)	69	25	20	18	19	0	70	8	1	1	3	2	5	.202	.281	.285	.567
21 Hou	AL	14	34	6	0	0	3	(1	2)	15	5	8	4	1	0	8	1	0	0	0	0	3	.176	.222	.441	.663
Postseason		35	113	26	7	0	3	(1	2)	42	11	13	8	8	2	30	4	0	0	0	2	1	.230	.304	.372	.676
10 ML YEARS		1053	3342	854	176	8	101	(55	46)	1349	400	397	389	247	10	758	39	35	12	41	28	83	.256	.313	.404	.717

Romy Gonzalez

Bats: R Throws: R Pos: 3B-4;RF-3;PH-3;2B-1;SS-1;LF-1   Ht: 6'1" Wt: 215 Born: 9/6/1996 Age: 25

Year	Team	Lg	G	AB	H	2B	3B	HR	(Hm	Rd)	TB	R	RBI	RC	TBB	IBB	SO	HBP	SH	SF	SB	CS	GDP	Avg	OBP	Slg	OPS
2021 Brham	AA	78	303	81	11	0	20	(-	-)	152	52	47	-	38	2	97	3	0	5	21	6	5	.267	.355	.502	.856
2021 Charllt	AAA	12	44	17	5	0	3	(-	-)	31	8	11	-	3	0	12	0	0	0	3	0	1	.386	.426	.705	1.130
2021 CWS	AL	10	32	8	3	0	0	(0	0)	11	4	2	3	1	0	11	0	0	0	0	0	1	.250	.273	.344	.616

Victor Gonzalez

Pitches: L Bats: L Pos: RP-43; SP-1   Ht: 6'0" Wt: 180 Born: 11/16/1995 Age: 26

			HOW MUCH PITCHED					WHAT HE GAVE UP									THE RESULTS								
Year	Team	Lg	G	GS	GF	IP	BFP	H	R	ER	HR	SH	SF	HB	TBB	IBB	SO	WP	W	L	Pct	Sv-Op	Hld	Vel	OPS	ERC	ERA
2021 OkCity	AAA	11	0	0	9.0	40	9	4	4	1	0	0	2	2	0	14	3	2	0	1.000	0--	-	-	.686	4.23	4.00
2020 LAD	NL	15	1	1	20.1	80	13	3	3	0	1	0	3	2	0	23	2	3	0	1.000	0-0	2	95	.428	1.29	1.33
2021 LAD	NL	44	1	5	35.1	155	32	14	14	3	1	1	3	19	2	33	1	3	1	.750	1-2	16	94	.709	4.26	3.57
Postseason		8	0	0	6.2	27	5	2	2	0	0	0	1	4	0	5	1	1	0	1.000	0-0	1	95	.638	2.96	2.70
2 ML YEARS		59	2	6	55.2	235	45	17	17	3	2	1	6	21	2	56	3	6	1	.857	1-2	18	95	.610	2.99	2.75

Niko Goodrum

Bats: B Throws: R Pos: SS-66;2B-9;CF-8;PH-8;LF-7;PR-2;1B-1;DH-1   Ht: 6'3" Wt: 215 Born: 2/28/1992 Age: 30

Year	Team	Lg	G	AB	H	2B	3B	HR	(Hm	Rd)	TB	R	RBI	RC	TBB	IBB	SO	HBP	SH	SF	SB	CS	GDP	Avg	OBP	Slg	OPS
2021 Toledo	AAA	14	54	10	0	0	0	(-	-)	10	7	2	-	7	0	16	0	0	1	1	0	1	.185	.274	.185	.459
2017 Min	AL	11	17	1	0	0	0	(0	0)	1	1	0	0	1	0	10	0	0	0	0	0	0	.059	.111	.059	.170
2018 Det	AL	131	444	109	29	3	16	(8	8)	192	55	53	63	42	1	132	4	0	2	12	4	9	.245	.315	.432	.747
2019 Det	AL	112	423	105	27	5	12	(4	8)	178	61	45	50	46	1	138	1	0	2	12	3	7	.248	.322	.421	.743
2020 Det	AL	43	158	29	7	1	5	(2	3)	53	15	20	13	18	0	69	0	0	3	7	1	4	.184	.263	.335	.598
2021 Det	AL	90	290	62	11	2	9	(1	8)	104	39	33	32	29	0	107	4	0	2	14	5	6	.214	.292	.359	.651
5 ML YEARS		387	1332	306	74	11	42	(15	27)	528	171	151	158	136	2	456	9	0	9	45	13	26	.230	.303	.396	.700

Brian Goodwin

Bats: L Throws: R Pos: RF-43;CF-27;LF-6;PH-3;DH-2;PR-2   Ht: 6'0" Wt: 205 Born: 11/2/1990 Age: 31

Year	Team	Lg	G	AB	H	2B	3B	HR	(Hm	Rd)	TB	R	RBI	RC	TBB	IBB	SO	HBP	SH	SF	SB	CS	GDP	Avg	OBP	Slg	OPS
2021 Charllt	AAA	24	86	21	4	0	3	(-	-)	34	12	11	-	9	0	31	0	0	0	2	2	1	.244	.316	.395	.711
2016 Was	NL	22	42	12	4	1	0	(0	0)	18	1	5	6	2	0	14	0	0	0	0	0	1	.286	.318	.429	.747
2017 Was	NL	74	251	63	21	4	13	(9	4)	125	41	30	31	23	2	69	1	0	3	6	0	3	.251	.313	.498	.811
2018 2 Tms		75	159	38	6	0	6	(2	4)	62	20	25	27	16	0	57	3	1	1	4	2	0	.239	.318	.390	.708
2019 LAA	AL	136	413	108	29	3	17	(10	7)	194	65	47	44	38	2	129	3	1	3	7	3	3	.262	.326	.470	.796

219

Year Team	Lg	G	AB	H	2B	3B	HR	(Hm Rd)	TB	R	RBI	RC	TBB	IBB	SO	HBP	SH	SF	SB	CS	GDP	Avg	OBP	Slg	OPS
2020 2 Tms		50	144	31	9	1	6	(5 1)	60	17	22	18	17	1	54	1	0	2	5	0	1	.215	.299	.417	.715
2021 CWS	AL	72	235	52	10	1	8	(5 3)	88	33	29	31	33	0	58	1	1	2	1	0	2	.221	.319	.374	.693
18 Was	NL	48	65	13	1	0	3	(1 2)	23	9	12	10	10	0	26	2	1	1	3	1	0	.200	.321	.354	.674
18 KC	AL	27	94	25	5	0	3	(1 2)	39	11	13	17	6	0	31	1	0	0	1	1	0	.266	.317	.415	.732
20 LAA	AL	30	95	23	7	1	4	(4 0)	44	12	17	15	12	1	35	1	0	1	1	0	0	.242	.330	.463	.793
20 Cin	NL	20	49	8	2	0	2	(1 1)	16	5	5	3	5	0	19	0	0	1	4	0	1	.163	.236	.327	.563
Postseason		3	1	0	0	0	0	(0 0)	0	0	0	0	0	0	0	0	0	0	0	0	0	.000	.000	.000	.000
6 ML YEARS		429	1244	304	79	7	50	(31 19)	547	177	158	170	129	5	381	9	3	10	23	5	10	.244	.318	.440	.757

Nick Gordon

Bats: L **Throws:** R **Pos:** CF-34;2B-17;SS-14;LF-11;PH-8;PR-4;3B-2;RF-1   **Ht:** 6'0" **Wt:** 160 **Born:** 10/24/1995 **Age:** 26

Year Team	Lg	G	AB	H	2B	3B	HR	(Hm Rd)	TB	R	RBI	RC	TBB	IBB	SO	HBP	SH	SF	SB	CS	GDP	Avg	OBP	Slg	OPS
2021 StPaul	AAA	18	71	20	0	1	3	(- -)	31	11	9	-	6	0	12	0	0	0	7	2	1	.282	.338	.437	.774
2021 Min	AL	73	200	48	9	1	4	(2 2)	71	19	23	26	12	0	55	3	0	1	10	1	7	.240	.292	.355	.647

Nolan Gorman

Bats: L **Throws:** R **Pos:** IF   **Ht:** 6'1" **Wt:** 210 **Born:** 5/10/2000 **Age:** 22

Year Team	Lg	G	AB	H	2B	3B	HR	(Hm Rd)	TB	R	RBI	RC	TBB	IBB	SO	HBP	SH	SF	SB	CS	GDP	Avg	OBP	Slg	OPS
2018 2 Tms	Low	63	237	69	13	1	17	(- -)	135	49	44	49	34	0	76	1	0	2	1	5	0	.291	.380	.570	.949
2019 2 Tms	Low	125	456	113	30	6	15	(- -)	200	65	62	67	45	3	152	9	0	2	2	0	5	.248	.326	.439	.765
2021 Sprgfld	AA	43	177	51	6	0	11	(- -)	90	26	27	-	18	0	52	0	0	0	4	0	2	.288	.354	.508	.862
2021 Memp	AAA	74	294	81	13	1	14	(- -)	138	44	48	-	19	2	60	2	0	3	3	0	5	.276	.321	.469	.790

Anthony Gose

Pitches: L **Bats:** L **Pos:** RP-6   GOASE   **Ht:** 6'0" **Wt:** 200 **Born:** 8/10/1990 **Age:** 31

Year Team	Lg	G	GS	GF	IP	BFP	H	R	ER	HR	SH	SF	HB	TBB	IBB	SO	WP	W	L	Pct	Sv-Op	Hld	Vel	OPS	ERC	ERA
2021 Clmbs	AAA	28	1	7	33.0	144	20	14	13	4	0	0	0	28	1	49	1	6	1	.857	2- -	-	-	.661	3.73	3.55
2021 Cle	AL	6	0	0	6.2	24	2	1	1	0	0	0	0	2	0	9	0	0	0	-	0-0	0	99	.303	0.57	1.35

Phil Gosselin

Bats: R **Throws:** R **Pos:** LF-39;3B-32;1B-23;PH-13;2B-4;DH-3;RF-1   GOSS-lin   **Ht:** 6'1" **Wt:** 188 **Born:** 10/3/1988 **Age:** 33

Year Team	Lg	G	AB	H	2B	3B	HR	(Hm Rd)	TB	R	RBI	RC	TBB	IBB	SO	HBP	SH	SF	SB	CS	GDP	Avg	OBP	Slg	OPS
2013 Atl	NL	4	6	2	0	0	0	(0 0)	2	2	0	1	1	1	2	0	0	0	0	0	0	.333	.429	.333	.762
2014 Atl	NL	46	128	34	4	0	1	(1 0)	41	17	3	10	5	0	27	2	1	0	2	2	1	.266	.304	.320	.624
2015 2 Tms	NL	44	106	33	9	1	3	(2 1)	53	19	15	22	9	0	16	2	0	1	2	1	2	.311	.373	.500	.873
2016 Ari	NL	122	220	61	12	1	2	(1 1)	81	26	13	24	15	0	46	1	2	2	3	0	0	.277	.324	.368	.692
2017 2 Tms		40	48	7	2	0	0	(0 0)	9	3	2	0	2	0	12	0	0	0	0	1	1	.146	.180	.188	.368
2018 Cin	NL	20	24	3	0	0	1	(1 0)	6	5	2	2	4	1	8	0	0	0	0	0	0	.125	.250	.250	.500
2019 Phi	NL	44	65	17	3	0	0	(0 0)	20	5	7	8	3	0	16	0	0	0	0	0	1	.262	.294	.308	.602
2020 Phi	NL	39	92	23	5	0	3	(2 1)	37	14	12	11	10	1	27	0	0	0	0	0	3	.250	.324	.402	.726
2021 LAA	AL	104	345	90	14	0	7	(3 4)	125	40	47	48	24	0	81	3	0	1	4	2	3	.261	.314	.362	.676
15 Atl	NL	20	40	13	4	0	0	(0 0)	17	2	2	6	2	0	6	0	0	0	2	0	0	.325	.357	.425	.782
15 Ari	NL	24	66	20	5	1	3	(2 1)	36	17	13	16	7	0	11	2	0	1	0	1	2	.303	.382	.545	.927
17 Pit	NL	28	40	6	1	0	0	(0 0)	7	3	2	0	2	0	9	0	0	0	0	1	1	.150	.190	.175	.365
17 Tex	AL	12	8	1	1	0	0	(0 0)	2	0	0	0	0	0	3	0	0	0	0	0	0	.125	.125	.250	.375
9 ML YEARS		463	1034	270	49	2	17	(10 7)	374	131	101	126	73	3	235	8	3	4	11	6	12	.261	.314	.362	.675

Ashton Goudeau

Pitches: R **Bats:** R **Pos:** RP-15; SP-1   **Ht:** 6'6" **Wt:** 220 **Born:** 7/23/1992 **Age:** 29

Year Team	Lg	G	GS	GF	IP	BFP	H	R	ER	HR	SH	SF	HB	TBB	IBB	SO	WP	W	L	Pct	Sv-Op	Hld	Vel	OPS	ERC	ERA
2021 Lsvlle	AAA	8	5	1	31.0	137	30	17	16	5	3	1	1	13	0	22	2	1	3	.250	0- -		-	.765	4.43	4.65
2020 Col	NL	4	0	2	8.1	39	15	7	7	3	0	2	1	2	0	2	1	0	0	-	0-0	0	93	1.226	12.28	7.56
2021 2 Tms	NL	16	1	3	34.1	141	24	16	16	4	3	0	2	17	3	22	1	2	1	.667	0-0	0	93	.681	3.08	4.19
21 Cin	NL	5	0	2	9.0	44	8	4	4	1	1	0	0	9	3	5	0	0	0	-	0-0	0	92	.837	5.13	4.00
21 Col	NL	11	1	1	25.1	97	16	12	12	3	2	0	2	8	0	17	1	2	1	.667	0-0	0	93	.615	2.37	4.26
2 ML YEARS		20	1	5	42.2	180	39	23	23	7	3	2	3	19	3	24	2	2	1	.667	0-0	0	93	.802	4.54	4.85

Yasmani Grandal

Bats: B **Throws:** R **Pos:** C-80;DH-9;1B-8;PH-2   yahz-MAH-nee gran-DAHL   **Ht:** 6'2" **Wt:** 225 **Born:** 11/8/1988 **Age:** 33

Year Team	Lg	G	AB	H	2B	3B	HR	(Hm Rd)	TB	R	RBI	RC	TBB	IBB	SO	HBP	SH	SF	SB	CS	GDP	Avg	OBP	Slg	OPS
2012 SD	NL	60	192	57	7	1	8	(3 5)	90	28	36	37	31	1	39	1	0	2	0	0	8	.297	.394	.469	.863
2013 SD	NL	28	88	19	8	0	1	(1 0)	30	13	9	12	18	2	18	1	0	1	0	0	3	.216	.352	.341	.692
2014 SD	NL	128	377	85	19	1	15	(7 8)	151	47	49	45	58	1	115	2	0	6	3	0	7	.225	.327	.401	.728
2015 LAD	NL	115	355	83	12	0	16	(8 8)	143	43	47	47	65	1	92	2	1	3	0	1	16	.234	.353	.403	.756
2016 LAD	NL	126	390	89	14	1	27	(20 7)	186	49	72	63	64	1	116	2	0	1	1	3	11	.228	.339	.477	.816
2017 LAD	NL	129	438	108	27	0	22	(13 9)	201	50	58	48	40	0	130	0	1	3	0	1	10	.247	.308	.459	.767
2018 LAD	NL	140	440	106	23	2	24	(11 13)	205	65	68	65	72	1	124	3	0	3	2	1	12	.241	.349	.466	.815

220

			BATTING																	RUNNING			AVERAGES			
Year Team	Lg	G	AB	H	2B	3B	HR	(Hm Rd)	TB	R	RBI	RC	TBB	IBB	SO	HBP	SH	SF	SB	CS	GDP	Avg	OBP	Slg	OPS
2019 Mil	NL	153	513	126	26	2	28	(13 15)	240	79	77	94	109	2	139	5	0	5	5	1	16	.246	.380	.468	.848
2020 CWS	AL	46	161	37	7	0	8	(3 5)	68	27	27	29	30	0	58	1	0	2	0	0	4	.230	.351	.422	.773
2021 CWS	AL	93	279	67	9	0	23	(14 9)	145	60	62	67	87	0	82	3	1	5	0	0	15	.240	.420	.520	.939
Postseason		36	88	11	1	0	5	(2 3)	27	6	12	7	21	0	39	0	1	0	0	0	2	.125	.294	.307	.600
10 ML YEARS		1018	3233	777	152	7	172	(93 79)	1459	461	505	507	574	9	913	20	3	31	11	7	100	.240	.355	.451	.807

Brusdar Graterol

Pitches: R **Bats:** R **Pos:** RP-33; SP-1   BROOS-dar   **Ht:** 6'1" **Wt:** 265 **Born:** 8/26/1998 **Age:** 23

		HOW MUCH PITCHED					WHAT HE GAVE UP								THE RESULTS						
Year Team	Lg	G	GS	GF	IP	BFP	H	R	ER	HR	SH	SF	HB	TBB	IBB	SO	WP	W	L	Pct	Sv-Op	Hld	Vel	OPS	ERC	ERA
2021 OkCity	AAA	17	0	2	16.2	69	12	12	12	1	0	0	2	5	0	20	3	2	2	.500	1--	-	-	.533	2.38	6.48
2019 Min	AL	10	0	4	9.2	40	10	5	5	1	0	1	1	2	1	10	2	1	1	.500	0-0	1	99	.714	3.90	4.66
2020 LAD	NL	23	2	1	23.1	88	18	9	8	1	0	2	3	3	0	13	0	1	2	.333	0-1	5	99	.560	2.17	3.09
2021 LAD	NL	34	1	6	33.1	150	34	18	17	2	0	0	5	13	6	27	2	3	0	1.000	0-2	4	100	.738	4.08	4.59
Postseason		10	0	2	8.2	33	6	3	3	0	0	0	0	1	0	6	0	0	0	-	1-1	3	100	.431	1.20	3.12
3 ML YEARS		67	3	11	66.1	278	62	32	30	4	0	3	9	18	7	50	4	5	3	.625	0-3	10	100	.678	3.36	4.07

Kendall Graveman

Pitches: R **Bats:** R **Pos:** RP-53   **Ht:** 6'2" **Wt:** 200 **Born:** 12/21/1990 **Age:** 31

		HOW MUCH PITCHED					WHAT HE GAVE UP								THE RESULTS						
Year Team	Lg	G	GS	GF	IP	BFP	H	R	ER	HR	SH	SF	HB	TBB	IBB	SO	WP	W	L	Pct	Sv-Op	Hld	Vel	OPS	ERC	ERA
2014 Tor	AL	5	0	1	4.2	18	4	2	2	0	0	0	0	0	0	4	1	0	0	-	0-0	0	93	.556	1.44	3.86
2015 Oak	AL	21	21	0	115.2	502	57	52	51	15	1	2	5	38	0	77	4	6	9	.400	0-0	0	91	.761	4.72	4.05
2016 Oak	AL	31	31	0	186.0	786	196	87	85	22	6	2	7	47	2	108	2	10	11	.476	0-0	0	93	.734	4.08	4.11
2017 Oak	AL	19	19	0	105.1	444	114	50	49	12	0	1	4	32	1	70	5	6	4	.600	0-0	0	93	.780	4.53	4.19
2018 Oak	AL	7	7	0	34.1	158	44	32	29	9	0	0	1	13	0	27	2	1	5	.167	0-0	0	94	.909	7.04	7.60
2020 Sea	AL	11	2	1	18.2	77	15	13	12	2	0	1	0	8	0	15	0	1	3	.250	0-1	5	95	.710	3.20	5.79
2021 2 Tms	AL	53	0	17	56.0	222	35	15	11	3	0	0	8	20	1	61	3	5	1	.833	10-15	11	97	.536	2.25	1.77
21 Sea	AL	30	0	14	33.0	121	15	7	3	2	0	0	3	8	0	34	2	4	0	1.000	10-12	4	97	.424	1.22	0.82
21 Hou	AL	23	0	3	23.0	101	20	8	8	1	0	0	5	12	1	27	1	1	1	.500	0-3	7	97	.676	4.28	3.13
7 ML YEARS		147	80	19	520.2	2207	534	256	240	63	3	10	25	158	4	362	17	29	33	.468	10-16	16	93	.740	4.22	4.15

Jon Gray

Pitches: R **Bats:** R **Pos:** SP-29   **Ht:** 6'4" **Wt:** 225 **Born:** 11/5/1991 **Age:** 30

		HOW MUCH PITCHED					WHAT HE GAVE UP								THE RESULTS						
Year Team	Lg	G	GS	GF	IP	BFP	H	R	ER	HR	SH	SF	HB	TBB	IBB	SO	WP	W	L	Pct	Sv-Op	Hld	Vel	OPS	ERC	ERA
2015 Col	NL	9	9	0	40.2	185	52	26	25	4	2	4	2	14	2	40	3	0	2	.000	0-0	0	94	.856	5.60	5.53
2016 Col	NL	29	29	0	168.0	712	153	92	86	18	5	5	12	59	2	185	7	10	10	.500	0-0	0	95	.703	3.71	4.61
2017 Col	NL	20	20	0	110.1	461	113	47	45	10	2	2	2	30	0	112	3	10	4	.714	0-0	0	96	.716	3.76	3.67
2018 Col	NL	31	31	0	172.1	743	180	102	98	27	4	3	6	52	1	183	6	12	9	.571	0-0	0	95	.773	4.44	5.12
2019 Col	NL	26	25	1	150.0	637	147	70	64	19	7	3	4	56	4	150	7	11	8	.579	0-0	0	96	.766	4.16	3.84
2020 Col	NL	8	8	0	39.0	174	45	31	29	6	0	1	2	11	0	22	2	2	4	.333	0-0	0	94	.815	4.99	6.69
2021 Col	NL	29	29	0	149.0	644	140	83	76	21	2	4	8	58	2	157	7	8	12	.400	0-0	0	95	.740	4.15	4.59
Postseason		1	1	0	1.1	11	7	4	4	1	0	0	0	0	0	2	0	0	1	.000	0-0	0	97	1.818	43.52	27.00
7 ML YEARS		152	151	1	829.1	3556	830	451	423	105	22	22	36	280	11	849	35	53	49	.520	0-0	0	95	.751	4.18	4.59

Josiah Gray

Pitches: R **Bats:** R **Pos:** SP-13; RP-1   **Ht:** 6'1" **Wt:** 190 **Born:** 12/21/1997 **Age:** 24

		HOW MUCH PITCHED					WHAT HE GAVE UP								THE RESULTS						
Year Team	Lg	G	GS	GF	IP	BFP	H	R	ER	HR	SH	SF	HB	TBB	IBB	SO	WP	W	L	Pct	Sv-Op	Hld	Vel	OPS	ERC	ERA
2021 2 Tms	NL	14	13	0	70.2	307	63	44	43	19	5	2	2	33	3	76	7	2	2	.500	0-0	0	95	.830	4.92	5.48
21 LAD	NL	2	1	0	8.0	35	7	6	6	4	0	0	0	5	1	13	1	0	0	-	0-0	0	95	.976	7.09	6.75
21 Was	NL	12	12	0	62.2	272	56	38	37	15	5	2	2	28	2	63	6	2	2	.500	0-0	0	95	.811	4.66	5.31

Sonny Gray

Pitches: R **Bats:** R **Pos:** SP-26   **Ht:** 5'10" **Wt:** 195 **Born:** 11/7/1989 **Age:** 32

		HOW MUCH PITCHED					WHAT HE GAVE UP								THE RESULTS						
Year Team	Lg	G	GS	GF	IP	BFP	H	R	ER	HR	SH	SF	HB	TBB	IBB	SO	WP	W	L	Pct	Sv-Op	Hld	Vel	OPS	ERC	ERA
2013 Oak	AL	12	10	0	64.0	261	51	22	19	4	0	3	0	20	0	67	2	5	3	.625	0-0	0	93	.570	2.42	2.67
2014 Oak	AL	33	33	0	219.0	899	187	84	75	15	8	5	7	74	2	183	15	14	10	.583	0-0	0	93	.627	2.99	3.08
2015 Oak	AL	31	31	0	208.0	831	166	71	63	17	1	4	2	59	0	169	13	14	7	.667	0-0	0	93	.590	2.53	2.73
2016 Oak	AL	22	22	0	117.0	517	133	80	74	18	0	7	2	42	0	94	15	5	11	.313	0-0	0	93	.818	5.16	5.69
2017 2 Tms	AL	27	27	0	162.1	678	139	79	64	19	1	2	3	57	1	153	11	10	12	.455	0-0	0	93	.668	3.26	3.55
2018 NYY	AL	30	23	2	130.1	582	138	73	71	14	1	5	8	57	0	123	9	11	9	.550	0-0	0	93	.768	4.85	4.90
2019 Cin	NL	31	31	0	175.1	708	122	59	56	17	6	5	7	68	1	205	7	11	8	.579	0-0	0	93	.605	2.57	2.87
2020 Cin	NL	11	11	0	56.0	235	42	26	23	4	0	2	0	26	0	72	7	5	3	.625	0-0	0	93	.607	2.90	3.70
2021 Cin	NL	26	26	0	135.1	575	115	67	63	19	2	2	8	50	1	155	9	7	9	.438	0-0	0	92	.687	3.58	4.19
17 Oak	AL	16	16	0	97.0	400	84	48	37	8	0	2	1	30	0	94	7	6	5	.545	0-0	0	93	.644	2.93	3.43
17 NYY	AL	11	11	0	65.1	278	55	31	27	11	1	0	2	27	1	59	4	4	7	.364	0-0	0	93	.702	3.77	3.72
Postseason		4	4	0	21.1	90	14	8	7	2	1	0	2	12	1	18	2	0	2	.000	0-0	0	93	.615	3.09	2.95
9 ML YEARS		223	214	2	1267.1	5286	1093	561	508	127	19	33	39	453	5	1221	88	82	72	.532	0-0	0	93	.661	3.28	3.61

Chad Green

Pitches: R **Bats:** L **Pos:** RP-67   **Ht:** 6'3" **Wt:** 215 **Born:** 5/24/1991 **Age:** 31

Year	Team	Lg	G	GS	GF	IP	BFP	H	R	ER	HR	SH	SF	HB	TBB	IBB	SO	WP	W	L	Pct	Sv-Op	Hld	Vel	OPS	ERC	ERA
2016	NYY	AL	12	8	4	45.2	198	49	26	24	12	1	1	1	15	0	52	1	2	4	.333	1-1	0	94	.852	5.46	4.73
2017	NYY	AL	40	1	4	69.0	253	34	14	14	4	2	1	2	17	0	103	3	5	0	1.000	0-1	9	96	.454	1.20	1.83
2018	NYY	AL	63	0	3	75.2	298	64	22	21	9	0	3	1	15	2	94	3	8	3	.727	0-4	12	96	.641	2.67	2.50
2019	NYY	AL	54	15	10	69.0	295	66	35	32	10	0	3	6	19	0	98	2	4	4	.500	2-2	4	96	.735	3.95	4.17
2020	NYY	AL	22	0	5	25.2	100	13	13	10	5	1	1	0	8	2	32	3	3	3	.500	1-3	6	95	.534	1.66	3.51
2021	NYY	AL	67	0	15	83.2	315	57	32	29	14	1	2	0	17	2	99	5	10	7	.588	6-12	18	96	.622	2.13	3.12
	Postseason		17	1	1	24.1	104	22	13	12	4	1	1	1	8	1	25	0	3	0	1.000	0-0	2	96	.753	3.72	4.44
	6 ML YEARS		258	24	41	368.2	1459	283	142	130	54	5	11	10	91	6	478	17	32	21	.604	10-23	49	96	.645	2.66	3.17

Conner Greene

Pitches: R **Bats:** R **Pos:** RP-23; SP-1   **Ht:** 6'4" **Wt:** 195 **Born:** 4/4/1995 **Age:** 27

Year	Team	Lg	G	GS	GF	IP	BFP	H	R	ER	HR	SH	SF	HB	TBB	IBB	SO	WP	W	L	Pct	Sv-Op	Hld	Vel	OPS	ERC	ERA
2021	Norfolk	AAA	9	3	1	28.0	137	38	25	23	7	0	0	0	17	0	28	4	1	3	.250	0- -	-		.918	8.35	7.39
2021	2 Tms		24	1	5	25.1	121	32	20	20	1	0	2	3	12	1	26	2	1	3	.250	0-4	1	96	.812	5.79	7.11
21	Bal	AL	22	1	3	23.1	113	30	20	20	1	0	2	3	12	1	24	1	1	3	.250	0-4	1	96	.836	6.17	7.71
21	LAD	NL	2	0	2	2.0	8	2	0	0	0	0	0	0	0	0	2	1	0	0	-	0-0	0	96	.500	1.95	0.00

Riley Greene

Bats: L **Throws:** L **Pos:** CF   **Ht:** 6'3" **Wt:** 200 **Born:** 9/28/2000 **Age:** 21

Year	Team	Lg	G	AB	H	2B	3B	HR	(Hm	Rd)	TB	R	RBI	RC	TBB	IBB	SO	HBP	SH	SF	SB	CS	GDP	Avg	OBP	Slg	OPS
2019	3 Tms	Low	57	221	60	8	3	5	(-	-)	89	34	28	33	22	0	63	5	0	3	5	0	4	.271	.347	.403	.749
2021	Erie	AA	84	326	97	16	5	16	(-	-)	171	59	54	-	41	1	102	4	0	2	12	1	3	.298	.381	.525	.905
2021	Toledo	AAA	36	145	42	7	3	7	(-	-)	76	32	27	-	19	2	47	2	0	1	3	0	3	.290	.377	.524	.901

Shane Greene

Pitches: R **Bats:** R **Pos:** RP-28   **Ht:** 6'4" **Wt:** 200 **Born:** 11/17/1988 **Age:** 33

Year	Team	Lg	G	GS	GF	IP	BFP	H	R	ER	HR	SH	SF	HB	TBB	IBB	SO	WP	W	L	Pct	Sv-Op	Hld	Vel	OPS	ERC	ERA
2014	NYY	AL	15	14	0	78.2	345	81	38	33	8	0	1	6	29	0	81	1	5	4	.556	0-0	0	93	.715	4.43	3.78
2015	Det	AL	18	16	1	83.2	373	103	67	64	13	2	4	6	27	4	50	1	4	8	.333	0-0	0	92	.897	5.83	6.88
2016	Det	AL	50	3	4	60.1	256	58	39	39	3	2	2	4	22	1	59	0	5	4	.556	2-3	16	94	.680	3.65	5.82
2017	Det	AL	71	0	26	67.2	283	50	21	20	6	0	1	4	34	4	73	1	4	3	.571	9-13	14	95	.631	3.14	2.66
2018	Det	AL	66	0	58	63.1	279	68	39	36	12	0	3	3	19	1	65	3	4	6	.400	32-38	0	94	.787	4.80	5.12
2019	2 Tms		65	0	37	62.2	252	46	22	16	8	1	1	3	17	1	64	0	0	3	.000	23-28	10	93	.598	2.51	2.30
2020	Atl	NL	28	0	6	27.2	109	22	9	8	2	1	1	2	9	1	21	0	1	0	1.000	0-0	9	92	.639	2.89	2.60
2021	2 Tms		28	0	7	23.2	113	25	19	19	6	0	0	4	14	0	24	1	0	1	.000	1-2	2	93	.886	7.06	7.23
19	Det	AL	38	0	32	38.0	151	21	11	5	5	1	0	1	12	1	43	0	0	2	.000	22-25	0	93	.504	1.70	1.18
19	Atl	NL	27	0	5	24.2	101	25	11	11	3	0	1	2	5	0	21	0	0	1	.000	1-3	10	92	.736	3.97	4.01
21	Atl	NL	19	0	5	17.0	83	22	16	16	5	0	0	1	9	0	17	0	0	1	.000	0-1	2	93	.947	8.09	8.47
21	LAD	NL	9	0	2	6.2	30	3	3	3	1	0	0	3	5	0	7	1	0	0	-	1-1	0	92	.685	4.53	4.05
	Postseason		8	0	3	8.2	37	10	2	2	0	0	0	0	2	1	9	1	0	0	-	0-1	0	93	.696	3.39	2.08
	8 ML YEARS		341	33	139	467.2	2010	453	254	235	58	6	13	32	171	12	437	7	23	29	.442	67-84	51	93	.733	4.18	4.52

Didi Gregorius

Bats: L **Throws:** R **Pos:** SS-101;PH-5   dee-dee greh-GORE-ee-us   **Ht:** 6'3" **Wt:** 205 **Born:** 2/18/1990 **Age:** 32

Year	Team	Lg	G	AB	H	2B	3B	HR	(Hm	Rd)	TB	R	RBI	RC	TBB	IBB	SO	HBP	SH	SF	SB	CS	GDP	Avg	OBP	Slg	OPS
2012	Cin	NL	8	20	6	0	0	0	(0	0)	6	1	2	2	0	0	5	0	1	0	0	0	0	.300	.300	.300	.600
2013	Ari	NL	103	357	90	16	3	7	(3	4)	133	47	28	42	37	5	65	6	2	1	0	2	4	.252	.332	.373	.704
2014	Ari	NL	80	270	61	9	5	6	(3	3)	98	35	27	37	22	3	52	3	2	2	3	0	1	.226	.290	.363	.653
2015	NYY	AL	155	525	139	24	2	9	(6	3)	194	57	56	64	33	0	85	11	3	6	5	3	4	.265	.318	.370	.688
2016	NYY	AL	153	562	155	32	2	20	(11	9)	251	68	70	71	19	2	82	6	5	5	7	1	9	.276	.304	.447	.751
2017	NYY	AL	136	534	153	27	0	25	(12	13)	255	73	87	84	25	1	70	3	0	7	3	1	7	.287	.318	.478	.796
2018	NYY	AL	134	504	135	23	5	27	(19	8)	249	89	86	79	48	3	69	7	1	9	10	6	8	.268	.335	.494	.829
2019	NYY	AL	82	324	77	14	2	16	(6	10)	143	47	61	45	17	1	53	1	0	2	1	2	5	.238	.276	.441	.718
2020	Phi	NL	60	215	61	10	2	10	(7	3)	105	34	40	38	15	3	28	4	1	2	3	2	4	.284	.339	.488	.827
2021	Phi	NL	103	368	77	16	2	13	(9	4)	136	35	54	31	25	1	67	8	0	7	3	0	5	.209	.270	.370	.639
	Postseason		28	101	26	3	1	4	(2	2)	43	11	16	16	9	3	22	0	1	1	0	0	0	.257	.315	.426	.741
	10 ML YEARS		1014	3679	954	171	23	133	(76	57)	1570	486	511	493	241	19	576	49	15	41	36	16	50	.259	.310	.427	.737

Grayson Greiner

Bats: R **Throws:** R **Pos:** C-31;PH-1   **Ht:** 6'6" **Wt:** 238 **Born:** 10/11/1992 **Age:** 29

Year	Team	Lg	G	AB	H	2B	3B	HR	(Hm	Rd)	TB	R	RBI	RC	TBB	IBB	SO	HBP	SH	SF	SB	CS	GDP	Avg	OBP	Slg	OPS
2021	Toledo	AAA	33	119	24	6	0	1	(-	-)	33	9	9	-	13	0	49	1	0	1	0	0	2	.202	.284	.277	.561
2018	Det	AL	30	96	21	6	0	0	(0	0)	27	9	12	13	17	0	32	0	0	3	0	1	0	.219	.328	.281	.609
2019	Det	AL	58	208	42	5	1	5	(1	4)	64	18	19	15	13	0	70	1	1	1	0	0	5	.202	.251	.308	.559
2020	Det	AL	18	51	6	2	0	3	(0	3)	17	8	8	3	3	0	20	1	0	0	0	0	0	.118	.182	.333	.515
2021	Det	AL	31	72	17	4	0	1	(0	1)	24	7	7	14	9	0	31	0	1	0	0	0	0	.236	.321	.333	.654
	4 ML YEARS		137	427	86	17	1	9	(1	8)	132	42	46	45	42	0	153	2	2	4	0	1	7	.201	.274	.309	.583

Zack Greinke

Pitches: R Bats: R Pos: SP-29; RP-1

GRAIN-key

Ht: 6'2" Wt: 200 Born: 10/21/1983 Age: 38

			HOW MUCH PITCHED					WHAT HE GAVE UP										THE RESULTS								
Year	Team	Lg	G	GS	GF	IP	BFP	H	R	ER	HR	SH	SF	HB	TBB	IBB	SO	WP	W	L	Pct	Sv-Op	Hld	Vel	OPS	ERC	ERA
2004	KC	AL	24	24	0	145.0	599	143	64	64	26	3	2	8	26	3	100	1	8	11	.421	0-0	0	89	.752	3.85	3.97
2005	KC	AL	33	33	0	183.0	829	233	125	118	23	4	4	13	53	0	114	4	5	17	.227	0-0	0	90	.846	5.71	5.80
2006	KC	AL	3	0	1	6.1	28	7	3	3	1	0	0	0	3	2	5	0	1	0	1.000	0-0	0	93	.757	4.93	4.26
2007	KC	AL	52	14	7	122.0	507	122	52	50	12	3	4	3	36	5	106	3	7	7	.500	1-1	12	94	.747	3.77	3.69
2008	KC	AL	32	32	0	202.1	851	202	87	78	21	2	4	4	56	1	183	8	13	10	.565	0-0	0	93	.715	3.68	3.47
2009	KC	AL	33	33	0	229.1	915	195	64	55	11	8	3	4	51	0	242	5	16	8	.667	0-0	0	94	.611	**2.39**	**2.16**
2010	KC	AL	33	33	0	220.0	919	219	114	102	18	6	7	7	55	1	181	4	10	14	.417	0-0	0	93	.696	3.48	4.17
2011	Mil	NL	28	28	0	171.2	715	161	82	73	19	6	1	4	45	0	201	10	16	6	.727	0-0	0	93	.708	3.35	3.83
2012 2 Tms			34	34	0	212.1	868	200	84	82	18	7	2	2	54	0	200	8	15	5	.750	0-0	0	92	.663	3.17	3.48
2013	LAD	NL	28	28	0	177.2	717	152	54	52	13	**13**	1	7	46	1	148	5	15	4	.789	0-0	0	92	.647	2.78	2.63
2014	LAD	NL	32	32	0	202.1	821	190	69	61	19	4	2	4	43	3	207	12	17	8	.680	0-0	0	92	.660	3.03	2.71
2015	LAD	NL	32	32	0	222.2	843	148	43	41	14	6	2	5	40	1	200	7	19	3	**.864**	0-0	0	92	.507	1.56	**1.66**
2016	Ari	NL	26	26	0	158.2	667	161	80	77	23	7	4	0	41	3	134	1	13	7	.650	0-0	0	91	.750	3.86	4.37
2017	Ari	NL	32	32	0	202.1	801	172	80	72	25	4	3	0	45	0	215	12	17	7	.708	0-0	0	91	.659	2.79	3.20
2018	Ari	NL	33	33	0	207.2	839	181	77	74	28	3	3	6	43	3	199	4	15	11	.577	0-0	0	90	.665	2.96	3.21
2019 2 Tms			33	33	0	208.2	810	175	73	68	21	5	4	4	30	2	187	2	18	5	.783	0-0	0	90	.623	2.39	2.93
2020	Hou	AL	12	12	0	67.0	273	67	30	30	6	0	1	1	9	0	67	3	3	3	.500	0-0	0	87	.687	3.04	4.03
2021	Hou	AL	30	29	0	171.0	697	164	82	79	30	2	5	2	36	0	120	3	11	6	.647	0-0	1	89	.725	3.68	4.16
12	Mil	NL	21	21	0	123.0	504	120	49	47	7	3	0	0	28	0	122	4	9	3	.750	0-0	0	92	.653	3.02	3.44
12	LAA	AL	13	13	0	89.1	364	80	35	35	11	4	2	2	26	0	78	4	6	2	.750	0-0	0	92	.679	3.38	3.53
19	Ari	NL	23	23	0	146.0	562	117	48	47	15	4	3	3	21	2	135	1	10	4	.714	0-0	0	90	.614	2.22	2.90
19	Hou	AL	10	10	0	62.2	248	58	25	21	6	1	1	1	9	0	52	1	8	1	.889	0-0	0	90	.644	2.79	3.02
Postseason			19	19	0	106.2	440	96	53	50	18	3	1	3	30	0	96	2	4	6	.400	0-0	0	91	.722	3.64	4.22
18 ML YEARS			530	488	8	3110.0	12699	2892	1263	1179	328	81	54	72	712	25	2809	92	219	132	.624	1-1	13	92	.682	3.17	3.41

Randal Grichuk

Bats: R Throws: R Pos: CF-96;RF-71;DH-12;PH-8

GRICH-ick

Ht: 6'2" Wt: 216 Born: 8/13/1991 Age: 30

						BATTING														RUNNING			AVERAGES			
Year	Team	Lg	G	AB	H	2B	3B	HR	(Hm	Rd)	TB	R	RBI	RC	TBB	IBB	SO	HBP	SH	SF	SB	CS	GDP	Avg	OBP	Slg	OPS
2014	StL	NL	47	110	27	6	1	3	(2	1)	44	11	8	7	5	0	31	0	1	0	0	2	4	.245	.278	.400	.678
2015	StL	NL	103	323	89	23	7	17	(10	7)	177	49	47	47	22	2	110	4	0	1	4	2	6	.276	.329	.548	.877
2016	StL	NL	132	446	107	29	3	24	(12	12)	214	66	68	62	28	0	141	3	0	1	5	4	9	.240	.289	.480	.769
2017	StL	NL	122	412	98	25	4	22	(13	9)	195	53	59	47	26	3	133	2	0	2	6	1	9	.238	.285	.473	.758
2018	Tor	AL	124	424	104	32	1	25	(17	8)	213	60	61	61	27	0	122	8	0	3	2	2	5	.245	.301	.502	.803
2019	Tor	AL	151	586	136	29	5	31	(19	12)	268	75	80	68	35	0	163	5	0	2	2	1	20	.232	.280	.457	.738
2020	Tor	AL	55	216	59	9	0	12	(7	5)	104	38	35	35	13	1	49	0	0	2	1	1	5	.273	.312	.481	.793
2021	Tor	AL	149	511	123	25	1	22	(11	11)	216	59	81	61	27	0	114	3	0	4	0	3	17	.241	.281	.423	.703
Postseason			15	50	9	0	0	3	(1	2)	18	5	4	2	2	0	22	0	0	0	0	0	0	.180	.212	.360	.572
8 ML YEARS			883	3028	743	178	21	156	(91	65)	1431	411	439	388	183	6	863	25	1	15	21	16	75	.245	.293	.473	.765

Trent Grisham

Bats: L Throws: L Pos: CF-127;PH-13

Ht: 5'11" Wt: 224 Born: 11/1/1996 Age: 25

						BATTING														RUNNING			AVERAGES			
Year	Team	Lg	G	AB	H	2B	3B	HR	(Hm	Rd)	TB	R	RBI	RC	TBB	IBB	SO	HBP	SH	SF	SB	CS	GDP	Avg	OBP	Slg	OPS
2019	Mil	NL	51	156	36	6	2	6	(3	3)	64	24	24	20	20	0	48	4	0	3	1	0	3	.231	.328	.410	.738
2020	SD	NL	59	215	54	8	3	10	(6	4)	98	42	26	35	31	0	64	3	1	1	10	1	1	.251	.352	.456	.808
2021	SD	NL	132	462	112	28	3	15	(4	11)	191	61	62	68	54	2	119	6	1	4	13	5	10	.242	.327	.413	.740
Postseason			7	25	3	1	0	0	(0	0)	4	2	2	4	5	0	13	1	0	0	0	0	0	.120	.290	.160	.450
3 ML YEARS			242	833	202	42	8	31	(13	18)	353	127	112	123	105	2	231	13	2	8	24	6	14	.242	.334	.424	.757

Robbie Grossman

Bats: B Throws: L Pos: LF-82;RF-73;DH-7;PH-3;PR-1

Ht: 6'0" Wt: 209 Born: 9/16/1989 Age: 32

						BATTING														RUNNING			AVERAGES			
Year	Team	Lg	G	AB	H	2B	3B	HR	(Hm	Rd)	TB	R	RBI	RC	TBB	IBB	SO	HBP	SH	SF	SB	CS	GDP	Avg	OBP	Slg	OPS
2013	Hou	AL	63	257	69	14	0	4	(3	1)	95	29	21	37	23	0	70	2	5	1	6	7	2	.268	.332	.370	.702
2014	Hou	AL	103	360	84	14	2	6	(2	4)	120	42	37	48	55	1	105	2	3	2	9	3	7	.233	.337	.333	.670
2015	Hou	AL	24	49	7	2	0	1	(1	0)	12	7	5	4	5	0	17	0	0	0	0	0	0	.143	.222	.245	.467
2016	Min	AL	99	332	93	19	1	11	(8	3)	147	49	37	52	55	0	96	2	0	0	2	3	3	.280	.386	.443	.828
2017	Min	AL	119	382	94	22	1	9	(5	4)	145	62	45	58	67	0	79	3	2	2	1	1	6	.246	.361	.380	.741
2018	Min	AL	129	396	108	27	1	5	(2	3)	152	50	48	62	60	0	83	2	2	5	0	1	2	.273	.367	.384	.751
2019	Oak	AL	138	420	101	21	3	6	(2	4)	146	57	38	58	59	2	86	1	0	2	9	4	7	.240	.334	.348	.682
2020	Oak	AL	51	166	40	12	2	8	(4	4)	80	23	23	27	21	2	38	5	0	0	8	1	1	.241	.344	.482	.826
2021	Det	AL	156	557	133	23	3	23	(12	11)	231	88	67	96	98	3	155	8	2	6	20	5	8	.239	.357	.415	.772
Postseason			8	25	5	2	0	0	(0	0)	7	3	0	2	3	0	8	0	0	0	0	0	0	.200	.286	.280	.566
9 ML YEARS			882	2919	729	154	13	73	(39	34)	1128	407	321	442	443	8	729	25	14	18	57	25	36	.250	.352	.386	.738

Robert Gsellman

Pitches: R Bats: R Pos: RP-16; SP-1

guh-ZELL-man

Ht: 6'4" Wt: 200 Born: 7/18/1993 Age: 28

				HOW MUCH PITCHED					WHAT HE GAVE UP										THE RESULTS								
Year	Team	Lg	G	GS	GF	IP	BFP	H	R	ER	HR	SH	SF	HB	TBB	IBB	SO	WP	W	L	Pct	Sv-Op	Hld	Vel	OPS	ERC	ERA
2016	NYM	NL	8	7	0	44.2	185	42	12	12	1	4	2	1	15	2	42	1	4	2	.667	0-0	0	94	.539	3.05	2.42
2017	NYM	NL	25	22	1	119.2	549	138	85	69	17	4	2	8	42	3	82	4	8	7	.533	0-1	1	93	.807	5.16	5.19
2018	NYM	NL	68	0	24	80.0	345	76	44	38	8	3	5	5	28	6	70	1	6	3	.667	13-19	15	94	.700	3.69	4.28

Year Team	Lg	G	GS	GF	IP	BFP	H	R	ER	HR	SH	SF	HB	TBB	IBB	SO	WP	W	L	Pct	Sv-Op	Hld	Vel	OPS	ERC	ERA
2019 NYM	NL	52	0	9	63.2	277	64	36	33	7	1	2	6	23	2	60	4	2	3	.400	1-5	7	95	.766	4.36	4.66
2020 NYM	NL	6	4	0	14.0	71	22	15	15	4	0	1	1	8	0	9	2	0	0	-	0-0	1	94	1.109	10.49	9.64
2021 NYM	NL	17	1	1	28.2	119	27	14	12	3	0	0	2	7	0	17	0	0	1	.000	0-0	1	94	.690	3.48	3.77
6 ML YEARS		176	34	35	350.2	1546	369	206	179	40	12	12	23	123	13	280	12	20	16	.556	14-25	25	94	.761	4.44	4.59

Reymin Guduan

Pitches: L Bats: L Pos: RP-11   rey-MEEN goo-DWAHN   **Ht: 6'4" Wt: 205 Born: 3/16/1992 Age: 30**

Year Team	Lg	G	GS	GF	IP	BFP	H	R	ER	HR	SH	SF	HB	TBB	IBB	SO	WP	W	L	Pct	Sv-Op	Hld	Vel	OPS	ERC	ERA
2021 LsVgs	AAA	30	0	10	32.0	145	39	20	18	2	0	1	0	14	1	34	4	4	3	.571	0--	-	-	.804	5.17	5.06
2017 Hou	AL	22	0	3	16.0	83	24	14	14	1	0	0	0	12	0	16	3	0	0	-	0-0	1	95	.899	8.22	7.88
2018 Hou	AL	3	0	2	3.1	11	1	1	1	1	0	0	0	0	0	4	0	0	0	-	0-0	0	95	.455	0.66	2.70
2019 Hou	AL	7	0	3	5.1	27	8	7	7	3	0	1	0	4	0	6	0	0	1	1.000	0-1	0	96	1.263	13.32	11.81
2021 Oak	AL	11	0	6	14.1	65	19	11	10	1	1	4	0	5	0	5	5	0	0	-	0-1	0	94	.848	5.58	6.28
4 ML YEARS		43	0	14	39.0	186	52	33	32	6	1	5	0	21	0	31	8	1	0	1.000	0-2	1	95	.904	7.09	7.38

Sean Guenther

Pitches: L Bats: L Pos: RP-14   **Ht: 5'11" Wt: 194 Born: 12/29/1995 Age: 26**

Year Team	Lg	G	GS	GF	IP	BFP	H	R	ER	HR	SH	SF	HB	TBB	IBB	SO	WP	W	L	Pct	Sv-Op	Hld	Vel	OPS	ERC	ERA
2021 Pnscla	AA	11	0	1	17.2	66	11	3	2	1	0	1	1	3	0	26	1	1	0	1.000	0--	-	-	.522	1.47	1.02
2021 Jaxnvl	AAA	15	1	3	22.2	93	21	14	12	2	0	2	2	4	0	28	0	3	1	.750	1--	-	-	.679	3.09	4.76
2021 Mia	NL	14	0	2	20.1	103	31	22	21	1	2	0	2	10	1	15	2	0	1	.000	0-0	0	93	.920	7.43	9.30

Deolis Guerra

Pitches: R Bats: R Pos: RP-53   day-OH-lis   **Ht: 6'5" Wt: 245 Born: 4/17/1989 Age: 33**

Year Team	Lg	G	GS	GF	IP	BFP	H	R	ER	HR	SH	SF	HB	TBB	IBB	SO	WP	W	L	Pct	Sv-Op	Hld	Vel	OPS	ERC	ERA
2015 Pit	NL	10	0	4	16.2	74	26	12	12	5	0	0	1	3	0	17	2	2	0	1.000	0-0	0	91	1.077	8.96	6.48
2016 LAA	AL	44	0	11	53.1	220	52	23	19	6	1	1	2	7	0	36	2	3	0	1.000	0-4	5	90	.671	3.08	3.21
2017 LAA	AL	19	0	5	25.0	105	20	13	13	4	0	1	0	12	0	22	2	2	2	.500	0-1	0	92	.729	3.70	4.68
2019 Mil	NL	1	0	0	0.2	6	4	4	4	1	0	1	0	0	0	0	0	0	0	-	0-0	0	92	2.067	61.64	54.00
2020 Phi	NL	9	0	5	7.1	36	10	9	7	3	0	0	2	2	0	8	0	1	3	.250	0-0	0	92	1.014	9.34	8.59
2021 Oak	AL	53	0	14	65.2	269	53	34	30	8	1	1	4	20	0	62	1	4	1	.800	0-0	3	91	.645	3.06	4.11
6 ML YEARS		136	0	39	168.2	710	165	95	85	27	2	4	9	44	0	145	7	12	6	.667	0-5	8	91	.741	4.03	4.54

Javy Guerra

Pitches: R Bats: R Pos: RP-6   **Ht: 6'1" Wt: 215 Born: 10/31/1985 Age: 36**

Year Team	Lg	G	GS	GF	IP	BFP	H	R	ER	HR	SH	SF	HB	TBB	IBB	SO	WP	W	L	Pct	Sv-Op	Hld	Vel	OPS	ERC	ERA
2011 LAD	NL	47	0	38	46.2	195	37	12	12	2	3	1	3	18	1	38	2	2	2	.500	21-23	0	94	.608	2.73	2.31
2012 LAD	NL	45	0	17	45.0	196	44	13	13	1	4	2	1	23	5	37	1	2	3	.400	8-13	4	93	.685	3.76	2.60
2013 LAD	NL	9	0	5	10.2	55	15	9	8	1	0	1	1	6	0	12	0	0	0	-	0-0	0	93	.826	7.24	6.75
2014 CWS	AL	42	0	10	46.1	198	41	15	15	3	2	4	5	20	5	38	2	2	4	.333	1-6	7	94	.696	3.60	2.91
2015 CWS	AL	3	0	0	1.2	7	2	0	0	0	0	0	0	1	0	0	0	0	0	-	0-0	1	92	.762	5.91	0.00
2016 LAA	AL	7	0	1	6.1	30	5	4	4	1	0	0	0	7	1	4	1	0	0	-	0-0	1	92	.842	6.80	5.68
2017 Mia	NL	16	0	5	21.0	88	23	8	7	2	1	0	0	7	1	12	0	1	1	.500	0-1	0	94	.757	4.40	3.00
2018 Mia	NL	32	0	12	35.2	162	42	27	22	4	2	1	3	12	2	30	3	1	1	.500	1-1	5	93	.835	5.12	5.55
2019 2 Tms		51	0	21	67.2	287	67	36	35	10	1	1	1	17	3	57	3	3	1	.750	2-2	5	93	.724	3.68	4.66
2020 Was	NL	14	0	2	15.2	70	19	7	7	2	0	0	0	7	0	13	0	0	0	-	0-0	5	92	.816	5.85	4.02
2021 Was	NL	6	0	1	6.0	37	12	13	11	3	1	1	3	3	0	4	1	0	1	.000	0-0	0	92	1.336	17.02	16.50
19 Tor	AL	11	0	6	14.0	59	12	6	6	1	1	0	1	5	1	15	0	0	0	-	1-1	1	93	.714	3.10	3.86
19 Was	NL	40	0	15	53.2	228	55	30	29	9	0	1	0	12	2	42	3	3	1	.750	1-1	4	93	.726	3.83	4.86
Postseason		2	0	2	3.0	15	6	1	1	1	0	0	0	0	0	1	0	0	0	-	0-0	0	93	1.067	10.41	3.00
11 ML YEARS		272	0	112	302.2	1325	307	144	134	29	14	11	18	121	18	245	13	11	13	.458	33-46	23	93	.741	4.26	3.98

Javy Guerra

Pitches: R Bats: L Pos: RP-4   **Ht: 6'0" Wt: 185 Born: 9/25/1995 Age: 26**

Year Team	Lg	G	GS	GF	IP	BFP	H	R	ER	HR	SH	SF	HB	TBB	IBB	SO	WP	W	L	Pct	Sv-Op	Hld	Vel	OPS	ERC	ERA
2019 SD	NL	8	0	1	8.2	36	7	5	5	3	1	0	1	3	0	6	0	0	0	-	0-0	0	98	.840	4.29	5.19
2020 SD	NL	14	0	5	13.1	67	25	16	15	1	0	1	1	5	0	12	2	1	0	1.000	0-0	2	98	.979	9.97	10.13
2021 SD	NL	4	0	0	3.2	18	4	2	2	0	0	0	0	2	0	3	0	0	0	-	0-0	0	98	.646	4.01	4.91
3 ML YEARS		26	0	6	25.2	121	36	23	22	4	0	2	1	10	0	21	2	1	0	1.000	0-0	2	98	.888	7.09	7.71

Junior Guerra

Pitches: R Bats: R Pos: RP-40; SP-1   **Ht: 6'0" Wt: 235 Born: 1/16/1985 Age: 37**

Year Team	Lg	G	GS	GF	IP	BFP	H	R	ER	HR	SH	SF	HB	TBB	IBB	SO	WP	W	L	Pct	Sv-Op	Hld	Vel	OPS	ERC	ERA
2015 CWS	AL	3	0	3	4.0	18	7	3	3	1	0	0	0	1	1	3	1	0	0	-	0-0	0	94	1.033	9.70	6.75
2016 Mil	NL	20	20	0	121.2	492	94	40	38	10	3	2	3	43	2	100	7	9	3	.750	0-0	0	93	.633	2.68	2.81
2017 Mil	NL	21	14	2	70.1	314	61	44	40	18	1	1	4	43	0	67	5	1	4	.200	0-0	0	92	.817	5.53	5.12
2018 Mil	NL	31	26	1	141.0	611	143	74	64	19	5	4	4	55	0	136	11	6	9	.400	0-1	0	93	.767	4.49	4.09

Year	Team	Lg	G	GS	GF	IP	BFP	H	R	ER	HR	SH	SF	HB	TBB	IBB	SO	WP	W	L	Pct	Sv-Op	Hld	Vel	OPS	ERC	ERA
						HOW MUCH PITCHED					WHAT HE GAVE UP											THE RESULTS					
2019	Mil	NL	72	0	11	83.2	344	58	35	33	11	3	2	4	36	2	77	5	9	5	.643	3-11	20	95	.639	2.90	3.55
2020	Ari	NL	25	0	5	23.2	103	17	10	8	1	2	1	2	15	2	21	2	1	2	.333	0-2	4	94	.638	3.18	3.04
2021	LAA	AL	41	1	14	65.1	307	67	45	44	6	0	2	3	46	1	61	9	5	2	.714	0-2	2	93	.757	5.50	6.06
Postseason			2	0	2	4.2	15	2	1	1	0	0	0	0	0	0	5	1	0	1	.000	0-0	0	94	.267	0.43	1.93
7 ML YEARS			213	61	36	509.2	2189	447	251	230	66	14	12	20	239	8	465	40	31	25	.554	3-15	27	93	.719	4.00	4.06

Vladimir Guerrero Jr.

Bats: R **Throws:** R **Pos:** 1B-133;DH-28;3B-1   **Ht:** 6'2" **Wt:** 250 **Born:** 3/16/1999 **Age:** 23

Year	Team	Lg	G	AB	H	2B	3B	HR	(Hm	Rd)	TB	R	RBI	RC	TBB	IBB	SO	HBP	SH	SF	SB	CS	GDP	Avg	OBP	Slg	OPS
									BATTING												RUNNING			AVERAGES			
2019	Tor	AL	123	464	126	26	2	15	(5	10)	201	52	69	67	46	0	91	2	0	2	0	1	17	.272	.339	.433	.772
2020	Tor	AL	60	221	58	13	2	9	(5	4)	102	34	33	30	20	1	38	2	0	0	1	0	6	.262	.329	.462	.791
2021	Tor	AL	161	604	188	29	1	48	(31	17)	363	123	111	136	86	7	110	6	0	2	4	1	20	.311	.401	.601	1.002
Postseason			2	7	1	0	0	0	(0	0)	1	0	0	0	0	0	4	1	0	0	0	0	0	.143	.250	.143	.393
3 ML YEARS			344	1289	372	68	5	72	(41	31)	666	209	213	233	152	8	239	10	0	4	5	2	43	.289	.367	.517	.884

Luis Guillorme

Bats: L **Throws:** R **Pos:** 3B-27;PH-19;2B-18;SS-11;PR-2   ghee-YOR-may   **Ht:** 5'10" **Wt:** 190 **Born:** 9/27/1994 **Age:** 27

Year	Team	Lg	G	AB	H	2B	3B	HR	(Hm	Rd)	TB	R	RBI	RC	TBB	IBB	SO	HBP	SH	SF	SB	CS	GDP	Avg	OBP	Slg	OPS
									BATTING												RUNNING			AVERAGES			
2018	NYM	NL	35	67	14	2	0	0	(0	0)	16	4	5	6	7	0	3	0	0	0	1	0	1	.209	.284	.239	.523
2019	NYM	NL	45	61	15	4	0	1	(1	0)	22	8	3	5	7	0	14	0	2	0	0	0	2	.246	.324	.361	.684
2020	NYM	NL	30	57	19	6	0	0	(0	0)	25	6	9	11	10	0	17	0	0	1	2	0	3	.333	.426	.439	.865
2021	NYM	NL	69	132	35	3	0	1	(0	1)	41	13	5	15	23	2	23	0	1	0	0	2	2	.265	.374	.311	.685
4 ML YEARS			179	317	83	15	0	2	(1	1)	104	31	22	37	47	2	57	0	3	1	3	2	8	.262	.356	.328	.684

Preston Guilmet

Pitches: R **Bats:** R **Pos:** RP-2   GILL-met   **Ht:** 6'2" **Wt:** 200 **Born:** 7/27/1987 **Age:** 34

Year	Team	Lg	G	GS	GF	IP	BFP	H	R	ER	HR	SH	SF	HB	TBB	IBB	SO	WP	W	L	Pct	Sv-Op	Hld	Vel	OPS	ERC	ERA
						HOW MUCH PITCHED					WHAT HE GAVE UP											THE RESULTS					
2021	Jaxnvl	AAA	31	0	6	51.2	204	36	24	22	8	0	1	1	13	0	67	3	5	2	.714	0--	-	-	.621	2.33	3.83
2013	Cle	AL	4	0	1	5.1	28	8	6	6	0	0	0	0	3	0	1	0	0	0	-	0-0	0	90	.873	6.48	10.13
2014	Bal	AL	10	0	4	10.1	43	8	6	6	2	0	1	0	2	0	12	1	0	1	.000	0-0	1	89	.633	2.47	5.23
2015	2 Tms		5	0	3	7.1	35	9	9	9	2	0	2	0	4	0	6	0	0	0	-	0-0	0	88	.923	7.27	11.05
2018	2 Tms		8	0	2	10.0	52	18	13	13	6	1	1	0	4	1	8	1	0	1	.000	0-0	1	91	1.388	13.32	11.70
2021	Mia	NL	2	0	1	2.0	7	2	1	1	1	0	0	0	0	0	1	0	0	0	-	0-0	1	89	1.000	5.45	4.50
15	TB	AL	3	0	2	5.1	23	5	3	3	1	0	1	0	2	0	5	0	0	0	-	0-0	0	88	.754	4.14	5.06
15	Mil	NL	2	0	1	2.0	12	4	6	6	1	0	1	0	2	0	1	0	0	0	-	0-0	0	88	1.278	17.51	27.00
18	StL	NL	2	0	0	2.0	13	7	5	5	2	0	1	0	0	0	3	1	0	1	.000	0-0	0	91	1.872	30.22	22.50
18	Tor	AL	6	0	2	8.0	39	11	8	8	4	1	0	0	4	1	5	0	0	0	-	0-0	1	91	1.218	9.71	9.00
5 ML YEARS			29	0	11	35.0	165	45	35	35	11	1	4	0	13	1	28	2	0	2	.000	0-0	2	89	.986	7.02	9.00

Yuli Gurriel

Bats: R **Throws:** R **Pos:** 1B-142;3B-1;DH-1   yoo-lee goo-REE-el   **Ht:** 6'0" **Wt:** 215 **Born:** 6/9/1984 **Age:** 38

Year	Team	Lg	G	AB	H	2B	3B	HR	(Hm	Rd)	TB	R	RBI	RC	TBB	IBB	SO	HBP	SH	SF	SB	CS	GDP	Avg	OBP	Slg	OPS
									BATTING												RUNNING			AVERAGES			
2016	Hou	AL	36	130	34	7	0	3	(1	2)	50	13	15	13	5	0	12	1	0	1	1	1	7	.262	.292	.385	.677
2017	Hou	AL	139	529	158	43	1	18	(8	10)	257	69	75	83	22	1	62	7	0	6	3	2	12	.299	.332	.486	.817
2018	Hou	AL	136	537	156	33	1	13	(10	3)	230	70	85	88	23	0	63	6	0	7	5	1	22	.291	.323	.428	.751
2019	Hou	AL	144	564	168	40	2	31	(19	12)	305	85	104	98	37	2	65	5	0	6	5	3	12	.298	.343	.541	.884
2020	Hou	AL	57	211	49	12	1	6	(3	3)	81	27	22	18	12	0	27	2	0	5	0	1	6	.232	.274	.384	.658
2021	Hou	AL	143	530	169	31	0	15	(8	7)	245	83	81	94	59	2	68	4	0	12	1	1	16	.319	.383	.462	.846
Postseason			57	216	51	12	1	5	(4	1)	80	19	25	25	19	1	23	2	0	2	1	0	5	.236	.301	.370	.672
6 ML YEARS			655	2501	734	166	5	86	(49	37)	1168	347	382	394	158	5	297	25	0	37	15	9	75	.293	.337	.467	.804

Lourdes Gurriel Jr.

Bats: R **Throws:** R **Pos:** LF-119;DH-14;1B-11;PH-4   goo-REE-el   **Ht:** 6'4" **Wt:** 215 **Born:** 10/10/1993 **Age:** 28

Year	Team	Lg	G	AB	H	2B	3B	HR	(Hm	Rd)	TB	R	RBI	RC	TBB	IBB	SO	HBP	SH	SF	SB	CS	GDP	Avg	OBP	Slg	OPS
									BATTING												RUNNING			AVERAGES			
2018	Tor	AL	65	249	70	8	0	11	(6	5)	111	30	35	30	9	1	59	2	1	2	1	2	2	.281	.309	.446	.755
2019	Tor	AL	84	314	87	19	2	20	(10	10)	170	52	50	51	20	0	86	5	1	3	6	4	4	.277	.327	.541	.869
2020	Tor	AL	57	208	64	14	0	11	(3	8)	111	28	33	37	14	0	48	0	0	2	3	1	7	.308	.348	.534	.882
2021	Tor	AL	141	500	138	28	2	21	(10	11)	233	62	84	82	32	1	102	2	1	6	1	3	8	.276	.319	.466	.785
Postseason			2	8	2	1	0	0	(0	0)	3	0	0	1	0	0	1	0	0	0	0	0	0	.250	.250	.375	.625
4 ML YEARS			347	1271	359	69	4	63	(29	34)	625	172	202	200	75	2	295	9	3	13	11	10	21	.282	.324	.492	.816

Taylor Gushue

Bats: B **Throws:** R **Pos:** C-1;1B-1;PH-1   GUSH-ooh   **Ht:** 6'1" **Wt:** 233 **Born:** 12/19/1993 **Age:** 28

Year	Team	Lg	G	AB	H	2B	3B	HR	(Hm	Rd)	TB	R	RBI	RC	TBB	IBB	SO	HBP	SH	SF	SB	CS	GDP	Avg	OBP	Slg	OPS
									BATTING												RUNNING			AVERAGES			
2021	Iowa	AAA	75	247	55	14	0	8	(-	-)	93	29	39	-	25	1	83	1	2	2	0	0	8	.223	.295	.377	.671
2021	ChC	NL	2	4	0	0	0	0	(0	0)	0	0	0	0	0	0	3	0	0	0	0	0	0	.000	.000	.000	.000

Jandel Gustave

Pitches: R Bats: R Pos: RP-14 yahn-DELL goo-STAH-vay Ht: 6'3" Wt: 220 Born: 10/12/1992 Age: 29

		HOW MUCH PITCHED			WHAT HE GAVE UP											THE RESULTS						
Year Team	Lg	G GS GF	IP	BFP	H	R	ER	HR	SH	SF	HB	TBB	IBB	SO	WP	W	L	Pct	Sv-Op	Hld	Vel	OPS	ERC	ERA
2021 Indy	AAA	15 0 13	15.0	62	12	6	6	0	0	0	1	5	0	18	0	1	0	1.000	5--	-	-	.233	2.36	3.60
2021 Nashv	AAA	6 0 3	6.0	21	3	1	1	0	0	0	1	5	0	8	0	1		.000	0--	-	-	.390	0.84	1.50
2016 Hou	AL	14 0 4	15.1	60	13	6	6	2	0	0	0	4	0	16	2	1	0	1.000	0-0	0	97	.676	3.04	3.52
2017 Hou	AL	6 0 2	5.0	25	5	4	3	0	0	0	0	7	0	2	0	0	0	-	0-0	0	96	.813	7.65	5.40
2019 SF	NL	23 0 4	24.1	99	18	11	8	1	1	3	0	9	0	14	0	0	0	-	1-2	4	96	.566	2.22	2.96
2021 Mil	NL	14 0 7	18.1	79	15	10	7	2	0	3	4	5	2	13	2	1	2	.333	0-1	0	97	.632	3.25	3.44
4 ML YEARS		57 0 17	63.0	263	51	31	24	5	1	6	4	25	2	45	4	2	2	.500	1-3	4	97	.636	3.10	3.43

Kelvin Gutierrez

Bats: R Throws: R Pos: 3B-84;1B-1;2B-1;PH-1;PR-1 Ht: 6'2" Wt: 215 Born: 8/28/1994 Age: 27

		BATTING																			RUNNING			AVERAGES			
Year Team	Lg	G	AB	H	2B	3B	HR	(Hm	Rd)	TB	R	RBI	RC	TBB	IBB	SO	HBP	SH	SF		SB	CS	GDP	Avg	OBP	Slg	OPS
2021 Norfolk	AAA	25	90	21	4	0	0	(-	-)	37	10	13	-	4	0	21	0	0	0		1	1	2	.233	.266	.411	.677
2019 KC	AL	20	73	19	2	1	1	(1	0)	26	4	11	9	5	0	24	0	0	1		1	0	2	.260	.304	.356	.660
2020 KC	AL	4	9	1	0	0	0	(0	0)	1	0	0	0	3	0	6	0	0	0		0	0	0	.111	.333	.111	.444
2021 2 Tms	AL	85	272	63	8	3	3	(1	2)	86	23	20	24	19	0	76	4	0	0		1	4		.232	.292	.316	.608
21 KC	AL	38	135	29	4	2	1	(0	1)	40	9	8	7	6	0	31	1	0	0		1		3	.215	.254	.296	.550
21 Bal	AL	47	137	34	4	1	2	(1	1)	46	14	12	17	13	0	45	3	0	0		1			.248	.327	.336	.663
3 ML YEARS		109	354	83	10	4	4	(2	2)	113	27	31	33	27	0	106	4	0	1		1	1	6	.234	.295	.319	.615

Vladimir Gutierrez

Pitches: R Bats: R Pos: SP-22 Ht: 6'1" Wt: 190 Born: 9/18/1995 Age: 26

		HOW MUCH PITCHED			WHAT HE GAVE UP											THE RESULTS						
Year Team	Lg	G GS GF	IP	BFP	H	R	ER	HR	SH	SF	HB	TBB	IBB	SO	WP	W	L	Pct	Sv-Op	Hld	Vel	OPS	ERC	ERA
2021 Cin	NL	22 22 0	114.0	496	115	61	60	20	4	4	4	46	0	88	3	9	6	.600	0-0	0	93	.805	4.83	4.74

Jorge Guzman

Pitches: R Bats: R Pos: RP-2 Ht: 6'1" Wt: 246 Born: 1/28/1996 Age: 26

		HOW MUCH PITCHED			WHAT HE GAVE UP											THE RESULTS						
Year Team	Lg	G GS GF	IP	BFP	H	R	ER	HR	SH	SF	HB	TBB	IBB	SO	WP	W	L	Pct	Sv-Op	Hld	Vel	OPS	ERC	ERA
2021 Jaxnvl	AAA	9 0 6	15.1	70	14	8	6	1	0	0	0	9	0	20	0	0	1	.000	4--	-	-	.656	3.90	3.52
2020 Mia	NL	1 0 0	1.0	7	2	2	2	2	0	0	1	1	0	0	0	0	0	-	0-0	0	97	2.171	41.82	18.00
2021 Mia	NL	2 0 0	1.2	15	4	6	6	0	0	0	0	6	1	3	0	0	0	-	0-0	0	96	1.222	25.60	32.40
2 ML YEARS		3 0 0	2.2	22	6	8	8	2	0	0	1	7	1	3	0	0	0	-			96	1.565	32.75	27.00

Ronald Guzman

Bats: L Throws: L Pos: 1B-4;LF-2;PH-2;DH-1 Ht: 6'5" Wt: 235 Born: 10/20/1994 Age: 27

		BATTING																			RUNNING			AVERAGES			
Year Team	Lg	G	AB	H	2B	3B	HR	(Hm	Rd)	TB	R	RBI	RC	TBB	IBB	SO	HBP	SH	SF		SB	CS	GDP	Avg	OBP	Slg	OPS
2018 Tex	AL	123	387	91	18	2	16	(7	9)	161	46	58	55	33	2	121	7	0	1		1	0	8	.235	.306	.416	.722
2019 Tex	AL	87	256	56	20	0	10	(2	8)	106	34	36	36	32	1	87	3	0	4		1	2	7	.219	.308	.414	.723
2020 Tex	AL	26	78	19	1	1	4	(3	1)	34	10	9	12	7	0	24	1	0	0		1	0	0	.244	.314	.436	.750
2021 Tex	AL	7	16	1	0	0	1	(1	0)	4	1	1	0	1	0	6	0	0	0		0	0	0	.063	.118	.250	.368
4 ML YEARS		243	737	167	39	3	31	(13	18)	305	91	104	103	73	3	238	11	0	5		3	2	15	.227	.304	.414	.718

Eric Haase

Bats: R Throws: R Pos: C-66;LF-22;DH-11;PH-6;1B-1;PR-1 Ht: 5'10" Wt: 210 Born: 12/18/1992 Age: 29

		BATTING																			RUNNING			AVERAGES			
Year Team	Lg	G	AB	H	2B	3B	HR	(Hm	Rd)	TB	R	RBI	RC	TBB	IBB	SO	HBP	SH	SF		SB	CS	GDP	Avg	OBP	Slg	OPS
2018 Cle	AL	9	16	2	0	0	0	(0	0)	2	0	1	1	0	0	6	1	0	0		0	0	1	.125	.176	.125	.301
2019 Cle	AL	10	16	1	0	0	1	(0	1)	4	1	3	1	1	0	8	0	0	0		0	0	0	.063	.118	.250	.368
2020 Det	AL	7	17	3	0	0	0	(0	0)	3	1	2	1	1	0	6	0	0	1		0	0	0	.176	.211	.176	.387
2021 Det	AL	98	351	81	12	1	22	(8	14)	161	48	61	43	26	0	119	2	0	2		2	0	11	.231	.286	.459	.745
4 ML YEARS		124	400	87	12	1	23	(8	15)	170	50	67	46	28	0	139	3	0	3		2	0	12	.218	.272	.425	.697

Josh Hader

Pitches: L Bats: L Pos: RP-60 Ht: 6'3" Wt: 180 Born: 4/7/1994 Age: 28

		HOW MUCH PITCHED			WHAT HE GAVE UP											THE RESULTS						
Year Team	Lg	G GS GF	IP	BFP	H	R	ER	HR	SH	SF	HB	TBB	IBB	SO	WP	W	L	Pct	Sv-Op	Hld	Vel	OPS	ERC	ERA
2017 Mil	NL	35 0 2	47.2	188	25	11	11	4	1	1	4	22	1	68	0	2	3	.400	0-1	12	94	.554	2.09	2.08
2018 Mil	NL	55 0 14	81.1	306	36	23	22	9	1	2	1	30	0	143	0	6	1	.857	12-17	21	95	.484	1.45	2.43
2019 Mil	NL	61 0 46	75.2	289	41	24	22	15	0	0	4	20	2	138	0	3	5	.375	37-**44**	6	96	.591	1.98	2.62
2020 Mil	NL	21 0 17	19.0	78	8	8	8	3	0	3	0	10	0	51	2	1	2	.333	**13-15**	0	95	.562	2.44	3.79
2021 Mil	NL	60 0 42	58.2	224	25	8	8	3	0	1	2	24	0	102	3	4	2	.667	34-35	0	96	.421	1.30	1.23
Postseason		9 0 2	12.1	45	7	3	2	0	1	0	1	2	0	20	0	0	1	.000	0-1	2	96	.398	1.16	1.46
5 ML YEARS		232 0 121	282.1	1085	135	74	71	34	2	4	14	106	3	482	5	16	13	.552	96-112	39	95	.518	1.68	2.26

Jake Hager

Bats: R **Throws:** R **Pos:** PH-6;2B-5;LF-2;SS-1;RF-1;PR-1   **Ht:** 6'1" **Wt:** 170 **Born:** 3/4/1993 **Age:** 29

Year	Team	Lg	G	AB	H	2B	3B	HR	(Hm	Rd)	TB	R	RBI	RC	TBB	IBB	SO	HBP	SH	SF	SB	CS	GDP	Avg	OBP	Slg	OPS
2021	Nashv	AAA	18	71	15	7	0	2	(-	-)	28	13	9	-	8	0	15	0	0	1	1	0	1	.211	.288	.394	.682
2021	Tacom	AAA	27	100	22	7	0	6	(-	-)	47	16	11	-	11	0	25	1	0	4	4	1	3	.220	.304	.470	.774
2021	Reno	AAA	27	97	21	7	0	4	(-	-)	40	14	16	-	10	0	32	0	0	2	2	0	1	.216	.284	.412	.697
2021	2 Tms	NL	14	26	3	0	0	0	(0	0)	3	2	2	1	4	0	14	0	0	0	0	0	0	.115	.233	.115	.349
21	NYM	NL	5	8	1	0	0	0	(0	0)	1	1	0	1	0	0	3	0	0	0	0	0	0	.125	.125	.125	.250
21	Ari	NL	9	18	2	0	0	0	(0	0)	2	1	2	0	4	0	11	0	0	0	0	0	0	.111	.273	.111	.384

Sam Haggerty

Bats: B **Throws:** R **Pos:** LF-20;RF-6;PH-5;2B-4;CF-3;PR-2;DH-1   **Ht:** 5'11" **Wt:** 175 **Born:** 5/26/1994 **Age:** 28

Year	Team	Lg	G	AB	H	2B	3B	HR	(Hm	Rd)	TB	R	RBI	RC	TBB	IBB	SO	HBP	SH	SF	SB	CS	GDP	Avg	OBP	Slg	OPS
2019	NYM	NL	11	4	0	0	0	0	(0	0)	0	2	0	0	0	0	3	0	0	0	0	0	0	.000	.000	.000	.000
2020	Sea	AL	13	50	13	4	0	1	(1	0)	20	7	6	10	4	0	16	0	0	0	4	0	0	.260	.315	.400	.715
2021	Sea	AL	35	86	16	3	0	2	(0	2)	25	15	5	5	6	0	28	1	1	0	5	1	0	.186	.247	.291	.538
	3 ML YEARS		59	140	29	7	0	3	(1	2)	45	24	11	15	10	0	47	1	1	0	9	1	1	.207	.265	.321	.586

Jesse Hahn

Pitches: R **Bats:** R **Pos:** RP-5   **Ht:** 6'5" **Wt:** 205 **Born:** 7/30/1989 **Age:** 32

Year	Team	Lg	G	GS	GF	IP	BFP	H	R	ER	HR	SH	SF	HB	TBB	IBB	SO	WP	W	L	Pct	Sv-Op	Hld	Vel	OPS	ERC	ERA
2014	SD	NL	14	12	2	73.1	306	57	26	25	4	3	1	4	32	1	70	4	7	4	.636	0-0	0	91	.623	2.91	3.07
2015	Oak	AL	16	16	0	96.2	406	88	46	36	5	1	2	8	25	1	64	7	6	6	.500	0-0	0	92	.623	3.00	3.35
2016	Oak	AL	9	9	0	46.1	203	57	32	31	8	1	1	0	19	1	23	2	2	4	.333	0-0	0	94	.860	6.22	6.02
2017	Oak	AL	14	13	1	69.2	316	78	46	41	4	3	6	3	27	0	55	2	3	6	.333	0-0	0	94	.748	4.46	5.30
2019	KC	AL	6	0	2	4.2	27	7	7	7	1	0	0	0	6	1	7	0	0	1	.000	0-0	0	95	1.053	11.57	13.50
2020	KC	AL	18	0	3	17.1	65	4	1	1	0	0	0	1	8	0	19	2	1	0	1.000	3-3	5	95	.289	0.74	0.52
2021	KC	AL	5	0	1	3.1	19	5	5	5	2	0	0	1	4	0	3	1	0	0	-	1-3	1	95	1.312	18.30	13.50
	7 ML YEARS		82	50	9	311.1	1342	296	163	146	24	8	10	17	121	4	241	18	19	21	.475	4-6	6	93	.689	3.78	4.22

David Hale

Pitches: R **Bats:** R **Pos:** RP-16; SP-1   **Ht:** 6'2" **Wt:** 210 **Born:** 9/27/1987 **Age:** 34

Year	Team	Lg	G	GS	GF	IP	BFP	H	R	ER	HR	SH	SF	HB	TBB	IBB	SO	WP	W	L	Pct	Sv-Op	Hld	Vel	OPS	ERC	ERA
2013	Atl	NL	2	2	0	11.0	46	11	1	1	0	0	0	1	0	0	14	0	1	0	1.000	0-0	0	91	.572	2.18	0.82
2014	Atl	NL	45	6	13	87.1	383	89	38	32	5	1	3	3	39	8	44	5	4	5	.444	0-0	4	91	.714	4.05	3.30
2015	Col	NL	17	12	0	78.1	346	95	56	53	14	3	2	2	20	2	61	11	5	5	.500	0-0	0	90	.861	5.33	6.09
2016	Col	NL	2	0	0	2.0	12	4	3	3	1	0	0	0	2	0	1	0	0	0	-	0-0	0	90	1.200	17.51	13.50
2018	2 Tms	NL	4	0	1	13.2	62	16	7	7	3	0	0	1	5	0	8	0	0	0	-	0-0	0	91	.891	6.11	4.61
2019	NYY	AL	20	0	10	37.2	157	39	13	13	2	0	1	1	7	1	23	2	3	0	1.000	2-2	0	93	.712	3.19	3.11
2020	2 Tms	NL	11	2	3	17.0	75	23	7	7	2	0	0	0	4	0	14	0	0	0	-	1-1	0	93	.867	5.69	3.71
2021	Phi	NL	17	1	8	26.2	116	30	20	19	5	0	0	1	9	1	21	2	0	2	.000	0-1	0	93	.835	5.35	6.41
18	NYY	AL	3	0	1	10.2	46	12	3	3	2	0	0	1	1	0	6	0	0	0	-	0-0	0	91	.804	4.42	2.53
18	Min	AL	1	0	0	3.0	16	4	4	4	1	0	0	0	4	0	2	0	0	0	-	0-0	0	92	1.167	13.17	12.00
20	NYY	AL	5	0	1	6.0	26	7	2	2	0	0	0	0	3	0	7	0	0	0	-	1-1	0	93	.776	4.92	3.00
20	Phi	NL	6	2	2	11.0	49	16	5	5	2	0	0	0	1	0	7	0	0	0	-	0-0	0	93	.909	6.06	4.09
	Postseason		1	0	1	0.1	1	0	0	0	0	0	0	0	0	0	0	0	0	0	-	0-0	0	92	.000	0.00	0.00
	8 ML YEARS		118	23	35	273.2	1197	307	145	135	32	4	6	8	87	12	186	20	13	12	.520	3-4	4	91	.787	4.60	4.44

DL Hall

Pitches: L **Bats:** L **Pos:** P   **Ht:** 6'2" **Wt:** 195 **Born:** 9/19/1998 **Age:** 23

Year	Team	Lg	G	GS	GF	IP	BFP	H	R	ER	HR	SH	SF	HB	TBB	IBB	SO	WP	W	L	Pct	Sv-Op	Hld	Vel	OPS	ERC	ERA
2017	Orioles	R	5	5	0	10.1	49	10	9	8	1	0	0	1	10	0	12	3	0	0	-	0- -	-	-	.672	6.82	6.97
2018	Dlmrva	A	22	20	0	94.1	391	68	31	22	6	6	2	5	42	0	100	0	2	7	.222	0- -	-	-	.749	2.72	2.10
2019	Frdrck	A+	19	17	1	80.2	346	53	33	31	3	1	5	6	54	0	116	0	4	5	.444	1- -	-	-	.592	3.09	3.46
2021	Bowie	AA	7	7	0	31.2	128	16	11	11	4	0	0	2	16	0	56	2	2	0	1.000	0- -	-	-	.538	2.29	3.13

Billy Hamilton

Bats: R **Throws:** R **Pos:** CF-47;LF-18;PR-12;PH-5;RF-2;DH-1   **Ht:** 6'0" **Wt:** 160 **Born:** 9/9/1990 **Age:** 31

Year	Team	Lg	G	AB	H	2B	3B	HR	(Hm	Rd)	TB	R	RBI	RC	TBB	IBB	SO	HBP	SH	SF	SB	CS	GDP	Avg	OBP	Slg	OPS
2013	Cin	NL	13	19	7	2	0	0	(0	0)	9	9	1	5	2	0	4	0	1	0	13	1	0	.368	.429	.474	.902
2014	Cin	NL	152	563	141	25	8	6	(3	3)	200	72	48	64	34	0	117	1	9	4	56	23	1	.250	.292	.355	.648
2015	Cin	NL	114	412	93	8	3	4	(2	2)	119	56	28	32	28	0	75	1	9	4	57	8	5	.226	.274	.289	.563
2016	Cin	NL	119	411	107	19	3	3	(2	1)	141	69	17	46	36	0	93	1	11	1	58	8	5	.260	.321	.343	.664
2017	Cin	NL	139	582	144	17	11	4	(3	1)	195	85	38	62	44	0	133	0	5	2	59	13	5	.247	.299	.335	.634
2018	Cin	NL	153	504	119	16	9	4	(4	0)	165	74	29	51	46	0	132	1	1	4	34	10	1	.236	.299	.327	.626
2019	2 Tms		119	316	69	14	2	0	(0	0)	87	41	15	29	32	1	87	0	3	2	22	6	1	.218	.289	.275	.564
2020	2 Tms	NL	31	32	4	0	0	0	(0	1)	7	10	2	2	2	0	7	0	1	0	6	2	0	.125	.171	.219	.390
2021	CWS	AL	71	127	28	8	3	2	(2	0)	48	23	11	9	4	0	47	0	3	1	9	0	1	.220	.242	.378	.620
19	KC	AL	93	275	58	12	2	0	(0	0)	74	32	12	22	25	0	74	0	3	2	18	5	1	.211	.275	.269	.544
19	Atl	NL	26	41	11	2	0	0	(0	0)	13	9	3	7	7	1	13	0	0	0	4	1	0	.268	.375	.317	.692

Year Team	Lg	G	AB	H	2B	3B	HR	(Hm	Rd)	TB	R	RBI	RC	TBB	IBB	SO	HBP	SH	SF	SB	CS	GDP	Avg	OBP	Slg	OPS
20 NYM	NL	17	22	1	0	0	0	(0	0)	1	4	1	0	1	0	3	0	1	1	3	1	0	.045	.083	.045	.129
20 ChC	NL	14	10	3	0	0	1	(0	1)	6	6	1	2	1	0	4	0	0	0	3	1	0	.300	.364	.600	.964
Postseason		3	0	0	0	0	0	(0	0)	0	2	0	0	1	0	0	0	0	0	1	0	0	-	1.000	-	-
9 ML YEARS		911	2966	712	109	39	24	(16	8)	971	439	189	300	228	1	695	4	43	19	314	71	19	.240	.293	.327	.621

J.D. Hammer

Pitches: R **Bats:** R **Pos:** RP-20

Ht: 6'3" **Wt:** 202 **Born:** 7/12/1994 **Age:** 27

Year Team	Lg	G	GS	GF	IP	BFP	H	R	ER	HR	SH	SF	HB	TBB	IBB	SO	WP	W	L	Pct	Sv-Op	Hld	Vel	OPS	ERC	ERA
2021 LV	AAA	18	0	7	21.2	93	15	7	6	2	1	0	2	12	0	34	1	2	0	1.000	1--	-	-	.597	3.26	2.49
2019 Phi	NL	20	0	7	19.0	81	15	8	8	2	0	0	0	12	0	13	1	1	0	1.000	0-1	0	94	.710	3.92	3.79
2021 Phi	NL	20	0	4	20.0	94	21	11	11	3	0	0	2	11	1	22	1	1	1	.500	0-0	0	94	.769	5.54	4.95
2 ML YEARS		40	0	11	39.0	175	36	19	19	5	0	0	2	23	1	35	2	2	1	.667	0-1	0	94	.742	4.74	4.38

Garrett Hampson

Bats: R **Throws:** R **Pos:** CF-91;2B-47;PH-24;SS-5;PR-4;3B-2

Ht: 5'11" **Wt:** 196 **Born:** 10/10/1994 **Age:** 27

Year Team	Lg	G	AB	H	2B	3B	HR	(Hm	Rd)	TB	R	RBI	RC	TBB	IBB	SO	HBP	SH	SF	SB	CS	GDP	Avg	OBP	Slg	OPS
2018 Col	NL	24	40	11	3	1	0	(0	0)	16	3	4	9	7	0	12	1	0	0	2	0	0	.275	.396	.400	.796
2019 Col	NL	105	299	74	9	4	8	(1	7)	115	40	27	29	24	1	88	0	2	2	15	3	2	.247	.302	.385	.686
2020 Col	NL	53	167	39	4	3	5	(3	2)	64	25	11	16	13	0	60	0	3	1	6	1	1	.234	.287	.383	.671
2021 Col	NL	147	453	106	21	6	11	(7	4)	172	69	33	49	33	2	118	3	3	2	17	7	6	.234	.289	.380	.669
Postseason		2	1	0	0	0	0	(0	0)	0	1	0	0	0	0	0	0	0	0	0	0	0	.000	.000	.000	.000
4 ML YEARS		329	959	230	37	14	24	(11	13)	367	137	75	103	77	3	278	4	8	5	40	11	9	.240	.298	.383	.680

Brad Hand

Pitches: L **Bats:** L **Pos:** RP-68

Ht: 6'3" **Wt:** 224 **Born:** 3/20/1990 **Age:** 32

Year Team	Lg	G	GS	GF	IP	BFP	H	R	ER	HR	SH	SF	HB	TBB	IBB	SO	WP	W	L	Pct	Sv-Op	Hld	Vel	OPS	ERC	ERA
2011 Fla	NL	12	12	0	60.0	263	53	32	28	10	4	3	1	35	1	38	0	1	8	.111	0-0	0	90	.789	4.68	4.20
2012 Mia	NL	1	1	0	3.2	23	6	7	7	1	0	0	0	6	1	3	0	0	1	.000	0-0	0	90	1.169	14.74	17.18
2013 Mia	NL	7	2	2	20.2	82	13	7	7	2	0	0	0	8	0	15	1	1	1	.500	0-0	0	93	.553	2.10	3.05
2014 Mia	NL	32	16	5	111.0	474	112	56	54	10	6	2	2	39	3	67	5	3	8	.273	1-1	0	92	.732	3.91	4.38
2015 Mia	NL	38	12	7	93.1	408	107	55	55	9	5	2	3	32	1	67	2	4	7	.364	0-0	2	92	.784	4.83	5.30
2016 SD	NL	82	0	16	89.1	364	63	32	29	8	2	2	1	36	4	111	7	4	4	.500	1-7	21	93	.589	2.44	2.92
2017 SD	NL	72	0	32	79.1	311	54	20	19	9	1	1	7	20	1	104	4	3	4	.429	21-26	16	94	.580	2.30	2.16
2018 2 Tms		69	0	42	72.0	301	52	28	22	8	2	0	9	28	2	106	2	2	5	.286	32-39	10	94	.656	3.03	2.75
2019 Cle	AL	60	0	54	57.1	242	53	21	21	6	1	0	4	18	5	84	0	6	4	.600	34-39	0	93	.695	3.50	3.30
2020 Cle	AL	23	0	21	22.0	86	13	8	5	0	0	1	2	4	0	29	1	2	1	.667	16-16	1	91	.486	1.21	2.05
2021 3 Tms		68	0	45	64.2	278	56	39	28	9	3	5	6	26	4	61	3	6	7	.462	21-29	3	93	.728	3.86	3.90
18 SD	NL	41	0	31	44.1	186	33	21	15	5	1	0	7	15	1	65	1	2	4	.333	24-29	3	94	.672	3.09	3.05
18 Cle	AL	28	0	11	27.2	115	19	7	7	3	1	0	2	13	1	41	1	0	1	.000	8-10	7	93	.632	2.94	2.28
21 Was	NL	41	0	36	42.2	182	31	22	17	5	3	3	5	18	4	42	1	5	5	.500	21-26	0	93	.655	3.04	3.04
21 Tor	AL	11	0	5	8.2	41	13	10	7	3	0	1	0	3	0	5	1	0	2	.000	0-1	0	93	1.012	8.98	7.27
21 NYM	NL	16	0	4	13.1	55	12	7	4	1	0	1	1	5	0	14	1	1	0	1.000	0-2	3	93	.744	3.68	2.70
Postseason		3	0	1	2.1	15	6	4	4	1	0	1	0	2	1	5	1	0	1	.000	0-1	0	92	1.283	19.40	15.43
11 ML YEARS		464	43	224	673.1	2832	582	305	275	72	24	16	35	252	22	685	25	32	50	.390	126-157	53	92	.688	3.44	3.68

Eric Hanhold

Pitches: R **Bats:** R **Pos:** RP-10

Ht: 6'5" **Wt:** 210 **Born:** 11/1/1993 **Age:** 28

Year Team	Lg	G	GS	GF	IP	BFP	H	R	ER	HR	SH	SF	HB	TBB	IBB	SO	WP	W	L	Pct	Sv-Op	Hld	Vel	OPS	ERC	ERA
2021 Norfolk	AAA	25	0	14	26.0	118	28	17	15	6	1	0	0	16	0	27	7	1	1	.500	4--	-	-	.911	6.53	5.19
2018 NYM	NL	3	0	0	2.1	13	4	2	2	0	0	0	1	1	0	2	0	0	0	-	0-0	0	96	.916	9.39	7.71
2021 Bal	AL	10	0	1	10.1	47	13	9	8	2	0	0	1	3	1	6	4	0	0	-	0-1	0	95	.827	6.08	6.97
2 ML YEARS		13	0	1	12.2	60	17	11	10	2	0	0	2	4	1	8	4	0	0	-	0-1	0	95	.846	6.71	7.11

Mitch Haniger

Bats: R **Throws:** R **Pos:** RF-123;DH-34

Ht: 6'2" **Wt:** 213 **Born:** 12/23/1990 **Age:** 31

Year Team	Lg	G	AB	H	2B	3B	HR	(Hm	Rd)	TB	R	RBI	RC	TBB	IBB	SO	HBP	SH	SF	SB	CS	GDP	Avg	OBP	Slg	OPS
2016 Ari	NL	34	109	25	2	1	5	(4	1)	44	9	17	16	12	2	27	1	0	1	0	0	3	.229	.309	.404	.713
2017 Sea	AL	96	369	104	25	2	16	(6	10)	181	58	47	55	31	0	93	9	1	0	5	4	9	.282	.352	.491	.843
2018 Sea	AL	157	596	170	38	4	26	(12	14)	294	90	93	102	70	4	148	10	0	7	8	2	8	.285	.366	.493	.859
2019 Sea	AL	63	246	54	13	1	15	(7	8)	114	46	32	35	30	1	81	0	0	3	4	0	3	.220	.314	.463	.778
2021 Sea	AL	157	620	157	23	2	39	(19	20)	301	110	100	105	54	2	169	9	0	8	1	0	12	.253	.318	.485	.804
5 ML YEARS		507	1940	510	101	10	101	(48	53)	934	313	289	313	197	9	518	34	1	18	18	6	35	.263	.339	.481	.820

Ian Happ

Bats: B **Throws:** R **Pos:** LF-65;CF-56;PH-25;RF-16;2B-8;3B-2;DH-1   **Ht:** 6'0" **Wt:** 205 **Born:** 8/12/1994 **Age:** 27

							BATTING													RUNNING			AVERAGES			
Year	Team	Lg	G	AB	H	2B	3B	HR	(Hm | Rd)	TB	R	RBI	RC	TBB	IBB	SO	HBP	SH	SF	SB	CS	GDP	Avg	OBP	Slg	OPS
2017	ChC	NL	115	364	92	17	3	24	(15 | 9)	187	62	68	57	39	5	129	4	2	4	8	4	12	.253	.328	.514	.842
2018	ChC	NL	142	387	90	19	2	15	(7 | 8)	158	56	44	56	70	9	167	3	0	2	8	4	6	.233	.353	.408	.761
2019	ChC	NL	58	140	37	7	1	11	(4 | 7)	79	25	30	30	15	0	39	0	0	1	2	0	1	.264	.333	.564	.898
2020	ChC	NL	57	198	51	11	1	12	(8 | 4)	100	27	28	35	30	1	63	2	1	0	1	3	1	.258	.361	.505	.866
2021	ChC	NL	148	465	105	20	1	25	(13 | 12)	202	63	66	75	62	0	156	5	2	1	9	2	12	.226	.323	.434	.757
	Postseason		8	15	5	0	0	1	(1 | 0)	8	1	1	0	2	0	6	0	0	0	0	0	0	.333	.412	.533	.945
	5 ML YEARS		520	1554	375	74	8	87	(47 | 40)	726	233	236	253	216	15	554	14	5	8	28	13	32	.241	.338	.467	.805

J.A. Happ

Pitches: L **Bats:** L **Pos:** SP-30   JAY   **Ht:** 6'5" **Wt:** 205 **Born:** 10/19/1982 **Age:** 39

			HOW MUCH PITCHED					WHAT HE GAVE UP										THE RESULTS							
Year	Team	Lg	G	GS	GF	IP	BFP	H	R	ER	HR	SH	SF	HB	TBB	IBB	SO	WP	W	L	Pct	Sv-Op	Hld	Vel	OPS	ERC	ERA
2007	Phi	NL	1	1	0	4.0	21	7	5	5	3	0	0	0	2	0	5	0	0	1	.000	0-0	0	88	1.323	15.13	11.25
2008	Phi	NL	8	4	1	31.2	138	28	13	13	3	2	1	1	14	1	26	1	1	0	1.000	0-0	1	89	.658	3.55	3.69
2009	Phi	NL	35	23	4	166.0	685	149	55	54	20	7	6	5	56	2	119	2	12	4	.750	0-0	0	90	.710	3.57	2.93
2010	2 Tms		16	16	0	87.1	374	73	37	33	8	5	4	1	47	1	70	4	6	4	.600	0-0	0	90	.688	3.69	3.40
2011	Hou	NL	28	28	0	156.1	698	157	103	93	21	12	8	2	83	5	134	3	6	15	.286	0-0	0	90	.806	4.86	5.35
2012	2 Tms		28	24	3	144.2	627	147	79	77	19	9	4	2	56	1	144	7	10	11	.476	0-0	1	90	.787	4.37	4.79
2013	Tor	AL	18	18	0	92.2	415	91	53	47	10	1	3	2	45	0	77	5	5	7	.417	0-0	0	91	.734	4.36	4.56
2014	Tor	AL	30	26	2	158.0	673	160	79	74	22	1	5	2	51	0	133	1	11	11	.500	0-0	0	93	.770	4.17	4.22
2015	2 Tms		32	31	0	172.0	717	173	71	69	16	2	0	2	45	4	151	6	11	8	.579	0-0	0	92	.698	3.56	3.61
2016	Tor	AL	32	32	0	195.0	796	168	72	69	22	2	2	6	60	0	163	3	20	4	.833	0-0	0	92	.665	3.22	3.18
2017	Tor	AL	25	25	0	145.1	626	145	64	57	18	1	4	0	46	1	142	4	10	11	.476	0-0	0	92	.700	3.81	3.53
2018	2 Tms		31	31	0	177.2	733	150	81	72	27	2	2	9	51	1	193	4	17	6	.739	0-0	0	92	.677	3.32	3.65
2019	NYY	AL	31	30	0	161.1	678	160	88	88	34	0	2	5	49	1	140	3	12	8	.600	0-0	0	91	.785	4.57	4.91
2020	NYY	AL	9	9	0	49.1	196	37	19	19	8	1	0	1	15	0	42	0	2	2	.500	0-0	0	91	.655	2.88	3.47
2021	2 Tms		30	30	0	152.1	671	177	100	98	30	2	3	3	48	0	122	4	10	8	.556	0-0	0	91	.851	5.45	5.79
10	Phi	NL	3	3	0	15.1	70	13	4	3	1	1	1	0	12	0	9	1	1	0	1.000	0-0	0	89	.702	4.40	1.76
10	Hou	NL	13	13	0	72.0	304	60	33	30	7	4	3	1	35	1	61	3	5	4	.556	0-0	0	90	.684	3.53	3.75
12	Hou	NL	18	18	0	104.1	457	112	58	56	17	7	2	1	39	0	98	5	7	9	.438	0-0	0	90	.818	4.86	4.83
12	Tor	AL	10	6	3	40.1	170	35	21	21	2	2	2	1	17	1	46	2	3	2	.600	0-0	1	91	.701	3.16	4.69
15	Sea	AL	21	20	0	108.2	468	121	58	56	13	1	0	2	32	3	82	4	4	6	.400	0-0	0	92	.764	4.49	4.64
15	Pit	NL	11	11	0	63.1	249	52	13	13	3	1	0	0	13	1	69	2	7	2	.778	0-0	0	92	.577	2.12	1.85
18	Tor	AL	20	20	0	114.0	475	99	61	53	17	1	1	4	35	0	130	1	10	6	.625	0-0	0	92	.677	3.43	4.18
18	NYY	AL	11	11	0	63.2	258	51	20	19	10	1	1	5	16	0	63	3	7	0	1.000	0-0	0	92	.676	3.11	2.69
21	Min	AL	19	19	0	98.1	445	125	76	74	21	0	3	3	31	0	77	3	5	6	.455	0-0	0	91	.906	6.31	6.77
21	StL	NL	11	11	0	54.0	226	52	24	24	9	2	0	0	17	0	45	1	5	2	.714	0-0	0	91	.743	4.00	4.00
	Postseason		15	4	1	27.2	134	36	18	18	6	0	0	0	16	0	26	1	1	4	.200	0-0	1	91	.871	7.50	5.86
15 ML YEARS			354	328	10	1893.2	8048	1822	919	868	261	47	44	41	668	16	1661	47	133	100	.571	0-0	2	91	.738	4.01	4.13

Blaine Hardy

Pitches: L **Bats:** L **Pos:** RP-1   **Ht:** 6'2" **Wt:** 218 **Born:** 3/14/1987 **Age:** 35

			HOW MUCH PITCHED					WHAT HE GAVE UP										THE RESULTS							
Year	Team	Lg	G	GS	GF	IP	BFP	H	R	ER	HR	SH	SF	HB	TBB	IBB	SO	WP	W	L	Pct	Sv-Op	Hld	Vel	OPS	ERC	ERA
2021	Nashv	AAA	29	8	1	67.0	272	55	25	20	10	1	0	0	27	1	61	4	6	6	.500	0- -	-	-	.684	3.51	2.69
2014	Det	AL	38	0	7	39.0	167	34	12	11	1	1	2	1	20	3	31	1	2	1	.667	0-1	4	89	.611	3.28	2.54
2015	Det	AL	70	0	11	61.1	265	61	23	21	2	3	4	1	22	2	55	5	5	3	.625	0-3	13	88	.704	3.38	3.08
2016	Det	AL	21	0	10	25.2	112	25	11	10	2	1	0	0	12	1	20	1	1	0	1.000	0-0	0	88	.707	3.95	3.51
2017	Det	AL	35	0	9	33.1	156	46	24	22	7	0	4	0	13	1	28	1	1	0	1.000	0-0	6	90	.925	7.12	5.94
2018	Det	AL	30	13	5	86.0	351	79	37	34	10	1	4	2	22	1	66	2	4	5	.444	1-1	2	88	.698	3.30	3.56
2019	Det	AL	39	0	3	44.1	182	38	24	22	10	1	4	0	13	0	29	3	1	1	.500	0-0	7	88	.751	3.66	4.47
2021	Mil	NL	1	0	1	1.0	7	3	3	2	0	1	0	0	1	0	1	0	0	1	.000	0-0	0	90	1.267	19.55	18.00
7 ML YEARS			234	13	46	290.2	1240	286	134	122	32	8	18	4	103	8	230	13	14	11	.560	1-5	32	89	.728	3.89	3.78

Bryce Harper

Bats: L **Throws:** R **Pos:** RF-139;DH-2;1B-1   **Ht:** 6'3" **Wt:** 210 **Born:** 10/16/1992 **Age:** 29

							BATTING													RUNNING			AVERAGES			
Year	Team	Lg	G	AB	H	2B	3B	HR	(Hm	Rd)	TB	R	RBI	RC	TBB	IBB	SO	HBP	SH	SF	SB	CS	GDP	Avg	OBP	Slg	OPS
2012	Was	NL	139	533	144	26	9	22	(10	12)	254	98	59	82	56	0	120	2	3	3	18	6	8	.270	.340	.477	.817
2013	Was	NL	118	424	116	24	3	20	(13	7)	206	71	58	73	61	4	94	5	3	4	11	4	4	.274	.368	.486	.854
2014	Was	NL	100	352	96	10	2	13	(5	8)	149	41	32	43	38	4	104	1	3	1	2	2	6	.273	.344	.423	.768
2015	Was	NL	153	521	172	38	1	42	(23	19)	338	118	99	138	124	15	131	5	0	4	15	4	15	.330	.460	.649	1.109
2016	Was	NL	147	506	123	24	2	24	(12	12)	223	84	86	90	108	20	117	3	0	10	21	10	11	.243	.373	.441	.814
2017	Was	NL	111	420	134	27	1	29	(12	17)	250	95	87	93	68	11	99	1	0	3	4	2	15	.319	.413	.595	1.008
2018	Was	NL	159	550	137	34	0	34	(17	17)	273	103	100	111	130	16	169	6	0	9	13	3	7	.249	.393	.496	.889
2019	Phi	NL	157	573	149	36	1	35	(20	15)	292	98	114	125	99	11	178	6	0	10	15	3	10	.260	.372	.510	.882
2020	Phi	NL	58	190	51	9	2	13	(7	6)	103	41	33	44	49	8	43	2	1	2	8	2	5	.268	.420	.542	.962
2021	Phi	NL	141	488	151	42	1	35	(19	16)	300	101	84	120	100	14	134	5	2	4	13	3	12	.309	.429	.615	1.044
	Postseason		19	76	16	4	1	5	(3	2)	37	12	10	12	11	1	23	1	0	1	4	0	0	.211	.315	.487	.801
	10 ML YEARS		1283	4557	1273	270	22	267	(138	129)	2388	850	752	919	833	103	1189	36	12	44	111	39	93	.279	.392	.524	.916

Ryne Harper

Pitches: R **Bats:** R **Pos:** RP-34   **Ht:** 6'3" **Wt:** 217 **Born:** 3/27/1989 **Age:** 3

Year	Team	Lg	G	GS	GF	IP	BFP	H	R	ER	HR	SH	SF	HB	TBB	IBB	SO	WP	W	L	Pct	Sv-Op	Hld	Vel	OPS	ERC	ERA
2021	Roch	AAA	13	0	5	19.2	82	16	12	8	2	0	0	1	8	0	23	1	1	1	.500	0- -	-	-	.661	3.32	3.66
2019	Min	AL	61	0	7	54.1	225	54	25	23	7	0	3	1	10	0	50	5	4	2	.667	1-4	12	89	.709	3.44	3.81
2020	Was	NL	23	0	12	23.2	110	29	21	20	5	0	0	1	9	2	25	2	1	0	1.000	0-0	1	88	.865	6.06	7.61
2021	Was	NL	34	0	10	35.2	148	28	16	16	6	0	1	2	14	1	31	0	0	2	.000	0-1	3	87	.687	3.52	4.04
	3 ML YEARS		118	0	29	113.2	483	111	62	59	18	0	4	4	33	3	106	7	5	4	.556	1-5	16	89	.738	3.98	4.67

Will Harris

Pitches: R **Bats:** R **Pos:** RP-8   **Ht:** 6'4" **Wt:** 236 **Born:** 8/28/1984 **Age:** 37

Year	Team	Lg	G	GS	GF	IP	BFP	H	R	ER	HR	SH	SF	HB	TBB	IBB	SO	WP	W	L	Pct	Sv-Op	Hld	Vel	OPS	ERC	ERA
2012	Col	NL	20	0	10	17.2	89	27	18	16	3	2	1	1	6	1	19	4	1	1	.500	0-0	3	91	.922	7.39	8.15
2013	Ari	NL	61	0	11	52.2	217	50	17	17	3	0	4	2	15	1	53	4	4	1	.800	0-1	4	92	.661	3.25	2.91
2014	Ari	NL	29	0	8	29.0	120	27	14	14	3	1	1	2	9	2	35	1	0	3	.000	0-1	3	92	.740	3.62	4.34
2015	Hou	AL	68	0	18	71.0	276	42	18	15	8	2	1	1	22	1	68	2	5	5	.500	2-6	13	92	.525	1.79	1.90
2016	Hou	AL	66	0	19	64.0	255	52	17	16	3	1	2	1	15	1	69	4	1	2	.333	12-15	28	92	.560	2.21	2.25
2017	Hou	AL	46	0	5	45.1	177	37	15	15	7	0	0	0	7	0	52	1	3	2	.600	2-4	20	92	.613	2.52	2.98
2018	Hou	AL	61	0	11	56.2	230	48	22	22	3	1	1	2	14	1	64	6	5	3	.625	0-3	16	92	.591	2.50	3.49
2019	Hou	AL	68	0	10	60.0	229	42	14	10	6	1	0	0	14	0	62	3	4	1	.800	4-5	26	88	.540	1.99	1.50
2020	Was	NL	20	0	5	17.2	84	21	9	6	3	0	0	0	9	0	21	1	0	1	.000	1-4	6	91	.797	5.96	3.06
2021	Was	NL	8	0	2	6.0	30	7	6	6	1	0	0	0	3	0	9	0	0	1	.000	0-0	1	90	.815	5.41	9.00
	Postseason		23	0	3	17.2	77	23	9	8	3	0	0	0	3	0	16	3	0	2	.000	1-3	10	92	.824	5.41	4.08
	10 ML YEARS		447	0	99	420.0	1707	353	150	137	40	8	10	9	114	7	452	26	23	20	.535	21-39	119	92	.621	2.77	2.94

Josh Harrison

Bats: R **Throws:** R **Pos:** 2B-102;3B-23;LF-19;SS-8;PH-3;CF-2;RF-1   **Ht:** 5'8" **Wt:** 190 **Born:** 7/8/1987 **Age:** 34

								BATTING														**RUNNING**			**AVERAGES**			
Year	Team	Lg	G	AB	H	2B	3B	HR	(Hm	Rd)	TB	R	RBI	RC	TBB	IBB	SO	HBP	SH	SF	SB	CS	GDP	Avg	OBP	Slg	OPS
2011	Pit	NL	65	195	53	13	2	1	(1	0)	73	21	16	19	3	0	24	0	5	1	4	1	6	.272	.281	.374	.656
2012	Pit	NL	104	249	58	9	5	3	(1	2)	86	34	16	22	10	0	37	7	7	3	7	3	3	.233	.279	.345	.624
2013	Pit	NL	60	88	22	1	2	3	(1	2)	36	10	14	11	2	0	10	3	2	0	2	0	4	.250	.290	.409	.699
2014	Pit	NL	143	520	164	38	7	13	(4	9)	255	77	52	84	22	1	81	4	2	2	18	7	6	.315	.347	.490	.837
2015	Pit	NL	114	418	120	29	1	4	(2	2)	163	57	28	48	19	1	71	7	3	2	10	8	4	.287	.327	.390	.717
2016	Pit	NL	131	487	138	25	7	4	(2	2)	189	57	59	61	18	0	76	5	4	8	19	4	10	.283	.311	.388	.699
2017	Pit	NL	128	486	132	26	2	16	(9	7)	210	66	47	65	28	2	90	23	2	3	12	4	5	.272	.339	.432	.771
2018	Pit	NL	97	344	86	13	1	8	(3	5)	125	41	37	42	18	1	68	5	2	5	3	0	8	.250	.293	.363	.656
2019	Det	AL	36	137	24	7	1	1	(1	0)	36	10	8	3	6	0	27	2	0	2	4	2	0	.175	.218	.263	.480
2020	Was	NL	33	79	22	2	0	3	(1	2)	33	11	14	12	6	0	12	4	0	2	1	2	2	.278	.352	.418	.769
2021	2 Tms		138	505	141	33	2	8	(4	4)	202	58	60	69	31	0	75	18	0	3	9	5	9	.279	.341	.400	.741
21	Was	NL	90	320	94	23	2	6	(2	4)	139	39	38	52	25	0	50	12	0	1	5	2	4	.294	.366	.434	.800
21	Oak	AL	48	185	47	10	0	2	(2	0)	63	19	22	17	6	0	25	6	0	2	4	3	5	.254	.296	.341	.637
	Postseason		4	7	2	0	0	0	(0	0)	2	1	0	0	0	0	2	1	0	0	0	1	0	.286	.375	.286	.661
	11 ML YEARS		1049	3508	960	196	30	64	(29	35)	1408	442	351	436	163	5	571	78	27	31	89	36	57	.274	.318	.401	.719

Monte Harrison

Bats: R **Throws:** R **Pos:** CF-4;RF-3;PH-3;PR-1   **Ht:** 6'3" **Wt:** 225 **Born:** 8/10/1995 **Age:** 26

								BATTING														**RUNNING**			**AVERAGES**			
Year	Team	Lg	G	AB	H	2B	3B	HR	(Hm	Rd)	TB	R	RBI	RC	TBB	IBB	SO	HBP	SH	SF	SB	CS	GDP	Avg	OBP	Slg	OPS
2021	Jaxnvl	AAA	74	269	65	8	1	15	(-	-)	120	47	52	-	31	0	121	6	0	2	24	3	5	.242	.331	.446	.777
2020	Mia	NL	32	47	8	1	0	1	(1	0)	12	8	3	1	4	0	26	0	0	0	6	0	0	.170	.235	.255	.491
2021	Mia	NL	9	10	2	1	0	0	(0	0)	3	0	0	0	0	0	3	0	1	0	1	1	0	.200	.200	.300	.500
	Postseason		2	0	0	0	0	0	(0	0)	0	0	0	0	0	0	0	0	0	0	1	0	0	-	-	-	-
	2 ML YEARS		41	57	10	2	0	1	(1	0)	15	8	3	1	4	0	29	0	1	0	6	1	0	.175	.230	.263	.493

Geoff Hartlieb

Pitches: R **Bats:** R **Pos:** RP-7   **Ht:** 6'5" **Wt:** 240 **Born:** 12/9/1993 **Age:** 28

Year	Team	Lg	G	GS	GF	IP	BFP	H	R	ER	HR	SH	SF	HB	TBB	IBB	SO	WP	W	L	Pct	Sv-Op	Hld	Vel	OPS	ERC	ERA
2021	Indy	AAA	9	0	2	9.2	38	5	2	2	1	0	0	0	4	0	13	1	1	1	.500	0- -	-	-	.502	1.70	1.86
2021	Syrcse	AAA	10	0	2	13.0	67	16	10	9	3	0	0	0	9	0	14	2	1	1	.500	0- -	-	-	.839	7.25	6.23
2019	Pit	NL	29	0	10	35.0	171	52	35	35	8	1	4	0	18	0	38	5	0	1	.000	0-0	2	96	1.020	8.67	9.00
2020	Pit	NL	21	0	1	22.1	101	16	11	9	1	0	1	3	19	0	19	2	1	0	1.000	0-0	5	94	.658	4.39	3.63
2021	2 Tms	NL	7	0	4	9.0	50	10	11	11	0	0	0	3	11	0	9	1	0	0	-	0-0	0	94	.897	8.56	11.00
21	Pit	NL	4	0	3	4.2	23	3	4	4	0	0	0	2	5	0	4	0	0	0	-	0-0	0	94	.747	5.54	7.71
21	NYM	NL	3	0	1	4.1	27	7	7	7	0	0	0	1	6	0	5	1	0	0	-	0-0	0	94	1.019	12.08	14.54
	3 ML YEARS		57	0	15	66.1	322	78	57	55	9	1	5	6	48	0	66	8	1	1	.500	0-0	7	95	.896	7.19	7.46

Ryan Hartman

Pitches: L Bats: L Pos: RP-1   Ht: 6'3" Wt: 234 Born: 4/21/1994 Age: 28

		HOW MUCH PITCHED					WHAT HE GAVE UP										THE RESULTS							
Year	Team	Lg	G	GS	GF	IP	BFP	H	R	ER	HR	SH	SF	HB	TBB	IBB	SO	WP	W	L	Pct	Sv-Op	Hld	Vel	OPS	ERC	ERA
2021	SgrLnd	AAA	13	12	0	62.2	265	62	36	35	16	1	1	2	18	0	59	2	3	3	.500	0- -	-	-	.833	4.75	5.03
2021	Norfolk	AAA	9	5	0	31.0	131	33	17	16	2	0	0	1	4	0	26	1	2	1	.667	0- -	-	-	.687	3.19	4.65
2021	Hou	AL	1	0	1	2.1	10	3	1	1	1	0	0	0	0	0	2	0	0	0	-	0-0	0	90	.900	6.14	3.86

Hunter Harvey

Pitches: R Bats: R Pos: RP-9   Ht: 6'3" Wt: 210 Born: 12/9/1994 Age: 27

		HOW MUCH PITCHED					WHAT HE GAVE UP										THE RESULTS							
Year	Team	Lg	G	GS	GF	IP	BFP	H	R	ER	HR	SH	SF	HB	TBB	IBB	SO	WP	W	L	Pct	Sv-Op	Hld	Vel	OPS	ERC	ERA
2021	Norfolk	AAA	8	1	0	10.0	51	19	11	9	2	1	0	0	2	1	7	1	2	1	.667	0- -	-	-	.982	9.32	8.10
2019	Bal	AL	7	0	1	6.1	26	3	1	1	1	0	0	0	4	0	11	0	1	0	1.000	0-1	1	98	.678	7.56	1.42
2020	Bal	AL	10	0	2	8.2	37	8	6	4	2	0	1	1	2	0	6	2	0	2	.000	0-0	4	97	.722	4.23	4.15
2021	Bal	AL	9	0	0	8.2	36	8	4	4	1	0	0	0	3	0	6	0	0	0	-	0-0	2	97	.760	3.58	4.15
	3 ML YEARS		26	0	3	23.2	99	19	11	9	4	0	1	1	9	0	23	2	1	2	.333	0-1	7	98	.725	3.52	3.42

Matt Harvey

Pitches: R Bats: R Pos: SP-28   Ht: 6'4" Wt: 220 Born: 3/27/1989 Age: 33

		HOW MUCH PITCHED					WHAT HE GAVE UP										THE RESULTS							
Year	Team	Lg	G	GS	GF	IP	BFP	H	R	ER	HR	SH	SF	HB	TBB	IBB	SO	WP	W	L	Pct	Sv-Op	Hld	Vel	OPS	ERC	ERA
2012	NYM	NL	10	10	0	59.1	245	42	19	18	5	3	3	3	26	0	70	3	3	5	.375	0-0	0	95	.631	2.75	2.73
2013	NYM	NL	26	26	0	178.1	690	135	46	45	7	5	4	4	31	1	191	2	9	5	.643	0-0	0	96	.530	1.76	2.27
2015	NYM	NL	29	29	0	189.1	755	156	62	57	18	7	2	5	37	2	188	4	13	8	.619	0-0	0	96	.609	2.44	2.71
2016	NYM	NL	17	17	0	92.2	402	111	65	50	8	5	4	1	25	1	76	4	4	10	.286	0-0	0	94	.797	4.65	4.86
2017	NYM	NL	19	18	0	92.2	431	110	70	69	21	3	2	6	47	3	67	6	5	7	.417	0-0	0	94	.890	6.87	6.70
2018	2 Tms	NL	32	28	2	155.0	663	165	87	85	27	6	5	6	37	2	131	2	7	9	.438	0-0	0	94	.783	4.42	4.94
2019	LAA	AL	12	12	0	59.2	266	63	48	47	13	1	4	3	29	0	39	3	3	5	.375	0-0	0	93	.887	5.91	7.09
2020	KC	AL	7	4	1	11.2	65	27	15	15	6	0	0	0	5	0	10	0	0	3	.000	0-0	0	93	1.309	17.52	11.57
2021	Bal	AL	28	28	0	127.2	582	160	96	89	19	2	2	5	37	1	95	3	6	14	.300	0-0	0	93	.830	5.51	6.27
18	NYM	NL	8	4	2	27.0	123	33	21	21	6	2	1	2	9	0	20	1	0	2	.000	0-0	0	93	.906	6.10	7.00
18	Cin	NL	24	24	0	128.0	540	132	66	64	21	4	3	5	28	2	111	1	7	7	.500	0-0	0	94	.756	4.08	4.50
	Postseason		4	4	0	26.2	109	21	10	9	2	0	1	1	8	1	27	0	2	0	1.000	0-0	0	95	.578	2.49	3.04
	9 ML YEARS		180	172	3	966.1	4099	969	498	475	124	32	26	33	274	10	867	27	50	66	.431	0-0	0	95	.733	3.94	4.42

Adam Haseley

Bats: L Throws: L Pos: CF-8;LF-2;PH-1   Ht: 6'1" Wt: 190 Born: 4/12/1996 Age: 26

								BATTING												RUNNING			AVERAGES			
Year	Team	Lg	G	AB	H	2B	3B	HR	(Hm	Rd)	TB	R	RBI	RC	TBB	IBB	SO	HBP	SH	SF	SB	CS	GDP	Avg	OBP	Slg	OPS
2021	LV	AAA	37	142	33	2	0	3	(-	-)	44	18	12	-	9	0	30	1	0	0	7	2	4	.232	.283	.310	.593
2021	2 Tms	Low	13	43	10	1	0	1	(-	-)	14	9	4	-	11	0	9	0	0	0	0	0	0	.233	.382	.326	.707
2019	Phi	NL	67	222	59	14	0	5	(3	2)	88	30	26	28	14	1	60	5	1	0	4	0	0	.266	.324	.396	.720
2020	Phi	NL	40	79	22	5	0	0	(0	0)	27	7	13	12	7	1	17	2	3	1	0	0	3	.278	.348	.342	.690
2021	Phi	NL	9	21	4	1	0	0	(0	0)	5	2	0	0	0	0	4	0	0	0	0	0	0	.190	.190	.238	.429
	3 ML YEARS		116	322	85	20	0	5	(3	2)	120	39	39	40	21	2	81	7	4	1	4	0	10	.264	.322	.373	.695

Thomas Hatch

Pitches: R Bats: R Pos: SP-2; RP-1   Ht: 6'1" Wt: 205 Born: 9/29/1994 Age: 27

		HOW MUCH PITCHED					WHAT HE GAVE UP										THE RESULTS							
Year	Team	Lg	G	GS	GF	IP	BFP	H	R	ER	HR	SH	SF	HB	TBB	IBB	SO	WP	W	L	Pct	Sv-Op	Hld	Vel	OPS	ERC	ERA
2021	Buffalo	AAA	15	14	0	64.2	273	58	33	29	10	1	2	7	19	0	70	2	2	6	.250	0- -	-	-	.756	3.88	4.04
2020	Tor	AL	17	1	1	26.1	109	18	11	8	2	0	0	2	13	0	23	0	3	1	.750	0-0	3	95	.601	2.90	2.73
2021	Tor	AL	3	2	0	9.1	45	11	7	7	2	0	0	1	6	0	8	2	0	1	.000	0-0	0	94	.953	7.58	6.75
	Postseason		2	0	1	2.0	6	0	0	0	0	0	0	0	0	0	1	0	0	0	-	0-0	0	-	.000	0.00	0.00
	2 ML YEARS		20	3	1	35.2	154	29	18	15	4	0	0	3	19	0	31	2	3	2	.600	0-0	3	95	.702	3.99	3.79

Ke'Bryan Hayes

Bats: R Throws: R Pos: 3B-95;PH-4   Ht: 5'10" Wt: 205 Born: 1/28/1997 Age: 25

								BATTING												RUNNING			AVERAGES			
Year	Team	Lg	G	AB	H	2B	3B	HR	(Hm	Rd)	TB	R	RBI	RC	TBB	IBB	SO	HBP	SH	SF	SB	CS	GDP	Avg	OBP	Slg	OPS
2017	Bradtn	A+	108	421	117	16	7	2	(-	-)	153	66	43	60	41	0	76	4	12	4	27	5	12	.278	.345	.363	.708
2018	Altna	AA	117	437	128	31	7	7	(-	-)	194	64	47	77	57	0	84	4	4	6	12	5	10	.293	.375	.444	.819
2019	Indy	AAA	110	427	113	30	2	10	(-	-)	177	64	53	64	43	0	90	5	1	4	12	1	8	.265	.336	.415	.751
2020	Pit	NL	24	85	32	7	2	5	(3	2)	58	17	11	24	9	2	20	1	0	0	1	0	2	.376	.442	.682	1.124
2021	Pit	NL	96	362	93	20	2	6	(2	4)	135	49	38	48	31	0	87	1	0	2	9	1	11	.257	.316	.373	.689
	2 ML YEARS		120	447	125	27	4	11	(5	6)	193	66	49	72	40	2	107	2	0	2	10	1	13	.280	.340	.432	.772

Austin Hays

Bats: R Throws: R Pos: LF-88;RF-54;PH-7;CF-6;PR-2   Ht: 6'0" Wt: 205 Born: 7/5/1995 Age: 26

						BATTING																RUNNING			AVERAGES			
Year	Team	Lg	G	AB	H	2B	3B	HR	(Hm	Rd)	TB	R	RBI	RC	TBB	IBB	SO	HBP	SH	SF	SB	CS	GDP	Avg	OBP	Slg	OPS
2017	Bal	AL	20	60	13	3	0	1	(0	1)	19	4	8	5	2	0	16	0	0	1	0	0	2	.217	.238	.317	.555
2019	Bal	AL	21	68	21	6	0	4	(2	2)	39	12	13	16	7	0	13	0	0	0	2	0	0	.309	.373	.574	.947
2020	Bal	AL	33	122	34	2	0	4	(1	3)	48	20	9	14	8	0	25	2	0	2	2	3	1	.279	.328	.393	.722
2021	Bal	AL	131	488	125	26	4	22	(13	9)	225	73	71	76	28	0	107	9	3	1	4	3	9	.256	.308	.461	.769
	4 ML YEARS		205	738	193	37	4	31	(16	15)	331	109	101	111	45	0	161	11	3	4	8	6	12	.262	.312	.449	.761

Louis Head

Pitches: R Bats: R Pos: RP-25; SP-2   Ht: 6'1" Wt: 180 Born: 4/23/1990 Age: 32

			HOW MUCH PITCHED					WHAT HE GAVE UP										THE RESULTS							
Year	Team	Lg	G	GS	GF	IP	BFP	H	R	ER	HR	SH	SF	HB	TBB	IBB	SO	WP	W	L	Pct	Sv-Op	Hld	Vel	OPS	ERC	ERA
2021	Drham	AAA	26	0	10	28.2	115	20	7	7	2	0	0	2	10	1	37	0	0	0	-	5-	-	-	.570	2.36	2.20
2021	TB	AL	27	2	12	35.0	134	21	10	9	2	0	2	3	9	0	32	1	2	0	1.000	0-0	0	94	.496	1.67	2.31

Andrew Heaney

Pitches: L Bats: L Pos: SP-23; RP-7   HEE-nee   Ht: 6'2" Wt: 200 Born: 6/5/1991 Age: 31

			HOW MUCH PITCHED					WHAT HE GAVE UP										THE RESULTS							
Year	Team	Lg	G	GS	GF	IP	BFP	H	R	ER	HR	SH	SF	HB	TBB	IBB	SO	WP	W	L	Pct	Sv-Op	Hld	Vel	OPS	ERC	ERA
2014	Mia	NL	7	5	2	29.1	126	32	19	19	6	2	0	3	7	0	20	2	0	3	.000	0-0	0	90	.847	5.17	5.83
2015	LAA	AL	18	18	0	105.2	438	99	41	41	9	1	3	6	28	1	78	4	6	4	.600	0-0	0	91	.679	3.35	3.49
2016	LAA	AL	1	1	0	6.0	25	7	4	4	2	0	0	0	0	0	7	0	0	1	.000	0-0	0	91	.840	4.78	6.00
2017	LAA	AL	5	5	0	21.2	101	27	17	17	12	2	0	0	9	0	27	2	1	2	.333	0-0	0	92	1.108	8.99	7.06
2018	LAA	AL	30	30	0	180.0	749	171	91	83	27	2	5	8	45	0	180	9	9	10	.474	0-0	0	92	.719	3.73	4.15
2019	LAA	AL	18	18	0	95.1	409	93	53	52	20	0	2	7	30	1	118	4	4	6	.400	0-0	0	93	.772	4.63	4.91
2020	LAA	AL	12	12	0	66.2	279	63	35	33	9	0	2	2	19	1	70	2	4	3	.571	0-0	0	92	.715	3.65	4.46
2021	2 Tms		30	23	2	129.2	558	130	85	84	29	0	4	6	41	0	150	4	8	9	.471	0-1	0	92	.804	4.78	5.83
21	LAA	AL	18	18	0	94.0	401	92	56	55	16	0	2	3	31	0	113	3	6	7	.462	0-0	0	92	.744	4.28	5.27
21	NYY	AL	12	5	2	35.2	157	38	29	29	13	0	2	3	10	0	37	1	2	2	.500	0-1	0	92	.959	6.12	7.32
	8 ML YEARS		121	112	4	634.1	2685	622	345	333	114	7	16	32	179	3	650	27	32	38	.457	0-1	0	92	.759	4.24	4.72

Taylor Hearn

Pitches: L Bats: L Pos: RP-31; SP-11   Ht: 6'6" Wt: 230 Born: 8/30/1994 Age: 27

			HOW MUCH PITCHED					WHAT HE GAVE UP										THE RESULTS							
Year	Team	Lg	G	GS	GF	IP	BFP	H	R	ER	HR	SH	SF	HB	TBB	IBB	SO	WP	W	L	Pct	Sv-Op	Hld	Vel	OPS	ERC	ERA
2019	Tex	AL	1	1	0	0.1	8	3	5	4	0	0	0	0	4	0	0	0	0	1	.000	0-0	0	92	1.875	131.5	108.0
2020	Tex	AL	14	0	3	17.1	76	13	8	7	2	0	1	1	11	0	23	2	0	0	-	0-0	0	95	.646	3.90	3.63
2021	Tex	AL	42	11	10	104.1	441	96	58	54	17	1	5	3	42	1	92	6	6	6	.500	0-1	1	95	.745	4.22	4.66
	3 ML YEARS		57	12	13	122.0	525	112	71	65	19	1	6	4	57	1	115	8	6	7	.462	0-1	1	95	.745	4.43	4.80

Jon Heasley

Pitches: R Bats: R Pos: SP-3   Ht: 6'3" Wt: 225 Born: 1/27/1997 Age: 25

			HOW MUCH PITCHED					WHAT HE GAVE UP										THE RESULTS							
Year	Team	Lg	G	GS	GF	IP	BFP	H	R	ER	HR	SH	SF	HB	TBB	IBB	SO	WP	W	L	Pct	Sv-Op	Hld	Vel	OPS	ERC	ERA
2021	NWArk	AA	22	21	0	105.1	433	95	42	39	18	0	2	7	34	0	120	4	7	3	.700	0- -	-	-	.729	4.08	3.33
2021	KC	AL	3	3	0	14.2	59	15	8	8	3	0	0	2	3	0	6	0	1	1	.500	0-0	0	94	.876	5.03	4.91

Nick Heath

Bats: L Throws: L Pos: CF-18;PR-3;PH-1   Ht: 6'1" Wt: 190 Born: 11/27/1993 Age: 28

						BATTING																RUNNING			AVERAGES			
Year	Team	Lg	G	AB	H	2B	3B	HR	(Hm	Rd)	TB	R	RBI	RC	TBB	IBB	SO	HBP	SH	SF	SB	CS	GDP	Avg	OBP	Slg	OPS
2021	Reno	AAA	59	193	48	9	5	5	(-	-)	82	36	27	-	25	0	76	3	0	4	19	4	0	.249	.338	.425	.763
2020	KC	AL	15	13	2	1	0	0	(0	0)	3	2	3	1	2	0	6	1	1	0	2	2	0	.154	.313	.231	.543
2021	Ari	NL	20	35	5	1	0	0	(0	0)	6	3	1	0	4	1	15	0	0	0	0	2	0	.143	.231	.171	.402
	2 ML YEARS		35	48	7	2	0	0	(0	0)	9	5	4	1	6	1	21	1	1	0	2	4	0	.146	.255	.188	.442

Austin Hedges

Bats: R Throws: R Pos: C-87;PH-1   Ht: 6'1" Wt: 223 Born: 8/18/1992 Age: 29

						BATTING																RUNNING			AVERAGES			
Year	Team	Lg	G	AB	H	2B	3B	HR	(Hm	Rd)	TB	R	RBI	RC	TBB	IBB	SO	HBP	SH	SF	SB	CS	GDP	Avg	OBP	Slg	OPS
2015	SD	NL	56	137	23	2	0	3	(2	1)	34	13	11	7	8	1	38	1	3	3	0	0	1	.168	.215	.248	.463
2016	SD	NL	8	24	3	1	0	0	(0	0)	4	2	1	0	0	0	7	1	0	0	0	1	0	.125	.154	.167	.321
2017	SD	NL	120	387	83	17	0	18	(9	9)	154	36	55	39	23	3	122	3	1	3	4	1	10	.214	.262	.398	.660
2018	SD	NL	91	303	70	14	2	14	(5	9)	130	29	37	28	21	3	90	1	0	1	3	0	9	.231	.282	.429	.711
2019	SD	NL	102	312	55	9	0	11	(3	8)	97	28	36	28	27	3	109	5	1	1	1	0	3	.176	.252	.311	.563
2020	2 Tms		35	69	10	1	0	3	(1	2)	20	7	6	3	6	0	23	2	5	1	1	1	3	.145	.231	.290	.521
2021	Cle	AL	88	286	51	7	0	10	(5	5)	88	32	31	20	15	1	87	1	7	3	1	0	7	.178	.220	.308	.527
20	SD	NL	29	57	9	1	0	3	(1	2)	19	7	6	3	6	0	18	2	5	1	1	1	3	.158	.258	.333	.591
20	Cle	AL	6	12	1	0	0	0	(0	0)	1	0	0	0	0	0	5	0	0	0	0	0	0	.083	.083	.083	.167
	Postseason		1	1	0	0	0	0	(0	0)	0	0	0	0	0	0	1	0	0	0	0	0	0	.000	.000	.000	.000
	7 ML YEARS		500	1518	295	51	2	59	(25	34)	527	147	177	125	100	11	476	14	18	13	10	3	33	.194	.249	.347	.596

Jonah Heim

Bats: B Throws: R Pos: C-78;DH-2;PH-2   Ht: 6'4" Wt: 220 Born: 6/27/1995 Age: 27

					BATTING														RUNNING			AVERAGES			
Year	Team	Lg	G	AB	H	2B	3B	HR	(Hm | Rd)	TB	R	RBI	RC	TBB	IBB	SO	HBP	SH	SF	SB	CS	GDP	Avg	OBP	Slg	OPS
2020	Oak	AL	13	38	8	0	0	0	(0 | 0)	8	5	5	5	3	0	3	0	0	0	0	0	1	.211	.268	.211	.479
2021	Tex	AL	82	265	52	13	0	10	(7 | 3)	95	22	32	23	15	0	58	1	1	3	3	1	8	.196	.239	.358	.598
	2 ML YEARS		95	303	60	13	0	10	(7 | 3)	103	27	37	28	18	0	61	1	1	3	3	1	9	.198	.243	.340	.583

Scott Heineman

Bats: R Throws: R Pos: PH-11;CF-8;1B-2;LF-2;RF-2;PR-1   Ht: 6'1" Wt: 220 Born: 12/4/1992 Age: 29

Year	Team	Lg	G	AB	H	2B	3B	HR	(Hm	Rd)	TB	R	RBI	RC	TBB	IBB	SO	HBP	SH	SF	SB	CS	GDP	Avg	OBP	Slg	OPS
2021	Lsvlle	AAA	17	61	17	3	1	1	(-	-)	25	10	4	-	5	0	12	2	0	0	4	1	1	.279	.353	.410	.763
2019	Tex	AL	25	75	16	6	0	2	(1	1)	28	8	7	7	9	0	20	1	0	1	1	2	3	.213	.306	.373	.679
2020	Tex	AL	24	52	8	3	0	1	(0	1)	14	6	7	4	2	0	11	0	0	0	3	0	1	.154	.185	.269	.454
2021	Cin	NL	19	30	3	0	0	2	(2	0)	9	5	3	1	3	0	15	1	0	0	0	0	1	.100	.206	.300	.506
	3 ML YEARS		68	157	27	9	0	5	(3	2)	51	19	17	12	14	0	46	2	0	1	4	2	5	.172	.249	.325	.573

Ryan Helsley

Pitches: R Bats: R Pos: RP-51   Ht: 6'2" Wt: 230 Born: 7/18/1994 Age: 27

			HOW MUCH PITCHED					WHAT HE GAVE UP										THE RESULTS							
Year	Team	Lg	G	GS	GF	IP	BFP	H	R	ER	HR	SH	SF	HB	TBB	IBB	SO	WP	W	L	Pct	Sv-Op	Hld	Vel	OPS	ERC	ERA
2019	StL	NL	24	0	4	36.2	153	34	13	12	5	1	1	0	12	2	32	2	2	0	1.000	0-1	1	98	.734	3.56	2.95
2020	StL	NL	12	0	4	12.0	52	8	8	7	3	0	1	0	8	1	10	0	1	1	.500	1-3	2	97	.769	4.53	5.25
2021	StL	NL	51	0	7	47.1	206	40	24	24	4	1	2	0	27	2	47	7	6	4	.600	1-3	10	97	.668	3.67	4.56
	Postseason		7	0	1	7.0	24	2	1	1	0	0	0	0	1	0	10	0	0	0	-	0-0	0	98	.255	0.34	1.29
	3 ML YEARS		87	0	15	96.0	411	82	45	43	12	2	3	1	47	5	89	9	9	5	.643	2-7	13	98	.706	3.74	4.03

Heath Hembree

Pitches: R Bats: R Pos: RP-60   HEHM-bree   Ht: 6'4" Wt: 220 Born: 1/13/1989 Age: 33

Year	Team	Lg	G	GS	GF	IP	BFP	H	R	ER	HR	SH	SF	HB	TBB	IBB	SO	WP	W	L	Pct	Sv-Op	Hld	Vel	OPS	ERC	ERA
2013	SF	NL	9	0	2	7.2	29	4	0	0	0	0	0	0	2	0	12	0	0	0	-	0-0	0	92	.392	1.02	0.00
2014	Bos	AL	6	0	3	10.0	43	11	5	5	1	0	0	0	5	2	6	1	0	0	-	0-0	0	92	.846	4.94	4.50
2015	Bos	AL	22	0	9	25.1	106	25	10	10	5	0	0	0	9	2	15	1	2	0	1.000	0-0	1	94	.795	4.46	3.55
2016	Bos	AL	38	0	8	51.0	223	51	23	15	6	0	1	0	17	1	47	0	4	1	.800	0-2	5	94	.695	3.78	2.65
2017	Bos	AL	62	0	8	62.0	271	72	29	25	10	1	2	1	18	0	70	2	2	3	.400	0-3	14	95	.803	5.07	3.63
2018	Bos	AL	67	0	10	60.0	260	53	30	28	10	0	5	1	27	1	76	4	4	1	.800	0-3	20	95	.734	4.05	4.20
2019	Bos	AL	45	0	14	39.2	173	34	20	17	7	0	0	3	18	2	46	2	1	0	1.000	2-3	4	94	.772	4.18	3.86
2020	2 Tms		22	0	2	19.0	90	26	19	19	9	0	1	0	8	0	20	0	3	0	1.000	0-1	3	94	1.159	10.17	9.00
2021	2 Tms	NL	60	0	21	58.0	243	45	39	36	12	0	0	2	24	1	83	2	2	7	.222	9-11	7	95	.712	3.68	5.59
20	Bos	AL	11	0	1	9.2	40	9	6	6	2	0	0	0	3	0	10	0	2	0	1.000	0-1	1	94	.786	4.08	5.59
20	Phi	NL	11	0	1	9.1	50	17	13	13	7	0	1	0	5	0	10	0	1	0	1.000	0-0	2	94	1.480	17.96	12.54
21	NYM	NL	15	0	5	15.2	64	13	6	6	2	0	0	0	5	1	15	1	0	0	-	1-1	1	95	.637	2.94	3.45
21	Cin	NL	45	0	16	42.1	179	32	33	30	10	0	0	2	19	0	68	1	2	7	.222	8-10	6	95	.739	3.97	6.38
	Postseason		4	0	2	4.2	16	0	0	0	0	0	0	0	5	0	3	0	0	0	-	0-0	0	94	.313	1.27	0.00
	9 ML YEARS		331	0	77	332.2	1438	321	175	155	60	1	9	9	128	9	375	12	18	12	.600	11-23	54	94	.769	4.41	4.19

Kyle Hendricks

Pitches: R Bats: R Pos: SP-32   Ht: 6'3" Wt: 190 Born: 12/7/1989 Age: 32

Year	Team	Lg	G	GS	GF	IP	BFP	H	R	ER	HR	SH	SF	HB	TBB	IBB	SO	WP	W	L	Pct	Sv-Op	Hld	Vel	OPS	ERC	ERA
2014	ChC	NL	13	13	0	80.1	321	72	24	22	4	4	1	4	15	2	47	0	7	2	.778	0-0	0	88	.610	2.61	2.46
2015	ChC	NL	32	32	0	180.0	739	166	82	79	17	6	0	8	43	1	167	3	8	7	.533	0-0	0	88	.677	3.18	3.95
2016	ChC	NL	31	30	0	190.0	745	142	53	45	15	4	3	8	44	1	170	5	16	8	.667	0-0	0	88	.581	**2.19**	**2.13**
2017	ChC	NL	24	24	0	139.2	570	126	49	47	17	6	1	2	40	1	123	0	7	5	.583	0-0	0	86	.670	3.34	3.03
2018	ChC	NL	33	33	0	199.0	812	184	82	76	22	7	7	9	44	4	161	0	14	11	.560	0-0	0	87	.685	3.22	3.44
2019	ChC	NL	30	30	0	177.0	730	168	78	68	19	8	5	9	32	1	150	1	11	10	.524	0-0	0	87	.687	3.17	3.46
2020	ChC	NL	12	12	0	81.1	315	73	26	26	10	0	2	1	8	1	64	1	6	5	.545	0-0	0	87	.632	2.62	2.88
2021	ChC	NL	32	32	0	181.0	785	**200**	101	96	31	6	3	13	44	3	131	2	14	7	.667	0-0	0	87	.811	4.80	4.77
	Postseason		12	11	0	57.2	242	53	22	20	10	2	1	3	16	1	51	0	2	4	.333	0-0	0	88	.726	3.79	3.12
	8 ML YEARS		207	206	0	1228.1	5017	1131	495	459	135	41	22	54	270	16	1013	12	83	55	.601	0-0	0	87	.678	3.19	3.36

Liam Hendriks

Pitches: R Bats: R Pos: RP-69   Ht: 6'0" Wt: 235 Born: 2/10/1989 Age: 33

Year	Team	Lg	G	GS	GF	IP	BFP	H	R	ER	HR	SH	SF	HB	TBB	IBB	SO	WP	W	L	Pct	Sv-Op	Hld	Vel	OPS	ERC	ERA
2011	Min	AL	4	4	0	23.1	100	29	16	16	3	0	1	0	6	0	16	1	0	2	.000	0-0	0	90	.866	5.26	6.17
2012	Min	AL	16	16	0	85.1	381	106	61	53	17	3	1	4	26	3	50	4	1	8	.111	0-0	0	90	.890	6.03	5.59
2013	Min	AL	10	8	1	47.1	224	67	39	36	10	0	2	3	14	1	34	1	1	3	.250	0-0	0	91	.907	7.16	6.85
2014	2 Tms	AL	9	6	0	32.2	143	38	21	19	3	0	2	3	7	0	23	1	1	2	.333	0-0	1	91	.786	4.56	5.23
2015	Tor	AL	58	0	14	64.2	261	59	23	21	3	0	2	2	11	1	71	4	5	0	1.000	0-2	5	95	.605	2.51	2.92
2016	Oak	AL	53	0	10	64.2	275	69	31	27	6	0	4	1	14	3	71	3	0	4	.000	0-1	10	94	.704	3.63	3.76
2017	Oak	AL	70	0	13	64.0	273	57	34	30	7	0	1	0	23	0	78	6	4	2	.667	1-4	16	95	.663	3.30	4.22
2018	Oak	AL	25	8	1	24.0	104	25	11	11	3	0	1	1	10	0	22	1	0	1	.000	0-0	0	94	.759	4.82	4.13
2019	Oak	AL	75	2	41	85.0	332	61	18	17	5	2	3	2	21	5	124	7	4	4	.500	25-32	8	96	.564	1.86	1.80

			HOW MUCH PITCHED					WHAT HE GAVE UP										THE RESULTS						
Year	Team	Lg	G	GS	GF	IP	BFP	H	R	ER	HR	SH	SF	HB	TBB	IBB	SO	WP	W	L	Pct	Sv-Op	Hld	Vel	OPS	ERC	ERA
2020	Oak	AL	24	0	20	25.1	92	14	6	5	1	1	1	0	3	1	37	0	3	1	.750	14-15	0	96	.405	0.95	1.78
2021	CWS	AL	69	0	58	71.0	267	45	23	20	11	0	0	1	7	1	113	6	8	3	.727	38-44	0	98	.517	1.53	2.54
14	Tor	AL	3	3	0	13.1	57	12	9	9	3	0	0	2	4	0	8	0	1	0	1.000	0-0	0	91	.767	4.58	6.08
14	KC	AL	6	3	0	19.1	86	26	12	10	0	0	2	1	3	0	15	1	0	2	.000	0-0	1	92	.799	4.52	4.66
	Postseason		8	1	4	12.2	51	12	7	7	2	0	1	0	2	0	16	0	1	1	.500	1-1	0	97	.684	3.23	4.97
	11 ML YEARS		413	44	158	587.1	2452	570	283	255	69	6	18	17	142	15	639	34	27	30	.474	78-98	40	94	.699	3.48	3.91

Ryan Hendrix

Pitches: R **Bats:** R **Pos:** RP-36   **Ht:** 6'3" **Wt:** 215 **Born:** 12/16/1994 **Age:** 27

			HOW MUCH PITCHED					WHAT HE GAVE UP										THE RESULTS						
Year	Team	Lg	G	GS	GF	IP	BFP	H	R	ER	HR	SH	SF	HB	TBB	IBB	SO	WP	W	L	Pct	Sv-Op	Hld	Vel	OPS	ERC	ERA
2021	Lsvlle	AAA	15	0	5	14.2	70	15	17	15	4	0	1	2	9	0	14	0	0	1	.000	0--	-	-	.886	6.89	9.20
2021	Cin	NL	36	0	9	31.2	142	33	23	21	8	0	2	1	16	2	35	6	5	1	.833	0-1	3	96	.881	5.93	5.97

Payton Henry

Bats: R **Throws:** R **Pos:** C-5   **Ht:** 6'2" **Wt:** 215 **Born:** 6/24/1997 **Age:** 25

								BATTING													RUNNING			AVERAGES			
Year	Team	Lg	G	AB	H	2B	3B	HR	(Hm	Rd)	TB	R	RBI	RC	TBB	IBB	SO	HBP	SH	SF	SB	CS	GDP	Avg	OBP	Slg	OPS
2021	Biloxi	AA	30	111	35	5	1	1	(-	-)	45	11	10	-	12	1	32	2	0	0	0	0	3	.315	.392	.405	.797
2021	Nashv	AAA	19	61	16	3	0	1	(-	-)	22	7	9	-	4	0	17	4	0	2	0	0	0	.262	.338	.361	.699
2021	Jaxnvl	AAA	22	69	13	2	0	4	(-	-)	27	7	8	-	10	0	26	1	0	0	0	0	4	.188	.300	.391	.691
2021	Mia	NL	5	15	4	1	0	0	(0	0)	5	0	0	1	1	0	5	0	0	0	0	0	1	.267	.313	.333	.646

Sam Hentges

Pitches: L **Bats:** L **Pos:** RP-18; SP-12   **Ht:** 6'6" **Wt:** 245 **Born:** 7/18/1996 **Age:** 25

			HOW MUCH PITCHED					WHAT HE GAVE UP										THE RESULTS						
Year	Team	Lg	G	GS	GF	IP	BFP	H	R	ER	HR	SH	SF	HB	TBB	IBB	SO	WP	W	L	Pct	Sv-Op	Hld	Vel	OPS	ERC	ERA
2021	Cle	AL	30	12	6	68.2	318	90	54	51	10	1	2	0	32	0	68	11	1	4	.200	0-0	0	94	.876	6.62	6.68

Guillermo Heredia

Bats: R **Throws:** L **Pos:** CF-108;LF-21;PH-16;PR-1   ghee-YAIR-moh   **Ht:** 5'10" **Wt:** 195 **Born:** 1/31/1991 **Age:** 31

								BATTING													RUNNING			AVERAGES			
Year	Team	Lg	G	AB	H	2B	3B	HR	(Hm	Rd)	TB	R	RBI	RC	TBB	IBB	SO	HBP	SH	SF	SB	CS	GDP	Avg	OBP	Slg	OPS
2016	Sea	AL	45	92	23	3	0	1	(1	0)	29	12	12	12	12	0	15	2	1	0	1	1	1	.250	.349	.315	.664
2017	Sea	AL	123	386	96	16	0	6	(4	2)	130	43	24	37	27	2	64	11	1	1	1	5	9	.249	.315	.337	.652
2018	Sea	AL	125	292	69	14	1	5	(1	4)	100	29	19	33	32	0	52	4	7	2	2	4	4	.236	.318	.342	.661
2019	TB	AL	89	204	46	13	0	5	(1	4)	74	31	20	20	18	0	60	6	2	1	2	2	4	.225	.306	.363	.668
2020	2 Tms	NL	15	33	7	0	0	2	(1	1)	13	6	5	4	3	0	9	0	0	0	1	0	0	.212	.278	.394	.672
2021	Atl	NL	120	305	67	26	0	5	(2	3)	108	46	26	34	32	3	81	9	0	1	0	0	5	.220	.311	.354	.665
20	Pit	NL	8	16	3	0	0	0	(0	0)	3	2	2	2	2	0	4	0	0	0	1	0	0	.188	.278	.188	.465
20	NYM	NL	7	17	4	0	0	2	(1	1)	10	4	3	2	1	0	5	0	0	0	0	0	0	.235	.278	.588	.866
	6 ML YEARS		517	1312	308	72	1	24	(10	14)	454	167	106	140	124	5	281	32	11	5	7	12	23	.235	.315	.346	.661

Jimmy Herget

Pitches: R **Bats:** R **Pos:** RP-18   **Ht:** 6'3" **Wt:** 170 **Born:** 9/9/1993 **Age:** 28

			HOW MUCH PITCHED					WHAT HE GAVE UP										THE RESULTS						
Year	Team	Lg	G	GS	GF	IP	BFP	H	R	ER	HR	SH	SF	HB	TBB	IBB	SO	WP	W	L	Pct	Sv-Op	Hld	Vel	OPS	ERC	ERA
2021	RdRck	AAA	27	0	15	37.2	157	28	14	11	5	0	2	0	12	0	48	0	2	2	.500	3- -	-	-	.583	2.50	2.63
2019	Cin	NL	5	0	4	6.1	26	8	3	3	2	0	0	0	3	0	0	0	0	0	-	0-0	0	93	1.119	8.76	4.26
2020	Tex	AL	20	1	6	19.2	87	13	7	7	2	1	1	2	14	1	17	0	1	0	1.000	0-1	1	93	.671	3.68	3.20
2021	2 Tms	AL	18	0	3	18.2	78	20	12	11	1	0	1	3	4	1	20	0	2	3	.400	0-2	1	91	.789	4.14	5.30
21	Tex	AL	4	0	1	4.0	18	5	5	4	1	0	0	1	0	0	2	0	1	0	1.000	0-0	1	91	.922	5.88	9.00
21	LAA	AL	14	0	2	14.2	60	15	7	7	0	0	1	2	4	1	18	0	1	3	.250	0-2	0	91	.746	3.64	4.30
	3 ML YEARS		43	1	13	44.2	191	41	22	21	5	1	2	5	21	2	37	0	3	3	.500	0-3	2	92	.785	4.49	4.23

Michael Hermosillo

Bats: R **Throws:** R **Pos:** PH-7;RF-6;CF-5;LF-2;PR-1   air-moh-SEE-yo   **Ht:** 6'0" **Wt:** 205 **Born:** 1/17/1995 **Age:** 27

								BATTING													RUNNING			AVERAGES			
Year	Team	Lg	G	AB	H	2B	3B	HR	(Hm	Rd)	TB	R	RBI	RC	TBB	IBB	SO	HBP	SH	SF	SB	CS	GDP	Avg	OBP	Slg	OPS
2021	Iowa	AAA	43	147	45	10	1	10	(-	-)	87	34	29	-	26	0	48	12	0	1	8	3	0	.306	.446	.592	1.038
2018	LAA	AL	31	57	12	4	0	1	(1	0)	19	7	1	3	8	0	17	2	0	0	1	0	0	.211	.274	.333	.608
2019	LAA	AL	18	36	5	1	1	0	(0	0)	8	7	3	3	5	0	19	4	0	1	2	0	1	.139	.304	.222	.527
2020	LAA	AL	7	8	2	0	0	0	(0	0)	2	0	2	1	1	0	1	0	0	1	1	0	0	.250	.300	.250	.550
2021	ChC	NL	16	36	7	2	0	3	(1	2)	18	5	7	3	1	0	12	1	0	0	0	0	3	.194	.237	.500	.737
	4 ML YEARS		72	137	26	7	1	4	(2	2)	47	19	13	10	10	0	49	7	0	2	3	1	4	.190	.276	.343	.619

Carlos Hernandez

Pitches: R Bats: R Pos: RP-13; SP-11   Ht: 6'4" Wt: 245 Born: 3/11/1997 Age: 25

Year Team	Lg	G	GS	GF	IP	BFP	H	R	ER	HR	SH	SF	HB	TBB	IBB	SO	WP	W	L	Pct	Sv-Op Hld	Vel	OPS	ERC	ERA
2021 Omha	AAA	6	6	0	26.1	113	28	15	13	6	0	1	3	6	0	26	1	2	1	.667	0- - -		.842	5.14	4.44
2020 KC	AL	5	3	0	14.2	67	19	9	8	4	0	1	0	6	0	13	0	1	0	.000	0-0 0	96	.955	7.75	4.91
2021 KC	AL	24	11	1	85.2	358	69	36	35	7	0	3	4	41	1	74	6	6	2	.750	0-0 0	97	.651	3.41	3.68
2 ML YEARS		29	14	1	100.1	425	88	45	43	11	0	3	5	47	1	87	6	6	3	.667	0-0 0	97	.700	3.98	3.86

Cesar Hernandez

Bats: B Throws: R Pos: 2B-142;DH-7;SS-1   Ht: 5'10" Wt: 195 Born: 5/23/1990 Age: 32

Year Team	Lg	G	AB	H	2B	3B	HR	(Hm	Rd)	TB	R	RBI	RC	TBB	IBB	SO	HBP	SH	SF	SB	CS	GDP	Avg	OBP	Slg	OPS
2013 Phi	NL	34	121	35	5	0	0	(0	0)	40	17	10	13	9	0	26	1	0	0	0	3	2	.289	.344	.331	.674
2014 Phi	NL	66	114	27	2	0	1	(1	0)	32	13	4	7	9	1	33	0	1	1	1	1	1	.237	.293	.281	.571
2015 Phi	NL	127	405	110	20	4	1	(1	0)	141	57	35	52	40	1	86	2	4	1	19	5	6	.272	.339	.348	.687
2016 Phi	NL	155	547	161	14	11	6	(4	2)	215	67	39	82	66	4	116	2	5	2	17	13	6	.294	.371	.393	.764
2017 Phi	NL	128	511	150	26	6	9	(6	3)	215	85	34	80	61	1	104	4	0	1	15	5	8	.294	.371	.421	.793
2018 Phi	NL	161	605	153	15	3	15	(7	8)	219	91	60	85	95	4	155	4	1	3	19	6	12	.253	.356	.362	.718
2019 Phi	NL	161	612	171	31	3	14	(7	7)	250	77	71	82	45	4	100	6	0	4	9	2	9	.279	.333	.408	.741
2020 Cle	AL	58	233	66	20	0	3	(3	0)	95	35	20	36	24	0	57	2	1	0	0	0	3	.283	.355	.408	.763
2021 2 Tms	AL	149	570	132	21	2	21	(12	9)	220	84	62	73	59	2	135	5	0	3	1	1	11	.232	.308	.386	.694
21 Cle	AL	96	376	87	17	2	18	(12	6)	162	60	47	56	38	0	90	4	0	0	0	0	6	.231	.307	.431	.738
21 CWS	AL	53	194	45	4	0	3	(0	3)	58	24	15	17	21	2	45	1	0	1	1	1	5	.232	.309	.299	.608
Postseason		2	8	3	1	0	0	(0	0)	4	2	1	2	1	0	3	0	0	0	0	0	0	.375	.444	.500	.944
9 ML YEARS		1039	3718	1005	154	29	70	(41	29)	1427	526	335	510	408	17	812	26	12	15	81	36	58	.270	.345	.384	.729

Darwinzon Hernandez

Pitches: L Bats: L Pos: RP-48   Ht: 6'2" Wt: 255 Born: 12/17/1996 Age: 25

Year Team	Lg	G	GS	GF	IP	BFP	H	R	ER	HR	SH	SF	HB	TBB	IBB	SO	WP	W	L	Pct	Sv-Op Hld	Vel	OPS	ERC	ERA
2019 Bos	AL	29	1	2	30.1	147	27	18	15	1	1	0	3	26	1	57	4	0	1	.000	0-0 2	96	.725	4.90	4.45
2020 Bos	AL	7	0	0	8.1	40	5	2	2	0	0	0	1	8	0	13	1	1	0	1.000	0-0 2	94	.511	3.46	2.16
2021 Bos	AL	48	0	5	40.0	182	29	17	15	5	1	2	5	31	0	54	3	2	2	.500	0-4 12	95	.702	4.64	3.38
3 ML YEARS		84	1	7	78.2	369	61	37	32	6	2	2	9	65	1	124	8	3	3	.500	0-4 16	95	.691	4.62	3.66

Elieser Hernandez

Pitches: R Bats: R Pos: SP-11   eh-LEE-eh-ser   Ht: 6'0" Wt: 214 Born: 5/3/1995 Age: 27

Year Team	Lg	G	GS	GF	IP	BFP	H	R	ER	HR	SH	SF	HB	TBB	IBB	SO	WP	W	L	Pct	Sv-Op Hld	Vel	OPS	ERC	ERA
2021 Jaxnvl	AAA	5	5	0	21.1	77	11	8	7	3	0	0	0	3	0	32	0	0	1	.000	0- - -		.493	1.23	2.95
2018 Mia	NL	32	6	6	65.2	284	68	38	38	11	3	2	2	27	3	45	1	2	7	.222	0-0 2	91	.809	4.94	5.21
2019 Mia	NL	21	15	1	82.1	353	76	49	46	20	3	1	9	26	1	85	2	3	5	.375	0-0 0	91	.820	4.69	5.03
2020 Mia	NL	6	6	0	25.2	106	21	10	9	5	0	0	2	5	0	34	0	1	0	1.000	0-0 0	91	.678	3.11	3.16
2021 Mia	NL	11	11	0	51.2	225	54	26	24	13	2	2	3	14	2	53	1	1	3	.250	0-0 0	91	.848	4.96	4.18
4 ML YEARS		70	38	7	225.1	968	219	123	117	49	8	5	16	72	6	217	4	7	15	.318	0-0 2	91	.808	4.64	4.67

Jonathan Hernandez

Pitches: R Bats: R Pos: P   Ht: 6'3" Wt: 190 Born: 7/6/1996 Age: 25

Year Team	Lg	G	GS	GF	IP	BFP	H	R	ER	HR	SH	SF	HB	TBB	IBB	SO	WP	W	L	Pct	Sv-Op Hld	Vel	OPS	ERC	ERA
2019 Tex	AL	9	2	1	16.2	78	14	10	8	3	0	1	0	13	0	19	1	2	1	.667	0-0 1	97	.721	4.94	4.32
2020 Tex	AL	27	0	5	31.0	125	24	10	10	2	1	2	4	8	0	31	0	5	1	.833	0-0 5	98	.618	2.65	2.90
2 ML YEARS		36	2	6	47.2	203	38	20	18	5	1	3	4	21	0	50	1	7	2	.778	0-0 6	97	.657	3.46	3.40

Kike Hernandez

Bats: R Throws: R Pos: CF-93;2B-47;SS-8;PH-3   kee-KAY   Ht: 5'11" Wt: 190 Born: 8/24/1991 Age: 30

Year Team	Lg	G	AB	H	2B	3B	HR	(Hm	Rd)	TB	R	RBI	RC	TBB	IBB	SO	HBP	SH	SF	SB	CS	GDP	Avg	OBP	Slg	OPS
2014 2 Tms		42	121	30	6	3	3	(1	2)	51	13	14	18	12	0	21	1	0	0	0	0	1	.248	.321	.421	.742
2015 LAD	NL	76	202	62	12	2	7	(5	2)	99	24	22	32	11	0	46	2	1	2	0	2	3	.307	.346	.490	.836
2016 LAD	NL	109	216	41	8	0	7	(5	2)	70	25	18	16	28	1	64	0	0	0	2	0	3	.190	.283	.324	.607
2017 LAD	NL	140	297	64	24	2	11	(7	4)	125	46	37	39	41	2	80	0	1	3	3	0	4	.215	.308	.421	.729
2018 LAD	NL	145	402	103	18	3	21	(14	7)	189	67	52	58	50	5	78	1	4	5	3	0	3	.256	.336	.470	.806
2019 LAD	NL	130	414	98	19	3	17	(8	9)	170	57	64	57	36	3	97	6	0	4	0	0	9	.237	.304	.411	.715
2020 LAD	NL	48	139	32	8	1	5	(4	1)	57	20	20	18	6	0	31	2	0	1	0	1	5	.230	.270	.410	.680
2021 Bos	AL	134	508	127	35	3	20	(10	10)	228	84	60	80	61	0	110	9	0	7	1	0	4	.250	.337	.449	.786
14 Hou	AL	24	81	23	4	2	1	(1	0)	34	10	8	14	8	0	11	0	0	0	0	0	1	.284	.348	.420	.768
14 Mia	NL	18	40	7	2	1	2	(0	2)	17	3	6	4	4	0	10	1	0	0	0	0	0	.175	.267	.425	.692
Postseason		58	122	26	3	0	8	(5	3)	53	17	18	16	18	2	34	2	0	0	3	2	2	.213	.324	.434	.758
8 ML YEARS		824	2299	557	129	15	91	(51	40)	989	336	287	318	245	11	527	21	6	22	13	5	32	.242	.318	.430	.748

Teoscar Hernandez

Bats: R **Throws:** R **Pos:** RF-110;LF-58;DH-11;CF-2;PH-1   tay-OH-skar   **Ht:** 6'2" **Wt:** 205 **Born:** 10/15/1992 **Age:** 29

Year Team	Lg	G	AB	H	2B	3B	HR	(Hm	Rd)	TB	R	RBI	RC	TBB	IBB	SO	HBP	SH	SF	SB	CS	GDP	Avg	OBP	Slg	OPS
2016 Hou	AL	41	100	23	7	0	4	(1	3)	42	15	11	11	11	1	28	0	0	1	0	2	5	.230	.304	.420	.724
2017 2 Tms	AL	27	88	23	6	0	8	(5	3)	53	16	20	15	6	0	36	0	0	0	0	1	0	.261	.305	.602	.908
2018 Tor	AL	134	476	114	29	7	22	(9	13)	223	67	57	60	41	0	163	3	0	3	5	5	14	.239	.302	.468	.771
2019 Tor	AL	125	417	96	19	2	26	(15	11)	197	58	65	67	45	1	153	1	0	1	6	3	8	.230	.306	.472	.778
2020 Tor	AL	50	190	55	7	0	16	(6	10)	110	33	34	31	14	0	63	1	0	1	6	1	4	.289	.340	.579	.919
2021 Tor	AL	143	550	163	29	0	32	(12	20)	288	92	116	104	36	1	148	7	0	2	12	4	5	.296	.346	.524	.870
17 Hou	AL	1	0	0	0	0	0	(0	0)	0	0	0	0	0	0	0	0	0	0	0	0	0	-	-	-	-
17 Tor	AL	26	88	23	6	0	8	(5	3)	53	16	20	15	6	0	36	0	0	0	0	1	0	.261	.305	.602	.908
Postseason		2	7	1	0	0	0	(0	0)	1	0	0	0	1	0	4	0	0	0	0	0	0	.143	.250	.143	.393
6 ML YEARS		520	1821	474	97	9	108	(48	60)	913	281	303	288	153	3	591	12	0	9	29	16	36	.260	.320	.501	.822

Yadiel Hernandez

Bats: L **Throws:** R **Pos:** PH-55;LF-48;RF-13   **Ht:** 5'10" **Wt:** 188 **Born:** 10/9/1987 **Age:** 34

Year Team	Lg	G	AB	H	2B	3B	HR	(Hm	Rd)	TB	R	RBI	RC	TBB	IBB	SO	HBP	SH	SF	SB	CS	GDP	Avg	OBP	Slg	OPS
2021 Roch	AAA	15	59	17	2	0	5	(-	-)	34	9	12	-	5	0	11	0	0	0	0	1	2	.288	.344	.576	.920
2020 Was	NL	12	26	5	3	0	1	(1	0)	11	3	6	4	1	0	12	0	0	1	0	0	0	.192	.214	.423	.637
2021 Was	NL	112	264	72	8	1	9	(3	6)	109	33	32	26	22	1	59	1	0	2	3	0	11	.273	.329	.413	.742
2 ML YEARS		124	290	77	11	1	10	(4	6)	120	36	38	30	23	1	71	1	0	3	3	0	11	.266	.319	.414	.732

Yonny Hernandez

Bats: B **Throws:** R **Pos:** 3B-29;2B-9;SS-6;DH-2;PH-1;PR-1   **Ht:** 5'9" **Wt:** 140 **Born:** 5/4/1998 **Age:** 24

Year Team	Lg	G	AB	H	2B	3B	HR	(Hm	Rd)	TB	R	RBI	RC	TBB	IBB	SO	HBP	SH	SF	SB	CS	GDP	Avg	OBP	Slg	OPS
2021 RdRck	AAA	61	192	48	7	2	1	(-	-)	62	42	13	-	51	0	44	7	1	0	21	10	1	.250	.424	.323	.747
2021 Tex	AL	43	143	31	5	0	0	(0	0)	36	15	6	13	17	0	32	4	1	1	11	2	2	.217	.315	.252	.567

Odubel Herrera

Bats: L **Throws:** R **Pos:** CF-104;LF-23;PH-9;RF-1   oh-DOO-bull   **Ht:** 5'11" **Wt:** 205 **Born:** 12/29/1991 **Age:** 30

Year Team	Lg	G	AB	H	2B	3B	HR	(Hm	Rd)	TB	R	RBI	RC	TBB	IBB	SO	HBP	SH	SF	SB	CS	GDP	Avg	OBP	Slg	OPS
2015 Phi	NL	147	495	147	30	3	8	(4	4)	207	64	41	66	28	0	129	8	5	1	16	8	6	.297	.344	.418	.762
2016 Phi	NL	159	583	167	21	6	15	(7	8)	245	87	49	93	63	7	134	6	2	2	25	7	6	.286	.361	.420	.781
2017 Phi	NL	138	526	148	42	3	14	(8	6)	238	67	56	63	31	4	126	4	0	2	8	5	13	.281	.325	.452	.778
2018 Phi	NL	148	550	140	19	3	22	(13	9)	231	64	71	71	38	3	122	7	1	1	5	2	11	.255	.310	.420	.730
2019 Phi	NL	39	126	28	10	1	1	(1	0)	43	12	16	13	11	0	33	1	0	1	2	2	0	.222	.288	.341	.629
2021 Phi	NL	124	450	117	27	2	13	(3	10)	187	59	51	58	29	0	77	6	1	5	6	1	6	.260	.310	.416	.726
6 ML YEARS		755	2730	747	149	18	73	(36	37)	1151	353	284	364	200	14	621	32	9	12	62	25	42	.274	.329	.422	.751

David Hess

Pitches: R **Bats:** R **Pos:** RP-14; SP-1   **Ht:** 6'1" **Wt:** 215 **Born:** 7/10/1993 **Age:** 28

Year Team	Lg	G	GS	GF	IP	BFP	H	R	ER	HR	SH	SF	HB	TBB	IBB	SO	WP	W	L	Pct	Sv-Op	Hld	Vel	OPS	ERC	ERA
2021 Drham	AAA	20	2	2	45.1	186	40	21	18	11	0	1	0	10	0	51	5	6	2	.750	0- -	-		.732	3.56	3.57
2018 Bal	AL	21	19	1	103.1	454	106	64	56	22	1	4	8	37	2	74	3	3	10	.231	0-0	0	92	.821	5.12	4.88
2019 Bal	AL	23	14	5	80.0	365	94	73	63	28	3	3	2	30	0	68	1	1	10	.091	0-0	0	93	.957	6.87	7.09
2020 Bal	AL	3	0	3	7.0	32	10	5	5	1	0	0	0	2	0	1	0	0	0	-	0-0	0	94	.975	6.54	6.43
2021 2 Tms		15	1	4	20.0	102	32	24	22	10	0	2	1	11	1	18	0	2	2	.500	0-2	2	94	1.215	12.32	9.90
21 Mia	NL	14	1	3	18.0	87	24	18	16	7	0	2	1	10	1	16	0	2	2	.500	0-2	2	94	1.105	9.40	8.00
21 TB	AL	1	0	1	2.0	15	8	6	6	3	0	0	0	1	0	2	0	0	0	-	0-0	0	93	1.814	44.87	27.00
4 ML YEARS		62	34	13	210.1	953	242	166	146	61	4	9	11	80	3	161	4	6	22	.214	0-2	2	93	.920	6.45	6.25

Codi Heuer

Pitches: R **Bats:** R **Pos:** RP-65   **Ht:** 6'5" **Wt:** 200 **Born:** 7/3/1996 **Age:** 25

Year Team	Lg	G	GS	GF	IP	BFP	H	R	ER	HR	SH	SF	HB	TBB	IBB	SO	WP	W	L	Pct	Sv-Op	Hld	Vel	OPS	ERC	ERA
2020 CWS	AL	21	0	4	23.2	92	12	4	4	1	0	1	0	9	0	25	0	3	0	1.000	1-1	5	98	.433	1.36	1.52
2021 2 Tms		65	0	11	67.1	281	65	34	32	7	4	3	2	23	3	56	6	7	4	.636	2-5	17	96	.731	3.81	4.28
21 CWS	AL	40	0	2	38.2	166	45	22	22	5	2	1	1	10	0	39	3	4	1	.800	0-0	13	97	.802	4.83	5.12
21 ChC	NL	25	0	9	28.2	115	20	12	10	2	2	2	1	13	3	17	3	3	3	.500	2-5	4	95	.620	2.54	3.14
Postseason		2	0	1	2.1	10	2	2	2	1	0	0	0	1	0	2	0	0	0	-	0-0	0	96	.856	5.50	7.71
2 ML YEARS		86	0	15	91.0	373	77	38	36	8	4	3	2	32	3	81	6	10	4	.714	3-6	22	96	.656	3.06	3.56

Jason Heyward

Bats: L **Throws:** L **Pos:** RF-97;PH-7;PR-1   **Ht:** 6'5" **Wt:** 240 **Born:** 8/9/1989 **Age:** 32

Year Team	Lg	G	AB	H	2B	3B	HR	(Hm	Rd)	TB	R	RBI	RC	TBB	IBB	SO	HBP	SH	SF	SB	CS	GDP	Avg	OBP	Slg	OPS
2010 Atl	NL	142	520	144	29	5	18	(9	9)	237	83	72	96	91	2	128	10	0	2	11	6	13	.277	.393	.456	.849
2011 Atl	NL	128	396	90	18	2	14	(5	9)	154	50	42	49	51	4	93	9	2	7	9	2	7	.227	.319	.389	.708
2012 Atl	NL	158	587	158	30	6	27	(9	18)	281	93	82	87	58	1	152	4	0	3	21	8	4	.269	.335	.479	.814
2013 Atl	NL	104	382	97	22	1	14	(10	4)	163	67	38	55	48	1	73	8	1	0	2	4	7	.254	.349	.427	.776

BATTING / RUNNING / AVERAGES

Year Team	Lg	G	AB	H	2B	3B	HR	(Hm	Rd)	TB	R	RBI	RC	TBB	IBB	SO	HBP	SH	SF	SB	CS	GDP	Avg	OBP	Slg	OPS
2014 Atl	NL	149	573	155	26	3	11	(5	6)	220	74	58	84	67	3	98	6	0	3	20	4	2	.271	.351	.384	.735
2015 StL	NL	154	547	160	33	4	13	(5	8)	240	79	60	78	56	4	90	2	0	3	23	3	13	.293	.359	.439	.797
2016 ChC	NL	142	530	122	27	1	7	(3	4)	172	61	49	53	54	0	93	5	1	2	11	4	12	.230	.306	.325	.631
2017 ChC	NL	126	432	112	15	4	11	(4	7)	168	59	59	60	41	1	67	3	2	2	4	4	8	.259	.326	.389	.715
2018 ChC	NL	127	440	119	23	4	8	(5	3)	174	67	57	67	42	1	60	2	2	2	1	1	7	.270	.335	.395	.731
2019 ChC	NL	147	513	129	20	4	21	(8	13)	220	78	62	74	68	5	110	5	0	3	8	3	12	.251	.343	.429	.772
2020 ChC	NL	50	147	39	6	2	6	(1	5)	67	20	22	30	30	1	37	2	0	2	2	0	1	.265	.392	.456	.848
2021 ChC	NL	104	323	69	15	2	8	(7	1)	112	35	30	32	27	1	68	3	0	0	5	1	4	.214	.280	.347	.627
Postseason		40	128	20	4	1	2	(0	2)	32	8	7	5	7	2	36	3	0	0	4	0	2	.156	.217	.250	.467
12 ML YEARS		1531	5390	1394	264	38	158	(71	87)	2208	766	631	765	633	24	1069	52	6	25	117	40	90	.259	.341	.410	.750

Aaron Hicks

Bats: B Throws: R Pos: CF-32;PH-2 Ht: 6'1" Wt: 205 Born: 10/2/1989 Age: 32

Year Team	Lg	G	AB	H	2B	3B	HR	(Hm	Rd)	TB	R	RBI	RC	TBB	IBB	SO	HBP	SH	SF	SB	CS	GDP	Avg	OBP	Slg	OPS
2013 Min	AL	81	281	54	11	3	8	(3	5)	95	37	27	25	24	0	84	2	4	2	9	3	0	.192	.259	.338	.597
2014 Min	AL	69	186	40	8	0	1	(0	1)	51	22	18	22	36	0	56	0	2	1	4	3	2	.215	.341	.274	.615
2015 Min	AL	97	352	90	11	3	11	(6	5)	140	48	33	45	34	2	66	2	0	2	13	3	6	.256	.323	.398	.721
2016 NYY	AL	123	327	71	13	1	8	(7	1)	110	32	31	28	30	1	68	0	1	3	3	4	7	.217	.281	.336	.617
2017 NYY	AL	88	301	80	18	0	15	(12	3)	143	54	52	52	51	0	67	3	1	5	10	5	8	.266	.372	.475	.847
2018 NYY	AL	137	480	119	18	3	27	(15	12)	224	90	79	94	90	1	111	3	2	6	11	2	1	.248	.366	.467	.833
2019 NYY	AL	59	221	52	10	0	12	(4	8)	98	41	36	34	31	0	72	0	1	2	3	1	2	.235	.325	.443	.769
2020 NYY	AL	54	169	38	10	2	6	(4	2)	70	28	21	32	41	1	38	1	0	0	4	1	4	.225	.379	.414	.793
2021 NYY	AL	32	108	21	3	0	4	(1	3)	36	13	14	10	14	0	30	2	0	2	0	0	3	.194	.294	.333	.627
Postseason		28	94	21	4	1	2	(1	1)	33	13	12	15	15	0	25	0	0	1	1	0	1	.223	.327	.351	.678
9 ML YEARS		740	2425	565	102	12	92	(52	40)	967	365	311	342	351	5	592	13	10	24	55	23	33	.233	.330	.399	.729

John Hicks

Bats: R Throws: R Pos: C-8;DH-2 Ht: 6'2" Wt: 230 Born: 8/31/1989 Age: 32

Year Team	Lg	G	AB	H	2B	3B	HR	(Hm	Rd)	TB	R	RBI	RC	TBB	IBB	SO	HBP	SH	SF	SB	CS	GDP	Avg	OBP	Slg	OPS
2021 RdRck	AAA	64	248	72	18	0	13	(-	-)	129	41	44	-	16	0	79	2	0	2	7	1	3	.290	.336	.520	.856
2015 Sea	AL	17	32	2	1	0	0	(0	0)	3	1	1	0	1	0	18	0	1	0	1	1	0	.063	.091	.094	.185
2016 Det	AL	1	2	1	1	0	0	(0	0)	2	1	0	0	0	0	0	0	0	0	0	0	0	.500	.500	1.000	1.500
2017 Det	AL	60	173	46	12	0	6	(3	3)	76	25	22	25	13	0	51	3	0	1	2	1	5	.266	.326	.439	.766
2018 Det	AL	81	288	75	12	1	9	(2	7)	116	35	32	35	22	0	84	0	1	1	0	1	9	.260	.312	.403	.715
2019 Det	AL	95	319	67	15	0	13	(6	7)	121	29	35	21	13	0	109	0	0	1	1	1	1	.210	.240	.379	.620
2021 Tex	AL	10	31	8	1	0	4	(1	3)	21	6	7	4	0	0	8	0	0	0	0	0	1	.258	.258	.677	.935
6 ML YEARS		264	845	199	42	1	32	(12	20)	339	97	97	85	49	0	270	3	2	3	4	4	22	.236	.279	.401	.680

Jordan Hicks

Pitches: R Bats: R Pos: RP-10 Ht: 6'2" Wt: 220 Born: 9/6/1996 Age: 25

Year Team	Lg	G	GS	GF	IP	BFP	H	R	ER	HR	SH	SF	HB	TBB	IBB	SO	WP	W	L	Pct	Sv-Op	Hld	Vel	OPS	ERC	ERA
2018 StL	NL	73	0	20	77.2	339	59	33	31	2	0	2	8	45	2	70	9	3	4	.429	6-13	24	101	.587	3.24	3.59
2019 StL	NL	29	0	21	28.2	110	16	10	10	2	0	0	1	11	0	31	2	2	2	.500	14-15	3	101	.510	1.80	3.14
2021 StL	NL	10	0	1	10.0	44	5	6	6	0	0	0	0	10	0	10	3	0	0	-	0-0	3	99	.576	2.87	5.40
3 ML YEARS		112	0	42	116.1	493	80	49	47	4	0	2	9	66	2	111	14	5	6	.455	20-28	30	101	.569	2.85	3.64

Kyle Higashioka

Bats: R Throws: R Pos: C-66;PH-2 he-gah-shi-oh-kah Ht: 6'1" Wt: 202 Born: 4/20/1990 Age: 32

Year Team	Lg	G	AB	H	2B	3B	HR	(Hm	Rd)	TB	R	RBI	RC	TBB	IBB	SO	HBP	SH	SF	SB	CS	GDP	Avg	OBP	Slg	OPS
2017 NYY	AL	9	18	0	0	0	0	(0	0)	0	2	0	0	2	0	6	0	0	0	0	0	0	.000	.100	.000	.100
2018 NYY	AL	29	72	12	2	0	3	(3	0)	23	6	6	2	6	0	16	1	0	0	0	0	2	.167	.241	.319	.560
2019 NYY	AL	18	56	12	5	0	3	(0	3)	26	8	11	7	0	0	26	0	0	1	0	0	1	.214	.211	.464	.675
2020 NYY	AL	16	48	12	1	0	4	(4	0)	25	7	10	8	0	0	11	0	0	0	0	0	0	.250	.250	.521	.771
2021 NYY	AL	67	193	35	10	0	10	(3	7)	75	20	29	20	17	0	59	0	0	1	0	0	4	.181	.246	.389	.635
Postseason		5	18	5	0	0	1	(0	1)	8	2	2	3	1	0	3	0	0	0	0	0	0	.278	.316	.444	.760
5 ML YEARS		139	387	71	18	0	20	(10	10)	149	43	56	37	25	0	118	1	0	2	0	0	7	.183	.234	.385	.619

P.J. Higgins

Bats: R Throws: R Pos: C-6;PH-4;1B-1 Ht: 5'10" Wt: 195 Born: 5/10/1993 Age: 29

Year Team	Lg	G	AB	H	2B	3B	HR	(Hm	Rd)	TB	R	RBI	RC	TBB	IBB	SO	HBP	SH	SF	SB	CS	GDP	Avg	OBP	Slg	OPS
2021 Iowa	AAA	11	39	13	2	1	1	(-	-)	20	7	6	-	8	0	11	1	0	0	0	0	0	.333	.458	.513	.971
2021 ChC	NL	9	23	1	0	0	0	(0	0)	1	1	0	0	2	0	8	0	0	0	0	0	2	.043	.120	.043	.163

Trevor Hildenberger

Pitches: R Bats: R Pos: RP-2   Ht: 6'2" Wt: 205 Born: 12/15/1990 Age: 31

			HOW MUCH PITCHED					WHAT HE GAVE UP											THE RESULTS						
Year	Team	Lg	G	GS	GF	IP	BFP	H	R	ER	HR	SH	SF	HB	TBB	IBB	SO	WP	W	L	Pct	Sv-Op	Hld	Vel	OPS	ERC	ERA
2021	Scrmto	AAA	20	2	5	23.0	102	18	13	12	1	0	0	6	13	1	23	2	2	1	.667	0- -	-	-	.664	4.07	4.70
2017	Min	AL	37	0	8	42.0	170	38	15	15	4	1	1	4	6	2	44	1	3	3	.500	1-3	12	89	.664	2.87	3.21
2018	Min	AL	73	0	20	73.0	319	75	46	44	12	3	3	2	26	9	70	2	4	6	.400	7-11	17	90	.803	4.37	5.42
2019	Min	AL	22	0	5	16.1	88	30	19	19	2	0	2	3	7	0	15	1	2	2	.500	1-1	6	88	1.033	10.46	10.47
2021	NYM	NL	2	0	1	2.1	14	3	4	4	1	0	0	1	3	0	4	1	0	0	-	0-0	0	89	1.100	14.93	15.43
	Postseason		1	0	0	1.1	7	1	1	1	0	0	0	0	2	1	0	0	0	0	-	0-0	0	91	.629	4.29	6.75
	4 ML YEARS		134	0	34	133.2	591	146	84	82	19	4	6	10	42	11	133	5	9	11	.450	9-15	35	89	.802	4.68	5.52

Derek Hill

Bats: R Throws: R Pos: CF-45;PH-3;PR-3;DH-2   Ht: 6'2" Wt: 190 Born: 12/30/1995 Age: 26

						BATTING															RUNNING			AVERAGES			
Year	Team	Lg	G	AB	H	2B	3B	HR	(Hm	Rd)	TB	R	RBI	RC	TBB	IBB	SO	HBP	SH	SF	SB	CS	GDP	Avg	OBP	Slg	OPS
2021	Toledo	AAA	34	125	40	5	3	4	(-	-)	63	21	15	-	10	0	39	2	3	1	4	1	2	.320	.377	.504	.881
2020	Det	AL	15	11	1	0	0	0	(0	0)	1	3	0	1	1	0	6	0	0	0	0	0	0	.091	.167	.091	.258
2021	Det	AL	49	139	36	3	3	3	(2	1)	54	19	14	18	10	0	42	1	0	0	6	3	2	.259	.313	.388	.702
	2 ML YEARS		64	150	37	3	3	3	(2	1)	55	22	14	19	11	0	48	1	0	0	6	3	2	.247	.302	.367	.669

Rich Hill

Pitches: L Bats: L Pos: SP-31; RP-1   Ht: 6'5" Wt: 221 Born: 3/11/1980 Age: 42

			HOW MUCH PITCHED					WHAT HE GAVE UP											THE RESULTS						
Year	Team	Lg	G	GS	GF	IP	BFP	H	R	ER	HR	SH	SF	HB	TBB	IBB	SO	WP	W	L	Pct	Sv-Op	Hld	Vel	OPS	ERC	ERA
2005	ChC	NL	10	4	1	23.2	115	25	24	24	3	1	0	1	17	1	21	0	0	2	.000	0-0	0	90	.794	5.81	9.13
2006	ChC	NL	17	16	1	99.1	417	83	51	46	16	8	3	2	39	1	90	3	6	7	.462	0-0	0	90	.725	3.59	4.17
2007	ChC	NL	32	32	0	195.0	812	170	89	85	27	9	4	12	63	3	183	1	11	8	.579	0-0	0	89	.699	3.56	3.92
2008	ChC	NL	5	5	0	19.2	89	13	9	9	2	0	2	1	18	0	15	1	1	0	1.000	0-0	0	88	.683	4.38	4.12
2009	Bal	AL	14	13	0	57.2	275	68	53	50	7	2	2	1	40	2	46	1	3	3	.500	0-0	0	88	.886	6.55	7.80
2010	Bos	AL	6	0	0	4.0	18	5	0	0	0	0	0	0	1	0	3	0	1	0	1.000	0-0	1	89	.627	4.05	0.00
2011	Bos	AL	9	0	3	8.0	30	3	0	0	0	0	0	1	3	0	12	1	0	0	-	0-0	3	91	.349	1.10	0.00
2012	Bos	AL	25	0	3	19.2	83	17	4	4	0	0	0	1	11	1	21	0	1	0	1.000	0-0	6	92	.685	3.24	1.83
2013	Cle	AL	63	0	3	38.2	182	38	30	27	3	1	2	2	29	6	51	6	1	2	.333	0-2	13	91	.719	5.07	6.28
2014	2 Tms	AL	16	0	2	5.1	29	7	2	2	0	0	0	0	6	1	9	0	0	0	-	0-0	1	90	.801	8.55	3.38
2015	Bos	AL	4	4	0	29.0	106	14	5	5	2	0	0	2	5	0	36	0	2	1	.667	0-0	0	90	.410	1.13	1.55
2016	2 Tms	AL	20	20	0	110.1	439	77	29	26	4	1	2	8	33	0	129	1	12	5	.706	0-0	0	90	.530	2.04	2.12
2017	LAD	NL	25	25	0	135.2	552	99	51	50	18	4	2	9	49	1	166	2	12	8	.600	0-0	0	89	.639	2.96	3.32
2018	LAD	NL	25	24	0	132.2	547	108	57	54	20	4	1	8	41	3	150	2	11	5	.688	0-0	0	89	.689	3.24	3.66
2019	LAD	NL	13	13	0	58.2	242	48	20	16	10	4	1	4	18	2	72	0	4	1	.800	0-0	0	88	.689	3.40	2.45
2020	Min	AL	8	8	0	38.2	156	28	13	13	3	0	1	1	17	0	31	1	2	2	.500	0-0	0	88	.601	2.89	3.03
2021	2 Tms	AL	32	31	0	158.2	661	137	70	68	21	3	5	16	55	0	150	3	7	8	.467	0-0	0	88	.718	3.80	3.86
14	LAA	AL	2	0	0	0.0	4	1	1	1	0	0	0	0	3	0	0	0	0	0	-	0-0	0	92	2.000	-	-
14	NYY	AL	14	0	2	5.1	25	6	1	1	0	0	0	0	3	1	9	0	0	0	-	0-0	1	90	.686	5.10	1.69
16	Oak	AL	14	14	0	76.0	311	55	22	19	2	0	1	8	28	0	90	0	9	3	.750	0-0	0	90	.559	2.44	2.25
16	LAD	NL	6	6	0	34.1	128	22	7	7	2	1	1	0	5	0	39	0	3	2	.600	0-0	0	90	.461	1.34	1.83
21	TB	AL	19	19	0	95.1	389	75	41	41	14	1	3	8	36	0	91	3	6	4	.600	0-0	0	88	.703	3.56	3.87
21	NYM	NL	13	12	0	63.1	272	62	29	27	7	2	2	8	19	0	59	0	1	4	.200	0-0	0	88	.740	4.16	3.84
	Postseason		13	12	1	53.0	234	41	18	18	5	3	1	4	32	3	65	1	1	2	.333	0-0	0	90	.643	3.71	3.06
	17 ML YEARS		324	195	13	1134.2	4753	940	507	479	136	37	25	69	445	21	1185	22	74	52	.587	0-2	24	89	.681	3.46	3.80

Tim Hill

Pitches: L Bats: R Pos: RP-78   Ht: 6'4" Wt: 200 Born: 2/10/1990 Age: 32

			HOW MUCH PITCHED					WHAT HE GAVE UP											THE RESULTS						
Year	Team	Lg	G	GS	GF	IP	BFP	H	R	ER	HR	SH	SF	HB	TBB	IBB	SO	WP	W	L	Pct	Sv-Op	Hld	Vel	OPS	ERC	ERA
2018	KC	AL	70	0	9	45.2	198	46	28	23	4	2	1	2	14	0	42	0	1	4	.200	2-4	13	91	.691	3.77	4.53
2019	KC	AL	46	0	4	39.2	161	31	17	16	4	1	0	4	13	2	39	0	2	0	1.000	1-2	9	90	.636	3.01	3.63
2020	SD	NL	23	0	3	18.0	79	17	9	9	3	0	0	2	6	1	20	1	3	0	1.000	0-0	5	91	.739	4.22	4.50
2021	SD	NL	78	0	10	59.2	255	51	34	24	9	2	2	6	23	5	56	1	6	6	.500	1-5	17	92	.704	3.81	3.62
	Postseason		3	0	0	2.1	10	1	1	0	0	0	0	1	1	0	3	0	0	0	-	0-0	0	91	.425	2.03	0.00
	4 ML YEARS		217	0	26	163.0	693	145	88	72	20	5	3	14	56	8	157	2	12	10	.545	4-11	44	91	.688	3.65	3.98

Sam Hilliard

Bats: L Throws: L Pos: CF-46;PH-20;LF-17;RF-11;DH-1;PR-1   Ht: 6'5" Wt: 236 Born: 2/21/1994 Age: 28

						BATTING															RUNNING			AVERAGES			
Year	Team	Lg	G	AB	H	2B	3B	HR	(Hm	Rd)	TB	R	RBI	RC	TBB	IBB	SO	HBP	SH	SF	SB	CS	GDP	Avg	OBP	Slg	OPS
2021	Albq	AAA	53	188	45	12	2	14	(-	-)	103	31	37	-	23	2	61	1	0	1	6	1	1	.239	.324	.548	.872
2019	Col	NL	27	77	21	4	2	7	(5	2)	50	13	13	17	9	0	23	1	0	0	2	0	1	.273	.356	.649	1.006
2020	Col	NL	36	105	22	2	2	6	(1	5)	46	13	10	12	9	0	42	0	0	0	3	0	0	.210	.272	.438	.710
2021	Col	NL	81	214	46	7	2	14	(6	8)	99	32	34	33	23	3	87	1	0	0	5	0	0	.215	.294	.463	.757
	3 ML YEARS		144	396	89	13	6	27	(12	15)	195	58	57	62	41	3	152	2	0	0	10	0	1	.225	.301	.492	.793

Keston Hiura

Bats: R **Throws:** R **Pos:** 1B-49;PH-13;2B-7;LF-1;PR-1

Ht: 6'0" **Wt:** 202 **Born:** 8/2/1996 **Age:** 25

Year	Team	Lg	G	AB	H	2B	3B	HR	(Hm	Rd)	TB	R	RBI	RC	TBB	IBB	SO	HBP	SH	SF	SB	CS	GDP	Avg	OBP	Slg	OPS
2021	Nashv	AAA	51	172	44	12	0	8	(-	-)	80	22	24		29	0	69	4	0	1	2	1	3	.256	.374	.465	.839
2019	Mil	NL	84	314	95	23	2	19	(10	9)	179	51	49	53	25	1	107	8	0	1	9	3	6	.303	.368	.570	.938
2020	Mil	NL	59	217	46	4	0	13	(6	7)	89	30	32	28	16	2	**85**	11	0	2	3	2	7	.212	.297	.410	.707
2021	Mil	NL	61	173	29	9	1	4	(3	1)	52	16	19	17	14	0	77	7	2	1	3	0	6	.168	.256	.301	.557
	Postseason		3	10	2	1	0	0	(0	0)	3	0	0		1	0	5	0	0	0	0	0	0	.200	.273	.300	.573
	3 ML YEARS		204	704	170	36	3	36	(19	17)	320	97	100	98	55	3	269	26	2	4	15	5	19	.241	.318	.455	.773

Nico Hoerner

Bats: R **Throws:** R **Pos:** 2B-30;SS-12;LF-3;CF-2;3B-1;PH-1

Ht: 6'1" **Wt:** 200 **Born:** 5/13/1997 **Age:** 25

Year	Team	Lg	G	AB	H	2B	3B	HR	(Hm	Rd)	TB	R	RBI	RC	TBB	IBB	SO	HBP	SH	SF	SB	CS	GDP	Avg	OBP	Slg	OPS
2019	ChC	NL	20	78	22	1	1	3	(3	0)	34	13	17	14	3	1	11	0	0	0	0	0	3	.282	.305	.436	.741
2020	ChC	NL	48	108	24	4	0	0	(0	0)	28	19	13	14	12	0	24	3	0	2	3	2	3	.222	.312	.259	.571
2021	ChC	NL	44	149	45	10	0	0	(0	0)	55	13	16	26	17	3	25	3	0	1	5	3	3	.302	.382	.369	.751
	3 ML YEARS		112	335	91	15	1	3	(3	0)	117	45	46	54	32	4	60	6	0	4	8	5	9	.272	.342	.349	.691

Jeff Hoffman

Pitches: R **Bats:** R **Pos:** RP-20; SP-11

Ht: 6'5" **Wt:** 235 **Born:** 1/8/1993 **Age:** 29

Year	Team	Lg	G	GS	GF	IP	BFP	H	R	ER	HR	SH	SF	HB	TBB	IBB	SO	WP	W	L	Pct	Sv-Op	Hld	Vel	OPS	ERC	ERA
2016	Col	NL	8	6	0	31.1	147	37	29	17	7	1	0	0	17	1	22	4	0	4	.000	0-0	0	94	.881	6.55	4.88
2017	Col	NL	23	16	3	99.1	440	106	66	65	15	3	5	4	40	1	82	2	6	5	.545	0-0	0	94	.833	4.97	5.89
2018	Col	NL	6	1	1	8.2	44	15	9	9	0	0	0	0	7	1	5	1	0	0	-	0-0	1	93	.986	9.88	9.35
2019	Col	NL	15	15	0	70.0	315	77	51	51	21	3	2	4	34	3	68	2	2	6	.250	0-0	0	94	.957	6.81	6.56
2020	Col	NL	16	0	5	21.1	104	32	23	22	3	0	2	2	9	1	20	4	2	1	.667	1-1	0	94	.985	7.93	9.28
2021	Cin	NL	31	11	7	73.0	335	70	41	37	12	1	2	5	45	2	79	9	3	5	.375	0-0	2	94	.795	5.37	4.56
	6 ML YEARS		99	49	16	303.2	1385	337	219	201	58	8	11	15	152	9	276	22	13	21	.382	1-1	3	94	.874	5.98	5.96

Bryan Holaday

HAHL-ih-daye

Bats: R **Throws:** R **Pos:** C-10;PH-3

Ht: 6'0" **Wt:** 203 **Born:** 11/19/1987 **Age:** 34

Year	Team	Lg	G	AB	H	2B	3B	HR	(Hm	Rd)	TB	R	RBI	RC	TBB	IBB	SO	HBP	SH	SF	SB	CS	GDP	Avg	OBP	Slg	OPS
2021	Reno	AAA	30	95	25	9	0	7	(-	-)	55	20	30		9	0	19	0	0	4	1	0	1	.263	.315	.579	.894
2012	Det	AL	6	12	3	1	0	0	(0	0)	4	3	0	1	0	0	2	0	1	0	0	0	0	.250	.250	.333	.583
2013	Det	AL	16	27	8	1	0	1	(1	0)	12	8	2	3	2	0	3	1	3	0	0	0	0	.296	.367	.444	.811
2014	Det	AL	62	156	36	5	1	0	(0	0)	43	14	15	11	8	0	37	1	2	4	1	1	4	.231	.266	.276	.542
2015	Det	AL	24	64	18	5	0	2	(1	1)	29	3	13	9	1	0	13	0	0	0	0	0	2	.281	.292	.453	.745
2016	2 Tms	AL	44	117	27	7	1	2	(1	1)	42	17	14	14	7	0	28	2	1	2	0	1	0	.231	.281	.359	.640
2017	Det	AL	13	29	7	2	0	0	(0	0)	9	1	2	2	0	0	1	0	0	0	0	0	2	.241	.241	.310	.552
2018	Mia	NL	61	151	31	5	0	1	(0	0)	39	7	16	10	10	2	29	2	1	2	0	0	0	.205	.261	.258	.519
2019	Mia	NL	43	115	32	6	0	4	(0	4)	50	12	12	14	11	2	21	1	1	1	0	1	5	.278	.344	.435	.779
2020	Bal	AL	21	31	5	1	0	0	(0	0)	6	5	4	2	0	0	9	0	0	0	0	0	0	.161	.212	.194	.406
2021	Ari	NL	13	31	6	2	0	0	(0	0)	8	2	1	2	1	0	15	2	0	0	0	0	0	.194	.265	.258	.523
16	Tex	AL	30	84	20	6	1	2	(1	1)	34	14	13	12	5	0	16	2	1	2	0	1	0	.238	.290	.405	.695
16	Bos	AL	14	33	7	1	0	0	(0	0)	8	3	1	2	2	0	12	0	0	0	0	0	1	.212	.257	.242	.500
	Postseason		1	2	0	0	0	0	(0	0)	0	0	0	0	0	0	1	0	0	0	0	0	0	.000	.000	.000	.000
	10 ML YEARS		303	733	173	35	2	10	(3	7)	242	72	79	68	42	4	158	9	9	9	1	3	17	.236	.282	.330	.613

Derek Holland

Pitches: L **Bats:** B **Pos:** RP-38; SP-1

Ht: 6'2" **Wt:** 223 **Born:** 10/9/1986 **Age:** 35

Year	Team	Lg	G	GS	GF	IP	BFP	H	R	ER	HR	SH	SF	HB	TBB	IBB	SO	WP	W	L	Pct	Sv-Op	Hld	Vel	OPS	ERC	ERA
2009	Tex	AL	33	21	0	138.1	611	160	98	94	26	2	3	4	47	0	107	3	8	13	.381	0-1	2	93	.856	5.52	6.12
2010	Tex	AL	14	10	2	57.1	253	55	30	26	6	0	2	4	24	0	54	0	3	4	.429	0-0	1	92	.727	4.17	4.08
2011	Tex	AL	32	32	0	198.0	843	201	97	87	22	1	3	6	67	1	162	2	16	5	.762	0-0	0	94	.724	4.15	3.95
2012	Tex	AL	29	27	1	175.1	730	162	100	91	32	5	4	3	52	0	145	1	12	7	.632	0-0	0	93	.745	3.86	4.67
2013	Tex	AL	33	33	0	213.0	894	210	90	81	20	8	9	3	64	0	189	9	10	9	.526	0-0	0	94	.711	3.64	3.42
2014	Tex	AL	6	5	0	37.0	145	34	8	6	2	1	0	2	5	1	25	1	2	0	1.000	0-0	0	92	.601	2.07	1.46
2015	Tex	AL	10	10	0	58.2	245	59	32	32	11	3	1	5	17	2	41	1	4	3	.571	0-0	0	93	.828	4.71	4.91
2016	Tex	AL	22	20	0	107.1	461	116	62	59	15	1	2	2	35	2	67	2	7	9	.438	0-0	0	92	.770	4.41	4.95
2017	CWS	AL	29	26	0	135.0	626	156	106	93	31	1	3	8	75	2	104	7	7	14	.333	0-0	0	91	.918	6.96	6.20
2018	SF	NL	36	30	1	171.1	727	154	74	68	19	**9**	7	4	67	6	169	2	7	9	.438	0-0	0	92	.718	3.58	3.57
2019	2 Tms	NL	51	8	19	84.1	376	82	61	57	20	7	2	4	45	2	82	1	2	5	.286	0-1	2	92	.852	5.64	6.08
2020	Pit	NL	12	5	3	40.2	179	42	33	31	12	0	0	3	15	0	45	0	1	3	.250	0-1	0	92	.876	5.84	6.86
2021	Det	AL	39	11	2	49.2	225	58	29	28	6	0	2	0	20	1	51	2	3	2	.600	0-0	4	93	.807	5.21	5.07
19	SF	NL	31	7	10	68.2	308	68	49	45	17	6	2	4	35	2	71	0	2	4	.333	0-0	2	92	.860	5.64	5.90
19	ChC	NL	20	1	9	15.2	68	14	12	12	3	1	0	0	10	0	11	1	0	1	.000	0-1	0	94	.814	5.23	6.89
	Postseason		14	5	2	37.2	161	37	23	21	10	0	0	1	16	0	24	2	3	1	.750	0-0	2	94	.870	5.47	5.02
	13 ML YEARS		346	228	38	1466.0	6315	1489	820	753	220	39	39	47	533	17	1241	33	82	83	.497	0-3	9	93	.775	4.50	4.62

Greg Holland

Pitches: R **Bats:** R **Pos:** RP-57   **Ht:** 5'10" **Wt:** 210 **Born:** 11/20/1985 **Age:** 36

Year	Team	Lg	G	GS	GF	IP	BFP	H	R	ER	HR	SH	SF	HB	TBB	IBB	SO	WP	W	L	Pct	Sv-Op	Hld	Vel	OPS	ERC	ERA
2010	KC	AL	15	0	10	18.2	87	23	15	14	3	1	0	0	8	0	23	2	0	1	.000	0-0	6	96	.835	5.88	6.75
2011	KC	AL	46	0	15	60.0	233	37	13	12	3	1	1	1	19	3	74	7	5	1	.833	4-6	18	95	.521	1.60	1.80
2012	KC	AL	67	0	36	67.0	289	58	22	22	2	4	3	0	34	7	91	3	7	4	.636	16-20	9	96	.653	3.07	2.96
2013	KC	AL	68	0	61	67.0	255	40	11	9	3	1	1	0	18	1	103	2	2	1	.667	47-50	1	96	.479	1.41	1.21
2014	KC	AL	65	0	60	62.1	240	37	13	10	3	1	1	0	20	0	90	9	1	3	.250	46-48	0	96	.472	1.54	1.44
2015	KC	AL	48	0	40	44.2	193	39	20	19	2	3	1	0	26	1	49	7	3	2	.600	32-37	0	94	.692	3.68	3.83
2017	Col	NL	61	0	58	57.1	235	40	24	23	7	0	1	1	26	1	70	7	3	6	.333	41-45	1	93	.623	2.86	3.61
2018	2 Tms	NL	56	0	13	46.1	212	43	30	24	2	1	0	1	32	2	47	0	2	2	.500	3-6	6	93	.697	4.33	4.66
2019	Ari	NL	40	0	27	35.2	152	25	18	18	5	0	2	0	24	2	41	6	1	2	.333	17-22	0	92	.687	3.71	4.54
2020	KC	AL	28	0	9	28.1	112	20	8	6	1	1	1	3	7	1	31	1	3	0	1.000	6-6	2	93	.580	1.98	1.91
2021	KC	AL	57	0	24	55.2	243	49	32	30	9	1	1	1	26	2	53	6	5	5	.375	8-12	8	93	.721	4.03	4.85
18	StL	NL	32	0	7	25.0	132	34	28	22	1	1	0	0	22	2	22	0	0	2	.000	0-3	2	93	.859	7.32	7.92
18	Was	NL	24	0	6	21.1	80	9	2	2	1	0	0	1	10	0	25	0	2	0	1.000	3-3	4	93	.438	1.48	0.84
	Postseason		12	0	11	11.2	49	7	3	3	0	0	0	0	6	2	15	1	0	0	-	7-7	0	95	.475	1.54	2.31
11 ML YEARS			551	0	353	543.0	2251	411	206	187	40	14	12	7	240	20	672	50	30	27	.526	220-252	45	95	.617	2.75	3.10

Jordan Holloway

Pitches: R **Bats:** R **Pos:** RP-9; SP-4   **Ht:** 6'6" **Wt:** 230 **Born:** 6/13/1996 **Age:** 26

Year	Team	Lg	G	GS	GF	IP	BFP	H	R	ER	HR	SH	SF	HB	TBB	IBB	SO	WP	W	L	Pct	Sv-Op	Hld	Vel	OPS	ERC	ERA
2021	Jaxnvl	AAA	8	6	0	31.1	134	29	20	17	5	0	1	2	14	0	29	1	0	5	.000	0--	-	-	.797	4.61	4.88
2020	Mia	NL	1	0	0	0.1	4	2	0	0	0	0	0	0	1	0	0	0	0	0	-	0-0	0	97	1.417	56.02	0.00
2021	Mia	NL	13	4	2	36.0	158	23	19	16	3	0	2	0	26	0	36	2	2	3	.400	0-0	0	96	.626	3.13	4.00
2 ML YEARS			14	4	2	36.1	162	25	19	16	3	0	2	0	27	0	36	2	2	3	.400	0-0	0	96	.644	3.45	3.96

Clay Holmes

Pitches: R **Bats:** R **Pos:** RP-69   **Ht:** 6'5" **Wt:** 245 **Born:** 3/27/1993 **Age:** 29

Year	Team	Lg	G	GS	GF	IP	BFP	H	R	ER	HR	SH	SF	HB	TBB	IBB	SO	WP	W	L	Pct	Sv-Op	Hld	Vel	OPS	ERC	ERA
2018	Pit	NL	11	4	6	26.1	129	30	21	20	2	0	1	2	23	1	21	4	1	3	.250	0-1	0	94	.824	6.99	6.84
2019	Pit	NL	35	0	10	50.0	240	45	36	31	5	0	0	9	36	1	56	4	1	2	.333	0-1	1	94	.743	5.32	5.58
2020	Pit	NL	1	0	0	1.1	6	2	0	0	0	0	0	0	0	0	1	0	0	0	-	0-0	0	92	.667	4.47	0.00
2021	2 Tms		69	0	15	70.0	292	53	32	28	5	1	1	4	29	2	78	9	8	4	.667	0-2	11	96	.580	2.80	3.60
21	Pit	NL	44	0	10	42.0	189	35	24	23	3	1	0	4	25	2	44	5	3	2	.600	0-0	6	96	.649	3.91	4.93
21	NYY	AL	25	0	5	28.0	103	18	8	5	2	0	1	0	4	0	34	4	5	2	.714	0-2	5	97	.458	1.40	1.61
4 ML YEARS			116	4	31	147.2	667	130	89	79	12	1	2	15	88	4	156	17	10	9	.526	0-4	12	95	.684	4.34	4.81

Brock Holt

Bats: L **Throws:** R **Pos:** 3B-69;PH-12;DH-5   **Ht:** 5'10" **Wt:** 180 **Born:** 6/11/1988 **Age:** 34

Year	Team	Lg	G	AB	H	2B	3B	HR	(Hm	Rd)	TB	R	RBI	RC	TBB	IBB	SO	HBP	SH	SF	SB	CS	GDP	Avg	OBP	Slg	OPS
2012	Pit	NL	24	65	19	2	1	0	(0	0)	23	6	3	10	4	0	14	0	2	1	0	0	1	.292	.329	.354	.682
2013	Bos	AL	26	59	12	2	0	0	(0	0)	14	9	11	7	7	0	4	0	3	3	1	0	0	.203	.275	.237	.513
2014	Bos	AL	106	449	126	23	5	4	(1	3)	171	68	29	56	33	0	98	2	5	3	12	2	7	.281	.331	.381	.711
2015	Bos	AL	129	454	127	27	6	2	(1	1)	172	56	45	65	46	0	97	3	4	2	8	1	7	.280	.349	.379	.727
2016	Bos	AL	94	290	74	16	0	7	(4	3)	111	45	34	36	27	0	58	3	1	3	4	3	5	.255	.322	.383	.705
2017	Bos	AL	64	140	28	6	0	0	(0	0)	34	20	7	12	19	0	34	3	0	2	2	1	3	.200	.305	.243	.548
2018	Bos	AL	109	321	89	18	2	7	(3	4)	132	41	46	48	37	2	73	7	0	2	7	7	7	.277	.362	.411	.774
2019	Bos	AL	87	259	77	14	2	3	(1	2)	104	38	31	40	28	1	57	4	0	4	1	0	4	.297	.369	.402	.771
2020	2 Tms	NL	37	95	20	6	0	0	(0	0)	26	12	5	8	9	0	24	1	0	1	1	0	3	.211	.283	.274	.557
2021	Tex	AL	77	235	49	13	1	2	(2	0)	70	21	23	25	23	0	49	1	0	1	5	1	5	.209	.281	.298	.579
20	Mil	NL	16	30	3	0	0	0	(0	0)	3	1	1	0	4	0	9	1	0	1	0	0	2	.100	.222	.100	.322
20	Was	NL	21	65	17	6	0	0	(0	0)	23	11	4	8	5	0	15	0	0	0	1	0	1	.262	.314	.354	.668
	Postseason		12	37	11	3	1	2	(0	2)	22	8	7	7	4	0	6	1	0	0	1	0	1	.297	.381	.595	.976
10 ML YEARS			753	2367	621	127	17	25	(12	13)	857	316	234	307	233	3	508	24	15	22	41	15	42	.262	.332	.362	.694

Brent Honeywell

Pitches: R **Bats:** R **Pos:** SP-2; RP-1   **Ht:** 6'2" **Wt:** 195 **Born:** 3/31/1995 **Age:** 27

Year	Team	Lg	G	GS	GF	IP	BFP	H	R	ER	HR	SH	SF	HB	TBB	IBB	SO	WP	W	L	Pct	Sv-Op	Hld	Vel	OPS	ERC	ERA
2021	Drham	AAA	31	13	5	81.2	335	74	40	36	13	0	1	3	24	0	67	5	5	4	.556	2--	-	-	.718	3.74	3.97
2021	TB	AL	3	2	0	4.1	21	5	4	4	2	0	0	0	3	0	4	0	0	0	-	0-0	0	94	.992	9.05	8.31

Rhys Hoskins

Bats: R **Throws:** R **Pos:** 1B-103;PH-6;DH-1   **Ht:** 6'4" **Wt:** 245 **Born:** 3/17/1993 **Age:** 29

Year	Team	Lg	G	AB	H	2B	3B	HR	(Hm	Rd)	TB	R	RBI	RC	TBB	IBB	SO	HBP	SH	SF	SB	CS	GDP	Avg	OBP	Slg	OPS
2017	Phi	NL	50	170	44	7	0	18	(10	8)	105	37	48	45	37	1	46	3	0	2	2	0	2	.259	.396	.618	1.014
2018	Phi	NL	153	558	137	38	0	34	(20	14)	277	89	96	97	87	2	150	9	0	5	5	3	7	.246	.354	.496	.850

Year	Team	Lg	G	AB	H	2B	3B	HR	(Hm	Rd)	TB	R	RBI	RC	TBB	IBB	SO	HBP	SH	SF	SB	CS	GDP	Avg	OBP	Slg	OPS
2019	Phi	NL	160	570	129	33	5	29	(16	13)	259	86	85	97	**116**	6	173	11	0	6	2	2	10	.226	.364	.454	.819
2020	Phi	NL	41	151	37	9	0	10	(4	6)	76	35	26	29	29	0	43	5	0	0	1	0	4	.245	.384	.503	.887
2021	Phi	NL	107	389	96	29	0	27	(9	18)	206	64	71	62	47	0	108	5	0	2	3	2	7	.247	.334	.530	.864
5 ML YEARS			511	1838	443	116	5	118	(59	59)	923	311	326	330	316	9	520	33	0	15	13	7	30	.241	.360	.502	.862

Eric Hosmer

Bats: L **Throws:** L **Pos:** 1B-131;PH-20;DH-2

HOZ-mur

Ht: 6'4" **Wt:** 226 **Born:** 10/24/1989 **Age:** 32

Year	Team	Lg	G	AB	H	2B	3B	HR	(Hm	Rd)	TB	R	RBI	RC	TBB	IBB	SO	HBP	SH	SF	SB	CS	GDP	Avg	OBP	Slg	OPS
2011	KC	AL	128	523	153	27	3	19	(3	16)	243	66	78	71	34	7	82	1	0	5	11	5	13	.293	.334	.465	.799
2012	KC	AL	152	535	124	22	2	14	(8	6)	192	65	60	61	56	4	95	2	0	5	16	1	10	.232	.304	.359	.663
2013	KC	AL	159	623	188	34	3	17	(10	7)	279	86	79	88	51	4	100	1	1	4	11	4	15	.302	.353	.448	.801
2014	KC	AL	131	503	136	35	1	9	(5	4)	200	54	58	62	35	4	93	3	0	6	4	2	12	.270	.318	.398	.716
2015	KC	AL	158	599	178	33	5	18	(10	8)	275	98	93	94	61	6	108	1	1	3	7	3	16	.297	.363	.459	.822
2016	KC	AL	158	605	161	24	1	25	(8	17)	262	80	104	87	57	5	132	1	0	4	5	3	18	.266	.328	.433	.761
2017	KC	AL	**162**	603	192	31	1	25	(16	9)	300	98	94	116	66	3	104	0	0	2	6	1	20	.318	.385	.498	.882
2018	SD	NL	157	613	155	31	2	18	(10	8)	244	72	69	77	62	10	142	1	0	1	7	4	18	.253	.322	.398	.720
2019	SD	NL	160	619	164	29	2	22	(11	11)	263	72	99	87	40	3	163	1	0	3	0	3	12	.265	.310	.425	.735
2020	SD	NL	38	143	41	6	0	9	(4	5)	74	23	36	27	9	0	28	2	0	2	4	0	3	.287	.333	.517	.851
2021	SD	NL	151	509	137	28	0	12	(7	5)	201	53	65	70	48	2	99	5	1	2	5	4	13	.269	.337	.395	.732
Postseason			37	148	38	6	1	4	(1	3)	58	21	33	22	13	2	38	0	0	4	1	1	2	.257	.309	.392	.701
11 ML YEARS			1554	5875	1629	300	20	188	(92	96)	2533	767	835	840	519	48	1146	22	3	39	76	30	150	.277	.336	.431	.767

Tanner Houck

Pitches: R **Bats:** R **Pos:** SP-13; RP-5

Ht: 6'5" **Wt:** 230 **Born:** 6/29/1996 **Age:** 26

Year	Team	Lg	G	GS	GF	IP	BFP	H	R	ER	HR	SH	SF	HB	TBB	IBB	SO	WP	W	L	Pct	Sv-Op	Hld	Vel	OPS	ERC	ERA
2021	Wrcstr	AAA	6	6	0	21.0	90	19	13	12	1	0	1	3	7	0	26	0	0	2	.000	0--	-	-	.689	3.48	5.14
2020	Bos	AL	3	3	0	17.0	63	6	2	1	0	0	1	0	9	0	21	1	3	0	1.000	0-0	0	92	.443	1.49	0.53
2021	Bos	AL	18	13	2	69.0	285	57	32	27	4	1	6	1	21	1	87	3	1	5	.167	1-1	1	94	.608	2.82	3.52
2 ML YEARS			21	16	2	86.0	348	63	34	28	5	1	7	1	30	1	108	4	4	5	.444	1-1	1	94	.579	2.53	2.93

Adrian Houser

Pitches: R **Bats:** R **Pos:** SP-26; RP-2

HOW-zer

Ht: 6'3" **Wt:** 222 **Born:** 2/2/1993 **Age:** 29

Year	Team	Lg	G	GS	GF	IP	BFP	H	R	ER	HR	SH	SF	HB	TBB	IBB	SO	WP	W	L	Pct	Sv-Op	Hld	Vel	OPS	ERC	ERA
2015	Mil	NL	2	0	2	2.0	8	1	0	0	0	0	0	2	0	0	0	0	0		-	0-0	0	94	.542	3.21	0.00
2018	Mil	NL	7	0	5	13.2	59	13	5	5	0	0	0	1	7	0	8	1	0	0		0-0	0	94	.728	3.89	3.29
2019	Mil	NL	35	18	3	111.1	462	101	49	46	14	3	3	5	37	2	117	2	6	7	.462	0-0	1	94	.710	3.68	3.72
2020	Mil	NL	12	11	1	56.0	246	63	41	33	8	0	0	4	21	0	44	1	1	6	.143	0-0	0	93	.815	5.41	5.30
2021	Mil	NL	28	26	0	142.1	599	118	61	51	12	6	1	9	64	0	105	9	10	6	.625	0-0	0	94	.662	3.51	3.22
Postseason			1	0	1	2.0	7	1	0	0	0	0	0	0	1	0	1	0	0	0		0-0	0	94	.452	1.62	0.00
5 ML YEARS			84	55	15	325.1	1374	296	156	135	34	9	4	19	131	2	274	13	17	19	.472	0-0	1	94	.709	3.90	3.73

Sam Howard

Pitches: L **Bats:** R **Pos:** RP-53; SP-1

Ht: 6'4" **Wt:** 195 **Born:** 3/5/1993 **Age:** 29

Year	Team	Lg	G	GS	GF	IP	BFP	H	R	ER	HR	SH	SF	HB	TBB	IBB	SO	WP	W	L	Pct	Sv-Op	Hld	Vel	OPS	ERC	ERA
2018	Col	NL	4	0	4	4.0	20	5	1	1	0	0	0	1	3	0	1	0	0	0		0-0	0	92	.888	7.36	2.25
2019	Col	NL	20	0	3	19.0	91	21	16	14	5	2	0	3	10	0	23	2	2	0	1.000	0-0	0	93	.895	7.04	6.63
2020	Pit	NL	22	0	4	21.0	90	17	10	9	4	0	1	3	9	0	27	0	2	3	.400	0-2	4	92	.764	4.34	3.86
2021	Pit	NL	54	1	5	45.0	199	34	29	28	7	1	2	3	32	1	60	2	3	4	.429	0-1	11	93	.727	4.58	5.60
4 ML YEARS			100	1	16	89.0	400	77	56	52	16	3	3	10	54	1	111	4	7	7	.500	0-3	15	93	.782	5.16	5.26

Spencer Howard

Pitches: R **Bats:** R **Pos:** SP-15; RP-4

Ht: 6'3" **Wt:** 210 **Born:** 7/28/1996 **Age:** 25

Year	Team	Lg	G	GS	GF	IP	BFP	H	R	ER	HR	SH	SF	HB	TBB	IBB	SO	WP	W	L	Pct	Sv-Op	Hld	Vel	OPS	ERC	ERA
2017	Wmspt	A-	9	9	0	28.1	123	22	15	14	0	0	0	2	18	0	40	5	1	1	.500	0--	-	-	.623	3.32	4.45
2018	Lakwd	A	23	23	0	112.0	465	101	52	47	6	1	4	0	40	0	147	15	9	8	.529	0--	-	-	.745	3.09	3.78
2019	3 Tms	Low	9	9	0	40.1	148	23	8	8	2	0	1	3	7	0	56	0	2	1	.667	0--	-	-	.432	1.35	1.79
2019	Rdng	AA	6	6	0	30.2	122	20	9	8	2	0	0	2	9	0	38	3	1	0	1.000	0--	-	-	.542	1.93	2.35
2021	LV	AAA	6	6	0	21.2	85	13	3	3	1	0	0	0	9	0	28	0	1	0	1.000	0--	-	-	.483	1.81	1.25
2020	Phi	NL	6	6	0	24.1	113	30	17	16	6	0	2	1	10	0	23	0	1	2	.333	0-0	0	94	.893	6.73	5.92
2021	2 Tms		19	15	1	49.2	229	53	45	41	7	0	2	3	27	0	52	5	0	5		0-0	0	94	.814	5.55	7.43
21	Phi	NL	11	7	1	28.1	127	25	19	18	2	0	1	3	17	0	31	2	0	2	.000	0-0	0	95	.751	4.39	5.72
21	Tex	AL	8	8	0	21.1	102	28	26	23	5	0	1	0	10	0	21	3	0	3	.000	0-0	0	94	.889	7.16	9.70
2 ML YEARS			25	21	1	74.0	342	83	62	57	13	0	4	4	37	0	75	5	1	7	.125	0-0	0	94	.841	5.94	6.93

Jared Hoying

Bats: L **Throws:** R **Pos:** LF-1;PH-1 **Ht:** 6'3" **Wt:** 205 **Born:** 5/18/1989 **Age:** 33

									BATTING												RUNNING			AVERAGES			
Year Team	Lg	G	AB	H	2B	3B	HR	(Hm	Rd)	TB	R	RBI	RC	TBB	IBB	SO	HBP	SH	SF	SB	CS	GDP	Avg	OBP	Slg	OPS
2016 Tex	AL	39	46	10	2	0	0	(0	0)	12	8	5	3	3	0	8	0	0	0	1	0	0	.217	.265	.261	.526
2017 Tex	AL	36	72	16	3	0	1	(1	0)	22	13	7	6	4	0	23	0	0	1	3	0	0	.222	.260	.306	.565
2021 Tor	AL	2	3	0	0	0	0	(0	0)	0	0	0	0	0	0	1	0	0	0	0	0	0	.000	.000	.000	.000
Postseason		2	1	0	0	0	0	(0	0)	0	1	0	0	0	0	1	0	0	0	0	0	0	.000	.000	.000	.000
3 ML YEARS		77	121	26	5	1	1	(1	0)	34	21	12	9	7	0	32	0	0	1	4	0	0	.215	.256	.281	.537

James Hoyt

Pitches: R **Bats:** R **Pos:** RP-9 **Ht:** 6'6" **Wt:** 230 **Born:** 9/30/1986 **Age:** 35

			HOW MUCH PITCHED				WHAT HE GAVE UP											THE RESULTS								
Year Team	Lg	G	GS	GF	IP	BFP	H	R	ER	HR	SH	SF	HB	TBB	IBB	SO	WP	W	L	Pct	Sv-Op	Hld	Vel	OPS	ERC	ERA
2021 Salt Lk	AAA	33	0	13	35.1	178	51	41	37	10	0	1	5	20	0	36	3	1	2	.333	3- -	-		1.045	9.81	9.42
2016 Hou	AL	22	0	7	22.0	91	16	12	11	5	1	1	1	9	1	28	3	1	1	.500	0-1	1	93	.707	3.55	4.50
2017 Hou	AL	43	0	7	49.1	211	51	24	24	7	0	0	2	14	0	66	4	1	0	1.000	0-0	7	93	.748	4.25	4.38
2018 Hou	AL	1	0	0	0.1	3	1	0	0	0	0	0	0	1	0	0	0	0	0	-	0-0	0	93	1.167	29.63	0.00
2019 Cle	AL	8	0	2	8.1	32	6	2	2	2	0	0	0	2	0	10	0	0	0	-	0-0	1	94	.717	2.87	2.16
2020 Mia	NL	24	0	3	14.2	62	9	2	2	1	0	1	1	8	1	20	2	2	0	1.000	0-0	5	88	.598	2.46	1.23
2021 LAA	AL	9	0	3	8.0	46	12	10	6	0	0	0	2	7	0	11	0	0	0	-	0-0	0	92	.916	8.91	6.75
Postseason		2	0	0	1.0	4	1	1	1	1	0	0	0	0	0	1	0	0	0	-	0-0	0	88	1.250	7.45	9.00
6 ML YEARS		107	0	22	102.2	445	95	50	45	15	1	2	6	41	2	135	9	4	1	.800	0-1	14	93	.738	4.14	3.94

Dakota Hudson

Pitches: R **Bats:** R **Pos:** SP-1; RP-1 **Ht:** 6'5" **Wt:** 215 **Born:** 9/15/1994 **Age:** 27

			HOW MUCH PITCHED				WHAT HE GAVE UP											THE RESULTS								
Year Team	Lg	G	GS	GF	IP	BFP	H	R	ER	HR	SH	SF	HB	TBB	IBB	SO	WP	W	L	Pct	Sv-Op	Hld	Vel	OPS	ERC	ERA
2018 StL	NL	26	0	2	27.1	118	19	9	8	0	0	2	1	18	0	19	2	4	1	.800	0-0	11	96	.559	2.82	2.63
2019 StL	NL	33	32	1	174.2	757	160	80	65	22	3	7	9	86	8	136	5	16	7	.696	1-1	0	94	.742	4.32	3.35
2020 StL	NL	8	8	0	39.0	151	24	13	12	5	0	0	1	15	1	31	0	3	2	.600	0-0	0	92	.583	2.34	2.77
2021 StL	NL	2	1	0	8.2	34	7	2	2	0	0	0	1	1	0	6	1	1	0	1.000	0-0	0	92	.546	1.90	2.08
Postseason		2	2	0	5.0	28	10	11	5	1	0	2	0	3	1	2	0	0	1	.000	0-0	0	93	1.160	11.75	9.00
4 ML YEARS		69	41	3	249.2	1060	210	104	87	27	3	9	12	120	9	192	8	24	10	.706	1-1	11	94	.693	3.74	3.14

Daniel Hudson

Pitches: R **Bats:** R **Pos:** RP-54 **Ht:** 6'3" **Wt:** 215 **Born:** 3/9/1987 **Age:** 35

			HOW MUCH PITCHED				WHAT HE GAVE UP											THE RESULTS								
Year Team	Lg	G	GS	GF	IP	BFP	H	R	ER	HR	SH	SF	HB	TBB	IBB	SO	WP	W	L	Pct	Sv-Op	Hld	Vel	OPS	ERC	ERA
2009 CWS	AL	6	2	1	18.2	82	16	9	7	3	0	1	1	9	0	14	1	1	1	.500	0-0	0	93	.711	4.15	3.38
2010 2 Tms		14	14	0	95.1	372	68	26	26	8	2	2	4	27	1	84	5	8	2	.800	0-0	0	93	.579	2.26	2.45
2011 Ari	NL	33	33	0	222.0	921	217	98	86	17	6	6	8	50	1	169	4	16	12	.571	0-0	0	93	.694	3.26	3.49
2012 Ari	NL	9	9	0	45.1	202	62	37	37	9	2	1	0	12	0	37	2	3	2	.600	0-0	0	95	.910	6.56	7.35
2014 Ari	NL	3	0	0	2.2	13	4	4	4	0	0	0	0	0	0	2	0	0	1	.000	0-0	0	95	.769	4.08	13.50
2015 Ari	NL	64	1	13	67.2	290	64	34	29	7	1	3	0	25	2	71	5	4	3	.571	4-6	20	96	.691	3.58	3.86
2016 Ari	NL	70	0	17	60.1	268	65	40	35	6	0	0	4	23	3	58	5	3	2	.600	5-7	17	96	.753	4.51	5.22
2017 Pit	NL	71	0	18	61.2	271	57	34	30	7	1	2	5	33	1	66	4	2	7	.222	0-2	21	96	.761	4.63	4.38
2018 LAD	NL	40	1	11	46.0	197	38	25	21	6	0	0	4	18	1	44	3	3	2	.600	0-1	3	95	.653	3.54	4.11
2019 2 Tms	NL	69	1	25	73.0	304	56	25	20	8	1	5	4	27	2	71	2	9	3	.750	8-12	11	96	.650	2.91	2.47
2020 Was	NL	21	0	15	20.2	92	15	15	14	6	1	0	3	11	0	28	0	3	2	.600	10-15	0	96	.786	4.83	6.10
2021 2 Tms	NL	54	0	8	51.2	210	40	22	19	8	0	4	0	16	1	75	3	5	3	.625	0-3	16	97	.672	2.81	3.31
10 CWS	AL	3	3	0	15.2	71	17	11	11	1	1	1	0	11	0	14	2	1	1	.500	0-0	0	93	.797	5.69	6.32
10	AL	11	11	0	79.2	301	51	15	15	7	1	1	4	16	1	70	3	7	1	.875	0-0	0	92	.531	1.70	1.69
19 Tor	AL	45	1	11	48.0	207	38	18	16	5	1	3	3	23	0	48	1	6	3	.667	2-4	8	96	.678	3.45	3.00
19 Was	NL	24	0	14	25.0	97	18	7	4	3	0	2	1	4	2	23	1	3	0	1.000	6-8	3	96	.593	1.93	1.44
21 Was	NL	31	0	2	32.2	127	23	9	8	4	0	2	0	7	0	48	1	4	1	.800	0-2	14	97	.575	2.00	2.20
21 SD	NL	23	0	6	19.0	83	17	13	11	4	0	2	0	9	1	27	2	1	2	.333	0-1	2	97	.827	4.37	5.21
Postseason		10	1	6	15.0	69	20	9	9	2	0	0	1	4	2	16	0	1	1	.500	4-4	1	96	.878	5.72	5.40
12 ML YEARS		454	61	108	765.0	3222	702	369	328	85	14	24	33	250	12	719	34	57	40	.588	27-46	88	95	.700	3.55	3.86

Tommy Hunter

Pitches: R **Bats:** R **Pos:** RP-3; SP-1 **Ht:** 6'3" **Wt:** 250 **Born:** 7/3/1986 **Age:** 35

			HOW MUCH PITCHED				WHAT HE GAVE UP											THE RESULTS								
Year Team	Lg	G	GS	GF	IP	BFP	H	R	ER	HR	SH	SF	HB	TBB	IBB	SO	WP	W	L	Pct	Sv-Op	Hld	Vel	OPS	ERC	ERA
2008 Tex	AL	3	3	0	11.0	63	23	20	20	4	0	1	4	3	0	9	0	0	2	.000	0-0	0	91	1.144	12.66	16.36
2009 Tex	AL	19	19	0	112.0	475	113	55	51	13	2	1	2	33	2	64	6	9	6	.600	0-0	0	89	.736	3.86	4.10
2010 Tex	AL	23	22	0	128.0	536	126	55	53	21	3	2	2	33	0	68	1	13	4	.765	0-0	0	90	.740	3.95	3.73
2011 2 Tms	AL	20	11	2	84.2	367	100	50	44	12	2	2	4	15	1	45	0	4	4	.500	0-1	1	92	.782	4.65	4.68
2012 Bal	AL	33	20	5	133.2	573	161	85	81	32	3	6	4	27	2	77	0	7	8	.467	0-1	0	96	.864	5.63	5.45
2013 Bal	AL	68	0	20	86.1	336	71	28	27	11	1	0	2	14	1	68	0	6	5	.545	4-6	21	96	.617	2.53	2.81
2014 Bal	AL	60	0	24	60.2	241	55	22	20	4	1	2	1	12	3	45	2	3	2	.600	11-17	12	96	.643	2.65	2.97
2015 2 Tms		58	0	17	60.1	249	61	29	28	7	1	3	1	14	2	47	2	4	2	.667	1-2	7	96	.711	3.65	4.18
2016 2 Tms	AL	33	0	8	34.0	139	35	13	12	1	1	0	2	8	1	23	0	2	2	.500	0-1	1	94	.678	3.43	3.18
2017 TB	AL	61	0	11	58.2	228	43	18	17	6	0	0	1	14	0	64	1	3	5	.375	1-1	25	96	.588	2.21	2.61
2018 Phi	NL	65	0	10	64.0	270	65	28	27	6	1	1	3	15	1	51	1	5	4	.556	4-6	25	96	.745	3.62	3.80
2019 Phi	NL	5	0	1	5.1	18	2	0	0	0	0	0	0	0	0	5	0	0	0	-	0-0	1	94	.222	0.31	0.00
2020 Phi	NL	24	0	1	24.2	102	22	11	11	2	1	0	3	6	0	25	0	0	1	.000	1-3	8	93	.698	3.27	4.01
2021 NYM	NL	4	1	0	8.0	33	4	0	0	0	1	0	1	3	0	6	1	0	0	-	0-0	0	92	.443	1.37	0.00

Scott Hurst

Bats: L Throws: R Pos: CF-6;PR-2;PH-1   Ht: 5'10" Wt: 175 Born: 3/25/1996 Age: 26

Year	Team	Lg	G	AB	H	2B	3B	HR	(Hm	Rd)	TB	R	RBI	RC	TBB	IBB	SO	HBP	SH	SF	SB	CS	GDP	Avg	OBP	Slg	OPS
2021	Memp	AAA	77	266	54	12	1	4	(-	-)	80	39	18	-	33	0	94	1	3	2	5	4	6	.203	.291	.301	.592
2021	StL	NL	7	5	0	0	0	0	(0	0)	0	0	0	0	0	0	1	0	0	0	0	0	0	.000	.000	.000	.000

Drew Hutchison

Pitches: R Bats: L Pos: RP-7; SP-2   Ht: 6'3" Wt: 215 Born: 8/22/1990 Age: 31

Year	Team	Lg	G	GS	GF	IP	BFP	H	R	ER	HR	SH	SF	HB	TBB	IBB	SO	WP	W	L	Pct	Sv-Op	Hld	Vel	OPS	ERC	ERA
2021	Toledo	AAA	19	19	0	88.1	379	78	42	37	8	1	1	6	41	0	89	7	8	3	.727	0- -	0	-	.688	3.91	3.77
2012	Tor	AL	11	11	0	58.2	257	59	31	30	8	1	1	5	20	0	49	1	5	3	.625	0-0	0	91	.759	4.43	4.60
2014	Tor	AL	32	32	0	184.2	786	173	92	92	23	4	10	7	60	1	184	4	11	13	.458	0-0	0	92	.723	3.70	4.48
2015	Tor	AL	30	28	0	150.1	664	179	103	93	22	0	6	11	44	0	129	7	13	5	.722	0-0	0	92	.825	5.44	5.57
2016	2 Tms		9	3	3	24.0	104	28	14	14	7	2	0	2	7	0	22	0	1	0	1.000	0-1	0	92	.903	6.24	5.25
2018	2 Tms		16	5	6	42.2	199	50	32	32	9	3	4	2	26	0	31	5	2	2	.500	0-0	0	90	.922	7.17	6.75
2021	Det	AL	9	2	0	21.1	91	20	11	5	1	1	2	0	11	0	10	1	3	1	.750	0-0	0	92	.682	3.89	2.11
16	Tor	AL	3	2	0	12.2	53	13	7	7	4	0	0	1	4	0	12	0	1	0	1.000	0-1	0	92	.923	5.98	4.97
16	Pit	NL	6	1	3	11.1	51	15	7	7	2	1	2	1	3	0	10	0	0	0	-	0-0	0	92	.880	6.50	5.56
18	Phi	NL	11	0	6	21.1	94	21	11	11	4	1	2	1	13	0	19	4	1	1	.500	0-0	0	91	.857	5.89	4.64
18	Tex	AL	5	5	0	21.1	105	29	21	21	5	2	2	1	13	0	12	1	1	1	.500	0-0	0	90	.981	8.50	8.86
6 ML YEARS			107	81	9	481.2	2101	509	283	266	69	10	25	27	168	1	425	18	35	24	.593	0-2	0	92	.785	4.74	4.97

Andy Ibanez

Bats: R Throws: R Pos: 2B-31;DH-16;1B-12;3B-11;PH-10;LF-1   Ht: 5'11" Wt: 205 Born: 4/3/1993 Age: 29

Year	Team	Lg	G	AB	H	2B	3B	HR	(Hm	Rd)	TB	R	RBI	RC	TBB	IBB	SO	HBP	SH	SF	SB	CS	GDP	Avg	OBP	Slg	OPS
2021	RdRck	AAA	30	114	39	11	1	7	(-	-)	73	21	27	-	12	1	18	2	0	1	1	0	1	.342	.411	.640	1.051
2021	Tex	AL	76	253	70	15	2	7	(5	2)	110	31	25	33	15	0	35	2	1	1	0	0	6	.277	.321	.435	.756

Jose Iglesias

Bats: R Throws: R Pos: SS-119;2B-18;PH-4;PR-2;DH-1   ee-GLAY-see-us   Ht: 5'11" Wt: 195 Born: 1/5/1990 Age: 32

Year	Team	Lg	G	AB	H	2B	3B	HR	(Hm	Rd)	TB	R	RBI	RC	TBB	IBB	SO	HBP	SH	SF	SB	CS	GDP	Avg	OBP	Slg	OPS
2011	Bos	AL	10	6	2	0	0	0	(0	0)	2	3	0	0	0	0	2	0	0	0	0	0	0	.333	.333	.333	.667
2012	Bos	AL	25	68	8	2	0	1	(0	1)	13	5	2	0	4	0	16	3	2	0	1	0	2	.118	.200	.191	.391
2013	2 Tms	AL	109	350	106	16	2	3	(1	2)	135	39	29	45	15	0	60	11	4	2	5	2	1	.303	.349	.386	.735
2015	Det	AL	120	416	125	17	3	2	(1	1)	154	44	23	47	25	2	44	6	4	3	11	8	10	.300	.347	.370	.717
2016	Det	AL	137	467	119	26	0	4	(1	3)	157	57	32	47	28	1	50	8	7	3	7	4	12	.255	.306	.336	.643
2017	Det	AL	130	463	118	33	1	6	(4	2)	171	56	54	54	21	0	65	1	3	1	7	4	6	.255	.288	.369	.657
2018	Det	AL	125	432	116	31	3	5	(3	2)	168	43	48	60	19	0	47	8	3	2	15	6	11	.269	.310	.389	.699
2019	Cin	NL	146	504	145	21	3	11	(9	2)	205	62	59	61	20	3	70	3	1	6	6	6	17	.288	.318	.407	.724
2020	Bal	AL	39	142	53	17	0	3	(1	2)	79	16	24	32	3	0	17	4	0	1	0	0	1	.373	.400	.556	.956
2021	2 Tms	AL	137	483	131	27	2	9	(5	4)	189	65	48	58	21	0	75	6	0	1	5	2	10	.271	.309	.391	.701
13	Bos	AL	63	215	71	10	2	1	(1	1)	88	27	19	34	11	0	30	6	3	2	3	1	4	.330	.376	.409	.785
13	Det	AL	46	135	35	6	0	2	(1	1)	47	12	10	11	4	0	30	5	4	0	2	1	3	.259	.306	.348	.654
21	LAA	AL	114	424	110	23	1	8	(5	3)	159	57	41	46	18	0	66	4	0	1	5	2	10	.259	.295	.375	.670
21	Bos	AL	23	59	21	4	1	1	(0	1)	30	8	7	12	3	0	9	2	0	0	0	0	0	.356	.406	.508	.915
Postseason			11	26	6	0	0	0	(0	0)	6	2	1	0	1	0	5	1	3	0	0	1	1	.231	.286	.231	.516
10 ML YEARS			978	3331	923	190	14	44	(25	19)	1273	390	319	404	156	6	446	50	24	15	57	32	76	.277	.318	.382	.700

Raisel Iglesias

Pitches: R Bats: R Pos: RP-65   rye-SELL   Ht: 6'2" Wt: 190 Born: 1/4/1990 Age: 32

Year	Team	Lg	G	GS	GF	IP	BFP	H	R	ER	HR	SH	SF	HB	TBB	IBB	SO	WP	W	L	Pct	Sv-Op	Hld	Vel	OPS	ERC	ERA
2015	Cin	NL	18	16	1	95.1	395	81	45	44	11	4	0	7	28	0	104	2	3	7	.300	0-0	0	92	.682	3.24	4.15
2016	Cin	NL	37	5	15	78.1	325	63	22	22	7	1	2	5	26	1	83	3	3	6	.600	6-8	7	93	.623	2.90	2.53
2017	Cin	NL	63	0	57	76.0	306	57	22	21	5	1	1	1	27	1	92	1	3	3	.500	28-30	0	96	.576	2.43	2.49
2018	Cin	NL	66	0	57	72.0	291	52	22	19	12	1	2	2	25	2	80	2	2	5	.286	30-34	0	95	.644	2.88	2.38
2019	Cin	NL	68	0	55	67.0	279	61	31	31	12	1	1	2	21	4	89	3	3	12	.200	34-40	3	95	.743	3.81	4.16
2020	Cin	NL	22	0	17	23.0	91	16	11	7	1	1	1	2	5	1	31	0	4	3	.571	8-10	2	96	.510	1.64	2.74
2021	LAA	AL	65	0	59	70.0	285	53	25	20	11	1	3	1	12	0	103	2	7	5	.583	34-39	0	94	.610	2.34	2.57
Postseason			2	0	0	1.2	10	2	4	3	2	0	0	1	0	0	3	0	0	0	-	0-0	0	98	1.643	23.20	16.20
7 ML YEARS			339	21	261	481.2	1960	383	178	164	59	10	10	19	144	9	582	13	25	37	.403	140-161	12	94	.641	2.87	3.06

Ender Inciarte

Bats: L Throws: L Pos: CF-37;PH-14;LF-4;PR-2   END-er in-see-ARR-tay   Ht: 5'11" Wt: 190 Born: 10/29/1990 Age: 31

Year Team	Lg	G	AB	H	2B	3B	HR	(Hm	Rd)	TB	R	RBI	RC	TBB	IBB	SO	HBP	SH	SF	SB	CS	GDP	Avg	OBP	Slg	OPS
2021 Lsvlle	AAA	15	59	17	3	0	0	(-	-)	20	7	7	-	6	0	10	0	0	0	0	1	0	.288	.354	.339	.693
2014 Ari	NL	118	418	116	18	2	4	(1	3)	150	54	27	49	25	0	53	0	4	0	19	3	3	.278	.318	.359	.677
2015 Ari	NL	132	524	159	27	5	6	(1	5)	214	73	45	69	26	0	58	4	2	5	21	10	8	.303	.338	.408	.747
2016 Atl	NL	131	522	152	24	7	3	(1	2)	199	85	29	58	45	5	68	4	5	2	16	7	8	.291	.351	.381	.732
2017 Atl	NL	158	662	201	27	5	11	(6	5)	271	93	57	95	49	3	94	0	3	4	22	9	8	.304	.350	.409	.759
2018 Atl	NL	156	597	158	27	6	10	(3	7)	227	83	61	70	49	1	86	6	4	4	28	14	6	.265	.325	.380	.705
2019 Atl	NL	65	199	49	11	2	5	(2	3)	79	30	24	32	26	2	41	4	0	1	7	1	1	.246	.343	.397	.740
2020 Atl	NL	46	116	22	2	1	1	(0	1)	29	17	10	9	12	0	25	0	1	2	4	1	0	.190	.262	.250	.512
2021 Atl	NL	52	79	17	2	0	2	(0	2)	25	11	10	7	7	0	22	0	2	1	1	0	1	.215	.276	.316	.592
Postseason		4	13	3	0	0	0	(0	0)	3	0	0	1	0	0	4	0	1	0	0	0	0	.231	.231	.231	.462
8 ML YEARS		858	3117	874	138	28	42	(14	28)	1194	446	263	389	239	11	447	18	21	19	118	45	35	.280	.333	.383	.716

Jonathan India

Bats: R Throws: R Pos: 2B-148;PH-4   Ht: 6'0" Wt: 200 Born: 12/15/1996 Age: 25

Year Team	Lg	G	AB	H	2B	3B	HR	(Hm	Rd)	TB	R	RBI	RC	TBB	IBB	SO	HBP	SH	SF	SB	CS	GDP	Avg	OBP	Slg	OPS
2021 Cin	NL	150	532	143	34	2	21	(9	12)	244	98	69	99	71	1	141	23	1	4	12	3	13	.269	.376	.459	.835

Cole Irvin

Pitches: L Bats: L Pos: SP-32   Ht: 6'4" Wt: 217 Born: 1/31/1994 Age: 28

Year Team	Lg	G	GS	GF	IP	BFP	H	R	ER	HR	SH	SF	HB	TBB	IBB	SO	WP	W	L	Pct	Sv-Op	Hld	Vel	OPS	ERC	ERA
2019 Phi	NL	16	3	1	41.2	181	45	28	27	7	1	2	3	13	1	31	1	2	1	.667	1-1	0	90	.796	4.96	5.83
2020 Phi	NL	3	0	1	3.2	22	11	7	7	1	0	0	0	1	0	4	0	0	1	.000	0-0	0	92	1.355	19.91	17.18
2021 Oak	AL	32	32	0	178.1	768	195	94	84	23	4	2	9	42	0	125	3	10	15	.400	0-0	0	91	.746	4.33	4.24
3 ML YEARS		51	35	2	223.2	971	251	129	118	31	5	4	12	56	1	160	4	12	17	.414	1-1	0	91	.770	4.64	4.75

Kyle Isbel

Bats: L Throws: R Pos: RF-14;CF-9;LF-4;PH-3;DH-2;PR-1   Ht: 5'11" Wt: 190 Born: 3/3/1997 Age: 25

Year Team	Lg	G	AB	H	2B	3B	HR	(Hm	Rd)	TB	R	RBI	RC	TBB	IBB	SO	HBP	SH	SF	SB	CS	GDP	Avg	OBP	Slg	OPS
2021 Omha	AAA	105	394	105	18	3	15	(-	-)	174	62	55	-	45	2	91	10	0	2	22	5	7	.266	.355	.442	.796
2021 KC	AL	28	76	21	5	2	1	(1	0)	33	16	7	13	7	0	23	0	0	0	2	0	0	.276	.337	.434	.772

Tyler Ivey

Pitches: R Bats: R Pos: SP-1   Ht: 6'4" Wt: 195 Born: 5/12/1996 Age: 26

Year Team	Lg	G	GS	GF	IP	BFP	H	R	ER	HR	SH	SF	HB	TBB	IBB	SO	WP	W	L	Pct	Sv-Op	Hld	Vel	OPS	ERC	ERA
2021 Hou	AL	1	1	0	4.2	20	6	4	4	1	0	0	0	1	0	3	1	0	0	-	0-0	0	90	.876	5.99	7.71

Alex Jackson

Bats: R Throws: R Pos: C-43;PH-10;RF-1;PR-1   Ht: 6'2" Wt: 215 Born: 12/25/1995 Age: 26

Year Team	Lg	G	AB	H	2B	3B	HR	(Hm	Rd)	TB	R	RBI	RC	TBB	IBB	SO	HBP	SH	SF	SB	CS	GDP	Avg	OBP	Slg	OPS
2021 Gwnntt	AAA	30	108	31	9	1	11	(-	-)	75	21	36	-	11	1	35	3	0	1	1	0	1	.287	.366	.694	1.060
2019 Atl	NL	4	13	0	0	0	0	(0	0)	0	0	0	1	1	1	5	1	0	0	0	0	1	.000	.133	.000	.133
2020 Atl	NL	5	7	2	1	0	0	(0	0)	3	0	0	0	0	0	4	0	0	0	0	0	1	.286	.286	.429	.714
2021 2 Tms	NL	52	131	18	4	0	3	(2	1)	31	13	12	11	13	1	73	7	0	0	0	0	0	.137	.252	.237	.488
21 Atl	NL	10	23	1	0	0	0	(0	0)	1	2	0	0	2	1	13	3	0	0	0	0	0	.043	.214	.043	.258
21 Mia	NL	42	108	17	4	0	3	(2	1)	30	11	12	11	11	0	60	4	0	0	0	0	0	.157	.260	.278	.538
3 ML YEARS		61	151	20	5	0	3	(2	1)	34	13	12	11	14	2	82	8	0	0	0	0	2	.132	.243	.225	.468

Andre Jackson

Pitches: R Bats: R Pos: RP-3   Ht: 6'3" Wt: 210 Born: 5/1/1996 Age: 26

Year Team	Lg	G	GS	GF	IP	BFP	H	R	ER	HR	SH	SF	HB	TBB	IBB	SO	WP	W	L	Pct	Sv-Op	Hld	Vel	OPS	ERC	ERA
2021 Tulsa	AA	15	13	0	63.1	253	46	24	23	12	0	0	4	20	0	75	4	3	2	.600	0-	-	-	.657	3.14	3.27
2021 OkCity	AAA	6	5	0	26.1	114	26	16	15	6	0	1	0	9	0	23	2	2	3	.400	0-	-	-	.778	4.55	5.13
2021 LAD	NL	3	0	1	11.2	50	10	3	3	1	2	0	0	6	0	10	0	0	1	.000	1-1	0	92	.714	3.63	2.31

Jay Jackson

Pitches: R Bats: R Pos: RP-22; SP-1   Ht: 6'1" Wt: 195 Born: 10/27/1987 Age: 34

Year Team	Lg	G	GS	GF	IP	BFP	H	R	ER	HR	SH	SF	HB	TBB	IBB	SO	WP	W	L	Pct	Sv-Op	Hld	Vel	OPS	ERC	ERA
2021 Scrmto	AAA	10	0	2	14.0	48	5	2	2	1	0	0	1	1	0	24	0	1	0	1.000	0- -	-	-	.295	0.52	1.29
2015 SD	NL	6	0	1	4.1	20	7	3	3	0	0	0	1	1	0	4	0	0	0	-	0-0	0	95	.874	6.40	6.23
2019 Mil	NL	28	0	9	30.1	132	22	15	15	6	1	2	2	18	1	47	0	1	0	1.000	0-0	2	94	.724	4.15	4.45
2021 SF	NL	23	1	4	21.2	90	15	9	9	3	1	1	0	12	0	28	0	2	1	.667	0-2	3	95	.685	3.28	3.74
3 ML YEARS		57	1	14	56.1	242	44	27	27	9	2	3	2	31	1	79	0	3	1	.750	0-2	5	95	.723	3.97	4.31

Luke Jackson

Pitches: R **Bats:** R **Pos:** RP-71
Ht: 6'2" **Wt:** 210 **Born:** 8/24/1991 **Age:** 30

Year	Team	Lg	G	GS	GF	IP	BFP	H	R	ER	HR	SH	SF	HB	TBB	IBB	SO	WP	W	L	Pct	Sv-Op	Hld	Vel	OPS	ERC	ERA
2015	Tex	AL	7	0	4	6.1	27	5	3	3	1	0	0	0	2	0	6	1	0	0	-	0-0	0	96	.619	2.81	4.26
2016	Tex	AL	8	0	2	11.2	62	22	14	14	4	0	1	0	8	0	3	0	0	0	-	0-0	0	94	1.201	13.93	10.80
2017	Atl	NL	43	0	17	50.2	224	55	26	26	4	1	2	4	19	4	33	4	2	0	1.000	0-0	1	95	.759	4.50	4.62
2018	Atl	NL	35	0	11	40.2	184	41	22	20	3	1	2	2	21	3	46	6	1	2	.333	1-2	3	94	.742	4.39	4.43
2019	Atl	NL	70	0	35	72.2	315	76	34	31	10	1	0	2	26	4	106	3	9	2	.818	18-25	9	96	.733	4.46	3.84
2020	Atl	NL	19	0	3	26.1	132	39	23	20	2	0	4	2	13	0	20	3	2	0	1.000	0-0	1	94	.852	7.39	6.84
2021	Atl	NL	71	0	5	63.2	261	45	15	14	6	1	2	2	29	2	70	3	2	2	.500	0-4	31	96	.609	2.78	1.98
	Postseason		3	0	0	2.2	18	6	4	3	1	0	0	1	2	0	6	0	0	0	-	0-0	1	96	1.167	17.71	10.13
	7 ML YEARS		253	0	77	272.0	1205	283	137	128	30	4	11	12	118	13	284	20	16	6	.727	19-31	45	95	.747	4.60	4.24

Josh James

Pitches: R **Bats:** R **Pos:** RP-5
Ht: 6'3" **Wt:** 234 **Born:** 3/8/1993 **Age:** 29

Year	Team	Lg	G	GS	GF	IP	BFP	H	R	ER	HR	SH	SF	HB	TBB	IBB	SO	WP	W	L	Pct	Sv-Op	Hld	Vel	OPS	ERC	ERA
2021	SgrLnd	AAA	18	0	4	17.2	76	13	4	3	0	0	0	4	6	0	24	5	1	2	.333	0- -	-	-	.545	2.54	1.53
2018	Hou	AL	6	3	0	23.0	90	15	6	6	3	0	0	2	7	0	29	0	2	0	1.000	0-0	2	97	.605	2.45	2.35
2019	Hou	AL	49	1	18	61.1	266	46	34	32	10	0	0	4	35	0	100	6	5	1	.833	1-3	6	97	.694	4.02	4.70
2020	Hou	AL	13	2	1	17.1	83	15	14	14	4	0	0	2	17	0	21	2	1	0	1.000	0-2	4	96	.894	7.35	7.27
2021	Hou	AL	5	0	5	5.0	21	4	3	3	1	0	0	0	2	0	8	2	0	0	-	0-0	0	95	.759	3.57	5.40
	Postseason		14	0	2	15.1	72	19	14	12	5	0	0	0	10	0	24	0	2	1	.667	0-2	0	98	1.000	8.67	7.04
	4 ML YEARS		73	6	24	106.2	461	80	57	55	18	0	0	8	61	0	158	10	8	1	.889	1-5	12	97	.714	4.13	4.64

Travis Jankowski

Bats: L **Throws:** R **Pos:** CF-45;PH-26;RF-8;LF-6;PR-4
Ht: 6'2" **Wt:** 190 **Born:** 6/15/1991 **Age:** 31

Year	Team	Lg	G	AB	H	2B	3B	HR	(Hm	Rd)	TB	R	RBI	RC	TBB	IBB	SO	HBP	SH	SF	SB	CS	GDP	Avg	OBP	Slg	OPS
2021	LV	AAA	19	56	17	4	0	0	(-	-)	21	16	7	-	15	1	9	0	1	0	4	3	0	.304	.451	.375	.826
2015	SD	NL	34	90	19	2	2	2	(0	2)	31	9	12	10	4	0	24	0	2	0	2	1	1	.211	.245	.344	.589
2016	SD	NL	131	335	82	13	2	2	(1	1)	105	53	12	34	42	0	100	2	3	0	30	12	5	.245	.332	.313	.646
2017	SD	NL	27	75	14	2	0	0	(0	0)	16	10	1	5	9	0	28	1	2	0	4	0	2	.187	.282	.213	.496
2018	SD	NL	117	347	90	12	3	4	(3	1)	120	45	17	42	37	0	73	1	2	0	24	7	7	.259	.332	.346	.678
2019	SD	NL	25	22	4	0	0	0	(0	0)	4	4	0	0	2	0	4	0	0	0	2	2	0	.182	.250	.182	.432
2020	Cin	NL	16	15	1	0	0	0	(0	0)	1	3	0	0	2	0	7	0	0	0	2	1	0	.067	.176	.067	.243
2021	Phi	NL	76	131	33	6	2	1	(1	0)	46	24	10	22	22	4	29	1	2	0	5	0	1	.252	.364	.351	.715
	Postseason		1	0	0	0	0	0	(0	0)	0	0	0	0	0	0	0	0	0	0	1	0	0	-	-	-	-
	7 ML YEARS		426	1015	243	35	9	9	(5	4)	323	148	52	113	118	4	265	5	11	0	69	23	17	.239	.322	.318	.640

Mickey Jannis

Pitches: R **Bats:** R **Pos:** RP-1
Ht: 5'9" **Wt:** 195 **Born:** 12/16/1987 **Age:** 34

Year	Team	Lg	G	GS	GF	IP	BFP	H	R	ER	HR	SH	SF	HB	TBB	IBB	SO	WP	W	L	Pct	Sv-Op	Hld	Vel	OPS	ERC	ERA
2021	Norfolk	AAA	13	5	3	47.0	206	45	30	26	6	1	5	3	25	0	29	7	0	5	.000	1- -	-	-	.792	4.91	4.98
2021	Bowie	AA	6	6	0	29.0	138	42	26	26	7	0	1	1	13	0	20	1	0	2	.000	0- -	-	-	1.007	8.49	8.07
2021	Bal	AL	1	0	0	3.1	21	8	7	7	3	0	0	0	4	0	1	0	0	0	-	0-0	0	88	1.689	27.99	18.90

Danny Jansen

Bats: R **Throws:** R **Pos:** C-69;PH-4;PR-3
Ht: 6'2" **Wt:** 225 **Born:** 4/15/1995 **Age:** 27

Year	Team	Lg	G	AB	H	2B	3B	HR	(Hm	Rd)	TB	R	RBI	RC	TBB	IBB	SO	HBP	SH	SF	SB	CS	GDP	Avg	OBP	Slg	OPS
2018	Tor	AL	31	81	20	6	0	3	(1	2)	35	12	8	14	9	0	17	4	0	1	0	0	1	.247	.347	.432	.779
2019	Tor	AL	107	347	72	12	1	13	(8	5)	125	41	43	40	31	1	79	4	1	1	0	1	8	.207	.279	.360	.640
2020	Tor	AL	43	120	22	3	0	6	(4	2)	43	18	20	17	21	0	31	2	3	1	0	0	0	.183	.313	.358	.671
2021	Tor	AL	70	184	41	13	0	11	(5	6)	87	32	28	24	17	0	44	3	1	0	0	0	4	.223	.299	.473	.772
	Postseason		2	5	2	0	0	2	(0	2)	8	2	2	1	0	0	0	0	0	0	0	0	0	.400	.400	1.600	2.000
	4 ML YEARS		251	732	155	34	1	33	(18	15)	290	103	99	95	78	1	171	13	5	3	0	1	14	.212	.298	.396	.694

Kenley Jansen

Pitches: R **Bats:** B **Pos:** RP-69
KEN-lee JANN-sen
Ht: 6'5" **Wt:** 265 **Born:** 9/30/1987 **Age:** 34

Year	Team	Lg	G	GS	GF	IP	BFP	H	R	ER	HR	SH	SF	HB	TBB	IBB	SO	WP	W	L	Pct	Sv-Op	Hld	Vel	OPS	ERC	ERA
2010	LAD	NL	25	0	8	27.0	109	12	2	2	0	1	0	1	15	1	41	1	1	0	1.000	4-4	5	94	.422	1.40	0.67
2011	LAD	NL	51	0	13	53.2	218	30	17	17	3	0	1	2	26	0	96	0	2	1	.667	5-6	9	94	.494	1.96	2.85
2012	LAD	NL	65	0	40	65.0	252	33	18	17	6	0	1	3	22	1	99	3	5	3	.625	25-32	8	92	.504	1.55	2.35
2013	LAD	NL	75	0	45	76.2	292	48	16	16	6	0	0	3	18	1	111	0	4	3	.571	28-32	16	94	.509	1.65	1.88
2014	LAD	NL	68	0	57	65.1	268	55	20	20	5	1	2	0	19	2	101	2	2	3	.400	44-49	0	94	.610	2.60	2.76
2015	LAD	NL	54	0	50	52.1	200	33	14	14	6	0	2	2	8	0	80	0	2	1	.667	36-38	1	93	.513	1.58	2.41
2016	LAD	NL	71	0	63	68.2	251	35	14	14	4	3	1	2	11	2	104	1	3	2	.600	47-53	0	94	.446	1.03	1.83
2017	LAD	NL	65	0	57	68.1	258	44	11	10	5	0	0	2	7	0	109	0	5	0	1.000	41-42	1	95	.476	1.35	1.32
2018	LAD	NL	69	0	59	71.2	289	54	28	24	13	0	1	2	17	1	82	0	1	5	.167	38-42	0	94	.635	2.68	3.01
2019	LAD	NL	62	0	51	63.0	263	51	28	26	9	0	3	4	16	0	80	2	5	3	.625	33-41	0	93	.653	2.92	3.71

HOW MUCH PITCHED						WHAT HE GAVE UP											THE RESULTS								
Year Team	Lg	G	GS	GF	IP	BFP	H	R	ER	HR	SH	SF	HB	TBB	IBB	SO	WP	W	L	Pct	Sv-Op	Hld	Vel	OPS	ERC	ERA
2020 LAD	NL	27	0	24	24.1	102	19	11	9	2	0	0	3	9	0	33	0	3	1	.750	11-13	0	92	.615	3.13	3.33
2021 LAD	NL	69	0	52	69.0	278	36	21	17	4	1	2	2	36	4	86	1	4	4	.500	38-43	0	94	.501	1.84	2.22
Postseason		49	0	39	56.1	218	30	17	15	6	0	0	3	17	2	78	0	1	2	.333	18-22	2	94	.507	1.60	2.40
12 ML YEARS		701	0	519	705.0	2780	450	200	186	63	6	13	26	204	12	1022	17	37	26	.587	350-395	39	94	.536	1.87	2.37

Cristian Javier

Pitches: R Bats: R Pos: RP-27; SP-9   Ht: 6'1" Wt: 213 Born: 3/26/1997 Age: 25

HOW MUCH PITCHED						WHAT HE GAVE UP											THE RESULTS								
Year Team	Lg	G	GS	GF	IP	BFP	H	R	ER	HR	SH	SF	HB	TBB	IBB	SO	WP	W	L	Pct	Sv-Op	Hld	Vel	OPS	ERC	ERA
2020 Hou	AL	12	10	0	54.1	214	36	21	21	11	0	2	2	18	0	54	4	5	2	.714	0-0	0	92	.652	2.83	3.48
2021 Hou	AL	36	9	5	101.1	424	67	41	40	16	1	2	7	53	1	130	6	4	1	.800	2-4	5	94	.655	3.35	3.55
Postseason		5	0	0	9.1	38	5	3	3	1	0	0	1	5	0	13	0	2	0	1.000	0-0	2	94	.602	2.62	2.89
2 ML YEARS		48	19	5	155.2	638	103	62	61	27	1	4	9	71	1	184	10	9	3	.750	2-4	5	93	.654	3.18	3.53

Griffin Jax

Pitches: R Bats: R Pos: SP-14; RP-4   Ht: 6'2" Wt: 195 Born: 11/22/1994 Age: 27

HOW MUCH PITCHED						WHAT HE GAVE UP											THE RESULTS								
Year Team	Lg	G	GS	GF	IP	BFP	H	R	ER	HR	SH	SF	HB	TBB	IBB	SO	WP	W	L	Pct	Sv-Op	Hld	Vel	OPS	ERC	ERA
2021 StPaul	AAA	8	8	0	40.2	170	37	17	17	2	0	1	0	16	0	36	0	4	1	.800	0--	-	-	.678	3.25	3.76
2021 Min	AL	18	14	2	82.0	360	82	62	58	23	0	6	5	29	1	65	6	4	5	.444	0-0	0	93	.860	5.32	6.37

Jon Jay

Bats: L Throws: L Pos: LF-5   Ht: 5'11" Wt: 200 Born: 3/15/1985 Age: 37

								BATTING													RUNNING			AVERAGES			
Year Team	Lg	G	AB	H	2B	3B	HR	(Hm	Rd)	TB	R	RBI	RC	TBB	IBB	SO	HBP	SH	SF		SB	CS	GDP	Avg	OBP	Slg	OPS
2021 Salt Lk	AAA	18	69	25	4	0	1	(-	-)	32	16	5	-	2	0	9	1	0	1		2	0	3	.362	.384	.464	.847
2010 StL	NL	105	287	86	19	2	4	(2	2)	121	47	27	40	24	0	50	3	8	1		2	4	5	.300	.359	.422	.780
2011 StL	NL	159	455	135	24	2	10	(5	5)	193	56	37	56	28	1	81	7	9	4		6	7	11	.297	.344	.424	.768
2012 StL	NL	117	443	135	22	4	4	(3	1)	177	70	40	65	34	3	71	15	9	1		19	7	9	.305	.373	.400	.773
2013 StL	NL	157	548	151	27	2	7	(2	5)	203	75	67	74	52	7	103	14	9	5		10	5	13	.276	.351	.370	.721
2014 StL	NL	140	413	125	16	3	3	(0	3)	156	52	46	57	28	3	78	20	3	4		6	3	17	.303	.372	.378	.750
2015 StL	NL	79	210	44	5	1	1	(0	1)	54	25	10	11	19	5	36	11	3	2		2	0	7	.210	.306	.257	.563
2016 SD	NL	90	347	101	26	1	2	(1	1)	135	49	26	55	19	0	78	6	1	0		2	0	5	.291	.339	.389	.728
2017 ChC	NL	141	379	112	18	3	2	(1	1)	142	65	34	58	37	3	80	12	3	2		6	2	11	.296	.374	.375	.749
2018 2 Tms		143	527	141	19	7	3	(2	1)	183	74	40	64	33	0	95	18	5	3		4	3	11	.268	.330	.347	.678
2019 CWS	AL	47	165	44	8	0	0	(0	0)	52	12	9	23	8	0	30	3	5	1		0	0	1	.267	.311	.315	.626
2020 Ari	NL	18	50	8	1	0	1	(1	0)	12	5	4	0	3	0	12	1	0	3		0	0	0	.160	.211	.240	.451
2021 LAA	AL	5	14	5	0	0	0	(0	0)	5	2	1	1	0	0	2	0	0	0		0	0	0	.357	.357	.357	.714
18 KC	AL	59	238	73	9	2	1	(1	0)	89	28	18	31	19	0	39	3	4	2		3	2	4	.307	.363	.374	.737
18 Ari	NL	84	289	68	10	5	2	(1	1)	94	46	22	33	14	0	56	15	1	1		1	1	7	.235	.304	.325	.629
Postseason		67	213	48	6	1	0	(0	0)	56	26	16	23	19	1	36	8	6	2		5	2	5	.225	.310	.263	.573
12 ML YEARS		1201	3838	1087	185	25	37	(17	20)	1433	532	341	504	285	22	716	110	55	26		55	33	90	.283	.348	.373	.721

Daulton Jefferies

Pitches: R Bats: L Pos: RP-4; SP-1   Ht: 6'0" Wt: 182 Born: 8/2/1995 Age: 26

HOW MUCH PITCHED						WHAT HE GAVE UP											THE RESULTS								
Year Team	Lg	G	GS	GF	IP	BFP	H	R	ER	HR	SH	SF	HB	TBB	IBB	SO	WP	W	L	Pct	Sv-Op	Hld	Vel	OPS	ERC	ERA
2021 LsVgs	AAA	15	15	0	77.0	332	90	44	42	13	0	5	4	11	0	68	1	5	1	.833	0--	-	-	.813	4.64	4.91
2020 Oak	AL	1	1	0	2.0	13	5	5	5	2	0	0	2	0	0	2	0	0	1	.000	0-0	0	94	1.538	27.53	22.50
2021 Oak	AL	5	1	1	15.0	58	11	6	6	1	0	0	1	4	0	8	1	1	0	1.000	0-0	0	94	.634	2.34	3.60
2 ML YEARS		6	2	1	17.0	71	16	11	11	3	0	0	1	6	0	9	1	1	1	.500	0-0	0	94	.793	4.43	5.82

Ryan Jeffers

Bats: R Throws: R Pos: C-84;PH-4;PR-1   Ht: 6'4" Wt: 235 Born: 6/3/1997 Age: 25

								BATTING													RUNNING			AVERAGES			
Year Team	Lg	G	AB	H	2B	3B	HR	(Hm	Rd)	TB	R	RBI	RC	TBB	IBB	SO	HBP	SH	SF		SB	CS	GDP	Avg	OBP	Slg	OPS
2021 StPaul	AAA	24	83	18	4	0	5	(-	-)	37	13	16	-	16	0	26	1	0	3		0	0	4	.217	.340	.446	.786
2020 Min	AL	26	55	15	0	0	3	(0	3)	24	5	7	8	5	0	19	2	0	0		0	0	0	.273	.355	.436	.791
2021 Min	AL	85	267	53	10	1	14	(8	6)	107	28	35	30	22	0	108	4	0	0		0	1	6	.199	.270	.401	.670
Postseason		2	5	0	0	0	0	(0	0)	0	0	0	0	0	0	2	0	0	0		0	0	0	.000	.000	.000	.000
2 ML YEARS		111	322	68	10	1	17	(11	6)	131	33	42	38	27	0	127	6	0	0		0	1	6	.211	.285	.407	.691

Jake Jewell

Pitches: R Bats: R Pos: RP-10   Ht: 6'2" Wt: 217 Born: 5/16/1993 Age: 29

HOW MUCH PITCHED						WHAT HE GAVE UP											THE RESULTS								
Year Team	Lg	G	GS	GF	IP	BFP	H	R	ER	HR	SH	SF	HB	TBB	IBB	SO	WP	W	L	Pct	Sv-Op	Hld	Vel	OPS	ERC	ERA
2021 Iowa	AAA	23	0	10	32.1	129	21	12	10	2	0	0	2	13	0	35	1	2	1	.667	4--	-	-	.612	2.48	2.78
2021 Scrmto	AAA	6	0	1	7.1	30	7	3	3	1	0	0	0	3	0	9	2	0	0		0--	-	-	.704	4.33	3.68
2018 LAA	AL	3	0	1	2.0	11	2	2	2	0	0	0	2	1	0	1	1	0	1	.000	0-0	0	96	.830	7.45	9.00
2019 LAA	AL	18	0	7	26.1	114	28	20	20	8	0	1	3	8	0	23	0	0	0		0-0	1	94	.901	6.10	6.84
2021 ChC	NL	10	0	3	10.0	51	18	12	11	5	0	0	0	5	0	10	1	0	2	.000	0-0	0	94	1.212	13.69	9.90
3 ML YEARS		31	0	11	38.1	176	48	34	33	13	0	1	5	14	0	34	2	0	3	.000	0-0	1	95	.990	8.02	7.75

Eloy Jimenez

Bats: R **Throws:** R **Pos:** LF-37;DH-18 eh-LOY he-MEN-ez **Ht:** 6'4" **Wt:** 240 **Born:** 11/27/1996 **Age:** 25

									BATTING												RUNNING			AVERAGES			
Year Team	Lg	G	AB	H	2B	3B	HR	(Hm	Rd)	TB	R	RBI	RC	TBB	IBB	SO	HBP	SH	SF	SB	CS	GDP	Avg	OBP	Slg	OPS
2021 Charlt	AAA	10	38	10	2	0	1	(-	-)	15	3	2		2	0	14	0	0	1	0	0	0	.263	.293	.395	.687
2019 CWS	AL	122	468	125	18	2	31	(12	19)	240	69	79	68	30	0	134	4	0	2	0	0	11	.267	.315	.513	.828
2020 CWS	AL	55	213	63	14	0	14	(8	6)	119	26	41	44	12	0	56	0	0	0	0	0	4	.296	.332	.559	.891
2021 CWS	AL	55	213	53	10	0	10	(2	8)	93	23	37	27	16	0	57	1	0	1	0	0	8	.249	.303	.437	.740
Postseason		1	2	1	1	0	0	(0	0)	2	0	0	0	0	0	0	0	0	0	0	0	0	.500	.500	1.000	1.500
3 ML YEARS		232	894	241	42	2	55	(22	33)	452	118	157	139	58	0	247	5	0	4	0	0	23	.270	.316	.506	.822

Joe Jimenez

Pitches: R **Bats:** R **Pos:** RP-52 he-MEN-ez **Ht:** 6'3" **Wt:** 277 **Born:** 1/17/1995 **Age:** 27

			HOW MUCH PITCHED					WHAT HE GAVE UP									THE RESULTS						
Year Team	Lg	G	GS	GF	IP	BFP	H	R	ER	HR	SH	SF	HB	TBB	IBB	SO	WP	W	L	Pct	Sv-Op Hld	Vel	OPS	ERC	ERA
2017 Det	AL	24	0	6	19.0	99	31	28	26	4	0	1	2	9	0	17	0	0	2	.000	0-1 -	95	.999	9.60	12.32
2018 Det	AL	68	0	17	62.2	267	53	34	30	5	0	2	3	22	3	78	3	5	4	.556	3-7 23	96	.645	2.95	4.31
2019 Det	AL	66	0	29	59.2	257	56	33	29	13	0	0	4	23	1	82	1	4	7	.364	9-14 15	95	.797	4.74	4.37
2020 Det	AL	25	0	9	22.2	101	25	19	18	7	0	2	5	6	0	22	1	1	3	.250	5-6 4	94	.936	6.68	7.15
2021 Det	AL	52	0	12	45.1	210	34	33	30	6	0	2	8	35	1	57	6	6	1	.857	1-2 5	95	.755	4.98	5.96
5 ML YEARS		235	0	73	209.1	934	199	147	133	35	0	7	22	95	5	256	11	16	17	.485	18-30 47	95	.781	4.83	5.72

Connor Joe

Bats: R **Throws:** R **Pos:** LF-32;PH-19;1B-14;DH-3 **Ht:** 6'0" **Wt:** 205 **Born:** 8/16/1992 **Age:** 29

									BATTING												RUNNING			AVERAGES			
Year Team	Lg	G	AB	H	2B	3B	HR	(Hm	Rd)	TB	R	RBI	RC	TBB	IBB	SO	HBP	SH	SF	SB	CS	GDP	Avg	OBP	Slg	OPS
2021 Albq	AAA	26	92	30	7	0	9	(-	-)	64	20	25	-	15	0	22	1	0	2	1	0	1	.326	.418	.696	1.114
2019 SF	NL	8	15	1	0	0	0	(0	0)	1	1	0	1	1	0	5	0	0	0	0	0	1	.067	.125	.067	.192
2021 Col	NL	63	179	51	9	0	8	(5	3)	84	23	35	41	26	0	41	3	0	3	0	0	1	.285	.379	.469	.848
2 ML YEARS		71	194	52	9	0	8	(5	3)	85	24	35	41	27	0	46	3	0	3	0	0	2	.268	.361	.438	.799

Daniel Johnson

Bats: L **Throws:** L **Pos:** RF-19;LF-9;PH-3;PR-2;DH-1 **Ht:** 5'10" **Wt:** 200 **Born:** 7/11/1995 **Age:** 26

									BATTING												RUNNING			AVERAGES			
Year Team	Lg	G	AB	H	2B	3B	HR	(Hm	Rd)	TB	R	RBI	RC	TBB	IBB	SO	HBP	SH	SF	SB	CS	GDP	Avg	OBP	Slg	OPS
2021 Clmbs	AAA	68	263	59	16	2	12	(-	-)	115	32	35	-	33	0	100	2	0	1	7	1	1	.224	.314	.437	.752
2020 Cle	AL	5	12	1	0	0	0	(0	0)	1	0	0	1	1	1	5	0	0	0	0	0	0	.083	.154	.083	.237
2021 Cle	AL	30	77	17	0	0	4	(2	2)	29	9	5	6	4	0	27	0	0	0	1	0	0	.221	.259	.377	.636
2 ML YEARS		35	89	18	0	0	4	(2	2)	30	9	5	7	5	1	32	0	0	0	1	0	0	.202	.245	.337	.582

DJ Johnson

Pitches: R **Bats:** L **Pos:** RP-4 **Ht:** 6'4" **Wt:** 230 **Born:** 8/30/1989 **Age:** 32

			HOW MUCH PITCHED					WHAT HE GAVE UP									THE RESULTS						
Year Team	Lg	G	GS	GF	IP	BFP	H	R	ER	HR	SH	SF	HB	TBB	IBB	SO	WP	W	L	Pct	Sv-Op Hld	Vel	OPS	ERC	ERA
2021 Clmbs	AAA	21	0	15	21.2	103	24	10	8	3	0	0	2	11	1	35	4	1	2	.333	6- - -	-	.793	5.54	3.32
2018 Col	NL	7	0	3	6.1	27	6	3	3	0	0	0	0	2	0	9	0	1	0	1.000	0-0 -	94	.536	2.73	4.26
2019 Col	NL	28	0	7	25.0	116	23	14	14	1	0	1	3	19	2	24	4	0	2	.000	0-0 4	93	.743	4.93	5.04
2021 2 Tms	AL	4	0	0	4.1	15	2	1	1	1	0	0	0	0	0	5	0	0	0	-	0-0 -	95	.467	0.97	2.08
21 Cle	AL	1	0	0	1.2	7	2	1	1	1	0	0	0	0	0	3	0	0	0	-	0-0 -	94	1.000	6.66	5.40
21 TB	AL	3	0	0	2.2	8	0	0	0	0	0	0	0	0	0	2	0	0	0	-	0-0 -	95	.000	0.00	0.00
Postseason		1	0	0	0.2	3	1	0	0	0	0	0	0	0	0	2	0	0	0	-	0-0 -	95	.667	4.47	0.00
3 ML YEARS		39	0	10	35.2	158	31	18	18	2	0	1	3	21	2	38	4	1	2	.333	0-0 4	94	.679	3.99	4.54

Pierce Johnson

Pitches: R **Bats:** R **Pos:** RP-61; SP-2 **Ht:** 6'2" **Wt:** 202 **Born:** 5/10/1991 **Age:** 31

			HOW MUCH PITCHED					WHAT HE GAVE UP									THE RESULTS						
Year Team	Lg	G	GS	GF	IP	BFP	H	R	ER	HR	SH	SF	HB	TBB	IBB	SO	WP	W	L	Pct	Sv-Op Hld	Vel	OPS	ERC	ERA
2017 ChC	NL	1	0	1	1.0	7	2	2	0	0	0	0	0	1	0	2	0	0	0	-	0-0 -	92	.762	10.22	0.00
2018 SF	NL	37	0	7	43.2	186	38	27	27	5	1	2	0	22	1	36	1	3	2	.600	0-0 1	94	.740	3.86	5.56
2020 SD	NL	24	0	7	20.0	80	15	7	6	2	0	1	0	9	0	27	1	3	1	.750	0-0 1	96	.643	3.04	2.70
2021 SD	NL	63	2	7	58.2	244	47	21	21	6	0	2	1	27	3	77	6	3	4	.429	0-2 9	96	.677	3.27	3.22
Postseason		5	0	0	4.0	18	3	2	2	0	0	0	1	2	0	7	0	0	0	-	0-0 -	96	.533	3.21	4.50
4 ML YEARS		125	2	21	123.1	517	102	57	54	13	1	5	1	59	4	142	8	9	7	.563	0-2 11	95	.695	3.49	3.94

Damon Jones

Pitches: L **Bats:** L **Pos:** RP-1 **Ht:** 6'5" **Wt:** 233 **Born:** 9/30/1994 **Age:** 27

			HOW MUCH PITCHED					WHAT HE GAVE UP									THE RESULTS						
Year Team	Lg	G	GS	GF	IP	BFP	H	R	ER	HR	SH	SF	HB	TBB	IBB	SO	WP	W	L	Pct	Sv-Op Hld	Vel	OPS	ERC	ERA
2021 LV	AAA	32	0	5	39.0	188	37	26	24	3	0	0	4	36	2	52	4	1	5	.167	1- - -	-	.754	6.05	5.54
2021 Phi	NL	1	0	0	0.1	4	1	0	0	0	0	0	0	2	0	0	0	0	0	-	0-0 -	94	1.250	44.74	0.00

JaCoby Jones

Bats: R **Throws:** R **Pos:** CF-30;PR-4;PH-3;LF-2   **Ht:** 6'2" **Wt:** 211 **Born:** 5/10/1992 **Age:** 30

Year	Team	Lg	G	AB	H	2B	3B	HR	(Hm	Rd)	TB	R	RBI	RC	TBB	IBB	SO	HBP	SH	SF	SB	CS	GDP	Avg	OBP	Slg	OPS
2021	Toledo	AAA	72	266	61	14	0	7	(-	-)	96	30	26	-	28	0	103	4	0	0	1	2	4	.229	.312	.361	.673
2016	Det	AL	13	28	6	3	0	0	(0	0)	9	3	2	2	0	0	12	0	0	0	0	0	1	.214	.214	.321	.536
2017	Det	AL	56	141	24	3	1	3	(2	1)	38	14	13	7	9	0	65	4	0	0	6	2	5	.170	.240	.270	.510
2018	Det	AL	129	429	89	22	6	11	(8	3)	156	54	34	36	24	0	142	11	1	2	13	5	9	.207	.266	.364	.630
2019	Det	AL	88	298	70	19	3	11	(7	4)	128	39	26	35	27	2	94	6	1	1	7	2	6	.235	.310	.430	.740
2020	Det	AL	30	97	26	9	0	5	(3	2)	50	19	14	14	7	0	34	3	0	1	1	1	1	.268	.333	.515	.849
2021	Det	AL	36	100	17	2	0	2	(1	1)	25	9	9	7	5	0	42	0	0	0	2	2	2	.170	.210	.250	.460
	6 ML YEARS		352	1093	232	58	10	32	(21	11)	406	138	98	101	72	2	389	24	2	4	29	12	24	.212	.275	.371	.646

Jahmai Jones

Bats: R **Throws:** R **Pos:** 2B-23;PR-3;PH-2   juh-MY   **Ht:** 6'0" **Wt:** 210 **Born:** 8/4/1997 **Age:** 24

Year	Team	Lg	G	AB	H	2B	3B	HR	(Hm	Rd)	TB	R	RBI	RC	TBB	IBB	SO	HBP	SH	SF	SB	CS	GDP	Avg	OBP	Slg	OPS
2021	Norfolk	AAA	70	255	62	9	3	11	(-	-)	110	34	37	-	35	0	68	2	0	2	11	3	9	.243	.337	.431	.768
2020	LAA	AL	3	7	3	0	0	0	(0	0)	3	2	1	2	0	0	2	0	0	0	0	0	0	.429	.429	.429	.857
2021	Bal	AL	26	67	10	3	0	0	(0	0)	13	5	3	3	4	0	26	1	0	0	1	0	1	.149	.208	.194	.402
	2 ML YEARS		29	74	13	3	0	0	(0	0)	16	7	4	5	4	0	28	1	0	0	1	0	1	.176	.228	.216	.444

Nate Jones

Pitches: R **Bats:** R **Pos:** RP-20   **Ht:** 6'5" **Wt:** 230 **Born:** 1/28/1986 **Age:** 36

Year	Team	Lg	G	GS	GF	IP	BFP	H	R	ER	HR	SH	SF	HB	TBB	IBB	SO	WP	W	L	Pct	Sv-Op	Hld	Vel	OPS	ERC	ERA
2012	CWS	AL	65	0	11	71.2	301	67	19	19	4	2	4	1	32	3	65	5	8	0	1.000	0-3	7	98	.686	3.67	2.39
2013	CWS	AL	70	0	17	78.0	315	69	40	36	5	3	6	1	26	1	89	8	4	5	.444	0-4	16	98	.659	3.09	4.15
2014	CWS	AL	2	0	0	0.0	5	2	4	4	0	0	0	0	3	0	0	0	0	0	-	0-1	0	96	2.500	-	-
2015	CWS	AL	19	0	3	19.0	72	12	7	7	5	2	0	0	6	0	27	0	2	2	.500	0-1	6	98	.695	2.87	3.32
2016	CWS	AL	71	0	11	70.2	274	48	20	18	7	2	2	3	15	3	80	7	5	3	.625	3-12	28	97	.552	1.87	2.29
2017	CWS	AL	11	0	1	11.2	49	9	3	3	1	1	0	1	6	1	15	1	1	0	1.000	0-0	4	97	.675	3.43	2.31
2018	CWS	AL	33	0	15	30.0	137	28	14	10	4	1	0	4	15	0	32	2	2	2	.500	5-8	6	97	.723	4.59	3.00
2019	CWS	AL	13	0	5	10.1	47	10	4	4	2	0	0	0	7	1	10	2	0	1	.000	1-1	2	95	.793	6.10	3.48
2020	Cin	NL	21	0	8	18.2	86	25	13	13	5	0	1	2	6	1	23	2	0	1	.000	0-0	4	96	.955	7.59	6.27
2021	2 Tms	NL	20	0	5	19.0	87	16	15	12	7	0	1	4	12	4	14	1	0	2	.000	0-1	5	96	.868	5.76	5.68
21	Atl	NL	12	0	4	10.1	50	8	6	4	3	0	0	1	10	4	7	1	0	2	.000	0-1	2	96	.842	6.12	3.48
21	LAD	NL	8	0	1	8.2	37	8	9	8	4	0	1	0	2	0	7	0	0	0	-	0-0	3	95	.888	5.00	8.31
	10 ML YEARS		325	0	76	329.0	1373	286	139	126	40	11	15	13	128	14	355	28	22	16	.579	9-31	78	97	.692	3.59	3.45

Taylor Jones

Bats: R **Throws:** R **Pos:** 1B-14;LF-10;DH-10;PH-6;PR-1   **Ht:** 6'7" **Wt:** 230 **Born:** 12/6/1993 **Age:** 28

Year	Team	Lg	G	AB	H	2B	3B	HR	(Hm	Rd)	TB	R	RBI	RC	TBB	IBB	SO	HBP	SH	SF	SB	CS	GDP	Avg	OBP	Slg	OPS
2021	SgrLnd	AAA	43	163	54	14	0	9	(-	-)	95	33	42	-	26	1	38	0	0	3	0	1	4	.331	.417	.583	.999
2020	Hou	AL	7	21	4	1	0	1	(0	1)	8	3	3	1	1	0	7	0	0	0	0	0	2	.190	.227	.381	.608
2021	Hou	AL	35	102	25	8	1	2	(2	0)	41	11	16	12	4	0	29	0	0	2	0	0	5	.245	.269	.402	.670
	2 ML YEARS		42	123	29	9	1	3	(2	1)	49	14	19	13	5	0	36	0	0	2	0	0	7	.236	.262	.398	.660

Matt Joyce

Bats: L **Throws:** R **Pos:** PH-30;LF-9;RF-9;PR-1   **Ht:** 6'2" **Wt:** 194 **Born:** 8/3/1984 **Age:** 37

Year	Team	Lg	G	AB	H	2B	3B	HR	(Hm	Rd)	TB	R	RBI	RC	TBB	IBB	SO	HBP	SH	SF	SB	CS	GDP	Avg	OBP	Slg	OPS
2008	Det	AL	92	242	61	16	3	12	(6	6)	119	40	33	36	31	0	65	2	0	2	0	2	3	.252	.339	.492	.831
2009	TB	AL	11	32	6	1	0	3	(2	1)	16	3	7	5	3	0	7	1	0	1	1	0	0	.188	.270	.500	.770
2010	TB	AL	77	216	52	15	3	10	(4	6)	103	30	40	41	40	2	55	2	0	3	2	2	2	.241	.360	.477	.837
2011	TB	AL	141	462	128	32	2	19	(11	8)	221	69	75	77	49	9	106	4	0	7	13	1	7	.277	.347	.478	.825
2012	TB	AL	124	399	96	18	3	17	(4	13)	171	55	59	59	55	4	102	6	1	1	4	3	10	.241	.341	.429	.747
2013	TB	AL	140	413	97	22	0	18	(8	10)	173	61	47	51	59	0	87	2	0	7	7	3	6	.235	.328	.419	.747
2014	TB	AL	140	418	106	23	2	9	(2	7)	160	51	52	52	62	4	111	4	0	9	2	5	11	.254	.349	.383	.732
2015	LAA	AL	93	247	43	12	1	5	(4	1)	72	17	21	15	30	1	67	4	1	2	0	3	5	.174	.272	.291	.564
2016	Pit	NL	140	231	56	10	1	13	(10	3)	107	45	42	47	59	4	67	3	0	1	1	1	9	.242	.403	.463	.866
2017	Oak	AL	141	469	114	33	0	25	(11	14)	222	78	68	70	66	0	113	2	0	7	4	1	10	.243	.335	.473	.808
2018	Oak	AL	83	207	43	9	0	7	(2	5)	73	34	15	20	35	2	53	1	1	2	0	2	3	.208	.322	.353	.675
2019	Atl	NL	129	200	59	10	0	7	(4	3)	90	32	23	39	38	0	45	0	0	0	0	0	3	.295	.408	.450	.858
2020	Mia	NL	46	127	32	4	0	2	(0	2)	42	16	14	17	20	0	41	0	0	1	1	0	3	.252	.351	.331	.682
2021	Phi	NL	43	55	5	1	0	2	(0	2)	12	6	7	3	12	2	16	1	0	1	0	0	2	.091	.261	.218	.479
	Postseason		22	53	8	2	0	1	(0	1)	13	1	5	3	4	0	18	0	0	0	1	0	0	.151	.211	.245	.456
	14 ML YEARS		1400	3718	898	206	15	149	(68	81)	1581	537	503	532	559	28	935	32	3	43	35	23	76	.242	.342	.425	.767

Aaron Judge

Bats: R Throws: R Pos: RF-114;CF-23;DH-22;PH-4   Ht: 6'7" Wt: 282 Born: 4/26/1992 Age: 30

Year	Team	Lg	G	AB	H	2B	3B	HR	(Hm	Rd)	TB	R	RBI	RC	TBB	IBB	SO	HBP	SH	SF	SB	CS	GDP	Avg	OBP	Slg	OPS
2016	NYY	AL	27	84	15	2	0	4	(3	1)	33	10	10	6	9	0	42	1	0	1	0	1	2	.179	.263	.345	.608
2017	NYY	AL	155	542	154	24	3	52	(33	19)	340	128	114	131	127	11	208	5	0	4	9	4	15	.284	.422	.627	1.049
2018	NYY	AL	112	413	115	22	0	27	(18	9)	218	77	67	82	76	3	152	4	0	5	6	3	10	.278	.392	.528	.919
2019	NYY	AL	102	378	103	18	1	27	(11	16)	204	75	55	70	64	4	141	3	0	1	3	2	11	.272	.381	.540	.921
2020	NYY	AL	28	101	26	3	0	9	(5	4)	56	23	22	19	10	0	32	2	0	0	1	0	5	.257	.336	.554	.891
2021	NYY	AL	148	550	158	24	0	39	(15	24)	299	89	98	115	75	2	158	3	0	5	6	1	16	.287	.373	.544	.916
	Postseason		34	131	30	4	0	11	(4	7)	67	24	22	22	23	0	51	0	0	1	2	1	2	.229	.342	.511	.853
6 ML YEARS			572	2068	571	93	4	158	(85	73)	1146	402	366	423	361	20	733	18	0	16	24	12	59	.276	.386	.554	.940

Jakob Junis

Pitches: R Bats: R Pos: RP-10; SP-6   Ht: 6'3" Wt: 220 Born: 9/16/1992 Age: 29

Year	Team	Lg	G	GS	GF	IP	BFP	H	R	ER	HR	SH	SF	HB	TBB	IBB	SO	WP	W	L	Pct	Sv-Op	Hld	Vel	OPS	ERC	ERA
2021	Omha	AAA	6	6	0	17.2	83	22	14	11	4	0	0	1	8	0	18	1	0	2	.000	0-	-	-	.914	6.93	5.60
2017	KC	AL	20	16	1	98.1	422	101	52	47	15	3	3	9	25	1	80	3	9	3	.750	0-0	0	91	.762	4.36	4.30
2018	KC	AL	30	30	0	177.0	758	182	94	86	32	4	8	15	43	1	164	9	9	12	.429	0-0	0	91	.773	4.49	4.37
2019	KC	AL	31	31	0	175.1	771	192	108	102	31	0	5	11	58	1	164	4	9	14	.391	0-0	0	92	.807	5.14	5.24
2020	KC	AL	8	6	0	25.1	114	35	18	18	7	0	1	2	6	1	19	2	0	2	.000	0-0	0	91	.958	7.50	6.39
2021	KC	AL	16	6	1	39.1	168	43	24	23	7	0	2	0	12	0	41	2	2	4	.333	0-2	0	91	.788	4.82	5.26
5 ML YEARS			105	89	2	515.1	2233	553	296	276	92	7	19	37	144	4	468	20	29	35	.453	0-2	1	91	.794	4.85	4.82

Janson Junk

Pitches: R Bats: R Pos: SP-4   Ht: 6'1" Wt: 177 Born: 1/15/1996 Age: 26

Year	Team	Lg	G	GS	GF	IP	BFP	H	R	ER	HR	SH	SF	HB	TBB	IBB	SO	WP	W	L	Pct	Sv-Op	Hld	Vel	OPS	ERC	ERA
2021	Smrst	AA	14	12	2	65.2	254	43	13	13	6	0	1	1	20	0	68	3	4	1	.800	1-	-	-	.549	2.01	1.78
2021	Rock	AA	5	5	0	27.1	121	32	21	16	5	0	1	0	7	0	29	1	2	2	.500	0-	-	-	.791	4.95	5.27
2021	LAA	AL	4	4	0	16.1	71	20	11	7	5	1	0	0	2	0	10	0	0	1	.000	0-0	0	93	.844	5.53	3.86

James Kaprielian

ka-PRELL-ee-an

Pitches: R Bats: R Pos: SP-21; RP-3   Ht: 6'3" Wt: 225 Born: 3/2/1994 Age: 28

Year	Team	Lg	G	GS	GF	IP	BFP	H	R	ER	HR	SH	SF	HB	TBB	IBB	SO	WP	W	L	Pct	Sv-Op	Hld	Vel	OPS	ERC	ERA
2020	Oak	AL	2	0	0	3.2	17	4	3	3	2	0	0	0	2	0	4	0	0	0	-	0-0	0	95	1.020	8.51	7.36
2021	Oak	AL	24	21	0	119.1	502	105	55	54	19	2	3	5	41	0	123	1	8	5	.615	0-0	0	93	.732	3.74	4.07
2 ML YEARS			26	21	0	123.0	519	109	58	57	21	2	3	5	43	0	127	1	8	5	.615	0-0	0	93	.741	3.87	4.17

James Karinchak

Pitches: R Bats: R Pos: RP-60   Ht: 6'3" Wt: 215 Born: 9/22/1995 Age: 26

Year	Team	Lg	G	GS	GF	IP	BFP	H	R	ER	HR	SH	SF	HB	TBB	IBB	SO	WP	W	L	Pct	Sv-Op	Hld	Vel	OPS	ERC	ERA
2021	Clmbs	AAA	6	0	1	5.0	20	2	2	2	1	0	0	0	3	0	7	1	1	1	.500	0-	-	-	.544	2.30	3.60
2019	Cle	AL	5	0	4	5.1	22	3	1	1	0	0	1	0	1	0	8	2	0	0	-	0-0	0	97	.382	0.90	1.69
2020	Cle	AL	27	0	4	27.0	109	14	9	8	1	1	4	0	16	1	53	5	1	2	.333	1-4	8	96	.505	1.87	2.67
2021	Cle	AL	60	0	26	55.1	235	35	27	25	9	0	2	2	32	0	78	3	7	4	.636	11-16	13	96	.645	3.27	4.07
	Postseason		1	0	0	0.0	3	1	1	1	1	0	0	0	2	0	0	0	0	0	-	0-0	0	96	5.000		
3 ML YEARS			92	0	34	87.2	366	52	37	34	10	1	7	2	49	1	139	10	8	6	.571	12-20	21	96	.588	2.63	3.49

Anthony Kay

Pitches: L Bats: L Pos: RP-6; SP-5   Ht: 6'0" Wt: 225 Born: 3/21/1995 Age: 27

Year	Team	Lg	G	GS	GF	IP	BFP	H	R	ER	HR	SH	SF	HB	TBB	IBB	SO	WP	W	L	Pct	Sv-Op	Hld	Vel	OPS	ERC	ERA
2021	Buffalo	AAA	8	8	0	26.1	126	31	30	26	5	0	1	4	13	0	29	4	0	4	.000	0-	-	-	.927	6.78	8.89
2019	Tor	AL	3	2	0	14.0	63	15	9	9	0	0	0	1	5	0	13	1	1	0	1.000	0-0	0	93	.649	3.75	5.79
2020	Tor	AL	13	0	0	21.0	98	22	13	12	3	0	2	0	14	1	22	0	2	0	1.000	0-0	2	94	.867	5.61	5.14
2021	Tor	AL	11	5	0	33.2	156	38	22	21	7	0	0	3	18	0	39	2	1	2	.333	0-0	0	95	.897	6.65	5.61
3 ML YEARS			27	7	0	68.2	317	75	44	42	10	0	2	4	37	1	74	3	4	2	.667	0-0	2	94	.837	5.70	5.50

Sean Kazmar Jr.

Bats: R Throws: R Pos: PH-2;DH-1;PR-1   Ht: 5'10" Wt: 185 Born: 8/5/1984 Age: 37

Year	Team	Lg	G	AB	H	2B	3B	HR	(Hm	Rd)	TB	R	RBI	RC	TBB	IBB	SO	HBP	SH	SF	SB	CS	GDP	Avg	OBP	Slg	OPS
2021	Gwnntt	AAA	82	252	55	9	0	9	(-	-)	91	29	26	-	17	1	43	1	0	2	3	0	6	.218	.268	.361	.629
2008	SD	NL	19	39	8	1	0	0	(0	0)	9	2	2	3	5	0	14	0	1	1	0	0	1	.205	.289	.231	.520
2021	Atl	NL	3	2	0	0	0	0	(0	0)	0	0	0	0	0	0	0	0	0	0	0	0	0	.000	.000	.000	.000
2 ML YEARS			22	41	8	1	0	0	(0	0)	9	2	2	3	5	0	14	0	1	1	0	0	1	.195	.277	.220	.496

Scott Kazmir

Pitches: L **Bats**: L **Pos**: SP-4; RP-1   KAZ-meer   **Ht**: 6'0" **Wt**: 185 **Born**: 1/24/1984 **Age**: 38

			HOW MUCH PITCHED					WHAT HE GAVE UP										THE RESULTS							
Year	Team	Lg	G	GS	GF	IP	BFP	H	R	ER	HR	SH	SF	HB	TBB	IBB	SO	WP	W	L	Pct	Sv-Op	Hld	Vel	OPS	ERC	ERA
2021	Scrmto	AAA	13	12	0	52.2	217	45	28	27	6	1	3	2	18	0	48	3	3	3	.500	0--	-	-	.688	3.34	4.61
2004	TB	AL	8	7	0	33.1	152	33	22	21	4	0	0	2	21	0	41	3	2	3	.400	0-0	0	94	.795	5.36	5.67
2005	TB	AL	32	32	0	186.0	818	172	90	78	12	6	9	10	**100**	3	174	7	10	9	.526	0-0	0	93	.721	4.13	3.77
2006	TB	AL	24	24	0	144.2	610	132	59	52	15	0	5	2	52	3	163	6	10	8	.556	0-0	0	92	.697	3.47	3.24
2007	TB	AL	34	**34**	0	206.2	887	196	91	80	18	6	3	7	89	1	**239**	10	13	9	.591	0-0	0	92	.711	3.97	3.48
2008	TB	AL	27	27	0	152.1	641	123	61	59	23	4	5	4	70	2	166	5	12	8	.600	0-0	0	92	.727	3.69	3.49
2009	2 Tms	AL	26	26	0	147.1	647	149	85	80	16	1	4	6	60	0	117	13	10	9	.526	0-0	0	91	.743	4.36	4.89
2010	LAA	AL	28	28	0	150.0	682	158	103	99	25	3	6	12	79	2	93	6	9	15	.375	0-0	0	91	.841	5.74	5.94
2011	LAA	AL	1	1	0	1.2	14	5	5	5	1	0	0	2	2	0	0	0	0	0	-	0-0	0	86	1.643	35.08	27.00
2013	Cle	AL	29	29	0	158.0	672	162	76	71	19	2	1	3	47	1	162	5	10	9	.526	0-0	0	92	.735	4.02	4.04
2014	Oak	AL	32	32	0	190.1	777	171	81	75	16	5	1	4	50	1	164	9	15	9	.625	0-0	0	91	.648	3.00	3.55
2015	2 Tms	AL	31	31	0	183.0	763	162	77	63	20	5	6	9	59	0	155	5	7	11	.389	0-0	0	91	.678	3.41	3.10
2016	LAD	NL	26	26	0	136.1	590	133	71	69	21	2	3	7	52	3	134	5	10	6	.625	0-0	0	92	.762	4.41	4.56
2021	SF	NL	5	4	0	11.1	55	15	9	8	3	0	0	0	6	1	10	0	0	1	.000	0-0	0	92	.951	7.59	6.35
	09 TB	AL	20	20	0	111.0	504	121	77	73	15	1	4	5	50	0	91	10	8	7	.533	0-0	0	91	.796	5.18	5.92
	09 LAA	AL	6	6	0	36.1	143	28	8	7	1	0	0	1	10	0	26	3	2	2	.500	0-0	0	93	.561	2.13	1.73
	15 Oak	AL	18	18	0	109.2	440	84	35	29	7	3	4	3	35	0	101	2	5	5	.500	0-0	0	91	.596	2.45	2.38
	15 Hou	AL	13	13	0	73.1	323	78	42	34	13	2	2	6	24	0	54	3	2	6	.250	0-0	0	91	.790	5.01	4.17
	Postseason		9	8	0	41.2	197	42	25	24	6	3	2	3	27	0	30	2	1	2	.333	0-0	0	92	.785	5.63	5.18
	13 ML YEARS		303	301	0	1701.0	7308	1611	830	760	193	34	43	68	687	17	1618	74	108	97	.527	0-0	0	92	.728	4.04	4.02

Keone Kela

Pitches: R **Bats**: R **Pos**: RP-12   KEY-oh-nee KELL-uh   **Ht**: 6'1" **Wt**: 220 **Born**: 4/16/1993 **Age**: 29

			HOW MUCH PITCHED					WHAT HE GAVE UP										THE RESULTS							
Year	Team	Lg	G	GS	GF	IP	BFP	H	R	ER	HR	SH	SF	HB	TBB	IBB	SO	WP	W	L	Pct	Sv-Op	Hld	Vel	OPS	ERC	ERA
2015	Tex	AL	68	0	11	60.1	243	52	18	16	4	1	0	0	18	0	68	6	7	5	.583	1-4	22	96	.615	2.79	2.39
2016	Tex	AL	35	0	2	34.0	150	30	23	23	6	2	1	3	17	0	45	2	5	1	.833	0-1	15	96	.779	4.68	6.09
2017	Tex	AL	39	0	13	38.2	151	18	12	12	4	0	0	1	17	1	51	1	4	1	.800	2-3	11	96	.479	1.64	2.79
2018	2 Tms		54	0	36	52.0	212	38	19	19	5	1	1	0	19	2	66	6	3	4	.429	24-26	4	97	.605	2.43	3.29
2019	Pit	NL	32	0	8	29.2	119	19	7	7	3	0	0	1	11	0	33	1	2	0	1.000	1-5	6	96	.606	2.23	2.12
2020	Pit	NL	3	0	1	2.0	10	3	1	1	0	0	0	0	3	0	3	0	0	0	-	0-0	0	96	1.067	10.88	4.50
2021	SD	NL	12	0	2	10.2	48	11	8	6	3	0	0	0	5	0	13	2	2	2	.500	0-2	1	95	.736	4.68	5.06
	18 Tex	AL	38	0	31	36.2	152	28	14	14	3	1	1	0	14	1	44	4	3	3	.500	24-25	0	97	.602	2.55	3.44
	18 Pit	NL	16	0	5	15.1	60	10	5	5	2	0	0	0	5	1	22	2	0	1	.000	0-1	4	97	.614	2.12	2.93
	Postseason		4	0	1	4.2	16	1	1	1	0	0	0	0	2	0	3	0	1	0	1.000	0-1	1	97	.473	1.27	1.93
	7 ML YEARS		243	0	73	227.1	933	171	88	84	26	4	2	5	86	3	279	18	23	13	.639	28-41	59	96	.627	2.82	3.33

Jarred Kelenic

Bats: L **Throws**: L **Pos**: CF-77; LF-14; RF-3; PH-1   KELL-nick   **Ht**: 6'1" **Wt**: 190 **Born**: 7/16/1999 **Age**: 22

			BATTING																RUNNING			AVERAGES			
Year	Team	Lg	G	AB	H	2B	3B	HR	(Hm | Rd)	TB	R	RBI	RC	TBB	IBB	SO	HBP	SH	SF	SB	CS	GDP	Avg	OBP	Slg	OPS
2018	2 Tms	Low	56	220	63	10	6	6	(- | -)	103	42	42	40	26	0	50	4	0	1	15	1	1	.286	.371	.468	.839
2019	2 Tms	Low	96	360	108	27	4	17	(- | -)	194	69	51	75	42	0	94	3	0	3	17	7	4	.300	.375	.539	.914
2019	Ark	AA	21	83	21	4	1	6	(- | -)	45	11	17	15	8	0	17	0	0	1	3	0	2	.253	.315	.542	.857
2021	Tacom	AAA	30	125	40	9	1	9	(- | -)	78	29	28	-	15	1	22	1	0	2	6	1	2	.320	.392	.624	1.016
2021	Sea	AL	93	337	61	13	1	14	(5 | 9)	118	41	43	29	36	0	106	3	0	1	6	4	5	.181	.265	.350	.615

Brad Keller

Pitches: R **Bats**: R **Pos**: SP-26   **Ht**: 6'5" **Wt**: 255 **Born**: 7/27/1995 **Age**: 26

			HOW MUCH PITCHED					WHAT HE GAVE UP										THE RESULTS							
Year	Team	Lg	G	GS	GF	IP	BFP	H	R	ER	HR	SH	SF	HB	TBB	IBB	SO	WP	W	L	Pct	Sv-Op	Hld	Vel	OPS	ERC	ERA
2018	KC	AL	41	20	2	140.1	583	133	50	48	7	0	3	2	50	1	96	8	9	6	.600	0-2	5	94	.653	3.39	3.08
2019	KC	AL	28	28	0	165.1	709	154	80	77	15	1	5	9	70	2	122	9	7	14	.333	0-0	0	93	.711	3.94	4.19
2020	KC	AL	9	9	0	54.2	215	39	16	15	2	0	3	2	17	0	35	1	5	3	.625	0-0	0	93	.513	2.06	2.47
2021	KC	AL	26	26	0	133.2	613	158	89	80	18	1	**9**	7	64	1	120	5	8	12	.400	0-0	0	94	.831	5.97	5.39
	4 ML YEARS		104	83	2	494.0	2120	484	235	220	42	2	20	20	201	4	373	23	29	35	.453	0-2	5	94	.708	4.07	4.01

Kyle Keller

Pitches: R **Bats**: R **Pos**: RP-32   **Ht**: 6'4" **Wt**: 205 **Born**: 4/28/1993 **Age**: 29

			HOW MUCH PITCHED					WHAT HE GAVE UP										THE RESULTS							
Year	Team	Lg	G	GS	GF	IP	BFP	H	R	ER	HR	SH	SF	HB	TBB	IBB	SO	WP	W	L	Pct	Sv-Op	Hld	Vel	OPS	ERC	ERA
2021	Indy	AAA	13	1	4	18.1	71	13	4	4	2	1	1	1	3	0	31	0	2	0	1.000	0--	-	-	.597	1.98	1.96
2019	Mia	NL	10	0	4	10.2	46	5	4	4	3	0	0	2	8	0	11	0	0	0	-	0-0	0	95	.715	4.53	3.38
2020	LAA	AL	2	0	1	2.1	13	3	2	2	0	0	0	0	2	0	1	1	0	0	-	0-0	0	95	.657	6.07	7.71
2021	Pit	NL	32	0	7	33.1	155	30	27	24	9	0	0	5	22	2	36	1	1	1	.500	0-0	2	95	.868	6.34	6.48
	3 ML YEARS		44	0	12	46.1	214	38	33	30	12	0	0	7	32	2	48	2	1	1	.500	0-0	2	95	.823	5.90	5.83

Mitch Keller

Pitches: R **Bats:** R **Pos:** SP-23

Ht: 6'2" **Wt:** 220 **Born:** 4/4/1996 **Age:** 26

			HOW MUCH PITCHED					WHAT HE GAVE UP											THE RESULTS						
Year	Team	Lg	G	GS	GF	IP	BFP	H	R	ER	HR	SH	SF	HB	TBB	IBB	SO	WP	W	L	Pct	Sv-Op	Hld	Vel	OPS	ERC	ERA
2021	Indy	AAA	8	6	0	28.0	128	27	18	10	2	0	2	1	13	1	39	2	1	1	.500	0--	-	-	.686	3.80	3.21
2019	Pit	NL	11	11	0	48.0	227	72	41	38	6	1	2	1	16	0	65	2	1	5	.167	0-0	0	95	.940	7.13	7.13
2020	Pit	NL	5	5	0	21.2	87	9	7	7	4	0	0	1	18	0	16	2	1	1	.500	0-0	0	94	.660	3.51	2.91
2021	Pit	NL	23	23	0	100.2	470	131	69	69	10	3	4	7	49	1	92	2	5	11	.313	0-0	0	94	.877	6.61	6.17
3 ML YEARS			39	39	0	170.1	784	212	117	114	20	4	6	9	83	1	173	6	7	17	.292	0-0	0	94	.874	6.34	6.02

Carson Kelly

Bats: R **Throws:** R **Pos:** C-91;PH-18

Ht: 6'2" **Wt:** 212 **Born:** 7/14/1994 **Age:** 27

										BATTING												RUNNING			AVERAGES			
Year	Team	Lg	G	AB	H	2B	3B	HR	(Hm	Rd)	TB	R	RBI	RC	TBB	IBB	SO	HBP	SH	SF	SB	CS	GDP	Avg	OBP	Slg	OPS
2016	StL	NL	10	13	2	1	0	0	(0	0)	3	1	1	0	0	0	2	1	0	0	0	0	0	.154	.214	.231	.445
2017	StL	NL	34	69	12	3	0	0	(0	0)	15	5	6	4	5	0	11	1	0	0	0	0	3	.174	.240	.217	.457
2018	StL	NL	19	35	4	0	0	0	(0	0)	4	1	3	1	3	0	7	1	3	0	0	0	0	.114	.205	.114	.319
2019	Ari	NL	111	314	77	19	0	18	(4	14)	150	46	47	46	48	10	79	2	0	1	0	0	11	.245	.348	.478	.826
2020	Ari	NL	39	122	27	5	0	5	(2	3)	47	11	19	16	6	0	29	1	0	0	0	0	4	.221	.264	.385	.649
2021	Ari	NL	98	304	73	11	1	13	(5	8)	125	41	46	45	44	1	74	6	0	5	0	0	10	.240	.343	.411	.754
6 ML YEARS			311	857	195	39	1	36	(11	25)	344	105	122	112	106	11	202	12	3	6	0	0	28	.228	.319	.401	.720

Joe Kelly

Pitches: R **Bats:** R **Pos:** RP-48

Ht: 6'1" **Wt:** 174 **Born:** 6/9/1988 **Age:** 34

			HOW MUCH PITCHED					WHAT HE GAVE UP											THE RESULTS						
Year	Team	Lg	G	GS	GF	IP	BFP	H	R	ER	HR	SH	SF	HB	TBB	IBB	SO	WP	W	L	Pct	Sv-Op	Hld	Vel	OPS	ERC	ERA
2012	StL	NL	24	6	4	107.0	457	112	50	42	10	4	1	3	36	2	75	4	5	7	.417	0-0	0	94	.740	4.17	3.53
2013	StL	NL	37	15	8	124.0	532	124	42	37	10	2	2	5	44	4	79	3	10	5	.667	0-1	2	95	.694	3.88	2.69
2014	2 Tms		17	17	0	96.1	415	88	48	45	8	2	4	7	42	0	66	3	6	4	.600	0-0	0	95	.693	3.92	4.20
2015	Bos	AL	25	25	0	134.1	587	145	76	72	15	0	5	6	49	0	110	9	10	6	.625	0-0	0	95	.769	4.68	4.82
2016	Bos	AL	20	6	6	40.0	188	44	23	23	5	0	4	2	24	0	48	0	4	0	1.000	0-1	2	96	.828	5.80	5.18
2017	Bos	AL	54	0	14	58.0	238	42	19	18	3	0	1	3	27	1	52	4	4	1	.800	0-4	13	99	.573	2.61	2.79
2018	Bos	AL	73	0	9	65.2	285	57	34	32	4	4	5	4	32	0	68	4	4	2	.667	2-7	21	98	.662	3.70	4.39
2019	LAD	NL	55	0	13	51.1	226	49	31	26	6	0	0	3	22	2	62	10	5	4	.556	1-6	8	98	.711	4.16	4.56
2020	LAD	NL	12	1	2	10.0	42	8	3	2	0	1	0	1	7	0	9	3	0	0	-	0-0	3	97	.681	3.57	1.80
2021	LAD	NL	48	0	7	44.0	182	28	16	14	3	0	2	4	15	1	50	0	2	0	1.000	2-3	10	98	.544	2.01	2.86
14	StL	NL	7	7	0	35.0	156	41	19	17	3	1	1	3	10	0	25	3	2	2	.500	0-0	0	95	.774	4.82	4.37
14	Bos	AL	10	10	0	61.1	259	47	29	28	5	1	3	4	32	0	41	0	4	2	.667	0-0	0	95	.641	3.43	4.11
Postseason			33	4	4	53.0	226	47	22	20	3	1	1	2	20	2	48	5	3	3	.500	1-1	2	97	.619	3.12	3.40
10 ML YEARS			365	80	63	730.2	3152	697	342	311	64	8	25	36	298	10	619	40	50	29	.633	5-22	59	96	.703	3.94	3.83

Merrill Kelly

Pitches: R **Bats:** R **Pos:** SP-27

Ht: 6'2" **Wt:** 202 **Born:** 10/14/1988 **Age:** 33

			HOW MUCH PITCHED					WHAT HE GAVE UP											THE RESULTS						
Year	Team	Lg	G	GS	GF	IP	BFP	H	R	ER	HR	SH	SF	HB	TBB	IBB	SO	WP	W	L	Pct	Sv-Op	Hld	Vel	OPS	ERC	ERA
2019	Ari	NL	32	32	0	183.1	777	184	95	90	29	2	5	2	57	4	158	4	13	14	.481	0-0	0	92	.761	4.16	4.42
2020	Ari	NL	5	5	0	31.1	125	26	9	9	5	0	0	1	5	1	29	0	3	2	.600	0-0	0	92	.651	2.68	2.59
2021	Ari	NL	27	27	0	158.0	667	163	82	78	21	6	4	4	41	3	130	2	7	11	.389	0-0	0	92	.748	4.00	4.44
3 ML YEARS			64	64	0	372.2	1569	373	186	177	55	8	9	7	103	8	317	6	23	27	.460	0-0	0	92	.747	3.96	4.27

Tony Kemp

Bats: L **Throws:** R **Pos:** 2B-89;LF-49;PH-16;PR-9;SS-1;DH-1

Ht: 5'6" **Wt:** 160 **Born:** 10/31/1991 **Age:** 30

										BATTING												RUNNING			AVERAGES			
Year	Team	Lg	G	AB	H	2B	3B	HR	(Hm	Rd)	TB	R	RBI	RC	TBB	IBB	SO	HBP	SH	SF	SB	CS	GDP	Avg	OBP	Slg	OPS
2016	Hou	AL	59	120	26	4	3	1	(1	0)	39	15	7	11	14	0	27	0	1	1	2	1	5	.217	.296	.325	.621
2017	Hou	AL	17	37	8	1	0	0	(0	0)	9	6	4	4	1	0	5	1	0	0	1	0	0	.216	.256	.243	.500
2018	Hou	AL	97	255	67	15	0	6	(1	5)	100	37	30	41	32	1	44	3	3	1	9	3	7	.263	.351	.392	.743
2019	2 Tms		110	245	52	9	4	8	(7	1)	93	31	29	28	23	1	47	6	1	4	4	4	4	.212	.291	.380	.671
2020	Oak	AL	49	93	23	5	0	0	(0	0)	28	15	4	11	15	0	14	3	1	2	3	1	0	.247	.363	.301	.664
2021	Oak	AL	131	330	92	16	3	8	(2	6)	138	54	37	65	52	0	51	6	4	5	8	2	5	.279	.382	.418	.800
19	Hou	AL	66	163	37	6	2	7	(6	1)	68	23	17	18	16	1	29	4	1	2	4	3	2	.227	.308	.417	.725
19	ChC	NL	44	82	15	3	2	1	(1	0)	25	8	12	10	7	0	18	2	0	2	0	1	2	.183	.258	.305	.563
Postseason			6	14	4	1	0	1	(1	0)	8	3	1	3	5	0	3	0	0	0	0	0	0	.286	.474	.571	1.045
6 ML YEARS			463	1080	268	50	10	23	(11	12)	407	158	111	160	137	2	188	19	10	13	27	11	18	.248	.339	.377	.716

Ian Kennedy

Pitches: R **Bats:** R **Pos:** RP-55

Ht: 6'0" **Wt:** 210 **Born:** 12/19/1984 **Age:** 37

			HOW MUCH PITCHED					WHAT HE GAVE UP											THE RESULTS						
Year	Team	Lg	G	GS	GF	IP	BFP	H	R	ER	HR	SH	SF	HB	TBB	IBB	SO	WP	W	L	Pct	Sv-Op	Hld	Vel	OPS	ERC	ERA
2007	NYY	AL	3	3	0	19.0	77	13	6	4	1	0	0	0	9	0	15	0	1	0	1.000	0-0	0	89	.565	2.42	1.89
2008	NYY	AL	10	9	1	39.2	194	50	37	36	5	1	4	1	26	0	27	3	0	4	.000	0-0	0	89	.917	6.93	8.17
2009	NYY	AL	1	0	0	1.0	6	0	0	0	0	0	0	1	2	0	1	0	0	0	-	0-0	1	92	.500	7.00	0.00
2010	Ari	NL	32	32	0	194.0	810	163	87	82	26	11	5	10	70	2	168	16	9	10	.474	0-0	0	89	.696	3.47	3.80
2011	Ari	NL	33	33	0	222.0	900	186	73	71	19	9	9	9	55	0	198	11	21	4	.840	0-0	0	90	.641	2.71	2.88
2012	Ari	NL	33	33	0	208.1	899	216	101	93	28	13	6	14	55	4	187	5	15	12	.556	0-0	0	90	.775	4.18	4.02
2013	2 Tms	NL	31	31	0	181.1	794	180	108	99	27	4	5	12	73	1	163	10	7	10	.412	0-0	0	90	.781	4.64	4.91

Year Team	Lg	G	GS	GF	IP	BFP	H	R	ER	HR	SH	SF	HB	TBB	IBB	SO	WP	W	L	Pct	Sv-Op	Hld	Vel	OPS	ERC	ERA
2014 SD	NL	33	33	0	201.0	846	189	85	81	16	9	8	4	70	4	207	11	13	13	.500	0-0	0	92	.698	3.47	3.63
2015 SD	NL	30	30	0	168.1	713	166	95	80	31	8	2	7	52	4	174	5	9	15	.375	0-0	0	91	.816	4.37	4.28
2016 KC	AL	33	33	0	195.2	818	173	81	80	33	1	5	13	66	1	184	4	11	11	.500	0-0	0	92	.722	3.94	3.68
2017 KC	AL	30	30	0	154.0	655	143	99	92	34	1	6	5	61	2	131	4	5	13	.278	0-0	0	92	.804	4.64	5.38
2018 KC	AL	22	22	0	119.2	518	125	66	62	20	4	2	1	40	2	105	4	3	9	.250	0-0	0	92	.779	4.51	4.66
2019 KC	AL	63	0	51	63.1	266	64	24	24	6	3	0	1	17	1	73	3	3	2	.600	30-34	1	94	.675	3.63	3.41
2020 KC	AL	15	1	1	14.0	69	20	17	14	7	1	0	1	5	1	15	0	0	2	.000	0-0	2	94	1.076	9.67	9.00
2021 2 Tms		55	0	44	56.1	228	45	21	20	12	1	0	2	17	3	62	0	3	1	.750	26-30	0	94	.700	3.41	3.20
13 Ari	NL	21	21	0	124.0	549	128	79	72	18	8	5	10	48	1	108	9	3	8	.273	0-0	0	90	.798	4.82	5.23
13 SD	NL	10	10	0	57.1	245	52	29	27	9	0	0	2	25	0	55	1	4	2	.667	0-0	0	90	.744	4.26	4.24
21 Tex	AL	32	0	25	32.1	126	27	9	9	5	0	0	0	7	2	35	0	0	0	-	16-17	0	94	.656	2.83	2.51
21 Phi	NL	23	0	19	24.0	102	18	12	11	7	1	0	2	10	1	27	0	3	1	.750	10-13	0	94	.758	4.22	4.13
Postseason		2	2	0	12.2	57	13	6	6	1	0	2	3	3	0	8	1	0	1	.000	0-0	0	92	.782	4.25	4.26
15 ML YEARS		424	290	97	1837.2	7793	1733	900	838	265	70	51	81	618	25	1710	76	100	106	.485	56-64	4	91	.743	3.96	4.10

Max Kepler

Bats: L **Throws:** L **Pos:** RF-97;CF-22;PH-7;DH-4 **Ht:** 6'4" **Wt:** 225 **Born:** 2/10/1993 **Age:** 29

Year Team	Lg	G	AB	H	2B	3B	HR	(Hm	Rd)	TB	R	RBI	RC	TBB	IBB	SO	HBP	SH	SF	SB	CS	GDP	Avg	OBP	Slg	OPS
2015 Min	AL	3	7	1	0	0	0	(0	0)	1	0	0	0	0	0	3	0	0	0	0	0	0	.143	.143	.143	.286
2016 Min	AL	113	396	93	20	2	17	(8	9)	168	52	63	52	42	3	93	3	1	5	6	2	2	.235	.309	.424	.734
2017 Min	AL	147	511	124	32	2	19	(9	10)	217	67	69	68	47	2	114	6	1	3	6	1	5	.243	.312	.425	.737
2018 Min	AL	156	532	119	30	4	20	(12	8)	217	80	58	65	71	2	96	5	0	3	4	5	8	.224	.319	.408	.727
2019 Min	AL	134	524	132	32	0	36	(17	19)	272	98	90	90	60	0	99	8	0	4	1	5	5	.252	.336	.519	.855
2020 Min	AL	48	171	39	9	0	9	(3	6)	75	27	23	27	22	0	36	2	0	1	3	0	1	.228	.321	.439	.760
2021 Min	AL	121	426	90	21	4	19	(11	8)	176	61	54	57	54	3	96	6	0	4	10	0	2	.211	.306	.413	.719
Postseason		6	18	1	1	0	0	(0	0)	2	1	0	1	7	0	4	0	0	0	0	0	0	.056	.320	.111	.431
7 ML YEARS		722	2567	598	144	12	120	(60	60)	1126	385	357	359	296	10	537	30	2	20	30	13	23	.233	.317	.439	.756

Clayton Kershaw

Pitches: L **Bats:** L **Pos:** SP-22 **Ht:** 6'4" **Wt:** 225 **Born:** 3/19/1988 **Age:** 34

Year Team	Lg	G	GS	GF	IP	BFP	H	R	ER	HR	SH	SF	HB	TBB	IBB	SO	WP	W	L	Pct	Sv-Op	Hld	Vel	OPS	ERC	ERA
2008 LAD	NL	22	21	0	107.2	470	109	51	51	11	3	3	1	52	3	100	7	5	5	.500	0-0	0	94	.756	4.53	4.26
2009 LAD	NL	31	30	1	171.0	701	119	55	53	7	11	2	1	91	4	185	11	8	8	.500	0-0	0	94	.588	2.60	2.79
2010 LAD	NL	32	32	0	204.1	848	160	73	66	13	8	4	7	81	9	212	5	13	10	.565	0-0	0	93	.615	2.72	2.91
2011 LAD	NL	33	33	0	233.1	912	174	66	59	15	11	2	3	54	2	248	5	21	5	.808	0-0	0	93	.554	2.00	2.28
2012 LAD	NL	33	33	0	227.2	901	170	70	64	16	18	4	5	63	5	229	6	14	9	.609	0-0	0	93	.593	2.20	2.53
2013 LAD	NL	33	33	0	236.0	908	164	55	48	11	8	3	3	52	2	232	12	16	9	.640	0-0	0	93	.521	1.65	1.83
2014 LAD	NL	27	27	0	198.1	749	139	42	39	9	6	1	2	31	0	239	7	21	3	.875	0-0	0	93	.521	1.53	1.77
2015 LAD	NL	33	33	0	232.2	890	163	62	55	15	4	0	5	42	1	301	9	16	7	.696	0-0	0	94	.521	1.67	2.13
2016 LAD	NL	21	21	0	149.0	544	97	31	28	8	4	1	2	11	1	172	5	12	4	.750	0-0	0	93	.472	1.23	1.69
2017 LAD	NL	27	27	0	175.0	679	136	49	45	23	4	3	0	30	0	202	4	18	4	.818	0-0	0	93	.604	2.27	2.31
2018 LAD	NL	26	26	0	161.1	650	139	55	49	17	3	2	2	29	0	155	10	9	5	.643	0-0	0	91	.630	2.56	2.73
2019 LAD	NL	29	28	0	178.1	706	145	63	60	28	6	1	1	41	0	189	7	16	5	.762	0-0	0	90	.664	2.86	3.03
2020 LAD	NL	10	10	0	58.1	221	41	18	14	8	0	1	1	8	0	62	0	6	2	.750	0-0	0	92	.591	1.90	2.16
2021 LAD	NL	22	22	0	121.2	488	103	51	48	15	3	0	3	21	0	144	7	10	8	.556	0-0	0	91	.636	2.62	3.55
Postseason		37	30	2	189.0	759	153	93	88	28	6	5	4	50	5	207	10	13	12	.520	1-2	1	93	.656	2.90	4.19
14 ML YEARS		379	376	1	2454.2	9667	1859	741	679	196	89	27	37	606	27	2670	95	185	84	.688	0-0	1	93	.583	2.19	2.49

Dallas Keuchel

Pitches: L **Bats:** L **Pos:** SP-30; RP-2 KY-kull **Ht:** 6'2" **Wt:** 205 **Born:** 1/1/1988 **Age:** 34

Year Team	Lg	G	GS	GF	IP	BFP	H	R	ER	HR	SH	SF	HB	TBB	IBB	SO	WP	W	L	Pct	Sv-Op	Hld	Vel	OPS	ERC	ERA
2012 Hou	NL	16	16	0	85.1	377	93	56	50	14	9	3	1	39	1	38	2	3	8	.273	0-0	0	88	.823	5.39	5.27
2013 Hou	AL	31	22	2	153.2	682	184	96	88	20	2	3	5	52	3	123	7	6	10	.375	0-0	2	89	.812	5.33	5.15
2014 Hou	AL	29	29	0	200.0	808	187	71	65	11	4	5	7	48	2	146	7	12	9	.571	0-0	0	90	.655	3.02	2.93
2015 Hou	AL	33	33	0	232.0	911	185	68	64	17	1	3	2	51	0	216	9	20	8	.714	0-0	0	90	.575	2.26	2.48
2016 Hou	AL	26	26	0	168.0	701	168	88	85	20	2	1	2	48	1	144	9	9	12	.429	0-0	0	89	.736	3.84	4.55
2017 Hou	AL	23	23	0	145.2	584	116	50	47	15	1	0	2	47	0	125	1	14	5	.737	0-0	0	89	.619	2.82	2.90
2018 Hou	AL	34	34	0	204.2	874	211	92	85	18	3	9	2	58	0	153	9	12	11	.522	0-0	0	89	.704	3.71	3.74
2019 Atl	NL	19	19	0	112.2	487	115	50	47	16	5	0	9	39	1	91	6	8	8	.500	0-0	0	88	.764	4.62	3.75
2020 CWS	AL	11	11	0	63.1	257	52	15	14	2	2	0	0	17	0	42	0	6	2	.750	0-0	0	87	.556	2.21	1.99
2021 CWS	AL	32	30	0	162.0	720	189	105	95	25	0	1	7	59	1	95	5	9	9	.500	0-0	0	88	.827	5.51	5.28
Postseason		13	12	1	63.0	264	58	29	26	10	4	1	0	20	3	56	1	4	3	.571	0-0	0	90	.727	3.61	3.71
10 ML YEARS		254	243	2	1527.1	6401	1500	691	640	158	29	25	37	458	9	1173	55	99	82	.547	0-0	2	89	.706	3.73	3.77

Mike Kickham

Pitches: L **Bats:** L **Pos:** RP-1 KICK-em **Ht:** 6'4" **Wt:** 220 **Born:** 12/12/1988 **Age:** 33

Year Team	Lg	G	GS	GF	IP	BFP	H	R	ER	HR	SH	SF	HB	TBB	IBB	SO	WP	W	L	Pct	Sv-Op	Hld	Vel	OPS	ERC	ERA
2021 OkCity	AAA	19	9	5	45.2	210	52	28	28	9	0	1	3	22	0	42	3	0	3	.000	0--	-	-	.856	6.24	5.52
2013 SF	NL	12	3	5	28.1	144	46	34	32	8	2	1	0	10	2	29	2	0	3	.000	0-0	0	90	1.036	8.75	10.16
2014 SF	NL	2	0	0	2.0	16	8	5	5	1	0	0	1	0	0	1	0	0	0	-	0-0	0	91	1.296	29.66	22.50
2020 Bos	AL	6	2	2	14.0	70	21	12	12	6	0	0	2	5	1	17	0	1	1	.500	0-0	0	89	1.083	10.10	7.71
2021 LAD	NL	1	0	1	2.0	12	5	3	3	1	0	0	1	2	0	2	0	0	0	-	0-0	0	88	1.483	23.45	13.50
4 ML YEARS		21	5	8	46.1	242	80	54	52	16	2	1	3	17	3	49	2	1	4	.200	0-0	0	90	1.088	10.51	10.10

Carter Kieboom

Bats: R **Throws:** R **Pos:** 3B-60;PH-3   **Ht:** 6'2" **Wt:** 215 **Born:** 9/3/1997 **Age:** 24

			BATTING																	**RUNNING**			**AVERAGES**			
Year Team	Lg	G	AB	H	2B	3B	HR	(Hm	Rd)	TB	R	RBI	RC	TBB	IBB	SO	HBP	SH	SF	SB	CS	GDP	Avg	OBP	Slg	OPS
2021 Roch	AAA	44	148	35	7	0	5	(-	-)	57	26	23	-	26	0	31	7	0	0	1	1	7	.236	.376	.385	.761
2019 Was	NL	11	39	5	0	0	2	(2	0)	11	4	2	0	4	1	16	0	0	0	0	0	0	.128	.209	.282	.491
2020 Was	NL	33	99	20	1	0	0	(0	0)	21	15	9	10	17	0	33	5	0	1	0	1	6	.202	.344	.212	.556
2021 Was	NL	62	217	45	6	0	6	(5	1)	69	26	20	14	25	2	62	5	0	2	0	0	9	.207	.301	.318	.619
3 ML YEARS		106	355	70	7	0	8	(7	1)	101	45	31	24	46	3	111	10	0	3	0	1	15	.197	.304	.285	.589

Kevin Kiermaier

Bats: L **Throws:** R **Pos:** CF-116;PR-6;PH-2;DH-1   KEER-my-urr   **Ht:** 6'1" **Wt:** 210 **Born:** 4/22/1990 **Age:** 32

			BATTING																	**RUNNING**			**AVERAGES**			
Year Team	Lg	G	AB	H	2B	3B	HR	(Hm	Rd)	TB	R	RBI	RC	TBB	IBB	SO	HBP	SH	SF	SB	CS	GDP	Avg	OBP	Slg	OPS
2013 TB	AL	1	0	0	0	0	0	(0	0)	0	0	0	0	0	0	0	0	0	0	0	0	0	-	-	-	-
2014 TB	AL	108	331	87	16	8	10	(4	6)	149	35	35	37	23	2	71	3	5	2	5	4	3	.263	.315	.450	.765
2015 TB	AL	151	505	133	25	12	10	(5	5)	212	62	40	66	24	0	95	2	2	2	18	5	7	.263	.298	.420	.718
2016 TB	AL	105	366	90	20	2	12	(5	7)	150	55	37	54	40	1	74	7	0	1	21	3	5	.246	.331	.410	.741
2017 TB	AL	98	380	105	15	3	15	(8	7)	171	56	39	53	31	2	99	5	4	1	16	7	3	.276	.338	.450	.788
2018 TB	AL	88	332	72	12	9	7	(4	3)	123	44	29	30	25	2	91	6	2	2	10	5	4	.217	.282	.370	.653
2019 TB	AL	129	447	102	20	7	14	(7	7)	178	60	55	56	26	2	104	5	1	1	19	5	8	.228	.278	.398	.676
2020 TB	AL	49	138	30	5	3	3	(0	3)	50	16	22	20	20	1	42	1	0	0	8	1	2	.217	.321	.362	.683
2021 TB	AL	122	348	90	19	7	4	(2	2)	135	54	37	47	33	2	99	5	0	4	9	5	4	.259	.328	.388	.716
Postseason		25	77	17	6	0	4	(2	2)	35	9	10	9	1	0	24	1	0	0	0	1	0	.221	.241	.455	.695
9 ML YEARS		851	2847	709	132	51	75	(35	40)	1168	382	294	363	222	12	675	34	14	13	106	35	36	.249	.310	.410	.720

Yusei Kikuchi

Pitches: L **Bats:** L **Pos:** SP-29   **Ht:** 6'0" **Wt:** 200 **Born:** 6/17/1991 **Age:** 31

			HOW MUCH PITCHED				**WHAT HE GAVE UP**									**THE RESULTS**							
Year Team	Lg	G	GS	GF	IP	BFP	H	R	ER	HR	SH	SF	HB	TBB	IBB	SO	WP	W	L	Pct	Sv-Op	Hld	Vel	OPS	ERC	ERA
2019 Sea	AL	32	32	0	161.2	721	195	109	98	36	0	5	6	50	0	116	5	6	11	.353	0-0	0	92	.888	5.97	5.46
2020 Sea	AL	9	9	0	47.0	194	41	27	27	3	0	2	0	20	0	47	3	2	4	.333	0-0	0	95	.681	3.31	5.17
2021 Sea	AL	29	29	0	157.0	666	145	82	77	27	1	1	5	62	0	163	6	7	9	.438	0-0	0	95	.751	4.28	4.41
3 ML YEARS		70	70	0	365.2	1581	381	218	202	66	1	8	11	132	0	326	14	15	24	.385	0-0	0	94	.805	4.88	4.97

Ha-seong Kim

Bats: R **Throws:** R **Pos:** PH-40;SS-35;3B-23;2B-21;PR-4   **Ht:** 5'9" **Wt:** 168 **Born:** 10/17/1995 **Age:** 26

			BATTING																	**RUNNING**			**AVERAGES**			
Year Team	Lg	G	AB	H	2B	3B	HR	(Hm	Rd)	TB	R	RBI	RC	TBB	IBB	SO	HBP	SH	SF	SB	CS	GDP	Avg	OBP	Slg	OPS
2021 SD	NL	117	267	54	12	2	8	(5	3)	94	27	34	24	22	1	71	4	2	3	6	1	6	.202	.270	.352	.622

Kwang-hyun Kim

Pitches: L **Bats:** L **Pos:** SP-21; RP-6   **Ht:** 6'2" **Wt:** 195 **Born:** 7/22/1988 **Age:** 33

			HOW MUCH PITCHED				**WHAT HE GAVE UP**									**THE RESULTS**							
Year Team	Lg	G	GS	GF	IP	BFP	H	R	ER	HR	SH	SF	HB	TBB	IBB	SO	WP	W	L	Pct	Sv-Op	Hld	Vel	OPS	ERC	ERA
2020 StL	NL	8	7	1	39.0	154	28	9	7	3	0	0	6	12	2	24	1	3	0	1.000	1-1	0	90	.584	2.09	1.62
2021 StL	NL	27	21	2	106.2	452	98	46	41	12	2	2	4	39	2	80	4	7	7	.500	1-1	0	89	.686	3.70	3.46
Postseason		1	1	0	3.2	18	5	3	3	0	0	2	0	2	0	2	0	0	0	-	0-0	0	90	.889	5.84	7.36
2 ML YEARS		35	28	3	145.2	606	126	55	48	15	2	2	4	51	4	104	5	10	7	.588	2-2	0	89	.660	3.24	2.97

Craig Kimbrel

Pitches: R **Bats:** R **Pos:** RP-63   KIM-brull   **Ht:** 6'0" **Wt:** 215 **Born:** 5/28/1988 **Age:** 34

			HOW MUCH PITCHED				**WHAT HE GAVE UP**									**THE RESULTS**							
Year Team	Lg	G	GS	GF	IP	BFP	H	R	ER	HR	SH	SF	HB	TBB	IBB	SO	WP	W	L	Pct	Sv-Op	Hld	Vel	OPS	ERC	ERA
2010 Atl	NL	21	0	7	20.2	88	9	2	1	0	0	0	1	16	1	40	4	4	0	1.000	1-1	2	95	.437	1.72	0.44
2011 Atl	NL	79	0	64	77.0	306	48	19	18	3	1	2	1	32	1	127	4	4	3	.571	46-54	0	96	.499	1.88	2.10
2012 Atl	NL	63	0	56	62.2	231	27	7	7	3	0	0	2	14	0	116	5	3	1	.750	42-45	0	97	.358	0.93	1.01
2013 Atl	NL	68	0	60	67.0	258	39	10	9	4	0	0	3	20	2	98	3	4	3	.571	50-54	0	97	.487	1.58	1.21
2014 Atl	NL	63	0	54	61.2	244	30	13	11	2	3	0	2	26	0	95	6	0	3	.000	47-51	0	97	.430	1.41	1.61
2015 SD	NL	61	0	53	59.1	239	40	19	17	6	0	0	1	22	1	87	4	4	2	.667	39-43	0	97	.569	2.31	2.58
2016 Bos	AL	57	0	47	53.0	220	28	22	20	4	1	1	4	30	0	83	6	2	6	.250	31-33	1	97	.539	2.32	3.40
2017 Bos	AL	67	0	51	69.0	254	33	11	11	6	1	0	4	14	0	126	5	5	0	1.000	35-39	1	98	.444	1.21	1.43
2018 Bos	AL	63	0	57	62.1	247	31	19	19	7	1	0	2	31	0	96	7	5	1	.833	42-47	0	97	.565	2.07	2.74
2019 ChC	NL	23	0	17	20.2	96	21	15	15	9	0	1	2	12	0	30	0	0	4	.000	13-16	0	96	1.019	7.90	6.53
2020 ChC	NL	18	0	11	15.1	69	10	9	9	2	0	0	2	12	1	28	4	0	1	.000	2-3	3	97	.693	4.20	5.28
2021 2 Tms	NL	63	0	43	59.2	235	31	19	15	6	0	3	3	23	1	100	8	4	5	.444	24-29	6	97	.514	1.76	2.26
21 ChC	NL	39	0	35	36.2	137	13	6	2	1	0	1	0	13	0	64	3	2	3	.400	23-25	0	97	.336	0.85	0.49
21 CWS	AL	24	0	8	23.0	98	18	13	13	5	0	2	3	10	1	36	5	2	2	.500	1-4	6	96	.774	4.27	5.09
Postseason		20	0	15	22.0	92	14	10	9	2	0	1	3	14	0	27	2	0	1	.000	7-7	1	98	.661	3.58	3.68
12 ML YEARS		646	0	520	628.1	2487	347	165	152	52	7	7	26	252	7	1026	56	35	29	.547	372-415	13	97	.513	1.84	2.18

Isiah Kiner-Falefa

Bats: R **Throws:** R **Pos:** SS-156;DH-1;PH-1;PR-1   **Ht:** 5'11" **Wt:** 190 **Born:** 3/23/1995 **Age:** 27

Year Team	Lg	G	AB	H	2B	3B	HR	(Hm	Rd)	TB	R	RBI	RC	TBB	IBB	SO	HBP	SH	SF	SB	CS	GDP	Avg	OBP	Slg	OPS
2018 Tex	AL	111	356	93	18	2	4	(0	4)	127	43	34	34	28	1	62	6	5	1	7	5	14	.261	.325	.357	.682
2019 Tex	AL	65	202	48	12	1	1	(0	1)	65	23	21	18	14	0	49	4	1	1	3	0	9	.238	.299	.322	.620
2020 Tex	AL	58	211	59	4	3	3	(1	2)	78	28	10	26	14	0	32	2	0	1	8	5	6	.280	.329	.370	.699
2021 Tex	AL	158	635	172	25	3	8	(6	2)	227	74	53	72	28	2	90	11	1	2	20	5	11	.271	.312	.357	.670
4 ML YEARS		392	1404	372	59	9	16	(7	9)	497	168	118	150	84	3	233	23	7	5	38	15	40	.265	.316	.354	.670

John King

Pitches: L **Bats:** L **Pos:** RP-27   **Ht:** 6'2" **Wt:** 215 **Born:** 9/14/1994 **Age:** 27

Year Team	Lg	G	GS	GF	IP	BFP	H	R	ER	HR	SH	SF	HB	TBB	IBB	SO	WP	W	L	Pct	Sv-Op	Hld	Vel	OPS	ERC	ERA
2020 Tex	AL	6	0	0	10.1	51	13	8	7	2	0	0	2	4	0	9	0	1	0	1.000	0-1	0	93	.839	6.83	6.10
2021 Tex	AL	27	0	6	46.0	193	41	24	18	3	1	0	4	12	1	40	2	7	5	.583	0-1	4	92	.626	3.00	3.52
2 ML YEARS		33	0	6	56.1	244	54	32	25	5	1	0	6	16	1	49	2	8	5	.615	0-2	4	92	.670	3.63	3.99

Michael King

Pitches: R **Bats:** R **Pos:** RP-16; SP-6   **Ht:** 6'3" **Wt:** 210 **Born:** 5/25/1995 **Age:** 27

Year Team	Lg	G	GS	GF	IP	BFP	H	R	ER	HR	SH	SF	HB	TBB	IBB	SO	WP	W	L	Pct	Sv-Op	Hld	Vel	OPS	ERC	ERA
2019 NYY	AL	1	0	0	2.0	9	2	1	0	0	0	0	0	0	0	1	0	0	0	-	0-0	0	92	.444	1.68	0.00
2020 NYY	AL	9	4	1	26.2	121	30	23	23	5	0	0	2	11	0	26	0	1	2	.333	0-0	0	93	.846	5.80	7.76
2021 NYY	AL	22	6	3	63.1	275	57	29	25	6	1	1	6	24	1	62	5	2	4	.333	0-0	2	94	.674	3.69	3.55
Postseason		1	0	1	2.0	6	0	0	0	0	0	0	0	0	0	1	0	0	0	-	0-0	0	94	.000	0.00	0.00
3 ML YEARS		32	10	4	92.0	405	89	53	48	11	1	1	8	35	1	89	5	3	6	.333	0-0	2	94	.720	4.22	4.70

Scott Kingery

Bats: R **Throws:** R **Pos:** PH-7;RF-5;2B-4;3B-1;LF-1;CF-1;PR-1   **Ht:** 5'10" **Wt:** 180 **Born:** 4/29/1994 **Age:** 28

Year Team	Lg	G	AB	H	2B	3B	HR	(Hm	Rd)	TB	R	RBI	RC	TBB	IBB	SO	HBP	SH	SF	SB	CS	GDP	Avg	OBP	Slg	OPS
2021 LV	AAA	23	72	13	4	2	0	(-	-)	21	11	5		13	0	27	1	0	2	3	1		.181	.307	.292	.598
2018 Phi	NL	147	452	102	23	2	8	(6	2)	153	55	35	39	24	1	126	3	0	5	10	3	3	.226	.267	.338	.605
2019 Phi	NL	126	458	118	34	4	19	(10	9)	217	64	55	63	34	1	147	5	1	2	15	4	3	.258	.315	.474	.788
2020 Phi	NL	36	113	18	5	0	3	(1	2)	32	12	6	6	9	0	35	1	1	0	0	0		.159	.228	.283	.511
2021 Phi	NL	15	19	1	0	0	0	(0	0)	1	1	0	0	0	0	12	0	0	0	0	0		.053	.053	.053	.105
4 ML YEARS		324	1042	239	62	6	30	(17	13)	403	132	96	108	67	2	320	9	2	7	25	7	6	.229	.280	.387	.667

Tyler Kinley

Pitches: R **Bats:** R **Pos:** RP-70   **Ht:** 6'4" **Wt:** 220 **Born:** 1/31/1991 **Age:** 31

Year Team	Lg	G	GS	GF	IP	BFP	H	R	ER	HR	SH	SF	HB	TBB	IBB	SO	WP	W	L	Pct	Sv-Op	Hld	Vel	OPS	ERC	ERA
2018 2 Tms		13	0	4	11.0	57	15	15	15	2	0	0	1	8	2	13	3	0	0	-	0-0	0	97	.942	8.25	12.27
2019 Mia	NL	52	0	13	49.1	221	43	20	20	5	1	2	1	36	2	46	3	3	1	.750	1-3	1	95	.723	4.71	3.65
2020 Col	NL	24	0	4	23.2	96	13	15	14	2	1	2	3	12	0	26	4	0	2	.000	0-0	4	96	.564	2.52	5.32
2021 Col	NL	70	0	7	70.1	295	59	37	37	12	1	2	2	26	1	68	4	3	2	.600	0-4	10	96	.720	3.60	4.73
18 AL		4	0	3	3.1	23	9	9	9	2	0	0	0	4	0	4	2	0	0	-	0-0	0	96	1.407	25.66	24.30
18 Mia	NL	9	0	1	7.2	34	6	6	6	0	0	0	1	4	2	9	1	0	0	-	0-0	0	97	.634	2.62	7.04
4 ML YEARS		159	0	28	154.1	669	130	87	86	21	3	6	7	82	5	153	14	6	5	.545	1-7	15	96	.719	4.09	5.02

Brandon Kintzler

Pitches: R **Bats:** R **Pos:** RP-28; SP-1   **Ht:** 5'10" **Wt:** 200 **Born:** 8/1/1984 **Age:** 37

Year Team	Lg	G	GS	GF	IP	BFP	H	R	ER	HR	SH	SF	HB	TBB	IBB	SO	WP	W	L	Pct	Sv-Op	Hld	Vel	OPS	ERC	ERA
2010 Mil	NL	7	0	2	7.1	33	10	6	6	2	1	0	0	4	1	9	1	0	1	.000	0-0	0	93	1.045	8.67	7.36
2011 Mil	NL	9	0	3	14.2	61	14	9	6	3	0	2	0	3	0	15	0	1	1	.500	0-0	0	93	.725	3.65	3.68
2012 Mil	NL	14	0	1	16.2	72	18	7	7	1	0	0	0	7	1	14	1	3	0	1.000	0-0	2	93	.732	4.30	3.78
2013 Mil	NL	71	0	11	77.0	305	66	26	23	2	4	2	1	16	2	58	1	3	3	.500	0-4	26	92	.567	2.21	2.69
2014 Mil	NL	64	0	13	58.1	239	62	22	21	8	4	1	0	16	3	31	1	3	3	.500	0-3	8	92	.781	4.28	3.24
2015 Mil	NL	7	0	4	7.0	36	12	6	5	1	0	0	0	5	0	7	1	0	1	.000	0-0	0	93	1.021	10.76	6.43
2016 Min	AL	54	0	36	54.1	224	59	22	19	5	0	0	2	8	1	35	0	0	2	.000	17-20	1	93	.705	3.68	3.15
2017 2 Tms		72	0	45	71.1	288	66	25	24	5	1	2	3	16	2	39	1	4	3	.571	29-35	10	93	.638	2.99	3.03
2018 2 Tms		70	0	15	60.2	263	67	31	31	5	1	2	4	22	5	43	1	3	3	.500	2-5	19	93	.787	4.62	4.60
2019 ChC	NL	62	0	10	57.0	227	45	18	17	5	1	4	1	13	3	48	0	3	3	.500	1-3	17	93	.632	2.47	2.68
2020 Mia	NL	24	0	21	24.1	101	21	7	6	3	0	1	0	11	3	14	0	2	3	.400	12-14	1	91	.710	3.57	2.22
2021 Phi	NL	29	1	6	29.2	141	45	23	21	7	0	1	1	8	2	22	0	2	1	.667	0-2	2	92	.963	7.72	6.37
17 Min	AL	45	0	41	45.1	182	41	15	14	3	0	2	1	11	1	27	1	2	2	.500	28-32	0	93	.626	2.97	2.78
17 Was	NL	27	0	4	26.0	106	25	10	10	2	1	0	1	5	1	12	0	2	1	.667	1-3	10	93	.659	3.04	3.46
18 Was	NL	45	0	8	42.2	175	40	17	17	2	1	0	3	13	3	31	1	1	2	.333	2-5	15	92	.689	3.28	3.59
18 ChC	NL	25	0	7	18.0	88	27	14	14	3	0	2	1	9	2	12	0	2	1	.667	0-0	4	93	.986	8.26	7.00
Postseason		6	0	4	6.1	24	4	2	2	0	1	0	1	2	0	7	0	0	1	.000	1-1	0	93	.654	1.99	2.84
12 ML YEARS		483	1	167	478.1	1990	485	202	186	47	11	12	15	129	23	335	7	24	24	.500	61-86	86	93	.717	3.75	3.50

Alex Kirilloff

Bats: L **Throws:** L **Pos:** 1B-29;RF-27;LF-13;PH-3;PR-1   **Ht:** 6'2" **Wt:** 195 **Born:** 11/9/1997 **Age:** 24

			BATTING																RUNNING			AVERAGES			
Year	Team	Lg	G	AB	H	2B	3B	HR	(Hm | Rd)	TB	R	RBI	RC	TBB	IBB	SO	HBP	SH	SF	SB	CS	GDP	Avg	OBP	Slg	OPS
2021	Min	AL	59	215	54	11	1	8	(6 | 2)	91	23	34	31	14	2	52	1	0	1	1	1	3	.251	.299	.423	.722
	Postseason		1	4	1	0	0	0	(0 | 0)	1	0	0	0	0	0	0	0	0	0	0	0	0	.250	.250	.250	.500

Alejandro Kirk

Bats: R **Throws:** R **Pos:** C-44;PH-9;DH-8   **Ht:** 5'8" **Wt:** 265 **Born:** 11/6/1998 **Age:** 23

Year	Team	Lg	G	AB	H	2B	3B	HR	(Hm	Rd)	TB	R	RBI	RC	TBB	IBB	SO	HBP	SH	SF	SB	CS	GDP	Avg	OBP	Slg	OPS
2021	Buffalo	AAA	14	49	17	3	0	2	(-	-)	26	7	13	-	5	0	9	0	0	2	0	0	0	.347	.393	.531	.923
2020	Tor	AL	9	24	9	2	0	1	(1	0)	14	4	3	5	1	0	4	0	0	0	0	0	0	.375	.400	.583	.983
2021	Tor	AL	60	165	40	8	0	8	(4	4)	72	19	24	22	19	0	22	3	0	2	0	0	7	.242	.328	.436	.764
	Postseason		1	3	1	0	0	0	(0	0)	1	0	0	0	0	0	0	0	0	0	0	0	0	.333	.333	.333	.667
	2 ML YEARS		69	189	49	10	0	9	(5	4)	86	23	27	27	20	0	26	3	0	2	0	0	7	.259	.336	.455	.791

Andrew Kittredge

Pitches: R **Bats:** R **Pos:** RP-53; SP-4   **Ht:** 6'1" **Wt:** 230 **Born:** 3/17/1990 **Age:** 32

			HOW MUCH PITCHED					WHAT HE GAVE UP										THE RESULTS								
Year	Team	Lg	G	GS	GF	IP	BFP	H	R	ER	HR	SH	SF	HB	TBB	IBB	SO	WP	W	L	Pct	Sv-Op	Hld	Vel	OPS	ERC	ERA
2017	TB	AL	15	0	2	15.1	66	13	4	3	2	1	0	0	6	1	14	1	0	1	.000	0-0	1	94	.665	3.19	1.76
2018	TB	AL	33	3	4	38.1	181	54	34	33	7	1	2	1	17	5	30	1	3	2	.600	0-0	0	93	.956	7.35	7.75
2019	TB	AL	37	7	10	49.2	210	51	25	23	7	0	2	2	12	0	58	2	1	0	1.000	0-0	2	95	.717	4.03	4.17
2020	TB	AL	8	1	1	8.0	31	8	2	2	0	0	0	0	2	0	3	0	0	0	-	1-1	1	94	.667	3.09	2.25
2021	TB	AL	57	4	15	71.2	282	55	21	15	7	1	1	3	15	5	77	5	9	3	.750	8-9	7	95	.592	2.23	1.88
	5 ML YEARS		150	15	32	183.0	770	181	86	76	23	3	6	6	52	11	182	9	13	6	.684	9-10	11	95	.719	3.79	3.74

Patrick Kivlehan

Bats: R **Throws:** R **Pos:** PH-3;RF-2   KIV-leh-hann   **Ht:** 6'2" **Wt:** 215 **Born:** 12/22/1989 **Age:** 32

Year	Team	Lg	G	AB	H	2B	3B	HR	(Hm	Rd)	TB	R	RBI	RC	TBB	IBB	SO	HBP	SH	SF	SB	CS	GDP	Avg	OBP	Slg	OPS
2021	ElPaso	AAA	86	315	82	18	0	21	(-	-)	163	49	69	-	26	0	94	2	0	3	4	3	4	.260	.318	.517	.835
2016	2 Tms	NL	8	21	4	0	0	1	(1	0)	7	5	2	3	2	0	11	1	0	0	0	0	0	.190	.292	.333	.625
2017	Cin	NL	115	178	37	5	1	9	(4	5)	71	23	26	20	22	1	61	3	0	1	1	2	2	.208	.304	.399	.703
2018	Ari	NL	9	13	3	0	2	0	(0	0)	7	3	0	2	0	0	6	1	0	0	0	0	0	.231	.286	.538	.824
2021	SD	NL	5	4	1	0	0	0	(0	0)	1	3	2	2	2	0	3	1	0	0	0	0	0	.250	.500	.250	.750
16	SD	NL	5	16	4	0	0	1	(1	0)	7	5	2	3	2	0	9	1	0	0	0	0	0	.250	.368	.438	.806
16	Cin	NL	3	5	0	0	0	0	(0	0)	0	0	0	0	0	0	2	0	0	0	0	0	0	.000	.000	.000	.000
	4 ML YEARS		137	216	45	5	3	10	(5	5)	86	34	30	27	26	1	81	6	0	2	1	2	2	.208	.308	.398	.706

Gabe Klobosits

Pitches: R **Bats:** L **Pos:** RP-11   **Ht:** 6'7" **Wt:** 270 **Born:** 5/16/1995 **Age:** 27

Year	Team	Lg	G	GS	GF	IP	BFP	H	R	ER	HR	SH	SF	HB	TBB	IBB	SO	WP	W	L	Pct	Sv-Op	Hld	Vel	OPS	ERC	ERA
2021	Hrsbrg	AA	15	0	8	20.0	79	13	3	2	1	0	0	0	8	3	26	0	2	1	.667	3--	-	-	.548	1.80	0.90
2021	Roch	AAA	15	0	9	17.1	72	13	3	2	0	1	0	2	4	0	19	0	1	1	.500	3--	-	-	.545	1.89	1.04
2021	Was	NL	11	0	2	11.1	52	13	8	7	0	0	0	1	5	1	5	2	0	1	.000	0-0	4	95	.713	4.47	5.56

Corey Kluber

Pitches: R **Bats:** R **Pos:** SP-16   CLUE-burr   **Ht:** 6'4" **Wt:** 215 **Born:** 4/10/1986 **Age:** 36

Year	Team	Lg	G	GS	GF	IP	BFP	H	R	ER	HR	SH	SF	HB	TBB	IBB	SO	WP	W	L	Pct	Sv-Op	Hld	Vel	OPS	ERC	ERA
2011	Cle	AL	3	0	2	4.1	25	6	4	4	0	0	0	2	3	0	5	1	0	0	-	0-0	0	92	.740	8.12	8.31
2012	Cle	AL	12	12	0	63.0	281	76	44	36	9	1	0	4	18	0	54	2	2	5	.286	0-0	0	93	.834	5.38	5.14
2013	Cle	AL	26	24	1	147.1	608	153	67	63	15	4	2	5	33	0	136	1	11	5	.688	0-0	0	93	.729	3.83	3.85
2014	Cle	AL	34	34	0	235.2	951	207	72	64	14	5	2	6	51	3	269	3	18	9	.667	0-0	0	93	.624	2.57	2.44
2015	Cle	AL	32	32	0	222.0	886	189	92	86	22	7	4	11	45	3	245	6	9	16	.360	0-0	0	93	.650	2.74	3.49
2016	Cle	AL	32	32	0	215.0	860	170	82	75	22	6	2	7	57	1	227	5	18	9	.667	0-0	0	92	.631	2.62	3.14
2017	Cle	AL	29	29	0	203.2	777	141	56	51	21	3	1	5	36	2	265	4	18	4	.818	0-0	0	93	.556	1.83	2.25
2018	Cle	AL	33	33	0	215.0	842	179	75	69	25	2	2	3	34	0	222	2	20	7	.741	0-0	0	92	.624	2.47	2.89
2019	Cle	AL	7	7	0	35.2	168	44	26	23	4	1	1	3	15	0	38	1	2	3	.400	0-0	0	92	.824	5.87	5.80
2020	Tex	AL	1	1	0	1.0	5	3	0	0	0	0	0	0	1	0	1	0	0	0	-	0-0	0	92	.333	1.26	0.00
2021	NYY	AL	16	16	0	80.0	341	74	37	34	8	1	3	5	33	0	82	3	5	3	.625	0-0	0	91	.704	4.00	3.83
	Postseason		9	9	0	45.1	194	44	20	20	10	0	1	5	13	0	47	0	4	3	.571	0-0	0	92	.787	4.75	3.97
	11 ML YEARS		225	220	3	1422.2	5742	1239	555	505	140	30	17	51	326	9	1544	28	103	61	.628	0-0	0	93	.652	2.88	3.19

Andrew Knapp

Bats: B **Throws:** R **Pos:** C-47;PH-13;1B-6;2B-1;PR-1   **Ht:** 6'1" **Wt:** 189 **Born:** 11/9/1991 **Age:** 30

Year	Team	Lg	G	AB	H	2B	3B	HR	(Hm	Rd)	TB	R	RBI	RC	TBB	IBB	SO	HBP	SH	SF	SB	CS	GDP	Avg	OBP	Slg	OPS
2017	Phi	NL	56	171	44	8	1	3	(2	1)	63	26	13	20	31	4	56	0	0	2	1	0	5	.257	.368	.368	.736
2018	Phi	NL	84	187	37	6	2	4	(1	3)	59	19	15	15	24	1	75	2	1	1	1	0	2	.198	.294	.316	.610

Year	Team	Lg	G	AB	H	2B	3B	HR	(Hm	Rd)	TB	R	RBI	RC	TBB	IBB	SO	HBP	SH	SF	SB	CS	GDP	Avg	OBP	Slg	OPS

BATTING / RUNNING / AVERAGES

Year	Team	Lg	G	AB	H	2B	3B	HR	(Hm	Rd)	TB	R	RBI	RC	TBB	IBB	SO	HBP	SH	SF	SB	CS	GDP	Avg	OBP	Slg	OPS
2019	Phi	NL	74	136	29	9	0	2	(0	2)	44	12	8	11	18	2	51	3	3	0	0	0	2	.213	.318	.324	.642
2020	Phi	NL	33	72	20	4	1	2	(0	2)	32	9	15	17	15	0	19	1	0	1	0	0	1	.278	.404	.444	.849
2021	Phi	NL	62	145	22	3	0	2	(1	1)	31	13	11	6	10	0	61	2	1	1	0	0	1	.152	.215	.214	.429
5 ML YEARS			309	711	152	30	4	13	(4	9)	229	79	62	69	98	7	262	8	5	5	2	0	11	.214	.314	.322	.636

Corey Knebel

Pitches: R **Bats:** R **Pos:** RP-23; SP-4   kuh-NAY-bull   **Ht:** 6'3" **Wt:** 224 **Born:** 11/26/1991 **Age:** 30

Year	Team	Lg	G	GS	GF	IP	BFP	H	R	ER	HR	SH	SF	HB	TBB	IBB	SO	WP	W	L	Pct	Sv-Op	Hld	Vel	OPS	ERC	ERA
2021	OkCity	AAA	6	1	0	5.2	23	4	1	1	0	0	0	1	1	0	11	1	0	0	-	0--	-	-	.594	1.76	1.59
2014	Det	AL	8	0	4	8.2	39	11	7	6	0	0	0	0	3	0	11	1	0	0	-	0-0	0	94	.776	4.65	6.23
2015	Mil	NL	48	0	15	50.1	209	44	18	18	8	0	0	2	17	1	58	1	0	0	-	0-1	3	95	.744	3.69	3.22
2016	Mil	NL	35	0	7	32.2	145	32	20	17	3	0	1	1	16	3	38	1	1	4	.200	2-4	13	95	.708	4.18	4.68
2017	Mil	NL	76	0	48	76.0	309	48	15	15	6	0	0	2	40	5	126	2	1	4	.200	39-45	11	97	.568	2.51	1.78
2018	Mil	NL	57	0	29	55.1	223	38	23	22	7	0	1	4	22	0	88	0	4	3	.571	16-19	6	97	.659	2.90	3.58
2020	Mil	NL	15	0	2	13.1	62	15	9	9	4	0	0	0	8	0	15	0	0	0	-	0-2	0	94	.927	7.20	6.08
2021	LAD	NL	27	4	3	25.2	101	16	8	7	2	0	1	0	9	1	30	0	4	0	1.000	3-5	7	96	.522	1.80	2.45
Postseason			9	0	1	10.0	33	2	1	1	0	0	0	1	3	0	14	0	1	0	1.000	1-1	3	97	.320	0.55	0.90
7 ML YEARS			266	4	108	262.0	1088	204	100	94	30	0	3	9	115	10	366	5	10	11	.476	60-76	40	96	.664	3.22	3.23

Reiss Knehr

Pitches: R **Bats:** L **Pos:** RP-7; SP-5   **Ht:** 6'2" **Wt:** 205 **Born:** 11/3/1996 **Age:** 25

Year	Team	Lg	G	GS	GF	IP	BFP	H	R	ER	HR	SH	SF	HB	TBB	IBB	SO	WP	W	L	Pct	Sv-Op	Hld	Vel	OPS	ERC	ERA
2021	SnAnt	AA	11	11	0	55.1	225	41	24	24	4	1	0	6	22	0	46	2	6	1	.857	0--	-	-	.629	2.99	3.90
2021	ElPaso	AAA	8	5	2	20.1	82	15	6	6	3	1	0	1	9	0	20	0	0	2	.000	1--	-	-	.731	3.45	2.66
2021	SD	NL	12	5	1	29.0	129	23	16	16	2	0	3	2	20	1	20	3	1	2	.333	0-0	0	94	.714	4.02	4.97

Dusten Knight

Pitches: R **Bats:** R **Pos:** RP-7   **Ht:** 6'0" **Wt:** 200 **Born:** 9/7/1990 **Age:** 31

Year	Team	Lg	G	GS	GF	IP	BFP	H	R	ER	HR	SH	SF	HB	TBB	IBB	SO	WP	W	L	Pct	Sv-Op	Hld	Vel	OPS	ERC	ERA
2021	Norfolk	AAA	34	0	22	37.1	145	28	12	12	5	0	0	0	13	1	37	3	2	2	.500	7--	-	-	.669	2.86	2.89
2021	Bal	AL	7	0	3	8.2	44	11	10	9	1	0	1	0	5	0	11	3	0	0	-	0-0	0	91	.837	6.06	9.35

Andrew Knizner

Bats: R **Throws:** R **Pos:** C-57;PH-10;PR-2;1B-1   KIZZ-ner   **Ht:** 6'1" **Wt:** 225 **Born:** 2/3/1995 **Age:** 27

Year	Team	Lg	G	AB	H	2B	3B	HR	(Hm	Rd)	TB	R	RBI	RC	TBB	IBB	SO	HBP	SH	SF	SB	CS	GDP	Avg	OBP	Slg	OPS
2019	StL	NL	18	53	12	2	0	2	(1	1)	20	7	7	7	4	0	14	1	0	0	2	0	3	.226	.293	.377	.670
2020	StL	NL	8	16	4	1	0	0	(0	0)	5	1	4	2	0	0	5	0	0	1	0	0	2	.250	.235	.313	.548
2021	StL	NL	63	161	28	7	0	1	(1	0)	38	18	9	6	20	2	39	4	0	0	0	0	7	.174	.281	.236	.517
3 ML YEARS			89	230	44	10	0	3	(2	1)	63	26	20	15	24	2	58	5	0	1	2	0	12	.191	.281	.274	.555

Brody Koerner

Pitches: R **Bats:** R **Pos:** RP-2   **Ht:** 6'2" **Wt:** 220 **Born:** 10/17/1993 **Age:** 28

Year	Team	Lg	G	GS	GF	IP	BFP	H	R	ER	HR	SH	SF	HB	TBB	IBB	SO	WP	W	L	Pct	Sv-Op	Hld	Vel	OPS	ERC	ERA
2021	S-WB	AAA	24	15	0	74.0	316	75	30	29	8	3	2	6	23	0	57	3	3	4	.429	0--	-	-	.722	4.23	3.53
2021	NYY	AL	2	0	2	3.0	13	2	1	1	0	0	0	1	2	0	1	0	0	0	-	0-0	0	89	.685	3.96	3.00

Adam Kolarek

Pitches: L **Bats:** L **Pos:** RP-12   **Ht:** 6'3" **Wt:** 215 **Born:** 1/14/1989 **Age:** 33

Year	Team	Lg	G	GS	GF	IP	BFP	H	R	ER	HR	SH	SF	HB	TBB	IBB	SO	WP	W	L	Pct	Sv-Op	Hld	Vel	OPS	ERC	ERA
2021	LsVgs	AAA	37	0	4	38.2	189	48	33	29	5	0	2	7	20	1	27	1	1	0	1.000	0--	-	-	.847	6.87	6.75
2017	TB	AL	12	0	5	8.1	40	9	6	6	2	1	0	4	4	2	4	1	1	0	1.000	0-0	2	88	.984	7.84	6.48
2018	TB	AL	31	0	5	34.1	141	38	15	15	0	0	1	1	5	1	19	0	1	0	1.000	2-4	10	90	.685	3.14	3.93
2019	2 Tms		80	0	18	55.0	229	48	22	20	7	0	0	3	16	4	45	1	6	3	.667	1-1	17	89	.669	3.23	3.27
2020	LAD	NL	20	0	3	19.0	72	11	2	2	1	0	1	0	4	0	13	2	3	0	1.000	1-1	3	89	.432	1.26	0.95
2021	Oak	AL	12	0	2	9.0	51	15	10	8	2	1	0	1	5	0	4	0	0	0	-	0-0	0	89	.943	9.73	8.00
19	TB	AL	54	0	15	43.1	184	39	19	19	6	0	0	3	14	4	36	1	4	3	.571	1-1	14	89	.700	3.58	3.95
19	LAD	NL	26	0	3	11.2	45	9	3	1	1	0	0	0	2	0	9	0	2	0	1.000	0-0	3	89	.547	2.01	0.77
Postseason			7	0	2	4.1	25	9	5	5	1	0	0	0	3	1	5	0	0	0	-	0-0	2	90	1.116	13.01	10.38
5 ML YEARS			155	0	33	125.2	533	121	55	51	12	2	2	9	34	7	85	5	11	3	.786	4-6	32	89	.687	3.51	3.65

Michael Kopech

Pitches: R Bats: R Pos: RP-40; SP-4　　　　　Ht: 6'3" Wt: 210 Born: 4/30/1996 Age: 26

Year	Team	Lg	G	GS	GF	IP	BFP	H	R	ER	HR	SH	SF	HB	TBB	IBB	SO	WP	W	L	Pct	Sv-Op	Hld	Vel	OPS	ERC	ERA
2017	Brham	AA	22	22	0	119.1	488	77	45	38	6	3	6	60	60	0	155	8	8	7	.533	0- -	-	-	.570	2.48	2.87
2018	Charllt	AAA	24	24	0	126.1	543	101	58	52	9	3	6	13	60	0	170	12	7	7	.500	0- -	-	-	.658	3.45	3.70
2018	CWS	AL	4	4	0	14.1	68	20	8	8	4	0	0	5	2	0	15	1	1	1	.500	0-0	0	95	1.004	8.42	5.02
2021	CWS	AL	44	4	1	69.1	285	54	27	27	9	0	3	1	24	1	103	3	4	3	.571	0-1	13	97	.651	2.88	3.50
2 ML YEARS			48	8	1	83.2	353	74	35	35	13	0	3	6	26	1	118	4	5	4	.556	0-1	13	97	.719	3.70	3.76

Jackson Kowar

Pitches: R Bats: R Pos: SP-8; RP-1　　　　　Ht: 6'5" Wt: 200 Born: 10/4/1996 Age: 25

Year	Team	Lg	G	GS	GF	IP	BFP	H	R	ER	HR	SH	SF	HB	TBB	IBB	SO	WP	W	L	Pct	Sv-Op	Hld	Vel	OPS	ERC	ERA
2021	Omha	AAA	17	16	1	80.2	338	66	31	31	7	0	0	4	34	0	115	14	9	4	.692	0- -	-	96	.658	3.29	3.46
2021	KC	AL	9	8	1	30.1	154	43	38	38	7	0	4	2	20	0	29	8	0	6	.000	0-0	0	96	1.008	9.14	11.27

Pete Kozma

Bats: R Throws: R Pos: SS-3　　　　　KAHZ-muh　　　　　Ht: 6'0" Wt: 190 Born: 4/11/1988 Age: 34

Year	Team	Lg	G	AB	H	2B	3B	HR	(Hm	Rd)	TB	R	RBI	RC	TBB	IBB	SO	HBP	SH	SF	SB	CS	GDP	Avg	OBP	Slg	OPS
2021	LsVgs	AAA	112	449	110	24	3	4	(-	-)	152	62	40	-	37	0	96	5	2	2	6	1	20	.245	.308	.339	.647
2011	StL	NL	16	17	3	1	0	0	(0	0)	4	2	1	2	4	0	4	0	1	0	0	0	0	.176	.333	.235	.569
2012	StL	NL	26	72	24	5	3	2	(0	2)	41	11	14	13	7	1	19	0	1	2	2	0	4	.333	.383	.569	.952
2013	StL	NL	143	410	89	20	0	1	(0	1)	112	44	35	39	34	8	91	0	1	3	3	1	6	.217	.275	.273	.548
2014	StL	NL	14	23	7	3	0	0	(0	0)	10	4	0	3	3	0	4	0	0	0	0	0	0	.304	.385	.435	.819
2015	StL	NL	76	99	15	0	0	0	(0	0)	15	15	2	4	10	2	21	1	1	0	3	1	0	.152	.236	.152	.388
2017	2 Tms	AL	39	45	5	0	0	1	(0	1)	8	6	2	1	3	0	20	2	1	0	0	1	0	.111	.200	.178	.378
2018	Det	AL	27	69	15	4	1	1	(0	1)	24	7	8	3	2	0	15	0	1	1	0	1	2	.217	.236	.348	.584
2021	Oak	AL	3	11	1	0	0	0	(0	0)	1	0	0	0	1	0	4	0	0	0	0	0	0	.091	.167	.091	.258
17	NYY	AL	11	9	1	0	0	0	(0	0)	1	2	0	0	1	0	2	0	0	0	0	0	0	.111	.200	.111	.311
17	Tex	AL	28	36	4	0	0	1	(0	1)	7	4	2	1	2	0	18	2	1	0	0	1	0	.111	.200	.194	.394
	Postseason		29	82	14	3	0	1	(0	1)	20	11	9	13	12	3	24	2	1	0	3	1	1	.171	.292	.244	.536
8 ML YEARS			344	746	159	33	4	5	(0	5)	215	89	62	65	64	11	178	3	6	6	8	4	12	.213	.276	.288	.564

Max Kranick

Pitches: R Bats: R Pos: SP-9　　　　　Ht: 6'3" Wt: 210 Born: 7/21/1997 Age: 24

Year	Team	Lg	G	GS	GF	IP	BFP	H	R	ER	HR	SH	SF	HB	TBB	IBB	SO	WP	W	L	Pct	Sv-Op	Hld	Vel	OPS	ERC	ERA
2021	Indy	AAA	12	12	0	54.1	231	53	30	25	6	1	2	2	16	0	45	0	4	4	.500	0- -	-	-	.718	3.71	4.14
2021	Pit	NL	9	9	0	38.2	182	47	28	27	4	1	2	4	19	3	32	2	2	3	.400	0-0	0	94	.855	6.02	6.28

Joey Krehbiel

Pitches: R Bats: R Pos: RP-6　　　　　KRAY-bull　　　　　Ht: 6'2" Wt: 185 Born: 12/20/1992 Age: 29

Year	Team	Lg	G	GS	GF	IP	BFP	H	R	ER	HR	SH	SF	HB	TBB	IBB	SO	WP	W	L	Pct	Sv-Op	Hld	Vel	OPS	ERC	ERA
2021	Drham	AAA	44	0	27	43.0	176	38	24	20	8	1	3	1	9	1	52	2	3	2	.600	4- -	-	-	.704	3.27	4.19
2018	Ari	NL	2	0	1	3.0	12	1	0	0	0	0	0	0	2	0	0	0	0	0	-	0-0	0	96	.350	1.26	0.00
2021	2 Tms	AL	6	0	1	8.1	34	5	4	4	1	0	0	0	5	0	7	1	0	0	-	0-0	2	96	.639	2.88	4.32
21	TB	AL	1	0	1	1.0	4	0	0	0	0	0	0	0	1	0	2	0	0	0	-	0-0	0	96	.250	0.95	0.00
21	Bal	AL	5	0	0	7.1	30	5	4	4	1	0	0	0	4	0	5	1	0	0	-	0-0	2	96	.685	3.22	4.91
2 ML YEARS			8	0	2	11.1	46	6	4	4	1	0	0	0	7	0	7	1	0	0	-	0-0	2	96	.565	2.37	3.18

Dean Kremer

Pitches: R Bats: R Pos: SP-13　　　　　Ht: 6'2" Wt: 200 Born: 1/7/1996 Age: 26

Year	Team	Lg	G	GS	GF	IP	BFP	H	R	ER	HR	SH	SF	HB	TBB	IBB	SO	WP	W	L	Pct	Sv-Op	Hld	Vel	OPS	ERC	ERA
2021	Norfolk	AAA	16	12	0	58.1	252	56	42	33	9	1	2	4	20	0	67	3	1	5	.167	0- -	-	-	.750	4.24	5.09
2020	Bal	AL	4	4	0	18.2	83	15	10	10	0	0	1	0	12	0	22	0	1	1	.500	0-0	0	93	.711	3.12	4.82
2021	Bal	AL	13	13	0	53.2	245	63	46	45	17	0	3	1	25	0	47	5	0	7	.000	0-0	0	93	.951	7.14	7.55
2 ML YEARS			17	17	0	72.1	328	78	56	55	17	0	4	1	37	0	69	5	1	8	.111	0-0	0	93	.892	6.04	6.84

Brooks Kriske

Pitches: R Bats: R Pos: RP-12　　　　　Ht: 6'3" Wt: 190 Born: 2/3/1994 Age: 28

Year	Team	Lg	G	GS	GF	IP	BFP	H	R	ER	HR	SH	SF	HB	TBB	IBB	SO	WP	W	L	Pct	Sv-Op	Hld	Vel	OPS	ERC	ERA
2021	S-WB	AAA	24	0	5	28.1	112	15	12	12	2	0	0	1	14	0	41	5	1	1	.500	1- -	-	-	.526	2.00	3.81
2020	NYY	AL	4	0	2	3.2	22	3	6	6	1	0	0	0	7	0	8	2	0	0	-	0-0	0	95	.855	10.28	14.73
2021	2 Tms	AL	12	0	8	11.1	56	17	19	18	7	1	1	1	6	0	11	5	2	1	.667	0-1	0	95	1.351	13.06	14.29
21	NYY	AL	8	0	8	7.2	41	12	14	13	5	1	1	1	6	0	7	5	1	1	.500	0-1	0	96	1.413	15.26	15.26
21	Bal	AL	4	0	0	3.2	15	5	5	5	2	0	0	0	0	0	4	0	1	0	1.000	0-0	0	95	1.200	8.01	12.27
2 ML YEARS			16	0	10	15.0	78	20	25	24	8	1	1	1	13	0	19	7	2	1	.667	0-1	0	95	1.232	12.44	14.40

Ian Krol

Pitches: L Bats: L Pos: RP-18   KROHL   Ht: 6'1" Wt: 210 Born: 5/9/1991 Age: 31

Year	Team	Lg	G	GS	GF	IP	BFP	H	R	ER	HR	SH	SF	HB	TBB	IBB	SO	WP	W	L	Pct	Sv-Op	Hld	Vel	OPS	ERC	ERA
2021	Toledo	AAA	20	1	9	25.2	108	20	8	7	4	0	0	2	12	0	31	2	2	0	1.000	4--	-	-	.683	3.85	2.45
2013	Was	NL	32	0	10	27.1	117	28	12	12	5	2	1	0	8	1	22	2	1	0	.667	0-1	2	93	.785	4.24	3.95
2014	Det	AL	45	0	5	32.2	154	42	23	18	6	0	1	2	13	4	28	1	0	0	-	1-4	10	92	.906	6.35	4.96
2015	Det	AL	33	0	6	28.0	129	31	19	18	4	2	0	2	17	1	26	0	2	3	.400	0-1	1	94	.847	6.23	5.79
2016	Atl	NL	63	0	7	51.0	217	54	19	18	4	1	1	3	13	3	56	5	2	0	1.000	0-2	10	94	.701	3.84	3.18
2017	Atl	NL	51	0	15	49.0	214	50	34	29	8	0	1	4	21	0	44	2	2	2	.500	0-0	3	93	.803	5.19	5.33
2018	LAA	AL	1	0	0	2.0	8	1	0	0	0	0	0	0	1	0	2	0	0	0	-	0-0	0	92	.393	1.41	0.00
2021	Det	AL	18	0	7	18.2	86	23	10	9	2	1	1	0	8	0	18	1	0	0	-	0-0	0	94	.838	5.53	4.49
	7 ML YEARS		243	0	50	208.2	925	229	117	104	29	6	5	11	81	9	196	11	8	6	.571	1-8	26	93	.799	5.02	4.49

Jack Kruger

Bats: R Throws: R Pos: C-1   Ht: 6'1" Wt: 195 Born: 10/26/1994 Age: 27

Year	Team	Lg	G	AB	H	2B	3B	HR	(Hm	Rd)	TB	R	RBI	RC	TBB	IBB	SO	HBP	SH	SF	SB	CS	GDP	Avg	OBP	Slg	OPS
2021	RdRck	AAA	44	152	40	7	1	2	(-	-)	55	16	14	-	10	0	32	0	0	0	1	1	1	.263	.309	.362	.670
2021	LAA	AL	1	0	0	0	0	0	(0	0)	0	0	0	0	0	0	0	0	0	0	0	0	0	-	-	-	-

Chad Kuhl

Pitches: R Bats: R Pos: SP-14; RP-14   cool   Ht: 6'3" Wt: 205 Born: 9/10/1992 Age: 29

Year	Team	Lg	G	GS	GF	IP	BFP	H	R	ER	HR	SH	SF	HB	TBB	IBB	SO	WP	W	L	Pct	Sv-Op	Hld	Vel	OPS	ERC	ERA
2016	Pit	NL	14	14	0	70.2	301	73	34	33	7	2	2	4	20	0	53	2	5	4	.556	0-0	0	93	.757	4.04	4.20
2017	Pit	NL	31	31	0	157.1	680	159	81	76	17	6	4	6	72	7	142	8	8	11	.421	0-0	0	96	.793	4.60	4.35
2018	Pit	NL	16	16	0	85.0	373	89	47	43	14	6	6	4	33	1	81	7	5	5	.500	0-0	0	95	.806	4.94	4.55
2020	Pit	NL	11	9	0	46.1	197	35	26	22	8	1	0	2	28	0	44	1	2	3	.400	0-0	0	94	.727	4.27	4.27
2021	Pit	NL	28	14	2	80.1	349	73	50	43	13	2	6	9	42	0	75	9	5	7	.417	0-2	4	94	.802	5.09	4.82
	5 ML YEARS		100	84	2	439.2	1900	429	238	217	59	17	18	25	195	8	395	27	25	30	.455	0-2	4	95	.785	4.63	4.44

Tommy La Stella

Bats: L Throws: R Pos: 2B-54;PH-23;3B-5;DH-2   Ht: 5'11" Wt: 180 Born: 1/31/1989 Age: 33

Year	Team	Lg	G	AB	H	2B	3B	HR	(Hm	Rd)	TB	R	RBI	RC	TBB	IBB	SO	HBP	SH	SF	SB	CS	GDP	Avg	OBP	Slg	OPS
2021	Scrmto	AAA	12	30	6	2	0	0	(-	-)	8	8	2	-	7	0	5	0	0	0	0	0	0	.200	.351	.267	.618
2014	Atl	NL	93	319	80	16	1	1	(1	0)	101	22	31	36	36	2	40	1	3	1	2	1	8	.251	.328	.317	.644
2015	ChC	NL	33	67	18	6	0	1	(1	0)	27	4	11	10	5	0	7	1	0	1	2	0	1	.269	.324	.403	.727
2016	ChC	NL	74	148	40	12	1	2	(1	1)	60	17	11	20	18	1	27	2	0	0	0	1	2	.270	.357	.405	.763
2017	ChC	NL	73	125	36	8	0	5	(0	5)	59	18	22	24	20	1	18	2	0	2	0	0	3	.288	.389	.472	.861
2018	ChC	NL	123	169	45	8	0	1	(1	0)	56	23	19	17	17	1	27	2	0	0	0	1	5	.266	.340	.331	.672
2019	LAA	AL	80	292	86	8	0	16	(11	5)	142	49	44	43	20	0	28	3	0	0	0	1	3	.295	.346	.486	.832
2020	2 Tms	AL	55	196	55	14	2	5	(2	3)	88	31	25	36	27	0	12	2	1	2	1	0	6	.281	.370	.449	.819
2021	SF	NL	76	220	55	11	1	7	(2	5)	89	26	27	31	18	1	26	1	0	1	0	0	4	.250	.308	.405	.713
20	LAA	AL	28	99	27	8	0	4	(2	2)	47	15	14	19	15	0	7	1	1	1	1	0	3	.273	.371	.475	.845
20	Oak	AL	27	97	28	6	2	1	(0	1)	41	16	11	17	12	0	5	1	0	1	0	0	3	.289	.369	.423	.792
	Postseason		19	40	8	1	0	1	(0	1)	12	5	2	4	3	0	7	1	0	0	0	0	1	.200	.273	.300	.573
	8 ML YEARS		607	1536	415	83	5	38	(18	20)	622	190	190	217	161	6	185	14	4	7	5	3	37	.270	.343	.405	.748

Asa Lacy

Pitches: L Bats: L Pos: P   Ht: 6'4" Wt: 215 Born: 6/2/1999 Age: 23

Year	Team	Lg	G	GS	GF	IP	BFP	H	R	ER	HR	SH	SF	HB	TBB	IBB	SO	WP	W	L	Pct	Sv-Op	Hld	Vel	OPS	ERC	ERA
2021	QuadC	A+	14	14	0	52.0	237	41	31	30	5	0	0	8	41	0	79	10	2	5	.286	0--	-	-	-	5.06	5.19

Tyler Ladendorf

Bats: R Throws: R Pos: PH-1   Ht: 5'11" Wt: 195 Born: 3/7/1988 Age: 34

Year	Team	Lg	G	AB	H	2B	3B	HR	(Hm	Rd)	TB	R	RBI	RC	TBB	IBB	SO	HBP	SH	SF	SB	CS	GDP	Avg	OBP	Slg	OPS
2021	Iowa	AAA	58	189	44	11	0	7	(-	-)	76	28	27	-	12	0	53	3	0	2	1	0	6	.233	.286	.402	.689
2015	Oak	AL	9	17	4	0	1	0	(0	0)	6	3	2	0	1	0	2	0	0	0	0	0	0	.235	.278	.353	.631
2016	Oak	AL	45	48	4	0	0	0	(0	0)	4	6	1	0	1	0	13	0	1	0	2	0	3	.083	.102	.083	.185
2021	ChC	NL	1	1	0	0	0	0	(0	0)	0	0	0	0	0	0	0	0	0	0	0	0	0	.000	.000	.000	.000
	3 ML YEARS		55	66	8	0	1	0	(0	0)	10	9	3	0	2	0	15	0	1	0	2	0	3	.121	.147	.152	.299

Juan Lagares

Bats: R Throws: R Pos: CF-62;RF-37;LF-23;PH-2;PR-1   luh-GAR-ess   Ht: 6'2" Wt: 219 Born: 3/17/1989 Age: 33

Year	Team	Lg	G	AB	H	2B	3B	HR	(Hm	Rd)	TB	R	RBI	RC	TBB	IBB	SO	HBP	SH	SF	SB	CS	GDP	Avg	OBP	Slg	OPS
2013	NYM	NL	121	392	95	21	5	4	(1	3)	138	35	34	36	20	4	96	2	5	2	6	3	6	.242	.281	.352	.633
2014	NYM	NL	116	416	117	24	3	4	(2	2)	159	46	47	53	20	1	87	7	3	6	13	4	6	.281	.321	.382	.703
2015	NYM	NL	143	441	116	16	5	6	(2	4)	158	47	41	51	16	2	87	4	1	3	7	3	6	.259	.289	.358	.647
2016	NYM	NL	79	142	34	7	2	3	(2	2)	54	15	9	12	11	1	27	2	4	1	4	2	6	.239	.301	.380	.682
2017	NYM	NL	94	252	63	16	2	3	(1	2)	92	37	15	20	14	0	56	3	2	1	7	3	6	.250	.296	.365	.661

Year	Team	Lg	G	AB	H	2B	3B	HR	(Hm	Rd)	TB	R	RBI	RC	TBB	IBB	SO	HBP	SH	SF	SB	CS	GDP	Avg	OBP	Slg	OPS
2018	NYM	NL	30	59	20	1	1	0	(0	0)	23	9	6	10	3	1	9	1	0	1	3	1	2	.339	.375	.390	.765
2019	NYM	NL	133	258	55	12	1	5	(2	3)	84	38	27	23	22	4	75	1	2	1	4	1	8	.213	.279	.326	.605
2020	NYM	NL	2	0	0	0	0	0	(0	0)	0	0	0	0	0	0	0	0	0	0	0	0	0	-	-	-	-
2021	LAA	NL	112	309	73	20	2	6	(1	5)	115	39	38	31	12	0	76	1	4	1	1	2	8	.236	.266	.372	.638
Postseason			13	23	8	2	0	0	(0	0)	10	7	0	3	1	0	3	0	1	0	2	0	0	.348	.375	.435	.810
9 ML YEARS			830	2269	571	117	21	31	(11	20)	823	266	217	236	118	13	513	22	21	16	45	19	46	.252	.293	.363	.656

Brady Lail

Pitches: R **Bats:** R **Pos:** RP-2   **Ht:** 6'2" **Wt:** 200 **Born:** 8/9/1993 **Age:** 28

			HOW MUCH PITCHED					WHAT HE GAVE UP										THE RESULTS							
Year	Team	Lg	G	GS	GF	IP	BFP	H	R	ER	HR	SH	SF	HB	TBB	IBB	SO	WP	W	L	Pct	Sv-Op	Hld	Vel	OPS	ERC	ERA
2021	LV	AAA	30	1	10	38.2	175	37	28	27	9	0	3	4	25	1	42	1	1	0	1.000	1- -	-	-	.909	6.37	6.28
2019	NYY	AL	1	0	0	2.2	10	2	3	3	1	0	0	0	1	0	2	0	0	0	-	0-0	0	92	.856	4.74	10.13
2020	2 Tms	AL	8	0	7	16.1	71	14	8	8	5	0	0	2	7	0	12	0	0	0	-	0-0	0	90	.249	5.31	4.41
2021	Sea	AL	2	0	2	2.0	10	4	3	3	1	0	0	0	0	0	1	0	0	0	-	0-0	0	93	1.200	11.88	13.50
20	CWS	AL	1	0	1	1.1	6	2	0	0	0	0	0	0	0	0	1	0	0	0	-	0-0	0	90	.667	4.47	0.00
20	Sea	AL	7	0	6	15.0	65	12	8	8	5	0	0	2	7	0	11	0	0	0	-	0-0	0	90	.823	5.38	4.80
3 ML YEARS			11	0	9	21.0	91	20	14	14	7	0	0	2	8	0	15	0	0	0	-	0-0	0	90	.861	5.80	6.00

Travis Lakins Sr.

Pitches: R **Bats:** R **Pos:** RP-23; SP-1   **Ht:** 6'1" **Wt:** 220 **Born:** 6/29/1994 **Age:** 28

			HOW MUCH PITCHED					WHAT HE GAVE UP										THE RESULTS							
Year	Team	Lg	G	GS	GF	IP	BFP	H	R	ER	HR	SH	SF	HB	TBB	IBB	SO	WP	W	L	Pct	Sv-Op	Hld	Vel	OPS	ERC	ERA
2019	Bos	AL	16	3	4	23.1	102	23	11	10	1	0	2	1	10	1	18	1	0	1	.000	0-0	1	94	.738	3.78	3.86
2020	Bal	AL	22	0	5	25.2	116	25	11	8	2	0	1	2	13	0	25	3	3	2	.600	1-1	1	93	.725	4.42	2.81
2021	Bal	AL	24	1	3	28.0	123	23	20	18	4	0	1	1	17	0	24	4	1	4	.200	0-1	3	93	.689	4.32	5.79
3 ML YEARS			62	4	12	77.0	341	71	42	36	7	0	4	4	40	1	67	8	4	7	.364	1-2	5	94	.716	4.19	4.21

Ryan LaMarre

Bats: R **Throws:** L **Pos:** LF-4;RF-4;CF-1;PH-1   la-MARR   **Ht:** 6'1" **Wt:** 215 **Born:** 11/21/1988 **Age:** 33

Year	Team	Lg	G	AB	H	2B	3B	HR	(Hm	Rd)	TB	R	RBI	RC	TBB	IBB	SO	HBP	SH	SF	SB	CS	GDP	Avg	OBP	Slg	OPS
2021	S-WB	AAA	57	193	52	11	2	6	(-	-)	85	24	30	-	26	1	58	7	0	0	14	5	4	.269	.376	.440	.817
2015	Cin	NL	21	25	2	0	0	0	(0	0)	2	2	0	0	0	0	9	0	1	0	0	0	1	.080	.080	.080	.160
2016	Bos	AL	6	5	0	0	0	0	(0	0)	0	1	0	0	1	0	2	0	0	0	0	0	0	.000	.167	.000	.167
2017	Oak	AL	3	7	0	0	0	0	(0	0)	0	0	0	0	1	0	3	0	0	0	0	0	0	.000	.125	.000	.125
2018	2 Tms	AL	76	165	46	11	0	2	(0	2)	63	15	18	19	10	0	53	2	0	3	2	2	3	.279	.322	.382	.704
2019	Min	AL	14	23	5	0	0	2	(1	1)	11	3	3	3	3	0	5	0	0	0	1	1	0	.217	.308	.478	.786
2021	NYY	AL	9	21	4	0	0	2	(1	1)	10	3	4	2	2	0	6	1	0	0	1	0	1	.190	.292	.476	.768
18	Min	AL	43	99	26	5	0	0	(0	0)	31	7	8	11	8	0	33	1	0	1	1	1	3	.263	.321	.313	.634
18	CWS	AL	33	66	20	6	0	2	(0	2)	32	8	10	8	2	0	20	1	0	2	1	1	0	.303	.324	.485	.809
6 ML YEARS			129	246	57	11	0	6	(2	4)	86	24	24	24	17	0	78	3	1	3	4	3	6	.232	.286	.350	.636

Jake Lamb

Bats: L **Throws:** R **Pos:** 3B-16;LF-16;PH-11;RF-9;DH-8;1B-3   **Ht:** 6'3" **Wt:** 215 **Born:** 10/9/1990 **Age:** 31

Year	Team	Lg	G	AB	H	2B	3B	HR	(Hm	Rd)	TB	R	RBI	RC	TBB	IBB	SO	HBP	SH	SF	SB	CS	GDP	Avg	OBP	Slg	OPS
2021	Charllt	AAA	16	61	15	5	0	3	(-	-)	29	6	8	-	8	0	15	0	0	0	0	0	1	.246	.333	.475	.809
2014	Ari	NL	37	126	29	4	1	4	(2	2)	47	15	11	7	6	0	37	0	0	1	1	1	4	.230	.263	.373	.636
2015	Ari	NL	107	350	92	15	5	6	(1	5)	135	38	34	39	36	3	97	1	0	3	3	2	5	.263	.331	.386	.716
2016	Ari	NL	151	523	130	31	9	29	(19	10)	266	81	91	84	64	5	154	3	0	4	6	1	13	.249	.332	.509	.840
2017	Ari	NL	149	536	133	30	4	30	(16	14)	261	89	105	90	87	13	152	7	0	5	6	4	15	.248	.357	.487	.844
2018	Ari	NL	56	207	46	8	0	6	(3	3)	72	34	31	26	26	0	65	1	0	1	1	2	4	.222	.307	.348	.655
2019	Ari	NL	78	187	36	8	2	6	(3	3)	66	26	30	27	32	1	55	5	0	2	1	0	4	.193	.323	.353	.676
2020	2 Tms	AL	31	88	17	5	0	3	(2	1)	31	7	10	11	8	0	25	3	0	0	1	0	1	.193	.283	.352	.635
2021	2 Tms	AL	55	144	28	4	0	7	(4	3)	53	25	19	14	22	0	51	2	0	2	0	0	4	.194	.306	.368	.674
20	Ari	NL	18	43	5	1	0	0	(0	0)	6	2	1	1	6	0	17	1	0	0	1	0	1	.116	.240	.140	.380
20	Oak	AL	13	45	12	4	0	3	(2	1)	25	5	9	10	2	0	8	2	0	0	0	0	0	.267	.327	.556	.882
21	CWS	AL	43	113	24	2	0	6	(4	2)	44	20	13	12	17	0	38	1	0	0	0	0	4	.212	.321	.389	.710
21	Tor	AL	12	31	4	2	0	1	(0	1)	9	5	6	2	5	0	13	1	0	2	0	0	0	.129	.256	.290	.547
8 ML YEARS			664	2161	511	105	21	91	(50	41)	931	315	331	298	281	22	636	22	0	21	18	11	50	.236	.328	.431	.758

Jimmy Lambert

Pitches: R **Bats:** R **Pos:** SP-3; RP-1   **Ht:** 6'2" **Wt:** 190 **Born:** 11/18/1994 **Age:** 27

			HOW MUCH PITCHED					WHAT HE GAVE UP										THE RESULTS							
Year	Team	Lg	G	GS	GF	IP	BFP	H	R	ER	HR	SH	SF	HB	TBB	IBB	SO	WP	W	L	Pct	Sv-Op	Hld	Vel	OPS	ERC	ERA
2021	Charllt	AAA	19	19	0	64.1	269	49	38	34	11	1	1	2	32	0	82	5	3	3	.500	0- -	-	-	.735	3.78	4.76
2020	CWS	AL	2	0	1	2.0	8	2	0	0	0	0	0	0	0	0	2	0	0	0	-	0-0	0	93	.500	1.95	0.00
2021	CWS	AL	4	3	0	13.0	60	16	9	9	3	0	1	2	6	0	10	0	1	1	.500	0-0	0	94	.949	7.66	6.23
2 ML YEARS			6	3	1	15.0	68	18	9	9	3	0	1	2	6	0	12	0	1	1	.500	0-0	0	94	.891	6.76	5.40

Peter Lambert

Pitches: R **Bats:** R **Pos:** SP-2   **Ht:** 6'2" **Wt:** 208 **Born:** 4/18/1997 **Age:** 25

			HOW MUCH PITCHED				WHAT HE GAVE UP											THE RESULTS						
Year	Team	Lg	G	GS	GF	IP	BFP	H	R	ER	HR	SH	SF	HB	TBB	IBB	SO	WP	W	L	Pct	Sv-Op	Hld	Vel	OPS	ERC	ERA
2019	Col	NL	19	19	0	89.1	420	119	74	72	18	4	3	6	36	3	57	5	3	7	.300	0-0	0	93	.958	7.11	7.25
2021	Col	NL	2	2	0	5.2	30	12	7	7	2	0	0	0	2	0	3	0	0	0	-	0-0	0	94	1.181	13.83	11.12
	2 ML YEARS		21	21	0	95.0	450	131	81	79	20	4	3	6	38	3	60	5	3	7	.300	0-0	0	93	.974	7.48	7.48

Dinelson Lamet

Pitches: R **Bats:** R **Pos:** RP-13; SP-9   dee-NEL-sun luh-MET   **Ht:** 6'3" **Wt:** 228 **Born:** 7/18/1992 **Age:** 29

			HOW MUCH PITCHED				WHAT HE GAVE UP											THE RESULTS						
Year	Team	Lg	G	GS	GF	IP	BFP	H	R	ER	HR	SH	SF	HB	TBB	IBB	SO	WP	W	L	Pct	Sv-Op	Hld	Vel	OPS	ERC	ERA
2017	SD	NL	21	21	0	114.1	485	88	63	58	18	1	5	6	54	2	139	9	7	8	.467	0-0	0	95	.707	3.64	4.57
2019	SD	NL	14	14	0	73.0	313	62	38	33	12	2	2	5	30	0	105	6	3	5	.375	0-0	0	96	.721	3.95	4.07
2020	SD	NL	12	12	0	69.0	267	39	18	16	5	0	1	4	20	0	93	1	3	1	.750	0-0	0	97	.496	1.60	2.09
2021	SD	NL	22	9	1	47.0	209	48	24	23	6	1	1	2	22	0	57	3	2	4	.333	0-0	1	96	.761	4.83	4.40
	4 ML YEARS		69	56	1	303.1	1274	237	143	130	41	4	9	17	126	2	394	19	15	18	.455	0-0	1	96	.674	3.37	3.86

Alex Lange

Pitches: R **Bats:** R **Pos:** RP-36   **Ht:** 6'3" **Wt:** 202 **Born:** 10/2/1995 **Age:** 26

			HOW MUCH PITCHED				WHAT HE GAVE UP											THE RESULTS						
Year	Team	Lg	G	GS	GF	IP	BFP	H	R	ER	HR	SH	SF	HB	TBB	IBB	SO	WP	W	L	Pct	Sv-Op	Hld	Vel	OPS	ERC	ERA
2021	Toledo	AAA	19	0	1	21.2	100	22	12	11	0	0	0	0	17	0	27	6	2	1	.667	1--	-	-	.751	4.96	4.57
2021	Det	AL	36	0	6	35.2	162	37	18	16	5	0	0	3	16	0	39	6	1	3	.250	1-3	6	96	.765	5.04	4.04

Trevor Larnach

Bats: L **Throws:** R **Pos:** LF-60;RF-20;PH-7   **Ht:** 6'4" **Wt:** 223 **Born:** 2/26/1997 **Age:** 25

			BATTING																			RUNNING			AVERAGES			
Year	Team	Lg	G	AB	H	2B	3B	HR	(Hm	Rd)	TB	R	RBI	RC	TBB	IBB	SO	HBP	SH	SF	SB	CS	GDP	Avg	OBP	Slg	OPS
2021	StPaul	AAA	14	51	9	1	0	3	(-	-)	19	13	7	-	6	0	21	5	0	0	0	0	2	.176	.323	.373	.695
2021	Min	AL	79	260	58	12	0	7	(4	3)	91	29	28	26	31	0	104	8	0	2	1	0	3	.223	.322	.350	.672

Jake Latz

Pitches: L **Bats:** R **Pos:** SP-1   **Ht:** 6'2" **Wt:** 185 **Born:** 4/8/1996 **Age:** 26

			HOW MUCH PITCHED				WHAT HE GAVE UP											THE RESULTS						
Year	Team	Lg	G	GS	GF	IP	BFP	H	R	ER	HR	SH	SF	HB	TBB	IBB	SO	WP	W	L	Pct	Sv-Op	Hld	Vel	OPS	ERC	ERA
2021	Frisco	AA	15	13	0	63.1	272	55	40	33	9	1	4	3	28	0	84	4	1	1	.500	0--	-	-	.724	3.97	4.69
2021	RdRck	AAA	6	5	0	29.0	129	30	18	11	5	0	1	1	12	0	29	2	1	0	1.000	0--	-	-	.794	4.92	3.41
2021	Tex	AL	1	1	0	4.2	19	5	3	3	3	0	0	0	0	0	4	0	0	1	.000	0-0	0	93	1.000	5.99	5.79

Eric Lauer

Pitches: L **Bats:** R **Pos:** SP-20; RP-4   **Ht:** 6'3" **Wt:** 228 **Born:** 6/3/1995 **Age:** 27

			HOW MUCH PITCHED				WHAT HE GAVE UP											THE RESULTS						
Year	Team	Lg	G	GS	GF	IP	BFP	H	R	ER	HR	SH	SF	HB	TBB	IBB	SO	WP	W	L	Pct	Sv-Op	Hld	Vel	OPS	ERC	ERA
2018	SD	NL	23	23	0	112.0	504	127	61	54	15	4	2	1	46	2	100	2	6	7	.462	0-0	0	91	.800	5.33	4.34
2019	SD	NL	30	29	0	149.2	651	158	82	74	20	3	3	5	51	4	138	4	8	10	.444	0-0	0	92	.760	4.47	4.45
2020	Mil	NL	4	2	0	11.0	61	17	16	16	2	0	1	2	9	0	12	1	0	2	.000	0-0	0	92	1.030	10.72	13.09
2021	Mil	NL	24	20	0	118.2	489	94	46	42	16	6	2	2	41	1	117	2	7	5	.583	0-0	0	93	.640	3.00	3.19
	4 ML YEARS		81	74	0	391.1	1705	396	205	186	53	13	8	15	147	7	367	9	21	24	.467	0-0	0	92	.746	4.40	4.28

Ramon Laureano

Bats: R **Throws:** R **Pos:** CF-75;RF-8;DH-5;PH-1   **Ht:** 5'11" **Wt:** 203 **Born:** 7/15/1994 **Age:** 27

			BATTING																			RUNNING			AVERAGES			
Year	Team	Lg	G	AB	H	2B	3B	HR	(Hm	Rd)	TB	R	RBI	RC	TBB	IBB	SO	HBP	SH	SF	SB	CS	GDP	Avg	OBP	Slg	OPS
2018	Oak	AL	48	156	45	12	1	5	(4	1)	74	27	19	29	16	0	50	2	0	2	7	1	0	.288	.358	.474	.832
2019	Oak	AL	123	434	125	29	0	24	(13	11)	226	79	67	69	27	0	123	11	1	8	13	2	7	.288	.340	.521	.860
2020	Oak	AL	54	183	39	8	1	6	(3	3)	67	27	25	28	24	0	58	12	0	3	2	1	7	.213	.338	.366	.704
2021	Oak	AL	88	341	84	21	2	14	(8	6)	151	43	39	49	27	0	98	9	0	1	12	5	4	.246	.317	.443	.760
	Postseason		9	32	6	1	0	2	(0	2)	13	4	6	3	2	0	10	0	0	0	0	0	1	.188	.229	.406	.635
	4 ML YEARS		313	1114	293	70	4	49	(28	21)	518	176	150	175	94	0	329	34	1	14	34	9	18	.263	.335	.465	.800

Ryan Lavarnway

Bats: R **Throws:** R **Pos:** C-8;PH-1   luh-VARN-way   **Ht:** 6'3" **Wt:** 239 **Born:** 8/7/1987 **Age:** 34

			BATTING																			RUNNING			AVERAGES			
Year	Team	Lg	G	AB	H	2B	3B	HR	(Hm	Rd)	TB	R	RBI	RC	TBB	IBB	SO	HBP	SH	SF	SB	CS	GDP	Avg	OBP	Slg	OPS
2021	Clmbs	AAA	47	169	43	7	0	13	(-	-)	89	26	40	-	18	1	54	1	0	0	0	0	3	.254	.330	.527	.856
2011	Bos	AL	17	39	9	2	0	2	(0	2)	17	5	8	4	4	0	10	0	0	0	0	0	1	.231	.302	.436	.738
2012	Bos	AL	46	153	24	8	0	2	(0	2)	38	11	12	4	11	0	41	0	0	2	0	0	4	.157	.211	.248	.459
2013	Bos	AL	25	77	23	7	0	1	(1	0)	33	8	14	11	2	0	17	2	0	1	0	0	3	.299	.329	.429	.758
2014	Bos	AL	9	10	0	0	0	0	(0	0)	0	0	0	0	0	0	3	0	0	0	0	0	0	.000	.000	.000	.000
2015	2 Tms		37	94	18	6	0	2	(0	2)	30	6	6	4	12	1	28	0	0	0	0	0	5	.191	.283	.319	.602
2017	Oak	AL	6	11	3	1	0	0	(0	0)	4	0	2	2	1	0	3	1	0	0	0	0	1	.273	.385	.364	.748
2018	Pit	NL	6	6	4	1	0	0	(0	0)	5	1	1	2	0	0	1	0	0	0	0	0	0	.667	.667	.833	1.500

			BATTING															RUNNING			AVERAGES			
Year	Team	Lg	G	AB	H	2B	3B	HR	(Hm | Rd)	TB	R	RBI	RC	TBB	IBB	SO	HBP	SH	SF	SB	CS	GDP	Avg	OBP	Slg	OPS
2019	Cin	NL	5	18	5	2	0	2	(2 | 0)	13	4	7	5	1	0	5	0	0	0	0	0	0	.278	.316	.722	1.038
2020	Mia	NL	5	11	4	0	0	0	(0 | 0)	4	0	0	1	0	0	2	0	0	0	0	0	0	.364	.364	.364	.727
2021	Cle	AL	9	28	7	3	0	0	(0 | 0)	10	2	0	2	1	0	10	0	1	0	0	0	0	.250	.276	.357	.633
15	Bal	AL	10	28	3	1	0	0	(0 | 0)	4	1	0	0	4	0	7	0	0	0	0	0	1	.107	.219	.143	.362
15	Atl	NL	27	66	15	5	0	2	(0 | 2)	26	5	6	4	8	1	21	0	0	0	0	0	4	.227	.311	.394	.705
10 ML YEARS			165	447	97	30	0	9	(3 | 6)	154	37	50	35	32	1	120	3	1	3	0	0	15	.217	.272	.345	.617

Derek Law

Pitches: R Bats: R Pos: RP-9 Ht: 6'3" Wt: 225 Born: 9/14/1990 Age: 31

			HOW MUCH PITCHED					WHAT HE GAVE UP										THE RESULTS						
Year	Team	Lg	G	GS	GF	IP	BFP	H	R	ER	HR	SH	SF	HB	TBB	IBB	SO	WP	W	L	Pct	Sv-Op	Hld	Vel	OPS	ERC	ERA
2021	StPaul	AAA	17	2	7	25.1	103	22	8	8	1	0	0	0	10	0	24	3	1	1	.500	4- -	-	-	.590	3.04	2.84
2016	SF	NL	61	0	12	55.0	214	44	13	13	3	0	0	0	9	0	50	1	4	2	.667	1-2	14	93	.570	1.93	2.13
2017	SF	NL	41	0	12	37.1	168	45	21	21	5	2	2	2	14	2	35	5	4	1	.800	4-6	5	94	.840	5.60	5.06
2018	SF	NL	7	0	4	13.1	66	16	13	11	2	0	1	1	8	0	12	1	1	0	1.000	0-0	0	94	.861	6.55	7.43
2019	Tor	AL	58	4	18	60.2	285	61	36	33	8	2	2	3	40	3	67	7	1	2	.333	5-6	8	94	.804	5.40	4.90
2021	Min	AL	9	0	4	15.0	67	16	7	7	2	0	1	0	8	0	14	1	0	0	-	0-0	0	94	.824	5.29	4.20
	Postseason		3	0	0	2.1	11	1	1	1	0	0	0	0	1	0	3	0	0	0	-	0-0	0	94	.282	0.88	3.86
5 ML YEARS			176	4	50	181.1	800	182	90	85	20	4	6	6	79	5	178	15	10	5	.667	10-14	27	94	.752	4.36	4.22

Justin Lawrence

Pitches: R Bats: R Pos: RP-19 Ht: 6'3" Wt: 213 Born: 11/25/1994 Age: 27

			HOW MUCH PITCHED					WHAT HE GAVE UP										THE RESULTS						
Year	Team	Lg	G	GS	GF	IP	BFP	H	R	ER	HR	SH	SF	HB	TBB	IBB	SO	WP	W	L	Pct	Sv-Op	Hld	Vel	OPS	ERC	ERA
2021	Albq	AAA	30	0	29	31.1	136	28	18	15	3	0	1	4	11	0	30	5	5	5	.500	13- -	-	-	.658	3.71	4.31
2021	Col	NL	19	0	4	16.2	86	21	16	16	0	1	3	0	19	1	17	2	1	0	1.000	0-1	2	97	.883	7.86	8.64

Wade LeBlanc

Pitches: L Bats: L Pos: SP-9; RP-9   lah-BLAHNK   Ht: 6'2" Wt: 195 Born: 8/7/1984 Age: 37

			HOW MUCH PITCHED					WHAT HE GAVE UP										THE RESULTS						
Year	Team	Lg	G	GS	GF	IP	BFP	H	R	ER	HR	SH	SF	HB	TBB	IBB	SO	WP	W	L	Pct	Sv-Op	Hld	Vel	OPS	ERC	ERA
2008	SD	NL	5	4	0	21.1	104	29	19	19	7	1	0	0	15	2	14	0	1	3	.250	0-0	0	86	1.086	9.57	8.02
2009	SD	NL	9	9	0	46.1	194	35	19	19	6	3	1	4	19	1	30	0	3	1	.750	0-0	0	85	.669	3.28	3.69
2010	SD	NL	26	25	0	146.0	625	157	69	69	24	7	2	2	51	5	110	2	8	12	.400	0-0	0	87	.818	4.84	4.25
2011	SD	NL	14	14	0	79.2	339	84	42	41	7	3	3	1	28	1	51	1	5	6	.455	0-0	0	87	.757	4.21	4.63
2012	Mia	NL	25	9	1	68.2	284	71	30	28	7	5	1	1	19	1	43	1	2	5	.286	0-0	1	87	.729	3.94	3.67
2013	2 Tms		17	7	1	55.0	259	72	40	33	7	2	1	3	20	3	33	0	1	5	.167	0-0	0	86	.855	5.97	5.40
2014	2 Tms	AL	11	3	3	29.2	121	27	13	13	2	0	2	2	7	2	21	1	1	1	.500	0-0	0	88	.625	2.96	3.94
2016	2 Tms		19	8	7	62.0	252	59	30	26	14	0	2	0	11	0	51	0	4	0	1.000	2-2	1	87	.776	3.72	3.77
2017	Pit		50	0	18	68.0	283	64	35	34	10	1	1	1	17	1	54	2	5	2	.714	1-3	4	87	.717	3.48	4.50
2018	Sea	AL	32	27	5	162.0	662	151	74	67	24	1	4	3	40	1	130	1	9	5	.643	0-0	0	86	.712	3.52	3.72
2019	Sea	AL	26	8	4	121.1	532	145	80	77	28	1	1	1	31	1	92	0	6	7	.462	0-0	0	86	.867	5.55	5.71
2020	Bal	AL	6	6	0	22.1	103	27	20	20	6	0	2	1	8	0	13	0	1	0	1.000	0-0	0	87	.882	6.46	8.06
2021	2 Tms		18	9	4	49.0	221	56	24	24	8	2	0	4	17	3	29	2	0	2	.000	0-0	0	88	.831	5.34	4.41
13	Mia	NL	13	7	0	48.2	222	63	30	28	6	2	1	2	15	2	31	0	1	5	.167	0-0	0	86	.834	5.67	5.18
13	Hou	AL	4	0	1	6.1	37	9	10	5	1	0	0	1	5	1	2	0	0	0	-	0-0	0	87	.986	8.25	7.11
14	LAA	AL	10	3	2	28.2	114	25	11	11	2	0	1	1	6	1	21	1	1	1	.500	0-0	0	88	.601	2.63	3.45
14	NYY	AL	1	0	1	1.0	7	2	2	2	0	0	1	1	1	1	0	0	0	0	-	0-0	0	89	1.071	13.81	18.00
16	Sea	AL	11	8	3	50.0	208	52	27	25	14	0	0	0	9	0	41	0	3	0	1.000	1-1	0	87	.841	4.58	4.50
16	Pit	NL	8	0	4	12.0	44	7	3	1	0	0	2	0	2	0	10	0	1	0	1.000	1-1	1	87	.455	1.03	0.75
21	Bal	AL	6	1	3	6.2	33	11	7	7	1	0	0	1	1	0	6	2	0	1	.000	0-0	0	88	.942	7.87	9.45
21	StL	NL	12	8	1	42.1	188	45	17	17	7	2	0	3	16	3	23	0	0	1	.000	0-0	0	88	.811	4.96	3.61
13 ML YEARS			258	129	43	931.1	3979	977	495	470	150	26	20	23	283	21	671	10	46	49	.484	3-5	6	87	.784	4.48	4.54

Jose Leclerc

Pitches: R Bats: R Pos: P   leh-KLURK   Ht: 6'0" Wt: 195 Born: 12/19/1993 Age: 28

			HOW MUCH PITCHED					WHAT HE GAVE UP										THE RESULTS						
Year	Team	Lg	G	GS	GF	IP	BFP	H	R	ER	HR	SH	SF	HB	TBB	IBB	SO	WP	W	L	Pct	Sv-Op	Hld	Vel	OPS	ERC	ERA
2016	Tex	AL	12	0	5	15.0	66	11	4	3	0	0	1	0	13	2	15	1	0	0	-	0-0	0	94	.710	3.46	1.80
2017	Tex	AL	47	0	15	45.2	200	23	21	20	4	0	0	3	40	1	60	5	2	3	.400	2-3	10	96	.585	3.28	3.94
2018	Tex	AL	59	0	21	57.2	223	24	16	10	1	4	0	3	25	1	85	0	2	3	.400	12-16	15	95	.431	1.21	1.56
2019	Tex	AL	70	3	40	68.2	299	52	34	33	7	3	2	6	39	1	100	7	2	4	.333	14-18	7	97	.701	3.68	4.33
2020	Tex	AL	2	0	2	2.0	10	2	1	1	0	0	0	0	2	0	3	0	0	0	-	1-1	0	95	.775	5.48	4.50
5 ML YEARS			190	3	83	189.0	798	112	76	67	12	7	3	12	119	5	263	15	6	10	.375	29-38	32	96	.598	2.70	3.19

Dylan Lee

Pitches: L Bats: L Pos: RP-2 Ht: 6'3" Wt: 214 Born: 8/1/1994 Age: 27

			HOW MUCH PITCHED					WHAT HE GAVE UP										THE RESULTS						
Year	Team	Lg	G	GS	GF	IP	BFP	H	R	ER	HR	SH	SF	HB	TBB	IBB	SO	WP	W	L	Pct	Sv-Op	Hld	Vel	OPS	ERC	ERA
2021	Gwnntt	AAA	34	0	7	45.2	172	29	11	8	4	2	1	1	6	0	52	1	5	1	.833	1- -	-	-	.520	1.43	1.58
2021	Atl	NL	2	0	0	2.0	9	3	2	2	1	0	0	0	0	0	3	0	0	0	-	0-0	0	93	1.222	8.13	9.00

Khalil Lee

Bats: L **Throws:** L **Pos:** RF-11;PR-2;PH-1   **Ht:** 5'10" **Wt:** 170 **Born:** 6/26/1998 **Age:** 24

										BATTING													RUNNING			AVERAGES			
Year Team	Lg	G	AB	H	2B	3B	HR	(Hm	Rd)	TB	R	RBI	RC	TBB	IBB	SO	HBP	SH	SF				SB	CS	GDP	Avg	OBP	Slg	OPS
2021 Syrcse	AAA	98	280	76	20	2	13	(-	-)	139	65	36	-	69	0	110	22	0	1				8	10	7	.271	.449	.496	.945
2021 NYM	NL	11	18	1	1	0	0	(0	0)	2	2	1	0	0	0	13	0	0	0				0	0	0	.056	.056	.111	.167

DJ LeMahieu

Bats: R **Throws:** R **Pos:** 2B-83;1B-55;3B-39;PH-2;DH-1   la-MAY-hugh   **Ht:** 6'4" **Wt:** 220 **Born:** 7/13/1988 **Age:** 33

								BATTING											RUNNING			AVERAGES			
Year Team	Lg	G	AB	H	2B	3B	HR	(Hm Rd)	TB	R	RBI	RC	TBB	IBB	SO	HBP	SH	SF	SB	CS	GDP	Avg	OBP	Slg	OPS
2011 ChC	NL	37	60	15	2	0	0	(0 0)	17	3	4	3	1	0	12	0	1	0	0	0	2	.250	.262	.283	.546
2012 Col	NL	81	229	68	12	4	2	(1 1)	94	26	22	28	13	4	42	0	3	2	1	2	8	.297	.332	.410	.742
2013 Col	NL	109	404	113	21	3	2	(1 1)	146	39	28	42	19	2	67	1	7	3	18	7	13	.280	.311	.361	.673
2014 Col	NL	149	494	132	15	5	5	(2 3)	172	59	42	47	33	7	97	2	7	2	10	10	13	.267	.315	.348	.663
2015 Col	NL	150	564	170	21	5	6	(3 3)	219	85	61	75	50	4	107	1	3	2	23	3	20	.301	.358	.388	.746
2016 Col	NL	146	552	192	32	8	11	(7 4)	273	104	66	104	66	2	80	3	8	6	11	7	19	.348	.416	.495	.911
2017 Col	NL	155	609	189	28	4	8	(5 3)	249	95	64	87	59	1	90	6	3	5	6	5	24	.310	.374	.409	.783
2018 Col	NL	128	533	147	32	2	15	(4 11)	228	90	62	72	37	0	82	2	2	7	6	5	14	.276	.321	.428	.749
2019 NYY	AL	145	602	197	33	2	26	(19 7)	312	109	102	122	46	0	90	2	1	4	5	2	14	.327	.375	.518	.893
2020 NYY	AL	50	195	71	10	2	10	(8 2)	115	41	27	46	18	0	21	2	0	1	3	0	3	.364	.421	.590	1.011
2021 NYY	AL	150	597	160	24	1	10	(5 5)	216	84	57	84	73	2	94	4	0	5	4	2	16	.268	.349	.362	.711
Postseason		21	92	25	5	0	3	(2 1)	39	14	11	13	10	0	15	0	0	1	0	1	2	.272	.340	.424	.764
11 ML YEARS		1300	4839	1454	230	36	95	(53 42)	2041	735	535	710	415	22	782	23	35	37	87	43	146	.300	.356	.422	.778

Sandy Leon

Bats: B **Throws:** R **Pos:** C-60;PH-21;3B-1;DH-1   lay-OHN   **Ht:** 5'10" **Wt:** 235 **Born:** 3/13/1989 **Age:** 33

								BATTING											RUNNING			AVERAGES			
Year Team	Lg	G	AB	H	2B	3B	HR	(Hm Rd)	TB	R	RBI	RC	TBB	IBB	SO	HBP	SH	SF	SB	CS	GDP	Avg	OBP	Slg	OPS
2012 Was	NL	12	30	8	2	0	0	(0 0)	10	2	2	2	4	0	11	2	0	0	0	0	1	.267	.389	.333	.722
2013 Was	NL	2	1	0	0	0	0	(0 0)	0	0	0	0	0	0	1	0	0	0	0	0	0	.000	.000	.000	.000
2014 Was	NL	20	64	10	1	0	1	(0 1)	14	7	3	2	6	0	20	0	0	0	0	0	1	.156	.229	.219	.447
2015 Bos	AL	41	114	21	2	0	0	(0 0)	23	8	3	1	7	1	28	1	6	0	0	1	4	.184	.238	.202	.439
2016 Bos	AL	78	252	78	17	2	7	(2 5)	120	36	35	44	23	1	66	2	4	2	0	0	4	.310	.369	.476	.845
2017 Bos	AL	85	271	61	14	0	7	(3 4)	96	32	39	32	25	1	74	1	1	3	0	0	5	.225	.290	.354	.644
2018 Bos	AL	89	265	47	12	0	5	(2 3)	74	30	22	17	15	0	75	4	3	1	1	0	6	.177	.232	.279	.511
2019 Bos	AL	65	172	33	3	0	5	(4 1)	51	14	19	15	13	0	47	1	4	1	0	0	0	.192	.251	.297	.548
2020 Cle	AL	25	66	9	1	0	2	(1 1)	16	4	4	3	14	0	21	1	0	0	0	0	2	.136	.296	.242	.539
2021 Mia	NL	84	202	37	5	0	4	(1 3)	54	15	14	5	12	0	65	3	1	2	0	0	2	.183	.237	.267	.505
Postseason		17	32	8	1	0	1	(0 1)	12	2	3	4	2	0	11	0	1	0	0	0	0	.250	.294	.375	.669
10 ML YEARS		501	1437	304	57	2	31	(13 18)	458	148	141	121	119	3	408	15	19	9	1	1	25	.212	.277	.319	.596

Dominic Leone

Pitches: R **Bats:** R **Pos:** RP-53; SP-4   LEE-own   **Ht:** 5'10" **Wt:** 215 **Born:** 10/26/1991 **Age:** 30

		HOW MUCH PITCHED					WHAT HE GAVE UP										THE RESULTS						
Year Team	Lg	G	GS	GF	IP	BFP	H	R	ER	HR	SH	SF	HB	TBB	IBB	SO	WP	W	L	Pct	Sv-Op Hld	Vel	OPS	ERC	ERA
2021 Scrmto	AAA	7	1	5	9.0	34	6	1	1	0	0	0	0	3	0	16	1	0	1	.000	2- - -		.458	1.66	1.00
2014 Sea	AL	57	0	3	66.1	272	52	18	16	4	1	3	3	25	3	70	4	8	2	.800	0-2 7	95	.624	2.71	2.17
2015 2 Tms		13	0	6	15.0	74	19	15	14	2	0	1	1	9	2	9	2	0	5	.000	0-1 1	93	.884	6.63	8.40
2016 Ari	NL	25	0	8	27.0	131	45	21	19	7	0	3	1	12	1	23	4	0	1	.000	0-1 0	93	1.095	10.37	6.33
2017 Tor	AL	65	0	6	70.1	279	51	22	20	6	0	3	0	23	3	81	8	3	0	1.000	1-5 11	94	.625	2.25	2.56
2018 StL	NL	29	0	8	24.0	106	27	12	12	3	1	3	0	8	3	26	0	1	2	.333	0-2 5	94	.727	4.43	4.50
2019 StL	NL	40	0	11	40.2	180	39	28	25	9	1	1	0	22	2	46	1	1	0	1.000	1-2 0	94	.822	5.20	5.53
2020 Cle	AL	12	0	4	9.2	47	14	9	9	3	0	0	0	5	0	16	1	0	0	-	0-0 3	95	1.023	9.14	8.38
2021 SF	NL	57	4	11	53.2	219	37	15	9	2	3	2	1	22	1	50	2	4	5	.444	2-4 15	95	.547	2.13	1.51
15 Sea	AL	10	0	5	11.1	54	11	9	8	1	0	0	0	9	2	7	2	0	4	.000	0-0 1	93	.770	4.93	6.35
15 Ari	NL	3	0	1	3.2	20	8	6	6	1	0	1	1	0	0	2	0	0	1	.000	0-1 0	93	1.172	12.63	14.73
8 ML YEARS		298	4	57	306.2	1308	284	140	124	36	6	16	6	126	15	321	22	17	15	.531	4-17 42	94	.723	3.83	3.64

Jon Lester

Pitches: L **Bats:** L **Pos:** SP-28   **Ht:** 6'4" **Wt:** 249 **Born:** 1/7/1984 **Age:** 38

		HOW MUCH PITCHED					WHAT HE GAVE UP										THE RESULTS						
Year Team	Lg	G	GS	GF	IP	BFP	H	R	ER	HR	SH	SF	HB	TBB	IBB	SO	WP	W	L	Pct	Sv-Op Hld	Vel	OPS	ERC	ERA
2006 Bos	AL	15	15	0	81.1	367	91	43	43	7	2	8	5	43	1	60	5	7	2	.778	0-0 0	90	.814	5.52	4.76
2007 Bos	AL	12	11	0	63.0	275	61	33	32	10	1	5	1	31	0	50	1	4	0	1.000	0-0 0	90	.753	4.78	4.57
2008 Bos	AL	33	33	0	210.1	874	202	78	75	14	6	3	10	66	1	152	3	16	6	.727	0-0 0	92	.688	3.55	3.21
2009 Bos	AL	32	32	0	203.1	843	186	80	77	20	2	6	3	64	0	225	6	15	8	.652	0-0 0	94	.667	3.35	3.41
2010 Bos	AL	32	32	0	208.0	861	167	81	75	14	6	6	10	83	0	225	4	19	9	.679	0-0 0	93	.628	3.00	3.25
2011 Bos	AL	31	31	0	191.2	799	166	77	74	20	2	2	11	75	0	182	4	15	9	.625	0-0 0	93	.690	3.62	3.47
2012 Bos	AL	33	33	0	205.1	876	216	117	110	25	5	7	4	68	2	166	6	9	14	.391	0-0 0	93	.773	4.36	4.82
2013 Bos	AL	33	33	0	213.1	903	209	94	89	19	1	1	7	67	0	177	5	15	8	.652	0-0 0	93	.703	3.69	3.75
2014 2 Tms	AL	32	32	0	219.2	885	194	76	60	16	6	5	5	48	0	220	3	16	11	.593	0-0 0	92	.635	2.70	2.46
2015 ChC	NL	32	32	0	205.0	828	183	83	76	16	5	4	7	47	0	207	8	11	12	.478	0-0 0	92	.661	2.88	3.34
2016 ChC	NL	32	32	0	202.2	796	154	57	55	21	4	4	6	52	0	197	4	19	5	.792	0-0 0	92	.602	2.47	2.44
2017 ChC	NL	32	32	0	180.2	763	179	101	87	26	4	4	4	60	3	180	3	13	8	.619	0-0 0	91	.750	4.16	4.33
2018 ChC	NL	32	32	0	181.2	761	174	75	67	24	7	3	6	64	1	149	4	18	6	.750	0-0 0	91	.733	4.07	3.32
2019 ChC	NL	31	31	0	171.2	764	205	101	85	26	4	5	5	52	0	165	3	13	10	.565	0-0 0	90	.815	5.27	4.46
2020 ChC	NL	12	12	0	61.0	265	64	35	35	11	0	7	3	17	0	42	2	3	3	.500	0-0 0	89	.777	4.56	5.16

Year	Team	Lg	G	GS	GF	IP	BFP	H	R	ER	HR	SH	SF	HB	TBB	IBB	SO	WP	W	L	Pct	Sv-Op	Hld	Vel	OPS	ERC	ERA
2021 2 Tms		NL	28	28	0	141.1	627	159	84	74	25	6	5	3	55	5	91	0	7	6	.538	0-0	0	88	.828	5.35	4.71
14	Bos	AL	21	21	0	143.0	580	128	52	40	9	5	2	4	32	0	149	2	10	7	.588	0-0	0	92	.637	2.73	2.52
14	Oak	AL	11	11	0	76.2	305	66	24	20	7	1	3	1	16	0	71	1	6	4	.600	0-0	0	91	.632	2.65	2.35
21	Was	NL	16	16	0	75.1	342	91	50	42	14	2	4	1	29	3	51	0	3	5	.375	0-0	0	89	.859	5.82	5.02
21	StL	NL	12	12	0	66.0	285	68	34	32	11	4	1	2	26	2	40	0	4	1	.800	0-0	0	88	.790	4.83	4.36
	Postseason		26	22	2	154.0	610	117	46	43	15	6	2	3	40	0	133	4	9	7	.563	0-0	0	93	.594	2.37	2.51
16 ML YEARS			452	451	0	2740.0	11487	2610	1215	1114	294	61	67	90	892	13	2488	63	200	117	.631	0-0	0	92	.708	3.73	3.66

Kyle Lewis

Bats: R **Throws:** R **Pos:** CF-34;DH-2

Ht: 6'4" **Wt:** 205 **Born:** 7/13/1995 **Age:** 26

					BATTING																	RUNNING			AVERAGES			
Year	Team	Lg	G	AB	H	2B	3B	HR	(Hm	Rd)	TB	R	RBI	RC	TBB	IBB	SO	HBP	SH	SF	SB	CS	GDP	Avg	OBP	Slg	OPS
2019	Sea	AL	18	71	19	5	0	6	(4	2)	42	10	13	13	3	0	29	0	0	1	0	0	0	.268	.293	.592	.885
2020	Sea	AL	58	206	54	3	0	11	(5	6)	90	37	28	31	34	0	71	0	0	2	5	1	5	.262	.364	.437	.801
2021	Sea	AL	36	130	32	4	0	5	(2	3)	51	15	11	21	16	0	37	1	0	0	2	0	1	.246	.333	.392	.726
3 ML YEARS			112	407	105	12	0	22	(11	11)	183	62	52	65	53	0	137	1	0	3	7	1	6	.258	.343	.450	.792

Royce Lewis

Bats: R **Throws:** R **Pos:** SS

Ht: 6'2" **Wt:** 200 **Born:** 6/5/1999 **Age:** 23

					BATTING																	RUNNING			AVERAGES			
Year	Team	Lg	G	AB	H	2B	3B	HR	(Hm	Rd)	TB	R	RBI	RC	TBB	IBB	SO	HBP	SH	SF	SB	CS	GDP	Avg	OBP	Slg	OPS
2017 2 Tms		Low	54	204	57	8	3	4	(-	-)	83	54	27	38	25	0	33	9	0	1	18	3	3	.279	.381	.407	.788
2018 2 Tms		Low	121	483	141	29	3	14	(-	-)	218	83	74	65	43	1	84	4	1	4	28	8	8	.292	.352	.451	.803
2019	FtMyrs	A+	94	383	91	17	3	10	(-	-)	144	55	35	46	27	1	90	3	0	5	16	8	5	.238	.289	.376	.665
2019	Pnscla	AA	33	134	31	9	1	2	(-	-)	48	18	14	15	11	0	33	1	0	2	6	2	0	.231	.291	.358	.649

Domingo Leyba

Bats: B **Throws:** R **Pos:** 2B-21;3B-10;PH-6

Ht: 5'11" **Wt:** 205 **Born:** 9/11/1995 **Age:** 26

					BATTING																	RUNNING			AVERAGES			
Year	Team	Lg	G	AB	H	2B	3B	HR	(Hm	Rd)	TB	R	RBI	RC	TBB	IBB	SO	HBP	SH	SF	SB	CS	GDP	Avg	OBP	Slg	OPS
2021	Norfolk	AAA	18	69	19	1	0	5	(-	-)	35	7	20	-	4	0	10	0	0	1	0	1	4	.275	.311	.507	.818
2021	RdRck	AAA	20	86	26	6	2	3	(-	-)	45	11	24	-	2	0	11	0	0	1	1	1	2	.302	.315	.523	.838
2019	Ari	NL	21	25	7	2	1	0	(0	0)	11	6	5	5	4	0	9	0	0	1	0	0	0	.280	.367	.440	.807
2021 2 Tms			34	87	10	1	0	1	(0	1)	14	6	4	1	8	0	23	1	0	0	0	0	4	.115	.198	.161	.359
21	Ari	NL	13	22	0	0	0	0	(0	0)	0	0	0	0	2	0	7	0	0	0	0	0	1	.000	.083	.000	.083
21	Bal	AL	21	65	10	1	0	1	(0	1)	14	6	4	1	6	0	16	1	0	0	0	0	3	.154	.236	.215	.451
2 ML YEARS			55	112	17	3	1	1	(0	1)	25	12	9	6	12	0	32	1	0	1	0	0	4	.152	.238	.223	.461

Tzu-Wei Lin

Bats: L **Throws:** R **Pos:** LF-1

zoo-way

Ht: 5'9" **Wt:** 180 **Born:** 2/15/1994 **Age:** 28

					BATTING																	RUNNING			AVERAGES			
Year	Team	Lg	G	AB	H	2B	3B	HR	(Hm	Rd)	TB	R	RBI	RC	TBB	IBB	SO	HBP	SH	SF	SB	CS	GDP	Avg	OBP	Slg	OPS
2017	Bos	AL	25	56	15	0	2	0	(0	0)	19	7	2	7	9	0	17	0	1	0	1	1	0	.268	.369	.339	.709
2018	Bos	AL	37	65	16	6	1	1	(0	1)	27	15	6	8	8	0	17	0	0	0	0	1	0	.246	.329	.415	.744
2019	Bos	AL	13	20	4	2	0	0	(0	0)	6	3	1	2	2	0	6	0	0	0	1	1	0	.200	.273	.300	.573
2020	Bos	AL	26	52	8	1	0	0	(0	0)	9	2	3	1	2	0	17	0	2	1	0	0	1	.154	.182	.173	.355
2021	Min	AL	1	0	0	0	0	0	(0	0)	0	0	0	0	0	0	0	0	0	0	0	0	0	-	-	-	-
5 ML YEARS			102	193	43	9	3	1	(0	1)	61	27	12	18	21	0	57	0	3	1	2	3	1	.223	.298	.316	.614

Josh Lindblom

Pitches: R **Bats:** R **Pos:** RP-8

LIN-bloom

Ht: 6'4" **Wt:** 240 **Born:** 6/15/1987 **Age:** 35

				HOW MUCH PITCHED				WHAT HE GAVE UP										THE RESULTS								
Year	Team	Lg	G	GS	GF	IP	BFP	H	R	ER	HR	SH	SF	HB	TBB	IBB	SO	WP	W	L	Pct	Sv-Op	Hld	Vel	OPS	ERC	ERA
2021	Nashv	AAA	21	19	0	99.2	424	97	37	35	10	4	4	2	26	1	109	6	5	4	.556	0--	-	-	.692	3.38	3.16
2011	LAD	NL	27	0	8	29.2	116	21	9	9	0	2	3	2	10	3	28	3	1	0	1.000	0-1	3	92	.572	1.90	2.73
2012 2 Tms		NL	74	0	18	71.0	304	61	31	28	13	2	0	4	35	2	70	2	3	5	.375	1-4	22	92	.753	4.47	3.55
2013	Tex	AL	8	5	2	31.1	137	35	19	19	4	0	0	1	12	2	21	2	1	3	.250	0-0	0	90	.788	4.64	5.46
2014	Oak	AL	1	1	0	4.2	22	5	2	2	1	0	0	1	2	0	2	0	0	0	-	0-0	0	91	.837	6.25	3.86
2017	Pit	NL	4	0	1	10.1	51	18	9	9	0	0	0	0	3	0	10	0	0	0	-	0-0	0	91	.849	7.25	7.84
2020	Mil	NL	12	10	1	45.1	191	42	26	26	8	0	1	4	16	0	52	2	2	4	.333	0-0	0	90	.732	4.02	5.16
2021	Mil	NL	8	0	5	16.2	85	23	18	18	5	0	1	3	10	0	17	3	0	0	-	0-0	0	90	1.086	9.77	9.72
12	LAD	NL	48	0	12	47.2	197	42	16	16	9	2	0	3	18	0	43	1	2	2	.500	0-2	15	92	.754	4.31	3.02
12	Phi	NL	26	0	6	23.1	107	19	15	12	4	0	0	1	17	2	27	1	1	3	.250	1-2	7	92	.750	4.77	4.63
7 ML YEARS			134	16	35	209.0	906	205	114	111	29	4	4	13	87	7	200	12	7	12	.368	1-5	25	91	.769	4.54	4.78

Francisco Lindor

Bats: B **Throws:** R **Pos:** SS-124;PH-2

lin-DOHR

Ht: 5'11" **Wt:** 190 **Born:** 11/14/1993 **Age:** 28

					BATTING																	RUNNING			AVERAGES			
Year	Team	Lg	G	AB	H	2B	3B	HR	(Hm	Rd)	TB	R	RBI	RC	TBB	IBB	SO	HBP	SH	SF	SB	CS	GDP	Avg	OBP	Slg	OPS
2015	Cle	AL	99	390	122	22	4	12	(8	4)	188	50	51	64	27	0	69	1	13	7	12	2	12	.313	.353	.482	.835
2016	Cle	AL	158	604	182	30	3	15	(6	9)	263	99	78	87	57	3	88	5	3	15	19	5	18	.301	.358	.435	.794
2017	Cle	AL	159	651	178	44	4	33	(16	17)	329	99	89	107	60	6	93	4	5	3	15	3	11	.273	.337	.505	.842
2018	Cle	AL	158	661	183	42	2	38	(20	18)	343	129	92	117	70	7	107	8	3	3	25	10	5	.277	.352	.519	.871

Year Team	Lg	G	AB	H	2B	3B	HR	(Hm	Rd)	TB	R	RBI	RC	TBB	IBB	SO	HBP	SH	SF	SB	CS	GDP	Avg	OBP	Slg	OPS
2019 Cle	AL	143	598	170	40	2	32	(14	18)	310	101	74	89	46	9	98	3	1	6	22	5	13	.284	.335	.518	.854
2020 Cle	AL	60	236	61	13	0	8	(3	5)	98	30	27	29	24	2	41	4	0	2	6	2	8	.258	.335	.415	.750
2021 NYM	NL	125	452	104	16	3	20	(12	8)	186	73	63	70	58	4	96	5	6	3	10	4	7	.230	.322	.412	.734
Postseason		25	95	25	4	0	5	(4	1)	44	11	12	14	9	2	27	0	1	0	1	3	3	.263	.327	.463	.790
7 ML YEARS		902	3592	1000	207	18	158	(79	79)	1717	581	474	563	342	31	592	30	31	39	109	31	74	.278	.343	.478	.821

Zack Littell

Pitches: R Bats: R Pos: RP-61; SP-2   lah-TELL   Ht: 6'4" Wt: 220 Born: 10/5/1995 Age: 26

			HOW MUCH PITCHED				WHAT HE GAVE UP										THE RESULTS								
Year Team	Lg	G	GS	GF	IP	BFP	H	R	ER	HR	SH	SF	HB	TBB	IBB	SO	WP	W	L	Pct	Sv-Op	Hld	Vel	OPS	ERC	ERA
2018 Min	AL	8	1	2	20.1	101	25	17	14	3	1	1	4	11	0	14	0	0	2	.000	0-0	0	92	.924	7.09	6.20
2019 Min	AL	29	0	7	37.0	146	34	12	11	4	1	0	0	9	1	32	0	6	0	1.000	0-1	1	94	.708	3.18	2.68
2020 Min	AL	6	0	3	6.1	31	12	7	7	5	0	0	1	3	0	3	1	0	0	-	0-0	0	94	1.516	19.87	9.95
2021 SF	NL	63	2	10	61.2	252	46	24	20	7	2	2	2	24	1	63	3	4	0	1.000	2-6	5	95	.662	2.88	2.92
Postseason		2	0	1	0.1	3	0	2	2	0	0	0	1	1	0	0	1	0	1	.000	0-0	0	95	.667	19.60	54.00
4 ML YEARS		106	4	21	125.1	530	117	60	52	19	4	3	7	47	2	112	4	10	2	.833	2-7	6	94	.773	4.22	3.73

Mauricio Llovera

Pitches: R Bats: R Pos: RP-6   yo-VAIR-uh   Ht: 5'11" Wt: 224 Born: 4/17/1996 Age: 26

			HOW MUCH PITCHED				WHAT HE GAVE UP										THE RESULTS								
Year Team	Lg	G	GS	GF	IP	BFP	H	R	ER	HR	SH	SF	HB	TBB	IBB	SO	WP	W	L	Pct	Sv-Op	Hld	Vel	OPS	ERC	ERA
2021 LV	AAA	31	3	10	47.1	206	40	21	20	5	1	1	4	22	2	44	3	2	2	.500	5--	-	-	.710	3.72	3.80
2020 Phi	NL	1	0	0	1.0	10	5	4	4	0	0	0	1	1	0	1	0	0	0	-	0-0	0	93	1.575	41.68	36.00
2021 Phi	NL	6	0	4	6.2	35	10	7	7	5	0	0	1	4	0	7	1	1	0	1.000	0-0	0	95	1.262	14.59	9.45
2 ML YEARS		7	0	4	7.2	45	15	11	11	5	0	0	2	5	0	8	1	1	0	1.000	0-0	0	94	1.331	18.32	12.91

Jonathan Loaisiga

Pitches: R Bats: R Pos: RP-57   loh-AYE-sig-ah   Ht: 5'11" Wt: 165 Born: 11/2/1994 Age: 27

			HOW MUCH PITCHED				WHAT HE GAVE UP										THE RESULTS								
Year Team	Lg	G	GS	GF	IP	BFP	H	R	ER	HR	SH	SF	HB	TBB	IBB	SO	WP	W	L	Pct	Sv-Op	Hld	Vel	OPS	ERC	ERA
2018 NYY	AL	9	4	2	24.2	108	26	17	14	3	0	0	0	12	0	33	0	2	0	1.000	0-0	0	96	.789	4.97	5.11
2019 NYY	AL	15	4	3	31.2	139	31	16	16	6	0	4	1	16	0	37	1	2	2	.500	0-1	0	97	.820	5.21	4.55
2020 NYY	AL	12	3	2	23.0	100	21	11	9	3	1	0	4	7	1	22	1	3	0	1.000	0-2	2	97	.740	4.00	3.52
2021 NYY	AL	57	0	8	70.2	283	56	19	17	3	2	2	3	16	0	69	4	9	4	.692	5-9	17	98	.548	2.16	2.17
Postseason		6	0	2	4.2	26	6	4	3	1	0	0	1	5	0	4	2	0	0	-	0-1	0	97	1.012	10.57	5.79
4 ML YEARS		93	11	15	150.0	630	134	63	56	15	3	6	8	51	1	161	6	16	6	.727	5-12	19	97	.677	3.46	3.36

Jose Lobaton

Bats: B Throws: R Pos: C-5;PH-1   LOE-bah-tone   Ht: 6'1" Wt: 212 Born: 10/21/1984 Age: 37

					BATTING															RUNNING			AVERAGES			
Year Team	Lg	G	AB	H	2B	3B	HR	(Hm	Rd)	TB	R	RBI	RC	TBB	IBB	SO	HBP	SH	SF	SB	CS	GDP	Avg	OBP	Slg	OPS
2021 Iowa	AAA	15	39	7	3	0	2	(-	-)	16	5	9	-	10	0	15	0	0	0	0	0	0	.179	.347	.410	.757
2009 SD	NL	7	17	3	0	0	0	(0	0)	3	0	0	0	0	0	5	0	0	0	0	0	1	.176	.176	.176	.353
2011 TB	AL	15	34	4	1	0	0	(0	0)	5	2	0	0	4	0	8	1	0	0	0	0	2	.118	.231	.147	.378
2012 TB	AL	69	167	37	10	0	2	(1	1)	53	16	20	19	24	1	46	2	2	2	0	1	6	.222	.323	.317	.640
2013 TB	AL	100	277	69	15	2	7	(5	2)	109	38	32	32	30	0	65	0	2	2	0	1	5	.249	.320	.394	.714
2014 Was	NL	66	214	50	9	0	2	(2	0)	65	18	12	13	15	1	61	1	0	0	0	0	5	.234	.287	.304	.591
2015 Was	NL	44	136	27	4	0	3	(1	2)	40	11	20	14	15	1	40	1	1	2	0	0	5	.199	.279	.294	.573
2016 Was	NL	39	99	23	3	1	3	(2	1)	37	10	8	9	12	1	18	1	1	1	0	0	4	.232	.319	.374	.692
2017 Was	NL	51	141	24	3	0	4	(1	3)	39	11	11	8	14	1	35	1	1	1	0	0	5	.170	.248	.277	.525
2018 NYM	NL	22	49	7	2	1	0	(0	0)	11	3	4	1	7	0	15	0	0	1	0	0	2	.143	.246	.224	.470
2021 ChC	NL	6	11	0	0	0	0	(0	0)	0	1	0	0	2	0	5	0	0	0	0	0	0	.000	.154	.000	.154
Postseason		9	18	5	0	0	2	(2	0)	11	2	4	2	0	0	4	0	0	0	0	0	1	.278	.278	.611	.889
10 ML YEARS		419	1145	244	47	4	21	(12	9)	362	110	107	96	123	5	298	7	7	9	0	2	35	.213	.291	.316	.607

Kyle Lobstein

Pitches: L Bats: L Pos: RP-3   LOB-steen   Ht: 6'3" Wt: 220 Born: 8/12/1989 Age: 32

			HOW MUCH PITCHED				WHAT HE GAVE UP										THE RESULTS								
Year Team	Lg	G	GS	GF	IP	BFP	H	R	ER	HR	SH	SF	HB	TBB	IBB	SO	WP	W	L	Pct	Sv-Op	Hld	Vel	OPS	ERC	ERA
2021 Roch	AAA	16	0	2	21.1	84	15	4	4	0	0	0	2	8	0	25	1	2	0	1.000	0--	-	-	.514	2.25	1.69
2021 Nashv	AAA	21	0	2	21.2	107	29	15	13	3	1	0	3	8	0	16	3	1	0	1.000	1--	-	-	.872	6.56	5.40
2014 Det	AL	7	6	1	39.1	164	35	20	19	3	1	1	0	14	2	27	0	1	2	.333	0-0	0	88	.665	3.07	4.35
2015 Det	AL	13	11	2	63.2	280	78	43	42	7	0	1	0	23	1	32	2	3	8	.273	0-0	0	86	.829	5.38	5.94
2016 Pit	NL	14	0	3	25.0	110	25	11	11	2	1	0	2	12	1	15	2	2	0	1.000	0-0	0	87	.758	4.56	3.96
2021 Was	NL	3	0	1	1.1	8	3	3	3	1	0	0	0	1	0	1	0	0	0	-	0-0	0	92	1.357	20.88	20.25
4 ML YEARS		37	17	7	129.1	562	141	77	75	13	2	2	2	50	4	75	4	6	10	.375	0-0	0	87	.775	4.60	5.22

Tim Locastro

Bats: R Throws: R Pos: CF-28;PH-16;LF-14;RF-9;PR-8

Ht: 6'1" Wt: 190 Born: 7/14/1992 Age: 29

								BATTING											RUNNING			AVERAGES			
Year	Team	Lg	G	AB	H	2B	3B	HR	(Hm | Rd)	TB	R	RBI	RC	TBB	IBB	SO	HBP	SH	SF	SB	CS	GDP	Avg	OBP	Slg	OPS
2017	LAD	NL	3	1	0	0	0	0	(0 | 0)	0	0	0	0	0	0	0	0	0	0	1	0	0	.000	.000	.000	.000
2018	LAD	NL	18	11	2	1	0	0	(0 | 0)	3	6	0	2	2	0	5	1	0	0	4	0	0	.182	.357	.273	.630
2019	Ari	NL	91	212	53	12	2	1	(0 | 1)	72	38	17	35	14	0	44	22	1	1	17	0	1	.250	.357	.340	.697
2020	Ari	NL	33	69	20	4	1	2	(1 | 1)	32	15	7	15	8	0	14	4	1	0	4	0	0	.290	.395	.464	.859
2021	2 Tms		64	139	25	4	0	2	(0 | 2)	35	15	7	7	7	0	33	9	0	1	5	3	2	.180	.263	.252	.515
21	Ari	NL	55	118	21	2	0	1	(0 | 1)	26	11	5	6	6	0	26	9	0	0	5	3	2	.178	.271	.220	.491
21	NYY	AL	9	21	4	2	0	1	(0 | 1)	9	4	2	1	1	0	7	0	0	1	0	0	0	.190	.217	.429	.646
	5 ML YEARS		209	432	100	21	3	5	(1 | 4)	142	74	31	59	31	0	96	36	2	2	31	3	3	.231	.333	.329	.662

Sammy Long

Pitches: L Bats: L Pos: RP-7; SP-5

Ht: 6'1" Wt: 185 Born: 7/8/1995 Age: 26

			HOW MUCH PITCHED					WHAT HE GAVE UP									THE RESULTS						
Year	Team	Lg	G	GS	GF	IP	BFP	H	R	ER	HR	SH	SF	HB	TBB	IBB	SO	WP	W	L	Pct	Sv-Op Hld	Vel	OPS	ERC	ERA
2021	Scrmto	AAA	11	3	2	26.1	102	16	6	6	2	0	0	0	9	0	31	1	1	0	1.000	0- - -	-	.525	1.77	2.05
2021	SF	NL	12	5	2	40.2	176	37	27	25	5	0	2	3	15	0	38	5	2	1	.667	0-0 0	93	.723	3.84	5.53

Shed Long Jr.

Bats: L Throws: R Pos: LF-25;2B-10;PH-2;DH-1

Ht: 5'8" Wt: 184 Born: 8/22/1995 Age: 26

								BATTING											RUNNING			AVERAGES			
Year	Team	Lg	G	AB	H	2B	3B	HR	(Hm | Rd)	TB	R	RBI	RC	TBB	IBB	SO	HBP	SH	SF	SB	CS	GDP	Avg	OBP	Slg	OPS
2019	Sea	AL	42	152	40	12	1	5	(1 | 4)	69	21	15	19	16	0	40	0	0	0	3	3	1	.263	.333	.454	.787
2020	Sea	AL	34	117	20	5	0	3	(0 | 3)	34	10	9	9	11	0	37	0	0	0	4	0	1	.171	.242	.291	.533
2021	Sea	AL	34	111	22	4	1	4	(3 | 1)	40	13	17	12	9	0	39	0	1	0	1	0	3	.198	.258	.360	.619
	3 ML YEARS		110	380	82	21	2	12	(4 | 8)	143	44	41	40	36	0	116	0	1	0	8	3	5	.216	.284	.376	.660

Evan Longoria

Bats: R Throws: R Pos: 3B-78;PH-6;PR-1

Ht: 6'1" Wt: 213 Born: 10/7/1985 Age: 36

								BATTING											RUNNING			AVERAGES			
Year	Team	Lg	G	AB	H	2B	3B	HR	(Hm | Rd)	TB	R	RBI	RC	TBB	IBB	SO	HBP	SH	SF	SB	CS	GDP	Avg	OBP	Slg	OPS
2008	TB	AL	122	448	122	31	2	27	(18 | 9)	238	67	85	72	46	4	122	6	0	8	7	0	8	.272	.343	.531	.874
2009	TB	AL	157	584	164	44	0	33	(16 | 17)	307	100	113	102	72	11	140	8	0	7	9	0	27	.281	.364	.526	.889
2010	TB	AL	151	574	169	46	5	22	(10 | 12)	291	96	104	99	72	12	124	5	0	10	15	5	15	.294	.372	.507	.879
2011	TB	AL	133	483	118	26	1	31	(14 | 17)	239	78	99	91	80	6	93	6	0	5	3	2	11	.244	.355	.495	.850
2012	TB	AL	74	273	79	14	0	17	(8 | 9)	144	39	55	55	33	6	61	3	0	3	2	3	14	.289	.369	.527	.896
2013	TB	AL	160	614	165	39	3	32	(15 | 17)	306	91	88	90	70	10	162	3	0	6	1	0	16	.269	.343	.498	.842
2014	TB	AL	162	624	158	26	1	22	(12 | 10)	252	83	91	83	57	11	133	9	1	9	5	0	15	.253	.320	.404	.724
2015	TB	AL	160	604	163	35	1	21	(10 | 11)	263	74	73	77	51	8	132	6	0	9	3	1	11	.270	.328	.435	.764
2016	TB	AL	160	633	173	41	4	36	(17 | 19)	330	81	98	95	42	6	144	3	0	7	0	3	13	.273	.318	.521	.840
2017	TB	AL	156	613	160	36	2	20	(10 | 10)	260	71	86	81	46	3	109	6	0	12	6	1	18	.261	.313	.424	.737
2018	SF	NL	125	480	117	25	4	16	(4 | 12)	198	51	54	46	22	3	101	5	0	5	3	1	11	.244	.281	.413	.694
2019	SF	NL	129	453	115	19	2	20	(6 | 14)	198	59	69	63	43	1	112	7	0	5	3	1	14	.254	.325	.437	.762
2020	SF	NL	53	193	49	10	1	7	(6 | 1)	82	26	28	16	11	0	39	2	0	3	0	1	10	.254	.297	.425	.722
2021	SF	NL	81	253	66	17	0	13	(5 | 8)	122	45	46	37	35	4	68	1	0	2	1	1	9	.261	.351	.482	.833
	Postseason		30	115	22	5	0	9	(4 | 5)	54	16	21	13	11	0	38	0	0	0	1	0	4	.191	.262	.470	.731
	14 ML YEARS		1823	6829	1818	409	26	317	(151 | 166)	3230	961	1089	1007	680	85	1540	70	1	91	58	19	192	.266	.335	.473	.808

Tim Lopes

Bats: R Throws: R Pos: PH-4;2B-3

Ht: 5'11" Wt: 180 Born: 6/24/1994 Age: 28

								BATTING											RUNNING			AVERAGES			
Year	Team	Lg	G	AB	H	2B	3B	HR	(Hm | Rd)	TB	R	RBI	RC	TBB	IBB	SO	HBP	SH	SF	SB	CS	GDP	Avg	OBP	Slg	OPS
2021	Nashv	AAA	93	327	74	16	4	11	(- | -)	131	52	39	-	34	0	92	5	0	4	9	3	4	.226	.305	.401	.706
2019	Sea	AL	41	111	30	7	0	1	(1 | 0)	40	11	12	16	15	0	29	1	0	1	6	3	1	.270	.359	.360	.720
2020	Sea	AL	46	143	34	12	0	2	(0 | 2)	52	16	15	16	6	0	34	2	0	0	5	0	2	.238	.278	.364	.642
2021	Mil	NL	7	10	1	0	0	0	(0 | 0)	1	1	0	0	1	0	4	0	0	0	0	1	0	.100	.182	.100	.282
	3 ML YEARS		94	264	65	19	0	3	(1 | 2)	93	28	27	32	22	0	67	3	0	1	11	4	3	.246	.310	.352	.663

Alejo Lopez

Bats: B Throws: R Pos: PH-9;2B-3;3B-3;LF-2;CF-1

Ht: 5'10" Wt: 170 Born: 5/5/1996 Age: 26

								BATTING											RUNNING			AVERAGES			
Year	Team	Lg	G	AB	H	2B	3B	HR	(Hm | Rd)	TB	R	RBI	RC	TBB	IBB	SO	HBP	SH	SF	SB	CS	GDP	Avg	OBP	Slg	OPS
2021	Chatt	AA	25	105	38	9	0	0	(- | -)	47	18	13	-	12	0	11	2	0	0	3	1	3	.362	.437	.448	.885
2021	Lsvlle	AAA	66	249	76	18	0	6	(- | -)	112	54	31	-	33	1	21	3	0	3	6	2	13	.305	.389	.450	.839
2021	Cin	NL	14	23	6	0	0	0	(0 | 0)	6	3	0	-	0	0	5	0	0	0	0	0	1	.261	.261	.261	.522

Jack Lopez

Bats: R Throws: R Pos: 2B-6;PR-1

Ht: 5'10" Wt: 160 Born: 12/16/1992 Age: 29

								BATTING											RUNNING			AVERAGES			
Year	Team	Lg	G	AB	H	2B	3B	HR	(Hm | Rd)	TB	R	RBI	RC	TBB	IBB	SO	HBP	SH	SF	SB	CS	GDP	Avg	OBP	Slg	OPS
2021	Wrcstr	AAA	65	213	56	13	1	3	(- | -)	80	26	33	-	18	0	52	5	0	3	14	1	6	.263	.331	.376	.706
2021	Bos	AL	7	13	2	2	0	0	(0 | 0)	4	2	0	-	1	0	6	0	2	0	0	0	0	.154	.214	.308	.522

Jorge Lopez

Pitches: R Bats: R Pos: SP-25; RP-8   Ht: 6'3" Wt: 200 Born: 2/10/1993 Age: 29

Year	Team	Lg		HOW MUCH PITCHED						WHAT HE GAVE UP											THE RESULTS						
			G	GS	GF	IP	BFP	H	R	ER	HR	SH	SF	HB	TBB	IBB	SO	WP	W	L	Pct	Sv-Op	Hld	Vel	OPS	ERC	ERA
2015	Mil	NL	2	2	0	10.0	46	14	6	6	0	0	0	1	5	0	10	1	1	1	.500	0-0	0	94	.860	6.87	5.40
2017	Mil	NL	1	0	1	2.0	10	4	1	1	0	0	0	0	1	0	0	0	0	0	-	0-0	0	95	1.056	10.75	4.50
2018	2 Tms		17	7	8	53.2	234	57	30	30	6	0	2	1	22	1	38	3	2	5	.286	0-0	0	94	.763	4.64	5.03
2019	KC	AL	39	18	8	123.2	548	140	94	87	27	0	7	10	42	0	109	6	4	9	.308	1-2	0	94	.864	5.85	6.33
2020	2 Tms	AL	10	6	1	39.0	174	46	32	29	7	1	3	3	12	1	28	4	2	2	.500	0-0	0	94	.817	5.61	6.69
2021	Bal	AL	33	25	2	121.2	555	142	83	82	21	1	3	10	56	2	112	9	3	14	.176	0-1	2	95	.860	6.25	6.07
18	Mil	NL	10	0	8	19.2	85	16	6	6	1	0	1	0	13	1	15	1	0	1	.000	0-0	0	94	.665	3.66	2.75
18	KC	AL	7	7	0	34.0	149	41	24	24	5	0	1	1	9	0	23	2	2	4	.333	0-0	0	93	.813	5.20	6.35
20	KC	AL	1	0	0	0.2	5	3	2	2	0	0	0	0	0	0	0	0	0	0	-	0-0	0	94	1.400	26.58	27.00
20	Bal	AL	9	6	1	38.1	169	43	30	27	7	1	3	3	12	1	28	4	2	2	.500	0-0	0	94	.799	5.32	6.34
	6 ML YEARS		102	58	20	350.0	1567	403	246	235	61	2	15	25	138	4	297	23	12	31	.279	1-3	2	94	.843	5.83	6.04

Nicky Lopez

Bats: L Throws: R Pos: SS-148;2B-4;PH-1;PR-1   Ht: 5'11" Wt: 180 Born: 3/13/1995 Age: 27

Year	Team	Lg				BATTING																RUNNING			AVERAGES			
			G	AB	H	2B	3B	HR	(Hm	Rd)	TB	R	RBI	RC	TBB	IBB	SO	HBP	SH	SF	SB	CS	GDP	Avg	OBP	Slg	OPS
2019	KC	AL	103	379	91	22	2	2	(1	1)	123	44	30	38	18	0	51	1	4	0	1	1	5	.240	.276	.325	.601
2020	KC	AL	56	169	34	8	0	1	(1	0)	45	15	13	12	18	0	41	2	3	0	0	5	1	.201	.286	.266	.552
2021	KC	AL	151	497	149	21	6	2	(1	1)	188	78	43	82	49	0	74	4	12	3	22	1	9	.300	.365	.378	.744
	3 ML YEARS		310	1045	274	51	8	5	(3	2)	356	137	86	132	85	0	166	7	19	3	23	7	15	.262	.321	.341	.662

Otto Lopez

Bats: R Throws: R Pos: PH-1   Ht: 5'10" Wt: 160 Born: 10/1/1998 Age: 23

Year	Team	Lg				BATTING																RUNNING			AVERAGES			
			G	AB	H	2B	3B	HR	(Hm	Rd)	TB	R	RBI	RC	TBB	IBB	SO	HBP	SH	SF	SB	CS	GDP	Avg	OBP	Slg	OPS
2021	Nham	AA	70	278	92	25	1	3	(-	-)	128	52	39	-	28	1	62	5	0	3	7	3	3	.331	.398	.460	.859
2021	Buffalo	AAA	39	155	46	7	3	2	(-	-)	65	33	24	-	11	1	23	4	1	2	14	0	4	.297	.355	.419	.774
2021	Tor	AL	1	1	0	0	0	0	(0	0)	0	0	0	0	0	0	1	0	0	0	0	0	0	.000	.000	.000	.000

Pablo Lopez

Pitches: R Bats: L Pos: SP-20   Ht: 6'4" Wt: 225 Born: 3/7/1996 Age: 26

Year	Team	Lg		HOW MUCH PITCHED						WHAT HE GAVE UP											THE RESULTS						
			G	GS	GF	IP	BFP	H	R	ER	HR	SH	SF	HB	TBB	IBB	SO	WP	W	L	Pct	Sv-Op	Hld	Vel	OPS	ERC	ERA
2018	Mia	NL	10	10	0	58.2	247	56	28	27	8	1	2	4	18	5	46	2	2	4	.333	0-0	0	92	.745	3.88	4.14
2019	Mia	NL	21	21	0	111.1	469	111	64	63	15	4	2	11	27	3	95	6	5	8	.385	0-0	0	94	.756	4.07	5.09
2020	Mia	NL	11	11	0	57.1	240	50	27	23	4	0	3	2	18	1	59	0	6	4	.600	0-0	0	94	.637	2.93	3.61
2021	Mia	NL	20	20	0	102.2	418	89	37	35	11	1	2	7	26	1	115	3	5	5	.500	0-0	0	94	.677	3.13	3.07
	Postseason		1	1	0	5.0	19	3	2	2	2	0	0	0	0	0	7	0	0	1	.000	0-0	0	95	.684	1.78	3.60
	4 ML YEARS		62	62	0	330.0	1374	306	156	148	38	6	9	24	89	10	315	11	18	21	.462	0-0	0	93	.709	3.53	4.04

Reynaldo Lopez

Pitches: R Bats: R Pos: RP-11; SP-9   ray-NAHL-doh   Ht: 6'1" Wt: 225 Born: 1/4/1994 Age: 28

Year	Team	Lg		HOW MUCH PITCHED						WHAT HE GAVE UP											THE RESULTS						
			G	GS	GF	IP	BFP	H	R	ER	HR	SH	SF	HB	TBB	IBB	SO	WP	W	L	Pct	Sv-Op	Hld	Vel	OPS	ERC	ERA
2021	Charllt	AAA	10	10	0	39.0	189	53	33	33	6	1	3	1	21	0	50	6	1	6	.143	0- -	-	-	.926	7.33	7.62
2016	Was	NL	11	6	1	44.0	201	47	27	24	4	3	2	0	22	2	42	5	5	3	.625	0-0	1	96	.772	4.60	4.91
2017	CWS	AL	8	8	0	47.2	207	49	29	25	7	0	2	1	14	0	30	3	3	3	.500	0-0	0	94	.741	4.12	4.72
2018	CWS	AL	32	32	0	188.2	799	165	88	82	25	0	9	10	75	1	151	7	7	10	.412	0-0	0	96	.713	3.80	3.91
2019	CWS	AL	33	33	0	184.0	809	203	119	110	35	2	5	8	65	0	169	5	10	15	.400	0-0	0	95	.833	5.33	5.38
2020	CWS	AL	8	8	0	26.1	121	28	21	19	9	1	0	1	15	0	24	1	1	3	.250	0-0	0	94	.944	7.17	6.49
2021	CWS	AL	20	9	3	57.2	222	42	27	22	10	0	4	0	13	0	55	1	4	4	.500	0-0	0	96	.667	2.48	3.43
	Postseason		1	0	0	2.0	9	2	1	1	0	0	0	0	1	0	3	0	0	0	-	0-0	0	96	.708	3.63	4.50
	6 ML YEARS		112	96	4	548.1	2359	534	311	282	90	6	22	20	204	3	471	22	30	38	.441	0-0	1	95	.769	4.40	4.63

Yoan Lopez

Pitches: R Bats: R Pos: RP-13   Ht: 6'3" Wt: 208 Born: 1/2/1993 Age: 29

Year	Team	Lg		HOW MUCH PITCHED						WHAT HE GAVE UP											THE RESULTS						
			G	GS	GF	IP	BFP	H	R	ER	HR	SH	SF	HB	TBB	IBB	SO	WP	W	L	Pct	Sv-Op	Hld	Vel	OPS	ERC	ERA
2021	Gwnntt	AAA	30	0	11	30.2	123	27	12	10	3	0	0	0	11	1	32	4	3	2	.600	2- -	-	-	.657	3.35	2.93
2018	Ari	NL	10	0	5	9.0	35	7	3	3	2	1	0	0	1	0	11	0	0	0	-	0-0	1	97	.720	2.47	3.00
2019	Ari	NL	70	0	13	60.2	246	52	27	23	11	1	4	0	17	2	42	1	2	7	.222	1-4	21	96	.728	3.32	3.41
2020	Ari	NL	20	0	7	19.2	87	21	15	13	4	0	0	0	9	2	16	0	0	1	.000	0-0	1	95	.870	5.30	5.95
2021	Ari	NL	13	0	5	12.1	61	18	10	9	3	0	1	0	6	2	13	0	0	0	-	0-3	2	96	1.005	7.96	6.57
	4 ML YEARS		113	0	30	101.2	429	98	55	48	20	2	5	0	33	6	82	1	2	8	.200	1-7	25	96	.795	4.13	4.25

Michael Lorenzen

Pitches: R Bats: R Pos: RP-27 Ht: 6'3" Wt: 217 Born: 1/4/1992 Age: 30

Year	Team	Lg	G	GS	GF	IP	BFP	H	R	ER	HR	SH	SF	HB	TBB	IBB	SO	WP	W	L	Pct	Sv-Op	Hld	Vel	OPS	ERC	ERA
2015	Cin	NL	27	21	1	113.1	515	131	70	68	18	2	1	6	57	6	83	4	4	9	.308	0-0	1	94	.882	6.09	5.40
2016	Cin	NL	35	0	4	50.0	202	41	16	16	5	0	0	6	13	0	48	2	2	1	.667	0-2	10	96	.630	3.11	2.88
2017	Cin	NL	70	0	14	83.0	361	78	43	41	9	2	1	4	34	5	80	12	8	4	.667	2-7	18	96	.695	3.89	4.45
2018	Cin	NL	45	3	10	81.0	344	78	32	28	6	2	3	3	34	2	54	2	4	2	.667	1-2	8	96	.707	3.95	3.11
2019	Cin	NL	73	0	16	83.1	343	68	29	27	9	4	2	2	28	1	85	2	1	4	.200	7-11	21	97	.644	2.96	2.92
2020	Cin	NL	18	2	5	33.2	147	30	17	16	3	1	1	1	17	1	35	2	3	1	.750	0-1	2	97	.691	3.84	4.28
2021	Cin	NL	27	0	5	29.0	125	26	18	18	2	1	1	1	14	0	21	5	1	2	.333	4-4	11	96	.673	3.75	5.59
	Postseason		2	0	1	2.2	11	2	0	0	0	0	0	1	0	0	6	1	0	0		0-0	0	97	.473	2.01	0.00
7 ML YEARS			295	26	52	473.1	2037	452	225	214	52	12	9	23	197	15	406	29	23	23	.500	14-27	71	95	.727	4.12	4.07

Aaron Loup

Pitches: L Bats: L Pos: RP-63; SP-2 LOOP Ht: 5'11" Wt: 210 Born: 12/19/1987 Age: 34

Year	Team	Lg	G	GS	GF	IP	BFP	H	R	ER	HR	SH	SF	HB	TBB	IBB	SO	WP	W	L	Pct	Sv-Op	Hld	Vel	OPS	ERC	ERA
2012	Tor	AL	33	0	3	30.2	117	26	10	9	0	2	1	0	2	0	21	1	0	2	.000	0-1	6	92	.547	1.59	2.64
2013	Tor	AL	64	0	12	69.1	282	66	23	19	5	2	4	7	13	4	53	2	4	6	.400	2-3	8	92	.670	3.20	2.47
2014	Tor	AL	71	0	15	68.2	283	50	25	24	4	3	3	6	30	5	56	5	4	4	.500	4-8	13	92	.647	2.75	3.15
2015	Tor	AL	60	0	6	42.1	186	47	24	21	6	2	0	6	7	0	46	0	2	5	.286	0-4	9	93	.776	4.54	4.46
2016	Tor	AL	21	0	2	14.1	62	15	8	8	2	0	3	3	4	0	15	3	0	0	-	0-1	1	91	.855	5.13	5.02
2017	Tor	AL	70	0	11	57.2	265	59	27	24	4	5	0	6	29	5	64	3	2	3	.400	0-0	6	92	.722	4.56	3.75
2018	2 Tms		59	0	8	39.2	183	48	23	20	4	0	3	4	14	0	44	0	0	0	-	0-0	11	92	.805	5.45	4.54
2019	SD	NL	4	0	1	3.1	14	2	0	0	0	0	1	1	1	0	5	0	0	0	-	0-0	1	92	.558	2.03	0.00
2020	TB	AL	24	0	6	25.0	96	17	9	7	3	2	1	3	4	0	22	0	3	2	.600	0-1	4	92	.635	2.16	2.52
2021	NYM	NL	65	2	6	56.2	218	37	9	6	1	1	4	4	16	0	57	0	6	0	1.000	0-4	16	92	.501	1.72	0.95
18	Tor	AL	50	0	7	35.2	166	44	21	18	4	0	3	3	13	0	42	0	0	0	-	0-0	9	92	.824	5.63	4.54
18	Phi	NL	9	0	1	4.0	17	4	2	2	0	0	0	1	1	0	2	0	0	0	-	0-0	2	91	.620	3.88	4.50
	Postseason		13	0	0	7.1	31	6	3	3	0	0	0	1	4	0	7	1	0	0	-	0-0	5	93	.624	3.58	3.68
10 ML YEARS			471	2	67	407.2	1706	367	158	138	29	17	20	40	120	14	383	14	21	22	.488	6-22	75	92	.674	3.28	3.05

Richard Lovelady

Pitches: L Bats: L Pos: RP-20 Ht: 6'0" Wt: 185 Born: 7/7/1995 Age: 26

Year	Team	Lg	G	GS	GF	IP	BFP	H	R	ER	HR	SH	SF	HB	TBB	IBB	SO	WP	W	L	Pct	Sv-Op	Hld	Vel	OPS	ERC	ERA
2021	Omha	AAA	7	0	0	8.1	33	5	1	1	0	0	0	1	4	1	9	1	0	0	-	0--	-		.553	2.00	1.08
2019	KC	AL	25	0	5	20.0	96	30	17	17	2	1	1	1	8	2	17	1	0	3	.000	0-1	2	94	.952	7.18	7.65
2020	KC	AL	1	0	0	1.0	4	1	1	1	1	0	0	0	1	0	0	0	0	0	-	0-0	0	92	1.833	17.98	9.00
2021	KC	AL	20	0	2	20.2	84	16	9	8	3	0	1	1	6	1	23	1	2	0	1.000	1-1	4	93	.616	2.85	3.48
3 ML YEARS			46	0	7	41.2	184	47	27	26	6	1	2	2	15	3	40	2	2	3	.400	1-2	6	93	.813	5.07	5.62

Brandon Lowe

Bats: L Throws: R Pos: 2B-133;PH-15;LF-10;RF-6;DH-3;1B-1 LAOW Ht: 5'10" Wt: 185 Born: 7/6/1994 Age: 27

Year	Team	Lg	G	AB	H	2B	3B	HR	(Hm	Rd)	TB	R	RBI	RC	TBB	IBB	SO	HBP	SH	SF	SB	CS	GDP	Avg	OBP	Slg	OPS
2018	TB	AL	43	129	30	6	2	6	(2	4)	58	16	25	21	16	0	38	2	0	1	2	1	3	.233	.324	.450	.774
2019	TB	AL	82	296	80	17	2	17	(8	9)	152	42	51	50	25	0	113	5	0	1	5	0	1	.270	.336	.514	.850
2020	TB	AL	56	193	52	9	2	14	(6	8)	107	36	37	39	25	0	58	4	0	2	3	0	2	.269	.362	.554	.916
2021	TB	AL	149	535	132	31	4	39	(19	20)	280	97	99	110	68	4	167	9	0	3	7	1	2	.247	.340	.523	.863
	Postseason		25	95	13	1	0	5	(2	3)	29	8	9	5	7	0	38	0	0	0	0	0	2	.137	.196	.305	.501
4 ML YEARS			330	1153	294	63	6	76	(35	41)	597	191	212	220	134	4	376	20	0	7	17	2	8	.255	.341	.518	.859

Josh Lowe

Bats: L Throws: R Pos: LF-1;RF-1 Ht: 6'4" Wt: 205 Born: 2/2/1998 Age: 24

Year	Team	Lg	G	AB	H	2B	3B	HR	(Hm	Rd)	TB	R	RBI	RC	TBB	IBB	SO	HBP	SH	SF	SB	CS	GDP	Avg	OBP	Slg	OPS
2017	BG	A	118	456	122	26	2	8	(-	-)	176	60	55	63	42	0	144	0	4	5	22	8	5	.268	.326	.386	.712
2018	Charltt	A+	105	399	95	25	3	6	(-	-)	144	62	47	51	47	2	117	4	1	4	18	6	2	.238	.322	.361	.682
2019	Mont	AA	121	448	113	23	4	18	(-	-)	198	70	62	73	59	0	132	3	6	3	30	9	1	.252	.341	.442	.783
2021	Drham	AAA	107	385	112	28	2	21	(-	-)	207	74	75		58	1	118	1	0	6	26	0	4	.291	.380	.538	.918
2021	TB	AL	2	1	1	0	0	0	(0	0)	1	0	0	1	0	0	0	0	0	0	1	0	0	1.000	1.000	1.000	2.000

Nathaniel Lowe

Bats: L Throws: R Pos: 1B-148;DH-8;PH-4;3B-1 Ht: 6'4" Wt: 220 Born: 7/7/1995 Age: 26

Year	Team	Lg	G	AB	H	2B	3B	HR	(Hm	Rd)	TB	R	RBI	RC	TBB	IBB	SO	HBP	SH	SF	SB	CS	GDP	Avg	OBP	Slg	OPS
2019	TB	AL	50	152	40	8	0	7	(4	3)	69	24	19	19	13	0	50	2	0	2	0	0	4	.263	.325	.454	.779
2020	TB	AL	21	67	15	2	0	4	(3	1)	29	10	11	8	9	2	28	0	0	0	1	0	2	.224	.316	.433	.749
2021	Tex	AL	157	557	147	24	3	18	(8	10)	231	75	72	96	80	2	162	2	0	3	8	0	13	.264	.357	.415	.771
	Postseason		1	3	0	0	0	0	(0	0)	0	0	0	0	0	0	2	0	0	0	0	0	0	.000	.000	.000	.000
3 ML YEARS			228	776	202	34	3	29	(15	14)	329	109	102	123	102	4	240	4	0	5	9	0	19	.260	.347	.424	.771

Jed Lowrie

LAU-ree

Bats: B Throws: R Pos: 2B-71;DH-58;PH-21;3B-1   Ht: 6'0" Wt: 180 Born: 4/17/1984 Age: 38

Year	Team	Lg	G	AB	H	2B	3B	HR	(Hm	Rd)	TB	R	RBI	RC	TBB	IBB	SO	HBP	SH	SF	SB	CS	GDP	Avg	OBP	Slg	OPS
2008	Bos	AL	81	260	67	25	3	2	(0	2)	104	34	46	35	35	0	68	1	2	8	1	0	8	.258	.339	.400	.739
2009	Bos	AL	32	68	10	2	0	2	(1	1)	18	5	11	5	6	0	20	0	0	2	0	0	0	.147	.211	.265	.475
2010	Bos	AL	55	171	49	14	0	9	(3	6)	90	31	24	32	25	0	25	1	0	1	1	1	2	.287	.381	.526	.907
2011	Bos	AL	88	309	78	14	4	6	(3	3)	118	40	36	33	23	2	60	2	1	6	1	1	6	.252	.303	.382	.685
2012	Hou	NL	97	340	83	18	0	16	(9	7)	149	43	42	45	43	0	65	2	0	2	2	0	3	.244	.331	.438	.769
2013	Oak	AL	154	603	175	45	2	15	(7	8)	269	80	75	88	50	3	91	2	3	4	1	0	17	.290	.344	.446	.791
2014	Oak	AL	136	502	125	29	3	6	(4	2)	178	59	50	52	51	5	79	5	2	6	0	0	14	.249	.321	.355	.676
2015	Hou	AL	69	230	51	14	0	9	(5	4)	92	35	30	29	28	5	43	3	0	2	1	0	3	.222	.312	.400	.712
2016	Oak	AL	87	338	89	12	1	2	(1	1)	109	30	27	36	26	0	65	1	0	4	0	0	10	.263	.314	.322	.637
2017	Oak	AL	153	567	157	49	3	14	(8	6)	254	86	69	94	73	2	100	2	0	3	0	1	10	.277	.360	.448	.808
2018	Oak	AL	157	596	159	37	1	23	(4	19)	267	78	99	106	78	1	128	3	0	3	0	0	8	.267	.353	.448	.801
2019	NYM	NL	9	7	0	0	0	0	(0	0)	0	0	0	0	1	0	4	0	0	0	0	0	0	.000	.125	.000	.125
2021	NYM	NL	139	457	112	28	0	14	(5	9)	182	55	69	72	49	1	108	2	0	4	0	0	8	.245	.318	.398	.717
	Postseason		23	64	9	2	0	1	(0	1)	14	7	5	4	7	0	17	1	1	1	0	0	1	.141	.233	.219	.452
	13 ML YEARS		1257	4448	1155	287	17	118	(50	68)	1830	576	578	627	488	19	856	24	8	44	7	3	89	.260	.333	.411	.745

Zac Lowther

Pitches: L Bats: L Pos: SP-6; RP-4   Ht: 6'2" Wt: 235 Born: 4/30/1996 Age: 26

			HOW MUCH PITCHED					WHAT HE GAVE UP										THE RESULTS							
Year	Team	Lg	G	GS	GF	IP	BFP	H	R	ER	HR	SH	SF	HB	TBB	IBB	SO	WP	W	L	Pct	Sv-Op	Hld	Vel	OPS	ERC	ERA
2021	Norfolk	AAA	8	8	0	30.1	144	33	23	22	4	1	0	3	16	0	33	4	0	5	.000	0- -	-	-	.791	5.58	6.53
2021	Bal	AL	10	6	2	29.2	138	36	23	22	6	0	0	4	13	0	30	1	1	3	.250	0-0	0	91	.880	6.94	6.67

Joey Lucchesi

loo-KAY-zee

Pitches: L Bats: L Pos: SP-8; RP-3   Ht: 6'5" Wt: 225 Born: 6/6/1993 Age: 29

			HOW MUCH PITCHED					WHAT HE GAVE UP										THE RESULTS							
Year	Team	Lg	G	GS	GF	IP	BFP	H	R	ER	HR	SH	SF	HB	TBB	IBB	SO	WP	W	L	Pct	Sv-Op	Hld	Vel	OPS	ERC	ERA
2018	SD	NL	26	26	0	130.0	548	125	63	59	23	3	4	4	43	2	145	4	8	9	.471	0-0	0	90	.766	4.24	4.08
2019	SD	NL	30	30	0	163.2	686	144	78	76	23	5	4	2	56	0	158	8	10	10	.500	0-0	0	90	.702	3.48	4.18
2020	SD	NL	3	2	0	5.2	32	13	5	5	0	0	1	2	2	0	5	0	0	1	.000	0-0	0	90	1.036	12.30	7.94
2021	NYM	NL	11	8	1	38.1	157	34	20	19	4	2	2	2	11	0	41	1	1	4	.200	0-0	0	91	.722	3.31	4.46
	4 ML YEARS		70	66	1	337.2	1423	316	166	159	50	10	11	9	112	2	349	13	19	24	.442	0-0	0	90	.737	3.87	4.24

Marco Luciano

Bats: R Throws: R Pos: SS   Ht: 6'2" Wt: 178 Born: 9/10/2001 Age: 20

Year	Team	Lg	G	AB	H	2B	3B	HR	(Hm	Rd)	TB	R	RBI	RC	TBB	IBB	SO	HBP	SH	SF	SB	CS	GDP	Avg	OBP	Slg	OPS
2019	2 Tms	Low	47	179	54	13	2	10	(-	-)	101	52	42	44	32	0	45	4	0	1	9	6	4	.302	.417	.564	.981
2021	2 Tms	Low	106	395	102	17	5	19	(-	-)	186	68	71	0	48	0	122	6	0	4	6	5	7	.258	.344	.471	.815

Jonathan Lucroy

LOO-croy

Bats: R Throws: R Pos: C-6;PH-1   Ht: 6'0" Wt: 200 Born: 6/13/1986 Age: 36

Year	Team	Lg	G	AB	H	2B	3B	HR	(Hm	Rd)	TB	R	RBI	RC	TBB	IBB	SO	HBP	SH	SF	SB	CS	GDP	Avg	OBP	Slg	OPS
2021	Gwnntt	AAA	31	91	20	4	0	2	(-	-)	30	10	16	-	17	0	20	3	0	3	0	0	2	.220	.351	.330	.681
2010	Mil	NL	75	277	70	9	0	4	(4	0)	91	24	26	23	18	1	44	1	0	1	4	2	9	.253	.300	.329	.628
2011	Mil	NL	136	430	114	16	1	12	(8	4)	168	45	59	50	29	0	99	2	4	3	2	1	7	.265	.313	.391	.703
2012	Mil	NL	96	316	101	17	4	12	(7	5)	162	46	58	61	22	1	44	4	1	3	4	1	12	.320	.368	.513	.881
2013	Mil	NL	147	521	146	25	6	18	(9	9)	237	59	82	78	46	2	69	5	0	8	9	1	16	.280	.340	.455	.795
2014	Mil	NL	153	585	176	53	2	13	(6	7)	272	73	69	90	66	3	71	2	0	2	4	4	13	.301	.373	.465	.837
2015	Mil	NL	103	371	98	20	3	7	(3	4)	145	51	43	46	36	0	64	1	1	6	1	0	18	.264	.326	.391	.717
2016	2 Tms		142	490	143	24	3	24	(15	9)	245	67	81	74	47	5	100	3	0	4	5	0	16	.292	.355	.500	.855
2017	2 Tms		123	423	112	21	3	6	(2	4)	157	45	40	53	46	6	51	8	0	4	1	0	16	.265	.345	.371	.716
2018	Oak	AL	126	415	100	21	1	4	(1	3)	135	41	51	44	29	1	65	3	1	6	0	0	12	.241	.291	.325	.617
2019	2 Tms		101	293	68	10	1	8	(6	2)	104	30	36	32	27	1	51	5	0	3	0	0	17	.232	.305	.355	.660
2020	Bos	AL	1	0	0	0	0	0	(0	0)	0	0	0	0	0	0	0	0	0	0	0	0	0	-	-	-	-
2021	2 Tms	NL	7	19	6	1	0	0	(0	0)	7	2	3	4	3	0	4	0	1	0	0	0	0	.316	.409	.368	.778
16	Mil	NL	95	338	101	17	3	13	(9	4)	163	48	50	46	33	3	70	1	0	4	5	0	12	.299	.359	.482	.841
16	Tex	AL	47	152	42	7	0	11	(6	5)	82	19	31	28	14	2	30	2	0	0	0	0	4	.276	.345	.539	.885
17	Tex	AL	77	281	68	15	0	4	(0	4)	95	27	27	28	19	0	32	4	0	2	1	0	10	.242	.297	.338	.635
17	Col	NL	46	142	44	6	3	2	(2	0)	62	18	13	25	27	6	19	4	0	2	0	0	6	.310	.429	.437	.865
19	LAA	AL	74	240	58	8	1	7	(5	2)	89	28	30	28	21	0	39	4	0	3	0	0	15	.242	.310	.371	.566
19	ChC	NL	27	53	10	2	0	1	(1	0)	15	2	6	4	6	1	12	1	0	0	0	0	2	.189	.283	.283	.566
21	Was	NL	5	14	5	1	0	0	(0	0)	6	2	2	2	0	0	2	0	0	0	0	0	0	.357	.357	.429	.786
21	Atl	NL	2	5	1	0	0	0	(0	0)	1	0	1	2	3	0	2	0	1	0	0	0	0	.200	.500	.200	.700
	Postseason		15	51	12	3	0	1	(1	0)	18	6	6	5	1	0	12	0	0	0	0	0	0	.235	.250	.353	.603
	12 ML YEARS		1210	4140	1134	217	24	108	(61	47)	1723	483	548	555	369	20	662	34	8	40	30	9	136	.274	.335	.416	.752

Lucas Luetge

Pitches: L Bats: L Pos: RP-56; SP-1

LIT-key

Ht: 6'4" **Wt:** 205 **Born:** 3/24/1987 **Age:** 35

Year	Team	Lg	G	GS	GF	IP	BFP	H	R	ER	HR	SH	SF	HB	TBB	IBB	SO	WP	W	L	Pct	Sv-Op	Hld	Vel	OPS	ERC	ERA
2012	Sea	AL	63	0	16	40.2	178	37	20	18	1	3	1	3	24	6	38	5	2	2	.500	2-3	12	89	.693	4.01	3.98
2013	Sea	AL	35	0	15	37.0	165	42	22	20	2	2	3	2	16	2	27	4	1	3	.250	0-0	1	91	.784	4.81	4.86
2014	Sea	AL	12	0	4	9.0	38	6	5	5	3	0	0	0	5	0	7	1	0	0	-	0-0	0	91	.744	4.31	5.00
2015	Sea	AL	1	0	1	2.1	8	0	0	0	0	0	0	0	2	0	2	0	0	0	-	0-0	0	91	.250	0.81	0.00
2021	NYY	AL	57	1	13	72.1	301	67	30	22	6	0	1	3	15	1	78	8	4	2	.667	1-3	3	88	.643	2.92	2.74
	5 ML YEARS		168	1	49	161.1	690	152	77	65	14	3	7	6	62	9	152	18	7	7	.500	3-6	16	90	.691	3.66	3.63

Seth Lugo

Pitches: R Bats: R Pos: RP-46

Ht: 6'4" **Wt:** 225 **Born:** 11/17/1989 **Age:** 32

Year	Team	Lg	G	GS	GF	IP	BFP	H	R	ER	HR	SH	SF	HB	TBB	IBB	SO	WP	W	L	Pct	Sv-Op	Hld	Vel	OPS	ERC	ERA
2016	NYM	NL	17	8	2	64.0	260	49	19	19	7	8	4	4	21	3	45	1	5	2	.714	0-0	0	92	.666	2.81	2.67
2017	NYM	NL	19	18	1	101.1	436	114	57	53	13	2	5	2	25	1	85	2	7	5	.583	0-0	0	91	.770	4.43	4.71
2018	NYM	NL	54	5	13	101.1	410	81	36	30	9	1	5	2	28	4	103	2	3	4	.429	3-4	11	94	.595	2.49	2.66
2019	NYM	NL	61	0	14	80.0	314	56	28	24	8	1	1	5	16	4	104	2	7	4	.636	6-11	21	94	.562	1.97	2.70
2020	NYM	NL	16	7	6	36.2	160	40	22	21	8	0	2	2	10	1	47	1	3	4	.429	3-5	0	93	.825	5.05	5.15
2021	NYM	NL	46	0	10	46.1	195	41	18	18	6	0	2	1	19	2	55	0	4	3	.571	1-4	13	94	.712	3.73	3.50
	6 ML YEARS		213	38	46	429.2	1775	381	180	165	51	12	19	16	119	15	439	8	29	22	.569	13-24	45	93	.676	3.20	3.46

Jordan Luplow

Bats: R Throws: R Pos: CF-22;1B-17;PH-12;RF-11;LF-6;DH-4;2B-1;3B-1

Ht: 6'1" **Wt:** 195 **Born:** 9/26/1993 **Age:** 28

Year	Team	Lg	G	AB	H	2B	3B	HR	(Hm	Rd)	TB	R	RBI	RC	TBB	IBB	SO	HBP	SH	SF	SB	CS	GDP	Avg	OBP	Slg	OPS
2017	Pit	NL	27	78	16	3	1	3	(3	0)	30	6	11	8	6	0	22	2	0	1	0	1	4	.205	.276	.385	.660
2018	Pit	NL	37	92	17	1	3	3	(3	0)	33	16	7	4	10	0	18	1	0	0	2	2	7	.185	.272	.359	.631
2019	Cle	AL	85	225	62	15	1	15	(8	7)	124	42	38	42	33	0	61	2	0	1	3	2	7	.276	.372	.551	.923
2020	Cle	AL	29	78	15	5	1	2	(1	1)	28	8	8	8	12	0	19	1	0	1	0	1	3	.192	.304	.359	.663
2021	2 Tms	AL	62	163	33	8	0	11	(5	6)	74	23	26	31	28	0	57	2	0	0	1	2	2	.202	.326	.454	.780
21	Cle	AL	36	98	17	5	0	7	(3	4)	43	12	20	22	21	0	31	2	0	0	0	2	1	.173	.331	.439	.769
21	TB	AL	26	65	16	3	0	4	(2	2)	31	11	8	9	7	0	26	0	0	0	1	0	1	.246	.319	.477	.796
	Postseason		1	2	1	1	0	0	(0	0)	2	0	2	1	0	0	0	0	0	0	0	0	0	.500	.500	1.000	1.500
	5 ML YEARS		240	636	143	32	6	34	(20	14)	289	95	92	93	89	0	177	8	0	3	6	8	23	.225	.326	.454	.780

Gavin Lux

Bats: L Throws: R Pos: SS-59;2B-27;LF-11;CF-6;PR-3;PH-2;3B-1;RF-1

Ht: 6'2" **Wt:** 190 **Born:** 11/23/1997 **Age:** 24

Year	Team	Lg	G	AB	H	2B	3B	HR	(Hm	Rd)	TB	R	RBI	RC	TBB	IBB	SO	HBP	SH	SF	SB	CS	GDP	Avg	OBP	Slg	OPS
2021	OkCity	AAA	17	68	19	4	0	1	(-	-)	26	18	10	-	6	0	15	0	0	0	0	0	1	.279	.338	.382	.720
2019	LAD	NL	23	75	18	4	1	2	(0	2)	30	12	9	10	7	0	24	0	0	0	2	0	0	.240	.305	.400	.705
2020	LAD	NL	19	63	11	2	0	3	(0	3)	22	8	8	8	6	0	19	0	0	0	1	0	0	.175	.246	.349	.596
2021	LAD	NL	102	335	81	12	4	7	(5	2)	122	49	46	48	41	3	83	3	0	2	4	1	3	.242	.328	.364	.692
	Postseason		5	10	2	0	0	1	(1	0)	5	1	1	1	1	0	7	0	0	0	0	0	0	.200	.273	.500	.773
	3 ML YEARS		144	473	110	18	5	12	(5	7)	174	69	63	66	54	3	126	3	0	2	7	1	3	.233	.314	.368	.682

Jesus Luzardo

Pitches: L Bats: L Pos: SP-18; RP-7

Ht: 6'0" **Wt:** 218 **Born:** 9/30/1997 **Age:** 24

Year	Team	Lg	G	GS	GF	IP	BFP	H	R	ER	HR	SH	SF	HB	TBB	IBB	SO	WP	W	L	Pct	Sv-Op	Hld	Vel	OPS	ERC	ERA
2021	LsVgs	AAA	8	8	0	29.0	135	33	24	21	3	0	1	5	15	0	26	3	2	2	.500	0--	-	-	.822	6.19	6.52
2019	Oak	AL	6	0	2	12.0	46	5	2	2	1	0	0	1	3	0	16	2	0	0	-	2-2	2	96	.434	1.13	1.50
2020	Oak	AL	12	9	1	59.0	248	58	27	27	9	1	1	3	17	1	59	3	3	2	.600	0-0	0	96	.745	4.11	4.12
2021	2 Tms		25	18	1	95.1	437	106	73	70	20	2	5	4	48	1	98	8	6	9	.400	0-0	1	96	.887	6.12	6.61
21	Oak	AL	13	6	1	38.0	173	46	32	29	11	1	1	0	16	0	40	3	2	4	.333	0-0	1	96	.915	6.84	6.87
21	Mia	NL	12	12	0	57.1	264	60	41	41	9	1	4	4	32	1	58	5	4	5	.444	0-0	0	95	.867	5.64	6.44
	Postseason		3	2	0	10.2	46	12	7	7	4	0	0	0	4	0	11	0	0	1	.000	0-0	0	96	.943	6.90	5.91
	3 ML YEARS		43	27	4	166.1	731	169	102	99	30	3	6	8	68	2	173	13	9	11	.450	2-2	3	96	.809	4.94	5.36

Jordan Lyles

Pitches: R Bats: R Pos: SP-30; RP-2

Ht: 6'5" **Wt:** 230 **Born:** 10/19/1990 **Age:** 31

Year	Team	Lg	G	GS	GF	IP	BFP	H	R	ER	HR	SH	SF	HB	TBB	IBB	SO	WP	W	L	Pct	Sv-Op	Hld	Vel	OPS	ERC	ERA
2011	Hou	NL	20	15	2	94.0	415	107	61	56	14	7	1	5	26	1	67	0	2	8	.200	0-0	0	90	.817	4.87	5.36
2012	Hou	NL	25	25	0	141.1	628	159	97	80	20	6	4	5	42	4	99	2	5	12	.294	0-0	0	92	.772	4.67	5.09
2013	Hou	AL	27	25	1	141.2	642	165	98	88	17	0	3	11	49	1	93	5	7	9	.438	1-1	1	92	.801	5.20	5.59
2014	Col	NL	22	22	0	126.2	546	127	64	61	12	4	3	8	46	1	90	6	7	4	.636	0-0	0	91	.750	4.17	4.33
2015	Col	NL	10	10	0	49.0	212	54	32	28	2	3	1	3	19	1	30	2	2	5	.286	0-0	0	92	.751	4.51	5.14
2016	Col	NL	40	5	7	58.2	273	69	46	38	4	1	2	4	28	2	32	5	4	5	.444	1-4	3	93	.790	5.32	5.83
2017	2 Tms	NL	38	5	12	69.2	324	96	64	60	16	2	1	4	22	1	55	4	1	5	.167	0-0	2	94	.948	7.24	7.75
2018	2 Tms	NL	35	8	10	87.2	371	83	42	40	12	3	4	3	38	3	84	5	3	4	.429	0-0	2	94	.718	3.78	4.11
2019	2 Tms	NL	28	28	0	141.0	599	131	72	65	25	2	3	1	55	2	146	4	12	8	.600	0-0	0	93	.767	4.18	4.15
2020	Tex	AL	12	9	0	57.2	266	67	49	45	12	1	5	2	23	0	36	3	1	6	.143	0-0	0	92	.841	5.82	7.02
2021	Tex	AL	32	30	1	180.0	769	194	104	103	38	2	7	7	56	0	146	9	10	13	.435	0-0	0	93	.834	5.20	5.15

Year Team	Lg	G	GS	GF	IP	BFP	H	R	ER	HR	SH	SF	HB	TBB	IBB	SO	WP	W	L	Pct	Sv-Op	Hld	Vel	OPS	ERC	ERA
17 Col	NL	33	0	12	46.2	211	61	37	36	11	1	1	4	12	1	33	2	0	2	.000	0-0	2	94	.921	6.72	6.94
17 SD	NL	5	5	0	23.0	113	35	24	24	5	1	0	0	10	0	22	2	1	3	.250	0-0	0	93	1.000	8.31	9.39
18 SD	NL	24	8	5	71.1	300	71	35	34	12	3	3	1	19	0	62	4	2	4	.333	0-0	2	93	.741	4.03	4.29
18 Mil	NL	11	0	5	16.1	71	12	7	6	0	0	1	2	9	3	22	1	1	0	1.000	0-0	0	94	.612	2.63	3.31
19 Pit	NL	17	17	0	82.1	361	88	53	49	16	1	1	1	33	1	90	4	5	7	.417	0-0	0	93	.853	5.20	5.36
19 Mil	NL	11	11	0	58.2	238	43	19	16	9	1	2	0	22	1	56	0	7	1	.875	0-0	0	93	.636	2.87	2.45
11 ML YEARS		289	182	33	1147.1	5045	1252	726	664	172	31	34	53	394	16	878	45	54	79	.406	2-5	8	92	.797	4.88	5.21

Daniel Lynch

Pitches: L Bats: L Pos: SP-15 Ht: 6'6" Wt: 200 Born: 11/17/1996 Age: 25

Year Team	Lg	G	GS	GF	IP	BFP	H	R	ER	HR	SH	SF	HB	TBB	IBB	SO	WP	W	L	Pct	Sv-Op	Hld	Vel	OPS	ERC	ERA
2021 Omha	AAA	12	11	0	57.0	257	74	39	37	10	0	3	3	18	0	62	4	4	3	.571	0--	-	-	.906	6.38	5.84
2021 KC	AL	15	15	0	68.0	311	80	46	43	9	1	4	4	31	0	55	4	4	6	.400	0-0	0	94	.836	5.85	5.69

Lance Lynn

Pitches: R Bats: B Pos: SP-28 Ht: 6'5" Wt: 270 Born: 5/12/1987 Age: 35

Year Team	Lg	G	GS	GF	IP	BFP	H	R	ER	HR	SH	SF	HB	TBB	IBB	SO	WP	W	L	Pct	Sv-Op	Hld	Vel	OPS	ERC	ERA
2011 StL	NL	18	2	2	34.2	136	25	12	12	3	1	0	1	11	1	40	1	1	1	.500	1-2	3	93	.591	2.37	3.12
2012 StL	NL	35	29	2	176.0	744	168	76	74	16	4	3	10	64	3	180	3	18	7	.720	0-0	1	93	.728	3.87	3.78
2013 StL	NL	33	33	0	201.2	856	189	92	89	14	11	8	11	76	0	198	6	15	10	.600	0-0	0	92	.701	3.67	3.97
2014 StL	NL	33	33	0	203.2	866	185	72	62	13	6	4	7	72	1	181	7	15	10	.600	0-0	0	92	.662	3.24	2.74
2015 StL	NL	31	31	0	175.1	751	172	66	59	13	9	2	5	68	5	167	2	12	11	.522	0-0	0	92	.708	3.83	3.03
2017 StL	NL	33	33	0	186.1	776	151	80	71	27	9	3	10	78	5	153	2	11	8	.579	0-0	0	92	.707	3.62	3.43
2018 2 Tms	AL	31	29	0	156.2	700	163	87	83	14	0	2	6	76	3	161	5	10	10	.500	0-0	0	93	.744	4.68	4.77
2019 Tex	AL	33	33	0	208.1	875	195	89	85	21	1	6	8	59	0	246	18	16	11	.593	0-0	0	94	.689	3.41	3.67
2020 Tex	AL	13	13	0	84.0	344	64	34	31	13	1	1	6	25	0	89	2	6	3	.667	0-0	0	93	.663	3.01	3.32
2021 CWS	AL	28	28	0	157.0	641	123	52	47	18	2	2	2	45	2	176	5	11	6	.647	0-0	0	93	.605	2.58	2.69
18 Min	AL	20	20	0	102.1	469	105	61	58	12	0	2	6	62	3	100	3	7	8	.467	0-0	0	93	.780	5.38	5.10
18 NYY	AL	11	9	0	54.1	231	58	26	25	2	0	0	0	14	0	61	2	3	2	.600	0-0	0	93	.676	3.44	4.14
Postseason		26	7	3	54.1	244	59	33	29	6	2	3	1	28	5	52	0	5	4	.556	0-0	3	94	.792	5.06	4.80
10 ML YEARS		288	264	4	1583.2	6689	1435	660	613	152	44	31	66	574	20	1591	51	115	77	.599	1-2	4	93	.690	3.53	3.48

Andres Machado

Pitches: R Bats: R Pos: RP-40 muh-CHAH-doe Ht: 6'0" Wt: 220 Born: 4/22/1993 Age: 29

Year Team	Lg	G	GS	GF	IP	BFP	H	R	ER	HR	SH	SF	HB	TBB	IBB	SO	WP	W	L	Pct	Sv-Op	Hld	Vel	OPS	ERC	ERA
2021 Roch	AAA	11	0	4	14.2	67	17	6	6	1	0	2	1	4	0	19	1	0	0	-	0--	-	-	.712	4.32	3.68
2017 KC	AL	2	0	1	3.2	24	10	9	9	2	0	0	1	3	0	1	0	0	0	-	0-0	0	96	1.399	23.02	22.09
2021 Was	NL	40	0	6	35.2	154	30	17	14	4	0	1	5	15	1	30	3	1	2	.333	0-3	10	95	.701	3.86	3.53
2 ML YEARS		42	0	7	39.1	178	40	26	23	6	0	1	5	18	1	31	3	1	2	.333	0-3	10	95	.795	5.24	5.26

Manny Machado

Bats: R Throws: R Pos: 3B-144;PH-6;DH-3 muh-CHAH-doe Ht: 6'3" Wt: 218 Born: 7/6/1992 Age: 29

Year Team	Lg	G	AB	H	2B	3B	HR	(Hm	Rd)	TB	R	RBI	RC	TBB	IBB	SO	HBP	SH	SF	SB	CS	GDP	Avg	OBP	Slg	OPS
2012 Bal	AL	51	191	50	8	3	7	(7	0)	85	24	26	29	9	0	38	0	1	1	2	0	6	.262	.294	.445	.739
2013 Bal	AL	156	667	189	51	3	14	(5	9)	288	88	71	87	29	0	113	2	9	3	6	7	15	.283	.314	.432	.746
2014 Bal	AL	82	327	91	14	0	12	(9	3)	141	38	32	44	20	2	68	3	2	2	2	0	13	.278	.324	.431	.755
2015 Bal	AL	162	633	181	30	1	35	(21	14)	318	102	86	107	70	2	111	4	2	4	20	8	17	.286	.359	.502	.861
2016 Bal	AL	157	640	188	40	1	37	(18	19)	341	105	96	103	48	9	120	3	0	5	0	3	14	.294	.343	.533	.876
2017 Bal	AL	156	630	163	33	1	33	(22	11)	297	81	95	94	50	3	115	1	0	9	9	4	17	.259	.310	.471	.782
2018 2 Tms		162	632	188	35	3	37	(24	13)	340	84	107	115	70	18	104	2	0	5	14	2	26	.297	.367	.538	.905
2019 SD	NL	156	587	150	21	2	32	(15	17)	271	81	85	86	65	3	128	6	0	3	5	3	24	.256	.334	.462	.796
2020 SD	NL	60	224	68	12	1	16	(13	3)	130	44	47	46	26	4	37	0	0	4	6	3	9	.304	.370	.580	.950
2021 SD	NL	153	564	157	31	2	28	(17	11)	276	92	106	109	63	10	102	2	0	11	12	3	10	.278	.347	.489	.836
18 Bal	AL	96	365	115	21	1	24	(17	7)	210	48	65	74	45	12	51	0	0	3	8	1	14	.315	.387	.575	.963
18 LAD	NL	66	267	73	14	2	13	(7	6)	130	36	42	41	25	6	53	2	0	2	6	1	12	.273	.338	.487	.825
Postseason		29	115	23	3	0	6	(2	4)	44	14	16	9	7	2	28	1	2	1	1	0	6	.200	.250	.383	.633
10 ML YEARS		1295	5095	1425	275	17	251	(151	100)	2487	739	751	820	450	51	936	23	14	47	76	33	151	.280	.338	.488	.826

Vimael Machin

Bats: L Throws: R Pos: SS-8;2B-3;3B-3;PH-2;PR-1 Ht: 5'11" Wt: 185 Born: 9/25/1993 Age: 28

Year Team	Lg	G	AB	H	2B	3B	HR	(Hm	Rd)	TB	R	RBI	RC	TBB	IBB	SO	HBP	SH	SF	SB	CS	GDP	Avg	OBP	Slg	OPS
2021 LsVgs	AAA	89	336	99	17	6	11	(-	-)	161	65	58	-	49	3	72	5	0	3	2	1	9	.295	.389	.479	.868
2020 Oak	AL	24	63	13	2	0	0	(0	0)	15	11	0	-	8	0	10	0	0	0	0	0	4	.206	.296	.238	.534
2021 Oak	AL	15	32	4	0	0	0	(0	0)	4	1	1	0	3	0	10	0	2	0	0	0	2	.125	.200	.125	.325
2 ML YEARS		39	95	17	2	0	0	(0	0)	19	12	1	0	11	0	20	0	2	0	0	0	6	.179	.264	.200	.464

Luis Madero

Pitches: R Bats: R Pos: RP-6

Ht: 6'1" Wt: 195 Born: 4/15/1997 Age: 25

			HOW MUCH PITCHED					WHAT HE GAVE UP												THE RESULTS								
Year	Team	Lg	G	GS	GF	IP	BFP	H	R	ER	HR	SH	SF	HB	TBB	IBB	SO	WP	W	L	Pct	Sv-Op	Hld	Vel	OPS	ERC	ERA
2021	Jaxnvl	AAA	17	7	1	57.0	240	46	28	18	4	1	0	1	24	0	58	2	7	3	.700	0--	-	-	.638	2.95	2.84
2021	Mia	NL	6	0	3	12.0	56	13	12	12	3	0	0	1	8	1	4	0	0	0	-	0-0	0	90	1.074	7.20	9.00

Nick Madrigal

Bats: R Throws: R Pos: 2B-53;PR-1

Ht: 5'8" Wt: 175 Born: 3/5/1997 Age: 25

						BATTING															RUNNING			AVERAGES			
Year	Team	Lg	G	AB	H	2B	3B	HR	(Hm	Rd)	TB	R	RBI	RC	TBB	IBB	SO	HBP	SH	SF	SB	CS	GDP	Avg	OBP	Slg	OPS
2018	3 Tms	Low	43	155	47	7	0	0	(-	-)	54	25	16	20	7	0	5	7	0	4	8	6	4	.303	.353	.348	.701
2019	WinSa	A+	49	191	52	10	2	2	(-	-)	72	20	27	30	17	2	6	6	1	3	17	4	6	.272	.346	.377	.723
2019	Brham	AA	42	164	56	11	2	1	(-	-)	74	30	16	30	14	0	5	2	0	0	14	6	1	.341	.400	.451	.851
2019	Charllt	AAA	29	118	39	6	1	1	(-	-)	50	26	12	20	13	0	5	1	1	1	4	3	3	.331	.398	.424	.822
2020	CWS	AL	29	103	35	3	0	0	(0	0)	38	8	11	16	4	0	7	2	0	0	2	1	5	.340	.376	.369	.745
2021	CWS	AL	54	200	61	10	4	2	(1	1)	85	30	21	30	11	0	17	3	0	1	1	2	3	.305	.349	.425	.774
	Postseason		3	12	3	0	0	0	(0	0)	3	1	0	0	0	0	0	0	0	0	0	0	0	.250	.250	.250	.500
	2 ML YEARS		83	303	96	13	4	2	(1	1)	123	38	32	46	15	0	24	5	0	1	3	3	8	.317	.358	.406	.764

Kenta Maeda

Pitches: R Bats: R Pos: SP-21

mah-AY-duh

Ht: 6'1" Wt: 185 Born: 4/11/1988 Age: 34

					HOW MUCH PITCHED			WHAT HE GAVE UP												THE RESULTS							
Year	Team	Lg	G	GS	GF	IP	BFP	H	R	ER	HR	SH	SF	HB	TBB	IBB	SO	WP	W	L	Pct	Sv-Op	Hld	Vel	OPS	ERC	ERA
2016	LAD	NL	32	32	0	175.2	716	150	72	68	20	0	3	8	50	6	179	6	16	11	.593	0-0	0	90	.649	3.09	3.48
2017	LAD	NL	29	25	1	134.1	557	121	68	63	22	6	4	5	34	1	140	4	13	6	.684	1-1	0	92	.714	3.48	4.22
2018	LAD	NL	39	20	4	125.1	532	115	58	53	13	2	3	5	43	4	153	2	8	10	.444	2-2	5	92	.706	3.51	3.81
2019	LAD	NL	37	26	3	153.2	624	114	70	69	22	2	3	4	51	1	169	3	10	8	.556	3-3	4	92	.642	2.79	4.04
2020	Min	AL	11	11	0	66.2	248	40	20	20	9	0	0	0	10	0	80	0	6	1	.857	0-0	0	91	.508	**1.48**	2.70
2021	Min	AL	21	21	0	106.1	453	106	60	55	16	1	1	7	32	1	113	3	6	5	.545	0-0	0	91	.755	4.28	4.66
	Postseason		25	4	2	37.2	159	29	12	12	2	0	0	2	15	2	44	2	2	1	.667	0-0	0	93	.620	2.60	2.87
	6 ML YEARS		169	135	8	762.0	3130	646	348	328	102	11	14	29	220	13	834	18	59	41	.590	6-6	9	91	.673	3.16	3.87

Tyler Mahle

Pitches: R Bats: R Pos: SP-33

Ht: 6'3" Wt: 210 Born: 9/29/1994 Age: 27

					HOW MUCH PITCHED			WHAT HE GAVE UP												THE RESULTS							
Year	Team	Lg	G	GS	GF	IP	BFP	H	R	ER	HR	SH	SF	HB	TBB	IBB	SO	WP	W	L	Pct	Sv-Op	Hld	Vel	OPS	ERC	ERA
2017	Cin	NL	4	4	0	20.0	92	19	6	6	0	2	0	4	11	1	14	1	1	2	.333	0-0	0	93	.684	4.27	2.70
2018	Cin	NL	23	23	0	112.0	507	125	68	62	22	5	3	3	53	7	110	1	7	9	.438	0-0	0	92	.848	5.77	4.98
2019	Cin	NL	25	25	0	129.2	556	136	82	74	25	2	2	6	34	0	129	2	3	12	.200	0-0	0	93	.775	4.61	5.14
2020	Cin	NL	10	9	0	47.2	201	34	21	19	6	0	4	4	21	0	60	2	2	2	.500	0-0	0	94	.666	3.13	3.59
2021	Cin	NL	33	33	0	180.0	759	158	78	75	24	9	2	10	64	0	210	4	13	6	.684	0-0	0	94	.705	3.67	3.75
	5 ML YEARS		95	94	0	489.1	2115	472	255	236	77	18	11	27	183	8	523	10	26	31	.456	0-0	0	93	.754	4.35	4.34

Luke Maile

Bats: R Throws: R Pos: C-12;PH-3;PR-1

MAY-lee

Ht: 6'3" Wt: 225 Born: 2/6/1991 Age: 31

						BATTING															RUNNING			AVERAGES			
Year	Team	Lg	G	AB	H	2B	3B	HR	(Hm	Rd)	TB	R	RBI	RC	TBB	IBB	SO	HBP	SH	SF	SB	CS	GDP	Avg	OBP	Slg	OPS
2021	Nashv	AAA	43	122	26	9	0	1	(-	-)	38	17	13	-	22	1	49	2	1	0	2	0	3	.213	.342	.311	.654
2015	TB	AL	15	35	6	3	0	0	(0	0)	9	2	2	0	0	0	8	0	0	0	0	0	3	.171	.171	.257	.429
2016	TB	AL	42	119	27	7	0	3	(2	1)	43	10	15	11	4	1	36	0	3	0	0	0	2	.227	.252	.361	.613
2017	Tor	AL	46	130	19	5	0	2	(1	1)	30	10	7	2	3	0	35	2	0	1	0	2	2	.146	.176	.231	.407
2018	Tor	AL	68	202	50	13	1	3	(2	1)	74	22	27	28	25	0	67	2	0	2	2	0	4	.248	.333	.366	.700
2019	Tor	AL	45	119	18	2	1	2	(2	0)	28	9	9	4	8	0	33	0	2	0	1	0	1	.151	.205	.235	.440
2021	Mil	NL	15	30	9	4	0	0	(0	0)	13	6	3	4	4	0	7	1	0	0	0	0	1	.300	.382	.433	.816
	6 ML YEARS		231	635	129	34	2	10	(7	3)	197	59	63	49	43	1	186	5	5	3	4	0	13	.203	.258	.310	.568

Martin Maldonado

Bats: R Throws: R Pos: C-123;1B-1;PH-1

mar-TEEN

Ht: 6'0" Wt: 230 Born: 8/16/1986 Age: 35

						BATTING															RUNNING			AVERAGES			
Year	Team	Lg	G	AB	H	2B	3B	HR	(Hm	Rd)	TB	R	RBI	RC	TBB	IBB	SO	HBP	SH	SF	SB	CS	GDP	Avg	OBP	Slg	OPS
2011	Mil	NL	3	1	0	0	0	0	(0	0)	0	0	0	0	0	0	1	0	0	0	0	0	0	.000	.000	.000	.000
2012	Mil	NL	78	233	62	9	0	8	(6	2)	95	22	30	28	17	0	56	2	4	0	1	1	5	.266	.321	.408	.729
2013	Mil	NL	67	183	31	7	1	4	(1	3)	52	13	22	14	13	1	53	3	3	0	0	0	2	.169	.236	.284	.520
2014	Mil	NL	52	111	26	5	0	4	(2	2)	43	14	16	14	11	1	32	3	1	0	0	0	4	.234	.320	.387	.707
2015	Mil	NL	79	229	48	7	0	4	(4	0)	67	19	22	20	23	3	65	1	1	2	0	1	6	.210	.282	.293	.575
2016	Mil	NL	76	208	42	7	0	8	(6	2)	73	21	21	23	35	9	56	6	3	1	1	0	6	.202	.332	.351	.683
2017	LAA	AL	138	429	95	19	1	14	(5	9)	158	43	38	37	15	1	119	18	8	1	0	2	12	.221	.276	.368	.645
2018	2 Tms	AL	119	373	84	18	1	9	(2	7)	131	39	44	36	16	0	98	11	2	2	0	1	8	.225	.276	.351	.627
2019	3 Tms	AL	105	333	71	19	0	12	(8	4)	126	46	27	29	32	1	86	6	2	1	0	0	11	.213	.293	.378	.671
2020	Hou	AL	47	135	29	4	0	6	(4	2)	51	19	24	27	27	0	51	1	2	0	1	0	2	.215	.350	.378	.727
2021	Hou	AL	125	373	64	10	1	12	(5	7)	112	40	36	28	47	1	127	5	0	1	0	0	9	.172	.272	.300	.573
18	LAA	AL	78	265	59	14	0	5	(2	3)	88	24	32	30	13	0	73	10	1	1	0	1	3	.223	.284	.332	.616
18	Hou	AL	41	108	25	4	1	4	(0	4)	43	15	12	8	3	0	25	1	1	1	0	0	5	.231	.257	.398	.655
19	KC	AL	74	238	54	15	0	6	(2	4)	87	26	17	21	17	0	55	5	2	1	0	0	9	.227	.291	.366	.657

Year Team	Lg	BATTING G	AB	H	2B	3B	HR	(Hm	Rd)	TB	R	RBI	RC	TBB	IBB	SO	HBP	SH	SF	RUNNING SB	CS	GDP	AVERAGES Avg	OBP	Slg	OPS
19 ChC	NL	4	11	0	0	0	0	(0	0)	0	0	0	0	2	1	5	0	0	0	0	0	0	.000	.154	.000	.154
19 Hou	AL	27	84	17	4	0	6	(6	0)	39	20	10	8	13	0	26	1	0	0	0	0	2	.202	.316	.464	.781
Postseason		27	74	14	4	0	3	(2	1)	27	11	4	4	5	0	31	2	2	0	0	0	2	.189	.259	.365	.624
11 ML YEARS		889	2608	552	105	4	81	(43	38)	908	276	280	258	236	17	744	56	26	8	3	5	65	.212	.290	.348	.638

Sean Manaea

muh-NIE-uh

Pitches: L **Bats:** R **Pos:** SP-32   **Ht:** 6'5" **Wt:** 245 **Born:** 2/1/1992 **Age:** 30

Year Team	Lg	HOW MUCH PITCHED G	GS	GF	IP	BFP	WHAT HE GAVE UP H	R	ER	HR	SH	SF	HB	TBB	IBB	SO	WP	THE RESULTS W	L	Pct	Sv-Op	Hld	Vel	OPS	ERC	ERA
2016 Oak	AL	25	24	0	144.2	594	135	65	62	20	4	4	4	37	1	124	3	7	9	.438	0-0	0	92	.713	3.53	3.86
2017 Oak	AL	29	29	0	158.2	692	167	88	77	18	1	2	10	32	1	140	8	12	10	.545	0-0	0	92	.763	4.51	4.37
2018 Oak	AL	27	27	0	160.2	654	141	67	64	21	4	2	8	32	1	108	9	12	9	.571	0-0	0	90	.663	3.02	3.59
2019 Oak	AL	5	5	0	29.2	109	16	4	4	3	0	0	2	7	0	30	1	4	0	1.000	0-0	0	90	.509	1.58	1.21
2020 Oak	AL	11	11	0	54.0	222	57	32	27	7	0	2	1	8	0	45	1	4	3	.571	0-0	0	90	.724	3.69	4.50
2021 Oak	AL	32	32	0	179.1	754	179	79	78	25	1	1	9	41	0	194	5	11	10	.524	0-0	0	92	.719	3.85	3.91
Postseason		2	2	0	6.1	28	9	8	8	5	0	0	0	1	0	7	0	0	2	.000	0-0	0	91	1.283	11.03	11.37
6 ML YEARS		129	128	0	727.0	3025	695	335	312	94	10	11	34	180	3	641	27	50	41	.549	0-0	0	92	.709	3.62	3.86

Trey Mancini

Bats: R **Throws:** R **Pos:** 1B-77;DH-68;PH-4   **Ht:** 6'3" **Wt:** 230 **Born:** 3/18/1992 **Age:** 30

Year Team	Lg	BATTING G	AB	H	2B	3B	HR	(Hm	Rd)	TB	R	RBI	RC	TBB	IBB	SO	HBP	SH	SF	RUNNING SB	CS	GDP	AVERAGES Avg	OBP	Slg	OPS
2016 Bal	AL	5	14	5	1	0	3	(3	0)	15	3	5	5	0	0	4	1	0	0	0	0	0	.357	.400	1.071	1.471
2017 Bal	AL	147	543	159	26	4	24	(11	13)	265	65	78	90	33	1	139	6	0	4	1	0	12	.293	.338	.488	.826
2018 Bal	AL	156	582	141	23	3	24	(13	11)	242	69	58	55	44	1	153	5	0	5	0	1	17	.242	.299	.416	.715
2019 Bal	AL	154	602	175	38	2	35	(18	17)	322	106	97	101	63	3	143	9	0	5	1	0	22	.291	.364	.535	.899
2021 Bal	AL	147	556	142	33	1	21	(14	7)	240	77	71	73	51	4	143	8	0	1	0	0	19	.255	.326	.432	.758
5 ML YEARS		609	2297	622	121	10	107	(59	48)	1084	320	309	324	191	9	582	29	0	15	2	1	70	.271	.333	.472	.804

Matt Manning

Pitches: R **Bats:** R **Pos:** SP-18   **Ht:** 6'6" **Wt:** 195 **Born:** 1/28/1998 **Age:** 24

Year Team	Lg	HOW MUCH PITCHED G	GS	GF	IP	BFP	WHAT HE GAVE UP H	R	ER	HR	SH	SF	HB	TBB	IBB	SO	WP	THE RESULTS W	L	Pct	Sv-Op	Hld	Vel	OPS	ERC	ERA
2017 2 Tms	Low	14	14	0	51.0	218	41	21	18	0	1	1	3	25	0	62	3	4	2	.667	0--	-	-	.605	2.87	3.18
2018 2 Tms	Low	20	20	0	107.0	442	79	39	38	7	2	3	3	47	0	141	6	7	7	.500	0--	-	-	.583	2.71	3.20
2019 Erie	AA	24	24	0	133.2	527	93	42	38	7	0	3	2	38	1	148	5	11	5	.688	0--	-	-	.540	1.87	2.56
2021 Toledo	AAA	7	7	0	32.1	144	40	29	29	11	1	1	0	10	0	36	2	1	3	.250	0--	-	-	.948	6.90	8.07
2021 Det	AL	18	18	0	85.1	385	96	59	55	10	0	4	3	33	0	57	1	4	7	.364	0-0	0	94	.789	4.93	5.80

Alek Manoah

Pitches: R **Bats:** R **Pos:** SP-20   **Ht:** 6'6" **Wt:** 260 **Born:** 1/9/1998 **Age:** 24

Year Team	Lg	HOW MUCH PITCHED G	GS	GF	IP	BFP	WHAT HE GAVE UP H	R	ER	HR	SH	SF	HB	TBB	IBB	SO	WP	THE RESULTS W	L	Pct	Sv-Op	Hld	Vel	OPS	ERC	ERA
2021 Tor	AL	20	20	0	111.2	459	77	44	40	12	0	2	16	40	0	127	0	9	2	.818	0-0	0	93	.604	2.87	3.22

Joe Mantiply

Pitches: L **Bats:** R **Pos:** RP-57   **Ht:** 6'4" **Wt:** 219 **Born:** 3/1/1991 **Age:** 31

Year Team	Lg	HOW MUCH PITCHED G	GS	GF	IP	BFP	WHAT HE GAVE UP H	R	ER	HR	SH	SF	HB	TBB	IBB	SO	WP	THE RESULTS W	L	Pct	Sv-Op	Hld	Vel	OPS	ERC	ERA
2021 Reno	AAA	5	0	4	4.2	19	4	2	1	1	0	0	1	0	0	10	0	0	1	.000	2--	-	-	.652	3.23	1.93
2016 Det	AL	5	0	3	2.2	16	7	5	5	1	1	0	0	2	1	2	0	0	0	-	0-0	0	88	1.446	19.98	16.88
2019 NYY	AL	1	0	0	3.0	14	3	3	3	1	0	0	0	2	0	2	0	1	0	1.000	0-0	0	89	1.024	6.85	9.00
2020 Ari	NL	4	0	1	2.1	15	3	4	4	0	0	0	0	4	0	2	0	0	0	-	0-0	0	91	.830	9.50	15.43
2021 Ari	NL	57	0	7	39.2	177	45	24	15	1	1	4	1	17	3	38	2	0	3	.000	0-2	11	91	.806	4.37	3.40
4 ML YEARS		67	0	11	47.2	222	58	36	27	3	2	4	1	25	4	44	2	1	3	.250	0-2	11	91	.866	5.47	5.10

Dillon Maples

Pitches: R **Bats:** R **Pos:** RP-28   **Ht:** 6'2" **Wt:** 230 **Born:** 5/9/1992 **Age:** 30

Year Team	Lg	HOW MUCH PITCHED G	GS	GF	IP	BFP	WHAT HE GAVE UP H	R	ER	HR	SH	SF	HB	TBB	IBB	SO	WP	THE RESULTS W	L	Pct	Sv-Op	Hld	Vel	OPS	ERC	ERA
2021 Iowa	AAA	17	1	1	19.0	90	14	12	12	3	0	2	4	18	0	23	1	3	1	.750	0--	-	-	.779	6.13	5.68
2017 ChC	NL	6	0	1	5.1	27	6	6	6	0	0	0	0	6	0	11	1	0	0	-	0-0	0	97	.825	6.99	10.13
2018 ChC	NL	9	0	1	5.1	29	7	7	7	2	0	0	2	5	0	9	2	1	0	1.000	0-0	0	97	1.210	12.98	11.81
2019 ChC	NL	14	0	3	11.2	54	6	7	7	2	0	0	4	10	0	18	0	1	0	1.000	0-0	0	97	.670	4.99	5.40
2020 ChC	NL	2	0	1	1.0	9	1	3	2	0	0	0	0	4	0	1	0	0	0	-	0-0	0	96	.956	16.22	18.00
2021 ChC	NL	28	0	10	31.1	139	15	10	9	2	0	2	8	25	0	40	5	1	0	1.000	0-0	0	95	.576	3.42	2.59
5 ML YEARS		59	0	16	54.2	258	35	33	31	6	0	2	14	50	0	79	8	3	1	1.000	0-0	0	96	.707	5.10	5.10

Tucupita Marcano

Bats: L **Throws:** R **Pos:** PH-12;2B-8;LF-4;RF-4;3B-1;PR-1   **Ht:** 6'0" **Wt:** 170 **Born:** 9/16/1999 **Age:** 22

Year	Team	Lg	G	AB	H	2B	3B	HR	(Hm	Rd)	TB	R	RBI	RC	TBB	IBB	SO	HBP	SH	SF	SB	CS	GDP	Avg	OBP	Slg	OPS
2021	ElPaso	AAA	45	172	47	7	2	6	(-	-)	76	31	27	-	27	0	26	0	0	3	4	4	1	.273	.366	.442	.808
2021	Indy	AAA	44	169	39	4	1	1	(-	-)	48	28	11	-	24	0	30	0	1	0	7	1	2	.231	.326	.284	.610
2021	SD	NL	25	44	8	1	0	0	(0	0)	9	7	3	1	6	0	9	0	0	0	0	0	2	.182	.280	.205	.485

Rafael Marchan

Bats: B **Throws:** R **Pos:** C-17;PH-4;1B-1   **Ht:** 5'9" **Wt:** 170 **Born:** 2/25/1999 **Age:** 23

Year	Team	Lg	G	AB	H	2B	3B	HR	(Hm	Rd)	TB	R	RBI	RC	TBB	IBB	SO	HBP	SH	SF	SB	CS	GDP	Avg	OBP	Slg	OPS
2021	LV	AAA	66	233	48	7	0	0	(-	-)	55	28	19	-	23	0	43	4	0	1	1	0	10	.206	.287	.236	.523
2020	Phi	NL	3	8	4	0	0	1	(0	0)	7	3	3	4	1	0	2	0	0	0	0	0	0	.500	.556	.875	1.431
2021	Phi	NL	20	52	12	1	1	1	(0	1)	18	7	4	4	4	0	10	0	0	0	0	0	1	.231	.286	.346	.632
	2 ML YEARS		23	60	16	1	1	2	(1	1)	25	10	7	8	5	0	12	0	0	0	0	0	1	.267	.323	.417	.740

Nick Margevicius

Pitches: L **Bats:** L **Pos:** SP-3; RP-2   mahr-GAH-vih-chus   **Ht:** 6'5" **Wt:** 220 **Born:** 6/18/1996 **Age:** 26

			HOW MUCH PITCHED					WHAT HE GAVE UP										THE RESULTS							
Year	Team	Lg	G	GS	GF	IP	BFP	H	R	ER	HR	SH	SF	HB	TBB	IBB	SO	WP	W	L	Pct	Sv-Op	Hld	Vel	OPS	ERC	ERA
2019	SD	NL	17	12	1	57.0	263	73	46	43	12	3	0	3	19	1	42	1	2	6	.250	0-0	0	88	.912	6.43	6.79
2020	Sea	AL	10	7	1	41.1	170	38	21	21	6	0	0	0	14	2	36	2	2	3	.400	0-1	0	90	.742	3.69	4.57
2021	Sea	AL	5	3	1	12.0	60	13	16	11	2	0	0	1	7	0	12	2	0	2	.000	0-0	0	90	.792	5.71	8.25
	3 ML YEARS		32	22	3	110.1	493	124	83	75	20	3	0	4	40	3	90	5	4	11	.267	0-1	0	89	.838	5.29	6.12

Manuel Margot

Bats: R **Throws:** R **Pos:** RF-86;LF-24;CF-24;PH-14;DH-3;PR-2   mar-GOH   **Ht:** 5'11" **Wt:** 180 **Born:** 9/28/1994 **Age:** 27

Year	Team	Lg	G	AB	H	2B	3B	HR	(Hm	Rd)	TB	R	RBI	RC	TBB	IBB	SO	HBP	SH	SF	SB	CS	GDP	Avg	OBP	Slg	OPS
2016	SD	NL	10	37	9	4	1	0	(0	0)	15	4	3	5	0	0	7	0	0	0	2	0	0	.243	.243	.405	.649
2017	SD	NL	126	487	128	18	7	13	(7	6)	199	53	39	55	35	0	106	2	1	4	17	7	6	.263	.313	.409	.721
2018	SD	NL	141	477	117	26	8	8	(5	3)	183	50	51	56	32	4	88	2	1	7	11	10	9	.245	.292	.384	.675
2019	SD	NL	151	398	93	19	3	12	(3	9)	154	59	37	47	38	1	88	2	3	0	20	4	6	.234	.304	.387	.691
2020	TB	AL	47	145	39	9	0	1	(1	0)	51	19	11	17	13	0	25	0	0	1	12	4	6	.269	.327	.352	.679
2021	TB	AL	125	421	107	18	3	10	(4	6)	161	55	57	57	37	2	70	1	1	4	13	8	4	.254	.313	.382	.696
	Postseason		19	58	16	1	0	5	(5	0)	32	10	11	11	5	0	19	1	1	0	2	1	0	.276	.344	.552	.895
	6 ML YEARS		600	1965	493	94	22	44	(20	24)	763	240	198	237	155	7	384	7	6	16	75	33	25	.251	.306	.388	.694

Jake Marisnick

Bats: R **Throws:** R **Pos:** CF-52;PH-42;LF-20;PR-3;RF-2   muh-RIZ-nick   **Ht:** 6'4" **Wt:** 220 **Born:** 3/30/1991 **Age:** 31

Year	Team	Lg	G	AB	H	2B	3B	HR	(Hm	Rd)	TB	R	RBI	RC	TBB	IBB	SO	HBP	SH	SF	SB	CS	GDP	Avg	OBP	Slg	OPS
2013	Mia	NL	40	109	20	2	1	1	(1	0)	27	6	5	7	6	0	27	1	1	1	3	1	1	.183	.231	.248	.478
2014	2 Tms		65	221	55	8	0	3	(3	0)	72	21	19	19	8	3	67	3	2	3	11	3	2	.249	.281	.326	.607
2015	Hou	AL	133	339	80	15	4	9	(4	5)	130	46	36	40	18	0	105	5	6	4	24	9	2	.236	.281	.383	.665
2016	Hou	AL	118	287	60	18	1	5	(1	4)	95	40	21	23	16	0	83	3	4	1	10	5	4	.209	.257	.331	.588
2017	Hou	AL	106	230	56	10	0	16	(10	6)	114	50	35	31	20	1	90	6	2	1	9	4	5	.243	.319	.496	.815
2018	Hou	AL	103	213	45	8	1	10	(2	8)	85	34	28	24	15	1	84	4	1	1	6	2	6	.211	.275	.399	.674
2019	Hou	AL	120	292	68	16	3	10	(5	5)	120	46	34	31	17	0	95	6	3	0	10	3	6	.233	.289	.411	.700
2020	NYM	NL	16	33	11	3	0	2	(1	1)	20	4	5	6	1	0	10	0	0	0	0	0	0	.333	.353	.606	.959
2021	2 Tms		99	176	38	7	3	5	(4	1)	66	21	24	20	11	0	65	7	2	2	4	1	4	.216	.286	.375	.661
14	Mia	NL	14	48	8	0	0	0	(0	0)	8	3	0	1	3	1	19	0	0	0	5	0	0	.167	.216	.167	.382
14	Hou	AL	51	173	47	8	0	3	(3	0)	64	18	19	18	5	2	48	3	2	3	6	3	2	.272	.299	.370	.669
21	ChC	NL	65	128	29	6	3	5	(4	1)	56	17	22	18	9	0	43	4	1	2	3	1	2	.227	.294	.438	.731
21	SD	NL	34	48	9	1	0	0	(0	0)	10	4	2	2	2	0	22	3	1	0	1	0	2	.188	.264	.208	.472
	Postseason		23	21	7	1	0	0	(0	0)	8	1	0	3	1	0	8	0	0	0	2	0	0	.333	.364	.381	.745
	9 ML YEARS		800	1900	433	87	13	61	(31	30)	729	268	207	201	112	5	626	35	21	13	77	28	30	.228	.282	.384	.665

Jose Marmolejos

Bats: L **Throws:** L **Pos:** 1B-14;LF-11;PH-9;DH-5;RF-2   marr-mo-LEH-hose   **Ht:** 6'2" **Wt:** 239 **Born:** 1/2/1993 **Age:** 29

Year	Team	Lg	G	AB	H	2B	3B	HR	(Hm	Rd)	TB	R	RBI	RC	TBB	IBB	SO	HBP	SH	SF	SB	CS	GDP	Avg	OBP	Slg	OPS
2021	Tacom	AAA	78	274	96	14	2	25	(-	-)	189	63	74	-	51	4	63	2	0	4	0	0	6	.350	.450	.690	1.140
2020	Sea	AL	35	107	22	4	0	6	(1	5)	44	12	18	15	7	0	32	1	0	0	0	1	2	.206	.261	.411	.672
2021	Sea	AL	41	106	17	4	0	4	(2	2)	33	11	12	7	15	0	39	0	0	1	0	0	0	.160	.262	.311	.574
	2 ML YEARS		76	213	39	8	0	10	(3	7)	77	23	30	22	22	0	71	1	0	1	0	1	2	.183	.262	.362	.623

German Marquez

Pitches: R Bats: R Pos: SP-32   hair-MAHN   Ht: 6'1" Wt: 230 Born: 2/22/1995 Age: 27

			HOW MUCH PITCHED					WHAT HE GAVE UP											THE RESULTS								
Year	Team	Lg	G	GS	GF	IP	BFP	H	R	ER	HR	SH	SF	HB	TBB	IBB	SO	WP	W	L	Pct	Sv-Op	Hld	Vel	OPS	ERC	ERA
2016	Col	NL	6	3	0	20.2	98	28	12	12	2	2	1	3	6	0	15	0	1	1	.500	0-0	0	93	.932	6.21	5.23
2017	Col	NL	29	29	0	162.0	701	174	82	79	25	5	4	8	49	3	147	6	11	7	.611	0-0	0	95	.806	4.67	4.39
2018	Col	NL	33	33	0	196.0	817	179	90	82	24	2	6	8	57	5	230	8	14	11	.560	0-0	0	95	.698	3.45	3.77
2019	Col	NL	28	28	0	174.0	721	174	96	92	29	6	4	5	35	0	175	14	12	5	.706	0-0	0	95	.740	3.86	4.76
2020	Col	NL	13	13	0	81.2	344	78	41	34	6	0	3	0	25	0	73	4	4	6	.400	0-0	0	95	.673	3.26	3.75
2021	Col	NL	32	32	0	180.0	756	165	92	88	21	5	0	4	64	5	176	15	12	11	.522	0-0	0	95	.699	3.61	4.40
	Postseason		1	1	0	5.0	22	7	2	2	1	0	0	0	1	0	5	0	0	1	.000	0-0	0	96	.840	6.52	3.60
	6 ML YEARS		141	138	0	814.1	3437	798	413	387	107	20	18	28	236	13	816	47	54	41	.568	0-0	0	95	.733	3.86	4.28

Deven Marrero

Bats: R Throws: R Pos: SS-4;PH-4;3B-3;1B-1;2B-1;PR-1   Ht: 6'0" Wt: 190 Born: 8/25/1990 Age: 31

			BATTING																	RUNNING			AVERAGES			
Year	Team	Lg	G	AB	H	2B	3B	HR	(Hm	Rd)	TB	R	RBI	RC	TBB	IBB	SO	HBP	SH	SF	SB	CS	GDP	Avg	OBP	Slg	OPS
2021	Jaxnvl	AAA	59	181	39	7	0	5	(-	-)	61	23	21	-	21	0	60	1	3	1	0	1	9	.215	.299	.337	.636
2015	Bos	AL	25	53	12	0	0	1	(0	1)	15	8	3	4	3	0	19	0	0	0	2	1	0	.226	.268	.283	.551
2016	Bos	AL	13	12	1	0	0	0	(0	0)	1	0	0	0	2	0	5	0	0	0	0	0	0	.083	.214	.083	.298
2017	Bos	AL	71	171	36	9	0	4	(1	3)	57	32	27	18	12	0	61	0	3	2	5	0	8	.211	.259	.333	.593
2018	Ari	NL	49	78	13	1	1	0	(0	0)	16	11	7	4	6	0	23	0	0	1	3	0	5	.167	.224	.205	.429
2019	Mia	NL	5	5	0	0	0	0	(0	0)	0	0	0	0	0	0	3	0	0	0	0	0	0	.000	.000	.000	.000
2021	Mia	NL	10	16	3	0	0	1	(1	0)	6	4	1	1	3	0	6	0	0	0	1	0	2	.188	.316	.375	.691
	Postseason		1	2	0	0	0	0	(0	0)	0	0	0	0	0	0	2	0	0	0	0	0	0	.000	.000	.000	.000
	6 ML YEARS		173	335	65	10	1	6	(2	4)	95	55	38	27	26	0	117	0	3	3	11	1	15	.194	.250	.284	.534

Brandon Marsh

Bats: L Throws: R Pos: CF-70   Ht: 6'4" Wt: 215 Born: 12/18/1997 Age: 24

			BATTING																	RUNNING			AVERAGES			
Year	Team	Lg	G	AB	H	2B	3B	HR	(Hm	Rd)	TB	R	RBI	RC	TBB	IBB	SO	HBP	SH	SF	SB	CS	GDP	Avg	OBP	Slg	OPS
2021	Salt Lk	AAA	24	94	24	5	3	3	(-	-)	44	26	8	-	16	0	29	0	0	0	2	0	1	.255	.364	.468	.832
2021	LAA	AL	70	236	60	12	3	2	(0	2)	84	27	19	26	20	0	91	2	1	1	6	1	3	.254	.317	.356	.673

Evan Marshall

Pitches: R Bats: R Pos: RP-27   Ht: 6'2" Wt: 235 Born: 4/18/1990 Age: 32

			HOW MUCH PITCHED					WHAT HE GAVE UP											THE RESULTS								
Year	Team	Lg	G	GS	GF	IP	BFP	H	R	ER	HR	SH	SF	HB	TBB	IBB	SO	WP	W	L	Pct	Sv-Op	Hld	Vel	OPS	ERC	ERA
2021	Charltt	AAA	5	0	2	4.1	17	4	1	1	0	0	0	0	3	0	6	0	0	0	-	0--	-	-	.912	4.70	2.08
2014	Ari	NL	57	0	11	49.1	210	50	17	15	3	2	1	2	17	3	54	3	4	4	.500	0-1	19	94	.709	3.76	2.74
2015	Ari	NL	13	0	4	13.1	61	20	9	9	3	0	0	0	5	1	7	1	0	2	.000	0-2	2	94	.999	8.27	6.08
2016	Ari	NL	15	0	8	15.1	79	28	18	15	2	0	0	1	8	2	9	1	0	1	.000	0-0	1	93	1.083	10.46	8.80
2017	Sea	AL	6	0	2	7.2	38	12	8	8	1	0	0	0	5	1	4	0	0	0	-	0-0	0	94	.993	8.94	9.39
2018	Cle	AL	10	0	1	7.0	37	12	6	6	0	0	0	1	4	0	9	1	0	0	-	0-1	3	93	.866	9.01	7.71
2019	CWS	AL	55	0	2	50.2	209	42	16	14	5	0	1	0	24	2	41	1	4	2	.667	0-4	19	94	.669	3.45	2.49
2020	CWS	AL	23	0	2	22.2	93	17	6	6	1	0	0	0	7	0	30	2	2	1	.667	0-2	8	93	.537	2.04	2.38
2021	CWS	AL	27	0	4	27.1	113	28	17	17	5	1	2	0	9	1	26	0	0	2	.000	0-4	6	93	.845	4.61	5.60
	Postseason		2	0	0	2.2	14	3	2	1	0	0	0	0	2	0	2	0	0	1	.000	0-0	1	94	.657	4.83	3.38
	8 ML YEARS		206	0	32	193.1	840	209	97	90	20	3	4	4	79	10	180	9	10	12	.455	0-14	58	94	.774	4.67	4.19

Jose Marte

Pitches: R Bats: R Pos: RP-4   Ht: 6'3" Wt: 180 Born: 6/14/1996 Age: 26

			HOW MUCH PITCHED					WHAT HE GAVE UP											THE RESULTS								
Year	Team	Lg	G	GS	GF	IP	BFP	H	R	ER	HR	SH	SF	HB	TBB	IBB	SO	WP	W	L	Pct	Sv-Op	Hld	Vel	OPS	ERC	ERA
2021	Eugene	A+	5	0	5	6.1	25	3	0	0	0	0	0	0	2	0	14	1	0	0	-	3--	-	-	-	0.95	0.00
2021	Rchmd	AA	19	0	7	22.2	101	21	11	9	0	0	1	0	15	1	36	3	2	0	1.000	1--	-	-	.686	3.87	3.57
2021	Salt Lk	AAA	6	0	2	7.0	35	10	8	7	0	1	0	2	3	0	7	1	1	1	.500	0--	-	-	.786	7.14	9.00
2021	LAA	AL	4	0	2	4.0	18	4	5	4	1	0	0	0	3	0	5	0	0	1	.000	0-1	0	97	.922	6.96	9.00

Ketel Marte

Bats: B Throws: R Pos: CF-71;2B-20;PH-8   kuh-TELL marr-TAY   Ht: 6'1" Wt: 210 Born: 10/12/1993 Age: 28

			BATTING																	RUNNING			AVERAGES			
Year	Team	Lg	G	AB	H	2B	3B	HR	(Hm	Rd)	TB	R	RBI	RC	TBB	IBB	SO	HBP	SH	SF	SB	CS	GDP	Avg	OBP	Slg	OPS
2015	Sea	AL	57	219	62	14	3	2	(1	1)	88	25	17	33	24	0	43	0	2	2	8	4	1	.283	.351	.402	.753
2016	Sea	AL	119	437	113	21	2	1	(1	0)	141	55	33	41	18	0	84	2	3	6	11	5	10	.259	.287	.323	.610
2017	Ari	NL	73	223	58	11	2	5	(1	4)	88	30	18	27	29	3	37	1	0	2	3	1	3	.260	.345	.395	.740
2018	Ari	NL	153	520	135	26	12	14	(8	6)	227	68	59	67	54	3	79	3	1	2	6	1	12	.260	.332	.437	.768
2019	Ari	NL	144	569	187	36	9	32	(13	19)	337	97	92	121	53	2	86	4	0	2	10	2	7	.329	.389	.592	.981
2020	Ari	NL	45	181	52	14	1	2	(1	1)	74	19	17	27	7	0	21	4	0	3	1	0	2	.287	.323	.409	.732
2021	Ari	NL	90	340	108	29	1	14	(7	7)	181	52	50	68	31	3	60	2	0	1	2	0	8	.318	.377	.532	.909
	Postseason		4	17	7	0	2	1	(0	1)	14	4	2	4	0	0	5	0	0	0	0	0	0	.412	.412	.824	1.235
	7 ML YEARS		681	2489	715	151	30	70	(32	38)	1136	346	286	384	216	11	410	16	6	18	41	13	43	.287	.346	.456	.802

Luis Marte

Bats: R Throws: R Pos: 2B-1;3B-1;SS-1;PH-1   Ht: 6'1" Wt: 188 Born: 12/15/1993 Age: 28

						BATTING															RUNNING			AVERAGES			
Year Team	Lg	G	AB	H	2B	3B	HR	(Hm Rd)	TB	R	RBI	RC	TBB	IBB	SO	HBP	SH	SF	SB	CS	GDP	Avg	OBP	Slg	OPS
2021 Jaxnvl	AAA	27	84	17	2	0	3	(- -)	28	7	11	-	2	0	20	0	0	2	3	1	1	.202	.216	.333	.549
2021 Mia	NL	4	6	1	0	0	0	(0 0)	1	2	0	0	1	0	2	0	0	0	0	0	0	.167	.286	.167	.452

Noelvi Marte

Bats: R Throws: R Pos: SS   Ht: 6'1" Wt: 181 Born: 10/16/2001 Age: 20

						BATTING															RUNNING			AVERAGES			
Year Team	Lg	G	AB	H	2B	3B	HR	(Hm Rd)	TB	R	RBI	RC	TBB	IBB	SO	HBP	SH	SF	SB	CS	GDP	Avg	OBP	Slg	OPS
2021 2 Tms	Low	107	444	121	28	2	17	(- -)	204	91	71	0	60	1	117	6	0	1	24	7	6	.273	.366	.459	.825

Starling Marte

marr-TAY

Bats: R Throws: R Pos: CF-119;PH-1   Ht: 6'1" Wt: 195 Born: 10/9/1988 Age: 33

						BATTING															RUNNING			AVERAGES			
Year Team	Lg	G	AB	H	2B	3B	HR	(Hm Rd)	TB	R	RBI	RC	TBB	IBB	SO	HBP	SH	SF	SB	CS	GDP	Avg	OBP	Slg	OPS
2012 Pit	NL	47	167	43	3	6	5	(3 2)	73	18	17	21	8	0	50	3	2	2	12	5	5	.257	.300	.437	.737
2013 Pit	NL	135	510	143	26	10	12	(5 7)	225	83	35	74	25	2	138	24	6	1	41	15	6	.280	.343	.441	.784
2014 Pit	NL	135	495	144	29	6	13	(5 8)	224	73	56	70	33	0	131	17	0	0	30	11	5	.291	.356	.453	.808
2015 Pit	NL	153	579	166	30	2	19	(10 9)	257	84	81	81	27	3	123	19	3	5	30	10	14	.287	.337	.444	.780
2016 Pit	NL	129	489	152	34	5	9	(2 7)	223	71	46	77	23	5	104	16	1	0	47	12	8	.311	.362	.456	.818
2017 Pit	NL	77	309	85	7	2	7	(5 2)	117	48	31	46	20	0	63	8	0	2	21	4	5	.275	.333	.379	.712
2018 Pit	NL	145	559	155	32	5	20	(8 12)	257	81	72	83	35	2	109	8	1	3	33	14	11	.277	.327	.460	.787
2019 Pit	NL	132	539	159	31	6	23	(9 14)	271	97	82	95	25	1	94	16	2	4	25	6	15	.295	.342	.503	.845
2020 2 Tms	NL	61	228	64	14	1	6	(2 4)	98	36	27	32	12	1	41	9	0	1	10	2	5	.281	.340	.430	.770
2021 2 Tms		120	467	145	27	3	12	(7 5)	214	89	55	89	43	2	99	13	1	2	47	5	6	.310	.383	.458	.841
20 Ari	NL	33	122	38	8	1	2	(0 2)	54	23	14	21	10	1	19	5	0	1	5	2	3	.311	.384	.443	.827
20 Mia	NL	28	106	26	6	0	4	(2 2)	44	13	13	11	2	0	22	4	0	0	5	0	2	.245	.286	.415	.701
21 Mia	NL	64	233	71	11	1	7	(3 4)	105	52	25	46	32	2	57	8	1	1	22	3	2	.305	.405	.451	.856
21 Oak	AL	56	234	74	16	2	5	(4 1)	109	37	30	43	11	0	42	5	0	1	25	2	4	.316	.359	.466	.824
Postseason		9	36	6	2	0	1	(0 1)	11	3	1	2	1	0	7	2	0	0	1	0	2	.167	.231	.306	.536
10 ML YEARS		1134	4342	1256	233	46	126	(56 70)	1959	680	502	668	251	16	952	133	16	20	296	84	80	.289	.346	.451	.797

Brett Martin

Pitches: L Bats: L Pos: RP-66   Ht: 6'4" Wt: 200 Born: 4/28/1995 Age: 27

		HOW MUCH PITCHED					WHAT HE GAVE UP											THE RESULTS							
Year Team	Lg	G	GS	GF	IP	BFP	H	R	ER	HR	SH	SF	HB	TBB	IBB	SO	WP	W	L	Pct	Sv-Op	Hld	Vel	OPS	ERC	ERA
2019 Tex	AL	51	2	7	62.1	280	72	38	33	7	0	3	2	18	2	62	3	2	3	.400	0-1	4	94	.745	4.54	4.76
2020 Tex	AL	15	0	4	14.2	61	8	5	3	2	0	1	0	9	0	8	1	1		.500	0-0	2	94	.612	2.67	1.84
2021 Tex	AL	66	0	24	62.1	264	67	31	22	5	4	0	0	14	4	42	4	4	4	.500	0-2	11	93	.686	3.54	3.18
3 ML YEARS		132	2	35	139.1	605	147	74	58	14	4	4	2	41	6	112	8	7	8	.467	0-3	17	94	.706	3.88	3.75

Chris Martin

Pitches: R Bats: R Pos: RP-46   Ht: 6'8" Wt: 225 Born: 6/2/1986 Age: 36

		HOW MUCH PITCHED					WHAT HE GAVE UP											THE RESULTS							
Year Team	Lg	G	GS	GF	IP	BFP	H	R	ER	HR	SH	SF	HB	TBB	IBB	SO	WP	W	L	Pct	Sv-Op	Hld	Vel	OPS	ERC	ERA
2014 Col	NL	16	0	1	15.2	69	22	12	12	2	0	0	0	4	0	14	1	0	0		0-0	3	94	.915	6.30	6.89
2015 NYY	AL	24	0	8	20.2	99	28	13	13	2	0	0	1	6	1	18	3	0	2	.000	1-1	5	94	.777	5.52	5.66
2018 Tex	AL	46	0	8	41.2	177	46	21	21	5	0	1	3	5	2	37	4	1	5	.167	0-3	14	95	.722	3.85	4.54
2019 2 Tms		58	0	20	55.2	216	52	23	21	9	0	2	0	5	0	65	0	1	3	.250	4-6	18	96	.675	2.98	3.40
2020 Atl	NL	19	0	3	18.0	66	8	3	2	1	0	0	1	3	1	20	0	1	1	.500	1-1	6	94	.375	0.89	1.00
2021 Atl	NL	46	0	24	43.1	181	49	20	19	4	2	1	3	6	1	33	0	2	4	.333	1-5	13	95	.726	4.03	3.95
19 Tex	AL	38	0	15	38.0	147	35	13	13	8	0	1	0	4	0	43	0	0	2	.000	4-5	12	96	.716	3.27	3.08
19 Atl	NL	20	0	5	17.2	69	17	10	8	1	0	1	0	1	0	22	0	1	1	.500	0-1	6	95	.589	2.36	4.08
Postseason		8	0	1	8.0	32	5	2	2	1	0	1	1	2	0	6	0	0	1	.000	0-0	1	95	.536	2.17	2.25
6 ML YEARS		209	0	48	195.0	808	205	92	88	23	2	4	8	29	5	187	8	5	15	.250	7-16	59	95	.705	3.63	4.06

Corbin Martin

Pitches: R Bats: R Pos: SP-3; RP-2   Ht: 6'2" Wt: 225 Born: 12/28/1995 Age: 26

		HOW MUCH PITCHED					WHAT HE GAVE UP											THE RESULTS							
Year Team	Lg	G	GS	GF	IP	BFP	H	R	ER	HR	SH	SF	HB	TBB	IBB	SO	WP	W	L	Pct	Sv-Op	Hld	Vel	OPS	ERC	ERA
2021 Reno	AAA	6	6	0	27.1	133	31	21	18	7	1	2	0	19	0	30	2	2	0	1.000	0--	-	-	.892	7.16	5.93
2019 Hou	AL	5	5	0	19.1	92	23	14	12	8	0	0	0	12	0	19	1	1	1	.500	0-0	0	95	1.030	8.64	5.59
2021 Ari	NL	5	3	0	16.0	86	23	19	19	5	2	1	1	14	0	13	0	0	3	.000	0-0	0	94	1.114	10.95	10.69
2 ML YEARS		10	8	0	35.1	178	46	33	31	13	2	1	1	26	0	32	1	1	4	.200	0-0	0	95	1.070	9.70	7.90

Jason Martin

Bats: L Throws: R Pos: LF-41;PH-15;CF-3;RF-3;PR-2;DH-1   Ht: 5'9" Wt: 185 Born: 9/5/1995 Age: 26

						BATTING															RUNNING			AVERAGES			
Year Team	Lg	G	AB	H	2B	3B	HR	(Hm Rd)	TB	R	RBI	RC	TBB	IBB	SO	HBP	SH	SF	SB	CS	GDP	Avg	OBP	Slg	OPS
2021 RdRck	AAA	38	125	31	4	2	10	(- -)	69	27	27	-	27	1	34	2	1	1	2	3	3	.248	.387	.552	.939

Year	Team	Lg	G	AB	H	2B	3B	HR	(Hm	Rd)	TB	R	RBI	RC	TBB	IBB	SO	HBP	SH	SF	SB	CS	GDP	Avg	OBP	Slg	OPS
2019	Pit	NL	20	36	9	2	0	0	(0	0)	11	5	2	5	4	0	10	0	0	0	2	0	0	.250	.325	.306	.631
2020	Pit	NL	7	9	0	0	0	0	(0	0)	0	2	0	0	2	0	4	0	0	0	0	0	0	.000	.182	.000	.182
2021	Tex	AL	58	144	30	3	0	6	(2	4)	51	14	17	15	8	0	41	0	1	1	3	1	1	.208	.248	.354	.603
3 ML YEARS			85	189	39	5	0	6	(2	4)	62	21	19	20	14	0	55	0	1	1	5	1	1	.206	.260	.328	.588

Richie Martin

Bats: R **Throws:** R **Pos:** SS-37;PH-1 **Ht:** 6'0" **Wt:** 190 **Born:** 12/22/1994 **Age:** 27

Year	Team	Lg	G	AB	H	2B	3B	HR	(Hm	Rd)	TB	R	RBI	RC	TBB	IBB	SO	HBP	SH	SF	SB	CS	GDP	Avg	OBP	Slg	OPS
2021	Norfolk	AAA	27	96	20	4	2	1	(-	-)	31	12	5	-	14	0	25	2	0	0	5	3	4	.208	.321	.323	.644
2019	Bal	AL	120	283	59	8	3	6	(3	3)	91	29	23	17	14	0	83	6	5	1	10	1	6	.208	.260	.322	.581
2021	Bal	AL	37	98	23	2	0	1	(0	1)	28	9	8	5	4	0	28	1	1	0	0	2	1	.235	.269	.286	.555
2 ML YEARS			157	381	82	10	3	7	(3	4)	119	38	31	22	18	0	111	7	6	2	10	3	7	.215	.262	.312	.575

Carlos Martinez

Pitches: R **Bats:** R **Pos:** SP-16 **Ht:** 6'0" **Wt:** 200 **Born:** 9/21/1991 **Age:** 30

			HOW MUCH PITCHED				WHAT HE GAVE UP										THE RESULTS							
Year	Team	Lg	G	GS	GF	IP	BFP	H	R	ER	HR	SH	SF	HB	TBB	IBB	SO	WP	W	L	Pct	Sv-Op	Hld	Vel	OPS	ERC	ERA
2013	StL	NL	21	1	5	28.1	124	31	16	16	1	1	1	3	9	1	24	0	2	1	.667	1-1	3	97	.704	4.20	5.08
2014	StL	NL	57	7	13	89.1	386	90	41	40	4	7	1	4	36	8	84	8	2	4	.333	1-6	17	97	.713	3.79	4.03
2015	StL	NL	31	29	1	179.2	755	168	65	60	13	9	4	8	63	5	184	8	14	7	.667	0-0	1	95	.687	3.51	3.01
2016	StL	NL	31	31	0	195.1	809	169	68	66	15	2	2	11	70	1	174	8	16	9	.640	0-0	0	96	.643	3.29	3.04
2017	StL	NL	32	32	0	205.0	858	179	93	83	27	4	2	8	71	3	217	9	12	11	.522	0-0	0	96	.694	3.51	3.64
2018	StL	NL	33	18	9	118.2	521	100	48	41	5	7	4	11	60	4	117	5	8	6	.571	5-5	3	94	.647	3.46	3.11
2019	StL	NL	48	0	38	48.1	200	39	18	17	2	1	1	3	18	1	53	2	4	2	.667	24-27	3	96	.590	2.77	3.17
2020	StL	NL	5	5	0	20.0	104	32	26	22	6	0	2	0	10	2	17	0	0	3	.000	0-0	0	93	1.045	9.41	9.90
2021	StL	NL	16	16	0	82.1	363	77	58	57	8	1	2	11	36	2	57	3	4	9	.308	0-0	0	93	.732	4.32	6.23
	Postseason		20	0	4	20.1	86	16	12	12	2	1	1	1	11	3	18	2	1	2	.333	0-1	5	97	.718	3.45	5.31
9 ML YEARS			274	139	66	967.0	4120	885	433	402	81	32	19	59	373	27	927	43	62	52	.544	31-39	27	95	.686	3.64	3.74

J.D. Martinez

Bats: R **Throws:** R **Pos:** DH-113;LF-30;RF-8 **Ht:** 6'3" **Wt:** 230 **Born:** 8/21/1987 **Age:** 34

Year	Team	Lg	G	AB	H	2B	3B	HR	(Hm	Rd)	TB	R	RBI	RC	TBB	IBB	SO	HBP	SH	SF	SB	CS	GDP	Avg	OBP	Slg	OPS
2011	Hou	NL	53	208	57	13	0	6	(3	3)	88	29	35	30	13	1	48	2	0	3	0	1	4	.274	.319	.423	.742
2012	Hou	NL	113	395	95	14	3	11	(5	6)	148	34	55	45	40	0	96	1	0	2	0	2	18	.241	.311	.375	.685
2013	Hou	AL	86	296	74	17	0	7	(4	3)	112	24	36	29	10	0	82	0	0	3	0	0	8	.250	.272	.378	.650
2014	Det	AL	123	441	139	30	3	23	(13	10)	244	57	76	75	30	5	126	3	0	6	6	3	8	.315	.358	.553	.912
2015	Det	AL	158	596	168	33	2	38	(20	18)	319	93	102	100	53	7	178	5	0	3	3	2	11	.282	.344	.535	.879
2016	Det	AL	120	460	141	35	2	22	(13	9)	246	69	68	77	49	2	128	3	0	5	1	2	13	.307	.373	.535	.908
2017	2 Tms		119	432	131	26	3	45	(27	18)	298	85	104	92	53	8	128	0	0	4	4	0	23	.303	.376	.690	1.066
2018	Bos	AL	150	569	188	37	2	43	(26	17)	358	111	130	138	69	11	146	4	0	7	6	1	19	.330	.402	.629	1.031
2019	Bos	AL	146	575	175	33	2	36	(18	18)	320	98	105	117	72	9	138	4	0	5	2	0	19	.304	.383	.557	.939
2020	Bos	AL	54	211	45	16	0	7	(4	3)	82	22	27	23	22	3	59	2	0	2	1	0	6	.213	.291	.389	.680
2021	Bos	AL	148	570	163	42	3	28	(14	14)	295	92	99	105	55	6	150	3	0	5	0	0	18	.286	.349	.518	.867
17	Det	AL	57	200	61	13	2	16	(11	5)	126	38	39	39	29	5	54	0	0	3	2	0	10	.305	.388	.630	1.018
17	Ari	NL	62	232	70	13	1	29	(16	13)	172	47	65	53	24	3	74	0	0	1	2	0	13	.302	.366	.741	1.107
	Postseason		21	77	22	3	0	6	(1	5)	43	10	20	18	11	3	21	0	0	2	0	1	1	.286	.367	.558	.925
11 ML YEARS			1270	4753	1376	296	20	266	(147	119)	2510	714	837	831	466	52	1279	27	0	45	25	11	147	.290	.353	.528	.881

Seth Martinez

Pitches: R **Bats:** R **Pos:** RP-3 **Ht:** 6'2" **Wt:** 200 **Born:** 8/29/1994 **Age:** 27

			HOW MUCH PITCHED				WHAT HE GAVE UP										THE RESULTS							
Year	Team	Lg	G	GS	GF	IP	BFP	H	R	ER	HR	SH	SF	HB	TBB	IBB	SO	WP	W	L	Pct	Sv-Op	Hld	Vel	OPS	ERC	ERA
2021	SgrLnd	AAA	35	0	2	56.2	227	34	21	18	5	0	2	3	20	0	76	3	5	3	.625	0--	-		.558	1.96	2.86
2021	Hou	AL	3	0	3	3.0	16	5	5	5	0	0	0	0	3	0	3	0	0	0	-	0-0	0	90	1.038	10.34	15.00

Nick Martini

Bats: L **Throws:** L **Pos:** PH-16;LF-7;RF-7;PR-1 **Ht:** 5'11" **Wt:** 205 **Born:** 6/27/1990 **Age:** 32

Year	Team	Lg	G	AB	H	2B	3B	HR	(Hm	Rd)	TB	R	RBI	RC	TBB	IBB	SO	HBP	SH	SF	SB	CS	GDP	Avg	OBP	Slg	OPS
2021	Iowa	AAA	78	270	72	9	3	11	(-	-)	120	56	40	-	42	1	70	11	0	0	2	1	6	.267	.387	.444	.831
2018	Oak	AL	55	152	45	9	3	1	(1	0)	63	26	19	30	21	1	36	5	0	1	0	0	0	.296	.397	.414	.811
2019	2 Tms		32	93	21	4	1	1	(0	1)	30	8	7	14	14	0	26	1	0	1	0	0	0	.226	.330	.323	.653
2021	ChC	NL	25	37	10	1	0	0	(0	0)	11	4	4	4	6	1	10	0	0	2	0	1	0	.270	.356	.297	.653
19	Oak	AL	6	11	1	0	0	1	(0	1)	4	1	2	2	2	0	5	0	0	0	0	0	0	.091	.231	.364	.594
19	SD	NL	26	82	20	4	1	0	(0	0)	26	7	5	12	12	0	21	1	0	1	0	0	0	.244	.344	.317	.661
	Postseason		1	4	1	0	0	0	(0	0)	1	0	0	0	0	0	2	0	0	0	0	0	0	.250	.250	.250	.500
3 ML YEARS			112	282	76	14	4	2	(1	1)	104	38	30	48	41	2	72	6	0	4	0	1	0	.270	.369	.369	.738

Jorge Mateo

Bats: R **Throws:** R **Pos:** PH-32;2B-18;SS-18;CF-11;3B-9;RF-7;LF-6;PR-5 **Ht:** 6'0" **Wt:** 182 **Born:** 6/23/1995 **Age:** 27

Year	Team	Lg	G	AB	H	2B	3B	HR	(Hm	Rd)	TB	R	RBI	RC	TBB	IBB	SO	HBP	SH	SF	SB	CS	GDP	Avg	OBP	Slg	OPS
2020	SD	NL	22	26	4	3	0	0	(0	0)	7	4	2	2	1	0	11	0	1	0	1	0	1	.154	.185	.269	.454
2021	2 Tms		89	194	48	11	1	4	(1	3)	73	19	14	22	9	0	55	4	1	1	10	3	1	.247	.293	.376	.670
21	SD	NL	57	87	18	4	0	2	(0	2)	28	10	6	7	2	0	27	3	1	0	5	0	1	.207	.250	.322	.572
21	Bal	AL	32	107	30	7	1	2	(1	1)	45	9	8	15	7	0	28	1	0	1	5	3	0	.280	.328	.421	.748
	2 ML YEARS		111	220	52	14	1	4	(1	3)	80	23	16	24	10	0	66	4	2	1	11	3	2	.236	.281	.364	.644

Jeff Mathis

Bats: R **Throws:** R **Pos:** C-3 **Ht:** 6'0" **Wt:** 205 **Born:** 3/31/1983 **Age:** 39

Year	Team	Lg	G	AB	H	2B	3B	HR	(Hm	Rd)	TB	R	RBI	RC	TBB	IBB	SO	HBP	SH	SF	SB	CS	GDP	Avg	OBP	Slg	OPS
2005	LAA	AL	5	3	1	0	0	0	(0	0)	1	1	0	0	0	0	1	0	0	0	0	0	0	.333	.333	.333	.667
2006	LAA	AL	23	55	8	2	0	2	(1	1)	16	9	6	4	7	1	14	0	0	1	0	0	0	.145	.238	.291	.529
2007	LAA	AL	59	171	36	12	0	4	(3	1)	60	24	23	13	15	0	49	2	3	4	0	1	3	.211	.276	.351	.627
2008	LAA	AL	94	283	55	8	0	9	(4	5)	90	35	42	33	30	4	90	3	8	4	2	2	1	.194	.275	.318	.593
2009	LAA	AL	84	237	50	8	0	5	(3	2)	73	26	28	24	22	0	73	4	8	1	2	3	2	.211	.288	.308	.596
2010	LAA	AL	68	205	40	6	1	3	(2	1)	57	19	18	10	6	0	59	1	3	3	3	0	3	.195	.219	.278	.497
2011	LAA	AL	93	247	43	12	0	3	(1	2)	64	18	22	12	15	2	75	2	14	3	1	2	3	.174	.225	.259	.484
2012	Tor	AL	71	211	46	13	0	8	(5	3)	83	25	27	18	9	0	68	0	6	1	1	0	2	.218	.249	.393	.642
2013	Mia	NL	73	232	42	7	1	5	(3	2)	66	14	29	15	21	4	76	1	1	1	0	0	5	.181	.251	.284	.535
2014	Mia	NL	64	175	35	7	0	2	(1	1)	48	12	12	11	15	2	64	0	5	0	0	0	2	.200	.263	.274	.537
2015	Mia	NL	32	93	15	4	1	2	(1	1)	27	9	12	3	7	1	24	0	0	3	0	0	0	.161	.214	.290	.504
2016	Mia	NL	41	126	30	4	1	2	(0	2)	42	12	15	10	4	0	36	1	1	0	0	0	1	.238	.267	.333	.601
2017	Ari	NL	60	186	40	10	2	2	(2	0)	60	13	11	14	14	1	61	2	1	0	1	0	6	.215	.277	.323	.600
2018	Ari	NL	69	195	39	9	1	1	(1	0)	53	15	20	15	20	1	66	0	1	2	0	0	7	.200	.272	.272	.544
2019	Tex	AL	88	228	36	9	0	2	(1	1)	51	17	12	9	15	1	87	0	0	1	1	0	2	.158	.209	.224	.433
2020	Tex	AL	24	62	10	1	1	3	(2	1)	22	6	9	7	5	0	24	0	0	1	0	0	0	.161	.221	.355	.575
2021	Atl	NL	3	9	0	0	0	0	(0	0)	0	0	0	0	0	0	5	0	0	0	0	0	0	.000	.000	.000	.000
	Postseason		13	29	11	5	0	1	(0	1)	19	3	4	5	1	0	8	0	1	0	0	0	0	.379	.400	.655	1.055
	17 ML YEARS		951	2718	526	112	8	53	(30	23)	813	255	286	198	205	17	872	16	51	25	12	8	39	.194	.252	.299	.551

Wyatt Mathisen

Bats: R **Throws:** R **Pos:** 1B-13;PH-11;3B-4;LF-2 **Ht:** 6'0" **Wt:** 217 **Born:** 12/30/1993 **Age:** 28

Year	Team	Lg	G	AB	H	2B	3B	HR	(Hm	Rd)	TB	R	RBI	RC	TBB	IBB	SO	HBP	SH	SF	SB	CS	GDP	Avg	OBP	Slg	OPS
2021	Drham	AAA	18	59	17	5	0	3	(-	-)	31	12	9	-	3	0	17	2	0	0	0	0	3	.288	.344	.525	.869
2021	Tacom	AAA	32	102	14	3	0	2	(-	-)	23	13	12	-	20	1	30	6	0	1	0	0	0	.137	.310	.225	.536
2021	Scrmto	AAA	19	64	15	3	0	5	(-	-)	33	13	11	-	7	0	20	2	0	0	0	0	0	.234	.329	.516	.844
2020	Ari	NL	9	27	6	0	0	2	(-	-)	12	5	5	5	5	0	12	1	0	0	0	0	0	.222	.364	.444	.808
2021	Ari	NL	23	42	5	0	0	1	(1	0)	8	3	8	3	5	0	21	3	0	1	0	0	0	.119	.255	.190	.445
	2 ML YEARS		32	69	11	0	0	3	(3	0)	20	8	13	8	10	0	33	4	0	1	0	0	0	.159	.298	.290	.587

Nick Maton

Bats: L **Throws:** R **Pos:** 2B-21;SS-20;PH-11;PR-1 **Ht:** 6'2" **Wt:** 178 **Born:** 2/18/1997 **Age:** 25

Year	Team	Lg	G	AB	H	2B	3B	HR	(Hm	Rd)	TB	R	RBI	RC	TBB	IBB	SO	HBP	SH	SF	SB	CS	GDP	Avg	OBP	Slg	OPS
2021	LV	AAA	60	197	39	11	2	5	(-	-)	69	29	27	-	35	0	58	4	2	2	3	2	3	.198	.328	.350	.678
2021	Phi	NL	52	117	30	7	1	2	(0	2)	45	16	14	17	10	0	39	2	1	1	2	0	0	.256	.323	.385	.708

Phil Maton

Pitches: R **Bats:** R **Pos:** RP-64; SP-1 **Ht:** 6'2" **Wt:** 206 **Born:** 3/25/1993 **Age:** 29

Year	Team	Lg	G	GS	GF	IP	BFP	H	R	ER	HR	SH	SF	HB	TBB	IBB	SO	WP	W	L	Pct	Sv-Op	Hld	Vel	OPS	ERC	ERA
2017	SD	NL	46	0	12	43.0	180	41	23	20	10	0	0	1	14	0	46	0	3	2	.600	1-1	8	93	.778	4.56	4.19
2018	SD	NL	45	0	12	47.1	214	50	25	23	7	3	2	1	23	1	55	4	0	2	.000	0-1	3	91	.757	4.55	4.37
2019	2 Tms		30	0	13	36.2	163	38	27	25	7	2	0	2	12	0	33	0	0	0	-	0-0	7	91	.806	4.72	6.14
2020	Cle	AL	23	0	4	21.2	96	23	14	11	4	0	0	4	6	1	32	1	3	3	.500	0-1	4	94	.716	4.18	4.57
2021	2 Tms		65	1	5	66.2	297	65	36	35	6	0	5	6	32	0	85	0	6	0	1.000	0-4	5	92	.772	4.52	4.73
19	SD	NL	21	0	5	24.1	115	34	22	21	6	2	0	1	6	0	20	1	0	0	-	0-0	2	91	.948	6.90	7.77
19	Cle	AL	9	0	8	12.1	48	4	5	4	1	0	0	1	6	0	13	2	0	0	-	0-0	0	90	.449	1.36	2.92
21	Cle	AL	38	1	3	41.1	178	36	21	21	4	0	3	3	20	0	61	0	2	0	1.000	0-1	3	92	.766	3.98	4.57
21	Hou	AL	27	0	2	25.1	119	29	15	14	2	0	2	3	12	0	24	0	4	0	1.000	0-3	2	91	.782	5.44	4.97
	Postseason		2	0	0	3.1	12	1	1	1	0	0	1	0	1	0	1	0	0	0	-	0-0	0	93	.367	0.57	2.70
	5 ML YEARS		209	1	46	215.1	950	217	125	114	27	4	6	15	87	2	251	8	12	7	.632	1-7	22	92	.770	4.55	4.76

Isaac Mattson

Pitches: R **Bats:** R **Pos:** RP-4 **Ht:** 6'2" **Wt:** 205 **Born:** 7/14/1995 **Age:** 26

Year	Team	Lg	G	GS	GF	IP	BFP	H	R	ER	HR	SH	SF	HB	TBB	IBB	SO	WP	W	L	Pct	Sv-Op	Hld	Vel	OPS	ERC	ERA
2021	Norfolk	AAA	17	0	6	16.1	78	24	13	12	3	1	0	1	6	0	22	2	0	2	.000	2- -	-	-	.960	7.77	6.61
2021	Bal	AL	4	0	3	4.1	23	5	3	3	0	0	0	0	5	0	3	1	0	0	-	0-0	0	93	.768	7.01	6.23

Steven Matz

Pitches: L Bats: R Pos: SP-29   Ht: 6'2" Wt: 201 Born: 5/29/1991 Age: 31

			HOW MUCH PITCHED					WHAT HE GAVE UP											THE RESULTS						
Year	Team	Lg	G	GS	GF	IP	BFP	H	R	ER	HR	SH	SF	HB	TBB	IBB	SO	WP	W	L	Pct	Sv-Op	Hld	Vel	OPS	ERC	ERA
2015	NYM	NL	6	6	0	35.2	149	34	9	9	4	1	1	1	10	0	34	0	4	0	1.000	0-0	0	94	.650	3.55	2.27
2016	NYM	NL	22	22	0	132.1	547	129	53	50	14	8	1	5	31	2	129	3	9	8	.529	0-0	0	94	.689	3.49	3.40
2017	NYM	NL	13	13	0	66.2	298	83	46	45	12	3	1	3	19	2	48	1	2	7	.222	0-0	0	93	.860	5.78	6.08
2018	NYM	NL	30	30	0	154.0	654	134	77	68	25	6	2	10	58	2	152	0	5	11	.313	0-0	0	93	.730	3.91	3.97
2019	NYM	NL	32	30	0	160.1	691	163	83	75	27	5	1	7	52	7	153	3	11	10	.524	0-0	1	93	.777	4.44	4.21
2020	NYM	NL	9	6	1	30.2	142	42	33	33	14	1	1	0	10	0	36	2	0	5	.000	0-0	0	95	1.069	8.76	9.68
2021	Tor	AL	29	29	0	150.2	647	158	70	64	18	0	1	6	43	0	144	5	14	7	.667	0-0	0	95	.725	4.18	3.82
	Postseason		3	3	0	14.2	64	17	6	6	0	0	0	0	4	1	13	0	0	1	.000	0-0	0	94	.678	3.60	3.68
	7 ML YEARS		141	136	1	730.1	3128	743	371	344	114	24	8	32	223	13	696	14	45	48	.484	0-0	1	94	.756	4.33	4.24

Tyler Matzek

Pitches: L Bats: L Pos: RP-69
MATT-zick   Ht: 6'3" Wt: 230 Born: 10/19/1990 Age: 31

			HOW MUCH PITCHED					WHAT HE GAVE UP											THE RESULTS						
Year	Team	Lg	G	GS	GF	IP	BFP	H	R	ER	HR	SH	SF	HB	TBB	IBB	SO	WP	W	L	Pct	Sv-Op	Hld	Vel	OPS	ERC	ERA
2014	Col	NL	20	19	1	117.2	503	120	53	53	9	4	3	3	44	1	91	3	6	11	.353	0-0	0	93	.749	4.06	4.05
2015	Col	NL	5	5	0	22.0	102	21	10	10	2	1	1	3	19	0	15	2	2	1	.667	0-0	0	92	.823	6.45	4.09
2020	Atl	NL	21	0	3	29.0	121	23	9	9	1	0	0	2	10	0	43	1	4	3	.571	0-2	1	94	.574	2.57	2.79
2021	Atl	NL	69	0	13	63.0	264	40	19	18	3	4	1	2	37	5	77	6	0	4	.000	0-0	24	96	.581	2.48	2.57
	Postseason		7	0	0	8.2	34	6	1	1	1	0	0	0	3	0	14	1	1	0	1.000	0-0	1	96	.587	2.42	1.04
	4 ML YEARS		115	24	17	231.2	990	204	91	90	15	9	5	10	110	6	226	12	12	19	.387	0-2	25	94	.691	3.61	3.50

Ronny Mauricio

Bats: B Throws: R Pos: SS   Ht: 6'3" Wt: 166 Born: 4/4/2001 Age: 21

			BATTING																			RUNNING			AVERAGES			
Year	Team	Lg	G	AB	H	2B	3B	HR	(Hm	Rd)	TB	R	RBI	RC	TBB	IBB	SO	HBP	SH	SF	SB	CS	GDP	Avg	OBP	Slg	OPS
2018	2 Tms	Low	57	227	62	16	3	3	(-	-)	93	32	35	27	13	0	40			7	2	6	3	.273	.304	.410	.713
2019	Columb	A	116	470	126	20	5	4	(-	-)	168	62	37	54	23	2	99	5	3	5	6	10	3	.268	.307	.357	.665
2021	Bklyn	A+	100	392	95	14	5	19	(-	-)	176	55	63	0	24	0	101	3	0	1	9	7	7	.242	.290	.449	.739

Dustin May

Pitches: R Bats: R Pos: SP-5   Ht: 6'6" Wt: 180 Born: 9/6/1997 Age: 24

			HOW MUCH PITCHED					WHAT HE GAVE UP											THE RESULTS						
Year	Team	Lg	G	GS	GF	IP	BFP	H	R	ER	HR	SH	SF	HB	TBB	IBB	SO	WP	W	L	Pct	Sv-Op	Hld	Vel	OPS	ERC	ERA
2019	LAD	NL	14	4	0	34.2	141	33	17	14	2	0	0	4	5	0	32	0	2	3	.400	0-1	4	96	.639	3.06	3.63
2020	LAD	NL	12	10	0	56.0	224	45	18	16	9	1	1	1	16	0	44	2	3	1	.750	0-0	0	98	.649	3.08	2.57
2021	LAD	NL	5	5	0	23.0	93	16	8	7	4	0	0	1	6	0	35	0	1	1	.500	0-0	0	98	.596	2.49	2.74
	Postseason		9	3	1	14.0	59	13	7	6	1	1	1	1	7	1	14	0	1	0	1.000	0-0	0	99	.770	4.22	3.86
	3 ML YEARS		31	19	0	113.2	458	94	43	37	15	1	1	6	27	0	111	2	6	5	.545	0-1	4	97	.635	2.96	2.93

Trevor May

Pitches: R Bats: R Pos: RP-68   Ht: 6'5" Wt: 240 Born: 9/23/1989 Age: 32

			HOW MUCH PITCHED					WHAT HE GAVE UP											THE RESULTS						
Year	Team	Lg	G	GS	GF	IP	BFP	H	R	ER	HR	SH	SF	HB	TBB	IBB	SO	WP	W	L	Pct	Sv-Op	Hld	Vel	OPS	ERC	ERA
2014	Min	AL	10	9	0	45.2	213	59	41	40	7	0	1	2	22	1	44	3	2	6	.333	0-0	0	92	.900	6.80	7.88
2015	Min	AL	48	16	9	114.2	492	127	53	51	11	3	4	4	26	2	110	4	8	9	.471	0-2	7	93	.752	4.06	4.00
2016	Min	AL	44	0	10	42.2	187	39	26	25	7	0	0	2	17	1	60	10	2	2	.500	0-2	6	94	.757	4.07	5.27
2018	Min	AL	24	1	6	25.1	103	21	9	9	4	2	0	1	5	0	36	1	4	1	.800	3-3	5	94	.646	2.85	3.20
2019	Min	AL	65	0	13	64.1	266	43	24	21	8	0	3	3	26	1	79	3	5	3	.625	2-4	17	96	.587	2.59	2.94
2020	Min	AL	24	0	4	23.1	96	20	11	10	5	0	1	0	7	0	38	2	1	0	1.000	2-2	8	96	.679	3.61	3.86
2021	NYM	NL	68	0	19	62.2	266	55	29	25	10	0	0	0	24	4	83	7	7	3	.700	4-7	16	97	.698	3.58	3.59
	Postseason		4	0	1	3.0	10	1	0	0	0	0	0	0	0	0	2	0	0	0	-	0-0	1	96	.200	0.25	0.00
	7 ML YEARS		283	26	61	378.2	1623	364	193	181	52	5	9	12	127	9	450	30	30	24	.556	11-20	59	94	.725	3.91	4.30

Cameron Maybin

Bats: R Throws: R Pos: CF-6;LF-4;RF-3   Ht: 6'3" Wt: 215 Born: 4/4/1987 Age: 35

			BATTING																			RUNNING			AVERAGES			
Year	Team	Lg	G	AB	H	2B	3B	HR	(Hm	Rd)	TB	R	RBI	RC	TBB	IBB	SO	HBP	SH	SF	SB	CS	GDP	Avg	OBP	Slg	OPS
2021	Iowa	AAA	10	39	4	1	0	1	(-	-)	8	5	3	-	4	0	14	0	0	1	1	0	1	.103	.186	.205	.391
2021	Syrcse	AAA	12	44	8	2	0	0	(-	-)	10	5	5	-	5	0	14	0	0	0	0	0	1	.182	.265	.227	.493
2007	Det	AL	24	49	7	3	0	1	(0	1)	13	8	2	2	3	0	21	1	0	0	5	0	0	.143	.208	.265	.473
2008	Fla	NL	8	32	16	2	0	0	(0	0)	18	9	2	8	3	0	8	0	1	0	4	0	0	.500	.543	.563	1.105
2009	Fla	NL	54	176	44	12	2	4	(1	3)	72	30	13	15	17	1	51	1	4	1	1	3	2	.250	.318	.409	.727
2010	Fla	NL	82	291	68	7	3	8	(5	3)	105	46	28	37	24	1	92	5	1	1	9	2	4	.234	.302	.361	.663
2011	SD	NL	137	516	136	24	8	9	(2	7)	203	82	40	69	44	2	125	2	4	2	40	8	6	.264	.323	.393	.716
2012	SD	NL	147	507	123	20	5	8	(3	5)	177	67	45	52	44	1	110	4	3	3	26	7	12	.243	.306	.349	.656
2013	SD	NL	14	51	8	1	0	1	(0	1)	12	7	5	5	4	1	9	1	1	0	4	1	3	.157	.232	.235	.467
2014	SD	NL	95	251	59	13	4	1	(0	1)	83	24	15	22	19	2	56	1	0	1	4	3	3	.235	.290	.331	.622
2015	Atl	NL	141	505	135	18	2	10	(5	5)	187	65	59	64	45	1	102	1	1	3	23	6	16	.267	.327	.370	.697
2016	Det	AL	94	349	110	14	5	4	(3	1)	146	65	43	60	36	0	69	3	2	1	15	6	8	.315	.383	.418	.801
2017	2 Tms	AL	114	395	90	20	2	10	(3	7)	144	63	35	51	51	1	94	2	1	1	33	8	12	.228	.318	.365	.683
2018	2 Tms	AL	129	342	85	14	2	4	(2	2)	115	32	28	38	38	1	75	2	0	2	10	5	7	.249	.326	.336	.662
2019	NYY	AL	82	239	68	17	0	11	(5	6)	118	48	32	36	30	0	72	0	0	0	9	6	5	.285	.364	.494	.858

Year Team	Lg	G	AB	H	2B	3B	HR	(Hm	Rd)	TB	R	RBI	RC	TBB	IBB	SO	HBP	SH	SF	SB	CS	GDP	Avg	OBP	Slg	OPS
2020 2 Tms		32	93	23	8	1	1	(1	0)	36	8	7	9	7	0	25	1	0	0	3	0	4	.247	.307	.387	.694
2021 NYM	NL	9	28	1	0	0	0	(0	0)	1	2	0	0	3	0	12	2	0	0	1	0	0	.036	.182	.036	.218
17 LAA	AL	93	336	79	19	1	6	(2	4)	118	57	22	42	48	1	78	2	0	1	29	5	11	.235	.333	.351	.685
17 Hou	AL	21	59	11	1	1	4	(1	3)	26	6	13	9	3	0	16	0	1	0	4	3	1	.186	.226	.441	.666
18 Mia	NL	99	251	63	12	1	3	(2	1)	86	20	20	20	32	1	55	2	0	2	8	5	3	.251	.338	.343	.681
18 Sea	AL	30	91	22	2	1	1	(0	1)	29	12	8	9	6	0	20	0	0	0	2	0	4	.242	.289	.319	.607
20 Det	AL	14	41	10	4	0	1	(1	0)	17	5	2	2	4	0	13	0	0	0	0	0	3	.244	.311	.415	.726
20 ChC	NL	18	52	13	4	1	0	(0	0)	19	3	5	7	3	0	12	0	1	0	3	0	1	.250	.304	.365	.669
Postseason		13	15	4	0	0	1	(0	1)	7	4	1	3	2	0	6	0	0	0	3	0	0	.267	.353	.467	.820
15 ML YEARS		1162	3824	973	173	34	72	(30	42)	1430	556	354	463	368	11	921	26	18	15	187	55	87	.254	.323	.374	.697

Marcelo Mayer

Bats: L **Throws:** R **Pos:** SS   **Ht:** 6'3" **Wt:** 188 **Born:** 12/12/2002 **Age:** 19

Year Team	Lg	G	AB	H	2B	3B	HR	(Hm	Rd)	TB	R	RBI	RC	TBB	IBB	SO	HBP	SH	SF	SB	CS	GDP	Avg	OBP	Slg	OPS
2021 RedSx	R	26	91	25	4	1	3	(-	-)	40	25	17	0	15	0	27	0	0	0	7	1	1	.275	.377	.440	.817

Mike Mayers

Pitches: R **Bats:** R **Pos:** RP-70; SP-2   MY-erz   **Ht:** 6'2" **Wt:** 220 **Born:** 12/6/1991 **Age:** 30

Year Team	Lg	G	GS	GF	IP	BFP	H	R	ER	HR	SH	SF	HB	TBB	IBB	SO	WP	W	L	Pct	Sv-Op	Hld	Vel	OPS	ERC	ERA
2016 StL	NL	4	1	0	5.1	35	16	16	16	3	0	1	1	3	0	2	0	1	1	.500	0-0	0	93	1.438	25.90	27.00
2017 StL	NL	3	0	1	4.2	25	8	8	6	2	0	2	0	4	1	3	0	0	0	-	0-0	0	94	1.427	13.79	11.57
2018 StL	NL	50	0	15	51.2	226	59	28	27	7	3	3	1	15	1	49	4	2	1	.667	1-1	6	96	.822	4.72	4.70
2019 StL	NL	16	0	4	19.0	88	21	14	14	3	0	0	1	11	2	16	1	0	1	1.000	0-0	1	95	.888	5.90	6.63
2020 LAA	AL	29	0	4	30.0	121	18	10	7	2	0	0	1	9	0	43	0	2	0	1.000	2-4	5	94	.484	1.59	2.10
2021 LAA	AL	72	2	9	75.0	315	71	32	32	11	1	1	3	26	0	90	0	5	5	.500	2-5	17	95	.748	4.10	3.84
6 ML YEARS		174	3	33	185.2	810	193	108	102	28	4	7	7	68	4	203	5	10	8	.556	5-10	29	95	.791	4.63	4.94

Jack Mayfield

Bats: R **Throws:** R **Pos:** 3B-68;SS-12;2B-9;PH-1;PR-1   **Ht:** 5'11" **Wt:** 190 **Born:** 9/30/1990 **Age:** 31

Year Team	Lg	G	AB	H	2B	3B	HR	(Hm	Rd)	TB	R	RBI	RC	TBB	IBB	SO	HBP	SH	SF	SB	CS	GDP	Avg	OBP	Slg	OPS
2021 Salt Lk	AAA	15	70	23	2	3	5	(-	-)	46	14	11	-	5	1	8	1	0	0	1	1	2	.329	.382	.657	1.039
2019 Hou	AL	26	64	10	5	0	2	(0	2)	21	8	5	3	1	0	16	0	0	0	0	0	0	.156	.169	.328	.497
2020 Hou	AL	21	42	8	1	0	0	(0	0)	9	5	3	1	2	0	14	1	1	1	0	0	1	.190	.239	.214	.453
2021 2 Tms	AL	87	266	58	15	0	10	(5	5)	103	30	39	29	17	0	68	3	3	1	5	0	6	.218	.272	.387	.659
21 LAA	AL	75	232	52	14	0	10	(5	5)	96	28	36	29	16	0	58	3	3	1	5	0	4	.224	.282	.414	.696
21 Sea	AL	12	34	6	1	0	0	(0	0)	7	2	3	0	1	0	10	0	0	0	0	0	2	.176	.200	.206	.406
3 ML YEARS		134	372	76	21	0	12	(5	7)	133	43	47	33	20	0	98	4	4	2	5	0	7	.204	.251	.358	.609

Tim Mayza

Pitches: L **Bats:** L **Pos:** RP-61   **Ht:** 6'3" **Wt:** 220 **Born:** 1/15/1992 **Age:** 30

Year Team	Lg	G	GS	GF	IP	BFP	H	R	ER	HR	SH	SF	HB	TBB	IBB	SO	WP	W	L	Pct	Sv-Op	Hld	Vel	OPS	ERC	ERA
2017 Tor	AL	19	0	7	17.0	79	24	15	13	3	0	0	0	4	0	27	0	1	0	1.000	0-0	2	94	.874	6.27	6.88
2018 Tor	AL	37	0	9	35.2	151	33	13	13	3	0	0	2	14	4	40	2	2	0	1.000	0-0	1	94	.695	3.61	3.28
2019 Tor	AL	68	0	5	51.1	227	45	29	28	8	1	2	1	27	2	55	4	1	3	.250	0-1	18	94	.741	4.20	4.91
2021 Tor	AL	61	0	10	53.0	210	40	21	20	5	1	0	3	12	0	57	2	5	2	.714	1-4	18	94	.572	2.34	3.40
4 ML YEARS		185	0	31	157.0	667	142	78	74	19	2	2	6	57	6	179	8	9	5	.643	1-5	39	94	.693	3.61	4.24

Nomar Mazara

Bats: L **Throws:** L **Pos:** RF-41;DH-7;PH-3   **Ht:** 6'4" **Wt:** 224 **Born:** 4/26/1995 **Age:** 27

Year Team	Lg	G	AB	H	2B	3B	HR	(Hm	Rd)	TB	R	RBI	RC	TBB	IBB	SO	HBP	SH	SF	SB	CS	GDP	Avg	OBP	Slg	OPS
2016 Tex	AL	145	516	137	13	3	20	(7	13)	216	59	64	67	39	1	112	6	0	7	0	2	12	.266	.320	.419	.739
2017 Tex	AL	148	554	140	30	2	20	(11	9)	234	64	101	87	55	6	127	4	0	3	2	2	12	.253	.323	.422	.745
2018 Tex	AL	128	489	116	25	1	20	(15	5)	213	61	77	67	40	2	116	4	0	3	1	0	13	.258	.317	.436	.753
2019 Tex	AL	116	429	115	27	1	19	(8	11)	201	69	66	60	28	2	108	6	0	6	4	1	5	.268	.318	.469	.786
2020 CWS	AL	42	136	31	6	0	1	(0	1)	40	13	15	16	10	0	44	3	0	0	0	1	0	.228	.295	.294	.589
2021 Det	AL	50	165	35	5	2	3	(2	1)	53	12	19	19	10	0	45	0	0	1	0	0	4	.212	.276	.321	.597
Postseason		4	12	4	1	0	0	(0	0)	5	1	2	2	1	0	6	0	0	0	0	0	0	.333	.385	.417	.801
6 ML YEARS		629	2289	584	106	9	83	(43	40)	957	278	342	316	187	11	552	23	0	20	7	6	46	.255	.315	.418	.733

Patrick Mazeika

Bats: L **Throws:** R **Pos:** C-24;PH-14;1B-1;DH-1   **Ht:** 6'3" **Wt:** 210 **Born:** 10/14/1993 **Age:** 28

Year Team	Lg	G	AB	H	2B	3B	HR	(Hm	Rd)	TB	R	RBI	RC	TBB	IBB	SO	HBP	SH	SF	SB	CS	GDP	Avg	OBP	Slg	OPS
2021 Syrcse	AAA	44	157	44	9	0	7	(-	-)	74	22	33	-	17	0	19	3	0	3	0	0	1	.280	.356	.471	.827
2021 NYM	NL	37	79	15	3	0	1	(0	1)	21	6	6	3	4	1	18	3	0	1	0	0	2	.190	.253	.266	.519

Chris Mazza

Pitches: R **Bats:** R **Pos:** RP-14   **Ht:** 6'4" **Wt:** 190 **Born:** 10/17/1989 **Age:** 32

			HOW MUCH PITCHED					WHAT HE GAVE UP										THE RESULTS						
Year	Team	Lg	G	GS	GF	IP	BFP	H	R	ER	HR	SH	SF	HB	TBB	IBB	SO	WP	W	L	Pct	Sv-Op	Hld	Vel	OPS	ERC	ERA
2021	Drham	AAA	25	3	3	36.0	150	26	14	13	3	0	0	4	13	1	44	2	4	1	.800	0- -	-	-	.595	2.69	3.25
2019	NYM	NL	9	0	6	16.1	74	21	10	10	0	0	1	4	5	0	11	0	1	1	.500	0-0	0	92	.905	5.81	5.51
2020	Bos	AL	9	6	0	30.0	136	34	18	16	3	0	1	2	15	0	29	4	1	2	.333	0-0	0	92	.790	5.61	4.80
2021	TB	AL	14	0	7	27.1	112	26	14	14	3	0	2	2	7	1	21	3	0	0	-	1-1	0	90	.718	3.64	4.61
	3 ML YEARS		32	6	13	73.2	322	81	42	40	6	0	4	8	27	1	61	7	2	3	.400	1-1	0	92	.791	4.91	4.89

Ryan McBroom

Bats: R **Throws:** L **Pos:** PH-6;DH-1   **Ht:** 6'3" **Wt:** 220 **Born:** 4/9/1992 **Age:** 30

			BATTING																		RUNNING			AVERAGES			
Year	Team	Lg	G	AB	H	2B	3B	HR	(Hm	Rd)	TB	R	RBI	RC	TBB	IBB	SO	HBP	SH	SF	SB	CS	GDP	Avg	OBP	Slg	OPS
2021	Omha	AAA	114	430	113	14	2	32	(-	-)	227	78	87	-	47	1	108	5	0	4	3	1	12	.263	.340	.528	.867
2019	KC	AL	23	75	22	5	0	0	(0	0)	27	8	6	7	7	0	25	1	0	0	0	0	3	.293	.361	.360	.721
2020	KC	AL	36	81	20	3	0	6	(3	3)	41	8	10	8	4	0	30	0	0	0	0	0	2	.247	.282	.506	.789
2021	KC	AL	7	8	2	0	0	0	(0	0)	2	1	0	1	1	0	6	0	0	0	0	0	0	.250	.333	.250	.583
	3 ML YEARS		66	164	44	8	0	6	(3	3)	70	17	16	16	12	0	61	1	0	0	0	0	5	.268	.322	.427	.749

James McCann

Bats: R **Throws:** R **Pos:** C-107;PH-13;1B-6;DH-1   **Ht:** 6'3" **Wt:** 220 **Born:** 6/13/1990 **Age:** 32

			BATTING																		RUNNING			AVERAGES			
Year	Team	Lg	G	AB	H	2B	3B	HR	(Hm	Rd)	TB	R	RBI	RC	TBB	IBB	SO	HBP	SH	SF	SB	CS	GDP	Avg	OBP	Slg	OPS
2014	Det	AL	9	12	3	1	0	0	(0	0)	4	2	0	1	0	0	2	0	0	0	1	0	0	.250	.250	.333	.583
2015	Det	AL	114	401	106	18	5	7	(5	2)	155	32	41	34	16	0	90	3	4	1	0	1	17	.264	.297	.387	.683
2016	Det	AL	105	344	76	9	1	12	(7	5)	123	31	48	30	23	0	109	2	1	3	0	1	12	.221	.272	.358	.629
2017	Det	AL	106	352	89	14	2	13	(8	5)	146	39	49	46	26	0	89	9	1	3	1	0	8	.253	.318	.415	.733
2018	Det	AL	118	427	94	16	0	8	(5	3)	134	31	39	31	26	0	116	2	0	2	0	3	9	.220	.267	.314	.581
2019	CWS	AL	118	439	120	26	1	18	(8	10)	202	62	60	67	30	1	137	6	1	0	4	1	10	.273	.328	.460	.789
2020	CWS	AL	31	97	28	3	0	7	(4	3)	52	20	15	16	8	0	30	4	0	2	1	1	2	.289	.360	.536	.896
2021	NYM	NL	121	375	87	12	1	10	(4	6)	131	29	46	37	32	1	115	2	0	3	1	2	12	.232	.294	.349	.643
	Postseason		2	6	1	0	0	0	(0	0)	1	1	0	0	0	0	3	1	0	0	0	0	0	.167	.286	.167	.452
	8 ML YEARS		722	2447	603	99	10	75	(41	34)	947	246	298	262	161	2	688	28	7	14	8	9	70	.246	.299	.387	.686

Jake McCarthy

Bats: L **Throws:** L **Pos:** CF-14;RF-6;PH-5;PR-1   **Ht:** 6'2" **Wt:** 215 **Born:** 7/30/1997 **Age:** 24

			BATTING																		RUNNING			AVERAGES			
Year	Team	Lg	G	AB	H	2B	3B	HR	(Hm	Rd)	TB	R	RBI	RC	TBB	IBB	SO	HBP	SH	SF	SB	CS	GDP	Avg	OBP	Slg	OPS
2021	Amrillo	AA	35	137	33	8	4	6	(-	-)	67	25	23	-	17	0	46	2	0	0	17	1	1	.241	.333	.489	.822
2021	Reno	AAA	50	191	50	6	7	9	(-	-)	97	38	31	-	20	0	49	0	0	1	12	3	0	.262	.330	.508	.838
2021	Ari	NL	24	59	13	3	0	2	(1	1)	22	11	4	5	8	0	23	2	1	0	3	2	0	.220	.333	.373	.706

Darren McCaughan

mih-CACK-en   **Ht:** 6'1" **Wt:** 200 **Born:** 3/18/1996 **Age:** 26

Pitches: R **Bats:** R **Pos:** SP-1; RP-1

			HOW MUCH PITCHED					WHAT HE GAVE UP											THE RESULTS						
Year	Team	Lg	G	GS	GF	IP	BFP	H	R	ER	HR	SH	SF	HB	TBB	IBB	SO	WP	W	L	Pct	Sv-Op	Hld	Vel	OPS	ERC	ERA
2021	Tacom	AAA	19	19	0	108.2	445	105	59	56	19	0	6	7	15	0	91	1	5	4	.556	0- -	-	-	.743	3.60	4.64
2021	Sea	AL	2	1	0	9.0	39	8	8	8	3	1	1	1	4	0	2	0	0	0	-	0-0	0	88	.936	5.79	8.00

Shane McClanahan

Pitches: L **Bats:** L **Pos:** SP-25   **Ht:** 6'1" **Wt:** 200 **Born:** 4/28/1997 **Age:** 25

			HOW MUCH PITCHED					WHAT HE GAVE UP											THE RESULTS						
Year	Team	Lg	G	GS	GF	IP	BFP	H	R	ER	HR	SH	SF	HB	TBB	IBB	SO	WP	W	L	Pct	Sv-Op	Hld	Vel	OPS	ERC	ERA
2021	TB	AL	25	25	0	123.1	517	120	49	47	14	2	0	2	37	0	141	9	10	6	.625	0-0	0	96	.697	3.71	3.43
	Postseason		4	0	2	4.1	24	8	5	4	2	0	1	0	2	0	4	0	0	0	-	0-0	0	97	1.131	12.37	8.31

Chas McCormick

Bats: R **Throws:** L **Pos:** LF-51;CF-33;RF-22;PR-10;PH-9;DH-3   **Ht:** 6'0" **Wt:** 208 **Born:** 4/19/1995 **Age:** 27

			BATTING																		RUNNING			AVERAGES			
Year	Team	Lg	G	AB	H	2B	3B	HR	(Hm	Rd)	TB	R	RBI	RC	TBB	IBB	SO	HBP	SH	SF	SB	CS	GDP	Avg	OBP	Slg	OPS
2021	Hou	AL	108	284	73	12	0	14	(7	7)	127	47	50	45	25	0	104	4	0	7	4	2	5	.257	.319	.447	.766

Lance McCullers Jr.

Pitches: R **Bats:** L **Pos:** SP-28   **Ht:** 6'1" **Wt:** 202 **Born:** 10/2/1993 **Age:** 28

			HOW MUCH PITCHED					WHAT HE GAVE UP											THE RESULTS						
Year	Team	Lg	G	GS	GF	IP	BFP	H	R	ER	HR	SH	SF	HB	TBB	IBB	SO	WP	W	L	Pct	Sv-Op	Hld	Vel	OPS	ERC	ERA
2015	Hou	AL	22	22	0	125.2	520	106	49	45	10	0	3	5	43	2	129	8	6	7	.462	0-0	0	94	.659	3.02	3.22
2016	Hou	AL	14	14	0	81.0	352	80	29	29	5	0	0	6	45	1	106	9	6	5	.545	0-0	0	94	.736	4.42	3.22
2017	Hou	AL	22	22	0	118.2	512	114	61	56	8	2	2	11	40	1	132	8	7	4	.636	0-0	0	94	.696	3.71	4.25
2018	Hou	AL	25	22	0	128.1	527	100	60	55	12	1	4	7	50	0	142	14	10	6	.625	0-0	1	94	.653	3.05	3.86

			HOW MUCH PITCHED						WHAT HE GAVE UP											THE RESULTS							
Year	Team	Lg	G	GS	GF	IP	BFP	H	R	ER	HR	SH	SF	HB	TBB	IBB	SO	WP	W	L	Pct	Sv-Op	Hld	Vel	OPS	ERC	ERA
2020	Hou	AL	11	11	0	55.0	227	44	29	24	5	1	1	5	20	0	56	0	3	3	.500	0-0	0	94	.710	3.19	3.93
2021	Hou	AL	28	28	0	162.1	684	122	59	57	11	1	1	10	76	0	185	7	13	5	.722	0-0	0	94	.628	3.08	3.16
	Postseason		14	7	1	46.2	192	35	22	17	9	0	0	8	15	0	53	2	1	2	.333	1-1	0	94	.693	3.75	3.28
6 ML YEARS			122	119	0	671.0	2822	566	287	266	53	5	11	38	274	4	750	46	45	30	.600	0-0	1	94	.671	3.34	3.57

Andrew McCutchen

Bats: R **Throws:** R **Pos:** LF-135;PH-11;DH-1

Ht: 5'11" **Wt:** 195 **Born:** 10/10/1986 **Age:** 35

			BATTING																			RUNNING			AVERAGES			
Year	Team	Lg	G	AB	H	2B	3B	HR	(Hm	Rd)	TB	R	RBI	RC	TBB	IBB	SO	HBP	SH	SF	SB	CS	GDP	Avg	OBP	Slg	OPS
2009	Pit	NL	108	433	124	26	9	12	(8	4)	204	74	54	78	54	2	83	2	0	4	22	5	3	.286	.365	.471	.836
2010	Pit	NL	154	570	163	35	5	16	(8	8)	256	94	56	86	70	1	89	5	1	7	33	10	6	.286	.365	.449	.814
2011	Pit	NL	158	572	148	34	5	23	(10	13)	261	87	89	102	89	3	126	9	2	6	23	10	7	.259	.364	.456	.820
2012	Pit	NL	157	593	194	29	6	31	(15	16)	328	107	96	125	70	13	132	5	0	5	20	12	9	.327	.400	.553	.953
2013	Pit	NL	157	583	185	38	5	21	(9	12)	296	97	84	105	78	12	101	9	0	4	27	10	13	.317	.404	.508	.911
2014	Pit	NL	146	548	172	38	6	25	(10	15)	297	89	83	109	84	8	115	10	0	6	18	3	9	.314	.410	.542	.952
2015	Pit	NL	157	566	165	36	3	23	(13	10)	276	91	96	120	98	12	133	12	0	3	11	5	9	.292	.401	.488	.889
2016	Pit	NL	153	598	153	26	3	24	(10	14)	257	81	79	83	69	7	143	5	0	3	6	7	15	.256	.336	.430	.766
2017	Pit	NL	156	570	159	30	2	28	(9	19)	277	94	88	98	73	5	116	4	0	3	11	5	10	.279	.363	.486	.849
2018	2 Tms		155	569	145	30	3	20	(7	13)	241	83	65	88	95	1	145	11	0	7	14	9	12	.255	.368	.424	.792
2019	Phi	NL	59	219	56	12	1	10	(5	5)	100	45	29	41	43	0	55	0	0	0	2	1	1	.256	.378	.457	.834
2020	Phi	NL	57	217	55	9	0	10	(5	5)	94	32	34	34	22	0	48	1	0	1	4	0	4	.253	.324	.433	.757
2021	Phi	NL	144	482	107	24	1	27	(12	15)	214	78	80	80	81	2	132	4	0	10	6	1	10	.222	.334	.444	.778
	18 SF		130	482	123	28	2	15	(5	10)	200	65	55	70	73	1	123	7	0	6	13	6	11	.255	.357	.415	.772
	18 NYY	AL	25	87	22	2	1	5	(2	3)	41	18	10	18	22	0	22	4	0	1	1	3	1	.253	.421	.471	.892
	Postseason		13	46	11	1	0	0	(0	0)	12	5	1	3	7	1	7	0	0	0	0	0	1	.239	.340	.261	.600
13 ML YEARS			1761	6520	1826	367	49	270	(121	149)	3101	1052	933	1149	926	66	1418	77	3	62	197	78	108	.280	.373	.476	.849

T.J. McFarland

Pitches: L **Bats:** L **Pos:** RP-38

Ht: 6'3" **Wt:** 200 **Born:** 6/8/1989 **Age:** 33

			HOW MUCH PITCHED					WHAT HE GAVE UP											THE RESULTS							
Year	Team	Lg	G	GS	GF	IP	BFP	H	R	ER	HR	SH	SF	HB	TBB	IBB	SO	WP	W	L	Pct	Sv-Op	Hld	Vel	OPS	ERC	ERA
2021	Roch	AAA	18	0	2	24.0	101	23	14	14	3	0	0	3	5	0	26	3	1	2	.333	1--	-	-	.683	3.76	5.25
2013	Bal	AL	38	1	8	74.2	331	83	37	35	7	2	1	0	28	5	58	2	4	1	.800	0-0	0	88	.737	4.40	4.22
2014	Bal	AL	37	1	14	58.2	255	70	22	18	2	5	0	4	13	2	34	0	4	2	.667	0-0	5	91	.739	4.23	2.76
2015	Bal	AL	30	0	7	40.1	188	52	26	22	4	0	0	0	18	5	26	3	2	2	.500	0-0	3	92	.814	5.68	4.91
2016	Bal	AL	16	0	3	24.2	112	33	19	19	3	0	3	2	10	2	7	1	2	2	.500	0-3	0	92	.928	6.74	6.93
2017	Ari	NL	43	1	22	54.0	241	65	42	32	4	2	3	2	17	6	29	2	4	5	.444	0-0	2	91	.757	4.65	5.33
2018	Ari	NL	47	0	21	72.0	292	64	18	16	4	1	1	0	22	3	42	2	2	2	.500	1-1	1	91	.631	2.82	2.00
2019	Ari	NL	51	0	13	56.0	250	71	35	30	6	2	2	1	20	5	35	1	0	0		0-0	9	89	.842	5.53	4.82
2020	Oak	AL	23	0	2	20.2	92	26	10	10	5	0	0	1	5	0	9	1	2	0	1.000	0-0	6	88	.894	6.20	4.35
2021	StL	NL	38	0	7	38.2	144	32	11	11	3	0	0	0	9	1	21	0	4	1	.800	0-1	15	89	.655	2.59	2.56
	Postseason		2	0	2	2.0	7	0	0	0	0	1	0	0	1	0	2	0	0	0		0-0	0	90	.143	0.27	0.00
9 ML YEARS			323	3	96	439.2	1905	496	220	193	38	12	10	10	142	29	261	12	24	15	.615	1-5	41	90	.757	4.42	3.95

Jake McGee

Pitches: L **Bats:** L **Pos:** RP-62

Ht: 6'4" **Wt:** 229 **Born:** 8/6/1986 **Age:** 35

			HOW MUCH PITCHED					WHAT HE GAVE UP											THE RESULTS							
Year	Team	Lg	G	GS	GF	IP	BFP	H	R	ER	HR	SH	SF	HB	TBB	IBB	SO	WP	W	L	Pct	Sv-Op	Hld	Vel	OPS	ERC	ERA
2010	TB	AL	8	0	3	5.0	20	2	1	1	0	0	0	0	3	0	6	0	0	0	-	0-0	0	94	.426	1.32	1.80
2011	TB	AL	37	0	9	28.0	124	30	14	14	5	1	0	0	12	1	27	0	5	2	.714	0-0	4	95	.801	5.09	4.50
2012	TB	AL	69	0	13	55.1	212	33	13	12	3	0	2	1	11	4	73	3	5	2	.714	0-2	19	96	.452	1.26	1.95
2013	TB	AL	71	0	6	62.2	260	52	28	28	8	1	3	1	22	5	75	4	5	3	.625	1-5	27	96	.659	3.07	4.02
2014	TB	AL	73	0	31	71.1	274	48	15	15	2	1	1	2	16	1	90	1	5	2	.714	19-23	14	96	.486	1.55	1.89
2015	TB	AL	39	0	6	37.1	147	27	11	10	3	0	1	1	8	1	48	1	1	2	.333	6-10	19	95	.544	1.92	2.41
2016	Col	NL	57	0	25	45.2	205	56	25	24	9	0	0	3	16	1	38	4	2	3	.400	15-19	4	93	.887	6.26	4.73
2017	Col	NL	62	0	13	57.1	229	47	23	23	4	1	1	1	16	0	58	5	0	2	.000	3-6	20	94	.624	2.59	3.61
2018	Col	NL	61	0	9	51.1	227	59	39	37	10	2	0	2	16	1	57	4	2	4	.333	1-3	14	94	.883	5.38	6.49
2019	Col	NL	45	0	10	41.1	180	47	25	20	11	0	3	3	11	1	35	0	0	2	.000	0-2	4	94	.903	5.83	4.35
2020	LAD	NL	24	0	4	20.1	79	14	6	6	2	1	0	0	3	0	33	0	3	1	.750	0-0	4	95	.565	1.59	2.66
2021	SF	NL	62	0	42	59.2	239	44	25	18	7	0	3	2	10	1	58	0	3	2	.600	31-36	8	95	.565	2.00	2.72
	Postseason		10	0	4	6.1	31	7	3	3	1	1	0	1	4	1	7	0	0	1	.000	0-0	2	96	.800	6.32	4.26
12 ML YEARS			608	0	171	535.1	2196	459	225	208	64	7	14	16	144	16	588	23	31	25	.554	76-106	137	95	.662	2.99	3.50

Kyle McGowin

Pitches: R **Bats:** R **Pos:** RP-27

Ht: 6'3" **Wt:** 202 **Born:** 11/27/1991 **Age:** 30

			HOW MUCH PITCHED					WHAT HE GAVE UP											THE RESULTS							
Year	Team	Lg	G	GS	GF	IP	BFP	H	R	ER	HR	SH	SF	HB	TBB	IBB	SO	WP	W	L	Pct	Sv-Op	Hld	Vel	OPS	ERC	ERA
2021	Roch	AAA	9	0	2	9.2	38	3	2	1	0	1	0	2	3	0	10	1	1	0	1.000	0--	-		.310	0.90	0.93
2018	Was	NL	5	1	2	7.2	34	6	5	5	2	0	1	0	5	0	8	2	0	0		0-0	0	91	.824	4.90	5.87
2019	Was	NL	7	1	4	16.0	76	22	19	18	7	1	1	1	4	0	18	4	0	0		1-1	0	91	1.012	8.33	10.13
2020	Was	NL	9	0	3	11.0	47	9	6	6	2	0	0	1	5	1	16	1	1	0	1.000	1-1	1	91	.655	3.63	4.91
2021	Was	NL	27	0	7	30.0	128	21	14	14	5	0	0	2	14	1	35	1	0	0		0-0	1	91	.646	3.26	4.20
4 ML YEARS			48	2	16	64.2	285	58	44	43	16	1	2	3	28	2	77	8	1	0	1.000	2-2	2	91	.768	4.66	5.98

Reese McGuire

Bats: L **Throws:** R **Pos:** C-73;PH-7;PR-2;DH-1 **Ht:** 6'0" **Wt:** 215 **Born:** 3/2/1995 **Age:** 27

																					BATTING																												RUNNING			AVERAGES			
Year	Team	Lg	G	AB	H	2B	3B	HR	(Hm	Rd)	TB	R	RBI	RC	TBB	IBB	SO	HBP	SH	SF	SB	CS	GDP	Avg	OBP	Slg	OPS
2018	Tor	AL	14	31	9	3	0	2	(1	1)	18	5	4	5	2	0	9	0	0	0	1	0	0	.290	.333	.581	.914
2019	Tor	AL	30	97	29	7	0	5	(4	1)	51	14	11	14	7	0	18	0	0	0	0	0	1	.299	.346	.526	.872
2020	Tor	AL	19	41	3	0	0	1	(0	1)	6	2	1	0	0	0	11	0	4	0	0	0	1	.073	.073	.146	.220
2021	Tor	AL	78	198	50	15	0	1	(0	1)	68	22	10	16	15	0	44	2	1	1	0	0	4	.253	.310	.343	.654
Postseason		1	0	0	0	0	0	0	(0	0)	0	0	0	0	0	0	0	0	0	0	0	0	0	-	-	-	-
4 ML YEARS		141	367	91	25	0	9	(5	4)	143	43	26	35	24	0	82	2	5	1	1	0	6	.248	.297	.390	.687

Collin McHugh

Pitches: R **Bats:** R **Pos:** RP-30; SP-7 mick-HYOO **Ht:** 6'2" **Wt:** 191 **Born:** 6/19/1987 **Age:** 35

			HOW MUCH PITCHED				WHAT HE GAVE UP										THE RESULTS							
Year	Team	Lg	G	GS	GF	IP	BFP	H	R	ER	HR	SH	SF	HB	TBB	IBB	SO	WP	W	L	Pct	Sv-Op	Hld	Vel	OPS	ERC	ERA
2012	NYM	NL	8	4	1	21.1	99	27	21	18	5	2	1	2	8	2	17	0	0	4	.000	0-0	0	90	1.044	6.83	7.59
2013	2 Tms	NL	7	5	2	26.0	125	45	29	29	6	2	2	0	5	0	11	0	0	4	.000	0-0	0	90	1.053	8.82	10.04
2014	Hou	AL	25	25	0	154.2	619	117	53	47	13	6	4	6	41	1	157	6	11	9	.550	0-0	0	92	.588	2.34	2.73
2015	Hou	AL	32	32	0	203.2	859	207	89	88	19	5	4	9	53	2	171	5	19	7	.731	0-0	0	90	.705	3.75	3.89
2016	Hou	AL	33	33	0	184.2	796	206	92	89	25	1	5	5	54	1	177	9	13	10	.565	0-0	0	90	.790	4.69	4.34
2017	Hou	AL	12	12	0	63.1	271	62	27	25	7	0	0	5	20	0	62	4	5	2	.714	0-0	0	90	.747	4.02	3.55
2018	Hou	AL	58	0	18	72.1	283	45	18	16	6	1	1	5	21	0	94	0	6	2	.750	0-1	12	92	.542	1.92	1.99
2019	Hou	AL	35	8	8	74.2	317	62	41	39	12	0	3	3	30	0	82	0	4	5	.444	0-0	4	91	.733	3.67	4.70
2021	TB	AL	37	7	11	64.0	247	48	15	11	3	1	0	2	12	2	74	2	6	1	.857	1-3	6	91	.541	1.83	1.55
13	NYM	NL	3	1	2	7.0	34	12	8	8	2	0	1	0	3	0	3	0	0	1	.000	0-0	0	91	1.141	10.77	10.29
13	Col	NL	4	4	0	19.0	91	33	21	21	4	2	1	0	2	0	8	0	0	3	.000	0-0	0	90	1.021	8.14	9.95
Postseason		8	2	3	20.0	77	11	8	8	3	0	0	2	6	0	14	0	2	1	.667	0-0	0	91	.551	2.12	3.60
9 ML YEARS		247	126	40	864.2	3616	819	385	362	96	18	20	37	244	8	845	26	64	44	.593	1-4	22	91	.706	3.56	3.77

Ryan McKenna

Bats: R **Throws:** R **Pos:** LF-50;CF-18;RF-18;PR-18;PH-8;DH-2;2B-1;3B-1 **Ht:** 5'11" **Wt:** 195 **Born:** 2/14/1997 **Age:** 25

											BATTING												RUNNING			AVERAGES			
Year	Team	Lg	G	AB	H	2B	3B	HR	(Hm	Rd)	TB	R	RBI	RC	TBB	IBB	SO	HBP	SH	SF	SB	CS	GDP	Avg	OBP	Slg	OPS
2021	Norfolk	AAA	27	101	31	3	1	11	(-	-)	69	25	23		21	0	33	0	0	1	7	3	0	.307	.423	.683	1.106
2021	Bal	AL	90	169	31	6	1	2	(5	-)	45	20	14	16	24	0	74	2	2	0	1	0	1	.183	.292	.266	.559

Triston McKenzie

Pitches: R **Bats:** R **Pos:** SP-24; RP-1 **Ht:** 6'5" **Wt:** 165 **Born:** 8/2/1997 **Age:** 24

			HOW MUCH PITCHED				WHAT HE GAVE UP										THE RESULTS							
Year	Team	Lg	G	GS	GF	IP	BFP	H	R	ER	HR	SH	SF	HB	TBB	IBB	SO	WP	W	L	Pct	Sv-Op	Hld	Vel	OPS	ERC	ERA
2021	Clmbs	AAA	5	5	0	21.1	91	18	8	7	5	0	0	0	12	0	23	0	1	1	.500	0- -	-	-	.785	4.87	2.95
2020	Cle	AL	8	6	0	33.1	127	21	12	12	6	0	0	1	9	0	42	0	2	1	.667	0-0	0	93	.612	2.32	3.24
2021	Cle	AL	25	24	0	120.0	495	84	66	66	21	0	1	3	58	0	136	2	5	9	.357	0-0	0	93	.676	3.38	4.95
Postseason		1	0	0	1.2	9	1	2	2	1	0	0	0	2	0	2	0	0	0	-	0-0	0	93	.905	7.86	10.80
2 ML YEARS		33	30	0	153.1	622	105	78	78	27	0	1	4	67	0	178	2	7	10	.412	0-0	0	92	.663	3.14	4.58

Billy McKinney

Bats: L **Throws:** L **Pos:** RF-48;PH-46;LF-27;1B-10;CF-3;PR-1 **Ht:** 6'1" **Wt:** 205 **Born:** 8/23/1994 **Age:** 27

											BATTING												RUNNING			AVERAGES			
Year	Team	Lg	G	AB	H	2B	3B	HR	(Hm	Rd)	TB	R	RBI	RC	TBB	IBB	SO	HBP	SH	SF	SB	CS	GDP	Avg	OBP	Slg	OPS
2018	2 Tms	AL	38	119	30	7	0	6	(5	1)	55	14	13	14	11	0	33	1	0	1	1	0	0	.252	.318	.462	.780
2019	Tor	AL	84	251	54	14	1	12	(7	5)	106	37	28	35	19	0	73	2	2	2	0	2	0	.215	.274	.422	.696
2020	Tor	AL	2	3	2	0	0	0	(0	0)	2	1	0	0	0	0	0	0	0	0	0	0	0	.667	.667	.667	1.333
2021	3 Tms	NL	116	265	51	11	3	9	(2	7)	95	32	27	25	32	2	79	1	0	2	2	0	3	.192	.280	.358	.638
18	NYY	AL	2	4	1	0	0	0	(0	0)	1	0	0	0	0	0	1	0	0	0	0	0	0	.250	.250	.250	.500
18	Tor	AL	36	115	29	7	0	6	(5	1)	54	14	13	14	11	0	32	1	0	1	1	0	0	.252	.320	.470	.790
21	Mil	NL	40	92	19	3	1	3	(0	3)	33	9	6	5	7	1	24	0	0	1	1	0	1	.207	.260	.359	.619
21	NYM	NL	39	91	20	6	1	5	(1	4)	43	15	14	14	11	0	31	0	0	0	1	0	1	.220	.304	.473	.776
21	LAD	NL	37	82	12	2	1	1	(1	0)	19	8	7	6	14	1	24	1	0	1	0	0	1	.146	.276	.232	.507
4 ML YEARS		240	638	137	32	4	27	(14	13)	258	84	68	74	62	2	185	4	2	5	3	2	3	.215	.286	.404	.691

Zach McKinstry

Bats: L **Throws:** R **Pos:** RF-23;2B-20;LF-14;3B-12;PH-7;PR-2 **Ht:** 6'0" **Wt:** 180 **Born:** 4/29/1995 **Age:** 27

											BATTING												RUNNING			AVERAGES			
Year	Team	Lg	G	AB	H	2B	3B	HR	(Hm	Rd)	TB	R	RBI	RC	TBB	IBB	SO	HBP	SH	SF	SB	CS	GDP	Avg	OBP	Slg	OPS
2021	OkCity	AAA	35	133	35	7	3	7	(-	-)	69	32	19	-	19	0	24	3	0	0	1	2	2	.263	.368	.519	.887
2020	LAD	NL	4	7	2	1	0	0	(0	0)	3	1	0	1	0	0	3	0	0	0	0	0	1	.286	.286	.429	.714
2021	LAD	NL	60	158	34	9	0	7	(5	2)	64	19	29	17	10	1	50	1	1	2	1	1	3	.215	.263	.405	.668
2 ML YEARS		64	165	36	10	0	7	(5	2)	67	20	29	18	10	1	53	1	1	2	1	1	4	.218	.264	.406	.670

Ryan McMahon

Bats: L Throws: R Pos: 3B-113;2B-52;PH-9;PR-2   Ht: 6'2" Wt: 219 Born: 12/14/1994 Age: 27

Year	Team	Lg	G	AB	H	2B	3B	HR	(Hm	Rd)	TB	R	RBI	RC	TBB	IBB	SO	HBP	SH	SF	SB	CS	GDP	Avg	OBP	Slg	OPS
2017	Col	NL	17	19	3	1	0	0	(0	0)	4	2	1	1	5	0	5	0	0	0	0	0	1	.158	.333	.211	.544
2018	Col	NL	91	181	42	9	1	5	(4	1)	68	17	19	23	18	2	64	2	0	1	1	0	0	.232	.307	.376	.683
2019	Col	NL	141	480	120	22	1	24	(18	6)	216	70	83	69	56	1	160	1	1	1	5	1	14	.250	.329	.450	.779
2020	Col	NL	52	172	37	6	1	9	(6	3)	72	23	26	24	18	0	66	2	0	1	0	1	4	.215	.295	.419	.714
2021	Col	NL	151	528	134	32	1	23	(12	11)	237	80	86	79	59	2	147	4	0	5	6	2	14	.254	.331	.449	.779
	Postseason		4	3	0	0	0	0	(0	0)	0	0	0	0	1	0	1	0	0	0	0	1	0	.000	.250	.000	.250
5 ML YEARS			452	1380	336	70	4	61	(40	21)	597	192	215	196	156	5	442	9	1	8	12	4	33	.243	.323	.433	.755

Jeff McNeil

Bats: L Throws: R Pos: 2B-79;LF-28;PH-17;3B-2;DH-2   Ht: 6'1" Wt: 195 Born: 4/8/1992 Age: 30

Year	Team	Lg	G	AB	H	2B	3B	HR	(Hm	Rd)	TB	R	RBI	RC	TBB	IBB	SO	HBP	SH	SF	SB	CS	GDP	Avg	OBP	Slg	OPS
2018	NYM	NL	63	225	74	11	6	3	(1	2)	106	35	19	39	14	1	24	5	4	0	7	1	2	.329	.381	.471	.852
2019	NYM	NL	133	510	162	38	1	23	(9	14)	271	83	75	103	35	4	75	21	0	1	5	6	5	.318	.384	.531	.916
2020	NYM	NL	52	183	57	14	0	4	(4	0)	83	19	23	30	20	2	24	3	0	3	0	2	3	.311	.383	.454	.836
2021	NYM	NL	120	386	97	19	1	7	(6	1)	139	48	35	36	29	0	58	10	0	1	3	0	10	.251	.319	.360	.679
4 ML YEARS			368	1304	390	82	8	37	(20	17)	599	185	152	208	98	5	181	39	4	5	15	9	20	.299	.364	.459	.824

Alex McRae

Pitches: R Bats: R Pos: RP-2   Ht: 6'2" Wt: 220 Born: 4/6/1993 Age: 29

Year	Team	Lg	G	GS	GF	IP	BFP	H	R	ER	HR	SH	SF	HB	TBB	IBB	SO	WP	W	L	Pct	Sv-Op	Hld	Vel	OPS	ERC	ERA
2021	Charllt	AAA	26	18	1	88.2	407	103	54	53	12	0	2	8	42	0	86	5	2	9	.182	0- -	-		.827	6.02	5.38
2018	Pit	NL	2	0	0	6.1	32	8	4	4	0	0	0	0	5	0	5	2	0	1	.000	0-0	0	92	.899	7.08	5.68
2019	Pit	NL	11	2	3	26.2	132	36	30	26	9	0	0	3	16	1	19	2	0	4	.000	0-0	0	93	1.027	9.60	8.78
2020	CWS	AL	2	0	1	3.0	10	1	0	0	0	0	0	0	0	0	2	0	0	0	-	0-0	0	92	.200	0.25	0.00
2021	CWS	AL	2	0	2	2.0	10	3	1	1	0	0	0	1	1	0	1	0	0	0	-	0-0	0	93	.733	6.48	4.50
4 ML YEARS			17	2	6	38.0	184	48	35	31	9	0	0	4	22	1	27	4	0	5	.000	0-0	0	93	.940	7.97	7.34

Austin Meadows

Bats: L Throws: L Pos: LF-78;DH-60;PH-11;RF-1   Ht: 6'3" Wt: 225 Born: 5/3/1995 Age: 27

Year	Team	Lg	G	AB	H	2B	3B	HR	(Hm	Rd)	TB	R	RBI	RC	TBB	IBB	SO	HBP	SH	SF	SB	CS	GDP	Avg	OBP	Slg	OPS
2018	2 Tms		59	178	51	9	2	6	(3	3)	82	19	17	23	10	2	40	1	0	2	5	1	4	.287	.325	.461	.785
2019	TB	AL	138	530	154	29	7	33	(13	20)	296	83	89	103	54	6	131	7	0	0	12	7	3	.291	.364	.558	.922
2020	TB	AL	36	132	27	8	1	4	(1	3)	49	19	13	13	17	0	50	1	0	2	2	1	0	.205	.296	.371	.667
2021	TB	AL	142	518	121	29	3	27	(10	17)	237	79	106	98	59	3	122	6	0	8	4	3	4	.234	.315	.458	.772
18	Pit	NL	49	154	45	8	2	5	(2	3)	72	16	13	20	8	2	35	1	0	2	4	1	1	.292	.327	.468	.795
18	TB	AL	10	24	6	1	0	1	(1	0)	10	3	4	3	2	0	5	0	0	0	1	0	0	.250	.308	.417	.724
	Postseason		22	74	10	2	0	2	(2	0)	18	6	5	2	5	0	28	0	0	0	0	0	1	.135	.190	.243	.433
4 ML YEARS			375	1358	353	75	13	70	(27	43)	664	200	225	237	140	11	343	15	0	12	23	12	8	.260	.333	.489	.822

John Means

Pitches: L Bats: L Pos: SP-26   Ht: 6'3" Wt: 235 Born: 4/24/1993 Age: 29

Year	Team	Lg	G	GS	GF	IP	BFP	H	R	ER	HR	SH	SF	HB	TBB	IBB	SO	WP	W	L	Pct	Sv-Op	Hld	Vel	OPS	ERC	ERA
2018	Bal	AL	1	0	1	3.1	16	6	5	5	1	0	0	0	0	0	4	0	0	0	-	0-0	0	90	1.125	11.50	13.50
2019	Bal	AL	31	27	1	155.0	637	138	68	62	23	0	3	5	38	0	121	5	12	11	.522	0-0	0	92	.702	3.31	3.60
2020	Bal	AL	10	10	0	43.2	176	36	22	22	12	0	1	4	7	0	42	2	2	4	.333	0-0	0	94	.718	3.61	4.53
2021	Bal	AL	26	26	0	146.2	590	125	64	59	30	1	2	4	26	0	134	3	6	9	.400	0-0	0	93	.690	3.14	3.62
4 ML YEARS			68	63	1	348.2	1419	305	159	148	66	1	6	13	71	0	301	10	20	24	.455	0-0	0	92	.704	3.32	3.82

Nick Mears

Pitches: R Bats: R Pos: RP-30   Ht: 6'2" Wt: 200 Born: 10/7/1996 Age: 25

Year	Team	Lg	G	GS	GF	IP	BFP	H	R	ER	HR	SH	SF	HB	TBB	IBB	SO	WP	W	L	Pct	Sv-Op	Hld	Vel	OPS	ERC	ERA
2021	Indy	AAA	17	0	7	18.2	82	16	12	11	2	1	0	2	9	0	25	0	2	2	.500	1- -	-		.676	4.03	5.30
2020	Pit	NL	4	0	2	5.0	26	4	3	3	1	0	1	0	7	0	7	1	0	0	-	0-0	0	96	.868	7.69	5.40
2021	Pit	NL	30	0	6	23.1	107	25	14	13	5	0	1	0	13	1	23	3	1	0	1.000	0-5	3	96	.818	5.86	5.01
2 ML YEARS			34	0	8	28.1	133	29	17	16	6	0	2	0	20	1	30	4	1	0	1.000	0-5	3	96	.828	6.19	5.08

Adonis Medina

Pitches: R Bats: R Pos: RP-3; SP-1   Ht: 6'1" Wt: 187 Born: 12/18/1996 Age: 25

Year	Team	Lg	G	GS	GF	IP	BFP	H	R	ER	HR	SH	SF	HB	TBB	IBB	SO	WP	W	L	Pct	Sv-Op	Hld	Vel	OPS	ERC	ERA
2021	LV	AAA	17	17	0	67.2	298	71	48	38	10	1	1	1	26	1	55	4	4	5	.444	0- -	-		.780	4.61	5.05
2020	Phi	NL	1	1	0	4.0	18	3	2	2	0	0	0	0	3	0	4	0	0	1	.000	0-0	0	92	.600	3.21	4.50
2021	Phi	NL	4	1	2	7.2	36	9	3	3	0	0	0	3	4	0	6	0	0	0	-	0-0	0	93	.858	6.73	3.52
2 ML YEARS			5	2	2	11.2	54	12	5	5	0	0	0	3	7	0	10	0	0	1	.000	0-0	0	93	.771	5.41	3.86

Trevor Megill

Pitches: R Bats: L Pos: RP-28 Ht: 6'8" Wt: 250 Born: 12/5/1993 Age: 28

		HOW MUCH PITCHED					WHAT HE GAVE UP											THE RESULTS						
Year	Team	Lg	G	GS	GF	IP	BFP	H	R	ER	HR	SH	SF	HB	TBB	IBB	SO	WP	W	L	Pct	Sv-Op	Hld	Vel	OPS	ERC	ERA
2021	Iowa	AAA	12	0	5	14.0	63	12	8	8	2	0	0	1	8	2	20	4	0	0	-	1--	-	-	.722	4.20	5.14
2021	ChC	NL	28	0	3	23.2	115	36	24	22	7	1	0	1	8	1	30	5	1	2	.333	0-0	1	96	1.014	8.63	8.37

Tylor Megill

Pitches: R Bats: R Pos: SP-18 Ht: 6'7" Wt: 230 Born: 7/28/1995 Age: 26

		HOW MUCH PITCHED					WHAT HE GAVE UP											THE RESULTS						
Year	Team	Lg	G	GS	GF	IP	BFP	H	R	ER	HR	SH	SF	HB	TBB	IBB	SO	WP	W	L	Pct	Sv-Op	Hld	Vel	OPS	ERC	ERA
2021	Bnghtn	AA	5	5	0	26.0	104	21	9	9	1	0	2	0	7	0	42	0	2	1	.667	0-0	-	-	.574	2.22	3.12
2021	NYM	NL	18	18	0	89.2	379	88	46	45	19	2	2	2	27	0	99	1	4	6	.400	0-0	0	95	.778	4.43	4.52

Ryan Meisinger

Pitches: R Bats: R Pos: RP-7 Ht: 6'4" Wt: 235 Born: 5/4/1994 Age: 28

		HOW MUCH PITCHED					WHAT HE GAVE UP											THE RESULTS						
Year	Team	Lg	G	GS	GF	IP	BFP	H	R	ER	HR	SH	SF	HB	TBB	IBB	SO	WP	W	L	Pct	Sv-Op	Hld	Vel	OPS	ERC	ERA
2021	Iowa	AAA	24	0	16	29.2	131	24	15	14	6	0	2	3	16	1	45	2	2	2	.500	3--	-	-	.746	4.57	4.25
2021	OkCity	AAA	9	0	3	9.0	39	8	2	1	2	0	0	1	3	0	12	0	1	0	1.000	0--	-	-	.765	4.38	1.00
2018	Bal	AL	18	1	2	21.0	87	18	15	15	6	1	1	0	10	0	21	4	2	1	.667	0-0	0	91	.886	5.01	6.43
2020	StL	NL	2	0	0	2.2	13	1	0	0	0	0	0	0	4	0	3	0	0	0	-	0-0	0	91	.587	5.54	0.00
2021	ChC	NL	7	0	2	7.1	38	11	10	10	2	1	1	0	5	0	6	1	0	0	-	0-0	0	92	1.013	9.76	12.27
	3 ML YEARS		27	1	4	31.0	138	30	25	25	8	2	2	1	19	0	30	5	2	1	.667	0-0	0	91	.903	6.20	7.26

Francisco Mejia

Bats: B Throws: R Pos: C-76;PH-6;DH-4;1B-2 Ht: 5'8" Wt: 188 Born: 10/27/1995 Age: 26

		BATTING																				RUNNING			AVERAGES			
Year	Team	Lg	G	AB	H	2B	3B	HR	(Hm	Rd)	TB	R	RBI	RC	TBB	IBB	SO	HBP	SH	SF	SB	CS	GDP	Avg	OBP	Slg	OPS
2017	Cle	AL	11	13	2	0	0	0	(0	0)	2	1	1	0	1	1	3	0	0	0	0	0	0	.154	.214	.154	.368
2018	2 Tms		21	56	10	2	0	3	(1	2)	21	6	8	5	5	0	19	1	0	0	0	0	2	.179	.258	.375	.633
2019	SD	NL	79	226	60	11	2	8	(3	5)	99	27	22	27	13	1	56	4	0	1	1	1	6	.265	.316	.438	.754
2020	SD	NL	17	39	3	1	0	1	(1	0)	7	5	2	0	1	0	9	2	0	0	0	0	1	.077	.143	.179	.322
2021	TB	AL	84	250	65	15	3	6	(2	4)	104	31	35	42	17	0	49	7	1	2	0	0	4	.260	.322	.416	.738
18	Cle	AL	1	2	0	0	0	0	(0	0)	0	0	0	0	2	0	0	0	0	0	0	0	0	.000	.500	.000	.500
18	SD	NL	20	54	10	2	0	3	(1	2)	21	6	8	5	3	0	19	1	0	0	0	0	2	.185	.241	.389	.630
	5 ML YEARS		212	584	140	29	5	18	(7	11)	233	70	68	74	37	2	136	14	1	3	1	1	13	.240	.299	.399	.698

Humberto Mejia

Pitches: R Bats: R Pos: SP-5 Ht: 6'4" Wt: 244 Born: 3/3/1997 Age: 25

		HOW MUCH PITCHED					WHAT HE GAVE UP											THE RESULTS						
Year	Team	Lg	G	GS	GF	IP	BFP	H	R	ER	HR	SH	SF	HB	TBB	IBB	SO	WP	W	L	Pct	Sv-Op	Hld	Vel	OPS	ERC	ERA
2021	Amrillo	AA	6	6	0	32.0	133	27	20	15	7	0	1	1	10	0	37	1	0	4	.000	0--	-	-	.765	3.73	4.22
2021	Reno	AAA	15	15	0	71.2	320	83	46	44	10	1	2	5	27	0	63	1	7	5	.583	0--	-	-	.834	5.54	5.53
2020	Mia	NL	3	3	0	10.0	49	13	8	6	3	0	0	1	6	0	11	0	0	2	.000	0-0	0	93	1.027	8.91	5.40
2021	Ari	NL	5	5	0	22.1	105	32	19	18	5	1	1	0	9	1	20	0	0	3	.000	0-0	0	92	1.096	7.69	7.25
	2 ML YEARS		8	8	0	32.1	154	45	27	24	8	1	1	1	15	1	31	0	0	5	.000	0-0	0	92	1.075	8.06	6.68

JC Mejia

Pitches: R Bats: R Pos: SP-11; RP-6 Ht: 6'5" Wt: 240 Born: 8/26/1996 Age: 25

		HOW MUCH PITCHED					WHAT HE GAVE UP											THE RESULTS						
Year	Team	Lg	G	GS	GF	IP	BFP	H	R	ER	HR	SH	SF	HB	TBB	IBB	SO	WP	W	L	Pct	Sv-Op	Hld	Vel	OPS	ERC	ERA
2021	Clmbs	AAA	8	6	0	23.0	108	23	19	19	8	0	0	3	15	0	25	2	0	3	.000	0--	-	-	.924	7.66	7.43
2021	Cle	AL	17	11	1	52.1	238	60	48	48	13	1	0	3	24	0	47	2	1	7	.125	0-0	0	93	.905	6.60	8.25

Mark Melancon

Pitches: R Bats: R Pos: RP-64 muh-LANN-sun Ht: 6'1" Wt: 215 Born: 3/28/1985 Age: 37

		HOW MUCH PITCHED					WHAT HE GAVE UP											THE RESULTS						
Year	Team	Lg	G	GS	GF	IP	BFP	H	R	ER	HR	SH	SF	HB	TBB	IBB	SO	WP	W	L	Pct	Sv-Op	Hld	Vel	OPS	ERC	ERA
2009	NYY	AL	13	0	4	16.1	74	13	8	7	0	0	0	4	10	0	10	3	0	1	.000	0-1	0	93	.665	3.94	3.86
2010	2 Tms		22	0	4	21.1	90	19	13	10	2	0	1	1	8	0	22	2	2	0	1.000	0-1	8	93	.674	3.53	4.22
2011	Hou	NL	71	0	47	74.1	309	65	28	23	5	2	0	2	26	6	66	1	8	4	.667	20-25	3	93	.631	2.98	2.78
2012	Bos	AL	41	0	17	45.0	194	45	31	31	8	1	2	3	12	1	41	2	0	2	.000	1-2	2	93	.754	4.24	6.20
2013	Pit	NL	72	0	24	71.0	279	60	15	11	1	1	0	1	8	0	70	6	3	2	.600	16-21	26	93	.511	1.78	1.39
2014	Pit	NL	72	0	48	71.0	277	51	15	15	2	1	1	3	11	1	71	3	3	5	.375	33-37	14	93	.473	1.54	1.90
2015	Pit	NL	78	0	63	76.2	293	57	22	19	4	1	1	2	14	2	62	3	3	2	.600	**51-53**	1	92	.541	1.82	2.23
2016	2 Tms		75	0	67	71.1	270	52	16	13	3	0	2	1	12	0	65	4	2	2	.500	47-51	0	92	.511	1.66	1.64
2017	SF	NL	32	0	18	30.0	130	37	16	15	3	0	0	1	6	0	29	2	1	2	.333	11-16	5	92	.794	4.78	4.50
2018	SF	NL	41	0	8	39.0	174	48	18	14	2	0	1	0	14	2	31	4	1	4	.200	3-7	8	92	.771	4.94	3.23
2019	2 Tms		66	0	34	67.1	284	71	28	27	4	0	1	2	18	2	68	4	5	2	.714	12-12	5	92	.678	3.69	3.61
2020	Atl	NL	23	0	19	22.2	95	22	8	7	1	1	1	2	7	3	14	1	2	1	.667	11-13	0	92	.639	3.38	2.78
2021	SD	NL	64	0	53	64.2	265	54	21	16	4	0	2	1	25	4	59	3	4	3	.571	**39-45**	0	92	.618	2.90	2.23
10	NYY	AL	2	0	2	4.0	19	7	5	4	1	0	1	0	0	0	3	0	0	0	-	0-0	0	93	.980	7.95	9.00
10	Hou	NL	20	0	2	17.1	71	12	8	6	1	0	0	1	8	0	19	2	2	0	1.000	0-1	8	93	.586	2.65	3.12
16	Pit	NL	45	0	39	41.2	163	31	10	7	2	0	2	1	9	0	38	1	1	1	.500	30-33	0	92	.516	1.89	1.51

Year	Team	Lg	G	GS	GF	IP	BFP	H	R	ER	HR	SH	SF	HB	TBB	IBB	SO	WP	W	L	Pct	Sv-Op	Hld	Vel	OPS	ERC	ERA
16	Was	NL	30	0	28	29.2	107	21	6	6	1	0	0	0	3	0	27	3	1	1	.500	17-18	0	92	.503	1.41	1.82
19	SF	NL	43	0	16	46.1	195	49	19	18	3	0	1	2	16	2	44	3	4	2	.667	1-1	5	92	.724	4.18	3.50
19	Atl	NL	23	0	18	21.0	89	22	9	9	1	0	0	0	2	0	24	1	1	0	1.000	11-11	0	93	.580	2.69	3.86
	Postseason		20	0	15	19.1	80	19	9	8	2	0	0	0	5	3	17	0	1	1	.500	5-7	0	93	.713	3.24	3.72
13 ML YEARS			670	0	406	670.2	2734	594	239	208	39	6	12	24	171	21	608	38	34	30	.531	244-284	72	93	.612	2.76	2.79

Keury Mella

Pitches: R Bats: R Pos: RP-2 — KAY-ooh-ree MAY-uh — Ht: 6'2" Wt: 234 Born: 8/2/1993 Age: 28

Year	Team	Lg	G	GS	GF	IP	BFP	H	R	ER	HR	SH	SF	HB	TBB	IBB	SO	WP	W	L	Pct	Sv-Op	Hld	Vel	OPS	ERC	ERA
2021	Reno	AAA	20	0	4	29.0	128	30	17	14	5	0	0	2	9	0	29	5	1	0	1.000	0--	-	-	.748	4.60	4.34
2021	Indy	AAA	16	0	6	19.0	84	17	16	15	1	0	0	1	12	0	23	3	2	0	1.000	3--	-	-	.752	4.30	7.11
2017	Cin	NL	2	0	1	4.0	19	5	3	3	1	0	0	0	2	1	1	0	0	0	-	0-0	0	96	.957	6.56	6.75
2018	Cin	NL	4	0	1	9.1	48	13	9	9	4	2	0	1	8	0	8	1	0	0	-	0-0	0	94	1.262	12.40	8.68
2019	Cin	NL	2	0	1	3.2	18	5	3	3	0	0	0	0	2	1	4	0	0	0	-	0-0	0	95	.826	5.31	7.36
2020	Ari	NL	11	0	3	10.0	42	10	3	2	1	0	1	0	3	1	10	1	2	0	1.000	0-0	0	95	.704	3.54	1.80
2021	Ari	NL	2	0	1	1.2	15	8	6	6	2	0	0	0	2	0	2	0	0	0	-	0-0	0	94	1.821	53.23	32.40
5 ML YEARS			21	0	7	28.2	142	41	24	23	8	2	1	1	17	3	25	2	2	0	1.000	0-0	0	95	1.050	9.06	7.22

Danny Mendick

Bats: R Throws: R Pos: 2B-28;SS-28;RF-8;PH-7;3B-4;LF-2;CF-1;PR-1 — Ht: 5'10" Wt: 195 Born: 9/28/1993 Age: 28

Year	Team	Lg	G	AB	H	2B	3B	HR	(Hm	Rd)	TB	R	RBI	RC	TBB	IBB	SO	HBP	SH	SF	SB	CS	GDP	Avg	OBP	Slg	OPS
2021	Charllt	AAA	22	83	22	3	0	2	(-	-)	31	15	7	-	7	0	15	1	0	0	1	0	1	.265	.330	.373	.703
2019	CWS	AL	16	39	12	0	0	2	(2	0)	18	6	4	6	1	0	11	0	0	0	0	0	1	.308	.325	.462	.787
2020	CWS	AL	33	107	26	4	1	3	(2	1)	41	11	6	6	6	0	25	0	0	1	0	1	3	.243	.281	.383	.664
2021	CWS	AL	71	164	36	5	0	2	(0	2)	47	14	20	22	18	0	42	2	1	1	0	1	1	.220	.303	.287	.589
3 ML YEARS			120	310	74	9	1	7	(4	3)	106	31	30	34	25	0	78	2	1	2	0	2	5	.239	.298	.342	.640

Conner Menez

Pitches: L Bats: L Pos: RP-7; SP-1 — Ht: 6'2" Wt: 206 Born: 5/29/1995 Age: 27

Year	Team	Lg	G	GS	GF	IP	BFP	H	R	ER	HR	SH	SF	HB	TBB	IBB	SO	WP	W	L	Pct	Sv-Op	Hld	Vel	OPS	ERC	ERA
2021	Scrmto	AAA	25	5	3	40.2	201	53	33	29	6	1	5	3	27	2	42	3	2	3	.400	1--	-	-	.894	7.62	6.42
2019	SF	NL	8	3	2	17.0	73	13	10	10	4	1	1	0	12	0	22	2	0	1	.000	0-0	0	91	.805	5.06	5.29
2020	SF	NL	7	0	3	11.1	45	6	4	3	2	1	0	1	5	0	8	0	1	0	1.000	0-0	0	92	.641	2.61	2.38
2021	SF	NL	8	1	0	14.0	62	16	10	6	2	0	1	0	3	0	15	0	1	0	1.000	0-0	1	91	.772	4.25	3.86
3 ML YEARS			23	4	5	42.1	180	35	24	19	8	2	2	1	20	0	45	2	2	1	.667	0-0	1	91	.753	4.10	4.04

Oscar Mercado

Bats: R Throws: R Pos: LF-45;RF-20;PH-10;CF-7;PR-3 — Ht: 6'2" Wt: 197 Born: 12/16/1994 Age: 27

Year	Team	Lg	G	AB	H	2B	3B	HR	(Hm	Rd)	TB	R	RBI	RC	TBB	IBB	SO	HBP	SH	SF	SB	CS	GDP	Avg	OBP	Slg	OPS
2021	Clmbs	AAA	45	171	37	13	1	5	(-	-)	67	29	23	-	23	0	32	6	1	2	9	1	2	.216	.327	.392	.719
2019	Cle	AL	115	438	118	25	3	15	(11	4)	194	70	54	69	28	0	84	5	7	4	15	4	9	.269	.318	.443	.761
2020	Cle	AL	36	86	11	1	0	1	(0	1)	15	6	6	1	5	0	27	0	1	0	3	0	0	.128	.174	.174	.348
2021	Cle	AL	72	214	48	11	1	6	(4	2)	79	27	19	29	21	0	42	2	1	0	7	1	1	.224	.300	.369	.669
	Postseason		1	1	0	0	0	0	(0	0)	0	0	0	0	0	0	1	0	0	0	0	0	0	.000	.000	.000	.000
3 ML YEARS			223	738	177	37	4	22	(15	7)	288	103	79	99	54	0	153	7	9	5	25	5	10	.240	.296	.390	.686

Yermin Mercedes

Bats: R Throws: R Pos: DH-61;PH-6;C-2;1B-1 — Ht: 5'11" Wt: 245 Born: 2/14/1993 Age: 29

Year	Team	Lg	G	AB	H	2B	3B	HR	(Hm	Rd)	TB	R	RBI	RC	TBB	IBB	SO	HBP	SH	SF	SB	CS	GDP	Avg	OBP	Slg	OPS
2021	Charllt	AAA	59	222	61	7	1	11	(-	-)	103	32	29	-	11	0	39	4	0	2	3	0	8	.275	.318	.464	.782
2020	CWS	AL	1	1	0	0	0	0	(0	0)	0	0	0	0	0	0	0	0	0	0	0	0	0	.000	.000	.000	.000
2021	CWS	AL	68	240	65	9	1	7	(4	3)	97	26	37	29	20	1	46	1	0	1	0	1	7	.271	.328	.404	.732
2 ML YEARS			69	241	65	9	1	7	(4	3)	97	26	37	29	20	1	46	1	0	1	0	1	7	.270	.327	.402	.729

Jordy Mercer

Bats: R Throws: R Pos: 2B-21;3B-14;PH-9;SS-6;1B-2;LF-1;DH-1;PR-1 — Ht: 6'3" Wt: 210 Born: 8/27/1986 Age: 35

Year	Team	Lg	G	AB	H	2B	3B	HR	(Hm	Rd)	TB	R	RBI	RC	TBB	IBB	SO	HBP	SH	SF	SB	CS	GDP	Avg	OBP	Slg	OPS
2012	Pit	NL	42	62	13	5	1	0	(1	0)	23	7	5	6	4	0	14	1	0	1	0	1	0	.210	.265	.371	.636
2013	Pit	NL	103	333	95	22	2	8	(1	7)	145	33	27	46	22	6	62	4	5	1	3	2	7	.285	.336	.435	.772
2014	Pit	NL	149	506	129	27	2	12	(3	9)	196	56	55	45	35	12	89	4	5	5	4	1	14	.255	.305	.387	.693
2015	Pit	NL	116	394	96	21	0	3	(0	3)	126	34	34	34	27	7	73	2	4	3	3	2	7	.244	.293	.320	.613
2016	Pit	NL	149	519	133	22	3	11	(4	7)	194	66	59	58	51	8	83	5	7	2	1	1	11	.256	.328	.374	.701
2017	Pit	NL	145	502	128	24	5	14	(5	9)	204	52	58	60	51	13	88	3	0	2	0	4	16	.255	.326	.406	.733
2018	Pit	NL	117	394	99	29	2	6	(1	5)	150	43	39	41	32	9	87	6	1	3	2	0	12	.251	.315	.381	.696
2019	Det	AL	74	256	69	16	0	9	(4	5)	112	24	22	28	13	1	57	2	0	0	0	0	4	.270	.310	.438	.747
2020	2 Tms	AL	9	20	4	0	0	0	(0	0)	4	2	0	1	2	0	2	0	0	0	0	0	1	.200	.273	.200	.473
2021	Was	NL	46	118	30	7	0	2	(2	0)	43	13	9	10	9	0	34	0	0	0	0	0	1	.254	.307	.364	.671

		BATTING																		RUNNING			AVERAGES			
Year Team	Lg	G	AB	H	2B	3B	HR	(Hm Rd)	TB	R	RBI	RC	TBB	IBB	SO	HBP	SH	SF	SB	CS	GDP	Avg	OBP	Slg	OPS
20 Det	AL	3	9	2	0	0	0	(0 0)	2	1	0	0	0	0	1	0	0	0	0	0	1	.222	.222	.222	.444
20 NYY	AL	6	11	2	0	0	0	(0 0)	2	1	0	1	2	0	1	0	0	0	0	0	0	.182	.308	.182	.490
Postseason		7	14	2	0	0	0	(0 0)	2	0	0	0	1	1	5	0	0	0	0	0	0	.143	.200	.143	.343
10 ML YEARS		950	3104	796	173	15	66	(21 45)	1197	330	308	329	246	56	589	27	22	17	13	11	73	.256	.315	.386	.701

Whit Merrifield

Bats: R **Throws:** R **Pos:** 2B-149;RF-18;LF-2;DH-2   **Ht:** 6'1" **Wt:** 195 **Born:** 1/24/1989 **Age:** 33

		BATTING																		RUNNING			AVERAGES			
Year Team	Lg	G	AB	H	2B	3B	HR	(Hm Rd)	TB	R	RBI	RC	TBB	IBB	SO	HBP	SH	SF	SB	CS	GDP	Avg	OBP	Slg	OPS
2016 KC	AL	81	311	88	22	3	2	(2 0)	122	44	29	38	19	1	72	0	1	1	8	3	1	.283	.323	.392	.716
2017 KC	AL	145	587	169	32	6	19	(13 6)	270	80	78	88	29	0	88	6	1	7	34	8	13	.288	.324	.460	.784
2018 KC	AL	158	632	192	43	3	12	(5 7)	277	88	60	103	61	2	114	6	2	6	45	10	12	.304	.367	.438	.806
2019 KC	AL	162	681	206	41	10	16	(4 12)	315	105	74	114	45	5	126	5	0	4	20	10	8	.302	.348	.463	.811
2020 KC	AL	60	248	70	12	0	9	(3 6)	109	38	30	41	12	0	33	4	0	1	12	3	3	.282	.325	.440	.764
2021 KC	AL	162	664	184	42	3	10	(5 5)	262	97	74	92	40	1	103	4	0	12	40	4	12	.277	.317	.395	.711
6 ML YEARS		768	3123	909	192	25	68	(32 36)	1355	452	345	476	206	9	536	25	4	31	159	38	49	.291	.337	.434	.771

Julian Merryweather

Pitches: R **Bats:** R **Pos:** RP-12; SP-1   **Ht:** 6'4" **Wt:** 215 **Born:** 10/14/1991 **Age:** 30

		HOW MUCH PITCHED				WHAT HE GAVE UP										THE RESULTS							
Year Team	Lg	G	GS	GF	IP	BFP	H	R	ER	HR	SH	SF	HB	TBB	IBB	SO	WP	W	L	Pct	Sv-Op	Hld	Vel	OPS	ERC	ERA
2020 Tor	AL	8	3	0	13.0	55	11	6	6	0	0	0	0	6	0	15	0	0	0	-	0-0	1	97	.595	2.79	4.15
2021 Tor	AL	13	1	4	13.0	55	13	7	7	4	0	1	1	4	0	12	2	0	1	.000	2-2	1	97	.837	5.58	4.85
2 ML YEARS		21	4	4	26.0	110	24	13	13	4	0	1	1	10	0	27	2	0	1	.000	2-2	2	97	.716	4.15	4.50

Max Meyer

Pitches: R **Bats:** L **Pos:** P   **Ht:** 6'0" **Wt:** 196 **Born:** 3/12/1999 **Age:** 23

		HOW MUCH PITCHED				WHAT HE GAVE UP										THE RESULTS							
Year Team	Lg	G	GS	GF	IP	BFP	H	R	ER	HR	SH	SF	HB	TBB	IBB	SO	WP	W	L	Pct	Sv-Op	Hld	Vel	OPS	ERC	ERA
2021 Pnscla	AA	20	20	0	101.0	416	84	35	27	7	0	1	3	40	0	113	9	6	3	.667	0- -	-	-	.652	3.11	2.41

Jake Meyers

Bats: R **Throws:** L **Pos:** CF-39;PH-6;LF-4;RF-3;DH-2;PR-2   **Ht:** 6'0" **Wt:** 200 **Born:** 6/18/1996 **Age:** 26

		BATTING																		RUNNING			AVERAGES			
Year Team	Lg	G	AB	H	2B	3B	HR	(Hm Rd)	TB	R	RBI	RC	TBB	IBB	SO	HBP	SH	SF	SB	CS	GDP	Avg	OBP	Slg	OPS
2021 SgrLnd	AAA	68	271	93	17	2	16	(- -)	162	52	51	-	25	0	59	6	0	2	10	3	3	.343	.408	.598	1.006
2021 Hou	AL	49	146	38	8	0	6	(3 3)	64	22	28	22	10	0	50	4	2	1	3	0	0	.260	.323	.438	.761

Keynan Middleton

Pitches: R **Bats:** R **Pos:** RP-31; SP-1   **Ht:** 6'3" **Wt:** 215 **Born:** 9/12/1993 **Age:** 28

		HOW MUCH PITCHED				WHAT HE GAVE UP										THE RESULTS							
Year Team	Lg	G	GS	GF	IP	BFP	H	R	ER	HR	SH	SF	HB	TBB	IBB	SO	WP	W	L	Pct	Sv-Op	Hld	Vel	OPS	ERC	ERA
2021 Tacom	AAA	7	1	1	7.2	32	7	3	2	1	0	0	0	2	0	13	0	1	0	1.000	0- -	-	-	.715	3.20	2.35
2017 LAA	AL	64	0	17	58.1	246	60	25	25	11	0	2	0	18	2	63	2	6	1	.857	3-5	10	97	.791	4.47	3.86
2018 LAA	AL	16	0	9	17.2	71	14	4	4	1	0	1	1	9	1	16	1	0	0	-	6-7	2	96	.688	3.42	2.04
2019 LAA	AL	11	0	0	7.2	33	4	1	1	0	0	0	0	7	0	6	1	0	0	-	0-0	0	94	.564	2.72	1.17
2020 LAA	AL	13	0	4	12.0	53	12	8	7	2	0	3	0	6	0	11	1	0	1	.000	0-0	2	97	.817	4.95	5.25
2021 Sea	AL	32	1	10	31.0	140	30	20	17	2	0	0	2	19	1	24	0	1	2	.333	4-4	3	95	.734	4.69	4.94
5 ML YEARS		136	1	40	126.2	543	120	58	54	16	0	6	3	59	4	120	5	7	4	.636	13-16	17	96	.754	4.34	3.84

Miles Mikolas

Pitches: R **Bats:** R **Pos:** SP-9   MIKE-uh-liss   **Ht:** 6'4" **Wt:** 230 **Born:** 8/23/1988 **Age:** 33

		HOW MUCH PITCHED				WHAT HE GAVE UP										THE RESULTS							
Year Team	Lg	G	GS	GF	IP	BFP	H	R	ER	HR	SH	SF	HB	TBB	IBB	SO	WP	W	L	Pct	Sv-Op	Hld	Vel	OPS	ERC	ERA
2021 Memp	AAA	5	5	0	19.1	73	17	5	5	2	0	0	0	3	0	13	1	1	1	.500	0- -	-	-	.645	2.70	2.33
2012 SD	NL	25	0	9	32.1	144	32	15	13	4	2	0	2	15	0	23	2	2	1	.667	0-1	1	93	.761	4.65	3.62
2013 SD	NL	2	0	1	1.2	7	0	0	0	0	0	0	1	1	0	1	0	0	0	-	0-0	0	94	.286	1.30	0.00
2014 Tex	AL	10	10	0	57.1	255	64	43	41	8	1	2	4	18	2	38	0	2	5	.286	0-0	0	93	.769	4.85	6.44
2018 StL	NL	32	32	0	200.2	808	186	70	63	16	8	4	7	29	4	146	2	18	4	.818	0-0	0	94	.628	2.70	2.83
2019 StL	NL	32	32	0	184.0	764	193	90	85	27	3	7	12	32	1	144	5	9	14	.391	0-0	0	94	.761	4.08	4.16
2021 StL	NL	9	9	0	44.2	186	43	24	21	6	2	1	2	11	0	31	1	2	3	.400	0-0	0	93	.710	3.68	4.23
Postseason		3	2	1	12.0	50	10	2	2	0	0	0	0	4	1	9	0	1	1	.500	0-0	0	94	.606	2.14	1.50
6 ML YEARS		110	83	10	520.2	2164	518	242	223	61	16	14	28	106	7	383	10	33	27	.550	0-1	1	94	.706	3.60	3.85

Wade Miley

Pitches: L **Bats:** L **Pos:** SP-28   MY-lee   **Ht:** 6'2" **Wt:** 220 **Born:** 11/13/1986 **Age:** 35

		HOW MUCH PITCHED				WHAT HE GAVE UP										THE RESULTS							
Year Team	Lg	G	GS	GF	IP	BFP	H	R	ER	HR	SH	SF	HB	TBB	IBB	SO	WP	W	L	Pct	Sv-Op	Hld	Vel	OPS	ERC	ERA
2011 Ari	NL	8	7	0	40.0	180	48	20	20	6	3	1	0	18	0	25	1	4	2	.667	0-0	0	90	.873	5.90	4.50
2012 Ari	NL	32	29	0	194.2	807	193	79	72	14	8	3	2	37	0	144	6	16	11	.593	0-0	0	91	.685	3.05	3.33
2013 Ari	NL	33	33	0	202.2	847	201	88	80	21	6	2	4	66	4	147	13	10	10	.500	0-0	0	91	.727	3.88	3.55
2014 Ari	NL	33	33	0	201.1	866	207	103	97	23	8	9	4	75	3	183	9	8	12	.400	0-0	0	91	.746	4.31	4.34

Year	Team	Lg	G	GS	GF	IP	BFP	H	R	ER	HR	SH	SF	HB	TBB	IBB	SO	WP	W	L	Pct	Sv-Op	Hld	Vel	OPS	ERC	ERA
2015	Bos	AL	32	32	0	193.2	831	201	98	96	17	3	2	4	64	0	147	10	11	11	.500	0-0	0	91	.740	4.01	4.46
2016	2 Tms		30	30	0	166.0	711	187	100	99	25	2	5	6	49	1	137	8	9	13	.409	0-0	0	90	.808	4.98	5.37
2017	Bal	AL	32	32	0	157.1	728	179	104	98	25	1	6	4	93	1	142	1	8	15	.348	0-0	0	91	.841	6.27	5.61
2018	Mil	NL	16	16	0	80.2	338	71	28	23	3	5	1	5	27	1	50	1	5	2	.714	0-0	0	91	.636	2.98	2.57
2019	Hou	AL	33	33	0	167.1	720	164	83	74	23	2	5	5	61	0	140	4	14	6	.700	0-0	0	91	.726	4.19	3.98
2020	Cin	NL	6	4	2	14.1	67	15	10	9	1	0	0	2	9	0	12	0	0	3	.000	0-0	0	90	.799	5.62	5.65
2021	Cin	NL	28	28	0	163.0	690	166	64	61	17	8	2	3	50	0	125	2	12	7	.632	0-0	0	90	.729	3.94	3.37
16	Sea	AL	19	19	0	112.0	469	117	62	62	18	2	3	3	34	1	82	5	7	8	.467	0-0	0	90	.786	4.58	4.98
16	Bal	AL	11	11	0	54.0	242	70	38	37	7	0	2	3	15	0	55	3	2	5	.286	0-0	0	90	.850	5.83	6.17
Postseason			5	4	0	17.1	72	14	5	4	2	0	0	0	5	0	10	0	0	0	-	0-0	0	91	.607	2.64	2.08
11 ML YEARS			283	277	2	1581.0	6785	1632	777	729	175	46	36	39	549	10	1252	55	97	92	.513	0-0	0	91	.747	4.23	4.15

Andrew Miller

Pitches: L Bats: L Pos: RP-40   Ht: 6'7" Wt: 200 Born: 5/21/1985 Age: 37

Year	Team	Lg	G	GS	GF	IP	BFP	H	R	ER	HR	SH	SF	HB	TBB	IBB	SO	WP	W	L	Pct	Sv-Op	Hld	Vel	OPS	ERC	ERA
2006	Det	AL	8	8	0	10.1	51	8	9	7	0	0	0	0	10	0	6	1	0	1	.000	0-0	1	94	.700	4.79	6.10
2007	Det	AL	13	13	0	64.0	309	73	43	40	8	3	1	7	39	0	56	4	5	5	.500	0-0	0	92	.821	6.31	5.63
2008	Fla	NL	29	20	1	107.1	492	120	78	70	7	10	7	4	56	4	89	4	6	10	.375	0-0	2	91	.798	5.04	5.87
2009	Fla	NL	20	14	1	80.0	366	85	52	43	7	6	4	2	43	1	59	10	3	5	.375	0-0	1	91	.792	4.90	4.84
2010	Fla	NL	9	7	1	32.2	171	51	34	31	6	5	2	1	26	2	28	5	1	5	.167	0-0	0	91	1.054	10.20	8.54
2011	Bos	AL	17	12	2	65.0	310	77	43	40	8	6	5	3	41	0	50	2	6	3	.667	0-0	0	93	.857	6.48	5.54
2012	Bos	AL	53	0	4	40.1	169	28	15	15	3	0	3	2	20	1	51	1	3	2	.600	0-0	13	95	.588	2.76	3.35
2013	Bos	AL	37	0	11	30.2	135	25	12	9	3	1	0	2	17	0	48	1	1	2	.333	0-1	6	95	.624	3.83	2.64
2014	2 Tms	AL	73	0	15	62.1	242	33	16	14	3	2	2	4	17	2	103	3	5	5	.500	1-2	22	94	.456	1.36	2.02
2015	NYY	AL	60	0	53	61.2	246	33	16	14	5	1	2	5	20	1	100	2	3	2	.600	36-38	0	94	.475	1.61	2.04
2016	2 Tms	AL	70	0	23	74.1	275	42	13	12	8	1	1	2	9	0	123	1	10	1	.909	12-14	25	95	.487	1.27	1.45
2017	Cle	AL	57	0	6	62.2	244	31	11	10	3	2	1	5	21	0	95	1	4	3	.571	2-4	27	94	.440	1.42	1.44
2018	Cle	AL	37	0	5	34.0	154	31	16	16	3	0	0	5	16	1	45	1	2	4	.333	2-5	10	93	.729	4.19	4.24
2019	StL	NL	73	0	11	54.2	236	45	32	27	11	0	1	8	27	1	70	4	5	6	.455	6-11	28	92	.739	4.81	4.45
2020	StL	NL	16	0	5	13.0	55	9	4	4	0	0	0	3	5	0	16	2	1	1	.500	4-5	2	90	.522	2.55	2.77
2021	StL	NL	40	0	6	36.0	164	41	19	19	5	2	1	5	16	1	40	1	0	0	-	0-0	4	88	.868	5.98	4.75
14	Bos	AL	50	0	12	42.1	170	25	13	11	2	2	2	4	13	2	69	2	3	5	.375	0-0	13	94	.492	1.62	2.34
14	Bal	AL	23	0	3	20.0	72	8	3	3	1	0	0	0	4	0	34	1	2	0	1.000	1-2	9	94	.375	0.86	1.35
16	NYY	AL	44	0	16	45.1	172	28	8	7	5	1	1	2	7	0	77	0	6	1	.857	9-11	16	95	.521	1.55	1.39
16	Cle	AL	26	0	7	29.0	103	14	5	5	3	0	0	0	2	0	46	1	4	0	1.000	3-3	9	95	.433	0.87	1.55
Postseason			29	0	3	38.2	148	20	4	4	3	1	1	3	13	2	54	1	2	1	.667	1-2	9	94	.491	1.59	0.93
16 ML YEARS			612	66	147	829.0	3619	732	413	371	80	39	30	61	383	14	979	44	55	55	.500	63-80	141	93	.695	3.86	4.03

Brad Miller

Bats: L Throws: R Pos: 1B-58;PH-56;RF-14;2B-13;3B-8;LF-6;DH-3   Ht: 6'2" Wt: 195 Born: 10/18/1989 Age: 32

Year	Team	Lg	G	AB	H	2B	3B	HR	(Hm	Rd)	TB	R	RBI	RC	TBB	IBB	SO	HBP	SH	SF	SB	CS	GDP	Avg	OBP	Slg	OPS
2013	Sea	AL	76	306	81	11	6	8	(3	5)	128	41	36	41	24	0	52	1	2	2	5	3	2	.265	.318	.418	.737
2014	Sea	AL	123	367	81	15	4	10	(4	6)	134	47	36	41	34	2	95	2	3	3	4	2	2	.221	.288	.365	.653
2015	Sea	AL	144	438	113	22	4	11	(6	5)	176	44	46	58	47	0	101	2	4	6	13	4	7	.258	.329	.402	.730
2016	TB	AL	152	548	133	29	6	30	(22	8)	264	73	81	74	47	0	149	3	0	3	6	4	5	.243	.304	.482	.786
2017	TB	AL	110	338	68	13	3	9	(6	3)	114	43	40	37	63	4	110	2	0	4	5	3	5	.201	.327	.337	.664
2018	2 Tms		75	230	57	13	2	7	(5	2)	95	21	29	27	22	1	82	0	0	0	0	0	4	.248	.311	.413	.724
2019	2 Tms		79	154	40	6	1	13	(6	7)	87	26	25	26	15	0	45	1	0	2	2	0	2	.260	.329	.565	.894
2020	StL	NL	48	142	33	8	1	7	(1	6)	64	21	25	25	25	1	46	3	0	1	1	0	2	.232	.357	.451	.807
2021	Phi	NL	140	331	75	9	3	20	(10	10)	150	53	49	52	45	2	112	1	0	0	3	0	7	.227	.321	.453	.774
18	TB	AL	48	156	40	10	1	5	(3	2)	67	16	21	18	16	0	51	0	0	2	0	0	2	.256	.322	.429	.751
18	Mil	NL	27	74	17	3	1	2	(2	0)	28	5	8	9	6	1	31	0	0	0	0	0	0	.230	.288	.378	.666
19	Cle	AL	13	36	9	3	0	1	(0	1)	15	4	4	7	4	0	10	0	0	0	1	0	0	.250	.325	.417	.742
19	Phi	NL	66	118	31	3	1	12	(6	6)	72	22	21	19	11	0	35	1	0	2	1	0	2	.263	.331	.610	.941
Postseason			1	1	0	0	0	0	(0	0)	0	0	0	0	0	0	0	0	0	0	0	0	0	.000	.000	.000	.000
9 ML YEARS			947	2854	681	126	30	115	(63	52)	1212	369	367	381	322	10	792	15	9	21	39	16	36	.239	.317	.425	.742

Brian Miller

Bats: L Throws: R Pos: LF-2;CF-2;RF-1;PH-1;PR-1   Ht: 6'1" Wt: 196 Born: 8/20/1995 Age: 26

Year	Team	Lg	G	AB	H	2B	3B	HR	(Hm	Rd)	TB	R	RBI	RC	TBB	IBB	SO	HBP	SH	SF	SB	CS	GDP	Avg	OBP	Slg	OPS
2021	Jaxnvl	AAA	111	388	101	15	3	2	(-	-)	128	51	34	-	33	0	87	2	7	4	36	7	7	.260	.319	.330	.648
2021	Mia	NL	5	11	3	0	0	0	(0	0)	3	1	0	1	0	0	3	0	0	0	0	0	0	.273	.273	.273	.545

Justin Miller

Pitches: R Bats: R Pos: RP-23   Ht: 6'3" Wt: 225 Born: 6/13/1987 Age: 35

Year	Team	Lg	G	GS	GF	IP	BFP	H	R	ER	HR	SH	SF	HB	TBB	IBB	SO	WP	W	L	Pct	Sv-Op	Hld	Vel	OPS	ERC	ERA
2021	Roch	AAA	13	0	10	16.1	62	9	2	1	0	1	1	0	4	1	29	2	1	0	1.000	5--	-	-	.374	1.02	0.55
2014	Det	AL	8	0	4	12.1	53	14	9	7	2	1	2	0	2	0	5	0	1	0	1.000	0-0	0	92	.829	4.21	5.11
2015	Col	NL	34	0	9	33.1	129	21	15	15	2	0	0	0	11	0	38	2	3	3	.500	1-2	7	94	.553	1.75	4.05
2016	Col	NL	40	0	13	42.2	194	50	27	27	6	0	3	2	20	0	45	3	1	1	.500	0-0	1	93	.885	5.92	5.70
2018	Was	NL	51	0	10	52.1	215	42	22	21	10	1	2	2	17	1	60	1	7	1	.875	2-3	11	94	.705	3.41	3.61
2019	Was	NL	17	0	5	15.2	65	16	8	7	5	1	0	2	4	0	11	0	0	1	1.000	0-1	4	92	.878	5.94	4.02

Year Team	Lg	G	GS	GF	IP	BFP	H	R	ER	HR	SH	SF	HB	TBB	IBB	SO	WP	W	L	Pct	Sv-Op	Hld	Vel	OPS	ERC	ERA
2021 2 Tms	NL	23	1	6	19.0	83	20	13	13	5	2	1	2	6	0	13	0	1	0	1.000	1-1	2	93	.873	5.68	6.16
21 Was	NL	5	0	1	3.0	15	5	5	5	3	1	0	1	1	0	4	0	0	0	—	0-0	1	93	1.505	15.61	15.00
21 StL	NL	18	0	5	16.0	68	15	8	8	2	1	1	2	5	0	9	0	1	0	1.000	1-1	1	93	.735	4.09	4.50
6 ML YEARS		173	0	47	175.1	739	163	94	90	30	5	8	8	60	1	172	6	14	5	.737	4-7	25	93	.767	4.14	4.62

Owen Miller

Bats: R **Throws:** R **Pos:** 2B-29;1B-18;3B-7;PH-5;DH-3;SS-1 **Ht:** 6'0" **Wt:** 185 **Born:** 11/15/1996 **Age:** 25

Year Team	Lg	G	AB	H	2B	3B	HR	(Hm	Rd)	TB	R	RBI	RC	TBB	IBB	SO	HBP	SH	SF	SB	CS	GDP	Avg	OBP	Slg	OPS
2021 Clmbs	AAA	48	182	54	12	1	7	(-	-)	89	25	22	-	21	0	52	2	0	1	0	0	6	.297	.374	.489	.863
2021 Cle	AL	60	191	39	8	0	4	(2	2)	59	17	18	9	9	0	54	1	0	1	2	0	7	.204	.243	.309	.551

Shelby Miller

Pitches: R **Bats:** R **Pos:** RP-13 **Ht:** 6'3" **Wt:** 225 **Born:** 10/10/1990 **Age:** 31

Year Team	Lg	G	GS	GF	IP	BFP	H	R	ER	HR	SH	SF	HB	TBB	IBB	SO	WP	W	L	Pct	Sv-Op	Hld	Vel	OPS	ERC	ERA
2021 Indy	AAA	10	1	1	14.0	56	10	7	6	1	0	0	0	3	0	22	1	2	1	.667	0- -	-		.515	1.72	3.86
2012 StL	NL	6	1	1	13.2	54	9	2	2	0	0	0	0	4	0	16	0	1	0	1.000	0-0	1	93	.463	1.65	1.32
2013 StL	NL	31	31	0	173.1	722	152	65	59	20	7	3	5	57	0	169	2	15	9	.625	0-0	0	94	.670	3.34	3.06
2014 StL	NL	32	31	0	183.0	764	160	78	76	22	7	4	2	73	4	127	4	10	9	.526	0-0	0	93	.698	3.56	3.74
2015 Atl	NL	33	33	0	205.1	860	183	82	69	13	8	4	6	73	8	171	5	6	17	.261	0-0	0	94	.663	3.12	3.02
2016 Ari	NL	20	20	0	101.0	460	127	72	69	14	3	3	2	42	3	70	3	3	12	.200	0-0	0	93	.867	6.03	6.15
2017 Ari	NL	4	4	0	22.0	99	20	10	10	1	0	0	0	12	1	20	1	2	2	.500	0-0	0	95	.668	3.53	4.09
2018 Ari	NL	5	4	0	16.0	79	24	21	19	5	0	1	0	8	0	19	1	0	4	.000	0-0	0	94	1.048	9.35	10.69
2019 Tex	AL	19	8	4	44.0	220	58	46	42	8	0	4	3	29	1	30	1	1	3	.250	0-1	1	94	.908	7.95	8.59
2021 2 Tms	NL	13	0	4	12.2	62	16	13	13	3	0	1	1	11	0	8	0	1	0	.000	0-0	1	94	1.023	9.68	9.24
21 ChC	NL	3	0	1	2.0	18	7	7	7	0	0	0	0	5	0	1	0	0	0	—	0-0	0	94	1.417	31.30	31.50
21 Pit	NL	10	0	3	10.2	44	9	6	6	3	0	1	1	6	0	7	0	1	0	.000	0-0	1	94	.877	5.98	5.06
Postseason		5	2	0	13.2	61	16	8	8	1	1	1	1	6	0	12	0	0	0	—	0-0	0	94	.768	5.46	5.27
9 ML YEARS		163	132	9	771.0	3320	749	389	359	86	25	20	20	309	17	630	17	38	57	.400	0-1	4	94	.729	4.07	4.19

Alec Mills

Pitches: R **Bats:** R **Pos:** SP-20; RP-12 **Ht:** 6'4" **Wt:** 205 **Born:** 11/30/1991 **Age:** 30

Year Team	Lg	G	GS	GF	IP	BFP	H	R	ER	HR	SH	SF	HB	TBB	IBB	SO	WP	W	L	Pct	Sv-Op	Hld	Vel	OPS	ERC	ERA
2016 KC	AL	3	0	2	3.1	19	3	5	5	0	0	0	1	5	0	4	0	0	0	—	0-0	0	92	.858	8.02	13.50
2018 ChC	NL	7	2	1	18.0	71	11	8	8	1	0	0	0	7	0	23	1	0	1	.000	0-0	0	91	.550	1.80	4.00
2019 ChC	NL	9	4	3	36.0	152	31	11	11	5	0	0	7	11	0	42	0	1	0	1.000	1-1	0	90	.718	4.03	2.75
2020 ChC	NL	11	11	0	62.1	252	53	31	31	13	0	1	2	19	0	46	0	5	5	.500	0-0	0	90	.741	3.80	4.48
2021 ChC	NL	32	20	4	119.0	517	137	75	67	16	4	2	7	34	2	87	4	6	7	.462	1-1	0	89	.798	5.01	5.07
5 ML YEARS		62	37	10	238.2	1011	235	130	122	35	4	3	17	76	2	202	5	12	13	.480	2-2	0	90	.756	4.32	4.60

Wyatt Mills

Pitches: R **Bats:** R **Pos:** RP-11 **Ht:** 6'4" **Wt:** 190 **Born:** 1/25/1995 **Age:** 27

Year Team	Lg	G	GS	GF	IP	BFP	H	R	ER	HR	SH	SF	HB	TBB	IBB	SO	WP	W	L	Pct	Sv-Op	Hld	Vel	OPS	ERC	ERA
2021 Tacom	AAA	23	1	7	28.2	114	19	12	10	2	0	0	1	7	1	51	1	4	2	.667	2- -	-	-	.510	1.67	3.14
2021 Sea	AL	11	0	4	12.2	64	19	14	14	1	0	2	1	7	0	11	1	0	0	—	0-0	0	93	.940	7.88	9.95

Hoby Milner

Pitches: L **Bats:** L **Pos:** RP-19 **Ht:** 6'3" **Wt:** 175 **Born:** 1/13/1991 **Age:** 31

Year Team	Lg	G	GS	GF	IP	BFP	H	R	ER	HR	SH	SF	HB	TBB	IBB	SO	WP	W	L	Pct	Sv-Op	Hld	Vel	OPS	ERC	ERA
2021 Nashv	AAA	30	0	9	32.0	120	19	6	6	2	0	2	2	2	0	48	1	1	1	.500	5- -	-	-	.423	1.15	1.69
2017 Phi	NL	37	0	5	31.1	139	30	7	7	2	2	1	4	16	3	22	0	0	0	—	0-1	7	89	.736	4.39	2.01
2018 2 Tms		14	0	3	7.1	38	9	8	6	3	0	0	1	5	1	8	0	0	0	—	0-0	1	89	.988	9.22	7.36
2019 TB	AL	4	0	1	3.2	17	4	3	3	0	0	0	1	1	0	3	0	0	0	—	0-0	1	88	.820	4.28	7.36
2020 LAA	AL	19	0	4	13.1	59	13	12	12	5	0	0	1	6	0	13	0	0	0	—	0-0	1	88	.897	6.45	8.10
2021 Mil	NL	19	0	10	21.2	99	30	15	13	8	1	0	2	3	0	30	0	0	0	—	0-0	1	89	.970	7.64	5.40
18 Phi	NL	10	0	2	4.2	25	6	4	4	1	0	0	1	3	1	4	0	0	0	—	0-0	0	89	.829	7.79	7.71
18 TB	AL	4	0	1	2.2	13	3	4	2	2	0	0	0	2	0	4	0	0	0	—	0-0	1	89	1.294	11.59	6.75
5 ML YEARS		93	0	23	77.1	352	86	45	41	18	3	1	9	31	4	76	0	0	0	—	0-1	11	89	.864	6.11	4.77

Tommy Milone

Pitches: L **Bats:** L **Pos:** RP-5; SP-1 **mah-LONE** **Ht:** 6'0" **Wt:** 215 **Born:** 2/16/1987 **Age:** 35

Year Team	Lg	G	GS	GF	IP	BFP	H	R	ER	HR	SH	SF	HB	TBB	IBB	SO	WP	W	L	Pct	Sv-Op	Hld	Vel	OPS	ERC	ERA
2021 Buffalo	AAA	8	4	0	13.2	55	9	6	4	2	1	0	0	5	0	9	2	0	0	—	0- -	-	-	.627	2.41	2.63
2011 Was	NL	5	5	0	26.0	110	28	11	11	2	3	2	2	4	2	15	0	1	0	1.000	0-0	0	88	.742	3.55	3.81
2012 Oak	AL	31	31	0	190.0	791	207	90	79	24	3	3	4	36	2	137	2	13	10	.565	0-0	0	88	.738	4.04	3.74
2013 Oak	AL	28	26	0	156.1	667	160	83	72	25	0	6	2	39	2	126	1	12	9	.571	0-0	0	87	.738	3.98	4.14
2014 2 Tms	AL	22	21	1	118.0	519	128	63	55	16	1	2	5	37	2	75	0	6	4	.600	0-0	0	87	.763	4.55	4.19
2015 Min	AL	24	23	1	128.2	543	128	64	56	17	6	7	1	36	1	91	3	9	5	.643	1-1	0	88	.731	3.79	3.92

Year	Team	Lg	G	GS	GF	IP	BFP	H	R	ER	HR	SH	SF	HB	TBB	IBB	SO	WP	W	L	Pct	Sv-Op	Hld	Vel	OPS	ERC	ERA
2016	Min	AL	19	12	3	69.1	311	84	53	44	15	4	3	1	22	3	49	3	3	5	.375	0-0	0	88	.857	5.77	5.71
2017	2 Tms	NL	17	8	2	48.1	221	65	43	41	15	2	0	0	14	3	38	0	1	3	.250	1-1	0	88	.970	7.12	7.63
2018	Was	NL	5	4	1	26.1	118	37	17	17	7	2	2	1	1	0	23	0	1	1	.500	0-0	0	87	.917	6.17	5.81
2019	Sea	AL	23	6	0	111.2	453	102	61	59	24	0	5	2	23	2	94	1	4	10	.286	0-0	0	87	.765	3.63	4.76
2020	2 Tms	NL	9	9	0	39.0	181	55	34	29	9	1	2	2	6	0	40	1	1	4	.200	0-0	0	86	.950	6.50	6.69
2021	Tor	AL	6	1	1	14.0	65	20	10	10	3	0	0	0	3	0	17	0	1	0	1.000	1-1	0	84	.934	6.57	6.43
14	Oak	AL	16	16	0	96.1	405	91	42	38	12	1	2	4	26	2	61	0	6	3	.667	0-0	0	87	.705	3.53	3.55
14	Min	AL	6	5	1	21.2	114	37	21	17	4	0	0	1	11	0	14	0				0-0	0	87	.969	9.76	7.06
17	Mil	NL	6	3	1	21.0	93	29	15	15	6	0	0	0	2	0	16	0	1	0	1.000	1-1	0	88	.905	6.32	6.43
17	NYM	NL	11	5	1	27.1	128	36	28	26	9	2	0	0	12	3	22	0	0	3	.000	0-0	0	88	1.021	7.74	8.56
20	Bal	AL	6	6	0	29.1	129	33	18	13	5	1	1	2	4	0	31	1	1	4	.200	0-0	0	86	.776	4.30	3.99
20	Atl	NL	3	3	0	9.2	52	22	16	16	4	0	1	0	2	0	9	0	0	0	-	0-0	0	86	1.380	14.68	14.90
Postseason			1	1	0	6.0	25	5	1	1	0	0	0	1	1	0	6	1	0	0	-	0-0	0	88	.584	2.26	1.50
11 ML YEARS			189	146	9	927.2	3979	1014	529	473	157	22	32	20	221	17	705	11	52	51	.505	3-3	1	87	.784	4.46	4.59

Juan Minaya

Pitches: R Bats: R Pos: RP-29   **Ht: 6'4" Wt: 210 Born: 9/18/1990 Age: 31**

Year	Team	Lg	G	GS	GF	IP	BFP	H	R	ER	HR	SH	SF	HB	TBB	IBB	SO	WP	W	L	Pct	Sv-Op	Hld	Vel	OPS	ERC	ERA
2021	StPaul	AAA	17	0	2	29.0	135	29	14	11	3	1	0	4	15	0	37	6	2	3	.400	0--	-		.782	5.00	3.41
2016	CWS	AL	11	0	3	10.1	47	10	6	5	0	0	0	0	5	0	6	0	1	0	1.000	0-0	0	94	.712	4.19	4.35
2017	CWS	AL	40	0	20	43.2	184	38	22	22	7	0	1	4	20	0	51	2	3	2	.600	9-10	2	94	.765	4.51	4.53
2018	CWS	AL	52	0	9	46.2	209	39	19	17	3	0	0	3	29	3	58	9	2	2	.500	1-4	8	95	.673	3.84	3.28
2019	CWS	AL	22	0	8	27.2	126	31	13	12	4	0	0	2	12	0	27	3	0	0	-	0-0	5	93	.857	5.51	3.90
2021	Min	AL	29	0	9	40.0	167	27	12	11	4	1	1	2	20	0	43	3	2	1	.667	0-0	7	95	.624	2.89	2.48
5 ML YEARS			154	0	49	168.1	733	145	72	67	18	1	2	13	86	3	185	17	8	5	.615	10-14	17	95	.720	4.06	3.58

Mike Minor

Pitches: L Bats: R Pos: SP-28   **Ht: 6'4" Wt: 210 Born: 12/26/1987 Age: 34**

Year	Team	Lg	G	GS	GF	IP	BFP	H	R	ER	HR	SH	SF	HB	TBB	IBB	SO	WP	W	L	Pct	Sv-Op	Hld	Vel	OPS	ERC	ERA
2010	Atl	NL	9	8	1	40.2	170	53	28	27	6	1	3	0	11	0	43	0	2	2	.600	0-0	0	91	.880	5.71	5.98
2011	Atl	NL	15	15	0	82.2	361	93	39	38	7	3	1	1	30	5	77	2	5	3	.625	0-0	0	91	.785	4.51	4.14
2012	Atl	NL	30	30	0	179.1	728	151	88	82	26	8	8	5	56	7	145	3	11	10	.524	0-0	0	90	.702	3.28	4.12
2013	Atl	NL	32	32	0	204.2	820	177	79	73	22	5	6	1	46	2	181	5	13	9	.591	0-0	0	90	.657	2.76	3.21
2014	Atl	NL	25	25	0	145.1	637	165	77	77	21	6	2	6	44	2	120	5	6	12	.333	0-0	0	90	.798	4.93	4.77
2017	KC	AL	65	0	13	77.2	307	57	23	22	5	3	1	1	22	3	88	5	6	6	.500	6-9	17	94	.585	2.07	2.55
2018	Tex	AL	28	28	0	157.0	640	138	76	73	25	1	6	8	38	1	132	3	12	8	.600	0-0	0	93	.733	3.40	4.18
2019	Tex	AL	32	32	0	208.1	863	190	86	83	30	3	6	7	68	1	200	2	14	10	.583	0-0	0	93	.704	3.78	3.59
2020	2 Tms	AL	12	11	0	56.2	239	50	36	35	11	0	1	1	20	0	62	0	1	6	.143	0-0	0	91	.712	3.90	5.56
2021	KC	AL	28	28	0	158.2	669	156	92	89	26	2	2	5	41	0	149	4	8	12	.400	0-0	0	91	.750	3.95	5.05
20	Tex	AL	7	7	0	35.1	155	35	23	22	7	0	1	0	13	0	35	0	0	5	.000	0-0	0	91	.742	4.45	5.60
20	Oak	AL	5	4	0	21.1	84	15	13	13	4	0	0	1	7	0	27	0	1	1	.500	0-0	0	91	.655	3.02	5.48
Postseason			4	1	0	10.0	40	10	1	1	0	1	0	2	2	0	7	0	1	0	1.000	0-0	0	92	.702	3.66	0.90
10 ML YEARS			276	209	14	1311.0	5449	1230	624	599	179	32	36	36	376	21	1197	29	79	78	.503	6-9	17	91	.722	3.64	4.11

A.J. Minter

Pitches: L Bats: L Pos: RP-61   **Ht: 6'0" Wt: 215 Born: 9/2/1993 Age: 28**

Year	Team	Lg	G	GS	GF	IP	BFP	H	R	ER	HR	SH	SF	HB	TBB	IBB	SO	WP	W	L	Pct	Sv-Op	Hld	Vel	OPS	ERC	ERA
2021	Gwnntt	AAA	7	0	7	7.1	25	0	0	0	0	0	0	0	3	0	10	1	0	0	-	6--	-		.120	0.19	0.00
2017	Atl	NL	16	0	3	15.0	60	13	5	5	1	0	0	0	2	0	26	0	0	1	.000	0-0	5	96	.595	2.15	3.00
2018	Atl	NL	65	0	31	61.1	260	57	23	22	3	1	1	2	22	1	69	5	4	3	.571	15-17	12	97	.642	3.27	3.23
2019	Atl	NL	36	0	12	29.1	147	36	23	23	3	1	1	1	23	5	35	5	3	4	.429	5-7	5	96	.857	6.73	7.06
2020	Atl	NL	22	0	6	21.2	85	15	3	2	1	1	0	0	9	2	24	1	1	1	.500	0-0	5	96	.606	2.15	0.83
2021	Atl	NL	61	0	4	52.1	221	44	27	22	2	0	4	1	20	0	57	0	3	6	.333	0-6	23	96	.644	2.77	3.78
Postseason			7	1	2	8.0	31	5	2	2	0	0	0	0	2	0	13	1	1	0	1.000	0-1	1	97	.674	2.38	2.25
5 ML YEARS			200	0	56	179.2	773	165	81	74	10	3	6	4	76	8	211	11	11	15	.423	20-30	50	96	.674	3.39	3.71

Anthony Misiewicz

Pitches: L Bats: R Pos: RP-66   mih-SEV-itch   **Ht: 6'1" Wt: 200 Born: 11/1/1994 Age: 27**

Year	Team	Lg	G	GS	GF	IP	BFP	H	R	ER	HR	SH	SF	HB	TBB	IBB	SO	WP	W	L	Pct	Sv-Op	Hld	Vel	OPS	ERC	ERA
2020	Sea	AL	21	0	1	20.0	83	20	9	9	2	0	0	1	6	1	25	2	0	2	.000	0-1	8	94	.746	3.92	4.05
2021	Sea	AL	66	0	11	54.2	236	61	30	28	7	1	1	1	15	2	53	6	5	5	.500	0-5	19	94	.759	4.44	4.61
2 ML YEARS			87	0	12	74.2	319	81	39	37	9	1	1	2	21	3	78	8	5	7	.417	0-6	27	94	.756	4.30	4.46

Bryan Mitchell

Pitches: R Bats: L Pos: RP-2   **Ht: 6'2" Wt: 215 Born: 4/19/1991 Age: 31**

Year	Team	Lg	G	GS	GF	IP	BFP	H	R	ER	HR	SH	SF	HB	TBB	IBB	SO	WP	W	L	Pct	Sv-Op	Hld	Vel	OPS	ERC	ERA
2021	LV	AAA	20	0	6	28.1	127	32	20	19	2	1	3	1	16	1	20	4	3	1	.750	1--	-		.823	5.52	6.04
2021	Jaxnvl	AAA	11	3	1	29.1	117	20	9	9	3	0	0	0	13	0	37	1	0	1	1.000	0--	-		.580	2.64	2.76
2014	NYY	AL	3	1	1	11.0	44	10	3	3	0	0	0	2	3	0	7	0	0	1	.000	0-0	0	94	.751	3.34	2.45
2015	NYY	AL	20	2	8	29.2	143	37	24	21	4	0	0	2	16	1	29	6	0	2	.000	1-1	1	96	.817	6.51	6.37

			HOW MUCH PITCHED				WHAT HE GAVE UP										THE RESULTS						
Year	Team	Lg	G	GS	GF	IP	BFP	H	R	ER	HR	SH	SF	HB	TBB	IBB	SO	WP	W	L	Pct	Sv-Op	Hld	Vel	OPS	ERC	ERA
2016	NYY	AL	5	5	0	25.0	107	26	13	9	1	1	0	0	12	0	11	0	1	2	.333	0-0	0	95	.741	4.32	3.24
2017	NYY	AL	20	1	8	32.2	153	42	24	21	1	0	0	1	13	1	17	2	1	1	.500	1-1	0	96	.783	5.40	5.79
2018	SD	NL	16	11	2	73.0	337	85	45	44	12	1	2	2	43	1	38	1	2	4	.333	0-0	0	94	.868	6.52	5.42
2021	Mia	NL	2	0	2	4.0	18	5	2	2	0	0	0	0	2	1	4	0	0	0		0-0	0	94	.826	4.82	4.50
	6 ML YEARS		66	20	21	175.1	802	205	111	100	19	2	2	7	89	4	106	9	4	10	.286	2-2	1	95	.818	5.74	5.13

Casey Mize

Pitches: R **Bats:** R **Pos:** SP-30   **Ht:** 6'3" **Wt:** 212 **Born:** 5/1/1997 **Age:** 25

			HOW MUCH PITCHED				WHAT HE GAVE UP										THE RESULTS						
Year	Team	Lg	G	GS	GF	IP	BFP	H	R	ER	HR	SH	SF	HB	TBB	IBB	SO	WP	W	L	Pct	Sv-Op	Hld	Vel	OPS	ERC	ERA
2018	2 Tms	Low	5	5	0	13.2	55	13	6	6	2	0	0	2	3	0	14	0	0	1	.000	0- -	-	-	.747	4.23	3.95
2019	Lkland	A+	6	6	0	30.2	107	11	3	3	0	1	0	1	5	0	30	0	2	0	1.000	0- -	-	-	.300	0.55	0.88
2019	Erie	AA	15	15	0	78.2	323	69	30	28	5	1	3	6	18	0	76	0	6	3	.667	0- -	-	-	.635	2.82	3.20
2020	Det	AL	7	7	0	28.1	133	29	25	22	7	0	0	5	13	0	26	2	0	3	.000	0-0	0	94	.832	6.13	6.99
2021	Det	AL	30	30	0	150.1	612	130	64	62	24	1	4	11	41	0	118	7	7	9	.438	0-0	0	94	.716	3.59	3.71
	2 ML YEARS		37	37	0	178.2	745	159	89	84	31	1	4	16	54	0	144	9	7	12	.368	0-0	0	94	.736	3.97	4.23

Yadier Molina

Bats: R **Throws:** R **Pos:** C-118;PH-3;1B-1   YAH-dee-air   **Ht:** 5'11" **Wt:** 225 **Born:** 7/13/1982 **Age:** 39

			BATTING																	RUNNING			AVERAGES			
Year	Team	Lg	G	AB	H	2B	3B	HR	(Hm	Rd)	TB	R	RBI	RC	TBB	IBB	SO	HBP	SH	SF	SB	CS	GDP	Avg	OBP	Slg	OPS
2004	StL	NL	51	135	36	6	0	2	(1	1)	48	12	15	15	13	3	20	0	2	1	0	1	4	.267	.329	.356	.684
2005	StL	NL	114	385	97	15	1	8	(6	2)	138	36	49	46	23	3	30	2	8	3	2	3	10	.252	.295	.358	.654
2006	StL	NL	129	417	90	26	0	6	(3	3)	134	29	49	35	26	2	41	8	8	2	1	2	15	.216	.274	.321	.595
2007	StL	NL	111	353	97	15	0	6	(4	2)	130	30	40	38	34	5	43	3	2	4	1	1	18	.275	.340	.368	.708
2008	StL	NL	124	444	135	18	0	7	(2	5)	174	37	56	57	32	4	29	1	3	5	0	2	21	.304	.349	.392	.740
2009	StL	NL	140	481	141	23	1	6	(5	1)	184	45	54	64	50	2	39	6	6	1	9	3	27	.293	.366	.383	.749
2010	StL	NL	136	465	122	19	0	6	(1	5)	159	34	62	55	42	6	51	7	2	5	8	4	19	.262	.329	.342	.671
2011	StL	NL	139	475	145	32	1	14	(5	9)	221	55	65	64	33	4	44	1	5	4	4	5	21	.305	.349	.465	.814
2012	StL	NL	138	505	159	28	0	22	(9	13)	253	65	76	91	45	4	55	5	3	5	12	3	10	.315	.373	.501	.874
2013	StL	NL	136	505	161	44	0	12	(5	7)	241	68	80	84	30	4	55	3	0	3	3	2	14	.319	.359	.477	.836
2014	StL	NL	110	404	114	21	0	7	(3	4)	156	40	38	47	28	4	55	6	1	6	1	1	14	.282	.333	.386	.719
2015	StL	NL	136	488	132	23	2	4	(3	1)	171	34	61	48	32	3	59	0	1	9	3	1	16	.270	.310	.350	.660
2016	StL	NL	147	534	164	38	1	8	(4	4)	228	56	58	74	39	1	63	6	0	2	3	2	22	.307	.360	.427	.787
2017	StL	NL	136	501	137	27	1	18	(7	11)	220	60	82	67	28	4	74	4	1	9	9	4	14	.273	.312	.439	.751
2018	StL	NL	123	459	120	20	0	20	(3	17)	200	55	74	65	29	0	66	9	0	6	4	3	15	.261	.314	.436	.750
2019	StL	NL	113	419	113	24	0	10	(4	6)	167	45	57	50	23	0	58	5	0	5	6	0	14	.270	.312	.399	.711
2020	StL	NL	42	145	38	2	0	4	(2	2)	52	12	16	16	6	0	21	3	1	1	0	0	7	.262	.303	.359	.662
2021	StL	NL	121	440	111	19	0	11	(5	6)	163	45	66	53	24	1	79	5	0	3	3	0	16	.252	.297	.370	.667
	Postseason		101	361	101	19	0	4	(2	2)	132	29	36	36	27	6	42	3	1	2	1	1	13	.280	.333	.366	.699
	18 ML YEARS		2146	7555	2112	400	7	171	(71	100)	3039	758	998	975	537	50	882	74	43	74	69	37	277	.280	.330	.402	.733

Sam Moll

Pitches: L **Bats:** L **Pos:** RP-8   **Ht:** 5'9" **Wt:** 190 **Born:** 1/3/1992 **Age:** 30

			HOW MUCH PITCHED				WHAT HE GAVE UP										THE RESULTS						
Year	Team	Lg	G	GS	GF	IP	BFP	H	R	ER	HR	SH	SF	HB	TBB	IBB	SO	WP	W	L	Pct	Sv-Op	Hld	Vel	OPS	ERC	ERA
2021	Reno	AAA	21	0	3	21.2	101	19	17	14	3	0	0	2	15	0	30	0	0	0		0- -	-	-	.749	5.08	5.82
2021	LsVgs	AAA	12	0	5	13.2	55	12	4	4	2	0	0	0	5	0	17	0	1	1	.500	2- -	-	-	.709	3.73	2.63
2017	Oak	AL	11	0	1	6.2	35	13	8	8	2	0	0	0	3	0	7	0	0	0		0-0	3	92	1.176	12.45	10.80
2021	Oak	AL	8	0	1	10.1	44	8	4	4	1	0	0	2	5	0	8	0	0	0		0-0	0	94	.638	3.98	3.48
	2 ML YEARS		19	0	2	17.0	79	21	12	12	3	0	0	2	8	0	15	0	0	0		0-0	3	93	.885	7.00	6.35

Yoan Moncada

Bats: B **Throws:** R **Pos:** 3B-138;DH-6   yo-AHN   **Ht:** 6'2" **Wt:** 225 **Born:** 5/27/1995 **Age:** 27

			BATTING																	RUNNING			AVERAGES			
Year	Team	Lg	G	AB	H	2B	3B	HR	(Hm	Rd)	TB	R	RBI	RC	TBB	IBB	SO	HBP	SH	SF	SB	CS	GDP	Avg	OBP	Slg	OPS
2016	Bos	AL	8	19	4	1	0	0	(0	0)	5	3	1	0	1	0	12	0	0	0	0	0	0	.211	.250	.263	.513
2017	CWS	AL	54	199	46	8	2	8	(4	4)	82	31	22	27	29	0	74	3	0	0	3	2	0	.231	.338	.412	.750
2018	CWS	AL	149	578	136	32	6	17	(10	7)	231	73	61	73	67	1	217	1	2	2	12	6	4	.235	.315	.400	.714
2019	CWS	AL	132	511	161	34	5	25	(16	9)	280	83	79	94	40	2	154	4	1	3	10	3	1	.315	.367	.548	.915
2020	CWS	AL	52	200	45	8	3	6	(5	1)	77	28	24	30	28	0	72	1	0	2	0	0	1	.225	.320	.385	.705
2021	CWS	AL	144	520	137	33	1	14	(12	2)	214	74	61	89	84	1	157	10	0	2	3	2	6	.263	.375	.412	.787
	Postseason		3	13	1	0	0	0	(0	0)	1	1	0	1	0	1	4	0	0	0	1	0	0	.077	.143	.077	.220
	6 ML YEARS		539	2027	529	116	17	70	(47	23)	889	292	248	313	249	4	686	19	3	9	28	13	12	.261	.346	.439	.784

Adalberto Mondesi

Bats: B **Throws:** R **Pos:** 3B-20;SS-11;DH-5;PR-1   **Ht:** 6'1" **Wt:** 200 **Born:** 7/27/1995 **Age:** 26

			BATTING																	RUNNING			AVERAGES			
Year	Team	Lg	G	AB	H	2B	3B	HR	(Hm	Rd)	TB	R	RBI	RC	TBB	IBB	SO	HBP	SH	SF	SB	CS	GDP	Avg	OBP	Slg	OPS
2021	Omha	AAA	14	49	10	1	0	2	(-	-)	17	8	2	-	2	0	13	0	0	0	5	1	0	.204	.235	.347	.582
2016	KC	AL	47	135	25	1	3	2	(0	2)	38	16	13	9	6	0	48	2	6	0	9	1	1	.185	.231	.281	.512
2017	KC	AL	25	53	9	1	0	1	(1	0)	13	4	3	0	3	0	22	0	4	0	5	2	2	.170	.214	.245	.460
2018	KC	AL	75	275	76	13	3	14	(7	7)	137	47	37	39	11	0	77	1	3	1	32	7	2	.276	.306	.498	.804
2019	KC	AL	102	415	109	20	**10**	9	(4	5)	176	58	62	60	19	0	132	0	3	6	43	7	6	.263	.291	.424	.715

	BATTING																			RUNNING			AVERAGES			
Year Team	Lg	G	AB	H	2B	3B	HR	(Hm Rd)	TB	R	RBI	RC	TBB	IBB	SO	HBP	SH	SF	SB	CS	GDP	Avg	OBP	Slg	OPS
2020 KC	AL	59	219	56	11	3	6	(4 2)	91	33	22	24	11	0	70	1	2	0	24	8	4	.256	.294	.416	.710
2021 KC	AL	35	126	29	8	1	6	(4 2)	57	19	17	17	6	0	43	1	3	0	15	1	2	.230	.271	.452	.723
Postseason		1	1	0	0	0	0	(0 0)	0	0	0	0	0	0	1	0	0	0	0	0	0	.000	.000	.000	.000
6 ML YEARS		343	1223	304	54	20	38	(20 18)	512	177	154	149	56	0	392	5	21	7	128	26	17	.249	.283	.419	.701

Mickey Moniak

Bats: L **Throws:** R **Pos:** CF-8;LF-6;PH-6;RF-3;PR-1   **Ht:** 6'2" **Wt:** 195 **Born:** 5/13/1998 **Age:** 24

		BATTING																		RUNNING			AVERAGES			
Year Team	Lg	G	AB	H	2B	3B	HR	(Hm Rd)	TB	R	RBI	RC	TBB	IBB	SO	HBP	SH	SF	SB	CS	GDP	Avg	OBP	Slg	OPS
2021 LV	AAA	98	356	87	15	8	14	(- -)	160	41	63	-	31	4	99	4	1	8	5	2	2	.244	.306	.449	.755
2020 Phi	NL	8	14	3	0	0	0	(0 0)	3	3	0	1	4	0	6	0	0	0	0	0	0	.214	.389	.214	.603
2021 Phi	NL	21	33	3	0	0	1	(1 0)	6	3	3	1	3	1	16	0	1	0	0	0	0	.091	.167	.182	.348
2 ML YEARS		29	47	6	0	0	1	(1 0)	9	6	3	2	7	1	22	0	1	0	0	0	0	.128	.241	.191	.432

Frankie Montas

Pitches: R **Bats:** R **Pos:** SP-32   MOHN-tahs   **Ht:** 6'2" **Wt:** 255 **Born:** 3/21/1993 **Age:** 29

		HOW MUCH PITCHED					WHAT HE GAVE UP										THE RESULTS							
Year Team	Lg	G	GS	GF	IP	BFP	H	R	ER	HR	SH	SF	HB	TBB	IBB	SO	WP	W	L	Pct	Sv-Op	Hld	Vel	OPS	ERC	ERA
2015 CWS	AL	7	2	2	15.0	66	14	8	8	1	0	0	0	9	1	20	0	0	2	.000	0-0	0	97	.699	4.16	4.80
2017 Oak	AL	23	0	5	32.0	152	39	25	25	10	0	0	3	20	0	36	1	0	0	.500	0-0	1	98	.974	8.72	7.03
2018 Oak	AL	13	11	0	65.0	283	74	34	28	5	2	3	2	21	0	43	5	5	4	.556	0-0	0	96	.796	4.55	3.88
2019 Oak	AL	16	16	0	96.0	394	84	35	28	8	0	2	4	23	1	103	5	9	2	.818	0-0	0	97	.646	2.82	2.63
2020 Oak	AL	11	11	0	53.0	237	57	35	33	10	0	2	1	23	0	60	2	3	5	.375	0-0	0	96	.806	5.33	5.60
2021 Oak	AL	32	32	0	187.0	778	164	79	70	20	2	4	7	57	1	207	11	13	9	.591	0-0	0	96	.666	3.21	3.37
Postseason		2	1	0	5.2	27	9	6	6	2	0	0	0	1	0	5	0	1	1	.500	0-0	0	97	.947	8.56	9.53
6 ML YEARS		102	72	8	448.0	1910	432	216	192	54	4	11	17	153	3	469	24	31	23	.574	0-0	1	96	.723	3.92	3.86

Rafael Montero

Pitches: R **Bats:** R **Pos:** RP-44   **Ht:** 6'0" **Wt:** 190 **Born:** 10/17/1990 **Age:** 31

		HOW MUCH PITCHED					WHAT HE GAVE UP										THE RESULTS							
Year Team	Lg	G	GS	GF	IP	BFP	H	R	ER	HR	SH	SF	HB	TBB	IBB	SO	WP	W	L	Pct	Sv-Op	Hld	Vel	OPS	ERC	ERA
2014 NYM	NL	10	8	1	44.1	194	44	21	20	8	0	0	0	23	0	42	0	1	3	.250	0-0	0	92	.825	5.16	4.06
2015 NYM	NL	5	1	1	10.0	46	9	6	5	0	1	0	0	5	3	13	0	1	0	1.000	0-0	0	92	.661	2.50	4.50
2016 NYM	NL	9	3	1	19.0	93	23	17	17	4	0	0	0	16	1	20	2	0	1	.000	0-0	0	93	.965	8.15	8.05
2017 NYM	NL	34	18	4	119.0	550	141	75	73	12	9	8	5	67	5	114	6	5	11	.313	0-0	0	94	.832	6.01	5.52
2019 Tex	AL	22	0	6	29.0	113	23	8	8	5	0	0	2	5	0	34	0	2	0	1.000	0-1	7	96	.671	2.89	2.48
2020 Tex	AL	17	0	16	17.2	72	12	11	8	2	1	0	1	6	0	19	0	0	1	.000	8-8	0	96	.652	2.43	4.08
2021 2 Tms	AL	44	0	18	49.1	225	59	40	35	4	1	3	5	17	1	42	4	5	4	.556	7-13	4	96	.784	5.18	6.39
21 Sea	AL	40	0	17	43.1	204	56	39	35	4	1	3	5	15	1	37	4	5	3	.625	7-13	4	96	.819	5.86	7.27
21 Hou	AL	4	0	1	6.0	21	3	1	0	0	0	0	0	2	0	5	0	0	1	.000	0-0	0	95	.449	1.20	0.00
7 ML YEARS		141	30	47	288.1	1293	311	178	166	35	12	11	13	139	10	284	12	13	21	.382	15-22	12	94	.801	5.17	5.18

Jordan Montgomery

Pitches: L **Bats:** L **Pos:** SP-30   **Ht:** 6'6" **Wt:** 228 **Born:** 12/27/1992 **Age:** 29

		HOW MUCH PITCHED					WHAT HE GAVE UP										THE RESULTS							
Year Team	Lg	G	GS	GF	IP	BFP	H	R	ER	HR	SH	SF	HB	TBB	IBB	SO	WP	W	L	Pct	Sv-Op	Hld	Vel	OPS	ERC	ERA
2017 NYY	AL	29	29	0	155.1	649	140	72	67	21	2	3	1	51	0	144	7	9	7	.563	0-0	0	92	.684	3.50	3.88
2018 NYY	AL	6	6	0	27.1	116	25	11	11	3	0	0	0	12	0	23	0	2	0	1.000	0-0	0	90	.675	3.85	3.62
2019 NYY	AL	2	1	0	4.0	19	7	3	3	1	0	0	0	0	0	5	0	0	0	-	0-0	0	92	1.053	7.95	6.75
2020 NYY	AL	10	10	0	44.0	193	48	27	25	7	0	0	2	9	0	47	3	2	3	.400	0-0	0	93	.749	4.25	5.11
2021 NYY	AL	30	30	0	157.1	661	150	73	67	19	1	7	2	51	0	162	12	6	7	.462	0-0	0	93	.688	3.72	3.83
Postseason		1	1	0	4.0	17	3	1	1	0	0	0	0	3	0	4	0	0	0	-	0-0	0	92	.639	3.44	2.25
5 ML YEARS		77	76	0	388.0	1638	370	186	173	51	3	10	5	123	0	381	22	19	17	.528	0-0	0	92	.697	3.74	4.01

Dylan Moore

Bats: R **Throws:** R **Pos:** 2B-66;LF-48;PH-11;3B-10;RF-9;SS-4;PR-3;DH-1   **Ht:** 6'0" **Wt:** 185 **Born:** 8/2/1992 **Age:** 29

		BATTING																		RUNNING			AVERAGES			
Year Team	Lg	G	AB	H	2B	3B	HR	(Hm Rd)	TB	R	RBI	RC	TBB	IBB	SO	HBP	SH	SF	SB	CS	GDP	Avg	OBP	Slg	OPS
2019 Sea	AL	113	247	51	14	2	9	(6 3)	96	31	28	29	25	0	93	9	1	0	11	9	6	.206	.302	.389	.691
2020 Sea	AL	38	137	35	9	0	8	(4 4)	68	26	17	22	14	0	43	8	0	0	12	5	4	.255	.358	.496	.855
2021 Sea	AL	126	332	60	11	2	12	(7 5)	111	42	43	40	40	0	111	4	0	1	21	5	6	.181	.276	.334	.610
3 ML YEARS		277	716	146	34	4	29	(17 12)	275	99	88	91	79	0	247	21	1	1	44	19	16	.204	.301	.384	.685

Matt Moore

Pitches: L **Bats:** L **Pos:** SP-13; RP-11   **Ht:** 6'3" **Wt:** 210 **Born:** 6/18/1989 **Age:** 33

		HOW MUCH PITCHED					WHAT HE GAVE UP										THE RESULTS							
Year Team	Lg	G	GS	GF	IP	BFP	H	R	ER	HR	SH	SF	HB	TBB	IBB	SO	WP	W	L	Pct	Sv-Op	Hld	Vel	OPS	ERC	ERA
2021 LV	AAA	5	5	0	19.1	87	20	10	10	5	0	0	1	11	0	22	0	0	2	.000	0--	-	-	.901	6.51	4.66
2011 TB	AL	3	1	0	9.1	40	9	3	3	1	0	0	0	3	0	15	2	1	0	1.000	0-0	1	96	.651	3.54	2.89
2012 TB	AL	31	31	0	177.1	759	158	85	75	18	3	4	7	81	5	175	8	11	11	.500	0-0	0	94	.706	3.83	3.81
2013 TB	AL	27	27	0	150.1	642	119	58	55	14	5	6	4	76	1	143	17	17	4	.810	0-0	0	92	.655	3.36	3.29
2014 TB	AL	2	2	0	10.0	44	10	3	3	1	0	0	0	5	0	6	0	0	2	.000	0-0	0	92	.777	4.48	2.70
2015 TB	AL	12	12	0	63.0	278	74	40	38	7	0	3	4	23	1	46	6	3	4	.429	0-0	0	92	.839	5.63	5.43

Year	Team	Lg	G	GS	GF	IP	BFP	H	R	ER	HR	SH	SF	HB	TBB	IBB	SO	WP	W	L	Pct	Sv-Op	Hld	Vel	OPS	ERC	ERA
						HOW MUCH PITCHED			**WHAT HE GAVE UP**												**THE RESULTS**						
2016	2 Tms		33	33	0	198.1	838	184	93	90	25	4	4	6	72	1	178	6	13	12	.520	0-0	0	93	.694	3.83	4.08
2017	SF	NL	32	31	1	174.1	790	200	**116**	**107**	27	6	4	7	67	3	148	10	6	**15**	.286	0-0	0	93	.835	5.33	5.52
2018	Tex	AL	39	12	10	102.0	471	128	82	77	19	1	4	5	41	1	86	6	3	8	.273	0-1	2	92	.911	6.43	6.79
2019	Det	AL	2	2	0	10.0	33	3	0	0	0	0	0	0	1	0	9	0	0	0		0-0	0	93	.215	0.32	0.00
2021	Phi	NL	24	13	5	73.0	334	78	54	51	15	8	1	2	38	4	63	3	2	4	.333	0-0	1	92	.871	5.71	6.29
16	TB	AL	21	21	0	130.0	549	125	62	59	20	3	2	5	40	0	109	3	7	7	.500	0-0	0	93	.716	4.02	4.08
16	SF	AL	12	12	0	68.1	289	59	31	31	5	1	2	1	32	1	69	3	6	5	.545	0-0	0	93	.651	3.47	4.08
	Postseason		5	3	0	24.1	97	14	11	9	2	0	1	2	8	1	25	2	1	1	.500	0-0	0	93	.550	1.78	3.33
	10 ML YEARS		205	164	16	967.2	4229	963	534	499	129	27	26	35	407	16	869	58	56	60	.483	0-1	4	93	.761	4.47	4.64

Colin Moran

Bats: L **Throws:** R **Pos:** 1B-84;PH-14;DH-3;3B-1   **Ht:** 6'4" **Wt:** 225 **Born:** 10/1/1992 **Age:** 29

Year	Team	Lg	G	AB	H	2B	3B	HR	(Hm	Rd)	TB	R	RBI	RC	TBB	IBB	SO	HBP	SH	SF	SB	CS	GDP	Avg	OBP	Slg	OPS
							BATTING															**RUNNING**			**AVERAGES**		
2016	Hou	AL	9	23	3	1	0	0	(0	0)	4	1	2	0	1	0	8	1	0	0	0	0	4	.130	.200	.174	.374
2017	Hou	AL	7	11	4	0	1	1	(0	1)	9	3	3	4	1	0	1	0	0	0	0	0	0	.364	.417	.818	1.235
2018	Pit	NL	144	415	115	19	1	11	(5	6)	169	49	58	55	39	4	82	4	0	7	0	2	6	.277	.340	.407	.747
2019	Pit	NL	149	466	129	30	1	13	(6	7)	200	46	80	69	30	4	117	3	0	4	0	1	13	.277	.322	.429	.751
2020	Pit	NL	52	178	44	10	0	10	(4	6)	84	28	23	22	19	0	52	2	0	1	0	0	9	.247	.325	.472	.797
2021	Pit	NL	99	318	82	12	0	10	(4	6)	124	29	50	42	36	0	87	2	0	3	1	0	6	.258	.334	.390	.724
	6 ML YEARS		460	1411	377	72	3	45	(19	26)	590	156	216	192	126	8	347	12	0	15	1	3	38	.267	.329	.418	.747

Jovani Moran

Pitches: L **Bats:** L **Pos:** RP-5   **Ht:** 6'1" **Wt:** 167 **Born:** 4/24/1997 **Age:** 25

Year	Team	Lg	G	GS	GF	IP	BFP	H	R	ER	HR	SH	SF	HB	TBB	IBB	SO	WP	W	L	Pct	Sv-Op	Hld	Vel	OPS	ERC	ERA
						HOW MUCH PITCHED			**WHAT HE GAVE UP**												**THE RESULTS**						
2021	Wich	AA	20	0	7	37.2	139	14	8	8	3	0	0	0	14	0	64	1	2	1	.667	2--	-	-	.409	1.11	1.91
2021	StPaul	AAA	15	0	3	29.2	122	14	11	10	3	1	0	3	18	2	45	2	2	1	.667	1--	-	-	.569	2.36	3.03
2021	Min	AL	5	0	0	8.0	38	9	7	7	0	0	0	0	7	0	10	1	0	0	-	0-0	0	93	.744	6.06	7.88

Adrian Morejon

Pitches: L **Bats:** L **Pos:** SP-2   moh-ray-HOHN   **Ht:** 5'11" **Wt:** 224 **Born:** 2/27/1999 **Age:** 23

Year	Team	Lg	G	GS	GF	IP	BFP	H	R	ER	HR	SH	SF	HB	TBB	IBB	SO	WP	W	L	Pct	Sv-Op	Hld	Vel	OPS	ERC	ERA
						HOW MUCH PITCHED			**WHAT HE GAVE UP**												**THE RESULTS**						
2019	SD	NL	5	2	1	8.0	42	15	9	9	1	0	0	0	3	0	9	0	0	0		0-0	0	96	1.044	9.51	10.13
2020	SD	NL	9	4	0	19.1	79	20	11	10	7	0	0	0	4	0	25	0	2	2	.500	0-0	0	97	.877	5.33	4.66
2021	SD	NL	2	2	0	4.2	20	5	2	2	2	0	0	0	2	0	3	0	0	0	-	0-0	0	96	.961	7.26	3.86
	Postseason		3	1	0	5.0	23	3	3	3	0	0	0	1	2	0	4	1	0	1	.000	0-0	0	97	.461	1.80	5.40
	3 ML YEARS		16	8	1	32.0	141	40	22	21	10	0	0	0	9	0	37	0	2	2	.500	0-0	0	97	.938	6.69	5.91

Mitch Moreland

Bats: L **Throws:** L **Pos:** DH-60;PH-17;1B-7   **Ht:** 6'3" **Wt:** 245 **Born:** 9/6/1985 **Age:** 36

Year	Team	Lg	G	AB	H	2B	3B	HR	(Hm	Rd)	TB	R	RBI	RC	TBB	IBB	SO	HBP	SH	SF	SB	CS	GDP	Avg	OBP	Slg	OPS
							BATTING															**RUNNING**			**AVERAGES**		
2010	Tex	AL	47	145	37	4	0	9	(3	6)	68	20	25	27	25	5	36	1	0	2	3	1	3	.255	.364	.469	.833
2011	Tex	AL	134	464	120	22	1	16	(7	9)	192	60	51	56	39	6	92	4	2	3	2	2	5	.259	.320	.414	.733
2012	Tex	AL	114	327	90	18	0	15	(10	5)	153	41	50	46	23	5	71	1	2	4	1	1	8	.275	.321	.468	.789
2013	Tex	AL	147	462	107	24	1	23	(10	13)	202	60	60	55	45	1	117	3	0	8	0	0	10	.232	.299	.437	.736
2014	Tex	AL	52	167	41	9	1	2	(1	1)	58	18	23	20	12	0	43	1	2	2	0	0	7	.246	.297	.347	.644
2015	Tex	AL	132	471	131	27	0	23	(9	14)	227	51	85	74	32	2	112	1	0	5	1	0	9	.278	.330	.482	.812
2016	Tex	AL	147	460	107	21	0	22	(13	9)	194	49	60	56	35	5	118	8	0	0	1	0	8	.233	.298	.422	.720
2017	Bos	AL	149	508	125	34	4	22	(10	12)	233	73	79	69	57	6	120	6	0	5	0	1	14	.246	.326	.443	.769
2018	Bos	AL	124	404	99	23	4	15	(6	9)	175	57	68	60	50	2	102	0	0	5	2	0	12	.245	.325	.433	.758
2019	Bos	AL	91	298	75	17	1	19	(8	11)	151	48	58	49	34	0	74	1	0	2	1	0	12	.252	.328	.507	.835
2020	2 Tms		42	136	36	9	0	10	(6	4)	75	22	29	27	15	2	32	1	0	0	0	0	5	.265	.342	.551	.894
2021	Oak	AL	81	229	52	11	1	10	(6	4)	95	28	30	26	18	0	58	2	0	3	0	0	5	.227	.286	.415	.701
20	Bos	AL	22	67	22	4	0	8	(5	3)	50	14	21	19	11	1	18	1	0	0	0	0	0	.328	.430	.746	1.177
20	SD	NL	20	69	14	5	0	2	(1	1)	25	8	8	8	4	1	14	0	0	0	0	0	5	.203	.247	.362	.609
	Postseason		52	135	35	10	4	4	(3	1)	57	17	19	21	12	1	32	2	1	0	0	0	3	.259	.329	.422	.751
	12 ML YEARS		1260	4071	1020	219	9	186	(89	97)	1815	527	618	565	385	34	975	35	6	39	11	5	97	.251	.318	.446	.764

Dauri Moreta

Pitches: R **Bats:** R **Pos:** RP-4   DOW-ree   **Ht:** 6'2" **Wt:** 185 **Born:** 4/15/1996 **Age:** 26

Year	Team	Lg	G	GS	GF	IP	BFP	H	R	ER	HR	SH	SF	HB	TBB	IBB	SO	WP	W	L	Pct	Sv-Op	Hld	Vel	OPS	ERC	ERA
						HOW MUCH PITCHED			**WHAT HE GAVE UP**												**THE RESULTS**						
2021	Chatt	AA	18	0	6	26.2	100	17	6	4	3	0	0	0	5	0	37	1	4	0	1.000	0--	-	-	.504	1.62	1.35
2021	Lsvlle	AAA	24	0	19	26.1	99	14	4	2	2	1	0	0	4	0	21	1	2	0	1.000	8--	-	-	.418	1.06	0.68
2021	Cin	NL	4	0	3	3.2	14	2	1	1	1	0	0	0	1	0	4	0	0	0	-	0-0	0	95	.599	2.19	2.45

Adam Morgan

Pitches: L Bats: L Pos: RP-34 **Ht: 6'1" Wt: 200 Born: 2/27/1990 Age: 32**

Year	Team	Lg	G	GS	GF	IP	BFP	H	R	ER	HR	SH	SF	HB	TBB	IBB	SO	WP	W	L	Pct	Sv-Op	Hld	Vel	OPS	ERC	ERA
2021	Iowa	AAA	15	0	6	16.1	65	10	5	4	1	0	0	4	3	1	21	0	0	1	.000	0- -	-	-	.503	1.89	2.20
2015	Phi	NL	15	15	0	84.1	352	88	45	42	14	1	3	4	17	0	49	2	5	7	.417	0-0	0	89	.775	4.21	4.48
2016	Phi	NL	23	21	0	113.1	507	141	81	76	23	3	4	4	29	3	95	2	2	11	.154	0-0	0	91	.880	5.72	6.04
2017	Phi	NL	37	0	6	54.2	229	51	25	25	10	0	0	4	18	2	63	1	3	3	.500	0-1	6	94	.737	3.92	4.12
2018	Phi	NL	67	0	9	49.1	214	49	25	21	5	0	2	0	22	3	50	3	0	2	.000	1-4	14	94	.698	4.14	3.83
2019	Phi	NL	40	0	0	29.2	120	20	14	13	4	0	0	3	10	1	29	0	3	3	.500	0-2	19	93	.621	2.68	3.94
2020	Phi	NL	17	0	4	13.0	58	14	8	8	3	0	0	0	6	0	16	0	0	1	.000	0-2	2	92	.845	5.72	5.54
2021	ChC	NL	34	0	6	25.1	108	22	15	12	6	0	2	1	12	0	28	0	2	1	.667	2-4	4	93	.829	4.79	4.26
	7 ML YEARS		233	36	26	369.2	1588	385	213	197	65	4	11	12	114	9	330	8	15	28	.349	3-13	45	91	.788	4.57	4.80

Eli Morgan

Pitches: R Bats: R Pos: SP-18 **Ht: 5'10" Wt: 190 Born: 5/13/1996 Age: 26**

Year	Team	Lg	G	GS	GF	IP	BFP	H	R	ER	HR	SH	SF	HB	TBB	IBB	SO	WP	W	L	Pct	Sv-Op	Hld	Vel	OPS	ERC	ERA
2021	Clmbs	AAA	5	5	0	22.1	92	20	10	10	1	1	0	1	11	0	21	1	0	1	.000	0- -	-	-	.681	3.86	4.03
2021	Cle	AL	18	18	0	89.1	379	90	54	53	20	2	1	4	22	0	81	0	5	7	.417	0-0	0	90	.809	4.50	5.34

Shawn Morimando

Pitches: L Bats: L Pos: RP-4 **Ht: 6'0" Wt: 206 Born: 11/20/1992 Age: 29**

Year	Team	Lg	G	GS	GF	IP	BFP	H	R	ER	HR	SH	SF	HB	TBB	IBB	SO	WP	W	L	Pct	Sv-Op	Hld	Vel	OPS	ERC	ERA
2021	Jaxnvl	AAA	18	16	1	89.2	382	90	45	43	17	0	1	2	31	0	86	3	3	4	.429	0- -	-	-	.770	4.63	4.32
2016	Cle	AL	2	0	0	4.2	27	9	6	6	2	0	0	0	5	0	5	0	0	0	-	0-0	0	90	1.291	17.18	11.57
2021	Mia	NL	4	0	1	10.1	54	18	11	11	2	0	1	0	5	0	9	0	0	0	-	0-0	0	91	1.072	9.75	9.58
	2 ML YEARS		6	0	1	15.0	81	27	17	17	4	0	1	0	10	0	14	0	0	0	-	0-0	0	91	1.143	11.92	10.20

Max Moroff

Bats: B Throws: R Pos: 2B-4;3B-1;PH-1 **Ht: 5'10" Wt: 190 Born: 5/13/1993 Age: 29**

Year	Team	Lg	G	AB	H	2B	3B	HR	(Hm	Rd)	TB	R	RBI	RC	TBB	IBB	SO	HBP	SH	SF	SB	CS	GDP	Avg	OBP	Slg	OPS
2016	Pit	NL	2	2	0	0	0	0	(0	0)	0	0	0	0	0	0	2	0	0	0	0	0	0	.000	.000	.000	.000
2017	Pit	NL	56	120	24	4	1	3	(3	0)	39	19	21	15	16	0	43	2	1	1	0	1	0	.200	.302	.325	.627
2018	Pit	NL	26	59	11	1	0	3	(2	1)	21	7	9	7	7	1	24	1	0	0	0	0	0	.186	.284	.356	.640
2019	Cle	AL	20	32	4	1	0	1	(1	0)	8	3	4	1	2	0	16	0	1	0	1	0	0	.125	.176	.250	.426
2021	StL	NL	6	16	1	0	0	0	(0	0)	1	0	1	0	0	0	10	0	0	0	0	0	0	.063	.063	.063	.125
	5 ML YEARS		110	229	40	6	1	7	(6	1)	69	29	35	23	25	1	95	3	2	1	1	1	0	.175	.264	.301	.565

Reyes Moronta

Pitches: R Bats: R Pos: RP-4 **Ht: 5'10" Wt: 265 Born: 1/6/1993 Age: 29**

Year	Team	Lg	G	GS	GF	IP	BFP	H	R	ER	HR	SH	SF	HB	TBB	IBB	SO	WP	W	L	Pct	Sv-Op	Hld	Vel	OPS	ERC	ERA
2021	Scrmto	AAA	23	2	1	17.1	91	21	19	19	3	1	1	0	22	0	18	2	0	1	.000	0- -	-	-	1.000	10.02	9.87
2017	SF	NL	7	0	1	6.2	29	6	2	2	1	0	0	0	3	1	11	0	0	0	-	0-1	0	96	.656	3.74	2.70
2018	SF	NL	69	0	9	65.0	262	34	20	18	4	1	3	0	37	4	79	5	5	2	.714	1-6	12	97	.507	1.93	2.49
2019	SF	NL	56	0	5	56.2	246	41	19	18	4	1	1	3	33	1	70	3	3	7	.300	0-5	15	97	.612	3.18	2.86
2021	SF	NL	4	0	0	4.0	13	1	1	1	1	0	0	0	0	0	2	0	0	0	-	0-0	2	94	.385	0.46	2.25
	4 ML YEARS		136	0	15	132.1	550	82	42	39	10	2	4	3	73	6	162	8	8	9	.471	1-12	29	97	.560	2.47	2.65

Charlie Morton

Pitches: R Bats: R Pos: SP-33 **Ht: 6'5" Wt: 215 Born: 11/12/1983 Age: 38**

Year	Team	Lg	G	GS	GF	IP	BFP	H	R	ER	HR	SH	SF	HB	TBB	IBB	SO	WP	W	L	Pct	Sv-Op	Hld	Vel	OPS	ERC	ERA
2008	Atl	NL	16	15	0	74.2	345	80	56	51	9	5	4	2	41	2	48	2	4	8	.333	0-0	0	91	.816	5.21	6.15
2009	Pit	NL	18	18	0	97.0	416	102	49	49	7	1	1	5	40	0	62	4	5	9	.357	0-0	0	91	.761	4.56	4.55
2010	Pit	NL	17	17	0	79.2	382	112	79	67	15	6	6	7	26	3	59	5	2	12	.143	0-0	0	93	.908	7.10	7.57
2011	Pit	NL	29	29	0	171.2	769	186	82	73	6	12	6	13	77	5	110	9	10	10	.500	0-0	0	91	.737	4.52	3.83
2012	Pit	NL	9	9	0	50.1	223	62	30	26	5	5	2	2	11	1	25	4	2	6	.250	0-0	0	90	.812	4.74	4.65
2013	Pit	NL	20	20	0	116.0	493	113	51	42	6	6	2	16	36	1	85	5	7	4	.636	0-0	0	93	.683	3.84	3.26
2014	Pit	NL	26	26	0	157.1	666	143	76	65	9	7	5	19	57	2	126	8	6	12	.333	0-0	0	91	.682	3.64	3.72
2015	Pit	NL	23	23	0	129.0	563	137	77	69	13	4	0	12	41	6	96	2	9	9	.500	0-0	0	92	.769	4.41	4.81
2016	Phi	NL	4	4	0	17.1	71	15	8	8	1	1	0	0	8	0	19	1	1	1	.500	0-0	0	94	.651	3.42	4.15
2017	Hou	AL	25	25	0	146.2	617	125	65	59	14	2	13	2	50	1	163	4	14	7	.667	0-0	0	95	.692	3.34	3.62
2018	Hou	AL	30	30	0	167.0	695	130	63	58	18	1	4	16	64	0	201	4	15	3	.833	0-0	0	96	.659	3.25	3.13
2019	TB	AL	33	33	0	194.2	790	154	71	66	15	1	3	12	57	0	240	5	16	6	.727	0-0	0	94	.623	2.67	3.05
2020	TB	AL	9	9	0	38.0	170	43	21	20	4	0	2	4	10	0	42	1	2	2	.500	0-0	0	93	.764	4.65	4.74
2021	Atl	NL	33	33	0	185.2	756	136	77	69	16	6	6	17	58	1	216	5	14	6	.700	0-0	0	95	.591	2.58	3.34
	Postseason		13	12	1	61.1	260	52	25	23	5	2	2	5	22	0	67	3	7	3	.700	0-0	0	95	.642	3.25	3.38
	14 ML YEARS		292	291	0	1625.0	6956	1538	805	722	138	57	43	138	576	22	1492	59	107	95	.530	0-0	0	93	.707	3.82	4.00

Taylor Motter

Bats: R **Throws:** R **Pos:** PH-8;3B-3;2B-2;RF-1;DH-1;PR-1 **Ht:** 6'1" **Wt:** 195 **Born:** 9/18/1989 **Age:** 32

Year	Team	Lg	G	AB	H	2B	3B	HR	Hm	Rd	TB	R	RBI	RC	TBB	IBB	SO	HBP	SH	SF	SB	CS	GDP	Avg	OBP	Slg	OPS
2021	Albq	AAA	68	214	71	16	1	24	-	-	161	54	57	-	49	3	50	2	0	2	0	0	11	.332	.457	.752	1.209
2021	Wrcstr	AAA	11	38	9	1	0	0	-	-	10	5	3	-	7	0	9	0	0	0	0	0	0	.237	.356	.263	.619
2016	TB	AL	34	80	15	3	0	2	0	2	24	11	9	7	11	0	19	1	0	1	0	1	1	.188	.290	.300	.590
2017	Sea	AL	92	258	51	12	0	7	5	2	84	29	26	21	21	0	62	0	0	1	12	1	9	.198	.257	.326	.583
2018	2 Tms	AL	17	34	5	0	0	1	1	0	8	2	2	2	4	0	8	0	0	0	1	0	0	.147	.237	.235	.472
2021	2 Tms		16	26	5	1	1	0	0	0	8	5	1	2	3	0	8	0	0	0	0	0	1	.192	.276	.308	.584
18	Sea	AL	8	15	4	0	0	1	1	0	7	2	1	2	2	0	5	0	0	0	0	0	0	.267	.353	.467	.820
18	Min	AL	9	19	1	0	0	0	0	0	1	0	1	0	2	0	3	0	0	0	1	0	0	.053	.143	.053	.195
21	Col	NL	13	20	3	0	0	0	0	0	3	2	0	0	2	0	6	0	0	0	0	0	1	.150	.227	.150	.377
21	Bos	AL	3	6	2	1	1	0	0	0	5	3	1	2	1	0	2	0	0	0	0	0	0	.333	.429	.833	1.262
	4 ML YEARS		159	398	76	16	1	10	6	4	124	47	38	32	39	0	97	1	0	2	13	2	11	.191	.264	.312	.575

Ryan Mountcastle

Bats: R **Throws:** R **Pos:** 1B-84;DH-41;LF-21;PH-3 **Ht:** 6'4" **Wt:** 230 **Born:** 2/18/1997 **Age:** 25

Year	Team	Lg	G	AB	H	2B	3B	HR	Hm	Rd	TB	R	RBI	RC	TBB	IBB	SO	HBP	SH	SF	SB	CS	GDP	Avg	OBP	Slg	OPS
2017	Frdrck	A+	88	360	113	35	1	15	-	-	195	63	47	66	14	2	61	3	0	2	8	2	9	.314	.343	.542	.885
2017	Bowie	AA	39	153	34	13	0	3	-	-	56	18	15	13	3	0	35	1	0	2	0	0	2	.222	.239	.366	.605
2018	Bowie	AA	102	394	117	19	4	13	-	-	183	63	59	64	26	2	79	3	0	5	2	0	10	.297	.341	.464	.806
2019	Norfolk	AAA	127	520	162	35	4	25	-	-	274	81	83	93	24	1	130	4	0	5	2	1	10	.312	.344	.527	.871
2020	Bal	AL	35	126	42	5	0	5	2	3	62	12	23	25	11	0	30	1	0	2	0	1	2	.333	.386	.492	.878
2021	Bal	AL	144	534	136	23	1	33	22	11	260	77	89	78	41	2	161	4	0	7	4	3	12	.255	.309	.487	.796
	2 ML YEARS		179	660	178	28	1	38	24	14	322	89	112	103	52	2	191	5	0	9	4	4	14	.270	.324	.488	.812

Mike Moustakas

Bats: L **Throws:** R **Pos:** 3B-44;PH-12;1B-11;2B-1 moo-STOCK-us **Ht:** 6'0" **Wt:** 225 **Born:** 9/11/1988 **Age:** 33

Year	Team	Lg	G	AB	H	2B	3B	HR	Hm	Rd	TB	R	RBI	RC	TBB	IBB	SO	HBP	SH	SF	SB	CS	GDP	Avg	OBP	Slg	OPS
2011	KC	AL	89	338	89	18	1	5	3	2	124	26	30	31	22	0	51	1	2	2	2	0	5	.263	.309	.367	.675
2012	KC	AL	149	563	136	34	1	20	10	10	232	69	73	64	39	4	124	7	0	5	5	2	4	.242	.296	.412	.708
2013	KC	AL	136	472	110	26	0	12	5	7	172	42	42	35	32	1	83	5	1	4	2	4	13	.233	.287	.364	.651
2014	KC	AL	140	457	97	21	1	15	5	10	165	45	54	44	35	1	74	3	1	4	1	0	12	.212	.271	.361	.632
2015	KC	AL	147	549	156	34	1	22	9	13	258	73	82	85	43	1	76	13	4	5	1	2	14	.284	.348	.470	.817
2016	KC	AL	27	104	25	6	0	7	4	3	52	12	13	10	9	0	13	0	0	0	0	1	5	.240	.301	.500	.801
2017	KC	AL	148	555	151	24	0	38	14	24	289	75	85	77	34	7	94	3	0	6	0	0	18	.272	.314	.521	.835
2018	2 Tms		152	573	144	33	1	28	14	14	263	66	95	89	49	5	103	7	0	6	4	1	13	.251	.315	.459	.774
2019	Mil	NL	143	523	133	30	1	35	14	21	270	80	87	82	53	5	98	6	0	2	3	0	12	.254	.329	.516	.845
2020	Cin	NL	44	139	32	9	0	8	4	4	65	13	27	26	18	1	36	4	0	2	1	0	5	.230	.331	.468	.799
2021	Cin	NL	62	183	38	12	0	6	3	3	68	21	22	20	18	0	46	2	0	3	0	0	6	.208	.282	.372	.653
18	KC	AL	98	378	94	21	1	20	9	11	177	46	62	54	30	3	63	5	0	4	3	0	10	.249	.309	.468	.778
18	Mil	NL	54	195	50	12	0	8	5	3	86	20	33	35	19	2	40	2	0	2	1	1	3	.256	.326	.441	.767
	Postseason		44	169	34	5	0	6	3	3	57	17	18	15	10	3	33	1	1	1	0	0	2	.201	.249	.337	.586
	11 ML YEARS		1237	4456	1111	247	6	196	85	111	1958	522	610	563	352	25	798	51	8	39	19	10	107	.249	.309	.439	.749

Kyle Muller

Pitches: L **Bats:** R **Pos:** SP-8; RP-1 **Ht:** 6'7" **Wt:** 250 **Born:** 10/7/1997 **Age:** 24

Year	Team	Lg	G	GS	GF	IP	BFP	H	R	ER	HR	SH	SF	HB	TBB	IBB	SO	WP	W	L	Pct	Sv-Op	Hld	Vel	OPS	ERC	ERA
2021	Gwnntt	AAA	16	16	0	76.2	329	62	36	29	9	1	5	1	39	0	85	15	5	4	.556	0- -	-	-	.671	3.58	3.40
2021	Atl	NL	9	8	0	36.2	155	26	17	17	2	2	2	2	20	1	37	9	2	4	.333	0-0	0	93	.608	2.91	4.17

Cedric Mullins II

Bats: L **Throws:** L **Pos:** CF-153;PH-8;DH-3 **Ht:** 5'8" **Wt:** 175 **Born:** 10/1/1994 **Age:** 27

Year	Team	Lg	G	AB	H	2B	3B	HR	Hm	Rd	TB	R	RBI	RC	TBB	IBB	SO	HBP	SH	SF	SB	CS	GDP	Avg	OBP	Slg	OPS
2018	Bal	AL	45	170	40	9	0	4	1	3	61	23	11	17	17	0	37	2	2	0	2	3	0	.235	.312	.359	.671
2019	Bal	AL	22	64	6	0	2	0	0	0	10	7	4	1	4	0	14	3	2	1	1	0	2	.094	.181	.156	.337
2020	Bal	AL	48	140	38	4	3	3	2	1	57	16	12	17	8	0	37	1	4	0	7	2	1	.271	.315	.407	.723
2021	Bal	AL	159	602	175	37	5	30	22	8	312	91	59	109	59	3	125	8	1	4	30	8	2	.291	.360	.518	.878
	4 ML YEARS		274	976	259	50	10	37	25	12	440	137	86	144	88	3	213	14	9	5	40	13	5	.265	.333	.451	.784

Max Muncy

Bats: L **Throws:** R **Pos:** 1B-122;2B-39;3B-7;PH-5;DH-1 **Ht:** 6'0" **Wt:** 215 **Born:** 8/25/1990 **Age:** 31

Year	Team	Lg	G	AB	H	2B	3B	HR	Hm	Rd	TB	R	RBI	RC	TBB	IBB	SO	HBP	SH	SF	SB	CS	GDP	Avg	OBP	Slg	OPS
2015	Oak	AL	45	102	21	8	1	3	1	2	40	14	9	9	9	0	31	0	0	1	0	0	0	.206	.268	.392	.660
2016	Oak	AL	51	113	21	2	0	2	1	1	29	13	8	10	20	1	24	0	0	0	0	0	2	.186	.308	.257	.565
2018	LAD	NL	137	395	104	17	2	35	20	15	230	75	79	87	79	6	131	5	0	2	3	0	4	.263	.391	.582	.973
2019	LAD	NL	141	487	122	22	1	35	13	22	251	101	98	93	90	1	149	8	0	4	4	1	5	.251	.374	.515	.889

Year	Team	Lg	G	AB	H	2B	3B	HR	(Hm	Rd)	TB	R	RBI	RC	TBB	IBB	SO	HBP	SH	SF	SB	CS	GDP	Avg	OBP	Slg	OPS
2020	LAD	NL	58	203	39	4	0	12	(7	5)	79	36	27	28	39	2	60	4	0	2	1	0	3	.192	.331	.389	.720
2021	LAD	NL	144	497	124	26	2	36	(23	13)	262	95	94	109	83	5	120	11	0	1	2	1	7	.249	.368	.527	.895
	Postseason		39	129	30	5	0	9	(5	4)	62	26	27	29	36	2	46	0	0	0	2	0	1	.233	.400	.481	.881
	6 ML YEARS		576	1797	431	79	6	123	(65	58)	891	334	315	336	320	15	515	28	0	10	10	2	21	.240	.361	.496	.857

Andres Munoz

Pitches: R **Bats:** R **Pos:** RP-1   ahn-DRAYS MOO-nyohs   **Ht:** 6'2" **Wt:** 243 **Born:** 1/16/1999 **Age:** 23

			HOW MUCH PITCHED					WHAT HE GAVE UP										THE RESULTS							
Year	Team	Lg	G	GS	GF	IP	BFP	H	R	ER	HR	SH	SF	HB	TBB	IBB	SO	WP	W	L	Pct	Sv-Op	Hld	Vel	OPS	ERC	ERA
2019	SD	NL	22	0	3	23.0	97	16	10	10	2	1	0	0	11	0	30	1	1	1	.500	1-2	8	100	.611	2.59	3.91
2021	Sea	AL	1	0	0	0.2	4	0	0	0	0	0	0	0	2	0	1	0	0	0	.500	0-0	0	100	.500	7.00	0.00
	2 ML YEARS		23	0	3	23.2	101	16	10	10	2	1	0	0	13	0	31	1	1	1	.500	1-2	8	100	.612	2.72	3.80

Yairo Munoz

Bats: R **Throws:** R **Pos:** 2B-3;LF-1;PR-1   JYE-roh MOON-yohs   **Ht:** 5'11" **Wt:** 200 **Born:** 1/23/1995 **Age:** 27

									BATTING												RUNNING			AVERAGES			
Year	Team	Lg	G	AB	H	2B	3B	HR	(Hm	Rd)	TB	R	RBI	RC	TBB	IBB	SO	HBP	SH	SF	SB	CS	GDP	Avg	OBP	Slg	OPS
2021	Wrcstr	AAA	85	341	108	16	4	8	(-	-)	156	44	36	-	14	0	49	2	1	3	18	5	6	.317	.344	.457	.802
2018	StL	NL	108	293	81	16	0	8	(1	7)	121	39	42	46	30	7	71	4	0	2	5	6	3	.276	.350	.413	.763
2019	StL	NL	88	172	46	7	1	2	(0	2)	61	20	13	19	7	0	37	1	0	1	8	3	5	.267	.298	.355	.653
2020	Bos	AL	12	45	15	5	0	1	(1	0)	23	6	4	7	0	0	11	0	0	0	2	0	1	.333	.333	.511	.844
2021	Bos	AL	5	11	1	0	0	0	(0	0)	1	0	0	0	0	0	2	0	0	0	0	0	0	.091	.091	.091	.182
	Postseason		1	1	0	0	0	0	(0	0)	0	0	0	0	0	0	1	0	0	0	0	0	0	.000	.000	.000	.000
	4 ML YEARS		213	521	143	28	1	11	(2	9)	206	65	59	72	37	7	121	5	0	3	15	9	9	.274	.327	.395	.722

Patrick Murphy

Pitches: R **Bats:** R **Pos:** RP-25   **Ht:** 6'5" **Wt:** 235 **Born:** 6/10/1995 **Age:** 27

			HOW MUCH PITCHED					WHAT HE GAVE UP										THE RESULTS							
Year	Team	Lg	G	GS	GF	IP	BFP	H	R	ER	HR	SH	SF	HB	TBB	IBB	SO	WP	W	L	Pct	Sv-Op	Hld	Vel	OPS	ERC	ERA
2021	Buffalo	AAA	10	0	0	14.2	58	8	1	0	0	0	0	0	8	0	17	0	1	1	.500	0- -	-	-	.476	1.71	0.00
2020	Tor	AL	4	0	2	6.0	25	6	1	1	0	0	0	0	2	0	5	0	0	0	-	0-0	0	97	.711	3.19	1.50
2021	2 Tms		25	0	4	28.0	128	31	18	16	3	0	0	4	10	0	29	3	0	3	.000	0-0	5	97	.764	5.07	5.14
21	Tor	AL	8	0	1	9.1	44	12	6	5	1	0	0	2	4	0	6	1	0	1	.000	0-0	1	97	.856	7.02	4.82
21	Was	NL	17	0	3	18.2	84	19	12	11	2	0	0	2	6	0	23	2	0	2	.000	0-0	4	97	.716	4.18	5.30
	2 ML YEARS		29	0	6	34.0	153	37	19	17	3	0	0	4	12	0	34	3	0	3	.000	0-0	5	97	.755	4.72	4.50

Sean Murphy

Bats: R **Throws:** R **Pos:** C-112;PH-7;DH-5   **Ht:** 6'3" **Wt:** 228 **Born:** 10/4/1994 **Age:** 27

									BATTING												RUNNING			AVERAGES			
Year	Team	Lg	G	AB	H	2B	3B	HR	(Hm	Rd)	TB	R	RBI	RC	TBB	IBB	SO	HBP	SH	SF	SB	CS	GDP	Avg	OBP	Slg	OPS
2019	Oak	AL	20	53	13	5	0	4	(1	3)	30	14	8	7	6	0	16	1	0	0	0	0	3	.245	.333	.566	.899
2020	Oak	AL	43	116	27	5	0	7	(3	4)	53	21	14	15	24	0	37	0	0	0	0	0	0	.233	.364	.457	.821
2021	Oak	AL	119	393	85	23	0	17	(6	11)	159	47	59	53	40	0	114	12	0	3	0	0	7	.216	.306	.405	.710
	Postseason		8	23	5	0	0	2	(2	0)	11	4	4	5	2	0	4	0	0	1	0	0	1	.217	.269	.478	.747
	3 ML YEARS		182	562	125	33	0	28	(10	18)	242	82	81	75	70	0	167	13	0	3	0	0	16	.222	.321	.431	.752

Tom Murphy

Bats: R **Throws:** R **Pos:** C-88;PH-8;DH-4;PR-2   **Ht:** 6'1" **Wt:** 218 **Born:** 4/3/1991 **Age:** 31

									BATTING												RUNNING			AVERAGES			
Year	Team	Lg	G	AB	H	2B	3B	HR	(Hm	Rd)	TB	R	RBI	RC	TBB	IBB	SO	HBP	SH	SF	SB	CS	GDP	Avg	OBP	Slg	OPS
2015	Col	NL	11	35	9	1	0	3	(3	0)	19	5	9	9	4	1	10	0	0	0	0	0	0	.257	.333	.543	.876
2016	Col	NL	21	44	12	2	0	5	(5	0)	29	8	13	10	4	0	19	1	0	0	1	0	0	.273	.347	.659	1.006
2017	Col	NL	12	24	1	1	0	0	(0	0)	2	1	1	0	2	1	9	0	0	0	0	0	0	.042	.115	.083	.199
2018	Col	NL	37	93	21	7	1	2	(1	1)	36	5	11	8	3	1	44	0	0	0	0	1	2	.226	.250	.387	.637
2019	Sea	AL	76	260	71	12	1	18	(6	12)	139	32	40	43	19	0	87	1	0	1	2	0	0	.273	.324	.535	.858
2021	Sea	AL	97	277	56	8	0	11	(10	1)	97	35	34	34	40	0	99	2	0	3	0	0	8	.202	.304	.350	.655
	6 ML YEARS		254	733	170	31	2	39	(25	14)	322	86	108	104	72	3	268	4	0	4	3	1	12	.232	.303	.439	.742

Joe Musgrove

Pitches: R **Bats:** R **Pos:** SP-31; RP-1   **Ht:** 6'5" **Wt:** 230 **Born:** 12/4/1992 **Age:** 29

			HOW MUCH PITCHED					WHAT HE GAVE UP										THE RESULTS							
Year	Team	Lg	G	GS	GF	IP	BFP	H	R	ER	HR	SH	SF	HB	TBB	IBB	SO	WP	W	L	Pct	Sv-Op	Hld	Vel	OPS	ERC	ERA
2016	Hou	AL	11	10	1	62.0	256	59	28	28	9	0	1	3	16	0	55	0	4	4	.500	0-0	0	92	.758	3.80	4.06
2017	Hou	AL	38	15	5	109.1	462	117	59	58	18	5	2	4	28	1	98	4	7	8	.467	2-4	5	93	.798	4.54	4.77
2018	Pit	NL	19	19	0	115.1	486	113	56	52	12	3	5	8	23	3	100	5	6	9	.400	0-0	0	93	.687	3.40	4.06
2019	Pit	NL	32	31	0	170.1	718	168	98	84	21	1	6	9	39	1	157	2	11	12	.478	0-0	1	92	.738	3.66	4.44
2020	Pit	NL	8	8	0	39.2	166	33	17	17	5	0	2	2	16	0	55	1	1	5	.167	0-0	0	93	.711	3.56	3.86
2021	SD	NL	32	31	1	181.1	748	142	68	64	22	3	6	18	54	3	203	3	11	9	.550	0-0	0	93	.652	3.00	3.18
	Postseason		7	0	3	6.2	27	6	6	6	3	0	1	0	1	1	3	0	1	0	1.000	0-0	1	95	.859	4.35	8.10
	6 ML YEARS		140	114	7	678.0	2836	632	326	303	87	12	22	44	176	8	668	15	40	47	.460	2-4	6	93	.717	3.58	4.02

Wil Myers

Bats: R **Throws:** R **Pos:** RF-118;PH-23;LF-13;DH-1   **Ht:** 6'3" **Wt:** 207 **Born:** 12/10/1990 **Age:** 31

								BATTING													RUNNING			AVERAGES			
Year	Team	Lg	G	AB	H	2B	3B	HR	(Hm	Rd)	TB	R	RBI	RC	TBB	IBB	SO	HBP	SH	SF	SB	CS	GDP	Avg	OBP	Slg	OPS
2013	TB	AL	88	335	98	23	0	13	(5	8)	160	50	53	52	33	6	91	1	0	4	5	2	10	.293	.354	.478	.831
2014	TB	AL	87	325	72	14	0	6	(2	4)	104	37	35	32	34	3	90	0	0	2	6	1	10	.222	.294	.320	.614
2015	SD	NL	60	225	57	13	1	8	(3	5)	96	40	29	35	27	0	55	1	0	0	5	2	2	.253	.336	.427	.763
2016	SD	NL	157	599	155	29	4	28	(18	10)	276	99	94	97	68	1	160	4	0	5	28	6	12	.259	.336	.461	.797
2017	SD	NL	155	567	138	29	3	30	(8	22)	263	80	74	80	70	3	180	5	0	7	20	6	15	.243	.328	.464	.792
2018	SD	NL	83	312	79	25	1	11	(6	5)	139	39	39	45	30	1	94	0	0	1	13	1	10	.253	.318	.446	.763
2019	SD	NL	155	435	104	22	1	18	(9	9)	182	58	53	54	51	0	168	2	1	1	16	7	12	.239	.321	.418	.739
2020	SD	NL	55	198	57	14	2	15	(11	4)	120	34	40	44	18	0	56	2	0	0	2	1	0	.288	.353	.606	.959
2021	SD	NL	146	442	113	24	2	17	(6	11)	192	56	63	65	54	2	141	0	0	4	8	5	9	.256	.334	.434	.768
	Postseason		11	42	7	1	0	2	(2	0)	14	4	5	3	5	1	15	0	0	0	1	0	0	.167	.255	.333	.589
	9 ML YEARS		986	3438	873	193	14	146	(68	78)	1532	493	480	504	385	16	1035	15	1	24	103	31	80	.254	.330	.446	.775

Tommy Nance

Pitches: R **Bats:** R **Pos:** RP-27   **Ht:** 6'6" **Wt:** 235 **Born:** 3/19/1991 **Age:** 31

			HOW MUCH PITCHED					WHAT HE GAVE UP										THE RESULTS							
Year	Team	Lg	G	GS	GF	IP	BFP	H	R	ER	HR	SH	SF	HB	TBB	IBB	SO	WP	W	L	Pct	Sv-Op	Hld	Vel	OPS	ERC	ERA
2021	Iowa	AAA	10	0	3	15.1	57	7	4	4	1	0	0	0	3	0	18	0	1	0	1.000	0- -	-	-	.398	0.92	2.35
2021	ChC	NL	27	0	6	28.2	127	25	23	23	5	0	1	3	13	0	30	7	1	1	.500	0-0	5	95	.741	4.42	7.22

Tyler Naquin

Bats: L **Throws:** R **Pos:** CF-92;LF-22;RF-21;PH-18;PR-1   NAY-kwin   **Ht:** 6'2" **Wt:** 195 **Born:** 4/24/1991 **Age:** 31

								BATTING													RUNNING			AVERAGES			
Year	Team	Lg	G	AB	H	2B	3B	HR	(Hm	Rd)	TB	R	RBI	RC	TBB	IBB	SO	HBP	SH	SF	SB	CS	GDP	Avg	OBP	Slg	OPS
2016	Cle	AL	116	321	95	18	5	14	(9	5)	165	52	43	53	36	4	112	4	2	2	6	3	4	.296	.372	.514	.886
2017	Cle	AL	19	37	8	2	0	0	(0	0)	10	4	1	2	2	0	9	0	0	1	0	1	1	.216	.250	.270	.520
2018	Cle	AL	61	174	46	7	0	3	(0	3)	62	22	23	21	6	1	42	2	0	1	1	1	1	.264	.295	.356	.651
2019	Cle	AL	89	274	79	19	0	10	(6	4)	128	34	34	36	14	2	66	2	2	2	4	2	8	.288	.325	.467	.792
2020	Cle	AL	40	133	29	8	1	4	(0	4)	51	15	20	14	5	0	40	1	0	2	0	1	3	.218	.248	.383	.632
2021	Cin	NL	127	411	111	24	2	19	(13	6)	196	52	70	67	35	1	106	5	0	3	5	3	5	.270	.333	.477	.809
	Postseason		13	31	5	2	0	0	(0	0)	7	0	3	1	1	1	18	0	1	0	0	0	0	.161	.188	.226	.413
	6 ML YEARS		452	1350	368	78	8	50	(28	22)	612	179	191	193	98	8	375	14	4	11	16	11	26	.273	.326	.453	.779

Omar Narvaez

Bats: L **Throws:** R **Pos:** C-111;PH-22;2B-1;DH-1   nar-VAH-es   **Ht:** 5'11" **Wt:** 220 **Born:** 2/10/1992 **Age:** 30

								BATTING													RUNNING			AVERAGES			
Year	Team	Lg	G	AB	H	2B	3B	HR	(Hm	Rd)	TB	R	RBI	RC	TBB	IBB	SO	HBP	SH	SF	SB	CS	GDP	Avg	OBP	Slg	OPS
2016	CWS	AL	34	101	27	4	0	1	(1	0)	34	13	10	15	14	1	14	0	0	2	0	0	0	.267	.350	.337	.687
2017	CWS	AL	90	253	70	10	0	2	(2	0)	86	23	14	33	38	1	45	1	3	0	0	0	8	.277	.373	.340	.713
2018	CWS	AL	97	280	77	14	1	9	(4	5)	120	30	30	43	38	1	65	2	2	0	0	2	5	.275	.366	.429	.794
2019	Sea	AL	132	428	119	12	0	22	(13	9)	197	63	55	66	47	1	92	4	0	3	0	0	5	.278	.353	.460	.813
2020	Mil	NL	40	108	19	4	0	2	(2	0)	29	8	10	13	16	0	39	2	0	0	0	0	1	.176	.294	.269	.563
2021	Mil	NL	123	391	104	20	0	11	(4	7)	157	54	49	59	41	3	84	7	0	6	0	0	13	.266	.342	.402	.743
	Postseason		2	1	0	0	0	0	(0	0)	0	0	0	0	0	0	1	0	0	0	0	0	0	.000	.000	.000	.000
	6 ML YEARS		516	1561	416	64	1	47	(26	21)	623	191	168	229	194	7	339	16	5	11	0	2	32	.266	.351	.399	.750

Packy Naughton

Pitches: L **Bats:** R **Pos:** SP-5; RP-2   **Ht:** 6'2" **Wt:** 195 **Born:** 4/16/1996 **Age:** 26

			HOW MUCH PITCHED					WHAT HE GAVE UP										THE RESULTS							
Year	Team	Lg	G	GS	GF	IP	BFP	H	R	ER	HR	SH	SF	HB	TBB	IBB	SO	WP	W	L	Pct	Sv-Op	Hld	Vel	OPS	ERC	ERA
2021	Salt Lk	AAA	13	9	0	56.2	244	69	30	30	7	0	0	0	13	0	53	4	2	2	.500	0- -	-	-	.804	4.85	4.76
2021	LAA	AL	7	5	0	22.2	108	27	18	16	3	0	0	1	14	1	12	0	0	4	.000	0-0	0	91	.808	6.44	6.35

Josh Naylor

Bats: L **Throws:** L **Pos:** RF-51;1B-15;DH-4;PH-3   **Ht:** 5'11" **Wt:** 250 **Born:** 6/22/1997 **Age:** 25

								BATTING													RUNNING			AVERAGES			
Year	Team	Lg	G	AB	H	2B	3B	HR	(Hm	Rd)	TB	R	RBI	RC	TBB	IBB	SO	HBP	SH	SF	SB	CS	GDP	Avg	OBP	Slg	OPS
2019	SD	NL	94	253	63	15	0	8	(4	4)	102	29	32	36	25	1	64	0	0	1	1	1	4	.249	.315	.403	.719
2020	2 Tms		40	97	24	3	1	1	(0	1)	32	13	6	9	5	0	12	1	0	0	1	0	2	.247	.291	.330	.621
2021	Cle	AL	69	233	59	13	0	7	(1	6)	93	28	21	24	14	1	45	2	0	0	1	0	7	.253	.301	.399	.700
20	SD	NL	18	36	10	0	1	1	(0	1)	15	4	4	4	1	0	4	1	0	0	1	0	2	.278	.316	.417	.733
20	Cle	AL	22	61	14	3	0	0	(0	0)	17	9	2	5	4	0	8	0	0	0	0	0	0	.230	.277	.279	.556
	Postseason		2	7	5	3	0	1	(1	0)	11	3	3	3	0	0	0	0	0	0	0	0	0	.714	.714	1.571	2.286
	3 ML YEARS		203	583	146	31	1	16	(5	11)	227	70	59	69	44	2	121	3	0	1	3	1	13	.250	.306	.389	.695

Nick Neidert

Pitches: R Bats: R Pos: SP-7; RP-1   NY-dert   Ht: 6'1" Wt: 202 Born: 11/20/1996 Age: 25

Year	Team	Lg	G	GS	GF	IP	BFP	H	R	ER	HR	SH	SF	HB	TBB	IBB	SO	WP	W	L	Pct	Sv-Op	Hld	Vel	OPS	ERC	ERA
2021	Jaxnvl	AAA	13	12	1	63.2	281	66	37	25	7	1	4	6	21	0	47	3	6	3	.667	0--	-	-	.724	4.40	3.53
2020	Mia	NL	4	0	1	8.1	34	10	5	5	1	0	0	0	2	0	4	0	0	0	-	0-0	0	92	.853	5.06	5.40
2021	Mia	NL	8	7	1	35.2	157	31	18	18	4	1	2	5	23	1	21	3	1	2	.333	0-0	0	92	.783	5.08	4.54
2 ML YEARS			12	7	2	44.0	191	41	23	23	5	1	2	5	25	1	25	3	1	2	.333	0-0	0	92	.798	5.09	4.70

Jimmy Nelson

Pitches: R Bats: R Pos: RP-27; SP-1   Ht: 6'6" Wt: 250 Born: 6/5/1989 Age: 33

Year	Team	Lg	G	GS	GF	IP	BFP	H	R	ER	HR	SH	SF	HB	TBB	IBB	SO	WP	W	L	Pct	Sv-Op	Hld	Vel	OPS	ERC	ERA
2013	Mil	NL	4	1	0	10.0	37	2	1	1	0	0	1	0	5	0	8	1	0	0	-	0-0	0	94	.286	0.64	0.90
2014	Mil	NL	14	12	1	69.1	311	82	42	38	6	1	2	8	19	0	57	4	2	9	.182	0-0	0	94	.793	4.96	4.93
2015	Mil	NL	30	30	0	177.1	752	163	89	81	18	4	7	13	65	4	148	11	11	13	.458	0-0	0	93	.704	3.79	4.11
2016	Mil	NL	32	32	0	179.1	807	186	108	92	25	7	4	17	86	2	140	8	8	16	.333	0-0	0	93	.791	5.29	4.62
2017	Mil	NL	29	29	0	175.1	728	171	75	68	16	4	2	9	48	1	199	6	12	6	.667	0-0	0	94	.689	3.64	3.49
2019	Mil	NL	10	3	2	22.0	105	25	18	17	4	0	0	2	17	1	26	1	0	2	.000	0-0	0	93	.966	7.63	6.95
2021	LAD	NL	28	1	5	29.0	116	14	8	6	0	1	0	4	13	0	44	4	1	2	.333	0-1	6	94	.453	1.56	1.86
7 ML YEARS			147	108	8	662.1	2856	643	341	303	69	17	16	53	253	8	622	35	34	48	.415	0-1	6	93	.728	4.20	4.12

Kyle Nelson

Pitches: L Bats: L Pos: RP-10   Ht: 6'1" Wt: 175 Born: 7/8/1996 Age: 25

Year	Team	Lg	G	GS	GF	IP	BFP	H	R	ER	HR	SH	SF	HB	TBB	IBB	SO	WP	W	L	Pct	Sv-Op	Hld	Vel	OPS	ERC	ERA
2021	Clmbs	AAA	24	0	2	24.2	115	22	22	19	1	0	2	0	20	0	30	1	0	1	.000	1--	-	-	.688	4.53	6.93
2020	Cle	AL	1	0	0	0.2	6	3	4	4	1	0	0	0	1	0	0	0	0	0	-	0-0	0	90	1.867	56.63	54.00
2021	Cle	AL	10	0	4	9.2	49	10	10	10	0	0	0	2	8	0	8	0	0	0	-	0-0	0	93	.716	5.81	9.31
2 ML YEARS			11	0	4	10.1	55	13	14	14	1	0	0	2	9	0	8	0	0	0	-	0-0	0	92	.845	8.23	12.19

Nick Nelson

Pitches: R Bats: R Pos: RP-9; SP-2   Ht: 6'1" Wt: 205 Born: 12/5/1995 Age: 26

Year	Team	Lg	G	GS	GF	IP	BFP	H	R	ER	HR	SH	SF	HB	TBB	IBB	SO	WP	W	L	Pct	Sv-Op	Hld	Vel	OPS	ERC	ERA
2021	S-WB	AAA	27	5	4	49.2	226	47	30	22	6	1	3	2	29	0	59	12	3	4	.429	1--	-	-	.750	4.73	3.99
2020	NYY	AL	11	0	4	20.2	90	20	13	11	4	0	1	0	11	0	18	0	1	0	1.000	0-0	0	96	.780	5.18	4.79
2021	NYY	AL	11	2	3	14.1	78	15	16	14	0	0	2	3	16	0	22	5	0	2	.000	0-1	0	96	.857	6.94	8.79
Postseason			2	0	1	2.0	7	1	0	0	0	0	0	0	0	0	2	0	0	0	-	0-0	0	97	.286	0.54	0.00
2 ML YEARS			22	2	7	35.0	168	35	29	25	4	0	3	3	27	0	40	5	1	2	.333	0-1	0	96	.817	5.97	6.43

Hector Neris

Pitches: R Bats: R Pos: RP-74   NAIR-ess   Ht: 6'2" Wt: 227 Born: 6/14/1989 Age: 33

Year	Team	Lg	G	GS	GF	IP	BFP	H	R	ER	HR	SH	SF	HB	TBB	IBB	SO	WP	W	L	Pct	Sv-Op	Hld	Vel	OPS	ERC	ERA
2014	Phi	NL	1	0	1	1.0	3	0	0	0	0	0	0	0	0	0	1	0	1	0	1.000	0-0	0	93	.000	0.00	0.00
2015	Phi	NL	32	0	8	40.1	170	38	19	17	8	1	0	4	10	0	41	3	2	2	.500	0-0	2	93	.772	4.21	3.79
2016	Phi	NL	79	0	13	80.1	328	59	26	23	9	1	2	3	30	3	102	4	4	4	.500	2-6	28	94	.620	2.73	2.58
2017	Phi	NL	74	0	56	74.2	320	68	26	25	9	1	2	6	26	3	86	2	4	5	.444	26-29	4	95	.689	3.74	3.01
2018	Phi	NL	53	0	28	47.2	203	46	27	27	11	2	0	1	16	1	76	5	1	3	.250	11-14	4	95	.803	4.55	5.10
2019	Phi	NL	68	0	49	67.2	275	45	24	22	10	1	2	6	24	1	89	2	3	6	.333	28-34	2	95	.613	2.74	2.93
2020	Phi	NL	24	0	13	21.2	103	24	15	11	0	0	0	0	13	2	27	3	2	2	.500	5-8	4	94	.670	4.36	4.57
2021	Phi	NL	74	0	29	74.1	310	55	34	30	12	1	1	4	32	3	98	4	4	7	.364	12-19	11	94	.677	3.32	3.63
8 ML YEARS			405	0	197	407.2	1712	335	171	155	59	7	7	24	151	13	520	23	21	29	.420	84-110	55	94	.681	3.45	3.42

Sheldon Neuse

Bats: R Throws: R Pos: 2B-13;PH-10;3B-8;LF-4;PR-2;RF-1;DH-1   Ht: 6'0" Wt: 232 Born: 12/10/1994 Age: 27

Year	Team	Lg	G	AB	H	2B	3B	HR	(Hm	Rd)	TB	R	RBI	RC	TBB	IBB	SO	HBP	SH	SF	SB	CS	GDP	Avg	OBP	Slg	OPS
2021	OkCity		76	308	91	13	3	13	(-	-)	149	57	56	-	29	0	80	1	0	4	5	0	10	.295	.354	.484	.838
2019	Oak	AL	25	56	14	3	0	0	(0	0)	17	3	7	5	4	0	19	0	0	2	0	0	2	.250	.295	.304	.599
2021	LAD	NL	33	65	11	1	0	3	(2	1)	21	6	4	0	1	0	26	0	0	0	1	1	2	.169	.182	.323	.505
2 ML YEARS			58	121	25	4	0	3	(2	1)	38	9	11	5	5	0	45	0	0	1	1	1	4	.207	.236	.314	.550

Tyler Nevin

Bats: R Throws: R Pos: LF-4;1B-2   Ht: 6'4" Wt: 225 Born: 5/29/1997 Age: 25

Year	Team	Lg	G	AB	H	2B	3B	HR	(Hm	Rd)	TB	R	RBI	RC	TBB	IBB	SO	HBP	SH	SF	SB	CS	GDP	Avg	OBP	Slg	OPS
2021	Norfolk	AAA	111	401	91	18	0	16	(-	-)	157	45	52	-	42	0	91	5	0	5	1	1	13	.227	.305	.392	.696
2021	Bal	AL	6	14	4	2	0	1	(0	1)	9	3	3	4	4	0	5	0	0	0	0	0	0	.286	.444	.643	1.087

Jake Newberry

Pitches: R Bats: R Pos: RP-4   Ht: 6'2" Wt: 200 Born: 11/20/1994 Age: 27

		HOW MUCH PITCHED					WHAT HE GAVE UP										THE RESULTS						
Year	Team	Lg	G	GS	GF	IP	BFP	H	R	ER	HR	SH	SF	HB	TBB	IBB	SO	WP	W	L	Pct	Sv-Op	Hld	Vel	OPS	ERC	ERA
2021	Omha	AAA	43	0	12	58.1	256	68	36	34	6	2	3	1	21	3	72	5	2	5	.286	2- -	-	-	.795	4.93	5.25
2018	KC	AL	14	0	3	13.1	60	13	8	7	3	0	0	0	9	0	11	1	2	0	1.000	0-0	1	94	.857	6.10	4.73
2019	KC	AL	27	0	6	31.0	137	29	13	13	7	0	3	1	16	2	29	0	1	0	1.000	0-1	4	94	.849	5.08	3.77
2020	KC	AL	20	0	6	22.0	94	20	12	10	3	0	2	2	12	0	24	3	1	0	1.000	1-1	1	93	.772	4.99	4.09
2021	KC	AL	4	0	1	4.1	24	10	8	8	2	0	0	0	3	0	5	1	0	0	-	0-0	0	94	1.399	19.39	16.62
	4 ML YEARS		65	0	16	70.2	315	72	41	38	15	0	5	3	40	2	69	5	4	0	1.000	1-2	6	94	.871	5.95	4.84

Sean Newcomb

Pitches: L Bats: L Pos: RP-32   Ht: 6'5" Wt: 255 Born: 6/12/1993 Age: 29

		HOW MUCH PITCHED					WHAT HE GAVE UP										THE RESULTS						
Year	Team	Lg	G	GS	GF	IP	BFP	H	R	ER	HR	SH	SF	HB	TBB	IBB	SO	WP	W	L	Pct	Sv-Op	Hld	Vel	OPS	ERC	ERA
2021	Gwnntt	AAA	14	0	12	15.2	60	9	3	3	1	0	0	1	3	0	27	2	3	0	1.000	3- -	-	-	.449	1.38	1.72
2017	Atl	NL	19	19	0	100.0	456	100	51	48	10	5	3	6	57	6	108	3	4	9	.308	0-0	0	94	.780	4.85	4.32
2018	Atl	NL	31	30	0	164.0	696	137	74	71	18	4	3	1	81	1	160	4	12	9	.571	0-0	0	93	.679	3.62	3.90
2019	Atl	NL	55	4	4	68.1	293	61	28	24	8	0	2	3	29	1	65	4	6	3	.667	1-3	16	94	.692	3.83	3.16
2020	Atl	NL	4	4	0	13.2	70	20	17	17	4	0	1	3	6	0	10	1	0	2	.000	0-0	0	93	.998	9.58	11.20
2021	Atl	NL	32	0	5	32.1	150	28	17	17	1	1	1	2	27	1	43	5	2	0	1.000	1-2	2	96	.719	4.66	4.73
	Postseason		6	1	1	8.1	28	2	2	1	0	1	0	0	3	0	6	0	1	0	1.000	0-0	1	96	.269	0.57	1.08
	5 ML YEARS		141	57	9	378.1	1665	346	187	177	41	10	10	15	200	9	386	17	24	23	.511	2-5	18	94	.726	4.27	4.21

Kevin Newman

Bats: R Throws: R Pos: SS-132;2B-15;PH-10   Ht: 6'0" Wt: 185 Born: 8/4/1993 Age: 28

								BATTING											RUNNING			AVERAGES			
Year	Team	Lg	G	AB	H	2B	3B	HR	(Hm | Rd)	TB	R	RBI	RC	TBB	IBB	SO	HBP	SH	SF	SB	CS	GDP	Avg	OBP	Slg	OPS
2018	Pit	NL	31	91	19	2	0	0	(0 | 0)	21	7	6	5	4	1	23	1	0	1	0	1	2	.209	.247	.231	.478
2019	Pit	NL	130	493	152	20	6	12	(3 | 9)	220	61	64	73	28	2	62	7	2	1	16	8	5	.308	.353	.446	.800
2020	Pit	NL	44	156	35	5	0	1	(0 | 1)	43	12	10	15	12	0	21	1	1	2	0	1	1	.224	.281	.276	.556
2021	Pit	NL	148	517	117	22	3	5	(2 | 3)	160	50	39	35	27	3	41	1	6	3	6	1	7	.226	.265	.309	.574
	4 ML YEARS		353	1257	323	49	9	18	(5 | 13)	444	130	119	128	71	6	147	10	9	7	22	11	15	.257	.300	.353	.654

Ljay Newsome

Pitches: R Bats: R Pos: RP-6; SP-1   Ht: 5'11" Wt: 210 Born: 11/8/1996 Age: 25

		HOW MUCH PITCHED					WHAT HE GAVE UP										THE RESULTS						
Year	Team	Lg	G	GS	GF	IP	BFP	H	R	ER	HR	SH	SF	HB	TBB	IBB	SO	WP	W	L	Pct	Sv-Op	Hld	Vel	OPS	ERC	ERA
2020	Sea	AL	5	4	0	15.2	68	20	9	9	4	0	0	1	1	0	9	0	0	1	.000	0-0	0	91	.914	5.62	5.17
2021	Sea	AL	7	1	4	14.2	69	20	14	13	5	1	1	0	3	1	16	1	1	1	.500	0-0	0	93	.978	6.74	7.98
	2 ML YEARS		12	5	4	30.1	137	40	23	22	9	1	1	1	4	1	25	1	1	2	.333	0-0	0	92	.946	6.16	6.53

Tomas Nido

Bats: R Throws: R Pos: C-52;PH-6;3B-1   Ht: 6'0" Wt: 211 Born: 4/12/1994 Age: 28

								BATTING											RUNNING			AVERAGES			
Year	Team	Lg	G	AB	H	2B	3B	HR	(Hm | Rd)	TB	R	RBI	RC	TBB	IBB	SO	HBP	SH	SF	SB	CS	GDP	Avg	OBP	Slg	OPS
2017	NYM	NL	5	10	3	1	0	0	(0 | 0)	4	0	3	2	0	0	2	0	0	0	0	0	0	.300	.300	.400	.700
2018	NYM	NL	34	84	14	3	0	1	(1 | 0)	20	10	9	2	4	0	27	0	0	2	0	0	4	.167	.200	.238	.438
2019	NYM	NL	50	136	26	5	0	4	(2 | 2)	43	9	14	5	7	2	37	0	1	0	0	0	4	.191	.231	.316	.547
2020	NYM	NL	7	24	7	1	0	2	(2 | 0)	14	4	6	4	2	0	6	0	0	0	0	0	2	.292	.346	.583	.929
2021	NYM	NL	58	153	34	5	1	3	(1 | 2)	50	16	13	12	5	1	44	3	0	0	1	0	4	.222	.261	.327	.588
	5 ML YEARS		154	407	84	15	1	10	(6 | 4)	131	39	45	25	18	3	116	3	1	2	1	0	14	.206	.244	.322	.566

Brandon Nimmo

Bats: L Throws: R Pos: CF-84;LF-10;PH-6   NIH-moe   Ht: 6'3" Wt: 206 Born: 3/27/1993 Age: 29

								BATTING											RUNNING			AVERAGES			
Year	Team	Lg	G	AB	H	2B	3B	HR	(Hm | Rd)	TB	R	RBI	RC	TBB	IBB	SO	HBP	SH	SF	SB	CS	GDP	Avg	OBP	Slg	OPS
2016	NYM	NL	32	73	20	1	0	1	(1 | 0)	24	12	6	9	6	0	20	1	0	0	0	0	0	.274	.338	.329	.666
2017	NYM	NL	69	177	46	11	1	5	(3 | 2)	74	26	21	26	33	1	60	2	1	2	2	0	3	.260	.379	.418	.797
2018	NYM	NL	140	433	114	28	8	17	(8 | 9)	209	77	47	84	80	2	140	22	0	0	9	6	8	.263	.404	.483	.886
2019	NYM	NL	69	199	44	11	1	8	(2 | 6)	81	34	29	38	46	2	71	5	1	3	3	0	1	.221	.375	.407	.783
2020	NYM	NL	55	186	52	8	3	8	(5 | 3)	90	33	18	33	33	0	43	6	0	0	1	2	1	.280	.404	.484	.888
2021	NYM	NL	92	325	95	17	3	8	(4 | 4)	142	51	28	58	54	0	79	5	2	0	5	4	3	.292	.401	.437	.838
	6 ML YEARS		457	1393	371	76	16	47	(23 | 24)	620	233	149	248	252	5	413	41	4	5	20	12	16	.266	.393	.445	.838

Vinny Nittoli

Pitches: R Bats: R Pos: RP-1   Ht: 6'1" Wt: 210 Born: 11/11/1990 Age: 31

		HOW MUCH PITCHED					WHAT HE GAVE UP										THE RESULTS						
Year	Team	Lg	G	GS	GF	IP	BFP	H	R	ER	HR	SH	SF	HB	TBB	IBB	SO	WP	W	L	Pct	Sv-Op	Hld	Vel	OPS	ERC	ERA
2021	Tacom	AAA	23	6	3	33.2	142	36	22	21	7	0	1	3	7	1	41	5	1	1	.500	0- -	-	-	.858	4.84	5.61
2021	StPaul	AAA	5	0	2	5.1	20	2	2	2	1	0	0	0	3	0	6	1	0	1	.000	1- -	-	-	.544	2.12	3.38
2021	Sea	AL	1	0	0	1.0	6	1	2	2	1	0	0	0	2	0	1	0	0	0	-	0-0	0	93	1.500	20.50	18.00

Stephen Nogosek

Pitches: R **Bats:** R **Pos:** RP-1 **Ht:** 6'2" **Wt:** 205 **Born:** 1/11/1995 **Age:** 27

Year	Team	Lg	G	GS	GF	IP	BFP	H	R	ER	HR	SH	SF	HB	TBB	IBB	SO	WP	W	L	Pct	Sv-Op	Hld	Vel	OPS	ERC	ERA
2021	Syrcse	AAA	26	0	12	33.0	151	35	23	20	2	0	3	0	16	2	47	2	1	5	.167	6--	-	-	.747	4.21	5.45
2019	NYM	NL	7	0	6	6.2	34	12	8	8	2	0	1	0	2	0	6	0	0	1	.000	0-0	0	95	1.057	10.23	10.80
2021	NYM	NL	1	0	0	3.0	12	3	2	2	2	0	0	0	0	0	5	0	0	1	.000	0-0	0	94	1.000	5.62	6.00
	2 ML YEARS		8	0	6	9.2	46	15	10	10	4	0	1	0	2	0	11	0	0	2	.000	0-0	0	95	1.044	8.95	9.31

John Nogowski

Bats: R **Throws:** L **Pos:** 1B-32;PH-23;RF-1 **Ht:** 6'0" **Wt:** 245 **Born:** 1/5/1993 **Age:** 29

Year	Team	Lg	G	AB	H	2B	3B	HR	(Hm	Rd)	TB	R	RBI	RC	TBB	IBB	SO	HBP	SH	SF	SB	CS	GDP	Avg	OBP	Slg	OPS
2021	Memp	AAA	36	128	25	4	0	3	(-	-)	38	16	14	-	15	1	31	5	0	0	3	0	5	.195	.304	.297	.601
2021	Indy	AAA	20	54	14	2	0	1	(-	-)	19	5	10	-	13	0	10	1	0	1	3	0	0	.259	.406	.352	.758
2020	StL	NL	1	4	1	0	0	0	(0	0)	1	0	0	0	0	0	1	0	0	0	0	0	0	.250	.250	.250	.500
2021	2 Tms	NL	52	129	30	7	0	1	(0	1)	40	14	14	14	12	0	22	1	0	1	0	1	2	.233	.301	.310	.611
21	StL	NL	19	18	1	0	0	0	(0	0)	1	2	0	0	1	0	2	1	0	0	0	0	1	.056	.150	.056	.206
21	Pit	NL	33	111	29	7	0	1	(0	1)	39	12	14	14	11	0	20	0	0	1	0	1	1	.261	.325	.351	.677
	2 ML YEARS		53	133	31	7	0	1	(0	1)	41	14	14	14	12	0	23	1	0	1	0	1	2	.233	.299	.308	.608

Aaron Nola

Pitches: R **Bats:** R **Pos:** SP-32 **Ht:** 6'2" **Wt:** 200 **Born:** 6/4/1993 **Age:** 29

Year	Team	Lg	G	GS	GF	IP	BFP	H	R	ER	HR	SH	SF	HB	TBB	IBB	SO	WP	W	L	Pct	Sv-Op	Hld	Vel	OPS	ERC	ERA
2015	Phi	NL	13	13	0	77.2	318	74	31	31	11	1	1	2	19	1	68	0	6	2	.750	0-0	0	91	.703	3.62	3.59
2016	Phi	NL	20	20	0	111.0	483	116	68	59	10	5	4	6	29	3	121	2	6	9	.400	0-0	0	90	.712	3.80	4.78
2017	Phi	NL	27	27	0	168.0	693	154	67	66	18	2	0	2	49	2	184	1	12	11	.522	0-0	0	92	.679	3.30	3.54
2018	Phi	NL	33	33	0	212.1	831	149	57	56	17	6	4	7	58	3	224	4	17	6	.739	0-0	0	92	.570	2.09	2.37
2019	Phi	NL	34	34	0	202.1	852	176	91	87	27	4	2	11	80	3	229	3	12	7	.632	0-0	0	93	.708	3.79	3.87
2020	Phi	NL	12	12	0	71.1	289	54	31	26	9	0	1	2	23	2	96	1	5	5	.500	0-0	0	92	.627	2.72	3.28
2021	Phi	NL	32	32	0	180.2	749	165	95	93	26	3	2	9	39	1	223	0	9	9	.500	0-0	0	93	.691	3.32	4.63
	7 ML YEARS		171	171	0	1023.1	4215	888	440	418	118	21	14	39	297	15	1145	11	67	49	.578	0-0	0	92	.668	3.17	3.68

Austin Nola

Bats: R **Throws:** R **Pos:** C-48;PH-6;2B-4;1B-1 **Ht:** 6'0" **Wt:** 197 **Born:** 12/28/1989 **Age:** 32

Year	Team	Lg	G	AB	H	2B	3B	HR	(Hm	Rd)	TB	R	RBI	RC	TBB	IBB	SO	HBP	SH	SF	SB	CS	GDP	Avg	OBP	Slg	OPS
2021	ElPaso	AAA	11	33	10	2	0	1	(-	-)	15	3	4	-	5	0	7	1	0	0	0	0	1	.303	.410	.455	.865
2019	Sea	AL	79	238	64	12	1	10	(1	9)	108	37	31	34	23	1	63	4	1	1	1	0	8	.269	.342	.454	.796
2020	2 Tms		48	161	44	9	1	7	(4	3)	76	24	28	27	18	1	34	3	0	2	0	0	3	.273	.353	.472	.825
2021	SD	NL	56	173	47	12	0	2	(2	0)	65	15	29	32	14	0	19	5	0	2	0	1	2	.272	.340	.376	.716
20	Sea	AL	29	98	30	5	1	5	(3	2)	52	15	19	19	9	1	17	2	0	1	0	0	1	.306	.373	.531	.903
20	SD	NL	19	63	14	4	0	2	(1	1)	24	9	9	8	9	0	17	1	0	1	0	0	2	.222	.324	.381	.705
	Postseason		6	17	2	0	0	0	(0	0)	2	2	3	1	4	0	7	0	0	2	0	0	0	.118	.261	.118	.379
	3 ML YEARS		183	572	155	33	2	19	(7	12)	249	76	88	93	55	2	116	12	1	5	1	1	13	.271	.345	.435	.780

Sean Nolin

Pitches: L **Bats:** L **Pos:** SP-5; RP-5 **Ht:** 6'4" **Wt:** 250 **Born:** 12/26/1989 **Age:** 32

Year	Team	Lg	G	GS	GF	IP	BFP	H	R	ER	HR	SH	SF	HB	TBB	IBB	SO	WP	W	L	Pct	Sv-Op	Hld	Vel	OPS	ERC	ERA
2021	Roch	AAA	12	10	1	48.1	205	48	20	20	7	0	1	6	15	0	54	0	3	3	.500	0--	-	-	.729	4.18	3.72
2013	Tor	AL	1	1	0	1.1	11	7	6	6	1	0	0	0	1	0	0	0	0	1	.000	0-0	0	89	1.927	52.56	40.50
2014	Tor	AL	1	0	1	1.0	4	1	1	1	0	0	0	0	0	0	0	0	0	0	-	0-0	0	93	1.250	7.45	9.00
2015	Oak	AL	6	6	0	29.0	134	35	19	17	4	1	5	0	12	0	15	3	1	2	.333	0-0	0	87	.793	5.49	5.28
2021	Was	NL	10	5	3	26.2	123	32	13	13	4	1	1	2	13	0	20	0	0	2	.000	0-0	0	91	.885	6.39	4.39
	4 ML YEARS		18	12	4	58.0	272	75	39	37	10	2	6	2	26	0	35	3	1	5	.167	0-0	0	89	.890	6.72	5.74

Lars Nootbaar

Bats: L **Throws:** R **Pos:** RF-26;PH-24;LF-9;PR-1 **Ht:** 6'3" **Wt:** 210 **Born:** 9/8/1997 **Age:** 24

Year	Team	Lg	G	AB	H	2B	3B	HR	(Hm	Rd)	TB	R	RBI	RC	TBB	IBB	SO	HBP	SH	SF	SB	CS	GDP	Avg	OBP	Slg	OPS
2021	Memp	AAA	35	117	36	2	1	6	(-	-)	58	21	19	-	17	3	25	2	0	0	1	3	0	.308	.404	.496	.900
2021	StL	NL	58	109	26	3	1	5	(1	4)	46	15	15	16	13	1	28	0	1	1	2	1	0	.239	.317	.422	.739

Daniel Norris

Pitches: L **Bats:** L **Pos:** RP-56 **Ht:** 6'2" **Wt:** 207 **Born:** 4/25/1993 **Age:** 29

Year	Team	Lg	G	GS	GF	IP	BFP	H	R	ER	HR	SH	SF	HB	TBB	IBB	SO	WP	W	L	Pct	Sv-Op	Hld	Vel	OPS	ERC	ERA
2014	Tor	AL	5	1	2	6.2	30	5	4	4	1	0	0	0	5	0	4	0	0	0	-	0-0	1	91	.667	4.31	5.40
2015	2 Tms	AL	13	13	0	60.0	251	53	31	25	9	1	4	2	19	0	45	3	3	2	.600	0-0	0	92	.732	3.55	3.75
2016	Det	AL	14	13	1	69.1	302	75	30	26	10	0	3	0	22	0	71	1	4	2	.667	0-0	0	93	.762	4.46	3.38
2017	Det	AL	22	18	1	101.2	460	120	64	60	12	2	3	3	44	3	86	1	5	8	.385	0-0	0	93	.840	5.48	5.31
2018	Det	AL	11	8	0	44.1	200	46	28	28	8	1	2	2	19	0	51	2	0	5	.000	0-0	0	90	.791	5.06	5.68
2019	Det	AL	32	29	0	144.1	610	154	75	72	25	5	3	4	38	0	125	5	3	13	.188	0-0	0	91	.797	4.58	4.49

Year	Team	Lg	G	GS	GF	IP	BFP	H	R	ER	HR	SH	SF	HB	TBB	IBB	SO	WP	W	L	Pct	Sv-Op	Hld	Vel	OPS	ERC	ERA
2020	Det	AL	14	1	1	27.2	116	25	10	10	2	0	0	0	7	0	28	0	3	1	.750	0-0	0	93	.639	2.74	3.25
2021	2 Tms		56	0	13	57.0	248	55	41	39	9	1	0	2	30	1	58	5	2	3	.400	1-4	7	93	.780	5.02	6.16
15	Tor	AL	5	5	0	23.1	103	23	11	10	3	1	2	2	12	0	18	2	1	1	.500	0-0	0	91	.816	5.10	3.86
15	Det	AL	8	8	0	36.2	148	30	20	15	6	0	2	0	7	0	27	1	2	1	.667	0-0	0	92	.674	2.64	3.86
21	Det	AL	38	0	10	36.2	157	38	25	24	4	0	0	2	15	1	40	3	1	3	.250	1-3	6	93	.757	4.70	5.89
21	Mil	NL	18	0	3	20.1	91	17	16	15	5	1	0	0	15	0	18	2	1	0	1.000	0-1	1	93	.822	5.60	6.64
8 ML YEARS			167	83	18	511.0	2217	533	283	264	76	10	16	13	184	4	468	17	20	34	.370	1-4	8	92	.781	4.60	4.65

Aaron Northcraft

Pitches: R Bats: R Pos: RP-5
Ht: 6'3" Wt: 229 Born: 5/28/1990 Age: 32

Year	Team	Lg	G	GS	GF	IP	BFP	H	R	ER	HR	SH	SF	HB	TBB	IBB	SO	WP	W	L	Pct	Sv-Op	Hld	Vel	OPS	ERC	ERA
2021	ElPaso	AAA	13	0	4	13.1	67	21	17	12	1	0	1	0	6	0	11	1	0	2	.000	1--	-	-	.886	7.40	8.10
2021	SD	NL	5	0	3	8.0	34	5	2	2	1	0	0	0	8	0	5	0	1	0	1.000	0-0	0	88	.729	4.82	2.25

James Norwood

Pitches: R Bats: R Pos: RP-5
Ht: 6'2" Wt: 215 Born: 12/24/1993 Age: 28

Year	Team	Lg	G	GS	GF	IP	BFP	H	R	ER	HR	SH	SF	HB	TBB	IBB	SO	WP	W	L	Pct	Sv-Op	Hld	Vel	OPS	ERC	ERA
2021	ElPaso	AAA	42	0	19	42.2	185	39	22	22	3	1	1	1	21	0	68	4	3	4	.429	4--	-	-	.735	3.84	4.64
2018	ChC	NL	11	0	5	11.0	54	14	7	5	0	0	2	0	5	0	10	1	0	1	.000	0-0	2	98	.714	4.75	4.09
2019	ChC	NL	9	0	3	9.1	44	9	4	3	1	0	0	0	8	0	11	1	0	1	.000	0-0	0	96	.803	5.76	2.89
2020	ChC	NL	3	0	0	1.2	9	4	3	3	0	0	0	0	1	0	1	1	0	0	-	0-0	0	97	1.181	14.52	16.20
2021	SD	NL	5	0	2	5.0	23	6	0	0	0	0	0	0	3	0	3	0	0	0	-	0-0	0	97	.741	5.34	0.00
4 ML YEARS			28	0	10	27.0	130	33	14	11	1	0	2	0	17	0	24	3	0	2	.000	0-0	2	97	.781	5.70	3.67

Jacob Nottingham

Bats: R Throws: R Pos: DH-5;1B-4;PH-4;C-3
Ht: 6'2" Wt: 220 Born: 4/3/1995 Age: 27

Year	Team	Lg	G	AB	H	2B	3B	HR	(Hm	Rd)	TB	R	RBI	RC	TBB	IBB	SO	HBP	SH	SF	SB	CS	GDP	Avg	OBP	Slg	OPS
2018	Mil	NL	9	20	4	1	0	0	(0	0)	5	2	0	1	4	0	8	0	0	0	0	0	0	.200	.333	.250	.583
2019	Mil	NL	9	6	2	0	0	1	(0	1)	5	1	4	3	0	0	2	1	0	0	0	0	0	.333	.429	.833	1.262
2020	Mil	NL	20	48	9	1	0	4	(3	1)	22	8	13	9	5	0	20	1	0	0	0	0	0	.188	.278	.458	.736
2021	2 Tms		15	40	6	1	0	3	(3	0)	16	5	6	4	2	0	20	2	0	1	0	0	0	.150	.222	.400	.622
21	Mil	NL	5	14	3	1	0	2	(2	0)	10	2	4	1	0	0	8	0	0	0	0	0	0	.214	.214	.714	.929
21	Sea	AL	10	26	3	0	0	1	(1	0)	6	3	2	0	2	0	12	2	0	1	0	0	0	.115	.226	.231	.457
Postseason			2	4	0	0	0	0	(0	0)	0	0	0	0	0	0	3	0	0	0	0	0	0	.000	.000	.000	.000
4 ML YEARS			53	114	21	3	0	8	(6	2)	48	16	23	14	11	0	50	4	0	1	0	0	1	.184	.277	.421	.698

Darien Nunez

Pitches: L Bats: L Pos: RP-5; SP-1
Ht: 6'2" Wt: 205 Born: 3/19/1993 Age: 29

Year	Team	Lg	G	GS	GF	IP	BFP	H	R	ER	HR	SH	SF	HB	TBB	IBB	SO	WP	W	L	Pct	Sv-Op	Hld	Vel	OPS	ERC	ERA
2021	OkCity	AAA	29	0	2	49.0	191	29	15	14	4	1	0	1	20	0	75	5	7	0	1.000	0--	-	-	.571	2.03	2.57
2021	LAD	NL	6	1	1	7.2	33	8	8	7	3	0	0	0	4	0	8	0	0	1	.000	0-1	0	94	1.019	7.34	8.22

Dom Nunez

Bats: L Throws: R Pos: C-77;PH-4;1B-1
Ht: 6'0" Wt: 212 Born: 1/17/1995 Age: 27

Year	Team	Lg	G	AB	H	2B	3B	HR	(Hm	Rd)	TB	R	RBI	RC	TBB	IBB	SO	HBP	SH	SF	SB	CS	GDP	Avg	OBP	Slg	OPS
2019	Col	NL	16	39	7	3	0	2	(2	0)	16	4	4	2	3	0	17	0	0	1	0	0	0	.179	.233	.410	.643
2021	Col	NL	81	228	43	12	3	10	(6	4)	91	31	33	27	34	4	91	0	0	1	0	0	0	.189	.293	.399	.692
2 ML YEARS			97	267	50	15	3	12	(8	4)	107	35	37	29	37	4	108	0	0	2	0	0	0	.187	.284	.401	.685

Renato Nunez

Bats: R Throws: R Pos: 1B-8;DH-6
Ht: 6'1" Wt: 220 Born: 4/4/1994 Age: 28

Year	Team	Lg	G	AB	H	2B	3B	HR	(Hm	Rd)	TB	R	RBI	RC	TBB	IBB	SO	HBP	SH	SF	SB	CS	GDP	Avg	OBP	Slg	OPS
2021	Toledo	AAA	74	265	77	14	2	20	(-	-)	155	59	64	-	31	0	76	11	0	4	1	0	7	.291	.383	.585	.968
2021	Nashv	AAA	18	62	12	2	0	1	(-	-)	17	6	4	-	5	0	16	2	0	0	0	0	1	.194	.275	.274	.550
2016	Oak	AL	9	15	2	0	0	0	(0	0)	2	0	1	0	0	0	3	0	0	0	0	0	0	.133	.133	.133	.267
2017	Oak	AL	8	15	3	0	0	1	(0	1)	6	1	3	3	1	0	8	0	0	0	0	0	0	.200	.250	.400	.650
2018	2 Tms	AL	73	236	61	14	0	8	(0	8)	99	28	22	26	19	0	62	4	0	2	0	0	4	.258	.322	.419	.741
2019	Bal	AL	151	541	132	24	0	31	(16	15)	249	72	90	81	44	1	143	10	0	4	1	1	9	.244	.311	.460	.771
2020	Bal	AL	52	195	50	10	0	12	(7	5)	96	29	31	26	17	0	64	3	0	1	0	0	0	.256	.324	.492	.816
2021	Det	AL	14	53	10	3	0	4	(1	3)	25	7	7	6	1	0	16	1	0	0	0	0	2	.189	.218	.472	.690
18	Tex	AL	13	36	6	1	0	1	(0	1)	10	2	2	1	3	0	12	1	0	1	0	0	0	.167	.244	.278	.522
18	Bal	AL	60	200	55	13	0	7	(0	7)	89	26	20	25	16	0	50	3	0	1	0	0	4	.275	.336	.445	.781
6 ML YEARS			307	1055	258	51	0	56	(24	32)	477	137	154	142	82	1	296	18	0	7	1	1	19	.245	.308	.452	.760

Bailey Ober

Pitches: R **Bats:** R **Pos:** SP-20
Ht: 6'9" **Wt:** 260 **Born:** 7/12/1995 **Age:** 26

		HOW MUCH PITCHED					WHAT HE GAVE UP										THE RESULTS						
Year	Team	Lg	G	GS	GF	IP	BFP	H	R	ER	HR	SH	SF	HB	TBB	IBB	SO	WP	W	L	Pct	Sv-Op	Hld	Vel	OPS	ERC	ERA
2021	Min	AL	20	20	0	92.1	379	92	45	43	20	0	3	1	19	0	96	1	3	3	.500	0-0	0	92	.784	4.13	4.19

Riley O'Brien

Pitches: R **Bats:** R **Pos:** SP-1
Ht: 6'4" **Wt:** 180 **Born:** 2/6/1995 **Age:** 27

Year	Team	Lg	G	GS	GF	IP	BFP	H	R	ER	HR	SH	SF	HB	TBB	IBB	SO	WP	W	L	Pct	Sv-Op	Hld	Vel	OPS	ERC	ERA
2021	Lsvlle	AAA	23	22	0	112.2	490	93	59	57	16	3	3	10	55	1	121	7	7	7	.500	0--	-	-	.725	4.05	4.55
2021	Cin	NL	1	1	0	1.1	9	2	2	2	2	0	0	0	3	0	2	0	0	1	.000	0-0	0	92	1.889	32.44	13.50

Darren O'Day

Pitches: R **Bats:** R **Pos:** RP-12
Ht: 6'4" **Wt:** 220 **Born:** 10/22/1982 **Age:** 39

Year	Team	Lg	G	GS	GF	IP	BFP	H	R	ER	HR	SH	SF	HB	TBB	IBB	SO	WP	W	L	Pct	Sv-Op	Hld	Vel	OPS	ERC	ERA
2008	LAA	AL	30	0	17	43.1	194	49	24	22	2	2	1	4	14	6	29	1	0	1	.000	0-0	1	87	.719	4.20	4.57
2009	2 Tms		68	0	15	58.2	233	41	14	12	3	1	3	5	18	1	56	1	2	1	.667	2-2	20	85	.543	2.20	1.84
2010	Tex	AL	72	0	14	62.0	240	43	15	14	5	1	3	5	12	2	45	0	6	2	.750	0-2	22	86	.548	1.93	2.03
2011	Tex	AL	16	0	7	16.2	74	17	10	10	7	1	1	2	5	0	18	0	0	1	.000	0-0	3	84	.929	6.45	5.40
2012	Bal	AL	69	0	10	67.0	263	49	17	17	6	3	1	3	14	2	69	0	7	1	.875	0-2	15	85	.613	2.06	2.28
2013	Bal	AL	68	0	18	62.0	247	47	16	15	7	1	1	5	15	1	59	1	5	3	.625	2-6	20	86	.617	2.60	2.18
2014	Bal	AL	68	0	18	68.2	271	42	14	13	6	1	2	8	19	4	73	0	5	2	.714	4-8	25	87	.550	1.92	1.70
2015	Bal	AL	68	0	19	65.1	257	47	13	11	5	0	1	5	14	1	82	0	6	2	.750	6-11	18	87	.540	2.09	1.52
2016	Bal	AL	34	0	6	31.0	131	25	13	13	6	0	0	1	13	2	38	0	3	1	.750	3-5	10	86	.717	3.70	3.77
2017	Bal	AL	64	0	16	60.1	240	41	24	23	8	0	1	3	24	2	76	0	2	3	.400	2-4	17	88	.609	2.79	3.43
2018	Bal	AL	20	0	10	20.0	83	18	9	8	3	0	0	3	4	1	27	0	0	2	.000	2-4	4	87	.722	3.61	3.60
2019	Atl	NL	8	0	0	5.1	21	3	1	1	0	0	0	1	1	0	6	0	0	0	-	0-0	0	87	.554	1.35	1.69
2020	Atl	NL	19	0	1	16.1	67	8	3	2	1	0	0	3	5	0	22	0	4	0	1.000	0-1	2	86	.442	1.57	1.10
2021	NYY	AL	12	0	1	10.2	46	9	4	4	2	0	0	1	4	0	11	0	0	0	-	0-0	4	86	.695	4.00	3.38
09	NYM	NL	4	0	1	3.0	17	5	2	0	0	0	1	1	1	0	2	0	0	0	-	0-0	0	84	.769	7.72	0.00
09	Tex	AL	64	0	14	55.2	216	36	12	12	3	1	2	4	17	1	54	1	2	1	.667	2-2	20	85	.526	1.95	1.94
	Postseason		30	0	1	20.1	82	16	10	10	4	1	0	2	6	1	21	0	0	3	.000	0-0	6	86	.694	3.53	4.43
	14 ML YEARS		616	0	152	587.1	2367	439	177	165	61	10	14	49	162	22	611	3	40	19	.678	21-45	161	86	.609	2.58	2.53

Joseph Odom

Bats: R **Throws:** R **Pos:** C-1;PH-1
Ht: 6'2" **Wt:** 215 **Born:** 1/9/1992 **Age:** 30

								BATTING													RUNNING			AVERAGES			
Year	Team	Lg	G	AB	H	2B	3B	HR	(Hm	Rd)	TB	R	RBI	RC	TBB	IBB	SO	HBP	SH	SF	SB	CS	GDP	Avg	OBP	Slg	OPS
2021	Drham	AAA	29	92	20	4	0	3	(-	-)	33	12	15	-	9	0	42	3	0	1	0	0	4	.217	.305	.359	.663
2020	Sea	AL	18	39	5	0	0	0	(0	0)	5	2	2	1	4	0	20	0	1	0	0	0	1	.128	.209	.128	.338
2021	TB	AL	2	2	0	0	0	0	(0	0)	0	0	0	0	0	0	1	0	0	0	0	0	0	.000	.000	.000	.000
	2 ML YEARS		20	41	5	0	0	0	(0	0)	5	2	2	1	4	0	21	0	1	0	0	0	1	.122	.200	.122	.322

Rougned Odor

Bats: L **Throws:** R **Pos:** 2B-74;3B-33;PH-9
ROOG-ned oh-DORE
Ht: 5'11" **Wt:** 200 **Born:** 2/3/1994 **Age:** 28

								BATTING													RUNNING			AVERAGES			
Year	Team	Lg	G	AB	H	2B	3B	HR	(Hm	Rd)	TB	R	RBI	RC	TBB	IBB	SO	HBP	SH	SF	SB	CS	GDP	Avg	OBP	Slg	OPS
2014	Tex	AL	114	386	100	14	7	9	(4	5)	155	39	48	46	17	1	71	5	6	3	4	7	7	.259	.297	.402	.698
2015	Tex	AL	120	426	111	21	9	16	(7	9)	198	54	61	62	23	2	79	14	2	5	6	7	3	.261	.316	.465	.781
2016	Tex	AL	150	605	164	33	4	33	(17	16)	304	89	88	77	19	0	135	4	0	4	14	7	6	.271	.296	.502	.798
2017	Tex	AL	162	607	124	21	3	30	(18	12)	241	79	75	61	32	5	162	8	0	4	15	6	13	.204	.252	.397	.649
2018	Tex	AL	129	474	120	23	2	18	(10	8)	201	76	63	67	43	2	127	11	2	5	12	12	5	.253	.326	.424	.751
2019	Tex	AL	145	522	107	30	1	30	(15	15)	229	77	93	77	52	2	178	5	1	5	11	9	4	.205	.283	.439	.721
2020	Tex	AL	38	138	23	4	0	10	(6	4)	57	15	30	16	7	0	47	1	0	2	0	1	2	.167	.209	.413	.623
2021	NYY	AL	102	322	65	12	0	15	(7	8)	122	42	39	38	27	2	100	11	1	0	0	1	3	.202	.286	.379	.665
	Postseason		8	28	7	1	0	2	(0	2)	14	9	4	5	3	0	5	2	0	0	1	0	0	.250	.364	.500	.864
	8 ML YEARS		960	3480	814	158	26	161	(84	77)	1507	471	497	444	220	14	899	59	12	24	62	50	43	.234	.289	.433	.722

Jake Odorizzi

Pitches: R **Bats:** R **Pos:** SP-23; RP-1
oh-duh-RIZZ-ee
Ht: 6'2" **Wt:** 190 **Born:** 3/27/1990 **Age:** 32

Year	Team	Lg	G	GS	GF	IP	BFP	H	R	ER	HR	SH	SF	HB	TBB	IBB	SO	WP	W	L	Pct	Sv-Op	Hld	Vel	OPS	ERC	ERA
2012	KC	AL	2	2	0	7.1	34	8	4	4	1	0	0	0	4	0	4	0	0	1	.000	0-0	0	90	.820	5.34	4.91
2013	TB	AL	7	4	2	29.2	122	28	13	13	3	0	1	2	8	0	22	1	0	1	.000	1-1	0	91	.744	3.62	3.94
2014	TB	AL	31	31	0	168.0	719	156	79	77	20	3	8	5	59	0	174	3	11	13	.458	0-0	0	90	.692	3.68	4.13
2015	TB	AL	28	28	0	169.1	700	149	65	63	18	4	3	3	46	0	150	5	9	9	.500	0-0	0	91	.680	3.02	3.35
2016	TB	AL	33	33	0	187.2	773	170	80	77	29	3	6	4	54	3	166	3	10	6	.625	0-0	0	92	.715	3.56	3.69
2017	TB	AL	28	28	0	143.1	604	117	80	66	30	2	7	2	61	1	127	1	10	8	.556	0-0	0	91	.736	3.91	4.14
2018	Min	AL	32	32	0	164.1	711	151	89	82	20	4	4	8	70	3	162	1	7	10	.412	0-0	0	91	.743	4.02	4.49
2019	Min	AL	30	30	0	159.0	658	139	65	62	16	4	4	4	53	0	178	4	15	7	.682	0-0	0	93	.671	3.25	3.51
2020	Min	AL	4	4	0	13.2	60	16	10	10	4	0	0	1	3	0	12	0	0	1	.000	0-0	0	93	.903	6.00	6.59
2021	Hou	AL	24	23	0	104.2	441	97	51	49	16	4	1	3	34	1	91	0	6	7	.462	0-0	0	92	.735	3.82	4.21
	Postseason		1	1	0	5.0	20	5	2	2	1	0	0	0	0	0	5	1	0	1	.000	0-0	0	93	.737	3.05	3.60
	10 ML YEARS		219	215	2	1147.0	4822	1031	536	503	157	24	34	32	392	8	1086	18	68	63	.519	1-1	0	92	.713	3.63	3.95

Brian O'Grady

Bats: L Throws: R Pos: PH-21;RF-10;LF-4;CF-2;1B-1   Ht: 6'2" Wt: 215 Born: 5/17/1992 Age: 30

Year	Team	Lg	G	AB	H	2B	3B	HR	(Hm	Rd)	TB	R	RBI	RC	TBB	IBB	SO	HBP	SH	SF	SB	CS	GDP	Avg	OBP	Slg	OPS
2021	ElPaso	AAA	70	268	72	19	5	13	(-	-)	140	40	40	-	33	2	80	4	0	3	10	3	1	.269	.354	.522	.876
2019	Cin	NL	28	42	8	2	1	2	(0	2)	18	4	3	4	4	0	17	2	0	0	1	0	0	.190	.292	.429	.720
2020	TB	AL	2	5	2	1	0	0	(0	0)	3	2	0	0	0	0	1	0	0	0	1	0	0	.400	.400	.600	1.000
2021	SD	NL	32	51	8	3	0	2	(1	1)	17	8	9	3	8	0	17	0	1	1	0	0	1	.157	.267	.333	.600
	3 ML YEARS		62	98	18	6	1	4	(1	3)	38	14	12	7	12	0	35	2	1	1	2	0	1	.184	.283	.388	.671

Ryan O'Hearn

Bats: L Throws: L Pos: DH-29;RF-25;1B-20;PH-15;LF-1   Ht: 6'3" Wt: 220 Born: 7/26/1993 Age: 28

Year	Team	Lg	G	AB	H	2B	3B	HR	(Hm	Rd)	TB	R	RBI	RC	TBB	IBB	SO	HBP	SH	SF	SB	CS	GDP	Avg	OBP	Slg	OPS
2021	Omha	AAA	19	72	27	4	0	12	(-	-)	67	22	25	-	9	1	15	1	0	0	3	0	1	.375	.451	.931	1.382
2018	KC	AL	44	149	39	10	2	12	(5	7)	89	23	30	33	20	0	45	1	0	0	0	0	0	.262	.353	.597	.950
2019	KC	AL	105	328	64	13	1	14	(6	8)	121	32	38	25	39	1	99	1	0	2	0	1	7	.195	.281	.369	.650
2020	KC	AL	42	113	22	6	0	2	(0	2)	34	7	18	14	18	2	37	0	0	1	0	0	0	.195	.303	.301	.604
2021	KC	AL	84	236	53	5	1	9	(1	8)	87	23	29	24	13	0	71	2	0	3	0	0	7	.225	.268	.369	.636
	4 ML YEARS		275	826	178	34	4	37	(12	25)	331	85	115	96	90	3	252	4	0	6	0	1	19	.215	.294	.401	.694

Shohei Ohtani

Bats: L Throws: R Pos: DH-126;PH-9;RF-6;LF-1   Ht: 6'4" Wt: 210 Born: 7/5/1994 Age: 27

Year	Team	Lg	G	AB	H	2B	3B	HR	(Hm	Rd)	TB	R	RBI	RC	TBB	IBB	SO	HBP	SH	SF	SB	CS	GDP	Avg	OBP	Slg	OPS
2018	LAA	AL	114	326	93	21	2	22	(15	7)	184	59	61	70	37	2	102	2	0	1	10	4	2	.285	.361	.564	.925
2019	LAA	AL	106	384	110	20	5	18	(11	7)	194	51	62	68	33	1	110	2	0	4	12	3	6	.286	.343	.505	.848
2020	LAA	AL	46	153	29	6	0	7	(4	3)	56	23	24	16	22	0	50	0	0	0	7	1	3	.190	.291	.366	.657
2021	LAA	AL	158	537	138	26	8	46	(26	20)	318	103	100	119	96	20	189	4	0	2	26	10	7	.257	.372	.592	.965
	4 ML YEARS		424	1400	370	73	15	93	(56	37)	752	236	247	273	188	23	451	8	0	7	55	18	18	.264	.353	.537	.890

Shohei Ohtani

Pitches: R Bats: L Pos: SP-23   Ht: 6'4" Wt: 210 Born: 7/5/1994 Age: 27

Year	Team	Lg	G	GS	GF	IP	BFP	H	R	ER	HR	SH	SF	HB	TBB	IBB	SO	WP	W	L	Pct	Sv-Op	Hld	Vel	OPS	ERC	ERA
2018	LAA	AL	10	10	0	51.2	211	38	19	19	6	0	1	1	22	0	63	5	4	2	.667	0-0	0	97	.621	2.96	3.31
2020	LAA	AL	2	2	0	1.2	16	3	7	7	0	0	0	0	8	0	3	1	0	1	.000	0-0	0	94	1.063	28.51	37.80
2021	LAA	AL	23	23	0	130.1	533	98	48	46	15	2	4	10	44	2	156	10	9	2	.818	0-0	0	96	.637	2.89	3.18
	3 ML YEARS		35	35	0	183.2	760	139	74	72	21	2	5	11	74	2	222	16	13	5	.722	0-0	0	96	.641	3.09	3.53

Steven Okert

Pitches: L Bats: L Pos: RP-34   Ht: 6'2" Wt: 202 Born: 7/9/1991 Age: 30

Year	Team	Lg	G	GS	GF	IP	BFP	H	R	ER	HR	SH	SF	HB	TBB	IBB	SO	WP	W	L	Pct	Sv-Op	Hld	Vel	OPS	ERC	ERA
2021	Jaxnvl	AAA	15	0	10	20.0	76	13	4	4	1	1	0	2	4	0	29	2	2	0	1.000	4--	-		.514	1.73	1.80
2016	SF	NL	16	0	3	14.0	58	14	5	5	2	0	0	4	1	0	14	0	0	1	-	0-1	2	92	.699	3.87	3.21
2017	SF	NL	44	0	3	27.0	118	24	18	17	3	3	2	3	11	2	22	0	1	1	.500	0-0	11	92	.755	3.83	5.67
2018	SF	NL	10	0	4	7.1	27	4	1	1	0	0	0	0	0	0	8	0	0	0	-	0-0	0	92	.444	0.94	1.23
2021	Mia	NL	34	0	5	36.0	142	22	12	11	5	1	2	4	15	2	40	4	3	1	.750	0-0	1	92	.649	2.78	2.75
	4 ML YEARS		104	0	15	84.1	345	64	36	34	11	4	4	7	30	5	84	4	4	2	.667	0-1	14	92	.676	3.07	3.63

Jared Oliva

Bats: R Throws: R Pos: RF-12;LF-5;PH-5;CF-2;PR-2   Ht: 6'2" Wt: 205 Born: 11/27/1995 Age: 26

Year	Team	Lg	G	AB	H	2B	3B	HR	(Hm	Rd)	TB	R	RBI	RC	TBB	IBB	SO	HBP	SH	SF	SB	CS	GDP	Avg	OBP	Slg	OPS
2021	Indy	AAA	60	210	54	11	3	2	(-	-)	77	25	23	-	17	1	64	5	0	0	10	3	8	.257	.328	.367	.694
2020	Pit	NL	6	16	3	0	0	0	(0	0)	3	0	0	0	0	0	6	0	0	0	1	0	0	.188	.188	.188	.375
2021	Pit	NL	20	40	7	2	0	0	(0	0)	9	4	2	1	3	1	10	0	0	0	2	0	0	.175	.233	.225	.458
	2 ML YEARS		26	56	10	2	0	0	(0	0)	12	4	2	1	3	1	16	0	0	0	3	0	0	.179	.220	.214	.435

Edward Olivares

Bats: R Throws: R Pos: RF-22;LF-11;PH-6;CF-4;PR-4;DH-1   Ht: 6'2" Wt: 190 Born: 3/6/1996 Age: 26

Year	Team	Lg	G	AB	H	2B	3B	HR	(Hm	Rd)	TB	R	RBI	RC	TBB	IBB	SO	HBP	SH	SF	SB	CS	GDP	Avg	OBP	Slg	OPS
2021	Omha	AAA	63	248	74	11	3	13	(-	-)	130	46	29	-	23	1	46	5	0	5	12	4	6	.298	.370	.524	.894
2020	2 Tms		31	96	23	2	1	3	(2	1)	36	9	10	8	4	0	25	0	0	1	0	2	1	.240	.267	.375	.642
2021	KC	AL	39	101	24	2	0	5	(1	4)	41	14	12	11	5	0	19	3	1	1	2	2	2	.238	.291	.406	.697
20	SD	NL	13	34	6	1	0	1	(1	0)	10	4	3	2	2	0	14	0	0	0	0	1	0	.176	.222	.294	.516
20	KC	AL	18	62	17	1	1	2	(1	1)	26	5	7	6	2	0	11	0	0	1	0	1	1	.274	.292	.419	.712
	2 ML YEARS		70	197	47	4	1	8	(3	5)	77	23	22	19	9	0	44	3	1	2	2	4	3	.239	.280	.391	.672

Matt Olson

Bats: L **Throws:** R **Pos:** 1B-152;DH-4   **Ht:** 6'5" **Wt:** 225 **Born:** 3/29/1994 **Age:** 28

Year	Team	Lg	G	AB	H	2B	3B	HR	(Hm	Rd)	TB	R	RBI	RC	TBB	IBB	SO	HBP	SH	SF	SB	CS	GDP	Avg	OBP	Slg	OPS
2016	Oak	AL	11	21	2	1	0	0	(0	0)	3	3	0	1	7	0	4	0	0	0	0	0	1	.095	.321	.143	.464
2017	Oak	AL	59	189	49	2	0	24	(12	12)	123	33	45	40	22	1	60	5	0	0	0	0	6	.259	.352	.651	1.003
2018	Oak	AL	**162**	580	143	33	0	29	(14	15)	263	85	84	86	70	3	163	8	0	2	2	1	13	.247	.335	.453	.788
2019	Oak	AL	127	483	129	26	0	36	(13	23)	263	73	91	92	51	7	138	12	0	1	0	0	11	.267	.351	.545	.896
2020	Oak	AL	60	210	41	4	1	14	(9	5)	89	28	42	34	34	2	77	1	0	0	1	0	2	.195	.310	.424	.734
2021	Oak	AL	156	565	153	35	0	39	(18	21)	305	101	111	107	88	12	113	9	0	11	4	1	17	.271	.371	.540	.911
	Postseason		9	28	4	0	0	2	(1	1)	10	4	3	1	8	0	11	0	0	0	0	0	2	.143	.333	.357	.690
	6 ML YEARS		575	2048	517	101	1	142	(66	76)	1046	323	373	360	272	25	555	35	0	14	7	2	50	.252	.348	.511	.859

Tyler O'Neill

Bats: R **Throws:** R **Pos:** LF-131;PH-6;DH-1   **Ht:** 5'11" **Wt:** 200 **Born:** 6/22/1995 **Age:** 27

Year	Team	Lg	G	AB	H	2B	3B	HR	(Hm	Rd)	TB	R	RBI	RC	TBB	IBB	SO	HBP	SH	SF	SB	CS	GDP	Avg	OBP	Slg	OPS
2018	StL	NL	61	130	33	5	0	9	(6	3)	65	29	23	24	7	0	57	3	0	2	2	0	0	.254	.303	.500	.803
2019	StL	NL	60	141	37	6	0	5	(4	1)	58	18	16	19	10	0	53	0	0	0	1	0	3	.262	.311	.411	.723
2020	StL	NL	50	139	24	5	0	7	(2	5)	50	20	19	15	15	0	43	2	0	1	3	1	3	.173	.261	.360	.621
2021	StL	NL	138	482	138	26	2	34	(15	19)	270	89	80	84	38	0	168	13	0	4	15	4	8	.286	.352	.560	.912
	Postseason		3	0	0	0	0	0	(0	0)	0	0	0	0	0	0	0	0	0	0	0	0	0	-	-	-	-
	4 ML YEARS		309	892	232	42	2	55	(27	28)	443	156	138	142	70	0	321	18	0	7	21	5	14	.260	.324	.497	.821

Kaleb Ort

Pitches: R **Bats:** R **Pos:** RP-1   **Ht:** 6'4" **Wt:** 240 **Born:** 2/5/1992 **Age:** 30

Year	Team	Lg	G	GS	GF	IP	BFP	H	R	ER	HR	SH	SF	HB	TBB	IBB	SO	WP	W	L	Pct	Sv-Op	Hld	Vel	OPS	ERC	ERA
2021	Wrcstr	AAA	42	0	35	45.1	200	40	19	15	4	1	2	5	20	2	62	1	1	3	.250	19--	-	-	.670	3.78	2.98
2021	Bos	AL	1	0	0	0.1	3	1	0	0	0	0	0	0	1	0	0	0	0	0	-	0-0	0	96	1.167	29.63	0.00

Oliver Ortega

Pitches: R **Bats:** R **Pos:** RP-8   **Ht:** 6'0" **Wt:** 165 **Born:** 10/2/1996 **Age:** 25

Year	Team	Lg	G	GS	GF	IP	BFP	H	R	ER	HR	SH	SF	HB	TBB	IBB	SO	WP	W	L	Pct	Sv-Op	Hld	Vel	OPS	ERC	ERA
2021	Rock	AA	25	0	13	30.2	139	33	28	21	3	1	0	1	13	0	46	6	2	3	.400	5--	-	-	.736	4.60	6.16
2021	Salt Lk	AAA	9	0	4	12.0	54	11	6	5	2	0	1	0	5	0	15	1	0	0	-	0--	-	-	.692	3.88	3.75
2021	LAA	AL	8	0	1	9.1	39	12	5	5	1	0	0	1	2	0	4	0	1	0	1.000	0-0	0	97	.829	5.94	4.82

Rafael Ortega

Bats: L **Throws:** R **Pos:** CF-73;PH-16;LF-13;RF-13;PR-1   **Ht:** 5'11" **Wt:** 180 **Born:** 5/15/1991 **Age:** 31

Year	Team	Lg	G	AB	H	2B	3B	HR	(Hm	Rd)	TB	R	RBI	RC	TBB	IBB	SO	HBP	SH	SF	SB	CS	GDP	Avg	OBP	Slg	OPS
2021	Iowa	AAA	16	64	16	3	0	4	(-	-)	31	11	11	-	8	0	13	0	0	0	1	1	1	.250	.333	.484	.818
2012	Col	NL	2	4	2	0	0	0	(0	0)	2	0	0	2	1	0	2	1	0	0	1	0	0	.500	.667	.500	1.167
2016	LAA	AL	66	185	43	8	0	1	(0	1)	54	24	16	19	13	0	23	0	3	0	8	3	5	.232	.283	.292	.575
2018	Mia	NL	41	133	31	3	1	0	(0	0)	36	10	7	10	10	0	23	0	0	0	5	2	5	.233	.287	.271	.557
2019	Atl	NL	34	88	18	3	0	2	(1	1)	27	7	10	8	8	0	22	0	0	0	3	0	2	.205	.271	.307	.578
2021	ChC	NL	103	296	86	14	2	11	(4	7)	137	44	33	56	30	1	70	2	2	0	12	6	3	.291	.360	.463	.823
	Postseason		4	3	0	0	0	0	(0	0)	0	1	0	0	0	0	1	0	0	0	0	0	0	.000	.000	.000	.000
	5 ML YEARS		246	706	180	28	3	14	(5	9)	256	85	66	95	62	1	140	3	5	0	29	11	15	.255	.318	.363	.680

Josh Osich

Pitches: L **Bats:** L **Pos:** RP-17   OH-sitch   **Ht:** 6'2" **Wt:** 235 **Born:** 9/3/1988 **Age:** 33

Year	Team	Lg	G	GS	GF	IP	BFP	H	R	ER	HR	SH	SF	HB	TBB	IBB	SO	WP	W	L	Pct	Sv-Op	Hld	Vel	OPS	ERC	ERA
2021	Lsville	AAA	11	2	2	15.0	62	11	9	9	2	0	0	0	6	0	15	0	0	2	.000	0--	-	-	.631	2.82	5.40
2015	SF	NL	35	0	6	28.2	120	24	12	7	4	1	1	0	8	0	27	2	2	0	1.000	0-2	11	96	.633	2.88	2.20
2016	SF	NL	59	0	9	36.1	160	31	20	19	7	1	0	3	19	1	25	2	1	3	.250	0-3	18	95	.769	4.65	4.71
2017	SF	NL	54	0	12	43.1	201	48	32	30	7	1	0	1	27	1	43	5	3	2	.600	0-1	6	95	.839	6.18	6.23
2018	SF	NL	12	0	2	12.0	61	20	11	11	2	0	0	2	7	0	10	3	0	0	-	0-1	2	95	1.052	10.94	8.25
2019	CWS	AL	57	0	14	67.2	272	62	38	35	15	0	1	0	15	1	61	3	4	0	1.000	0-1	2	94	.752	3.72	4.66
2020	2 Tms		17	1	3	18.1	86	21	16	13	6	0	0	2	5	0	24	0	1	1	.500	0-0	1	92	.832	6.16	6.38
2021	Cin	NL	17	0	3	14.1	60	15	9	8	4	0	0	0	5	0	9	0	2	0	1.000	1-3	3	94	.842	5.58	5.02
20	Bos	AL	13	1	3	15.2	70	16	10	10	6	0	0	1	5	0	20	0	1	1	.500	0-0	1	92	.846	5.92	5.74
20	ChC	NL	4	0	0	2.2	16	5	6	3	0	0	0	1	0	0	4	0	0	0	-	0-0	0	93	.775	7.22	10.13
	7 ML YEARS		251	1	49	220.2	960	221	138	123	45	3	2	8	86	3	199	15	13	6	.684	1-11	43	95	.790	4.90	5.02

Corey Oswalt

Pitches: R Bats: R Pos: RP-2; SP-1   Ht: 6'5" Wt: 250 Born: 9/3/1993 Age: 28

				HOW MUCH PITCHED			WHAT HE GAVE UP											THE RESULTS						
Year	Team	Lg	G	GS	GF	IP	BFP	H	R	ER	HR	SH	SF	HB	TBB	IBB	SO	WP	W	L	Pct	Sv-Op	Hld	Vel	OPS	ERC	ERA
2021	Syrcse	AAA	6	2	3	13.0	54	12	6	6	4	0	0	1	3	0	15	0	1	1	.500	2--	-	-	.796	4.65	4.15
2018	NYM	NL	17	12	2	64.2	282	69	43	42	14	1	0	4	20	1	45	4	3	3	.500	0-0	1	90	.806	5.14	5.85
2019	NYM	NL	2	0	0	6.2	34	9	9	9	1	0	0	0	6	1	5	0	0	1	.000	0-0	0	92	1.013	8.55	12.15
2020	NYM	NL	4	1	2	13.0	55	14	7	7	3	0	0	1	2	0	11	0	0	0	-	0-0	0	92	.886	4.71	4.85
2021	NYM	NL	3	1	0	10.1	42	12	4	4	1	0	0	0	2	0	10	1	1	1	.500	0-0	0	92	.808	4.37	3.48
	4 ML YEARS		26	14	4	94.2	413	104	63	62	19	1	0	5	30	2	71	5	4	5	.444	0-0	1	91	.833	5.23	5.89

Adam Ottavino

Pitches: R Bats: B Pos: RP-69   ott-tah-VEE-no   Ht: 6'5" Wt: 246 Born: 11/22/1985 Age: 36

				HOW MUCH PITCHED			WHAT HE GAVE UP											THE RESULTS						
Year	Team	Lg	G	GS	GF	IP	BFP	H	R	ER	HR	SH	SF	HB	TBB	IBB	SO	WP	W	L	Pct	Sv-Op	Hld	Vel	OPS	ERC	ERA
2010	StL	NL	5	3	0	22.1	110	37	21	21	5	1	0	0	9	1	12	1	0	2	.000	0-0	0	93	1.072	9.22	8.46
2012	Col	NL	53	0	6	79.0	339	76	42	40	9	3	1	1	34	7	81	8	5	1	.833	0-2	6	94	.717	4.01	4.56
2013	Col	NL	51	0	5	78.1	335	73	27	23	5	6	4	2	31	5	78	9	1	3	.250	0-0	8	91	.672	3.42	2.64
2014	Col	NL	75	0	16	65.0	272	67	26	26	6	2	3	4	16	1	70	4	1	4	.200	1-6	21	94	.735	3.87	3.60
2015	Col	NL	10	0	5	10.1	35	3	0	0	0	0	0	1	2	0	13	0	1	0	1.000	3-3	3	96	.265	0.56	0.00
2016	Col	NL	34	0	19	27.0	107	18	9	8	3	0	0	2	7	0	35	4	1	3	.250	7-12	4	94	.528	2.17	2.67
2017	Col	NL	63	0	11	53.1	243	48	30	30	8	0	3	4	39	2	63	8	2	3	.400	0-2	21	94	.786	5.51	5.06
2018	Col	NL	75	0	16	77.2	309	41	25	21	5	1	5	6	36	5	112	7	6	4	.600	6-11	34	94	.509	1.89	2.43
2019	NYY	AL	73	0	7	66.1	283	47	17	14	5	0	3	2	40	3	88	3	6	5	.545	2-9	28	94	.624	3.13	1.90
2020	NYY	AL	24	0	4	18.1	85	20	12	12	2	0	1	1	9	0	25	1	2	3	.400	0-3	2	93	.772	5.13	5.89
2021	Bos	AL	69	0	15	62.0	276	55	31	29	5	2	2	7	35	2	71	4	7	3	.700	11-17	22	94	.728	4.34	4.21
	Postseason		12	0	1	7.2	42	10	7	6	1	0	0	0	7	1	7	3	0	1	.000	0-1	0	94	.885	7.50	7.04
	11 ML YEARS		532	3	104	559.2	2394	485	240	224	53	15	22	30	258	26	648	49	32	31	.508	30-65	149	94	.687	3.69	3.60

Glenn Otto

Pitches: R Bats: R Pos: SP-6   Ht: 6'3" Wt: 240 Born: 3/11/1996 Age: 26

				HOW MUCH PITCHED			WHAT HE GAVE UP											THE RESULTS						
Year	Team	Lg	G	GS	GF	IP	BFP	H	R	ER	HR	SH	SF	HB	TBB	IBB	SO	WP	W	L	Pct	Sv-Op	Hld	Vel	OPS	ERC	ERA
2021	Smrst	AA	11	10	0	65.1	253	46	23	23	6	1	3	2	14	0	103	4	6	3	.667	0--	-	-	.577	1.97	3.17
2021	Tex	AL	6	6	0	23.1	111	32	24	24	2	1	0	2	8	0	28	1	0	3	.000	0-0	0	93	.872	6.19	9.26

Connor Overton

Pitches: R Bats: L Pos: RP-6; SP-3   Ht: 6'0" Wt: 190 Born: 7/24/1993 Age: 28

				HOW MUCH PITCHED			WHAT HE GAVE UP											THE RESULTS						
Year	Team	Lg	G	GS	GF	IP	BFP	H	R	ER	HR	SH	SF	HB	TBB	IBB	SO	WP	W	L	Pct	Sv-Op	Hld	Vel	OPS	ERC	ERA
2021	Buffalo	AAA	21	7	0	57.2	232	52	14	13	3	2	1	6	10	0	50	4	2	1	.667	0--	-	-	.638	2.84	2.03
2021	2 Tms		9	3	2	15.1	63	14	8	8	2	0	2	0	5	0	15	1	0	1	.000	0-0	0	92	.712	3.57	4.70
21	Tor	AL	4	0	2	6.2	24	4	0	0	0	0	0	0	2	0	4	1	0	0	-	0-0	0	93	.432	1.41	0.00
21	Pit	NL	5	3	0	8.2	39	10	8	8	2	0	2	0	3	0	11	0	0	1	.000	0-0	0	92	.892	5.58	8.31

Johan Oviedo

Pitches: R Bats: R Pos: SP-13; RP-1   Ht: 6'5" Wt: 245 Born: 3/2/1998 Age: 24

				HOW MUCH PITCHED			WHAT HE GAVE UP											THE RESULTS						
Year	Team	Lg	G	GS	GF	IP	BFP	H	R	ER	HR	SH	SF	HB	TBB	IBB	SO	WP	W	L	Pct	Sv-Op	Hld	Vel	OPS	ERC	ERA
2021	Memp	AAA	11	11	0	51.2	233	53	37	36	7	0	0	5	27	0	56	3	1	6	.143	0--	-	-	.773	5.43	6.27
2020	StL	NL	5	5	0	24.2	112	24	18	15	3	0	2	5	10	0	16	4	0	3	.000	0-0	0	95	.780	4.84	5.47
2021	StL	NL	14	13	0	62.1	288	61	39	34	8	1	1	6	37	2	51	2	0	5	.000	0-0	0	95	.774	5.21	4.91
	2 ML YEARS		19	18	0	87.0	400	85	57	49	11	1	3	11	47	2	67	6	0	8	.000	0-0	0	95	.776	5.10	5.07

Luis Oviedo

Pitches: R Bats: R Pos: RP-21; SP-1   Ht: 6'4" Wt: 235 Born: 5/15/1999 Age: 23

				HOW MUCH PITCHED			WHAT HE GAVE UP											THE RESULTS						
Year	Team	Lg	G	GS	GF	IP	BFP	H	R	ER	HR	SH	SF	HB	TBB	IBB	SO	WP	W	L	Pct	Sv-Op	Hld	Vel	OPS	ERC	ERA
2021	Pit	NL	22	1	12	29.2	147	33	32	29	4	0	2	2	26	1	31	2	1	2	.333	0-0	0	94	.885	7.21	8.80

Hunter Owen

Bats: R Throws: R Pos: PH-2;RF-1   Ht: 5'11" Wt: 200 Born: 9/22/1993 Age: 28

							BATTING														RUNNING			AVERAGES			
Year	Team	Lg	G	AB	H	2B	3B	HR	(Hm	Rd)	TB	R	RBI	RC	TBB	IBB	SO	HBP	SH	SF	SB	CS	GDP	Avg	OBP	Slg	OPS
2021	Indy	AAA	96	324	75	11	0	20	(-	-)	146	54	53	-	29	2	124	6	0	3	2	2	5	.231	.304	.451	.754
2021	Pit	NL	3	4	0	0	0	0	(0	0)	0	0	0	0	0	0	3	1	0	0	0	0	0	.000	.200	.000	.200

Chris Owings

Bats: R **Throws:** R **Pos:** PH-9;2B-3;LF-3;RF-3;3B-1;SS-1;CF-1;DH-1

Ht: 5'10" **Wt:** 185 **Born:** 8/12/1991 **Age:** 30

Year	Team	Lg	G	AB	H	2B	3B	HR	(Hm	Rd)	TB	R	RBI	RC	TBB	IBB	SO	HBP	SH	SF	SB	CS	GDP	Avg	OBP	Slg	OPS
2013	Ari	NL	20	55	16	5	0	0	(0	0)	21	5	5	7	6	1	10	0	0	0	2	0	0	.291	.361	.382	.742
2014	Ari	NL	91	310	81	15	6	6	(1	5)	126	34	26	38	16	0	67	2	2	2	8	1	4	.261	.300	.406	.706
2015	Ari	NL	147	515	117	27	5	4	(3	1)	166	59	43	41	26	3	144	1	7	3	16	4	9	.227	.264	.322	.587
2016	Ari	NL	119	437	121	24	11	5	(5	0)	182	52	49	60	20	4	87	5	2	2	21	2	8	.277	.315	.416	.731
2017	Ari	NL	97	362	97	25	1	12	(8	4)	160	41	51	48	17	0	87	1	0	4	12	2	3	.268	.299	.442	.741
2018	Ari	NL	106	281	58	15	0	4	(3	1)	85	34	22	25	24	4	75	2	0	2	11	4	4	.206	.272	.302	.574
2019	2 Tms	AL	67	180	25	6	1	3	(0	3)	42	13	14	7	14	0	78	2	0	0	5	2	2	.139	.209	.233	.443
2020	Col	NL	17	41	11	1	0	2	(2	0)	18	9	5	6	3	0	11	0	0	0	1	0	0	.268	.318	.439	.757
2021	Col	NL	21	43	14	4	3	1	(0	1)	27	9	5	11	7	1	15	0	0	0	2	1	0	.326	.420	.628	1.048
19	KC	AL	41	135	18	4	1	2	(0	2)	30	9	9	4	8	0	55	2	0	0	4	1	1	.133	.193	.222	.415
19	Bos	AL	26	45	7	2	0	1	(0	1)	12	4	5	3	6	0	23	0	0	0	1	1	1	.156	.255	.267	.522
9 ML YEARS			685	2224	540	122	27	37	(22	15)	827	256	220	243	133	13	574	13	13	13	78	16	30	.243	.288	.372	.660

Marcell Ozuna

Bats: R **Throws:** R **Pos:** LF-48

oh-ZUNE-uh

Ht: 6'1" **Wt:** 225 **Born:** 11/12/1990 **Age:** 31

Year	Team	Lg	G	AB	H	2B	3B	HR	(Hm	Rd)	TB	R	RBI	RC	TBB	IBB	SO	HBP	SH	SF	SB	CS	GDP	Avg	OBP	Slg	OPS
2013	Mia	NL	70	275	73	17	4	3	(0	3)	107	31	32	35	13	0	57	2	1	0	5	1	6	.265	.303	.389	.693
2014	Mia	NL	153	565	152	26	5	23	(12	11)	257	72	85	74	41	1	164	1	0	5	3	1	12	.269	.317	.455	.772
2015	Mia	NL	123	459	119	27	0	10	(2	8)	176	47	44	48	30	1	110	3	0	2	2	3	10	.259	.308	.383	.691
2016	Mia	NL	148	557	148	23	6	23	(12	11)	252	75	76	69	43	2	115	4	0	4	0	3	11	.266	.321	.452	.773
2017	Mia	NL	159	613	191	30	2	37	(22	15)	336	93	124	117	64	4	144	0	0	2	1	3	18	.312	.376	.548	.924
2018	StL	NL	148	582	163	16	2	23	(13	10)	252	69	88	86	38	2	110	3	0	4	3	0	21	.280	.325	.433	.758
2019	StL	NL	130	485	117	23	1	29	(13	16)	229	80	89	73	62	2	114	1	0	1	12	2	21	.241	.328	.472	.800
2020	Atl	NL	60	228	77	14	0	18	(8	10)	145	38	56	58	38	3	60	0	0	1	0	0	3	.338	.431	.636	1.067
2021	Atl	NL	48	188	40	6	0	7	(5	2)	67	21	26	21	19	0	46	1	0	0	0	0	6	.213	.288	.356	.645
Postseason			21	88	25	7	0	5	(5	0)	47	14	16	13	3	0	27	1	0	0	0	0	2	.284	.315	.534	.849
9 ML YEARS			1039	3952	1080	182	20	173	(87	86)	1821	526	620	581	348	15	920	15	1	19	26	13	97	.273	.333	.461	.794

Cristian Pache

Bats: R **Throws:** R **Pos:** CF-22;PR-1

PAH-chay

Ht: 6'2" **Wt:** 215 **Born:** 11/19/1998 **Age:** 23

Year	Team	Lg	G	AB	H	2B	3B	HR	(Hm	Rd)	TB	R	RBI	RC	TBB	IBB	SO	HBP	SH	SF	SB	CS	GDP	Avg	OBP	Slg	OPS
2017	Rome	A	119	469	132	13	8	0	(-	-)	161	60	42	57	39	1	104	0	4	2	32	14	6	.281	.335	.343	.679
2018	Florida	A+	93	369	105	20	5	8	(-	-)	159	46	40	49	15	2	69	0	0	2	7	6	5	.285	.311	.431	.742
2018	Missi	AA	29	104	27	3	1	1	(-	-)	35	10	7	9	5	0	28	0	0	0	0	2	1	.260	.294	.337	.630
2019	Missi	AA	104	392	109	28	8	11	(-	-)	186	50	53	61	34	1	104	4	1	2	8	11	7	.278	.340	.474	.815
2019	Gwnntt	AAA	26	95	26	8	1	1	(-	-)	39	13	8	13	9	0	18	0	1	0	0	0	3	.274	.337	.411	.747
2021	Gwnntt	AAA	84	303	80	15	0	10	(-	-)	125	48	38	-	30	0	93	1	1	0	9	5	2	.264	.332	.413	.745
2020	Atl	NL	2	4	1	0	0	0	(0	0)	1	0	0	0	0	0	2	0	0	0	0	0	0	.250	.250	.250	.500
2021	Atl	NL	22	63	7	3	0	1	(0	1)	13	6	4	1	2	0	25	1	2	0	0	0	1	.111	.152	.206	.358
Postseason			12	22	4	1	0	1	(1	0)	8	4	4	2	3	0	4	0	0	0	0	0	1	.182	.280	.364	.644
2 ML YEARS			24	67	8	3	0	1	(0	1)	14	6	4	1	2	0	27	1	2	0	0	0	1	.119	.157	.209	.366

Chris Paddack

Pitches: R **Bats:** R **Pos:** SP-22;RP-1

Ht: 6'5" **Wt:** 217 **Born:** 1/8/1996 **Age:** 26

Year	Team	Lg	G	GS	GF	IP	BFP	H	R	ER	HR	SH	SF	HB	TBB	IBB	SO	WP	W	L	Pct	Sv-Op	Hld	Vel	OPS	ERC	ERA
2019	SD	NL	26	26	0	140.2	568	107	58	52	23	4	3	6	31	1	153	1	9	7	.563	0-0	0	94	.635	2.62	3.33
2020	SD	NL	12	12	0	59.0	245	60	33	31	14	0	2	2	12	0	58	0	4	5	.444	0-0	0	94	.817	4.46	4.73
2021	SD	NL	23	22	0	108.1	459	115	67	61	15	7	2	1	22	1	99	2	7	7	.500	0-0	0	95	.750	3.87	5.07
Postseason			1	1	0	2.1	15	8	6	6	1	0	1	0	0	0	1	0	0	1	.000	0-0	0	94	1.533	22.85	23.14
3 ML YEARS			61	60	0	308.0	1272	282	158	144	52	11	7	9	65	2	310	3	20	19	.513	0-0	0	94	.712	3.38	4.21

Kevin Padlo

Bats: R **Throws:** R **Pos:** 3B-6;1B-3;PH-1;PR-1

Ht: 6'2" **Wt:** 210 **Born:** 7/15/1996 **Age:** 25

Year	Team	Lg	G	AB	H	2B	3B	HR	(Hm	Rd)	TB	R	RBI	RC	TBB	IBB	SO	HBP	SH	SF	SB	CS	GDP	Avg	OBP	Slg	OPS
2021	Drham	AAA	69	253	49	11	0	12	(-	-)	96	41	37	-	25	1	93	2	0	2	5	1	1	.194	.270	.379	.649
2021	Tacom	AAA	22	86	29	3	1	8	(-	-)	58	22	21	-	16	0	16	0	0	1	1	1	1	.337	.437	.674	1.111
2021	2 Tms	AL	10	13	1	1	0	0	(0	0)	2	1	0	0	2	0	9	0	0	0	0	0	0	.077	.200	.154	.354
21	TB	AL	9	12	1	1	0	0	(0	0)	2	1	0	0	2	0	8	0	0	0	0	0	0	.083	.214	.167	.381
21	Sea	AL	1	1	0	0	0	0	(0	0)	0	0	0	0	0	0	1	0	0	0	0	0	0	.000	.000	.000	.000

Emilio Pagan

Pitches: R **Bats:** L **Pos:** RP-67

Ht: 6'2" **Wt:** 208 **Born:** 5/7/1991 **Age:** 31

Year	Team	Lg	G	GS	GF	IP	BFP	H	R	ER	HR	SH	SF	HB	TBB	IBB	SO	WP	W	L	Pct	Sv-Op	Hld	Vel	OPS	ERC	ERA
2017	Sea	AL	34	0	9	50.1	196	39	20	20	8	7	2	1	8	0	56	1	2	3	.400	0-1	8	94	.610	2.32	3.22
2018	Oak	AL	55	0	17	62.0	262	55	30	30	13	0	1	3	19	1	63	3	3	1	.750	0-0	6	94	.767	3.92	4.35
2019	TB	AL	66	0	29	70.0	267	45	19	18	12	0	1	1	13	1	96	3	4	2	.667	20-28	7	96	.590	1.91	2.31

Year Team	Lg	G	GS	GF	IP	BFP	H	R	ER	HR	SH	SF	HB	TBB	IBB	SO	WP	W	L	Pct	Sv-Op	Hld	Vel	OPS	ERC	ERA
2020 SD	NL	22	0	5	22.0	87	14	11	11	4	0	1	0	9	0	23	0	0	1	.000	2-7	7	95	.641	2.73	4.50
2021 SD	NL	67	0	10	63.1	263	56	35	34	16	0	1	2	18	0	69	0	4	3	.571	0-5	17	95	.801	4.07	4.83
Postseason		9	0	1	8.0	36	7	3	2	2	0	0	0	4	0	5	0	1	0	1.000	0-0	2	97	.774	4.58	2.25
5 ML YEARS		244	0	70	267.2	1075	209	115	111	52	1	6	7	67	2	307	7	13	10	.565	22-41	45	95	.692	2.99	3.73

Josh Palacios

Bats: L Throws: R Pos: RF-8;LF-4;CF-2;DH-1;PH-1   **Ht: 6'1" Wt: 198 Born: 7/30/1995 Age: 26**

Year Team	Lg	G	AB	H	2B	3B	HR	(Hm	Rd)	TB	R	RBI	RC	TBB	IBB	SO	HBP	SH	SF	SB	CS	GDP	Avg	OBP	Slg	OPS
2021 Buffalo	AAA	16	54	13	2	0	0	(-	-)	15	7	2	-	5	0	16	4	0	0	1	2	0	.241	.349	.278	.627
2021 Tor	AL	13	35	7	0	0	0	(0	0)	7	7	4	3	3	0	11	2	1	1	0	0	0	.200	.293	.200	.493

Joe Panik

Bats: L Throws: R Pos: 3B-32;PH-30;2B-27;1B-9;DH-3   PAN-ick   **Ht: 6'1" Wt: 205 Born: 10/30/1990 Age: 31**

Year Team	Lg	G	AB	H	2B	3B	HR	(Hm	Rd)	TB	R	RBI	RC	TBB	IBB	SO	HBP	SH	SF	SB	CS	GDP	Avg	OBP	Slg	OPS
2014 SF	NL	73	269	82	10	2	1	(0	1)	99	31	18	33	16	0	33	0	1	1	0	0	4	.305	.343	.368	.711
2015 SF	NL	100	382	119	27	2	8	(4	4)	174	59	37	60	38	0	42	5	3	4	3	2	7	.312	.378	.455	.833
2016 SF	NL	127	464	111	21	7	10	(3	7)	176	67	62	56	50	5	47	4	3	5	5	0	14	.239	.315	.379	.695
2017 SF	NL	138	511	147	28	5	10	(0	10)	215	60	53	73	46	4	54	5	3	8	4	1	10	.288	.347	.421	.768
2018 SF	NL	102	358	91	14	1	4	(1	3)	119	38	24	31	26	3	30	3	1	4	2	0	10	.254	.307	.332	.639
2019 2 Tms	NL	142	438	107	21	2	5	(1	4)	147	50	39	51	43	2	47	4	2	4	4	2	6	.244	.315	.336	.651
2020 Tor	AL	41	120	27	6	0	1	(0	1)	36	18	7	14	20	0	27	1	0	0	0	0	9	.225	.340	.300	.640
2021 2 Tms	NL	95	236	49	9	0	3	(1	2)	67	17	18	20	17	1	34	2	1		2	0	6	.208	.266	.284	.550
19 SF	NL	103	344	81	17	1	3	(0	3)	109	33	27	37	36	2	38	3	1	4	4	2	5	.235	.310	.317	.627
19 NYM	NL	39	94	26	4	1	2	(1	1)	38	17	12	14	7	0	9	1	1	0	0	0	1	.277	.333	.404	.738
21 Tor	AL	42	114	28	6	0	2	(1	1)	40	9	11	15	8	0	14	0	0	0	0	0	1	.246	.293	.351	.644
21 Mia	NL	53	122	21	3	0	1	(0	1)	27	8	7	5	9	1	20	2	1		2	0	5	.172	.241	.221	.462
Postseason		23	92	24	4	2	1	(1	0)	35	10	10	11	7	0	10	0	1	1	0	0	1	.261	.310	.380	.690
8 ML YEARS		818	2778	733	136	19	42	(10	32)	1033	340	258	338	256	15	314	24	14	27	22	7	64	.264	.328	.372	.700

Enoli Paredes

Pitches: R Bats: R Pos: RP-12   **Ht: 5'11" Wt: 171 Born: 9/28/1995 Age: 26**

Year Team	Lg	G	GS	GF	IP	BFP	H	R	ER	HR	SH	SF	HB	TBB	IBB	SO	WP	W	L	Pct	Sv-Op	Hld	Vel	OPS	ERC	ERA
2021 SgrLnd	AAA	25	0	9	26.1	124	26	12	12	6	0	0	4	19	0	38	5	1	0	1.000	1--	-	-	.841	7.08	4.10
2020 Hou	AL	22	0	4	20.2	90	18	9	7	1	1	1	1	11	0	20	0	3	3	.500	0-2	4	96	.666	3.69	3.05
2021 Hou	AL	12	0	1	8.2	53	7	10	6	0	0	1	2	17	0	15	1	0	0	-	0-0	2	95	.763	8.84	6.23
Postseason		7	0	1	7.0	29	3	4	4	1	1	0	2	4	0	9	0	0	0	-	0-1	2	96	.594	3.09	5.14
2 ML YEARS		34	0	5	29.1	143	25	19	13	1	1	2	3	28	0	35	1	3	3	.500	0-2	6	96	.706	5.17	3.99

Isaac Paredes

Bats: R Throws: R Pos: 2B-10;3B-8;SS-5   **Ht: 5'11" Wt: 213 Born: 2/18/1999 Age: 23**

Year Team	Lg	G	AB	H	2B	3B	HR	(Hm	Rd)	TB	R	RBI	RC	TBB	IBB	SO	HBP	SH	SF	SB	CS	GDP	Avg	OBP	Slg	OPS
2021 Toledo	AAA	72	253	67	10	2	11	(-	-)	114	39	42	-	56	0	47	2	0	4	0	0	11	.265	.397	.451	.847
2020 Det	AL	34	100	22	4	0	1	(0	1)	29	7	6	8	8	0	24	0	0	0	0	0	1	.220	.278	.290	.568
2021 Det	AL	23	72	15	3	1	1	(1	0)	23	7	5	5	10	1	11	1	0	2	0	0	4	.208	.306	.319	.625
2 ML YEARS		57	172	37	7	1	2	(1	1)	52	14	11	13	18	1	35	1	0	2	0	0	5	.215	.290	.302	.592

Hoy Park

Bats: L Throws: R Pos: 2B-16;PH-10;3B-9;SS-8;LF-4;CF-2;RF-2   **Ht: 6'1" Wt: 175 Born: 4/7/1996 Age: 26**

Year Team	Lg	G	AB	H	2B	3B	HR	(Hm	Rd)	TB	R	RBI	RC	TBB	IBB	SO	HBP	SH	SF	SB	CS	GDP	Avg	OBP	Slg	OPS
2021 Smrst	AA	10	31	6	1	0	1	(-	-)	10	4	3	-	6	0	3	0	1	1	3	0	0	.194	.316	.323	.638
2021 S-WB	AAA	48	171	56	9	1	10	(-	-)	97	44	29	-	46	3	46	3	2	1	8	4	3	.327	.475	.567	1.042
2021 2 Tms		45	128	25	5	2	3	(1	2)	43	16	14	14	18	1	38	1	1	1	1	1	4	.195	.297	.336	.633
21 NYY	AL	1	1	0	0	0	0	(0	0)	0	0	0	0	0	0	0	0	0	0	0	0	0	.000	.000	.000	.000
21 Pit	NL	44	127	25	5	2	3	(1	2)	43	16	14	14	18	1	38	1	1	1	1	1	4	.197	.299	.339	.638

Blake Parker

Pitches: R Bats: R Pos: RP-47   **Ht: 6'3" Wt: 225 Born: 6/19/1985 Age: 37**

Year Team	Lg	G	GS	GF	IP	BFP	H	R	ER	HR	SH	SF	HB	TBB	IBB	SO	WP	W	L	Pct	Sv-Op	Hld	Vel	OPS	ERC	ERA
2021 Clmbs	AAA	12	0	8	11.0	40	2	0	0	0	0	0	0	5	0	15	1	0	0	-	4--	-	-	.238	0.54	0.00
2012 ChC	NL	7	0	0	6.0	32	10	7	4	3	0	0	0	5	1	6	0	0	0	-	0-0	0	92	1.172	14.02	6.00
2013 ChC	NL	49	0	18	46.1	195	39	17	14	4	0	1	2	15	1	55	2	1	2	.333	1-1	7	92	.626	2.91	2.72
2014 ChC	NL	18	0	10	21.0	91	24	13	12	3	0	1	0	4	0	24	1	1	1	.500	0-0	1	91	.784	4.24	5.14
2016 2 Tms	AL	17	0	5	17.1	79	17	9	9	1	0	0	2	9	1	15	0	1	0	1.000	1-1	0	92	.707	4.41	4.67
2017 LAA	AL	71	0	17	67.1	264	40	20	19	7	1	4	1	16	0	86	4	3	3	.500	8-11	15	94	.527	1.60	2.54
2018 LAA	AL	67	0	21	66.1	276	63	24	24	12	0	1	3	19	1	70	8	2	1	.667	14-17	6	92	.751	4.10	3.26
2019 2 Tms	AL	60	2	21	61.1	255	53	32	31	13	2	3	4	22	0	65	4	3	3	.500	10-11	13	91	.746	4.15	4.55
2020 Phi	NL	14	1	4	16.0	69	12	7	7	1	0	1	0	9	2	25	0	1	0	1.000	0-1	1	91	.677	3.24	2.81

Year	Team	Lg	G	GS	GF	IP	BFP	H	R	ER	HR	SH	SF	HB	TBB	IBB	SO	WP	W	L	Pct	Sv-Op	Hld	Vel	OPS	ERC	ERA
2021	Cle	AL	47	0	13	43.2	185	43	15	15	5	0	2	2	14	0	37	1	2	1	.667	0-0	4	91	.714	3.99	3.09
16	Sea	AL	1	0	0	1.0	5	1	0	0	0	0	0	0	1	0	0	0	0	0		0-0	0	93	.650	5.48	0.00
16	NYY	AL	16	0	5	16.1	74	16	9	9	1	0	0	2	8	1	15	0	1	0	1.000	1-1	0	92	.711	4.35	4.96
19	Min	AL	37	0	19	36.1	157	34	18	17	7	0	1	2	16	0	34	4	1	2	.333	10-11	9	92	.773	4.79	4.21
19	Phi	NL	23	2	2	25.0	98	19	14	14	6	2	1	1	6	0	31	0	2	1	.667	0-0	4	91	.703	3.24	5.04
9 ML YEARS			350	3	129	345.1	1436	301	144	133	50	3	12	13	113	6	383	20	16	11	.593	34-42	47	92	.694	3.51	3.47

Gerardo Parra

Bats: L **Throws:** L **Pos:** PH-29;LF-19;CF-8;RF-3;PR-3 heh-RAHR-doh PAR-uh **Ht:** 5'11" **Wt:** 210 **Born:** 5/6/1987 **Age:** 35

Year	Team	Lg	G	AB	H	2B	3B	HR	(Hm	Rd)	TB	R	RBI	RC	TBB	IBB	SO	HBP	SH	SF	SB	CS	GDP	Avg	OBP	Slg	OPS
2021	Roch	AAA	21	72	16	3	1	1	(-	-)	24	10	12	-	19	0	17	0	0	0	1	2	5	.222	.385	.333	.718
2009	Ari	NL	120	455	132	21	8	5	(4	1)	184	59	60	58	25	1	89	1	4	6	5	7	18	.290	.324	.404	.729
2010	Ari	NL	133	364	95	19	6	3	(1	2)	135	31	30	38	23	10	76	2	3	1	1	0	8	.261	.308	.371	.679
2011	Ari	NL	141	445	130	20	8	8	(3	5)	190	55	46	71	43	16	82	3	0	2	15	1	8	.292	.357	.427	.784
2012	Ari	NL	133	385	105	21	2	7	(5	2)	151	58	36	50	33	4	77	4	6	2	15	9	4	.273	.335	.392	.727
2013	Ari	NL	156	601	161	43	4	10	(6	4)	242	79	48	69	48	3	100	3	7	4	10	10	12	.268	.323	.403	.726
2014	2 Tms	NL	150	529	138	22	4	9	(3	6)	195	64	40	46	32	5	100	5	6	2	9	7	10	.261	.308	.369	.677
2015	2 Tms		155	547	159	36	5	14	(8	6)	247	83	51	71	28	3	92	5	4	5	14	4	8	.291	.328	.452	.780
2016	Col	NL	102	368	93	27	5	2	(5	2)	147	45	39	29	9	1	73	1	1	2	6	4	16	.253	.271	.399	.671
2017	Col	NL	115	392	121	24	1	10	(6	4)	177	56	71	56	20	0	67	4	0	9	2	5	13	.309	.341	.452	.793
2018	Col	NL	142	401	114	17	0	6	(3	3)	149	52	53	57	32	3	75	2	1	4	11	4	6	.284	.342	.372	.714
2019	2 Tms	NL	119	274	64	14	1	9	(4	5)	107	38	48	38	19	3	59	5	1	2	8	3	7	.234	.293	.391	.684
2021	Was	NL	53	97	23	5	0	2	(2	0)	34	13	10	8	6	0	30	2	1	1	1	1	3	.237	.292	.351	.643
14	Ari	NL	104	406	105	18	3	6	(2	4)	147	51	30	37	24	3	72	4	4	2	5	5	6	.259	.305	.362	.667
14	Mil	NL	46	123	33	4	1	3	(1	2)	48	13	10	9	8	2	28	1	2	0	4	2	4	.268	.318	.390	.708
15	Mil	NL	100	323	106	24	5	9	(4	5)	167	53	31	47	20	2	57	3	1	4	9	3	7	.328	.369	.517	.886
15	Bal	AL	55	224	53	12	0	5	(4	1)	80	30	20	24	8	1	35	2	3	1	5	1	1	.237	.268	.357	.625
19	SF	NL	30	86	17	3	0	1	(0	1)	23	8	6	7	8	2	18	2	0	1	2	1	0	.198	.278	.267	.546
19	Was	NL	89	188	47	11	1	8	(4	4)	84	30	42	31	11	1	41	3	1	1	6	2	7	.250	.300	.447	.747
	Postseason		16	36	8	1	0	0	(0	0)	9	4	1	3	3	0	10	0	0	0	0	0	0	.222	.282	.250	.532
12 ML YEARS			1519	4858	1335	269	42	90	(50	40)	1958	633	532	591	318	49	920	40	35	39	97	55	113	.275	.322	.403	.725

Luis Patino

Pitches: R **Bats:** R **Pos:** SP-15; RP-4 **Ht:** 6'1" **Wt:** 192 **Born:** 10/26/1999 **Age:** 22

Year	Team	Lg	G	GS	GF	IP	BFP	H	R	ER	HR	SH	SF	HB	TBB	IBB	SO	WP	W	L	Pct	Sv-Op	Hld	Vel	OPS	ERC	ERA
2017	Padres	R	9	8	0	40.0	168	32	14	11	2	0	0	2	16	0	43	4	2	1	.667	0- -	-	-	.638	2.84	2.48
2018	FtWyn	A	17	17	0	83.1	330	65	25	20	1	2	2	5	24	0	98	13	6	3	.667	0- -	-	-	.573	2.25	2.16
2019	Lk Els	A+	18	17	0	87.0	357	61	30	26	4	0	4	1	34	0	113	8	6	8	.429	0- -	-	-	.592	2.15	2.69
2021	Drham	AAA	7	7	0	29.1	122	23	10	10	2	0	1	2	11	0	41	0	3	1	.750	0- -	-	-	.610	2.87	3.07
2020	SD	NL	11	1	0	17.1	85	18	10	10	3	0	1	0	14	0	21	1	1	0	1.000	0-0	0	97	.788	5.66	5.19
2021	TB	AL	19	15	0	77.1	333	69	40	37	12	0	3	3	29	2	74	7	5	3	.625	0-0	0	96	.696	3.79	4.31
	Postseason		3	0	1	2.2	12	2	1	1	0	0	0	0	2	0	0	0	0	0	-	0-0	1	97	.733	3.21	3.38
2 ML YEARS			30	16	1	94.2	418	87	50	47	15	0	3	4	43	2	95	8	6	3	.667	0-0	0	96	.715	4.29	4.47

Spencer Patton

Pitches: R **Bats:** R **Pos:** RP-42 **Ht:** 6'1" **Wt:** 200 **Born:** 2/20/1988 **Age:** 34

Year	Team	Lg	G	GS	GF	IP	BFP	H	R	ER	HR	SH	SF	HB	TBB	IBB	SO	WP	W	L	Pct	Sv-Op	Hld	Vel	OPS	ERC	ERA
2021	RdRck	AAA	11	0	6	12.0	45	6	0	0	0	0	0	0	6	0	12	0	2	0	1.000	4- -	-	-	.497	1.51	0.00
2014	Tex	AL	9	0	2	9.1	35	6	1	1	0	0	0	0	2	0	8	0	1	0	1.000	0-0	2	92	.441	1.29	0.96
2015	Tex	AL	27	0	6	24.0	109	24	24	24	5	1	0	4	12	0	28	1	1	1	.500	0-0	3	92	.870	6.04	9.00
2016	ChC	NL	16	0	7	21.1	101	20	16	13	3	0	0	1	14	0	22	0	1	1	.500	0-0	1	92	.719	5.01	5.48
2021	Tex	AL	42	0	13	42.1	172	36	20	18	4	0	0	0	15	0	48	1	2	2	.500	2-5	11	93	.653	3.12	3.83
4 ML YEARS			94	0	28	97.0	417	86	61	56	12	1	0	5	43	0	106	2	5	4	.556	2-5	17	93	.705	3.98	5.20

David Paulino

Pitches: R **Bats:** R **Pos:** RP-1 **Ht:** 6'6" **Wt:** 240 **Born:** 2/6/1994 **Age:** 28

Year	Team	Lg	G	GS	GF	IP	BFP	H	R	ER	HR	SH	SF	HB	TBB	IBB	SO	WP	W	L	Pct	Sv-Op	Hld	Vel	OPS	ERC	ERA
2021	LV	AAA	30	7	8	70.0	307	61	36	34	8	1	6	8	31	1	77	7	4	3	.571	2- -	-	-	.695	4.00	4.37
2016	Hou	AL	3	1	1	7.0	29	6	4	4	0	0	0	1	3	0	2	2	0	1	.000	0-0	0	92	.665	3.40	5.14
2017	Hou	AL	6	6	0	29.0	128	36	21	21	8	0	0	0	7	0	34	5	2	0	1.000	0-0	0	93	.686	6.08	6.52
2018	Tor	AL	7	0	4	6.2	28	6	2	1	1	0	1	0	2	0	6	0	1	0	1.000	0-0	0	93	.686	3.40	1.35
2021	Phi	NL	1	0	1	2.0	9	3	2	2	1	0	0	0	0	0	0	0	0	0	-	0-0	0	95	1.111	8.13	9.00
4 ML YEARS			17	7	6	44.2	194	51	29	28	10	0	1	1	12	0	42	7	3	1	.750	0-0	0	93	.857	5.33	5.64

James Paxton

Pitches: L Bats: L Pos: SP-1

Ht: 6'4" Wt: 227 Born: 11/6/1988 Age: 33

Year	Team	Lg	G	GS	GF	IP	BFP	H	R	ER	HR	SH	SF	HB	TBB	IBB	SO	WP	W	L	Pct	Sv-Op	Hld	Vel	OPS	ERC	ERA
2013	Sea	AL	4	4	0	24.0	94	15	5	4	2	0	0	0	7	2	21	0	3	0	1.000	0-0	0	95	.533	1.61	1.50
2014	Sea	AL	13	13	0	74.0	303	60	29	25	3	3	1	1	29	2	59	7	6	4	.600	0-0	0	95	.612	2.69	3.04
2015	Sea	AL	13	13	0	67.0	297	67	34	29	8	0	3	0	29	1	56	5	3	4	.429	0-0	0	94	.704	4.22	3.90
2016	Sea	AL	20	20	0	121.0	511	134	62	51	9	4	0	5	24	3	117	5	6	7	.462	0-0	0	97	.717	3.70	3.79
2017	Sea	AL	24	24	0	136.0	552	113	47	45	9	1	5	3	37	1	156	15	12	5	.706	0-0	0	95	.602	2.56	2.98
2018	Sea	AL	28	28	0	160.1	645	134	67	67	23	2	2	1	42	0	208	8	11	6	.647	0-0	0	95	.662	2.98	3.76
2019	NYY	AL	29	29	0	150.2	633	138	71	64	23	2	4	2	55	0	186	7	15	6	.714	0-0	0	95	.732	3.90	3.82
2020	NYY	AL	5	5	0	20.1	90	23	17	15	4	0	1	1	7	0	26	2	1	1	.500	0-0	0	92	.875	5.53	6.64
2021	Sea	AL	1	1	0	1.1	9	0	1	1	0	0	0	0	1	0	2	1	0	0	-	0-0	0	94	.200	0.57	6.75
	Postseason		3	3	0	13.0	58	13	5	5	2	0	0	0	7	0	20	1	1	0	1.000	0-0	0	96	.776	5.01	3.46
9 ML YEARS			137	137	0	754.2	3130	684	333	301	81	8	22	9	231	9	831	50	57	33	.633	0-0	0	95	.675	3.28	3.59

Joel Payamps

Pitches: R Bats: R Pos: RP-36; SP-1

Ht: 6'2" Wt: 225 Born: 4/7/1994 Age: 28

Year	Team	Lg	G	GS	GF	IP	BFP	H	R	ER	HR	SH	SF	HB	TBB	IBB	SO	WP	W	L	Pct	Sv-Op	Hld	Vel	OPS	ERC	ERA
2021	Omha	AAA	8	0	5	8.0	39	10	5	4	0	0	0	0	4	0	14	0	1	0	1.000	2--	-	-	.816	4.86	4.50
2019	Ari	NL	2	0	1	4.0	17	4	2	2	0	1	0	0	3	0	3	0	0	0	-	0-0	0	93	.745	5.14	4.50
2020	Ari	NL	2	0	1	3.0	13	2	2	1	0	0	0	0	3	0	2	0	0	0	-	0-0	0	94	.685	3.96	3.00
2021	2 Tms	AL	37	1	9	50.1	205	44	22	19	6	0	0	1	14	2	38	1	1	3	.250	0-0	0	95	.667	3.10	3.40
21	Tor	AL	22	0	8	30.0	119	21	10	9	3	0	0	1	11	2	22	0	0	2	.000	0-0	0	95	.586	2.47	2.70
21	KC	AL	15	1	1	20.1	86	23	12	10	3	0	0	0	3	0	16	1	1	1	.500	0-0	0	95	.772	4.08	4.43
3 ML YEARS			41	1	11	57.1	235	50	26	22	6	1	0	1	20	2	43	1	1	3	.250	0-0	0	95	.674	3.29	3.45

Tyler Payne

Bats: R Throws: R Pos: C-1;PH-1

Ht: 5'11" Wt: 210 Born: 10/25/1992 Age: 29

										BATTING												RUNNING			AVERAGES			
Year	Team	Lg	G	AB	H	2B	3B	HR	(Hm	Rd)	TB	R	RBI	RC	TBB	IBB	SO	HBP	SH	SF	SB	CS	GDP	Avg	OBP	Slg	OPS
2021	Tenn	AA	60	213	49	14	1	4	(-	-)	77	26	30	-	17	0	67	2	0	3	1	0	4	.230	.289	.362	.651
2021	ChC	NL	1	2	0	0	0	0	(0	0)	0	0	0	0	0	0	2	0	0	0	0	0	0	.000	.000	.000	.000

Mark Payton

Bats: L Throws: L Pos: PH-21;RF-4;LF-1

Ht: 5'8" Wt: 180 Born: 12/7/1991 Age: 30

										BATTING												RUNNING			AVERAGES			
Year	Team	Lg	G	AB	H	2B	3B	HR	(Hm	Rd)	TB	R	RBI	RC	TBB	IBB	SO	HBP	SH	SF	SB	CS	GDP	Avg	OBP	Slg	OPS
2021	Lsvlle	AAA	35	139	39	7	2	4	(-	-)	62	19	14	-	11	1	23	0	0	1	4	1	4	.281	.331	.446	.777
2021	Syrcse	AAA	36	133	40	10	1	1	(-	-)	55	19	14	-	18	1	23	2	0	2	2	2	1	.301	.387	.414	.801
2020	Cin	NL	8	18	3	1	0	0	(0	0)	4	0	0	0	2	0	5	0	0	0	1	0	1	.167	.250	.222	.472
2021	Cin	NL	24	22	4	0	0	0	(0	0)	4	2	0	1	2	0	7	0	0	0	0	0	0	.182	.250	.182	.432
2 ML YEARS			32	40	7	1	0	0	(0	0)	8	2	0	1	4	0	12	0	0	0	1	0	1	.175	.250	.200	.450

Brad Peacock

Pitches: R Bats: R Pos: SP-1; RP-1

Ht: 6'1" Wt: 207 Born: 2/2/1988 Age: 34

Year	Team	Lg	G	GS	GF	IP	BFP	H	R	ER	HR	SH	SF	HB	TBB	IBB	SO	WP	W	L	Pct	Sv-Op	Hld	Vel	OPS	ERC	ERA
2021	Clmbs	AAA	11	10	0	34.0	160	39	30	29	6	0	3	5	14	0	38	0	0	4	.000	0--	-	-	.826	6.05	7.68
2011	Was	NL	3	2	0	12.0	48	7	1	1	0	0	0	0	6	0	4	1	2	0	1.000	0-1	0	93	.437	1.71	0.75
2013	Hou	AL	18	14	1	83.1	365	78	51	48	15	1	1	3	37	0	77	4	5	6	.455	0-0	2	93	.779	4.54	5.18
2014	Hou	AL	28	24	3	131.2	589	136	80	69	20	0	6	4	70	4	119	6	4	9	.308	0-0	1	92	.801	5.29	4.72
2015	Hou	AL	1	1	0	5.0	22	5	3	3	0	0	1	1	2	0	3	0	0	1	.000	0-0	0	90	.808	4.20	5.40
2016	Hou	AL	10	5	3	31.2	127	21	15	13	6	0	0	0	14	0	28	2	0	1	.000	0-0	0	92	.700	3.04	3.69
2017	Hou	AL	34	21	7	132.0	546	100	46	44	10	1	0	3	57	0	161	6	13	2	.867	0-0	1	92	.615	2.83	3.00
2018	Hou	AL	61	1	20	65.0	272	56	26	25	11	0	1	3	20	0	96	5	3	5	.375	3-6	10	93	.722	3.55	3.46
2019	Hou	AL	23	15	1	91.2	383	78	43	42	15	0	3	5	31	0	96	1	7	6	.538	0-0	0	92	.725	3.65	4.12
2020	Hou	AL	3	0	0	2.1	12	3	2	2	0	0	0	1	1	0	3	0	0	0	-	0-0	0	90	.817	6.63	7.71
2021	Bos	AL	2	1	1	5.1	26	6	9	9	2	0	0	1	3	0	3	0	0	1	.000	0-0	0	91	1.021	8.41	15.19
	Postseason		12	2	2	18.0	80	16	9	9	2	0	0	1	8	0	23	1	0	0	-	1-1	2	93	.721	3.78	4.12
10 ML YEARS			183	84	36	560.0	2390	490	276	256	79	2	12	21	241	4	590	25	34	31	.523	3-7	13	92	.724	3.91	4.11

Matt Peacock

Pitches: R Bats: R Pos: RP-27; SP-8

Ht: 6'1" Wt: 185 Born: 2/27/1994 Age: 28

Year	Team	Lg	G	GS	GF	IP	BFP	H	R	ER	HR	SH	SF	HB	TBB	IBB	SO	WP	W	L	Pct	Sv-Op	Hld	Vel	OPS	ERC	ERA
2021	Reno	AAA	5	0	5	4.0	19	7	6	6	2	0	0	0	0	0	3	0	1	1	.500	1--	-	-	1.158	9.97	13.50
2021	Ari	NL	35	8	12	86.1	386	107	55	47	13	2	3	1	28	5	50	2	5	7	.417	0-0	0	93	.848	5.49	4.90

Nate Pearson

Pitches: R Bats: R Pos: RP-11; SP-1

Ht: 6'6" Wt: 250 Born: 8/20/1996 Age: 25

Year	Team	Lg	G	GS	GF	IP	BFP	H	R	ER	HR	SH	SF	HB	TBB	IBB	SO	WP	W	L	Pct	Sv-Op	Hld	Vel	OPS	ERC	ERA
2017	2 Tms	Low	8	8	0	20.0	71	7	2	2	0	0	0	0	5	0	26	2	0	0	-	0--	-	-	.305	0.61	0.90
2019	Dnedin	A+	6	6	0	21.0	75	10	2	2	2	0	0	0	3	0	35	0	3	0	1.000	0--	-	-	.409	0.99	0.86
2019	Nham	AA	16	16	0	62.2	244	41	18	18	4	0	0	2	21	0	69	6	1	4	.200	0--	-	-	.538	2.02	2.59
2021	Buffalo	AAA	12	6	1	30.2	129	21	15	15	4	0	1	4	13	0	44	5	1	3	.250	0--	-	-	.655	3.14	4.40
2020	Tor	AL	5	4	0	18.0	81	14	15	12	5	0	1	0	13	0	16	1	1	0	1.000	0-0	0	96	.781	5.30	6.00
2021	Tor	AL	12	1	4	15.0	71	14	8	7	2	0	0	0	12	1	20	5	1	1	.500	0-0	0	98	.756	5.30	4.20
	Postseason		1	0	0	2.0	6	0	0	0	0	0	0	0	0	0	5	0	0	0	-	0-0	0	98	.000	0.00	0.00
	2 ML YEARS		17	5	4	33.0	152	28	23	19	7	0	1	0	25	1	36	6	2	1	.667	0-0	0	97	.769	5.32	5.18

Joc Pederson

Bats: L Throws: L Pos: LF-66;RF-39;CF-26;PH-25;1B-1;DH-1   JOCK

Ht: 6'1" Wt: 220 Born: 4/21/1992 Age: 30

Year	Team	Lg	G	AB	H	2B	3B	HR	(Hm	Rd)	TB	R	RBI	RC	TBB	IBB	SO	HBP	SH	SF	SB	CS	GDP	Avg	OBP	Slg	OPS
2014	LAD	NL	18	28	4	0	0	0	(0	0)	4	1	0	1	9	0	11	0	1	0	0	0	1	.143	.351	.143	.494
2015	LAD	NL	151	480	101	19	1	26	(13	13)	200	67	54	62	92	6	170	9	2	2	4	7	5	.210	.346	.417	.763
2016	LAD	NL	137	406	100	26	0	25	(13	12)	201	64	68	71	63	4	130	4	1	2	6	2	5	.246	.352	.495	.847
2017	LAD	NL	102	273	58	20	0	11	(8	3)	111	44	35	35	39	1	68	10	0	1	4	3	7	.212	.331	.407	.738
2018	LAD	NL	148	395	98	27	3	25	(13	12)	206	65	56	55	40	3	85	4	1	3	1	5	6	.248	.321	.522	.843
2019	LAD	NL	149	450	112	16	3	36	(24	12)	242	83	74	82	50	2	111	12	0	1	1	1	4	.249	.339	.538	.876
2020	LAD	NL	43	121	23	4	0	7	(2	5)	48	21	16	15	11	0	34	5	0	0	1	0	5	.190	.285	.397	.681
2021	2 Tms	NL	137	429	102	19	3	18	(7	11)	181	55	61	59	39	0	117	8	0	5	2	3	9	.238	.310	.422	.732
21	ChC	NL	73	256	59	11	2	11	(5	6)	107	35	39	34	22	0	74	5	0	4	2	3	5	.230	.300	.418	.718
21	Atl	NL	64	173	43	8	1	7	(2	5)	74	20	22	25	17	0	43	3	0	1	0	0	4	.249	.325	.428	.752
	Postseason		64	151	41	8	0	9	(5	4)	76	25	20	25	15	3	49	3	1	0	2	0	3	.272	.349	.503	.852
	8 ML YEARS		885	2582	598	131	10	148	(80	68)	1193	400	364	380	343	16	726	52	5	15	19	21	42	.232	.332	.462	.794

Elvis Peguero

Pitches: R Bats: R Pos: RP-3

Ht: 6'5" Wt: 208 Born: 3/20/1997 Age: 25

Year	Team	Lg	G	GS	GF	IP	BFP	H	R	ER	HR	SH	SF	HB	TBB	IBB	SO	WP	W	L	Pct	Sv-Op	Hld	Vel	OPS	ERC	ERA
2021	Smrst	AA	6	0	2	12.0	48	6	4	2	1	0	0	0	5	0	17	0	1	0	1.000	0--	-	-	.462	1.54	1.50
2021	HudVal	A+	15	0	4	32.1	131	22	10	9	2	0	0	0	11	0	40	0	3	1	.750	2--	-	-	-	1.94	2.51
2021	LAA	AL	3	0	0	2.1	17	7	7	7	0	0	0	1	3	0	1	0	0	1	.000	0-0	0	96	1.493	24.54	27.00

Felix Pena

Pitches: R Bats: R Pos: RP-2

Ht: 6'2" Wt: 220 Born: 2/25/1990 Age: 32

Year	Team	Lg	G	GS	GF	IP	BFP	H	R	ER	HR	SH	SF	HB	TBB	IBB	SO	WP	W	L	Pct	Sv-Op	Hld	Vel	OPS	ERC	ERA
2021	Salt Lk	AAA	31	7	6	68.1	313	82	64	61	14	0	3	3	27	0	59	8	5	4	.556	0--	-	-	.922	6.16	8.03
2016	ChC	NL	11	0	2	9.0	35	5	4	4	1	0	0	0	3	1	13	1	0	0	-	1-1	2	93	.479	1.57	4.00
2017	ChC	NL	25	0	15	34.1	155	35	21	20	8	0	0	2	18	1	37	3	1	0	1.000	0-0	1	94	.866	5.88	5.24
2018	LAA	AL	19	17	1	92.2	389	87	45	44	12	1	4	4	28	0	85	7	3	5	.375	0-0	0	92	.699	3.73	4.18
2019	LAA	AL	22	7	1	96.1	407	80	56	49	16	0	1	6	34	0	101	8	8	3	.727	0-0	1	92	.696	3.60	4.58
2020	LAA	AL	25	0	5	26.2	115	27	12	12	2	0	0	1	8	0	29	3	3	0	1.000	2-5	4	94	.672	3.67	4.05
2021	LAA	AL	2	0	0	1.2	16	7	7	7	0	0	0	0	4	0	2	1	0	0	-	0-0	0	92	1.438	36.78	37.80
	6 ML YEARS		104	24	24	260.2	1117	241	145	135	39	1	5	13	95	2	267	23	15	8	.652	3-6	8	93	.721	4.01	4.66

David Peralta

Bats: L Throws: L Pos: LF-137;PH-20;DH-1;PR-1

Ht: 6'1" Wt: 210 Born: 8/14/1987 Age: 34

Year	Team	Lg	G	AB	H	2B	3B	HR	(Hm	Rd)	TB	R	RBI	RC	TBB	IBB	SO	HBP	SH	SF	SB	CS	GDP	Avg	OBP	Slg	OPS
2014	Ari	NL	88	329	94	12	9	8	(5	3)	148	40	36	38	16	0	60	1	1	1	6	3	9	.286	.320	.450	.770
2015	Ari	NL	149	462	144	26	10	17	(8	9)	241	61	78	83	44	2	107	4	0	7	9	4	7	.312	.371	.522	.893
2016	Ari	NL	48	171	43	9	5	4	(3	1)	74	23	15	15	8	1	42	3	0	1	2	0	3	.251	.295	.433	.728
2017	Ari	NL	140	525	154	31	3	14	(8	6)	233	82	57	77	43	1	94	6	0	3	8	4	7	.293	.352	.444	.796
2018	Ari	NL	146	560	164	25	5	30	(16	14)	289	75	87	104	48	4	124	4	0	2	4	0	14	.293	.352	.516	.868
2019	Ari	NL	99	382	105	29	3	12	(6	6)	176	48	57	62	35	3	87	5	0	1	0	0	9	.275	.343	.461	.804
2020	Ari	NL	54	203	61	10	1	5	(2	3)	88	19	34	33	13	0	45	0	0	2	1	0	4	.300	.339	.433	.773
2021	Ari	NL	150	487	126	30	8	8	(5	3)	196	57	63	69	46	3	92	3	0	2	2	1	9	.259	.325	.402	.728
	Postseason		4	18	4	0	0	0	(0	0)	4	2	0	1	1	0	1	0	0	0	0	0	1	.222	.263	.222	.485
	8 ML YEARS		874	3119	891	172	44	98	(53	45)	1445	405	427	481	253	14	651	26	1	19	32	12	62	.286	.342	.463	.806

Freddy Peralta

Pitches: R Bats: R Pos: SP-27; RP-1

Ht: 5'11" Wt: 199 Born: 6/4/1996 Age: 26

Year	Team	Lg	G	GS	GF	IP	BFP	H	R	ER	HR	SH	SF	HB	TBB	IBB	SO	WP	W	L	Pct	Sv-Op	Hld	Vel	OPS	ERC	ERA
2018	Mil	NL	16	14	1	78.1	321	49	37	37	8	1	1	4	40	1	96	3	6	4	.600	0-0	0	91	.622	2.71	4.25
2019	Mil	NL	39	8	3	85.0	382	87	58	50	15	3	1	2	37	1	115	3	7	3	.700	1-2	5	94	.790	4.86	5.29
2020	Mil	NL	15	1	2	29.1	125	22	14	13	2	1	1	3	12	0	47	2	3	1	.750	0-1	3	93	.622	2.88	3.99
2021	Mil	NL	28	27	0	144.1	580	84	47	45	14	2	1	11	56	1	195	4	10	5	.667	0-0	0	93	.561	2.12	2.81
	Postseason		2	2	0	4.0	16	1	1	1	1	0	0	0	3	0	7	0	0	0	-	0-0	0	93	.558	2.39	2.25
	4 ML YEARS		98	50	6	337.0	1408	242	156	145	39	4	20	145	3	453	12	26	13	.667	1-3	8	93	.643	2.96	3.87

Wandy Peralta

Pitches: L Bats: L Pos: RP-55; SP-1

Ht: 6'0" Wt: 217 Born: 7/27/1991 Age: 30

		HOW MUCH PITCHED			WHAT HE GAVE UP												THE RESULTS							
Year Team	Lg	G	GS	GF	IP	BFP	H	R	ER	HR	SH	SF	HB	TBB	IBB	SO	WP	W	L	Pct	Sv-Op	Hld	Vel	OPS	ERC	ERA
2016 Cin	NL	10	0	3	7.1	39	11	7	7	1	0	0	1	7	0	5	0	0	0	-	0-0	2	95	1.036	10.93	8.59
2017 Cin	NL	69	0	10	64.2	263	53	28	27	8	2	3	1	24	1	57	4	3	4	.429	0-2	16	96	.681	3.24	3.76
2018 Cin	NL	59	0	6	45.1	227	58	32	27	2	1	1	2	31	2	31	0	2	2	.500	0-0	7	96	.783	6.37	5.36
2019 2 Tms	NL	47	0	11	39.2	172	40	25	25	11	0	3	2	16	3	32	0	1	1	.500	0-1	3	95	.860	5.56	5.67
2020 SF	NL	25	0	9	27.1	114	22	13	10	3	0	1	2	11	0	25	0	1	1	.500	0-1	1	95	.657	3.40	3.29
2021 2 Tms		56	1	14	51.0	219	49	24	19	6	0	2	1	21	1	43	4	5	4	.556	5-6	5	95	.709	4.08	3.35
19 Cin	NL	39	0	11	34.0	151	36	23	23	10	0	3	2	15	3	27	0	1	1	.500	0-1	2	95	.893	6.17	6.09
19 SF	NL	8	0	0	5.2	21	4	2	2	1	0	0	0	1	0	5	0	0	0	-	0-0	1	95	.638	2.27	3.18
21 SF	NL	10	0	6	8.1	37	11	5	5	1	0	1	0	3	0	8	1	2	1	.667	2-3	0	96	.863	6.15	5.40
21 NYY	AL	46	1	8	42.2	182	38	19	14	5	0	1	1	18	1	35	3	3	3	.500	3-3	5	95	.677	3.72	2.95
6 ML YEARS		266	1	53	235.1	1034	233	129	115	31	3	10	9	110	7	193	8	12	12	.500	5-10	34	96	.749	4.63	4.40

Wily Peralta

Pitches: R Bats: R Pos: SP-18; RP-1

pah-RALL-tah

Ht: 6'1" Wt: 255 Born: 5/8/1989 Age: 33

		HOW MUCH PITCHED			WHAT HE GAVE UP												THE RESULTS							
Year Team	Lg	G	GS	GF	IP	BFP	H	R	ER	HR	SH	SF	HB	TBB	IBB	SO	WP	W	L	Pct	Sv-Op	Hld	Vel	OPS	ERC	ERA
2021 Toledo	AAA	6	6	0	19.2	80	15	6	6	2	0	0	1	8	0	21	1	1	0	1.000	0--	-	-	.652	3.10	2.75
2012 Mil	NL	6	5	1	29.0	113	24	8	8	0	3	0	0	11	0	23	1	2	1	.667	0-0	0	96	.601	2.61	2.48
2013 Mil	NL	32	32	0	183.1	802	187	107	89	19	11	3	7	73	3	129	12	11	15	.423	0-0	0	95	.722	4.32	4.37
2014 Mil	NL	32	32	0	198.2	838	198	88	78	23	9	3	7	61	0	154	7	17	11	.607	0-0	0	96	.714	3.98	3.53
2015 Mil	NL	20	20	0	108.2	478	130	60	57	14	4	3	4	37	2	60	5	5	10	.333	0-0	0	94	.844	5.40	4.72
2016 Mil	NL	23	23	0	127.2	554	152	73	69	19	6	4	3	43	1	93	0	7	11	.389	0-0	0	95	.855	5.52	4.86
2017 Mil	NL	19	8	4	57.1	269	73	51	50	10	1	3	1	32	2	52	5	5	4	.556	0-0	0	94	.947	7.07	7.85
2018 KC	AL	37	0	30	34.1	149	28	14	14	4	1	2	1	23	1	35	4	1	0	1.000	14-14	1	96	.737	4.37	3.67
2019 KC	AL	42	0	23	40.1	176	45	28	26	7	1	2	2	19	1	24	0	2	4	.333	2-5	5	94	.864	6.01	5.80
2021 Det	AL	19	18	0	93.2	402	87	41	32	12	2	5	4	38	0	58	1	4	5	.444	0-0	1	94	.738	4.07	3.07
9 ML YEARS		230	138	58	873.0	3781	924	470	423	108	38	25	29	337	10	628	35	54	61	.470	16-19	7	95	.777	4.70	4.36

Jose Peraza

Bats: R Throws: R Pos: 2B-36;PH-23;3B-9;SS-1;LF-1;PR-1 per-AH-zuh

Ht: 6'0" Wt: 210 Born: 4/30/1994 Age: 28

		BATTING																	RUNNING			AVERAGES			
Year Team	Lg	G	AB	H	2B	3B	HR	(Hm	Rd)	TB	R	RBI	RC	TBB	IBB	SO	HBP	SH	SF	SB	CS	GDP	Avg	OBP	Slg	OPS
2021 Syrcse	AAA	10	37	10	2	0	0	(-	-)	12	5	4	-	2	0	2	0	0	0	1	0	0	.270	.308	.324	.632
2015 LAD	NL	7	22	4	1	1	0	(0	0)	7	3	1	2	2	1	2	0	1	0	3	0	0	.182	.250	.318	.568
2016 Cin	NL	72	241	78	8	2	3	(1	2)	99	25	25	32	7	0	33	5	0	3	21	10	3	.324	.352	.411	.762
2017 Cin	NL	143	487	126	9	4	5	(3	2)	158	50	37	43	20	1	70	7	3	1	23	8	7	.259	.297	.324	.622
2018 Cin	NL	157	632	182	31	4	14	(7	7)	263	85	58	79	29	4	75	9	8	5	23	6	12	.288	.326	.416	.742
2019 Cin	NL	141	376	90	18	2	6	(4	2)	130	37	33	34	17	0	58	8	0	2	7	6	9	.239	.285	.346	.631
2020 Bos	AL	34	111	25	8	1	1	(1	0)	38	13	8	8	5	0	18	3	0	1	1	1	3	.225	.275	.342	.617
2021 NYM	NL	64	142	29	7	0	6	(3	3)	54	21	20	16	9	0	26	3	0	0	1	0	5	.204	.266	.380	.647
7 ML YEARS		618	2011	534	82	14	35	(19	16)	749	234	182	214	89	6	282	35	12	12	79	31	39	.266	.306	.372	.679

Angel Perdomo

Pitches: L Bats: L Pos: RP-19

Ht: 6'8" Wt: 265 Born: 5/7/1994 Age: 28

		HOW MUCH PITCHED			WHAT HE GAVE UP												THE RESULTS							
Year Team	Lg	G	GS	GF	IP	BFP	H	R	ER	HR	SH	SF	HB	TBB	IBB	SO	WP	W	L	Pct	Sv-Op	Hld	Vel	OPS	ERC	ERA
2021 Nashv	AAA	14	1	5	14.0	52	8	3	2	1	1	0	0	4	0	25	2	1	0	1.000	0--	-	-	.491	1.52	1.29
2020 Mil	NL	3	0	1	2.2	19	3	7	6	0	0	0	1	7	1	5	0	0	0	-	0-0	0	95	1.033	13.65	20.25
2021 Mil	NL	19	0	8	17.0	79	12	12	12	4	0	1	2	16	2	28	1	1	0	1.000	0-0	0	94	.813	5.90	6.35
2 ML YEARS		22	0	9	19.2	98	15	19	18	4	0	1	3	23	3	33	1	1	0	1.000	0-0	0	94	.855	6.98	8.24

Geraldo Perdomo

Bats: B Throws: R Pos: SS-10;PH-1

Ht: 6'2" Wt: 203 Born: 10/22/1999 Age: 22

		BATTING																	RUNNING			AVERAGES			
Year Team	Lg	G	AB	H	2B	3B	HR	(Hm	Rd)	TB	R	RBI	RC	TBB	IBB	SO	HBP	SH	SF	SB	CS	GDP	Avg	OBP	Slg	OPS
2018 3 Tms	Low	57	211	68	7	5	4	(-	-)	97	43	24	48	39	3	44	5	1	1	24	6	3	.322	.438	.460	.897
2019 2 Tms	Low	116	407	112	21	3	3	(-	-)	148	63	47	73	70	0	67	15	3	4	26	13	8	.275	.397	.364	.761
2021 Amrillo	AA	82	286	66	8	5	6	(-	-)	102	51	32	-	47	0	81	7	2	2	8	4	5	.231	.351	.357	.708
2021 Ari	NL	11	31	8	3	1	0	(0	0)	13	5	1	3	6	2	6	0	0	0	0	0	0	.258	.378	.419	.798

Cionel Perez

Pitches: L Bats: R Pos: RP-25

see-oh-NEHL

Ht: 5'11" Wt: 162 Born: 4/21/1996 Age: 26

		HOW MUCH PITCHED			WHAT HE GAVE UP												THE RESULTS							
Year Team	Lg	G	GS	GF	IP	BFP	H	R	ER	HR	SH	SF	HB	TBB	IBB	SO	WP	W	L	Pct	Sv-Op	Hld	Vel	OPS	ERC	ERA
2021 Lsvlle	AAA	30	0	10	29.1	123	24	12	10	1	1	0	0	12	1	40	1	1	2	.333	2--	-	-	.586	2.62	3.07
2018 Hou	AL	8	0	3	11.1	45	6	5	5	3	0	0	0	7	0	12	0	0	0	-	0-0	0	95	.684	3.56	3.97
2019 Hou	AL	5	0	3	9.0	40	11	10	10	3	0	0	0	2	0	7	0	1	1	.500	0-0	0	95	.904	6.18	10.00
2020 Hou	AL	7	0	1	6.1	32	7	2	2	0	0	0	0	6	1	8	0	0	0	-	0-0	2	95	.675	5.57	2.84
2021 Cin	NL	25	0	5	24.0	111	21	21	17	5	0	1	0	20	1	25	1	1	2	.333	0-0	2	96	.814	5.85	6.38
4 ML YEARS		45	0	12	50.2	228	45	38	34	11	0	1	0	35	2	52	1	2	3	.400	0-0	2	96	.788	5.40	6.04

Francisco Perez

Pitches: L **Bats:** B **Pos:** RP-4
Ht: 6'2" **Wt:** 215 **Born:** 7/20/1997 **Age:** 24

				HOW MUCH PITCHED			WHAT HE GAVE UP											THE RESULTS						
Year	Team	Lg	G	GS	GF	IP	BFP	H	R	ER	HR	SH	SF	HB	TBB	IBB	SO	WP	W	L	Pct	Sv-Op	Hld	Vel	OPS	ERC	ERA
2021	Akron	AA	11	0	4	27.0	98	8	2	2	0	0	1	0	9	1	46	0	3	0	1.000	2--	-	-	.287	0.58	0.67
2021	Clmbs	AAA	18	0	5	25.2	113	18	9	9	2	0	0	2	19	0	35	3	1	0	1.000	1--	-	-	.639	3.89	3.16
2021	Cle	AL	4	0	1	6.2	28	6	3	3	0	0	1	0	3	0	5	0	0	0	-	0-0	0	93	.613	3.08	4.05

Hernan Perez

Bats: R **Throws:** R **Pos:** 2B-3;PH-3;1B-2;LF-1;RF-1
air-NAHN
Ht: 6'1" **Wt:** 213 **Born:** 3/26/1991 **Age:** 31

									BATTING													RUNNING			AVERAGES			
Year	Team	Lg	G	AB	H	2B	3B	HR	(Hm	Rd)	TB	R	RBI	RC	TBB	IBB	SO	HBP	SH	SF	SB	CS	GDP	Avg	OBP	Slg	OPS
2021	Nashv	AAA	23	84	30	6	0	3	(-	-)	45	8	18	-	6	0	16	0	0	1	4	1	3	.357	.396	.536	.931
2012	Det	AL	2	2	1	0	0	0	(0	0)	1	1	0	0	0	0	0	0	0	0	0	0	0	.500	.500	.500	1.000
2013	Det	AL	34	66	13	0	1	0	(0	0)	15	13	5	4	2	0	15	0	2	1	1	0	2	.197	.217	.227	.445
2014	Det	AL	8	5	1	0	0	0	(0	0)	1	1	0	0	1	0	1	0	0	0	0	0	0	.200	.333	.200	.533
2015	2 Tms		112	263	64	15	2	1	(0	1)	86	14	21	23	5	1	59	0	3	1	5	1	6	.243	.257	.327	.584
2016	Mil	NL	123	404	110	18	3	13	(7	6)	173	50	56	56	18	0	94	1	3	4	34	7	6	.272	.302	.428	.730
2017	Mil	NL	136	432	112	19	3	14	(7	7)	179	47	51	49	20	1	79	0	2	4	13	4	8	.259	.289	.414	.704
2018	Mil	NL	132	316	80	11	2	9	(5	4)	122	36	29	33	17	1	71	0	1	1	11	3	6	.253	.290	.386	.676
2019	Mil	NL	91	232	53	11	0	8	(3	5)	88	29	18	12	11	0	66	0	2	1	5	1	9	.228	.262	.379	.642
2020	ChC	NL	3	6	1	0	0	0	(0	0)	1	0	0	0	0	0	2	0	0	0	0	0	0	.167	.167	.167	.333
2021	Was	NL	10	19	1	0	0	0	(0	0)	1	1	0	0	2	0	10	0	0	0	0	0	0	.053	.143	.053	.195
15	Det	AL	22	33	2	0	0	0	(0	0)	2	1	0	0	1	0	11	0	0	0	1	0	2	.061	.088	.061	.149
15	Mil	NL	90	230	62	15	2	1	(0	1)	84	13	21	23	4	1	48	0	3	1	4	1	4	.270	.281	.365	.646
	Postseason		13	16	3	2	0	0	(0	0)	5	1	2	1	1	0	3	0	0	1	2	2	1	.188	.222	.313	.535
	10 ML YEARS		651	1745	436	74	11	45	(22	23)	667	192	180	177	76	3	397	1	12	12	69	16	37	.250	.280	.382	.662

Martin Perez

Pitches: L **Bats:** L **Pos:** SP-22; RP-14
mar-TEEN
Ht: 6'0" **Wt:** 200 **Born:** 4/4/1991 **Age:** 31

				HOW MUCH PITCHED				WHAT HE GAVE UP										THE RESULTS								
Year	Team	Lg	G	GS	GF	IP	BFP	H	R	ER	HR	SH	SF	HB	TBB	IBB	SO	WP	W	L	Pct	Sv-Op	Hld	Vel	OPS	ERC	ERA
2012	Tex	AL	12	6	2	38.0	177	47	26	23	3	1	2	1	25	1	25	5	1	4	.200	0-0	0	92	.819	5.33	5.45
2013	Tex	AL	20	20	0	124.1	529	129	55	50	15	2	3	3	37	1	84	9	10	6	.625	0-0	0	93	.728	4.14	3.62
2014	Tex	AL	8	8	0	51.1	207	50	25	25	3	1	0	1	19	1	35	1	4	3	.571	0-0	0	90	.743	3.82	4.38
2015	Tex	AL	14	14	0	78.2	339	88	45	39	3	0	3	2	24	1	48	1	3	6	.333	0-0	0	92	.729	4.04	4.46
2016	Tex	AL	33	33	0	198.2	855	205	110	97	18	9	8	4	76	0	103	3	10	11	.476	0-0	0	93	.741	4.24	4.39
2017	Tex	AL	32	32	0	185.0	811	221	108	99	23	4	3	6	63	3	115	4	13	12	.520	0-0	0	93	.812	5.35	4.82
2018	Tex	AL	22	15	3	85.1	397	116	68	59	16	1	5	2	36	1	52	3	2	7	.222	0-1	2	93	.916	7.19	6.22
2019	Min	AL	32	29	0	165.1	737	184	104	94	23	3	5	3	67	1	135	3	10	7	.588	0-0	0	94	.785	5.07	5.12
2020	Bos	AL	12	12	0	62.0	262	55	33	31	8	1	4	3	28	0	46	2	3	5	.375	0-0	0	92	.744	4.13	4.50
2021	Bos	AL	36	22	6	114.0	509	136	71	60	19	1	4	9	36	2	97	2	7	8	.467	0-1	1	93	.838	5.68	4.74
	Postseason		1	1	0	5.0	21	6	4	4	0	1	0	0	3	1	2	0	0	1	.000	0-0	0	92	.921	5.47	7.20
	10 ML YEARS		221	191	11	1102.2	4823	1231	645	577	131	23	33	35	401	10	740	33	63	69	.477	0-1	3	93	.785	4.89	4.71

Michael Perez

Bats: L **Throws:** R **Pos:** C-58;PH-11;1B-1
Ht: 5'10" **Wt:** 195 **Born:** 8/7/1992 **Age:** 29

									BATTING													RUNNING			AVERAGES			
Year	Team	Lg	G	AB	H	2B	3B	HR	(Hm	Rd)	TB	R	RBI	RC	TBB	IBB	SO	HBP	SH	SF	SB	CS	GDP	Avg	OBP	Slg	OPS
2018	TB	AL	24	74	21	5	0	1	(0	1)	29	9	11	9	3	0	19	0	1	2	0	0	0	.284	.304	.392	.696
2019	TB	AL	22	46	10	5	0	0	(0	0)	15	6	2	6	8	0	19	1	0	0	0	0	0	.217	.345	.326	.672
2020	TB	AL	38	84	14	3	0	1	(1	0)	20	7	13	6	5	0	27	1	0	3	0	0	3	.167	.237	.238	.475
2021	Pit	NL	70	210	30	8	1	7	(4	3)	61	19	21	8	19	1	68	2	0	4	0	1	4	.143	.221	.290	.511
	Postseason		8	7	2	0	0	1	(0	1)	5	1	3	3	0	0	2	0	0	0	0	0	0	.286	.286	.714	1.000
	4 ML YEARS		154	414	75	21	1	9	(5	4)	125	41	47	28	37	1	133	4	1	9	0	1	7	.181	.253	.302	.555

Oliver Perez

Pitches: L **Bats:** L **Pos:** RP-5
Ht: 6'3" **Wt:** 225 **Born:** 8/15/1981 **Age:** 40

				HOW MUCH PITCHED				WHAT HE GAVE UP										THE RESULTS								
Year	Team	Lg	G	GS	GF	IP	BFP	H	R	ER	HR	SH	SF	HB	TBB	IBB	SO	WP	W	L	Pct	Sv-Op	Hld	Vel	OPS	ERC	ERA
2002	SD	NL	16	15	0	90.0	387	71	37	35	13	5	3	5	48	1	94	3	4	5	.444	0-0	0	91	.702	3.93	3.50
2003	2 Tms	NL	24	24	0	126.2	579	129	80	77	22	5	2	4	77	3	141	7	4	10	.286	0-0	0	93	.830	5.66	5.47
2004	Pit	NL	30	30	0	196.0	805	145	71	65	22	9	5	9	81	2	239	2	12	10	.545	0-0	0	93	.655	2.99	2.98
2005	Pit	NL	20	20	0	103.0	471	102	68	67	23	5	4	6	70	1	97	3	7	5	.583	0-0	0	91	.874	6.44	5.85
2006	2 Tms	NL	22	22	0	112.2	529	129	90	82	20	5	10	4	68	0	102	5	3	13	.188	0-0	0	90	.865	6.62	6.55
2007	NYM	NL	29	29	0	177.0	765	153	90	70	22	4	7	7	79	1	174	6	15	10	.600	0-0	0	91	.696	3.76	3.56
2008	NYM	NL	34	34	0	194.0	847	167	100	91	24	9	7	11	105	4	180	9	10	7	.588	0-0	0	91	.725	4.21	4.22
2009	NYM	NL	14	14	0	66.0	324	69	51	50	12	5	4	4	58	2	62	2	3	4	.429	0-0	0	90	.897	7.16	6.82
2010	NYM	NL	17	7	4	46.1	234	54	37	35	9	1	3	4	42	3	37	4	0	5	.000	0-0	0	88	.935	8.27	6.80
2012	Sea	AL	33	0	6	29.2	123	27	7	7	1	1	1	0	10	2	24	2	1	3	.250	0-2	5	94	.628	2.82	2.12
2013	Sea	AL	61	0	22	53.0	229	50	23	22	6	1	0	1	26	3	74	1	3	3	.500	2-3	8	92	.731	4.23	3.74
2014	Ari	AL	68	0	11	58.2	256	50	25	19	5	4	0	7	24	2	51	3	3	4	.429	0-1	15	91	.679	3.53	2.91
2015	2 Tms		70	0	15	41.0	183	39	24	19	4	4	1	4	15	2	51	3	2	4	.333	0-3	10	92	.681	3.81	4.17
2016	Was	NL	64	0	7	40.0	182	38	22	22	4	1	1	7	20	3	46	5	2	3	.400	0-1	15	92	.751	4.72	4.95
2017	Was	NL	50	0	8	33.0	143	32	17	17	4	0	1	4	12	1	39	1	0	0	-	1-1	12	93	.772	4.32	4.64
2018	Cle	AL	51	0	1	32.1	120	17	6	5	1	0	1	2	7	3	43	1	2	2	.500	0-0	15	91	.417	1.12	1.39
2019	Cle	AL	67	0	4	40.2	173	38	20	18	5	0	1	3	12	2	48	1	2	4	.333	1-5	22	92	.733	3.64	3.98
2020	Cle	AL	21	0	2	18.0	72	13	5	4	0	0	1	3	6	3	14	0	1	1	.500	1-2	3	90	.564	2.17	2.00

Year	Team	Lg	G	GS	GF	IP	BFP	H	R	ER	HR	SH	SF	HB	TBB	IBB	SO	WP	W	L	Pct	Sv-Op	Hld	Vel	OPS	ERC	ERA
			HOW MUCH PITCHED					**WHAT HE GAVE UP**											**THE RESULTS**								
2021	Cle	AL	5	0	3	3.2	18	5	1	0	0	0	0	0	1	1	4	0	0	1	.000	0-0	0	89	.627	4.01	0.00
03	SD	NL	19	19	0	103.2	473	103	65	62	20	4	2	3	65	2	117	6	4	7	.364	0-0	0	92	.836	5.74	5.38
03	Pit	NL	5	5	0	23.0	106	26	15	15	2	1	0	1	12	1	24	1	0	3	.000	0-0	0	93	.806	5.29	5.87
06	Pit	NL	15	15	0	76.0	364	88	64	56	13	5	8	3	51	0	61	4	2	10	.167	0-0	0	90	.877	6.85	6.63
06	NYM	NL	7	7	0	36.2	165	41	26	26	7	0	2	3	17	0	41	1	1	3	.250	0-0	0	91	.838	6.16	6.38
15	Ari	NL	48	0	11	29.0	128	25	12	10	2	1	0	4	11	1	37	2	2	1	.667	0-3	7	92	.627	3.38	3.10
15	Hou	AL	22	0	4	12.0	55	14	12	9	2	0	0	0	4	1	14	1	0	3	.000	0-0	3	92	.798	4.89	6.75
Postseason			11	2	2	16.2	71	18	7	7	3	3	0	2	5	1	10	0	2	0	1.000	0-0	3	93	.859	5.30	3.78
19 ML YEARS			696	195	83	1461.2	6440	1328	774	705	197	56	51	87	761	40	1545	58	73	93	.440	5-18	105	91	.747	4.47	4.34

Roberto Perez

Bats: R Throws: R Pos: C-43;1B-1;PH-1 **Ht: 5'11" Wt: 220 Born: 12/23/1988 Age: 33**

Year	Team	Lg	G	AB	H	2B	3B	HR	(Hm	Rd)	TB	R	RBI	RC	TBB	IBB	SO	HBP	SH	SF	SB	CS	GDP	Avg	OBP	Slg	OPS
			BATTING																		**RUNNING**			**AVERAGES**			
2014	Cle	AL	29	85	23	5	0	1	(1	0)	31	10	4	8	5	0	26	0	5	0	0	0	2	.271	.311	.365	.676
2015	Cle	AL	70	184	42	9	1	7	(4	3)	74	30	21	24	33	1	64	1	5	2	0	0	9	.228	.348	.402	.751
2016	Cle	AL	61	153	28	6	1	3	(1	2)	45	14	17	17	23	0	44	0	5	3	0	0	4	.183	.285	.294	.579
2017	Cle	AL	73	217	45	12	0	8	(6	2)	81	22	38	26	26	0	71	0	4	1	0	1	4	.207	.291	.373	.664
2018	Cle	AL	62	179	30	9	1	2	(1	1)	47	16	19	12	21	0	70	1	7	2	1	0	6	.168	.256	.263	.519
2019	Cle	AL	119	389	93	9	1	24	(12	12)	176	46	63	56	45	1	127	4	7	4	0	0	12	.239	.321	.452	.774
2020	Cle	AL	32	97	16	2	0	1	(0	1)	21	6	5	5	11	0	38	2	0	0	0	0	2	.165	.264	.216	.480
2021	Cle	AL	44	141	21	3	0	7	(3	4)	45	13	17	13	17	0	56	1	2	0	1	0	1	.149	.245	.319	.564
Postseason			21	59	13	1	0	4	(3	1)	26	6	10	8	9	0	20	1	2	0	0	0	2	.220	.333	.441	.774
8 ML YEARS			490	1445	298	55	4	53	(28	25)	520	157	184	161	181	2	496	10	35	12	2	1	40	.206	.297	.360	.657

Salvador Perez

Bats: R Throws: R Pos: C-124;DH-40;PH-1 **Ht: 6'3" Wt: 255 Born: 5/10/1990 Age: 32**

Year	Team	Lg	G	AB	H	2B	3B	HR	(Hm	Rd)	TB	R	RBI	RC	TBB	IBB	SO	HBP	SH	SF	SB	CS	GDP	Avg	OBP	Slg	OPS
			BATTING																		**RUNNING**			**AVERAGES**			
2011	KC	AL	39	148	49	8	2	3	(1	2)	70	20	21	26	7	0	20	1	0	2	0	0	5	.331	.361	.473	.834
2012	KC	AL	76	289	87	16	0	11	(3	8)	136	38	39	36	12	3	27	1	0	3	0	0	14	.301	.328	.471	.798
2013	KC	AL	138	496	145	25	3	13	(6	7)	215	48	79	77	21	2	63	4	0	5	0	0	13	.292	.323	.433	.757
2014	KC	AL	150	578	150	28	2	17	(8	9)	233	57	70	55	22	2	85	3	0	3	1	0	22	.260	.289	.403	.692
2015	KC	AL	142	531	138	25	0	21	(9	12)	226	52	70	60	13	4	82	4	0	5	1	0	23	.260	.280	.426	.706
2016	KC	AL	139	514	127	28	2	22	(11	11)	225	57	64	61	22	3	119	8	0	2	0	0	12	.247	.288	.438	.725
2017	KC	AL	129	471	126	24	1	27	(6	21)	233	57	80	65	17	3	95	5	0	5	1	0	23	.268	.297	.495	.792
2018	KC	AL	129	510	120	23	0	27	(11	16)	224	52	80	58	17	0	108	12	0	5	1	1	19	.235	.274	.439	.713
2020	KC	AL	37	150	50	12	0	11	(5	6)	95	22	32	29	3	0	36	2	0	1	1	0	0	.333	.353	.633	.986
2021	KC	AL	161	620	169	24	0	**48**	(27	21)	337	88	**121**	103	28	4	170	13	0	14	1	0	14	.273	.316	.544	.859
Postseason			31	116	27	4	0	5	(3	2)	46	14	14	10	5	0	19	3	0	0	0	0	3	.233	.282	.397	.679
10 ML YEARS			1140	4307	1161	213	10	200	(87	113)	1994	491	656	570	162	21	805	53	0	35	6	1	145	.270	.302	.463	.765

Dillon Peters

Pitches: L Bats: L Pos: SP-6 **Ht: 5'11" Wt: 190 Born: 8/31/1992 Age: 29**

Year	Team	Lg	G	GS	GF	IP	BFP	H	R	ER	HR	SH	SF	HB	TBB	IBB	SO	WP	W	L	Pct	Sv-Op	Hld	Vel	OPS	ERC	ERA
			HOW MUCH PITCHED					**WHAT HE GAVE UP**											**THE RESULTS**								
2021	Salt Lk	AAA	8	8	0	41.1	179	47	21	20	12	0	0	0	13	0	48	2	2	2	.500	0- -	-	-	.907	5.94	4.35
2021	Indy	AAA	5	2	0	12.0	48	4	2	2	2	0	0	2	6	0	15	0	1	0	1.000	0- -	-	-	.500	2.03	1.50
2017	Mia	NL	6	6	0	31.1	139	32	18	18	3	0	0	2	19	1	27	3	1	2	.333	0-0	0	91	.771	5.38	5.17
2018	Mia	NL	7	5	2	27.2	129	34	22	22	4	1	1	1	15	0	17	3	2	2	.500	0-0	0	91	.868	6.59	7.16
2019	LAA	AL	17	12	1	72.0	327	85	50	43	18	1	2	5	26	1	55	1	4	4	.500	0-0	0	91	.926	6.34	5.38
2020	LAA	AL	1	1	0	1.2	9	3	4	3	2	0	0	0	0	0	2	0	0	0	-	0-0	0	91	1.333	14.27	16.20
2021	Pit	NL	6	6	0	26.2	117	26	12	11	2	0	0	1	10	0	23	0	1	2	.333	0-0	0	91	.731	3.72	3.71
5 ML YEARS			37	30	3	159.1	721	180	106	97	29	2	3	9	70	2	124	7	8	10	.444	0-0	0	91	.861	5.83	5.48

DJ Peters

Bats: R Throws: R Pos: CF-29;LF-22;RF-16;PH-7;PR-3;DH-2 **Ht: 6'6" Wt: 225 Born: 12/12/1995 Age: 26**

Year	Team	Lg	G	AB	H	2B	3B	HR	(Hm	Rd)	TB	R	RBI	RC	TBB	IBB	SO	HBP	SH	SF	SB	CS	GDP	Avg	OBP	Slg	OPS
			BATTING																		**RUNNING**			**AVERAGES**			
2021	OkCity	AAA	50	180	42	9	2	4	(-	-)	67	24	19	-	20	0	58	3	0	1	1	1	2	.233	.319	.372	.691
2021	2 Tms		70	223	44	9	1	13	(8	5)	94	29	38	27	12	4	82	2	0	3	2	0	4	.197	.242	.422	.663
21	LAD	NL	18	26	5	2	0	1	(1	0)	10	5	4	4	8	4	14	0	0	0	0	0	0	.192	.382	.385	.767
21	Tex	AL	52	197	39	7	1	12	(7	5)	84	24	34	23	4	0	68	2	0	3	2	0	4	.198	.218	.426	.645

David Peterson

Pitches: L Bats: L Pos: SP-15 **Ht: 6'6" Wt: 240 Born: 9/3/1995 Age: 26**

Year	Team	Lg	G	GS	GF	IP	BFP	H	R	ER	HR	SH	SF	HB	TBB	IBB	SO	WP	W	L	Pct	Sv-Op	Hld	Vel	OPS	ERC	ERA
			HOW MUCH PITCHED					**WHAT HE GAVE UP**											**THE RESULTS**								
2020	NYM	NL	10	9	0	49.2	205	36	20	19	5	0	0	3	24	0	40	1	6	2	.750	0-0	0	92	.644	3.20	3.44
2021	NYM	NL	15	15	0	66.2	287	64	44	41	11	2	0	5	29	0	69	6	2	6	.250	0-0	0	93	.798	4.85	5.54
2 ML YEARS			25	24	0	116.1	492	100	64	60	16	2	0	8	53	0	109	7	8	8	.500	0-0	0	92	.734	4.12	4.64

Jace Peterson

Bats: L **Throws:** R **Pos:** 2B-35;1B-26;PH-19;RF-17;3B-11;LF-11;SS-1 JAYCE **Ht:** 6'0" **Wt:** 215 **Born:** 5/9/1990 **Age:** 32

Year	Team	Lg	G	AB	H	2B	3B	HR	(Hm	Rd)	TB	R	RBI	RC	TBB	IBB	SO	HBP	SH	SF	SB	CS	GDP	Avg	OBP	Slg	OPS
2021	Nashv	AAA	17	55	13	4	0	5	(-	-)	32	12	19	-	9	0	19	0	0	0	1	0	2	.236	.344	.582	.926
2014	SD	NL	27	53	6	0	0	0	(0	0)	6	3	0	0	2	1	18	1	2	0	2	0	1	.113	.161	.113	.274
2015	Atl	NL	152	528	126	23	5	6	(1	5)	177	55	52	56	56	4	120	3	7	3	12	10	5	.239	.314	.335	.649
2016	Atl	NL	115	350	89	16	1	7	(3	4)	128	45	29	42	52	2	69	1	2	3	5	5	9	.254	.350	.366	.715
2017	Atl	NL	89	186	40	9	2	2	(2	0)	59	15	17	20	27	3	48	1	1	0	3	0	4	.215	.318	.317	.635
2018	2 Tms	AL	96	210	42	13	2	3	(2	1)	68	21	28	26	31	0	58	3	1	1	13	3	8	.200	.310	.324	.634
2019	Bal	AL	29	100	22	3	1	2	(0	0)	33	14	11	13	6	0	24	1	0	1	4	1	1	.220	.269	.330	.599
2020	Mil	NL	26	45	9	1	0	2	(1	1)	16	6	5	10	15	0	20	0	0	1	1	0	0	.200	.393	.356	.749
2021	Mil	NL	94	259	64	11	1	6	(1	5)	95	36	31	41	38	0	68	3	0	2	10	1	1	.247	.348	.367	.714
18	NYY	AL	3	10	3	0	0	0	(0	0)	3	0	0	1	1	0	3	0	0	0	0	1	0	.300	.364	.300	.664
18	Bal	AL	93	200	39	13	2	3	(2	1)	65	21	28	25	30	0	55	3	1	1	13	2	8	.195	.308	.325	.633
	Postseason		1	0	0	0	0	0	(0	0)	0	0	0	0	1	0	0	0	0	0	0	0	0	-	1.000	-	-
	8 ML YEARS		628	1731	398	76	12	28	(12	16)	582	195	173	208	227	10	425	13	13	11	50	20	29	.230	.322	.336	.658

Yusmeiro Petit

Pitches: R **Bats:** R **Pos:** RP-78 yooz-MAY-roh peh-TEET **Ht:** 6'1" **Wt:** 252 **Born:** 11/22/1984 **Age:** 37

Year	Team	Lg	G	GS	GF	IP	BFP	H	R	ER	HR	SH	SF	HB	TBB	IBB	SO	WP	W	L	Pct	Sv-Op	Hld	Vel	OPS	ERC	ERA
2006	Fla	NL	15	1	5	26.1	129	46	28	28	7	1	1	0	9	1	20	0	1	1	.500	0-0	0	89	1.125	10.07	9.57
2007	Ari	NL	14	10	2	57.0	243	58	30	29	12	1	1	0	18	1	40	0	3	4	.429	0-0	0	87	.830	4.56	4.58
2008	Ari	NL	19	8	6	56.1	229	45	29	27	12	4	2	1	14	2	42	3	3	5	.375	0-0	0	87	.704	3.08	4.31
2009	Ari	NL	23	17	2	89.2	407	102	62	58	19	3	0	0	34	1	74	3	3	10	.231	0-0	0	87	.837	5.44	5.82
2012	SF	NL	1	0	0	4.2	22	7	2	2	0	1	0	0	4	0	1	0	0	0	-	0-0	0	88	.936	9.14	3.86
2013	SF	NL	8	7	0	48.0	196	46	19	19	4	2	0	0	11	1	47	0	4	1	.800	0-0	0	88	.660	3.08	3.56
2014	SF	NL	39	12	14	117.0	461	97	51	48	12	0	3	1	22	5	133	0	5	5	.500	0-0	0	89	.635	2.40	3.69
2015	SF	NL	42	1	15	76.0	316	75	32	31	11	1	6	1	15	2	59	3	1	1	.500	1-1	0	88	.743	3.48	3.67
2016	Was	NL	36	1	16	62.0	265	67	33	31	12	3	1	0	15	3	49	3	3	5	.375	1-2	1	89	.793	4.42	4.50
2017	LAA	AL	60	1	10	91.1	354	69	32	28	9	1	1	1	18	4	101	0	5	2	.714	4-5	14	90	.571	2.07	2.76
2018	Oak	AL	74	0	12	93.0	368	76	32	31	13	1	5	0	18	4	76	1	7	3	.700	0-2	16	89	.649	2.52	3.00
2019	Oak	AL	80	0	6	83.0	308	57	25	25	11	1	3	0	10	0	71	2	5	3	.625	0-1	29	88	.579	1.71	2.71
2020	Oak	AL	26	0	6	21.2	88	19	4	4	3	0	0	0	5	0	17	0	2	1	.667	0-0	7	88	.639	2.99	1.66
2021	Oak	AL	78	0	10	78.0	313	69	35	34	12	2	1	1	12	1	37	1	8	3	.727	2-8	22	88	.659	2.86	3.92
	Postseason		10	0	0	19.2	79	17	9	9	2	0	0	1	5	2	19	1	3	0	1.000	0-0	0	89	.702	2.92	4.12
	14 ML YEARS		515	59	104	904.0	3699	833	414	395	137	21	26	5	205	25	767	17	50	44	.532	8-19	89	88	.707	3.28	3.93

Jake Petricka

Pitches: R **Bats:** R **Pos:** RP-7 puh-TRICH-kuh **Ht:** 6'4" **Wt:** 218 **Born:** 6/5/1988 **Age:** 34

Year	Team	Lg	G	GS	GF	IP	BFP	H	R	ER	HR	SH	SF	HB	TBB	IBB	SO	WP	W	L	Pct	Sv-Op	Hld	Vel	OPS	ERC	ERA
2021	Salt Lk	AAA	21	0	3	34.0	148	38	16	16	5	0	1	1	10	0	33	1	5	2	.714	0--	-	-	.816	4.77	4.24
2013	CWS	AL	16	0	3	19.1	85	20	7	7	0	1	1	1	10	1	10	4	1	1	.500	0-0	1	93	.688	4.18	3.26
2014	CWS	AL	67	0	33	73.0	307	67	24	24	3	3	4	2	33	4	55	2	1	6	.143	14-18	10	94	.671	3.52	2.96
2015	CWS	AL	62	0	18	52.0	220	56	21	21	2	3	1	1	18	4	33	2	4	3	.571	2-3	12	94	.716	3.91	3.63
2016	CWS	AL	9	0	1	8.0	39	8	5	4	1	1	0	0	8	0	7	3	0	0	-	0-0	1	94	.854	6.76	4.50
2017	CWS	AL	27	0	7	25.2	122	39	21	20	6	0	1	1	6	0	26	3	1	1	.500	0-1	3	94	.947	7.66	7.01
2018	Tor	AL	41	0	5	45.2	208	59	28	23	6	1	0	5	16	0	41	5	3	1	.750	0-0	1	95	.897	6.44	4.53
2019	Mil	NL	6	0	1	8.0	36	6	3	3	0	1	0	0	6	1	3	1	0	0	-	0-0	0	93	.643	3.00	3.38
2021	LAA	AL	7	0	1	6.0	32	6	10	10	1	0	1	1	7	1	8	1	0	1	.000	0-1	1	93	.872	8.01	15.00
	8 ML YEARS		235	0	74	237.2	1049	261	119	112	19	9	9	11	104	11	183	21	10	13	.435	16-24	28	94	.773	4.82	4.24

Tommy Pham

Bats: R **Throws:** R **Pos:** LF-113;PH-30;CF-11;DH-3;RF-1 FAM **Ht:** 6'1" **Wt:** 223 **Born:** 3/8/1988 **Age:** 34

Year	Team	Lg	G	AB	H	2B	3B	HR	(Hm	Rd)	TB	R	RBI	RC	TBB	IBB	SO	HBP	SH	SF	SB	CS	GDP	Avg	OBP	Slg	OPS
2014	StL	NL	6	2	0	0	0	0	(0	0)	0	0	0	0	0	0	2	0	0	0	0	0	0	.000	.000	.000	.000
2015	StL	NL	52	153	41	7	5	5	(1	4)	73	28	18	26	19	1	41	0	0	1	2	0	1	.268	.347	.477	.824
2016	StL	NL	78	159	36	7	0	9	(3	6)	70	26	17	21	20	1	71	3	1	0	2	2	3	.226	.324	.440	.764
2017	StL	NL	128	444	136	22	2	23	(6	17)	231	95	73	93	71	0	117	10	2	3	25	7	18	.306	.411	.520	.931
2018	2 Tms	AL	137	494	136	18	6	21	(9	12)	229	102	63	76	67	2	140	6	0	3	15	7	18	.275	.367	.464	.830
2019	TB	AL	145	567	155	33	2	21	(11	10)	255	77	68	86	81	4	123	5	0	1	25	4	22	.273	.369	.450	.818
2020	SD	NL	31	109	23	2	0	3	(0	3)	34	13	12	14	15	0	27	1	0	0	6	0	2	.211	.312	.312	.624
2021	SD	NL	155	475	109	24	2	15	(5	10)	182	74	49	55	78	3	128	4	0	4	14	6	10	.229	.340	.383	.724
18	StL	NL	98	351	87	11	6	14	(6	8)	140	67	41	45	42	1	97	2	0	1	10	6	12	.248	.331	.399	.730
18	TB	AL	39	143	49	7	6	7	(3	4)	89	35	22	31	25	1	43	4	0	2	5	1	6	.343	.448	.622	1.071
	Postseason		15	54	19	2	0	3	(2	1)	30	5	6	9	2	0	11	0	0	0	4	0	3	.352	.375	.556	.931
	8 ML YEARS		732	2403	636	113	17	97	(35	62)	1074	415	300	371	351	11	649	29	3	12	89	26	74	.265	.364	.447	.810

David Phelps

Pitches: R Bats: R Pos: RP-10; SP-1   Ht: 6'2" Wt: 198 Born: 10/9/1986 Age: 35

			HOW MUCH PITCHED					WHAT HE GAVE UP										THE RESULTS						
Year	Team	Lg	G	GS	GF	IP	BFP	H	R	ER	HR	SH	SF	HB	TBB	IBB	SO	WP	W	L	Pct	Sv-Op	Hld	Vel	OPS	ERC	ERA
2012	NYY	AL	33	11	5	99.2	414	81	38	37	14	4	3	6	38	2	96	2	4	4	.500	0-0	2	91	.682	3.48	3.34
2013	NYY	AL	22	12	3	86.2	376	88	50	48	8	1	2	5	35	1	79	2	6	5	.545	0-1	1	90	.749	4.38	4.98
2014	NYY	AL	32	17	5	113.0	497	115	62	55	13	4	3	7	46	2	92	2	5	5	.500	1-1	5	90	.753	4.52	4.38
2015	Mia	NL	23	19	1	112.0	482	119	59	56	11	2	5	4	33	0	77	2	4	8	.333	0-0	0	90	.729	4.13	4.50
2016	Mia	NL	64	5	6	86.2	352	61	23	22	6	1	2	2	38	6	114	0	7	6	.538	4-10	25	94	.582	2.47	2.28
2017	2 Tms		54	0	5	55.2	238	51	23	21	5	2	2	1	26	3	62	0	4	5	.444	0-8	21	94	.693	3.82	3.40
2019	2 Tms		41	1	4	34.1	147	31	14	13	5	0	1	1	17	1	36	3	2	1	.667	1-5	5	93	.755	4.36	3.41
2020	2 Tms	NL	22	0	4	20.2	85	19	16	15	7	0	0	1	5	0	31	1	2	4	.333	0-2	6	94	.813	4.78	6.53
2021	Tor	AL	11	1	1	10.1	42	8	2	1	0	0	0	1	4	0	15	0	0	0	-	0-0	4	94	.553	2.60	0.87
17	Mia	NL	44	0	4	47.0	197	42	20	18	5	2	1	0	21	3	51	0	2	4	.333	0-6	18	94	.699	3.68	3.45
17	Sea	AL	10	0	1	8.2	41	9	3	3	0	0	1	1	5	0	11	0	2	1	.667	0-2	3	94	.660	4.54	3.12
19	Tor	AL	17	1	1	17.1	71	14	7	7	3	0	0	1	7	1	18	1	0	0	-	0-2	4	92	.754	3.77	3.63
19	ChC	NL	24	0	3	17.0	76	17	7	6	2	0	1	0	10	0	18	2	2	1	.667	1-3	1	93	.755	4.98	3.18
20	Mil	NL	12	0	3	13.0	48	7	5	4	2	0	0	1	2	0	20	1	2	3	.400	0-1	4	94	.497	1.56	2.77
20	Phi	NL	10	0	1	7.2	37	12	11	11	5	0	0	0	3	0	11	0	0	1	.000	0-1	2	94	1.229	12.43	12.91
	Postseason		3	0	1	3.1	19	7	4	3	0	0	0	0	1	0	2	0	0	2	.000	0-0	0	90	1.032	8.97	8.10
	9 ML YEARS		302	66	34	619.0	2633	573	287	268	69	14	18	28	242	15	602	12	34	38	.472	6-27	69	91	.708	3.87	3.90

Brett Phillips

Bats: L Throws: R Pos: CF-52;RF-46;LF-19;PR-16;PH-6;DH-2   Ht: 6'0" Wt: 195 Born: 5/30/1994 Age: 28

							BATTING														RUNNING			AVERAGES			
Year	Team	Lg	G	AB	H	2B	3B	HR	(Hm	Rd)	TB	R	RBI	RC	TBB	IBB	SO	HBP	SH	SF	SB	CS	GDP	Avg	OBP	Slg	OPS
2017	Mil	NL	37	87	24	3	0	4	(2	2)	39	9	12	14	9	2	34	1	1	0	5	0	0	.276	.351	.448	.799
2018	2 Tms		51	134	25	4	3	2	(1	1)	41	15	11	10	11	0	61	1	0	1	1	1	2	.187	.252	.306	.558
2019	KC	AL	30	65	9	2	0	2	(1	1)	17	7	6	2	10	0	23	0	2	2	3	0	1	.138	.247	.262	.508
2020	2 Tms	AL	35	51	10	0	2	2	(1	1)	20	10	5	6	8	0	15	0	0	0	6	1	0	.196	.305	.392	.697
2021	TB	AL	119	253	52	9	4	13	(6	7)	108	50	44	40	33	0	113	2	2	2	14	3	3	.206	.300	.427	.727
18	Mil	NL	15	22	4	0	1	0	(0	0)	6	2	4	2	2	0	11	0	0	0	0	0	1	.182	.250	.273	.523
18	KC	AL	36	112	21	4	2	2	(1	1)	35	13	7	8	9	0	50	1	0	1	1	1	1	.188	.252	.313	.565
20	KC	AL	18	31	7	0	1	1	(0	1)	12	8	2	3	3	0	8	0	0	0	3	1	0	.226	.294	.387	.681
20	TB	AL	17	20	3	0	1	1	(1	0)	8	2	3	3	5	0	7	0	0	0	3	0	0	.150	.320	.400	.720
	Postseason		7	3	1	0	0	0	(0	0)	1	0	1	1	0	0	1	0	0	0	1	0	0	.333	.333	.333	.667
	5 ML YEARS		272	590	120	18	9	23	(11	12)	225	91	78	72	71	2	246	4	5	5	29	5	6	.203	.291	.381	.672

Evan Phillips

Pitches: R Bats: R Pos: RP-8   Ht: 6'2" Wt: 215 Born: 9/11/1994 Age: 27

			HOW MUCH PITCHED					WHAT HE GAVE UP											THE RESULTS						
Year	Team	Lg	G	GS	GF	IP	BFP	H	R	ER	HR	SH	SF	HB	TBB	IBB	SO	WP	W	L	Pct	Sv-Op	Hld	Vel	OPS	ERC	ERA
2021	Norfolk	AAA	18	0	3	25.0	106	21	16	14	5	0	2	0	14	1	35	2	1	1	.500	0- -	-	-	.797	4.55	5.04
2018	2 Tms		9	1	4	11.2	59	13	19	17	5	0	0	1	10	0	8	1	0	1	.000	0-0	0	94	1.073	9.76	13.11
2019	Bal	AL	25	0	2	28.0	140	32	20	20	2	1	2	5	20	0	40	2	0	1	.000	0-0	3	94	.821	6.59	6.43
2020	Bal	AL	14	0	3	14.1	69	14	8	8	1	0	0	3	10	0	20	1	1	1	.500	0-0	2	95	.695	5.67	5.02
2021	2 Tms		8	0	5	13.1	58	11	6	5	1	0	0	1	5	1	11	1	1	1	.500	1-1	0	95	.601	2.91	3.38
18	Atl	NL	4	0	4	6.1	29	6	6	6	3	0	0	0	4	0	3	0	0	0	-	0-0	0	94	.985	7.41	8.53
18	Bal	AL	5	1	0	5.1	30	7	13	11	2	0	0	1	6	0	5	1	0	1	.000	0-0	0	94	1.162	12.53	18.56
21	TB	AL	1	0	1	3.0	12	3	1	1	1	0	0	0	0	0	2	0	0	0	-	1-1	0	96	.750	3.79	3.00
21	LAD	NL	7	0	4	10.1	46	8	5	4	0	0	0	1	5	1	9	1	1	1	.500	0-0	0	95	.554	2.55	3.48
	4 ML YEARS		56	1	14	67.1	326	70	53	50	9	1	2	10	45	1	79	5	2	4	.333	1-1	5	94	.799	6.12	6.68

Kevin Pillar

Bats: R Throws: R Pos: CF-57;LF-52;PH-26;RF-22;PR-1   pih-LAHR   Ht: 6'0" Wt: 200 Born: 1/4/1989 Age: 33

							BATTING														RUNNING			AVERAGES			
Year	Team	Lg	G	AB	H	2B	3B	HR	(Hm	Rd)	TB	R	RBI	RC	TBB	IBB	SO	HBP	SH	SF	SB	CS	GDP	Avg	OBP	Slg	OPS
2013	Tor	AL	36	102	21	4	0	3	(1	2)	34	11	13	9	4	0	29	2	2	0	0	1	0	.206	.250	.333	.583
2014	Tor	AL	53	116	31	9	0	2	(2	0)	46	19	7	8	4	0	28	1	0	1	1	2	3	.267	.295	.397	.692
2015	Tor	AL	159	586	163	31	2	12	(6	6)	234	76	56	73	28	1	85	5	4	5	25	4	9	.278	.314	.399	.713
2016	Tor	AL	146	548	146	35	2	7	(3	4)	206	59	53	66	24	0	90	6	3	3	14	6	12	.266	.303	.376	.679
2017	Tor	AL	154	587	150	37	1	16	(6	10)	237	72	42	58	33	0	95	6	3	3	15	6	13	.256	.300	.404	.704
2018	Tor	AL	142	512	129	40	2	15	(11	4)	218	65	59	59	18	0	98	6	0	6	14	3	6	.252	.282	.426	.708
2019	2 Tms		161	611	158	37	3	21	(11	10)	264	83	88	76	18	4	89	9	0	7	14	5	15	.259	.287	.432	.719
2020	2 Tms		54	208	60	12	3	6	(2	4)	96	34	26	29	13	1	41	2	0	0	5	2	4	.288	.336	.462	.798
2021	NYM	NL	124	325	75	11	2	15	(6	9)	135	40	47	40	11	0	81	10	0	1	4	3	5	.231	.277	.415	.692
19	Tor	AL	5	16	1	0	0	0	(0	0)	1	1	1	0	0	0	3	0	0	0	0	0	0	.063	.059	.063	.121
19	SF	NL	156	595	157	37	3	21	(11	10)	263	82	87	76	18	4	86	9	0	6	14	5	15	.264	.293	.442	.735
20	Bos	AL	30	117	32	7	2	4	(2	2)	55	20	13	14	8	0	23	1	0	0	1	1	4	.274	.325	.470	.795
20	Col	NL	24	91	28	5	1	2	(0	2)	41	14	13	15	5	1	18	1	0	0	4	1	0	.308	.351	.451	.801
	Postseason		20	74	15	6	0	2	(0	2)	27	7	8	8	5	1	14	0	0	1	3	1	1	.203	.250	.365	.615
	9 ML YEARS		1029	3595	933	216	15	97	(48	49)	1470	459	391	418	153	6	636	47	12	26	92	32	69	.260	.297	.409	.705

Manny Pina

Bats: R **Throws:** R **Pos:** C-65;PH-17   PEEN-yah   **Ht:** 6'0" **Wt:** 222 **Born:** 6/5/1987 **Age:** 35

Year	Team	Lg	G	AB	H	2B	3B	HR	(Hm	Rd)	TB	R	RBI	RC	TBB	IBB	SO	HBP	SH	SF	SB	CS	GDP	Avg	OBP	Slg	OPS
2011	KC	AL	4	14	3	2	0	0	(0	0)	5	2	0	1	1	0	2	0	0	0	0	0	1	.214	.267	.357	.624
2012	KC	AL	1	2	0	0	0	0	(0	0)	0	0	0	0	0	0	0	0	0	0	0	0	0	.000	.000	.000	.000
2016	Mil	NL	33	71	18	4	0	2	(1	1)	28	4	12	8	10	0	15	0	0	0	0	1	2	.254	.346	.394	.740
2017	Mil	NL	107	330	92	21	0	9	(6	3)	140	45	43	46	20	0	79	5	1	3	2	0	8	.279	.327	.424	.751
2018	Mil	NL	98	306	77	13	2	9	(6	3)	121	39	28	27	21	3	62	5	1	4	2	0	13	.252	.307	.395	.702
2019	Mil	NL	76	158	36	8	0	7	(5	2)	65	10	25	20	16	1	50	4	0	1	0	0	1	.228	.313	.411	.724
2020	Mil	NL	15	39	9	1	0	2	(2	0)	16	4	5	6	3	0	11	3	0	0	0	0	0	.231	.333	.410	.744
2021	Mil	NL	75	180	34	6	0	13	(4	9)	79	27	33	28	22	0	38	5	0	1	0	0	4	.189	.293	.439	.732
	Postseason		5	7	3	1	0	0	(0	0)	4	1	0	3	5	0	1	0	0	0	0	0	0	.429	.667	.571	1.238
	8 ML YEARS		409	1100	269	55	2	42	(24	18)	454	131	146	136	93	4	257	22	2	9	4	1	29	.245	.314	.413	.726

Chad Pinder

Bats: R **Throws:** R **Pos:** RF-39;LF-17;PH-14;SS-8;2B-7;3B-6;DH-2   **Ht:** 6'2" **Wt:** 210 **Born:** 3/29/1992 **Age:** 30

Year	Team	Lg	G	AB	H	2B	3B	HR	(Hm	Rd)	TB	R	RBI	RC	TBB	IBB	SO	HBP	SH	SF	SB	CS	GDP	Avg	OBP	Slg	OPS
2016	Oak	AL	22	51	12	4	0	1	(0	1)	19	4	4	5	3	0	14	0	0	1	0	0	1	.235	.273	.373	.645
2017	Oak	AL	87	282	67	15	1	15	(10	5)	129	36	42	37	18	0	92	5	0	3	2	1	7	.238	.292	.457	.750
2018	Oak	AL	110	298	77	12	1	13	(6	7)	130	43	27	35	27	1	88	6	2	0	0	2	4	.258	.332	.436	.769
2019	Oak	AL	124	341	82	21	0	13	(6	7)	142	45	47	43	20	0	88	5	1	3	0	1	11	.240	.290	.416	.706
2020	Oak	AL	24	56	13	3	0	2	(0	2)	22	8	8	8	5	0	13	0	0	0	0	0	3	.232	.295	.393	.688
2021	Oak	AL	75	214	52	16	1	6	(2	4)	88	30	27	25	16	0	62	2	0	1	1	0	6	.243	.300	.411	.712
	Postseason		7	22	7	1	0	2	(1	1)	14	2	7	7	3	1	6	0	0	1	0	0	1	.318	.385	.636	1.021
	6 ML YEARS		442	1242	303	71	3	50	(24	26)	530	166	155	153	89	1	357	18	3	8	3	4	32	.244	.302	.427	.729

Michael Pineda

Pitches: R **Bats:** R **Pos:** SP-21; RP-1   pah-NAY-dah   **Ht:** 6'7" **Wt:** 280 **Born:** 1/18/1989 **Age:** 33

Year	Team	Lg	G	GS	GF	IP	BFP	H	R	ER	HR	SH	SF	HB	TBB	IBB	SO	WP	W	L	Pct	Sv-Op	Hld	Vel	OPS	ERC	ERA
2011	Sea	AL	28	28	0	171.0	696	133	76	71	18	4	3	5	55	1	173	9	9	10	.474	0-0	0	95	.621	2.73	3.74
2014	NYY	AL	13	13	0	76.1	290	56	18	16	5	2	1	0	7	0	59	3	5	5	.500	0-0	0	92	.526	1.51	1.89
2015	NYY	AL	27	27	0	160.2	668	176	83	78	21	4	6	3	21	0	156	4	12	10	.545	0-0	0	93	.752	3.82	4.37
2016	NYY	AL	32	32	0	175.2	756	184	98	94	27	0	3	6	53	1	207	7	6	12	.333	0-0	0	94	.784	4.45	4.82
2017	NYY	AL	17	17	0	96.1	410	103	55	47	20	0	4	2	21	0	92	5	8	4	.667	0-0	0	94	.769	4.52	4.39
2019	Min	AL	26	26	0	146.0	600	141	68	65	23	2	7	5	28	1	140	8	11	5	.688	0-0	0	93	.721	3.58	4.01
2020	Min	AL	5	5	0	26.2	111	25	10	10	0	0	2	1	7	0	25	0	2	0	1.000	0-0	0	92	.604	2.69	3.38
2021	Min	AL	22	21	0	109.1	458	114	49	44	17	3	2	2	21	1	88	1	9	8	.529	0-0	0	91	.755	3.90	3.62
	8 ML YEARS		170	169	0	962.0	3989	932	457	425	131	15	28	24	213	4	940	37	62	54	.534	0-0	0	93	.712	3.53	3.98

Stephen Piscotty

Bats: R **Throws:** R **Pos:** RF-67;PH-17;DH-5;PR-1   **Ht:** 6'4" **Wt:** 211 **Born:** 1/14/1991 **Age:** 31

Year	Team	Lg	G	AB	H	2B	3B	HR	(Hm	Rd)	TB	R	RBI	RC	TBB	IBB	SO	HBP	SH	SF	SB	CS	GDP	Avg	OBP	Slg	OPS
2015	StL	NL	63	233	71	15	4	7	(4	3)	115	29	39	41	20	2	56	1	0	2	2	1	7	.305	.359	.494	.853
2016	StL	NL	153	582	159	35	3	22	(13	9)	266	86	85	97	51	0	133	12	1	2	7	5	14	.273	.343	.457	.800
2017	StL	NL	107	341	80	16	1	9	(1	8)	125	40	39	43	52	2	87	5	0	3	3	6	11	.235	.342	.367	.708
2018	Oak	AL	151	546	146	41	0	27	(10	17)	268	78	88	87	42	0	114	12	0	5	2	0	21	.267	.331	.491	.821
2019	Oak	AL	93	357	89	17	1	13	(8	5)	147	46	44	42	29	0	84	3	1	3	2	0	13	.249	.309	.412	.720
2020	Oak	AL	45	159	36	6	0	5	(1	4)	57	17	29	21	9	0	53	1	1	1	4	0	4	.226	.271	.358	.629
2021	Oak	AL	72	173	38	8	0	5	(2	3)	61	14	16	21	13	0	48	2	0	0	1	0	2	.220	.282	.353	.635
	Postseason		8	26	7	1	0	3	(1	2)	17	5	6	8	3	0	11	0	0	0	0	0	1	.269	.345	.654	.999
	7 ML YEARS		684	2391	619	138	9	88	(39	49)	1039	310	340	352	216	4	575	36	3	16	21	12	72	.259	.328	.435	.762

Nick Pivetta

Pitches: R **Bats:** R **Pos:** SP-30; RP-1   **Ht:** 6'5" **Wt:** 214 **Born:** 2/14/1993 **Age:** 29

Year	Team	Lg	G	GS	GF	IP	BFP	H	R	ER	HR	SH	SF	HB	TBB	IBB	SO	WP	W	L	Pct	Sv-Op	Hld	Vel	OPS	ERC	ERA
2017	Phi	NL	26	26	0	133.0	584	144	91	89	25	4	4	1	57	0	140	11	8	10	.444	0-0	0	94	.846	5.52	6.02
2018	Phi	NL	33	32	1	164.0	694	163	91	87	24	8	5	5	51	0	188	8	7	14	.333	0-0	0	95	.743	4.15	4.77
2019	Phi	NL	30	13	8	93.2	421	103	64	56	20	4	4	4	39	2	89	4	4	6	.400	1-1	1	95	.866	5.67	5.38
2020	2 Tms		5	2	0	15.2	71	18	12	12	4	0	1	1	6	0	17	1	2	0	1.000	0-0	0	93	.924	6.28	6.89
2021	Bos	AL	31	30	1	155.0	661	137	80	78	24	2	4	5	65	2	175	9	9	8	.529	1-1	0	95	.731	3.98	4.53
20	Phi	NL	3	0	0	5.2	29	10	10	10	3	0	1	1	1	0	4	1	0	0	-	0-0	1	94	1.375	12.33	15.88
20	Bos	AL	2	2	0	10.0	42	8	2	2	1	0	0	0	5	0	13	0	2	0	1.000	0-0	0	92	.607	3.39	1.80
	5 ML YEARS		125	103	10	561.1	2431	565	338	322	97	18	21	19	218	4	609	33	30	38	.441	2-2	2	95	.791	4.72	5.16

Kevin Plawecki

Bats: R **Throws:** R **Pos:** C-53;PH-6;DH-5;1B-2   plah-WEH-kee   **Ht:** 6'2" **Wt:** 208 **Born:** 2/26/1991 **Age:** 31

							BATTING														RUNNING			AVERAGES			
Year	Team	Lg	G	AB	H	2B	3B	HR	(Hm	Rd)	TB	R	RBI	RC	TBB	IBB	SO	HBP	SH	SF	SB	CS	GDP	Avg	OBP	Slg	OPS
2015	NYM	NL	73	233	51	9	0	3	(1	2)	69	18	21	22	17	4	60	4	1	3	0	0	4	.219	.280	.296	.576
2016	NYM	NL	48	132	26	6	0	1	(0	1)	35	6	11	11	17	2	33	2	0	0	0	0	1	.197	.298	.265	.563
2017	NYM	NL	37	100	26	5	0	3	(3	0)	40	11	13	15	14	2	17	3	0	1	1	0	2	.260	.364	.400	.764
2018	NYM	NL	79	238	50	13	2	7	(5	2)	88	33	30	25	28	2	65	9	1	1	0	1	12	.210	.315	.370	.685
2019	Cle	AL	60	158	35	10	0	3	(3	0)	54	13	17	14	12	0	31	3	0	1	0	1	4	.222	.287	.342	.629
2020	Bos	AL	24	82	28	5	1	1	(1	0)	38	8	17	17	5	0	14	2	0	0	1	0	4	.341	.393	.463	.857
2021	Bos	AL	64	157	45	7	0	3	(3	0)	61	15	15	21	12	0	26	3	1	0	0	0	4	.287	.349	.389	.737
	7 ML YEARS		385	1100	261	55	3	21	(16	5)	385	104	124	125	105	10	246	26	3	6	2	2	31	.237	.317	.350	.667

Zach Plesac

Pitches: R **Bats:** R **Pos:** SP-25   **Ht:** 6'3" **Wt:** 220 **Born:** 1/21/1995 **Age:** 27

			HOW MUCH PITCHED				WHAT HE GAVE UP										THE RESULTS							
Year	Team	Lg	G	GS	GF	IP	BFP	H	R	ER	HR	SH	SF	HB	TBB	IBB	SO	WP	W	L	Pct	Sv-Op	Hld	Vel	OPS	ERC	ERA
2019	Cle	AL	21	21	0	115.2	475	102	52	49	19	2	0	3	40	0	88	1	8	6	.571	0-0	0	94	.744	3.82	3.81
2020	Cle	AL	8	8	0	55.1	206	38	14	14	8	0	0	1	6	0	57	0	4	2	.667	0-0	0	93	.565	1.78	2.28
2021	Cle	AL	25	25	0	142.2	598	137	79	74	23	1	3	7	34	1	100	5	10	6	.625	0-0	0	93	.735	3.79	4.67
	3 ML YEARS		54	54	0	313.2	1279	277	145	137	50	3	3	11	80	1	245	6	22	14	.611	0-0	0	93	.710	3.42	3.93

Adam Plutko

Pitches: R **Bats:** R **Pos:** RP-37; SP-1   PLET-ko   **Ht:** 6'3" **Wt:** 215 **Born:** 10/3/1991 **Age:** 30

			HOW MUCH PITCHED				WHAT HE GAVE UP										THE RESULTS							
Year	Team	Lg	G	GS	GF	IP	BFP	H	R	ER	HR	SH	SF	HB	TBB	IBB	SO	WP	W	L	Pct	Sv-Op	Hld	Vel	OPS	ERC	ERA
2021	Norfolk	AAA	9	0	2	10.2	49	12	10	10	4	0	0	1	5	0	12	1	0	1	.000	0- -	-		.972	7.66	8.44
2016	Cle	AL	2	0	1	3.2	18	5	3	3	1	0	0	0	2	0	3	1	0	0	-	0-0	0	91	.951	8.17	7.36
2018	Cle	AL	17	12	4	76.2	326	78	45	45	21	1	2	1	23	1	60	3	4	5	.444	1-1	0	91	.869	5.00	5.28
2019	Cle	AL	21	20	0	109.1	462	115	61	59	22	0	2	4	26	2	78	0	7	5	.583	0-0	0	91	.802	4.55	4.86
2020	Cle	AL	10	4	5	27.2	116	30	15	15	5	1	0	1	7	0	15	0	2	2	.500	1-1	0	91	.826	4.79	4.88
2021	Bal	AL	38	1	3	56.1	255	65	43	42	17	1	4	3	27	1	44	3	1	2	.333	1-3	5	92	.988	7.20	6.71
	5 ML YEARS		88	37	13	273.2	1177	293	167	164	66	3	8	9	85	4	200	7	14	14	.500	3-5	5	91	.864	5.27	5.39

Colin Poche

Pitches: L **Bats:** L **Pos:** P   poh-SHAY   **Ht:** 6'3" **Wt:** 225 **Born:** 1/17/1994 **Age:** 28

			HOW MUCH PITCHED				WHAT HE GAVE UP										THE RESULTS							
Year	Team	Lg	G	GS	GF	IP	BFP	H	R	ER	HR	SH	SF	HB	TBB	IBB	SO	WP	W	L	Pct	Sv-Op	Hld	Vel	OPS	ERC	ERA
2019	TB	AL	51	0	8	51.2	207	33	27	27	9	1	0	5	19	1	72	2	5	5	.500	2-6	16	93	.650	2.88	4.70
	Postseason		5	0	3	4.1	15	2	1	1	1	0	0	0	0	0	6	0	0	0	-	0-0	0	93	.467	0.97	2.08

Gregory Polanco

Bats: L **Throws:** L **Pos:** RF-92;PH-15   poh-LAHN-koh   **Ht:** 6'5" **Wt:** 240 **Born:** 9/14/1991 **Age:** 30

							BATTING														RUNNING			AVERAGES			
Year	Team	Lg	G	AB	H	2B	3B	HR	(Hm	Rd)	TB	R	RBI	RC	TBB	IBB	SO	HBP	SH	SF	SB	CS	GDP	Avg	OBP	Slg	OPS
2021	Buffalo	AAA	20	72	23	5	0	6	(-	-)	46	9	17	-	7	0	17	2	0	0	5	0	1	.319	.395	.639	1.034
2014	Pit	NL	89	277	65	9	0	7	(5	2)	95	50	33	32	30	1	59	0	2	2	14	5	1	.235	.307	.343	.650
2015	Pit	NL	153	593	152	35	6	9	(6	3)	226	83	52	73	55	6	121	1	1	2	27	10	5	.256	.320	.381	.701
2016	Pit	NL	144	527	136	34	4	22	(9	13)	244	79	86	73	53	6	119	0	1	6	17	6	13	.258	.323	.463	.786
2017	Pit	NL	108	379	95	20	0	11	(7	4)	148	39	35	39	27	4	60	3	0	1	8	1	5	.251	.305	.391	.695
2018	Pit	NL	130	461	117	32	6	23	(12	11)	230	75	81	76	61	5	117	3	0	7	12	2	11	.254	.340	.499	.839
2019	Pit	NL	42	153	37	8	1	6	(3	3)	65	23	17	17	12	1	49	1	0	0	3	1	4	.242	.301	.425	.726
2020	Pit	NL	50	157	24	6	0	7	(4	3)	51	12	22	12	13	0	65	0	0	3	3	1	1	.153	.214	.325	.539
2021	Pit	NL	107	336	70	12	2	11	(3	8)	119	38	36	32	36	2	104	2	0	8	14	1	8	.208	.283	.354	.637
	Postseason		1	4	0	0	0	0	(0	0)	0	0	0	0	0	0	2	0	0	0	0	0	0	.000	.000	.000	.000
	8 ML YEARS		823	2883	696	156	19	96	(49	47)	1178	399	362	354	287	25	694	10	4	29	98	27	48	.241	.309	.409	.718

Jorge Polanco

Bats: B **Throws:** R **Pos:** 2B-120;SS-39;DH-8;PH-5;PR-1   poh-LAHN-koh   **Ht:** 5'11" **Wt:** 208 **Born:** 7/5/1993 **Age:** 28

							BATTING														RUNNING			AVERAGES			
Year	Team	Lg	G	AB	H	2B	3B	HR	(Hm	Rd)	TB	R	RBI	RC	TBB	IBB	SO	HBP	SH	SF	SB	CS	GDP	Avg	OBP	Slg	OPS
2014	Min	AL	5	6	2	1	1	0	(0	0)	5	2	3	4	2	0	2	0	0	0	0	0	0	.333	.500	.833	1.333
2015	Min	AL	4	10	3	0	0	0	(0	0)	3	1	1	3	2	0	1	0	0	0	1	0	0	.300	.417	.300	.717
2016	Min	AL	69	245	69	15	4	4	(1	3)	104	24	27	36	17	0	46	3	2	3	4	3	3	.282	.332	.424	.757
2017	Min	AL	133	488	125	30	3	13	(4	9)	200	60	74	68	41	1	78	2	7	6	13	5	7	.256	.313	.410	.723
2018	Min	AL	77	302	87	18	3	6	(1	5)	129	38	42	50	25	0	62	2	3	1	7	7	5	.288	.345	.427	.773
2019	Min	AL	153	631	186	40	7	22	(9	13)	306	107	79	112	60	2	116	4	2	7	4	3	11	.295	.356	.485	.841
2020	Min	AL	55	209	54	8	0	4	(2	2)	74	22	19	23	13	0	35	1	2	1	4	2	7	.258	.304	.354	.658
2021	Min	AL	152	588	158	35	2	33	(11	22)	296	97	98	112	45	0	118	5	0	6	11	6	4	.269	.323	.503	.826
	Postseason		6	22	5	0	0	1	(0	1)	8	3	2	3	4	0	5	1	0	0	1	0	0	.227	.370	.364	.734
	8 ML YEARS		648	2479	684	147	20	82	(28	54)	1117	351	343	408	205	3	458	17	16	24	44	26	37	.276	.332	.451	.783

A.J. Pollock

Bats: R **Throws:** R **Pos:** LF-103;PH-15;CF-8   **Ht:** 6'1" **Wt:** 210 **Born:** 12/5/1987 **Age:** 34

Year	Team	Lg	G	AB	H	2B	3B	HR	(Hm	Rd)	TB	R	RBI	RC	TBB	IBB	SO	HBP	SH	SF	SB	CS	GDP	Avg	OBP	Slg	OPS
2012	Ari	NL	31	81	20	4	1	2	(2	0)	32	8	8	9	9	1	11	0	1	2	1	2	2	.247	.315	.395	.710
2013	Ari	NL	137	443	119	28	5	8	(3	5)	181	64	38	58	33	1	82	2	3	1	12	3	5	.269	.322	.409	.730
2014	Ari	NL	75	265	80	19	6	7	(7	0)	132	41	24	43	19	0	46	2	1	0	14	3	4	.302	.353	.498	.851
2015	Ari	NL	157	609	192	39	6	20	(9	11)	303	111	76	106	53	0	89	2	0	9	39	7	19	.315	.367	.498	.865
2016	Ari	NL	12	41	10	0	0	2	(0	2)	16	9	4	5	5	0	8	0	0	0	4	0	1	.244	.326	.390	.716
2017	Ari	NL	112	425	113	33	6	14	(9	5)	200	73	49	66	35	1	71	6	0	0	20	6	8	.266	.330	.471	.801
2018	Ari	NL	113	413	106	21	5	21	(11	10)	200	61	65	57	31	2	100	8	1	7	13	2	6	.257	.316	.484	.800
2019	LAD	NL	86	308	82	15	1	15	(9	6)	144	49	47	50	23	1	74	7	0	7	5	1	7	.266	.327	.468	.795
2020	LAD	NL	55	196	54	9	0	16	(9	7)	111	30	34	29	12	1	45	0	0	2	2	2	6	.276	.314	.566	.881
2021	LAD	NL	117	384	114	27	1	21	(12	9)	206	53	69	73	30	4	80	6	0	2	9	1	4	.297	.355	.536	.892
	Postseason		23	68	12	3	1	1	(0	1)	20	8	5	4	5	0	22	1	0	0	1	0	2	.176	.243	.294	.537
	10 ML YEARS		895	3165	890	195	31	126	(71	55)	1525	499	414	496	250	11	606	33	6	27	119	27	62	.281	.338	.482	.819

Drew Pomeranz

Pitches: L **Bats:** R **Pos:** RP-27   POMM-er-anze   **Ht:** 6'5" **Wt:** 246 **Born:** 11/22/1988 **Age:** 33

			HOW MUCH PITCHED					WHAT HE GAVE UP										THE RESULTS							
Year	Team	Lg	G	GS	GF	IP	BFP	H	R	ER	HR	SH	SF	HB	TBB	IBB	SO	WP	W	L	Pct	Sv-Op	Hld	Vel	OPS	ERC	ERA
2011	Col	NL	4	4	0	18.1	77	19	11	11	0	1	0	1	5	0	13	1	2	1	.667	0-0	0	90	.700	3.36	5.40
2012	Col	NL	22	22	0	96.2	434	97	57	53	14	8	4	4	46	2	83	8	2	9	.182	0-0	0	91	.775	4.78	4.93
2013	Col	NL	8	4	0	21.2	105	25	15	15	4	1	1	1	19	1	19	0	0	4	.000	0-0	0	91	.951	8.04	6.23
2014	Oak	AL	20	10	4	69.0	278	51	22	18	7	1	0	1	26	0	64	0	5	4	.556	0-0	0	91	.586	2.70	2.35
2015	Oak	AL	53	9	9	86.0	357	71	44	35	8	4	5	3	31	1	82	2	5	6	.455	3-6	12	91	.651	3.05	3.66
2016	2 Tms		31	30	0	170.2	703	137	65	63	22	3	3	1	65	3	186	10	11	12	.478	0-0	0	90	.658	3.13	3.32
2017	Bos	AL	32	32	0	173.2	740	166	69	64	19	2	6	4	69	0	174	6	17	6	.739	0-0	0	91	.712	4.00	3.32
2018	Bos	AL	26	11	5	74.0	344	87	53	50	12	0	3	4	44	1	66	4	2	6	.250	0-0	1	89	.894	6.73	6.08
2019	2 Tms	NL	46	18	5	104.0	455	105	58	56	21	2	2	4	44	0	137	1	2	10	.167	2-2	12	93	.804	5.13	4.85
2020	SD	NL	20	0	5	18.2	73	9	3	3	1	0	1	0	10	0	29	0	1	0	1.000	4-5	9	95	.454	1.71	1.45
2021	SD	NL	27	0	2	25.2	102	19	6	5	2	0	2	0	10	1	30	1	1	0	1.000	0-0	13	94	.618	2.55	1.75
16	SD	NL	17	17	0	102.0	411	67	30	28	8	2	3	1	41	2	115	7	8	7	.533	0-0	0	90	.555	2.17	2.47
16	Bos	AL	14	13	1	68.2	292	70	35	35	14	1	0	0	24	1	71	3	3	5	.375	0-0	0	91	.799	4.73	4.59
19	SF	NL	21	17	0	77.2	355	89	51	49	17	2	1	4	36	0	92	1	2	9	.182	0-0	0	92	.872	6.32	5.68
19	Mil	NL	25	1	4	26.1	100	16	7	7	4	0	1	0	8	0	45	0	0	1	.000	2-2	12	94	.570	2.07	2.39
	Postseason		9	1	0	11.2	54	12	8	6	3	1	3	1	6	1	14	0	0	1	.000	0-0	3	94	.893	5.98	4.63
	11 ML YEARS		289	140	30	858.1	3668	786	403	373	110	22	27	23	369	9	883	33	48	58	.453	9-13	47	91	.720	4.02	3.91

Cody Ponce

Pitches: R **Bats:** R **Pos:** RP-13; SP-2   **Ht:** 6'6" **Wt:** 255 **Born:** 4/25/1994 **Age:** 28

			HOW MUCH PITCHED					WHAT HE GAVE UP										THE RESULTS							
Year	Team	Lg	G	GS	GF	IP	BFP	H	R	ER	HR	SH	SF	HB	TBB	IBB	SO	WP	W	L	Pct	Sv-Op	Hld	Vel	OPS	ERC	ERA
2021	Indy	AAA	15	8	3	57.1	242	55	30	30	8	2	2	3	18	0	59	2	1	4	.200	0--	-		.736	4.01	4.71
2020	Pit	NL	5	3	1	17.0	66	12	7	6	5	0	0	0	6	0	12	0	1	1	.500	0-0	0	93	.806	3.62	3.18
2021	Pit	NL	15	2	1	38.1	179	56	34	30	8	1	3	1	11	1	36	2	0	6	.000	0-0	0	93	.996	7.31	7.04
	2 ML YEARS		20	5	2	55.1	245	68	41	36	13	1	3	1	17	1	48	2	1	7	.125	0-0	0	93	.944	6.13	5.86

Daniel Ponce de Leon

Pitches: R **Bats:** R **Pos:** RP-22; SP-2   **Ht:** 6'3" **Wt:** 200 **Born:** 1/16/1992 **Age:** 30

			HOW MUCH PITCHED					WHAT HE GAVE UP										THE RESULTS							
Year	Team	Lg	G	GS	GF	IP	BFP	H	R	ER	HR	SH	SF	HB	TBB	IBB	SO	WP	W	L	Pct	Sv-Op	Hld	Vel	OPS	ERC	ERA
2021	Memp	AAA	5	5	0	9.0	36	3	0	0	0	0	0	0	8	0	9	0	0	0	-	0--	-		.448	1.83	0.00
2018	StL	NL	11	4	2	33.0	132	24	10	10	2	0	1	1	13	0	31	0	0	2	.000	1-1	0	93	.596	2.54	2.73
2019	StL	NL	13	8	1	48.2	203	36	21	20	6	0	1	2	26	3	52	1	1	2	.333	0-0	0	93	.666	3.46	3.70
2020	StL	NL	9	8	1	32.2	143	23	18	18	8	0	2	0	20	0	45	0	1	3	.250	0-0	0	93	.744	4.43	4.96
2021	StL	NL	24	2	9	33.1	158	32	24	23	5	1	3	5	22	1	24	2	1	1	.500	2-3	0	93	.840	5.74	6.21
	Postseason		2	0	1	3.0	15	4	4	4	2	0	0	0	2	0	6	0	0	1	.000	0-0	0	95	1.246	12.01	12.00
	4 ML YEARS		57	22	13	147.2	636	115	73	71	21	1	5	10	81	4	152	4	3	8	.273	3-4	0	93	.710	3.95	4.33

Zach Pop

Pitches: R **Bats:** R **Pos:** RP-50   **Ht:** 6'4" **Wt:** 220 **Born:** 9/20/1996 **Age:** 25

			HOW MUCH PITCHED					WHAT HE GAVE UP										THE RESULTS							
Year	Team	Lg	G	GS	GF	IP	BFP	H	R	ER	HR	SH	SF	HB	TBB	IBB	SO	WP	W	L	Pct	Sv-Op	Hld	Vel	OPS	ERC	ERA
2021	Mia	NL	50	0	10	54.2	246	54	29	25	3	1	0	8	24	2	51	2	1	0	1.000	0-1	1	95	.713	4.30	4.12

Sean Poppen

Pitches: R **Bats:** R **Pos:** RP-24   **Ht:** 6'3" **Wt:** 210 **Born:** 3/15/1994 **Age:** 28

			HOW MUCH PITCHED					WHAT HE GAVE UP										THE RESULTS							
Year	Team	Lg	G	GS	GF	IP	BFP	H	R	ER	HR	SH	SF	HB	TBB	IBB	SO	WP	W	L	Pct	Sv-Op	Hld	Vel	OPS	ERC	ERA
2021	Drham	AAA	19	0	9	28.1	112	23	7	5	1	0	1	0	11	0	30	1	2	3	.400	2--	-		.574	2.75	1.59
2019	Min	AL	4	0	3	8.1	36	10	7	7	1	0	0	0	5	0	9	0	0	0	-	0-0	0	95	.997	6.83	7.56
2020	Min	AL	6	0	4	7.2	35	9	4	4	0	0	0	0	4	0	10	3	0	0	-	0-0	1	94	.759	4.80	4.70
2021	3 Tms		24	0	6	22.2	110	31	18	13	2	0	0	3	9	2	26	2	1	1	.500	1-1	1	94	.860	6.44	5.16

Year	Team	Lg				HOW MUCH PITCHED					WHAT HE GAVE UP							THE RESULTS						
			G	GS	GF	IP	BFP	H	R	ER	HR	SH	SF	HB	TBB	IBB	SO	WP	W	L	Pct	Sv-Op	Hld	Vel	OPS	ERC	ERA
21	Pit	NL	3	0	1	4.2	26	11	7	4	1	0	0	1	2	0	4	0	0	0	-	0-0	0	94	1.278	16.48	7.71
21	TB	AL	1	0	1	0.2	2	0	0	0	0	0	0	0	0	0	1	0	0	0	-	0-0	0	93	.000	0.00	0.00
21	Ari	NL	20	0	4	17.1	82	20	11	9	1	0	0	2	7	2	21	2	1	1	.500	1-1	0	94	.751	4.71	4.67
	3 ML YEARS		34	0	13	38.2	181	50	29	24	3	0	0	3	18	2	45	5	1	1	.500	1-1	2	94	.867	6.18	5.59

Buster Posey

Bats: R **Throws:** R **Pos:** C-106;PH-10;DH-1   **Ht:** 6'1" **Wt:** 213 **Born:** 3/27/1987 **Age:** 35

Year	Team	Lg						BATTING													RUNNING			AVERAGES			
			G	AB	H	2B	3B	HR	(Hm	Rd)	TB	R	RBI	RC	TBB	IBB	SO	HBP	SH	SF	SB	CS	GDP	Avg	OBP	Slg	OPS
2009	SF	NL	7	17	2	0	0	0	(0	0)	2	1	0	0	0	0	4	0	0	0	0	0	0	.118	.118	.118	.235
2010	SF	NL	108	406	124	23	2	18	(6	12)	205	58	67	70	30	5	55	4	0	3	0	2	12	.305	.357	.505	.862
2011	SF	NL	45	162	46	5	0	4	(1	3)	63	17	21	26	18	3	30	4	0	1	3	0	4	.284	.368	.389	.756
2012	SF	NL	148	530	178	39	1	24	(7	17)	291	78	103	111	69	7	96	2	0	9	1	1	19	.336	.408	.549	.957
2013	SF	NL	148	520	153	34	1	15	(8	7)	234	61	72	77	60	8	70	8	0	7	2	1	15	.294	.371	.450	.821
2014	SF	NL	147	547	170	28	2	22	(11	11)	268	72	89	94	47	5	69	3	0	8	0	1	16	.311	.364	.490	.854
2015	SF	NL	150	557	177	28	0	19	(6	13)	262	74	95	96	56	10	52	3	0	7	2	0	17	.318	.379	.470	.849
2016	SF	NL	146	539	155	33	2	14	(7	7)	234	82	80	82	64	7	68	3	0	8	6	1	18	.288	.362	.434	.796
2017	SF	NL	140	494	158	34	0	12	(3	9)	228	62	67	84	61	13	66	8	0	5	6	1	19	.320	.400	.462	.861
2018	SF	NL	105	398	113	22	1	5	(4	1)	152	47	41	58	45	3	53	3	0	2	3	2	12	.284	.359	.382	.741
2019	SF	NL	114	405	104	24	0	7	(1	6)	149	43	38	49	34	1	71	4	1	1	0	0	18	.257	.320	.368	.688
2021	SF	NL	113	395	120	23	0	18	(7	11)	197	68	56	71	56	5	87	1	0	2	0	0	15	.304	.390	.499	.889
	Postseason		53	206	51	4	0	4	(1	3)	67	17	23	21	23	5	41	1	0	2	1	1	4	.248	.323	.325	.649
	12 ML YEARS		1371	4970	1500	293	9	158	(61	97)	2285	663	729	818	540	67	721	43	1	53	23	9	163	.302	.372	.460	.831

Cody Poteet

Pitches: R **Bats:** R **Pos:** SP-7   **Ht:** 6'1" **Wt:** 190 **Born:** 7/30/1994 **Age:** 27

Year	Team	Lg				HOW MUCH PITCHED					WHAT HE GAVE UP							THE RESULTS						
			G	GS	GF	IP	BFP	H	R	ER	HR	SH	SF	HB	TBB	IBB	SO	WP	W	L	Pct	Sv-Op	Hld	Vel	OPS	ERC	ERA
2021	Mia	NL	7	7	0	30.2	132	25	17	17	7	0	0	0	16	0	32	1	2	3	.400	0-0	0	94	.768	4.36	4.99

Yohel Pozo

Bats: R **Throws:** R **Pos:** DH-17;C-2;PH-2   **Ht:** 6'0" **Wt:** 201 **Born:** 6/14/1997 **Age:** 25

Year	Team	Lg						BATTING													RUNNING			AVERAGES			
			G	AB	H	2B	3B	HR	(Hm	Rd)	TB	R	RBI	RC	TBB	IBB	SO	HBP	SH	SF	SB	CS	GDP	Avg	OBP	Slg	OPS
2021	RdRck	AAA	74	303	103	17	2	21	(-	-)	187	44	71	-	7	0	40	1	0	1	0	0	11	.340	.356	.617	.973
2021	Tex	AL	21	74	21	4	0	1	(1	0)	28	8	9	12	3	0	10	0	0	0	0	0	1	.284	.312	.378	.690

Ryan Pressly

Pitches: R **Bats:** R **Pos:** RP-64   **Ht:** 6'2" **Wt:** 206 **Born:** 12/15/1988 **Age:** 33

Year	Team	Lg				HOW MUCH PITCHED					WHAT HE GAVE UP							THE RESULTS						
			G	GS	GF	IP	BFP	H	R	ER	HR	SH	SF	HB	TBB	IBB	SO	WP	W	L	Pct	Sv-Op	Hld	Vel	OPS	ERC	ERA
2013	Min	AL	49	0	18	76.2	315	71	37	33	5	2	3	0	27	1	49	7	3	3	.500	0-0	1	93	.677	3.31	3.87
2014	Min	AL	25	0	5	28.1	122	30	10	9	3	2	3	1	8	2	14	1	2	0	1.000	0-1	2	93	.779	3.98	2.86
2015	Min	AL	27	0	6	27.2	119	27	9	9	0	1	1	0	12	1	22	2	3	2	.600	0-0	4	94	.645	3.31	2.93
2016	Min	AL	72	0	10	75.1	328	79	34	31	8	4	2	2	23	2	67	7	6	7	.462	1-6	13	95	.725	4.01	3.70
2017	Min	AL	57	0	10	61.1	252	52	34	32	10	2	1	3	19	5	61	5	2	3	.400	0-1	6	96	.697	3.41	4.70
2018	2 Tms	AL	77	0	11	71.0	292	57	21	20	6	1	2	3	22	1	101	8	2	1	.667	2-8	21	96	.604	2.71	2.54
2019	Hou	AL	55	0	8	54.1	211	37	15	14	6	0	1	0	12	0	72	4	2	3	.400	3-8	31	96	.543	1.85	2.32
2020	Hou	AL	23	0	15	21.0	91	21	10	8	2	0	0	1	7	1	29	1	1	3	.250	12-16	1	95	.728	3.85	3.43
2021	Hou	AL	64	0	49	64.0	250	49	19	16	4	1	0	0	13	1	81	3	5	3	.625	26-28	1	95	.546	1.92	2.25
18	Min	AL	51	0	7	47.2	208	46	19	18	5	1	2	2	19	1	69	6	1	1	.500	0-8	8	96	.699	3.99	3.40
18	Hou	AL	26	0	4	23.1	84	11	2	2	1	0	0	1	3	0	32	2	1	0	1.000	2-4	13	96	.379	0.88	0.77
	Postseason		22	0	8	18.0	80	20	11	10	0	1	0	0	7	1	21	4	2	0	1.000	4-4	3	95	.647	3.78	5.00
	9 ML YEARS		449	0	132	479.2	1980	423	189	172	44	13	13	10	143	14	496	38	26	25	.510	44-68	79	95	.652	3.03	3.23

David Price

Pitches: L **Bats:** L **Pos:** RP-28; SP-11   **Ht:** 6'5" **Wt:** 215 **Born:** 8/26/1985 **Age:** 36

Year	Team	Lg				HOW MUCH PITCHED					WHAT HE GAVE UP							THE RESULTS						
			G	GS	GF	IP	BFP	H	R	ER	HR	SH	SF	HB	TBB	IBB	SO	WP	W	L	Pct	Sv-Op	Hld	Vel	OPS	ERC	ERA
2008	TB	AL	5	1	0	14.0	57	9	4	3	1	0	1	1	4	0	12	0	0	0	-	0-0	1	94	.501	1.86	1.93
2009	TB	AL	23	23	0	128.1	557	119	72	63	17	3	2	4	54	0	102	2	10	7	.588	0-0	0	93	.716	4.05	4.42
2010	TB	AL	32	31	0	208.2	861	170	71	63	15	4	3	5	79	1	188	5	19	6	.760	0-0	0	95	.637	2.91	2.72
2011	TB	AL	34	34	0	224.1	918	192	93	87	22	4	7	9	63	5	218	2	12	13	.480	0-0	0	95	.659	2.97	3.49
2012	TB	AL	31	31	0	211.0	836	173	63	60	16	2	3	5	59	2	205	8	20	5	.800	0-0	0	96	.602	2.67	2.56
2013	TB	AL	27	27	0	186.2	740	178	78	69	16	1	2	3	27	0	151	0	10	8	.556	0-0	0	96	.661	2.89	3.33
2014	2 Tms	AL	34	34	0	248.1	1009	230	100	90	25	4	3	5	38	1	271	2	15	12	.556	0-0	0	93	.647	2.79	3.26
2015	2 Tms	AL	32	32	0	220.1	888	190	70	60	17	4	8	3	47	2	225	4	18	5	.783	0-0	0	94	.621	2.54	2.45
2016	Bos	AL	35	35	0	230.0	951	227	106	102	30	8	7	7	50	2	228	4	17	9	.654	0-0	0	94	.721	3.63	3.99
2017	Bos	AL	16	11	1	74.2	317	65	30	28	8	0	2	4	24	0	76	2	6	3	.667	0-0	1	94	.652	3.25	3.38
2018	Bos	AL	30	30	0	176.0	722	151	75	70	25	4	4	10	50	0	177	1	16	7	.696	0-0	0	93	.691	3.38	3.58
2019	Bos	AL	22	22	0	107.1	458	109	57	51	15	0	1	3	32	0	128	3	7	5	.583	0-0	0	92	.755	4.13	4.28
2021	LAD	NL	39	11	5	73.2	326	79	35	33	8	3	2	4	26	2	58	1	5	2	.714	1-1	1	93	.766	4.48	4.03
14	TB	AL	23	23	0	170.2	689	156	68	59	20	3	3	5	23	1	189	2	11	8	.579	0-0	0	93	.647	2.79	3.11
14	Det	AL	11	11	0	77.2	320	74	32	31	5	1	0	0	15	0	82	0	4	4	.500	0-0	0	93	.647	2.77	3.59

Year	Team	Lg	G	GS	GF	IP	BFP	H	R	ER	HR	SH	SF	HB	TBB	IBB	SO	WP	W	L	Pct	Sv-Op	Hld	Vel	OPS	ERC	ERA
15	Det	AL	21	21	0	146.0	592	133	50	41	13	4	5	3	29	2	138	3	9	4	.692	0-0	0	94	.654	2.83	2.53
15	Tor	AL	11	11	0	74.1	296	57	20	19	4	0	3	0	18	0	87	1	9	1	.900	0-0	0	95	.555	2.00	2.30
	Postseason		23	14	5	99.1	414	91	53	51	16	0	2	3	28	1	91	1	5	9	.357	1-1	0	94	.707	3.65	4.62
13 ML YEARS			360	322	6	2103.1	8640	1892	854	779	215	34	45	63	553	14	2039	40	155	82	.654	1-1	3	94	.667	3.14	3.33

Jurickson Profar

Bats: B Throws: R Pos: LF-36;PH-36;RF-29;1B-20;CF-20;2B-10   JURR-ick-sun PRO-farr   Ht: 6'0" Wt: 184 Born: 2/20/1993 Age: 29

Year	Team	Lg	G	AB	H	2B	3B	HR	(Hm	Rd)	TB	R	RBI	RC	TBB	IBB	SO	HBP	SH	SF	SB	CS	GDP	Avg	OBP	Slg	OPS
2012	Tex	AL	9	17	3	2	0	1	(0	1)	8	2	2	1	0	0	4	0	0	0	0	0	1	.176	.176	.471	.647
2013	Tex	AL	85	286	67	11	0	6	(3	3)	96	30	26	30	26	0	63	5	6	1	2	4	1	.234	.308	.336	.644
2016	Tex	AL	90	272	65	6	3	5	(4	1)	92	35	20	30	30	0	61	3	2	0	2	1	7	.239	.321	.338	.660
2017	Tex	AL	22	58	10	2	0	0	(0	0)	12	8	5	5	9	0	14	1	2	0	1	1	0	.172	.294	.207	.501
2018	Tex	AL	146	524	133	35	6	20	(11	9)	240	82	77	88	54	1	88	12	0	4	10	0	9	.254	.335	.458	.793
2019	Oak	AL	139	459	100	24	2	20	(11	9)	188	65	67	58	48	2	75	8	0	3	9	1	12	.218	.301	.410	.711
2020	SD	NL	56	180	50	6	0	7	(2	5)	77	28	25	30	15	0	28	4	1	2	7	1	1	.278	.343	.428	.771
2021	SD	NL	137	353	80	17	2	4	(2	2)	113	47	33	36	49	1	65	6	1	2	10	5	12	.227	.329	.320	.649
	Postseason		8	20	7	0	0	0	(0	0)	7	1	0	2	0	0	3	0	0	0	0	0	0	.350	.350	.350	.700
8 ML YEARS			684	2149	508	103	13	63	(33	30)	826	297	255	278	231	4	398	39	12	12	41	13	43	.236	.320	.384	.704

Austin Pruitt

Pitches: R Bats: R Pos: RP-6   Ht: 5'10" Wt: 185 Born: 8/31/1989 Age: 32

Year	Team	Lg	G	GS	GF	IP	BFP	H	R	ER	HR	SH	SF	HB	TBB	IBB	SO	WP	W	L	Pct	Sv-Op	Hld	Vel	OPS	ERC	ERA
2021	SgrLnd	AAA	5	2	0	7.1	28	7	3	3	1	0	0	0	1	0	6	0	1	0	1.000	0--	-	-	.730	3.23	3.68
2021	Jaxnvl	AAA	7	0	1	8.2	36	7	7	3	1	0	2	0	2	0	9	0	1	0	1.000	0--	-	-	.625	2.39	3.12
2017	TB	AL	30	8	7	83.0	371	103	55	49	11	0	5	0	22	2	66	4	7	5	.583	1-2	1	92	.827	5.36	5.31
2018	TB	AL	23	0	11	69.2	291	72	40	36	7	1	4	1	16	0	42	1	2	3	.400	4-5	0	92	.712	3.67	4.65
2019	TB	AL	14	2	4	47.0	193	47	23	23	7	2	2	0	12	2	39	1	3	0	1.000	0-0	0	92	.761	3.84	4.40
2021	2 Tms		6	0	3	7.1	29	7	3	3	2	0	0	1	0	0	5	0	0	1	.000	0-0	0	92	.776	3.93	3.68
21	Hou	AL	2	0	1	2.2	12	3	2	2	2	0	0	1	0	0	1	0	0	1	.000	0-0	0	92	1.152	9.34	6.75
21	Mia	NL	4	0	2	4.2	17	4	1	1	0	0	0	0	0	0	4	0	0	0	-	0-0	0	92	.529	1.52	1.93
4 ML YEARS			73	10	25	207.0	884	229	121	111	27	4	6	7	50	4	152	6	12	9	.571	5-7	1	92	.773	4.38	4.83

Albert Pujols

Bats: R Throws: R Pos: 1B-76;PH-44;DH-2;3B-1   POO-holes   Ht: 6'3" Wt: 235 Born: 1/16/1980 Age: 42

Year	Team	Lg	G	AB	H	2B	3B	HR	(Hm	Rd)	TB	R	RBI	RC	TBB	IBB	SO	HBP	SH	SF	SB	CS	GDP	Avg	OBP	Slg	OPS
2001	StL	NL	161	590	194	47	4	37	(18	19)	360	112	130	132	69	6	93	9	1	7	1	3	21	.329	.403	.610	1.013
2002	StL	NL	157	590	185	40	2	34	(14	20)	331	118	127	121	72	13	69	9	0	4	2	4	20	.314	.394	.561	.955
2003	StL	NL	157	591	212	51	1	43	(21	22)	394	137	124	160	79	12	65	10	0	5	5	1	13	.359	.439	.667	1.106
2004	StL	NL	154	592	196	51	2	46	(18	28)	389	133	123	143	84	12	52	7	0	9	5	5	21	.331	.415	.657	1.072
2005	StL	NL	161	591	195	38	2	41	(23	18)	360	129	117	139	97	27	65	9	0	3	16	2	19	.330	.430	.609	1.039
2006	StL	NL	143	535	177	33	1	49	(24	25)	359	119	137	146	92	28	50	4	0	3	7	2	20	.331	.431	.671	1.102
2007	StL	NL	158	565	185	38	1	32	(12	20)	321	99	103	118	99	22	58	7	0	8	2	6	27	.327	.429	.568	.997
2008	StL	NL	148	524	187	44	0	37	(19	18)	342	100	116	130	104	34	54	5	0	5	7	3	16	.357	.462	.653	1.114
2009	StL	NL	160	568	186	45	1	47	(22	25)	374	124	135	145	115	44	64	9	0	8	16	4	23	.327	.443	.658	1.101
2010	StL	NL	159	587	183	39	1	42	(17	25)	350	115	118	131	103	38	76	4	0	4	14	4	23	.312	.414	.596	1.011
2011	StL	NL	147	579	173	29	0	37	(16	21)	313	105	99	100	61	15	58	4	0	7	9	1	29	.299	.366	.541	.906
2012	LAA	AL	154	607	173	50	0	30	(14	16)	313	85	105	100	52	16	76	5	0	6	8	1	19	.285	.343	.516	.859
2013	LAA	AL	99	391	101	19	0	17	(8	9)	171	49	64	54	40	8	55	5	0	7	1	1	18	.258	.330	.437	.767
2014	LAA	AL	159	633	172	37	1	28	(13	15)	295	89	105	86	48	11	71	4	0	9	5	1	28	.272	.324	.466	.790
2015	LAA	AL	157	602	147	22	0	40	(20	20)	289	85	95	82	50	10	72	6	0	3	5	3	15	.244	.307	.480	.787
2016	LAA	AL	152	593	159	19	0	31	(18	13)	271	71	119	91	49	6	75	2	0	4	4	0	24	.268	.323	.457	.780
2017	LAA	AL	149	593	143	17	0	23	(13	10)	229	53	101	66	37	5	93	2	0	4	3	0	26	.241	.286	.386	.672
2018	LAA	AL	117	465	114	20	0	19	(10	9)	191	50	64	55	28	3	65	2	0	3	1	0	12	.245	.289	.411	.700
2019	LAA	AL	131	491	120	22	0	23	(9	14)	211	55	93	69	43	1	68	3	0	4	3	0	21	.244	.305	.430	.734
2020	LAA	AL	39	152	34	8	0	6	(4	2)	60	15	25	15	9	1	25	1	0	1	0	0	4	.224	.270	.395	.665
2021	2 Tms		109	275	65	3	0	17	(10	7)	119	29	50	36	14	3	45	5	0	2	2	0	14	.236	.284	.433	.717
21	LAA	AL	24	86	17	0	0	5	(2	3)	32	9	12	7	3	1	13	3	0	0	1	0	4	.198	.250	.372	.622
21	LAD	NL	85	189	48	3	0	12	(8	4)	87	20	38	29	11	2	32	2	0	2	1	0	10	.254	.299	.460	.759
	Postseason		77	279	90	18	1	19	(7	12)	167	55	54	68	49	20	40	5	0	1	1	2	6	.323	.431	.599	1.030
21 ML YEARS			2971	11114	3301	672	16	679	(323	356)	6042	1872	2150	2119	1345	315	1349	113	1	117	116	41	413	.297	.375	.544	.919

A.J. Puk

Pitches: L Bats: L Pos: RP-12   Ht: 6'7" Wt: 248 Born: 4/25/1995 Age: 27

Year	Team	Lg	G	GS	GF	IP	BFP	H	R	ER	HR	SH	SF	HB	TBB	IBB	SO	WP	W	L	Pct	Sv-Op	Hld	Vel	OPS	ERC	ERA
2021	LsVgs	AAA	29	4	2	48.2	226	61	40	33	12	0	4	2	19	0	58	5	1	-	.286	1--	-	-	.905	6.77	6.10
2019	Oak	AL	10	0	4	11.1	47	10	4	4	1	0	0	0	5	0	13	2	2	0	1.000	0-1	2	97	.652	3.60	3.18
2021	Oak	AL	12	0	3	13.1	65	18	9	9	1	0	0	1	6	0	16	2	0	3	.000	0-2	0	96	.764	6.31	6.08
2 ML YEARS			22	0	3	24.2	112	28	13	13	2	0	0	1	11	0	29	4	2	3	.400	0-3	2	96	.717	5.03	4.74

Kevin Quackenbush

Pitches: R Bats: R Pos: RP-1 **Ht:** 6'4" **Wt:** 235 **Born:** 11/28/1988 **Age:** 33

		HOW MUCH PITCHED				WHAT HE GAVE UP												THE RESULTS					
Year Team	Lg	G	GS	GF	IP	BFP	H	R	ER	HR	SH	SF	HB	TBB	IBB	SO	WP	W	L	Pct	Sv-Op	Hld	Vel	OPS	ERC	ERA
2021 OkCity	AAA	43	0	40	41.2	177	33	13	8	1	0	1	2	21	0	46	0	1	7	.125	21--	-		.617	3.01	1.73
2014 SD	NL	56	0	18	54.1	222	42	15	15	2	1	3	2	18	4	56	1	3	3	.500	6-7	10	91	.568	2.25	2.48
2015 SD	NL	57	0	19	58.1	243	52	28	26	6	1	4	1	20	3	58	0	3	2	.600	0-1	2	91	.670	3.28	4.01
2016 SD	NL	60	0	17	59.2	253	55	27	26	8	2	2	0	22	2	42	2	7	7	.500	2-3	9	91	.743	3.67	3.92
2017 SD	NL	20	0	4	26.1	125	32	23	23	5	0	1	1	16	0	23	3	0	2	.000	0-0	1	91	.869	7.14	7.86
2018 Cin	NL	10	0	1	9.0	45	13	11	11	3	0	0	0	6	1	7	0	0	1	.000	0-0	0	90	1.063	9.85	11.00
2021 LAD	NL	1	0	0	0.1	4	3	1	1	0	0	0	0	0	0	1	0	0	0	-	0-0	0	88	1.750	67.29	27.00
6 ML YEARS		204	0	59	208.0	892	197	105	102	24	4	10	4	82	10	187	6	13	15	.464	8-11	22	91	.718	3.85	4.41

Cal Quantrill

Pitches: R Bats: L Pos: SP-22; RP-18 **Ht:** 6'3" **Wt:** 195 **Born:** 2/10/1995 **Age:** 27

		HOW MUCH PITCHED				WHAT HE GAVE UP												THE RESULTS					
Year Team	Lg	G	GS	GF	IP	BFP	H	R	ER	HR	SH	SF	HB	TBB	IBB	SO	WP	W	L	Pct	Sv-Op	Hld	Vel	OPS	ERC	ERA
2019 SD	NL	23	18	0	103.0	443	106	61	59	15	2	3	3	28	2	89	3	6	8	.429	0-0	1	94	.741	4.07	5.16
2020 2 Tms		18	3	2	32.0	135	31	12	8	4	1	0	3	8	1	31	0	2	0	1.000	1-2	2	95	.701	3.81	2.25
2021 Cle	AL	40	22	2	149.2	616	129	55	48	16	4	4	9	47	0	121	3	8	3	.727	0-0	1	94	.675	3.31	2.89
20 SD	NL	10	1	1	17.1	74	17	6	5	2	1	0	2	6	1	18	0	2	0	1.000	1-1	1	95	.727	4.32	2.60
20 Cle	AL	8	2	1	14.2	61	14	6	3	2	0	0	1	2	0	13	0	0	0	-	0-1	1	95	.669	3.24	1.84
Postseason		1	0	1	0.1	2	0	0	0	0	0	0	0	1	0	1	0	0	0	-	0-0	0	95	.500	7.00	0.00
3 ML YEARS		81	43	4	284.2	1194	266	128	115	35	7	7	15	83	3	241	6	16	11	.593	1-2	4	94	.703	3.64	3.64

Jose Quijada

kee-HAH-dah

Pitches: L Bats: L Pos: RP-26 **Ht:** 5'11" **Wt:** 215 **Born:** 11/9/1995 **Age:** 26

		HOW MUCH PITCHED				WHAT HE GAVE UP												THE RESULTS					
Year Team	Lg	G	GS	GF	IP	BFP	H	R	ER	HR	SH	SF	HB	TBB	IBB	SO	WP	W	L	Pct	Sv-Op	Hld	Vel	OPS	ERC	ERA
2021 Salt Lk	AAA	22	0	13	29.1	116	17	8	5	2	0	0	0	11	0	37	0	3	1	.750	1--	-		.484	1.67	1.53
2019 Mia	NL	34	0	9	29.2	144	27	20	19	10	1	0	4	26	3	44	2	2	3	.400	1-2	4	93	.974	7.81	5.76
2020 LAA	AL	6	0	1	3.2	20	6	4	3	1	0	1	1	2	0	5	0	0	1	.000	0-1	1	93	1.013	11.40	7.36
2021 LAA	AL	26	0	2	25.2	110	20	14	13	2	0	0	1	15	1	38	1	0	2	.000	0-0	4	94	.657	3.53	4.56
3 ML YEARS		66	0	12	59.0	274	53	38	35	13	1	1	6	43	4	88	3	2	6	.250	1-3	9	93	.844	6.04	5.34

Roman Quinn

Bats: B Throws: R Pos: CF-21;PH-5;RF-4;LF-2;PR-1 **Ht:** 5'10" **Wt:** 175 **Born:** 5/14/1993 **Age:** 29

		BATTING																	RUNNING			AVERAGES			
Year Team	Lg	G	AB	H	2B	3B	HR	(Hm	Rd)	TB	R	RBI	RC	TBB	IBB	SO	HBP	SH	SF	SB	CS	GDP	Avg	OBP	Slg	OPS
2016 Phi	NL	15	57	15	4	0	0	(0	0)	19	10	6	9	8	0	19	2	2	0	5	1	0	.263	.373	.333	.706
2018 Phi	NL	50	131	34	6	4	2	(1	1)	54	13	12	15	10	0	35	1	1	0	10	4	1	.260	.317	.412	.729
2019 Phi	NL	44	108	23	3	1	4	(3	1)	40	18	11	15	12	0	34	1	1	0	8	0	2	.213	.298	.370	.668
2020 Phi	NL	41	108	23	3	1	2	(2	0)	34	14	7	9	5	0	39	2	1	0	12	0	0	.213	.261	.315	.576
2021 Phi	NL	28	52	9	2	2	0	(0	0)	15	8	2	4	6	0	19	4	0	0	4	3	0	.173	.306	.288	.595
5 ML YEARS		178	456	104	18	8	8	(6	2)	162	63	38	52	41	0	146	10	5	0	39	8	3	.228	.306	.355	.661

Jose Quintana

KIN-tahn-ah

Pitches: L Bats: R Pos: RP-19; SP-10 **Ht:** 6'1" **Wt:** 220 **Born:** 1/24/1989 **Age:** 33

		HOW MUCH PITCHED				WHAT HE GAVE UP												THE RESULTS					
Year Team	Lg	G	GS	GF	IP	BFP	H	R	ER	HR	SH	SF	HB	TBB	IBB	SO	WP	W	L	Pct	Sv-Op	Hld	Vel	OPS	ERC	ERA
2012 CWS	AL	25	22	2	136.1	568	142	62	57	14	5	1	3	42	4	81	10	6	6	.500	0-0	0	90	.754	4.13	3.76
2013 CWS	AL	33	33	0	200.0	832	188	83	78	23	3	6	5	56	2	164	2	9	7	.563	0-0	0	91	.695	3.47	3.51
2014 CWS	AL	32	32	0	200.1	830	197	87	74	10	4	6	2	52	3	178	7	9	11	.450	0-0	0	92	.662	3.15	3.32
2015 CWS	AL	32	32	0	206.1	862	218	81	77	16	4	4	8	44	4	177	5	9	10	.474	0-0	0	92	.722	3.67	3.36
2016 CWS	AL	32	32	0	208.0	837	192	76	74	22	2	2	4	50	1	181	10	13	12	.520	0-0	0	92	.687	3.23	3.20
2017 2 Tms		32	32	0	188.2	790	170	92	87	23	1	3	10	61	4	207	8	11	11	.500	0-0	0	92	.701	3.57	4.15
2018 ChC	NL	32	32	0	174.1	739	162	81	78	25	8	2	3	68	3	158	3	13	11	.542	0-0	0	92	.737	4.00	4.03
2019 ChC	NL	32	31	0	171.0	745	191	100	89	20	5	13	2	46	0	152	11	13	9	.591	0-0	0	91	.763	4.32	4.68
2020 ChC	NL	4	1	0	10.0	41	10	5	5	1	0	0	0	3	0	12	1	0	0	-	0-0	0	91	.738	3.80	4.50
2021 2 Tms		29	10	5	63.0	297	74	50	45	12	0	2	1	35	1	85	7	0	3	.000	0-0	2	92	.853	6.40	6.43
17 CWS	AL	18	18	0	104.1	444	98	55	52	14	1	2	2	40	1	109	7	4	8	.333	0-0	0	92	.735	3.97	4.49
17 ChC	NL	14	14	0	84.1	346	72	37	35	9	0	1	8	21	3	98	1	7	3	.700	0-0	0	92	.659	3.08	3.74
21 LAA	AL	24	10	5	53.1	254	66	45	40	9	0	2	1	29	0	73	5	0	3	.000	0-0	2	92	.860	6.62	6.75
21 SF	NL	5	0	0	9.2	43	8	5	5	3	0	0	0	6	1	12	2	0	0	-	0-0	0	92	.812	5.22	4.66
Postseason		4	3	0	13.1	57	11	9	8	1	0	2	0	5	0	12	0	0	1	.000	0-1	1	92	.621	2.76	5.40
10 ML YEARS		283	257	7	1558.0	6541	1544	717	664	166	32	39	38	457	22	1395	64	83	80	.509	0-0	2	92	.719	3.75	3.84

Tanner Rainey

Pitches: R Bats: R Pos: RP-38 **Ht:** 6'2" **Wt:** 247 **Born:** 12/25/1992 **Age:** 29

		HOW MUCH PITCHED				WHAT HE GAVE UP												THE RESULTS					
Year Team	Lg	G	GS	GF	IP	BFP	H	R	ER	HR	SH	SF	HB	TBB	IBB	SO	WP	W	L	Pct	Sv-Op	Hld	Vel	OPS	ERC	ERA
2021 Roch	AAA	8	1	1	7.2	31	3	2	2	1	0	0	0	5	0	15	0	1	0	1.000	0--	-		.489	2.04	1.98
2018 Cin	NL	8	0	2	7.0	45	13	19	19	4	0	0	0	12	1	7	0	0	0	-	0-0	0	98	1.462	21.19	24.43
2019 Was	NL	52	0	7	48.1	214	32	22	21	6	2	0	4	38	2	74	7	2	3	.400	0-3	9	98	.696	4.13	3.91

Year	Team	Lg	G	GS	GF	IP	BFP	H	R	ER	HR	SH	SF	HB	TBB	IBB	SO	WP	W	L	Pct	Sv-Op	Hld	Vel	OPS	ERC	ERA
2020	Was	NL	20	0	1	20.1	75	8	6	6	4	0	0	1	7	1	32	3	1	1	.500	0-0	9	97	.542	1.60	2.66
2021	Was	NL	38	0	8	31.2	151	29	27	26	6	0	1	3	25	1	42	0	1	3	.250	3-6	10	96	.836	6.11	7.39
	Postseason		9	0	1	6.2	28	3	5	5	1	0	0	0	5	0	6	1	0	0	-	0-0	2	99	.547	2.75	6.75
	4 ML YEARS		118	0	18	107.1	485	82	74	72	20	2	2	8	82	5	155	10	4	7	.364	3-9	28	97	.781	5.03	6.04

Cal Raleigh

Bats: B **Throws:** R **Pos:** C-43;PH-6
Ht: 6'3" **Wt:** 215 **Born:** 11/26/1996 **Age:** 25

			BATTING																				RUNNING			AVERAGES			
Year	Team	Lg	G	AB	H	2B	3B	HR	(Hm	Rd)	TB	R	RBI	RC	TBB	IBB	SO	HBP	SH	SF		SB	CS	GDP	Avg	OBP	Slg	OPS
2021	Tacom	AAA	44	176	57	21	1	9	(-	-)	107	34	36	-	14	0	25	4	0	5		3	2	5	.324	.377	.608	.985
2021	Sea	AL	47	139	25	12	0	2	(1	1)	43	6	13	7	7	0	52	1	0	1		0	0	3	.180	.223	.309	.532

Brooks Raley

Pitches: L **Bats:** L **Pos:** RP-58
RAIL-ee
Ht: 6'3" **Wt:** 200 **Born:** 6/29/1988 **Age:** 34

Year	Team	Lg	G	GS	GF	IP	BFP	H	R	ER	HR	SH	SF	HB	TBB	IBB	SO	WP	W	L	Pct	Sv-Op	Hld	Vel	OPS	ERC	ERA
2012	ChC	NL	5	5	0	24.1	116	33	23	22	7	1	0	0	11	0	16	0	1	2	.333	0-0	0	88	.931	7.87	8.14
2013	ChC	NL	9	0	1	14.0	61	11	9	8	2	1	1	2	8	0	14	0	0	0	-	0-0	0	89	.758	4.48	5.14
2020	2 Tms		21	0	7	20.0	84	13	12	11	3	1	0	4	6	0	27	0	0	1	.000	1-1	6	90	.633	2.82	4.95
2021	Hou		58	0	9	49.0	205	43	30	26	6	1	0	3	16	0	65	1	2	3	.400	2-5	9	91	.666	3.51	4.78
20	Cin	NL	4	0	2	4.0	22	5	4	4	0	0	0	3	2	0	6	0	0	0	-	0-0	0	91	.866	8.02	9.00
20	Hou	AL	17	0	5	16.0	62	8	8	7	3	1	0	1	4	0	21	0	0	1	.000	1-1	6	90	.552	1.69	3.94
	Postseason		6	0	1	5.2	26	4	2	2	0	0	2	1	5	1	9	0	0	1	.000	0-0	1	91	.774	3.88	3.18
	4 ML YEARS		93	5	17	107.1	466	100	74	67	18	4	1	9	41	0	122	1	3	6	.333	3-6	15	89	.738	4.40	5.62

Luke Raley

Bats: L **Throws:** R **Pos:** RF-16;LF-13;PH-9
Ht: 6'4" **Wt:** 235 **Born:** 9/19/1994 **Age:** 27

			BATTING																				RUNNING			AVERAGES			
Year	Team	Lg	G	AB	H	2B	3B	HR	(Hm	Rd)	TB	R	RBI	RC	TBB	IBB	SO	HBP	SH	SF		SB	CS	GDP	Avg	OBP	Slg	OPS
2021	OkCity	AAA	68	258	75	14	2	18	(-	-)	147	58	66	-	25	0	73	18	0	1		7	3	2	.291	.391	.570	.960
2021	LAD	NL	33	66	12	1	0	2	(0	2)	19	5	4	4	2	1	25	4	0	0		0	0	1	.182	.250	.288	.538

Erasmo Ramirez

Pitches: R **Bats:** R **Pos:** RP-17
eh-RASS-moh
Ht: 6'0" **Wt:** 220 **Born:** 5/2/1990 **Age:** 32

Year	Team	Lg	G	GS	GF	IP	BFP	H	R	ER	HR	SH	SF	HB	TBB	IBB	SO	WP	W	L	Pct	Sv-Op	Hld	Vel	OPS	ERC	ERA
2021	Toledo	AAA	5	0	0	8.0	32	4	3	3	0	0	0	0	3	0	10	4	1	0	1.000	0-	-	-	.391	1.13	3.38
2012	Sea	AL	16	8	2	59.0	238	47	26	22	6	1	5	3	12	1	48	0	1	3	.250	0-0	0	93	.616	2.42	3.36
2013	Sea	AL	14	13	0	72.1	321	79	44	40	12	0	3	3	26	0	57	0	5	3	.625	0-0	0	92	.772	5.04	4.98
2014	Sea	AL	17	14	0	75.1	338	82	44	44	13	1	1	6	34	2	60	3	1	6	.143	0-0	0	91	.815	5.68	5.26
2015	TB	AL	34	27	5	163.1	666	145	73	68	16	1	1	9	40	0	126	3	11	6	.647	0-0	0	91	.655	3.11	3.75
2016	TB	AL	64	1	16	90.2	378	90	39	38	14	7	2	4	26	5	63	7	7	11	.389	2-6	15	91	.766	4.13	3.77
2017	2 Tms	AL	37	19	4	131.1	539	123	70	64	22	2	7	2	31	2	109	1	5	6	.455	1-2	6	92	.733	3.58	4.39
2018	Sea	AL	10	10	0	45.2	202	52	35	33	14	0	4	3	12	0	33	0	2	4	.333	0-0	0	90	.916	6.02	6.50
2019	Bos	AL	1	0	1	3.0	15	4	4	4	2	1	0	1	1	0	1	0	0	0	-	0-0	0	90	1.345	12.01	12.00
2020	NYM	NL	6	0	3	14.1	53	8	1	1	1	0	0	4	4	0	9	0	0	0	-	1-1	0	90	.471	1.45	0.63
2021	Det	AL	17	0	3	26.2	109	24	17	17	4	0	2	1	16	0	20	0	1	1	.500	0-0	0	92	.681	3.15	5.74
17	TB	AL	26	8	4	69.1	282	66	39	37	10	1	2	1	16	1	55	1	4	3	.571	1-2	6	92	.719	3.53	4.80
17	Sea	AL	11	11	0	62.0	257	57	31	27	12	1	5	1	15	1	54	0	1	3	.250	0-0	0	92	.749	3.62	3.92
	10 ML YEARS		216	92	31	681.2	2859	654	353	331	104	13	25	32	191	10	526	14	33	40	.452	4-9	21	91	.732	3.91	4.37

Harold Ramirez

Bats: R **Throws:** R **Pos:** LF-49;RF-34;CF-20;PH-4;PR-3;DH-2;1B-1
Ht: 5'10" **Wt:** 232 **Born:** 9/6/1994 **Age:** 27

			BATTING																				RUNNING			AVERAGES			
Year	Team	Lg	G	AB	H	2B	3B	HR	(Hm	Rd)	TB	R	RBI	RC	TBB	IBB	SO	HBP	SH	SF		SB	CS	GDP	Avg	OBP	Slg	OPS
2019	Mia	NL	119	421	116	20	3	11	(5	6)	175	54	50	52	18	1	91	5	0	1		2	1	8	.276	.312	.416	.728
2020	Mia	NL	3	10	2	0	0	0	(0	0)	2	2	1	1	1	0	2	0	0	0		0	1	0	.200	.273	.200	.473
2021	Cle	AL	99	339	91	21	4	7	(1	6)	135	33	41	48	14	1	56	5	0	3		3	1	10	.268	.305	.398	.703
	3 ML YEARS		221	770	209	41	4	18	(6	12)	312	89	92	101	33	2	149	10	0	4		5	3	18	.271	.308	.405	.714

Jose Ramirez

Bats: B **Throws:** R **Pos:** 3B-133;DH-19;PH-1
Ht: 5'9" **Wt:** 190 **Born:** 9/17/1992 **Age:** 29

			BATTING																				RUNNING			AVERAGES			
Year	Team	Lg	G	AB	H	2B	3B	HR	(Hm	Rd)	TB	R	RBI	RC	TBB	IBB	SO	HBP	SH	SF		SB	CS	GDP	Avg	OBP	Slg	OPS
2013	Cle	AL	15	12	4	0	1	0	(0	0)	6	5	0	2	2	0	2	0	0	0		0	1	0	.333	.429	.500	.929
2014	Cle	AL	68	237	62	10	2	2	(1	1)	82	27	17	25	13	0	35	1	**13**	2		10	1	3	.262	.300	.346	.646
2015	Cle	AL	97	315	69	14	3	6	(1	5)	107	50	27	32	32	0	39	1	5	2		10	4	5	.219	.291	.340	.631
2016	Cle	AL	152	565	176	46	3	11	(8	3)	261	84	76	101	44	1	62	4	1	4		22	7	10	.312	.363	.462	.825
2017	Cle	AL	152	585	186	**56**	6	29	(10	19)	341	107	83	113	52	5	69	3	0	5		17	5	13	.318	.374	.583	.957
2018	Cle	AL	157	578	156	38	4	39	(19	20)	319	110	105	130	106	15	80	8	0	6		34	6	2	.270	.387	.552	.939
2019	Cle	AL	129	482	123	33	3	23	(8	15)	231	68	83	74	52	3	74	2	0	6		24	4	8	.255	.327	.479	.806

		BATTING																				RUNNING			AVERAGES			
Year	Team	Lg	G	AB	H	2B	3B	HR	(Hm	Rd)	TB	R	RBI	RC	TBB	IBB	SO	HBP	SH	SF	SB	CS	GDP	Avg	OBP	Slg	OPS
2020	Cle	AL	58	219	64	16	1	17	(8	9)	133	45	46	52	31	0	43	3	0	1	10	3	2	.292	.386	.607	.993
2021	Cle	AL	152	552	147	32	5	36	(21	15)	297	111	103	116	72	10	87	7	0	5	27	4	13	.266	.355	.538	.893
	Postseason		25	94	20	5	0	1	(0	1)	28	9	8	7	8	1	19	0	0	0	0	1	2	.213	.275	.298	.572
	9 ML YEARS		980	3545	987	245	28	163	(76	87)	1777	607	540	647	404	34	491	29	19	31	154	35	56	.278	.354	.501	.855

Nick Ramirez

Pitches: L **Bats:** L **Pos:** RP-13   **Ht:** 6'4" **Wt:** 232 **Born:** 8/1/1989 **Age:** 32

			HOW MUCH PITCHED					WHAT HE GAVE UP										THE RESULTS							
Year	Team	Lg	G	GS	GF	IP	BFP	H	R	ER	HR	SH	SF	HB	TBB	IBB	SO	WP	W	L	Pct	Sv-Op	Hld	Vel	OPS	ERC	ERA
2021	ElPaso	AAA	34	2	2	46.1	202	46	26	24	5	0	0	1	16	0	49	2	2	2	.500	1--	-	-	.679	3.87	4.66
2019	Det	AL	46	0	7	79.2	348	76	45	36	11	1	3	1	35	4	74	6	5	4	.556	0-1	1	90	.748	4.16	4.07
2020	Det	AL	5	0	1	10.2	46	8	7	7	3	0	1	1	4	0	11	0	0	0	-	0-0	0	90	.708	3.99	5.91
2021	SD	NL	13	0	5	20.1	91	23	15	13	2	0	1	0	7	2	14	0	1	1	.500	0-0	0	90	.739	4.31	5.75
	3 ML YEARS		64	0	13	110.2	485	107	67	56	16	1	5	2	46	6	99	6	6	5	.545	0-1	1	90	.743	4.17	4.55

Noe Ramirez

Pitches: R **Bats:** R **Pos:** RP-38   no-EH   **Ht:** 6'3" **Wt:** 205 **Born:** 12/22/1989 **Age:** 32

			HOW MUCH PITCHED					WHAT HE GAVE UP										THE RESULTS							
Year	Team	Lg	G	GS	GF	IP	BFP	H	R	ER	HR	SH	SF	HB	TBB	IBB	SO	WP	W	L	Pct	Sv-Op	Hld	Vel	OPS	ERC	ERA
2021	Reno	AAA	8	0	0	9.0	40	8	8	8	3	0	2	0	5	1	12	1	2	0	1.000	0--	-	-	.901	5.45	8.00
2015	Bos	AL	17	0	3	13.0	61	13	12	6	3	0	0	2	7	0	13	1	0	1	.000	0-0	4	90	.803	6.15	4.15
2016	Bos	AL	14	0	7	13.0	61	16	9	9	4	0	2	2	8	1	15	0	0	0	-	0-0	0	90	1.059	9.08	6.23
2017	2 Tms	AL	12	0	1	13.0	49	6	5	4	2	0	0	0	5	0	14	0	0	0	-	0-0	0	90	.520	1.68	2.77
2018	LAA	AL	69	1	12	83.1	353	75	43	42	15	0	0	6	30	3	95	4	7	5	.583	1-4	5	90	.750	4.16	4.54
2019	LAA	AL	51	7	10	67.2	280	59	30	30	9	0	1	5	20	1	79	2	5	4	.556	0-0	3	89	.698	3.48	3.99
2020	LAA	AL	21	0	3	21.0	85	15	7	7	2	0	1	1	9	2	14	1	1	0	1.000	0-1	0	89	.618	2.73	3.00
2021	2 Tms	AL	38	0	7	36.0	147	23	14	12	3	1	2	3	12	0	29	2	0	2	.000	1-3	10	89	.547	2.12	3.00
17	Bos	AL	2	0	1	4.2	18	3	2	2	2	0	0	0	1	0	4	0	0	0	-	0-0	0	89	.752	3.21	3.86
17	LAA	AL	10	0	0	8.1	31	3	3	2	0	0	0	0	4	0	10	0	0	0	-	0-0	0	90	.374	1.02	2.16
21	LAA	AL	2	0	1	3.1	15	5	2	2	1	0	0	0	1	0	0	0	0	0	-	0-0	0	89	1.114	8.71	5.40
21	Ari	NL	36	0	6	32.2	132	18	12	10	2	1	2	3	11	0	29	2	0	2	.000	1-3	10	89	.479	1.64	2.76
	7 ML YEARS		222	8	43	247.0	1036	207	120	110	38	1	6	19	91	7	259	10	13	12	.520	2-8	22	90	.706	3.70	4.01

Roel Ramirez

Pitches: R **Bats:** R **Pos:** RP-1   **Ht:** 6'0" **Wt:** 235 **Born:** 5/26/1995 **Age:** 27

			HOW MUCH PITCHED					WHAT HE GAVE UP										THE RESULTS							
Year	Team	Lg	G	GS	GF	IP	BFP	H	R	ER	HR	SH	SF	HB	TBB	IBB	SO	WP	W	L	Pct	Sv-Op	Hld	Vel	OPS	ERC	ERA
2021	Memp	AAA	20	0	6	29.0	115	26	17	14	2	0	2	0	8	1	32	5	0	1	.000	1--	-	-	.648	2.91	4.34
2021	Syrcse	AAA	11	0	5	12.0	64	16	14	11	3	1	0	1	10	0	15	2	0	2	.000	2--	-	-	.965	9.36	8.25
2020	StL	NL	1	0	0	0.2	8	6	6	6	4	0	0	0	1	0	1	1	0	0	-	0-0	0	92	3.446	200.7	81.00
2021	StL	NL	1	0	0	0.1	4	1	3	3	0	0	0	0	2	0	0	0	0	0	-	0-0	0	94	1.250	44.74	81.00
	2 ML YEARS		2	0	0	1.0	12	7	9	9	4	0	0	0	3	0	1	1	0	0	-	0-0	0	93	2.944	144.0	81.00

Yefry Ramirez

Pitches: R **Bats:** R **Pos:** RP-1   Jefry   **Ht:** 6'2" **Wt:** 215 **Born:** 11/28/1993 **Age:** 28

			HOW MUCH PITCHED					WHAT HE GAVE UP										THE RESULTS							
Year	Team	Lg	G	GS	GF	IP	BFP	H	R	ER	HR	SH	SF	HB	TBB	IBB	SO	WP	W	L	Pct	Sv-Op	Hld	Vel	OPS	ERC	ERA
2021	OkCity	AAA	24	21	0	106.0	476	109	72	62	14	1	3	7	50	0	105	6	5	4	.556	0--	-	-	.759	5.00	5.26
2018	Bal	AL	17	12	2	65.1	294	64	44	43	11	2	3	4	36	1	62	5	1	8	.111	0-0	0	93	.802	5.30	5.92
2019	2 Tms	AL	13	1	7	24.1	119	30	24	20	4	0	2	4	16	0	27	2	0	2	.000	0-0	0	93	.936	7.91	7.40
2021	LAD	NL	1	0	1	2.0	6	0	0	0	0	0	0	0	1	0	2	0	0	0	-	0-0	0	93	.167	0.32	0.00
19	Bal	AL	4	1	2	10.1	49	11	9	8	2	0	2	2	9	0	11	1	0	2	.000	0-0	0	93	1.005	8.56	6.97
19	Pit	NL	9	0	5	14.0	70	19	15	12	2	0	0	2	7	0	16	1	0	0	-	0-0	0	93	.892	7.45	7.71
	3 ML YEARS		31	13	10	91.2	419	94	68	63	15	2	5	8	53	1	91	7	1	10	.091	0-0	0	93	.830	5.80	6.19

Yohan Ramirez

Pitches: R **Bats:** R **Pos:** RP-25   **Ht:** 6'4" **Wt:** 190 **Born:** 5/6/1995 **Age:** 27

			HOW MUCH PITCHED					WHAT HE GAVE UP										THE RESULTS							
Year	Team	Lg	G	GS	GF	IP	BFP	H	R	ER	HR	SH	SF	HB	TBB	IBB	SO	WP	W	L	Pct	Sv-Op	Hld	Vel	OPS	ERC	ERA
2021	Tacom	AAA	15	0	5	17.1	76	12	8	8	2	0	0	3	13	0	24	1	0	0	-	0--	-	-	.685	4.65	4.15
2020	Sea	AL	16	0	7	20.2	94	9	6	6	3	0	1	4	20	1	26	2	0	0	-	3-3	1	96	.626	4.07	2.61
2021	Sea	AL	25	0	15	27.2	114	18	14	12	6	3	0	3	12	0	35	2	1	3	.250	2-2	0	95	.693	3.50	3.90
	2 ML YEARS		41	0	22	48.1	208	27	20	18	9	3	1	7	32	1	61	4	1	3	.250	5-5	1	96	.667	3.78	3.35

AJ Ramos

Pitches: R **Bats:** R **Pos:** RP-4   **Ht:** 5'10" **Wt:** 200 **Born:** 9/20/1986 **Age:** 35

			HOW MUCH PITCHED					WHAT HE GAVE UP										THE RESULTS							
Year	Team	Lg	G	GS	GF	IP	BFP	H	R	ER	HR	SH	SF	HB	TBB	IBB	SO	WP	W	L	Pct	Sv-Op	Hld	Vel	OPS	ERC	ERA
2021	Salt Lk	AAA	42	0	12	53.0	245	55	35	31	9	0	2	3	26	1	76	4	0	2	.000	2--	-	-	.810	5.21	5.26
2012	Mia	NL	11	0	4	9.1	40	8	4	4	2	0	0	1	4	0	13	0	0	0	-	0-1	1	94	.754	4.65	3.86
2013	Mia	NL	68	0	18	80.0	338	58	32	28	4	1	3	2	43	3	86	1	3	4	.429	0-4	11	93	.603	2.80	3.15
2014	Mia	NL	68	0	12	64.0	270	36	16	15	1	3	1	3	43	7	73	7	7	0	1.000	0-3	20	91	.543	2.19	2.11
2015	Mia	NL	71	0	51	70.1	277	45	18	18	6	1	2	3	26	0	87	2	2	4	.333	32-38	4	93	.562	2.21	2.30

Year	Team	Lg	G	GS	GF	IP	BFP	H	R	ER	HR	SH	SF	HB	TBB	IBB	SO	WP	W	L	Pct	Sv-Op	Hld	Vel	OPS	ERC	ERA
2016	Mia	NL	67	0	52	64.0	278	52	21	20	1	2	4	4	35	3	73	6	1	4	.200	40-43	2	92	.600	3.15	2.81
2017	2 Tms	NL	61	0	55	58.2	258	49	27	26	7	1	1	2	34	1	72	7	2	4	.333	27-30	1	92	.694	4.06	3.99
2018	NYM	NL	28	0	5	19.2	88	17	14	14	3	0	1	0	15	0	22	1	2	2	.500	0-0	0	91	.766	5.22	6.41
2020	Col	NL	3	0	0	2.2	15	4	1	1	1	0	0	0	3	0	1	0	0	0	-	0-0	0	92	1.133	12.97	3.38
2021	LAA	AL	4	0	3	4.2	16	0	0	0	0	0	0	0	2	0	3	0	0	0	-	0-0	0	91	.125	0.20	0.00
17	Mia	NL	40	0	38	39.2	171	30	17	16	4	1	0	2	22	1	47	4	2	4	.333	20-22	0	92	.646	3.46	3.63
17	NYM	NL	21	0	17	19.0	87	19	10	10	3	0	1	0	12	0	25	3	0	0	-	7-8	1	92	.789	5.39	4.74
	9 ML YEARS		381	0	200	373.1	1580	269	133	126	25	8	12	15	205	14	430	24	17	18	.486	99-119	46	92	.613	3.00	3.04

Henry Ramos

Bats: B **Throws:** R **Pos:** RF-8;PH-6;LF-5

Ht: 6'0" **Wt:** 215 **Born:** 4/15/1992 **Age:** 30

							BATTING															RUNNING			AVERAGES			
Year	Team	Lg	G	AB	H	2B	3B	HR	(Hm	Rd)	TB	R	RBI	RC	TBB	IBB	SO	HBP	SH	SF	SB	CS	GDP	Avg	OBP	Slg	OPS
2021	Reno	AAA	75	256	95	16	1	12	(-	-)	149	62	57	-	29	0	48	5	0	4	4	5	5	.371	.439	.582	1.021
2021	Ari	NL	18	50	10	2	0	1	(0	1)	15	5	8	6	4	0	12	0	0	1	0	0	1	.200	.255	.300	.555

Wilson Ramos

Bats: R **Throws:** R **Pos:** C-34;DH-11;PH-1

Ht: 6'1" **Wt:** 241 **Born:** 8/10/1987 **Age:** 34

							BATTING															RUNNING			AVERAGES			
Year	Team	Lg	G	AB	H	2B	3B	HR	(Hm	Rd)	TB	R	RBI	RC	TBB	IBB	SO	HBP	SH	SF	SB	CS	GDP	Avg	OBP	Slg	OPS
2021	Clmbs	AAA	16	60	19	3	0	3	(-	-)	31	6	9	-	1	0	6	0	0	0	0	0	4	.317	.328	.517	.845
2010	2 Tms		22	79	22	7	0	1	(1	0)	32	5	5	10	2	0	12	1	0	0	0	0	2	.278	.305	.405	.710
2011	Was	NL	113	389	104	22	1	15	(8	7)	173	48	52	43	38	8	76	2	4	2	0	2	19	.267	.334	.445	.779
2012	Was	NL	25	83	22	2	0	3	(1	2)	33	11	10	12	12	2	19	0	0	1	0	0	1	.265	.354	.398	.752
2013	Was	NL	78	287	78	9	0	16	(6	10)	135	29	59	40	15	1	42	0	0	1	0	1	12	.272	.307	.470	.777
2014	Was	NL	88	341	91	12	0	11	(3	8)	136	32	47	35	17	2	57	0	0	3	0	0	17	.267	.299	.399	.698
2015	Was	NL	128	475	109	16	0	15	(10	5)	170	41	68	39	21	2	101	0	0	8	0	0	16	.229	.258	.358	.616
2016	Was	NL	131	482	148	25	0	22	(12	10)	239	58	80	78	35	2	79	2	0	4	0	0	17	.307	.354	.496	.850
2017	TB	AL	64	208	54	6	0	11	(3	8)	93	19	35	27	10	2	36	0	0	3	0	0	11	.260	.290	.447	.737
2018	2 Tms		111	382	117	22	1	15	(6	9)	186	39	70	70	32	2	80	0	0	2	0	0	20	.306	.358	.487	.845
2019	NYM	NL	141	473	136	19	1	14	(8	6)	197	52	73	70	44	5	69	4	0	3	1	0	16	.288	.351	.416	.768
2020	NYM	NL	45	142	34	6	0	5	(1	4)	55	13	15	11	10	0	31	2	0	1	0	0	5	.239	.297	.387	.684
2021	2 Tms	AL	44	151	31	5	0	8	(4	4)	60	15	20	11	9	0	36	0	0	1	0	0	2	.205	.248	.397	.646
10	Min	AL	7	27	8	3	0	0	(0	0)	11	2	1	3	0	0	3	1	0	0	0	0	1	.296	.321	.407	.729
10	Was	NL	15	52	14	4	0	1	(1	0)	21	3	4	7	2	0	9	0	0	0	0	0	1	.269	.296	.404	.700
18	TB	AL	78	293	87	14	0	14	(6	8)	143	30	53	50	22	1	61	0	0	0	0	0	17	.297	.346	.488	.834
18	Phi	NL	33	89	30	8	1	1	(0	1)	43	9	17	20	10	1	19	0	0	2	0	0	3	.337	.396	.483	.879
21	Det	AL	35	120	24	5	0	6	(2	4)	47	12	13	8	6	0	29	0	0	1	0	0	1	.200	.238	.392	.630
21	Cle	AL	9	31	7	0	0	2	(2	0)	13	3	7	3	3	0	7	0	0	0	0	0	1	.226	.286	.419	.705
	Postseason		4	17	2	0	0	0	(0	0)	2	1	0	0	1	0	6	0	1	0	0	0	1	.118	.167	.118	.284
	12 ML YEARS		990	3492	946	151	2	136	(63	73)	1509	362	534	446	245	26	638	11	4	29	1	3	138	.271	.318	.432	.750

Drew Rasmussen

Pitches: R **Bats:** R **Pos:** RP-25; SP-10

Ht: 6'1" **Wt:** 211 **Born:** 7/27/1995 **Age:** 26

				HOW MUCH PITCHED					WHAT HE GAVE UP											THE RESULTS						
Year	Team	Lg	G	GS	GF	IP	BFP	H	R	ER	HR	SH	SF	HB	TBB	IBB	SO	WP	W	L	Pct	Sv-Op	Hld	Vel	OPS	ERC	ERA
2021	Drham	AAA	8	1	2	11.1	42	5	0	0	0	0	0	2	2	0	23	0	2	0	1.000	1--	-		.425	1.00	0.00
2020	Mil	NL	12	0	3	15.1	71	17	10	10	3	0	0	0	9	0	21	0	1	0	1.000	0-0	0	98	.834	6.18	5.87
2021	2 Tms		35	10	9	76.0	307	57	27	24	5	1	1	0	25	2	73	4	4	1	.800	1-1	1	97	.575	2.25	2.84
21	Mil	NL	15	0	7	17.0	77	13	11	8	2	0	0	0	12	2	25	2	0	1	.000	1-1	0	97	.679	3.74	4.24
21	TB	AL	20	10	2	59.0	230	44	16	16	3	1	1	0	13	0	48	2	4	0	1.000	0-0	1	97	.542	1.85	2.44
	Postseason		1	0	1	1.0	4	1	0	0	0	0	0	0	0	0	2	0	0	0	-	0-0	0		.750	1.95	0.00
	2 ML YEARS		47	10	12	91.1	378	74	37	34	8	1	1	0	34	2	94	4	5	1	.833	1-1	1	97	.623	2.82	3.35

Corey Ray

Bats: L **Throws:** L **Pos:** RF-1;PH-1

Ht: 6'0" **Wt:** 196 **Born:** 9/22/1994 **Age:** 27

							BATTING															RUNNING			AVERAGES			
Year	Team	Lg	G	AB	H	2B	3B	HR	(Hm	Rd)	TB	R	RBI	RC	TBB	IBB	SO	HBP	SH	SF	SB	CS	GDP	Avg	OBP	Slg	OPS
2021	Nashv	AAA	39	146	40	11	2	6	(-	-)	73	18	19	-	10	0	45	1	0	0	2	0	0	.274	.325	.500	.825
2021	Mil	NL	1	2	0	0	0	0	(0	0)	0	1	0	0	1	0	1	0	0	0	0	0	0	.000	.333	.000	.333

Robbie Ray

Pitches: L **Bats:** L **Pos:** SP-32

Ht: 6'2" **Wt:** 215 **Born:** 10/1/1991 **Age:** 30

				HOW MUCH PITCHED					WHAT HE GAVE UP											THE RESULTS						
Year	Team	Lg	G	GS	GF	IP	BFP	H	R	ER	HR	SH	SF	HB	TBB	IBB	SO	WP	W	L	Pct	Sv-Op	Hld	Vel	OPS	ERC	ERA
2014	Det	AL	9	6	1	28.2	136	43	26	26	1	1	1	0	11	0	19	2	1	4	.200	0-0	1	91	.993	7.72	8.16
2015	Ari	NL	23	23	0	127.2	545	121	56	50	9	7	6	8	49	3	119	2	5	12	.294	0-0	0	93	.731	3.75	3.52
2016	Ari	NL	32	32	0	174.1	776	185	105	95	24	3	2	6	71	4	218	8	8	15	.348	0-0	0	94	.770	4.78	4.90
2017	Ari	NL	28	28	0	162.0	665	116	57	52	23	4	3	5	71	3	218	8	15	5	.750	0-0	0	94	.646	3.08	2.89
2018	Ari	NL	24	24	0	123.2	526	97	55	54	19	1	4	5	70	3	165	6	6	2	.750	0-0	0	94	.706	4.08	3.93
2019	Ari	NL	33	33	0	174.1	747	150	91	84	30	11	4	5	84	5	235	7	12	8	.600	0-0	0	92	.766	4.19	4.34
2020	2 Tms		12	11	0	51.2	251	53	40	38	13	0	2	1	45	1	68	6	2	5	.286	0-0	0	94	.917	7.42	6.62
2021	Tor	AL	32	32	0	193.1	773	150	62	61	33	1	2	4	52	0	248	5	13	7	.650	0-0	0	95	.667	2.91	2.84

Year	Team	Lg	G	GS	GF	IP	BFP	H	R	ER	HR	SH	SF	HB	TBB	IBB	SO	WP	W	L	Pct	Sv-Op	Hld	Vel	OPS	ERC	ERA
20	Ari	NL	7	7	0	31.0	154	31	27	27	9	0	2	1	31	1	43	6	1	4	.200	0-0	0	94	.967	8.23	7.84
20	Tor	AL	5	4	0	20.2	97	22	13	11	4	0	0	0	14	0	25	0	1	1	.500	0-0	0	94	.841	6.26	4.79
	Postseason		3	1	0	9.2	41	7	6	6	0	0	0	1	5	0	14	5	0	2	.000	0-0	0	94	.603	2.74	5.59
8 ML YEARS			193	189	1	1035.2	4419	915	492	460	156	28	21	34	453	19	1290	43	62	58	.517	0-0	1	94	.735	4.03	4.00

Colin Rea

Pitches: R **Bats:** R **Pos:** RP-1   ray   **Ht:** 6'5" **Wt:** 235 **Born:** 7/1/1990 **Age:** 31

Year	Team	Lg	G	GS	GF	IP	BFP	H	R	ER	HR	SH	SF	HB	TBB	IBB	SO	WP	W	L	Pct	Sv-Op	Hld	Vel	OPS	ERC	ERA
2021	Nashv	AAA	7	7	0	35.2	142	33	9	9	2	0	0	1	4	0	35	1	4	2	.667	0--	-	-	.589	2.45	2.27
2015	SD	NL	6	6	0	31.2	133	29	16	15	2	1	2	1	11	0	26	0	2	2	.500	0-0	0	91	.700	3.29	4.26
2016	2 Tms	NL	20	19	0	102.2	454	102	63	55	12	4	2	8	44	4	80	0	5	5	.500	0-0	0	92	.768	4.50	4.82
2020	ChC	NL	9	2	3	14.0	62	15	9	9	3	0	1	0	2	0	10	0	1	1	.500	0-0	1	93	.715	3.88	5.79
2021	Mil	NL	1	0	1	6.0	24	7	5	5	2	0	1	0	0	0	5	0	0	0		0-0	0	93	.944	5.00	7.50
16	SD	NL	19	18	0	99.1	443	101	63	55	12	3	2	8	44	4	76	0	5	5	.500	0-0	0	92	.782	4.73	4.98
16	Mia	NL	1	1	0	3.1	11	1	0	0	0	1	0	0	0	0	4	0	0	0		0-0	0	90	.200	0.21	0.00
4 ML YEARS			36	27	4	154.1	673	153	93	84	19	5	6	9	57	4	121	0	8	8	.500	0-0	1	92	.757	4.22	4.90

J.T. Realmuto

Bats: R **Throws:** R **Pos:** C-118;1B-16;PH-9;DH-3   ray-al-MOO-toh   **Ht:** 6'1" **Wt:** 212 **Born:** 3/18/1991 **Age:** 31

									BATTING													RUNNING			AVERAGES			
Year	Team	Lg	G	AB	H	2B	3B	HR	(Hm	Rd)	TB	R	RBI	RC	TBB	IBB	SO	HBP	SH	SF	SB	CS	GDP	Avg	OBP	Slg	OPS
2014	Mia	NL	11	29	7	1	1	0	(0	0)	10	4	9	4	1	0	8	0	0	0	0	0	2	.241	.267	.345	.611
2015	Mia	NL	126	441	114	21	7	10	(6	4)	179	49	47	44	19	2	70	2	1	4	8	4	11	.259	.290	.406	.696
2016	Mia	NL	137	509	154	31	0	11	(3	8)	218	60	48	63	28	1	100	5	0	3	12	4	12	.303	.343	.428	.771
2017	Mia	NL	141	532	148	31	5	17	(5	12)	240	68	65	74	36	4	106	8	0	3	8	2	13	.278	.332	.451	.783
2018	Mia	NL	125	477	132	30	3	21	(8	13)	231	74	74	74	38	0	104	10	0	4	3	2	9	.277	.340	.484	.825
2019	Phi	NL	145	538	148	36	3	25	(16	9)	265	92	83	78	41	2	123	5	0	9	9	1	12	.275	.328	.493	.820
2020	Phi	NL	47	173	46	6	0	11	(8	3)	85	33	32	28	16	0	48	6	0	0	4	1	3	.266	.349	.491	.840
2021	Phi	NL	134	476	125	25	4	17	(12	5)	209	64	73	80	48	5	129	11	0	2	13	3	8	.263	.343	.439	.782
8 ML YEARS			866	3175	874	181	23	112	(58	54)	1437	444	431	445	227	14	688	47	1	24	57	17	70	.275	.331	.453	.783

Josh Reddick

Bats: L **Throws:** R **Pos:** RF-36;PH-16;CF-4;PR-2;LF-1   **Ht:** 6'2" **Wt:** 197 **Born:** 2/19/1987 **Age:** 35

									BATTING													RUNNING			AVERAGES			
Year	Team	Lg	G	AB	H	2B	3B	HR	(Hm	Rd)	TB	R	RBI	RC	TBB	IBB	SO	HBP	SH	SF	SB	CS	GDP	Avg	OBP	Slg	OPS
2021	Reno	AAA	11	46	14	2	0	2	(-	-)	22	9	8	-	5	0	7	0	0	1	0	0	0	.304	.365	.478	.844
2021	Syrcse	AAA	11	33	6	1	0	1	(-	-)	10	4	4	-	4	0	13	1	0	0	0	0	0	.182	.289	.303	.593
2009	Bos	AL	27	59	10	4	0	2	(0	2)	20	5	4	4	2	0	17	1	0	0	0	0	0	.169	.210	.339	.549
2010	Bos	AL	29	62	12	3	1	1	(1	0)	20	5	5	1	1	0	15	0	0	0	1	0	1	.194	.206	.323	.529
2011	Bos	AL	87	254	71	18	3	7	(2	5)	116	41	28	33	19	1	50	1	0	4	1	2	1	.280	.327	.457	.784
2012	Oak	AL	156	611	148	29	5	32	(18	14)	283	85	85	73	55	8	151	2	1	4	11	1	15	.242	.305	.463	.768
2013	Oak	AL	114	385	87	19	2	12	(2	10)	146	54	56	53	46	1	86	2	1	7	9	2	4	.226	.307	.379	.686
2014	Oak	AL	109	363	96	16	7	12	(5	7)	162	53	54	54	28	0	63	1	0	3	1	1	3	.264	.316	.446	.763
2015	Oak	AL	149	526	143	25	4	20	(7	13)	236	67	77	83	49	1	65	0	1	2	10	2	7	.272	.333	.449	.781
2016	2 Tms		115	398	112	17	1	10	(5	5)	161	53	37	54	39	5	56	0	0	3	8	3	8	.281	.345	.405	.749
2017	Hou	AL	134	477	150	34	4	13	(6	7)	231	77	82	88	43	1	72	0	1	12	7	3	9	.314	.363	.484	.847
2018	Hou	AL	134	433	105	13	2	17	(6	11)	173	63	47	50	49	3	77	0	1	2	7	2	9	.242	.318	.400	.718
2019	Hou	AL	141	501	138	19	3	14	(6	8)	205	57	56	65	36	1	66	0	1	9	5	2	9	.275	.319	.409	.728
2020	Hou	AL	56	188	46	11	1	4	(1	3)	71	22	23	25	20	0	42	0	0	1	1	0	5	.245	.316	.378	.693
2021	Ari	NL	54	151	39	11	0	2	(2	0)	56	15	21	18	6	0	31	0	0	1	0	0	4	.258	.285	.371	.656
16	Oak	AL	68	243	72	11	1	8	(3	5)	109	33	28	42	28	5	34	0	0	1	5	0	7	.296	.368	.449	.816
16	LAD	NL	47	155	40	6	0	2	(2	0)	52	20	9	12	11	0	22	0	0	0	3	3	1	.258	.307	.335	.643
	Postseason		74	227	47	3	0	4	(0	4)	62	23	12	15	17	3	55	0	0	3	0	0	7	.207	.262	.273	.535
13 ML YEARS			1305	4408	1157	219	33	146	(61	85)	1880	597	575	601	393	21	791	7	6	46	61	18	75	.262	.321	.426	.747

Cody Reed

Pitches: L **Bats:** L **Pos:** RP-12   **Ht:** 6'5" **Wt:** 230 **Born:** 4/15/1993 **Age:** 29

Year	Team	Lg	G	GS	GF	IP	BFP	H	R	ER	HR	SH	SF	HB	TBB	IBB	SO	WP	W	L	Pct	Sv-Op	Hld	Vel	OPS	ERC	ERA
2016	Cin	NL	10	10	0	47.2	230	67	47	39	12	1	1	4	19	2	43	1	0	7	.000	0-0	0	93	.968	8.00	7.36
2017	Cin	NL	12	1	3	17.2	79	11	11	10	3	0	0	0	19	3	17	2	1	1	.500	1-1	0	94	.780	4.97	5.09
2018	Cin	NL	17	7	2	43.0	188	45	21	19	5	2	2	2	15	0	42	2	1	3	.250	0-0	1	92	.729	4.41	3.98
2019	Cin	NL	3	0	1	6.1	25	6	1	1	0	0	0	0	1	1	7	1	0	0		0-0	0	94	.530	2.11	1.42
2020	2 Tms		11	0	5	12.0	55	11	6	6	2	0	0	1	8	0	12	1	0	1	.000	0-0	0	94	.798	5.50	4.50
2021	TB	AL	12	0	5	9.2	42	8	5	4	1	1	0	1	6	0	7	0	0	1	.000	0-0	3	93	.719	4.53	3.72
20	Cin	NL	9	0	4	9.1	46	10	6	6	2	0	0	1	8	0	10	1	0	1	.000	0-0	0	95	.927	7.84	5.79
20	TB	AL	2	0	1	2.2	9	1	0	0	0	0	0	0	0	0	2	0	0	0		0-0	0	94	.222	0.31	0.00
6 ML YEARS			65	18	16	136.1	619	148	91	79	23	4	3	8	68	6	128	8	2	13	.133	1-1	4	93	.823	5.67	5.22

Jake Reed

Pitches: R **Bats:** R **Pos:** RP-9; SP-1   **Ht:** 6'2" **Wt:** 195 **Born:** 9/29/1992 **Age:** 29

Year	Team	Lg	G	GS	GF	IP	BFP	H	R	ER	HR	SH	SF	HB	TBB	IBB	SO	WP	W	L	Pct	Sv-Op	Hld	Vel	OPS	ERC	ERA
2021	Salt Lk	AAA	8	0	5	10.2	52	13	10	10	1	1	0	1	6	0	17	1	0	0	-	1--	-	-	.888	6.22	8.44
2021	OkCity	AAA	9	0	4	10.1	43	12	3	3	1	1	0	1	1	0	11	1	0	0	-	0--	-	-	.733	4.25	2.61
2021	Syrcse	AAA	6	0	0	6.2	25	5	2	2	1	0	0	1	0	0	7	0	0	0	-	0--	-	-	.657	2.22	2.70
2021	2 Tms	NL	10	1	3	10.0	43	10	6	4	1	1	0	0	2	1	10	0	0	1	.000	0-1	0	88	.636	3.00	3.60
21	LAD	NL	6	1	2	5.1	24	5	3	2	1	1	0	0	2	1	5	0	0	0	-	0-1	0	88	.733	3.67	3.38
21	NYM	NL	4	0	1	4.2	19	5	3	2	0	0	0	0	0	0	5	0	0	1	.000	0-0	0	88	.526	2.27	3.86

Jakson Reetz

Bats: R **Throws:** R **Pos:** C-1;PH-1   **Ht:** 6'0" **Wt:** 205 **Born:** 1/3/1996 **Age:** 26

Year	Team	Lg	G	AB	H	2B	3B	HR	(Hm	Rd)	TB	R	RBI	RC	TBB	IBB	SO	HBP	SH	SF	SB	CS	GDP	Avg	OBP	Slg	OPS
2021	Hrsbrg	AA	64	221	42	13	0	4	(-	-)	67	31	18	-	24	0	69	10	0	0	1	1	2	.190	.298	.303	.601
2021	Roch	AAA	12	33	5	2	0	2	(-	-)	13	3	8	-	3	0	12	3	0	1	0	0	0	.152	.275	.394	.669
2021	Was	NL	2	2	1	1	0	0	(0	0)	2	1	0	1	0	0	0	0	0	0	0	0	0	.500	.500	1.000	1.500

Rob Refsnyder

Bats: R **Throws:** R **Pos:** CF-22;LF-20;RF-9;PH-7;PR-3;DH-1   REF-snide-er   **Ht:** 6'0" **Wt:** 205 **Born:** 3/26/1991 **Age:** 31

Year	Team	Lg	G	AB	H	2B	3B	HR	(Hm	Rd)	TB	R	RBI	RC	TBB	IBB	SO	HBP	SH	SF	SB	CS	GDP	Avg	OBP	Slg	OPS
2021	StPaul	AAA	18	66	21	5	0	5	(-	-)	41	13	14	-	12	0	13	1	0	1	0	0	2	.318	.425	.621	1.046
2015	NYY	AL	16	43	13	3	0	2	(1	1)	22	3	5	6	3	1	7	0	0	0	2	0	3	.302	.348	.512	.859
2016	NYY	AL	58	152	38	9	0	0	(0	0)	47	25	12	14	18	2	30	1	0	3	2	1	5	.250	.328	.309	.637
2017	2 Tms	AL	52	88	15	2	1	0	(0	0)	19	8	0	0	8	1	17	1	0	0	4	1	4	.170	.247	.216	.463
2018	TB	AL	40	84	14	3	0	2	(0	2)	23	10	5	6	18	0	26	0	0	0	0	2	5	.167	.314	.274	.588
2020	Tex	AL	15	30	6	1	0	0	(0	0)	7	4	1	2	2	0	11	1	0	1	0	0	0	.200	.265	.233	.498
2021	Min	AL	51	139	34	7	0	2	(1	1)	47	21	12	16	17	0	40	0	0	1	1	0	4	.245	.325	.338	.663
17	NYY	AL	20	37	5	1	1	0	(0	0)	8	3	0	0	3	0	8	0	0	0	2	0	2	.135	.200	.216	.416
17	Tor	AL	32	51	10	1	0	0	(0	0)	11	5	0	0	5	1	9	1	0	0	2	1	2	.196	.281	.216	.496
	Postseason		1	3	0	0	0	0	(0	0)	0	0	0	0	0	0	0	0	0	0	0	0	0	.000	.000	.000	.000
	6 ML YEARS		232	536	120	25	1	6	(2	4)	165	71	35	44	66	4	131	3	0	5	9	4	19	.224	.310	.308	.618

Sean Reid-Foley

Pitches: R **Bats:** R **Pos:** RP-12   **Ht:** 6'3" **Wt:** 230 **Born:** 8/30/1995 **Age:** 26

Year	Team	Lg	G	GS	GF	IP	BFP	H	R	ER	HR	SH	SF	HB	TBB	IBB	SO	WP	W	L	Pct	Sv-Op	Hld	Vel	OPS	ERC	ERA
2021	Syrcse	AAA	10	0	1	11.1	44	5	3	3	1	0	1	0	5	0	19	0	0	0	-	0--	-	-	.464	1.47	2.38
2018	Tor	AL	7	7	0	33.1	150	31	23	19	6	0	1	1	21	0	42	3	2	4	.333	0-0	0	94	.794	5.32	5.13
2019	Tor	AL	9	6	0	31.2	150	33	20	15	5	0	1	2	21	0	28	3	2	4	.333	0-0	0	93	.818	6.01	4.26
2020	Tor	AL	5	0	2	6.2	30	3	3	1	0	0	0	0	6	1	6	0	1	0	1.000	0-0	0	95	.425	1.93	1.35
2021	NYM	NL	12	0	1	20.2	92	22	15	12	3	0	0	0	9	2	26	1	2	1	.667	0-0	0	94	.771	4.70	5.23
	4 ML YEARS		33	13	3	92.1	422	89	61	47	14	0	2	3	57	3	102	7	7	9	.438	0-0	0	93	.773	5.14	4.58

Zach Reks

Bats: L **Throws:** R **Pos:** LF-3;PH-3;RF-2;PR-1   **Ht:** 6'2" **Wt:** 190 **Born:** 11/12/1993 **Age:** 28

Year	Team	Lg	G	AB	H	2B	3B	HR	(Hm	Rd)	TB	R	RBI	RC	TBB	IBB	SO	HBP	SH	SF	SB	CS	GDP	Avg	OBP	Slg	OPS
2021	OkCity	AAA	85	313	90	24	1	19	(-	-)	173	69	67	-	46	0	105	8	0	2	0	1	8	.288	.390	.553	.943
2021	LAD	NL	6	10	0	0	0	0	(0	0)	0	2	0	0	0	0	7	0	0	0	0	0	0	.000	.000	.000	.000

Anthony Rendon

Bats: R **Throws:** R **Pos:** 3B-57;DH-1   ren-DOAN   **Ht:** 6'1" **Wt:** 200 **Born:** 6/6/1990 **Age:** 32

Year	Team	Lg	G	AB	H	2B	3B	HR	(Hm	Rd)	TB	R	RBI	RC	TBB	IBB	SO	HBP	SH	SF	SB	CS	GDP	Avg	OBP	Slg	OPS
2013	Was	NL	98	351	93	23	1	7	(3	4)	139	40	35	43	31	3	69	5	2	5	1	1	7	.265	.329	.396	.725
2014	Was	NL	153	613	176	39	6	21	(10	11)	290	111	83	97	58	2	104	5	2	5	17	3	11	.287	.351	.473	.824
2015	Was	NL	80	311	82	16	0	5	(3	2)	113	43	25	39	36	0	70	4	0	4	1	2	8	.264	.344	.363	.707
2016	Was	NL	156	567	153	38	2	20	(11	9)	255	91	85	95	65	2	117	7	0	6	12	6	5	.270	.348	.450	.797
2017	Was	NL	147	508	153	41	1	25	(14	11)	271	81	100	115	84	6	82	7	0	6	7	2	7	.301	.403	.533	.937
2018	Was	NL	136	529	163	44	2	24	(10	14)	283	88	92	99	55	5	82	5	0	8	2	1	5	.308	.374	.535	.909
2019	Was	NL	146	545	174	44	3	34	(20	14)	326	117	126	130	80	8	86	12	0	9	5	1	13	.319	.412	.598	1.010
2020	LAA	AL	52	189	54	11	1	9	(9	0)	94	29	31	38	38	2	31	5	0	0	0	0	10	.286	.418	.497	.915
2021	LAA	AL	58	217	52	13	0	6	(2	4)	83	24	34	23	29	2	41	1	0	2	0	0	11	.240	.329	.382	.712
	Postseason		31	117	33	8	0	5	(1	4)	56	16	21	22	18	3	19	0	0	3	1	0	2	.282	.370	.479	.848
	9 ML YEARS		1026	3830	1100	269	16	151	(82	69)	1854	624	611	679	476	30	682	51	4	47	45	16	77	.287	.369	.484	.854

Hunter Renfroe

Bats: R **Throws:** R **Pos:** RF-138;CF-8;PH-2;DH-1   **Ht:** 6'1" **Wt:** 230 **Born:** 1/28/1992 **Age:** 30

Year	Team	Lg	G	AB	H	2B	3B	HR	(Hm	Rd)	TB	R	RBI	RC	TBB	IBB	SO	HBP	SH	SF	SB	CS	GDP	Avg	OBP	Slg	OPS
2016	SD	NL	11	35	13	3	0	4	(4	0)	28	8	14	10	1	1	5	0	0	0	0	0	1	.371	.389	.800	1.189
2017	SD	NL	122	445	103	25	1	26	(14	12)	208	51	58	48	27	1	140	6	0	1	3	0	4	.231	.284	.467	.751
2018	SD	NL	117	403	100	23	1	26	(13	13)	203	53	68	58	30	2	109	3	0	5	2	1	9	.248	.302	.504	.805
2019	SD	NL	140	440	95	19	1	33	(14	19)	215	64	64	57	46	1	154	2	0	6	5	0	6	.216	.289	.489	.778
2020	TB	AL	42	122	19	5	0	8	(5	3)	48	18	22	13	14	0	37	2	0	1	2	0	3	.156	.252	.393	.645
2021	Bos	AL	144	521	135	33	0	31	(14	17)	261	89	96	78	44	0	130	1	0	6	1	2	6	.259	.315	.501	.816
	Postseason		12	23	4	1	0	2	(2	0)	11	2	7	3	1	0	11	0	0	0	0	0	0	.174	.208	.478	.687
	6 ML YEARS		576	1966	465	108	3	128	(64	64)	963	283	322	264	162	5	575	14	0	19	13	3	29	.237	.297	.490	.786

Luis Rengifo

Bats: B **Throws:** R **Pos:** SS-26;RF-14;3B-12;PH-5;2B-4;LF-1   ren-HEE-foh   **Ht:** 5'10" **Wt:** 195 **Born:** 2/26/1997 **Age:** 25

Year	Team	Lg	G	AB	H	2B	3B	HR	(Hm	Rd)	TB	R	RBI	RC	TBB	IBB	SO	HBP	SH	SF	SB	CS	GDP	Avg	OBP	Slg	OPS
2021	Salt Lk	AAA	53	207	68	16	4	8	(-	-)	116	46	32	-	17	1	32	3	0	1	13	5	3	.329	.386	.560	.946
2019	LAA	AL	108	357	85	18	3	7	(1	6)	130	44	33	45	40	0	93	5	1	3	2	5	6	.238	.321	.364	.685
2020	LAA	AL	33	90	14	1	0	1	(0	1)	18	12	3	2	14	0	26	0	2	0	3	1	2	.156	.269	.200	.469
2021	LAA	AL	54	174	35	1	0	6	(3	3)	54	22	18	10	9	0	38	2	3	2	1	0	3	.201	.246	.310	.556
	3 ML YEARS		195	621	134	20	3	14	(4	10)	202	78	54	57	63	0	157	7	6	5	6	6	11	.216	.293	.325	.618

Alex Reyes

Pitches: R **Bats:** R **Pos:** RP-69   **Ht:** 6'4" **Wt:** 220 **Born:** 8/29/1994 **Age:** 27

			HOW MUCH PITCHED					WHAT HE GAVE UP										THE RESULTS							
Year	Team	Lg	G	GS	GF	IP	BFP	H	R	ER	HR	SH	SF	HB	TBB	IBB	SO	WP	W	L	Pct	Sv-Op Hld	Vel	OPS	ERC	ERA
2016	StL	NL	12	5	3	46.0	189	33	8	8	1	1	1	0	23	1	52	3	4	1	.800	1-1 1	97	.578	2.43	1.57
2018	StL	NL	1	1	0	4.0	15	3	0	0	0	0	1	2	0	2	0	0	0	-	0-0 0	95	.650	3.97	0.00
2019	StL	NL	4	0	0	3.0	17	2	5	5	1	0	1	0	6	0	1	1	0	1	.000	0-0 2	97	.971	10.79	15.00
2020	StL	NL	15	1	5	19.2	86	14	10	7	1	1	0	0	14	1	27	2	2	1	.667	1-1 2	98	.611	3.22	3.20
2021	StL	NL	69	0	54	72.1	317	46	32	26	9	0	1	2	52	1	95	10	10	8	.556	29-34 3	97	.609	3.48	3.24
	Postseason		2	0	2	3.1	15	2	3	1	1	0	0	0	2	1	3	0	0	0	-	1-1 0	99	.651	3.21	2.70
	5 ML YEARS		101	7	62	145.0	624	98	55	46	12	2	3	3	97	3	177	16	16	11	.593	31-36 8	97	.609	3.24	2.86

Franmil Reyes

Bats: R **Throws:** R **Pos:** DH-103;RF-11;PH-1   **Ht:** 6'5" **Wt:** 265 **Born:** 7/7/1995 **Age:** 26

Year	Team	Lg	G	AB	H	2B	3B	HR	(Hm	Rd)	TB	R	RBI	RC	TBB	IBB	SO	HBP	SH	SF	SB	CS	GDP	Avg	OBP	Slg	OPS
2018	SD	NL	87	261	73	9	0	16	(8	8)	130	36	31	37	24	0	80	0	0	0	0	0	5	.280	.340	.498	.838
2019	2 Tms		150	494	123	19	0	37	(25	12)	253	69	81	71	47	1	156	0	0	7	0	0	15	.249	.310	.512	.822
2020	Cle	AL	59	211	58	10	0	9	(2	7)	95	27	34	32	24	0	69	1	0	5	0	0	6	.275	.344	.450	.795
2021	Cle	AL	115	418	106	18	2	30	(16	14)	218	57	85	70	43	3	149	2	0	3	4	1	13	.254	.324	.522	.846
19	SD	NL	99	321	82	9	0	27	(17	10)	172	43	46	41	29	1	93	0	0	4	0	0	12	.255	.314	.536	.849
19	Cle	AL	51	173	41	10	0	10	(8	2)	81	26	35	30	18	0	63	0	0	3	0	0	3	.237	.304	.468	.772
	Postseason		2	7	0	0	0	0	(0	0)	0	2	0	0	2	0	5	0	0	0	0	0	0	.000	.222	.000	.222
	4 ML YEARS		411	1384	360	56	2	92	(51	41)	696	189	231	210	138	4	454	3	0	15	4	1	39	.260	.325	.503	.828

Pablo Reyes

Bats: R **Throws:** R **Pos:** 3B-28;PH-24;PR-5;2B-2;SS-2;LF-1;DH-1   **Ht:** 5'8" **Wt:** 175 **Born:** 9/5/1993 **Age:** 28

Year	Team	Lg	G	AB	H	2B	3B	HR	(Hm	Rd)	TB	R	RBI	RC	TBB	IBB	SO	HBP	SH	SF	SB	CS	GDP	Avg	OBP	Slg	OPS
2021	Nashv	AAA	31	122	29	7	0	3	(-	-)	45	25	15	-	14	0	22	1	0	4	1	3	1	.238	.312	.369	.681
2018	Pit	NL	18	58	17	2	0	3	(0	3)	28	9	7	7	5	0	11	0	0	0	1	2	.293	.349	.483	.832
2019	Pit	NL	71	143	29	7	2	2	(1	1)	46	18	19	16	13	0	36	1	0	0	1	1	0	.203	.274	.322	.596
2021	Mil	NL	53	78	20	5	0	1	(1	0)	28	12	3	8	9	1	15	0	0	0	4	0	2	.256	.333	.359	.692
	3 ML YEARS		142	279	66	14	2	6	(2	4)	102	39	29	31	27	1	62	1	0	0	5	2	4	.237	.306	.366	.672

Victor Reyes

Bats: B **Throws:** R **Pos:** RF-43;CF-20;PH-8;PR-8;DH-4;LF-1   **Ht:** 6'5" **Wt:** 194 **Born:** 10/5/1994 **Age:** 27

Year	Team	Lg	G	AB	H	2B	3B	HR	(Hm	Rd)	TB	R	RBI	RC	TBB	IBB	SO	HBP	SH	SF	SB	CS	GDP	Avg	OBP	Slg	OPS
2021	Toledo	AAA	20	78	30	7	2	1	(-	-)	44	13	10	-	10	0	17	2	0	1	5	2	2	.385	.462	.564	1.026
2018	Det	AL	100	212	47	5	3	1	(0	1)	61	35	12	12	5	0	46	0	1	1	9	1	4	.222	.239	.288	.526
2019	Det	AL	69	276	84	16	5	3	(2	1)	119	29	25	35	14	0	64	0	0	2	9	3	3	.304	.336	.431	.767
2020	Det	AL	57	202	56	7	2	4	(1	3)	79	30	14	23	9	0	45	2	0	0	8	2	4	.277	.315	.391	.706
2021	Det	AL	76	209	54	10	4	5	(4	1)	87	26	22	25	8	0	55	0	2	1	5	1	2	.258	.284	.416	.701
	4 ML YEARS		302	899	241	38	14	13	(7	6)	346	120	73	95	36	0	210	2	3	4	31	7	15	.268	.296	.385	.681

Bryan Reynolds

Bats: B Throws: R Pos: CF-137;LF-17;PH-9;DH-1   Ht: 6'3" Wt: 210 Born: 1/27/1995 Age: 27

							BATTING												RUNNING			AVERAGES			
Year	Team	Lg	G	AB	H	2B	3B	HR	(Hm | Rd)	TB	R	RBI	RC	TBB	IBB	SO	HBP	SH	SF	SB	CS	GDP	Avg	OBP	Slg	OPS
2019	Pit	NL	134	491	154	37	4	16	(8 | 8)	247	83	68	89	46	0	121	6	0	3	3	2	9	.314	.377	.503	.880
2020	Pit	NL	55	185	35	6	2	7	(4 | 3)	66	24	19	22	21	0	57	1	0	0	1	1	2	.189	.275	.357	.632
2021	Pit	NL	159	559	169	35	8	24	(12 | 12)	292	93	90	112	75	9	119	8	0	4	5	2	10	.302	.390	.522	.912
	3 ML YEARS		348	1235	358	78	14	47	(24 | 23)	605	200	177	223	142	9	297	15	0	7	9	5	21	.290	.368	.490	.858

Garrett Richards

Pitches: R Bats: R Pos: SP-22; RP-18   Ht: 6'2" Wt: 210 Born: 5/27/1988 Age: 34

			HOW MUCH PITCHED					WHAT HE GAVE UP										THE RESULTS							
Year	Team	Lg	G	GS	GF	IP	BFP	H	R	ER	HR	SH	SF	HB	TBB	IBB	SO	WP	W	L	Pct	Sv-Op	Hld	Vel	OPS	ERC	ERA
2011	LAA	AL	7	3	2	14.0	62	16	11	9	4	0	0	0	7	0	9	2	0	2	.000	0-0	0	95	.989	6.97	5.79
2012	LAA	AL	30	9	4	71.0	318	77	46	37	7	2	4	3	34	1	47	2	4	3	.571	1-3	5	95	.793	5.04	4.69
2013	LAA	AL	47	17	6	145.0	620	151	73	67	12	9	3	1	44	4	101	11	7	8	.467	1-2	5	95	.699	3.78	4.16
2014	LAA	AL	26	26	0	168.2	678	124	51	49	5	0	3	7	51	1	164	22	13	4	.765	0-0	0	96	.529	2.06	2.61
2015	LAA	AL	32	32	0	207.1	865	181	94	84	20	6	10	5	76	2	176	17	15	12	.556	0-0	0	96	.664	3.32	3.65
2016	LAA	AL	6	6	0	34.2	148	31	16	9	2	2	0	1	15	1	34	3	1	3	.250	0-0	0	96	.683	3.39	2.34
2017	LAA	AL	6	6	0	27.2	108	18	8	7	1	1	0	0	7	0	27	2	0	2	.000	0-0	0	96	.494	1.49	2.28
2018	LAA	AL	16	16	0	76.1	324	64	43	31	11	1	0	1	34	0	87	15	5	4	.556	0-0	0	96	.688	3.69	3.66
2019	SD	NL	3	3	0	8.2	41	10	8	8	2	1	0	0	6	0	11	1	0	1	.000	0-0	0	95	1.076	7.31	8.31
2020	SD	NL	14	10	2	51.1	213	47	23	23	7	0	1	2	17	0	46	3	2	2	.500	0-0	1	95	.724	3.80	4.03
2021	Bos	AL	40	22	4	136.2	617	158	86	74	19	0	5	5	60	1	115	7	7	8	.467	3-3	5	94	.829	5.60	4.87
	Postseason		4	0	0	2.2	12	1	2	2	0	0	0	0	2	0	4	1	0	1	.000	0-0	0	95	.450	1.42	6.75
	11 ML YEARS		227	150	18	941.1	3994	877	459	398	90	22	26	25	351	10	817	85	54	49	.524	5-8	13	95	.692	3.65	3.81

Trevor Richards

Pitches: R Bats: R Pos: RP-53   Ht: 6'2" Wt: 195 Born: 5/15/1993 Age: 29

			HOW MUCH PITCHED					WHAT HE GAVE UP										THE RESULTS							
Year	Team	Lg	G	GS	GF	IP	BFP	H	R	ER	HR	SH	SF	HB	TBB	IBB	SO	WP	W	L	Pct	Sv-Op	Hld	Vel	OPS	ERC	ERA
2021	Drhm	AAA	7	0	2	7.1	26	3	0	0	0	0	0	1	0	12	0	1	0	1.000	0- -	-		.274	0.55	0.00
2018	Mia	NL	25	25	0	126.1	547	121	65	62	15	5	4	5	54	5	130	8	4	9	.308	0-0	0	91	.754	4.18	4.42
2019	2 Tms		30	23	1	135.1	580	127	63	61	19	5	4	5	56	6	127	4	6	12	.333	0-0	1	91	.749	4.16	4.06
2020	TB	AL	9	4	1	32.0	150	44	24	21	6	1	1	0	11	0	27	1	0	0		0-0	0	91	.880	6.66	5.91
2021	3 Tms		53	0	10	64.1	251	40	26	25	12	1	0	0	22	1	78	8	7	2	.778	1-6	6	93	.612	2.40	3.50
19	Mia	NL	23	20	1	112.0	483	104	56	56	16	4	4	5	51	6	103	4	3	12	.200	0-0	1	91	.759	4.32	4.50
19	TB	AL	7	3	0	23.1	97	23	7	5	3	1	0	0	5	0	24	0	3	0	1.000	0-0	0	90	.693	3.43	1.93
21	TB	AL	6	0	2	12.0	47	9	6	6	2	0	0	0	3	0	16	1	1	1		1-1	0	92	.642	2.62	4.50
21	Mil	NL	15	0	3	19.2	82	15	7	7	3	1	0	0	9	1	25	6	3	0	1.000	0-2	0	93	.685	3.27	3.20
21	Tor	AL	32	0	5	32.2	122	16	13	12	7	0	0	0	10	0	37	1	4	2	.667	0-3	5	93	.552	1.82	3.31
	4 ML YEARS		117	52	12	358.0	1528	332	178	169	52	12	9	10	143	12	362	21	17	23	.425	1-6	7	91	.741	4.04	4.25

JT Riddle

Bats: L Throws: R Pos: SS-3;PR-1   Ht: 6'1" Wt: 190 Born: 10/12/1991 Age: 30

							BATTING												RUNNING			AVERAGES			
Year	Team	Lg	G	AB	H	2B	3B	HR	(Hm	Rd)	TB	R	RBI	RC	TBB	IBB	SO	HBP	SH	SF	SB	CS	GDP	Avg	OBP	Slg	OPS
2021	StPaul	AAA	91	317	64	13	2	7	(-	-)	102	42	40	-	23	1	62	7	0	3	3	3	9	.202	.269	.322	.590
2017	Mia	NL	70	228	57	13	1	3	(2	1)	81	20	31	24	12	2	50	0	2	5	0	2	6	.250	.282	.355	.637
2018	Mia	NL	102	308	71	10	4	9	(4	5)	116	28	36	31	20	1	67	0	3	1	0	3	4	.231	.277	.377	.653
2019	Mia	NL	51	132	25	6	0	6	(3	3)	49	15	12	7	5	1	42	0	0	0	0	0	3	.189	.230	.371	.601
2020	Pit	NL	23	67	10	2	0	1	(0	1)	15	8	1	0	2	0	13	0	0	0	1	0	0	.149	.174	.224	.398
2021	Min	AL	4	6	2	0	0	0	(0	0)	2	1	0	0	0	0	0	0	0	0	0	0	0	.333	.333	.333	.667
	5 ML YEARS		250	741	165	31	5	19	(9	10)	263	72	80	62	39	4	172	2	5	6	1	5	13	.223	.261	.355	.616

Stephen Ridings

Pitches: R Bats: R Pos: RP-5   Ht: 6'8" Wt: 220 Born: 8/14/1995 Age: 26

			HOW MUCH PITCHED					WHAT HE GAVE UP										THE RESULTS							
Year	Team	Lg	G	GS	GF	IP	BFP	H	R	ER	HR	SH	SF	HB	TBB	IBB	SO	WP	W	L	Pct	Sv-Op	Hld	Vel	OPS	ERC	ERA
2021	Smrst	AA	14	0	10	19.0	70	8	2	1	0	0	0	3	2	0	30	3	4	0	1.000	2- -	-		.355	0.77	0.47
2021	S-WB	AAA	8	0	6	10.0	40	8	6	3	2	0	0	0	2	0	12	0	1	0	1.000	1- -	-		.618	2.80	2.70
2021	NYY	AL	5	0	0	5.0	20	4	2	1	0	1	0	0	2	0	7	0	0	0		0-0	1	97	.728	2.46	1.80

Austin Riley

Bats: R Throws: R Pos: 3B-156;1B-10;PH-2;RF-1   Ht: 6'3" Wt: 240 Born: 4/2/1997 Age: 25

							BATTING												RUNNING			AVERAGES			
Year	Team	Lg	G	AB	H	2B	3B	HR	(Hm	Rd)	TB	R	RBI	RC	TBB	IBB	SO	HBP	SH	SF	SB	CS	GDP	Avg	OBP	Slg	OPS
2019	Atl	NL	80	274	62	11	1	18	(11	7)	129	41	49	38	16	3	108	5	0	2	0	2	4	.226	.279	.471	.750
2020	Atl	NL	51	188	45	7	1	8	(3	5)	78	24	27	24	16	1	49	1	0	1	0	0	1	.239	.301	.415	.716
2021	Atl	NL	160	590	179	33	1	33	(13	20)	313	91	107	111	52	2	168	12	0	8	0	1	11	.303	.367	.531	.898
	Postseason		12	45	8	0	0	1	(0	1)	11	4	4	2	3	1	18	1	0	0	0	0	0	.178	.245	.244	.489
	3 ML YEARS		291	1052	286	51	3	59	(27	32)	520	156	183	173	84	6	325	18	0	11	0	3	20	.272	.333	.494	.827

Edwin Rios

Bats: L **Throws:** R **Pos:** 1B-10;PH-10;3B-6;RF-2;DH-1 **Ht:** 6'3" **Wt:** 220 **Born:** 4/21/1994 **Age:** 28

								BATTING												RUNNING			AVERAGES			
Year	Team	Lg	G	AB	H	2B	3B	HR	(Hm Rd)	TB	R	RBI	RC	TBB	IBB	SO	HBP	SH	SF	SB	CS	GDP	Avg	OBP	Slg	OPS
2019	LAD	NL	28	47	13	2	1	4	(0 4)	29	10	8	10	9	0	21	0	0	0	0	0	1	.277	.393	.617	1.010
2020	LAD	NL	32	76	19	6	0	8	(4 4)	49	13	17	15	4	0	18	2	0	1	0	0	2	.250	.301	.645	.946
2021	LAD	NL	25	51	4	0	0	1	(0 1)	7	4	1	0	7	0	18	2	0	0	0	0	3	.078	.217	.137	.354
	Postseason		7	14	2	0	0	2	(0 2)	8	2	3	1	3	0	8	0	0	1	0	0	0	.143	.278	.571	.849
	3 ML YEARS		85	174	36	8	1	13	(4 9)	85	27	26	25	20	0	57	4	0	1	0	0	6	.207	.302	.489	.790

Yacksel Rios

Pitches: R **Bats:** R **Pos:** RP-23 **Ht:** 6'3" **Wt:** 215 **Born:** 6/27/1993 **Age:** 29

			HOW MUCH PITCHED					WHAT HE GAVE UP									THE RESULTS								
Year	Team	Lg	G	GS	GF	IP	BFP	H	R	ER	HR	SH	SF	HB	TBB	IBB	SO	WP	W	L	Pct	Sv-Op Hld	Vel	OPS	ERC	ERA
2021	Drham	AAA	12	0	7	13.2	49	8	2	1	1	0	0	0	2	0	17	1	2	0	1.000	2--	-	.481	1.26	0.66
2017	Phi	NL	13	0	7	16.1	73	15	8	8	4	1	0	0	9	1	17	0	1	0	1.000	0-0 0	94	.825	5.06	4.41
2018	Phi	NL	36	0	10	36.0	165	43	28	27	6	0	1	2	15	2	36	2	3	2	.600	0-0 2	96	.853	5.90	6.75
2019	2 Tms	NL	14	0	5	13.0	65	16	13	10	4	1	2	3	8	0	12	1	1	0	1.000	0-0 1	96	1.049	9.16	6.92
2020	Pit	NL	3	0	1	4.0	17	3	4	4	0	0	0	1	2	0	3	0	0	0	-	0-0 1	95	.639	3.44	9.00
2021	2 Tms	AL	23	0	6	27.1	114	18	13	13	3	0	1	1	16	0	23	4	3	0	1.000	0-0 1	97	.684	3.34	4.28
19	Phi	NL	4	0	3	2.2	19	6	7	4	2	1	1	1	3	0	2	1	0	0	-	0-0 0	96	1.632	24.00	13.50
19	Pit	NL	10	0	2	10.1	46	10	6	6	2	0	1	2	5	0	10	0	1	0	1.000	0-0 1	96	.843	5.87	5.23
21	Sea	AL	3	0	0	3.0	16	5	3	3	0	0	0	1	2	0	2	1	0	0	-	0-0 0	97	1.115	10.34	9.00
21	Bos	AL	20	0	6	24.1	98	13	10	10	3	0	1	1	14	0	21	3	3	0	1.000	0-0 1	97	.615	2.64	3.70
	5 ML YEARS		89	0	29	96.2	434	95	66	62	17	2	4	8	50	3	91	7	8	2	.800	0-0 5	96	.824	5.30	5.77

Webster Rivas

Bats: R **Throws:** R **Pos:** C-24;PH-2 **Ht:** 6'1" **Wt:** 219 **Born:** 8/8/1990 **Age:** 31

								BATTING												RUNNING			AVERAGES			
Year	Team	Lg	G	AB	H	2B	3B	HR	(Hm Rd)	TB	R	RBI	RC	TBB	IBB	SO	HBP	SH	SF	SB	CS	GDP	Avg	OBP	Slg	OPS
2021	ElPaso	AAA	52	163	41	8	0	5	(- -)	64	19	15	-	22	1	39	0	0	1	0	0	7	.252	.339	.393	.731
2021	SD	NL	24	68	15	2	0	2	(0 2)	23	8	4	3	8	0	16	0	1	0	0	0	6	.221	.303	.338	.641

Alfonso Rivas III

Bats: L **Throws:** L **Pos:** PH-6;1B-5;LF-5;RF-5 **Ht:** 5'11" **Wt:** 190 **Born:** 9/13/1996 **Age:** 25

								BATTING												RUNNING			AVERAGES			
Year	Team	Lg	G	AB	H	2B	3B	HR	(Hm Rd)	TB	R	RBI	RC	TBB	IBB	SO	HBP	SH	SF	SB	CS	GDP	Avg	OBP	Slg	OPS
2021	Iowa	AAA	58	197	56	13	0	4	(- -)	81	22	32	-	35	1	49	5	0	0	0	1	9	.284	.405	.411	.816
2021	ChC	NL	18	44	14	1	0	1	(0 1)	18	7	3	6	4	0	16	1	0	0	0	0	1	.318	.388	.409	.797

Emmanuel Rivera

Bats: R **Throws:** R **Pos:** 3B-28;1B-1 **Ht:** 6'2" **Wt:** 225 **Born:** 6/29/1996 **Age:** 26

								BATTING												RUNNING			AVERAGES			
Year	Team	Lg	G	AB	H	2B	3B	HR	(Hm Rd)	TB	R	RBI	RC	TBB	IBB	SO	HBP	SH	SF	SB	CS	GDP	Avg	OBP	Slg	OPS
2021	Omha	AAA	59	240	67	12	2	18	(- -)	137	46	52	-	18	0	55	3	0	2	3	0	7	.279	.335	.571	.905
2021	KC	AL	29	90	23	4	0	1	(0 1)	30	13	5	9	8	0	21	0	0	0	2	0	2	.256	.316	.333	.650

Rene Rivera

Bats: R **Throws:** R **Pos:** C-24;PH-1 ruh-NAY **Ht:** 5'10" **Wt:** 215 **Born:** 7/31/1983 **Age:** 38

								BATTING												RUNNING			AVERAGES			
Year	Team	Lg	G	AB	H	2B	3B	HR	(Hm Rd)	TB	R	RBI	RC	TBB	IBB	SO	HBP	SH	SF	SB	CS	GDP	Avg	OBP	Slg	OPS
2004	Sea	AL	2	3	0	0	0	0	(0 0)	0	0	0	0	0	0	1	0	0	0	0	0	0	.000	.000	.000	.000
2005	Sea	AL	16	48	19	3	0	1	(0 1)	25	3	6	8	1	0	11	0	1	0	0	0	0	.396	.408	.521	.929
2006	Sea	AL	35	99	15	4	0	2	(1 1)	25	8	4	4	3	0	29	1	3	0	1	0	2	.152	.184	.253	.437
2011	Min	AL	45	104	15	3	0	1	(0 1)	21	9	5	3	8	0	32	1	0	1	0	0	0	.144	.211	.202	.412
2013	SD	NL	23	67	17	3	1	0	(0 0)	22	4	7	6	2	1	16	0	0	2	0	0	1	.254	.268	.328	.596
2014	SD	NL	103	294	74	18	1	11	(1 10)	127	27	44	41	27	3	76	3	3	2	0	0	6	.252	.319	.432	.751
2015	TB	AL	110	298	53	14	0	5	(4 1)	82	16	26	16	11	0	86	3	5	2	0	0	4	.178	.213	.275	.489
2016	NYM	NL	65	185	41	4	0	6	(4 2)	63	12	26	19	16	3	54	3	1	2	0	0	4	.222	.291	.341	.632
2017	2 Tms	NL	74	218	55	9	0	10	(5 5)	94	23	35	29	14	3	70	3	1	1	0	1	4	.252	.305	.431	.736
2018	2 Tms		33	86	20	4	0	4	(2 2)	36	8	11	8	4	0	35	1	0	0	0	0	3	.233	.275	.419	.693
2019	NYM	NL	9	17	4	0	0	1	(1 0)	7	2	3	4	3	0	4	0	0	0	0	0	0	.235	.350	.412	.762
2020	NYM	NL	2	4	1	0	0	0	(0 0)	1	0	0	0	0	0	3	0	0	0	0	0	0	.250	.250	.250	.500
2021	2 Tms	NL	25	69	16	3	0	2	(0 2)	25	8	9	7	4	0	29	2	3	0	0	0	4	.232	.293	.362	.656
17	NYM	NL	54	174	40	4	0	8	(3 5)	68	15	23	18	9	3	54	3	0	1	0	1	3	.230	.278	.391	.669
17	ChC	NL	20	44	15	5	0	2	(2 0)	26	8	12	11	5	0	16	0	1	0	0	0	1	.341	.408	.591	.999
18	LAA	AL	30	82	20	4	0	4	(2 2)	36	8	11	8	4	0	32	1	0	0	0	0	3	.244	.287	.439	.726
18	Atl	NL	3	4	0	0	0	0	(0 0)	0	0	0	0	0	0	3	0	0	0	0	0	0	.000	.000	.000	.000
21	Cle	AL	21	55	13	3	0	2	(0 2)	22	6	9	7	4	0	24	1	3	0	0	0	2	.236	.300	.400	.700
21	Was	NL	4	14	3	0	0	0	(0 0)	3	2	0	0	0	0	5	1	0	0	0	0	2	.214	.267	.214	.481
	Postseason		1	3	1	0	0	0	(0 0)	1	0	0	0	0	0	0	0	0	0	0	0	0	.333	.333	.333	.627
	13 ML YEARS		542	1492	330	65	2	43	(18 25)	528	120	176	145	93	10	446	17	17	10	1	1	30	.221	.273	.354	.627

Sebastian Rivero

Bats: R **Throws:** R **Pos:** C-17   **Ht:** 6'1" **Wt:** 210 **Born:** 11/16/1998 **Age:** 23

					BATTING																RUNNING			AVERAGES			
Year	Team	Lg	G	AB	H	2B	3B	HR	(Hm	Rd)	TB	R	RBI	RC	TBB	IBB	SO	HBP	SH	SF	SB	CS	GDP	Avg	OBP	Slg	OPS
2021	Omha	AAA	42	150	39	7	1	3	(-	-)	57	18	26	-	10	1	45	3	0	0	2	1	3	.260	.319	.380	.699
2021	KC	AL	17	40	7	2	0	0	(0	0)	9	1	3	0	3	0	15	1	0	0	0	0	1	.175	.250	.225	.475

Anthony Rizzo

Bats: L **Throws:** L **Pos:** 1B-139;PH-2;2B-1   **Ht:** 6'3" **Wt:** 240 **Born:** 8/8/1989 **Age:** 32

					BATTING																RUNNING			AVERAGES			
Year	Team	Lg	G	AB	H	2B	3B	HR	(Hm	Rd)	TB	R	RBI	RC	TBB	IBB	SO	HBP	SH	SF	SB	CS	GDP	Avg	OBP	Slg	OPS
2011	SD	NL	49	128	18	8	1	1	(1	0)	31	9	9	7	21	1	46	4	0	0	2	1	2	.141	.281	.242	.523
2012	ChC	NL	87	337	96	15	0	15	(7	8)	156	44	48	57	27	1	62	3	0	1	3	2	7	.285	.342	.463	.805
2013	ChC	NL	160	606	141	40	2	23	(13	10)	254	71	80	74	76	7	127	6	0	2	6	5	12	.233	.323	.419	.742
2014	ChC	NL	140	524	150	28	1	32	(14	18)	276	89	78	99	73	7	116	15	0	4	5	4	8	.286	.386	.527	.913
2015	ChC	NL	160	586	163	38	3	31	(11	20)	300	94	101	115	78	9	105	30	0	7	17	6	9	.278	.387	.512	.899
2016	ChC	NL	155	583	170	43	4	32	(12	20)	317	94	109	119	74	8	108	16	0	3	3	5	13	.292	.385	.544	.928
2017	ChC	NL	157	572	156	32	3	32	(15	17)	290	99	109	116	91	11	90	24	0	4	10	4	21	.273	.392	.507	.899
2018	ChC	NL	153	566	160	29	1	25	(13	12)	266	74	101	97	70	15	80	20	0	9	6	4	11	.283	.376	.470	.846
2019	ChC	NL	146	512	150	29	3	27	(13	14)	266	89	94	111	71	3	86	27	0	3	5	2	15	.293	.405	.520	.924
2020	ChC	NL	58	203	45	6	0	11	(4	7)	84	26	24	25	28	4	38	10	0	2	3	1	6	.222	.342	.414	.755
2021	2 Tms		141	496	123	23	3	22	(10	12)	218	73	61	75	52	2	87	23	0	5	6	2	15	.248	.344	.440	.783
21	ChC	NL	92	323	80	16	3	14	(7	7)	144	41	40	49	36	2	59	14	0	3	4	2	10	.248	.346	.446	.792
21	NYY	AL	49	173	43	7	0	8	(3	5)	74	32	21	26	16	0	28	9	0	2	2	0	5	.249	.340	.428	.768
	Postseason		39	146	30	6	0	6	(3	3)	54	16	18	16	12	2	38	4	0	0	2	0	4	.205	.284	.370	.654
	11 ML YEARS		1406	5113	1372	291	21	251	(113	138)	2458	762	814	895	661	68	945	178	0	40	66	36	119	.268	.369	.481	.850

Tanner Roark

Pitches: R **Bats:** R **Pos:** RP-2; SP-1   **Ht:** 6'2" **Wt:** 238 **Born:** 10/5/1986 **Age:** 35
ROW-ark

			HOW MUCH PITCHED					WHAT HE GAVE UP										THE RESULTS							
Year	Team	Lg	G	GS	GF	IP	BFP	H	R	ER	HR	SH	SF	HB	TBB	IBB	SO	WP	W	L	Pct	Sv-Op	Hld	Vel	OPS	ERC	ERA
2021	Gwnntt	AAA	24	3	4	46.1	188	38	11	11	2	1	0	3	16	0	44	3	4	1	.800	3--	-	-	.626	2.85	2.14
2013	Was	NL	14	5	1	53.2	204	38	11	9	1	3	2	0	11	0	40	0	7	1	.875	0-0	0	93	.473	1.54	1.51
2014	Was	NL	31	31	0	198.2	798	178	64	63	16	5	2	6	39	1	138	0	15	10	.600	0-0	0	91	.632	2.76	2.85
2015	Was	NL	40	12	8	111.0	467	119	55	54	17	4	4	5	26	3	70	0	4	7	.364	1-2	4	93	.784	4.39	4.38
2016	Was	NL	34	33	0	210.0	855	173	72	66	17	10	1	13	73	4	172	6	16	10	.615	0-0	1	92	.634	3.08	2.83
2017	Was	NL	32	30	0	181.1	776	178	105	94	23	3	2	6	64	5	166	3	13	11	.542	0-0	0	92	.729	4.06	4.67
2018	Was	NL	31	30	1	180.1	760	181	90	87	24	4	6	10	50	3	146	5	9	15	.375	0-0	0	91	.741	4.07	4.34
2019	2 Tms		31	31	0	165.1	722	180	84	80	28	0	2	13	51	1	158	3	10	10	.500	0-0	0	92	.806	5.05	4.35
2020	Tor	AL	11	11	0	47.2	220	60	39	36	14	0	1	2	23	0	41	2	2	3	.400	0-0	0	91	1.000	7.85	6.80
2021	Tor	AL	3	1	1	7.0	31	7	7	5	3	0	0	0	2	0	5	0	0	1	.000	0-0	0	91	.877	5.51	6.43
19	Cin	NL	21	21	0	110.1	484	119	55	52	14	0	1	9	38	1	108	0	6	7	.462	0-0	0	92	.774	4.84	4.24
19	Oak	AL	10	10	0	55.0	238	61	29	28	14	0	1	4	13	0	50	3	4	3	.571	0-0	0	92	.868	5.44	4.58
	Postseason		3	1	1	7.0	35	10	3	3	2	0	0	1	3	1	4	0	1	0	1.000	0-0	0	94	.916	8.56	3.86
	9 ML YEARS		227	184	11	1155.0	4833	1114	527	494	143	29	20	55	339	17	936	19	76	68	.528	1-2	6	92	.717	3.83	3.85

Luis Robert

Bats: R **Throws:** R **Pos:** CF-67;DH-1   **Ht:** 6'2" **Wt:** 220 **Born:** 8/3/1997 **Age:** 24

					BATTING																RUNNING			AVERAGES			
Year	Team	Lg	G	AB	H	2B	3B	HR	(Hm	Rd)	TB	R	RBI	RC	TBB	IBB	SO	HBP	SH	SF	SB	CS	GDP	Avg	OBP	Slg	OPS
2020	CWS	AL	56	202	47	8	0	11	(6	5)	88	33	31	30	20	0	73	1	0	2	9	2	4	.233	.302	.436	.738
2021	CWS	AL	68	275	93	22	1	13	(8	5)	156	42	43	53	14	1	61	5	0	2	6	1	4	.338	.378	.567	.946
	Postseason		3	13	4	0	0	1	(0	1)	7	2	2	1	0	0	4	0	0	0	0	0	0	.308	.308	.538	.846
	2 ML YEARS		124	477	140	30	1	24	(14	10)	244	75	74	83	34	1	134	6	0	4	15	3	8	.294	.345	.512	.857

Daniel Robertson

Bats: R **Throws:** R **Pos:** 3B-24;PH-16;2B-9;SS-8;1B-3;PR-1   **Ht:** 5'11" **Wt:** 210 **Born:** 3/22/1994 **Age:** 28

					BATTING																RUNNING			AVERAGES			
Year	Team	Lg	G	AB	H	2B	3B	HR	(Hm	Rd)	TB	R	RBI	RC	TBB	IBB	SO	HBP	SH	SF	SB	CS	GDP	Avg	OBP	Slg	OPS
2021	Nashv	AAA	28	78	9	3	0	0	(-	-)	12	6	3	-	10	0	25	0	0	0	0	0	3	.115	.216	.154	.370
2017	TB	AL	75	218	45	7	2	5	(4	1)	71	22	19	23	29	0	73	4	1	2	1	1	5	.206	.308	.326	.634
2018	TB	AL	88	282	74	16	0	9	(5	4)	117	46	34	40	43	0	77	13	0	2	2	2	7	.262	.382	.415	.797
2019	TB	AL	74	207	44	9	1	2	(0	2)	61	23	19	16	24	0	59	6	0	0	2	2	10	.213	.312	.295	.607
2020	SF	NL	13	21	7	0	0	0	(0	0)	7	4	2	4	3	0	6	0	0	0	0	0	0	.333	.417	.333	.750
2021	Mil	NL	50	73	12	2	0	2	(1	1)	20	10	4	5	12	1	28	3	1	1	0	0	1	.164	.303	.274	.577
	5 ML YEARS		300	801	182	34	3	18	(10	8)	276	105	78	88	111	1	243	26	2	5	5	5	23	.227	.338	.345	.683

David Robertson

Pitches: R **Bats:** R **Pos:** RP-11; SP-1   **Ht:** 5'11" **Wt:** 195 **Born:** 4/9/1985 **Age:** 37

			HOW MUCH PITCHED					WHAT HE GAVE UP										THE RESULTS							
Year	Team	Lg	G	GS	GF	IP	BFP	H	R	ER	HR	SH	SF	HB	TBB	IBB	SO	WP	W	L	Pct	Sv-Op	Hld	Vel	OPS	ERC	ERA
2021	Drham	AAA	6	0	1	6.0	22	4	1	0	0	0	0	1	2	0	12	1	0	0	-	0--	-	-	.473	1.73	0.00
2008	NYY	AL	25	0	8	30.1	131	29	18	18	3	0	3	0	15	2	36	1	4	0	1.000	0-0	0	91	.690	4.12	5.34
2009	NYY	AL	45	0	20	43.2	191	36	19	16	4	0	0	1	23	1	63	6	2	1	.667	1-1	5	92	.685	3.51	3.30
2010	NYY	AL	64	0	10	61.1	273	59	26	26	5	5	3	3	33	6	71	7	4	5	.444	1-3	14	92	.721	4.29	3.82
2011	NYY	AL	70	0	8	66.2	272	40	9	8	1	1	0	1	35	6	100	6	4	0	1.000	1-4	34	93	.506	1.85	1.08

Year	Team	Lg	G	GS	GF	IP	BFP	H	R	ER	HR	SH	SF	HB	TBB	IBB	SO	WP	W	L	Pct	Sv-Op	Hld	Vel	OPS	ERC	ERA
			HOW MUCH PITCHED					**WHAT HE GAVE UP**											**THE RESULTS**								
2012	NYY	AL	65	0	17	60.2	248	52	19	18	5	0	1	1	19	0	81	1	2	7	.222	2-5	30	92	.638	2.95	2.67
2013	NYY	AL	70	0	9	66.1	262	51	15	15	5	3	0	2	18	1	77	1	5	1	.833	3-5	33	92	.584	2.37	2.04
2014	NYY	AL	63	0	55	64.1	259	45	23	22	7	1	0	1	23	2	96	0	4	5	.444	39-44	0	92	.588	2.41	3.08
2015	CWS	AL	60	0	53	63.1	250	46	27	24	7	0	0	1	13	2	86	4	6	5	.545	34-41	0	92	.573	2.00	3.41
2016	CWS	AL	62	0	48	62.1	267	53	24	24	6	3	2	1	32	4	75	1	5	3	.625	37-44	0	91	.684	3.63	3.47
2017	2 Tms	AL	61	0	34	68.1	264	35	14	14	6	0	1	3	23	5	98	7	9	2	.818	14-16	8	91	.488	1.50	1.84
2018	NYY	AL	69	0	11	69.2	283	46	30	25	7	4	1	0	26	1	91	1	8	3	.727	5-9	21	92	.595	2.15	3.23
2019	Phi	NL	7	0	3	6.2	33	8	4	4	1	0	0	0	6	0	6	0	0	1	.000	0-0	2	92	.869	7.88	5.40
2021	TB	AL	12	1	1	12.0	50	11	7	6	2	0	0	0	4	0	16	0	0	0	-	0-2	2	92	.713	3.81	4.50
17	CWS	AL	31	0	28	33.1	132	21	10	10	4	0	0	2	11	3	47	3	4	2	.667	13-14	0	91	.577	2.14	2.70
17	NYY	AL	30	0	6	35.0	132	14	4	4	2	0	1	1	12	2	51	4	5	0	1.000	1-2	8	92	.399	1.05	1.03
	Postseason		30	0	9	33.2	136	26	13	13	4	1	0	1	10	3	40	2	5	0	1.000	0-1	3	92	.637	2.59	3.48
	13 ML YEARS		673	1	277	675.2	2783	511	235	220	59	17	11	14	270	30	896	40	53	33	.616	137-174	149	92	.613	2.70	2.93

Hansel Robles

Pitches: R Bats: R Pos: RP-72   Ht: 6'0" Wt: 220 Born: 8/13/1990 Age: 31

Year	Team	Lg	G	GS	GF	IP	BFP	H	R	ER	HR	SH	SF	HB	TBB	IBB	SO	WP	W	L	Pct	Sv-Op	Hld	Vel	OPS	ERC	ERA
			HOW MUCH PITCHED					**WHAT HE GAVE UP**											**THE RESULTS**								
2015	NYM	NL	57	0	7	54.0	217	37	27	22	8	1	1	2	18	1	61	2	4	3	.571	0-4	12	96	.659	2.57	3.67
2016	NYM	NL	68	0	15	77.2	331	69	32	30	7	1	5	1	36	4	85	3	6	4	.600	1-3	13	95	.703	3.62	3.48
2017	NYM	NL	46	0	9	56.2	247	47	31	31	10	3	2	5	29	2	60	2	7	5	.583	0-2	5	95	.750	4.38	4.92
2018	2 Tms		53	0	14	56.0	242	53	26	23	9	2	3	2	25	1	59	2	2	3	.400	2-3	8	96	.771	4.53	3.70
2019	LAA	AL	71	1	51	72.2	283	58	20	20	6	2	3	0	16	1	75	4	5	1	.833	23-27	2	97	.595	2.28	2.48
2020	LAA	AL	18	0	16	16.2	80	19	20	19	4	1	1	1	10	0	20	1	0	2	.000	1-3	0	96	.917	6.96	10.26
2021	2 Tms		72	0	21	69.0	297	58	39	34	8	1	0	5	37	3	76	4	3	5	.375	14-16	17	97	.735	4.10	4.43
18	NYM	NL	16	0	3	19.2	88	21	11	11	7	1	1	1	10	1	23	1	2	2	.500	0-0	2	95	.981	7.12	5.03
18	LAA	AL	37	0	11	36.1	154	32	15	12	2	1	2	1	15	0	36	1	0	1	.000	2-3	6	97	.654	3.27	2.97
21	Min	AL	45	0	16	44.0	188	37	28	24	6	1	0	3	24	1	43	2	3	4	.429	10-12	14	97	.761	4.35	4.91
21	Bos	AL	27	0	5	25.0	109	21	11	10	2	0	0	2	13	2	33	2	0	1	.000	4-4	3	97	.692	3.68	3.60
	Postseason		3	0	2	3.0	9	0	0	0	0	0	0	0	0	0	4	0	0	0	-	0-0	0	97	.000	0.00	0.00
	7 ML YEARS		385	1	122	402.2	1697	341	195	179	52	11	15	16	171	12	436	18	27	23	.540	41-58	57	96	.711	3.65	4.00

Victor Robles

Bats: R Throws: R Pos: CF-104;PH-9   Ht: 6'0" Wt: 205 Born: 5/19/1997 Age: 25

Year	Team	Lg	G	AB	H	2B	3B	HR	(Hm	Rd)	TB	R	RBI	RC	TBB	IBB	SO	HBP	SH	SF	SB	CS	GDP	Avg	OBP	Slg	OPS
						BATTING															**RUNNING**			**AVERAGES**			
2021	Roch	AAA	20	75	25	8	1	4	(-	-)	47	13	8	-	5	0	22	2	1	0	6	1	0	.333	.390	.627	1.017
2017	Was	NL	13	24	6	1	2	0	(0	0)	11	2	4	3	0	0	6	2	1	0	0	1	2	.250	.308	.458	.766
2018	Was	NL	21	59	17	3	1	3	(2	1)	31	8	10	10	4	0	12	2	0	1	3	2	2	.288	.348	.525	.874
2019	Was	NL	155	546	139	33	3	17	(10	7)	229	86	65	79	35	3	140	25	6	5	28	9	6	.255	.326	.419	.745
2020	Was	NL	52	168	37	5	1	3	(2	1)	53	20	15	18	9	0	53	9	1	2	4	1	0	.220	.293	.315	.608
2021	Was	NL	107	315	64	21	1	2	(2	0)	93	37	19	30	33	3	85	16	4	1	8	6	7	.203	.310	.295	.605
	Postseason		14	42	9	1	1	1	(1	0)	15	9	3	3	2	0	16	1	1	0	1	0	2	.214	.267	.357	.624
	5 ML YEARS		348	1112	263	63	8	25	(16	9)	417	153	113	140	81	6	296	54	12	9	43	19	17	.237	.317	.375	.692

Jacob Robson

Bats: L Throws: R Pos: LF-3;CF-1;PH-1;PR-1   Ht: 5'10" Wt: 182 Born: 11/20/1994 Age: 27

Year	Team	Lg	G	AB	H	2B	3B	HR	(Hm	Rd)	TB	R	RBI	RC	TBB	IBB	SO	HBP	SH	SF	SB	CS	GDP	Avg	OBP	Slg	OPS
						BATTING															**RUNNING**			**AVERAGES**			
2021	Erie	AA	18	66	28	9	2	2	(-	-)	47	17	10	-	14	0	21	1	1	0	4	1	0	.424	.531	.712	1.243
2021	Toledo	AAA	73	223	61	10	3	5	(-	-)	92	35	27	-	43	0	96	3	0	0	14	9	2	.274	.398	.413	.810
2021	Det	AL	4	7	0	0	0	0	(0	0)	0	1	0	0	0	0	4	0	0	0	0	0	0	.000	.000	.000	.000

Brendan Rodgers

Bats: R Throws: R Pos: 2B-81;SS-26;PH-6   Ht: 6'0" Wt: 204 Born: 8/9/1996 Age: 25

Year	Team	Lg	G	AB	H	2B	3B	HR	(Hm	Rd)	TB	R	RBI	RC	TBB	IBB	SO	HBP	SH	SF	SB	CS	GDP	Avg	OBP	Slg	OPS
						BATTING															**RUNNING**			**AVERAGES**			
2019	Col	NL	25	76	17	2	0	0	(0	0)	19	8	7	5	4	0	27	1	0	0	0	0	2	.224	.272	.250	.522
2020	Col	NL	7	21	2	1	0	0	(0	0)	3	1	2	0	0	0	6	0	0	0	0	0	0	.095	.095	.143	.238
2021	Col	NL	102	387	110	21	3	15	(3	12)	182	49	51	58	19	0	84	7	0	2	0	0	8	.284	.328	.470	.798
	3 ML YEARS		134	484	129	24	3	15	(3	12)	204	58	60	63	23	0	117	8	0	2	0	0	10	.267	.309	.421	.731

Carlos Rodon

Pitches: L Bats: L Pos: SP-24   Ht: 6'3" Wt: 245 Born: 12/10/1992 Age: 29

roh-DON

Year	Team	Lg	G	GS	GF	IP	BFP	H	R	ER	HR	SH	SF	HB	TBB	IBB	SO	WP	W	L	Pct	Sv-Op	Hld	Vel	OPS	ERC	ERA
			HOW MUCH PITCHED					**WHAT HE GAVE UP**											**THE RESULTS**								
2015	CWS	AL	26	23	1	139.1	607	130	63	58	11	6	5	6	71	0	139	7	9	6	.600	0-0	0	93	.725	4.25	3.75
2016	CWS	AL	28	28	0	165.0	715	176	82	74	23	4	6	6	54	3	168	11	9	10	.474	0-0	0	93	.763	4.57	4.04
2017	CWS	AL	12	12	0	69.1	297	64	35	32	12	1	2	3	31	0	76	4	2	5	.286	0-0	0	93	.770	4.57	4.15
2018	CWS	AL	20	20	0	120.2	511	97	61	56	15	0	2	12	55	1	90	4	6	8	.429	0-0	0	93	.698	3.80	4.18
2019	CWS	AL	7	7	0	34.2	158	33	22	20	4	0	2	1	17	0	46	5	3	2	.600	0-0	0	92	.714	4.19	5.19
2020	CWS	AL	4	2	0	7.2	35	9	7	7	1	0	0	1	3	0	6	1	0	2	.000	0-1	0	93	.920	5.87	8.22
2021	CWS	AL	24	24	0	132.2	534	91	39	35	13	3	5	8	36	1	185	7	13	5	.722	0-0	0	95	.560	2.14	2.37
	Postseason		1	0	0	0.0	3	1	2	2	0	0	0	0	2	1	0	0	0	0	-	0-0	0	96	3.000	-	-
	7 ML YEARS		121	116	1	669.1	2857	600	309	282	79	14	22	39	267	5	710	39	42	38	.525	0-1	0	94	.705	3.84	3.79

Chris Rodriguez

Pitches: R **Bats:** R **Pos:** RP-13; SP-2

Ht: 6'2" **Wt:** 185 **Born:** 7/20/1998 **Age:** 23

Year	Team	Lg	G	GS	GF	IP	BFP	H	R	ER	HR	SH	SF	HB	TBB	IBB	SO	WP	W	L	Pct	Sv-Op	Hld	Vel	OPS	ERC	ERA
2021	Rock	AA	5	5	0	12.2	58	15	9	6	1	0	0	0	5	0	17	2	0	0		0- -	-	-	.684	4.83	4.26
2021	LAA	AL	15	2	1	29.2	134	28	14	12	0	0	0	4	15	0	29	1	2	1	.667	0-1	2	96	.664	3.90	3.64

Eduardo Rodriguez

Pitches: L **Bats:** L **Pos:** SP-31; RP-1

Ht: 6'2" **Wt:** 231 **Born:** 4/7/1993 **Age:** 29

Year	Team	Lg	G	GS	GF	IP	BFP	H	R	ER	HR	SH	SF	HB	TBB	IBB	SO	WP	W	L	Pct	Sv-Op	Hld	Vel	OPS	ERC	ERA
2015	Bos	AL	21	21	0	121.2	522	120	55	52	13	5	4	4	37	1	98	4	10	6	.625	0-0	0	94	.701	3.73	3.85
2016	Bos	AL	20	20	0	107.0	458	99	58	56	16	1	4	3	40	1	100	0	3	7	.300	0-0	0	93	.728	3.96	4.71
2017	Bos	AL	25	24	1	137.1	582	126	66	64	19	1	3	5	50	1	150	1	6	7	.462	0-0	0	93	.736	3.87	4.19
2018	Bos	AL	27	23	1	129.2	553	119	56	55	16	0	3	4	45	1	146	1	13	5	.722	0-0	0	93	.681	3.63	3.82
2019	Bos	AL	34	34	0	203.1	859	195	88	86	24	2	5	7	75	2	213	3	19	6	.760	0-0	0	93	.714	4.03	3.81
2021	Bos	AL	32	31	0	157.2	675	172	87	83	19	2	2	2	47	0	185	0	13	8	.619	0-0	0	93	.766	4.41	4.74
	Postseason		8	1	2	10.0	44	7	9	9	2	0	0	2	5	1	11	0	0	0		0-0	1	94	.697	4.04	8.10
6 ML YEARS			159	153	1	856.2	3649	831	410	396	107	11	21	25	294	6	892	9	64	39	.621	0-0	0	93	.722	3.96	4.16

Grayson Rodriguez

Pitches: R **Bats:** L **Pos:** P

Ht: 6'5" **Wt:** 220 **Born:** 11/16/1999 **Age:** 22

Year	Team	Lg	G	GS	GF	IP	BFP	H	R	ER	HR	SH	SF	HB	TBB	IBB	SO	WP	W	L	Pct	Sv-Op	Hld	Vel	OPS	ERC	ERA
2018	Orioles	R	9	8	0	19.1	80	17	6	3	0	0	1	0	7	0	20	2	0	2	.000	0- -	-	-	.674	2.64	1.40
2019	Dlmrva	A	20	20	0	94.0	377	57	30	28	4	0	4	4	36	0	129	8	10	4	.714	0- -	-	-	.337	1.80	2.68
2021	Abrdn	A+	5	5	0	23.1	88	11	4	4	2	0	0	3	5	0	40	1	3	0	1.000	0- -	-	-		1.35	1.54
2021	Bowie	AA	18	18	0	79.2	310	47	26	23	8	0	0	3	22	0	121	3	6	1	.857	0- -	-	-	.539	1.70	2.60

Jefry Rodriguez

Pitches: R **Bats:** R **Pos:** RP-13; SP-1

Ht: 6'6" **Wt:** 232 **Born:** 7/26/1993 **Age:** 28

Year	Team	Lg	G	GS	GF	IP	BFP	H	R	ER	HR	SH	SF	HB	TBB	IBB	SO	WP	W	L	Pct	Sv-Op	Hld	Vel	OPS	ERC	ERA
2021	Roch	AAA	11	10	0	41.1	176	34	24	20	4	2	0	2	21	0	43	6	2	0	1.000	0- -	-	-	.679	3.72	4.35
2018	Was	AL	14	8	1	52.0	233	43	35	33	8	3	1	3	37	5	39	2	3	3	.500	0-0	0	95	.784	4.81	5.71
2019	Cle	AL	10	8	1	46.2	203	48	26	24	5	1	3	0	21	1	33	4	1	5	.167	0-0	0	94	.769	4.49	4.63
2021	Was	NL	14	1	10	24.1	112	25	16	16	6	0	0	1	17	0	20	4	0	0		0-0	0	95	.852	6.92	5.92
3 ML YEARS			38	17	12	123.0	548	116	77	73	19	4	4	4	75	6	92	10	4	8	.333	0-0	0	95	.792	5.09	5.34

Joely Rodriguez

Pitches: L **Bats:** L **Pos:** RP-52

joe-EL-ee

Ht: 6'1" **Wt:** 200 **Born:** 11/14/1991 **Age:** 30

Year	Team	Lg	G	GS	GF	IP	BFP	H	R	ER	HR	SH	SF	HB	TBB	IBB	SO	WP	W	L	Pct	Sv-Op	Hld	Vel	OPS	ERC	ERA
2016	Phi	NL	12	0	1	9.2	39	8	3	3	0	0	0	1	4	1	7	0	0	0		0-0	3	95	.598	2.91	2.79
2017	Phi	NL	26	0	4	27.0	134	37	26	19	4	1	0	4	15	3	18	0	1	2	.333	0-2	3	93	.930	7.81	6.33
2020	Tex	AL	12	0	2	12.2	52	8	3	3	0	1	0	0	5	0	17	1	0	0		0-1	3	95	.494	1.56	2.13
2021	2 Tms	AL	52	0	8	46.1	207	53	27	24	4	2	5	0	18	1	47	3	2	3	.400	1-3	13	94	.739	4.67	4.66
21	Tex	AL	31	0	6	27.1	128	32	19	18	3	1	2	0	12	1	30	1	1	3	.250	1-2	9	94	.748	5.01	5.93
21	NYY	AL	21	0	2	19.0	79	21	8	6	1	1	3	0	6	0	17	2	1	0	1.000	0-1	4	94	.723	4.18	2.84
4 ML YEARS			102	0	15	95.2	432	106	59	49	8	4	5	5	42	5	89	4	3	5	.375	1-6	22	94	.755	4.82	4.61

Julio Rodriguez

Bats: R **Throws:** R **Pos:** RF

Ht: 6'3" **Wt:** 180 **Born:** 12/29/2000 **Age:** 21

Year	Team	Lg	G	AB	H	2B	3B	HR	(Hm	Rd)	TB	R	RBI	RC	TBB	IBB	SO	HBP	SH	SF	SB	CS	GDP	Avg	OBP	Slg	OPS
2019	2 Tms	Low	84	328	107	26	4	12	(-	-)	177	63	69	68	25	1	76	11	0	3	1	3	10	.326	.390	.540	.929
2021	Ark	AA	46	174	63	11	0	7	(-	-)	95	35	26	-	29	1	37	3	0	0	16	4	2	.362	.461	.546	1.007
2021	Everett	A+	28	117	38	8	2	6	(-	-)	68	29	21	0	14	0	29	3	0	0	5	1	3	.325	.410	.581	.992

Manuel Rodriguez

Pitches: R **Bats:** R **Pos:** RP-20

Ht: 5'11" **Wt:** 210 **Born:** 8/6/1996 **Age:** 25

Year	Team	Lg	G	GS	GF	IP	BFP	H	R	ER	HR	SH	SF	HB	TBB	IBB	SO	WP	W	L	Pct	Sv-Op	Hld	Vel	OPS	ERC	ERA
2021	Tenn	AA	13	0	10	13.1	59	8	5	3	1	0	1	3	10	0	19	0	1	1	.500	4- -	-	-	.600	3.92	2.03
2021	Iowa	AAA	7	0	3	7.1	28	6	0	0	0	0	0	0	2	0	8	0	0	0		1- -	-	-	.516	2.18	0.00
2021	ChC	NL	20	0	8	17.2	83	18	18	12	3	0	0	1	12	1	16	1	3	3	.500	1-1	1	97	.816	5.94	6.11

Nivaldo Rodriguez

Pitches: R Bats: R Pos: RP-4 · Ht: 6'1" Wt: 214 Born: 4/16/1997 Age: 25

Year Team	Lg	G	GS	GF	IP	BFP	H	R	ER	HR	SH	SF	HB	TBB	IBB	SO	WP	W	L	Pct	Sv-Op	Hld	Vel	OPS	ERC	ERA
2021 SgrLnd	AAA	10	6	1	27.1	128	33	19	18	5	0	0	0	16	0	25	3	2	1	.667	0- -	-		.883	6.76	5.93
2021 Toledo	AAA	12	4	1	29.2	134	33	22	16	6	0	1	0	12	0	17	2	2	1	.667	0- -	-		.807	5.37	4.85
2020 Hou	AL	5	0	3	8.2	46	15	7	6	3	0	1	0	6	1	8	1	0	1	.000	0-0	0	93	1.123	12.18	6.23
2021 Hou	AL	4	0	4	7.1	31	4	2	2	2	0	0	3	4	0	3	0	0	0		0-0	0	92	.813	5.22	2.45
2 ML YEARS		9	0	7	16.0	77	19	9	8	5	0	1	3	10	1	11	1	0	1	.000	0-0	0	92	1.003	8.83	4.50

Richard Rodriguez

Pitches: R Bats: R Pos: RP-64 · Ht: 6'4" Wt: 220 Born: 3/4/1990 Age: 32

Year Team	Lg	G	GS	GF	IP	BFP	H	R	ER	HR	SH	SF	HB	TBB	IBB	SO	WP	W	L	Pct	Sv-Op	Hld	Vel	OPS	ERC	ERA
2017 Bal	AL	5	0	1	5.2	31	12	9	9	4	0	0	1	3	1	3	0	0	0	-	0-0	0	94	1.516	19.81	14.29
2018 Pit	NL	63	0	20	69.1	279	55	19	19	5	1	1	5	19	3	88	11	4	3	.571	0-0	15	93	.596	2.58	2.47
2019 Pit	NL	72	0	12	65.1	285	65	30	27	14	0	1	2	23	3	63	1	4	5	.444	1-5	16	93	.751	4.62	3.72
2020 Pit	NL	24	0	15	23.1	93	15	8	7	3	0	1	2	5	0	34	3	3	2	.600	4-5	2	93	.537	2.00	2.70
2021 2 Tms	NL	64	0	36	64.1	251	50	21	21	8	0	0	2	10	1	42	4	5	4	.556	14-17	8	93	.619	2.26	2.94
21 Pit	NL	37	0	33	38.1	145	27	12	12	2	0	0	1	5	0	33	2	4	2	.667	14-17	0	93	.523	1.54	2.82
21 Atl	NL	27	0	3	26.0	106	23	9	9	6	0	0	1	5	1	9	2	1	2	.333	0-0	8	93	.754	3.53	3.12
5 ML YEARS		228	0	84	228.0	939	197	87	83	34	1	3	12	60	8	230	19	16	14	.533	19-27	41	93	.673	3.27	3.28

Chaz Roe

Pitches: R Bats: R Pos: RP-1 · ROW · Ht: 6'5" Wt: 190 Born: 10/9/1986 Age: 35

Year Team	Lg	G	GS	GF	IP	BFP	H	R	ER	HR	SH	SF	HB	TBB	IBB	SO	WP	W	L	Pct	Sv-Op	Hld	Vel	OPS	ERC	ERA
2021 Drham	AAA	7	0	0	6.1	28	6	6	5	0	0	1	0	3	0	7	0	0	0	-	0- -	-		.655	3.27	7.11
2013 Ari	NL	21	0	4	22.1	95	18	10	10	3	2	1	0	13	3	24	1	1	0	1.000	0-2	1	91	.726	3.78	4.03
2014 NYY	AL	3	0	2	2.0	13	3	3	2	0	1	0	0	3	0	4	1	0	0		0-0	0	91	1.239	9.89	9.00
2015 Bal	AL	36	0	6	41.1	177	44	19	19	4	1	1	1	17	2	38	1	4	2	.667	0-1	4	93	.798	4.62	4.14
2016 2 Tms		30	0	11	29.2	124	22	12	12	2	0	2	1	14	1	37	1	2	0	1.000	0-1	3	93	.672	2.82	3.64
2017 2 Tms		12	0	3	10.2	44	7	5	3	1	0	0	1	5	0	13	1	0	0		0-0	1	93	.585	2.84	2.53
2018 TB	AL	61	0	6	50.1	203	35	21	20	6	1	0	8	16	1	53	1	1	3	.250	1-2	31	92	.629	2.90	3.58
2019 TB	AL	71	0	11	51.0	229	49	27	23	3	0	1	1	31	2	65	3	1	3	.250	1-5	23	92	.704	4.36	4.06
2020 TB	AL	10	0	4	9.1	39	10	4	3	0	0	1	1	3	0	9	0	2	0	1.000	1-1	2	91	.771	4.08	2.89
2021 TB	AL	1	0	0	0.2	4	1	2	2	0	0	0	0	1	0	2	0	0	0		0-0	0	92	1.500	10.76	27.00
16 Bal	AL	9	0	6	9.2	44	8	4	4	2	0	0	0	7	0	11	1	1	0	1.000	0-0	0	92	.800	5.07	3.72
16 Atl	AL	21	0	5	20.0	80	14	8	8	0	0	2	1	7	1	26	0	1	0	1.000	0-1	3	93	.604	1.86	3.60
17 Atl	NL	3	0	0	2.0	13	3	4	2	0	0	0	0	2	0	1	0	0	0		0-0	0	93	.762	9.89	9.00
17 TB	AL	9	0	3	8.2	31	4	1	1	1	0	0	1	3	0	12	1	0	0		0-0	1	93	.512	1.51	1.04
Postseason		3	0	0	2.2	12	3	2	2	0	0	0	0	1	0	2	0	0	0	-	0-0	0	94	.697	3.84	6.75
9 ML YEARS		245	0	47	217.1	928	189	103	94	19	4	7	13	103	9	245	8	11	8	.579	3-12	66	92	.710	3.76	3.89

Jake Rogers

Bats: R Throws: R Pos: C-37;3B-1;PH-1 · Ht: 6'1" Wt: 201 Born: 4/18/1995 Age: 27

Year Team	Lg	G	AB	H	2B	3B	HR	(Hm	Rd)	TB	R	RBI	RC	TBB	IBB	SO	HBP	SH	SF	SB	CS	GDP	Avg	OBP	Slg	OPS
2019 Det	AL	35	112	14	3	0	4	(3	1)	29	11	8	4	13	0	51	1	2	0	0	0	3	.125	.222	.259	.481
2021 Det	AL	38	113	27	5	3	6	(3	3)	56	17	17	17	11	0	46	0	3	0	1	0	0	.239	.306	.496	.802
2 ML YEARS		73	225	41	8	3	10	(6	4)	85	28	25	21	24	0	97	1	5	0	1	0	3	.182	.264	.378	.642

Josh Rogers

Pitches: L Bats: L Pos: SP-6 · Ht: 6'3" Wt: 210 Born: 7/10/1994 Age: 27

Year Team	Lg	G	GS	GF	IP	BFP	H	R	ER	HR	SH	SF	HB	TBB	IBB	SO	WP	W	L	Pct	Sv-Op	Hld	Vel	OPS	ERC	ERA
2021 Roch	AAA	14	13	0	73.0	314	75	32	30	8	0	2	4	21	0	49	1	7	3	.700	0- -	-		.726	4.05	3.70
2018 Bal	AL	3	3	0	11.2	56	17	11	11	2	0	1	0	5	0	6	0	1	2	.333	0-0	0	90	.953	7.52	8.49
2019 Bal	AL	5	0	1	14.1	69	18	14	14	7	0	0	4	6	0	5	0	0	1	.000	0-0	0	89	1.118	10.35	8.79
2021 Was	NL	6	6	0	35.2	151	32	13	13	7	1	1	2	14	0	22	0	2	2	.500	0-0	0	90	.756	4.40	3.28
3 ML YEARS		14	9	1	61.2	276	67	38	38	16	1	2	6	25	0	33	0	3	5	.375	0-0	0	90	.885	6.24	5.55

Taylor Rogers

Pitches: L Bats: L Pos: RP-40 · Ht: 6'3" Wt: 190 Born: 12/17/1990 Age: 31

Year Team	Lg	G	GS	GF	IP	BFP	H	R	ER	HR	SH	SF	HB	TBB	IBB	SO	WP	W	L	Pct	Sv-Op	Hld	Vel	OPS	ERC	ERA
2016 Min	AL	57	0	8	61.1	264	63	29	27	7	0	1	5	16	3	64	1	3	1	.750	0-0	9	93	.719	3.99	3.96
2017 Min	AL	69	0	7	55.2	237	52	20	19	6	2	0	3	21	5	49	1	7	3	.700	0-4	30	93	.693	3.76	3.07
2018 Min	AL	72	0	6	68.1	260	49	20	20	3	1	3	2	16	3	75	0	1	2	.333	2-4	18	93	.553	1.83	2.63
2019 Min	AL	60	0	36	69.0	278	58	20	20	8	3	0	6	11	2	90	2	2	4	.333	30-36	10	95	.625	2.70	2.61
2020 Min	AL	21	0	16	20.0	91	26	14	9	2	0	0	1	4	0	24	1	2	4	.333	9-11	2	95	.806	5.07	4.05
2021 Min	AL	40	0	15	40.1	166	38	18	15	4	2	2	0	8	2	59	3	2	4	.333	9-13	6	96	.651	2.88	3.35
Postseason		4	0	0	3.1	14	4	2	2	0	0	0	0	1	0	4	0	0	0	-	0-0	0	95	.742	4.29	5.40
6 ML YEARS		319	0	88	314.2	1296	286	121	110	30	8	6	17	76	15	361	8	17	18	.486	50-68	77	94	.658	3.09	3.15

Trevor Rogers

Pitches: L Bats: L Pos: SP-25   Ht: 6'5" Wt: 217 Born: 11/13/1997 Age: 24

Year	Team	Lg	G	GS	GF	IP	BFP	H	R	ER	HR	SH	SF	HB	TBB	IBB	SO	WP	W	L	Pct	Sv-Op	Hld	Vel	OPS	ERC	ERA
2020	Mia	NL	7	7	0	28.0	130	32	20	19	5	0	2	2	13	0	39	0	1	2	.333	0-0	0	94	.866	5.99	6.11
2021	Mia	NL	25	25	0	133.0	550	107	46	39	6	6	2	5	46	2	157	4	7	8	.467	0-0	0	95	.609	2.58	2.64
	Postseason		1	0	0	1.2	10	4	3	2	0	0	0	0	1	0	2	0	0	0	-	0-0	0	96	1.167	13.02	10.80
2 ML YEARS			32	32	0	161.0	680	139	66	58	11	6	4	7	59	2	196	4	8	10	.444	0-0	0	94	.658	3.11	3.24

Tyler Rogers

Pitches: R Bats: R Pos: RP-80   Ht: 6'3" Wt: 181 Born: 12/17/1990 Age: 31

Year	Team	Lg	G	GS	GF	IP	BFP	H	R	ER	HR	SH	SF	HB	TBB	IBB	SO	WP	W	L	Pct	Sv-Op	Hld	Vel	OPS	ERC	ERA
2019	SF	NL	17	0	4	17.2	70	12	3	2	0	1	0	1	3	0	16	1	2	0	1.000	0-2	5	82	.463	1.37	1.02
2020	SF	NL	29	0	6	28.0	123	31	16	14	2	1	0	4	6	0	27	0	3	3	.500	3-6	10	83	.711	4.27	4.50
2021	SF	NL	80	0	18	81.0	326	74	23	20	5	1	2	5	13	0	55	0	7	1	.875	13-19	30	83	.611	2.73	2.22
3 ML YEARS			126	0	28	126.2	519	117	42	36	7	3	2	10	22	0	98	1	12	4	.750	16-27	45	83	.614	2.82	2.56

Jose Rojas

Bats: L Throws: R Pos: RF-25;2B-14;3B-12;LF-9;PH-9;1B-2;PR-2;DH-1   Ht: 6'0" Wt: 200 Born: 2/24/1993 Age: 29

Year	Team	Lg	G	AB	H	2B	3B	HR	(Hm	Rd)	TB	R	RBI	RC	TBB	IBB	SO	HBP	SH	SF	SB	CS	GDP	Avg	OBP	Slg	OPS
2021	Salt Lk	AAA	55	216	56	11	1	8	(-	-)	93	32	34	-	23	1	38	0	0	2	4	1	3	.259	.328	.431	.758
2021	LAA	AL	61	168	35	14	0	6	(4	2)	67	26	15	18	15	0	50	1	0	0	2	1	2	.208	.277	.399	.676

Josh Rojas

Bats: L Throws: R Pos: 2B-55;SS-42;RF-37;LF-18;PH-16;3B-14;PR-1   Ht: 6'1" Wt: 207 Born: 6/30/1994 Age: 28

Year	Team	Lg	G	AB	H	2B	3B	HR	(Hm	Rd)	TB	R	RBI	RC	TBB	IBB	SO	HBP	SH	SF	SB	CS	GDP	Avg	OBP	Slg	OPS
2019	Ari	NL	41	138	30	7	2	2	(2	0)	43	17	16	15	18	0	41	1	0	0	4	2	3	.217	.312	.312	.624
2020	Ari	NL	17	61	11	0	0	0	(0	0)	11	9	2	2	7	0	16	0	0	2	1	1	1	.180	.257	.180	.437
2021	Ari	NL	139	484	128	32	3	11	(6	5)	199	69	44	66	58	1	137	0	1	3	9	4	7	.264	.341	.411	.752
3 ML YEARS			197	683	169	39	3	13	(8	5)	253	95	62	83	83	1	194	1	1	5	14	7	11	.247	.328	.370	.698

Miguel Rojas

Bats: R Throws: R Pos: SS-128;PH-8   Ht: 6'0" Wt: 188 Born: 2/24/1989 Age: 33

Year	Team	Lg	G	AB	H	2B	3B	HR	(Hm	Rd)	TB	R	RBI	RC	TBB	IBB	SO	HBP	SH	SF	SB	CS	GDP	Avg	OBP	Slg	OPS
2014	LAD	NL	85	149	27	3	0	1	(0	1)	33	16	9	6	10	1	28	2	1	0	0	0	5	.181	.242	.221	.464
2015	Mia	NL	60	142	40	7	1	1	(1	0)	52	13	17	15	11	1	16	0	2	2	0	1	4	.282	.329	.366	.695
2016	Mia	NL	123	194	48	12	0	1	(0	1)	63	27	14	14	11	2	27	1	6	2	2	1	10	.247	.288	.325	.613
2017	Mia	NL	90	272	79	16	2	1	(1	0)	102	37	26	32	27	5	32	4	1	2	2	1	6	.290	.361	.375	.736
2018	Mia	NL	153	488	123	13	0	11	(4	7)	169	44	53	51	24	2	69	9	2	4	6	3	23	.252	.297	.346	.643
2019	Mia	NL	132	483	137	29	1	5	(3	2)	183	52	46	63	32	2	62	5	1	5	9	5	15	.284	.331	.379	.710
2020	Mia	NL	40	125	38	10	1	4	(2	2)	62	20	20	28	16	2	18	2	0	1	5	1	1	.304	.392	.496	.888
2021	Mia	NL	132	495	131	30	3	9	(4	5)	194	66	48	64	37	0	74	5	1	1	13	3	10	.265	.322	.392	.713
	Postseason		6	19	3	0	0	1	(0	1)	6	2	1	0	1	1	3	1	0	0	0	0	0	.158	.238	.316	.554
8 ML YEARS			815	2348	623	120	8	33	(15	18)	858	275	233	273	168	15	326	28	14	16	37	15	74	.265	.320	.365	.685

Jordan Romano

Pitches: R Bats: R Pos: RP-62   Ht: 6'5" Wt: 225 Born: 4/21/1993 Age: 29

Year	Team	Lg	G	GS	GF	IP	BFP	H	R	ER	HR	SH	SF	HB	TBB	IBB	SO	WP	W	L	Pct	Sv-Op	Hld	Vel	OPS	ERC	ERA
2019	Tor	AL	17	0	2	15.1	75	17	14	13	4	0	0	4	9	0	21	0	0	2	.000	0-0	5	95	.884	7.90	7.63
2020	Tor	AL	15	0	3	14.2	57	8	3	2	2	0	0	0	5	0	21	0	2	1	.667	2-3	5	97	.517	1.77	1.23
2021	Tor	AL	62	0	43	63.0	253	41	17	15	7	1	0	1	25	0	85	2	7	1	.875	23-24	5	98	.576	2.37	2.14
3 ML YEARS			94	0	48	93.0	385	66	34	30	13	1	0	5	39	0	127	2	9	4	.692	25-27	15	97	.625	3.04	2.90

Sal Romano

Pitches: R Bats: L Pos: RP-19   Ht: 6'5" Wt: 255 Born: 10/12/1993 Age: 28

Year	Team	Lg	G	GS	GF	IP	BFP	H	R	ER	HR	SH	SF	HB	TBB	IBB	SO	WP	W	L	Pct	Sv-Op	Hld	Vel	OPS	ERC	ERA
2021	S-WB	AAA	25	0	10	30.1	131	36	18	12	1	0	3	1	5	0	25	2	1	1	.500	2--	-	-	.678	3.82	3.56
2017	Cin	NL	16	16	0	87.0	384	91	49	43	9	6	4	4	37	2	73	5	5	8	.385	0-0	0	95	.799	4.61	4.45
2018	Cin	NL	39	25	1	145.2	644	155	92	86	23	3	4	4	53	6	105	7	8	11	.421	0-0	2	94	.784	4.69	5.31
2019	Cin	NL	12	0	4	16.1	77	22	14	14	4	0	1	1	8	1	16	1	1	0	1.000	2-2	1	96	1.029	8.05	7.71
2020	Cin	NL	2	0	1	1.1	4	0	0	0	0	0	0	0	0	0	0	0	1	0	1.000	0-0	0	95	.000	0.00	0.00
2021	3 Tms	NL	19	0	6	25.0	118	31	20	17	5	0	1	1	11	2	17	0	0	2	.000	0-0	1	94	.855	6.32	6.12
21	Cin	NL	14	0	5	20.2	91	20	14	12	4	0	0	0	9	2	12	0	0	0	-	0-0	0	93	.746	4.44	5.23
21	NYY	AL	4	0	0	3.1	20	7	2	2	0	0	1	0	2	0	5	0	0	1	.000	0-0	1	95	1.029	12.26	5.40
21	Mil	NL	1	0	1	1.0	7	4	4	3	1	0	0	1	0	0	0	0	0	1	.000	0-0	0	95	1.714	34.98	27.00
5 ML YEARS			88	41	12	275.1	1227	299	175	160	41	9	11	10	109	11	211	13	15	21	.417	2-2	4	95	.808	4.95	5.23

Jhon Romero

Pitches: R **Bats:** R **Pos:** RP-5 **Ht:** 5'10" **Wt:** 195 **Born:** 1/17/1995 **Age:** 27

			HOW MUCH PITCHED				WHAT HE GAVE UP										THE RESULTS							
Year	Team	Lg	G	GS	GF	IP	BFP	H	R	ER	HR	SH	SF	HB	TBB	IBB	SO	WP	W	L	Pct	Sv-Op	Hld	Vel	OPS	ERC	ERA
2021	Hrsbrg	AA	33	0	9	47.2	199	45	17	15	5	1	0	3	10	1	58	2	2	4	.333	2- -	-	-	.660	3.25	2.83
2021	Roch	AAA	5	0	0	7.1	27	5	1	1	0	0	0	0	1	0	11	0	0	0	-	0- -	-	-	.568	1.78	1.23
2021	Was	NL	5	0	1	4.0	17	5	2	2	0	0	1	0	0	0	3	0	0	0	-	0-0	0	95	.857	3.14	4.50

JoJo Romero

Pitches: L **Bats:** L **Pos:** RP-11 **Ht:** 5'11" **Wt:** 200 **Born:** 9/9/1996 **Age:** 25

			HOW MUCH PITCHED				WHAT HE GAVE UP										THE RESULTS							
Year	Team	Lg	G	GS	GF	IP	BFP	H	R	ER	HR	SH	SF	HB	TBB	IBB	SO	WP	W	L	Pct	Sv-Op	Hld	Vel	OPS	ERC	ERA
2020	Phi	NL	12	0	2	10.2	47	13	10	9	1	1	0	2	2	0	10	0	0	0	-	0-0	4	95	.822	5.30	7.59
2021	Phi	NL	11	0	1	9.0	44	12	8	7	4	0	0	1	4	1	8	0	0	0	-	0-0	3	94	1.053	9.26	7.00
	2 ML YEARS		23	0	3	19.2	91	25	18	16	5	1	0	3	6	1	18	0	0	0	-	0-0	7	95	.933	7.07	7.32

Andrew Romine

Bats: B **Throws:** R **Pos:** SS-16;PH-8;2B-2;PR-1 ROW-mine **Ht:** 6'1" **Wt:** 190 **Born:** 12/24/1985 **Age:** 36

			BATTING																	RUNNING			AVERAGES			
Year	Team	Lg	G	AB	H	2B	3B	HR	(Hm	Rd)	TB	R	RBI	RC	TBB	IBB	SO	HBP	SH	SF	SB	CS	GDP	Avg	OBP	Slg	OPS
2021	Iowa	AAA	57	197	58	7	2	1	(-	-)	72	28	15	-	18	0	40	2	7	0	2	4	6	.294	.359	.365	.725
2010	LAA	AL	5	11	1	0	0	0	(0	0)	1	0	0	0	0	0	4	0	0	0	0	0	0	.091	.091	.091	.182
2011	LAA	AL	10	16	2	0	0	0	(0	0)	2	2	0	0	1	0	6	0	1	0	1	0	0	.125	.176	.125	.301
2012	LAA	AL	12	17	7	0	0	0	(0	0)	7	2	1	5	3	0	3	0	1	0	1	0	0	.412	.500	.412	.912
2013	LAA	AL	47	108	28	3	0	0	(0	0)	31	9	10	12	7	0	24	1	6	1	1	0	2	.259	.308	.287	.595
2014	Det	AL	94	251	57	6	0	2	(1	1)	69	30	12	17	18	0	60	0	4	0	12	2	5	.227	.279	.275	.554
2015	Det	AL	109	184	47	5	0	2	(0	2)	58	25	15	13	11	1	46	3	4	1	10	5	4	.255	.307	.315	.622
2016	Det	AL	109	174	41	5	2	2	(1	1)	56	21	16	15	13	0	38	4	3	0	8	0	5	.236	.304	.322	.626
2017	Det	AL	124	318	74	17	2	4	(3	1)	107	45	25	27	22	0	67	4	2	2	6	4	7	.233	.289	.336	.625
2018	Sea	AL	75	119	25	2	1	0	(0	0)	29	15	2	4	7	0	39	1	4	0	1	0	2	.210	.260	.244	.504
2020	Tex	AL	2	4	1	0	0	0	(0	0)	2	1	0	0	0	0	1	0	0	0	0	0	0	.250	.250	.500	.750
2021	ChC	NL	26	60	11	2	0	1	(1	0)	16	7	5	4	4	0	24	0	0	0	0	1	1	.183	.234	.267	.501
	Postseason		3	11	2	0	0	0	(0	0)	2	0	0	0	0	0	4	0	0	0	0	0	0	.182	.182	.182	.364
	11 ML YEARS		613	1262	294	41	5	11	(6	5)	378	157	86	97	86	1	312	13	26	4	40	12	26	.233	.288	.300	.587

Austin Romine

Bats: R **Throws:** R **Pos:** C-21;PH-9 ROW-mine **Ht:** 6'1" **Wt:** 216 **Born:** 11/22/1988 **Age:** 33

			BATTING																	RUNNING			AVERAGES			
Year	Team	Lg	G	AB	H	2B	3B	HR	(Hm	Rd)	TB	R	RBI	RC	TBB	IBB	SO	HBP	SH	SF	SB	CS	GDP	Avg	OBP	Slg	OPS
2011	NYY	AL	9	19	3	0	0	0	(0	0)	3	2	0	0	1	0	5	0	0	0	0	0	0	.158	.200	.158	.358
2013	NYY	AL	60	135	28	9	0	1	(0	1)	40	15	10	8	8	0	37	1	3	1	1	0	7	.207	.255	.296	.551
2014	NYY	AL	7	13	3	1	0	0	(0	0)	4	2	1	2	0	0	4	0	0	0	0	0	0	.231	.231	.308	.538
2015	NYY	AL	1	2	0	0	0	0	(0	0)	0	0	0	0	0	0	0	0	0	0	0	0	0	.000	.000	.000	.000
2016	NYY	AL	62	165	40	11	0	4	(1	3)	63	17	26	19	7	1	31	0	1	3	1	0	7	.242	.269	.382	.650
2017	NYY	AL	80	229	50	9	1	2	(2	0)	67	19	21	18	16	0	57	2	2	3	0	0	7	.218	.272	.293	.565
2018	NYY	AL	77	242	59	12	0	10	(3	7)	101	30	42	32	17	0	67	2	1	3	1	0	10	.244	.295	.417	.713
2019	NYY	AL	73	228	64	12	0	8	(2	6)	100	29	35	30	10	0	50	0	1	1	1	1	7	.281	.310	.439	.748
2020	Det	AL	37	130	31	5	0	2	(1	1)	42	12	17	13	4	0	47	0	0	1	0	0	3	.238	.259	.323	.582
2021	ChC	NL	28	60	13	2	0	1	(1	0)	18	5	5	2	2	0	22	0	0	0	0	0	4	.217	.242	.300	.542
	Postseason		3	2	0	0	0	0	(0	0)	0	0	0	0	0	0	0	0	0	0	0	0	0	.000	.000	.000	.000
	10 ML YEARS		434	1223	291	61	1	28	(10	18)	438	131	157	124	65	1	320	5	8	12	4	1	45	.238	.277	.358	.635

Sergio Romo

Pitches: R **Bats:** R **Pos:** RP-66 **Ht:** 5'11" **Wt:** 185 **Born:** 3/4/1983 **Age:** 39

			HOW MUCH PITCHED				WHAT HE GAVE UP											THE RESULTS							
Year	Team	Lg	G	GS	GF	IP	BFP	H	R	ER	HR	SH	SF	HB	TBB	IBB	SO	WP	W	L	Pct	Sv-Op	Hld	Vel	OPS	ERC	ERA
2008	SF	NL	29	0	8	34.0	130	16	13	8	3	2	1	3	8	1	33	0	3	1	.750	0-0	5	89	.470	1.27	2.12
2009	SF	NL	45	0	9	34.0	143	30	15	15	1	2	0	1	11	0	41	2	5	2	.714	2-2	10	90	.631	2.76	3.97
2010	SF	NL	68	0	13	62.0	247	46	16	15	6	2	2	4	14	2	70	0	5	3	.625	0-4	21	89	.599	2.26	2.18
2011	SF	NL	65	0	16	48.0	175	29	8	8	2	2	0	0	5	1	70	0	3	1	.750	1-2	23	89	.458	1.08	1.50
2012	SF	NL	69	0	27	55.1	215	37	11	11	5	2	0	3	10	1	63	2	4	2	.667	14-15	23	88	.525	1.72	1.79
2013	SF	NL	65	0	52	60.1	250	53	20	17	5	1	1	1	12	3	58	1	5	8	.385	38-43	0	88	.614	2.47	2.54
2014	SF	NL	64	0	35	58.0	230	43	24	24	9	2	0	4	12	2	59	2	6	4	.600	23-28	11	88	.622	2.54	3.72
2015	SF	NL	70	0	14	57.1	230	51	20	19	3	2	1	2	10	2	71	4	0	5	.000	2-4	34	87	.622	2.37	2.98
2016	SF	NL	40	0	13	30.2	117	26	9	9	5	0	0	0	7	1	33	1	1	0	1.000	4-4	14	86	.709	3.13	2.64
2017	2 Tms		55	0	12	55.2	224	42	23	22	9	2	0	2	19	2	59	2	3	1	.750	0-11	11	86	.661	2.97	3.56
2018	TB	AL	73	5	38	67.1	284	65	31	31	11	2	2	2	20	0	75	2	3	4	.429	25-33	9	86	.718	4.02	4.14
2019	2 Tms		65	0	33	60.1	249	50	27	23	7	0	4	2	17	3	60	3	2	1	.667	20-23	17	86	.649	2.83	3.43
2020	Min	AL	24	0	7	20.0	87	16	9	9	3	0	1	3	7	0	23	0	1	2	.333	5-6	10	86	.667	3.58	4.05
2021	Oak	AL	66	0	18	61.2	259	56	33	32	7	1	2	2	21	2	60	1	1	1	.500	3-7	12	86	.709	3.73	4.67
	17 LAD	NL	30	0	8	25.0	108	23	17	17	7	0	0	0	12	1	31	0	1	1	.500	0-0	7	87	.845	5.15	6.12
	17 TB	AL	25	0	4	30.2	116	19	6	5	2	0	1	1	7	1	28	2	2	0	1.000	0-1	4	86	.494	1.54	1.47
	19 Mia	NL	38	0	28	37.2	156	33	18	15	4	0	3	0	13	3	33	2	2	1	.667	17-18	1	86	.673	3.12	3.58
	19 Min	AL	27	0	5	22.2	93	17	9	8	3	0	1	2	4	0	27	1	0	0	-	3-5	16	86	.608	2.35	3.18
	Postseason		30	0	13	26.0	106	22	13	10	4	0	0	0	6	0	23	1	3	2	.600	4-7	4	88	.634	2.89	3.46
	14 ML YEARS		798	5	295	704.2	2840	560	259	243	78	17	13	27	173	20	775	20	42	35	.545	137-172	200	88	.623	2.57	3.10

Angel Rondon

Pitches: R **Bats:** R **Pos:** RP-2 **Ht:** 6'1" **Wt:** 205 **Born:** 12/1/1997 **Age:** 24

Year	Team	Lg	G	GS	GF	IP	BFP	H	R	ER	HR	SH	SF	HB	TBB	IBB	SO	WP	W	L	Pct	Sv-Op	Hld	Vel	OPS	ERC	ERA
2021	Memp	AAA	19	13	0	76.2	339	85	46	39	15	2	3	3	22	0	68	1	6	4	.600	0--	-	-	.805	4.99	4.58
2021	StL	NL	2	0	1	2.0	7	1	0	0	0	0	0	0	1	0	1	0	0	0	-	0-0	0	93	.452	1.62	0.00

Jose Rondon

Bats: R **Throws:** R **Pos:** PH-44;3B-7;RF-7;2B-2;LF-2;DH-2;PR-2;1B-1   rohn-DOHN **Ht:** 6'1" **Wt:** 215 **Born:** 3/3/1994 **Age:** 28

Year	Team	Lg	G	AB	H	2B	3B	HR	(Hm	Rd)	TB	R	RBI	RC	TBB	IBB	SO	HBP	SH	SF	SB	CS	GDP	Avg	OBP	Slg	OPS
2021	Memp	AAA	21	85	20	3	0	6	(-	-)	41	14	19	-	8	0	22	0	0	0	0	0	4	.235	.301	.482	.783
2016	SD	NL	8	25	3	0	0	0	(0	0)	3	1	1	1	1	0	4	0	0	0	0	0	1	.120	.154	.120	.274
2018	CWS	AL	42	100	23	6	0	6	(2	4)	47	15	14	11	7	0	30	0	0	0	2	1	3	.230	.280	.470	.750
2019	2 Tms	AL	56	143	28	3	0	3	(3	0)	40	10	9	7	11	0	38	2	1	0	0	0	4	.196	.263	.280	.543
2021	StL	NL	63	80	21	3	0	3	(2	1)	33	13	9	11	8	0	17	0	0	2	2	0	1	.263	.322	.413	.735
19	CWS	AL	55	142	28	3	0	3	(3	0)	40	10	9	7	11	0	38	2	1	0	0	0	4	.197	.265	.282	.546
19	Bal	AL	1	1	0	0	0	0	(0	0)	0	0	0	0	0	0	0	0	0	0	0	0	0	.000	.000	.000	.000
	4 ML YEARS		169	348	75	12	0	12	(7	5)	123	39	33	30	27	0	89	2	1	2	4	1	9	.216	.274	.353	.628

Brent Rooker

Bats: R **Throws:** R **Pos:** LF-38;DH-10;RF-8;PH-6 **Ht:** 6'3" **Wt:** 225 **Born:** 11/1/1994 **Age:** 27

Year	Team	Lg	G	AB	H	2B	3B	HR	(Hm	Rd)	TB	R	RBI	RC	TBB	IBB	SO	HBP	SH	SF	SB	CS	GDP	Avg	OBP	Slg	OPS
2021	StPaul	AAA	62	220	54	8	1	20	(-	-)	124	40	49	-	38	2	80	6	0	3	1	2	7	.245	.367	.564	.931
2020	Min	AL	7	19	6	2	0	1	(0	1)	11	4	5	5	0	0	5	2	0	0	0	0	1	.316	.381	.579	.960
2021	Min	AL	58	189	38	10	0	9	(6	3)	75	25	16	18	15	0	70	9	0	0	0	0	1	.201	.291	.397	.688
	2 ML YEARS		65	208	44	12	0	10	(6	4)	86	29	21	23	15	0	75	11	0	0	0	0	1	.212	.299	.413	.713

Ben Rortvedt

Bats: L **Throws:** R **Pos:** C-39;PH-2;PR-1 **Ht:** 5'10" **Wt:** 205 **Born:** 9/25/1997 **Age:** 24

Year	Team	Lg	G	AB	H	2B	3B	HR	(Hm	Rd)	TB	R	RBI	RC	TBB	IBB	SO	HBP	SH	SF	SB	CS	GDP	Avg	OBP	Slg	OPS
2021	StPaul	AAA	34	122	31	6	0	5	(-	-)	52	18	22	-	10	0	35	3	0	1	0	0	3	.254	.324	.426	.750
2021	Min	AL	39	89	15	1	0	3	(2	1)	25	8	7	2	6	0	29	1	2	0	0	0	2	.169	.229	.281	.510

Amed Rosario

Bats: R **Throws:** R **Pos:** SS-121;CF-18;PH-6;DH-3 **Ht:** 6'2" **Wt:** 190 **Born:** 11/20/1995 **Age:** 26

Year	Team	Lg	G	AB	H	2B	3B	HR	(Hm	Rd)	TB	R	RBI	RC	TBB	IBB	SO	HBP	SH	SF	SB	CS	GDP	Avg	OBP	Slg	OPS
2017	NYM	NL	46	165	41	4	4	4	(1	3)	65	16	10	14	3	0	49	2	0	0	7	3	3	.248	.271	.394	.665
2018	NYM	NL	154	554	142	26	8	9	(4	5)	211	76	51	60	29	4	119	3	3	3	24	11	9	.256	.295	.381	.676
2019	NYM	NL	157	616	177	30	7	15	(8	7)	266	75	72	79	31	2	124	3	2	3	19	10	13	.287	.323	.432	.755
2020	NYM	NL	46	143	36	3	1	4	(0	4)	53	20	15	10	4	0	34	0	0	0	1	1	5	.252	.272	.371	.643
2021	Cle	AL	141	550	155	25	6	11	(5	6)	225	77	57	82	31	0	120	3	0	4	13	0	12	.282	.321	.409	.731
	5 ML YEARS		544	2028	551	88	26	43	(18	25)	820	264	205	245	98	6	446	11	5	10	63	25	42	.272	.307	.404	.712

Eddie Rosario

Bats: L **Throws:** R **Pos:** LF-100;PH-7;DH-6;RF-1 **Ht:** 6'1" **Wt:** 180 **Born:** 9/28/1991 **Age:** 30

Year	Team	Lg	G	AB	H	2B	3B	HR	(Hm	Rd)	TB	R	RBI	RC	TBB	IBB	SO	HBP	SH	SF	SB	CS	GDP	Avg	OBP	Slg	OPS
2021	Gwnntt	AAA	13	51	10	2	0	4	(-	-)	24	7	16	-	2	0	6	0	0	0	0	0	2	.196	.226	.471	.697
2015	Min	AL	122	453	121	18	15	13	(10	3)	208	60	50	58	15	3	118	0	3	3	11	6	5	.267	.289	.459	.748
2016	Min	AL	92	335	90	17	2	10	(4	6)	141	52	32	35	12	2	91	2	2	3	5	2	4	.269	.295	.421	.716
2017	Min	AL	151	542	157	33	2	27	(20	7)	275	79	78	77	35	1	106	0	4	8	9	8	10	.290	.328	.507	.836
2018	Min	AL	138	559	161	31	2	24	(15	9)	268	87	77	79	30	5	104	0	1	2	8	2	9	.288	.323	.479	.803
2019	Min	AL	137	562	155	28	1	32	(12	20)	281	91	109	88	22	2	86	0	0	6	3	1	10	.276	.300	.500	.800
2020	Min	AL	57	210	54	7	0	13	(6	7)	100	31	42	37	19	2	34	0	0	2	3	1	3	.257	.316	.476	.792
2021	2 Tms		111	379	98	19	3	14	(6	8)	165	42	62	55	26	0	61	1	2	4	11	3	4	.259	.305	.435	.740
21	Cle	AL	78	283	72	15	1	7	(2	5)	110	29	46	38	17	0	47	1	2	3	9	2	3	.254	.296	.389	.685
21	Atl	NL	33	96	26	4	2	7	(4	3)	55	13	16	17	9	0	14	0	0	1	2	1	1	.271	.330	.573	.903
	Postseason		6	23	5	1	0	2	(1	1)	12	2	3	1	1	0	6	0	0	0	0	0	1	.217	.250	.522	.772
	7 ML YEARS		808	3040	836	153	25	133	(73	60)	1438	442	450	429	159	15	600	3	12	28	50	23	40	.275	.309	.473	.782

Trevor Rosenthal

Pitches: R **Bats:** R **Pos:** P **Ht:** 6'2" **Wt:** 230 **Born:** 5/29/1990 **Age:** 32

Year	Team	Lg	G	GS	GF	IP	BFP	H	R	ER	HR	SH	SF	HB	TBB	IBB	SO	WP	W	L	Pct	Sv-Op	Hld	Vel	OPS	ERC	ERA
2012	StL	NL	19	0	7	22.2	89	14	7	7	2	1	0	1	7	0	25	1	0	2	.000	0-0	3	98	.513	1.89	2.78
2013	StL	NL	74	0	15	75.1	311	63	25	22	4	0	3	6	20	0	108	3	2	4	.333	3-8	29	97	.608	2.68	2.63
2014	StL	NL	72	0	59	70.1	308	57	25	25	2	2	4	4	42	5	87	1	2	6	.250	45-51	2	97	.641	3.36	3.20
2015	StL	NL	68	0	57	68.2	287	62	16	16	3	1	0	1	25	3	83	7	2	4	.333	48-51	0	98	.619	3.04	2.10
2016	StL	NL	45	0	27	40.1	197	48	22	20	3	1	0	3	29	0	56	0	2	4	.333	14-18	0	97	.792	6.59	4.46
2017	StL	NL	50	0	16	47.2	202	37	20	18	3	1	3	2	20	0	76	2	3	4	.429	11-13	12	98	.572	2.80	3.40
2019	2 Tms		22	0	8	15.1	85	11	24	23	0	1	1	4	26	0	17	9	0	1	.000	0-0	1	98	.715	7.67	13.50

Year Team	Lg	G	GS	GF	IP	BFP	H	R	ER	HR	SH	SF	HB	TBB	IBB	SO	WP	W	L	Pct	Sv-Op	Hld	Vel	OPS	ERC	ERA
2020 2 Tms		23	0	18	23.2	91	12	6	5	2	0	1	1	8	0	38	0	1	0	1.000	11-12	1	98	.527	1.54	1.90
19 Was	NL	12	0	5	6.1	43	8	16	16	0	0	1	3	15	0	5	5	0	1	.000	0-0	1	98	.938	15.78	22.74
19 Det	AL	10	0	3	9.0	42	3	8	7	0	1	0	1	11	0	12	4	0	0	-	0-0	1	98	.504	3.04	7.00
20 KC	AL	14	0	9	13.2	56	9	5	5	2	0	0	1	7	0	21	0	0	0	-	7-7	1	98	.699	3.32	3.29
20 SD	NL	9	0	9	10.0	35	3	1	0	0	0	1	0	1	0	17	0	1	0	1.000	4-5	0	98	.266	0.30	0.00
Postseason		27	0	19	30.0	125	20	8	8	1	0	0	1	16	3	48	1	1	0	1.000	8-10	2	98	.583	2.34	2.40
8 ML YEARS		373	0	207	364.0	1570	304	145	136	19	10	9	22	177	8	490	23	12	25	.324	132-153	49	97	.632	3.34	3.36

Joe Ross

Pitches: R Bats: R Pos: SP-19; RP-1   **Ht: 6'4" Wt: 223 Born: 5/21/1993 Age: 29**

Year Team	Lg	G	GS	GF	IP	BFP	H	R	ER	HR	SH	SF	HB	TBB	IBB	SO	WP	W	L	Pct	Sv-Op	Hld	Vel	OPS	ERC	ERA
2015 Was	NL	16	13	1	76.2	314	64	33	31	7	3	1	2	21	0	69	1	5	5	.500	0-0	0	93	.628	2.74	3.64
2016 Was	NL	19	19	0	105.0	447	108	43	40	9	7	3	6	29	3	93	2	7	5	.583	0-0	0	93	.713	3.84	3.43
2017 Was	NL	13	13	0	73.2	323	88	44	41	16	5	0	1	20	2	68	2	5	3	.625	0-0	0	91	.867	5.54	5.01
2018 Was	NL	3	3	0	16.0	68	17	10	9	3	0	0	2	4	0	7	0	0	2	.000	0-0	0	93	.870	5.09	5.06
2019 Was	NL	27	9	3	64.0	295	74	41	39	7	3	1	4	33	1	57	2	4	4	.500	0-2	2	94	.829	5.79	5.48
2021 Was	NL	20	19	0	108.0	460	98	57	50	17	3	2	8	34	4	109	0	5	9	.357	0-0	0	94	.708	3.81	4.17
Postseason		3	2	0	9.2	42	9	8	8	3	0	0	2	4	0	4	1	0	1	.000	0-0	0	95	.885	6.34	7.45
6 ML YEARS		98	76	4	443.1	1907	449	228	210	59	21	7	23	141	10	403	7	26	28	.481	0-2	2	93	.748	4.22	4.26

Zac Rosscup

ROSS-cup

Pitches: L Bats: R Pos: RP-4   **Ht: 6'2" Wt: 220 Born: 6/9/1988 Age: 34**

Year Team	Lg	G	GS	GF	IP	BFP	H	R	ER	HR	SH	SF	HB	TBB	IBB	SO	WP	W	L	Pct	Sv-Op	Hld	Vel	OPS	ERC	ERA
2021 Albq	AAA	30	0	8	29.0	124	21	9	8	1	0	1	3	14	0	41	8	1	0	1.000	5--	-	-	.599	2.81	2.48
2013 ChC	NL	10	0	3	6.2	30	3	1	1	1	0	0	0	7	1	7	0	0	0	-	0-0	0	93	.638	3.56	1.35
2014 ChC	NL	18	0	5	13.1	66	14	14	14	2	0	0	0	12	1	21	0	1	0	1.000	0-0	1	92	.875	6.54	9.45
2015 ChC	NL	33	0	6	26.2	118	26	13	13	5	2	0	0	13	0	29	1	2	1	.667	0-2	6	93	.860	4.85	4.39
2017 2 Tms	NL	10	0	2	7.2	32	9	4	4	2	0	0	0	0	0	10	0	0	0	-	0-0	1	93	.806	4.37	4.70
2018 LAD	NL	17	0	5	11.1	47	9	6	6	3	0	0	0	4	0	20	0	0	1	.000	0-1	1	92	.718	3.75	4.76
2019 3 Tms		28	0	2	18.0	94	22	15	10	2	0	0	0	19	1	26	3	2	0	1.000	0-1	5	92	.863	8.06	5.00
2021 Col	NL	4	0	4	3.0	13	3	1	1	1	0	1	1	1	0	4	0	0	0	-	0-0	0	91	.985	7.42	3.00
17 ChC	NL	1	0	0	0.2	2	0	0	0	0	0	0	0	0	0	0	0	0	0	-	0-0	0		.000	0.00	0.00
17 Col	NL	9	0	2	7.0	30	9	4	4	2	0	0	0	0	0	10	0	0	0	-	0-0	1	93	.862	5.20	5.14
19 Sea	AL	19	0	1	14.0	69	13	8	5	1	0	0	0	14	1	20	2	2	0	1.000	0-1	5	92	.719	5.54	3.21
19 Tor	AL	2	0	0	1.0	8	3	4	3	0	0	0	0	2	0	2	0	0	0	-	0-0	0	93	1.292	24.59	27.00
19 LAD	NL	7	0	1	3.0	17	6	3	2	1	0	0	0	3	0	4	1	0	0	-	0-0	0	93	1.244	16.63	6.00
7 ML YEARS		120	0	27	86.2	400	86	54	49	16	2	1	1	56	3	117	4	5	2	.714	0-4	14	93	.832	5.58	5.09

Ramon Rosso

Pitches: R Bats: R Pos: RP-7   **Ht: 6'4" Wt: 240 Born: 6/9/1996 Age: 26**

Year Team	Lg	G	GS	GF	IP	BFP	H	R	ER	HR	SH	SF	HB	TBB	IBB	SO	WP	W	L	Pct	Sv-Op	Hld	Vel	OPS	ERC	ERA
2021 LV	AAA	19	3	3	28.0	126	24	22	14	2	0	4	3	18	1	26	5	0	2	.000	0--	-	-	.704	4.36	4.50
2020 Phi	NL	7	1	3	9.2	46	9	7	7	1	0	0	1	8	0	11	3	0	1	.000	0-0	0	94	.824	5.83	6.52
2021 Phi	NL	7	0	2	8.0	35	10	6	5	2	0	0	0	3	0	7	2	0	0	-	0-0	0	95	.903	6.85	5.63
2 ML YEARS		14	1	5	17.2	81	19	13	12	3	0	0	1	11	0	18	5	0	1	.000	0-0	0	94	.861	6.32	6.11

Ben Rowen

Pitches: R Bats: R Pos: RP-8   **Ht: 6'4" Wt: 200 Born: 11/15/1988 Age: 33**

Year Team	Lg	G	GS	GF	IP	BFP	H	R	ER	HR	SH	SF	HB	TBB	IBB	SO	WP	W	L	Pct	Sv-Op	Hld	Vel	OPS	ERC	ERA
2021 Salt Lk	AAA	20	0	3	29.1	127	32	23	22	2	1	4	3	8	0	17	0	1	2	.333	0--	-	-	.810	4.30	6.75
2014 Tex	AL	8	0	4	8.2	39	10	4	4	0	1	2	0	4	3	7	0	0	0	-	0-0	0	79	.743	3.81	4.15
2016 Mil	NL	4	0	1	3.0	19	10	6	5	0	0	0	0	0	0	2	0	0	0	-	0-0	0	80	1.053	17.08	15.00
2021 LAA	AL	8	0	5	11.1	49	12	8	7	3	0	1	2	2	0	8	0	0	0	-	0-0	0	80	.872	5.40	5.56
3 ML YEARS		20	0	10	23.0	107	32	18	16	3	1	3	2	6	3	17	0	0	0	-	0-0	0	80	.862	6.15	6.26

Michael Rucker

Pitches: R Bats: R Pos: RP-20   **Ht: 6'1" Wt: 195 Born: 4/27/1994 Age: 28**

Year Team	Lg	G	GS	GF	IP	BFP	H	R	ER	HR	SH	SF	HB	TBB	IBB	SO	WP	W	L	Pct	Sv-Op	Hld	Vel	OPS	ERC	ERA
2021 Iowa	AAA	19	0	2	39.1	167	44	22	21	8	0	0	2	9	1	49	0	3	0	1.000	0--	-	-	.842	5.04	4.81
2021 ChC	NL	20	0	6	28.1	126	32	25	22	5	0	1	2	11	0	30	0	0	0	-	1-2	0	95	.839	5.71	6.99

Darin Ruf

Bats: R **Throws:** R **Pos:** PH-48;1B-44;LF-33;RF-5;DH-2 ROUGH **Ht:** 6'2" **Wt:** 232 **Born:** 7/28/1986 **Age:** 35

Year	Team	Lg	G	AB	H	2B	3B	HR	(Hm	Rd)	TB	R	RBI	RC	TBB	IBB	SO	HBP	SH	SF	SB	CS	GDP	Avg	OBP	Slg	OPS
2012	Phi	NL	12	33	11	2	1	3	(1	2)	24	4	10	5	2	1	12	0	0	2	0	0	1	.333	.351	.727	1.079
2013	Phi	NL	73	251	62	11	0	14	(11	3)	115	36	30	33	33	1	91	7	0	2	0	0	4	.247	.348	.458	.806
2014	Phi	NL	52	102	24	8	0	3	(3	0)	41	13	8	9	8	0	32	4	1	2	0	0	2	.235	.310	.402	.712
2015	Phi	NL	106	268	63	12	0	12	(6	6)	111	30	39	34	21	0	69	5	0	3	1	0	7	.235	.300	.414	.714
2016	Phi	NL	43	83	17	2	0	3	(1	2)	28	8	9	4	4	0	25	0	0	5	0	1	5	.205	.236	.337	.573
2020	SF	NL	40	87	24	6	0	5	(4	1)	45	11	18	18	13	0	23	0	0	0	1	0	1	.276	.370	.517	.887
2021	SF	NL	117	262	71	13	2	16	(5	11)	136	41	43	45	46	2	87	3	0	1	2	0	8	.271	.385	.519	.904
	7 ML YEARS		443	1086	272	54	4	56	(31	25)	500	143	157	148	127	4	339	19	1	12	4	1	28	.250	.336	.460	.796

Jose Ruiz

Pitches: R **Bats:** R **Pos:** RP-59 **Ht:** 6'1" **Wt:** 245 **Born:** 10/21/1994 **Age:** 27

Year	Team	Lg	G	GS	GF	IP	BFP	H	R	ER	HR	SH	SF	HB	TBB	IBB	SO	WP	W	L	Pct	Sv-Op	Hld	Vel	OPS	ERC	ERA
2017	SD	NL	1	0	1	1.0	4	0	0	0	0	0	0	0	1	0	1	0	0	0	-	0-0	0	95	.250	0.95	0.00
2018	CWS	AL	6	0	2	4.1	21	5	2	2	1	0	0	0	3	0	6	2	0	0	-	0-0	0	96	.825	7.12	4.15
2019	CWS	AL	40	0	16	40.0	198	56	27	25	6	2	2	2	24	2	35	4	1	4	.200	0-1	1	96	.924	7.89	5.63
2020	CWS	AL	5	0	4	4.0	14	2	1	1	1	0	0	0	0	0	5	0	0	0	-	0-1	0	97	.500	1.13	2.25
2021	CWS	AL	59	0	23	65.0	271	51	26	22	8	1	2	0	25	1	63	2	1	3	.250	0-1	4	97	.648	2.93	3.05
	5 ML YEARS		111	1	46	114.1	508	114	56	50	16	3	4	2	53	3	110	8	2	7	.222	0-3	5	97	.753	4.56	3.94

Keibert Ruiz

Bats: B **Throws:** R **Pos:** C-23;PH-7 **Ht:** 6'0" **Wt:** 225 **Born:** 7/20/1998 **Age:** 23

Year	Team	Lg	G	AB	H	2B	3B	HR	(Hm	Rd)	TB	R	RBI	RC	TBB	IBB	SO	HBP	SH	SF	SB	CS	GDP	Avg	OBP	Slg	OPS
2017	2 Tms	Low	101	376	119	23	2	8	(-	-)	170	58	51	70	25	2	53	4	1	5	0	0	12	.316	.361	.452	.813
2018	Tulsa	AA	101	377	100	14	0	12	(-	-)	150	44	47	51	26	1	33	9	0	3	0	1	14	.265	.325	.398	.723
2019	Tulsa	AA	76	276	70	9	0	4	(-	-)	91	33	25	33	28	2	21	4	0	2	0	0	10	.254	.329	.330	.659
2021	OkCity	AAA	52	206	64	18	0	16	(-	-)	130	39	45	-	23	0	27	1	0	1	0	0	4	.311	.381	.631	1.012
2021	Roch	AAA	20	78	24	6	0	5	(-	-)	45	11	14	-	7	1	6	0	0	0	0	0	1	.308	.365	.577	.942
2020	LAD	NL	2	8	2	0	0	1	(0	1)	5	1	1	1	0	0	3	0	0	0	0	0	0	.250	.250	.625	.875
2021	2 Tms	NL	29	88	24	3	0	3	(0	3)	36	10	15	9	6	0	9	2	0	0	0	0	3	.273	.333	.409	.742
21	LAD	NL	6	7	1	0	0	1	(0	1)	4	1	1	0	0	0	5	0	0	0	0	0	0	.143	.143	.571	.714
21	Was	NL	23	81	23	3	0	2	(0	2)	32	9	14	9	6	0	4	2	0	0	0	0	3	.284	.348	.395	.743
	2 ML YEARS		31	96	26	3	0	4	(0	4)	41	11	16	10	6	0	12	2	0	0	0	0	3	.271	.327	.427	.754

Rio Ruiz

Bats: L **Throws:** R **Pos:** PH-28;2B-20;3B-17;LF-2;1B-1;DH-1;PR-1 **Ht:** 6'2" **Wt:** 220 **Born:** 5/22/1994 **Age:** 28

Year	Team	Lg	G	AB	H	2B	3B	HR	(Hm	Rd)	TB	R	RBI	RC	TBB	IBB	SO	HBP	SH	SF	SB	CS	GDP	Avg	OBP	Slg	OPS
2021	Albq	AAA	59	224	68	20	1	7	(-	-)	111	38	28	-	20	0	39	2	0	3	3	1	6	.304	.361	.496	.857
2016	Atl	NL	5	7	2	0	1	0	(0	0)	4	1	2	2	0	0	2	0	0	0	1	0	0	.286	.286	.571	.857
2017	Atl	NL	53	150	29	5	0	4	(2	2)	46	22	19	15	19	1	41	1	0	3	1	0	4	.193	.283	.307	.590
2018	Atl	NL	14	12	1	0	0	0	(0	0)	1	1	0	0	2	0	5	1	0	0	0	0	0	.083	.267	.083	.350
2019	Bal	AL	127	370	86	13	2	12	(6	6)	139	35	46	50	40	0	88	0	1	2	0	1	12	.232	.306	.376	.682
2020	Bal	AL	54	185	41	11	0	9	(4	5)	79	25	32	23	17	1	46	0	1	2	1	2	4	.222	.286	.427	.713
2021	2 Tms		62	125	21	4	0	3	(0	3)	34	11	10	6	12	0	38	1	1	2	2	0	3	.168	.243	.272	.515
21	Bal	AL	32	90	15	3	0	3	(0	3)	27	10	6	4	9	0	29	1	1	0	2	0	3	.167	.250	.300	.550
21	Col	NL	30	35	6	1	0	0	(0	0)	7	1	4	2	3	0	9	0	0	2	0	0	0	.171	.225	.200	.425
	6 ML YEARS		315	849	180	33	3	28	(12	16)	303	95	109	96	90	2	220	3	3	8	5	3	23	.212	.287	.357	.644

Adley Rutschman

Bats: B **Throws:** R **Pos:** C **Ht:** 6'2" **Wt:** 220 **Born:** 2/6/1998 **Age:** 24

Year	Team	Lg	G	AB	H	2B	3B	HR	(Hm	Rd)	TB	R	RBI	RC	TBB	IBB	SO	HBP	SH	SF	SB	CS	GDP	Avg	OBP	Slg	OPS
2019	3 Tms	Low	37	130	33	8	1	4	(-	-)	55	19	26	20	20	1	27	1	0	3	1	0	2	.254	.351	.423	.774
2021	Bowie	AA	80	295	80	16	0	18	(-	-)	150	61	55	-	55	2	57	5	0	2	1	1	5	.271	.392	.508	.901
2021	Norfolk	AAA	38	138	44	9	2	5	(-	-)	72	22	20	-	22	0	29	2	0	2	2	2	1	.319	.415	.522	.936

Joe Ryan

Pitches: R **Bats:** R **Pos:** SP-5 **Ht:** 6'2" **Wt:** 205 **Born:** 6/5/1996 **Age:** 26

Year	Team	Lg	G	GS	GF	IP	BFP	H	R	ER	HR	SH	SF	HB	TBB	IBB	SO	WP	W	L	Pct	Sv-Op	Hld	Vel	OPS	ERC	ERA
2021	Drham	AAA	12	11	0	57.0	215	35	25	23	8	0	2	3	10	0	75	3	4	3	.571	0- -	-	-	.568	1.76	3.63
2021	Min	AL	5	5	0	26.2	100	16	12	12	4	0	0	0	5	0	30	1	2	1	.667	0-0	0	91	.557	1.62	4.05

Kyle Ryan

Pitches: L Bats: L Pos: RP-13 **Ht: 6'5" Wt: 215 Born: 9/25/1991 Age: 30**

Year	Team	Lg	G	GS	GF	IP	BFP	H	R	ER	HR	SH	SF	HB	TBB	IBB	SO	WP	W	L	Pct	Sv-Op	Hld	Vel	OPS	ERC	ERA
2021	Iowa	AAA	19	0	6	25.0	93	16	7	7	2	0	1	0	7	1	24	0	2	0	1.000	1--	-	-	.518	1.77	2.52
2014	Det	AL	6	1	1	10.1	41	10	3	3	0	0	0	0	2	0	4	0	2	0	1.000	0-0	0	89	.626	2.57	2.61
2015	Det	AL	16	6	3	56.1	237	60	29	28	9	2	1	1	20	0	30	1	2	4	.333	0-0	0	88	.795	4.94	4.47
2016	Det	AL	56	0	14	55.2	226	48	21	19	2	2	1	3	15	5	35	1	4	2	.667	0-1	4	89	.636	2.55	3.07
2017	Det	AL	8	0	0	5.2	29	9	5	5	0	0	1	0	7	1	1	0	0	0	-	0-1	4	90	1.028	11.19	7.94
2019	ChC	NL	73	0	12	61.0	260	55	26	24	5	0	3	1	29	2	58	1	4	2	.667	0-2	14	90	.669	3.75	3.54
2020	ChC	NL	18	0	2	15.2	66	16	9	9	5	0	1	0	6	0	11	0	1	0	1.000	1-1	4	88	.900	5.84	5.17
2021	ChC	NL	13	0	4	13.1	62	17	10	10	3	1	1	0	6	1	8	1	0	0	-	1-1	0	88	.951	6.73	6.75
7 ML YEARS			190	7	36	218.0	921	215	103	98	24	5	7	5	85	9	147	4	13	8	.619	2-6	26	89	.738	4.14	4.05

Hyun-Jin Ryu

he-YUN-jin ree-YOO

Pitches: L Bats: R Pos: SP-31 **Ht: 6'3" Wt: 255 Born: 3/25/1987 Age: 35**

Year	Team	Lg	G	GS	GF	IP	BFP	H	R	ER	HR	SH	SF	HB	TBB	IBB	SO	WP	W	L	Pct	Sv-Op	Hld	Vel	OPS	ERC	ERA
2013	LAD	NL	30	30	0	192.0	783	182	67	64	15	7	3	1	49	4	154	5	14	8	.636	0-0	0	90	.660	3.13	3.00
2014	LAD	NL	26	26	0	152.0	631	152	60	57	8	6	2	3	29	2	139	2	14	7	.667	0-0	0	91	.658	3.00	3.38
2016	LAD	NL	1	1	0	4.2	24	8	6	6	1	0	0	0	2	1	4	0	0	1	.000	0-0	0	90	1.144	9.03	11.57
2017	LAD	NL	25	24	1	126.2	541	128	58	53	22	4	1	4	45	3	116	4	5	9	.357	1-1	0	90	.792	4.61	3.77
2018	LAD	NL	15	15	0	82.1	324	68	23	18	9	1	0	1	15	1	89	0	7	3	.700	0-0	0	91	.622	2.45	1.97
2019	LAD	NL	29	29	0	182.2	723	160	53	47	17	8	2	4	24	2	163	0	14	5	.737	0-0	0	91	.622	2.45	2.32
2020	Tor	AL	12	12	0	67.0	275	60	22	20	6	1	0	1	17	0	72	1	5	2	.714	0-0	0	90	.636	2.94	2.69
2021	Tor	AL	31	31	0	169.0	701	170	85	82	24	1	3	2	37	0	143	2	14	10	.583	0-0	0	92	.733	3.73	4.37
Postseason			9	9	0	41.2	180	49	25	21	5	0	0	0	9	2	35	0	3	3	.500	0-0	0	90	.749	4.37	4.54
8 ML YEARS			169	168	1	976.1	4002	928	374	347	102	28	11	16	218	13	880	14	73	45	.619	1-1	0	90	.681	3.21	3.20

Casey Sadler

Pitches: R Bats: R Pos: RP-42 **Ht: 6'3" Wt: 205 Born: 7/13/1990 Age: 31**

Year	Team	Lg	G	GS	GF	IP	BFP	H	R	ER	HR	SH	SF	HB	TBB	IBB	SO	WP	W	L	Pct	Sv-Op	Hld	Vel	OPS	ERC	ERA
2014	Pit	NL	6	0	2	10.1	49	12	9	9	0	0	2	1	5	0	7	1	0	1	.000	0-0	0	92	.782	4.80	7.84
2015	Pit	NL	1	1	0	5.0	19	4	2	2	1	0	0	0	1	0	5	0	1	0	1.000	0-0	0	91	.763	2.98	3.60
2018	Pit	NL	2	0	1	4.1	25	9	7	4	0	0	0	0	3	0	3	1	0	0	-	0-0	0	93	1.116	11.14	8.31
2019	2 Tms		33	1	16	46.1	194	41	14	11	5	2	1	4	13	2	31	0	4	0	1.000	1-2	2	93	.664	3.30	2.14
2020	2 Tms		17	0	2	19.1	86	15	13	11	3	1	0	0	12	0	21	5	1	2	.333	0-0	5	93	.715	3.94	5.12
2021	Sea	AL	42	0	2	40.1	145	19	4	3	1	0	1	1	10	0	37	2	0	1	.000	0-0	15	93	.402	1.03	0.67
19	TB	AL	9	0	8	19.1	79	16	5	4	2	0	0	1	5	0	11	0	0	0	-	0-0	0	93	.621	2.83	1.86
19	LAD	NL	24	1	8	27.0	115	25	9	7	3	2	1	3	8	2	20	0	4	0	1.000	1-2	2	94	.695	3.64	2.33
20	ChC	NL	10	0	1	9.1	44	8	6	6	2	1	0	0	8	0	9	3	0	0	-	0-0	4	93	.801	5.86	5.79
20	Sea	AL	7	0	1	10.0	42	7	7	5	1	0	0	0	4	0	12	2	1	2	.333	0-0	1	93	.630	2.39	4.50
6 ML YEARS			101	2	23	125.2	518	100	49	40	10	3	4	6	44	2	104	9	6	4	.600	1-2	22	93	.634	2.82	2.86

Chris Sale

SAIL

Pitches: L Bats: L Pos: SP-9 **Ht: 6'6" Wt: 183 Born: 3/30/1989 Age: 33**

Year	Team	Lg	G	GS	GF	IP	BFP	H	R	ER	HR	SH	SF	HB	TBB	IBB	SO	WP	W	L	Pct	Sv-Op	Hld	Vel	OPS	ERC	ERA
2010	CWS	AL	21	0	8	23.1	92	15	5	5	2	1	0	0	10	0	32	1	2	1	.667	4-4	2	96	.546	2.30	1.93
2011	CWS	AL	58	0	17	71.0	288	52	22	22	6	3	0	2	27	3	79	2	2	2	.500	8-10	16	95	.612	2.55	2.79
2012	CWS	AL	30	29	0	192.0	772	167	66	65	19	1	3	6	51	5	192	6	17	8	.680	0-1	0	92	.660	3.00	3.05
2013	CWS	AL	30	30	0	214.1	866	184	81	73	23	2	4	14	46	2	226	8	11	14	.440	0-0	0	93	.636	2.92	3.07
2014	CWS	AL	26	26	0	174.0	685	129	48	42	13	2	3	11	39	2	208	3	12	4	.750	0-0	0	94	.567	2.18	2.17
2015	CWS	AL	31	31	0	208.2	854	185	88	79	23	2	4	13	42	0	274	7	13	11	.542	0-0	0	94	.649	3.00	3.41
2016	CWS	AL	32	32	0	226.2	907	190	88	84	27	5	3	17	45	2	233	2	17	10	.630	0-0	0	93	.651	2.88	3.34
2017	Bos	AL	32	32	0	214.1	851	165	73	69	24	2	4	8	43	0	308	3	17	8	.680	0-0	0	94	.603	2.33	2.90
2018	Bos	AL	27	27	0	158.0	617	102	39	37	11	0	4	14	34	0	237	4	12	4	.750	0-0	0	95	.532	1.76	2.11
2019	Bos	AL	25	25	0	147.1	612	123	80	72	24	2	4	13	37	0	218	2	6	11	.353	0-0	0	93	.695	3.31	4.40
2021	Bos	AL	9	9	0	42.2	183	45	19	15	6	0	0	4	12	1	52	0	5	1	.833	0-0	0	94	.752	4.60	3.16
Postseason			7	4	1	25.0	107	24	16	16	5	0	0	1	9	0	36	0	1	2	.333	0-0	1	94	.751	4.54	5.76
11 ML YEARS			321	241	25	1672.1	6727	1357	609	563	178	20	28	102	386	15	2059	38	114	74	.606	12-15	18	94	.628	2.71	3.03

Adrian Sampson

Pitches: R Bats: R Pos: SP-5; RP-5 **Ht: 6'2" Wt: 210 Born: 10/7/1991 Age: 30**

Year	Team	Lg	G	GS	GF	IP	BFP	H	R	ER	HR	SH	SF	HB	TBB	IBB	SO	WP	W	L	Pct	Sv-Op	Hld	Vel	OPS	ERC	ERA
2021	Iowa	AAA	16	14	0	81.2	361	92	47	45	19	1	2	7	33	1	61	2	4	5	.444	0--	-	-	.901	6.33	4.96
2016	Sea	AL	1	1	0	4.2	21	8	4	4	2	0	0	0	1	0	2	0	0	1	.000	0-0	0	91	1.129	11.33	7.71
2018	Tex	AL	5	4	0	23.0	96	24	13	11	6	0	1	2	4	0	15	2	0	3	.000	0-0	0	91	.829	4.92	4.30
2019	Tex	AL	35	15	4	125.1	563	156	86	82	29	0	2	9	36	1	101	4	6	8	.429	0-0	0	93	.925	6.36	5.89
2021	ChC	NL	10	5	0	35.1	145	30	15	11	8	1	0	6	8	0	28	1	1	2	.333	0-0	0	92	.767	4.15	2.80
4 ML YEARS			51	25	4	188.1	825	218	118	108	45	1	3	17	49	1	146	7	7	14	.333	0-0	0	92	.892	5.85	5.16

Aaron Sanchez

Pitches: R **Bats:** R **Pos:** SP-7; RP-2 **Ht:** 6'4" **Wt:** 210 **Born:** 7/1/1992 **Age:** 29

			HOW MUCH PITCHED						WHAT HE GAVE UP										THE RESULTS								
Year	Team	Lg	G	GS	GF	IP	BFP	H	R	ER	HR	SH	SF	HB	TBB	IBB	SO	WP	W	L	Pct	Sv-Op	Hld	Vel	OPS	ERC	ERA
2021 Scrmto	AAA		6	6	0	17.1	85	24	16	15	4	0	2	1	10	0	11	3	1	1	.500	0--	-	-	1.023	8.58	7.79
2014 Tor	AL		24	0	6	33.0	121	14	5	4	1	2	0	1	9	0	27	1	2	2	.500	3-3	7	97	.367	0.96	1.09
2015 Tor	AL		41	11	4	92.1	380	74	35	33	9	2	1	3	44	2	61	8	7	6	.538	0-1	10	95	.666	3.47	3.22
2016 Tor	AL		30	30	0	192.0	790	161	69	64	15	1	2	5	63	0	161	5	15	2	.882	0-0	0	95	.625	2.90	3.00
2017 Tor	AL		8	8	0	36.0	167	42	24	17	6	0	0	1	20	0	24	1	1	3	.250	0-0	0	95	.836	6.36	4.25
2018 Tor	AL		20	20	0	105.0	474	106	62	57	11	0	4	7	58	2	86	4	4	6	.400	0-0	0	94	.768	5.02	4.89
2019 2 Tms	AL		27	27	0	131.1	605	145	92	86	20	0	4	11	68	2	115	7	5	14	.263	0-0	0	94	.828	5.88	5.89
2021 SF	NL		9	7	1	35.1	156	32	12	12	2	0	4		15	0	26	0	1	1	.500	0-0	0	90	.655	3.71	3.06
19 Tor	AL		23	23	0	112.2	524	131	82	76	15	0	3	10	59	2	99	7	3	14	.176	0-0	0	94	.835	6.16	6.07
19 Hou	AL		4	4	0	18.2	81	14	10	10	5	0	1	1	9	0	16	0	2	0	1.000	0-0	0	92	.782	4.22	4.82
Postseason			11	2	1	19.0	77	12	8	7	2	2	0	0	8	0	16	1	2	0	1.000	0-0	0	96	.565	2.24	3.32
7 ML YEARS			159	103	11	625.0	2693	574	299	273	64	5	11	32	277	6	500	26	35	34	.507	3-4	17	94	.704	4.01	3.93

Adrian Sanchez

Bats: R **Throws:** R **Pos:** 2B-9;PH-5;3B-2;RF-1;PR-1 **Ht:** 6'0" **Wt:** 208 **Born:** 8/16/1990 **Age:** 31

					BATTING															RUNNING			AVERAGES			
Year	Team	Lg	G	AB	H	2B	3B	HR	(Hm	Rd)	TB	R	RBI	RC	TBB	IBB	SO	HBP	SH	SF	SB	CS	GDP	Avg	OBP	Slg	OPS
2021 Roch	AAA		44	155	48	8	0	4	(-	-)	68	20	19	-	11	0	28	1	3	0	4	2	5	.310	.359	.439	.798
2017 Was	NL		34	71	19	7	0	0	(0	0)	26	6	11	9	1	0	25	1	2	0	0	2	2	.268	.288	.366	.654
2018 Was	NL		28	58	16	2	1	0	(0	0)	20	8	3	5	1	0	8	0	0	0	0	0	0	.276	.288	.345	.633
2019 Was	NL		28	31	7	0	0	0	(0	0)	7	3	1	1	1	0	10	0	0	0	0	0	0	.226	.250	.226	.476
2021 Was	NL		16	35	9	2	0	0	(0	0)	11	5	1	2	3	1	4	0	0	0	0	0	2	.257	.316	.314	.630
4 ML YEARS			106	195	51	11	1	0	(0	0)	64	22	16	17	6	1	47	1	2	0	0	2	4	.262	.287	.328	.615

Ali Sanchez

Bats: R **Throws:** R **Pos:** C-2 **Ht:** 6'1" **Wt:** 200 **Born:** 1/20/1997 **Age:** 25

					BATTING															RUNNING			AVERAGES			
Year	Team	Lg	G	AB	H	2B	3B	HR	(Hm	Rd)	TB	R	RBI	RC	TBB	IBB	SO	HBP	SH	SF	SB	CS	GDP	Avg	OBP	Slg	OPS
2021 Memp	AAA		70	251	69	10	0	4	(-	-)	91	24	22	-	18	0	47	0	0	1	0	2	14	.275	.322	.363	.685
2020 NYM	NL		5	9	1	0	0	0	(0	0)	1	0	0	0	0	0	3	0	0	0	0	0	0	.111	.200	.111	.311
2021 StL	NL		2	4	2	2	0	0	(0	0)	4	0	0	0	0	0	0	0	0	0	0	0	0	.500	.500	1.000	1.500
2 ML YEARS			7	13	3	2	0	0	(0	0)	5	0	0	0	0	0	3	0	0	0	0	0	2	.231	.286	.385	.670

Anibal Sanchez

Pitches: R **Bats:** R **Pos:** P **Ht:** 6'0" **Wt:** 205 **Born:** 2/27/1984 **Age:** 38

ah-NEE-bahl

			HOW MUCH PITCHED						WHAT HE GAVE UP										THE RESULTS								
Year	Team	Lg	G	GS	GF	IP	BFP	H	R	ER	HR	SH	SF	HB	TBB	IBB	SO	WP	W	L	Pct	Sv-Op	Hld	Vel	OPS	ERC	ERA
2006 Fla	NL		18	17	0	114.1	469	90	39	36	9	3	1	4	46	1	72	4	10	3	.769	0-0	0	91	.635	2.96	2.83
2007 Fla	NL		6	6	0	30.0	151	43	17	16	3	2	2	2	19	1	14	3	2	1	.667	0-0	0	90	.930	7.90	4.80
2008 Fla	NL		10	10	0	51.2	241	54	35	32	7	4	2	6	27	2	50	1	2	5	.286	0-0	0	90	.788	5.40	5.57
2009 Fla	NL		16	16	0	86.0	383	84	39	37	10	2	2	1	46	5	71	0	4	8	.333	0-0	0	91	.756	4.51	3.87
2010 Fla	NL		32	32	0	195.0	841	192	89	77	10	13	3	7	70	5	157	7	13	12	.520	0-0	0	91	.680	3.56	3.55
2011 Fla	NL		32	32	0	196.1	830	187	85	80	20	12	1	5	64	8	202	4	8	9	.471	0-0	0	92	.711	3.57	3.67
2012 2 Tms			31	31	0	195.2	820	200	95	84	20	5	7	5	48	3	167	7	9	13	.409	0-0	0	92	.716	3.70	3.86
2013 Det	AL		29	29	0	182.0	746	156	56	52	9	4	4	2	54	1	202	9	14	8	.636	0-0	0	93	.616	2.63	2.57
2014 Det	AL		22	21	0	126.0	514	108	55	48	4	3	4	3	30	1	102	5	8	5	.615	0-0	0	92	.599	2.35	3.43
2015 Det	AL		25	25	0	157.0	660	152	89	87	29	5	2	1	49	1	138	5	10	10	.500	0-0	0	92	.768	4.14	4.99
2016 Det	AL		35	26	3	153.1	668	171	108	100	30	4	6	5	53	1	135	7	7	13	.350	0-0	0	91	.828	5.40	5.87
2017 Det	AL		28	17	6	105.1	482	139	81	75	26	2	3	4	29	1	104	5	3	7	.300	0-0	0	91	.906	6.66	6.41
2018 Atl	NL		25	24	0	136.2	553	106	48	43	15	7	2	3	42	0	135	3	6	5	.538	0-0	0	91	.633	2.71	2.83
2019 Was	NL		30	30	0	166.0	712	153	77	71	22	1	2	4	58	10	134	1	11	8	.579	0-0	0	90	.709	3.53	3.85
2020 Was	NL		11	11	0	53.0	245	70	40	39	10	0	0	3	18	2	43	0	4	5	.444	0-0	0	90	.907	6.74	6.62
12 Mia	NL		19	19	0	121.0	504	119	59	53	12	4	5	2	33	2	110	4	5	7	.417	0-0	0	91	.717	3.55	3.94
12 Det	AL		12	12	0	74.2	316	81	36	31	8	1	2	3	15	1	57	3	4	6	.400	0-0	0	93	.714	3.91	3.74
Postseason			11	10	0	61.1	256	51	22	20	9	1	1	2	19	1	64	4	3	6	.333	0-0	1	92	.677	3.16	2.93
15 ML YEARS			350	327	9	1948.1	8315	1905	953	877	225	67	42	56	653	42	1726	60	112	113	.498	0-0	0	91	.723	3.87	4.05

Cristopher Sanchez

Pitches: L **Bats:** L **Pos:** RP-6; SP-1 **Ht:** 6'1" **Wt:** 165 **Born:** 12/12/1996 **Age:** 25

			HOW MUCH PITCHED						WHAT HE GAVE UP										THE RESULTS								
Year	Team	Lg	G	GS	GF	IP	BFP	H	R	ER	HR	SH	SF	HB	TBB	IBB	SO	WP	W	L	Pct	Sv-Op	Hld	Vel	OPS	ERC	ERA
2021 LV	AAA		19	17	0	73.0	325	58	39	38	4	0	0	2	48	0	89	4	5	6	.455	0--	-	-	.623	3.64	4.68
2021 Phi	NL		7	1	0	12.2	59	16	8	7	1	2	0	0	7	0	13	0	1	0	1.000	0-0	0	94	.864	6.15	4.97

Gary Sanchez

Bats: R **Throws:** R **Pos:** C-110;PH-11;DH-5 **Ht:** 6'2" **Wt:** 230 **Born:** 12/2/1992 **Age:** 29

					BATTING															RUNNING			AVERAGES			
Year	Team	Lg	G	AB	H	2B	3B	HR	(Hm	Rd)	TB	R	RBI	RC	TBB	IBB	SO	HBP	SH	SF	SB	CS	GDP	Avg	OBP	Slg	OPS
2015 NYY	AL		2	2	0	0	0	0	(0	0)	0	0	0	0	0	0	1	0	0	0	0	0	0	.000	.000	.000	.000
2016 NYY	AL		53	201	60	12	0	20	(10	10)	132	34	42	40	24	2	57	2	0	2	1	0	5	.299	.376	.657	1.032
2017 NYY	AL		122	471	131	20	0	33	(15	18)	250	79	90	81	40	1	120	10	0	4	2	1	9	.278	.345	.531	.876
2018 NYY	AL		89	323	60	17	0	18	(8	10)	131	51	53	41	46	0	94	3	0	2	1	0	10	.186	.291	.406	.697

								BATTING														RUNNING			AVERAGES			
Year Team	Lg	G	AB	H	2B	3B	HR	(Hm	Rd)	TB	R	RBI	RC	TBB	IBB	SO	HBP	SH	SF		SB	CS	GDP	Avg	OBP	Slg	OPS
2019 NYY	AL	106	396	92	12	1	34	(19	15)	208	62	77	64	40	3	125	9	0	1		0	1	3	.232	.316	.525	.841
2020 NYY	AL	49	156	23	4	0	10	(7	3)	57	19	24	12	18	0	64	4	0	0		0	0	6	.147	.253	.365	.618
2021 NYY	AL	117	383	78	13	1	23	(15	8)	162	54	54	50	52	3	121	5	0	0		5	0	14	.204	.307	.423	.730
Postseason		30	110	19	3	0	7	(3	4)	43	11	19	10	6	0	44	1	0	3		0	0	3	.173	.217	.391	.608
7 ML YEARS		538	1932	444	78	2	138	(74	64)	940	299	340	288	220	9	582	33	0	9		4	2	47	.230	.318	.487	.804

Jesus Sanchez

Bats: L **Throws:** R **Pos:** RF-41;LF-21;PH-3   **Ht:** 6'3" **Wt:** 222 **Born:** 10/7/1997 **Age:** 24

								BATTING														RUNNING			AVERAGES			
Year Team	Lg	G	AB	H	2B	3B	HR	(Hm	Rd)	TB	R	RBI	RC	TBB	IBB	SO	HBP	SH	SF		SB	CS	GDP	Avg	OBP	Slg	OPS
2021 Jaxnvl	AAA	37	141	49	5	4	10	(-	-)	92	23	31	-	12	1	29	2	0	0		1	0	2	.348	.406	.652	1.059
2020 Mia	NL	10	25	1	0	0	0	(0	0)	2	1	2	0	4	0	11	0	0	0		0	0	1	.040	.172	.080	.252
2021 Mia	NL	64	227	57	8	2	14	(7	7)	111	27	36	38	20	3	78	3	0	1		0	1	2	.251	.319	.489	.808
2 ML YEARS		74	252	58	9	2	14	(7	7)	113	28	38	38	24	3	89	3	0	1		0	1	3	.230	.304	.448	.752

Miguel Sanchez

Pitches: R **Bats:** R **Pos:** RP-28   **Ht:** 6'3" **Wt:** 205 **Born:** 12/31/1993 **Age:** 28

		HOW MUCH PITCHED				WHAT HE GAVE UP										THE RESULTS							
Year Team	Lg	G	GS	GF	IP	BFP	H	R	ER	HR	SH	SF	HB	TBB	IBB	SO	WP	W	L	Pct	Sv-Op	Hld	Vel	OPS	ERC	ERA
2021 Nashv	AAA	19	0	4	25.0	106	22	15	10	3	0	0	1	9	0	24	4	2	0	1.000	0- -	-	-	.698	3.52	3.60
2021 Mil	NL	28	0	11	26.0	120	27	14	12	4	1	2	2	14	2	23	2	2	1	.667	0-1	0	94	.807	5.37	4.15

Sixto Sanchez

Pitches: R **Bats:** R **Pos:** P   **Ht:** 6'0" **Wt:** 234 **Born:** 7/29/1998 **Age:** 23

		HOW MUCH PITCHED				WHAT HE GAVE UP										THE RESULTS							
Year Team	Lg	G	GS	GF	IP	BFP	H	R	ER	HR	SH	SF	HB	TBB	IBB	SO	WP	W	L	Pct	Sv-Op	Hld	Vel	OPS	ERC	ERA
2017 2 Tms	Low	18	18	0	95.0	375	73	35	32	2	2	3	4	18	0	84	5	5	7	.417	0- -	-	-	.436	1.81	3.03
2018 Clrwtr	A+	8	8	0	46.2	188	39	14	13	1	0	1	2	11	0	45	0	4	3	.571	0- -	-	-	.604	2.28	2.51
2019 Jaxnvl	AA	18	18	0	103.0	411	87	33	29	5	2	0	3	19	0	97	0	8	4	.667	0- -	-	-	.600	2.26	2.53
2020 Mia	NL	7	7	0	39.0	158	36	15	15	3	0	1	2	11	1	33	1	3	2	.600	0-0	0	98	.643	3.32	3.46
Postseason		2	2	0	8.0	38	8	4	4	0	0	1	2	5	0	8	0	0	1	.000	0-0	0	98	.695	5.15	4.50

Nick Sandlin

Pitches: R **Bats:** R **Pos:** RP-34   **Ht:** 5'11" **Wt:** 175 **Born:** 1/10/1997 **Age:** 25

		HOW MUCH PITCHED				WHAT HE GAVE UP										THE RESULTS							
Year Team	Lg	G	GS	GF	IP	BFP	H	R	ER	HR	SH	SF	HB	TBB	IBB	SO	WP	W	L	Pct	Sv-Op	Hld	Vel	OPS	ERC	ERA
2021 Cle	AL	34	0	4	33.2	141	21	15	11	2	0	1	4	17	0	48	1	1	1	.500	0-1	5	95	.584	2.63	2.94

Pablo Sandoval

Bats: B **Throws:** R **Pos:** PH-61;DH-6;1B-2;3B-1;PR-1   **Ht:** 5'10" **Wt:** 268 **Born:** 8/11/1986 **Age:** 35

								BATTING														RUNNING			AVERAGES			
Year Team	Lg	G	AB	H	2B	3B	HR	(Hm	Rd)	TB	R	RBI	RC	TBB	IBB	SO	HBP	SH	SF		SB	CS	GDP	Avg	OBP	Slg	OPS
2008 SF	NL	41	145	50	10	1	3	(1	2)	71	24	24	24	4	1	14	1	0	4		0	0	6	.345	.357	.490	.847
2009 SF	NL	153	572	189	44	5	25	(13	12)	318	79	90	113	52	13	83	4	0	5		5	5	10	.330	.387	.556	.943
2010 SF	NL	152	563	151	34	3	13	(9	4)	230	61	63	55	47	12	81	1	0	5		3	2	26	.268	.323	.409	.732
2011 SF	NL	117	426	134	26	3	23	(7	16)	235	55	70	72	32	9	63	0	1	7		2	4	12	.315	.357	.552	.909
2012 SF	NL	108	396	112	25	2	12	(7	5)	177	59	63	60	38	4	59	1	0	7		1	1	13	.283	.342	.447	.789
2013 SF	NL	141	525	146	27	2	14	(6	8)	219	52	79	78	47	5	79	6	0	6		0	0	19	.278	.341	.417	.758
2014 SF	NL	157	588	164	26	3	16	(9	7)	244	68	73	78	39	6	85	4	0	7		0	0	16	.279	.324	.415	.739
2015 Bos	AL	126	470	115	25	1	10	(4	6)	172	43	47	46	25	1	73	7	1	2		0	0	14	.245	.292	.366	.658
2016 Bos	AL	3	6	0	0	0	0	(0	0)	0	0	0	0	1	0	4	0	0	0		0	0	0	.000	.143	.000	.143
2017 2 Tms		79	259	57	11	0	9	(4	5)	95	27	32	20	16	0	53	1	0	3		0	1	11	.220	.265	.367	.632
2018 SF	NL	92	230	57	10	1	9	(6	3)	96	22	40	31	19	2	52	2	0	1		0	0	9	.248	.310	.417	.727
2019 SF	NL	108	272	73	23	0	14	(6	8)	138	42	41	38	18	2	67	1	2	3		1	0	8	.268	.313	.507	.820
2020 2 Tms	NL	34	84	18	1	0	1	(0	1)	22	5	6	5	8	0	19	1	0	1		0	0	3	.214	.287	.262	.549
2021 Atl	NL	69	73	13	0	0	4	(2	2)	25	11	11	8	11	0	25	2	0	0		0	0	2	.178	.302	.342	.645
17 Bos	AL	32	99	21	2	0	4	(2	2)	35	10	12	9	8	0	24	0	0	1		0	1	4	.212	.269	.354	.622
17 SF	NL	47	160	36	9	0	5	(2	3)	60	17	20	11	8	0	29	1	0	2		0	0	7	.225	.263	.375	.638
20 SF	NL	33	82	18	1	0	1	(0	1)	22	5	6	5	6	0	18	1	0	1		0	0	3	.220	.278	.268	.546
20 Atl	NL	1	2	0	0	0	0	(0	0)	0	0	0	0	2	0	1	0	0	0		0	0	0	.000	.500	.000	.500
Postseason		42	157	53	13	0	6	(3	3)	84	21	20	27	10	3	24	3	0	1		0	0	7	.338	.386	.535	.921
14 ML YEARS		1380	4609	1279	262	21	153	(74	79)	2042	548	639	628	357	55	757	31	4	51		12	13	149	.278	.330	.443	.773

Patrick Sandoval

Pitches: L **Bats:** L **Pos:** SP-14; RP-3   **Ht:** 6'3" **Wt:** 190 **Born:** 10/18/1996 **Age:** 25

		HOW MUCH PITCHED				WHAT HE GAVE UP										THE RESULTS							
Year Team	Lg	G	GS	GF	IP	BFP	H	R	ER	HR	SH	SF	HB	TBB	IBB	SO	WP	W	L	Pct	Sv-Op	Hld	Vel	OPS	ERC	ERA
2019 LAA	AL	10	9	0	39.1	169	35	22	22	6	2	1	1	19	0	42	0	0	4	.000	0-0	0	93	.754	4.28	5.03
2020 LAA	AL	9	6	0	36.2	159	37	26	23	10	0	0	0	12	0	33	2	1	5	.167	0-0	0	93	.818	4.92	5.65
2021 LAA	AL	17	14	2	87.0	363	69	38	35	11	0	2	4	36	0	94	3	3	6	.333	1-1	0	93	.649	3.36	3.62
3 ML YEARS		36	29	2	163.0	691	141	86	80	27	2	3	5	67	0	169	9	4	15	.211	1-1	0	93	.715	3.93	4.42

Reiver Sanmartin

Pitches: L **Bats:** L **Pos:** SP-2 **Ht:** 6'2" **Wt:** 160 **Born:** 4/15/1996 **Age:** 26

			HOW MUCH PITCHED				WHAT HE GAVE UP									THE RESULTS							
Year	Team	Lg	G	GS	GF	IP	BFP	H	R	ER	HR	SH	SF	HB	TBB	IBB	SO	WP	W	L	Pct	Sv-Op	Hld	Vel	OPS	ERC	ERA
2021	Lsvlle	AAA	21	14	0	82.1	343	80	40	36	6	2	0	2	23	0	89	4	8	2	.800	0- -	-	-	.656	3.39	3.94
2021	Cin	NL	2	2	0	11.2	47	12	2	2	0	0	0	0	2	0	11	1	2	0	1.000	0-0	0	89	.653	2.78	1.54

Miguel Sano

Bats: R **Throws:** R **Pos:** 1B-118;DH-11;3B-9;PH-5;PR-1 sah-NO **Ht:** 6'4" **Wt:** 272 **Born:** 5/11/1993 **Age:** 29

						BATTING														RUNNING			AVERAGES			
Year	Team	Lg	G	AB	H	2B	3B	HR	(Hm	Rd)	TB	R	RBI	RC	TBB	IBB	SO	HBP	SH	SF	SB	CS	GDP	Avg	OBP	Slg	OPS
2015	Min	AL	80	279	75	17	1	18	(10	8)	148	46	52	62	53	1	119	1	0	2	1	1	4	.269	.385	.530	.916
2016	Min	AL	116	437	103	22	1	25	(11	14)	202	57	66	62	54	1	178	1	0	3	1	0	8	.236	.319	.462	.781
2017	Min	AL	114	424	112	15	2	28	(12	16)	215	75	77	71	54	5	173	4	0	1	0	0	12	.264	.352	.507	.859
2018	Min	AL	71	266	53	14	0	13	(7	6)	106	32	41	28	31	0	115	0	0	2	0	0	7	.199	.281	.398	.679
2019	Min	AL	105	380	94	19	2	34	(14	20)	219	76	79	74	55	0	159	3	0	1	0	1	5	.247	.346	.576	.923
2020	Min	AL	53	186	38	12	0	13	(6	7)	89	31	25	22	18	1	90	1	0	0	0	0	3	.204	.278	.478	.757
2021	Min	AL	135	470	105	24	0	30	(17	13)	219	68	75	60	59	2	183	2	0	1	2	1	13	.223	.312	.466	.778
	Postseason		5	19	2	0	0	1	(0	1)	5	1	1	0	1	0	9	0	0	0	0	0	0	.105	.150	.263	.413
	7 ML YEARS		674	2442	580	123	6	161	(77	84)	1198	385	415	379	324	10	1017	12	0	10	4	3	52	.238	.329	.491	.819

Carlos Santana

Bats: B **Throws:** R **Pos:** 1B-136;DH-19;PH-3 **Ht:** 5'11" **Wt:** 215 **Born:** 4/8/1986 **Age:** 36

						BATTING														RUNNING			AVERAGES			
Year	Team	Lg	G	AB	H	2B	3B	HR	(Hm	Rd)	TB	R	RBI	RC	TBB	IBB	SO	HBP	SH	SF	SB	CS	GDP	Avg	OBP	Slg	OPS
2010	Cle	AL	46	150	39	13	0	6	(2	4)	70	23	22	25	37	2	29	1	0	4	3	0	3	.260	.401	.467	.868
2011	Cle	AL	155	552	132	35	2	27	(14	13)	252	84	79	81	97	7	133	2	0	7	5	3	15	.239	.351	.457	.808
2012	Cle	AL	143	507	128	27	2	18	(7	11)	213	72	76	77	91	4	101	3	0	8	3	5	21	.252	.365	.420	.785
2013	Cle	AL	154	541	145	39	1	20	(12	8)	246	75	74	93	93	6	110	4	0	4	3	1	7	.268	.377	.455	.832
2014	Cle	AL	152	541	125	25	0	27	(13	14)	231	68	85	88	113	5	124	3	0	3	5	2	13	.231	.365	.427	.792
2015	Cle	AL	154	550	127	29	2	19	(6	13)	217	72	85	80	108	8	122	3	0	5	11	3	20	.231	.357	.395	.752
2016	Cle	AL	158	582	151	31	3	34	(20	14)	290	89	87	104	99	0	99	2	0	5	5	2	18	.259	.366	.498	.865
2017	Cle	AL	154	571	148	37	3	23	(11	12)	260	90	79	89	88	6	94	6	0	2	5	1	11	.259	.363	.455	.818
2018	Phi	NL	161	560	128	28	2	24	(13	11)	232	82	86	87	110	6	93	1	0	8	2	1	12	.229	.352	.414	.766
2019	Cle	AL	158	573	161	30	1	34	(19	15)	295	110	93	114	108	12	108	3	0	4	0	0	13	.281	.397	.515	.911
2020	Cle	AL	60	206	41	7	0	8	(5	3)	72	34	30	35	47	1	43	1	0	1	0	0	5	.199	.349	.350	.699
2021	KC	AL	158	565	121	15	0	19	(7	12)	193	66	69	66	86	3	102	3	0	5	2	0	15	.214	.319	.342	.660
	Postseason		23	83	16	2	0	4	(1	3)	30	9	8	10	12	0	19	1	0	0	0	0	1	.193	.302	.361	.664
	12 ML YEARS		1653	5898	1446	316	16	259	(129	130)	2571	865	865	939	1077	60	1158	32	0	54	48	18	150	.245	.362	.436	.798

Danny Santana

Bats: B **Throws:** R **Pos:** 1B-14;CF-13;LF-7;PH-4;PR-3;DH-2 **Ht:** 5'11" **Wt:** 195 **Born:** 11/7/1990 **Age:** 31

						BATTING														RUNNING			AVERAGES			
Year	Team	Lg	G	AB	H	2B	3B	HR	(Hm	Rd)	TB	R	RBI	RC	TBB	IBB	SO	HBP	SH	SF	SB	CS	GDP	Avg	OBP	Slg	OPS
2014	Min	AL	101	405	129	27	7	7	(3	4)	191	70	40	72	19	0	98	3	2	1	20	4	3	.319	.353	.472	.824
2015	Min	AL	91	261	56	10	5	0	(0	0)	76	30	21	16	6	1	68	3	7	0	8	4	7	.215	.241	.291	.532
2016	Min	AL	75	233	56	10	2	2	(0	2)	76	29	14	18	12	0	55	1	1	1	12	9	1	.240	.279	.326	.606
2017	2 Tms		82	168	34	10	2	4	(3	1)	60	19	23	17	8	1	41	1	1	0	7	0	3	.202	.243	.357	.600
2018	Atl	NL	15	28	5	3	0	0	(0	0)	8	4	2	2	3	0	11	1	0	1	1	1	0	.179	.281	.286	.567
2019	Tex	AL	130	474	134	23	6	28	(19	9)	253	81	81	83	25	2	151	6	0	5	21	6	8	.283	.324	.534	.857
2020	Tex	AL	15	55	8	4	0	1	(0	1)	15	6	7	4	7	0	24	0	0	1	2	0	1	.145	.238	.273	.511
2021	Bos	AL	38	116	21	2	1	5	(2	3)	40	15	14	13	10	0	30	1	0	0	4	2	0	.181	.252	.345	.597
17	Min	AL	13	25	5	1	0	1	(1	0)	9	3	1	0	1	0	8	0	0	0	1	0	1	.200	.231	.360	.591
17	Atl	NL	69	143	29	9	2	3	(2	1)	51	16	22	17	7	1	33	1	1	0	6	0	2	.203	.245	.357	.602
	8 ML YEARS		547	1740	443	89	23	47	(27	20)	719	254	202	225	90	4	478	16	11	8	75	26	23	.255	.296	.413	.709

Dennis Santana

Pitches: R **Bats:** R **Pos:** RP-55 **Ht:** 6'2" **Wt:** 190 **Born:** 4/12/1996 **Age:** 26

			HOW MUCH PITCHED				WHAT HE GAVE UP									THE RESULTS							
Year	Team	Lg	G	GS	GF	IP	BFP	H	R	ER	HR	SH	SF	HB	TBB	IBB	SO	WP	W	L	Pct	Sv-Op	Hld	Vel	OPS	ERC	ERA
2018	LAD	NL	1	0	0	3.2	19	6	5	5	0	1	0	1	1	0	4	1	1	0	1.000	0-0	0	93	1.007	7.52	12.27
2019	LAD	NL	3	0	1	5.0	27	6	4	4	1	0	1	2	4	0	6	1	0	0	-	0-0	0	93	.994	9.44	7.20
2020	LAD	NL	12	0	7	17.0	73	15	11	10	4	0	0	2	7	0	18	1	1	2	.333	0-1	0	94	.782	4.93	5.29
2021	2 Tms		55	0	12	54.2	237	48	31	26	4	1	1	3	32	2	46	4	2	4	.333	0-2	6	95	.692	4.16	4.28
21	LAD	NL	16	0	5	15.0	74	18	11	10	0	0	3	3	11	1	8	2	0	0	-	0-0	1	95	.766	6.55	6.00
21	Tex	AL	39	0	7	39.2	163	30	20	16	4	1	1	0	21	1	38	2	2	4	.333	0-2	5	96	.658	3.31	3.63
	4 ML YEARS		71	0	20	80.1	356	75	51	45	9	2	2	8	44	2	74	7	4	6	.400	0-3	6	95	.749	4.79	5.04

Edgar Santana

Pitches: R **Bats:** R **Pos:** RP-41 **Ht:** 6'2" **Wt:** 205 **Born:** 10/16/1991 **Age:** 30

			HOW MUCH PITCHED				WHAT HE GAVE UP									THE RESULTS							
Year	Team	Lg	G	GS	GF	IP	BFP	H	R	ER	HR	SH	SF	HB	TBB	IBB	SO	WP	W	L	Pct	Sv-Op	Hld	Vel	OPS	ERC	ERA
2017	Pit	NL	19	0	2	18.0	81	16	8	7	1	2	0	1	12	1	20	0	0	0	-	0-0	2	95	.780	4.72	3.50
2018	Pit	NL	69	0	11	66.1	271	61	25	24	7	1	1	3	12	2	54	3	3	4	.429	0-7	20	95	.659	2.96	3.26
2021	Atl	NL	41	0	13	42.2	175	37	20	17	7	1	0	0	12	1	33	1	3	0	1.000	0-0	3	94	.664	3.25	3.59
	3 ML YEARS		129	0	26	127.0	527	114	53	48	16	3	1	4	36	4	107	4	6	4	.600	0-7	25	95	.679	3.30	3.40

Ervin Santana

Pitches: R **Bats:** R **Pos:** RP-36; SP-2 **Ht:** 6'2" **Wt:** 175 **Born:** 12/12/1982 **Age:** 39

			HOW MUCH PITCHED					WHAT HE GAVE UP									THE RESULTS						
Year	Team	Lg	G	GS	GF	IP	BFP	H	R	ER	HR	SH	SF	HB	TBB	IBB	SO	WP	W	L	Pct	Sv-Op	Hld	Vel	OPS	ERC	ERA
2005	LAA	AL	23	23	0	133.2	583	139	73	69	17	1	4	8	47	2	99	4	12	8	.600	0-0	0	93	.781	4.51	4.65
2006	LAA	AL	33	33	0	204.0	846	181	106	97	21	4	10	11	70	2	141	10	16	8	.667	0-0	0	93	.707	3.51	4.28
2007	LAA	AL	28	26	1	150.0	675	174	103	96	26	3	2	8	58	3	126	7	7	14	.333	0-0	0	92	.854	5.69	5.76
2008	LAA	AL	32	32	0	219.0	897	198	89	85	23	3	5	8	47	2	214	5	16	7	.696	0-0	0	94	.651	3.00	3.49
2009	LAA	AL	24	23	0	139.2	614	159	83	78	24	2	1	10	47	4	107	4	8	8	.500	0-0	1	92	.833	5.47	5.03
2010	LAA	AL	33	33	0	222.2	954	221	104	97	27	8	8	12	73	2	169	11	17	10	.630	0-0	0	92	.744	4.10	3.92
2011	LAA	AL	33	33	0	228.2	949	207	95	86	26	4	7	8	72	4	178	10	11	12	.478	0-0	0	93	.693	3.45	3.38
2012	LAA	AL	30	30	0	178.0	764	165	109	102	**39**	2	2	9	61	2	133	4	9	13	.409	0-0	0	92	.774	4.38	5.16
2013	KC	AL	32	32	0	211.0	859	190	85	76	26	2	3	6	51	3	161	6	9	10	.474	0-0	0	92	.668	3.19	3.24
2014	Atl	NL	31	31	0	196.0	817	193	90	86	16	12	**12**	4	63	4	179	9	14	10	.583	0-0	0	92	.724	3.68	3.95
2015	Min	AL	17	17	0	108.0	457	104	50	48	12	4	2	4	36	2	82	3	7	5	.583	0-0	0	92	.729	3.82	4.00
2016	Min	AL	30	30	0	181.1	748	168	78	68	19	1	5	4	53	2	149	11	7	11	.389	0-0	0	93	.682	3.39	3.38
2017	Min	AL	33	33	0	211.1	864	177	85	77	31	4	4	8	61	2	167	12	16	8	.667	0-0	0	93	.678	3.21	3.28
2018	Min	AL	5	5	0	24.2	114	31	22	22	9	0	3	2	9	0	16	0	0	1	.000	0-0	0	89	1.038	7.88	8.03
2019	CWS	AL	3	3	0	13.1	64	19	14	14	6	0	2	0	6	0	5	1	0	2	.000	0-0	0	90	1.212	9.79	9.45
2021	KC	AL	38	2	19	65.1	277	65	35	34	9	0	2	2	22	1	52	7	2	2	.500	0-0	0	94	.768	4.20	4.68
	Postseason		9	3	3	24.2	112	24	21	18	6	1	1	3	11	1	14	0	2	2	.500	0-0	0	94	.811	5.47	6.57
16 ML YEARS			425	386	20	2486.2	10482	2391	1221	1135	331	50	72	104	776	35	1978	104	151	129	.539	0-0	1	93	.733	3.90	4.11

Anthony Santander

Bats: B **Throws:** R **Pos:** RF-81;DH-21;PH-6;LF-4 sahn-tahn-DARE **Ht:** 6'2" **Wt:** 235 **Born:** 10/19/1994 **Age:** 27

			BATTING																RUNNING			AVERAGES			
Year	Team	Lg	G	AB	H	2B	3B	HR	(Hm | Rd)	TB	R	RBI	RC	TBB	IBB	SO	HBP	SH	SF	SB	CS	GDP	Avg	OBP	Slg	OPS
2017	Bal	AL	13	30	8	3	0	0	(0 | 0)	11	1	2	2	0	0	8	0	0	1	0	0	0	.267	.258	.367	.625
2018	Bal	AL	33	101	20	5	1	1	(0 | 1)	30	8	6	10	6	0	21	1	0	1	1	0	1	.198	.250	.297	.547
2019	Bal	AL	93	380	99	20	1	20	(10 | 10)	181	46	59	55	19	0	86	2	1	3	1	2	1	.261	.297	.476	.773
2020	Bal	AL	37	153	40	13	1	11	(8 | 3)	88	24	32	28	10	3	25	2	0	0	0	1	2	.261	.315	.575	.890
2021	Bal	AL	110	406	98	24	0	18	(15 | 3)	176	54	50	40	23	0	101	4	1	4	1	1	11	.241	.286	.433	.720
5 ML YEARS			286	1070	265	65	3	50	(33 | 17)	486	133	149	135	58	3	241	9	2	8	3	4	15	.248	.290	.454	.744

Hector Santiago

Pitches: L **Bats:** R **Pos:** RP-12; SP-1 **Ht:** 6'0" **Wt:** 215 **Born:** 12/16/1987 **Age:** 34

			HOW MUCH PITCHED					WHAT HE GAVE UP									THE RESULTS						
Year	Team	Lg	G	GS	GF	IP	BFP	H	R	ER	HR	SH	SF	HB	TBB	IBB	SO	WP	W	L	Pct	Sv-Op	Hld	Vel	OPS	ERC	ERA
2011	CWS	AL	2	0	1	5.1	18	1	0	0	0	0	0	0	1	1	2	1	0	0		0-0	0	94	.170	0.16	0.00
2012	CWS	AL	42	4	19	70.1	306	54	26	26	10	2	1	7	40	1	79	5	4	1	.800	4-6	4	93	.680	4.11	3.33
2013	CWS	AL	34	23	4	149.0	656	137	69	59	17	3	3	15	72	2	137	2	4	9	.308	0-0	0	92	.739	4.43	3.56
2014	LAA	AL	30	24	2	127.1	544	120	63	53	15	1	3	3	53	3	108	5	6	9	.400	0-0	1	91	.698	4.02	3.75
2015	LAA	AL	33	32	0	180.2	776	156	80	72	**29**	4	4	10	71	5	162	1	9	9	.500	0-0	0	90	.723	3.82	3.59
2016	2 Tms	AL	33	33	0	182.0	785	169	100	95	33	5	6	5	**79**	0	144	3	13	10	.565	0-0	0	91	.774	4.48	4.70
2017	Min	AL	15	14	1	70.1	311	70	44	44	15	0	1	5	31	0	51	0	4	8	.333	0-0	0	91	.782	5.33	5.63
2018	CWS	AL	49	7	27	102.0	460	101	54	50	16	1	3	5	60	3	103	1	6	3	.667	2-2	0	91	.807	5.38	4.41
2019	2 Tms	AL	19	2	11	33.2	163	42	26	25	8	0	1	0	22	0	40	0	1	1	.500	0-0	0	92	.950	7.71	6.68
2021	Sea	AL	13	1	6	26.1	117	27	10	10	2	0	1	0	11	0	30	0	1	1	.500	0-0	0	91	.715	4.01	3.42
16 LAA		AL	22	22	0	120.2	515	104	61	57	20	3	4	4	57	0	107	2	10	4	.714	0-0	0	92	.736	4.20	4.25
16 Min		AL	11	11	0	61.1	270	65	39	38	13	2	2	1	22	0	37	1	3	6	.333	0-0	0	91	.843	5.05	5.58
19 NYM		NL	8	0	6	8.0	38	10	6	6	1	0	0	0	5	0	6	0	1	0	1.000	0-0	0	92	.940	6.73	6.75
19 CWS		AL	11	2	5	25.2	125	32	20	19	7	0	1	0	17	0	34	0	0	1	.000	0-0	0	92	.953	8.01	6.66
	Postseason		1	0	0	1.1	7	1	2	2	1	0	0	0	2	0	0	0	0	0	-	0-0	0	91	1.229	12.98	13.50
10 ML YEARS			270	140	71	947.0	4136	877	472	434	145	16	23	50	440	15	856	18	48	51	.485	6-8	5	91	.749	4.47	4.12

Tony Santillan

Pitches: R **Bats:** R **Pos:** RP-22; SP-4 **Ht:** 6'3" **Wt:** 240 **Born:** 4/15/1997 **Age:** 25

			HOW MUCH PITCHED					WHAT HE GAVE UP									THE RESULTS						
Year	Team	Lg	G	GS	GF	IP	BFP	H	R	ER	HR	SH	SF	HB	TBB	IBB	SO	WP	W	L	Pct	Sv-Op	Hld	Vel	OPS	ERC	ERA
2021	Lsvlle	AAA	13	6	4	38.0	152	25	10	9	5	0	0	0	15	0	51	4	1	3	.250	2--	-	-	.614	2.47	2.13
2021	Cin	NL	26	4	5	43.1	190	34	15	14	7	1	4	7	21	0	56	1	1	3	.250	0-0	0	95	.729	4.24	2.91

Antonio Santos

Pitches: R **Bats:** R **Pos:** RP-7 **Ht:** 6'3" **Wt:** 223 **Born:** 10/6/1996 **Age:** 25

			HOW MUCH PITCHED					WHAT HE GAVE UP									THE RESULTS						
Year	Team	Lg	G	GS	GF	IP	BFP	H	R	ER	HR	SH	SF	HB	TBB	IBB	SO	WP	W	L	Pct	Sv-Op	Hld	Vel	OPS	ERC	ERA
2021	Albq	AAA	33	2	4	45.0	207	54	40	39	10	0	3	3	23	0	32	5	0	5	.000	0--	-	-	.920	7.12	7.80
2020	Col	NL	3	1	0	6.0	35	14	11	11	1	0	0	2	4	0	4	0	0	1	.000	0-0	0	93	1.330	17.82	16.50
2021	Col	NL	7	0	4	11.1	46	9	7	6	1	0	0	0	5	0	10	2	0	1	.000	0-0	0	96	.670	3.14	4.76
2 ML YEARS			10	1	4	17.1	81	23	18	17	2	0	0	2	9	0	14	2	0	2	.000	0-0	0	95	.948	7.45	8.83

Gregory Santos

Pitches: R Bats: R Pos: RP-3 Ht: 6'2" Wt: 190 Born: 8/28/1999 Age: 22

			HOW MUCH PITCHED					WHAT HE GAVE UP											THE RESULTS						
Year	Team	Lg	G	GS	GF	IP	BFP	H	R	ER	HR	SH	SF	HB	TBB	IBB	SO	WP	W	L	Pct	Sv-Op	Hld	Vel	OPS	ERC	ERA
2018	SlKzr	A-	12	12	0	49.2	227	64	34	25	3	1	3	0	15	0	46	7	2	5	.286	0--	-	-	.779	4.94	4.53
2019	Augsta	A	8	8	0	34.2	143	34	16	11	4	0	0	0	16	0	26	0	1	5	.167	0--	-	-	.458	3.56	2.86
2021	Scrmto	AAA	14	0	1	15.2	73	16	9	9	1	0	0	3	9	0	15	3	1	1	.500	0--	-	-	.744	5.40	5.17
2021	SF	NL	3	0	1	2.0	13	5	6	5	3	0	0	0	2	0	3	0	0	2	.000	0-0	1	98	1.811	33.45	22.50

Tayler Saucedo

Pitches: L Bats: L Pos: RP-29 Ht: 6'5" Wt: 185 Born: 6/18/1993 Age: 29

			HOW MUCH PITCHED					WHAT HE GAVE UP											THE RESULTS						
Year	Team	Lg	G	GS	GF	IP	BFP	H	R	ER	HR	SH	SF	HB	TBB	IBB	SO	WP	W	L	Pct	Sv-Op	Hld	Vel	OPS	ERC	ERA
2021	Buffalo	AAA	11	0	0	17.1	64	13	4	4	0	0	0	2	2	1	23	1	2	1	.667	0--	-	-	.532	1.68	2.08
2021	Tor	AL	29	0	9	25.2	109	22	14	13	1	0	1	2	10	0	19	2	0	0	-	0-2	1	94	.666	3.13	4.56

Hirokazu Sawamura

Pitches: R Bats: R Pos: RP-55 Ht: 6'0" Wt: 212 Born: 4/3/1988 Age: 34

			HOW MUCH PITCHED					WHAT HE GAVE UP											THE RESULTS						
Year	Team	Lg	G	GS	GF	IP	BFP	H	R	ER	HR	SH	SF	HB	TBB	IBB	SO	WP	W	L	Pct	Sv-Op	Hld	Vel	OPS	ERC	ERA
2021	Bos	AL	55	0	4	53.0	233	45	24	18	9	0	1	2	32	6	61	8	5	1	.833	0-1	10	96	.768	4.50	3.06

Josh Sborz

Pitches: R Bats: R Pos: RP-63 Ht: 6'3" Wt: 215 Born: 12/17/1993 Age: 28

			HOW MUCH PITCHED					WHAT HE GAVE UP											THE RESULTS						
Year	Team	Lg	G	GS	GF	IP	BFP	H	R	ER	HR	SH	SF	HB	TBB	IBB	SO	WP	W	L	Pct	Sv-Op	Hld	Vel	OPS	ERC	ERA
2019	LAD	NL	7	0	6	9.0	40	10	8	8	2	0	1	0	4	0	7	0	0	1	.000	0-0	0	95	.921	5.84	8.00
2020	LAD	NL	4	0	3	4.1	16	2	1	1	1	0	0	0	1	0	2	0	0	0	-	0-0	0	96	.588	1.53	2.08
2021	Tex	AL	63	0	16	59.0	257	52	29	26	7	0	3	0	32	1	69	8	4	3	.571	1-4	9	97	.710	4.05	3.97
	3 ML YEARS		74	0	25	72.1	313	64	38	35	10	0	4	0	37	1	78	8	4	4	.500	1-4	9	97	.731	4.10	4.35

Mac Sceroler

Pitches: R Bats: R Pos: RP-5 Ht: 6'3" Wt: 215 Born: 4/9/1995 Age: 27

			HOW MUCH PITCHED					WHAT HE GAVE UP											THE RESULTS						
Year	Team	Lg	G	GS	GF	IP	BFP	H	R	ER	HR	SH	SF	HB	TBB	IBB	SO	WP	W	L	Pct	Sv-Op	Hld	Vel	OPS	ERC	ERA
2021	Chatt	AA	10	7	0	36.1	173	48	39	34	7	0	0	3	11	0	38	6	1	4	.200	0--	-	-	.879	6.41	8.42
2021	Bal	AL	5	0	3	7.2	48	15	15	12	6	0	0	1	7	0	11	1	0	0	-	0-0	0	93	1.429	19.63	14.09

Scott Schebler

Bats: L Throws: R Pos: CF-4;RF-4;LF-3;PH-3;PR-1 SHEB-ler Ht: 6'1" Wt: 228 Born: 10/6/1990 Age: 31

			BATTING																		RUNNING			AVERAGES			
Year	Team	Lg	G	AB	H	2B	3B	HR	(Hm	Rd)	TB	R	RBI	RC	TBB	IBB	SO	HBP	SH	SF	SB	CS	GDP	Avg	OBP	Slg	OPS
2021	Salt Lk	AAA	69	255	55	14	0	11	(-	-)	102	31	40	-	12	0	86	12	0	1	3	1	5	.216	.295	.400	.695
2015	LAD	NL	19	36	9	0	0	3	(1	2)	18	6	4	4	3	1	13	1	0	0	2	1	0	.250	.325	.500	.825
2016	Cin	NL	82	257	68	12	2	9	(5	4)	111	36	40	36	19	2	59	6	0	0	2	4	5	.265	.330	.432	.762
2017	Cin	NL	141	473	110	25	2	30	(13	17)	229	63	67	58	39	5	125	14	0	5	5	3	7	.233	.307	.484	.791
2018	Cin	NL	107	380	97	19	0	17	(7	10)	167	55	49	47	39	1	99	9	0	2	4	2	5	.255	.337	.439	.777
2019	Cin	NL	30	81	10	2	0	2	(1	1)	18	11	7	3	14	0	27	0	0	0	0	1	3	.123	.253	.222	.475
2020	Atl	NL	1	1	0	0	0	0	(0	0)	0	0	0	0	0	0	0	0	0	0	0	0	0	.000	.000	.000	.000
2021	LAA	AL	14	34	5	3	0	0	(0	0)	8	3	0	0	0	0	17	0	0	0	0	0	0	.147	.147	.235	.382
	7 ML YEARS		394	1262	299	61	4	61	(27	34)	551	174	167	148	114	9	340	30	0	7	13	11	20	.237	.314	.437	.750

Max Scherzer

Pitches: R Bats: R Pos: SP-30 SHERR-zer Ht: 6'3" Wt: 208 Born: 7/27/1984 Age: 37

			HOW MUCH PITCHED					WHAT HE GAVE UP											THE RESULTS						
Year	Team	Lg	G	GS	GF	IP	BFP	H	R	ER	HR	SH	SF	HB	TBB	IBB	SO	WP	W	L	Pct	Sv-Op	Hld	Vel	OPS	ERC	ERA
2008	Ari	NL	16	7	2	56.0	237	48	24	19	5	4	2	5	21	1	66	2	0	4	.000	0-0	0	94	.649	3.45	3.05
2009	Ari	NL	30	30	0	170.1	741	166	94	78	20	5	6	10	63	1	174	5	9	11	.450	0-0	0	94	.751	4.12	4.12
2010	Det	AL	31	31	0	195.2	800	174	84	76	20	5	6	10	70	1	184	8	12	11	.522	0-0	0	93	.700	3.56	3.50
2011	Det	AL	33	33	0	195.0	833	207	101	96	29	3	7	7	56	1	174	12	15	9	.625	0-0	0	93	.781	4.48	4.43
2012	Det	AL	32	32	0	187.2	787	179	82	78	23	5	1	5	60	2	231	2	16	7	.696	0-0	0	94	.721	3.77	3.74
2013	Det	AL	32	32	0	214.1	836	152	73	69	18	2	8	4	56	0	240	6	21	3	.875	0-0	0	93	.583	2.07	2.90
2014	Det	AL	33	33	0	220.1	904	196	80	77	18	4	8	6	63	1	252	10	18	5	.783	0-0	0	93	.663	3.04	3.15
2015	Was	NL	33	33	0	228.2	899	176	74	71	27	11	2	5	34	2	276	10	14	12	.538	0-0	0	94	.600	2.11	2.79
2016	Was	NL	34	34	0	228.1	902	165	77	75	31	7	3	6	56	2	284	2	20	7	.741	0-0	0	94	.619	2.35	2.96
2017	Was	NL	31	31	0	200.2	780	126	62	56	22	4	1	11	55	2	268	4	16	6	.727	0-0	0	94	.566	1.98	2.51
2018	Was	NL	33	33	0	220.2	866	150	66	62	23	4	2	12	51	4	300	4	18	7	.720	0-0	0	95	.580	2.02	2.53
2019	Was	NL	27	27	0	172.1	693	144	59	56	18	0	2	6	33	2	243	0	11	7	.611	0-0	0	95	.637	2.58	2.92
2020	Was	NL	12	12	0	67.1	295	70	30	28	10	0	2	1	23	1	92	6	5	4	.556	0-0	0	94	.742	4.36	3.74
2021	2 Tms	NL	30	30	0	179.1	693	119	53	49	23	2	1	10	36	0	236	2	15	4	.789	0-0	0	94	.570	2.01	2.46
	21 Was	NL	19	19	0	111.0	428	71	36	34	18	1	1	8	28	0	147	0	8	4	.667	0-0	0	94	.604	2.35	2.76
	21 LAD	NL	11	11	0	68.1	265	48	17	15	5	1	0	2	8	0	89	2	7	0	1.000	0-0	0	95	.515	1.54	1.98
	Postseason		22	18	0	112.0	463	81	45	42	12	3	0	7	46	3	137	5	7	5	.583	0-0	2	94	.639	2.88	3.38
	14 ML YEARS		407	398	2	2536.2	10266	2072	959	890	287	56	50	96	677	20	3020	73	190	97	.662	0-0	0	94	.650	2.82	3.16

Clarke Schmidt

Pitches: R **Bats:** R **Pos:** SP-1; RP-1　　　　　　　　**Ht:** 6'1" **Wt:** 209 **Born:** 2/20/1996 **Age:** 26

			HOW MUCH PITCHED					WHAT HE GAVE UP											THE RESULTS						
Year	Team	Lg	G	GS	GF	IP	BFP	H	R	ER	HR	SH	SF	HB	TBB	IBB	SO	WP	W	L	Pct	Sv-Op	Hld	Vel	OPS	ERC	ERA
2021	S-WB	AAA	5	4	0	19.2	89	22	11	6	3	0	0	1	7	0	28	0	0	1	.000	0--	-	-	.744	5.05	2.75
2020	NYY	AL	3	1	2	6.1	33	7	5	5	0	0	0	2	5	0	7	1	0	1	.000	0-0	0	95	.770	6.52	7.11
2021	NYY	AL	2	1	1	6.1	38	11	8	4	1	1	0	1	5	0	6	0	0	0		0-0	0	93	.976	10.94	5.68
	2 ML YEARS		5	2	3	12.2	71	18	13	9	1	1	0	3	10	0	13	1	0	1	.000	0-0	0	94	.881	8.69	6.39

Jonathan Schoop

Bats: R **Throws:** R **Pos:** 1B-114;2B-38;DH-15;3B-1　　　SCOPE　　　　**Ht:** 6'1" **Wt:** 247 **Born:** 10/16/1991 **Age:** 30

			BATTING																		RUNNING			AVERAGES			
Year	Team	Lg	G	AB	H	2B	3B	HR	(Hm	Rd)	TB	R	RBI	RC	TBB	IBB	SO	HBP	SH	SF	SB	CS	GDP	Avg	OBP	Slg	OPS
2013	Bal	AL	5	14	4	0	0	1	(1	0)	7	5	1	1	1	0	2	0	0	0	0	0	2	.286	.333	.500	.833
2014	Bal	AL	137	455	95	18	0	16	(5	11)	161	48	45	32	13	0	122	8	5	0	2	0	12	.209	.244	.354	.598
2015	Bal	AL	86	305	85	17	0	15	(9	6)	147	34	39	40	9	0	79	4	1	2	2	0	9	.279	.306	.482	.788
2016	Bal	AL	162	615	164	38	1	25	(13	12)	279	82	82	72	21	0	137	8	0	3	1	2	16	.267	.298	.454	.752
2017	Bal	AL	160	622	182	35	0	32	(18	14)	313	92	105	100	35	0	142	11	0	7	1	0	20	.293	.338	.503	.841
2018	2 Tms		131	473	110	22	1	21	(12	9)	197	61	61	45	19	2	115	4	1	4	1	1	11	.233	.266	.416	.682
2019	Min	AL	121	433	111	23	1	23	(7	16)	205	61	59	52	20	1	116	10	0	1	1	1	13	.256	.304	.473	.777
2020	Det	AL	44	162	45	4	2	8	(6	2)	77	26	23	23	8	0	39	4	0	2	0	0	8	.278	.324	.475	.799
2021	Det	AL	156	623	173	30	1	22	(11	11)	271	85	84	86	37	0	133	6	0	8	2	0	15	.278	.320	.435	.755
18	Bal	AL	85	349	85	18	1	17	(9	8)	156	45	40	34	12	1	74	3	1	2	0	1	8	.244	.273	.447	.720
18	Mil	NL	46	124	25	4	0	4	(3	1)	41	16	21	11	7	1	41	1	0	2	1	0	3	.202	.246	.331	.577
	Postseason		14	35	4	1	0	0	(0	0)	5	3	2	2	3	0	10	0	0	0	2	0	1	.114	.184	.143	.327
	9 ML YEARS		1002	3702	969	187	6	163	(82	81)	1657	494	499	451	163	3	885	55	7	27	10	4	106	.262	.301	.448	.748

John Schreiber

Pitches: R **Bats:** R **Pos:** RP-1　　　　　　　　**Ht:** 6'2" **Wt:** 210 **Born:** 3/5/1994 **Age:** 28

			HOW MUCH PITCHED					WHAT HE GAVE UP											THE RESULTS						
Year	Team	Lg	G	GS	GF	IP	BFP	H	R	ER	HR	SH	SF	HB	TBB	IBB	SO	WP	W	L	Pct	Sv-Op	Hld	Vel	OPS	ERC	ERA
2021	Wrcstr	AAA	31	8	5	63.0	267	60	23	20	3	0	1	1	23	0	61	1	2	3	.400	1--	-	-	.666	3.39	2.86
2019	Det	AL	13	0	3	13.0	59	16	9	9	3	0	0	1	4	0	19	1	2	0	1.000	0-1	1	92	.837	6.34	6.23
2020	Det	AL	15	0	2	15.2	70	19	11	11	2	0	1	1	4	1	14	0	0	1	.000	0-1	1	90	.827	5.02	6.32
2021	Bos	AL	1	0	0	3.0	13	4	1	1	0	0	0	0	1	0	5	0	0	0		0-0	0	92	.885	5.24	3.00
	3 ML YEARS		29	0	5	31.2	142	39	21	21	5	0	1	2	9	1	38	1	2	1	.667	0-2	2	91	.837	5.58	5.97

Max Schrock

Bats: L **Throws:** R **Pos:** LF-23;PH-19;3B-9;2B-8;1B-5;RF-1　　　　**Ht:** 5'9" **Wt:** 185 **Born:** 10/12/1994 **Age:** 27

			BATTING																		RUNNING			AVERAGES			
Year	Team	Lg	G	AB	H	2B	3B	HR	(Hm	Rd)	TB	R	RBI	RC	TBB	IBB	SO	HBP	SH	SF	SB	CS	GDP	Avg	OBP	Slg	OPS
2021	Lsvlle	AAA	38	128	37	4	0	6	(-	-)	59	14	19	-	7	1	25	2	0	1	0	0	2	.289	.333	.461	.794
2020	StL	NL	11	17	3	0	0	1	(0	1)	6	1	1	0	0	0	6	0	0	0	0	0	0	.176	.176	.353	.529
2021	Cin	NL	53	125	36	7	2	3	(2	1)	56	19	14	20	8	1	24	0	0	1	1	1	0	.288	.328	.448	.776
	2 ML YEARS		64	142	39	7	2	4	(2	2)	62	20	15	20	8	1	30	0	0	1	1	1	0	.275	.311	.437	.748

Kyle Schwarber

Bats: L **Throws:** R **Pos:** LF-87;DH-14;1B-10;PH-4　　　SHWAR-burr　　　**Ht:** 6'0" **Wt:** 229 **Born:** 3/5/1993 **Age:** 29

			BATTING																		RUNNING			AVERAGES			
Year	Team	Lg	G	AB	H	2B	3B	HR	(Hm	Rd)	TB	R	RBI	RC	TBB	IBB	SO	HBP	SH	SF	SB	CS	GDP	Avg	OBP	Slg	OPS
2015	ChC	NL	69	232	57	6	1	16	(7	9)	113	52	43	39	36	1	77	4	0	1	3	3	4	.246	.355	.487	.842
2016	ChC	NL	2	4	0	0	0	0	(0	0)	0	0	0	0	1	0	2	0	0	0	0	0	0	.000	.200	.000	.200
2017	ChC	NL	129	422	89	16	1	30	(18	12)	197	67	59	55	59	1	150	5	0	0	1	1	6	.211	.315	.467	.782
2018	ChC	NL	137	428	102	14	3	26	(11	15)	200	64	61	65	78	20	140	1	1	2	4	3	6	.238	.356	.467	.823
2019	ChC	NL	155	529	132	29	3	38	(18	20)	281	82	92	92	70	5	156	5	0	6	2	3	6	.250	.339	.531	.871
2020	ChC	NL	59	191	36	6	0	11	(5	6)	75	30	24	27	30	1	66	3	0	1	0	3	3	.188	.308	.393	.701
2021	2 Tms		113	399	106	19	0	32	(21	11)	221	76	71	83	64	1	127	6	0	2	1	1	4	.266	.374	.554	.928
21	Was	NL	72	265	67	9	0	25	(17	8)	151	42	53	49	31	1	88	5	0	2	1	1	4	.253	.340	.570	.910
21	Bos	AL	41	134	39	10	0	7	(4	3)	70	34	18	34	33	0	39	1	0	0	0	0	0	.291	.435	.522	.957
	Postseason		24	66	19	1	0	6	(4	2)	38	10	11	12	13	0	19	0	0	0	1	0	1	.288	.405	.576	.981
	7 ML YEARS		664	2205	522	90	8	153	(80	73)	1087	371	350	361	338	29	718	24	1	11	12	11	29	.237	.343	.493	.836

Frank Schwindel

Bats: R **Throws:** R **Pos:** 1B-52;DH-8;PH-7　　　　　　**Ht:** 6'1" **Wt:** 220 **Born:** 6/29/1992 **Age:** 30

			BATTING																		RUNNING			AVERAGES			
Year	Team	Lg	G	AB	H	2B	3B	HR	(Hm	Rd)	TB	R	RBI	RC	TBB	IBB	SO	HBP	SH	SF	SB	CS	GDP	Avg	OBP	Slg	OPS
2021	LsVgs	AAA	45	189	60	11	0	16	(-	-)	119	41	41	-	13	0	35	2	0	3	0	0	6	.317	.362	.630	.992
2019	KC	AL	6	15	1	0	0	0	(0	0)	1	0	0	0	0	0	2	0	0	0	0	0	0	.067	.067	.067	.133
2021	2 Tms		64	242	79	20	1	14	(7	7)	143	44	43	48	16	2	41	1	0	0	2	1	4	.326	.371	.591	.962
21	Oak	AL	8	20	3	1	0	1	(1	0)	7	2	3	2	0	0	5	0	0	0	0	0	0	.150	.150	.350	.500
21	ChC	NL	56	222	76	19	1	13	(6	7)	136	42	40	46	16	2	36	1	0	0	2	1	4	.342	.389	.613	1.002
	2 ML YEARS		70	257	80	20	1	14	(7	7)	144	44	43	48	16	2	43	1	0	0	2	1	4	.311	.354	.560	.914

Tanner Scott

Pitches: L Bats: R Pos: RP-62
Ht: 6'0" Wt: 235 Born: 7/22/1994 Age: 27

Year	Team	Lg	G	GS	GF	IP	BFP	H	R	ER	HR	SH	SF	HB	TBB	IBB	SO	WP	W	L	Pct	Sv-Op	Hld	Vel	OPS	ERC	ERA
2017	Bal	AL	2	0	1	1.2	9	2	2	0	0	0	0	0	2	0	2	0	0	0	-	0-0	0	98	.873	7.49	10.80
2018	Bal	AL	53	0	8	53.1	240	55	33	32	6	1	1	1	28	1	76	7	3	3	.500	0-3	5	97	.777	4.86	5.40
2019	Bal	AL	28	0	5	26.1	122	28	17	14	4	0	0	2	19	2	37	2	1	1	.500	0-1	2	96	.847	6.54	4.78
2020	Bal	AL	25	0	6	20.2	86	12	5	3	1	0	0	3	10	0	23	4	0	0		1-2	5	96	.524	2.37	1.31
2021	Bal	AL	62	0	12	54.0	251	48	34	31	6	0	3	6	37	1	70	10	5	4	.556	0-2	16	97	.714	4.99	5.17
	5 ML YEARS		170	0	32	156.0	708	145	91	82	17	1	4	12	96	4	208	23	9	8	.529	1-8	28	97	.738	4.84	4.73

Andre Scrubb

Pitches: R Bats: R Pos: RP-18
Ht: 6'4" Wt: 270 Born: 1/13/1995 Age: 27

Year	Team	Lg	G	GS	GF	IP	BFP	H	R	ER	HR	SH	SF	HB	TBB	IBB	SO	WP	W	L	Pct	Sv-Op	Hld	Vel	OPS	ERC	ERA
2021	SgrLnd	AAA	14	0	1	14.0	63	6	2	2	0	1	0	2	13	0	17	2	0	0	-	0- -			.488	2.68	1.29
2020	Hou	AL	20	0	4	23.2	102	15	5	5	1	1	2	0	20	1	24	1	1	0	1.000	1-1	2	93	.587	3.33	1.90
2021	Hou	AL	18	0	4	19.2	86	15	11	11	5	0	2	0	14	0	21	2	1	1	.500	0-2	2	94	.780	5.12	5.03
	Postseason		4	0	2	4.0	18	4	1	1	0	0	0	0	2	0	7	0	0	0		0-0	0	95	.771	5.46	2.25
	2 ML YEARS		38	0	9	43.1	188	30	16	16	6	1	4	0	34	1	45	3	2	1	.667	1-3	4	93	.678	4.15	3.32

Connor Seabold

Pitches: R Bats: R Pos: SP-1
Ht: 6'2" Wt: 190 Born: 1/24/1996 Age: 26

Year	Team	Lg	G	GS	GF	IP	BFP	H	R	ER	HR	SH	SF	HB	TBB	IBB	SO	WP	W	L	Pct	Sv-Op	Hld	Vel	OPS	ERC	ERA
2021	Wrcstr	AAA	10	10	0	49.0	207	39	23	20	6	1	0	6	17	0	52	2	3	3	.500	0- -	-		.671	3.35	3.67
2021	Bos	AL	1	1	0	3.0	12	3	2	2	1	0	0	0	2	0	0	0	0	0		0-0	0	90	1.117	8.08	6.00

Corey Seager

Bats: L Throws: R Pos: SS-92;PH-4 SEE-gurr
Ht: 6'4" Wt: 215 Born: 4/27/1994 Age: 28

Year	Team	Lg	G	AB	H	2B	3B	HR	(Hm	Rd)	TB	R	RBI	RC	TBB	IBB	SO	HBP	SH	SF	SB	CS	GDP	Avg	OBP	Slg	OPS
2015	LAD	NL	27	98	33	8	1	4	(3	1)	55	17	17	19	14	1	19	1	0	0	2	0	2	.337	.425	.561	.986
2016	LAD	NL	157	627	193	40	5	26	(18	8)	321	105	72	110	54	1	133	4	0	2	3	3	12	.308	.365	.512	.877
2017	LAD	NL	145	539	159	33	0	22	(12	10)	258	85	77	104	67	5	131	4	0	3	4	2	14	.295	.375	.479	.854
2018	LAD	NL	26	101	27	5	1	2	(1	1)	40	13	13	17	11	1	17	2	0	1	0	0	2	.267	.348	.396	.744
2019	LAD	NL	134	489	133	44	1	19	(9	10)	236	82	87	81	44	3	98	4	0	4	1	0	8	.272	.335	.483	.817
2020	LAD	NL	52	212	65	12	1	15	(7	8)	124	38	41	36	17	0	37	1	0	2	1	0	1	.307	.358	.585	.943
2021	LAD	NL	95	353	108	22	3	16	(9	7)	184	54	57	74	48	2	66	5	0	3	1	1	8	.306	.394	.521	.915
	Postseason		49	185	46	8	1	11	(5	6)	89	32	30	27	22	0	53	2	0	2	3	0	6	.249	.332	.481	.813
	7 ML YEARS		636	2419	718	164	12	104	(59	45)	1218	394	364	441	255	17	501	21	0	15	12	6	54	.297	.367	.504	.870

Kyle Seager

Bats: L Throws: R Pos: 3B-149;DH-10;PH-2 SEE-gurr
Ht: 6'0" Wt: 216 Born: 11/3/1987 Age: 34

Year	Team	Lg	G	AB	H	2B	3B	HR	(Hm	Rd)	TB	R	RBI	RC	TBB	IBB	SO	HBP	SH	SF	SB	CS	GDP	Avg	OBP	Slg	OPS
2011	Sea	AL	53	182	47	13	0	3	(0	3)	69	22	13	16	13	0	36	2	2	2	3	1	4	.258	.312	.379	.691
2012	Sea	AL	155	594	154	35	1	20	(5	15)	251	62	86	88	46	1	110	5	2	4	13	5	9	.259	.316	.423	.738
2013	Sea	AL	160	615	160	32	2	22	(8	14)	262	79	69	90	68	1	122	7	0	5	9	3	8	.260	.338	.426	.764
2014	Sea	AL	159	590	158	27	4	25	(16	9)	268	71	96	96	52	3	118	8	1	3	7	5	12	.268	.334	.454	.788
2015	Sea	AL	161	623	166	37	0	26	(7	19)	281	85	74	75	54	6	98	4	0	4	6	6	17	.266	.328	.451	.779
2016	Sea	AL	158	597	166	36	3	30	(11	19)	298	89	99	110	69	10	108	8	0	2	3	1	18	.278	.359	.499	.859
2017	Sea	AL	154	578	144	33	1	27	(12	15)	260	72	88	84	58	6	110	8	0	6	2	1	6	.249	.323	.450	.773
2018	Sea	AL	155	583	129	36	1	22	(8	14)	233	62	78	59	38	3	138	5	0	4	2	2	10	.221	.273	.400	.673
2019	Sea	AL	106	393	94	19	1	23	(10	13)	184	55	63	57	44	0	86	4	0	2	2	2	12	.239	.321	.468	.789
2020	Sea	AL	60	203	49	12	0	9	(4	5)	88	35	40	37	32	3	33	7	0	6	5	0	4	.241	.355	.433	.788
2021	Sea	AL	159	603	128	29	1	35	(13	22)	264	73	101	91	59	2	161	4	0	4	3	1	7	.212	.285	.438	.723
	11 ML YEARS		1480	5561	1395	309	14	242	(94	148)	2458	705	807	803	533	35	1120	63	5	42	55	27	107	.251	.321	.442	.763

Jean Segura

Bats: R Throws: R Pos: 2B-128;PH-3;SS-1 JEEN seh-GOO-ruh
Ht: 5'10" Wt: 220 Born: 3/17/1990 Age: 32

Year	Team	Lg	G	AB	H	2B	3B	HR	(Hm	Rd)	TB	R	RBI	RC	TBB	IBB	SO	HBP	SH	SF	SB	CS	GDP	Avg	OBP	Slg	OPS
2012	2 Tms		45	151	39	4	3	0	(0	0)	49	19	14	16	13	1	23	0	1	1	7	1	1	.258	.315	.325	.640
2013	Mil	NL	146	588	173	20	10	12	(7	5)	249	74	49	72	25	1	84	6	2	2	44	13	11	.294	.329	.423	.752
2014	Mil	NL	146	513	126	14	6	5	(3	2)	167	61	31	45	28	5	70	4	10	2	20	9	13	.246	.289	.326	.614
2015	Mil	NL	142	560	144	16	5	6	(4	2)	188	57	50	57	13	2	93	6	3	2	25	6	14	.257	.281	.336	.616
2016	Ari	NL	153	637	203	41	7	20	(12	8)	318	102	64	107	39	1	101	12	4	4	33	10	6	.319	.368	.499	.867
2017	Sea	AL	125	524	157	30	2	11	(7	4)	224	80	45	71	34	3	83	6	0	1	22	8	14	.300	.349	.427	.776
2018	Sea	AL	144	586	178	29	3	10	(7	3)	243	91	63	77	32	2	69	4	4	6	20	11	17	.304	.341	.415	.755
2019	Phi	NL	144	576	161	37	4	12	(9	3)	242	79	60	79	30	1	73	8	1	3	10	2	11	.280	.323	.420	.743
2020	Phi	NL	54	192	51	5	2	7	(5	2)	81	28	25	28	23	2	45	1	1	0	2	2	6	.266	.347	.422	.769
2021	Phi	NL	131	514	149	27	3	14	(6	8)	224	76	58	75	39	3	78	9	1	4	9	3	16	.290	.348	.436	.784
12	LAA	AL	1	3	0	0	0	0	(0	0)	0	0	0	0	0	0	2	0	0	0	0	0	0	.000	.000	.000	.000
12	Mil	NL	44	148	39	4	3	0	(0	0)	49	19	14	16	13	3	21	0	1	1	7	1	1	.264	.321	.331	.652
	10 ML YEARS		1230	4841	1381	223	45	97	(60	37)	1985	667	459	627	276	23	719	56	27	23	192	65	115	.285	.330	.410	.740

Sam Selman

Pitches: L **Bats:** R **Pos:** RP-25   **Ht:** 6'2" **Wt:** 198 **Born:** 11/14/1990 **Age:** 31

			HOW MUCH PITCHED					WHAT HE GAVE UP											THE RESULTS								
Year Team	Lg	G	GS	GF	IP	BFP	H	R	ER	HR	SH	SF	HB	TBB	IBB	SO	WP	W	L	Pct	Sv-Op	Hld	Vel	OPS	ERC	ERA
2021 Scrmto	AAA	17	2	5	22.1	97	13	10	10	0	0	1	0	19	1	24	0	1	0	1.000	1--	-		.564	2.71	4.03
2019 SF	NL	10	0	3	10.1	44	6	5	5	2	1	0	2	6	0	10	0	0	0	-	0-1	1	90	.697	3.89	4.35
2020 SF	NL	24	0	8	19.1	82	13	8	8	2	1	0	2	9	0	23	2	1	1	.500	1-1	3	91	.611	2.92	3.72
2021 2 Tms		25	0	9	25.0	110	20	17	16	3	0	3	5	12	1	19	0	0	1	.000	0-1	1	91	.692	4.12	5.76
21 SF	NL	7	0	2	8.0	33	4	4	4	2	0	0	1	4	0	8	0	0	0	-	0-1	0	91	.666	3.17	4.50
21 LAA	AL	18	0	7	17.0	77	16	13	12	1	0	3	4	8	1	11	0	0	1	.000	0-0	1	91	.702	4.54	6.35
3 ML YEARS		59	0	20	54.2	236	39	30	29	7	2	3	9	27	1	52	2	1	2	.333	1-3	5	91	.664	3.64	4.77

Marcus Semien

Bats: R **Throws:** R **Pos:** 2B-147;SS-21;DH-1   SIM-ee-inn   **Ht:** 6'0" **Wt:** 195 **Born:** 9/17/1990 **Age:** 31

								BATTING											RUNNING			AVERAGES			
Year Team	Lg	G	AB	H	2B	3B	HR	(Hm Rd)	TB	R	RBI	RC	TBB	IBB	SO	HBP	SH	SF	SB	CS	GDP	Avg	OBP	Slg	OPS
2013 CWS	AL	21	69	18	4	0	2	(2 0)	28	7	7	7	1	0	22	0	0	1	2	2	1	.261	.268	.406	.673
2014 CWS	AL	64	231	54	10	2	6	(4 2)	86	30	28	31	21	0	70	1	2	0	3	0	6	.234	.300	.372	.673
2015 Oak	AL	155	556	143	23	7	15	(5 10)	225	65	45	57	42	1	132	1	1	1	11	5	16	.257	.310	.405	.715
2016 Oak	AL	159	568	135	27	2	27	(10 17)	247	72	75	77	51	1	139	0	1	1	10	2	12	.238	.300	.435	.735
2017 Oak	AL	85	342	85	19	1	10	(5 5)	136	53	40	48	38	0	85	2	1	3	12	1	3	.249	.325	.398	.722
2018 Oak	AL	159	632	161	35	2	15	(6 9)	245	89	70	85	61	1	131	1	2	7	14	6	12	.255	.318	.388	.706
2019 Oak	AL	162	657	187	43	7	33	(15 18)	343	123	92	136	87	2	102	2	0	1	10	8	11	.285	.369	.522	.892
2020 Oak	AL	53	211	47	9	1	7	(2 5)	79	28	23	30	25	0	50	0	0	0	4	0	3	.223	.305	.374	.679
2021 Tor	AL	162	652	173	39	2	45	(22 23)	351	115	102	112	66	0	146	3	0	3	15	1	9	.265	.334	.538	.872
Postseason		9	35	13	1	0	2	(1 1)	20	7	4	9	5	0	4	0	0	0	0	0	0	.371	.450	.571	1.021
9 ML YEARS		1020	3918	1003	209	24	160	(71 89)	1740	582	482	583	392	5	877	10	7	17	81	25	73	.256	.324	.444	.768

Antonio Senzatela

Pitches: R **Bats:** R **Pos:** SP-28   **Ht:** 6'1" **Wt:** 236 **Born:** 1/21/1995 **Age:** 27

			HOW MUCH PITCHED					WHAT HE GAVE UP											THE RESULTS								
Year Team	Lg	G	GS	GF	IP	BFP	H	R	ER	HR	SH	SF	HB	TBB	IBB	SO	WP	W	L	Pct	Sv-Op	Hld	Vel	OPS	ERC	ERA
2017 Col	NL	36	20	3	134.2	564	128	72	70	18	4	5	4	47	1	102	1	10	5	.667	0-0	1	94	.756	4.00	4.68
2018 Col	NL	23	13	2	90.1	390	94	45	44	10	1	3	3	30	1	69	1	6	6	.500	0-0	0	94	.763	4.22	4.38
2019 Col	NL	25	25	0	124.2	582	161	99	93	19	4	3	4	57	5	76	1	11	11	.500	0-0	0	94	.890	6.53	6.71
2020 Col	NL	12	12	0	73.1	303	71	29	28	9	0	2	4	18	0	41	0	5	3	.625	0-0	0	94	.716	3.72	3.44
2021 Col	NL	28	28	0	156.2	670	178	84	77	12	3	6	9	32	1	105	4	4	10	.286	0-0	0	95	.749	4.14	4.42
Postseason		1	1	0	5.0	19	3	2	2	1	0	0	0	2	0	1	2	0	0	-	0-0	0	94	.616	2.72	3.60
5 ML YEARS		124	98	5	579.2	2509	632	329	312	68	12	19	24	184	8	393	7	36	35	.507	0-0	1	94	.781	4.56	4.84

Nick Senzel

Bats: R **Throws:** R **Pos:** CF-29;2B-8;PH-4;3B-3;PR-1   **Ht:** 6'1" **Wt:** 205 **Born:** 6/29/1995 **Age:** 27

								BATTING											RUNNING			AVERAGES			
Year Team	Lg	G	AB	H	2B	3B	HR	(Hm Rd)	TB	R	RBI	RC	TBB	IBB	SO	HBP	SH	SF	SB	CS	GDP	Avg	OBP	Slg	OPS
2021 Lsvlle	AAA	10	35	10	3	1	0	(- -)	15	5	2		2	0	2	0	0	1	0	0	1	.286	.316	.429	.744
2019 Cin	NL	104	375	96	20	4	12	(7 5)	160	55	42	49	30	0	101	3	0	1	14	5	6	.256	.315	.427	.742
2020 Cin	NL	23	70	13	6	0	2	(2 0)	25	8	8	7	6	0	15	0	0	1	2	1	2	.186	.247	.357	.604
2021 Cin	NL	36	111	28	4	0	1	(1 0)	35	18	8	12	12	0	16	0	0	1	2	5	3	.252	.323	.315	.638
Postseason		2	7	2	0	0	0	(0 0)	2	0	0	0	0	0	2	0	0	0	0	0	0	.286	.286	.286	.571
3 ML YEARS		163	556	137	30	4	15	(10 5)	220	81	58	68	48	0	132	3	0	3	18	11	11	.246	.308	.396	.704

Luis Severino

Pitches: R **Bats:** R **Pos:** RP-4   **Ht:** 6'2" **Wt:** 218 **Born:** 2/20/1994 **Age:** 28

			HOW MUCH PITCHED					WHAT HE GAVE UP											THE RESULTS								
Year Team	Lg	G	GS	GF	IP	BFP	H	R	ER	HR	SH	SF	HB	TBB	IBB	SO	WP	W	L	Pct	Sv-Op	Hld	Vel	OPS	ERC	ERA
2015 NYY	AL	11	11	0	62.1	255	53	21	20	9	0	0	2	22	0	56	2	5	3	.625	0-0	0	95	.705	3.57	2.89
2016 NYY	AL	22	11	3	71.0	312	78	48	46	11	0	0	3	25	1	66	3	3	8	.273	0-0	1	96	.812	5.00	5.83
2017 NYY	AL	31	31	0	193.1	783	150	73	64	21	3	2	6	51	0	230	6	14	6	.700	0-0	0	98	.603	2.53	2.98
2018 NYY	AL	32	32	0	191.1	780	173	76	72	19	1	2	5	46	0	220	8	19	8	.704	0-0	0	98	.666	3.06	3.39
2019 NYY	AL	3	3	0	12.0	48	6	2	2	0	0	0	1	6	0	17	0	1	1	.500	0-0	0	96	.442	1.62	1.50
2021 NYY	AL	4	0	1	6.0	22	2	0	0	0	0	0	1	1	0	8	0	1	0	1.000	0-1	1	95	.332	0.69	0.00
Postseason		8	8	0	31.1	144	31	18	18	7	0	1	0	19	0	31	0	1	3	.250	0-0	0	97	.799	5.66	5.17
6 ML YEARS		103	88	4	536.0	2200	462	220	204	60	4	4	18	151	1	597	19	43	26	.623	0-0	2	97	.661	3.08	3.43

Pedro Severino

Bats: R **Throws:** R **Pos:** C-109;DH-4;PH-3   **Ht:** 6'1" **Wt:** 235 **Born:** 7/20/1993 **Age:** 28

								BATTING											RUNNING			AVERAGES			
Year Team	Lg	G	AB	H	2B	3B	HR	(Hm Rd)	TB	R	RBI	RC	TBB	IBB	SO	HBP	SH	SF	SB	CS	GDP	Avg	OBP	Slg	OPS
2015 Was	NL	2	4	1	1	0	0	(0 0)	2	1	0	0	0	0	1	0	0	0	0	0	0	.250	.250	.500	.750
2016 Was	NL	16	28	9	2	0	2	(1 1)	17	6	4	5	5	0	3	1	0	0	0	0	0	.321	.441	.607	1.048
2017 Was	NL	17	29	5	1	0	0	(0 0)	6	0	3	2	2	1	10	0	0	0	0	0	0	.172	.226	.207	.433
2018 Was	NL	70	190	32	9	0	2	(2 0)	47	14	15	12	18	4	47	4	0	1	1	0	3	.168	.254	.247	.501
2019 Bal	AL	96	305	76	13	0	13	(7 6)	128	37	44	39	29	0	73	4	1	2	3	1	5	.249	.321	.420	.740

			BATTING																RUNNING			AVERAGES			
Year Team	Lg	G	AB	H	2B	3B	HR	(Hm Rd)	TB	R	RBI	RC	TBB	IBB	SO	HBP	SH	SF	SB	CS	GDP	Avg	OBP	Slg	OPS
2020 Bal	AL	48	160	40	5	1	5	(3 2)	62	17	21	20	16	0	40	1	1	0	1	0	3	.250	.322	.388	.710
2021 Bal	AL	113	379	94	18	1	11	(8 3)	145	32	46	48	34	1	109	1	0	5	1	0	9	.248	.308	.383	.690
Postseason		4	10	1	1	0	0	(0 0)	2	1	0	0	0	0	3	0	0	0	0	0	0	.100	.100	.200	.300
7 ML YEARS		362	1095	257	49	1	33	(21 12)	407	107	133	126	104	6	283	11	2	8	5	1	20	.235	.305	.372	.677

Paul Sewald

Pitches: R Bats: R Pos: RP-62

Ht: 6'3" Wt: 207 Born: 5/26/1990 Age: 32

		HOW MUCH PITCHED					WHAT HE GAVE UP											THE RESULTS							
Year Team	Lg	G	GS	GF	IP	BFP	H	R	ER	HR	SH	SF	HB	TBB	IBB	SO	WP	W	L	Pct	Sv-Op	Hld	Vel	OPS	ERC	ERA
2017 NYM	NL	57	0	12	65.1	275	58	36	33	8	3	3	3	21	2	69	3	0	6	.000	0-3	13	91	.706	3.41	4.55
2018 NYM	NL	46	0	9	56.1	253	62	39	38	8	2	3	1	23	2	58	1	0	7	.000	2-4	2	90	.820	4.93	6.07
2019 NYM	NL	17	0	6	19.2	80	18	10	10	3	1	1	1	3	0	22	0	1	1	.500	1-1	0	91	.724	3.17	4.58
2020 NYM	NL	5	0	1	6.0	35	12	9	9	1	0	1	1	4	0	2	0	0	0	-	0-0	0	92	1.072	13.03	13.50
2021 Sea	AL	62	0	18	64.2	264	42	24	22	10	0	0	0	24	5	104	2	10	3	.769	11-16	16	92	.590	2.29	3.06
5 ML YEARS		187	0	46	212.0	907	192	118	112	30	6	8	6	75	9	255	6	11	17	.393	14-24	31	91	.719	3.63	4.75

Bryan Shaw

Pitches: R Bats: B Pos: RP-81

Ht: 6'1" Wt: 226 Born: 11/8/1987 Age: 34

		HOW MUCH PITCHED					WHAT HE GAVE UP											THE RESULTS							
Year Team	Lg	G	GS	GF	IP	BFP	H	R	ER	HR	SH	SF	HB	TBB	IBB	SO	WP	W	L	Pct	Sv-Op	Hld	Vel	OPS	ERC	ERA
2011 Ari	NL	33	0	8	28.1	122	30	9	8	2	0	0	4	8	1	24	1	1	0	1.000	0-0	5	91	.699	4.31	2.54
2012 Ari	NL	64	0	19	59.1	252	60	29	23	4	4	2	2	24	3	41	4	1	6	.143	2-4	10	92	.747	4.08	3.49
2013 Cle	AL	70	0	11	75.0	316	60	31	27	4	4	2	4	28	2	73	5	7	3	.700	1-5	12	91	.586	2.71	3.24
2014 Cle	AL	80	0	16	76.1	313	61	26	22	6	5	2	2	22	4	64	4	5	5	.500	2-9	24	93	.602	2.45	2.59
2015 Cle	AL	74	0	19	64.0	265	59	24	21	8	1	0	1	19	1	54	3	3	3	.500	2-6	23	93	.693	3.47	2.95
2016 Cle	AL	75	0	9	66.2	275	56	26	24	8	2	1	1	28	3	69	2	2	5	.286	1-4	25	93	.686	3.47	3.24
2017 Cle	AL	79	0	16	76.2	312	71	36	30	5	1	1	0	22	3	73	3	4	6	.400	3-6	26	94	.653	3.01	3.52
2018 Col	NL	61	0	14	54.2	257	70	43	36	9	1	3	1	28	1	54	8	4	6	.400	0-5	13	93	.896	6.79	5.93
2019 Col	NL	70	0	18	72.0	311	69	44	43	12	1	1	5	29	1	58	1	3	2	.600	1-6	12	93	.798	4.61	5.38
2020 Sea	AL	6	0	1	6.0	38	13	12	12	1	0	1	1	6	0	4	0	1	0	1.000	0-1	0	93	1.293	15.93	18.00
2021 Cle	AL	81	0	10	77.1	334	69	33	30	10	1	0	1	38	0	71	6	6	7	.462	2-8	20	93	.712	4.08	3.49
Postseason		19	0	2	22.0	89	19	8	6	2	0	1	0	6	3	22	1	2	1	.667	0-0	5	95	.622	2.63	2.45
11 ML YEARS		693	0	141	656.1	2795	618	313	276	69	20	13	22	252	19	585	37	37	43	.463	14-54	174	93	.711	3.82	3.78

Travis Shaw

Bats: L Throws: R Pos: 3B-48;1B-31;PH-24;DH-4

Ht: 6'4" Wt: 230 Born: 4/16/1990 Age: 32

			BATTING																RUNNING			AVERAGES			
Year Team	Lg	G	AB	H	2B	3B	HR	(Hm Rd)	TB	R	RBI	RC	TBB	IBB	SO	HBP	SH	SF	SB	CS	GDP	Avg	OBP	Slg	OPS
2021 Nashv	AAA	11	33	9	1	0	2	(- -)	16	6	8	-	7	0	8	1	0	0	0	0	2	.273	.415	.485	.899
2015 Bos	AL	65	226	61	10	0	13	(8 5)	110	31	36	35	18	1	57	2	0	2	0	1	1	.270	.327	.487	.813
2016 Bos	AL	145	480	116	34	2	16	(7 9)	202	63	71	64	43	4	133	3	0	4	5	1	10	.242	.306	.421	.726
2017 Mil	NL	144	538	147	34	1	31	(13 18)	276	84	101	93	60	6	138	4	1	3	10	0	20	.273	.349	.513	.862
2018 Mil	NL	152	498	120	23	1	32	(16 16)	239	73	86	84	78	6	108	4	1	6	5	2	7	.241	.345	.480	.825
2019 Mil	NL	86	230	36	5	0	7	(3 4)	62	22	16	11	36	3	89	4	0	0	0	0	5	.157	.281	.270	.551
2020 Tor	AL	50	163	39	10	0	6	(3 3)	67	17	17	19	16	0	50	0	0	1	0	0	4	.239	.306	.411	.717
2021 2 Tms		84	220	44	11	0	9	(6 3)	82	20	39	24	24	0	68	3	2	1	0	0	2	.200	.286	.373	.659
21 Mil	NL	56	178	34	8	0	6	(4 2)	60	14	28	15	19	0	51	3	1	1	0	0	2	.191	.279	.337	.616
21 Bos	AL	28	42	10	3	0	3	(2 1)	22	6	11	9	5	0	17	0	1	0	0	0	0	.238	.319	.524	.843
Postseason		13	36	10	2	1	1	(1 0)	17	2	2	3	5	1	11	0	0	0	1	0	0	.278	.366	.472	.838
7 ML YEARS		726	2355	563	127	3	114	(56 58)	1038	310	366	330	275	20	643	20	4	17	20	4	49	.239	.322	.441	.762

Gavin Sheets

Bats: L Throws: L Pos: DH-22;RF-13;1B-10;PH-9;LF-4

Ht: 6'5" Wt: 230 Born: 4/23/1996 Age: 26

			BATTING																RUNNING			AVERAGES			
Year Team	Lg	G	AB	H	2B	3B	HR	(Hm Rd)	TB	R	RBI	RC	TBB	IBB	SO	HBP	SH	SF	SB	CS	GDP	Avg	OBP	Slg	OPS
2021 Charllt	AAA	60	227	67	15	0	11	(- -)	115	36	46	-	25	0	55	0	0	2	1	1	2	.295	.362	.507	.869
2021 CWS	AL	54	160	40	8	0	11	(8 3)	81	23	34	30	16	0	40	2	0	1	0	0	4	.250	.324	.506	.830

Jordan Sheffield

Pitches: R Bats: R Pos: RP-30

Ht: 5'10" Wt: 190 Born: 6/1/1995 Age: 27

		HOW MUCH PITCHED					WHAT HE GAVE UP											THE RESULTS							
Year Team	Lg	G	GS	GF	IP	BFP	H	R	ER	HR	SH	SF	HB	TBB	IBB	SO	WP	W	L	Pct	Sv-Op	Hld	Vel	OPS	ERC	ERA
2021 Col	NL	30	0	12	29.1	116	19	11	11	2	0	1	2	13	0	20	4	0	0	-	0-0	4	96	.563	2.54	3.38

Justus Sheffield

Pitches: L Bats: L Pos: SP-15; RP-6

Ht: 5'10" Wt: 195 Born: 5/13/1996 Age: 26

		HOW MUCH PITCHED					WHAT HE GAVE UP											THE RESULTS							
Year Team	Lg	G	GS	GF	IP	BFP	H	R	ER	HR	SH	SF	HB	TBB	IBB	SO	WP	W	L	Pct	Sv-Op	Hld	Vel	OPS	ERC	ERA
2018 NYY	AL	3	0	2	2.2	14	4	3	3	1	0	0	0	3	0	0	1	0	0	-	0-0	0	94	1.227	13.94	10.13
2019 Sea	AL	8	7	0	36.0	168	44	22	22	5	1	0	3	18	0	37	3	0	1	.000	0-0	0	93	.881	6.51	5.50
2020 Sea	AL	10	10	0	55.1	232	52	23	22	2	0	2	3	20	0	48	1	4	3	.571	0-0	0	92	.628	3.43	3.58
2021 Sea	AL	21	15	0	80.1	385	105	69	61	14	1	4	5	43	1	63	5	7	8	.467	0-0	0	92	.913	7.36	6.83
4 ML YEARS		42	32	2	174.1	799	205	117	108	22	2	6	11	84	1	148	10	11	12	.478	0-0	0	92	.827	5.94	5.58

Jimmie Sherfy

Pitches: R **Bats:** R **Pos:** RP-14   **Ht:** 6'0" **Wt:** 175 **Born:** 12/27/1991 **Age:** 30

Year	Team	Lg	G	GS	GF	IP	BFP	H	R	ER	HR	SH	SF	HB	TBB	IBB	SO	WP	W	L	Pct	Sv-Op	Hld	Vel	OPS	ERC	ERA
2021	Scrmto	AAA	6	0	2	7.2	28	3	0	0	0	0	0	0	1	0	11	0	1	0	1.000	0- -	-	-	.328	0.49	0.00
2017	Ari	NL	11	0	2	10.2	37	5	0	0	0	0	0	0	2	0	9	0	2	0	1.000	1-1	2	94	.418	0.80	0.00
2018	Ari	NL	15	0	3	16.1	69	8	3	3	1	0	2	2	10	1	17	0	0	0	-	0-0	1	93	.490	2.24	1.65
2019	Ari	NL	17	0	4	18.1	83	23	12	12	4	1	1	0	5	0	22	0	1	0	1.000	1-2	0	92	.867	6.10	5.89
2021	2 Tms	NL	14	0	7	15.0	63	12	8	7	3	1	1	2	4	0	12	1	2	1	.667	0-0	0	94	.672	3.57	4.20
21	SF	NL	10	0	4	10.2	46	9	5	5	2	1	1	1	4	0	9	1	1	0	1.000	0-0	0	94	.696	4.00	4.22
21	LAD	NL	4	0	3	4.1	17	3	3	2	1	0	0	1	0	0	3	0	1	1	.500	0-0	0	94	.610	2.55	4.15
	Postseason		2	0	1	1.0	8	5	4	4	0	0	0	0	0	0	1	0	0	0	-	0-0	0	93	1.625	30.85	36.00
	4 ML YEARS		57	0	16	60.1	252	48	23	22	8	2	3	5	21	1	60	1	5	1	.833	2-3	3	93	.653	3.26	3.28

Ryan Sherriff

Pitches: L **Bats:** L **Pos:** RP-16   **Ht:** 6'1" **Wt:** 190 **Born:** 5/25/1990 **Age:** 32

Year	Team	Lg	G	GS	GF	IP	BFP	H	R	ER	HR	SH	SF	HB	TBB	IBB	SO	WP	W	L	Pct	Sv-Op	Hld	Vel	OPS	ERC	ERA
2021	Drham	AAA	31	2	5	25.0	102	15	7	6	1	0	0	1	14	1	27	1	5	3	.625	1- -	-	-	.524	2.30	2.16
2017	StL	NL	13	0	2	14.1	60	13	5	5	2	0	0	1	4	0	15	0	2	1	.667	0-0	1	92	.682	3.62	3.14
2018	StL	NL	5	0	0	5.2	27	8	4	4	1	0	0	1	2	0	3	0	0	0	-	0-0	1	91	.949	7.89	6.35
2020	TB	AL	10	0	3	9.2	34	6	0	0	0	0	0	0	2	0	2	0	1	0	1.000	1-1	1	91	.423	1.29	0.00
2021	TB	AL	16	0	6	14.2	72	14	11	9	0	0	1	4	9	0	16	2	0	1	.000	1-2	1	92	.668	4.71	5.52
	Postseason		2	0	0	2.0	7	0	0	0	0	0	0	0	1	0	1	0	0	0	-	0-0	0	91	.143	0.27	0.00
	4 ML YEARS		44	0	11	44.1	193	41	20	18	3	0	1	6	17	0	36	2	3	2	.600	2-3	4	92	.669	3.88	3.65

Matt Shoemaker

Pitches: R **Bats:** R **Pos:** SP-11; RP-5   SHOO-may-kerr   **Ht:** 6'2" **Wt:** 225 **Born:** 9/27/1986 **Age:** 35

Year	Team	Lg	G	GS	GF	IP	BFP	H	R	ER	HR	SH	SF	HB	TBB	IBB	SO	WP	W	L	Pct	Sv-Op	Hld	Vel	OPS	ERC	ERA
2021	Scrmto	AAA	8	7	1	42.1	180	49	27	25	7	1	1	3	7	0	43	2	3	3	.500	0- -	-	-	.871	4.84	5.31
2013	LAA	AL	1	1	0	5.0	19	2	0	0	0	0	0	0	2	0	5	1	0	0	-	0-0	0	91	.328	0.95	0.00
2014	LAA	AL	27	20	5	136.0	543	122	49	46	14	3	5	4	24	0	124	5	16	4	.800	0-0	0	91	.658	2.84	3.04
2015	LAA	AL	25	24	1	135.1	569	135	70	67	24	4	4	4	35	2	116	3	7	10	.412	0-0	0	90	.758	4.12	4.46
2016	LAA	AL	27	27	0	160.0	668	166	71	69	18	2	5	7	30	1	143	2	9	13	.409	0-0	0	91	.723	3.71	3.88
2017	LAA	AL	14	14	0	77.2	326	73	41	39	15	1	1	4	28	0	69	2	6	3	.667	0-0	0	92	.788	4.52	4.52
2018	LAA	AL	7	7	0	31.0	130	29	17	17	3	0	0	1	10	0	33	3	2	2	.500	0-0	0	91	.694	3.54	4.94
2019	Tor	AL	5	5	0	28.2	108	16	7	5	3	0	0	1	9	0	24	1	3	0	1.000	0-0	0	91	.547	1.77	1.57
2020	Tor	AL	6	6	0	28.2	115	22	16	15	8	1	0	0	9	0	26	0	1	1	.000	0-0	0	92	.739	3.60	4.71
2021	Min	AL	16	11	4	60.1	284	73	56	54	15	2	5	3	27	1	40	1	3	8	.273	0-0	0	92	.903	6.71	8.06
	Postseason		2	2	0	9.0	34	7	1	1	0	1	0	0	0	0	8	0	0	0	-	0-0	0	92	.455	1.21	1.00
	9 ML YEARS		128	115	10	662.2	2762	638	327	312	100	13	20	24	174	4	580	18	46	41	.529	0-0	0	91	.733	3.82	4.24

Zack Short

Bats: R **Throws:** R **Pos:** SS-52;PR-6;3B-3;PH-3;2B-2;DH-1   **Ht:** 5'10" **Wt:** 180 **Born:** 5/29/1995 **Age:** 27

Year	Team	Lg	G	AB	H	2B	3B	HR	(Hm	Rd)	TB	R	RBI	RC	TBB	IBB	SO	HBP	SH	SF	SB	CS	GDP	Avg	OBP	Slg	OPS
2021	Toledo	AAA	46	157	37	7	0	9	(-	-)	71	30	29	-	33	0	47	7	0	1	1	1	1	.236	.389	.452	.841
2021	Det	AL	61	156	22	4	0	6	(4	2)	44	21	20	9	22	1	59	0	0	6	2	0	4	.141	.239	.282	.521

Chasen Shreve

Pitches: L **Bats:** L **Pos:** RP-57   CHAY-sen shreev   **Ht:** 6'4" **Wt:** 180 **Born:** 7/12/1990 **Age:** 31

Year	Team	Lg	G	GS	GF	IP	BFP	H	R	ER	HR	SH	SF	HB	TBB	IBB	SO	WP	W	L	Pct	Sv-Op	Hld	Vel	OPS	ERC	ERA
2014	Atl	NL	15	0	4	12.1	50	10	1	1	0	1	0	0	3	0	15	1	0	0	-	0-0	5	91	.526	1.88	0.73
2015	NYY	AL	59	0	13	58.1	251	49	21	20	10	2	0	1	33	2	64	4	6	2	.750	0-1	10	91	.738	4.39	3.09
2016	NYY	AL	37	0	11	33.0	142	29	19	19	8	1	0	3	13	0	33	0	2	1	.667	1-1	1	92	.823	4.70	5.18
2017	NYY	AL	44	0	15	45.1	198	35	20	19	8	0	2	0	25	3	58	4	4	1	.800	0-1	1	93	.712	3.71	3.77
2018	2 Tms		60	0	20	52.2	235	53	28	23	11	0	4	1	27	0	62	2	3	4	.429	1-1	6	92	.832	5.43	3.93
2019	StL	NL	3	0	1	2.0	10	2	2	2	0	0	0	1	1	0	2	0	1	0	1.000	0-0	1	91	.900	5.48	9.00
2020	NYM	NL	17	0	1	25.0	102	17	12	11	4	0	1	0	12	0	34	0	1	0	1.000	0-0	1	92	.655	3.07	3.96
2021	Pit	NL	57	0	5	56.1	235	43	20	20	7	0	3	1	28	0	45	0	3	3	.500	0-2	11	92	.681	3.42	3.20
18	NYY	AL	40	0	13	38.0	170	39	23	18	8	0	2	1	18	0	46	2	2	2	.500	1-1	3	92	.831	5.40	4.26
18	StL	NL	20	0	7	14.2	65	14	5	5	3	0	2	0	9	0	16	0	1	2	.333	0-0	3	92	.835	5.52	3.07
	8 ML YEARS		292	0	69	285.0	1223	238	123	115	48	4	10	7	142	5	313	11	20	11	.645	2-6	33	92	.736	4.07	3.63

Magneuris Sierra

Bats: L **Throws:** L **Pos:** CF-54;PH-41;PR-20;LF-16;RF-8   mag-NEW-rees   **Ht:** 5'11" **Wt:** 178 **Born:** 4/7/1996 **Age:** 26

Year	Team	Lg	G	AB	H	2B	3B	HR	(Hm	Rd)	TB	R	RBI	RC	TBB	IBB	SO	HBP	SH	SF	SB	CS	GDP	Avg	OBP	Slg	OPS
2017	StL	NL	22	60	19	0	0	0	(0	0)	19	10	5	10	4	0	14	0	0	0	2	2	0	.317	.359	.317	.676
2018	Mia	NL	54	147	28	3	0	0	(0	0)	31	10	7	6	6	1	39	0	3	0	3	2	0	.190	.222	.211	.433
2019	Mia	NL	15	40	14	1	1	0	(0	0)	17	5	1	5	2	0	7	0	0	0	3	3	0	.350	.381	.425	.806

Year Team	Lg	G	AB	H	2B	3B	HR	(Hm	Rd)	TB	R	RBI	RC	TBB	IBB	SO	HBP	SH	SF	SB	CS	GDP	Avg	OBP	Slg	OPS
2020 Mia	NL	19	44	11	3	1	0	(0	0)	16	8	7	8	5	0	9	1	2	1	4	1	0	.250	.333	.364	.697
2021 Mia	NL	123	209	48	6	1	0	(0	0)	56	27	5	15	15	4	50	0	1	0	11	0	1	.230	.281	.268	.549
Postseason		5	11	3	1	0	0	(0	0)	4	1	1	1	0	0	4	0	0	0	0	0	0	.273	.273	.364	.636
5 ML YEARS		233	500	120	13	3	0	(0	0)	139	60	25	44	32	5	119	1	6	1	23	8	1	.240	.287	.278	.565

Andrelton Simmons

Bats: R Throws: R Pos: SS-131;PR-2;PH-1   ANN-drel-ton   Ht: 6'2" Wt: 195 Born: 9/4/1989 Age: 32

Year Team	Lg	G	AB	H	2B	3B	HR	(Hm	Rd)	TB	R	RBI	RC	TBB	IBB	SO	HBP	SH	SF	SB	CS	GDP	Avg	OBP	Slg	OPS
2012 Atl	NL	49	166	48	8	2	3	(3	0)	69	17	19	23	12	1	21	1	0	3	1	0	5	.289	.335	.416	.751
2013 Atl	NL	157	606	150	27	6	17	(5	12)	240	76	59	60	40	1	55	3	5	4	6	5	16	.248	.296	.396	.692
2014 Atl	NL	146	540	132	18	4	7	(3	4)	179	44	46	41	32	4	60	0	2	2	4	5	25	.244	.286	.331	.617
2015 Atl	NL	147	535	142	23	2	4	(2	2)	181	60	44	48	39	6	48	6	1	2	5	3	19	.265	.321	.338	.660
2016 LAA	AL	124	448	126	22	2	4	(0	4)	164	48	44	52	28	0	38	2	1	4	10	1	16	.281	.324	.366	.690
2017 LAA	AL	158	589	164	38	2	14	(10	4)	248	77	69	91	47	0	67	3	0	8	19	6	20	.278	.331	.421	.752
2018 LAA	AL	146	554	162	26	5	11	(1	10)	231	68	75	80	35	2	44	5	1	5	10	2	17	.292	.337	.417	.754
2019 LAA	AL	103	398	105	19	0	7	(5	2)	145	47	40	36	24	1	37	2	0	0	10	2	21	.264	.309	.364	.673
2020 LAA	AL	30	118	35	7	0	0	(0	0)	42	19	10	15	8	0	16	1	0	0	2	0	5	.297	.346	.356	.702
2021 Min	AL	131	412	92	12	0	3	(3	0)	113	37	31	35	32	0	62	3	3	1	1	0	14	.223	.283	.274	.558
Postseason		5	16	4	1	0	0	(0	0)	5	0	2	1	2	0	3	0	1	0	0	0	1	.250	.333	.313	.646
10 ML YEARS		1191	4366	1156	200	23	70	(36	34)	1612	493	437	481	297	15	448	26	13	29	68	24	158	.265	.313	.369	.683

Lucas Sims

Pitches: R Bats: R Pos: RP-47   Ht: 6'2" Wt: 225 Born: 5/10/1994 Age: 28

		HOW MUCH PITCHED					WHAT HE GAVE UP										THE RESULTS							
Year Team	Lg	G	GS	GF	IP	BFP	H	R	ER	HR	SH	SF	HB	TBB	IBB	SO	WP	W	L	Pct	Sv-Op	Hld	Vel	OPS	ERC	ERA
2021 Lsvlle	AAA	5	2	0	4.2	22	6	2	2	2	1	0	0	3	0	4	2	0	0	-	0- --	-	-	1.095	9.91	3.86
2017 Atl	NL	14	10	1	57.2	255	64	37	36	9	5	1	4	23	2	44	0	3	6	.333	0-0	1	92	.869	5.43	5.62
2018 2 Tms		9	0	2	15.2	77	15	13	13	3	0	0	2	13	1	16	0	0	0	-	0-1	0	92	.825	6.59	7.47
2019 Cin	NL	24	4	2	43.0	177	31	22	22	8	1	1	2	19	0	57	1	2	1	.667	0-0	3	94	.711	3.49	4.60
2020 Cin	NL	20	0	5	25.2	103	13	10	7	3	0	0	3	11	0	34	0	3	0	1.000	0-2	5	94	.554	2.17	2.45
2021 Cin	NL	47	0	13	47.0	195	34	26	23	6	0	3	4	18	3	76	2	5	3	.625	7-10	9	95	.658	2.92	4.40
18 Atl	NL	6	0	2	10.1	52	12	9	9	2	0	0	1	8	1	10	0	0	0	-	0-1	0	93	.869	7.45	7.84
18 Cin	NL	3	0	0	5.1	25	3	4	4	1	0	0	1	5	0	6	0	0	0	-	0-0	0	92	.728	5.00	6.75
Postseason		2	0	0	2.2	9	0	0	0	0	0	0	0	1	0	5	0	0	0	-	0-0	0	95	.111	0.16	0.00
5 ML YEARS		114	14	23	189.0	807	157	108	101	29	6	5	15	84	6	227	3	13	10	.565	7-13	18	93	.739	3.95	4.81

Brady Singer

Pitches: R Bats: R Pos: SP-27   Ht: 6'5" Wt: 215 Born: 8/4/1996 Age: 25

		HOW MUCH PITCHED					WHAT HE GAVE UP										THE RESULTS							
Year Team	Lg	G	GS	GF	IP	BFP	H	R	ER	HR	SH	SF	HB	TBB	IBB	SO	WP	W	L	Pct	Sv-Op	Hld	Vel	OPS	ERC	ERA
2020 KC	AL	12	12	0	64.1	263	52	29	29	8	0	2	2	23	0	61	5	4	5	.444	0-0	0	93	.649	3.19	4.06
2021 KC	AL	27	27	0	128.1	586	146	81	70	14	0	3	11	53	1	131	3	5	10	.333	0-0	0	94	.773	5.28	4.91
2 ML YEARS		39	39	0	192.2	849	198	110	99	22	0	5	13	76	1	192	8	9	15	.375	0-0	0	94	.734	4.56	4.62

Jose Siri

Bats: R Throws: R Pos: RF-9;CF-5;LF-4;PR-4;PH-2   Ht: 6'2" Wt: 175 Born: 7/22/1995 Age: 26

Year Team	Lg	G	AB	H	2B	3B	HR	(Hm	Rd)	TB	R	RBI	RC	TBB	IBB	SO	HBP	SH	SF	SB	CS	GDP	Avg	OBP	Slg	OPS
2021 SgrLnd	AAA	94	362	115	29	4	16	(-	-)	200	70	72	-	26	0	122	5	1	3	24	3	5	.318	.369	.552	.921
2021 Hou	AL	21	46	14	0	1	4	(1	3)	28	10	9	11	1	0	17	2	0	0	3	1	0	.304	.347	.609	.956

Chance Sisco

Bats: L Throws: R Pos: C-25;PH-2;DH-1   Ht: 6'3" Wt: 210 Born: 2/24/1995 Age: 27

Year Team	Lg	G	AB	H	2B	3B	HR	(Hm	Rd)	TB	R	RBI	RC	TBB	IBB	SO	HBP	SH	SF	SB	CS	GDP	Avg	OBP	Slg	OPS
2021 Norfolk	AAA	12	44	9	3	0	1	(-	-)	15	7	4	-	7	0	17	1	0	0	0	0	1	.205	.327	.341	.668
2021 Syrcse	AAA	34	106	21	6	1	5	(-	-)	44	15	14	-	12	1	26	4	0	0	0	0	5	.198	.303	.415	.718
2017 Bal	AL	10	18	6	2	0	2	(1	1)	14	3	4	6	3	0	7	1	0	0	0	0	0	.333	.455	.778	1.232
2018 Bal	AL	63	160	29	8	0	2	(2	0)	43	13	16	13	13	0	66	11	0	0	1	0	2	.181	.288	.269	.557
2019 Bal	AL	59	167	35	7	0	8	(3	5)	66	29	20	21	22	0	61	9	0	1	0	1	5	.210	.333	.395	.729
2020 Bal	AL	36	98	21	4	0	4	(3	1)	37	11	10	12	17	0	41	6	0	0	0	0	1	.214	.364	.378	.741
2021 2 Tms		28	74	11	3	0	0	(0	0)	14	5	4	3	7	0	21	2	0	0	0	0	1	.149	.241	.189	.430
21 Bal	AL	23	65	10	2	0	0	(0	0)	12	4	3	3	6	0	18	2	0	0	0	0	1	.154	.247	.185	.431
21 NYM	NL	5	9	1	1	0	0	(0	0)	2	1	1	0	1	0	3	0	0	0	0	0	0	.111	.200	.222	.422
5 ML YEARS		196	517	102	24	0	16	(9	7)	174	61	54	55	62	0	196	29	0	0	1	1	9	.197	.317	.337	.654

Brandyn Sittinger

Pitches: R Bats: R Pos: RP-5   Ht: 6'1" Wt: 200 Born: 6/6/1994 Age: 2?

			HOW MUCH PITCHED					WHAT HE GAVE UP										THE RESULTS							
Year	Team	Lg	G	GS	GF	IP	BFP	H	R	ER	HR	SH	SF	HB	TBB	IBB	SO	WP	W	L	Pct	Sv-Op	Hld	Vel	OPS	ERC	ERA
2021	Amrillo	AA	12	0	5	16.0	60	11	7	7	2	0	1	0	3	0	21	2	0	1	.000	1--	-	-	.573	1.91	3.94
2021	Reno	AAA	23	0	8	23.1	100	18	11	11	2	0	0	0	14	0	32	1	1	1	.500	4--	-	-	.657	3.49	4.24
2021	Ari	NL	5	0	0	4.2	21	5	4	4	3	0	1	1	2	0	1	0	0	1	.000	0-2	0	94	1.263	10.16	7.71

Tarik Skubal

Pitches: L Bats: L Pos: SP-29; RP-2   Ht: 6'3" Wt: 240 Born: 11/20/1996 Age: 2?

			HOW MUCH PITCHED					WHAT HE GAVE UP										THE RESULTS							
Year	Team	Lg	G	GS	GF	IP	BFP	H	R	ER	HR	SH	SF	HB	TBB	IBB	SO	WP	W	L	Pct	Sv-Op	Hld	Vel	OPS	ERC	ERA
2018	3 Tms	Low	9	1	3	22.1	82	15	3	1	0	0	0	0	4	1	33	1	3	0	1.000	2--	-	-	.536	1.29	0.40
2019	Lkland	A+	15	15	0	80.1	320	62	29	23	5	1	0	4	19	0	97	4	4	5	.444	0--	-	-	.591	2.25	2.58
2019	Erie	AA	9	9	0	42.1	170	25	13	10	2	0	2	1	18	0	82	1	2	3	.400	0--	-	-	.527	1.83	2.13
2020	Det	AL	8	7	0	32.0	134	28	21	20	9	0	2	2	11	0	37	0	1	4	.200	0-0	0	94	.802	4.65	5.63
2021	Det	AL	31	29	1	149.1	634	141	76	72	35	1	4	6	47	0	164	4	8	12	.400	0-0	0	94	.782	4.47	4.34
	2 ML YEARS		39	36	1	181.1	768	169	97	92	44	1	6	8	58	0	201	4	9	16	.360	0-0	0	94	.786	4.50	4.57

Austin Slater

Bats: R Throws: R Pos: CF-77;PH-48;LF-37;RF-24;PR-5;DH-1   Ht: 6'1" Wt: 204 Born: 12/13/1992 Age: 2?

			BATTING																				RUNNING			AVERAGES			
Year	Team	Lg	G	AB	H	2B	3B	HR	(Hm	Rd)	TB	R	RBI	RC	TBB	IBB	SO	HBP	SH	SF		SB	CS	GDP	Avg	OBP	Slg	OPS
2017	SF	NL	34	117	33	3	1	3	(0	3)	47	15	16	17	8	0	29	2	0	0		3		.282	.339	.402	.740
2018	SF	NL	74	199	50	6	1	1	(0	1)	61	21	23	23	20	2	69	5	0	1		7	0	5	.251	.333	.307	.640
2019	SF	NL	68	168	40	9	3	5	(2	3)	70	20	21	28	22	1	59	2	0	0		1	0	1	.238	.333	.417	.750
2020	SF	NL	31	85	24	2	1	5	(2	3)	43	18	7	18	16	0	22	2	1	0		8	1	2	.282	.408	.506	.914
2021	SF	NL	129	274	66	12	1	12	(5	7)	116	39	32	37	28	2	84	4	0	0		15	2	7	.241	.320	.423	.744
	5 ML YEARS		336	843	213	32	7	26	(9	17)	337	113	99	123	94	5	263	15	1	1		31	3	18	.253	.338	.400	.738

Aaron Slegers

Pitches: R Bats: R Pos: RP-29   Ht: 6'10" Wt: 260 Born: 9/4/1992 Age: 2?

			HOW MUCH PITCHED					WHAT HE GAVE UP										THE RESULTS							
Year	Team	Lg	G	GS	GF	IP	BFP	H	R	ER	HR	SH	SF	HB	TBB	IBB	SO	WP	W	L	Pct	Sv-Op	Hld	Vel	OPS	ERC	ERA
2021	Salt Lk	AAA	16	5	2	28.0	136	43	25	20	9	0	0	2	10	0	12	0	0	1	.000	0--	-	-	1.058	9.41	6.43
2017	Min	AL	4	3	0	15.1	62	12	12	11	3	0	0	0	6	0	9	0	0	1	.000	0-0	0	91	.689	3.48	6.46
2018	Min	AL	4	2	1	13.2	60	17	8	8	3	0	0	1	2	0	6	0	1	1	.500	0-0	0	90	.877	5.59	5.27
2019	TB	AL	1	0	1	3.0	12	3	1	1	1	0	0	1	0	0	5	0	0	0	-	1-1	0	90	.879	5.79	3.00
2020	TB	AL	11	1	3	26.0	101	18	10	10	1	1	0	2	5	2	19	0	0	0	-	2-2	2	91	.487	1.63	3.46
2021	LAA	AL	29	0	5	31.0	149	43	24	24	6	1	0	1	15	0	25	1	2	2	.500	0-2	0	92	.944	7.68	6.97
	Postseason		3	0	2	5.0	21	4	1	1	0	0	0	0	2	1	3	0	0	0	-	0-0	0	92	.496	2.03	1.80
	5 ML YEARS		49	6	10	89.0	385	93	55	54	14	2	0	5	28	2	59	1	3	4	.429	3-5	4	91	.769	4.58	5.46

Devin Smeltzer

Pitches: L Bats: R Pos: RP-1   Ht: 6'3" Wt: 195 Born: 9/7/1995 Age: 26

			HOW MUCH PITCHED					WHAT HE GAVE UP										THE RESULTS							
Year	Team	Lg	G	GS	GF	IP	BFP	H	R	ER	HR	SH	SF	HB	TBB	IBB	SO	WP	W	L	Pct	Sv-Op	Hld	Vel	OPS	ERC	ERA
2019	Min	AL	11	6	2	49.0	202	50	23	21	8	0	0	1	12	0	38	1	2	2	.500	1-1	1	89	.777	4.18	3.86
2020	Min	AL	7	1	2	16.0	72	19	12	12	2	1	0	1	5	0	15	0	2	0	1.000	0-0	0	88	.829	5.20	6.75
2021	Min	AL	1	0	1	4.2	17	1	1	0	0	0	1	2	1	0	3	0	0	0	-	0-0	0	86	.312	0.95	0.00
	Postseason		1	0	0	3.1	14	2	0	0	0	0	0	0	3	0	4	0	0	0	-	0-0	0	89	.539	3.21	0.00
	3 ML YEARS		19	7	5	69.2	291	70	36	33	10	1	1	4	18	0	56	1	4	2	.667	1-1	1	89	.767	4.13	4.26

Burch Smith

Pitches: R Bats: R Pos: RP-31   Ht: 6'4" Wt: 225 Born: 4/12/1990 Age: 32

			HOW MUCH PITCHED					WHAT HE GAVE UP										THE RESULTS							
Year	Team	Lg	G	GS	GF	IP	BFP	H	R	ER	HR	SH	SF	HB	TBB	IBB	SO	WP	W	L	Pct	Sv-Op	Hld	Vel	OPS	ERC	ERA
2013	SD	NL	10	7	3	36.1	167	39	26	26	9	1	0	0	21	1	46	0	1	3	.250	0-0	0	92	.899	6.27	6.44
2018	KC	AL	38	6	16	78.0	358	90	60	60	15	2	4	4	40	2	77	0	1	6	.143	0-0	0	93	.873	6.38	6.92
2019	2 Tms	NL	17	0	6	21.1	106	26	14	13	3	1	0	1	14	2	20	1	0	1	.000	0-1	0	93	.857	6.56	5.48
2020	Oak	AL	6	0	3	12.0	44	7	3	3	1	0	0	0	4	0	13	0	2	0	1.000	1-1	0	94	.461	1.11	2.25
2021	Oak	AL	31	0	10	43.1	188	49	27	26	5	0	1	1	11	0	28	2	1	1	.500	0-1	4	94	.764	4.40	5.40
	19 Mil	NL	7	0	4	12.2	65	16	11	11	3	0	0	1	10	2	14	1	0	1	.000	0-0	0	93	.952	8.37	7.82
	19 SF	NL	10	0	2	8.2	41	10	3	2	0	1	0	0	4	0	6	0	0	0	-	0-1	0	93	.711	4.19	2.08
	5 ML YEARS		102	13	38	191.0	863	211	130	128	33	4	5	6	87	5	184	3	5	11	.313	1-3	5	93	.830	5.51	6.03

Caleb Smith

Pitches: L Bats: R Pos: RP-32; SP-13   Ht: 6'0" Wt: 207 Born: 7/28/1991 Age: 30

			HOW MUCH PITCHED					WHAT HE GAVE UP										THE RESULTS							
Year	Team	Lg	G	GS	GF	IP	BFP	H	R	ER	HR	SH	SF	HB	TBB	IBB	SO	WP	W	L	Pct	Sv-Op	Hld	Vel	OPS	ERC	ERA
2017	NYY	AL	9	2	6	18.2	86	21	16	16	4	0	1	0	10	1	18	1	0	1	.000	0-0	0	94	.854	6.09	7.71
2018	Mia	NL	16	16	0	77.1	326	63	36	36	10	2	2	3	33	2	88	0	5	6	.455	0-0	0	93	.694	3.46	4.19
2019	Mia	NL	28	28	0	153.1	646	128	82	77	33	2	5	6	60	2	168	6	10	11	.476	0-0	0	92	.755	4.01	4.52
2020	2 Tms	NL	5	4	0	14.0	60	6	4	4	3	0	0	0	12	0	15	0	0	0	-	0-0	0	92	.613	3.44	2.57

Year Team	Lg	G	GS	GF	IP	BFP	H	R	ER	HR	SH	SF	HB	TBB	IBB	SO	WP	W	L	Pct	Sv-Op	Hld	Vel	OPS	ERC	ERA
2021 Ari	NL	45	13	4	113.2	500	93	64	61	20	1	0	6	63	3	124	2	4	9	.308	0-2	2	91	.726	4.31	4.83
20 Mia	NL	1	1	0	3.0	15	1	1	1	1	0	0	0	6	0	3	0	0	0	-	0-0	0	92	.911	9.13	3.00
20 Ari	NL	4	3	0	11.0	45	5	3	3	2	0	0	0	6	0	12	0	0	0	-	0-0	0	92	.526	2.21	2.45
5 ML YEARS		103	63	10	377.0	1618	311	202	194	70	5	8	15	178	8	413	9	19	27	.413	0-2	2	92	.734	4.07	4.63

Dominic Smith

Bats: L **Throws:** L **Pos:** LF-114;PH-26;1B-15;DH-2 **Ht:** 6'0" **Wt:** 239 **Born:** 6/15/1995 **Age:** 27

					BATTING															RUNNING			AVERAGES			
Year Team	Lg	G	AB	H	2B	3B	HR	(Hm	Rd)	TB	R	RBI	RC	TBB	IBB	SO	HBP	SH	SF	SB	CS	GDP	Avg	OBP	Slg	OPS
2017 NYM	NL	49	167	33	6	0	9	(4	5)	66	17	26	19	14	0	49	1	0	1	0	0	5	.198	.262	.395	.658
2018 NYM	NL	56	143	32	11	1	5	(4	1)	60	14	11	9	4	0	47	2	0	0	0	0	2	.224	.255	.420	.675
2019 NYM	NL	89	177	50	10	0	11	(3	8)	93	35	25	26	19	0	44	1	0	0	1	2	5	.282	.355	.525	.881
2020 NYM	NL	50	177	56	21	1	10	(5	5)	109	27	42	35	14	0	45	5	0	3	0	0	2	.316	.377	.616	.993
2021 NYM	NL	145	446	109	20	0	11	(3	8)	162	43	58	48	32	2	112	9	0	6	2	1	13	.244	.304	.363	.667
5 ML YEARS		389	1110	280	68	2	46	(19	27)	490	136	162	137	83	2	297	18	0	10	3	3	27	.252	.312	.441	.753

Drew Smith

Pitches: R **Bats:** R **Pos:** RP-30; SP-1 **Ht:** 6'2" **Wt:** 190 **Born:** 9/24/1993 **Age:** 28

		HOW MUCH PITCHED					WHAT HE GAVE UP											THE RESULTS							
Year Team	Lg	G	GS	GF	IP	BFP	H	R	ER	HR	SH	SF	HB	TBB	IBB	SO	WP	W	L	Pct	Sv-Op	Hld	Vel	OPS	ERC	ERA
2018 NYM	NL	27	0	8	28.0	120	34	11	11	2	0	2	2	6	0	18	1	1	1	.500	0-2	4	96	.795	4.77	3.54
2020 NYM	NL	8	0	3	7.0	29	6	6	5	2	0	0	0	2	1	7	1	0	1	.000	0-0	2	95	.757	3.75	6.43
2021 NYM	NL	31	1	10	41.1	165	28	13	11	7	0	1	2	16	4	41	0	3	1	.750	0-0	1	95	.676	2.85	2.40
3 ML YEARS		66	1	21	76.1	314	68	30	27	11	0	3	4	24	5	66	2	4	3	.571	0-2	7	96	.730	3.61	3.18

Joe Smith

Pitches: R **Bats:** R **Pos:** RP-50 **Ht:** 6'2" **Wt:** 211 **Born:** 3/22/1984 **Age:** 38

		HOW MUCH PITCHED					WHAT HE GAVE UP											THE RESULTS							
Year Team	Lg	G	GS	GF	IP	BFP	H	R	ER	HR	SH	SF	HB	TBB	IBB	SO	WP	W	L	Pct	Sv-Op	Hld	Vel	OPS	ERC	ERA
2007 NYM	NL	54	0	14	44.1	205	48	18	17	3	2	0	7	21	4	45	2	3	2	.600	0-0	10	86	.757	5.04	3.45
2008 NYM	NL	82	0	12	63.1	271	51	28	25	4	4	0	4	31	4	52	1	6	3	.667	0-3	18	89	.658	3.23	3.55
2009 Cle	AL	37	0	5	34.0	142	30	16	13	4	1	1	0	13	0	30	2	0	0	-	0-1	10	90	.707	3.49	3.44
2010 Cle	AL	53	0	7	40.0	170	30	18	17	4	1	0	1	24	2	32	0	2	2	.500	0-1	17	91	.659	3.53	3.83
2011 Cle	AL	71	0	13	67.0	267	52	16	15	1	2	2	2	21	1	45	2	3	3	.500	0-3	16	90	.541	2.19	2.01
2012 Cle	AL	72	0	12	67.0	278	53	27	22	4	1	1	2	25	4	53	1	7	4	.636	0-3	21	89	.594	2.60	2.96
2013 Cle	AL	70	0	20	63.0	259	54	17	16	5	3	0	3	23	2	54	3	6	2	.750	3-8	25	90	.643	3.23	2.29
2014 LAA	AL	76	0	26	74.2	285	45	16	15	4	3	0	6	15	3	68	4	7	2	.778	15-19	18	89	.491	1.47	1.81
2015 LAA	AL	70	0	13	65.1	271	64	26	26	4	2	1	2	19	4	57	1	5	5	.500	5-9	32	89	.684	3.36	3.58
2016 2 Tms		54	0	19	52.0	217	47	20	20	8	1	1	6	18	3	40	0	2	5	.286	6-9	7	88	.716	4.19	3.46
2017 2 Tms	AL	59	0	3	54.0	214	46	20	20	4	1	1	1	10	1	71	0	3	0	1.000	1-2	21	89	.601	2.40	3.33
2018 Hou	AL	56	0	13	45.2	180	34	20	19	7	0	2	2	12	0	46	1	5	1	.833	0-2	11	88	.645	2.75	3.74
2019 Hou	AL	28	0	4	25.0	96	19	6	5	2	0	0	0	5	0	22	0	1	0	1.000	0-1	4	88	.569	2.04	1.80
2021 2 Tms	AL	50	0	12	39.2	173	47	23	22	5	2	2	3	8	2	34	2	4	4	.500	0-3	4	86	.801	4.75	4.99
16 LAA	AL	38	0	16	37.2	160	36	16	16	4	1	1	5	13	3	25	0	1	4	.200	6-9	6	88	.697	4.15	3.82
16 ChC	NL	16	0	3	14.1	57	11	4	4	4	0	0	1	5	0	15	0	1	1	.500	0-0	1	89	.769	4.20	2.51
17 Tor	AL	38	0	1	35.2	144	30	13	13	3	1	1	1	10	1	51	0	3	0	1.000	0-1	13	89	.623	2.78	3.28
17 Cle	AL	21	0	2	18.1	70	16	7	7	1	0	0	0	0	0	20	0	0	0	-	1-1	8	89	.557	1.72	3.44
21 Hou	AL	27	0	10	21.2	103	35	18	18	4	2	1	3	4	0	17	2	1	1	.500	0-0	1	87	.996	8.38	7.48
21 Sea	AL	23	0	2	18.0	70	12	5	4	1	0	1	0	4	2	17	0	3	3	.500	0-3	3	86	.521	1.45	2.00
Postseason		18	0	4	14.0	54	8	4	4	2	0	1	0	3	1	13	0	0	1	.000	0-0	2	89	.484	1.47	2.57
14 ML YEARS		832	0	173	735.0	3028	620	271	252	59	23	11	39	245	30	649	19	54	33	.621	30-64	214	89	.641	3.02	3.09

Kevan Smith

Bats: R **Throws:** R **Pos:** C-31;PH-2 **Ht:** 6'4" **Wt:** 230 **Born:** 6/28/1988 **Age:** 34

					BATTING															RUNNING			AVERAGES			
Year Team	Lg	G	AB	H	2B	3B	HR	(Hm	Rd)	TB	R	RBI	RC	TBB	IBB	SO	HBP	SH	SF	SB	CS	GDP	Avg	OBP	Slg	OPS
2016 CWS	AL	7	16	2	0	0	0	(0	0)	2	2	0	0	0	0	6	0	0	0	0	0	1	.125	.125	.125	.250
2017 CWS	AL	87	276	78	17	0	4	(4	0)	107	23	30	29	9	0	46	3	2	3	0	0	9	.283	.309	.388	.697
2018 CWS	AL	52	171	50	6	0	3	(1	2)	65	21	21	25	10	0	18	5	0	1	1	0	5	.292	.348	.380	.728
2019 LAA	AL	67	191	48	12	0	5	(1	4)	75	21	20	19	16	0	37	3	0	1	2	0	8	.251	.318	.393	.710
2020 TB	AL	17	31	8	3	0	1	(1	0)	14	3	8	7	5	0	11	1	0	0	0	0	1	.258	.378	.452	.830
2021 2 Tms		33	95	16	3	0	0	(0	0)	19	8	3	3	10	3	31	0	0	0	0	0	3	.168	.248	.200	.448
21 TB	AL	3	4	1	0	0	0	(0	0)	1	2	0	0	0	0	2	0	0	0	0	0	0	.250	.250	.250	.500
21 Atl	NL	30	91	15	3	0	0	(0	0)	18	6	3	3	10	3	29	0	0	0	0	0	3	.165	.248	.198	.445
6 ML YEARS		263	780	202	41	0	13	(7	6)	282	78	82	83	50	3	149	12	2	5	3	0	27	.259	.312	.362	.673

Kevin Smith

Bats: R **Throws:** R **Pos:** 3B-14;PH-2;PR-2;1B-1;LF-1;DH-1 **Ht:** 6'0" **Wt:** 190 **Born:** 7/4/1996 **Age:** 25

					BATTING															RUNNING			AVERAGES			
Year Team	Lg	G	AB	H	2B	3B	HR	(Hm	Rd)	TB	R	RBI	RC	TBB	IBB	SO	HBP	SH	SF	SB	CS	GDP	Avg	OBP	Slg	OPS
2021 Buffalo	AAA	90	338	96	26	4	19	(-	-)	187	61	66	-	43	1	93	3	2	3	18	3	5	.284	.367	.553	.920
2021 Tor	AL	18	32	3	0	0	1	(0	1)	6	2	1	0	3	0	11	1	0	0	0	0	0	.094	.194	.188	.382

Pavin Smith

Bats: L **Throws:** L **Pos:** 1B-54;RF-54;CF-39;PH-23;LF-22 **Ht:** 6'2" **Wt:** 208 **Born:** 2/6/1996 **Age:** 26

										BATTING											RUNNING			AVERAGES			
Year	Team	Lg	G	AB	H	2B	3B	HR	(Hm	Rd)	TB	R	RBI	RC	TBB	IBB	SO	HBP	SH	SF	SB	CS	GDP	Avg	OBP	Slg	OPS
2020	Ari	NL	12	37	10	0	1	1	(1	0)	15	7	4	5	5	0	8	0	0	2	1	0	0	.270	.341	.405	.746
2021	Ari	NL	145	498	133	27	4	11	(6	5)	201	68	49	66	42	1	106	4	0	1	1	0	11	.267	.328	.404	.732
	2 ML YEARS		157	535	143	27	5	12	(7	5)	216	75	53	71	47	1	114	4	0	3	2	0	11	.267	.329	.404	.733

Riley Smith

Pitches: R **Bats:** R **Pos:** RP-18; SP-6 **Ht:** 6'1" **Wt:** 207 **Born:** 1/15/1995 **Age:** 27

			HOW MUCH PITCHED					WHAT HE GAVE UP											THE RESULTS							
Year	Team	Lg	G	GS	GF	IP	BFP	H	R	ER	HR	SH	SF	HB	TBB	IBB	SO	WP	W	L	Pct	Sv-Op	Hld	Vel	OPS	ERC	ERA
2020	Ari	NL	6	0	5	18.1	70	15	3	3	1	1	0	0	5	0	18	0	2	0	1.000	0-0	0	93	.602	2.53	1.47
2021	Ari	NL	24	6	4	67.1	301	86	46	45	10	1	2	4	15	2	36	0	1	4	.200	1-1	0	93	.873	5.50	6.01
	2 ML YEARS		30	6	9	85.2	371	101	49	48	11	2	2	4	20	2	54	0	3	4	.429	1-1	0	93	.823	4.82	5.04

Will Smith

Pitches: L **Bats:** R **Pos:** RP-71 **Ht:** 6'5" **Wt:** 255 **Born:** 7/10/1989 **Age:** 32

			HOW MUCH PITCHED					WHAT HE GAVE UP											THE RESULTS							
Year	Team	Lg	G	GS	GF	IP	BFP	H	R	ER	HR	SH	SF	HB	TBB	IBB	SO	WP	W	L	Pct	Sv-Op	Hld	Vel	OPS	ERC	ERA
2012	KC	AL	16	16	0	89.2	396	111	54	53	12	2	5	1	33	1	59	4	6	9	.400	0-0	0	90	.853	5.75	5.32
2013	KC	AL	19	1	4	33.1	131	24	16	12	6	0	4	1	7	0	43	0	2	1	.667	0-3	6	91	.631	2.47	3.24
2014	Mil	NL	78	0	6	65.2	286	62	31	27	6	1	1	3	31	6	86	7	1	3	.250	1-6	30	93	.737	4.02	3.70
2015	Mil	NL	76	0	11	63.1	264	52	23	19	5	1	2	1	24	1	91	5	2	7	.778	0-4	20	93	.649	2.91	2.70
2016	2 Tms	NL	53	0	4	40.1	167	31	19	15	3	1	1	1	18	1	48	3	2	4	.333	0-5	23	92	.637	2.92	3.35
2018	SF	NL	54	0	27	53.0	210	37	18	15	3	2	2	0	15	4	71	2	2	3	.400	14-18	6	93	.533	1.74	2.55
2019	SF	NL	63	0	52	65.1	257	46	20	20	10	0	1	0	21	2	96	3	6	0	1.000	34-38	0	93	.618	2.54	2.76
2020	Atl	NL	18	0	1	16.0	62	11	8	8	7	0	0		4	0	18	0	2	2	.500	0-1	5	93	.794	3.74	4.50
2021	Atl	NL	71	0	60	68.0	283	49	27	26	11	0	2	5	28	2	87	3	3	7	.300	37-43	0	93	.693	3.24	3.44
16	Mil	NL	27	0	3	22.0	92	18	13	9	3	1	1	1	9	1	22	3	1	3	.250	0-4	12	92	.708	3.48	3.68
16	SF	NL	26	0	1	18.1	75	13	6	6	0	0	0	0	9	0	26	0	1	1	.500	0-1	11	92	.551	2.26	2.95
	Postseason		9	0	0	7.1	29	3	4	3	1	0	0	0	3	0	8	0	2	2	.500	0-2	2	94	.438	1.42	3.68
	9 ML YEARS		448	17	165	494.2	2056	423	216	195	63	7	18	12	181	17	599	27	31	31	.500	86-118	90	92	.693	3.39	3.55

Will Smith

Bats: R **Throws:** R **Pos:** C-117;PH-13;DH-3;1B-1;3B-1 **Ht:** 5'10" **Wt:** 195 **Born:** 3/28/1995 **Age:** 27

										BATTING											RUNNING			AVERAGES			
Year	Team	Lg	G	AB	H	2B	3B	HR	(Hm	Rd)	TB	R	RBI	RC	TBB	IBB	SO	HBP	SH	SF	SB	CS	GDP	Avg	OBP	Slg	OPS
2019	LAD	NL	54	170	43	9	0	15	(7	8)	97	30	42	38	18	1	52	5	0	3	2	1	0	.253	.337	.571	.907
2020	LAD	NL	37	114	33	9	0	8	(7	1)	66	23	25	27	20	1	22	2	0	2	0	0	2	.289	.401	.579	.980
2021	LAD	NL	130	414	107	19	2	25	(13	12)	205	71	76	73	58	4	101	18	0	11	3	0	11	.258	.365	.495	.860
	Postseason		22	82	15	4	0	2	(1	1)	25	7	13	8	9	2	29	0	0	0	0	0	0	.183	.264	.305	.569
	3 ML YEARS		221	698	183	37	2	48	(27	21)	368	124	143	138	96	6	175	25	0	15	5	0	16	.262	.365	.527	.892

Drew Smyly

Pitches: L **Bats:** L **Pos:** SP-23; RP-6   SMY-lee   **Ht:** 6'2" **Wt:** 188 **Born:** 6/13/1989 **Age:** 33

			HOW MUCH PITCHED					WHAT HE GAVE UP											THE RESULTS							
Year	Team	Lg	G	GS	GF	IP	BFP	H	R	ER	HR	SH	SF	HB	TBB	IBB	SO	WP	W	L	Pct	Sv-Op	Hld	Vel	OPS	ERC	ERA
2012	Det	AL	23	18	0	99.1	416	93	49	44	12	2	3	2	33	1	94	3	4	3	.571	0-0	1	92	.732	3.68	3.99
2013	Det	AL	63	0	9	76.0	303	62	20	20	4	0	1	1	17	1	81	5	6	0	1.000	2-6	21	91	.601	2.21	2.37
2014	2 Tms	AL	28	25	0	153.0	618	136	57	55	18	1	3	1	42	2	133	8	9	10	.474	0-0	1	90	.688	3.17	3.24
2015	TB	AL	12	12	0	66.2	275	58	24	23	11	1	1	1	20	0	77	2	5	2	.714	0-0	0	90	.701	3.45	3.11
2016	TB	AL	30	30	0	175.1	738	174	103	95	32	5	11	2	49	2	167	10	7	12	.368	0-0	0	90	.763	4.13	4.88
2019	2 Tms	AL	25	21	1	114.0	514	126	83	79	32	2	2	2	55	0	120	7	4	7	.364	1-1	0	91	.916	6.49	6.24
2020	SF	NL	7	5	0	26.1	111	20	11	10	2	0	1	0	9	0	42	1	0	1	.000	0-0	0	94	.558	2.32	3.42
2021	Atl	NL	29	23	2	126.2	546	133	69	63	27	5	3	2	41	3	117	5	11	4	.733	0-0	0	92	.806	4.87	4.48
14	Det	AL	21	18	0	105.1	445	111	48	46	14	0	3	1	31	1	89	4	6	9	.400	0-0	1	90	.770	4.26	3.93
14	TB	AL	7	7	0	47.2	173	25	9	9	4	1	0	0	11	1	44	4	3	1	.750	0-0	0	90	.476	1.28	1.70
19	Tex	AL	13	9	1	51.1	251	64	49	48	19	0	2	1	34	0	52	5	1	5	.167	1-1	0	91	1.021	8.95	8.42
19	Phi	AL	12	12	0	62.2	263	62	34	31	13	2	0	1	21	0	68	2	3	2	.600	0-0	0	92	.820	4.64	4.45
	Postseason		10	0	1	7.0	30	3	3	2	0	0	0	0	6	1	7	0	1	0	1.000	0-0	2	91	.467	1.81	2.57
	8 ML YEARS		217	134	12	837.1	3521	802	416	389	138	16	25	11	266	9	831	41	46	39	.541	3-7	23	91	.749	4.00	4.18

Kirby Snead

Pitches: L **Bats:** L **Pos:** RP-7 **Ht:** 6'1" **Wt:** 218 **Born:** 10/7/1994 **Age:** 27

			HOW MUCH PITCHED					WHAT HE GAVE UP											THE RESULTS							
Year	Team	Lg	G	GS	GF	IP	BFP	H	R	ER	HR	SH	SF	HB	TBB	IBB	SO	WP	W	L	Pct	Sv-Op	Hld	Vel	OPS	ERC	ERA
2021	Buffalo	AAA	35	1	11	39.0	152	21	11	7	1	0	1	1	14	0	54	0	2	0	1.000	4--	-	-	.453	1.41	1.62
2021	Tor	AL	7	0	2	7.2	30	7	3	2	0	0	0	1	2	0	7	1	0	1	.000	0-0	0	93	.667	3.16	2.35

Blake Snell

Pitches: L Bats: L Pos: SP-27

Ht: 6'4" Wt: 225 Born: 12/4/1992 Age: 29

Year	Team	Lg	G	GS	GF	IP	BFP	H	R	ER	HR	SH	SF	HB	TBB	IBB	SO	WP	W	L	Pct	Sv-Op	Hld	Vel	OPS	ERC	ERA
2016	TB	AL	19	19	0	89.0	401	93	44	35	5	2	2	0	51	0	98	6	6	8	.429	0-0	0	94	.728	4.69	3.54
2017	TB	AL	24	24	0	129.1	547	113	65	58	15	4	1	0	59	1	119	8	5	7	.417	0-0	0	94	.707	3.71	4.04
2018	TB	AL	31	31	0	180.2	700	112	41	38	16	2	3	1	64	2	221	13	21	5	.808	0-0	0	96	.554	1.95	1.89
2019	TB	AL	23	23	0	107.0	441	96	53	51	14	0	1	1	40	1	147	11	6	8	.429	0-0	0	96	.702	3.72	4.29
2020	TB	AL	11	11	0	50.0	203	42	19	18	10	1	0	0	18	0	63	7	4	2	.667	0-0	0	95	.726	3.77	3.24
2021	SD	NL	27	27	0	128.2	550	101	61	60	16	5	1	3	69	1	170	7	7	6	.538	0-0	0	95	.692	3.66	4.20
	Postseason		9	7	1	35.0	138	24	11	11	6	0	1	0	14	0	44	2	2	3	.400	1-1	0	96	.633	2.93	2.83
6 ML YEARS			135	135	0	684.2	2842	557	283	260	76	14	8	5	301	5	818	52	49	36	.576	0-0	0	95	.670	3.34	3.42

Nick Snyder

Pitches: R Bats: R Pos: RP-4

Ht: 6'4" Wt: 190 Born: 10/10/1995 Age: 26

Year	Team	Lg	G	GS	GF	IP	BFP	H	R	ER	HR	SH	SF	HB	TBB	IBB	SO	WP	W	L	Pct	Sv-Op	Hld	Vel	OPS	ERC	ERA
2021	Frisco	AA	13	0	7	16.1	62	12	4	3	1	0	1	0	1	0	25	1	0	1	.000	1--	-	-	.476	1.42	1.65
2021	Hkry	A+	10	0	7	12.1	44	8	3	3	2	0	0	0	3	0	17	0	0	0	-	3--	-	-	-	2.27	2.19
2021	RdRck	AAA	5	0	4	4.1	17	3	3	3	1	0	0	0	1	0	5	0	1	0	1.000	0--	-	-	.735	2.55	6.23
2021	Tex	AL	4	0	2	3.2	15	3	2	2	0	0	0	0	3	0	1	0	0	0	-	0-0	1	99	.733	4.38	4.91

Eric Sogard

Bats: L Throws: R Pos: 2B-43;PH-31;3B-10;SS-4;1B-1   SO-guard

Ht: 5'10" Wt: 180 Born: 5/22/1986 Age: 36

Year	Team	Lg	G	AB	H	2B	3B	HR	(Hm	Rd)	TB	R	RBI	RC	TBB	IBB	SO	HBP	SH	SF	SB	CS	GDP	Avg	OBP	Slg	OPS
2010	Oak	AL	4	7	3	0	0	0	(0	0)	3	0	0	1	2	0	1	0	0	0	0	1	0	.429	.556	.429	.984
2011	Oak	AL	27	70	14	3	0	2	(0	2)	23	7	4	3	4	0	13	0	0	0	0	0	2	.200	.243	.329	.572
2012	Oak	AL	37	102	17	3	1	2	(0	2)	28	8	7	7	5	0	17	0	1	0	2	0	1	.167	.206	.275	.480
2013	Oak	AL	130	368	98	24	3	2	(0	2)	134	45	35	43	27	2	51	5	6	4	10	5	4	.266	.322	.364	.686
2014	Oak	AL	117	291	65	10	0	1	(1	0)	78	38	22	27	31	0	37	1	4	2	11	4	6	.223	.298	.268	.567
2015	Oak	AL	120	372	92	12	3	1	(1	0)	113	40	37	36	23	1	50	2	3	1	6	1	9	.247	.294	.304	.598
2017	Mil	NL	94	249	68	15	1	3	(2	1)	94	37	18	37	45	2	37	4	1	0	3	3	7	.273	.393	.378	.770
2018	Mil	NL	55	97	13	3	0	0	(0	0)	16	7	2	7	12	1	23	2	1	1	3	0	3	.134	.241	.165	.406
2019	2 Tms		110	396	115	23	2	13	(8	5)	181	59	40	67	38	2	63	2	3	3	8	0	4	.290	.353	.457	.810
2020	Mil	NL	43	115	24	5	0	1	(0	1)	32	10	10	13	11	0	20	1	0	1	0	0	1	.209	.281	.278	.560
2021	ChC	NL	78	169	42	6	1	1	(0	1)	53	16	12	16	9	1	30	0	0	2	3	1	5	.249	.283	.314	.597
2019	Tor	AL	73	287	86	17	2	10	(6	4)	137	45	30	52	29	0	47	1	3	3	6	0	2	.300	.363	.477	.840
2019	TB	AL	37	109	29	6	0	3	(2	1)	44	14	10	15	9	2	16	1	0	0	2	0	2	.266	.328	.404	.731
	Postseason		8	20	3	0	0	1	(0	1)	6	2	2	1	2	0	4	0	1	0	0	0	0	.150	.227	.300	.527
11 ML YEARS			815	2236	551	104	11	26	(13	13)	755	267	187	252	207	9	342	17	19	14	46	15	42	.246	.313	.338	.651

Nick Solak

Bats: R Throws: R Pos: 2B-121;DH-5;PH-2

Ht: 5'11" Wt: 185 Born: 1/11/1995 Age: 27

Year	Team	Lg	G	AB	H	2B	3B	HR	(Hm	Rd)	TB	R	RBI	RC	TBB	IBB	SO	HBP	SH	SF	SB	CS	GDP	Avg	OBP	Slg	OPS
2021	RdRck	AAA	22	85	30	6	0	1	(-	-)	39	15	6	-	7	0	16	1	0	0	0	1	4	.353	.409	.459	.867
2019	Tex	AL	33	116	34	6	1	5	(3	2)	57	19	17	25	15	1	29	4	0	2	2	0	2	.293	.393	.491	.884
2020	Tex	AL	58	209	56	10	0	2	(0	2)	72	27	23	30	18	0	42	2	0	4	7	1	6	.268	.326	.344	.671
2021	Tex	AL	127	458	111	18	2	11	(6	5)	166	57	49	53	34	0	107	15	2	2	7	5	11	.242	.314	.362	.677
3 ML YEARS			218	783	201	34	3	18	(9	9)	295	103	89	108	67	1	178	21	2	6	16	6	19	.257	.330	.377	.706

Donovan Solano

Bats: R Throws: R Pos: 2B-91;PH-18;SS-2;PR-1   sol-ON-oh

Ht: 5'8" Wt: 210 Born: 12/17/1987 Age: 34

Year	Team	Lg	G	AB	H	2B	3B	HR	(Hm	Rd)	TB	R	RBI	RC	TBB	IBB	SO	HBP	SH	SF	SB	CS	GDP	Avg	OBP	Slg	OPS
2012	Mia	NL	93	285	84	11	3	2	(0	2)	107	29	28	35	21	1	58	2	3	5	0	0	5	.295	.342	.375	.717
2013	Mia	NL	102	361	90	13	1	3	(0	3)	114	33	34	38	23	3	57	7	2	2	3	1	11	.249	.305	.316	.621
2014	Mia	NL	111	310	78	11	1	3	(1	2)	100	26	28	35	19	0	61	3	7	1	1	2	5	.252	.300	.323	.623
2015	Mia	NL	55	90	17	3	1	0	(0	0)	22	6	7	3	1	0	18	2	1	0	0	0	4	.189	.215	.244	.459
2016	NYY	AL	9	22	5	2	0	1	(0	1)	10	5	2	3	1	0	3	0	0	0	0	0	0	.227	.261	.455	.715
2019	SF	NL	81	215	71	13	1	4	(0	4)	98	27	23	36	10	0	49	1	0	2	0	1	4	.330	.360	.456	.815
2020	SF	NL	54	190	62	15	1	3	(3	0)	88	22	29	36	10	0	39	2	0	1	0	0	3	.326	.365	.463	.828
2021	SF	NL	101	307	86	17	0	7	(3	4)	124	35	31	40	25	2	58	7	1	4	2	0	8	.280	.344	.404	.748
8 ML YEARS			606	1780	493	85	8	23	(7	16)	663	183	182	226	110	6	343	24	14	15	13	4	39	.277	.325	.372	.698

Jorge Soler

Bats: R Throws: R Pos: RF-96;DH-47;PH-7   HOR-hay so-LAIR

Ht: 6'4" Wt: 235 Born: 2/25/1992 Age: 30

Year	Team	Lg	G	AB	H	2B	3B	HR	(Hm	Rd)	TB	R	RBI	RC	TBB	IBB	SO	HBP	SH	SF	SB	CS	GDP	Avg	OBP	Slg	OPS
2014	ChC	NL	24	89	26	8	1	5	(1	4)	51	11	20	15	6	0	24	0	0	2	1	0	3	.292	.330	.573	.903
2015	ChC	NL	101	366	96	18	1	10	(7	3)	146	39	47	43	32	5	121	3	0	3	3	1	9	.262	.324	.399	.723
2016	ChC	NL	86	227	54	9	0	12	(6	6)	99	37	31	31	31	0	66	3	0	3	0	0	5	.238	.333	.436	.769
2017	KC	AL	35	97	14	5	0	2	(2	0)	25	7	6	5	12	1	36	1	0	0	0	0	3	.144	.245	.258	.503
2018	KC	AL	61	223	59	18	0	9	(5	4)	104	27	28	32	28	0	69	4	0	2	3	1	6	.265	.354	.466	.820
2019	KC	AL	162	589	156	33	1	48	(21	27)	335	95	117	109	73	3	178	10	0	4	3	1	16	.265	.354	.569	.922

Year	Team	Lg	G	AB	H	2B	3B	HR	(Hm	Rd)	TB	R	RBI	RC	TBB	IBB	SO	HBP	SH	SF	SB	CS	GDP	Avg	OBP	Slg	OPS
2020	KC	AL	43	149	34	8	0	8	(4	4)	66	17	24	24	19	0	60	3	0	1	0	0	3	.228	.326	.443	.769
2021	2 Tms		149	516	115	27	0	27	(13	14)	223	74	70	66	67	0	142	6	0	5	0	0	12	.223	.316	.432	.749
21	KC	AL	94	308	59	16	0	13	(7	6)	114	38	37	29	38	0	97	5	0	3	0	0	9	.192	.288	.370	.658
21	Atl		55	208	56	11	0	14	(6	8)	109	36	33	37	29	0	45	1	0	2	0	0	3	.269	.358	.524	.882
	Postseason		15	32	11	3	1	3	(2	1)	25	6	5	9	9	0	9	0	0	0	0	0	1	.344	.488	.781	1.269
	8 ML YEARS		661	2256	554	126	3	121	(59	62)	1049	307	343	325	268	9	696	30	0	20	10	3	59	.246	.331	.465	.796

Peter Solomon

Pitches: R Bats: R Pos: RP-6   **Ht: 6'4" Wt: 211 Born: 8/16/1996 Age: 2**

Year	Team	Lg	G	GS	GF	IP	BFP	H	R	ER	HR	SH	SF	HB	TBB	IBB	SO	WP	W	L	Pct	Sv-Op	Hld	Vel	OPS	ERC	ERA
2021	SgrLnd	AAA	21	18	1	97.2	426	89	55	51	16	1	2	2	42	0	112	8	8	1	.889	1- -	-	-	.719	4.13	4.70
2021	Hou	AL	6	0	3	14.0	55	10	2	2	0	0	1	0	8	0	10	2	1	0	1.000	0-0	0	92	.610	2.73	1.29

Joakim Soria

wah-KEEM SORE-ee-uh

Pitches: R Bats: R Pos: RP-41   **Ht: 6'3" Wt: 205 Born: 5/18/1984 Age: 38**

Year	Team	Lg	G	GS	GF	IP	BFP	H	R	ER	HR	SH	SF	HB	TBB	IBB	SO	WP	W	L	Pct	Sv-Op	Hld	Vel	OPS	ERC	ERA
2007	KC	AL	62	0	38	69.0	270	46	20	19	3	1	3	1	19	3	75	2	2	3	.400	17-21	9	91	.510	1.63	2.48
2008	KC	AL	63	0	57	67.1	260	39	13	12	5	2	2	6	19	1	66	1	2	3	.400	42-45	0	91	.503	1.72	1.60
2009	KC	AL	47	0	41	53.0	222	44	14	13	5	1	2	2	16	1	69	3	3	2	.600	30-33	0	92	.614	2.80	2.21
2010	KC	AL	66	0	56	65.2	270	53	13	13	4	3	4	2	16	1	71	3	1	2	.333	43-46	0	92	.568	2.27	1.78
2011	KC	AL	60	0	47	60.1	256	60	29	27	7	3	2	2	17	0	60	1	5	5	.500	28-35	0	91	.709	3.80	4.03
2013	Tex	AL	26	0	9	23.2	101	18	10	10	2	1	0	1	14	2	28	2	1	0	1.000	0-0	6	91	.624	3.45	3.80
2014	2 Tms	AL	48	0	37	44.1	182	38	19	16	2	1	2	2	6	2	48	1	2	4	.333	18-20	1	90	.605	2.04	3.25
2015	2 Tms	AL	72	0	40	67.2	272	55	20	19	8	1	1	2	19	1	64	5	3	1	.750	24-30	11	92	.628	2.87	2.53
2016	KC	AL	70	0	18	66.2	293	70	31	30	10	4	2	2	27	0	68	2	5	8	.385	1-8	20	93	.800	4.86	4.05
2017	KC	AL	59	0	10	56.0	232	49	24	23	1	0	1	1	20	2	64	4	4	3	.571	1-8	20	93	.592	2.73	3.70
2018	2 Tms	AL	66	0	29	60.2	255	53	24	21	4	1	0	2	16	1	75	2	3	4	.429	16-21	13	92	.619	2.68	3.12
2019	Oak	AL	71	1	21	69.0	278	51	33	33	9	1	2	3	20	1	79	5	2	4	.333	1-6	21	93	.608	2.61	4.30
2020	Oak	AL	22	0	4	22.1	96	18	8	7	1	0	3	0	10	3	24	0	2	2	.500	2-3	4	92	.581	2.55	2.82
2021	2 Tms	AL	41	0	20	37.1	159	39	21	21	6	0	1	1	12	0	40	2	1	4	.200	6-9	5	93	.810	4.60	5.06
14	Tex	AL	35	0	32	33.1	133	25	12	10	0	1	1	1	4	1	42	0	1	3	.250	17-19	0	90	.521	1.38	2.70
14	Det	AL	13	0	5	11.0	49	13	7	6	2	0	1	1	2	1	6	1	1	1	.500	1-1	1	91	.838	4.92	4.91
15	Det	AL	43	0	35	41.0	165	32	13	13	8	1	0	2	11	1	36	0	3	1	.750	23-26	0	92	.665	3.15	2.85
15	Pit	NL	29	0	5	26.2	107	23	7	6	0	0	1	0	8	0	28	5	0	0	-	1-4	11	92	.571	2.39	2.03
18	CWS	AL	40	0	29	38.2	164	35	13	11	2	1	0	1	10	1	49	1	0	3	.000	16-19	2	92	.591	2.68	2.56
18	Mil	NL	26	0	0	22.0	91	18	11	10	2	0	0	1	6	0	26	1	3	1	.750	0-2	11	93	.668	2.69	4.09
21	Ari	NL	31	0	20	29.1	125	31	14	14	4	0	1	1	8	0	31	1	1	4	.200	6-8	3	93	.798	4.29	4.30
21	Tor	AL	10	0	0	8.0	34	8	7	7	2	0	0	0	4	0	9	1	0	0	-	0-1	2	92	.853	5.82	7.88
	Postseason		14	0	2	10.2	53	14	12	12	1	0	0	0	8	1	12	0	1	1	.500	0-1	2	93	.860	7.15	10.13
	14 ML YEARS		773	1	427	763.0	3146	633	279	264	67	19	25	27	231	18	831	33	36	45	.444	229-285	110	92	.625	2.80	3.11

Mike Soroka

suh-ROH-kah

Pitches: R Bats: R Pos: P   **Ht: 6'5" Wt: 225 Born: 8/4/1997 Age: 24**

Year	Team	Lg	G	GS	GF	IP	BFP	H	R	ER	HR	SH	SF	HB	TBB	IBB	SO	WP	W	L	Pct	Sv-Op	Hld	Vel	OPS	ERC	ERA
2018	Atl	NL	5	5	0	25.2	113	30	14	10	1	1	1	0	7	0	21	2	2	1	.667	0-0	0	93	.744	4.02	3.51
2019	Atl	NL	29	29	0	174.2	701	153	56	52	14	3	2	7	41	1	142	3	13	4	.765	0-0	0	92	.628	2.86	2.68
2020	Atl	NL	3	3	0	13.2	57	11	7	6	0	0	1	0	7	0	8	1	0	1	.000	0-0	0	92	.578	3.12	3.95
	Postseason		1	1	0	7.0	23	2	1	1	0	0	1	0	0	0	7	0	0	0	-	0-0	0	93	.223	0.19	1.29
	3 ML YEARS		37	37	0	214.0	871	194	77	68	15	4	3	8	55	1	171	6	15	6	.714	0-0	0	92	.641	3.01	2.86

Edmundo Sosa

Bats: R Throws: R Pos: SS-71;2B-25;PH-14;3B-9;CF-1;PR-1   **Ht: 6'0" Wt: 210 Born: 3/6/1996 Age: 26**

Year	Team	Lg	G	AB	H	2B	3B	HR	(Hm	Rd)	TB	R	RBI	RC	TBB	IBB	SO	HBP	SH	SF	SB	CS	GDP	Avg	OBP	Slg	OPS
2018	StL	NL	3	2	0	0	0	0	(0	0)	0	1	0	0	1	0	1	0	0	0	0	0	0	.000	.333	.000	.333
2019	StL	NL	8	8	2	0	0	0	(0	0)	2	2	0	1	1	0	2	1	0	0	1	0	0	.250	.400	.250	.650
2021	StL	NL	113	288	78	8	4	6	(2	4)	112	39	27	36	17	2	63	17	1	2	4	4	8	.271	.346	.389	.735
	3 ML YEARS		124	298	80	8	4	6	(2	4)	114	42	27	37	19	2	66	18	1	2	5	4	8	.268	.347	.383	.730

Gregory Soto

Pitches: L Bats: L Pos: RP-62   **Ht: 6'1" Wt: 234 Born: 2/11/1995 Age: 27**

Year	Team	Lg	G	GS	GF	IP	BFP	H	R	ER	HR	SH	SF	HB	TBB	IBB	SO	WP	W	L	Pct	Sv-Op	Hld	Vel	OPS	ERC	ERA
2019	Det	AL	33	7	9	57.2	276	74	39	37	9	0	3	0	33	1	45	5	0	5	.000	0-1	0	95	.884	6.86	5.77
2020	Det	AL	27	0	6	23.0	98	16	11	11	2	0	0	2	13	0	29	3	0	1	.000	2-3	4	97	.605	3.30	4.30
2021	Det	AL	62	0	38	63.2	276	46	30	24	7	1	2	1	40	2	76	11	6	3	.667	18-19	7	98	.635	3.46	3.39
	3 ML YEARS		122	7	53	144.1	650	136	80	72	18	1	5	3	86	3	150	19	6	9	.400	20-23	13	97	.738	4.71	4.49

Juan Soto

Bats: L **Throws:** L **Pos:** RF-144;PH-5;DH-2   **Ht:** 6'2" **Wt:** 224 **Born:** 10/25/1998 **Age:** 23

Year	Team	Lg	G	AB	H	2B	3B	HR	(Hm	Rd)	TB	R	RBI	RC	TBB	IBB	SO	HBP	SH	SF	SB	CS	GDP	Avg	OBP	Slg	OPS
2018	Was	NL	116	414	121	25	1	22	(6	16)	214	77	70	73	79	10	99	0	1	0	5	2	9	.292	.406	.517	.923
2019	Was	NL	150	542	153	32	5	34	(18	16)	297	110	110	117	108	3	132	3	0	6	12	1	11	.282	.401	.548	.949
2020	Was	NL	47	154	54	14	0	13	(4	9)	107	39	37	53	41	12	28	1	0	0	6	2	1	**.351**	**.490**	**.695**	**1.185**
2021	Was	NL	151	502	157	20	2	29	(15	14)	268	111	95	127	145	23	93	2	0	5	9	7	23	.313	.465	.534	.999
	Postseason		17	65	18	3	0	5	(2	3)	36	12	14	12	9	2	21	1	0	0	1	0	0	.277	.373	.554	.927
	4 ML YEARS		464	1612	485	91	8	98	(38	60)	886	337	312	370	373	48	352	6	1	11	32	12	44	.301	.432	.550	.981

Steven Souza Jr.

Bats: R **Throws:** R **Pos:** RF-8;PH-7;LF-5   SOO-zuh   **Ht:** 6'4" **Wt:** 225 **Born:** 4/24/1989 **Age:** 33

Year	Team	Lg	G	AB	H	2B	3B	HR	(Hm	Rd)	TB	R	RBI	RC	TBB	IBB	SO	HBP	SH	SF	SB	CS	GDP	Avg	OBP	Slg	OPS
2021	OkCity	AAA	54	182	50	14	1	11	(-	-)	99	38	33	-	33	1	58	4	0	1	4	0	0	.275	.395	.544	.939
2014	Was	NL	21	23	3	0	0	2	(1	1)	9	2	2	1	3	0	7	0	0	0	0	0	1	.130	.231	.391	.622
2015	TB	AL	110	373	84	15	1	16	(6	10)	149	59	40	40	46	0	144	5	1	1	12	6	7	.225	.318	.399	.717
2016	TB	AL	120	430	106	17	1	17	(7	10)	176	58	49	53	31	0	159	5	0	2	7	6	5	.247	.303	.409	.713
2017	TB	AL	148	523	125	21	2	30	(14	16)	240	78	78	85	84	2	179	7	2	1	16	4	9	.239	.351	.459	.810
2018	Ari	NL	72	241	53	15	3	5	(3	2)	89	21	29	29	28	0	75	3	0	0	6	1	4	.220	.309	.369	.678
2020	ChC	NL	11	27	4	2	0	1	(1	0)	9	3	5	3	4	0	15	0	0	0	1	0	0	.148	.258	.333	.591
2021	LAD	NL	17	33	5	1	1	1	(0	1)	11	2	3	1	2	0	14	1	0	0	0	0	2	.152	.222	.333	.556
	7 ML YEARS		499	1650	380	71	8	72	(32	40)	683	223	206	212	198	2	593	21	3	4	42	17	28	.230	.320	.414	.734

Gabe Speier

Pitches: L **Bats:** L **Pos:** RP-7   **Ht:** 5'11" **Wt:** 200 **Born:** 4/12/1995 **Age:** 27

			HOW MUCH PITCHED					WHAT HE GAVE UP										THE RESULTS						
Year	Team	Lg	G	GS	GF	IP	BFP	H	R	ER	HR	SH	SF	HB	TBB	IBB	SO	WP	W	L	Pct	Sv-Op	Hld	Vel	OPS	ERC	ERA
2021	Omha	AAA	45	0	14	45.1	191	45	15	15	5	0	0	4	9	2	57	3	3	0	1.000	5- -	-	-	.663	3.58	2.98
2019	KC	AL	9	0	1	7.1	33	5	6	6	2	0	0	0	6	0	10	1	0	0	-	0-0	1	95	.778	5.10	7.36
2020	KC	AL	8	0	3	5.2	30	9	5	5	1	0	0	0	4	0	6	0	0	1	.000	0-0	1	92	.794	9.58	7.94
2021	KC	AL	7	0	1	7.2	33	10	3	1	0	0	0	1	0	0	5	0	0	0	-	0-0	0	94	.646	4.03	1.17
	3 ML YEARS		24	0	5	20.2	96	24	14	12	3	0	0	1	10	0	21	1	0	1	.000	0-0	2	94	.788	5.84	5.23

Shea Spitzbarth

Pitches: R **Bats:** R **Pos:** RP-5   **Ht:** 6'1" **Wt:** 215 **Born:** 10/4/1994 **Age:** 27

			HOW MUCH PITCHED					WHAT HE GAVE UP										THE RESULTS						
Year	Team	Lg	G	GS	GF	IP	BFP	H	R	ER	HR	SH	SF	HB	TBB	IBB	SO	WP	W	L	Pct	Sv-Op	Hld	Vel	OPS	ERC	ERA
2021	Indy	AAA	42	0	17	46.2	191	35	15	11	4	0	1	2	21	2	41	1	3	3	.500	2- -	-	-	.609	2.99	2.12
2021	Pit	NL	5	0	4	5.0	22	4	2	2	1	0	0	1	2	0	1	0	0	0	-	0-0	1	92	.687	4.36	3.60

George Springer

Bats: R **Throws:** R **Pos:** CF-40;DH-38;RF-4   **Ht:** 6'3" **Wt:** 221 **Born:** 9/19/1989 **Age:** 32

Year	Team	Lg	G	AB	H	2B	3B	HR	(Hm	Rd)	TB	R	RBI	RC	TBB	IBB	SO	HBP	SH	SF	SB	CS	GDP	Avg	OBP	Slg	OPS
2014	Hou	AL	78	295	68	8	1	20	(5	15)	138	45	51	45	39	4	114	9	0	2	5	2	4	.231	.336	.468	.804
2015	Hou	AL	102	388	107	19	2	16	(9	7)	178	59	41	60	50	0	109	8	2	3	16	4	4	.276	.367	.459	.826
2016	Hou	AL	**162**	644	168	29	5	29	(13	16)	294	116	82	100	88	2	178	11	0	1	9	**10**	12	.261	.359	.457	.815
2017	Hou	AL	140	548	155	29	0	34	(16	18)	286	112	85	99	64	1	111	11	0	4	5	7	11	.283	.367	.522	.889
2018	Hou	AL	140	544	144	26	0	22	(12	10)	236	102	71	84	64	0	122	5	0	3	6	4	12	.265	.346	.434	.780
2019	Hou	AL	122	479	140	20	6	39	(18	21)	283	96	96	103	67	1	113	6	0	2	6	2	6	.292	.383	.591	.974
2020	Hou	AL	51	189	50	6	2	14	(6	8)	102	37	32	42	24	0	38	5	0	2	1	2	3	.265	.359	.540	.899
2021	Tor	AL	78	299	79	19	1	22	(15	7)	166	59	50	55	37	1	79	4	0	1	4	1	6	.264	.352	.555	.907
	Postseason		63	260	70	15	0	19	(9	10)	142	43	38	48	31	1	71	1	0	0	4	1	4	.269	.349	.546	.895
	8 ML YEARS		873	3386	911	156	14	196	(94	102)	1683	626	508	588	433	9	864	59	2	20	52	32	64	.269	.360	.497	.857

Jeffrey Springs

Pitches: L **Bats:** L **Pos:** RP-43   **Ht:** 6'3" **Wt:** 218 **Born:** 9/20/1992 **Age:** 29

			HOW MUCH PITCHED					WHAT HE GAVE UP										THE RESULTS						
Year	Team	Lg	G	GS	GF	IP	BFP	H	R	ER	HR	SH	SF	HB	TBB	IBB	SO	WP	W	L	Pct	Sv-Op	Hld	Vel	OPS	ERC	ERA
2018	Tex	AL	18	2	4	32.0	141	32	14	12	4	1	0	1	14	1	31	3	1	1	.500	0-1	2	91	.744	4.44	3.38
2019	Tex	AL	25	0	7	32.1	155	38	23	23	4	0	2	0	23	0	32	0	4	1	.800	0-0	1	92	.884	6.57	6.40
2020	Bos	AL	16	0	4	20.1	99	30	18	16	5	0	1	0	7	1	28	2	0	2	.000	0-1	0	92	.973	7.87	7.08
2021	TB	AL	43	0	9	44.2	179	35	21	17	9	1	2	0	14	1	63	3	5	1	.833	2-4	10	93	.720	3.21	3.43
	4 ML YEARS		102	2	28	129.1	574	135	76	68	22	2	5	2	58	3	154	8	10	5	.667	2-6	14	92	.814	5.03	4.73

Jacob Stallings

Bats: R **Throws:** R **Pos:** C-104;PH-8;1B-1   **Ht:** 6'5" **Wt:** 225 **Born:** 12/22/1989 **Age:** 32

Year	Team	Lg	G	AB	H	2B	3B	HR	(Hm	Rd)	TB	R	RBI	RC	TBB	IBB	SO	HBP	SH	SF	SB	CS	GDP	Avg	OBP	Slg	OPS
2016	Pit	NL	5	15	6	1	0	0	(0	0)	7	0	2	3	0	0	4	0	0	0	1	0	0	.400	.400	.467	.867
2017	Pit	NL	5	14	5	2	0	0	(0	0)	7	3	3	3	2	1	2	0	0	0	0	0	0	.357	.438	.500	.938
2018	Pit	NL	14	37	8	0	0	0	(0	0)	8	2	5	3	0	0	9	0	0	1	0	0	2	.216	.268	.216	.485

Year	Team	Lg	G	AB	H	2B	3B	HR	(Hm	Rd)	TB	R	RBI	RC	TBB	IBB	SO	HBP	SH	SF	SB	CS	GDP	Avg	OBP	Slg	OPS
2019	Pit	NL	71	191	50	5	0	6	(1	5)	73	26	13	18	16	5	40	2	1	0	0	0	3	.262	.325	.382	.708
2020	Pit	NL	42	125	31	7	0	3	(3	0)	47	13	18	18	15	0	40	0	2	1	0	0	2	.248	.326	.376	.702
2021	Pit	NL	112	374	92	20	1	8	(5	3)	138	38	53	49	49	0	85	2	0	2	0	0	10	.246	.335	.369	.704
	6 ML YEARS		249	756	192	35	1	17	(9	8)	280	82	94	94	85	6	180	4	3	4	1	0	17	.254	.331	.370	.701

Craig Stammen

Pitches: R **Bats:** R **Pos:** RP-63; SP-4   STAMM-enn   **Ht:** 6'2" **Wt:** 228 **Born:** 3/9/1984 **Age:** 38

Year	Team	Lg	G	GS	GF	IP	BFP	H	R	ER	HR	SH	SF	HB	TBB	IBB	SO	WP	W	L	Pct	Sv-Op	Hld	Vel	OPS	ERC	ERA
2009	Was	NL	19	19	0	105.2	448	112	67	60	14	4	3	3	24	1	48	7	4	7	.364	0-0	0	89	.774	4.03	5.11
2010	Was	NL	35	19	3	128.0	562	151	78	73	18	3	5	6	41	4	85	3	4	4	.500	0-0	1	90	.814	4.79	5.13
2011	Was	NL	7	0	2	10.1	38	3	1	1	0	0	0	0	4	0	12	1	1	1	.500	0-0	1	91	.272	0.67	0.87
2012	Was	NL	59	0	15	88.1	370	70	27	23	7	5	1	2	36	4	87	3	6	1	.857	1-2	10	92	.636	2.84	2.34
2013	Was	NL	55	0	14	81.2	339	78	30	25	4	8	4	2	27	3	79	2	7	6	.538	0-1	7	92	.682	3.32	2.76
2014	Was	NL	49	0	15	72.2	304	78	34	31	5	3	1	3	14	2	56	1	4	5	.444	0-0	7	92	.708	3.61	3.84
2015	Was	NL	5	0	0	4.0	17	2	0	0	0	0	1	0	3	1	3	0	0	0	-	0-0	2	92	.525	1.66	0.00
2017	SD	NL	60	0	9	80.1	329	68	29	28	12	2	0	2	28	3	74	2	2	3	.400	0-2	11	92	.684	3.46	3.14
2018	SD	NL	73	0	7	79.0	317	65	25	24	3	2	1	3	17	3	88	3	8	3	.727	0-5	23	92	.583	2.17	2.73
2019	SD	NL	76	0	12	82.0	339	80	36	30	13	0	3	2	15	2	73	0	8	7	.533	4-13	31	93	.719	3.51	3.29
2020	SD	NL	24	0	6	24.0	105	27	16	15	2	2	0	2	4	0	20	0	4	2	.667	0-1	5	92	.702	3.97	5.63
2021	SD	NL	67	4	4	88.1	355	79	31	30	13	1	2	3	13	1	83	3	6	3	.667	1-2	7	92	.652	2.94	3.06
	Postseason		10	1	0	11.2	55	13	7	7	1	1	1	3	4	1	9	1	0	0	-	0-0	1	92	.805	5.14	5.40
	12 ML YEARS		529	42	87	844.1	3523	813	374	340	86	32	22	23	226	24	708	25	54	42	.563	6-26	105	91	.700	3.44	3.62

Ryne Stanek

Pitches: R **Bats:** R **Pos:** RP-72   **Ht:** 6'4" **Wt:** 226 **Born:** 7/26/1991 **Age:** 30

Year	Team	Lg	G	GS	GF	IP	BFP	H	R	ER	HR	SH	SF	HB	TBB	IBB	SO	WP	W	L	Pct	Sv-Op	Hld	Vel	OPS	ERC	ERA
2017	TB	AL	21	0	4	20.0	95	26	13	13	6	0	1	0	12	2	29	4	0	0	-	0-1	4	98	.985	8.31	5.85
2018	TB	AL	59	29	16	66.1	263	45	23	22	8	0	0	1	27	1	81	5	2	3	.400	0-0	8	98	.618	2.64	2.98
2019	2 Tms		63	27	12	77.0	327	61	39	34	11	0	3	0	39	3	89	5	0	4	.000	1-5	7	98	.688	3.56	3.97
2020	Mia	NL	9	0	3	10.0	48	11	8	8	3	0	0	0	8	1	11	0	0	0	-	0-0	0	96	.921	7.82	7.20
2021	Hou	AL	72	0	13	68.1	290	46	32	26	8	0	1	5	37	3	83	6	3	5	.375	2-4	21	98	.615	3.15	3.42
19	TB	AL	41	27	3	55.2	228	44	24	21	7	0	2	0	20	1	61	2	0	2	.000	0-0	2	98	.654	2.93	3.40
19	Mia	AL	22	0	9	21.1	99	17	15	13	4	0	1	0	19	2	28	3	0	2	.000	1-5	5	98	.769	5.31	5.48
	Postseason		2	0	1	2.0	9	0	0	0	0	0	0	0	3	0	3	1	0	0	-	0-0	0	98	.333	1.96	0.00
	5 ML YEARS		224	56	42	241.2	1023	189	115	103	36	0	5	6	123	10	293	20	5	12	.294	3-10	40	98	.688	3.67	3.84

Giancarlo Stanton

Bats: R **Throws:** R **Pos:** DH-108;RF-16;LF-10;PH-5   john-CAHR-loh   **Ht:** 6'6" **Wt:** 245 **Born:** 11/8/1989 **Age:** 32

Year	Team	Lg	G	AB	H	2B	3B	HR	(Hm	Rd)	TB	R	RBI	RC	TBB	IBB	SO	HBP	SH	SF	SB	CS	GDP	Avg	OBP	Slg	OPS
2010	Fla	NL	100	359	93	21	1	22	(7	15)	182	45	59	56	34	6	123	2	0	1	5	2	7	.259	.326	.507	.833
2011	Fla	NL	150	516	135	30	5	34	(16	18)	277	79	87	81	70	6	166	9	0	6	5	5	11	.262	.356	.537	.893
2012	Mia	NL	123	449	130	30	1	37	(16	21)	273	75	86	79	46	9	143	5	0	1	6	2	5	.290	.361	.608	.969
2013	Mia	NL	116	425	106	26	0	24	(15	9)	204	62	62	66	74	5	140	4	0	1	1	0	10	.249	.365	.480	.845
2014	Mia	NL	145	539	155	31	1	37	(24	13)	299	89	105	109	94	24	170	3	0	2	13	1	16	.288	.395	.555	.950
2015	Mia	NL	74	279	74	12	1	27	(13	14)	169	47	67	54	34	6	95	2	0	3	4	2	5	.265	.346	.606	.952
2016	Mia	NL	119	413	99	20	1	27	(13	14)	202	56	74	56	50	5	140	4	0	2	0	0	6	.240	.326	.489	.815
2017	Mia	NL	159	597	168	32	0	59	(31	28)	377	123	132	117	85	13	163	7	0	3	2	2	13	.281	.376	.631	1.007
2018	NYY	AL	158	617	164	34	1	38	(20	18)	314	102	100	98	70	5	211	6	0	10	5	0	17	.266	.343	.509	.852
2019	NYY	AL	18	59	17	3	0	3	(2	1)	29	8	13	14	12	0	24	0	0	0	0	0	1	.288	.403	.492	.894
2020	NYY	AL	23	76	19	7	0	4	(1	3)	38	12	11	14	15	1	27	2	0	0	1	1	4	.250	.387	.500	.887
2021	NYY	AL	139	510	139	19	0	35	(15	20)	263	64	97	91	63	1	157	3	0	3	0	0	22	.273	.354	.516	.870
	Postseason		17	60	16	1	0	8	(2	6)	41	12	16	12	9	0	22	0	0	2	1	0	3	.267	.352	.683	1.035
	12 ML YEARS		1324	4839	1299	265	11	347	(173	174)	2627	762	893	835	647	81	1559	49	0	33	42	15	117	.268	.358	.543	.901

Cody Stashak

Pitches: R **Bats:** R **Pos:** RP-15   **Ht:** 6'2" **Wt:** 180 **Born:** 6/4/1994 **Age:** 28

Year	Team	Lg	G	GS	GF	IP	BFP	H	R	ER	HR	SH	SF	HB	TBB	IBB	SO	WP	W	L	Pct	Sv-Op	Hld	Vel	OPS	ERC	ERA
2019	Min	AL	18	1	4	25.0	104	29	9	9	3	0	1	1	1	0	25	0	0	1	.000	0-0	1	92	.773	3.82	3.24
2020	Min	AL	11	0	1	15.0	57	11	5	5	2	0	0	0	3	0	17	1	1	0	1.000	0-0	5	92	.635	2.22	3.00
2021	Min	AL	15	0	1	15.2	75	16	12	12	2	0	2	1	10	0	26	1	0	0	-	0-0	2	91	.779	5.42	6.89
	Postseason		3	0	0	3.2	16	4	3	3	3	0	0	0	1	0	1	0	0	1	.000	0-0	0	92	1.179	8.92	7.36
	3 ML YEARS		44	1	6	55.2	236	56	26	26	7	0	3	2	14	0	68	2	1	1	.500	0-0	8	91	.743	3.81	4.20

Max Stassi

Bats: R **Throws:** R **Pos:** C-86;PH-2   STASS-ee   **Ht:** 5'10" **Wt:** 200 **Born:** 3/15/1991 **Age:** 31

Year	Team	Lg	G	AB	H	2B	3B	HR	(Hm	Rd)	TB	R	RBI	RC	TBB	IBB	SO	HBP	SH	SF	SB	CS	GDP	Avg	OBP	Slg	OPS
2013	Hou	AL	3	7	2	0	0	0	(0	0)	2	0	1	0	0	0	2	1	0	0	0	0	1	.286	.375	.286	.661
2014	Hou	AL	7	20	7	2	0	0	(0	0)	9	2	4	4	0	0	6	0	0	0	0	0	0	.350	.350	.450	.800
2015	Hou	AL	11	15	6	0	0	1	(1	0)	9	4	2	3	1	0	5	0	1	0	0	0	1	.400	.438	.600	1.038
2016	Hou	AL	9	13	1	0	0	0	(0	0)	1	1	0	0	0	0	5	0	0	0	0	0	0	.077	.077	.077	.154

Year Team	Lg	G	AB	H	2B	3B	HR	(Hm	Rd)	TB	R	RBI	RC	TBB	IBB	SO	HBP	SH	SF	SB	CS	GDP	Avg	OBP	Slg	OPS
2017 Hou	AL	14	24	4	1	0	2	(1	1)	11	5	4	3	6	0	4	0	0	1	0	0	2	.167	.323	.458	.781
2018 Hou	AL	88	221	50	13	0	8	(1	7)	87	28	27	33	23	0	74	6	0	0	0	0	6	.226	.316	.394	.710
2019 2 Tms	AL	51	132	18	1	0	1	(0	1)	22	7	5	2	12	0	49	1	0	2	0	0	3	.136	.211	.167	.378
2020 LAA	AL	31	90	25	2	0	7	(3	4)	48	12	20	18	11	0	21	1	0	3	0	0	5	.278	.352	.533	.886
2021 LAA	AL	87	282	68	11	1	13	(9	4)	120	45	35	40	28	0	101	8	0	1	0	0	8	.241	.326	.426	.752
19 Hou	AL	31	90	15	1	0	1	(0	1)	19	4	3	2	7	0	34	1	0	0	0	0	1	.167	.235	.211	.446
19 LAA	AL	20	42	3	0	0	0	(0	0)	3	3	2	0	5	0	15	0	0	2	0	0	2	.071	.163	.071	.235
9 ML YEARS		301	804	181	30	1	32	(15	17)	309	104	98	103	81	0	267	17	1	7	0	0	26	.225	.307	.384	.691

Josh Staumont

Pitches: R Bats: R Pos: RP-64   Ht: 6'3" Wt: 200 Born: 12/21/1993 Age: 28

		HOW MUCH PITCHED					WHAT HE GAVE UP										THE RESULTS							
Year Team	Lg	G	GS	GF	IP	BFP	H	R	ER	HR	SH	SF	HB	TBB	IBB	SO	WP	W	L	Pct	Sv-Op	Hld	Vel	OPS	ERC	ERA
2019 KC	AL	16	0	7	19.1	88	21	13	6	4	0	0	1	10	1	15	0	0	0	-	0-1	0	96	.870	6.01	3.72
2020 KC	AL	26	0	3	25.2	112	20	8	7	2	0	0	3	16	0	37	1	2	1	.667	0-0	8	98	.639	4.06	2.45
2021 KC	AL	64	0	19	65.2	264	43	24	21	6	0	0	2	27	1	72	4	4	3	.571	5-5	16	97	.566	2.37	2.88
3 ML YEARS		106	0	29	110.2	464	84	45	36	12	0	0	6	53	2	124	5	6	4	.600	5-6	24	97	.642	3.33	2.93

Drew Steckenrider

Pitches: R Bats: R Pos: RP-62   Ht: 6'4" Wt: 217 Born: 1/10/1991 Age: 31

		HOW MUCH PITCHED					WHAT HE GAVE UP										THE RESULTS							
Year Team	Lg	G	GS	GF	IP	BFP	H	R	ER	HR	SH	SF	HB	TBB	IBB	SO	WP	W	L	Pct	Sv-Op	Hld	Vel	OPS	ERC	ERA
2017 Mia	NL	37	0	7	34.2	151	30	13	9	4	0	1	0	18	1	54	1	1	1	.500	1-1	0	95	.674	3.80	2.34
2018 Mia	NL	71	0	17	64.2	272	55	29	28	7	0	1	2	27	5	74	0	4	4	.500	5-10	19	95	.664	3.39	3.90
2019 Mia	NL	15	0	4	14.1	58	9	10	10	6	0	0	1	5	0	14	0	0	2	.000	0-1	3	95	.778	4.00	6.28
2021 Sea	AL	62	0	20	67.2	267	52	16	15	5	1	2	4	17	2	58	0	5	2	.714	14-17	7	94	.608	2.38	2.00
4 ML YEARS		185	0	48	181.1	748	146	68	62	22	1	4	7	67	8	200	1	10	9	.526	20-29	39	95	.655	3.14	3.08

Justin Steele

Pitches: L Bats: L Pos: RP-11; SP-9   Ht: 6'2" Wt: 205 Born: 7/11/1995 Age: 26

		HOW MUCH PITCHED					WHAT HE GAVE UP										THE RESULTS							
Year Team	Lg	G	GS	GF	IP	BFP	H	R	ER	HR	SH	SF	HB	TBB	IBB	SO	WP	W	L	Pct	Sv-Op	Hld	Vel	OPS	ERC	ERA
2021 Iowa	AAA	9	5	0	27.1	110	14	6	4	1	0	1	1	13	1	29	3	2	0	1.000	0- -	-	-	.455	1.59	1.32
2021 ChC	NL	20	9	2	57.0	248	50	29	27	12	1	0	5	27	2	59	0	4	4	.500	0-0	1	93	.769	4.76	4.26

Trevor Stephan

Pitches: R Bats: R Pos: RP-43   Ht: 6'5" Wt: 225 Born: 11/25/1995 Age: 26

		HOW MUCH PITCHED					WHAT HE GAVE UP										THE RESULTS							
Year Team	Lg	G	GS	GF	IP	BFP	H	R	ER	HR	SH	SF	HB	TBB	IBB	SO	WP	W	L	Pct	Sv-Op	Hld	Vel	OPS	ERC	ERA
2021 Cle	AL	43	0	13	63.1	282	58	32	31	15	0	1	3	31	1	75	0	3	1	.750	1-1	3	96	.796	5.00	4.41

Robert Stephenson

Pitches: R Bats: R Pos: RP-49   Ht: 6'3" Wt: 205 Born: 2/24/1993 Age: 29

		HOW MUCH PITCHED					WHAT HE GAVE UP										THE RESULTS							
Year Team	Lg	G	GS	GF	IP	BFP	H	R	ER	HR	SH	SF	HB	TBB	IBB	SO	WP	W	L	Pct	Sv-Op	Hld	Vel	OPS	ERC	ERA
2016 Cin	NL	8	8	0	37.0	170	41	26	25	9	0	0	4	19	1	31	2	2	3	.400	0-0	0	93	.893	6.78	6.08
2017 Cin	NL	25	11	6	84.2	383	81	52	44	12	5	6	2	53	3	86	5	5	6	.455	1-1	0	94	.805	5.06	4.68
2018 Cin	NL	4	3	0	11.2	63	17	12	12	2	0	1	0	12	3	11	2	0	2	.000	0-0	0	93	1.040	9.71	9.26
2019 Cin	NL	57	0	16	64.2	262	43	30	27	9	0	1	0	24	4	81	3	3	2	.600	0-4	11	95	.634	2.33	3.76
2020 Cin	NL	10	0	4	10.0	43	11	11	11	8	0	0	1	3	0	13	0	0	0	-	0-0	1	95	1.246	10.14	9.90
2021 Col	NL	49	0	10	46.0	197	42	20	16	5	1	2	2	18	0	52	3	2	1	.667	1-2	4	97	.724	3.77	3.13
6 ML YEARS		153	22	36	254.0	1118	235	151	135	45	6	10	9	129	11	274	15	12	14	.462	2-7	16	94	.794	4.68	4.78

Tyler Stephenson

Bats: R Throws: R Pos: C-78;PH-44;1B-23;LF-1;PR-1   Ht: 6'4" Wt: 225 Born: 8/16/1996 Age: 25

		BATTING																		RUNNING			AVERAGES			
Year Team	Lg	G	AB	H	2B	3B	HR	(Hm	Rd)	TB	R	RBI	RC	TBB	IBB	SO	HBP	SH	SF	SB	CS	GDP	Avg	OBP	Slg	OPS
2020 Cin	NL	8	17	5	0	0	2	(2	0)	11	4	6	3	2	0	9	1	0	0	0	0	0	.294	.400	.647	1.047
2021 Cin	NL	132	350	100	21	0	10	(5	5)	151	56	45	52	41	1	75	6	0	5	0	0	11	.286	.366	.431	.797
2 ML YEARS		140	367	105	21	0	12	(7	5)	162	60	51	55	43	1	84	7	0	5	0	0	11	.286	.367	.441	.809

Andrew Stevenson

Bats: L Throws: L Pos: PH-51;CF-31;LF-24;RF-11;PR-5   Ht: 6'0" Wt: 192 Born: 6/1/1994 Age: 28

		BATTING																		RUNNING			AVERAGES			
Year Team	Lg	G	AB	H	2B	3B	HR	(Hm	Rd)	TB	R	RBI	RC	TBB	IBB	SO	HBP	SH	SF	SB	CS	GDP	Avg	OBP	Slg	OPS
2021 Roch	AAA	15	55	24	4	0	2	(-	-)	34	11	8	-	3	0	11	0	0	0	2	0	0	.436	.466	.618	1.084
2017 Was	NL	37	57	9	2	0	0	(0	0)	11	5	1	1	7	0	20	0	2	0	1	0	0	.158	.250	.193	.443
2018 Was	NL	57	75	19	2	0	1	(1	0)	24	9	13	11	6	0	23	1	1	3	1	1	0	.253	.306	.320	.626
2019 Was	NL	30	30	11	1	1	0	(0	0)	14	4	0	6	6	0	11	1	0	0	0	1	1	.367	.486	.467	.953

Year Team	Lg	G	AB	H	2B	3B	HR	(Hm Rd)	TB	R	RBI	RC	TBB	IBB	SO	HBP	SH	SF	SB	CS	GDP	Avg	OBP	Slg	OPS
2020 Was	NL	15	41	15	1	1	2	(2 0)	30	11	12	13	5	0	11	1	0	0	2	0	0	.366	.447	.732	1.179
2021 Was	NL	109	192	44	6	0	5	(3 2)	65	22	23	18	13	2	61	5	2	1	1	1	3	.229	.294	.339	.632
Postseason		1	0	0	0	0	0	(0 0)	0	1	0	0	0	0	0	0	0	0	0	0	0	-	-	-	-
5 ML YEARS		248	395	98	18	2	8	(6 2)	144	51	49	49	37	2	126	8	5	4	5	3	4	.248	.322	.365	.687

D.J. Stewart

Bats: L **Throws:** R **Pos:** LF-39;RF-33;PH-19;DH-13 **Ht:** 6'0" **Wt:** 210 **Born:** 11/30/1993 **Age:** 28

Year Team	Lg	G	AB	H	2B	3B	HR	(Hm Rd)	TB	R	RBI	RC	TBB	IBB	SO	HBP	SH	SF	SB	CS	GDP	Avg	OBP	Slg	OPS
2018 Bal	AL	17	40	10	3	0	3	(2 1)	22	8	10	8	4	0	12	2	0	1	2	1	0	.250	.340	.550	.890
2019 Bal	AL	44	126	30	6	0	4	(1 3)	48	15	15	17	14	1	26	1	0	1	1	2	3	.238	.317	.381	.698
2020 Bal	AL	31	88	17	2	0	7	(4 3)	40	13	15	18	20	2	38	2	2	0	0	0	0	.193	.355	.455	.809
2021 Bal	AL	100	270	55	10	0	12	(7 5)	101	39	33	35	44	1	89	4	0	0	0	0	3	.204	.324	.374	.698
4 ML YEARS		192	524	112	21	0	26	(14 12)	211	75	73	78	82	2	165	9	2	2	3	3	6	.214	.329	.403	.732

Kohl Stewart

Pitches: R **Bats:** R **Pos:** SP-3; RP-1 **Ht:** 6'3" **Wt:** 200 **Born:** 10/7/1994 **Age:** 27

		HOW MUCH PITCHED					WHAT HE GAVE UP										THE RESULTS							
Year Team	Lg	G	GS	GF	IP	BFP	H	R	ER	HR	SH	SF	HB	TBB	IBB	SO	WP	W	L	Pct	Sv-Op Hld	Vel	OPS	ERC	ERA
2021 Iowa	AAA	6	5	0	26.0	100	16	10	10	3	0	1	1	6	0	26	0	2	3	.400	0- -	-		.556	1.76	3.46
2018 Min	AL	8	4	0	36.2	159	34	16	15	1	0	0	3	18	0	24	4	2	1	.667	0-0	0	93	.672	3.87	3.68
2019 Min	AL	9	2	5	25.1	109	29	18	18	5	0	0	1	8	0	10	6	2	2	.500	0-0	1	92	.869	5.59	6.39
2021 ChC	NL	4	3	0	13.2	64	17	12	8	2	1	0	2	6	0	11	0	1	1	.500	0-0	0	91	.851	6.73	5.27
3 ML YEARS		21	9	5	75.2	332	80	46	41	8	1	0	6	32	0	45	10	5	4	.556	0-0	1	92	.773	4.94	4.88

Jonathan Stiever

Pitches: R **Bats:** R **Pos:** RP-1 **Ht:** 6'2" **Wt:** 210 **Born:** 5/12/1997 **Age:** 25

		HOW MUCH PITCHED					WHAT HE GAVE UP										THE RESULTS							
Year Team	Lg	G	GS	GF	IP	BFP	H	R	ER	HR	SH	SF	HB	TBB	IBB	SO	WP	W	L	Pct	Sv-Op Hld	Vel	OPS	ERC	ERA
2021 Charltt	AAA	17	17	0	74.0	335	80	51	48	13	0	2	3	28	0	88	12	5	5	.500	0- -	-		.825	5.02	5.84
2020 CWS	AL	2	2	0	6.1	29	7	7	7	4	0	0	0	4	0	3	0	0	0	.000	0-0	0	92	1.139	10.13	9.95
2021 CWS	AL	1	0	0	0.0	4	4	3	3	0	0	0	0	0	0	0	0	0	0	-	0-0	0	93	2.000	-	-
2 ML YEARS		3	2	0	6.1	33	11	10	10	4	0	0	0	4	0	3	0	0	1	.000	0-0	0	93	1.248	15.14	14.21

Robert Stock

Pitches: R **Bats:** L **Pos:** SP-3 **Ht:** 6'1" **Wt:** 214 **Born:** 11/21/1989 **Age:** 32

		HOW MUCH PITCHED					WHAT HE GAVE UP										THE RESULTS							
Year Team	Lg	G	GS	GF	IP	BFP	H	R	ER	HR	SH	SF	HB	TBB	IBB	SO	WP	W	L	Pct	Sv-Op Hld	Vel	OPS	ERC	ERA
2021 Iowa	AAA	9	2	3	19.2	82	17	10	9	4	0	0	1	4	0	25	0	0	3	.000	0- -	-		.719	3.31	4.12
2018 SD	NL	32	0	6	39.2	166	37	13	11	1	1	0	2	13	1	38	3	1	1	.500	0-1	4	98	.615	3.11	2.50
2019 SD	NL	10	0	4	10.2	56	14	14	12	2	0	0	1	8	0	15	4	1	0	1.000	0-1	0	98	.900	8.30	10.13
2020 Bos	NL	10	0	4	13.1	62	16	9	7	0	1	1	0	10	0	14	3	0	1	.000	0-0	0	97	.826	6.08	4.73
2021 2 Tms	NL	3	3	0	9.0	45	10	8	8	3	0	0	1	9	0	9	1	0	2	.000	0-0	0	96	1.016	10.15	8.00
21 ChC	NL	1	1	0	4.0	22	4	5	5	1	0	0	1	6	0	3	1	0	1	.000	0-0	0	96	1.033	11.62	11.25
21 NYM	NL	2	2	0	5.0	23	6	3	3	2	0	0	0	3	0	6	0	0	1	.000	0-0	0	96	.991	8.79	5.40
4 ML YEARS		55	3	14	72.2	329	77	44	38	6	2	1	4	40	1	76	11	2	4	.333	0-2	4	97	.753	5.12	4.71

Troy Stokes Jr.

Bats: R **Throws:** R **Pos:** RF-4;PH-4 **Ht:** 5'9" **Wt:** 205 **Born:** 2/2/1996 **Age:** 26

Year Team	Lg	G	AB	H	2B	3B	HR	(Hm Rd)	TB	R	RBI	RC	TBB	IBB	SO	HBP	SH	SF	SB	CS	GDP	Avg	OBP	Slg	OPS
2021 Indy	AAA	29	71	12	2	1	2	(- -)	22	11	5	-	11	0	18	2	0	0	4	0	0	.169	.298	.310	.607
2021 Nashv	AAA	67	133	27	5	2	2	(- -)	42	18	9	-	16	0	36	3	0	0	5	2	4	.203	.303	.316	.618
2021 Pit	NL	8	18	2	1	0	0	(0 0)	3	2	2	1	1	0	5	1	0	0	1	0	0	.111	.200	.167	.367

Trevor Story

Bats: R **Throws:** R **Pos:** SS-138;PH-3;DH-1 **Ht:** 6'2" **Wt:** 213 **Born:** 11/15/1992 **Age:** 29

Year Team	Lg	G	AB	H	2B	3B	HR	(Hm Rd)	TB	R	RBI	RC	TBB	IBB	SO	HBP	SH	SF	SB	CS	GDP	Avg	OBP	Slg	OPS
2016 Col	NL	97	372	101	21	4	27	(16 11)	211	67	72	67	35	2	130	5	2	1	8	5	5	.272	.341	.567	.909
2017 Col	NL	145	503	120	32	3	24	(13 11)	230	68	82	66	49	4	191	2	0	1	7	2	12	.239	.308	.457	.765
2018 Col	NL	157	598	174	42	6	37	(26 11)	339	88	108	107	47	3	168	7	0	4	27	6	12	.291	.348	.567	.914
2019 Col	NL	145	588	173	38	5	35	(24 11)	326	111	85	113	58	0	174	7	0	3	23	8	3	.294	.363	.554	.917
2020 Col	NL	59	235	68	13	4	11	(5 6)	122	41	28	35	24	1	63	0	0	0	15	3	5	.289	.355	.519	.874
2021 Col	NL	142	526	132	34	5	24	(11 13)	248	88	75	83	53	2	139	11	0	5	20	6	7	.251	.329	.471	.801
Postseason		5	22	7	2	0	1	(0 1)	12	3	1	2	0	0	7	0	0	0	0	0	0	.318	.318	.545	.864
6 ML YEARS		745	2822	768	180	27	158	(95 63)	1476	463	450	471	266	12	865	32	2	14	100	30	44	.272	.340	.523	.863

Matt Strahm

Pitches: L **Bats:** R **Pos:** RP-5; SP-1   **Ht:** 6'2" **Wt:** 190 **Born:** 11/12/1991 **Age:** 30

Year	Team	Lg	G	GS	GF	IP	BFP	H	R	ER	HR	SH	SF	HB	TBB	IBB	SO	WP	W	L	Pct	Sv-Op	Hld	Vel	OPS	ERC	ERA
2016	KC	AL	21	0	1	22.0	88	13	4	3	0	0	0	1	11	1	30	1	2	2	.500	0-0	6	94	.484	1.84	1.23
2017	KC	AL	24	3	3	34.2	154	30	22	21	6	2	0	3	22	2	37	3	2	5	.286	0-0	5	94	.779	5.10	5.45
2018	SD	NL	41	5	5	61.1	245	39	16	14	6	1	1	3	21	1	69	2	3	4	.429	0-0	7	93	.564	2.12	2.05
2019	SD	NL	46	16	4	114.2	487	121	61	60	22	4	1	7	22	4	118	3	6	11	.353	0-1	6	92	.787	4.35	4.71
2020	SD	NL	19	0	2	20.2	83	14	6	6	3	0	0	5	4	0	15	1	0	1	.000	0-2	3	93	.615	2.82	2.61
2021	SD	NL	6	1	0	6.2	36	15	6	6	0	1	0	0	1	1	4	0	0	1	.000	0-1	0	93	1.045	9.49	8.10
	Postseason		4	0	0	2.1	16	7	3	3	0	0	1	0	2	1	2	0	0	0	-	0-0	0	94	1.255	17.62	11.57
	6 ML YEARS		157	25	15	260.0	1093	232	115	110	37	8	3	19	81	9	273	10	13	24	.351	0-4	27	93	.709	3.65	3.81

Stephen Strasburg

Pitches: R **Bats:** R **Pos:** SP-5   **Ht:** 6'5" **Wt:** 240 **Born:** 7/20/1988 **Age:** 33

Year	Team	Lg	G	GS	GF	IP	BFP	H	R	ER	HR	SH	SF	HB	TBB	IBB	SO	WP	W	L	Pct	Sv-Op	Hld	Vel	OPS	ERC	ERA
2010	Was	NL	12	12	0	68.0	274	56	25	22	5	2	2	0	17	0	92	2	5	3	.625	0-0	0	97	.596	2.41	2.91
2011	Was	NL	5	5	0	24.0	88	15	5	4	0	1	1	0	2	0	24	0	1	1	.500	0-0	0	96	.398	0.97	1.50
2012	Was	NL	28	28	0	159.1	653	136	62	56	15	6	4	4	48	1	197	5	15	6	.714	0-0	0	96	.649	2.97	3.16
2013	Was	NL	30	30	0	183.0	731	136	71	61	16	5	1	12	56	1	191	7	8	9	.471	0-0	0	95	.588	2.58	3.00
2014	Was	NL	34	34	0	215.0	868	198	86	75	23	9	4	5	43	4	242	7	14	11	.560	0-0	0	95	.672	3.02	3.14
2015	Was	NL	23	23	0	127.1	523	115	56	49	14	5	1	3	26	0	155	4	11	7	.611	0-0	0	95	.653	2.92	3.46
2016	Was	NL	24	24	0	147.2	598	119	59	59	15	5	1	2	44	1	183	2	15	4	.789	0-0	0	96	.637	2.72	3.60
2017	Was	NL	28	28	0	175.1	701	131	55	49	13	2	4	7	47	5	204	3	15	4	.789	0-0	0	96	.581	2.22	2.52
2018	Was	NL	22	22	0	130.0	544	118	59	54	18	1	5	8	38	2	156	5	10	7	.588	0-0	0	95	.711	3.62	3.74
2019	Was	NL	33	33	0	209.0	841	161	79	77	24	3	4	10	56	4	251	8	18	6	.750	0-0	0	94	.620	2.62	3.32
2020	Was	NL	2	2	0	5.0	23	8	6	6	1	0	0	0	1	0	2	0	0	1	.000	0-0	0	92	.937	7.85	10.80
2021	Was	NL	5	5	0	21.2	95	16	12	11	4	0	0	1	14	2	21	0	1	2	.333	0-0	0	92	.714	4.17	4.57
	Postseason		9	8	0	55.1	218	44	13	9	4	2	2	1	8	1	71	1	6	2	.750	0-0	0	95	.562	1.95	1.46
	12 ML YEARS		246	246	0	1465.1	5939	1209	575	523	148	39	27	52	392	20	1718	43	113	61	.649	0-0	0	95	.634	2.77	3.21

Chris Stratton

Pitches: R **Bats:** R **Pos:** RP-68   **Ht:** 6'2" **Wt:** 205 **Born:** 8/22/1990 **Age:** 31

Year	Team	Lg	G	GS	GF	IP	BFP	H	R	ER	HR	SH	SF	HB	TBB	IBB	SO	WP	W	L	Pct	Sv-Op	Hld	Vel	OPS	ERC	ERA
2016	SF	NL	7	0	7	10.0	43	11	4	4	1	0	0	0	5	0	6	0	1	0	1.000	0-0	0	91	.767	5.31	3.60
2017	SF	NL	13	10	1	58.2	256	59	25	24	5	2	3	1	28	0	51	2	4	4	.500	1-2	0	92	.738	4.42	3.68
2018	SF	NL	28	26	1	145.0	625	153	87	82	19	3	6	2	54	1	112	6	10	10	.500	0-0	0	92	.791	4.59	5.09
2019	2 Tms		35	5	7	76.0	344	93	50	47	13	0	1	0	33	1	69	2	1	3	.250	0-0	0	92	.873	6.10	5.57
2020	Pit	NL	27	0	3	30.0	131	26	19	13	3	0	2	0	13	0	39	1	2	1	.667	0-0	2	93	.651	3.34	3.90
2021	Pit	NL	68	0	18	79.1	337	70	34	32	9	0	3	1	33	2	86	3	7	1	.875	8-13	7	93	.675	3.57	3.63
19	LAA	AL	7	5	0	29.1	144	43	28	28	6	0	1	0	18	0	22	1	0	2	.000	0-0	0	91	1.000	8.90	8.59
19	Pit	NL	28	0	7	46.2	200	50	22	19	7	0	0	0	15	1	47	1	1	1	.500	0-0	0	93	.784	4.50	3.66
	6 ML YEARS		178	41	37	399.0	1736	412	219	202	50	5	15	4	166	4	363	14	25	19	.568	9-17	12	92	.766	4.55	4.56

Myles Straw

Bats: R **Throws:** R **Pos:** CF-156;PH-2;PR-2   **Ht:** 5'10" **Wt:** 178 **Born:** 10/17/1994 **Age:** 27

Year	Team	Lg	G	AB	H	2B	3B	HR	(Hm	Rd)	TB	R	RBI	RC	TBB	IBB	SO	HBP	SH	SF	SB	CS	GDP	Avg	OBP	Slg	OPS
2018	Hou	AL	9	9	3	0	0	1	(0	1)	6	4	1	2	1	0	0	0	0	0	2	0	0	.333	.400	.667	1.067
2019	Hou	AL	56	108	29	4	2	0	(0	0)	37	27	7	17	19	0	24	0	1	0	8	1	2	.269	.378	.343	.721
2020	Hou	AL	33	82	17	4	0	0	(0	0)	21	8	8	8	4	0	22	0	0	0	6	2	0	.207	.244	.256	.500
2021	2 Tms		158	564	153	29	1	4	(2	2)	196	86	48	72	67	0	121	2	1	4	30	6	13	.271	.349	.348	.696
21	Hou	AL	98	325	85	13	1	2	(1	1)	106	44	34	39	38	0	71	2	1	4	17	5	7	.262	.339	.326	.665
21	Cle	AL	60	239	68	16	0	2	(1	1)	90	42	14	33	29	0	50	0	0	0	13	1	6	.285	.362	.377	.739
	Postseason		8	0	0	0	0	0	(0	0)	0	1	0	0	0	0	0	0	0	0	1	0	0	-	-	-	-
	4 ML YEARS		256	763	202	37	3	5	(2	3)	260	125	64	99	91	0	167	2	2	4	46	9	15	.265	.343	.341	.684

Hunter Strickland

Pitches: R **Bats:** R **Pos:** RP-57   **Ht:** 6'3" **Wt:** 225 **Born:** 9/24/1988 **Age:** 33

Year	Team	Lg	G	GS	GF	IP	BFP	H	R	ER	HR	SH	SF	HB	TBB	IBB	SO	WP	W	L	Pct	Sv-Op	Hld	Vel	OPS	ERC	ERA
2014	SF	NL	9	0	5	7.0	25	5	0	0	0	0	0	0	0	0	9	0	1	0	1.000	1-1	1	98	.440	1.08	0.00
2015	SF	NL	55	0	11	51.1	191	34	14	14	4	0	0	2	10	1	50	1	3	3	.500	0-2	20	97	.543	1.72	2.45
2016	SF	NL	72	0	14	61.0	250	50	21	21	4	0	3	2	19	3	57	3	3	3	.500	3-8	18	97	.589	2.61	3.10
2017	SF	NL	68	0	17	61.1	268	59	20	18	4	1	3	2	29	4	58	3	4	3	.571	1-3	21	96	.702	3.91	2.64
2018	SF	NL	49	0	35	45.1	201	43	25	20	5	2	3	1	21	2	37	4	3	5	.375	14-18	0	95	.758	4.03	3.97
2019	2 Tms		28	0	3	24.1	105	22	15	15	6	0	0	3	8	0	18	1	2	1	.667	2-3	10	96	.809	4.72	5.55
2020	NYM	NL	4	0	2	3.1	16	5	4	3	0	1	0	0	1	0	4	0	0	1	.000	0-0	0	95	.842	5.66	8.10
2021	3 Tms		57	0	19	58.2	242	46	21	17	8	1	1	2	22	0	58	3	3	2	.600	0-0	0	95	.670	3.18	2.61
19	Sea	AL	4	0	2	3.1	13	2	3	3	1	0	0	1	0	0	3	0	0	1	.000	2-3	0	96	.731	2.70	8.10
19	Was	NL	24	0	1	21.0	92	20	12	12	5	0	0	2	8	0	15	1	2	0	1.000	0-0	10	96	.820	5.05	5.14
21	TB	AL	13	0	7	16.0	66	14	4	3	1	0	0	0	6	0	16	1	0	0	-	0-0	0	95	.653	3.09	1.69
21	LAA	AL	9	0	2	6.1	34	11	9	7	3	1	0	0	4	0	4	0	0	0	-	0-0	0	95	1.248	13.14	9.95
21	Mil	NL	35	0	10	36.1	142	21	8	7	4	0	1	2	12	0	38	2	3	2	.600	0-0	0	95	.546	1.95	1.73
	Postseason		13	0	7	13.0	54	14	11	11	9	0	0	4	4	0	14	1	1	0	1.000	1-2	1	97	1.193	8.64	7.62
	8 ML YEARS		342	0	106	312.1	1298	264	120	108	31	4	11	12	110	10	291	15	19	18	.514	21-35	72	96	.664	3.15	3.11

Spencer Strider

Pitches: R **Bats:** R **Pos:** RP-2   **Ht:** 6'0" **Wt:** 195 **Born:** 10/28/1998 **Age:** 23

			HOW MUCH PITCHED			WHAT HE GAVE UP										THE RESULTS						
Year	Team	Lg	G	GS	GF	IP	BFP	H	R	ER	HR	SH	SF	HB	TBB	IBB	SO	WP	W	L	Pct	Sv-Op	Hld	Vel	OPS	ERC	ERA
2021	Missi	AA	14	14	0	63.0	266	48	34	33	6	0	3	6	29	0	94	7	3	7	.300	0--	-	-	.676	3.36	4.71
2021	2 Tms	Low	7	0	0	30.0	119	15	5	5	1	0	0	0	11	0	56	0	0	0	-	0--	-	-		1.25	1.50
2021	Atl	NL	2	0	0	2.1	9	2	1	1	1	0	0	0	1	0	0	0	1	0	1.000	0-0	0	98	.958	6.17	3.86

Ross Stripling

Pitches: R **Bats:** R **Pos:** SP-19; RP-5   **Ht:** 6'3" **Wt:** 220 **Born:** 11/23/1989 **Age:** 32

			HOW MUCH PITCHED					WHAT HE GAVE UP											THE RESULTS							
Year	Team	Lg	G	GS	GF	IP	BFP	H	R	ER	HR	SH	SF	HB	TBB	IBB	SO	WP	W	L	Pct	Sv-Op	Hld	Vel	OPS	ERC	ERA
2016	LAD	NL	22	14	4	100.0	419	96	46	44	10	3	1	1	30	3	74	6	5	9	.357	0-0	0	90	.709	3.46	3.96
2017	LAD	NL	49	2	12	74.1	304	69	31	31	10	2	3	0	19	4	74	2	3	5	.375	2-5	4	93	.691	3.29	3.75
2018	LAD	NL	33	21	2	122.0	503	123	42	41	18	2	0	1	22	2	136	3	8	6	.571	0-0	3	92	.722	3.58	3.02
2019	LAD	NL	32	15	4	90.2	370	84	40	35	11	0	4	2	20	0	93	4	4	4	.500	0-0	3	91	.699	3.22	3.47
2020	2 Tms		12	9	1	49.1	220	56	37	32	13	2	0	1	18	0	40	1	3	3	.500	1-1	0	92	.882	5.97	5.84
2021	Tor	AL	24	19	1	101.1	431	99	55	54	23	1	3	2	30	0	94	0	5	7	.417	0-0	0	92	.793	4.43	4.80
20	LAD	NL	7	7	0	33.2	150	38	26	21	12	2	0	1	11	0	27	1	3	1	.750	0-0	0	92	.933	6.43	5.61
20	Tor	AL	5	2	1	15.2	70	18	11	11	1	0	0	0	7	0	13	0	0	2	.000	1-1	0	92	.770	4.87	6.32
	Postseason		12	0	4	9.2	43	14	7	6	0	0	2	0	2	0	5	1	0	0	-	0-0	0		.834	5.25	5.59
	6 ML YEARS		172	80	24	537.2	2247	527	251	237	85	10	11	7	139	9	511	16	28	34	.452	3-6	10	91	.741	3.82	3.97

Marcus Stroman

Pitches: R **Bats:** R **Pos:** SP-33   **Ht:** 5'7" **Wt:** 180 **Born:** 5/1/1991 **Age:** 31

			HOW MUCH PITCHED					WHAT HE GAVE UP											THE RESULTS							
Year	Team	Lg	G	GS	GF	IP	BFP	H	R	ER	HR	SH	SF	HB	TBB	IBB	SO	WP	W	L	Pct	Sv-Op	Hld	Vel	OPS	ERC	ERA
2014	Tor	AL	26	20	1	130.2	534	125	56	53	7	0	2	3	28	1	111	9	11	6	.647	1-1	0	94	.633	2.93	3.65
2015	Tor	AL	4	4	0	27.0	103	20	5	5	2	0	0	1	6	0	18	2	4	0	1.000	0-0	0	92	.554	2.16	1.67
2016	Tor	AL	32	32	0	204.0	855	209	104	99	21	2	2	4	54	0	166	9	9	10	.474	0-0	0	93	.720	3.81	4.37
2017	Tor	AL	33	33	0	201.0	834	201	82	69	21	0	4	6	62	1	164	3	13	9	.591	0-0	0	93	.715	3.97	3.09
2018	Tor	AL	19	19	0	102.1	449	115	68	63	9	2	3	2	36	0	77	3	4	9	.308	0-0	0	92	.759	4.59	5.54
2019	2 Tms		32	32	0	184.1	774	183	77	66	18	1	2	1	58	1	159	7	10	13	.435	0-0	0	92	.697	3.73	3.22
2021	NYM	NL	33	33	0	179.0	730	161	70	60	17	6	8	7	44	2	158	7	10	13	.435	0-0	0	92	.655	3.07	3.02
19	Tor	AL	21	21	0	124.2	513	118	50	41	10	0	1	0	35	0	99	4	6	11	.353	0-0	0	93	.656	3.23	2.96
19	NYM	NL	11	11	0	59.2	261	65	27	25	8	1	1	1	23	1	60	3	4	2	.667	0-0	0	92	.781	4.84	3.77
	Postseason		5	5	0	30.2	128	29	16	15	4	0	1	0	7	0	21	2	1	1	.500	0-0	0	93	.690	3.24	4.40
	7 ML YEARS		179	173	1	1028.1	4279	1014	462	415	95	11	21	24	288	5	853	40	61	60	.504	1-1	0	93	.693	3.61	3.63

Pedro Strop

Pitches: R **Bats:** R **Pos:** RP-2   STROPE   **Ht:** 6'1" **Wt:** 220 **Born:** 6/13/1985 **Age:** 37

			HOW MUCH PITCHED					WHAT HE GAVE UP											THE RESULTS							
Year	Team	Lg	G	GS	GF	IP	BFP	H	R	ER	HR	SH	SF	HB	TBB	IBB	SO	WP	W	L	Pct	Sv-Op	Hld	Vel	OPS	ERC	ERA
2009	Tex	AL	7	0	3	7.0	30	6	6	6	0	0	0	0	4	0	9	0	0	0	-	0-0	0	95	.679	3.27	7.71
2010	Tex	AL	15	0	5	10.2	60	17	12	12	2	1	0	1	11	0	11	5	0	0	-	0-0	1	95	1.109	11.92	10.13
2011	2 Tms	AL	23	0	6	22.0	90	15	5	5	0	2	1	1	10	0	21	2	2	1	.667	0-2	4	94	.519	2.15	2.05
2012	Bal	AL	70	0	17	66.1	283	52	18	18	2	1	1	4	37	2	58	5	5	2	.714	3-10	24	97	.613	3.22	2.44
2013	2 Tms		66	0	22	57.1	254	45	30	29	5	7	0	6	26	2	66	8	2	5	.286	1-4	17	96	.663	3.21	4.55
2014	ChC	NL	65	0	13	61.0	244	40	19	15	2	0	1	4	25	3	71	6	2	4	.333	2-6	21	95	.535	2.12	2.21
2015	ChC	NL	76	0	12	68.0	270	39	24	22	5	1	3	4	29	6	81	6	2	6	.250	3-5	28	95	.538	1.94	2.91
2016	ChC	NL	54	0	8	47.1	187	27	16	15	4	0	2	4	15	1	60	7	2	2	.500	0-4	21	95	.561	1.78	2.85
2017	ChC	NL	69	0	8	60.1	250	45	22	19	4	2	1	3	26	1	65	7	5	4	.556	0-4	21	96	.619	2.78	2.83
2018	ChC	NL	60	0	20	59.2	240	38	15	15	4	1	1	5	21	3	57	3	6	1	.857	13-17	9	95	.541	2.06	2.26
2019	ChC	NL	50	0	27	41.2	178	33	24	23	6	0	1	5	20	1	49	4	2	5	.286	10-16	13	94	.734	4.01	4.97
2020	Cin	NL	4	0	0	2.1	15	1	3	1	0	0	1	0	6	0	3	1	0	0	-	0-0	1	92	.592	7.50	3.86
2021	ChC	NL	2	0	0	2.0	10	2	0	0	0	0	0	0	2	0	3	0	1	0	1.000	0-0	0	92	.650	5.48	0.00
11	Tex	AL	11	0	4	9.2	44	7	4	4	1	1	1	1	7	0	9	2	0	0	-	0-1	0	94	.555	3.34	3.72
11	Bal	AL	12	0	2	12.1	46	8	1	1	0	1	0	0	3	0	12	0	2	1	1.000	0-1	4	95	.483	1.39	0.73
13	Bal	AL	29	0	15	22.1	111	23	19	18	4	4	0	2	15	2	24	5	0	3	.000	0-3	3	96	.861	5.81	7.25
13	ChC	NL	37	0	7	35.0	143	22	11	11	1	3	0	4	11	0	42	3	2	2	.500	1-1	14	96	.520	1.80	2.83
	Postseason		22	0	2	19.1	75	9	4	4	1	1	0	4	7	0	14	1	1	0	1.000	0-0	4	95	.524	1.76	1.86
	13 ML YEARS		561	0	141	505.2	2111	360	194	180	34	15	12	37	232	19	554	54	29	30	.492	32-68	153	95	.605	2.76	3.20

Garrett Stubbs

Bats: L **Throws:** R **Pos:** C-14; PH-5; LF-2; PR-1   **Ht:** 5'10" **Wt:** 170 **Born:** 5/26/1993 **Age:** 29

			BATTING																			RUNNING			AVERAGES			
Year	Team	Lg	G	AB	H	2B	3B	HR	(Hm	Rd)	TB	R	RBI	RC	TBB	IBB	SO	HBP	SH	SF	SB	CS	GDP	Avg	OBP	Slg	OPS
2021	SgrLnd	AAA	35	109	30	5	0	2	(-	-)	41	24	15	-	27	0	28	1	0	2	4	0	0	.275	.417	.376	.793
2019	Hou	AL	19	35	7	3	0	0	(0	0)	10	8	2	1	4	0	7	0	0	0	1	0	1	.200	.282	.286	.568
2020	Hou	AL	14	8	1	0	0	0	(0	0)	1	1	1	0	0	0	0	0	1	1	0	1	0	.125	.111	.125	.236
2021	Hou	AL	18	34	6	2	0	0	(0	0)	8	2	3	2	2	0	7	0	2	0	0	0	0	.176	.222	.235	.458
	Postseason		1	0	0	0	0	0	(0	0)	0	0	0	0	0	0	0	0	0	0	0	0	0	-	-	-	-
	3 ML YEARS		51	77	14	5	0	0	(0	0)	19	11	6	3	6	0	14	0	3	1	1	1	1	.182	.238	.247	.485

Eugenio Suarez

Bats: R **Throws:** R **Pos:** 3B-104;SS-34;PH-10   ay-yoo-HAY-nee-oh SWAH-rez   **Ht:** 5'11" **Wt:** 213 **Born:** 7/18/1991 **Age:** 30

Year	Team	Lg	G	AB	H	2B	3B	HR	(Hm	Rd)	TB	R	RBI	RC	TBB	IBB	SO	HBP	SH	SF	SB	CS	GDP	Avg	OBP	Slg	OPS
2014	Det	AL	85	244	59	9	1	4	(2	2)	82	33	23	30	22	1	67	5	5	1	3	2	3	.242	.316	.336	.652
2015	Cin	NL	97	372	104	19	2	13	(4	9)	166	42	48	49	17	0	94	3	4	2	4	1	7	.280	.315	.446	.761
2016	Cin	NL	159	565	140	25	2	21	(10	11)	232	78	70	77	51	0	155	8	0	3	11	5	10	.248	.317	.411	.728
2017	Cin	NL	156	534	139	25	2	26	(21	5)	246	87	82	81	84	1	147	9	0	5	4	5	16	.260	.367	.461	.828
2018	Cin	NL	143	527	149	22	2	34	(19	15)	277	79	104	95	64	7	142	9	0	6	1	1	20	.283	.366	.526	.892
2019	Cin	NL	159	575	156	22	2	49	(24	25)	329	87	103	103	70	4	**189**	11	0	6	3	2	12	.271	.358	.572	.930
2020	Cin	NL	57	198	40	8	0	15	(5	**10**)	93	29	38	32	30	1	67	2	0	1	2	0	5	.202	.312	.470	.781
2021	Cin	NL	145	505	100	23	2	31	(15	16)	216	71	79	53	56	0	171	8	0	5	0	1	14	.198	.286	.428	.713
	Postseason		3	10	2	0	0	0	(0	0)	2	0	0	0	1	0	4	0	0	0	0	0	0	.200	.273	.200	.473
	8 ML YEARS		1001	3520	887	153	11	193	(100	93)	1641	506	547	520	394	14	1032	55	9	29	28	17	87	.252	.334	.466	.800

Jose Suarez

Pitches: L **Bats:** L **Pos:** SP-14; RP-9   **Ht:** 5'10" **Wt:** 225 **Born:** 1/3/1998 **Age:** 24

Year	Team	Lg	G	GS	GF	IP	BFP	H	R	ER	HR	SH	SF	HB	TBB	IBB	SO	WP	W	L	Pct	Sv-Op	Hld	Vel	OPS	ERC	ERA
2019	LAA	AL	19	15	0	81.0	375	100	67	64	23	1	2	10	33	1	72	5	2	6	.250	0-0	0	92	.948	7.55	7.11
2020	LAA	AL	2	2	0	2.1	23	10	10	10	1	0	0	1	5	0	2	1	0	2	.000	0-0	0	93	1.578	44.98	38.57
2021	LAA	AL	23	14	2	98.1	413	85	45	41	11	2	2	4	36	1	85	4	8	8	.500	0-0	0	93	.686	3.42	3.75
	3 ML YEARS		44	31	2	181.2	811	195	122	115	35	3	4	15	74	2	159	10	10	16	.385	0-0	0	92	.830	5.55	5.70

Ranger Suarez

Pitches: L **Bats:** L **Pos:** RP-27; SP-12   **Ht:** 6'1" **Wt:** 217 **Born:** 8/26/1995 **Age:** 26

Year	Team	Lg	G	GS	GF	IP	BFP	H	R	ER	HR	SH	SF	HB	TBB	IBB	SO	WP	W	L	Pct	Sv-Op	Hld	Vel	OPS	ERC	ERA
2018	Phi	NL	4	3	0	15.0	69	21	14	9	3	1	0	0	6	1	11	0	1	1	.500	0-0	0	92	.945	7.33	5.40
2019	Phi	NL	37	0	8	48.2	205	52	18	17	6	3	2	1	12	2	42	1	6	1	.857	0-1	6	92	.739	4.07	3.14
2020	Phi	NL	3	0	1	4.0	26	10	9	9	1	0	0	1	4	0	1	0	0	1	.000	0-0	0	91	1.291	20.74	20.25
2021	Phi	NL	39	12	13	106.0	418	73	20	16	4	3	1	5	33	3	107	1	8	5	.615	4-7	0	93	.523	1.94	1.36
	4 ML YEARS		83	15	22	173.2	718	156	61	51	14	7	3	7	55	6	161	2	15	8	.652	4-8	6	93	.652	3.21	2.64

Wander Suero

Pitches: R **Bats:** R **Pos:** RP-45   **Ht:** 6'4" **Wt:** 216 **Born:** 9/15/1991 **Age:** 30

Year	Team	Lg	G	GS	GF	IP	BFP	H	R	ER	HR	SH	SF	HB	TBB	IBB	SO	WP	W	L	Pct	Sv-Op	Hld	Vel	OPS	ERC	ERA
2021	Roch	AAA	10	1	1	9.2	42	11	9	9	0	0	2	0	3	1	11	0	2	1	.667	0- -	-	-	.793	3.60	8.38
2018	Was	NL	40	0	11	47.2	200	43	20	19	4	1	1	4	15	2	47	3	4	1	.800	0-0	2	92	.719	3.38	3.59
2019	Was	NL	78	0	10	71.1	296	64	36	36	5	0	3	3	26	3	81	2	6	9	.400	1-7	19	93	.666	3.34	4.54
2020	Was	NL	22	0	2	23.2	102	20	10	10	1	0	1	3	10	2	28	2	2	0	1.000	0-0	6	91	.642	3.25	3.80
2021	Was	NL	45	0	8	42.2	190	45	35	30	11	0	2	4	15	1	44	5	2	3	.400	0-3	6	92	.858	5.64	6.33
	Postseason		4	0	2	2.0	8	2	1	1	1	0	0	0	0	0	2	0	0	0	-	0-0	0	93	1.000	4.70	4.50
	4 ML YEARS		185	0	31	185.1	788	172	101	95	21	1	7	14	66	8	200	12	14	13	.519	1-10	33	92	.723	3.85	4.61

Cole Sulser

Pitches: R **Bats:** R **Pos:** RP-60   **Ht:** 6'1" **Wt:** 190 **Born:** 3/12/1990 **Age:** 32

Year	Team	Lg	G	GS	GF	IP	BFP	H	R	ER	HR	SH	SF	HB	TBB	IBB	SO	WP	W	L	Pct	Sv-Op	Hld	Vel	OPS	ERC	ERA
2019	TB	AL	7	0	4	7.1	29	5	0	0	0	0	0	0	3	0	9	0	0	0	-	0-0	0	93	.507	1.90	0.00
2020	Bal	AL	19	0	9	22.2	100	17	18	14	2	2	0	0	17	1	19	1	1	5	.167	5-8	1	94	.705	3.87	5.56
2021	Bal	AL	60	0	18	63.1	257	48	20	19	5	1	1	0	23	0	73	6	5	4	.556	8-11	6	93	.596	2.53	2.70
	3 ML YEARS		86	0	31	93.1	386	70	38	33	7	3	1	0	43	1	101	7	6	9	.400	13-19	7	93	.617	2.79	3.18

Brent Suter

Pitches: L **Bats:** L **Pos:** RP-60; SP-1   SOO-ter   **Ht:** 6'4" **Wt:** 213 **Born:** 8/29/1989 **Age:** 32

Year	Team	Lg	G	GS	GF	IP	BFP	H	R	ER	HR	SH	SF	HB	TBB	IBB	SO	WP	W	L	Pct	Sv-Op	Hld	Vel	OPS	ERC	ERA
2016	Mil	NL	14	2	4	21.2	91	25	8	8	3	1	0	1	5	0	15	1	2	2	.500	0-0	2	84	.773	4.90	3.32
2017	Mil	NL	22	14	1	81.2	341	83	33	31	8	1	1	2	22	2	64	1	3	2	.600	0-0	0	86	.702	3.75	3.42
2018	Mil	NL	20	18	0	101.1	424	102	55	50	18	5	1	4	19	2	84	1	8	7	.533	0-0	0	87	.754	3.88	4.44
2019	Mil	NL	9	0	0	18.1	65	10	1	1	1	0	0	0	1	0	15	0	4	0	1.000	0-0	2	88	.435	0.88	0.49
2020	Mil	NL	16	4	3	31.2	129	30	13	11	4	0	0	1	5	0	38	0	2	0	1.000	0-0	2	86	.645	3.14	3.13
2021	Mil	NL	61	1	9	73.1	313	72	34	25	9	2	0	1	24	3	69	1	12	5	.706	1-9	8	87	.714	3.80	3.07
	Postseason		2	1	0	2.2	18	4	3	3	0	0	0	0	5	0	0	0	0	1	.000	0-0	0	86	1.038	11.70	10.13
	6 ML YEARS		142	39	15	328.0	1363	322	144	126	43	9	2	9	76	7	285	4	31	16	.660	1-9	14	86	.707	3.61	3.46

Kurt Suzuki

Bats: R **Throws:** R **Pos:** C-69;PH-6;PR-1 **Ht:** 5'11" **Wt:** 210 **Born:** 10/4/1983 **Age:** 38

							BATTING													RUNNING			AVERAGES			
Year	Team	Lg	G	AB	H	2B	3B	HR	(Hm | Rd)	TB	R	RBI	RC	TBB	IBB	SO	HBP	SH	SF	SB	CS	GDP	Avg	OBP	Slg	OPS
2007	Oak	AL	68	213	53	13	0	7	(4 | 3)	87	27	39	33	24	0	39	3	3	5	0	0	4	.249	.327	.408	.735
2008	Oak	AL	148	530	148	25	1	7	(5 | 2)	196	54	42	66	44	2	69	11	2	1	2	3	20	.279	.346	.370	.716
2009	Oak	AL	147	570	156	37	1	15	(8 | 7)	240	74	88	77	28	0	59	8	1	7	8	2	14	.274	.313	.421	.734
2010	Oak	AL	131	495	120	18	2	13	(8 | 5)	181	55	71	54	33	3	49	12	0	4	3	2	22	.242	.303	.366	.669
2011	Oak	AL	134	460	109	26	0	14	(8 | 6)	177	54	44	42	38	1	64	7	3	7	2	2	14	.237	.301	.385	.686
2012	2 Tms		118	408	96	20	0	6	(3 | 3)	134	36	43	39	20	3	73	5	4	5	2	0	5	.235	.276	.328	.605
2013	2 Tms		94	285	66	13	1	5	(2 | 3)	96	25	32	34	22	6	35	3	2	4	2	0	2	.232	.290	.337	.627
2014	Min	AL	131	452	130	34	0	3	(1 | 2)	173	37	61	65	34	0	46	9	1	7	0	1	9	.288	.345	.383	.727
2015	Min	AL	131	433	104	17	0	5	(3 | 2)	136	36	50	46	29	4	59	7	6	4	0	0	14	.240	.296	.314	.610
2016	Min	AL	106	345	89	24	1	8	(4 | 4)	139	34	49	45	18	0	48	5	1	4	0	0	5	.258	.301	.403	.704
2017	Atl	NL	81	276	78	13	0	19	(8 | 11)	148	38	50	49	17	2	39	13	1	2	0	0	5	.283	.351	.536	.887
2018	Atl	NL	105	347	94	24	0	12	(5 | 7)	154	45	50	45	22	0	43	13	0	6	0	0	6	.271	.332	.444	.776
2019	Was	NL	85	280	74	11	0	17	(10 | 7)	136	37	63	53	20	1	36	6	0	3	0	1	10	.264	.324	.486	.809
2020	Was	NL	33	111	30	8	0	2	(0 | 2)	44	15	17	11	11	0	19	4	0	3	1	0	4	.270	.349	.396	.745
2021	LAA	AL	72	219	49	8	0	6	(3 | 3)	75	17	16	21	12	0	44	11	2	3	0	0	7	.224	.294	.342	.636
12	Oak	AL	75	262	57	15	0	1	(1 | 0)	75	19	18	16	9	0	53	3	2	2	1	0	3	.218	.250	.286	.536
12	Was	NL	43	146	39	5	0	5	(2 | 3)	59	17	25	23	11	3	20	2	2	3	1	0	2	.267	.321	.404	.725
13	Was	NL	79	252	56	11	1	3	(0 | 3)	78	19	25	26	20	6	32	3	2	4	2	0	2	.222	.283	.310	.593
13	Oak	AL	15	33	10	2	0	2	(2 | 0)	18	6	7	8	2	0	3	0	0	0	0	0	0	.303	.343	.545	.888
	Postseason		19	55	9	0	0	1	(0 | 1)	12	2	5	4	6	0	16	1	0	0	0	0	3	.164	.258	.218	.476
	15 ML YEARS		1584	5424	1396	291	6	139	(72 | 67)	2116	584	715	680	372	22	722	117	26	65	20	11	145	.257	.315	.390	.705

Dansby Swanson

Bats: R **Throws:** R **Pos:** SS-159;PH-2 **Ht:** 6'1" **Wt:** 190 **Born:** 2/11/1994 **Age:** 28

							BATTING													RUNNING			AVERAGES			
Year	Team	Lg	G	AB	H	2B	3B	HR	(Hm	Rd)	TB	R	RBI	RC	TBB	IBB	SO	HBP	SH	SF	SB	CS	GDP	Avg	OBP	Slg	OPS
2016	Atl	NL	38	129	39	7	1	3	(1	2)	57	20	17	17	13	5	34	0	1	2	3	0	2	.302	.361	.442	.803
2017	Atl	NL	144	488	113	23	2	6	(2	4)	158	59	51	55	59	10	120	0	0	4	3	3	7	.232	.312	.324	.636
2018	Atl	NL	136	478	114	25	4	14	(7	7)	189	51	59	59	44	15	122	2	6	3	10	4	5	.238	.304	.395	.699
2019	Atl	NL	127	483	121	26	3	17	(8	9)	204	77	65	61	51	2	124	5	1	5	10	5	7	.251	.325	.422	.748
2020	Atl	NL	60	237	65	15	0	10	(6	4)	110	49	35	40	22	0	71	4	0	1	5	0	0	.274	.345	.464	.809
2021	Atl	NL	160	588	146	33	2	27	(14	13)	264	78	88	85	52	4	167	5	1	7	9	3	7	.248	.311	.449	.760
	Postseason		17	63	19	5	1	3	(2	1)	35	9	11	14	6	1	23	0	0	1	2	0	0	.302	.357	.556	.913
	6 ML YEARS		665	2403	598	129	12	77	(38	39)	982	334	315	317	241	36	638	16	9	22	40	15	28	.249	.319	.409	.727

Erik Swanson

Pitches: R **Bats:** R **Pos:** RP-31; SP-2 **Ht:** 6'3" **Wt:** 220 **Born:** 9/4/1993 **Age:** 28

			HOW MUCH PITCHED				WHAT HE GAVE UP											THE RESULTS							
Year	Team	Lg	G	GS	GF	IP	BFP	H	R	ER	HR	SH	SF	HB	TBB	IBB	SO	WP	W	L	Pct	Sv-Op	Hld	Vel	OPS	ERC	ERA
2019	Sea	AL	27	6	7	58.0	245	56	41	37	17	0	1	2	12	1	52	2	1	5	.167	2-2	5		.803	4.38	5.74
2020	Sea	AL	9	0	2	7.2	37	11	12	11	3	0	1	2	2	0	9	1	0	2	.000	0-1	1	96	1.093	9.84	12.91
2021	Sea	AL	33	2	5	35.1	144	28	18	13	5	0	1	1	10	1	35	0	0	3	.000	1-3	5	95	.672	2.83	3.31
	3 ML YEARS		69	10	14	101.0	426	95	71	61	25	0	3	5	24	2	96	3	1	10	.091	3-6	7	94	.783	4.17	5.44

Anthony Swarzak

Pitches: R **Bats:** R **Pos:** RP-13   SWORE-zack   **Ht:** 6'4" **Wt:** 215 **Born:** 9/10/1985 **Age:** 36

			HOW MUCH PITCHED				WHAT HE GAVE UP											THE RESULTS							
Year	Team	Lg	G	GS	GF	IP	BFP	H	R	ER	HR	SH	SF	HB	TBB	IBB	SO	WP	W	L	Pct	Sv-Op	Hld	Vel	OPS	ERC	ERA
2021	Omha	AAA	9	0	7	9.1	33	7	3	3	2	0	0	0	0	0	14	0	1	0	1.000	4--	-		.606	2.04	2.89
2009	Min	AL	12	12	0	59.0	268	76	43	41	12	1	1	2	20	0	34	0	3	7	.300	0-0	0	90	.879	6.50	6.25
2011	Min	AL	27	11	2	102.0	441	111	53	49	9	2	3	6	26	1	55	3	4	7	.364	0-0	0	91	.724	4.11	4.32
2012	Min	AL	44	5	9	96.2	413	106	57	54	15	3	6	0	31	8	62	3	3	6	.333	0-1	1	92	.798	4.63	5.03
2013	Min	AL	48	0	8	96.0	387	89	33	31	7	2	5	1	22	1	69	1	3	2	.600	0-2	3	92	.649	2.94	2.91
2014	Min	AL	50	4	11	86.0	378	100	48	44	5	1	2	0	28	5	47	0	3	2	.600	0-1	3	92	.752	4.29	4.60
2015	Cle	AL	10	0	3	13.1	61	18	9	5	1	0	0	0	4	1	13	0	0	0	-	0-0	0	92	.799	5.34	3.38
2016	NYY	AL	26	0	6	31.0	124	28	19	19	10	0	1	1	7	0	31	1	1	2	.333	0-1	1	93	.847	4.51	5.52
2017	2 Tms		70	0	6	77.1	303	58	21	20	6	1	3	2	22	4	91	2	6	4	.600	2-5	27	95	.595	2.29	2.33
2018	NYM	NL	29	0	12	26.1	116	28	18	18	6	0	1	1	14	0	31	2	0	2	.000	4-5	2	94	.861	6.32	6.15
2019	2 Tms		59	0	8	53.1	234	52	30	27	12	0	0	0	27	3	52	2	3	4	.429	4-7	17	93	.792	5.18	4.56
2021	2 Tms		13	0	6	12.1	56	20	13	13	4	0	0	1	1	0	9	0	0	1	.000	0-0	0	93	1.097	8.97	9.49
17	CWS	AL	41	0	5	48.1	186	37	12	12	2	0	2	0	13	2	52	2	4	3	.571	1-3	10	94	.555	2.06	2.23
17	Mil	NL	29	0	1	29.0	117	21	9	8	4	1	1	2	9	2	39	0	2	1	.667	1-2	17	95	.660	2.69	2.48
19	Sea	AL	15	0	7	13.2	64	14	11	8	6	0	0	0	8	1	17	1	2	2	.500	3-6	0	94	.933	7.19	5.27
19	Atl	NL	44	0	1	39.2	170	38	19	19	6	0	0	0	19	2	35	1	1	2	.333	1-1	17	93	.739	4.51	4.31
21	Ari	NL	6	0	1	4.2	21	7	5	5	1	0	0	0	1	0	4	0	0	1	.000	0-0	0	93	1.031	7.39	9.64
21	KC	AL	7	0	5	7.2	35	13	8	8	3	0	0	1	0	0	5	0	0	0	-	0-0	0	93	1.135	9.96	9.39
	11 ML YEARS		388	32	71	653.1	2781	686	344	321	87	10	22	14	202	23	494	14	26	37	.413	10-22	54	92	.755	4.30	4.42

Noah Syndergaard

Pitches: R Bats: L Pos: SP-2

sin-DER-gard

Ht: 6'6" Wt: 242 Born: 8/29/1992 Age: 29

Year Team	Lg	G	GS	GF	IP	BFP	H	R	ER	HR	SH	SF	HB	TBB	IBB	SO	WP	W	L	Pct	Sv-Op	Hld	Vel	OPS	ERC	ERA
2015 NYM	NL	24	24	0	150.0	603	126	60	54	19	5	3	8	31	2	166	6	9	7	.563	0-0	0	97	.645	2.70	3.24
2016 NYM	NL	31	30	0	183.2	744	168	61	53	11	3	4	2	43	2	218	10	14	9	.609	0-0	0	98	.639	2.79	2.60
2017 NYM	NL	7	7	0	30.1	124	29	14	10	0	1	1	1	3	1	34	3	1	2	.333	0-0	0	98	.573	2.13	2.97
2018 NYM	NL	25	25	0	154.1	644	148	55	52	9	3	3	7	39	2	155	2	13	4	.765	0-0	0	97	.651	3.16	3.03
2019 NYM	NL	32	32	0	197.2	825	194	101	94	24	3	8	6	50	2	202	4	10	8	.556	0-0	0	98	.714	3.66	4.28
2021 NYM	NL	2	2	0	2.0	8	3	2	2	1	0	0	0	0	0	2	0	0	1	.000	0-0	0	95	1.250	9.22	9.00
Postseason		5	4	0	26.0	103	17	7	7	0	1	0	0	11	1	36	1	2	1	.667	0-0	1	98	.505	1.75	2.42
6 ML YEARS		121	120	0	718.0	2948	668	293	265	64	15	19	19	166	9	777	25	47	31	.603	0-0	1	98	.663	3.07	3.32

Thomas Szapucki

Pitches: L Bats: R Pos: RP-1

Ht: 6'2" Wt: 181 Born: 6/12/1996 Age: 26

Year Team	Lg	G	GS	GF	IP	BFP	H	R	ER	HR	SH	SF	HB	TBB	IBB	SO	WP	W	L	Pct	Sv-Op	Hld	Vel	OPS	ERC	ERA
2021 Syrcse	AAA	10	9	1	41.2	193	42	28	19	5	2	1	2	28	0	41	4	0	4	.000	0--	-	-	.783	5.56	4.10
2021 NYM	NL	1	0	0	3.2	20	7	6	6	2	0	0	0	3	0	4	0	0	0	-	0-0	0	91	1.382	17.09	14.73

Jameson Taillon

Pitches: R Bats: R Pos: SP-29

TIE-yohn

Ht: 6'5" Wt: 230 Born: 11/18/1991 Age: 30

Year Team	Lg	G	GS	GF	IP	BFP	H	R	ER	HR	SH	SF	HB	TBB	IBB	SO	WP	W	L	Pct	Sv-Op	Hld	Vel	OPS	ERC	ERA
2016 Pit	NL	18	18	0	104.0	418	99	40	39	13	4	1	3	17	1	85	1	5	4	.556	0-0	0	94	.702	3.21	3.38
2017 Pit	NL	25	25	0	133.2	587	152	69	66	11	8	4	4	46	3	125	7	8	7	.533	0-0	0	95	.789	4.61	4.44
2018 Pit	NL	32	32	0	191.0	785	179	69	68	20	4	2	6	46	2	179	2	14	10	.583	0-0	0	95	.681	3.26	3.20
2019 Pit	NL	7	7	0	37.1	158	34	24	17	4	0	1	2	8	1	30	1	2	3	.400	0-0	0	95	.680	2.98	4.10
2021 NYY	AL	29	29	0	144.1	603	130	73	69	24	1	5	6	44	1	140	4	8	6	.571	0-0	0	94	.721	3.74	4.30
5 ML YEARS		111	111	0	610.1	2551	594	275	259	72	17	13	21	161	10	559	15	37	30	.552	0-0	0	95	.718	3.64	3.82

Domingo Tapia

Pitches: R Bats: R Pos: RP-34

Ht: 6'3" Wt: 263 Born: 8/4/1991 Age: 30

Year Team	Lg	G	GS	GF	IP	BFP	H	R	ER	HR	SH	SF	HB	TBB	IBB	SO	WP	W	L	Pct	Sv-Op	Hld	Vel	OPS	ERC	ERA
2021 Tacom	AAA	5	0	0	6.1	24	2	3	1	0	1	0	0	2	1	6	0	0	0	-	0--	-	-	.269	0.50	1.42
2021 Omha	AAA	18	0	7	22.0	100	20	12	11	4	0	0	1	15	0	22	1	1	0	1.000	2--	-	-	.753	5.49	4.50
2020 Bos	AL	5	0	0	4.1	19	4	1	1	1	0	0	0	2	0	4	0	0	0	-	0-0	0	99	.786	4.71	2.08
2021 2 Tms	AL	34	0	1	33.2	135	25	10	10	1	0	0	0	15	2	26	2	4	1	.800	0-3	7	97	.571	2.42	2.67
21 Sea	AL	2	0	1	2.0	11	4	0	0	0	0	0	0	1	0	1	0	0	0	-	0-0	0	98	.855	9.72	0.00
21 KC	AL	32	0	0	31.2	124	21	10	10	1	0	0	0	14	2	25	2	4	1	.800	0-3	7	97	.546	2.06	2.84
2 ML YEARS		39	0	1	38.0	154	29	11	11	2	0	0	0	17	2	30	2	4	1	.800	0-3	7	98	.598	2.67	2.61

Raimel Tapia

Bats: L Throws: L Pos: LF-118;PH-16;RF-4;CF-3

rye-MELL

Ht: 6'3" Wt: 175 Born: 2/4/1994 Age: 28

Year Team	Lg	G	AB	H	2B	3B	HR	(Hm	Rd)	TB	R	RBI	RC	TBB	IBB	SO	HBP	SH	SF	SB	CS	GDP	Avg	OBP	Slg	OPS
2016 Col	NL	22	38	10	0	0	0	(0	0)	10	4	3	5	2	0	11	0	0	1	3	0	0	.263	.293	.263	.556
2017 Col	NL	70	160	46	12	2	2	(1	1)	68	27	16	20	8	1	36	2	1	0	5	2	3	.288	.329	.425	.754
2018 Col	NL	25	25	5	2	1	1	(0	1)	12	6	6	5	2	0	7	0	0	0	0	0	0	.200	.259	.480	.739
2019 Col	NL	138	426	117	23	5	9	(6	3)	177	54	44	54	21	0	100	0	0	0	9	3	2	.275	.309	.415	.724
2020 Col	NL	51	184	59	8	2	1	(0	1)	74	26	17	33	14	0	38	2	1	3	8	2	3	.321	.369	.402	.772
2021 Col	NL	133	487	133	26	2	6	(6	0)	181	69	50	67	40	2	70	1	1	4	20	6	8	.273	.327	.372	.699
Postseason		1	1	1	0	0	0	(0	0)	1	0	1		0	0	0	0	0	0	0	0	0	1.000	1.000	1.000	2.000
6 ML YEARS		439	1320	370	71	12	19	(13	6)	522	186	136	184	87	3	262	5	3	8	45	13	16	.280	.325	.395	.721

Stephen Tarpley

Pitches: L Bats: R Pos: RP-1

Ht: 6'0" Wt: 202 Born: 2/17/1993 Age: 29

Year Team	Lg	G	GS	GF	IP	BFP	H	R	ER	HR	SH	SF	HB	TBB	IBB	SO	WP	W	L	Pct	Sv-Op	Hld	Vel	OPS	ERC	ERA
2021 Syrcse	AAA	9	0	1	8.2	53	20	17	15	3	1	1	2	6	0	10	1	1	2	.333	0--	-	-	1.306	18.17	15.58
2018 NYY	AL	10	0	3	9.0	40	6	3	3	0	0	0	0	6	0	13	0	0	0	-	0-0	0	93	.506	2.46	3.00
2019 NYY	AL	21	1	3	24.2	120	34	20	19	6	0	0	2	15	1	34	5	1	0	1.000	2-2	2	92	.988	8.99	6.93
2020 Mia	NL	12	0	3	11.0	53	11	12	11	2	2	1	3	8	2	11	0	2	2	.500	1-1	2	91	.944	6.98	9.00
2021 NYM	NL	1	0	0	0.0	4	1	2	2	0	0	0	1	2	0	0	0	0	0	-	0-0	0	91	2.000		
Postseason		1	0	1	1.0	8	4	3	3	0	0	0	0	1	0	1	1	0	0	-	0-0	0	93	1.339	27.72	27.00
4 ML YEARS		44	1	9	44.2	217	52	37	35	8	2	1	6	31	3	58	5	3	2	.600	3-3	4	92	.900	7.43	7.05

Dillon Tate

Pitches: R **Bats:** R **Pos:** RP-62   **Ht:** 6'2" **Wt:** 195 **Born:** 5/1/1994 **Age:** 28

		HOW MUCH PITCHED					WHAT HE GAVE UP											THE RESULTS						
Year	Team	Lg	G	GS	GF	IP	BFP	H	R	ER	HR	SH	SF	HB	TBB	IBB	SO	WP	W	L	Pct	Sv-Op	Hld	Vel	OPS	ERC	ERA
2019	Bal	AL	16	0	5	21.0	93	18	15	15	3	0	1	5	9	0	20	2	0	2	.000	0-0	1	94	.729	4.64	6.43
2020	Bal	AL	12	0	1	16.2	64	9	7	6	1	0	2	2	5	0	14	1	1	1	.500	0-0	2	94	.486	1.66	3.24
2021	Bal	AL	62	0	19	67.2	287	61	35	33	7	2	6	7	23	0	49	7	0	6	.000	3-5	7	96	.713	3.74	4.39
	3 ML YEARS		90	0	25	105.1	444	88	57	54	11	2	9	14	37	0	83	10	1	9	.100	3-5	10	95	.684	3.55	4.61

Fernando Tatis Jr.

Bats: R **Throws:** R **Pos:** SS-102;RF-20;CF-7;PH-4;DH-1   **Ht:** 6'3" **Wt:** 217 **Born:** 1/2/1999 **Age:** 23

							BATTING													RUNNING			AVERAGES			
Year	Team	Lg	G	AB	H	2B	3B	HR	(Hm Rd)	TB	R	RBI	RC	TBB	IBB	SO	HBP	SH	SF	SB	CS	GDP	Avg	OBP	Slg	OPS
2019	SD	NL	84	334	106	13	6	22	(10 12)	197	61	53	73	30	1	110	5	0	3	16	6	4	.317	.379	.590	.969
2020	SD	NL	59	224	62	11	2	17	(8 9)	128	50	45	48	27	1	61	5	0	1	11	3	6	.277	.366	.571	.937
2021	SD	NL	130	478	135	31	0	**42**	(18 24)	292	99	97	110	62	6	153	2	0	4	25	4	5	.282	.364	.611	.975
	Postseason		6	22	7	2	0	2	(2 0)	15	5	5	5	5	1	7	0	0	0	1	1	0	.318	.444	.682	1.126
	3 ML YEARS		273	1036	303	55	8	81	(36 45)	617	210	195	231	119	8	324	12	0	8	52	13	15	.292	.369	.596	.965

Mike Tauchman

Bats: L **Throws:** L **Pos:** LF-45;PH-18;RF-14;CF-12;PR-7;DH-1   **Ht:** 6'2" **Wt:** 220 **Born:** 12/3/1990 **Age:** 31

							BATTING													RUNNING			AVERAGES			
Year	Team	Lg	G	AB	H	2B	3B	HR	(Hm Rd)	TB	R	RBI	RC	TBB	IBB	SO	HBP	SH	SF	SB	CS	GDP	Avg	OBP	Slg	OPS
2021	Scrmto	AAA	38	115	32	9	2	3	(- -)	54	25	18	-	20	0	30	3	0	3	2	1	2	.278	.390	.470	.860
2017	Col	NL	31	27	6	0	1	0	(0 0)	8	2	2	2	5	0	10	0	0	0	1	2	1	.222	.344	.296	.640
2018	Col	NL	21	32	3	1	0	0	(0 0)	4	5	0	0	4	0	15	0	1	0	1	0	0	.094	.194	.125	.319
2019	NYY	AL	87	260	72	18	1	13	(7 6)	131	46	47	50	34	0	71	1	0	1	6	0	9	.277	.361	.504	.865
2020	NYY	AL	43	95	23	6	0	0	(0 0)	29	18	14	13	14	3	26	1	0	1	6	0	3	.242	.342	.305	.648
2021	2 Tms		75	166	30	5	0	4	(0 4)	47	22	15	17	23	0	58	1	1	0	3	3	0	.181	.284	.283	.567
21	NYY	AL	11	14	3	1	0	0	(0 0)	4	1	0	2	1	0	6	0	1	0	2	0	0	.214	.267	.286	.552
21	SF	NL	64	152	27	4	0	4	(0 4)	43	21	15	15	22	0	52	1	0	0	1	3	0	.178	.286	.283	.569
	Postseason		1	0	0	0	0	0	(0 0)	0	1	0	0	0	0	0	0	0	0	0	0	0	-	-	-	-
	5 ML YEARS		257	580	134	30	2	17	(7 10)	219	93	78	82	80	3	180	3	2	2	17	5	13	.231	.326	.378	.704

Leody Taveras

Bats: B **Throws:** R **Pos:** CF-48;PH-2   **Ht:** 6'2" **Wt:** 195 **Born:** 9/8/1998 **Age:** 23

							BATTING													RUNNING			AVERAGES			
Year	Team	Lg	G	AB	H	2B	3B	HR	(Hm Rd)	TB	R	RBI	RC	TBB	IBB	SO	HBP	SH	SF	SB	CS	GDP	Avg	OBP	Slg	OPS
2021	RdRck	AAA	87	322	79	19	2	17	(- -)	153	57	55	-	49	3	95	2	2	6	13	5	2	.245	.343	.475	.818
2020	Tex	AL	33	119	27	6	1	4	(2 2)	47	20	6	15	14	0	43	0	1	0	8	0	0	.227	.308	.395	.703
2021	Tex	AL	49	174	28	6	2	3	(2 1)	47	14	9	6	9	0	60	1	1	0	10	1	3	.161	.207	.270	.477
	2 ML YEARS		82	293	55	12	3	7	(4 3)	94	34	15	21	23	0	103	1	2	0	18	1	3	.188	.249	.321	.570

Blake Taylor

Pitches: L **Bats:** L **Pos:** RP-51   **Ht:** 6'3" **Wt:** 220 **Born:** 8/17/1995 **Age:** 26

			HOW MUCH PITCHED					WHAT HE GAVE UP											THE RESULTS						
Year	Team	Lg	G	GS	GF	IP	BFP	H	R	ER	HR	SH	SF	HB	TBB	IBB	SO	WP	W	L	Pct	Sv-Op	Hld	Vel	OPS	ERC	ERA
2020	Hou	AL	22	0	5	20.2	87	13	7	5	2	0	0	0	12	1	17	1	2	1	.667	1-2	5	94	.567	2.64	2.18
2021	Hou	AL	51	0	10	42.2	188	38	19	15	6	1	2	0	22	2	41	5	4	4	.500	0-5	5	93	.720	4.04	3.16
	Postseason		8	0	1	5.2	25	5	1	1	1	0	1	1	2	0	4	0	1	0	1.000	0-0	0	94	.749	4.37	1.59
	2 ML YEARS		73	0	15	63.1	275	51	26	20	8	1	2	0	34	3	58	6	6	5	.545	1-7	10	93	.672	3.56	2.84

Chris Taylor

Bats: R **Throws:** R **Pos:** CF-61;2B-46;LF-30;SS-23;3B-11;PH-9;RF-8   **Ht:** 6'1" **Wt:** 196 **Born:** 8/29/1990 **Age:** 31

							BATTING													RUNNING			AVERAGES			
Year	Team	Lg	G	AB	H	2B	3B	HR	(Hm Rd)	TB	R	RBI	RC	TBB	IBB	SO	HBP	SH	SF	SB	CS	GDP	Avg	OBP	Slg	OPS
2014	Sea	AL	47	136	39	8	0	0	(0 0)	47	16	9	18	11	0	39	2	1	1	5	2	3	.287	.347	.346	.692
2015	Sea	AL	37	94	16	3	1	0	(0 0)	21	9	1	1	6	0	31	0	2	0	3	2	0	.170	.220	.223	.443
2016	2 Tms		36	61	13	2	2	1	(0 1)	22	8	7	5	4	1	15	0	0	0	0	0	0	.213	.262	.361	.622
2017	LAD	NL	140	514	148	34	5	21	(7 14)	255	85	72	88	50	0	142	3	0	1	17	4	2	.288	.354	.496	.850
2018	LAD	NL	155	536	136	35	8	17	(10 7)	238	85	63	75	55	0	**178**	9	0	4	9	6	5	.254	.331	.444	.775
2019	LAD	NL	124	366	96	29	4	12	(8 4)	169	52	52	60	37	3	115	4	2	5	8	0	6	.262	.333	.462	.794
2020	LAD	NL	56	185	50	10	2	8	(5 3)	88	30	32	36	26	0	55	2	1	0	3	2	3	.270	.366	.476	.842
2021	LAD	NL	148	507	129	25	4	20	(13 7)	222	92	73	84	63	2	167	8	1	3	13	1	5	.254	.344	.438	.782
16	Sea	AL	2	3	1	0	0	0	(0 0)	1	0	0	0	0	0	2	0	0	0	0	0	0	.333	.333	.333	.667
16	LAD	NL	34	58	12	2	2	1	(0 1)	21	8	7	5	4	1	13	0	0	0	0	0	3	.207	.258	.362	.620
	Postseason		51	164	39	9	2	5	(3 2)	67	27	13	24	28	0	51	1	0	0	1	1	0	.238	.352	.409	.761
	8 ML YEARS		743	2399	627	146	26	79	(43 36)	1062	377	309	367	252	6	742	28	7	14	58	17	27	.261	.337	.443	.779

Josh Taylor

Pitches: L Bats: L Pos: RP-61

Ht: 6'5" Wt: 245 Born: 3/2/1993 Age: 29

			HOW MUCH PITCHED					WHAT HE GAVE UP										THE RESULTS							
Year	Team	Lg	G	GS	GF	IP	BFP	H	R	ER	HR	SH	SF	HB	TBB	IBB	SO	WP	W	L	Pct	Sv-Op	Hld	Vel	OPS	ERC	ERA
2019	Bos	AL	52	1	8	47.1	194	40	17	16	5	0	1	2	16	1	62	3	2	2	.500	0-1	4	95	.642	3.22	3.04
2020	Bos	AL	8	0	1	7.1	36	7	8	8	2	0	1	1	5	0	7	0	1	1	.500	0-2	1	94	.861	6.56	9.82
2021	Bos	AL	61	0	12	47.2	209	45	18	18	2	0	0	3	23	3	60	2	1	0	1.000	1-1	15	95	.662	3.80	3.40
	3 ML YEARS		121	1	21	102.1	439	92	43	42	9	0	1	6	44	4	129	5	4	3	.571	1-4	20	95	.669	3.72	3.69

Michael A. Taylor

Bats: R Throws: R Pos: CF-139;DH-2;PH-2;PR-1

Ht: 6'4" Wt: 215 Born: 3/26/1991 Age: 31

									BATTING												RUNNING			AVERAGES			
Year	Team	Lg	G	AB	H	2B	3B	HR	(Hm	Rd)	TB	R	RBI	RC	TBB	IBB	SO	HBP	SH	SF	SB	CS	GDP	Avg	OBP	Slg	OPS
2014	Was	NL	17	39	8	3	0	1	(0	1)	14	5	5	3	3	0	17	1	0	0	0	2	1	.205	.279	.359	.638
2015	Was	NL	138	472	108	15	2	14	(6	8)	169	49	63	60	35	9	158	1	1	2	16	3	5	.229	.282	.358	.640
2016	Was	NL	76	221	51	11	0	7	(1	6)	83	28	16	20	14	0	77	1	0	1	14	3	2	.231	.278	.376	.654
2017	Was	NL	118	399	108	23	3	19	(11	8)	194	55	53	57	29	3	137	1	1	2	17	7	3	.271	.320	.486	.806
2018	Was	NL	134	353	80	23	3	6	(2	4)	126	46	28	33	29	2	116	1	2	0	24	6	9	.227	.287	.357	.644
2019	Was	NL	53	88	22	7	0	1	(1	0)	32	10	3	7	7	0	34	0	2	0	6	0	0	.250	.305	.364	.669
2020	Was	NL	38	92	18	6	0	5	(2	3)	39	11	16	9	6	0	27	1	0	0	0	0	2	.196	.253	.424	.676
2021	KC	AL	142	483	118	16	1	12	(7	5)	172	58	54	50	33	0	144	5	2	5	14	7	9	.244	.297	.356	.653
	Postseason		16	38	12	0	0	4	(1	3)	24	7	10	11	4	0	13	1	0	0	0	0	0	.316	.395	.632	1.027
	8 ML YEARS		716	2147	513	103	9	65	(30	35)	829	262	238	239	156	14	710	11	8	10	91	28	31	.239	.293	.386	.679

Tyrone Taylor

Bats: R Throws: R Pos: LF-37;RF-29;PH-26;CF-16

Ht: 6'0" Wt: 194 Born: 1/22/1994 Age: 28

									BATTING												RUNNING			AVERAGES			
Year	Team	Lg	G	AB	H	2B	3B	HR	(Hm	Rd)	TB	R	RBI	RC	TBB	IBB	SO	HBP	SH	SF	SB	CS	GDP	Avg	OBP	Slg	OPS
2019	Mil	NL	15	10	4	2	0	0	(0	0)	6	1	1	3	1	0	1	1	0	0	0	0	0	.400	.500	.600	1.100
2020	Mil	NL	22	38	9	4	0	2	(0	2)	19	6	6	5	2	0	8	1	0	0	0	0	1	.237	.293	.500	.793
2021	Mil	NL	93	243	60	9	3	12	(9	3)	111	33	43	36	20	1	59	7	0	1	6	1	6	.247	.321	.457	.778
	Postseason		2	5	0	0	0	0	(0	0)	0	0	0	0	0	0	3	0	0	0	0	0	0	.000	.000	.000	.000
	3 ML YEARS		130	291	73	15	3	14	(9	5)	136	40	50	44	23	1	68	9	0	1	6	1	7	.251	.324	.467	.791

Julio Teheran

Pitches: R Bats: R Pos: SP-1

tay-RAHN

Ht: 6'2" Wt: 205 Born: 1/27/1991 Age: 31

			HOW MUCH PITCHED					WHAT HE GAVE UP										THE RESULTS							
Year	Team	Lg	G	GS	GF	IP	BFP	H	R	ER	HR	SH	SF	HB	TBB	IBB	SO	WP	W	L	Pct	Sv-Op	Hld	Vel	OPS	ERC	ERA
2011	Atl	NL	5	3	0	19.2	87	21	11	11	4	2	1	0	8	0	10	1	1	1	.500	0-0	0	93	.828	5.19	5.03
2012	Atl	NL	2	1	0	6.1	24	5	4	4	0	0	0	1	1	0	5	0	0	0	-	0-0	0	92	.467	1.64	5.68
2013	Atl	NL	30	30	0	185.2	774	173	69	66	22	8	5	13	45	4	170	2	14	8	.636	0-0	0	92	.700	3.45	3.20
2014	Atl	NL	33	33	0	221.0	884	188	82	71	22	13	4	4	51	4	186	1	14	13	.519	0-0	0	90	.639	2.71	2.89
2015	Atl	NL	33	33	0	200.2	843	189	99	90	27	10	3	9	73	3	171	2	11	8	.579	0-0	0	91	.737	4.07	4.04
2016	Atl	NL	30	30	0	188.0	758	157	70	67	22	4	1	9	41	2	167	7	7	10	.412	0-0	0	91	.650	2.79	3.21
2017	Atl	NL	32	32	0	188.1	812	186	103	94	31	7	3	7	72	3	151	6	11	13	.458	0-0	0	91	.772	4.52	4.49
2018	Atl	NL	31	31	0	175.2	724	122	80	77	26	3	5	9	84	3	162	2	9	9	.500	0-0	0	90	.672	3.25	3.94
2019	Atl	NL	33	33	0	174.2	754	148	81	74	22	6	5	14	83	3	162	5	10	11	.476	0-0	0	90	.717	3.99	3.81
2020	LAA	AL	10	9	0	31.1	149	39	35	35	12	0	3	2	16	0	20	1	0	4	.000	0-0	0	89	1.023	8.56	10.05
2021	Det	AL	1	1	0	5.0	20	4	1	1	1	0	0	0	3	0	3	0	1	0	1.000	0-0	0	90	.821	4.85	1.80
	Postseason		4	1	2	6.0	29	10	7	7	1	0	2	0	2	1	9	1	0	2	.000	0-0	0	93	1.014	8.24	10.50
	11 ML YEARS		240	236	0	1396.1	5829	1232	635	590	189	53	30	67	477	22	1207	27	78	77	.503	0-0	0	91	.707	3.62	3.80

Anderson Tejeda

Bats: B Throws: R Pos: 3B-5;2B-1

Ht: 6'0" Wt: 200 Born: 5/1/1998 Age: 24

									BATTING												RUNNING			AVERAGES			
Year	Team	Lg	G	AB	H	2B	3B	HR	(Hm	Rd)	TB	R	RBI	RC	TBB	IBB	SO	HBP	SH	SF	SB	CS	GDP	Avg	OBP	Slg	OPS
2021	RdRck	AAA	28	99	15	1	1	3	(-	-)	27	13	12	-	11	0	47	0	1	0	8	2	1	.152	.236	.273	.509
2021	Frisco	AA	47	175	35	8	0	9	(-	-)	70	19	20	-	15	0	82	1	1	0	2	1	1	.200	.267	.400	.667
2020	Tex	AL	23	75	19	4	1	3	(0	3)	34	7	8	7	2	0	30	0	0	0	4	1	2	.253	.273	.453	.726
2021	Tex	AL	5	16	1	0	0	0	(0	0)	1	1	0	0	1	0	10	0	0	0	1	0	0	.063	.118	.063	.180
	2 ML YEARS		28	91	20	4	1	3	(0	3)	35	8	8	7	3	0	40	0	0	0	5	1	2	.220	.245	.385	.629

Rowdy Tellez

Bats: L Throws: L Pos: 1B-65;PH-26;DH-19

Ht: 6'4" Wt: 255 Born: 3/16/1995 Age: 27

									BATTING												RUNNING			AVERAGES			
Year	Team	Lg	G	AB	H	2B	3B	HR	(Hm	Rd)	TB	R	RBI	RC	TBB	IBB	SO	HBP	SH	SF	SB	CS	GDP	Avg	OBP	Slg	OPS
2021	Buffalo	AAA	13	47	14	4	0	4	(-	-)	30	8	11	-	6	0	11	2	0	0	0	0	1	.298	.400	.638	1.038
2018	Tor	AL	23	70	22	9	0	4	(3	1)	43	10	14	17	2	0	21	0	0	1	0	0	0	.314	.329	.614	.943
2019	Tor	AL	111	370	84	19	0	21	(12	9)	166	49	54	47	29	3	116	7	0	3	1	1	9	.227	.293	.449	.742
2020	Tor	AL	35	113	32	5	0	8	(5	3)	61	20	23	22	11	1	20	1	0	2	0	1	1	.283	.346	.540	.886
2021	2 Tms		106	297	72	14	2	11	(4	7)	123	34	36	33	23	4	65	4	0	1	0	0	3	.242	.305	.414	.719
21	Tor	AL	50	139	29	4	1	4	(1	3)	47	12	8	7	9	1	33	3	0	0	0	0	3	.209	.272	.338	.610
21	Mil	NL	56	158	43	10	1	7	(3	4)	76	22	28	26	14	3	32	1	0	1	0	0	3	.272	.333	.481	.814
	Postseason		1	1	1	0	0	0	(0	0)	1	1	0	1	0	0	0	0	0	0	0	0	0	1.000	1.000	1.000	2.000
	4 ML YEARS		275	850	210	47	2	44	(24	20)	393	113	127	119	65	8	222	12	0	7	1	2	16	.247	.307	.462	.770

Ryan Tepera

Pitches: R Bats: R Pos: RP-65

tuh-PAIR-uh

Ht: 6'1" Wt: 195 Born: 11/3/1987 Age: 34

			HOW MUCH PITCHED				WHAT HE GAVE UP											THE RESULTS						
Year	Team	Lg	G	GS	GF	IP	BFP	H	R	ER	HR	SH	SF	HB	TBB	IBB	SO	WP	W	L	Pct	Sv-Op Hld	Vel	OPS	ERC	ERA
2015	Tor	AL	32	0	12	33.0	128	23	14	12	8	0	3	6	0	22	2	0	2	.000	1-1 0	95	.670	2.87	3.27
2016	Tor	AL	20	0	13	18.1	85	17	8	6	1	1	0	3	8	1	18	3	0	0	.000	0-0 1	95	.635	3.81	2.95
2017	Tor	AL	73	0	12	77.2	319	57	35	31	7	1	1	8	31	4	81	5	7	1	.875	2-4 17	95	.633	2.94	3.59
2018	Tor	AL	68	0	19	64.2	263	55	27	26	9	0	3	4	24	1	68	5	5	5	.500	7-15 19	95	.738	3.77	3.62
2019	Tor	AL	23	1	7	21.2	91	20	12	12	5	1	2	0	8	2	14	2	0	2	.000	0-0 2	94	.824	4.29	4.98
2020	ChC	NL	21	0	1	20.2	89	17	9	9	2	0	1	1	12	0	31	1	0	1	.000	0-1 2	94	.684	4.01	3.92
2021	2 Tms		65	0	7	61.1	240	35	19	19	4	0	4	4	19	1	74	4	0	2	.000	2-5 21	93	.514	1.63	2.79
21	ChC	NL	43	0	3	43.1	165	22	14	14	3	0	3	3	12	0	50	1	0	2	.000	1-3 15	94	.469	1.41	2.91
21	CWS	AL	22	0	4	18.0	75	13	5	5	1	0	1	1	7	1	24	3	0	0	-	1-2 6	93	.613	2.36	2.50
	Postseason		3	0	1	3.0	17	5	4	4	0	0	3	0	3	0	2	2	0	0	-	0-0 0	93	1.016	9.70	12.00
	7 ML YEARS		302	1	71	297.1	1215	224	124	115	36	3	11	23	108	9	308	22	12	14	.462	12-26 61	95	.655	3.03	3.48

Curtis Terry

Bats: R Throws: R Pos: DH-12;1B-1

Ht: 6'2" Wt: 258 Born: 10/6/1996 Age: 25

							BATTING														RUNNING			AVERAGES			
Year	Team	Lg	G	AB	H	2B	3B	HR	(Hm	Rd)	TB	R	RBI	RC	TBB	IBB	SO	HBP	SH	SF	SB	CS	GDP	Avg	OBP	Slg	OPS
2021	RdRck	AAA	97	356	100	24	2	22	(-	-)	194	58	75	-	29	0	92	14	0	3	3	1	12	.281	.356	.545	.901
2021	Tex	AL	13	45	4	2	0	0	(0	0)	6	3	1	0	2	0	15	1	0	0	0	0	0	.089	.146	.133	.279

Matt Thaiss

Bats: L Throws: R Pos: 1B-2;PH-1

THICE

Ht: 6'0" Wt: 215 Born: 5/6/1995 Age: 27

							BATTING														RUNNING			AVERAGES			
Year	Team	Lg	G	AB	H	2B	3B	HR	(Hm	Rd)	TB	R	RBI	RC	TBB	IBB	SO	HBP	SH	SF	SB	CS	GDP	Avg	OBP	Slg	OPS
2021	Salt Lk	AAA	101	379	106	23	4	17	(-	-)	188	71	69	-	60	3	92	6	0	4	2	1	8	.280	.383	.496	.879
2019	LAA	AL	53	147	31	7	0	8	(8	0)	62	17	23	20	17	0	52	0	0	0	0	0	4	.211	.293	.422	.714
2020	LAA	AL	8	21	3	0	0	1	(0	1)	6	3	1	0	4	0	8	0	0	0	0	0	1	.143	.280	.286	.566
2021	LAA	AL	3	7	1	0	0	0	(0	0)	1	1	0	0	1	0	1	0	0	0	0	0	0	.143	.250	.143	.393
	3 ML YEARS		64	175	35	7	0	9	(8	1)	69	21	24	20	22	0	61	0	0	0	0	0	5	.200	.289	.394	.684

Caleb Thielbar

Pitches: L Bats: R Pos: RP-59

THEEL-bar

Ht: 6'0" Wt: 205 Born: 1/31/1987 Age: 35

			HOW MUCH PITCHED				WHAT HE GAVE UP											THE RESULTS						
Year	Team	Lg	G	GS	GF	IP	BFP	H	R	ER	HR	SH	SF	HB	TBB	IBB	SO	WP	W	L	Pct	Sv-Op Hld	Vel	OPS	ERC	ERA
2013	Min	AL	49	0	16	46.0	171	24	11	9	4	0	1	0	14	4	39	1	3	2	.600	0-0 1	90	.530	1.38	1.76
2014	Min	AL	54	0	7	47.2	206	51	19	18	3	1	6	1	16	1	35	0	2	1	.667	0-1 7	89	.738	4.01	3.40
2015	Min	AL	6	0	1	5.0	20	5	3	3	0	1	0	0	6	0	5	1	0	0	-	0-0 1	90	.579	1.95	5.40
2020	Min	AL	17	0	3	20.0	82	14	6	5	0	0	0	0	9	0	22	2	2	1	.667	0-0 1	91	.500	2.05	2.25
2021	Min	AL	59	0	14	64.0	266	55	24	23	8	3	3	3	20	1	77	3	7	0	1.000	0-0 12	91	.697	3.29	3.23
	Postseason		1	0	1	0.1	2	1	0	0	0	0	0	0	0	0	0	0	0	0	-	0-0 0	91	1.000	14.52	0.00
	5 ML YEARS		185	0	41	182.2	745	149	63	58	15	5	10	4	59	6	178	7	14	4	.778	0-1 22	90	.645	2.73	2.86

Alek Thomas

Bats: L Throws: L Pos: CF

Ht: 5'11" Wt: 175 Born: 4/28/2000 Age: 22

							BATTING														RUNNING			AVERAGES			
Year	Team	Lg	G	AB	H	2B	3B	HR	(Hm	Rd)	TB	R	RBI	RC	TBB	IBB	SO	HBP	SH	SF	SB	CS	GDP	Avg	OBP	Slg	OPS
2018	2 Tms	Low	56	246	82	14	6	2	(-	-)	114	50	27	46	24	0	37	1	0	0	12	5	4	.333	.395	.463	.858
2019	2 Tms	Low	114	447	134	23	7	10	(-	-)	201	76	55	81	52	2	105	6	0	1	15	11	7	.300	.379	.450	.829
2021	Amarillo	AA	72	286	81	18	8	10	(-	-)	145	54	41	-	37	0	65	5	0	1	8	6	3	.283	.374	.507	.881
2021	Reno	AAA	33	144	54	11	4	8	(-	-)	97	32	18	-	15	0	33	2	0	0	5	5	1	.375	.441	.674	1.115

Dillon Thomas

Bats: L Throws: L Pos: LF-2;CF-1;RF-1;PH-1

Ht: 6'1" Wt: 215 Born: 12/10/1992 Age: 29

							BATTING														RUNNING			AVERAGES			
Year	Team	Lg	G	AB	H	2B	3B	HR	(Hm	Rd)	TB	R	RBI	RC	TBB	IBB	SO	HBP	SH	SF	SB	CS	GDP	Avg	OBP	Slg	OPS
2021	Tacom	AAA	90	318	86	18	1	12	(-	-)	142	67	45	-	40	1	112	18	0	1	11	1	5	.270	.382	.447	.829
2021	Sea	AL	4	9	1	0	0	0	(0	0)	1	2	2	1	0	0	7	0	0	0	0	0	0	.111	.111	.111	.222

Lane Thomas

Bats: R Throws: R Pos: CF-42;PH-16;LF-12;RF-10;2B-2;PR-2

Ht: 6'0" Wt: 185 Born: 8/23/1995 Age: 26

							BATTING														RUNNING			AVERAGES			
Year	Team	Lg	G	AB	H	2B	3B	HR	(Hm	Rd)	TB	R	RBI	RC	TBB	IBB	SO	HBP	SH	SF	SB	CS	GDP	Avg	OBP	Slg	OPS
2021	Memp	AAA	30	113	30	5	2	4	(-	-)	51	18	20	-	12	0	35	1	0	1	3	2	2	.265	.339	.451	.790
2019	StL	NL	34	38	12	0	1	4	(3	1)	26	6	12	12	4	0	8	2	0	0	1	1	1	.316	.409	.684	1.093
2020	StL	NL	18	36	4	2	0	1	(1	0)	9	5	2	1	4	0	13	0	0	0	0	0	1	.111	.200	.250	.450
2021	2 Tms	NL	77	226	53	15	2	7	(4	3)	93	35	28	33	37	1	63	0	0	1	6	3	6	.235	.341	.412	.752
21	StL	NL	32	48	5	1	0	0	(0	0)	6	2	1	1	10	1	17	0	0	0	2	1	1	.104	.259	.125	.384
21	Was	NL	45	178	48	14	2	7	(4	3)	87	33	27	32	27	0	46	0	0	1	4	2	5	.270	.364	.489	.853
	3 ML YEARS		129	300	69	17	3	12	(8	4)	128	46	42	46	45	1	84	2	0	1	7	4	8	.230	.333	.427	.760

Keegan Thompson

Pitches: R **Bats:** R **Pos:** RP-26; SP-6   **Ht:** 6'1" **Wt:** 210 **Born:** 3/13/1995 **Age:** 27

		HOW MUCH PITCHED					WHAT HE GAVE UP											THE RESULTS							
Year Team	Lg	G	GS	GF	IP	BFP	H	R	ER	HR	SH	SF	HB	TBB	IBB	SO	WP	W	L	Pct	Sv-Op	Hld	Vel	OPS	ERC	ERA
2021 ChC	NL	32	6	5	53.1	243	48	22	20	9	2	1	2	31	1	55	4	3	3	.500	1-2	1	94	.745	4.70	3.38

Mason Thompson

Pitches: R **Bats:** R **Pos:** RP-31   **Ht:** 6'7" **Wt:** 223 **Born:** 2/20/1998 **Age:** 24

		HOW MUCH PITCHED					WHAT HE GAVE UP											THE RESULTS							
Year Team	Lg	G	GS	GF	IP	BFP	H	R	ER	HR	SH	SF	HB	TBB	IBB	SO	WP	W	L	Pct	Sv-Op	Hld	Vel	OPS	ERC	ERA
2021 ElPaso	AAA	23	0	12	26.2	110	25	18	17	4	0	0	0	8	0	24	1	3	2	.600	7--	-	-	.741	3.71	5.74
2021 2 Tms	NL	31	0	5	24.2	121	32	15	11	4	2	0	1	15	1	23	3	1	3	.250	0-3	6	96	.801	7.24	4.01
21 SD	NL	4	0	1	3.0	13	4	1	1	0	0	0	0	1	0	2	2	0	0	-	0-0	1	98	.801	5.24	3.00
21 Was	NL	27	0	4	21.2	108	28	14	10	4	2	0	1	14	1	21	1	1	3	.250	0-3	5	96	.889	7.53	4.15

Ryan Thompson

Pitches: R **Bats:** R **Pos:** RP-36   **Ht:** 6'5" **Wt:** 210 **Born:** 6/26/1992 **Age:** 30

		HOW MUCH PITCHED					WHAT HE GAVE UP											THE RESULTS							
Year Team	Lg	G	GS	GF	IP	BFP	H	R	ER	HR	SH	SF	HB	TBB	IBB	SO	WP	W	L	Pct	Sv-Op	Hld	Vel	OPS	ERC	ERA
2020 TB	AL	25	1	3	26.1	114	29	15	13	4	0	0	0	8	0	23	0	1	2	.333	1-1	4	91	.749	4.61	4.44
2021 TB	AL	36	0	2	34.0	134	26	11	9	3	0	0	2	9	2	37	1	3	2	.600	0-4	11	91	.642	2.47	2.38
Postseason		9	1	1	9.1	38	7	2	2	1	0	1	1	4	0	10	0	0	1	.000	0-0	3	92	.628	3.42	1.93
2 ML YEARS		61	1	5	60.1	248	55	26	22	7	0	0	2	17	2	60	1	4	4	.500	1-5	15	91	.691	3.36	3.28

Trayce Thompson

Bats: R **Throws:** R **Pos:** RF-8;CF-3;PH-3;LF-2   **Ht:** 6'3" **Wt:** 225 **Born:** 3/15/1991 **Age:** 31

		BATTING																		RUNNING			AVERAGES			
Year Team	Lg	G	AB	H	2B	3B	HR	(Hm	Rd)	TB	R	RBI	RC	TBB	IBB	SO	HBP	SH	SF	SB	CS	GDP	Avg	OBP	Slg	OPS
2021 Iowa	AAA	88	305	71	14	1	21	(-	-)	150	48	63	-	45	0	116	7	0	1	3	1	5	.233	.344	.492	.835
2015 CWS	AL	44	122	36	8	3	5	(3	2)	65	17	16	20	13	0	26	0	0	0	1	0	3	.295	.363	.533	.896
2016 LAD	NL	80	236	53	11	0	13	(9	4)	103	31	32	26	26	0	66	0	0	0	5	1	3	.225	.302	.436	.738
2017 LAD	NL	27	49	6	2	1	1	(0	1)	13	6	2	1	6	1	23	0	0	0	0	0	0	.122	.218	.265	.483
2018 2 Tms	AL	51	128	15	3	0	3	(2	1)	27	15	9	6	7	1	50	0	1	1	3	1	0	.117	.162	.211	.373
2021 ChC	NL	15	28	7	1	0	4	(1	3)	20	6	9	8	7	0	11	0	0	0	2	0	2	.250	.400	.714	1.114
18 Oak	AL	3	7	1	0	0	0	(0	0)	1	1	0	0	0	0	4	0	0	0	0	0	0	.143	.143	.143	.286
18 CWS	AL	48	121	14	3	0	3	(2	1)	26	14	9	6	7	1	46	0	1	1	3	1	0	.116	.163	.215	.378
5 ML YEARS		217	563	117	25	4	26	(15	11)	228	75	68	55	59	2	176	0	1	1	11	2	8	.208	.283	.405	.687

Zach Thompson

Pitches: R **Bats:** R **Pos:** SP-14; RP-12   **Ht:** 6'7" **Wt:** 230 **Born:** 10/23/1993 **Age:** 28

		HOW MUCH PITCHED					WHAT HE GAVE UP											THE RESULTS							
Year Team	Lg	G	GS	GF	IP	BFP	H	R	ER	HR	SH	SF	HB	TBB	IBB	SO	WP	W	L	Pct	Sv-Op	Hld	Vel	OPS	ERC	ERA
2021 Jaxnvl	AAA	8	0	4	15.0	69	22	11	11	4	0	1	1	2	0	21	1	0	0	-	1--	-	-	.993	7.27	6.60
2021 Mia	NL	26	14	2	75.0	315	63	35	27	6	3	3		28	1	66	5	3	7	.300	0-0	0	92	.675	3.09	3.24

Trent Thornton

Pitches: R **Bats:** R **Pos:** RP-34; SP-3   **Ht:** 6'0" **Wt:** 195 **Born:** 9/30/1993 **Age:** 28

		HOW MUCH PITCHED					WHAT HE GAVE UP											THE RESULTS							
Year Team	Lg	G	GS	GF	IP	BFP	H	R	ER	HR	SH	SF	HB	TBB	IBB	SO	WP	W	L	Pct	Sv-Op	Hld	Vel	OPS	ERC	ERA
2021 Buffalo	AAA	9	0	5	9.1	37	8	2	0	0	0	0	0	2	0	7	0	1	0	1.000	2--	-	-	.585	2.06	0.00
2019 Tor	AL	32	29	0	154.1	677	156	87	83	24	1	7	5	61	0	149	5	6	9	.400	0-0	0	93	.768	4.60	4.84
2020 Tor	AL	3	3	0	5.2	33	15	7	7	0	0	1	0	3	0	6	0	0	0	-	0-0	0	94	1.166	15.41	11.12
2021 Tor	AL	37	3	4	49.0	216	54	33	26	12	1	1	4	16	1	52	3	1	3	.250	0-0	0	92	.880	5.75	4.78
3 ML YEARS		72	35	4	209.0	926	225	127	116	36	2	9	9	80	1	207	8	7	12	.368	0-0	0	93	.808	5.11	5.00

Lewis Thorpe

Pitches: L **Bats:** R **Pos:** SP-4; RP-1   **Ht:** 6'1" **Wt:** 218 **Born:** 11/23/1995 **Age:** 26

		HOW MUCH PITCHED					WHAT HE GAVE UP											THE RESULTS							
Year Team	Lg	G	GS	GF	IP	BFP	H	R	ER	HR	SH	SF	HB	TBB	IBB	SO	WP	W	L	Pct	Sv-Op	Hld	Vel	OPS	ERC	ERA
2021 StPaul	AAA	6	2	0	17.0	71	12	9	9	1	0	0	1	7	0	12	0	1	2	.333	0--	-	-	.583	2.47	4.76
2019 Min	AL	12	3	2	27.2	124	38	19	19	3	0	1	0	10	0	31	3	3	2	.600	0-2	0	91	.918	6.41	6.18
2020 Min	AL	7	1	3	16.1	77	24	12	11	4	0	0	0	10	0	10	0	0	1	.000	0-0	0	90	1.039	9.70	6.06
2021 Min	AL	5	4	1	15.1	66	14	11	8	2	0	0	0	7	0	6	1	0	2	.000	0-0	0	89	.708	4.01	4.70
3 ML YEARS		24	7	7	59.1	267	76	42	38	9	0	1	0	27	0	47	4	3	5	.375	0-2	0	90	.900	6.58	5.76

Ty Tice

Pitches: R **Bats:** L **Pos:** RP-5   **Ht:** 5'9" **Wt:** 185 **Born:** 7/4/1996 **Age:** 25

		HOW MUCH PITCHED					WHAT HE GAVE UP											THE RESULTS							
Year Team	Lg	G	GS	GF	IP	BFP	H	R	ER	HR	SH	SF	HB	TBB	IBB	SO	WP	W	L	Pct	Sv-Op	Hld	Vel	OPS	ERC	ERA
2021 Gwnntt	AAA	11	0	2	11.0	49	13	9	9	4	0	1	0	5	0	8	2	1	0	1.000	0--	-	-	.972	7.58	7.36

		HOW MUCH PITCHED						WHAT HE GAVE UP											THE RESULTS							
Year	Team	Lg	G	GS	GF	IP	BFP	H	R	ER	HR	SH	SF	HB	TBB	IBB	SO	WP	W	L	Pct	Sv-Op	Hld	Vel	OPS	ERC	ERA
2021	Reno	AAA	10	0	5	8.1	42	9	10	10	2	0	1	3	7	0	10	1	0	1	.000	0--	-	-	1.001	9.47	10.80
2021	2 Tms		5	0	3	8.0	39	10	4	4	1	0	0	1	5	0	6	0	0	0	-	0-0	0	94	.865	7.27	4.50
21	Tor	AL	4	0	2	7.0	34	9	4	4	1	0	0	1	4	0	6	0	0	0	-	0-0	0	94	.895	7.54	5.14
21	Atl	NL	1	0	1	1.0	5	1	0	0	0	0	0	0	1	0	0	0	0	0	-	0-0	0	93	.650	5.48	0.00

Jesus Tinoco

Pitches: R **Bats:** R **Pos:** RP-1   hay-SOOS tih-NO-ko   **Ht:** 6'4" **Wt:** 258 **Born:** 4/30/1995 **Age:** 27

		HOW MUCH PITCHED						WHAT HE GAVE UP											THE RESULTS							
Year	Team	Lg	G	GS	GF	IP	BFP	H	R	ER	HR	SH	SF	HB	TBB	IBB	SO	WP	W	L	Pct	Sv-Op	Hld	Vel	OPS	ERC	ERA
2021	Albq	AAA	34	2	5	52.1	242	64	35	35	6	1	6	1	26	0	55	5	3	2	.600	0--	-	-	.873	5.99	6.02
2019	Col	NL	24	0	3	36.0	161	36	23	19	12	0	1	1	22	1	28	1	0	3	.000	1-1	2	94	.965	6.94	4.75
2020	2 Tms	NL	6	0	3	8.2	32	3	1	1	0	0	0	0	7	0	6	2	0	0	-	0-0	0	94	.433	1.80	1.04
2021	Col	NL	1	0	0	1.1	10	5	5	5	3	0	0	1	1	0	0	0	0	0	-	0-0	0	93	2.450	65.75	33.75
20	Mia	NL	3	0	1	5.0	15	0	0	0	0	0	0	0	3	0	3	0	0	0	-	0-0	0	94	.200	0.45	0.00
20	Col	NL	3	0	2	3.2	17	3	1	1	0	0	0	0	4	0	3	2	0	0	-	0-0	0	94	.643	5.09	2.45
	3 ML YEARS		31	0	6	46.0	203	44	29	25	15	0	1	2	30	1	34	3	0	3	.000	1-1	2	94	.957	7.00	4.89

Ka'ai Tom

Bats: L **Throws:** R **Pos:** LF-32;PH-10;RF-4;PR-3;DH-2   kuh-EYE   **Ht:** 5'9" **Wt:** 185 **Born:** 5/29/1994 **Age:** 28

			BATTING																RUNNING			AVERAGES			
Year	Team	Lg	G	AB	H	2B	3B	HR	(Hm | Rd)	TB	R	RBI	RC	TBB	IBB	SO	HBP	SH	SF	SB	CS	GDP	Avg	OBP	Slg	OPS
2021	Indy	AAA	23	58	11	1	0	2	(- | -)	18	6	7	-	5	0	19	4	0	0	0	0	1	.190	.299	.310	.609
2021	2 Tms		48	108	15	2	1	2	(1 | 1)	25	10	12	9	17	1	36	5	0	3	1	0	1	.139	.278	.231	.510
21	Oak	AL	9	16	1	0	0	0	(0 | 0)	1	1	1	0	0	0	6	0	0	0	0	0	0	.063	.063	.063	.125
21	Pit	NL	39	92	14	2	1	2	(1 | 1)	24	9	11	9	17	1	30	5	0	3	1	0	1	.152	.308	.261	.569

Josh Tomlin

Pitches: R **Bats:** R **Pos:** RP-35   **Ht:** 6'1" **Wt:** 190 **Born:** 10/19/1984 **Age:** 37

			HOW MUCH PITCHED						WHAT HE GAVE UP											THE RESULTS							
Year	Team	Lg	G	GS	GF	IP	BFP	H	R	ER	HR	SH	SF	HB	TBB	IBB	SO	WP	W	L	Pct	Sv-Op	Hld	Vel	OPS	ERC	ERA
2010	Cle	AL	12	12	0	73.0	301	72	38	37	10	3	3	3	19	3	43	1	6	4	.600	0-0	0	89	.773	3.89	4.56
2011	Cle	AL	26	26	0	165.1	662	157	80	78	24	1	3	3	21	2	89	3	12	7	.632	0-0	0	88	.712	3.11	4.25
2012	Cle	AL	21	16	0	103.1	452	126	74	73	18	2	3	3	25	3	56	4	5	8	.385	0-0	0	89	.860	5.34	6.36
2013	Cle	AL	1	0	0	2.0	9	2	0	0	0	0	0	0	0	0	0	0	0	0	-	0-0	0	90	.500	1.68	0.00
2014	Cle	AL	25	16	6	104.0	446	120	66	55	18	1	3	1	14	3	94	6	6	9	.400	0-0	0	89	.781	4.28	4.76
2015	Cle	AL	10	10	0	65.2	251	47	22	22	13	0	0	2	8	0	57	1	7	2	.778	0-0	0	88	.642	2.24	3.02
2016	Cle	AL	30	29	1	174.0	725	187	97	85	36	4	4	3	20	2	118	4	13	9	.591	0-0	0	88	.778	4.06	4.40
2017	Cle	AL	26	26	0	141.0	585	166	80	78	23	0	3	4	14	0	109	1	10	9	.526	0-0	0	88	.807	4.49	4.98
2018	Cle	AL	32	9	19	70.1	321	92	52	48	25	0	2	4	12	1	46	5	2	5	.286	0-0	0	88	.947	6.86	6.14
2019	Atl	NL	51	1	21	79.1	320	82	35	33	14	4	2	0	7	0	51	2	2	1	.667	2-4	7	89	.744	3.53	3.74
2020	Atl	NL	17	5	2	39.2	163	40	22	21	6	1	1	1	8	2	36	1	2	2	.500	0-0	1	88	.737	3.75	4.76
2021	Atl	NL	35	0	6	49.1	218	69	36	36	10	1	1	1	5	0	37	0	4	0	1.000	0-0	1	88	.894	6.02	6.57
	Postseason		10	4	3	27.0	104	21	12	12	2	0	0	0	5	0	21	0	3	1	.750	0-0	1	88	.563	2.04	4.00
	12 ML YEARS		286	150	55	1067.0	4453	1160	602	566	197	16	25	25	153	16	736	28	69	56	.552	2-4	9	88	.786	4.17	4.77

Justin Topa

Pitches: R **Bats:** R **Pos:** RP-4   **Ht:** 6'4" **Wt:** 200 **Born:** 3/7/1991 **Age:** 31

			HOW MUCH PITCHED						WHAT HE GAVE UP											THE RESULTS							
Year	Team	Lg	G	GS	GF	IP	BFP	H	R	ER	HR	SH	SF	HB	TBB	IBB	SO	WP	W	L	Pct	Sv-Op	Hld	Vel	OPS	ERC	ERA
2021	Nashv	AAA	10	0	3	9.0	36	7	3	3	0	0	0	0	2	0	9	1	1	0	1.000	0--	-	-	.456	1.68	3.00
2020	Mil	NL	6	0	2	7.2	30	7	3	2	1	0	0	0	0	0	12	0	0	1	.000	0-0	0	98	.633	2.25	2.35
2021	Mil	NL	4	0	0	3.1	23	12	11	11	2	0	0	1	1	1	1	0	0	0	-	0-0	0	96	1.520	27.35	29.70
	Postseason		1	0	0	2.0	7	1	0	0	0	0	0	0	1	0	1	0	0	0	-	0-0	0	97	.452	1.62	0.00
	2 ML YEARS		10	0	2	11.0	53	19	14	13	3	0	0	1	1	1	13	0	0	1	.000	0-0	0	97	1.012	8.26	10.64

Spencer Torkelson

Bats: R **Throws:** R **Pos:** IF   **Ht:** 6'1" **Wt:** 220 **Born:** 8/26/1999 **Age:** 22

			BATTING																RUNNING			AVERAGES			
Year	Team	Lg	G	AB	H	2B	3B	HR	(Hm | Rd)	TB	R	RBI	RC	TBB	IBB	SO	HBP	SH	SF	SB	CS	GDP	Avg	OBP	Slg	OPS
2021	Erie	AA	50	175	46	10	0	14	(- | -)	98	33	36	-	30	0	50	3	0	4	1	1	4	.263	.373	.560	.933
2021	Toledo	AAA	35	131	31	7	1	10	(- | -)	70	31	25	-	18	1	33	3	0	3	0	0	4	.237	.335	.534	.870
2021	Wmich	A+	31	109	34	11	1	5	(- | -)	62	21	28	0	24	0	28	4	0	4	3	2	4	.312	.440	.569	1.009

Abraham Toro

Bats: B **Throws:** R **Pos:** 2B-58;3B-32;PH-4;1B-2;PR-1   **Ht:** 6'0" **Wt:** 206 **Born:** 12/20/1996 **Age:** 25

			BATTING																RUNNING			AVERAGES			
Year	Team	Lg	G	AB	H	2B	3B	HR	(Hm | Rd)	TB	R	RBI	RC	TBB	IBB	SO	HBP	SH	SF	SB	CS	GDP	Avg	OBP	Slg	OPS
2021	SgrLnd	AAA	17	54	19	5	1	2	(- | -)	32	10	11	-	11	0	8	3	0	0	2	1	2	.352	.485	.593	1.078
2019	Hou	AL	25	78	17	3	2	2	(1 | 1)	30	13	9	8	9	0	19	1	0	1	1	1	2	.218	.303	.385	.688
2020	Hou	AL	33	87	13	2	0	3	(1 | 2)	24	13	9	5	3	0	23	7	0	0	1	1	1	.149	.237	.276	.513
2021	2 Tms	AL	95	335	80	12	0	11	(6 | 5)	125	45	46	47	31	0	54	7	0	2	6	3	5	.239	.315	.373	.688

Year	Team	Lg	G	AB	H	2B	3B	HR	(Hm	Rd)	TB	R	RBI	RC	TBB	IBB	SO	HBP	SH	SF	SB	CS	GDP	Avg	OBP	Slg	OPS
21	Hou	AL	35	109	23	1	0	6	(2	4)	42	17	20	15	9	0	21	3	0	1	3	1	1	.211	.287	.385	.672
21	Sea	AL	60	226	57	11	0	5	(4	1)	83	28	26	32	22	0	33	4	0	1	3	2	4	.252	.328	.367	.695
	Postseason		1	0	0	0	0	0	(0	0)	0	0	0	0	1	0	0	0	0	0	0	0	0	-	1.000	-	-
3 ML YEARS			153	500	110	17	2	16	(8	8)	179	71	64	60	43	0	96	15	0	3	8	5	8	.220	.299	.358	.657

Luis Torrens

Bats: R **Throws:** R **Pos:** DH-59;C-35;PH-12;1B-5;3B-2   **Ht:** 6'0" **Wt:** 208 **Born:** 5/2/1996 **Age:** 26

Year	Team	Lg	G	AB	H	2B	3B	HR	(Hm	Rd)	TB	R	RBI	RC	TBB	IBB	SO	HBP	SH	SF	SB	CS	GDP	Avg	OBP	Slg	OPS
2021	Tacom	AAA	19	73	16	4	0	6	(-	-)	38	12	19	-	10	0	22	1	0	1	0	0	2	.219	.318	.521	.838
2017	SD	NL	56	123	20	3	1	0	(0	0)	25	7	7	4	12	3	30	1	3	0	0	0	4	.163	.243	.203	.446
2019	SD	NL	7	14	3	1	0	0	(0	0)	4	2	0	1	2	0	6	0	0	0	0	0	1	.214	.313	.286	.598
2020	2 Tms		25	70	18	5	0	1	(1	0)	26	5	6	7	7	0	15	0	1	0	0	0	1	.257	.325	.371	.696
2021	Sea	AL	108	346	84	16	2	15	(7	8)	149	39	47	46	28	1	99	1	0	3	0	0	8	.243	.299	.431	.730
20	SD	NL	7	11	3	1	0	0	(0	0)	4	0	0	1	1	0	2	0	1	0	0	0	0	.273	.333	.364	.697
20	Sea	AL	18	59	15	4	0	1	(1	0)	22	5	6	6	6	0	13	0	0	0	0	0	1	.254	.323	.373	.696
4 ML YEARS			196	553	125	25	3	16	(8	8)	204	53	60	58	49	4	150	2	4	3	0	0	14	.226	.290	.369	.659

Gleyber Torres

Bats: R **Throws:** R **Pos:** SS-108;2B-19;PH-4   **Ht:** 6'1" **Wt:** 205 **Born:** 12/13/1996 **Age:** 25

Year	Team	Lg	G	AB	H	2B	3B	HR	(Hm	Rd)	TB	R	RBI	RC	TBB	IBB	SO	HBP	SH	SF	SB	CS	GDP	Avg	OBP	Slg	OPS
2018	NYY	AL	123	431	117	16	1	24	(13	11)	207	54	77	78	42	3	122	5	1	5	6	2	8	.271	.340	.480	.820
2019	NYY	AL	144	546	152	26	0	38	(20	18)	292	96	90	101	48	3	129	3	1	6	5	2	10	.278	.337	.535	.871
2020	NYY	AL	42	136	33	8	0	3	(1	2)	50	17	16	18	22	0	28	2	0	0	1	0	5	.243	.356	.368	.724
2021	NYY	AL	127	459	119	22	0	9	(6	3)	168	50	51	59	50	1	104	1	2	4	14	6	12	.259	.331	.366	.697
	Postseason		21	76	26	5	0	5	(2	3)	46	14	15	19	12	0	15	0	0	0	4	0	3	.342	.432	.605	1.037
4 ML YEARS			436	1572	421	72	1	74	(40	34)	717	217	234	256	162	7	383	11	4	15	26	10	35	.268	.338	.456	.794

Ronald Torreyes

Bats: R **Throws:** R **Pos:** 3B-50;SS-44;PH-19;2B-11;CF-1   toh-RAY-ess   **Ht:** 5'8" **Wt:** 155 **Born:** 9/2/1992 **Age:** 29

Year	Team	Lg	G	AB	H	2B	3B	HR	(Hm	Rd)	TB	R	RBI	RC	TBB	IBB	SO	HBP	SH	SF	SB	CS	GDP	Avg	OBP	Slg	OPS
2015	LAD	NL	8	6	2	1	0	0	(0	0)	3	1	1	2	1	0	1	0	1	0	0	0	0	.333	.429	.500	.929
2016	NYY	AL	72	155	40	7	4	1	(0	1)	58	20	12	19	10	0	20	1	1	1	2	1	4	.258	.305	.374	.680
2017	NYY	AL	108	315	92	15	1	3	(2	1)	118	35	36	37	11	0	43	1	5	4	2	0	9	.292	.314	.375	.689
2018	NYY	AL	41	100	28	7	1	0	(0	0)	37	9	7	12	2	0	16	0	0	0	0	0	3	.280	.294	.370	.664
2019	Min	AL	7	16	3	0	0	0	(0	0)	3	3	1	0	0	0	3	1	0	0	1	0	0	.188	.235	.188	.423
2020	Phi	NL	4	7	1	1	0	0	(0	0)	2	1	0	0	0	0	0	0	0	0	0	0	0	.143	.143	.286	.429
2021	Phi	NL	112	318	77	10	1	7	(3	4)	110	30	41	38	19	2	41	1	5	1	2	1	7	.242	.286	.346	.632
	Postseason		2	1	0	0	0	0	(0	0)	0	0	0	0	0	0	1	0	0	0	0	0	0	.000	.000	.000	.000
7 ML YEARS			352	917	243	41	7	11	(5	6)	331	99	98	108	43	2	124	4	12	6	7	2	24	.265	.299	.361	.660

Touki Toussaint

Pitches: R **Bats:** R **Pos:** SP-10; RP-1   TOO-key TOO-sahnt   **Ht:** 6'3" **Wt:** 215 **Born:** 6/20/1996 **Age:** 26

			HOW MUCH PITCHED					WHAT HE GAVE UP										THE RESULTS							
Year	Team	Lg	G	GS	GF	IP	BFP	H	R	ER	HR	SH	SF	HB	TBB	IBB	SO	WP	W	L	Pct	Sv-Op Hld	Vel	OPS	ERC	ERA
2021	Gwnntt	AAA	5	4	0	17.2	74	10	8	8	1	0	0	3	11	0	26	0	2	1	.667	0- - -		.591	2.98	4.08
2018	Atl	NL	7	5	1	29.0	123	18	13	13	1	1	0	2	21	1	32	1	2	1	.667	0-0 0	93	.619	3.05	4.03
2019	Atl	NL	24	1	3	41.2	198	44	28	26	5	2	0	7	26	2	45	6	4	0	1.000	0-0 2	93	.810	6.05	5.62
2020	Atl	NL	7	5	0	24.1	120	27	28	24	7	1	0	5	16	0	30	2	0	2	.000	0-0 0	94	.954	8.17	8.88
2021	Atl	NL	11	10	1	50.0	216	43	28	25	11	2	2	6	22	1	48	2	3	3	.500	0-0 0	93	.777	4.77	4.50
	Postseason		2	0	0	3.0	13	1	0	0	0	0	0	0	4	0	2	0	1	0	1.000	0-0 0	95	.607	3.31	0.00
4 ML YEARS			49	21	5	145.0	657	132	97	88	24	6	2	20	85	4	155	11	9	6	.600	0-0 2	93	.791	5.32	5.46

Wilfredo Tovar

Bats: R **Throws:** R **Pos:** 2B-4;PH-2   will-FRAY-doe TOE-varr   **Ht:** 5'7" **Wt:** 180 **Born:** 8/11/1991 **Age:** 30

Year	Team	Lg	G	AB	H	2B	3B	HR	(Hm	Rd)	TB	R	RBI	RC	TBB	IBB	SO	HBP	SH	SF	SB	CS	GDP	Avg	OBP	Slg	OPS
2021	Syrcse	AAA	96	340	97	16	0	7	(-	-)	134	52	50	-	45	0	43	3	0	4	13	4	19	.285	.370	.394	.764
2013	NYM	NL	7	15	3	0	0	0	(0	0)	3	1	2	2	1	1	3	1	2	0	1	0	2	.200	.294	.200	.494
2014	NYM	NL	2	3	0	0	0	0	(0	0)	0	0	0	0	0	0	0	0	0	0	0	0	0	.000	.000	.000	.000
2019	LAA	AL	31	83	16	5	0	0	(0	0)	21	5	5	4	5	0	15	0	0	0	0	0	0	.193	.239	.253	.492
2021	NYM	NL	6	11	2	0	0	0	(0	0)	2	0	1	2	1	0	4	0	0	0	0	0	0	.182	.250	.182	.432
4 ML YEARS			46	112	21	5	0	0	(0	0)	26	6	8	8	7	1	22	1	2	0	1	0	2	.188	.242	.232	.474

Taylor Trammell

Bats: L **Throws:** L **Pos:** CF-37;LF-14;PR-1   **Ht:** 6'2" **Wt:** 213 **Born:** 9/13/1997 **Age:** 24

Year	Team	Lg	G	AB	H	2B	3B	HR	(Hm	Rd)	TB	R	RBI	RC	TBB	IBB	SO	HBP	SH	SF	SB	CS	GDP	Avg	OBP	Slg	OPS
2021	Tacom	AAA	71	274	72	15	1	12	(-	-)	125	43	49	-	40	1	74	5	0	4	8	2	1	.263	.362	.456	.818
2021	Sea	AL	51	156	25	7	0	8	(3	5)	56	23	18	12	17	0	75	3	2	0	2	3	1	.160	.256	.359	.615

Blake Treinen

Pitches: R **Bats:** R **Pos:** RP-72
TRY-nen
Ht: 6'5" **Wt:** 225 **Born:** 6/30/1988 **Age:** 34

			HOW MUCH PITCHED					WHAT HE GAVE UP											THE RESULTS							
Year	Team	Lg	G	GS	GF	IP	BFP	H	R	ER	HR	SH	SF	HB	TBB	IBB	SO	WP	W	L	Pct	Sv-Op	Hld	Vel	OPS	ERC	ERA
2014	Was	NL	15	7	6	50.2	214	57	17	14	1	0	0	2	13	1	30	1	2	3	.400	0-0	0	95	.678	3.86	2.49
2015	Was	NL	60	0	17	67.2	280	62	32	29	4	1	1	2	32	6	65	4	2	5	.286	0-3	10	96	.692	3.76	3.86
2016	Was	NL	73	0	17	67.0	263	51	19	17	5	2	2	0	31	6	63	1	4	1	.800	1-3	22	95	.648	2.92	2.28
2017	2 Tms		72	0	35	75.2	325	80	35	33	6	0	3	5	25	3	74	4	3	6	.333	16-21	10	97	.736	4.24	3.93
2018	Oak	AL	68	0	58	80.1	315	46	12	7	2	1	0	1	21	3	100	6	9	2	.818	38-43	5	97	.417	1.21	0.78
2019	Oak	AL	57	0	35	58.2	266	58	33	32	9	1	1	1	37	1	59	1	6	5	.545	16-21	3	97	.778	5.39	4.91
2020	LAD	NL	27	0	3	25.2	107	23	15	11	1	0	1	2	8	1	22	2	3	3	.500	1-2	9	97	.621	3.03	3.86
2021	LAD	NL	72	0	10	72.1	286	46	20	16	5	0	1	3	25	1	85	3	6	5	.545	7-11	**32**	97	.512	1.97	1.99
17	Was	NL	37	0	11	37.2	169	48	24	24	3	0	3	3	13	1	32	1	0	2	.000	3-5	5	97	.832	5.71	5.73
17	Oak	AL	35	0	24	38.0	156	32	11	9	3	0	0	2	12	2	42	3	3	4	.429	13-16	5	97	.633	2.92	2.13
	Postseason		15	0	1	16.0	66	14	11	11	2	0	1	2	3	0	15	1	2	2	.500	1-1	3	97	.738	3.22	6.19
	8 ML YEARS		444	7	181	498.0	2056	423	183	159	33	5	9	16	192	22	498	22	35	30	.538	79-104	86	97	.631	3.09	2.87

Alan Trejo

Bats: R **Throws:** R **Pos:** PH-11;2B-10;SS-9;PR-1
Ht: 6'2" **Wt:** 205 **Born:** 5/30/1996 **Age:** 26

					BATTING														RUNNING			AVERAGES			
Year	Team	Lg	G	AB	H	2B	3B	HR	(Hm Rd)	TB	R	RBI	RC	TBB	IBB	SO	HBP	SH	SF	SB	CS	GDP	Avg	OBP	Slg	OPS
2021	Albq	AAA	85	315	90	34	6	16	(- -)	184	54	69	-	23	0	75	1	2	3	2	3	2	.286	.333	.584	.917
2021	Col	NL	28	46	10	2	0	1	(1 0)	15	7	3	1	3	1	15	0	0	1	0	0	2	.217	.260	.326	.586

Jose Trevino

Bats: R **Throws:** R **Pos:** C-88;PH-2
treh-VEEN-yo
Ht: 5'11" **Wt:** 210 **Born:** 11/28/1992 **Age:** 29

					BATTING														RUNNING			AVERAGES			
Year	Team	Lg	G	AB	H	2B	3B	HR	(Hm Rd)	TB	R	RBI	RC	TBB	IBB	SO	HBP	SH	SF	SB	CS	GDP	Avg	OBP	Slg	OPS
2018	Tex	AL	3	8	2	0	0	0	(0 0)	2	0	3	2	0	0	1	0	0	0	0	0	1	.250	.250	.250	.500
2019	Tex	AL	40	120	31	9	0	2	(1 1)	46	18	13	11	3	0	27	0	1	2	0	0	6	.258	.272	.383	.655
2020	Tex	AL	24	76	19	8	0	2	(0 2)	33	10	9	9	3	0	15	1	1	2	0	0	1	.250	.280	.434	.715
2021	Tex	AL	89	285	68	14	0	5	(3 2)	97	23	30	23	12	1	57	0	2	3	1	1	13	.239	.267	.340	.607
	4 ML YEARS		156	489	120	31	0	9	(4 5)	178	51	55	45	18	1	100	1	4	7	1	1	21	.245	.270	.364	.634

Lou Trivino

Pitches: R **Bats:** R **Pos:** RP-71
Ht: 6'5" **Wt:** 235 **Born:** 10/1/1991 **Age:** 30

					HOW MUCH PITCHED					WHAT HE GAVE UP										THE RESULTS							
Year	Team	Lg	G	GS	GF	IP	BFP	H	R	ER	HR	SH	SF	HB	TBB	IBB	SO	WP	W	L	Pct	Sv-Op	Hld	Vel	OPS	ERC	ERA
2018	Oak	AL	69	1	10	74.0	299	53	24	24	8	1	1	2	31	4	82	4	8	3	.727	4-9	23	98	.603	2.76	2.92
2019	Oak	AL	61	0	10	60.0	269	61	40	35	7	2	3	3	31	2	57	7	4	6	.400	0-5	17	97	.782	4.90	5.25
2020	Oak	AL	20	0	9	23.1	93	16	10	10	3	0	0	0	10	0	26	1	0	0	-	0-1	0	96	.605	2.76	3.86
2021	Oak	AL	71	0	44	73.2	310	58	32	26	5	2	1	4	34	2	67	7	7	8	.467	22-26	8	96	.622	3.12	3.18
	Postseason		5	0	1	5.2	22	2	1	1	1	0	0	2	2	0	6	0	0	0	-	0-0	1	97	.551	2.44	1.59
	4 ML YEARS		221	1	73	231.0	971	188	106	95	23	5	5	9	106	8	232	19	19	17	.528	26-41	48	97	.658	3.40	3.70

Chadwick Tromp

Bats: R **Throws:** R **Pos:** C-8;PR-3
Ht: 5'8" **Wt:** 221 **Born:** 3/21/1995 **Age:** 27

					BATTING														RUNNING			AVERAGES			
Year	Team	Lg	G	AB	H	2B	3B	HR	(Hm Rd)	TB	R	RBI	RC	TBB	IBB	SO	HBP	SH	SF	SB	CS	GDP	Avg	OBP	Slg	OPS
2021	Scrmto	AAA	55	192	43	12	0	6	(- -)	73	23	24	-	10	0	47	1	0	1	0	0	4	.224	.265	.380	.645
2020	SF	NL	24	61	13	1	0	4	(2 2)	26	11	10	4	1	0	20	0	0	2	0	0	3	.213	.219	.426	.645
2021	SF	NL	9	18	4	0	0	1	(0 1)	7	1	2	2	0	0	4	0	0	0	0	0	1	.222	.222	.389	.611
	2 ML YEARS		33	79	17	1	0	5	(2 3)	33	12	12	6	1	0	24	0	0	2	0	0	4	.215	.220	.418	.637

Nick Tropeano

Pitches: R **Bats:** R **Pos:** RP-5
TROH-pee-ah-no
Ht: 6'4" **Wt:** 205 **Born:** 8/27/1990 **Age:** 31

					HOW MUCH PITCHED					WHAT HE GAVE UP										THE RESULTS							
Year	Team	Lg	G	GS	GF	IP	BFP	H	R	ER	HR	SH	SF	HB	TBB	IBB	SO	WP	W	L	Pct	Sv-Op	Hld	Vel	OPS	ERC	ERA
2021	Syrcse	AAA	5	1	2	11.0	45	6	2	2	0	1	0	1	7	0	10	0	1	0	1.000	0-	-	-	.568	2.29	1.64
2021	OkCity	AAA	8	5	0	22.2	107	27	19	14	4	0	2	2	10	0	25	1	1	0	1.000	0-	-	-	.881	6.19	5.56
2014	Hou	AL	4	4	0	21.2	91	19	12	11	0	1	1	1	9	1	13	1	1	3	.250	0-0	0	90	.626	2.92	4.57
2015	LAA	AL	8	7	0	37.2	161	40	18	16	2	2	1	0	10	0	38	0	3	2	.600	0-0	0	91	.700	3.53	3.82
2016	LAA	AL	13	13	0	68.1	296	70	27	27	14	1	3	2	31	1	68	4	3	2	.600	0-0	0	91	.843	5.41	3.56
2018	LAA	AL	14	14	0	76.0	316	68	41	40	16	0	2	2	31	2	64	2	5	6	.455	0-0	0	90	.807	4.45	4.74
2019	LAA	AL	3	1	0	13.2	66	18	15	15	6	0	1	2	6	0	10	0	0	1	.000	0-0	0	91	1.061	9.62	9.88
2020	Pit	NL	7	0	2	15.2	66	14	2	2	1	0	1	4	6	0	19	1	1	0	1.000	0-0	0	91	.676	2.89	1.15
2021	2 Tms		5	0	1	8.0	34	8	3	2	1	1	0	0	3	0	2	1	1	0	1.000	0-0	0	90	.767	4.19	2.25
21	SF	NL	4	0	1	6.0	23	4	2	1	0	1	0	0	2	0	2	1	1	0	1.000	0-0	0	90	.523	1.64	1.50
21	NYM	NL	1	0	0	2.0	11	4	1	1	1	0	0	0	1	0	0	0	0	0	-	0-0	0	90	1.255	14.72	4.50
	7 ML YEARS		54	39	3	241.0	1030	237	118	113	40	5	8	8	94	4	214	9	14	14	.500	0-0	0	91	.791	4.57	4.22

Mike Trout

Bats: R Throws: R Pos: CF-36

Ht: 6'2" Wt: 235 Born: 8/7/1991 Age: 30

Year	Team	Lg	G	AB	H	2B	3B	HR	(Hm	Rd)	TB	R	RBI	RC	TBB	IBB	SO	HBP	SH	SF	SB	CS	GDP	Avg	OBP	Slg	OPS
2011	LAA	AL	40	123	27	6	0	5	(1	4)	48	20	16	14	9	0	30	2	0	1	4	0	2	.220	.281	.390	.672
2012	LAA	AL	139	559	182	27	8	30	(16	14)	315	129	83	127	67	4	139	6	0	7	49	5	7	.326	.399	.564	.963
2013	LAA	AL	157	589	190	39	9	27	(13	14)	328	109	97	141	110	10	136	9	0	8	33	7	8	.323	.432	.557	.988
2014	LAA	AL	157	602	173	39	9	36	(19	17)	338	115	111	131	83	6	184	10	0	10	16	2	6	.287	.377	.561	.939
2015	LAA	AL	159	575	172	32	6	41	(20	21)	339	104	90	131	92	14	158	10	0	5	11	7	11	.299	.402	.590	.991
2016	LAA	AL	159	549	173	32	5	29	(14	15)	302	123	100	137	116	12	137	11	0	5	30	7	5	.315	.441	.550	.991
2017	LAA	AL	114	402	123	25	3	33	(20	13)	253	92	72	110	94	15	90	7	0	4	22	4	8	.306	.442	.629	1.071
2018	LAA	AL	140	471	147	24	4	39	(17	22)	296	101	79	140	122	25	124	10	0	4	24	2	5	.312	.460	.628	1.088
2019	LAA	AL	134	470	137	27	2	45	(21	24)	303	110	104	132	110	14	120	16	0	4	11	2	5	.291	.438	.645	1.083
2020	LAA	AL	53	199	56	9	2	17	(10	7)	120	41	46	49	35	4	56	3	0	4	1	1	1	.281	.390	.603	.993
2021	LAA	AL	36	117	39	8	1	8	(5	3)	73	23	18	36	27	5	41	2	0	0	2	2	0	.333	.466	.624	1.090
	Postseason		3	12	1	0	0	1	(0	1)	4	1	1	0	3	0	2	0	0	0	0	1	0	.083	.267	.333	.600
11 ML YEARS			1288	4656	1419	268	49	310	(156	154)	2715	967	816	1148	865	109	1215	86	0	52	203	37	58	.305	.419	.583	1.002

Yoshi Tsutsugo

Bats: L Throws: R Pos: 1B-31;RF-20;PH-20;LF-10;DH-9   yo-shee-toh-mo tsoo-tsoo-go

Ht: 6'1" Wt: 225 Born: 11/26/1991 Age: 30

Year	Team	Lg	G	AB	H	2B	3B	HR	(Hm	Rd)	TB	R	RBI	RC	TBB	IBB	SO	HBP	SH	SF	SB	CS	GDP	Avg	OBP	Slg	OPS
2021	OkCity	AAA	43	148	38	7	0	10	(-	-)	75	28	32	-	26	0	32	1	0	5	0	0	6	.257	.361	.507	.868
2020	TB	AL	51	157	31	5	1	8	(4	4)	62	27	24	22	26	1	50	1	0	1	0	0	5	.197	.314	.395	.708
2021	3 Tms		81	230	50	12	1	8	(3	5)	88	27	32	32	29	0	72	1	1	1	0	1	3	.217	.307	.383	.689
21	TB	AL	26	78	13	4	0	0	(0	0)	17	5	5	4	8	0	27	0	1	0	0	0	1	.167	.244	.218	.462
21	LAD	NL	12	25	3	0	0	0	(0	0)	3	2	2	2	6	0	12	0	0	0	0	0	0	.120	.290	.120	.410
21	Pit	NL	43	127	34	8	1	8	(3	5)	68	20	25	26	15	0	33	1	0	1	0	1	2	.268	.347	.535	.883
	Postseason		8	16	2	0	0	0	(0	0)	2	0	0	0	0	0	3	0	0	0	0	0	1	.125	.125	.125	.250
2 ML YEARS			132	387	81	17	2	16	(7	9)	150	54	56	54	55	1	122	2	1	2	0	1	8	.209	.309	.388	.697

Cole Tucker

Bats: B Throws: R Pos: SS-17;RF-12;PH-10;2B-9;CF-2;1B-1

Ht: 6'3" Wt: 205 Born: 7/3/1996 Age: 25

Year	Team	Lg	G	AB	H	2B	3B	HR	(Hm	Rd)	TB	R	RBI	RC	TBB	IBB	SO	HBP	SH	SF	SB	CS	GDP	Avg	OBP	Slg	OPS
2021	Indy	AAA	61	220	49	11	2	6	(-	-)	82	33	20	-	41	0	58	2	0	0	9	3	4	.223	.350	.373	.723
2019	Pit	NL	56	147	31	10	3	2	(1	1)	53	16	13	14	10	1	40	1	1	0	4	0	3	.211	.266	.361	.626
2020	Pit	NL	37	109	24	3	0	1	(0	1)	30	17	8	6	5	0	31	0	1	1	1	0	1	.220	.252	.275	.527
2021	Pit	NL	43	117	26	4	2	2	(1	1)	40	15	12	14	13	0	33	0	0	1	2	2	2	.222	.298	.342	.640
3 ML YEARS			136	373	81	17	5	5	(2	3)	123	48	33	34	28	1	104	1	2	2	3	2	7	.217	.272	.330	.602

Kyle Tucker

Bats: L Throws: R Pos: RF-133;CF-4;DH-4;PH-1

Ht: 6'4" Wt: 199 Born: 1/17/1997 Age: 25

Year	Team	Lg	G	AB	H	2B	3B	HR	(Hm	Rd)	TB	R	RBI	RC	TBB	IBB	SO	HBP	SH	SF	SB	CS	GDP	Avg	OBP	Slg	OPS
2018	Hou	AL	28	64	9	2	1	0	(0	0)	13	10	4	0	6	0	13	2	0	0	1	1	1	.141	.236	.203	.439
2019	Hou	AL	22	67	18	6	0	4	(1	3)	36	15	11	10	4	1	20	1	0	0	5	0	1	.269	.319	.537	.857
2020	Hou	AL	58	209	56	12	6	9	(4	5)	107	33	42	44	18	2	46	0	0	1	8	1	2	.268	.325	.512	.837
2021	Hou	AL	140	506	149	37	3	30	(15	15)	282	83	92	97	53	5	90	1	0	5	14	2	10	.294	.359	.557	.917
	Postseason		22	61	17	0	0	1	(0	1)	20	6	6	7	5	0	15	0	0	1	1	0	1	.279	.328	.328	.656
4 ML YEARS			248	846	232	57	10	43	(20	23)	438	141	149	151	81	8	169	4	0	6	28	4	14	.274	.338	.518	.856

Spencer Turnbull

Pitches: R Bats: R Pos: SP-9

Ht: 6'3" Wt: 210 Born: 9/18/1992 Age: 29

			HOW MUCH PITCHED					WHAT HE GAVE UP									THE RESULTS							
Year	Team	Lg	G	GS	GF	IP	BFP	H	R	ER	HR	SH	SF	HB	TBB	IBB	SO	WP	W	L	Pct	Sv-Op	Hld	Vel	OPS	ERC	ERA
2018	Det	AL	4	3	0	16.1	69	17	11	11	1	0	0	4	0	15	1	0	2	.000	0-0	1	94	.658	3.41	6.06
2019	Det	AL	30	30	0	148.1	656	154	86	76	14	1	4	16	59	1	146	9	3	17	.150	0-0	0	94	.763	4.69	4.61
2020	Det	AL	11	11	0	56.2	242	47	25	25	2	2	1	2	29	1	51	0	4	4	.500	0-0	0	94	.662	3.24	3.97
2021	Det	AL	9	9	0	50.0	201	37	18	16	2	1	1	5	12	0	44	0	4	2	.667	0-0	0	94	.556	2.14	2.88
4 ML YEARS			54	53	0	271.1	1168	255	140	128	19	4	6	23	104	2	256	10	11	25	.306	0-0	1	94	.700	3.79	4.25

Justin Turner

Bats: R Throws: R Pos: 3B-143;PH-11;DH-4

Ht: 5'11" Wt: 202 Born: 11/23/1984 Age: 37

Year	Team	Lg	G	AB	H	2B	3B	HR	(Hm	Rd)	TB	R	RBI	RC	TBB	IBB	SO	HBP	SH	SF	SB	CS	GDP	Avg	OBP	Slg	OPS
2009	Bal	AL	12	18	3	0	0	0	(0	0)	3	2	3	1	4	0	3	0	0	0	0	0	1	.167	.318	.167	.485
2010	2 Tms		9	17	1	1	0	0	(0	0)	2	1	0	0	1	0	3	0	0	0	0	0	0	.059	.111	.118	.229
2011	NYM	NL	117	435	113	30	0	4	(3	1)	155	49	51	59	39	2	59	10	2	1	7	2	9	.260	.334	.356	.690
2012	NYM	NL	94	171	46	13	1	2	(2	0)	67	20	19	19	9	0	24	4	0	1	1	1	9	.269	.319	.392	.711
2013	NYM	NL	86	200	56	13	1	2	(0	2)	77	12	16	17	11	1	34	1	1	1	0	1	6	.280	.319	.385	.704
2014	LAD	NL	109	288	98	21	1	7	(5	2)	142	46	43	55	28	1	58	4	0	2	6	1	6	.340	.404	.493	.897
2015	LAD	NL	126	385	113	26	1	16	(8	8)	189	55	60	65	36	1	71	13	1	4	5	2	10	.294	.370	.491	.861
2016	LAD	NL	151	556	153	34	3	27	(11	16)	274	79	90	96	48	4	107	10	0	8	4	1	16	.275	.339	.493	.832
2017	LAD	NL	130	457	147	32	0	21	(10	11)	242	72	71	95	59	5	56	19	1	7	7	1	12	.322	.415	.530	.945
2018	LAD	NL	103	365	114	31	1	14	(9	5)	189	62	52	71	47	3	54	12	0	2	2	1	10	.312	.406	.518	.924

Year	Team	Lg	G	AB	H	2B	3B	HR	(Hm	Rd)	TB	R	RBI	RC	TBB	IBB	SO	HBP	SH	SF	SB	CS	GDP	Avg	OBP	Slg	OPS
2019	LAD	NL	135	479	139	24	0	27	(14	13)	244	80	67	84	51	1	88	14	0	5	2	0	11	.290	.372	.509	.881
2020	LAD	NL	42	150	46	9	1	4	(4	0)	69	26	23	32	18	0	26	6	0	1	1	0	2	.307	.400	.460	.860
2021	LAD	NL	151	533	148	22	0	27	(13	14)	251	87	87	90	61	0	98	12	0	6	3	0	12	.278	.361	.471	.832
10	Bal	AL	5	9	0	0	0	0	(0	0)	0	0	0	0	0	0	3	0	0	0	0	0	0	.000	.000	.000	.000
10	NYM	NL	4	8	1	1	0	0	(0	0)	2	1	0	0	1	0	0	0	0	0	0	0	0	.125	.222	.250	.472
Postseason			72	268	79	19	1	12	(5	7)	136	40	41	56	33	1	48	11	0	2	5	0	3	.295	.392	.507	.899
13 ML YEARS			1265	4054	1177	256	9	151	(79	72)	1904	591	582	684	412	15	681	105	5	38	38	10	104	.290	.368	.470	.837

Trea Turner

TRAY

Bats: R Throws: R Pos: SS-98;2B-49;PH-1   Ht: 6'2" Wt: 185 Born: 6/30/1993 Age: 29

Year	Team	Lg	G	AB	H	2B	3B	HR	(Hm	Rd)	TB	R	RBI	RC	TBB	IBB	SO	HBP	SH	SF	SB	CS	GDP	Avg	OBP	Slg	OPS
2015	Was	NL	27	40	9	1	0	1	(0	1)	13	5	1	2	4	0	12	0	0	0	2	2	0	.225	.295	.325	.620
2016	Was	NL	73	307	105	14	8	13	(7	6)	174	53	40	62	14	0	59	1	0	2	33	6	1	.342	.370	.567	.937
2017	Was	NL	98	412	117	24	6	11	(6	5)	186	75	45	67	30	0	80	4	0	1	46	8	4	.284	.338	.451	.789
2018	Was	NL	162	664	180	27	6	19	(10	9)	276	103	73	105	69	3	132	5	2	0	43	9	7	.271	.344	.416	.760
2019	Was	NL	122	521	155	37	5	19	(11	8)	259	96	57	87	43	2	113	3	0	2	35	5	10	.298	.353	.497	.850
2020	Was	NL	59	233	78	15	4	12	(5	7)	137	46	41	52	22	0	36	2	0	2	12	4	5	.335	.394	.588	.982
2021	2 Tms	NL	148	595	195	34	3	28	(16	12)	319	107	77	109	41	2	110	6	0	4	32	5	18	.328	.375	.536	.911
21	Was	NL	96	388	125	17	3	18	(10	8)	202	66	49	66	26	0	77	4	0	2	21	3	13	.322	.369	.521	.890
21	LAD	NL	52	207	70	17	0	10	(6	4)	117	41	28	43	15	2	33	2	0	2	11	2	5	.338	.385	.565	.950
Postseason			27	116	27	5	0	1	(1	0)	35	16	4	8	9	1	33	0	0	1	4	0	1	.233	.286	.302	.587
7 ML YEARS			689	2772	839	152	32	103	(55	48)	1364	485	334	484	223	7	542	21	2	11	203	39	45	.303	.358	.492	.850

Kyle Tyler

Pitches: R Bats: R Pos: RP-5   Ht: 6'0" Wt: 185 Born: 12/27/1996 Age: 25

Year	Team	Lg	G	GS	GF	IP	BFP	H	R	ER	HR	SH	SF	HB	TBB	IBB	SO	WP	W	L	Pct	Sv-Op	Hld	Vel	OPS	ERC	ERA
2021	Rock	AA	15	12	2	72.0	300	64	31	27	8	0	0	3	22	0	73	5	5	2	.714	1--	-	-	.660	3.33	3.38
2021	Salt Lk	AAA	5	2	2	14.0	63	20	8	8	1	0	0	0	3	0	19	0	1	2	.333	0--	-	-	.782	5.65	5.14
2021	LAA	AL	5	0	3	12.1	52	8	4	4	1	0	2	2	6	0	6	0	0	0	-	0-0	0	91	.593	3.00	2.92

Edwin Uceta

Pitches: R Bats: R Pos: RP-13; SP-1   Ht: 6'0" Wt: 155 Born: 1/9/1998 Age: 24

Year	Team	Lg	G	GS	GF	IP	BFP	H	R	ER	HR	SH	SF	HB	TBB	IBB	SO	WP	W	L	Pct	Sv-Op	Hld	Vel	OPS	ERC	ERA
2021	OkCity	AAA	9	3	0	26.2	121	27	16	15	4	0	2	3	12	0	35	2	2	3	.400	0--	-	-	.837	5.10	5.06
2021	LAD	NL	14	1	5	20.1	92	19	18	15	3	2	3	0	12	1	25	1	0	3	.000	0-0	0	93	.758	4.62	6.64

Duane Underwood Jr.

Pitches: R Bats: R Pos: RP-43   Ht: 6'2" Wt: 210 Born: 7/20/1994 Age: 27

Year	Team	Lg	G	GS	GF	IP	BFP	H	R	ER	HR	SH	SF	HB	TBB	IBB	SO	WP	W	L	Pct	Sv-Op	Hld	Vel	OPS	ERC	ERA
2018	ChC	NL	1	1	0	4.0	16	2	1	1	1	0	0	0	3	0	3	0	0	1	.000	0-0	0	92	.697	3.91	2.25
2019	ChC	NL	12	0	1	11.2	51	13	7	7	2	0	0	1	3	0	13	1	0	0	-	0-0	0	95	.865	5.01	5.40
2020	ChC	NL	17	0	3	20.2	88	25	13	13	5	0	1	1	6	1	27	2	1	0	1.000	0-0	1	95	.939	6.33	5.66
2021	Pit	NL	43	0	6	72.2	320	77	40	35	9	0	4	4	27	1	65	3	2	3	.400	0-0	2	94	.776	4.66	4.33
4 ML YEARS			73	1	10	109.0	475	117	61	56	17	0	5	6	39	2	108	6	3	4	.429	0-0	3	94	.814	4.97	4.62

Justin Upton

Bats: R Throws: R Pos: LF-87;CF-1;DH-1;PH-1   Ht: 6'1" Wt: 215 Born: 8/25/1987 Age: 34

Year	Team	Lg	G	AB	H	2B	3B	HR	(Hm	Rd)	TB	R	RBI	RC	TBB	IBB	SO	HBP	SH	SF	SB	CS	GDP	Avg	OBP	Slg	OPS
2007	Ari	NL	43	140	31	8	3	2	(2	0)	51	17	11	13	11	4	37	1	0	0	2	0	3	.221	.283	.364	.647
2008	Ari	NL	108	356	89	19	6	15	(12	3)	165	52	42	47	54	6	121	4	0	3	1	4	3	.250	.353	.463	.816
2009	Ari	NL	138	526	158	30	7	26	(14	12)	280	84	86	94	55	3	137	2	1	4	20	5	10	.300	.366	.532	.899
2010	Ari	NL	133	495	135	27	3	17	(8	9)	219	73	69	73	64	5	152	4	1	7	18	8	20	.273	.356	.442	.799
2011	Ari	NL	159	592	171	39	5	31	(20	11)	313	105	88	103	59	9	126	19	0	4	21	9	8	.289	.369	.529	.898
2012	Ari	NL	150	554	155	24	5	17	(11	6)	238	107	67	82	63	5	121	5	0	6	18	8	7	.280	.355	.430	.785
2013	Atl	NL	149	558	147	27	2	27	(13	14)	259	94	70	84	75	4	161	5	1	4	8	1	12	.263	.354	.464	.818
2014	Atl	NL	154	566	153	34	2	29	(18	11)	278	77	102	84	60	1	171	6	0	8	8	4	10	.270	.342	.491	.833
2015	SD	NL	150	542	136	26	3	26	(15	11)	246	85	81	85	68	5	159	4	0	5	19	5	10	.251	.336	.454	.790
2016	Det	AL	153	570	140	28	2	31	(14	17)	265	81	87	77	50	3	179	4	0	2	9	4	15	.246	.310	.465	.775
2017	2 Tms	AL	152	557	152	44	0	35	(17	18)	301	100	109	109	74	3	180	3	0	1	14	5	9	.273	.361	.540	.901
2018	LAA	AL	145	533	137	18	1	30	(22	8)	247	80	85	79	64	1	176	10	0	6	8	2	12	.257	.344	.463	.808
2019	LAA	AL	63	219	47	8	0	12	(5	7)	91	34	40	30	32	0	78	0	0	5	1	1	5	.215	.309	.416	.724
2020	LAA	AL	42	147	30	5	0	9	(5	4)	62	20	22	17	11	0	43	7	0	1	0	2	6	.204	.289	.422	.711
2021	LAA	AL	89	318	67	12	0	17	(13	4)	130	47	41	37	39	0	107	1	0	3	4	1	11	.211	.296	.409	.705
17	Det	AL	125	459	128	37	0	28	(13	15)	249	81	94	98	57	2	147	3	0	1	10	5	6	.279	.362	.542	.904
17	Atl	AL	27	98	24	7	0	7	(4	3)	52	19	15	11	17	1	33	0	0	0	4	0	3	.245	.357	.531	.888
Postseason			15	48	11	2	1	2	(0	2)	21	7	4	7	10	0	13	2	0	0	1	0	0	.229	.383	.438	.821
15 ML YEARS			1828	6673	1748	349	38	324	(189	135)	3145	1056	1000	1014	779	49	1948	75	3	59	151	59	141	.262	.343	.471	.814

Jose Urena

Pitches: R **Bats:** R **Pos:** SP-18; RP-8
oo-RAY-nuh
Ht: 6'2" **Wt:** 208 **Born:** 9/12/1991 **Age:** 30

Year	Team	Lg	G	GS	GF	IP	BFP	H	R	ER	HR	SH	SF	HB	TBB	IBB	SO	WP	W	L	Pct	Sv-Op	Hld	Vel	OPS	ERC	ERA
2015	Mia	NL	20	9	4	61.2	274	73	37	36	5	3	5	3	25	2	28	2	1	5	.167	0-1	0	94	.818	5.27	5.25
2016	Mia	NL	28	12	4	83.2	373	91	59	57	11	3	4	6	29	6	58	0	4	9	.308	1-3	1	95	.800	4.70	6.13
2017	Mia	NL	34	28	2	169.2	724	152	77	72	26	5	3	14	64	4	113	5	14	7	.667	0-0	0	95	.735	4.07	3.82
2018	Mia	NL	31	31	0	174.0	712	155	78	77	19	5	4	12	51	8	130	2	9	12	.429	0-0	0	96	.690	3.40	3.98
2019	Mia	NL	24	13	8	84.2	369	99	53	49	13	1	2	2	26	3	62	2	4	10	.286	3-5	0	96	.818	5.16	5.21
2020	Mia	NL	5	5	0	23.1	104	22	15	14	4	0	0	2	13	0	15	1	0	3	.000	0-0	0	95	.783	5.31	5.40
2021	Det	AL	26	18	1	100.2	456	119	70	65	14	0	2	4	42	0	67	4	4	8	.333	0-0	1	94	.837	5.68	5.81
7 ML YEARS			168	116	19	697.2	3012	711	389	370	92	17	20	43	250	23	473	16	36	54	.400	4-9	2	95	.767	4.47	4.77

Julio Urias

Pitches: L **Bats:** L **Pos:** SP-32
oo-ree-AHS
Ht: 6'0" **Wt:** 225 **Born:** 8/12/1996 **Age:** 25

Year	Team	Lg	G	GS	GF	IP	BFP	H	R	ER	HR	SH	SF	HB	TBB	IBB	SO	WP	W	L	Pct	Sv-Op	Hld	Vel	OPS	ERC	ERA
2016	LAD	NL	18	15	1	77.0	336	81	32	29	5	4	1	4	31	0	84	3	5	2	.714	0-0	0	93	.728	4.37	3.39
2017	LAD	NL	5	5	0	23.1	102	23	15	14	1	2	0	1	14	1	11	1	0	2	.000	0-0	0	93	.768	4.61	5.40
2018	LAD	NL	3	0	3	4.0	13	1	0	0	0	0	0	0	0	0	7	0	0	0	-	0-0	0	93	.154	0.14	0.00
2019	LAD	NL	37	8	7	79.2	326	59	28	22	7	0	1	5	27	1	85	2	4	3	.571	4-5	5	95	.603	2.60	2.49
2020	LAD	NL	11	10	0	55.0	224	45	20	20	5	0	1	0	18	0	45	2	3	0	1.000	0-0	0	94	.608	2.78	3.27
2021	LAD	NL	32	32	0	185.2	745	151	67	61	19	7	2	7	38	3	195	2	20	3	.870	0-0	0	94	.614	2.48	2.96
Postseason			18	3	4	38.2	148	24	13	12	5	1	0	0	9	0	39	1	6	2	.750	1-1	1	94	.531	1.73	2.79
6 ML YEARS			106	70	11	424.2	1746	360	162	146	37	13	5	17	128	5	427	10	32	10	.762	4-5	5	94	.638	2.94	3.09

Luis Urias

Bats: R **Throws:** R **Pos:** 3B-68;SS-68;2B-25;PH-10
oo-REE-ahs
Ht: 5'9" **Wt:** 186 **Born:** 6/3/1997 **Age:** 25

Year	Team	Lg	G	AB	H	2B	3B	HR	(Hm	Rd)	TB	R	RBI	RC	TBB	IBB	SO	HBP	SH	SF	SB	CS	GDP	Avg	OBP	Slg	OPS
2018	SD	NL	12	48	10	1	0	2	(1	1)	17	5	5	6	3	0	10	1	0	1	1	0	0	.208	.264	.354	.618
2019	SD	NL	71	215	48	8	1	4	(1	3)	70	27	24	22	25	0	56	9	0	0	0	1	8	.223	.329	.326	.655
2020	Mil	NL	41	109	26	4	1	0	(0	0)	32	11	11	11	10	0	32	1	0	0	2	2	4	.239	.308	.294	.602
2021	Mil	NL	150	490	122	25	1	23	(11	12)	218	77	75	80	63	3	116	10	1	3	5	1	9	.249	.345	.445	.789
Postseason			1	2	1	0	0	0	(0	0)	1	0	0	0	1	0	0	0	0	0	0	0	0	.500	.667	.500	1.167
4 ML YEARS			274	862	206	38	3	29	(13	16)	337	120	115	119	101	3	214	21	1	4	8	4	21	.239	.332	.391	.723

Ramon Urias

Bats: R **Throws:** R **Pos:** SS-48;2B-32;3B-10;PH-7
Ht: 6'0" **Wt:** 190 **Born:** 6/3/1994 **Age:** 28

Year	Team	Lg	G	AB	H	2B	3B	HR	(Hm	Rd)	TB	R	RBI	RC	TBB	IBB	SO	HBP	SH	SF	SB	CS	GDP	Avg	OBP	Slg	OPS
2021	Norfolk	AAA	24	89	23	6	1	4	(-	-)	43	14	12	-	9	0	25	2	1	0	1	1	2	.258	.340	.483	.823
2020	Bal	AL	10	25	9	2	0	1	(0	1)	14	3	3	6	2	0	6	0	0	0	0	0	1	.360	.407	.560	.967
2021	Bal	AL	85	262	73	14	0	7	(4	3)	108	33	38	46	28	0	76	6	0	0	1	2	3	.279	.361	.412	.774
2 ML YEARS			95	287	82	16	0	8	(4	4)	122	36	41	52	30	0	82	6	0	0	1	2	4	.286	.365	.425	.790

Jose Urquidy

Pitches: R **Bats:** R **Pos:** SP-20
Ht: 6'0" **Wt:** 217 **Born:** 5/1/1995 **Age:** 27

Year	Team	Lg	G	GS	GF	IP	BFP	H	R	ER	HR	SH	SF	HB	TBB	IBB	SO	WP	W	L	Pct	Sv-Op	Hld	Vel	OPS	ERC	ERA
2019	Hou	AL	9	7	0	41.0	167	38	18	18	6	2	0	0	7	0	40	4	2	1	.667	0-0	0	93	.678	3.05	3.95
2020	Hou	AL	5	5	0	29.2	116	22	9	9	4	0	0	1	8	0	17	0	1	1	.500	0-0	0	93	.594	2.63	2.73
2021	Hou	AL	20	20	0	107.0	423	87	43	43	17	2	1	2	19	0	90	2	8	3	.727	0-0	0	93	.663	2.67	3.62
Postseason			8	4	1	25.2	108	21	9	8	5	0	1	1	8	0	24	0	1	1	.500	0-0	0	94	.676	3.41	2.81
3 ML YEARS			34	32	0	177.2	706	147	70	70	27	4	1	3	34	0	147	6	11	5	.688	0-0	0	93	.655	2.75	3.55

Gio Urshela

Bats: R **Throws:** R **Pos:** 3B-96;SS-28;PH-6
urr-SHELL-ah
Ht: 6'0" **Wt:** 215 **Born:** 10/11/1991 **Age:** 30

Year	Team	Lg	G	AB	H	2B	3B	HR	(Hm	Rd)	TB	R	RBI	RC	TBB	IBB	SO	HBP	SH	SF	SB	CS	GDP	Avg	OBP	Slg	OPS
2015	Cle	AL	81	267	60	8	1	6	(3	3)	88	25	21	19	18	0	58	2	1	0	0	1	9	.225	.279	.330	.608
2017	Cle	AL	67	156	35	7	0	1	(0	1)	45	14	15	10	8	0	22	0	1	0	0	0	6	.224	.262	.288	.551
2018	Tor	AL	19	43	10	1	0	1	(1	0)	14	7	3	2	2	0	10	1	0	0	0	0	1	.233	.283	.326	.608
2019	NYY	AL	132	442	139	34	0	21	(8	13)	236	73	74	80	25	1	87	5	0	4	1	1	13	.314	.355	.534	.889
2020	NYY	AL	43	151	45	11	0	6	(6	0)	74	24	30	31	18	0	25	1	0	4	1	0	6	.298	.368	.490	.858
2021	NYY	AL	116	420	112	18	2	14	(6	8)	176	42	49	50	20	0	109	1	0	1	1	0	16	.267	.301	.419	.720
Postseason			21	73	15	1	0	3	(0	3)	25	8	8	8	4	0	17	0	1	1	0	0	1	.205	.244	.342	.586
6 ML YEARS			458	1479	401	79	3	49	(24	25)	633	185	192	192	91	1	311	10	2	9	3	2	51	.271	.316	.428	.744

Pat Valaika

Bats: R **Throws:** R **Pos:** 2B-72;SS-17;1B-6;PH-6;LF-3;PR-3;3B-2   **Ht:** 6'0" **Wt:** 200 **Born:** 9/9/1992 **Age:** 29

Year	Team	Lg	G	AB	H	2B	3B	HR	(Hm	Rd)	TB	R	RBI	RC	TBB	IBB	SO	HBP	SH	SF	SB	CS	GDP	Avg	OBP	Slg	OPS
2021	Norfolk	AAA	22	80	18	1	0	2	(-	-)	25	9	7	-	2	0	22	0	0	0	0	0	0	.225	.244	.313	.556
2016	Col	NL	13	19	5	1	0	1	(0	1)	9	3	2	1	0	0	8	0	0	0	0	0	0	.263	.263	.474	.737
2017	Col	NL	110	182	47	11	0	13	(9	4)	97	28	40	31	7	0	53	0	5	1	0	0	1	.258	.284	.533	.817
2018	Col	NL	68	122	19	5	0	2	(1	1)	30	8	5	2	9	0	30	0	2	0	0	0	4	.156	.214	.246	.460
2019	Col	NL	40	79	15	5	1	1	(1	0)	25	11	4	8	7	0	34	0	0	0	0	0	0	.190	.256	.316	.572
2020	Bal	AL	52	141	39	4	0	8	(5	3)	67	24	16	16	8	0	34	0	1	0	0	2	3	.277	.315	.475	.791
2021	Bal	AL	91	259	52	8	0	5	(2	3)	75	17	25	17	16	0	76	2	1	3	1	1	4	.201	.250	.290	.540
	Postseason		2	2	1	1	0	0	(0	0)	2	0	0	-	1	0	0	0	0	0	0	0	0	.500	.500	1.000	1.500
	6 ML YEARS		374	802	177	34	1	30	(18	12)	303	91	92	75	47	0	235	2	9	4	1	3	13	.221	.264	.378	.642

Cesar Valdez

Pitches: R **Bats:** R **Pos:** RP-39   **Ht:** 6'2" **Wt:** 225 **Born:** 3/17/1985 **Age:** 37

Year	Team	Lg	G	GS	GF	IP	BFP	H	R	ER	HR	SH	SF	HB	TBB	IBB	SO	WP	W	L	Pct	Sv-Op	Hld	Vel	OPS	ERC	ERA
2021	Norfolk	AAA	9	0	1	12.2	50	10	3	2	0	0	0	1	3	1	12	0	0	1	.000	0--	-	-	.541	2.00	1.42
2010	Ari	NL	9	2	3	20.0	97	29	19	17	2	0	0	1	10	2	13	3	1	2	.333	0-0	0	89	.889	7.29	7.65
2017	2 Tms	AL	11	4	5	30.2	142	41	29	26	7	0	0	1	11	1	21	1	1	1	.500	0-0	0	88	.988	7.11	7.63
2020	Bal	AL	9	0	7	14.1	53	7	3	2	0	0	1	0	3	0	12	1	1	1	.500	3-3	0	86	.413	0.84	1.26
2021	Bal	AL	39	0	16	46.0	210	62	32	30	8	0	1	1	14	2	45	2	2	2	.500	8-13	0	85	.892	6.33	5.87
17	Oak	AL	4	1	2	9.1	44	14	10	10	4	0	0	0	4	0	5	0	0	0	-	0-0	0	88	1.134	10.35	9.64
17	Tor	AL	7	3	3	21.1	96	27	19	16	3	0	0	1	7	1	16	1	1	1	.500	0-0	0	88	.921	5.81	6.75
	4 ML YEARS		68	6	31	111.0	500	139	83	75	17	0	2	3	38	5	91	7	5	6	.455	11-16	0	87	.868	5.77	6.08

Framber Valdez

Pitches: L **Bats:** L **Pos:** SP-22   **Ht:** 5'11" **Wt:** 239 **Born:** 11/19/1993 **Age:** 28

Year	Team	Lg	G	GS	GF	IP	BFP	H	R	ER	HR	SH	SF	HB	TBB	IBB	SO	WP	W	L	Pct	Sv-Op	Hld	Vel	OPS	ERC	ERA
2018	Hou	AL	8	5	0	37.0	154	22	10	9	3	0	0	4	24	0	34	5	4	1	.800	0-0	0	92	.595	3.20	2.19
2019	Hou	AL	26	8	7	70.2	329	74	51	46	9	0	4	4	44	0	68	4	4	7	.364	0-0	0	93	.790	5.65	5.86
2020	Hou	AL	11	10	0	70.2	288	63	32	28	5	1	3	5	16	0	76	6	5	3	.625	0-0	0	93	.635	2.94	3.57
2021	Hou	AL	22	22	0	134.2	572	110	52	47	12	1	1	11	58	1	125	9	11	6	.647	0-0	0	93	.641	3.42	3.14
	Postseason		4	3	1	24.0	90	14	5	5	3	0	0	0	10	0	26	0	3	1	.750	0-0	0	93	.579	2.30	1.88
	4 ML YEARS		67	45	7	313.0	1343	269	145	130	29	2	8	24	142	1	303	24	24	17	.585	0-0	0	93	.671	3.76	3.74

Phillips Valdez

Pitches: R **Bats:** R **Pos:** RP-28   **Ht:** 6'2" **Wt:** 160 **Born:** 11/16/1991 **Age:** 30

Year	Team	Lg	G	GS	GF	IP	BFP	H	R	ER	HR	SH	SF	HB	TBB	IBB	SO	WP	W	L	Pct	Sv-Op	Hld	Vel	OPS	ERC	ERA
2021	Wrcstr	AAA	15	0	5	14.2	62	13	6	6	2	0	0	4	8	0	18	0	1	0	1.000	1--	-	-	.709	4.40	3.68
2019	Tex	AL	11	0	2	16.0	75	17	7	7	3	0	1	2	9	0	18	1	0	0	-	0-0	0	92	.818	6.26	3.94
2020	Bos	AL	24	0	5	30.1	137	33	16	11	3	0	1	3	16	0	30	0	1	1	.500	0-1	4	92	.790	5.61	3.26
2021	Bos	AL	28	0	15	40.0	177	35	29	26	4	1	3	7	19	1	35	5	2	0	1.000	1-1	2	93	.700	4.31	5.85
	3 ML YEARS		63	0	22	86.1	389	85	52	44	10	1	5	12	44	1	83	6	3	1	.750	1-2	6	92	.755	5.11	4.59

Breyvic Valera

Bats: B **Throws:** R **Pos:** 3B-21;2B-10;PH-10;PR-5;DH-1   **Ht:** 5'11" **Wt:** 190 **Born:** 1/8/1992 **Age:** 30

Year	Team	Lg	G	AB	H	2B	3B	HR	(Hm	Rd)	TB	R	RBI	RC	TBB	IBB	SO	HBP	SH	SF	SB	CS	GDP	Avg	OBP	Slg	OPS
2021	Buffalo	AAA	41	150	47	11	1	3	(-	-)	69	29	28	-	24	0	19	2	0	4	7	4	5	.313	.406	.460	.866
2017	StL	NL	5	10	1	0	0	0	(0	0)	1	0	0	0	1	0	0	0	0	0	0	0	0	.100	.182	.100	.282
2018	2 Tms	AL	32	64	15	0	1	0	(0	0)	17	8	8	10	7	0	13	0	2	2	1	0	0	.234	.301	.266	.567
2019	2 Tms	AL	17	47	11	2	1	1	(1	0)	18	7	6	8	4	0	7	1	0	0	0	0	0	.234	.308	.383	.691
2021	Tor	AL	39	87	22	6	0	1	(1	0)	31	10	15	12	8	0	12	0	1	1	0	0	0	.253	.313	.356	.669
18	LAD	NL	20	29	5	0	0	0	(0	0)	5	4	4	3	4	0	4	0	1	0	1	0	0	.172	.273	.172	.445
18	Bal	AL	12	35	10	0	1	0	(0	0)	12	4	4	7	3	0	9	0	1	2	0	0	0	.286	.325	.343	.668
19	NYY	AL	12	32	7	1	1	0	(0	0)	10	5	3	5	4	0	5	1	0	0	0	0	0	.219	.324	.313	.637
19	Tor	AL	5	15	4	1	0	0	(0	0)	5	2	3	3	0	0	2	0	0	0	0	0	0	.267	.267	.533	.800
	4 ML YEARS		93	208	49	8	2	2	(2	0)	67	25	29	30	20	0	32	1	3	3	2	0	2	.236	.302	.322	.624

Josh VanMeter

Bats: L **Throws:** R **Pos:** 2B-52;PH-40;3B-25;1B-1;LF-1;RF-1   **Ht:** 5'11" **Wt:** 194 **Born:** 3/10/1995 **Age:** 27

Year	Team	Lg	G	AB	H	2B	3B	HR	(Hm	Rd)	TB	R	RBI	RC	TBB	IBB	SO	HBP	SH	SF	SB	CS	GDP	Avg	OBP	Slg	OPS
2021	Reno	AAA	19	67	26	6	0	9	(-	-)	59	23	20	-	23	0	21	0	0	1	1	0	0	.388	.538	.881	1.419
2019	Cin	NL	95	228	54	13	1	8	(3	5)	93	33	23	28	29	0	56	2	0	1	9	3	5	.237	.327	.408	.735
2020	2 Tms	NL	26	70	9	3	0	2	(2	0)	18	9	6	5	7	0	24	2	0	0	1	0	0	.129	.228	.257	.485
2021	Ari	NL	112	274	58	17	2	6	(5	1)	97	26	36	37	33	0	83	1	0	2	3	2	5	.212	.297	.354	.651
20	Cin	NL	14	34	2	1	0	1	(1	0)	6	3	1	0	3	0	16	1	0	0	1	0	0	.059	.158	.176	.334
20	Bal	AL	12	36	7	2	0	1	(1	0)	12	6	5	5	4	0	8	1	0	0	0	0	0	.194	.293	.333	.626
	3 ML YEARS		233	572	121	33	3	16	(10	6)	208	68	65	70	69	0	163	5	0	3	13	5	10	.212	.300	.364	.664

Ildemaro Vargas

Bats: B Throws: R Pos: PH-12;3B-10;2B-9;SS-5;LF-2;DH-1 Ht: 6'0" Wt: 180 Born: 7/16/1991 Age: 30

Year Team	Lg	G	AB	H	2B	3B	HR	(Hm	Rd)	TB	R	RBI	RC	TBB	IBB	SO	HBP	SH	SF	SB	CS	GDP	Avg	OBP	Slg	OPS
2021 Reno	AAA	57	249	78	21	0	10	(-	-)	129	50	39	-	16	2	27	0	0	3	3	1	6	.313	.351	.518	.869
2017 Ari	NL	12	13	4	1	0	0	(0	0)	5	4	4	2	0	0	3	0	0	0	0	0	1	.308	.308	.385	.692
2018 Ari	NL	14	19	4	0	0	1	(0	1)	7	2	4	4	1	0	4	0	0	0	1	0	1	.211	.250	.368	.618
2019 Ari	NL	92	201	54	9	1	6	(2	4)	83	25	24	26	9	0	24	0	0	1	1	0	6	.269	.299	.413	.712
2020 3 Tms		24	51	10	1	1	1	(0	1)	16	6	3	2	2	0	10	0	0	1	1	0	2	.196	.222	.314	.536
2021 3 Tms	NL	34	77	12	3	1	0	(0	0)	17	7	7	3	6	1	17	0	0	1	1	0	2	.156	.217	.221	.438
20 Ari	NL	8	20	3	0	0	0	(0	0)	3	2	0	0	1	0	5	0	0	0	0	0	1	.150	.190	.150	.340
20 Min	AL	10	22	5	1	1	0	(0	0)	8	3	2	1	1	0	2	0	0	0	0	0	1	.227	.250	.364	.614
20 ChC	NL	6	9	2	0	0	1	(0	1)	5	1	1	1	0	0	3	0	0	1	1	0		.222	.222	.556	.778
21 ChC	NL	9	21	3	2	0	0	(0	0)	5	3	2	1	3	0	7	0	0	1	1	0	1	.143	.250	.238	.488
21 Pit	NL	7	13	1	0	0	0	(0	0)	1	0	1	0	0	0	3	0	0	0	0	0		.077	.077	.077	.154
21 Ari	NL	18	43	8	1	1	0	(0	0)	11	4	4	2	3	1	7	0	0	0	0	0	0	.186	.239	.256	.495
5 ML YEARS		176	361	84	14	3	8	(2	6)	128	44	42	37	18	1	58	0	0	2	3	0	12	.233	.268	.355	.622

Daulton Varsho

Bats: L Throws: R Pos: C-41;CF-30;PH-17;LF-12;RF-12;PR-4 Ht: 5'10" Wt: 207 Born: 7/2/1996 Age: 25

Year Team	Lg	G	AB	H	2B	3B	HR	(Hm	Rd)	TB	R	RBI	RC	TBB	IBB	SO	HBP	SH	SF	SB	CS	GDP	Avg	OBP	Slg	OPS
2021 Reno	AAA	18	80	25	6	1	9	(-	-)	60	18	25	-	7	0	16	0	0	0	2	0	2	.313	.368	.750	1.118
2020 Ari	NL	37	101	19	5	2	3	(1	2)	37	16	9	8	12	0	33	2	0	0	3	1	1	.188	.287	.366	.653
2021 Ari	NL	95	284	70	17	2	11	(2	9)	124	41	38	41	30	3	67	0	1	0	6	0	4	.246	.318	.437	.755
2 ML YEARS		132	385	89	22	4	14	(3	11)	161	57	47	49	42	3	100	2	1	0	9	1	5	.231	.310	.418	.728

Andrew Vasquez

Pitches: L Bats: L Pos: RP-2 Ht: 6'6" Wt: 228 Born: 9/14/1993 Age: 28

Year Team	Lg	G	GS	GF	IP	BFP	H	R	ER	HR	SH	SF	HB	TBB	IBB	SO	WP	W	L	Pct	Sv-Op	Hld	Vel	OPS	ERC	ERA
2021 StPaul	AAA	33	0	12	42.1	182	21	21	17	5	0	0	13	22	0	68	1	4	0	1.000	0- -	-	-	.593	3.06	3.61
2021 OkCity	AAA	5	0	0	5.0	22	5	2	2	0	0	0	2	2	0	9	0	0	0		0- -	-	-	.618	3.28	3.60
2018 Min	AL	9	0	0	5.0	26	5	4	3	0	0	0	3	2	0	7	0	1	0	1.000	0-0	0	90	.766	5.24	5.40
2019 Min	AL	1	0	0	0.0	3	0	3	3	0	0	0	1	2	0	0	0	0	0		0-0	0	85	-	-	-
2021 LAD	NL	2	0	1	1.2	6	1	1	0	0	0	1	0	0	0	3	0	0	0		0-1	0	91	.333	0.75	0.00
3 ML YEARS		12	0	1	6.2	35	6	8	6	0	0	0	4	4	0	10	0	1	0	1.000	0-1	0	90	.733	5.48	8.10

Andrew Vaughn

Bats: R Throws: R Pos: LF-95;RF-18;1B-15;DH-6;PH-6;3B-2;PR-2;2B-1 Ht: 6'0" Wt: 215 Born: 4/3/1998 Age: 24

Year Team	Lg	G	AB	H	2B	3B	HR	(Hm	Rd)	TB	R	RBI	RC	TBB	IBB	SO	HBP	SH	SF	SB	CS	GDP	Avg	OBP	Slg	OPS
2019 3 Tms	Low	55	205	57	17	0	6	(-	-)	92	33	36	36	30	0	38	7	0	3	1	0	9	.278	.384	.449	.832
2021 CWS	AL	127	417	98	22	0	15	(8	7)	165	56	48	45	41	0	101	6	0	5	1	1	14	.235	.309	.396	.705

Christian Vazquez

Bats: R Throws: R Pos: C-132;PH-6;DH-3;2B-2;3B-2;PR-2;1B-1 VAZ-kehz Ht: 5'9" Wt: 205 Born: 8/21/1990 Age: 31

Year Team	Lg	G	AB	H	2B	3B	HR	(Hm	Rd)	TB	R	RBI	RC	TBB	IBB	SO	HBP	SH	SF	SB	CS	GDP	Avg	OBP	Slg	OPS
2014 Bos	AL	55	175	42	9	0	1	(1	0)	54	15	20	19	19	1	33	0	3	4	0	0	4	.240	.308	.309	.617
2016 Bos	AL	57	172	39	9	1	1	(1	0)	53	21	12	11	10	1	39	2	0	0	0	0	3	.227	.277	.308	.585
2017 Bos	AL	99	324	94	18	2	5	(4	1)	131	43	32	41	17	0	64	3	0	1	7	2	14	.290	.330	.404	.735
2018 Bos	AL	80	251	52	10	0	3	(2	1)	71	24	16	13	13	1	41	4	1	0	4	1	4	.207	.257	.283	.540
2019 Bos	AL	138	482	133	26	1	23	(8	15)	230	66	72	69	33	3	101	0	3	3	4	2	17	.276	.320	.477	.798
2020 Bos	AL	47	173	49	9	0	7	(5	2)	79	22	23	25	16	0	43	0	0	0	4	3	6	.283	.344	.457	.801
2021 Bos	AL	138	458	118	23	1	6	(3	3)	161	51	49	47	33	0	84	2	1	4	8	4	15	.258	.308	.352	.659
Postseason		14	43	10	1	0	1	(0	1)	14	5	2	2	3	0	10	0	0	0	0	0	0	.233	.283	.326	.608
7 ML YEARS		614	2035	527	104	5	46	(21	25)	779	242	224	225	141	6	405	11	8	12	27	12	64	.259	.309	.383	.692

Vince Velasquez

Pitches: R Bats: R Pos: SP-21; RP-4 Ht: 6'3" Wt: 212 Born: 6/7/1992 Age: 30

Year Team	Lg	G	GS	GF	IP	BFP	H	R	ER	HR	SH	SF	HB	TBB	IBB	SO	WP	W	L	Pct	Sv-Op	Hld	Vel	OPS	ERC	ERA
2015 Hou	AL	19	7	5	55.2	231	50	28	27	5	0	0	2	21	0	58	3	1	1	.500	0-0	0	95	.720	3.58	4.37
2016 Phi	NL	24	24	0	131.0	551	129	64	60	21	9	5	1	45	1	152	3	8	6	.571	0-0	0	94	.765	4.25	4.12
2017 Phi	NL	15	15	0	72.0	315	74	44	41	15	2	2	3	34	1	68	2	2	7	.222	0-0	0	94	.851	5.58	5.13
2018 Phi	NL	31	30	1	146.2	630	138	83	79	16	7	3	8	59	1	161	9	9	12	.429	0-0	0	94	.747	4.04	4.85
2019 Phi	NL	33	23	2	117.1	516	120	69	64	26	3	3	9	43	2	130	3	7	8	.467	0-0	0	94	.833	5.21	4.91
2020 Phi	NL	9	7	0	34.0	154	36	21	21	5	0	3	1	17	1	46	5	1	1	.500	0-0	0	94	.804	5.51	5.56
2021 2 Tms	NL	25	21	1	94.1	417	91	68	66	23	1	0	4	49	2	101	2	3	9	.250	0-0	0	93	.872	5.58	6.30
21 Phi	NL	21	17	1	81.2	361	76	55	54	17	1	0	4	45	2	85	2	3	6	.333	0-0	0	93	.842	5.27	5.95
21 SD	NL	4	4	0	12.2	56	15	13	12	6	0	0	0	4	0	16	0	0	3	.000	0-0	0	93	1.051	7.55	8.53
7 ML YEARS		156	127	9	651.0	2814	638	377	358	111	22	13	30	268	8	716	24	31	44	.413	0-0	2	94	.797	4.71	4.95

Andrew Velazquez

Bats: B Throws: R Pos: SS-28;PR-2   Ht: 5'9" Wt: 170 Born: 7/14/1994 Age: 27

Year	Team	Lg	G	AB	H	2B	3B	HR	(Hm	Rd)	TB	R	RBI	RC	TBB	IBB	SO	HBP	SH	SF	SB	CS	GDP	Avg	OBP	Slg	OPS
2021	S-WB	AAA	77	264	72	20	3	7	(-	-)	119	40	46	-	37	1	87	1	2	2	29	3	4	.273	.362	.451	.813
2018	TB	AL	13	10	3	1	0	0	(0	0)	4	3	0	3	1	0	3	1	0	0	1	0	0	.300	.417	.400	.817
2019	2 Tms	AL	15	23	2	2	0	0	(0	0)	4	3	0	0	1	0	13	0	0	0	1	0	0	.087	.125	.174	.299
2020	Bal	AL	40	63	10	1	1	0	(0	0)	13	11	3	3	10	0	23	0	4	0	4	2	2	.159	.274	.206	.480
2021	NYY	AL	28	67	15	4	1	1	(1	0)	24	11	6	5	1	0	23	0	0	0	4	1	1	.224	.235	.358	.594
19	TB	AL	10	12	1	1	0	0	(0	0)	2	2	0	0	0	0	6	0	0	0	0	0	0	.083	.083	.167	.250
19	Cle	AL	5	11	1	1	0	0	(0	0)	2	1	0	0	1	0	7	0	0	0	1	0	0	.091	.167	.182	.348
	4 ML YEARS		96	163	30	8	2	1	(1	0)	45	28	9	11	13	0	62	1	4	0	10	3	3	.184	.249	.276	.525

Alex Verdugo

Bats: L Throws: L Pos: LF-90;CF-42;RF-24;PH-6;DH-1   Ht: 6'0" Wt: 192 Born: 5/15/1996 Age: 26

Year	Team	Lg	G	AB	H	2B	3B	HR	(Hm	Rd)	TB	R	RBI	RC	TBB	IBB	SO	HBP	SH	SF	SB	CS	GDP	Avg	OBP	Slg	OPS
2017	LAD	NL	15	23	4	0	0	1	(1	0)	7	1	1	0	2	0	4	0	0	0	0	1	1	.174	.240	.304	.544
2018	LAD	NL	37	77	20	6	0	1	(0	1)	29	11	4	6	8	0	14	0	1	0	0	0	4	.260	.329	.377	.706
2019	LAD	NL	106	343	101	22	2	12	(5	7)	163	43	44	51	26	1	49	2	0	6	4	1	8	.294	.342	.475	.817
2020	Bos	AL	53	201	62	16	0	6	(2	4)	96	36	15	31	17	1	45	2	0	1	4	0	4	.308	.367	.478	.844
2021	Bos	AL	146	544	157	32	2	13	(6	7)	232	88	63	85	51	6	96	4	0	5	6	2	11	.289	.351	.426	.777
	5 ML YEARS		357	1188	344	76	4	33	(14	19)	527	179	127	173	104	8	208	8	1	12	14	4	28	.290	.348	.444	.791

Justin Verlander

Pitches: R Bats: R Pos: P   Ht: 6'5" Wt: 235 Born: 2/20/1983 Age: 39

Year	Team	Lg	G	GS	GF	IP	BFP	H	R	ER	HR	SH	SF	HB	TBB	IBB	SO	WP	W	L	Pct	Sv-Op	Hld	Vel	OPS	ERC	ERA
2005	Det	AL	2	2	0	11.1	54	15	9	9	1	0	0	1	5	0	7	1	0	2	.000	0-0	0	95	.868	6.41	7.15
2006	Det	AL	30	30	0	186.0	776	187	78	75	21	2	4	6	60	1	124	5	17	9	.654	0-0	0	95	.741	4.12	3.63
2007	Det	AL	32	32	0	201.2	866	181	88	82	20	3	1	19	67	3	183	17	18	6	.750	0-0	0	95	.668	3.53	3.66
2008	Det	AL	33	33	0	201.0	880	195	119	108	18	4	6	14	87	8	163	6	11	17	.393	0-0	0	94	.715	4.17	4.84
2009	Det	AL	35	35	0	240.0	982	219	99	92	20	6	4	6	63	5	269	8	19	9	.679	0-0	0	96	.665	3.06	3.45
2010	Det	AL	33	33	0	224.1	925	190	89	84	14	6	8	6	71	0	219	11	18	9	.667	0-0	0	95	.630	2.79	3.37
2011	Det	AL	34	34	0	251.0	969	174	73	67	24	2	3	3	57	0	250	7	24	5	.828	0-0	0	95	.555	1.92	2.40
2012	Det	AL	33	33	0	238.1	956	192	81	70	19	4	3	5	60	2	239	2	17	8	.680	0-0	0	94	.601	2.45	2.64
2013	Det	AL	34	34	0	218.1	925	212	94	84	19	2	6	4	75	1	217	3	13	12	.520	0-0	0	93	.691	3.68	3.46
2014	Det	AL	32	32	0	206.0	893	223	114	104	18	6	5	5	65	1	159	5	15	12	.556	0-0	0	92	.756	4.19	4.54
2015	Det	AL	20	20	0	133.1	535	113	56	50	13	1	4	5	32	1	113	2	5	8	.385	0-0	0	93	.634	2.75	3.38
2016	Det	AL	34	34	0	227.2	903	171	81	77	30	4	7	8	57	1	254	6	16	9	.640	0-0	0	93	.630	2.54	3.04
2017	2 Tms	AL	33	33	0	206.0	849	170	80	77	27	1	4	4	72	4	219	5	15	8	.652	0-0	0	95	.660	3.19	3.36
2018	Hou	AL	34	34	0	214.0	833	156	63	60	28	2	5	8	37	0	290	5	16	9	.640	0-0	0	95	.602	2.16	2.52
2019	Hou	AL	34	34	0	223.0	847	137	66	64	36	0	2	6	42	0	300	4	21	6	.778	0-0	0	95	.579	1.80	2.58
2020	Hou	AL	1	1	0	6.0	21	3	2	2	2	0	0	0	1	0	7	0	1	0	1.000	0-0	0	95	.640	1.95	3.00
17	Det	AL	28	28	0	172.0	729	153	76	73	23	1	4	3	67	4	176	5	10	8	.556	0-0	0	95	.693	3.67	3.82
17	Hou	AL	5	5	0	34.0	120	17	4	4	4	0	0	1	5	0	43	0	5	0	1.000	0-0	0	95	.464	1.22	1.06
	Postseason		31	30	0	187.2	754	140	74	71	26	2	3	3	60	0	205	8	14	11	.560	0-0	0	95	.629	2.73	3.40
	16 ML YEARS		454	454	0	2988.0	12214	2538	1192	1105	310	43	64	98	851	27	3013	87	226	129	.637	0-0	0	94	.652	2.97	3.33

Alex Vesia

Pitches: L Bats: L Pos: RP-41   Ht: 6'1" Wt: 209 Born: 4/11/1996 Age: 26

Year	Team	Lg	G	GS	GF	IP	BFP	H	R	ER	HR	SH	SF	HB	TBB	IBB	SO	WP	W	L	Pct	Sv-Op	Hld	Vel	OPS	ERC	ERA
2021	OkCity	AAA	9	0	2	9.0	32	3	1	1	0	0	0	1	3	0	19	0	0	0	-	2- -	-		.326	0.92	1.00
2020	Mia	NL	5	0	4	4.1	27	7	10	9	3	0	0	0	7	0	5	0	0	1	.000	0-0	1	92	1.319	19.97	18.69
2021	LAD	NL	41	0	7	40.0	161	17	17	10	6	0	2	2	22	3	54	0	3	1	.750	1-2	9	94	.551	2.04	2.25
	2 ML YEARS		46	0	7	44.1	188	24	27	19	9	0	2	2	29	3	59	0	3	2	.600	1-2	10	93	.654	3.27	3.86

Will Vest

Pitches: R Bats: R Pos: RP-32   Ht: 6'0" Wt: 180 Born: 6/6/1995 Age: 27

Year	Team	Lg	G	GS	GF	IP	BFP	H	R	ER	HR	SH	SF	HB	TBB	IBB	SO	WP	W	L	Pct	Sv-Op	Hld	Vel	OPS	ERC	ERA
2021	Toledo	AAA	21	0	10	23.2	103	27	14	14	3	1	0	0	8	0	25	0	1	3	.250	2- -	-		.790	4.86	5.32
2021	Sea	AL	32	0	4	35.0	156	38	25	24	2	1	2	3	18	0	27	3	1	0	1.000	0-0	6	94	.812	5.19	6.17

Matt Vierling

Bats: R Throws: R Pos: PH-14;1B-9;CF-8;LF-7;RF-6   Ht: 6'3" Wt: 205 Born: 9/16/1996 Age: 25

Year	Team	Lg	G	AB	H	2B	3B	HR	(Hm	Rd)	TB	R	RBI	RC	TBB	IBB	SO	HBP	SH	SF	SB	CS	GDP	Avg	OBP	Slg	OPS
2021	Rdng	AA	24	87	30	6	1	6	(-	-)	56	16	16	-	12	0	18	1	0	2	5	1	2	.345	.422	.644	1.065
2021	LV	AAA	56	207	51	6	1	5	(-	-)	74	25	31	-	24	0	47	3	0	3	5	1	3	.246	.329	.357	.687
2021	Phi	NL	34	71	23	3	1	2	(1	1)	34	11	6	11	4	1	20	1	0	1	2	0	1	.324	.364	.479	.843

Ryan Vilade

Bats: R **Throws:** R **Pos:** LF-2;PR-1 **Ht:** 6'2" **Wt:** 226 **Born:** 2/18/1999 **Age:** 23

Year	Team	Lg	G	AB	H	2B	3B	HR	(Hm	Rd)	TB	R	RBI	RC	TBB	IBB	SO	HBP	SH	SF	SB	CS	GDP	Avg	OBP	Slg	OPS
2021	Albq	AAA	112	451	128	27	5	7	(-	-)	186	79	43	-	36	1	88	1	2	5	12	4	10	.284	.335	.412	.747
2021	Col	NL	3	6	0	0	0	0	(0	0)	0	0	0	-	1	0	1	0	0	0	0	0	0	.000	.143	.000	.143

Jonathan Villar

Bats: B **Throws:** R **Pos:** 3B-97;SS-26;PH-18;2B-9;PR-1   vee-YARR **Ht:** 6'0" **Wt:** 233 **Born:** 5/2/1991 **Age:** 31

Year	Team	Lg	G	AB	H	2B	3B	HR	(Hm	Rd)	TB	R	RBI	RC	TBB	IBB	SO	HBP	SH	SF	SB	CS	GDP	Avg	OBP	Slg	OPS
2013	Hou	AL	58	210	51	9	2	1	(0	1)	67	26	8	22	24	1	71	0	7	0	18	8	5	.243	.321	.319	.640
2014	Hou	AL	87	263	55	13	2	7	(3	4)	93	31	27	24	19	1	80	2	4	1	17	4	4	.209	.267	.354	.620
2015	Hou	AL	53	116	33	7	1	2	(0	2)	48	18	11	15	10	0	29	0	1	1	7	2	3	.284	.339	.414	.752
2016	Mil	NL	156	589	168	38	3	19	(6	13)	269	92	63	102	79	4	174	2	5	4	62	18	7	.285	.369	.457	.826
2017	Mil	NL	122	403	97	18	1	11	(7	4)	150	49	40	45	30	1	132	0	2	1	23	8	4	.241	.293	.372	.665
2018	2 Tms		141	466	121	14	1	14	(6	8)	179	54	46	67	41	0	138	4	4	2	35	5	13	.260	.325	.384	.709
2019	Bal	AL	162	642	176	33	5	24	(16	8)	291	111	73	100	61	0	176	4	2	4	40	9	8	.274	.339	.453	.792
2020	2 Tms		52	185	43	5	0	2	(1	1)	54	13	15	15	19	1	54	0	1	2	16	5	2	.232	.301	.292	.593
2021	NYM	NL	142	454	113	18	2	18	(9	9)	189	63	42	52	46	2	132	3	2	0	14	7	6	.249	.322	.416	.738
18	Mil	NL	87	257	67	10	1	6	(2	4)	97	26	22	29	19	0	80	2	0	1	14	2	9	.261	.315	.377	.693
18	Bal	AL	54	209	54	4	0	8	(4	4)	82	28	24	38	22	0	58	3	1	1	21	3	4	.258	.336	.392	.729
20	Mia	NL	30	116	30	4	0	2	(1	1)	40	10	9	9	10	1	32	0	1	0	9	5	2	.259	.315	.345	.660
20	Tor	AL	22	69	13	1	0	0	(0	0)	14	3	6	6	9	0	22	0	0	2	7	0	0	.188	.278	.203	.481
	Postseason		2	2	0	0	0	0	(0	0)	0	1	0	0	0	0	1	0	0	0	1	0	1	.000	.000	.000	.000
9 ML YEARS			973	3328	857	155	17	98	(48	50)	1340	457	325	442	329	10	986	16	25	15	232	66	52	.258	.326	.403	.729

Nick Vincent

Pitches: R **Bats:** R **Pos:** RP-7 **Ht:** 5'10" **Wt:** 185 **Born:** 7/12/1986 **Age:** 35

			HOW MUCH PITCHED					WHAT HE GAVE UP										THE RESULTS								
Year	Team	Lg	G	GS	GF	IP	BFP	H	R	ER	HR	SH	SF	HB	TBB	IBB	SO	WP	W	L	Pct	Sv-Op	Hld	Vel	OPS	ERC	ERA
2021	RdRck	AAA	15	0	3	15.1	74	18	10	7	1	0	1	0	7	0	22	1	0	0	-	0--	-	-	.732	4.69	4.11
2021	StPaul	AAA	24	0	14	31.2	137	27	20	16	8	1	2	4	7	0	38	0	3	1	.750	6--	-	-	.735	3.84	4.55
2012	SD	NL	27	0	3	26.1	105	19	5	5	2	1	0	1	7	0	28	1	2	0	1.000	0-1	5	90	.551	2.13	1.71
2013	SD	NL	45	0	7	46.1	180	33	11	11	1	4	0	2	11	3	49	0	6	3	.667	1-1	10	90	.525	1.67	2.14
2014	SD	NL	63	0	7	55.0	215	44	22	22	5	3	0	2	11	1	62	1	1	2	.333	0-2	20	90	.626	2.39	3.60
2015	SD	NL	26	0	8	23.0	100	25	8	6	0	0	1	0	10	1	22	0	1	0	1.000	0-2	0	90	.698	3.95	2.35
2016	Sea	AL	60	0	15	60.1	247	53	26	25	11	1	1	1	15	5	65	0	4	4	.500	3-9	17	90	.700	3.28	3.73
2017	Sea	AL	69	0	7	64.2	262	62	23	23	3	4	4	0	13	5	50	0	3	3	.500	0-2	29	90	.643	2.67	3.20
2018	Sea	AL	62	1	8	56.1	239	50	28	25	7	1	2	3	15	4	56	0	4	4	.500	0-2	15	90	.662	3.11	3.99
2019	2 Tms	NL	32	1	8	44.2	194	47	23	22	8	0	2	4	12	3	47	0	1	4	.200	0-0	1	89	.785	4.63	4.43
2020	Mia	NL	21	0	8	22.1	92	23	11	11	5	0	0	1	6	0	17	0	1	2	.333	3-3	0	89	.844	4.94	4.43
2021	Min	AL	7	0	1	12.2	47	6	1	1	1	0	0	1	5	0	9	0	0	0	-	0-0	0	89	.499	1.71	0.71
19	SF	NL	18	1	4	30.2	138	36	20	19	7	0	1	3	8	2	30	0	0	2	.000	0-0	0	89	.856	5.67	5.58
19	Phi	NL	14	0	4	14.0	56	11	3	3	1	0	1	1	4	1	17	0	1	2	.333	0-0	1	89	.606	2.56	1.93
	Postseason		1	0	1	1.0	4	1	0	0	0	0	0	0	0	0	1	0	0	0	-	0-0	0	90	1.000	1.95	0.00
10 ML YEARS			412	2	72	411.2	1681	362	158	151	43	14	10	15	105	22	405	2	23	23	.500	7-22	97	90	.661	2.98	3.30

Daniel Vogelbach

Bats: L **Throws:** R **Pos:** 1B-59;PH-36;DH-3   VOH-guhl-back **Ht:** 6'0" **Wt:** 270 **Born:** 12/17/1992 **Age:** 29

Year	Team	Lg	G	AB	H	2B	3B	HR	(Hm	Rd)	TB	R	RBI	RC	TBB	IBB	SO	HBP	SH	SF	SB	CS	GDP	Avg	OBP	Slg	OPS
2021	Nashv	AAA	18	48	15	0	0	3	(-	-)	24	8	8	-	16	0	13	0	0	1	0	0	4	.313	.477	.500	.977
2016	Sea	AL	8	12	1	0	0	0	(0	0)	1	0	0	0	1	0	6	0	0	0	0	0	0	.083	.154	.083	.237
2017	Sea	AL	16	28	6	1	0	0	(0	0)	7	0	2	2	3	0	9	0	0	0	0	0	2	.214	.290	.250	.540
2018	Sea	AL	37	87	18	2	0	4	(2	2)	32	9	13	11	13	0	26	2	0	0	0	0	4	.207	.324	.368	.691
2019	Sea	AL	144	462	96	17	0	30	(12	18)	203	73	76	72	92	2	149	2	0	2	0	0	4	.208	.341	.439	.780
2020	3 Tms		39	115	24	3	0	6	(4	2)	45	16	16	15	20	1	33	1	0	0	0	0	3	.209	.331	.391	.722
2021	Mil	NL	93	215	47	8	0	9	(5	4)	82	30	24	30	43	1	57	0	0	0	0	0	6	.219	.349	.381	.730
20	Sea	AL	18	53	5	1	0	2	(1	1)	12	3	4	3	11	1	13	0	0	0	0	0	1	.094	.250	.226	.476
20	Tor	AL	2	4	0	0	0	0	(0	0)	0	0	0	0	1	0	2	0	0	0	0	0	0	.000	.000	.000	.000
20	Mil	NL	19	58	19	2	0	4	(3	1)	33	13	12	12	8	0	18	1	0	0	0	0	2	.328	.418	.569	.987
	Postseason		2	5	1	1	0	0	(0	0)	2	1	0	0	0	0	2	0	0	0	0	0	0	.200	.200	.400	.600
6 ML YEARS			337	919	192	31	0	49	(23	26)	370	128	131	130	172	4	280	5	0	2	0	0	19	.209	.336	.403	.739

Stephen Vogt

Bats: L **Throws:** R **Pos:** C-63;PH-18;1B-2   VOTE **Ht:** 6'0" **Wt:** 216 **Born:** 11/1/1984 **Age:** 37

Year	Team	Lg	G	AB	H	2B	3B	HR	(Hm	Rd)	TB	R	RBI	RC	TBB	IBB	SO	HBP	SH	SF	SB	CS	GDP	Avg	OBP	Slg	OPS
2012	TB	AL	18	25	0	0	0	0	(0	0)	0	0	0	0	2	0	2	0	0	0	0	0	0	.000	.074	.000	.074
2013	Oak	AL	47	135	34	6	1	4	(3	1)	54	18	16	15	9	1	28	0	2	2	0	1	2	.252	.295	.400	.695
2014	Oak	AL	84	269	75	10	2	9	(4	5)	116	26	35	38	16	2	39	1	0	1	1	0	2	.279	.321	.431	.752
2015	Oak	AL	136	445	116	21	3	18	(5	13)	197	58	71	75	56	6	97	2	0	8	0	2	9	.261	.341	.443	.783
2016	Oak	AL	137	490	123	30	2	14	(4	10)	199	54	56	51	35	3	83	4	0	3	0	0	6	.251	.305	.406	.711
2017	2 Tms		99	279	65	15	1	12	(6	6)	118	25	40	33	21	1	56	0	1	2	1	1	2	.233	.285	.423	.708
2019	SF	NL	99	255	67	24	2	10	(3	7)	125	30	40	42	20	1	66	1	0	4	3	1	1	.263	.314	.490	.804
2020	Ari	NL	26	72	12	5	0	1	(0	1)	20	6	7	5	8	0	18	0	0	0	0	0	0	.167	.247	.278	.525
2021	2 Tms	NL	78	210	41	6	1	7	(3	4)	70	24	25	20	26	2	56	0	1	1	0	0	4	.195	.283	.333	.616

Year Team	Lg	G	AB	H	2B	3B	HR	(Hm	Rd)	TB	R	RBI	RC	TBB	IBB	SO	HBP	SH	SF	SB	CS	GDP	Avg	OBP	Slg	OPS
17 Oak	AL	54	157	34	8	1	4	(1	3)	56	12	20	19	16	1	31	0	0	1	0	1	1	.217	.287	.357	.644
17 Mil	NL	45	122	31	7	0	8	(5	3)	62	13	20	14	5	0	25	0	1	1	0	0	1	.254	.281	.508	.789
21 Ari	NL	52	132	28	6	1	5	(1	4)	51	17	17	16	18	1	36	0	1	0	0	0	2	.212	.307	.386	.693
21 Atl	NL	26	78	13	0	0	2	(2	0)	19	7	8	4	8	1	20	0	0	1	0	0	0	.167	.241	.244	.485
Postseason		6	19	3	0	1	0	(0	0)	5	2	1	1	2	0	8	0	0	0	0	0	0	.158	.238	.263	.501
9 ML YEARS		724	2180	533	117	12	75	(28	47)	899	241	290	279	193	16	445	8	4	22	4	5	25	.244	.305	.412	.718

Luke Voit

Bats: R **Throws:** R **Pos:** 1B-42;DH-13;PH-13 **Ht:** 6'3" **Wt:** 255 **Born:** 2/13/1991 **Age:** 31

Year Team	Lg	G	AB	H	2B	3B	HR	(Hm	Rd)	TB	R	RBI	RC	TBB	IBB	SO	HBP	SH	SF	SB	CS	GDP	Avg	OBP	Slg	OPS
2017 StL	NL	62	114	28	9	0	4	(4	0)	49	18	18	12	7	0	31	0	0	0	0	0	0	.246	.306	.430	.736
2018 2 Tms		47	143	46	5	0	15	(7	8)	96	30	36	40	17	0	43	1	0	0	0	0	3	.322	.398	.671	1.069
2019 NYY	AL	118	429	113	21	1	21	(7	14)	199	72	62	79	71	2	142	9	1	0	0	0	12	.263	.378	.464	.842
2020 NYY	AL	56	213	59	5	0	22	(16	6)	130	41	52	46	17	0	54	3	0	1	0	0	4	.277	.338	.610	.948
2021 NYY	AL	68	213	51	7	1	11	(6	5)	93	26	35	27	21	0	74	7	0	0	0	0	12	.239	.328	.437	.764
18 StL	NL	8	11	2	0	0	1	(1	0)	5	2	3	2	2	0	4	0	0	0	0	0	0	.182	.308	.455	.762
18 NYY	AL	39	132	44	5	0	14	(6	8)	91	28	33	38	15	0	39	1	0	0	0	0	3	.333	.405	.689	1.095
Postseason		12	42	9	3	1	1	(1	0)	17	7	6	7	8	0	13	0	0	0	0	0	0	.214	.340	.405	.745
5 ML YEARS		351	1112	297	47	2	73	(40	33)	567	187	203	204	133	2	344	23	0	2	0	0	35	.267	.357	.510	.867

Anthony Volpe

Bats: R **Throws:** R **Pos:** SS **Ht:** 5'11" **Wt:** 180 **Born:** 4/28/2001 **Age:** 21

Year Team	Lg	G	AB	H	2B	3B	HR	(Hm	Rd)	TB	R	RBI	RC	TBB	IBB	SO	HBP	SH	SF	SB	CS	GDP	Avg	OBP	Slg	OPS
2021 2 Tms	Low	109	412	121	35	6	27	(-	-)	249	113	86	0	78	1	101	18	0	5	33	9	5	.294	.423	.604	1.027

Jason Vosler

Bats: L **Throws:** R **Pos:** 3B-19;PH-17;1B-3;2B-3;LF-2;PR-2;RF-1;DH-1 **Ht:** 6'1" **Wt:** 220 **Born:** 9/6/1993 **Age:** 28

Year Team	Lg	G	AB	H	2B	3B	HR	(Hm	Rd)	TB	R	RBI	RC	TBB	IBB	SO	HBP	SH	SF	SB	CS	GDP	Avg	OBP	Slg	OPS
2021 Scrmto	AAA	67	245	71	14	1	15	(-	-)	132	49	50	-	33	0	42	6	0	6	0	0	1	.290	.379	.539	.918
2021 SF	NL	41	73	13	4	0	3	(1	2)	26	12	9	5	7	1	21	1	0	1	2	0	5	.178	.256	.356	.612

Austin Voth

Pitches: R **Bats:** R **Pos:** RP-48; SP-1 **Ht:** 6'2" **Wt:** 211 **Born:** 6/26/1992 **Age:** 30

	HOW MUCH PITCHED					WHAT HE GAVE UP										THE RESULTS								
Year Team	Lg	G	GS	GF	IP	BFP	H	R	ER	HR	SH	SF	HB	TBB	IBB	SO	WP	W	L	Pct	Sv-Op	Hld	Vel	OPS	ERC	ERA
2018 Was	NL	4	2	0	12.1	55	12	9	9	3	1	1	0	6	0	11	1	1	1	.500	0-0	0	91	.780	5.19	6.57
2019 Was	NL	9	8	0	43.2	174	33	16	16	5	1	2	3	13	2	44	0	2	1	.667	0-0	0	93	.677	2.74	3.30
2020 Was	NL	11	11	0	49.2	225	57	36	35	14	0	0	4	18	2	44	1	2	5	.286	0-0	0	92	.923	6.38	6.34
2021 Was	NL	49	1	8	57.1	248	57	35	34	10	3	2	1	28	5	59	1	4	1	.800	0-5	7	94	.818	4.97	5.34
4 ML YEARS		73	22	8	163.0	702	159	96	94	32	5	5	8	65	9	158	3	9	8	.529	0-5	7	93	.814	4.76	5.19

Joey Votto

VAH-toe

Bats: L **Throws:** R **Pos:** 1B-123;DH-3;PH-3 **Ht:** 6'2" **Wt:** 220 **Born:** 9/10/1983 **Age:** 38

Year Team	Lg	G	AB	H	2B	3B	HR	(Hm	Rd)	TB	R	RBI	RC	TBB	IBB	SO	HBP	SH	SF	SB	CS	GDP	Avg	OBP	Slg	OPS
2007 Cin	NL	24	84	27	7	0	4	(4	0)	46	11	17	17	5	1	15	0	0	0	1	0	0	.321	.360	.548	.907
2008 Cin	NL	151	526	156	32	3	24	(14	10)	266	69	84	91	59	9	102	2	0	2	7	5	7	.297	.368	.506	.874
2009 Cin	NL	131	469	151	38	1	25	(14	11)	266	82	84	99	70	10	106	4	0	1	4	1	8	.322	.414	.567	.981
2010 Cin	NL	150	547	177	36	2	37	(18	19)	328	106	113	132	91	8	125	7	0	3	16	5	11	.324	.424	.600	1.024
2011 Cin	NL	161	599	185	40	3	29	(13	16)	318	101	103	131	110	15	129	4	0	6	8	6	20	.309	.416	.531	.947
2012 Cin	NL	111	374	126	44	0	14	(10	4)	212	59	56	97	94	18	85	5	0	2	5	3	8	.337	.474	.567	1.041
2013 Cin	NL	162	581	177	30	3	24	(11	13)	285	101	73	121	135	19	138	4	0	6	6	3	15	.305	.435	.491	.926
2014 Cin	NL	62	220	56	16	0	6	(6	0)	90	32	23	36	47	2	49	3	0	2	1	1	5	.255	.390	.409	.799
2015 Cin	NL	158	545	171	33	2	29	(14	15)	295	95	80	135	143	15	135	5	0	2	11	3	11	.314	.459	.541	1.000
2016 Cin	NL	158	556	181	34	2	29	(16	13)	306	101	97	130	108	15	120	5	0	8	8	1	16	.326	.434	.550	.985
2017 Cin	NL	162	559	179	34	1	36	(20	16)	323	106	100	139	134	20	83	8	0	6	5	1	16	.320	.454	.578	1.032
2018 Cin	NL	145	503	143	28	2	12	(8	4)	211	67	67	98	108	6	101	9	0	3	2	0	15	.284	.417	.419	.837
2019 Cin	NL	142	525	137	32	1	15	(4	11)	216	79	47	72	76	2	123	4	0	3	5	0	14	.261	.357	.411	.768
2020 Cin	NL	54	186	42	8	0	11	(10	1)	83	32	22	26	37	1	43	0	0	0	0	0	5	.226	.354	.446	.800
2021 Cin	NL	129	448	119	23	1	36	(20	16)	252	73	99	101	77	6	127	4	0	4	1	0	7	.266	.375	.563	.938
Postseason		11	41	10	0	0	0	(0	0)	10	3	1	3	5	1	12	0	0	1	0	0	1	.244	.319	.244	.563
15 ML YEARS		1900	6722	2027	435	21	331	(182	149)	3497	1114	1065	1425	1294	147	1481	64	0	48	80	29	158	.302	.416	.520	.937

Michael Wacha

Pitches: R **Bats:** R **Pos:** SP-23; RP-6
WAHK-ah
Ht: 6'6" **Wt:** 215 **Born:** 7/1/1991 **Age:** 30

Year	Team	Lg	G	GS	GF	IP	BFP	H	R	ER	HR	SH	SF	HB	TBB	IBB	SO	WP	W	L	Pct	Sv-Op	Hld	Vel	OPS	ERC	ERA
2013	StL	NL	15	9	2	64.2	260	52	20	20	5	1	3	0	19	0	65	3	4	1	.800	0-1	0	93	.603	2.52	2.78
2014	StL	NL	19	19	0	107.0	447	95	41	38	6	1	2	5	33	0	94	2	5	6	.455	0-0	0	93	.636	3.00	3.20
2015	StL	NL	30	30	0	181.1	762	162	74	68	19	8	3	6	58	4	153	4	17	7	.708	0-0	0	94	.672	3.28	3.38
2016	StL	NL	27	24	1	138.0	606	159	86	78	15	4	5	1	45	6	114	6	7	7	.500	0-0	0	93	.800	4.66	5.09
2017	StL	NL	30	30	0	165.2	701	170	82	76	17	3	4	3	55	3	158	3	12	9	.571	0-0	0	95	.735	4.07	4.13
2018	StL	NL	15	15	0	84.1	355	68	36	30	9	4	5	2	36	0	71	2	8	2	.800	0-0	0	94	.646	3.24	3.20
2019	StL	NL	29	24	0	126.2	562	143	71	67	26	6	5	3	55	4	104	2	6	7	.462	0-0	0	93	.865	5.88	4.76
2020	NYM	NL	8	7	0	34.0	156	46	26	25	9	0	0	2	7	0	37	0	1	4	.200	0-0	0	94	.951	6.76	6.62
2021	TB	AL	29	23	1	124.2	528	132	73	70	23	1	4	4	31	0	121	5	3	5	.375	0-0	1	94	.784	4.54	5.05
	Postseason		7	6	1	35.1	144	24	16	16	7	0	0	1	16	4	38	0	4	3	.571	0-0	0	94	.694	3.15	4.08
	9 ML YEARS		202	181	4	1026.1	4377	1027	509	472	129	28	31	26	339	17	917	31	63	48	.568	0-1	1	94	.738	4.06	4.14

Brandon Waddell

Pitches: L **Bats:** L **Pos:** RP-9
Ht: 6'3" **Wt:** 180 **Born:** 6/3/1994 **Age:** 28

Year	Team	Lg	G	GS	GF	IP	BFP	H	R	ER	HR	SH	SF	HB	TBB	IBB	SO	WP	W	L	Pct	Sv-Op	Hld	Vel	OPS	ERC	ERA
2021	Memp	AAA	8	0	1	10.0	41	10	3	2	1	0	1	0	3	0	10	0	2	0	1.000	0- -	-		.777	3.80	1.80
2020	Pit	NL	2	0	1	3.1	14	2	1	1	0	0	0	0	3	0	2	0	0	0	-	0-0	0	93	.619	2.03	2.70
2021	3 Tms		9	0	5	9.1	51	14	8	7	2	0	0	0	9	0	7	1	0	1	.000	0-0	0	93	1.070	10.56	6.75
21	Min	AL	4	0	2	4.0	25	10	6	5	2	0	0	0	3	0	1	0	0	1	.000	0-0	0	93	1.429	20.19	11.25
21	Bal	AL	1	0	1	1.0	4	0	0	0	0	0	0	0	1	0	0	0	0	0	-	0-0	0	93	.250	0.95	0.00
21	StL	NL	4	0	2	4.1	22	4	2	2	0	0	0	0	5	0	6	1	0	0	-	0-0	0	93	.762	5.62	4.15
	2 ML YEARS		11	0	6	12.2	65	16	9	8	2	0	0	0	11	0	9	1	0	1	.000	0-0	0	93	.971	7.97	5.68

Konner Wade

Pitches: R **Bats:** L **Pos:** RP-7
Ht: 6'3" **Wt:** 195 **Born:** 12/3/1991 **Age:** 30

Year	Team	Lg	G	GS	GF	IP	BFP	H	R	ER	HR	SH	SF	HB	TBB	IBB	SO	WP	W	L	Pct	Sv-Op	Hld	Vel	OPS	ERC	ERA
2021	Norfolk	AAA	20	6	1	73.0	293	57	28	24	11	1	7	2	18	1	50	1	4	2	.667	0- -	-		.649	2.72	2.96
2021	Bal	AL	7	0	2	12.1	64	23	16	16	3	0	0	0	5	1	11	0	0	0	-	0-0	0	90	1.048	10.70	11.68

Tyler Wade

Bats: L **Throws:** R **Pos:** SS-31;PR-28;3B-27;2B-19;CF-10;LF-8;RF-7;DH-3;PH-2
Ht: 6'1" **Wt:** 188 **Born:** 11/23/1994 **Age:** 27

Year	Team	Lg	G	AB	H	2B	3B	HR	(Hm	Rd)	TB	R	RBI	RC	TBB	IBB	SO	HBP	SH	SF	SB	CS	GDP	Avg	OBP	Slg	OPS
2017	NYY	AL	30	58	9	4	0	0	(0	0)	13	7	2	1	5	0	19	0	0	2	1	1	2	.155	.222	.224	.446
2018	NYY	AL	36	66	11	4	0	1	(0	1)	18	8	5	4	4	0	23	0	0	0	1	0	1	.167	.214	.273	.487
2019	NYY	AL	43	94	23	3	1	2	(2	0)	34	16	11	12	11	0	28	1	2	0	7	0	0	.245	.330	.362	.692
2020	NYY	AL	52	88	15	3	0	3	(3	0)	27	19	10	10	12	0	22	3	1	1	4	1	1	.170	.288	.307	.595
2021	NYY	AL	103	127	34	5	1	0	(0	0)	41	31	5	17	16	1	37	1	0	0	17	6	3	.268	.354	.323	.677
	Postseason		4	0	0	0	0	0	(0	0)	0	1	0	0	1	0	0	0	0	0	0	0	0	-	1.000	-	-
	5 ML YEARS		264	433	92	19	2	6	(5	1)	133	81	33	44	48	1	129	5	3	1	30	8	7	.212	.298	.307	.605

LaMonte Wade Jr.

Bats: L **Throws:** L **Pos:** RF-52;LF-42;1B-31;PH-22;CF-2
lah-MONT
Ht: 6'1" **Wt:** 205 **Born:** 1/1/1994 **Age:** 28

Year	Team	Lg	G	AB	H	2B	3B	HR	(Hm	Rd)	TB	R	RBI	RC	TBB	IBB	SO	HBP	SH	SF	SB	CS	GDP	Avg	OBP	Slg	OPS
2021	Scrmto	AAA	14	45	11	2	0	3	(-	-)	22	12	8	-	14	1	13	0	0	0	0	1	1	.244	.424	.489	.913
2019	Min	AL	26	56	11	2	1	2	(1	1)	21	10	5	9	11	0	9	2	0	0	1	0	0	.196	.348	.375	.723
2020	Min	AL	16	39	9	3	0	0	(0	0)	12	3	1	5	4	0	9	1	1	0	1	0	0	.231	.318	.308	.626
2021	SF	NL	109	336	85	17	3	18	(12	6)	162	52	56	63	33	1	89	5	4	3	6	1	3	.253	.326	.482	.808
	3 ML YEARS		151	431	105	22	4	20	(13	7)	195	65	62	77	48	1	107	8	4	3	7	3	3	.244	.329	.452	.781

Adam Wainwright

Pitches: R **Bats:** R **Pos:** SP-32
Ht: 6'7" **Wt:** 230 **Born:** 8/30/1981 **Age:** 40

Year	Team	Lg	G	GS	GF	IP	BFP	H	R	ER	HR	SH	SF	HB	TBB	IBB	SO	WP	W	L	Pct	Sv-Op	Hld	Vel	OPS	ERC	ERA
2005	StL	NL	2	0	1	2.0	9	2	3	3	1	0	0	0	1	0	0	0	0	0	-	0-0	0	91	.958	7.30	13.50
2006	StL	NL	61	0	10	75.0	309	64	26	26	6	4	1	4	22	2	72	3	2	1	.667	3-5	17	91	.644	2.92	3.12
2007	StL	NL	32	32	0	202.0	882	212	93	83	13	9	5	9	70	4	136	6	14	12	.538	0-0	0	89	.721	4.01	3.70
2008	StL	NL	20	20	0	132.0	544	122	51	47	12	6	4	3	34	1	91	3	11	3	.786	0-0	0	90	.688	3.14	3.20
2009	StL	NL	34	34	0	233.0	970	216	75	68	17	10	5	3	66	1	212	7	19	8	.704	0-0	0	91	.646	3.08	2.63
2010	StL	NL	33	33	0	230.1	910	186	68	62	15	13	6	4	56	2	213	2	20	11	.645	0-0	0	91	.604	2.36	2.42
2012	StL	NL	32	32	0	198.2	831	196	96	87	15	9	6	6	52	3	184	5	14	13	.519	0-0	0	90	.701	3.41	3.94
2013	StL	NL	34	34	0	241.2	956	223	83	79	15	13	2	6	35	2	219	5	19	9	.679	0-0	0	91	.636	2.60	2.94
2014	StL	NL	32	32	0	227.0	898	184	64	60	10	8	3	7	50	5	179	4	20	9	.690	0-0	0	90	.580	2.20	2.38
2015	StL	NL	7	4	2	28.0	111	25	7	5	0	2	0	4	4	0	20	0	2	1	.667	0-0	0	90	.590	1.97	1.61
2016	StL	NL	33	33	0	198.2	847	220	108	102	22	8	9	5	59	4	161	1	13	9	.591	0-0	0	90	.785	4.50	4.62
2017	StL	NL	24	23	0	123.1	546	140	73	70	14	5	1	5	45	4	96	2	12	5	.706	0-0	0	90	.794	4.93	5.11
2018	StL	NL	8	8	0	40.1	181	41	21	20	5	3	2	2	18	1	40	1	2	4	.333	0-0	0	89	.753	4.60	4.46
2019	StL	NL	31	31	0	171.2	745	181	83	80	22	6	5	8	64	2	153	2	14	10	.583	0-0	0	90	.782	4.64	4.19

			HOW MUCH PITCHED					WHAT HE GAVE UP										THE RESULTS							
Year	Team	Lg	G	GS	GF	IP	BFP	H	R	ER	HR	SH	SF	HB	TBB	IBB	SO	WP	W	L	Pct	Sv-Op	Hld	Vel	OPS	ERC	ERA
2020	StL	NL	10	10	0	65.2	262	54	25	23	9	0	1	2	15	0	54	0	5	3	.625	0-0	0	89	.640	2.85	3.15
2021	StL	NL	32	32	0	206.1	828	168	72	70	21	3	1	9	50	3	174	4	17	7	.708	0-0	0	89	.627	2.67	3.05
	Postseason		28	15	9	109.0	443	101	38	35	10	3	2	2	20	1	118	4	4	5	.444	4-5	0	91	.655	2.86	2.89
	16 ML YEARS		425	358	13	2375.2	9829	2234	948	885	197	99	51	73	641	39	2004	45	184	105	.637	3-5	17	90	.679	3.25	3.35

Christian Walker

Bats: R **Throws:** R **Pos:** 1B-107;PH-14;DH-1   **Ht:** 6'0" **Wt:** 208 **Born:** 3/28/1991 **Age:** 31

					BATTING																RUNNING			AVERAGES			
Year	Team	Lg	G	AB	H	2B	3B	HR	(Hm	Rd)	TB	R	RBI	RC	TBB	IBB	SO	HBP	SH	SF	SB	CS	GDP	Avg	OBP	Slg	OPS
2014	Bal	AL	6	18	3	1	0	1	(1	0)	7	1	1	0	1	0	9	0	0	0	0	0	0	.167	.211	.389	.599
2015	Bal	AL	7	9	1	0	0	0	(0	0)	1	0	0	1	3	0	4	0	0	0	0	0	0	.111	.333	.111	.444
2017	Ari	NL	11	12	3	1	0	2	(2	0)	10	2	2	2	1	0	5	2	0	0	0	0	0	.250	.400	.833	1.233
2018	Ari	NL	37	49	8	2	0	3	(2	1)	19	6	6	3	3	0	22	1	0	0	1	0	1	.163	.226	.388	.614
2019	Ari	NL	152	529	137	26	1	29	(16	13)	252	86	73	83	67	6	155	6	0	1	8	1	11	.259	.348	.476	.825
2020	Ari	NL	57	218	59	18	1	7	(5	2)	100	35	34	34	19	0	50	3	0	3	1	1	6	.271	.333	.459	.792
2021	Ari	NL	115	401	98	23	1	10	(3	7)	153	55	46	48	38	1	106	4	0	2	0	0	8	.244	.315	.382	.696
	Postseason		2	1	1	0	0	0	(0	0)	1	0	0		0	0	0	1	0	0	0	0	0	1.000	1.000	1.000	2.000
	7 ML YEARS		385	1236	309	71	3	52	(29	23)	542	185	162	171	132	7	351	16	0	6	10	2	26	.250	.329	.439	.767

Taijuan Walker

Pitches: R **Bats:** R **Pos:** SP-29; RP-1   TIE-wahn   **Ht:** 6'4" **Wt:** 235 **Born:** 8/13/1992 **Age:** 29

			HOW MUCH PITCHED					WHAT HE GAVE UP										THE RESULTS							
Year	Team	Lg	G	GS	GF	IP	BFP	H	R	ER	HR	SH	SF	HB	TBB	IBB	SO	WP	W	L	Pct	Sv-Op	Hld	Vel	OPS	ERC	ERA
2013	Sea	AL	3	3	0	15.0	60	11	7	6	0	0	2	0	4	0	12	0	1	0	1.000	0-0	0	95	.546	1.63	3.60
2014	Sea	AL	8	5	2	38.0	160	31	12	11	2	0	0	3	18	1	34	2	2	3	.400	0-0	0	95	.642	3.34	2.61
2015	Sea	AL	29	29	0	169.2	706	163	92	86	25	4	5	9	40	1	157	4	11	8	.579	0-0	0	94	.717	3.74	4.56
2016	Sea	AL	25	25	0	134.1	573	129	75	63	27	3	3	8	37	2	119	4	8	11	.421	0-0	0	94	.767	4.20	4.22
2017	Ari	NL	28	28	0	157.1	684	148	76	61	17	5	8	9	61	7	146	7	9	9	.500	0-0	0	94	.732	3.85	3.49
2018	Ari	NL	3	3	0	13.0	56	15	5	5	1	0	0	0	5	0	9	0	0	0	-	0-0	0	94	.749	4.88	3.46
2019	Ari	NL	1	1	0	1.0	4	1	0	0	0	0	0	0	0	0	1	0	0	0	-	0-0	0	93	.750	1.95	0.00
2020	2 Tms		11	11	0	53.1	225	43	23	16	8	0	1	4	19	0	50	1	4	3	.571	0-0	0	93	.661	3.42	2.70
2021	NYM	NL	30	29	0	159.0	654	133	84	79	26	2	3	4	55	0	146	5	7	11	.389	0-0	0	94	.694	3.51	4.47
20	Sea	AL	5	5	0	27.0	112	21	13	12	5	0	1	3	8	0	25	0	2	2	.500	0-0	0	93	.676	3.42	4.00
20	Tor	AL	6	6	0	26.1	113	22	10	4	3	0	0	1	11	0	25	1	2	1	.667	0-0	0	93	.647	3.41	1.37
	Postseason		1	1	0	1.0	9	4	4	4	1	0	0	0	2	1	3	0	0	1	.000	0-0	0	93	1.810	44.27	36.00
	9 ML YEARS		138	134	2	740.2	3122	674	374	327	106	14	22	37	239	11	674	23	42	45	.483	0-0	0	94	.714	3.73	3.97

Chad Wallach

Bats: R **Throws:** R **Pos:** C-20;PH-3;PR-1   **Ht:** 6'2" **Wt:** 246 **Born:** 11/4/1991 **Age:** 30

					BATTING																RUNNING			AVERAGES			
Year	Team	Lg	G	AB	H	2B	3B	HR	(Hm	Rd)	TB	R	RBI	RC	TBB	IBB	SO	HBP	SH	SF	SB	CS	GDP	Avg	OBP	Slg	OPS
2021	Jaxnvl	AAA	31	103	21	2	0	7	(-	-)	44	11	17	-	23	0	35	4	0	0	0	0	3	.204	.369	.427	.796
2021	Salt Lk	AAA	35	133	30	7	0	7	(-	-)	58	28	21	-	18	1	41	1	0	1	0	0	7	.226	.320	.436	.756
2017	Cin	NL	6	11	1	0	0	0	(0	0)	1	0	0	0	0	0	5	0	0	0	0	0	0	.091	.091	.091	.182
2018	Mia	NL	15	45	8	1	0	1	(1	0)	12	4	5	4	4	0	23	2	1	0	0	0	0	.178	.275	.267	.541
2019	Mia	NL	19	48	12	3	0	1	(1	0)	18	4	3	5	6	0	12	0	0	0	0	0	0	.250	.333	.375	.708
2020	Mia	NL	15	44	10	3	0	1	(1	0)	16	4	6	7	3	0	12	0	1	0	0	0	1	.227	.277	.364	.640
2021	Mia	NL	23	60	12	2	1	0	(1	0)	16	2	6	3	3	0	32	1	0	2	0	0	1	.200	.242	.267	.509
	Postseason		5	14	1	0	0	0	(0	0)	1	1	0	0	0	0	6	0	0	0	0	0	0	.071	.071	.071	.143
	5 ML YEARS		78	208	43	9	1	3	(3	0)	63	14	20	19	16	0	84	3	2	2	0	0	2	.207	.271	.303	.574

Taylor Walls

Bats: B **Throws:** R **Pos:** SS-49;2B-3;PR-3;3B-1;DH-1;PH-1   **Ht:** 5'10" **Wt:** 185 **Born:** 7/10/1996 **Age:** 25

					BATTING																RUNNING			AVERAGES			
Year	Team	Lg	G	AB	H	2B	3B	HR	(Hm	Rd)	TB	R	RBI	RC	TBB	IBB	SO	HBP	SH	SF	SB	CS	GDP	Avg	OBP	Slg	OPS
2021	Drham	AAA	47	158	40	7	1	8	(-	-)	73	38	28	-	37	2	54	2	0	2	10	3	2	.253	.397	.462	.859
2021	TB	AL	54	152	32	10	0	1	(1	0)	45	15	15	17	23	0	49	0	1	0	4	2	3	.211	.314	.296	.610

Jared Walsh

Bats: L **Throws:** L **Pos:** 1B-128;RF-18;PH-1;PR-1   **Ht:** 6'0" **Wt:** 210 **Born:** 7/30/1993 **Age:** 28

					BATTING																RUNNING			AVERAGES			
Year	Team	Lg	G	AB	H	2B	3B	HR	(Hm	Rd)	TB	R	RBI	RC	TBB	IBB	SO	HBP	SH	SF	SB	CS	GDP	Avg	OBP	Slg	OPS
2019	LAA	AL	34	79	16	5	1	1	(1	0)	26	6	5	8	6	1	35	2	0	0	0	0	0	.203	.276	.329	.605
2020	LAA	AL	32	99	29	4	2	9	(4	5)	64	19	26	21	5	0	15	1	0	3	0	0	0	.293	.324	.646	.971
2021	LAA	AL	144	530	147	34	1	29	(15	14)	270	70	98	97	48	6	152	4	0	3	2	1	7	.277	.340	.509	.850
	3 ML YEARS		210	708	192	43	4	39	(20	19)	360	95	129	126	59	7	202	7	0	6	2	1	7	.271	.331	.508	.839

Donovan Walton

Bats: L **Throws:** R **Pos:** 2B-14;LF-5;3B-2;SS-2;PH-2;PR-2;DH-1   **Ht:** 5'10" **Wt:** 175 **Born:** 5/25/1994 **Age:** 28

Year	Team	Lg	G	AB	H	2B	3B	HR	(Hm	Rd)	TB	R	RBI	RC	TBB	IBB	SO	HBP	SH	SF	SB	CS	GDP	Avg	OBP	Slg	OPS
2021	Tacom	AAA	66	271	84	19	1	13	(-	-)	144	49	59	-	33	1	35	11	0	5	0	3	6	.310	.400	.531	.931
2019	Sea	AL	7	16	3	0	0	0	(0	0)	3	2	2	1	3	0	5	0	0	0	0	1	0	.188	.316	.188	.503
2020	Sea	AL	5	13	2	1	0	0	(0	0)	3	0	3	0	1	0	5	0	0	0	0	1	1	.154	.214	.231	.445
2021	Sea	AL	24	63	13	2	1	2	(1	1)	23	6	7	6	4	0	15	0	2	0	1	0	1	.206	.254	.365	.619
	3 ML YEARS		36	92	18	3	1	2	(1	1)	29	8	12	7	8	0	25	0	2	0	1	2	2	.196	.260	.315	.575

Andrew Wantz

Pitches: R **Bats:** R **Pos:** RP-21   **Ht:** 6'4" **Wt:** 235 **Born:** 10/13/1995 **Age:** 26

Year	Team	Lg	G	GS	GF	IP	BFP	H	R	ER	HR	SH	SF	HB	TBB	IBB	SO	WP	W	L	Pct	Sv-Op	Hld	Vel	OPS	ERC	ERA
2021	Salt Lk	AAA	12	5	2	30.1	116	22	9	6	2	0	0	6			30	2	1	0	1.000	0- -	-	-	.541	1.79	1.78
2021	LAA	AL	21	0	3	27.1	120	23	17	15	5	0	0	3	11	1	38	1	1	0	1.000	0-1	0	93	.711	4.03	4.94

Taylor Ward

Bats: R **Throws:** R **Pos:** RF-51;LF-18;CF-12;C-1;PR-1   **Ht:** 6'1" **Wt:** 200 **Born:** 12/14/1993 **Age:** 28

Year	Team	Lg	G	AB	H	2B	3B	HR	(Hm	Rd)	TB	R	RBI	RC	TBB	IBB	SO	HBP	SH	SF	SB	CS	GDP	Avg	OBP	Slg	OPS
2021	Salt Lk	AAA	13	49	21	9	0	4	(-	-)	42	15	10	-	9	1	12	1	0	0	0	0	0	.429	.525	.857	1.383
2018	LAA	AL	40	135	24	3	0	6	(4	2)	45	14	15	14	9	0	45	3	0	0	2	0	0	.178	.245	.333	.578
2019	LAA	AL	20	42	8	3	0	1	(1	0)	14	4	2	2	6	0	23	0	0	0	1	0	0	.190	.292	.333	.625
2020	LAA	AL	34	94	26	6	2	0	(0	0)	36	16	5	14	8	0	28	0	0	0	2	0	1	.277	.333	.383	.716
2021	LAA	AL	65	208	52	15	0	8	(7	1)	91	33	33	35	20	0	55	6	2	1	1	1	4	.250	.332	.438	.769
	4 ML YEARS		159	479	110	27	2	15	(12	3)	186	67	55	65	43	0	151	9	2	1	5	1	6	.230	.305	.388	.693

Art Warren

Pitches: R **Bats:** R **Pos:** RP-26   **Ht:** 6'3" **Wt:** 230 **Born:** 3/23/1993 **Age:** 29

Year	Team	Lg	G	GS	GF	IP	BFP	H	R	ER	HR	SH	SF	HB	TBB	IBB	SO	WP	W	L	Pct	Sv-Op	Hld	Vel	OPS	ERC	ERA
2021	Lsvlle	AAA	15	0	7	16.0	72	18	10	9	1	0	0	0	5	1	30	4	1	2	.333	2- -	-	-	.708	3.89	5.06
2019	Sea	AL	6	0	2	5.1	21	2	0	0	0	0	0	0	2	0	5	1	1	0	1.000	0-0	1	95	.296	0.81	0.00
2021	Cin	NL	26	0	6	21.0	82	11	3	3	1	1	0	1	8	1	34	0	3	0	1.000	0-0	1	95	.483	1.51	1.29
	2 ML YEARS		32	0	8	26.1	103	13	3	3	1	1	0	1	10	1	39	1	4	0	1.000	0-0	2	95	.444	1.35	1.03

Austin Warren

Pitches: R **Bats:** R **Pos:** RP-16   **Ht:** 6'0" **Wt:** 170 **Born:** 2/5/1996 **Age:** 26

Year	Team	Lg	G	GS	GF	IP	BFP	H	R	ER	HR	SH	SF	HB	TBB	IBB	SO	WP	W	L	Pct	Sv-Op	Hld	Vel	OPS	ERC	ERA
2021	Salt Lk	AAA	22	1	3	36.1	166	42	26	25	5	0	2	2	18	0	45	1	2	3	.400	1- -	-	-	.846	5.95	6.19
2021	LAA	AL	16	0	1	20.1	84	16	5	4	0	0	0	1	5	0	20	0	3	0	1.000	1-1	2	94	.544	1.90	1.77

Spenser Watkins

Pitches: R **Bats:** R **Pos:** SP-10; RP-6   **Ht:** 6'2" **Wt:** 185 **Born:** 8/27/1992 **Age:** 29

Year	Team	Lg	G	GS	GF	IP	BFP	H	R	ER	HR	SH	SF	HB	TBB	IBB	SO	WP	W	L	Pct	Sv-Op	Hld	Vel	OPS	ERC	ERA
2021	Norfolk	AAA	8	6	0	35.2	147	28	16	14	6	2	2	0	11	0	30	3	1	2	.333	0- -	-	-	.678	2.93	3.53
2021	Bal	AL	16	10	4	54.2	255	74	50	49	14	1	3	2	19	0	35	4	2	7	.222	0-0	0	91	.970	7.33	8.07

Tony Watson

Pitches: L **Bats:** L **Pos:** RP-62   **Ht:** 6'3" **Wt:** 224 **Born:** 5/30/1985 **Age:** 37

Year	Team	Lg	G	GS	GF	IP	BFP	H	R	ER	HR	SH	SF	HB	TBB	IBB	SO	WP	W	L	Pct	Sv-Op	Hld	Vel	OPS	ERC	ERA
2011	Pit	NL	43	0	6	41.0	174	34	18	18	6	2	1	1	20	4	37	0	2	2	.500	0-1	10	91	.711	3.75	3.95
2012	Pit	NL	68	0	10	53.1	215	37	21	20	5	2	2	1	23	1	53	1	5	2	.714	0-2	16	94	.623	2.62	3.38
2013	Pit	NL	67	0	14	71.2	280	51	19	19	5	3	1	6	12	1	54	2	3	1	.750	2-4	22	94	.544	1.88	2.39
2014	Pit	NL	78	0	3	77.1	305	64	16	14	5	5	3	6	15	0	81	0	10	2	.833	2-9	34	94	.613	2.54	1.63
2015	Pit	NL	77	0	4	75.1	293	55	17	16	3	1	3	4	17	1	62	1	4	1	.800	1-3	41	94	.525	1.92	1.91
2016	Pit	NL	70	0	27	67.2	272	52	26	23	10	4	3	3	20	1	58	0	2	5	.286	15-20	23	94	.672	3.06	3.06
2017	2 Tms	NL	71	0	23	66.2	291	72	26	25	9	5	2	5	20	7	53	0	7	4	.636	10-18	14	94	.764	4.50	3.38
2018	SF	NL	72	0	10	66.0	261	54	19	19	4	2	4	1	14	3	72	0	4	6	.400	0-4	32	92	.599	2.21	2.59
2019	SF	NL	60	0	4	54.0	231	56	26	25	9	2	0	5	12	1	41	1	2	2	.500	0-3	25	93	.757	4.36	4.17
2020	SF	NL	21	0	4	18.0	73	13	8	5	3	0	1	1	3	0	15	0	1	0	1.000	2-2	10	90	.571	2.24	2.50
2021	2 Tms	NL	62	0	4	57.1	225	40	26	25	4	0	0	0	18	1	44	0	7	4	.636	0-3	19	92	.543	2.03	3.92
17	Pit	NL	47	0	22	46.2	209	57	20	19	7	3	2	3	14	4	35	0	5	3	.625	10-17	6	93	.824	5.45	3.66
17	LAD	NL	24	0	1	20.0	82	15	6	6	2	2	0	2	6	3	18	0	2	1	.667	0-1	8	94	.607	2.52	2.70
21	LAA	AL	36	0	4	33.0	135	25	18	17	3	0	0	0	14	1	25	0	3	3	.500	0-3	12	92	.595	2.79	4.64
21	SF	NL	26	0	0	24.1	90	15	8	8	1	0	0	0	4	0	19	0	4	1	.800	0-0	7	93	.467	1.26	2.96
	Postseason		16	0	0	12.0	48	9	4	3	1	0	0	2	2	0	5	0	2	0	1.000	0-0	4	94	.566	2.43	2.25
	11 ML YEARS		689	0	109	648.1	2620	528	222	209	63	27	18	33	174	20	570	5	47	29	.618	32-69	246	93	.630	2.74	2.90

Ryan Weathers

Pitches: L Bats: R Pos: SP-18; RP-12   Ht: 6'1" Wt: 230 Born: 12/17/1999 Age: 22

Year Team	Lg	G	GS	GF	IP	BFP	H	R	ER	HR	SH	SF	HB	TBB	IBB	SO	WP	W	L	Pct	Sv-Op	Hld	Vel	OPS	ERC	ERA
2021 SD	NL	30	18	1	94.2	401	101	57	56	20	5	1	3	30	1	72	2	4	7	.364	1-1	0	94	.836	5.15	5.32
Postseason		1	0	0	1.1	6	0	0	0	0	0	0	0	2	0	1	0	0	0	-	0-0	0	95	.333	1.96	0.00

Luke Weaver

Pitches: R Bats: R Pos: SP-13   Ht: 6'2" Wt: 183 Born: 8/21/1993 Age: 28

Year Team	Lg	G	GS	GF	IP	BFP	H	R	ER	HR	SH	SF	HB	TBB	IBB	SO	WP	W	L	Pct	Sv-Op	Hld	Vel	OPS	ERC	ERA
2016 StL	NL	9	8	0	36.1	167	46	29	23	7	2	3	2	12	0	45	1	1	4	.200	0-0	0	92	.870	6.23	5.70
2017 StL	NL	13	10	0	60.1	252	59	27	26	7	1	1	1	17	1	72	0	7	2	.778	0-0	0	93	.699	3.66	3.88
2018 StL	NL	30	25	3	136.1	609	150	83	75	19	9	1	3	54	2	121	3	7	11	.389	0-0	0	94	.786	4.93	4.95
2019 Ari	NL	12	12	0	64.1	260	55	22	21	6	0	1	3	14	1	69	0	4	3	.571	0-0	0	94	.645	2.73	2.94
2020 Ari	NL	12	12	0	52.0	236	63	39	38	10	0	1	1	18	0	55	0	1	9	.100	0-0	0	94	.871	5.78	6.58
2021 Ari	NL	13	13	0	65.2	275	58	34	31	11	3	1	1	20	3	62	0	3	6	.333	0-0	0	94	.761	3.45	4.25
6 ML YEARS		89	80	3	415.0	1799	431	234	214	60	15	8	11	135	7	424	4	23	35	.397	0-0	0	94	.768	4.35	4.64

Jacob Webb

Pitches: R Bats: R Pos: RP-34   Ht: 6'2" Wt: 210 Born: 8/15/1993 Age: 28

Year Team	Lg	G	GS	GF	IP	BFP	H	R	ER	HR	SH	SF	HB	TBB	IBB	SO	WP	W	L	Pct	Sv-Op	Hld	Vel	OPS	ERC	ERA
2021 Gwnntt	AAA	24	0	19	24.0	99	17	9	8	2	1	2	1	7	0	34	2	1	2	.333	6--	-	-	.573	2.13	3.00
2019 Atl	NL	36	0	12	32.1	131	24	10	5	4	1	0	1	12	0	28	3	4	0	1.000	2-4	9	95	.661	2.89	1.39
2020 Atl	NL	8	0	4	10.0	40	7	2	0	0	0	0	0	5	1	10	0	0	0	-	0-0	0	94	.529	2.16	0.00
2021 Atl	NL	34	0	15	34.1	153	38	22	16	4	1	1	1	14	4	33	3	5	4	.556	1-2	0	94	.790	4.74	4.19
Postseason		3	0	0	3.0	16	5	3	3	1	0	0	1	1	0	6	0	0	0	-	0-0	0	95	1.080	11.45	9.00
3 ML YEARS		78	0	31	76.2	324	69	34	21	8	2	1	2	31	5	71	6	9	4	.692	3-6	9	95	.706	3.59	2.47

Logan Webb

Pitches: R Bats: R Pos: SP-26; RP-1   Ht: 6'1" Wt: 220 Born: 11/18/1996 Age: 25

Year Team	Lg	G	GS	GF	IP	BFP	H	R	ER	HR	SH	SF	HB	TBB	IBB	SO	WP	W	L	Pct	Sv-Op	Hld	Vel	OPS	ERC	ERA
2019 SF	NL	8	8	0	39.2	174	44	25	23	5	0	1	1	14	0	37	4	2	3	.400	0-0	0	93	.795	4.81	5.22
2020 SF	NL	13	11	0	54.1	246	61	38	33	4	0	1	7	24	1	46	3	3	4	.429	0-0	0	93	.806	5.31	5.47
2021 SF	NL	27	26	0	148.1	596	128	53	50	18	3	3	8	36	0	158	2	11	3	.786	0-0	1	93	.622	2.76	3.03
3 ML YEARS		48	45	0	242.1	1016	233	116	106	18	3	5	16	74	1	241	9	16	10	.615	0-0	1	93	.695	3.62	3.94

Tyler Webb

Pitches: L Bats: L Pos: RP-22   Ht: 6'5" Wt: 240 Born: 7/20/1990 Age: 31

Year Team	Lg	G	GS	GF	IP	BFP	H	R	ER	HR	SH	SF	HB	TBB	IBB	SO	WP	W	L	Pct	Sv-Op	Hld	Vel	OPS	ERC	ERA
2021 Memp	AAA	18	0	3	21.2	98	17	15	14	5	0	0	2	14	0	32	1	0	2	.000	0--	-	-	.727	5.06	5.82
2017 2 Tms		9	0	3	8.0	36	9	5	5	2	0	0	0	5	1	8	0	0	0	-	0-1	0	91	.905	6.96	5.63
2018 2 Tms	NL	22	0	5	20.1	90	22	15	10	3	1	0	1	9	2	15	0	0	1	.000	0-0	0	90	.828	5.17	4.43
2019 StL	NL	65	0	11	55.0	221	33	23	23	7	2	2	2	23	3	48	2	2	1	.667	1-1	8	90	.593	2.29	3.76
2020 StL	NL	21	0	5	21.2	87	17	5	5	2	1	1	0	7	0	19	1	1	1	.500	1-3	2	90	.600	2.62	2.08
2021 StL	NL	22	0	4	16.1	92	22	26	24	1	1	1	0	19	1	14	1	0	0	-	0-0	2	91	.887	8.55	13.22
17 NYY	AL	7	0	2	6.0	23	3	3	3	1	0	0	0	4	0	5	0	0	0	-	0-0	0	91	.673	3.11	4.50
17 Mil	NL	2	0	1	2.0	13	6	2	2	1	0	0	0	1	1	3	0	0	0	-	0-1	0	92	1.288	21.60	9.00
18 SD	NL	4	0	1	5.0	24	6	7	7	2	0	0	0	3	0	4	0	0	1	.000	0-0	0	89	1.042	8.40	12.60
18 StL	NL	18	0	4	15.1	66	16	8	3	1	1	0	1	6	2	11	0	0	0	-	0-0	0	90	.750	4.17	1.76
Postseason		6	0	1	4.0	19	5	4	3	0	0	0	1	1	1	5	0	0	0	-	0-0	0	91	.721	4.53	6.75
5 ML YEARS		139	0	28	121.1	526	103	74	67	15	5	4	3	63	7	104	4	3	3	.500	2-5	12	90	.706	3.84	4.97

Ryan Weber

Pitches: R Bats: R Pos: RP-4   Ht: 6'1" Wt: 175 Born: 8/12/1990 Age: 31

Year Team	Lg	G	GS	GF	IP	BFP	H	R	ER	HR	SH	SF	HB	TBB	IBB	SO	WP	W	L	Pct	Sv-Op	Hld	Vel	OPS	ERC	ERA
2021 Wrcstr	AAA	7	6	0	35.0	147	35	22	18	5	1	1	3	10	0	33	1	2	2	.500	0--	-	-	.753	4.36	4.63
2021 Tacom	AAA	9	9	0	54.1	213	49	24	22	7	0	1	2	2	0	53	1	4	2	.667	0--	-	-	.643	2.49	3.64
2015 Atl	NL	5	5	0	28.1	109	25	15	15	3	0	0	2	6	0	19	0	0	3	.000	0-0	0	90	.699	3.26	4.76
2016 Atl	NL	16	2	6	36.1	157	46	22	22	7	1	0	2	5	2	23	1	1	1	.500	0-1	0	91	.877	5.40	5.45
2017 Sea	AL	1	1	0	3.2	14	3	1	1	0	0	0	0	0	0	0	0	0	0	-	0-0	0	90	.500	1.32	2.45
2018 TB	AL	2	0	0	5.1	25	5	5	3	0	0	1	1	2	0	1	0	0	1	.000	0-0	0	89	.701	3.36	5.06
2019 Bos	AL	18	3	8	40.2	185	48	25	23	5	1	0	3	8	0	29	2	4	4	.333	0-0	0	89	.789	4.63	5.09
2020 Bos	AL	17	5	3	43.0	185	44	23	21	8	1	1	3	14	0	27	1	1	3	.250	0-0	5	89	.807	4.84	4.40
2021 3 Tms		4	0	3	9.2	45	15	13	13	5	0	1	1	4	0	8	0	0	0	-	0-0	0	89	1.265	12.59	12.10
21 Bos	AL	1	0	0	5.2	30	13	11	11	4	0	1	0	2	0	7	0	0	0	-	0-0	0	89	1.500	19.62	17.47
21 Mil	NL	1	0	1	1.0	3	1	0	0	0	0	0	0	0	0	1	0	0	0	-	0-0	0	89	.667	7.20	0.00
21 Sea	AL	2	0	2	3.0	12	1	2	2	1	0	0	1	2	0	1	0	0	0	-	0-0	0	89	.778	4.68	6.00
7 ML YEARS		63	16	20	167.0	716	186	104	98	28	3	3	12	39	2	107	4	4	12	.250	0-1	5	89	.819	4.86	5.28

Jordan Weems

Pitches: R Bats: L Pos: RP-7
Ht: 6'3" Wt: 175 Born: 11/7/1992 Age: 29

Year	Team	Lg	G	GS	GF	IP	BFP	H	R	ER	HR	SH	SF	HB	TBB	IBB	SO	WP	W	L	Pct	Sv-Op	Hld	Vel	OPS	ERC	ERA
2021	LsVgs	AAA	15	0	8	14.2	66	17	12	12	6	0	0	2	6	0	17	1	0	2	.000	1--	-	-	1.086	8.30	7.36
2021	Reno	AAA	15	0	6	13.2	60	15	11	11	3	0	1	0	8	0	9	0	1	1	.500	0--	-	-	.887	6.65	7.24
2020	Oak	AL	9	0	4	14.0	58	10	5	5	1	0	1	0	7	0	18	2	0	0	-	0-0	0	95	.593	2.74	3.21
2021	2 Tms		7	0	3	5.2	30	6	10	10	2	0	0	1	6	1	7	1	0	1	.000	0-1	0	95	1.086	9.73	15.88
21	Oak	AL	5	0	3	4.1	18	2	3	3	1	0	0	0	3	0	4	0	0	0	-	0-0	0	95	.678	3.11	6.23
21	Ari	NL	2	0	0	1.1	12	4	7	7	1	0	0	1	3	1	3	1	0	1	.000	0-1	0	95	1.792	38.10	47.25
	Postseason		1	0	0	0.0	3	2	2	2	0	0	0	0	1	0	0	0	0	0	-	0-0	0	95	2.000	-	-
	2 ML YEARS		16	0	7	19.2	88	16	15	15	3	0	1	1	13	1	25	3	0	1	.000	0-1	0	95	.752	4.51	6.86

Patrick Weigel

Pitches: R Bats: R Pos: RP-3
Ht: 6'6" Wt: 240 Born: 7/8/1994 Age: 27

Year	Team	Lg	G	GS	GF	IP	BFP	H	R	ER	HR	SH	SF	HB	TBB	IBB	SO	WP	W	L	Pct	Sv-Op	Hld	Vel	OPS	ERC	ERA
2021	Nashv	AAA	36	1	6	43.1	216	47	40	35	6	3	1	3	38	1	48	9	2	1	.667	2--	-	-	.885	7.27	7.27
2020	Atl	NL	1	0	0	0.2	7	2	2	2	0	0	1	0	3	0	0	1	0	0	-	0-0	0	94	1.714	37.18	27.00
2021	Mil	NL	3	0	1	4.0	21	4	2	2	1	0	0	1	4	0	9	1	0	0	-	0-0	0	94	.866	8.80	4.50
	2 ML YEARS		4	0	1	4.2	28	6	4	4	1	0	1	1	7	0	9	2	0	0	-	0-0	0	94	1.026	12.58	7.71

Colton Welker

Bats: R Throws: R Pos: PH-12;3B-5;1B-2
Ht: 6'1" Wt: 235 Born: 10/9/1997 Age: 24

Year	Team	Lg	G	AB	H	2B	3B	HR	(Hm	Rd)	TB	R	RBI	RC	TBB	IBB	SO	HBP	SH	SF	SB	CS	GDP	Avg	OBP	Slg	OPS
2021	Albq	AAA	23	84	24	5	1	3	(-	-)	40	13	18	-	12	0	20	1	0	1	0	0	0	.286	.378	.476	.854
2021	Col	NL	19	37	7	1	0	0	(0	0)	8	7	2	2	3	0	11	0	0	0	0	0	1	.189	.250	.216	.466

Alexander Wells

Pitches: L Bats: L Pos: SP-8; RP-3
Ht: 6'1" Wt: 195 Born: 2/27/1997 Age: 25

Year	Team	Lg	G	GS	GF	IP	BFP	H	R	ER	HR	SH	SF	HB	TBB	IBB	SO	WP	W	L	Pct	Sv-Op	Hld	Vel	OPS	ERC	ERA
2021	Norfolk	AAA	13	10	1	54.2	219	49	23	20	6	0	0	0	7	0	48	0	6	3	.667	0--	-	-	.622	2.53	3.29
2021	Bal	AL	11	8	2	42.2	197	53	32	32	10	0	1	3	16	0	26	0	2	3	.400	0-0	0	89	.885	6.71	6.75

Tyler Wells

Pitches: R Bats: R Pos: RP-44
Ht: 6'8" Wt: 255 Born: 8/26/1994 Age: 27

Year	Team	Lg	G	GS	GF	IP	BFP	H	R	ER	HR	SH	SF	HB	TBB	IBB	SO	WP	W	L	Pct	Sv-Op	Hld	Vel	OPS	ERC	ERA
2021	Bal	AL	44	0	18	57.0	224	40	27	26	9	1	2	1	12	0	65	1	2	3	.400	4-7	1	95	.603	2.20	4.11

J.B. Wendelken

Pitches: R Bats: R Pos: RP-46
Ht: 6'1" Wt: 242 Born: 3/24/1993 Age: 29

Year	Team	Lg	G	GS	GF	IP	BFP	H	R	ER	HR	SH	SF	HB	TBB	IBB	SO	WP	W	L	Pct	Sv-Op	Hld	Vel	OPS	ERC	ERA
2016	Oak	AL	8	0	3	12.2	64	18	15	14	3	0	0	0	9	0	12	2	0	0	-	0-0	0	93	.931	9.17	9.95
2018	Oak	AL	13	0	3	16.2	62	8	1	1	1	0	0	0	5	0	14	1	0	0	-	0-0	1	95	.438	1.20	0.54
2019	Oak	AL	27	0	4	32.2	131	21	14	13	2	1	1	2	9	2	34	2	3	1	.750	0-1	9	95	.543	1.69	3.58
2020	Oak	AL	21	0	6	25.0	106	17	8	5	2	0	1	0	11	0	31	2	1	1	.500	0-0	2	95	.546	2.30	1.80
2021	2 Tms		46	0	15	43.2	194	44	24	21	4	0	0	0	22	3	39	4	4	3	.571	2-3	6	94	.712	4.32	4.33
21	Oak	AL	26	0	6	25.0	117	29	15	12	2	0	0	0	13	2	26	4	2	1	.667	0-1	2	94	.734	5.05	4.32
21	Ari	NL	20	0	9	18.2	77	15	9	9	2	0	0	0	9	1	13	0	2	2	.500	2-2	4	95	.679	3.37	4.34
	Postseason		4	0	0	4.2	21	5	6	2	1	0	0	0	1	0	4	0	0	1	.000	0-1	1	94	.736	4.17	3.86
	5 ML YEARS		115	0	31	130.2	557	108	62	54	12	1	2	2	56	5	130	11	8	5	.615	2-4	10	94	.634	3.13	3.72

Joey Wendle

Bats: L Throws: R Pos: 3B-107;SS-25;2B-16;PH-7;PR-5
Ht: 6'1" Wt: 195 Born: 4/26/1990 Age: 32

Year	Team	Lg	G	AB	H	2B	3B	HR	(Hm	Rd)	TB	R	RBI	RC	TBB	IBB	SO	HBP	SH	SF	SB	CS	GDP	Avg	OBP	Slg	OPS
2016	Oak	AL	28	96	25	1	0	1	(0	1)	29	11	11	10	6	0	16	0	0	2	2	0	3	.260	.298	.302	.600
2017	Oak	AL	8	13	4	1	0	1	(0	1)	8	3	5	4	1	1	3	0	0	0	0	0	0	.308	.357	.615	.973
2018	TB	AL	139	487	146	33	6	7	(2	5)	212	62	61	70	37	4	96	9	2	10	16	4	11	.300	.354	.435	.789
2019	TB	AL	75	238	55	13	2	3	(2	1)	81	32	19	23	14	0	47	0	3	0	8	3	4	.231	.293	.340	.633
2020	TB	AL	50	168	48	9	2	4	(1	3)	73	24	17	24	10	1	35	0	0	1	8	2	1	.286	.342	.435	.777
2021	TB	AL	136	460	122	31	4	11	(2	9)	194	73	54	59	28	4	113	10	0	3	8	6	9	.265	.319	.422	.741
	Postseason		25	68	13	3	0	0	(0	0)	16	9	6	3	3	0	21	1	0	1	1	0	3	.191	.233	.235	.468
	6 ML YEARS		436	1462	400	88	14	27	(7	20)	597	205	167	190	96	10	310	32	2	19	42	15	28	.274	.328	.408	.736

Zack Wheeler

Pitches: R **Bats:** L **Pos:** SP-32   **Ht:** 6'4" **Wt:** 195 **Born:** 5/30/1990 **Age:** 32

		HOW MUCH PITCHED					WHAT HE GAVE UP											THE RESULTS							
Year	Team	Lg	G	GS	GF	IP	BFP	H	R	ER	HR	SH	SF	HB	TBB	IBB	SO	WP	W	L	Pct	Sv-Op	Hld	Vel	OPS	ERC	ERA
2013	NYM	NL	17	17	0	100.0	431	90	42	38	10	3	7	4	46	2	84	6	7	5	.583	0-0	0	94	.696	3.88	3.42
2014	NYM	NL	32	32	0	185.1	794	167	84	73	14	5	3	11	79	3	187	9	11	11	.500	0-0	0	95	.678	3.68	3.54
2017	NYM	NL	17	17	0	86.1	386	97	53	50	15	0	1	3	40	1	81	1	3	7	.300	0-0	0	95	.828	5.81	5.21
2018	NYM	NL	29	29	0	182.1	744	150	69	67	14	8	4	9	55	0	179	2	12	7	.632	0-0	0	96	.611	2.81	3.31
2019	NYM	NL	31	31	0	195.1	828	196	93	86	22	8	7	2	50	4	195	5	11	8	.579	0-0	0	97	.694	3.57	3.96
2020	Phi	NL	11	11	0	71.0	288	67	26	23	3	1	0	7	16	2	53	0	4	2	.667	0-0	0	97	.662	3.16	2.92
2021	Phi	NL	32	32	0	213.1	849	169	72	66	16	7	3	8	46	1	247	6	14	10	.583	0-0	0	97	.586	2.29	2.78
	7 ML YEARS		169	169	0	1033.2	4320	936	439	403	94	32	25	44	332	13	1026	29	62	50	.554	0-0	0	96	.665	3.35	3.51

Eli White

Bats: R **Throws:** R **Pos:** LF-30;CF-22;RF-11;PR-5;2B-3;DH-1   **Ht:** 6'3" **Wt:** 195 **Born:** 6/26/1994 **Age:** 28

						BATTING															RUNNING			AVERAGES			
Year	Team	Lg	G	AB	H	2B	3B	HR	(Hm	Rd)	TB	R	RBI	RC	TBB	IBB	SO	HBP	SH	SF	SB	CS	GDP	Avg	OBP	Slg	OPS
2021	RdRck	AAA	20	67	23	2	1	3	(-	-)	36	19	11	-	12	0	20	1	0	0	3	1	0	.343	.450	.537	.987
2020	Tex	AL	19	48	9	2	0	0	(0	0)	11	5	3	2	3	0	16	0	0	1	1	1	0	.188	.231	.229	.460
2021	Tex	AL	64	198	35	6	1	6	(1	5)	61	26	15	14	18	0	66	4	0	0	4	3	2	.177	.259	.308	.567
	2 ML YEARS		83	246	44	8	1	6	(1	5)	72	31	18	16	21	0	82	4	0	1	5	4	2	.179	.254	.293	.546

Evan White

Bats: R **Throws:** L **Pos:** 1B-30   **Ht:** 6'3" **Wt:** 220 **Born:** 4/26/1996 **Age:** 26

						BATTING															RUNNING			AVERAGES			
Year	Team	Lg	G	AB	H	2B	3B	HR	(Hm	Rd)	TB	R	RBI	RC	TBB	IBB	SO	HBP	SH	SF	SB	CS	GDP	Avg	OBP	Slg	OPS
2020	Sea	AL	54	182	32	7	0	8	(2	6)	63	19	26	22	18	0	84	1	0	1	1	2	3	.176	.252	.346	.599
2021	Sea	AL	30	97	14	3	0	2	(1	1)	23	8	9	5	6	0	31	1	0	0	0	0	1	.144	.202	.237	.439
	2 ML YEARS		84	279	46	10	0	10	(3	7)	86	27	35	27	24	0	115	2	0	1	1	2	4	.165	.235	.308	.544

Mitch White

Pitches: R **Bats:** R **Pos:** RP-17; SP-4   **Ht:** 6'3" **Wt:** 210 **Born:** 12/28/1994 **Age:** 27

		HOW MUCH PITCHED					WHAT HE GAVE UP											THE RESULTS							
Year	Team	Lg	G	GS	GF	IP	BFP	H	R	ER	HR	SH	SF	HB	TBB	IBB	SO	WP	W	L	Pct	Sv-Op	Hld	Vel	OPS	ERC	ERA
2021	OkCity	AAA	10	7	0	32.0	135	28	9	6	1	0	0	0	12	0	39	2	1	0	1.000	0--	-	-	.613	2.81	1.69
2020	LAD	NL	2	0	2	3.0	11	1	0	0	0	0	0	0	1	0	2	0	1	0	1.000	0-0	0	94	.282	0.69	0.00
2021	LAD	NL	21	4	6	46.2	197	38	28	19	6	1	2	0	17	1	49	3	1	3	.250	0-2	0	95	.637	3.00	3.66
	2 ML YEARS		23	4	8	49.2	208	39	28	19	6	1	2	0	18	1	51	3	2	3	.400	0-2	0	94	.618	2.80	3.44

Kodi Whitley

Pitches: R **Bats:** R **Pos:** RP-25   **Ht:** 6'3" **Wt:** 220 **Born:** 2/21/1995 **Age:** 27

		HOW MUCH PITCHED					WHAT HE GAVE UP											THE RESULTS							
Year	Team	Lg	G	GS	GF	IP	BFP	H	R	ER	HR	SH	SF	HB	TBB	IBB	SO	WP	W	L	Pct	Sv-Op	Hld	Vel	OPS	ERC	ERA
2021	Sprgfld	AA	6	1	1	4.2	22	5	8	7	1	0	1	0	3	0	8	0	1	2	.333	0--	-	-	.919	6.25	13.50
2021	Memp	AAA	12	0	9	16.0	66	11	4	3	1	0	1	1	7	0	21	0	3	0	1.000	3--	-	-	.586	2.55	1.69
2020	StL	NL	4	0	1	4.2	17	2	1	1	1	0	0	0	1	0	5	0	0	0	-	0-0	0	94	.489	1.34	1.93
2021	StL	NL	25	0	6	25.1	101	15	8	7	1	0	2	0	12	0	27	1	0	0	-	0-0	4	94	.497	1.90	2.49
	Postseason		1	0	1	0.1	2	1	1	1	1	0	0	0	0	0	0	0	0	0	-	0-0	0	94	2.500	47.50	27.00
	2 ML YEARS		29	0	7	30.0	118	17	9	8	2	0	2	0	13	0	32	1	0	0	-	0-0	4	94	.497	1.82	2.40

Garrett Whitlock

Pitches: R **Bats:** R **Pos:** RP-46   **Ht:** 6'5" **Wt:** 225 **Born:** 6/11/1996 **Age:** 26

		HOW MUCH PITCHED					WHAT HE GAVE UP											THE RESULTS							
Year	Team	Lg	G	GS	GF	IP	BFP	H	R	ER	HR	SH	SF	HB	TBB	IBB	SO	WP	W	L	Pct	Sv-Op	Hld	Vel	OPS	ERC	ERA
2021	Bos	AL	46	0	11	73.1	298	64	22	16	6	0	3	3	17	2	81	3	8	4	.667	2-5	14	96	.631	2.77	1.96

Rowan Wick

Pitches: R **Bats:** L **Pos:** RP-22   **Ht:** 6'3" **Wt:** 234 **Born:** 11/9/1992 **Age:** 29

		HOW MUCH PITCHED					WHAT HE GAVE UP											THE RESULTS							
Year	Team	Lg	G	GS	GF	IP	BFP	H	R	ER	HR	SH	SF	HB	TBB	IBB	SO	WP	W	L	Pct	Sv-Op	Hld	Vel	OPS	ERC	ERA
2021	Iowa	AAA	5	0	1	4.1	22	6	5	5	0	0	0	0	3	1	8	1	0	0	-	0--	-	-	.830	6.09	10.38
2018	SD	NL	10	0	3	8.1	38	13	6	6	1	0	0	0	1	0	7	0	0	1	.000	0-0	0	95	.936	6.41	6.48
2019	ChC	NL	31	0	7	33.1	140	22	13	9	0	1	0	3	16	1	35	0	2	0	1.000	2-2	5	96	.528	2.18	2.43
2020	ChC	NL	19	0	6	17.1	74	18	6	6	1	0	0	0	6	1	20	0	1	0	1.000	4-4	5	95	.721	3.71	3.12
2021	ChC	NL	22	0	8	23.0	100	17	12	11	1	0	1	1	14	0	29	1	0	1	.000	5-8	2	95	.576	3.18	4.30
	4 ML YEARS		82	0	24	82.0	352	70	37	32	3	1	1	4	37	2	91	1	2	3	.400	11-14	12	95	.632	3.16	3.51

Taylor Widener

Pitches: R **Bats:** L **Pos:** SP-13; RP-10   **Ht:** 6'0" **Wt:** 203 **Born:** 10/24/1994 **Age:** 27

Year	Team	Lg	G	GS	GF	IP	BFP	H	R	ER	HR	SH	SF	HB	TBB	IBB	SO	WP	W	L	Pct	Sv-Op	Hld	Vel	OPS	ERC	ERA
2020	Ari	NL	12	0	4	20.0	88	14	10	10	5	0	0	3	12	1	22	0	0	1	.000	0-0	-	95	.782	4.73	4.50
2021	Ari	NL	23	13	0	70.1	319	65	38	34	14	3	2	7	37	3	73	1	0	2	.667	0-0	1	93	.800	5.11	4.35
2 ML YEARS			35	13	4	90.1	407	79	48	44	19	3	2	10	49	4	95	1	2	2	.500	0-0	2	93	.796	5.03	4.38

Brad Wieck

Pitches: L **Bats:** L **Pos:** RP-15   **Ht:** 6'8" **Wt:** 257 **Born:** 10/14/1991 **Age:** 30

Year	Team	Lg	G	GS	GF	IP	BFP	H	R	ER	HR	SH	SF	HB	TBB	IBB	SO	WP	W	L	Pct	Sv-Op	Hld	Vel	OPS	ERC	ERA
2021	Iowa	AAA	6	0	0	7.2	39	5	6	4	0	1	1	3	8	0	12	0	0	1	.000	0- -	-	-	.729	5.10	4.70
2018	SD	NL	5	0	0	7.0	24	3	1	1	1	0	0	0	0	0	10	0	0	0	-	0-0	0	92	.417	0.70	1.29
2019	2 Tms	NL	44	0	5	34.2	148	28	23	22	8	0	1	3	13	0	49	1	2	2	.500	0-2	9	94	.748	4.05	5.71
2020	ChC	NL	1	0	0	1.0	5	1	2	2	1	0	0	0	1	0	2	0	0	0	-	0-0	0	91	1.400	14.27	18.00
2021	ChC	NL	15	0	5	17.0	71	10	0	0	0	0	0	0	10	0	28	0	0	0	-	0-0	1	93	.495	1.94	0.00
19	SD	NL	30	0	3	24.2	110	26	19	18	7	0	1	1	9	0	31	0	0	1	.000	0-2	8	94	.863	5.62	6.57
19	ChC	NL	14	0	2	10.0	38	2	4	4	1	0	0	2	4	0	18	1	2	1	.667	0-0	1	94	.398	1.14	3.60
4 ML YEARS			65	0	10	59.2	248	42	26	25	10	0	1	3	24	0	89	1	2	2	.500	0-2	10	93	.655	3.07	3.77

Stevie Wilkerson

Bats: B **Throws:** R **Pos:** 2B-26; LF-3; PH-3; PR-2; RF-1   **Ht:** 6'2" **Wt:** 200 **Born:** 1/11/1992 **Age:** 30

Year	Team	Lg	G	AB	H	2B	3B	HR	(Hm	Rd)	TB	R	RBI	RC	TBB	IBB	SO	HBP	SH	SF	SB	CS	GDP	Avg	OBP	Slg	OPS
2021	Norfolk	AAA	36	123	30	6	0	2	(-	-)	42	17	7	-	21	0	39	0	1	1	0	0	7	.244	.352	.341	.693
2018	Bal	AL	16	46	8	3	0	0	(0	0)	11	2	3	3	3	0	16	0	0	1	1	0	0	.174	.224	.239	.464
2019	Bal	AL	119	329	74	18	2	10	(6	4)	126	41	35	33	22	0	108	7	1	2	3	3	5	.225	.286	.383	.669
2021	Bal	AL	31	72	12	3	0	0	(0	0)	15	5	2	2	3	0	30	1	0	0	2	0	0	.167	.211	.208	.419
3 ML YEARS			166	447	94	24	2	10	(6	4)	152	48	40	38	28	0	154	8	1	2	6	3	5	.210	.268	.340	.608

Devin Williams

Pitches: R **Bats:** R **Pos:** RP-58   **Ht:** 6'2" **Wt:** 200 **Born:** 9/21/1994 **Age:** 27

Year	Team	Lg	G	GS	GF	IP	BFP	H	R	ER	HR	SH	SF	HB	TBB	IBB	SO	WP	W	L	Pct	Sv-Op	Hld	Vel	OPS	ERC	ERA
2019	Mil	NL	13	0	1	13.2	67	18	9	6	2	1	0	2	6	0	14	1	0	0	-	0-0	2	96	.894	6.97	3.95
2020	Mil	NL	22	0	1	27.0	100	8	4	1	1	0	0	1	9	0	53	3	4	1	.800	0-0	9	97	.339	0.76	0.33
2021	Mil	NL	58	0	6	54.0	226	36	17	15	5	1	1	2	28	0	87	2	8	2	.800	3-6	23	95	.587	2.81	2.50
3 ML YEARS			93	0	8	94.2	393	62	30	22	8	2	1	5	43	0	154	6	12	3	.800	3-6	34	96	.575	2.52	2.09

Justin Williams

Bats: L **Throws:** R **Pos:** RF-24; LF-19; PH-13   **Ht:** 6'1" **Wt:** 235 **Born:** 8/20/1995 **Age:** 26

Year	Team	Lg	G	AB	H	2B	3B	HR	(Hm	Rd)	TB	R	RBI	RC	TBB	IBB	SO	HBP	SH	SF	SB	CS	GDP	Avg	OBP	Slg	OPS
2021	Memp	AAA	20	72	18	2	1	5	(-	-)	37	7	13	-	1	0	21	1	0	0	1	0	2	.250	.270	.514	.784
2018	TB	AL	1	1	0	0	0	0	(0	0)	0	0	0	0	0	0	0	0	0	0	0	0	1	.000	.000	.000	.000
2020	StL	NL	3	5	1	0	0	0	(0	0)	1	0	0	0	1	0	2	0	0	0	0	0	0	.200	.333	.200	.533
2021	StL	NL	51	119	19	0	0	4	(0	4)	31	10	11	9	17	5	46	1	0	0	0	1	2	.160	.270	.261	.531
3 ML YEARS			55	125	20	0	0	4	(0	4)	32	10	11	9	18	5	48	1	0	0	0	1	3	.160	.271	.256	.527

Luke Williams

Bats: R **Throws:** R **Pos:** PH-23; CF-15; 2B-8; 3B-8; LF-7; 1B-6; SS-5; RF-3   **Ht:** 6'1" **Wt:** 186 **Born:** 8/9/1996 **Age:** 25

Year	Team	Lg	G	AB	H	2B	3B	HR	(Hm	Rd)	TB	R	RBI	RC	TBB	IBB	SO	HBP	SH	SF	SB	CS	GDP	Avg	OBP	Slg	OPS
2021	LV	AAA	28	109	31	5	2	0	(-	-)	40	19	13	-	11	0	26	1	0	3	6	3	4	.284	.347	.367	.714
2021	Phi	NL	58	98	24	4	0	1	(1	0)	31	8	6	10	10	0	23	0	0	0	2	2	2	.245	.315	.316	.631

Mason Williams

Bats: L **Throws:** R **Pos:** CF-15; PH-2; LF-1   **Ht:** 6'1" **Wt:** 195 **Born:** 8/21/1991 **Age:** 30

Year	Team	Lg	G	AB	H	2B	3B	HR	(Hm	Rd)	TB	R	RBI	RC	TBB	IBB	SO	HBP	SH	SF	SB	CS	GDP	Avg	OBP	Slg	OPS
2021	Syrcse	AAA	68	204	58	13	0	5	(-	-)	86	31	29	-	15	0	48	2	1	3	7	0	2	.284	.335	.422	.756
2015	NYY	AL	8	21	6	3	0	1	(0	1)	12	3	3	4	1	0	3	0	0	0	0	0	0	.286	.318	.571	.890
2016	NYY	AL	12	27	8	1	0	0	(0	0)	9	4	2	3	1	0	12	0	1	0	0	0	0	.296	.321	.333	.655
2017	NYY	AL	5	16	4	0	0	0	(0	0)	4	3	1	1	1	0	2	0	0	0	2	0	0	.250	.294	.250	.544
2018	Cin	NL	51	123	36	5	1	2	(2	0)	49	10	6	11	7	1	29	0	2	0	1	2	5	.293	.331	.398	.729
2019	Bal	AL	11	30	8	1	0	0	(0	0)	9	4	2	2	3	0	6	0	0	1	1	0	0	.267	.324	.300	.624
2020	Bal	AL	10	18	2	0	1	0	(0	0)	4	0	0	0	0	0	9	0	0	1	0	1	0	.111	.111	.222	.333
2021	NYM	NL	17	33	7	1	0	1	(0	1)	11	3	1	1	4	1	9	0	0	0	0	1	1	.212	.297	.333	.631
7 ML YEARS			114	268	71	11	2	4	(2	2)	98	27	15	22	17	2	70	0	3	1	4	4	6	.265	.308	.366	.673

Nick Williams

Bats: L **Throws:** L **Pos:** LF-3;DH-1;PR-1   **Ht:** 6'3" **Wt:** 215 **Born:** 9/8/1993 **Age:** 28

Year	Team	Lg	G	AB	H	2B	3B	HR	(Hm	Rd)	TB	R	RBI	RC	TBB	IBB	SO	HBP	SH	SF	SB	CS	GDP	Avg	OBP	Slg	OPS
2021	Charllt	AAA	39	126	33	7	1	4	(-	-)	54	15	13	-	7	0	36	3	1	1	4	0	1	.262	.314	.429	.742
2017	Phi	NL	83	313	90	14	4	12	(6	6)	148	45	55	47	20	0	97	6	0	4	1	2	8	.288	.338	.473	.811
2018	Phi	NL	140	407	104	12	3	17	(9	8)	173	53	50	50	32	2	111	9	0	0	3	2	4	.256	.324	.425	.749
2019	Phi	NL	67	106	16	4	0	2	(1	1)	26	9	5	1	4	0	43	2	0	0	0	0	1	.151	.196	.245	.442
2021	CWS	AL	4	10	0	0	0	0	(0	0)	0	2	0	0	1	0	4	2	0	0	0	0	1	.000	.231	.000	.231
	4 ML YEARS		294	836	210	30	7	31	(16	15)	347	109	110	98	57	2	255	19	0	4	4	4	14	.251	.312	.415	.727

Taylor Williams

Pitches: R **Bats:** B **Pos:** RP-11   **Ht:** 5'11" **Wt:** 185 **Born:** 7/21/1991 **Age:** 30

Year	Team	Lg	G	GS	GF	IP	BFP	H	R	ER	HR	SH	SF	HB	TBB	IBB	SO	WP	W	L	Pct	Sv-Op	Hld	Vel	OPS	ERC	ERA
2021	ElPaso	AAA	9	0	0	13.1	61	12	10	10	5	1	0	3	8	0	16	0	2	0	1.000	0- -	-	-	.955	7.53	6.75
2017	Mil	NL	5	0	5	4.2	20	4	1	1	0	0	0	0	2	0	4	0	0	0		0-0	0	96	.633	2.67	1.93
2018	Mil	NL	56	0	10	53.0	236	53	28	25	6	4	2	1	25	4	57	4	1	3	.250	0-1	4	96	.747	4.34	4.25
2019	Mil	NL	10	0	4	14.2	73	22	17	16	1	0	0	2	7	2	15	1	1	1	.500	0-1	0	95	.878	7.50	9.82
2020	2 Tms		15	0	9	14.2	67	14	10	10	1	0	0	3	7	1	20	6	1	1	.500	6-6	1	95	.709	4.52	6.14
2021	2 Tms	NL	11	0	4	11.2	55	12	7	6	1	0	1	2	8	0	9	2	0	0		0-0	1	94	.809	6.06	4.63
	20	Sea	AL	14	0	9	13.2	62	12	9	9	1	0	0	3	7	1	19	6	1	1	.500	6-6	1	95	.682	4.32	5.93
	20	SD	NL	1	0	0	1.0	5	2	1	1	0	0	0	0	0	0	1	0	0	0		0-0	0	96	1.000	7.48	9.00
	21	SD	NL	5	0	0	5.1	23	3	1	1	0	0	0	2	3	0	6	0	0	0		0-0	0	94	.514	3.05	1.69
	21	Mia	NL	6	0	4	6.1	32	9	6	5	1	0	1	0	5	0	3	2	0	0		0-0	0	93	1.014	8.95	7.11
	5 ML YEARS		97	0	32	98.2	451	105	63	58	9	4	3	8	49	7	105	13	3	5	.375	6-8	6	95	.766	4.92	5.29

Trevor Williams

Pitches: R **Bats:** R **Pos:** SP-15; RP-8   **Ht:** 6'3" **Wt:** 235 **Born:** 4/25/1992 **Age:** 30

Year	Team	Lg	G	GS	GF	IP	BFP	H	R	ER	HR	SH	SF	HB	TBB	IBB	SO	WP	W	L	Pct	Sv-Op	Hld	Vel	OPS	ERC	ERA
2016	Pit	NL	7	1	1	12.2	61	19	13	11	4	0	0	0	5	0	11	0	1	1	.500	0-1	0	93	1.054	8.89	7.82
2017	Pit	NL	31	25	1	150.1	642	145	73	68	14	8	4	9	52	4	117	2	7	9	.438	0-0	0	92	.715	3.82	4.07
2018	Pit	NL	31	31	0	170.2	701	146	64	59	15	6	4	4	55	3	126	4	14	10	.583	0-0	0	90	.659	3.00	3.11
2019	Pit	NL	26	26	0	145.2	636	162	93	87	27	6	8	7	44	3	113	2	7	9	.438	0-0	0	91	.851	5.11	5.38
2020	Pit	NL	11	11	0	55.1	252	66	42	38	15	1	3	4	21	0	49	1	2	8	.200	0-0	0	91	.905	6.74	6.18
2021	2 Tms	NL	23	15	3	91.0	405	105	51	44	11	3	1	3	31	0	90	0	4	2	.667	0-0	0	91	.808	4.98	4.35
	21	ChC	NL	13	12	0	58.2	264	68	37	33	10	0	1	2	22	0	61	0	4	2	.667	0-0	0	91	.833	5.53	5.06
	21	NYM	NL	10	3	3	32.1	141	37	14	11	1	3	0	1	9	0	29	0	0	0		0-0	0	91	.762	4.02	3.06
	6 ML YEARS		129	109	5	625.2	2697	643	336	307	86	24	20	27	208	10	506	9	35	39	.473	0-1	0	91	.772	4.38	4.42

Bryse Wilson

Pitches: R **Bats:** R **Pos:** SP-16   **Ht:** 6'2" **Wt:** 225 **Born:** 12/20/1997 **Age:** 24

Year	Team	Lg	G	GS	GF	IP	BFP	H	R	ER	HR	SH	SF	HB	TBB	IBB	SO	WP	W	L	Pct	Sv-Op	Hld	Vel	OPS	ERC	ERA
2021	Gwnntt	AAA	10	9	1	55.1	235	61	26	26	8	2	0	2	16	0	42	3	5	2	.714	0- -	-	-	.813	4.79	4.23
2018	Atl	NL	3	1	2	7.0	33	8	5	5	0	0	1	0	6	2	6	0	1	0	1.000	0-0	0	95	.886	5.54	6.43
2019	Atl	NL	6	4	1	20.0	93	26	18	16	5	2	0	0	10	1	16	1	1	1	.500	0-0	0	95	1.050	7.50	7.20
2020	Atl	NL	6	2	2	15.2	73	18	7	7	2	0	0	1	9	0	15	0	1	0	1.000	1-1	0	94	.828	6.18	4.02
2021	2 Tms	NL	16	16	0	74.0	322	85	45	44	15	2	4	1	22	3	46	2	3	7	.300	0-0	0	93	.843	5.26	5.35
	21	Atl	NL	8	8	0	33.2	153	45	23	22	7	1	2	1	12	2	23	1	2	3	.400	0-0	0	93	.914	6.89	5.88
	21	Pit	NL	8	8	0	40.1	169	40	22	22	8	1	2	0	10	1	23	1	1	4	.200	0-0	0	93	.778	4.01	4.91
	Postseason		1	1	0	6.0	20	1	1	1	1	0	0	0	1	0	5	0	1	0	1.000	0-0	0	95	.311	0.46	1.50
	4 ML YEARS		31	23	5	116.2	521	137	75	72	22	4	5	2	47	6	83	3	6	8	.429	1-1	0	94	.880	5.80	5.55

Cody Wilson

Bats: R **Throws:** R **Pos:** PH-1   **Ht:** 6'2" **Wt:** 200 **Born:** 7/4/1996 **Age:** 25

Year	Team	Lg	G	AB	H	2B	3B	HR	(Hm	Rd)	TB	R	RBI	RC	TBB	IBB	SO	HBP	SH	SF	SB	CS	GDP	Avg	OBP	Slg	OPS
2021	Hrsbrg	AA	17	52	6	1	1	0	(-	-)	9	2	1	-	6	0	14	0	0	0	0	2	2	.115	.207	.173	.380
2021	Roch	AAA	33	102	13	2	1	0	(-	-)	17	10	7	-	12	0	38	1	2	0	7	2	2	.127	.226	.167	.393
2021	Was	NL	1	1	0	0	0	0	(0	0)	0	0	0	0	0	0	0	0	0	0	0	0	0	.000	.000	.000	.000

Jacob Wilson

Bats: R **Throws:** R **Pos:** 3B-6;2B-4;LF-1;PH-1;PR-1   **Ht:** 5'11" **Wt:** 219 **Born:** 7/29/1990 **Age:** 31

Year	Team	Lg	G	AB	H	2B	3B	HR	(Hm	Rd)	TB	R	RBI	RC	TBB	IBB	SO	HBP	SH	SF	SB	CS	GDP	Avg	OBP	Slg	OPS
2021	LsVgs	AAA	49	184	53	17	2	14	(-	-)	116	39	46	-	26	0	43	5	0	3	0	0	5	.288	.385	.630	1.016
2021	SgrLnd	AAA	19	71	13	0	0	1	(-	-)	16	4	6	-	6	0	17	1	0	1	0	0	3	.183	.253	.225	.479
2021	2 Tms	AL	12	20	3	1	1	0	(0	0)	6	3	1	0	1	0	3	0	0	0	0	0	1	.150	.190	.300	.490
	21	Oak	AL	6	7	1	0	0	0	(0 | 0)	1	1	0	0	0	0	1	0	0	0	0	0	0	.143	.143	.143	.286
	21	Hou	AL	6	13	2	1	1	0	(0 | 0)	5	2	1	0	1	0	2	0	0	0	0	0	1	.154	.214	.385	.599

Justin Wilson

Pitches: L **Bats:** L **Pos:** RP-42   **Ht:** 6'2" **Wt:** 205 **Born:** 8/18/1987 **Age:** 34

Year Team	Lg	G	GS	GF	IP	BFP	H	R	ER	HR	SH	SF	HB	TBB	IBB	SO	WP	W	L	Pct	Sv-Op	Hld	Vel	OPS	ERC	ERA
2012 Pit	NL	8	0	3	4.2	26	10	1	1	0	1	0	0	3	0	7	1	0	0	-	0-0	0	94	1.111	11.83	1.93
2013 Pit	NL	58	0	8	73.2	295	50	17	17	4	3	1	3	28	1	59	5	6	1	.857	0-3	14	95	.543	2.20	2.08
2014 Pit	NL	70	0	15	60.0	256	49	30	28	4	0	0	3	30	5	61	4	3	4	.429	0-3	16	95	.643	3.29	4.20
2015 NYY	AL	74	0	3	61.0	244	49	21	21	3	2	0	2	20	0	66	4	5	0	1.000	0-2	29	95	.602	2.63	3.10
2016 Det	AL	66	0	10	58.2	251	61	29	27	6	1	0	1	17	2	65	4	4	5	.444	1-6	25	95	.708	3.87	4.14
2017 2 Tms		65	0	30	58.0	248	40	23	22	5	0	1	1	35	1	80	4	4	4	.500	13-16	9	96	.633	3.08	3.41
2018 ChC	NL	71	0	12	54.2	236	45	22	21	5	0	1	0	33	1	69	4	4	5	.444	0-3	16	95	.682	3.81	3.46
2019 NYM	NL	45	0	9	39.0	166	33	12	11	4	0	0	2	19	1	44	4	4	2	.667	4-5	9	95	.670	3.78	2.54
2020 NYM	NL	23	0	2	19.2	86	18	10	8	1	1	0	1	9	1	23	3	2	1	.667	0-0	10	95	.623	3.55	3.66
2021 2 Tms		42	0	13	34.0	149	32	22	20	6	0	0	1	16	0	29	2	1	1	.500	0-1	4	94	.766	4.66	5.29
17 Det	AL	42	0	26	40.1	157	22	12	12	5	0	1	0	16	0	55	3	3	4	.429	13-15	8	96	.563	1.91	2.68
17 ChC	NL	23	0	4	17.2	91	18	11	10	0	0	0	1	19	1	25	1	1	0	1.000	0-1	1	96	.756	5.98	5.09
21 NYY	AL	21	0	7	18.0	83	18	17	15	5	0	0	1	9	0	15	1	1	1	.500	0-1	2	93	.584	5.84	7.50
21 Cin	NL	21	0	6	16.0	66	14	5	5	1	0	0	0	7	0	14	1	0	0	-	0-0	2	94	.623	3.38	2.81
Postseason		6	0	1	5.1	21	3	1	1	0	0	0	0	3	0	4	1	0	0	-	0-0	0	96	.452	1.87	1.69
10 ML YEARS		522	0	105	463.1	1957	387	187	176	38	8	3	14	210	12	503	35	33	23	.589	18-39	132	95	.652	3.34	3.42

Trey Wingenter

Pitches: R **Bats:** R **Pos:** P   **Ht:** 6'7" **Wt:** 237 **Born:** 4/15/1994 **Age:** 28

Year Team	Lg	G	GS	GF	IP	BFP	H	R	ER	HR	SH	SF	HB	TBB	IBB	SO	WP	W	L	Pct	Sv-Op	Hld	Vel	OPS	ERC	ERA
2018 SD	NL	22	0	5	19.0	81	13	8	8	3	0	1	1	11	0	27	1	0	0	-	0-2	5	97	.647	3.62	3.79
2019 SD	NL	51	1	8	51.0	218	34	32	32	5	1	2	5	28	0	72	4	1	3	.250	1-4	16	96	.633	3.16	5.65
2 ML YEARS		73	1	13	70.0	299	47	40	40	8	1	3	6	39	0	99	5	1	3	.250	1-6	21	96	.637	3.29	5.14

Jesse Winker

Bats: L **Throws:** L **Pos:** LF-101;RF-5;DH-5;PH-5;CF-1   **Ht:** 6'3" **Wt:** 215 **Born:** 8/17/1993 **Age:** 28

Year Team	Lg	G	AB	H	2B	3B	HR	(Hm	Rd)	TB	R	RBI	RC	TBB	IBB	SO	HBP	SH	SF	SB	CS	GDP	Avg	OBP	Slg	OPS
2017 Cin	NL	47	121	36	7	0	7	(2	5)	64	21	15	18	15	0	24	0	1	0	1	1	2	.298	.375	.529	.904
2018 Cin	NL	89	281	84	16	0	7	(6	1)	121	38	43	54	49	4	46	2	1	1	0	0	6	.299	.405	.431	.836
2019 Cin	NL	113	338	91	17	2	16	(10	6)	160	51	38	48	38	2	60	8	0	1	0	2	10	.269	.357	.473	.830
2020 Cin	NL	54	149	38	7	0	12	(8	4)	81	27	23	31	28	0	46	5	0	1	1	0	3	.255	.388	.544	.932
2021 Cin	NL	110	423	129	32	1	24	(13	11)	235	77	71	90	53	1	75	9	0	0	1	0	14	.305	.394	.556	.949
Postseason		2	6	1	0	0	0	(0	0)	1	0	0	0	1	0	2	1	0	0	0	0	0	.167	.375	.167	.542
5 ML YEARS		413	1312	378	79	3	66	(39	27)	661	214	190	241	183	7	251	24	2	2	3	3	35	.288	.385	.504	.888

Dan Winkler

Pitches: R **Bats:** R **Pos:** RP-47   **Ht:** 6'3" **Wt:** 205 **Born:** 2/2/1990 **Age:** 32

Year Team	Lg	G	GS	GF	IP	BFP	H	R	ER	HR	SH	SF	HB	TBB	IBB	SO	WP	W	L	Pct	Sv-Op	Hld	Vel	OPS	ERC	ERA
2015 Atl	NL	2	0	0	1.2	8	2	2	2	2	0	0	0	1	0	2	0	0	0	-	0-0	0	89	1.518	14.99	10.80
2016 Atl	NL	3	0	0	2.1	8	0	0	0	0	0	0	0	1	0	4	0	0	0	-	0-0	0	92	.125	0.20	0.00
2017 Atl	NL	16	0	1	14.1	53	7	4	4	1	1	0	0	6	0	18	0	1	1	.500	0-0	4	94	.511	1.57	2.51
2018 Atl	NL	69	0	11	60.1	255	52	27	23	3	1	1	5	20	1	69	2	4	0	1.000	2-5	23	93	.645	2.99	3.43
2019 Atl	NL	27	0	4	21.2	93	18	14	12	5	0	0	1	11	0	22	1	3	1	.750	0-1	6	93	.804	4.67	4.98
2020 ChC	NL	18	0	4	18.1	76	11	7	6	3	1	0	1	11	0	18	0	0	0	-	0-1	1	93	.624	3.35	2.95
2021 ChC	NL	47	0	11	39.2	190	32	24	23	5	0	1	9	30	1	40	3	1	3	.250	0-1	6	93	.747	5.31	5.22
Postseason		1	0	1	1.0	4	0	0	0	0	0	0	1	0	0	2	0	0	0	-	0-0	0	93	.250	0.95	0.00
7 ML YEARS		182	0	31	158.1	683	122	78	70	19	3	2	16	80	2	173	6	9	5	.643	2-8	40	93	.687	3.71	3.98

Patrick Wisdom

Bats: R **Throws:** R **Pos:** 3B-77;LF-15;PH-15;1B-13;RF-3   **Ht:** 6'2" **Wt:** 220 **Born:** 8/27/1991 **Age:** 30

Year Team	Lg	G	AB	H	2B	3B	HR	(Hm	Rd)	TB	R	RBI	RC	TBB	IBB	SO	HBP	SH	SF	SB	CS	GDP	Avg	OBP	Slg	OPS
2018 StL	NL	32	50	13	1	0	4	(3	1)	26	11	10	8	6	0	19	2	0	0	2	1	1	.260	.362	.520	.882
2019 Tex	AL	9	26	4	1	0	0	(0	0)	5	1	1	1	1	0	15	0	0	0	0	0	0	.154	.185	.192	.377
2020 ChC	NL	2	2	0	0	0	0	(0	0)	0	0	0	0	0	0	0	0	0	0	0	0	0	.000	.000	.000	.000
2021 ChC	NL	106	338	78	13	0	28	(13	15)	175	54	61	48	32	1	153	4	0	0	4	1	7	.231	.305	.518	.823
4 ML YEARS		149	416	95	15	0	32	(16	16)	206	66	72	57	39	1	187	6	1	0	6	2	8	.228	.304	.495	.799

Matt Wisler

Pitches: R **Bats:** R **Pos:** RP-48   WISS-lurr   **Ht:** 6'3" **Wt:** 215 **Born:** 9/12/1992 **Age:** 29

Year Team	Lg	G	GS	GF	IP	BFP	H	R	ER	HR	SH	SF	HB	TBB	IBB	SO	WP	W	L	Pct	Sv-Op	Hld	Vel	OPS	ERC	ERA
2015 Atl	NL	20	19	0	109.0	478	119	59	57	16	4	5	4	40	4	72	0	8	8	.500	0-0	0	93	.819	4.91	4.71
2016 Atl	NL	27	26	1	156.2	671	159	90	87	26	2	3	4	49	4	115	5	7	13	.350	1-1	0	93	.756	4.32	5.00
2017 Atl	NL	20	1	8	32.1	153	43	31	30	5	2	3	2	13	0	22	0	0	1	.000	0-0	0	93	.971	6.68	8.35
2018 2 Tms	NL	18	3	3	40.0	166	41	20	19	8	1	3	0	7	0	32	1	1	1	.500	0-1	0	92	.781	3.95	4.28
2019 2 Tms		44	8	7	51.1	224	56	34	32	10	1	1	0	16	0	63	3	3	4	.429	0-3	8	93	.813	4.85	5.61
2020 Min	AL	18	4	3	25.1	107	15	3	3	4	0	1	0	14	0	35	1	0	1	.000	1-2	3	92	.564	2.59	1.07
2021 2 Tms		48	0	8	48.2	195	41	24	20	8	1	1	0	11	1	62	1	3	5	.375	1-4	10	92	.672	2.79	3.70

Year	Team	Lg	G	GS	GF	IP	BFP	H	R	ER	HR	SH	SF	HB	TBB	IBB	SO	WP	W	L	Pct	Sv-Op	Hld	Vel	OPS	ERC	ERA
18	Atl	NL	7	3	1	26.2	112	30	16	16	6	0	1	0	5	0	21	1	1	1	.500	0-0	0	93	.850	4.82	5.40
18	Cin	NL	11	0	2	13.1	54	11	4	3	2	1	2	0	2	0	11	0	0	0	-	0-1	0	92	.633	2.41	2.03
19	SD	NL	21	0	5	29.0	129	34	17	17	5	1	1	0	10	0	34	3	2	2	.500	0-2	4	93	.822	5.35	5.28
19	Sea	AL	23	8	2	22.1	95	22	17	15	5	0	0	0	6	0	29	0	1	2	.333	0-1	4	93	.800	4.21	6.04
21	SF	NL	21	0	4	19.1	82	19	13	13	4	0	1	0	6	0	26	0	1	2	.333	0-1	3	92	.798	4.32	6.05
21	TB	AL	27	0	4	29.1	113	22	11	7	2	0	2	1	5	1	36	1	2	3	.400	1-3	7	91	.581	1.89	2.15
7 ML YEARS			195	61	30	463.1	1994	474	261	248	73	10	18	13	150	8	401	13	22	33	.400	3-11	21	93	.778	4.37	4.82

Bobby Witt Jr.

Bats: R Throws: R Pos: SS   Ht: 6'1" Wt: 200 Born: 6/14/2000 Age: 22

								BATTING														RUNNING			AVERAGES			
Year	Team	Lg	G	AB	H	2B	3B	HR	(Hm	Rd)	TB	R	RBI	RC	TBB	IBB	SO	HBP	SH	SF	SB	CS	GDP	Avg	OBP	Slg	OPS
2019	Royals	R	37	164	43	2	5	1	(-	-)	58	30	27	21	13	0	35	1	0	2	9	1	4	.262	.317	.354	.670
2021	NWArk	AA	61	244	72	11	4	16	(-	-)	139	44	51	-	25	0	67	6	0	4	14	7	1	.295	.369	.570	.939
2021	Omha	AAA	59	241	71	24	0	17	(-	-)	146	53	44	-	24	1	60	2	1	2	15	2	0	.295	.361	.606	.966

Nick Wittgren

Pitches: R Bats: R Pos: RP-59; SP-1   Ht: 6'2" Wt: 216 Born: 5/29/1991 Age: 31

			HOW MUCH PITCHED					WHAT HE GAVE UP											THE RESULTS						
Year	Team	Lg	G	GS	GF	IP	BFP	H	R	ER	HR	SH	SF	HB	TBB	IBB	SO	WP	W	L	Pct	Sv-Op	Hld	Vel	OPS	ERC	ERA
2016	Mia	NL	48	0	9	51.2	213	50	18	18	6	3	2	1	10	2	42	1	4	3	.571	0-2	5	92	.671	3.21	3.14
2017	Mia	NL	38	0	3	42.1	182	46	22	22	5	0	3	0	13	1	43	2	3	1	.750	0-0	5	92	.800	4.29	4.68
2018	Mia	NL	32	0	6	33.2	148	29	13	11	1	1	1	1	15	3	31	2	2	1	.667	0-0	4	92	.629	2.86	2.94
2019	Cle	AL	55	0	13	57.2	231	47	22	18	10	0	0	0	15	1	60	0	5	1	.833	4-6	12	92	.676	2.99	2.81
2020	Cle	AL	25	0	6	23.2	98	18	9	9	4	1	0	5	6	2	28	0	2	0	1.000	0-1	10	93	.706	3.37	3.42
2021	Cle	AL	60	1	13	62.1	258	61	38	35	13	2	3	2	17	5	61	2	2	9	.182	1-1	9	92	.800	4.26	5.05
Postseason			1	0	1	1.1	6	0	0	0	0	0	0	0	2	0	3	0	0	0	-	0-0	0	94	.333	1.96	0.00
6 ML YEARS			258	1	50	271.1	1130	251	122	113	39	7	9	9	76	14	265	7	18	15	.545	5-10	46	92	.720	3.54	3.75

Asher Wojciechowski

Pitches: R Bats: R Pos: SP-1   wo-juh-HOW-ski   Ht: 6'4" Wt: 235 Born: 12/21/1988 Age: 33

			HOW MUCH PITCHED					WHAT HE GAVE UP											THE RESULTS						
Year	Team	Lg	G	GS	GF	IP	BFP	H	R	ER	HR	SH	SF	HB	TBB	IBB	SO	WP	W	L	Pct	Sv-Op	Hld	Vel	OPS	ERC	ERA
2021	Tacom	AAA	5	5	0	17.0	78	21	11	11	2	0	0	1	6	0	27	0	0	1	.000	0--	-	-	.782	5.57	5.82
2015	Hou	AL	5	3	2	16.1	79	23	13	13	2	0	2	0	7	0	16	1	0	1	.000	0-0	0	91	.965	6.66	7.16
2017	Cin	AL	25	8	2	62.1	279	71	48	45	14	5	2	5	19	1	64	1	4	3	.571	0-0	2	93	.899	5.65	6.50
2019	Bal	AL	17	16	0	82.1	361	80	46	45	17	1	0	9	28	0	80	3	4	8	.333	0-0	0	91	.808	4.81	4.92
2020	Bal	AL	10	7	2	37.0	168	45	29	28	11	0	4	1	15	0	31	0	1	3	.250	0-0	0	91	.963	7.04	6.81
2021	NYY	AL	1	1	0	4.0	19	3	2	2	1	0	0	1	3	0	4	0	0	0	-	0-0	0	91	.902	6.10	4.50
5 ML YEARS			58	35	6	202.0	906	222	138	133	45	6	8	16	72	1	195	5	9	15	.375	0-0	2	92	.880	5.64	5.93

Tony Wolters

Bats: L Throws: R Pos: C-8;PH-5;2B-2;LF-1;PR-1   WAHL-ters   Ht: 5'10" Wt: 195 Born: 6/9/1992 Age: 30

								BATTING														RUNNING			AVERAGES			
Year	Team	Lg	G	AB	H	2B	3B	HR	(Hm	Rd)	TB	R	RBI	RC	TBB	IBB	SO	HBP	SH	SF	SB	CS	GDP	Avg	OBP	Slg	OPS
2021	Iowa	AAA	38	115	30	4	0	4	(-	-)	46	18	17	-	18	1	33	4	1	0	1	1	1	.261	.380	.400	.780
2021	OkCity	AAA	26	93	20	6	1	2	(-	-)	34	10	13	-	8	0	20	5	0	1	0	1	4	.215	.308	.366	.674
2016	Col	NL	71	205	53	15	2	3	(2	1)	81	27	30	30	21	2	53	0	4	0	4	1	1	.259	.327	.395	.723
2017	Col	NL	83	229	55	8	1	0	(0	0)	65	30	16	25	33	9	55	2	2	0	0	1	9	.240	.341	.284	.625
2018	Col	NL	74	182	31	4	4	3	(1	2)	52	19	27	18	26	2	33	6	0	2	2	0	6	.170	.292	.286	.577
2019	Col	NL	121	359	94	17	2	1	(0	1)	118	42	42	42	36	5	68	3	8	2	0	1	9	.262	.337	.329	.666
2020	Col	NL	42	100	23	4	0	0	(0	0)	27	10	8	11	6	0	30	1	2	0	0	0	1	.230	.280	.270	.550
2021	ChC	NL	14	24	3	0	0	0	(0	0)	3	3	0	1	5	0	12	0	1	0	0	1	1	.125	.276	.125	.401
Postseason			3	3	2	0	0	0	(0	0)	2	0	1	0	0	0	0	0	0	0	0	0	0	.667	.667	.667	1.333
6 ML YEARS			405	1099	259	48	9	7	(3	4)	346	131	123	127	127	18	251	17	11	8	6	4	27	.236	.322	.315	.637

Connor Wong

Bats: R Throws: R Pos: C-5;DH-1;PH-1;PR-1   Ht: 6'1" Wt: 181 Born: 5/19/1996 Age: 26

								BATTING														RUNNING			AVERAGES			
Year	Team	Lg	G	AB	H	2B	3B	HR	(Hm	Rd)	TB	R	RBI	RC	TBB	IBB	SO	HBP	SH	SF	SB	CS	GDP	Avg	OBP	Slg	OPS
2021	Wrcstr	AAA	48	190	47	12	0	7	(-	-)	80	19	25	-	9	0	57	0	0	0	7	1	2	.247	.281	.421	.702
2021	Bos	AL	6	13	4	1	1	0	(0	0)	7	3	1	2	1	0	7	0	0	0	0	0	0	.308	.357	.538	.896

Kean Wong

Bats: L Throws: R Pos: PH-12;2B-10;3B-6;LF-4;RF-4;PR-3   Ht: 5'9" Wt: 189 Born: 4/17/1995 Age: 27

								BATTING														RUNNING			AVERAGES			
Year	Team	Lg	G	AB	H	2B	3B	HR	(Hm	Rd)	TB	R	RBI	RC	TBB	IBB	SO	HBP	SH	SF	SB	CS	GDP	Avg	OBP	Slg	OPS
2021	Salt Lk	AAA	46	189	64	10	2	4	(-	-)	90	31	22	-	14	2	32	0	0	0	10	3	4	.339	.384	.476	.860
2019	2 Tms	AL	7	18	3	0	0	0	(0	0)	3	2	0	0	0	0	6	0	0	0	0	1	0	.167	.167	.167	.333
2021	LAA	AL	32	60	10	2	1	0	(0	0)	14	3	6	1	2	0	17	0	4	0	0	0	0	.167	.194	.233	.427
19	TB	AL	6	14	3	0	0	0	(0	0)	3	1	0	0	0	0	5	0	0	0	0	1	0	.214	.214	.214	.429
19	LAA	AL	1	4	0	0	0	0	(0	0)	0	1	0	0	0	0	1	0	0	0	0	0	0	.000	.000	.000	.000
2 ML YEARS			39	78	13	2	1	0	(0	0)	17	5	6	1	2	0	23	0	4	0	0	2	0	.167	.188	.218	.405

Kolten Wong

Bats: L **Throws:** R **Pos:** 2B-113;PH-5   COLT-enn   **Ht:** 5'7" **Wt:** 185 **Born:** 10/10/1990 **Age:** 31

Year	Team	Lg	G	AB	H	2B	3B	HR	(Hm	Rd)	TB	R	RBI	RC	TBB	IBB	SO	HBP	SH	SF	SB	CS	GDP	Avg	OBP	Slg	OPS
2013	StL	NL	32	59	9	1	0	0	(0	0)	10	6	0	0	3	0	12	0	0	0	3	0	2	.153	.194	.169	.363
2014	StL	NL	113	402	100	14	3	12	(10	2)	156	52	42	41	21	3	71	4	5	1	20	4	12	.249	.292	.388	.680
2015	StL	NL	150	557	146	28	4	11	(5	6)	215	71	61	67	36	2	95	15	0	5	15	8	10	.262	.321	.386	.707
2016	StL	NL	121	313	75	7	7	5	(3	2)	111	39	23	36	34	2	52	9	0	5	7	0	3	.240	.327	.355	.682
2017	StL	NL	108	354	101	27	3	4	(3	1)	146	55	42	56	41	11	60	12	1	3	8	2	4	.285	.376	.412	.788
2018	StL	NL	127	353	88	18	2	9	(6	3)	137	41	38	46	31	3	60	14	6	3	6	5	6	.249	.332	.388	.720
2019	StL	NL	148	478	136	25	4	11	(1	10)	202	61	59	81	47	5	83	13	6	5	24	4	2	.285	.361	.423	.784
2020	StL	NL	53	181	48	4	2	1	(0	1)	59	26	16	30	20	1	30	4	2	1	5	2	1	.265	.350	.326	.675
2021	Mil	NL	116	445	121	32	2	14	(8	6)	199	70	50	73	31	1	83	13	0	3	12	5	2	.272	.335	.447	.783
	Postseason		31	97	20	8	1	5	(3	2)	45	10	15	11	5	2	17	0	1	1	4	0	3	.206	.243	.464	.707
9 ML YEARS			968	3142	824	156	27	67	(36	31)	1235	421	331	430	264	28	546	84	20	26	100	30	42	.262	.333	.393	.726

Alex Wood

Pitches: L **Bats:** R **Pos:** SP-26   **Ht:** 6'4" **Wt:** 215 **Born:** 1/12/1991 **Age:** 31

Year	Team	Lg	G	GS	GF	IP	BFP	H	R	ER	HR	SH	SF	HB	TBB	IBB	SO	WP	W	L	Pct	Sv-Op	Hld	Vel	OPS	ERC	ERA
2013	Atl	NL	31	11	9	77.2	327	76	29	27	3	4	1	3	27	1	77	4	3	3	.500	0-0	1	92	.670	3.40	3.13
2014	Atl	NL	35	24	2	171.2	694	151	58	53	16	7	3	6	45	1	170	5	11	11	.500	0-0	2	90	.651	3.04	2.78
2015	2 Tms	NL	32	32	0	189.2	801	198	86	81	15	15	3	4	59	4	139	6	12	12	.500	0-0	0	89	.724	3.94	3.84
2016	LAD	NL	14	10	0	60.1	255	56	30	25	5	0	2	3	20	0	66	4	1	4	.200	0-0	1	91	.660	3.49	3.73
2017	LAD	NL	27	25	0	152.1	614	123	50	46	15	4	0	6	38	6	151	2	16	3	**.842**	0-0	1	92	.620	2.58	2.72
2018	LAD	NL	33	27	0	151.2	637	143	70	62	14	3	7	8	40	5	135	2	9	7	.563	0-0	1	90	.664	3.32	3.68
2019	Cin	NL	7	7	0	35.2	153	41	25	23	11	2	0	1	9	0	30	0	1	3	.250	0-0	0	90	.926	6.02	5.80
2020	LAD	NL	9	2	2	12.2	65	17	11	9	2	0	0	3	6	1	15	1	0	1	.000	0-0	1	91	.918	7.50	6.39
2021	SF	NL	26	26	0	138.2	585	125	63	59	14	0	1	16	39	1	152	7	10	4	.714	0-0	0	92	.680	3.52	3.83
15	Atl	NL	20	20	0	119.1	509	132	50	47	8	11	1	2	36	2	90	5	7	6	.538	0-0	0	89	.729	4.15	3.54
15	LAD	NL	12	12	0	70.1	292	66	36	34	7	4	2	2	23	2	49	1	5	6	.455	0-0	0	88	.714	3.58	4.35
	Postseason		20	2	4	33.0	139	27	17	13	9	0	0	3	11	5	36	1	1	2	.333	0-0	6	92	.775	4.04	3.55
9 ML YEARS			214	164	13	990.1	4131	930	422	385	95	37	20	48	283	19	935	31	63	48	.568	0-0	6	90	.683	3.45	3.50

Hunter Wood

Pitches: R **Bats:** R **Pos:** RP-5   **Ht:** 6'1" **Wt:** 175 **Born:** 8/12/1993 **Age:** 28

Year	Team	Lg	G	GS	GF	IP	BFP	H	R	ER	HR	SH	SF	HB	TBB	IBB	SO	WP	W	L	Pct	Sv-Op	Hld	Vel	OPS	ERC	ERA
2017	TB	AL	1	0	1	0.1	1	0	0	0	0	0	0	0	0	0	0	0				0-0	0	90	.000	0.00	0.00
2018	TB	AL	29	8	3	41.0	179	42	17	17	4	1	1	0	18	1	42	0	1	1	.500	0-0	4	94	.727	4.31	3.73
2019	2 Tms	AL	36	2	9	45.1	195	46	20	15	7	0	1	1	12	1	39	5	1	1	.500	1-1	2	94	.721	3.96	2.98
2021	Tex	AL	5	0	1	5.0	19	2	2	2	1	0	1	0	2	0	5	1	0	0		0-0	1	93	.586	1.65	3.60
19	TB	AL	19	2	4	29.0	120	26	11	8	4	0	1	1	7	1	24	1	1	1	.500	1-1	1	93	.677	3.20	2.48
19	Cle	AL	17	0	5	16.1	75	20	9	7	3	0	0	0	5	0	15	4	0	0	-	0-0	1	94	.790	5.40	3.86
4 ML YEARS			71	10	14	91.2	394	90	39	34	12	1	3	1	32	2	86	6	2	2	.500	1-1	7	94	.715	3.95	3.34

Jake Woodford

Pitches: R **Bats:** R **Pos:** RP-18; SP-8   **Ht:** 6'4" **Wt:** 215 **Born:** 10/28/1996 **Age:** 25

Year	Team	Lg	G	GS	GF	IP	BFP	H	R	ER	HR	SH	SF	HB	TBB	IBB	SO	WP	W	L	Pct	Sv-Op	Hld	Vel	OPS	ERC	ERA
2021	Memp	AAA	7	7	0	34.0	152	41	21	17	4	0	2	1	12	0	25	1	2	3	.400	0- -	-		.837	4.16	4.50
2020	StL	NL	12	1	4	21.0	85	20	13	13	7	0	1	0	5	0	16	1	1	0	1.000	0-0	0	93	.826	4.76	5.57
2021	StL	NL	26	8	4	67.2	293	66	32	30	7	0	7	8	25	0	50	2	3	4	.429	0-0	0	92	.741	4.35	3.99
2 ML YEARS			38	9	8	88.2	378	86	45	43	14	0	8	8	30	0	66	3	4	4	.500	0-0	0	92	.762	4.49	4.36

Brandon Woodruff

Pitches: R **Bats:** L **Pos:** SP-30   **Ht:** 6'4" **Wt:** 243 **Born:** 2/10/1993 **Age:** 29

Year	Team	Lg	G	GS	GF	IP	BFP	H	R	ER	HR	SH	SF	HB	TBB	IBB	SO	WP	W	L	Pct	Sv-Op	Hld	Vel	OPS	ERC	ERA
2017	Mil	NL	8	8	0	43.0	180	43	23	23	5	1	0	3	14	1	32	0	2	3	.400	0-0	0	94	.719	4.16	4.81
2018	Mil	NL	19	4	4	42.1	176	36	18	17	4	0	1	2	14	0	47	1	3	0	1.000	1-1	2	95	.641	3.14	3.61
2019	Mil	NL	22	22	0	121.2	493	109	49	49	12	2	2	5	30	0	143	1	11	3	.786	0-0	0	96	.650	3.13	3.62
2020	Mil	NL	13	**13**	0	73.2	293	55	26	25	9	0	1	4	18	0	91	1	3	5	.375	0-0	0	97	.604	2.51	3.05
2021	Mil	NL	30	30	0	179.1	708	130	54	51	18	4	4	7	43	0	211	2	9	10	.474	0-0	0	96	.573	2.21	2.56
	Postseason		6	3	1	21.0	79	14	7	6	1	1	0	2	3	1	32	0	1	2	.333	0-0	0	96	.504	1.57	2.57
5 ML YEARS			92	77	4	460.0	1854	373	170	165	48	7	8	21	119	1	524	5	28	21	.571	1-1	2	96	.619	2.75	3.23

Brandon Workman

Pitches: R **Bats:** R **Pos:** RP-29   **Ht:** 6'5" **Wt:** 235 **Born:** 8/13/1988 **Age:** 33

Year	Team	Lg	G	GS	GF	IP	BFP	H	R	ER	HR	SH	SF	HB	TBB	IBB	SO	WP	W	L	Pct	Sv-Op	Hld	Vel	OPS	ERC	ERA
2021	Wrcstr	AAA	7	0	2	7.0	27	3	1	1	0	0	0	0	4	0	10	0	0	0	-	1- -	-	-	.390	1.40	1.29
2013	Bos	AL	20	3	5	41.2	180	44	23	23	5	2	1	0	15	1	47	1	6	3	.667	0-1	1	92	.751	4.34	4.97
2014	Bos	AL	19	15	2	87.0	378	88	57	50	11	3	3	1	36	0	70	2	1	10	.091	0-0	1	90	.748	4.43	5.17
2017	Bos	AL	33	0	8	39.2	162	37	17	14	7	2	1	1	11	2	37	1	1	1	.500	0-1	4	92	.782	3.83	3.18
2018	Bos	AL	43	0	4	41.1	167	34	15	15	6	0	3	0	16	0	37	0	6	1	.857	0-0	7	91	.705	3.46	3.27

Year	Team	Lg	G	GS	GF	IP	BFP	H	R	ER	HR	SH	SF	HB	TBB	IBB	SO	WP	W	L	Pct	Sv-Op	Hld	Vel	OPS	ERC	ERA
2019	Bos	AL	73	0	30	71.2	286	29	18	15	1	1	3	2	45	4	104	4	10	1	.909	16-22	15	93	.433	1.47	1.88
2020	2 Tms		21	0	15	19.2	101	31	14	13	4	0	0	0	13	2	23	0	1	4	.200	9-12	1	93	1.004	9.52	5.95
2021	2 Tms		29	0	9	28.0	136	36	20	17	4	0	0	0	21	2	25	1	1	2	.333	0-0	4	91	.906	7.61	5.46
20	Bos	AL	7	0	6	6.2	31	8	3	3	0	0	0	0	4	0	8	0	0	0	—	4-4	0	93	.683	5.28	4.05
20	Phi	NL	14	0	9	13.0	70	23	11	10	4	0	0	0	9	2	15	0	1	4	.200	5-8	1	93	1.146	11.90	6.92
21	ChC	NL	10	0	2	8.0	43	12	9	6	2	0	0	0	7	0	11	1	0	2	.000	0-0	2	91	.997	10.48	6.75
21	Bos	AL	19	0	7	20.0	93	24	11	11	2	0	0	0	14	2	14	0	1	0	1.000	0-0	2	91	.864	6.50	4.95
	Postseason		10	0	0	9.2	48	14	6	5	2	1	0	0	6	1	7	0	0	1	.000	0-0	1	92	.938	8.49	4.66
	7 ML YEARS		238	18	73	329.0	1410	299	164	147	38	8	11	4	157	11	343	9	26	22	.542	25-36	33	92	.720	4.00	4.02

Kyle Wright

Pitches: R **Bats:** R **Pos:** SP-2   **Ht:** 6'4" **Wt:** 215 **Born:** 10/2/1995 **Age:** 26

Year	Team	Lg	G	GS	GF	IP	BFP	H	R	ER	HR	SH	SF	HB	TBB	IBB	SO	WP	W	L	Pct	Sv-Op	Hld	Vel	OPS	ERC	ERA
2021	Gwnntt	AAA	23	23	0	130.0	542	112	52	46	9	0	1	6	44	0	129	12	9	5	.643	0--	-	-	.651	3.06	3.18
2018	Atl	NL	4	0	1	6.0	28	4	3	3	2	0	0	0	6	0	5	0	0	0	—	0-0	0	94	.812	6.25	4.50
2019	Atl	NL	7	4	2	19.2	93	24	19	19	4	0	0	1	13	1	18	2	0	3	.000	0-0	0	95	.966	7.64	8.69
2020	Atl	NL	8	8	0	38.0	168	35	23	22	7	0	0	0	24	1	30	1	2	4	.333	0-0	0	94	.782	5.19	5.21
2021	Atl	NL	2	2	0	6.1	35	7	7	7	2	1	1	4	5	0	6	1	0	1	.000	0-0	0	93	1.096	10.97	9.95
	Postseason		2	2	0	6.2	33	8	7	7	2	0	0	1	4	0	7	0	1	1	.500	0-0	0	94	.965	8.28	9.45
	4 ML YEARS		21	14	3	70.0	324	70	52	51	15	1	1	5	48	2	59	4	2	8	.200	0-0	0	94	.868	6.44	6.56

Mike Wright Jr.

Pitches: R **Bats:** R **Pos:** RP-13   **Ht:** 6'6" **Wt:** 240 **Born:** 1/3/1990 **Age:** 32

Year	Team	Lg	G	GS	GF	IP	BFP	H	R	ER	HR	SH	SF	HB	TBB	IBB	SO	WP	W	L	Pct	Sv-Op	Hld	Vel	OPS	ERC	ERA
2021	Charllt	AAA	16	16	0	95.1	392	71	38	36	11	1	3	8	29	0	90	3	7	5	.583	0--	-	-	.635	2.74	3.40
2015	Bal	AL	12	9	0	44.2	204	52	30	30	9	0	2	5	18	3	26	2	3	5	.375	0-0	0	93	.887	6.20	6.04
2016	Bal	AL	18	12	5	74.2	328	81	53	48	12	1	5	9	26	0	50	2	3	4	.429	0-0	0	93	.850	5.38	5.79
2017	Bal	AL	13	0	4	25.0	109	26	16	16	5	0	1	3	7	0	28	1	0	0	—	0-0	0	94	.830	5.01	5.76
2018	Bal	AL	48	2	16	84.1	388	101	55	52	12	1	6	7	36	1	74	4	4	2	.667	0-0	1	93	.837	6.00	5.55
2019	2 Tms	AL	19	0	9	29.1	147	44	30	26	6	0	2	2	12	1	30	2	0	1	.000	1-2	0	93	.959	8.05	7.98
2021	CWS	AL	13	0	5	18.0	81	17	12	11	1	0	1	2	11	0	11	2	0	1	.000	0-0	0	91	.744	4.76	5.50
19	Bal	AL	10	0	4	13.1	66	20	14	14	5	0	1	1	7	0	14	1	0	1	.000	1-2	0	93	1.091	10.62	9.45
19	Sea	AL	9	0	5	16.0	81	24	16	12	1	0	1	1	5	1	16	1	0	0	—	0-0	0	93	.857	6.12	6.75
	6 ML YEARS		123	23	39	276.0	1257	321	196	183	45	2	17	28	110	5	219	13	10	13	.435	1-2	1	93	.857	5.91	5.97

Austin Wynns

Bats: R **Throws:** R **Pos:** C-44;1B-1;PH-1   **Ht:** 6'0" **Wt:** 190 **Born:** 12/10/1990 **Age:** 31

Year	Team	Lg	G	AB	H	2B	3B	HR	(Hm	Rd)	TB	R	RBI	RC	TBB	IBB	SO	HBP	SH	SF	SB	CS	GDP	Avg	OBP	Slg	OPS
2021	Norfolk	AAA	15	48	16	2	0	3	(-	-)	27	7	9		7	0	11	3	1	0	0	0	1	.333	.448	.563	1.011
2018	Bal	AL	42	110	28	2	0	4	(1	3)	42	16	11	9	5	0	25	0	3	0	0	0	7	.255	.287	.382	.669
2019	Bal	AL	28	70	15	1	0	1	(0	1)	19	8	5	4	3	0	14	0	1	0	0	0	2	.214	.247	.271	.518
2021	Bal	AL	45	130	24	4	0	4	(1	3)	40	14	14	9	8	0	31	0	1	0	1	0	6	.185	.232	.308	.540
	3 ML YEARS		115	310	67	7	0	9	(2	7)	101	38	30	22	16	0	70	0	5	0	1	0	15	.216	.255	.326	.580

Miguel Yajure

Pitches: R **Bats:** R **Pos:** SP-3; RP-1   yuh-HOO-ray   **Ht:** 6'1" **Wt:** 220 **Born:** 5/1/1998 **Age:** 24

Year	Team	Lg	G	GS	GF	IP	BFP	H	R	ER	HR	SH	SF	HB	TBB	IBB	SO	WP	W	L	Pct	Sv-Op	Hld	Vel	OPS	ERC	ERA
2018	CtnSC	A	14	14	0	64.2	270	64	38	28	3	3	3	0	15	0	56	3	4	3	.571	0--	-	-	.836	2.99	3.90
2019	Tampa	A+	22	18	2	127.2	512	110	47	32	5	0	4	7	28	0	122	9	8	6	.571	0--	-	-	.616	2.53	2.26
2021	Indy	AAA	9	9	0	43.2	174	33	17	15	6	0	1	2	13	0	40	3	2	3	.400	0--	-	-	.649	2.85	3.09
2020	NYY	AL	3	0	3	7.0	29	3	1	1	1	0	0	1	5	0	8	1	0	0	—	0-0	0	92	.571	3.09	1.29
2021	Pit	NL	4	3	0	15.0	68	17	14	14	6	0	0	1	7	0	11	0	0	2	.000	0-0	0	91	1.034	7.85	8.40
	2 ML YEARS		7	3	3	22.0	97	20	15	15	7	0	0	2	12	0	19	1	0	2	.000	0-0	0	91	.905	6.22	6.14

Jordan Yamamoto

Pitches: R **Bats:** R **Pos:** SP-1; RP-1   **Ht:** 6'0" **Wt:** 185 **Born:** 5/11/1996 **Age:** 26

Year	Team	Lg	G	GS	GF	IP	BFP	H	R	ER	HR	SH	SF	HB	TBB	IBB	SO	WP	W	L	Pct	Sv-Op	Hld	Vel	OPS	ERC	ERA
2021	Syrcse	AAA	6	5	0	17.2	77	18	8	8	4	0	0	1	9	0	18	1	0	2	.000	0--	-	-	.816	5.35	4.08
2019	Mia	NL	15	15	0	78.2	325	54	42	39	11	0	2	5	36	1	82	5	4	5	.444	0-0	0	92	.647	3.10	4.46
2020	Mia	NL	4	3	0	11.1	67	27	24	23	8	0	1	0	7	0	13	0	0	1	.000	0-0	0	90	1.491	21.05	18.26
2021	NYM	NL	2	1	0	6.2	33	10	6	3	0	0	0	2	2	0	3	0	1	1	.500	0-0	0	90	.804	7.12	4.05
	3 ML YEARS		21	19	0	96.2	425	91	72	65	19	0	3	7	45	1	98	5	5	7	.417	0-0	0	91	.793	4.97	6.05

Hyeon-jong Yang

Pitches: L Bats: L Pos: RP-8; SP-4 Ht: 6'0" Wt: 200 Born: 3/1/1988 Age: 34

			HOW MUCH PITCHED			WHAT HE GAVE UP										THE RESULTS						
Year	Team	Lg	G	GS	GF	IP	BFP	H	R	ER	HR	SH	SF	HB	TBB	IBB	SO	WP	W	L	Pct	Sv-Op	Hld	Vel	OPS	ERC	ERA
2021	RdRck	AAA	10	9	0	45.0	195	52	32	28	10	0	3	1	10	0	42	3	0	3	.000	0- --	-	-	.876	5.17	5.60
2021	Tex	AL	12	4	1	35.1	160	42	24	22	9	0	1	1	16	0	25	2	0	3	.000	0-0	0	90	.904	6.81	5.60

Ryan Yarbrough

Pitches: L Bats: R Pos: SP-21; RP-9 Ht: 6'5" Wt: 205 Born: 12/31/1991 Age: 30

Year	Team	Lg	G	GS	GF	IP	BFP	H	R	ER	HR	SH	SF	HB	TBB	IBB	SO	WP	W	L	Pct	Sv-Op	Hld	Vel	OPS	ERC	ERA
2018	TB	AL	38	6	3	147.1	628	140	70	64	18	1	1	8	50	6	128	1	16	6	.727	0-0	0	89	.730	3.86	3.91
2019	TB	AL	28	14	1	141.2	563	121	69	65	15	0	3	9	20	2	117	0	11	6	.647	0-0	0	88	.650	2.60	4.13
2020	TB	AL	11	9	0	55.2	234	54	22	22	5	2	2	7	12	1	44	2	1	4	.200	0-0	0	87	.689	3.61	3.56
2021	TB	AL	30	21	0	155.0	653	163	96	88	25	4	3	9	27	2	117	1	9	7	.563	0-0	0	86	.764	4.08	5.11
	Postseason		8	2	1	17.2	74	18	6	6	5	0	0	1	5	0	8	0	2	0	1.000	0-0	0	88	.854	5.34	3.06
	4 ML YEARS		107	50	4	499.2	2078	478	257	239	63	7	9	33	109	11	406	4	37	23	.617	0-0	0	88	.714	3.53	4.30

Eric Yardley

Pitches: R Bats: R Pos: RP-17 Ht: 6'0" Wt: 170 Born: 8/18/1990 Age: 31

Year	Team	Lg	G	GS	GF	IP	BFP	H	R	ER	HR	SH	SF	HB	TBB	IBB	SO	WP	W	L	Pct	Sv-Op	Hld	Vel	OPS	ERC	ERA
2021	Nashv	AAA	37	0	8	34.1	151	35	13	12	2	0	2	6	8	1	29	2	4	1	.800	0- --	-	-	.665	3.80	3.15
2019	SD	NL	10	0	2	11.2	52	12	5	3	1	2	0	1	3	0	7	0	0	1	.000	0-0	0	86	.668	3.73	2.31
2020	Mil	NL	24	0	4	23.1	97	19	6	4	2	0	1	1	10	0	19	0	2	0	1.000	0-2	1	88	.662	3.29	1.54
2021	Mil	NL	17	0	5	18.2	89	24	15	14	3	1	1	3	10	2	5	1	0	0	-	0-1	1	87	.975	7.52	6.75
	Postseason		1	0	0	2.1	7	0	0	0	0	0	0	0	2	0	0	0	0	0	-	0-0	0	88	.000	0.00	0.00
	3 ML YEARS		51	0	11	53.2	238	55	26	21	6	3	2	5	23	2	31	1	2	1	.667	0-3	2	87	.778	4.74	3.52

Mike Yastrzemski

Bats: L Throws: L Pos: RF-115;CF-34;PH-19;PR-1 yuh-STREM-skee Ht: 5'10" Wt: 178 Born: 8/23/1990 Age: 31

						BATTING															RUNNING			AVERAGES			
Year	Team	Lg	G	AB	H	2B	3B	HR	(Hm	Rd)	TB	R	RBI	RC	TBB	IBB	SO	HBP	SH	SF	SB	CS	GDP	Avg	OBP	Slg	OPS
2019	SF	NL	107	371	101	22	3	21	(8	13)	192	64	55	61	32	1	107	4	1	3	2	4	4	.272	.334	.518	.852
2020	SF	NL	54	192	57	14	4	10	(6	4)	109	39	35	43	30	2	55	3	0	0	2	1	2	.297	.400	.568	.968
2021	SF	NL	139	468	105	28	3	25	(8	17)	214	75	71	67	51	4	131	9	1	3	4	0	3	.224	.311	.457	.768
	3 ML YEARS		300	1031	263	64	10	56	(22	34)	515	178	161	171	113	7	293	16	2	6	8	5	9	.255	.336	.500	.836

Kirby Yates

Pitches: R Bats: L Pos: P Ht: 5'10" Wt: 205 Born: 3/25/1987 Age: 35

Year	Team	Lg	G	GS	GF	IP	BFP	H	R	ER	HR	SH	SF	HB	TBB	IBB	SO	WP	W	L	Pct	Sv-Op	Hld	Vel	OPS	ERC	ERA
2014	TB	AL	37	0	12	36.0	156	33	16	15	4	0	1	3	15	3	42	2	0	2	.000	1-2	0	92	.699	3.94	3.75
2015	TB	AL	20	0	10	20.1	92	23	18	18	10	0	0	1	7	0	21	0	1	0	1.000	0-0	0	92	1.004	7.58	7.97
2016	NYY	AL	41	0	11	41.1	184	41	24	24	5	1	1	4	19	1	50	1	2	1	.667	0-2	3	93	.746	4.77	5.23
2017	2 Tms		62	0	12	56.2	231	44	28	25	12	0	1	2	19	2	88	0	4	5	.444	1-4	20	94	.698	3.42	3.97
2018	SD	NL	65	0	28	63.0	250	41	15	15	6	0	3	4	17	0	90	2	5	3	.625	12-13	16	94	.527	2.00	2.14
2019	SD	NL	60	0	51	60.2	243	41	14	8	2	1	1	7	13	1	101	2	0	5	.000	41-44	0	94	.515	1.72	1.19
2020	SD	NL	6	0	3	4.1	25	7	6	6	1	0	1	0	4	0	8	2	0	1	.000	2-2	1	94	.940	10.86	12.46
17	LAA	AL	1	0	0	1.0	5	2	2	2	2	0	0	0	0	0	1	0	0	0	-	0-0	0	94	2.000	25.07	18.00
17	SD	NL	61	0	12	55.2	226	42	26	23	10	0	1	2	19	2	87	0	4	5	.444	1-4	20	94	.666	3.13	3.72
	7 ML YEARS		291	0	127	282.1	1181	230	121	111	40	2	8	21	94	7	400	9	12	17	.414	57-67	39	93	.660	3.31	3.54

Christian Yelich

Bats: L Throws: R Pos: LF-107;PH-10;DH-4;RF-1 YELL-itch Ht: 6'3" Wt: 195 Born: 12/5/1991 Age: 30

						BATTING															RUNNING			AVERAGES			
Year	Team	Lg	G	AB	H	2B	3B	HR	(Hm	Rd)	TB	R	RBI	RC	TBB	IBB	SO	HBP	SH	SF	SB	CS	GDP	Avg	OBP	Slg	OPS
2013	Mia	NL	62	240	69	12	1	4	(0	4)	95	34	16	35	31	1	66	1	0	1	10	0	4	.288	.370	.396	.766
2014	Mia	NL	144	582	165	30	6	9	(2	7)	234	94	54	87	70	3	137	3	3	2	21	7	9	.284	.362	.402	.764
2015	Mia	NL	126	476	143	30	2	7	(1	6)	198	63	44	64	47	2	101	2	0	0	16	5	13	.300	.366	.416	.782
2016	Mia	NL	155	578	172	38	3	21	(8	13)	279	78	98	89	72	4	138	4	0	5	9	4	20	.298	.376	.483	.859
2017	Mia	NL	156	602	170	36	2	18	(7	11)	264	100	81	99	80	4	137	6	0	6	16	2	13	.282	.369	.439	.807
2018	Mil	NL	147	574	187	34	7	36	(22	14)	343	118	110	128	68	2	135	7	0	2	22	4	14	.326	.402	.598	1.000
2019	Mil	NL	130	489	161	29	3	44	(27	17)	328	100	97	126	80	16	118	8	0	3	30	2	8	.329	.429	.671	1.100
2020	Mil	NL	58	200	41	7	1	12	(6	6)	86	39	22	28	46	2	76	1	0	4	4	2	4	.205	.356	.430	.786
2021	Mil	NL	117	399	99	19	2	9	(6	3)	149	70	51	67	70	5	113	3	0	3	9	3	5	.248	.362	.373	.736
	Postseason		12	45	9	2	0	2	(2	0)	17	7	3	4	11	1	11	0	0	0	2	0	2	.200	.357	.378	.735
	9 ML YEARS		1095	4140	1207	235	27	160	(79	81)	1976	696	573	723	564	39	1021	35	3	22	137	29	90	.292	.379	.477	.857

Huascar Ynoa

Pitches: R Bats: R Pos: SP-17; RP-1

WAH-scar ee-NOH-ah

Ht: 6'2" Wt: 220 Born: 5/28/1998 Age: 24

Year	Team	Lg	G	GS	GF	IP	BFP	H	R	ER	HR	SH	SF	HB	TBB	IBB	SO	WP	W	L	Pct	Sv-Op	Hld	Vel	OPS	ERC	ERA
2019	Atl	NL	2	0	1	3.0	16	6	6	6	1	0	0	0	1	0	3	0	0	0	-	0-0	0	98	1.171	12.18	18.00
2020	Atl	NL	9	5	1	21.2	100	23	14	14	2	0	2	2	13	1	17	2	0	0	-	0-0	0	95	.802	5.50	5.82
2021	Atl	NL	18	17	0	91.0	372	76	42	41	14	1	2	4	25	1	100	4	4	6	.400	0-0	0	97	.701	3.20	4.05
	Postseason		1	0	0	4.0	18	1	0	0	0	0	0	1	4	0	4	0	0	0	-	0-0	0	96	.410	2.38	0.00
	3 ML YEARS		29	22	2	115.2	488	105	62	61	17	1	4	6	39	2	120	6	4	6	.400	0-0	0	96	.737	3.81	4.75

Alex Young

Pitches: L Bats: L Pos: RP-38; SP-2

Ht: 6'3" Wt: 220 Born: 9/9/1993 Age: 28

Year	Team	Lg	G	GS	GF	IP	BFP	H	R	ER	HR	SH	SF	HB	TBB	IBB	SO	WP	W	L	Pct	Sv-Op	Hld	Vel	OPS	ERC	ERA
2021	Clmbs	AAA	7	0	1	8.0	34	8	5	5	1	1	0	0	4	0	6	2	0	0	-	0--	-	-	.812	4.85	5.63
2019	Ari	NL	17	15	0	83.1	349	72	40	33	14	3	0	4	27	4	71	2	7	5	.583	0-0	0	89	.710	3.58	3.56
2020	Ari	NL	15	7	0	46.1	204	51	30	28	11	0	5	1	14	0	39	1	2	4	.333	0-0	1	91	.872	5.24	5.44
2021	2 Tms		40	2	12	52.0	246	65	43	38	12	2	2	3	27	4	43	3	2	6	.250	0-2	5	90	.927	7.23	6.58
21	Ari	NL	30	2	7	41.2	193	50	34	29	11	2	2	1	20	3	38	2	2	6	.250	0-2	3	90	.913	6.81	6.26
21	Cle	AL	10	0	5	10.1	53	15	9	9	1	0	0	2	7	1	5	1	0	0	-	0-0	1	91	.976	8.78	7.84
	3 ML YEARS		72	24	12	181.2	799	188	113	99	37	5	7	8	68	8	153	6	11	15	.423	0-2	5	90	.818	4.98	4.90

Andy Young

Bats: R Throws: R Pos: PH-36;2B-21;3B-2;LF-1;DH-1

Ht: 6'0" Wt: 200 Born: 5/10/1994 Age: 28

Year	Team	Lg	G	AB	H	2B	3B	HR	(Hm	Rd)	TB	R	RBI	RC	TBB	IBB	SO	HBP	SH	SF	SB	CS	GDP	Avg	OBP	Slg	OPS
2021	Reno	AAA	48	194	59	20	2	11	(-	-)	116	43	41	-	20	0	78	8	0	2	2	0	6	.304	.388	.598	.986
2020	Ari	NL	12	26	5	2	0	1	(0	1)	10	3	4	4	5	0	10	3	0	0	0	0	3	.192	.382	.385	.767
2021	Ari	NL	58	91	19	7	0	6	(2	4)	44	13	15	12	6	0	45	6	0	1	0	0	3	.209	.298	.484	.782
	2 ML YEARS		70	117	24	9	0	7	(2	5)	54	16	19	16	11	0	55	9	0	1	0	0	3	.205	.319	.462	.780

Daniel Zamora

Pitches: L Bats: L Pos: RP-4

Ht: 6'3" Wt: 195 Born: 4/15/1993 Age: 29

Year	Team	Lg	G	GS	GF	IP	BFP	H	R	ER	HR	SH	SF	HB	TBB	IBB	SO	WP	W	L	Pct	Sv-Op	Hld	Vel	OPS	ERC	ERA
2021	Tacom	AAA	27	1	6	35.0	154	37	23	17	5	0	1	0	15	1	46	1	3	0	1.000	1--	-	-	.765	4.77	4.37
2018	NYM	NL	16	0	4	9.0	36	6	3	3	1	1	0	1	3	1	16	0	1	0	1.000	0-0	5	89	.641	2.45	3.00
2019	NYM	NL	17	0	3	8.2	41	10	5	5	1	0	1	1	5	1	8	0	0	1	.000	0-0	0	89	.861	6.09	5.19
2021	Sea	AL	4	0	1	4.1	18	5	4	3	1	0	0	0	1	0	3	0	2	0	1.000	0-0	0	90	.922	5.39	6.23
	3 ML YEARS		37	0	8	22.0	95	21	12	11	3	1	1	2	9	2	27	0	3	1	.750	0-0	5	89	.792	4.38	4.50

Seby Zavala

Bats: R Throws: R Pos: C-33;PH-3;DH-1;PR-1

Ht: 5'11" Wt: 205 Born: 8/28/1993 Age: 28

Year	Team	Lg	G	AB	H	2B	3B	HR	(Hm	Rd)	TB	R	RBI	RC	TBB	IBB	SO	HBP	SH	SF	SB	CS	GDP	Avg	OBP	Slg	OPS
2021	Charllt	AAA	40	143	26	5	0	8	(-	-)	55	19	20	-	19	0	72	1	0	3	0	1	4	.182	.277	.385	.662
2019	CWS	AL	5	12	1	0	0	0	(0	0)	1	1	0	0	0	0	9	0	0	0	0	0	0	.083	.083	.083	.167
2021	CWS	AL	37	93	17	3	0	5	(4	1)	35	15	15	10	6	0	41	1	4	0	0	0	1	.183	.240	.376	.616
	2 ML YEARS		42	105	18	3	0	5	(4	1)	36	16	15	10	6	0	50	1	4	0	0	0	1	.171	.223	.343	.566

Angel Zerpa

Pitches: L Bats: L Pos: SP-1

Ht: 6'0" Wt: 220 Born: 9/27/1999 Age: 22

Year	Team	Lg	G	GS	GF	IP	BFP	H	R	ER	HR	SH	SF	HB	TBB	IBB	SO	WP	W	L	Pct	Sv-Op	Hld	Vel	OPS	ERC	ERA
2021	QuadC	A+	8	8	0	41.2	167	32	12	12	2	0	0	8	0	53	0	4	0	1.000	0--	-	-	-	1.77	2.59
2021	NWArk	AA	13	13	0	45.1	200	51	30	30	7	0	2	1	19	0	54	8	0	3	.000	0--	-	-	.799	5.45	5.96
2021	KC	AL	1	1	0	5.0	20	3	2	0	0	1	1	0	1	0	4	0	0	1	.000	0-0	0	94	.446	1.06	0.00

T.J. Zeuch

Pitches: R Bats: R Pos: SP-3; RP-2

ZOYK

Ht: 6'7" Wt: 245 Born: 8/1/1995 Age: 26

Year	Team	Lg	G	GS	GF	IP	BFP	H	R	ER	HR	SH	SF	HB	TBB	IBB	SO	WP	W	L	Pct	Sv-Op	Hld	Vel	OPS	ERC	ERA
2021	Buffalo	AAA	12	9	1	58.0	253	65	34	26	8	0	2	4	13	0	42	3	2	3	.400	0--	-	-	.777	4.55	4.03
2021	Memp	AAA	9	5	1	38.1	162	36	22	21	6	0	1	1	15	0	35	5	2	0	1.000	1--	-	-	.721	4.25	4.93
2019	Tor	AL	5	3	0	22.2	99	22	13	12	2	0	0	0	11	0	20	2	1	2	.333	0-0	0	92	.731	4.15	4.76
2020	Tor	AL	3	1	1	11.1	47	9	2	2	1	0	0	0	4	0	3	0	1	0	1.000	0-0	0	92	.625	2.68	1.59
2021	Tor	AL	5	3	0	15.0	74	21	16	11	6	0	0	0	9	0	8	0	0	2	.000	0-0	0	94	1.082	9.94	6.60
	3 ML YEARS		13	7	1	49.0	220	52	31	25	9	0	0	0	24	0	31	2	2	4	.333	0-0	0	93	.825	5.37	4.59

Bradley Zimmer

Bats: L **Throws:** R **Pos:** CF-54;RF-43;PH-5;LF-3;PR-3;DH-1   **Ht:** 6'4" **Wt:** 185 **Born:** 11/27/1992 **Age:** 29

							BATTING													RUNNING			AVERAGES			
Year	Team	Lg	G	AB	H	2B	3B	HR	(Hm | Rd)	TB	R	RBI	RC	TBB	IBB	SO	HBP	SH	SF	SB	CS	GDP	Avg	OBP	Slg	OPS
2021	Clmbs	AAA	18	60	16	3	0	1	(- | -)	22	9	8	-	10	0	26	5	0	0	4	2	0	.267	.413	.367	.780
2017	Cle	AL	101	299	72	15	2	8	(5 | 3)	115	41	39	37	26	1	99	4	0	3	18	1	5	.241	.307	.385	.692
2018	Cle	AL	34	106	24	5	0	2	(1 | 1)	35	14	9	9	7	0	44	1	0	0	4	1	1	.226	.281	.330	.611
2019	Cle	AL	9	13	0	0	0	0	(0 | 0)	0	1	0	0	1	0	7	0	0	0	0	0	0	.000	.071	.000	.071
2020	Cle	AL	20	37	6	0	0	1	(1 | 0)	9	3	3	3	7	0	14	5	0	1	2	1	2	.162	.360	.243	.603
2021	Cle	AL	99	299	68	9	1	8	(4 | 4)	103	44	35	38	30	0	122	15	0	4	15	3	3	.227	.325	.344	.669
	5 ML YEARS		263	754	170	29	3	19	(11 | 8)	262	103	86	87	71	1	286	25	0	8	39	6	11	.225	.310	.347	.658

Kyle Zimmer

Pitches: R **Bats:** R **Pos:** RP-50; SP-2   **Ht:** 6'3" **Wt:** 225 **Born:** 9/13/1991 **Age:** 30

			HOW MUCH PITCHED					WHAT HE GAVE UP										THE RESULTS						
Year	Team	Lg	G	GS	GF	IP	BFP	H	R	ER	HR	SH	SF	HB	TBB	IBB	SO	WP	W	L	Pct	Sv-Op	Hld	Vel	OPS	ERC	ERA
2021	Omha	AAA	8	0	0	9.0	36	7	3	3	0	0	0	0	4	0	11	1	1	1	.500	0- -	-		.524	2.51	3.00
2019	KC	AL	15	0	3	18.1	102	28	22	22	2	0	0	0	19	0	18	2	0	1	.000	0-0	0	97	.991	10.03	10.80
2020	KC	AL	16	1	4	23.0	91	14	4	4	0	0	0	1	10	0	26	2	1	0	1.000	0-0	0	94	.537	1.78	1.57
2021	KC	AL	52	2	9	54.0	223	46	32	29	7	0	4	0	30	1	46	9	4	1	.800	2-3	10	94	.738	4.25	4.83
	3 ML YEARS		83	3	16	95.1	416	88	58	55	9	0	4	1	59	1	90	13	5	2	.714	2-3	10	95	.753	4.59	5.19

Ryan Zimmerman

Bats: R **Throws:** R **Pos:** PH-58;1B-54;DH-3   **Ht:** 6'3" **Wt:** 215 **Born:** 9/28/1984 **Age:** 37

							BATTING													RUNNING			AVERAGES			
Year	Team	Lg	G	AB	H	2B	3B	HR	(Hm	Rd)	TB	R	RBI	RC	TBB	IBB	SO	HBP	SH	SF	SB	CS	GDP	Avg	OBP	Slg	OPS
2005	Was	NL	20	58	23	10	0	0	(0	0)	33	6	6	9	3	0	12	0	0	1	0	0	1	.397	.419	.569	.988
2006	Was	NL	157	614	176	47	3	20	(10	10)	289	84	110	101	61	7	120	2	1	4	11	8	15	.287	.351	.471	.822
2007	Was	NL	162	653	174	43	5	24	(11	13)	299	99	91	83	61	3	125	3	0	5	4	1	26	.266	.330	.458	.788
2008	Was	NL	106	428	121	24	1	14	(7	7)	189	51	51	48	31	1	71	3	0	4	1	1	12	.283	.333	.442	.774
2009	Was	NL	157	610	178	37	3	33	(17	16)	320	110	106	96	72	9	119	2	0	9	2	0	22	.292	.364	.525	.888
2010	Was	NL	142	525	161	32	0	25	(9	16)	268	85	85	97	69	6	98	4	0	5	4	1	16	.307	.388	.510	.899
2011	Was	NL	101	395	114	21	2	12	(7	5)	175	52	49	58	41	4	73	1	0	3	3	1	14	.289	.355	.443	.798
2012	Was	NL	145	578	163	36	1	25	(16	9)	276	93	95	84	57	8	116	2	0	4	5	2	**20**	.282	.346	.478	.824
2013	Was	NL	147	568	156	26	2	26	(7	19)	264	84	79	83	60	2	133	2	0	3	6	0	16	.275	.344	.465	.809
2014	Was	NL	61	214	60	19	1	5	(1	4)	96	26	38	32	22	0	37	0	0	6	0	0	6	.280	.342	.449	.790
2015	Was	NL	95	346	86	25	1	16	(9	7)	161	43	73	49	33	0	79	1	0	10	1	0	13	.249	.308	.465	.773
2016	Was	NL	115	427	93	18	1	15	(9	6)	158	60	46	36	29	1	104	5	0	6	4	1	12	.218	.272	.370	.642
2017	Was	NL	144	524	159	33	0	36	(19	17)	300	90	108	94	44	1	126	3	0	5	1	0	16	.303	.358	.573	.930
2018	Was	NL	85	288	76	21	2	13	(7	6)	140	33	51	41	30	1	55	3	0	2	1	1	10	.264	.337	.486	.824
2019	Was	NL	52	171	44	9	0	6	(2	4)	71	20	27	22	17	0	39	0	0	4	0	0	4	.257	.321	.415	.736
2021	Was	NL	110	255	62	16	0	14	(6	8)	120	27	46	27	16	0	77	0	0	2	0	0	9	.243	.286	.471	.756
	Postseason		35	117	32	7	0	5	(3	2)	54	10	17	19	10	0	30	0	0	1	1	0	2	.274	.328	.462	.790
	16 ML YEARS		1799	6654	1846	417	22	284	(137	147)	3159	963	1061	960	646	43	1384	31	1	69	43	16	212	.277	.341	.475	.816

Bruce Zimmermann

Pitches: L **Bats:** L **Pos:** SP-13; RP-1   **Ht:** 6'1" **Wt:** 215 **Born:** 2/9/1995 **Age:** 27

			HOW MUCH PITCHED					WHAT HE GAVE UP										THE RESULTS						
Year	Team	Lg	G	GS	GF	IP	BFP	H	R	ER	HR	SH	SF	HB	TBB	IBB	SO	WP	W	L	Pct	Sv-Op	Hld	Vel	OPS	ERC	ERA
2020	Bal	AL	2	1	1	7.0	31	6	6	6	2	0	0	2	2	0	7	2	0	0	-	0-0	0	91	.767	5.18	7.71
2021	Bal	AL	14	13	0	64.1	285	75	37	36	14	1	2	2	22	0	56	0	4	5	.444	0-0	0	91	.841	5.83	5.04
	2 ML YEARS		16	14	1	71.1	316	81	43	42	16	1	2	4	24	0	63	2	4	5	.444	0-0	0	91	.834	5.76	5.30

Jordan Zimmermann

Pitches: R **Bats:** R **Pos:** RP-2   **Ht:** 6'2" **Wt:** 225 **Born:** 5/23/1986 **Age:** 36

			HOW MUCH PITCHED					WHAT HE GAVE UP										THE RESULTS						
Year	Team	Lg	G	GS	GF	IP	BFP	H	R	ER	HR	SH	SF	HB	TBB	IBB	SO	WP	W	L	Pct	Sv-Op	Hld	Vel	OPS	ERC	ERA
2009	Was	NL	16	16	0	91.1	391	95	51	47	10	5	3	4	29	0	92	0	3	5	.375	0-0	0	93	.760	4.25	4.63
2010	Was	NL	7	7	0	31.0	135	31	20	17	8	1	1	2	10	1	27	0	1	2	.333	0-0	0	92	.817	5.02	4.94
2011	Was	NL	26	26	0	161.1	662	154	62	57	12	8	2	7	31	2	124	3	8	11	.421	0-0	0	93	.671	3.02	3.18
2012	Was	NL	32	32	0	195.2	805	186	69	64	18	8	4	8	43	2	153	3	12	8	.600	0-0	0	94	.686	3.22	2.94
2013	Was	NL	32	32	0	213.1	865	192	81	77	19	9	4	7	40	0	161	3	**19**	9	.679	0-0	0	94	.654	2.79	3.25
2014	Was	NL	32	32	0	199.2	800	185	67	59	13	5	3	6	29	0	182	4	14	5	.737	0-0	0	94	.631	2.64	2.66
2015	Was	NL	33	**33**	0	201.2	831	204	89	82	24	8	2	8	39	3	164	2	13	10	.565	0-0	0	93	.699	3.63	3.66
2016	Det	AL	19	18	1	105.1	450	118	63	57	14	1	5	2	26	0	66	3	9	7	.563	0-0	0	92	.804	4.48	4.87
2017	Det	AL	29	29	0	160.0	713	204	111	108	29	3	8	7	44	2	103	3	8	13	.381	0-0	0	92	.888	6.00	6.08
2018	Det	AL	25	25	0	131.1	556	140	76	66	28	2	5	2	26	0	111	1	8	7	.467	0-0	0	91	.800	4.42	4.52
2019	Det	AL	23	23	0	112.0	504	145	89	86	19	3	4	6	25	2	82	3	1	13	.071	0-0	0	90	.877	5.74	6.91
2020	Det	AL	3	2	0	5.2	28	11	6	5	0	0	0	0	2	0	6	0	0	0	-	0-0	0	89	.964	9.33	7.94
2021	Mil	NL	2	0	1	5.2	26	8	5	5	1	0	0	1	2	0	0	0	0	0	-	0-0	0	89	1.032	8.21	7.94
	Postseason		3	2	0	12.2	47	10	6	6	1	1	0	0	1	0	11	0	0	1	.000	0-0	0	94	.550	1.80	4.26
	13 ML YEARS		279	275	2	1614.0	6766	1673	789	730	195	53	41	60	346	12	1271	25	95	91	.511	0-0	0	93	.737	3.84	4.07

Tyler Zuber

Pitches: R **Bats:** R **Pos:** RP-31 **Ht:** 5'11" **Wt:** 195 **Born:** 6/16/1995 **Age:** 27

			HOW MUCH PITCHED					WHAT HE GAVE UP												THE RESULTS							
Year	Team	Lg	G	GS	GF	IP	BFP	H	R	ER	HR	SH	SF	HB	TBB	IBB	SO	WP	W	L	Pct	Sv-Op	Hld	Vel	OPS	ERC	ERA
2021	Omha	AAA	28	0	22	28.2	116	15	10	9	3	0	1	0	16	3	43	1	1	3	.250	8- -	-	-	.550	2.07	2.83
2020	KC	AL	23	0	8	22.0	99	15	11	10	4	1	1	1	20	1	30	1	1	2	.333	0-0	0	94	.736	5.05	4.09
2021	KC	AL	31	0	6	27.1	123	26	20	19	6	0	1	1	17	1	25	2	0	3	.000	0-0	4	95	.819	5.71	6.26
	2 ML YEARS		54	0	14	49.1	222	41	31	29	10	1	2	2	37	2	55	3	1	5	.167	0-0	4	94	.784	5.42	5.29

Mike Zunino

Bats: R **Throws:** R **Pos:** C-105;PH-5 zoo-NEE-no **Ht:** 6'2" **Wt:** 235 **Born:** 3/25/1991 **Age:** 31

			BATTING																			RUNNING			AVERAGES			
Year	Team	Lg	G	AB	H	2B	3B	HR	(Hm	Rd)	TB	R	RBI	RC	TBB	IBB	SO	HBP	SH	SF	SB	CS	GDP	Avg	OBP	Slg	OPS
2013	Sea	AL	52	173	37	5	0	5	(3	2)	57	22	14	13	16	0	49	3	0	1	1	0	5	.214	.290	.329	.620
2014	Sea	AL	131	438	87	20	2	22	(10	12)	177	51	60	39	17	1	158	17	0	4	0	3	12	.199	.254	.404	.658
2015	Sea	AL	112	350	61	11	0	11	(6	5)	105	28	28	14	21	0	132	5	8	2	0	1	6	.174	.230	.300	.530
2016	Sea	AL	55	164	34	7	0	12	(9	3)	77	16	31	28	21	0	65	6	0	1	0	0	0	.207	.318	.470	.787
2017	Sea	AL	124	387	97	25	0	25	(14	11)	197	52	64	55	39	0	160	8	0	1	1	0	8	.251	.331	.509	.840
2018	Sea	AL	113	373	75	18	0	20	(5	15)	153	37	44	29	24	0	150	6	0	2	0	0	7	.201	.259	.410	.669
2019	TB	AL	90	266	44	10	1	9	(5	4)	83	30	32	18	20	0	98	3	0	0	0	0	4	.165	.232	.312	.544
2020	TB	AL	28	75	11	4	0	4	(1	3)	27	8	10	7	6	0	37	3	0	0	0	0	0	.147	.238	.360	.598
2021	TB	AL	109	333	72	11	2	33	(14	19)	186	64	62	55	34	0	132	7	0	1	0	0	7	.216	.301	.559	.860
	Postseason		19	53	9	0	0	4	(4	0)	21	4	8	4	1	0	27	1	0	1	0	0	1	.170	.196	.396	.593
	9 ML YEARS		814	2559	518	111	5	141	(67	74)	1062	308	345	258	198	1	981	58	8	12	2	4	49	.202	.274	.415	.689

Baserunning Data

Bill James

The Baserunning Data is perhaps the most fun section of this book, for me. I often write the introduction to the Baserunning Data, because I just enjoy nosing around in it and finding stuff that I didn't know. The data is just so clean and clear, and, here's the thing, it never messes with your head. It tells you *specifically* stuff that you already knew *generally*, which makes you feel like you're a smart guy and you understand this stuff. I remember when Prince Fielder was in the majors, he would have baserunning data that would crack you up. I think one year he went 0-for-45 at going from first to third on a single. The man was lucky if he could get from first to third on a double.

When Chase Utley was in the majors, he would lead the league in almost any off-beat statistic that you could come up with, including the baserunning numbers. If you would check who was the best in the majors at going from first to third on a single or scoring from first on a double or whatever, it seemed like it was always Chase Utley.

My task here, then, is to help you understand this stuff well enough that you also can enjoy looking through it.

Going from first to third on a single. An average major league player in 2021 went first-to-third on a single 29% of the time, based on the guys in this chart; I think it is usually 28%, but that may include pitchers, who only go from first to third on a single when being chased by an animal they suspect may have rabies.

Miami Second Baseman Jazz Chisholm went first-to-third on a single 14 times in 18 tries in 2021, the highest percentage of any player (78%). Don't feel bad if you didn't know that Miami's second baseman was Jazz Chisholm; I didn't know it, either, and this is what I do for a living. That's only 18 opportunities, though, and you'd probably need 25 opportunities to qualify if this was a championship that people qualified for, so the leader among players with 25 opportunities was Cleveland's superstar third baseman, José Ramírez, who was 18-for-28. Ramírez was 9.8 bases better than an average baserunner in this area, the best in the majors; Tommy Edman was second at 9.1, and Jazz Chisholm third at 8.7.

The worst in the majors in this area was DJ LeMahieu, who was 6-for-42 going first-to-third on a single, or 6.3 bases worse than average. LeMahieu's advance frequency was probably held down because the Yankees have all of those right-handed bangers who probably hit most of their singles to left field, I am guessing, and you don't go first-to-third on a single to left as often as you do on a single to right. All statistics have outside influences; you never have pure data.

Here's a weird fact: Victor Robles of Washington did not go first-to-third on a single all year; he was 0-for-14. Victor Robles, as you probably know, is a fast guy, a speed guy. Why he was 0-for-14 in this area, I have no idea.

Another weird one. One of my favorite players, Jackie Bradley Jr., also did not go first-to-third on a single all year. He was 0-for-5. He was only on first when a single was hit 5 times all season! Jackie historically has been very, very good at going from first to third on a single, with a career figure of 39% despite playing most of his career in Fenway Park, where it is difficult to go from first to third on a single to left. A big contributor here is that Jackie had a terrible year with the bat, but still, one would expect that, given the number of times he was on first base after a single, walk or hit batsman, there should have been 12-15 times when somebody hit a single. Jackie is still a tremendous baserunner.

His career may be over now, I don't know, but the best player in the majors at going first-to-third, career data, is Dexter Fowler, at 54%. Elvis Andrus (another one of my favorite players) is the only other player over 50%, and some guy named "Trout" is third at 48%. Alex Avila, Pablo Sandoval, Mike Moustakas and Yadier Molina are at the bottom of the chart.

Vladimir Guerrero Jr. was on first base when a single was hit 51 times in 2021, the most of any major league player. His advancement percentage was very low.

Scoring from Second on a Single: An average player scores from second on a single 59% of the time. Yan Gomes, of all people, was 10-for-11 at scoring from second on a single, the highest percentage of any player with at least

10 chances. Gomes is a veteran catcher who is decidedly not a fast runner. Ronald Acuña was 13-for-15, which makes more sense, and the young wonder Wander Franco was 12-for-14; he seems to do everything well. José Ramírez was also 16-for-19 here.

In terms of net gain, the number one man was Tim Anderson, who was 19-for-23, which is 5.4 bases better than average. Pittsburgh center fielder Bryan Reynolds was the only other guy who was +5. Cincinnati's Nick Castellanos was the worst in the majors, 5-for-18.

An average major league player has about 60% as many chances to score from second on a single as he does to go first-to-third on a single. Whit Merrifield, who steals a lot of bases and thus is on second base a lot, had the most opportunities to score on a single, 32, but for whatever reason was just 18-for-32, a below-average percentage.

In career data, the best in the majors is Elvis Andrus. Andrus is 38 bases better than average here, +38.4. No other active major leaguer is +25.

Albert Pujols has been really good in this area, +23 bases. Albert used to run OK, but he was never fast, and it has been a long, long time since he was young. But sometimes guys who aren't fast are better baserunners than you think they are.

One reason I love this data is that it spreads out so quickly. If the norm is 29%, some guys will be over 50%, some guys under 10%—not as a fluke, but just because there are very real separations in ability in this area, which manifest themselves quickly in performance data. That's not the way it is in a lot of the data that we struggle with. We're measuring something REAL here, something that actually matters. It doesn't matter a tremendous amount; you can't win the pennant by baserunning. One team hits home runs; the other one steals bases, the home run-hitting team wins; that's just the way it is.

But at the same time, baserunning has value. You can't reliably track that value through secondary inferences, because the effects aren't large enough, but you CAN track it directly, because the data works. That's why it's so neat.

Well, this article is getting a little too long, so I'd better cut through the back lawns to make it a little quicker. A player scores from first base on a double 42, 44% of the time, but there are less than half as many opportunities to do that as to score from second on a single. Cincinnati rookie Jonathan India was the only major league player to have 20 opportunities. Trea Turner was the best in the majors at this in 2021, 9-for-11, while Yandy Diaz was the worst, 3-for-17. I love Yandy, too, because he is a very serious-looking player. He always looks like "I'm not out here to mess around. I'm here to play baseball."

Another thing we measure is "Bases Taken". There are an array of events which are documented in the stat sheets, but which are not documented in the official records as BASERUNNING events, although they are. There are five such events: Wild Pitches, Balks, Passed Balls, Sacrifice Flies, and runners moving up on Defensive Indifference.

The view which is encouraged by the official records is that, "Well, that was just a wild pitch. It was something the pitcher did, but ANYBODY would have moved up on that pitch." But when you watch the game, you realize that that is not true. Runners move up on Wild Pitches when they are alert enough to do so. There are lots of potential wild pitches on which runners miss the opportunity to advance.

You wouldn't want to document those events one by one, because the numbers would be so small that the totals would just be litter. But when you add them all together, they're meaningful. There were 4,500 such events in the major leagues last year, or 150 per team, or almost one per game.

Whit Merrifield led the majors in Bases Taken, with 34. That's not surprising; Whit leads in all kinds of things like that. But some of the names near the top of the list are players who were near the bottom of other lists: Nick Castellanos (27), DJ LeMahieu (26). Mark Canha had 25; he's not really somebody you would think of here. I remember David Ortiz, early in his career, did well in this category. He never could run, but he reacted quickly. When the ball got away from the catcher, he moved.

There's a lot more stuff to find in this data, but I suppose I had better let you find it yourself. Make the effort; you'll enjoy it.

2021 Baserunning

Player	1st to 3rd Moved	Chances	2nd to Home Moved	Chances	1st to Home Moved	Chances	Bases Taken	Out Adv	Doubled Off	BR Outs	GDP	GDP Opps	BR Gain	SB Gain	Net Gain
Abreu, Jose	11	26	12	16	2	7	19	3	2	5	28	158	-11	+1	-10
Acuna Jr., Ronald	8	16	13	15	3	5	11	2	1	3	0	34	+10	+5	+15
Adames, Willy	12	21	15	23	4	7	10	3	2	5	9	108	-1	-3	-4
Adrianza, Ehire	3	8	4	5	2	2	9	1	0	1	4	51	+7	0	+7
Aguilar, Jesus	5	23	6	9	1	7	6	2	0	2	11	97	-10	0	-10
Ahmed, Nick	10	22	8	10	1	1	12	2	1	3	9	89	+4	+3	+7
Akiyama, Shogo	3	7	4	5	2	2	4	0	0	0	1	36	+7	-4	+3
Alberto, Hanser	1	5	3	8	0	0	7	0	1	1	1	38	+2	+1	+3
Albies, Ozzie	7	17	18	27	3	4	22	2	1	3	4	115	+19	+12	+31
Alcantara, Sergio	2	5	3	5	1	1	7	0	1	1	3	45	+4	+3	+7
Alfaro, Jorge	1	15	5	6	1	2	12	1	3	4	8	58	-7	+6	-1
Almonte, Abraham	3	12	3	5	0	0	5	2	0	2	2	31	-2	-1	-3
Alonso, Pete	7	26	4	14	1	4	14	2	1	3	20	152	-13	+3	-10
Altuve, Jose	16	45	12	20	4	11	25	5	3	8	9	104	-3	-1	-4
Alvarez, Yordan	6	31	15	23	6	10	10	0	0	0	16	127	+1	+1	+2
Anderson, Brian	6	19	2	5	0	4	11	0	0	0	4	37	+5	+5	+10
Anderson, Tim	10	24	19	23	6	8	17	1	2	3	5	75	+15	+4	+19
Andrus, Elvis	10	23	18	23	4	5	15	1	3	4	14	99	+2	+8	+10
Andujar, Miguel	3	8	2	3	1	1	5	0	0	0	8	38	0	-2	-2
Aquino, Aristides	4	8	1	3	2	3	3	1	0	2	0	37	0	-2	-2
Arenado, Nolan	16	31	4	8	2	8	15	4	0	4	20	141	-5	+2	-3
Arozarena, Randy	9	27	12	18	4	10	21	0	1	1	9	115	+15	0	+15
Arraez, Luis	7	20	8	13	3	10	28	1	1	2	9	62	+13	-2	+11
Arroyo, Christian	5	11	2	2	1	2	5	0	0	0	1	22	+7	+1	+8
Astudillo, Willians	4	10	1	4	0	2	3	0	0	0	12	40	-8	0	-8
Baddoo, Akil	10	26	12	20	1	2	12	2	1	3	5	67	+2	+10	+12
Bader, Harrison	3	11	4	10	1	1	16	1	1	2	4	86	+8	+1	+9
Baez, Javier	9	20	8	10	4	6	21	2	2	4	12	121	+10	+8	+18
Barnes, Austin	2	13	3	5	0	1	6	0	0	0	6	53	+1	+1	+2
Barnhart, Tucker	2	12	6	11	1	7	7	0	0	0	8	75	-2	0	-2
Bauers, Jake	4	12	0	3	0	1	3	1	1	2	1	49	-4	+4	0
Beaty, Matt	2	12	4	6	3	5	2	0	1	1	3	60	-1	-2	-3
Bell, Josh	11	37	10	14	3	10	13	5	0	5	22	146	-16	0	-16
Bellinger, Cody	3	11	6	8	3	4	8	2	0	2	2	66	+6	+1	+7
Belt, Brandon	7	18	6	12	1	7	7	1	0	1	9	76	-3	-1	-4
Benintendi, Andrew	7	24	8	12	4	7	17	4	1	5	2	90	+5	-10	-5
Berti, Jon	3	10	9	12	2	4	19	0	1	1	7	50	+13	0	+13
Betts, Mookie	7	26	15	18	5	11	22	4	0	4	5	72	+9	0	+9
Bichette, Bo	12	35	20	29	5	9	13	3	2	5	10	118	-2	+23	+21
Biggio, Cavan	2	14	6	8	1	1	6	2	1	3	4	52	-5	+1	-4
Blackmon, Charlie	6	40	10	17	7	13	15	3	2	5	8	112	-8	+3	-5
Bogaerts, Xander	14	31	11	19	3	12	18	3	0	3	13	117	+2	+3	+5
Bohm, Alec	7	26	3	12	2	12	11	3	0	3	12	94	-13	+4	-9
Bote, David	2	12	7	11	0	3	8	1	0	1	13	77	-6	-2	-8
Bradley Jr., Jackie	0	5	6	7	4	6	14	0	0	0	8	80	+12	+5	+17
Bradley, Bobby	3	17	4	7	1	4	3	1	1	2	3	53	-6	0	-6
Brantley, Michael	5	32	8	15	5	15	20	0	0	0	11	106	+7	+1	+8
Bregman, Alex	3	20	6	13	3	9	10	2	0	2	13	98	-9	+1	-8
Brinson, Lewis	3	13	5	8	3	4	7	2	0	2	5	47	-1	-1	-2
Brosseau, Mike	2	5	6	10	0	3	2	3	0	3	1	32	-7	+2	-5
Brown, Seth	3	9	3	10	0	4	12	2	1	3	1	64	+2	+2	+4
Bryant, Kris	12	28	10	14	5	7	14	0	1	1	9	116	+14	+6	+20
Buxton, Byron	2	5	5	6	0	1	13	0	2	2	0	45	+10	+7	+17
Cabrera, Asdrubal	6	23	7	10	0	3	5	3	1	5	8	68	-16	+1	-15
Cabrera, Miguel	6	26	5	10	1	10	9	2	0	2	21	120	-17	0	-17
Cain, Lorenzo	6	17	6	9	2	3	8	0	0	0	5	58	+8	+9	+17
Calhoun, Kole	2	10	3	4	1	3	3	1	0	1	2	34	-1	+1	0
Calhoun, Willie	1	8	2	6	2	3	8	3	0	3	6	52	-7	-4	-11
Candelario, Jeimer	7	37	12	21	6	12	24	3	2	5	10	132	+1	0	+1
Canha, Mark	12	33	10	18	3	7	25	5	0	5	9	87	+3	+8	+11
Caratini, Victor	2	18	3	9	1	5	8	2	1	3	13	67	-18	+2	-16
Carlson, Dylan	10	35	15	19	5	8	17	3	1	5	5	95	+5	0	+5
Carpenter, Matt	2	9	2	7	0	0	6	1	1	2	1	45	-2	+2	0

2021 Baserunning

Player	1st to 3rd Moved	Chances	2nd to Home Moved	Chances	1st to Home Moved	Chances	Bases Taken	Out Adv	Doubled Off	BR Outs	GDP	GDP Opps	BR Gain	SB Gain	Net Gain
Casali, Curt	1	8	3	6	1	3	7	1	0	1	3	47	+1	0	+1
Castellanos, Nick	6	22	5	18	6	12	27	2	2	4	16	141	+1	+1	+2
Castro, Harold	5	18	6	14	1	4	9	2	2	4	7	68	-10	-1	-11
Castro, Jason	1	5	2	4	1	5	4	0	0	0	4	35	-1	0	-1
Castro, Starlin	2	14	4	8	0	5	4	1	1	2	6	61	-11	-2	-13
Castro, Willi	10	22	8	11	2	3	14	2	0	2	5	82	+12	+1	+13
Cave, Jake	2	8	1	2	1	1	5	0	0	0	0	23	+5	-1	+4
Chang, Yu	3	7	4	6	3	3	4	0	1	1	4	43	+2	+1	+3
Chapman, Matt	14	32	8	10	6	8	11	4	0	4	6	118	+8	-1	+7
Chisholm Jr., Jazz	14	18	9	14	2	2	20	2	2	4	3	59	+16	+7	+23
Choi, Ji-Man	1	11	3	4	0	1	7	1	0	1	5	50	-2	0	-2
Collins, Zack	1	12	6	12	2	3	5	1	0	1	4	51	-2	-1	-3
Conforto, Michael	5	25	4	14	4	8	12	1	1	2	14	124	-7	+1	-6
Contreras, William	2	7	1	1	0	3	4	0	0	0	3	38	+2	0	+2
Contreras, Willson	10	21	7	13	3	6	14	7	2	9	11	88	-17	-3	-20
Cooper, Garrett	1	14	5	12	0	5	6	3	0	3	6	41	-15	-1	-16
Correa, Carlos	7	40	13	21	4	11	13	3	0	3	16	135	-11	0	-11
Crawford, Brandon	11	34	10	16	3	7	18	4	0	4	8	121	+5	+5	+10
Crawford, J.P.	6	35	10	23	0	1	25	2	1	3	10	90	-2	-9	-11
Cron, C.J.	9	26	10	13	4	12	9	3	0	3	11	104	-5	+1	-4
Cronenworth, Jake	8	26	15	26	3	9	20	1	1	2	8	124	+10	-2	+8
Cruz, Nelson	4	24	10	15	1	7	11	3	0	3	14	133	-9	+3	-6
Culberson, Charlie	6	11	2	4	0	1	5	1	0	1	3	48	+3	+5	+8
d'Arnaud, Travis	2	5	2	4	1	1	5	0	1	1	7	47	-2	0	-2
Dahl, David	2	7	3	6	1	2	3	1	1	2	3	37	-5	0	-5
Dalbec, Bobby	5	16	3	7	3	7	8	3	0	3	3	78	-1	+2	+1
Davis, J.D.	1	12	2	6	0	2	7	0	4	4	4	46	-12	+1	-11
Daza, Yonathan	5	17	6	8	1	3	7	1	0	1	9	61	-2	0	-2
De La Cruz, Bryan	6	15	2	2	0	0	4	0	1	1	8	44	-3	-1	-4
DeJong, Paul	3	23	3	4	1	5	8	0	0	0	6	73	+1	+2	+3
Devers, Rafael	12	30	19	29	6	14	19	3	1	4	13	129	+5	-5	0
Diaz, Aledmys	1	12	6	8	0	3	10	1	0	2	7	66	-3	-2	-5
Diaz, Elias	2	11	6	10	0	5	7	1	0	1	15	76	-10	0	-10
Diaz, Isan	3	10	3	6	1	3	8	0	0	1	2	47	+4	-1	+3
Diaz, Yandy	9	24	9	14	3	17	17	2	3	5	11	100	-7	-1	-8
Dickerson, Alex	2	11	3	7	2	5	10	1	0	1	7	68	+1	+1	+2
Dickerson, Corey	6	19	5	7	1	1	5	2	0	2	8	64	-5	-4	-9
Difo, Wilmer	6	14	4	7	1	2	3	1	0	1	2	42	+1	+1	+2
Donaldson, Josh	13	36	5	12	2	8	19	1	1	2	22	109	-5	0	-5
Dozier, Hunter	6	21	17	21	2	4	11	2	0	2	12	98	+2	-3	-1
Dubon, Mauricio	0	4	2	5	0	1	7	2	0	2	5	37	-5	0	-5
Duffy, Matt	6	17	6	10	3	7	16	0	0	0	16	57	+3	+6	+9
Duggar, Steven	1	8	7	11	3	4	12	0	0	0	4	69	+12	+7	+19
Duvall, Adam	4	13	3	9	1	6	14	5	0	5	7	102	-6	+5	-1
Dyson, Jarrod	4	8	0	0	0	0	9	1	2	3	1	23	0	0	0
Eaton, Adam	3	8	4	5	3	3	11	2	1	3	6	55	+2	+3	+5
Edman, Tommy	19	34	18	28	4	8	21	3	0	3	4	87	+20	+20	+40
Escobar, Alcides	9	24	8	16	0	0	13	0	0	0	2	61	+13	+3	+16
Escobar, Eduardo	8	22	8	14	2	11	11	3	1	4	3	132	+2	+1	+3
Espinal, Santiago	6	9	3	5	4	8	7	0	1	1	4	47	+5	+4	+9
Evans, Phillip	6	14	2	4	1	3	4	1	0	1	3	37	0	+1	+1
Farmer, Kyle	5	20	9	12	5	7	14	2	0	2	16	110	0	-4	-4
Fletcher, David	7	22	12	19	9	14	25	1	0	1	10	91	+18	+9	+27
Flores, Wilmer	7	26	5	13	1	4	10	3	0	3	11	84	-10	+1	-9
Fraley, Jake	5	15	3	8	1	2	6	1	0	1	3	55	+1	+6	+7
France, Ty	12	36	11	19	3	5	18	5	1	6	13	126	-7	0	-7
Franco, Maikel	3	14	2	6	1	4	7	1	0	1	12	77	-7	0	-7
Franco, Wander	7	17	12	14	2	4	14	2	0	2	2	61	+14	0	+14
Frazier, Adam	9	41	18	26	1	9	26	5	0	5	10	88	-2	0	-2
Frazier, Clint	2	9	3	8	0	1	4	0	0	0	8	36	-6	+2	-4
Freeman, Freddie	18	40	13	20	11	17	22	2	0	3	11	132	+17	+2	+19
Fuentes, Joshua	5	8	4	6	1	1	9	0	0	0	5	60	+11	0	+11
Gallo, Joey	9	34	13	17	6	10	13	0	1	1	6	108	+12	+6	+18
Galvis, Freddy	4	17	8	13	1	3	14	0	0	0	6	73	+10	+1	+11

2021 Baserunning

Player	1st to 3rd		2nd to Home		1st to Home		Bases Taken	Out Adv	Doubled Off	BR Outs	GDP	GDP Opps	BR Gain	SB Gain	Net Gain
	Moved	Chances	Moved	Chances	Moved	Chances									
Gamel, Ben	6	19	8	12	2	5	14	1	0	1	7	75	+8	-9	-1
Garcia, Adolis	3	15	11	14	3	7	20	5	2	7	15	147	-6	+6	0
Garcia, Avisail	3	20	9	11	4	6	8	1	0	1	12	101	-2	0	-2
Garcia, Leury	15	26	9	13	3	5	11	2	0	2	12	115	+8	+2	+10
Garcia, Luis	3	8	4	5	0	1	9	0	0	0	8	57	+5	-4	+1
Gardner, Brett	1	14	4	8	4	7	22	2	3	5	3	84	+4	+4	+8
Garver, Mitch	2	6	5	10	1	3	3	0	0	0	4	52	0	-1	-1
Gimenez, Andres	3	5	4	6	0	2	10	1	0	1	1	35	+8	+11	+19
Goldschmidt, Paul	11	28	18	25	1	7	20	2	0	2	13	139	+11	+12	+23
Gomes, Yan	6	18	10	11	0	3	5	0	0	0	15	83	-3	0	-3
Gonzalez, Erik	3	10	2	4	0	2	3	0	3	3	4	32	-10	-2	-12
Gonzalez, Marwin	7	19	5	10	1	4	7	3	0	3	8	55	-8	-1	-9
Goodrum, Niko	6	15	5	9	2	2	11	2	0	2	6	52	+3	+4	+7
Goodwin, Brian	5	20	3	5	1	2	6	3	1	4	2	58	-6	+1	-5
Gordon, Nick	3	6	2	3	0	0	7	0	0	0	7	35	+2	+8	+10
Gosselin, Phil	11	22	4	10	2	8	8	2	0	2	3	76	+4	0	+4
Grandal, Yasmani	6	27	4	13	1	7	7	3	1	4	15	95	-23	0	-23
Gregorius, Didi	7	14	5	10	2	5	8	2	0	2	8	93	+1	+3	+4
Grichuk, Randal	7	22	3	7	1	5	13	3	1	4	17	103	-13	-6	-19
Grisham, Trent	8	17	13	18	3	6	16	0	0	0	10	89	+15	+3	+18
Grossman, Robbie	12	41	9	17	7	11	17	1	0	1	8	107	+10	+10	+20
Guerrero Jr., Vladimir	9	51	10	20	9	16	19	1	1	2	20	137	-7	+2	-5
Guillorme, Luis	3	4	2	3	1	3	5	0	1	1	2	25	+2	-4	-2
Gurriel Jr., Lourdes	3	21	8	13	0	8	22	1	1	2	8	98	+6	-5	+1
Gurriel, Yuli	12	37	9	15	5	14	19	2	0	2	16	120	+1	-1	0
Gutierrez, Kelvin	7	12	1	3	1	4	9	2	1	4	4	48	-4	-2	-6
Haase, Eric	3	12	2	4	1	5	14	1	2	3	11	88	-3	+2	-1
Hampson, Garrett	10	17	7	13	6	7	18	0	0	0	6	91	+23	+3	+26
Haniger, Mitch	8	33	11	18	2	10	18	3	1	4	12	123	-4	+1	-3
Happ, Ian	3	19	3	6	3	6	9	2	0	2	12	98	-7	+5	-2
Harper, Bryce	10	39	8	17	6	10	16	7	1	8	12	119	-18	+7	-11
Harrison, Josh	7	25	9	11	4	9	14	6	1	7	9	96	-11	-1	-12
Hayes, Ke'Bryan	3	19	8	14	1	3	13	2	0	2	11	77	-4	+7	+3
Hays, Austin	5	23	12	17	2	7	15	3	1	4	9	101	-2	-2	-4
Hedges, Austin	2	4	1	4	1	4	8	1	0	1	7	64	+1	+1	+2
Heim, Jonah	4	5	2	5	1	4	5	1	1	2	8	57	-5	+1	-4
Heredia, Guillermo	4	8	10	12	2	4	18	1	0	1	5	74	+18	0	+18
Hernandez, Cesar	8	37	10	18	2	8	19	0	0	0	11	101	+6	-1	+5
Hernandez, Kike	9	25	10	15	8	12	21	0	1	1	4	85	+22	+1	+23
Hernandez, Teoscar	11	25	11	18	4	10	20	1	0	2	5	122	+18	+4	+22
Hernandez, Yadiel	2	15	6	12	0	4	7	1	0	1	11	63	-9	+3	-6
Hernandez, Yonny	1	9	6	7	2	2	1	1	0	1	2	20	-3	+7	+4
Herrera, Odubel	6	22	7	15	2	6	17	3	0	3	6	73	+1	+4	+5
Heyward, Jason	6	10	3	6	3	3	11	1	0	1	4	63	+11	+3	+14
Higashioka, Kyle	2	8	1	3	1	2	4	1	0	1	4	43	-1	0	-1
Hill, Derek	1	3	4	4	1	1	6	0	0	0	2	25	+7	0	+7
Hilliard, Sam	2	6	2	2	0	2	10	1	1	2	0	45	+6	+5	+11
Hiura, Keston	1	6	0	2	0	1	8	0	0	0	6	34	+1	+3	+4
Hoerner, Nico	1	6	2	5	1	2	7	3	0	3	3	25	-7	-1	-8
Holt, Brock	1	7	2	7	2	5	7	2	0	2	5	35	-7	+3	-4
Hoskins, Rhys	4	14	6	12	2	5	12	3	3	6	7	77	-11	-1	-12
Hosmer, Eric	6	27	6	13	2	9	19	3	1	4	13	81	-10	-3	-13
Ibanez, Andy	1	10	3	5	1	3	12	2	1	3	6	54	-3	0	-3
Iglesias, Jose	7	19	12	20	4	12	18	4	2	6	10	88	-7	+1	-6
India, Jonathan	6	29	11	18	9	22	26	3	1	4	13	99	0	+6	+6
Jankowski, Travis	2	8	7	11	0	2	4	0	0	0	1	25	+2	+5	+7
Jansen, Danny	2	5	6	8	1	3	3	1	0	1	4	42	0	0	0
Jeffers, Ryan	1	9	2	5	1	5	2	1	1	1	6	45	-9	-2	-11
Jimenez, Eloy	0	7	1	3	1	3	5	0	1	1	8	51	-6	0	-6
Joe, Connor	6	15	2	5	3	5	2	0	0	0	1	24	+2	0	+2
Judge, Aaron	5	28	13	20	3	10	19	2	2	4	16	146	-5	+4	-1
Kelenic, Jarred	2	7	4	7	1	4	9	0	1	1	5	76	+4	-2	+2
Kelly, Carson	5	23	7	10	0	4	6	0	0	0	10	72	-3	0	-3
Kemp, Tony	13	33	6	9	5	6	17	3	0	3	2	69	+14	+4	+18

2021 Baserunning

Player	1st to 3rd Moved	Chances	2nd to Home Moved	Chances	1st to Home Moved	Chances	Bases Taken	Out Adv	Doubled Off	BR Outs	GDP	GDP Opps	BR Gain	SB Gain	Net Gain
Kepler, Max	6	16	6	10	2	4	17	0	0	0	2	72	+19	+10	+29
Kieboom, Carter	4	16	2	7	3	5	3	1	0	1	9	65	-7	0	-7
Kiermaier, Kevin	9	19	5	6	2	3	14	2	0	2	4	72	+12	-1	+11
Kim, Ha-seong	4	14	1	4	0	1	3	0	0	0	6	67	-1	+4	+3
Kiner-Falefa, Isiah	11	36	8	15	2	9	24	2	1	4	11	88	0	+10	+10
Kirilloff, Alex	2	8	2	4	3	4	7	3	0	3	3	50	-2	-1	-3
Kirk, Alejandro	1	7	1	3	0	1	6	0	0	0	7	36	-2	0	-2
Knizner, Andrew	0	9	2	4	2	3	6	0	1	1	7	36	-5	0	-5
La Stella, Tommy	0	11	3	4	0	1	6	1	1	2	4	28	-7	0	-7
Lagares, Juan	6	12	8	13	1	3	11	1	1	2	8	60	+2	-3	-1
Larnach, Trevor	0	16	2	5	1	3	10	3	0	3	3	65	-5	+1	-4
Laureano, Ramon	6	15	0	6	2	3	15	2	1	3	4	70	+4	+2	+6
LeMahieu, DJ	6	42	14	22	2	9	26	0	0	1	16	105	+2	0	+2
Leon, Sandy	0	13	1	5	0	2	3	0	0	0	2	26	-5	0	-5
Lindor, Francisco	14	33	6	12	2	6	15	0	1	1	7	116	+13	+2	+15
Locastro, Tim	3	11	1	5	2	2	7	0	1	1	2	23	+1	-1	0
Longoria, Evan	2	12	8	13	2	6	7	1	1	2	9	49	-8	-1	-9
Lopez, Nicky	6	30	11	14	8	11	28	1	0	1	9	101	+22	+20	+42
Lowe, Brandon	9	20	9	11	3	7	20	0	1	1	2	82	+23	+5	+28
Lowe, Nathaniel	3	30	11	21	2	5	19	3	2	5	13	111	-13	+8	-5
Lowrie, Jed	6	16	7	16	2	8	11	0	0	0	8	93	+4	0	+4
Luplow, Jordan	2	4	3	8	0	4	4	0	0	0	2	38	+1	-3	-2
Lux, Gavin	11	17	8	11	4	6	14	1	0	1	3	75	+20	+2	+22
Machado, Manny	12	31	8	18	3	7	20	3	1	4	10	107	+2	+6	+8
Madrigal, Nick	3	11	9	10	2	2	7	0	0	0	3	40	+9	-3	+6
Maldonado, Martin	1	16	7	11	0	6	7	3	1	4	9	71	-17	0	-17
Mancini, Trey	8	35	10	18	4	12	21	4	2	6	19	107	-16	0	-16
Margot, Manuel	8	16	2	5	2	6	18	3	0	3	4	86	+10	-3	+7
Marisnick, Jake	6	10	1	2	1	2	6	1	0	1	4	45	+5	+2	+7
Marsh, Brandon	2	5	5	8	2	2	4	0	0	0	3	47	+5	+4	+9
Marte, Ketel	3	17	9	14	4	8	7	3	0	3	8	61	-9	+2	-7
Marte, Starling	11	24	15	19	7	8	16	1	3	4	6	109	+13	+37	+50
Martinez, J.D.	6	20	14	21	5	12	19	2	2	4	18	150	-2	0	-2
Mateo, Jorge	2	5	3	5	0	1	6	0	1	1	1	38	+3	+4	+7
Mayfield, Jack	2	9	5	9	2	4	6	3	2	5	6	56	-13	+5	-8
Mazara, Nomar	2	6	3	4	0	1	3	0	0	0	4	41	+2	0	+2
McCann, James	1	17	2	3	2	4	4	2	0	2	12	77	-14	-3	-17
McCormick, Chas	4	14	6	11	2	3	11	1	2	3	5	69	0	0	0
McCutchen, Andrew	7	23	9	15	3	5	13	0	0	0	10	103	+8	+4	+12
McGuire, Reese	3	10	7	9	3	4	3	0	0	0	4	35	+3	0	+3
McKenna, Ryan	2	6	3	5	2	3	11	0	0	0	1	31	+11	+1	+12
McKinney, Billy	2	12	3	7	1	2	10	1	1	2	3	51	+1	+2	+3
McMahon, Ryan	9	20	6	14	7	9	14	3	1	4	14	102	-4	+2	-2
McNeil, Jeff	4	23	3	10	2	5	7	2	0	2	10	84	-11	+3	-8
Meadows, Austin	15	28	3	6	5	10	17	4	2	6	4	99	+6	-2	+4
Mejia, Francisco	0	8	7	8	0	3	2	1	2	3	4	37	-12	0	-12
Mendick, Danny	4	10	3	4	1	3	5	2	1	3	1	38	-2	-2	-4
Mercado, Oscar	2	12	2	7	5	6	7	0	0	0	1	38	+6	+5	+11
Mercedes, Yermin	1	6	1	4	4	9	8	1	0	1	7	58	-1	-2	-3
Merrifield, Whit	10	31	18	32	3	10	34	3	2	5	12	113	+9	+32	+41
Meyers, Jake	1	8	3	6	2	3	2	0	0	0	0	32	+2	+3	+5
Miller, Brad	2	15	8	14	0	3	11	1	2	3	7	72	-5	+3	-2
Miller, Owen	2	6	2	4	0	0	2	2	0	2	7	33	-10	+2	-8
Molina, Yadier	1	12	3	12	1	4	8	1	1	2	16	84	-18	+3	-15
Moncada, Yoan	10	34	14	18	3	7	21	3	1	4	6	108	+9	-1	+8
Moore, Dylan	4	12	4	7	2	3	9	3	0	3	6	57	-3	+11	+8
Moran, Colin	3	25	0	7	0	5	8	5	0	5	6	70	-21	+1	-20
Moreland, Mitch	1	10	2	6	0	3	5	0	1	1	5	46	-5	0	-5
Mountcastle, Ryan	8	30	12	12	4	8	12	2	1	3	12	101	0	-2	-2
Moustakas, Mike	3	9	4	7	2	3	2	0	1	1	6	43	-4	0	-4
Mullins II, Cedric	9	27	15	19	4	8	22	3	1	4	2	97	+15	+14	+29
Muncy, Max	11	38	7	17	2	4	25	0	0	1	7	120	+17	0	+17
Murphy, Sean	6	19	3	8	3	6	11	3	2	5	7	90	-7	0	-7
Murphy, Tom	2	14	4	8	4	4	6	0	1	1	8	60	-3	0	-3

2021 Baserunning

Player	1st to 3rd Moved	Chances	2nd to Home Moved	Chances	1st to Home Moved	Chances	Bases Taken	Out Adv	Doubled Off	BR Outs	GDP	GDP Opps	BR Gain	SB Gain	Net Gain
Myers, Wil	4	19	13	18	4	8	16	2	0	2	9	92	+6	-2	+4
Naquin, Tyler	4	13	10	10	1	3	9	1	1	2	9	103	+3	-1	+2
Narvaez, Omar	10	32	11	18	2	6	10	3	0	3	13	89	-8	0	-8
Naylor, Josh	4	12	8	10	1	5	9	2	0	2	7	42	-1	+1	0
Newman, Kevin	11	23	8	12	3	8	19	0	0	0	7	122	+23	+4	+27
Nimmo, Brandon	11	25	9	16	4	7	9	3	1	4	3	59	-1	-3	-4
Nola, Austin	2	9	2	5	2	3	5	0	0	0	2	35	+3	-2	+1
Nunez, Dom	3	7	9	10	1	4	7	1	0	1	0	44	+9	0	+9
O'Hearn, Ryan	2	11	1	3	0	1	3	0	0	0	7	49	-4	0	-4
O'Neill, Tyler	7	23	15	19	3	3	16	1	0	1	8	89	+14	+7	+21
Odor, Rougned	5	16	8	10	4	4	5	0	1	1	3	70	+7	-2	+5
Ohtani, Shohei	6	26	15	23	2	7	12	3	1	4	7	119	-3	+6	+3
Olson, Matt	8	28	12	17	7	11	16	6	1	7	17	133	-12	+2	-10
Ortega, Rafael	4	16	2	9	6	9	9	1	1	2	3	47	-1	0	-1
Ozuna, Marcell	0	4	2	3	0	2	6	0	0	0	6	43	0	0	0
Panik, Joe	2	9	1	2	1	5	8	2	0	2	9	52	-6	+2	-4
Pederson, Joc	8	19	2	7	5	8	14	2	0	2	9	83	+4	-4	0
Peralta, David	4	19	12	15	2	6	18	0	2	2	9	107	+8	0	+8
Perez, Michael	1	8	2	4	1	2	5	0	0	0	4	54	+3	-2	+1
Perez, Salvador	3	25	5	13	2	7	18	3	0	3	14	158	-4	+1	-3
Peters, DJ	4	10	2	2	2	3	4	1	0	1	4	46	+2	+2	+4
Peterson, Jace	3	8	6	8	3	5	10	2	1	3	1	47	+4	+8	+12
Pham, Tommy	7	25	9	14	4	8	15	1	2	3	10	83	-2	+2	0
Phillips, Brett	2	7	7	11	7	7	7	2	0	2	3	49	+4	+8	+12
Pillar, Kevin	1	9	6	9	1	4	5	0	1	1	5	76	0	-2	-2
Pina, Manny	2	9	1	4	0	1	6	1	1	2	4	44	-4	0	-4
Pinder, Chad	3	6	6	10	1	4	7	1	0	1	6	37	0	+1	+1
Piscotty, Stephen	2	6	5	9	1	2	3	2	0	2	2	26	-4	+1	-3
Plawecki, Kevin	3	13	4	7	1	5	4	0	0	0	4	34	-1	0	-1
Polanco, Gregory	4	16	6	7	2	6	7	0	0	0	8	86	+5	+12	+17
Polanco, Jorge	10	25	11	19	2	5	16	1	1	2	4	104	+12	-1	+11
Pollock, A.J.	4	15	5	10	2	3	5	0	0	0	4	67	+2	+7	+9
Posey, Buster	3	22	8	17	4	8	9	2	1	3	15	85	-17	0	-17
Profar, Jurickson	11	23	6	10	3	7	14	3	0	3	12	79	0	0	0
Pujols, Albert	0	11	0	4	0	0	8	1	0	1	14	67	-11	+2	-9
Ramirez, Harold	6	18	5	8	3	7	15	1	1	2	10	73	+3	+1	+4
Ramirez, Jose	18	28	16	19	3	7	14	3	0	4	13	131	+9	+19	+28
Realmuto, J.T.	11	23	6	9	5	5	21	2	1	3	8	100	+15	+7	+22
Refsnyder, Rob	0	11	2	6	0	1	8	0	0	0	4	31	0	+1	+1
Rendon, Anthony	1	14	4	4	2	4	4	0	1	1	11	52	-9	0	-9
Renfroe, Hunter	6	26	8	19	1	5	9	4	1	5	6	107	-13	-3	-16
Reyes, Franmil	4	15	2	8	0	2	7	3	0	3	13	77	-16	+2	-14
Reyes, Victor	6	8	2	3	2	3	9	2	0	2	2	26	+6	+3	+9
Reynolds, Bryan	13	32	17	20	7	10	24	4	1	5	10	144	+16	+1	+17
Riley, Austin	11	41	8	12	4	12	8	5	0	5	11	118	-15	-2	-17
Rizzo, Anthony	10	21	6	15	0	6	17	2	0	2	15	129	+1	+2	+3
Robert, Luis	1	13	3	7	0	4	9	0	1	1	4	50	-2	+4	+2
Robles, Victor	0	14	6	12	1	3	9	2	0	2	7	59	-8	-4	-12
Rodgers, Brendan	3	11	6	10	1	6	8	0	2	2	8	83	-4	0	-4
Rojas, Jose	1	4	3	6	1	4	3	1	0	1	2	32	-2	0	-2
Rojas, Josh	8	22	13	16	5	7	22	1	1	2	7	86	+18	+1	+19
Rojas, Miguel	7	21	10	14	3	5	15	3	2	5	10	75	-5	+7	+2
Rooker, Brent	1	7	4	5	0	1	5	0	0	0	1	42	+6	0	+6
Rosario, Amed	10	24	12	18	6	11	20	3	0	3	12	109	+9	+13	+22
Rosario, Eddie	3	13	7	13	0	2	7	2	1	3	4	65	-6	+5	-1
Ruf, Darin	7	19	4	9	0	2	10	1	1	2	8	61	-3	+2	-1
Sanchez, Gary	4	18	5	7	2	6	9	3	0	3	14	82	-11	0	-11
Sanchez, Jesus	3	10	2	9	0	1	2	1	0	1	2	46	-5	-2	-7
Sano, Miguel	5	25	10	17	1	2	10	1	0	1	13	97	-4	0	-4
Santana, Carlos	11	35	2	10	3	8	16	2	0	2	12	118	-1	+2	+1
Santander, Anthony	3	19	8	11	5	7	15	2	0	2	11	99	+5	-1	+4
Schoop, Jonathan	11	37	13	19	1	7	21	3	3	6	15	103	-9	+2	-7
Schwarber, Kyle	7	27	4	12	4	8	8	3	0	3	4	76	-6	-1	-7
Schwindel, Frank	2	12	5	12	0	2	3	0	0	0	4	52	-3	0	-3

2021 Baserunning

Player	1st to 3rd Moved	Chances	2nd to Home Moved	Chances	1st to Home Moved	Chances	Bases Taken	Out Adv	Doubled Off	BR Outs	GDP	GDP Opps	BR Gain	SB Gain	Net Gain
Seager, Corey	7	28	6	10	3	8	13	1	0	1	8	74	+3	-1	+2
Seager, Kyle	5	27	9	23	2	5	19	6	1	7	7	146	-8	+1	-7
Segura, Jean	9	18	12	17	4	10	17	2	1	3	16	92	-1	+3	+2
Semien, Marcus	14	37	12	18	7	12	22	3	1	4	9	126	+13	+13	+26
Severino, Pedro	4	21	2	9	1	7	12	2	2	4	9	72	-14	0	-14
Shaw, Travis	0	6	3	6	1	4	5	2	0	2	2	58	-3	0	-3
Sheets, Gavin	1	9	3	7	0	0	1	1	0	1	4	43	-6	0	-6
Sierra, Magneuris	3	8	11	16	3	4	6	1	1	2	1	24	+2	+11	+13
Simmons, Andrelton	6	18	5	9	3	6	17	2	0	3	14	77	-2	+1	-1
Slater, Austin	4	8	4	8	4	6	11	0	0	0	7	44	+7	+11	+18
Smith, Dominic	5	12	6	18	3	6	10	2	0	2	13	117	-5	0	-5
Smith, Pavin	6	28	14	25	3	13	19	3	0	3	11	90	-4	+1	-3
Smith, Will	6	24	3	13	3	11	16	5	1	7	11	114	-18	+3	-15
Sogard, Eric	2	8	2	3	2	3	5	3	0	3	5	31	-7	+1	-6
Solak, Nick	11	23	9	12	5	7	20	2	1	3	11	102	+12	-3	+9
Solano, Donovan	5	13	7	12	2	5	9	0	1	1	8	73	+2	+2	+4
Soler, Jorge	4	33	10	22	1	9	17	3	1	4	12	102	-15	0	-15
Sosa, Edmundo	5	12	6	10	1	2	11	2	0	2	8	56	0	-4	-4
Soto, Juan	13	50	15	26	5	12	24	4	1	5	23	166	-10	-5	-15
Springer, George	3	14	6	12	1	4	13	1	4	5	6	49	-10	+2	-8
Stallings, Jacob	1	21	2	9	0	3	11	0	2	2	10	82	-12	0	-12
Stanton, Giancarlo	3	25	3	9	1	6	18	2	0	2	22	121	-12	0	-12
Stassi, Max	4	17	3	8	1	7	10	1	0	2	8	74	-5	0	-5
Stephenson, Tyler	3	16	3	9	5	11	16	2	1	4	11	93	-7	0	-7
Stevenson, Andrew	1	12	5	7	2	4	11	0	0	0	3	33	+7	-1	+6
Stewart, D.J.	10	30	8	10	1	1	10	0	2	2	3	54	+7	0	+7
Story, Trevor	5	21	17	21	6	10	11	2	2	4	7	116	+2	+8	+10
Straw, Myles	11	29	15	24	3	5	30	2	0	2	13	115	+18	+18	+36
Suarez, Eugenio	5	29	6	14	1	5	12	3	2	5	14	132	-16	-2	-18
Suzuki, Kurt	2	12	0	3	0	0	3	0	0	0	7	44	-5	0	-5
Swanson, Dansby	9	30	11	19	4	8	15	0	1	1	7	109	+10	+3	+13
Tapia, Raimel	10	30	11	17	3	6	19	0	2	2	8	59	+7	+8	+15
Tatis Jr., Fernando	11	23	4	6	0	3	23	2	1	3	5	90	+15	+17	+32
Tauchman, Mike	2	4	1	4	3	4	4	2	0	2	0	25	-1	-3	-4
Taylor, Chris	11	29	12	24	4	8	14	1	0	1	5	123	+12	+11	+23
Taylor, Michael A.	8	22	11	19	3	5	16	2	0	2	9	78	+5	0	+5
Taylor, Tyrone	3	9	4	4	0	0	6	1	0	1	6	56	+2	+4	+6
Tellez, Rowdy	2	10	1	4	1	3	3	0	0	0	6	63	-3	0	-3
Thomas, Lane	3	16	7	12	1	3	11	0	2	2	6	36	-3	0	-3
Toro, Abraham	2	19	6	11	4	9	8	1	1	2	5	79	-3	0	-3
Torrens, Luis	2	14	3	7	3	5	6	0	0	0	8	69	-1	0	-1
Torres, Gleyber	8	22	8	11	2	4	9	0	3	3	12	105	-4	+2	-2
Torreyes, Ronald	3	16	6	8	0	1	10	0	0	0	7	83	+7	0	+7
Trevino, Jose	2	10	4	7	0	2	2	1	1	2	13	54	-16	-1	-17
Trout, Mike	1	6	3	4	3	6	7	0	0	0	0	24	+8	+2	+10
Tsutsugo, Yoshi	0	7	4	10	2	5	3	0	0	0	3	47	-2	-2	-4
Tucker, Kyle	9	22	10	15	3	6	21	1	0	1	10	128	+18	+10	+28
Turner, Justin	7	27	10	20	1	7	16	1	0	1	12	138	+2	+3	+5
Turner, Trea	11	22	15	25	9	11	21	0	1	2	18	100	+8	+22	+30
Upton, Justin	1	9	2	4	4	6	5	0	2	2	11	76	-8	+2	-6
Urias, Luis	9	22	7	10	2	8	15	4	1	5	9	96	-4	+3	-1
Urias, Ramon	1	13	4	6	1	4	13	1	1	2	3	60	+3	-3	0
Urshela, Gio	1	17	5	10	4	14	11	3	0	3	16	98	-16	+1	-15
Valaika, Pat	1	11	1	3	1	2	5	0	0	0	4	40	0	-1	-1
VanMeter, Josh	3	15	1	3	3	7	6	2	0	2	5	57	-5	-1	-6
Varsho, Daulton	5	12	2	7	6	8	12	0	1	1	4	71	+10	+6	+16
Vaughn, Andrew	6	20	8	14	0	4	10	2	1	3	14	106	-10	-1	-11
Vazquez, Christian	2	26	6	11	2	4	14	5	0	5	15	91	-18	0	-18
Verdugo, Alex	8	36	6	15	5	10	20	2	2	4	11	109	-4	+2	-2
Villar, Jonathan	7	18	6	11	3	4	10	2	0	3	6	93	+1	0	+1
Vogelbach, Daniel	1	10	5	8	1	6	6	4	0	4	6	42	-14	0	-14
Vogt, Stephen	3	5	6	9	0	2	8	0	0	0	2	45	+10	0	+10
Voit, Luke	1	14	3	7	0	0	5	0	0	0	12	52	-9	0	-9
Votto, Joey	4	23	5	10	3	12	14	1	1	2	7	96	-1	+1	0

2021 Baserunning

Player	1st to 3rd Moved	1st to 3rd Chances	2nd to Home Moved	2nd to Home Chances	1st to Home Moved	1st to Home Chances	Bases Taken	Out Adv	Doubled Off	BR Outs	GDP	GDP Opps	BR Gain	SB Gain	Net Gain
Wade Jr., LaMonte	4	12	4	8	0	2	13	2	0	2	3	50	+4	+4	+8
Wade, Tyler	2	5	8	11	1	2	18	0	1	1	3	19	+13	+5	+18
Walker, Christian	10	27	6	10	2	5	8	0	0	0	8	81	+5	0	+5
Walls, Taylor	1	8	2	5	0	0	7	0	1	1	3	31	0	0	0
Walsh, Jared	2	24	10	18	1	3	20	2	0	2	7	108	+5	0	+5
Ward, Taylor	3	12	3	5	3	6	3	2	0	2	4	34	-6	-1	-7
Wendle, Joey	6	21	7	12	5	7	11	2	0	2	9	89	+1	-4	-3
White, Eli	3	9	4	7	2	2	7	0	0	0	2	34	+7	-2	+5
Winker, Jesse	6	32	4	12	2	8	19	7	1	8	14	106	-22	+1	-21
Wisdom, Patrick	4	17	5	9	0	0	7	0	0	0	7	61	+2	+2	+4
Wong, Kolten	6	17	8	16	4	8	14	3	2	5	2	64	-2	+2	0
Yastrzemski, Mike	5	18	11	17	3	7	15	1	1	2	3	104	+12	+4	+16
Yelich, Christian	9	30	9	13	3	6	10	2	1	3	5	98	+2	+3	+5
Zimmer, Bradley	5	14	10	16	0	5	5	3	3	6	3	53	-15	+9	-6
Zimmerman, Ryan	3	14	4	8	1	2	7	1	1	2	9	71	-5	0	-5
Zunino, Mike	3	12	5	8	2	5	14	0	0	0	7	67	+10	0	+10

Career Baserunning
Players with 1000 Career Games
(Data goes back to 2002)

Player	1st to 3rd Moved	Chances	2nd to Home Moved	Chances	1st to Home Moved	Chances	Bases Taken	Out Adv	Doubled Off	BR Outs	GDP	GDP Opps	BR Gain	SB Gain	Net Gain
Abreu, Jose	58	225	69	113	28	73	123	26	9	36	148	1021	-75	+1	-74
Altuve, Jose	109	315	133	225	50	89	211	49	13	65	158	1135	-49	+101	+52
Andrus, Elvis	192	383	180	240	70	105	287	32	26	59	175	1368	+167	+103	+270
Arenado, Nolan	89	258	81	125	25	57	113	17	7	24	141	1080	-6	-12	-18
Avila, Alex	30	183	40	99	9	49	74	17	16	33	83	690	-113	-8	-121
Belt, Brandon	70	273	83	142	22	70	133	32	6	38	51	963	+14	+4	+18
Blackmon, Charlie	89	322	114	176	41	73	176	26	11	38	53	703	+51	+24	+75
Bogaerts, Xander	113	239	97	140	48	86	146	28	5	33	100	944	+71	+36	+107
Bradley Jr., Jackie	64	163	60	95	25	50	105	9	6	15	56	716	+73	+37	+110
Brantley, Michael	86	318	87	157	42	104	186	15	5	21	127	1125	+52	+60	+112
Bruce, Jay	69	268	86	166	34	74	141	27	8	35	101	1294	+20	-15	+5
Cabrera, Asdrubal	109	362	133	221	39	100	228	61	10	76	177	1488	-65	+27	-38
Cabrera, Miguel	148	684	191	360	50	176	277	53	14	69	342	2272	-200	-3	-203
Cain, Lorenzo	97	229	104	151	41	59	151	16	10	26	105	822	+77	+104	+181
Calhoun, Kole	68	201	73	121	32	71	152	25	7	32	68	747	+48	+3	+51
Carpenter, Matt	90	319	97	180	28	69	153	34	14	48	36	763	-3	-7	-10
Castellanos, Nick	49	181	57	116	21	58	135	21	16	37	85	919	-21	-20	-41
Castro, Starlin	81	305	107	167	40	88	144	25	13	38	177	1186	-69	-15	-84
Crawford, Brandon	63	257	98	153	24	56	162	22	4	26	104	1113	+50	-23	+27
Cruz, Nelson	69	365	101	176	18	96	180	32	12	44	161	1483	-74	+15	-59
Donaldson, Josh	79	264	77	128	29	78	164	26	15	41	116	1006	-12	+22	+10
Escobar, Alcides	107	292	138	205	49	69	174	16	14	30	112	1043	+102	+89	+191
Escobar, Eduardo	66	202	52	99	26	52	113	23	5	28	53	832	+34	-9	+25
Fowler, Dexter	164	302	120	181	40	70	210	51	29	81	59	842	+55	+13	+68
Frazier, Todd	71	212	61	111	33	65	135	32	10	43	95	924	-14	-3	-17
Freeman, Freddie	107	357	137	216	47	120	192	27	8	36	127	1366	+50	+5	+55
Galvis, Freddy	49	180	72	104	16	38	106	20	5	25	83	813	+10	+15	+25
Gardner, Brett	119	311	124	199	51	86	262	24	22	46	58	1059	+177	+146	+323
Goldschmidt, Paul	108	327	132	206	48	97	202	13	6	19	127	1298	+128	+74	+202
Gonzalez, Marwin	46	185	47	87	19	54	99	23	4	28	83	677	-43	-15	-58
Grandal, Yasmani	41	181	31	86	9	67	73	21	7	30	100	768	-119	-3	-122
Gregorius, Didi	66	204	80	114	31	50	104	15	2	17	50	779	+82	+4	+86
Harper, Bryce	100	273	90	164	65	115	152	48	20	68	93	1166	-42	+33	-9
Harrison, Josh	61	167	86	115	30	58	115	21	11	33	57	611	+27	+17	+44
Hernandez, Cesar	63	231	74	115	35	71	130	14	10	24	58	586	+27	+9	+36
Heyward, Jason	125	326	126	192	55	84	185	22	7	29	91	1163	+145	+37	+182
Hosmer, Eric	83	334	120	195	47	88	162	30	16	48	150	1193	-54	+16	-38
Jay, Jon	87	276	108	140	37	62	135	21	7	29	90	723	+45	-11	+34
Joyce, Matt	69	218	86	127	34	61	109	15	9	24	76	850	+45	-11	+34
LeMahieu, DJ	68	262	112	183	43	94	177	12	12	25	146	900	+1	+1	+2
Longoria, Evan	85	344	137	214	38	98	184	19	14	34	192	1538	-6	+20	+14
Lowrie, Jed	56	238	86	143	27	80	144	19	3	22	89	959	+35	+1	+36
Lucroy, Jonathan	44	198	65	124	22	64	100	26	11	39	136	876	-121	+12	-109
Machado, Manny	82	252	93	163	32	62	172	30	10	40	151	1115	-15	+10	-5
Marte, Starling	89	212	116	158	38	64	144	30	13	43	80	839	+39	+128	+167
Martinez, J.D.	60	247	79	153	25	85	137	18	12	30	147	1098	-65	+3	-62
Maybin, Cameron	66	175	102	140	41	61	126	15	17	33	87	777	+41	+77	+118
McCutchen, Andrew	113	437	154	237	54	112	180	20	12	33	108	1286	+54	+41	+95
Molina, Yadier	72	401	99	223	20	101	173	33	15	50	277	1605	-236	-5	-241
Moreland, Mitch	37	206	61	114	14	57	95	12	11	24	98	888	-51	+1	-50
Moustakas, Mike	38	230	70	129	15	60	112	23	9	32	107	983	-66	-1	-67
Ozuna, Marcell	83	228	60	104	30	58	102	15	4	20	97	847	+18	0	+18
Parra, Gerardo	78	231	116	169	31	61	159	46	9	56	113	961	-24	-13	-37
Perez, Salvador	38	193	65	131	12	57	93	16	3	19	145	937	-85	+4	-81
Pillar, Kevin	58	162	65	105	28	50	97	9	6	15	69	742	+53	+28	+81
Posey, Buster	65	289	86	178	34	104	169	17	7	24	163	1103	-45	+5	-40
Pujols, Albert	185	610	219	333	60	163	305	76	23	102	392	2675	-167	+39	-128
Reddick, Josh	81	234	64	117	32	65	141	12	12	26	75	947	+63	+25	+88
Rendon, Anthony	65	233	93	133	35	66	135	11	7	18	77	801	+67	+13	+80
Rizzo, Anthony	81	282	84	156	21	93	160	40	16	56	119	1287	-68	-6	-74
Sandoval, Pablo	45	273	74	139	15	59	143	24	7	32	149	1032	-77	-14	-91

Career Baserunning
Players with 1000 Career Games
(Data goes back to 2002)

Player	1st to 3rd Moved	Chances	2nd to Home Moved	Chances	1st to Home Moved	Chances	Bases Taken	Out Adv	Doubled Off	BR Outs	GDP	GDP Opps	BR Gain	SB Gain	Net Gain
Santana, Carlos	98	368	107	188	41	115	191	35	8	45	150	1319	-33	+12	-21
Schoop, Jonathan	54	153	62	97	18	49	114	15	9	24	106	737	-6	+2	-4
Seager, Kyle	86	260	90	166	25	62	161	34	11	46	107	1195	-1	+1	0
Segura, Jean	91	225	121	165	35	66	177	25	23	49	115	829	+11	+62	+73
Semien, Marcus	59	187	86	118	37	55	124	19	4	23	73	751	+58	+31	+89
Simmons, Andrelton	70	199	86	123	23	61	127	18	7	27	158	902	-33	+20	-13
Stanton, Giancarlo	46	233	76	140	23	68	158	25	4	30	117	1147	-3	+12	+9
Suarez, Eugenio	48	219	48	106	16	41	86	21	5	28	87	825	-64	-6	-70
Suzuki, Kurt	74	295	89	176	31	74	124	18	2	21	145	1178	-22	-2	-24
Trout, Mike	163	337	133	191	47	79	196	18	18	37	58	1088	+190	+129	+319
Turner, Justin	82	258	85	146	21	70	131	22	6	31	104	990	-9	+18	+9
Upton, Justin	131	372	149	213	66	111	177	25	19	44	141	1540	+81	+33	+114
Votto, Joey	119	507	133	253	44	147	205	48	24	73	158	1592	-132	+22	-110
Yelich, Christian	91	250	113	158	42	64	133	15	10	25	90	921	+72	+79	+151
Zimmerman, Ryan	110	364	144	218	55	111	190	27	8	35	212	1577	+24	+11	+35

2002-2021 MLB Averages

1st to 3rd	2nd to Home	1st to Home
28%	59%	44%

2021 Team Baserunning

Team	1st to 3rd Moved	1st to 3rd Chances	2nd to Home Moved	2nd to Home Chances	1st to Home Moved	1st to Home Chances	Bases Taken	Out Adv	Doubled Off	BR Outs	GDP	GDP Opps	BR Gain	SB Gain	Net Gain
Kansas City Royals	73	268	95	166	32	74	183	19	9	29	100	1053	+28	+58	+86
Los Angeles Dodgers	83	286	92	172	37	82	183	17	5	25	95	1190	+53	+31	+84
St Louis Cardinals	84	261	98	159	25	55	158	21	5	27	99	1066	+33	+45	+78
Tampa Bay Rays	84	237	100	149	37	90	182	24	10	34	75	1094	+70	+4	+74
Atlanta Braves	77	242	103	162	33	77	172	22	7	31	105	1031	-8	+75	+67
Cleveland Indians	84	241	97	168	29	73	149	24	9	34	119	1083	+29	+32	+61
San Diego Padres	87	263	94	161	26	74	186	20	7	27	98	1098	+31	+30	+61
Colorado Rockies	79	254	101	158	43	89	146	16	10	26	103	1156	+13	+39	+52
Philadelphia Phillies	79	250	87	158	34	79	167	24	9	33	99	1074	+13	+39	+52
Oakland Athletics	100	272	95	164	42	79	169	34	12	46	120	1074	+25	+24	+49
Minnesota Twins	69	251	82	147	22	64	187	15	7	23	111	1103	+2	+41	+43
Toronto Blue Jays	79	279	100	167	38	88	177	22	12	35	99	1150	+28	+11	+39
Arizona D-Backs	82	278	113	172	36	88	153	18	9	28	113	1083	0	+38	+38
Detroit Tigers	87	295	101	168	27	66	176	24	12	36	94	976	-12	+48	+36
Miami Marlins	82	260	88	148	25	63	145	21	12	34	117	1101	-14	+38	+24
San Francisco Giants	67	255	95	182	31	80	167	24	6	30	107	1050	-5	+27	+22
Los Angeles Angels	66	231	92	162	43	94	149	21	8	30	113	1123	-28	+48	+20
Texas Rangers	65	233	84	141	29	66	155	25	11	37	102	1253	-20	+40	+20
Milwaukee Brewers	76	250	96	156	31	76	139	27	9	36	136	1049	-11	+21	+10
Houston Astros	75	318	113	191	39	107	185	22	6	29	105	1177	0	+8	+8
Baltimore Orioles	66	268	97	147	27	73	178	22	14	36	154	1140	+5	-2	+3
Boston Red Sox	93	293	101	177	39	100	176	29	11	39	133	1246	-25	+27	+2
New York Yankees	55	265	95	159	29	76	181	14	11	26	139	1144	-12	+12	0
Chicago Cubs	76	241	70	136	36	68	150	21	6	27	92	1097	-19	+17	-2
Chicago White Sox	89	300	117	175	38	82	164	25	13	38	123	1194	-6	0	-6
Pittsburgh Pirates	76	295	87	150	22	69	157	21	9	30	129	1277	-35	+16	-19
Seattle Mariners	60	253	73	154	24	57	148	25	10	35	158	1236	-55	+2	-53
New York Mets	75	248	66	150	27	61	126	19	11	31			-48	-12	-60
Cincinnati Reds	59	255	80	156	47	117	173	25	13	40			-76	+4	-72
Washington Nationals	74	312	108	194	26	77	158	25	7	32					
MLB Totals	2301	7954	2820	4849	974	2344	4939	666	279	964	3319	33747			

Stolen Base Times

Alex Vigderman

It's 2021. We might be past the cliche "chicks dig the long ball." But we know that home runs dominate baseball culture, and interestingly enough this section that has nothing to do with home runs shows that to be true.

If I were to ask you which players hit the ball hardest on average this season, you'd have a pretty good shot of nailing the leader. (Check out the Hard Hit Balls section to find out!) That's because home runs make the highlight reel, and we revere the biggest blasts of the year.

Try this. Think of the fastest basestealers in the game, the players you'd expect to top this list. Then check your work on the next page.

OK, are you back? Good.

Names like Byron Buxton, Trevor Story, Trea Turner, and Whit Merrifield aren't big surprises. But it's exciting to see a name like Sam Haggerty getting top billing. He's the kind of player that you'd probably have to be a *Seattle Times* writer to have thought of.

Haggerty only has 150-some plate appearances to his name and has been a below-average hitter, but that doesn't mean that he doesn't have a particular set of skills that make him a nightmare for opponents. From 2017-19 he stole a smidge under 100 bases in a smidge under 300 games across three levels of the minors, and these timing numbers line up with that kind of production on the basepaths.

Go on, take a look at the rest of the list. Next time you'll ace the pop quiz.

Stolen Base Times - 2B Only

Runner	Timed Attempts	Average
Haggerty, Sam	6	3.48
Sierra, Magneuris	7	3.52
Buxton, Byron	8	3.53
Story, Trevor	12	3.53
Edman, Tommy	24	3.53
Mondesi, Adalberto	7	3.54
Laureano, Ramon	6	3.55
Turner, Trea	22	3.55
Dyson, Jarrod	7	3.55
Rojas, Josh	13	3.55
India, Jonathan	8	3.56
Moore, Dylan	17	3.56
Merrifield, Whit	17	3.56
Straw, Myles	23	3.56
Slater, Austin	12	3.57
Rosario, Amed	11	3.57
Alfaro, Jorge	7	3.57
Chisholm Jr., Jazz	19	3.57
Bichette, Bo	16	3.58
Hampson, Garrett	13	3.58
Berti, Jon	8	3.58
Wade, Tyler	18	3.58
Anderson, Tim	15	3.58
Mullins II, Cedric	28	3.59
Rosario, Eddie	9	3.59
Kiermaier, Kevin	10	3.59
Marte, Starling	35	3.59
Segura, Jean	8	3.59
Fraley, Jake	6	3.59
Robles, Victor	7	3.59
Acuna Jr., Ronald	16	3.59
Hill, Derek	6	3.60
Gordon, Nick	7	3.60
Kiner-Falefa, Isiah	15	3.60
Polanco, Jorge	8	3.60
Ramirez, Jose	20	3.60
Tapia, Raimel	17	3.60
Alford, Anthony	9	3.61
Duggar, Steven	7	3.61
Goldschmidt, Paul	6	3.61
Grisham, Trent	9	3.61
Taveras, Leody	10	3.61
Baddoo, Akil	17	3.62
Pham, Tommy	14	3.62
Castro, Willi	10	3.62
Zimmer, Bradley	15	3.63
Wendle, Joey	11	3.63
Wong, Kolten	11	3.63
Nimmo, Brandon	6	3.64
Mateo, Jorge	7	3.64
Benintendi, Andrew	8	3.64
Marsh, Brandon	6	3.64
Gimenez, Andres	9	3.64
Arozarena, Randy	25	3.65
Bader, Harrison	8	3.65
Machado, Manny	9	3.65
Villar, Jonathan	10	3.65
Fletcher, David	12	3.66
Margot, Manuel	10	3.66
O'Neill, Tyler	17	3.66
Garcia, Adolis	11	3.66
Sosa, Edmundo	7	3.67
Cain, Lorenzo	8	3.67
Polanco, Gregory	13	3.67
Peterson, Jace	9	3.67
Myers, Wil	6	3.68
Albies, Ozzie	15	3.68
Bryant, Kris	7	3.68
Phillips, Brett	13	3.68
Swanson, Dansby	8	3.68
Hayes, Ke'Bryan	7	3.68

Runner	Timed Attempts	Average
Tatis Jr., Fernando	22	3.68
Ohtani, Shohei	23	3.68
Kelenic, Jarred	9	3.68
Harper, Bryce	6	3.69
Goodrum, Niko	10	3.69
Kepler, Max	8	3.70
Lindor, Francisco	10	3.70
Andrus, Elvis	9	3.70
Taylor, Michael A.	10	3.70
Tucker, Kyle	12	3.71
Lopez, Nicky	14	3.72
Grossman, Robbie	16	3.72
Yelich, Christian	9	3.72
Baez, Javier	12	3.73
Ahmed, Nick	6	3.73
Realmuto, J.T.	7	3.74
Ortega, Rafael	9	3.74
Profar, Jurickson	10	3.74
Solak, Nick	7	3.74
Semien, Marcus	8	3.75
Betts, Mookie	10	3.75
Hernandez, Teoscar	9	3.76
Crawford, J.P.	9	3.77
Toro, Abraham	8	3.77
Hernandez, Yonny	9	3.78
Soto, Juan	8	3.81
Rojas, Miguel	7	3.81
Torres, Gleyber	12	3.83
Vazquez, Christian	6	3.84
Gamel, Ben	7	3.86
Frazier, Adam	8	3.90

Pitcher's Repertoires

Bill James

See, the trouble with this book, Louie, is that there is too much information in it. So I've added a little more.

I am quite serious in saying that the problem with this book is that there is too much information in it. Louie is just an imaginary gangster that I talk to sometimes about my problems. But there is so much information in this book that you can't possibly absorb more than 1% of it in a one-hour sitting, and really, nobody has time to give the book 100 sittings. There is so much information here that if you explained it all, strung it all out into paragraphs, it would be like 10,000 pages. Literally. "Scott Alexander, a 31-year-old pitcher with the Los Angeles Dodgers, had a 2.93 ERA in 2021 and 2.92 the previous season, despite which he has been unable to find regular major league work, spending most of his time on the injured list or on rehab assignments. He does not have an impressive fastball, averaging just 92.2 miles per hour, but throws the fastball 75% of the time, his other two options being a slider (17%) and a change (8%). It is one of the thinner repertoires in the major leagues." See, that's just one pitcher with information from just a couple of sections of the book, including this one, and there are dozens of sections of the book, and there were 804 pitchers who pitched in the majors last year, so…do the math. It would go on forever. I tell ya, Louie, it's a problem. It prevents the people who buy the book from getting full value OUT of the book, because they are buried so deep in these little sand pebbles of knowledge that they can't get out. Kind of like what you did with that guy who ratted on you after the Tucson job. Oh, sorry; I shouldn't have brought that up.

What we hope that you will do with this book is to make a little list of players that you are interested in—a mental list is fine—and use this book to get a deeper understanding of those players. This section of the book will tell you how hard he throws, and what his secondary pitches are and how often he throws them and when the last time he had Tommy John surgery was. If he is a relief pitcher, there is a section of the book that will tell you how many relief games he pitched, and how often he entered the game in the early innings, and how many times he pitched on consecutive days, and how many long outings he had, and what the leverage index was (which indicates whether he was used in crucial situations or in games when the score was not close), and how many inherited runners he faced and how many of them scored, and, if he had Saves, how many of them were Easy Saves and how many were Tough Saves, and a bunch of other stuff—just on that chart. Another section will give you his career batting record; another section, his career fielding record, and whether he is good at holding runners. We're planning to add a section detailing what kind of underwear he wears and how often he uses underarm deodorant. Joking.

I did add a section, however. This is a stat that I invented a little more than 10 years ago and thought that I had put in the book years ago, but apparently I didn't. It is called the Pitch Mix Index. It is a measure of how much the pitcher mixes up his pitches. If he just relies on one or two pitches, he'll have a low number. If he can throw whatever he wants to throw, like Hyun-Jin Ryu or Max Scherzer or Corbin Burnes or Nathan Eovaldi, he'll have a high number. I'll give you the formula later, because I don't want Louie to beat it out of me.

When I first figured this, eleven years ago, there was one pitcher, Shaun Marcum of Toronto, who had *by far* the highest number in the majors. It was around four. There wasn't anybody else who had a number higher than three.

I would bet that Shaun Marcum threw harder than you do, but I wouldn't give odds on it. Marcum was a true junkballer, with what barely qualified as a major league fastball in 2010, and would probably get you cut from your high school team in 2021—yet, by mixing up his pitches, he was able to get hitters out and win games. He was a very good third starter.

Studying the issue then, I found that pitchers who mixed up their pitches were more successful than those who used a limited pallet. This was somewhat contrary to the thinking of the time. The dominant belief of pitching coaches at the time was that you didn't want to get beat with your second- or third-best pitch. There were always a few veteran pitchers who would develop a deeper repertoire, like Orlando Hernandez, David Cone and John Burkett, but it wasn't something that was generally encouraged.

To walk you back further in time than you might really want to go, in the 1930s and 1940s a pitcher who came to the major leagues was expected to be able to throw any pitch that was called, and was also expected to be able to vary his arm angle. He was expected to be able to throw a knuckleball, a hard curve, a slow curve, a sidearm curve.

There were no pitching coaches at that time. From 1948 to 1953, however, every team or almost every team hired a pitching coach. Almost immediately, pitching coaches started shaving the repertoire. They convinced people to stop throwing knuckleballs if they had other options. They replaced the idea of throwing from a variety of angles with the dominant concept of "repeatability". It was crucial for a pitcher to be able to repeat his delivery. It was the thickest chapter in the pitching coach's bible: Repeat your delivery.

This sounds dismissive of pitching coaches, and I apologize for that. Pitching Coaches of course made giant contributions to the forward progress of major league pitchers, and some other time we'll discuss those. But in 2010, the dominant theme of the profession was: don't get beat with your third best pitch.

But I—and apparently many other people—discovered that pitchers who threw a mixed repertoire were actually more effective than those who threw only a couple of pitches. In ten years there has been a sea change in the thinking on this issue. Now, developing and using secondary pitches to keep the batter off stride is just the way it is done. Whereas 10 years ago Shaun Marcum had the highest pitch index in the major leagues (by far) with a number somewhere around 4.00, now there are MANY pitchers whose numbers are over 4.00. It's common. I wish that we had documented this change in the game in the pages of these handbooks, but we missed the chance to do that, and I don't suppose it matters.

Well, I promised Louie I would explain how you figure this "pitch mix" number. Let's say that a pitcher throws 40% fastballs, 30% sliders, 20% changeups and 10% buttered biscuits. You take the square root of .40, which is .632456, the square root of .3 (.547723), the square root of .2 (.447214) and the square root of .1 (.316228). You add those four square roots together, you get 1.944. You square 1.944, and you get 3.78. So he would have a Pitch Mix Index of 3.78.

If a pitcher has four pitches and throws them all equally, he has a Pitch Mix Index of 4.00. If he has three pitches and throws them all equally, he has a Pitch Mix Index of 3.00.

Andrew Kittredge had a really good year last year with a Pitch Mix Index of 2.27. There used to be top relievers with Pitch Mix Indexes of 1.50, and knuckleball pitchers have Pitch Mix Indexes just barely over 1.00. Thanks for reading. I hope that this contributes to your understanding of the game.

Player	Tommy John SX	Fastball Velocity	Fastball	Slider	Change	Cutter	Curve	Splitter	Other	PMI
Abbott, Cory	-	92.7	59%	-	6%	18%	17%	-		3.43
Abreu, Albert	-	98.0	49%	35%	16%	-	<1%	-		2.99
Abreu, Bryan	-	95.7	45%	38%	-	-	17%	-		2.89
Adams, Austin	-	94.1	13%	87%	-	-	-	-		1.67
Akin, Keegan	-	92.1	57%	19%	19%	-	4%	-		3.38
Albers, Andrew	Jan `09	88.4	64%	15%	15%	-	7%	-		3.34
Alcala, Jorge	-	97.4	43%	41%	16%	-	-	-		2.87
Alcantara, Sandy	-	97.9	50%	24%	23%	-	3%	-		3.40
Alexander, Tyler	-	90.4	36%	15%	18%	31%	-	-		3.88
Alexy, A.J.	-	93.4	54%	19%	18%	-	8%	-		3.56
Allard, Kolby	-	91.6	47%	-	17%	25%	11%	-		3.72
Allen, Logan	-	92.7	43%	32%	16%	-	9%	-		3.69
Almonte, Yency	-	94.1	49%	41%	10%	-	-	-		2.75
Alvarado, Jose	-	99.4	81%	16%	-	-	3%	-		2.20
Alvarez, Jose	-	91.3	58%	11%	28%	3%	-	-		3.23
Alzolay, Adbert	-	93.9	46%	38%	7%	7%	3%	-		3.95
Anderson, Brett	July `11	89.1	46%	8%	25%	8%	13%	-		4.42
Anderson, Chase	-	91.5	40%	-	29%	22%	9%	-		3.77
Anderson, Drew	Apr `15	92.6	49%	20%	14%	-	16%	-		3.73
Anderson, Ian	-	94.6	47%	-	31%	-	21%	-		2.92
Anderson, Shaun	-	93.4	36%	61%	2%	-	2%	-		2.69
Anderson, Tyler	-	90.2	48%	-	25%	27%	<1%	-		3.20
Andriese, Matt	-	91.8	48%	6%	33%	-	13%	-		3.49
Antone, Tejay	Aug `21 Apr `17	96.8	32%	34%	-	-	34%	-		3.00
Arihara, Kohei	-	90.9	46%	18%	13%	13%	2%	8%		5.09
Armstrong, Shawn	-	93.9	55%	<1%	-	38%	7%	-		2.80
Arrieta, Jake	-	91.4	54%	-	7%	24%	15%	-		3.53
Ashby, Aaron	-	96.6	36%	39%	21%	-	4%	-		3.55
Banda, Anthony	June `18	94.1	48%	<1%	37%	-	14%	-		3.15
Baragar, Caleb	-	92.8	81%	18%	-	-	<1%	-		1.97
Bard, Daniel	-	97.5	48%	46%	5%	-	-	-		2.59
Barlow, Joe	-	94.5	47%	41%	-	-	13%	-		2.81
Barlow, Scott	June `12	95.4	33%	46%	-	-	20%	-		2.92
Barnes, Charlie	-	89.8	44%	24%	29%	-	2%	-		3.43
Barnes, Jacob	-	94.7	56%	<1%	-	36%	-	7%		2.77
Barnes, Matt	-	95.9	50%	-	2%	-	48%	-		2.35
Barria, Jaime	-	93.1	55%	37%	8%	-	-	-		2.68
Bass, Anthony	-	95.4	49%	50%	-	-	-	<1%		2.25
Bassitt, Chris	May `16	93.0	55%	8%	10%	21%	6%	-		4.20
Bauer, Trevor	-	94.0	46%	19%	3%	21%	11%	-		4.29
Bednar, David	-	96.8	56%	-	-	-	24%	21%		2.85
Bedrosian, Cam	May `11	92.9	50%	25%	-	-	-	25%		2.91
Bender, Anthony	-	96.9	53%	46%	<1%	-	-	-		2.23
Benjamin, Wes	Apr `14	91.3	44%	29%	13%	-	15%	-		3.76
Berrios, Jose	-	94.0	56%	-	13%	-	31%	-		2.77
Bickford, Phil	-	93.9	64%	35%	-	-	-	<1%		2.13
Bieber, Shane	-	92.8	35%	26%	5%	3%	31%	-		4.18
Bielak, Brandon	-	93.8	56%	17%	11%	5%	10%	-		4.18
Blackburn, Paul	-	91.0	48%	26%	14%	-	12%	-		3.70
Bleier, Richard	-	90.1	63%	13%	1%	24%	-	-		3.05
Borucki, Ryan	Mar `13	95.3	58%	-	9%	33%	-	-		2.67
Bowden, Ben	-	92.5	71%	11%	19%	-	-	-		2.55
Boxberger, Brad	-	93.6	56%	24%	20%	-	-	-		2.84
Boyd, Matthew	-	92.0	48%	22%	22%	-	8%	-		3.66
Brach, Brad	-	93.6	51%	13%	36%	-	-	-		2.80
Bradley, Archie	-	94.0	70%	-	14%	-	16%	-		2.58

415

Player	Tommy John SX	Fastball Velocity	Fastball	Slider	Change	Cutter	Curve	Splitter	Other	PMI
Brault, Steven	-	90.7	54%	21%	21%	-	4%	-		3.43
Brentz, Jake	-	97.0	59%	28%	13%	-	-	-		2.74
Brogdon, Connor	-	96.0	45%	-	36%	19%	-	-		2.91
Brothers, Rex	-	94.5	66%	34%	-	-	-	-		1.95
Brubaker, JT	-	93.2	49%	34%	6%	-	10%	-		3.46
Bubic, Kris	-	90.9	52%	-	31%	-	17%	-		2.86
Buehler, Walker	Aug `15	95.4	52%	14%	5%	16%	13%	-		4.33
Bumgarner, Madison	-	90.4	36%	34%	8%	-	22%	-		3.74
Bummer, Aaron	Aug `15	95.4	62%	29%	<1%	8%	-	-		2.85
Bundy, Dylan	June `13	90.8	51%	21%	14%	-	14%	-		3.68
Burnes, Corbin	-	96.9	11%	9%	10%	52%	18%	-		4.37
Burr, Ryan	June `19	94.7	50%	10%	-	40%	-	-		2.73
Cabrera, Edward	-	96.7	39%	20%	24%	-	18%	-		3.91
Cabrera, Genesis	-	97.7	64%	-	17%	-	19%	-		2.71
Cahill, Trevor	-	89.8	36%	18%	24%	-	22%	-		3.93
Campbell, Paul	-	92.7	47%	29%	6%	-	19%	-		3.59
Canning, Griffin	-	93.6	41%	27%	21%	-	11%	-		3.81
Carrasco, Carlos	Sept `11	93.3	51%	20%	24%	-	5%	-		3.51
Castellanos, Humberto	-	90.5	57%	26%	11%	6%	-	-		3.39
Castillo, Diego	-	94.7	34%	66%	-	-	-	-		1.94
Castillo, Luis	-	97.3	52%	17%	30%	-	-	-		2.86
Castro, Anthony	May `15	95.3	52%	-	<1%	-	47%	-		2.25
Castro, Miguel	-	98.1	42%	35%	23%	-	-	-		2.95
Cease, Dylan	July `14	96.7	47%	31%	7%	-	15%	-		3.61
Cessa, Luis	-	93.6	31%	57%	12%	-	-	-		2.75
Chacin, Jhoulys	-	92.8	42%	35%	4%	20%	-	-		3.50
Chafin, Andrew	June `09	92.0	73%	26%	<1%	-	-	-		1.97
Chapman, Aroldis	-	98.5	62%	27%	-	-	-	11%		2.68
Chargois, JT	Sept `13	96.3	40%	60%	-	-	-	-		1.98
Chatwood, Tyler	July `14 Jan `06	95.6	54%	-	4%	36%	6%	-		3.15
Chavez, Jesse	-	91.2	40%	10%	10%	39%	-	-		3.61
Cimber, Adam	-	87.1	68%	32%	-	-	-	-		1.93
Cishek, Steve	-	90.1	61%	39%	<1%	-	-	-		2.11
Cisnero, Jose	May `14	96.6	66%	28%	6%	-	-	-		2.52
Civale, Aaron	-	91.6	33%	11%	-	26%	16%	14%		4.81
Clarke, Taylor	Jan `13	95.6	53%	29%	16%	-	2%	-		3.26
Clase, Emmanuel	-	100.3	70%	30%	-	-	-	-		1.92
Claudio, Alex	-	85.5	48%	27%	25%	-	-	-		2.93
Clay, Sam	-	92.4	66%	24%	9%	-	-	-		2.60
Cleavinger, Garrett	-	95.8	54%	46%	-	-	-	-		2.00
Clippard, Tyler	-	88.9	43%	-	34%	2%	5%	15%		4.04
Cobb, Alex	May `15	92.8	47%	1%	37%	-	15%	-		3.21
Cole, Gerrit	-	97.7	48%	22%	14%	-	16%	-		3.75
Colome, Alex	-	93.8	29%	-	-	71%	-	-		1.91
Coonrod, Sam	Sept `17	98.0	73%	15%	8%	4%	-	-		2.98
Corbin, Patrick	Mar `14	92.5	56%	38%	4%	<1%	<1%	-		2.97
Cortes, Nestor	-	90.7	47%	23%	10%	-	20%	-		3.72
Cotton, Jharel	Mar `18	93.2	46%	14%	30%	1%	8%	-		4.02
Coulombe, Danny	Mar `11	90.4	33%	42%	-	-	25%	-		2.97
Cousins, Jake	-	95.5	38%	61%	2%	-	-	-		2.30
Crichton, Stefan	-	90.9	69%	28%	3%	-	-	-		2.36
Crick, Kyle	-	92.6	39%	61%	<1%	-	-	-		2.16
Crismatt, Nabil	-	89.9	25%	-	51%	-	24%	-		2.90
Crochet, Garrett	-	96.7	64%	28%	8%	-	-	-		2.59
Crowe, Wil	Apr `15	93.6	47%	25%	18%	-	11%	-		3.72
Cueto, Johnny	Aug `18	91.8	52%	12%	24%	12%	2%	-		4.05

Player	Tommy John SX	Fastball Velocity	Pitch Repertoire							PMI
			Fastball	Slider	Change	Cutter	Curve	Splitter	Other	
Curtiss, John	Sept '21	95.0	50%	50%	-	-	-	-		2.00
	Aug '12									
Darvish, Yu	Mar '15	94.5	30%	22%	<1%	34%	9%	4%		4.72
Davies, Zach	-	88.0	53%	<1%	32%	8%	7%	-		3.64
Davis, Austin	-	93.7	52%	38%	10%	-	-	-		2.73
Davis, Wade	-	92.6	47%	-	2%	32%	20%	-		3.30
De Geus, Brett	-	93.8	56%	-	<1%	24%	19%	-		3.05
De Jong, Chase	-	93.0	49%	23%	5%	-	24%	-		3.54
De Los Santos, Enyel	-	94.9	68%	21%	11%	-	-	-		2.60
deGrom, Jacob	Oct '10	99.3	57%	33%	9%	-	<1%	-		2.86
DeSclafani, Anthony	-	94.1	46%	36%	10%	-	8%	-		3.54
Detmers, Reid	-	92.9	45%	24%	5%	-	26%	-		3.57
Detwiler, Ross	-	91.7	51%	37%	4%	-	8%	-		3.26
Diaz, Edwin	-	98.8	62%	38%	-	-	-	-		1.97
Diaz, Miguel	-	94.5	46%	2%	52%	-	-	-		2.36
Diaz, Yennsy	-	95.4	65%	8%	28%	-	-	-		2.58
Diekman, Jake	-	95.4	67%	32%	<1%	-	-	-		2.17
Diplan, Marcos	-	93.7	62%	-	11%	-	27%	-		2.67
Dobnak, Randy	-	91.7	59%	33%	7%	-	-	-		2.62
Dolis, Rafael	July '07	94.8	65%	23%	-	-	-	12%		2.67
Doolittle, Sean	-	93.1	81%	14%	5%	-	<1%	-		2.36
Doval, Camilo	-	98.7	42%	58%	-	-	-	-		1.99
Duffey, Tyler	-	92.5	49%	-	-	-	51%	-		2.00
Duffy, Danny	June '12	93.7	56%	18%	15%	-	11%	-		3.58
Dugger, Robert	-	91.4	43%	21%	4%	-	33%	-		3.53
Dunn, Justin	-	93.7	52%	15%	<1%	-	32%	-		3.09
Dunning, Dane	Mar '19	90.4	53%	21%	13%	8%	5%	-		4.20
Eflin, Zach	-	92.6	54%	13%	11%	11%	11%	-		4.36
Eickhoff, Jerad	-	90.1	49%	29%	7%	-	15%	-		3.59
Ellis, Chris	-	93.8	48%	31%	9%	-	12%	-		3.59
Enns, Dietrich	June '14	94.3	59%	36%	3%	<1%	2%	-		3.03
Eovaldi, Nathan	Aug '16	96.9	42%	14%	-	12%	19%	13%		4.68
	May '07									
Eshelman, Thomas	-	86.6	49%	26%	15%	-	11%	-		3.68
Espino, Paolo	-	89.0	55%	16%	4%	-	24%	-		3.40
Estevez, Carlos	-	97.1	66%	15%	19%	-	-	-		2.68
Evans, Demarcus	-	91.0	61%	14%	-	25%	-	-		2.75
Fairbanks, Pete	Aug '17	97.2	58%	42%	<1%	-	-	-		2.13
	Jan '11									
Falter, Bailey	-	91.8	68%	-	6%	24%	3%	-		2.93
Familia, Jeurys	-	96.7	73%	24%	-	-	-	3%		2.31
Faria, Jake	-	92.3	56%	8%	21%	-	16%	-		3.51
Farmer, Buck	-	94.1	48%	-	26%	-	27%	-		2.94
Farrell, Luke	-	91.4	40%	52%	-	-	6%	2%		3.03
Fedde, Erick	June '14	93.9	43%	23%	10%	23%	-	-		3.77
Feliz, Michael	-	93.8	58%	34%	8%	-	-	-		2.63
Fernandez, Junior	-	97.7	48%	21%	32%	-	-	-		2.92
Feyereisen, J.P.	-	93.1	52%	29%	20%	-	-	-		2.88
Finnegan, Kyle	-	95.6	68%	19%	-	-	-	12%		2.61
Flaherty, Jack	-	93.3	57%	28%	2%	-	13%	-		3.17
Fleming, Josh	-	91.2	46%	-	22%	27%	5%	-		3.56
Flexen, Chris	July '14	92.8	40%	-	15%	29%	15%	-		3.83
Floro, Dylan	-	93.7	63%	-	24%	13%	-	-		2.71
Foltynewicz, Mike	-	93.6	51%	24%	13%	-	12%	-		3.65
Foster, Matt	-	93.6	64%	10%	22%	3%	-	-		3.16
Freeland, Kyle	-	91.4	42%	23%	16%	-	20%	-		3.86
Fried, Max	Aug '14	93.9	50%	22%	2%	-	26%	-		3.35
Fry, Paul	-	92.9	55%	45%	<1%	-	-	-		2.13

417

Player	Tommy John SX	Fastball Velocity	Pitch Repertoire							PMI
			Fastball	Slider	Change	Cutter	Curve	Splitter	Other	
Fulmer, Carson	-	93.2	40%	-	15%	24%	21%	-		3.87
Fulmer, Michael	Mar `19	95.7	46%	40%	11%	-	3%	-		3.32
Funkhouser, Kyle	-	95.6	62%	30%	8%	-	-	-		2.61
Gallegos, Giovanny	Jan `11	94.5	53%	43%	5%	-	-	-		2.54
Gallen, Zac	-	93.4	55%	9%	17%	7%	12%	-		4.27
Gant, John	-	91.8	49%	15%	23%	7%	6%	-		4.31
Garcia, Bryan	Feb `18	94.0	56%	26%	18%	-	-	-		2.83
Garcia, Jarlin	-	93.2	50%	25%	24%	-	-	-		2.91
Garcia, Luis	-	93.3	45%	12%	11%	22%	9%	-		4.55
Garcia, Luis	-	98.3	59%	29%	-	-	-	12%		2.72
Garcia, Yimi	Oct `16	95.9	46%	18%	6%	30%	-	-		3.61
Garrett, Amir	-	94.8	49%	51%	-	-	-	-		2.00
Garrett, Braxton	June `17	90.0	49%	22%	12%	-	17%	-		3.71
Garza, Justin	May `15	94.8	54%	9%	8%	29%	-	-		3.45
Garza, Ralph	-	91.1	48%	31%	8%	9%	3%	-		4.10
Gausman, Kevin	-	94.6	53%	6%	5%	-	-	37%		3.21
German, Domingo	Mar `15	93.5	44%	-	22%	-	34%	-		2.95
Gibson, Kyle	Sept `11	92.5	46%	16%	13%	15%	9%	-		4.56
Gil, Luis	-	96.1	53%	39%	7%	-	-	-		2.65
Gilbert, Logan	-	95.3	62%	24%	8%	-	7%	-		3.29
Gilbert, Tyler	-	89.7	41%	-	6%	45%	8%	-		3.38
Gilbreath, Lucas	-	93.4	63%	35%	-	-	-	2%		2.35
Ginkel, Kevin	-	94.7	59%	40%	<1%	-	-	-		2.15
Giolito, Lucas	Aug `12	93.9	44%	21%	32%	-	3%	-		3.46
Givens, Mychal	-	94.8	47%	16%	38%	-	-	-		2.86
Glasnow, Tyler	Aug `21	97.0	52%	32%	3%	-	14%	-		3.30
Gomber, Austin	-	91.6	41%	24%	19%	-	16%	-		3.87
Gonsolin, Tony	-	93.8	44%	26%	-	-	9%	22%		3.73
Gonzales, Marco	Apr `16	88.4	51%	-	20%	14%	15%	-		3.71
Gonzalez, Chi Chi	July `17	91.8	53%	32%	10%	-	6%	-		3.40
Gonzalez, Victor	Jan `17	94.4	55%	45%	-	-	-	-		1.99
Goudeau, Ashton	-	92.7	45%	-	22%	-	33%	-		2.94
Graterol, Brusdar	Aug `15	100.0	61%	31%	-	7%	-	-		2.61
Graveman, Kendall	July `18	96.6	72%	21%	7%	-	<1%	-		2.68
Gray, Jon	-	94.9	48%	38%	8%	-	6%	-		3.40
Gray, Josiah	-	94.6	52%	20%	3%	-	25%	-		3.40
Gray, Sonny	-	92.4	53%	15%	3%	5%	23%	-		4.03
Green, Chad	-	95.7	66%	-	-	-	34%	-		1.95
Greene, Conner	-	95.9	48%	31%	9%	-	12%	-		3.58
Greene, Shane	May `08	92.7	35%	28%	8%	30%	-	-		3.77
Greinke, Zack	-	88.9	46%	15%	22%	-	17%	-		3.79
Gsellman, Robert	-	94.0	63%	19%	16%	-	1%	-		3.09
Guenther, Sean	-	93.1	57%	34%	9%	-	-	-		2.68
Guerra, Deolis	-	90.8	46%	-	31%	14%	9%	-		3.66
Guerra, Junior	-	92.8	56%	12%	-	-	16%	16%		3.59
Gutierrez, Vladimir	-	93.3	47%	23%	12%	-	18%	-		3.74
Hader, Josh	-	96.4	65%	28%	7%	-	-	-		2.55
Hale, David	-	92.8	56%	20%	24%	-	-	-		2.85
Hammer, J.D.	-	94.0	61%	37%	-	-	2%	-		2.32
Hand, Brad	-	93.0	57%	43%	-	-	-	-		1.99
Happ, J.A.	-	90.6	71%	12%	-	-	4%	12%		3.06
Harper, Ryne	-	86.6	22%	-	-	-	78%	-		1.83
Harvey, Matt	Oct `13	93.2	55%	19%	12%	-	14%	-		3.60
Head, Louis	-	93.7	52%	47%	<1%	-	-	-		2.20
Heaney, Andrew	July `16	92.0	59%	23%	18%	-	-	-		2.79
Hearn, Taylor	-	94.8	68%	20%	12%	-	-	-		2.62
Helsley, Ryan	-	97.5	56%	-	3%	35%	7%	-		3.11
Hembree, Heath	-	95.3	52%	47%	-	-	<1%	-		2.19

Player	Tommy John SX	Fastball Velocity	Pitch Repertoire							PMI
			Fastball	Slider	Change	Cutter	Curve	Splitter	Other	
Hendricks, Kyle	-	87.3	61%	-	28%	-	12%	-		2.71
Hendriks, Liam	-	97.7	69%	22%	-	-	9%	-		2.56
Hendrix, Ryan	-	96.4	44%	-	<1%	-	55%	-		2.20
Hentges, Sam	July `16	94.4	51%	24%	<1%	-	25%	-		3.09
Hernandez, Carlos	-	97.2	56%	16%	9%	-	19%	-		3.56
Hernandez, Darwinzon	-	94.9	74%	21%	-	-	5%	-		2.38
Hernandez, Elieser	-	90.9	54%	34%	11%	-	-	-		2.76
Hess, David	-	94.0	58%	38%	4%	-	-	-		2.46
Heuer, Codi	-	95.9	56%	23%	20%	-	-	-		2.84
Hill, Rich	June `11	88.0	50%	7%	-	3%	38%	3%		3.66
Hill, Tim	-	91.7	84%	15%	<1%	-	-	-		1.81
Hoffman, Jeff	May `14	94.3	56%	21%	12%	-	11%	-		3.55
Holland, Derek	-	93.0	57%	27%	9%	-	7%	-		3.38
Holland, Greg	Oct `15	92.8	40%	48%	<1%	-	12%	-		2.89
Holloway, Jordan	June `17	95.6	46%	41%	3%	-	11%	-		3.27
Holmes, Clay	Mar `14	96.1	59%	28%	-	-	13%	-		2.75
Houck, Tanner	-	94.1	56%	37%	-	-	-	7%		2.64
Houser, Adrian	July `16	93.7	68%	7%	11%	-	14%	-		3.24
Howard, Sam	-	93.5	43%	55%	2%	-	-	-		2.35
Howard, Spencer	-	94.2	64%	14%	9%	5%	8%	-		3.95
Hudson, Daniel	June `13 July `12	97.0	68%	29%	3%	-	-	-		2.34
Iglesias, Raisel	-	96.4	45%	31%	24%	-	-	-		2.95
Irvin, Cole	Feb `14	90.7	60%	15%	22%	-	3%	-		3.25
Jackson, Jay	-	94.8	35%	65%	<1%	-	-	-		2.15
Jackson, Luke	-	95.9	36%	52%	-	-	13%	-		2.80
Jansen, Kenley	-	93.9	27%	15%	-	58%	-	-		2.79
Javier, Cristian	-	93.6	59%	27%	6%	-	8%	-		3.28
Jax, Griffin	-	92.7	46%	31%	14%	-	9%	-		3.64
Jimenez, Joe	-	94.7	54%	33%	13%	-	-	-		2.79
Johnson, Pierce	-	95.5	33%	-	-	-	67%	-		1.94
Junis, Jakob	-	90.9	30%	41%	3%	26%	-	-		3.51
Kaprielian, James	Apr `17	93.0	59%	17%	16%	-	8%	-		3.48
Karinchak, James	-	95.9	68%	-	-	-	32%	-		1.93
Kay, Anthony	Oct `16	94.6	58%	8%	11%	11%	11%	-		4.21
Keller, Brad	-	93.9	60%	35%	5%	-	-	-		2.54
Keller, Kyle	-	94.6	56%	-	-	-	44%	-		1.99
Keller, Mitch	-	93.9	57%	24%	5%	-	15%	-		3.39
Kelly, Joe	-	97.7	41%	-	16%	-	43%	-		2.88
Kelly, Merrill	-	91.8	50%	<1%	17%	15%	18%	-		3.85
Kennedy, Ian	-	94.1	83%	-	8%	4%	5%	-		2.63
Kershaw, Clayton	-	90.7	37%	47%	<1%	-	15%	-		3.11
Keuchel, Dallas	-	87.9	40%	7%	29%	24%	-	-		3.71
Kikuchi, Yusei	-	95.2	36%	19%	-	35%	-	10%		3.79
Kim, Kwang-hyun	Jan `17	89.1	42%	38%	-	-	9%	12%		3.61
Kimbrel, Craig	-	96.5	59%	-	-	-	41%	-		1.98
King, John	Jan `17	92.3	57%	14%	19%	10%	-	-		3.53
King, Michael	-	94.1	62%	13%	12%	3%	10%	-		3.93
Kinley, Tyler	-	96.0	43%	53%	4%	-	-	-		2.51
Kintzler, Brandon	-	92.1	75%	14%	11%	-	-	-		2.47
Kittredge, Andrew	-	95.3	54%	45%	-	-	-	<1%		2.19
Kluber, Corey	-	90.6	30%	-	14%	27%	29%	-		3.92
Knebel, Corey	Apr `19	96.4	58%	-	-	-	42%	-		1.99
Knehr, Reiss	-	93.5	55%	15%	23%	-	8%	-		3.53
Kopech, Michael	Sept `18	97.4	64%	27%	3%	-	6%	-		3.00
Kowar, Jackson	-	95.7	55%	13%	30%	-	1%	-		3.14
Kranick, Max	-	94.2	49%	31%	7%	-	12%	-		3.55
Kremer, Dean	-	92.6	56%	-	8%	21%	16%	-		3.52

Player	Tommy John SX	Fastball Velocity	Pitch Repertoire							PMI
			Fastball	Slider	Change	Cutter	Curve	Splitter	Other	
Kuhl, Chad	Sept `18	94.2	39%	46%	4%	-	11%	-		3.38
Lakins, Travis	-	93.4	37%	-	6%	38%	19%	-		3.63
Lamet, Dinelson	Apr `18	95.5	48%	51%	1%	-	-	-		2.30
Lange, Alex	-	96.4	45%	<1%	15%	-	39%	-		2.99
Lauer, Eric	-	92.6	45%	11%	11%	19%	15%	-		4.60
LeBlanc, Wade	-	87.7	40%	-	23%	27%	11%	-		3.81
Leone, Dominic	-	95.5	49%	28%	-	24%	-	-		2.92
Lester, Jon	-	88.4	47%	-	18%	27%	8%	-		3.67
Littell, Zack	-	95.0	58%	-	-	37%	-	5%		2.55
Loaisiga, Jonathan	May `16	98.4	59%	-	18%	-	23%	-		2.80
Long, Sammy	-	92.7	43%	-	20%	2%	34%	-		3.39
Lopez, Jorge	-	95.2	58%	6%	13%	-	24%	-		3.40
Lopez, Pablo	Nov `13	94.0	45%	-	32%	13%	10%	-		3.64
Lopez, Reynaldo	-	95.8	58%	34%	4%	-	5%	-		3.06
Lorenzen, Michael	-	96.5	36%	14%	18%	29%	2%	-		4.40
Loup, Aaron	-	92.4	52%	7%	9%	33%	-	-		3.40
Lowther, Zac	-	90.8	54%	13%	17%	-	16%	-		3.64
Lucchesi, Joey	June `21	91.1	59%	-	35%	4%	-	1%		2.85
Luetge, Lucas	June `17	88.4	-	23%	-	62%	15%	-		2.74
Lugo, Seth	-	93.8	54%	14%	3%	-	28%	-		3.32
Luzardo, Jesus	Mar `16	95.5	51%	29%	20%	-	<1%	-		3.02
Lyles, Jordan	-	92.8	48%	26%	7%	-	18%	-		3.62
Lynch, Daniel	-	93.7	52%	29%	16%	-	3%	-		3.34
Lynn, Lance	Nov `15	93.5	62%	30%	<1%	-	3%	4%		3.07
Machado, Andres	Jan `15	94.7	71%	19%	10%	-	-	-		2.55
Maeda, Kenta	-	90.5	31%	36%	28%	-	4%	-		3.59
Mahle, Tyler	-	94.1	53%	31%	-	-	-	16%		2.84
Manaea, Sean	-	92.2	60%	16%	24%	-	-	-		2.76
Manning, Matt	-	93.7	61%	15%	13%	-	11%	-		3.47
Manoah, Alek	-	93.4	63%	28%	10%	-	-	-		2.65
Mantiply, Joe	Mar `18	91.2	51%	30%	18%	-	-	-		2.87
Maples, Dillon	-	95.3	52%	36%	-	-	12%	-		2.79
Marquez, German	-	94.8	53%	25%	2%	-	20%	-		3.30
Marshall, Evan	-	93.1	37%	-	35%	-	28%	-		2.99
Martin, Brett	-	93.4	54%	25%	-	-	21%	-		2.86
Martin, Chris	-	94.8	53%	16%	-	19%	-	12%		3.65
Martinez, Carlos	-	92.7	42%	15%	13%	21%	8%	-		4.63
Maton, Phil	-	91.7	45%	18%	-	5%	32%	-		3.53
Matz, Steven	May `10	94.5	52%	8%	23%	-	17%	-		3.59
Matzek, Tyler	-	96.1	71%	23%	-	-	7%	-		2.48
May, Dustin	May `21	98.0	59%	-	-	18%	23%	-		2.80
May, Trevor	Mar `17	96.6	60%	25%	15%	-	-	-		2.76
Mayers, Mike	-	94.6	38%	32%	<1%	30%	-	-		3.13
Mayza, Tim	Sept `19	94.1	71%	29%	-	-	-	-		1.91
Mazza, Chris	-	90.5	33%	29%	2%	36%	-	-		3.46
McClanahan, Shane	Oct `15	96.5	41%	35%	-	-	16%	8%		3.68
McCullers Jr., Lance	Nov `18	94.0	34%	24%	14%	3%	25%	-		4.52
McFarland, T.J.	-	88.9	69%	8%	23%	-	-	-		2.55
McGee, Jake	July `08	94.9	90%	10%	-	-	-	-		1.60
McGowin, Kyle	-	91.0	31%	69%	-	-	-	-		1.93
McHugh, Collin	-	90.6	11%	53%	<1%	33%	3%	-		3.39
McKenzie, Triston	-	92.1	61%	19%	1%	-	18%	-		3.11
Means, John	-	92.8	48%	8%	27%	-	16%	-		3.64
Mears, Nick	-	95.6	64%	-	-	-	36%	-		1.96
Megill, Trevor	May `13	96.4	67%	18%	-	-	16%	-		2.67
Megill, Tylor	-	94.7	58%	19%	21%	-	3%	-		3.30
Mejia, Humberto	-	92.0	63%	16%	16%	-	5%	-		3.31
Mejia, JC	-	92.7	58%	24%	12%	-	7%	-		3.40

Player	Tommy John SX	Fastball Velocity	Pitch Repertoire							PMI
			Fastball	Slider	Change	Cutter	Curve	Splitter	Other	
Melancon, Mark	Oct `06	92.2	11%	-	<1%	55%	34%	-		2.88
Middleton, Keynan	May `18	95.4	58%	30%	12%	-	-	-		2.74
Mikolas, Miles	-	93.1	50%	26%	7%	-	18%	-		3.58
Miley, Wade	-	89.8	18%	5%	27%	47%	4%	-		4.15
Miller, Andrew	-	88.5	35%	65%	-	-	-	-		1.96
Mills, Alec	July `13	89.0	60%	13%	17%	-	10%	-		3.47
Milner, Hoby	-	89.2	56%	36%	8%	-	-	-		2.66
Minaya, Juan	-	95.2	51%	4%	45%	-	-	-		2.49
Minor, Mike	-	91.0	43%	22%	20%	-	16%	-		3.85
Minter, A.J.	Mar `15	96.1	42%	44%	13%	-	-	-		2.83
Misiewicz, Anthony	-	94.4	35%	-	-	34%	31%	-		3.00
Mize, Casey	-	93.6	52%	28%	-	-	7%	13%		3.51
Montas, Frankie	-	96.3	58%	19%	-	-	-	22%		2.81
Montero, Rafael	Mar `18	95.5	62%	19%	19%	-	-	-		2.76
Montgomery, Jordan	June `18	92.5	38%	-	24%	14%	24%	-		3.88
Moore, Matt	Apr `14	92.5	57%	-	19%	9%	15%	-		3.52
Morgan, Adam	-	92.6	35%	48%	7%	-	10%	-		3.50
Morgan, Eli	-	90.4	50%	21%	23%	2%	4%	-		3.98
Morton, Charlie	June `12	95.3	49%	-	5%	9%	37%	-		3.35
Muller, Kyle	-	93.4	42%	35%	2%	-	21%	-		3.37
Murphy, Patrick	July `12	96.7	66%	-	1%	-	33%	-		2.26
Musgrove, Joe	-	93.3	27%	28%	5%	17%	24%	-		4.67
Nance, Tommy	Jan `13	95.4	62%	11%	-	-	27%	-		2.68
Naughton, Packy	Jan `13	90.6	57%	13%	28%	-	2%	-		3.22
Neidert, Nick	-	91.8	47%	31%	12%	-	10%	-		3.63
Nelson, Jimmy	Aug `21	93.9	33%	33%	-	-	34%	-		3.00
Neris, Hector	-	94.4	56%	4%	-	-	-	41%		2.47
Newcomb, Sean	-	95.7	58%	26%	<1%	-	16%	-		3.06
Nola, Aaron	-	92.7	52%	-	20%	2%	27%	-		3.27
Nolin, Sean	Aug `16	90.7	47%	-	16%	24%	14%	-		3.76
Norris, Daniel	-	92.8	47%	23%	30%	-	-	-		2.93
Ober, Bailey	Mar `15	92.4	58%	18%	13%	-	11%	-		3.52
Odorizzi, Jake	-	92.2	55%	10%	22%	7%	5%	-		4.12
Ohtani, Shohei	Oct `18	95.7	44%	22%	-	13%	4%	18%		4.41
Okert, Steven	-	92.2	40%	60%	-	-	-	-		1.98
Ottavino, Adam	May `15	95.0	48%	48%	1%	2%	-	-		2.70
Otto, Glenn	-	92.7	49%	35%	6%	-	10%	-		3.44
Oviedo, Johan	-	94.9	54%	24%	11%	-	12%	-		3.58
Oviedo, Luis	-	94.3	51%	21%	6%	-	22%	-		3.57
Paddack, Chris	Aug `16	94.9	59%	-	26%	2%	12%	-		3.16
Pagan, Emilio	-	95.0	61%	38%	1%	-	-	-		2.25
Parker, Blake	-	90.7	46%	-	-	11%	8%	34%		3.57
Patino, Luis	-	95.7	64%	26%	5%	-	5%	-		3.09
Patton, Spencer	-	93.4	57%	34%	10%	-	-	-		2.71
Payamps, Joel	-	94.7	60%	30%	10%	-	-	-		2.68
Peacock, Matt	-	93.4	68%	25%	7%	-	-	-		2.52
Peralta, Freddy	-	93.4	53%	26%	10%	-	11%	-		3.55
Peralta, Wandy	-	95.2	37%	14%	49%	-	-	-		2.83
Peralta, Wily	Jan `07	93.9	55%	22%	-	-	-	23%		2.86
Perdomo, Angel	-	94.4	65%	23%	12%	-	-	-		2.67
Perez, Cionel	-	96.0	64%	28%	8%	-	-	-		2.59
Perez, Martin	May `14	93.0	39%	-	24%	29%	8%	-		3.76
Peters, Dillon	July `14	90.8	52%	-	32%	-	16%	-		2.85
Peterson, David	-	92.6	58%	25%	16%	-	<1%	-		3.02
Petit, Yusmeiro	-	87.7	45%	-	18%	24%	14%	-		3.79
Pineda, Michael	July `17	90.7	54%	29%	17%	-	-	-		2.84
Pivetta, Nick	-	94.8	52%	22%	3%	-	24%	-		3.37
Plesac, Zach	Apr `16	92.9	42%	23%	24%	-	11%	-		3.80

Player	Tommy John SX	Fastball Velocity	Pitch Repertoire							PMI
			Fastball	Slider	Change	Cutter	Curve	Splitter	Other	
Plutko, Adam	-	91.6	50%	11%	-	32%	7%	-		3.50
Pomeranz, Drew	-	94.0	75%	-	-	-	25%	-		1.86
Ponce de Leon, Daniel	-	93.1	72%	-	12%	12%	4%	-		3.04
Ponce, Cody	-	93.2	42%	14%	8%	19%	17%	-		4.64
Pop, Zach	May `19	95.4	68%	32%	-	-	-	-		1.93
Poppen, Sean	-	94.3	53%	38%	9%	-	-	-		2.72
Poteet, Cody	-	93.6	49%	19%	18%	-	14%	-		3.74
Pressly, Ryan	-	95.5	40%	36%	-	-	24%	-		2.97
Price, David	-	92.9	53%	-	25%	20%	2%	-		3.30
Quantrill, Cal	Mar `15	94.3	51%	31%	14%	-	4%	-		3.43
Quijada, Jose	-	93.7	73%	13%	14%	-	-	-		2.52
Quintana, Jose	-	91.6	59%	13%	15%	-	14%	-		3.53
Rainey, Tanner	-	96.4	65%	35%	-	-	-	-		1.96
Raley, Brooks	-	90.8	22%	29%	4%	32%	13%	-		4.52
Ramirez, Erasmo	-	92.4	45%	3%	8%	44%	-	-		3.17
Ramirez, Noe	-	89.2	37%	33%	30%	-	-	-		2.99
Ramirez, Yohan	-	95.5	54%	46%	-	-	-	-		2.00
Rasmussen, Drew	Aug `17 Mar `16	97.1	65%	30%	2%	-	2%	-		2.78
Ray, Robbie	-	94.8	60%	31%	3%	-	6%	-		3.08
Reid-Foley, Sean	-	93.7	64%	24%	12%	-	-	-		2.69
Reyes, Alex	Feb `17	96.7	55%	28%	9%	-	8%	-		3.45
Richards, Garrett	July `18	94.4	54%	27%	7%	-	12%	-		3.48
Richards, Trevor	-	92.8	57%	14%	29%	-	-	-		2.78
Rios, Yacksel	-	97.2	61%	22%	<1%	-	<1%	16%		3.12
Robles, Hansel	-	96.8	56%	15%	-	-	-	30%		2.80
Rodon, Carlos	May `19	95.4	59%	27%	12%	-	2%	-		3.14
Rodriguez, Chris	-	95.8	65%	6%	5%	-	24%	-		3.10
Rodriguez, Eduardo	-	92.6	52%	8%	23%	17%	-	-		3.61
Rodriguez, Jefry	-	94.6	75%	-	3%	-	22%	-		2.25
Rodriguez, Joely	-	94.1	58%	4%	37%	-	-	-		2.49
Rodriguez, Richard	-	93.1	86%	14%	-	-	-	-		1.69
Rogers, Josh	July `19 Apr `13	90.5	51%	36%	13%	-	-	-		2.80
Rogers, Taylor	-	95.8	46%	54%	-	-	-	-		2.00
Rogers, Trevor	-	94.6	58%	15%	28%	-	-	-		2.78
Rogers, Tyler	-	82.7	57%	43%	-	-	-	-		1.99
Romano, Jordan	Mar `15	97.6	63%	37%	-	-	-	-		1.96
Romano, Sal	-	93.7	62%	36%	-	-	1%	-		2.28
Romo, Sergio	-	85.5	33%	56%	11%	-	-	-		2.74
Ross, Joe	July `17	93.5	62%	31%	7%	-	-	-		2.58
Rucker, Michael	-	95.1	37%	12%	7%	24%	20%	-		4.66
Ruiz, Jose	-	97.0	59%	1%	4%	-	35%	-		2.81
Ryan, Joe	-	91.3	66%	16%	10%	-	8%	-		3.29
Ryu, Hyun-Jin	Jan `04	90.0	36%	7%	26%	19%	13%	-		4.66
Sadler, Casey	Nov `15	93.1	28%	41%	-	-	31%	-		2.98
Sale, Chris	Mar `20	93.6	49%	32%	19%	-	-	-		2.90
Sampson, Adrian	July `09	91.9	59%	17%	25%	-	-	-		2.79
Sanchez, Aaron	-	90.0	48%	-	22%	-	31%	-		2.92
Sanchez, Miguel	-	94.2	38%	11%	51%	-	-	-		2.76
Sandlin, Nick	-	94.5	51%	46%	-	-	-	2%		2.39
Sandoval, Patrick	-	93.3	43%	17%	30%	-	10%	-		3.74
Santana, Dennis	-	95.4	48%	31%	21%	-	-	-		2.91
Santana, Edgar	Oct `18	94.3	65%	35%	-	-	-	-		1.95
Santana, Ervin	-	93.4	46%	52%	3%	-	-	-		2.43
Santiago, Hector	-	90.9	67%	8%	26%	-	-	-		2.55
Santillan, Tony	-	95.0	47%	47%	6%	-	-	-		2.63
Saucedo, Tayler	-	93.7	56%	22%	10%	-	11%	-		3.53

Player	Tommy John SX	Fastball Velocity	Pitch Repertoire							PMI
			Fastball	Slider	Change	Cutter	Curve	Splitter	Other	
Sawamura, Hirokazu	-	96.1	46%	15%	-	-	-	39%		2.86
Sborz, Josh	-	96.8	54%	29%	-	-	16%	-		2.83
Scherzer, Max	-	94.3	47%	19%	15%	9%	10%	-		4.52
Scott, Tanner	-	96.8	48%	52%	-	-	-	-		2.00
Scrubb, Andre	-	94.0	-	5%	-	54%	42%	-		2.53
Selman, Sam	-	91.0	55%	45%	-	-	-	-		1.99
Senzatela, Antonio	-	94.6	56%	32%	6%	-	6%	-		3.26
Sewald, Paul	-	92.4	58%	42%	<1%	-	-	-		2.07
Shaw, Bryan	-	92.9	1%	11%	4%	78%	6%	-		3.15
Sheffield, Jordan	Apr `13	96.4	65%	-	17%	-	18%	-		2.70
Sheffield, Justus	-	92.4	47%	32%	21%	-	-	-		2.92
Shoemaker, Matt	-	91.7	41%	26%	-	-	-	33%		2.97
Shreve, Chasen	-	91.6	40%	23%	-	-	-	37%		2.96
Sims, Lucas	-	95.1	41%	42%	<1%	-	17%	-		3.01
Singer, Brady	-	93.7	58%	38%	4%	-	-	-		2.49
Skubal, Tarik	Apr `16	94.4	56%	23%	12%	-	7%	3%		3.96
Slegers, Aaron	-	91.7	58%	33%	8%	-	-	-		2.66
Smith, Burch	Apr `15	93.5	69%	2%	14%	-	15%	-		3.01
Smith, Caleb	-	91.4	48%	30%	15%	-	8%	-		3.60
Smith, Drew	Mar `19	95.0	56%	-	5%	32%	8%	-		3.24
Smith, Joe	-	86.4	63%	35%	2%	-	-	-		2.34
Smith, Riley	-	92.9	58%	14%	17%	-	11%	-		3.54
Smith, Will	Mar `17	92.8	47%	41%	-	-	12%	-		2.79
Smyly, Drew	July `17	92.1	47%	-	-	11%	42%	-		2.78
Snell, Blake	-	95.2	52%	24%	10%	-	13%	-		3.60
Soria, Joakim	Apr `12 Jan `03	92.9	60%	21%	-	-	4%	14%		3.32
Soto, Gregory	-	98.3	62%	38%	-	-	-	-		1.97
Springs, Jeffrey	-	93.4	42%	30%	28%	-	-	-		2.98
Stammen, Craig	-	92.3	48%	-	<1%	22%	30%	-		3.15
Stanek, Ryne	-	97.7	60%	19%	-	-	-	22%		2.79
Staumont, Josh	-	96.6	65%	-	-	-	35%	-		1.95
Steckenrider, Drew	May `13	94.1	66%	18%	16%	-	-	-		2.68
Steele, Justin	Aug `17	93.1	66%	16%	2%	-	16%	-		3.08
Stephan, Trevor	-	96.2	60%	32%	8%	-	-	-		2.64
Stephenson, Robert	-	96.5	49%	46%	<1%	-	4%	-		2.75
Strasburg, Stephen	Sept `10	91.9	54%	-	16%	-	30%	-		2.83
Stratton, Chris	-	93.0	48%	14%	13%	-	25%	-		3.70
Strickland, Hunter	May `13	94.8	57%	41%	-	-	-	2%		2.38
Stripling, Ross	Apr `14	91.9	51%	18%	15%	-	15%	-		3.71
Stroman, Marcus	-	92.0	45%	23%	16%	14%	2%	-		4.30
Suarez, Jose	-	92.7	48%	-	28%	-	24%	-		2.93
Suarez, Ranger	-	93.2	68%	8%	24%	-	-	-		2.54
Suero, Wander	-	92.1	-	-	16%	76%	8%	-		2.42
Sulser, Cole	Jan `15 Apr `11	93.3	51%	13%	33%	-	2%	-		3.27
Suter, Brent	July `18	87.4	77%	9%	9%	-	5%	-		2.88
Swanson, Erik	-	94.8	60%	19%	-	-	-	21%		2.79
Taillon, Jameson	Aug `19 Apr `14	94.0	55%	20%	6%	-	19%	<1%		3.57
Tapia, Domingo	May `15	97.3	73%	21%	6%	-	-	-		2.43
Tate, Dillon	-	95.5	61%	24%	16%	-	-	-		2.76
Taylor, Blake	July `15	93.1	72%	28%	-	-	-	-		1.89
Taylor, Josh	-	94.6	49%	46%	-	-	5%	-		2.57
Tepera, Ryan	-	93.3	44%	<1%	-	45%	-	10%		2.99
Thielbar, Caleb	-	91.3	49%	34%	-	-	16%	-		2.87
Thompson, Keegan	June `15	93.9	48%	-	2%	27%	23%	-		3.39
Thompson, Mason	Mar `15	96.2	85%	14%	1%	-	-	-		1.96

Player	Tommy John SX	Fastball Velocity	Fastball	Slider	Change	Cutter	Curve	Splitter	Other	PMI
Thompson, Ryan	Jan '18	91.0	56%	38%	1%	5%	-	-		2.91
Thompson, Zach	-	92.2	35%	-	13%	35%	17%	-		3.82
Thornton, Trent	-	93.7	42%	4%	6%	22%	26%	-		4.30
Tomlin, Josh	Aug '12	88.9	23%	-	1%	47%	29%	-		3.31
Toussaint, Touki	-	92.8	52%	-	-	-	27%	21%		2.89
Treinen, Blake	-	97.5	35%	35%	<1%	30%	-	-		3.10
Trivino, Lou	-	95.8	60%	-	12%	16%	11%	-		3.47
Turnbull, Spencer	July '21	94.2	61%	24%	7%	-	8%	-		3.32
Uceta, Edwin	-	92.9	45%	-	41%	-	14%	-		2.85
Underwood Jr., Duane	-	94.0	46%	2%	27%	-	25%	-		3.33
Urena, Jose	-	94.0	64%	23%	13%	-	-	-		2.70
Urias, Julio	-	94.1	48%	-	17%	-	34%	-		2.88
Urquidy, Jose	Jan '17	92.6	55%	19%	18%	-	7%	-		3.53
Valdez, Cesar	-	85.1	20%	5%	75%	-	-	-		2.37
Valdez, Framber	-	92.5	57%	-	12%	-	31%	-		2.75
Valdez, Phillips	-	92.7	40%	11%	49%	-	-	-		2.76
Velasquez, Vince	Sept '10	93.1	55%	14%	15%	-	17%	-		3.62
Vesia, Alex	-	93.9	72%	18%	10%	-	-	-		2.52
Vest, Will	Jan '16	93.6	57%	23%	20%	-	-	-		2.83
Voth, Austin	-	94.2	60%	14%	<1%	-	27%	-		2.92
Wacha, Michael	-	93.8	40%	-	29%	25%	6%	-		3.68
Wainwright, Adam	Feb '11	89.1	38%	-	6%	22%	34%	-		3.67
Walker, Taijuan	Apr '18	94.2	57%	19%	-	2%	7%	14%		3.93
Wantz, Andrew	-	93.3	46%	17%	8%	29%	-	-		3.65
Watkins, Spenser	-	90.8	47%	-	6%	31%	16%	-		3.57
Watson, Tony	-	92.4	43%	24%	33%	-	-	-		2.96
Weathers, Ryan	-	94.0	62%	30%	8%	-	-	-		2.62
Weaver, Luke	-	93.7	62%	-	30%	6%	2%	-		2.96
Webb, Jacob	Apr '15	94.1	45%	9%	46%	-	-	-		2.73
Webb, Logan	June '16	92.9	47%	28%	23%	3%	-	-		3.42
Webb, Tyler	Jan '08	90.7	68%	14%	19%	-	-	-		2.63
Wells, Alex	-	88.5	51%	16%	14%	-	19%	-		3.70
Wells, Tyler	May '19	95.2	59%	27%	10%	-	4%	-		3.27
Wendelken, J.B.	Oct '16	94.1	64%	23%	10%	-	3%	-		3.09
Wheeler, Zack	Mar '15	97.1	61%	25%	3%	-	11%	<1%		3.42
White, Mitch	Nov '13	94.5	53%	18%	1%	-	28%	-		3.22
Whitley, Kodi	Mar '16	93.7	57%	15%	28%	-	-	-		2.79
Whitlock, Garrett	July '19	96.0	63%	17%	21%	-	-	-		2.73
Wick, Rowan	-	94.7	62%	5%	-	12%	22%	-		3.30
Widener, Taylor	-	92.6	67%	17%	16%	-	-	-		2.67
Williams, Devin	Mar '17	95.4	35%	1%	64%	-	-	-		2.27
Williams, Trevor	-	91.1	60%	21%	10%	-	9%	-		3.41
Wilson, Bryse	-	93.0	64%	5%	20%	-	12%	-		3.26
Wilson, Justin	-	93.6	58%	6%	-	36%	-	-		2.58
Winkler, Dan	July '14	93.5	35%	7%	-	58%	-	-		2.62
Wisler, Matt	-	91.5	9%	91%	-	-	-	-		1.58
Wittgren, Nick	-	92.5	57%	11%	23%	10%	-	-		3.50
Wood, Alex	Jan '09	91.8	46%	32%	22%	-	-	-		2.93
Woodford, Jake	-	91.7	60%	22%	5%	-	13%	-		3.36
Woodruff, Brandon	-	96.5	60%	9%	14%	-	16%	-		3.46
Workman, Brandon	June '15	91.1	36%	-	-	14%	51%	-		2.82
Yang, Hyeon-jong	-	90.0	46%	23%	27%	-	4%	-		3.53
Yarbrough, Ryan	-	86.5	14%	18%	28%	40%	-	-		3.83
Ynoa, Huascar	-	96.5	45%	48%	7%	-	-	-		2.64
Young, Alex	-	90.3	41%	-	19%	21%	19%	-		3.88
Zimmer, Kyle	-	94.1	51%	37%	2%	-	10%	-		3.20
Zimmermann, Bruce	-	91.5	42%	19%	26%	-	13%	-		3.82
Zuber, Tyler	-	94.6	58%	30%	6%	-	6%	-		3.23

Relief Pitching

Sarah Thompson

There are plenty of ways to evaluate relief pitching, which adds yet another wrinkle of complication to the tall order of building a great, or even just acceptable, bullpen.

Saves and blown saves are a little too black-and-white for my taste and ignore a great deal of nuance that lives in closing games or keeping your team in the game. Not all save situations are created equal, nor are all saves.

White Sox closer Liam Hendriks led MLB relievers in Tough Saves (see the Glossary for exactly what that means) in 2021. He went 4-for-4 in Tough Save opportunities, yet blew 3 Easy Saves and 3 Regular Saves. But he was perfect when needed most.

I'm interested in trying to figure out who may not be as great as their surface-level stats may indicate.

Before the trade deadline, Ian Kennedy was with the Rangers. As a closer, he boasted a 2.51 ERA and collected 16 saves in 17 opportunities. Considering those numbers, it certainly feels like he's on the elite side of the closer spectrum. Yet, 13 of these were considered easy, and three were considered regular saves. He was only put into one tough situation, and he did not record that save. Eighty-one percent of his saves with Texas were considered easy, the highest proportion among MLB closers.

The Phillies, needing a bona fide closer after Archie Bradley and Hector Neris began to falter in high-leverage situations, acquired Kennedy (and others) at the trade deadline for two prospects and a former top-100 prospect who hadn't been living up to expectations in his sophomore season.

Kennedy wasn't necessarily *bad*, but he wasn't the closer many thought the Phillies were getting. In the red pinstripes, he pitched to a 4.13 ERA and collected 10 saves in 13 save opportunities. He was actually 2-for-2 in tough save opportunities, but 5-for-6 in easy save situations and 3-for-5 in regular save opportunities. When he closes out a one-run game against the Dodgers, the acquisition is a win. When he allows a 2-run home run with one strike left to throw in the ninth against the Rockies, and then another home run right after that, it's not so much a win anymore. Those home runs in the 9th were only part of the story of his .758 opposing OPS with the Phillies.

The solution isn't exactly clear cut. You want your closer to be 100% (or close to it) on easy saves, yet a reliever who *only* gets easy saves may not be what their ERA or SV% indicates.

As always, there's more than meets the eye to building a bullpen, and the more we know, the better equipped we are to make decisions. It's impossible to predict the exact ups and downs of a relief pitcher, but we can still try.

Arizona Diamondbacks

Pitcher	Pos	T	Usage					Inherited Runners			Saves			Relief Results						
			Rel G	Early Entry	Cons Days	Long	Lev Ind	#	Scrd	Pct	Easy	Reg	Tough	Clean	BS Win	BS	Holds	Sv/Hld Pct	Opp OPS	Rel ERA
Ramirez, Noe	SU	R	36	1	7	1	1.3	6	1	.17	1 - 3	0 - 0	0 - 0	29	0	2	10	.85	.479	2.76
Mantiply, Joe	LT	L	57	22	16	2	1.2	50	10	.20	0 - 0	0 - 1	0 - 1	37	0	2	11	.85	.806	3.40
Buchter, Ryan	LT	L	18	4	5	2	0.6	11	3	.27	0 - 0	0 - 1	0 - 0	10	0	1	0	.00	.978	6.61
Smith, Caleb	LM	L	32	15	4	17	0.8	13	2	.15	0 - 1	0 - 1	0 - 0	20	0	2	2	.50	.615	2.70
De Geus, Brett	LM	R	28	8	4	5	0.9	15	5	.33	0 - 0	0 - 1	0 - 1	13	1	2	3	.60	.921	6.56
Young, Alex	LM	L	28	15	4	7	0.9	21	10	.48	0 - 0	0 - 1	0 - 1	13	0	2	3	.60	.875	5.45
Peacock, Matt	LM	R	27	13	2	15	0.8	6	1	.17	0 - 0	0 - 0	0 - 0	10	0	0	0		.786	4.64
Smith, Riley	LM	R	18	11	1	9	0.5	8	2	.25	0 - 0	1 - 1	0 - 0	6	0	0	0	1.00	.839	4.89
Clarke, Taylor	UR	R	43	7	9	6	1.2	10	3	.30	0 - 0	0 - 1	0 - 0	22	0	1	7	.88	.776	4.98
Ginkel, Kevin	UR	R	32	8	5	3	0.6	8	3	.38	0 - 0	0 - 1	0 - 0	19	0	1	6	.86	.904	6.35
Soria, Joakim	UR	R	31	0	7	0	1.1	1	1	1.00	6 - 6	0 - 2	0 - 0	23	0	2	3	.82	.798	4.30
Crichton, Stefan	UR	R	31	3	5	0	1.2	10	4	.40	3 - 3	1 - 1	0 - 0	17	0	0	5	1.00	.914	7.33
Clippard, Tyler	UR	R	26	1	4	0	1.8	2	2	1.00	5 - 6	1 - 3	0 - 0	18	0	3	3	.75	.727	3.20
Faria, Jake	UR	R	21	5	4	4	0.6	3	1	.33	0 - 0	0 - 0	0 - 0	13	0	0	0		.880	5.95
Bukauskas, J.B.	UR	R	21	6	4	1	0.8	12	6	.50	0 - 0	0 - 0	0 - 1	10	0	1	1	.50	.971	7.79
Poppen, Sean	UR	R	20	8	4	1	0.7	11	5	.45	0 - 0	0 - 1	0 - 0	14	0	0	1	1.00	.751	4.67
Wendelken, J.B.	UR	R	20	1	3	2	1.4	0	0	.00	2 - 2	0 - 0	0 - 0	15	0	0	4	1.00	.679	4.34
Lopez, Yoan	UR	R	13	2	1	1	0.8	6	1	.17	0 - 0	0 - 1	0 - 2	5	0	3	2	.40	1.005	6.57
Widener, Taylor	UR	R	10	3	0	1	1.1	1	1	1.00	0 - 0	0 - 0	0 - 0	7	0	0	1	1.00	.900	4.82

Atlanta Braves

Pitcher	Pos	T	Usage					Inherited Runners			Saves			Relief Results						
			Rel G	Early Entry	Cons Days	Long	Lev Ind	#	Scrd	Pct	Easy	Reg	Tough	Clean	BS Win	BS	Holds	Sv/Hld Pct	Opp OPS	Rel ERA
Smith, Will	CL	L	71	0	20	3	2.2	2	1	.50	24 - 26	13 - 17	0 - 0	51	1	6	0	.86	.693	3.44
Jackson, Luke	SU	R	71	12	15	2	1.3	27	7	.26	0 - 0	0 - 3	0 - 1	55	0	4	31	.89	.609	1.98
Matzek, Tyler	SU	R	69	16	14	4	1.2	29	3	.10	0 - 0	0 - 0	0 - 0	54	0	0	24	1.00	.581	2.57
Minter, A.J.	SU	L	61	14	15	1	1.5	25	4	.16	0 - 0	0 - 5	0 - 1	42	1	6	23	.79	.644	3.78
Martin, Chris	SU	R	46	3	5	1	1.4	3	2	.67	1 - 3	0 - 1	0 - 1	31	1	4	13	.78	.726	3.95
Rodriguez, Richard	SU	R	27	5	7	1	1.2	1	0	.00	0 - 0	0 - 0	0 - 0	20	0	0	8	1.00	.754	3.12
Dayton, Grant	LT	L	13	4	1	4	0.5	14	5	.36	0 - 0	0 - 0	0 - 0	6	0	0	1	1.00	.854	6.23
Newcomb, Sean	LM	L	32	14	3	9	0.7	15	9	.60	1 - 1	0 - 1	0 - 0	18	0	1	2	.75	.719	4.73
Chavez, Jesse	LM	R	26	18	3	3	1.0	12	5	.42	0 - 0	0 - 0	0 - 1	17	0	1	2	.67	.518	2.03
Santana, Edgar	UR	R	41	16	7	4	0.5	13	5	.38	0 - 0	0 - 0	0 - 0	26	0	0	3	1.00	.664	3.59
Tomlin, Josh	UR	R	35	14	2	13	0.4	12	4	.33	0 - 0	0 - 0	0 - 0	19	0	0	1	1.00	.894	6.57
Webb, Jacob	UR	R	34	13	8	5	1.0	23	9	.39	0 - 0	0 - 1	1 - 1	21	0	1	0	.50	.790	4.19
Greene, Shane	UR	R	19	6	2	2	0.7	0	0	.00	0 - 0	0 - 1	0 - 0	11	0	1	2	.67	.947	8.47
Jones, Nate	UR	R	12	4	2	1	1.8	10	4	.40	0 - 0	0 - 0	0 - 1	5	0	1	2	.67	.842	3.48

Baltimore Orioles

Pitcher	Pos	T	Usage					Inherited Runners			Saves			Relief Results						
			Rel G	Early Entry	Cons Days	Long	Lev Ind	#	Scrd	Pct	Easy	Reg	Tough	Clean	BS Win	BS	Holds	Sv/Hld Pct	Opp OPS	Rel ERA
Scott, Tanner	LT	L	62	14	11	6	1.4	38	14	.37	0 - 0	0 - 1	0 - 1	39	0	2	16	.89	.714	5.17
Fry, Paul	LT	L	52	12	8	4	1.3	24	6	.25	1 - 1	0 - 0	1 - 3	36	0	2	11	.87	.637	6.08

Baltimore Orioles

Pitcher	Pos	T	Usage					Inherited Runners			Saves			Relief Results						
			Rel G	Early Entry	Cons Days	Long	Lev Ind	#	Scrd	Pct	Easy	Reg	Tough	Clean	BS Win	BS	Holds	Sv/Hld Pct	Opp OPS	Rel ERA
Plutko, Adam	LM	R	37	24	3	19	0.9	36	13	.36	0-1	1-1	0-1	15	0	2	5	.75	.948	6.18
Lakins, Travis	LM	R	23	10	3	6	0.9	10	2	.20	0-0	0-0	0-1	13	0	1	3	.75	.682	5.81
Diplan, Marcos	LM	R	23	15	2	8	0.7	18	8	.44	0-0	0-0	0-0	10	0	0	1	1.00	.712	4.50
Greene, Conner	LM	R	21	10	4	3	1.0	8	2	.25	0-1	0-2	0-1	11	1	4	1	.20	.844	8.06
Armstrong, Shawn	LM	R	20	7	3	5	0.4	11	9	.82	0-0	0-1	0-0	7	0	1	1	.50	.970	8.55
Abad, Fernando	LM	L	16	9	2	3	0.6	12	5	.42	0-0	0-0	0-0	7	0	0	2	1.00	.819	5.60
Tate, Dillon	UR	R	62	20	9	10	0.9	53	25	.47	1-1	1-1	1-3	32	0	2	7	.83	.713	4.39
Sulser, Cole	UR	R	60	17	10	9	1.1	35	11	.31	3-3	5-7	0-1	39	0	3	6	.82	.596	2.70
Wells, Tyler	UR	R	44	14	6	12	0.9	28	9	.32	2-2	2-4	0-1	26	0	3	1	.63	.603	4.11
Valdez, Cesar	UR	R	39	7	6	10	1.3	14	7	.50	5-5	2-6	1-2	19	0	5	0	.62	.892	5.87
Hanhold, Eric	UR	R	10	8	1	3	0.7	8	6	.75	0-0	0-0	0-1	4	0	1	0	.00	.827	6.97

Boston Red Sox

Pitcher	Pos	T	Usage					Inherited Runners			Saves			Relief Results						
			Rel G	Early Entry	Cons Days	Long	Lev Ind	#	Scrd	Pct	Easy	Reg	Tough	Clean	BS Win	BS	Holds	Sv/Hld Pct	Opp OPS	Rel ERA
Barnes, Matt	CL	R	60	2	17	5	1.8	12	4	.33	11-12	12-16	1-2	41	0	6	0	.80	.641	3.79
Ottavino, Adam	SU	R	69	2	19	7	1.8	33	8	.24	4-5	5-8	2-4	46	1	6	22	.85	.728	4.21
Hernandez, Darwinzon	SU	L	48	14	12	1	1.2	27	8	.30	0-0	0-1	0-3	35	0	4	12	.75	.702	3.38
Whitlock, Garrett	SU	R	46	19	1	22	1.3	25	6	.24	0-0	2-4	0-1	28	1	3	14	.84	.631	1.96
Taylor, Josh	LT	L	61	20	17	4	1.2	46	11	.24	0-0	0-0	1-1	46	0	0	15	1.00	.662	3.40
Davis, Austin	LT	L	19	6	5	2	0.8	12	5	.42	0-0	0-1	0-1	12	1	2	2	.50	.773	4.86
Sawamura, Hirokazu	LM	R	55	30	8	8	1.0	35	6	.17	0-0	0-1	0-0	13	0	0	10	.91	.768	3.06
Valdez, Phillips	LM	R	28	9	7	10	0.6	15	5	.33	1-1	0-0	0-0	19	0	0	2	1.00	.700	5.85
Robles, Hansel	LM	R	27	14	10	2	0.9	14	4	.29	2-2	1-1	1-1	19	0	0	3	1.00	.692	3.60
Andriese, Matt	LM	R	26	11	0	12	0.9	6	6	1.00	1-2	0-1	0-1	9	1	3	3	.57	.942	6.03
Richards, Garrett	LM	R	18	8	4	7	0.9	8	1	.13	1-1	2-2	0-0	10	0	0	2	1.00	.659	3.42
Rios, Yacksel	UR	R	20	9	2	4	0.4	8	3	.38	0-0	0-0	0-0	14	0	0	1	1.00	.615	3.70
Workman, Brandon	UR	R	19	5	4	3	0.6	11	5	.45	0-0	0-0	0-0	11	0	0	2	1.00	.864	4.95
Perez, Martin	UR	L	14	4	2	2	0.9	1	1	1.00	0-0	0-0	0-0	6	0	0	1	1.00	.795	4.50
Brasier, Ryan	UR	R	13	5	6	1	1.1	11	2	.18	0-0	0-0	0-0	9	0	0	3	1.00	.742	1.50
Brice, Austin	UR	R	13	5	1	3	0.4	6	5	.83	0-0	0-0	0-0	7	0	0	0		.843	6.59

Chicago Cubs

Pitcher	Pos	T	Usage					Inherited Runners			Saves			Relief Results						
			Rel G	Early Entry	Cons Days	Long	Lev Ind	#	Scrd	Pct	Easy	Reg	Tough	Clean	BS Win	BS	Holds	Sv/Hld Pct	Opp OPS	Rel ERA
Kimbrel, Craig	CL	R	39	0	11	4	2.1	16	0	.00	13-13	8-9	2-3	34	0	2	0	.92	.336	0.49
Chafin, Andrew	SU	L	43	3	6	0	1.2	20	5	.25	0-0	0-0	0-1	37	0	1	17	.94	.461	2.06
Tepera, Ryan	SU	R	43	8	8	2	1.2	31	7	.23	0-0	0-0	1-3	32	0	2	15	.89	.469	2.91
Wieck, Brad	LT	L	15	4	4	3	0.2	1	0	.00	0-0	0-0	0-0	15	0	0	1	1.00	.495	0.00
Ryan, Kyle	LT	L	13	5	2	2	0.6	7	5	.71	1-1	0-0	0-0	5	0	0	0	1.00	.951	6.75
Steele, Justin	LT	L	11	7	0	4	0.9	10	3	.30	0-0	0-0	0-0	7	0	0	1	1.00	.584	2.03
Brothers, Rex	LM	L	57	30	11	6	0.8	29	10	.34	0-0	0-0	1-1	35	0	0	8	1.00	.746	5.26
Morgan, Adam	LM	L	34	16	8	2	0.9	25	10	.40	1-1	1-1	0-2	21	0	2	4	.75	.829	4.26
Thompson, Keegan	LM	R	26	18	3	13	1.1	10	6	.60	0-0	1-1	0-1	15	1	1	1	.67	.692	2.43
Rucker, Michael	LM	R	20	11	2	10	0.6	13	4	.31	0-0	0-1	1-1	8	0	1	0	.50	.839	6.99
Winkler, Dan	UR	R	47	13	9	6	1.1	23	8	.35	0-0	0-1	0-0	35	0	1	6	.86	.747	5.22

Chicago Cubs

Pitcher	Pos	T	Usage					Inherited Runners			Saves			Relief Results						
			Rel G	Early Entry	Cons Days	Long	Lev Ind	#	Scrd	Pct	Easy	Reg	Tough	Clean	BS Win	BS	Holds	Sv/Hld Pct	Opp OPS	Rel ERA
Maples, Dillon	UR	R	28	5	6	8	0.3	10	3	.30	0-0	0-0	0-0	19	0	0	0		.576	2.59
Megill, Trevor	UR	R	28	12	3	0	0.7	11	7	.64	0-0	0-0	0-0	15	0	0	1	1.00	1.014	8.37
Nance, Tommy	UR	R	27	11	3	2	0.6	9	4	.44	0-0	0-0	0-0	15	0	0	5	1.00	.741	7.22
Heuer, Codi	UR	R	25	5	4	6	1.8	13	4	.31	0-1	2-3	0-1	15	0	3	4	.67	.620	3.14
Wick, Rowan	UR	R	22	1	4	3	1.6	2	1	.50	2-3	3-5	0-0	15	0	3	2	.70	.576	4.30
Rodriguez, Manuel	UR	R	20	7	1	1	1.2	8	4	.50	0-0	1-1	0-0	11	0	0	1	1.00	.816	6.11
Effross, Scott	UR	R	14	6	3	2	0.9	10	5	.50	0-0	0-1	0-0	7	0	1	3	.75	.716	3.68
Mills, Alec	UR	R	12	6	0	7	0.9	4	0	.00	1-1	0-0	0-0	5	0	0	0	1.00	.896	6.41
Adam, Jason	UR	R	12	4	2	2	0.6	4	3	.75	0-0	0-0	0-0	8	0	0	2	1.00	.795	5.91
Workman, Brandon	UR	R	10	4	2	2	0.9	1	0	.00	0-0	0-0	0-0	7	0	0	2	1.00	.997	6.75
Jewell, Jake	UR	R	10	4	2	5	0.4	7	4	.57	0-0	0-0	0-0	3	0	0	0		1.212	9.90

Chicago White Sox

Pitcher	Pos	T	Usage					Inherited Runners			Saves			Relief Results						
			Rel G	Early Entry	Cons Days	Long	Lev Ind	#	Scrd	Pct	Easy	Reg	Tough	Clean	BS Win	BS	Holds	Sv/Hld Pct	Opp OPS	Rel ERA
Hendriks, Liam	CL	R	69	0	17	8	1.5	30	3	.10	22-25	12-15	4-4	51	4	6	0	.86	.517	2.54
Bummer, Aaron	SU	L	62	10	12	7	1.4	20	7	.35	1-2	1-4	0-2	43	0	6	21	.79	.560	3.51
Kopech, Michael	SU	R	40	19	4	19	1.0	8	2	.25	0-0	0-1	0-0	27	0	1	13	.93	.692	3.90
Heuer, Codi	SU	R	40	11	7	4	1.1	23	4	.17	0-0	0-0	0-0	27	0	0	13	1.00	.802	5.12
Marshall, Evan	SU	R	27	11	5	4	1.3	23	10	.43	0-1	0-1	0-2	13	0	4	6	.60	.845	5.60
Kimbrel, Craig	SU	R	24	1	7	1	1.4	1	1	1.00	1-2	0-2	0-0	14	1	3	6	.70	.774	5.09
Tepera, Ryan	SU	R	22	4	6	1	1.1	5	3	.60	1-1	0-1	0-0	16	0	1	6	.88	.613	2.50
Crochet, Garrett	LT	L	54	18	4	9	1.2	24	8	.33	0-0	0-1	0-0	39	0	1	12	.92	.598	2.82
Ruiz, Jose	UR	R	59	19	10	9	0.5	22	14	.64	0-0	0-0	0-1	35	0	1	4	.80	.648	3.05
Foster, Matt	UR	R	37	14	5	10	0.7	24	9	.38	0-0	0-1	1-1	19	0	1	2	.75	.811	6.00
Burr, Ryan	UR	R	33	14	6	5	0.7	12	6	.50	0-0	0-1	0-0	24	1	1	3	.75	.686	2.60
Wright Jr., Mike	UR	R	13	4	1	7	0.5	2	0	.00	0-0	0-0	0-0	6	0	0	0		.744	5.50
Lopez, Reynaldo	UR	R	11	5	1	7	0.7	1	0	.00	0-0	0-0	0-0	7	0	0	0		.516	2.21

Cincinnati Reds

Pitcher	Pos	T	Usage					Inherited Runners			Saves			Relief Results						
			Rel G	Early Entry	Cons Days	Long	Lev Ind	#	Scrd	Pct	Easy	Reg	Tough	Clean	BS Win	BS	Holds	Sv/Hld Pct	Opp OPS	Rel ERA
Givens, Mychal	CL	R	23	1	6	1	1.9	6	4	.67	4-5	4-4	0-1	17	0	2	3	.85	.740	4.22
Sims, Lucas	SU	R	47	10	8	7	1.9	21	6	.29	3-3	3-5	1-2	33	0	3	9	.84	.658	4.40
Hembree, Heath	SU	R	45	8	14	6	1.3	18	4	.22	2-2	6-7	0-1	24	0	2	6	.88	.739	6.38
Brach, Brad	SU	R	35	5	6	1	1.3	15	6	.40	0-0	0-1	0-1	18	0	2	10	.85	.804	6.30
Lorenzen, Michael	SU	R	27	2	8	5	1.5	7	3	.43	2-2	1-1	1-1	19	0	0	11	1.00	.673	5.59
Antone, Tejay	SU	R	23	9	4	9	1.7	21	8	.38	0-0	2-4	1-3	15	1	4	8	.73	.508	2.14
Garrett, Amir	LT	L	63	13	15	1	1.2	24	8	.33	3-4	2-3	2-4	39	0	4	7	.78	.799	6.04
Perez, Cionel	LT	L	25	11	4	4	0.6	12	5	.42	0-0	0-0	0-0	14	0	0	0		.814	6.38
Osich, Josh	LT	L	17	4	7	1	1.2	8	4	.50	1-1	0-1	2-0	11	0	2	3	.67	.842	5.02
Doolittle, Sean	LM	L	45	9	6	2	1.0	20	12	.60	0-1	1-2	0-2	27	0	4	4	.56	.832	4.46
Hendrix, Ryan	LM	R	36	14	8	4	0.7	21	9	.43	0-1	0-0	0-0	19	0	1	3	.75	.881	5.97
Santillan, Tony	LM	R	22	13	2	4	0.9	13	2	.15	0-0	0-0	0-0	17	0	0	0		.620	2.36
Wilson, Justin	LM	L	21	7	3	1	0.6	9	3	.33	0-0	0-0	0-0	16	0	0	2	1.00	.623	2.81
Hoffman, Jeff	LM	R	20	7	2	9	0.8	10	5	.50	0-0	0-0	0-0	11	0	0	2	1.00	.809	3.54
Fulmer, Carson	LM	R	20	7	3	8	0.3	3	1	.33	0-0	0-3	0-0	10	0	0	1	1.00	.794	6.66
Warren, Art	UR	R	26	4	7	0	0.9	9	0	.00	0-0	0-0	0-0	24	0	0	1	1.00	.483	1.29
Cessa, Luis	UR	R	24	7	4	2	0.9	12	3	.25	0-0	0-0	0-0	17	0	0	3	1.00	.658	2.05
Romano, Sal	UR	R	14	5	1	6	0.3	4	0	.00	0-0	0-0	0-0	7	0	0	0		.746	5.23

Cleveland Indians

Pitcher	Pos	T	Usage					Inherited Runners			Saves			Relief Results						
			Rel G	Early Entry	Cons Days	Long	Lev Ind	#	Scrd	Pct	Easy	Reg	Tough	Clean	BS Win	BS	Holds	Sv/Hld Pct	Opp OPS	Rel ERA
Clase, Emmanuel	CL	R	71	1	20	1	1.6	6	1	.17	17-17	6-11	1-1	58	1	5	6	.86	.481	1.29
Shaw, Bryan	SU	R	81	15	26	7	1.3	36	10	.28	1-2	0-3	1-3	55	1	6	20	.79	.712	3.49
Karinchak, James	SU	R	60	1	16	2	1.9	23	5	.22	4-6	7-9	0-1	43	1	5	13	.83	.645	4.07
Nelson, Kyle	LT	L	10	4	1	2	0.4	6	2	.33	0-0	0-0	0-0	6	0	0	0		.716	9.31
Young, Alex	LT	L	10	3	1	1	0.7	6	3	.50	0-0	0-0	0-0	4	0	0	1	1.00	.976	7.84
Stephan, Trevor	LM	R	43	22	1	26	0.5	16	6	.38	1-1	0-0	0-0	22	0	0	3	1.00	.796	4.41
Maton, Phil	LM	R	37	20	5	9	0.8	28	12	.43	0-0	0-1	0-0	21	1	1	3	.75	.759	4.50
Sandlin, Nick	LM	R	34	21	3	5	0.9	21	9	.43	0-0	0-1	0-0	23	0	1	5	.83	.584	2.94
Garza, Justin	LM	R	21	13	0	10	0.6	13	9	.69	0-0	0-1	0-0	6	0	1	0	.00	.790	4.71
Quantrill, Cal	LM	R	18	9	1	8	1.0	5	2	.40	0-0	0-0	0-0	12	0	0	1	1.00	.669	1.88
Hentges, Sam	LM	L	18	7	2	8	0.8	4	3	.75	0-0	0-0	0-0	12	0	0	0		.872	4.88
Wittgren, Nick	UR	R	59	15	7	9	1.1	14	2	.14	1-1	0-0	0-0	37	0	0	9	1.00	.787	4.82
Parker, Blake	UR	R	47	13	7	4	0.7	17	6	.35	0-0	0-0	0-0	33	0	0	4	1.00	.714	3.09

Colorado Rockies

Pitcher	Pos	T	Usage					Inherited Runners			Saves			Relief Results						
			Rel G	Early Entry	Cons Days	Long	Lev Ind	#	Scrd	Pct	Easy	Reg	Tough	Clean	BS Win	BS	Holds	Sv/Hld Pct	Opp OPS	Rel ERA
Bard, Daniel	CL	R	67	4	14	10	1.9	5	0	.00	15-18	5-9	0-1	42	3	8	4	.75	.800	5.21
Estevez, Carlos	SU	R	64	2	12	3	1.7	18	6	.33	6-6	4-9	1-2	40	1	6	15	.81	.804	4.38
Chacin, Jhoulys	SU	R	45	15	7	16	1.1	13	7	.54	0-0	0-2	0-0	28	0	2	17	.89	.703	4.33
Gilbreath, Lucas	LT	L	46	17	4	4	0.7	22	6	.27	1-1	0-0	0-0	31	0	0	4	1.00	.622	3.24
Bowden, Ben	LT	L	39	15	5	8	0.5	18	7	.39	0-1	0-0	0-0	19	0	1	1	.50	.880	6.56
Kinley, Tyler	UR	R	70	20	10	5	1.0	42	19	.45	0-0	0-1	0-3	42	1	4	10	.71	.720	4.73
Stephenson, Robert	UR	R	49	15	9	3	0.8	36	13	.36	0-0	1-2	0-0	27	1	1	4	.83	.724	3.13
Almonte, Yency	UR	R	48	15	7	9	0.9	26	6	.23	0-1	0-2	0-0	27	0	3	3	.50	.844	7.55
Givens, Mychal	UR	R	31	3	7	2	1.7	10	5	.50	0-0	0-1	0-0	22	0	1	8	.89	.751	2.73
Sheffield, Jordan	UR	R	30	7	3	3	0.6	8	1	.13	0-0	0-0	0-0	23	0	0	4	1.00	.563	3.84
Lawrence, Justin	UR	R	19	7	3	2	1.1	9	6	.67	0-0	0-1	0-0	9	0	1	2	.67	.883	8.64
Goudeau, Ashton	UR	R	10	9	0	7	0.7	6	2	.33	0-0	0-0	0-0	3	0	0	0		.642	4.84

Detroit Tigers

Pitcher	Pos	T	Usage					Inherited Runners			Saves			Relief Results						
			Rel G	Early Entry	Cons Days	Long	Lev Ind	#	Scrd	Pct	Easy	Reg	Tough	Clean	BS Win	BS	Holds	Sv/Hld Pct	Opp OPS	Rel ERA
Soto, Gregory	CL	L	62	2	14	12	2.0	21	9	.43	12-12	5-5	1-2	43	0	1	7	.96	.635	3.39
Fulmer, Michael	CL	R	48	8	3	7	1.5	24	11	.46	6-7	5-6	3-5	32	0	4	9	.85	.712	2.53
Cisnero, Jose	SU	R	67	9	15	5	1.5	27	7	.26	2-3	1-4	1-1	43	1	4	18	.85	.672	3.65
Krol, Ian	LT	L	18	6	4	4	0.4	12	8	.67	0-0	0-0	0-0	10	0	0	0		.838	4.34
Funkhouser, Kyle	LM	R	55	29	11	15	1.4	28	5	.18	1-2	0-2	0-1	40	0	4	9	.71	.691	3.69
Norris, Daniel	LM	L	38	15	5	4	0.9	20	7	.35	0-0	1-2	0-1	22	0	2	6	.78	.757	5.89
Holland, Derek	LM	L	38	15	2	10	0.6	10	3	.30	0-0	0-0	0-0	26	0	0	4	1.00	.804	4.79
Farmer, Buck	LM	R	36	16	8	8	0.4	17	7	.41	0-0	0-0	0-1	21	0	1	2	.67	.886	6.37
Alexander, Tyler	LM	L	26	15	2	10	0.8	8	1	.13	0-0	0-0	0-0	12	0	0	3	1.00	.742	4.54
Ramirez, Erasmo	LM	R	17	9	0	5	0.6	4	0	.00	0-0	0-0	0-0	7	0	0	0		.681	5.74
Jimenez, Joe	UR	R	52	15	9	3	0.8	20	8	.40	1-2	0-0	0-0	34	0	1	5	.86	.755	5.96
Garcia, Bryan	UR	R	39	14	8	5	0.8	13	3	.23	0-0	1-2	1-1	19	0	1	3	.83	.947	7.55
Lange, Alex	UR	R	36	15	3	4	0.9	22	12	.55	0-0	1-2	0-1	23	0	2	6	.78	.765	4.04
Foley, Jason	UR	R	11	5	1	1	0.7	2	1	.50	0-0	0-0	0-0	7	0	0	2	1.00	.761	2.61

Houston Astros

Pitcher	Pos	T	Usage					Inherited Runners			Saves			Relief Results						
			Rel G	Early Entry	Cons Days	Long	Lev Ind	#	Scrd	Pct	Easy	Reg	Tough	Clean	BS Win	BS	Holds	Sv/Hld Pct	Opp OPS	Rel ERA
Pressly, Ryan	CL	R	64	0	17	5	1.7	10	2	.20	14-14	12-14	0-0	49	0	2	1	.93	.546	2.25
Stanek, Ryne	SU	R	72	8	12	6	1.4	16	3	.19	2-2	0-2	0-0	51	1	2	21	.92	.615	3.42
Abreu, Bryan	SU	R	31	15	4	10	1.2	17	7	.41	1-1	0-2	0-2	16	0	4	7	.67	.754	5.75
Javier, Cristian	SU	R	27	16	0	20	1.0	10	5	.50	1-2	1-1	0-1	10	0	2	5	.78	.691	3.93
Graveman, Kendall	SU	R	23	0	3	4	1.8	7	4	.57	0-0	0-1	0-2	16	0	3	7	.70	.676	3.13
Raley, Brooks	LT	L	58	18	9	4	1.1	37	15	.41	0-0	2-2	0-3	35	0	3	9	.79	.666	4.78
Taylor, Blake	LT	L	51	10	10	4	1.0	26	8	.31	0-0	0-3	0-2	35	1	5	5	.50	.720	3.16
Emanuel, Kent	LT	L	10	3	1	2	0.3	5	2	.40	0-0	0-0	0-0	5	0	0	1	1.00	.631	2.55
Bielak, Brandon	LM	R	26	13	2	14	0.7	12	4	.33	0-0	1-2	0-0	12	0	1	2	.75	.712	4.47
Smith, Joe	UR	R	27	4	4	2	0.4	14	9	.64	0-0	0-0	0-0	15	0	0	1	1.00	.996	7.48
Maton, Phil	UR	R	27	12	6	3	1.1	15	5	.33	0-0	0-0	0-3	17	0	3	2	.40	.763	4.97
Garcia, Yimi	UR	R	23	7	4	2	1.0	11	1	.09	0-0	0-0	0-0	15	0	0	2	1.00	.646	5.48
Scrubb, Andre	UR	R	18	5	3	3	0.7	12	4	.33	0-1	0-0	0-1	10	0	2	2	.50	.780	5.03
Paredes, Enoli	UR	R	12	3	0	4	1.1	5	3	.60	0-0	0-0	0-0	7	0	0	2	1.00	.763	6.23

Kansas City Royals

Pitcher	Pos	T	Usage					Inherited Runners			Saves			Relief Results						
			Rel G	Early Entry	Cons Days	Long	Lev Ind	#	Scrd	Pct	Easy	Reg	Tough	Clean	BS Win	BS	Holds	Sv/Hld Pct	Opp OPS	Rel ERA
Barlow, Scott	CL	R	71	6	20	7	1.6	25	13	.52	11-12	5-6	0-4	50	3	6	14	.83	.626	2.42
Brentz, Jake	SU	L	72	15	21	8	1.1	27	10	.37	1-1	1-4	0-2	44	0	5	15	.77	.665	3.66
Staumont, Josh	SU	R	64	17	10	6	1.2	20	5	.25	2-2	3-3	0-0	48	0	0	16	1.00	.566	2.88
Holland, Greg	SU	R	57	5	13	8	1.2	19	8	.42	6-7	1-2	1-3	38	0	4	8	.80	.721	4.85
Tapia, Domingo	SU	R	32	16	5	3	1.3	21	4	.19	0-0	0-1	0-2	23	1	3	7	.70	.546	2.84
Santana, Ervin	LM	R	36	15	2	17	0.5	15	2	.13	0-0	0-0	0-0	20	0	0	0		.770	4.55
Lovelady, Richard	LM	L	20	8	4	4	0.9	15	5	.33	0-0	1-1	0-0	13	0	0	4	1.00	.616	3.48
Payamps, Joel	LM	R	14	10	1	6	1.1	12	6	.50	0-0	0-0	0-0	5	0	0	0		.748	4.50
Hernandez, Carlos	LM	R	13	9	0	8	1.0	7	3	.43	0-0	0-0	0-0	3	0	0	0		.672	3.95
Zimmer, Kyle	UR	R	50	23	5	7	0.9	32	10	.31	0-0	2-2	0-1	29	0	1	10	.92	.743	5.29
Davis, Wade	UR	R	40	7	5	8	0.4	8	0	.00	1-1	0-1	1-1	24	0	1	2	.80	.798	6.75
Zuber, Tyler	UR	R	31	13	6	1	0.7	22	6	.27	0-0	0-0	0-0	15	0	0	4	1.00	.819	6.26
Junis, Jakob	UR	R	10	4	1	2	0.8	1	0	.00	0-0	0-2	0-0	5	1	2	0	.00	.982	6.75

Los Angeles Angels

Pitcher	Pos	T	Usage					Inherited Runners			Saves			Relief Results						
			Rel G	Early Entry	Cons Days	Long	Lev Ind	#	Scrd	Pct	Easy	Reg	Tough	Clean	BS Win	BS	Holds	Sv/Hld Pct	Opp OPS	Rel ERA
Iglesias, Raisel	CL	R	65	0	16	6	1.9	24	5	.21	13-14	17-18	4-7	45	3	5	0	.87	.610	2.57
Cishek, Steve	SU	R	74	24	14	9	1.1	61	26	.43	0-1	0-1	0-2	46	0	4	21	.84	.668	3.42
Mayers, Mike	SU	R	70	13	14	7	1.2	34	14	.41	1-2	1-2	0-1	49	0	3	17	.86	.735	3.53
Watson, Tony	SU	R	36	8	4	2	1.3	23	2	.09	0-1	0-2	0-0	26	0	3	12	.80	.595	4.64
Claudio, Alex	LT	L	41	14	10	4	0.5	21	8	.38	0-0	0-0	1-1	25	0	2	2	1.00	.840	5.51
Quintana, Jose	LT	L	14	5	0	5	0.9	11	3	.27	0-0	0-0	0-0	7	0	0	2	1.00	.777	3.93
Guerra, Junior	LM	R	40	18	6	26	0.4	27	12	.44	0-0	0-2	0-0	17	1	2	2	.50	.739	5.74
Slegers, Aaron	LM	R	29	14	3	5	0.9	21	13	.62	0-0	0-1	0-1	16	1	2	2	.50	.944	6.97
Quijada, Jose	LM	L	26	14	2	3	0.9	21	6	.29	0-0	0-0	0-0	16	0	0	4	1.00	.657	4.56
Wantz, Andrew	LM	R	21	14	0	8	0.8	19	7	.37	0-0	0-0	0-1	13	0	1	0	.00	.711	4.94
Selman, Sam	LM	L	18	8	2	3	0.7	10	5	.50	0-0	0-0	0-0	11	0	0	1	1.00	.702	6.35
Warren, Austin	LM	R	16	8	0	2	1.1	13	3	.23	0-0	1-1	0-0	13	0	0	2	1.00	.544	1.77
Rodriguez, Chris	LM	R	13	10	0	6	1.1	10	2	.20	0-1	0-0	0-0	5	0	1	2	.67	.645	3.66
Herget, Jimmy	UR	R	14	8	1	2	0.9	11	3	.27	0-0	0-0	0-1	7	0	2	0	.00	.746	4.30

Los Angeles Dodgers

Pitcher	Pos	T	Rel G	Early Entry	Cons Days	Long	Lev Ind	#	Scrd	Pct	Easy	Reg	Tough	Clean	BS Win	BS	Holds	Sv/Hld Pct	Opp OPS	Rel ERA
Jansen, Kenley	CL	R	69	0	20	5	2.2	18	2	.11	21 - 22	14 - 17	3 - 4	55	0	5	0	.88	.501	2.22
Treinen, Blake	SU	R	72	3	21	1	1.6	29	4	.14	5 - 6	2 - 3	0 - 2	54	2	4	32	.91	.512	1.99
Gonzalez, Victor	SU	L	43	13	14	1	1.5	39	12	.31	0 - 1	1 - 1	0 - 0	26	1	1	16	.94	.693	3.38
Knebel, Corey	SU	R	23	7	2	1	1.3	6	0	.00	1 - 3	1 - 1	1 - 1	19	1	2	7	.83	.498	2.70
Price, David	LT	L	28	9	4	7	0.9	5	1	.20	1 - 1	0 - 0	0 - 0	17	0	0	1	1.00	.864	4.18
Cleavinger, Garrett	LT	L	21	4	3	3	1.1	6	2	.33	0 - 0	0 - 0	0 - 1	12	0	1	0	.00	.890	3.18
Alexander, Scott	LT	L	18	4	5	1	1.1	6	1	.17	0 - 0	0 - 0	0 - 1	14	0	1	2	.67	.669	2.93
Bickford, Phil	LM	R	56	24	16	3	1.1	22	1	.05	1 - 1	0 - 2	0 - 0	43	0	2	9	.83	.600	2.50
Vesia, Alex	LM	L	41	22	9	2	1.2	19	4	.21	0 - 0	0 - 0	1 - 2	31	0	1	9	.91	.551	2.25
Bruihl, Justin	LM	L	19	11	4	1	1.0	12	1	.08	0 - 0	0 - 0	0 - 0	16	0	0	3	1.00	.556	3.38
Kelly, Joe	UR	R	48	12	11	3	1.1	20	2	.10	0 - 1	2 - 2	0 - 0	36	0	1	10	.92	.544	2.86
Graterol, Brusdar	UR	R	33	14	10	2	1.3	17	2	.12	0 - 1	0 - 1	0 - 0	21	0	2	4	.67	.712	4.18
Nelson, Jimmy	UR	R	27	6	1	4	1.4	4	1	.25	0 - 0	0 - 1	0 - 0	21	0	1	6	.86	.436	1.98
White, Mitch	UR	R	17	5	2	7	0.7	7	6	.86	0 - 1	0 - 0	0 - 1	10	0	2	0	.00	.541	2.35
Santana, Dennis	UR	R	16	4	4	2	1.0	6	2	.33	0 - 0	0 - 0	0 - 0	11	0	0	1	1.00	.766	6.00
Uceta, Edwin	UR	R	13	2	1	7	0.7	5	3	.60	0 - 0	0 - 0	0 - 0	6	0	0	0		.679	6.38

Miami Marlins

Pitcher	Pos	T	Rel G	Early Entry	Cons Days	Long	Lev Ind	#	Scrd	Pct	Easy	Reg	Tough	Clean	BS Win	BS	Holds	Sv/Hld Pct	Opp OPS	Rel ERA
Floro, Dylan	CL	R	68	0	16	7	1.9	9	3	.33	9 - 10	4 - 8	2 - 3	53	1	6	11	.81	.576	2.81
Garcia, Yimi	CL	R	39	0	7	1	2.3	5	0	.00	7 - 8	7 - 9	1 - 1	28	0	3	2	.85	.729	3.47
Bass, Anthony	SU	R	69	6	18	2	1.3	16	4	.25	0 - 1	0 - 2	0 - 1	47	0	4	19	.83	.734	3.73
Bleier, Richard	SU	L	68	17	18	1	1.3	31	10	.32	0 - 2	0 - 1	0 - 3	49	0	6	20	.77	.603	2.95
Guenther, Sean	LT	L	14	8	1	4	0.4	2	0	.00	0 - 0	0 - 0	0 - 0	5	0	0	0		.920	9.30
Pop, Zach	LM	R	50	28	7	9	0.6	20	12	.60	0 - 0	0 - 1	0 - 0	30	0	1	1	.50	.713	4.12
Detwiler, Ross	LM	L	41	22	7	4	0.6	13	5	.38	0 - 0	0 - 0	0 - 0	29	0	0	1	1.00	.573	2.87
Okert, Steven	LM	L	34	19	7	8	0.8	20	3	.15	0 - 0	0 - 0	0 - 0	21	0	0	1	1.00	.649	2.75
Curtiss, John	LM	R	34	15	4	6	0.7	15	7	.47	0 - 0	0 - 0	0 - 0	23	0	0	1	1.00	.647	2.37
Cimber, Adam	LM	R	33	16	8	3	0.9	15	3	.20	0 - 0	0 - 0	0 - 0	22	0	0	0		.643	2.88
Campbell, Paul	LM	R	15	9	2	7	0.8	9	3	.33	0 - 0	0 - 0	0 - 0	5	0	0	0		.787	5.87
Bender, Anthony	UR	R	59	21	14	7	1.3	22	7	.32	1 - 1	2 - 3	0 - 1	41	1	2	12	.88	.643	2.83
Hess, David	UR	R	13	7	2	4	1.1	10	7	.70	0 - 0	0 - 1	0 - 1	4	1	2	2	.50	.933	4.76
Thompson, Zach	UR	R	12	8	0	1	0.9	8	3	.38	0 - 0	0 - 0	0 - 0	9	0	0	0		.737	3.18

Milwaukee Brewers

Pitcher	Pos	T	Rel G	Early Entry	Cons Days	Long	Lev Ind	#	Scrd	Pct	Easy	Reg	Tough	Clean	BS Win	BS	Holds	Sv/Hld Pct	Opp OPS	Rel ERA
Hader, Josh	CL	L	60	0	18	3	1.9	8	3	.38	24 - 24	10 - 11	0 - 0	52	0	1	0	.97	.421	1.23
Boxberger, Brad	SU	R	71	13	18	4	1.5	30	8	.27	2 - 3	1 - 5	1 - 1	54	0	5	23	.84	.618	3.34
Williams, Devin	SU	R	58	3	13	3	1.8	5	2	.40	3 - 4	0 - 2	0 - 0	45	0	3	23	.90	.587	2.50
Feyereisen, J.P.	SU	R	21	0	5	1	1.3	8	0	.00	0 - 0	0 - 2	0 - 0	16	0	2	9	.82	.538	3.26
Perdomo, Angel	LT	L	19	4	1	4	0.5	8	1	.13	0 - 0	0 - 0	0 - 0	11	0	0	0		.813	6.35
Norris, Daniel	LT	L	18	4	3	5	0.4	5	4	.80	0 - 1	0 - 0	0 - 0	11	0	1	1	.50	.822	6.64
Suter, Brent	LM	L	60	29	10	17	1.2	24	10	.42	0 - 1	1 - 7	0 - 1	33	1	8	8	.53	.711	2.79
Strickland, Hunter	LM	R	35	15	3	5	0.6	11	3	.27	0 - 0	0 - 0	0 - 0	28	0	0	1	1.00	.546	1.73
Milner, Hoby	LM	L	19	5	3	7	0.3	7	3	.43	0 - 0	0 - 0	0 - 0	12	0	0	1	1.00	.970	5.40
Cousins, Jake	UR	R	30	10	7	4	1.1	11	4	.36	0 - 0	0 - 0	0 - 0	22	0	0	7	1.00	.582	2.70
Sanchez, Miguel	UR	R	28	4	4	7	0.5	9	3	.33	0 - 0	0 - 1	0 - 0	17	0	1	0	.00	.807	4.15
Yardley, Eric	UR	R	17	5	1	4	0.7	2	2	1.00	0 - 0	0 - 1	0 - 0	9	0	1	1	.50	.975	6.75
Richards, Trevor	UR	R	15	6	2	7	0.9	8	1	.13	0 - 0	0 - 2	0 - 0	11	0	2	0	.00	.685	3.20
Rasmussen, Drew	UR	R	15	6	2	5	1.1	6	1	.17	0 - 0	0 - 0	1 - 1	10	0	0	0	1.00	.679	4.24
Gustave, Jandel	UR	R	14	4	0	5	0.8	5	1	.20	0 - 0	0 - 1	0 - 0	8	1	1	0	.00	.632	3.44

Minnesota Twins

Pitcher	Pos	T	Usage					Inherited Runners			Saves			Relief Results						
			Rel G	Early Entry	Cons Days	Long	Lev Ind	#	Scrd	Pct	Easy	Reg	Tough	Clean	BS Win	BS	Holds	Sv/Hld Pct	Opp OPS	Rel ERA
Colome, Alex	CL	R	67	3	19	9	1.7	12	4	.33	11 - 15	6 - 9	0 - 0	45	1	7	5	.76	.740	4.15
Duffey, Tyler	SU	R	64	16	11	5	1.5	26	11	.42	3 - 3	0 - 2	0 - 0	44	0	2	22	.93	.619	3.18
Robles, Hansel	SU	R	45	6	11	5	1.9	8	3	.38	7 - 7	3 - 5	0 - 0	27	1	2	14	.92	.761	4.91
Rogers, Taylor	SU	L	40	3	7	4	2.0	15	8	.53	5 - 6	2 - 4	2 - 3	27	0	4	8	.81	.651	3.35
Thielbar, Caleb	LT	L	59	20	10	14	1.0	27	15	.56	0 - 0	0 - 0	0 - 0	40	0	0	12	1.00	.697	3.23
Coulombe, Danny	LT	L	28	7	3	4	0.8	5	1	.20	0 - 0	0 - 1	0 - 0	17	0	1	2	.67	.714	3.58
Minaya, Juan	LM	R	29	13	2	9	1.0	8	0	.00	0 - 0	0 - 0	0 - 0	22	0	0	7	1.00	.624	2.48
Farrell, Luke	LM	R	19	9	1	6	0.6	3	0	.00	0 - 0	0 - 0	0 - 0	15	0	0	1	1.00	.741	3.04
Stashak, Cody	LM	R	15	12	1	4	0.9	9	6	.67	0 - 0	0 - 0	0 - 0	7	0	0	2	1.00	.779	6.89
Alcala, Jorge	UR	R	59	21	8	2	1.0	21	6	.29	0 - 0	1 - 5	0 - 0	39	1	4	11	.75	.644	3.92
Garza, Ralph	UR	R	18	3	4	1	0.6	6	0	.00	0 - 0	1 - 2	0 - 0	12	0	1	2	.75	.626	3.26
Barraclough, Kyle	UR	R	10	5	2	6	0.7	5	2	.40	0 - 0	0 - 0	0 - 0	4	0	0	1	1.00	.877	5.54

New York Mets

Pitcher	Pos	T	Usage					Inherited Runners			Saves			Relief Results						
			Rel G	Early Entry	Cons Days	Long	Lev Ind	#	Scrd	Pct	Easy	Reg	Tough	Clean	BS Win	BS	Holds	Sv/Hld Pct	Opp OPS	Rel ERA
Diaz, Edwin	CL	R	63	0	13	5	2.2	7	0	.00	14 - 16	17 - 20	1 - 2	47	1	6	0	.84	.580	3.45
May, Trevor	SU	R	68	6	17	6	1.3	7	3	.43	3 - 4	1 - 2	0 - 1	49	0	3	16	.87	.698	3.59
Loup, Aaron	SU	L	63	25	18	2	1.5	48	16	.33	0 - 0	0 - 1	0 - 3	45	0	4	16	.80	.506	1.01
Lugo, Seth	SU	R	46	10	10	6	1.7	12	7	.58	0 - 1	1 - 1	0 - 2	32	1	3	13	.82	.712	3.50
Hand, Brad	LT	L	16	5	4	1	1.1	6	5	.83	0 - 0	0 - 1	0 - 1	9	0	2	3	.60	.744	2.70
Castro, Miguel	LM	R	67	31	11	9	1.0	20	4	.20	0 - 0	0 - 2	0 - 0	46	0	2	9	.82	.626	3.56
Smith, Drew	LM	R	30	11	3	7	0.6	11	1	.09	0 - 0	0 - 0	0 - 0	19	0	0	1	1.00	.679	2.52
Diaz, Yennsy	LM	R	20	8	5	8	0.4	3	0	.00	0 - 0	0 - 0	0 - 0	12	0	0	0		.788	5.40
Gsellman, Robert	LM	R	16	12	2	9	0.6	16	4	.25	0 - 0	0 - 0	0 - 0	7	0	0	1	1.00	.647	3.71
Reid-Foley, Sean	LM	R	12	9	0	8	0.8	2	2	1.00	0 - 0	0 - 0	0 - 0	5	0	0	0		.771	5.23
Familia, Jeurys	UR	R	65	18	16	5	1.2	31	11	.35	0 - 0	0 - 4	1 - 3	43	3	6	11	.67	.767	3.94
Barnes, Jacob	UR	R	19	7	2	5	0.6	10	5	.50	0 - 0	2 - 2	0 - 0	12	0	0	1	1.00	.856	6.27
Hembree, Heath	UR	R	15	4	3	2	0.6	0	0	.00	1 - 1	0 - 0	0 - 0	12	0	0	1	1.00	.637	3.45

New York Yankees

Pitcher	Pos	T	Usage					Inherited Runners			Saves			Relief Results						
			Rel G	Early Entry	Cons Days	Long	Lev Ind	#	Scrd	Pct	Easy	Reg	Tough	Clean	BS Win	BS	Holds	Sv/Hld Pct	Opp OPS	Rel ERA
Chapman, Aroldis	CL	L	61	0	16	5	2.0	3	0	.00	19 - 20	11 - 14	0 - 0	47	2	4	1	.89	.678	3.36
Green, Chad	SU	R	67	17	9	16	1.6	32	7	.22	3 - 4	2 - 4	1 - 4	44	1	6	18	.80	.622	3.12
Loaisiga, Jonathan	SU	R	57	18	6	14	1.7	35	6	.17	1 - 1	2 - 5	2 - 3	45	0	4	17	.85	.548	2.17
Britton, Zack	SU	L	22	1	5	1	2.0	3	2	.67	1 - 1	0 - 2	0 - 1	10	0	3	11	.80	.802	5.89
Wilson, Justin	LT	L	21	4	0	1	0.9	7	0	.00	0 - 0	0 - 1	0 - 0	12	0	1	2	.67	.883	7.50
Rodriguez, Joely	LT	L	21	9	5	2	0.7	14	6	.43	0 - 0	0 - 1	0 - 0	12	0	1	4	.80	.723	2.84
Luetge, Lucas	LM	L	56	29	7	16	0.9	33	12	.36	0 - 0	1 - 3	0 - 0	33	0	2	3	.67	.647	2.69
Peralta, Wandy	LM	L	45	15	12	3	1.2	30	4	.13	1 - 1	1 - 1	1 - 1	28	0	0	5	1.00	.682	3.07
Abreu, Albert	LM	R	28	13	2	11	0.8	22	8	.36	0 - 0	0 - 0	1 - 1	15	0	0	3	1.00	.749	5.15
King, Michael	LM	R	16	13	0	11	0.8	9	3	.33	0 - 0	0 - 0	0 - 0	8	0	0	2	1.00	.578	2.33
Cessa, Luis	UR	R	29	8	3	8	0.5	7	2	.29	0 - 0	0 - 0	0 - 0	19	0	0	1	1.00	.605	2.82
Holmes, Clay	UR	R	25	9	5	1	1.6	5	1	.20	0 - 1	0 - 1	0 - 0	17	1	2	5	.71	.458	1.61
O'Day, Darren	UR	R	12	3	1	0	1.6	1	1	1.00	0 - 0	0 - 0	0 - 0	8	0	0	4	1.00	.695	3.38

Oakland Athletics

Pitcher	Pos	T	Usage					Inherited Runners			Saves			Relief Results						
			Rel G	Early Entry	Cons Days	Long	Lev Ind	#	Scrd	Pct	Easy	Reg	Tough	Clean	BS Win	BS	Holds	Sv/Hld Pct	Opp OPS	Rel ERA
Trivino, Lou	CL	R	71	4	15	9	1.8	16	2	.13	17 - 17	4 - 8	1 - 1	53	0	4	8	.88	.622	3.18
Petit, Yusmeiro	SU	R	78	22	18	6	1.2	45	15	.33	2 - 4	0 - 2	0 - 2	53	1	6	22	.80	.659	3.92
Diekman, Jake	SU	L	67	6	13	8	1.4	17	7	.41	2 - 3	5 - 10	0 - 1	45	0	7	14	.75	.715	3.86
Chafin, Andrew	SU	L	28	2	7	1	1.6	9	5	.56	3 - 3	2 - 2	0 - 2	21	1	2	5	.83	.597	1.53
Kolarek, Adam	LT	L	12	4	3	2	0.4	9	6	.67	0 - 0	0 - 0	0 - 0	4	0	0	0		.943	8.00
Puk, A.J.	LT	L	12	3	1	2	0.6	2	0	.00	0 - 0	0 - 2	0 - 0	8	0	2	0	.00	.764	6.08
Guduan, Reymin	LT	L	11	0	1	3	0.2	3	2	.67	0 - 0	0 - 0	0 - 1	5	0	1	0	.00	.848	6.28
Smith, Burch	LM	R	31	14	2	9	0.6	14	6	.43	0 - 0	0 - 1	0 - 0	17	0	1	4	.80	.764	5.40
Romo, Sergio	UR	R	66	8	12	4	1.1	24	12	.50	2 - 4	1 - 1	0 - 2	42	0	4	12	.79	.709	4.67
Guerra, Deolis	UR	R	53	22	11	12	0.6	20	6	.30	0 - 0	0 - 0	0 - 0	35	0	0	3	1.00	.645	4.11
Wendelken, J.B.	UR	R	26	6	6	3	0.8	11	3	.27	0 - 0	0 - 1	0 - 0	14	1	1	2	.67	.734	4.32
Acevedo, Domingo	UR	R	10	2	1	1	0.2	0	0	.00	0 - 0	0 - 0	0 - 0	7	0	0	0		.770	3.27

Philadelphia Phillies

Pitcher	Pos	T	Usage					Inherited Runners			Saves			Relief Results						
			Rel G	Early Entry	Cons Days	Long	Lev Ind	#	Scrd	Pct	Easy	Reg	Tough	Clean	BS Win	BS	Holds	Sv/Hld Pct	Opp OPS	Rel ERA
Neris, Hector	CL	R	74	14	18	14	1.5	25	10	.40	6 - 8	5 - 9	1 - 2	52	0	7	11	.77	.677	3.63
Kennedy, Ian	CL	R	23	0	5	7	2.0	5	1	.20	5 - 6	3 - 5	2 - 2	15	1	3	0	.77	.758	4.13
Alvarado, Jose	SU	L	64	13	16	7	1.8	32	6	.19	2 - 3	3 - 4	0 - 1	43	1	3	16	.88	.707	4.20
Bradley, Archie	SU	R	53	9	12	7	1.3	19	6	.32	2 - 3	0 - 1	0 - 1	34	2	3	13	.83	.743	3.71
Coonrod, Sam	SU	R	40	10	8	5	1.2	15	10	.67	0 - 0	2 - 6	0 - 0	23	0	4	8	.71	.706	4.05
Suarez, Ranger	LT	L	27	10	4	9	1.1	22	5	.23	2 - 3	1 - 2	1 - 2	15	1	3	0	.57	.483	1.12
Romero, JoJo	LT	L	11	5	3	1	1.1	6	5	.83	0 - 0	0 - 0	0 - 0	5	0	0	3	1.00	1.053	7.00
De Los Santos, Enyel	LM	R	26	8	1	8	0.6	12	8	.67	0 - 1	0 - 1	0 - 0	11	0	2	1	.33	.929	6.75
Falter, Bailey	LM	L	21	11	0	9	0.6	13	6	.46	0 - 0	0 - 0	0 - 0	10	0	0	2	1.00	.692	5.12
Hammer, J.D.	LM	R	20	10	4	5	0.6	11	8	.73	0 - 0	0 - 0	0 - 0	15	0	0	0		.769	4.95
Hale, David	LM	R	16	6	1	8	0.5	16	11	.69	0 - 0	0 - 1	0 - 0	5	0	1	0	.00	.842	6.85
Brogdon, Connor	UR	R	55	21	13	10	1.1	16	6	.38	1 - 2	0 - 1	0 - 2	37	0	4	10	.73	.643	3.49
Kintzler, Brandon	UR	R	28	9	2	4	0.8	15	6	.40	0 - 2	0 - 0	0 - 0	15	0	2	2	.50	.954	6.28
Moore, Matt	UR	L	11	5	1	4	0.9	4	1	.25	0 - 0	0 - 0	0 - 0	3	0	0	1	1.00	.729	5.40
Bedrosian, Cam	UR	R	10	4	0	2	0.9	5	1	.20	0 - 0	0 - 1	0 - 0	6	0	1	1	.50	.791	5.00

Pittsburgh Pirates

Pitcher	Pos	T	Usage					Inherited Runners			Saves			Relief Results						
			Rel G	Early Entry	Cons Days	Long	Lev Ind	#	Scrd	Pct	Easy	Reg	Tough	Clean	BS Win	BS	Holds	Sv/Hld Pct	Opp OPS	Rel ERA
Rodriguez, Richard	CL	R	37	0	6	4	1.7	7	2	.29	8 - 8	6 - 8	0 - 1	29	0	3	0	.82	.523	2.82
Bednar, David	SU	R	61	5	8	6	1.0	21	2	.10	1 - 1	2 - 3	0 - 1	49	0	2	13	.89	.577	2.23
Shreve, Chasen	LT	L	57	23	12	8	0.9	28	10	.36	0 - 0	0 - 1	0 - 1	40	0	2	11	.85	.681	3.20
Davis, Austin	LT	L	10	3	1	2	0.8	4	2	.50	0 - 1	0 - 0	0 - 0	5	0	1	2	.67	.702	5.59
Howard, Sam	LM	L	53	26	10	7	1.0	27	4	.15	0 - 0	0 - 1	0 - 0	36	0	1	11	.92	.740	5.73
Holmes, Clay	LM	R	44	23	6	8	0.9	23	10	.43	0 - 0	0 - 0	0 - 0	28	0	0	6	1.00	.649	4.93
Underwood Jr., Duane	LM	R	43	27	1	22	0.6	16	10	.63	0 - 0	0 - 0	0 - 0	20	0	0	2	1.00	.776	4.33
Keller, Kyle	LM	R	32	15	3	9	0.5	9	3	.33	0 - 0	0 - 0	0 - 0	16	0	0	2	1.00	.868	6.48
Banda, Anthony	LM	L	25	15	2	5	0.8	8	3	.38	0 - 0	0 - 1	0 - 1	16	0	2	4	.67	.752	3.42
Ponce, Cody	LM	R	13	13	0	12	0.7	1	1	1.00	0 - 0	0 - 0	0 - 0	3	0	0	0		.924	5.97
Stratton, Chris	UR	R	68	22	10	16	1.1	17	4	.24	5 - 6	3 - 6	0 - 1	49	1	5	7	.75	.675	3.63
Mears, Nick	UR	R	30	10	5	5	1.0	22	13	.59	0 - 0	0 - 1	0 - 4	18	1	5	3	.38	.818	5.01
Crick, Kyle	UR	R	27	2	0	0	1.2	3	1	.33	0 - 0	0 - 0	0 - 0	19	0	1	6	.86	.558	4.44
Oviedo, Luis	UR	R	21	7	0	9	0.4	1	0	.00	0 - 0	0 - 0	0 - 0	11	0	0	0		.814	7.22
Kuhl, Chad	UR	R	14	3	0	2	1.1	0	0	.00	0 - 1	0 - 1	0 - 0	9	0	2	4	.67	1.037	6.75
Miller, Shelby	UR	R	10	3	0	2	0.7	2	0	.00	0 - 0	0 - 0	0 - 0	6	0	0	1	1.00	.877	5.06

San Diego Padres

Pitcher	Pos	T	Usage Rel G	Early Entry	Cons Days	Long	Lev Ind	Inherited Runners #	Scrd	Pct	Saves Easy	Reg	Tough	Clean	BS Win	BS	Holds	Sv/Hld Pct	Opp OPS	Rel ERA
Melancon, Mark	CL	R	64	1	16	6	2.2	4	2	.50	24-26	14-18	1-1	47	1	6	0	.87	.618	2.23
Pagan, Emilio	SU	R	67	3	11	6	1.1	12	4	.33	0-4	0-1	0-0	48	0	5	17	.77	.801	4.83
Pomeranz, Drew	SU	L	27	1	1	2	1.2	2	1	.50	0-0	0-0	0-0	21	0	0	13	1.00	.618	1.75
Hill, Tim	LT	L	78	32	22	2	1.3	48	12	.25	1-1	0-3	0-1	54	1	4	17	.82	.704	3.62
Ramirez, Nick	LT	L	13	6	2	6	0.7	2	0	.00	0-0	0-0	0-0	7	0	0	0		.739	5.75
Stammen, Craig	LM	R	63	37	9	17	0.9	22	12	.55	0-0	1-2	0-0	41	0	1	7	.89	.627	2.80
Crismatt, Nabil	LM	R	45	24	6	26	0.6	14	6	.43	0-0	0-0	0-0	25	0	0	1	1.00	.761	3.76
Diaz, Miguel	LM	R	23	12	5	10	0.6	7	1	.14	1-1	0-0	0-0	15	0	0	1	1.00	.732	3.65
Weathers, Ryan	LM	L	12	9	0	8	0.8	0	0	.00	0-0	1-1	0-0	6	0	0	0	1.00	.637	2.49
Adams, Austin	UR	R	65	18	13	4	1.0	18	5	.28	0-0	0-1	0-0	46	1	1	10	.91	.610	4.10
Johnson, Pierce	UR	R	61	25	11	6	1.0	13	1	.08	0-0	0-2	0-0	45	0	2	9	.82	.663	3.18
Hudson, Daniel	UR	R	23	3	4	2	1.0	10	5	.50	0-0	0-1	0-0	10	1	1	2	.67	.827	5.21
Lamet, Dinelson	UR	R	13	8	1	4	0.9	1	0	.00	0-0	0-0	0-0	6	0	0	1	1.00	.747	5.09
Kela, Keone	UR	R	12	5	0	2	1.1	0	0	.00	0-0	0-2	0-0	8	0	2	1	.33	.736	5.06

San Francisco Giants

Pitcher	Pos	T	Usage Rel G	Early Entry	Cons Days	Long	Lev Ind	Inherited Runners #	Scrd	Pct	Saves Easy	Reg	Tough	Clean	BS Win	BS	Holds	Sv/Hld Pct	Opp OPS	Rel ERA
McGee, Jake	CL	L	62	0	17	2	2.0	3	1	.33	19-21	12-14	0-1	46	0	5	8	.89	.565	2.72
Rogers, Tyler	SU	R	80	2	25	4	1.9	10	3	.30	8-10	5-8	0-1	67	1	6	30	.88	.611	2.22
Leone, Dominic	SU	R	53	8	19	2	1.3	12	4	.33	1-1	0-1	1-2	40	1	2	15	.89	.566	1.30
Doval, Camilo	SU	R	29	4	8	2	1.3	14	5	.36	2-3	1-2	0-1	21	0	3	5	.73	.599	3.00
Baragar, Caleb	SU	L	25	8	4	1	1.0	5	0	.00	1-1	1-1	0-1	20	0	1	7	.90	.693	1.57
Garcia, Jarlin	LT	L	58	27	11	10	1.0	29	12	.41	1-2	0-0	0-1	36	1	2	11	.86	.635	2.62
Watson, Tony	LT	L	26	2	6	0	1.1	2	0	.00	0-0	0-0	0-0	22	0	0	7	1.00	.467	2.96
Peralta, Wandy	LT	L	10	2	2	1	1.5	4	2	.50	1-1	0-1	1-1	6	1	1	0	.67	.863	5.40
Alvarez, Jose	LM	L	66	29	17	7	0.8	37	7	.19	0-0	0-0	0-0	49	0	0	8	1.00	.529	2.14
Jackson, Jay	LM	R	22	13	4	2	0.9	13	3	.23	0-1	0-1	0-0	18	1	2	3	.60	.620	2.53
Littell, Zack	UR	R	61	26	17	6	1.1	23	7	.30	0-0	1-3	1-3	43	0	4	5	.64	.635	2.37
Wisler, Matt	UR	R	21	8	5	1	0.6	13	8	.62	0-0	0-1	0-0	11	0	1	3	.75	.798	6.05
Brebbia, John	UR	R	18	6	2	3	0.6	7	6	.86	0-0	0-0	0-0	9	0	0	1	1.00	.917	5.89
Castro, Kervin	UR	R	10	3	2	3	0.8	7	3	.43	0-0	0-0	0-0	7	0	0	0		.609	0.00
Sherfy, Jimmie	UR	R	10	1	3	3	0.2	0	0	.00	0-0	0-0	0-0	7	0	0	0		.696	4.22

Seattle Mariners

Pitcher	Pos	T	Usage Rel G	Early Entry	Cons Days	Long	Lev Ind	Inherited Runners #	Scrd	Pct	Saves Easy	Reg	Tough	Clean	BS Win	BS	Holds	Sv/Hld Pct	Opp OPS	Rel ERA
Graveman, Kendall	CL	R	30	3	4	3	1.8	6	0	.00	3-3	7-9	0-0	25	0	2	4	.88	.424	0.82
Misiewicz, Anthony	SU	L	66	19	16	3	1.2	22	6	.27	0-0	0-5	0-0	47	0	5	19	.79	.759	4.61
Steckenrider, Drew	SU	R	62	12	11	6	1.3	18	6	.33	7-7	6-8	1-2	48	0	3	7	.88	.608	2.00
Sewald, Paul	SU	R	62	4	17	10	1.6	22	3	.14	6-8	2-3	3-5	47	1	5	16	.84	.590	3.06
Sadler, Casey	SU	R	42	19	11	1	1.1	19	3	.16	0-0	0-0	0-0	35	0	0	15	1.00	.402	0.67
Chargois, JT	SU	R	31	21	4	4	1.2	29	8	.28	0-0	0-1	0-1	19	1	2	9	.82	.618	3.00
Castillo, Diego	SU	R	24	0	6	1	1.7	4	2	.50	2-3	0-3	0-0	17	1	4	7	.69	.639	2.86
Santiago, Hector	LT	L	12	5	2	9	0.5	2	0	.00	0-0	0-0	0-0	7	0	0	0		.706	3.47
Doolittle, Sean	LT	L	11	5	2	1	0.6	6	1	.17	0-0	0-0	0-0	8	0	0	1	1.00	.661	4.76
Montero, Rafael	LM	R	40	7	5	8	1.5	11	2	.18	4-5	3-7	0-1	20	1	6	4	.65	.819	7.27
Vest, Will	LM	R	32	19	6	7	0.8	23	6	.26	0-0	0-0	0-0	19	0	0	6	1.00	.812	6.17
Swanson, Erik	UR	R	31	8	5	2	1.1	8	2	.25	0-1	0-1	1-1	20	0	2	5	.75	.692	3.52
Middleton, Keynan	UR	R	31	7	2	2	0.9	5	0	.00	2-2	1-1	1-1	22	0	0	3	1.00	.686	3.60
Ramirez, Yohan	UR	R	25	7	3	4	0.6	11	5	.45	0-0	1-1	1-1	16	0	0	0	1.00	.693	3.90
Smith, Joe	UR	R	23	11	4	0	1.2	18	7	.39	0-0	0-1	0-2	17	1	3	3	.50	.521	2.00
Mills, Wyatt	UR	R	11	6	1	4	0.2	6	3	.50	0-0	0-0	0-0	4	0	0	0		.940	9.95

St Louis Cardinals

Pitcher	Pos	T	Usage					Inherited Runners			Saves			Relief Results						
			Rel G	Early Entry	Cons Days	Long	Lev Ind	#	Scrd	Pct	Easy	Reg	Tough	Clean	BS Win	BS	Holds	Sv/Hld Pct	Opp OPS	Rel ERA
Reyes, Alex	CL	R	70	6	13	11	1.7	15	10	.67	19 - 21	9 - 11	1 - 2	51	0	5	3	.86	.609	3.24
Gallegos, Giovanny	SU	R	73	4	17	10	1.7	25	3	.12	7 - 8	6 - 10	1 - 4	55	1	8	24	.83	.551	3.02
Cabrera, Genesis	SU	L	71	6	18	6	1.3	43	17	.40	0 - 1	0 - 1	0 - 1	49	0	3	28	.90	.628	3.73
McFarland, T.J.	SU	L	38	12	12	3	1.1	25	8	.32	0 - 0	0 - 0	0 - 1	29	0	1	15	.94	.655	2.56
Garcia, Luis	SU	R	34	11	7	2	1.1	10	4	.40	1 - 1	0 - 1	1 - 1	25	0	1	11	.93	.550	3.24
Miller, Andrew	LT	L	40	19	4	2	0.6	16	4	.25	0 - 0	0 - 0	0 - 0	25	0	0	4	1.00	.868	4.75
Helsley, Ryan	LM	R	51	25	6	5	1.1	31	4	.13	0 - 1	0 - 1	1 - 1	36	0	2	10	.85	.668	4.56
Ponce de Leon, Daniel	LM	R	22	8	3	10	0.7	5	3	.60	0 - 0	1 - 2	1 - 1	11	0	1	0	.67	.762	5.00
Webb, Tyler	LM	L	22	11	7	5	0.7	20	10	.50	0 - 0	0 - 0	0 - 0	7	0	0	2	1.00	.887	13.22
Woodford, Jake	LM	R	18	13	2	10	0.7	25	15	.60	0 - 0	0 - 0	0 - 0	5	0	0	0		.763	3.82
Whitley, Kodi	UR	R	25	6	5	2	0.6	16	7	.44	0 - 0	0 - 0	0 - 0	16	0	0	4	1.00	.497	2.49
Miller, Justin	UR	R	18	5	1	0	0.5	12	2	.17	0 - 0	0 - 0	1 - 1	12	0	0	1	1.00	.735	4.50
Fernandez, Junior	UR	R	18	5	0	6	0.1	8	5	.63	0 - 0	0 - 0	0 - 0	12	0	0	0		.864	5.66
Elledge, Seth	UR	R	11	5	1	2	0.2	10	8	.80	0 - 0	0 - 0	0 - 0	4	0	0	0		.869	4.63
Gant, John	UR	R	11	4	2	2	1.2	5	0	.00	0 - 0	0 - 0	0 - 0	9	0	0	1	1.00	.541	1.54
Hicks, Jordan	UR	R	10	4	0	2	0.5	1	0	.00	0 - 0	0 - 0	0 - 0	6	0	0	3	1.00	.576	5.40

Tampa Bay Rays

Pitcher	Pos	T	Usage					Inherited Runners			Saves			Relief Results						
			Rel G	Early Entry	Cons Days	Long	Lev Ind	#	Scrd	Pct	Easy	Reg	Tough	Clean	BS Win	BS	Holds	Sv/Hld Pct	Opp OPS	Rel ERA
Castillo, Diego	CL	R	37	2	10	2	1.9	10	1	.10	7 - 7	7 - 9	0 - 0	28	0	2	3	.89	.613	2.72
Kittredge, Andrew	SU	R	53	20	4	9	1.5	29	15	.52	4 - 4	3 - 3	1 - 2	32	0	1	7	.94	.566	1.65
Fairbanks, Pete	SU	R	47	5	9	5	1.7	5	0	.00	4 - 4	1 - 3	0 - 0	35	0	2	14	.90	.659	3.59
Springs, Jeffrey	SU	L	43	12	8	8	1.1	15	6	.40	1 - 1	1 - 1	0 - 2	25	0	2	10	.86	.720	3.43
Thompson, Ryan	SU	R	36	12	7	2	2.0	26	8	.31	0 - 0	0 - 2	0 - 2	24	0	4	11	.73	.642	2.38
McHugh, Collin	SU	R	30	14	0	16	1.2	3	1	.33	0 - 0	1 - 3	0 - 0	20	1	2	6	.78	.586	1.90
Wisler, Matt	SU	R	27	6	3	5	1.7	10	3	.30	0 - 0	1 - 3	0 - 0	18	1	2	7	.80	.581	2.15
Chargois, JT	SU	R	25	9	5	1	1.3	9	4	.44	0 - 0	0 - 1	0 - 2	18	0	3	6	.67	.672	1.90
Sherriff, Ryan	LT	L	16	5	3	3	0.7	6	3	.50	0 - 0	1 - 1	0 - 1	9	0	1	1	.67	.668	5.52
Reed, Cody	LT	L	12	1	3	0	0.7	3	0	.00	0 - 0	0 - 0	0 - 0	9	0	0	3	1.00	.719	3.72
Feyereisen, J.P.	LM	R	34	11	5	7	1.3	10	2	.20	3 - 3	0 - 1	0 - 0	24	1	1	6	.90	.656	2.45
Conley, Adam	LM	L	17	12	3	4	0.6	7	1	.14	0 - 0	0 - 0	0 - 0	13	0	0	0		.653	2.29
Fleming, Josh	LM	L	15	10	0	11	0.9	4	0	.00	0 - 0	1 - 1	0 - 0	5	0	0	3	1.00	.653	3.75
Head, Louis	UR	R	25	5	5	7	0.4	8	0	.00	0 - 0	0 - 0	0 - 0	21	0	0	0		.456	1.91
Mazza, Chris	UR	R	14	5	1	8	0.4	5	0	.00	0 - 0	1 - 1	0 - 0	9	0	0	0	1.00	.718	4.61
Strickland, Hunter	UR	R	13	1	2	4	0.6	3	1	.33	0 - 0	0 - 0	0 - 0	9	0	0	1	1.00	.653	1.69
Robertson, David	UR	R	11	0	1	1	1.3	0	0	.00	0 - 1	0 - 1	0 - 0	7	0	2	2	.50	.730	4.91
Armstrong, Shawn	UR	R	11	5	1	7	0.5	4	1	.25	0 - 0	0 - 0	0 - 0	6	0	0	1	1.00	.719	4.50
Rasmussen, Drew	UR	R	10	5	0	7	1.0	3	0	.00	0 - 0	0 - 0	0 - 0	6	0	0	1	1.00	.677	3.71

Texas Rangers

Pitcher	Pos	T	Usage Rel G	Early Entry	Cons Days	Long	Lev Ind	Inherited Runners #	Scrd	Pct	Saves Easy	Reg	Tough	Clean	BS Win	BS	Holds	Sv/Hld Pct	Opp OPS	Rel ERA
Kennedy, Ian	CL	R	32	0	6	2	1.5	4	1	.25	12 - 12	4 - 4	0 - 1	24	0	1	0	.94	.656	2.51
Barlow, Joe	CL	R	31	3	5	3	1.1	8	3	.38	7 - 7	4 - 5	0 - 0	25	0	1	3	.93	.433	1.55
Patton, Spencer	SU	R	42	1	5	4	1.1	7	3	.43	1 - 1	1 - 3	0 - 1	29	1	3	11	.81	.653	3.83
Rodriguez, Joely	SU	L	31	1	2	3	1.5	11	3	.27	1 - 1	0 - 0	0 - 1	20	0	1	9	.91	.748	5.93
Martin, Brett	LT	L	66	13	9	4	1.0	49	18	.37	0 - 1	0 - 0	0 - 1	39	0	2	11	.85	.686	3.18
Benjamin, Wes	LT	L	11	8	0	6	0.7	5	2	.40	0 - 0	0 - 0	0 - 1	4	0	1	0	.00	.822	6.62
Santana, Dennis	LM	R	39	15	7	9	1.0	29	3	.10	0 - 0	0 - 1	0 - 1	28	0	2	5	.71	.658	3.63
Hearn, Taylor	LM	L	31	13	0	19	0.9	10	3	.30	0 - 0	0 - 1	0 - 0	15	0	1	1	.50	.698	3.54
King, John	LM	L	27	13	0	12	1.1	11	3	.27	0 - 0	0 - 0	0 - 1	16	0	1	4	.80	.626	3.52
Evans, Demarcus	LM	R	25	11	2	8	0.7	11	4	.36	0 - 0	0 - 1	0 - 1	15	0	2	2	.50	.760	5.13
Cotton, Jharel	LM	R	23	11	1	10	0.6	9	3	.33	0 - 0	0 - 0	0 - 0	13	0	0	3	1.00	.659	3.52
De Geus, Brett	LM	R	19	6	0	10	0.4	15	4	.27	0 - 0	0 - 0	0 - 0	10	0	0	0		.840	8.44
Allard, Kolby	LM	L	15	11	0	10	0.7	11	5	.45	0 - 0	0 - 0	0 - 0	6	0	0	1	1.00	.798	5.45
Sborz, Josh	UR	R	63	11	9	8	1.0	21	8	.38	0 - 0	0 - 1	1 - 3	39	0	3	9	.77	.710	3.97

Toronto Blue Jays

Pitcher	Pos	T	Usage Rel G	Early Entry	Cons Days	Long	Lev Ind	Inherited Runners #	Scrd	Pct	Saves Easy	Reg	Tough	Clean	BS Win	BS	Holds	Sv/Hld Pct	Opp OPS	Rel ERA
Romano, Jordan	CL	R	62	0	11	5	1.5	15	6	.40	15 - 15	8 - 8	0 - 1	46	0	1	5	.97	.576	2.14
Mayza, Tim	SU	L	61	15	11	2	1.1	37	8	.22	0 - 1	0 - 1	1 - 2	46	0	3	18	.86	.572	3.40
Chatwood, Tyler	SU	R	30	7	4	2	1.5	15	5	.33	1 - 1	0 - 0	0 - 1	22	0	1	10	.92	.599	5.46
Saucedo, Tayler	LT	L	29	9	7	3	0.5	16	5	.31	0 - 0	0 - 1	0 - 1	19	0	2	1	.33	.666	4.56
Borucki, Ryan	LT	L	24	8	3	0	0.7	11	3	.27	0 - 1	0 - 0	0 - 0	14	0	1	1	.50	.738	4.94
Hand, Brad	LT	L	11	2	1	0	0.9	6	2	.33	0 - 0	0 - 0	0 - 1	5	0	1	0	.00	1.012	7.27
Thornton, Trent	LM	R	34	18	1	14	0.8	13	3	.23	0 - 0	0 - 0	0 - 0	16	0	0	0		.843	4.95
Richards, Trevor	LM	R	32	10	5	4	1.0	15	3	.20	0 - 0	0 - 1	0 - 2	24	0	3	5	.63	.552	3.31
Payamps, Joel	LM	R	22	7	2	7	0.8	7	2	.29	0 - 0	0 - 0	0 - 0	15	0	0	0		.586	2.70
Cimber, Adam	UR	R	39	10	7	1	0.9	24	7	.29	1 - 1	0 - 0	0 - 0	27	0	0	5	1.00	.567	1.69
Dolis, Rafael	UR	R	39	6	4	3	1.0	15	6	.40	2 - 3	0 - 0	1 - 1	25	0	1	3	.86	.730	5.63
Castro, Anthony	UR	R	25	9	2	4	1.0	14	2	.14	1 - 2	0 - 0	0 - 0	14	0	1	1	.67	.745	4.74
Merryweather, Julian	UR	R	12	3	0	2	1.3	5	2	.40	1 - 1	1 - 1	0 - 0	7	0	0	1	1.00	.853	5.25
Phelps, David	UR	R	11	1	1	1	1.3	3	1	.33	0 - 0	0 - 0	0 - 0	7	0	0	4	1.00	.580	0.96
Pearson, Nate	UR	R	11	3	0	2	0.5	1	0	.00	0 - 0	0 - 0	0 - 0	8	0	0	0		.663	2.84
Soria, Joakim	UR	R	10	1	0	0	1.0	1	0	.00	0 - 0	0 - 1	0 - 0	7	0	1	2	.67	.853	7.88
Barnes, Jacob	UR	R	10	4	0	4	0.2	6	0	.00	0 - 0	0 - 0	0 - 0	6	0	0	0		.816	6.30

Washington Nationals

Pitcher	Pos	T	Usage Rel G	Early Entry	Cons Days	Long	Lev Ind	Inherited Runners #	Scrd	Pct	Saves Easy	Reg	Tough	Clean	BS Win	BS	Holds	Sv/Hld Pct	Opp OPS	Rel ERA
Hand, Brad	CL	L	41	0	16	6	2.2	4	1	.25	13 - 14	8 - 12	0 - 0	27	1	5	0	.81	.655	3.59
Finnegan, Kyle	SU	R	68	18	18	9	1.5	25	12	.48	5 - 6	6 - 7	0 - 1	45	0	3	13	.89	.748	3.55
Machado, Andres	SU	R	40	15	15	1	1.2	27	12	.44	0 - 0	0 - 2	0 - 1	25	0	3	10	.77	.701	3.53
Rainey, Tanner	SU	R	38	7	9	4	1.4	14	5	.36	3 - 3	0 - 2	0 - 1	24	1	3	10	.81	.836	7.39
Hudson, Daniel	SU	R	31	1	9	2	1.6	11	4	.36	0 - 0	0 - 1	0 - 1	23	1	2	14	.88	.575	2.20

Washington Nationals

Pitcher	Pos	T	Usage					Inherited Runners			Saves			Relief Results						
			Rel G	Early Entry	Cons Days	Long	Lev Ind	#	Scrd	Pct	Easy	Reg	Tough	Clean	BS Win	BS	Holds	Sv/Hld Pct	Opp OPS	Rel ERA
Thompson, Mason	SU	R	27	9	4	2	1.2	15	6	.40	0 - 0	0 - 1	0 - 2	17	0	3	5	.63	.889	4.15
Clay, Sam	LT	L	58	24	13	3	1.0	23	6	.26	0 - 0	0 - 1	0 - 0	33	0	1	11	.92	.792	5.60
Baldonado, Alberto	LT	L	14	8	4	1	1.5	8	3	.38	0 - 1	0 - 2	0 - 1	8	0	4	3	.43	.818	8.44
McGowin, Kyle	LM	R	27	11	7	5	0.6	8	3	.38	0 - 0	0 - 0	0 - 0	17	0	0	1	1.00	.646	4.20
Voth, Austin	UR	R	48	19	7	12	1.0	15	7	.47	0 - 1	0 - 2	0 - 2	30	2	5	7	.58	.841	5.53
Suero, Wander	UR	R	45	19	14	7	0.8	16	6	.38	0 - 1	0 - 0	0 - 2	22	0	3	6	.67	.858	6.33
Harper, Ryne	UR	R	34	10	8	6	0.5	18	1	.06	0 - 1	0 - 0	0 - 0	26	0	1	3	.75	.687	4.04
Murphy, Patrick	UR	R	17	7	2	3	1.1	5	1	.20	0 - 0	0 - 0	0 - 0	9	0	0	4	1.00	.716	5.30
Espino, Paolo	UR	R	16	4	1	4	0.8	6	3	.50	0 - 0	1 - 1	0 - 0	10	0	0	0	1.00	.616	3.42
Rodriguez, Jefry	UR	R	13	4	2	7	0.2	1	1	1.00	0 - 0	0 - 0	0 - 0	5	0	0	0		.914	7.08
Klobosits, Gabe	UR	R	11	5	2	2	1.2	3	3	1.00	0 - 0	0 - 0	0 - 0	5	0	0	4	1.00	.713	5.56

Openers

Alex Vigderman

"Have you watched Ted Lasso?"
"You heard about these NFTs?"
"Collin McHugh."

All of these were openers in 2021. That last flavor isn't as big a deal as it was a couple years ago. We're not spending as much time starting up conversations with strangers, and MLB teams aren't quite as taken with the hot new in-game tactic as they were in 2018 and 2019.

That isn't to say that we suddenly returned to the days of yore, when men were men and starting pitchers were their own closers. We're just not seeing as many cases of the Opener tactic being used.

For years, we floated between 1-2% of starts being at most 3 innings and at most 3 earned runs allowed. That description includes opener games, but also allows for more typical "bullpen games." In 2018, the rate of such games more than doubled, to 5%. Since 2019, we've been above 7%. So we're seeing a lot of intentionally short outings, openers or not.

For those of you who haven't checked in with us in a while, we define an opener game as one where a traditional short-stint reliever starts the game and is then followed by a traditional starter. That pitcher then serves as a bulk-innings pitcher, to use a new term. The opener is *relieving* the next pitcher of the burden of facing the meat of the order the first time through.

As you take a look at the ERAs, keep in mind that these guys are facing the meat of the lineup and then ducking out, so they'll perform worse than they would in a more typical role, when they might face other hitters.

Opener Usage

By Team					
Team	2018	2019	2020	2021	Total
Tampa Bay Rays	39	35	3	17	94
Los Angeles Angels	0	27	0	1	28
Seattle Mariners	1	24	0	1	26
Toronto Blue Jays	1	15	3	2	21
Texas Rangers	3	9	3	1	16
New York Yankees	0	10	0	1	11
Oakland Athletics	7	3	0	0	10
Los Angeles Dodgers	1	1	1	5	8
Minnesota Twins	7	0	0	1	8
Baltimore Orioles	2	3	0	1	6
Miami Marlins	0	0	0	4	4
New York Mets	0	0	0	4	4
San Francisco Giants	0	1	1	2	4
Pittsburgh Pirates	0	3	0	1	4
San Diego Padres	0	2	0	1	3
Houston Astros	1	2	0	0	3
Arizona Diamondbacks	0	1	0	0	1
Chicago White Sox	0	1	0	0	1
Philadelphia Phillies	0	1	0	0	1
Washington Nationals	0	1	0	0	1
Milwaukee Brewers	1	0	0	0	1
St Louis Cardinals	0	0	0	0	0
Cleveland Indians	0	0	0	0	0
Detroit Tigers	0	0	0	0	0
Kansas City Royals	0	0	0	0	0
Boston Red Sox	0	0	0	0	0
Atlanta Braves	0	0	0	0	0
Chicago Cubs	0	0	0	0	0
Cincinnati Reds	0	0	0	0	0
Colorado Rockies	0	0	0	0	0
Total	63	139	11	42	255

Appearances By Pitcher						
Pitcher	2018	2019	2020	2021	Total	ERA
Ryne Stanek	20	22	0	0	42	3.36
Diego Castillo	6	6	0	0	12	4.41
Wilmer Font	0	10	0	0	10	5.51
Hunter Wood	8	2	0	0	10	3.18
Andrew Kittredge	1	4	0	4	9	7.82
Chad Green	0	8	0	0	8	2.53
Matt Wisler	0	8	0	0	8	0.00
Liam Hendriks	6	2	0	0	8	2.25
Collin McHugh	0	0	0	7	7	0.00
Noe Ramirez	0	7	0	0	7	6.48
Cam Bedrosian	0	7	0	0	7	2.57
Taylor Cole	0	6	0	0	6	11.05
Matt Carasiti	0	5	0	0	5	10.38
Gabriel Moya	5	0	0	0	5	3.00
John Curtiss	0	0	3	0	3	2.70
Julian Merryweather	0	0	3	0	3	3.60
Luis Garcia	0	2	1	0	3	3.00
Jesse Chavez	0	3	0	0	3	0.00
Luke Bard	0	3	0	0	3	3.00
Jose Leclerc	0	3	0	0	3	2.45
Sergio Romo	3	0	0	0	3	3.00
Noah Syndergaard	0	0	0	2	2	9.00
Brent Honeywell	0	0	0	2	2	9.00
Louis Head	0	0	0	2	2	9.00
Zack Littell	0	0	0	2	2	36.00
David Phelps	0	1	0	1	2	0.00
Cory Gearrin	0	2	0	0	2	18.00
Derek Law	0	2	0	0	2	5.40
Sam Tuivailala	0	2	0	0	2	0.00
Tayler Scott	0	2	0	0	2	27.00
Austin Adams	0	2	0	0	2	16.20
Jimmy Yacabonis	0	2	0	0	2	3.00
Montana DuRapau	0	2	0	0	2	10.13
Gerson Bautista	0	2	0	0	2	13.50
Nick Vincent	1	1	0	0	2	9.00
Connor Sadzeck	2	0	0	0	2	0.00
Pierce Johnson	0	0	0	1	1	0.00
Danny Coulombe	0	0	0	1	1	5.40
Keynan Middleton	0	0	0	1	1	45.00
Miguel Castro	0	0	0	1	1	0.00
Corey Knebel	0	0	0	1	1	0.00
Junior Guerra	0	0	0	1	1	27.00
Ross Detwiler	0	0	0	1	1	0.00
Anthony Bass	0	0	0	1	1	9.00
David Robertson	0	0	0	1	1	0.00
Aaron Loup	0	0	0	1	1	0.00
Trent Thornton	0	0	0	1	1	0.00
Anthony Bender	0	0	0	1	1	0.00
Nick Nelson	0	0	0	1	1	18.00
Brusdar Graterol	0	0	0	1	1	18.00
Darien Nunez	0	0	0	1	1	9.00
Luis Patino	0	0	0	1	1	0.00
Spencer Howard	0	0	0	1	1	0.00
Justin Bruihl	0	0	0	1	1	0.00
Adam Plutko	0	0	0	1	1	36.00
Zach Thompson	0	0	0	1	1	9.00
Jake Reed	0	0	0	1	1	9.00
Sam Howard	0	0	0	1	1	0.00

Pitchers Fielding & Holding Runners, and Hitters Pitching

Sarah Thompson

When a batter hits a rocket right back at the pitcher, a couple of things could happen—the pitcher gets hit, he hits the deck and puts his trust in his defense, or he snags it and throws to a base if necessary. Here, we're going to highlight the players who more often than not succeed in the latter outcome.

In this section, we're singing the praises of pitchers like Dallas Keuchel, Taijuan Walker, Max Fried, and Zack Wheeler. Their commonalities lie in how well they field.

Dallas Keuchel saved the most runs of any pitcher with his fielding this season, saving 12 runs for the White Sox. Year after year, he excels at holding runners—he's only ever had a negative Stolen Based Runs Saved total once (his first season in MLB, 2012). This season, he's saved two runs by holding baserunners. The rest of those Runs Saved come from regular fielding. He's saved 10 plays on his gloveside, four straight on, and cost his team only one play on his armside. Pitchers are athletes. Even those on the wrong side of 30.

Ryan Weathers was outstanding at holding runners in his debut season. He's picked off eight runners, which exceeds the next-best pickoff count by four (Max Fried, 4). Weathers also has one assist catching a baserunner stealing and only two stolen bases allowed to his name.

What about hitters who have answered the call to record the last few outs of a blowout?

Sandy León, who is usually receiving pitches instead of throwing them, was called to pitch on six separate occasions, facing 26 batters. He allowed only seven hits, four of which were extra base hits. Half (1) of his strikeouts were swinging strikes, which trails only utility-man Hernán Pérez, who had two swinging Ks.

Harold Castro, Tigers utility-man, has the best track record of the bunch—a 0.00 ERA in 3 outings that total 2 2/3 IP.

In total, 61 non-pitchers had to take the mound this season, eclipsing 2019's total of 56. Forty-seven of those pitchers recorded at least three outs, just shy of 2019's record of 52.

Pitchers Fielding and Holding Runners

Pitcher	Inn	PO	A	E	DP	Pct	SBA	CS	PCS	PPO	CS%	RS
Abad, Fernando	17.2	0	3	0	0	1.000	0	0	0	0	-	0
Abbott, Cory	17.1	2	1	0	0	1.000	3	0	0	0	.00	0
Abreu, Albert	36.2	6	3	0	0	1.000	5	0	0	0	.00	-1
Abreu, Bryan	36.0	7	3	0	1	1.000	2	0	0	1	.00	1
Acevedo, D.	11.0	1	3	0	0	1.000	0	0	0	1	-	0
Adam, Jason	10.2	1	0	0	0	1.000	1	1	0	0	1.00	0
Adams, Austin L	52.2	2	5	0	0	1.000	6	1	0	0	.17	-1
Adon, Joan	5.1	0	0	0	0	-	0	0	0	0	-	0
Aguilar, Miguel	7.0	0	1	0	0	1.000	0	0	0	0	-	0
Akin, Keegan	95.0	0	6	0	1	1.000	2	2	1	0	1.00	0
Alaniz, R.J.	2.2	0	0	0	0	-	0	0	0	0	-	0
Albers, Andrew	19.0	1	1	0	0	1.000	0	0	0	0	-	-1
Alcala, Jorge	59.2	4	3	0	0	1.000	4	0	0	1	.00	0
Alcantara, Sandy	205.2	24	26	4	1	.926	18	5	0	1	.28	-2
Alexander, Scott	15.1	4	1	0	1	1.000	5	0	0	0	.00	-2
Alexander, Tyler	106.1	2	6	0	0	1.000	2	0	0	0	.00	-1
Alexy, A.J.	23.0	0	4	0	0	1.000	0	0	0	1	-	2
Allard, Kolby	124.2	2	7	0	0	1.000	6	0	0	1	.00	-2
Allen, Logan	50.1	3	4	0	0	1.000	3	1	0	0	.33	-1
Allgeyer, Nick	1.0	0	0	0	0	-	0	0	0	0	-	0
Almonte, Yency	47.2	3	1	0	0	1.000	5	0	0	0	.00	-2
Altavilla, Dan	1.1	0	0	0	0	-	0	0	0	0	-	0
Alvarado, Jose	55.2	3	5	1	1	.889	6	2	2	0	.33	-1
Alvarez, Jose	64.2	2	11	2	0	.867	6	1	1	1	.17	0
Alzolay, Adbert	125.2	19	11	0	2	1.000	12	2	0	0	.17	0
Anderson, Brett	96.0	1	13	2	1	.875	2	1	1	0	.50	-1
Anderson, Chase	48.0	8	11	0	1	1.000	1	0	0	0	.00	2
Anderson, Drew	22.0	1	3	0	1	1.000	3	0	0	0	.00	0
Anderson, Ian	128.1	8	16	1	2	.960	6	0	0	0	.00	-2
Anderson, Nick	6.0	0	0	1	0	.000	0	0	0	0	-	-1
Anderson, Shaun	23.1	1	2	0	0	1.000	0	0	0	0	-	0
Anderson, Tanner	5.0	0	2	0	1	1.000	0	0	0	0	-	1
Anderson, Tyler	167.0	9	26	3	3	.921	9	1	1	0	.11	2
Andriese, Matt	48.1	1	3	0	0	1.000	3	0	0	0	.00	-1
Antone, Tejay	33.2	5	2	0	1	1.000	3	0	0	0	.00	0
Archer, Chris	19.1	0	0	0	0	-	0	0	0	0	-	-1
Arihara, Kohei	40.2	3	2	0	1	1.000	0	0	0	0	-	0
Armstrong, Shawn	36.0	0	3	1	0	.750	1	0	0	0	.00	1
Arrieta, Jake	98.2	3	6	4	0	.692	11	2	0	0	.18	-3
Ashby, Aaron	31.2	1	3	1	0	.800	3	0	0	0	.00	-2
Avila, Pedro	4.0	0	0	0	0	-	0	0	0	0	-	0
Avilan, Luis	5.0	0	0	0	0	-	0	0	0	0	-	0
Axford, John	0.1	0	0	0	0	-	0	0	0	0	-	0
Baez, Pedro	4.1	0	0	0	0	-	0	0	0	0	-	0
Baker, Bryan	1.0	0	0	0	0	-	0	0	0	0	-	0
Baldonado, A.	10.2	0	1	0	0	1.000	0	0	0	0	-	0
Banda, Anthony	33.2	1	0	1	0	.500	0	0	0	0	-	0
Baragar, Caleb	23.0	2	2	0	1	1.000	1	1	0	0	1.00	0
Bard, Daniel	65.2	1	2	1	0	.750	10	3	0	0	.30	-1
Barlow, Joe	29.0	2	1	0	0	1.000	1	0	0	0	.00	0
Barlow, Scott	74.1	1	6	0	0	1.000	4	0	0	1	.00	0
Barnes, Charlie	38.0	0	4	0	0	1.000	2	1	0	0	.50	0
Barnes, Jacob	28.2	2	3	0	0	1.000	3	1	0	0	.33	1
Barnes, Matt	54.2	0	3	0	0	1.000	8	1	0	0	.13	-2
Barraclough, Kyle	13.0	3	0	0	0	1.000	3	0	0	0	.00	-1
Barreda, Manny	2.2	0	0	0	0	-	0	0	0	0	-	0
Barria, Jaime	56.2	1	3	0	0	1.000	2	0	0	0	.00	0
Bass, Anthony	61.1	6	6	1	0	.923	5	4	1	1	.80	1
Bassitt, Chris	157.1	4	11	1	0	.938	10	3	0	0	.30	-1
Bauer, Trevor	107.2	3	6	1	0	.900	15	3	0	0	.20	-1
Baumann, Mike	10.0	0	1	0	0	1.000	0	0	0	0	-	0
Baz, Shane	13.1	0	0	0	0	-	0	0	0	0	-	0
Bazardo, Eduard	3.0	0	0	0	0	-	0	0	0	0	-	0
Beasley, Jeremy	9.1	2	1	0	0	1.000	3	0	0	0	.00	0
Bednar, David	60.2	2	3	0	0	1.000	5	2	0	0	.40	-1
Bedrosian, Cam	25.0	2	2	0	0	1.000	0	0	0	0	-	0
Beede, Tyler	1.0	0	0	0	0	-	0	0	0	0	-	0
Bellatti, Andrew	3.1	0	0	2	0	.000	0	0	0	0	-	-1
Bender, Anthony	61.1	1	8	2	3	.818	5	3	0	0	.60	3
Benjamin, Wes	22.2	0	0	0	0	-	0	0	0	0	-	0
Bergen, Travis	10.2	0	1	0	0	1.000	0	0	0	0	-	0

Pitcher	Inn	PO	A	E	DP	Pct	SBA	CS	PCS	PPO	CS%	RS
Berrios, Jose	192.0	13	23	4	5	.900	7	5	1	2	.71	5
Betances, Dellin	1.0	0	0	0	0	-	3	0	0	0	.00	-1
Bettinger, Alec	10.0	1	0	0	0	1.000	0	0	0	0	-	0
Biagini, Joe	3.0	0	0	0	0	-	0	0	0	0	-	0
Bickford, Phil	51.1	2	1	0	1	1.000	8	2	0	0	.25	-2
Biddle, Jesse	10.2	0	3	0	0	1.000	2	0	0	0	.00	0
Bieber, Shane	96.2	4	8	0	0	1.000	7	4	0	1	.57	2
Bielak, Brandon	50.0	2	5	1	0	.875	2	1	0	0	.50	0
Blackburn, Paul	38.1	1	3	1	0	.800	2	1	0	0	.50	-1
Bleier, Richard	58.0	6	8	0	0	1.000	3	0	0	0	.00	0
Blewett, Scott	5.0	0	0	0	0	-	0	0	0	0	-	0
Bolanos, Ronald	6.1	0	0	0	0	-	0	0	0	0	-	0
Borucki, Ryan	23.2	0	4	0	0	1.000	0	0	0	0	-	0
Bostick, Akeem	1.0	0	0	0	0	-	0	0	0	0	-	0
Bowden, Ben	35.2	0	1	1	0	.500	0	0	0	0	-	-2
Boxberger, Brad	64.2	4	4	1	0	.889	3	0	0	0	.00	-1
Boyd, Matthew	78.2	4	9	0	1	1.000	2	1	1	0	.50	1
Brach, Brad	30.0	2	5	2	1	.778	7	1	0	0	.14	0
Bradley, Archie	51.0	2	4	0	0	1.000	2	0	0	0	.00	0
Brasier, Ryan	12.0	1	1	0	0	1.000	1	1	0	0	1.00	-1
Brault, Steven	27.2	0	6	0	0	1.000	1	0	0	0	.00	2
Brebbia, John	18.1	1	0	0	0	1.000	1	0	0	0	.00	0
Brennan, Brandon	3.0	0	0	0	0	-	1	1	0	0	1.00	0
Brentz, Jake	64.0	1	8	0	0	1.000	2	1	0	0	.50	2
Brewer, Colten	1.0	0	0	0	0	-	1	0	0	0	.00	0
Brice, Austin	13.2	1	1	0	0	1.000	1	0	0	0	.00	-1
Britton, Zack	18.1	0	3	0	2	1.000	2	0	0	0	.00	0
Brogdon, Connor	57.2	7	7	0	1	1.000	6	0	0	0	.00	0
Brothers, Rex	53.0	1	2	0	0	1.000	6	0	0	0	.00	-2
Brubaker, JT	124.1	6	15	1	2	.955	5	4	0	1	.80	2
Bruihl, Justin	18.2	0	3	0	0	1.000	1	1	0	0	1.00	0
Bubic, Kris	130.0	3	9	1	2	.923	4	3	0	0	.75	-1
Buchter, Ryan	16.1	0	3	0	0	1.000	2	1	1	0	.50	1
Buehler, Walker	207.2	10	25	1	1	.972	15	3	1	0	.20	-1
Bukauskas, J.B.	17.1	0	1	0	0	1.000	2	1	0	0	.50	0
Bumgarner, M.	146.1	6	13	1	0	.950	15	4	3	0	.27	0
Bummer, Aaron	56.1	2	9	1	2	.917	7	2	1	0	.29	-1
Bundy, Dylan	90.2	3	6	0	0	1.000	6	0	0	0	.00	0
Burdi, Zack	10.0	0	1	0	0	1.000	3	0	0	0	.00	0
Burnes, Corbin	167.0	9	18	1	0	.964	20	2	0	0	.10	-2
Burr, Ryan	36.2	2	2	0	1	1.000	3	0	0	0	.00	-2
Burrows, Beau	11.0	0	0	0	0	-	1	1	0	0	1.00	0
Bush, Matt	4.0	0	0	0	0	-	0	0	0	0	-	0
Cabrera, Edward	26.1	0	3	0	1	1.000	2	1	0	0	.50	0
Cabrera, Genesis	70.0	6	4	0	1	1.000	2	0	0	0	.00	-1
Cahill, Trevor	37.0	2	5	2	0	.778	3	0	0	0	.00	0
Camarena, Daniel	9.1	0	2	0	0	1.000	2	0	0	0	.00	0
Campbell, Paul	26.2	4	1	0	0	1.000	2	1	0	0	.50	0
Canning, Griffin	62.2	4	8	1	1	.923	6	1	0	3	.17	2
Carlton, Drew	3.2	0	0	0	0	-	1	1	0	0	1.00	0
Carrasco, Carlos	53.2	5	6	1	1	.917	1	0	0	0	.00	0
Castano, Daniel	20.1	2	3	2	0	.714	2	0	0	0	.00	0
Castellani, Ryan	3.1	1	0	0	0	1.000	1	1	0	0	1.00	0
Castellanos, H.	45.2	4	7	0	0	1.000	1	0	0	0	.00	0
Castillo, Diego	58.1	1	4	1	0	.833	6	1	0	1	.17	-2
Castillo, Luis	187.2	17	16	1	5	.971	9	4	0	0	.44	1
Castro, Anthony	24.2	4	2	0	0	1.000	1	0	0	0	.00	0
Castro, Kervin	13.1	0	1	0	0	1.000	0	0	0	0	-	0
Castro, Miguel	70.1	8	8	1	0	.941	12	2	0	0	.17	-2
Cease, Dylan	165.2	5	8	3	1	.813	24	2	0	0	.08	-7
Cessa, Luis	64.2	7	7	0	0	1.000	2	1	0	0	.50	0
Chacin, Jhoulys	64.1	6	9	0	0	1.000	7	2	0	0	.29	0
Chafin, Andrew	68.2	6	8	1	1	.933	1	0	0	0	.00	0
Chapman, Aroldis	56.1	0	3	3	0	.500	6	1	1	0	.17	-1
Chargois, JT	53.2	3	3	0	0	1.000	4	3	0	0	.75	0
Chatwood, Tyler	32.0	3	3	1	0	.857	1	0	0	0	.00	0
Chavez, Jesse	33.2	1	4	1	0	.833	2	0	0	0	.00	1
Cimber, Adam	71.2	3	12	2	0	.882	3	2	0	1	.67	2
Cishek, Steve	68.1	3	8	1	1	.917	3	2	0	2	.67	0
Cisnero, Jose	61.2	4	4	1	0	.889	2	0	0	0	.00	-2
Civale, Aaron	124.1	7	15	0	1	1.000	8	4	0	0	.50	2

2021 Fielding and Holding Runners

Pitcher	Inn	PO	A	E	DP	Pct	SBA	CS	PCS	PPO	CS%	RS
Clarke, Taylor	43.1	1	5	0	0	1.000	2	0	0	0	.00	0
Clase, Emmanuel	69.2	9	9	1	1	.947	4	0	0	0	.00	0
Claudio, Alex	32.2	6	2	0	0	1.000	2	1	1	0	.50	0
Clay, Sam	45.0	1	4	0	0	1.000	1	0	0	0	.00	0
Cleavinger, Garrett	18.0	2	1	0	0	1.000	3	0	0	0	.00	-1
Clippard, Tyler	25.1	0	0	0	0	-	3	0	0	0	.00	0
Cobb, Alex	93.1	10	14	1	0	.960	6	0	0	1	.00	2
Cody, Kyle	11.1	0	0	0	0	-	3	0	0	0	.00	-2
Cole, A.J.	8.0	0	0	0	0	-	0	0	0	0	-	0
Cole, Gerrit	181.1	10	11	0	1	1.000	9	0	0	1	.00	0
Coleman, Dylan	6.1	0	0	0	0	-	0	0	0	0	-	0
Colome, Alex	65.0	1	4	3	0	.625	12	1	1	0	.08	-3
Conley, Adam	19.2	4	1	0	0	1.000	2	1	0	0	.50	0
Contreras, Roansy	3.0	0	0	0	0	-	1	1	0	0	1.00	0
Coonrod, Sam	42.1	1	4	1	0	.833	2	0	0	0	.00	-1
Corbin, Patrick	171.2	9	29	0	1	1.000	18	5	3	0	.28	1
Cortes, Nestor	93.0	3	4	0	1	1.000	5	0	0	0	.00	-1
Cotton, Jharel	30.2	1	1	0	0	1.000	1	0	0	0	.00	0
Coulombe, Danny	34.1	0	6	0	0	1.000	5	3	3	0	.60	1
Cousins, Jake	30.0	1	3	0	0	1.000	9	1	0	0	.11	-1
Crawford, Kutter	2.0	0	0	0	0	-	1	0	0	0	.00	0
Crichton, Stefan	23.1	2	3	0	2	1.000	2	0	0	0	.00	0
Crick, Kyle	24.1	0	3	0	0	1.000	6	0	0	0	.00	-1
Crismatt, Nabil	81.1	5	7	1	0	.923	8	3	0	0	.38	-1
Criswell, Cooper	1.1	0	0	0	0	-	0	0	0	0	-	0
Crochet, Garrett	54.1	0	3	3	0	.500	7	1	0	0	.14	-3
Crouse, Hans	7.0	0	0	0	0	-	0	0	0	0	-	0
Crowe, Wil	116.2	5	10	0	1	1.000	2	1	0	1	.50	1
Cueto, Johnny	114.2	12	14	3	1	.897	0	0	0	3	-	1
Curtiss, John	44.1	0	6	1	1	.857	3	0	0	0	.00	0
Darvish, Yu	166.1	14	8	0	1	1.000	16	1	0	0	.06	-2
Davidson, Tucker	20.0	0	1	0	0	1.000	0	0	0	0	-	0
Davies, Zach	148.0	13	22	0	2	1.000	9	3	0	2	.33	6
Davis, Austin	26.1	0	2	0	0	1.000	3	0	0	0	.00	0
Davis, Wade	42.2	2	2	0	0	1.000	4	0	0	0	.00	-1
Dayton, Grant	13.0	1	3	0	0	1.000	0	0	0	0	-	-1
De Geus, Brett	50.0	3	8	1	1	.917	3	0	0	2	.00	-1
De Jong, Chase	43.2	1	8	1	2	.900	0	0	0	0	-	1
De Leon, Jose	18.1	1	2	0	0	1.000	0	0	0	0	-	0
De Los Santos, E.	35.1	2	2	1	0	.800	0	0	0	1	-	-1
deGrom, Jacob	92.0	6	7	0	0	1.000	6	1	0	0	.17	0
Del Pozo, Miguel	5.1	0	2	0	0	1.000	0	0	0	0	-	1
DeSclafani, A.	167.2	8	16	0	1	1.000	11	4	1	0	.36	2
Detmers, Reid	20.2	0	2	0	0	1.000	8	0	0	0	.00	-1
Detwiler, Ross	52.1	4	4	1	0	.889	5	0	0	0	.00	1
Devenski, Chris	7.1	0	1	0	0	1.000	5	0	0	0	.00	-1
Diaz, Edwin	62.2	4	5	0	0	1.000	10	4	0	0	.40	0
Diaz, Jhonathan	13.0	1	2	0	1	1.000	0	0	0	0	-	0
Diaz, Miguel	42.0	1	6	1	1	.875	2	0	0	0	.00	2
Diaz, Yennsy	25.0	1	1	0	0	1.000	3	1	0	0	.33	0
Dickson, Brandon	2.0	0	0	0	0	-	0	0	0	0	-	0
Diekman, Jake	60.2	2	3	0	0	1.000	9	4	1	0	.44	0
Diplan, Marcos	30.0	0	2	0	0	1.000	0	0	0	0	-	0
Dobnak, Randy	50.2	2	6	0	0	1.000	2	1	0	0	.50	-1
Dohy, Kyle	1.0	0	0	0	0	-	0	0	0	0	-	0
Dolis, Rafael	32.0	1	2	0	0	1.000	5	0	0	0	.00	-1
Dominguez, S.	1.0	0	0	0	0	-	0	0	0	0	-	0
Doolittle, Sean	49.2	2	1	0	0	1.000	7	3	1	0	.43	0
Doval, Camilo	27.0	0	3	0	0	1.000	0	0	0	0	-	-1
Duffey, Tyler	62.1	1	2	1	0	.750	2	2	0	0	1.00	0
Duffy, Danny	61.0	1	5	0	1	1.000	1	1	0	0	1.00	0
Dugger, Robert	25.2	2	1	0	0	1.000	2	0	0	1	.00	-1
Dunn, Justin	50.1	4	2	1	0	.857	10	0	0	0	.00	-3
Dunning, Dane	117.2	5	7	0	2	1.000	7	2	0	0	.29	-2
Duplantier, Jon	13.0	0	1	0	0	1.000	0	0	0	0	-	-1
Edwards Jr., Carl	5.2	0	0	0	0	-	0	0	0	0	-	0
Effross, Scott	14.2	0	1	0	0	1.000	5	2	1	0	.40	-1
Eflin, Zach	105.2	7	16	1	4	.958	1	0	0	0	.00	2
Eickhoff, Jerad	19.2	3	4	0	1	1.000	0	0	0	0	-	1
Elledge, Seth	11.2	1	0	0	0	1.000	1	1	0	0	1.00	0
Ellis, Chris	29.1	0	2	0	0	1.000	6	2	1	0	.33	0
Emanuel, Kent	17.2	3	1	0	0	1.000	0	0	0	0	-	0
Enns, Dietrich	22.1	0	2	0	0	1.000	3	2	2	0	.67	1
Eovaldi, Nathan	182.1	13	23	0	2	1.000	10	0	0	0	.00	0
Eshelman, T.	27.2	1	1	0	0	1.000	1	1	0	0	1.00	-1
Espinal, Raynel	2.0	0	1	0	0	1.000	0	0	0	0	-	0
Espino, Paolo	109.2	9	11	0	0	1.000	5	1	0	0	.20	1
Estevez, Carlos	61.2	5	5	0	1	1.000	2	0	0	0	.00	-2
Evans, Demarcus	26.1	0	1	0	0	1.000	0	0	0	0	-	0
Fairbanks, Pete	42.2	4	2	0	0	1.000	10	2	0	0	.20	-2
Falter, Bailey	33.2	0	2	0	0	1.000	1	1	0	0	1.00	0
Familia, Jeurys	59.1	3	7	0	0	1.000	2	0	0	0	.00	0
Faria, Jake	32.2	7	1	0	0	1.000	2	0	0	0	.00	0
Farmer, Buck	35.1	0	3	0	1	1.000	1	0	0	0	.00	0
Farrell, Luke	24.2	1	1	0	0	1.000	2	0	0	0	.00	-1
Fedde, Erick	133.1	12	19	0	0	1.000	22	6	0	0	.27	0
Feliz, Michael	20.0	1	0	0	1	1.000	2	1	0	0	.50	-1
Feliz, Neftali	4.0	1	0	0	0	1.000	0	0	0	0	-	0
Feltner, Ryan	6.1	1	0	0	0	1.000	0	0	0	0	-	0
Fernandez, Julian	6.2	2	0	0	0	1.000	1	0	0	0	.00	0
Fernandez, Junior	20.2	0	2	0	0	1.000	0	0	0	0	-	-1
Feyereisen, J.P.	56.0	6	2	0	0	1.000	5	1	0	0	.20	1
Fiers, Mike	9.1	0	1	0	0	1.000	0	0	0	0	-	0
Finnegan, Kyle	66.0	5	6	0	0	1.000	11	2	0	0	.18	-1
Flaa, Jay	2.2	0	0	0	0	-	0	0	0	0	-	0
Flaherty, Jack	78.1	7	6	1	0	.929	3	3	1	0	1.00	3
Fleming, Josh	104.1	10	20	0	1	1.000	1	0	0	0	.00	3
Fletcher, Aaron	3.2	0	0	0	0	-	0	0	0	0	-	0
Flexen, Chris	179.2	21	25	0	1	1.000	5	1	0	3	.20	5
Flores Jr., B.	0.0	0	0	0	0	-	0	0	0	0	-	0
Floro, Dylan	64.0	6	3	0	0	1.000	3	1	0	0	.33	-2
Foley, Jason	10.1	0	0	0	0	-	2	1	0	0	.50	0
Foltynewicz, Mike	139.0	4	13	1	0	.944	5	3	0	1	.60	1
Foster, Matt	39.0	0	4	0	1	1.000	3	1	0	0	.33	1
Frankoff, Seth	14.2	1	4	0	1	1.000	2	1	0	0	.50	0
Freeland, Kyle	120.2	5	10	0	3	1.000	12	4	1	0	.33	-3
Frias, Luis	3.1	0	0	0	0	-	0	0	0	0	-	0
Fried, Max	165.2	8	37	1	3	.978	11	3	3	4	.27	6
Fry, Jace	6.2	0	2	0	1	1.000	2	1	1	0	.50	0
Fry, Paul	47.1	1	6	0	0	1.000	3	0	0	0	.00	-1
Fulmer, Carson	25.2	0	1	0	0	1.000	2	0	0	0	.00	-1
Fulmer, Michael	69.2	5	3	1	0	.889	6	0	0	0	.00	-2
Funkhouser, Kyle	68.1	5	7	1	0	.923	4	1	0	0	.25	1
Gallegos, G.	80.1	4	8	1	1	.923	5	2	0	1	.40	1
Gallen, Zac	121.1	4	11	1	0	.938	2	1	0	0	.50	2
Gant, John	110.0	4	16	2	3	.909	11	0	0	0	.00	2
Garcia, Bryan	39.1	0	3	1	0	.750	3	0	0	0	.00	1
Garcia, Deivi	8.1	0	0	0	0	-	0	0	0	0	-	0
Garcia, Edgar	14.2	0	1	0	0	1.000	2	0	0	0	.00	0
Garcia, Jarlin	68.2	3	11	0	0	1.000	9	5	3	0	.56	3
Garcia, Luis (STL)	33.1	2	4	0	0	1.000	1	1	0	0	1.00	0
Garcia, Luis (HOU)	155.1	10	10	2	1	.909	22	8	0	0	.36	-3
Garcia, Rony	3.2	0	0	0	0	-	1	1	0	0	1.00	0
Garcia, Yimi	57.2	3	5	1	0	.889	2	0	0	0	.00	0
Garrett, Amir	47.2	4	5	0	1	1.000	5	0	0	0	.00	0
Garrett, Braxton	34.0	0	7	1	0	.875	0	0	0	0	-	1
Garza, Justin	28.2	2	3	0	1	1.000	1	0	0	0	.00	0
Garza, Ralph	30.1	1	3	0	0	1.000	0	0	0	0	-	1
Gausman, Kevin	192.0	13	19	1	1	.970	11	2	0	2	.18	3
German, Domingo	98.1	2	6	2	0	.800	7	1	0	0	.14	-3
Gibaut, Ian	6.2	0	0	0	0	-	0	0	0	0	-	0
Gibson, Kyle	182.0	11	23	1	2	.971	5	3	0	1	.60	2
Gil, Luis	29.1	0	2	0	0	1.000	0	0	0	0	-	0
Gilbert, Logan	119.1	5	9	0	0	1.000	10	0	0	0	.00	-1
Gilbert, Tyler	40.0	4	7	0	2	1.000	4	2	1	0	.50	1
Gilbreath, Lucas	42.2	1	4	0	0	1.000	0	0	0	0	-	0
Ginkel, Kevin	28.1	3	0	0	0	1.000	1	1	0	0	1.00	-2
Giolito, Lucas	178.2	1	10	0	0	1.000	16	1	1	2	.06	-2
Givens, Mychal	51.0	6	5	0	0	1.000	11	4	1	0	.36	1
Glasnow, Tyler	88.0	6	3	0	0	1.000	8	2	0	0	.25	-1
Godley, Zack	3.1	0	0	1	0	.000	0	0	0	0	-	0
Gomber, Austin	115.1	1	7	1	1	.889	2	1	0	0	.50	0
Gonsalves, S.	4.1	0	0	0	0	-	0	0	0	0	-	0
Gonsolin, Tony	55.2	5	4	0	0	1.000	2	2	0	0	1.00	0
Gonzales, Marco	143.1	6	18	2	0	.923	10	3	1	1	.30	4
Gonzalez, Chi Chi	101.2	13	12	1	2	.962	4	2	1	0	.50	0

2021 Fielding and Holding Runners

Pitcher	Inn	PO	A	E	DP	Pct	SBA	CS	PCS	PPO	CS%	RS
Gonzalez, Victor	35.1	1	6	0	1	1.000	3	1	0	0	.33	1
Gose, Anthony	6.2	0	2	0	0	1.000	0	0	0	0	-	0
Goudeau, Ashton	34.1	2	4	0	1	1.000	3	1	0	0	.33	0
Graterol, Brusdar	33.1	5	10	0	1	1.000	2	1	0	0	.50	2
Graveman, K.	56.0	0	4	0	0	1.000	6	2	0	0	.33	0
Gray, Jon	149.0	11	7	2	0	.900	10	2	0	0	.20	-2
Gray, Josiah	70.2	3	6	0	2	1.000	6	1	1	0	.17	1
Gray, Sonny	135.1	13	19	0	2	1.000	11	0	0	0	.00	0
Green, Chad	83.2	1	4	0	0	1.000	7	5	0	0	.71	1
Greene, Conner	25.1	0	3	0	0	1.000	5	1	0	0	.20	0
Greene, Shane	23.2	1	0	0	0	1.000	1	0	0	0	.00	0
Greinke, Zack	171.0	17	20	0	6	1.000	8	1	0	0	.13	5
Gsellman, Robert	28.2	5	7	0	1	1.000	2	1	1	0	.50	1
Guduan, Reymin	14.1	2	1	0	0	1.000	0	0	0	0	-	0
Guenther, Sean	20.1	2	1	0	0	1.000	0	0	0	0	-	-1
Guerra, Deolis	65.2	3	4	1	1	.875	10	0	0	0	.00	-3
Guerra, Javy (SD)	3.2	0	0	0	0	-	0	0	0	0	-	0
Guerra, Javy (WAS)	6.0	2	1	0	0	1.000	0	0	0	0	-	0
Guerra, Junior	65.1	3	10	0	2	1.000	3	0	0	0	.00	1
Guilmet, Preston	2.0	0	0	0	0	-	0	0	0	0	-	0
Gustave, Jandel	18.1	0	1	0	0	1.000	0	0	0	0	-	-1
Gutierrez, Vladimir	114.0	10	14	2	1	.923	15	1	1	1	.07	-1
Guzman, Jorge	1.2	0	0	0	0	-	1	0	0	0	.00	0
Hader, Josh	58.2	1	3	0	0	1.000	6	1	0	0	.17	-1
Hahn, Jesse	3.1	1	1	0	0	1.000	0	0	0	0	-	1
Hale, David	26.2	1	5	0	0	1.000	2	0	0	0	.00	1
Hammer, J.D.	20.0	2	0	1	0	.667	0	0	0	0	-	-1
Hand, Brad	64.2	0	7	1	0	.889	7	0	0	0	.00	-1
Hanhold, Eric	10.1	0	1	0	0	1.000	4	0	0	0	.00	-1
Happ, J.A.	152.1	5	8	1	0	.929	9	1	0	0	.11	-1
Hardy, Blaine	1.0	0	0	0	0	-	0	0	0	0	-	0
Harper, Ryne	35.2	3	4	0	0	1.000	2	1	0	0	.50	0
Harris, Will	6.0	0	0	0	0	-	0	0	0	0	-	0
Hartlieb, Geoff	9.0	0	0	0	0	-	0	0	0	0	-	0
Hartman, Ryan	2.1	0	0	0	0	-	0	0	0	0	-	0
Harvey, Hunter	8.2	1	0	0	0	1.000	1	1	0	0	1.00	0
Harvey, Matt	127.2	7	13	1	1	.952	17	2	0	0	.12	0
Hatch, Thomas	9.1	0	0	1	0	.000	0	0	0	0	-	0
Head, Louis	35.0	3	1	1	0	.800	3	1	0	0	.33	1
Heaney, Andrew	129.2	8	5	0	0	1.000	4	0	0	0	.00	-3
Hearn, Taylor	104.1	1	7	1	0	.889	8	1	1	0	.13	0
Heasley, Jon	14.2	0	1	0	0	1.000	1	1	0	1	1.00	1
Helsley, Ryan	47.1	3	8	0	0	1.000	1	0	0	0	.00	1
Hembree, Heath	58.0	3	2	0	1	1.000	5	1	0	0	.20	0
Hendricks, Kyle	181.0	17	20	0	1	1.000	10	1	0	1	.10	1
Hendriks, Liam	71.0	4	1	0	0	1.000	6	0	0	0	.00	-1
Hendrix, Ryan	31.2	3	1	0	0	1.000	1	1	0	0	1.00	-1
Hentges, Sam	68.2	0	10	0	0	1.000	5	0	0	0	.00	0
Herget, Jimmy	18.2	1	2	0	0	1.000	4	0	0	0	.00	0
Hernandez, Carlos	85.2	4	8	1	2	.923	2	1	0	0	.50	0
Hernandez, D.	40.0	1	2	0	0	1.000	4	2	0	0	.50	0
Hernandez, E.	51.2	6	5	0	0	1.000	2	1	0	0	.50	0
Hess, David	20.0	0	0	0	0	-	0	0	0	0	-	RS
Heuer, Codi	67.1	3	6	0	0	1.000	5	2	0	0	.40	0
Hicks, Jordan	10.0	1	4	0	0	1.000	2	1	1	0	.50	0
Hildenberger, T.	2.1	0	0	0	0	-	0	0	0	0	-	0
Hill, Rich	158.2	2	17	1	0	.950	14	5	2	0	.36	0
Hill, Tim	59.2	3	13	0	0	1.000	0	0	0	0	-	1
Hoffman, Jeff	73.0	4	5	3	2	.750	3	0	0	1	.00	-2
Holland, Derek	49.2	3	4	1	0	.875	3	1	0	0	.33	-2
Holland, Greg	55.2	7	5	1	0	.923	1	0	0	0	.00	-2
Holloway, Jordan	36.0	3	4	0	0	1.000	2	0	0	0	.00	1
Holmes, Clay	70.0	7	11	0	0	1.000	2	0	0	0	.00	2
Honeywell, Brent	4.1	1	1	0	0	1.000	1	0	0	0	.00	0
Houck, Tanner	69.0	1	7	0	0	1.000	7	0	0	0	.00	-1
Houser, Adrian	142.1	5	31	0	1	1.000	25	6	1	0	.24	1
Howard, Sam	45.0	1	5	1	0	.857	3	0	0	0	.00	1
Howard, Spencer	49.2	2	4	0	0	1.000	6	1	0	0	.17	0
Hoyt, James	8.0	0	0	0	0	-	0	0	0	0	-	0
Hudson, Dakota	8.2	0	1	0	0	1.000	1	0	0	0	.00	0
Hudson, Daniel	51.2	1	6	0	0	1.000	1	0	0	0	.00	1
Hunter, Tommy	8.0	0	0	0	0	-	0	0	0	0	-	0
Hutchison, Drew	21.1	2	5	0	1	1.000	3	2	0	0	.67	0

Pitcher	Inn	PO	A	E	DP	Pct	SBA	CS	PCS	PPO	CS%	RS
Iglesias, Raisel	70.0	6	6	1	0	.923	3	0	0	0	.00	0
Irvin, Cole	178.1	6	20	1	2	.963	3	1	1	0	.33	1
Ivey, Tyler	4.2	0	1	0	0	1.000	1	0	0	0	.00	0
Jackson, Andre	11.2	2	2	0	0	1.000	0	0	0	0	-	0
Jackson, Jay	21.2	0	1	0	0	1.000	1	0	0	0	.00	0
Jackson, Luke	63.2	2	3	0	0	1.000	8	1	0	0	.13	-1
James, Josh	5.0	0	0	0	0	-	0	0	0	0	-	0
Jannis, Mickey	3.1	0	0	0	0	-	1	1	0	0	1.00	0
Jansen, Kenley	69.0	4	2	0	0	1.000	10	0	0	0	.00	-2
Javier, Cristian	101.1	4	1	0	0	1.000	5	1	0	0	.20	0
Jax, Griffin	82.0	0	2	2	0	.500	9	1	0	0	.11	-3
Jefferies, Daulton	15.0	0	3	0	0	1.000	1	0	0	0	.00	1
Jewell, Jake	10.0	0	1	0	0	1.000	1	1	0	0	1.00	0
Jimenez, Joe	45.1	3	0	2	0	.600	9	1	0	0	.11	-2
Johnson, DJ	4.1	0	0	0	0	-	0	0	0	0	-	0
Johnson, Pierce	58.2	2	4	0	1	1.000	3	1	1	0	.33	0
Jones, Damon	0.1	0	0	0	0	-	0	0	0	0	-	0
Jones, Nate	19.0	1	0	0	0	1.000	0	0	0	0	-	-1
Junis, Jakob	39.1	2	4	0	1	1.000	1	1	0	0	1.00	1
Junk, Janson	16.1	4	2	0	0	1.000	2	0	0	0	.00	0
Kaprielian, James	119.1	5	6	2	2	.846	9	0	0	1	.00	-3
Karinchak, James	55.1	1	1	0	0	1.000	7	0	0	0	.00	-2
Kay, Anthony	33.2	1	4	0	0	1.000	2	2	0	0	1.00	0
Kazmir, Scott	11.1	1	0	0	0	1.000	0	0	0	0	-	0
Kela, Keone	10.2	1	0	0	0	1.000	1	0	0	0	.00	0
Keller, Brad	133.2	6	7	0	0	1.000	9	4	0	0	.44	-3
Keller, Kyle	33.1	0	2	0	0	1.000	1	0	0	0	.00	0
Keller, Mitch	100.2	4	10	0	1	1.000	11	3	1	0	.27	1
Kelly, Joe	44.0	2	4	0	0	1.000	2	0	0	0	.00	0
Kelly, Merrill	158.0	13	16	0	2	1.000	13	4	0	2	.31	2
Kennedy, Ian	56.1	3	0	0	1	1.000	0	0	0	0	-	0
Kershaw, Clayton	121.2	4	14	0	0	1.000	12	5	3	1	.42	1
Keuchel, Dallas	162.0	7	41	1	3	.980	6	4	2	0	.67	12
Kickham, Mike	2.0	0	0	0	0	-	0	0	0	0	-	0
Kikuchi, Yusei	157.0	6	13	0	1	1.000	7	3	1	0	.43	3
Kim, Kwang-hyun	106.2	6	14	1	0	.952	4	3	2	0	.75	4
Kimbrel, Craig	59.2	2	2	0	0	1.000	7	1	0	0	.14	-1
King, John	46.0	2	7	1	0	.900	0	0	0	0	.00	0
King, Michael	63.1	3	7	0	0	1.000	0	0	0	0	-	1
Kinley, Tyler	70.1	6	4	0	0	1.000	3	0	0	0	.00	1
Kintzler, Brandon	29.2	3	5	0	1	1.000	2	0	0	0	.00	1
Kittredge, Andrew	71.2	3	2	1	0	.833	5	1	0	0	.20	-1
Klobosits, Gabe	11.1	0	2	0	0	1.000	2	0	0	0	.00	0
Kluber, Corey	80.0	4	5	1	0	.900	14	2	0	0	.14	-3
Knebel, Corey	25.2	3	2	0	1	1.000	1	0	0	0	.00	0
Knehr, Reiss	29.0	0	2	0	0	1.000	3	0	0	0	.00	0
Knight, Dusten	8.2	0	0	0	0	-	0	0	0	0	-	0
Koerner, Brody	3.0	0	1	0	0	1.000	0	0	0	0	-	0
Kolarek, Adam	9.0	1	1	0	0	1.000	0	0	0	0	-	-2
Kopech, Michael	69.1	1	1	0	0	1.000	10	0	0	0	.00	-3
Kowar, Jackson	30.1	0	7	0	0	1.000	2	0	0	1	.00	1
Kranick, Max	38.2	2	5	0	0	1.000	4	1	0	0	.25	0
Krehbiel, Joey	8.1	1	1	0	0	1.000	1	0	0	0	-	0
Kremer, Dean	53.2	2	4	0	0	1.000	1	1	0	0	1.00	0
Kriske, Brooks	11.1	0	2	0	0	1.000	1	0	0	0	.00	0
Krol, Ian	18.2	1	2	1	0	.750	0	0	0	0	-	0
Kuhl, Chad	80.1	3	8	1	4	.917	7	2	0	0	.29	0
Lail, Brady	2.0	0	0	0	0	-	1	0	0	0	.00	0
Lakins, Travis	28.0	1	4	0	0	1.000	4	1	0	0	.25	2
Lambert, Jimmy	13.0	0	0	0	0	-	2	0	0	0	.00	0
Lambert, Peter	5.2	0	1	0	0	1.000	0	0	0	0	-	0
Lamet, Dinelson	47.0	5	2	0	0	1.000	4	0	0	0	.00	-1
Lange, Alex	35.2	3	2	0	0	1.000	4	0	0	0	.00	-1
Latz, Jake	4.2	0	1	0	0	1.000	0	0	0	0	-	0
Lauer, Eric	118.2	4	15	2	1	.905	4	1	1	3	.25	4
Law, Derek	15.0	1	1	0	0	1.000	0	0	0	0	.00	0
Lawrence, Justin	16.2	0	2	0	0	1.000	1	0	0	0	.00	-1
LeBlanc, Wade	49.0	4	4	0	0	1.000	1	1	0	0	1.00	1
Lee, Dylan	2.0	0	0	0	0	-	0	0	0	0	-	0
Leone, Dominic	53.2	2	7	0	1	1.000	0	0	0	0	-	0
Lester, Jon	141.1	9	17	0	1	1.000	16	5	0	0	.31	-1
Lindblom, Josh	16.2	0	0	0	0	-	1	0	0	0	.00	0
Littell, Zack	61.2	6	7	1	0	.929	2	1	0	1	.50	0

Pitcher	Inn	PO	A	E	DP	Pct	SBA	CS	PCS	PPO	CS%	RS
Llovera, Mauricio	6.2	0	1	0	0	1.000	0	0	0	0	-	0
Loaisiga, Jonathan	70.2	4	11	1	0	.938	3	0	0	0	.00	1
Lobstein, Kyle	1.1	0	0	0	0	-	0	0	0	0	-	0
Long, Sammy	40.2	1	4	0	0	1.000	4	1	1	0	.25	0
Lopez, Jorge	121.2	8	10	0	0	1.000	5	3	0	0	.60	-2
Lopez, Pablo	102.2	4	9	0	1	1.000	3	1	0	0	.33	0
Lopez, Reynaldo	57.2	1	5	2	0	.750	8	6	1	1	.75	1
Lopez, Yoan	12.1	2	0	0	0	1.000	2	0	0	0	.00	0
Lorenzen, Michael	29.0	4	5	0	1	1.000	0	0	0	0	-	0
Loup, Aaron	56.2	2	12	0	1	1.000	4	2	2	0	.50	1
Lovelady, Richard	20.2	1	5	0	0	1.000	1	1	0	0	1.00	1
Lowther, Zac	29.2	1	3	0	0	1.000	0	0	0	0	-	-1
Lucchesi, Joey	38.1	3	2	0	0	1.000	3	1	1	0	.33	-1
Luetge, Lucas	72.1	3	5	0	0	1.000	5	0	0	0	.00	0
Lugo, Seth	46.1	6	3	1	0	.900	0	0	0	0	-	0
Luzardo, Jesus	95.1	6	11	0	0	1.000	4	1	1	0	.25	4
Lyles, Jordan	180.0	8	15	0	0	1.000	23	3	0	0	.13	-1
Lynch, Daniel	68.0	1	4	0	1	1.000	2	0	0	0	.00	-1
Lynn, Lance	157.0	3	5	2	0	.800	18	3	0	0	.17	-3
Machado, Andres	35.2	2	1	0	0	1.000	3	1	0	0	.33	-1
Madero, Luis	12.0	4	0	0	0	1.000	2	0	0	0	.00	0
Maeda, Kenta	106.1	6	10	1	2	.941	4	1	0	0	.25	0
Mahle, Tyler	180.0	21	15	0	2	1.000	5	3	1	1	.60	2
Manaea, Sean	179.1	6	16	1	1	.957	5	2	0	0	.40	-1
Manning, Matt	85.1	10	9	0	1	1.000	9	2	0	0	.22	2
Manoah, Alek	111.2	6	3	1	0	.900	1	1	0	0	1.00	1
Mantiply, Joe	39.2	2	6	0	1	1.000	6	5	1	0	.83	0
Maples, Dillon	31.1	3	2	0	0	1.000	6	1	0	0	.17	-1
Margevicius, Nick	12.0	0	1	0	1	1.000	1	0	0	0	.00	0
Marquez, German	180.0	14	24	2	1	.950	12	4	0	0	.33	1
Marshall, Evan	27.1	2	4	0	0	1.000	1	0	0	1	.00	1
Marte, Jose	4.0	0	0	0	0	-	2	1	0	0	.50	0
Martin, Brett	62.1	1	10	2	0	.846	2	0	0	0	.00	0
Martin, Chris	43.1	3	2	0	0	1.000	6	1	0	1	.17	0
Martin, Corbin	16.0	1	1	0	0	1.000	0	0	0	0	-	0
Martinez, Carlos	82.1	10	9	1	0	.950	5	1	0	0	.20	-2
Martinez, Seth	3.0	0	0	0	0	-	0	0	0	0	-	0
Maton, Phil	66.2	4	8	1	0	.923	8	3	2	0	.38	0
Mattson, Isaac	4.1	0	0	0	0	-	0	0	0	0	-	0
Matz, Steven	150.2	5	22	1	1	.964	7	1	1	0	.14	3
Matzek, Tyler	63.0	2	6	0	2	1.000	2	1	1	0	.50	2
May, Dustin	23.0	2	2	0	0	1.000	3	1	0	0	.33	0
May, Trevor	62.2	0	3	0	0	1.000	3	0	0	0	.00	0
Mayers, Mike	75.0	3	4	0	0	1.000	3	1	0	0	.33	-1
Mayza, Tim	53.0	1	7	0	0	1.000	3	0	0	0	.00	1
Mazza, Chris	27.1	1	1	1	0	.667	1	0	0	0	.00	0
McCaughan, D.	9.0	1	0	0	0	1.000	0	0	0	0	-	0
McClanahan, S.	123.1	1	14	0	0	1.000	10	3	2	0	.30	2
McCullers Jr., L.	162.1	15	13	0	0	1.000	8	6	0	0	.75	3
McFarland, T.J.	38.2	2	0	0	0	1.000	0	0	0	0	-	-1
McGee, Jake	59.2	3	3	1	0	.857	1	0	0	0	.00	0
McGowin, Kyle	30.0	2	0	0	0	1.000	4	0	0	0	.00	-1
McHugh, Collin	64.0	1	3	0	0	1.000	0	0	0	1	-	0
McKenzie, Triston	120.0	5	12	0	0	1.000	8	3	2	1	.38	2
McRae, Alex	2.0	0	0	0	0	-	1	0	0	0	.00	0
Means, John	146.2	3	10	1	0	.929	2	2	0	1	1.00	0
Mears, Nick	23.1	3	1	0	0	1.000	4	0	0	0	.00	-2
Medina, Adonis	7.2	1	1	0	1	1.000	1	0	0	0	.00	0
Megill, Trevor	23.2	0	4	1	1	.800	0	0	0	0	-	1
Megill, Tylor	89.2	6	5	0	0	1.000	3	0	0	1	.00	-1
Meisinger, Ryan	7.1	0	0	0	0	-	1	0	0	0	.00	0
Mejia, Humberto	22.1	1	0	0	0	1.000	1	0	0	0	.00	0
Mejia, JC	52.1	3	6	0	0	1.000	1	0	0	0	.00	0
Melancon, Mark	64.2	3	11	1	2	.933	0	0	0	0	-	2
Mella, Keury	1.2	0	0	0	0	-	0	0	0	0	-	0
Menez, Conner	14.0	0	1	1	0	.500	0	0	0	0	-	-1
Merryweather, J.	13.0	0	1	0	0	1.000	0	0	0	0	-	0
Middleton, Keynan	31.0	0	1	0	0	1.000	8	0	0	0	.00	-1
Mikolas, Miles	44.2	4	9	0	0	1.000	0	0	0	0	-	1
Miley, Wade	163.0	3	30	2	3	.943	5	3	3	3	.60	3
Miller, Andrew	36.0	1	5	0	2	1.000	4	1	0	0	.25	0
Miller, Justin	19.0	0	1	0	0	1.000	1	0	0	0	.00	-1
Miller, Shelby	12.2	0	1	0	0	1.000	1	1	0	0	1.00	0

Pitcher	Inn	PO	A	E	DP	Pct	SBA	CS	PCS	PPO	CS%	RS
Mills, Alec	119.0	9	13	1	2	.957	8	1	0	0	.13	-1
Mills, Wyatt	12.2	1	2	0	0	1.000	0	0	0	0	-	0
Milner, Hoby	21.2	0	2	0	0	1.000	1	1	0	0	1.00	0
Milone, Tommy	14.0	1	0	0	0	1.000	0	0	0	0	-	-1
Minaya, Juan	40.0	2	5	0	0	1.000	2	0	0	0	.00	-1
Minor, Mike	158.2	1	7	1	0	.889	6	3	1	0	.50	1
Minter, A.J.	52.1	3	5	2	0	.800	7	3	2	0	.43	0
Misiewicz, A.	54.2	2	4	0	0	1.000	0	0	0	0	-	0
Mitchell, Bryan	4.0	0	1	0	0	1.000	0	0	0	0	-	0
Mize, Casey	150.1	9	17	1	1	.963	9	6	1	0	.67	3
Moll, Sam	10.1	0	3	0	1	1.000	1	1	1	0	1.00	-1
Montas, Frankie	187.0	10	17	1	2	.964	11	5	0	0	.45	3
Montero, Rafael	49.1	4	5	0	1	1.000	7	0	0	0	.00	-1
Montgomery, J.	157.1	2	18	1	0	.952	12	5	3	0	.42	-1
Moore, Matt	73.0	4	8	1	0	.923	1	0	0	1	.00	0
Moran, Jovani	8.0	0	0	0	0	-	0	0	0	0	-	-1
Morejon, Adrian	4.2	0	1	0	0	1.000	0	0	0	0	-	0
Moreta, Dauri	3.2	0	0	0	0	-	0	0	0	0	-	0
Morgan, Adam	25.1	2	3	0	2	1.000	2	0	0	0	.00	0
Morgan, Eli	89.1	1	11	0	2	1.000	2	0	0	0	.00	1
Morimando, S.	10.1	1	0	0	0	1.000	0	0	0	0	-	0
Moronta, Reyes	4.0	3	0	0	0	1.000	0	0	0	0	-	0
Morton, Charlie	185.2	9	15	3	0	.889	7	0	0	0	.00	-1
Muller, Kyle	36.2	0	2	0	0	1.000	2	0	0	0	.00	0
Munoz, Andres	0.2	0	0	0	0	-	1	0	0	0	.00	0
Murphy, Patrick	28.0	2	2	0	0	1.000	3	0	0	0	.00	-1
Musgrove, Joe	181.1	21	18	1	0	.975	7	1	0	0	.14	2
Nance, Tommy	28.2	4	2	0	1	1.000	4	1	0	0	.25	0
Naughton, Packy	22.2	2	5	0	0	1.000	0	0	0	0	-	1
Neidert, Nick	35.2	5	2	0	1	1.000	1	0	0	0	.00	1
Nelson, Jimmy	29.0	1	2	0	0	1.000	5	0	0	0	.00	-1
Nelson, Kyle	9.2	0	1	0	0	1.000	0	0	0	0	-	0
Nelson, Nick	14.1	0	1	0	0	1.000	1	0	0	0	.00	0
Neris, Hector	74.1	5	5	0	0	1.000	7	2	0	1	.29	0
Newberry, Jake	4.1	0	1	0	1	1.000	0	0	0	0	-	0
Newcomb, Sean	32.1	1	5	0	0	1.000	2	2	1	0	1.00	1
Newsome, Ljay	14.2	0	0	0	0	-	3	0	0	0	.00	0
Nittoli, Vinny	1.0	0	0	0	0	-	0	0	0	0	-	0
Nogosek, Stephen	3.0	0	0	0	0	-	0	0	0	0	-	0
Nola, Aaron	180.2	16	8	2	0	.923	9	2	1	0	.22	-2
Nolin, Sean	26.2	0	1	0	0	1.000	3	1	0	0	.33	-1
Norris, Daniel	57.0	4	0	1	0	.800	4	2	0	0	.50	-1
Northcraft, Aaron	8.0	1	2	0	0	1.000	0	0	0	0	-	1
Norwood, James	5.0	0	0	0	0	-	0	0	0	0	-	0
Nunez, Darien	7.2	0	2	0	0	1.000	2	1	1	0	.50	0
Ober, Bailey	92.1	3	7	0	1	1.000	6	3	1	0	.50	2
O'Brien, Riley	1.1	0	0	0	0	-	0	0	0	0	-	0
O'Day, Darren	10.2	0	1	0	0	1.000	0	0	0	0	-	0
Odorizzi, Jake	104.2	7	15	1	1	.957	5	2	1	1	.40	3
Ohtani, Shohei	130.1	11	6	1	0	.944	4	2	0	0	.50	2
Okert, Steven	36.0	0	1	0	0	1.000	1	1	1	0	1.00	0
Ort, Kaleb	0.1	0	0	0	0	-	0	0	0	0	-	0
Ortega, Oliver	9.1	1	1	0	0	1.000	2	1	0	0	.50	0
Osich, Josh	14.1	4	2	0	0	1.000	2	1	0	0	.50	0
Oswalt, Corey	10.1	0	2	0	0	1.000	2	2	0	1	1.00	1
Ottavino, Adam	62.0	0	7	3	0	.700	25	3	1	1	.12	-5
Otto, Glenn	23.1	0	3	0	0	1.000	3	0	0	0	.00	0
Overton, Connor	15.1	1	3	0	0	1.000	0	0	0	0	-	0
Oviedo, Johan	62.1	6	6	1	0	.923	3	1	0	0	.33	-2
Oviedo, Luis	29.2	2	2	0	1	1.000	5	0	0	0	.00	-1
Paddack, Chris	108.1	8	10	1	0	.947	7	2	0	0	.29	-1
Pagan, Emilio	63.1	4	0	1	0	.800	3	1	0	0	.33	0
Paredes, Enoli	8.2	0	1	1	0	.500	1	0	0	0	.00	0
Parker, Blake	43.2	3	2	0	0	1.000	7	2	1	0	.29	-1
Patino, Luis	77.1	0	5	2	0	.714	2	0	0	0	.00	0
Patton, Spencer	42.1	5	3	0	0	1.000	3	1	0	0	.33	-1
Paulino, David	2.0	0	0	0	0	-	0	0	0	0	-	0
Paxton, James	1.1	0	0	0	0	-	0	0	0	0	-	0
Payamps, Joel	50.1	0	5	0	0	1.000	1	1	0	0	1.00	0
Peacock, Brad	5.1	0	0	0	0	-	0	0	0	0	-	0
Peacock, Matt	86.1	14	13	0	0	1.000	3	2	1	0	.67	-1
Pearson, Nate	15.0	0	0	0	0	-	0	0	0	0	-	0
Peguero, Elvis	2.1	0	0	0	0	-	1	0	0	0	.00	0

Pitcher	Inn	PO	A	E	DP	Pct	SBA	CS	PCS	PPO	CS%	RS
						2021 Fielding and Holding Runners						
Pena, Felix	1.2	0	0	0	0	-	0	0	0	0	-	0
Peralta, Freddy	144.1	11	7	4	0	.818	11	4	0	0	.36	-3
Peralta, Wandy	51.0	3	9	0	1	1.000	0	0	0	0	-	1
Peralta, Wily	93.2	5	4	2	0	.818	9	2	0	0	.22	-1
Perdomo, Angel	17.0	0	2	1	0	.667	4	2	1	0	.50	-1
Perez, Cionel	24.0	0	4	0	0	1.000	3	2	1	0	.67	1
Perez, Francisco	6.2	0	0	0	0	-	0	0	0	0	-	0
Perez, Martin	114.0	3	14	0	2	1.000	7	3	1	0	.43	1
Perez, Oliver	3.2	0	0	0	0	-	0	0	0	0	-	0
Peters, Dillon	26.2	1	3	0	0	1.000	1	0	0	0	.00	1
Peterson, David	66.2	5	8	0	1	1.000	5	3	1	1	.60	1
Petit, Yusmeiro	78.0	3	6	0	0	1.000	5	1	0	0	.20	-1
Petricka, Jake	6.0	0	1	0	0	1.000	1	0	0	0	.00	0
Phelps, David	10.1	0	0	0	0	-	0	0	0	0	-	0
Phillips, Evan	13.1	0	0	0	0	-	1	0	0	0	.00	0
Pineda, Michael	109.1	2	11	1	1	.929	15	5	2	0	.33	1
Pivetta, Nick	155.0	7	8	3	0	.833	11	0	0	0	.00	-2
Plesac, Zach	142.2	16	12	2	0	.933	4	1	0	1	.25	1
Plutko, Adam	56.1	3	5	0	0	1.000	2	2	0	0	1.00	2
Pomeranz, Drew	25.2	0	3	0	0	1.000	3	1	1	0	.33	0
Ponce, Cody	38.1	2	1	0	0	1.000	2	0	0	0	.00	-1
Ponce de Leon, D.	33.1	4	2	1	0	.857	0	0	0	0	-	0
Pop, Zach	54.2	5	5	0	0	1.000	2	0	0	0	.00	-2
Poppen, Sean	22.2	0	0	2	0	.000	0	0	0	0	-	-2
Poteet, Cody	30.2	2	2	0	1	1.000	2	0	0	0	.00	0
Pressly, Ryan	64.0	4	5	1	1	.900	2	0	0	0	.00	-1
Price, David	73.2	3	9	1	0	.923	3	2	0	0	.67	1
Pruitt, Austin	7.1	0	0	0	0	-	0	0	0	0	-	0
Puk, A.J.	13.1	0	2	0	0	1.000	0	0	0	0	-	1
Quackenbush, K.	0.1	0	0	0	0	-	0	0	0	0	-	0
Quantrill, Cal	149.2	8	19	1	3	.964	7	1	0	0	.14	3
Quijada, Jose	25.2	0	2	0	0	1.000	1	1	0	1	1.00	1
Quintana, Jose	63.0	5	6	1	0	.917	6	1	1	0	.17	0
Rainey, Tanner	31.2	0	0	0	0	-	1	0	0	0	.00	-1
Raley, Brooks	49.0	4	9	0	2	1.000	3	1	0	0	.33	2
Ramirez, Erasmo	26.2	2	2	0	0	1.000	1	1	0	1	1.00	0
Ramirez, Nick	20.1	2	1	0	0	1.000	0	0	0	0	-	0
Ramirez, Noe	36.0	2	2	0	0	1.000	6	0	0	0	.00	-1
Ramirez, Roel	0.1	0	0	0	0	-	0	0	0	0	-	0
Ramirez, Yefry	2.0	0	0	0	0	-	0	0	0	0	-	0
Ramirez, Yohan	27.2	1	2	0	0	1.000	1	0	0	0	.00	-1
Ramos, AJ	4.2	0	0	0	0	-	0	0	0	0	-	0
Rasmussen, Drew	76.0	4	5	0	0	1.000	4	0	0	0	.00	0
Ray, Robbie	193.1	4	15	1	1	.950	29	4	2	0	.14	-2
Rea, Colin	6.0	0	0	0	0	-	0	0	0	0	-	0
Reed, Cody	9.2	2	1	0	0	1.000	2	0	0	0	.00	0
Reed, Jake	10.0	0	1	0	0	1.000	1	0	0	0	.00	0
Reid-Foley, Sean	20.2	0	2	1	0	.667	0	0	0	0	-	-1
Reyes, Alex	72.1	4	7	2	1	.846	9	1	0	0	.11	0
Richards, Garrett	136.2	7	11	2	2	.900	9	2	0	0	.22	-2
Richards, Trevor	64.1	1	6	0	0	1.000	3	3	0	0	1.00	1
Ridings, Stephen	5.0	1	0	1	0	.500	0	0	0	0	-	-1
Rios, Yacksel	27.1	0	6	0	0	1.000	3	1	1	1	.33	2
Roark, Tanner	7.0	0	0	0	0	-	4	0	0	0	.00	-1
Robertson, David	12.0	1	1	0	0	1.000	1	1	1	0	1.00	0
Robles, Hansel	69.0	4	5	1	0	.900	6	1	0	0	.17	0
Rodon, Carlos	132.2	3	5	2	0	.800	11	0	0	0	.00	-4
Rodriguez, Chris	29.2	2	0	0	0	1.000	5	1	0	0	.20	0
Rodriguez, E.	157.2	1	14	0	1	1.000	4	2	0	0	.50	0
Rodriguez, Jefry	24.1	0	1	0	0	1.000	1	1	0	0	1.00	0
Rodriguez, Joely	46.1	2	11	1	1	.929	6	1	1	0	.17	-2
Rodriguez, Manuel	17.2	1	3	1	0	.800	1	0	0	0	.00	0
Rodriguez, N.	7.1	0	2	0	0	1.000	0	0	0	0	-	1
Rodriguez, R.	64.1	0	1	0	0	1.000	1	1	0	0	1.00	-1
Roe, Chaz	0.2	0	0	0	0	-	0	0	0	0	-	0
Rogers, Josh	35.2	0	4	0	1	1.000	0	0	0	0	-	1
Rogers, Taylor	40.1	1	4	0	0	1.000	1	0	0	0	.00	0
Rogers, Trevor	133.0	6	15	3	0	.875	12	3	1	0	.25	3
Rogers, Tyler	81.0	9	17	0	4	1.000	6	2	0	0	.33	-4
Romano, Jordan	63.0	2	7	0	0	1.000	12	3	0	0	.25	-1
Romano, Sal	25.0	0	5	0	2	1.000	2	0	0	0	.00	0
Romero, Jhon	4.0	0	1	0	0	1.000	0	0	0	0	-	0
Romero, JoJo	9.0	2	1	0	0	1.000	0	0	0	0	-	0

Pitcher	Inn	PO	A	E	DP	Pct	SBA	CS	PCS	PPO	CS%	RS
						2021 Fielding and Holding Runners						
Romo, Sergio	61.2	3	4	1	1	.875	11	1	0	1	.09	0
Rondon, Angel	2.0	0	0	0	0	-	0	0	0	0	-	0
Ross, Joe	108.0	4	14	0	2	1.000	7	2	0	0	.29	1
Rosscup, Zac	3.0	0	1	0	0	1.000	0	0	0	0	-	0
Rosso, Ramon	8.0	0	1	0	0	1.000	0	0	0	0	-	0
Rowen, Ben	11.1	1	1	1	0	.667	0	0	0	0	-	0
Rucker, Michael	28.1	0	1	0	1	1.000	4	0	0	0	.00	-2
Ruiz, Jose	65.0	1	2	1	0	.750	4	0	0	0	.00	0
Ryan, Joe	26.2	1	1	1	0	.667	2	0	0	0	.00	0
Ryan, Kyle	13.1	0	4	0	0	1.000	0	0	0	0	-	1
Ryu, Hyun-Jin	169.0	1	10	0	0	1.000	2	1	1	0	.50	-2
Sadler, Casey	40.1	1	5	1	2	.857	1	0	0	0	.00	0
Sale, Chris	42.2	0	6	0	0	1.000	2	1	0	0	.50	0
Sampson, Adrian	35.1	1	3	0	2	1.000	1	0	0	0	.00	0
Sanchez, Aaron	35.1	2	7	0	1	1.000	5	0	0	0	.00	0
Sanchez, C.	12.2	0	2	2	0	.500	2	0	0	0	.00	-2
Sanchez, Miguel	26.0	3	2	0	0	1.000	1	0	0	0	.00	0
Sandlin, Nick	33.2	0	4	0	1	1.000	2	1	0	0	.50	0
Sandoval, Patrick	87.0	3	7	0	0	1.000	2	2	0	0	1.00	0
Sanmartin, Reiver	11.2	1	2	0	0	1.000	0	0	0	0	-	0
Santana, Dennis	54.2	2	2	1	1	.800	7	1	0	0	.14	-2
Santana, Edgar	42.2	3	6	0	0	1.000	7	3	0	0	.43	0
Santana, Ervin	65.1	6	4	1	1	.909	2	0	0	0	.00	-2
Santiago, Hector	26.1	4	0	0	0	1.000	1	0	0	0	.00	0
Santillan, Tony	43.1	1	4	1	0	.833	3	2	1	0	.67	-1
Santos, Antonio	11.1	1	0	0	0	1.000	1	0	0	0	.00	-1
Santos, Gregory	2.0	0	0	0	0	-	0	0	0	0	-	0
Saucedo, Tayler	25.2	0	6	0	0	1.000	3	0	0	0	.00	1
Sawamura, H.	53.0	1	3	0	0	1.000	0	0	0	0	-	-1
Sborz, Josh	59.0	3	5	0	2	1.000	10	2	1	0	.20	-1
Sceroler, Mac	7.2	0	1	1	0	.500	0	0	0	0	-	0
Scherzer, Max	179.1	8	10	0	0	1.000	13	7	0	0	.54	1
Schmidt, Clarke	6.1	0	1	0	0	1.000	1	0	0	0	.00	-1
Schreiber, John	3.0	0	0	0	0	-	0	0	0	0	-	0
Scott, Tanner	54.0	1	4	0	0	1.000	0	0	0	0	-	0
Scrubb, Andre	19.2	0	2	0	1	1.000	2	1	0	0	.50	0
Seabold, Connor	3.0	0	0	0	0	-	0	0	0	0	-	0
Selman, Sam	25.0	0	2	0	0	1.000	3	1	1	0	.33	1
Senzatela, Antonio	156.2	7	24	0	2	1.000	4	1	0	0	.25	2
Severino, Luis	6.0	1	0	0	0	1.000	0	0	0	0	-	0
Sewald, Paul	64.2	4	4	2	0	.800	4	0	0	0	.00	-1
Shaw, Bryan	77.1	5	7	1	0	.923	2	1	0	0	.50	0
Sheffield, Jordan	29.1	3	3	0	1	1.000	2	2	1	0	1.00	0
Sheffield, Justus	80.1	5	11	1	2	.941	12	3	2	0	.25	-1
Sherfy, Jimmie	15.0	0	1	0	0	1.000	1	0	0	0	.00	-1
Sherriff, Ryan	14.2	0	2	0	0	1.000	0	0	0	0	-	1
Shoemaker, Matt	60.1	7	5	1	0	.923	7	0	0	2	.00	-1
Shreve, Chasen	56.1	3	5	0	0	1.000	0	0	0	0	-	0
Sims, Lucas	47.0	0	3	0	0	1.000	3	1	0	0	.33	0
Singer, Brady	128.1	9	5	6	1	.700	14	4	1	0	.29	-6
Sittinger, Brandyn	4.2	0	1	0	0	1.000	1	1	1	0	1.00	0
Skubal, Tarik	149.1	4	15	3	0	.864	9	4	2	0	.44	1
Slegers, Aaron	31.0	1	4	0	0	1.000	12	2	0	0	.17	-1
Smeltzer, Devin	4.2	1	0	0	0	1.000	0	0	0	0	-	0
Smith, Burch	43.1	1	3	1	0	.800	0	0	0	0	-	0
Smith, Caleb	113.2	3	8	2	0	.846	8	2	2	0	.25	0
Smith, Drew	41.1	2	1	0	1	1.000	4	1	0	0	.25	0
Smith, Joe	39.2	2	6	0	0	1.000	3	1	1	1	.33	1
Smith, Riley	67.1	6	9	0	0	1.000	4	2	1	0	.50	2
Smith, Will	68.0	2	4	0	0	1.000	1	0	0	0	.00	1
Smyly, Drew	126.2	3	24	1	2	.964	11	5	5	0	.45	3
Snead, Kirby	7.2	1	0	1	0	1.000	1	1	0	0	1.00	0
Snell, Blake	128.2	4	9	0	2	1.000	22	3	2	0	.14	-4
Snyder, Nick	3.2	0	0	0	0	-	0	0	0	0	-	0
Solomon, Peter	14.0	2	1	0	0	1.000	1	1	0	1	1.00	0
Soria, Joakim	37.1	1	2	0	0	1.000	1	0	0	0	.00	0
Soto, Gregory	63.2	1	7	0	0	1.000	1	0	0	0	.00	0
Speier, Gabe	7.2	1	1	0	0	1.000	1	1	1	0	1.00	0
Spitzbarth, Shea	5.0	0	0	0	0	-	0	0	0	0	-	0
Springs, Jeffrey	44.2	1	2	0	0	1.000	0	0	0	1	-	0
Stammen, Craig	88.1	7	9	0	2	1.000	13	1	0	0	.08	-4
Stanek, Ryne	68.1	2	4	0	2	1.000	3	0	0	0	.00	0
Stashak, Cody	15.2	0	1	0	0	1.000	0	0	0	0	-	0

Pitcher	Inn	PO	A	E	DP	Pct	SBA	CS	PCS	PPO	CS%	RS
2021 Fielding and Holding Runners												
Staumont, Josh	65.2	2	2	1	0	.800	2	0	0	0	.00	-1
Steckenrider, Drew	67.2	6	1	0	0	1.000	3	0	0	0	.00	-3
Steele, Justin	57.0	1	9	0	1	1.000	6	1	0	0	.17	1
Stephan, Trevor	63.1	6	2	2	0	.800	8	1	0	0	.13	-1
Stephenson, R.	46.0	2	3	1	0	.833	4	0	0	0	.00	-2
Stewart, Kohl	13.2	2	3	0	0	1.000	0	0	0	0	-	0
Stiever, Jonathan	0.0	0	0	0	0	-	0	0	0	0	-	0
Stock, Robert	9.0	1	1	0	0	1.000	1	0	0	0	.00	0
Strahm, Matt	6.2	1	0	0	0	1.000	0	0	0	0	-	-1
Strasburg, S.	21.2	1	3	0	0	1.000	2	0	0	0	.00	0
Stratton, Chris	79.1	6	2	0	0	1.000	2	0	0	0	.00	0
Strickland, Hunter	58.2	1	2	0	0	1.000	6	0	0	0	.00	-1
Strider, Spencer	2.1	1	0	0	0	1.000	0	0	0	0	-	0
Stripling, Ross	101.1	2	8	0	0	1.000	6	2	0	0	.33	1
Stroman, Marcus	179.0	20	29	2	1	.961	17	7	0	0	.41	1
Strop, Pedro	2.0	0	0	0	0	-	0	0	0	0	-	0
Suarez, Jose	98.1	6	5	1	0	.917	6	0	0	0	.00	-1
Suarez, Ranger	106.0	10	24	1	1	.971	3	1	1	0	.33	6
Suero, Wander	42.2	0	2	0	1	1.000	0	0	0	0	-	0
Sulser, Cole	63.1	6	4	0	0	1.000	2	0	0	0	.00	2
Suter, Brent	73.1	7	9	0	0	1.000	1	1	0	0	1.00	1
Swanson, Erik	35.1	2	0	1	0	.667	4	1	0	0	.25	0
Swarzak, Anthony	12.1	1	1	0	0	1.000	0	0	0	0	-	0
Syndergaard, N.	2.0	0	0	0	0	-	0	0	0	0	-	0
Szapucki, Thomas	3.2	1	1	0	0	1.000	0	0	0	0	-	0
Taillon, Jameson	144.1	5	9	0	0	1.000	18	3	1	0	.17	-2
Tapia, Domingo	33.2	0	2	0	0	1.000	2	1	0	0	.50	0
Tarpley, Stephen	0.0	0	0	0	0	-	0	0	0	0	-	0
Tate, Dillon	67.2	5	14	1	1	.950	5	2	1	0	.40	1
Taylor, Blake	42.2	1	2	1	0	.750	0	0	0	0	-	-2
Taylor, Josh	47.2	0	2	0	0	1.000	3	1	1	0	.33	-1
Teheran, Julio	5.0	0	1	0	0	1.000	0	0	0	0	-	0
Tepera, Ryan	61.1	0	5	1	0	.833	4	1	0	0	.25	-1
Thielbar, Caleb	64.0	3	4	0	0	1.000	3	1	1	0	.33	-1
Thompson, K.	53.1	4	0	0	0	1.000	3	0	0	0	.00	-1
Thompson, Mason	24.2	0	1	2	0	.333	3	0	0	0	.00	-3
Thompson, Ryan	34.0	2	3	0	0	1.000	2	0	0	0	.00	1
Thompson, Zach	75.0	2	10	1	2	.923	3	1	1	1	.33	1
Thornton, Trent	49.0	0	4	0	0	1.000	7	3	0	0	.43	0
Thorpe, Lewis	15.1	2	2	0	0	1.000	1	0	0	0	.00	0
Tice, Ty	8.0	2	0	0	0	1.000	0	0	0	0	-	0
Tinoco, Jesus	1.1	0	0	0	0	-	1	1	0	0	1.00	0
Tomlin, Josh	49.1	4	6	0	0	1.000	3	1	0	1	.33	2
Topa, Justin	3.1	0	0	0	0	-	1	0	0	0	.00	0
Toussaint, Touki	50.0	2	6	1	0	.889	4	0	0	0	.00	-2
Treinen, Blake	72.1	3	12	0	0	1.000	20	3	1	2	.15	1
Trivino, Lou	73.2	5	5	0	2	1.000	9	2	0	0	.22	0
Tropeano, Nick	8.0	1	1	0	0	1.000	0	0	0	0	-	0
Turnbull, Spencer	50.0	6	6	0	0	1.000	5	1	0	0	.20	-2
Tyler, Kyle	12.1	1	2	0	0	1.000	0	0	0	0	-	0
Uceta, Edwin	20.1	0	3	0	1	1.000	1	0	0	0	.00	0
Underwood Jr., D.	72.2	3	4	1	1	.875	8	1	0	0	.13	-2
Urena, Jose	100.2	10	5	1	1	.938	11	6	0	0	.55	1
Urias, Julio	185.2	3	18	0	0	1.000	5	3	1	0	.60	2
Urquidy, Jose	107.0	6	6	0	0	1.000	4	2	0	0	.50	-1
Valdez, Cesar	46.0	1	1	0	0	1.000	1	1	0	0	1.00	-2
Valdez, Framber	134.2	5	7	1	0	.923	5	0	0	1	.00	-5
Valdez, Phillips	40.0	5	6	0	1	1.000	3	1	0	0	.33	1
Vasquez, Andrew	1.2	0	1	0	0	1.000	0	0	0	0	-	0
Velasquez, Vince	94.1	3	3	0	0	1.000	12	4	0	0	.33	-1
Vesia, Alex	40.0	0	0	1	0	.000	2	1	0	0	.50	-1
Vest, Will	35.0	4	6	1	2	.909	1	1	0	0	1.00	1
Vincent, Nick	12.2	0	1	1	0	.500	0	0	0	0	-	0
Voth, Austin	57.1	7	5	0	1	1.000	5	4	0	0	.80	1
Wacha, Michael	124.2	7	8	0	2	1.000	7	2	1	0	.29	-1
Waddell, Brandon	9.1	0	0	0	0	-	0	0	0	0	-	0
Wade, Konner	12.1	2	0	0	0	1.000	0	0	0	0	-	0
Wainwright, Adam	206.1	19	16	2	2	.946	6	3	1	0	.50	3
Walker, Taijuan	159.0	16	33	2	1	.961	11	4	1	3	.36	7
Wantz, Andrew	27.1	1	0	0	0	1.000	1	1	0	0	1.00	0
Warren, Art	21.0	0	1	0	0	1.000	4	0	0	0	.00	-1
Warren, Austin	20.1	4	3	0	0	1.000	2	0	0	0	.00	1
Watkins, Spenser	54.2	4	3	0	0	1.000	4	2	1	0	.50	1

Pitcher	Inn	PO	A	E	DP	Pct	SBA	CS	PCS	PPO	CS%	RS
2021 Fielding and Holding Runners												
Watson, Tony	57.1	4	6	2	2	.833	4	0	0	0	.00	-1
Weathers, Ryan	94.2	4	18	2	0	.917	3	1	1	8	.33	3
Weaver, Luke	65.2	3	3	1	0	.857	5	0	0	2	.00	-1
Webb, Jacob	34.1	1	3	3	0	.571	3	1	1	0	.33	-2
Webb, Logan	148.1	14	23	0	2	1.000	11	1	0	1	.09	1
Webb, Tyler	16.1	1	0	0	0	1.000	2	1	0	0	.50	0
Weber, Ryan	9.2	2	0	0	0	1.000	1	0	0	0	.00	0
Weems, Jordan	5.2	0	0	0	0	-	0	0	0	0	-	0
Weigel, Patrick	4.0	0	1	0	0	1.000	0	0	0	0	-	0
Wells, Alex	42.2	1	5	2	0	.750	4	1	0	0	.25	1
Wells, Tyler	57.0	1	3	0	0	1.000	2	0	0	0	.00	0
Wendelken, J.B.	43.2	2	3	0	1	1.000	2	1	0	0	.50	0
Wheeler, Zack	213.1	20	26	2	4	.958	7	3	0	0	.43	5
White, Mitch	46.2	4	6	1	0	.909	7	1	0	0	.14	-2
Whitley, Kodi	25.1	3	1	0	0	1.000	0	0	0	0	-	0
Whitlock, Garrett	73.1	3	5	0	0	1.000	5	2	2	0	.40	0
Wick, Rowan	23.0	0	2	0	0	1.000	1	0	0	0	.00	-1
Widener, Taylor	70.1	6	7	0	1	1.000	4	1	0	0	.25	1
Wieck, Brad	17.0	1	0	0	0	1.000	1	0	0	0	.00	0
Williams, Devin	54.0	2	3	0	0	1.000	6	2	0	0	.33	0
Williams, Taylor	11.2	2	1	0	0	1.000	1	0	0	0	.00	0
Williams, Trevor	91.0	11	7	0	1	1.000	5	2	0	1	.40	0
Wilson, Bryse	74.0	5	7	3	0	.800	6	1	0	0	.17	-1
Wilson, Justin	34.0	1	0	0	0	1.000	2	0	0	0	.00	0
Winkler, Dan	39.2	3	4	1	0	.875	2	0	0	0	.00	0
Wisler, Matt	48.2	1	3	0	0	1.000	5	1	1	0	.20	-1
Wittgren, Nick	62.1	5	3	0	0	1.000	2	1	0	0	.50	-1
Wojciechowski, A.	4.0	0	0	0	0	-	0	0	0	0	-	0
Wood, Alex	138.2	7	11	0	1	1.000	3	2	1	0	.67	-1
Wood, Hunter	5.0	0	1	0	0	1.000	0	0	0	0	-	0
Woodford, Jake	67.2	3	9	1	0	.923	3	2	1	1	.67	1
Woodruff, Brandon	179.1	10	19	2	2	.935	8	5	0	0	.63	2
Workman, B.	28.0	3	4	0	0	1.000	9	4	3	0	.44	0
Wright, Kyle	6.1	0	0	0	0	-	1	0	0	0	.00	0
Wright Jr., Mike	18.0	1	4	0	0	1.000	1	1	0	0	1.00	0
Yajure, Miguel	15.0	0	2	0	0	1.000	3	0	0	0	.00	-1
Yamamoto, Jordan	6.2	0	0	1	0	.000	1	0	0	0	.00	0
Yang, Hyeon-jong	35.1	4	1	0	1	1.000	0	0	0	0	-	0
Yarbrough, Ryan	155.0	6	18	0	1	1.000	10	3	1	0	.30	0
Yardley, Eric	18.2	0	9	0	1	1.000	1	0	0	0	.00	2
Ynoa, Huascar	91.0	5	11	0	1	1.000	7	1	0	0	.14	1
Young, Alex	52.0	3	4	0	0	1.000	0	0	0	0	-	0
Zamora, Daniel	4.1	1	0	0	0	1.000	0	0	0	0	-	0
Zerpa, Angel	5.0	0	2	0	0	1.000	0	0	0	0	-	0
Zeuch, T.J.	15.0	1	0	1	0	.500	0	0	0	0	-	-1
Zimmer, Kyle	54.0	4	5	0	3	1.000	3	1	0	0	.33	0
Zimmermann, B.	64.1	1	4	0	0	1.000	4	2	0	1	.50	0
Zimmermann, J.	5.2	0	1	0	0	1.000	0	0	0	0	-	0
Zuber, Tyler	27.1	1	3	0	0	1.000	0	0	0	0	-	0

Hitters Pitching

Player	2021 Pitching											Career Pitching										
	G	W	L	Sv	IP	H	R	ER	BB	SO	ERA	G	W	L	Sv	IP	H	R	ER	BB	SO	ERA
Adrianza, Ehire	-	-	-	-	-	-	-	-	-	-	-	2	0	0	0	2.0	6	4	4	0	1	18.00
Alberto, Hanser	1	-	-	-	0.1	-	-	-	-	-	0.00	2	0	0	0	1.1	1	2	2	2	0	13.50
Alcantara, Sergio	1	-	-	-	0.1	-	-	-	-	-	0.00	1	0	0	0	0.1	0	0	0	0	0	0.00
Almora Jr., Albert	1	-	-	-	1.0	1	3	3	1	-	27.00	1	0	0	0	1.0	1	3	3	1	0	27.00
Arauz, Jonathan	1	-	-	-	1.0	2	1	1	-	-	9.00	1	0	0	0	1.0	2	1	1	0	0	9.00
Arcia, Orlando	-	-	-	-	-	-	-	-	-	-	-	2	0	0	0	2.0	4	4	4	1	0	18.00
Arroyo, Christian	1	-	-	-	1.0	1	2	-	1	-	0.00	1	0	0	0	1.0	1	2	0	1	0	0.00
Arteaga, Humberto	-	-	-	-	-	-	-	-	-	-	-	1	0	0	0	1.2	2	1	1	1	0	5.40
Astudillo, Willians	4	-	-	-	4.0	1	1	1	2	-	2.25	5	0	0	0	5.0	6	6	6	2	0	10.80
Avila, Alex	-	-	-	-	-	-	-	-	-	-	-	3	0	0	0	4.0	3	1	1	1	1	2.25
Bemboom, Anthony	1	-	-	-	1.0	3	2	2	-	-	18.00	2	0	0	0	2.0	3	2	2	1	0	9.00
Blandino, Alex	4	-	-	-	3.2	4	5	4	4	1	9.82	5	0	0	0	4.2	5	5	4	4	3	7.71
Brantly, Rob	-	-	-	-	-	-	-	-	-	-	-	1	0	0	0	1.0	1	1	1	0	0	9.00
Brosseau, Mike	-	-	-	-	-	-	-	-	-	-	-	4	0	0	0	4.1	5	2	2	0	1	4.15
Burns, Andy	1	-	-	-	1.0	3	2	2	-	1	18.00	1	0	0	0	1.0	3	2	2	0	1	18.00
Butera, Drew	-	-	-	-	-	-	-	-	-	-	-	7	0	0	0	6.0	8	5	5	4	5	7.50
Cabrera, Asdrubal	2	-	-	-	1.1	1	-	-	-	-	0.00	2	0	0	0	1.1	1	0	0	0	0	0.00
Caratini, Victor	-	-	-	-	-	-	-	-	-	-	-	4	0	0	0	4.0	5	4	4	1	0	9.00
Carpenter, Matt	1	-	-	-	1.1	2	-	-	-	-	0.00	1	0	0	0	1.1	2	0	0	0	0	0.00
Castro, Harold	3	-	-	-	2.2	-	-	-	3	-	0.00	3	0	0	0	2.2	0	0	0	3	0	0.00
Cronenworth, Jake	1	-	-	-	0.2	1	-	-	-	1	0.00	1	0	0	0	0.2	1	0	0	0	1	0.00
Culberson, Charlie	2	-	-	-	2.0	2	-	-	-	-	0.00	6	0	0	0	5.1	6	1	1	2	1	1.69
Davis, J.D.	-	-	-	-	-	-	-	-	-	-	-	3	0	0	0	2.2	2	1	1	1	4	3.38
Davis, Taylor	-	-	-	-	-	-	-	-	-	-	-	1	0	0	0	1.0	3	0	0	0	0	0.00
Difo, Wilmer	2	-	-	-	2.0	9	8	8	3	1	36.00	2	0	0	0	2.0	9	8	8	3	1	36.00
Drury, Brandon	1	-	-	-	0.2	3	2	2	1	-	27.00	1	0	0	0	0.2	3	2	2	1	0	27.00
Duffy, Matt	1	-	-	-	0.1	-	-	-	-	-	0.00	1	0	0	0	0.1	0	0	0	0	0	0.00
Eaton, Adam	1	-	-	-	1.0	2	-	-	-	-	0.00	1	0	0	0	1.0	2	0	0	0	0	0.00
Escobar, Eduardo	-	-	-	-	-	-	-	-	-	-	-	1	0	0	0	1.0	1	0	0	0	0	0.00
Espinal, Santiago	-	-	-	-	-	-	-	-	-	-	-	2	0	0	0	2.0	3	2	2	1	0	9.00
Evans, Phillip	1	-	-	-	1.0	-	-	-	-	-	0.00	1	0	0	0	1.0	0	0	0	0	0	0.00
Farmer, Kyle	-	-	-	-	-	-	-	-	-	-	-	1	0	0	0	1.1	1	0	0	0	0	0.00
Ford, Mike	-	-	-	-	-	-	-	-	-	-	-	1	0	0	0	2.0	6	5	5	0	1	22.50
France, Ty	-	-	-	-	-	-	-	-	-	-	-	2	0	0	0	2.0	2	1	1	0	0	4.50
Frazier, Todd	-	-	-	-	-	-	-	-	-	-	-	1	0	0	0	1.0	0	0	0	0	1	0.00
Freeman, Mike	1	-	-	-	0.1	-	-	-	-	1	0.00	3	0	0	0	3.1	5	3	3	0	1	8.10
Fuentes, Joshua	1	-	-	-	1.0	1	-	-	-	-	0.00	1	0	0	0	1.0	1	0	0	0	0	0.00
Garcia, Leury	-	-	-	-	-	-	-	-	-	-	-	2	0	1	0	2.0	2	2	2	2	1	9.00
Garcia, Robel	1	-	-	-	1.0	5	4	4	-	-	36.00	1	0	0	0	1.0	5	4	4	0	0	36.00
Garver, Mitch	-	-	-	-	-	-	-	-	-	-	-	1	0	0	0	1.0	1	0	0	0	0	0.00
Gonzalez, Marwin	1	-	-	-	1.0	-	-	-	-	-	0.00	1	0	0	0	1.0	0	0	0	0	0	0.00
Gonzalez, Romy	1	-	-	-	0.1	-	-	-	-	1	0.00	1	0	0	0	0.1	0	0	0	0	1	0.00
Guillorme, Luis	1	-	-	-	1.0	3	2	2	1	-	18.00	2	0	0	0	2.0	3	2	2	1	0	9.00
Happ, Ian	-	-	-	-	-	-	-	-	-	-	-	1	0	0	0	1.0	1	0	0	0	0	0.00
Harrison, Josh	-	-	-	-	-	-	-	-	-	-	-	1	0	0	0	0.1	0	0	0	0	0	0.00
Hernandez, Kike	-	-	-	-	-	-	-	-	-	-	-	1	0	1	0	0.1	1	3	3	2	0	81.00
Holaday, Bryan	1	-	-	-	1.0	1	1	1	1	-	9.00	6	0	0	0	5.0	7	4	4	1	1	7.20
Holt, Brock	1	-	-	-	1.0	1	-	-	-	-	0.00	3	0	0	0	2.1	6	2	2	0	0	7.71
Hoying, Jared	-	-	-	-	-	-	-	-	-	-	-	1	0	0	0	1.0	1	1	1	0	0	9.00
Jay, Jon	-	-	-	-	-	-	-	-	-	-	-	1	0	0	0	1.0	1	0	0	0	0	0.00
Kelly, Carson	-	-	-	-	-	-	-	-	-	-	-	1	0	0	0	1.0	1	0	0	0	0	0.00
Kingery, Scott	-	-	-	-	-	-	-	-	-	-	-	1	0	0	0	1.1	4	2	2	0	0	13.50
Knapp, Andrew	1	-	-	-	0.1	-	-	-	-	-	0.00	1	0	0	0	0.1	0	0	0	0	0	0.00
La Stella, Tommy	-	-	-	-	-	-	-	-	-	-	-	1	0	0	0	1.1	3	1	1	0	0	6.75
Ladendorf, Tyler	-	-	-	-	-	-	-	-	-	-	-	1	0	0	0	1.0	1	0	0	1	0	0.00
LaMarre, Ryan	-	-	-	-	-	-	-	-	-	-	-	2	0	0	0	1.2	3	1	1	0	0	5.40
Leon, Sandy	6	-	-	-	6.0	7	5	5	1	2	7.50	6	0	0	0	6.0	7	5	5	1	2	7.50
Lin, Tzu-Wei	-	-	-	-	-	-	-	-	-	-	-	1	0	0	0	1.0	4	3	3	0	0	27.00
Lopes, Tim	-	-	-	-	-	-	-	-	-	-	-	1	0	0	0	1.0	2	2	2	1	0	18.00
Luplow, Jordan	1	-	-	-	1.0	2	1	1	-	-	9.00	1	0	0	0	1.0	2	1	1	0	0	9.00
Maile, Luke	1	-	-	-	1.0	2	1	1	-	-	9.00	3	0	0	0	3.0	3	1	1	0	3	3.00
Maldonado, Martin	-	-	-	-	-	-	-	-	-	-	-	1	0	0	0	1.0	1	0	0	0	0	0.00
Martini, Nick	-	-	-	-	-	-	-	-	-	-	-	1	0	0	0	1.0	0	0	0	2	1	0.00
Mathis, Jeff	-	-	-	-	-	-	-	-	-	-	-	5	0	1	0	5.0	8	5	5	1	2	9.00
Mathisen, Wyatt	1	-	-	-	1.0	1	-	-	-	-	0.00	1	0	0	0	1.0	1	0	0	0	0	0.00
Maton, Nick	1	-	-	-	0.1	-	-	-	-	1	0.00	1	0	0	0	0.1	0	0	0	0	1	0.00
Mayfield, Jack	1	-	-	-	0.1	-	-	-	-	-	0.00	1	0	0	0	0.1	0	0	0	0	0	0.00
Mejia, Francisco	2	-	-	-	2.0	6	6	6	-	-	27.00	2	0	0	0	2.0	6	6	6	0	0	27.00

Hitters Pitching

Player	2021 Pitching											Career Pitching										
	G	W	L	Sv	IP	H	R	ER	BB	SO	ERA	G	W	L	Sv	IP	H	R	ER	BB	SO	ERA
Mendick, Danny	1	-	-	-	1.0	1	-	-	-	1	0.00	1	0	0	0	1.0	1	0	0	0	1	0.00
Mercedes, Yermin	1	-	-	-	1.0	3	1	1	2	-	9.00	1	0	0	0	1.0	3	1	1	2	0	9.00
Moore, Dylan	-	-	-	-	-	-	-	-	-	-		1	0	0	0	1.0	5	4	4	2	0	36.00
Moreland, Mitch	1	-	-	-	1.0	1	-	-	-	1	0.00	3	0	0	0	3.0	3	0	0	0	2	0.00
Motter, Taylor	-	-	-	-	-	-	-	-	-	-		2	0	0	0	1.1	2	1	1	1	1	6.75
Murphy, Tom	-	-	-	-	-	-	-	-	-	-		3	0	0	0	3.0	1	2	2	1	2	6.00
Nogowski, John	3	-	-	-	3.0	8	5	5	-	-	15.00	3	0	0	0	3.0	8	5	5	0	0	15.00
Owings, Chris	-	-	-	-	-	-	-	-	-	-		1	0	0	0	1.2	6	4	4	1	0	21.60
Parra, Gerardo	-	-	-	-	-	-	-	-	-	-		1	0	0	0	0.0	1	5	5	4	0	-
Peralta, David	1	-	-	-	1.0	4	3	3	-	1	27.00	1	0	0	0	1.0	4	3	3	0	1	27.00
Peraza, Jose	-	-	-	-	-	-	-	-	-	-		3	0	0	0	1.2	3	1	1	0	0	5.40
Perez, Hernan	2	-	-	-	2.0	1	-	-	-	2	0.00	9	0	0	0	9.1	11	6	6	4	5	5.79
Peterson, Jace	2	-	-	-	2.0	4	2	2	1	2	9.00	3	0	0	0	3.0	10	6	6	1	3	18.00
Phillips, Brett	1	-	-	-	1.0	2	1	1	2	-	9.00	1	0	0	0	1.0	2	1	1	2	0	9.00
Pillar, Kevin	1	-	-	-	0.1	-	-	-	-	-	0.00	1	0	0	0	0.1	0	0	0	0	0	0.00
Plawecki, Kevin	1	-	-	-	1.0	-	-	-	-	-	0.00	6	0	0	0	6.2	5	4	4	1	0	5.40
Quinn, Roman	-	-	-	-	-	-	-	-	-	-		3	0	1	0	5.0	13	10	10	5	1	18.00
Reddick, Josh	1	-	-	-	0.2	2	1	1	1	-	13.50	1	0	0	0	0.2	2	1	1	1	0	13.50
Rizzo, Anthony	1	-	-	-	0.2	-	-	-	1	1	0.00	2	0	0	0	1.0	0	0	0	1	1	0.00
Robertson, Daniel	1	-	-	-	1.0	1	-	-	-	-	0.00	3	0	0	0	3.0	2	0	0	0	0	0.00
Rogers, Jake	1	-	-	-	1.0	2	2	2	1	-	18.00	1	0	0	0	1.0	2	2	2	1	0	18.00
Romine, Andrew	1	-	-	-	1.0	2	1	1	-	1	9.00	8	0	0	0	6.2	12	9	9	5	2	12.15
Romine, Austin	-	-	-	-	-	-	-	-	-	-		1	0	0	0	1.0	4	3	3	0	0	27.00
Rondon, Jose	-	-	-	-	-	-	-	-	-	-		1	0	0	0	1.0	2	0	0	0	0	0.00
Ruf, Darin	1	-	-	-	1.0	3	2	2	-	-	18.00	1	0	0	0	1.0	3	2	2	0	0	18.00
Sandoval, Pablo	-	-	-	-	-	-	-	-	-	-		2	0	0	0	2.0	0	0	0	0	0	0.00
Schrock, Max	2	-	-	-	1.2	-	-	-	-	1	0.00	3	0	0	0	2.2	0	0	0	0	1	0.00
Slater, Austin	1	-	-	-	0.1	-	-	-	1	-	0.00	1	0	0	0	0.1	0	0	0	1	0	0.00
Sogard, Eric	5	-	-	-	4.1	7	3	3	-	1	6.23	5	0	0	0	4.1	7	3	3	0	1	6.23
Stallings, Jacob	-	-	-	-	-	-	-	-	-	-		1	0	0	0	1.0	0	0	0	0	0	0.00
Stassi, Max	-	-	-	-	-	-	-	-	-	-		1	0	0	0	0.1	0	0	0	0	0	0.00
Tauchman, Mike	1	-	-	-	1.0	3	1	1	-	-	9.00	1	0	0	0	1.0	3	1	1	0	0	9.00
Tom, Ka'ai	1	-	-	-	1.0	1	-	-	-	-	0.00	1	0	0	0	1.0	1	0	0	0	0	0.00
Torreyes, Ronald	2	-	-	-	2.2	6	4	4	-	1	13.50	2	0	0	0	2.2	6	4	4	0	1	13.50
Turner, Justin	1	-	-	-	1.0	2	-	-	-	-	0.00	1	0	0	0	1.0	2	0	0	0	0	0.00
Valaika, Pat	2	-	-	-	1.1	-	-	-	-	-	0.00	2	0	0	0	1.1	0	0	0	0	0	0.00
Walsh, Jared	-	-	-	-	-	-	-	-	-	-		5	0	0	0	5.0	3	1	1	6	5	1.80
Wilkerson, Stevie	1	-	-	-	1.0	2	1	1	-	-	9.00	5	0	0	1	6.1	8	5	5	0	1	7.11
Wynns, Austin	1	-	-	-	1.0	1	1	1	-	-	9.00	1	0	0	0	1.0	1	1	1	0	0	9.00

Pitchers Hitting

Brian Reiff

Fear not, fans of substandard hitting performances. The Pitchers Hitting section is back!

With the universal Designated Hitter rule in place for the 2020 season, we felt as though the four total plate appearances pitchers not named Shohei Ohtani weren't really enough to warrant an entire section of last year's book. But with the rule rolled back this year, pitchers once again have been given the opportunity to impress readers of this book with their hitting prowess.

The off-year from hitting certainly didn't do anything to improve pitchers' hitting performances. Pitchers combined for a .285 OPS at the plate, which, while not as bad when comparing to MLB-wide offensive performance, was still the worst mark in the league's history.

Only one pitcher with at least 10 plate appearances had a batting average north of .300: Mets ace Jacob deGrom. The clear NL Cy Young favorite before his injury, deGrom is certainly better known for his arm, having pitched to a sterling 1.94 ERA over the past four seasons. If not for his injury, he could have failed to record a single hit all season and still have generated more value for his team than any other pitcher this season. As it is, his .758 OPS led all pitchers with at least 10 plate appearances, supplementing what could have been a truly historic season.

Speaking of going hitless, one of the frontrunners for the NL Cy Young in deGrom's absence did just that. The Dodgers' Max Scherzer, traded midseason from the Nationals, failed to record a hit in any of the 59 at-bats he accumulated between his two clubs, the most hitless at-bats for any player in a season since Bob Buhl had 70 in 1962 for the Braves and Cubs. That said, when someone pitches as well as Scherzer (or deGrom for that matter), they can be forgiven for their shortcomings at the plate.

Pitchers Hitting
Pitchers with 10+ PA or 10+ Total Bases in 2021

Pitcher	B	AB	H	2B	3B	HR	R	RBI	BB	SO	SH	GDP	Avg	OBP	Slg	OPS
Alcantara, Sandy	R	58	2	1	0	0	0	0	3	45	2	0	.034	.097	.052	.148
Alzolay, Adbert	R	31	2	1	0	0	1	0	1	13	1	1	.065	.094	.097	.191
Anderson, Brett	L	28	0	0	0	0	2	1	4	14	2	3	.000	.125	.000	.125
Anderson, Chase	R	11	0	0	0	0	0	0	0	6	3	0	.000	.000	.000	.000
Anderson, Ian	R	37	2	1	0	0	0	0	1	29	3	0	.054	.079	.081	.160
Anderson, Tyler	L	39	4	0	0	1	1	1	1	29	0	0	.103	.125	.179	.304
Arrieta, Jake	R	23	3	0	0	0	3	0	2	16	4	0	.130	.231	.130	.361
Bauer, Trevor	R	30	1	0	0	0	0	1	1	11	3	0	.033	.065	.033	.098
Brubaker, JT	R	38	3	0	0	0	0	3	4	15	1	2	.079	.167	.079	.246
Buehler, Walker	R	69	7	2	0	0	5	3	5	45	8	0	.101	.162	.130	.293
Bumgarner, Madison	R	39	4	1	0	0	3	3	9	29	2	0	.103	.280	.128	.408
Burnes, Corbin	R	52	8	0	0	0	1	4	3	26	4	0	.154	.200	.154	.354
Carrasco, Carlos	R	15	0	0	0	0	0	0	0	10	4	0	.000	.000	.000	.000
Castillo, Luis	R	49	8	2	0	0	1	2	1	23	9	1	.163	.180	.204	.384
Corbin, Patrick	L	53	7	0	0	0	1	0	3	24	7	0	.132	.179	.132	.311
Crismatt, Nabil	R	10	0	0	0	0	0	0	0	6	1	0	.000	.000	.000	.000
Crowe, Wil	R	35	2	1	0	0	2	0	1	14	4	0	.057	.108	.086	.194
Cueto, Johnny	R	29	2	0	0	0	1	0	3	9	5	0	.069	.156	.069	.225
Darvish, Yu	R	53	5	2	0	0	2	1	0	25	1	2	.094	.111	.132	.243
Davies, Zach	R	34	6	0	0	0	2	2	0	8	10	0	.176	.176	.176	.353
De Jong, Chase	L	12	1	1	0	0	1	0	0	5	3	0	.083	.083	.167	.250
deGrom, Jacob	R	33	12	1	0	0	4	6	0	9	0	0	.364	.364	.394	.758
DeSclafani, Anthony	R	51	2	1	0	0	2	1	4	33	7	0	.039	.109	.059	.168
Eflin, Zach	R	29	0	0	0	0	1	1	1	15	6	0	.000	.065	.000	.065
Espino, Paolo	R	30	5	0	0	0	2	0	0	15	3	0	.167	.167	.167	.333
Fedde, Erick	R	36	0	0	0	0	0	1	1	14	5	0	.000	.026	.000	.026
Flaherty, Jack	R	17	2	0	0	1	2	3	5	7	3	0	.118	.304	.294	.598
Freeland, Kyle	L	33	6	1	0	0	3	4	2	17	4	0	.182	.222	.212	.434
Fried, Max	L	55	15	3	0	0	7	5	4	18	8	0	.273	.322	.327	.649
Gallen, Zac	R	32	6	2	0	0	2	3	1	18	9	1	.188	.212	.250	.462
Gant, John	R	13	0	0	0	0	0	0	0	8	5	0	.000	.000	.000	.000
Garrett, Braxton	R	11	2	0	0	0	1	0	0	4	0	0	.182	.182	.182	.364
Gausman, Kevin	L	54	10	0	0	0	6	4	2	31	5	0	.185	.211	.185	.396
Gibson, Kyle	R	29	4	0	0	1	3	2	0	10	1	0	.138	.138	.241	.379
Gomber, Austin	L	32	3	0	0	0	0	1	1	13	9	1	.094	.121	.094	.215
Gonsolin, Tony	R	17	3	1	0	0	2	0	1	8	1	0	.176	.222	.235	.458
Gonzalez, Chi Chi	R	31	5	1	0	0	3	1	1	16	2	0	.161	.188	.194	.381
Gray, Jon	R	47	5	0	0	0	2	3	0	32	3	0	.106	.106	.106	.213
Gray, Josiah	R	22	1	0	0	0	0	0	1	12	1	0	.045	.087	.045	.132
Gray, Sonny	R	41	6	0	0	0	4	0	1	10	1	1	.146	.167	.146	.313
Gutierrez, Vladimir	R	33	3	0	0	0	3	1	2	14	7	0	.091	.143	.091	.234
Happ, J.A.	L	14	0	0	0	0	0	0	1	5	0	0	.000	.067	.000	.067
Hendricks, Kyle	R	52	6	1	0	0	3	1	2	26	7	0	.115	.148	.135	.283
Hernandez, Elieser	R	14	1	0	0	0	1	0	0	7	4	0	.071	.071	.071	.143
Hill, Rich	L	24	3	0	0	0	0	0	0	10	2	2	.125	.125	.125	.250
Hoffman, Jeff	R	15	2	0	0	0	1	1	0	3	1	0	.133	.133	.133	.267
Holloway, Jordan	R	10	1	0	0	0	0	0	0	6	0	0	.100	.100	.100	.200
Houser, Adrian	R	42	3	0	0	2	2	2	2	30	2	0	.071	.114	.214	.328
Keller, Mitch	R	28	3	0	0	0	2	0	2	14	2	0	.107	.167	.107	.274
Kelly, Merrill	R	47	3	1	0	0	1	1	4	27	7	1	.064	.137	.085	.222
Kershaw, Clayton	L	36	8	0	0	0	2	3	1	11	2	0	.222	.243	.222	.465
Kim, Kwang-hyun	L	26	3	1	0	0	0	2	0	9	2	0	.115	.148	.154	.302
Kranick, Max	R	12	0	0	0	0	0	0	0	5	2	0	.000	.000	.000	.000
Kuhl, Chad	R	21	1	0	0	0	1	0	1	11	2	0	.048	.091	.048	.139
Lauer, Eric	R	26	4	0	0	1	3	4	3	15	6	1	.154	.258	.269	.527
LeBlanc, Wade	L	11	0	0	0	0	0	0	0	3	2	0	.000	.000	.000	.000
Lester, Jon	L	48	8	2	0	1	3	3	2	24	1	0	.167	.200	.271	.471
Long, Sammy	L	10	1	0	0	0	0	0	0	4	1	0	.100	.100	.100	.200
Lopez, Pablo	L	33	2	2	0	0	2	0	0	17	2	1	.061	.061	.121	.182
Lucchesi, Joey	L	10	0	0	0	0	1	0	1	7	0	0	.000	.091	.000	.091
Luzardo, Jesus	L	15	0	0	0	0	1	0	4	6	1	0	.000	.211	.000	.211
Mahle, Tyler	R	55	3	0	0	0	1	1	4	19	7	2	.055	.119	.055	.173
Marquez, German	R	53	14	5	0	1	5	9	0	13	7	0	.264	.264	.415	.679
Martinez, Carlos	R	24	2	1	0	0	1	0	0	15	1	0	.083	.083	.125	.208
Megill, Tylor	R	28	6	3	0	0	1	0	1	17	2	0	.214	.241	.321	.563
Miley, Wade	L	54	10	3	0	0	9	3	3	13	2	0	.185	.228	.241	.469
Mills, Alec	R	32	1	1	0	0	1	0	0	26	4	0	.031	.031	.063	.094
Moore, Matt	L	19	0	0	0	0	0	0	0	13	1	0	.000	.000	.000	.000

Pitchers Hitting

Pitchers with 10+ PA or 10+ Total Bases in 2021

Pitcher	B	AB	H	2B	3B	HR	R	RBI	BB	SO	SH	GDP	Avg	OBP	Slg	OPS
Morton, Charlie	R	55	7	1	0	0	5	1	0	31	7	0	.127	.127	.145	.273
Muller, Kyle	R	11	1	0	0	0	0	0	1	7	1	0	.091	.167	.091	.258
Musgrove, Joe	R	51	7	2	0	0	2	1	1	23	4	0	.137	.151	.176	.327
Neidert, Nick	R	11	0	0	0	0	0	0	1	5	0	0	.000	.083	.000	.083
Nola, Aaron	R	49	7	2	0	0	5	4	6	29	7	0	.143	.232	.184	.416
Oviedo, Johan	R	20	3	0	0	0	3	2	2	9	0	0	.150	.227	.150	.377
Paddack, Chris	R	35	1	0	0	0	0	0	1	26	5	0	.029	.081	.029	.110
Peacock, Matt	R	16	4	0	0	0	3	2	1	4	0	1	.250	.294	.250	.544
Peralta, Freddy	R	43	4	0	0	0	1	0	1	22	1	1	.093	.114	.093	.207
Peterson, David	L	16	1	1	0	0	2	0	0	10	3	0	.063	.118	.125	.243
Poteet, Cody	R	10	1	0	0	0	1	1	0	3	1	0	.100	.100	.100	.200
Price, David	L	15	4	1	0	0	1	2	0	3	2	0	.267	.250	.333	.583
Rogers, Josh	L	12	0	0	0	0	0	0	1	4	1	0	.000	.077	.000	.077
Rogers, Trevor	L	43	3	0	0	0	0	0	1	27	2	0	.070	.091	.070	.161
Ross, Joe	R	32	8	0	0	0	1	3	1	14	5	0	.250	.294	.250	.544
Sanchez, Aaron	R	10	0	0	0	0	0	0	0	7	0	0	.000	.000	.000	.000
Scherzer, Max	R	59	0	0	0	0	0	1	0	28	3	1	.000	.000	.000	.000
Senzatela, Antonio	R	39	2	0	0	0	1	1	0	19	12	0	.051	.051	.051	.103
Smith, Caleb	R	22	2	1	0	0	2	0	1	14	1	0	.091	.167	.136	.303
Smith, Riley	R	16	0	0	0	0	0	0	0	11	1	0	.000	.000	.000	.000
Smyly, Drew	L	41	3	0	0	0	0	0	0	19	2	0	.073	.073	.073	.146
Snell, Blake	L	34	4	0	0	0	1	0	0	17	3	1	.118	.118	.118	.235
Steele, Justin	L	13	2	0	0	0	3	0	0	4	0	1	.154	.154	.154	.308
Stroman, Marcus	R	51	5	2	0	0	2	1	4	24	3	0	.098	.164	.137	.301
Suarez, Ranger	L	16	3	2	0	0	2	1	1	5	5	0	.188	.278	.313	.590
Thompson, Zach	R	15	2	1	0	0	0	0	0	9	3	0	.133	.133	.200	.333
Toussaint, Touki	R	15	0	0	0	0	1	0	2	9	1	0	.000	.118	.000	.118
Urias, Julio	L	59	12	2	0	0	5	9	0	22	10	1	.203	.217	.237	.454
Velasquez, Vince	R	23	2	0	0	0	0	3	2	9	5	0	.087	.160	.087	.247
Wainwright, Adam	R	57	7	2	0	0	1	4	3	25	14	2	.123	.167	.158	.325
Walker, Taijuan	R	47	5	0	0	0	0	1	1	29	2	1	.106	.143	.106	.249
Weathers, Ryan	R	27	4	0	0	1	3	1	1	7	0	0	.148	.179	.259	.438
Weaver, Luke	R	19	2	0	0	0	1	1	1	12	2	0	.105	.150	.105	.255
Webb, Logan	R	46	6	2	1	1	7	7	2	21	5	1	.130	.167	.283	.449
Wheeler, Zack	L	68	11	2	0	0	1	3	0	39	5	1	.162	.162	.191	.353
White, Mitch	R	15	0	0	0	0	1	0	1	11	0	0	.000	.063	.000	.063
Widener, Taylor	L	16	1	0	0	0	1	0	1	11	1	0	.063	.118	.063	.180
Williams, Trevor	R	25	5	0	0	0	1	1	1	9	2	0	.200	.231	.200	.431
Wilson, Bryse	R	21	1	0	0	0	1	1	0	9	3	0	.048	.091	.048	.139
Wood, Alex	R	38	0	0	0	0	0	0	5	26	4	0	.000	.116	.000	.116
Woodford, Jake	R	18	2	0	0	0	0	0	0	9	2	0	.111	.111	.111	.222
Woodruff, Brandon	L	52	6	0	0	0	0	2	3	28	3	0	.115	.164	.115	.279
Ynoa, Huascar	R	32	7	1	0	2	3	6	0	15	0	0	.219	.219	.438	.656

Career Pitchers Hitting
Active Pitchers with 100+ PAs in their careers

Pitcher	B	AB	H	2B	3B	HR	R	RBI	BB	SO	SH	GDP	Avg	OBP	Slg	OPS
Anderson, Chase	R	275	25	2	0	0	6	10	4	146	31	3	.091	.110	.098	.209
Anderson, Tyler	L	157	15	0	0	2	11	5	9	93	16	3	.096	.150	.134	.283
Buehler, Walker	R	171	19	2	0	1	11	6	11	99	13	0	.111	.165	.140	.305
Bumgarner, Madison	R	633	109	19	0	19	54	65	49	284	42	5	.172	.232	.292	.524
Cahill, Trevor	R	191	23	3	1	0	7	12	5	67	20	2	.120	.143	.147	.289
Castillo, Luis	R	199	22	4	0	0	8	5	4	89	20	2	.111	.128	.131	.259
Chacin, Jhoulys	R	361	65	8	0	2	16	22	11	88	31	3	.180	.205	.219	.424
Chatwood, Tyler	R	205	42	5	1	0	17	17	8	52	29	1	.205	.235	.239	.474
Cole, Gerrit	R	251	41	2	0	3	17	15	6	112	28	4	.163	.186	.207	.393
Corbin, Patrick	L	410	62	9	3	0	30	23	21	169	38	4	.151	.194	.188	.382
Cueto, Johnny	R	545	55	1	0	0	27	18	17	178	90	6	.101	.129	.103	.232
Darvish, Yu	R	152	15	4	0	1	4	5	3	83	8	4	.099	.121	.145	.266
Davies, Zach	R	215	27	4	0	0	15	9	9	81	38	2	.126	.161	.144	.305
deGrom, Jacob	L	383	78	9	0	3	27	29	17	116	23	8	.204	.238	.251	.488
DeSclafani, Anthony	R	257	29	3	0	1	7	12	9	144	16	2	.113	.142	.136	.279
Eflin, Zach	R	167	21	3	0	1	10	6	1	94	15	2	.126	.136	.162	.298
Eovaldi, Nathan	R	153	12	0	0	0	9	2	7	97	14	0	.078	.119	.078	.197
Foltynewicz, Mike	R	201	14	3	0	0	8	9	1	127	24	2	.070	.074	.085	.158
Freeland, Kyle	L	173	22	4	0	1	12	8	8	102	16	1	.127	.165	.168	.332
Gose, Anthony	L	1128	271	47	19	12	155	69	101	353	11	27	.240	.309	.348	.656
Gray, Jon	R	242	22	4	0	1	11	13	11	147	28	2	.091	.130	.120	.250
Greinke, Zack	R	521	117	29	1	9	49	34	26	114	47	8	.225	.262	.336	.598
Happ, J.A.	L	211	20	2	0	1	13	6	11	91	31	1	.095	.140	.118	.258
Harvey, Matt	R	255	27	7	0	1	8	14	4	108	16	10	.106	.120	.145	.265
Hendricks, Kyle	R	358	37	5	0	0	12	16	11	178	33	3	.103	.135	.117	.252
Hill, Rich	L	256	29	5	0	0	4	13	3	111	12	4	.113	.130	.133	.263
Kennedy, Ian	R	321	42	11	1	1	21	18	33	154	42	3	.131	.213	.181	.394
Kershaw, Clayton	L	698	113	11	1	1	46	40	34	211	110	15	.162	.205	.185	.390
Lester, Jon	L	366	42	10	0	4	27	31	21	162	34	6	.115	.162	.175	.337
Lyles, Jordan	R	223	25	4	0	2	16	15	11	115	14	5	.112	.157	.157	.314
Lynn, Lance	B	283	24	5	0	0	15	7	12	159	35	2	.085	.128	.102	.230
Maeda, Kenta	R	179	28	4	0	1	12	14	1	42	35	3	.156	.161	.196	.357
Marquez, German	R	212	51	11	1	2	19	30	0	59	32	3	.241	.241	.330	.571
Martinez, Carlos	R	249	46	9	0	1	14	23	2	87	18	3	.185	.199	.233	.432
Matz, Steven	R	176	30	3	1	3	8	13	7	50	15	4	.170	.201	.250	.451
Miley, Wade	L	297	47	8	0	1	22	15	13	80	30	4	.158	.194	.195	.389
Miller, Shelby	R	203	22	10	1	1	16	7	12	109	34	3	.108	.165	.182	.347
Minor, Mike	R	217	25	6	0	2	13	10	9	100	16	2	.115	.150	.171	.321
Morton, Charlie	R	321	27	5	0	0	9	7	3	170	44	4	.084	.092	.100	.192
Nelson, Jimmy	R	191	19	2	0	0	3	7	4	116	13	1	.099	.118	.110	.228
Nola, Aaron	R	271	24	6	0	0	15	12	21	158	24	4	.089	.156	.111	.267
Peralta, Wily	R	201	20	4	0	1	8	11	8	83	23	4	.100	.133	.134	.267
Quintana, Jose	R	156	12	1	0	0	4	7	3	84	24	4	.077	.094	.083	.177
Ray, Robbie	L	237	34	6	0	1	11	9	4	116	26	3	.143	.157	.181	.338
Ross, Joe	R	157	29	4	0	0	7	5	6	69	10	4	.185	.224	.210	.434
Ryu, Hyun-Jin	R	217	38	8	1	1	19	12	12	96	32	1	.175	.222	.235	.457
Scherzer, Max	R	464	78	6	0	1	31	30	13	161	49	5	.168	.194	.188	.381
Strasburg, Stephen	R	440	67	10	0	4	23	29	24	153	56	6	.152	.198	.202	.400
Syndergaard, Noah	L	222	34	7	0	6	14	15	15	144	13	2	.153	.206	.266	.472
Teheran, Julio	R	382	56	6	0	1	10	26	9	112	67	3	.147	.169	.170	.339
Velasquez, Vince	R	157	32	2	0	1	9	8	6	49	17	5	.204	.233	.236	.469
Wacha, Michael	R	251	23	2	0	0	16	9	9	125	29	3	.092	.123	.100	.222
Wainwright, Adam	R	742	143	39	2	10	55	75	27	249	74	11	.193	.220	.291	.511
Wheeler, Zack	L	288	44	9	0	1	13	18	5	128	27	2	.153	.172	.194	.367
Williams, Trevor	R	146	18	0	0	0	8	6	9	57	18	1	.123	.174	.123	.297
Wood, Alex	R	276	23	2	0	0	8	12	14	171	33	3	.083	.128	.091	.218

Lords of the Flies

Sarah Thompson

Just as we all expected—a home run leaderboard topped by a catcher and a player with both a Hall-of-Fame legacy and enormous public expectations, followed by a pitcher and a second baseman coming off a sub-.700 OPS season. Power came from all kinds of interesting places this season.

Salvador Perez is your Big Fly king, blasting 48 fly balls over the fence in 2021. He never hit a cheapy, either—his shortest home run went 330 feet, and he has the fourth-most homers that went at least 400 feet (28). Setting a record for most home runs hit by a player whose primary position was catcher and dethroning one of the best catchers in baseball history in the process is a pretty impressive feat. It doesn't get much cooler than that.

Until you remember the other history being made this season—pitcher Shohei Ohtani was only two home runs shy of the MLB lead. Ohtani tops a different leaderboard—the number of home runs hit at least 400 feet, with 34. That composes 74% of his total HR count. One of those 400-footers was hit in a game in which he pitched 8 innings and struck out 8. He allowed a home run in the 5th and hit his own in the 8th.

Jorge Soler didn't hit as many home runs as some (27), but he has the largest proportion of home runs hit that were at least 400 feet. Twenty-three of his 27 dingers were hit that far—the rest were hit between the meager distances of 380 and 399.

In the tables that follow, batted balls are grouped by their distance. Each group includes balls within 10 feet in either direction of the distance listed. The 390 group contains balls hit anywhere between 380 and 399 feet. The Long column includes the total number of long fly ball outs (hit at least 300 feet), and the HR column excludes inside-the-park home runs.

The tables include only players who have hit at least 15 home runs or at least 50 long fly outs.

Long Outs and Home Runs

Player	Long Out Distances						Home Run Distances					
	330	350	370	390	400+	Long	330	350	370	390	400+	HR
Guerrero Jr., Vladimir	27	9	11	5	0	66	0	3	5	9	31	48
Perez, Salvador	14	12	10	7	2	55	0	3	11	6	28	48
Ohtani, Shohei	16	13	6	4	0	57	0	1	5	6	34	46
Semien, Marcus	29	18	12	7	0	92	1	4	12	14	14	45
Tatis Jr., Fernando	8	11	8	6	0	48	1	0	3	7	31	42
Lowe, Brandon	15	11	10	4	0	59	0	4	7	5	23	39
Haniger, Mitch	15	19	10	7	0	62	0	0	8	9	22	39
Judge, Aaron	22	11	13	4	1	60	0	5	3	9	22	39
Olson, Matt	20	13	12	5	1	68	0	2	4	12	21	39
Devers, Rafael	11	15	10	3	1	57	0	1	2	9	26	38
Duvall, Adam	14	4	11	6	0	48	0	0	5	7	26	38
Gallo, Joey	11	5	6	3	1	32	1	2	3	10	22	38
Alonso, Pete	14	16	14	4	3	69	0	1	5	8	23	37
Muncy, Max	11	11	13	7	1	58	0	0	5	4	27	36
Votto, Joey	12	11	8	6	0	50	0	1	7	7	21	36
Ramirez, Jose	21	15	11	6	0	72	0	6	7	10	13	36
Stanton, Giancarlo	10	11	3	2	0	38	0	4	3	5	23	35
Seager, Kyle	22	24	15	7	3	91	0	4	2	7	22	35
O'Neill, Tyler	11	11	5	3	1	38	0	0	5	5	24	34
Harper, Bryce	11	10	7	7	0	48	0	2	4	6	22	34
Castellanos, Nick	18	16	11	4	0	69	0	2	5	7	20	34
Arenado, Nolan	29	20	21	4	1	88	0	2	9	16	7	34
Alvarez, Yordan	15	17	9	2	3	62	0	3	4	3	23	33
Riley, Austin	6	13	7	3	1	44	0	0	6	7	20	33
Zunino, Mike	8	3	5	4	0	28	0	4	5	7	17	33
Polanco, Jorge	25	13	12	7	0	76	0	2	4	11	16	33
Mountcastle, Ryan	19	16	6	5	0	57	0	4	2	12	15	33
Schwarber, Kyle	12	4	6	3	0	34	0	0	3	6	23	32
Cruz, Nelson	16	14	8	5	2	62	0	1	6	4	21	32
Hernandez, Teoscar	26	10	8	3	0	63	0	3	3	8	18	32
Goldschmidt, Paul	23	16	16	9	2	88	0	0	3	2	26	31
Renfroe, Hunter	8	8	7	4	1	43	0	0	5	2	24	31
Freeman, Freddie	20	14	15	3	0	70	0	0	3	6	22	31
Suarez, Eugenio	12	9	8	4	1	51	0	2	2	9	18	31
Baez, Javier	6	7	3	3	1	29	0	2	3	9	17	31
Garcia, Adolis	15	12	15	3	3	60	0	1	9	4	17	31
Altuve, Jose	24	16	8	5	0	73	2	3	7	12	7	31
Reyes, Franmil	5	6	7	4	1	26	0	4	1	2	23	30
Sano, Miguel	10	7	2	3	0	31	0	3	3	1	23	30
Abreu, Jose	15	11	7	5	0	51	0	3	3	5	19	30
Albies, Ozzie	21	23	13	8	0	85	0	0	5	9	16	30
Tucker, Kyle	25	18	10	7	4	76	0	3	5	8	14	30
Mullins II, Cedric	15	16	9	6	0	63	0	1	3	14	12	30
Belt, Brandon	6	9	4	2	1	28	1	0	8	2	18	29
Garcia, Avisail	7	8	5	6	0	38	0	3	2	7	17	29
Bichette, Bo	17	8	9	5	0	55	0	0	5	9	15	29
Walsh, Jared	9	8	7	2	0	32	0	1	4	10	14	29
Soto, Juan	13	14	6	4	0	45	0	2	5	8	14	29
Cron, C.J.	13	10	7	2	0	49	0	1	0	7	20	28
Turner, Trea	18	14	7	7	0	61	0	1	2	5	20	28
Escobar, Eduardo	20	14	10	8	0	65	1	0	3	5	19	28
Wisdom, Patrick	8	5	5	2	0	28	0	0	3	8	17	28
Martinez, J.D.	16	17	16	7	1	72	1	3	1	7	16	28
Machado, Manny	17	16	15	5	1	75	0	2	4	7	15	28
Soler, Jorge	9	13	11	4	1	54	0	0	0	4	23	27
Chapman, Matt	7	11	6	6	2	47	0	1	0	5	21	27
Bell, Josh	14	8	4	5	0	40	0	0	2	6	19	27
Hoskins, Rhys	12	13	3	2	1	48	0	1	4	3	19	27
McCutchen, Andrew	9	12	11	7	0	56	0	1	5	5	16	27
Swanson, Dansby	17	12	6	9	0	66	0	0	4	9	14	27
Turner, Justin	21	26	18	3	0	78	0	2	3	13	9	27
Donaldson, Josh	15	9	9	4	2	50	0	0	3	4	19	26
Meadows, Austin	24	16	6	10	0	71	2	0	5	7	12	26
Correa, Carlos	8	16	6	7	1	52	1	3	6	8	7	26
Yastrzemski, Mike	13	9	11	4	0	51	0	2	2	6	15	25
Dalbec, Bobby	12	6	5	5	0	38	0	1	4	7	13	25
Adames, Willy	16	8	9	8	2	56	0	2	4	7	12	25
Happ, Ian	12	11	3	4	0	38	0	0	6	8	11	25
Smith, Will	18	15	10	5	0	56	0	2	4	9	10	25
Bryant, Kris	16	21	7	2	0	56	0	2	6	7	10	25
Acuna Jr., Ronald	10	4	6	4	0	32	0	1	2	3	18	24
Story, Trevor	16	13	8	8	4	62	0	1	2	4	17	24
Reynolds, Bryan	20	22	5	3	1	65	0	0	2	8	14	24

Long Outs and Home Runs

Player	Long Out Distances						Home Run Distances					
	330	350	370	390	400+	Long	330	350	370	390	400+	HR
Winker, Jesse	12	6	7	7	0	45	0	0	3	7	14	24
Crawford, Brandon	15	17	10	6	0	59	0	1	5	6	12	24
McMahon, Ryan	13	13	12	5	2	63	0	0	3	5	15	23
Sanchez, Gary	5	8	3	3	0	29	0	1	4	3	15	23
Bogaerts, Xander	10	12	9	7	0	52	0	2	4	2	15	23
Grandal, Yasmani	6	7	3	3	0	28	0	0	4	6	13	23
Betts, Mookie	13	22	9	6	1	61	0	1	3	8	11	23
Urias, Luis	16	12	8	7	0	54	0	0	2	12	9	23
Grossman, Robbie	28	14	8	5	0	82	0	3	4	8	8	23
Rizzo, Anthony	18	8	7	3	0	54	0	0	4	5	13	22
Springer, George	8	6	6	2	0	25	0	3	2	5	12	22
Grichuk, Randal	17	13	7	4	1	58	0	0	6	4	12	22
Aguilar, Jesus	22	16	14	1	1	74	0	1	4	7	10	22
Schoop, Jonathan	15	13	3	3	1	50	0	0	5	8	9	22
Hays, Austin	12	15	7	5	1	48	0	1	4	7	9	22
Haase, Eric	11	3	1	1	1	29	0	0	5	1	15	21
India, Jonathan	14	12	7	3	0	44	0	0	2	5	14	21
Contreras, Willson	15	12	3	5	0	41	0	0	2	5	14	21
Mancini, Trey	17	8	8	2	0	51	0	0	4	3	14	21
Pollock, A.J.	10	12	8	4	0	52	0	0	3	5	13	21
Gurriel Jr., Lourdes	13	9	7	8	0	52	1	0	3	5	12	21
Hernandez, Cesar	24	9	14	5	0	65	0	2	3	6	10	21
Miller, Brad	5	10	3	2	1	27	0	2	2	4	12	20
Arozarena, Randy	11	7	6	3	0	37	0	3	2	3	12	20
Taylor, Chris	20	6	12	0	0	54	0	0	2	7	11	20
Brown, Seth	10	4	5	0	1	32	0	3	2	4	11	20
Hernandez, Kike	20	19	10	7	1	72	0	2	4	6	8	20
Lindor, Francisco	11	14	10	5	0	60	0	2	3	9	6	20
Santana, Carlos	21	16	11	7	2	74	0	2	1	1	15	19
Buxton, Byron	3	4	2	1	0	19	0	1	0	5	13	19
Naquin, Tyler	12	4	10	1	0	36	0	0	2	5	12	19
DeJong, Paul	11	14	7	2	1	45	0	1	2	5	11	19
Cronenworth, Jake	14	16	6	4	1	59	0	0	1	8	10	19
Kepler, Max	17	12	10	4	1	55	0	2	2	6	9	19
Pederson, Joc	11	11	13	5	2	53	0	0	2	3	13	18
Lowe, Nathaniel	19	10	6	6	0	56	0	0	2	3	13	18
Santander, Anthony	9	10	3	3	1	38	0	0	1	6	11	18
France, Ty	11	10	16	1	0	61	0	0	2	6	10	18
Villar, Jonathan	6	8	7	1	0	28	0	0	2	7	9	18
Wade Jr., LaMonte	14	13	5	3	0	42	0	1	5	3	9	18
Carlson, Dylan	25	9	11	5	2	73	0	1	2	7	8	18
Diaz, Elias	5	12	5	4	1	35	0	2	1	7	8	18
Flores, Wilmer	12	15	8	2	0	52	0	1	3	7	7	18
Posey, Buster	5	7	7	0	1	33	0	1	5	7	5	18
Murphy, Sean	12	8	7	1	1	38	0	0	2	3	12	17
Chisholm Jr., Jazz	12	8	3	2	0	39	0	0	3	2	12	17
Upton, Justin	7	5	7	1	0	25	0	0	4	2	11	17
Pujols, Albert	12	6	6	1	0	31	0	1	2	4	10	17
Myers, Wil	14	3	9	3	1	42	0	3	1	5	8	17
Benintendi, Andrew	15	17	19	7	1	81	0	0	4	8	5	17
Anderson, Tim	20	10	4	4	0	48	0	0	4	9	4	17
Canha, Mark	14	10	12	2	1	53	0	2	5	6	4	17
Realmuto, J.T.	16	5	6	4	0	46	0	4	3	7	3	17
Seager, Corey	10	12	8	4	0	48	0	0	1	6	9	16
Dozier, Hunter	21	12	6	5	0	61	0	0	1	7	8	16
Ruf, Darin	7	6	2	1	1	24	0	0	3	5	8	16
Candelario, Jeimer	11	9	15	5	0	53	1	1	3	3	8	16
Farmer, Kyle	18	16	8	5	0	62	0	0	2	7	7	16
Bader, Harrison	8	9	9	1	0	35	0	1	2	6	7	16
Vaughn, Andrew	16	9	9	10	0	53	0	2	0	3	10	15
Odor, Rougned	9	5	4	4	0	30	1	0	3	1	10	15
Rodgers, Brendan	6	12	5	5	0	37	0	0	1	5	9	15
Cabrera, Miguel	15	15	10	3	2	59	0	2	2	4	7	15
Pham, Tommy	16	12	7	7	2	57	0	0	1	8	6	15
Pillar, Kevin	15	7	3	4	1	40	0	0	3	6	6	15
Torrens, Luis	9	6	6	2	0	33	1	0	5	4	5	15
Grisham, Trent	10	12	6	2	1	45	1	0	4	6	4	15
Gurriel, Yuli	28	20	6	3	0	66	0	1	1	9	3	15
Moncada, Yoan	13	10	8	3	0	50	0	1	1	3	9	14
Rosario, Eddie	10	11	8	7	0	52	0	1	3	4	6	14
Lowrie, Jed	21	14	14	7	0	61	0	0	3	6	5	14
Wong, Kolten	19	12	10	3	0	57	0	0	4	6	4	14
Verdugo, Alex	8	7	8	5	0	51	0	2	0	2	9	13
Blackmon, Charlie	19	11	12	1	2	61	0	0	1	4	8	13
Diaz, Yandy	15	14	8	6	0	59	0	2	2	3	6	13
Taylor, Michael A.	20	11	5	5	0	61	0	1	1	4	6	12

457

Long Outs and Home Runs

Player	Long Out Distances						Home Run Distances					
	330	350	370	390	400+	Long	330	350	370	390	400+	HR
Edman, Tommy	16	20	13	5	0	71	0	0	2	1	8	11
Smith, Pavin	14	14	12	6	0	58	0	1	1	1	8	11
Hampson, Garrett	16	14	13	8	2	62	0	1	2	1	7	11
Smith, Dominic	16	16	11	3	0	59	0	0	3	3	5	11
Molina, Yadier	23	15	16	4	0	69	0	1	3	3	4	11
Narvaez, Omar	14	13	4	4	0	56	0	0	1	7	3	11
Toro, Abraham	15	8	8	5	0	52	0	2	4	2	3	11
Merrifield, Whit	27	20	17	4	0	98	0	1	2	5	2	10
LeMahieu, DJ	22	9	7	6	1	60	1	2	3	3	1	10
Rojas, Miguel	16	7	8	1	0	54	0	0	1	3	5	9
Torres, Gleyber	9	11	9	8	1	51	0	2	0	3	4	9
Iglesias, Jose	13	17	6	0	0	53	0	0	1	5	3	9
Crawford, J.P.	15	15	4	1	0	53	0	2	2	3	2	9
Brantley, Michael	12	10	10	4	0	51	0	0	2	1	5	8
Harrison, Josh	11	20	15	4	0	69	0	0	2	2	4	8
Kiner-Falefa, Isiah	16	15	8	3	0	60	0	0	1	4	3	8
Kemp, Tony	10	15	6	2	0	52	0	5	2	1	0	8
Vazquez, Christian	13	10	9	2	0	58	0	0	1	4	1	6
Newman, Kevin	18	14	11	2	0	67	0	1	0	3	1	5
Frazier, Adam	19	18	7	0	0	61	0	0	2	3	0	5
Straw, Myles	15	14	8	1	0	59	1	1	1	0	1	4
Andrus, Elvis	10	24	6	3	1	60	0	0	1	0	2	3
Arraez, Luis	18	17	6	3	0	64	0	0	0	1	1	2

Hard Hit Balls

Lindsay Zeck

Both home runs and the hard-hit ball rate were down this season:

Season	Home Runs	Hard-Hit Rate
2019	6,776	38.0%
2020	6,325*	33.2%
2021	5,944	32.1%

*Home Run total prorated due to shortened 2020 season

Many of this season's home run leaders show up at the top of this section's leaderboard for hard hit ball percentage. Salvador Perez, Shohei Ohtani, Fernando Tatis Jr., and Aaron Judge all finished in the top 10 of both home runs and hard-hit rate. However, Evan Longoria, who hit 43.3% of his balls in play hard (10th overall), hit only 13 home runs. Conversely, Marcus Semien, who finished the season with the fourth-most home runs (45), finished 93rd on this section's leaderboard with a 36.0% hard hit rate.

There were also players who went against the declining hard-hit balls trend. Juan Lagares more than doubled his combined 2019-2020 hard-hit balls percentage (18.8% to 37.8%). Joey Votto finished sixth on the leaderboard, increasing his 2019-2020 percentage by just over 10 points.

For the second season in a row, Tatis Jr. led all of MLB in hard-hit percentage at 48%. His .898 slugging percentage on balls in play (including home runs), trailed only three players: Patrick Wisdom (.946), Mike Zunino (.925), and Ohtani (.914).

Wisdom, as the MLB leader in slugging percentage on balls in play, also hit 28 home runs. He hit a home run in 7.5 percent of his plate appearances. Out of all players with at least 250 plate appearances, he trailed only Zunino (8.8%), Tatis Jr. (7.7%), Brandon Belt (7.6%), and Byron Buxton (7.5%, just ahead of Wisdom).

This section includes the leaderboard of hard, medium, and soft hit rates, reported by batted ball. It also includes count and slugging percentage for each. Players with at least 250 plate appearances in 2021 are included.

Hard Hit Balls
Highest Percentage of Hard Hit Balls - Players with 250+ PA in 2021

Player	In Play	Hard Count	Hard SLG	Medium Count	Medium SLG	Soft Count	Soft SLG	Hard Pct	Medium Pct	Soft Pct	SLG
Tatis Jr., Fernando	329	158	1.506	122	.342	49	.327	48.0%	37.1%	14.9%	.898
Judge, Aaron	397	186	1.268	177	.314	34	.353	46.9%	44.6%	8.6%	.763
Sano, Miguel	288	131	1.454	114	.237	43	.070	45.5%	39.6%	14.9%	.763
Wisdom, Patrick	185	84	1.702	74	.365	27	.185	45.4%	40.0%	14.6%	.946
Ohtani, Shohei	350	158	1.618	154	.359	38	.237	45.1%	44.0%	10.9%	.914
Votto, Joey	325	146	1.379	153	.320	26	.154	44.9%	47.1%	8.0%	.785
Perez, Salvador	454	199	1.423	194	.254	61	.148	43.8%	42.7%	13.4%	.749
Reyes, Franmil	272	119	1.496	111	.327	42	.167	43.8%	40.8%	15.4%	.810
Harper, Bryce	360	156	1.374	158	.458	46	.370	43.3%	43.9%	12.8%	.847
Longoria, Evan	187	81	1.175	92	.275	14	.214	43.3%	49.2%	7.5%	.659
Miller, Brad	219	94	1.287	93	.258	32	.156	42.9%	42.5%	14.6%	.685
O'Neill, Tyler	318	136	1.614	137	.321	45	.289	42.8%	43.1%	14.2%	.860
Buxton, Byron	173	74	1.635	75	.307	24	.333	42.8%	43.4%	13.9%	.879
Thomas, Lane	164	70	.928	67	.388	27	.111	42.7%	40.9%	16.5%	.571
Grandal, Yasmani	203	86	1.458	87	.250	30	.100	42.4%	42.9%	14.8%	.736
Guerrero Jr., Vladimir	496	207	1.415	236	.284	53	.113	41.7%	47.6%	10.7%	.735
Stanton, Giancarlo	356	148	1.442	151	.295	57	.123	41.6%	42.4%	16.0%	.745
Goldschmidt, Paul	472	195	1.155	220	.352	57	.175	41.3%	46.6%	12.1%	.664
Seager, Corey	290	119	1.145	138	.292	33	.303	41.0%	47.6%	11.4%	.641
Betts, Mookie	385	158	1.117	174	.272	53	.151	41.0%	45.2%	13.8%	.597
Machado, Manny	473	193	1.101	207	.245	73	.260	40.8%	43.8%	15.4%	.597
Zunino, Mike	202	82	1.866	70	.420	50	.080	40.6%	34.7%	24.8%	.925
Turner, Justin	441	179	.971	212	.360	50	.120	40.6%	48.1%	11.3%	.577
Moncada, Yoan	365	148	.905	164	.401	53	.283	40.5%	44.9%	14.5%	.590
Castellanos, Nick	416	168	1.354	198	.378	50	.200	40.4%	47.6%	12.0%	.746
Ruf, Darin	176	71	1.451	82	.333	23	.261	40.3%	46.6%	13.1%	.777
Donaldson, Josh	351	141	1.225	167	.265	43	.116	40.2%	47.6%	12.3%	.633
Devers, Rafael	451	181	1.307	192	.363	78	.167	40.1%	42.6%	17.3%	.711
Marte, Ketel	281	112	1.108	135	.393	34	.147	39.9%	48.0%	12.1%	.646
Ramirez, Jose	470	187	1.196	197	.364	86	.070	39.8%	41.9%	18.3%	.639
Jeffers, Ryan	159	63	1.238	72	.278	24	.375	39.6%	45.3%	15.1%	.673
Bote, David	222	88	.816	95	.196	39	.179	39.6%	42.8%	17.6%	.440
Alvarez, Yordan	395	156	1.297	188	.366	51	.314	39.5%	47.6%	12.9%	.727
Marsh, Brandon	147	58	.845	83	.420	6	.167	39.5%	56.5%	4.1%	.579
Muncy, Max	378	149	1.369	181	.289	48	.125	39.4%	47.9%	12.7%	.695
Tucker, Kyle	421	165	1.195	213	.373	43	.186	39.2%	50.6%	10.2%	.678
Contreras, Willson	279	109	1.234	135	.323	35	.171	39.1%	48.4%	12.5%	.658
Schwarber, Kyle	274	107	1.733	125	.248	42	.190	39.1%	45.6%	15.3%	.813
Soto, Juan	414	162	1.222	186	.341	66	.182	39.1%	44.9%	15.9%	.655
Garcia, Adolis	391	152	1.293	203	.313	36	.194	38.9%	51.9%	9.2%	.682
Zimmerman, Ryan	180	70	1.309	77	.338	33	.152	38.9%	42.8%	18.3%	.674
Bradley, Bobby	149	58	1.466	71	.338	20	.050	38.9%	47.7%	13.4%	.747
Martinez, J.D.	425	165	1.172	215	.439	45	.244	38.8%	50.6%	10.6%	.702
Acuna Jr., Ronald	217	84	1.646	105	.333	28	.286	38.7%	48.4%	12.9%	.835
Belt, Brandon	223	86	1.812	102	.324	35	.200	38.6%	45.7%	15.7%	.874
Choi, Ji-Man	171	66	1.045	78	.397	27	.222	38.6%	45.6%	15.8%	.620
McMahon, Ryan	386	149	1.109	188	.341	49	.224	38.6%	48.7%	12.7%	.622
Freeman, Freddie	495	190	1.122	247	.305	58	.259	38.4%	49.9%	11.7%	.613
Story, Trevor	392	150	1.228	186	.333	56	.143	38.3%	47.4%	14.3%	.641
Cruz, Nelson	396	151	1.297	181	.303	64	.156	38.1%	45.7%	16.2%	.659
Murphy, Tom	181	69	1.060	75	.311	37	.081	38.1%	41.4%	20.4%	.545
Bohm, Alec	273	104	.843	136	.299	33	.121	38.1%	49.8%	12.1%	.483
Sanchez, Jesus	150	57	1.446	73	.384	20	.100	38.0%	48.7%	13.3%	.745
Rodgers, Brendan	305	116	1.191	135	.246	54	.222	38.0%	44.3%	17.7%	.601
Pujols, Albert	232	88	1.045	104	.206	40	.150	37.9%	44.8%	17.2%	.517
Alonso, Pete	438	166	1.364	204	.264	68	.191	37.9%	46.6%	15.5%	.671
Gallo, Joey	286	108	1.701	135	.304	43	.116	37.8%	47.2%	15.0%	.800
Lagares, Juan	238	90	.809	110	.358	38	.132	37.8%	46.2%	16.0%	.494
Dalbec, Bobby	262	99	1.586	137	.346	26	.077	37.8%	52.3%	9.9%	.789
Nunez, Dom	138	52	1.412	62	.258	24	.125	37.7%	44.9%	17.4%	.664
Adames, Willy	342	129	1.302	165	.360	48	.250	37.7%	48.2%	14.0%	.701
Pollock, A.J.	306	115	1.281	149	.318	42	.310	37.6%	48.7%	13.7%	.678
Bell, Josh	400	150	1.195	202	.265	48	.125	37.5%	50.5%	12.0%	.597
Garcia, Avisail	345	129	1.315	164	.273	52	.288	37.4%	47.5%	15.1%	.665
Abreu, Jose	433	162	1.289	218	.289	53	.113	37.4%	50.3%	12.2%	.643
Wade Jr., LaMonte	254	95	1.301	130	.272	29	.241	37.4%	51.2%	11.4%	.656
Smith, Will	324	121	1.333	164	.269	39	.256	37.3%	50.6%	12.0%	.655
Haniger, Mitch	459	171	1.347	201	.299	87	.195	37.3%	43.8%	19.0%	.667
Cabrera, Miguel	363	135	.908	186	.324	42	.119	37.2%	51.2%	11.6%	.514
Soler, Jorge	378	140	1.252	180	.250	58	.086	37.0%	47.6%	15.3%	.598
Pham, Tommy	351	130	.977	172	.290	49	.143	37.0%	49.0%	14.0%	.524
Tsutsugo, Yoshi	160	59	.949	79	.312	22	.364	36.9%	49.4%	13.8%	.557

460

Hard Hit Balls

Highest Percentage of Hard Hit Balls - Players with 250+ PA in 2021

Player	In Play	Hard		Medium		Soft		Overall			
		Count	SLG	Count	SLG	Count	SLG	Hard Pct	Medium Pct	Soft Pct	SLG
Seager, Kyle	446	164	1.142	207	.302	75	.227	36.8%	46.4%	16.8%	.597
Conforto, Michael	304	112	.911	149	.306	43	.209	36.8%	49.0%	14.1%	.517
Baez, Javier	321	118	1.569	142	.298	61	.393	36.8%	44.2%	19.0%	.780
Lowrie, Jed	353	130	.977	181	.292	42	.095	36.8%	51.3%	11.9%	.521
Polanco, Gregory	240	88	.988	104	.248	48	.250	36.7%	43.3%	20.0%	.513
Hernandez, Teoscar	404	148	1.243	204	.446	52	.269	36.6%	50.5%	12.9%	.716
Correa, Carlos	445	163	1.110	207	.368	75	.187	36.6%	46.5%	16.9%	.613
Dozier, Hunter	339	124	1.082	173	.320	42	.143	36.6%	51.0%	12.4%	.577
Heim, Jonah	211	77	.959	78	.234	56	.107	36.5%	37.0%	26.5%	.459
Winker, Jesse	348	127	1.252	166	.392	55	.200	36.5%	47.7%	15.8%	.675
McCutchen, Andrew	357	130	1.214	172	.314	55	.145	36.4%	48.2%	15.4%	.611
Bichette, Bo	507	184	1.154	248	.333	75	.240	36.3%	48.9%	14.8%	.616
Haase, Eric	234	85	1.518	115	.230	34	.176	36.3%	49.1%	14.5%	.694
Olson, Matt	463	168	1.404	205	.328	90	.144	36.3%	44.3%	19.4%	.675
Alfaro, Jorge	196	71	.944	93	.280	32	.250	36.2%	47.4%	16.3%	.515
Farmer, Kyle	392	142	.943	190	.323	60	.150	36.2%	48.5%	15.3%	.521
Cron, C.J.	357	129	1.430	167	.335	61	.180	36.1%	46.8%	17.1%	.705
Bryant, Kris	380	137	1.299	179	.316	64	.203	36.1%	47.1%	16.8%	.653
Naquin, Tyler	308	111	1.264	151	.302	46	.261	36.0%	49.0%	14.9%	.643
Upton, Justin	214	77	1.342	101	.232	36	.139	36.0%	47.2%	16.8%	.616
Semien, Marcus	509	183	1.464	249	.258	77	.286	36.0%	48.9%	15.1%	.694
Walsh, Jared	381	137	1.419	176	.345	68	.250	36.0%	46.2%	17.8%	.714
Duvall, Adam	342	123	1.719	155	.214	64	.172	36.0%	45.3%	18.7%	.743
Renfroe, Hunter	397	143	1.371	179	.341	75	.120	36.0%	45.1%	18.9%	.668
Santander, Anthony	310	111	1.155	145	.284	54	.167	35.8%	46.8%	17.4%	.577
Aguilar, Jesus	363	130	1.086	181	.318	52	.212	35.8%	49.9%	14.3%	.579
McCormick, Chas	187	67	1.364	98	.337	22	.273	35.8%	52.4%	11.8%	.706
Realmuto, J.T.	349	125	1.130	162	.296	62	.355	35.8%	46.4%	17.8%	.602
VanMeter, Josh	193	69	.882	94	.355	30	.133	35.8%	48.7%	15.5%	.508
Lowe, Nathaniel	398	142	1.057	198	.337	58	.276	35.7%	49.7%	14.6%	.585
Hayes, Ke'Bryan	277	99	.848	126	.331	52	.192	35.7%	45.5%	18.8%	.491
Walker, Christian	297	106	.905	147	.363	44	.114	35.7%	49.5%	14.8%	.519
Tellez, Rowdy	233	83	1.122	113	.248	37	.081	35.6%	48.5%	15.9%	.530
Torrens, Luis	250	89	1.314	118	.246	43	.163	35.6%	47.2%	17.2%	.603
Kepler, Max	334	119	1.094	160	.234	55	.200	35.6%	47.9%	16.5%	.533
Alcantara, Sergio	149	53	.923	71	.304	25	.120	35.6%	47.7%	16.8%	.493
Robert, Luis	216	77	1.307	111	.468	28	.214	35.6%	51.4%	13.0%	.729
Hernandez, Kike	405	144	1.107	199	.337	62	.113	35.6%	49.1%	15.3%	.573
Urias, Ramon	186	66	.939	86	.453	34	.206	35.5%	46.2%	18.3%	.581
Vaughn, Andrew	321	114	.982	163	.290	44	.227	35.5%	50.8%	13.7%	.522
Lowe, Brandon	371	131	1.569	174	.326	66	.303	35.3%	46.9%	17.8%	.761
Hampson, Garrett	340	120	.815	178	.362	42	.286	35.3%	52.4%	12.4%	.513
Ramirez, Harold	286	101	.911	136	.256	49	.184	35.3%	47.6%	17.1%	.477
Riley, Austin	430	152	1.424	194	.383	84	.313	35.3%	45.1%	19.5%	.742
Bogaerts, Xander	423	149	1.075	207	.438	67	.224	35.2%	48.9%	15.8%	.627
Diaz, Elias	279	98	1.206	124	.274	57	.105	35.1%	44.4%	20.4%	.565
Meadows, Austin	404	142	1.252	192	.230	70	.286	35.1%	47.5%	17.3%	.598
Smith, Dominic	340	119	.896	180	.287	41	.195	35.0%	52.9%	12.1%	.485
Turner, Trea	489	171	1.214	235	.389	83	.289	35.0%	48.1%	17.0%	.658
Benintendi, Andrew	403	141	.971	217	.355	45	.200	35.0%	53.8%	11.2%	.551
Urias, Luis	378	132	1.206	174	.310	72	.097	34.9%	46.0%	19.0%	.583
Gomes, Yan	272	95	1.084	135	.269	42	.190	34.9%	49.6%	15.4%	.542
Yelich, Christian	289	101	.899	142	.326	46	.304	34.9%	49.1%	15.9%	.521
Suarez, Eugenio	339	118	1.448	168	.224	53	.208	34.8%	49.6%	15.6%	.647
Albies, Ozzie	508	177	1.218	259	.333	72	.139	34.8%	51.0%	14.2%	.613
Phillips, Brett	144	50	1.440	77	.370	17	.353	34.7%	53.5%	11.8%	.750
Escobar, Eduardo	426	148	1.291	206	.293	72	.111	34.7%	48.4%	16.9%	.609
Diaz, Yandy	384	133	.802	192	.311	59	.271	34.6%	50.0%	15.4%	.474
Smith, Pavin	393	136	.874	178	.365	79	.228	34.6%	45.3%	20.1%	.513
Diaz, Aledmys	232	80	.938	112	.357	40	.100	34.5%	48.3%	17.2%	.513
Brantley, Michael	417	144	.799	216	.363	57	.211	34.5%	51.8%	13.7%	.493
Reynolds, Bryan	443	153	1.250	223	.377	67	.284	34.5%	50.3%	15.1%	.665
DeJong, Paul	255	88	1.291	125	.192	42	.095	34.5%	49.0%	16.5%	.549
Springer, George	221	76	1.579	102	.396	43	.140	34.4%	46.2%	19.5%	.755
Calhoun, Willie	227	78	.744	119	.339	30	.033	34.4%	52.4%	13.2%	.438
Hoskins, Rhys	283	97	1.629	150	.291	36	.139	34.3%	53.0%	12.7%	.733
Happ, Ian	312	107	1.274	156	.312	49	.388	34.3%	50.0%	15.7%	.654
Zimmer, Bradley	181	62	1.117	92	.322	27	.259	34.3%	50.8%	14.9%	.582
Dickerson, Corey	269	92	.891	123	.311	54	.315	34.2%	45.7%	20.1%	.511
Pederson, Joc	317	108	1.114	164	.364	45	.111	34.1%	51.7%	14.2%	.580
India, Jonathan	396	135	1.231	199	.354	62	.161	34.1%	50.3%	15.7%	.624
Mancini, Trey	414	141	1.107	196	.332	77	.260	34.1%	47.3%	18.6%	.581
Taylor, Tyrone	185	63	1.111	89	.386	33	.212	34.1%	48.1%	17.8%	.603

Hard Hit Balls
Highest Percentage of Hard Hit Balls - Players with 250+ PA in 2021

Player	In Play	Hard Count	Hard SLG	Medium Count	Medium SLG	Soft Count	Soft SLG	Hard Pct	Medium Pct	Soft Pct	SLG
Bradley Jr., Jackie	258	88	.851	131	.194	39	.051	34.1%	50.8%	15.1%	.396
Brown, Seth	194	66	1.754	86	.212	42	.071	34.0%	44.3%	21.6%	.703
Gamel, Ben	241	82	.975	129	.368	30	.267	34.0%	53.5%	12.4%	.562
Murphy, Sean	282	96	1.213	133	.250	53	.226	34.0%	47.2%	18.8%	.570
Wong, Kolten	365	124	1.106	192	.258	49	.286	34.0%	52.6%	13.4%	.550
O'Hearn, Ryan	168	57	.911	88	.360	23	.217	33.9%	52.4%	13.7%	.527
Nimmo, Brandon	248	84	.964	115	.389	49	.347	33.9%	46.4%	19.8%	.577
Mountcastle, Ryan	380	129	1.376	189	.387	62	.258	33.9%	49.7%	16.3%	.697
Varsho, Daulton	218	74	1.189	100	.323	44	.091	33.9%	45.9%	20.2%	.571
Santana, Carlos	467	158	.904	225	.186	84	.119	33.8%	48.2%	18.0%	.418
Cooper, Garrett	148	50	1.320	77	.382	21	.238	33.8%	52.0%	14.2%	.680
Gurriel, Yuli	474	160	.929	234	.395	80	.150	33.8%	49.4%	16.9%	.530
Anderson, Tim	409	138	1.051	214	.366	57	.421	33.7%	52.3%	13.9%	.605
Stallings, Jacob	291	98	.847	148	.315	45	.200	33.7%	50.9%	15.5%	.478
Grichuk, Randal	401	135	1.159	199	.278	67	.119	33.7%	49.6%	16.7%	.544
Arenado, Nolan	504	170	1.212	245	.342	89	.112	33.7%	48.6%	17.7%	.590
Larnach, Trevor	158	53	1.245	85	.241	20	.250	33.5%	53.8%	12.7%	.583
France, Ty	471	158	1.052	232	.323	81	.210	33.5%	49.3%	17.2%	.546
Barnhart, Tucker	251	84	.927	134	.323	33	.273	33.5%	53.4%	13.1%	.516
Vogelbach, Daniel	158	53	1.094	84	.238	21	.190	33.5%	53.2%	13.3%	.519
Polanco, Jorge	476	159	1.297	250	.327	67	.164	33.4%	52.5%	14.1%	.630
Candelario, Jeimer	422	141	.979	208	.404	73	.342	33.4%	49.3%	17.3%	.585
Blackmon, Charlie	426	142	.851	201	.352	83	.253	33.3%	47.2%	19.5%	.499
Swanson, Dansby	429	143	1.324	232	.303	54	.204	33.3%	54.1%	12.6%	.627
Odor, Rougned	223	74	1.216	108	.234	41	.171	33.2%	48.4%	18.4%	.550
Mullins II, Cedric	482	160	1.258	250	.378	72	.264	33.2%	51.9%	14.9%	.654
Hernandez, Yadiel	207	68	.970	119	.347	20	.150	32.9%	57.5%	9.7%	.532
Marte, Starling	371	122	1.058	179	.373	70	.271	32.9%	48.2%	18.9%	.579
Kelly, Carson	235	77	1.040	117	.342	41	.195	32.8%	49.8%	17.4%	.543
Moreland, Mitch	174	57	1.268	99	.237	18	.056	32.8%	56.9%	10.3%	.556
Taylor, Michael A.	346	113	.892	190	.303	43	.395	32.7%	54.9%	12.4%	.507
Molina, Yadier	364	119	.814	193	.335	52	.058	32.7%	53.0%	14.3%	.452
Gurriel Jr., Lourdes	405	132	1.138	221	.319	52	.308	32.6%	54.6%	12.8%	.585
Cabrera, Asdrubal	233	76	.946	122	.325	35	.114	32.6%	52.4%	15.0%	.493
Laureano, Ramon	244	79	1.392	124	.260	41	.220	32.4%	50.8%	16.8%	.621
Hosmer, Eric	413	134	.925	191	.328	88	.182	32.4%	46.2%	21.3%	.490
Lindor, Francisco	365	118	1.162	195	.225	52	.154	32.3%	53.4%	14.2%	.522
Peralta, David	397	128	.890	199	.354	70	.186	32.2%	50.1%	17.6%	.496
Rizzo, Anthony	414	133	1.143	223	.271	58	.121	32.1%	53.9%	14.0%	.533
Arozarena, Randy	364	117	1.357	181	.393	66	.258	32.1%	49.7%	18.1%	.677
Dickerson, Alex	207	66	1.303	96	.250	45	.200	31.9%	46.4%	21.7%	.575
McKinney, Billy	188	60	1.203	98	.206	30	.133	31.9%	52.1%	16.0%	.511
Pillar, Kevin	245	78	1.218	113	.286	54	.148	31.8%	46.1%	22.0%	.553
Schwindel, Frank	201	64	1.484	87	.448	50	.180	31.8%	43.3%	24.9%	.711
Diaz, Isan	170	54	.788	87	.271	29	.103	31.8%	51.2%	17.1%	.404
Crawford, Brandon	383	121	1.385	203	.396	59	.169	31.6%	53.0%	15.4%	.667
Canha, Mark	393	124	1.048	203	.289	66	.197	31.6%	51.7%	16.8%	.514
Rosario, Eddie	324	102	1.061	166	.293	56	.232	31.5%	51.2%	17.3%	.519
Taylor, Chris	344	108	1.336	184	.359	52	.269	31.4%	53.5%	15.1%	.653
Bregman, Alex	299	94	.859	158	.372	47	.213	31.4%	52.8%	15.7%	.498
Wendle, Joey	350	110	1.000	189	.390	51	.235	31.4%	54.0%	14.6%	.559
Baddoo, Akil	294	92	1.198	150	.392	52	.250	31.3%	51.0%	17.7%	.619
Severino, Pedro	275	86	1.048	128	.392	61	.131	31.3%	46.5%	22.2%	.537
Alberto, Hanser	221	69	.806	122	.314	30	.200	31.2%	55.2%	13.6%	.451
Caratini, Victor	235	73	.857	126	.280	36	.167	31.1%	53.6%	15.3%	.437
Shaw, Travis	155	48	1.362	72	.214	35	.086	31.0%	46.5%	22.6%	.539
Flores, Wilmer	336	104	1.173	184	.254	48	.125	31.0%	54.8%	14.3%	.523
Stewart, D.J.	181	56	1.339	81	.284	44	.068	30.9%	44.8%	24.3%	.558
Ibanez, Andy	220	68	.970	119	.314	33	.242	30.9%	54.1%	15.0%	.505
Chisholm Jr., Jazz	324	100	1.337	167	.274	57	.368	30.9%	51.5%	17.6%	.618
Sanchez, Gary	262	81	1.469	141	.255	40	.175	30.9%	53.8%	15.3%	.618
Goodrum, Niko	185	57	1.164	110	.327	18	.222	30.8%	59.5%	9.7%	.568
Altuve, Jose	517	159	1.173	260	.363	98	.184	30.8%	50.3%	19.0%	.576
Bellinger, Cody	224	69	.909	124	.250	31	.129	30.8%	55.4%	13.8%	.430
Garcia, Luis	198	61	1.148	105	.200	32	.188	30.8%	53.0%	16.2%	.490
Moran, Colin	234	72	1.056	127	.331	35	.200	30.8%	54.3%	15.0%	.537
Verdugo, Alex	452	139	.921	253	.379	60	.167	30.8%	56.0%	13.3%	.519
Goodwin, Brian	179	55	1.018	100	.296	24	.125	30.7%	55.9%	13.4%	.497
Castro, Starlin	257	79	.701	136	.381	42	.310	30.7%	52.9%	16.3%	.466
Gutierrez, Kelvin	196	60	.633	104	.413	32	.156	30.6%	53.1%	16.3%	.439
Heyward, Jason	255	78	.885	114	.281	63	.175	30.6%	44.7%	24.7%	.439
Hays, Austin	385	118	1.205	204	.378	63	.127	30.6%	53.0%	16.4%	.591
Posey, Buster	310	95	1.309	168	.395	47	.170	30.6%	54.2%	15.2%	.640

Hard Hit Balls
Highest Percentage of Hard Hit Balls - Players with 250+ PA in 2021

Player	In Play	Hard Count	Hard SLG	Medium Count	Medium SLG	Soft Count	Soft SLG	Hard Pct	Medium Pct	Soft Pct	SLG
Bader, Harrison	284	87	1.337	136	.259	61	.311	30.6%	47.9%	21.5%	.599
Biggio, Cavan	177	54	1.096	104	.267	19	.263	30.5%	58.8%	10.7%	.517
Schoop, Jonathan	498	152	1.180	240	.286	106	.255	30.5%	48.2%	21.3%	.553
Lux, Gavin	254	77	.711	145	.424	32	.219	30.3%	57.1%	12.6%	.484
Stassi, Max	182	55	1.509	98	.340	29	.138	30.2%	53.8%	15.9%	.663
Heredia, Guillermo	225	68	.896	110	.382	47	.128	30.2%	48.9%	20.9%	.482
Yastrzemski, Mike	341	103	1.510	189	.296	49	.102	30.2%	55.4%	14.4%	.635
Chapman, Matt	336	101	1.582	169	.252	66	.258	30.1%	50.3%	19.6%	.651
Fraley, Jake	146	44	1.140	70	.279	32	.344	30.1%	47.9%	21.9%	.552
Herrera, Odubel	379	114	.947	202	.345	63	.190	30.1%	53.3%	16.6%	.501
Trevino, Jose	233	70	.897	125	.279	38	.053	30.0%	53.6%	16.3%	.425
Toro, Abraham	283	85	.929	149	.197	49	.347	30.0%	52.7%	17.3%	.445
Myers, Wil	305	91	1.422	157	.312	57	.281	29.8%	51.5%	18.7%	.638
Margot, Manuel	356	106	.885	189	.290	61	.246	29.8%	53.1%	17.1%	.459
McCann, James	263	78	.987	144	.319	41	.268	29.7%	54.8%	15.6%	.504
Stephenson, Tyler	280	83	1.037	163	.377	34	.176	29.6%	58.2%	12.1%	.549
Grisham, Trent	348	103	1.088	189	.389	56	.143	29.6%	54.3%	16.1%	.557
Cronenworth, Jake	483	143	1.128	261	.339	79	.190	29.6%	54.0%	16.4%	.547
Cain, Lorenzo	210	62	.918	112	.348	36	.222	29.5%	53.3%	17.1%	.493
Solano, Donovan	254	75	.973	148	.306	31	.258	29.5%	58.3%	12.2%	.498
Duggar, Steven	180	53	1.264	111	.414	16	.250	29.4%	61.7%	8.9%	.650
Solak, Nick	355	104	1.000	185	.269	66	.212	29.3%	52.1%	18.6%	.473
Rojas, Josh	351	103	1.049	208	.395	40	.275	29.3%	59.3%	11.4%	.573
Kelenic, Jarred	232	68	1.224	121	.223	43	.209	29.3%	52.2%	18.5%	.511
Anderson, Brian	168	49	1.061	94	.340	25	.160	29.2%	56.0%	14.9%	.524
Edman, Tommy	552	161	.849	303	.304	88	.250	29.2%	54.9%	15.9%	.454
Franco, Wander	245	71	.971	134	.418	40	.150	29.0%	54.7%	16.3%	.533
Villar, Jonathan	324	94	1.319	158	.314	72	.222	29.0%	48.8%	22.2%	.587
Chang, Yu	169	49	1.306	82	.358	38	.211	29.0%	48.5%	22.5%	.601
Slater, Austin	190	55	1.255	107	.374	28	.250	28.9%	56.3%	14.7%	.611
McNeil, Jeff	329	95	.702	178	.331	56	.232	28.9%	54.1%	17.0%	.421
Kim, Ha-seong	201	58	1.071	98	.274	45	.178	28.9%	48.8%	22.4%	.480
Gardner, Brett	298	86	1.060	147	.297	65	.154	28.9%	49.3%	21.8%	.488
Galvis, Freddy	284	82	1.148	138	.313	64	.156	28.9%	48.6%	22.5%	.520
Rosario, Amed	434	125	.917	236	.415	73	.219	28.8%	54.4%	16.8%	.523
Segura, Jean	441	127	1.040	215	.329	99	.253	28.8%	48.8%	22.4%	.514
Castro, Harold	252	72	.493	152	.465	28	.393	28.6%	60.3%	11.1%	.465
Carlson, Dylan	398	114	1.152	233	.385	51	.412	28.6%	58.5%	12.8%	.609
Franco, Maikel	313	89	1.067	162	.189	62	.145	28.4%	51.8%	19.8%	.432
Gosselin, Phil	265	75	.773	146	.352	44	.364	28.3%	55.1%	16.6%	.473
Arraez, Luis	386	109	.667	244	.326	33	.333	28.2%	63.2%	8.5%	.424
Harrison, Josh	433	122	.811	249	.337	62	.323	28.2%	57.5%	14.3%	.470
Naylor, Josh	188	53	1.189	106	.255	29	.103	28.2%	56.4%	15.4%	.495
Urshela, Gio	312	88	1.115	176	.392	48	.208	28.2%	56.4%	15.4%	.566
Kiermaier, Kevin	253	71	.855	124	.467	58	.328	28.1%	49.0%	22.9%	.542
Hernandez, Cesar	438	123	1.057	244	.318	71	.197	28.1%	55.7%	16.2%	.506
Gonzalez, Marwin	200	56	.873	106	.305	38	.105	28.0%	53.0%	19.0%	.424
Maldonado, Martin	247	69	1.029	145	.264	33	.091	27.9%	58.7%	13.4%	.455
Valaika, Pat	187	52	.800	100	.276	35	.229	27.8%	53.5%	18.7%	.410
Ortega, Rafael	228	63	1.254	130	.398	35	.200	27.6%	57.0%	15.4%	.606
LeMahieu, DJ	508	139	.797	296	.305	73	.233	27.4%	58.3%	14.4%	.429
Grossman, Robbie	410	112	1.279	236	.306	62	.306	27.3%	57.6%	15.1%	.575
Mayfield, Jack	202	55	1.145	93	.382	54	.111	27.2%	46.0%	26.7%	.520
Andrus, Elvis	423	115	.583	230	.354	78	.167	27.2%	54.4%	18.4%	.382
Kiner-Falefa, Isiah	548	149	.709	313	.337	86	.200	27.2%	57.1%	15.7%	.417
Brinson, Lewis	204	55	1.200	105	.282	44	.182	27.0%	51.5%	21.6%	.510
Eaton, Adam	188	50	.920	105	.280	33	.273	26.6%	55.9%	17.6%	.454
Garcia, Leury	332	88	.782	193	.394	51	.333	26.5%	58.1%	15.4%	.491
Duffy, Matt	227	60	.867	138	.350	29	.345	26.4%	60.8%	12.8%	.487
Merrifield, Whit	573	150	.772	354	.383	69	.246	26.2%	61.8%	12.0%	.467
Culberson, Charlie	188	49	.917	108	.400	31	.267	26.1%	57.4%	16.5%	.514
Kemp, Tony	288	75	.918	175	.405	38	.079	26.0%	60.8%	13.2%	.495
Torres, Gleyber	361	93	.891	209	.363	59	.203	25.8%	57.9%	16.3%	.473
Ahmed, Nick	333	86	.977	189	.301	58	.121	25.8%	56.8%	17.4%	.445
Fuentes, Joshua	207	53	1.058	115	.287	39	.179	25.6%	55.6%	18.8%	.461
Narvaez, Omar	313	80	1.013	172	.381	61	.230	25.6%	55.0%	19.5%	.511
Bauers, Jake	204	52	.692	117	.299	35	.200	25.5%	57.4%	17.2%	.382
Lopez, Nicky	438	110	.713	258	.380	70	.257	25.1%	58.9%	16.0%	.444
Berti, Jon	175	44	.837	107	.314	24	.167	25.1%	61.1%	13.7%	.424
Daza, Yonathan	248	62	.806	145	.312	41	.341	25.0%	58.5%	16.5%	.444
Peterson, Jace	193	48	1.064	119	.339	26	.192	24.9%	61.7%	13.5%	.497
Rojas, Miguel	423	105	.962	238	.354	80	.125	24.8%	56.3%	18.9%	.461
Iglesias, Jose	409	101	.881	231	.348	77	.260	24.7%	56.5%	18.8%	.463

Hard Hit Balls
Highest Percentage of Hard Hit Balls - Players with 250+ PA in 2021

Player	In Play	Hard Count	Hard SLG	Medium Count	Medium SLG	Soft Count	Soft SLG	Hard Pct	Medium Pct	Soft Pct	Overall SLG
Tapia, Raimel	422	104	.853	223	.345	95	.189	24.6%	52.8%	22.5%	.434
Sosa, Edmundo	228	56	1.000	128	.344	44	.295	24.6%	56.1%	19.3%	.498
Gregorius, Didi	308	75	1.082	161	.301	72	.139	24.4%	52.3%	23.4%	.452
Mejia, Francisco	204	49	1.204	111	.333	44	.205	24.0%	54.4%	21.6%	.517
Moore, Dylan	222	53	1.377	115	.237	54	.204	23.9%	51.8%	24.3%	.502
Frazier, Adam	512	122	.738	300	.385	90	.367	23.8%	58.6%	17.6%	.467
Robles, Victor	235	56	.804	126	.339	53	.132	23.8%	53.6%	22.6%	.404
Mercedes, Yermin	195	46	1.239	116	.287	33	.212	23.6%	59.5%	16.9%	.500
Holt, Brock	187	44	.767	114	.298	29	.103	23.5%	61.0%	15.5%	.376
Profar, Jurickson	291	68	.864	156	.310	67	.119	23.4%	53.6%	23.0%	.392
Vazquez, Christian	379	86	.802	215	.348	78	.244	22.7%	56.7%	20.6%	.430
Crawford, J.P.	510	115	.894	292	.363	103	.205	22.5%	57.3%	20.2%	.461
Panik, Joe	204	46	.667	113	.259	45	.178	22.5%	55.4%	22.1%	.332
Hedges, Austin	209	47	1.217	117	.241	45	.133	22.5%	56.0%	21.5%	.442
Newman, Kevin	485	107	.714	287	.254	91	.154	22.1%	59.2%	18.8%	.336
Castro, Willi	310	68	1.104	173	.327	69	.232	21.9%	55.8%	22.3%	.477
Straw, Myles	448	98	.594	301	.419	49	.286	21.9%	67.2%	10.9%	.442
Escobar, Alcides	267	55	.907	152	.409	60	.317	20.6%	56.9%	22.5%	.490
Simmons, Andrelton	354	66	.712	209	.254	79	.177	18.6%	59.0%	22.3%	.323
Torreyes, Ronald	283	49	1.042	169	.287	65	.200	17.3%	59.7%	23.0%	.397
Fletcher, David	573	99	.616	341	.302	133	.308	17.3%	59.5%	23.2%	.359
All MLB	121699	39100	1.114	62566	.319	20033	.200	32.1%	51.4%	16.5%	.555

RBI Percentages

Mark Simon

In 2019, Connor Joe was a Rule V pick by the Reds from the Dodgers, who was then obtained by the Giants late in spring training and was made their Opening Day left fielder.

Joe went 1-for-15 in eight games, was returned to the Dodgers two weeks into the season, and didn't see the majors again in 2019.

But in 2021, he made it back with the Rockies. If you look at the next page, you'll see that he's the third name from the top on a list in which the next three names below Joe's are Bryce Harper, Shohei Ohtani, and Juan Soto.

That's some small sample size fun for you. Joe had 35 RBI in 179 at-bats. He went 16-for-40 and drove in 25 runs with runners in scoring position.

If you're not familiar with RBI opportunities, there's a glossary in the back of the book and a full explanation is in there. In short, it creates a system that measures how effective you are at driving in runs, with the additional context of knowing how many you could have driven in.

Here's one scenario. Reds outfielder Nick Castellanos had 100 RBI in 531 at-bats. Mariners outfielder Mitch Haniger had 100 in 620 at-bats. Knowing nothing else, you might think that Castellanos' season was more efficient.

But if you look at our lists, you'll see that they had about the same number of RBI opportunities (the Mariners offense had a rough year). Haniger did well given what his teammates presented him.

I'll close by pointing out the only player with an RBI percentage less than 10%—Magneuris Sierra. He had 5 RBI in 209 at-bats. If he's looking for encouragement, he should look to Connor Joe. The 2022 season may give him a fresh start.

RBI Percentages by Batter

Player	AB	RBI	RBI Opps	Pct
Tatis Jr., Fernando	478	97	200.6	.484
Joe, Connor	179	35	76.5	.458
Hernandez, Teoscar	550	116	254.1	.457
Harper, Bryce	488	84	185.8	.452
Ohtani, Shohei	537	100	223.5	.447
Soto, Juan	502	95	215.3	.441
Machado, Manny	564	106	241.7	.439
Duvall, Adam	513	113	259.7	.435
Votto, Joey	448	99	229.1	.432
Acuna Jr., Ronald	297	52	121.2	.429
Polanco, Jorge	588	98	229.6	.427
Walsh, Jared	530	98	229.7	.427
Schwindel, Frank	242	43	101.2	.425
Cron, C.J.	470	92	217.9	.422
Wade Jr., LaMonte	336	56	132.7	.422
Abreu, Jose	566	117	278.0	.421
Gurriel Jr., Lourdes	500	84	199.6	.421
Lowe, Brandon	535	99	235.6	.420
Muncy, Max	497	94	224.6	.419
Bichette, Bo	640	102	244.3	.418
Pollock, A.J.	384	69	164.9	.418
Meadows, Austin	518	106	255.3	.415
Garcia, Avisail	461	86	207.7	.414
Rosario, Eddie	379	62	149.6	.414
Nola, Austin	173	29	70.2	.413
Springer, George	299	50	121.7	.411
Buxton, Byron	235	32	78.1	.410
Guerrero Jr., Vladimir	604	111	270.6	.410
Aguilar, Jesus	449	93	227.3	.409
Albies, Ozzie	629	106	258.9	.409
Ramirez, Jose	552	103	252.2	.408
Judge, Aaron	550	98	240.6	.407
Perez, Salvador	620	121	298.9	.405
Castellanos, Nick	531	100	247.4	.404
Haniger, Mitch	620	100	247.7	.404
Seager, Corey	353	57	141.6	.403
Grandal, Yasmani	279	62	154.4	.402
Sheets, Gavin	160	34	84.6	.402
Baddoo, Akil	413	55	137.0	.401
Marte, Ketel	340	50	124.8	.401
Altuve, Jose	601	83	207.9	.399
Crawford, Brandon	483	90	225.7	.399
McCormick, Chas	284	50	126.1	.397
Schwarber, Kyle	399	71	179.0	.397
Ward, Taylor	208	33	83.3	.396
Fraley, Jake	214	36	91.2	.395
Belt, Brandon	325	59	149.7	.394
Reyes, Franmil	418	85	216.5	.393
Goldschmidt, Paul	603	99	253.4	.391
Riley, Austin	590	107	273.5	.391
Bradley, Bobby	245	41	105.1	.390
Winker, Jesse	423	71	181.9	.390
Zunino, Mike	333	62	159.0	.390
Stanton, Giancarlo	510	97	249.6	.389
Devers, Rafael	591	113	291.0	.388
Naquin, Tyler	411	70	180.6	.388
Semien, Marcus	652	102	262.7	.388
Freeman, Freddie	600	83	214.6	.387
Reynolds, Bryan	559	90	233.4	.386
Robert, Luis	275	43	111.4	.386
Franco, Wander	281	39	101.4	.385
Hays, Austin	488	71	184.5	.385
Olson, Matt	565	111	289.8	.383
Baez, Javier	502	87	227.6	.382
Benintendi, Andrew	493	73	191.2	.382
Hilliard, Sam	214	34	88.9	.382
Kirilloff, Alex	215	34	89.0	.382
McCutchen, Andrew	482	80	209.4	.382

Player	AB	RBI	RBI Opps	Pct
Beaty, Matt	204	40	105.1	.381
Murphy, Sean	393	59	154.9	.381
Chang, Yu	237	39	102.6	.380
Renfroe, Hunter	521	96	252.6	.380
Martinez, J.D.	570	99	261.5	.379
Urias, Luis	490	75	197.8	.379
Arenado, Nolan	593	105	278.1	.378
Seager, Kyle	603	101	267.4	.378
Turner, Trea	595	77	203.7	.378
Arroyo, Christian	164	25	66.3	.377
Dalbec, Bobby	417	78	206.7	.377
Cooper, Garrett	215	33	87.7	.376
McKinstry, Zach	158	29	77.1	.376
Tucker, Kyle	506	92	244.7	.376
Mejia, Francisco	250	35	93.4	.375
Pina, Manny	180	33	87.9	.375
Sanchez, Jesus	227	36	96.1	.375
Escobar, Eduardo	549	90	240.5	.374
Gurriel, Yuli	530	81	216.5	.374
Jimenez, Eloy	213	37	99.1	.373
Alvarez, Yordan	537	104	279.7	.372
Cruz, Nelson	513	86	231.3	.372
O'Neill, Tyler	482	80	215.6	.371
Luplow, Jordan	163	28	75.6	.370
Taylor, Tyrone	243	43	116.1	.370
Correa, Carlos	555	92	249.0	.369
Hoskins, Rhys	389	71	192.3	.369
Turner, Justin	533	87	235.6	.369
Choi, Ji-Man	258	45	123.1	.366
Mountcastle, Ryan	534	89	243.6	.365
Anderson, Tim	527	61	167.4	.364
Bryant, Kris	513	73	200.3	.364
Lindor, Francisco	452	63	173.1	.364
Longoria, Evan	253	46	126.5	.364
Betts, Mookie	466	58	159.7	.363
Urias, Ramon	262	38	104.6	.363
Bregman, Alex	348	55	151.8	.362
Realmuto, J.T.	476	73	201.7	.362
Yastrzemski, Mike	468	71	196.3	.362
Schoop, Jonathan	623	84	233.0	.361
Toro, Abraham	335	46	127.3	.361
Smith, Will	414	76	211.4	.360
Diaz, Aledmys	294	45	125.5	.359
Phillips, Brett	253	44	122.5	.359
Adrianza, Ehire	182	28	78.3	.358
Donaldson, Josh	457	72	201.2	.358
Garver, Mitch	207	34	95.2	.357
Pujols, Albert	275	50	140.1	.357
Wisdom, Patrick	338	61	170.7	.357
Adames, Willy	497	73	205.1	.356
Arozarena, Randy	529	69	193.9	.356
Molina, Yadier	440	66	185.4	.356
Blackmon, Charlie	514	78	219.6	.355
Posey, Buster	395	56	157.6	.355
Story, Trevor	526	75	212.1	.354
India, Jonathan	532	69	195.2	.353
Swanson, Dansby	588	88	249.5	.353
Bogaerts, Xander	529	79	224.7	.352
Pederson, Joc	429	61	173.4	.352
Ramirez, Harold	339	41	116.5	.352
Rodgers, Brendan	387	51	144.9	.352
Cabrera, Miguel	472	75	214.4	.350
Chisholm Jr., Jazz	464	53	151.8	.349
Gallo, Joey	498	77	220.5	.349
Gosselin, Phil	345	47	134.6	.349
Marte, Starling	467	55	157.5	.349
Happ, Ian	465	66	189.6	.348
McMahon, Ryan	528	86	246.8	.348

466

Player	AB	RBI	RBI Opps	Pct
La Stella, Tommy	220	27	77.9	.347
Ortega, Rafael	296	33	95.1	.347
Alonso, Pete	561	94	271.4	.346
Anderson, Brian	233	28	81.0	.346
Brown, Seth	281	48	138.7	.346
Lowrie, Jed	457	69	199.6	.346
Contreras, Willson	413	57	165.0	.345
Mercedes, Yermin	240	37	107.1	.345
Pillar, Kevin	325	47	136.3	.345
Higashioka, Kyle	193	29	84.2	.344
Peters, DJ	223	38	110.4	.344
Torrens, Luis	346	47	136.6	.344
Jeffers, Ryan	267	35	101.9	.343
Yelich, Christian	399	51	148.8	.343
Garcia, Adolis	581	90	263.3	.342
Ozuna, Marcell	188	26	76.0	.342
Canha, Mark	519	61	179.1	.341
Grichuk, Randal	511	81	237.4	.341
Wong, Kolten	445	50	146.8	.341
Bell, Josh	498	88	259.1	.340
Diaz, Yandy	465	64	188.2	.340
Gomes, Yan	349	52	152.9	.340
Taylor, Chris	507	73	214.9	.340
Lowe, Nathaniel	557	72	212.8	.338
Varsho, Daulton	284	38	112.3	.338
Haase, Eric	351	61	180.8	.337
Tsutsugo, Yoshi	230	32	95.0	.337
VanMeter, Josh	274	36	106.9	.337
France, Ty	571	73	217.1	.336
Nunez, Dom	228	33	98.1	.336
Voit, Luke	213	35	104.1	.336
Grisham, Trent	462	62	184.9	.335
Marisnick, Jake	176	24	71.7	.335
Mayfield, Jack	266	39	116.3	.335
Carlson, Dylan	542	65	194.5	.334
Contreras, William	163	23	68.9	.334
Margot, Manuel	421	57	170.9	.334
Reyes, Victor	209	22	65.8	.334
Torreyes, Ronald	318	41	123.0	.333
Bader, Harrison	367	50	150.5	.332
Chapman, Matt	529	72	217.9	.330
Lux, Gavin	335	46	139.3	.330
Soler, Jorge	516	70	212.1	.330
Cain, Lorenzo	257	36	109.7	.328
Grossman, Robbie	557	67	204.1	.328
Myers, Wil	442	63	192.3	.328
Ruf, Darin	262	43	131.2	.328
Stallings, Jacob	374	53	161.8	.328
Jansen, Danny	184	28	85.6	.327
Mullins II, Cedric	602	59	180.5	.327
Peralta, David	487	63	194.0	.325
Stephenson, Tyler	350	45	138.4	.325
Thomas, Lane	226	28	86.1	.325
Peterson, Jace	259	31	95.6	.324
Reddick, Josh	151	21	64.9	.324
Moran, Colin	318	50	155.0	.323
Shaw, Travis	220	39	120.6	.323
Dickerson, Alex	283	38	118.3	.321
Hernandez, Cesar	570	62	193.4	.321
Hernandez, Kike	508	60	187.1	.321
Cronenworth, Jake	567	71	221.8	.320
Slater, Austin	274	32	100.0	.320
Kelly, Carson	304	46	144.0	.319
Mancini, Trey	556	71	222.7	.319
Merrifield, Whit	664	74	232.1	.319
Miller, Brad	331	49	154.1	.318
Farmer, Kyle	483	63	199.0	.317
Kepler, Max	426	54	170.6	.317
Kirk, Alejandro	165	24	75.6	.317

Player	AB	RBI	RBI Opps	Pct
Rizzo, Anthony	496	61	192.3	.317
Madrigal, Nick	200	21	66.4	.316
Sanchez, Gary	383	54	170.7	.316
Sano, Miguel	470	75	237.7	.316
Candelario, Jeimer	557	67	212.8	.315
Kemp, Tony	330	37	117.9	.314
DeJong, Paul	356	45	143.7	.313
Heim, Jonah	265	32	102.2	.313
Stevenson, Andrew	192	23	73.5	.313
Laureano, Ramon	341	39	125.0	.312
Segura, Jean	514	58	186.1	.312
Verdugo, Alex	544	63	201.9	.312
Narvaez, Omar	391	49	157.5	.311
Suarez, Eugenio	505	79	253.9	.311
Zimmerman, Ryan	255	46	148.1	.311
Ibanez, Andy	253	25	80.7	.310
Garcia, Leury	415	54	175.0	.309
Moreland, Mitch	229	30	97.1	.309
Rendon, Anthony	217	34	110.0	.309
Rojas, Miguel	495	48	155.5	.309
Barnhart, Tucker	348	48	155.7	.308
Hosmer, Eric	509	65	211.2	.308
Eaton, Adam	254	30	98.0	.306
Harrison, Josh	505	60	196.3	.306
Hayes, Ke'Bryan	362	38	124.1	.306
Tapia, Raimel	487	50	163.5	.306
Lagares, Juan	309	38	124.7	.305
Flores, Wilmer	389	53	174.5	.304
Herrera, Odubel	450	51	168.0	.304
Pinder, Chad	214	27	88.8	.304
Gordon, Nick	200	23	76.2	.302
Conforto, Michael	406	55	182.8	.301
Duggar, Steven	268	35	116.2	.301
Odor, Rougned	322	39	129.7	.301
Zimmer, Bradley	299	35	116.3	.301
Moncada, Yoan	520	61	203.3	.300
Urshela, Gio	420	49	163.5	.300
Bohm, Alec	380	47	157.1	.299
Edman, Tommy	641	56	187.6	.299
Kiermaier, Kevin	348	37	123.8	.299
Moore, Dylan	332	43	143.8	.299
Rosario, Amed	550	57	190.6	.299
Arraez, Luis	428	42	141.1	.298
Santana, Carlos	565	69	232.3	.297
Castro, Harold	315	37	125.1	.296
Davis, J.D.	179	23	77.7	.296
Dubon, Mauricio	175	22	74.4	.296
Franco, Maikel	377	47	158.8	.296
Torres, Gleyber	459	51	172.3	.296
Biggio, Cavan	250	27	91.4	.295
Casali, Curt	200	26	88.1	.295
Difo, Wilmer	219	24	81.3	.295
Mendick, Danny	164	20	67.9	.295
Escobar, Alcides	319	28	95.1	.294
Stassi, Max	282	35	119.6	.293
Castro, Starlin	315	38	130.1	.292
Galvis, Freddy	356	40	136.9	.292
Kiner-Falefa, Isiah	635	53	181.2	.292
Taylor, Michael A.	483	54	185.1	.292
Brosseau, Mike	150	18	61.9	.291
Goodwin, Brian	235	29	99.7	.291
Holt, Brock	235	23	79.1	.291
Severino, Pedro	379	46	157.9	.291
Vogelbach, Daniel	215	24	82.4	.291
Walker, Christian	401	46	158.1	.291
Brinson, Lewis	274	33	113.6	.290
Iglesias, Jose	483	48	165.4	.290
Nimmo, Brandon	325	28	96.7	.290
Ramos, Wilson	151	20	68.9	.290

467

Player	AB	RBI	RBI Opps	Pct
Aquino, Aristides	174	23	79.6	.289
Brantley, Michael	469	47	162.5	.289
Cabrera, Asdrubal	309	42	145.5	.289
Moustakas, Mike	183	22	76.1	.289
De La Cruz, Bryan	199	19	65.9	.288
Diaz, Elias	338	44	152.8	.288
Gregorius, Didi	368	54	187.7	.288
LeMahieu, DJ	597	57	197.6	.288
Trammell, Taylor	156	18	62.6	.288
d'Arnaud, Travis	209	26	90.7	.287
Fuentes, Joshua	271	33	115.0	.287
McCann, James	375	46	160.5	.287
Culberson, Charlie	247	22	76.9	.286
Kelenic, Jarred	337	43	150.9	.285
Santander, Anthony	406	50	175.4	.285
Crawford, J.P.	619	54	190.4	.284
Goodrum, Niko	290	33	116.3	.284
Tellez, Rowdy	297	36	127.0	.283
Collins, Zack	195	26	92.3	.282
Gonzalez, Erik	220	21	74.4	.282
Stewart, D.J.	270	33	117.0	.282
Upton, Justin	318	41	145.4	.282
Solano, Donovan	307	31	110.5	.281
Calhoun, Willie	260	25	89.2	.280
Murphy, Tom	277	34	121.5	.280
O'Hearn, Ryan	236	29	103.7	.280
Duffy, Matt	289	30	107.6	.279
Daza, Yonathan	301	30	108.0	.278
Vogt, Stephen	210	25	89.8	.278
Pham, Tommy	475	49	177.7	.276
Smith, Dominic	446	58	210.5	.276
Walls, Taylor	152	15	54.4	.276
Alberto, Hanser	241	24	87.4	.275
Smith, Pavin	498	49	178.4	.275
Trevino, Jose	285	30	109.0	.275
Caratini, Victor	313	39	142.3	.274
Piscotty, Stephen	173	16	58.3	.274
Wendle, Joey	460	54	196.9	.274
Mazara, Nomar	165	19	69.7	.273
Solak, Nick	458	49	179.4	.273
Alfaro, Jorge	295	30	110.9	.271
Barnes, Austin	200	23	84.9	.271
Hernandez, Yadiel	264	32	118.0	.271
Kim, Ha-seong	267	34	125.5	.271
Vazquez, Christian	458	49	181.3	.270
Gimenez, Andres	188	16	59.8	.268
Valaika, Pat	259	25	93.2	.268
Dozier, Hunter	487	54	202.0	.267
Gardner, Brett	387	39	145.8	.267
Plawecki, Kevin	157	15	56.2	.267
Lopez, Nicky	497	43	161.9	.266
Sosa, Edmundo	288	27	103.1	.262
Hedges, Austin	286	31	118.7	.261
Mercado, Oscar	214	19	72.7	.261
Rojas, Josh	484	44	169.2	.260
Heyward, Jason	323	30	116.9	.257
Bote, David	291	35	136.7	.256
Vaughn, Andrew	417	48	187.3	.256
Frazier, Adam	577	43	169.5	.254
Fletcher, David	626	47	187.2	.251
Bellinger, Cody	315	36	144.0	.250
Naylor, Josh	233	21	83.9	.250
Polanco, Gregory	336	36	144.1	.250
Short, Zack	156	20	80.4	.249
Dickerson, Corey	336	29	117.1	.248
Villar, Jonathan	454	42	170.0	.247
Nido, Tomas	153	13	53.1	.245
Gonzalez, Marwin	276	28	114.8	.244
Straw, Myles	564	48	196.5	.244

Player	AB	RBI	RBI Opps	Pct
Castro, Willi	413	38	156.3	.243
Cave, Jake	164	13	53.4	.243
Rooker, Brent	189	16	65.9	.243
Astudillo, Willians	208	21	86.8	.242
McKinney, Billy	265	27	111.5	.242
Rengifo, Luis	174	18	74.4	.242
McKenna, Ryan	169	14	58.4	.240
Marsh, Brandon	236	19	79.4	.239
Rojas, Jose	168	15	62.9	.238
Dahl, David	205	18	75.9	.237
Heredia, Guillermo	305	26	109.6	.237
Hampson, Garrett	453	33	140.1	.236
Tauchman, Mike	166	15	63.6	.236
Akiyama, Shogo	162	12	51.0	.235
Berti, Jon	233	19	80.9	.235
Calhoun, Kole	166	17	72.8	.234
Espinal, Santiago	222	17	72.5	.234
Gutierrez, Kelvin	272	20	85.5	.234
Hiura, Keston	173	19	81.1	.234
McNeil, Jeff	386	35	149.8	.234
Larnach, Trevor	260	28	120.2	.233
Garcia, Luis	236	22	95.4	.231
Panik, Joe	236	18	77.9	.231
Profar, Jurickson	353	33	142.7	.231
Ahmed, Nick	434	38	165.2	.230
Carpenter, Matt	207	21	91.2	.230
Maldonado, Martin	373	36	156.3	.230
Miller, Owen	191	18	79.0	.228
Simmons, Andrelton	412	31	136.9	.226
Perez, Michael	210	21	93.3	.225
Suzuki, Kurt	219	16	72.1	.222
Alcantara, Sergio	220	17	77.4	.220
Gamel, Ben	340	26	118.0	.220
White, Eli	198	15	68.7	.218
Evans, Phillip	214	16	74.8	.214
Newman, Kevin	517	39	182.3	.214
Mateo, Jorge	194	14	65.9	.212
Frazier, Clint	183	15	71.7	.209
Andrus, Elvis	497	37	178.8	.207
Sogard, Eric	169	12	57.9	.207
Andujar, Miguel	154	12	58.2	.206
Diaz, Isan	239	17	89.6	.190
Kieboom, Carter	217	20	106.1	.189
Robles, Victor	315	19	107.1	.177
Bauers, Jake	282	19	108.9	.174
Bradley Jr., Jackie	387	29	168.5	.172
Leon, Sandy	202	14	84.0	.167
Taveras, Leody	174	9	59.8	.151
Knizner, Andrew	161	9	62.3	.144
McGuire, Reese	198	10	71.0	.141
Sierra, Magneuris	209	5	51.9	.096

468

Pinch Hitting

Brian Reiff

The Fountain of Youth has been found. Turns out it's been on the bench in Dodger Stadium all along.

Albert Pujols, once universally considered the best hitter in baseball, has had his fair share of difficulties since his high-profile move to the west coast. Finally, after posting a .622 OPS through 24 games in 2021, he was cut by the Angels and soon joined the crosstown Dodgers.

With his new team, he posted his best numbers since 2016, but it was as a pinch hitter where he truly shined. Pujols went 14-for-37 with two home runs as a pinch hitter, good for a .955 OPS that was more than 200 points better than the .715 mark he posted as a first baseman for the Dodgers. Small sample sizes, yes, but Pujols did admirably well given he had just 39 plate appearances as a pinch hitter prior to this season.

As impressive as Pujols' stat line was, there were others who surpassed it. The Pirates' Wilmer Difo, whose 65 pinch-hit plate appearances were third most in MLB, slashed .286/.369/.536 as a pinch hitter. Austin Slater of the Giants had an OPS of 1.148 while tying for the MLB lead with four pinch-hit home runs, leading them to an MLB-record 18 pinch-hit home runs.

Arguably the most impressive performance in the following charts was that of Ji-Man Choi, who reached base in 9 of his 10 times at the plate as a pinch hitter for the Rays. Also of note was Mets catcher Patrick Mazeika, whose two walk-off pinch-hit plate appearances (both fielder's choices!) led MLB.

The tables on the accompanying page includes all players with at least 10 pinch-hit plate appearances or total bases this season, or at least 100 pinch-hit plate appearances in their careers.

Pinch Hitting
Pinch Hitters with 10+ PAs or 10+ Total Bases in 2021

Batter	B	AB	H	2B	3B	HR	RBI	TBB	IBB	SO	GDP	Avg	OBP	Slg	OPS
Adams, Matt	L	15	2	1	0	0	1	0	0	4	1	.133	.133	.200	.333
Adams, Riley	R	12	0	0	0	0	0	1	0	9	1	.000	.143	.000	.143
Adrianza, Ehire	B	64	16	5	0	3	12	8	0	12	0	.250	.333	.469	.802
Aguilar, Jesus	R	12	3	1	0	0	3	2	0	4	0	.250	.333	.333	.667
Akiyama, Shogo	L	32	6	2	0	0	1	1	0	7	0	.188	.278	.250	.528
Alberto, Hanser	R	22	7	1	2	0	5	1	0	6	0	.318	.333	.545	.879
Alcantara, Sergio	B	11	3	1	0	1	3	1	0	3	0	.273	.333	.636	.970
Alfaro, Jorge	R	12	4	1	0	0	2	0	0	1	0	.333	.385	.417	.801
Alford, Anthony	R	11	4	1	0	0	0	1	0	5	0	.364	.417	.455	.871
Almonte, Abraham	B	20	4	2	0	1	5	3	0	6	1	.200	.304	.450	.754
Almora Jr., Albert	R	14	0	0	0	0	0	0	0	6	1	.000	.000	.000	.000
Aquino, Aristides	R	22	5	2	0	0	3	4	1	13	0	.227	.321	.318	.640
Arcia, Orlando	R	13	2	2	0	0	2	2	0	2	0	.154	.267	.308	.574
Arraez, Luis	L	10	2	0	0	0	1	1	0	2	0	.200	.273	.200	.473
Barnes, Austin	R	21	7	2	0	2	5	1	0	7	0	.333	.364	.714	1.078
Barnhart, Tucker	L	10	1	0	0	0	1	2	0	5	1	.100	.308	.100	.408
Bauers, Jake	L	26	6	2	0	1	4	3	0	7	0	.231	.333	.423	.756
Beaty, Matt	L	50	9	0	0	1	4	5	0	15	0	.180	.305	.240	.545
Bell, Josh	B	15	5	1	0	1	2	2	0	3	0	.333	.412	.600	1.012
Belt, Brandon	L	9	2	0	0	2	3	2	0	4	2	.222	.364	.889	1.253
Berti, Jon	R	11	1	0	0	0	0	5	0	4	0	.091	.375	.091	.466
Blackmon, Charlie	L	13	5	0	0	0	3	0	0	5	0	.385	.467	.385	.851
Blandino, Alex	R	12	3	0	0	0	1	0	0	7	0	.250	.308	.250	.558
Blankenhorn, Travis	L	15	3	1	0	1	4	1	0	6	0	.200	.250	.467	.717
Bote, David	R	13	2	0	0	0	2	2	0	6	0	.154	.250	.154	.404
Bradley Jr., Jackie	L	19	0	0	0	0	0	1	0	9	1	.000	.050	.000	.050
Brinson, Lewis	R	12	3	1	0	0	0	0	0	4	0	.250	.250	.333	.583
Brosseau, Mike	R	8	0	0	0	0	1	2	0	5	0	.000	.200	.000	.200
Brown, Seth	L	27	6	1	0	1	6	1	0	8	0	.222	.241	.370	.612
Cabrera, Asdrubal	B	28	2	1	0	0	4	5	0	8	1	.071	.200	.107	.307
Calhoun, Kole	L	11	3	1	0	0	1	1	0	1	0	.273	.333	.364	.697
Camargo, Johan	B	12	0	0	0	0	0	2	0	5	0	.000	.143	.000	.143
Caratini, Victor	B	14	4	0	0	0	3	2	0	4	1	.286	.375	.286	.661
Carpenter, Matt	L	60	9	4	0	2	9	14	0	22	1	.150	.329	.317	.646
Casali, Curt	R	13	1	0	0	0	1	2	0	9	0	.077	.200	.077	.277
Castro, Harold	L	14	3	0	0	0	2	1	0	5	0	.214	.267	.214	.481
Castro, Jason	L	18	7	2	0	1	6	5	0	8	0	.389	.522	.667	1.188
Chang, Yu	R	17	3	0	0	1	2	0	0	6	0	.176	.176	.353	.529
Chirinos, Robinson	R	17	3	0	0	1	3	2	0	9	1	.176	.263	.353	.616
Choi, Ji-Man	L	8	7	2	0	1	9	2	0	0	0	.875	.900	1.500	2.400
Conforto, Michael	L	8	2	1	0	1	3	3	1	1	0	.250	.455	.750	1.205
Contreras, Willson	R	8	2	1	0	0	1	4	0	2	0	.250	.538	.375	.913
Cooper, Garrett	R	10	3	0	0	0	1	5	0	3	0	.300	.563	.300	.863
Cron, C.J.	R	7	3	1	0	0	1	3	0	2	0	.429	.600	.571	1.171
Davis, J.D.	R	21	9	3	0	0	2	1	0	5	0	.429	.455	.571	1.026
Davis, Khris	R	14	5	1	0	2	4	1	0	4	1	.357	.400	.857	1.257
Daza, Yonathan	R	25	9	1	0	0	4	3	0	3	1	.360	.433	.400	.833
Dean, Austin	R	10	2	0	0	0	1	4	0	3	0	.200	.400	.200	.600
Diaz, Aledmys	R	8	3	0	0	0	1	2	0	2	1	.375	.500	.375	.875
Diaz, Elias	R	16	1	0	0	0	3	2	0	5	0	.063	.158	.063	.220
Diaz, Isan	L	22	4	2	0	0	0	1	0	9	1	.182	.217	.273	.490
Dickerson, Alex	L	29	6	2	0	3	3	4	0	8	2	.207	.343	.586	.929
Dickerson, Corey	L	16	5	1	0	0	3	1	0	4	1	.313	.333	.375	.708
Difo, Wilmer	B	56	16	1	2	3	12	8	0	13	0	.286	.369	.536	.905
Drury, Brandon	R	30	11	3	0	3	9	1	0	5	0	.367	.387	.767	1.154
Dubon, Mauricio	R	15	3	2	0	0	1	0	0	4	0	.200	.200	.333	.533
Duffy, Matt	R	23	8	1	0	0	1	1	0	6	3	.348	.400	.391	.791
Duggar, Steven	L	23	3	1	0	0	0	4	0	8	2	.130	.259	.174	.433
Duvall, Adam	R	11	4	2	0	2	3	0	0	6	0	.364	.364	1.091	1.455
Espinal, Santiago	R	11	2	0	0	0	0	1	0	2	0	.182	.250	.182	.432
Estrada, Thairo	R	16	2	0	0	1	1	0	0	3	0	.125	.176	.313	.489
Evans, Phillip	R	15	4	1	0	1	3	3	0	4	0	.267	.450	.533	.983
Flores, Wilmer	R	33	8	2	0	2	8	5	0	6	1	.242	.359	.485	.844
Fraley, Jake	L	16	3	0	0	0	0	0	0	6	0	.188	.235	.188	.423
Frazier, Adam	L	11	1	0	0	0	1	2	0	2	0	.091	.231	.091	.322
Freeman, Mike	L	10	0	0	0	0	0	0	0	3	1	.000	.000	.000	.000
Fuentes, Joshua	R	21	5	1	0	1	4	0	0	8	0	.238	.238	.429	.667
Gamel, Ben	L	21	2	1	0	0	1	2	0	9	1	.095	.174	.143	.317

Pinch Hitting
Pinch Hitters with 10+ PAs or 10+ Total Bases in 2021

Batter	B	AB	H	2B	3B	HR	RBI	TBB	IBB	SO	GDP	Avg	OBP	Slg	OPS
Garcia, Avisail	R	10	3	0	0	0	0	5	1	2	0	.300	.533	.300	.833
Garcia, Robel	B	9	3	0	0	0	1	1	0	3	0	.333	.400	.333	.733
Garver, Mitch	R	9	1	1	0	0	0	2	0	4	0	.111	.273	.222	.495
Gonzalez, Erik	R	12	2	0	0	0	2	1	0	8	0	.167	.231	.167	.397
Gosselin, Phil	R	13	2	0	0	0	1	0	0	4	0	.154	.154	.154	.308
Grisham, Trent	L	11	1	1	0	0	0	1	0	4	0	.091	.167	.182	.348
Guillorme, Luis	L	18	3	1	0	0	1	1	0	5	0	.167	.211	.222	.433
Hampson, Garrett	R	24	5	1	1	2	3	0	0	9	1	.208	.208	.583	.792
Happ, Ian	B	23	4	2	0	0	4	2	0	7	2	.174	.240	.261	.501
Heineman, Scott	R	9	0	0	0	0	0	2	0	6	1	.000	.182	.000	.182
Heredia, Guillermo	R	12	3	0	0	0	0	3	0	4	0	.250	.438	.250	.688
Hernandez, Yadiel	L	50	13	2	0	1	5	3	0	12	0	.260	.309	.360	.669
Hilliard, Sam	L	20	6	0	1	2	5	0	0	6	0	.300	.300	.700	1.000
Hiura, Keston	R	13	1	1	0	0	0	0	0	7	0	.077	.077	.154	.231
Holt, Brock	L	10	2	0	0	0	0	2	0	5	0	.200	.333	.200	.533
Hosmer, Eric	L	19	3	2	0	0	1	1	0	4	0	.158	.200	.263	.463
Ibanez, Andy	R	9	3	1	0	0	0	1	0	2	0	.333	.400	.444	.844
Inciarte, Ender	L	13	2	1	0	0	2	1	0	7	0	.154	.214	.231	.445
Jackson, Alex	R	9	1	0	0	0	0	1	0	6	0	.111	.200	.111	.311
Jankowski, Travis	L	21	5	0	0	0	1	4	1	3	0	.238	.360	.238	.598
Joe, Connor	R	19	3	0	0	1	3	0	0	5	0	.158	.158	.316	.474
Joyce, Matt	L	21	1	1	0	0	1	7	1	10	0	.048	.310	.095	.406
Kelly, Carson	R	16	2	0	0	1	1	1	0	7	0	.125	.176	.313	.489
Kemp, Tony	L	13	3	1	0	0	1	2	0	3	0	.231	.313	.308	.620
Kim, Ha-seong	R	35	4	0	0	1	2	4	0	14	1	.114	.200	.200	.400
Knapp, Andrew	B	13	2	0	0	0	2	0	0	7	0	.154	.154	.154	.308
Knizner, Andrew	R	8	2	0	0	0	2	1	0	3	0	.250	.400	.250	.650
La Stella, Tommy	L	23	6	0	0	0	2	0	0	3	0	.261	.261	.261	.522
Lamb, Jake	L	8	0	0	0	0	0	2	0	5	0	.000	.273	.000	.273
Leon, Sandy	B	18	3	0	0	0	1	2	0	7	0	.167	.286	.167	.452
Locastro, Tim	R	13	2	0	0	1	3	1	0	4	0	.154	.313	.385	.697
Lowe, Brandon	L	11	3	0	0	1	3	3	0	3	0	.273	.467	.545	1.012
Lowrie, Jed	B	21	4	2	0	0	1	0	0	5	0	.190	.190	.286	.476
Luplow, Jordan	R	10	0	0	0	0	0	2	0	7	0	.000	.167	.000	.167
Marcano, Tucupita	L	10	2	0	0	0	0	2	0	3	1	.200	.333	.200	.533
Margot, Manuel	R	12	1	0	0	0	1	2	1	1	0	.083	.214	.083	.298
Marisnick, Jake	R	39	8	2	0	0	2	3	0	17	1	.205	.262	.256	.518
Martin, Jason	L	14	3	1	0	0	1	0	0	6	0	.214	.214	.286	.500
Martini, Nick	L	14	2	1	0	0	1	1	0	6	0	.143	.200	.214	.414
Mateo, Jorge	R	29	4	1	0	0	1	0	0	13	0	.138	.194	.172	.366
Mathisen, Wyatt	R	9	1	0	0	0	0	1	0	4	0	.111	.273	.111	.384
Maton, Nick	L	8	0	0	0	0	1	2	0	4	0	.000	.200	.000	.200
Mazeika, Patrick	L	13	2	0	0	0	3	1	0	2	0	.154	.214	.154	.368
McCann, James	R	11	4	2	0	1	5	1	0	5	1	.364	.385	.818	1.203
McCutchen, Andrew	R	9	1	0	0	1	4	2	0	5	0	.111	.273	.444	.717
McKinney, Billy	L	38	10	1	0	0	4	4	0	15	0	.263	.341	.289	.630
McNeil, Jeff	L	15	5	2	0	0	2	2	0	5	0	.333	.412	.467	.878
Meadows, Austin	L	7	2	1	0	0	3	3	1	0	0	.286	.455	.429	.883
Mercado, Oscar	R	9	4	1	0	0	0	1	0	3	0	.444	.500	.556	1.056
Miller, Brad	L	51	14	4	0	2	5	5	0	16	1	.275	.339	.471	.810
Moore, Dylan	R	8	2	0	0	1	3	3	0	3	0	.250	.455	.625	1.080
Moran, Colin	L	12	4	0	0	0	3	2	0	3	2	.333	.429	.333	.762
Moreland, Mitch	L	17	5	0	0	0	2	0	0	3	1	.294	.294	.294	.588
Moustakas, Mike	L	11	2	1	0	0	0	1	0	3	1	.182	.250	.273	.523
Myers, Wil	R	21	6	1	0	0	3	2	0	5	3	.286	.348	.333	.681
Naquin, Tyler	L	15	2	0	1	0	3	2	0	5	0	.133	.278	.267	.544
Narvaez, Omar	L	19	2	0	0	0	1	1	0	7	0	.105	.182	.105	.287
Neuse, Sheldon	R	10	2	0	0	1	1	0	0	4	0	.200	.200	.500	.700
Newman, Kevin	R	8	1	0	0	0	1	0	0	1	1	.125	.111	.125	.236
Nogowski, John	R	21	2	0	0	0	1	1	0	3	1	.095	.174	.095	.269
Nootbaar, Lars	L	19	3	1	0	1	3	4	0	5	0	.158	.304	.368	.673
O'Grady, Brian	L	17	3	2	0	1	2	3	0	5	0	.176	.300	.471	.771
O'Hearn, Ryan	L	14	3	0	0	1	3	1	0	4	0	.214	.267	.429	.695
Ortega, Rafael	L	15	7	1	0	1	3	0	0	1	0	.467	.467	.733	1.200
Panik, Joe	L	27	1	0	0	0	1	2	0	3	2	.037	.133	.037	.170
Park, Hoy	L	8	1	0	0	0	0	1	0	1	0	.125	.222	.125	.347
Parra, Gerardo	L	25	6	1	0	0	1	4	0	8	1	.240	.345	.280	.625
Payton, Mark	L	18	3	0	0	0	0	2	0	5	0	.167	.250	.167	.417
Pederson, Joc	L	22	4	2	1	0	4	2	0	6	2	.182	.280	.364	.644

471

Pinch Hitting
Pinch Hitters with 10+ PAs or 10+ Total Bases in 2021

Batter	B	AB	H	2B	3B	HR	RBI	TBB	IBB	SO	GDP	Avg	OBP	Slg	OPS
Peralta, David	L	17	8	0	1	0	5	3	0	2	0	.471	.550	.588	1.138
Peraza, Jose	R	18	6	2	0	1	5	3	0	3	0	.333	.478	.611	1.089
Perez, Michael	L	11	3	0	0	1	3	0	0	4	1	.273	.273	.545	.818
Peterson, Jace	L	17	3	0	0	0	0	2	0	3	0	.176	.263	.176	.440
Pham, Tommy	R	28	9	2	0	0	3	2	1	7	0	.321	.367	.393	.760
Pillar, Kevin	R	23	4	0	0	1	2	1	0	8	0	.174	.240	.304	.544
Pina, Manny	R	14	2	0	0	1	2	3	0	4	0	.143	.294	.357	.651
Pinder, Chad	R	11	6	1	0	2	9	3	0	3	1	.545	.643	1.182	1.825
Piscotty, Stephen	R	15	2	0	0	0	1	1	0	3	1	.133	.235	.133	.369
Polanco, Gregory	L	13	2	0	0	0	0	2	0	8	0	.154	.267	.154	.421
Pollock, A.J.	R	13	4	0	0	0	2	2	0	3	0	.308	.400	.308	.708
Posey, Buster	R	9	1	0	0	0	0	1	0	4	1	.111	.200	.111	.311
Profar, Jurickson	B	30	3	1	0	0	1	6	0	4	2	.100	.250	.133	.383
Pujols, Albert	R	39	14	0	0	2	10	3	1	9	1	.359	.395	.513	.908
Reddick, Josh	L	16	2	1	0	1	2	0	0	3	1	.125	.125	.375	.500
Reyes, Pablo	R	17	2	0	0	0	0	6	0	5	0	.118	.348	.118	.465
Rios, Edwin	L	10	0	0	0	0	0	0	0	6	0	.000	.000	.000	.000
Robertson, Daniel	R	10	0	0	0	0	0	6	0	9	0	.000	.375	.000	.375
Rojas, Josh	L	13	1	0	0	0	0	3	1	7	0	.077	.250	.077	.327
Rondon, Jose	R	39	12	1	0	3	6	3	0	9	0	.308	.349	.564	.913
Ruf, Darin	R	39	6	1	0	1	6	6	1	18	1	.154	.292	.256	.548
Ruiz, Rio	L	24	5	2	0	0	2	2	0	8	0	.208	.259	.292	.551
Sanchez, Gary	R	8	1	0	0	1	2	3	0	2	0	.125	.364	.500	.864
Sandoval, Pablo	B	51	6	0	0	4	11	8	0	19	2	.118	.262	.353	.615
Schrock, Max	L	17	7	1	1	0	2	2	0	4	0	.412	.474	.588	1.062
Shaw, Travis	L	18	2	1	0	0	0	5	0	7	0	.111	.304	.167	.471
Sierra, Magneuris	L	40	9	0	1	0	0	1	0	7	1	.225	.244	.275	.519
Slater, Austin	R	38	11	2	1	4	13	9	1	11	0	.289	.438	.711	1.148
Smith, Dominic	L	23	7	3	0	0	5	3	0	8	1	.304	.385	.435	.819
Smith, Pavin	L	21	4	1	0	0	0	1	0	4	1	.190	.261	.238	.499
Smith, Will	R	9	1	0	0	1	4	1	1	5	0	.111	.308	.444	.752
Sogard, Eric	L	29	10	2	0	0	4	2	1	2	0	.345	.387	.414	.801
Solano, Donovan	R	15	5	3	0	2	4	2	0	2	0	.333	.444	.933	1.378
Sosa, Edmundo	R	14	3	0	0	0	0	0	0	3	1	.214	.214	.214	.429
Stephenson, Tyler	R	40	9	2	0	3	12	1	0	12	2	.225	.256	.500	.756
Stevenson, Andrew	L	47	15	0	0	2	4	2	0	14	2	.319	.347	.447	.794
Stewart, D.J.	L	17	2	1	0	0	0	1	0	8	0	.118	.167	.176	.343
Suarez, Eugenio	R	10	1	1	0	0	0	0	0	6	0	.100	.100	.200	.300
Tapia, Raimel	L	12	3	0	1	0	1	4	1	2	4	.250	.438	.417	.854
Tauchman, Mike	L	16	2	0	0	0	0	2	0	8	0	.125	.222	.125	.347
Taylor, Tyrone	R	19	6	1	0	2	5	4	0	7	0	.316	.462	.684	1.146
Tellez, Rowdy	L	21	5	1	1	2	6	4	1	10	0	.238	.346	.667	1.013
Thomas, Lane	R	13	2	1	0	0	0	3	0	6	0	.154	.313	.231	.543
Tom, Ka'ai	L	8	1	0	0	0	1	2	0	3	0	.125	.300	.125	.425
Torrens, Luis	R	12	5	1	0	1	2	0	0	2	0	.417	.417	.750	1.167
Torreyes, Ronald	R	17	7	1	0	1	6	1	0	1	0	.412	.444	.647	1.092
Trejo, Alan	R	11	4	1	0	0	0	0	0	4	0	.364	.364	.455	.818
Tsutsugo, Yoshi	L	15	5	2	0	3	5	3	0	4	0	.333	.444	1.067	1.511
Tucker, Cole	B	9	2	0	0	0	0	1	0	3	0	.222	.300	.222	.522
Turner, Justin	R	10	2	1	0	1	1	0	0	2	0	.200	.273	.600	.873
Urias, Luis	R	10	2	1	0	1	5	0	0	5	0	.200	.200	.600	.800
Valera, Breyvic	B	9	2	1	0	0	0	1	0	4	0	.222	.300	.333	.633
VanMeter, Josh	L	33	2	1	0	0	2	7	0	13	1	.061	.225	.091	.316
Vargas, Ildemaro	B	12	2	0	0	0	1	0	0	2	0	.167	.167	.167	.333
Varsho, Daulton	L	15	5	1	0	0	1	2	0	4	0	.333	.412	.400	.812
Vierling, Matt	R	12	3	0	0	1	1	2	1	4	1	.250	.357	.500	.857
Villar, Jonathan	B	17	3	1	0	0	2	1	0	7	0	.176	.222	.235	.458
Vogelbach, Daniel	L	28	5	0	0	1	5	7	0	10	1	.179	.343	.286	.629
Vogt, Stephen	L	14	4	1	0	0	2	3	0	5	0	.286	.412	.357	.769
Voit, Luke	R	11	2	0	0	1	1	2	0	6	1	.182	.308	.455	.762
Vosler, Jason	L	13	3	0	0	1	3	3	0	6	1	.231	.353	.462	.814

Pinch Hitting

Pinch Hitters with 10+ PAs or 10+ Total Bases in 2021

Batter	B	AB	H	2B	3B	HR	RBI	TBB	IBB	SO	GDP	Avg	OBP	Slg	OPS
Wade Jr., LaMonte	L	20	4	0	0	1	2	1	1	9	0	.200	.273	.350	.623
Walker, Christian	R	13	3	2	0	0	1	0	0	4	0	.231	.286	.385	.670
Welker, Colton	R	10	1	1	0	0	1	2	0	4	1	.100	.250	.200	.450
Williams, Justin	L	9	3	0	0	1	3	3	0	3	0	.333	.538	.667	1.205
Williams, Luke	R	22	4	0	0	0	1	1	0	8	1	.182	.217	.182	.399
Wisdom, Patrick	R	13	4	1	0	1	2	2	0	4	0	.308	.400	.615	1.015
Wong, Kean	L	10	0	0	0	0	2	1	0	3	0	.000	.091	.000	.091
Yastrzemski, Mike	L	17	4	2	0	1	3	1	0	8	0	.235	.316	.529	.845
Yelich, Christian	L	8	1	0	0	0	1	1	0	3	1	.125	.200	.125	.325
Young, Andy	R	30	7	2	0	3	6	4	0	19	1	.233	.361	.600	.961
Zimmerman, Ryan	R	56	12	5	0	2	6	1	0	18	1	.214	.224	.411	.635

Career Pinch Hitting
Active Pinch Hitters with 100+ PAs in their careers

Batter	B	AB	H	2B	3B	HR	RBI	TBB	IBB	SO	GDP	Avg	OBP	Slg	OPS
Adams, Matt	L	235	58	11	0	11	50	11	3	80	5	.247	.281	.434	.715
Adrianza, Ehire	B	148	35	12	1	3	19	12	0	32	1	.236	.298	.392	.690
Aguilar, Jesus	R	135	30	7	0	5	21	16	0	48	6	.222	.303	.385	.688
Almora Jr., Albert	R	116	19	3	0	1	14	3	1	23	6	.164	.189	.216	.404
Barnes, Austin	R	100	23	5	0	2	14	10	0	34	4	.230	.319	.340	.659
Cabrera, Asdrubal	B	84	18	4	0	3	18	16	2	24	6	.214	.337	.369	.706
Carpenter, Matt	L	125	25	10	0	5	31	26	0	48	2	.200	.338	.400	.738
Culberson, Charlie	R	147	35	5	3	6	29	6	0	42	6	.238	.269	.435	.705
Dickerson, Alex	L	84	22	3	0	6	17	14	2	23	5	.262	.376	.512	.888
Dickerson, Corey	L	113	26	8	1	0	12	7	4	33	2	.230	.273	.319	.591
Difo, Wilmer	B	126	27	2	2	3	15	17	0	31	0	.214	.306	.333	.639
Flores, Wilmer	R	123	29	7	0	7	26	15	1	30	1	.236	.326	.463	.790
Fowler, Dexter	B	90	22	5	1	3	11	15	0	30	0	.244	.358	.422	.781
Frazier, Adam	L	88	22	5	0	1	7	14	0	10	2	.250	.371	.341	.712
Gosselin, Phil	R	184	45	8	0	1	13	13	2	58	2	.245	.291	.304	.596
Grandal, Yasmani	B	88	19	3	0	4	19	19	0	38	3	.216	.355	.386	.742
Harrison, Josh	R	121	21	3	1	3	14	4	0	23	2	.174	.205	.289	.494
Hernandez, Kike	R	162	33	8	0	6	20	17	3	52	1	.204	.276	.364	.640
Jay, Jon	L	152	42	3	1	3	19	14	1	37	7	.276	.356	.368	.725
Joyce, Matt	L	301	60	17	1	8	41	64	4	94	10	.199	.341	.342	.684
La Stella, Tommy	L	187	51	14	0	1	25	26	1	30	5	.273	.373	.364	.737
Miller, Brad	L	136	29	7	1	3	13	11	1	49	3	.213	.277	.346	.623
Moreland, Mitch	L	115	33	5	0	4	25	15	2	29	4	.287	.374	.435	.809
Parra, Gerardo	L	220	52	10	1	2	29	15	2	53	6	.236	.290	.318	.608
Pederson, Joc	L	121	23	7	1	4	15	22	0	37	2	.190	.317	.364	.681
Perez, Hernan	R	103	20	5	1	1	8	8	0	27	4	.194	.252	.291	.544
Ruf, Darin	R	125	17	1	0	5	15	10	1	52	3	.136	.218	.264	.482
Sandoval, Pablo	B	178	45	13	0	7	33	16	3	56	6	.253	.323	.444	.767
Sogard, Eric	L	108	28	5	0	0	9	17	2	16	4	.259	.357	.306	.663
Solano, Donovan	R	132	33	3	3	2	13	7	0	31	2	.250	.308	.364	.671
Stevenson, Andrew	L	112	34	3	1	3	12	11	0	37	3	.304	.362	.429	.791
Tapia, Raimel	L	98	24	3	3	5	21	9	1	28	7	.245	.315	.490	.805
Turner, Justin	R	182	47	11	0	7	39	16	1	36	8	.258	.322	.434	.756
Valaika, Pat	R	109	29	11	0	6	22	7	0	42	3	.266	.305	.532	.837
Vogt, Stephen	L	112	21	7	1	2	13	20	3	34	0	.188	.306	.321	.627
Zimmerman, Ryan	R	102	25	9	0	4	19	4	1	27	2	.245	.275	.451	.726

Productive Outs

Bill James

Eric Hosmer is the Babe Ruth of Productive Outs. Almost all analytical systems undervalue Eric Hosmer because we do not give him credit for the fact that he is significantly better than anybody else at moving runners with his outs. I suspect that the term "Productive Outs" more or less defines itself, but if it does not, a Productive Out is an out that moves a baserunner. An unproductive out is an out by a hitter which occurs in a situation in which the batter COULD have made an out that advanced a runner, but didn't. Only a fairly small percentage of outs have any chance to become Productive Outs. If a batter makes an out with the bases empty, that out by definition is neither productive nor unproductive, and the third out of an inning is by definition neither productive nor unproductive. Assuming that half of all outs are made with the bases empty and a third of outs are third outs, only about one-third of outs are classed as either productive or unproductive, and, since there are more runners on base when there are two out than when there are none out, the percentage is actually a little lower than that.

Anyway, Eric Hosmer's rate of Productive Outs is kind of eye-popping. He had 37 Productive Outs in 2021, 43 Unproductive Outs. At first one suspects this must be some kind of misprint. 37 of 80 is 46%. An average hitter has only 23.5% Productive Outs. Hosmer last year was basically twice the league norm.

The 37 Productive Outs did not lead the majors. Whit Merrifield had 38, but Merrifield was 38 for 113, which is still a good percentage. Merrifield led the league in Outs Made; he should have some productive ones. (Merrifield, by the way, has quite an impressive collection of Black Ink notes. He has led his league three times in games played, three times in at bats, twice in hits, once in doubles, once in triples, three times in stolen bases, once in Sacrifice Flies, and, we now know, at least once in Productive Outs. There are players in the Hall of Fame who never led their league in any batting category.)

Anyway, Hosmer was 18 productive outs better than average, which was easily the best in the majors. Raimel Tapia, Anthony Rizzo and Harold Castro were all +13, and they were second-third-fourth. In his career, Hosmer is +85 bases compared to an average out-maker, which is second on the career list; Elvis Andrus is +89, but Andrus bunts. Bunts are productive outs, but that's a different thing. Hosmer doesn't bunt; he moves runners without bunting. Hosmer's career percentage is really good, too.

How valuable is that, and should he get credit for it in things like WAR and other metrics?

Well, making outs is not a good thing in general. A productive out doesn't increase your expected runs scored in the inning; it usually decreases it—but it doesn't decrease it by nearly as much as an unproductive out. But EVERYBODY makes outs; that's not the appropriate standard here.

Almost all outs are costly. But all analytical systems reduce their estimates of a player's value when he makes an out. If you reduce a player's value by the same amount when he makes a productive out as you do when he makes an unproductive out, then you are missing some value.

With a runner on first and nobody out, a team can expect to score about .441 runs in the inning. With a runner on first and one out, the expectation drops to .284, a cost of .157 runs. But with a runner on SECOND and one out, the expectation drops to only .418, a cost of .023 runs. In that particular situation, having a productive out as opposed to an unproductive out eliminates 85% of the cost of the out. In that case, the value of a productive out as opposed to an unproductive out is .134 runs.

Usually it is not 85%, and usually it is not .134 runs; usually it is less than that. Moving a runner from second to third with the first out of an inning actually is not costly; that actually is a benefit to the team, so in that case the productive out eliminates more than 100% of the cost of the out.

In general, the value of a productive out as opposed to an unproductive out is about .10 to .11 runs, I believe. Eric Hosmer is about +18 on productive outs vs. an average player making the same number of outs, so that would add about two runs to his value. It's not a huge deal, but it's two runs. In sabermetrics, we chase down values a fifth of that size. It's an actual, documentable skill at which he excels year-in and year-out, as Anthony Rizzo does, and he should get credit for it.

On a team level, the best team at making productive as opposed to unproductive outs was Eric Hosmer's San Diego Padres, who had a productive out percentage of .295, make them +58 as compared to an average team. Their manager got fired. I was sorry to see that; Jayce Tingler is a fine person and a fine manager, and I don't often say things like that about somebody from the University of Missouri. Let us hope that, like Gabe Kapler, he gets hired by the right team for him, and goes out and kicks butt next year.

Anyway, the point was that being good at making productive as opposed to unproductive outs didn't really do them a hell of a lot of good. You wouldn't really expect that it would; +58 in this area is only +6 or 7 runs, which isn't going to turn your season around, and then there is this issue: if you emphasize making productive outs too much, you could be encouraging the wrong thing. Eric Hosmer hit .269 with 12 homers, 65 RBI and a .732 OPS, and you're really not paying him $21 million a year to do that.

On the other hand, the WORST team in this area was the Baltimore Orioles, -39 compared to an average team, and that didn't seem to do them a lot of good, either. There is not an obvious correlation between success in this area and overall team success—but in evaluating individuals, it could still be counted.

Manufactured Run Contributions

First of all, Manufactured Run Contributions are totally different from Manufactured Runs. For the past several years, the people who have written this section, introducing the data, have referred to Manufactured Run Contributions as Manufactured Runs. I don't know how this got started or why it has been so hard to stop it, but in any case it has.

A Manufactured Run is a run that results from teams moving runners along other than by playing station-to-station baseball. The term, which I think was popularized by Tim McCarver although it may have been used occasionally before McCarver was a national broadcaster, refers to runs that teams create by being aggressive on the bases or hitting behind the runner or something like that. The term came to be fairly widely used, but there was no exact definition of it, thus no way to study it. You can't study Manufactured Runs unless you know what one is. In 2007, for the 2008 Handbook, we developed a specific definition, and we have printed the data ever since.

Any run that scores on a home run is not a manufactured run. A run that scores as a result of three singles is not a manufactured run, or a run that scores as a result of a walk and two singles or two walks and a single…not a manufactured run, because three of the four bases are directly accounted for by batter's actions.

On the other hand, if a team makes a run out of TWO events—two singles, or a walk and a single…that's a manufactured run. Walk, single, runner goes to third, scores on a ground ball, that's a manufactured run. A batter hits a single, steals second, scores on another single…that's a manufactured run. The full definition is in the Glossary at the back of the book.

No one has ever argued with us about the definition, because frankly nobody has ever taken that much of an interest in the concept It's never really caught on. We'll keep putting the data out there; maybe it will catch on sometime later.

Anyway, the difference between a Manufactured Run and a Manufactured Run Contribution is somewhat like the difference between a Home Run and an RBI. A Manufactured Run, like a home run, is the whole thing. A Manufactured Run Contribution, like an RBI, is just a part of it. A Manufactured Run is a TEAM thing. A MR-Contribution is an INDIVIDUAL thing.

The team which manufactured the most runs in 2021 was the Kansas City Royals (175), followed by the Tampa Bay Rays (164). The teams which manufactured the fewest runs were the Seattle Mariners (105) and the New York Mets (106).

Manufactured Runs are at least vaguely related to Productive Outs, and I think there is a visible connection between Productive Outs and Manufactured Runs, on the team level. As we said about Productive Outs, there doesn't appear to be a real obvious connection between Manufactured Runs *on the offensive side* and team success. Sometimes Manufacturing Runs is something you do when you don't have good hitters.

Manufactured Runs can be studied from both an offensive and a defensive standpoint—that is, as there are teams which are good at putting parts of a run together into whole runs, there are also teams which are good at preventing the other team from doing this. From a defensive standpoint, this may be more closely tied to team success. The major league teams which were best at preventing Manufactured Runs in 2021 were San Francisco (92 Manufactured Runs by the Opposition), Houston (99), Toronto (99), the Dodgers (106) and the Braves (109). As you are probably aware, those are all really good teams.

From an individual perspective, the player who contributed to the most Manufactured Runs (MR-Con) was Whit Merrifield (33), while Giancarlo Stanton contributed to only 5. It's just not his thing, you know? I think that's a really insightful descriptive fact, don't you? 33 Manufactured Run Contributions versus 5. It's not just coincidence, or who is around you in the batting order; it says something important about how you play the game.

Finally, this question. As the major leagues become more and more dominated by home run hitters, have Manufactured Runs become less common?

Yes. Yes, I'm afraid they have. In 2007, when we introduced the concept, there were just short of 5,000 Manufactured Runs in the major league season (4,956). In 2021, there just short of 4,000 (3,979). Over the fourteen years, there has been a 20% decline in the number of Manufactured Runs.

Players with the most Manufactured Runs, Productive Outs, & Unproductive Outs

Manufactured Runs	
Merrifield, Whit	33
Lopez, Nicky	30
Altuve, Jose	30
Tapia, Raimel	29
Kiner-Falefa, Isiah	28
Marte, Starling	24
Ramirez, Jose	23
Turner, Trea	23
Straw, Myles	23
Canha, Mark	23
Edman, Tommy	23
Rosario, Amed	22
Fletcher, David	22
Frazier, Adam	21
Soto, Juan	21
Lowe, Brandon	21
Reynolds, Bryan	21
Kemp, Tony	20
Bogaerts, Xander	20
Machado, Manny	20
Anderson, Tim	20
Rojas, Josh	20
Garcia, Leury	20
Semien, Marcus	20
Tatis Jr., Fernando	20
Verdugo, Alex	19
ONeill, Tyler'	19
Ohtani, Shohei	19
Taylor, Michael A.	19
Chisholm Jr., Jazz	19
Baddoo, Akil	18
Urias, Luis	18
Devers, Rafael	18
Arozarena, Randy	18
LeMahieu, DJ	17
Andrus, Elvis	17
Adames, Willy	17
Albies, Ozzie	17
Hampson, Garrett	17
Garcia, Adolis	17
Bichette, Bo	17
Grossman, Robbie	17
Rojas, Miguel	17
Lindor, Francisco	17
Betts, Mookie	16
Ahmed, Nick	16
Story, Trevor	16
Mullins II, Cedric	16
Baez, Javier	16
India, Jonathan	16

Productive Outs	
Merrifield, Whit	38
Hosmer, Eric	37
Rizzo, Anthony	35
Santana, Carlos	34
Abreu, Jose	34
Cronenworth, Jake	33
Blackmon, Charlie	32
Lopez, Nicky	32
Albies, Ozzie	31
Olson, Matt	31
Verdugo, Alex	31
McMahon, Ryan	30
Garcia, Leury	30
Perez, Salvador	30
Newman, Kevin	29
Reynolds, Bryan	29
Bichette, Bo	28
Carlson, Dylan	28
Soto, Juan	28
Gurriel, Yuli	28
Garcia, Adolis	27
Rosario, Amed	27
Diaz, Yandy	27
Fletcher, David	27
Peralta, David	27
Devers, Rafael	27
Edman, Tommy	27
Tapia, Raimel	27
Cruz, Nelson	27
Lindor, Francisco	26
Castro, Harold	26
Freeman, Freddie	26
Ramirez, Jose	26
Grossman, Robbie	25
Seager, Kyle	25
Herrera, Odubel	25
Lowe, Nathaniel	25
Bell, Josh	25
Castellanos, Nick	25
Arenado, Nolan	25
LeMahieu, DJ	24
Gardner, Brett	24
Gregorius, Didi	24
Polanco, Jorge	24
Yelich, Christian	24
Straw, Myles	24
Chapman, Matt	24
Kiner-Falefa, Isiah	24
France, Ty	24

Unproductive Outs	
Garcia, Adolis	111
Goldschmidt, Paul	106
Seager, Kyle	96
Escobar, Eduardo	95
Alonso, Pete	94
Perez, Salvador	94
Arenado, Nolan	93
Martinez, J.D.	90
Chapman, Matt	89
Olson, Matt	88
Suarez, Eugenio	88
Abreu, Jose	87
Alvarez, Yordan	87
Turner, Justin	86
Semien, Marcus	84
Castellanos, Nick	83
Cruz, Nelson	83
Machado, Manny	83
Taylor, Chris	82
Judge, Aaron	81
Story, Trevor	81
Lindor, Francisco	80
Renfroe, Hunter	80
Reynolds, Bryan	80
Santana, Carlos	80
Newman, Kevin	80
Moncada, Yoan	79
Mountcastle, Ryan	79
Sano, Miguel	79
Mancini, Trey	78
Duvall, Adam	78
Adames, Willy	78
Smith, Dominic	78
Haniger, Mitch	78
Muncy, Max	78
Arozarena, Randy	77
Soto, Juan	77
Riley, Austin	77
Lowe, Nathaniel	76
Yastrzemski, Mike	76
Bell, Josh	75
Dozier, Hunter	75
Baez, Javier	75
Merrifield, Whit	75
Ramirez, Jose	75
Correa, Carlos	74
Guerrero Jr., Vladimir	74
Grichuk, Randal	74
Villar, Jonathan	74
France, Ty	74

Manufactured Runs, Productive Outs, & Unproductive Outs Produced by Team

Team	Manufactured Runs	Productive Outs	Unproductive Outs
Arizona Diamondbacks	129	222	762
Atlanta Braves	122	213	700
Baltimore Orioles	114	180	743
Boston Red Sox	149	241	722
Chicago White Sox	143	227	757
Chicago Cubs	128	236	718
Cincinnati Reds	107	219	775
Cleveland Indians	143	222	694
Colorado Rockies	146	269	722
Detroit Tigers	129	214	687
Houston Astros	139	228	758
Kansas City Royals	175	263	706
Los Angeles Dodgers	134	222	756
Los Angeles Angels	143	222	708
Miami Marlins	119	197	688
Milwaukee Brewers	146	225	718
Minnesota Twins	121	209	699
New York Yankees	117	184	726
New York Mets	106	210	749
Oakland Athletics	159	236	695
Philadelphia Phillies	129	244	713
Pittsburgh Pirates	142	239	736
San Diego Padres	142	286	684
San Francisco Giants	109	205	763
Seattle Mariners	105	179	736
St Louis Cardinals	132	236	699
Tampa Bay Rays	164	220	760
Texas Rangers	124	214	699
Toronto Blue Jays	131	200	706
Washington Nationals	132	219	733

Manufactured Runs, Productive Outs, & Unproductive Outs Allowed by Team

Team	Manufactured Runs	Productive Outs	Unproductive Outs
Arizona Diamondbacks	142	281	747
Atlanta Braves	109	249	690
Baltimore Orioles	132	224	749
Boston Red Sox	160	222	774
Chicago White Sox	147	215	658
Chicago Cubs	138	247	751
Cincinnati Reds	146	229	753
Cleveland Indians	123	190	752
Colorado Rockies	122	241	761
Detroit Tigers	146	258	747
Houston Astros	99	218	756
Kansas City Royals	175	216	734
Los Angeles Dodgers	106	228	703
Los Angeles Angels	174	201	730
Miami Marlins	138	220	727
Milwaukee Brewers	135	219	698
Minnesota Twins	148	233	714
New York Yankees	135	209	712
New York Mets	120	205	655
Oakland Athletics	127	195	735
Philadelphia Phillies	113	205	696
Pittsburgh Pirates	135	233	772
San Diego Padres	136	213	718
San Francisco Giants	92	209	705
Seattle Mariners	131	211	748
St Louis Cardinals	139	259	750
Tampa Bay Rays	121	194	679
Texas Rangers	147	235	680
Toronto Blue Jays	99	172	741
Washington Nationals	144	250	677

Managers

Mark Simon

As a fan of the TV show *Jeopardy*, I've greatly enjoyed the recent run of dominance by one of the game's all-time best players, Matt Amodio (whose hobby happens to be studying baseball stats).

What made Amodio so impressive was not just his knowledge base, but in how he managed a game. He played aggressively, picked the bottom clues first, hunted down Daily Doubles, and then made big wagers on them. He bet on himself and his team (his brain cells) to come through as needed.

In the 2021 baseball season, the game manager most similar to Amodio was Gabe Kapler of the Giants.

Kapler has come a long way from his two rough seasons with the Phillies. In two seasons with the Giants he's changed things up a little bit and maxed out on what he's gotten from his team.

The Giants have led the majors in pinch-hitter usage in each of the last two seasons by a considerable margin and in 2021, they finished with 68 more than the next-closest team.

And Kapler made big bets on his entire bench this year. Seven different players had at least 20 pinch-hit at-bats. The Giants also led the NL in defensive substitutions with 48.

But Kapler took it a step further. He and his coaching staff established in-game platoons that were meant to go beyond one moment in a game. The Giants had 116 substitutes (including relievers) enter a game this season and record at least two plate appearances. No other team had more than 90.

Kapler's other version of managing aggressively was in the composition and use of his bullpen, a mix of lefties, righties, and unusual arm angles (Tyler Rogers). The Giants used relievers on consecutive days 146 times, more than any other team. And those pitchers were great! They had an MLB-low 1.48 ERA in those situations.

Amodio's strategy was a winning one and had considerable staying power. Kapler's had enough staying power to get through 2021 with 107 wins for the Giants. Whether it will work for the long term will be a greater challenge.

Content Management

If you like our work, there are plenty of other outlets at which you can find more of it.

The SIS Baseball Podcast features interviews with notable players (Byron Buxton, Cedric Mullins, Matt Chapman) and notable people who cover baseball (Joe Sheehan, Tyler Kepner), and provides insight into different baseball work being done at our company. It can be found wherever you subscribe to podcasts.

Our blog (SportsInfoSolutionsBlog.com) features articles and research written by our R&D team and our Baseball Operations Department. Topics include examinations of player and team performance as well as statistical updates and leaderboards.

You can also follow us on Twitter at @SportsInfo_SIS and on Instagram at @sportsinfosolutions.

Brad Ausmus

Year	Team	Lg	G	LINEUPS		SUBSTITUTION			PITCHER USAGE						TACTICS				INTENTIONAL BB				RESULTS		
				LUp	PL%	PH	PR	DS	Quick	Slow	LO	RCD	LS	Rel	SBA	SacA	RM	PO	#	Good	NG	Bomb	W	L	Pct
2014	Tigers	AL	162	103	.51	79	43	44	28	55	43	99	1	473	147	32	144	13	34	17	17	5	90	72	.556
2015	Tigers	AL	161	122	.47	83	38	50	33	59	30	131	4	505	134	37	161	7	32	18	14	7	74	87	.460
2016	Tigers	AL	161	111	.48	89	31	50	41	37	18	93	4	476	87	21	95	3	25	12	13	6	86	75	.534
2017	Tigers	AL	162	131	.50	103	30	24	28	52	17	97	6	510	99	16	104	3	42	26	16	8	64	98	.395
2019	Angels	AL	162	153	.57	98	27	44	34	29	0	105	5	589	85	4	78	1	11	5	6	4	72	90	.444
	162-Game Average			124	.50	91	34	43	33	47	22	105	4	512	111	22	117	5	29	16	13	6	77	85	.475

Dusty Baker

Year	Team	Lg	G	LINEUPS		SUBSTITUTION			PITCHER USAGE						TACTICS				INTENTIONAL BB				RESULTS		
				LUp	PL%	PH	PR	DS	Quick	Slow	LO	RCD	LS	Rel	SBA	SacA	RM	PO	#	Good	NG	Bomb	W	L	Pct
1994	Giants	NL	115	76	.53	177	16	9	29	25	2	86	12	288	154	88		78	40	24	16	8	55	60	.478
1995	Giants	NL	144	97	.41	230	36	13	32	50	8	90	8	381	184	101		77	51	32	19	14	67	77	.465
1996	Giants	NL	162	129	.51	250	17	15	24	58	15	94	8	425	166	103		96	60	37	23	15	68	94	.420
1997	Giants	NL	162	114	.71	212	17	22	46	25	17	132	4	481	170	85		93	57	36	21	12	90	72	.556
1998	Giants	NL	163	130	.62	224	20	12	43	38	8	113	5	433	153	111		41	68	42	26	9	89	74	.546
1999	Giants	NL	162	119	.62	233	16	16	30	51	27	111		450	165	113		40	41	25	16	10	86	76	.531
2000	Giants	NL	162	82	.56	233	26	22	38	50	25	91	3	384	118	86		37	26	17	9	2	97	65	.599
2001	Giants	NL	162	122	.48	261	22	19	40	48	10	114	4	439	99	95		45	49	33	16	6	90	72	.556
2002	Giants	NL	162	118	.43	223	32	38	29	56	53	106	8	417	95	89	42	41	44	28	16	10	95	66	.590
2003	Cubs	NL	162	114	.49	272	25	43	24	58	65	111	3	420	104	93	31	24	36	23	13	4	88	74	.543
2004	Cubs	NL	162	113	.44	254	16	19	37	41	42	129	8	460	94	108	71	62	33	22	11	7	89	73	.549
2005	Cubs	NL	162	121	.59	240	21	29	40	46	36	103	2	457	104	88	107	70	48	27	21	7	79	83	.488
2006	Cubs	NL	162	133	.56	271	9	26	45	39	22	165	2	542	170	108	139	46	44	28	16	11	66	96	.407
2008	Reds	NL	162	119	.58	285	28	27	26	63	39	124	2	507	132	100	101	37	40	28	12	4	74	88	.457
2009	Reds	NL	162	130	.45	252	15	35	30	62	35	115	1	478	136	120	118	23	36	29	7	4	78	84	.481
2010	Reds	NL	162	120	.46	258	19	49	36	41	22	140	0	502	136	91	157	13	32	22	10	9	91	71	.562
2011	Reds	NL	162	142	.42	240	29	42	34	51	20	115	0	501	147	102	226	33	47	26	21	5	79	83	.488
2012	Reds	NL	162	121	.43	201	19	39	33	39	30	78	4	425	114	108	148	19	33	22	11	3	97	65	.599
2013	Reds	NL	162	95	.54	236	20	27	39	40	14	99	3	461	102	110	157	21	28	23	5	3	90	72	.556
2016	Nationals	NL	162	112	.57	220	20	27	35	45	21	119	4	508	160	59	161	3	43	28	15	9	95	67	.586
2017	Nationals	NL	162	124	.59	241	33	26	22	53	27	90	2	487	138	57	113	3	39	29	10	6	97	65	.599
2020	Astros	AL	60	49	.48	28	13	7	14	15	1	24	0	193	33	7	36	3	7	4	3	1	29	31	.483
2021	Astros	AL	162	133	.50	94	27	22	38	45	2	81	4	512	69	14	96	0	12	8	4	1	95	67	.586
	162-Game Average			119	.52	234	23	27	35	47	25	110	4	462	134	93	119	41	42	27	15	7	86	76	.531

Rocco Baldelli

Year	Team	Lg	G	LINEUPS		SUBSTITUTION			PITCHER USAGE						TACTICS				INTENTIONAL BB				RESULTS		
				LUp	PL%	PH	PR	DS	Quick	Slow	LO	RCD	LS	Rel	SBA	SacA	RM	PO	#	Good	NG	Bomb	W	L	Pct
2019	Twins	AL	162	145	.62	84	24	35	42	43	1	94	16	524	49	16	56	4	10	9	1	1	101	61	.623
2020	Twins	AL	60	56	.65	29	19	20	14	11	1	29	0	202	21	3	18	0	0	0	0	0	36	24	.600
2021	Twins	AL	162	149	.61	112	28	27	50	50	1	84	6	529	69	11	70	0	13	7	6	3	73	89	.451
	162-Game Average			148	.62	95	30	35	45	44	1	87	9	529	59	13	61	2	10	7	3	2	89	73	.549

Jeff Banister

Year	Team	Lg	G	LINEUPS		SUBSTITUTION			PITCHER USAGE						TACTICS				INTENTIONAL BB				RESULTS		
				LUp	PL%	PH	PR	DS	Quick	Slow	LO	RCD	LS	Rel	SBA	SacA	RM	PO	#	Good	NG	Bomb	W	L	Pct
2015	Rangers	AL	162	127	.57	94	51	46	40	47	11	122	0	498	140	66	158	5	29	19	10	5	88	74	.543
2016	Rangers	AL	162	124	.55	84	58	38	47	44	7	85	1	479	135	26	136	3	16	5	11	8	95	67	.586
2017	Rangers	AL	162	134	.54	66	40	20	39	40	6	71	7	464	157	35	153	0	22	9	13	10	78	84	.481
2018	Rangers	AL	152	122	.61	74	40	21	29	44	1	63	3	465	108	42	135	1	22	13	9	6	64	88	.421
	162-Game Average			129	.57	81	48	32	39	44	6	86	3	484	137	43	148	2	23	12	11	7	83	79	.512

Rod Barajas

Year	Team	Lg	G	LINEUPS		SUBSTITUTION			PITCHER USAGE						TACTICS				INTENTIONAL BB				RESULTS		
				LUp	PL%	PH	PR	DS	Quick	Slow	LO	RCD	LS	Rel	SBA	SacA	RM	PO	#	Good	NG	Bomb	W	L	Pct
2019	Padres	NL	8	8	.69	28	2	1	5	0	0	4	0	34	4	2	8	0	0	0	0	0	1	7	.125
	162-Game Average			162	.69	567	41	20	101	0	0	81	0	689	81	41	162	0	0	0	0	0	20	142	.123

David Bell

Year	Team	Lg	G	LINEUPS		SUBSTITUTION			PITCHER USAGE						TACTICS				INTENTIONAL BB				RESULTS		
				LUp	PL%	PH	PR	DS	Quick	Slow	LO	RCD	LS	Rel	SBA	SacA	RM	PO	#	Good	NG	Bomb	W	L	Pct
2019	Reds	NL	162	140	.55	319	28	46	36	43	9	104	10	535	118	44	111	1	31	25	6	5	75	87	.463
2020	Reds	NL	60	54	.68	68	17	16	13	18	5	28	1	168	38	1	32	1	6	4	2	2	31	29	.517
2021	Reds	NL	162	133	.56	303	23	33	22	56	2	111	6	579	60	49	68	0	30	23	7	3	83	79	.512
	162-Game Average			138	.57	291	29	40	30	49	7	103	7	541	91	40	89	1	28	22	6	4	80	82	.494

Bud Black

Year	Team	Lg	G	LINEUPS		SUBSTITUTION			PITCHER USAGE						TACTICS				INTENTIONAL BB				RESULTS		
				LUp	PL%	PH	PR	DS	Quick	Slow	LO	RCD	LS	Rel	SBA	SacA	RM	PO	#	Good	NG	Bomb	W	L	Pct
2007	Padres	NL	163	115	.62	279	18	13	63	28	13	122	0	485	79	85	73	56	48	28	20	11	89	74	.546
2008	Padres	NL	162	113	.63	286	25	20	55	36	17	109	0	491	53	75	78	31	61	30	31	17	63	99	.389
2009	Padres	NL	162	137	.64	264	8	34	50	37	8	118	5	527	111	99	84	55	58	42	16	6	75	87	.463
2010	Padres	NL	162	135	.61	285	16	45	55	33	10	132	7	499	174	99	135	31	51	35	16	8	90	72	.556
2011	Padres	NL	162	140	.58	288	20	43	40	36	10	110	2	490	214	69	184	41	56	31	25	13	71	91	.438
2012	Padres	NL	162	132	.74	280	26	35	45	49	11	126	5	529	201	89	162	21	48	34	14	7	76	86	.469
2013	Padres	NL	162	145	.66	271	24	37	35	46	4	102	1	488	152	78	122	12	31	20	11	8	76	86	.469
2014	Padres	NL	162	157	.74	313	23	29	49	33	13	104	1	481	125	74	116	15	32	24	8	4	77	85	.475
2015	Padres	NL	65	50	.54	113	6	6	8	25	3	40	0	199	54	24	46	2	15	11	4	0	32	33	.492
2017	Rockies	NL	162	111	.51	261	19	14	44	36	4	100	2	549	93	76	149	4	20	14	6	3	87	75	.537
2018	Rockies	NL	163	126	.56	276	20	19	29	49	5	103	1	518	128	65	137	2	24	16	8	5	91	72	.558
2019	Rockies	NL	162	141	.60	305	8	13	27	58	1	114	3	590	102	71	96	5	33	21	12	3	71	91	.438
2020	Rockies	NL	60	52	.60	51	10	9	5	20	0	31	2	189	51	11	37	2	5	3	2	1	26	34	.433
2021	Rockies	NL	161	143	.55	280	13	13	35	51	0	83	1	543	99	64	92	7	19	12	7	4	74	87	.460
	162-Game Average			133	.62	278	18	26	42	42	8	109	2	515	128	77	118	22	39	25	14	7	78	84	.481

Bruce Bochy

Year	Team	Lg	G	LINEUPS		SUBSTITUTION			PITCHER USAGE						TACTICS				INTENTIONAL BB				RESULTS		
				LUp	PL%	PH	PR	DS	Quick	Slow	LO	RCD	LS	Rel	SBA	SacA	RM	PO	#	Good	NG	Bomb	W	L	Pct
1995	Padres	NL	144	96	.59	262	30	23	44	41	17	38	3	337	170	68		38	37	19	18	11	70	74	.486
1996	Padres	NL	162	114	.52	289	29	15	51	33	10	67	12	411	164	73		65	47	29	18	12	91	71	.562
1997	Padres	NL	162	111	.60	291	26	9	45	45	3	81	11	426	200	84		58	37	20	17	11	76	86	.469
1998	Padres	NL	162	108	.65	280	62	44	44	45	9	81	12	369	116	84		27	45	31	14	10	98	64	.605
1999	Padres	NL	162	137	.60	298	51	21	44	36	4	68	5	403	241	60		29	48	29	19	13	74	88	.457
2000	Padres	NL	162	134	.52	285	44	14	41	47	14	105	5	443	184	52		27	50	21	29	13	76	86	.469
2001	Padres	NL	162	116	.60	255	54	27	32	47	6	85	10	422	173	43		23	54	31	23	13	79	83	.488
2002	Padres	NL	162	123	.66	259	44	56	39	40	17	106	4	459	115	63	74	14	61	38	23	14	66	96	.407
2003	Padres	NL	162	134	.58	339	20	29	34	43	16	100	3	473	115	63	41	6	52	33	19	12	64	98	.395
2004	Padres	NL	162	96	.54	261	28	47	47	32	15	76	3	437	77	75	96	14	39	24	15	10	87	75	.537
2005	Padres	NL	162	128	.58	285	31	49	46	36	23	87	1	456	143	89	111	16	45	33	12	8	82	80	.506
2006	Padres	NL	162	111	.60	264	64	48	43	42	24	111	2	475	154	77	110	21	63	43	20	10	88	74	.543
2007	Giants	NL	162	128	.72	264	50	45	26	50	36	132	2	466	152	86	119	10	41	29	12	3	71	91	.438
2008	Giants	NL	162	134	.68	276	32	39	24	59	42	97	6	478	154	77	155	5	59	40	19	8	72	90	.444
2009	Giants	NL	162	134	.65	231	21	52	42	40	32	84	8	457	106	93	118	5	49	32	17	10	88	74	.543
2010	Giants	NL	162	126	.55	224	45	70	29	37	40	118	12	477	87	102	144	12	58	41	17	8	92	70	.568
2011	Giants	NL	162	138	.62	245	49	42	38	38	44	108	3	480	136	79	175	11	46	36	10	6	86	76	.531
2012	Giants	NL	162	112	.75	220	32	55	22	50	31	136	9	526	157	87	176	15	42	30	12	5	94	68	.580
2013	Giants	NL	162	109	.70	263	19	45	33	52	23	143	4	524	93	78	164	7	64	46	18	6	76	86	.469
2014	Giants	NL	162	131	.66	236	29	64	45	41	19	102	1	475	83	53	147	12	35	25	10	9	88	74	.543
2015	Giants	NL	162	124	.63	230	12	21	45	32	11	137	2	557	129	54	173	8	28	20	8	3	84	78	.519
2016	Giants	NL	162	121	.66	268	7	29	31	42	28	148	4	575	115	54	178	6	30	25	5	4	87	75	.537
2017	Giants	NL	162	136	.61	298	22	12	22	59	20	93	2	502	110	51	135	3	42	29	13	11	64	98	.395
2018	Giants	NL	162	140	.59	305	16	30	36	38	6	100	0	549	111	43	139	2	37	25	12	5	73	89	.451
2019	Giants	NL	162	141	.67	362	11	25	34	43	4	94	2	587	75	37	101	4	26	16	10	4	77	85	.475
	162-Game Average			124	.62	273	33	37	38	43	20	100	5	474	135	69	131	18	46	30	16	9	80	82	.494

Aaron Boone

Year	Team	Lg	G	LINEUPS		SUBSTITUTION			PITCHER USAGE						TACTICS				INTENTIONAL BB				RESULTS		
				LUp	PL%	PH	PR	DS	Quick	Slow	LO	RCD	LS	Rel	SBA	SacA	RM	PO	#	Good	NG	Bomb	W	L	Pct
2018	Yankees	AL	162	137	.54	71	14	24	45	32	4	75	5	508	84	17	113	3	9	4	5	3	100	62	.617
2019	Yankees	AL	162	155	.48	57	24	32	43	27	1	80	5	545	77	19	81	2	12	9	3	1	103	59	.636
2020	Yankees	AL	60	57	.48	36	15	20	18	17	3	26	1	174	34	4	39	0	5	5	0	0	33	27	.550
2021	Yankees	AL	162	146	.50	94	45	45	50	31	3	73	3	512	81	11	80	6	10	6	4	2	92	70	.568
	162-Game Average			147	.50	77	29	36	46	32	3	75	4	516	82	15	93	3	11	7	4	2	97	65	.599

Mickey Callaway

Year	Team	Lg	G	LINEUPS		SUBSTITUTION			PITCHER USAGE						TACTICS				INTENTIONAL BB				RESULTS		
				LUp	PL%	PH	PR	DS	Quick	Slow	LO	RCD	LS	Rel	SBA	SacA	RM	PO	#	Good	NG	Bomb	W	L	Pct
2018	Mets	NL	162	151	.58	258	17	30	41	43	11	72	10	501	110	39	119	6	32	17	15	9	77	85	.475
2019	Mets	NL	162	132	.50	273	42	65	35	57	16	87	6	502	83	42	102	10	40	27	13	6	86	76	.531
	162-Game Average			142	.54	266	30	48	38	50	14	80	8	502	97	41	111	8	36	22	14	8	82	81	.503

Kevin Cash

Year	Team	Lg	G	LUp	PL%	PH	PR	DS	Quick	Slow	LO	RCD	LS	Rel	SBA	SacA	RM	PO	#	Good	NG	Bomb	W	L	Pct
				LINEUPS		SUBSTITUTION			PITCHER USAGE						TACTICS				INTENTIONAL BB				RESULTS		
2015	Rays	AL	162	137	.62	219	23	38	72	33	10	134	3	530	132	27	173	2	23	17	6	3	80	82	.494
2016	Rays	AL	162	142	.55	103	11	28	42	52	18	100	8	485	97	24	146	12	25	16	9	4	68	94	.420
2017	Rays	AL	162	126	.57	123	21	24	39	47	16	89	9	511	122	24	143	12	37	25	12	8	80	82	.494
2018	Rays	AL	162	151	.58	109	25	33	50	18	5	115	10	553	179	37	190	2	34	20	14	9	90	72	.556
2019	Rays	AL	162	152	.59	131	31	43	50	18	0	136	6	603	131	11	166	3	27	14	13	8	96	66	.593
2020	Rays	AL	60	59	.68	66	14	24	22	9	0	35	3	219	57	1	38	1	4	3	1	0	40	20	.667
2021	Rays	AL	162	158	.67	120	36	55	66	37	2	71	10	531	130	6	142	3	27	16	11	7	100	62	.617
162-Game Average				145	.60	137	25	38	54	34	8	107	8	539	133	20	157	5	28	17	10	6	87	75	.537

Alex Cora

Year	Team	Lg	G	LUp	PL%	PH	PR	DS	Quick	Slow	LO	RCD	LS	Rel	SBA	SacA	RM	PO	#	Good	NG	Bomb	W	L	Pct
				LINEUPS		SUBSTITUTION			PITCHER USAGE						TACTICS				INTENTIONAL BB				RESULTS		
2018	Red Sox	AL	162	134	.55	96	22	31	58	44	5	101	4	535	156	8	183	1	8	4	4	1	108	54	.667
2019	Red Sox	AL	162	135	.57	123	29	18	45	52	16	134	3	632	98	26	140	2	22	14	8	6	84	78	.519
2021	Red Sox	AL	162	141	.56	95	23	27	36	44	1	116	8	563	61	15	79	0	31	21	10	6	92	70	.568
162-Game Average				137	.56	105	25	25	46	47	7	117	5	577	105	16	134	1	20	13	7	4	95	67	.586

Craig Counsell

Year	Team	Lg	G	LUp	PL%	PH	PR	DS	Quick	Slow	LO	RCD	LS	Rel	SBA	SacA	RM	PO	#	Good	NG	Bomb	W	L	Pct
				LINEUPS		SUBSTITUTION			PITCHER USAGE						TACTICS				INTENTIONAL BB				RESULTS		
2015	Brewers	NL	137	106	.54	247	14	30	30	47	3	85	1	424	99	56	106	2	30	26	4	3	61	76	.445
2016	Brewers	NL	162	123	.55	284	4	22	40	41	1	115	3	513	237	71	160	0	33	16	17	8	73	89	.451
2017	Brewers	NL	162	123	.53	285	18	44	58	33	5	124	5	550	169	56	159	0	45	30	15	9	86	76	.531
2018	Brewers	NL	163	137	.54	288	17	77	64	29	0	105	18	559	156	38	148	1	34	22	12	7	96	67	.589
2019	Brewers	NL	162	134	.64	317	14	56	60	26	1	97	17	588	126	29	78	3	28	22	6	2	89	73	.549
2020	Brewers	NL	60	53	.62	65	14	16	15	11	0	18	1	189	26	0	22	0	1	1	0	0	29	31	.483
2021	Brewers	NL	162	138	.62	294	13	39	44	29	2	92	2	533	103	35	66	0	19	13	6	2	95	67	.586
162-Game Average				131	.57	286	15	46	50	35	2	102	8	539	147	46	119	1	31	21	10	5	85	77	.525

Terry Francona

Year	Team	Lg	G	LUp	PL%	PH	PR	DS	Quick	Slow	LO	RCD	LS	Rel	SBA	SacA	RM	PO	#	Good	NG	Bomb	W	L	Pct
				LINEUPS		SUBSTITUTION			PITCHER USAGE						TACTICS				INTENTIONAL BB				RESULTS		
1997	Phillies	NL	162	98	.66	288	19	28	28	54	22	102	9	409	148	91		30	42	23	19	9	68	94	.420
1998	Phillies	NL	162	84	.53	256	20	19	34	57	20	88	7	385	142	85		16	27	10	17	8	75	87	.463
1999	Phillies	NL	162	85	.51	239	13	31	29	41	16	111	7	441	160	81		27	24	14	10	6	77	85	.475
2000	Phillies	NL	162	108	.53	278	17	14	38	43	25	102	5	414	132	89		16	32	22	10	7	65	97	.401
2004	Red Sox	AL	162	141	.65	116	65	58	41	48	32	105	8	437	98	18	91	28	28	22	6	4	98	64	.605
2005	Red Sox	AL	162	104	.67	110	46	37	25	55	30	99	3	442	57	21	79	11	28	18	10	5	95	67	.586
2006	Red Sox	AL	162	116	.59	93	54	49	36	44	13	94	9	454	74	33	98	16	25	11	14	7	86	76	.531
2007	Red Sox	AL	162	109	.60	84	34	23	41	35	32	89	4	451	120	45	90	14	20	14	6	4	96	66	.593
2008	Red Sox	AL	162	131	.59	62	40	40	50	30	20	90	11	466	155	40	87	8	17	10	7	4	95	67	.586
2009	Red Sox	AL	162	113	.58	85	47	28	36	50	30	68	6	463	165	29	68	9	24	15	9	6	95	67	.586
2010	Red Sox	AL	162	143	.62	125	48	34	32	63	49	84	3	443	85	36	125	26	30	17	13	4	89	73	.549
2011	Red Sox	AL	162	123	.67	89	44	11	52	46	27	89	4	444	144	29	163	34	11	6	5	2	90	72	.556
2013	Indians	AL	162	121	.75	78	45	24	47	34	18	122	2	540	153	41	158	3	26	15	11	6	92	70	.568
2014	Indians	AL	162	133	.78	123	16	24	37	37	18	150	7	573	131	58	128	3	51	29	22	13	85	77	.525
2015	Indians	AL	161	127	.75	138	21	13	40	36	23	85	4	476	114	63	87	4	27	20	7	5	81	80	.503
2016	Indians	AL	161	101	.73	144	27	29	47	39	18	103	3	504	165	44	126	2	34	22	12	7	94	67	.584
2017	Indians	AL	162	131	.73	93	43	50	48	31	20	106	4	497	111	35	95	2	15	11	4	3	102	60	.630
2018	Indians	AL	162	105	.75	97	74	42	29	48	23	121	10	508	171	44	152	6	29	19	10	7	91	71	.562
2019	Indians	AL	162	132	.73	101	25	15	30	44	29	89	9	522	138	57	100	2	19	11	8	7	93	69	.574
2020	Indians	AL	60	48	.74	37	18	10	8	18	2	27	2	181	35	14	33	0	8	4	4	1	35	25	.583
2021	Indians	AL	162	141	.63	89	17	19	43	45	5	91	3	535	126	25	98	0	12	7	5	1	80	82	.494
162-Game Average				118	.65	132	36	29	38	44	23	99	6	471	129	48	109	13	26	16	10	6	88	74	.543

Ron Gardenhire

Year	Team	Lg	G	LUp	PL%	PH	PR	DS	Quick	Slow	LO	RCD	LS	Rel	SBA	SacA	RM	PO	#	Good	NG	Bomb	W	L	Pct
				LINEUPS		SUBSTITUTION			PITCHER USAGE						TACTICS				INTENTIONAL BB				RESULTS		
2002	Twins	AL	161	111	.69	141	36	42	54	25	10	84	1	435	141	48	44	11	24	16	8	4	94	67	.584
2003	Twins	AL	162	126	.63	144	50	26	49	33	13	85	2	399	138	59	37	14	35	16	19	6	90	72	.556
2004	Twins	AL	162	131	.59	129	45	29	56	21	20	106	4	435	162	66	121	18	27	15	12	7	92	70	.568
2005	Twins	AL	162	135	.58	104	45	26	50	21	5	87	1	396	146	59	138	16	38	28	10	3	83	79	.512
2006	Twins	AL	162	97	.62	93	36	21	60	31	3	82	5	421	143	48	130	11	25	14	11	4	96	66	.593
2007	Twins	AL	162	139	.63	104	42	25	45	30	8	99	4	438	142	45	148	11	33	14	19	9	79	83	.488
2008	Twins	AL	163	103	.64	109	26	12	47	29	5	115	3	485	144	73	143	17	38	25	13	8	88	75	.540
2009	Twins	AL	163	129	.63	83	54	34	43	25	12	115	3	480	117	62	100	21	20	9	11	6	87	76	.534

				LINEUPS		SUBSTITUTION			PITCHER USAGE						TACTICS				INTENTIONAL BB				RESULTS		
Year	Team	Lg	G	LUp	PL%	PH	PR	DS	Quick	Slow	LO	RCD	LS	Rel	SBA	SacA	RM	PO	#	Good	NG	Bomb	W	L	Pct
2010	Twins	AL	162	112	.62	86	**55**	30	**57**	28	5	106	1	465	96	47	140	14	19	12	7	4	94	68	.580
2011	Twins	AL	162	150	.58	93	**48**	21	34	44	17	82	1	457	131	44	170	5	37	21	16	9	63	**99**	.389
2012	Twins	AL	162	121	.62	64	45	24	42	31	4	82	1	499	172	49	207	10	43	27	16	6	66	**96**	.407
2013	Twins	AL	162	139	.66	103	42	28	41	43	6	78	1	511	85	37	137	14	31	13	18	7	66	96	.407
2014	Twins	AL	162	132	.64	97	44	23	40	40	2	82	2	491	135	31	149	5	24	11	13	6	70	**92**	.432
2018	Tigers	AL	162	144	.56	75	60	8	40	39	1	99	3	542	100	25	121	6	20	11	9	7	64	98	.395
2019	Tigers	AL	161	155	.48	68	**42**	7	45	46	2	87	0	577	77	19	93	**7**	24	13	11	6	47	**114**	.292
2020	Tigers	AL	50	44	.55	26	21	7	16	12	0	24	0	191	18	1	18	0	1	0	1	1	21	29	.420
	162-Game Average			129	.61	99	45	24	47	33	7	92	2	472	127	47	124	12	29	16	13	6	78	84	.481

John Gibbons

				LINEUPS		SUBSTITUTION			PITCHER USAGE						TACTICS				INTENTIONAL BB				RESULTS		
Year	Team	Lg	G	LUp	PL%	PH	PR	DS	Quick	Slow	LO	RCD	LS	Rel	SBA	SacA	RM	PO	#	Good	NG	Bomb	W	L	Pct
2004	Blue Jays	AL	50	36	.68	42	3	2	16	8	7	22	1	130	34	2	47	21	11	5	6	3	20	30	.400
2005	Blue Jays	AL	162	124	.66	**148**	11	37	**55**	18	9	77	12	432	107	28	128	45	29	13	16	9	80	82	.494
2006	Blue Jays	AL	162	120	.53	112	32	40	59	33	17	94	**16**	482	98	20	127	40	56	32	**24**	12	87	75	.537
2007	Blue Jays	AL	162	131	.46	**139**	**48**	33	45	37	31	75	9	420	79	35	99	37	34	17	17	6	83	79	.512
2008	Blue Jays	AL	74	60	.48	53	15	18	12	20	12	43	0	205	70	23	39	10	26	16	10	6	35	39	.473
2013	Blue Jays	AL	162	136	.63	124	31	24	**55**	44	14	69	2	487	153	41	160	4	33	17	16	6	74	88	.457
2014	Blue Jays	AL	162	128	.72	**202**	41	49	45	37	20	73	**8**	449	99	49	161	6	23	17	6	2	83	79	.512
2015	Blue Jays	AL	162	129	.48	97	41	47	46	37	13	85	6	469	111	45	152	2	20	10	10	3	93	69	.574
2016	Blue Jays	AL	162	141	.44	90	37	54	39	30	6	98	6	487	78	33	109	1	10	6	4	3	89	73	.549
2017	Blue Jays	AL	162	136	.56	**126**	39	33	41	33	8	100	4	**578**	77	35	132	4	25	14	11	5	76	86	.469
2018	Blue Jays	AL	162	**154**	.59	128	38	28	27	49	2	111	3	590	77	8	120	6	19	13	6	4	73	89	.451
	162-Game Average			133	.56	129	34	37	45	35	14	87	7	484	101	33	130	18	29	16	13	6	81	81	.500

Joe Girardi

				LINEUPS		SUBSTITUTION			PITCHER USAGE						TACTICS				INTENTIONAL BB				RESULTS		
Year	Team	Lg	G	LUp	PL%	PH	PR	DS	Quick	Slow	LO	RCD	LS	Rel	SBA	SacA	RM	PO	#	Good	NG	Bomb	W	L	Pct
2006	Marlins	NL	162	117	.50	250	44	**66**	46	40	28	76	3	438	168	97	108	42	58	37	21	7	78	84	.481
2008	Yankees	AL	162	114	.63	97	37	42	**60**	37	12	88	10	475	157	38	**173**	36	37	22	15	8	89	73	.549
2009	Yankees	AL	162	106	.73	97	**61**	42	36	45	27	88	**13**	461	139	44	83	33	28	14	14	9	**103**	59	.636
2010	Yankees	AL	162	114	.72	117	44	31	43	39	33	76	3	430	133	47	152	20	37	26	11	4	95	67	.586
2011	Yankees	AL	162	94	.69	72	41	53	51	36	21	88	2	465	193	50	151	26	43	30	13	4	**97**	65	.599
2012	Yankees	AL	162	107	.70	149	33	48	37	53	21	115	7	485	120	47	145	10	32	17	15	6	**95**	67	.586
2013	Yankees	AL	162	141	.59	119	15	29	42	50	23	82	4	428	146	49	131	4	34	20	14	6	85	77	.525
2014	Yankees	AL	162	142	.74	100	27	33	51	28	10	95	7	475	138	44	132	8	23	10	13	9	84	78	.519
2015	Yankees	AL	162	126	.79	118	50	57	48	34	9	80	**10**	497	88	32	92	6	16	8	8	4	87	75	.537
2016	Yankees	AL	162	143	.72	85	32	48	53	44	8	99	7	483	94	35	89	3	15	9	6	4	84	78	.519
2017	Yankees	AL	162	140	.56	112	22	10	49	29	9	79	7	477	112	28	117	3	18	11	7	4	91	71	.562
2020	Phillies	NL	60	51	.59	46	7	7	9	13	4	27	1	189	43	13	28	0	12	6	6	3	28	32	.467
2021	Phillies	NL	162	135	.59	276	10	44	36	52	**9**	89	6	525	96	**66**	87	0	37	27	10	5	82	80	.506
	162-Game Average			124	.66	132	34	41	45	40	17	87	6	471	132	48	120	15	32	19	12	6	89	73	.549

Andy Green

				LINEUPS		SUBSTITUTION			PITCHER USAGE						TACTICS				INTENTIONAL BB				RESULTS		
Year	Team	Lg	G	LUp	PL%	PH	PR	DS	Quick	Slow	LO	RCD	LS	Rel	SBA	SacA	RM	PO	#	Good	NG	Bomb	W	L	Pct
2016	Padres	NL	162	130	.56	249	29	25	46	53	6	119	4	510	170	48	138	3	44	26	18	9	68	**94**	.420
2017	Padres	NL	162	138	.55	238	10	38	45	43	5	101	2	517	122	63	119	2	28	18	10	4	71	91	.438
2018	Padres	NL	162	146	.62	264	21	38	45	49	5	84	6	535	131	49	109	0	28	17	11	6	66	96	.407
2019	Padres	NL	154	139	.45	263	11	51	52	31	0	99	5	509	103	42	93	0	19	14	5	3	69	85	.448
	162-Game Average			140	.54	257	18	38	48	45	4	102	4	524	133	51	116	1	30	19	11	6	69	93	.426

A.J. Hinch

				LINEUPS		SUBSTITUTION			PITCHER USAGE						TACTICS				INTENTIONAL BB				RESULTS		
Year	Team	Lg	G	LUp	PL%	PH	PR	DS	Quick	Slow	LO	RCD	LS	Rel	SBA	SacA	RM	PO	#	Good	NG	Bomb	W	L	Pct
2009	Diamondbacks	NL	133	115	.63	222	10	13	24	50	24	61	5	392	113	64	41	5	24	12	12	4	58	75	.436
2010	Diamondbacks	NL	79	56	.53	120	7	4	12	40	21	39	1	207	58	19	51	7	19	9	10	9	31	48	.392
2015	Astros	AL	162	**151**	.63	122	40	37	33	41	19	97	0	482	**169**	31	128	6	17	11	6	2	86	76	.531
2016	Astros	AL	162	143	.55	118	35	27	42	35	9	87	1	500	146	38	137	5	19	11	8	6	84	78	.519
2017	Astros	AL	162	144	.56	73	29	39	**57**	35	3	83	8	519	140	21	148	6	17	12	5	3	**101**	61	.623
2018	Astros	AL	162	144	.54	92	34	39	31	35	10	80	4	510	97	9	154	2	4	3	1	0	**103**	59	.636
2019	Astros	AL	162	134	.46	81	41	26	38	30	7	92	2	492	94	15	96	0	0	0	0	0	**107**	55	.660
2021	Tigers	AL	162	153	.71	72	41	18	61	35	1	85	8	577	113	16	92	0	10	4	6	3	77	85	.475
	162-Game Average			142	.58	123	32	28	41	41	13	85	4	503	127	29	116	4	15	8	7	4	89	73	.549

Clint Hurdle

Year	Team	Lg	G	LINEUPS		SUBSTITUTION			PITCHER USAGE						TACTICS				INTENTIONAL BB				RESULTS		
				LUp	PL%	PH	PR	DS	Quick	Slow	LO	RCD	LS	Rel	SBA	SacA	RM	PO	#	Good	NG	Bomb	W	L	Pct
2002	Rockies	NL	140	100	.52	274	28	41	33	45	17	104	3	437	139	46	50	13	38	22	16	11	67	73	.479
2003	Rockies	NL	162	108	.47	317	17	32	35	40	5	87	4	500	100	82	26	16	51	31	20	13	74	88	.457
2004	Rockies	NL	162	131	.57	289	18	35	36	63	20	74	1	473	77	128	67	12	84	54	30	12	68	94	.420
2005	Rockies	NL	162	135	.60	273	21	40	42	60	17	89	2	459	97	114	119	22	54	28	26	15	67	95	.414
2006	Rockies	NL	162	111	.49	259	17	22	34	52	17	107	2	499	135	156	114	28	81	45	36	23	76	86	.469
2007	Rockies	NL	163	96	.51	283	32	29	45	37	13	112	1	529	131	112	109	26	61	30	31	14	90	73	.552
2008	Rockies	NL	162	131	.49	253	20	31	40	43	16	85	2	485	178	111	116	43	49	31	18	6	74	88	.457
2009	Rockies	NL	46	42	.60	73	8	10	11	14	3	31	0	135	45	26	34	3	11	8	3	1	18	28	.391
2011	Pirates	NL	162	134	.60	278	26	63	58	27	1	134	3	549	160	101	173	20	65	39	26	13	72	90	.444
2012	Pirates	NL	162	133	.55	270	26	60	50	33	3	74	2	483	125	82	120	17	30	18	12	3	79	83	.488
2013	Pirates	NL	162	127	.51	289	24	61	61	25	7	76	3	465	136	83	172	20	26	22	4	2	94	68	.580
2014	Pirates	NL	162	123	.50	322	28	38	47	40	7	91	0	452	151	85	187	24	43	26	17	7	88	74	.543
2015	Pirates	NL	162	108	.50	269	48	76	39	40	9	124	1	500	143	81	173	9	38	31	7	3	98	64	.605
2016	Pirates	NL	162	125	.41	293	39	73	57	36	1	119	4	525	155	55	154	9	28	15	13	6	78	83	.484
2017	Pirates	NL	162	138	.51	277	23	37	42	39	6	110	8	502	103	59	124	7	32	17	15	7	75	87	.463
2018	Pirates	NL	161	128	.62	267	14	27	44	36	1	88	6	480	108	45	119	2	43	32	11	6	82	79	.509
2019	Pirates	NL	161	131	.67	281	30	38	40	49	0	85	7	548	93	60	117	16	22	15	7	5	69	92	.429
	162-Game Average			124	.53	283	26	44	44	42	9	99	3	497	129	88	122	18	47	29	18	9	79	83	.488

Brandon Hyde

Year	Team	Lg	G	LINEUPS		SUBSTITUTION			PITCHER USAGE						TACTICS				INTENTIONAL BB				RESULTS		
				LUp	PL%	PH	PR	DS	Quick	Slow	LO	RCD	LS	Rel	SBA	SacA	RM	PO	#	Good	NG	Bomb	W	L	Pct
2011	Marlins	NL	1	1	.44	0	0	0	0	0	1	0	3	0	0	0	1	0	1	1	0	0	0	1	.000
2019	Orioles	AL	162	150	.70	126	26	42	30	35	1	73	11	533	114	34	82	0	11	5	6	4	54	108	.333
2020	Orioles	AL	60	58	.56	44	21	14	15	10	0	31	4	207	33	15	32	0	2	1	1	1	25	35	.417
2021	Orioles	AL	162	147	.60	86	32	32	41	45	1	75	6	569	77	19	66	0	12	7	5	3	52	110	.321
	162-Game Average			150	.63	108	33	37	36	38	1	76	9	552	94	29	76	0	11	6	5	3	55	107	.340

Gabe Kapler

Year	Team	Lg	G	LINEUPS		SUBSTITUTION			PITCHER USAGE						TACTICS				INTENTIONAL BB				RESULTS		
				LUp	PL%	PH	PR	DS	Quick	Slow	LO	RCD	LS	Rel	SBA	SacA	RM	PO	#	Good	NG	Bomb	W	L	Pct
2018	Phillies	NL	162	138	.66	295	22	38	38	38	3	117	11	596	95	46	65	0	35	25	10	5	80	82	.494
2019	Phillies	NL	162	106	.55	312	11	21	28	48	3	121	9	564	96	50	69	0	38	31	7	4	81	81	.500
2020	Giants	NL	60	53	.66	73	13	31	17	20	1	50	1	236	27	3	25	0	2	2	0	0	29	31	.483
2021	Giants	NL	162	148	.66	407	26	48	42	29	1	146	2	599	80	47	80	0	20	11	9	2	107	55	.660
	162-Game Average			132	.63	323	21	41	37	40	2	129	7	592	88	43	71	0	28	20	8	3	88	74	.543

Tony LaRussa

Year	Team	Lg	G	LINEUPS		SUBSTITUTION			PITCHER USAGE						TACTICS				INTENTIONAL BB				RESULTS		
				LUp	PL%	PH	PR	DS	Quick	Slow	LO	RCD	LS	Rel	SBA	SacA	RM	PO	#	Good	NG	Bomb	W	L	Pct
1994	Athletics	AL	114	97	.62	89	28	14	43	21	5	60	4	308	130	31		32	30	20	10	4	51	63	.447
1995	Athletics	AL	144	120	.54	113	38	24	33	38	19	46	7	358	158	42		42	26	18	8	4	67	77	.465
1996	Cardinals	NL	162	120	.52	246	25	13	32	48	24	90	8	413	207	117		41	43	28	15	7	88	74	.543
1997	Cardinals	NL	162	146	.54	307	17	18	34	42	16	81	2	399	224	77		79	34	26	8	2	73	89	.451
1998	Cardinals	NL	162	146	.52	259	7	18	62	31	13	82	14	429	174	85		34	38	25	13	8	83	79	.512
1999	Cardinals	NL	161	138	.47	264	32	28	50	41	13	96	14	454	182	103		30	38	20	18	11	75	86	.466
2000	Cardinals	NL	162	137	.53	240	35	25	40	31	11	63	18	386	138	107		34	28	21	7	6	95	67	.586
2001	Cardinals	NL	162	117	.47	256	26	13	46	36	7	140	7	485	126	102		25	36	21	15	4	93	69	.574
2002	Cardinals	NL	162	117	.52	340	27	41	58	33	23	110	6	472	128	106	75	13	39	25	14	8	97	65	.599
2003	Cardinals	NL	162	126	.50	352	28	51	38	49	36	113	9	460	114	108	56	9	36	28	8	2	85	77	.525
2004	Cardinals	NL	162	119	.53	275	25	69	30	48	31	120	16	469	158	88	158	9	24	17	7	4	105	57	.648
2005	Cardinals	NL	162	138	.55	270	25	48	40	38	22	88	4	436	119	92	153	9	27	16	11	7	100	62	.617
2006	Cardinals	NL	161	131	.56	272	11	53	50	34	21	95	6	469	91	86	123	13	35	21	14	3	83	78	.516
2007	Cardinals	NL	162	148	.60	317	19	37	46	44	8	102	5	516	89	85	120	23	25	10	15	11	78	84	.481
2008	Cardinals	NL	162	140	.64	275	26	57	52	40	16	101	11	506	105	87	114	18	21	13	8	1	86	76	.531
2009	Cardinals	NL	162	126	.52	289	12	51	55	38	17	102	8	481	106	93	91	17	23	15	8	1	91	71	.562
2010	Cardinals	NL	162	135	.55	292	16	28	52	40	16	80	5	455	120	87	151	22	32	17	15	8	86	76	.531
2011	Cardinals	NL	162	126	.57	262	36	86	47	44	20	94	8	468	96	101	179	17	44	23	21	14	90	72	.556
2021	White Sox	AL	162	153	.61	83	22	41	36	49	8	86	9	512	77	32	104	0	16	10	6	2	93	69	.574
	162-Game Average			133	.54	258	24	38	45	40	18	94	9	456	137	88	120	25	32	20	12	6	87	75	.537

Torey Lovullo

Year	Team	Lg	G	LUp	PL%	PH	PR	DS	Quick	Slow	LO	RCD	LS	Rel	SBA	SacA	RM	PO	#	Good	NG	Bomb	W	L	Pct
				LINEUPS		**SUBSTITUTION**			**PITCHER USAGE**						**TACTICS**				**INTENTIONAL BB**				**RESULTS**		
2015	Red Sox	AL	48	40	.58	17	17	4	9	16	10	28	0	149	35	10	32	0	5	3	2	1	28	20	.583
2017	Diamondbacks	NL	162	129	.55	254	28	36	34	45	6	116	2	513	133	50	85	3	45	32	13	6	93	69	.574
2018	Diamondbacks	NL	162	144	.66	258	13	32	31	45	2	**143**	2	573	104	60	92	3	43	29	14	4	82	80	.506
2019	Diamondbacks	NL	162	126	.66	256	21	46	32	38	0	105	9	557	102	49	105	5	38	19	**19**	8	85	77	.525
2020	Diamondbacks	NL	60	56	.69	27	12	3	11	16	0	31	1	200	30	2	14	0	20	**13**	7	**5**	25	35	.417
2021	Diamondbacks	NL	162	**157**	.74	339	22	17	34	54	0	95	2	565	59	40	67	6	45	30	15	7	52	**110**	.321
	162-Game Average			140	.65	247	24	30	32	46	4	111	3	548	99	45	85	4	42	27	15	7	78	84	.481

Joe Maddon

Year	Team	Lg	G	LUp	PL%	PH	PR	DS	Quick	Slow	LO	RCD	LS	Rel	SBA	SacA	RM	PO	#	Good	NG	Bomb	W	L	Pct
				LINEUPS		**SUBSTITUTION**			**PITCHER USAGE**						**TACTICS**				**INTENTIONAL BB**				**RESULTS**		
1996	Angels	AL	22	19	.64	21	5	0	7	6	6	10	3	48	11	20		6	4	3	1	1	8	14	.364
1998	Angels	AL	8	4	.57	2	4	0	1	5	3	5	3	12	2	7		0	1	0	1	0	6	2	.750
1999	Angels	AL	29	19	.58	29	4	1	6	0	4	20	0	85	23	12		7	3	1	2	1	19	10	.655
2006	Devil Rays	AL	162	**145**	.54	81	26	51	41	39	16	79	10	444	186	51	132	48	39	19	20	13	61	**101**	.377
2007	Devil Rays	AL	162	122	.53	80	19	16	31	**56**	19	113	1	483	179	40	118	**50**	31	18	13	4	66	**96**	.407
2008	Rays	AL	162	115	.69	**133**	16	39	48	37	14	112	7	448	**192**	31	113	26	29	15	14	8	97	65	.599
2009	Rays	AL	162	123	.66	**140**	21	18	28	51	23	**139**	3	510	**255**	29	99	15	22	10	12	7	84	78	.519
2010	Rays	AL	162	129	.67	**174**	31	18	41	34	26	135	2	491	219	45	166	12	34	**28**	6	3	**96**	66	.593
2011	Rays	AL	162	130	.67	137	16	31	34	36	47	112	6	438	217	42	187	6	38	23	15	6	91	71	.562
2012	Rays	AL	162	**151**	.62	156	37	52	43	38	33	123	3	472	178	40	181	7	35	25	10	6	90	72	.556
2013	Rays	AL	163	**147**	.64	**193**	27	**56**	52	38	16	111	6	485	111	26	117	6	38	21	17	11	92	71	.564
2014	Rays	AL	162	130	.58	171	23	15	44	35	26	110	3	494	90	54	143	2	27	20	7	3	77	85	.475
2015	Cubs	NL	162	119	.60	**288**	22	32	41	31	14	129	2	552	132	48	**180**	3	38	22	16	**10**	97	65	.599
2016	Cubs	NL	162	130	.62	236	19	35	56	29	13	100	3	503	100	54	111	6	24	19	5	3	**103**	58	.640
2017	Cubs	NL	162	143	.65	296	7	**51**	47	30	10	85	3	531	93	54	122	1	29	18	11	7	92	70	.568
2018	Cubs	NL	163	152	.61	280	18	48	41	44	5	120	2	**600**	104	56	130	1	33	25	8	6	95	68	.583
2019	Cubs	NL	162	140	.56	244	15	43	40	41	7	103	4	576	69	46	87	3	16	11	5	3	84	78	.519
2020	Angels	AL	60	52	.53	20	13	15	16	17	1	51	**6**	228	29	6	37	2	**8**	**6**	2	1	26	34	.433
2021	Angels	AL	162	146	.50	74	12	41	46	36	6	80	**10**	562	105	34	117	**11**	18	9	9	**9**	77	85	.475
	162-Game Average			134	.61	175	21	36	42	38	18	110	5	506	146	44	133	13	30	19	11	6	86	76	.531

Dave Martinez

Year	Team	Lg	G	LUp	PL%	PH	PR	DS	Quick	Slow	LO	RCD	LS	Rel	SBA	SacA	RM	PO	#	Good	NG	Bomb	W	L	Pct
				LINEUPS		**SUBSTITUTION**			**PITCHER USAGE**						**TACTICS**				**INTENTIONAL BB**				**RESULTS**		
2018	Nationals	NL	162	125	.61	295	23	26	31	**62**	**22**	123	4	562	152	55	91	3	37	24	13	6	82	80	.506
2019	Nationals	NL	162	106	.49	253	15	19	32	41	13	**136**	8	530	145	77	81	0	41	31	10	6	93	69	.574
2020	Nationals	NL	60	54	.61	31	13	7	8	**27**	**5**	47	0	202	45	9	35	0	**22**	**13**	9	**5**	26	34	.433
2021	Nationals	NL	162	128	.56	284	14	21	32	53	1	135	5	569	82	57	93	1	**46**	27	19	**11**	65	97	.401
	162-Game Average			123	.56	256	19	22	31	54	12	131	5	553	126	59	89	1	43	28	15	8	79	83	.488

Mike Matheny

Year	Team	Lg	G	LUp	PL%	PH	PR	DS	Quick	Slow	LO	RCD	LS	Rel	SBA	SacA	RM	PO	#	Good	NG	Bomb	W	L	Pct
				LINEUPS		**SUBSTITUTION**			**PITCHER USAGE**						**TACTICS**				**INTENTIONAL BB**				**RESULTS**		
2012	Cardinals	NL	162	122	.62	286	**37**	33	53	37	8	118	5	506	128	95	144	16	28	13	15	7	88	74	.543
2013	Cardinals	NL	162	89	.56	237	30	41	42	49	25	114	**4**	483	67	73	125	6	26	20	6	6	**97**	65	.599
2014	Cardinals	NL	162	119	.56	258	21	35	53	32	17	119	5	485	89	81	155	10	35	20	15	7	90	72	.556
2015	Cardinals	NL	162	135	.52	274	46	41	**51**	29	11	**142**	**8**	515	107	60	168	15	37	29	8	3	**100**	62	.617
2016	Cardinals	NL	162	**146**	.50	284	**39**	42	42	39	8	95	2	481	61	56	107	21	35	19	16	8	86	76	.531
2017	Cardinals	NL	162	144	.45	295	21	30	45	34	5	106	8	546	112	68	125	8	50	33	17	11	83	79	.512
2018	Cardinals	NL	93	69	.47	140	13	34	20	22	3	61	5	321	55	38	57	1	24	13	11	6	47	46	.505
2020	Royals	AL	60	52	.50	50	15	10	19	15	2	**52**	2	232	**69**	16	**40**	0	7	4	3	**3**	26	34	.433
2021	Royals	AL	162	133	.56	80	32	33	30	**54**	3	98	5	556	**157**	42	139	0	16	9	7	4	74	88	.457
	162-Game Average			127	.53	240	32	38	45	39	10	114	6	519	106	67	133	10	32	20	12	7	87	75	.537

Don Mattingly

Year	Team	Lg	G	LUp	PL%	PH	PR	DS	Quick	Slow	LO	RCD	LS	Rel	SBA	SacA	RM	PO	#	Good	NG	Bomb	W	L	Pct
				LINEUPS		**SUBSTITUTION**			**PITCHER USAGE**						**TACTICS**				**INTENTIONAL BB**				**RESULTS**		
2011	Dodgers	NL	161	140	.57	233	29	44	45	40	30	86	1	461	166	93	181	13	48	27	21	12	82	79	.509
2012	Dodgers	NL	162	127	.59	247	22	43	51	39	20	118	2	506	148	105	153	8	**62**	**38**	24	**15**	86	76	.531
2013	Dodgers	NL	162	**145**	.55	210	18	47	40	30	18	118	3	504	106	99	131	10	44	28	16	7	92	70	.568
2014	Dodgers	NL	162	124	.51	237	17	62	49	31	15	107	9	496	**188**	67	168	2	35	20	15	8	94	68	.580
2015	Dodgers	NL	161	136	.70	276	20	45	50	30	13	119	1	508	93	67	136	2	32	18	14	5	91	70	.565
2016	Marlins	NL	161	111	.48	281	28	69	48	35	10	145	1	559	99	63	101	2	**62**	**42**	20	**14**	79	82	.491
2017	Marlins	NL	162	98	.52	271	9	20	43	32	4	120	5	**580**	121	66	125	2	59	39	20	12	77	85	.475
2018	Marlins	NL	161	137	.46	283	19	53	47	43	2	114	0	546	76	45	121	1	**73**	**40**	**33**	**19**	63	98	.391

Year	Team	Lg	G	LINEUPS LUp	PL%	SUBSTITUTION PH	PR	DS	PITCHER USAGE Quick	Slow	LO	RCD	LS	Rel	TACTICS SBA	SacA	RM	PO	INT BB #	Good	NG	Bomb	RESULTS W	L	Pct
2019	Marlins	NL	162	**143**	.43	293	24	25	34	48	3	112	1	539	85	49	124	0	**52**	33	19	9	57	105	.352
2020	Marlins	NL	60	55	.54	37	15	14	20	12	0	40	3	215	65	8	36	0	14	8	6	3	31	29	.517
2021	Marlins	NL	162	147	.50	271	**36**	22	41	23	2	112	2	595	135	46	**143**	0	43	22	**21**	4	67	95	.414
	162-Game Average			132	.53	255	23	43	45	35	11	115	2	532	124	68	137	4	51	30	20	10	79	83	.488

Lloyd McClendon

Year	Team	Lg	G	LINEUPS LUp	PL%	SUBSTITUTION PH	PR	DS	PITCHER USAGE Quick	Slow	LO	RCD	LS	Rel	TACTICS SBA	SacA	RM	PO	INT BB #	Good	NG	Bomb	RESULTS W	L	Pct
2001	Pirates	NL	162	131	.51	255	17	32	45	38	2	85	5	410	166	83		52	74	44	30	19	62	100	.383
2002	Pirates	NL	162	121	.45	261	38	**65**	**62**	30	3	98	2	458	135	93	73	67	**93**	**61**	32	**22**	72	89	.447
2003	Pirates	NL	162	114	.57	315	27	59	46	35	27	114	10	457	123	99	55	**73**	58	34	24	13	75	87	.463
2004	Pirates	NL	161	114	.50	278	13	58	**50**	40	26	133	1	464	103	100	91	61	64	37	27	**16**	72	89	.447
2005	Pirates	NL	136	123	.53	218	8	19	37	34	15	86	5	357	84	62	83	37	60	32	28	16	55	81	.404
2014	Mariners	AL	162	141	.69	93	48	33	**61**	21	11	87	3	497	138	48	187	**30**	36	21	15	9	87	75	.537
2015	Mariners	AL	162	140	.63	133	52	50	53	31	10	114	5	509	114	49	148	**30**	41	23	**18**	**10**	76	86	.469
2020	Tigers	AL	8	8	.56	5	4	3	2	3	0	5	0	27	7	0	7	0	1	0	1	0	2	6	.250
	162-Game Average			130	.56	227	30	46	52	34	14	105	5	462	127	78	110	51	62	37	25	15	73	89	.451

Bob Melvin

Year	Team	Lg	G	LINEUPS LUp	PL%	SUBSTITUTION PH	PR	DS	PITCHER USAGE Quick	Slow	LO	RCD	LS	Rel	TACTICS SBA	SacA	RM	PO	INT BB #	Good	NG	Bomb	RESULTS W	L	Pct
2003	Mariners	AL	162	111	.62	81	62	33	27	46	43	56	6	366	145	44	37	5	24	14	10	4	93	69	.574
2004	Mariners	AL	162	**151**	.59	109	**66**	26	26	63	43	82	5	414	152	56	123	24	32	18	14	8	63	99	.389
2005	Diamondbacks	NL	162	120	.68	**310**	26	38	26	56	36	123	**11**	458	93	93	101	30	43	27	16	9	77	85	.475
2006	Diamondbacks	NL	162	114	.72	278	11	35	37	42	15	86	0	461	106	83	61	30	44	28	16	8	76	86	.469
2007	Diamondbacks	NL	162	146	.57	243	11	61	35	42	31	96	2	469	133	74	70	25	38	30	8	4	**90**	72	.556
2008	Diamondbacks	NL	162	134	.57	263	27	30	41	39	16	102	0	444	81	87	79	28	41	27	14	9	82	80	.506
2009	Diamondbacks	NL	29	29	.62	47	6	8	7	4	3	17	0	91	29	17	13	3	3	1	2	2	12	17	.414
2011	Athletics	AL	99	87	.71	33	13	17	24	23	18	59	2	283	103	34	87	23	9	5	4	3	47	52	.475
2012	Athletics	AL	162	132	.71	111	17	18	**63**	29	5	93	2	462	154	41	116	30	34	21	13	6	94	68	.580
2013	Athletics	AL	162	133	.77	166	14	35	48	28	7	84	7	447	102	32	74	8	23	18	5	3	96	66	.593
2014	Athletics	AL	162	137	.77	187	38	44	45	30	11	100	7	441	103	22	74	16	28	20	8	4	88	74	.543
2015	Athletics	AL	162	137	.65	161	24	35	53	36	10	100	**10**	487	107	17	130	20	19	8	11	8	68	**94**	.420
2016	Athletics	AL	162	141	.64	135	28	39	**55**	36	7	96	3	492	73	19	79	5	28	14	**14**	8	69	93	.426
2017	Athletics	AL	162	137	.60	**126**	19	32	39	46	5	117	4	525	79	16	85	9	17	12	5	4	75	87	.463
2018	Athletics	AL	162	121	.55	**138**	16	23	49	22	1	115	9	578	56	10	74	8	19	14	5	3	97	65	.599
2019	Athletics	AL	162	138	.53	117	11	34	36	30	4	123	10	547	70	10	72	4	19	12	7	4	97	65	.599
2020	Athletics	AL	60	50	.53	32	17	10	12	9	1	34	4	181	29	2	33	1	6	4	2	1	36	24	.600
2021	Athletics	AL	162	153	.58	**158**	31	21	21	34	3	93	5	504	108	20	102	0	11	7	4	2	86	76	.531
	162-Game Average			134	.64	167	27	33	40	38	16	98	5	473	107	42	88	17	27	17	10	6	83	79	.512

Paul Molitor

Year	Team	Lg	G	LINEUPS LUp	PL%	SUBSTITUTION PH	PR	DS	PITCHER USAGE Quick	Slow	LO	RCD	LS	Rel	TACTICS SBA	SacA	RM	PO	INT BB #	Good	NG	Bomb	RESULTS W	L	Pct
2015	Twins	AL	162	124	.59	75	34	27	51	27	7	123	4	520	108	44	132	5	34	20	14	8	83	79	.512
2016	Twins	AL	162	**148**	.61	72	25	18	33	57	4	117	4	**533**	123	47	157	5	26	13	13	**8**	59	**103**	.364
2017	Twins	AL	162	137	.71	104	22	31	54	32	4	95	8	520	123	46	164	4	37	19	**18**	**11**	85	77	.525
2018	Twins	AL	162	145	.70	102	21	23	35	43	14	104	3	566	74	21	134	5	**34**	18	**16**	**11**	78	84	.481
	162-Game Average			139	.65	88	26	25	43	40	7	110	5	535	107	40	147	5	33	18	15	10	76	86	.469

Charlie Montoyo

Year	Team	Lg	G	LINEUPS LUp	PL%	SUBSTITUTION PH	PR	DS	PITCHER USAGE Quick	Slow	LO	RCD	LS	Rel	TACTICS SBA	SacA	RM	PO	INT BB #	Good	NG	Bomb	RESULTS W	L	Pct
2019	Blue Jays	AL	162	158	.59	79	25	15	47	26	1	87	10	591	71	18	86	6	25	**20**	5	0	67	95	.414
2020	Blue Jays	AL	60	56	.53	37	14	15	14	15	0	26	4	226	39	9	28	**3**	7	4	3	0	32	28	.533
2021	Blue Jays	AL	162	133	.42	100	39	42	37	32	5	62	5	536	101	14	117	4	10	6	4	3	91	71	.562
	162-Game Average			146	.51	91	33	30	41	31	3	74	8	571	89	17	97	5	18	13	5	1	80	82	.494

Bryan Price

Year	Team	Lg	G	LINEUPS LUp	PL%	SUBSTITUTION PH	PR	DS	PITCHER USAGE Quick	Slow	LO	RCD	LS	Rel	TACTICS SBA	SacA	RM	PO	INT BB #	Good	NG	Bomb	RESULTS W	L	Pct
2014	Reds	NL	162	130	.54	220	21	33	35	37	26	82	3	428	174	87	135	9	23	21	12	5	76	86	.469
2015	Reds	NL	162	118	.57	263	16	26	42	48	**15**	102	2	521	172	63	144	**28**	42	29	13	7	64	**98**	.395
2016	Reds	NL	162	109	.52	230	17	23	37	39	10	67	3	484	190	**81**	163	**26**	31	23	8	5	68	94	.420

Year	Team	Lg	G	LINEUPS		SUBSTITUTION			PITCHER USAGE						TACTICS				INTENTIONAL BB				RESULTS		
				LUp	PL%	PH	PR	DS	Quick	Slow	LO	RCD	LS	Rel	SBA	SacA	RM	PO	#	Good	NG	Bomb	W	L	Pct
2017	Reds	NL	162	94	.59	241	13	25	37	42	7	64	13	504	159	68	128	17	37	23	14	7	68	94	.420
2018	Reds	NL	18	18	.60	29	2	1	2	7	0	10	1	61	10	8	13	3	8	6	2	1	3	15	.167
	162-Game Average			114	.55	239	17	26	37	42	14	79	5	486	171	75	142	20	37	25	12	6	68	94	.420

Tom Prince

Year	Team	Lg	G	LINEUPS		SUBSTITUTION			PITCHER USAGE						TACTICS				INTENTIONAL BB				RESULTS		
				LUp	PL%	PH	PR	DS	Quick	Slow	LO	RCD	LS	Rel	SBA	SacA	RM	PO	#	Good	NG	Bomb	W	L	Pct
2019	Pirates	NL	1	1	.25	1	0	0	0	0	0	0	0	2	0	0	0	0	0	0	0	0	0	1	.000
	162-Game Average			162	.25	162	0	0	0	0	0	0	0	324	0	0	0	0	0	0	0	0	0	162	.000

Rick Renteria

Year	Team	Lg	G	LINEUPS		SUBSTITUTION			PITCHER USAGE						TACTICS				INTENTIONAL BB				RESULTS		
				LUp	PL%	PH	PR	DS	Quick	Slow	LO	RCD	LS	Rel	SBA	SacA	RM	PO	#	Good	NG	Bomb	W	L	Pct
2014	Cubs	NL	162	137	.63	275	9	20	50	42	12	103	1	537	105	77	106	5	37	23	14	8	73	89	.451
2017	White Sox	AL	162	150	.57	86	26	9	31	58	6	108	2	520	102	47	133	1	36	19	17	9	67	95	.414
2018	White Sox	AL	162	142	.60	90	30	25	18	66	9	99	5	553	139	28	126	10	25	15	10	6	62	100	.383
2019	White Sox	AL	161	143	.66	87	27	27	32	48	7	91	4	536	91	35	103	5	30	16	14	5	72	89	.447
2020	White Sox	AL	60	51	.49	22	24	8	15	17	3	37	3	224	28	2	31	0	6	1	5	2	35	25	.583
	162-Game Average			143	.60	128	27	20	33	53	8	100	3	543	107	43	114	5	31	17	14	7	71	91	.438

Jim Riggleman

Year	Team	Lg	G	LINEUPS		SUBSTITUTION			PITCHER USAGE						TACTICS				INTENTIONAL BB				RESULTS		
				LUp	PL%	PH	PR	DS	Quick	Slow	LO	RCD	LS	Rel	SBA	SacA	RM	PO	#	Good	NG	Bomb	W	L	Pct
1994	Padres	NL	117	93	.63	184	28	19	11	5	3	53	10	273	116	80		52	62	34	28	11	47	70	.402
1995	Cubs	NL	144	92	.56	196	9	30	15	8	13	119	12	414	142	90		53	68	45	23	12	73	71	.507
1996	Cubs	NL	162	87	.54	326	34	21	17	11	7	114	11	439	158	79		65	55	33	22	10	68	94	.420
1997	Cubs	NL	162	127	.50	280	40	44	13	5	2	113	9	441	176	103		74	51	38	13	6	68	94	.420
1998	Cubs	NL	163	104	.60	273	26	35	16	14	20	133	6	449	109	89		26	48	22	26	15	90	73	.552
1999	Cubs	NL	162	122	.61	312	25	30	16	19	8	105	4	441	104	94		20	48	21	27	15	67	95	.414
2008	Mariners	AL	90	70	.60	75	30	22	21	25	19	50	4	272	57	27	88	10	25	17	8	3	36	54	.400
2009	Nationals	NL	75	60	.51	115	15	33	24	16	4	63	6	250	59	44	36	8	33	17	16	8	33	42	.440
2010	Nationals	NL	162	131	.58	271	33	67	50	32	9	101	5	494	151	101	158	13	57	37	20	10	69	93	.426
2011	Nationals	NL	75	59	.58	105	22	23	24	15	2	54	5	220	80	47	89	3	22	16	6	3	38	37	.507
2018	Reds	NL	144	113	.65	215	16	34	31	40	4	93	15	483	100	68	138	10	52	30	22	9	64	80	.444
	162-Game Average			118	.58	262	31	40	26	21	10	111	10	465	139	91	151	37	58	34	23	11	74	88	.457

Dave Roberts

Year	Team	Lg	G	LINEUPS		SUBSTITUTION			PITCHER USAGE						TACTICS				INTENTIONAL BB				RESULTS		
				LUp	PL%	PH	PR	DS	Quick	Slow	LO	RCD	LS	Rel	SBA	SacA	RM	PO	#	Good	NG	Bomb	W	L	Pct
2015	Padres	NL	1	1	.63	3	0	0	0	1	0	2	0	3	1	0	0	0	1	0	0	0	0	1	.000
2016	Dodgers	NL	162	120	.69	325	11	26	60	26	6	143	5	606	71	45	120	2	51	36	15	10	91	71	.562
2017	Dodgers	NL	162	147	.64	345	10	30	82	22	3	104	18	536	105	45	97	3	33	23	10	6	104	58	.642
2018	Dodgers	NL	163	155	.67	362	16	51	64	29	3	112	9	593	99	51	87	0	39	26	13	5	92	71	.564
2019	Dodgers	NL	162	139	.62	309	13	16	57	28	2	108	9	545	67	61	44	3	24	12	12	8	106	56	.654
2020	Dodgers	NL	60	57	.56	41	5	11	24	7	0	37	0	249	37	3	32	0	4	2	2	2	43	17	.717
2021	Dodgers	NL	162	146	.53	280	17	35	56	37	8	136	7	600	82	34	67	0	43	33	10	7	106	56	.654
	162-Game Average			142	.62	309	13	31	64	28	4	119	9	582	86	45	83	1	36	25	12	7	101	61	.623

Ron Roenicke

Year	Team	Lg	G	LINEUPS		SUBSTITUTION			PITCHER USAGE						TACTICS				INTENTIONAL BB				RESULTS		
				LUp	PL%	PH	PR	DS	Quick	Slow	LO	RCD	LS	Rel	SBA	SacA	RM	PO	#	Good	NG	Bomb	W	L	Pct
2011	Brewers	NL	162	105	.45	260	31	36	36	43	31	92	1	434	125	104	141	14	16	9	7	4	96	66	.593
2012	Brewers	NL	162	110	.45	322	20	25	36	50	23	149	1	512	197	91	152	8	20	12	8	2	83	79	.512
2013	Brewers	NL	162	125	.47	275	15	34	39	47	7	96	2	501	192	86	157	6	29	22	7	6	74	88	.457
2014	Brewers	NL	162	115	.44	253	19	37	33	48	12	114	1	478	145	92	127	11	20	16	4	4	82	80	.506
2015	Brewers	NL	25	24	.39	48	4	5	3	9	2	15	0	72	14	18	17	2	6	5	1	1	7	18	.280
2020	Red Sox	AL	60	52	.57	22	7	2	22	12	0	26	0	232	40	3	25	1	4	2	2	1	24	36	.400
	162-Game Average			117	.46	261	21	31	37	46	17	109	1	493	158	87	137	9	21	15	6	4	81	81	.500

Luis Rojas

Year	Team	Lg	G	LINEUPS		SUBSTITUTION			PITCHER USAGE						TACTICS				INTENTIONAL BB				RESULTS		
				LUp	PL%	PH	PR	DS	Quick	Slow	LO	RCD	LS	Rel	SBA	SacA	RM	PO	#	Good	NG	Bomb	W	L	Pct
2020	Mets	NL	60	53	.60	37	19	19	14	15	2	33	4	197	30	3	35	5	7	2	5	3	26	34	.433
2021	Mets	NL	162	133	.65	292	16	36	63	27	1	107	4	543	80	53	79	1	21	15	6	2	77	85	.475
	162-Game Average			136	.64	240	26	40	56	31	2	102	6	540	80	41	83	4	20	12	8	4	75	87	.463

David Ross

Year	Team	Lg	G	LUp	PL%	PH	PR	DS	Quick	Slow	LO	RCD	LS	Rel	SBA	SacA	RM	PO	#	Good	NG	Bomb	W	L	Pct
2020	Cubs	NL	60	54	.61	51	16	23	12	14	1	27	3	188	34	0	46	0	7	4	3	1	34	26	.567
2021	Cubs	NL	162	138	.59	309	15	23	41	43	0	95	7	599	123	47	103	0	25	15	10	8	71	91	.438
	162-Game Average			140	.60	263	23	34	39	42	1	89	7	574	115	34	109	0	23	14	9	7	77	85	.475

Mike Scioscia

Year	Team	Lg	G	LUp	PL%	PH	PR	DS	Quick	Slow	LO	RCD	LS	Rel	SBA	SacA	RM	PO	#	Good	NG	Bomb	W	L	Pct
2000	Angels	AL	162	75	.62	110	41	4	56	42	6	95	9	441	145	63		40	44	28	16	7	82	80	.506
2001	Angels	AL	162	130	.62	118	30	8	29	41	5	81	9	384	168	66		50	47	22	25	12	75	87	.463
2002	Angels	AL	162	102	.64	162	57	26	36	33	34	88	8	400	168	62	52	30	24	15	9	5	99	63	.611
2003	Angels	AL	162	130	.64	134	54	40	50	48	11	60	4	375	190	64	79	25	38	26	12	3	77	85	.475
2004	Angels	AL	162	126	.57	94	32	44	37	40	22	61	11	343	189	70	229	33	27	18	9	3	92	70	.568
2005	Angels	AL	162	124	.65	92	37	37	47	37	24	88	9	379	218	58	160	43	24	15	9	4	95	67	.586
2006	Angels	AL	162	114	.63	103	45	38	38	49	21	99	9	380	205	37	166	22	27	18	9	6	89	73	.549
2007	Angels	AL	162	127	.66	103	26	19	39	40	14	94	4	396	194	41	166	44	22	12	10	5	94	68	.580
2008	Angels	AL	162	125	.63	74	30	36	37	48	21	87	1	383	177	39	151	31	32	22	10	6	100	62	.617
2009	Angels	AL	162	123	.69	80	26	37	47	47	33	91	1	434	211	55	137	40	35	22	13	6	97	65	.599
2010	Angels	AL	162	133	.59	96	31	23	41	52	48	76	0	410	156	58	223	28	33	17	16	8	80	82	.494
2011	Angels	AL	162	129	.64	88	14	24	31	37	55	57	1	386	187	69	212	46	34	25	9	5	86	76	.531
2012	Angels	AL	162	121	.55	73	33	47	37	47	31	96	8	444	167	61	236	33	20	11	9	7	89	73	.549
2013	Angels	AL	162	118	.56	88	26	39	31	44	29	130	8	496	116	48	205	41	36	19	17	11	78	84	.481
2014	Angels	AL	162	125	.58	123	46	59	49	39	22	141	0	543	120	35	189	14	41	31	10	5	98	64	.605
2015	Angels	AL	162	125	.53	117	62	73	38	38	12	145	4	518	86	41	168	15	45	34	11	9	85	77	.525
2016	Angels	AL	162	133	.45	98	54	57	47	32	12	99	2	527	189	38	211	14	27	19	8	5	74	88	.457
2017	Angels	AL	162	116	.52	109	38	24	57	26	4	92	8	543	180	23	208	11	25	14	11	7	80	82	.494
2018	Angels	AL	162	132	.50	114	33	34	58	19	3	102	7	601	111	16	134	3	17	9	8	1	80	82	.494
	162-Game Average			121	.59	104	38	35	42	40	21	94	5	441	163	50	172	30	31	20	12	6	87	75	.537

Scott Servais

Year	Team	Lg	G	LUp	PL%	PH	PR	DS	Quick	Slow	LO	RCD	LS	Rel	SBA	SacA	RM	PO	#	Good	NG	Bomb	W	L	Pct
2016	Mariners	AL	162	114	.72	166	33	43	42	38	8	93	7	476	84	36	79	1	30	16	14	6	86	76	.531
2017	Mariners	AL	162	120	.52	93	29	18	55	32	3	98	7	527	124	26	99	4	28	15	13	7	78	84	.481
2018	Mariners	AL	162	124	.54	103	42	28	44	42	3	122	3	537	116	43	91	7	21	15	6	4	89	73	.549
2019	Mariners	AL	162	153	.58	82	33	35	33	37	4	58	3	538	162	17	100	7	25	11	14	7	68	94	.420
2020	Mariners	AL	60	59	.56	26	9	7	7	14	0	12	2	189	66	5	37	0	7	6	1	1	27	33	.450
2021	Mariners	AL	162	132	.60	102	12	26	37	43	1	105	7	584	88	19	80	2	23	16	7	3	90	72	.556
	162-Game Average			131	.59	107	29	29	41	38	4	91	5	531	119	27	90	4	25	15	10	5	82	80	.506

Derek Shelton

Year	Team	Lg	G	LUp	PL%	PH	PR	DS	Quick	Slow	LO	RCD	LS	Rel	SBA	SacA	RM	PO	#	Good	NG	Bomb	W	L	Pct
2020	Pirates	NL	60	57	.65	26	15	5	16	18	2	26	0	209	27	7	31	2	3	1	2	0	19	41	.317
2021	Pirates	NL	162	150	.66	290	4	15	48	47	0	64	1	583	90	48	129	0	26	17	9	4	61	101	.377
	162-Game Average			151	.66	231	14	15	47	47	1	66	1	578	85	40	117	1	21	13	8	3	58	104	.358

Mike Shildt

Year	Team	Lg	G	LUp	PL%	PH	PR	DS	Quick	Slow	LO	RCD	LS	Rel	SBA	SacA	RM	PO	#	Good	NG	Bomb	W	L	Pct
2018	Cardinals	NL	69	58	.49	117	22	30	21	11	1	44	3	244	40	29	82	0	25	16	9	2	41	28	.594
2019	Cardinals	NL	162	97	.48	268	30	44	47	33	9	111	10	542	145	57	154	2	41	29	12	4	91	71	.562
2020	Cardinals	NL	58	54	.60	32	9	11	19	13	1	25	4	176	28	5	36	0	8	6	2	1	30	28	.517
2021	Cardinals	NL	162	107	.47	258	11	32	43	39	2	99	5	556	111	55	95	0	30	22	8	3	90	72	.556
	162-Game Average			114	.49	242	26	42	47	34	5	100	8	545	116	52	132	1	37	26	11	4	91	71	.562

Buck Showalter

Year	Team	Lg	G	LUp	PL%	PH	PR	DS	Quick	Slow	LO	RCD	LS	Rel	SBA	SacA	RM	PO	#	Good	NG	Bomb	W	L	Pct
1994	Yankees	AL	113	79	.59	95	31	3	24	30	0	38	7	241	95	34		22	24	13	11	4	70	43	.619
1995	Yankees	AL	145	107	.68	124	30	20	29	42	37	57	6	302	80	27		29	21	14	7	1	79	65	.549
1998	Diamondbacks	NL	162	124	.62	252	17	15	34	40	7	43	6	368	111	68		13	32	16	16	9	65	97	.401
1999	Diamondbacks	NL	162	97	.63	220	20	17	37	48	25	74	3	382	176	75		15	48	29	19	8	100	62	.617
2000	Diamondbacks	NL	162	99	.60	250	32	11	46	26	18	74	3	382	141	89		10	53	28	25	16	85	77	.525
2003	Rangers	AL	162	133	.61	88	51	41	35	33	12	93	7	494	90	35	80	14	45	24	21	14	71	91	.438
2004	Rangers	AL	162	120	.64	86	15	24	53	30	12	82	10	468	105	30	88	5	29	19	10	3	89	73	.549

Year	Team	Lg	G	LINEUPS		SUBSTITUTION			PITCHER USAGE						TACTICS				INTENTIONAL BB				RESULTS		
				LUp	PL%	PH	PR	DS	Quick	Slow	LO	RCD	LS	Rel	SBA	SacA	RM	PO	#	Good	NG	Bomb	W	L	Pct
2005	Rangers	AL	162	98	.59	57	22	11	42	39	17	79	8	454	82	11	103	5	31	10	21	16	79	83	.488
2006	Rangers	AL	162	95	.57	39	34	22	41	27	10	85	4	489	77	30	72	8	18	11	7	5	80	82	.494
2010	Orioles	AL	57	42	.74	20	11	13	23	9	10	24	1	144	38	13	31	1	10	9	1	1	34	23	.596
2011	Orioles	AL	162	117	.53	60	39	27	43	40	14	61	2	478	106	32	133	6	42	31	11	5	69	93	.426
2012	Orioles	AL	162	120	.62	78	28	31	37	42	10	88	0	492	87	46	145	6	36	25	11	5	93	69	.574
2013	Orioles	AL	162	100	.65	90	23	21	31	39	19	84	4	473	108	37	104	4	32	11	21	13	85	77	.525
2014	Orioles	AL	162	120	.49	77	29	51	37	34	17	89	2	479	64	50	101	10	25	16	9	4	96	66	.593
2015	Orioles	AL	162	145	.60	89	21	35	35	41	6	76	8	453	69	26	95	10	27	12	15	8	81	81	.500
2016	Orioles	AL	162	125	.53	74	31	33	36	50	16	68	9	443	32	21	55	10	23	13	10	5	89	73	.549
2017	Orioles	AL	162	115	.44	95	31	40	27	57	21	93	3	492	45	19	40	8	21	15	6	5	75	87	.463
2018	Orioles	AL	162	152	.55	98	30	31	27	47	7	58	8	490	103	23	75	2	29	21	8	6	47	115	.290
	162-Game Average			117	.59	112	29	26	38	40	15	75	6	445	95	39	91	10	32	19	14		82	80	.506

Brian Snitker

Year	Team	Lg	G	LINEUPS		SUBSTITUTION			PITCHER USAGE						TACTICS				INTENTIONAL BB				RESULTS		
				LUp	PL%	PH	PR	DS	Quick	Slow	LO	RCD	LS	Rel	SBA	SacA	RM	PO	#	Good	NG	Bomb	W	L	Pct
2016	Braves	NL	124	85	.62	214	8	14	31	36	7	96	1	456	83	64	118	7	40	23	17	10	59	65	.476
2017	Braves	NL	162	108	.58	268	38	16	31	52	8	101	1	530	108	76	139	3	39	27	12	9	72	90	.444
2018	Braves	NL	162	103	.65	254	24	21	50	39	8	92	2	553	126	59	137	7	43	32	11	5	90	72	.556
2019	Braves	NL	162	95	.60	265	20	33	44	35	1	96	6	575	117	34	91	3	33	27	6	3	97	65	.599
2020	Braves	NL	60	51	.48	29	9	10	23	12	0	26	1	228	27	3	46	1	13	8	5	2	35	25	.583
2021	Braves	NL	161	100	.51	273	10	37	31	42	1	106	0	581	78	39	107	0	34	23	11	0	88	73	.547
	162-Game Average			106	.58	254	21	26	41	42	5	101	2	570	105	54	124	4	39	27	12	6	86	76	.531

Jayce Tingler

Year	Team	Lg	G	LINEUPS		SUBSTITUTION			PITCHER USAGE						TACTICS				INTENTIONAL BB				RESULTS		
				LUp	PL%	PH	PR	DS	Quick	Slow	LO	RCD	LS	Rel	SBA	SacA	RM	PO	#	Good	NG	Bomb	W	L	Pct
2020	Padres	NL	60	56	.59	44	10	13	23	9	1	27	0	218	68	14	46	0	2	1	1	0	37	23	.617
2021	Padres	NL	162	140	.57	307	13	27	47	36	3	106	4	624	149	42	130	0	33	26	7	2	79	83	.488
	162-Game Average			143	.58	256	17	29	51	33	3	97	3	614	158	41	128	0	26	20	6	1	85	77	.525

Don Wakamatsu

Year	Team	Lg	G	LINEUPS		SUBSTITUTION			PITCHER USAGE						TACTICS				INTENTIONAL BB				RESULTS		
				LUp	PL%	PH	PR	DS	Quick	Slow	LO	RCD	LS	Rel	SBA	SacA	RM	PO	#	Good	NG	Bomb	W	L	Pct
2009	Mariners	AL	162	138	.51	58	31	19	50	27	18	76	1	410	122	61	91	4	13	3	10	6	85	77	.525
2010	Mariners	AL	112	93	.61	49	21	12	37	21	20	39	2	254	129	40	124	17	25	11	14	7	42	70	.375
2018	Rangers	AL	10	10	.59	7	2	1	5	0	0	8	0	41	1	0	3	0	1	0	1	1	3	7	.300
	162-Game Average			137	.55	65	31	18	52	27	22	70	2	402	144	58	124	12	22	8	14	8	74	88	.457

Chris Woodward

Year	Team	Lg	G	LINEUPS		SUBSTITUTION			PITCHER USAGE						TACTICS				INTENTIONAL BB				RESULTS		
				LUp	PL%	PH	PR	DS	Quick	Slow	LO	RCD	LS	Rel	SBA	SacA	RM	PO	#	Good	NG	Bomb	W	L	Pct
2019	Rangers	AL	162	150	.62	82	14	19	32	48	24	70	2	499	169	19	115	0	11	4	7	5	78	84	.481
2020	Rangers	AL	60	58	.62	30	10	9	13	29	4	29	1	204	63	5	35	0	3	2	1	1	22	38	.367
2021	Rangers	AL	162	145	.61	89	14	4	38	44	2	50	0	507	135	24	123	1	11	4	7	2	60	102	.370
	162-Game Average			149	.62	85	16	14	35	51	13	63	1	510	155	20	115	0	11	4	6	3	68	95	.417

Ned Yost

Year	Team	Lg	G	LINEUPS		SUBSTITUTION			PITCHER USAGE						TACTICS				INTENTIONAL BB				RESULTS		
				LUp	PL%	PH	PR	DS	Quick	Slow	LO	RCD	LS	Rel	SBA	SacA	RM	PO	#	Good	NG	Bomb	W	L	Pct
2003	Brewers	NL	162	97	.44	304	22	39	23	59	18	90	6	460	138	85	40	23	43	28	15	9	68	94	.420
2004	Brewers	NL	161	131	.60	283	25	20	39	41	27	63	2	423	178	79	108	8	27	16	11	8	67	94	.416
2005	Brewers	NL	162	99	.46	259	18	35	26	41	42	71	2	395	113	89	97	50	52	23	29	10	81	81	.500
2006	Brewers	NL	162	106	.48	238	12	14	33	44	18	77	4	427	108	80	82	16	34	14	20	12	75	87	.463
2007	Brewers	NL	162	109	.60	259	11	41	37	42	18	117	7	492	128	74	94	19	37	28	9	9	83	79	.512
2008	Brewers	NL	150	74	.48	217	5	16	37	39	23	69	5	399	141	61	105	31	30	17	13	7	83	67	.553
2010	Royals	AL	127	80	.57	56	25	6	22	39	20	65	0	332	127	40	128	18	25	16	9	5	55	72	.433
2011	Royals	AL	162	87	.57	38	28	16	42	42	21	56	7	420	211	65	203	19	42	27	15	5	71	91	.438
2012	Royals	AL	162	118	.57	60	34	15	48	37	10	108	1	500	170	37	149	25	44	29	15	11	72	90	.444
2013	Royals	AL	162	127	.60	79	48	39	43	44	21	72	2	427	185	48	168	25	21	12	9	5	86	76	.531
2014	Royals	AL	162	101	.52	51	63	46	37	51	19	93	1	451	189	45	159	3	14	7	7	3	89	73	.549
2015	Royals	AL	162	83	.57	40	40	26	51	42	13	90	3	493	138	45	126	5	10	7	3	1	95	67	.586
2016	Royals	AL	162	108	.54	50	38	12	49	44	10	85	2	472	156	55	130	0	8	6	2	2	81	81	.500
2017	Royals	AL	162	86	.53	48	29	25	53	31	2	120	0	538	122	20	110	0	24	14	10	6	80	82	.494

Year	Team	Lg	G	LINEUPS		SUBSTITUTION			PITCHER USAGE						TACTICS				INTENTIONAL BB				RESULTS		
				LUp	PL%	PH	PR	DS	Quick	Slow	LO	RCD	LS	Rel	SBA	SacA	RM	PO	#	Good	NG	Bomb	W	L	Pct
2018	Royals	AL	162	150	.58	48	7	12	32	52	6	75	0	483	155	42	136	1	28	15	13	7	58	104	.358
2019	Royals	AL	162	132	.56	58	25	16	30	52	5	85	3	520	156	32	92	0	25	15	10	5	59	103	.364
	162-Game Average			107	.54	133	27	24	38	45	18	85	3	461	154	57	123	15	30	17	12	7	77	85	.475

Categories of this record are Games Managed (G), Number of Different Lineups Used (LUp), the percentage of players who had the platoon advantage at the start of the game (PL%), Pinch Hitters Used (PH), Pinch Runners Used (PR), Defensive Substitutes Used (DS), Quick Hooks (Quick), Slow Hooks (Slow), Long Outings by Starting Pitchers (LO), Relievers Used on Consecutive Days (RCD), Long Saves (LS), Relievers Used (Rel), Stolen Base Attempts (SBA), Sacrifice Bunt Attempts (SacA), Runners Moving with the Pitch (RM), Pitchouts ordered (PO), Intentional Walks issued (#), Intentional Walks resulting in a Good Outcome (Good), Intentional Walks resulting Not in a Good Outcome (NG), Intentional Walks Blowing Up on the Manager (Bomb), Wins (W), Losses (L), and Winning Percentage (Pct).

2021 American League Managers

Manager	G	LINEUPS		SUBSTITUTION			PITCHER USAGE						TACTICS				INTENTIONAL BB				RESULTS		
		LUp	PL%	PH	PR	DS	Quick	Slow	LO	RCD	LS	Rel	SBA	SacA	RM	PO	#	Good	NG	Bomb	W	L	Pct
Brandon Hyde, Bal	162	147	.60	86	32	32	41	45	1	75	6	569	77	19	66	0	12	7	5	3	52	110	.321
Alex Cora, Bos	162	141	.56	95	23	27	36	44	1	116	8	563	61	15	79	0	31	21	10	6	92	70	.568
Terry Francona, Cle	162	141	.63	89	17	19	43	45	5	91	3	535	126	25	98	0	12	7	5	1	80	82	.494
Tony LaRussa, CWS	162	153	.61	83	22	41	36	49	8	86	9	577	77	32	104	0	16	10	6	2	93	69	.574
A.J. Hinch, Det	162	153	.71	72	41	18	61	35	1	85	8	577	113	16	92	0	10	4	6	3	77	85	.475
Dusty Baker, Hou	162	133	.50	94	27	22	38	45	2	81	4	512	69	14	96	0	12	8	4	1	95	67	.586
Mike Matheny, KC	162	133	.56	80	32	33	30	54	3	98	5	556	157	42	139	0	16	9	7	4	74	88	.457
Joe Maddon, LAA	162	146	.50	74	12	41	46	36	6	80	10	562	105	34	117	11	18	9	9	9	77	85	.475
Rocco Baldelli, Min	162	149	.61	112	28	27	50	50	0	84	6	529	69	11	70	0	13	7	6	3	73	89	.451
Aaron Boone, NYY	162	146	.50	94	45	45	50	31	3	73	3	512	81	11	80	6	10	6	4	2	92	70	.568
Bob Melvin, Oak	162	153	.58	158	31	21	21	34	3	93	5	504	108	20	102	0	11	7	4	2	86	76	.531
Scott Servais, Sea	162	132	.60	102	12	26	37	43	1	105	7	584	88	19	80	2	23	16	7	3	90	72	.556
Kevin Cash, TB	162	158	.67	120	36	55	66	37	2	71	10	531	130	6	142	3	27	16	11	7	100	62	.617
Chris Woodward, Tex	162	145	.61	89	14	4	38	44	2	50	0	507	135	24	123	1	11	4	7	3	60	102	.370
Charlie Montoyo, Tor	162	133	.42	100	39	42	37	32	5	62	5	536	101	14	117	4	10	6	4	3	91	71	.562
162-Game Average		144	.58	97	27	30	42	42	3	83	6	539	100	20	100	2	15	9	6	3	82	80	.506

2021 National League Managers

Manager	G	LINEUPS		SUBSTITUTION			PITCHER USAGE						TACTICS				INTENTIONAL BB				RESULTS		
		LUp	PL%	PH	PR	DS	Quick	Slow	LO	RCD	LS	Rel	SBA	SacA	RM	PO	#	Good	NG	Bomb	W	L	Pct
Torey Lovullo, Ari	162	157	.74	339	22	17	34	54	0	95	2	565	59	40	67	6	45	30	15	7	52	110	.321
Brian Snitker, Atl	161	100	.51	273	10	37	31	42	1	106	0	581	78	39	107	0	34	23	11	0	88	73	.547
David Ross, ChC	162	138	.59	309	15	23	41	43	0	95	7	599	123	47	103	0	25	15	10	8	71	91	.438
David Bell, Cin	162	133	.56	303	23	33	22	56	2	111	6	579	60	49	68	0	30	23	7	3	83	79	.512
Bud Black, Col	161	143	.55	280	13	13	35	51	0	83	1	543	99	64	92	7	19	12	7	4	74	87	.460
Dave Roberts, LAD	162	146	.53	280	17	35	56	37	8	136	7	600	82	34	67	0	43	33	10	7	106	56	.654
Don Mattingly, Mia	162	147	.50	271	36	22	41	23	2	112	2	595	135	46	143	0	43	22	21	4	67	95	.414
Craig Counsell, Mil	162	138	.62	294	13	39	44	29	2	92	2	533	103	35	66	0	19	13	6	2	95	67	.586
Luis Rojas, NYM	162	133	.65	292	16	36	63	27	1	107	4	525	80	53	79	1	21	15	6	2	77	85	.475
Joe Girardi, Phi	162	135	.59	276	14	44	36	52	9	89	6	525	96	66	87	0	37	27	10	5	82	80	.506
Derek Shelton, Pit	162	150	.66	290	4	15	48	47	0	64	1	583	90	48	129	0	26	17	9	4	61	101	.377
Jayce Tingler, SD	162	140	.57	307	13	27	47	36	3	106	4	624	149	42	130	0	33	26	7	2	79	83	.488
Gabe Kapler, SF	162	148	.66	407	26	48	42	29	1	146	2	599	80	47	80	0	20	11	9	2	107	55	.660
Mike Shildt, StL	162	107	.47	258	11	32	43	39	2	99	5	556	111	55	95	0	30	22	8	3	90	72	.556
Dave Martinez, Was	162	128	.56	284	14	21	32	53	1	135	5	569	82	57	93	1	46	27	19	11	65	97	.401
162-Game Average		136	.58	298	16	29	41	41	2	105	4	573	95	48	94	1	31	21	10	4	80	82	.494

Ballparks and Park Indices

Brian Reiff

As a case study in park factors, let us consider Nolan Arenado.

In 2021, Arenado put up some of the worst numbers of his career. If you discount his rookie season and the shortened 2020 season, Arenado set career lows in batting average, on-base percentage and slugging percentage, and his 151 hits, 34 home runs and 105 RBIs were the fewest he had in a season in which he played at least 120 games. While the numbers he put up were still respectable, they were nowhere close to what he had been putting up in years prior.

Of course, in every season before this one, Arenado had played his home baseball in Coors Field, the most hitter-friendly ballpark in MLB. As you can see in the next few pages, between 2019 and 2021, Coors Field had a Runs factor of 134, meaning it inflated run totals by 34 percent. No other park had a Runs factor above 116 during that same span.

Meanwhile, Busch Stadium, where Arenado played his home games this year, has a three-year Runs factor of 89 (fifth lowest in MLB over that span) and a one-year factor of 82 (tied second lowest). Basically, he went from the best hitters' park of the modern game to one of the worst. His OPS on the road (.885, the second-highest mark of his career) was actually higher than it was at home (.722, the lowest of his career).

How did that affect him? Well, between 2015 and 2019, Arenado consistently finished with an OPS+ between 124 and 133, meaning after adjusting for park factors, his OPS was between 24 and 33 percent better than the average hitter. In 2021, he finished with a 121 OPS+.

That goes to show the impact that a given ballpark can have on a player's stat line. Arenado posted an OPS (.807) below .890 in a full season for the first time since 2014 and still had a comparable OPS+ to previous years thanks to his home park's run suppression and the MLB-wide offensive decline. Discount both park factors and Arenado at your own peril.

Arizona Diamondbacks - Chase Field Surface: FieldTurf
LF: 330   CF: 407   RF: 334

| | 2021 Season | | | | | | | 2019-2021 | | | | | | |
| | Home Games | | | Away Games | | | | Home Games | | | Away Games | | | |
	D'Backs	Opp	Total	D'Backs	Opp	Total	Index	D'Backs	Opp	Total	D'Backs	Opp	Total	Index
G	81	81	162	81	81	162		192	192	384	192	192	384	
Avg	.251	.269	.260	.222	.265	.243	107	.251	.257	.254	.236	.259	.247	103
AB	2728	2902	5630	2761	2644	5405	104	6466	6796	13262	6653	6321	12974	102
R	369	442	811	310	451	761	107	924	954	1878	837	977	1814	104
H	684	780	1464	613	700	1313	112	1626	1749	3375	1572	1637	3209	105
2B	169	184	353	139	143	282	120	366	385	751	331	349	680	108
3B	20	20	40	11	25	36	107	54	45	99	29	40	69	140
HR	69	101	170	75	131	206	79	195	255	450	227	290	517	85
BB	269	255	524	268	300	568	89	653	613	1266	605	693	1298	95
SO	699	656	1355	766	582	1348	97	1549	1690	3239	1737	1499	3236	98
Foul Outs	58	64	122	68	71	139	84	127	145	272	133	159	292	91
E	48	35	83	52	53	105	79	110	116	226	111	108	219	103
E-Infield	20	12	32	20	28	48	67	47	45	92	45	52	97	95
LHB-Avg	.262	.265	.263	.228	.266	.243	108	.256	.254	.255	.228	.257	.240	106
LHB-HR	46	44	90	42	54	96	91	103	107	210	102	113	215	95
RHB-Avg	.232	.271	.257	.213	.264	.243	106	.246	.260	.254	.246	.260	.254	100
RHB-HR	23	57	80	33	77	110	69	92	148	240	125	177	302	78

Atlanta Braves - Trust Park
LF: 335   CF: 400   RF: 325

| | 2021 Season | | | | | | | 2019-2021 | | | | | | |
| | Home Games | | | Away Games | | | | Home Games | | | Away Games | | | |
	Braves	Opp	Total	Braves	Opp	Total	Index	Braves	Opp	Total	Braves	Opp	Total	Index
G	80	80	160	81	81	162		191	191	382	192	192	384	
Avg	.248	.228	.238	.239	.241	.240	99	.259	.245	.252	.249	.246	.248	102
AB	2625	2695	5320	2738	2584	5322	101	6305	6532	12837	6692	6304	12996	99
R	404	352	756	386	304	690	111	1026	859	1885	967	828	1795	106
H	652	614	1266	655	622	1277	100	1630	1599	3229	1665	1552	3217	101
2B	139	119	258	130	124	254	102	344	304	648	332	286	618	106
3B	10	11	21	10	10	20	105	26	25	51	26	29	55	94
HR	116	96	212	123	87	210	101	299	225	524	292	230	522	102
BB	271	251	523	278	265	543	96	721	624	1346	686	660	1346	101
SO	731	733	1464	722	684	1406	104	1720	1688	3408	1773	1628	3401	101
Foul Outs	42	50	92	56	42	98	94	106	114	220	136	112	248	90
E	39	38	77	33	33	66	118	103	121	224	81	92	173	130
E-Infield	15	16	31	7	11	18	174	46	44	90	19	34	53	171
LHB-Avg	.261	.225	.242	.239	.234	.236	102	.260	.243	.252	.257	.241	.250	101
LHB-HR	39	39	78	43	30	73	110	100	90	190	99	82	181	111
RHB-Avg	.242	.230	.236	.239	.245	.242	97	.257	.246	.251	.243	.249	.246	102
RHB-HR	77	57	134	80	57	137	96	199	135	334	193	148	341	96

Baltimore Orioles - Oriole Park at Camden Yards
LF: 333   CF: 410   RF: 318

| | 2021 Season | | | | | | | 2019-2021 | | | | | | |
| | Home Games | | | Away Games | | | | Home Games | | | Away Games | | | |
	Orioles	Opp	Total	Orioles	Opp	Total	Index	Orioles	Opp	Total	Orioles	Opp	Total	Index
G	81	81	162	81	81	162		195	195	390	189	189	378	
Avg	.251	.275	.264	.227	.270	.248	106	.249	.272	.261	.242	.264	.253	103
AB	2684	2877	5561	2736	2685	5421	103	6488	6916	13404	6554	6334	12888	101
R	362	507	869	297	449	746	116	862	1197	2059	800	1034	1834	109
H	675	792	1467	621	726	1347	109	1615	1879	3494	1583	1672	3255	104
2B	131	148	279	135	143	278	98	309	356	665	311	339	650	98
3B	8	10	18	7	14	21	84	27	26	53	20	39	59	86
HR	122	155	277	73	103	176	153	281	373	654	204	269	473	133
BB	228	282	510	223	281	504	99	552	653	1205	525	663	1188	98
SO	690	654	1344	764	580	1344	97	1632	1549	3181	1771	1420	3191	96
Foul Outs	54	62	116	73	70	143	79	141	153	294	156	153	309	91
E	31	39	70	43	35	78	90	106	114	220	119	111	230	93
E-Infield	14	14	28	18	14	32	88	39	42	81	41	42	83	95
LHB-Avg	.252	.269	.262	.218	.260	.240	109	.241	.262	.252	.227	.251	.239	105
LHB-HR	42	50	92	23	27	50	186	105	128	233	79	91	170	135
RHB-Avg	.251	.278	.265	.231	.276	.252	105	.254	.278	.266	.250	.272	.261	102
RHB-HR	80	105	185	50	76	126	141	176	245	421	125	178	303	132

Boston Red Sox - Fenway Park
LF: 310   CF: 420   RF:302

| | 2021 Season | | | | | | | 2019-2021 | | | | | | |
| | Home Games | | | Away Games | | | | Home Games | | | Away Games | | | |
	Red Sox	Opp	Total	Red Sox	Opp	Total	Index	Red Sox	Opp	Total	Red Sox	Opp	Total	Index
G	81	81	162	81	81	162		191	191	382	193	193	386	
Avg	.281	.268	.274	.241	.246	.244	112	.278	.264	.271	.253	.253	.253	107
AB	2720	2832	5552	2775	2638	5413	103	6543	6739	13282	6805	6482	13287	101
R	470	402	872	359	347	706	124	1061	1017	2078	961	911	1872	112
H	764	759	1523	670	650	1320	115	1816	1779	3595	1724	1640	3364	108
2B	192	173	365	138	133	271	131	468	416	884	325	327	652	136
3B	14	9	23	9	11	20	112	33	26	59	24	27	51	116
HR	108	90	198	111	86	197	98	258	236	494	287	253	540	92
BB	266	266	532	246	280	526	99	651	716	1367	638	687	1325	103
SO	624	778	1402	762	749	1511	90	1568	1868	3436	1745	1829	3574	96
Foul Outs	59	46	105	69	53	122	84	105	106	211	153	114	267	79
E	48	51	99	60	47	107	93	132	122	254	109	115	224	115
E-Infield	16	20	36	27	17	44	82	55	50	105	52	46	98	108
LHB-Avg	.282	.253	.267	.228	.231	.230	116	.274	.255	.264	.250	.238	.245	108
LHB-HR	32	21	53	40	26	66	83	87	80	167	111	89	200	85
RHB-Avg	.281	.276	.278	.248	.255	.252	111	.280	.269	.274	.255	.261	.258	106
RHB-HR	76	69	145	71	60	131	105	171	156	327	176	164	340	95

Chicago Cubs - Wrigley Field
LF: 355   CF: 400   RF:353

| | 2021 Season | | | | | | | 2019-2021 | | | | | | |
| | Home Games | | | Away Games | | | | Home Games | | | Away Games | | | |
	Cubs	Opp	Total	Cubs	Opp	Total	Index	Cubs	Opp	Total	Cubs	Opp	Total	Index
G	81	81	162	81	81	162		195	195	390	189	189	378	
Avg	.240	.256	.248	.233	.254	.244	102	.244	.244	.244	.237	.256	.247	99
AB	2582	2810	5392	2724	2621	5345	101	6234	6639	12873	6451	6223	12674	98
R	369	428	797	336	411	747	107	905	866	1771	879	930	1809	95
H	619	719	1338	636	667	1303	103	1523	1618	3141	1532	1595	3127	97
2B	100	136	236	125	147	272	86	282	304	586	295	334	629	92
3B	17	5	22	9	9	18	121	39	23	62	21	22	43	142
HR	111	131	242	99	104	203	118	264	257	521	276	247	523	98
BB	264	277	541	238	319	557	96	701	611	1312	611	701	1312	98
SO	792	694	1486	804	664	1468	100	1765	1748	3513	1859	1577	3436	101
Foul Outs	37	27	64	47	42	89	71	78	69	147	109	109	218	66
E	41	49	90	46	41	87	103	108	104	212	127	102	229	90
E-Infield	24	19	43	18	19	37	116	49	47	96	52	47	99	94
LHB-Avg	.248	.252	.250	.228	.254	.241	104	.251	.240	.245	.234	.260	.247	99
LHB-HR	39	59	98	35	50	85	119	111	102	213	121	103	224	96
RHB-Avg	.234	.259	.247	.237	.255	.246	100	.240	.246	.243	.240	.253	.247	99
RHB-HR	72	72	144	64	54	118	117	153	155	308	155	144	299	99

Chicago White Sox - Guaranteed Rate Field
LF: 330   CF: 400   RF:334

| | 2021 Season | | | | | | | 2019-2021 | | | | | | |
| | Home Games | | | Away Games | | | | Home Games | | | Away Games | | | |
	White Sox	Opp	Total	White Sox	Opp	Total	Index	White Sox	Opp	Total	White Sox	Opp	Total	Index
G	80	80	160	82	82	164		190	190	380	193	193	386	
Avg	.260	.215	.237	.253	.243	.248	96	.259	.232	.245	.259	.255	.257	95
AB	2559	2609	5168	2798	2651	5449	97	6186	6365	12551	6747	6341	13088	97
R	407	295	702	389	341	730	99	896	842	1738	914	872	1786	99
H	666	561	1227	707	644	1351	93	1603	1474	3077	1747	1617	3364	93
2B	116	100	216	159	99	258	88	283	249	532	346	311	657	84
3B	12	10	22	10	16	26	89	17	15	32	31	33	64	52
HR	106	102	208	84	80	164	134	248	283	531	220	208	428	129
BB	300	227	527	286	258	544	102	581	649	1230	562	635	1197	107
SO	638	804	1442	751	784	1535	99	1657	1753	3410	1852	1670	3522	101
Foul Outs	50	66	116	60	57	117	105	116	145	261	137	139	276	99
E	45	60	105	52	47	99	109	120	136	256	133	126	259	100
E-Infield	23	32	55	17	24	41	138	57	67	124	55	49	104	121
LHB-Avg	.243	.209	.225	.227	.245	.236	95	.235	.217	.225	.237	.257	.248	91
LHB-HR	46	40	86	22	29	51	163	81	101	182	46	80	126	148
RHB-Avg	.271	.220	.246	.267	.242	.255	97	.273	.242	.258	.271	.254	.263	98
RHB-HR	60	62	122	51	62	113	120	167	182	349	174	128	302	122

Cincinnati Reds - Great American Ballpark
LF: 328   CF: 404   RF:325

	2021 Season							2019-2021						
	Home Games			Away Games				Home Games			Away Games			
	Reds	Opp	Total	Reds	Opp	Total	Index	Reds	Opp	Total	Reds	Opp	Total	Index
G	81	81	162	81	81	162		189	189	378	195	195	390	
Avg	.263	.252	.258	.236	.236	.236	109	.252	.239	.245	.231	.234	.233	105
AB	2675	2812	5487	2748	2628	5376	102	6170	6447	12617	6545	6255	12800	102
R	448	413	861	338	347	685	126	924	900	1824	806	814	1620	116
H	704	710	1414	648	620	1268	112	1556	1538	3094	1514	1463	2977	107
2B	151	146	297	144	115	259	112	299	313	612	307	285	592	105
3B	7	10	17	6	20	26	64	13	18	31	30	41	71	44
HR	129	121	250	93	85	178	138	298	282	580	241	205	446	132
BB	309	309	618	244	308	552	110	670	680	1350	614	686	1300	105
SO	726	802	1528	699	722	1421	105	1695	1926	3621	1700	1765	3465	106
Foul Outs	53	52	105	41	36	77	134	113	132	245	104	104	208	119
E	42	47	89	49	32	81	110	96	97	193	113	94	207	96
E-Infield	19	21	40	17	16	33	121	37	46	83	39	42	81	106
LHB-Avg	.265	.244	.254	.250	.220	.235	108	.256	.234	.244	.229	.234	.232	105
LHB-HR	58	52	110	38	38	76	143	122	143	265	95	95	190	137
RHB-Avg	.262	.259	.261	.226	.248	.236	110	.249	.243	.246	.233	.234	.233	105
RHB-HR	71	69	140	55	47	102	134	176	139	315	146	110	256	128

Cleveland Indians - Progressive Field
LF: 325   CF: 405   RF:325

	2021 Season							2019-2021						
	Home Games			Away Games				Home Games			Away Games			
	Indians	Opp	Total	Indians	Opp	Total	Index	Indians	Opp	Total	Indians	Opp	Total	Index
G	80	80	160	82	82	164		191	191	382	193	193	386	
Avg	.238	.242	.240	.238	.238	.238	101	.241	.239	.240	.242	.236	.239	100
AB	2543	2685	5228	2789	2652	5441	98	6114	6457	12571	6602	6300	12902	98
R	339	359	698	378	368	746	96	841	800	1641	893	793	1686	98
H	606	650	1256	663	631	1294	99	1472	1544	3016	1597	1485	3082	99
2B	114	135	249	134	131	265	98	300	351	651	330	313	643	104
3B	12	5	17	10	11	21	84	19	20	39	26	25	51	78
HR	101	112	213	102	104	206	108	233	260	493	252	231	483	105
BB	226	250	476	227	272	499	99	610	559	1169	645	570	1215	99
SO	663	696	1359	724	695	1419	100	1576	1807	3383	1660	1713	3373	103
Foul Outs	56	40	96	63	68	131	76	134	115	249	152	165	317	81
E	51	49	100	35	53	88	116	106	113	219	93	107	200	111
E-Infield	29	20	49	16	24	40	126	54	47	101	34	48	82	124
LHB-Avg	.231	.238	.235	.237	.230	.233	101	.238	.236	.237	.243	.227	.235	101
LHB-HR	42	43	85	39	44	83	105	114	108	222	123	99	222	104
RHB-Avg	.243	.246	.244	.238	.245	.241	101	.243	.241	.242	.241	.243	.242	100
RHB-HR	59	69	128	63	60	123	110	119	152	271	129	132	261	106

Colorado Rockies - Coors Field
LF: 347   CF: 415   RF:350

	2021 Season							2019-2021						
	Home Games			Away Games				Home Games			Away Games			
	Rockies	Opp	Total	Rockies	Opp	Total	Index	Rockies	Opp	Total	Rockies	Opp	Total	Index
G	81	81	162	80	80	160		192	192	384	191	191	382	
Avg	.280	.256	.268	.217	.264	.240	111	.288	.281	.284	.225	.259	.242	118
AB	2730	2788	5518	2644	2589	5233	104	6619	6880	13499	6472	6256	12728	106
R	456	407	863	283	389	672	127	1109	1164	2273	740	943	1683	134
H	764	713	1477	574	684	1258	116	1909	1931	3840	1459	1621	3080	124
2B	171	148	319	104	143	247	122	386	407	793	296	328	624	120
3B	25	18	43	9	13	22	185	67	59	126	24	35	59	201
HR	104	98	202	78	98	176	109	271	285	556	198	264	462	113
BB	235	265	500	256	274	530	89	571	647	1218	570	686	1256	91
SO	604	625	1229	752	644	1396	83	1519	1479	2998	1883	1447	3330	85
Foul Outs	56	43	99	36	54	90	104	115	105	220	136	123	259	80
E	37	48	85	36	37	73	115	109	131	240	104	105	209	114
E-Infield	19	19	38	12	14	26	144	47	51	98	34	45	79	123
LHB-Avg	.268	.255	.261	.221	.274	.249	104	.289	.273	.281	.234	.266	.250	112
LHB-HR	41	39	80	25	44	69	106	118	118	236	79	113	192	115
RHB-Avg	.288	.257	.273	.215	.256	.234	117	.288	.288	.288	.218	.253	.235	122
RHB-HR	63	59	122	53	54	107	111	153	167	320	119	151	270	113

Detroit Tigers - Comerica Park
LF: 345   CF: 420   RF: 330

| | 2021 Season | | | | | | | 2019-2021 | | | | | | |
| | Home Games | | | Away Games | | | | Home Games | | | Away Games | | | |
	Tigers	Opp	Total	Tigers	Opp	Total	Index	Tigers	Opp	Total	Tigers	Opp	Total	Index
G	81	81	162	81	81	162		189	189	378	192	192	384	
Avg	.242	.243	.242	.242	.261	.251	97	.244	.262	.253	.239	.265	.252	101
AB	2610	2762	5372	2766	2685	5451	99	6215	6661	12876	6603	6377	12980	101
R	335	344	679	362	412	774	88	731	991	1722	797	998	1795	97
H	631	670	1301	668	700	1368	95	1516	1748	3264	1579	1688	3267	101
2B	109	142	251	127	117	244	104	283	352	635	323	319	642	100
3B	26	19	45	11	9	20	228	64	53	117	26	26	52	227
HR	81	73	154	98	126	224	70	172	256	428	218	284	502	86
BB	247	293	540	243	278	521	105	501	657	1158	527	642	1169	100
SO	717	638	1355	797	621	1418	97	1729	1519	3248	1947	1552	3499	94
Foul Outs	66	77	143	51	62	113	128	147	168	315	131	125	256	124
E	36	36	72	47	39	86	84	115	89	204	107	102	209	99
E-Infield	19	13	32	25	19	44	73	51	35	86	47	42	89	98
LHB-Avg	.233	.225	.230	.241	.267	.253	91	.240	.246	.243	.244	.273	.258	94
LHB-HR	30	19	49	35	53	88	56	55	71	126	66	97	163	75
RHB-Avg	.248	.253	.251	.242	.257	.250	100	.246	.273	.260	.236	.260	.248	105
RHB-HR	51	54	105	63	73	136	79	117	185	302	152	187	339	92

Houston Astros - Minute Maid Park
LF: 315   CF: 409   RF: 326

| | 2021 Season | | | | | | | 2019-2021 | | | | | | |
| | Home Games | | | Away Games | | | | Home Games | | | Away Games | | | |
	Astros	Opp	Total	Astros	Opp	Total	Index	Astros	Opp	Total	Astros	Opp	Total	Index
G	81	81	162	81	81	162		190	190	380	194	194	388	
Avg	.267	.222	.244	.268	.234	.252	97	.270	.218	.244	.262	.236	.250	98
AB	2727	2782	5509	2866	2607	5473	101	6348	6478	12826	6850	6344	13194	99
R	427	327	754	436	331	767	98	1048	740	1788	1014	833	1847	99
H	727	618	1345	769	611	1380	97	1715	1411	3126	1797	1495	3292	97
2B	148	121	269	151	115	266	100	352	254	606	373	311	684	91
3B	12	7	19	2	6	8	236	31	21	52	23	25	48	111
HR	105	99	204	116	88	204	99	284	254	538	294	233	527	105
BB	296	282	578	273	267	540	106	713	586	1299	693	628	1321	101
SO	589	768	1357	633	688	1321	102	1359	1919	3278	1469	1734	3203	105
Foul Outs	50	49	99	59	56	115	86	120	115	235	152	138	290	83
E	38	41	79	33	37	70	113	79	108	187	83	89	172	111
E-Infield	15	17	32	9	19	28	114	27	44	71	28	42	70	104
LHB-Avg	.276	.232	.251	.269	.225	.246	102	.282	.210	.240	.269	.225	.245	98
LHB-HR	38	40	78	50	26	76	98	88	111	199	98	90	188	103
RHB-Avg	.262	.215	.240	.268	.240	.256	94	.264	.225	.246	.259	.244	.252	98
RHB-HR	67	59	126	66	62	128	100	196	143	339	196	143	339	106

Kansas City Royals - Kauffman Stadium
LF: 330   CF: 410   RF: 330

| | 2021 Season | | | | | | | 2019-2021 | | | | | | |
| | Home Games | | | Away Games | | | | Home Games | | | Away Games | | | |
	Royals	Opp	Total	Royals	Opp	Total	Index	Royals	Opp	Total	Royals	Opp	Total	Index
G	81	81	162	81	81	162		191	191	382	193	193	386	
Avg	.261	.264	.263	.236	.243	.239	110	.258	.271	.264	.237	.253	.245	108
AB	2701	2815	5516	2726	2599	5325	104	6353	6715	13068	6558	6246	12804	103
R	379	414	793	307	374	681	116	845	1012	1857	780	917	1697	111
H	705	744	1449	644	631	1275	114	1639	1817	3456	1551	1583	3134	111
2B	136	149	285	115	110	225	122	335	354	689	294	284	578	117
3B	18	12	30	11	12	23	126	43	30	73	33	27	60	119
HR	76	84	160	87	105	192	80	170	219	389	223	267	490	78
BB	223	263	486	198	328	526	89	531	632	1163	518	752	1270	90
SO	600	656	1256	658	688	1346	90	1472	1499	2971	1718	1592	3310	88
Foul Outs	55	51	106	54	61	115	89	136	115	251	118	133	251	98
E	48	65	113	36	36	72	157	101	130	231	87	106	193	121
E-Infield	22	26	48	14	17	31	155	46	52	98	36	43	79	125
LHB-Avg	.250	.255	.253	.250	.235	.243	104	.245	.273	.261	.227	.249	.238	109
LHB-HR	16	38	54	31	42	73	70	38	97	135	63	108	171	76
RHB-Avg	.267	.270	.268	.228	.247	.238	113	.265	.269	.267	.242	.256	.249	107
RHB-HR	60	46	106	56	63	119	87	132	122	254	160	159	319	79

Los Angeles Angels - Angel Stadium of Anaheim
LF: 330   CF: 400   RF:330

| | 2021 Season | | | | | | | 2019-2021 | | | | | | |
| | Home Games | | | Away Games | | | | Home Games | | | Away Games | | | |
	Angels	Opp	Total	Angels	Opp	Total	Index	Angels	Opp	Total	Angels	Opp	Total	Index
G	82	82	164	80	80	160		192	192	384	192	192	384	
Avg	.253	.245	.249	.237	.257	.247	101	.253	.247	.250	.239	.256	.247	101
AB	2691	2829	5520	2746	2646	5392	100	6393	6720	13113	6606	6341	12947	101
R	387	402	789	336	402	738	104	951	987	1938	835	1006	1841	105
H	681	692	1373	650	681	1331	101	1620	1659	3279	1580	1623	3203	102
2B	127	132	259	138	151	289	88	321	317	638	309	356	665	95
3B	10	7	17	13	6	19	87	26	21	47	26	30	56	83
HR	105	104	209	85	84	169	121	267	283	550	228	254	482	113
BB	243	319	562	221	273	494	111	665	710	1375	624	657	1281	106
SO	704	748	1452	690	705	1395	102	1561	1756	3317	1599	1624	3223	102
Foul Outs	55	34	89	61	56	117	74	131	104	235	152	131	283	82
E	49	31	80	39	52	91	86	120	86	206	96	125	221	93
E-Infield	23	13	36	13	24	37	95	52	41	93	38	63	101	92
LHB-Avg	.251	.243	.247	.242	.261	.252	98	.247	.243	.245	.238	.256	.247	99
LHB-HR	47	42	89	42	33	75	119	126	122	248	100	95	195	123
RHB-Avg	.254	.245	.250	.234	.255	.244	102	.257	.249	.253	.240	.256	.248	102
RHB-HR	58	62	120	43	51	94	123	141	161	302	128	159	287	105

Los Angeles Dodgers - Dodger Stadium
LF: 330   CF: 395   RF:330

| | 2021 Season | | | | | | | 2019-2021 | | | | | | |
| | Home Games | | | Away Games | | | | Home Games | | | Away Games | | | |
	Dodgers	Opp	Total	Dodgers	Opp	Total	Index	Dodgers	Opp	Total	Dodgers	Opp	Total	Index
G	81	81	162	81	81	162		192	192	384	192	192	384	
Avg	.244	.208	.226	.244	.207	.226	100	.257	.212	.234	.247	.218	.233	100
AB	2597	2706	5303	2848	2629	5477	97	6243	6435	12678	6737	6275	13012	97
R	411	268	679	419	293	712	95	1026	637	1663	1039	750	1789	93
H	634	564	1198	696	543	1239	97	1603	1364	2967	1664	1368	3032	98
2B	125	113	238	122	114	236	104	316	256	572	330	279	609	96
3B	9	4	13	15	5	20	67	18	11	29	32	29	61	49
HR	140	91	231	97	70	167	143	347	229	576	287	183	470	126
BB	301	208	509	312	278	590	89	692	449	1141	756	574	1330	88
SO	682	833	1515	726	766	1492	105	1511	1900	3411	1724	1735	3459	101
Foul Outs	51	64	115	65	52	117	102	119	138	257	128	107	235	112
E	40	39	79	49	47	96	82	103	99	202	132	109	241	84
E-Infield	17	12	29	20	21	41	71	42	34	76	53	50	103	74
LHB-Avg	.228	.201	.214	.232	.210	.221	97	.251	.204	.228	.247	.220	.234	97
LHB-HR	54	36	90	34	34	68	132	160	86	246	152	86	238	108
RHB-Avg	.255	.214	.235	.253	.204	.230	102	.262	.218	.238	.247	.217	.232	103
RHB-HR	86	55	141	63	36	99	151	187	143	330	135	97	232	144

Miami Marlins - Marlins Park   Surface: FieldTurf
LF: 344   CF: 400   RF:335

| | 2021 Season | | | | | | | 2019-2021 | | | | | | |
| | Home Games | | | Away Games | | | | Home Games | | | Away Games | | | |
	Marlins	Opp	Total	Marlins	Opp	Total	Index	Marlins	Opp	Total	Marlins	Opp	Total	Index
G	81	81	162	81	81	162		188	188	376	196	196	392	
Avg	.238	.222	.230	.227	.261	.243	94	.241	.237	.239	.234	.254	.244	98
AB	2643	2756	5399	2705	2574	5279	102	6166	6412	12578	6629	6332	12961	101
R	324	314	638	299	387	686	93	748	857	1605	753	956	1709	98
H	630	611	1241	614	671	1285	97	1489	1521	3010	1553	1607	3160	99
2B	99	144	243	127	161	288	82	263	355	618	310	348	658	97
3B	17	14	31	6	17	23	132	30	34	64	16	31	47	140
HR	71	79	150	87	83	170	86	161	215	376	203	265	468	83
BB	222	273	495	228	256	484	100	502	670	1172	534	700	1234	98
SO	747	764	1511	806	617	1423	104	1702	1668	3370	1857	1542	3399	102
Foul Outs	60	47	107	53	45	98	107	109	144	253	115	128	243	107
E	63	51	114	59	32	91	125	118	113	231	138	120	258	93
E-Infield	29	23	52	27	19	46	113	43	44	87	59	58	117	78
LHB-Avg	.218	.237	.228	.215	.271	.244	93	.211	.249	.234	.222	.272	.251	93
LHB-HR	24	39	63	28	42	70	89	45	92	137	52	121	173	81
RHB-Avg	.250	.211	.231	.234	.253	.243	95	.253	.228	.242	.239	.241	.240	101
RHB-HR	47	40	87	59	41	100	85	116	123	239	151	144	295	84

Milwaukee Brewers - Miller Park
LF: 344   CF: 400   RF:345

	2021 Season							2019-2021						
	Home Games			Away Games				Home Games			Away Games			
	Brewers	Opp	Total	Brewers	Opp	Total	Index	Brewers	Opp	Total	Brewers	Opp	Total	Index
G	81	81	162	81	81	162		191	191	382	193	193	386	
Avg	.222	.224	.223	.244	.211	.228	98	.235	.227	.231	.240	.237	.238	97
AB	2587	2755	5342	2775	2545	5320	100	6149	6479	12628	6675	6312	12987	98
R	350	346	696	388	277	665	105	859	845	1704	895	808	1703	101
H	575	618	1193	676	538	1214	98	1446	1473	2919	1600	1493	3093	95
2B	115	94	209	140	106	246	85	287	243	530	330	287	617	88
3B	9	13	22	9	5	14	156	19	32	51	21	32	53	99
HR	95	90	185	99	78	177	104	260	240	500	259	220	479	107
BB	313	290	603	273	247	520	115	742	653	1395	694	643	1337	107
SO	712	845	1557	753	773	1526	102	1769	1965	3734	1841	1764	3605	107
Foul Outs	67	55	122	52	40	92	132	131	147	278	125	112	237	121
E	49	44	93	45	58	103	90	108	113	221	118	110	228	98
E-Infield	19	14	33	17	23	40	83	45	48	93	42	40	82	115
LHB-Avg	.224	.222	.223	.236	.209	.225	99	.238	.226	.232	.236	.243	.239	97
LHB-HR	36	29	65	39	25	64	103	124	88	212	124	96	220	99
RHB-Avg	.220	.226	.224	.252	.213	.231	97	.233	.228	.230	.243	.232	.237	97
RHB-HR	59	61	120	60	53	113	104	136	152	288	135	124	259	115

Minnesota Twins - Target Field
LF: 339   CF: 411   RF:328

	2021 Season							2019-2021						
	Home Games			Away Games				Home Games			Away Games			
	Twins	Opp	Total	Twins	Opp	Total	Index	Twins	Opp	Total	Twins	Opp	Total	Index
G	81	81	162	81	81	162		193	193	386	191	191	382	
Avg	.239	.252	.245	.244	.258	.251	98	.250	.251	.250	.258	.254	.256	98
AB	2650	2810	5460	2781	2650	5431	101	6417	6757	13174	6683	6301	12984	100
R	365	409	774	364	425	789	98	947	902	1849	990	901	1891	97
H	633	707	1340	678	685	1363	98	1605	1695	3300	1721	1601	3322	98
2B	125	168	293	146	133	279	104	339	355	694	331	301	632	108
3B	9	7	16	8	15	23	69	23	23	46	20	27	47	96
HR	112	121	233	116	118	234	99	292	245	537	334	254	588	90
BB	276	231	507	249	253	502	100	654	546	1200	582	560	1142	104
SO	673	657	1330	732	660	1392	95	1596	1724	3320	1671	1591	3262	100
Foul Outs	70	45	115	51	55	106	108	166	116	282	140	154	294	95
E	58	40	98	49	43	92	107	114	98	212	124	105	229	92
E-Infield	28	13	41	21	21	42	98	51	35	86	54	57	111	77
LHB-Avg	.240	.270	.255	.244	.268	.256	100	.259	.262	.260	.254	.252	.253	103
LHB-HR	37	49	86	33	46	79	112	107	88	195	122	94	216	92
RHB-Avg	.238	.240	.239	.243	.252	.248	97	.243	.243	.243	.261	.256	.258	94
RHB-HR	75	72	147	83	72	155	92	185	157	342	212	160	372	88

New York Mets - Citi Field
LF: 335   CF: 408   RF:330

	2021 Season							2019-2021						
	Home Games			Away Games				Home Games			Away Games			
	Mets	Opp	Total	Mets	Opp	Total	Index	Mets	Opp	Total	Mets	Opp	Total	Index
G	81	81	162	81	81	162		191	191	382	193	193	386	
Avg	.243	.219	.231	.234	.252	.243	95	.249	.232	.240	.255	.259	.257	94
AB	2477	2567	5044	2733	2608	5341	94	6121	6366	12487	6736	6412	13148	96
R	303	284	587	333	384	717	82	810	781	1591	903	932	1835	88
H	603	563	1166	639	658	1297	90	1522	1479	3001	1716	1658	3374	90
2B	108	105	213	120	135	255	88	282	296	578	332	344	676	90
3B	8	5	13	10	14	24	57	16	13	29	26	30	56	55
HR	77	93	170	99	97	196	92	244	239	483	260	236	496	103
BB	246	251	497	249	224	473	111	588	603	1191	620	591	1211	104
SO	655	767	1422	737	686	1423	106	1563	1908	3471	1711	1639	3350	109
Foul Outs	53	34	87	59	57	116	79	125	101	226	123	123	246	97
E	37	40	77	58	47	105	73	100	98	198	126	111	237	84
E-Infield	16	14	30	19	21	40	75	40	31	71	51	45	96	75
LHB-Avg	.257	.211	.235	.224	.247	.234	100	.263	.231	.248	.254	.255	.254	97
LHB-HR	35	41	76	44	42	86	93	101	98	199	118	90	208	103
RHB-Avg	.229	.226	.227	.244	.256	.250	91	.236	.233	.235	.255	.261	.258	91
RHB-HR	42	52	94	55	55	110	91	143	141	284	142	146	288	102

New York Yankees - Yankee Stadium
LF: 318   CF: 408   RF:314

	2021 Season							2019-2021						
	Home Games			Away Games			Index	Home Games			Away Games			Index
	Yankees	Opp	Total	Yankees	Opp	Total		Yankees	Opp	Total	Yankees	Opp	Total	
G	81	81	162	81	81	162		193	193	386	191	191	382	
Avg	.232	.226	.229	.242	.236	.239	96	.251	.229	.240	.253	.249	.251	95
AB	2570	2721	5291	2761	2665	5426	98	6212	6502	12714	6617	6346	12963	97
R	353	328	681	358	341	699	97	984	763	1747	985	915	1900	91
H	597	615	1212	669	628	1297	93	1559	1489	3048	1673	1583	3256	93
2B	97	100	197	116	132	248	81	261	268	529	329	336	665	81
3B	4	4	8	8	11	19	43	17	12	29	19	27	46	64
HR	106	113	219	116	83	199	113	316	267	583	306	260	566	105
BB	323	264	587	298	228	526	114	723	586	1309	718	581	1299	103
SO	725	825	1550	757	744	1501	106	1650	1909	3559	1749	1722	3471	105
Foul Outs	41	59	100	47	58	105	98	109	127	236	121	132	253	95
E	48	29	77	50	40	90	86	119	91	210	129	108	237	88
E-Infield	20	11	31	23	15	38	82	52	26	78	56	39	95	81
LHB-Avg	.199	.209	.205	.214	.227	.221	93	.218	.225	.222	.227	.242	.235	94
LHB-HR	26	45	71	27	25	52	143	72	103	175	78	85	163	110
RHB-Avg	.245	.235	.240	.254	.240	.247	97	.264	.231	.248	.263	.254	.259	96
RHB-HR	80	68	148	89	58	147	102	244	164	408	228	175	403	103

Oakland Athletics - RingCentral Coliseum
LF: 330   CF: 400   RF:330

	2021 Season							2019-2021						
	Home Games			Away Games			Index	Home Games			Away Games			Index
	Athletics	Opp	Total	Athletics	Opp	Total		Athletics	Opp	Total	Athletics	Opp	Total	
G	81	81	162	81	81	162		192	192	384	192	192	384	
Avg	.229	.243	.236	.246	.252	.249	95	.237	.237	.237	.245	.251	.248	96
AB	2585	2825	5410	2810	2683	5493	98	6208	6650	12858	6656	6363	13019	99
R	339	331	670	404	356	760	88	861	743	1604	1001	856	1857	86
H	591	687	1278	692	675	1367	93	1469	1579	3048	1628	1596	3224	95
2B	123	126	249	148	121	269	94	320	298	618	334	283	617	101
3B	10	7	17	9	11	20	86	28	16	44	25	28	53	84
HR	87	91	178	112	100	212	85	242	201	443	285	260	545	82
BB	282	196	478	263	243	506	96	696	504	1200	665	577	1242	98
SO	676	680	1356	673	652	1325	104	1528	1627	3155	1683	1510	3193	100
Foul Outs	68	101	169	62	63	125	137	185	214	399	148	152	300	135
E	38	47	85	34	49	83	102	92	109	201	86	116	202	100
E-Infield	14	11	25	16	21	37	68	41	35	76	37	50	87	87
LHB-Avg	.245	.241	.243	.244	.243	.244	100	.235	.240	.238	.242	.246	.244	97
LHB-HR	39	37	76	51	33	84	93	83	87	170	98	110	208	81
RHB-Avg	.221	.244	.233	.247	.257	.252	92	.237	.236	.237	.246	.254	.249	95
RHB-HR	48	54	102	61	67	128	80	159	114	273	187	150	337	83

Philadelphia Phillies - Citizens Bank Park
LF: 329   CF: 401   RF:329

	2021 Season							2019-2021						
	Home Games			Away Games			Index	Home Games			Away Games			Index
	Phillies	Opp	Total	Phillies	Opp	Total		Phillies	Opp	Total	Phillies	Opp	Total	
G	81	81	162	81	81	162		194	194	388	190	190	380	
Avg	.244	.238	.241	.236	.250	.243	99	.250	.252	.251	.240	.261	.250	101
AB	2611	2764	5375	2755	2654	5409	99	6370	6701	13071	6515	6259	12774	100
R	363	362	725	371	383	754	96	947	909	1856	867	941	1808	101
H	637	658	1295	651	663	1314	99	1595	1692	3287	1562	1631	3193	101
2B	123	131	254	139	134	273	94	323	297	620	340	334	674	90
3B	17	10	27	7	18	25	109	37	28	65	23	31	54	118
HR	95	104	199	103	96	199	101	266	285	551	229	253	482	112
BB	285	251	536	279	258	537	100	713	614	1327	642	626	1268	102
SO	684	790	1474	718	690	1408	105	1637	1771	3408	1698	1633	3331	100
Foul Outs	59	65	124	54	56	110	113	167	155	322	125	101	226	139
E	49	46	95	45	53	98	97	112	127	239	115	129	244	96
E-Infield	19	22	41	24	21	45	91	45	60	105	48	46	94	109
LHB-Avg	.237	.233	.235	.239	.235	.237	99	.249	.257	.253	.244	.252	.248	102
LHB-HR	45	42	87	48	41	89	99	113	127	240	106	104	210	113
RHB-Avg	.250	.242	.246	.234	.263	.248	99	.251	.250	.250	.237	.267	.251	100
RHB-HR	50	62	112	55	55	110	102	153	158	311	123	149	272	111

Pittsburgh Pirates - PNC Park
LF: 325   CF: 399   RF:320

| | 2021 Season | | | | | | | 2019-2021 | | | | | | |
| | Home Games | | | Away Games | | | | Home Games | | | Away Games | | | |
	Pirates	Opp	Total	Pirates	Opp	Total	Index	Pirates	Opp	Total	Pirates	Opp	Total	Index
G	81	81	162	81	81	162		193	193	386	191	191	382	
Avg	.245	.257	.251	.228	.264	.246	102	.251	.254	.252	.242	.266	.254	99
AB	2619	2774	5393	2717	2605	5322	101	6402	6722	13124	6523	6223	12746	102
R	330	396	726	279	437	716	101	836	1001	1837	750	1041	1791	102
H	642	712	1354	619	688	1307	104	1605	1707	3312	1578	1655	3233	101
2B	130	160	290	110	138	248	115	343	419	762	288	330	618	120
3B	21	17	38	14	15	29	129	45	33	78	34	36	70	108
HR	58	89	147	66	124	190	76	156	248	404	190	286	476	82
BB	280	318	598	249	288	537	110	603	753	1356	518	686	1204	109
SO	635	647	1282	693	665	1358	93	1460	1680	3140	1602	1611	3213	95
Foul Outs	41	56	97	45	49	94	102	98	114	212	130	113	243	85
E	33	36	69	37	41	78	88	125	115	240	113	113	226	105
E-Infield	13	12	25	16	15	31	81	49	42	91	45	44	89	101
LHB-Avg	.251	.252	.251	.239	.276	.256	98	.260	.255	.258	.247	.274	.260	99
LHB-HR	39	37	76	45	59	104	73	94	102	196	106	134	240	81
RHB-Avg	.239	.260	.251	.216	.255	.237	106	.241	.253	.248	.237	.260	.249	100
RHB-HR	19	52	71	21	65	86	80	62	146	208	84	152	236	84

San Diego Padres - PETCO Park
LF: 336   CF: 396   RF:322

| | 2021 Season | | | | | | | 2019-2021 | | | | | | |
| | Home Games | | | Away Games | | | | Home Games | | | Away Games | | | |
	Padres	Opp	Total	Padres	Opp	Total	Index	Padres	Opp	Total	Padres	Opp	Total	Index
G	81	81	162	81	81	162		194	194	388	190	190	380	
Avg	.241	.227	.234	.244	.248	.246	95	.237	.230	.234	.248	.256	.252	93
AB	2630	2772	5402	2754	2608	5362	101	6250	6627	12877	6497	6256	12753	99
R	355	328	683	374	380	754	91	833	810	1643	903	928	1831	88
H	634	629	1263	671	648	1319	96	1482	1525	3007	1610	1602	3212	92
2B	137	127	264	136	146	282	93	288	323	611	312	333	645	94
3B	10	6	16	11	15	26	61	23	16	39	34	33	67	58
HR	86	97	183	94	108	202	90	242	235	477	252	255	507	93
BB	329	238	567	257	278	535	105	702	565	1267	592	584	1176	107
SO	669	827	1496	655	690	1345	110	1699	1884	3583	1685	1673	3358	106
Foul Outs	62	44	106	62	46	108	97	130	106	236	157	105	262	89
E	47	42	89	35	47	82	109	115	108	223	116	102	218	100
E-Infield	24	18	42	10	25	35	120	50	37	87	30	46	76	112
LHB-Avg	.256	.215	.235	.239	.239	.239	98	.246	.220	.232	.247	.259	.253	92
LHB-HR	32	35	67	29	40	69	96	67	87	154	66	102	168	90
RHB-Avg	.230	.236	.233	.247	.255	.251	93	.232	.238	.235	.248	.254	.251	94
RHB-HR	54	62	116	65	68	133	87	175	148	323	186	153	339	95

San Francisco Giants - Oracle Park
LF: 339   CF: 391   RF:309

| | 2021 Season | | | | | | | 2020-2021 | | | | | | |
| | Home Games | | | Away Games | | | | Home Games | | | Away Games | | | |
	Giants	Opp	Total	Giants	Opp	Total	Index	Giants	Opp	Total	Giants	Opp	Total	Index
G	81	81	162	81	81	162		114	114	228	108	108	216	
Avg	.254	.227	.240	.244	.233	.239	101	.259	.231	.245	.246	.235	.241	102
AB	2641	2761	5402	2821	2691	5512	98	3738	3882	7620	3743	3538	7281	99
R	381	309	690	423	285	708	97	561	467	1028	542	424	966	101
H	671	627	1298	689	627	1316	99	970	895	1865	922	833	1755	101
2B	148	120	268	123	119	242	113	213	181	394	165	155	320	118
3B	14	18	32	11	11	22	148	23	25	48	16	18	34	135
HR	104	67	171	137	84	221	79	155	101	256	167	119	286	86
BB	317	195	512	285	221	506	103	445	311	756	352	315	667	108
SO	704	727	1431	757	698	1455	100	961	1040	2001	999	873	1872	102
Foul Outs	40	48	88	56	70	126	71	56	72	128	72	91	163	75
E	47	37	84	33	40	73	115	64	50	114	58	51	109	99
E-Infield	25	13	38	16	20	36	106	35	19	54	30	28	58	88
LHB-Avg	.250	.228	.239	.246	.230	.238	100	.257	.225	.241	.246	.230	.239	101
LHB-HR	58	24	82	73	32	105	81	81	38	119	88	44	132	90
RHB-Avg	.258	.227	.241	.243	.236	.239	101	.261	.235	.247	.247	.240	.243	102
RHB-HR	46	43	89	64	52	116	77	74	63	137	79	75	154	82

Seattle Mariners - T-Mobile Park
LF: 331 CF: 405 RF:326

	2021 Season							2019-2021						
	Home Games			Away Games				Home Games			Away Games			
	Mariners	Opp	Total	Mariners	Opp	Total	Index	Mariners	Opp	Total	Mariners	Opp	Total	Index
G	81	81	162	81	81	162		186	186	372	198	198	396	
Avg	.214	.232	.223	.237	.263	.250	89	.224	.240	.232	.237	.267	.252	92
AB	2580	2780	5360	2775	2710	5485	98	6008	6437	12445	6776	6671	13447	99
R	329	340	669	368	408	776	86	793	883	1676	916	1061	1977	90
H	552	644	1196	657	712	1369	87	1343	1542	2885	1606	1780	3386	91
2B	100	129	229	133	159	292	80	259	306	565	316	415	731	84
3B	7	6	13	4	20	24	55	16	16	32	28	44	72	48
HR	94	99	193	105	98	203	97	224	266	490	274	270	544	97
BB	278	223	501	257	262	519	99	647	556	1203	683	664	1347	97
SO	751	702	1453	741	626	1367	109	1770	1557	3327	1848	1479	3327	108
Foul Outs	73	69	142	57	62	119	122	141	159	300	137	146	283	115
E	37	37	74	42	30	72	103	109	96	205	125	88	213	102
E-Infield	15	15	30	18	13	31	97	43	37	80	56	38	94	91
LHB-Avg	.196	.226	.209	.235	.237	.236	89	.211	.242	.224	.237	.250	.243	92
LHB-HR	41	41	82	54	33	87	98	97	99	196	130	97	227	93
RHB-Avg	.232	.235	.234	.239	.277	.261	90	.236	.238	.238	.237	.276	.259	92
RHB-HR	53	58	111	51	65	116	97	127	167	294	144	173	317	100

St Louis Cardinals - Busch Stadium
LF: 336 CF: 400 RF:335

	2021 Season							2019-2021						
	Home Games			Away Games				Home Games			Away Games			
	Cardinals	Opp	Total	Cardinals	Opp	Total	Index	Cardinals	Opp	Total	Cardinals	Opp	Total	Index
G	81	81	162	81	81	162		189	189	378	193	193	386	
Avg	.241	.227	.234	.246	.241	.243	96	.245	.225	.235	.241	.242	.241	97
AB	2598	2705	5303	2753	2576	5329	100	6042	6278	12320	6510	6131	12641	100
R	307	314	621	399	358	757	82	813	709	1522	897	854	1751	89
H	627	613	1240	676	621	1297	96	1481	1413	2894	1568	1481	3049	97
2B	127	117	244	134	135	269	91	273	263	536	307	305	612	90
3B	8	8	16	14	9	23	70	28	15	43	25	25	50	88
HR	77	73	150	121	79	200	75	191	196	387	268	216	484	82
BB	228	269	497	250	339	589	85	627	607	1234	617	750	1367	93
SO	632	628	1260	709	597	1306	97	1489	1508	2997	1749	1580	3329	92
Foul Outs	65	53	118	59	46	105	113	147	119	266	128	104	232	118
E	36	44	80	48	47	95	84	89	113	202	94	118	212	97
E-Infield	8	14	22	18	16	34	65	28	40	68	36	47	83	84
LHB-Avg	.235	.224	.229	.208	.242	.228	100	.248	.223	.234	.228	.241	.236	99
LHB-HR	10	31	41	20	30	50	78	40	88	128	68	89	157	82
RHB-Avg	.244	.228	.237	.259	.240	.251	94	.244	.226	.236	.247	.242	.245	96
RHB-HR	67	42	109	101	49	150	75	151	108	259	200	127	327	82

Tampa Bay Rays - Tropicana Field Surface: FieldTurf
LF: 315 CF: 404 RF:322

	2021 Season							2019-2021						
	Home Games			Away Games				Home Games			Away Games			
	Rays	Opp	Total	Rays	Opp	Total	Index	Rays	Opp	Total	Rays	Opp	Total	Index
G	81	81	162	81	81	162		191	191	382	193	193	386	
Avg	.241	.213	.227	.243	.250	.247	92	.243	.220	.231	.250	.244	.247	93
AB	2628	2695	5323	2879	2759	5638	94	6288	6479	12767	6822	6501	13323	97
R	401	259	660	456	392	848	78	901	669	1570	1014	867	1881	84
H	634	574	1208	701	690	1391	87	1527	1424	2951	1705	1589	3294	91
2B	137	116	253	151	128	279	96	330	287	617	354	304	658	98
3B	19	5	24	16	18	34	75	40	24	64	36	31	67	100
HR	95	76	171	127	108	235	77	227	196	423	292	239	531	83
BB	306	209	515	279	227	506	108	707	507	1214	663	550	1213	104
SO	757	793	1550	785	685	1470	112	1808	1915	3723	1835	1736	3571	109
Foul Outs	75	64	139	60	51	111	133	158	151	309	143	117	260	124
E	43	56	99	37	63	100	99	96	106	202	104	134	238	86
E-Infield	14	29	43	12	25	37	116	39	54	93	42	47	89	106
LHB-Avg	.228	.213	.222	.250	.242	.247	90	.236	.215	.227	.252	.231	.244	93
LHB-HR	45	20	65	67	35	102	66	107	65	172	143	75	218	81
RHB-Avg	.256	.213	.230	.236	.254	.246	93	.249	.222	.234	.248	.251	.250	94
RHB-HR	50	56	106	60	73	133	86	120	131	251	149	164	313	85

Texas Rangers - Globe Life Field Surface: FieldTurf
LF: 329   CF: 407   RF:326

	2021 Season							2020-2021						
	Home Games			Away Games				Home Games			Away Games			
	Rangers	Opp	Total	Rangers	Opp	Total	Index	Rangers	Opp	Total	Rangers	Opp	Total	Index
G	81	81	162	81	81	162		111	111	222	111	111	222	
Avg	.237	.248	.243	.227	.266	.246	99	.235	.244	.240	.221	.262	.241	99
AB	2642	2817	5459	2763	2651	5414	101	3586	3831	7417	3755	3618	7373	101
R	320	388	708	305	427	732	97	443	533	976	406	594	1000	98
H	627	698	1325	627	704	1331	100	844	934	1778	830	947	1777	100
2B	109	127	236	116	122	238	98	147	167	314	158	165	323	97
3B	7	11	18	17	8	25	71	13	16	29	20	16	36	80
HR	91	103	194	76	129	205	94	118	142	260	111	171	282	92
BB	211	247	458	222	266	488	93	305	379	684	295	370	665	102
SO	645	632	1277	736	607	1343	94	907	910	1817	1022	818	1840	98
Foul Outs	59	64	123	59	62	121	101	79	90	169	85	84	169	99
E	42	35	77	41	41	82	94	60	55	115	63	54	117	98
E-Infield	17	16	33	15	14	29	114	26	24	50	24	21	45	111
LHB-Avg	.226	.250	.238	.219	.251	.234	102	.223	.245	.234	.210	.245	.227	103
LHB-HR	38	42	80	33	41	74	102	57	57	114	54	56	110	95
RHB-Avg	.245	.246	.246	.232	.274	.253	97	.244	.243	.244	.228	.272	.250	97
RHB-HR	53	61	114	43	88	131	89	61	85	146	57	115	172	89

Toronto Blue Jays - Rogers Centre Surface: FieldTurf
LF: 328   CF: 400   RF:328

	2021 Season							2019-2021						
	Home Games			Away Games				Home Games			Away Games			
	Blue Jays	Opp	Total	Blue Jays	Opp	Total	Index	Blue Jays	Opp	Total	Blue Jays	Opp	Total	Index
G	35	35	70	127	127	254		116	116	232	268	268	536	
Avg	.268	.222	.245	.265	.239	.253	97	.241	.248	.245	.256	.249	.253	97
AB	1156	1186	2342	4320	4151	8471	100	3853	4093	7946	9139	8861	18000	102
R	187	130	317	659	533	1192	96	546	560	1106	1328	1243	2571	99
H	310	263	573	1145	994	2139	97	929	1014	1943	2341	2210	4551	99
2B	70	49	119	215	199	414	104	199	212	411	460	481	941	99
3B	4	1	5	9	18	27	67	16	10	26	22	41	63	93
HR	56	40	96	206	169	375	93	192	174	366	405	344	749	111
BB	94	73	167	402	401	803	75	347	373	720	861	955	1816	90
SO	217	332	549	1001	1136	2137	93	937	1039	1976	2303	2280	4583	98
Foul Outs	29	39	68	72	101	173	142	100	110	210	143	217	360	132
E	13	12	25	77	73	150	60	59	46	105	166	165	331	73
E-Infield	3	6	9	32	30	62	53	21	20	41	73	66	139	68
LHB-Avg	.259	.196	.217	.226	.232	.230	95	.230	.246	.239	.236	.240	.238	100
LHB-HR	3	9	12	17	56	73	76	63	74	137	87	130	217	138
RHB-Avg	.270	.231	.252	.274	.243	.261	97	.246	.249	.248	.264	.256	.260	95
RHB-HR	53	31	84	189	113	302	94	129	100	229	318	214	532	99

Washington Nationals - Nationals Park
LF: 336   CF: 403   RF:335

	2021 Season							2019-2021						
	Home Games			Away Games				Home Games			Away Games			
	Nationals	Opp	Total	Nationals	Opp	Total	Index	Nationals	Opp	Total	Nationals	Opp	Total	Index
G	81	81	162	81	81	162		195	195	390	189	189	378	
Avg	.265	.249	.257	.251	.260	.255	101	.265	.253	.259	.258	.252	.255	101
AB	2596	2712	5308	2789	2649	5438	98	6345	6694	13039	6520	6183	12703	99
R	350	397	747	374	423	797	94	947	931	1878	943	914	1857	99
H	687	676	1363	701	688	1389	98	1682	1692	3374	1685	1560	3245	101
2B	130	128	258	142	123	265	100	356	325	681	326	308	634	105
3B	8	8	16	12	11	23	71	27	19	46	32	24	56	80
HR	95	121	216	87	126	213	104	255	280	535	224	263	487	107
BB	271	256	527	302	292	594	91	682	626	1308	667	655	1322	96
SO	602	669	1271	701	677	1378	94	1488	1732	3220	1574	1633	3207	98
Foul Outs	45	72	117	40	59	99	121	137	153	290	113	141	254	111
E	54	56	110	42	56	98	112	118	120	238	104	113	217	106
E-Infield	24	24	48	22	27	49	98	54	51	105	56	48	104	98
LHB-Avg	.262	.247	.254	.255	.244	.249	102	.263	.260	.262	.255	.246	.250	105
LHB-HR	46	47	93	52	43	95	94	104	116	220	105	93	198	104
RHB-Avg	.267	.251	.259	.249	.271	.259	100	.266	.247	.257	.260	.257	.259	99
RHB-HR	49	74	123	35	83	118	111	151	164	315	119	170	289	109

507

2021 American League Ballpark Index Rankings

Home Park	TOTALS												LHB		RHB	
	Avg	AB	R	H	2B	3B	HR	BB	SO	FO	E	E-Inf	Avg	HR	Avg	HR
Red Sox (Fenway Park)	112	103	124	115	131	112	98	99	90	84	93	82	116	83	111	105
Orioles (Oriole Park at Camden Yards)	106	103	116	109	98	84	153	99	97	79	90	88	109	186	105	141
Royals (Kauffman Stadium)	110	104	116	114	122	126	80	89	90	89	157	155	104	70	113	87
Angels (Angel Stadium of Anaheim)	101	100	104	101	88	87	121	111	102	74	86	95	98	119	102	123
White Sox (Guaranteed Rate Field)	96	97	99	93	88	89	134	102	99	105	109	138	95	163	97	120
Astros (Minute Maid Park)	97	101	98	97	100	236	99	106	102	86	113	114	102	98	94	100
Twins (Target Field)	98	101	98	98	104	69	99	100	95	108	107	98	100	112	97	92
Yankees (Yankee Stadium)	96	98	97	93	81	43	113	114	106	98	86	82	93	143	97	102
Rangers (Globe Life Field)	99	101	97	100	98	71	94	93	94	101	94	114	102	102	97	89
Blue Jays (Rogers Centre)	97	100	96	97	104	67	93	75	93	142	60	53	95	76	97	94
Indians (Progressive Field)	101	98	96	99	98	84	108	99	100	76	116	126	101	105	101	110
Athletics (RingCentral Coliseum)	95	98	88	93	94	86	85	96	104	137	102	68	100	93	92	80
Tigers (Comerica Park)	97	99	88	95	104	228	70	105	97	128	84	73	91	56	100	79
Mariners (T-Mobile Park)	89	98	86	87	80	55	97	99	109	122	103	97	89	98	90	97
Rays (Tropicana Field)	92	94	78	87	96	75	77	108	112	133	99	116	90	66	93	86

2021 National League Ballpark Index Rankings

Home Park	TOTALS												LHB		RHB	
	Avg	AB	R	H	2B	3B	HR	BB	SO	FO	E	E-Inf	Avg	HR	Avg	HR
Rockies (Coors Field)	111	104	127	116	122	185	109	89	83	104	115	144	104	106	117	111
Reds (Great American Ballpark)	109	102	126	112	112	64	138	110	105	134	110	121	108	143	110	134
Braves (Trust Park)	99	101	111	100	102	105	101	96	104	94	118	174	102	110	97	96
Cubs (Wrigley Field)	102	101	107	103	86	121	118	96	100	71	103	116	104	119	100	117
Diamondbacks (Chase Field)	107	104	107	112	120	107	79	89	97	84	79	67	108	91	106	69
Brewers (Miller Park)	98	100	105	98	85	156	104	115	102	132	90	83	99	103	97	104
Pirates (PNC Park)	102	101	101	104	115	129	76	110	93	102	88	81	98	73	106	80
Giants (Oracle Park)	101	98	97	99	113	148	79	103	100	71	115	106	100	81	101	77
Phillies (Citizens Bank Park)	99	99	96	99	94	109	101	100	105	113	97	91	99	99	99	102
Dodgers (Dodger Stadium)	100	97	95	97	104	67	143	89	105	102	82	71	97	132	102	151
Nationals (Nationals Park)	101	98	94	98	100	71	104	91	94	121	112	98	102	94	100	111
Marlins (Marlins Park)	94	102	93	97	82	132	86	100	104	107	125	113	93	89	95	85
Padres (PETCO Park)	95	101	91	96	93	61	90	105	110	97	109	120	98	96	93	87
Cardinals (Busch Stadium)	96	100	82	96	91	70	75	85	97	113	84	65	100	78	94	75
Mets (Citi Field)	95	94	82	90	88	57	92	111	106	79	73	75	100	93	91	91

2021 AL Home Runs

Home Park	Index
Orioles	153
White Sox	134
Angels	121
Yankees	113
Indians	108
Astros	99
Twins	99
Red Sox	98
Mariners	97
Rangers	94
Blue Jays	93
Athletics	85
Royals	80
Rays	77
Tigers	70

2021 AL LHB Home Runs

Home Park	Index
Orioles	186
White Sox	163
Yankees	143
Angels	119
Twins	112
Indians	105
Rangers	102
Mariners	98
Astros	98
Athletics	93
Red Sox	83
Blue Jays	76
Royals	70
Rays	66
Tigers	56

2021 AL RHB Home Runs

Home Park	Index
Orioles	141
Angels	123
White Sox	120
Indians	110
Red Sox	105
Yankees	102
Astros	100
Mariners	97
Blue Jays	94
Twins	92
Rangers	89
Royals	87
Rays	86
Athletics	80
Tigers	79

2021 NL Home Runs

Home Park	Index
Dodgers	143
Reds	138
Cubs	118
Rockies	109
Brewers	104
Nationals	104
Braves	101
Phillies	101
Mets	92
Padres	90
Marlins	86
Diamondbacks	79
Giants	79
Pirates	76
Cardinals	75

2021 NL LHB Home Runs

Home Park	Index
Reds	143
Dodgers	132
Cubs	119
Braves	110
Rockies	106
Brewers	103
Phillies	99
Padres	96
Nationals	94
Mets	93
Diamondbacks	91
Marlins	89
Giants	81
Cardinals	78
Pirates	73

2021 NL RHB Home Runs

Home Park	Index
Dodgers	151
Reds	134
Cubs	117
Nationals	111
Rockies	111
Brewers	104
Phillies	102
Braves	96
Mets	91
Padres	87
Marlins	85
Pirates	80
Giants	77
Cardinals	75
Diamondbacks	69

2021 AL Avg	
Home Park	Index
Red Sox	112
Royals	110
Orioles	106
Indians	101
Angels	101
Rangers	99
Twins	98
Blue Jays	97
Astros	97
Tigers	97
Yankees	96
White Sox	96
Athletics	95
Rays	92
Mariners	89

2021 AL LHB Avg	
Home Park	Index
Red Sox	116
Orioles	109
Royals	104
Astros	102
Rangers	102
Indians	101
Twins	100
Athletics	100
Angels	98
White Sox	95
Blue Jays	95
Yankees	93
Tigers	91
Rays	90
Mariners	89

2021 AL RHB Avg	
Home Park	Index
Royals	113
Red Sox	111
Orioles	105
Angels	102
Indians	101
Tigers	100
Rangers	97
Yankees	97
Blue Jays	97
Twins	97
White Sox	97
Astros	94
Rays	93
Athletics	92
Mariners	90

2021 NL Avg	
Home Park	Index
Rockies	111
Reds	109
Diamondbacks	107
Pirates	102
Cubs	102
Giants	101
Nationals	101
Dodgers	100
Phillies	99
Braves	99
Brewers	98
Cardinals	96
Mets	95
Padres	95
Marlins	94

2021 NL LHB Avg	
Home Park	Index
Diamondbacks	108
Reds	108
Rockies	104
Cubs	104
Braves	102
Nationals	102
Mets	100
Giants	100
Cardinals	100
Brewers	99
Phillies	99
Pirates	98
Padres	98
Dodgers	97
Marlins	93

2021 NL RHB Avg	
Home Park	Index
Rockies	117
Reds	110
Pirates	106
Diamondbacks	106
Dodgers	102
Giants	101
Cubs	100
Nationals	100
Phillies	99
Braves	97
Brewers	97
Marlins	95
Cardinals	94
Padres	93
Mets	91

2021 AL Doubles	
Home Park	Index
Red Sox	131
Royals	122
Twins	104
Tigers	104
Blue Jays	104
Astros	100
Rangers	98
Orioles	98
Indians	98
Rays	96
Athletics	94
White Sox	88
Angels	88
Yankees	81
Mariners	80

2021 AL Triples	
Home Park	Index
Astros	236
Tigers	228
Royals	126
Red Sox	112
White Sox	89
Angels	87
Athletics	86
Indians	84
Orioles	84
Rays	75
Rangers	71
Twins	69
Blue Jays	67
Mariners	55
Yankees	43

2021 AL Errors	
Home Park	Index
Royals	157
Indians	116
Astros	113
White Sox	109
Twins	107
Mariners	103
Athletics	102
Rays	99
Rangers	94
Red Sox	93
Orioles	90
Angels	86
Yankees	86
Tigers	84
Blue Jays	60

2021 NL Doubles	
Home Park	Index
Rockies	122
Diamondbacks	120
Pirates	115
Giants	113
Reds	112
Dodgers	104
Braves	102
Nationals	100
Phillies	94
Padres	93
Cardinals	91
Mets	88
Cubs	86
Brewers	85
Marlins	82

2021 NL Triples	
Home Park	Index
Rockies	185
Brewers	156
Giants	148
Marlins	132
Pirates	129
Cubs	121
Phillies	109
Diamondbacks	107
Braves	105
Nationals	71
Cardinals	70
Dodgers	67
Reds	64
Padres	61
Mets	57

2021 NL Errors	
Home Park	Index
Marlins	125
Braves	118
Giants	115
Rockies	115
Nationals	112
Reds	110
Padres	109
Cubs	103
Phillies	97
Brewers	90
Pirates	88
Cardinals	84
Dodgers	82
Diamondbacks	79
Mets	73

2019-2021 American League Ballpark Index Rankings

Home Park	Avg	AB	R	H	2B	3B	HR	BB	SO	FO	E	E-Inf	LHB Avg	LHB HR	RHB Avg	RHB HR
Royals (Kauffman Stadium)	108	103	111	111	117	119	78	90	88	98	121	125	109	76	107	79
Red Sox (Fenway Park)	107	101	112	108	136	116	92	103	96	79	115	108	108	85	106	95
Orioles (Oriole Park at Camden Yards)	103	101	109	104	98	86	133	98	96	91	93	95	105	135	102	132
Angels (Angel Stadium of Anaheim)	101	101	105	102	95	83	113	106	102	82	93	92	99	123	102	105
Tigers (Comerica Park)	101	101	97	101	100	227	86	100	94	124	99	98	94	75	105	92
Indians (Progressive Field)	100	98	98	99	104	78	105	99	103	81	111	124	101	104	100	106
Rangers (Globe Life Field)[1]	99	101	98	100	97	80	92	102	98	99	98	111	103	95	97	89
Twins (Target Field)	98	100	97	98	108	96	90	104	100	95	92	77	103	92	94	88
Astros (Minute Maid Park)	98	99	99	97	91	111	105	101	105	83	111	104	98	103	98	106
Blue Jays (Rogers Centre)	97	102	99	99	99	93	111	90	98	132	73	68	100	138	95	99
Athletics (RingCentral Coliseum)	96	99	86	95	101	84	82	98	100	135	100	87	97	81	95	83
Yankees (Yankee Stadium)	95	97	91	93	81	64	105	103	105	95	88	81	94	110	96	103
White Sox (Guaranteed Rate Field)	95	97	99	93	84	52	129	107	101	99	100	121	91	148	98	122
Rays (Tropicana Field)	93	97	84	91	98	100	83	104	109	124	86	106	93	81	94	85
Mariners (T-Mobile Park)	92	99	90	91	84	48	97	97	108	115	102	91	92	93	92	100

2019-2021 National League Ballpark Index Rankings

Home Park	Avg	AB	R	H	2B	3B	HR	BB	SO	FO	E	E-Inf	LHB Avg	LHB HR	RHB Avg	RHB HR
Rockies (Coors Field)	118	106	134	124	120	201	113	91	85	80	114	123	112	115	122	113
Reds (Great American Ballpark)	105	102	116	107	105	44	132	105	106	119	96	106	105	137	105	128
Diamondbacks (Chase Field)	103	102	104	105	108	140	85	95	98	91	103	95	106	95	100	78
Braves (Trust Park)	102	99	106	101	106	94	102	101	101	90	130	171	101	111	102	96
Giants (Oracle Park)[1]	102	99	101	101	118	135	86	108	102	75	99	88	101	90	102	82
Nationals (Nationals Park)	101	99	98	101	105	80	107	96	98	111	106	98	105	104	99	109
Phillies (Citizens Bank Park)	101	100	101	101	90	118	112	102	100	139	96	109	102	113	100	111
Dodgers (Dodger Stadium)	100	97	93	98	96	49	126	88	101	112	84	74	97	108	103	144
Pirates (PNC Park)	99	102	102	101	120	108	82	109	95	85	105	101	99	81	100	84
Cubs (Wrigley Field)	99	98	95	97	92	142	98	98	101	66	90	94	99	96	99	99
Marlins (Marlins Park)	98	101	98	99	97	140	83	98	102	107	93	78	93	81	101	84
Cardinals (Busch Stadium)	97	100	89	97	90	88	82	93	92	118	97	84	99	82	96	82
Brewers (Miller Park)	97	98	101	95	88	99	107	107	107	121	98	115	97	99	97	115
Mets (Citi Field)	94	96	88	90	90	55	103	104	109	97	84	75	97	103	91	102
Padres (PETCO Park)	93	99	88	92	94	58	93	107	106	89	100	112	92	90	94	95

2019-2021 AL Home Runs

Home Park	Index
Orioles	133
White Sox	129
Angels	113
Blue Jays	111
Yankees	105
Astros	105
Indians	105
Mariners	97
Rangers[1]	92
Red Sox	92
Twins	90
Tigers	86
Rays	83
Athletics	82
Royals	78

2019-2021 AL LHB Home Runs

Home Park	Index
White Sox	148
Blue Jays	138
Orioles	135
Angels	123
Yankees	110
Indians	104
Astros	103
Rangers[1]	95
Mariners	93
Twins	92
Red Sox	85
Athletics	81
Rays	81
Royals	76
Tigers	75

2019-2021 AL RHB Home Runs

Home Park	Index
Orioles	132
White Sox	122
Astros	106
Indians	106
Angels	105
Yankees	103
Mariners	100
Blue Jays	99
Red Sox	95
Tigers	92
Rangers[1]	89
Twins	88
Rays	85
Athletics	83
Royals	79

2019-2021 NL Home Runs

Home Park	Index
Reds	132
Dodgers	126
Rockies	113
Phillies	112
Brewers	107
Nationals	107
Mets	103
Braves	102
Cubs	98
Padres	93
Giants[1]	86
Diamondbacks	85
Marlins	83
Pirates	82
Cardinals	82

2019-2021 NL LHB Home Runs

Home Park	Index
Reds	137
Rockies	115
Phillies	113
Braves	111
Dodgers	108
Nationals	104
Mets	103
Brewers	99
Cubs	96
Diamondbacks	95
Giants[1]	90
Padres	90
Cardinals	82
Pirates	81
Marlins	81

2019-2021 NL RHB Home Runs

Home Park	Index
Dodgers	144
Reds	128
Brewers	115
Rockies	113
Phillies	111
Nationals	109
Mets	102
Cubs	99
Braves	96
Padres	95
Pirates	84
Marlins	84
Cardinals	82
Giants[1]	82
Diamondbacks	78

1. 2020-2021 only

2019-2021 AL Avg	
Home Park	Index
Royals	108
Red Sox	107
Orioles	103
Angels	101
Tigers	101
Indians	100
Rangers[1]	99
Twins	98
Astros	98
Blue Jays	97
Athletics	96
Yankees	95
White Sox	95
Rays	93
Mariners	92

2019-2021 AL LHB Avg	
Home Park	Index
Royals	109
Red Sox	108
Orioles	105
Rangers[1]	103
Twins	103
Indians	101
Blue Jays	100
Angels	99
Astros	98
Athletics	97
Yankees	94
Tigers	94
Rays	93
Mariners	92
White Sox	91

2019-2021 AL RHB Avg	
Home Park	Index
Royals	107
Red Sox	106
Tigers	105
Angels	102
Orioles	102
Indians	100
White Sox	98
Astros	98
Rangers[1]	97
Yankees	96
Blue Jays	95
Athletics	95
Twins	94
Rays	94
Mariners	92

2019-2021 NL Avg	
Home Park	Index
Rockies	118
Reds	105
Diamondbacks	103
Braves	102
Giants[1]	102
Nationals	101
Phillies	101
Dodgers	100
Pirates	99
Cubs	99
Marlins	98
Cardinals	97
Brewers	97
Mets	94
Padres	93

2019-2021 NL LHB Avg	
Home Park	Index
Rockies	112
Diamondbacks	106
Reds	105
Nationals	105
Phillies	102
Giants[1]	101
Braves	101
Cubs	99
Pirates	99
Cardinals	99
Mets	97
Dodgers	97
Brewers	97
Marlins	93
Padres	92

2019-2021 NL RHB Avg	
Home Park	Index
Rockies	122
Reds	105
Dodgers	103
Braves	102
Giants[1]	102
Marlins	101
Diamondbacks	100
Pirates	100
Phillies	100
Nationals	99
Cubs	99
Brewers	97
Cardinals	96
Padres	94
Mets	91

2019-2021 AL Doubles	
Home Park	Index
Red Sox	136
Royals	117
Twins	108
Indians	104
Athletics	101
Tigers	100
Blue Jays	99
Orioles	98
Rays	98
Rangers[1]	97
Angels	95
Astros	91
White Sox	84
Mariners	84
Yankees	81

2019-2021 AL Triples	
Home Park	Index
Tigers	227
Royals	119
Red Sox	116
Astros	111
Rays	100
Twins	96
Blue Jays	93
Orioles	86
Athletics	84
Angels	83
Rangers[1]	80
Indians	78
Yankees	64
White Sox	52
Mariners	48

2019-2021 AL Errors	
Home Park	Index
Royals	121
Red Sox	115
Astros	111
Indians	111
Mariners	102
White Sox	100
Athletics	100
Tigers	99
Rangers[1]	98
Angels	93
Orioles	93
Twins	92
Yankees	88
Rays	86
Blue Jays	73

2019-2021 NL Doubles	
Home Park	Index
Rockies	120
Pirates	120
Giants[1]	118
Diamondbacks	108
Braves	106
Reds	105
Nationals	105
Marlins	97
Dodgers	96
Padres	94
Cubs	92
Mets	90
Phillies	90
Cardinals	90
Brewers	88

2019-2021 NL Triples	
Home Park	Index
Rockies	201
Cubs	142
Diamondbacks	140
Marlins	140
Giants[1]	135
Phillies	118
Pirates	108
Brewers	99
Braves	94
Cardinals	88
Nationals	80
Padres	58
Mets	55
Dodgers	49
Reds	44

2019-2021 NL Errors	
Home Park	Index
Braves	130
Rockies	114
Nationals	106
Pirates	105
Diamondbacks	103
Padres	100
Giants[1]	99
Brewers	98
Cardinals	97
Reds	96
Phillies	96
Marlins	93
Cubs	90
Mets	84
Dodgers	84

Lefty/Righty

Mark Simon

Remember last year when Ryan Tepera got an accidental MVP Award vote from a voter who meant to vote for Trea Turner?

While I'm not here to endorse the inadvertent usage of one's vote, I do think it would be a nice tribute for someone like Cubs and Athletics pitcher Andrew Chafin to get recognition for his season.

MLB changed its rules to all but eliminate pitchers of Chafin's ilk, basically striking the term LOOGY from our vocabulary with the three-batter minimum (inning-ending plays notwithstanding).

Baseball players adapted as they do, and in the survival of the fittest, it was pitchers like Chafin and Aaron Loup of the Mets who emerged as the most valuable in 2021 when you look at their statistical ledgers.

In 2019 (pre-rule change), Chafin faced 60% left-handed hitters and 40% right-handed hitters (135 out of 225 were lefties). He could survive by being very good against lefties and alright versus righties, which he was. He pitched to a 3.76 ERA.

But in 2021, Chafin's batters-faced splits flipped. He faced 39% left-handed hitters and 61% right-handed hitters (104 out of 266 were lefties) because he was now required to face more than one batter in most instances.

To be useful to his team, Chafin had to get right-handed hitters out. In other words, he had to be a LARMOGY (which stands for "Lefty and Righty Many Outs Guy"—I don't think that's catching on). Chafin did that and then some in 2021.

Right-handed batters slashed .196/.247/.304 against Chafin in 2021. And he was his usual very good self against left-handed hitters (.170/.250/.223).

Chafin's slider was a putaway pitch against both left and right-handed hitters.

Lefties were 3-for-33 in at-bats ending in one. Right-handed batters were 4-for-43.

We selected Chafin for this essay because he had the highest Baseball-Reference WAR among lefty relievers not named Ranger Suarez or Josh Hader.

There's plenty of good data to be mined from the accompanying tables from this section whether you're interested in checking out your favorite former LOOGY-turned LARMOGY or looking up data on some of the game's top stars.

For example:

- Get yourself a lefty hitter who can hit home runs against lefty pitchers like Matt Olson can. Olson's 22 home runs versus lefties matched his total from 2017 to 2020 combined.

- The head of the class when it came to right-handed pitchers against left-handed hitters were Liam Hendriks (.433 OPS) and Emmanuel Clase (.440). And no starting pitcher was near Jacob deGrom's .442.

The following pages include platoon splits for all hitters with at least 100 plate appearances and pitchers with at least 100 batters faced in 2021. It contains batting average, on-base percentage, and slugging percentage, along with a count of at-bats, hits, doubles, triples, home runs, RBI, walks, and strikeouts for hitters against both right- and left-handed pitchers.

The lists are alphabetical by last name. At the end of each set are MLB season numbers for context. If you're looking for split leaderboards, they can be found in the next section in the book.

Batters vs. Left-Handed and Right-Handed Pitchers

Batter	vs	Avg	AB	H	2B	3B	HR	RBI	BB	SO	OBP	Slg
Abreu, Jose	L	.294	136	40	7	1	11	30	11	29	.366	.603
Bats Right	R	.251	430	108	23	1	19	87	50	114	.346	.442
Acuna Jr., Ronald	L	.302	63	19	3	0	6	16	15	14	.432	.635
Bats Right	R	.278	234	65	16	1	18	36	34	71	.384	.585
Adames, Willy	L	.235	149	35	8	0	8	18	19	52	.321	.450
Bats Right	R	.273	348	95	24	1	17	55	38	104	.344	.494
Adell, Jo	L	.250	44	11	0	1	3	9	1	9	.267	.500
Bats Right	R	.244	86	21	5	1	1	17	7	23	.309	.360
Adrianza, Ehire	L	.240	50	12	2	0	1	7	8	9	.345	.340
Bats Both	R	.250	132	33	7	2	4	21	13	33	.320	.424
Aguilar, Jesus	L	.259	112	29	6	0	5	19	17	28	.358	.446
Bats Right	R	.261	337	88	17	0	17	74	29	65	.318	.463
Ahmed, Nick	L	.252	143	36	15	3	3	14	13	29	.316	.462
Bats Right	R	.206	291	60	15	0	2	24	21	75	.262	.278
Akiyama, Shogo	L	.240	25	6	1	0	0	1	5	5	.387	.280
Bats Left	R	.197	137	27	7	0	0	11	9	35	.260	.248
Alberto, Hanser	L	.286	119	34	10	2	2	15	4	12	.317	.454
Bats Right	R	.254	122	31	10	1	0	9	0	14	.264	.352
Albies, Ozzie	L	.323	164	53	14	1	9	33	8	24	.354	.585
Bats Both	R	.237	465	110	26	6	21	73	39	104	.295	.454
Alcantara, Sergio	L	.145	69	10	1	1	0	3	9	19	.247	.188
Bats Both	R	.232	151	35	5	2	5	14	21	55	.329	.391
Alfaro, Jorge	L	.259	85	22	8	0	3	11	2	29	.276	.459
Bats Right	R	.238	210	50	7	1	1	19	9	70	.286	.295
Alford, Anthony	L	.156	45	7	1	0	3	5	4	20	.240	.378
Bats Right	R	.273	88	24	5	1	2	6	8	38	.347	.420
Almonte, Abraham	L	.133	30	4	2	0	0	2	3	9	.212	.200
Bats Both	R	.237	118	28	10	0	5	17	23	29	.359	.449
Alonso, Pete	L	.237	169	40	5	1	16	32	26	43	.342	.562
Bats Right	R	.273	392	107	22	2	21	62	34	84	.345	.500
Altuve, Jose	L	.278	187	52	12	0	7	21	16	27	.335	.455
Bats Right	R	.278	414	115	20	1	24	62	50	64	.357	.505
Alvarez, Yordan	L	.283	205	58	12	0	13	39	18	53	.349	.532
Bats Left	R	.274	332	91	23	1	20	65	32	92	.344	.530
Anderson, Brian	L	.158	57	9	1	0	1	5	2	26	.200	.228
Bats Right	R	.278	176	49	8	0	6	23	24	39	.377	.426
Anderson, Tim	L	.319	138	44	9	1	4	16	5	30	.343	.486
Bats Right	R	.306	389	119	20	1	13	45	17	89	.336	.463
Andrus, Elvis	L	.190	163	31	6	0	0	10	12	32	.251	.227
Bats Right	R	.269	334	90	19	2	3	27	19	49	.315	.365
Andujar, Miguel	L	.222	63	14	1	0	2	4	3	16	.258	.333
Bats Right	R	.275	91	25	1	0	4	8	4	12	.302	.418
Aquino, Aristides	L	.198	81	16	2	0	6	13	15	28	.316	.444
Bats Right	R	.183	93	17	4	1	4	10	12	47	.283	.376
Arenado, Nolan	L	.295	112	33	6	0	9	26	9	19	.341	.589
Bats Right	R	.245	481	118	28	3	25	79	41	77	.306	.472
Arozarena, Randy	L	.302	202	61	13	2	10	22	26	61	.386	.535
Bats Right	R	.257	327	84	19	1	10	47	30	109	.337	.413
Arraez, Luis	L	.253	99	25	5	1	0	9	13	20	.333	.323
Bats Left	R	.307	329	101	12	5	2	33	30	28	.364	.392
Arroyo, Christian	L	.329	70	23	5	0	3	10	2	17	.356	.529
Bats Right	R	.213	94	20	7	0	3	15	6	27	.302	.383
Astudillo, Willians	L	.241	83	20	4	0	3	12	2	5	.264	.398
Bats Right	R	.232	125	29	4	0	4	9	1	7	.256	.360
Baddoo, Akil	L	.214	98	21	1	1	0	11	9	33	.278	.245
Bats Left	R	.273	315	86	19	6	13	44	36	89	.346	.495
Bader, Harrison	L	.243	70	17	4	0	4	8	4	16	.293	.471
Bats Right	R	.273	297	81	17	1	12	42	23	69	.331	.458
Baez, Javier	L	.291	127	37	6	0	9	21	13	43	.375	.551
Bats Right	R	.256	375	96	12	2	22	66	15	141	.299	.475
Barnes, Austin	L	.212	66	14	1	0	3	6	4	19	.278	.364
Bats Right	R	.216	134	29	7	0	3	17	16	37	.309	.336
Barnhart, Tucker	L	.255	55	14	4	0	1	7	2	17	.288	.382
Bats Left	R	.246	293	72	17	0	6	41	27	83	.322	.365
Bauers, Jake	L	.231	65	15	2	0	0	3	4	26	.275	.262
Bats Left	R	.203	217	44	5	0	4	16	26	52	.294	.281
Beaty, Matt	L	.350	20	7	0	0	1	5	1	4	.409	.500
Bats Left	R	.261	184	48	4	1	6	35	19	40	.358	.391
Bell, Josh	L	.245	151	37	7	0	9	26	30	25	.368	.470
Bats Both	R	.268	347	93	17	1	18	62	35	76	.337	.478
Bellinger, Cody	L	.116	86	10	0	1	1	4	10	20	.208	.174
Bats Left	R	.183	229	42	9	1	9	32	21	74	.252	.349
Belt, Brandon	L	.246	61	15	1	0	4	11	11	15	.373	.459
Bats Left	R	.280	264	74	13	2	25	48	37	88	.379	.629
Benintendi, Andrew	L	.303	145	44	11	1	3	23	7	27	.340	.455
Bats Left	R	.264	348	92	16	1	14	50	29	70	.318	.437
Berti, Jon	L	.161	87	14	3	0	2	6	16	24	.288	.264
Bats Right	R	.240	146	35	7	1	2	13	16	37	.325	.342
Betts, Mookie	L	.266	124	33	7	1	6	15	21	29	.374	.484
Bats Right	R	.263	342	90	22	2	17	43	47	57	.365	.488
Bichette, Bo	L	.340	150	51	8	0	8	22	14	28	.396	.553
Bats Right	R	.286	490	140	22	1	21	80	26	109	.327	.463
Biggio, Cavan	L	.200	60	12	3	0	0	5	8	24	.290	.250
Bats Left	R	.232	190	44	7	1	7	22	29	54	.332	.389
Blackmon, Charlie	L	.287	136	39	4	0	3	18	19	25	.386	.382
Bats Left	R	.265	378	100	21	4	10	60	35	66	.337	.421
Bogaerts, Xander	L	.284	183	52	8	0	7	30	28	45	.376	.443
Bats Right	R	.301	346	104	26	1	16	49	34	68	.367	.520
Bohm, Alec	L	.289	121	35	6	0	4	19	12	36	.358	.438
Bats Right	R	.228	259	59	9	0	3	28	19	75	.279	.297
Bote, David	L	.213	89	19	4	1	4	16	9	25	.290	.416
Bats Right	R	.193	202	39	6	1	4	19	18	48	.270	.292
Bradley, Bobby	L	.162	68	11	3	0	5	12	7	31	.269	.426
Bats Left	R	.226	177	40	7	0	11	29	18	68	.303	.452
Bradley Jr., Jackie	L	.169	65	11	0	1	1	6	10	24	.282	.246
Bats Left	R	.161	322	52	14	2	5	23	18	108	.226	.264
Brantley, Michael	L	.219	169	37	8	1	2	14	8	24	.261	.314
Bats Left	R	.363	300	109	21	2	6	33	25	29	.418	.507
Bregman, Alex	L	.300	120	36	5	0	4	19	19	19	.397	.442
Bats Right	R	.254	228	58	12	0	8	36	25	34	.332	.412
Brinson, Lewis	L	.256	90	23	5	0	4	12	6	26	.302	.444
Bats Right	R	.212	184	39	9	0	5	21	7	46	.244	.342
Brosseau, Mike	L	.234	94	22	6	0	4	14	13	30	.321	.426
Bats Right	R	.107	56	6	3	0	1	4	2	23	.167	.214
Brown, Seth	L	.136	22	3	0	0	1	2	3	7	.231	.273
Bats Left	R	.220	259	57	13	1	19	46	20	82	.278	.498
Bryant, Kris	L	.284	134	38	7	0	9	22	19	38	.373	.537
Bats Right	R	.259	379	98	25	2	16	51	43	97	.346	.462
Buxton, Byron	L	.325	80	26	9	0	5	6	4	22	.372	.625
Bats Right	R	.297	155	46	14	0	14	26	9	40	.351	.658
Cabrera, Asdrubal	L	.257	109	28	9	0	2	16	12	25	.333	.394
Bats Both	R	.215	200	43	12	0	5	26	24	55	.301	.350
Cabrera, Miguel	L	.269	134	36	3	0	3	19	15	33	.340	.358
Bats Right	R	.251	338	85	13	0	12	56	25	85	.306	.396
Cain, Lorenzo	L	.206	68	14	4	0	1	12	10	11	.308	.309
Bats Right	R	.275	189	52	9	0	7	24	16	37	.337	.434
Calhoun, Kole	L	.122	41	5	2	0	0	4	2	10	.163	.171
Bats Left	R	.272	125	34	6	0	5	13	13	31	.338	.440
Calhoun, Willie	L	.236	55	13	3	1	1	6	3	5	.300	.382
Bats Left	R	.254	205	52	7	2	5	19	18	29	.313	.380
Cameron, Daz	L	.175	40	7	3	0	1	4	3	14	.233	.325
Bats Right	R	.206	63	13	2	0	3	9	7	24	.306	.381
Candelario, Jeimer	L	.273	161	44	14	1	3	16	10	38	.324	.429
Bats Both	R	.270	396	107	28	2	13	51	55	97	.362	.449
Canha, Mark	L	.221	181	40	9	1	7	23	23	41	.329	.398
Bats Right	R	.237	338	80	13	3	10	38	54	87	.373	.382
Caratini, Victor	L	.271	70	19	1	0	1	10	4	23	.316	.329
Bats Both	R	.214	243	52	8	0	6	29	31	59	.307	.321
Carlson, Dylan	L	.341	123	42	8	0	5	19	12	32	.394	.528
Bats Both	R	.243	419	102	23	4	13	46	45	120	.328	.411
Carpenter, Matt	L	.056	18	1	0	0	0	1	4	9	.217	.056
Bats Left	R	.180	189	34	11	1	3	20	31	68	.314	.296
Casali, Curt	L	.102	49	5	2	0	1	4	6	18	.214	.204
Bats Right	R	.245	151	37	9	1	4	22	20	48	.345	.397
Castellanos, Nick	L	.306	144	44	11	0	10	28	10	32	.355	.590
Bats Right	R	.310	387	120	27	1	24	72	31	89	.365	.571
Castro, Harold	L	.214	42	9	1	0	0	1	0	10	.214	.238
Bats Left	R	.293	273	80	12	1	3	36	14	62	.324	.377
Castro, Jason	L	.180	50	9	2	0	1	4	4	19	.281	.280
Bats Left	R	.263	99	26	5	0	7	17	21	35	.392	.525
Castro, Starlin	L	.349	83	29	6	0	0	11	5	20	.382	.422
Bats Right	R	.259	232	60	14	0	3	27	21	42	.316	.358
Castro, Willi	L	.281	128	36	8	1	1	15	5	22	.311	.383
Bats Both	R	.193	285	55	7	5	8	23	18	87	.256	.337
Cave, Jake	L	.122	41	5	0	0	0	2	0	17	.122	.122
Bats Left	R	.211	123	26	6	1	3	11	10	45	.287	.350
Chang, Yu	L	.226	124	28	6	2	4	18	6	36	.265	.403
Bats Right	R	.230	113	26	8	1	5	21	5	33	.269	.451
Chapman, Matt	L	.228	180	41	3	1	14	30	25	66	.317	.489
Bats Right	R	.201	349	70	12	2	13	42	55	136	.312	.358
Chisholm Jr., Jazz	L	.237	139	33	7	1	4	13	7	50	.282	.388
Bats Left	R	.252	325	82	13	3	14	40	27	95	.312	.440

Batters vs. Left-Handed and Right-Handed Pitchers

Batter	vs	Avg	AB	H	2B	3B	HR	RBI	BB	SO	OBP	Slg
Choi, Ji-Man	L	.186	70	13	5	0	0	5	7	30	.269	.257
Bats Left	R	.245	188	46	9	0	11	40	38	57	.374	.468
Clement, Ernie	L	.225	40	9	0	0	3	3	2	5	.279	.450
Bats Right	R	.235	81	19	4	0	0	6	5	14	.287	.284
Collins, Zack	L	.176	51	9	2	0	1	6	7	21	.276	.275
Bats Left	R	.222	144	32	11	0	3	20	27	48	.349	.361
Conforto, Michael	L	.205	122	25	2	0	1	9	19	37	.336	.246
Bats Left	R	.243	284	69	18	0	13	46	40	67	.348	.444
Contreras, William	L	.188	32	6	0	0	2	3	4	15	.297	.375
Bats Right	R	.221	131	29	4	1	6	20	15	39	.304	.405
Contreras, Willson	L	.284	116	33	5	0	8	23	14	33	.356	.534
Bats Right	R	.219	297	65	15	0	13	34	38	105	.333	.401
Cooper, Garrett	L	.344	64	22	2	0	4	11	6	20	.408	.563
Bats Right	R	.258	151	39	8	1	5	22	24	48	.369	.424
Cordero, Franchy	L	.188	16	3	0	0	0	1	1	6	.235	.188
Bats Left	R	.189	111	21	6	0	1	8	7	45	.237	.270
Correa, Carlos	L	.290	186	54	12	1	5	22	32	32	.398	.446
Bats Right	R	.274	369	101	22	0	21	70	43	84	.348	.504
Crawford, Brandon	L	.244	135	33	6	0	6	27	12	38	.300	.422
Bats Left	R	.319	348	111	24	3	18	63	44	67	.401	.560
Crawford, J.P.	L	.274	252	69	14	0	4	28	15	48	.324	.377
Bats Left	R	.272	367	100	23	0	5	26	43	66	.348	.376
Cron, C.J.	L	.311	132	41	12	0	8	30	15	34	.393	.583
Bats Right	R	.269	338	91	19	1	20	62	45	83	.368	.509
Cronenworth, Jake	L	.270	178	48	13	2	4	21	13	31	.337	.433
Bats Left	R	.265	389	103	20	5	17	50	42	59	.342	.473
Cruz, Nelson	L	.316	171	54	8	0	10	28	15	39	.375	.538
Bats Right	R	.240	342	82	13	1	22	58	36	87	.314	.477
Culberson, Charlie	L	.346	133	46	12	2	4	17	6	24	.376	.556
Bats Right	R	.123	114	14	3	0	1	5	11	40	.206	.175
Dahl, David	L	.102	59	6	2	0	0	2	3	20	.156	.136
Bats Left	R	.253	146	37	9	0	4	16	7	39	.284	.397
Dalbec, Bobby	L	.278	176	49	9	3	11	39	11	65	.326	.551
Bats Right	R	.212	241	51	12	2	14	39	17	91	.278	.452
d'Arnaud, Travis	L	.256	39	10	4	0	1	2	8	7	.396	.436
Bats Right	R	.212	170	36	10	0	6	24	9	46	.254	.376
Davis, J.D.	L	.241	54	13	2	0	1	6	10	23	.354	.333
Bats Right	R	.304	125	38	10	0	4	17	14	45	.397	.480
Daza, Yonathan	L	.296	108	32	5	1	1	10	7	23	.339	.389
Bats Right	R	.275	193	53	7	1	1	20	14	37	.329	.337
De La Cruz, Bryan	L	.347	49	17	3	0	2	2	6	11	.418	.531
Bats Right	R	.280	150	42	4	2	3	17	12	42	.335	.393
DeJong, Paul	L	.163	80	13	3	0	4	7	8	30	.256	.350
Bats Right	R	.207	276	57	7	1	15	38	27	73	.292	.402
Devers, Rafael	L	.278	227	63	11	0	6	28	20	41	.345	.405
Bats Left	R	.280	364	102	26	1	32	85	42	102	.357	.621
Diaz, Aledmys	L	.265	102	27	9	0	4	20	7	19	.318	.471
Bats Right	R	.255	192	49	10	0	4	25	9	43	.316	.370
Diaz, Elias	L	.242	120	29	6	0	6	13	15	27	.326	.442
Bats Right	R	.248	218	54	12	1	12	31	15	33	.301	.477
Diaz, Isan	L	.169	77	13	2	0	0	3	7	21	.244	.195
Bats Left	R	.204	162	33	7	0	4	14	27	52	.314	.321
Diaz, Lewin	L	.179	39	7	0	1	1	1	0	14	.179	.308
Bats Left	R	.217	83	18	4	0	7	12	6	19	.270	.518
Diaz, Yandy	L	.288	191	55	12	0	6	25	25	33	.367	.445
Bats Right	R	.234	274	64	8	1	7	39	44	52	.344	.347
Dickerson, Alex	L	.286	21	6	0	0	1	4	5	5	.444	.429
Bats Left	R	.229	262	60	10	2	12	34	18	71	.291	.420
Dickerson, Corey	L	.234	47	11	3	1	0	3	5	12	.302	.340
Bats Left	R	.277	289	80	15	4	6	26	20	56	.330	.419
Difo, Wilmer	L	.234	64	15	3	0	0	2	3	20	.269	.281
Bats Both	R	.284	155	44	4	3	4	22	17	34	.353	.426
Donaldson, Josh	L	.257	140	36	5	0	13	28	25	41	.371	.571
Bats Right	R	.243	317	77	21	0	13	44	49	73	.343	.432
Dozier, Hunter	L	.204	137	28	9	0	3	9	18	47	.304	.336
Bats Right	R	.220	350	77	18	6	13	45	25	107	.278	.417
Dubon, Mauricio	L	.250	68	17	3	0	3	8	5	11	.301	.426
Bats Right	R	.234	107	25	6	0	2	14	4	30	.263	.346
Duffy, Matt	L	.270	89	24	4	0	0	5	11	15	.363	.315
Bats Right	R	.295	200	59	8	0	5	25	14	48	.355	.410
Duggar, Steven	L	.233	43	10	1	0	1	5	7	16	.340	.326
Bats Left	R	.262	225	59	13	5	7	30	20	72	.328	.458
Duran, Jarren	L	.185	27	5	0	1	0	2	0	9	.179	.259
Bats Left	R	.225	80	18	3	1	2	8	4	31	.262	.363
Duvall, Adam	L	.178	129	23	5	0	6	24	13	48	.254	.357
Bats Right	R	.245	384	94	12	2	32	89	22	126	.291	.536

Batter	vs	Avg	AB	H	2B	3B	HR	RBI	BB	SO	OBP	Slg
Dyson, Jarrod	L	.179	28	5	1	1	0	1	1	11	.207	.286
Bats Left	R	.215	107	23	6	1	0	9	9	22	.274	.290
Eaton, Adam	L	.178	45	8	2	0	0	3	3	11	.224	.222
Bats Left	R	.206	209	43	8	2	6	27	19	60	.294	.349
Edman, Tommy	L	.267	146	39	12	1	6	16	8	21	.308	.486
Bats Both	R	.261	495	129	29	2	5	40	30	74	.308	.358
Engel, Adam	L	.200	45	9	2	0	2	3	2	11	.265	.378
Bats Right	R	.282	78	22	7	0	5	15	9	20	.374	.564
Escobar, Alcides	L	.280	93	26	10	0	0	4	5	19	.356	.387
Bats Right	R	.292	226	66	11	2	4	24	12	37	.333	.412
Escobar, Eduardo	L	.295	149	44	9	0	9	25	9	20	.340	.537
Bats Both	R	.238	400	95	17	5	19	65	39	104	.305	.448
Espinal, Santiago	L	.348	92	32	5	0	0	7	7	11	.394	.402
Bats Right	R	.285	130	37	8	1	2	10	15	19	.363	.408
Estrada, Thairo	L	.236	55	13	2	0	2	9	5	10	.300	.382
Bats Right	R	.303	66	20	2	0	5	13	4	13	.361	.561
Evans, Phillip	L	.242	62	15	1	0	1	6	10	15	.365	.306
Bats Right	R	.191	152	29	4	0	4	10	18	38	.289	.296
Farmer, Kyle	L	.257	113	29	4	0	7	10	6	20	.311	.478
Bats Right	R	.265	370	98	18	2	9	53	16	77	.318	.397
Fletcher, David	L	.316	193	61	11	1	2	17	15	12	.365	.415
Bats Right	R	.238	433	103	16	2	0	30	16	48	.266	.284
Flores, Wilmer	L	.288	139	40	7	0	6	19	10	24	.336	.468
Bats Right	R	.248	250	62	9	1	12	34	31	32	.334	.436
Fraley, Jake	L	.169	71	12	1	0	1	6	14	30	.306	.225
Bats Left	R	.231	143	33	6	0	8	30	32	41	.374	.441
France, Ty	L	.311	193	60	9	1	9	33	13	34	.366	.508
Bats Right	R	.280	378	106	23	0	9	40	33	72	.369	.413
Franco, Maikel	L	.198	121	24	9	0	2	13	7	25	.244	.322
Bats Right	R	.215	256	55	13	0	9	34	13	42	.257	.371
Franco, Wander	L	.357	98	35	8	2	4	16	11	10	.418	.602
Bats Both	R	.251	183	46	10	3	3	23	13	27	.308	.388
Frazier, Adam	L	.274	164	45	9	2	3	17	11	31	.343	.409
Bats Left	R	.317	413	131	27	3	2	26	37	38	.378	.412
Frazier, Clint	L	.188	69	13	1	0	1	3	13	27	.317	.246
Bats Right	R	.184	114	21	8	0	4	12	19	38	.316	.360
Freeman, Freddie	L	.257	171	44	6	1	7	20	16	31	.333	.427
Bats Left	R	.317	429	136	19	1	24	63	69	76	.416	.534
Fuentes, Joshua	L	.238	84	20	6	1	2	12	7	21	.297	.405
Bats Right	R	.219	187	41	5	0	5	21	5	44	.238	.326
Gallagher, Cam	L	.229	35	8	1	0	0	1	3	4	.289	.257
Bats Right	R	.260	77	20	5	0	1	6	5	16	.301	.364
Gallo, Joey	L	.200	180	36	6	1	11	24	34	83	.339	.428
Bats Left	R	.198	318	63	7	0	27	53	77	130	.357	.475
Galvis, Freddy	L	.268	112	30	7	0	5	16	5	20	.297	.464
Bats Both	R	.230	244	56	8	1	9	24	22	57	.304	.381
Gamel, Ben	L	.237	97	23	5	1	1	7	5	28	.283	.340
Bats Left	R	.251	243	61	13	2	7	19	46	77	.370	.407
Garcia, Adolis	L	.232	203	47	11	0	10	32	8	72	.263	.433
Bats Right	R	.249	378	94	15	2	21	58	24	122	.298	.466
Garcia, Avisail	L	.279	104	29	8	0	6	19	20	24	.406	.529
Bats Right	R	.258	357	92	10	0	23	67	18	97	.305	.479
Garcia, Leury	L	.282	124	35	7	1	1	20	7	33	.319	.379
Bats Both	R	.261	291	76	15	3	4	34	34	64	.342	.375
Garcia, Luis	L	.297	64	19	7	0	1	7	2	12	.318	.453
Bats Left	R	.221	172	38	11	2	5	15	9	31	.260	.395
Garcia, Robel	L	.278	18	5	0	0	0	1	4	7	.409	.278
Bats Both	R	.125	88	11	3	0	1	7	4	35	.170	.193
Gardner, Brett	L	.253	95	24	2	0	1	6	12	30	.345	.305
Bats Left	R	.212	292	62	14	4	9	33	48	70	.321	.380
Garver, Mitch	L	.215	93	20	4	0	6	16	10	32	.286	.452
Bats Right	R	.289	114	33	11	0	7	18	21	39	.413	.570
Gimenez, Andres	L	.194	36	7	2	0	1	3	2	8	.237	.333
Bats Left	R	.224	152	34	8	0	4	13	9	46	.292	.355
Goldschmidt, Paul	L	.350	123	43	11	1	8	30	13	28	.413	.650
Bats Right	R	.279	480	134	25	1	23	69	54	108	.353	.479
Gomes, Yan	L	.314	121	38	9	0	7	22	2	25	.328	.562
Bats Right	R	.219	228	50	6	1	7	30	17	53	.288	.346
Gonzalez, Erik	L	.294	68	20	2	0	2	12	5	11	.342	.412
Bats Right	R	.204	152	31	5	1	0	9	3	29	.218	.250
Gonzalez, Marwin	L	.250	84	21	9	0	2	9	4	14	.284	.429
Bats Both	R	.177	192	34	5	0	3	19	16	64	.271	.250
Goodrum, Niko	L	.274	95	26	3	1	2	10	11	33	.352	.389
Bats Both	R	.185	195	36	8	1	7	23	18	74	.263	.344
Goodwin, Brian	L	.136	59	8	0	0	0	6	5	18	.200	.136
Bats Left	R	.250	176	44	10	1	8	23	28	40	.356	.455

Batters vs. Left-Handed and Right-Handed Pitchers

Batter	vs	Avg	AB	H	2B	3B	HR	RBI	BB	SO	OBP	Slg
Gordon, Nick	L	.244	45	11	0	0	0	4	1	13	.277	.244
Bats Left	R	.239	155	37	9	1	4	19	11	42	.296	.387
Gosselin, Phil	L	.275	142	39	5	0	2	15	13	23	.344	.352
Bats Right	R	.251	203	51	9	0	5	32	11	58	.292	.369
Grandal, Yasmani	L	.266	64	17	0	0	6	16	29	21	.484	.547
Bats Both	R	.233	215	50	9	0	17	46	58	61	.398	.512
Gregorius, Didi	L	.157	89	14	3	0	3	14	7	19	.264	.292
Bats Left	R	.226	279	63	13	2	10	40	18	48	.272	.394
Grichuk, Randal	L	.246	138	34	9	0	6	18	8	25	.291	.442
Bats Right	R	.239	373	89	16	1	16	63	19	89	.277	.416
Grisham, Trent	L	.261	115	30	3	2	5	24	16	26	.372	.452
Bats Left	R	.236	347	82	25	1	10	38	38	93	.311	.401
Grossman, Robbie	L	.279	172	48	6	2	8	27	27	42	.380	.477
Bats Both	R	.221	385	85	17	1	15	40	71	113	.347	.387
Guerrero Jr., Vladimir	L	.295	146	43	3	0	11	19	27	24	.405	.541
Bats Right	R	.317	458	145	26	1	37	92	59	86	.400	.620
Guillorme, Luis	L	.265	34	9	0	0	0	1	3	7	.324	.265
Bats Left	R	.265	98	26	3	0	1	4	20	16	.390	.327
Gurriel, Yuli	L	.326	181	59	13	0	8	34	23	17	.394	.530
Bats Right	R	.315	349	110	18	0	7	47	36	51	.378	.427
Gurriel Jr., Lourdes	L	.269	145	39	8	1	5	23	8	33	.301	.441
Bats Right	R	.279	355	99	20	1	16	61	24	69	.326	.476
Gutierrez, Kelvin	L	.253	75	19	3	1	2	8	5	22	.309	.400
Bats Right	R	.223	197	44	5	2	1	12	14	54	.285	.284
Haase, Eric	L	.283	120	34	4	0	11	25	6	38	.315	.592
Bats Right	R	.203	231	47	8	1	11	36	20	81	.272	.390
Hamilton, Billy	L	.229	48	11	3	2	2	5	2	19	.260	.500
Bats Right	R	.215	79	17	5	1	0	6	2	28	.232	.304
Hampson, Garrett	L	.271	144	39	9	3	5	13	13	26	.335	.479
Bats Right	R	.217	309	67	12	3	6	20	20	92	.267	.333
Haniger, Mitch	L	.286	203	58	8	1	16	35	21	52	.349	.571
Bats Right	R	.237	417	99	15	1	23	65	33	117	.303	.444
Happ, Ian	L	.213	108	23	6	0	3	12	13	38	.301	.352
Bats Both	R	.230	357	82	14	1	22	54	49	118	.329	.459
Harper, Bryce	L	.257	152	39	8	1	4	12	34	54	.397	.401
Bats Left	R	.333	336	112	34	0	31	72	66	80	.444	.711
Harrison, Josh	L	.295	146	43	8	0	3	25	6	19	.360	.411
Bats Right	R	.273	359	98	25	2	5	35	25	56	.333	.396
Hayes, Ke'Bryan	L	.279	111	31	8	2	1	12	8	23	.325	.414
Bats Right	R	.247	251	62	12	0	5	26	23	64	.312	.355
Hays, Austin	L	.308	198	61	11	2	11	30	10	33	.346	.551
Bats Right	R	.221	290	64	15	2	11	41	18	74	.283	.400
Hedges, Austin	L	.179	84	15	2	0	4	7	5	26	.222	.345
Bats Right	R	.178	202	36	5	0	6	24	10	61	.219	.292
Heim, Jonah	L	.253	75	19	6	0	3	13	3	19	.275	.453
Bats Both	R	.174	190	33	7	0	7	19	12	39	.225	.321
Heredia, Guillermo	L	.258	89	23	12	0	1	7	8	19	.330	.427
Bats Right	R	.204	216	44	14	0	4	19	24	62	.304	.324
Hernandez, Cesar	L	.215	181	39	7	0	13	25	20	39	.297	.470
Bats Both	R	.239	389	93	14	2	8	37	39	96	.313	.347
Hernandez, Kike	L	.260	196	51	13	1	10	25	31	41	.361	.490
Bats Right	R	.244	312	76	22	2	10	35	30	69	.321	.423
Hernandez, Teoscar	L	.372	129	48	12	0	12	38	8	28	.407	.744
Bats Right	R	.273	421	115	17	0	20	78	28	120	.327	.456
Hernandez, Yadiel	L	.300	80	24	3	1	4	13	6	23	.349	.513
Bats Left	R	.261	184	48	5	0	5	19	16	36	.320	.370
Hernandez, Yonny	L	.182	44	8	1	0	0	1	3	6	.234	.205
Bats Both	R	.232	99	23	4	0	0	5	14	26	.347	.273
Herrera, Odubel	L	.252	139	35	9	0	3	12	6	26	.305	.381
Bats Left	R	.264	311	82	18	2	10	39	23	51	.313	.431
Heyward, Jason	L	.235	68	16	3	0	1	8	5	15	.297	.324
Bats Left	R	.208	255	53	12	2	7	22	22	53	.276	.353
Hicks, Aaron	L	.242	33	8	1	0	3	7	2	11	.278	.545
Bats Both	R	.173	75	13	2	0	1	7	12	19	.300	.240
Higashioka, Kyle	L	.234	64	15	3	0	5	16	4	16	.275	.516
Bats Right	R	.155	129	20	7	0	5	13	13	43	.232	.326
Hill, Derek	L	.311	61	19	2	2	1	5	2	15	.333	.459
Bats Right	R	.218	78	17	1	1	2	9	8	27	.299	.333
Hilliard, Sam	L	.255	51	13	1	0	4	8	6	21	.333	.510
Bats Left	R	.202	163	33	6	2	10	26	17	66	.282	.448
Hiura, Keston	L	.130	54	7	1	0	1	5	5	25	.203	.204
Bats Right	R	.185	119	22	8	1	3	14	9	52	.279	.345
Hoerner, Nico	L	.244	45	11	2	0	0	4	8	6	.352	.289
Bats Right	R	.327	104	34	8	0	0	12	9	19	.397	.404
Holt, Brock	L	.171	41	7	0	0	0	3	1	9	.190	.171
Bats Left	R	.216	194	42	13	1	2	20	22	40	.298	.325

Batter	vs	Avg	AB	H	2B	3B	HR	RBI	BB	SO	OBP	Slg
Hoskins, Rhys	L	.250	128	32	11	0	10	24	18	34	.360	.570
Bats Right	R	.245	261	64	18	0	17	47	29	74	.321	.510
Hosmer, Eric	L	.262	149	39	9	0	3	19	5	27	.293	.383
Bats Left	R	.272	360	98	19	0	9	46	43	72	.354	.400
Ibanez, Andy	L	.344	93	32	8	0	3	12	3	10	.371	.527
Bats Right	R	.238	160	38	7	2	4	13	12	25	.293	.381
Iglesias, Jose	L	.297	148	44	8	1	4	17	9	22	.338	.446
Bats Right	R	.260	335	87	19	1	5	31	12	53	.297	.367
India, Jonathan	L	.297	138	41	10	0	3	14	18	28	.390	.435
Bats Right	R	.259	394	102	24	2	18	55	53	113	.372	.467
Jackson, Alex	L	.086	35	3	0	0	0	1	5	18	.200	.086
Bats Right	R	.156	96	15	4	0	3	11	8	55	.270	.292
Jankowski, Travis	L	.300	20	6	0	1	0	1	1	6	.333	.400
Bats Left	R	.243	111	27	6	1	1	9	21	23	.368	.342
Jansen, Danny	L	.150	60	9	2	0	3	6	6	16	.250	.333
Bats Right	R	.258	124	32	11	0	8	22	11	28	.324	.540
Jeffers, Ryan	L	.225	89	20	3	0	5	13	10	36	.303	.427
Bats Right	R	.185	178	33	7	1	9	22	12	72	.253	.388
Jimenez, Eloy	L	.170	53	9	2	0	2	6	5	16	.254	.321
Bats Right	R	.275	160	44	8	0	8	31	11	41	.320	.475
Joe, Connor	L	.306	49	15	0	0	4	12	7	9	.390	.551
Bats Right	R	.277	130	36	9	0	4	23	19	32	.375	.438
Jones, JaCoby	L	.150	40	6	0	0	0	4	3	16	.209	.150
Bats Right	R	.183	60	11	2	0	2	5	2	26	.210	.317
Jones, Taylor	L	.367	30	11	5	0	0	5	1	10	.375	.533
Bats Right	R	.194	72	14	3	1	2	11	3	19	.224	.347
Judge, Aaron	L	.298	161	48	3	0	15	32	24	44	.394	.596
Bats Right	R	.283	389	110	21	0	24	66	51	114	.364	.522
Kelenic, Jarred	L	.168	131	22	5	0	2	13	12	40	.238	.252
Bats Left	R	.189	206	39	8	1	12	30	24	66	.282	.413
Kelly, Carson	L	.313	112	35	4	1	9	27	19	19	.410	.607
Bats Right	R	.198	192	38	7	0	4	19	25	55	.302	.297
Kemp, Tony	L	.240	75	18	1	0	2	10	17	18	.402	.333
Bats Left	R	.290	255	74	15	3	6	27	35	33	.375	.443
Kepler, Max	L	.157	115	18	4	1	2	8	11	26	.248	.261
Bats Left	R	.232	311	72	17	3	17	46	43	70	.327	.469
Kieboom, Carter	L	.178	73	13	0	0	3	8	12	14	.318	.301
Bats Right	R	.222	144	32	6	0	3	12	13	48	.292	.326
Kiermaier, Kevin	L	.268	112	30	5	2	0	11	7	36	.328	.348
Bats Left	R	.254	236	60	14	5	4	26	26	63	.328	.407
Kim, Ha-seong	L	.222	81	18	7	0	2	14	7	21	.289	.383
Bats Right	R	.194	186	36	5	2	6	20	15	50	.262	.339
Kiner-Falefa, Isiah	L	.233	202	47	9	0	2	12	7	27	.271	.307
Bats Right	R	.289	433	125	16	3	6	41	21	63	.331	.381
Kirilloff, Alex	L	.279	68	19	4	0	3	11	3	15	.310	.471
Bats Left	R	.238	147	35	7	1	5	23	11	37	.294	.401
Kirk, Alejandro	L	.314	51	16	2	0	4	11	6	6	.400	.588
Bats Right	R	.211	114	24	6	0	4	13	13	16	.295	.368
Knapp, Andrew	L	.125	48	6	1	0	0	2	2	21	.160	.146
Bats Both	R	.165	97	16	2	0	2	9	8	40	.241	.247
Knizner, Andrew	L	.089	45	4	1	0	0	1	3	14	.163	.111
Bats Right	R	.207	116	24	6	0	1	8	17	25	.324	.284
La Stella, Tommy	L	.240	25	6	1	0	0	2	1	3	.269	.280
Bats Left	R	.251	195	49	10	1	7	25	17	23	.313	.421
Lagares, Juan	L	.252	111	28	11	1	3	11	5	24	.288	.450
Bats Right	R	.227	198	45	9	1	3	27	7	52	.254	.328
Lamb, Jake	L	.208	24	5	1	0	0	3	2	10	.269	.250
Bats Left	R	.192	120	23	3	0	7	16	20	41	.313	.392
Larnach, Trevor	L	.183	82	15	2	0	2	8	6	34	.244	.280
Bats Left	R	.242	178	43	10	0	5	20	25	70	.355	.382
Laureano, Ramon	L	.304	115	35	9	1	3	11	11	24	.380	.478
Bats Right	R	.217	226	49	12	1	11	28	16	74	.285	.425
LeMahieu, DJ	L	.266	188	50	7	0	2	18	23	22	.343	.335
Bats Right	R	.269	409	110	17	1	8	39	50	72	.352	.374
Leon, Sandy	L	.228	57	13	2	0	0	1	6	12	.313	.263
Bats Both	R	.166	145	24	3	0	4	13	6	53	.206	.269
Lewis, Kyle	L	.242	33	8	1	0	1	3	2	5	.286	.364
Bats Right	R	.247	97	24	3	0	4	8	14	32	.348	.402
Lindor, Francisco	L	.240	146	35	5	2	5	16	15	22	.311	.404
Bats Both	R	.225	306	69	11	1	15	47	43	74	.328	.415
Locastro, Tim	L	.184	49	9	3	0	2	5	2	12	.298	.367
Bats Right	R	.178	90	16	1	0	0	2	5	21	.242	.189
Long Jr., Shed	L	.163	49	8	2	1	1	6	3	16	.212	.306
Bats Left	R	.226	62	14	2	0	3	11	6	23	.294	.403
Longoria, Evan	L	.318	66	21	3	0	6	13	15	11	.451	.636
Bats Right	R	.241	187	45	14	0	7	33	20	57	.311	.428

Batters vs. Left-Handed and Right-Handed Pitchers

Batter	vs	Avg	AB	H	2B	3B	HR	RBI	BB	SO	OBP	Slg
Lopez, Nicky	L	.288	125	36	3	2	1	15	9	20	.336	.368
Bats Left	R	.304	372	113	18	4	1	28	40	54	.375	.382
Lowe, Brandon	L	.198	172	34	5	0	10	27	14	64	.261	.401
Bats Left	R	.270	363	98	26	0	29	72	54	103	.375	.581
Lowe, Nathaniel	L	.277	184	51	8	1	4	19	23	55	.357	.397
Bats Left	R	.257	373	96	16	2	14	53	57	107	.356	.424
Lowrie, Jed	L	.259	162	42	8	0	3	23	16	38	.322	.364
Bats Both	R	.237	295	70	20	0	11	46	33	70	.316	.417
Lux, Gavin	L	.188	85	16	2	0	1	5	12	24	.286	.247
Bats Left	R	.260	250	65	10	4	6	41	29	59	.343	.404
Machado, Manny	L	.246	134	33	9	0	5	14	27	20	.374	.425
Bats Right	R	.288	430	124	22	2	23	92	36	82	.338	.509
Madrigal, Nick	L	.373	59	22	4	1	2	5	4	4	.413	.576
Bats Right	R	.277	141	39	6	3	0	16	7	13	.322	.362
Maldonado, Martin	L	.212	113	24	1	1	5	18	11	37	.294	.372
Bats Right	R	.154	260	40	9	0	7	18	36	90	.263	.269
Mancini, Trey	L	.288	198	57	14	1	11	35	22	46	.363	.535
Bats Right	R	.237	358	85	19	0	10	36	29	97	.305	.374
Margot, Manuel	L	.273	187	51	11	1	4	22	20	26	.346	.406
Bats Right	R	.239	234	56	7	2	6	35	17	44	.286	.363
Marisnick, Jake	L	.259	81	21	4	2	2	11	5	28	.311	.432
Bats Right	R	.179	95	17	3	1	3	13	6	37	.264	.326
Marmolejos, Jose	L	.111	9	1	0	0	0	0	2	3	.273	.111
Bats Left	R	.165	97	16	4	0	4	12	13	36	.261	.330
Marsh, Brandon	L	.260	77	20	1	0	0	3	3	30	.288	.273
Bats Left	R	.252	159	40	11	3	2	16	17	61	.330	.396
Marte, Ketel	L	.387	106	41	13	0	8	23	7	14	.435	.736
Bats Both	R	.286	234	67	16	1	6	27	24	46	.351	.440
Marte, Starling	L	.273	150	41	8	0	5	14	11	37	.335	.427
Bats Right	R	.328	317	104	19	3	7	41	32	62	.404	.473
Martin, Jason	L	.108	37	4	0	0	0	0	0	10	.108	.108
Bats Left	R	.243	107	26	3	0	6	17	8	31	.293	.439
Martinez, J.D.	L	.279	204	57	11	2	9	36	20	45	.341	.485
Bats Right	R	.290	366	106	31	1	19	63	35	105	.354	.536
Mateo, Jorge	L	.254	71	18	4	1	1	6	3	22	.284	.380
Bats Right	R	.244	123	30	7	0	3	8	6	33	.299	.374
Maton, Nick	L	.325	40	13	2	0	2	5	2	15	.357	.525
Bats Left	R	.221	77	17	5	1	0	9	8	24	.307	.312
Mayfield, Jack	L	.223	94	21	3	0	5	13	7	23	.282	.415
Bats Right	R	.215	172	37	12	0	5	26	10	45	.266	.372
Mazara, Nomar	L	.095	21	2	0	0	0	3	2	8	.174	.095
Bats Left	R	.229	144	33	5	2	3	16	13	37	.291	.354
McCann, James	L	.257	113	29	5	0	4	19	13	34	.336	.407
Bats Right	R	.221	262	58	7	1	6	27	19	81	.275	.324
McCormick, Chas	L	.244	78	19	5	0	5	18	10	28	.330	.500
Bats Right	R	.262	206	54	7	0	9	32	15	76	.314	.427
McCutchen, Andrew	L	.293	164	48	7	1	15	32	28	36	.405	.622
Bats Right	R	.186	318	59	17	0	12	48	53	96	.298	.352
McGuire, Reese	L	.175	40	7	3	0	0	0	2	14	.214	.250
Bats Left	R	.272	158	43	12	0	1	10	13	30	.333	.367
McKenna, Ryan	L	.154	78	12	2	0	1	9	9	31	.250	.218
Bats Right	R	.209	91	19	4	1	1	5	15	43	.327	.308
McKinstry, Zach	L	.224	49	11	4	0	1	9	4	15	.283	.367
Bats Left	R	.211	109	23	5	0	6	20	6	35	.254	.422
McMahon, Ryan	L	.229	153	35	7	0	4	21	17	46	.312	.353
Bats Left	R	.264	375	99	25	1	19	65	42	101	.338	.488
McNeil, Jeff	L	.253	99	25	3	1	0	8	8	19	.327	.303
Bats Left	R	.251	287	72	16	0	7	27	21	39	.316	.380
Meadows, Austin	L	.198	167	33	7	0	3	25	15	43	.270	.293
Bats Left	R	.251	351	88	22	3	24	81	44	79	.336	.536
Mejia, Francisco	L	.276	105	29	5	0	3	10	10	22	.339	.410
Bats Both	R	.248	145	36	10	3	3	25	7	27	.311	.421
Mendick, Danny	L	.219	73	16	0	0	1	8	7	20	.288	.260
Bats Right	R	.220	91	20	5	0	1	12	11	22	.314	.308
Mercado, Oscar	L	.294	85	25	6	0	2	6	11	14	.381	.435
Bats Right	R	.178	129	23	5	1	4	13	10	28	.243	.326
Mercedes, Yermin	L	.338	65	22	4	1	2	11	5	6	.386	.523
Bats Right	R	.246	175	43	5	0	5	26	15	40	.307	.360
Mercer, Jordy	L	.304	46	14	4	0	0	1	2	14	.333	.391
Bats Right	R	.222	72	16	3	0	2	8	7	20	.291	.347
Merrifield, Whit	L	.276	181	50	14	0	3	18	11	24	.316	.403
Bats Right	R	.277	483	134	28	3	7	56	29	79	.317	.391
Meyers, Jake	L	.304	56	17	6	0	3	12	1	20	.328	.571
Bats Right	R	.233	90	21	2	0	3	16	9	30	.320	.356
Miller, Brad	L	.169	77	13	1	0	4	13	3	32	.200	.338
Bats Left	R	.244	254	62	8	3	16	36	42	80	.354	.488

Batter	vs	Avg	AB	H	2B	3B	HR	RBI	BB	SO	OBP	Slg
Miller, Owen	L	.198	81	16	2	0	2	9	4	25	.235	.296
Bats Right	R	.209	110	23	6	0	2	9	5	29	.248	.318
Molina, Yadier	L	.278	72	20	8	0	3	16	7	11	.338	.514
Bats Right	R	.247	368	91	11	0	8	50	17	68	.288	.342
Moncada, Yoan	L	.252	135	34	8	0	2	10	13	51	.344	.356
Bats Both	R	.268	385	103	25	1	12	51	71	106	.385	.431
Mondesi, Adalberto	L	.256	39	10	2	0	3	8	1	11	.293	.538
Bats Both	R	.218	87	19	6	1	3	9	5	32	.261	.414
Moore, Dylan	L	.206	136	28	4	0	6	16	21	33	.316	.368
Bats Right	R	.163	196	32	7	2	6	27	19	78	.247	.311
Moran, Colin	L	.171	82	14	2	0	2	9	11	23	.284	.268
Bats Left	R	.288	236	68	10	0	8	41	25	64	.352	.432
Moreland, Mitch	L	.154	39	6	1	0	2	7	4	14	.227	.333
Bats Left	R	.242	190	46	10	1	8	23	14	44	.298	.432
Mountcastle, Ryan	L	.266	188	50	8	1	13	36	16	55	.316	.527
Bats Right	R	.249	346	86	15	0	20	53	25	106	.305	.465
Moustakas, Mike	L	.086	35	3	1	0	0	1	5	11	.214	.114
Bats Left	R	.236	148	35	11	0	6	21	13	35	.299	.432
Mullins II, Cedric	L	.277	224	62	12	0	9	20	17	46	.337	.451
Bats Left	R	.299	378	113	25	5	21	39	42	79	.372	.558
Muncy, Max	L	.276	134	37	4	1	11	27	20	26	.394	.567
Bats Left	R	.240	363	87	22	1	25	67	63	94	.359	.512
Murphy, Sean	L	.194	124	24	4	0	5	15	12	38	.282	.347
Bats Right	R	.227	269	61	19	0	12	44	28	76	.317	.431
Murphy, Tom	L	.232	142	33	5	0	8	22	26	50	.357	.437
Bats Right	R	.170	135	23	3	0	3	12	14	49	.245	.259
Myers, Wil	L	.271	118	32	9	0	4	11	21	32	.379	.449
Bats Right	R	.250	324	81	15	2	13	52	33	109	.317	.429
Naquin, Tyler	L	.197	61	12	1	0	1	6	8	18	.300	.262
Bats Left	R	.283	350	99	23	2	18	64	27	88	.339	.514
Narvaez, Omar	L	.152	66	10	1	0	1	7	4	16	.222	.212
Bats Left	R	.289	325	94	19	0	10	42	37	68	.365	.440
Naylor, Josh	L	.193	83	16	3	0	1	5	5	21	.247	.265
Bats Left	R	.287	150	43	10	0	6	16	9	24	.331	.473
Newman, Kevin	L	.221	163	36	9	1	3	9	9	8	.259	.344
Bats Right	R	.229	354	81	13	2	2	30	18	33	.267	.294
Nido, Tomas	L	.200	40	8	1	0	1	2	2	9	.238	.300
Bats Right	R	.230	113	26	4	1	2	11	3	35	.269	.336
Nimmo, Brandon	L	.306	98	30	4	1	1	7	19	27	.429	.398
Bats Left	R	.286	227	65	13	2	7	21	35	52	.389	.454
Nogowski, John	L	.262	42	11	3	0	0	3	4	7	.326	.333
Bats Right	R	.218	87	19	4	0	1	11	8	15	.289	.299
Nola, Austin	L	.348	69	24	6	0	0	12	5	7	.387	.435
Bats Right	R	.221	104	23	6	0	2	17	9	12	.311	.337
Nootbaar, Lars	L	.273	22	6	3	0	1	3	2	6	.320	.545
Bats Left	R	.230	87	20	0	1	4	12	11	22	.316	.391
Nunez, Dom	L	.158	38	6	0	0	2	3	3	15	.220	.316
Bats Left	R	.195	190	37	12	3	8	30	31	76	.306	.416
Odor, Rougned	L	.227	97	22	2	0	6	12	10	26	.324	.433
Bats Left	R	.191	225	43	10	0	9	27	17	74	.269	.356
O'Hearn, Ryan	L	.161	31	5	0	0	0	1	2	10	.235	.161
Bats Left	R	.234	205	48	5	1	9	28	11	61	.273	.400
Ohtani, Shohei	L	.263	198	52	10	5	18	34	23	69	.344	.636
Bats Left	R	.254	339	86	16	3	28	66	73	120	.388	.566
Olivares, Edward	L	.205	44	9	0	0	1	4	3	10	.271	.273
Bats Right	R	.263	57	15	2	0	4	8	2	9	.306	.509
Olson, Matt	L	.270	222	60	9	0	22	50	26	46	.354	.608
Bats Left	R	.271	343	93	26	0	17	61	62	67	.382	.496
O'Neill, Tyler	L	.289	83	24	8	0	7	14	13	28	.388	.639
Bats Right	R	.286	399	114	18	2	27	66	25	140	.344	.544
Ortega, Rafael	L	.128	47	6	0	0	0	0	11	20	.293	.128
Bats Left	R	.321	249	80	14	2	11	33	19	50	.374	.526
Ozuna, Marcell	L	.188	48	9	2	0	2	3	4	13	.250	.354
Bats Right	R	.221	140	31	4	0	5	23	15	33	.301	.357
Panik, Joe	L	.102	49	5	2	0	0	0	7	9	.228	.143
Bats Left	R	.235	187	44	7	0	3	18	10	25	.276	.321
Park, Hoy	L	.292	24	7	1	2	1	6	3	7	.370	.625
Bats Left	R	.173	104	18	4	0	2	8	15	31	.281	.269
Pederson, Joc	L	.265	98	26	5	0	2	17	10	25	.348	.378
Bats Left	R	.230	331	76	14	3	16	44	29	92	.298	.435
Peralta, David	L	.267	86	23	8	1	1	12	5	16	.315	.419
Bats Left	R	.257	401	103	22	7	7	51	41	76	.327	.399
Peraza, Jose	L	.175	63	11	4	0	3	11	3	11	.224	.381
Bats Right	R	.228	79	18	3	0	3	9	6	15	.299	.380
Perez, Michael	L	.154	26	4	1	0	0	0	8	8	.353	.192
Bats Left	R	.141	184	26	7	1	7	21	11	60	.198	.304

Batters vs. Left-Handed and Right-Handed Pitchers

Batter	vs	Avg	AB	H	2B	3B	HR	RBI	BB	SO	OBP	Slg
Perez, Roberto	L	.173	52	9	0	0	4	9	8	18	.295	.404
Bats Right	R	.135	89	12	3	0	3	8	9	38	.214	.270
Perez, Salvador	L	.302	172	52	4	0	18	36	8	40	.342	.640
Bats Right	R	.261	448	117	20	0	30	85	20	130	.306	.507
Peters, DJ	L	.148	81	12	2	0	3	11	6	31	.211	.284
Bats Right	R	.225	142	32	7	1	10	27	6	51	.260	.500
Peterson, Jace	L	.271	48	13	1	0	0	6	5	14	.333	.292
Bats Left	R	.242	211	51	10	1	6	25	33	54	.351	.384
Pham, Tommy	L	.202	124	25	5	0	4	10	28	36	.351	.339
Bats Right	R	.239	351	84	19	2	11	39	50	92	.337	.399
Phillips, Brett	L	.110	73	8	1	0	1	3	9	41	.207	.164
Bats Left	R	.244	180	44	8	4	12	41	24	72	.337	.533
Pillar, Kevin	L	.240	121	29	4	0	6	11	2	26	.256	.421
Bats Right	R	.225	204	46	7	2	9	36	9	55	.288	.412
Pina, Manny	L	.221	77	17	4	0	6	15	12	12	.348	.506
Bats Right	R	.165	103	17	2	0	7	18	10	26	.250	.388
Pinder, Chad	L	.291	103	30	7	1	5	18	10	27	.360	.524
Bats Right	R	.198	111	22	9	0	1	9	6	35	.244	.306
Piscotty, Stephen	L	.256	90	23	6	0	2	7	8	17	.323	.389
Bats Right	R	.181	83	15	2	0	3	9	5	31	.236	.313
Plawecki, Kevin	L	.310	71	22	2	0	2	10	5	9	.372	.423
Bats Right	R	.267	86	23	5	0	1	5	7	17	.330	.360
Polanco, Gregory	L	.172	93	16	3	0	0	9	8	36	.236	.204
Bats Left	R	.222	243	54	9	2	11	27	28	68	.301	.412
Polanco, Jorge	L	.273	198	54	15	1	9	32	8	34	.308	.495
Bats Both	R	.267	390	104	20	1	24	66	37	84	.330	.508
Pollock, A.J.	L	.288	125	36	7	0	7	17	12	26	.360	.512
Bats Right	R	.301	259	78	20	1	14	52	18	54	.353	.548
Posey, Buster	L	.368	106	39	9	0	6	18	12	22	.429	.623
Bats Right	R	.280	289	81	14	0	12	38	44	65	.376	.453
Profar, Jurickson	L	.154	78	12	3	0	1	6	10	15	.247	.231
Bats Both	R	.247	275	68	14	2	3	27	39	50	.352	.345
Pujols, Albert	L	.294	136	40	3	0	13	34	8	21	.336	.603
Bats Right	R	.180	139	25	0	0	4	16	6	24	.233	.266
Raleigh, Cal	L	.219	32	7	3	0	0	2	1	9	.265	.313
Bats Both	R	.168	107	18	9	0	2	11	6	43	.211	.308
Ramirez, Harold	L	.288	118	34	12	0	2	12	7	19	.333	.441
Bats Right	R	.258	221	57	9	1	5	29	7	37	.289	.376
Ramirez, Jose	L	.289	190	55	12	0	11	30	19	28	.355	.526
Bats Both	R	.254	362	92	20	5	25	73	53	59	.355	.544
Ramos, Wilson	L	.175	40	7	1	0	1	4	3	10	.233	.275
Bats Right	R	.216	111	24	4	0	7	16	6	26	.254	.441
Realmuto, J.T.	L	.241	137	33	12	0	3	14	17	39	.333	.394
Bats Right	R	.271	339	92	13	4	14	59	31	90	.346	.457
Reddick, Josh	L	.184	49	9	3	0	0	2	1	11	.200	.245
Bats Left	R	.294	102	30	8	0	2	19	5	20	.324	.431
Refsnyder, Rob	L	.304	56	17	2	0	1	5	8	14	.391	.393
Bats Right	R	.205	83	17	5	0	1	7	9	26	.280	.301
Rendon, Anthony	L	.194	67	13	3	0	2	8	12	9	.313	.328
Bats Right	R	.260	150	39	10	0	4	26	17	32	.337	.407
Renfroe, Hunter	L	.276	181	50	11	0	11	33	25	41	.365	.519
Bats Right	R	.250	340	85	22	0	20	63	19	89	.286	.491
Rengifo, Luis	L	.212	52	11	0	0	1	4	3	12	.263	.269
Bats Both	R	.197	122	24	1	0	5	14	6	26	.238	.328
Reyes, Franmil	L	.260	127	33	6	0	9	22	18	43	.356	.520
Bats Right	R	.251	291	73	12	2	21	63	25	106	.309	.522
Reyes, Victor	L	.323	65	21	4	1	2	10	3	14	.353	.508
Bats Both	R	.229	144	33	6	3	3	12	5	41	.253	.375
Reynolds, Bryan	L	.325	166	54	17	1	4	24	23	43	.403	.512
Bats Both	R	.293	393	115	18	7	20	66	52	76	.385	.527
Riley, Austin	L	.274	135	37	12	0	3	18	9	42	.322	.430
Bats Right	R	.312	455	142	21	1	30	89	43	126	.380	.560
Rizzo, Anthony	L	.325	151	49	6	0	7	21	11	17	.398	.503
Bats Left	R	.214	345	74	17	3	15	40	41	70	.321	.412
Robert, Luis	L	.397	63	25	7	0	6	16	4	13	.441	.794
Bats Right	R	.321	212	68	15	1	7	27	10	48	.360	.500
Robles, Victor	L	.176	91	16	3	0	1	4	14	27	.330	.242
Bats Right	R	.214	224	48	18	1	1	15	19	58	.300	.317
Rodgers, Brendan	L	.317	101	32	8	0	8	19	3	14	.349	.634
Bats Right	R	.273	286	78	13	3	7	32	16	70	.320	.413
Rogers, Jake	L	.256	43	11	2	2	3	7	3	13	.304	.605
Bats Right	R	.229	70	16	3	1	3	10	8	33	.308	.429
Rojas, Jose	L	.237	38	9	4	0	2	4	5	11	.341	.500
Bats Left	R	.200	130	26	10	0	4	11	10	39	.257	.369
Rojas, Josh	L	.277	130	36	7	0	4	13	15	41	.352	.423
Bats Left	R	.260	354	92	25	3	7	31	43	96	.338	.407
Rojas, Miguel	L	.317	142	45	12	0	4	18	17	18	.399	.486
Bats Right	R	.244	353	86	18	3	5	30	20	56	.288	.354
Rooker, Brent	L	.212	66	14	5	0	2	4	6	22	.316	.379
Bats Right	R	.195	123	24	5	0	7	12	9	48	.277	.407
Rosario, Amed	L	.313	176	55	9	3	5	22	12	33	.356	.483
Bats Right	R	.267	374	100	16	3	6	35	19	87	.305	.374
Rosario, Eddie	L	.265	113	30	3	1	2	23	4	20	.288	.363
Bats Left	R	.256	266	68	16	2	12	39	22	41	.312	.466
Ruf, Darin	L	.283	113	32	6	1	9	21	24	28	.414	.593
Bats Right	R	.262	149	39	7	1	7	22	22	59	.360	.463
Sanchez, Gary	L	.230	113	26	7	0	8	19	16	30	.331	.504
Bats Right	R	.193	270	52	6	1	15	35	36	91	.297	.389
Sanchez, Jesus	L	.257	70	18	2	1	4	8	5	26	.316	.486
Bats Left	R	.248	157	39	6	1	10	28	15	52	.320	.490
Sano, Miguel	L	.238	151	36	4	0	5	18	23	50	.339	.364
Bats Right	R	.216	319	69	20	0	25	57	36	133	.299	.514
Santana, Carlos	L	.283	173	49	4	0	4	20	15	21	.342	.376
Bats Both	R	.184	392	72	11	0	15	49	71	81	.309	.327
Santana, Danny	L	.179	28	5	1	0	1	7	4	9	.281	.321
Bats Both	R	.182	88	16	1	1	4	7	6	21	.242	.352
Santander, Anthony	L	.257	148	38	10	0	4	12	7	49	.293	.405
Bats Both	R	.233	258	60	14	0	14	38	16	52	.282	.450
Schoop, Jonathan	L	.333	177	59	10	0	9	33	15	40	.383	.542
Bats Right	R	.256	446	114	20	1	13	51	22	93	.295	.392
Schrock, Max	L	.100	10	1	1	0	0	2	1	4	.182	.200
Bats Left	R	.304	115	35	6	2	3	12	7	20	.341	.470
Schwarber, Kyle	L	.268	123	33	4	0	4	11	21	43	.389	.398
Bats Left	R	.264	276	73	15	0	28	60	43	84	.366	.623
Schwindel, Frank	L	.324	71	23	5	1	6	11	9	11	.400	.676
Bats Right	R	.327	171	56	15	0	8	32	7	30	.358	.556
Seager, Corey	L	.330	115	38	7	0	6	22	6	27	.371	.548
Bats Left	R	.294	238	70	15	3	10	35	42	39	.404	.508
Seager, Kyle	L	.219	219	48	9	0	13	32	13	64	.261	.438
Bats Left	R	.208	384	80	20	1	22	69	46	97	.298	.438
Segura, Jean	L	.313	163	51	11	1	6	21	17	22	.379	.503
Bats Right	R	.279	351	98	16	2	8	37	22	56	.333	.405
Semien, Marcus	L	.243	177	43	8	1	10	30	17	43	.313	.469
Bats Right	R	.274	475	130	31	1	35	72	49	103	.342	.564
Senzel, Nick	L	.333	18	6	1	0	0	1	1	3	.350	.389
Bats Right	R	.237	93	22	3	0	1	7	11	13	.317	.301
Severino, Pedro	L	.293	147	43	6	0	7	20	12	34	.342	.476
Bats Right	R	.220	232	51	12	0	4	26	22	75	.287	.323
Shaw, Travis	L	.154	39	6	2	0	1	2	6	12	.283	.282
Bats Left	R	.210	181	38	9	0	8	37	18	56	.287	.392
Sheets, Gavin	L	.111	18	2	0	0	0	2	1	8	.158	.111
Bats Left	R	.268	142	38	8	0	11	32	15	32	.344	.556
Short, Zack	L	.134	67	9	2	0	3	8	12	21	.259	.299
Bats Right	R	.146	89	13	2	0	3	12	10	38	.223	.270
Sierra, Magneuris	L	.245	49	12	0	0	0	1	0	11	.245	.245
Bats Left	R	.225	160	36	6	1	0	4	15	39	.291	.275
Simmons, Andrelton	L	.245	147	36	5	0	2	11	14	23	.315	.320
Bats Right	R	.211	265	56	7	0	1	20	18	39	.266	.249
Slater, Austin	L	.284	169	48	10	0	10	24	21	37	.373	.521
Bats Right	R	.171	105	18	2	1	2	8	7	47	.230	.267
Smith, Dominic	L	.312	125	39	7	0	2	20	11	28	.367	.416
Bats Left	R	.218	321	70	13	0	9	38	21	84	.280	.343
Smith, Pavin	L	.239	134	32	3	1	1	19	13	31	.309	.299
Bats Left	R	.277	364	101	24	3	10	30	29	75	.336	.442
Smith, Will	L	.231	121	28	4	0	6	11	15	26	.319	.413
Bats Right	R	.270	293	79	15	2	19	65	43	75	.383	.529
Sogard, Eric	L	.214	42	9	0	0	0	4	3	4	.267	.214
Bats Left	R	.260	127	33	6	1	1	8	6	26	.289	.346
Solak, Nick	L	.266	139	37	6	0	3	21	12	29	.354	.374
Bats Right	R	.232	319	74	12	2	8	28	22	78	.296	.357
Solano, Donovan	L	.301	113	34	5	0	5	16	7	17	.344	.478
Bats Right	R	.268	194	52	12	0	2	15	18	41	.344	.361
Soler, Jorge	L	.224	143	32	5	0	12	16	22	42	.335	.510
Bats Right	R	.223	373	83	22	0	15	54	45	100	.309	.402
Sosa, Edmundo	L	.217	69	15	2	3	1	9	4	13	.304	.377
Bats Right	R	.288	219	63	6	1	5	18	13	50	.359	.393
Soto, Juan	L	.280	193	54	7	0	10	35	40	42	.403	.472
Bats Left	R	.333	309	103	13	2	19	60	105	51	.500	.573
Springer, George	L	.282	78	22	4	1	5	13	12	26	.391	.551
Bats Right	R	.258	221	57	15	0	17	37	25	53	.337	.557
Stallings, Jacob	L	.200	135	27	5	0	4	21	14	29	.272	.326
Bats Right	R	.272	239	65	15	1	4	32	35	56	.370	.393

Batters vs. Left-Handed and Right-Handed Pitchers

Batter	vs	Avg	AB	H	2B	3B	HR	RBI	BB	SO	OBP	Slg
Stanton, Giancarlo	L	.271	144	39	3	0	10	26	24	42	.386	.500
Bats Right	R	.273	366	100	16	0	25	71	39	115	.341	.522
Stassi, Max	L	.194	67	13	4	0	2	7	10	25	.299	.343
Bats Right	R	.256	215	55	7	1	11	28	18	76	.335	.451
Stephenson, Tyler	L	.291	127	37	9	0	4	18	13	20	.357	.457
Bats Right	R	.283	223	63	12	0	6	27	28	55	.371	.417
Stevenson, Andrew	L	.214	28	6	0	0	2	7	1	5	.233	.429
Bats Left	R	.232	164	38	6	0	3	16	12	56	.304	.323
Stewart, D.J.	L	.220	41	9	0	0	0	4	5	14	.319	.220
Bats Left	R	.201	229	46	10	0	12	29	39	75	.325	.402
Story, Trevor	L	.297	145	43	13	3	9	27	13	30	.360	.614
Bats Right	R	.234	381	89	21	2	15	48	40	109	.318	.417
Straw, Myles	L	.243	181	44	5	0	0	11	21	41	.322	.271
Bats Right	R	.285	383	109	24	1	4	37	46	80	.361	.384
Suarez, Eugenio	L	.172	134	23	6	0	6	14	16	53	.268	.351
Bats Right	R	.208	371	77	17	0	25	65	40	118	.292	.456
Suzuki, Kurt	L	.242	99	24	3	0	5	9	4	17	.312	.424
Bats Right	R	.208	120	25	5	0	1	7	8	27	.279	.275
Swanson, Dansby	L	.237	131	31	9	0	7	25	12	31	.299	.466
Bats Right	R	.252	457	115	24	2	20	63	40	136	.315	.444
Tapia, Raimel	L	.292	130	38	7	0	0	16	6	17	.321	.346
Bats Left	R	.266	357	95	19	2	6	40	34	53	.329	.381
Tatis Jr., Fernando	L	.284	116	33	9	0	9	21	17	36	.373	.595
Bats Right	R	.282	362	102	22	0	33	76	45	117	.362	.616
Tauchman, Mike	L	.182	33	6	1	0	0	1	6	15	.325	.212
Bats Left	R	.180	133	24	4	0	4	14	17	43	.273	.301
Taveras, Leody	L	.182	55	10	3	0	1	4	2	22	.211	.291
Bats Both	R	.151	119	18	3	2	2	5	7	38	.205	.261
Taylor, Chris	L	.296	152	45	13	2	6	25	17	51	.371	.526
Bats Right	R	.237	355	84	12	2	14	48	46	116	.333	.400
Taylor, Michael A.	L	.295	139	41	6	0	4	21	11	44	.344	.424
Bats Right	R	.224	344	77	10	1	8	33	22	100	.277	.328
Taylor, Tyrone	L	.298	84	25	2	0	5	10	3	22	.337	.500
Bats Right	R	.220	159	35	7	3	7	33	17	37	.313	.434
Tellez, Rowdy	L	.276	58	16	1	0	2	7	3	12	.333	.397
Bats Left	R	.234	239	56	13	2	9	29	20	53	.298	.418
Thomas, Lane	L	.381	63	24	7	2	1	8	15	14	.500	.603
Bats Right	R	.178	163	29	8	0	6	20	22	49	.274	.337
Toro, Abraham	L	.250	108	27	5	0	0	8	11	21	.336	.296
Bats Both	R	.233	227	53	7	0	11	38	20	33	.304	.410
Torrens, Luis	L	.275	142	39	9	1	9	23	8	34	.341	.542
Bats Right	R	.221	204	45	7	1	6	24	20	65	.291	.353
Torres, Gleyber	L	.293	140	41	6	0	5	15	14	28	.359	.443
Bats Right	R	.245	319	78	16	0	4	36	36	76	.318	.332
Torreyes, Ronald	L	.284	116	33	6	0	3	17	9	16	.341	.414
Bats Right	R	.218	202	44	4	1	4	24	10	25	.254	.307
Trammell, Taylor	L	.098	51	5	2	0	1	4	6	26	.207	.196
Bats Left	R	.190	105	20	5	0	7	14	11	49	.280	.438
Trevino, Jose	L	.189	90	17	6	0	0	3	4	12	.223	.256
Bats Right	R	.262	195	51	8	0	5	27	8	45	.286	.379
Trout, Mike	L	.265	34	9	1	0	0	2	12	12	.468	.294
Bats Right	R	.361	83	30	7	1	8	16	15	29	.465	.759
Tsutsugo, Yoshi	L	.258	66	17	3	1	2	9	3	21	.286	.424
Bats Left	R	.201	164	33	9	0	6	23	26	51	.314	.366
Tucker, Cole	L	.161	31	5	1	0	0	1	3	9	.235	.194
Bats Both	R	.244	86	21	3	2	2	11	10	24	.320	.395
Tucker, Kyle	L	.286	185	53	11	2	13	44	14	25	.332	.578
Bats Left	R	.299	321	96	26	1	17	48	39	65	.375	.545
Turner, Justin	L	.258	159	41	7	0	10	30	15	27	.328	.491
Bats Right	R	.286	374	107	15	0	17	57	46	71	.375	.463
Turner, Trea	L	.392	153	60	12	2	11	32	11	19	.437	.712
Bats Right	R	.305	442	135	22	1	17	45	30	91	.353	.475
Upton, Justin	L	.225	89	20	2	0	7	15	17	31	.355	.483
Bats Right	R	.205	229	47	10	0	10	26	22	76	.272	.380
Urias, Luis	L	.243	115	28	5	0	7	18	14	23	.331	.470
Bats Right	R	.251	375	94	20	1	16	57	49	93	.349	.437
Urias, Ramon	L	.235	119	28	5	0	5	15	12	36	.311	.403
Bats Right	R	.315	143	45	9	0	2	23	16	40	.402	.420
Urshela, Gio	L	.293	133	39	9	1	4	13	3	37	.312	.466
Bats Right	R	.254	287	73	9	1	10	36	17	72	.296	.397
Valaika, Pat	L	.214	103	22	2	0	2	11	8	24	.265	.291
Bats Right	R	.192	156	30	6	0	3	14	8	52	.240	.288
VanMeter, Josh	L	.326	43	14	2	1	1	12	4	12	.383	.488
Bats Left	R	.190	231	44	15	1	5	24	29	71	.281	.329
Varsho, Daulton	L	.293	82	24	5	0	3	11	8	16	.356	.463
Bats Left	R	.228	202	46	12	2	8	27	22	51	.304	.426

Batter	vs	Avg	AB	H	2B	3B	HR	RBI	BB	SO	OBP	Slg
Vaughn, Andrew	L	.269	119	32	10	0	8	17	21	32	.383	.555
Bats Right	R	.221	298	66	12	0	7	31	20	69	.277	.332
Vazquez, Christian	L	.219	151	33	7	0	2	12	7	29	.250	.305
Bats Right	R	.277	307	85	16	1	4	37	26	55	.335	.375
Verdugo, Alex	L	.228	189	43	5	0	2	12	9	35	.269	.286
Bats Left	R	.321	355	114	27	2	11	51	42	61	.392	.501
Villar, Jonathan	L	.281	146	41	7	0	3	9	11	43	.331	.390
Bats Both	R	.234	308	72	11	2	15	33	35	89	.318	.429
Vogelbach, Daniel	L	.097	31	3	0	0	1	3	3	10	.176	.194
Bats Left	R	.239	184	44	8	0	8	21	40	47	.375	.413
Vogt, Stephen	L	.293	41	12	1	0	1	7	6	14	.383	.390
Bats Left	R	.172	169	29	5	1	6	18	20	42	.258	.320
Voit, Luke	L	.259	81	21	1	1	3	14	10	23	.348	.407
Bats Right	R	.227	132	30	6	0	8	21	11	51	.315	.455
Votto, Joey	L	.215	144	31	8	1	5	27	19	47	.313	.389
Bats Left	R	.289	304	88	15	0	31	72	58	80	.403	.645
Wade, Tyler	L	.325	40	13	0	1	0	1	2	10	.357	.375
Bats Left	R	.241	87	21	5	0	0	4	14	27	.353	.299
Wade Jr., LaMonte	L	.135	37	5	2	0	0	2	2	14	.200	.189
Bats Left	R	.268	299	80	15	3	18	54	31	75	.341	.528
Walker, Christian	L	.240	121	29	9	0	0	9	18	27	.345	.314
Bats Right	R	.246	280	69	14	1	10	37	20	79	.300	.411
Walls, Taylor	L	.230	61	14	3	0	0	6	9	18	.329	.279
Bats Both	R	.198	91	18	7	0	1	9	14	31	.305	.308
Walsh, Jared	L	.170	182	31	4	0	10	30	9	54	.208	.357
Bats Left	R	.333	348	116	30	1	19	68	39	98	.405	.589
Ward, Taylor	L	.303	66	20	4	0	2	11	8	14	.395	.455
Bats Right	R	.225	142	32	11	0	6	22	12	41	.302	.430
Wendle, Joey	L	.202	119	24	4	2	2	11	11	35	.284	.319
Bats Left	R	.287	341	98	27	2	9	43	17	78	.332	.457
White, Eli	L	.133	75	10	2	0	1	4	10	23	.253	.200
Bats Right	R	.203	123	25	4	1	5	11	8	43	.263	.374
Williams, Justin	L	.133	15	2	0	0	0	3	4	7	.316	.133
Bats Left	R	.163	104	17	0	0	4	8	13	39	.263	.279
Winker, Jesse	L	.176	102	18	2	0	3	15	15	28	.288	.284
Bats Left	R	.346	321	111	30	1	21	56	38	47	.428	.642
Wisdom, Patrick	L	.223	103	23	5	0	8	15	14	52	.316	.505
Bats Right	R	.234	235	55	8	0	20	46	18	101	.300	.523
Wong, Kolten	L	.297	138	41	6	2	4	17	7	22	.333	.457
Bats Left	R	.261	307	80	26	0	10	33	24	61	.336	.443
Wynns, Austin	L	.256	39	10	0	0	1	7	3	8	.310	.333
Bats Right	R	.154	91	14	4	0	3	7	5	23	.198	.297
Yastrzemski, Mike	L	.170	112	19	4	0	2	7	11	33	.254	.259
Bats Left	R	.242	356	86	24	3	23	64	40	98	.328	.520
Yelich, Christian	L	.187	107	20	4	2	2	12	17	38	.294	.318
Bats Left	R	.292	292	79	15	0	7	39	53	75	.387	.394
Zimmer, Bradley	L	.211	76	16	1	0	1	5	7	30	.295	.263
Bats Left	R	.233	223	52	8	1	7	30	23	92	.335	.372
Zimmerman, Ryan	L	.291	110	32	11	0	7	24	5	35	.319	.582
Bats Right	R	.207	145	30	5	0	7	22	11	42	.261	.386
Zunino, Mike	L	.342	114	39	8	2	16	30	14	36	.419	.868
Bats Right	R	.151	219	33	3	0	17	32	20	96	.240	.397
AL	L	.252	-	-	-	-	-	-	-	-	.320	.420
	R	.242	-	-	-	-	-	-	-	-	.314	.412
NL	L	.245	-	-	-	-	-	-	-	-	.321	.407
	R	.241	-	-	-	-	-	-	-	-	.317	.407
MLB	L	.249	-	-	-	-	-	-	-	-	.321	.414
	R	.242	-	-	-	-	-	-	-	-	.316	.409

Pitchers vs. Left-Handed and Right-Handed Batters

Pitcher	vs	Avg	AB	H	2B	3B	HR	RBI	BB	SO	OBP	Slg
Abreu, Albert	L	.208	48	10	1	0	5	15	11	15	.356	.542
Throws Right	R	.205	83	17	5	0	3	10	8	20	.289	.373
Abreu, Bryan	L	.302	53	16	4	0	0	1	6	15	.393	.377
Throws Right	R	.224	85	19	5	0	4	27	12	21	.320	.424
Adams, Austin L	L	.197	71	14	3	1	1	13	10	28	.368	.310
Throws Right	R	.133	105	14	7	0	0	7	25	48	.364	.200
Akin, Keegan	L	.304	102	31	6	1	4	17	8	27	.357	.500
Throws Left	R	.285	277	79	15	1	13	44	32	55	.357	.487
Alcala, Jorge	L	.214	84	18	2	0	6	13	9	28	.287	.452
Throws Right	R	.214	126	27	3	0	4	15	4	33	.246	.333
Alcantara, Sandy	L	.229	401	92	25	1	14	43	33	94	.290	.401
Throws Right	R	.215	367	79	15	2	7	32	17	107	.265	.324
Alexander, Tyler	L	.193	88	17	0	1	2	5	8	20	.273	.284
Throws Left	R	.272	327	89	20	1	14	38	20	67	.315	.468
Allard, Kolby	L	.246	130	32	3	0	10	27	8	34	.300	.500
Throws Left	R	.262	366	96	13	2	19	49	23	70	.307	.464
Allen, Logan	L	.342	38	13	1	0	2	8	1	4	.375	.526
Throws Left	R	.280	161	45	8	0	10	23	16	33	.352	.516
Almonte, Yency	L	.299	87	26	6	1	3	15	15	20	.408	.494
Throws Right	R	.223	94	21	4	0	6	26	14	27	.333	.457
Alvarado, Jose	L	.123	73	9	0	0	1	6	14	20	.304	.164
Throws Left	R	.266	124	33	7	0	4	17	33	48	.428	.419
Alvarez, Jose	L	.220	118	26	2	1	0	12	6	16	.256	.254
Throws Left	R	.214	126	27	3	1	2	11	13	26	.288	.302
Alzolay, Adbert	L	.269	227	61	13	0	20	39	20	53	.333	.590
Throws Right	R	.206	247	51	6	1	5	20	14	75	.257	.300
Anderson, Brett	L	.303	76	23	2	0	2	11	5	16	.353	.408
Throws Left	R	.270	293	79	23	1	9	31	23	42	.320	.447
Anderson, Chase	L	.174	92	16	3	1	4	9	13	16	.290	.359
Throws Right	R	.357	98	35	11	1	6	19	7	19	.402	.673
Anderson, Ian	L	.205	229	47	7	0	10	23	23	58	.277	.367
Throws Right	R	.236	246	58	16	0	6	24	30	66	.321	.374
Anderson, Tyler	L	.265	162	43	5	3	3	14	9	26	.302	.389
Throws Left	R	.261	486	127	25	3	24	66	29	108	.301	.473
Andriese, Matt	L	.342	79	27	3	1	3	20	3	17	.375	.519
Throws Right	R	.311	122	38	5	1	4	18	10	33	.368	.467
Antone, Tejay	L	.172	58	10	1	0	2	10	6	22	.273	.293
Throws Right	R	.130	54	7	1	0	1	5	7	20	.242	.204
Arihara, Kohei	L	.250	68	17	6	2	3	7	7	8	.329	.529
Throws Right	R	.304	92	28	8	0	8	23	6	16	.363	.652
Armstrong, Shawn	L	.327	55	18	2	0	7	20	7	17	.406	.745
Throws Right	R	.228	92	21	5	1	3	14	8	27	.297	.402
Arrieta, Jake	L	.319	207	66	11	1	11	33	31	42	.407	.541
Throws Right	R	.320	203	65	15	0	13	44	13	41	.368	.586
Ashby, Aaron	L	.375	16	6	0	0	0	2	3	7	.500	.375
Throws Left	R	.184	103	19	2	0	4	14	9	32	.248	.320
Banda, Anthony	L	.224	49	11	0	0	1	4	7	9	.316	.286
Throws Left	R	.322	87	28	8	0	5	16	6	23	.375	.586
Bard, Daniel	L	.319	135	43	13	2	7	25	18	40	.406	.600
Throws Right	R	.208	125	26	2	0	1	8	18	40	.331	.248
Barlow, Joe	L	.143	42	6	0	0	0	3	5	11	.224	.143
Throws Right	R	.109	55	6	3	0	2	7	7	16	.210	.273
Barlow, Scott	L	.235	115	27	3	0	3	11	16	38	.336	.339
Throws Right	R	.214	159	34	14	0	1	20	12	53	.267	.321
Barnes, Charlie	L	.258	31	8	1	0	0	5	4	5	.351	.290
Throws Left	R	.314	121	38	10	0	4	20	12	15	.390	.496
Barnes, Matt	L	.156	64	10	2	0	2	10	12	28	.295	.281
Throws Right	R	.230	135	31	4	0	6	14	8	56	.278	.393
Barria, Jaime	L	.313	83	26	4	0	3	8	7	9	.367	.470
Throws Right	R	.303	145	44	10	0	5	21	12	26	.363	.476
Bass, Anthony	L	.300	100	30	3	0	10	20	10	18	.374	.630
Throws Right	R	.195	128	25	4	1	1	7	14	40	.273	.266
Bassitt, Chris	L	.196	280	55	10	1	11	29	20	79	.255	.357
Throws Right	R	.238	303	72	19	0	4	20	19	80	.299	.340
Bauer, Trevor	L	.220	191	42	9	2	12	25	18	58	.290	.476
Throws Right	R	.146	199	29	5	0	7	8	19	79	.227	.276
Bednar, David	L	.178	90	16	3	0	2	7	8	29	.253	.278
Throws Right	R	.190	126	24	6	3	3	10	11	48	.254	.357
Bender, Anthony	L	.247	89	22	7	0	2	10	10	15	.333	.393
Throws Right	R	.180	128	23	5	2	3	15	10	56	.255	.320
Benjamin, Wes	L	.414	29	12	1	0	3	8	7	3	.514	.759
Throws Left	R	.262	65	17	3	0	3	14	10	16	.360	.446
Berrios, Jose	L	.254	346	88	25	3	15	42	28	106	.315	.474
Throws Right	R	.193	368	71	15	0	7	35	17	98	.249	.291
Bickford, Phil	L	.222	54	12	3	0	2	5	9	12	.348	.389
Throws Right	R	.186	129	24	2	1	5	8	10	47	.248	.333

Pitcher	vs	Avg	AB	H	2B	3B	HR	RBI	BB	SO	OBP	Slg
Bieber, Shane	L	.249	181	45	11	1	6	18	21	76	.337	.420
Throws Right	R	.210	186	39	7	0	5	15	12	58	.260	.328
Bielak, Brandon	L	.256	86	22	1	0	1	11	8	22	.316	.302
Throws Right	R	.252	103	26	8	0	4	17	13	24	.347	.447
Blackburn, Paul	L	.333	69	23	4	1	3	9	6	13	.403	.551
Throws Right	R	.309	94	29	3	1	5	15	4	13	.337	.521
Bleier, Richard	L	.211	90	19	2	0	1	8	1	23	.215	.267
Throws Left	R	.262	122	32	6	0	3	13	5	21	.305	.385
Bowden, Ben	L	.309	68	21	3	1	3	11	9	21	.390	.515
Throws Left	R	.271	85	23	8	1	3	20	12	21	.367	.494
Boxberger, Brad	L	.139	108	15	1	0	1	7	17	38	.266	.176
Throws Right	R	.240	121	29	5	1	7	21	8	45	.306	.471
Boyd, Matthew	L	.270	74	20	1	0	3	11	4	16	.304	.405
Throws Left	R	.250	228	57	13	1	6	22	19	51	.323	.395
Brach, Brad	L	.250	44	11	3	0	3	10	8	9	.358	.523
Throws Right	R	.257	74	19	5	0	2	13	10	24	.353	.405
Bradley, Archie	L	.227	88	20	5	1	2	7	15	20	.340	.375
Throws Right	R	.282	110	31	5	1	3	17	7	20	.339	.427
Brault, Steven	L	.133	15	2	2	0	0	0	2	2	.278	.267
Throws Left	R	.316	98	31	5	4	3	18	10	17	.380	.541
Brentz, Jake	L	.116	69	8	0	0	2	6	17	21	.292	.203
Throws Left	R	.231	160	37	9	2	5	21	20	55	.333	.406
Brogdon, Connor	L	.218	110	24	5	0	3	12	9	24	.273	.345
Throws Right	R	.223	103	23	7	0	3	13	9	26	.292	.379
Brothers, Rex	L	.179	78	14	3	0	3	12	17	31	.347	.333
Throws Left	R	.235	115	27	6	0	6	19	18	44	.348	.443
Brubaker, JT	L	.269	234	63	12	0	14	32	19	58	.329	.500
Throws Right	R	.239	251	60	10	2	14	38	19	71	.309	.462
Bubic, Kris	L	.238	80	19	6	2	4	12	11	18	.337	.513
Throws Left	R	.251	407	102	17	1	18	49	48	96	.336	.430
Buehler, Walker	L	.201	383	77	18	2	9	25	33	102	.267	.329
Throws Right	R	.198	364	72	18	0	10	32	19	110	.245	.330
Bumgarner, Madison	L	.193	119	23	2	0	7	14	11	35	.276	.387
Throws Left	R	.256	434	111	31	2	17	63	28	89	.309	.454
Bummer, Aaron	L	.151	73	11	0	0	0	4	2	32	.173	.151
Throws Left	R	.230	135	31	1	0	3	18	27	43	.371	.304
Bundy, Dylan	L	.238	147	35	7	1	7	24	16	32	.313	.442
Throws Right	R	.263	205	54	15	0	13	30	18	52	.336	.527
Burnes, Corbin	L	.220	322	71	12	2	3	18	17	120	.263	.298
Throws Right	R	.179	290	52	5	1	4	23	17	114	.232	.245
Burr, Ryan	L	.246	57	14	1	0	2	7	15	14	.397	.368
Throws Right	R	.206	68	14	2	0	1	8	6	19	.276	.279
Cabrera, Edward	L	.259	54	14	1	1	4	10	12	14	.412	.537
Throws Right	R	.233	43	10	4	0	2	7	7	14	.365	.465
Cabrera, Genesis	L	.261	92	24	7	0	1	16	15	29	.387	.370
Throws Left	R	.178	157	28	9	0	2	24	21	48	.276	.274
Cahill, Trevor	L	.349	63	22	4	1	3	12	8	12	.423	.587
Throws Right	R	.238	84	20	2	0	1	14	6	20	.287	.298
Campbell, Paul	L	.286	49	14	2	0	3	10	5	11	.375	.510
Throws Right	R	.290	62	18	3	1	2	10	5	15	.343	.468
Canning, Griffin	L	.252	107	27	6	0	4	15	18	23	.360	.421
Throws Right	R	.273	139	38	6	2	10	23	10	39	.325	.561
Carrasco, Carlos	L	.245	102	25	6	0	3	18	9	21	.301	.392
Throws Right	R	.296	115	34	8	0	9	18	9	29	.347	.600
Castellanos, Humberto	L	.256	86	22	6	1	5	16	9	12	.326	.523
Throws Right	R	.299	87	26	3	0	2	8	6	17	.358	.402
Castillo, Diego	L	.203	69	14	1	0	6	14	11	20	.337	.478
Throws Right	R	.190	137	26	5	0	3	11	6	55	.230	.292
Castillo, Luis	L	.245	347	85	18	4	7	38	54	96	.349	.380
Throws Right	R	.264	364	96	16	3	12	45	21	96	.312	.423
Castro, Anthony	L	.211	38	8	4	0	1	7	2	12	.244	.395
Throws Right	R	.254	59	15	3	0	3	6	6	20	.353	.458
Castro, Miguel	L	.198	126	25	3	0	2	7	17	33	.313	.270
Throws Right	R	.180	128	23	4	0	5	18	26	44	.327	.328
Cease, Dylan	L	.226	310	70	7	3	11	35	30	113	.304	.374
Throws Right	R	.220	313	69	15	0	9	35	38	113	.307	.355
Cessa, Luis	L	.202	104	21	4	1	5	12	5	28	.239	.404
Throws Right	R	.250	136	34	6	0	0	14	14	26	.320	.294
Chacin, Jhoulys	L	.202	119	24	4	4	3	14	19	21	.312	.378
Throws Right	R	.242	120	29	8	0	5	20	9	26	.292	.433
Chafin, Andrew	L	.170	94	16	0	1	1	4	8	21	.250	.223
Throws Left	R	.196	148	29	7	0	3	17	11	43	.247	.304
Chapman, Aroldis	L	.116	43	5	1	0	1	5	7	22	.269	.209
Throws Left	R	.200	155	31	7	0	8	16	31	75	.333	.400
Chargois, JT	L	.147	68	10	2	0	2	8	14	24	.306	.265
Throws Right	R	.233	120	28	8	1	3	15	6	29	.290	.392

Pitchers vs. Left-Handed and Right-Handed Batters

Pitcher	vs	Avg	AB	H	2B	3B	HR	RBI	BB	SO	OBP	Slg
Chatwood, Tyler	L	.244	45	11	3	0	0	8	12	14	.404	.311
Throws Right	R	.200	75	15	3	0	2	11	9	24	.318	.320
Chavez, Jesse	L	.173	52	9	4	0	0	3	7	15	.267	.250
Throws Right	R	.191	68	13	3	1	0	9	4	21	.233	.265
Cimber, Adam	L	.184	87	16	4	1	1	8	12	21	.287	.287
Throws Right	R	.259	174	45	6	1	1	19	4	30	.297	.322
Cishek, Steve	L	.209	86	18	6	0	0	15	22	29	.386	.279
Throws Right	R	.253	170	43	8	0	2	30	19	35	.332	.335
Cisnero, Jose	L	.260	77	20	3	0	2	13	16	26	.385	.377
Throws Right	R	.208	149	31	6	0	4	18	15	36	.293	.329
Civale, Aaron	L	.215	228	49	6	1	11	21	15	59	.264	.395
Throws Right	R	.257	230	59	12	3	12	30	16	40	.311	.491
Clarke, Taylor	L	.301	73	22	6	0	1	8	5	12	.346	.425
Throws Right	R	.283	106	30	8	0	3	12	9	27	.336	.443
Clase, Emmanuel	L	.179	123	22	1	0	1	5	8	33	.229	.211
Throws Right	R	.209	139	29	3	1	1	8	8	41	.252	.266
Claudio, Alex	L	.275	69	19	5	0	4	10	6	19	.333	.522
Throws Left	R	.281	64	18	5	0	2	13	9	11	.370	.453
Clay, Sam	L	.250	84	21	2	0	2	10	8	21	.330	.345
Throws Left	R	.333	102	34	7	0	2	14	14	13	.425	.461
Clippard, Tyler	L	.279	43	12	2	1	3	9	5	9	.354	.581
Throws Right	R	.192	52	10	3	0	0	4	6	12	.306	.250
Cobb, Alex	L	.228	171	39	5	1	1	18	22	45	.320	.287
Throws Right	R	.251	183	46	10	1	4	22	11	53	.298	.383
Cole, Gerrit	L	.216	292	63	11	1	13	28	21	124	.271	.394
Throws Right	R	.229	385	88	16	0	11	36	20	119	.264	.356
Colome, Alex	L	.302	106	32	6	0	5	24	15	27	.395	.500
Throws Right	R	.237	152	36	8	0	3	16	8	31	.279	.349
Coonrod, Sam	L	.247	73	18	3	0	2	8	9	21	.329	.370
Throws Right	R	.247	93	23	3	0	3	15	6	27	.311	.376
Corbin, Patrick	L	.228	145	33	4	2	2	14	14	42	.294	.324
Throws Left	R	.302	527	159	28	2	35	95	46	101	.359	.562
Cortes, Nestor	L	.228	79	18	6	1	2	7	4	25	.274	.405
Throws Left	R	.214	266	57	8	0	12	20	21	78	.273	.380
Cotton, Jharel	L	.208	48	10	2	0	1	6	4	13	.291	.313
Throws Right	R	.257	70	18	3	0	1	7	11	17	.354	.343
Coulombe, Danny	L	.250	44	11	0	0	3	6	3	11	.298	.455
Throws Left	R	.276	87	24	8	0	2	10	4	22	.308	.437
Cousins, Jake	L	.146	41	6	1	0	0	3	13	19	.386	.171
Throws Right	R	.167	60	10	1	0	3	5	6	25	.254	.333
Crichton, Stefan	L	.400	30	12	1	0	1	6	6	5	.513	.533
Throws Right	R	.304	69	21	6	0	2	12	6	12	.372	.478
Crick, Kyle	L	.147	34	5	2	0	0	3	7	9	.333	.206
Throws Right	R	.196	46	9	0	0	0	4	12	12	.377	.196
Crismatt, Nabil	L	.295	139	41	7	0	3	20	12	27	.355	.410
Throws Right	R	.258	178	46	9	0	7	22	12	44	.330	.427
Crochet, Garrett	L	.171	70	12	2	0	0	4	12	25	.301	.200
Throws Left	R	.236	127	30	5	1	2	17	15	40	.313	.339
Crowe, Wil	L	.239	197	47	10	2	9	30	30	53	.346	.447
Throws Right	R	.304	260	79	10	2	16	42	27	58	.376	.542
Cueto, Johnny	L	.274	234	64	13	5	8	28	21	51	.336	.474
Throws Right	R	.299	211	63	10	1	7	26	9	47	.335	.455
Curtiss, John	L	.260	73	19	4	0	2	13	2	19	.276	.397
Throws Right	R	.232	99	23	4	1	4	17	10	25	.309	.414
Darvish, Yu	L	.222	306	68	18	3	14	35	22	86	.281	.438
Throws Right	R	.221	317	70	17	2	14	39	22	113	.278	.420
Davies, Zach	L	.251	239	60	19	0	10	36	44	44	.369	.456
Throws Right	R	.302	338	102	22	1	15	54	31	70	.366	.506
Davis, Wade	L	.257	70	18	1	0	6	15	8	20	.333	.529
Throws Right	R	.280	93	26	5	0	2	13	11	18	.351	.398
De Geus, Brett	L	.377	77	29	6	1	4	22	11	15	.467	.636
Throws Right	R	.266	124	33	4	2	2	26	14	26	.361	.379
De Jong, Chase	L	.300	100	30	9	3	7	18	13	19	.381	.660
Throws Right	R	.253	75	19	6	0	4	9	6	20	.317	.493
De Los Santos, Enyel	L	.279	68	19	3	0	5	14	11	26	.380	.544
Throws Right	R	.300	80	24	9	0	3	19	7	22	.385	.525
deGrom, Jacob	L	.128	149	19	6	2	4	7	6	69	.167	.275
Throws Right	R	.130	161	21	7	0	2	6	5	77	.155	.211
DeSclafani, Anthony	L	.248	303	75	13	1	10	30	21	74	.298	.396
Throws Right	R	.204	323	66	9	1	9	26	21	78	.255	.322
Detmers, Reid	L	.318	22	7	0	0	2	7	0	7	.375	.591
Throws Left	R	.288	66	19	6	0	3	9	11	12	.390	.515
Detwiler, Ross	L	.237	76	18	5	0	2	8	10	21	.348	.382
Throws Left	R	.213	122	26	6	2	8	24	10	41	.292	.492
Diaz, Edwin	L	.165	109	18	4	1	2	12	14	44	.276	.275
Throws Right	R	.223	112	25	5	0	1	15	9	45	.315	.295

Pitcher	vs	Avg	AB	H	2B	3B	HR	RBI	BB	SO	OBP	Slg
Diaz, Miguel	L	.172	64	11	4	1	3	9	11	17	.293	.406
Throws Right	R	.227	88	20	3	1	5	10	8	29	.292	.455
Diaz, Yennsy	L	.267	45	12	1	1	3	5	4	7	.327	.533
Throws Right	R	.245	53	13	1	0	2	10	8	14	.349	.377
Diekman, Jake	L	.229	83	19	4	1	1	8	17	32	.379	.337
Throws Left	R	.200	140	28	2	1	9	25	17	51	.289	.421
Diplan, Marcos	L	.209	43	9	2	0	1	9	2	7	.244	.326
Throws Right	R	.203	64	13	2	0	5	13	13	17	.333	.469
Dobnak, Randy	L	.327	98	32	6	1	6	17	5	9	.365	.592
Throws Right	R	.296	115	34	11	0	5	21	7	18	.333	.522
Dolis, Rafael	L	.213	47	10	3	1	0	8	11	19	.373	.319
Throws Right	R	.244	78	19	4	0	2	14	16	20	.381	.372
Doolittle, Sean	L	.222	90	20	5	2	2	20	7	30	.276	.389
Throws Left	R	.288	104	30	8	0	5	14	16	23	.390	.510
Doval, Camilo	L	.220	41	9	1	0	3	5	3	15	.289	.463
Throws Right	R	.172	58	10	1	0	1	5	6	22	.250	.241
Duffey, Tyler	L	.253	75	19	3	1	2	13	14	20	.385	.400
Throws Right	R	.197	147	29	4	0	2	13	14	41	.265	.265
Duffy, Danny	L	.217	46	10	0	0	3	4	3	16	.265	.413
Throws Left	R	.228	184	42	8	2	3	13	19	49	.300	.342
Dugger, Robert	L	.293	41	12	2	0	1	4	6	7	.383	.415
Throws Right	R	.344	64	22	4	2	3	21	6	12	.397	.609
Dunn, Justin	L	.200	95	19	1	1	5	13	21	26	.350	.389
Throws Right	R	.202	89	18	3	0	1	5	8	23	.287	.270
Dunning, Dane	L	.279	204	57	20	0	4	22	17	49	.345	.436
Throws Right	R	.271	255	69	9	1	9	33	26	65	.345	.420
Eflin, Zach	L	.264	201	53	11	2	7	23	8	49	.294	.443
Throws Right	R	.286	220	63	18	0	8	24	8	50	.317	.477
Eickhoff, Jerad	L	.432	44	19	4	0	7	14	6	5	.509	1.000
Throws Right	R	.239	46	11	4	0	2	9	4	8	.314	.457
Ellis, Chris	L	.139	36	5	0	0	2	4	7	9	.279	.306
Throws Right	R	.232	69	16	4	0	1	3	7	14	.321	.333
Eovaldi, Nathan	L	.241	323	78	25	3	4	32	15	90	.280	.375
Throws Right	R	.263	396	104	29	1	11	39	20	105	.305	.424
Eshelman, Thomas	L	.225	40	9	2	0	2	8	5	6	.304	.425
Throws Right	R	.338	74	25	7	0	4	12	5	5	.388	.595
Espino, Paolo	L	.280	218	61	16	2	6	23	11	38	.313	.454
Throws Right	R	.230	204	47	9	0	13	29	14	54	.281	.466
Estevez, Carlos	L	.287	122	35	8	1	4	14	8	32	.323	.467
Throws Right	R	.300	120	36	5	0	4	21	13	28	.375	.442
Evans, Demarcus	L	.333	39	13	3	0	1	9	9	8	.458	.487
Throws Right	R	.177	62	11	3	0	3	10	7	25	.268	.371
Fairbanks, Pete	L	.343	70	24	5	0	2	7	9	21	.425	.500
Throws Right	R	.167	96	16	2	1	0	8	12	35	.257	.208
Falter, Bailey	L	.288	52	15	1	0	1	8	3	17	.339	.365
Throws Left	R	.244	78	19	3	1	4	13	3	17	.277	.462
Familia, Jeurys	L	.270	100	27	7	0	5	16	14	33	.365	.490
Throws Right	R	.231	130	30	6	0	5	19	13	39	.306	.392
Faria, Jake	L	.297	64	19	3	2	2	8	8	15	.375	.500
Throws Right	R	.274	73	20	4	1	3	14	5	17	.333	.479
Farmer, Buck	L	.298	47	14	2	0	4	12	9	14	.431	.596
Throws Right	R	.268	97	26	3	0	5	15	12	23	.363	.454
Farrell, Luke	L	.265	34	9	2	0	0	1	5	9	.359	.324
Throws Right	R	.288	66	19	4	1	4	10	8	16	.365	.561
Fedde, Erick	L	.290	272	79	12	1	13	38	25	59	.352	.485
Throws Right	R	.258	252	65	17	0	10	41	23	69	.321	.444
Feyereisen, J.P.	L	.235	81	19	5	1	3	15	13	18	.337	.432
Throws Right	R	.147	116	17	3	1	2	8	20	35	.270	.241
Finnegan, Kyle	L	.207	116	24	3	1	5	21	21	31	.328	.379
Throws Right	R	.288	139	40	7	0	4	29	13	37	.357	.424
Flaherty, Jack	L	.195	149	29	6	0	4	11	15	39	.275	.315
Throws Right	R	.204	137	28	5	0	8	19	11	46	.281	.416
Fleming, Josh	L	.277	112	31	3	0	6	20	3	28	.308	.464
Throws Left	R	.265	298	79	19	1	5	33	28	37	.329	.386
Flexen, Chris	L	.235	319	75	14	2	10	37	13	59	.265	.386
Throws Right	R	.296	371	110	20	3	9	36	27	66	.346	.439
Floro, Dylan	L	.236	110	26	5	0	1	9	17	18	.336	.309
Throws Right	R	.201	134	27	6	0	1	13	8	44	.246	.269
Foltynewicz, Mike	L	.271	247	67	16	2	18	36	23	40	.337	.571
Throws Right	R	.250	288	72	18	0	17	46	13	57	.296	.490
Foster, Matt	L	.286	70	20	2	0	3	14	3	18	.333	.443
Throws Right	R	.264	87	23	3	0	6	16	10	22	.333	.506
Freeland, Kyle	L	.303	132	40	5	0	4	22	9	23	.357	.432
Throws Left	R	.276	337	93	23	0	16	32	29	82	.336	.487
Fried, Max	L	.240	154	37	7	2	5	15	12	45	.298	.409
Throws Left	R	.223	458	102	21	0	10	39	29	113	.277	.334

Pitchers vs. Left-Handed and Right-Handed Batters

Pitcher	vs	Avg	AB	H	2B	3B	HR	RBI	BB	SO	OBP	Slg
Fry, Paul	L	.229	70	16	2	0	3	12	15	21	.365	.386
Throws Left	R	.202	104	21	1	0	0	10	20	39	.349	.212
Fulmer, Carson	L	.233	43	10	2	0	1	4	8	12	.365	.349
Throws Right	R	.291	55	16	3	1	2	11	5	12	.365	.491
Fulmer, Michael	L	.190	121	23	4	0	3	14	7	39	.256	.298
Throws Right	R	.309	149	46	6	1	4	24	13	34	.366	.443
Funkhouser, Kyle	L	.248	105	26	2	1	2	14	18	30	.357	.343
Throws Right	R	.216	148	32	2	2	4	17	20	33	.318	.338
Gallegos, Giovanny	L	.176	136	24	7	1	3	11	10	48	.231	.309
Throws Right	R	.190	142	27	6	0	3	15	10	47	.265	.296
Gallen, Zac	L	.252	242	61	11	2	5	24	23	64	.323	.376
Throws Right	R	.213	221	47	11	0	14	35	26	75	.299	.452
Gant, John	L	.223	175	39	9	2	5	22	38	42	.363	.383
Throws Right	R	.240	233	56	8	2	5	21	33	50	.344	.356
Garcia, Bryan	L	.364	66	24	6	0	6	17	15	10	.488	.727
Throws Right	R	.247	97	24	6	0	4	16	10	22	.324	.433
Garcia, Jarlin	L	.173	104	18	7	0	1	11	9	27	.243	.269
Throws Left	R	.213	141	30	11	0	8	18	9	41	.265	.461
Garcia, Luis	L	.289	45	13	4	0	2	6	5	14	.353	.511
Throws Right	R	.152	79	12	2	0	0	4	3	20	.190	.177
Garcia, Luis	L	.279	287	80	17	0	13	37	25	75	.340	.474
Throws Right	R	.182	286	52	14	1	6	20	25	92	.247	.301
Garcia, Yimi	L	.253	91	23	4	1	6	15	10	21	.327	.516
Throws Right	R	.213	122	26	6	1	2	14	8	39	.260	.328
Garrett, Amir	L	.226	84	19	2	0	3	12	15	35	.343	.357
Throws Left	R	.267	101	27	8	0	6	19	14	26	.357	.525
Garrett, Braxton	L	.394	33	13	3	0	0	3	4	7	.487	.485
Throws Left	R	.293	99	29	5	0	3	12	16	25	.388	.434
Garza, Justin	L	.279	43	12	1	0	2	9	10	8	.415	.442
Throws Right	R	.231	65	15	4	0	3	12	8	21	.311	.431
Gausman, Kevin	L	.214	355	76	14	3	8	26	26	113	.266	.338
Throws Right	R	.206	360	74	15	1	12	35	24	114	.262	.353
German, Domingo	L	.214	173	37	7	0	7	16	9	48	.253	.376
Throws Right	R	.251	207	52	9	3	10	28	18	50	.316	.469
Gibson, Kyle	L	.259	355	92	20	2	10	34	31	73	.327	.411
Throws Right	R	.206	320	66	12	0	7	29	33	82	.283	.309
Gil, Luis	L	.167	42	7	0	0	1	2	8	13	.300	.238
Throws Right	R	.194	67	13	1	0	3	4	11	25	.316	.343
Gilbert, Logan	L	.239	213	51	13	0	5	25	17	57	.293	.371
Throws Right	R	.243	251	61	17	2	12	31	11	71	.290	.470
Gilbert, Tyler	L	.115	52	6	1	0	0	3	6	8	.207	.135
Throws Left	R	.250	88	22	5	1	4	13	7	17	.306	.466
Gilbreath, Lucas	L	.228	79	18	4	0	4	12	14	24	.347	.430
Throws Left	R	.188	80	15	0	0	1	5	9	20	.267	.225
Ginkel, Kevin	L	.317	41	13	3	1	5	12	9	12	.451	.805
Throws Right	R	.239	71	17	5	0	2	12	5	19	.299	.394
Giolito, Lucas	L	.221	312	69	13	2	9	30	29	97	.287	.362
Throws Right	R	.217	350	76	14	2	18	33	23	104	.267	.423
Givens, Mychal	L	.214	84	18	5	0	2	10	20	19	.362	.345
Throws Right	R	.250	100	25	7	0	5	16	7	35	.306	.470
Glasnow, Tyler	L	.139	137	19	8	0	4	9	8	54	.186	.285
Throws Right	R	.205	176	36	5	1	6	14	19	69	.282	.347
Gomber, Austin	L	.223	121	27	5	0	5	14	8	30	.269	.388
Throws Left	R	.235	319	75	16	1	15	40	33	83	.312	.433
Gonsolin, Tony	L	.213	122	26	6	0	3	9	18	35	.314	.336
Throws Right	R	.185	81	15	4	0	5	10	16	30	.320	.420
Gonzales, Marco	L	.210	143	30	4	0	6	14	5	29	.240	.364
Throws Left	R	.242	392	95	29	2	23	49	37	79	.313	.503
Gonzalez, Chi Chi	L	.305	220	67	12	2	6	31	17	29	.357	.459
Throws Right	R	.317	189	60	23	0	12	43	11	27	.367	.630
Gonzalez, Victor	L	.200	70	14	2	0	1	10	8	9	.296	.271
Throws Left	R	.295	61	18	4	0	2	15	11	24	.411	.459
Graterol, Brusdar	L	.286	49	14	7	0	2	9	8	10	.417	.551
Throws Right	R	.244	82	20	4	0	0	4	5	17	.303	.293
Graveman, Kendall	L	.253	91	23	4	0	3	13	12	27	.352	.396
Throws Right	R	.117	103	12	1	0	0	5	8	34	.222	.126
Gray, Jon	L	.235	324	76	14	5	11	41	38	79	.320	.410
Throws Right	R	.258	248	64	13	0	10	29	20	78	.322	.431
Gray, Josiah	L	.221	122	27	5	0	9	24	18	32	.324	.484
Throws Right	R	.252	143	36	5	2	10	18	15	44	.325	.524
Gray, Sonny	L	.208	236	49	8	4	8	33	28	80	.300	.377
Throws Right	R	.239	276	66	7	1	11	31	22	75	.305	.391
Green, Chad	L	.200	125	25	5	0	6	13	8	40	.246	.384
Throws Right	R	.188	170	32	8	1	8	24	9	59	.228	.388
Greene, Conner	L	.313	32	10	3	0	0	2	6	8	.410	.406
Throws Right	R	.306	72	22	6	0	1	11	6	18	.378	.431

Pitcher	vs	Avg	AB	H	2B	3B	HR	RBI	BB	SO	OBP	Slg
Greinke, Zack	L	.199	256	51	8	0	8	23	15	45	.241	.324
Throws Right	R	.285	396	113	21	0	22	55	21	75	.323	.505
Gsellman, Robert	L	.261	46	12	2	0	1	5	4	7	.333	.370
Throws Right	R	.238	63	15	4	0	2	11	3	10	.284	.397
Guenther, Sean	L	.447	38	17	3	1	0	5	4	3	.512	.579
Throws Left	R	.275	51	14	5	0	1	14	6	12	.362	.431
Guerra, Deolis	L	.217	106	23	5	0	3	12	8	35	.284	.349
Throws Right	R	.219	137	30	5	0	5	16	12	27	.289	.365
Guerra, Junior	L	.304	92	28	5	0	3	19	28	19	.467	.457
Throws Right	R	.238	164	39	7	0	3	28	18	42	.319	.335
Gutierrez, Vladimir	L	.255	212	54	12	2	13	31	27	33	.336	.514
Throws Right	R	.271	225	61	14	0	7	23	19	55	.336	.427
Hader, Josh	L	.133	45	6	1	0	0	1	5	23	.220	.156
Throws Left	R	.125	152	19	3	0	3	10	19	79	.230	.204
Hale, David	L	.167	42	7	2	0	2	9	6	9	.286	.357
Throws Right	R	.359	64	23	5	0	3	18	3	12	.388	.578
Hand, Brad	L	.225	71	16	3	1	1	7	10	18	.329	.338
Throws Left	R	.240	167	40	7	1	8	32	16	43	.316	.437
Happ, J.A.	L	.250	132	33	3	2	3	15	8	33	.298	.371
Throws Left	R	.298	483	144	32	4	27	75	40	89	.352	.549
Harper, Ryne	L	.258	62	16	2	0	2	4	6	13	.329	.387
Throws Right	R	.174	69	12	3	0	4	10	8	18	.269	.391
Harvey, Matt	L	.261	241	63	17	1	9	35	16	48	.317	.452
Throws Right	R	.329	295	97	16	3	10	48	21	47	.374	.505
Head, Louis	L	.146	48	7	1	0	1	1	5	9	.255	.229
Throws Right	R	.194	72	14	2	0	1	7	4	23	.241	.264
Heaney, Andrew	L	.260	127	33	9	0	5	12	10	32	.321	.449
Throws Left	R	.255	380	97	19	1	24	62	31	118	.316	.500
Hearn, Taylor	L	.198	116	23	1	1	5	14	11	34	.277	.353
Throws Left	R	.267	273	73	15	0	12	35	31	58	.340	.454
Helsley, Ryan	L	.250	64	16	3	0	0	8	10	12	.342	.297
Throws Right	R	.214	112	24	5	0	4	11	17	35	.318	.366
Hembree, Heath	L	.253	79	20	7	0	7	18	8	29	.322	.608
Throws Right	R	.181	138	25	3	0	5	16	16	54	.276	.312
Hendricks, Kyle	L	.287	317	91	21	4	16	39	34	62	.362	.530
Throws Right	R	.271	402	109	22	1	15	49	10	69	.303	.443
Hendriks, Liam	L	.133	128	17	3	0	5	10	3	58	.159	.273
Throws Right	R	.215	130	28	1	0	6	16	4	55	.239	.362
Hendrix, Ryan	L	.212	52	11	4	1	3	10	6	13	.295	.500
Throws Right	R	.310	71	22	2	0	5	15	10	22	.395	.549
Hentges, Sam	L	.258	66	17	2	0	1	8	6	14	.319	.333
Throws Left	R	.336	217	73	17	0	9	43	26	54	.404	.539
Hernandez, Carlos	L	.184	141	26	2	1	3	14	22	34	.303	.277
Throws Right	R	.254	169	43	7	1	4	18	19	40	.332	.379
Hernandez, Darwinzon	L	.204	54	11	3	0	2	4	13	24	.371	.370
Throws Left	R	.202	89	18	2	0	3	16	18	30	.351	.326
Hernandez, Elieser	L	.282	110	31	7	1	11	18	11	23	.350	.664
Throws Right	R	.245	94	23	6	0	2	8	3	30	.280	.372
Heuer, Codi	L	.302	106	32	9	2	5	15	4	24	.339	.566
Throws Right	R	.231	143	33	2	0	2	15	19	32	.315	.287
Hill, Rich	L	.187	139	26	5	0	2	13	19	39	.297	.266
Throws Left	R	.251	443	111	27	1	19	52	36	111	.323	.445
Hill, Tim	L	.210	119	25	5	0	3	18	10	28	.293	.328
Throws Left	R	.252	103	26	1	1	6	17	13	28	.342	.456
Hoffman, Jeff	L	.261	134	35	11	0	7	19	28	32	.405	.500
Throws Right	R	.236	148	35	4	1	5	19	17	47	.313	.378
Holland, Derek	L	.257	74	19	6	1	1	8	6	17	.313	.405
Throws Left	R	.305	128	39	6	1	5	19	14	34	.372	.484
Holland, Greg	L	.205	88	18	5	1	5	11	14	26	.320	.455
Throws Right	R	.246	126	31	4	0	4	22	12	27	.309	.373
Holloway, Jordan	L	.193	57	11	3	1	1	9	8	16	.288	.333
Throws Right	R	.164	73	12	4	0	2	6	18	20	.326	.301
Holmes, Clay	L	.272	81	22	3	0	3	18	13	18	.388	.420
Throws Right	R	.176	176	31	2	0	2	15	16	60	.249	.222
Houck, Tanner	L	.231	121	28	4	1	2	11	11	33	.309	.331
Throws Right	R	.215	135	29	5	0	2	13	10	54	.284	.296
Houser, Adrian	L	.273	227	62	11	2	4	22	35	41	.370	.392
Throws Right	R	.192	291	56	7	0	8	26	29	64	.285	.299
Howard, Sam	L	.158	76	12	3	0	1	6	14	25	.293	.237
Throws Left	R	.259	85	22	3	0	6	18	18	35	.396	.506
Howard, Spencer	L	.216	88	19	3	2	3	14	13	26	.324	.398
Throws Right	R	.312	109	34	4	2	4	22	14	26	.394	.495
Hudson, Daniel	L	.256	78	20	5	0	2	8	7	27	.310	.397
Throws Right	R	.179	112	20	8	0	6	17	9	48	.236	.411
Iglesias, Raisel	L	.223	112	25	5	0	5	10	3	41	.239	.402
Throws Right	R	.194	144	28	3	0	6	16	9	62	.245	.340

Pitchers vs. Left-Handed and Right-Handed Batters

Pitcher	vs	Avg	AB	H	2B	3B	HR	RBI	BB	SO	OBP	Slg
Irvin, Cole	L	.289	180	52	11	0	5	17	11	35	.333	.433
Throws Left	R	.270	530	143	24	1	18	66	31	90	.319	.421
Jackson, Luke	L	.196	92	18	6	0	0	3	16	24	.315	.261
Throws Right	R	.200	135	27	3	0	6	19	13	46	.276	.356
Jansen, Kenley	L	.169	118	20	4	0	3	14	15	38	.267	.280
Throws Right	R	.136	118	16	3	0	1	8	21	48	.270	.186
Javier, Cristian	L	.230	148	34	4	0	6	16	31	44	.368	.378
Throws Right	R	.155	213	33	7	1	10	25	22	86	.249	.338
Jax, Griffin	L	.254	126	32	11	0	7	21	15	24	.340	.508
Throws Right	R	.258	194	50	10	0	16	40	14	41	.310	.557
Jimenez, Joe	L	.219	64	14	3	1	2	12	15	22	.378	.391
Throws Right	R	.198	101	20	7	0	4	14	20	35	.359	.386
Johnson, Pierce	L	.230	100	23	5	0	3	6	14	39	.330	.370
Throws Right	R	.211	114	24	9	0	3	11	13	38	.287	.368
Junis, Jakob	L	.294	85	25	5	0	4	13	8	21	.351	.494
Throws Right	R	.261	69	18	2	0	3	5	4	20	.297	.420
Kaprielian, James	L	.266	222	59	15	2	11	33	31	53	.360	.500
Throws Right	R	.201	229	46	9	2	8	18	10	70	.240	.362
Karinchak, James	L	.158	114	18	3	1	4	15	17	48	.267	.307
Throws Right	R	.200	85	17	3	0	5	16	15	30	.327	.412
Kay, Anthony	L	.341	41	14	3	1	5	11	7	15	.438	.829
Throws Left	R	.255	94	24	6	0	2	9	11	24	.352	.383
Keller, Brad	L	.301	276	83	14	1	9	40	31	72	.375	.457
Throws Right	R	.293	256	75	13	1	9	40	33	48	.374	.457
Keller, Kyle	L	.255	55	14	3	1	4	14	9	15	.369	.564
Throws Right	R	.219	73	16	2	0	5	11	13	21	.367	.452
Keller, Mitch	L	.345	197	68	18	1	2	32	27	33	.419	.477
Throws Right	R	.300	210	63	11	1	8	31	22	59	.382	.476
Kelly, Joe	L	.183	71	13	5	0	1	10	8	20	.259	.296
Throws Right	R	.167	90	15	2	1	2	4	7	30	.257	.278
Kelly, Merrill	L	.235	294	69	15	2	7	31	21	55	.283	.371
Throws Right	R	.296	318	94	16	2	14	43	20	75	.344	.491
Kennedy, Ian	L	.231	91	21	3	0	6	11	10	28	.307	.462
Throws Right	R	.205	117	24	3	0	6	12	7	34	.262	.385
Kershaw, Clayton	L	.178	129	23	3	0	1	12	6	37	.215	.225
Throws Left	R	.242	331	80	19	1	14	37	15	107	.281	.432
Keuchel, Dallas	L	.304	135	41	6	2	4	17	11	28	.361	.467
Throws Left	R	.286	517	148	28	3	21	74	48	67	.353	.474
Kikuchi, Yusei	L	.147	136	20	2	0	5	11	10	40	.205	.272
Throws Left	R	.271	461	125	26	2	22	58	52	123	.351	.479
Kim, Kwang-hyun	L	.156	90	14	4	0	0	3	12	26	.252	.200
Throws Left	R	.267	315	84	11	1	12	38	27	54	.331	.422
Kimbrel, Craig	L	.143	98	14	3	1	3	10	7	49	.220	.286
Throws Right	R	.157	108	17	2	0	3	8	16	51	.262	.259
King, John	L	.140	57	8	1	0	0	1	5	15	.246	.158
Throws Left	R	.277	119	33	5	1	3	17	7	25	.323	.412
King, Michael	L	.256	82	21	5	0	4	12	9	24	.351	.463
Throws Right	R	.225	160	36	6	0	2	11	15	38	.302	.300
Kinley, Tyler	L	.195	128	25	4	3	5	23	19	35	.302	.391
Throws Right	R	.250	136	34	5	1	7	28	7	33	.290	.456
Kintzler, Brandon	L	.283	53	15	1	1	1	9	1	7	.291	.396
Throws Right	R	.385	78	30	7	0	6	14	7	15	.442	.705
Kittredge, Andrew	L	.200	75	15	5	0	2	9	10	20	.302	.347
Throws Right	R	.214	187	40	6	0	5	23	5	57	.241	.326
Kluber, Corey	L	.218	119	26	4	0	0	7	9	38	.286	.252
Throws Right	R	.267	180	48	8	1	8	26	24	44	.357	.456
Knebel, Corey	L	.140	43	6	1	0	1	4	6	12	.245	.233
Throws Right	R	.208	48	10	2	0	1	3	3	18	.250	.313
Knehr, Reiss	L	.182	44	8	3	1	1	4	6	6	.288	.364
Throws Right	R	.250	60	15	4	0	1	11	14	14	.390	.367
Kopech, Michael	L	.176	108	19	2	2	5	9	7	54	.222	.370
Throws Right	R	.235	149	35	5	2	4	16	17	49	.315	.376
Kowar, Jackson	L	.333	54	18	5	0	4	18	11	10	.426	.648
Throws Right	R	.338	74	25	6	0	3	19	9	19	.419	.541
Kranick, Max	L	.333	78	26	8	0	1	10	13	17	.436	.474
Throws Right	R	.269	78	21	6	0	3	14	6	15	.333	.462
Kremer, Dean	L	.261	88	23	4	0	6	13	14	26	.356	.511
Throws Right	R	.313	128	40	9	0	11	25	11	21	.369	.641
Kuhl, Chad	L	.257	136	35	7	0	8	26	21	36	.372	.485
Throws Right	R	.247	154	38	10	0	5	19	21	39	.344	.409
Lakins, Travis	L	.244	45	11	2	0	0	4	6	9	.327	.289
Throws Right	R	.203	59	12	0	0	4	10	11	15	.338	.407
Lamet, Dinelson	L	.315	89	28	8	0	2	10	8	24	.378	.472
Throws Right	R	.213	94	20	2	0	4	9	14	33	.318	.362
Lange, Alex	L	.239	67	16	2	1	2	8	7	16	.320	.388
Throws Right	R	.276	76	21	4	0	3	17	9	23	.368	.447

Pitcher	vs	Avg	AB	H	2B	3B	HR	RBI	BB	SO	OBP	Slg
Lauer, Eric	L	.228	101	23	3	1	1	10	15	21	.328	.307
Throws Left	R	.211	337	71	9	0	15	35	26	96	.270	.371
LeBlanc, Wade	L	.288	66	19	5	0	4	14	2	8	.329	.545
Throws Left	R	.280	132	37	8	1	4	10	15	21	.362	.447
Leone, Dominic	L	.154	78	12	2	0	1	6	13	23	.283	.218
Throws Right	R	.223	112	25	6	0	1	6	9	27	.276	.304
Lester, Jon	L	.246	118	29	6	0	3	13	7	19	.287	.373
Throws Left	R	.295	440	130	27	0	22	63	48	72	.366	.507
Littell, Zack	L	.250	80	20	5	2	2	11	11	25	.344	.438
Throws Right	R	.183	142	26	7	0	5	17	13	38	.255	.338
Loaisiga, Jonathan	L	.238	105	25	4	1	1	9	9	26	.299	.324
Throws Right	R	.200	155	31	2	0	2	11	7	43	.244	.252
Long, Sammy	L	.164	61	10	1	1	1	6	7	19	.246	.262
Throws Left	R	.284	95	27	9	0	4	14	8	19	.355	.505
Lopez, Jorge	L	.294	201	59	15	1	11	37	29	45	.392	.542
Throws Right	R	.292	284	83	13	0	10	33	27	67	.365	.444
Lopez, Pablo	L	.245	192	47	14	0	3	10	15	44	.301	.365
Throws Right	R	.221	190	42	7	2	8	22	11	71	.284	.405
Lopez, Reynaldo	L	.219	96	21	6	1	4	11	7	22	.269	.427
Throws Right	R	.193	109	21	6	0	6	15	6	33	.229	.413
Lorenzen, Michael	L	.226	62	14	3	0	2	10	9	10	.319	.371
Throws Right	R	.261	46	12	2	0	0	4	5	11	.346	.304
Loup, Aaron	L	.167	84	14	1	0	1	10	5	20	.226	.214
Throws Left	R	.211	109	23	3	1	0	7	11	37	.290	.257
Lowther, Zac	L	.440	25	11	2	0	1	3	3	6	.500	.640
Throws Left	R	.260	96	25	4	0	5	15	10	24	.355	.458
Lucchesi, Joey	L	.276	29	8	2	0	0	1	2	9	.344	.345
Throws Left	R	.236	110	26	6	2	4	17	9	32	.295	.436
Luetge, Lucas	L	.196	92	18	5	0	2	7	1	25	.204	.315
Throws Left	R	.259	189	49	9	1	4	28	14	53	.319	.381
Lugo, Seth	L	.237	76	18	2	1	3	11	15	21	.359	.408
Throws Right	R	.237	97	23	6	0	3	14	4	34	.272	.392
Luzardo, Jesus	L	.253	91	23	5	2	2	5	11	25	.340	.418
Throws Left	R	.289	287	83	19	2	18	55	37	73	.370	.557
Lyles, Jordan	L	.260	281	73	15	2	14	33	33	51	.335	.477
Throws Right	R	.291	416	121	19	1	24	66	23	95	.335	.514
Lynch, Daniel	L	.161	31	5	1	0	0	2	2	6	.229	.194
Throws Left	R	.313	240	75	14	2	9	35	29	49	.389	.500
Lynn, Lance	L	.227	291	66	13	0	10	28	31	84	.302	.375
Throws Right	R	.192	297	57	7	1	8	18	14	92	.230	.303
Machado, Andres	L	.200	60	12	1	1	1	13	7	15	.290	.300
Throws Right	R	.247	73	18	5	0	3	9	8	15	.353	.438
Maeda, Kenta	L	.258	209	54	11	2	8	26	17	57	.330	.445
Throws Right	R	.257	202	52	9	0	8	20	15	56	.312	.421
Mahle, Tyler	L	.198	333	66	13	1	6	24	34	115	.276	.297
Throws Right	R	.270	341	92	18	2	18	43	30	95	.342	.493
Manaea, Sean	L	.204	167	34	3	0	7	21	7	58	.243	.347
Throws Left	R	.271	535	145	30	2	18	54	34	136	.323	.436
Manning, Matt	L	.253	158	40	10	2	5	26	17	24	.320	.437
Throws Right	R	.301	186	56	13	0	5	26	16	33	.364	.452
Manoah, Alek	L	.228	202	46	6	0	8	26	28	68	.333	.376
Throws Right	R	.156	199	31	7	0	4	15	12	59	.244	.251
Mantiply, Joe	L	.261	69	18	3	2	0	9	9	24	.346	.362
Throws Left	R	.318	85	27	8	3	1	12	8	14	.368	.518
Maples, Dillon	L	.087	46	4	1	0	0	4	16	21	.377	.109
Throws Right	R	.190	58	11	2	0	2	7	9	19	.314	.328
Marquez, German	L	.265	366	97	22	0	9	44	43	78	.345	.399
Throws Right	R	.215	316	68	13	1	12	39	21	98	.268	.377
Marshall, Evan	L	.205	39	8	2	1	1	8	5	9	.289	.385
Throws Right	R	.323	62	20	5	0	4	17	4	17	.358	.597
Martin, Brett	L	.255	94	24	2	0	1	11	4	18	.286	.309
Throws Left	R	.283	152	43	8	0	4	26	10	24	.327	.414
Martin, Chris	L	.303	76	23	4	0	2	8	4	15	.346	.434
Throws Right	R	.280	93	26	3	0	2	14	2	18	.306	.376
Martinez, Carlos	L	.261	180	47	12	0	4	33	18	30	.337	.394
Throws Right	R	.226	133	30	5	2	4	16	18	27	.350	.383
Maton, Phil	L	.233	116	27	9	1	3	24	12	33	.321	.405
Throws Right	R	.268	138	37	12	1	3	22	20	52	.362	.435
Matz, Steven	L	.276	134	37	3	2	3	17	9	43	.324	.396
Throws Left	R	.261	463	121	21	1	15	45	34	101	.319	.408
Matzek, Tyler	L	.239	92	22	7	0	1	8	10	28	.314	.348
Throws Left	R	.141	128	18	5	0	2	8	27	49	.297	.227
May, Trevor	L	.240	104	25	3	1	6	15	12	39	.319	.462
Throws Right	R	.217	138	30	3	2	4	9	12	44	.280	.355
Mayers, Mike	L	.250	124	31	6	0	5	17	16	47	.338	.419
Throws Right	R	.250	160	40	8	2	6	19	10	43	.302	.438

Pitchers vs. Left-Handed and Right-Handed Batters

Pitcher	vs	Avg	AB	H	2B	3B	HR	RBI	BB	SO	OBP	Slg
Mayza, Tim	L	.181	72	13	0	0	1	6	3	23	.224	.222
Throws Left	R	.221	122	27	3	1	4	18	9	34	.286	.361
Mazza, Chris	L	.205	39	8	2	0	1	6	5	12	.319	.333
Throws Right	R	.290	62	18	2	1	2	8	2	9	.308	.452
McClanahan, Shane	L	.293	92	27	2	0	2	7	5	29	.330	.380
Throws Left	R	.242	384	93	21	0	12	36	32	112	.304	.391
McCullers Jr., Lance	L	.223	283	63	16	1	6	27	45	85	.340	.350
Throws Right	R	.188	313	59	10	2	7	19	31	100	.270	.300
McFarland, T.J.	L	.167	48	8	1	0	2	6	1	12	.184	.313
Throws Left	R	.276	87	24	6	1	1	10	8	9	.337	.402
McGee, Jake	L	.197	66	13	3	0	0	3	4	17	.254	.242
Throws Left	R	.196	158	31	6	0	7	22	6	41	.226	.367
McGowin, Kyle	L	.222	54	12	1	0	4	8	8	19	.344	.463
Throws Right	R	.155	58	9	3	0	1	7	6	16	.234	.259
McHugh, Collin	L	.163	80	13	2	1	0	3	5	32	.230	.213
Throws Right	R	.230	152	35	4	1	3	11	7	42	.264	.329
McKenzie, Triston	L	.203	207	42	12	0	8	22	28	63	.304	.377
Throws Right	R	.186	226	42	7	0	13	34	30	73	.283	.389
Means, John	L	.229	118	27	6	0	3	4	7	28	.272	.356
Throws Left	R	.223	439	98	15	1	27	54	19	106	.261	.446
Mears, Nick	L	.282	39	11	0	0	3	11	5	8	.356	.513
Throws Right	R	.259	54	14	3	0	2	14	8	15	.355	.426
Megill, Trevor	L	.273	44	12	1	0	1	5	4	19	.347	.364
Throws Right	R	.393	61	24	5	1	6	19	4	11	.431	.803
Megill, Tylor	L	.315	165	52	8	1	13	26	16	44	.383	.612
Throws Right	R	.200	180	36	6	0	6	19	11	55	.244	.333
Mejia, Humberto	L	.364	44	16	7	2	3	10	3	11	.396	.818
Throws Right	R	.320	50	16	6	1	2	7	6	9	.393	.600
Mejia, JC	L	.328	122	40	10	0	10	29	13	21	.397	.656
Throws Right	R	.227	88	20	4	0	3	13	11	26	.327	.375
Melancon, Mark	L	.150	100	15	4	0	0	3	9	24	.220	.190
Throws Right	R	.285	137	39	5	0	4	16	16	35	.359	.409
Middleton, Keynan	L	.231	39	9	2	0	1	7	11	9	.400	.359
Throws Right	R	.263	80	21	6	0	1	11	8	15	.344	.375
Mikolas, Miles	L	.273	88	24	4	0	2	11	9	14	.350	.386
Throws Right	R	.232	82	19	4	0	4	11	2	17	.250	.427
Miley, Wade	L	.218	124	27	3	0	3	12	7	30	.265	.315
Throws Left	R	.276	503	139	32	2	14	46	43	95	.335	.431
Miller, Andrew	L	.182	66	12	2	1	1	4	4	25	.257	.288
Throws Left	R	.392	74	29	6	1	4	15	12	15	.489	.662
Mills, Alec	L	.326	215	70	16	0	11	31	20	39	.401	.553
Throws Right	R	.263	255	67	11	0	5	25	14	48	.299	.365
Minaya, Juan	L	.250	48	12	2	0	1	5	10	12	.373	.354
Throws Right	R	.158	95	15	6	0	3	7	10	31	.252	.316
Minor, Mike	L	.253	91	23	5	1	2	9	5	26	.313	.396
Throws Left	R	.252	528	133	30	3	24	73	36	123	.301	.456
Minter, A.J.	L	.200	85	17	6	0	0	8	10	30	.276	.271
Throws Left	R	.245	110	27	10	1	2	13	10	27	.311	.409
Misiewicz, Anthony	L	.261	92	24	4	0	2	11	5	23	.303	.370
Throws Left	R	.294	126	37	8	0	5	14	10	30	.346	.476
Mize, Casey	L	.256	262	67	11	4	17	37	25	56	.322	.523
Throws Right	R	.215	293	63	9	1	7	23	16	62	.276	.324
Montas, Frankie	L	.225	346	78	20	2	8	33	37	112	.301	.364
Throws Right	R	.238	361	86	13	1	12	42	20	95	.288	.380
Montero, Rafael	L	.276	76	21	6	0	3	21	10	12	.371	.474
Throws Right	R	.309	123	38	7	0	1	14	7	30	.356	.390
Montgomery, Jordan	L	.227	132	30	1	0	4	11	6	31	.271	.326
Throws Left	R	.256	468	120	20	0	15	55	45	131	.317	.395
Moore, Matt	L	.289	90	26	3	0	3	9	8	19	.347	.422
Throws Left	R	.267	195	52	19	0	12	38	30	44	.368	.549
Morgan, Adam	L	.125	56	7	2	1	1	8	6	20	.219	.250
Throws Left	R	.405	37	15	3	0	5	11	6	8	.477	.892
Morgan, Eli	L	.261	138	36	11	0	8	17	7	25	.311	.514
Throws Right	R	.257	210	54	13	0	12	29	15	56	.308	.490
Morton, Charlie	L	.183	312	57	8	3	7	26	27	116	.273	.295
Throws Right	R	.221	357	79	9	0	9	44	31	100	.289	.322
Muller, Kyle	L	.188	32	6	0	0	1	6	3	8	.278	.281
Throws Left	R	.206	97	20	6	0	1	7	17	29	.325	.299
Musgrove, Joe	L	.230	343	79	14	4	14	37	28	101	.307	.417
Throws Right	R	.194	324	63	13	0	8	29	26	102	.266	.309
Nance, Tommy	L	.167	54	9	2	0	3	13	5	17	.233	.370
Throws Right	R	.286	56	16	2	1	2	9	8	13	.403	.464
Naughton, Packy	L	.296	27	8	0	0	1	4	2	4	.345	.407
Throws Left	R	.288	66	19	3	0	2	10	12	8	.405	.424
Neidert, Nick	L	.300	60	18	5	0	2	11	14	10	.443	.483
Throws Right	R	.197	66	13	3	0	2	6	9	11	.312	.333

Pitcher	vs	Avg	AB	H	2B	3B	HR	RBI	BB	SO	OBP	Slg
Nelson, Jimmy	L	.174	46	8	1	0	0	3	8	18	.309	.196
Throws Right	R	.115	52	6	3	0	0	3	5	26	.233	.173
Neris, Hector	L	.223	121	27	7	0	6	16	26	45	.358	.430
Throws Right	R	.185	151	28	4	1	6	25	6	53	.236	.344
Newcomb, Sean	L	.244	41	10	2	0	0	7	8	17	.392	.293
Throws Left	R	.231	78	18	5	1	1	14	19	26	.378	.359
Nola, Aaron	L	.221	349	77	15	4	14	52	17	121	.265	.407
Throws Right	R	.254	347	88	14	1	12	34	22	102	.306	.403
Nolin, Sean	L	.297	37	11	1	1	2	7	4	5	.381	.541
Throws Left	R	.304	69	21	4	1	2	6	9	15	.388	.478
Norris, Daniel	L	.205	83	17	2	0	3	14	10	28	.305	.337
Throws Left	R	.288	132	38	8	0	6	25	20	30	.382	.485
Ober, Bailey	L	.288	160	46	9	0	8	17	13	41	.345	.494
Throws Right	R	.235	196	46	7	3	12	24	6	55	.254	.485
Odorizzi, Jake	L	.250	176	44	17	1	5	19	23	42	.337	.443
Throws Right	R	.238	223	53	3	2	11	29	11	49	.282	.417
Ohtani, Shohei	L	.235	243	57	11	0	12	21	25	70	.305	.428
Throws Right	R	.178	230	41	12	0	3	15	19	86	.266	.270
Okert, Steven	L	.140	50	7	1	0	1	2	4	20	.241	.220
Throws Left	R	.214	70	15	5	0	4	11	11	20	.325	.457
Ottavino, Adam	L	.274	84	23	10	0	0	10	11	27	.384	.393
Throws Right	R	.219	146	32	6	0	5	22	24	44	.337	.363
Otto, Glenn	L	.452	31	14	4	1	0	8	3	6	.500	.645
Throws Right	R	.261	69	18	3	1	2	14	5	22	.329	.420
Oviedo, Johan	L	.272	125	34	7	1	4	18	23	20	.393	.440
Throws Right	R	.229	118	27	6	0	4	14	14	31	.328	.381
Oviedo, Luis	L	.302	53	16	5	1	3	13	14	14	.449	.604
Throws Right	R	.266	64	17	3	0	1	14	12	17	.385	.359
Paddack, Chris	L	.214	215	46	11	1	5	28	13	47	.258	.344
Throws Right	R	.325	212	69	11	3	10	30	9	52	.354	.547
Pagan, Emilio	L	.210	105	22	8	1	7	17	9	33	.270	.505
Throws Right	R	.248	137	34	10	0	9	20	9	36	.304	.518
Parker, Blake	L	.215	93	20	1	1	3	9	4	24	.247	.344
Throws Right	R	.311	74	23	5	0	2	10	10	13	.398	.459
Patino, Luis	L	.274	124	34	7	0	5	17	21	22	.378	.452
Throws Right	R	.201	174	35	5	0	7	19	8	52	.243	.351
Patton, Spencer	L	.318	66	21	5	0	0	10	12	16	.423	.394
Throws Right	R	.165	91	15	3	0	4	11	3	32	.191	.330
Payamps, Joel	L	.176	68	12	3	0	2	5	5	13	.233	.309
Throws Right	R	.262	122	32	7	0	4	20	9	25	.318	.418
Peacock, Matt	L	.327	162	53	12	2	8	31	14	13	.380	.574
Throws Right	R	.284	190	54	10	1	5	23	14	37	.332	.426
Peralta, Freddy	L	.157	274	43	7	2	8	20	33	93	.257	.285
Throws Right	R	.174	236	41	16	0	6	25	23	102	.266	.318
Peralta, Wandy	L	.246	69	17	2	1	1	5	8	19	.333	.348
Throws Left	R	.254	126	32	4	0	5	23	13	24	.319	.405
Peralta, Wily	L	.192	172	33	7	2	5	18	17	33	.270	.343
Throws Right	R	.300	180	54	10	1	7	22	21	25	.374	.483
Perez, Cionel	L	.222	36	8	0	1	2	9	5	9	.317	.444
Throws Left	R	.241	54	13	2	0	3	10	15	16	.400	.444
Perez, Martin	L	.253	95	24	7	0	1	9	3	18	.311	.358
Throws Left	R	.308	364	112	17	2	18	54	33	79	.368	.514
Peters, Dillon	L	.200	20	4	3	0	1	3	1	5	.238	.500
Throws Left	R	.256	86	22	5	2	1	8	9	18	.333	.395
Peterson, David	L	.281	64	18	2	0	2	5	6	22	.361	.406
Throws Left	R	.246	187	46	13	1	9	30	23	47	.338	.471
Petit, Yusmeiro	L	.219	114	25	5	1	6	16	6	15	.256	.439
Throws Right	R	.242	182	44	3	1	6	29	6	22	.268	.368
Pineda, Michael	L	.290	186	54	11	2	8	19	7	32	.316	.500
Throws Right	R	.246	244	60	15	0	9	25	14	56	.290	.418
Pivetta, Nick	L	.233	227	53	10	1	9	25	31	69	.330	.405
Throws Right	R	.235	358	84	21	1	15	51	34	106	.304	.425
Plesac, Zach	L	.234	252	59	14	1	7	26	25	44	.304	.381
Throws Right	R	.260	300	78	19	0	16	43	9	56	.294	.483
Plutko, Adam	L	.337	83	28	4	2	6	18	5	21	.391	.651
Throws Right	R	.270	137	37	11	0	11	33	22	23	.364	.591
Pomeranz, Drew	L	.156	32	5	1	0	0	2	3	14	.222	.188
Throws Left	R	.241	58	14	2	1	2	3	7	16	.318	.414
Ponce, Cody	L	.338	68	23	8	1	6	21	3	10	.356	.750
Throws Right	R	.347	95	33	10	0	2	14	8	26	.400	.516
Ponce de Leon, Daniel	L	.267	60	16	4	0	4	12	11	12	.380	.533
Throws Right	R	.239	67	16	8	0	1	10	11	12	.372	.403
Pop, Zach	L	.220	82	18	6	2	2	20	11	18	.312	.415
Throws Right	R	.275	131	36	4	0	1	15	13	33	.375	.328
Poteet, Cody	L	.197	61	12	4	0	5	12	5	16	.258	.508
Throws Right	R	.236	55	13	3	0	2	5	11	16	.364	.400

Pitchers vs. Left-Handed and Right-Handed Batters

Pitcher	vs	Avg	AB	H	2B	3B	HR	RBI	BB	SO	OBP	Slg
Pressly, Ryan	L	.194	108	21	7	0	1	6	5	40	.230	.287
Throws Right	R	.219	128	28	2	0	3	14	8	41	.265	.305
Price, David	L	.276	105	29	7	1	2	11	9	20	.353	.419
Throws Left	R	.270	185	50	12	0	6	24	17	38	.330	.432
Quantrill, Cal	L	.214	276	59	16	2	8	21	26	74	.279	.373
Throws Right	R	.254	276	70	7	1	8	25	21	47	.326	.373
Quijada, Jose	L	.263	38	10	3	0	1	5	6	13	.378	.421
Throws Left	R	.179	56	10	2	0	1	6	9	25	.292	.268
Quintana, Jose	L	.152	79	12	2	0	2	5	11	36	.264	.253
Throws Left	R	.344	180	62	13	0	10	36	24	49	.417	.583
Rainey, Tanner	L	.212	52	11	3	1	3	8	9	19	.359	.481
Throws Right	R	.257	70	18	2	1	3	19	16	23	.391	.443
Raley, Brooks	L	.195	77	15	2	0	0	3	4	35	.262	.221
Throws Left	R	.259	108	28	4	0	6	32	12	30	.333	.463
Ramirez, Erasmo	L	.324	37	12	1	0	3	9	1	9	.350	.595
Throws Right	R	.188	64	12	2	1	1	2	4	11	.232	.297
Ramirez, Noe	L	.211	57	12	2	0	1	4	7	9	.297	.298
Throws Right	R	.153	72	11	3	0	2	9	5	20	.232	.278
Ramirez, Yohan	L	.235	34	8	0	0	3	8	4	10	.333	.500
Throws Right	R	.161	62	10	2	0	3	11	8	25	.278	.339
Rasmussen, Drew	L	.202	104	21	5	1	1	9	7	27	.252	.298
Throws Right	R	.205	176	36	5	1	4	17	18	46	.277	.313
Ray, Robbie	L	.187	134	25	6	0	6	7	6	44	.227	.366
Throws Left	R	.216	580	125	25	3	27	54	46	204	.276	.409
Reyes, Alex	L	.155	129	20	2	0	5	26	30	43	.319	.287
Throws Right	R	.195	133	26	2	0	4	10	22	52	.312	.301
Richards, Garrett	L	.257	210	54	14	1	5	25	24	42	.331	.405
Throws Right	R	.309	337	104	21	2	14	52	36	73	.381	.507
Richards, Trevor	L	.149	94	14	1	0	6	10	12	34	.245	.351
Throws Right	R	.194	134	26	4	1	6	18	10	44	.250	.373
Robles, Hansel	L	.219	105	23	5	1	5	17	22	29	.354	.429
Throws Right	R	.235	149	35	12	0	3	19	15	47	.325	.376
Rodon, Carlos	L	.240	104	25	3	1	1	5	5	35	.275	.317
Throws Left	R	.175	377	66	12	0	12	33	31	150	.249	.302
Rodriguez, Chris	L	.213	47	10	2	0	0	3	6	11	.327	.255
Throws Right	R	.265	68	18	6	0	0	5	9	18	.367	.353
Rodriguez, Eduardo	L	.258	132	34	9	0	5	19	5	47	.295	.439
Throws Left	R	.282	490	138	32	1	14	53	42	138	.337	.437
Rodriguez, Jefry	L	.250	44	11	1	0	1	7	4	6	.313	.341
Throws Right	R	.280	50	14	0	0	5	9	13	14	.438	.580
Rodriguez, Joely	L	.203	59	12	1	0	1	8	7	20	.288	.271
Throws Left	R	.339	121	41	4	0	3	19	11	27	.380	.446
Rodriguez, Richard	L	.214	117	25	6	1	6	15	4	24	.246	.436
Throws Right	R	.205	122	25	5	1	2	8	6	18	.248	.311
Rogers, Josh	L	.143	42	6	0	0	0	1	2	8	.200	.143
Throws Left	R	.286	91	26	5	0	7	12	12	14	.371	.571
Rogers, Taylor	L	.170	53	9	3	0	2	9	1	29	.185	.340
Throws Left	R	.287	101	29	4	0	2	15	7	30	.327	.386
Rogers, Trevor	L	.259	112	29	5	0	0	7	17	39	.359	.304
Throws Left	R	.206	378	78	26	0	6	33	29	118	.269	.323
Rogers, Tyler	L	.179	140	25	4	0	1	9	6	24	.230	.229
Throws Right	R	.297	165	49	7	0	4	15	7	31	.329	.412
Romano, Jordan	L	.140	93	13	2	0	2	5	7	43	.208	.226
Throws Right	R	.211	133	28	6	0	5	14	18	42	.305	.368
Romo, Sergio	L	.235	85	20	1	1	3	8	12	18	.330	.376
Throws Right	R	.240	150	36	9	0	6	31	9	42	.290	.420
Ross, Joe	L	.254	201	51	11	0	10	32	25	57	.349	.458
Throws Right	R	.222	212	47	6	0	7	20	9	52	.262	.349
Rucker, Michael	L	.271	59	16	4	0	2	12	2	17	.295	.441
Throws Right	R	.302	53	16	3	0	3	12	9	13	.415	.528
Ruiz, Jose	L	.208	101	21	8	0	6	18	12	22	.289	.465
Throws Right	R	.211	142	30	6	0	2	18	13	41	.276	.296
Ryan, Joe	L	.149	47	7	2	0	3	6	4	12	.216	.383
Throws Right	R	.188	48	9	3	0	1	6	1	18	.204	.313
Ryu, Hyun-Jin	L	.255	141	36	11	1	2	15	8	30	.295	.390
Throws Left	R	.259	517	134	27	2	22	63	29	113	.299	.447
Sadler, Casey	L	.116	43	5	2	0	1	1	4	14	.208	.233
Throws Right	R	.156	90	14	0	1	0	4	6	23	.206	.178
Sale, Chris	L	.154	26	4	1	0	0	1	0	8	.154	.192
Throws Left	R	.291	141	41	4	1	6	13	12	44	.363	.461
Sampson, Adrian	L	.226	62	14	4	0	3	8	6	15	.304	.435
Throws Right	R	.235	68	16	2	0	5	7	2	13	.307	.485
Sanchez, Aaron	L	.217	60	13	3	0	2	9	8	11	.319	.367
Throws Right	R	.247	77	19	2	1	0	3	7	15	.333	.299
Sanchez, Miguel	L	.265	49	13	3	0	3	7	5	6	.339	.510
Throws Right	R	.269	52	14	3	0	1	7	9	17	.381	.385

Pitcher	vs	Avg	AB	H	2B	3B	HR	RBI	BB	SO	OBP	Slg
Sandlin, Nick	L	.146	41	6	3	1	1	9	6	14	.286	.341
Throws Right	R	.192	78	15	2	0	1	9	11	34	.304	.256
Sandoval, Patrick	L	.151	93	14	2	0	4	11	5	28	.216	.301
Throws Left	R	.241	228	55	4	2	7	17	31	66	.333	.368
Santana, Dennis	L	.232	82	19	4	1	2	13	14	20	.344	.378
Throws Right	R	.246	118	29	2	0	2	16	18	26	.357	.314
Santana, Edgar	L	.172	64	11	2	0	0	0	7	10	.254	.203
Throws Right	R	.265	98	26	2	0	7	20	5	23	.301	.500
Santana, Ervin	L	.275	102	28	5	0	7	14	13	22	.353	.529
Throws Right	R	.248	149	37	11	2	2	19	9	30	.298	.389
Santiago, Hector	L	.290	31	9	3	0	1	3	4	12	.361	.484
Throws Left	R	.243	74	18	5	0	1	6	7	18	.309	.351
Santillan, Tony	L	.242	66	16	0	2	2	8	11	21	.386	.394
Throws Right	R	.198	91	18	4	0	5	9	10	35	.283	.407
Saucedo, Tayler	L	.139	36	5	1	0	0	0	4	12	.244	.167
Throws Left	R	.283	60	17	8	0	1	13	6	7	.353	.467
Sawamura, Hirokazu	L	.218	55	12	4	0	2	4	14	18	.377	.400
Throws Right	R	.231	143	33	9	0	7	18	18	43	.323	.441
Sborz, Josh	L	.271	85	23	5	1	4	13	10	26	.344	.494
Throws Right	R	.212	137	29	5	0	3	14	22	43	.317	.314
Scherzer, Max	L	.192	317	61	12	1	10	26	26	108	.266	.331
Throws Right	R	.177	327	58	9	1	13	23	10	128	.211	.330
Scott, Tanner	L	.203	69	14	3	0	0	12	15	28	.341	.246
Throws Left	R	.250	136	34	1	1	6	24	22	42	.373	.404
Senzatela, Antonio	L	.294	303	89	23	3	5	33	18	43	.340	.439
Throws Right	R	.281	317	89	16	1	7	38	14	62	.317	.404
Sewald, Paul	L	.165	97	16	2	1	5	11	17	42	.289	.361
Throws Right	R	.183	142	26	5	0	5	12	7	62	.221	.324
Shaw, Bryan	L	.225	151	34	8	1	2	10	20	34	.316	.331
Throws Right	R	.245	143	35	5	0	8	28	18	37	.333	.448
Sheffield, Jordan	L	.220	59	13	1	0	1	5	8	11	.319	.288
Throws Right	R	.146	41	6	1	0	1	4	5	9	.255	.244
Sheffield, Justus	L	.266	79	21	5	0	2	14	12	17	.366	.405
Throws Left	R	.332	253	84	19	0	12	48	31	46	.409	.549
Shoemaker, Matt	L	.331	121	40	8	0	8	25	16	17	.403	.595
Throws Right	R	.264	125	33	6	0	7	27	11	23	.331	.480
Shreve, Chasen	L	.200	90	18	4	0	3	15	12	21	.288	.344
Throws Left	R	.221	113	25	8	0	4	12	16	24	.321	.398
Sims, Lucas	L	.214	70	15	0	0	4	13	11	33	.341	.386
Throws Right	R	.190	100	19	11	0	2	12	7	43	.245	.360
Singer, Brady	L	.268	272	73	14	1	11	49	33	77	.361	.449
Throws Right	R	.296	247	73	7	2	3	22	20	54	.356	.377
Skubal, Tarik	L	.264	110	29	8	0	1	7	7	28	.311	.364
Throws Left	R	.240	466	112	20	0	34	64	40	136	.305	.502
Slegers, Aaron	L	.395	38	15	5	0	3	9	8	4	.500	.763
Throws Right	R	.298	94	28	6	0	3	21	7	21	.353	.457
Smith, Burch	L	.316	57	18	5	0	2	13	7	8	.391	.509
Throws Right	R	.256	117	30	7	0	3	18	4	20	.285	.393
Smith, Caleb	L	.250	128	32	7	0	7	23	11	36	.324	.469
Throws Left	R	.203	301	61	12	0	13	37	52	88	.326	.372
Smith, Drew	L	.145	62	9	2	0	4	6	10	19	.270	.371
Throws Right	R	.226	84	19	7	0	3	6	6	22	.286	.417
Smith, Joe	L	.250	40	10	1	0	0	8	1	8	.273	.275
Throws Right	R	.314	118	37	8	1	5	25	7	26	.362	.525
Smith, Riley	L	.280	107	30	7	0	5	16	5	14	.319	.486
Throws Right	R	.326	172	56	19	2	5	30	10	22	.370	.547
Smith, Will	L	.212	66	14	1	1	3	12	9	22	.308	.394
Throws Left	R	.192	182	35	13	1	8	15	19	65	.283	.407
Smyly, Drew	L	.285	137	39	10	0	8	21	7	37	.315	.533
Throws Left	R	.263	357	94	13	0	19	41	34	80	.330	.459
Snell, Blake	L	.144	111	16	5	0	2	11	10	48	.215	.243
Throws Left	R	.235	361	85	21	1	14	47	59	122	.347	.416
Soria, Joakim	L	.314	51	16	5	0	3	5	4	11	.375	.588
Throws Right	R	.245	94	23	6	1	3	16	8	29	.301	.426
Soto, Gregory	L	.183	71	13	2	0	0	9	10	23	.284	.211
Throws Left	R	.205	161	33	5	0	7	22	30	53	.330	.366
Springs, Jeffrey	L	.263	57	15	4	1	3	8	5	19	.317	.526
Throws Left	R	.190	105	20	2	1	6	15	9	44	.252	.400
Stammen, Craig	L	.224	143	32	4	0	7	13	6	32	.257	.399
Throws Right	R	.244	193	47	7	0	6	27	7	51	.277	.373
Stanek, Ryne	L	.245	98	24	2	0	6	14	18	30	.368	.449
Throws Right	R	.148	149	22	5	0	2	15	19	53	.260	.221
Staumont, Josh	L	.208	96	20	2	0	2	12	14	28	.321	.292
Throws Right	R	.165	139	23	6	0	4	12	13	44	.237	.295
Steckenrider, Drew	L	.178	107	19	4	0	1	7	14	24	.268	.243
Throws Right	R	.243	136	33	10	0	4	13	3	34	.280	.404

Pitchers vs. Left-Handed and Right-Handed Batters

Pitcher	vs	Avg	AB	H	2B	3B	HR	RBI	BB	SO	OBP	Slg
Steele, Justin	L	.098	41	4	1	0	1	3	10	18	.275	.195
Throws Left	R	.264	174	46	7	0	11	24	17	41	.347	.494
Stephan, Trevor	L	.239	109	26	5	0	4	12	16	30	.341	.394
Throws Right	R	.230	139	32	8	0	11	23	15	45	.312	.525
Stephenson, Robert	L	.241	83	20	2	3	3	17	6	28	.292	.446
Throws Right	R	.242	91	22	4	1	2	13	12	24	.336	.374
Stratton, Chris	L	.260	131	34	6	0	4	14	18	38	.349	.397
Throws Right	R	.213	169	36	5	1	5	20	15	48	.277	.343
Strickland, Hunter	L	.250	76	19	5	0	1	3	8	10	.321	.355
Throws Right	R	.193	140	27	7	0	7	15	14	48	.274	.393
Stripling, Ross	L	.218	147	32	7	2	7	15	16	42	.299	.435
Throws Right	R	.270	248	67	14	0	16	36	14	52	.308	.520
Stroman, Marcus	L	.239	326	78	8	2	8	28	23	71	.296	.350
Throws Right	R	.245	339	83	15	1	9	34	21	87	.290	.375
Suarez, Jose	L	.315	92	29	8	0	5	15	10	19	.394	.565
Throws Left	R	.202	277	56	15	0	6	24	26	66	.274	.321
Suarez, Ranger	L	.109	101	11	2	0	0	4	8	37	.182	.129
Throws Left	R	.225	275	62	7	1	4	18	25	70	.298	.302
Suero, Wander	L	.273	77	21	4	0	5	13	10	20	.356	.519
Throws Right	R	.261	92	24	6	0	6	19	5	24	.320	.522
Sulser, Cole	L	.186	113	21	5	1	1	8	13	31	.270	.274
Throws Right	R	.227	119	27	4	0	4	15	10	42	.285	.361
Suter, Brent	L	.215	93	20	3	1	3	17	9	24	.291	.366
Throws Left	R	.269	193	52	11	0	6	21	15	45	.322	.420
Swanson, Erik	L	.234	64	15	2	0	3	8	5	16	.290	.406
Throws Right	R	.191	68	13	2	3	2	8	5	19	.253	.397
Taillon, Jameson	L	.225	231	52	9	0	12	27	30	61	.313	.420
Throws Right	R	.247	316	78	18	1	12	42	14	79	.288	.424
Tapia, Domingo	L	.194	36	7	2	0	0	3	6	7	.310	.250
Throws Right	R	.214	84	18	3	0	1	9	9	19	.290	.286
Tate, Dillon	L	.235	81	19	4	0	4	21	13	16	.337	.432
Throws Right	R	.250	168	42	10	1	3	31	10	33	.307	.375
Taylor, Blake	L	.123	65	8	3	0	2	7	7	26	.208	.262
Throws Left	R	.306	98	30	6	0	4	17	15	15	.391	.490
Taylor, Josh	L	.146	82	12	1	0	0	0	7	28	.222	.159
Throws Left	R	.327	101	33	7	0	2	23	16	32	.429	.455
Tepera, Ryan	L	.135	74	10	2	0	1	7	8	30	.226	.203
Throws Right	R	.180	139	25	5	2	3	19	11	44	.250	.309
Thielbar, Caleb	L	.214	84	18	6	0	3	12	4	26	.253	.393
Throws Left	R	.242	153	37	10	0	5	21	16	51	.320	.405
Thompson, Keegan	L	.240	100	24	4	0	6	11	16	23	.345	.460
Throws Right	R	.226	106	24	5	0	3	14	15	32	.331	.358
Thompson, Mason	L	.222	36	8	2	0	2	4	11	7	.404	.444
Throws Right	R	.358	67	24	3	0	2	11	4	16	.403	.493
Thompson, Ryan	L	.200	20	4	1	0	1	2	2	5	.304	.400
Throws Right	R	.214	103	22	7	1	2	13	7	32	.270	.359
Thompson, Zach	L	.262	130	34	12	2	3	14	17	29	.353	.454
Throws Right	R	.196	148	29	7	0	3	15	11	37	.253	.304
Thornton, Trent	L	.241	58	14	4	0	2	8	7	20	.323	.414
Throws Right	R	.294	136	40	8	1	10	18	9	32	.353	.588
Tomlin, Josh	L	.305	82	25	5	1	2	9	2	15	.329	.463
Throws Right	R	.341	129	44	8	1	8	28	3	22	.353	.605
Toussaint, Touki	L	.208	72	15	2	0	5	12	13	17	.348	.444
Throws Right	R	.250	112	28	4	0	6	15	9	31	.320	.446
Treinen, Blake	L	.140	107	15	4	0	2	3	15	40	.262	.234
Throws Right	R	.207	150	31	0	0	3	13	10	45	.256	.267
Trivino, Lou	L	.282	110	31	6	0	3	10	19	23	.388	.418
Throws Right	R	.176	159	28	5	0	2	12	15	44	.263	.245
Turnbull, Spencer	L	.176	91	16	2	1	2	6	6	22	.250	.286
Throws Right	R	.231	91	21	5	0	0	8	6	22	.290	.286
Underwood Jr., Duane	L	.296	125	37	9	0	7	25	12	24	.362	.536
Throws Right	R	.250	160	40	8	2	2	22	15	41	.318	.363
Urena, Jose	L	.325	197	64	15	2	8	35	23	18	.397	.543
Throws Right	R	.261	211	55	14	0	6	28	19	49	.328	.412
Urias, Julio	L	.210	181	38	9	0	8	15	5	56	.247	.392
Throws Left	R	.222	510	113	24	0	11	46	33	139	.272	.333
Urquidy, Jose	L	.190	168	32	8	1	5	17	10	39	.235	.339
Throws Right	R	.238	231	55	12	1	12	25	9	51	.273	.455
Valdez, Cesar	L	.266	79	21	3	0	3	10	9	17	.348	.418
Throws Right	R	.357	115	41	11	1	5	28	5	28	.380	.600
Valdez, Framber	L	.225	80	18	2	0	3	8	12	26	.354	.363
Throws Left	R	.219	421	92	14	1	9	36	46	99	.305	.321
Valdez, Phillips	L	.311	61	19	3	0	1	14	5	13	.353	.410
Throws Right	R	.186	86	16	2	0	3	18	14	22	.343	.314
Velasquez, Vince	L	.297	145	43	8	4	7	22	21	40	.386	.552
Throws Right	R	.221	217	48	14	0	16	36	28	61	.321	.507

Pitcher	vs	Avg	AB	H	2B	3B	HR	RBI	BB	SO	OBP	Slg
Vesia, Alex	L	.123	65	8	3	0	1	6	8	29	.240	.215
Throws Left	R	.129	70	9	2	0	5	10	14	25	.267	.371
Vest, Will	L	.279	61	17	6	0	1	13	5	10	.348	.426
Throws Right	R	.296	71	21	7	0	1	13	13	17	.407	.437
Voth, Austin	L	.267	101	27	4	0	6	16	18	18	.380	.485
Throws Right	R	.265	113	30	9	0	4	22	10	41	.323	.451
Wacha, Michael	L	.243	185	45	8	0	8	23	13	42	.300	.416
Throws Right	R	.287	303	87	17	1	15	43	18	79	.327	.498
Wainwright, Adam	L	.229	397	91	22	2	10	35	26	86	.285	.370
Throws Right	R	.209	368	77	12	0	11	31	24	88	.264	.332
Walker, Taijuan	L	.192	250	48	11	0	10	31	32	63	.284	.356
Throws Right	R	.250	340	85	14	0	16	42	23	83	.302	.432
Wantz, Andrew	L	.282	39	11	0	0	3	13	7	12	.391	.513
Throws Right	R	.182	66	12	4	0	2	11	4	26	.260	.333
Watkins, Spenser	L	.296	108	32	7	1	5	20	8	20	.350	.519
Throws Right	R	.344	122	42	10	1	9	29	11	15	.394	.664
Watson, Tony	L	.195	82	16	2	0	2	6	7	21	.258	.293
Throws Left	R	.192	125	24	5	0	2	11	11	23	.257	.280
Weathers, Ryan	L	.291	117	34	6	0	4	14	5	21	.325	.444
Throws Left	R	.273	245	67	13	0	16	38	25	51	.344	.522
Weaver, Luke	L	.245	102	25	7	2	6	15	10	17	.310	.529
Throws Right	R	.224	147	33	7	4	5	18	10	45	.278	.429
Webb, Jacob	L	.254	59	15	4	2	0	7	7	12	.328	.390
Throws Right	R	.299	77	23	2	0	4	20	7	21	.365	.481
Webb, Logan	L	.260	265	69	12	1	4	27	22	66	.320	.358
Throws Right	R	.210	281	59	10	1	5	21	14	92	.262	.306
Wells, Alexander	L	.292	48	14	1	1	1	4	4	12	.358	.417
Throws Left	R	.302	129	39	6	0	9	26	12	14	.368	.558
Wells, Tyler	L	.167	72	12	1	1	1	9	5	27	.218	.250
Throws Right	R	.206	136	28	4	1	8	25	7	38	.248	.426
Wendelken, J.B.	L	.292	72	21	2	0	2	9	13	13	.400	.403
Throws Right	R	.230	100	23	6	0	2	13	9	26	.294	.350
Wheeler, Zack	L	.213	422	90	15	3	8	28	29	133	.270	.320
Throws Right	R	.218	363	79	14	0	8	35	17	114	.259	.322
White, Mitch	L	.230	87	20	4	0	3	12	9	24	.299	.379
Throws Right	R	.200	90	18	3	0	3	16	8	25	.263	.333
Whitley, Kodi	L	.200	35	7	1	0	0	1	4	11	.275	.229
Throws Right	R	.154	52	8	1	0	1	6	8	16	.262	.231
Whitlock, Garrett	L	.293	99	29	6	0	4	15	7	24	.349	.475
Throws Right	R	.199	176	35	8	0	2	8	10	57	.243	.278
Wick, Rowan	L	.182	44	8	0	0	0	9	7	15	.302	.182
Throws Right	R	.231	39	9	1	0	1	3	7	14	.348	.333
Widener, Taylor	L	.256	133	34	11	0	8	20	20	34	.365	.519
Throws Right	R	.226	137	31	5	0	6	15	17	39	.325	.394
Williams, Devin	L	.190	100	19	2	1	4	9	19	38	.322	.350
Throws Right	R	.181	94	17	2	0	1	9	9	49	.260	.234
Williams, Trevor	L	.272	184	50	15	1	5	19	17	41	.340	.446
Throws Right	R	.302	182	55	10	2	6	25	14	49	.354	.478
Wilson, Bryse	L	.279	154	43	7	0	9	17	14	18	.339	.500
Throws Right	R	.302	139	42	11	0	6	20	8	28	.336	.511
Winkler, Dan	L	.229	70	16	5	0	1	8	12	19	.353	.343
Throws Right	R	.200	80	16	4	0	4	18	18	21	.390	.400
Wisler, Matt	L	.246	69	17	3	2	2	12	3	27	.267	.435
Throws Right	R	.216	111	24	6	0	4	17	8	35	.275	.378
Wittgren, Nick	L	.320	97	31	10	0	6	22	11	21	.396	.608
Throws Right	R	.219	137	30	2	1	7	15	6	40	.248	.401
Wood, Alex	L	.258	124	32	4	0	3	10	8	29	.311	.363
Throws Left	R	.230	405	93	20	3	11	42	31	123	.307	.375
Woodford, Jake	L	.317	123	39	5	2	5	23	7	21	.353	.512
Throws Right	R	.208	130	27	6	0	2	20	18	29	.325	.300
Woodruff, Brandon	L	.182	330	60	6	1	10	19	26	111	.245	.297
Throws Right	R	.219	320	70	10	2	8	31	17	100	.267	.338
Yang, Hyeon-jong	L	.293	41	12	2	1	2	7	4	3	.356	.537
Throws Left	R	.297	101	30	3	0	7	18	12	22	.374	.535
Yarbrough, Ryan	L	.235	119	28	5	0	2	12	9	34	.295	.328
Throws Left	R	.275	491	135	32	2	23	78	18	83	.309	.489
Ynoa, Huascar	L	.211	152	32	12	1	5	15	10	45	.261	.401
Throws Right	R	.234	188	44	8	1	9	25	15	55	.301	.431
Young, Alex	L	.284	81	23	1	1	5	13	11	22	.370	.506
Throws Left	R	.321	131	42	8	1	7	40	16	21	.401	.557
Zimmer, Kyle	L	.179	78	14	2	0	1	9	15	23	.302	.244
Throws Right	R	.288	111	32	6	0	6	25	15	23	.370	.505
Zimmermann, Bruce	L	.321	53	17	2	0	3	6	6	14	.390	.528
Throws Left	R	.283	205	58	8	0	11	27	16	42	.338	.483
Zuber, Tyler	L	.308	52	16	4	0	5	12	6	11	.390	.673
Throws Right	R	.192	52	10	0	0	1	8	11	14	.328	.250

Pitchers vs. Left-Handed and Right-Handed Batters

Pitcher	vs	Avg	AB	H	2B	3B	HR	RBI	BB	SO	OBP	Slg
AL	L	.240	-	-	-	-	-	-	-	-	.319	.405
	R	.249	-	-	-	-	-	-	-	-	.316	.419
NL	L	.239	-	-	-	-	-	-	-	-	.320	.404
	R	.244	-	-	-	-	-	-	-	-	.315	.411
MLB	L	.240	-	-	-	-	-	-	-	-	.319	.404
	R	.247	-	-	-	-	-	-	-	-	.315	.415

2021 Leaderboards

Mark Simon

I love me some unheralded statistical leaders.

You can find a bunch on the next few pages. Let me provide a helpful guide.

- Rays catcher Mike Zunino DESTROYED left-handed pitching this season. He slashed .342/.419/.868 with 16 home runs in 114 at-bats against lefties. His 1.287 OPS was well-ahead of the next-closest player.

  Zunino significantly struggled against right-handed pitching (.151 batting average). But against lefties, he was an MVP-caliber player.

- Brewers outfielder Avisaíl García was a hacker and he had the results to back it up. García led the NL in first-pitch swing percentage at just shy of 50%. No other player in the league was even close to his percentage.

- German Márquez won't be happy if there's a universal DH. He was the pitcher OPS leader after hitting .264 with 5 doubles and a home run in 2021.

- Mariners starting pitcher Chris Flexen entered 2021 with an 8.07 career ERA and plenty of doubters after spending the 2020 season in Korea. But while overseas, Flexen made himself into a good pitcher. He led the majors by inducing 22 groundball double plays and finished 14-6 with a 3.61 ERA for a team that contended until the season's final day.

- Braves reliever Tyler Matzek had 24 holds and no blown saves. He led NL pitchers in hold + save percentage. That's an unheralded bullpen success story on a division-winning team for 2021. Similarly, Josh Staumont was perfect for the Royals in 21 opportunities. He netted five saves and 16 holds.

Your turn to look for some. Have fun!

2021 American League Batting Leaders

Batting Average
(minimum 502 PA)

Gurriel, Yuli	.319
Brantley, Michael	.311
Guerrero Jr., Vladimir	.311
Anderson, Tim	.309
Lopez, Nicky	.300
Bichette, Bo	.298
Hernandez, Teoscar	.296
Bogaerts, Xander	.295
Tucker, Kyle	.294
France, Ty	.291

On Base Percentage
(minimum 502 PA)

Guerrero Jr., Vladimir	.401
Gurriel, Yuli	.383
Moncada, Yoan	.375
Judge, Aaron	.373
Ohtani, Shohei	.372
Olson, Matt	.371
Bogaerts, Xander	.370
France, Ty	.368
Correa, Carlos	.366
Lopez, Nicky	.365

Slugging Average
(minimum 502 PA)

Guerrero Jr., Vladimir	.601
Ohtani, Shohei	.592
Tucker, Kyle	.557
Judge, Aaron	.544
Perez, Salvador	.544
Olson, Matt	.540
Semien, Marcus	.538
Devers, Rafael	.538
Ramirez, Jose	.538
Alvarez, Yordan	.531

Home Runs

Guerrero Jr., Vladimir	48
Perez, Salvador	48
Ohtani, Shohei	46
Semien, Marcus	45
Haniger, Mitch	39
Judge, Aaron	39
Lowe, Brandon	39
Olson, Matt	39
Devers, Rafael	38
Gallo, Joey	38

Games

Merrifield, Whit	162
Semien, Marcus	162
Guerrero Jr., Vladimir	161
Perez, Salvador	161
Crawford, J.P.	160
Bichette, Bo	159
Mullins II, Cedric	159
Seager, Kyle	159
3 tied with	158

Plate Appearances

Semien, Marcus	724
Merrifield, Whit	720
Guerrero Jr., Vladimir	698
Haniger, Mitch	691
Bichette, Bo	690
Crawford, J.P.	687
LeMahieu, DJ	679
Altuve, Jose	678
Kiner-Falefa, Isiah	677
Mullins II, Cedric	675

At Bats

Merrifield, Whit	664
Semien, Marcus	652
Bichette, Bo	640
Kiner-Falefa, Isiah	635
Fletcher, David	626
Schoop, Jonathan	623
Haniger, Mitch	620
Perez, Salvador	620
Crawford, J.P.	619
Guerrero Jr., Vladimir	604

Hits

Bichette, Bo	191
Guerrero Jr., Vladimir	188
Merrifield, Whit	184
Mullins II, Cedric	175
Schoop, Jonathan	173
Semien, Marcus	173
Kiner-Falefa, Isiah	172
Crawford, J.P.	169
Gurriel, Yuli	169
Perez, Salvador	169

Singles

Kiner-Falefa, Isiah	136
Fletcher, David	132
Bichette, Bo	131
Merrifield, Whit	129
LeMahieu, DJ	125
Crawford, J.P.	123
Gurriel, Yuli	123
Lopez, Nicky	120
Schoop, Jonathan	120
Straw, Myles	119

Doubles

Candelario, Jeimer	42
Martinez, J.D.	42
Merrifield, Whit	42
Semien, Marcus	39
Crawford, J.P.	37
Devers, Rafael	37
Mullins II, Cedric	37
Tucker, Kyle	37
4 tied with	35

Triples

Ohtani, Shohei	8
Baddoo, Akil	7
Kiermaier, Kevin	7
Arraez, Luis	6
Castro, Willi	6
Dozier, Hunter	6
Lopez, Nicky	6
Rosario, Amed	6
4 tied with	5

Total Bases

Guerrero Jr., Vladimir	363
Semien, Marcus	351
Perez, Salvador	337
Devers, Rafael	318
Ohtani, Shohei	318
Mullins II, Cedric	312
Bichette, Bo	310
Olson, Matt	305
Haniger, Mitch	301
Judge, Aaron	299

Runs Scored

Guerrero Jr., Vladimir	123
Bichette, Bo	121
Altuve, Jose	117
Semien, Marcus	115
Ramirez, Jose	111
Haniger, Mitch	110
Correa, Carlos	104
Ohtani, Shohei	103
Devers, Rafael	101
Olson, Matt	101

RBI

Perez, Salvador	121
Abreu, Jose	117
Hernandez, Teoscar	116
Devers, Rafael	113
Guerrero Jr., Vladimir	111
Olson, Matt	111
Meadows, Austin	106
Alvarez, Yordan	104
Ramirez, Jose	103
2 tied with	102

Walks

Gallo, Joey	111
Grossman, Robbie	98
Ohtani, Shohei	96
Olson, Matt	88
Grandal, Yasmani	87
Guerrero Jr., Vladimir	86
Santana, Carlos	86
Moncada, Yoan	84
Chapman, Matt	80
Lowe, Nate	80

Strikeouts

Gallo, Joey	213
Chapman, Matt	202
Garcia, Adolis	194
Ohtani, Shohei	189
Sano, Miguel	183
Arozarena, Randy	170
Perez, Salvador	170
Haniger, Mitch	169
Lowe, Brandon	167
Lowe, Nate	162

2021 American League Batting Leaders

Intentional Walks	
Ohtani, Shohei	20
Olson, Matt	12
Cruz, Nelson	10
Ramirez, Jose	10
Devers, Rafael	7
Guerrero Jr., Vladimir	7
Martinez, J.D.	6
Verdugo, Alex	6
Walsh, Jared	6
3 tied with	5

BA Bases Loaded	
(minimum 10 PA)	
Hernandez, Teoscar	.643
Cabrera, Miguel	.625
Baddoo, Akil	.600
Gosselin, Phil	.600
Voit, Luke	.600
Hays, Austin	.556
Gurriel Jr., Lourdes	.545
Walsh, Jared	.538
7 tied with	.500

Sacrifice Hits	
Lopez, Nicky	12
Garcia, Leury	9
Hedges, Austin	7
Fletcher, David	6
Gardner, Brett	5
8 tied with	4

Sacrifice Flies	
Gurriel, Yuli	12
Merrifield, Whit	12
Olson, Matt	11
Abreu, Jose	10
Cabrera, Miguel	9
Chapman, Matt	9
Cruz, Nelson	9
4 tied with	8

BA Close & Late	
(minimum 50 PA)	
Castro, Jason	.375
Judge, Aaron	.364
Lopez, Nicky	.344
Mancini, Trey	.344
Torres, Gleyber	.329
Gurriel, Yuli	.319
Laureano, Ramon	.319
Castro, Harold	.315
Arozarena, Randy	.313
Polanco, Jorge	.307

Batting Average w/ RISP	
(minimum 100 PA)	
Gurriel Jr., Lourdes	.368
Baddoo, Akil	.359
Lowrie, Jed	.342
Bichette, Bo	.340
Martinez, J.D.	.335
Hays, Austin	.333
Polanco, Jorge	.333
Judge, Aaron	.331
Walsh, Jared	.325
Hernandez, Teoscar	.323

SLG vs. LHP	
(minimum 125 PA)	
Zunino, Mike	.868
Hernandez, Teoscar	.744
Perez, Salvador	.640
Ohtani, Shohei	.636
Olson, Matt	.608
Abreu, Jose	.603
Judge, Aaron	.596
Haase, Eric	.592
Tucker, Kyle	.578
2 tied with	.571

SLG vs. RHP	
(minimum 377 PA)	
Devers, Rafael	.621
Guerrero Jr., Vladimir	.620
Walsh, Jared	.589
Lowe, Brandon	.581
Ohtani, Shohei	.566
Semien, Marcus	.564
Mullins II, Cedric	.558
Ramirez, Jose	.544
Meadows, Austin	.536
Martinez, J.D.	.536

Leadoff Hitters OBP	
(minimum 150 PA)	
Arozarena, Randy	.397
Arraez, Luis	.368
Canha, Mark	.364
Lowe, Brandon	.364
Springer, George	.361
Straw, Myles	.360
Mullins II, Cedric	.360
LeMahieu, DJ	.350
Altuve, Jose	.350
Crawford, J.P.	.345

Cleanup Hitters SLG	
(minimum 150 PA)	
Meadows, Austin	.574
Gallo, Joey	.571
Devers, Rafael	.540
Bichette, Bo	.536
Alvarez, Yordan	.534
Bogaerts, Xander	.531
Stanton, Giancarlo	.529
Perez, Salvador	.520
Hernandez, Teoscar	.510
Donaldson, Josh	.496

BA vs. LHP	
(minimum 125 PA)	
Hernandez, Teoscar	.372
Culberson, Charlie	.346
Zunino, Mike	.342
Bichette, Bo	.340
Schoop, Jonathan	.333
Gurriel, Yuli	.326
Anderson, Tim	.319
Fletcher, David	.316
Cruz, Nelson	.316
Rosario, Amed	.313

BA vs. RHP	
(minimum 377 PA)	
Walsh, Jared	.333
Verdugo, Alex	.321
Guerrero Jr., Vladimir	.317
Gurriel, Yuli	.315
Anderson, Tim	.306
Lopez, Nicky	.304
Bogaerts, Xander	.301
Mullins II, Cedric	.299
Martinez, J.D.	.290
Kiner-Falefa, Isiah	.289

Home BA	
(minimum 251 PA)	
Guerrero Jr., Vladimir	.332
Tucker, Kyle	.332
Gurriel, Yuli	.328
Anderson, Tim	.325
Bogaerts, Xander	.316
Bichette, Bo	.315
Verdugo, Alex	.312
France, Ty	.302
Lopez, Nicky	.297
Perez, Salvador	.297

Away BA	
(minimum 251 PA)	
Hernandez, Teoscar	.321
Judge, Aaron	.314
Gurriel, Yuli	.311
Wendle, Joey	.311
Lopez, Nicky	.302
Benintendi, Andrew	.302
Crawford, J.P.	.296
Garcia, Leury	.296
Arraez, Luis	.293
Anderson, Tim	.293

OBP vs. LHP	
(minimum 125 PA)	
Zunino, Mike	.419
Hernandez, Teoscar	.407
Guerrero Jr., Vladimir	.405
Correa, Carlos	.398
Bregman, Alex	.397
Bichette, Bo	.396
Gurriel, Yuli	.394
Judge, Aaron	.394
Arozarena, Randy	.386
Stanton, Giancarlo	.386

OBP vs. RHP	
(minimum 377 PA)	
Walsh, Jared	.405
Guerrero Jr., Vladimir	.400
Verdugo, Alex	.392
Ohtani, Shohei	.388
Moncada, Yoan	.385
Olson, Matt	.382
Gurriel, Yuli	.378
Lopez, Nicky	.375
Lowe, Brandon	.375
Canha, Mark	.373

2021 American League Batting Leaders

Stolen Bases

Merrifield, Whit	40
Mullins II, Cedric	30
Straw, Myles	30
Ramirez, Jose	27
Ohtani, Shohei	26
Bichette, Bo	25
Marte, Starling	25
Lopez, Nicky	22
Moore, Dylan	21
3 tied with	20

Caught Stealing

Arozarena, Randy	10
Ohtani, Shohei	10
Benintendi, Andrew	9
Margot, Manuel	8
Mullins II, Cedric	8
Anderson, Tim	7
Taylor, Michael A.	7
6 tied with	6

Highest SB Success Pct
(minimum 15 SBA)

Bichette, Bo	96.2
Lopez, Nicky	95.7
Mondesi, Adalberto	93.8
Semien, Marcus	93.8
Marte, Starling	92.6
Merrifield, Whit	90.9
Tucker, Kyle	87.5
Ramirez, Jose	87.1
3 tied with	83.3

Lowest SB Success Pct
(minimum 15 SBA)

Benintendi, Andrew	47.1
Margot, Manuel	61.9
Polanco, Jorge	64.7
Arozarena, Randy	66.7
Dyson, Jarrod	66.7
Taylor, Michael A.	66.7
Torres, Gleyber	70.0
Laureano, Ramon	70.6
Anderson, Tim	72.0
Ohtani, Shohei	72.2

Steals of Third

Merrifield, Whit	16
Hamilton, Billy	6
Lopez, Nicky	6
Mondesi, Adalberto	6
Canha, Mark	5
Laureano, Ramon	5
Ramirez, Jose	5
Straw, Myles	5
4 tied with	4

Grounded Into DP

Abreu, Jose	28
Donaldson, Josh	22
Stanton, Giancarlo	22
Cabrera, Miguel	21
Guerrero Jr., Vladimir	20
Mancini, Trey	19
Martinez, J.D.	18
Grichuk, Randal	17
Olson, Matt	17
6 tied with	16

Grounded Into DP Pct
(minimum 50 GIDP Ops)

Brown, Seth	1.56
Mullins II, Cedric	2.06
Benintendi, Andrew	2.22
Lowe, Brandon	2.44
Kepler, Max	2.78
Kemp, Tony	2.90
Franco, Wander	3.28
Goodwin, Brian	3.45
Gardner, Brett	3.57
2 tied with	3.85

Hit By Pitch

Canha, Mark	27
France, Ty	27
Abreu, Jose	22
Solak, Nick	15
Zimmer, Bradley	15
Arozarena, Randy	14
Perez, Salvador	13
Murphy, Sean	12
3 tied with	11

Pitches Seen

Semien, Marcus	2923
Grossman, Robbie	2817
Crawford, J.P.	2791
Haniger, Mitch	2775
Olson, Matt	2774
Santana, Carlos	2706
Lowe, Nate	2691
Chapman, Matt	2675
Ramirez, Jose	2675
LeMahieu, DJ	2660

At Bats Per Home Run
(minimum 502 PA)

Ohtani, Shohei	11.7
Guerrero Jr., Vladimir	12.6
Perez, Salvador	12.9
Gallo, Joey	13.1
Lowe, Brandon	13.7
Judge, Aaron	14.1
Olson, Matt	14.5
Semien, Marcus	14.5
Stanton, Giancarlo	14.6
Ramirez, Jose	15.3

Highest GB/FB Ratio
(minimum 502 PA)

Anderson, Tim	2.51
Lopez, Nicky	2.37
Kiner-Falefa, Isiah	2.06
LeMahieu, DJ	2.03
Lowe, Nate	1.99
Rosario, Amed	1.83
Solak, Nick	1.80
Verdugo, Alex	1.74
Fletcher, David	1.73
Brantley, Michael	1.65

Lowest GB/FB Ratio
(minimum 502 PA)

Meadows, Austin	0.54
Seager, Kyle	0.63
Grossman, Robbie	0.64
Gallo, Joey	0.64
Semien, Marcus	0.64
Chapman, Matt	0.65
Hernandez, Kike	0.71
Polanco, Jorge	0.72
Tucker, Kyle	0.76
Lowe, Brandon	0.78

Pitches Per Plate App
(minimum 502 PA)

Chapman, Matt	4.30
Gallo, Joey	4.24
Canha, Mark	4.23
Moncada, Yoan	4.21
Ramirez, Jose	4.21
Grossman, Robbie	4.20
Judge, Aaron	4.19
Lowe, Nate	4.19
Stanton, Giancarlo	4.19
Straw, Myles	4.16

Pct Pitches Taken
(minimum 1500 Pitches)

Grandal, Yasmani	68.1
Gardner, Brett	62.5
Grossman, Robbie	61.7
Straw, Myles	59.7
Gallo, Joey	59.5
Canha, Mark	59.5
Moore, Dylan	58.8
LeMahieu, DJ	58.6
Bregman, Alex	58.5
Kemp, Tony	58.0

Best BPS on OutZ
(minimum 502 PA)

Gurriel, Yuli	.746
Gurriel Jr., Lourdes	.632
Bogaerts, Xander	.628
Tucker, Kyle	.626
Guerrero Jr., Vladimir	.614
Brantley, Michael	.586
Altuve, Jose	.582
Candelario, Jeimer	.574
Fletcher, David	.570
Arozarena, Randy	.569

Worst BPS on OutZ
(minimum 502 PA)

Gallo, Joey	.279
Seager, Kyle	.318
Dozier, Hunter	.327
Sano, Miguel	.330
Grichuk, Randal	.335
Martinez, J.D.	.346
Taylor, Michael A.	.349
Torres, Gleyber	.352
Chapman, Matt	.358
France, Ty	.359

2021 American League Batting Leaders

Best OPS vs Fastballs
(minimum 251 PA)

Guerrero Jr., Vladimir	1.087
Sano, Miguel	.976
Judge, Aaron	.975
Semien, Marcus	.973
Bogaerts, Xander	.948
Donaldson, Josh	.938
Brantley, Michael	.935
Ohtani, Shohei	.928
Tucker, Kyle	.918
Gallo, Joey	.912

Best OPS vs Curveballs
(minimum 50 PA)

Guerrero Jr., Vladimir	1.137
Lowe, Brandon	1.097
Moncada, Yoan	1.093
Bichette, Bo	1.048
LeMahieu, DJ	.901
Mullins II, Cedric	.900
Devers, Rafael	.893
Alvarez, Yordan	.885
Walsh, Jared	.858
Grossman, Robbie	.851

Best OPS vs Changeups
(minimum 50 PA)

Cabrera, Miguel	1.139
Correa, Carlos	1.125
Abreu, Jose	1.096
Dalbec, Bobby	1.089
Grichuk, Randal	1.061
Lowe, Nate	1.047
Anderson, Tim	1.017
Gurriel, Yuli	.993
Rosario, Amed	.961
Benintendi, Andrew	.958

Best OPS vs Sliders
(minimum 32 PA)

Franco, Wander	1.216
Kemp, Tony	1.169
Marte, Starling	1.121
Grandal, Yasmani	1.104
Ohtani, Shohei	1.101
Olson, Matt	1.081
Ward, Taylor	1.051
Stanton, Giancarlo	.971
Rendon, Anthony	.970
2 tied with	.962

OPS
(minimum 502 PA)

Guerrero Jr., Vladimir	1.002
Ohtani, Shohei	.965
Tucker, Kyle	.917
Judge, Aaron	.916
Olson, Matt	.911
Ramirez, Jose	.893
Devers, Rafael	.890
Mullins II, Cedric	.878
Alvarez, Yordan	.877
Semien, Marcus	.873

OPS First Half
(minimum 260 PA)

Guerrero Jr., Vladimir	1.089
Ohtani, Shohei	1.062
Olson, Matt	.938
Bogaerts, Xander	.930
Cruz, Nelson	.930
Martinez, J.D.	.926
Gallo, Joey	.923
Mullins II, Cedric	.921
Devers, Rafael	.913
Judge, Aaron	.901

OPS Second Half
(minimum 201 PA)

Tucker, Kyle	1.029
Springer, George	.965
Lowe, Brandon	.959
Judge, Aaron	.937
Arozarena, Randy	.935
Perez, Salvador	.932
Hernandez, Teoscar	.925
Ramirez, Jose	.919
Polanco, Jorge	.914
Guerrero Jr., Vladimir	.905

OPS by Catchers
(minimum 251 PA)

Grandal, Yasmani	.948
Perez, Salvador	.872
Zunino, Mike	.850
Stassi, Max	.757
Sanchez, Gary	.756
Murphy, Sean	.716
Severino, Pedro	.701
Haase, Eric	.689
Jeffers, Ryan	.666
Vazquez, Christian	.649

OPS by First Basemen
(minimum 251 PA)

Guerrero Jr., Vladimir	1.017
Olson, Matt	.933
France, Ty	.842
Gurriel, Yuli	.839
Walsh, Jared	.837
Abreu, Jose	.834
Mountcastle, Ryan	.821
Diaz, Yandy	.788
Sano, Miguel	.785
Dalbec, Bobby	.768

OPS by Second Basemen
(minimum 251 PA)

Semien, Marcus	.886
Lowe, Brandon	.851
Altuve, Jose	.840
Polanco, Jorge	.814
Lowrie, Jed	.792
LeMahieu, DJ	.720
Merrifield, Whit	.695
Hernandez, Cesar	.691
Solak, Nick	.688
Fletcher, David	.627

OPS by Third Basemen
(minimum 251 PA)

Devers, Rafael	.902
Ramirez, Jose	.889
Donaldson, Josh	.871
Candelario, Jeimer	.796
Moncada, Yoan	.785
Bregman, Alex	.766
Wendle, Joey	.761
Seager, Kyle	.739
Chapman, Matt	.715
Urshela, Gio	.696

OPS by Shortstops
(minimum 251 PA)

Bogaerts, Xander	.855
Bichette, Bo	.853
Correa, Carlos	.850
Anderson, Tim	.806
Franco, Wander	.795
Lopez, Nicky	.737
Galvis, Freddy	.723
Rosario, Amed	.722
Crawford, J.P.	.715
Torres, Gleyber	.671

OPS by Left Fielders
(minimum 251 PA)

Arozarena, Randy	.843
Gurriel Jr., Lourdes	.834
Brantley, Michael	.803
Grossman, Robbie	.774
Benintendi, Andrew	.774
Verdugo, Alex	.772
Vaughn, Andrew	.740
Hays, Austin	.724
Meadows, Austin	.722
Canha, Mark	.720

OPS by Center Fielders
(minimum 251 PA)

Buxton, Byron	.997
Robert, Luis	.930
Mullins II, Cedric	.879
Marte, Starling	.824
Garcia, Adolis	.819
Laureano, Ramon	.758
Gardner, Brett	.721
Kiermaier, Kevin	.720
Straw, Myles	.698
Grichuk, Randal	.696

OPS by Right Fielders
(minimum 251 PA)

Judge, Aaron	.969
Hernandez, Teoscar	.899
Tucker, Kyle	.890
Gallo, Joey	.844
Renfroe, Hunter	.824
Haniger, Mitch	.801
Grossman, Robbie	.790
Santander, Anthony	.742
Kepler, Max	.733
Margot, Manuel	.725

OPS by Designated Hitters
(minimum 125 PA)

Ohtani, Shohei	.981
Martinez, J.D.	.945
Stanton, Giancarlo	.843
Mancini, Trey	.842
Meadows, Austin	.831
Cruz, Nelson	.830
Perez, Salvador	.827
Reyes, Franmil	.822
Haniger, Mitch	.813
Brantley, Michael	.805

2021 American League Batting Leaders

OPS Batting Left vs. LHP
(minimum 125 PA)

Player	OPS
Ohtani, Shohei	.980
Olson, Matt	.962
Tucker, Kyle	.910
Alvarez, Yordan	.881
Benintendi, Andrew	.795
Mullins II, Cedric	.788
Gallo, Joey	.767
Lowe, Nate	.754
Devers, Rafael	.751
Lopez, Nicky	.704

OPS Batting Left vs. RHP
(minimum 377 PA)

Player	OPS
Walsh, Jared	.994
Devers, Rafael	.978
Lowe, Brandon	.956
Ohtani, Shohei	.954
Mullins II, Cedric	.931
Ramirez, Jose	.899
Verdugo, Alex	.893
Olson, Matt	.877
Meadows, Austin	.871
Polanco, Jorge	.838

OPS Batting Right vs. LHP
(minimum 125 PA)

Player	OPS
Zunino, Mike	1.287
Hernandez, Teoscar	1.151
Judge, Aaron	.990
Perez, Salvador	.982
Abreu, Jose	.969
Bichette, Bo	.950
Guerrero Jr., Vladimir	.946
Donaldson, Josh	.943
Vaughn, Andrew	.938
Culberson, Charlie	.932

OPS Batting Right vs. RHP
(minimum 377 PA)

Player	OPS
Guerrero Jr., Vladimir	1.020
Semien, Marcus	.906
Martinez, J.D.	.888
Bogaerts, Xander	.887
Judge, Aaron	.886
Stanton, Giancarlo	.863
Altuve, Jose	.862
Correa, Carlos	.853
Perez, Salvador	.812
Gurriel, Yuli	.805

OPS vs. LHP
(minimum 125 PA)

Player	OPS
Zunino, Mike	1.287
Hernandez, Teoscar	1.151
Judge, Aaron	.990
Perez, Salvador	.982
Ohtani, Shohei	.980
Abreu, Jose	.969
Olson, Matt	.962
Bichette, Bo	.950
Guerrero Jr., Vladimir	.946
Donaldson, Josh	.943

OPS vs. RHP
(minimum 377 PA)

Player	OPS
Guerrero Jr., Vladimir	1.020
Walsh, Jared	.994
Devers, Rafael	.978
Lowe, Brandon	.956
Ohtani, Shohei	.954
Mullins II, Cedric	.931
Semien, Marcus	.906
Ramirez, Jose	.899
Verdugo, Alex	.893
Martinez, J.D.	.888

RC Per 27 Outs vs. LHP
(minimum 125 PA)

Zunino, Mike	11.3
Hernandez, Teoscar	10.3
Bichette, Bo	8.7
Judge, Aaron	8.5
Gurriel, Yuli	7.8
Culberson, Charlie	7.6
Schoop, Jonathan	7.3
Ohtani, Shohei	7.3
France, Ty	7.3
2 tied with	7.2

RC Per 27 Outs vs. RHP
(minimum 377 PA)

Walsh, Jared	9.9
Lowe, Brandon	8.8
Guerrero Jr., Vladimir	8.6
Meadows, Austin	8.2
Ramirez, Jose	7.8
Devers, Rafael	7.5
Ohtani, Shohei	7.5
Verdugo, Alex	7.4
Mullins II, Cedric	7.3
Moncada, Yoan	6.8

Highest RBI %
(minimum 502 PA)

Player	RBI %
Hernandez, Teoscar	45.76
Ohtani, Shohei	44.74
Walsh, Jared	42.66
Polanco, Jorge	42.50
Abreu, Jose	42.09
Gurriel Jr., Lourdes	42.08
Lowe, Brandon	42.02
Bichette, Bo	41.75
Meadows, Austin	41.52
Guerrero Jr., Vladimir	41.02

Lowest RBI %
(minimum 502 PA)

Player	RBI %
Andrus, Elvis	20.69
Fletcher, David	25.11
Lopez, Nicky	26.56
Dozier, Hunter	26.73
Solak, Nick	27.31
Crawford, J.P.	28.36
LeMahieu, DJ	28.85
Brantley, Michael	28.92
Kiner-Falefa, Isiah	29.09
Taylor, Michael A.	29.17

Highest Strikeout per PA
(minimum 502 PA)

Gallo, Joey	.346
Sano, Miguel	.344
Chapman, Matt	.325
Garcia, Adolis	.312
Ohtani, Shohei	.296
Dozier, Hunter	.284
Arozarena, Randy	.281
Mountcastle, Ryan	.275
Taylor, Michael A.	.273
Lowe, Brandon	.272

Lowest Strikeout per PA
(minimum 502 PA)

Fletcher, David	.090
Brantley, Michael	.104
Gurriel, Yuli	.112
Lopez, Nicky	.131
Kiner-Falefa, Isiah	.133
Altuve, Jose	.134
Ramirez, Jose	.137
LeMahieu, DJ	.138
Merrifield, Whit	.143
Iglesias, Jose	.147

Home Runs At Home

Guerrero Jr., Vladimir	31
Perez, Salvador	27
Ohtani, Shohei	26
Gallo, Joey	22
Mountcastle, Ryan	22
Mullins II, Cedric	22
Semien, Marcus	22
Ramirez, Jose	21
4 tied with	19

Home Runs Away

Judge, Aaron	24
Semien, Marcus	23
Devers, Rafael	22
Polanco, Jorge	22
Seager, Kyle	22
Olson, Matt	21
Perez, Salvador	21
6 tied with	20

Longest Avg Home Run
(min 10 over the wall)

Player	Ft
Soler, Jorge	429
Buxton, Byron	419
Peters, DJ	417
Ohtani, Shohei	416
Stanton, Giancarlo	414
Renfroe, Hunter	413
Sano, Miguel	413
Robert, Luis	413
Lowe, Nate	413
Sheets, Gavin	412

Shortest Avg Home Run
(min 10 over the wall)

Player	Ft
Maldonado, Martin	377
Toro, Abraham	382
Gurriel, Yuli	384
Baddoo, Akil	385
Bregman, Alex	386
Canha, Mark	386
Correa, Carlos	387
Anderson, Tim	387
Murphy, Tom	387
Solak, Nick	387

2021 American League Batting Leaders

Under Age 26: AB Per HR
(minimum 300 PA)

Guerrero Jr., Vladimir	12.6
Devers, Rafael	15.6
Mountcastle, Ryan	16.2
Alvarez, Yordan	16.3
Tucker, Kyle	16.9
Bichette, Bo	22.1
Torrens, Luis	23.1
Kelenic, Jarred	24.1
Vaughn, Andrew	27.8
Toro, Abraham	30.5

Under Age 26: OPS
(minimum 300 PA)

Guerrero Jr., Vladimir	1.002
Tucker, Kyle	.917
Devers, Rafael	.890
Alvarez, Yordan	.877
Bichette, Bo	.828
Franco, Wander	.810
Mountcastle, Ryan	.796
Verdugo, Alex	.777
Baddoo, Akil	.766
Arraez, Luis	.733

Under Age 26: RC/27 Outs
(minimum 300 PA)

Guerrero Jr., Vladimir	8.2
Tucker, Kyle	6.8
Franco, Wander	6.6
Devers, Rafael	6.5
Bichette, Bo	6.5
Alvarez, Yordan	6.2
Baddoo, Akil	5.9
Verdugo, Alex	5.5
Rosario, Amed	5.2
Arraez, Luis	5.2

Longest Home Run

Sano, Miguel, 8/25	495
Mercedes, Yermin, 4/8	485
Sano, Miguel, 8/18	475
Cordero, Franchy, 5/23	474
Sano, Miguel, 7/28	473
Brown, Seth, 7/10	472
Stanton, Giancarlo, 8/27	472
Zunino, Mike, 5/11	472
Stanton, Giancarlo, 4/5	471
Zimmer, Bradley, 8/9	471

Swing and Miss %
(minimum 1500 Pitches Seen)

Gallo, Joey	38.4
Zunino, Mike	38.0
Dalbec, Bobby	37.3
Sano, Miguel	36.9
Ohtani, Shohei	34.2
Haase, Eric	34.0
Garcia, Adolis	33.2
Perez, Salvador	32.6
Reyes, Franmil	32.4
Lowe, Brandon	32.0

Highest First Swing %
(minimum 502 PA)

Bichette, Bo	44.9
Lowe, Brandon	43.9
Tucker, Kyle	41.2
Perez, Salvador	41.1
Guerrero Jr., Vladimir	40.6
Mountcastle, Ryan	39.1
Cruz, Nelson	39.0
Martinez, J.D.	38.9
Anderson, Tim	38.8
Devers, Rafael	38.2

Lowest First Swing %
(minimum 502 PA)

Ramirez, Jose	13.5
Bogaerts, Xander	16.3
Solak, Nick	17.2
Canha, Mark	17.4
Rosario, Amed	17.5
Stanton, Giancarlo	18.2
Moncada, Yoan	18.5
Verdugo, Alex	18.9
Kiner-Falefa, Isiah	20.5
LeMahieu, DJ	21.0

Home RC Per 27 Outs
(minimum 251 PA)

Guerrero Jr., Vladimir	9.8
Tucker, Kyle	8.9
Ohtani, Shohei	8.7
France, Ty	7.7
Bichette, Bo	7.5
Devers, Rafael	7.3
Ramirez, Jose	7.2
Martinez, J.D.	7.1
Bogaerts, Xander	7.1
Altuve, Jose	7.1

Road RC Per 27 Outs
(minimum 251 PA)

Hernandez, Teoscar	8.9
Judge, Aaron	8.8
Polanco, Jorge	7.5
Canha, Mark	7.4
Lowe, Brandon	7.3
Seager, Kyle	7.2
Wendle, Joey	7.2
Ramirez, Jose	7.1
Stanton, Giancarlo	7.0
Alvarez, Yordan	6.5

Lead Changing RBI

Perez, Salvador	40
Olson, Matt	38
Seager, Kyle	37
Devers, Rafael	34
Guerrero Jr., Vladimir	34
Meadows, Austin	34
Correa, Carlos	33
France, Ty	33
Hernandez, Teoscar	33
Judge, Aaron	32

2021 National League Batting Leaders

Batting Average
(minimum 502 PA)

Turner, Trea	.328
Soto, Juan	.313
Harper, Bryce	.309
Castellanos, Nick	.309
Frazier, Adam	.305
Riley, Austin	.303
Reynolds, Bryan	.302
Freeman, Freddie	.300
Crawford, Brandon	.298
Goldschmidt, Paul	.294

On Base Percentage
(minimum 502 PA)

Soto, Juan	.465
Harper, Bryce	.429
Freeman, Freddie	.393
Reynolds, Bryan	.390
India, Jonathan	.376
Votto, Joey	.375
Cron, C.J.	.375
Turner, Trea	.375
Crawford, Brandon	.373
Muncy, Max	.368

Slugging Average
(minimum 502 PA)

Harper, Bryce	.615
Tatis Jr., Fernando	.611
Castellanos, Nick	.576
Votto, Joey	.563
O'Neill, Tyler	.560
Turner, Trea	.536
Soto, Juan	.534
Riley, Austin	.531
Cron, C.J.	.530
Muncy, Max	.527

Home Runs

Tatis Jr., Fernando	42
Duvall, Adam	38
Alonso, Pete	37
Muncy, Max	36
Votto, Joey	36
Harper, Bryce	35
Arenado, Nolan	34
Castellanos, Nick	34
O'Neill, Tyler	34
Riley, Austin	33

Games

Riley, Austin	160
Swanson, Dansby	160
Edman, Tommy	159
Freeman, Freddie	159
Reynolds, Bryan	159
Goldschmidt, Paul	158
Arenado, Nolan	157
Albies, Ozzie	156
Frazier, Adam	155
Pham, Tommy	155

Plate Appearances

Freeman, Freddie	695
Edman, Tommy	691
Albies, Ozzie	686
Goldschmidt, Paul	679
Riley, Austin	662
Soto, Juan	654
Arenado, Nolan	653
Swanson, Dansby	653
Reynolds, Bryan	646
Turner, Trea	646

At Bats

Edman, Tommy	641
Albies, Ozzie	629
Goldschmidt, Paul	603
Freeman, Freddie	600
Turner, Trea	595
Arenado, Nolan	593
Riley, Austin	590
Swanson, Dansby	588
Frazier, Adam	577
Cronenworth, Jake	567

Hits

Turner, Trea	195
Freeman, Freddie	180
Riley, Austin	179
Goldschmidt, Paul	177
Frazier, Adam	176
Reynolds, Bryan	169
Edman, Tommy	168
Castellanos, Nick	164
Albies, Ozzie	163
2 tied with	157

Singles

Frazier, Adam	130
Turner, Trea	130
Freeman, Freddie	122
Edman, Tommy	113
Riley, Austin	112
Goldschmidt, Paul	108
Soto, Juan	106
Segura, Jean	105
Reynolds, Bryan	102
2 tied with	99

Doubles

Harper, Bryce	42
Edman, Tommy	41
Albies, Ozzie	40
Castellanos, Nick	38
Frazier, Adam	36
Goldschmidt, Paul	36
Reynolds, Bryan	35
4 tied with	34

Triples

Peralta, David	8
Reynolds, Bryan	8
Albies, Ozzie	7
Cronenworth, Jake	7
Hampson, Garrett	6
Duggar, Steven	5
Escobar, Eduardo	5
Frazier, Adam	5
Story, Trevor	5
8 tied with	4

Total Bases

Turner, Trea	319
Riley, Austin	313
Goldschmidt, Paul	310
Albies, Ozzie	307
Castellanos, Nick	306
Freeman, Freddie	302
Harper, Bryce	300
Arenado, Nolan	293
Reynolds, Bryan	292
Tatis Jr., Fernando	292

Runs Scored

Freeman, Freddie	120
Soto, Juan	111
Turner, Trea	107
Albies, Ozzie	103
Goldschmidt, Paul	102
Harper, Bryce	101
Tatis Jr., Fernando	99
India, Jonathan	98
Castellanos, Nick	95
Muncy, Max	95

RBI

Duvall, Adam	113
Riley, Austin	107
Albies, Ozzie	106
Machado, Manny	106
Arenado, Nolan	105
Castellanos, Nick	100
Goldschmidt, Paul	99
Votto, Joey	99
Tatis Jr., Fernando	97
Soto, Juan	95

Walks

Soto, Juan	145
Harper, Bryce	100
Freeman, Freddie	85
Muncy, Max	83
McCutchen, Andrew	81
Pham, Tommy	78
Votto, Joey	77
Reynolds, Bryan	75
India, Jonathan	71
Yelich, Christian	70

Strikeouts

Baez, Javier	184
Duvall, Adam	174
Suarez, Eugenio	171
O'Neill, Tyler	168
Riley, Austin	168
Swanson, Dansby	167
Taylor, Chris	167
Happ, Ian	156
Tatis Jr., Fernando	153
Wisdom, Patrick	153

2021 National League Batting Leaders

Intentional Walks	
Soto, Juan	23
Freeman, Freddie	15
Harper, Bryce	14
Machado, Manny	10
Reynolds, Bryan	9
Arenado, Nolan	8
Caratini, Victor	8
7 tied with	6

BA Bases Loaded
(minimum 10 PA)

Naquin, Tyler	.700
Stephenson, Tyler	.571
Tatis Jr., Fernando	.556
Beaty, Matt	.500
Harper, Bryce	.500
Torreyes, Ronald	.500
Turner, Trea	.500
Segura, Jean	.462
Lindor, Francisco	.455
Peralta, David	.455

Sacrifice Hits	
Wainwright, Adam	14
Senzatela, Antonio	12
Davies, Zach	10
Urias, Julio	10
Castillo, Luis	9
Gallen, Zac	9
Gomber, Austin	9
Buehler, Walker	8
Fried, Max	8
9 tied with	7

Sacrifice Flies	
Machado, Manny	11
Smith, Will	11
Carlson, Dylan	8
Polanco, Gregory	8
Riley, Austin	8
6 tied with	7

BA Close & Late
(minimum 50 PA)

Adames, Willy	.388
Seager, Corey	.379
Wade Jr., LaMonte	.362
Crawford, Brandon	.319
Winker, Jesse	.311
Hoskins, Rhys	.310
Castellanos, Nick	.309
Riley, Austin	.306
Hernandez, Yadiel	.300
Aguilar, Jesus	.299

Batting Average w/ RISP
(minimum 100 PA)

Soto, Juan	.396
Tatis Jr., Fernando	.364
Crawford, Brandon	.353
Freeman, Freddie	.352
Muncy, Max	.346
Machado, Manny	.344
Winker, Jesse	.341
Seager, Corey	.338
Goldschmidt, Paul	.331
Harper, Bryce	.330

SLG vs. LHP
(minimum 125 PA)

Turner, Trea	.712
Goldschmidt, Paul	.650
McCutchen, Andrew	.622
Story, Trevor	.614
Kelly, Carson	.607
Tatis Jr., Fernando	.595
Ruf, Darin	.593
Castellanos, Nick	.590
Albies, Ozzie	.585
Cron, C.J.	.583

SLG vs. RHP
(minimum 377 PA)

Harper, Bryce	.711
Tatis Jr., Fernando	.616
Soto, Juan	.573
Castellanos, Nick	.571
Riley, Austin	.560
Crawford, Brandon	.560
O'Neill, Tyler	.544
Duvall, Adam	.536
Freeman, Freddie	.534
Reynolds, Bryan	.527

Leadoff Hitters OBP
(minimum 150 PA)

Nimmo, Brandon	.393
Acuna Jr., Ronald	.392
India, Jonathan	.383
Ortega, Rafael	.378
Frazier, Adam	.377
Betts, Mookie	.370
Pham, Tommy	.364
Thomas, Lane	.361
Villar, Jonathan	.360
Turner, Trea	.358

Cleanup Hitters SLG
(minimum 150 PA)

Machado, Manny	.638
Votto, Joey	.611
Riley, Austin	.548
Smith, Will	.527
Albies, Ozzie	.526
Arenado, Nolan	.513
Bell, Josh	.495
Alonso, Pete	.489
Garcia, Avisail	.482
Duvall, Adam	.466

BA vs. LHP
(minimum 125 PA)

Turner, Trea	.392
Goldschmidt, Paul	.350
Carlson, Dylan	.341
Reynolds, Bryan	.325
Albies, Ozzie	.323
Rojas, Miguel	.317
Segura, Jean	.313
Kelly, Carson	.313
Smith, Dominic	.312
Cron, C.J.	.311

BA vs. RHP
(minimum 377 PA)

Harper, Bryce	.333
Soto, Juan	.333
Crawford, Brandon	.319
Frazier, Adam	.317
Freeman, Freddie	.317
Riley, Austin	.312
Castellanos, Nick	.310
Turner, Trea	.305
Reynolds, Bryan	.293
Machado, Manny	.288

Home BA
(minimum 251 PA)

Castellanos, Nick	.359
Turner, Trea	.336
Harper, Bryce	.329
Cron, C.J.	.326
Frazier, Adam	.315
Crawford, Brandon	.307
Carlson, Dylan	.306
Freeman, Freddie	.304
O'Neill, Tyler	.303
Segura, Jean	.302

Away BA
(minimum 251 PA)

Soto, Juan	.333
Tatis Jr., Fernando	.323
Turner, Trea	.320
Riley, Austin	.319
Reynolds, Bryan	.314
Goldschmidt, Paul	.301
Freeman, Freddie	.296
Frazier, Adam	.296
Harper, Bryce	.291
Crawford, Brandon	.289

OBP vs. LHP
(minimum 125 PA)

Turner, Trea	.437
Ruf, Darin	.414
Goldschmidt, Paul	.413
Kelly, Carson	.410
Garcia, Avisail	.406
McCutchen, Andrew	.405
Soto, Juan	.403
Reynolds, Bryan	.403
Rojas, Miguel	.399
Harper, Bryce	.397

OBP vs. RHP
(minimum 377 PA)

Soto, Juan	.500
Harper, Bryce	.444
Freeman, Freddie	.416
Crawford, Brandon	.401
Reynolds, Bryan	.385
Riley, Austin	.380
Frazier, Adam	.378
Turner, Justin	.375
India, Jonathan	.372
Cron, C.J.	.368

2021 National League Batting Leaders

Stolen Bases

Turner, Trea	32
Edman, Tommy	30
Tatis Jr., Fernando	25
Chisholm Jr., Jazz	23
Marte, Starling	22
Albies, Ozzie	20
Story, Trevor	20
Tapia, Raimel	20
Baez, Javier	18
2 tied with	17

Caught Stealing

Chisholm Jr., Jazz	8
Hampson, Garrett	7
Soto, Juan	7
Villar, Jonathan	7
8 tied with	6

Highest SB Success Pct
(minimum 15 SBA)

Polanco, Gregory	93.3
Slater, Austin	88.2
Marte, Starling	88.0
Cain, Lorenzo	86.7
Turner, Trea	86.5
Tatis Jr., Fernando	86.2
Edman, Tommy	85.7
Albies, Ozzie	83.3
3 tied with	81.3

Lowest SB Success Pct
(minimum 15 SBA)

Soto, Juan	56.3
Betts, Mookie	66.7
Frazier, Adam	66.7
Ortega, Rafael	66.7
Profar, Jurickson	66.7
Villar, Jonathan	66.7
Pham, Tommy	70.0
Wong, Kolten	70.6
Hampson, Garrett	70.8
Grisham, Trent	72.2

Steals of Third

Turner, Trea	7
Baez, Javier	5
Chisholm Jr., Jazz	5
Harper, Bryce	5
India, Jonathan	5
Crawford, Brandon	4
Hampson, Garrett	4
Pollock, A.J.	4
Tatis Jr., Fernando	4
3 tied with	3

Grounded Into DP

Soto, Juan	23
Bell, Josh	22
Alonso, Pete	20
Arenado, Nolan	20
Turner, Trea	18
Castellanos, Nick	16
Duffy, Matt	16
Farmer, Kyle	16
Molina, Yadier	16
Segura, Jean	16

Grounded Into DP Pct
(minimum 50 GIDP Ops)

Escobar, Eduardo	2.27
Yastrzemski, Mike	2.88
Bellinger, Cody	3.03
Wong, Kolten	3.13
Escobar, Alcides	3.28
Albies, Ozzie	3.48
Marte, Starling	3.70
Lux, Gavin	4.00
Taylor, Chris	4.07
Edman, Tommy	4.60

Hit By Pitch

India, Jonathan	23
Farmer, Kyle	18
Smith, Will	18
Sosa, Edmundo	17
Robles, Victor	16
Contreras, Willson	14
Rizzo, Anthony	14
4 tied with	13

Pitches Seen

Goldschmidt, Paul	2751
Freeman, Freddie	2688
India, Jonathan	2643
Edman, Tommy	2612
Albies, Ozzie	2608
Soto, Juan	2601
Riley, Austin	2595
Swanson, Dansby	2578
Carlson, Dylan	2530
Reynolds, Bryan	2493

At Bats Per Home Run
(minimum 502 PA)

Tatis Jr., Fernando	11.4
Votto, Joey	12.4
Duvall, Adam	13.5
Muncy, Max	13.8
Harper, Bryce	13.9
O'Neill, Tyler	14.2
Alonso, Pete	15.2
Castellanos, Nick	15.6
Garcia, Avisail	15.9
Baez, Javier	16.2

Highest GB/FB Ratio
(minimum 502 PA)

Tapia, Raimel	4.10
Hosmer, Eric	2.15
Peralta, David	2.10
Bell, Josh	2.02
Soto, Juan	1.83
Segura, Jean	1.81
Rojas, Josh	1.77
Villar, Jonathan	1.58
Chisholm Jr., Jazz	1.57
Blackmon, Charlie	1.53

Lowest GB/FB Ratio
(minimum 502 PA)

Duvall, Adam	0.56
Arenado, Nolan	0.63
Albies, Ozzie	0.65
Escobar, Eduardo	0.67
Aguilar, Jesus	0.71
Yastrzemski, Mike	0.72
Votto, Joey	0.76
Suarez, Eugenio	0.78
Turner, Justin	0.80
Betts, Mookie	0.81

Pitches Per Plate App
(minimum 502 PA)

Pham, Tommy	4.23
Rojas, Josh	4.21
Happ, Ian	4.21
India, Jonathan	4.19
Votto, Joey	4.19
Suarez, Eugenio	4.17
Grisham, Trent	4.11
Muncy, Max	4.11
Taylor, Chris	4.10
Carlson, Dylan	4.09

Pct Pitches Taken
(minimum 1500 Pitches)

Soto, Juan	65.0
Muncy, Max	62.4
Pham, Tommy	61.8
India, Jonathan	61.0
Betts, Mookie	59.6
Stephenson, Tyler	59.6
Grisham, Trent	59.5
Yelich, Christian	58.6
McCutchen, Andrew	58.3
Smith, Will	58.1

Best BPS on OutZ
(minimum 502 PA)

Harper, Bryce	.722
Freeman, Freddie	.709
Turner, Trea	.651
Arenado, Nolan	.611
Riley, Austin	.596
Escobar, Eduardo	.596
Machado, Manny	.591
Castellanos, Nick	.583
Votto, Joey	.580
Aguilar, Jesus	.574

Worst BPS on OutZ
(minimum 502 PA)

Pham, Tommy	.230
Taylor, Chris	.239
Happ, Ian	.286
Bryant, Kris	.294
Blackmon, Charlie	.296
Lindor, Francisco	.302
Story, Trevor	.309
McCutchen, Andrew	.340
Suarez, Eugenio	.342
Duvall, Adam	.346

2021 National League Batting Leaders

Best OPS vs Fastballs
(minimum 251 PA)

Soto, Juan	1.158
Harper, Bryce	1.077
Muncy, Max	1.059
Votto, Joey	1.048
Castellanos, Nick	1.034
Cron, C.J.	1.008
Turner, Trea	1.007
Reynolds, Bryan	1.005
Tatis Jr., Fernando	.991
Crawford, Brandon	.986

Best OPS vs Curveballs
(minimum 50 PA)

Duvall, Adam	1.188
Riley, Austin	1.054
Crawford, Brandon	1.009
Happ, Ian	.962
Votto, Joey	.957
Turner, Trea	.917
Story, Trevor	.898
Turner, Justin	.865
Albies, Ozzie	.864
McMahon, Ryan	.850

Best OPS vs Changeups
(minimum 50 PA)

Arenado, Nolan	1.233
Riley, Austin	1.095
Harper, Bryce	1.077
Winker, Jesse	1.044
Belt, Brandon	1.020
Segura, Jean	1.004
Goldschmidt, Paul	.979
Wade Jr., LaMonte	.944
Freeman, Freddie	.943
Smith, Pavin	.936

Best OPS vs Sliders
(minimum 32 PA)

Acuna Jr., Ronald	1.148
Bell, Josh	1.088
Alonso, Pete	1.074
Belt, Brandon	1.055
Nimmo, Brandon	1.055
Aguilar, Jesus	1.032
Ruf, Darin	1.004
Wong, Kolten	1.004
Harper, Bryce	.994
Cronenworth, Jake	.976

OPS
(minimum 502 PA)

Harper, Bryce	1.044
Soto, Juan	.999
Tatis Jr., Fernando	.975
Castellanos, Nick	.939
Votto, Joey	.938
Reynolds, Bryan	.912
O'Neill, Tyler	.912
Turner, Trea	.911
Cron, C.J.	.905
Riley, Austin	.898

OPS First Half
(minimum 260 PA)

Tatis Jr., Fernando	1.020
Acuna Jr., Ronald	.990
Muncy, Max	.972
Castellanos, Nick	.969
Crawford, Brandon	.921
Winker, Jesse	.921
Schwarber, Kyle	.910
Reynolds, Bryan	.906
Harper, Bryce	.899
Turner, Justin	.889

OPS Second Half
(minimum 201 PA)

Harper, Bryce	1.188
Soto, Juan	1.164
Votto, Joey	1.057
Goldschmidt, Paul	1.020
Seager, Corey	1.009
Schwindel, Frank	1.002
Riley, Austin	.976
Cron, C.J.	.974
Turner, Trea	.946
O'Neill, Tyler	.942

OPS by Catchers
(minimum 251 PA)

Posey, Buster	.913
Smith, Will	.875
Stephenson, Tyler	.856
Realmuto, J.T.	.804
Diaz, Elias	.803
Narvaez, Omar	.776
Contreras, Willson	.774
Kelly, Carson	.768
Stallings, Jacob	.715
Nunez, Dom	.695

OPS by First Basemen
(minimum 251 PA)

Belt, Brandon	.967
Votto, Joey	.940
Cron, C.J.	.905
Freeman, Freddie	.896
Goldschmidt, Paul	.887
Hoskins, Rhys	.872
Alonso, Pete	.852
Muncy, Max	.843
Bell, Josh	.834
Rizzo, Anthony	.792

OPS by Second Basemen
(minimum 251 PA)

India, Jonathan	.838
Cronenworth, Jake	.823
Albies, Ozzie	.799
Rodgers, Brendan	.794
Wong, Kolten	.791
Segura, Jean	.790
Frazier, Adam	.787
Chisholm Jr., Jazz	.734
Harrison, Josh	.727
Solano, Donovan	.710

OPS by Third Basemen
(minimum 251 PA)

Riley, Austin	.916
Longoria, Evan	.835
Machado, Manny	.832
Turner, Justin	.831
McMahon, Ryan	.815
Wisdom, Patrick	.814
Urias, Luis	.809
Arenado, Nolan	.802
Escobar, Eduardo	.785
Suarez, Eugenio	.748

OPS by Shortstops
(minimum 251 PA)

Tatis Jr., Fernando	1.003
Seager, Corey	.925
Turner, Trea	.906
Crawford, Brandon	.898
Adames, Willy	.895
Story, Trevor	.811
Baez, Javier	.772
Farmer, Kyle	.766
Swanson, Dansby	.763
Escobar, Alcides	.748

OPS by Left Fielders
(minimum 251 PA)

Winker, Jesse	.981
O'Neill, Tyler	.927
Schwarber, Kyle	.910
Gamel, Ben	.889
Pollock, A.J.	.869
McCutchen, Andrew	.777
Yelich, Christian	.761
Pham, Tommy	.744
Pederson, Joc	.727
Peralta, David	.709

OPS by Center Fielders
(minimum 251 PA)

Reynolds, Bryan	.934
Marte, Ketel	.879
Marte, Starling	.854
Nimmo, Brandon	.840
Ortega, Rafael	.816
Bader, Harrison	.785
Duggar, Steven	.785
Grisham, Trent	.750
Cain, Lorenzo	.742
Naquin, Tyler	.710

OPS by Right Fielders
(minimum 251 PA)

Harper, Bryce	1.046
Soto, Juan	1.008
Acuna Jr., Ronald	.998
Castellanos, Nick	.940
Betts, Mookie	.819
Garcia, Avisail	.817
Carlson, Dylan	.791
Yastrzemski, Mike	.770
Duvall, Adam	.765
Myers, Wil	.764

OPS by Pitchers
(minimum 50 PA)

Marquez, German	.679
Fried, Max	.569
Miley, Wade	.486
Webb, Logan	.459
Urias, Julio	.454
Bumgarner, Madison	.427
Nola, Aaron	.402
Gausman, Kevin	.399
Castillo, Luis	.384
Wheeler, Zack	.358

2021 National League Batting Leaders

OPS Batting Left vs. LHP
(minimum 125 PA)

Muncy, Max	.961
Soto, Juan	.875
Grisham, Trent	.824
Harper, Bryce	.798
Wong, Kolten	.790
Smith, Dominic	.783
Rojas, Josh	.775
Cronenworth, Jake	.769
Blackmon, Charlie	.768
Freeman, Freddie	.760

OPS Batting Left vs. RHP
(minimum 377 PA)

Harper, Bryce	1.155
Soto, Juan	1.073
Crawford, Brandon	.961
Freeman, Freddie	.949
Reynolds, Bryan	.911
Muncy, Max	.871
Naquin, Tyler	.853
Yastrzemski, Mike	.848
McMahon, Ryan	.826
Bell, Josh	.815

OPS Batting Right vs. LHP
(minimum 125 PA)

Turner, Trea	1.150
Goldschmidt, Paul	1.063
McCutchen, Andrew	1.027
Kelly, Carson	1.018
Ruf, Darin	1.007
Cron, C.J.	.977
Story, Trevor	.974
Tatis Jr., Fernando	.968
Castellanos, Nick	.945
Albies, Ozzie	.940

OPS Batting Right vs. RHP
(minimum 377 PA)

Tatis Jr., Fernando	.978
Riley, Austin	.941
Castellanos, Nick	.936
O'Neill, Tyler	.888
Cron, C.J.	.877
Betts, Mookie	.853
Machado, Manny	.847
Alonso, Pete	.845
India, Jonathan	.839
Turner, Justin	.837

OPS vs. LHP
(minimum 125 PA)

Turner, Trea	1.150
Goldschmidt, Paul	1.063
McCutchen, Andrew	1.027
Kelly, Carson	1.018
Ruf, Darin	1.007
Cron, C.J.	.977
Story, Trevor	.974
Tatis Jr., Fernando	.968
Muncy, Max	.961
Castellanos, Nick	.945

OPS vs. RHP
(minimum 377 PA)

Harper, Bryce	1.155
Soto, Juan	1.073
Tatis Jr., Fernando	.978
Crawford, Brandon	.961
Freeman, Freddie	.949
Riley, Austin	.941
Castellanos, Nick	.936
Reynolds, Bryan	.911
O'Neill, Tyler	.888
Cron, C.J.	.877

RC Per 27 Outs vs. LHP
(minimum 125 PA)

Turner, Trea	10.1
Kelly, Carson	9.4
Goldschmidt, Paul	9.1
Cron, C.J.	8.6
Albies, Ozzie	8.5
McCutchen, Andrew	8.1
Rojas, Miguel	7.8
Taylor, Chris	7.8
Carlson, Dylan	7.7
Contreras, Willson	7.7

RC Per 27 Outs vs. RHP
(minimum 377 PA)

Harper, Bryce	10.2
Soto, Juan	9.9
Freeman, Freddie	8.5
Tatis Jr., Fernando	8.4
Crawford, Brandon	8.4
Riley, Austin	7.4
Muncy, Max	7.4
Reynolds, Bryan	7.3
Machado, Manny	7.2
Realmuto, J.T.	6.7

Highest RBI %
(minimum 502 PA)

Tatis Jr., Fernando	48.35
Harper, Bryce	45.21
Soto, Juan	44.12
Machado, Manny	43.86
Votto, Joey	43.21
Cron, C.J.	42.22
Muncy, Max	41.85
Garcia, Avisail	41.41
Albies, Ozzie	40.94
Aguilar, Jesus	40.92

Lowest RBI %
(minimum 502 PA)

Newman, Kevin	21.39
Villar, Jonathan	24.71
Rojas, Josh	26.00
Smith, Pavin	27.47
Pham, Tommy	27.57
Edman, Tommy	29.96
Tapia, Raimel	30.58
Hosmer, Eric	30.78
Rojas, Miguel	30.87
Suarez, Eugenio	31.11

Highest Strikeout per PA
(minimum 502 PA)

Baez, Javier	.336
Duvall, Adam	.314
O'Neill, Tyler	.313
Suarez, Eugenio	.298
Happ, Ian	.292
Taylor, Chris	.287
Chisholm Jr., Jazz	.286
Tatis Jr., Fernando	.280
Villar, Jonathan	.261
Swanson, Dansby	.256

Lowest Strikeout per PA
(minimum 502 PA)

Newman, Kevin	.074
Frazier, Adam	.108
Tapia, Raimel	.131
Edman, Tommy	.137
Rojas, Miguel	.137
Segura, Jean	.138
Cronenworth, Jake	.140
Soto, Juan	.142
Arenado, Nolan	.147
Freeman, Freddie	.154

Home Runs At Home

Castellanos, Nick	23
Muncy, Max	23
Votto, Joey	20
Baez, Javier	19
Cron, C.J.	19
Harper, Bryce	19
Tatis Jr., Fernando	18
Albies, Ozzie	17
Machado, Manny	17
Schwarber, Kyle	17

Home Runs Away

Alonso, Pete	25
Tatis Jr., Fernando	24
Duvall, Adam	22
Arenado, Nolan	20
Riley, Austin	20
O'Neill, Tyler	19
Soto, Juan	19
Hoskins, Rhys	18
3 tied with	17

Longest Avg Home Run
(min 10 over the wall)

Hilliard, Sam	422
Cron, C.J.	420
Acuna Jr., Ronald	419
Soler, Jorge	418
Story, Trevor	417
Sanchez, Jesus	417
Duvall, Adam	416
Tatis Jr., Fernando	416
Goldschmidt, Paul	415
Hosmer, Eric	415

Shortest Avg Home Run
(min 10 over the wall)

Ortega, Rafael	376
Realmuto, J.T.	382
Grisham, Trent	386
Arenado, Nolan	386
Posey, Buster	387
Gregorius, Didi	392
Bryant, Kris	392
Dickerson, Alex	392
Wong, Kolten	392
Flores, Wilmer	393

2021 National League Batting Leaders

Under Age 26: AB Per HR
(minimum 300 PA)

Tatis Jr., Fernando	11.4
Acuna Jr., Ronald	12.4
Soto, Juan	17.3
Riley, Austin	17.9
Albies, Ozzie	21.0
Urias, Luis	21.3
India, Jonathan	25.3
Chisholm Jr., Jazz	25.8
Rodgers, Brendan	25.8
Varsho, Daulton	25.8

Under Age 26: OPS
(minimum 300 PA)

Soto, Juan	.999
Acuna Jr., Ronald	.990
Tatis Jr., Fernando	.975
Riley, Austin	.898
India, Jonathan	.835
Albies, Ozzie	.799
Rodgers, Brendan	.798
Stephenson, Tyler	.797
Urias, Luis	.789
Carlson, Dylan	.780

Under Age 26: RC/27 Outs
(minimum 300 PA)

Soto, Juan	8.8
Tatis Jr., Fernando	8.1
Acuna Jr., Ronald	7.4
Riley, Austin	6.8
India, Jonathan	6.3
Albies, Ozzie	5.8
Urias, Luis	5.5
Rodgers, Brendan	5.3
Carlson, Dylan	5.2
Stephenson, Tyler	5.1

Longest Home Run

Pham, Tommy, 8/17	486
Duvall, Adam, 9/20	483
Acuna Jr., Ronald, 4/27	481
Ozuna, Marcell, 4/29	479
McMahon, Ryan, 5/15	478
Duvall, Adam, 9/2	477
Tatis Jr., Fernando, 6/16	477
Story, Trevor, 9/28	475
Raley, Luke, 9/22	472
Goldschmidt, Paul, 6/26	470

Swing and Miss %
(minimum 1500 Pitches Seen)

Wisdom, Patrick	40.2
Baez, Javier	39.7
Bradley Jr., Jackie	33.8
Tatis Jr., Fernando	33.8
O'Neill, Tyler	33.8
Contreras, Willson	33.8
Garcia, Avisail	32.6
Taylor, Chris	31.8
Harper, Bryce	31.3
Happ, Ian	31.1

Highest First Swing %
(minimum 502 PA)

Garcia, Avisail	48.2
Albies, Ozzie	41.1
Castellanos, Nick	40.9
McMahon, Ryan	40.5
Crawford, Brandon	40.0
Baez, Javier	38.8
Tatis Jr., Fernando	38.6
Harper, Bryce	38.5
Freeman, Freddie	38.4
Reynolds, Bryan	38.2

Lowest First Swing %
(minimum 502 PA)

Aguilar, Jesus	9.0
India, Jonathan	14.8
Betts, Mookie	18.0
Cronenworth, Jake	18.9
Muncy, Max	19.3
Pham, Tommy	19.5
Smith, Will	19.9
Goldschmidt, Paul	20.5
Edman, Tommy	20.8
Smith, Pavin	21.5

Home RC Per 27 Outs
(minimum 251 PA)

Castellanos, Nick	10.3
Cron, C.J.	10.3
Harper, Bryce	10.1
Votto, Joey	9.4
Muncy, Max	8.7
Soto, Juan	8.2
Crawford, Brandon	7.7
Turner, Trea	7.3
Freeman, Freddie	6.9
Realmuto, J.T.	6.9

Road RC Per 27 Outs
(minimum 251 PA)

Tatis Jr., Fernando	10.0
Soto, Juan	9.3
Reynolds, Bryan	8.3
Freeman, Freddie	7.8
Alonso, Pete	7.8
Harper, Bryce	7.4
Riley, Austin	7.4
Duvall, Adam	7.4
Goldschmidt, Paul	7.2
Crawford, Brandon	6.9

Lead Changing RBI

Albies, Ozzie	36
Arenado, Nolan	35
Machado, Manny	33
Blackmon, Charlie	32
Goldschmidt, Paul	32
Votto, Joey	31
Crawford, Brandon	30
6 tied with	29

2021 American League Pitching Leaders

Earned Run Average
(minimum 162 IP)

Ray, Robbie	2.84
McCullers Jr., Lance	3.16
Cole, Gerrit	3.23
Montas, Frankie	3.37
Berrios, Jose	3.52
Giolito, Lucas	3.53
Flexen, Chris	3.61
Eovaldi, Nathan	3.75
Cease, Dylan	3.91
Manaea, Sean	3.91

Winning Percentage
(minimum 15 Decisions)

Bassitt, Chris	.750
McCullers Jr., Lance	.722
Rodon, Carlos	.722
Civale, Aaron	.706
Flexen, Chris	.700
Cole, Gerrit	.667
Matz, Steven	.667
Cease, Dylan	.650
Ray, Robbie	.650
3 tied with	.647

Opponent Batting Average
(minimum 120 IP)

Rodon, Carlos	.189
McKenzie, Triston	.194
McCullers Jr., Lance	.205
Ohtani, Shohei	.207
Lynn, Lance	.209
Ray, Robbie	.210
Bassitt, Chris	.218
Giolito, Lucas	.219
Valdez, Framber	.220
Berrios, Jose	.223

Baserunners Per 9 IP
(minimum 120 IP)

Rodon, Carlos	9.16
Means, John	9.51
Ray, Robbie	9.59
Cole, Gerrit	9.63
Lynn, Lance	9.75
Giolito, Lucas	10.02
Bassitt, Chris	10.13
Berrios, Jose	10.27
Civale, Aaron	10.35
Ohtani, Shohei	10.50

Games

Shaw, Bryan	81
Petit, Yusmeiro	78
Cishek, Steve	74
Brentz, Jake	72
Mayers, Mike	72
Robles, Hansel	72
Stanek, Ryne	72
Barlow, Scott	71
Clase, Emmanuel	71
Trivino, Lou	71

Games Started

Berrios, Jose	32
Cease, Dylan	32
Eovaldi, Nathan	32
Irvin, Cole	32
Manaea, Sean	32
Montas, Frankie	32
Ray, Robbie	32
4 tied with	31

Complete Games

Cole, Gerrit	2
Manaea, Sean	2
17 tied with	1

Shutouts

Manaea, Sean	2
Bassitt, Chris	1
Cease, Dylan	1
Cole, Gerrit	1
Kluber, Corey	1
Lynn, Lance	1
Means, John	1
Rodon, Carlos	1
Ryu, Hyun-Jin	1
Turnbull, Spencer	1

Wins

Cole, Gerrit	16
Flexen, Chris	14
Matz, Steven	14
Ryu, Hyun-Jin	14
Cease, Dylan	13
McCullers Jr., Lance	13
Montas, Frankie	13
Ray, Robbie	13
Rodon, Carlos	13
Rodriguez, Eduardo	13

Losses

Irvin, Cole	15
Harvey, Matt	14
Lopez, Jorge	14
Lyles, Jordan	13
Allard, Kolby	12
Foltynewicz, Mike	12
Keller, Brad	12
Minor, Mike	12
Skubal, Tarik	12
5 tied with	10

No Decisions

Montgomery, Jordan	17
Taillon, Jameson	15
Wacha, Michael	15
Mize, Casey	14
Ober, Bailey	14
Gilbert, Logan	13
Kikuchi, Yusei	13
Pivetta, Nick	13
8 tied with	12

Wild Pitches

Cease, Dylan	13
Giolito, Lucas	12
Montgomery, Jordan	12
Hentges, Sam	11
Montas, Frankie	11
Soto, Gregory	11
Ohtani, Shohei	10
Scott, Tanner	10
10 tied with	9

Strikeouts

Ray, Robbie	248
Cole, Gerrit	243
Cease, Dylan	226
Montas, Frankie	207
Berrios, Jose	204
Giolito, Lucas	201
Eovaldi, Nathan	195
Manaea, Sean	194
3 tied with	185

Walks Allowed

McCullers Jr., Lance	76
Cease, Dylan	68
Pivetta, Nick	65
Keller, Brad	64
Kikuchi, Yusei	62
Richards, Garrett	60
Bubic, Kris	59
Keuchel, Dallas	59
McKenzie, Triston	58
Valdez, Framber	58

Intentional Walks Allowed

Sawamura, Hirokazu	6
Cishek, Steve	5
Fleming, Josh	5
Kittredge, Andrew	5
Sewald, Paul	5
Wittgren, Nick	5
Martin, Brett	4
7 tied with	3

Hit Batters

Manoah, Alek	16
Berrios, Jose	15
Bassitt, Chris	11
Mize, Casey	11
Singer, Brady	11
Valdez, Framber	11
Lopez, Jorge	10
McCullers Jr., Lance	10
Ohtani, Shohei	10
7 tied with	9

2021 American League Pitching Leaders

Runs Allowed		Hits Allowed		Doubles Allowed		Home Runs Allowed	
Keuchel, Dallas	105	Irvin, Cole	195	Eovaldi, Nathan	54	Lyles, Jordan	38
Lyles, Jordan	104	Lyles, Jordan	194	Rodriguez, Eduardo	41	Foltynewicz, Mike	35
Harvey, Matt	96	Keuchel, Dallas	189	Berrios, Jose	40	Skubal, Tarik	35
Yarbrough, Ryan	96	Flexen, Chris	185	Ryu, Hyun-Jin	38	Ray, Robbie	33
Irvin, Cole	94	Eovaldi, Nathan	182	Yarbrough, Ryan	37	Greinke, Zack	30
Minor, Mike	92	Manaea, Sean	179	Irvin, Cole	35	Means, John	30
Keller, Brad	89	Rodriguez, Eduardo	172	Minor, Mike	35	Allard, Kolby	29
Rodriguez, Eduardo	87	Ryu, Hyun-Jin	170	Richards, Garrett	35	Gonzales, Marco	29
Foltynewicz, Mike	86	Greinke, Zack	164	4 tied with	34	Heaney, Andrew	29
Richards, Garrett	86	Montas, Frankie	164			2 tied with	27

Run Support Per Nine IP		% Pitches In Strike Zone		Pitches Per Start		Pitches Per Batter	
(minimum 120 IP)		(minimum 120 IP)		(minimum 20 GS)		(minimum 120 IP)	
Matz, Steven	7.95	Manaea, Sean	46.5	McCullers Jr., Lance	99.6	Irvin, Cole	3.49
Ryu, Hyun-Jin	7.30	Bassitt, Chris	46.5	Cole, Gerrit	99.0	Valdez, Framber	3.65
Cease, Dylan	6.85	Eovaldi, Nathan	46.1	Ray, Robbie	98.2	Plesac, Zach	3.69
Civale, Aaron	6.73	Matz, Steven	45.5	Giolito, Lucas	95.8	Greinke, Zack	3.70
Keuchel, Dallas	6.50	Skubal, Tarik	45.0	Berrios, Jose	95.1	Bassitt, Chris	3.74
Heaney, Andrew	6.32	Richards, Garrett	43.8	Valdez, Framber	95.0	Wacha, Michael	3.74
McClanahan, Shane	5.98	Allard, Kolby	43.6	Montas, Frankie	94.6	Richards, Garrett	3.78
Garcia, Luis	5.97	Ohtani, Shohei	43.4	Minor, Mike	93.6	McClanahan, Shane	3.78
Eovaldi, Nathan	5.82	Kikuchi, Yusei	43.2	Lynn, Lance	93.1	Keuchel, Dallas	3.79
Valdez, Framber	5.75	Wacha, Michael	43.0	Heaney, Andrew	93.1	Flexen, Chris	3.79

Quality Starts		Batters Faced		Innings Pitched		Most Pitches in a Game	
Ray, Robbie	23	Berrios, Jose	781	Ray, Robbie	193.1	Cole, Gerrit	129
Montas, Frankie	20	Montas, Frankie	778	Berrios, Jose	192.0	Lyles, Jordan	124
Cole, Gerrit	18	Ray, Robbie	773	Montas, Frankie	187.0	Bieber, Shane	121
Berrios, Jose	17	Lyles, Jordan	769	Eovaldi, Nathan	182.1	Bieber, Shane	119
Bassitt, Chris	16	Irvin, Cole	768	Cole, Gerrit	181.1	Lynn, Lance	117
6 tied with	15	Eovaldi, Nathan	764	Lyles, Jordan	180.0	Ohtani, Shohei	117
		Manaea, Sean	754	Flexen, Chris	179.2	Turnbull, Spencer	117
		Flexen, Chris	741	Manaea, Sean	179.1	Cole, Gerrit	116
		Cole, Gerrit	726	Giolito, Lucas	178.2	Sandoval, Patrick	115
		2 tied with	720	Irvin, Cole	178.1	10 tied with	114

Stolen Bases Allowed		Caught Stealing Off		Stolen Base Pct Allowed		Pickoffs	
				(minimum 162 IP)			
Ray, Robbie	25	Garcia, Luis	8	McCullers Jr., Lance	25.0	Berrios, Jose	3
Cease, Dylan	22	Lopez, Reynaldo	6	Berrios, Jose	28.6	Canning, Griffin	3
Ottavino, Adam	22	McCullers Jr., Lance	6	Keuchel, Dallas	33.3	Coulombe, Danny	3
Lyles, Jordan	20	Mize, Casey	6	Ryu, Hyun-Jin	50.0	Flexen, Chris	3
Giolito, Lucas	15	Urena, Jose	6	Montas, Frankie	54.5	Giolito, Lucas	3
Harvey, Matt	15	Berrios, Jose	5	Manaea, Sean	60.0	McKenzie, Triston	3
Lynn, Lance	15	Green, Chad	5	Irvin, Cole	66.7	Montgomery, Jordan	3
Taillon, Jameson	15	Montas, Frankie	5	Flexen, Chris	80.0	17 tied with	2
Garcia, Luis	14	Montgomery, Jordan	5	Ray, Robbie	86.2		
Kluber, Corey	12	Pineda, Michael	5	Lyles, Jordan	87.0		

2021 American League Pitching Leaders

Strikeouts Per 9 IP
(minimum 120 IP)

Rodon, Carlos	12.55
Cease, Dylan	12.28
Cole, Gerrit	12.06
Ray, Robbie	11.54
Ohtani, Shohei	10.77
Rodriguez, Eduardo	10.56
Heaney, Andrew	10.41
McClanahan, Shane	10.29
McCullers Jr., Lance	10.26
McKenzie, Triston	10.20

Opp On-Base Percentage
(minimum 120 IP)

Rodon, Carlos	.255
Means, John	.263
Ray, Robbie	.267
Lynn, Lance	.267
Cole, Gerrit	.267
Giolito, Lucas	.277
Bassitt, Chris	.278
Berrios, Jose	.281
Ohtani, Shohei	.286
Civale, Aaron	.288

Opp Slugging Average
(minimum 120 IP)

Rodon, Carlos	.306
McCullers Jr., Lance	.324
Valdez, Framber	.327
Lynn, Lance	.338
Bassitt, Chris	.348
Ohtani, Shohei	.351
Cease, Dylan	.364
Montas, Frankie	.372
Cole, Gerrit	.372
Quantrill, Cal	.373

Opponent OPS
(minimum 120 IP)

Rodon, Carlos	.560
Lynn, Lance	.605
Bassitt, Chris	.626
McCullers Jr., Lance	.628
Ohtani, Shohei	.637
Cole, Gerrit	.639
Valdez, Framber	.641
Berrios, Jose	.661
Montas, Frankie	.666
Ray, Robbie	.667

Home Runs Per Nine IP
(minimum 120 IP)

McCullers Jr., Lance	0.72
Eovaldi, Nathan	0.74
Valdez, Framber	0.80
Bassitt, Chris	0.86
Rodon, Carlos	0.88
Flexen, Chris	0.95
Quantrill, Cal	0.96
Montas, Frankie	0.96
Singer, Brady	0.98
McClanahan, Shane	1.02

Batting Average vs. LHB
(minimum 125 BF)

Hendriks, Liam	.133
Glasnow, Tyler	.139
Kikuchi, Yusei	.147
Karinchak, James	.158
Clase, Emmanuel	.179
Hernandez, Carlos	.182
Sulser, Cole	.186
Ray, Robbie	.187
Fulmer, Michael	.190
Urquidy, Jose	.190

Batting Average vs. RHB
(minimum 225 BF)

Javier, Cristian	.155
Manoah, Alek	.156
Rodon, Carlos	.175
Ohtani, Shohei	.178
Garcia, Luis	.182
McKenzie, Triston	.186
McCullers Jr., Lance	.188
Lynn, Lance	.192
Berrios, Jose	.193
Kaprielian, James	.201

Opp BA w/ RISP
(minimum 125 BF)

Ray, Robbie	.161
Mize, Casey	.162
McCullers Jr., Lance	.164
Quantrill, Cal	.167
Bassitt, Chris	.177
Cole, Gerrit	.184
Garcia, Luis	.185
Kikuchi, Yusei	.195
Cease, Dylan	.197
Skubal, Tarik	.198

OBP vs. Leadoff Hitter
(minimum 120 BF)

Means, John	.252
Manaea, Sean	.258
Montas, Frankie	.259
Taillon, Jameson	.261
Flexen, Chris	.269
Ray, Robbie	.273
Valdez, Framber	.273
Rodon, Carlos	.276
Harvey, Matt	.277
Ryu, Hyun-Jin	.278

Strikeouts / Walks Ratio
(minimum 120 IP)

Cole, Gerrit	5.93
Eovaldi, Nathan	5.57
Means, John	5.15
Rodon, Carlos	5.14
Ray, Robbie	4.77
Manaea, Sean	4.73
Berrios, Jose	4.53
Yarbrough, Ryan	4.33
Bassitt, Chris	4.08
Rodriguez, Eduardo	3.94

Highest GB/FB Ratio
(minimum 120 IP)

Valdez, Framber	4.73
Keuchel, Dallas	2.18
McCullers Jr., Lance	2.09
Lopez, Jorge	1.80
Singer, Brady	1.80
Keller, Brad	1.65
Kikuchi, Yusei	1.60
McClanahan, Shane	1.54
Richards, Garrett	1.47
Bubic, Kris	1.47

Lowest GB/FB Ratio
(minimum 120 IP)

McKenzie, Triston	0.62
Gonzales, Marco	0.67
Taillon, Jameson	0.69
Means, John	0.70
Heaney, Andrew	0.74
Cease, Dylan	0.75
Giolito, Lucas	0.78
Rodon, Carlos	0.84
Ray, Robbie	0.84
Lynn, Lance	0.89

Sacrifice Flies Allowed

Keller, Brad	9
Cease, Dylan	7
Flexen, Chris	7
Lyles, Jordan	7
Montgomery, Jordan	7
Cole, Gerrit	6
Jax, Griffin	6
Tate, Dillon	6
13 tied with	5

Sacrifice Hits Allowed

Irvin, Cole	4
Martin, Brett	4
Odorizzi, Jake	4
Quantrill, Cal	4
8 tied with	3

GIDP Induced

Flexen, Chris	22
Keuchel, Dallas	21
Bubic, Kris	20
Greinke, Zack	18
Irvin, Cole	18
Lyles, Jordan	18
Quantrill, Cal	18
Kikuchi, Yusei	17
Mize, Casey	17
Richards, Garrett	17

GIDP Per Nine IP
(minimum 120 IP)

Bubic, Kris	1.38
Keuchel, Dallas	1.17
Richards, Garrett	1.12
Flexen, Chris	1.10
Quantrill, Cal	1.08
Lopez, Jorge	1.04
Mize, Casey	1.02
Kikuchi, Yusei	0.97
Greinke, Zack	0.95
Keller, Brad	0.94

2021 American League Pitching Leaders

Saves

Hendriks, Liam	38
Iglesias, Raisel	34
Chapman, Aroldis	30
Pressly, Ryan	26
Barnes, Matt	24
Clase, Emmanuel	24
Romano, Jordan	23
Trivino, Lou	22
Soto, Gregory	18
Colome, Alex	17

Blown Saves

Colome, Alex	7
Diekman, Jake	7
10 tied with	6

Save Pct
(minimum 20 Save Ops)

Romano, Jordan	95.8
Pressly, Ryan	92.9
Chapman, Aroldis	88.2
Iglesias, Raisel	87.2
Hendriks, Liam	86.4
Trivino, Lou	84.6
Clase, Emmanuel	82.8
Barnes, Matt	80.0
Barlow, Scott	72.7
Castillo, Diego	72.7

Save Opportunities

Hendriks, Liam	44
Iglesias, Raisel	39
Chapman, Aroldis	34
Barnes, Matt	30
Clase, Emmanuel	29
Pressly, Ryan	28
Trivino, Lou	26
Colome, Alex	24
Romano, Jordan	24
2 tied with	22

Easy Saves

Hendriks, Liam	22
Chapman, Aroldis	19
Clase, Emmanuel	17
Trivino, Lou	17
Romano, Jordan	15
Iglesias, Raisel	14
Pressly, Ryan	14
Kennedy, Ian	13
Soto, Gregory	12
3 tied with	11

Regular Saves

Iglesias, Raisel	16
Barnes, Matt	12
Hendriks, Liam	12
Pressly, Ryan	12
Chapman, Aroldis	11
Romano, Jordan	8
Castillo, Diego	7
Graveman, Kendall	7
4 tied with	6

Tough Saves

Hendriks, Liam	4
Iglesias, Raisel	4
Fulmer, Michael	3
Sewald, Paul	3
Loaisiga, Jonathan	2
Ottavino, Adam	2
Rogers, Taylor	2
25 tied with	1

Holds Adjusted Saves %
(minimum 20 Save Ops + Holds)

Staumont, Josh	100.0
Romano, Jordan	96.6
Soto, Gregory	96.2
Robles, Hansel	93.9
Pressly, Ryan	93.1
Duffey, Tyler	92.6
Stanek, Ryne	92.0
Fairbanks, Pete	90.5
Chapman, Aroldis	88.6
Trivino, Lou	88.2

Relief Wins

Green, Chad	10
Sewald, Paul	10
Kittredge, Andrew	9
Loaisiga, Jonathan	9
Hendriks, Liam	8
Petit, Yusmeiro	8
Whitlock, Garrett	8
8 tied with	7

Relief Losses

Trivino, Lou	8
Wittgren, Nick	8
Green, Chad	7
Shaw, Bryan	7
Alcala, Jorge	6
Fairbanks, Pete	6
Tate, Dillon	6
12 tied with	5

Relief Games

Shaw, Bryan	81
Petit, Yusmeiro	78
Cishek, Steve	74
Brentz, Jake	72
Robles, Hansel	72
Stanek, Ryne	72
Barlow, Scott	71
Clase, Emmanuel	71
Trivino, Lou	71
Mayers, Mike	70

Holds

Duffey, Tyler	22
Ottavino, Adam	22
Petit, Yusmeiro	22
Bummer, Aaron	21
Cishek, Steve	21
Stanek, Ryne	21
Shaw, Bryan	20
Misiewicz, Anthony	19
3 tied with	18

Relief Innings

Green, Chad	83.2
Petit, Yusmeiro	78.0
Shaw, Bryan	77.1
Barlow, Scott	74.1
Trivino, Lou	73.2
Whitlock, Garrett	73.1
Mayers, Mike	71.1
Hendriks, Liam	71.0
Loaisiga, Jonathan	70.2
Luetge, Lucas	70.1

Inherited Runners Scrd %
(minimum 25 IR)

Hendriks, Liam	10.0
Santana, Dennis	10.3
Peralta, Wandy	13.3
Loaisiga, Jonathan	17.1
Sawamura, Hirokazu	17.1
Funkhouser, Kyle	17.9
Mayza, Tim	21.6
Green, Chad	21.9
Taylor, Josh	23.9
Whitlock, Garrett	24.0

Relief Opp On Base Pct
(minimum 50 IP)

Hendriks, Liam	.199
Green, Chad	.236
Wells, Tyler	.238
Clase, Emmanuel	.241
Iglesias, Raisel	.243
Pressly, Ryan	.249
Sewald, Paul	.251
Kittredge, Andrew	.259
Alcala, Jorge	.263
Mayza, Tim	.263

Relief Opp Slugging Avg
(minimum 50 IP)

Clase, Emmanuel	.240
Bummer, Aaron	.250
Graveman, Kendall	.253
Loaisiga, Jonathan	.281
Crochet, Garrett	.289
Staumont, Josh	.294
Pressly, Ryan	.297
Kittredge, Andrew	.307
Mayza, Tim	.309
Trivino, Lou	.310

2021 American League Pitching Leaders

Relief Opp BA Vs LHB (minimum 50 AB)	
Brentz, Jake	.116
Taylor, Blake	.123
Hendriks, Liam	.133
Romano, Jordan	.140
King, John	.140
Taylor, Josh	.146
Chargois, JT	.147
Bummer, Aaron	.151
Barnes, Matt	.156
Hearn, Taylor	.157

Relief Opp BA Vs RHB (minimum 50 AB)	
Barlow, Joe	.109
Graveman, Kendall	.117
Suarez, Jose	.141
Stanek, Ryne	.148
Feyereisen, J.P.	.150
Sadler, Casey	.156
Minaya, Juan	.158
Wisler, Matt	.159
Richards, Trevor	.160
Ramirez, Yohan	.161

Relief Opp Batting Average (minimum 50 IP)	
Hendriks, Liam	.174
Sewald, Paul	.176
Karinchak, James	.176
Graveman, Kendall	.180
Romano, Jordan	.181
Chapman, Aroldis	.182
Staumont, Josh	.183
Stanek, Ryne	.186
Wells, Tyler	.192
Green, Chad	.193

Relief Earned Run Average (minimum 50 IP)	
Clase, Emmanuel	1.29
Kittredge, Andrew	1.65
Graveman, Kendall	1.77
McHugh, Collin	1.90
Whitlock, Garrett	1.96
Steckenrider, Drew	2.00
Romano, Jordan	2.14
Loaisiga, Jonathan	2.17
Pressly, Ryan	2.25
Barlow, Scott	2.42

Rel OBP 1st Batter Faced (minimum 40 BF)	
Hendriks, Liam	.145
Chargois, JT	.179
Patton, Spencer	.190
Sadler, Casey	.190
Iglesias, Raisel	.200
Kopech, Michael	.200
Wells, Tyler	.205
Kittredge, Andrew	.208
Mayza, Tim	.217
Whitlock, Garrett	.217

Rel Opp BA w/ Runners On (minimum 50 IP)	
Romano, Jordan	.155
Javier, Cristian	.163
Sawamura, Hirokazu	.168
Castillo, Diego	.176
Chapman, Aroldis	.176
Trivino, Lou	.177
Stanek, Ryne	.177
Sborz, Josh	.178
Whitlock, Garrett	.178
Graveman, Kendall	.180

Relief Opp BA w/ RISP (minimum 50 IP)	
Romano, Jordan	.097
Brentz, Jake	.125
Whitlock, Garrett	.139
Bickford, Phil	.140
Sawamura, Hirokazu	.143
Steckenrider, Drew	.143
Clase, Emmanuel	.145
Chapman, Aroldis	.148
Javier, Cristian	.154
Karinchak, James	.162

Fastest Avg Fastball-Relief (minimum 50 IP)	
Clase, Emmanuel	100.3
Chapman, Aroldis	98.5
Loaisiga, Jonathan	98.4
Soto, Gregory	98.3
Hendriks, Liam	97.7
Kopech, Michael	97.7
Stanek, Ryne	97.7
Romano, Jordan	97.6
Alcala, Jorge	97.4
Ruiz, Jose	97.0

Fastest Average Fastball (minimum 120 IP)	
Cole, Gerrit	97.7
Eovaldi, Nathan	96.9
Cease, Dylan	96.7
McClanahan, Shane	96.5
Montas, Frankie	96.3
Ohtani, Shohei	95.7
Rodon, Carlos	95.4
Lopez, Jorge	95.2
Kikuchi, Yusei	95.2
Pivetta, Nick	94.8

Slowest Average Fastball (minimum 120 IP)	
Yarbrough, Ryan	86.5
Keuchel, Dallas	87.9
Gonzales, Marco	88.4
Greinke, Zack	88.9
Ryu, Hyun-Jin	90.0
Irvin, Cole	90.7
Bubic, Kris	90.9
Minor, Mike	91.0
Civale, Aaron	91.6
Allard, Kolby	91.6

Pitches 100+ Velocity	
Clase, Emmanuel	598
Chapman, Aroldis	179
Soto, Gregory	111
Loaisiga, Jonathan	98
Cole, Gerrit	96
Hernandez, Carlos	59
Kopech, Michael	55
Romano, Jordan	53
Gose, Anthony	37
Pearson, Nate	32

Pitches 95+ Velocity	
Montas, Frankie	1698
Cole, Gerrit	1418
Cease, Dylan	1316
Eovaldi, Nathan	1223
Ray, Robbie	1162
Gilbert, Logan	1002
Lopez, Jorge	931
Pivetta, Nick	902
Rodon, Carlos	894
Green, Chad	784

Pitches Less Than 80 MPH	
Yarbrough, Ryan	1136
Hill, Rich	1133
Ryu, Hyun-Jin	618
Gonzales, Marco	604
Maton, Phil	588
Romo, Sergio	585
Valdez, Cesar	556
Valdez, Framber	555
Heaney, Andrew	530
Bubic, Kris	498

Lowest % Fastballs (minimum 120 IP)	
Yarbrough, Ryan	13.5
Civale, Aaron	32.9
McCullers Jr., Lance	34.0
Kikuchi, Yusei	36.0
Ryu, Hyun-Jin	36.0
Montgomery, Jordan	38.2
Wacha, Michael	39.9
Flexen, Chris	40.0
Keuchel, Dallas	40.1
McClanahan, Shane	40.8

Highest % Fastballs (minimum 120 IP)	
Lynn, Lance	62.5
McKenzie, Triston	61.4
Manaea, Sean	60.2
Irvin, Cole	60.0
Keller, Brad	59.8
Ray, Robbie	59.8
Heaney, Andrew	59.3
Rodon, Carlos	58.6
Montas, Frankie	58.3
Singer, Brady	57.9

Highest % Curveballs (minimum 120 IP)	
Valdez, Framber	30.8
Berrios, Jose	30.5
McCullers Jr., Lance	25.0
Pivetta, Nick	23.7
Lopez, Jorge	23.7
Montgomery, Jordan	23.7
Taillon, Jameson	19.0
Eovaldi, Nathan	18.8
Lyles, Jordan	18.2
McKenzie, Triston	18.1

2021 American League Pitching Leaders

Highest % Changeups
(minimum 120 IP)

Giolito, Lucas	31.8
Bubic, Kris	30.8
Wacha, Michael	29.2
Keuchel, Dallas	28.6
Yarbrough, Ryan	28.0
Means, John	27.3
Ryu, Hyun-Jin	25.5
Montgomery, Jordan	24.4
Plesac, Zach	24.2
Manaea, Sean	24.2

Highest % Sliders
(minimum 120 IP)

Singer, Brady	38.1
Keller, Brad	34.8
McClanahan, Shane	34.8
Ray, Robbie	31.0
Quantrill, Cal	30.6
Cease, Dylan	30.6
Lynn, Lance	30.3
Mize, Casey	28.0
Richards, Garrett	27.4
Rodon, Carlos	27.2

Balks

11 tied with	2

Strikeout/Hit Ratio
(minimum 50 IP)

Chapman, Aroldis	2.69
Hendriks, Liam	2.51
Sewald, Paul	2.48
Glasnow, Tyler	2.24
Karinchak, James	2.23
Romano, Jordan	2.07
Barnes, Matt	2.05
Rodon, Carlos	2.03
Iglesias, Raisel	1.94
Javier, Cristian	1.94

Opp OPS vs Fastballs
(minimum 251 BF)

Rodon, Carlos	.536
Bassitt, Chris	.583
Manoah, Alek	.585
Lynn, Lance	.596
Valdez, Framber	.636
Bubic, Kris	.649
Ray, Robbie	.650
Cole, Gerrit	.653
Gilbert, Logan	.653
Taillon, Jameson	.664

Opp OPS vs Curveballs
(minimum 100 BF)

German, Domingo	.446
Eovaldi, Nathan	.464
McCullers Jr., Lance	.502
Duffey, Tyler	.538
Valdez, Framber	.580
Hill, Rich	.583
Montgomery, Jordan	.615
Pivetta, Nick	.649
Bieber, Shane	.679
Berrios, Jose	.692

Opp OPS vs Changeups
(minimum 100 BF)

Sulser, Cole	.440
Suarez, Jose	.503
Flexen, Chris	.514
Sandoval, Patrick	.544
Peralta, Wandy	.566
Montgomery, Jordan	.570
Greinke, Zack	.593
Cole, Gerrit	.614
Matz, Steven	.617
Cobb, Alex	.618

Opp OPS vs Sliders
(minimum 64 BF)

Clase, Emmanuel	.320
Garcia, Luis	.370
Pressly, Ryan	.402
Rodon, Carlos	.430
Castillo, Diego	.458
Bieber, Shane	.467
Javier, Cristian	.468
Rasmussen, Drew	.480
Santana, Ervin	.486
Soto, Gregory	.488

Earned Runs

Lyles, Jordan	103
Keuchel, Dallas	95
Harvey, Matt	89
Minor, Mike	89
Yarbrough, Ryan	88
Foltynewicz, Mike	84
Heaney, Andrew	84
Irvin, Cole	84
Rodriguez, Eduardo	83
2 tied with	82

Hits Per Nine Innings
(minimum 120 IP)

Rodon, Carlos	6.17
McKenzie, Triston	6.30
McCullers Jr., Lance	6.76
Ohtani, Shohei	6.77
Ray, Robbie	6.98
Lynn, Lance	7.05
Bassitt, Chris	7.26
Giolito, Lucas	7.30
Valdez, Framber	7.35
Berrios, Jose	7.45

2021 National League Pitching Leaders

Earned Run Average (minimum 162 IP)	
Burnes, Corbin	2.43
Scherzer, Max	2.46
Buehler, Walker	2.47
Woodruff, Brandon	2.56
Wheeler, Zack	2.78
Gausman, Kevin	2.81
Urias, Julio	2.96
Stroman, Marcus	3.02
Fried, Max	3.04
Wainwright, Adam	3.05

Winning Percentage (minimum 15 Decisions)	
Urias, Julio	.870
Buehler, Walker	.800
Scherzer, Max	.789
Smyly, Drew	.733
Wainwright, Adam	.708
Suter, Brent	.706
Gausman, Kevin	.700
Morton, Charlie	.700
Burnes, Corbin	.688
Mahle, Tyler	.684

Opponent Batting Average (minimum 120 IP)	
Peralta, Freddy	.165
Scherzer, Max	.185
Buehler, Walker	.199
Woodruff, Brandon	.200
Burnes, Corbin	.201
Morton, Charlie	.203
Gausman, Kevin	.210
Musgrove, Joe	.213
Snell, Blake	.214
Wheeler, Zack	.215

Baserunners Per 9 IP (minimum 120 IP)	
Scherzer, Max	8.28
Burnes, Corbin	8.78
Buehler, Walker	8.97
Woodruff, Brandon	9.03
Kershaw, Clayton	9.40
Wheeler, Zack	9.41
Peralta, Freddy	9.42
Urias, Julio	9.50
Gausman, Kevin	9.56
Wainwright, Adam	9.90

Games	
Rogers, Tyler	80
Hill, Tim	78
Neris, Hector	74
Gallegos, Giovanny	73
Treinen, Blake	72
Boxberger, Brad	71
Cabrera, Genesis	71
Jackson, Luke	71
Smith, Will	71
2 tied with	70

Games Started	
Alcantara, Sandy	33
Buehler, Walker	33
Castillo, Luis	33
Gausman, Kevin	33
Mahle, Tyler	33
Morton, Charlie	33
Stroman, Marcus	33
7 tied with	32

Complete Games	
Marquez, German	3
Wainwright, Adam	3
Wheeler, Zack	3
DeSclafani, Anthony	2
Fried, Max	2
Musgrove, Joe	2
14 tied with	1

Shutouts	
DeSclafani, Anthony	2
Fried, Max	2
Musgrove, Joe	2
Wheeler, Zack	2
10 tied with	1

Wins	
Urias, Julio	20
Wainwright, Adam	17
Buehler, Walker	16
Scherzer, Max	15
Fried, Max	14
Gausman, Kevin	14
Hendricks, Kyle	14
Morton, Charlie	14
Wheeler, Zack	14
2 tied with	13

Losses	
Castillo, Luis	16
Corbin, Patrick	16
Alcantara, Sandy	15
Arrieta, Jake	14
Alzolay, Adbert	13
Brubaker, JT	13
Stroman, Marcus	13
Davies, Zach	12
Gray, Jon	12
5 tied with	11

No Decisions	
Lester, Jon	15
Davies, Zach	14
Mahle, Tyler	14
Nola, Aaron	14
Senzatela, Antonio	14
Snell, Blake	14
Buehler, Walker	13
Crowe, Wil	13
Gausman, Kevin	13
Morton, Charlie	13

Wild Pitches	
Marquez, German	15
Reyes, Alex	10
Alvarado, Jose	9
Cabrera, Genesis	9
Darvish, Yu	9
Gray, Sonny	9
Hoffman, Jeff	9
Houser, Adrian	9
Kuhl, Chad	9
Muller, Kyle	9

Strikeouts	
Wheeler, Zack	247
Scherzer, Max	236
Burnes, Corbin	234
Gausman, Kevin	227
Nola, Aaron	223
Morton, Charlie	216
Buehler, Walker	212
Woodruff, Brandon	211
Mahle, Tyler	210
Musgrove, Joe	203

Walks Allowed	
Castillo, Luis	75
Davies, Zach	75
Snell, Blake	69
Houser, Adrian	64
Mahle, Tyler	64
Marquez, German	64
Smith, Caleb	63
Corbin, Patrick	60
Gray, Jon	58
Morton, Charlie	58

Intentional Walks Allowed	
Bickford, Phil	7
Bass, Anthony	6
Fedde, Erick	6
Graterol, Brusdar	6
9 tied with	5

Hit Batters	
Adams, Austin L	24
Musgrove, Joe	18
Morton, Charlie	17
Wood, Alex	16
Hendricks, Kyle	13
Bumgarner, Madison	11
Martinez, Carlos	11
Peralta, Freddy	11
3 tied with	10

2021 National League Pitching Leaders

Runs Allowed

Corbin, Patrick	114
Hendricks, Kyle	101
Davies, Zach	99
Nola, Aaron	95
Castillo, Luis	94
Marquez, German	92
Arrieta, Jake	91
Fedde, Erick	90
Alcantara, Sandy	85
3 tied with	84

Hits Allowed

Hendricks, Kyle	200
Corbin, Patrick	192
Castillo, Luis	181
Senzatela, Antonio	178
Alcantara, Sandy	171
Wheeler, Zack	169
Wainwright, Adam	168
Miley, Wade	166
Marquez, German	165
Nola, Aaron	165

Doubles Allowed

Hendricks, Kyle	43
Davies, Zach	41
Alcantara, Sandy	40
Senzatela, Antonio	39
Buehler, Walker	36
Darvish, Yu	35
Gonzalez, Chi Chi	35
Marquez, German	35
Miley, Wade	35
2 tied with	34

Home Runs Allowed

Corbin, Patrick	37
Hendricks, Kyle	31
Brubaker, JT	28
Darvish, Yu	28
Smyly, Drew	27
Nola, Aaron	26
Walker, Taijuan	26
4 tied with	25

Run Support Per Nine IP
(minimum 120 IP)

Urias, Julio	7.17
Miley, Wade	6.63
Fried, Max	6.36
Smyly, Drew	6.32
Mahle, Tyler	5.90
Lester, Jon	5.86
Kershaw, Clayton	5.84
Morton, Charlie	5.77
Fedde, Erick	5.67
Webb, Logan	5.64

% Pitches In Strike Zone
(minimum 120 IP)

Urias, Julio	45.4
Senzatela, Antonio	44.8
Bumgarner, Madison	44.6
Darvish, Yu	44.1
Walker, Taijuan	43.9
DeSclafani, Anthony	43.4
Woodruff, Brandon	43.3
Fried, Max	43.3
Gray, Jon	43.0
Wood, Alex	42.8

Pitches Per Start
(minimum 20 GS)

Wheeler, Zack	100.2
Mahle, Tyler	96.8
Castillo, Luis	95.9
Wainwright, Adam	95.9
Buehler, Walker	95.5
Scherzer, Max	94.0
Alcantara, Sandy	93.8
Woodruff, Brandon	93.7
Musgrove, Joe	92.9
Nola, Aaron	92.8

Pitches Per Batter
(minimum 120 IP)

Hendricks, Kyle	3.58
Senzatela, Antonio	3.59
Brubaker, JT	3.61
Kelly, Merrill	3.64
Corbin, Patrick	3.66
Freeland, Kyle	3.66
Marquez, German	3.69
Alcantara, Sandy	3.70
Kershaw, Clayton	3.70
Wainwright, Adam	3.71

Quality Starts

Buehler, Walker	27
Alcantara, Sandy	23
Wainwright, Adam	22
Gausman, Kevin	20
Wheeler, Zack	20
Woodruff, Brandon	20
Fried, Max	19
Hendricks, Kyle	19
Morton, Charlie	19
3 tied with	18

Batters Faced

Wheeler, Zack	849
Alcantara, Sandy	837
Wainwright, Adam	828
Buehler, Walker	815
Castillo, Luis	803
Hendricks, Kyle	785
Gausman, Kevin	775
Mahle, Tyler	759
Marquez, German	756
Morton, Charlie	756

Innings Pitched

Wheeler, Zack	213.1
Buehler, Walker	207.2
Wainwright, Adam	206.1
Alcantara, Sandy	205.2
Gausman, Kevin	192.0
Castillo, Luis	187.2
Morton, Charlie	185.2
Urias, Julio	185.2
Musgrove, Joe	181.1
Hendricks, Kyle	181.0

Most Pitches in a Game

Bauer, Trevor	126
Snell, Blake	122
Cueto, Johnny	118
Wheeler, Zack	118
Bauer, Trevor	117
Nola, Aaron	117
Nola, Aaron	116
Bauer, Trevor	115
Burnes, Corbin	115
8 tied with	114

Stolen Bases Allowed

Houser, Adrian	19
Snell, Blake	19
Burnes, Corbin	18
Treinen, Blake	17
Fedde, Erick	16
Darvish, Yu	15
Gutierrez, Vladimir	14
Alcantara, Sandy	13
Corbin, Patrick	13
3 tied with	12

Caught Stealing Off

Scherzer, Max	7
Stroman, Marcus	7
Fedde, Erick	6
Houser, Adrian	6
8 tied with	5

Stolen Base Pct Allowed
(minimum 162 IP)

Woodruff, Brandon	37.5
Mahle, Tyler	40.0
Miley, Wade	40.0
Urias, Julio	40.0
Scherzer, Max	46.2
Wainwright, Adam	50.0
Castillo, Luis	55.6
Wheeler, Zack	57.1
Stroman, Marcus	58.8
DeSclafani, Anthony	63.6

Pickoffs

Weathers, Ryan	9
Fried, Max	7
Miley, Wade	6
Smyly, Drew	5
Kershaw, Clayton	4
Lauer, Eric	4
Walker, Taijuan	4
5 tied with	3

2021 National League Pitching Leaders

Strikeouts Per 9 IP	
(minimum 120 IP)	
Burnes, Corbin	12.61
Peralta, Freddy	12.16
Snell, Blake	11.89
Scherzer, Max	11.84
Nola, Aaron	11.11
Darvish, Yu	10.77
Kershaw, Clayton	10.65
Gausman, Kevin	10.64
Rogers, Trevor	10.62
Woodruff, Brandon	10.59

Opp On-Base Percentage	
(minimum 120 IP)	
Scherzer, Max	.239
Burnes, Corbin	.248
Woodruff, Brandon	.256
Buehler, Walker	.256
Peralta, Freddy	.261
Kershaw, Clayton	.262
Gausman, Kevin	.264
Wheeler, Zack	.265
Urias, Julio	.266
Wainwright, Adam	.275

Opp Slugging Average	
(minimum 120 IP)	
Burnes, Corbin	.273
Peralta, Freddy	.300
Morton, Charlie	.309
Woodruff, Brandon	.317
Rogers, Trevor	.318
Wheeler, Zack	.321
Buehler, Walker	.329
Scherzer, Max	.331
Webb, Logan	.332
Houser, Adrian	.340

Opponent OPS	
(minimum 120 IP)	
Burnes, Corbin	.521
Peralta, Freddy	.561
Scherzer, Max	.570
Woodruff, Brandon	.573
Buehler, Walker	.586
Wheeler, Zack	.586
Morton, Charlie	.591
Gausman, Kevin	.609
Rogers, Trevor	.609
Urias, Julio	.614

Home Runs Per Nine IP	
(minimum 120 IP)	
Burnes, Corbin	0.38
Rogers, Trevor	0.41
Webb, Logan	0.55
Wheeler, Zack	0.68
Senzatela, Antonio	0.69
Houser, Adrian	0.76
Morton, Charlie	0.78
Fried, Max	0.81
Buehler, Walker	0.82
Stroman, Marcus	0.85

Batting Average vs. LHB	
(minimum 125 BF)	
deGrom, Jacob	.128
Boxberger, Brad	.139
Treinen, Blake	.140
Reyes, Alex	.155
Peralta, Freddy	.157
Diaz, Edwin	.165
Jansen, Kenley	.169
Gallegos, Giovanny	.176
Kershaw, Clayton	.178
Rogers, Tyler	.179

Batting Average vs. RHB	
(minimum 225 BF)	
Peralta, Freddy	.174
Scherzer, Max	.177
Burnes, Corbin	.179
Houser, Adrian	.192
Musgrove, Joe	.194
Buehler, Walker	.198
Smith, Caleb	.203
DeSclafani, Anthony	.204
Gausman, Kevin	.206
Rogers, Trevor	.206

Opp BA w/ RISP	
(minimum 125 BF)	
Woodruff, Brandon	.135
Gausman, Kevin	.154
Hendricks, Kyle	.182
Wainwright, Adam	.184
Buehler, Walker	.190
Miley, Wade	.198
Houser, Adrian	.200
Mahle, Tyler	.217
Webb, Logan	.224
Rogers, Trevor	.230

OBP vs. Leadoff Hitter	
(minimum 120 BF)	
Peralta, Freddy	.209
Gray, Sonny	.223
Wheeler, Zack	.226
Lauer, Eric	.232
Gausman, Kevin	.240
Urias, Julio	.246
Burnes, Corbin	.253
Woodruff, Brandon	.257
Morton, Charlie	.260
Alcantara, Sandy	.262

Strikeouts / Walks Ratio	
(minimum 120 IP)	
Burnes, Corbin	6.88
Kershaw, Clayton	6.86
Scherzer, Max	6.56
Nola, Aaron	5.72
Wheeler, Zack	5.37
Urias, Julio	5.13
Woodruff, Brandon	4.91
Gausman, Kevin	4.54
Darvish, Yu	4.52
Webb, Logan	4.39

Highest GB/FB Ratio	
(minimum 120 IP)	
Webb, Logan	3.29
Houser, Adrian	2.79
Castillo, Luis	2.30
Marquez, German	1.96
Stroman, Marcus	1.92
Alcantara, Sandy	1.92
Senzatela, Antonio	1.91
Wood, Alex	1.90
Fried, Max	1.87
Miley, Wade	1.82

Lowest GB/FB Ratio	
(minimum 120 IP)	
Scherzer, Max	0.69
Peralta, Freddy	0.70
Bumgarner, Madison	0.74
Darvish, Yu	0.82
Urias, Julio	0.98
Nola, Aaron	1.00
Smyly, Drew	1.00
Walker, Taijuan	1.02
Snell, Blake	1.06
Rogers, Trevor	1.13

Sacrifice Flies Allowed	
Stroman, Marcus	8
Bumgarner, Madison	7
Woodford, Jake	7
Arrieta, Jake	6
Kuhl, Chad	6
Morton, Charlie	6
Musgrove, Joe	6
Senzatela, Antonio	6
6 tied with	5

Sacrifice Hits Allowed	
Corbin, Patrick	10
Cueto, Johnny	10
Mahle, Tyler	9
Castillo, Luis	8
Davies, Zach	8
Fedde, Erick	8
Miley, Wade	8
Moore, Matt	8
4 tied with	7

GIDP Induced	
Castillo, Luis	20
Corbin, Patrick	19
Senzatela, Antonio	19
Houser, Adrian	18
Mills, Alec	18
Webb, Logan	18
Alcantara, Sandy	17
Buehler, Walker	17
Kuhl, Chad	17
Stroman, Marcus	17

GIDP Per Nine IP	
(minimum 120 IP)	
Freeland, Kyle	1.19
Houser, Adrian	1.14
Senzatela, Antonio	1.09
Webb, Logan	1.09
Corbin, Patrick	1.00
Castillo, Luis	0.96
Lester, Jon	0.89
Miley, Wade	0.88
Stroman, Marcus	0.85
2 tied with	0.80

2021 National League Pitching Leaders

Saves			Blown Saves			Save Pct			Save Opportunities	
						(minimum 20 Save Ops)				
Melancon, Mark	39		Bard, Daniel	8		Hader, Josh	97.1		Melancon, Mark	45
Jansen, Kenley	38		Gallegos, Giovanny	8		Kimbrel, Craig	92.0		Jansen, Kenley	43
Smith, Will	37		Suter, Brent	8		Jansen, Kenley	88.4		Smith, Will	43
Hader, Josh	34		Hand, Brad	7		Melancon, Mark	86.7		Diaz, Edwin	38
Diaz, Edwin	32		Neris, Hector	7		McGee, Jake	86.1		McGee, Jake	36
McGee, Jake	31		9 tied with	6		Smith, Will	86.0		Hader, Josh	35
Reyes, Alex	29					Reyes, Alex	85.3		Reyes, Alex	34
Kimbrel, Craig	23					Diaz, Edwin	84.2		Bard, Daniel	28
Hand, Brad	21					Hand, Brad	75.0		Hand, Brad	28
Bard, Daniel	20					2 tied with	71.4		Kimbrel, Craig	25

Easy Saves			Regular Saves			Tough Saves			Holds Adjusted Saves %	
									(minimum 20 Save Ops + Holds)	
Hader, Josh	24		Diaz, Edwin	17		Jansen, Kenley	3		Matzek, Tyler	100.0
Melancon, Mark	24		Jansen, Kenley	14		Floro, Dylan	2		Hader, Josh	97.1
Smith, Will	24		Melancon, Mark	14		Kennedy, Ian	2		Kimbrel, Craig	92.0
Jansen, Kenley	21		Smith, Will	13		Kimbrel, Craig	2		Treinen, Blake	90.7
McGee, Jake	19		McGee, Jake	12		26 tied with	1		Cabrera, Genesis	90.3
Reyes, Alex	19		Hader, Josh	10					Williams, Devin	89.7
Bard, Daniel	15		Reyes, Alex	9					Finnegan, Kyle	88.9
Diaz, Edwin	14		Garcia, Yimi	8					Jackson, Luke	88.6
Hand, Brad	13		Hand, Brad	8					McGee, Jake	88.6
Kimbrel, Craig	13		Kimbrel, Craig	8					Jansen, Kenley	88.4

Relief Wins			Relief Losses			Relief Games			Holds	
Suter, Brent	12		Finnegan, Kyle	9		Rogers, Tyler	80		Treinen, Blake	32
Reyes, Alex	10		Bard, Daniel	8		Hill, Tim	78		Jackson, Luke	31
Familia, Jeurys	9		Bass, Anthony	8		Neris, Hector	74		Rogers, Tyler	30
Williams, Devin	8		Reyes, Alex	8		Gallegos, Giovanny	73		Cabrera, Genesis	28
Alvarado, Jose	7		Garcia, Yimi	7		Treinen, Blake	72		Gallegos, Giovanny	24
Bard, Daniel	7		Hembree, Heath	7		Boxberger, Brad	71		Matzek, Tyler	24
Bradley, Archie	7		Neris, Hector	7		Cabrera, Genesis	71		Boxberger, Brad	23
May, Trevor	7		Smith, Will	7		Jackson, Luke	71		Minter, A.J.	23
Rogers, Tyler	7		4 tied with	6		Smith, Will	71		Williams, Devin	23
Stratton, Chris	7					Kinley, Tyler	70		Bleier, Richard	20

Relief Innings			Inherited Runners Scrd %			Relief Opp On Base Pct			Relief Opp Slugging Avg	
			(minimum 25 IR)			(minimum 50 IP)			(minimum 50 IP)	
Crismatt, Nabil	81.1		Matzek, Tyler	10.3		Hader, Josh	.228		Hader, Josh	.193
Rogers, Tyler	81.0		Gallegos, Giovanny	12.0		McGee, Jake	.234		Jansen, Kenley	.233
Gallegos, Giovanny	80.1		Helsley, Ryan	12.9		Rodriguez, Richard	.247		Loup, Aaron	.240
Stammen, Craig	80.1		Treinen, Blake	13.8		Gallegos, Giovanny	.249		Adams, Austin L	.244
Stratton, Chris	79.1		Howard, Sam	14.8		Stammen, Craig	.249		Treinen, Blake	.253
Neris, Hector	74.1		Minter, A.J.	16.0		Bednar, David	.253		Alvarez, Jose	.268
Underwood Jr., Duane	72.2		Alvarado, Jose	18.8		Garcia, Jarlin	.256		Matzek, Tyler	.277
Reyes, Alex	72.1		Alvarez, Jose	18.9		Treinen, Blake	.259		Diaz, Edwin	.285
Treinen, Blake	72.1		Mantiply, Joe	20.0		Alvarez, Jose	.261		Floro, Dylan	.287
Suter, Brent	71.0		Tepera, Ryan	22.6		Loup, Aaron	.266		Williams, Devin	.294

2021 National League Pitching Leaders

Relief Opp BA Vs LHB (minimum 50 AB)		Relief Opp BA Vs RHB (minimum 50 AB)		Relief Opp Batting Average (minimum 50 IP)		Relief Earned Run Average (minimum 50 IP)	
Kimbrel, Craig	.100	Nelson, Jimmy	.100	Hader, Josh	.127	Loup, Aaron	1.01
Tepera, Ryan	.100	Kimbrel, Craig	.113	Jansen, Kenley	.153	Hader, Josh	1.23
Vesia, Alex	.123	Hader, Josh	.125	Adams, Austin L	.159	Jackson, Luke	1.98
Alvarado, Jose	.123	Vesia, Alex	.129	Reyes, Alex	.176	Treinen, Blake	1.99
Morgan, Adam	.125	Antone, Tejay	.130	Treinen, Blake	.179	Alvarez, Jose	2.14
Smith, Drew	.136	Adams, Austin L	.133	Matzek, Tyler	.182	Jansen, Kenley	2.22
Boxberger, Brad	.139	Ashby, Aaron	.133	Gallegos, Giovanny	.183	Rogers, Tyler	2.22
Okert, Steven	.140	Jansen, Kenley	.136	Bednar, David	.185	Bednar, David	2.23
Treinen, Blake	.140	Matzek, Tyler	.141	Williams, Devin	.186	Melancon, Mark	2.23
Leone, Dominic	.143	Strickland, Hunter	.145	Castro, Miguel	.190	Littell, Zack	2.37

Rel OBP 1st Batter Faced (minimum 40 BF)		Rel Opp BA w/ Runners On (minimum 50 IP)		Relief Opp BA w/ RISP (minimum 50 IP)		Fastest Avg Fastball-Relief (minimum 50 IP)	
Alvarez, Jose	.152	Hader, Josh	.103	Hader, Josh	.087	Alvarado, Jose	99.4
Vesia, Alex	.171	Bickford, Phil	.139	Treinen, Blake	.111	Diaz, Edwin	98.8
McGee, Jake	.177	Adams, Austin L	.141	Smith, Will	.119	Castro, Miguel	98.1
Hudson, Daniel	.185	Shreve, Chasen	.147	Boxberger, Brad	.129	Cabrera, Genesis	97.7
Chafin, Andrew	.186	Garcia, Jarlin	.149	Bednar, David	.132	Bard, Daniel	97.5
Rodriguez, Richard	.203	Littell, Zack	.150	Bickford, Phil	.143	Treinen, Blake	97.5
Treinen, Blake	.208	Jansen, Kenley	.151	May, Trevor	.148	Estevez, Carlos	97.1
Boxberger, Brad	.214	Treinen, Blake	.161	Matzek, Tyler	.149	Hudson, Daniel	97.0
Familia, Jeurys	.231	Bednar, David	.165	Jackson, Luke	.152	Bender, Anthony	96.9
Gallegos, Giovanny	.233	Johnson, Pierce	.168	Reyes, Alex	.156	Bednar, David	96.8

Fastest Average Fastball (minimum 120 IP)		Slowest Average Fastball (minimum 120 IP)		Pitches 100+ Velocity		Pitches 95+ Velocity	
Alcantara, Sandy	97.9	Hendricks, Kyle	87.3	Alvarado, Jose	396	Wheeler, Zack	1940
Castillo, Luis	97.3	Davies, Zach	88.0	deGrom, Jacob	314	Woodruff, Brandon	1651
Wheeler, Zack	97.1	Lester, Jon	88.4	Graterol, Brusdar	231	Castillo, Luis	1619
Burnes, Corbin	96.9	Wainwright, Adam	89.1	Diaz, Edwin	169	Alcantara, Sandy	1542
Woodruff, Brandon	96.5	Miley, Wade	89.8	Alcantara, Sandy	122	Buehler, Walker	1328
Buehler, Walker	95.4	Bumgarner, Madison	90.4	Hicks, Jordan	75	Burnes, Corbin	1292
Morton, Charlie	95.3	Kershaw, Clayton	90.7	Doval, Camilo	47	Morton, Charlie	1162
Snell, Blake	95.2	Freeland, Kyle	91.4	Helsley, Ryan	41	Snell, Blake	944
Gray, Jon	94.9	Kelly, Merrill	91.8	Castro, Miguel	40	Gausman, Kevin	912
Marquez, German	94.8	Wood, Alex	91.8	Coonrod, Sam	39	Alvarado, Jose	907

Pitches Less Than 80 MPH		Lowest % Fastballs (minimum 120 IP)		Highest % Fastballs (minimum 120 IP)		Highest % Curveballs (minimum 120 IP)	
Hill, Rich	1133	Burnes, Corbin	10.8	Houser, Adrian	67.6	Smyly, Drew	41.9
Wainwright, Adam	1051	Miley, Wade	17.5	Wheeler, Zack	60.7	Morton, Charlie	36.7
Davies, Zach	868	Musgrove, Joe	26.9	Hendricks, Kyle	60.5	Urias, Julio	34.2
Espino, Paolo	681	Darvish, Yu	30.4	Woodruff, Brandon	60.4	Wainwright, Adam	34.1
Fried, Max	663	Bumgarner, Madison	36.5	Rogers, Trevor	57.7	Nola, Aaron	27.0
Smyly, Drew	645	Kershaw, Clayton	36.8	Walker, Taijuan	57.4	Fried, Max	25.6
Mills, Alec	641	Wainwright, Adam	37.9	Corbin, Patrick	56.4	Musgrove, Joe	23.6
Nola, Aaron	640	Freeland, Kyle	41.6	Senzatela, Antonio	56.1	Gray, Sonny	23.4
Scherzer, Max	542	Fedde, Erick	43.3	Gallen, Zac	55.0	Bumgarner, Madison	21.7
Hendricks, Kyle	530	Stroman, Marcus	44.9	Peralta, Freddy	53.1	Anderson, Ian	21.1

2021 National League Pitching Leaders

Highest % Changeups
(minimum 120 IP)

Davies, Zach	32.4
Anderson, Ian	31.4
Castillo, Luis	30.5
Hendricks, Kyle	27.8
Rogers, Trevor	27.5
Miley, Wade	27.2
Alcantara, Sandy	23.3
Webb, Logan	23.1
Wood, Alex	22.1
Nola, Aaron	19.8

Highest % Sliders
(minimum 120 IP)

Kershaw, Clayton	47.5
Corbin, Patrick	38.2
Gray, Jon	37.9
Alzolay, Adbert	37.7
DeSclafani, Anthony	35.7
Brubaker, JT	34.2
Bumgarner, Madison	34.0
Senzatela, Antonio	31.7
Wood, Alex	31.5
Mahle, Tyler	31.1

Balks

Alzolay, Adbert	3
Anderson, Brett	2
Garcia, Jarlin	2
Gutierrez, Vladimir	2
Hader, Josh	2
Jansen, Kenley	2
Littell, Zack	2
Minter, A.J.	2
Santana, Edgar	2
Senzatela, Antonio	2

Strikeout/Hit Ratio
(minimum 50 IP)

Hader, Josh	4.08
deGrom, Jacob	3.65
Adams, Austin L	2.71
Williams, Devin	2.42
Jansen, Kenley	2.39
Peralta, Freddy	2.32
Diaz, Edwin	2.07
Reyes, Alex	2.07
Scherzer, Max	1.98
3 tied with	1.93

Opp OPS vs Fastballs
(minimum 251 BF)

Suarez, Ranger	.475
Scherzer, Max	.566
Peralta, Freddy	.571
Buehler, Walker	.573
Wainwright, Adam	.573
Wheeler, Zack	.580
DeSclafani, Anthony	.595
Houser, Adrian	.596
Woodruff, Brandon	.600
Alcantara, Sandy	.623

Opp OPS vs Curveballs
(minimum 100 BF)

Burnes, Corbin	.294
Musgrove, Joe	.442
Woodruff, Brandon	.442
Urias, Julio	.444
Morton, Charlie	.468
Fried, Max	.577
Espino, Paolo	.587
Wainwright, Adam	.606
Marquez, German	.613
Johnson, Pierce	.660

Opp OPS vs Changeups
(minimum 100 BF)

Scherzer, Max	.468
Williams, Devin	.495
Brogdon, Connor	.510
Urias, Julio	.515
Anderson, Brett	.520
Woodruff, Brandon	.522
Rogers, Trevor	.550
Lester, Jon	.573
Gomber, Austin	.576
Castillo, Luis	.645

Opp OPS vs Sliders
(minimum 64 BF)

Treinen, Blake	.315
deGrom, Jacob	.343
Cousins, Jake	.406
Burnes, Corbin	.434
Rogers, Tyler	.457
Bauer, Trevor	.461
Diaz, Edwin	.464
May, Trevor	.486
Scherzer, Max	.491
Walker, Taijuan	.500

Earned Runs

Corbin, Patrick	111
Hendricks, Kyle	96
Davies, Zach	95
Nola, Aaron	93
Marquez, German	88
Castillo, Luis	83
Arrieta, Jake	81
Fedde, Erick	81
Walker, Taijuan	79
2 tied with	78

Hits Per Nine Innings
(minimum 120 IP)

Peralta, Freddy	5.24
Scherzer, Max	5.97
Buehler, Walker	6.46
Woodruff, Brandon	6.52
Morton, Charlie	6.59
Burnes, Corbin	6.63
Gausman, Kevin	7.03
Musgrove, Joe	7.05
Snell, Blake	7.06
Wheeler, Zack	7.13

2021 American League Fielding Leaders

2B Pivot %
(minimum 98 G)

Polanco, Jorge	0.723
Lowe, Brandon	0.720
Hernandez, Cesar	0.692
Semien, Marcus	0.663
Fletcher, David	0.636
Altuve, Jose	0.634
Merrifield, Whit	0.632
Solak, Nick	0.589

SS Pivot %
(minimum 98 G)

Anderson, Tim	0.651
Lopez, Nicky	0.610
Bogaerts, Xander	0.596
Bichette, Bo	0.577
Kiner-Falefa, Isiah	0.548
Simmons, Andrelton	0.544
Torres, Gleyber	0.543
Crawford, J.P.	0.541
Rosario, Amed	0.500
Andrus, Elvis	0.485

Highest Pct CS by Catchers
(minimum 500 INN or 50 SBA)

Perez, Salvador	41.0
Maldonado, Martin	38.3
McGuire, Reese	31.0
Haase, Eric	29.4
Hedges, Austin	24.4
Murphy, Sean	22.6
Vazquez, Christian	21.4
Heim, Jonah	20.5
Mejia, Francisco	19.2
Suzuki, Kurt	18.6

Lowest Pct CS by Catchers
(minimum 500 INN or 50 SBA)

Sanchez, Gary	9.1
Murphy, Tom	10.2
Stassi, Max	12.0
Trevino, Jose	13.0
Higashioka, Kyle	13.2
Collins, Zack	13.5
Zunino, Mike	14.5
Jeffers, Ryan	14.8
Grandal, Yasmani	15.3
Severino, Pedro	16.2

2B Double Play %
(minimum 98 G)

Hernandez, Cesar	0.630
Lowe, Brandon	0.618
Semien, Marcus	0.600
Merrifield, Whit	0.563
Polanco, Jorge	0.545
Fletcher, David	0.541
Altuve, Jose	0.500
Solak, Nick	0.483

3B Double Play %
(minimum 98 G)

Ramirez, Jose	0.630
Chapman, Matt	0.619
Seager, Kyle	0.600
Candelario, Jeimer	0.458
Wendle, Joey	0.450
Moncada, Yoan	0.448
Devers, Rafael	0.421
Franco, Maikel	0.366

SS Double Play %
(minimum 98 G)

Anderson, Tim	0.671
Crawford, J.P.	0.626
Bogaerts, Xander	0.625
Kiner-Falefa, Isiah	0.589
Bichette, Bo	0.574
Simmons, Andrelton	0.554
Lopez, Nicky	0.545
Rosario, Amed	0.539
Torres, Gleyber	0.522
Andrus, Elvis	0.514

Errors

Bichette, Bo	24
Devers, Rafael	22
Kiner-Falefa, Isiah	19
Torres, Gleyber	19
Iglesias, Jose	17
Polanco, Jorge	17
Moncada, Yoan	16
Sano, Miguel	16
Andrus, Elvis	15
Ramirez, Jose	15

Fielding Errors

Devers, Rafael	12
Sano, Miguel	12
Bichette, Bo	11
Ramirez, Jose	11
Dalbec, Bobby	10
Polanco, Jorge	10
Seager, Kyle	10
4 tied with	9

Throwing Errors

Bichette, Bo	13
Kiner-Falefa, Isiah	11
Devers, Rafael	10
Iglesias, Jose	10
Torres, Gleyber	10
Crawford, J.P.	9
Wendle, Joey	9
Odor, Rougned	8
Semien, Marcus	8
5 tied with	7

Range Factor for 2B
(minimum 98 games)

Merrifield, Whit	4.77
Fletcher, David	4.58
Polanco, Jorge	4.24
Altuve, Jose	3.87
Lowe, Brandon	3.76
Solak, Nick	3.76
Semien, Marcus	3.75
Hernandez, Cesar	3.51

Range Factor for 3B
(minimum 98 games)

Wendle, Joey	3.02
Chapman, Matt	3.01
Devers, Rafael	2.88
Seager, Kyle	2.69
Candelario, Jeimer	2.65
Franco, Maikel	2.55
Ramirez, Jose	2.51
Moncada, Yoan	2.48

Range Factor for SS
(minimum 98 games)

Kiner-Falefa, Isiah	4.30
Simmons, Andrelton	4.03
Bogaerts, Xander	3.96
Correa, Carlos	3.91
Crawford, J.P.	3.89
Lopez, Nicky	3.84
Bichette, Bo	3.77
Anderson, Tim	3.62
Andrus, Elvis	3.60
Rosario, Amed	3.57

2021 National League Fielding Leaders

2B Pivot %
(minimum 98 G)

Frazier, Adam	0.680
Segura, Jean	0.663
Wong, Kolten	0.607
Albies, Ozzie	0.596
India, Jonathan	0.560
Edman, Tommy	0.507

SS Pivot %
(minimum 98 G)

Rojas, Miguel	0.693
Farmer, Kyle	0.643
Gregorius, Didi	0.635
Story, Trevor	0.619
Turner, Trea	0.613
Tatis Jr., Fernando	0.581
Ahmed, Nick	0.566
Newman, Kevin	0.559
Swanson, Dansby	0.557
Baez, Javier	0.537

Highest Pct CS by Catchers
(minimum 500 INN or 50 SBA)

Diaz, Elias	38.9
Gomes, Yan	34.1
Molina, Yadier	33.3
Posey, Buster	24.4
McCann, James	22.0
Smith, Will	20.9
Barnhart, Tucker	20.4
Realmuto, J.T.	20.0
Stallings, Jacob	19.6
Kelly, Carson	19.5

Lowest Pct CS by Catchers
(minimum 500 INN or 50 SBA)

Casali, Curt	10.5
Caratini, Victor	11.3
Stephenson, Tyler	15.0
Vogt, Stephen	15.9
Barnes, Austin	16.3
Nunez, Dom	17.3
Contreras, Willson	17.9
Narvaez, Omar	19.5
Kelly, Carson	19.5
Stallings, Jacob	19.6

2B Double Play %
(minimum 98 G)

Frazier, Adam	0.552
Segura, Jean	0.534
Wong, Kolten	0.526
India, Jonathan	0.442
Albies, Ozzie	0.435
Edman, Tommy	0.387

3B Double Play %
(minimum 98 G)

Machado, Manny	0.424
Bohm, Alec	0.400
Arenado, Nolan	0.398
Turner, Justin	0.391
McMahon, Ryan	0.368
Escobar, Eduardo	0.366
Suarez, Eugenio	0.364
Riley, Austin	0.300

SS Double Play %
(minimum 98 G)

Rojas, Miguel	0.667
Story, Trevor	0.620
Farmer, Kyle	0.607
Newman, Kevin	0.606
Gregorius, Didi	0.564
DeJong, Paul	0.562
Tatis Jr., Fernando	0.560
Baez, Javier	0.560
Swanson, Dansby	0.544
Ahmed, Nick	0.540

Errors

Baez, Javier	24
Chisholm Jr., Jazz	24
Urias, Luis	24
Tatis Jr., Fernando	22
Gregorius, Didi	18
Suarez, Eugenio	17
Bohm, Alec	16
Turner, Trea	16
3 tied with	15

Fielding Errors

Chisholm Jr., Jazz	16
Suarez, Eugenio	12
Gregorius, Didi	10
Bohm, Alec	9
Castro, Starlin	9
Escobar, Eduardo	9
Segura, Jean	9
Tatis Jr., Fernando	9
Turner, Trea	9
3 tied with	8

Throwing Errors

Urias, Luis	19
Baez, Javier	17
Tatis Jr., Fernando	13
Story, Trevor	11
India, Jonathan	9
Machado, Manny	9
Riley, Austin	9
Villar, Jonathan	9
4 tied with	8

Range Factor for 2B
(minimum 98 games)

Segura, Jean	4.66
Edman, Tommy	4.39
India, Jonathan	4.36
Albies, Ozzie	4.11
Frazier, Adam	4.07
Wong, Kolten	3.77

Range Factor for 3B
(minimum 98 games)

Arenado, Nolan	2.83
Suarez, Eugenio	2.66
Riley, Austin	2.64
Machado, Manny	2.57
McMahon, Ryan	2.49
Bohm, Alec	2.39
Escobar, Eduardo	2.25
Turner, Justin	2.25

Range Factor for SS
(minimum 98 games)

Baez, Javier	4.47
Ahmed, Nick	4.13
Story, Trevor	4.12
Rojas, Miguel	3.98
DeJong, Paul	3.97
Crawford, Brandon	3.92
Gregorius, Didi	3.89
Lindor, Francisco	3.80
Newman, Kevin	3.77
Swanson, Dansby	3.68

2021 Active Career Batting Leaders

Batting Average
(minimum 1000 PA)

Cabrera, Miguel	.310
Altuve, Jose	.308
Trout, Mike	.305
Turner, Trea	.303
Posey, Buster	.302
Votto, Joey	.302
Bichette, Bo	.301
Soto, Juan	.301
LeMahieu, DJ	.300
Blackmon, Charlie	.300

On Base Percentage
(minimum 1000 PA)

Soto, Juan	.432
Trout, Mike	.419
Votto, Joey	.416
Nimmo, Brandon	.393
Harper, Bryce	.392
Goldschmidt, Paul	.389
Cabrera, Miguel	.387
Judge, Aaron	.386
Winker, Jesse	.385
Freeman, Freddie	.384

Slugging Average
(minimum 1000 PA)

Tatis Jr., Fernando	.596
Trout, Mike	.583
Judge, Aaron	.554
Soto, Juan	.550
Acuna Jr., Ronald	.549
Pujols, Albert	.544
Stanton, Giancarlo	.543
Alonso, Pete	.542
Ohtani, Shohei	.537
Arenado, Nolan	.535

Home Runs

Pujols, Albert	679
Cabrera, Miguel	502
Cruz, Nelson	449
Stanton, Giancarlo	347
Votto, Joey	331
Upton, Justin	324
Bruce, Jay	319
Longoria, Evan	317
Trout, Mike	310
Zimmerman, Ryan	284

Games

Pujols, Albert	2971
Cabrera, Miguel	2587
Molina, Yadier	2146
Votto, Joey	1900
Cruz, Nelson	1882
Upton, Justin	1828
Longoria, Evan	1823
Cabrera, Asdrubal	1822
Zimmerman, Ryan	1799
Andrus, Elvis	1798

At Bats

Pujols, Albert	11114
Cabrera, Miguel	9625
Molina, Yadier	7555
Cruz, Nelson	6910
Andrus, Elvis	6863
Longoria, Evan	6829
Votto, Joey	6722
Upton, Justin	6673
Zimmerman, Ryan	6654
Cabrera, Asdrubal	6632

Hits

Pujols, Albert	3301
Cabrera, Miguel	2987
Molina, Yadier	2112
Votto, Joey	2027
Cruz, Nelson	1913
Andrus, Elvis	1864
Zimmerman, Ryan	1846
McCutchen, Andrew	1826
Longoria, Evan	1818
Altuve, Jose	1777

Total Bases

Pujols, Albert	6042
Cabrera, Miguel	5124
Cruz, Nelson	3639
Votto, Joey	3497
Longoria, Evan	3230
Zimmerman, Ryan	3159
Upton, Justin	3145
McCutchen, Andrew	3101
Molina, Yadier	3039
Freeman, Freddie	2934

Doubles

Pujols, Albert	672
Cabrera, Miguel	597
Votto, Joey	435
Zimmerman, Ryan	417
Longoria, Evan	409
Cabrera, Asdrubal	401
Molina, Yadier	400
Freeman, Freddie	367
McCutchen, Andrew	367
Cruz, Nelson	351

Triples

Fowler, Dexter	82
Gardner, Brett	73
Escobar, Alcides	56
Blackmon, Charlie	52
Kiermaier, Kevin	51
Andrus, Elvis	50
McCutchen, Andrew	49
Trout, Mike	49
Eaton, Adam	46
Marte, Starling	46

Runs Scored

Pujols, Albert	1872
Cabrera, Miguel	1505
Votto, Joey	1114
Upton, Justin	1056
McCutchen, Andrew	1052
Cruz, Nelson	1031
Freeman, Freddie	969
Trout, Mike	967
Zimmerman, Ryan	963
Longoria, Evan	961

RBI

Pujols, Albert	2150
Cabrera, Miguel	1804
Cruz, Nelson	1238
Longoria, Evan	1089
Votto, Joey	1065
Zimmerman, Ryan	1061
Upton, Justin	1000
Molina, Yadier	998
Bruce, Jay	951
Freeman, Freddie	941

Walks

Pujols, Albert	1345
Votto, Joey	1294
Cabrera, Miguel	1199
Santana, Carlos	1077
McCutchen, Andrew	926
Trout, Mike	865
Goldschmidt, Paul	837
Harper, Bryce	833
Upton, Justin	779
Freeman, Freddie	777

Intentional Walks

Pujols, Albert	315
Cabrera, Miguel	235
Votto, Joey	147
Trout, Mike	109
Goldschmidt, Paul	107
Harper, Bryce	103
Freeman, Freddie	102
Longoria, Evan	85
Stanton, Giancarlo	81
Cruz, Nelson	76

Hit By Pitch

Rizzo, Anthony	178
Marte, Starling	133
Suzuki, Kurt	117
Pujols, Albert	113
Jay, Jon	110
Abreu, Jose	105
Turner, Justin	105
Bryant, Kris	87
Trout, Mike	86
Blackmon, Charlie	85

Strikeouts

Upton, Justin	1948
Cabrera, Miguel	1930
Cruz, Nelson	1751
Bruce, Jay	1572
Stanton, Giancarlo	1559
Longoria, Evan	1540
Votto, Joey	1481
McCutchen, Andrew	1418
Goldschmidt, Paul	1404
Zimmerman, Ryan	1384

2021 Active Career Batting Leaders

Sacrifice Hits		Sacrifice Flies		Stolen Bases		Seasons Played	
Kershaw, Clayton	110	Pujols, Albert	117	Andrus, Elvis	317	Pujols, Albert	21
Andrus, Elvis	103	Cabrera, Miguel	95	Hamilton, Billy	314	Cabrera, Miguel	19
Cueto, Johnny	90	Longoria, Evan	91	Marte, Starling	296	Perez, Oliver	19
Escobar, Alcides	87	Molina, Yadier	74	Gardner, Brett	274	Greinke, Zack	18
Wainwright, Adam	74	Zimmerman, Ryan	69	Dyson, Jarrod	266	Molina, Yadier	18
Gardner, Brett	69	Suzuki, Kurt	65	Altuve, Jose	261	Cruz, Nelson	17
Teheran, Julio	67	McCutchen, Andrew	62	Villar, Jonathan	232	Hill, Rich	17
Strasburg, Stephen	56	Cabrera, Asdrubal	61	Trout, Mike	203	Mathis, Jeff	17
Jay, Jon	55	Upton, Justin	59	Turner, Trea	203	5 tied with	16
2 tied with	51	Arenado, Nolan	57	McCutchen, Andrew	197		

At Bats Per Home Run (minimum 1000 AB)		Grounded Into DP		Highest SB Success Pct (minimum 100 SBA)		Lowest SB Success Pct (minimum 100 SBA)	
Gallo, Joey	12.7	Pujols, Albert	413	Trout, Mike	84.6	Odor, Rougned	55.4
Tatis Jr., Fernando	12.8	Cabrera, Miguel	342	Dyson, Jarrod	84.4	Bruce, Jay	61.9
Alonso, Pete	12.9	Molina, Yadier	277	Turner, Trea	83.9	Castro, Starlin	63.1
Judge, Aaron	13.1	Zimmerman, Ryan	212	Mondesi, Adalberto	83.1	Parra, Gerardo	63.8
Stanton, Giancarlo	13.9	Longoria, Evan	192	Yelich, Christian	82.5	Rizzo, Anthony	64.7
Sanchez, Gary	14.0	Cabrera, Asdrubal	177	Betts, Mookie	82.0	Molina, Yadier	65.1
Schwarber, Kyle	14.4	Castro, Starlin	177	Cain, Lorenzo	81.7	Frazier, Todd	65.8
Olson, Matt	14.4	Andrus, Elvis	175	Hamilton, Billy	81.6	LeMahieu, DJ	66.9
Acuna Jr., Ronald	14.4	Posey, Buster	163	Pollock, A.J.	81.5	Fowler, Dexter	68.7
Muncy, Max	14.6	Cruz, Nelson	161	Ramirez, Jose	81.5	Hernandez, Cesar	69.2

Strikeouts / Walks Ratio (minimum 1000 AB)		At Bats Per GIDP (minimum 1000 AB)		OPS (minimum 1000 PA)		Secondary Average (minimum 1000 PA)	
Soto, Juan	.944	Kingery, Scott	173.7	Trout, Mike	1.002	Trout, Mike	.508
Pujols, Albert	1.003	Meadows, Austin	169.8	Soto, Juan	.981	Soto, Juan	.500
Santana, Carlos	1.075	Moncada, Yoan	168.9	Tatis Jr., Fernando	.965	Gallo, Joey	.475
Bregman, Alex	1.122	Gallo, Joey	167.8	Judge, Aaron	.940	Tatis Jr., Fernando	.468
Votto, Joey	1.145	Buxton, Byron	161.5	Votto, Joey	.937	Judge, Aaron	.464
La Stella, Tommy	1.149	Hamilton, Billy	156.1	Acuna Jr., Ronald	.925	Acuna Jr., Ronald	.457
Ramirez, Jose	1.215	Lowe, Brandon	144.1	Cabrera, Miguel	.920	Harper, Bryce	.452
Panik, Joe	1.227	DeShields, Delino	140.6	Pujols, Albert	.919	Ohtani, Shohei	.446
Betts, Mookie	1.270	Albies, Ozzie	124.6	Harper, Bryce	.916	Hoskins, Rhys	.440
Posey, Buster	1.335	Goodwin, Brian	124.4	Goldschmidt, Paul	.911	Muncy, Max	.440

Highest Strikeout per PA (minimum 1000 PA)		Lowest Strikeout per PA (minimum 1000 PA)		Plate Appearances		At Bats Per RBI (minimum 1000 AB)	
Gallo, Joey	.369	Simmons, Andrelton	.095	Pujols, Albert	12690	Soto, Juan	5.2
Sano, Miguel	.365	Fletcher, David	.099	Cabrera, Miguel	10993	Pujols, Albert	5.2
Zunino, Mike	.346	Panik, Joe	.101	Molina, Yadier	8284	Aguilar, Jesus	5.2
Alfaro, Jorge	.338	La Stella, Tommy	.106	Votto, Joey	8128	Tatis Jr., Fernando	5.3
Jones, JaCoby	.326	Molina, Yadier	.106	Cruz, Nelson	7737	Cabrera, Miguel	5.3
Souza Jr., Steven	.316	Pujols, Albert	.106	Longoria, Evan	7671	Stanton, Giancarlo	5.4
Happ, Ian	.308	Brantley, Michael	.108	Andrus, Elvis	7620	Lowe, Brandon	5.4
Goodrum, Niko	.307	Gurriel, Yuli	.109	Upton, Justin	7592	Arenado, Nolan	5.4
Taylor, Michael A.	.304	Newman, Kevin	.109	McCutchen, Andrew	7588	Voit, Luke	5.5
Marisnick, Jake	.301	Alberto, Hanser	.117	Zimmerman, Ryan	7402	Alonso, Pete	5.5

2021 Active Career Pitching Leaders

Earned Run Average (minimum 750 IP)	
Kershaw, Clayton	2.49
deGrom, Jacob	2.50
Sale, Chris	3.03
Soria, Joakim	3.11
Clippard, Tyler	3.13
Scherzer, Max	3.16
Kluber, Corey	3.20
Cole, Gerrit	3.20
Ryu, Hyun-Jin	3.20
Strasburg, Stephen	3.21

Winning Percentage (minimum 100 Decisions)	
Kershaw, Clayton	.688
Scherzer, Max	.662
Price, David	.654
Cole, Gerrit	.650
Strasburg, Stephen	.649
Wainwright, Adam	.637
Lester, Jon	.631
Kluber, Corey	.628
Greinke, Zack	.624
Rodriguez, Eduardo	.621

Opponent Batting Average (minimum 750 IP)	
Clippard, Tyler	.198
Kershaw, Clayton	.209
deGrom, Jacob	.213
Darvish, Yu	.218
Sale, Chris	.219
Scherzer, Max	.221
Soria, Joakim	.223
Strasburg, Stephen	.223
Hill, Rich	.225
Maeda, Kenta	.226

Baserunners Per 9 IP (minimum 750 IP)	
Kershaw, Clayton	9.17
deGrom, Jacob	9.25
Sale, Chris	9.93
Scherzer, Max	10.09
Strasburg, Stephen	10.15
Kluber, Corey	10.22
Clippard, Tyler	10.25
Cole, Gerrit	10.29
Petit, Yusmeiro	10.38
Bumgarner, Madison	10.45

Games	
Smith, Joe	832
Clippard, Tyler	803
Romo, Sergio	798
Soria, Joakim	773
Jansen, Kenley	701
Perez, Oliver	695
Shaw, Bryan	693
Watson, Tony	689
Robertson, David	673
Melancon, Mark	670

Games Started	
Greinke, Zack	488
Lester, Jon	451
Scherzer, Max	398
Santana, Ervin	386
Kershaw, Clayton	376
Wainwright, Adam	358
Cueto, Johnny	329
Happ, J.A.	328
Price, David	322
Bumgarner, Madison	321

Complete Games	
Wainwright, Adam	27
Kershaw, Clayton	25
Santana, Ervin	21
Kluber, Corey	18
Cueto, Johnny	17
Greinke, Zack	17
Price, David	17
Bumgarner, Madison	16
Sale, Chris	16
Lester, Jon	15

Shutouts	
Kershaw, Clayton	15
Santana, Ervin	11
Wainwright, Adam	11
Cueto, Johnny	8
Holland, Derek	8
Kluber, Corey	8
Bumgarner, Madison	7
4 tied with	5

Wins	
Greinke, Zack	219
Lester, Jon	200
Scherzer, Max	190
Kershaw, Clayton	185
Wainwright, Adam	184
Price, David	155
Santana, Ervin	151
Cueto, Johnny	135
Happ, J.A.	133
Bumgarner, Madison	127

Losses	
Greinke, Zack	132
Santana, Ervin	129
Lester, Jon	117
Bumgarner, Madison	106
Kennedy, Ian	106
Wainwright, Adam	105
Happ, J.A.	100
Cahill, Trevor	99
3 tied with	97

Innings Pitched	
Greinke, Zack	3110.0
Lester, Jon	2740.0
Scherzer, Max	2536.2
Santana, Ervin	2486.2
Kershaw, Clayton	2454.2
Wainwright, Adam	2375.2
Price, David	2103.1
Cueto, Johnny	2034.1
Bumgarner, Madison	2034.0
Happ, J.A.	1893.2

Batters Faced	
Greinke, Zack	12699
Lester, Jon	11487
Santana, Ervin	10482
Scherzer, Max	10266
Wainwright, Adam	9829
Kershaw, Clayton	9667
Price, David	8640
Cueto, Johnny	8454
Bumgarner, Madison	8310
Happ, J.A.	8048

Strikeouts	
Scherzer, Max	3020
Greinke, Zack	2809
Kershaw, Clayton	2670
Lester, Jon	2488
Sale, Chris	2059
Price, David	2039
Wainwright, Adam	2004
Santana, Ervin	1978
Bumgarner, Madison	1948
Strasburg, Stephen	1718

Walks Allowed	
Lester, Jon	892
Santana, Ervin	776
Perez, Oliver	761
Greinke, Zack	712
Kazmir, Scott	687
Scherzer, Max	677
Happ, J.A.	668
Wainwright, Adam	641
Kennedy, Ian	618
Cahill, Trevor	615

Hit Batters	
Morton, Charlie	138
Cueto, Johnny	111
Santana, Ervin	104
Sale, Chris	102
Scherzer, Max	96
Lester, Jon	90
Perez, Oliver	87
Kennedy, Ian	81
Bumgarner, Madison	79
Wainwright, Adam	73

Wild Pitches	
Santana, Ervin	104
Cahill, Trevor	100
Kershaw, Clayton	95
Greinke, Zack	92
Gray, Sonny	88
Richards, Garrett	85
Arrieta, Jake	79
Kennedy, Ian	76
Kazmir, Scott	74
Scherzer, Max	73

2021 Active Career Pitching Leaders

Saves	
Kimbrel, Craig	372
Jansen, Kenley	350
Chapman, Aroldis	306
Melancon, Mark	244
Soria, Joakim	229
Holland, Greg	220
Diaz, Edwin	173
Colome, Alex	155
Britton, Zack	154
Axford, John	144

Save Pct	
(minimum 50 Save Ops)	
Kimbrel, Craig	89.6
Chapman, Aroldis	89.0
Jansen, Kenley	88.6
Britton, Zack	88.5
Davis, Wade	87.6
Kennedy, Ian	87.5
Holland, Greg	87.3
Iglesias, Raisel	87.0
Diaz, Edwin	86.1
Melancon, Mark	85.9

Home Runs Allowed	
Santana, Ervin	331
Greinke, Zack	328
Lester, Jon	294
Scherzer, Max	287
Kennedy, Ian	265
Happ, J.A.	261
Bumgarner, Madison	229
Holland, Derek	220
Cueto, Johnny	217
Price, David	215

Strikeouts Per 9 IP	
(minimum 750 IP)	
Ray, Robbie	11.21
Sale, Chris	11.08
Darvish, Yu	11.07
deGrom, Jacob	10.74
Scherzer, Max	10.72
Miller, Andrew	10.63
Strasburg, Stephen	10.55
Cole, Gerrit	10.39
Nola, Aaron	10.07
Paxton, James	9.91

Opp On-Base Percentage	
(minimum 750 IP)	
Kershaw, Clayton	.261
deGrom, Jacob	.262
Sale, Chris	.275
Scherzer, Max	.279
Strasburg, Stephen	.280
Clippard, Tyler	.281
Kluber, Corey	.283
Petit, Yusmeiro	.284
Cole, Gerrit	.285
Soria, Joakim	.285

Opp Slugging Average	
(minimum 750 IP)	
Kershaw, Clayton	.322
deGrom, Jacob	.328
Soria, Joakim	.340
Sale, Chris	.353
Strasburg, Stephen	.353
Clippard, Tyler	.355
Wheeler, Zack	.359
Gray, Sonny	.359
Martinez, Carlos	.364
Miller, Andrew	.367

Hits Per Nine Innings	
(minimum 750 IP)	
Clippard, Tyler	6.42
Kershaw, Clayton	6.82
deGrom, Jacob	7.00
Darvish, Yu	7.29
Sale, Chris	7.30
Scherzer, Max	7.35
Strasburg, Stephen	7.43
Hill, Rich	7.46
Soria, Joakim	7.47
Maeda, Kenta	7.63

Home Runs Per Nine IP	
(minimum 750 IP)	
Kershaw, Clayton	0.72
Wainwright, Adam	0.75
Martinez, Carlos	0.75
Morton, Charlie	0.76
deGrom, Jacob	0.77
Soria, Joakim	0.79
Wheeler, Zack	0.82
Stroman, Marcus	0.83
Richards, Garrett	0.86
Wood, Alex	0.86

Strikeouts / Walks Ratio	
(minimum 750 IP)	
Sale, Chris	5.33
deGrom, Jacob	5.10
Tomlin, Josh	4.81
Kluber, Corey	4.74
Cole, Gerrit	4.49
Scherzer, Max	4.46
Pineda, Michael	4.41
Kershaw, Clayton	4.41
Strasburg, Stephen	4.38
Bumgarner, Madison	4.06

Stolen Base Pct Allowed	
(minimum 750 IP)	
Cueto, Johnny	44.0
Rodriguez, Eduardo	44.8
Miley, Wade	46.4
LeBlanc, Wade	50.8
Greinke, Zack	52.4
Kershaw, Clayton	52.4
Ryu, Hyun-Jin	53.3
Davies, Zach	55.0
Wood, Alex	56.3
Wainwright, Adam	57.3

GIDP Induced	
Lester, Jon	250
Greinke, Zack	242
Wainwright, Adam	228
Santana, Ervin	190
Keuchel, Dallas	187
Kershaw, Clayton	170
Gibson, Kyle	165
Morton, Charlie	162
Perez, Martin	155
Cueto, Johnny	154

GIDP Per Nine IP	
(minimum 750 IP)	
Chatwood, Tyler	1.35
Perez, Martin	1.27
Gibson, Kyle	1.11
Keuchel, Dallas	1.10
Anderson, Brett	1.06
Stroman, Marcus	1.04
Peralta, Wily	1.02
Martinez, Carlos	1.01
Hunter, Tommy	0.93
Roark, Tanner	0.90

Complete Game %	
(minimum 100 GS)	
Kluber, Corey	0.08
Wainwright, Adam	0.08
Kershaw, Clayton	0.07
Sale, Chris	0.07
Santana, Ervin	0.05
Carrasco, Carlos	0.05
Price, David	0.05
Cueto, Johnny	0.05
Bumgarner, Madison	0.05
Keuchel, Dallas	0.05

Quality Start Pct	
(minimum 100 GS)	
deGrom, Jacob	74.2
Kershaw, Clayton	72.1
Sale, Chris	67.6
Cole, Gerrit	67.1
Scherzer, Max	64.8
Wainwright, Adam	63.1
Price, David	63.0
Greinke, Zack	62.9
Bumgarner, Madison	62.0
Strasburg, Stephen	61.8

Walks Per 9 IP	
(minimum 750 IP)	
Tomlin, Josh	1.29
Zimmermann, Jordan	1.93
Hendricks, Kyle	1.98
Pineda, Michael	1.99
Ryu, Hyun-Jin	2.01
Hunter, Tommy	2.04
Petit, Yusmeiro	2.04
Greinke, Zack	2.06
Kluber, Corey	2.06
Sale, Chris	2.08

Games Finished	
Kimbrel, Craig	520
Jansen, Kenley	519
Chapman, Aroldis	465
Soria, Joakim	427
Melancon, Mark	406
Holland, Greg	353
Cishek, Steve	300
Romo, Sergio	295
Axford, John	286
Robertson, David	277

2021 American League Bill James Leaders

Top Game Scores

Pitcher	Date	Opp	IP	H	R	ER	BB	SO	GS
Means, John, Bal	5/5	Sea	9.0	0	0	0	0	12	99
Kluber, Corey, NYY	5/19	Tex	9.0	0	0	0	1	9	95
Rodon, Carlos, CWS	4/14	Cle	9.0	0	0	0	0	7	94
Turnbull, Spencer, Det	5/18	Sea	9.0	0	0	0	2	9	94
Bassitt, Chris, Oak	5/27	LAA	9.0	2	0	0	1	9	91
Bieber, Shane, Cle	4/13	CWS	9.0	3	0	0	1	11	91
Cole, Gerrit, NYY	7/10	Hou	9.0	3	0	0	2	12	91
McKenzie, Triston, Cle	8/15	Det	8.0	1	0	0	0	11	91
Civale, Aaron, Cle	6/11	Sea	8.0	1	0	0	1	11	90
Manoah, Alek, Tor	9/13	TB	8.0	1	0	0	0	10	90
Sandoval, Patrick, LAA	7/24	Min	8.2	1	1	1	1	13	90

Worst Game Scores

Pitcher	Date	Opp	IP	H	R	ER	BB	SO	GS
Fleming, Josh, TB	8/11	Bos	3.1	11	10	10	6	3	-5
Foltynewicz, Mike, Tex	7/18	Tor	1.2	8	10	10	2	0	-3
Anderson, Tyler, Sea	9/25	LAA	2.0	9	9	9	1	0	1
Happ, J.A., Min	7/28	Det	3.0	10	9	9	4	2	1
Flexen, Chris, Sea	5/21	SD	1.2	10	8	8	1	1	3
Albers, Andrew, Min	9/4	TB	3.0	10	9	9	1	2	4
Shoemaker, Matt, Min	6/4	KC	0.1	6	9	8	2	1	4
Giolito, Lucas, CWS	4/19	Bos	1.0	8	8	7	2	0	5
Lynch, Daniel, KC	5/8	CWS	0.2	7	8	8	1	0	5
Dobnak, Randy, Min	6/9	NYY	4.2	11	8	8	3	0	7
Happ, J.A., Min	5/12	CWS	3.1	9	9	9	2	3	7
Mejia, JC, Cle	8/4	Tor	2.1	7	8	8	4	0	7

Runs Created

Guerrero Jr., Vladimir	136
Ohtani, Shohei	119
Ramirez, Jose	116
Judge, Aaron	115
Bichette, Bo	114
Polanco, Jorge	112
Semien, Marcus	112
Devers, Rafael	111
Lowe, Brandon	110
2 tied with	109

Runs Created Per 27 Outs

Guerrero Jr., Vladimir	8.2
Ohtani, Shohei	7.5
Judge, Aaron	7.3
Ramirez, Jose	7.1
Lowe, Brandon	7.1
Hernandez, Teoscar	6.9
Tucker, Kyle	6.8
Polanco, Jorge	6.6
Devers, Rafael	6.5
Mullins II, Cedric	6.5

Offensive Winning %

Guerrero Jr., Vladimir	.747
Lowe, Brandon	.739
Ohtani, Shohei	.720
Judge, Aaron	.717
Ramirez, Jose	.711
Tucker, Kyle	.693
Meadows, Austin	.689
Hernandez, Teoscar	.677
Olson, Matt	.677
Polanco, Jorge	.674

Secondary Average

(minimum 502 PA)

Ohtani, Shohei	.562
Gallo, Joey	.494
Ramirez, Jose	.451
Guerrero Jr., Vladimir	.439
Olson, Matt	.432
Lowe, Brandon	.417
Judge, Aaron	.404
Semien, Marcus	.397
Tucker, Kyle	.395
Donaldson, Josh	.389

Isolated Power

(minimum 502 PA)

Ohtani, Shohei	.335
Guerrero Jr., Vladimir	.290
Lowe, Brandon	.277
Semien, Marcus	.273
Ramirez, Jose	.272
Perez, Salvador	.271
Olson, Matt	.269
Tucker, Kyle	.263
Gallo, Joey	.259
Devers, Rafael	.259

Power / Speed Number

(minimum 502 PA)

Ohtani, Shohei	33.2
Ramirez, Jose	30.9
Mullins II, Cedric	30.0
Bichette, Bo	26.9
Semien, Marcus	22.5
Grossman, Robbie	21.4
Garcia, Adolis	21.1
Arozarena, Randy	20.0
Tucker, Kyle	19.1
Anderson, Tim	17.5

Speed Scores

Mullins II, Cedric	8.35
Merrifield, Whit	7.80
Bichette, Bo	7.45
Margot, Manuel	7.44
Straw, Myles	7.39
Kepler, Max	7.25
Anderson, Tim	7.22
Tucker, Kyle	7.20
Ohtani, Shohei	7.16
Ramirez, Jose	6.92

Cheap Wins

Keuchel, Dallas	5
Pivetta, Nick	4
Plesac, Zach	4
Richards, Garrett	3
10 tied with	2

Tough Losses

Berrios, Jose	6
Allard, Kolby	5
Foltynewicz, Mike	5
Lyles, Jordan	5
Montas, Frankie	5
Sandoval, Patrick	5
5 tied with	4

2021 National League Bill James Leaders

Top Game Scores

Pitcher	Date	Opp	IP	H	R	ER	BB	SO	GS
deGrom, Jacob, NYM	4/23	Was	9.0	2	0	0	0	15	98
Musgrove, Joe, SD	4/9	Tex	9.0	0	0	0	0	10	97
Burnes, Corbin, Mil	9/11	Cle	8.0	0	0	0	1	14	95
Miley, Wade, Cin	5/7	Cle	9.0	0	0	0	1	8	94
Nola, Aaron, Phi	4/18	StL	9.0	2	0	0	0	10	93
Wheeler, Zack, Phi	8/8	NYM	9.0	2	0	0	1	11	93
DeSclafani, Anthony, SF	6/11	Was	9.0	2	0	0	1	8	90
Wainwright, Adam, StL	8/11	Pit	9.0	2	0	0	0	7	90
6 tied with									89

Worst Game Scores

Pitcher	Date	Opp	IP	H	R	ER	BB	SO	GS
Bettinger, Alec, Mil	5/2	LAD	4.0	11	11	11	2	0	-6
Martinez, Carlos, StL	6/2	LAD	0.2	6	10	10	4	1	-3
Alcantara, Sandy, Mia	8/6	Col	3.2	10	10	10	2	1	0
DeSclafani, Anthony, SF	5/23	LAD	2.2	9	10	10	3	3	0
Corbin, Patrick, Was	4/15	Ari	2.0	6	10	9	4	1	3
Smith, Caleb, Ari	7/10	LAD	1.0	6	9	9	3	1	3
Gomber, Austin, Col	4/26	SF	1.2	7	9	9	4	3	4
Eickhoff, Jerad, NYM	7/27	Atl	3.1	7	10	10	5	4	5
Paddack, Chris, SD	7/7	Was	2.0	9	9	8	1	2	5
Castillo, Luis, Cin	4/1	StL	3.1	8	10	8	2	0	6
Hendricks, Kyle, ChC	8/12	Mil	4.0	11	9	9	1	3	6

Runs Created

Soto, Juan	127
Freeman, Freddie	123
Harper, Bryce	120
Reynolds, Bryan	112
Riley, Austin	111
Tatis Jr., Fernando	110
Machado, Manny	109
Muncy, Max	109
Turner, Trea	109
Goldschmidt, Paul	108

Runs Created Per 27 Outs

Harper, Bryce	8.8
Soto, Juan	8.8
Tatis Jr., Fernando	8.1
Votto, Joey	7.8
Muncy, Max	7.5
Freeman, Freddie	7.4
Crawford, Brandon	7.4
Reynolds, Bryan	7.2
Cron, C.J.	7.1
Castellanos, Nick	6.8

Offensive Winning %

Soto, Juan	.807
Harper, Bryce	.796
Tatis Jr., Fernando	.792
Muncy, Max	.741
Crawford, Brandon	.736
Reynolds, Bryan	.727
Freeman, Freddie	.721
Machado, Manny	.718
Goldschmidt, Paul	.713
Votto, Joey	.707

Secondary Average
(minimum 502 PA)

Harper, Bryce	.537
Soto, Juan	.528
Tatis Jr., Fernando	.510
Votto, Joey	.471
Muncy, Max	.449
McCutchen, Andrew	.402
Betts, Mookie	.391
O'Neill, Tyler	.384
Cron, C.J.	.379
Alonso, Pete	.369

Isolated Power
(minimum 502 PA)

Tatis Jr., Fernando	.328
Harper, Bryce	.305
Votto, Joey	.297
Muncy, Max	.278
O'Neill, Tyler	.274
Castellanos, Nick	.267
Duvall, Adam	.263
Alonso, Pete	.257
Cron, C.J.	.249
Arenado, Nolan	.239

Power / Speed Number
(minimum 502 PA)

Tatis Jr., Fernando	31.3
Turner, Trea	29.9
Albies, Ozzie	24.0
Baez, Javier	22.8
Story, Trevor	21.8
O'Neill, Tyler	20.8
Chisholm Jr., Jazz	20.2
Harper, Bryce	19.0
Goldschmidt, Paul	17.3
Machado, Manny	16.8

Speed Scores

Hampson, Garrett	8.05
Albies, Ozzie	7.73
Story, Trevor	7.52
Yastrzemski, Mike	7.49
Edman, Tommy	7.28
Tatis Jr., Fernando	7.13
Taylor, Chris	7.05
Turner, Trea	7.00
Betts, Mookie	6.95
Grisham, Trent	6.79

Cheap Wins

Morton, Charlie	3
Wainwright, Adam	3
Luzardo, Jesus	2
Musgrove, Joe	2
Nola, Aaron	2
Paddack, Chris	2
Urias, Julio	2
Weathers, Ryan	2
Wheeler, Zack	2
28 tied with	1

Tough Losses

Castillo, Luis	8
Alcantara, Sandy	6
Alzolay, Adbert	6
Woodruff, Brandon	6
Darvish, Yu	5
Musgrove, Joe	5
Bauer, Trevor	4
Smith, Caleb	4
Stroman, Marcus	4
Wheeler, Zack	4

Additional Bill James Leaders

Top AL Batter Game Scores

Batter	Date	Opp	AB	R	H	HR	RBI	RC	GS
Zavala, Seby, CWS	7/31	Cle	4	4	4	3	6	5.77	123
Gurriel Jr., Lourdes, Tor	9/12	Bal	3	5	2	2	7	4.33	118
Grandal, Yasmani, CWS	8/27	ChC	6	2	4	2	8	4.59	111
Lowe, Brandon, TB	10/2	NYY	5	3	3	3	7	4.53	110
Mountcastle, Ryan, Bal	6/19	Tor	4	3	4	3	4	5.77	108
Martinez, J.D., Bos	4/11	Bal	6	4	4	3	4	5.26	108
Guerrero Jr., Vlad, Tor	4/27	Was	4	3	3	3	7	4.15	106
Schoop, Jonathan, Det	6/4	CWS	4	2	4	2	5	5.50	105
Rosario, Amed, Cle	8/31	KC	5	2	5	2	5	5.39	104
Dalbec, Bobby, Bos	8/26	Min	4	3	3	2	7	3.72	102
Schwarber, Kyle, Bos	9/22	NYY	4	4	3	2	4	4.54	100
Benintendi, Andrew, KC	9/10	Min	5	3	4	2	5	4.43	99

Worst AL Batter Game Scores

Batter	Date	Opp	AB	R	H	SO	DP	RC	GS
Perez, Salvador, KC	4/11	CWS	5	0	0	3	1	-1.18	3
Cabrera, Miguel, Det	5/4	Bos	5	0	0	2	2	-1.17	3
Bruce, Jay, NYY	4/14	Tor	4	0	0	2	1	-1.10	4
Martinez, J.D., Bos	5/2	Tex	4	0	0	2	2	-1.10	4
Zunino, Mike, TB	9/5	Min	4	0	0	1	2	-1.08	4
Bregman, Alex, Hou	4/20	Col	4	0	0	1	2	-1.08	4
Short, Zack, Det	7/23	KC	4	0	0	1	2	-1.08	4
Lamb, Jake, CWS	8/21	TB	4	0	0	1	2	-1.08	4
Candelario, Jeimer, Det	4/4	Cle	4	0	0	1	1	-1.08	4
Garver, Mitch, Min	5/15	Oak	4	0	0	1	1	-1.08	4
Rizzo, Anthony, NYY	8/7	Sea	4	0	0	1	2	-1.08	4
Grichuk, Randal, Tor	8/20	Det	4	0	0	1	2	-1.08	4

Top NL Batter Game Scores

Batter	Date	Opp	AB	R	H	HR	RBI	RC	GS
Urias, Luis, Mil	8/12	ChC	6	5	5	2	5	6.31	128
Albies, Ozzie, Atl	6/30	NYM	6	4	5	2	7	4.80	118
Duvall, Adam, Mia	4/13	Atl	5	4	4	2	7	4.78	118
Winker, Jesse, Cin	5/21	Mil	4	4	4	3	6	6.29	113
Winker, Jesse, Cin	6/6	Stl	4	3	3	3	6	5.28	113
Tatis Jr., Fernando, SD	6/25	Ari	5	4	4	3	4	5.53	110
Lindor, Francisco, NYM	9/12	NYY	4	3	3	3	5	5.28	108
McMahon, Ryan, Col	4/6	Ari	6	3	4	3	4	5.67	107
Castellanos, Nick, Cin	5/2	ChC	6	4	5	2	4	5.16	107
Ortega, Rafael, ChC	8/1	Was	4	3	4	3	5	5.12	106
Tatis Jr., Fernando, SD	5/23	Sea	3	3	3	2	6	4.38	103
Peralta, David, Ari	4/22	Cin	6	2	5	1	7	4.23	102

Worst NL Batter Game Scores

Batter	Date	Opp	AB	R	H	SO	DP	RC	GS
Grisham, Trent, SD	7/17	Was	5	0	0	1	2	-1.15	3
De La Cruz, Bryan, Mia	9/29	NYM	4	0	0	2	2	-1.10	4
Bote, David, ChC	9/28	Pit	4	0	0	1	2	-1.08	4
Berti, Jon, Mia	6/6	Pit	4	0	0	1	1	-1.08	4
Smith, Dominic, NYM	6/11	SD	4	0	0	1	2	-1.08	4
Aguilar, Jesus, Mia	6/24	Was	4	0	0	1	1	-1.08	4
Bote, David, ChC	8/23	Col	4	0	0	1	2	-1.08	4
Riley, Austin, Atl	6/9	Phi	4	0	0	0	1	-1.06	4
Albies, Ozzie, Atl	6/12	Mia	4	0	0	1	1	-1.06	4
Pham, Tommy, SD	5/17	Col	4	0	0	0	1	-1.06	4
Smith, Pavin, Ari	4/28	SD	4	0	0	0	2	-1.06	4
Harper, Bryce, Phi	9/3	Mia	4	0	0	0	2	-1.06	4

AL Batters Win Shares

Judge, Aaron	31
Lowe, Brandon	30
Polanco, Jorge	29
Ramirez, Jose	29
France, Ty	28
Guerrero Jr., Vladimir	28
Perez, Salvador	28
Haniger, Mitch	27
3 tied with	26

NL Batters Win Shares

Crawford, Brandon	31
Harper, Bryce	31
Soto, Juan	31
Goldschmidt, Paul	28
Reynolds, Bryan	28
Tatis Jr., Fernando	28
Freeman, Freddie	27
Machado, Manny	27
Muncy, Max	27
Turner, Trea	26

AL Pitchers Win Shares

Ray, Robbie	17
Cole, Gerrit	16
Hendriks, Liam	16
Clase, Emmanuel	15
Iglesias, Raisel	15
Lynn, Lance	15
Romano, Jordan	14
Barlow, Scott	14
Rodon, Carlos	14
Eovaldi, Nathan	14

NL Pitchers Win Shares

Wheeler, Zack	19
Buehler, Walker	18
Burnes, Corbin	16
Gausman, Kevin	16
Hader, Josh	16
Scherzer, Max	16
Suarez, Ranger	16
Urias, Julio	16
Wainwright, Adam	16
2 tied with	15

Career Batters Win Shares

Pujols, Albert	494
Cabrera, Miguel	420
Votto, Joey	333
Trout, Mike	319
McCutchen, Andrew	299
Molina, Yadier	297
Freeman, Freddie	270
Cruz, Nelson	259
Goldschmidt, Paul	251
Posey, Buster	243

Career Pitchers Win Shares

Greinke, Zack	236
Kershaw, Clayton	215
Scherzer, Max	205
Lester, Jon	182
Wainwright, Adam	172
Price, David	148
Sale, Chris	148
Jansen, Kenley	140
Santana, Ervin	137
Kimbrel, Craig	136

AL Component ERA
(minimum 162 IP)

Cole, Gerrit	2.77
Ray, Robbie	2.91
Berrios, Jose	2.92
Giolito, Lucas	3.03
McCullers Jr., Lance	3.08
Montas, Frankie	3.21
Eovaldi, Nathan	3.24
Cease, Dylan	3.54
Greinke, Zack	3.68
Ryu, Hyun-Jin	3.73

NL Component ERA
(minimum 162 IP)

Burnes, Corbin	1.81
Scherzer, Max	2.01
Buehler, Walker	2.13
Woodruff, Brandon	2.21
Wheeler, Zack	2.29
Gausman, Kevin	2.48
Urias, Julio	2.48
Morton, Charlie	2.58
Wainwright, Adam	2.67
Alcantara, Sandy	2.76

Fielding Statistics

Sarah Thompson

For the second year in a row, a Colorado Rockies third baseman leads MLB in Defensive Runs Saved. Ryan McMahon filled Nolan Arenado's shoes at the hot corner tremendously, saving 13 runs at third. He saved 9 runs at second, combining for 22 Runs Saved.

At third, McMahon saved an equal amount of runs with his arm and his range (5), but where he really set himself apart from the rest were his Good Fielding Plays and Defensive Misplays.

His 21 GFPs were good for tied third at the position, with Austin Riley (25) and Arenado (24) ahead of him.

However, the players with more GFPs than him made many more mistakes. Riley had 22 Defensive Misplays and 14 errors. Arenado had 19 DMs and 11 errors. McMahon made only 10 DMs and five errors when playing third.

When accounting for the difference among GFPs, DMs, and errors, McMahon had a "net" of 6 at third, which led all MLB third basemen.

In the tables below, you'll find each player's DRS at their position and the components that factor into their Runs Saved total. This differs among positions—for all positions, the PART system is used, and each player's total ART (Air, Range, Throwing Runs Saved) is listed.

Every position accrues run value from Good Fielding Plays and Defensive Misplays and errors as well. All infielders are evaluated on their performance in double play situations (GDP), but only first and third basemen have a column for runs saved on bunts. Defensive Runs Saved considers Outfield Arm Runs Saved ("Throws") for outfielders in the Runs Saved total. Catchers can accrue Runs Saved by framing ("SZ") and preventing stolen bases ("SB"). The column "Other" for catchers combines Bunt Runs Saved and Adjusted Earned Runs Saved.

First Basemen - Regulars

Player	Tm	G	GS	Inn	PO	A	E	DP	Pct.	Bases Saved	Runs Saved ART	GFP/ DME	Bunts/ GDP	Total
Goldschmidt, Paul	StL	153	153	1313	1144	106	2	111	.998	+3	7	3	-1	9
Muncy, Max	LAD	122	101	901	771	47	2	48	.998	+6	5	1	0	6
Olson, Matt	Oak	152	152	1339	1156	73	6	98	.995	-1	3	2	1	6
Alonso, Pete	NYM	148	148	1244	978	98	8	98	.993	+4	5	0	0	5
France, Ty	Sea	106	101	915	740	73	1	78	.999	+1	4	-1	2	5
Gurriel, Yuli	Hou	142	139	1222	1057	86	6	95	.995	-2	4	0	1	5
Walker, Christian	Ari	107	99	866	744	66	6	64	.993	+8	8	-1	-3	4
Votto, Joey	Cin	123	122	1043	853	99	7	91	.993	-1	3	1	0	4
Aguilar, Jesus	Mia	113	112	962	824	83	8	94	.991	-2	5	-2	0	3
Cron, C.J.	Col	130	129	1095	1040	90	10	103	.991	+2	2	0	1	3
Guerrero Jr., Vladimir	Tor	133	133	1144	1026	46	8	90	.993	+1	4	-2	0	2
Freeman, Freddie	Atl	159	158	1358	1252	101	3	95	.998	0	-1	3	0	2
Santana, Carlos	KC	136	136	1167	1001	50	7	117	.993	+3	-2	2	1	1
Bell, Josh	Was	119	116	983	819	73	5	71	.994	-2	-2	2	-1	-1
Abreu, Jose	CWS	135	134	1153	980	35	5	93	.995	-3	-3	1	1	-1
Walsh, Jared	LAA	128	119	1065	896	73	5	96	.995	0	0	-1	-1	-2
Lowe, Nathaniel	Tex	148	144	1269	1164	54	11	119	.991	+2	-1	-1	-1	-3
Schoop, Jonathan	Det	114	103	906	826	58	7	79	.992	0	-3	-2	1	-4
Hosmer, Eric	SD	131	129	1113	909	92	7	97	.993	-4	-5	1	0	-4
Belt, Brandon	SF	93	85	765	681	56	3	60	.996	0	-5	0	1	-4
Sano, Miguel	Min	118	114	996	878	43	13	94	.986	-4	-4	0	-1	-5
Rizzo, Anthony	TOT	139	137	1190	968	118	6	98	.995	-2	-6	1	-1	-6
Hoskins, Rhys	Phi	103	99	855	735	79	4	81	.995	-3	-5	-1	-1	-7
Dalbec, Bobby	Bos	123	111	969	828	51	11	79	.988	-3	-6	-1	0	-7

Second Basemen - Regulars

Player	Tm	G	GS	Inn	PO	A	E	DP	Pct.	Range	Bases Saved	Runs Saved ART	GFP/ DME	GDP	Total
Merrifield, Whit	KC	149	147	1256	283	382	8	103	.988	4.77	+3	10	2	2	14
Semien, Marcus	Tor	147	146	1246	202	317	8	86	.985	3.75	+1	11	-1	1	11
Fletcher, David	LAA	142	140	1212	262	354	6	86	.990	4.58	+8	8	3	0	11
Frazier, Adam	TOT	140	134	1160	212	312	5	77	.991	4.07	0	2	3	2	7
Edman, Tommy	StL	130	115	1032	195	308	5	64	.990	4.39	+13	9	0	-3	6
Wong, Kolten	Mil	113	108	937	164	229	2	51	.995	3.77	+2	6	0	0	6
Segura, Jean	Phi	128	127	1080	224	335	11	85	.981	4.66	-9	4	0	1	5
Cronenworth, Jake	SD	94	89	791	142	213	5	60	.986	4.04	+6	2	1	2	5
Polanco, Jorge	Min	120	112	971	164	294	12	70	.974	4.24	-5	3	-1	1	3
Albies, Ozzie	Atl	156	156	1359	231	389	8	75	.987	4.11	+3	4	-2	-1	1
India, Jonathan	Cin	148	144	1248	269	336	15	78	.976	4.36	+9	2	-1	-1	0
Harrison, Josh	TOT	102	91	799	147	195	5	48	.986	3.85	-3	-1	1	0	0
Altuve, Jose	Hou	144	143	1263	199	344	8	76	.985	3.87	+2	-2	0	-1	-3
Solak, Nick	Tex	121	120	1051	169	270	5	63	.989	3.76	-9	-3	1	-4	-6
Lowe, Brandon	TB	133	120	1093	187	270	11	78	.976	3.76	-4	-7	-1	1	-7
Hernandez, Cesar	TOT	142	142	1227	175	303	12	73	.976	3.51	+1	-9	-3	1	-11

Third Basemen - Regulars

Player	Tm	G	GS	Inn	PO	A	E	DP	Pct.	Range	Bases Saved	Runs Saved ART	GFP/ DME	Bunts/ GDP	Total
Hayes, Ke'Bryan	Pit	95	89	766	73	173	3	28	.988	2.89	+11	13	1	2	16
Riley, Austin	Atl	156	153	1327	89	300	14	18	.965	2.64	+2	12	1	0	13
McMahon, Ryan	Col	113	95	849	64	171	5	16	.979	2.49	+10	11	1	1	13
Chapman, Matt	Oak	150	150	1315	166	274	6	40	.987	3.01	+3	9	-1	2	10
Ramirez, Jose	Cle	133	132	1141	105	213	15	34	.955	2.51	+9	9	0	1	10
Machado, Manny	SD	144	144	1238	94	261	13	34	.965	2.57	+7	6	1	-1	6
Arenado, Nolan	StL	155	155	1312	125	287	11	38	.974	2.83	+11	6	0	0	6
Moncada, Yoan	CWS	138	138	1182	90	236	16	28	.953	2.48	-6	2	0	1	3
Bregman, Alex	Hou	90	90	783	59	158	8	13	.964	2.50	-5	1	1	0	2
Wendle, Joey	TB	107	82	766	81	176	11	22	.959	3.02	+3	1	1	0	2
Donaldson, Josh	Min	92	91	761	71	187	13	19	.952	3.05	-6	-1	1	1	1
Turner, Justin	LAD	143	135	1174	82	211	12	18	.961	2.25	+7	-3	0	1	-2
Suarez, Eugenio	Cin	104	102	886	69	193	9	21	.967	2.66	+2	1	-1	-3	-3
Escobar, Eduardo	TOT	99	93	767	40	152	11	17	.946	2.25	-1	0	-2	-1	-3
Candelario, Jeimer	Det	142	142	1238	91	273	9	30	.976	2.65	-4	-4	1	0	-3
Seager, Kyle	Sea	149	148	1303	99	291	14	43	.965	2.69	+4	-5	1	1	-3
Urshela, Gio	NYY	96	85	755	56	175	10	26	.959	2.75	-8	-7	1	2	-4
Franco, Maikel	Bal	99	97	820	66	166	8	15	.967	2.55	-9	-7	0	-1	-8

Player	Tm	G	GS	Inn	PO	A	E	DP	Pct.	Range	Bases Saved	Runs Saved ART	GFP/ DME	Bunts/ GDP	Total
Devers, Rafael	Bos	151	151	1299	147	269	22	37	.950	2.88	-2	-12	-2	1	-13
Bohm, Alec	Phi	103	98	834	67	154	15	17	.936	2.39	-4	-14	0	1	-13

Shortstops - Regulars

Player	Tm	G	GS	Inn	PO	A	E	DP	Pct.	Range	Bases Saved	Runs Saved ART	GFP/ DME	GDP	Total
Correa, Carlos	Hou	148	147	1305	183	384	11	70	.981	3.91	+4	18	3	-1	20
Simmons, Andrelton	Min	131	126	1092	167	322	12	67	.976	4.03	+8	15	0	0	15
Kiner-Falefa, Isiah	Tex	156	155	1360	214	436	19	98	.972	4.30	-3	12	-2	0	10
Story, Trevor	Col	138	138	1175	190	348	14	91	.975	4.12	-2	9	0	0	9
Crawford, J.P.	Sea	160	159	1412	222	388	12	89	.981	3.89	+2	5	0	3	8
Newman, Kevin	Pit	132	123	1074	164	286	3	62	.993	3.77	0	8	-2	1	7
Crawford, Brandon	SF	135	130	1166	168	340	9	68	.983	3.92	+6	7	0	-1	6
DeJong, Paul	StL	107	100	873	129	256	8	51	.980	3.97	+9	6	0	0	6
Rojas, Miguel	Mia	128	124	1073	191	283	11	80	.977	3.98	+6	1	1	3	5
Lindor, Francisco	NYM	124	122	1029	160	275	10	58	.978	3.80	+6	5	-1	0	4
Ahmed, Nick	Ari	127	118	1028	170	302	9	59	.981	4.13	+1	4	1	-1	4
Anderson, Tim	CWS	122	122	1048	152	270	10	59	.977	3.62	-1	2	-1	2	3
Baez, Javier	TOT	100	98	835	152	263	20	53	.954	4.47	+3	2	0	1	3
Lopez, Nicky	KC	148	141	1234	156	371	7	77	.987	3.84	+7	1	2	0	3
Farmer, Kyle	Cin	121	115	1009	128	270	5	53	.988	3.55	-3	0	1	1	2
Bichette, Bo	Tor	148	148	1271	169	364	24	73	.957	3.77	-4	-1	3	0	2
Turner, Trea	TOT	98	98	818	107	225	11	40	.968	3.65	+5	1	0	0	1
Adames, Willy	TOT	136	131	1150	153	332	15	63	.970	3.80	+8	0	0	1	1
Seager, Corey	LAD	92	90	803	104	202	8	22	.975	3.43	+3	3	-1	-2	0
Bogaerts, Xander	Bos	138	137	1169	152	362	9	76	.983	3.96	-1	-9	2	2	-5
Tatis Jr., Fernando	SD	102	101	842	113	217	21	45	.940	3.53	-7	-6	-1	1	-6
Swanson, Dansby	Atl	159	158	1372	185	376	10	64	.982	3.68	0	-11	3	1	-7
Rosario, Amed	Cle	121	118	1020	112	292	10	59	.976	3.57	-13	-7	-2	0	-9
Andrus, Elvis	Oak	143	141	1246	161	337	15	61	.971	3.60	+3	-8	-1	-1	-10
Gregorius, Didi	Phi	101	98	848	131	236	18	49	.953	3.89	-8	-9	-1	0	-10
Torres, Gleyber	NYY	108	104	916	121	236	18	37	.952	3.51	-5	-9	-1	0	-10
Iglesias, Jose	TOT	119	114	993	122	259	16	44	.960	3.45	-6	-20	0	-2	-22

Left Fielders - Regulars

Player	Tm	G	GS	Inn	PO	A	E	DP	Pct.	Range	Bases Saved	Runs Saved R/P	GFP/ DME	Throws	Total
O'Neill, Tyler	StL	131	129	1105	221	7	9	1	.962	1.86	+21	6	1	4	11
Tapia, Raimel	Col	118	110	952	173	7	3	0	.984	1.70	+14	4	0	3	7
Benintendi, Andrew	KC	129	129	1116	225	6	3	1	.987	1.86	+7	2	4	1	7
Gurriel Jr., Lourdes	Tor	119	115	944	169	12	4	2	.978	1.73	-15	-5	4	7	6
Pollock, A.J.	LAD	103	92	806	167	4	0	1	1.000	1.91	+11	1	2	0	3
Rosario, Eddie	TOT	100	96	818	171	4	3	1	.983	1.93	+6	3	0	-1	2
Peralta, David	Ari	137	123	1075	277	2	3	0	.989	2.34	+1	3	1	-4	0
Yelich, Christian	Mil	107	103	894	170	5	1	0	.994	1.76	+8	2	1	-4	-1
Pham, Tommy	SD	113	108	899	190	2	2	1	.990	1.92	-7	-1	-1	-2	-4
Winker, Jesse	Cin	101	98	832	150	4	2	0	.987	1.67	-12	-3	0	-2	-5
Smith, Dominic	NYM	114	107	860	159	2	1	0	.994	1.69	-3	-3	0	-2	-5
McCutchen, Andrew	Phi	135	131	1099	189	4	4	0	.980	1.58	-14	-6	1	-2	-7
Canha, Mark	Oak	106	93	806	137	1	3	0	.979	1.54	-1	-3	-3	-4	-10

Center Fielders - Regulars

Player	Tm	G	GS	Inn	PO	A	E	DP	Pct.	Range	Bases Saved	Runs Saved R/P	GFP/ DME	Throws	Total
Taylor, Michael A.	KC	139	135	1186	351	11	3	3	.992	2.75	+21	12	2	5	19
Bader, Harrison	StL	103	101	887	289	4	3	1	.990	2.97	+28	15	0	0	15
Kiermaier, Kevin	TB	116	101	895	229	1	1	0	.996	2.31	+28	10	1	2	13
Grisham, Trent	SD	127	118	1043	274	2	4	1	.986	2.38	+9	7	-1	2	8
Straw, Myles	TOT	156	149	1338	386	6	2	2	.995	2.64	+23	6	0	-2	4
Herrera, Odubel	Phi	104	92	819	188	5	2	2	.990	2.12	-2	1	0	1	2
Robles, Victor	Was	104	93	792	215	5	0	1	1.000	2.50	-5	-4	1	3	0
Mullins II, Cedric	Bal	153	146	1264	389	7	6	2	.985	2.82	+16	2	1	-4	-1
Gardner, Brett	NYY	105	92	816	205	2	0	1	1.000	2.28	+3	0	0	-1	-1
Marte, Starling	TOT	119	117	1023	280	8	3	3	.990	2.53	-4	-5	-1	2	-4
Reynolds, Bryan	Pit	137	131	1134	324	3	2	1	.994	2.60	-23	-4	0	-1	-5

Right Fielders - Regulars

Player	Tm	G	GS	Inn	PO	A	E	DP	Pct.	Range	Bases Saved	Runs Saved R/P	GFP/DME	Throws	Total
Gallo, Joey	TOT	92	89	765	192	9	4	3	.980	2.37	+8	2	3	7	12
Tucker, Kyle	Hou	133	126	1129	246	6	2	2	.992	2.01	+21	11	2	-2	11
Judge, Aaron	NYY	114	101	912	206	8	3	2	.986	2.11	+4	2	4	5	11
Kepler, Max	Min	97	90	786	169	5	0	1	1.000	1.99	+11	5	1	3	9
Garcia, Avisail	Mil	121	117	1007	201	4	6	0	.972	1.83	+11	3	0	5	8
Yastrzemski, Mike	SF	115	90	832	208	1	1	0	.995	2.26	+12	10	-1	-4	5
Heyward, Jason	ChC	97	92	784	157	3	0	1	1.000	1.84	+12	7	-2	-1	4
Soto, Juan	Was	144	144	1226	295	5	6	1	.980	2.20	+16	7	-2	-1	4
Betts, Mookie	LAD	98	86	752	151	1	2	1	.987	1.82	+2	4	1	-1	4
Renfroe, Hunter	Bos	138	133	1166	242	16	12	3	.956	1.99	-4	-3	0	3	0
Blackmon, Charlie	Col	137	134	1144	211	14	2	3	.991	1.77	+6	-1	1	-2	-2
Hernandez, Teoscar	Tor	110	105	881	220	7	3	1	.987	2.32	-4	-4	-1	3	-2
Haniger, Mitch	Sea	123	122	1081	270	3	3	0	.989	2.27	-3	0	1	-4	-3
Conforto, Michael	NYM	117	111	956	192	7	5	2	.975	1.87	-8	-3	-1	0	-4
Harper, Bryce	Phi	139	138	1174	214	10	1	1	.996	1.72	-25	-12	1	5	-6
Castellanos, Nick	Cin	135	134	1123	226	7	2	0	.991	1.87	-8	-3	-1	-3	-7
Polanco, Gregory	Pit	92	91	785	191	2	4	0	.980	2.21	-13	-2	-1	-5	-8
Myers, Wil	SD	118	107	934	181	1	0	1	1.000	1.75	-6	-6	1	-3	-8
Soler, Jorge	TOT	96	95	752	141	3	3	0	.980	1.72	-11	-7	-2	-2	-11

Catchers - Regulars

Player	Tm	G	GS	Inn	PO	A	E	DP	PB	Pct.	SB Att	CS	Pit CS	CS Pct	Cat ERA	Stk Sav	Runs Saved GFP/DME	SB	SZ	Other	Total
Stallings, Jacob	Pit	104	103	892	868	49	5	3	0	.995	56	11	1	.20	4.88	44	9	0	5	7	21
Hedges, Austin	Cle	87	85	744	721	44	2	7	2	.997	41	10	4	.24	3.95	32	4	1	4	3	12
Murphy, Sean	Oak	112	104	923	873	42	6	6	1	.993	53	12	1	.23	3.99	46	-1	2	5	4	10
Stassi, Max	LAA	86	80	703	697	25	4	1	8	.994	50	6	2	.12	4.63	81	1	-1	10	0	10
Diaz, Elias	Col	98	87	775	699	48	4	5	8	.995	36	14	2	.39	4.63	-19	1	6	-2	4	9
Trevino, Jose	Tex	88	81	713	644	27	6	3	4	.991	46	6	1	.13	5.05	45	3	0	5	0	8
Contreras, Willson	ChC	116	112	936	885	57	7	6	3	.993	56	10	2	.18	4.48	-25	4	0	-3	7	8
Zunino, Mike	TB	105	97	860	909	37	5	3	10	.995	55	8	5	.15	3.58	65	-3	1	8	1	7
Molina, Yadier	StL	118	118	1001	869	49	3	11	6	.997	39	13	5	.33	4.04	-14	2	3	-2	3	6
Heim, Jonah	Tex	78	73	641	557	25	3	3	3	.995	39	8	1	.21	4.52	41	-2	2	5	1	6
Gomes, Yan	TOT	92	90	771	730	44	8	3	3	.990	60	17	2	.28	4.34	-44	4	3	-5	3	5
Vazquez, Christian	Bos	132	119	1051	1136	58	7	6	10	.994	70	15	3	.21	3.14	65	-1	1	8	-3	5
Smith, Will	LAD	117	111	1005	1101	43	6	1	9	.995	91	19	5	.21	4.75	36	3	-4	4	1	4
Jeffers, Ryan	Min	84	77	671	626	30	4	2	6	.994	54	8	5	.15	4.00	6	3	0	0	0	3
Narvaez, Omar	Mil	111	100	886	1005	52	6	2	5	.994	77	15	2	.19	3.31	35	-3	0	4	2	3
Kelly, Carson	Ari	91	80	707	617	29	5	3	8	.992	41	8	2	.20	4.84	-13	1	-1	-2	4	2
Murphy, Tom	Sea	88	83	728	664	24	7	2	6	.990	49	5	4	.10	4.19	7	0	0	1	0	1
Barnhart, Tucker	Cin	102	97	846	880	47	2	4	3	.998	54	11	6	.20	4.70	13	5	-1	2	-6	0
Realmuto, J.T.	Phi	118	112	973	1057	30	1	5	6	.999	35	7	3	.20	4.47	12	3	0	1	-4	0
Grandal, Yasmani	CWS	80	76	627	687	23	8	2	7	.989	59	9	3	.15	3.62	5	-2	-1	1	1	-1
Maldonado, Martin	Hou	123	118	1011	1049	44	8	9	7	.993	47	18	1	.38	3.82	-20	1	2	-2	-3	-2
Posey, Buster	SF	106	102	892	884	31	3	3	2	.997	41	10	4	.24	3.58	8	2	1	1	-9	-5
Perez, Salvador	KC	124	120	1003	975	61	2	12	1	.998	39	16	2	.41	4.67	-96	1	5	-11	0	-5
McCann, James	NYM	107	97	826	877	33	6	2	8	.993	59	13	4	.22	4.00	-3	-2	1	0	-4	-5
Caratini, Victor	SD	101	87	787	851	34	2	3	6	.998	53	6	4	.11	4.01	-37	2	-3	-4	-1	-6
Nunez, Dom	Col	77	74	622	581	28	3	1	6	.995	52	9	2	.17	5.06	8	-1	-2	1	-4	-6
Severino, Pedro	Bal	109	102	883	797	31	4	2	10	.995	37	6	3	.16	5.38	-70	-8	-2	-8	9	-9
Sanchez, Gary	NYY	110	100	879	932	54	6	1	8	.994	55	5	5	.09	4.01	-9	-5	-1	-1	-3	-10

Player	Pos	G	GS	Inn	Pct.	DRS
Abreu, J	3B	1	0	0	-	0
Acuna Jr., R	CF	2	1	13	1.000	0
	RF	80	79	662	.985	2
Adams, M	1B	7	7	50	1.000	1
Adell, J	LF	25	17	158	1.000	-3
	RF	19	18	145	1.000	4
Adrianza, E	2B	7	4	37	1.000	-1
	3B	16	8	81	1.000	1
	SS	5	1	18	1.000	0
	LF	6	5	44	1.000	-1
	CF	1	0	2	1.000	0
	RF	14	11	108	1.000	-1
Aguilar, J	3B	2	0	2	1.000	0
Akiyama, S	LF	9	4	48	.889	-1
	CF	48	29	295	.987	-3
	RF	4	0	7	1.000	0
Alberto, H	2B	31	12	135	.952	0
	3B	49	30	294	.955	0
	SS	17	11	101	1.000	0
Alcantara, S	2B	22	18	159	.975	0
	3B	3	2	17	.800	0
	SS	55	44	388	.970	2
Alfaro, J	1B	3	2	17	1.000	-1
	LF	21	18	142	.913	0
Alford, A	LF	32	28	253	1.000	1
	CF	6	5	40	.833	-1
	RF	1	1	9	1.000	1
Allen, G	LF	5	0	18	1.000	0
	CF	4	3	28	1.000	-1
	RF	8	8	59	1.000	0
Almonte, A	LF	40	36	297	.966	-8
	RF	4	1	21	-	0
Almora Jr., A	LF	3	0	3	1.000	0
	CF	32	10	112	.974	0
	RF	1	1	5	1.000	0
Alvarez, E	2B	4	3	27	1.000	0
	3B	17	17	144	.909	0
Alvarez, Y	LF	41	39	319	.981	-2
Amburgey, T	RF	2	2	11	1.000	0
Anderson, B	3B	65	63	555	.970	3
	SS	1	0	6	1.000	0
Andreoli, J	LF	3	0	6	1.000	0
	CF	2	0	4	1.000	0
	RF	2	0	4	-	0
Andujar, M	1B	2	2	17	1.000	0
	3B	4	3	27	1.000	0
	LF	37	37	306	.985	-1
Aquino, A	LF	35	24	210	.919	0
	CF	14	5	60	1.000	-1
	RF	27	11	132	1.000	1
Arauz, J	2B	12	9	68	.935	0
	3B	2	1	9	1.000	0
	SS	13	9	91	.971	0
Arcia, O	2B	1	1	9	.800	-1
	3B	3	2	18	1.000	1
	SS	5	3	33	.929	0
	LF	14	13	102	.966	1
Arozarena, R	LF	81	69	612	.991	7
	CF	1	0	3	-	0
	RF	53	48	410	1.000	-4
Arraez, L	2B	48	35	321	.987	2
	3B	55	46	415	.957	5
	LF	27	23	165	1.000	3
Arroyo, C	1B	1	1	3	1.000	0
	2B	51	43	387	1.000	5
	SS	2	0	2	1.000	0
Arteaga, H	SS	1	1	9	1.000	0
Astudillo, W	1B	27	22	201	1.000	0
	2B	4	2	16	.833	0
	3B	29	22	205	.969	-4
	RF	1	1	5	1.000	0
Avila, A	2B	1	1	5	1.000	0
Baddoo, A	LF	56	46	407	.988	1
	CF	66	58	513	.988	-4
	RF	5	3	33	1.000	1
Baez, J	2B	35	32	286	.968	3
Barnes, A	2B	7	0	18	.833	-1
Barnhart, T	1B	2	0	4	1.000	0
Barrera, L	LF	2	1	9	-	-1
	CF	1	0	1	1.000	0
	RF	2	1	9	1.000	1
Barrero, J	2B	2	1	11	.875	0

Player	Pos	G	GS	Inn	Pct.	DRS
	SS	9	7	65	.971	-1
	CF	7	5	40	1.000	2
Bauers, J	1B	54	37	354	1.000	2
	LF	21	13	126	1.000	2
	RF	23	20	175	1.000	2
Beaty, M	1B	21	16	116	1.000	1
	3B	5	0	11	.800	-1
	LF	28	20	162	.917	-4
	RF	20	8	86	.923	-3
Beer, S	1B	1	1	6	1.000	-1
Bell, J	LF	9	5	52	1.000	2
	RF	1	1	8	-	0
Bellinger, C	1B	4	2	20	.923	-1
	CF	87	74	675	.988	-1
	RF	7	4	40	1.000	-1
Bemboom, A	LF	1	0	2	1.000	0
Berti, J	2B	27	17	181	.987	0
	3B	46	41	336	.927	2
	SS	2	1	8	1.000	0
	LF	7	4	30	1.000	0
	CF	4	0	12	1.000	0
	RF	1	0	3	-	0
Betts, M	2B	7	5	46	1.000	1
	CF	30	25	212	.980	0
Biggio, C	1B	7	3	34	1.000	0
	2B	7	4	40	1.000	-1
	3B	52	49	412	.935	2
	LF	1	1	9	-	0
	RF	15	13	117	1.000	1
Bishop, B	LF	8	1	20	1.000	0
Blandino, A	1B	17	8	87	1.000	0
	2B	5	1	15	1.000	0
	3B	9	2	31	1.000	1
	SS	1	0	-	-	0
	LF	3	0	7	1.000	0
Blankenhorn, T	2B	6	1	16	.700	-2
	LF	1	0	3	1.000	0
	RF	1	0	1	1.000	0
Bohm, A	1B	7	3	34	.963	-2
Bolt, S	LF	6	1	20	1.000	-1
	CF	16	9	92	1.000	3
	RF	4	2	20	1.000	0
Bonifacio, J	LF	2	0	3	1.000	0
	CF	3	3	18	1.000	-1
Bote, D	2B	61	54	469	.991	-1
	3B	24	21	173	.947	1
Bradley, B	1B	68	65	543	.990	-1
Bradley Jr., J	LF	14	11	88	1.000	1
	CF	89	79	722	1.000	9
	RF	17	9	105	1.000	2
Brantley, M	LF	84	80	667	.992	2
	RF	8	8	61	1.000	-1
Brantly, R	1B	1	1	9	1.000	0
Brinson, L	LF	51	35	332	.976	5
	CF	33	31	240	.983	-2
	RF	4	3	28	1.000	0
Brosseau, M	1B	10	2	36	.974	1
	2B	27	22	184	1.000	5
	3B	23	16	140	.974	1
	LF	1	0	6	1.000	0
	RF	1	0	3	-	0
Brown, S	1B	6	3	30	.967	-2
	LF	19	10	98	1.000	5
	CF	4	2	20	1.000	1
	RF	75	50	472	.984	1
Bruce, J	1B	10	10	84	1.000	0
Brujan, V	2B	4	4	29	.941	-2
	LF	1	0	1	-	0
	CF	1	0	4	-	-1
	RF	2	2	16	1.000	0
Bryant, K	1B	12	10	92	.989	1
	3B	55	47	386	.946	-2
	SS	1	0	2	1.000	-1
	LF	48	35	310	.983	-1
	CF	19	13	110	1.000	0
	RF	39	33	276	.982	-2
Burger, J	3B	8	7	62	1.000	1
Burns, A	1B	2	0	5	1.000	0
	2B	3	2	13	1.000	0
	3B	2	0	6	1.000	-1
Buxton, B	CF	60	59	510	.994	10
Cabrera, A	1B	19	15	122	.991	0

Player	Pos	G	GS	Inn	Pct.	DRS
	3B	65	55	489	.940	1
	SS	1	0	1	-	0
Cabrera, M	1B	44	44	367	.997	-4
Cain, L	CF	70	69	593	.994	6
Calhoun, K	RF	39	36	309	.972	0
Calhoun, W	LF	41	38	321	1.000	-1
Camargo, J	1B	1	0	2	1.000	0
	2B	1	0	6	1.000	0
	3B	1	0	2	-	0
Cameron, D	LF	1	0	2	1.000	0
	CF	15	12	110	1.000	0
	RF	18	15	139	1.000	-2
Campbell, E	1B	1	1	8	1.000	0
	3B	2	2	18	1.000	0
Canha, M	1B	2	0	2	1.000	0
	CF	23	21	188	1.000	0
	RF	27	20	175	1.000	0
Canning, G	LF	1	0	2	-	0
Caratini, V	1B	5	0	7	1.000	-1
	3B	2	0	2	-	0
Carlson, D	LF	9	8	68	1.000	0
	CF	60	59	501	.986	-2
	RF	87	78	675	.987	3
Carpenter, M	1B	14	9	90	.988	-1
	2B	34	29	215	.974	-7
	3B	6	4	38	1.000	-1
Casali, C	1B	3	0	4	1.000	0
Castillo, I	2B	1	0	4	-	0
	3B	1	0	2	1.000	0
Castro, H	1B	15	7	78	1.000	-1
	2B	33	25	233	.992	0
	3B	12	11	94	.938	-1
	SS	43	34	291	1.000	-5
	LF	3	1	12	1.000	0
	CF	2	2	12	1.000	-2
Castro, R	2B	20	19	148	.951	-3
	3B	5	4	32	1.000	0
Castro, S	3B	85	84	715	.946	2
	SS	1	1	5	1.000	0
Castro, W	2B	91	81	714	.978	-8
	SS	20	19	157	.968	-2
	LF	10	10	84	1.000	-2
Cave, J	LF	37	16	178	1.000	-1
	CF	29	18	168	.979	-1
	RF	11	7	66	.960	-1
Celestino, G	LF	1	0	1	-	0
	CF	22	20	152	.951	-2
	RF	2	0	11	1.000	2
Chang, Y	1B	49	41	340	.991	0
	2B	8	3	37	.955	0
	3B	21	13	120	.974	1
	SS	7	6	55	1.000	-1
Chapman, M	SS	3	0	4	1.000	-1
Chavis, M	1B	9	5	57	.981	0
	2B	29	20	182	.989	1
	3B	4	3	29	1.000	0
	RF	1	1	4	1.000	-1
Chirinos, R	2B	2	0	2	-	0
Chisholm Jr., J	2B	91	87	739	.959	5
	SS	37	31	278	.925	-4
Choi, J	1B	73	67	587	.996	-4
Clement, E	2B	22	22	188	.976	-1
	3B	16	13	112	1.000	1
	SS	1	1	3	-	-1
	LF	2	0	8	-	0
Collins, Z	1B	1	0	1	1.000	0
Contreras, W	3B	1	0	1	-	0
	LF	1	0	1	-	0
Cooper, G	1B	19	14	132	1.000	3
	RF	41	39	315	.984	-5
Cordero, F	1B	8	8	65	1.000	0
	LF	33	27	240	.956	2
	RF	2	1	10	1.000	-1
Craig, W	1B	18	16	140	.991	-3
Cronenworth, J	1B	24	20	171	.994	1
	SS	41	36	327	.977	-1
Cruz, N	1B	1	1	7	1.000	0
Cruz, O	SS	2	2	18	1.000	0
Culberson, C	1B	4	3	27	1.000	1
	2B	4	3	26	1.000	0
	3B	68	60	516	.966	4
	SS	3	3	25	.800	0

Player	Pos	G	GS	Inn	Pct.	DRS
	LF	6	5	42	1.000	-1
	RF	1	0	2	1.000	0
Dahl, D	LF	31	27	242	1.000	-4
	CF	1	1	8	1.000	0
	RF	12	11	91	1.000	3
Dalbec, B	3B	14	4	52	.944	-1
	SS	2	0	4	1.000	0
Davis, J	3B	50	48	383	.960	-7
Davis, J	LF	2	1	8	1.000	0
	RF	1	1	7	1.000	1
Davis, J	LF	3	0	4	-	0
	CF	55	25	248	1.000	1
Davis, K	LF	3	2	17	1.000	0
Daza, Y	LF	12	10	79	1.000	0
	CF	57	46	405	.991	-3
	RF	22	15	138	1.000	7
De Goti, A	2B	2	2	16	1.000	0
De La Cruz, B	LF	16	11	99	1.000	2
	CF	24	23	199	.983	-1
	RF	23	19	175	.957	1
Dean, A	LF	6	3	32	1.000	-1
	RF	3	1	12	1.000	0
Deichmann, G	LF	2	0	5	1.000	0
	RF	7	6	52	.909	1
DeShields, D	LF	3	3	21	1.000	1
	CF	18	10	92	.967	-2
Devers, J	2B	13	7	65	1.000	0
	SS	5	4	29	.900	-3
Devers, R	2B	2	0	3	1.000	0
Diaz, A	1B	12	10	94	1.000	0
	2B	13	9	87	.976	3
	3B	30	28	248	.988	6
	SS	9	7	59	.947	-1
	LF	15	11	93	1.000	0
	RF	1	1	6	-	0
Diaz, I	2B	35	33	270	.982	-4
	3B	37	30	279	.934	-3
Diaz, L	1B	32	29	259	1.000	9
Diaz, Y	1B	81	66	604	.996	0
	2B	1	0	1	-	0
	3B	58	52	443	.983	-9
Dickerson, A	LF	82	69	552	.982	-5
Dickerson, C	LF	77	69	586	.991	-1
	CF	10	9	62	.938	0
	RF	5	3	22	1.000	1
Difo, W	2B	28	14	151	.972	-1
	3B	18	12	95	.935	-3
	SS	4	3	29	1.000	0
	CF	4	3	30	.917	-1
	RF	8	7	53	.875	-4
Dorow, R	3B	3	2	20	1.000	0
Dozier, H	1B	19	12	122	1.000	0
	3B	57	52	423	.956	-12
	LF	14	13	96	1.000	0
	RF	60	50	454	.982	-9
Drury, B	1B	3	1	14	1.000	-1
	2B	2	2	15	1.000	0
	3B	7	5	40	.938	-2
	LF	6	4	25	1.000	1
	RF	6	5	31	1.000	0
Dubon, M	2B	20	6	87	.976	-2
	3B	12	3	51	.917	0
	SS	21	18	151	.952	2
	CF	27	13	133	1.000	2
Duffy, M	1B	2	0	4	1.000	0
	2B	21	17	146	.987	2
	3B	56	47	416	.973	1
	SS	2	2	31	1.000	0
	LF	3	3	22	1.000	0
Duggar, S	LF	4	1	13	1.000	0
	CF	93	66	599	.988	5
	RF	1	0	3	1.000	0
Duran, J	LF	1	1	8	1.000	0
	CF	28	25	215	1.000	-5
Duvall, A	LF	51	48	407	.968	6
	CF	30	25	211	1.000	4
	RF	78	59	537	.992	9
Dyson, J	LF	20	6	83	1.000	1
	CF	38	20	195	1.000	3
	RF	34	7	115	.970	4
Eaton, A	1B	1	0	1	1.000	0
	LF	2	1	9	-	0

Player	Pos	G	GS	Inn	Pct.	DRS
	RF	79	67	587	.970	-2
Edman, T	SS	4	3	26	1.000	1
	RF	41	35	284	.970	0
Ellis, D	2B	4	4	24	1.000	-1
	3B	17	15	137	1.000	-3
Engel, A	LF	4	2	17	1.000	1
	CF	26	24	212	1.000	5
	RF	10	8	71	.950	0
Escobar, A	2B	17	17	134	1.000	1
	SS	61	58	503	.969	-3
Escobar, E	1B	18	14	126	1.000	-1
	2B	42	31	284	.992	-1
	SS	1	0	2	-	0
Espinal, S	3B	81	62	552	.980	8
Estrada, T	2B	16	7	81	.977	0
	3B	4	1	19	1.000	1
	SS	19	14	132	.962	-3
	LF	4	4	27	1.000	0
	RF	1	1	6	-	0
Evans, P	1B	20	15	135	.984	2
	3B	14	12	102	.967	2
	LF	16	13	113	.933	-1
	RF	15	12	102	.900	-4
Fairchild, S	LF	2	1	9	1.000	0
	CF	5	2	18	1.000	1
	RF	1	1	6	1.000	0
Fargas, J	LF	2	2	17	1.000	1
	CF	12	10	83	1.000	1
	RF	2	1	8	1.000	0
Farmer, K	1B	5	2	23	1.000	-1
	2B	9	3	41	1.000	1
	3B	10	8	66	.929	0
	LF	2	0	2	-	0
Fisher, D	LF	1	0	3	-	0
	RF	1	1	11	1.000	0
Fletcher, D	SS	20	16	145	.971	2
Flores, W	1B	34	21	182	.988	1
	2B	30	22	182	.985	-1
	3B	58	51	431	.941	-1
Florial, E	CF	11	7	64	1.000	0
Ford, M	1B	21	18	157	1.000	-1
Fowler, D	RF	7	6	50	1.000	-1
Fowler, D	CF	12	12	94	1.000	0
	RF	1	0	1	1.000	0
Fraley, J	LF	51	36	333	.986	5
	CF	14	14	132	.976	0
	RF	6	6	53	1.000	-1
France, T	2B	21	19	153	.972	-1
	3B	5	5	39	.857	-2
Franco, M	1B	2	0	8	1.000	0
Franco, W	2B	1	1	8	1.000	0
	3B	8	7	62	.810	-1
	SS	63	61	543	.977	6
Frazier, A	LF	12	5	55	1.000	0
Frazier, C	LF	37	30	255	1.000	-6
	RF	33	26	220	.976	-5
Frazier, T	1B	4	3	32	1.000	-1
	3B	3	2	18	1.000	0
Freeland, K	RF	1	0	1	-	0
Freeman, M	1B	9	2	26	1.000	0
	2B	2	0	6	1.000	0
	3B	7	2	28	1.000	1
	SS	12	8	75	.950	1
	LF	1	0	0	-	0
	CF	3	0	1	1.000	0
Friedl, T	LF	5	2	24	1.000	0
	CF	6	6	50	.818	-2
Fuentes, J	1B	32	9	125	.982	1
	3B	60	56	452	.963	10
	LF	2	0	3	1.000	0
Gallo, J	LF	51	46	414	.968	3
Galvis, F	1B	1	0	1	1.000	0
	2B	2	2	15	1.000	0
	3B	32	18	154	.956	3
	SS	82	79	648	.979	-4
Gamel, B	1B	4	0	9	1.000	0
	LF	73	66	561	1.000	-5
	CF	20	11	108	1.000	-4
	RF	18	12	118	1.000	-1
Garcia, A	LF	9	8	66	1.000	0
	CF	79	76	668	.986	3
	RF	51	50	448	.992	13

Player	Pos	G	GS	Inn	Pct.	DRS
Garcia, A	CF	1	1	9	1.000	0
Garcia, L	2B	36	33	278	.972	-2
	3B	11	8	74	.952	1
	SS	19	18	156	1.000	-1
	LF	26	8	111	.955	1
	CF	26	22	164	1.000	0
	RF	34	28	235	.979	-1
Garcia, L	2B	59	55	458	.962	2
	SS	8	7	68	.920	-3
Garcia, R	1B	2	0	2	1.000	0
	2B	9	6	59	1.000	0
	3B	15	10	102	.962	-1
	SS	13	8	81	.974	-1
Gardner, B	LF	35	21	223	.980	-2
Garlick, K	LF	12	9	85	1.000	0
	CF	5	2	22	1.000	0
	RF	18	13	117	1.000	0
Garver, M	1B	4	1	9	.857	-1
Giambrone, T	2B	4	3	28	.941	0
Gimenez, A	2B	25	23	197	.991	-2
	SS	42	36	322	.965	5
Gittens, C	1B	13	10	89	1.000	1
Gonzalez, E	1B	13	10	84	1.000	1
	3B	38	31	282	.969	5
	SS	17	12	100	.962	-1
Gonzalez, L	LF	2	1	7	-	-1
	RF	3	2	17	1.000	0
Gonzalez, M	1B	14	11	113	.982	1
	2B	39	32	277	.958	-2
	3B	11	8	80	.960	-1
	SS	12	9	85	.949	2
	LF	12	8	70	1.000	1
	RF	2	2	18	1.000	0
Gonzalez, R	2B	1	1	8	.800	-1
	3B	4	3	26	1.000	0
	SS	1	0	2	1.000	0
	LF	1	1	7	-	0
	RF	3	2	18	1.000	0
Goodrum, N	1B	1	0	0	-	0
	2B	8	8	69	1.000	0
	SS	66	60	534	.969	-6
	LF	7	6	44	.900	-1
	CF	8	4	39	1.000	-1
Goodwin, B	LF	6	2	23	.900	0
	CF	27	27	205	1.000	-4
	RF	43	33	314	.985	-6
Gordon, N	2B	17	13	110	.977	1
	3B	2	0	2	.667	0
	SS	14	8	75	1.000	0
	LF	11	7	64	1.000	-2
	CF	34	24	223	1.000	-1
	RF	1	0	3	1.000	0
Gosselin, P	1B	23	21	171	1.000	-1
	2B	4	4	26	.923	-1
	3B	32	24	210	.955	-3
	LF	39	36	302	1.000	-3
	RF	1	0	1	-	0
Grandal, Y	1B	8	5	54	1.000	0
Grichuk, R	CF	96	87	735	1.000	-2
	RF	71	34	330	1.000	6
Grossman, R	LF	82	76	668	1.000	-4
	RF	73	69	585	1.000	-4
Guerrero Jr., V	3B	1	0	2	-	0
Guillorme, L	2B	18	13	114	1.000	0
	3B	27	18	154	.927	-2
	SS	11	5	58	.897	-1
Gurriel, Y	3B	1	0	2	-	0
Gurriel Jr., L	1B	11	7	68	1.000	1
Gushue, T	1B	1	0	5	1.000	0
Gutierrez, K	1B	1	0	2	1.000	1
	2B	1	0	1	-	0
	3B	84	74	662	.944	-1
Guzman, R	1B	4	3	28	1.000	0
	LF	2	1	2	-	0
Haase, E	1B	1	0	2	1.000	0
	LF	22	20	169	.968	0
Hager, J	2B	5	5	42	1.000	0
	SS	1	0	1	1.000	0
	LF	2	0	5	-	0
	RF	1	1	8	1.000	0
Haggerty, S	2B	4	1	16	1.000	0
	LF	20	15	130	1.000	2

All Other Fielders

Player	Pos	G	GS	Inn	Pct.	DRS
	CF	3	2	19	1.000	0
	RF	6	4	38	1.000	-2
Hamilton, B	LF	18	5	68	1.000	1
	CF	47	22	241	1.000	1
	RF	2	1	13	1.000	0
Hampson, G	2B	47	30	288	1.000	4
	3B	2	1	8	1.000	0
	SS	5	2	21	.900	-1
	CF	91	74	649	1.000	0
Happ, I	2B	8	4	35	.917	-1
	3B	2	0	1	-	0
	LF	65	52	459	1.000	2
	CF	56	52	439	1.000	-2
	RF	16	11	95	1.000	-2
Harper, B	1B	1	0	0	-	0
Harrison, J	3B	23	15	137	.957	1
	SS	8	7	57	.857	-2
	LF	19	15	122	.952	-2
	CF	2	2	10	.667	-1
	RF	1	1	7	-	0
Harrison, M	CF	4	2	20	1.000	1
	RF	3	0	3	1.000	1
Haseley, A	LF	2	0	5	1.000	0
	CF	8	7	46	1.000	-1
Hays, A	LF	88	75	662	1.000	4
	CF	6	3	30	.889	0
	RF	54	42	360	1.000	10
Heath, N	CF	18	9	89	1.000	0
Heineman, S	1B	2	0	7	1.000	0
	LF	2	0	2	1.000	0
	CF	8	7	53	1.000	0
	RF	2	0	3	1.000	0
Heredia, G	LF	21	2	43	1.000	0
	CF	108	82	719	.985	1
Hermosillo, M	LF	2	1	11	1.000	0
	CF	5	3	29	1.000	1
	RF	6	3	32	1.000	1
Hernandez, C	SS	1	0	2	-	0
Hernandez, K	2B	47	45	367	.976	0
	SS	8	4	37	1.000	2
	CF	93	81	716	.978	14
Hernandez, T	LF	58	24	250	.952	0
	CF	2	1	7	-	0
Hernandez, Y	LF	48	46	374	.990	-9
	RF	13	10	86	1.000	1
Hernandez, Y	2B	9	8	73	.976	2
	3B	29	28	242	.988	4
	SS	6	4	39	1.000	2
Herrera, O	LF	23	14	142	.963	-1
	RF	1	1	9	-	0
Hicks, A	CF	32	30	273	.983	-4
Higgins, P	1B	1	0	5	1.000	0
Hill, D	CF	45	41	341	.990	-7
Hilliard, S	LF	17	10	86	1.000	0
	CF	46	38	323	1.000	0
	RF	11	7	70	1.000	-2
Hiura, K	1B	49	42	357	.991	1
	2B	7	4	36	1.000	0
	LF	1	0	3	1.000	0
Hoerner, N	2B	30	30	251	.992	4
	3B	1	0	0	-	0
	SS	12	12	98	.979	0
	LF	3	1	13	1.000	-1
	CF	2	0	3	1.000	0
Holt, B	3B	69	57	516	.978	4
Hoying, J	LF	1	1	6	-	0
Hurst, S	CF	6	0	10	1.000	0
Ibanez, A	1B	12	11	92	1.000	2
	2B	31	28	248	.983	4
	3B	11	10	86	.963	2
	LF	1	1	9	1.000	0
Iglesias, J	2B	18	14	123	.978	0
Inciarte, E	LF	4	0	4	-	0
	CF	37	17	169	1.000	1
Isbel, K	LF	4	1	19	1.000	0
	CF	9	7	64	1.000	0
	RF	14	12	101	1.000	0
Jackson, A	RF	1	0	1	-	0
Jankowski, T	LF	6	3	29	1.000	0
	CF	45	26	248	1.000	-4
	RF	8	1	24	1.000	0
Jay, J	LF	5	3	29	1.000	0

All Other Fielders

Player	Pos	G	GS	Inn	Pct.	DRS
Jimenez, E	LF	37	37	304	.984	1
Joe, C	1B	14	13	101	.982	2
	LF	32	27	238	.968	4
Johnson Jr., D	LF	9	7	59	.923	0
	RF	19	16	132	.969	0
Jones, J	LF	2	1	11	1.000	-1
	CF	30	26	237	1.000	-1
Jones, J	2B	23	19	156	.966	-1
Jones, T	1B	14	8	87	1.000	2
	LF	10	8	75	1.000	2
Joyce, M	LF	9	4	37	1.000	1
	RF	9	5	50	1.000	0
Judge, A	CF	23	21	158	1.000	-1
Kelenic, J	LF	14	14	123	.960	-3
	CF	77	75	675	.986	-16
	RF	3	2	18	1.000	1
Kemp, T	2B	89	53	520	.980	0
	SS	1	0	2	1.000	0
	LF	49	37	337	1.000	2
Kepler, M	CF	22	19	164	1.000	-5
Kieboom, C	3B	60	59	507	.958	-8
Kim, H	2B	21	20	148	1.000	5
	3B	23	18	166	.982	4
	SS	35	25	260	.970	9
Kingery, S	2B	4	1	12	.800	-1
	3B	1	0	5	1.000	-1
	LF	1	0	1	-	0
	CF	1	0	3	-	0
	RF	5	1	12	1.000	1
Kirilloff, A	1B	29	25	214	1.000	1
	LF	13	11	93	.958	-2
	RF	27	19	172	1.000	1
Kivlehan, P	RF	2	2	12	1.000	0
Knapp, A	1B	6	0	6	1.000	0
	2B	1	0	1	1.000	0
Knizner, A	1B	1	0	2	1.000	0
Kozma, P	SS	3	3	25	1.000	2
La Stella, T	2B	54	47	404	.995	-3
	3B	5	5	32	1.000	0
Lagares, J	LF	23	7	84	1.000	1
	CF	62	51	470	1.000	2
	RF	37	25	230	1.000	-1
LaMarre, R	LF	4	4	27	1.000	0
	CF	1	1	8	1.000	0
	RF	4	2	18	.667	-1
Lamb, J	1B	3	3	16	.929	-1
	3B	16	12	110	.972	2
	LF	16	13	84	1.000	0
	RF	9	8	67	1.000	-2
Larnach, T	LF	60	51	466	.971	-2
	RF	20	18	145	1.000	4
Laureano, R	CF	75	75	653	.990	3
	RF	8	8	71	1.000	1
Lee, K	RF	11	4	45	1.000	0
LeMahieu, D	1B	55	33	321	.997	0
	2B	83	77	663	.993	-2
	3B	39	36	299	.930	-1
Leon, S	3B	1	0	1	-	0
Lewis, K	CF	34	34	294	.989	-1
Leyba, D	2B	21	16	136	.983	-3
	3B	10	8	70	1.000	0
Lin, T	LF	1	0	2	-	0
Locastro, T	LF	14	10	75	1.000	0
	CF	28	21	178	1.000	-1
	RF	9	3	41	1.000	1
Long Jr., S	2B	10	9	71	1.000	0
	LF	25	22	198	1.000	-3
Longoria, E	3B	78	67	611	.974	-1
Lopes, T	2B	3	1	17	1.000	0
Lopez, A	2B	3	1	10	1.000	0
	3B	3	2	15	.667	-1
	LF	2	0	4	-	0
	CF	1	0	0	-	0
Lopez, J	2B	6	5	41	.962	1
Lopez, N	2B	4	3	27	1.000	2
Lorenzen, M	CF	1	0	1	-	0
	RF	1	0	1	1.000	0
Lowe, B	1B	1	0	1	1.000	0
	LF	10	6	43	1.000	-1
	RF	6	5	45	.933	-2
Lowe, J	LF	1	0	2	1.000	0
	RF	1	1	7	1.000	0

All Other Fielders

Player	Pos	G	GS	Inn	Pct.	DRS
Lowe, N	3B	1	0	1	1.000	0
Lowrie, J	2B	71	69	585	.986	-11
	3B	1	0	3	1.000	0
Luplow, J	1B	17	14	107	1.000	1
	2B	1	0	1	-	0
	3B	1	0	1	-	0
	LF	6	5	39	1.000	-2
	CF	22	19	155	1.000	-2
	RF	11	6	65	1.000	0
Lux, G	2B	27	26	206	.988	4
	3B	1	1	6	.500	0
	SS	59	50	471	.966	0
	LF	11	10	86	1.000	-3
	CF	6	6	45	1.000	0
	RF	1	0	3	-	-1
Machin, V	2B	3	3	23	1.000	1
	3B	3	1	10	.500	0
	SS	8	7	58	.944	-1
Madrigal, N	2B	53	53	452	.973	-4
Maldonado, M	1B	1	1	9	1.000	0
Mancini, T	1B	77	75	641	.998	-1
Marcano, T	2B	8	5	42	1.000	2
	3B	1	0	2	-	0
	LF	4	2	16	1.000	0
	RF	4	2	16	.500	-1
Marchan, R	1B	1	0	1	-	0
Margot, M	LF	24	12	123	1.000	4
	CF	24	22	182	.983	3
	RF	86	70	657	.984	6
Marisnick, J	LF	20	6	78	1.000	2
	CF	52	30	283	.974	1
	RF	2	1	11	1.000	0
Marmolejos, J	1B	14	13	112	.980	-1
	LF	11	11	83	1.000	-1
	RF	2	2	15	1.000	-1
Marrero, D	1B	1	0	0	-	0
	2B	1	1	9	1.000	0
	3B	3	2	19	1.000	0
	SS	4	1	14	1.000	0
Marsh, B	CF	70	63	568	.994	-3
Marte, K	2B	20	14	129	.958	0
	CF	71	67	567	.987	-15
Marte, L	2B	1	1	8	1.000	-1
	3B	1	0	3	1.000	0
	SS	1	1	7	1.000	0
Martin, J	LF	41	34	318	.987	0
	CF	3	3	25	1.000	0
	RF	3	0	5	1.000	0
Martin, R	SS	37	29	263	.955	-7
Martinez, J	LF	30	28	247	.983	2
	RF	8	7	52	1.000	0
Martini, N	LF	7	2	22	1.000	1
	RF	7	4	42	1.000	-2
Mateo, J	2B	18	12	112	.982	1
	3B	9	0	27	1.000	0
	SS	18	15	120	.980	-1
	LF	6	2	28	1.000	0
	CF	11	6	67	1.000	0
	RF	7	3	46	1.000	0
Mathisen, W	1B	13	6	68	1.000	1
	3B	4	0	6	-	0
	LF	2	2	10	1.000	0
Maton, N	2B	21	15	144	1.000	-1
	SS	20	16	145	.933	-3
Maybin, C	LF	4	3	18	1.000	1
	CF	6	4	40	1.000	0
	RF	3	2	19	1.000	0
Mayfield, J	2B	9	8	67	1.000	1
	3B	68	59	529	.957	-1
	SS	12	10	88	.971	-2
Mazara, N	RF	41	39	332	.957	0
Mazeika, P	1B	1	1	6	1.000	0
McCann, J	1B	6	5	45	1.000	1
McCarthy, J	CF	14	12	103	1.000	1
	RF	6	3	49	1.000	0
McCormick, C	LF	51	20	250	1.000	5
	CF	33	29	253	.983	2
	RF	22	20	183	1.000	7
McKenna, R	2B	1	0	0	-	0
	3B	1	0	1	-	0
	LF	50	24	236	1.000	6
	CF	18	13	108	1.000	-1

Player	Pos	G	GS	Inn	Pct.	DRS
	RF	18	12	114	.944	-3
McKinney, B	1B	10	3	38	1.000	0
	LF	27	20	178	1.000	2
	CF	3	0	2	1.000	0
	RF	48	41	358	.986	4
McKinstry, Z	2B	20	10	112	.902	-2
	3B	12	6	65	1.000	0
	LF	14	5	42	1.000	-2
	RF	23	18	147	1.000	-1
McMahon, R	2B	52	44	368	.990	9
McNeil, J	2B	79	73	606	.976	4
	3B	2	0	5	1.000	0
	LF	28	26	217	.960	1
Meadows, A	LF	78	72	616	.991	-1
	RF	1	1	8	.500	-2
Mejia, F	1B	2	1	11	1.000	0
Mendick, D	2B	28	21	196	.988	-3
	3B	4	1	11	1.000	-1
	SS	28	22	195	1.000	0
	LF	2	0	2	-	0
	CF	1	0	5	-	0
	RF	8	7	49	1.000	1
Mercado, O	LF	45	36	344	1.000	4
	CF	7	6	40	1.000	1
	RF	20	14	124	.970	0
Mercedes, Y	1B	1	1	4	.000	0
Mercer, J	1B	2	0	3	1.000	0
	2B	21	19	158	.941	-1
	3B	14	10	95	.926	-1
	SS	6	0	15	1.000	1
	LF	1	0	0	-	0
Merrifield, W	LF	2	2	17	1.000	0
	RF	18	11	100	1.000	-2
Meyers, J	LF	4	2	16	1.000	0
	CF	39	31	293	.987	3
	RF	3	3	24	1.000	1
Miller, B	1B	58	47	392	.992	1
	2B	13	8	74	1.000	1
	3B	8	4	38	1.000	-2
	LF	6	5	37	1.000	-1
	RF	14	12	97	.882	-4
Miller, B	LF	2	2	17	1.000	0
	CF	2	1	11	1.000	0
	RF	1	0	1	-	0
Miller, O	1B	18	18	162	.986	-4
	2B	29	25	220	.982	1
	3B	7	4	35	.900	-2
	SS	1	1	8	1.000	0
Molina, Y	1B	1	0	3	1.000	0
Mondesi, A	3B	20	20	175	.964	-1
	SS	11	10	82	1.000	-1
Moniak, M	LF	6	0	9	-	0
	CF	8	7	53	1.000	1
	RF	3	0	6	-	-1
Moore, D	2B	66	56	507	.987	4
	3B	10	4	48	1.000	3
	SS	4	2	18	1.000	-1
	LF	48	34	285	1.000	3
	RF	9	5	50	.909	1
Moran, C	1B	84	81	669	.992	-3
	3B	1	0	1	-	0
Moreland, M	1B	7	7	61	1.000	0
Moroff, M	2B	4	2	19	1.000	-1
	3B	1	1	9	.667	-1
Motter, T	2B	2	1	11	.750	0
	3B	3	2	16	1.000	1
	RF	1	1	8	1.000	1
Mountcastle, R	1B	84	82	704	.998	-1
	LF	21	18	144	.964	-5
Moustakas, M	1B	11	7	57	1.000	2
	2B	1	1	11	-	0
	3B	44	41	349	.948	-6
Muncy, M	2B	39	31	254	.991	2
	3B	7	3	27	1.000	0
Munoz, Y	2B	3	1	20	1.000	0
	LF	1	1	9	-	0
Musgrove, J	LF	1	1	0	1.000	1
Myers, W	LF	13	10	87	1.000	0
Naquin, T	LF	22	13	131	.962	-1
	CF	92	78	645	.986	-6
	RF	21	15	137	.958	-2
Narvaez, O	2B	1	0	1	-	-1

Player	Pos	G	GS	Inn	Pct.	DRS
Naylor, J	1B	15	11	97	.978	1
	RF	51	50	423	.977	-2
Neuse, S	2B	13	7	72	.923	0
	3B	8	3	34	1.000	0
	LF	4	3	25	1.000	0
	RF	1	0	2	-	0
Nevin, T	1B	2	2	14	.857	-1
	LF	4	3	23	1.000	0
Newman, K	2B	15	11	92	1.000	-1
Nido, T	3B	1	0	2	-	0
Nimmo, B	LF	10	3	33	1.000	1
	CF	84	82	679	.995	4
Nogowski, J	1B	32	28	238	1.000	3
	RF	1	0	1	-	0
Nola, A	1B	1	1	9	1.000	0
	2B	4	0	6	1.000	0
Nootbaar, L	LF	9	4	41	1.000	1
	RF	26	19	181	.960	1
Nottingham, J	1B	4	4	33	1.000	0
Nunez, D	1B	1	0	0	-	0
Nunez, R	1B	8	8	67	1.000	-1
Odor, R	2B	74	60	540	.962	-3
	3B	33	29	247	.940	0
O'Grady, B	1B	1	0	2	1.000	0
	LF	4	2	23	1.000	1
	CF	2	0	4	1.000	1
	RF	10	7	62	1.000	1
OHearn, R'	1B	20	13	117	.973	0
	LF	1	1	5	-	0
	RF	25	22	167	1.000	-1
Ohtani, S	LF	1	0	1	-	0
	RF	6	0	7	-	0
Oliva, J	LF	5	2	21	1.000	1
	CF	2	0	2	1.000	0
	RF	12	7	65	1.000	-3
Olivares, E	LF	11	10	84	1.000	0
	CF	4	3	24	.667	0
	RF	22	14	135	.963	0
Ortega, R	LF	13	3	42	1.000	1
	CF	73	63	535	.992	-2
	RF	13	7	71	.941	1
Owen, H	RF	1	1	5	-	0
Owings, C	2B	3	3	26	1.000	1
	3B	1	0	3	-	0
	SS	1	1	9	1.000	1
	LF	3	2	19	1.000	0
	CF	1	1	5	1.000	-1
	RF	3	3	19	1.000	-1
Ozuna, M	LF	48	48	411	1.000	4
Pache, C	CF	22	20	168	.977	0
Padlo, K	1B	3	0	4	1.000	0
	3B	6	4	36	.929	0
Palacios, J	LF	4	2	26	1.000	0
	CF	2	2	17	1.000	1
	RF	8	7	49	1.000	0
Panik, J	1B	9	7	62	.983	0
	2B	27	21	186	1.000	1
	3B	32	27	226	.896	-9
Paredes, I	2B	10	9	80	.978	-1
	3B	8	8	71	1.000	0
	SS	5	4	39	.938	-1
Park, H	2B	16	12	112	.982	0
	3B	9	8	61	1.000	-1
	SS	8	8	58	1.000	-1
	LF	4	3	26	1.000	0
	CF	4	2	16	1.000	0
	RF	2	1	10	1.000	0
Parra, G	LF	19	11	113	.909	-1
	CF	8	4	46	1.000	-2
	RF	3	2	17	1.000	0
Payton, M	LF	1	0	3	1.000	0
	RF	4	0	9	.800	-1
Pederson, J	1B	1	0	1	-	0
	LF	66	63	518	.989	-4
	CF	26	24	194	1.000	-2
	RF	39	21	206	1.000	0
Peraza, J	2B	36	32	257	1.000	0
	3B	9	5	47	.917	0
	SS	1	0	1	-	0
	LF	1	0	1	-	0
Perdomo, G	SS	10	9	81	.976	1
Perez, H	1B	2	1	8	1.000	0

Player	Pos	G	GS	Inn	Pct.	DRS
	2B	3	2	15	1.000	0
	LF	1	1	5	1.000	0
	RF	1	1	7	1.000	0
Perez, M	1B	1	0	1	-	0
Perez, R	1B	1	0	2	1.000	0
Peters, D	LF	22	18	162	1.000	2
	CF	29	22	210	1.000	1
	RF	16	15	130	1.000	0
Peterson, J	1B	26	7	102	.965	0
	2B	35	28	254	.991	-3
	3B	11	9	76	.938	0
	SS	1	0	0	-	0
	LF	11	7	66	1.000	2
	RF	17	15	119	1.000	-1
Pham, T	CF	11	10	91	1.000	-1
	RF	1	1	7	1.000	0
Phillips, B	LF	19	0	31	1.000	2
	CF	52	39	372	.984	3
	RF	46	35	310	.978	6
Pillar, K	LF	52	16	183	1.000	2
	CF	57	49	402	1.000	-1
	RF	22	17	135	1.000	-2
Pinder, C	2B	7	5	44	1.000	0
	3B	6	4	34	.938	0
	SS	8	4	40	1.000	-2
	LF	17	15	125	1.000	0
	RF	39	29	244	.982	-1
Piscotty, S	RF	67	49	417	1.000	-6
Plawecki, K	1B	2	0	2	1.000	0
Polanco, J	SS	39	26	237	.948	-1
Pollock, A	CF	8	5	48	1.000	0
Profar, J	1B	20	12	127	.991	2
	2B	10	6	60	.935	-4
	LF	36	28	257	.982	1
	CF	20	19	148	1.000	-3
	RF	29	24	195	.943	-2
Pujols, A	1B	76	57	506	.993	-4
	3B	1	0	1	-	0
Quinn, R	LF	2	1	10	1.000	0
	CF	21	10	106	1.000	2
	RF	4	3	23	1.000	1
Raley, L	LF	13	7	78	1.000	0
	RF	16	8	81	1.000	0
Ramirez, H	1B	1	0	5	1.000	0
	LF	49	43	361	1.000	-3
	CF	20	19	150	.971	-5
	RF	34	28	241	.986	0
Ramos, H	LF	5	5	40	.833	-2
	RF	8	6	62	1.000	-1
Ray, C	RF	1	0	5	1.000	0
Realmuto, J	1B	16	7	65	.984	0
Reddick, J	LF	1	0	5	1.000	0
	CF	4	2	20	1.000	1
	RF	36	32	276	.984	-4
Refsnyder, R	LF	20	10	101	1.000	0
	CF	22	20	181	.980	-2
	RF	9	7	60	1.000	0
Reks, Z	LF	3	2	12	1.000	1
	RF	2	0	6	1.000	0
Rendon, A	3B	57	57	497	.993	-6
Renfroe, H	CF	8	6	47	1.000	-1
Rengifo, L	2B	4	3	26	.941	0
	3B	12	9	83	.828	-1
	SS	26	25	227	.981	1
	LF	1	0	1	-	0
	RF	14	9	87	.960	-2
Reyes, F	RF	11	11	76	1.000	-1
Reyes, P	2B	2	2	16	1.000	0
	3B	28	12	130	.966	0
	SS	2	2	16	1.000	1
	LF	1	2	0	1.000	0
Reyes, V	LF	1	1	9	-	-1
	CF	20	19	163	1.000	-4
	RF	43	36	332	.989	-1
Reynolds, B	LF	17	17	139	1.000	0
Riddle, J	SS	3	2	16	1.000	0
Riley, A	1B	10	3	47	1.000	0
	RF	1	0	2	-	-1
Rios, E	1B	10	5	55	1.000	0
	3B	6	5	46	.917	-1
	RF	2	1	8	-	0
Rivas III, A	1B	5	3	28	1.000	0

Player	Pos	G	GS	Inn	Pct.	DRS
	LF	5	3	31	.900	0
	RF	5	5	37	1.000	-1
Rivera, E	1B	1	1	9	1.000	0
	3B	28	26	222	.934	1
Rizzo, A	2B	1	0	0	-	0
Robert, L	CF	67	67	575	.976	4
Robertson, D	1B	3	0	6	1.000	1
	2B	9	3	38	.957	-2
	3B	24	4	75	.952	-1
	SS	8	6	58	1.000	0
Robson, J	LF	3	1	14	1.000	0
	CF	1	0	4	-	0
Rodgers, B	2B	81	78	661	.988	-5
	SS	26	18	164	.984	1
Rogers, J	3B	1	0	1	-	0
Rojas, J	1B	2	0	4	.833	0
	2B	14	10	96	.975	-3
	3B	12	11	88	.974	-1
	LF	9	1	36	1.000	0
	RF	25	20	169	1.000	-2
Rojas, J	2B	55	37	356	.976	-4
	3B	14	7	66	.905	-2
	SS	42	33	283	.939	-13
	LF	18	12	92	1.000	0
	RF	37	27	248	.964	2
Romine, A	2B	2	1	12	1.000	0
	SS	16	14	118	.967	1
Rondon, J	1B	1	0	2	-	0
	2B	2	1	11	1.000	0
	3B	7	1	27	.933	-1
	LF	2	0	9	1.000	1
	RF	7	6	47	1.000	-2
Rooker, B	LF	38	35	264	1.000	-6
	RF	8	7	54	.900	-3
Rosario, A	CF	18	14	123	1.000	-2
Rosario, E	RF	1	0	1	-	0
Ruf, D	1B	44	31	301	.997	2
	LF	33	26	197	1.000	-1
	RF	5	3	30	1.000	3
Ruiz, R	1B	1	1	8	1.000	0
	2B	20	17	154	.976	-2
	3B	17	8	87	1.000	2
	LF	2	0	3	-	0
Sanchez, A	2B	9	7	69	1.000	1
	3B	2	1	10	1.000	1
	RF	1	0	1	-	0
Sanchez, J	LF	21	20	183	.977	-1
	RF	41	41	344	.952	5
Sandoval, P	1B	2	0	4	1.000	0
	3B	1	0	1	-	0
Sano, M	3B	9	3	37	.750	-3
Santana, D	1B	14	11	98	1.000	-1
	LF	7	4	43	1.000	1
	CF	13	12	104	1.000	0
Santander, A	LF	4	4	29	1.000	2
	RF	81	78	669	.994	-3
Schebler, S	LF	3	2	17	1.000	0
	CF	4	3	31	1.000	0
	RF	4	3	28	1.000	0
Schoop, J	2B	38	38	313	.984	0
	3B	1	0	1	1.000	0
Schrock, M	1B	5	2	23	1.000	-1
	2B	8	5	47	1.000	-1
	3B	9	2	24	1.000	-1
	LF	23	18	149	.939	-1
	RF	1	1	7	1.000	0
Schwarber, K	1B	10	9	75	.985	-3
	LF	87	86	724	.981	-5
Schwindel, F	1B	52	50	429	.998	-4
Segura, J	SS	1	0	1	-	0
Semien, M	SS	21	14	134	.984	1
Senzel, N	2B	8	6	46	.875	0
	3B	3	2	19	1.000	1
	CF	29	21	191	.978	-2
Shaw, T	1B	31	8	108	.976	-2
	3B	48	45	360	.952	-2
Sheets, G	1B	10	10	81	.983	-2
	LF	4	3	23	-	0
	RF	13	11	82	.941	-2
Short, Z	2B	2	1	11	.917	1
	3B	3	1	15	1.000	0
	SS	52	45	399	.982	-1

Player	Pos	G	GS	Inn	Pct.	DRS
Sierra, M	LF	16	6	71	.938	0
	CF	54	36	336	.989	7
	RF	8	2	25	1.000	0
Siri, J	LF	4	2	21	1.000	0
	CF	5	5	39	.875	-1
	RF	9	4	42	1.000	0
Slater, A	LF	37	9	124	1.000	0
	CF	77	39	386	1.000	0
	RF	24	7	93	1.000	2
Smith, D	1B	15	7	71	.981	2
Smith, K	1B	1	1	5	1.000	0
	3B	14	8	78	.950	0
	LF	1	1	6	-	0
Smith, P	1B	54	42	369	.994	0
	LF	22	9	96	.952	0
	CF	39	29	252	.984	-10
	RF	53	42	345	1.000	-1
Smith, W	1B	1	0	2	1.000	0
	3B	1	0	2	.000	-1
Sogard, E	1B	1	0	0	-	0
	2B	43	32	285	.992	-1
	3B	10	3	36	.917	0
	SS	4	3	22	1.000	1
Solano, D	2B	91	78	687	.978	-7
	SS	2	0	6	1.000	0
Sosa, E	2B	25	15	139	.987	2
	3B	9	1	31	1.000	1
	SS	71	59	518	.961	8
	CF	1	0	0	-	0
Souza Jr., S	LF	5	1	13	-	0
	RF	8	7	54	1.000	1
Springer, G	CF	40	40	328	.978	-1
	RF	4	0	6	1.000	0
Stallings, J	1B	1	0	1	1.000	0
Stanton, G	LF	10	10	71	1.000	0
	RF	16	16	129	.966	0
Stephenson, T	1B	23	17	147	.993	-1
	LF	1	0	1	-	-1
Stevenson, A	LF	24	12	123	1.000	0
	CF	31	24	208	.960	1
	RF	11	3	42	1.000	0
Stewart, D	LF	39	36	281	.963	-3
	RF	33	29	249	.968	-6
Stokes Jr., T	RF	4	4	36	1.000	1
Stubbs, G	LF	2	0	3	1.000	0
Suarez, E	SS	34	32	285	.936	-6
Tapia, R	CF	3	2	15	1.000	1
	RF	4	1	17	1.000	0
Tatis Jr., F	CF	7	7	56	.944	0
	RF	20	16	151	1.000	0
Tauchman, M	LF	45	22	229	.979	5
	CF	12	11	82	1.000	0
	RF	14	11	77	1.000	1
Taveras, L	CF	48	46	402	.977	6
Taylor, C	2B	46	33	294	.964	2
	3B	11	9	81	.842	-3
	SS	23	19	154	.973	0
	LF	30	16	170	.968	-1
	CF	61	48	423	.991	-4
	RF	8	7	70	1.000	1
Taylor, T	LF	37	24	230	1.000	2
	CF	16	13	112	1.000	3
	RF	29	20	183	1.000	2
Tejeda, A	2B	1	0	1	-	0
	3B	5	5	43	1.000	1
Tellez, R	1B	65	57	485	.987	-4
Terry, C	1B	1	1	8	1.000	0
Thaiss, M	2B	2	2	16	1.000	0
Thomas, D	LF	2	0	3	1.000	0
	CF	1	1	8	1.000	1
	RF	1	1	11	1.000	0
Thomas, L	2B	2	0	3	1.000	0
	LF	12	5	54	1.000	0
	CF	42	41	357	.967	-2
	RF	10	6	63	1.000	1
Thompson, T	LF	2	0	1	-	0
	CF	3	2	17	1.000	0
	RF	8	6	54	1.000	1
Tom, K	LF	32	31	253	1.000	1
	RF	4	3	26	1.000	0
Toro, A	1B	2	2	17	1.000	0
	2B	58	58	525	.975	-1

Player	Pos	G	GS	Inn	Pct.	DRS
	3B	32	29	263	.963	2
Torrens, L	1B	5	5	39	.971	1
	3B	2	0	2	1.000	0
Torres, G	2B	19	19	169	.986	-2
Torreyes, R	2B	11	4	48	.957	-1
	3B	50	40	354	1.000	2
	SS	44	38	333	.978	-1
	CF	1	0	2	1.000	0
Tovar, W	2B	4	1	24	1.000	0
Trammell, T	LF	14	12	104	1.000	-2
	CF	37	36	313	1.000	0
Trejo, A	2B	10	6	54	.926	0
	SS	9	2	28	1.000	1
Trout, M	CF	36	36	295	1.000	-4
Tsutsugo, Y	1B	31	20	189	1.000	-1
	LF	10	8	74	1.000	1
	RF	20	20	150	.964	-5
Tucker, C	1B	1	0	1	1.000	0
	2B	9	8	66	1.000	1
	SS	17	14	117	.942	-4
	CF	2	1	11	1.000	0
	RF	12	5	59	1.000	-1
Tucker, K	CF	4	4	28	.889	-1
Turner, T	2B	49	48	437	.973	3
Upton, J	LF	87	86	687	.984	-11
	CF	1	0	1	-	0
Urias, L	2B	25	16	136	.984	-3
	3B	68	58	508	.940	6
	SS	68	59	536	.935	-3
Urias, R	2B	32	27	213	.954	-1
	3B	10	10	75	1.000	2
	SS	48	36	344	.953	-1
Urshela, G	SS	28	24	200	.970	-1
Valaika, P	1B	6	3	34	1.000	0
	2B	72	58	505	1.000	-4
	3B	2	1	9	1.000	0
	SS	17	11	101	.980	-5
	LF	3	0	9	1.000	0
Valera, B	2B	10	4	48	1.000	-3
	3B	21	17	140	1.000	1
VanMeter, J	1B	1	1	6	1.000	0
	2B	52	46	372	.976	-2
	3B	25	19	183	.885	-2
	LF	1	0	1	1.000	0
	RF	1	0	3	1.000	0
Vargas, I	2B	9	7	56	1.000	1
	3B	10	7	60	.941	-1
	SS	5	3	32	.909	0
	LF	2	1	9	1.000	0
Varsho, D	LF	12	6	61	1.000	4
	CF	30	21	199	.985	-2
	RF	12	9	78	1.000	2
Vaughn, A	1B	15	10	100	.987	-2
	2B	1	1	8	1.000	0
	3B	2	1	10	1.000	-1
	LF	95	86	720	.985	-2
	RF	18	14	118	.955	-3
Vazquez, C	1B	1	0	2	1.000	0
	2B	2	0	5	1.000	-1
	3B	2	0	4	-	0
Velazquez, A	SS	28	20	180	.963	0
Verdugo, A	LF	90	79	678	.992	7
	CF	42	38	337	.975	-7
	RF	24	19	173	.967	1
Vierling, M	1B	9	6	55	1.000	-1
	LF	7	2	21	1.000	-1
	CF	8	6	50	1.000	1
	RF	6	1	16	1.000	0
Vilade, R	LF	2	2	16	1.000	0
Villar, J	2B	9	8	63	.964	-2
	3B	97	86	748	.933	-4
	SS	26	23	199	1.000	4
Vogelbach, D	1B	59	52	408	.997	-4
Vogt, S	1B	2	0	4	1.000	0
Voit, L	1B	42	42	344	.983	-2
Vosler, J	1B	3	1	13	1.000	-1
	2B	3	2	15	1.000	0
	3B	19	14	121	.906	-4
	LF	2	1	5	1.000	0
	RF	1	0	1	-	0
Wade, T	2B	19	6	63	.950	-5
	3B	27	9	108	.939	0

All Other Fielders

Player	Pos	G	GS	Inn	Pct.	DRS
	SS	31	14	139	1.000	-4
	LF	8	4	40	1.000	1
	CF	10	1	24	1.000	1
	RF	7	1	29	1.000	2
Wade Jr., L	1B	31	24	191	.977	-2
	LF	42	17	187	.978	2
	CF	2	2	13	1.000	-1
	RF	52	40	343	1.000	0
Walls, T	2B	3	2	23	1.000	-1
	3B	1	1	7	-	0
	SS	49	41	378	.968	10
Walsh, J	RF	18	17	148	.957	-1
Walton, D	2B	14	11	101	.981	-1
	3B	2	1	10	.667	0
	SS	2	1	10	1.000	1
	LF	5	4	35	.857	0
Ward, T	LF	18	8	85	.947	-1
	CF	12	9	56	1.000	0
	RF	51	42	368	.989	-3
Welker, C	1B	2	2	18	1.000	0
	3B	5	5	44	1.000	0
Wendle, J	2B	16	13	117	1.000	2
	SS	25	23	199	1.000	6
White, E	2B	3	3	25	1.000	-1
	LF	30	28	248	.983	4
	CF	22	18	160	1.000	-2
	RF	11	6	63	.944	0
White, E	1B	30	28	238	.992	2
Wilkerson, S	2B	26	18	164	.968	1
	LF	3	1	12	1.000	-1
	RF	1	0	1	1.000	0
Williams, J	LF	19	16	140	1.000	4
	RF	24	17	155	.939	-3
Williams, L	1B	6	0	9	1.000	0
	2B	8	5	44	1.000	1
	3B	8	3	33	.900	0
	SS	5	2	18	1.000	-1
	LF	7	2	25	1.000	0
	CF	15	11	73	.923	0
	RF	3	0	7	1.000	-1
Williams, M	LF	1	0	2	-	0
	CF	15	10	89	1.000	1
Williams, N	LF	3	3	28	1.000	-1
Wilson, J	2B	4	2	16	1.000	0
	3B	6	4	33	1.000	0
	LF	1	1	6	1.000	0
Winker, J	CF	1	1	6	-	0
	RF	5	1	16	1.000	-1
Wisdom, P	1B	13	8	74	.988	0
	3B	77	63	573	.962	4
	LF	15	12	98	1.000	0
	RF	3	2	15	1.000	0
Wolters, T	2B	2	0	1	-	0
	LF	1	0	0	-	0
Wong, K	2B	10	5	62	1.000	-1
	3B	6	3	25	1.000	0
	LF	4	2	17	1.000	-1
	RF	4	3	21	1.000	3
Wynns, A	1B	1	0	1	1.000	0
Yastrzemski, M	CF	34	29	227	1.000	2
Yelich, C	RF	1	0	3	-	0
Young, A	2B	21	16	138	.969	-10
	3B	2	0	3	.000	-1
	LF	1	1	5	.500	0
Zimmer, B	LF	3	2	18	1.000	1
	CF	54	45	395	1.000	1
	RF	43	37	347	.988	1
Zimmerman, R	1B	54	45	401	1.000	5

All Other Catchers

Player	Tm	G	GS	Inn	PO	A	E	DP	PB	Pct.	SB Att	CS	Pit CS	CS Pct	Cat ERA	Stk Sav	GFP/ DME	SB	SZ	Other	Total
																		Runs Saved			
Adams, Riley	TOT	34	27	237	226	19	1	0	0	.996	27	3	0	.11	5.57	-36	0	-1	-4	-1	-6
Alfaro, Jorge	Mia	61	57	476	467	19	2	1	13	.996	20	8	1	.40	4.05	35	-6	2	4	-2	-2
Allen, Austin	Oak	2	2	16	18	3	1	0	0	.955	4	2	0	.50	6.19	0	0	1	0	0	1
Astudillo, Willians	Min	10	4	41	33	2	0	1	1	1.000	2	1	0	.50	5.27	-4	0	0	0	0	0
Avila, Alex	Was	27	27	232	235	9	1	3	0	.996	14	4	2	.29	3.69	-11	2	1	-1	2	4
Barnes, Austin	LAD	52	51	442	515	15	6	3	3	.989	43	7	3	.16	2.81	25	1	0	3	1	5
Barrera, Tres	Was	29	27	233	222	12	2	2	2	.992	20	1	0	.05	5.41	6	1	-2	1	-1	-1
Bart, Joey	SF	1	1	9	8	0	0	0	0	1.000	0	0	0	-	4.00	0	0	0	0	0	0
Bemboom, Anthony	LAA	7	7	61	71	1	2	0	0	.973	4	0	1	.00	4.45	2	0	-1	0	0	-1
Brantly, Rob	NYY	5	4	37	37	3	0	0	0	1.000	5	2	0	.40	3.19	0	-1	1	0	0	0
Butera, Drew	LAA	12	12	98	99	2	0	0	3	1.000	2	1	0	.50	5.60	-14	0	0	-2	0	-2
Campusano, Luis	SD	9	9	75	85	1	0	0	1	1.000	4	0	0	.00	3.24	3	1	-1	0	-1	-1
Casali, Curt	SF	64	55	509	502	18	4	2	4	.992	19	2	3	.11	2.72	2	-1	-2	0	5	2
Castillo, Erick	ChC	4	2	21	15	3	0	2	0	1.000	5	1	0	.20	2.57	-2	0	1	0	0	1
Castro, Jason	Hou	52	37	355	363	13	2	1	3	.995	31	4	0	.13	3.82	-4	-1	-2	-1	0	-4
Chirinos, Robinson	ChC	27	21	191	188	7	1	2	4	.995	24	4	0	.17	6.51	4	-1	-1	1	-1	-2
Ciuffo, Nick	Bal	2	2	17	14	0	0	0	0	1.000	1	0	1	.00	5.82	-2	0	0	0	0	0
Collins, Zack	CWS	73	55	506	611	29	4	1	3	.994	52	7	2	.13	4.02	-67	-3	-1	-8	-6	-18
Contreras, William	Atl	49	47	416	411	21	2	0	7	.995	19	2	8	.11	4.16	-29	-1	-1	-3	-2	-7
d'Arnaud, Travis	Atl	57	53	471	485	29	1	0	3	.998	28	2	3	.07	3.92	21	4	-2	3	-1	4
Davis, Taylor	Pit	2	2	16	11	0	0	0	0	1.000	1	0	0	.00	6.19	3	0	0	0	0	0
Fortes, Nick	Mia	7	4	44	50	5	1	1	4	.982	8	2	0	.25	5.32	-6	-2	0	-1	0	-3
Gallagher, Cam	KC	46	33	309	281	13	5	0	1	.983	17	4	0	.24	3.99	36	3	-1	4	0	6
Garcia, Aramis	Oak	30	26	232	217	9	2	0	4	.991	10	2	2	.20	3.64	4	-4	0	0	1	-3
Garneau, Dustin	Det	20	19	165	142	9	2	1	3	.987	14	5	0	.36	3.82	0	-1	1	0	0	0
Garver, Mitch	Min	59	53	452	426	12	1	2	4	.998	27	3	2	.11	4.74	-1	1	-1	0	0	0
Godoy, Jose	Sea	14	11	95	97	4	2	0	0	.981	6	0	0	.00	5.49	0	1	0	0	0	1
Greiner, Grayson	Det	31	25	214	201	7	2	0	3	.990	19	4	1	.21	5.05	-14	-1	0	-2	-2	-5
Gushue, Taylor	ChC	1	0	1	1	0	0	0	0	1.000	0	0	0	-	0.00	0	0	0	0	0	0
Haase, Eric	Det	66	61	543	487	23	5	3	7	.990	34	10	1	.29	4.12	-29	-1	1	-3	0	-3
Henry, Payton	Mia	5	5	38	43	1	0	0	1	1.000	1	0	0	.00	4.70	2	0	0	0	0	0
Hicks, John	Tex	8	6	52	45	4	0	0	0	1.000	2	0	1	.00	3.96	-1	0	0	0	0	0
Higashioka, Kyle	NYY	66	58	519	609	18	3	1	6	.995	38	5	0	.13	3.38	26	1	-2	3	3	5
Higgins, P.J.	ChC	6	5	46	54	3	0	1	1	1.000	2	1	0	.50	1.76	1	0	0	0	0	0
Holaday, Bryan	Ari	10	10	85	76	2	1	0	0	.987	6	1	1	.17	6.67	-10	0	0	-1	0	-1
Jackson, Alex	TOT	43	37	325	307	17	3	1	3	.991	14	4	1	.29	4.82	-5	0	1	0	-1	0
Jansen, Danny	Tor	69	54	481	522	17	2	3	0	.996	23	4	1	.17	4.21	-6	2	1	-1	-2	0
Kirk, Alejandro	Tor	44	40	338	353	17	2	1	2	.995	31	5	1	.16	3.09	-16	-1	-1	-2	1	-3
Knapp, Andrew	Phi	47	37	331	340	16	1	1	4	.997	22	2	0	.09	3.84	-15	-3	-3	-2	0	-8
Knizner, Andrew	StL	57	43	407	368	21	3	4	1	.992	21	4	1	.19	3.81	-33	1	0	-4	0	-3
Kruger, Jack	LAA	1	0	1	1	0	0	0	0	1.000	0	0	0	-	0.00	0	0	0	0	0	0
Lavarnway, Ryan	Cle	8	8	71	76	0	3	0	0	.962	1	0	0	.00	4.84	-3	0	0	0	0	0
Leon, Sandy	Mia	60	48	437	444	20	3	3	4	.994	27	5	3	.19	3.23	4	1	0	1	1	3
Lobaton, Jose	ChC	5	3	29	28	1	0	0	1	1.000	7	0	0	.00	9.00	-4	0	-1	0	0	-1
Lucroy, Jonathan	TOT	6	6	50	52	1	0	0	1	1.000	4	0	0	.00	3.96	-2	-1	0	0	0	-1
Maile, Luke	Mil	12	7	72	82	5	0	0	0	1.000	4	1	1	.25	2.86	-1	0	0	0	0	0
Marchan, Rafael	Phi	17	13	115	107	6	1	0	1	.991	5	2	1	.40	5.32	-9	0	1	-1	0	0
Mathis, Jeff	Atl	3	3	26	23	1	0	0	1	1.000	2	0	0	.00	4.15	2	0	0	0	0	0
Mazeika, Patrick	NYM	24	18	168	166	11	2	1	2	.989	9	2	1	.22	3.96	1	0	0	0	1	1
McGuire, Reese	Tor	73	61	522	547	16	0	2	4	1.000	29	9	2	.31	4.10	24	0	1	3	-2	2
Mejia, Francisco	TB	76	64	583	554	33	4	1	4	.993	26	5	4	.19	3.86	17	-1	1	2	0	2
Mercedes, Yermin	CWS	2	0	2	2	0	0	0	0	1.000	0	0	0	-	0.00	0	0	0	0	0	0
Nido, Tomas	NYM	52	45	366	415	23	5	5	2	.989	20	11	1	.55	3.69	42	-1	5	5	1	10
Nola, Austin	SD	48	46	399	428	14	1	3	4	.998	29	3	1	.10	3.92	1	1	-2	0	0	-1
Nottingham, Jacob	TOT	3	3	25	22	2	0	0	2	1.000	0	0	0	-	8.64	-1	-1	0	0	0	-1
Odom, Joseph	TB	1	0	2	2	0	0	0	0	1.000	0	0	0	-	0.00	0	0	0	0	0	0
Payne, Tyler	ChC	1	0	3	2	0	0	0	0	1.000	0	0	0	-	0.00	0	0	0	0	0	0
Perez, Michael	Pit	58	57	488	457	20	3	4	2	.994	26	6	1	.23	5.40	-12	2	0	-1	-2	-1
Perez, Roberto	Cle	43	43	364	375	11	4	1	3	.990	19	3	0	.16	4.40	-3	1	-2	0	0	-1
Pina, Manny	Mil	65	52	452	511	27	3	1	3	.994	36	10	1	.28	3.68	11	3	2	1	1	7
Plawecki, Kevin	Bos	53	40	337	382	12	2	1	3	.995	37	0	3	.00	4.46	18	-2	-4	2	1	-3
Pozo, Yohel	Tex	2	2	18	15	0	0	0	0	1.000	1	0	0	.00	7.50	0	0	0	0	0	0
Raleigh, Cal	Sea	43	36	333	303	8	1	0	5	.997	23	4	1	.17	4.57	13	-1	0	2	-2	-1
Ramos, Wilson	TOT	34	31	264	237	11	0	2	4	1.000	24	3	1	.13	5.07	-30	-4	0	-4	-1	-9
Reetz, Jakson	Was	1	0	2	4	0	0	0	0	1.000	0	0	0	-	0.00	0	0	0	0	0	0
Rivas, Webster	SD	24	20	169	152	9	0	1	0	1.000	15	4	0	.27	5.28	-3	0	1	0	-1	0
Rivera, Rene	TOT	24	21	186	200	15	3	1	4	.986	20	8	1	.40	6.34	-14	-2	2	-2	-2	-4
Rivero, Sebastian	KC	17	9	106	95	8	0	0	2	1.000	6	1	1	.17	6.37	-2	0	0	0	0	0
Rogers, Jake	Det	37	35	311	289	17	1	3	3	.997	13	7	1	.54	3.97	-8	-2	2	-1	2	1
Romine, Austin	ChC	21	14	132	121	3	1	0	1	.992	9	1	0	.11	6.14	-6	1	-1	-1	0	-1
Rortvedt, Ben	Min	39	28	256	244	14	3	2	2	.989	14	5	2	.36	5.13	21	2	1	3	-1	5
Ruiz, Keibert	TOT	23	20	182	181	13	1	1	0	.995	11	2	0	.18	4.85	5	1	0	0	0	1
Sanchez, Ali	StL	2	1	9	7	0	0	0	0	1.000	0	0	0	-	8.00	0	0	0	0	0	0
Sisco, Chance	TOT	25	21	179	173	12	0	0	3	1.000	13	6	1	.46	5.33	-21	0	2	-2	0	0
Smith, Kevan	TOT	31	28	238	242	11	1	0	4	.996	10	2	0	.20	2.92	3	-2	0	0	1	-1
Stephenson, Tyler	Cin	78	65	588	661	22	0	4	7	1.000	40	6	2	.15	3.99	12	-1	0	1	3	3
Stubbs, Garrett	Hou	14	7	79	76	2	0	0	0	1.000	2	2	1	1.00	3.08	-1	-1	1	0	0	0
Suzuki, Kurt	LAA	69	63	557	597	33	10	5	7	.984	43	8	0	.19	4.56	-51	-3	-2	-6	-1	-12
Torrens, Luis	Sea	35	32	285	278	12	1	0	1	.997	25	3	0	.12	3.86	-25	-2	0	-3	1	-4

Player	Tm	G	GS	Inn	PO	A	E	DP	PB	Pct.	SB Att	CS	Pit CS	CS Pct	Cat ERA	Stk Sav	Runs Saved GFP/ DME	SB	SZ	Other	Total
Tromp, Chadwick	SF	8	4	45	51	1	0	0	0	1.000	6	1	0	.17	2.42	2	0	-1	0	0	-1
Varsho, Daulton	Ari	41	37	319	284	13	3	2	4	.990	19	4	3	.21	5.39	-23	-1	-1	-3	-1	-6
Vogt, Stephen	TOT	63	57	496	445	28	2	2	5	.996	44	7	7	.16	4.79	0	1	-1	0	0	0
Wallach, Chad	Mia	20	18	159	161	3	2	1	4	.988	14	1	0	.07	3.57	4	-1	-1	0	-2	-4
Ward, Taylor	LAA	1	0	2	2	0	0	0	0	1.000	1	0	0	.00	27.00	0	0	0	0	0	0
Wolters, Tony	ChC	8	5	54	65	3	0	1	0	1.000	8	1	1	.13	4.64	3	0	-1	0	0	-1
Wong, Connor	Bos	5	3	31	31	1	0	0	0	1.000	1	1	0	1.00	4.35	0	0	1	0	0	1
Wynns, Austin	Bal	44	39	342	288	18	1	1	0	.997	29	11	0	.38	7.15	-35	0	1	-4	-3	-6
Zavala, Seby	CWS	33	31	268	296	12	1	0	8	.997	26	2	1	.08	3.46	9	-2	-2	1	1	-2

Runs Saved Multi-Year Summary

Lindsay Zeck

The three biggest offensive names on the Cubs were traded this season. Javier Báez (Gold Glove and four-time Fielding Bible Award winner), Anthony Rizzo (four-time Gold Glove winner and Fielding Bible Award winner), and Kris Bryant all had a rough defensive season compared to their norm.

Bryant and Rizzo had their worst defensive season yet costing their teams five and six runs, respectively. Rizzo had never before finished a season in the negative. Báez saved six runs, tying his 2020 shortened season total, a far cry from his MLB-leading 32 runs saved in 2019.

Nolan Arenado—a name that has become synonymous with great defense with his eight Gold Gloves and four Fielding Bible Awards—saw a decline in Defensive Runs Saved in his first season with St. Louis. His six runs saved was his lowest total ever, including the shortened 2020 season during which he saved more than double his 2021 total (13).

Ryan McMahon and Josh Fuentes served as ample defensive replacements with their 23 combined runs saved at third base, with 13 and 10, respectively. The 25 combined runs saved for Rockies' third basemen (including one each for Rio Ruiz and Taylor Motter) was the highest position total in the National League. McMahon also saved nine runs at second base which gave him a league-leading 22 Runs Saved.

Another Gold-Glover, Joey Gallo, was traded this season from the Rangers to the Yankees. He, unlike the traded players mentioned above, saved a personal best 15 total runs. His efforts contributed to the Rangers right fielders saving the most runs of any position for any team in baseball.

Prior to his trade to the Yankees, Joey Gallo saved 13 runs in right field for the Rangers. Adolis García took his place after the trade deadline and also saved 13. Garcia and Gallo's 26 Runs Saved, along with 3 from David Dahl and 1 from DJ Peters, totaled 30 runs saved at the position. Gallo finished the season with the second-most Runs Saved of all right fielders, trailing only García.

Please note that some of these numbers have been modified since our last Handbook for 2017 and beyond due to a disconnect between the timing of a play and what is shown on the broadcast. For more on this, please use your phone to scan the QR code below.

Milestone Approaching

Shortstop Andrelton Simmons will enter 2022 with 197 career Defensive Runs Saved, only three runs behind Adrián Beltré for the most by a player since SIS began tracking the stat in 2003. This is particularly impressive considering that Simmons has played more than 8,000 fewer innings than Beltre in that time.

Defensive Runs Saved By Season

Player	YOB	Pos 1	Pos 2	<17	17	18	19	20	21
Abreu, Jose	1987	1B		-14	1	-1	-3	5	-1
Adames, Willy	1995	SS				-8	8	2	1
Aguilar, Jesus	1990	1B		-2	-1	8	0	0	3
Ahmed, Nick	1990	SS		24	6	28	16	4	4
Albies, Ozzie	1997	2B			1	13	9	-1	1
Alfaro, Jorge	1993	C		-1	-6	4	-2	-7	-3
Almora Jr., Albert	1994	CF		3	2	12	-3	0	0
Alonso, Pete	1994	1B					1	-5	5
Altuve, Jose	1990	2B		-35	-1	2	-1	-3	-3
Anderson, Tim	1993	SS		3	-23	12	-6	2	3
Andrus, Elvis	1988	SS		-5	12	3	-9	-3	-10
Arcia, Orlando	1994	SS		4	4	7	-2	-4	1
Arenado, Nolan	1991	3B		65	17	12	23	13	6
Bader, Harrison	1994	CF			2	16	15	1	15
Baez, Javier	1992	SS	2B	12	3	10	32	6	6
Barnhart, Tucker	1991	C		-2	15	-8	4	8	0
Bell, Josh	1992	1B		-11	-5	-8	-6	-1	1
Belt, Brandon	1988	1B		26	10	10	0	0	-4
Benintendi, Andrew	1994	LF		1	9	6	-2	2	7
Betts, Mookie	1992	RF	CF	46	30	18	20	10	5
Bichette, Bo	1998	SS					5	0	2
Blackmon, Charlie	1986	CF	RF	-16	-8	-26	-8	0	-2
Bogaerts, Xander	1992	SS		-24	-11	-8	-9	-4	-5
Bohm, Alec	1996	3B						-6	-15
Bradley Jr., Jackie	1990	CF		34	14	4	0	5	12
Brantley, Michael	1987	LF		0	6	-2	10	4	1
Bregman, Alex	1994	3B		6	-3	5	10	1	2
Bruce, Jay	1987	RF		30	4	-7	3	2	0
Bryant, Kris	1992	3B	CF	5	-2	-1	-2	2	-5
Buxton, Byron	1993	CF		7	22	2	8	11	10
Cabrera, Miguel	1983	1B		-79	-11	-5	-1		-4
Cain, Lorenzo	1986	CF		81	6	20	19	1	6
Calhoun, Kole	1987	RF		1	2	0	-6	0	0
Candelario, Jeimer	1993	3B		1	-8	-11	-1	5	-3
Canha, Mark	1989	LF	CF	-4	-5	-4	-6	1	-11
Caratini, Victor	1993	C			1	2	-1	1	-7
Castellanos, Nick	1992	RF	3B	-26	-28	-19	-9	-4	-7
Castro, Jason	1987	C		4	11	1	-7	-1	-4
Castro, Starlin	1990	2B	3B	-38	-6	-10	3	1	2
Castro, Willi	1997	2B					-3	-10	-12
Chapman, Matt	1993	3B			15	23	28	3	9
Chirinos, Robinson	1984	C		-2	1	-10	4	-5	-2
Chisholm Jr., Jazz	1998	2B	SS					0	1
Conforto, Michael	1993	RF	LF	11	-3	-5	-1	0	-4
Contreras, Willson	1992	C		-1	0	3	-2	1	8
Correa, Carlos	1994	SS		10	10	11	9	7	20
Crawford, Brandon	1987	SS		72	10	-4	-10	1	6
Crawford, J.P.	1995	SS			5	-2	0	6	8
Cron, C.J.	1990	1B		-4	6	1	1	0	3
Cronenworth, Jake	1994	2B	SS					1	5
Dalbec, Bobby	1995	1B						-1	-8
d'Arnaud, Travis	1989	C		-10	-2	-1	-6	-7	4
DeJong, Paul	1993	SS			-1	6	24	0	6
DeShields, Delino	1992	CF		-10	3	8	5	0	-1
Devers, Rafael	1996	3B			-5	-11	-5	-4	-13
Diaz, Elias	1990	C		0	-3	-1	-21	0	9
Dickerson, Corey	1989	LF		-9	1	15	-5	-2	0
Donaldson, Josh	1985	3B		19	-1	-3	10	-1	1
Duvall, Adam	1988	LF	CF	15	11	16	2	0	19
Dyson, Jarrod	1984	CF		52	15	9	15	-3	8
Eaton, Adam	1988	RF		20	-6	-4	-2	-7	-2
Edman, Tommy	1995	2B	RF				10	7	7
Engel, Adam	1991	CF				0	7	4	0
Escobar, Alcides	1986	SS		16	-11	-28			-2
Escobar, Eduardo	1989	3B	2B	-19	-8	-4	-1	0	-5
Farmer, Kyle	1990	SS			0	2	0	3	2
Fletcher, David	1994	2B			7	11	5	13
France, Ty	1994	1B				-4	1	2
Franco, Maikel	1992	3B		-18	0	-10	1	0	-8
Frazier, Adam	1991	2B		-3	-2	8	5	7	7
Frazier, Todd	1986	3B		10	3	9	1	2	-1
Freeman, Freddie	1989	1B		0	4	8	-1	1	2
Gallo, Joey	1993	RF	LF	-1	-4	4	5	13	15
Galvis, Freddy	1989	SS		-9	5	2	12	0	-1
Garcia, Avisail	1991	RF		-14	-1	-2	3	-4	8
Gardner, Brett	1983	LF	CF	100	21	12	7	1	-3
Goldschmidt, Paul	1987	1B		25	14	5	0	1	9
Gomes, Yan	1987	C		32	-1	4	5	-3	5
Grandal, Yasmani	1988	C		38	18	12	-3	6	-1
Gregorius, Didi	1990	SS		-3	8	2	-9	-2	-10
Grichuk, Randal	1991	CF	RF	17	2	2	-4	-8	4
Grisham, Trent	1996	CF					4	7	8
Grossman, Robbie	1989	LF	RF	-17	-1	-4	2	-2	-5
Guerrero Jr., Vladimir	1999	1B					-3	-4	2
Gurriel, Yuli	1984	1B		4	-1	3	3	2	5
Gurriel Jr., Lourdes	1993	LF				-11	-2	-4	7
Hamilton, Billy	1990	CF		42	13	7	8	2	2
Haniger, Mitch	1990	RF		-1	7	8	3		-3
Harper, Bryce	1992	RF		20	6	-21	11	-1	-6
Harrison, Josh	1987	2B		28	10	0	-1	2	-4
Hayes, Ke'Bryan	1997	3B						4	16
Hedges, Austin	1992	C		4	21	10	20	0	12
Heredia, Guillermo	1991	CF		4	7	-5	2	2	1
Hernandez, Cesar	1990	2B		-14	-2	-5	0	6	-11
Hernandez, Kike	1991	CF	2B	9	5	5	14	10	16
Hernandez, Teoscar	1992	RF	LF	0	0	-12	-7	-2	-2
Herrera, Odubel	1991	CF		20	9	-8	-3		1
Heyward, Jason	1989	RF	CF	116	18	9	6	1	4
Hicks, Aaron	1989	CF		6	15	-7	-1	-8	-4
Hoskins, Rhys	1993	1B	LF		1	-20	3	-5	-7
Hosmer, Eric	1989	1B		-8	-5	2	-6	3	-4
Iglesias, Jose	1990	SS		15	-5	0	5	-2	-22
Inciarte, Ender	1990	CF		61	4	16	-1	-1	1
Judge, Aaron	1992	RF		0	8	16	21	3	10
Kelly, Carson	1994	C		0	2	-1	0	-2	2
Kepler, Max	1993	RF	CF	8	5	15	6	1	4
Kiermaier, Kevin	1990	CF		77	20	13	12	10	13
Kiner-Falefa, Isiah	1995	SS				2	-5	10	10
Lamb, Jake	1990	3B		10	-8	2	1	-4	-5
LeMahieu, DJ	1988	2B		28	14	18	3	0	-3
Leon, Sandy	1989	C		8	15	11	-1	0	3
Lindor, Francisco	1993	SS		13	7	6	9	3	4
Longoria, Evan	1985	3B		77	8	1	7	2	-1
Lopez, Nicky	1995	SS	2B				-2	7	5
Lowe, Brandon	1994	2B				0	1	1	-10
Lowe, Nathaniel	1995	1B					-2	2	-3
Lowrie, Jed	1984	2B		-40	-6	-10			-12
Lucroy, Jonathan	1986	C		92	-15	-11	-14	0	-1
Machado, Manny	1992	3B	SS	75	9	-5	-3	7	6
Maldonado, Martin	1986	C		45	22	2	6	-1	-2
Margot, Manuel	1994	CF	RF	4	8	7	6	3	13
Marisnick, Jake	1991	CF		53	3	12	7	-3	3
Marte, Starling	1988	CF	LF	63	6	4	-8	-2	-4
Mazara, Nomar	1995	RF		-7	-8	-7	-1	2	0
McCann, James	1990	C		-1	-2	-2	4	5	-4
McCutchen, Andrew	1986	CF	LF	-51	-9	-2	-5	-7	-7
McMahon, Ryan	1994	3B	2B		0	6	7	2	22
Mercer, Jordy	1986	SS		-6	-12	-5	-9	0	-1
Merrifield, Whit	1989	2B		4	-2	-1	2	-2	12
Molina, Yadier	1982	C		165	5	-3	1	1	6
Moncada, Yoan	1995	3B	2B	-2	6	-10	0	-2	3
Moreland, Mitch	1985	1B		8	9	5	1	2	0
Mountcastle, Ryan	1997	1B						-2	-6
Moustakas, Mike	1988	3B		4	-11	-2	-4	-3	-4
Mullins II, Cedric	1994	CF				-6	1	0	-1
Muncy, Max	1990	1B	2B	-2		-3	9	0	8
Murphy, Sean	1994	C					-1	2	10
Murphy, Tom	1991	C		-3	-1	-1	7		1
Myers, Wil	1990	1B	RF	-6	2	4	-10	-2	-8
Narvaez, Omar	1992	C		-2	-7	-14	-18	2	2
Newman, Kevin	1993	SS			-5	-5	-4	6
Odor, Rougned	1994	2B	3B	-19	2	7	-8	-5	-3

Player	YOB	Position		DRS By Season					
		1	2	<17	17	18	19	20	21
Olson, Matt	1994	1B		0	8	8	12	3	6
O'Neill, Tyler	1995	LF				4	0	9	11
Ozuna, Marcell	1990	LF	CF	2	6	3	3	-2	4
Panik, Joe	1990	2B	3B	11	-7	-4	-7	-5	-8
Peralta, David	1987	LF	RF	-2	4	0	7	-1	0
Perez, Roberto	1988	C		22	15	4	30	6	-1
Perez, Salvador	1990	C		26	0	1		3	-5
Pham, Tommy	1988	LF	CF	-3	12	-2	2	-1	-5
Pillar, Kevin	1989	CF		52	14	-3	-8	-2	-1
Pina, Manny	1987	C		-1	14	6	7	4	7
Piscotty, Stephen	1991	RF		-4	6	-6	2	2	-6
Polanco, Gregory	1991	RF		11	2	-2	-4	1	-8
Polanco, Jorge	1993	SS	2B	-11	-8	-8	-10	-4	2
Pollock, A.J.	1987	CF	LF	29	6	2	-11	-3	2
Posey, Buster	1987	C		91	4	10	13		-5
Ramirez, Jose	1992	3B		14	6	-2	0	-6	10
Ramos, Wilson	1987	C		32	-3	-6	-11	-1	-9
Realmuto, J.T.	1991	C		-13	2	-1	11	-2	0
Reddick, Josh	1987	RF		55	8	7	9	-3	-3
Rendon, Anthony	1990	3B		19	9	2	6	-1	-6
Renfroe, Hunter	1992	RF		-1	0	4	19	-2	-1
Reynolds, Bryan	1995	CF	LF				7	6	-5
Riley, Austin	1997	3B					4	-10	13
Rizzo, Anthony	1989	1B		50	11	6	5	4	-6
Robles, Victor	1997	CF			2	2	25	-4	0
Rojas, Miguel	1989	SS		16	5	6	-1	1	5
Rosario, Amed	1995	SS			-6	-9	-3	-2	-11
Rosario, Eddie	1991	LF		12	-11	10	-11	3	2
Sanchez, Gary	1992	C		3	0	4	-2	-4	-10
Sano, Miguel	1993	1B	3B	-14	-3	-6	-13	-5	-8
Santana, Carlos	1986	1B		-67	7	4	-1	6	1
Schoop, Jonathan	1991	2B	1B	19	14	14	-2	1	-4
Schwarber, Kyle	1993	LF		-6	-7	6	-2	-3	-8
Seager, Corey	1994	SS		-7	7	-1	-1	-2	0
Seager, Kyle	1987	3B		26	7	-3	8	-3	-3
Segura, Jean	1990	SS	2B	15	1	-2	-3	2	5
Semien, Marcus	1990	SS	2B	-5	-2	11	7	-6	12
Severino, Pedro	1993	C		1	0	1	-12	1	-9
Shaw, Travis	1990	3B		7	-1	12	-2	0	-4
Simmons, Andrelton	1989	SS		118	41	17	8	-2	15
Smith, Dominic	1995	LF			-5	-4	-2	-1	-3
Smith, Will	1995	C					4	-2	4
Solak, Nick	1995	2B					-2	-13	-6
Soler, Jorge	1992	RF		-12	-3	-13	-9	-1	-11
Soto, Juan	1998	LF	RF			-4	2	-9	4
Souza Jr., Steven	1989	RF		-1	5	-2		1	1
Springer, George	1989	RF	CF	12	1	-2	12	3	-1
Stallings, Jacob	1989	C		0	-1	0	14	7	21
Stanton, Giancarlo	1989	RF		34	11	5	-1		0
Stassi, Max	1991	C		1	1	10	3	1	10
Story, Trevor	1992	SS		14	12	7	21	6	9
Straw, Myles	1994	CF				0	3	-1	4
Suarez, Eugenio	1991	3B	SS	-12	4	-1	-6	-4	-9
Suzuki, Kurt	1983	C		-53	3	-7	-15	-5	-12
Swanson, Dansby	1994	SS		2	-4	9	-2	9	-7
Tapia, Raimel	1994	LF		0	-7	0	-2	1	8
Tatis Jr., Fernando	1999	SS					-3	0	-6
Taylor, Michael A.	1991	CF		6	12	14	-1	-2	19
Torres, Gleyber	1996	SS	2B			3	-14	-9	-12
Trevino, Jose	1992	C				0	0	0	8
Trout, Mike	1991	CF		8	-3	6	-4	-9	-4
Tucker, Kyle	1997	RF				-1	4	5	10
Turner, Justin	1984	3B		-5	4	3	-5	-1	-2
Turner, Trea	1993	SS	2B	2	2	8	4	-5	4
Upton, Justin	1987	LF		-7	7	-1	-13	-4	-11
Urshela, Gio	1991	3B		-1	1	-4	0	5	-5
Vazquez, Christian	1990	C		20	10	-1	6	1	4
Villar, Jonathan	1991	2B	3B	-15	0	7	-6	-2	-2
Vogt, Stephen	1984	C		-15	-8		-4	2	-1
Votto, Joey	1983	1B		25	18	10	7	-7	4
Walker, Christian	1991	1B		-1	-1	0	9	-1	4
Walsh, Jared	1993	1B					1	-2	-3
Wendle, Joey	1990	3B	2B	3	0	10	2	2	10

Player	YOB	Position		DRS By Season					
		1	2	<17	17	18	19	20	21
Winker, Jesse	1993	LF			-5	-12	-1	1	-6
Wolters, Tony	1992	C		4	0	14	10	-2	-1
Wong, Kolten	1990	2B		17	-3	13	17	5	6
Yastrzemski, Mike	1990	RF	CF				7	2	7
Yelich, Christian	1991	LF	CF	17	-11	1	-2	-6	-1
Zimmerman, Ryan	1984	1B		44	-8	5	5		5
Zunino, Mike	1991	C		25	4	11	8	-2	7

Win Shares

Mark Simon

In the absence of a summing or sorting function that would allow you to look at the columns on the accompanying pages and discern some totals and ranks, I can tell you that…

Shohei Ohtani led MLB with 38 Win Shares **in 2021**. Aaron Judge, Brandon Crawford, Juan Soto and Bryce Harper tied for second with 31.

Soto has the most Win Shares over **the last two seasons** with 45, one more than Freddie Freeman. The AL leader is Brandon Lowe, which is interesting because he doesn't necessarily come to mind as the best player in the AL over the last two seasons. But by this stat, he is.

Freeman takes the lead with 72 Win Shares if we're calculating a "**last three seasons**" leaderboard. Soto's second at 69, followed by Marcus Semien (68), Bryce Harper (67), DJ LeMahieu (65), and Jorge Polanco (61). Polanco being a top-five player the last three seasons is a surprise… but as Bill James likes to point out—stats are supposed to surprise you.

Freeman also leads with 98 Win Shares **over the last four seasons** (meaning 2018 to 2021). Freddie's agents may want to take a look at this given that it provides some sabermetric solidification to his Hall-of-Fame case.

I'm sure you were waiting for Mike Trout to take over—and he barely does here. **Over the last five seasons**, he's at 121 Win Shares. Freeman has 120. Props too to Mookie Betts (118) and Jose Ramirez (114), the only other players within 10 Win Shares.

This is where it gets kind of boring…Trout is the Win Shares leader since 2017, 2016, 2015, 2014, 2013, 2012, 2011, 2010, and 2009. He didn't even play in 2009 or 2010, but he's amassed so many Win Shares that he tops the list regardless.

To close, we'll circle back to 2008, which gets us to someone other than Trout. It's Joey Votto, who leads with 330 Win Shares. Trout is second, of course, at 319, followed by Miguel Cabrera (300), Robinson Cano (299), and Andrew McCutchen (299).

Had Trout been fully healthy in 2021, he'd probably have led since 2008 as well.

Catch Him If You Can

Speaking of winning, one of the things illustrative of the Giants success this season was that they could sub in anyone and still be effective.

Case in point, they went 41-13 when Buster Posey's backup, Curt Casali, was their starting catcher this season. Correlation doesn't necessarily equal causation here, but things are going pretty well when you can sit a potential future Hall-of-Famer for a batter with a .210 batting average and .663 OPS. It helped that Casali did well by the pitching staff—he caught five straight shutouts in one stretch.

Casali finished with 6 Win Shares.

Player	<12	12	13	14	15	16	17	18	19	20	21	Career
WIN SHARES BY YEAR												
Abreu, Jose				29	27	20	24	17	20	10	19	166
Acuna Jr., Ronald								19	28	9	14	70
Adames, Willy								8	15	9	22	54
Adams, Matt		1	12	15	3	9	11	8	6	0	0	65
Adrianza, Ehire			0	1	3	1	6	7	7	1	5	31
Aguilar, Jesus				0	1	0	9	19	7	8	15	59
Ahmed, Nick				1	8	3	4	15	17	6	7	61
Albies, Ozzie							8	18	29	5	25	85
Alcantara, Sandy							0	2	12	2	12	28
Alfaro, Jorge						0	5	12	10	4	5	36
Almora Jr., Albert						5	11	13	3	1	0	33
Alonso, Pete									24	5	20	49
Altuve, Jose	2	17	11	30	27	36	35	23	17	2	25	225
Alvarez, Jose			0	0	5	3	3	7	6	1	6	31
Alvarez, Yordan									14	0	18	32
Anderson, Brett	21	3	0	3	8	0	1	3	11	3	3	56
Anderson, Brian							2	27	13	12	8	62
Anderson, Chase				6	5	6	14	8	7	0	0	46
Anderson, Ian										3	9	12
Anderson, Tim						10	7	13	19	7	23	79
Anderson, Tyler						8	5	8	0	3	7	31
Andrus, Elvis	55	23	15	13	21	26	25	7	17	1	9	212
Archer, Chris			0	10	11	14	8	10	6	3	1	63
Arcia, Orlando						4	18	5	12	5	2	46
Arenado, Nolan			9	12	26	26	26	28	24	2	23	176
Arozarena, Randy									1	4	21	26
Arraez, Luis									14	7	15	36
Arrieta, Jake	10	0	3	12	27	16	11	8	6	2	0	95
Avila, Alex	37	15	6	14	6	2	13	3	6	1	2	105
Baddoo, Akil											18	18
Bader, Harrison							2	13	9	4	15	43
Baez, Javier			2	1	14	15	24	19	3	20		98
Baez, Pedro			2	4	6	6	4	8	2	0		32
Barlow, Scott								1	5	2	14	22
Barnes, Austin					1	1	13	3	3	3	4	28
Barnes, Matt				0	1	5	7	7	7	2	10	39
Barnhart, Tucker				1	4	12	14	9	9	5	11	65
Bassitt, Chris					2	4	0	3	9	6	13	37
Bauer, Trevor		0	0	5	8	11	12	18	11	10	9	84
Beaty, Matt									9	1	8	18
Bednar, David									0	0	9	9
Bell, Josh						3	16	15	24	2	12	72
Bellinger, Cody							23	19	31	9	3	85
Belt, Brandon	5	17	24	5	20	24	12	14	15	7	17	160
Benintendi, Andrew						4	19	24	15	0	16	78
Berrios, Jose						0	10	12	13	4	13	52
Betances, Dellin	0		0	14	14	12	9	9	0	0	0	58
Betts, Mookie				8	23	29	26	36	25	13	18	178
Bichette, Bo									6	6	24	36
Bieber, Shane								7	19	11	8	45
Biggio, Cavan									14	10	5	29
Blackmon, Charlie	1	1	7	16	20	22	33	25	21	7	16	169
Bogaerts, Xander			1	7	22	19	16	27	25	6	25	148
Boxberger, Brad		2	1	8	8	1	3	6	1	1	8	39
Boyd, Matthew					0	5	4	8	10	0	4	31
Brach, Brad	0	3	1	5	9	12	11	4	2	0	0	47
Bradley, Archie					0	6	12	7	9	4	5	43
Bradley Jr., Jackie			1	5	10	19	14	16	10	5	5	85
Brantley, Michael	19	18	21	31	21	1	10	16	21	9	13	180
Bregman, Alex						10	23	36	31	6	11	117
Britton, Zack	6	3	1	17	15	19	6	5	9	4	0	85
Bruce, Jay	54	18	21	10	10	18	21	10	5	1	0	168
Bryant, Kris					30	32	26	15	23	3	19	148
Buehler, Walker							0	10	13	2	18	43
Bumgarner, Madison	21	11	12	16	17	19	8	9	11	0	5	129
Bundy, Dylan		0				7	11	3	6	5	1	33
Burnes, Corbin								5	0	7	16	28
Buxton, Byron					2	5	14	1	11	5	14	52
Cabrera, Asdrubal	71	19	12	15	11	21	17	20	16	4	6	212
Cabrera, Miguel	233	32	37	28	26	25	7	5	9	9	9	420
Cain, Lorenzo	6	7	12	19	27	13	24	25	11	1	9	154
Calhoun, Kole		0	8	20	21	19	17	8	14	7	1	115
Camargo, Johan							7	16	5	1	0	29

Player	<12	12	13	14	15	16	17	18	19	20	21	Career
WIN SHARES BY YEAR												
Candelario, Jeimer						0	4	11	4	9	22	50
Canha, Mark					12	0	1	12	19	11	20	75
Carlson, Dylan										2	20	22
Carpenter, Matt	0	9	35	27	30	21	20	28	11	3	4	188
Carrasco, Carlos	8		0	12	14	12	18	15	3	6	0	88
Casali, Curt				2	4	2	1	4	6	4	6	29
Castellanos, Nick			0	13	13	15	18	26	16	3	20	124
Castillo, Diego								5	7	4	8	24
Castillo, Luis							6	6	16	6	11	45
Castro, Harold								0	6	2	8	16
Castro, Jason	4	8	18	10	7	9	12	1	7	3	6	85
Castro, Starlin	37	23	7	20	13	15	13	18	11	1	8	166
Cease, Dylan									2	3	11	16
Chacin, Jhoulys	22	4	15	2	2	5	10	12	0	0	6	78
Chafin, Andrew				1	8	0	5	4	4	0	10	32
Chapman, Aroldis	6	21	12	13	13	15	9	12	10	2	10	123
Chapman, Matt							11	25	25	5	14	80
Chatwood, Tyler	3	3	11	1		11	8	2	6	1	1	47
Chavez, Jesse	4	0	3	7	6	3	3	12	5	0	4	47
Chirinos, Robinson	1		0	11	4	6	10	13	11	0	3	59
Chisholm Jr., Jazz										1	13	14
Choi, Ji-Man						0	1	6	14	4	11	36
Cishek, Steve	7	10	14	10	3	11	6	10	8	1	5	85
Civale, Aaron									6	4	9	19
Clase, Emmanuel									3		15	18
Claudio, Alex				1	1	5	12	5	4	1	1	30
Clippard, Tyler	29	11	10	10	9	7	3	7	6	3	2	97
Cobb, Alex	3	6	13	13		0	12	3	0	2	7	59
Cole, Gerrit			8	7	18	6	10	16	22	6	16	109
Colome, Alex			1	2	6	12	12	9	12	5	5	64
Conforto, Michael					8	6	20	21	20	8	12	95
Contreras, Willson						9	17	14	13	9	14	76
Cooper, Garrett							1	1	9	6	8	25
Corbin, Patrick		4	13		5	5	11	15	16	2	1	72
Correa, Carlos					18	26	26	12	13	6	23	124
Cortes, Nestor								0	1	0	8	9
Crawford, Brandon	5	13	11	22	20	21	13	18	13	6	31	173
Crawford, J.P.							2	5	10	8	26	51
Cron, C.J.				8	9	14	10	12	12	2	18	85
Cronenworth, Jake										7	22	29
Cruz, Nelson	65	17	16	22	26	21	24	22	22	8	16	259
Cueto, Johnny	37	21	5	22	12	19	6	4	0	2	5	133
Dahl, David						6		9	12	1	1	29
Dalbec, Bobby										3	11	14
d'Arnaud, Travis			1	8	11	3	10	1	15	6	3	58
Darvish, Yu		14	18	10		8	12	1	9	9	6	87
Davies, Zach					2	8	13	1	11	6	2	43
Davis, J.D.							1	1	14	4	8	28
Davis, Khris				6	12	11	15	20	23	8	0	96
Davis, Wade	16	7	2	15	19	11	12	0	0	0		94
deGrom, Jacob				11	15	11	11	20	21	6	13	108
DeJong, Paul							13	16	20	6	9	64
DeSclafani, Anthony					0	7	7	3	10	0	12	39
DeShields, Delino					16	2	10	6	10	3	1	48
Devenski, Chris						11	10	3	3	0	0	27
Devers, Rafael							7	9	24	6	25	71
Diaz, Aledmys						18	4	12	7	1	8	50
Diaz, Edwin						8	10	18	3	4	10	53
Diaz, Elias					0	0	2	11	5	1	7	26
Diaz, Yandy							3	3	7	5	17	35
Dickerson, Alex						0	8		6	5	8	27
Dickerson, Corey			4	15	8	9	18	16	10	3	5	88
Diekman, Jake		1	3	4	4	7	2	4	3	4	5	37
Difo, Wilmer					0	2	8	6	3	0	6	25
Donaldson, Josh	0	8	32	27	32	28	25	7	25	3	17	204
Doolittle, Sean		5	8	11	2	4	11	12	9	0	3	65
Dozier, Hunter							0	1	16	3	6	26
Drury, Brandon					0	9	12	0	4	0	2	27
Duffy, Danny	1	2	3	12	7	15	10	6	7	2	6	71
Duffy, Matt				2	22	5		18	4		9	60
Duggar, Steven								5	6	0	9	20
Duvall, Adam				0	2	16	12	5	4	4	19	62
Dyson, Jarrod	4	8	7	9	6	12	8	4	10	1	1	70

Player	<12	12	13	14	15	16	17	18	19	20	21	Career
Eaton, Adam		2	5	20	24	24	5	12	16	4	5	117
Edman, Tommy									12	5	20	37
Eovaldi, Nathan	2	3	5	4	9	6		5	1	3	14	52
Escobar, Alcides	24	14	10	20	15	13	14	4			11	125
Escobar, Eduardo	0	2	2	13	14	7	14	20	22	2	17	113
Familia, Jeurys		0	0	9	15	16	2	9	1	2	4	58
Farmer, Kyle							0	2	4	2	12	20
Fiers, Mike	0	8	0	7	9	7	3	12	12	3	0	61
Flaherty, Jack							0	9	17	2	6	34
Fletcher, David							8	18	7	17		50
Flexen, Chris							0	0	0		13	13
Flores, Wilmer			2	7	16	9	8	11	8	5	12	78
Floro, Dylan					0	0	7	3	3	10		23
Foltynewicz, Mike				0	0	6	5	14	5	0	2	32
Fowler, Dexter	44	15	13	16	22	22	16	3	17	2	0	170
Fraley, Jake									0	0	11	11
France, Ty								5	7	28		40
Franco, Maikel				1	13	17	6	13	7	8	1	66
Franco, Wander											15	15
Frazier, Adam					5	13	12	15	3	21		69
Frazier, Todd	3	13	15	20	13	15	13	12	18	3	0	125
Freeland, Kyle							11	21	0	5	8	45
Freeman, Freddie	19	18	35	28	22	28	22	26	28	17	27	270
Fried, Max							1	2	12	5	15	35
Fulmer, Michael					14	10	4		0	9		37
Gallegos, Giovanny					0	1	9	3	13			26
Gallo, Joey				2	0	16	13	11	6	19		67
Galvis, Freddy		3	4	2	15	16	18	14	12	4	6	94
Gamel, Ben				1	13	9	7	2	8			40
Garcia, Adolis						0			0	13		13
Garcia, Avisail		1	5	4	10	11	22	6	13	3	17	92
Garcia, Leury		2	1	1	1	8	9	8	2	13		45
Garcia, Luis									1	11		12
Gardner, Brett	45	2	22	19	19	17	19	13	17	5	11	189
Garver, Mitch						1	11	18	1	9		40
Gausman, Kevin		1	6	5	12	9	9	1	4	16		63
Gibson, Kyle		0	8	12	4	7	13	7	2	11		64
Giolito, Lucas				0	4	1	15	5	13			38
Givens, Mychal				4	7	10	5	5	1	7		39
Glasnow, Tyler					1	1	4	8	7			25
Goldschmidt, Paul	6	17	36	20	35	25	29	25	21	9	28	251
Gomes, Yan		2	14	18	5	4	12	9	8	2	9	83
Gonzales, Marco				2	0		1	10	11	5	9	38
Gonzalez, Marwin		2	2	6	8	7	26	13	12	4	4	84
Goodrum, Niko						0	13	7	2	7		29
Goodwin, Brian					1	6	6	10	3	5		31
Gosselin, Phil			0	2	6	3	0	0	1	1	9	22
Grandal, Yasmani		11	4	12	15	19	12	17	24	7	16	137
Graveman, Kendall			0	5	9	6	0		1	11		32
Gray, Jon				1	9	10	7	12	1	8		48
Gray, Sonny		5	13	16	0	10	6	17	5	8		80
Green, Chad				2	9	9	4	3	11			38
Greene, Shane			4	0	3	9	5	11	3	0		35
Gregorius, Didi		0	10	9	17	16	18	21	11	9	5	116
Greinke, Zack	84	16	17	15	26	10	18	17	21	3	9	236
Grichuk, Randal				1	12	13	7	13	8	8	10	72
Grisham, Trent								3	7	14		24
Grossman, Robbie			7	10	0	10	10	13	11	7	22	90
Guerra, Junior				0	10	1	5	9	2	2		29
Guerrero Jr., Vlad									11	5	28	44
Gurriel, Yuli					2	18	19	20	2	19		80
Gurriel Jr., Lourdes							8	9	9	16		42
Haase, Eric						0	0	0		11		11
Hader, Josh						6	14	16	4	16		56
Hamilton, Billy			2	15	5	9	10	8	3	1	1	54
Hampson, Garrett							2	3	2	8		15
Hand, Brad	1	0	1	3	1	8	14	12	11	6	7	64
Haniger, Mitch						3	12	28	7		27	77
Happ, Ian						12	12	7	9	16		56
Happ, J.A.	24	5	3	7	10	18	10	14	6	3		103
Harper, Bryce		21	19	9	38	20	22	23	27	9	31	219
Harris, Will		0	5	1	9	11	5	5	10	1	0	47
Harrison, Josh	5	4	3	25	12	15	15	9	1	2	14	105

Player	<12	12	13	14	15	16	17	18	19	20	21	Career
Hayes, Ke'Bryan										5	11	16
Hays, Austin						0		2	13			19
Heaney, Andrew			0	8	0	8	4	3	4			27
Hedges, Austin			2	0	8	5	4	1	5			25
Hendricks, Kyle			7	8	17	11	13	12	7	7		82
Hendriks, Liam	0	0	0	0	5	3	5	1	17	16		53
Heredia, Guillermo					3	6	7	3	1	7		27
Hernandez, Cesar			3	1	12	24	18	22	16	8	16	120
Hernandez, Kike			5	9	2	9	13	12	4	17		71
Hernandez, Teoscar				2	3	11	12	7	22			57
Herrera, Odubel				16	25	10	14	2		11		78
Heyward, Jason	34	22	14	23	21	12	14	16	13	9	4	182
Hicks, Aaron			4	4	11	4	11	22	7	7	1	71
Hill, Rich	21	3	0	1	4	12	11	7	5	3	7	74
Holland, Greg	9	11	18	15	7		12	5	4	5	5	91
Holt, Brock		3	1	12	14	6	2	11	8	1	4	62
Hoskins, Rhys						10	22	18	6	13		69
Hosmer, Eric	13	10	18	14	22	17	30	16	17	6	13	176
Houser, Adrian				0			1	7	1	10		19
Hudson, Daniel	26	0		0	4	4	3	2	11	1	5	56
Hunter, Tommy	21	4	10	8	4	3	8	6	1	2	2	69
Iglesias, Jose	0	1	13		12	13	11	15	12	8	10	95
Iglesias, Raisel					4	7	14	11	9	6	15	66
Inciarte, Ender			10	15	14	22	17	7	1	2		88
India, Jonathan											22	22
Jackson, Luke					0	0	2	2	10	0	9	23
Jansen, Kenley	12	15	16	11	12	17	19	10	10	4	14	140
Jay, Jon	21	15	17	16	3	12	12	11	4	0	0	111
Jimenez, Eloy									12	9	4	25
Joe, Connor								0		8		8
Joyce, Matt	36	13	11	10	1	11	14	3	8	3	0	110
Judge, Aaron						0	29	19	16	4	31	99
Kazmir, Scott	55		8	10	11	4				0		88
Kela, Keone				8	2	6	8	4	0	0		28
Keller, Brad							12	9	5	4		30
Kelly, Carson					0	1	0	11	3	8		23
Kelly, Joe		5	9	5	6	2	7	5	3	1	5	48
Kemp, Tony					1	1	9	5	3	18		37
Kennedy, Ian	33	11	2	9	4	14	3	4	10	0	9	99
Kepler, Max				0	8	12	13	19	6	11		69
Kershaw, Clayton	55	19	22	22	21	16	19	12	15	6	8	215
Keuchel, Dallas		0	3	16	22	6	13	11	7	7	4	89
Kiermaier, Kevin		0	9	19	13	13	7	11	6	10		88
Kimbrel, Craig	21	18	17	16	11	9	19	14	0	1	10	136
Kiner-Falefa, Isiah								5	2	5	16	28
Kintzler, Brandon	1	2	8	4	0	7	11	4	7	3	0	47
Kittredge, Andrew							2	0	3	1	10	16
Kluber, Corey	0	1	9	21	14	20	23	20	1	0	5	114
Knebel, Corey				0	4	2	17	8		0	4	35
La Stella, Tommy			9	3	4	5	2	8	7	7		45
Lagares, Juan			7	15	13	2	2	3	2	0	4	48
Lamb, Jake				1	9	16	17	4	4	3	2	56
Lauer, Eric								4	6	0	9	19
Laureano, Ramon							9	17	7	11		44
LeBlanc, Wade	10	4	0	2		4	4	10	3	0	2	39
LeMahieu, DJ	0	6	8	9	14	22	20	19	33	12	20	163
Leon, Sandy		0	0	1	3	12	9	6	3	1	3	38
Lester, Jon	75	8	12	18	13	18	9	14	8	2	5	182
Lindor, Francisco				14	21	27	30	19	6	20		137
Loaisiga, Jonathan								1	1	2	12	16
Longoria, Evan	96	14	24	21	18	20	18	7	14	1	9	242
Lopez, Nicky									6	3	21	30
Lorenzen, Michael				2	4	6	7	12	3	3		37
Loup, Aaron		3	7	7	1	0	4	1	1	3	9	36
Lowe, Brandon							6	14	11	30		61
Lowe, Nathaniel								3	1	19		23
Lowrie, Jed	21	11	23	11	6	8	22	29	0		16	147
Lucroy, Jonathan	19	15	19	26	10	22	11	10	5	0	1	138
Lugo, Seth					6	3	8	12	2	4		35
Lux, Gavin									2	2	12	16
Lyles, Jordan	0	1	2	6	1	2	1	4	8	0	6	31
Lynn, Lance	2	11	7	16	12		11	6	18	7	15	105
Machado, Manny		7	20	12	27	28	19	28	18	11	27	197

WIN SHARES BY YEAR

Player	<12	12	13	14	15	16	17	18	19	20	21	Career
Madrigal, Nick										4	8	12
Maeda, Kenta						11	7	5	10	7	4	44
Mahle, Tyler							1	3	2	4	13	23
Maldonado, Martin	0	7	3	4	5	7	11	11	6	7	8	69
Manaea, Sean						7	8	9	4	2	11	41
Mancini, Trey						1	19	6	17		10	53
Manoah, Alek											9	9
Margot, Manuel						1	13	10	9	4	13	50
Marisnick, Jake			2	5	9	3	6	5	7	1	4	42
Marquez, German						1	11	16	13	6	13	60
Marte, Ketel					9	7	6	16	29	5	14	86
Marte, Starling		5	20	17	20	17	10	21	21	6	21	158
Martinez, Carlos			1	4	14	16	12	10	9	0	0	66
Martinez, J.D.	6	7	3	19	25	17	20	33	22	2	19	173
Matz, Steven					4	9	0	4	8	0	11	36
May, Trevor				0	7	2		4	7	2	6	28
Maybin, Cameron	30	13	0	5	16	14	10	9	8	2	0	107
Mazara, Nomar						16	16	10	10	3	3	58
McCann, James				0	10	9	10	6	16	5	9	65
McClanahan, Shane											8	8
McCormick, Chas											10	10
McCullers Jr., Lance					8	6	5	7		2	13	41
McCutchen, Andrew	68	40	34	33	35	17	22	20	8	6	16	299
McGee, Jake	2	8	5	15	7	4	7	0	2	3	12	65
McHugh, Collin			0	0	13	13	8	4	9		8	59
McMahon, Ryan							0	4	11	4	14	33
McNeil, Jeff								11	24	6	6	47
Meadows, Austin								5	23	2	22	52
Means, John								0	10	2	10	22
Mejia, Francisco							0	1	5	1	11	18
Melancon, Mark	13	0	15	15	17	16	3	3	8	3	12	105
Mercer, Jordy		2	13	10	8	13	12	9	5	0	1	73
Merrifield, Whit						8	21	22	21	9	21	102
Mikolas, Miles		2	0	0			17	8			1	28
Miley, Wade	2	14	10	7	9	3	4	7	11	0	14	81
Miller, Andrew	6	4	2	9	13	19	11	3	4	2	1	74
Miller, Brad			10	11	15	15	6	5	6	5	11	84
Minor, Mike	3	7	13	3			11	11	18	0	6	72
Mize, Casey										0	9	9
Molina, Yadier	110	29	29	19	16	21	19	18	16	4	16	297
Moncada, Yoan						0	6	13	23	6	22	70
Mondesi, Adalberto						2	1	8	12	5	3	31
Montas, Frankie					0		0	3	8	0	13	24
Montgomery, Jordan							9	2	0	1	9	21
Moore, Dylan									5	5	10	20
Moran, Colin						0	1	13	14	2	7	37
Moreland, Mitch	14	9	10	3	16	10	12	12	8	5	4	103
Morton, Charlie	12	0	6	4	2	1	10	13	18	2	13	81
Mountcastle, Ryan										5	13	18
Moustakas, Mike	4	14	5	9	21	1	15	19	19	5	2	114
Mullins II, Cedric								2	1	3	22	28
Muncy, Max					1	2		21	22	5	27	78
Murphy, Sean									2	5	14	21
Musgrove, Joe						3	4	5	7	2	12	33
Myers, Wil			14	6	9	19	19	10	10	10	13	110
Naquin, Tyler						13	0	5	8	2	12	40
Narvaez, Omar						3	7	10	14	4	15	53
Nelson, Jimmy				1	0	8	4	13	0		3	29
Neris, Hector				0	2	11	11	3	13	2	8	50
Newman, Kevin								1	16	2	6	25
Nimmo, Brandon						2	6	22	8	6	15	59
Nola, Aaron					4	3	12	22	14	4	8	67
Nola, Austin									7	8	8	23
O'Day, Darren	20	10	8	10	12	3	6	1	1	2	1	74
Odor, Rougned				11	16	18	8	13	13	3	9	91
Odorizzi, Jake		0	1	7	11	11	7	7	12	0	5	61
Ohtani, Shohei								20	12	1	38	71
Olson, Matt						0	9	19	21	8	26	83
O'Neill, Tyler								6	3	3	22	34
Ortega, Rafael		1					3			1	1	14
Ottavino, Adam	0	5	7	6	4	5	3	14	8	1	8	61
Owings, Chris			2	8	6	11	9	3	2	1	3	45
Ozuna, Marcell			8	19	10	15	29	19	14	13	4	131

Player	<12	12	13	14	15	16	17	18	19	20	21	Career
Pagan, Emilio							4	3	15	2	3	27
Panik, Joe				10	17	13	15	6	11	3	4	79
Parker, Blake		0	4	0		1	10	7	5	1	4	32
Parra, Gerardo	34	9	15	6	14	2	9	12	7		1	109
Paxton, James		3	5	3	5	11	11	9	0	0		47
Peacock, Brad	2		2	2	0	1	12	5	6	0	0	30
Pederson, Joc				0	15	19	7	11	17	3	11	83
Peralta, David			7	20	2	16	23	13	6	11		98
Peralta, Freddy								4	3	2	12	21
Peralta, Wily	3	5	12	3	4	0	4	1			6	38
Peraza, Jose					0	7	5	14	5	1	3	35
Perez, Hernan	0	1	0	4	11	9	7	2	0		0	34
Perez, Martin		1	8	2	3	9	9	1	6	3	5	47
Perez, Roberto				2	7	5	8	2	18	3	3	48
Perez, Salvador	7	10	23	17	18	16	13	18		7	28	157
Peterson, Jace				1	14	9	3	4	2	2	9	44
Petit, Yusmeiro	7	0	2	4	3	2	10	8	10	3	7	56
Pham, Tommy				0	7	4	21	17	17	2	9	77
Phelps, David	7	3	4	3	12	4			3	2	2	40
Phillips, Brett							3	1	1	2	10	17
Pillar, Kevin			1	1	15	15	9	11	16	5	8	81
Pina, Manny	0	0				2	12	8	5	2	7	36
Pinder, Chad						1	7	8	8	2	5	31
Pineda, Michael	10			8	7	6	5		9	2	7	54
Piscotty, Stephen					11	22	7	21	7	4	4	76
Pivetta, Nick							1	5	2	1	9	18
Plawecki, Kevin					7	3	4	5	4	4	5	32
Polanco, Gregory				8	17	14	6	18	2	1	4	70
Polanco, Jorge				1	1	8	14	11	26	6	29	96
Pollock, A.J.		2	14	10	27	1	15	13	10	5	18	115
Pomeranz, Drew	1	4	0	5	5	12	15		0	4	4	54
Posey, Buster	29	38	24	30	29	24	22	15	12		20	243
Pressly, Ryan			4	2	3	6	3	8	9	2	13	50
Price, David	37	19	12	16	19	14	7	14	6		4	148
Profar, Jurickson		0	5			6	1	16	10	6	5	49
Pujols, Albert	373	25	10	19	18	17	7	8	10	1	6	494
Quantrill, Cal									3	3	12	18
Quintana, Jose		9	13	12	15	15	10	9	6	0	1	90
Ramirez, Harold									9	0	10	19
Ramirez, Jose			1	7	4	22	28	29	17	11	29	148
Ramos, AJ			0	5	8	14	11	6	0	0	1	45
Ramos, Wilson	16	3	8	10	11	24	6	19	15	1	2	115
Ray, Robbie			0	6	7	17	7	8	1		17	63
Realmuto, J.T.					1	10	19	25	22	6	22	124
Reddick, Josh	8	16	13	13	17	12	21	10	12	5	3	130
Rendon, Anthony			12	26	9	22	29	22	31	7	4	162
Renfroe, Hunter						2	9	12	11	2	15	51
Reyes, Alex						6		1	0	2	11	20
Reyes, Franmil								8	13	4	13	38
Reynolds, Bryan									19	3	28	50
Richards, Garrett	0	1	6	13	14	2	2	4	0	3	6	51
Riley, Austin									6	4	23	33
Rivera, Rene	6		2	14	5	6	7	3	1	0	2	46
Rizzo, Anthony	0	12	14	28	32	29	25	22	25	5	15	207
Roark, Tanner			7	15	4	17	7	8	8	0	0	66
Robert, Luis										7	13	20
Robertson, David	20	7	12	12	13	10	13	9	0		0	96
Robles, Hansel					3	6	3	3	15	0	6	36
Robles, Victor							1	2	15	3	4	25
Rodgers, Brendan									1	0	12	13
Rodon, Carlos					9	8	3	6	1	0	14	41
Rodriguez, Eduardo					8	4	8	10	15		9	54
Rodriguez, Richard							0	8	5	4	11	28
Rogers, Taylor						4	7	8	13	2	5	39
Rogers, Trevor										0	10	10
Rogers, Tyler									3	2	14	19
Rojas, Josh									2	0	11	13
Rojas, Miguel				1	4	3	8	13	12	10	14	65
Romano, Jordan									0	3	14	17
Romo, Sergio	25	11	9	8	5	4	4	7	11	3	3	90
Rosario, Amed							2	14	19	1	20	56
Rosario, Eddie					12	5	14	16	17	9	11	84
Ruf, Darin		1	8	1	7	0				4	11	32

Player	<12	12	13	14	15	16	17	18	19	20	21	Career
Ryu, Hyun-Jin			13	9		0	7	7	18	5	10	69
Sale, Chris	16	19	15	17	15	17	20	18	7		4	148
Sanchez, Aaron				6	6	17	1	4	2		2	38
Sanchez, Gary					0	11	16	8	15	2	11	63
Sandoval, Pablo	65	18	22	21	6	0	2	6	8	0	1	149
Sano, Miguel					16	11	14	4	17	4	9	75
Santana, Carlos	29	21	26	22	13	19	17	19	24	6	8	204
Santana, Danny				18	3	1	3	0	15	0	2	42
Santana, Ervin	74	2	14	9	7	11	17	0	0		3	137
Santiago, Hector	1	7	8	5	11	7	2	5	0		2	48
Schebler, Scott					1	7	9	8	1	0	0	26
Scherzer, Max	36	14	20	18	18	20	21	22	16	4	16	205
Schoop, Jonathan			0	6	9	18	26	8	9	6	19	101
Schwarber, Kyle					10	0	10	15	18	6	19	78
Schwindel, Frank										0	11	11
Seager, Corey					6	29	31	4	20	9	21	120
Seager, Kyle	3	24	23	28	17	30	20	14	11	10	25	205
Segura, Jean		4	21	13	12	23	16	24	15	6	20	154
Semien, Marcus			2	7	10	21	11	21	36	8	24	140
Senzatela, Antonio							9	5	2	7	8	31
Severino, Luis					5	1	16	16	1		1	40
Severino, Pedro					0	2	0	4	6	4	13	29
Sewald, Paul							2	0	1	0	11	14
Shaw, Bryan	3	4	7	8	7	7	7	0	5	0	6	54
Shaw, Travis					7	12	22	21	3	3	4	72
Shoemaker, Matt			1	11	5	9	4	1	3	1	0	35
Simmons, Andrelton		8	19	13	14	14	24	22	6	2	7	129
Slater, Austin							3	4	7	4	8	26
Smith, Dominic							3	1	5	7	8	24
Smith, Joe	22	6	9	14	8	4	6	4	3		2	78
Smith, Pavin										1	11	12
Smith, Will		2	3	4	7	3		10	14	1	11	55
Smith, Will									10	7	18	35
Smyly, Drew		6	10	10	5	4			3	2	6	46
Snell, Blake						5	6	22	6	4	6	49
Sogard, Eric	1	1	10	7	8		8	1	15	3	3	57
Solak, Nick									5	6	10	21
Solano, Donovan		8	9	10	1	1			10	7	10	56
Soler, Jorge				4	10	7	0	6	18	4	10	59
Soria, Joakim	64		2	6	10	5	6	8	5	3	2	111
Sosa, Edmundo									0	0	10	10
Soto, Gregory									1	1	9	11
Soto, Juan								15	24	14	31	84
Souza Jr., Steven				0	7	10	19	5		0	0	41
Springer, George				10	13	23	24	19	25	10	11	135
Stallings, Jacob						1	1	1	4	4	13	24
Stammen, Craig	8	9	7	4	1		7	10	9	1	7	63
Stanton, Giancarlo	32	19	15	31	14	12	29	18	3	2	20	195
Stassi, Max			0	1	1	0	0	9	1	4	8	24
Staumont, Josh									1	2	9	12
Steckenrider, Drew							3	4	0		12	19
Stephenson, Tyler										1	12	13
Story, Trevor						13	13	26	22	7	16	97
Strasburg, Stephen	7	14	11	13	8	11	17	7	19	0	1	108
Stratton, Chris						1	4	3	3	2	9	22
Straw, Myles								1	4	1	17	23
Strickland, Hunter				2	5	7	7	4	1	0	5	31
Stripling, Ross						4	5	8	6	0	4	27
Stroman, Marcus				9	3	10	16	2	14		12	66
Strop, Pedro	3	10	5	6	8	5	7	12	4	0	0	60
Suarez, Eugenio				9	10	16	16	21	21	6	8	107
Suarez, Ranger								0	6	0	16	22
Sulser, Cole									1	1	9	11
Suter, Brent						2	6	4	4	3	7	26
Suzuki, Kurt	59	10	6	14	8	7	12	10	11	2	3	142
Swanson, Dansby						4	10	15	15	10	17	71
Syndergaard, Noah					9	18	2	11	9		0	49
Taillon, Jameson						6	6	14	1		8	35
Tapia, Raimel						1	3	1	7	6	10	28
Tatis Jr., Fernando									18	12	28	58
Taylor, Chris				5	1	1	23	17	13	9	20	89
Taylor, Michael A.				1	14	4	14	5	0	1	9	48
Taylor, Tyrone									1	1	8	10

Player	<12	12	13	14	15	16	17	18	19	20	21	Career
Teheran, Julio	0	0	12	15	8	13	7	9	11	0	1	76
Tepera, Ryan					2	1	8	7	1	1	7	27
Tomlin, Josh	13	0	0	2	6	10	6	0	6	2	1	46
Toro, Abraham									1	0	12	13
Torrens, Luis							1		0	1	10	12
Torres, Gleyber								19	28	3	14	64
Torreyes, Ronald					1	5	7	3	0	0	8	24
Treinen, Blake				4	3	8	7	19	4	2	12	59
Trivino, Lou								8	2	1	11	22
Trout, Mike	3	38	40	40	42	35	29	39	33	10	10	319
Tucker, Kyle								0	2	11	22	35
Turner, Justin	15	4	3	18	18	25	24	19	20	8	21	175
Turner, Trea					0	17	17	25	19	13	26	117
Upton, Justin	68	16	21	21	21	14	22	17	4	2	5	211
Urias, Julio						5	0	0	9	4	16	34
Urias, Luis								1	4	2	19	26
Urias, Ramon										1	9	10
Urshela, Gio					3		1	0	21	8	13	46
Valdez, Framber								4	1	4	10	19
Vazquez, Christian				4		3	11	4	15	5	9	51
Verdugo, Alex							0	1	11	5	16	33
Villar, Jonathan			3	5	4	24	8	15	19	2	12	92
Vincent, Nick		3	6	4	1	5	6	4	2	1	2	34
Vogt, Stephen		0	4	8	18	9	6		11	1	3	60
Voit, Luke							2	10	17	9	5	43
Votto, Joey	112	27	30	8	33	33	33	22	11	3	21	333
Wacha, Michael			4	7	14	2	8	6	4	0	2	47
Wade Jr., LaMonte									2	1	15	18
Wainwright, Adam	74	9	16	23	3	10	6	1	9	5	16	172
Walker, Christian			0	0			0	0	16	5	7	28
Walker, Taijuan			1	3	6	5	11	1	0	4	5	36
Walsh, Jared									1	4	22	27
Watson, Tony	3	5	8	11	12	9	7	9	3	3	6	76
Webb, Logan									1	1	12	14
Wendle, Joey						2	1	19	5	7	14	48
Wheeler, Zack			5	8			1	11	12	5	19	61
Whitlock, Garrett											11	11
Williams, Devin									0	5	8	13
Williams, Trevor						0	7	13	4	0	4	28
Wilson, Justin		0	8	2	7	5	10	4	6	2	2	46
Winker, Jesse							3	12	8	5	18	46
Wisdom, Patrick								2	0	0	10	12
Wolters, Tony						5	5	3	10	2	0	25
Wong, Kolten			1	10	18	9	14	12	24	8	18	114
Wood, Alex			4	13	8	2	15	6	0	0	8	56
Woodruff, Brandon							2	3	11	6	15	37
Workman, Brandon			2	0			3	5	15	1	1	27
Yastrzemski, Mike									14	10	16	40
Yelich, Christian			8	22	15	21	23	34	33	4	15	175
Zimmer, Bradley							8	2	0	0	8	18
Zimmerman, Ryan	114	22	23	8	10	3	18	7	3		3	211
Zimmermann, Jordan	15	15	15	16	11	4	3	5	0	0	0	84
Zunino, Mike			2	11	5	8	14	7	5	2	14	68

Instant Replay

Mark Simon

We've had a new phenomenon in baseball since the advent of instant replay challenges, that of the delayed celebration.

That's what we're dubbing instances in which there was a replay review on the final play of the game that was favorable for the winning team.

There were 38 such instances in 2021, easily the most in a season since replay was instituted in 2014.

Those aren't part of our tracking on the accompanying page, but from a storytelling perspective, those were the moments that intrigued us the most.

Those calls instituted by umpire review were overturned only 6 times out of those 38 instances. That's a much lower percentage than on team-requested reviews, which makes sense given that there's a "let's make absolutely sure" component to checking a game-ending play.

The NL West was essentially decided by a replay review that was upheld.

The Giants and Dodgers played an epic 11-inning game on September 3, which ended when Trea Turner's throw to first base was caught off the bag by first baseman Will Smith. Buster Posey was ruled safe, the call stood, the Giants won, and won the division by one game.

As for what's on the next page, you'll see that all Replay Reviews were overturned 48% of the time, which was up from both 2019 (45%) and 2020 (43%) and basically matched the 2018 percentage.

The Giants led MLB in requested reviews with 59. The Twins had the biggest differential with 31 challenges overturned and only 11 opposing challenges that went against them. And the Reds had the highest challenge success rate, 76%.

2021 Instant Replay Summary

Replay Type	Total Replays	Overturned	Percent
Force Play	561	335	59.7
Tag Play	520	228	43.8
Hit By Pitch	104	53	51.0
Fair or Foul	68	12	17.6
Boundary Call (Home Run)	43	8	18.6
Trap or Catch	29	13	44.8
Fan Interference	27	6	22.2
Home Plate Collision	21	2	9.5
Catcher's Interference	17	11	64.7
Slide Interference	13	4	30.8
Missed Base	9	5	55.6
Rules Check	8	0	0.0
Stadium Boundary	8	4	50.0
Runner Placement	4	0	0.0
Record Keeping	4	2	50.0
Passed Runner	1	0	0.0
Tag-Up Play	1	0	0.0
Timing Play	1	1	100.0

2021 Challenges

Team	Challenges	Overturned	Pct	Opponent Challenges	Overturned	Pct	Net
Minnesota Twins	56	31	55.4	31	11	35.5	20
San Francisco Giants	59	33	55.9	48	24	50.0	9
Washington Nationals	40	24	60.0	37	15	40.5	9
Toronto Blue Jays	61	31	50.8	50	23	46.0	8
Cleveland Indians	42	27	64.3	43	21	48.8	6
Colorado Rockies	41	25	61.0	43	20	46.5	5
Cincinnati Reds	42	32	76.2	41	27	65.9	5
New York Mets	45	25	55.6	37	20	54.1	5
Houston Astros	42	18	42.9	34	14	41.2	4
Boston Red Sox	33	20	60.6	39	16	41.0	4
San Diego Padres	52	23	44.2	47	21	44.7	2
St Louis Cardinals	39	23	59.0	42	21	50.0	2
Arizona Diamondbacks	45	17	37.8	31	16	51.6	1
Los Angeles Angels	57	27	47.4	49	27	55.1	0
Seattle Mariners	35	20	57.1	43	21	48.8	-1
Miami Marlins	51	21	41.2	44	22	50.0	-1
Texas Rangers	50	26	52.0	55	27	49.1	-1
Chicago Cubs	50	26	52.0	47	28	59.6	-2
Detroit Tigers	38	20	52.6	41	24	58.5	-4
Tampa Bay Rays	38	12	31.6	40	16	40.0	-4
Pittsburgh Pirates	39	21	53.8	44	26	59.1	-5
Chicago White Sox	27	15	55.6	39	20	51.3	-5
Baltimore Orioles	40	16	40.0	43	22	51.2	-6
New York Yankees	36	17	47.2	46	23	50.0	-6
Philadelphia Phillies	41	16	39.0	47	22	46.8	-6
Oakland Athletics	40	17	42.5	45	24	53.3	-7
Atlanta Braves	34	15	44.1	42	22	52.4	-7
Los Angeles Dodgers	49	18	36.7	51	26	51.0	-8
Milwaukee Brewers	27	13	48.1	42	21	50.0	-8
Kansas City Royals	37	21	56.8	45	30	66.7	-9

2021 Projections Review

Mark Simon

Kris Bryant hit .206 with a .644 OPS during an injury-bothered 34 games with the Cubs in 2020.

Ha!, said our projections system, as it calculated Bryant's numbers for 2021.

Bryant's track record was a good one as he headed into his age-29 season. He averaged 141 games and 28 home runs and 81 RBIs from 2015 to 2019.

As such, our projection took that into consideration, weighted that in combination with the weirdness that was 2020 and projected the following:

141 games, 26 home runs, 76 RBI.

Bryant's actual numbers in 2021:

144 games, 25 home runs and 73 RBI.

Kris Bryant

Label	G	AB	R	H	D	T	HR	RBI	BB	SO	SB	Avg	Slg
Act	144	513	86	136	32	2	25	73	62	135	10	.265	.481
Proj	141	529	94	139	32	3	26	76	72	149	3	.263	.482

Two other veterans with long track records that we did well by projections-wise were Josh Donaldson and Paul Goldschmidt.

The system's evaluation was that Donaldson was aging and thus in decline, but that he still had a meaningful amount of power in his bat. Our system was within one of his hit total and one of his RBI total, while nailing his home runs exactly. The biggest miss there was in games and at-bats, which underestimated him by 11 and 13, respectively.

Josh Donaldson

Label	G	AB	R	H	D	T	HR	RBI	BB	SO	SB	Avg	Slg
Act	135	457	73	113	26	0	26	72	74	114	0	.247	.475
Proj	124	444	78	112	25	1	26	73	77	123	2	.252	.489

Goldschmidt was another player that had a power dip in 2020, but whose home run total of 31 our system matched exactly. Thank his MVP-caliber September/October, in which he hit nine home runs, for that.

This one was a good call. We said he would hit .287 and slug .504. He exceeded those expectations by just a little, going .294 and .514.

Paul Goldschmidt

Label	G	AB	R	H	D	T	HR	RBI	BB	SO	SB	Avg	Slg
Act	158	603	102	177	36	2	31	99	67	136	12	.294	.514
Proj	161	593	96	170	32	2	31	94	96	158	5	.287	.504

I like those three because in each instance, we had reason as human beings to feel a little nervous about what these players had done and could do.

A projection system doesn't feel nervousness. It just executes against the ideas that serve as its foundation over and over and over.

Perhaps you're good at that. If so, I'm guessing you do well in your fantasy leagues. If I could have maintained that same level of objectivity, I would have done better in mine (I say that every year). But alas.

The projection I most remembered from editing last year's Handbook was that for Vladimir Guerrero Jr. We're an impatient society these days, and there was disappointment that Guerrero "only" hit .272 with 15 home runs as a 20-year-old and didn't quite reach an .800 OPS at age 21.

The projection system sensed better days ahead. It projected 26 home runs and an .836 OPS. The latter would beat Vlad's OPS from his first two seasons by 58 points.

So I don't consider this one a miss. I think it was a win for the system, which puts stock in minor league numbers and considers an aging curve by which a player who plays regularly at 20 is going to develop well as he ages.

We just didn't realize quite how well.

Vladimir Guerrero Jr.

Label	G	AB	R	H	D	T	HR	RBI	BB	SO	SB	Avg	Slg
Act	161	604	123	188	29	1	48	111	86	110	4	.311	.601
Proj	157	582	80	165	34	2	26	98	58	100	2	.284	.483

Most of the projection "misses" have some sort of major injury connection to them, like Mike Trout. The system isn't designed to make a guess that Trout is going to play in only 36 games.

But there are a few players whose offensive craters we just didn't see coming, like Nationals outfielder Victor Robles.

Victor Robles

Label	G	AB	R	H	D	T	HR	RBI	BB	SO	SB	Avg	Slg
Act	107	315	37	64	21	1	2	19	33	85	8	.203	.295
Proj	150	519	76	130	29	3	13	56	36	138	17	.250	.393

If we're going to be wrong on someone by that much, it feels better to be wrong in a Cedric Mullins kind of way.

No one could have predicted this.

Cedric Mullins

Label	G	AB	R	H	D	T	HR	RBI	BB	SO	SB	Avg	Slg
Act	159	602	91	175	37	5	30	59	59	125	30	.291	.518
Proj	129	427	62	101	19	5	11	38	35	101	17	.237	.382

In the end, this is how we roll with projections. Take pride in the ones that our system nailed. Wonder where it went wrong on the ones that the system didn't. And try to find silver linings in the bad misses.

I'm intrigued that our projection system was as skeptical as it was for Madison Bumgarner given his pre-2020 track record. He only once had an ERA above 3.40 with the Giants, but that 3.90 in 2019 and a 6.48 in nine starts in 2020 produced a projection of a 4.53 ERA in 2021 (playing in Arizona probably had something to do with it too).

The system was right on with him across the board.

Madison Bumgarner

Label	G	GS	IP	H	HR	BB	SO	HB	W	L	Pct	Sv	BR/9	ERA
Actual	26	26	146.3	134	24	39	124	11	7	10	.412	0	11.3	4.67
Projected	28	28	150.0	156	27	39	130	9	8	9	.471	0	12.2	4.53

On a more positive note, the system did great at projecting a great, Yankees starter Gerrit Cole. It just missed getting his ERA, baserunners per 9 and strikeouts per 9 exactly right, and as a bonus, it nailed his win-loss record.

Gerrit Cole

Label	G	GS	IP	H	HR	BB	SO	HB	W	L	Pct	Sv	BR/9	ERA
Act	30	30	181.3	151	24	41	243	2	16	8	.667	0	9.6	3.23
Proj	33	33	210.0	163	30	55	277	5	16	8	.667	0	9.6	3.20

Here's one that I'm scoring as a very good projection even though the system missed on his innings pitched by more than 50. Somehow, it divined that Clayton Kershaw was in for a statistical letdown and his highest ERA since his debut season of 2008.

It was right. Scarily right on his ERA and baserunners per 9 innings. This is one that makes me feel good about what we've built.

Clayton Kershaw

Label	G	GS	IP	H	HR	BB	SO	HB	W	L	Pct	Sv	BR/9	ERA
Act	22	22	121.7	103	15	21	144	3	10	8	.556	0	9.4	3.55
Proj	29	29	173.0	149	27	34	177	2	13	6	.684	0	9.6	3.58

As for the misses, there were certainly plenty. Predicting pitching is reaalllllllly hard. The system didn't come close on Joe Musgrove, Marcus Stroman, Frankie Montas or Adam Wainwright, among others.

The system was off on Zack Wheeler, which I find interesting given that from 2018 to 2020, Wheeler had a 3.53 ERA. But the projections thought that Wheeler still had a little 2017 in him. Maybe Wheeler's low strikeout numbers in 2020 scared it?

Anyways, our projections had Wheeler reverting. It didn't see his breakthrough coming.

Zack Wheeler

Label	G	GS	IP	H	HR	BB	SO	HB	W	L	Pct	Sv	BR/9	ERA
Act	32	32	213.3	169	16	46	247	8	14	10	.583	0	9.4	2.78
Proj	30	30	188.0	191	21	54	163	9	11	10	.524	0	12.2	4.14

I do want to bring one up that I think was a case of decent process, bad results, and that would be Casey Mize.

Our system divined that he would have a home run problem in 2021, based on his allowing seven in 28 1/3 innings in 2020. He did.

It overprojected both Mize's strikeouts and his walks. Working just off his strikeouts, walks, and home runs allowed in 2021, Mize had a 4.71 FIP.

Had that been Mize's ERA, our projection would have been pretty good. But a Tigers defense that was among the worst in baseball in 2021 was respectable when Mize was on the mound.

Mize also held opponents to a .162 batting average with runners in scoring position. He basically bulldogged his way to an ERA that was much better than it probably would have been under most circumstances. So it's hard to feel bad about that projection being off.

Meanwhile, the human element is that we can feel good for Mize who goes into this offseason with something good to build on for 2022.

Casey Mize

Label	G	GS	IP	H	HR	BB	SO	HB	W	L	Pct	Sv	BR/9	ERA
Act	30	30	150.3	130	24	41	118	11	7	9	.438	0	10.9	3.71
Proj	31	31	167.0	182	25	58	157	19	7	12	.368	0	14.0	4.80

Again, the good, the bad, the silver linings. This is how I look at projections.

Lastly, you're wondering—How does the SIS projection system do?

We can answer that. I looked at the last three seasons worth of projections against actual results and gave each projection a grade.

"Great" projections like Bryant and Bumgarner scored a 950 or better when using Bill James Similarity Scores. "Good" ones like Kershaw scored 900 or better. "Bad" ones like Mullins scored below 800.

My biggest takeaway from this is that it was tough to really nail a pitcher this year, which isn't surprising given that this season followed one shortened by a pandemic. And boy is it a lot easier to miss on a pitcher than it is on a hitter.

	Great	Great or Good	Bad
2018 Hitters	17%	62%	17%
2019 Hitters	15%	58%	18%
2021 Hitters	19%	58%	17%
2018 Pitchers	16%	49%	28%
2019 Pitchers	12%	49%	29%
2021 Pitchers	9%	47%	27%

Hope this all gives you some things to consider as you study the ones for 2022.

2022 Hitter Projections

Hitter	Team	Age	G	AB	H	2B	3B	HR	R	RBI	RC	RC27	BB	SO	SB	CS	SB%	Avg	OBP	Slg	OPS
Abreu, Jose	CWS	35	154	601	160	34	2	30	85	110	93	5.5	50	150	1	0	1.00	.266	.339	.479	.818
Acuna Jr., Ronald	Atl	24	147	559	158	32	3	39	116	92	118	7.5	80	166	27	8	.77	.283	.383	.560	.943
Adames, Willy	Mil	26	151	546	134	28	3	23	79	70	75	4.7	60	172	6	4	.60	.245	.322	.434	.756
Adams, Riley	Was	26	70	217	42	11	1	9	31	27	23	3.5	28	87	0	0	.00	.194	.319	.378	.697
Adell, Jo	LAA	23	137	506	112	25	2	23	66	76	58	3.8	35	182	8	1	.89	.221	.278	.415	.693
Adrianza, Ehire	Atl	32	86	148	36	8	1	3	22	17	17	4.0	15	35	0	0	.00	.243	.321	.372	.693
Aguilar, Jesus	Mia	32	134	420	110	20	0	21	52	74	65	5.4	46	98	0	0	.00	.262	.339	.460	.799
Ahmed, Nick	Ari	32	133	467	110	27	3	10	56	53	51	3.7	39	109	7	3	.70	.236	.299	.370	.669
Akiyama, Shogo	Cin	34	66	115	25	5	0	0	11	7	9	2.4	12	29	2	2	.50	.217	.302	.261	.563
Alberto, Hanser	KC	29	112	353	99	20	2	6	41	38	42	4.2	9	42	3	2	.60	.280	.306	.399	.705
Albies, Ozzie	Atl	25	158	640	175	41	7	27	102	91	103	5.7	49	131	19	4	.83	.273	.329	.486	.815
Alcantara, Sergio	ChC	25	89	269	62	9	2	5	35	23	30	3.7	37	84	4	1	.80	.230	.326	.335	.660
Alfaro, Jorge	Mia	29	108	333	80	13	1	8	33	40	33	3.4	15	117	6	1	.86	.240	.289	.357	.647
Alford, Anthony	Pit	27	63	130	28	6	1	5	17	15	15	3.8	14	56	4	1	.80	.215	.306	.392	.698
Allen, Nick	Oak	23	65	115	27	5	1	3	14	15	13	3.8	8	32	3	0	1.00	.235	.290	.374	.664
Alonso, Pete	NYM	27	155	574	146	28	2	43	87	108	103	6.2	68	148	2	0	1.00	.254	.349	.535	.883
Altuve, Jose	Hou	32	137	515	147	29	2	21	90	68	86	6.0	53	84	5	2	.71	.285	.358	.472	.830
Alvarez, Yordan	Hou	25	144	547	154	37	1	38	95	117	110	7.3	63	152	2	0	1.00	.282	.363	.561	.924
Amaya, Miguel	ChC	23	80	252	53	12	0	4	32	28	26	3.4	46	81	3	0	1.00	.210	.354	.306	.659
Anderson, Brian	Mia	29	123	423	105	22	2	13	54	57	55	4.5	45	117	5	1	.83	.248	.336	.402	.738
Anderson, Tim	CWS	29	140	579	181	33	3	20	92	63	96	6.2	24	138	16	5	.76	.313	.343	.484	.827
Andrus, Elvis	Oak	33	121	406	107	22	2	6	50	39	47	4.1	27	68	9	3	.75	.264	.316	.372	.688
Andujar, Miguel	NYY	27	50	105	28	6	0	4	13	14	14	4.8	6	19	0	0	.00	.267	.313	.438	.751
Aquino, Aristides	Cin	28	70	142	31	5	1	9	19	20	19	4.5	15	52	1	0	1.00	.218	.297	.458	.755
Arenado, Nolan	StL	31	151	568	158	33	2	35	81	99	103	6.5	56	96	2	1	.67	.278	.346	.528	.874
Arias, Gabriel	Cle	22	134	482	112	25	3	12	54	51	51	3.6	34	141	3	0	1.00	.232	.290	.371	.661
Arozarena, Randy	TB	27	147	550	136	31	3	19	93	69	74	4.6	59	173	17	7	.71	.247	.340	.418	.758
Arraez, Luis	Min	25	128	469	149	26	4	5	66	47	75	6.1	47	52	3	2	.60	.318	.382	.422	.804
Arroyo, Christian	Bos	27	91	330	83	21	1	10	41	45	40	4.2	21	83	2	1	.67	.252	.312	.412	.724
Astudillo, Willians	Min	30	71	178	49	8	0	6	19	21	22	4.4	4	11	0	0	.00	.275	.306	.421	.728
Baddoo, Akil	Det	23	137	466	110	22	9	14	69	65	63	4.6	56	134	21	4	.84	.236	.318	.412	.730
Bader, Harrison	StL	28	134	408	100	20	2	17	59	50	53	4.5	36	116	9	4	.69	.245	.320	.429	.749
Baez, Javier	NYM	29	143	507	121	26	2	26	75	72	64	4.3	28	174	12	4	.75	.239	.289	.452	.741
Barnes, Austin	LAD	32	84	239	52	11	1	7	34	27	26	3.6	29	66	2	1	.67	.218	.315	.360	.675
Barnhart, Tucker	Cin	31	110	331	78	18	1	8	34	41	38	3.9	35	89	0	0	.00	.236	.316	.369	.685
Barrero, Jose	Cin	24	142	528	128	22	2	25	72	80	69	4.5	41	164	12	2	.86	.242	.312	.434	.745
Bart, Joey	SF	25	91	303	66	13	1	9	37	40	29	3.1	19	119	0	0	.00	.218	.280	.356	.636
Beaty, Matt	LAD	29	84	158	42	9	0	4	22	23	20	4.5	13	32	1	1	.50	.266	.345	.399	.743
Bell, Josh	Was	29	145	473	122	25	2	24	69	78	77	5.7	63	105	0	0	.00	.258	.348	.471	.819
Bellinger, Cody	LAD	26	145	518	128	26	3	31	84	83	85	5.7	68	136	9	2	.82	.247	.337	.488	.825
Belt, Brandon	SF	34	132	434	108	25	2	24	68	64	73	5.8	67	127	3	2	.60	.249	.356	.482	.837
Benintendi, Andrew	KC	27	137	469	130	29	3	16	66	70	73	5.5	48	100	8	4	.67	.277	.348	.454	.802
Berti, Jon	Mia	32	95	266	63	10	3	5	41	25	31	3.9	33	73	9	3	.75	.237	.332	.353	.686
Betts, Mookie	LAD	29	146	576	166	39	3	32	114	83	116	7.3	79	102	13	3	.81	.288	.382	.533	.915
Bichette, Bo	Tor	24	159	646	193	39	3	28	108	99	114	6.5	45	144	23	3	.88	.299	.349	.498	.848
Biggio, Cavan	Tor	27	115	379	82	17	2	15	56	55	50	4.4	68	132	6	1	.86	.216	.340	.391	.731
Blackmon, Charlie	Col	35	156	594	178	34	6	24	101	83	106	6.6	54	115	3	2	.60	.300	.368	.498	.866
Bogaerts, Xander	Bos	29	154	585	167	41	2	23	98	92	102	6.3	67	123	6	1	.86	.285	.364	.480	.844
Bohm, Alec	Phi	25	128	397	103	20	1	10	52	51	51	4.5	38	109	4	1	.80	.259	.329	.390	.719
Bote, David	ChC	29	108	276	64	12	1	10	33	37	33	4.0	30	77	1	1	.50	.232	.318	.391	.710
Bradley Jr., Jackie	Mil	32	103	276	58	13	2	7	36	29	27	3.2	27	88	5	2	.71	.210	.294	.348	.642
Bradley, Bobby	Cle	26	120	395	79	17	1	25	51	65	47	3.9	40	163	0	0	.00	.200	.283	.438	.721
Brantley, Michael	Hou	35	141	543	161	35	2	12	78	66	83	5.6	44	70	2	0	1.00	.297	.355	.435	.789
Bregman, Alex	Hou	28	140	504	139	34	2	23	87	83	91	6.5	76	82	2	1	.67	.276	.378	.488	.866
Brinson, Lewis	Mia	28	87	238	52	11	2	7	24	27	23	3.2	15	71	2	1	.67	.218	.273	.370	.643
Brosseau, Mike	TB	28	74	177	40	9	1	7	24	24	21	4.1	17	57	2	0	1.00	.226	.312	.407	.718
Brown, Seth	Oak	29	65	121	27	7	1	6	16	20	15	4.2	9	41	1	0	1.00	.223	.282	.446	.729
Brujan, Vidal	TB	24	125	449	108	28	2	11	66	55	56	4.2	41	94	22	2	.92	.241	.307	.385	.692
Bryant, Kris	SF	30	134	459	121	30	2	25	82	64	76	5.8	60	124	6	2	.75	.264	.363	.475	.838
Burger, Jake	CWS	26	78	242	53	11	2	10	28	31	26	3.6	16	85	0	0	.00	.219	.276	.405	.681
Buxton, Byron	Min	28	113	407	106	28	3	23	68	58	65	5.6	26	117	13	2	.87	.260	.314	.514	.828
Cabrera, Asdrubal	Cin	36	85	246	61	14	1	8	33	34	32	4.5	25	60	1	0	1.00	.248	.322	.411	.733
Cabrera, Miguel	Det	39	112	340	88	14	0	11	36	47	44	4.5	34	85	0	0	.00	.259	.332	.397	.729
Cain, Lorenzo	Mil	36	100	346	92	17	1	8	49	33	46	4.7	34	69	13	3	.81	.266	.337	.390	.727
Calhoun, Kole	Ari	34	130	446	109	22	2	20	67	59	63	4.8	51	116	3	1	.75	.244	.329	.437	.766
Calhoun, Willie	Tex	27	70	182	46	9	1	6	21	22	23	4.4	15	29	0	0	.00	.253	.317	.412	.729
Campusano, Luis	SD	23	78	241	55	13	1	9	24	24	28	3.9	19	71	1	0	1.00	.228	.298	.402	.701
Candelario, Jeimer	Det	28	146	533	137	35	4	17	70	68	77	5.1	63	139	1	1	.50	.257	.342	.433	.776
Canha, Mark	Oak	33	142	469	112	24	2	17	79	60	64	4.6	65	123	7	2	.78	.239	.357	.407	.764
Caratini, Victor	SD	28	105	278	68	13	0	7	30	34	33	4.0	30	71	1	0	1.00	.245	.327	.367	.694
Carlson, Dylan	StL	23	152	550	145	34	5	20	84	72	84	5.4	60	154	3	1	.75	.264	.347	.453	.800
Carpenter, Matt	StL	36	73	141	31	8	1	5	21	17	19	4.5	24	46	1	0	1.00	.220	.345	.397	.742
Casali, Curt	SF	33	77	203	46	9	0	6	21	26	23	3.7	24	64	0	0	.00	.227	.317	.360	.677
Castellanos, Nick	Cin	30	151	575	163	43	3	32	91	92	103	6.4	45	143	2	2	.50	.283	.343	.536	.879
Castro, Harold	Det	28	119	402	108	16	2	5	41	39	43	3.8	17	93	2	1	.67	.269	.302	.356	.657
Castro, Jason	Hou	35	70	191	40	10	0	8	26	22	23	3.9	27	71	0	0	.00	.209	.314	.387	.701
Castro, Willi	Det	25	112	355	92	17	4	10	49	41	45	4.4	22	96	7	2	.78	.259	.313	.414	.727
Cave, Jake	Min	29	70	135	32	7	1	4	18	16	15	3.8	10	48	1	1	.50	.237	.299	.393	.692
Chang, Yu	Cle	26	60	166	36	9	1	6	21	23	18	3.6	13	55	1	0	1.00	.217	.282	.392	.673

2022 Hitter Projections

Hitter	Team	Age	G	AB	H	2B	3B	HR	R	RBI	RC	RC27	BB	SO	SB	CS	SB%	Avg	OBP	Slg	OPS
Chapman, Matt	Oak	29	152	554	121	28	3	29	85	78	74	4.4	71	196	2	2	.50	.218	.314	.437	.751
Chavis, Michael	Pit	26	95	298	69	13	1	15	41	43	35	4.0	19	103	3	2	.60	.232	.291	.433	.724
Chirinos, Robinson	ChC	38	65	192	39	8	1	8	25	26	21	3.6	23	71	0	0	.00	.203	.311	.380	.691
Chisholm Jr., Jazz	Mia	24	139	484	112	19	5	22	71	62	62	4.2	43	162	22	7	.76	.231	.301	.428	.728
Choi, Ji-Man	TB	31	102	287	65	17	1	10	36	42	38	4.4	44	91	0	0	.00	.226	.335	.397	.733
Collins, Zack	CWS	27	73	197	40	10	0	7	25	30	23	3.8	35	77	1	0	1.00	.203	.326	.360	.687
Conforto, Michael	NYM	29	136	464	118	25	1	21	70	70	72	5.4	67	126	2	1	.67	.254	.362	.448	.810
Contreras, William	Atl	24	94	310	74	13	1	15	39	44	41	4.5	29	93	0	0	.00	.239	.312	.432	.744
Contreras, Willson	ChC	30	124	409	98	22	1	20	60	60	57	4.8	48	128	3	3	.50	.240	.338	.445	.783
Cooper, Garrett	Mia	31	115	416	109	22	1	14	53	58	58	4.9	43	122	1	1	.50	.262	.340	.421	.760
Correa, Carlos	Hou	27	148	552	152	33	2	25	88	93	95	6.2	73	126	1	0	1.00	.275	.364	.478	.842
Crawford, Brandon	SF	35	149	520	132	31	3	18	69	77	72	4.8	53	121	7	4	.64	.254	.329	.429	.758
Crawford, J.P.	Sea	27	151	582	144	30	3	9	78	59	67	3.9	66	120	4	3	.57	.247	.330	.356	.686
Cron, C.J.	Col	32	138	460	128	27	1	27	64	87	82	6.4	46	116	1	1	.50	.278	.359	.517	.876
Cronenworth, Jake	SD	28	146	545	149	32	5	18	86	67	83	5.4	55	95	5	2	.71	.273	.349	.450	.798
Cruz, Nelson	TB	41	143	532	134	22	1	30	78	86	81	5.3	57	145	2	0	1.00	.252	.334	.466	.801
Cruz, Oneil	Pit	23	140	480	124	22	3	33	95	94	81	5.9	41	161	16	3	.84	.258	.318	.523	.841
Culberson, Charlie	Tex	33	62	106	24	5	1	2	11	11	10	3.2	7	29	2	1	.67	.226	.281	.349	.630
Dahl, David	Ari	28	66	178	47	11	2	5	23	22	23	4.6	11	47	1	1	.50	.264	.311	.433	.743
Dalbec, Bobby	Bos	27	137	466	106	21	3	27	60	84	63	4.6	44	180	2	0	1.00	.227	.308	.459	.767
d'Arnaud, Travis	Atl	33	103	351	87	18	0	12	42	49	43	4.3	30	90	0	0	.00	.248	.313	.402	.714
Davis, Brennen	ChC	22	80	250	55	15	0	15	42	38	34	4.5	26	102	2	0	1.00	.220	.313	.460	.773
Davis, J.D.	NYM	29	131	434	109	25	1	17	56	59	62	4.9	50	142	2	0	1.00	.251	.339	.431	.770
Daza, Yonathan	Col	28	71	158	44	8	1	2	15	14	19	4.4	10	31	1	0	1.00	.278	.325	.380	.705
De La Cruz, Bryan	Mia	25	147	505	129	23	5	12	63	52	63	4.4	47	137	3	1	.75	.255	.323	.392	.715
DeJong, Paul	StL	28	125	431	100	21	1	21	58	61	55	4.3	40	126	4	2	.67	.232	.310	.432	.742
Devers, Rafael	Bos	25	158	630	174	42	2	36	106	116	110	6.2	59	151	5	4	.56	.276	.344	.521	.865
Diaz, Aledmys	Hou	31	93	290	73	18	1	9	36	38	36	4.3	20	58	0	0	.00	.252	.311	.414	.725
Diaz, Elias	Col	31	106	320	85	17	0	13	40	43	45	5.0	25	60	0	0	.00	.266	.323	.441	.763
Diaz, Lewin	Mia	25	75	226	52	14	1	12	27	33	29	4.3	14	61	0	0	.00	.230	.278	.460	.738
Diaz, Yandy	TB	30	120	398	104	19	1	9	54	45	54	4.7	58	80	1	1	.50	.261	.358	.382	.740
Dickerson, Alex	SF	32	116	309	77	16	2	13	45	44	43	4.8	28	78	1	0	1.00	.249	.324	.440	.764
Dickerson, Corey	Tor	33	112	346	91	21	3	9	40	37	44	4.4	21	73	4	3	.57	.263	.309	.419	.728
Donaldson, Josh	Min	36	136	481	120	26	1	28	79	75	83	6.0	82	128	1	0	1.00	.249	.364	.482	.847
Downs, Jeter	Bos	23	135	459	123	20	1	17	72	68	66	5.0	44	100	7	2	.78	.268	.341	.427	.768
Dozier, Hunter	KC	30	132	426	99	24	4	15	53	50	53	4.1	42	135	4	3	.57	.232	.307	.413	.720
Dubon, Mauricio	SF	27	80	190	50	9	1	5	24	20	24	4.4	14	40	3	1	.75	.263	.320	.400	.720
Duffy, Matt	ChC	31	72	184	49	8	0	3	23	18	22	4.2	17	40	4	1	.80	.266	.338	.359	.697
Duggar, Steven	SF	28	91	223	54	13	2	5	31	24	28	4.2	22	75	7	1	.88	.242	.313	.386	.699
Duran, Jarren	Bos	25	143	515	108	18	5	7	70	40	41	2.6	29	167	15	2	.88	.210	.256	.305	.561
Duvall, Adam	Atl	33	137	456	104	21	2	31	65	87	63	4.7	36	148	3	1	.75	.228	.293	.487	.780
Dyson, Jarrod	Tor	37	69	112	25	4	1	1	15	7	10	3.0	10	24	7	2	.78	.223	.293	.304	.596
Edman, Tommy	StL	27	148	548	152	31	5	13	79	55	77	5.0	37	96	21	4	.84	.277	.330	.423	.753
Engel, Adam	CWS	30	96	269	59	13	2	7	33	25	26	3.2	18	82	10	3	.77	.219	.286	.361	.646
Escobar, Alcides	Was	35	91	328	82	17	1	5	41	30	33	3.5	16	67	3	1	.75	.250	.293	.354	.647
Escobar, Eduardo	Mil	33	136	481	117	24	4	23	63	72	66	4.7	41	110	1	0	1.00	.243	.307	.453	.760
Espinal, Santiago	Tor	27	122	378	107	22	1	6	48	45	52	5.0	35	67	8	2	.80	.283	.347	.394	.741
Estrada, Thairo	SF	26	78	175	47	9	1	6	25	24	24	4.9	12	37	3	1	.75	.269	.326	.434	.761
Evans, Phillip	Pit	29	50	96	23	5	0	2	11	9	11	3.8	10	23	0	0	.00	.240	.318	.354	.672
Farmer, Kyle	Cin	31	134	389	102	21	1	12	44	48	48	4.3	22	84	2	2	.50	.262	.320	.414	.734
Fletcher, David	LAA	28	141	523	145	27	2	3	66	43	60	4.1	34	58	10	3	.77	.277	.324	.354	.678
Flores, Wilmer	SF	30	145	493	136	29	1	22	66	73	78	5.7	42	75	1	0	1.00	.276	.339	.473	.812
Fortes, Nick	Mia	25	46	124	32	5	1	5	15	19	18	5.0	11	28	2	0	1.00	.258	.328	.435	.764
Fowler, Dexter	LAA	36	60	150	35	7	1	5	23	18	20	4.4	22	44	3	1	.75	.233	.339	.393	.732
Fraley, Jake	Sea	27	60	133	32	7	1	6	20	22	21	5.3	21	45	5	1	.83	.241	.353	.444	.796
France, Ty	Sea	27	141	500	138	29	1	19	72	74	74	5.4	40	105	0	0	.00	.276	.356	.452	.808
Franco, Maikel	Atl	29	60	180	44	10	0	7	19	26	22	4.2	13	32	0	0	.00	.244	.299	.417	.716
Franco, Wander	TB	21	152	603	168	36	6	18	106	94	91	5.4	50	83	8	1	.89	.279	.339	.448	.787
Frazier, Adam	SD	30	152	538	145	31	4	7	71	49	66	4.3	46	77	6	5	.55	.270	.336	.381	.717
Frazier, Clint	NYY	27	77	196	43	11	1	7	27	23	23	4.0	24	66	2	1	.67	.219	.314	.393	.707
Freeman, Freddie	Atl	32	161	605	183	38	3	32	112	100	127	7.8	89	121	7	3	.70	.302	.399	.534	.933
Friedl, T.J.	Cin	26	70	150	36	5	1	4	21	12	17	3.9	15	31	3	1	.75	.240	.325	.367	.692
Fuentes, Joshua	Col	29	71	156	35	7	1	4	17	18	14	3.1	7	44	0	0	.00	.224	.262	.359	.621
Gallo, Joey	NYY	28	135	428	87	16	1	32	71	67	67	5.1	83	186	4	1	.80	.203	.339	.470	.809
Galvis, Freddy	Phi	32	103	361	88	17	2	12	43	41	43	4.0	26	84	2	1	.67	.244	.300	.402	.702
Gamel, Ben	Pit	30	101	281	72	16	2	5	39	27	36	4.4	34	83	3	3	.50	.256	.341	.381	.721
Garcia, Adolis	Tex	29	141	507	114	24	3	24	69	75	57	3.8	27	176	10	3	.77	.225	.272	.426	.698
Garcia, Avisail	Mil	31	134	449	116	22	1	22	61	70	64	4.9	36	120	6	4	.60	.258	.326	.459	.785
Garcia, Leury	CWS	31	125	437	113	19	3	7	61	46	49	3.9	31	105	6	2	.75	.259	.315	.364	.679
Garcia, Luis	Was	22	141	473	126	24	2	17	62	50	62	4.7	26	94	2	1	.67	.266	.306	.433	.739
Gardner, Brett	NYY	38	128	365	83	15	3	9	54	36	42	3.9	49	90	4	1	.80	.227	.324	.359	.683
Garver, Mitch	Min	31	83	243	62	15	1	12	36	36	39	5.5	30	81	1	1	.50	.255	.344	.473	.817
Gimenez, Andres	Cle	23	108	286	69	15	2	8	38	31	32	3.8	17	83	9	2	.82	.241	.304	.392	.696
Goldschmidt, Paul	StL	34	161	593	167	32	2	31	96	94	110	6.7	80	147	9	2	.82	.282	.372	.499	.871
Gomes, Yan	Oak	34	115	414	99	20	1	15	50	55	48	3.9	28	103	1	0	1.00	.239	.298	.401	.699
Gonzalez, Erik	Pit	30	59	126	29	6	1	2	12	12	11	3.0	6	32	1	1	.50	.230	.271	.341	.612
Gonzalez, Marwin	Hou	33	98	278	65	14	1	9	32	36	32	3.8	23	74	2	1	.67	.234	.304	.388	.692
Goodrum, Niko	Det	30	107	345	74	16	3	10	44	38	36	3.4	33	124	11	4	.73	.214	.289	.365	.654
Goodwin, Brian	CWS	31	85	251	57	13	1	9	32	30	30	4.0	27	78	3	1	.75	.227	.305	.394	.699
Gordon, Nick	Min	26	81	235	56	12	2	4	27	24	25	3.5	15	66	9	2	.82	.238	.292	.357	.650
Gorman, Nolan	StL	22	138	510	124	19	1	24	64	71	63	4.2	32	144	4	1	.80	.243	.289	.425	.715

2022 Hitter Projections

Hitter	Team	Age	G	AB	H	2B	3B	HR	R	RBI	RC	RC27	BB	SO	SB	CS	SB%	Avg	OBP	Slg	OPS
Gosselin, Phil	LAA	33	93	218	53	10	1	4	26	26	23	3.6	18	54	2	1	.67	.243	.304	.353	.657
Grandal, Yasmani	CWS	33	126	442	106	20	1	30	70	76	81	6.2	92	134	1	1	.50	.240	.375	.493	.869
Greene, Riley	Det	21	139	507	125	18	4	27	89	91	74	5.0	53	183	8	2	.80	.247	.325	.458	.783
Gregorius, Didi	Phi	32	133	485	122	23	2	19	63	74	61	4.4	33	81	4	2	.67	.252	.309	.425	.733
Grichuk, Randal	Tor	30	146	523	128	29	2	26	67	78	68	4.5	31	132	1	1	.50	.245	.292	.457	.749
Grisham, Trent	SD	25	128	371	91	19	3	14	53	52	54	4.9	51	101	10	3	.77	.245	.344	.426	.770
Grossman, Robbie	Det	32	142	458	111	24	3	15	66	53	66	4.9	75	120	13	4	.76	.242	.355	.406	.761
Guerrero Jr., Vladimir	Tor	23	155	573	169	32	2	40	98	108	122	7.8	74	103	3	1	.75	.295	.381	.567	.949
Guillorme, Luis	NYM	27	94	214	56	9	0	2	24	17	25	4.1	30	41	1	1	.50	.262	.355	.332	.687
Gurriel Jr., Lourdes	Tor	28	146	542	150	32	2	25	70	91	83	5.4	33	121	2	2	.50	.277	.323	.482	.805
Gurriel, Yuli	Hou	38	134	460	126	27	1	13	64	66	63	4.9	36	62	1	1	.50	.274	.332	.422	.754
Gutierrez, Kelvin	Bal	27	75	213	48	7	2	4	20	22	20	3.2	16	62	1	0	1.00	.225	.286	.333	.619
Guzman, Ronald	Tex	27	85	245	57	12	1	9	30	30	29	4.0	23	74	1	1	.50	.233	.306	.400	.706
Haase, Eric	Det	29	105	357	76	13	2	19	46	55	42	3.9	31	139	2	0	1.00	.213	.281	.420	.701
Hamilton, Billy	CWS	31	78	190	42	7	2	2	28	11	18	3.0	15	58	14	3	.82	.221	.278	.311	.589
Hampson, Garrett	Col	27	133	396	99	19	6	11	55	51	51	4.4	33	109	14	4	.78	.250	.311	.412	.723
Haniger, Mitch	Sea	31	148	569	142	28	2	31	90	85	85	5.2	57	159	2	1	.67	.250	.329	.469	.798
Happ, Ian	ChC	27	144	532	120	25	2	26	76	78	73	4.6	74	182	8	3	.73	.226	.326	.427	.752
Harper, Bryce	Phi	29	154	553	153	36	2	37	105	102	123	7.9	114	153	13	3	.81	.277	.405	.550	.954
Harrison, Josh	Oak	34	117	367	96	20	2	7	41	40	43	4.1	22	62	5	2	.71	.262	.323	.384	.707
Hayes, Ke'Bryan	Pit	25	150	564	145	35	4	13	79	63	75	4.6	55	142	12	2	.86	.257	.327	.402	.730
Hays, Austin	Bal	26	135	479	121	25	2	23	70	69	64	4.6	28	113	4	2	.67	.253	.305	.457	.762
Hedges, Austin	Cle	29	91	179	38	7	0	7	19	22	17	3.2	11	55	1	0	1.00	.212	.262	.369	.630
Heim, Jonah	Tex	27	88	265	62	14	0	10	26	36	30	3.9	20	56	2	1	.67	.234	.290	.400	.690
Heredia, Guillermo	Atl	31	91	207	48	12	0	4	29	18	21	3.5	20	52	1	1	.50	.232	.318	.348	.665
Hernandez, Cesar	CWS	32	140	527	135	23	3	16	73	53	70	4.7	59	120	3	1	.75	.256	.337	.402	.739
Hernandez, Kike	Bos	30	135	435	110	28	2	17	68	58	64	5.1	50	99	1	0	1.00	.253	.338	.444	.782
Hernandez, Teoscar	Tor	29	145	536	141	28	2	29	80	90	83	5.4	43	159	10	4	.71	.263	.324	.485	.809
Hernandez, Yadiel	Was	34	84	178	47	7	0	7	23	24	25	5.0	18	47	1	0	1.00	.264	.335	.421	.756
Hernandez, Yonny	Tex	24	85	281	65	10	1	1	40	17	30	3.6	49	68	16	1	.94	.231	.361	.285	.646
Herrera, Odubel	Phi	30	120	420	110	23	3	13	54	49	56	4.6	31	83	5	2	.71	.262	.320	.424	.744
Heyward, Jason	ChC	32	130	421	103	19	3	12	55	49	53	4.3	47	98	5	2	.71	.245	.326	.390	.716
Hicks, Aaron	NYY	32	90	267	62	13	1	12	43	38	39	4.9	44	69	3	1	.75	.232	.345	.423	.768
Higashioka, Kyle	NYY	32	68	198	44	10	0	10	22	30	24	4.0	16	59	0	0	.00	.222	.284	.424	.708
Hill, Derek	Det	26	49	141	32	5	1	3	21	14	14	3.2	10	50	4	1	.80	.227	.288	.340	.628
Hilliard, Sam	Col	28	85	214	43	8	2	11	28	28	24	3.7	21	88	5	1	.83	.201	.275	.411	.687
Hiura, Keston	Mil	25	65	172	38	9	1	8	22	22	21	4.0	16	70	2	1	.67	.221	.306	.424	.730
Hoerner, Nico	ChC	25	135	457	121	26	2	4	59	47	53	4.1	42	83	10	5	.67	.265	.339	.357	.695
Holt, Brock	Tex	34	65	132	32	7	0	2	16	14	14	3.7	14	29	2	1	.67	.242	.324	.341	.665
Hoskins, Rhys	Phi	29	143	530	127	32	2	34	86	95	90	5.8	82	150	4	2	.67	.240	.351	.500	.851
Hosmer, Eric	SD	32	146	500	128	24	1	15	60	64	63	4.4	46	108	4	3	.57	.256	.322	.398	.720
Ibanez, Andy	Tex	29	105	348	92	19	1	11	43	37	46	4.7	26	65	1	0	1.00	.264	.321	.420	.740
Iglesias, Jose	Bos	32	128	451	125	29	2	8	55	51	56	4.5	21	67	4	2	.67	.277	.318	.404	.722
India, Jonathan	Cin	25	150	533	142	31	1	25	99	73	90	6.0	75	142	10	2	.83	.266	.381	.469	.850
Isbel, Kyle	KC	25	122	409	94	18	3	12	58	47	47	3.8	38	114	13	2	.87	.230	.306	.377	.683
Jackson, Alex	Mia	26	60	157	31	7	0	9	19	25	17	3.5	13	67	0	0	.00	.197	.284	.414	.698
Jankowski, Travis	Phi	31	85	146	34	5	1	1	22	9	15	3.4	20	36	6	2	.75	.233	.329	.301	.631
Jansen, Danny	Tor	27	78	218	53	11	0	11	31	31	31	4.9	25	49	0	0	.00	.243	.335	.445	.780
Jeffers, Ryan	Min	25	81	211	47	8	0	13	24	28	27	4.2	18	80	0	0	.00	.223	.296	.445	.742
Jimenez, Eloy	CWS	25	142	547	148	29	1	30	70	90	85	5.6	37	152	0	0	.00	.271	.320	.492	.812
Joe, Connor	Col	29	95	280	73	16	1	13	39	43	45	5.7	39	75	1	1	.50	.261	.361	.464	.825
Jones, Nolan	Cle	24	138	480	97	26	2	16	70	57	53	3.6	67	177	8	2	.80	.202	.307	.365	.672
Judge, Aaron	NYY	30	134	508	140	24	1	34	91	89	100	7.0	79	162	5	2	.71	.276	.377	.528	.905
Jung, Josh	Tex	24	135	499	128	29	3	32	74	99	81	5.7	41	151	2	0	1.00	.257	.323	.519	.842
Kelenic, Jarred	Sea	24	145	516	124	27	2	28	71	80	75	4.9	55	143	11	4	.73	.240	.318	.463	.781
Kelly, Carson	Ari	27	114	351	85	17	0	15	44	48	48	4.7	45	85	0	0	.00	.242	.337	.419	.755
Kemp, Tony	Oak	30	124	344	93	17	3	6	50	35	47	4.8	43	56	7	3	.70	.270	.360	.390	.749
Kepler, Max	Min	29	130	443	106	25	3	21	67	62	65	5.0	54	96	7	2	.78	.239	.330	.451	.781
Kieboom, Carter	Was	24	133	479	112	20	1	15	65	58	58	4.1	62	135	2	1	.67	.234	.338	.374	.711
Kiermaier, Kevin	TB	32	129	386	89	17	5	7	54	40	41	3.5	35	106	10	4	.71	.231	.303	.355	.658
Kiner-Falefa, Isiah	Tex	27	148	548	145	24	3	7	62	46	61	3.9	34	88	15	5	.75	.265	.319	.358	.677
Kirilloff, Alex	Min	24	125	457	132	23	2	20	56	70	74	5.9	32	110	3	1	.75	.289	.341	.479	.820
Kirk, Alejandro	Tor	23	84	259	71	15	0	11	31	45	41	5.6	27	44	0	0	.00	.274	.349	.459	.809
Knapp, Andrew	Phi	30	70	152	30	6	1	3	16	13	13	2.8	18	59	0	0	.00	.197	.291	.309	.600
Knizner, Andrew	StL	27	66	170	41	8	0	3	20	16	18	3.6	16	39	0	0	.00	.241	.321	.341	.662
La Stella, Tommy	SF	33	95	332	88	17	1	9	46	39	45	4.8	34	42	0	0	.00	.265	.339	.404	.742
Lagares, Juan	LAA	33	66	120	29	7	1	2	16	12	12	3.4	6	30	1	1	.50	.242	.283	.367	.650
Laureano, Ramon	Oak	27	128	450	113	26	3	19	66	58	64	4.9	41	134	12	4	.75	.251	.330	.449	.779
Lee, Khalil	NYM	24	80	204	44	10	1	6	31	21	24	3.9	33	80	4	1	.80	.216	.350	.363	.712
LeMahieu, DJ	NYY	33	151	605	174	30	2	13	94	67	87	5.2	62	96	4	2	.67	.288	.358	.408	.766
Leon, Sandy	Mia	33	75	184	36	7	0	4	17	17	14	2.5	15	57	0	0	.00	.196	.264	.299	.563
Lewis, Kyle	Sea	26	114	421	106	21	1	19	61	69	63	5.2	54	144	6	1	.86	.252	.340	.442	.781
Lewis, Royce	Min	23	102	361	83	25	1	9	53	43	40	3.7	29	103	8	2	.80	.230	.291	.380	.670
Lindor, Francisco	NYM	28	149	586	151	33	3	26	91	74	89	5.3	64	113	13	4	.76	.258	.337	.457	.794
Locastro, Tim	NYY	29	78	156	37	8	1	3	24	11	16	3.5	10	35	5	1	.83	.237	.328	.359	.687
Long Jr., Shed	Sea	26	46	97	22	4	1	3	12	11	11	3.8	9	31	1	0	1.00	.227	.292	.381	.674
Longoria, Evan	SF	36	115	417	107	24	2	18	55	61	59	5.0	36	101	1	1	.50	.257	.322	.453	.775
Lopez, Nicky	KC	27	149	492	132	20	4	3	65	41	58	4.2	48	77	15	3	.83	.268	.338	.343	.682
Lowe, Brandon	TB	27	148	542	135	30	2	37	90	102	93	5.9	66	174	6	1	.86	.249	.340	.517	.857
Lowe, Josh	TB	24	110	384	94	22	2	17	58	59	58	5.2	47	133	16	2	.89	.245	.329	.445	.774
Lowe, Nathaniel	Tex	26	148	518	134	26	2	20	76	76	80	5.4	76	151	4	1	.80	.259	.357	.432	.789

2022 Hitter Projections

Hitter	Team	Age	G	AB	H	2B	3B	HR	R	RBI	RC	RC27	BB	SO	SB	CS	SB%	Avg	OBP	Slg	OPS
Lowrie, Jed	Oak	38	98	246	60	14	1	7	30	32	31	4.3	27	58	0	0	.00	.244	.321	.394	.715
Luplow, Jordan	TB	28	87	241	53	14	1	12	34	32	33	4.5	34	73	2	2	.50	.220	.324	.436	.759
Lux, Gavin	LAD	24	127	440	120	22	4	15	71	60	69	5.6	52	116	5	1	.83	.273	.352	.443	.795
Machado, Manny	SD	29	159	601	165	33	2	33	90	100	104	6.2	65	114	10	3	.77	.275	.348	.501	.849
Madrigal, Nick	ChC	25	133	485	144	24	5	5	72	51	66	5.0	31	39	6	2	.75	.297	.348	.398	.746
Maldonado, Martin	Hou	35	111	310	61	12	1	9	35	31	28	2.9	32	102	0	0	.00	.197	.284	.329	.614
Mancini, Trey	Bal	30	140	530	139	29	2	23	74	69	78	5.2	47	139	0	0	.00	.262	.330	.455	.785
Margot, Manuel	TB	27	115	313	77	16	3	7	39	33	37	3.9	27	59	10	5	.67	.246	.308	.383	.691
Marisnick, Jake	SD	31	97	221	48	12	1	7	33	26	22	3.3	15	80	4	2	.67	.217	.285	.376	.661
Marsh, Brandon	LAA	24	130	483	112	25	4	8	64	45	54	3.8	53	176	12	1	.92	.232	.312	.350	.662
Marte, Ketel	Ari	28	135	530	154	36	6	18	76	66	89	6.2	47	91	4	1	.80	.291	.353	.483	.836
Marte, Starling	Oak	33	147	574	159	32	4	16	93	67	83	5.1	41	119	34	8	.81	.277	.342	.430	.773
Martinez, J.D.	Bos	34	133	468	131	32	2	24	75	82	84	6.5	50	127	1	0	1.00	.280	.353	.511	.864
Mayfield, Jack	LAA	31	66	134	31	7	0	5	17	18	15	3.8	9	34	2	0	1.00	.231	.285	.396	.680
McCann, James	NYM	32	116	377	85	15	1	11	39	45	38	3.4	30	117	1	1	.50	.225	.290	.358	.648
McCormick, Chas	Hou	27	87	259	62	9	2	10	39	40	34	4.4	29	81	4	1	.80	.239	.325	.405	.731
McCutchen, Andrew	Phi	35	135	461	110	23	1	22	72	66	68	5.0	69	122	5	2	.71	.239	.343	.436	.779
McGuire, Reese	Tor	27	70	162	37	8	1	3	17	15	16	3.4	14	37	0	0	.00	.228	.298	.346	.643
McKinney, Billy	LAD	27	78	176	39	9	2	6	21	19	21	3.9	18	52	1	0	1.00	.222	.297	.398	.695
McKinstry, Zach	LAD	27	51	99	24	5	1	4	14	15	13	4.6	9	28	1	0	1.00	.242	.312	.434	.746
McMahon, Ryan	Col	27	145	486	123	28	1	24	67	77	74	5.2	53	146	5	2	.71	.253	.330	.463	.793
McNeil, Jeff	NYM	30	140	497	139	30	2	14	70	59	71	5.2	39	79	4	2	.67	.280	.348	.433	.781
Meadows, Austin	TB	27	118	388	95	23	3	19	58	65	57	5.0	41	96	4	2	.67	.245	.323	.466	.790
Mejia, Francisco	TB	26	81	211	51	12	1	6	25	25	24	3.9	14	46	0	0	.00	.242	.304	.393	.698
Mendick, Danny	CWS	28	77	184	42	8	0	4	20	19	18	3.4	18	46	2	1	.67	.228	.304	.337	.641
Mercado, Oscar	Cle	27	65	143	34	7	1	4	20	14	17	4.0	13	33	5	1	.83	.238	.310	.385	.695
Mercedes, Yermin	CWS	29	62	200	51	8	1	8	23	30	26	4.6	15	42	1	0	1.00	.255	.313	.425	.738
Mercer, Jordy	Was	35	64	161	39	9	1	4	18	16	19	3.9	13	38	0	0	.00	.242	.303	.385	.688
Merrifield, Whit	KC	33	148	606	174	39	4	13	86	66	88	5.2	40	103	28	7	.80	.287	.336	.429	.765
Meyers, Jake	Hou	26	123	394	89	15	1	14	53	55	43	3.6	33	131	5	1	.83	.226	.300	.376	.676
Miller, Brad	Phi	32	96	211	48	9	2	12	31	32	31	4.9	28	70	2	1	.67	.227	.321	.460	.781
Molina, Yadier	StL	39	120	429	112	21	0	12	44	57	51	4.1	24	76	2	1	.67	.261	.309	.394	.703
Moncada, Yoan	CWS	27	143	516	131	28	4	17	75	65	75	5.0	71	166	4	2	.67	.254	.351	.422	.773
Mondesi, Adalberto	KC	26	120	440	109	21	7	17	61	57	59	4.5	22	145	42	7	.86	.248	.287	.443	.730
Moore, Dylan	Sea	29	114	307	63	15	2	11	39	36	33	3.4	32	98	15	5	.75	.205	.295	.375	.669
Moran, Colin	Pit	29	116	348	87	17	1	11	38	48	44	4.4	34	95	1	1	.50	.250	.322	.399	.722
Moreland, Mitch	Oak	36	85	235	53	12	1	10	30	34	29	4.1	23	61	0	0	.00	.226	.300	.413	.713
Mountcastle, Ryan	Bal	25	146	513	135	26	2	30	70	84	79	5.4	35	152	3	2	.60	.263	.315	.497	.812
Moustakas, Mike	Cin	33	105	326	80	19	0	18	42	49	47	5.0	30	71	1	0	1.00	.245	.317	.469	.786
Mullins II, Cedric	Bal	27	156	586	152	30	6	24	86	57	88	5.2	54	130	24	5	.83	.259	.328	.454	.782
Muncy, Max	LAD	31	140	460	114	21	1	32	83	78	83	6.2	79	125	2	1	.67	.248	.367	.507	.874
Murphy, Sean	Oak	27	119	399	88	24	1	17	55	57	49	4.1	45	117	0	0	.00	.221	.315	.414	.729
Murphy, Tom	Sea	31	65	208	41	9	1	9	24	26	21	3.3	21	77	0	0	.00	.197	.277	.380	.657
Myers, Wil	SD	31	151	494	120	29	2	22	68	70	70	4.8	57	160	9	4	.69	.243	.324	.443	.767
Naquin, Tyler	Cin	31	120	372	98	20	2	16	47	55	53	5.0	28	102	3	2	.60	.263	.322	.457	.779
Narvaez, Omar	Mil	30	125	395	107	20	0	11	49	44	56	5.0	46	90	0	0	.00	.271	.354	.405	.759
Naylor, Josh	Cle	25	131	458	121	26	1	15	59	56	63	4.8	40	91	2	1	.67	.264	.327	.424	.751
Newman, Kevin	Pit	28	120	383	102	19	2	5	43	33	43	4.0	24	43	5	2	.71	.266	.315	.366	.680
Nido, Tomas	NYM	28	63	156	35	7	0	3	15	17	13	2.9	7	41	1	0	1.00	.224	.262	.327	.589
Nimmo, Brandon	NYM	29	129	456	117	23	4	12	72	46	67	5.1	77	119	5	3	.63	.257	.377	.404	.780
Nola, Austin	SD	32	101	348	90	19	1	8	39	44	44	4.4	34	68	1	1	.50	.259	.337	.388	.725
Nootbaar, Lars	StL	24	65	123	31	3	1	5	17	15	17	4.8	16	32	2	1	.67	.252	.343	.415	.757
Nunez, Dom	Col	27	70	177	34	8	1	8	22	24	20	3.6	25	69	0	0	.00	.192	.296	.384	.680
Odor, Rougned	NYY	28	103	314	69	14	1	16	42	43	37	3.9	25	97	1	1	.50	.220	.290	.424	.713
O'Hearn, Ryan	KC	28	76	167	37	8	1	8	18	24	21	4.2	17	52	1	0	1.00	.222	.297	.425	.722
Ohtani, Shohei	LAA	27	144	504	125	26	5	40	86	94	99	6.6	79	171	20	7	.74	.248	.353	.558	.911
Olivares, Edward	KC	26	120	397	101	17	2	17	56	50	54	4.7	30	90	11	2	.85	.254	.320	.436	.755
Olson, Matt	Oak	28	155	555	139	29	1	36	86	100	95	5.9	78	139	3	1	.75	.250	.351	.501	.852
O'Neill, Tyler	StL	27	140	488	120	22	2	31	78	82	74	5.2	42	174	11	3	.79	.246	.316	.490	.806
Ortega, Rafael	ChC	31	105	319	78	16	3	9	43	31	40	4.3	32	73	9	3	.75	.245	.315	.398	.713
Ozuna, Marcell	Atl	31	98	315	86	15	1	16	46	55	52	5.9	34	76	2	1	.67	.273	.346	.479	.825
Pache, Cristian	Atl	23	129	438	99	25	2	14	54	53	48	3.7	32	155	5	1	.83	.226	.282	.388	.670
Park, Hoy	Pit	26	45	153	38	7	1	4	24	18	22	4.8	27	47	3	1	.75	.248	.368	.386	.754
Pederson, Joc	Atl	30	116	313	74	16	1	17	49	46	44	4.8	34	85	1	1	.50	.236	.325	.457	.782
Peralta, David	Ari	34	138	472	126	27	5	12	58	61	65	4.9	41	98	2	1	.67	.267	.331	.422	.752
Peraza, Jose	NYM	28	87	213	54	10	1	4	24	19	23	3.7	11	34	3	1	.75	.254	.303	.366	.669
Peraza, Oswald	NYY	22	142	511	130	1	0	17	67	35	57	3.9	35	119	21	3	.88	.254	.302	.356	.658
Perdomo, Geraldo	Ari	22	140	448	93	10	4	7	61	44	40	2.9	58	144	4	1	.80	.208	.308	.295	.603
Perez, Michael	Pit	29	56	97	20	5	0	3	9	12	9	3.1	9	30	0	0	.00	.206	.280	.351	.631
Perez, Roberto	Cle	33	102	246	48	9	0	9	24	32	24	3.1	30	89	1	0	1.00	.195	.288	.341	.629
Perez, Salvador	KC	32	139	518	139	26	0	34	66	90	80	5.5	22	137	1	0	1.00	.268	.311	.515	.826
Peterson, Jace	Mil	32	110	347	78	17	3	9	46	42	42	4.1	50	96	10	2	.83	.225	.328	.369	.696
Pham, Tommy	SD	34	134	487	119	23	2	16	76	56	67	4.7	73	133	13	5	.72	.244	.349	.398	.747
Phillips, Brett	TB	28	105	228	41	7	3	8	32	27	22	3.1	30	100	10	2	.83	.180	.278	.342	.620
Pillar, Kevin	NYM	33	112	330	80	19	2	12	41	39	38	3.9	14	70	4	2	.67	.242	.286	.421	.707
Pina, Manny	Mil	35	75	179	43	8	0	9	21	25	24	4.5	16	43	0	0	.00	.240	.317	.436	.752
Pinder, Chad	Oak	30	86	210	50	12	1	7	28	26	24	3.9	15	62	1	1	.50	.238	.298	.405	.703
Piscotty, Stephen	Oak	31	75	189	46	11	0	7	23	25	24	4.4	17	50	1	0	1.00	.243	.316	.413	.728
Plawecki, Kevin	Bos	31	68	167	43	9	0	4	17	21	20	4.2	14	31	0	0	.00	.257	.330	.383	.713
Polanco, Gregory	Tor	30	81	206	48	11	1	9	24	27	27	4.4	19	62	7	1	.88	.233	.301	.427	.728
Polanco, Jorge	Min	28	150	568	153	35	4	26	81	84	88	5.5	47	112	9	5	.64	.269	.330	.482	.812

596

2022 Hitter Projections

Hitter	Team	Age	G	AB	H	2B	3B	HR	R	RBI	RC	RC27	BB	SO	SB	CS	SB%	Avg	OBP	Slg	OPS
Pollock, A.J.	LAD	34	132	484	135	30	2	29	71	74	85	6.3	37	107	8	2	.80	.279	.339	.529	.868
Posey, Buster	SF	35	111	402	111	23	0	12	55	50	60	5.4	48	81	0	0	.00	.276	.358	.423	.781
Profar, Jurickson	SD	29	117	313	74	16	1	7	42	34	36	3.9	37	57	7	2	.78	.236	.329	.361	.690
Pujols, Albert	LAD	42	81	220	56	8	0	11	22	36	29	4.6	14	36	1	0	1.00	.255	.305	.441	.746
Raleigh, Cal	Sea	25	100	333	80	28	1	12	36	44	42	4.3	22	92	2	0	1.00	.240	.295	.438	.734
Ramirez, Harold	Cle	27	102	309	85	18	1	7	35	37	39	4.5	16	61	3	1	.75	.275	.321	.408	.729
Ramirez, Jose	Cle	29	155	584	164	42	4	35	104	102	118	7.2	76	93	24	5	.83	.281	.369	.546	.916
Ramos, Heliot	SF	22	132	461	101	22	3	19	60	61	52	3.7	36	172	7	2	.78	.219	.281	.403	.685
Ramos, Wilson	Cle	34	55	176	46	8	0	7	18	27	23	4.6	12	34	0	0	.00	.261	.312	.426	.738
Realmuto, J.T.	Phi	31	138	516	133	30	3	18	77	73	71	4.8	45	133	10	3	.77	.258	.329	.432	.761
Rendon, Anthony	LAA	32	127	444	127	32	2	20	72	79	84	6.9	64	81	1	0	1.00	.286	.383	.502	.886
Renfroe, Hunter	Bos	30	141	486	121	29	1	28	74	82	72	5.1	40	134	2	1	.67	.249	.310	.486	.796
Rengifo, Luis	LAA	25	66	173	41	7	1	5	24	18	20	3.9	16	39	4	1	.80	.237	.309	.376	.685
Reyes, Franmil	Cle	26	141	490	122	22	1	35	69	91	80	5.7	51	166	3	1	.75	.249	.322	.512	.835
Reyes, Victor	Det	27	129	436	119	23	5	9	57	46	56	4.6	22	105	12	2	.86	.273	.311	.411	.721
Reynolds, Bryan	Pit	27	158	553	159	34	5	23	88	83	100	6.6	70	131	4	2	.67	.288	.375	.492	.866
Riley, Austin	Atl	25	158	595	163	33	1	35	90	107	101	6.1	52	177	0	0	.00	.274	.342	.509	.852
Rizzo, Anthony	NYY	32	139	463	121	24	2	22	68	71	74	5.6	58	84	4	2	.67	.261	.368	.464	.832
Robert, Luis	CWS	24	147	559	159	35	3	29	91	86	97	6.3	38	151	15	1	.94	.284	.341	.513	.854
Robles, Victor	Was	25	111	321	77	20	2	7	44	30	37	3.9	28	89	9	4	.69	.240	.328	.380	.708
Rodgers, Brendan	Col	25	148	560	152	31	2	21	67	74	78	5.0	32	131	1	0	1.00	.271	.322	.446	.769
Rodriguez, Julio	Sea	21	140	502	137	25	0	26	89	87	87	6.1	64	126	16	3	.84	.273	.362	.478	.840
Rogers, Jake	Det	27	51	125	24	5	1	6	18	18	14	3.5	14	52	1	0	1.00	.192	.284	.392	.676
Rojas, Josh	Ari	28	135	471	119	29	3	14	70	54	66	4.8	59	130	10	4	.71	.253	.337	.416	.753
Rojas, Miguel	Mia	33	139	510	134	28	2	9	62	53	61	4.2	38	77	10	4	.71	.263	.321	.378	.700
Rooker, Brent	Min	27	53	116	26	6	0	6	15	16	15	4.2	11	46	0	0	.00	.224	.313	.431	.744
Rosario, Amed	Cle	26	145	531	147	26	5	11	72	58	68	4.6	29	117	12	4	.75	.277	.318	.407	.725
Rosario, Eddie	Atl	30	130	454	121	25	2	21	64	73	66	5.1	28	80	8	3	.73	.267	.311	.469	.780
Ruf, Darin	SF	35	111	279	69	14	1	14	40	43	44	5.4	40	91	2	0	1.00	.247	.348	.455	.803
Ruiz, Keibert	Was	23	93	316	83	15	0	15	37	46	46	5.1	26	41	0	0	.00	.263	.325	.453	.777
Ruiz, Rio	Col	28	67	141	33	7	1	4	16	18	16	3.9	13	36	1	0	1.00	.234	.303	.383	.686
Rutschman, Adley	Bal	24	122	450	118	23	2	25	73	73	77	6.0	59	114	2	0	1.00	.262	.355	.489	.844
Sanchez, Gary	NYY	29	120	387	88	16	1	25	56	63	56	4.9	46	122	0	0	.00	.227	.319	.468	.787
Sanchez, Jesus	Mia	24	143	507	120	21	2	25	58	80	66	4.4	47	165	1	1	.50	.237	.309	.434	.743
Sano, Miguel	Min	29	131	457	102	23	1	30	70	77	67	4.9	58	186	1	1	.50	.223	.313	.475	.788
Santana, Carlos	KC	36	143	485	122	22	1	20	72	64	74	5.3	80	91	2	0	1.00	.252	.361	.425	.786
Santana, Danny	Bos	31	53	133	33	7	1	7	20	19	18	4.7	9	40	4	2	.67	.248	.301	.474	.774
Santander, Anthony	Bal	27	120	422	107	26	2	21	55	60	59	4.8	25	101	1	1	.50	.254	.302	.474	.775
Schoop, Jonathan	Det	30	136	482	130	24	1	19	66	66	66	4.8	26	111	1	0	1.00	.270	.317	.442	.758
Schwarber, Kyle	Bos	29	142	482	118	24	1	33	81	81	84	6.0	76	154	2	2	.50	.245	.355	.504	.859
Schwindel, Frank	ChC	30	140	545	138	31	1	24	66	81	70	4.5	28	115	2	1	.67	.253	.295	.446	.740
Seager, Corey	LAD	28	135	521	152	37	2	25	84	82	98	6.9	60	104	2	1	.67	.292	.370	.514	.885
Seager, Kyle	Sea	34	146	502	117	26	1	25	64	78	67	4.5	51	125	3	1	.75	.233	.311	.438	.750
Segura, Jean	Phi	32	148	570	161	31	3	14	83	61	79	5.0	41	91	9	4	.69	.282	.339	.421	.760
Semien, Marcus	Tor	31	154	594	151	34	2	30	92	80	91	5.3	62	130	11	3	.79	.254	.327	.470	.796
Senzel, Nick	Cin	26	80	213	58	12	2	6	31	23	30	5.0	20	45	4	3	.57	.272	.338	.432	.770
Severino, Pedro	Bal	28	104	356	85	16	1	12	33	42	42	4.0	31	96	1	0	1.00	.239	.303	.390	.694
Shaw, Travis	Bos	32	86	220	51	12	0	10	27	34	29	4.5	27	65	0	0	.00	.232	.321	.423	.744
Sheets, Gavin	CWS	26	115	404	101	19	0	20	50	63	57	4.9	39	108	1	0	1.00	.250	.319	.446	.765
Sierra, Magneuris	Mia	26	115	209	50	8	2	1	26	12	19	3.1	13	49	9	2	.82	.239	.287	.311	.598
Simmons, Andrelton	Min	32	114	373	94	18	1	4	42	37	39	3.6	28	51	2	0	1.00	.252	.309	.338	.647
Siri, Jose	Hou	26	131	474	101	14	5	21	62	63	51	3.5	35	184	19	4	.83	.213	.274	.397	.671
Slater, Austin	SF	29	127	377	96	21	2	14	51	49	55	5.1	43	116	15	3	.83	.255	.342	.432	.774
Smith, Dominic	NYM	27	128	370	92	21	1	11	43	50	45	4.2	29	94	1	1	.50	.249	.314	.400	.714
Smith, Pavin	Ari	26	139	484	129	29	4	14	68	59	69	5.1	47	101	1	0	1.00	.267	.335	.430	.765
Smith, Will	LAD	27	131	419	105	21	1	28	69	81	73	6.0	58	110	2	0	1.00	.251	.360	.506	.866
Solak, Nick	Tex	27	130	448	115	20	1	14	62	54	57	4.4	40	110	6	2	.75	.257	.333	.400	.732
Solano, Donovan	SF	34	105	360	100	22	1	7	40	41	46	4.6	22	74	1	0	1.00	.278	.330	.403	.733
Soler, Jorge	Atl	30	140	474	112	25	0	28	67	71	72	5.2	63	147	1	0	1.00	.236	.335	.466	.801
Sosa, Edmundo	StL	26	113	348	88	15	3	9	45	38	39	3.9	18	84	3	2	.60	.253	.318	.391	.708
Soto, Juan	Was	23	150	536	164	32	2	34	115	112	136	9.4	139	106	10	5	.67	.306	.451	.563	1.014
Springer, George	Tor	32	136	527	140	26	2	32	93	80	91	6.0	63	128	6	4	.60	.266	.353	.505	.858
Stallings, Jacob	Pit	32	121	409	101	24	1	10	47	54	50	4.2	43	99	0	0	.00	.247	.325	.384	.708
Stanton, Giancarlo	NYY	32	122	443	118	21	0	29	65	81	80	6.4	58	142	1	0	1.00	.266	.356	.510	.867
Stassi, Max	LAA	31	110	355	77	14	1	14	47	43	40	3.7	38	125	0	0	.00	.217	.307	.380	.687
Stephenson, Tyler	Cin	25	133	375	102	21	0	11	59	53	54	5.2	44	85	0	0	.00	.272	.359	.416	.775
Stevenson, Andrew	Was	28	80	154	38	7	1	3	20	16	17	3.7	12	47	2	1	.67	.247	.310	.364	.673
Stewart, D.J.	Bal	28	95	249	54	12	1	11	36	35	32	4.3	36	78	1	0	1.00	.217	.328	.406	.733
Story, Trevor	Col	29	154	604	169	40	6	36	100	95	114	6.7	60	171	20	6	.77	.280	.353	.545	.897
Straw, Myles	Cle	27	140	557	145	25	3	3	85	46	67	4.2	67	125	29	5	.85	.260	.342	.332	.674
Suarez, Eugenio	Cin	30	130	425	100	19	1	28	62	70	65	5.2	52	140	1	1	.50	.235	.329	.482	.811
Suzuki, Kurt	LAA	38	75	228	55	11	0	7	25	30	25	3.8	15	41	0	0	.00	.241	.311	.382	.692
Swaggerty, Travis	Pit	24	90	281	72	10	0	14	53	40	43	5.3	33	65	12	2	.86	.256	.347	.441	.788
Swanson, Dansby	Atl	28	158	608	154	35	3	24	86	86	86	4.9	60	170	9	3	.75	.253	.325	.439	.765
Tapia, Raimel	Col	28	132	449	125	25	4	7	59	45	60	4.7	32	81	16	4	.80	.278	.329	.399	.728
Tatis Jr., Fernando	SD	23	144	554	157	30	4	47	113	109	124	8.0	67	172	27	5	.84	.283	.367	.606	.973
Tauchman, Mike	SF	31	70	132	28	7	1	3	18	14	14	3.4	16	39	1	0	1.00	.212	.302	.348	.650
Taveras, Leody	Tex	23	70	181	38	9	2	6	22	20	20	3.5	18	61	6	2	.75	.210	.285	.381	.666
Taylor, Chris	LAD	31	152	522	131	32	4	20	83	71	76	5.0	60	167	10	3	.77	.251	.336	.443	.779
Taylor, Michael A.	KC	31	135	452	110	24	2	12	58	51	52	3.9	34	144	11	4	.73	.243	.301	.385	.686
Taylor, Tyrone	Mil	28	90	254	60	11	2	11	31	34	31	4.2	19	59	4	1	.80	.236	.302	.425	.727

597

2022 Hitter Projections

Hitter	Team	Age	G	AB	H	2B	3B	HR	R	RBI	RC	RC27	BB	SO	SB	CS	SB%	Avg	OBP	Slg	OPS
Tellez, Rowdy	Mil	27	113	340	82	19	1	16	43	49	46	4.7	32	87	0	0	.00	.241	.316	.444	.760
Thomas, Alek	Ari	22	142	528	127	24	5	18	75	62	66	4.3	49	149	8	2	.80	.241	.313	.407	.721
Thomas, Lane	Was	26	136	503	114	25	5	17	70	71	62	4.1	60	163	10	4	.71	.227	.314	.398	.712
Torkelson, Spencer	Det	22	141	501	131	27	1	34	90	98	91	6.4	65	153	2	0	1.00	.261	.357	.523	.879
Toro, Abraham	Sea	25	130	464	121	27	2	16	67	70	65	4.9	47	92	7	4	.64	.261	.343	.431	.774
Torrens, Luis	Sea	26	85	226	51	12	1	9	25	32	27	4.0	22	64	0	0	.00	.226	.297	.407	.704
Torres, Gleyber	NYY	25	140	516	139	26	1	19	69	74	77	5.2	58	120	12	5	.71	.269	.348	.434	.782
Torreyes, Ronald	Phi	29	90	198	49	8	1	4	21	23	21	3.6	11	28	1	0	1.00	.247	.290	.359	.649
Trammell, Taylor	Sea	24	55	164	34	7	1	6	21	21	18	3.5	19	61	3	1	.75	.207	.301	.372	.673
Trevino, Jose	Tex	29	86	252	60	13	0	5	24	26	24	3.2	12	52	1	1	.50	.238	.273	.349	.622
Trout, Mike	LAA	30	118	437	125	25	3	32	94	81	106	8.8	99	125	8	2	.80	.286	.429	.577	1.005
Tsutsugo, Yoshi	Pit	30	85	275	61	14	1	12	38	42	36	4.3	38	82	0	0	.00	.222	.321	.411	.732
Tucker, Cole	Pit	25	78	199	44	8	2	4	26	17	21	3.5	23	58	5	1	.83	.221	.305	.342	.647
Tucker, Kyle	Hou	25	150	541	149	33	4	31	87	98	99	6.5	55	117	15	2	.88	.275	.346	.523	.869
Turner, Justin	LAD	37	146	536	152	30	1	25	85	78	93	6.3	60	100	2	0	1.00	.284	.370	.483	.854
Turner, Trea	LAD	28	153	618	184	36	5	28	105	75	113	6.7	50	121	29	5	.85	.298	.355	.508	.863
Upton, Justin	LAA	34	82	226	50	9	0	12	34	34	29	4.2	27	77	2	1	.67	.221	.310	.420	.730
Urias, Luis	Mil	25	154	502	125	25	3	20	73	63	72	4.9	63	124	5	2	.71	.249	.345	.430	.776
Urias, Ramon	Bal	28	85	251	63	16	0	8	31	33	33	4.5	25	75	1	1	.50	.251	.333	.410	.744
Urshela, Gio	NYY	30	131	451	121	26	1	13	53	55	58	4.6	26	105	1	0	1.00	.268	.313	.417	.729
Valaika, Pat	Bal	29	92	214	46	9	0	7	21	22	19	3.0	12	66	1	1	.50	.215	.260	.355	.615
VanMeter, Josh	Ari	27	90	217	51	13	1	8	27	28	29	4.5	27	65	3	1	.75	.235	.322	.415	.737
Varsho, Daulton	Ari	25	110	328	84	20	3	18	56	50	54	5.7	34	79	5	1	.83	.256	.330	.500	.830
Vaughn, Andrew	CWS	24	140	503	127	30	0	22	68	61	72	4.9	52	121	1	1	.50	.252	.332	.443	.775
Vazquez, Christian	Bos	31	135	473	123	26	1	10	57	53	56	4.1	34	96	7	4	.64	.260	.314	.383	.696
Verdugo, Alex	Bos	26	148	549	156	35	2	14	78	64	82	5.4	51	98	6	2	.75	.284	.349	.432	.781
Vilade, Ryan	Col	23	91	323	72	14	2	3	36	21	27	2.8	21	79	4	1	.80	.223	.277	.307	.583
Villar, Jonathan	NYM	31	130	425	100	18	2	13	57	40	50	3.9	43	127	15	5	.75	.235	.310	.379	.689
Vogelbach, Daniel	Mil	29	84	203	47	8	0	9	28	29	29	4.8	38	57	0	0	.00	.232	.355	.404	.759
Vogt, Stephen	Atl	37	55	129	29	7	1	5	14	16	16	4.1	13	33	0	0	.00	.225	.296	.411	.707
Voit, Luke	NYY	31	123	438	112	20	2	23	65	69	67	5.4	48	135	0	0	.00	.256	.341	.468	.809
Votto, Joey	Cin	38	142	496	129	27	2	27	77	76	90	6.4	88	129	1	0	1.00	.260	.377	.486	.863
Wade Jr., LaMonte	SF	28	122	374	89	16	2	16	52	48	52	4.7	50	96	6	2	.75	.238	.337	.420	.757
Wade, Tyler	NYY	27	95	201	46	9	2	2	32	14	21	3.4	21	59	14	4	.78	.229	.308	.323	.631
Walker, Christian	Ari	31	105	351	86	20	1	14	50	46	47	4.6	33	100	1	0	1.00	.245	.317	.427	.744
Walker, Steele	Tex	25	80	203	49	8	2	8	26	30	25	4.3	15	54	3	0	1.00	.241	.300	.419	.719
Walsh, Jared	LAA	28	147	529	136	31	1	30	74	94	83	5.5	50	162	2	1	.67	.257	.328	.490	.818
Ward, Taylor	LAA	28	99	305	79	18	1	13	46	40	47	5.4	38	89	4	1	.80	.259	.352	.452	.805
Waters, Drew	Atl	23	90	279	63	17	1	7	40	25	31	3.7	25	103	10	2	.83	.226	.296	.369	.666
Welker, Colton	Col	24	93	324	75	17	0	9	35	42	36	3.7	31	89	1	0	1.00	.231	.303	.367	.670
Wendle, Joey	TB	32	132	432	105	25	4	8	59	45	46	3.7	26	104	7	3	.70	.243	.300	.375	.675
White, Evan	Sea	26	110	355	83	14	1	19	48	54	45	4.3	28	124	2	1	.67	.234	.295	.439	.735
Winker, Jesse	Cin	28	138	470	133	30	1	23	70	69	86	6.6	64	93	1	1	.50	.283	.379	.498	.877
Wisdom, Patrick	ChC	30	138	444	90	19	1	27	62	70	53	3.9	43	193	5	1	.83	.203	.280	.432	.713
Witt Jr., Bobby	KC	22	149	551	142	33	6	39	92	101	98	6.2	47	168	16	2	.89	.258	.324	.552	.876
Wong, Kolten	Mil	31	141	497	128	28	4	13	71	56	65	4.5	46	94	12	5	.71	.258	.339	.408	.747
Yastrzemski, Mike	SF	31	142	489	118	29	4	23	78	71	71	4.9	54	144	4	2	.67	.241	.325	.458	.784
Yelich, Christian	Mil	30	134	442	118	24	2	19	79	66	76	6.0	71	125	11	3	.79	.267	.373	.459	.833
Zavala, Seby	CWS	28	52	150	25	6	0	6	17	18	11	2.3	12	73	0	0	.00	.167	.238	.327	.564
Zimmer, Bradley	Cle	29	69	140	30	6	1	4	19	16	15	3.5	15	59	5	1	.83	.214	.317	.357	.674
Zimmerman, Ryan	Was	37	57	103	25	6	0	5	13	16	14	4.6	8	29	0	0	.00	.243	.297	.447	.744
Zunino, Mike	TB	31	103	305	64	13	1	21	42	49	40	4.3	29	121	0	0	.00	.210	.291	.466	.757

2022 Pitcher Projections

Pitcher	Team	Age	G	GS	IP	H	HR	BB	SO	HB	W	L	Pct	Sv	BR/9	ERA
Abad, Fernando	Bal	36	30	0	35	43	5	9	30	0	2	2	.500	0	13.4	4.63
Abbott, Cory	ChC	26	20	0	46	46	9	25	55	2	2	3	.400	0	14.3	4.79
Adams, Austin	SD	31	61	0	51	36	3	31	73	15	3	3	.500	0	14.5	3.83
Akin, Keegan	Bal	27	24	24	117	123	17	52	113	3	6	7	.462	0	13.7	4.62
Alcala, Jorge	Min	26	53	0	57	58	9	19	59	2	3	3	.500	0	12.5	4.26
Alcantara, Sandy	Mia	26	33	33	202	174	22	63	189	9	10	12	.455	0	11.0	3.72
Alexander, Scott	LAD	32	40	0	39	37	4	14	26	1	3	2	.600	0	12.0	4.23
Alexander, Tyler	Det	27	37	21	136	162	24	33	115	8	6	10	.375	0	13.4	4.87
Alexy, A.J.	Tex	24	18	18	90	62	12	47	95	5	5	5	.500	0	11.4	3.87
Allard, Kolby	Tex	24	31	16	120	130	19	37	103	4	5	8	.385	0	12.8	4.54
Allen, Logan	Cle	25	16	11	66	74	11	30	60	5	3	5	.375	0	14.9	5.18
Almonte, Yency	Col	28	47	0	54	55	9	27	50	4	3	3	.500	0	14.3	5.00
Alvarado, Jose	Phi	27	64	0	54	44	5	41	65	5	3	3	.500	0	15.0	4.33
Alvarez, Jose	SF	33	75	0	72	71	5	23	50	1	4	4	.500	0	11.9	4.02
Alzolay, Adbert	ChC	27	29	29	151	138	28	52	158	7	7	9	.438	0	11.7	4.14
Anderson, Brett	Mil	34	30	17	91	97	11	25	55	3	4	6	.400	0	12.4	4.45
Anderson, Chase	Tex	34	15	11	70	74	15	26	56	3	3	5	.375	0	13.2	5.01
Anderson, Ian	Atl	24	29	29	163	143	19	76	173	3	10	8	.556	0	12.3	3.94
Anderson, Nick	TB	31	40	0	40	36	7	10	49	1	2	2	.500	18	10.6	3.57
Anderson, Tyler	Sea	32	28	28	155	157	28	42	124	3	7	10	.412	0	11.7	4.39
Ashby, Aaron	Mil	24	22	22	110	93	11	54	156	4	7	5	.583	0	12.4	3.54
Banda, Anthony	Pit	28	50	0	56	65	9	23	53	3	2	4	.333	0	14.6	4.98
Bard, Daniel	Col	37	68	0	67	71	9	36	77	7	3	4	.429	12	15.3	4.84
Barlow, Joe	Tex	26	55	0	53	33	4	25	60	1	3	3	.500	25	10.0	3.20
Barlow, Scott	KC	29	69	0	73	66	9	29	87	3	4	4	.500	26	12.1	3.80
Barnes, Charlie	Min	26	13	13	56	67	6	21	42	5	3	4	.429	0	14.9	5.06
Barnes, Matt	Bos	32	62	0	56	44	7	25	82	3	4	2	.667	22	11.6	3.40
Barria, Jaime	LAA	25	19	19	83	94	15	23	60	3	4	5	.444	0	13.0	4.88
Bass, Anthony	Mia	34	67	0	61	53	8	22	54	2	3	4	.429	0	11.4	3.99
Bassitt, Chris	Oak	33	28	28	164	150	20	46	157	12	9	9	.500	0	11.4	3.86
Bauer, Trevor	LAD	31	25	25	161	120	23	54	196	9	12	6	.667	0	10.2	3.40
Baz, Shane	TB	23	26	26	128	93	21	25	179	10	8	6	.571	0	9.0	3.23
Bednar, David	Pit	27	57	0	66	53	7	22	83	2	4	3	.571	19	10.5	3.23
Bender, Anthony	Mia	27	55	0	56	45	5	19	63	5	3	3	.500	2	11.1	3.44
Berrios, Jose	Tor	28	32	32	196	177	25	49	201	12	13	9	.591	0	10.9	3.70
Bickford, Phil	LAD	26	48	0	45	34	5	15	56	3	3	2	.600	0	10.4	3.35
Bieber, Shane	Cle	27	29	29	183	151	22	47	239	5	12	8	.600	0	10.0	3.14
Bielak, Brandon	Hou	26	28	0	55	51	7	23	51	2	3	3	.500	0	12.4	4.19
Blackburn, Paul	Oak	28	21	11	60	71	8	17	48	2	3	4	.429	0	13.5	4.65
Bleier, Richard	Mia	35	66	0	56	54	4	8	39	3	3	3	.500	0	10.4	3.68
Boxberger, Brad	Mil	34	71	0	65	51	10	30	78	4	4	4	.500	0	11.8	3.86
Boyd, Matthew	Det	31	16	16	82	82	15	24	79	6	4	5	.444	0	12.3	4.34
Bradley, Archie	Phi	29	57	0	58	59	6	24	51	3	3	3	.500	0	13.3	4.35
Brasier, Ryan	Bos	34	41	0	40	41	5	14	37	1	2	2	.500	0	12.6	4.17
Brault, Steven	Pit	30	13	13	55	55	7	27	44	4	2	4	.333	0	14.1	4.83
Brentz, Jake	KC	27	68	0	60	53	7	37	69	5	3	4	.429	0	14.3	4.43
Brogdon, Connor	Phi	27	52	0	54	44	8	18	54	1	3	3	.500	0	10.5	3.71
Brothers, Rex	ChC	34	50	0	47	42	8	37	66	5	2	3	.400	0	16.1	4.98
Brown, Hunter	Hou	23	15	15	73	70	9	38	95	2	4	4	.500	0	13.6	4.07
Brubaker, JT	Pit	28	18	18	95	95	14	30	95	7	5	6	.455	0	12.5	4.22
Bubic, Kris	KC	24	25	25	131	130	22	57	118	7	6	8	.429	0	13.3	4.67
Buehler, Walker	LAD	27	33	33	211	168	23	54	219	7	16	7	.696	0	9.8	3.32
Bumgarner, Madison	Ari	32	28	28	176	180	32	48	148	12	8	11	.421	0	12.3	4.50
Bummer, Aaron	CWS	28	66	0	60	45	3	27	73	3	4	3	.571	0	11.3	3.26
Bundy, Dylan	LAA	29	18	18	96	97	19	33	93	5	5	6	.455	0	12.7	4.55
Burnes, Corbin	Mil	27	28	28	175	140	18	48	237	7	12	7	.632	0	10.0	3.01
Burr, Ryan	CWS	28	38	0	41	36	5	21	36	1	2	2	.500	0	12.7	4.29
Cabrera, Edward	Mia	24	16	16	73	63	14	41	95	5	3	5	.375	0	13.4	4.38
Cabrera, Genesis	StL	25	67	0	71	60	9	37	78	4	4	4	.500	0	12.8	4.08
Canning, Griffin	LAA	26	13	13	72	69	11	30	74	3	4	4	.500	0	12.8	4.32
Carrasco, Carlos	NYM	35	26	26	140	134	22	44	151	3	8	8	.500	0	11.6	3.92
Castellanos, Humberto	Ari	24	23	23	110	102	20	30	94	8	6	7	.462	0	11.5	4.24
Castillo, Diego	Sea	28	61	0	60	41	7	20	73	4	4	3	.571	15	9.8	3.20
Castillo, Luis	Cin	29	31	31	192	176	24	75	200	6	12	9	.571	0	12.0	3.96
Castro, Kervin	SF	23	33	0	37	28	2	16	46	1	3	2	.600	0	10.9	3.12
Castro, Miguel	NYM	27	71	0	72	55	8	42	78	4	4	4	.500	0	12.6	4.01
Cease, Dylan	CWS	26	31	31	168	148	23	73	211	6	10	9	.526	0	12.3	3.86
Cessa, Luis	Cin	30	57	0	70	66	8	22	60	1	4	3	.571	12	11.4	3.92
Chacin, Jhoulys	Col	34	55	0	74	79	13	31	56	2	3	5	.375	0	13.6	4.99
Chafin, Andrew	Oak	32	71	0	75	65	7	24	72	2	4	4	.500	8	10.9	3.61
Chapman, Aroldis	NYY	34	58	0	56	36	6	33	91	3	4	2	.667	33	11.6	3.19
Chargois, JT	TB	31	61	0	60	48	7	24	60	5	3	3	.500	0	11.6	3.84
Chavez, Jesse	Atl	38	40	0	44	40	6	14	45	1	3	2	.600	0	11.3	3.85
Chirinos, Yonny	TB	28	18	6	84	80	13	21	72	3	4	5	.444	0	11.1	4.03
Cimber, Adam	Tor	31	75	0	74	72	5	17	51	6	5	4	.556	0	11.6	3.88
Cishek, Steve	LAA	36	67	0	69	61	7	36	64	7	4	4	.500	0	13.6	4.31
Cisnero, Jose	Det	33	59	0	56	51	6	27	57	4	3	3	.500	0	13.2	4.18
Civale, Aaron	Cle	27	29	29	174	171	27	44	144	6	9	11	.450	0	11.4	4.15
Clarke, Taylor	Ari	29	39	0	36	37	5	13	31	1	2	2	.500	0	12.8	4.38

2022 Pitcher Projections

Pitcher	Team	Age	G	GS	IP	H	HR	BB	SO	HB	W	L	Pct	Sv	BR/9	ERA
Clase, Emmanuel	Cle	24	71	0	73	59	3	17	77	0	5	3	.625	28	9.4	2.91
Clay, Sam	Was	29	48	0	37	44	2	20	32	4	2	2	.500	0	16.5	5.11
Clevinger, Mike	SD	31	24	24	140	111	14	47	158	2	10	6	.625	0	10.3	3.32
Clippard, Tyler	Ari	37	44	0	44	36	6	14	43	3	2	2	.500	11	10.8	3.80
Cobb, Alex	LAA	34	21	21	122	125	17	41	113	4	7	7	.500	0	12.5	4.28
Cole, Gerrit	NYY	31	32	32	190	148	25	47	249	4	14	7	.667	0	9.4	3.05
Colome, Alex	Min	33	71	0	72	68	8	25	62	4	4	4	.500	24	12.1	4.05
Conley, Adam	TB	32	32	0	39	34	6	18	36	3	2	2	.500	0	12.7	4.39
Contreras, Roansy	Pit	22	10	10	52	43	6	14	68	3	3	3	.500	0	10.4	3.63
Coonrod, Sam	Phi	29	42	0	42	41	6	18	44	3	2	2	.500	0	13.3	4.40
Corbin, Patrick	Was	32	30	30	179	195	29	59	161	3	9	11	.450	0	12.9	4.55
Cortes, Nestor	NYY	27	22	22	110	95	19	34	118	3	7	6	.538	0	10.8	3.84
Cotton, Jharel	Tex	30	42	0	58	50	7	26	66	2	3	3	.500	0	12.1	3.86
Coulombe, Danny	Min	32	40	0	46	48	8	13	50	2	2	3	.400	0	12.3	4.21
Cousins, Jake	Mil	27	30	0	33	20	4	17	49	4	2	1	.667	0	11.2	3.30
Crismatt, Nabil	SD	27	46	0	80	84	12	25	76	6	4	5	.444	0	12.9	4.45
Crochet, Garrett	CWS	23	60	0	61	50	3	27	73	2	4	3	.571	0	11.7	3.32
Crowe, Wil	Pit	27	27	27	125	134	23	59	115	5	5	9	.357	0	14.3	5.04
Cueto, Johnny	SF	36	19	19	101	110	15	31	84	4	5	6	.455	0	12.9	4.54
Curtiss, John	Mil	29	43	0	45	43	6	18	46	2	2	3	.400	0	12.6	4.10
Darvish, Yu	SD	35	29	29	160	133	26	45	188	8	10	7	.588	0	10.5	3.57
Davidson, Tucker	Atl	26	12	12	62	59	6	28	63	2	4	3	.571	0	12.9	4.08
Davies, Zach	ChC	29	29	29	146	155	23	64	111	4	6	10	.375	0	13.7	4.90
Davis, Wade	KC	36	39	0	41	45	8	19	37	2	2	3	.400	0	14.5	5.16
deGrom, Jacob	NYM	34	27	27	176	114	15	35	246	4	14	5	.737	0	7.8	2.40
DeSclafani, Anthony	SF	32	30	30	158	157	26	45	140	4	8	9	.471	0	11.7	4.19
Detmers, Reid	LAA	22	18	18	95	101	16	35	90	6	5	6	.455	0	13.5	4.55
Detwiler, Ross	SD	36	48	0	48	49	10	18	46	4	2	3	.400	0	13.3	4.88
Diaz, Edwin	NYM	28	59	0	61	43	7	23	92	7	4	3	.571	33	10.8	3.10
Diaz, Miguel	SD	27	23	0	40	39	8	22	45	1	2	3	.400	0	14.0	4.84
Diekman, Jake	Oak	35	68	0	63	50	7	36	83	6	4	4	.500	8	13.1	3.82
Dobnak, Randy	Min	27	25	25	133	142	14	38	86	6	7	8	.467	0	12.6	4.40
Dominguez, Seranthony	Phi	27	40	0	42	36	5	20	47	3	3	2	.600	0	12.6	3.86
Doolittle, Sean	Sea	35	48	0	47	45	8	17	49	2	2	3	.400	0	12.3	4.21
Doval, Camilo	SF	24	60	0	60	49	7	33	83	4	4	3	.571	25	12.9	3.78
Duffey, Tyler	Min	31	62	0	64	55	8	24	67	3	4	3	.571	5	11.5	3.81
Duffy, Danny	LAD	33	13	13	70	63	12	27	71	2	5	3	.625	0	11.8	4.14
Dunn, Justin	Sea	26	18	18	100	94	14	52	100	6	5	7	.417	0	13.7	4.50
Dunning, Dane	Tex	27	28	28	138	142	13	51	134	8	7	9	.438	0	13.1	4.14
Effross, Scott	ChC	28	46	0	52	50	8	14	54	5	2	3	.400	0	11.9	4.07
Eflin, Zach	Phi	28	24	24	144	149	22	33	135	4	8	8	.500	0	11.6	4.08
Ellis, Chris	Bal	29	18	18	87	97	17	42	79	5	3	6	.333	0	14.9	5.33
Eovaldi, Nathan	Bos	32	32	32	185	188	23	40	190	8	11	9	.550	0	11.5	3.79
Espino, Paolo	Was	35	25	25	127	140	23	34	107	3	6	8	.429	0	12.5	4.58
Estevez, Carlos	Col	29	68	0	68	82	13	24	69	3	3	5	.375	23	14.4	5.10
Fairbanks, Pete	TB	28	50	0	45	39	5	20	60	1	3	2	.600	4	12.0	3.58
Falter, Bailey	Phi	25	25	0	42	42	6	10	47	1	3	2	.600	0	11.4	3.69
Familia, Jeurys	NYM	32	71	0	64	58	7	33	70	3	3	4	.429	0	13.2	4.15
Fedde, Erick	Was	29	32	28	146	162	23	56	127	5	7	9	.438	0	13.7	4.81
Feyereisen, J.P.	TB	29	50	0	54	41	7	29	53	1	3	3	.500	5	11.8	4.00
Fiers, Mike	Oak	37	19	19	115	120	21	31	76	6	5	8	.385	0	12.3	4.70
Finnegan, Kyle	Was	30	67	0	69	65	7	34	72	2	4	4	.500	25	13.2	4.11
Flaherty, Jack	StL	26	27	27	151	112	21	50	171	9	10	7	.588	0	10.2	3.49
Fleming, Josh	TB	26	25	8	85	92	11	23	59	3	4	5	.444	0	12.5	4.45
Flexen, Chris	Sea	27	32	32	180	203	25	47	132	4	8	12	.400	0	12.7	4.53
Floro, Dylan	Mia	31	67	0	66	61	4	24	60	1	3	4	.429	28	11.7	3.73
Foltynewicz, Mike	Tex	30	22	22	119	121	22	36	90	6	5	8	.385	0	12.3	4.62
Foster, Matt	CWS	27	32	0	35	33	6	11	39	1	2	2	.500	0	11.6	4.01
Freeland, Kyle	Col	29	27	27	148	164	24	50	118	5	7	9	.438	0	13.3	4.74
Fried, Max	Atl	28	29	29	183	169	18	55	176	8	12	9	.571	0	11.4	3.76
Fry, Paul	Bal	29	49	0	45	40	4	28	52	4	2	3	.400	0	14.4	4.20
Fulmer, Michael	Det	29	61	0	76	83	11	26	73	4	3	5	.375	15	13.4	4.56
Funkhouser, Kyle	Det	28	65	0	75	81	8	44	70	3	3	5	.375	3	15.4	4.92
Gallegos, Giovanny	StL	30	74	0	79	53	8	20	92	4	6	3	.667	19	8.8	2.94
Gallen, Zac	Ari	26	27	27	157	136	22	60	178	6	9	8	.529	0	11.6	3.80
Gant, John	Min	29	39	20	105	94	10	61	89	4	6	6	.500	0	13.6	4.37
Garcia, Bryan	Det	27	28	0	30	32	5	15	24	1	1	2	.333	0	14.4	5.10
Garcia, Deivi	NYY	23	12	12	55	62	11	32	60	5	2	4	.333	0	16.2	5.57
Garcia, Jarlin	SF	29	62	0	74	64	11	24	66	2	4	4	.500	0	10.9	3.92
Garcia, Luis	StL	35	58	0	59	58	9	21	59	3	3	3	.500	0	12.5	4.20
Garcia, Yimi	Hou	31	61	0	59	50	12	17	60	3	3	3	.500	0	10.7	3.95
Garrett, Amir	Cin	30	57	0	46	40	7	26	58	1	3	2	.600	0	13.1	4.21
Garza, Ralph	Min	28	39	0	44	34	5	21	45	3	3	2	.600	0	11.9	3.88
Gausman, Kevin	SF	31	33	33	194	174	25	54	218	5	12	10	.545	0	10.8	3.56
German, Domingo	NYY	29	21	21	115	107	22	34	118	3	7	6	.538	0	11.3	4.05
Gibson, Kyle	Phi	34	31	31	186	188	24	70	161	9	10	11	.476	0	12.9	4.38
Gil, Luis	NYY	24	16	16	78	58	11	45	104	3	5	4	.556	0	12.7	3.86
Gilbert, Logan	Sea	25	27	27	131	120	16	32	140	7	8	7	.533	0	10.9	3.60
Gilbert, Tyler	Ari	28	19	19	97	80	11	31	79	4	6	5	.545	0	10.7	3.84
Gilbreath, Lucas	Col	26	46	0	43	35	6	23	45	1	2	2	.500	0	12.3	4.12
Giles, Ken	Sea	31	40	0	40	32	5	12	56	0	3	2	.600	12	9.9	3.09

600

2022 Pitcher Projections

Pitcher	Team	Age	G	GS	IP	H	HR	BB	SO	HB	W	L	Pct	Sv	BR/9	ERA
Giolito, Lucas	CWS	27	31	31	181	149	26	61	204	5	11	9	.550	0	10.7	3.62
Givens, Mychal	Cin	32	56	0	54	45	9	26	61	2	3	3	.500	15	12.2	4.10
Gomber, Austin	Col	28	25	25	130	130	21	48	126	4	7	7	.500	0	12.6	4.33
Gonsolin, Tony	LAD	28	14	12	57	43	7	25	60	1	4	2	.667	0	10.9	3.68
Gonzales, Marco	Sea	30	29	29	185	179	27	47	142	7	9	11	.450	0	11.3	4.13
Gonzalez, Chi Chi	Col	30	18	13	67	83	13	23	41	4	3	5	.375	0	14.8	5.58
Gonzalez, Victor	LAD	26	42	0	41	39	4	16	42	4	3	2	.600	0	13.0	4.07
Gore, MacKenzie	SD	23	20	20	108	112	14	68	123	4	5	7	.417	0	15.3	4.84
Gose, Anthony	Cle	31	30	0	30	21	4	13	40	2	2	1	.667	0	10.8	3.43
Goudeau, Ashton	Col	29	23	1	55	64	8	21	38	2	3	4	.429	0	14.2	5.08
Graterol, Brusdar	LAD	23	51	0	53	45	4	18	48	6	4	2	.667	0	11.7	3.78
Graveman, Kendall	Hou	31	57	0	60	52	8	23	61	6	3	3	.500	5	12.2	4.08
Gray, Jon	Col	30	30	30	154	161	26	57	154	7	8	9	.471	0	13.1	4.53
Gray, Josiah	Was	24	26	26	137	116	25	54	153	5	8	7	.533	0	11.5	4.01
Gray, Sonny	Cin	32	28	28	156	135	19	64	174	9	10	8	.556	0	12.0	3.87
Green, Chad	NYY	31	67	0	82	65	13	19	97	2	6	3	.667	0	9.4	3.34
Greene, Conner	Bal	27	38	0	41	48	6	25	38	3	2	3	.400	0	16.7	5.60
Greene, Hunter	Cin	22	24	24	125	113	20	50	162	9	8	6	.571	0	12.4	3.93
Greinke, Zack	Hou	38	26	26	146	143	22	28	110	3	9	8	.529	0	10.7	4.02
Guerra, Deolis	Oak	33	58	0	73	63	10	22	71	4	4	4	.500	0	11.0	3.80
Guerra, Junior	LAA	37	40	0	62	62	9	34	55	3	3	4	.429	0	14.4	4.87
Gutierrez, Vladimir	Cin	26	22	22	113	117	21	43	95	7	6	7	.462	0	13.3	4.86
Hader, Josh	Mil	28	59	0	59	30	8	23	100	3	5	2	.714	34	8.5	2.48
Hand, Brad	NYM	32	70	0	63	53	7	24	68	6	4	3	.571	0	11.9	3.79
Happ, J.A.	StL	39	30	30	135	141	23	42	108	4	7	8	.467	0	12.5	4.54
Harper, Ryne	Was	33	45	0	44	45	6	15	43	2	2	2	.500	0	12.7	4.30
Harvey, Matt	Bal	33	23	23	103	131	21	31	77	4	4	7	.364	0	14.5	5.42
Head, Louis	TB	32	36	0	44	39	5	16	47	4	2	2	.500	0	12.1	3.85
Heaney, Andrew	NYY	31	16	16	84	82	16	25	93	4	5	5	.500	0	11.9	4.13
Hearn, Taylor	Tex	27	34	16	129	123	18	55	119	5	6	9	.400	0	12.8	4.33
Helsley, Ryan	StL	27	48	0	47	39	6	25	46	1	3	2	.600	0	12.4	4.07
Hembree, Heath	NYM	33	57	0	58	47	12	25	77	3	3	3	.500	0	11.6	3.90
Hendricks, Kyle	ChC	32	31	31	179	190	26	40	133	10	8	12	.400	0	12.1	4.33
Hendriks, Liam	CWS	33	68	0	70	50	8	11	103	1	6	2	.750	36	8.0	2.40
Hernandez, Carlos	KC	25	23	23	117	110	17	48	104	7	6	7	.462	0	12.7	4.39
Hernandez, Darwinzon	Bos	25	47	0	41	34	3	34	57	5	2	2	.500	0	16.0	4.39
Hernandez, Elieser	Mia	27	23	23	110	96	20	31	123	8	5	7	.417	0	11.0	3.86
Heuer, Codi	ChC	25	66	0	69	63	5	24	60	2	4	4	.500	19	11.6	3.76
Hicks, Jordan	StL	25	48	0	50	34	2	34	50	3	3	2	.600	9	12.8	3.74
Hill, Rich	NYM	42	31	29	146	130	22	53	135	13	8	9	.471	0	12.1	4.19
Hill, Tim	SD	32	76	0	59	51	7	21	56	6	3	3	.500	0	11.9	3.95
Hoffman, Jeff	Cin	29	31	0	45	46	9	23	48	3	2	3	.400	0	14.4	5.00
Holland, Derek	Det	35	44	0	58	63	11	25	57	3	2	4	.333	0	14.1	4.97
Holland, Greg	KC	36	46	0	48	44	7	23	46	1	3	3	.500	0	12.8	4.32
Holmes, Clay	NYY	29	73	0	74	66	6	37	79	5	4	4	.500	0	13.1	3.99
Houck, Tanner	Bos	26	27	27	139	126	12	53	165	15	9	7	.563	0	12.6	3.74
Houser, Adrian	Mil	29	25	25	138	133	16	58	108	9	7	9	.438	0	13.0	4.41
Howard, Sam	Pit	29	49	0	45	38	6	25	55	3	2	3	.400	0	13.2	4.10
Howard, Spencer	Tex	25	22	22	110	103	13	51	121	5	5	7	.417	0	13.0	4.09
Hudson, Dakota	StL	27	25	25	131	114	11	58	96	7	7	7	.500	0	12.3	4.16
Hudson, Daniel	SD	35	57	0	52	39	8	20	67	3	3	2	.600	0	10.7	3.49
Iglesias, Raisel	LAA	32	66	0	72	60	12	17	97	2	5	3	.625	33	9.9	3.25
Irvin, Cole	Oak	28	31	31	171	195	23	40	122	7	8	11	.421	0	12.7	4.50
Jackson, Luke	Atl	30	73	0	70	66	7	32	77	3	4	4	.500	0	13.0	3.99
Jansen, Kenley	LAD	34	68	0	68	48	9	29	82	3	5	2	.714	35	10.6	3.47
Javier, Cristian	Hou	25	34	8	110	71	15	54	138	6	7	5	.583	0	10.7	3.47
Jax, Griffin	Min	27	13	13	60	62	10	21	48	3	3	4	.429	0	12.9	4.65
Jefferies, Daulton	Oak	26	14	14	73	80	11	12	61	4	4	4	.500	0	11.8	4.20
Jimenez, Joe	Det	27	52	0	48	42	8	26	58	6	2	3	.400	0	13.9	4.50
Johnson, Pierce	SD	31	63	0	63	49	7	30	78	1	4	3	.571	0	11.4	3.54
Kaprielian, James	Oak	28	23	23	124	117	22	42	127	5	6	7	.462	0	11.9	4.17
Karinchak, James	Cle	26	47	0	47	33	6	28	72	1	3	2	.600	10	11.9	3.45
Keller, Brad	KC	26	26	26	143	145	15	61	119	6	7	9	.438	0	13.3	4.38
Keller, Mitch	Pit	26	27	27	130	142	14	61	132	6	6	8	.429	0	14.5	4.57
Kelly, Joe	LAD	34	50	0	46	37	4	19	50	3	3	2	.600	0	11.5	3.63
Kelly, Merrill	Ari	33	27	27	158	168	26	44	129	4	8	10	.444	0	12.3	4.45
Kennedy, Ian	Phi	37	59	0	59	57	11	19	62	2	3	3	.500	26	11.9	4.20
Kershaw, Clayton	LAD	34	23	23	119	101	18	23	130	2	9	4	.692	0	9.5	3.41
Keuchel, Dallas	CWS	34	31	29	153	177	20	52	95	6	7	10	.412	0	13.8	4.91
Kikuchi, Yusei	Sea	31	28	28	142	143	26	54	136	4	7	9	.438	0	12.7	4.53
Kim, Kwang-hyun	StL	33	19	19	93	84	12	34	67	3	5	5	.500	0	11.7	4.22
Kimbrel, Craig	CWS	34	63	0	62	39	10	28	98	4	4	3	.571	8	10.3	3.13
King, Michael	NYY	27	22	0	54	52	7	17	54	4	3	3	.500	0	12.2	4.02
Kinley, Tyler	Col	31	74	0	76	69	11	35	73	3	4	4	.500	0	12.7	4.27
Kirby, George	Sea	24	10	10	56	59	0	17	58	2	3	3	.500	0	12.5	3.48
Kittredge, Andrew	TB	32	60	0	74	65	8	18	77	3	4	4	.500	11	10.5	3.48
Kluber, Corey	NYY	36	18	18	90	84	11	32	91	5	5	5	.500	0	12.1	3.99
Knebel, Corey	LAD	30	40	0	42	31	6	16	53	2	3	1	.750	0	10.5	3.45
Kopech, Michael	CWS	26	50	0	75	62	9	30	107	4	5	3	.625	0	11.5	3.40
Kowar, Jackson	KC	25	18	18	81	80	11	37	101	4	4	5	.444	0	13.4	4.17
Kremer, Dean	Bal	26	17	17	85	95	16	35	85	3	4	6	.400	0	14.1	4.98

601

2022 Pitcher Projections

Pitcher	Team	Age	G	GS	IP	H	HR	BB	SO	HB	W	L	Pct	Sv	BR/9	ERA
Kuhl, Chad	Pit	29	25	15	80	73	13	42	75	6	4	5	.444	0	13.6	4.73
Lamet, Dinelson	SD	29	22	22	123	101	15	49	154	7	8	6	.571	0	11.5	3.60
Lange, Alex	Det	26	36	0	36	39	4	21	40	2	2	2	.500	3	15.5	4.75
Lauer, Eric	Mil	27	26	26	140	127	21	53	141	5	8	8	.500	0	11.9	4.04
Leone, Dominic	SF	30	73	0	70	61	9	31	75	1	4	4	.500	5	12.0	3.91
Lester, Jon	StL	38	26	26	126	146	20	45	86	4	6	8	.429	0	13.9	5.04
Liberatore, Matthew	StL	22	20	20	106	110	20	29	103	4	6	6	.500	0	12.1	4.38
Littell, Zack	SF	26	66	0	72	70	9	30	71	3	4	4	.500	0	12.9	4.19
Loaisiga, Jonathan	NYY	27	60	0	74	67	9	20	74	4	5	4	.556	0	11.1	3.74
Lodolo, Nick	Cin	24	18	18	94	87	8	24	99	11	6	4	.600	0	11.7	3.45
Long, Sammy	SF	26	14	0	35	30	3	12	39	1	2	2	.500	0	11.1	3.36
Lopez, Jorge	Bal	29	33	17	99	115	20	41	87	7	4	7	.364	0	14.8	5.41
Lopez, Pablo	Mia	26	27	27	147	130	18	40	154	10	7	9	.438	0	11.0	3.68
Lopez, Reynaldo	CWS	28	29	15	90	91	16	34	89	3	5	5	.500	0	12.8	4.45
Lorenzen, Michael	Cin	30	47	0	53	48	5	23	46	2	3	3	.500	9	12.4	4.05
Loup, Aaron	NYM	34	69	0	62	48	4	18	60	6	4	3	.571	0	10.5	3.39
Luetge, Lucas	NYY	35	55	0	71	67	6	17	74	4	5	3	.625	0	11.2	3.53
Lugo, Seth	NYM	32	55	0	57	50	7	20	66	2	3	3	.500	0	11.4	3.64
Luzardo, Jesus	Mia	24	20	20	96	96	13	40	99	6	4	7	.364	0	13.3	4.36
Lyles, Jordan	Tex	31	31	31	188	207	40	63	151	6	7	14	.333	0	13.2	5.00
Lynch, Daniel	KC	25	23	23	105	130	17	41	98	6	4	7	.364	0	15.2	5.23
Lynn, Lance	CWS	35	29	29	168	150	22	53	181	6	10	8	.556	0	11.2	3.73
Machado, Andres	Was	29	65	0	60	62	9	26	54	6	3	4	.429	0	14.1	4.80
Mahle, Tyler	Cin	27	33	33	192	178	32	71	216	10	11	10	.524	0	12.1	4.08
Manaea, Sean	Oak	30	31	31	174	165	24	38	177	8	10	9	.526	0	10.9	3.73
Manning, Matt	Det	24	26	26	127	142	18	45	108	3	6	9	.400	0	13.5	4.65
Manoah, Alek	Tor	24	26	26	140	95	15	46	166	21	10	6	.625	0	10.4	3.36
Mantiply, Joe	Ari	31	63	0	43	46	4	16	43	2	2	3	.400	0	13.4	4.19
Marquez, Brailyn	ChC	23	15	15	72	67	9	43	72	2	5	5	.500	0	14.0	4.88
Marquez, German	Col	27	29	29	164	166	23	53	160	4	9	9	.500	0	12.2	4.12
Marshall, Evan	CWS	32	36	0	32	30	3	12	32	0	2	2	.500	0	11.8	3.74
Martin, Brett	Tex	27	63	0	63	78	6	18	48	1	3	4	.429	0	13.9	4.65
Martin, Chris	Atl	36	48	0	47	49	5	7	41	2	3	2	.600	0	11.1	3.81
Martinez, Carlos	StL	30	25	15	85	84	9	39	65	9	4	5	.444	0	14.0	4.66
Maton, Phil	Hou	29	69	0	69	65	8	29	86	6	4	4	.500	0	13.0	3.91
Matz, Steven	Tor	31	29	29	156	170	28	47	144	7	8	9	.471	0	12.9	4.62
Matzek, Tyler	Atl	31	71	0	66	48	4	37	80	3	4	3	.571	0	12.0	3.49
May, Dustin	LAD	24	15	15	77	65	7	21	83	6	6	3	.667	0	10.8	3.43
May, Trevor	NYM	32	69	0	65	52	10	26	84	1	4	3	.571	0	10.9	3.50
Mayers, Mike	LAA	30	68	0	78	73	11	27	91	3	5	4	.556	5	11.9	3.84
Mayza, Tim	Tor	30	57	0	56	50	7	18	59	4	4	3	.571	0	11.4	3.78
McClanahan, Shane	TB	25	28	28	137	142	18	42	155	2	7	8	.467	0	12.2	3.91
McCullers Jr., Lance	Hou	28	29	29	178	135	15	76	197	11	12	8	.600	0	11.2	3.51
McFarland, T.J.	StL	33	64	0	67	67	8	18	47	3	4	4	.500	0	11.8	4.20
McGee, Jake	SF	35	56	0	56	51	10	12	55	2	3	3	.500	15	10.4	3.86
McHugh, Collin	TB	35	38	7	66	50	6	17	73	3	4	3	.571	0	9.7	3.18
McKenzie, Triston	Cle	24	26	26	145	109	24	64	164	4	8	8	.500	0	11.0	3.79
Means, John	Bal	29	28	28	160	155	30	33	141	6	9	9	.500	0	10.9	4.09
Megill, Trevor	ChC	28	42	0	40	44	6	17	51	2	2	3	.400	0	14.2	4.51
Megill, Tylor	NYM	26	21	21	104	93	17	32	125	3	6	5	.545	0	11.1	3.74
Melancon, Mark	SD	37	57	0	60	59	4	22	52	2	4	3	.571	32	12.5	3.95
Merryweather, Julian	Tor	30	35	0	40	43	6	14	42	3	2	2	.500	0	13.5	4.51
Mikolas, Miles	StL	33	15	15	83	86	11	17	60	4	5	5	.500	0	11.6	4.20
Miley, Wade	Cin	35	26	26	155	167	19	53	119	5	8	9	.471	0	13.1	4.47
Miller, Andrew	StL	37	38	0	35	32	5	16	40	5	2	2	.500	0	13.6	4.37
Mills, Alec	ChC	30	27	27	143	159	22	45	111	7	6	10	.375	0	13.3	4.75
Minaya, Juan	Min	31	44	0	61	56	8	31	67	5	3	3	.500	0	13.6	4.28
Minor, Mike	KC	34	28	28	164	162	27	45	150	6	9	9	.500	0	11.7	4.15
Minter, A.J.	Atl	28	57	0	54	47	4	22	60	1	4	2	.667	0	11.7	3.61
Misiewicz, Anthony	Sea	27	62	0	51	58	8	15	49	1	2	3	.400	0	13.1	4.50
Mize, Casey	Det	25	30	30	155	151	24	45	126	13	7	10	.412	0	12.1	4.33
Montas, Frankie	Oak	29	31	31	195	184	23	62	207	7	11	11	.500	0	11.7	3.79
Montero, Rafael	Hou	31	40	0	44	47	4	14	40	4	2	2	.500	0	13.3	4.30
Montgomery, Jordan	NYY	29	29	29	156	152	21	48	158	3	9	8	.529	0	11.7	3.93
Moore, Matt	Phi	33	24	12	77	86	17	39	69	3	3	5	.375	0	15.0	5.50
Morgan, Adam	ChC	32	45	0	36	30	6	14	39	3	2	2	.500	0	11.8	4.03
Morgan, Eli	Cle	26	23	23	116	122	22	38	108	5	5	8	.385	0	12.8	4.58
Morton, Charlie	Atl	38	33	33	188	163	18	61	208	17	12	9	.571	0	11.5	3.62
Muller, Kyle	Atl	24	18	18	88	78	10	52	96	3	5	5	.500	0	13.6	4.25
Musgrove, Joe	SD	29	31	31	188	161	24	55	203	15	12	9	.571	0	11.1	3.67
Nelson, Jimmy	LAD	33	35	0	35	25	4	19	48	4	3	1	.750	0	12.3	3.69
Neris, Hector	Phi	33	75	0	75	63	11	32	96	4	5	4	.556	8	11.9	3.77
Nola, Aaron	Phi	29	31	31	179	158	23	50	212	8	12	8	.600	0	10.9	3.52
Norris, Daniel	Mil	29	51	0	58	54	10	24	58	2	3	4	.429	0	12.4	4.35
Ober, Bailey	Min	26	28	28	129	120	21	28	140	1	8	6	.571	0	10.4	3.65
Odorizzi, Jake	Hou	32	26	26	118	113	16	40	110	4	7	6	.538	0	12.0	4.07
Ohtani, Shohei	LAA	27	22	22	125	97	14	46	148	9	8	6	.571	0	10.9	3.48
Okert, Steven	Mia	30	46	0	49	41	8	16	59	4	2	3	.400	0	11.2	3.74
Ottavino, Adam	Bos	36	66	0	61	50	6	33	71	5	4	3	.571	5	13.0	3.95
Oviedo, Johan	StL	24	10	10	48	51	6	27	46	5	2	3	.400	0	15.6	5.07
Oviedo, Luis	Pit	23	40	0	48	53	7	27	52	3	2	3	.400	0	15.6	5.07

2022 Pitcher Projections

Pitcher	Team	Age	G	GS	IP	H	HR	BB	SO	HB	W	L	Pct	Sv	BR/9	ERA
Paddack, Chris	SD	26	23	23	119	115	19	25	114	3	7	6	.538	0	10.8	3.85
Pagan, Emilio	SD	31	64	0	63	51	13	19	69	2	4	3	.571	0	10.3	3.81
Parker, Blake	Cle	37	55	0	55	50	9	20	54	2	3	3	.500	0	11.8	4.12
Patino, Luis	TB	22	25	25	122	107	18	48	132	6	7	7	.500	0	11.9	3.95
Patton, Spencer	Tex	34	52	0	56	46	5	22	60	0	3	3	.500	4	10.9	3.52
Payamps, Joel	KC	28	39	0	55	56	6	16	47	2	3	3	.500	0	12.1	4.04
Pearson, Nate	Tor	25	25	25	122	92	18	64	150	7	8	6	.571	0	12.0	3.86
Peralta, Freddy	Mil	26	27	27	140	97	16	58	190	9	9	6	.600	0	10.5	3.25
Peralta, Wandy	NYY	30	59	0	55	56	7	24	46	2	3	3	.500	0	13.4	4.50
Peralta, Wily	Det	33	24	24	126	129	18	56	88	5	5	9	.357	0	13.6	4.82
Perez, Martin	Bos	31	39	15	113	129	18	41	90	6	5	7	.417	0	14.0	4.98
Peters, Dillon	Pit	29	11	11	53	59	10	19	51	2	2	4	.333	0	13.6	4.84
Peterson, David	NYM	26	15	15	64	65	8	28	63	4	3	4	.429	0	13.6	4.43
Petit, Yusmeiro	Oak	37	76	0	77	70	12	13	44	1	4	5	.444	0	9.8	4.04
Pineda, Michael	Min	33	23	23	115	120	17	25	93	3	6	6	.500	0	11.6	4.16
Pivetta, Nick	Bos	29	29	29	151	145	24	61	164	5	9	8	.529	0	12.6	4.20
Plesac, Zach	Cle	27	28	28	164	152	24	40	127	7	9	10	.474	0	10.9	4.03
Poche, Colin	TB	28	35	0	35	28	4	12	43	1	2	2	.500	0	10.5	3.34
Pomeranz, Drew	SD	33	35	0	38	34	7	19	45	1	2	2	.500	0	12.8	4.26
Ponce, Cody	Pit	28	23	0	54	58	9	19	52	3	2	4	.333	0	13.3	4.67
Pop, Zach	Mia	25	55	0	60	55	3	26	56	8	3	4	.429	0	13.4	4.03
Pressly, Ryan	Hou	33	62	0	62	50	6	15	77	1	5	2	.714	32	9.6	3.02
Price, David	LAD	36	36	11	80	81	11	26	71	4	5	4	.556	0	12.5	4.28
Puk, A.J.	Oak	27	18	18	87	100	17	31	102	4	4	6	.400	0	14.0	4.76
Quantrill, Cal	Cle	27	28	28	155	153	20	47	128	8	8	10	.444	0	12.1	4.17
Quintana, Jose	SF	33	29	6	57	59	8	24	64	1	3	3	.500	0	13.3	4.35
Rainey, Tanner	Was	29	35	0	32	24	5	23	45	2	2	2	.500	0	13.8	4.22
Raley, Brooks	Hou	34	57	0	51	44	8	16	65	4	3	2	.600	0	11.3	3.68
Ramirez, Noe	Ari	32	47	0	44	38	6	16	41	3	2	2	.500	0	11.7	3.96
Rasmussen, Drew	TB	26	23	23	111	96	10	41	124	3	7	6	.538	0	11.4	3.52
Ray, Robbie	Tor	30	32	32	195	169	36	72	244	5	12	9	.571	0	11.4	3.85
Reyes, Alex	StL	27	68	0	73	48	9	53	94	2	4	4	.500	15	12.7	3.89
Richards, Garrett	Bos	34	51	0	70	78	11	30	59	2	3	5	.375	10	14.1	4.95
Richards, Trevor	Tor	29	63	0	70	64	11	23	74	1	4	3	.571	0	11.3	3.91
Robles, Hansel	Bos	31	73	0	72	66	10	34	75	4	4	4	.500	15	13.0	4.26
Rodon, Carlos	CWS	29	26	26	143	108	16	46	185	9	10	6	.625	0	10.3	3.19
Rodriguez, Eduardo	Bos	29	32	32	162	159	19	52	181	4	10	8	.556	0	11.9	3.79
Rodriguez, Joely	NYY	30	55	0	51	53	3	20	52	1	3	3	.500	0	13.1	3.90
Rodriguez, Manuel	ChC	25	35	0	35	30	4	23	39	4	1	2	.333	0	14.7	4.63
Rodriguez, Richard	Atl	32	68	0	69	62	11	15	57	3	4	3	.571	6	10.4	3.94
Rodriguez, Yerry	Tex	24	10	10	55	53	6	23	66	4	3	3	.500	0	13.1	4.01
Rogers, Josh	Was	27	15	15	83	101	18	27	54	4	3	6	.333	0	14.3	5.53
Rogers, Tyler	SF	31	78	0	83	79	6	20	61	6	5	4	.556	9	11.4	3.85
Romano, Jordan	Tor	29	66	0	67	54	10	25	83	3	4	3	.571	29	11.0	3.59
Romo, Sergio	Oak	39	65	0	64	59	10	21	61	3	3	4	.429	4	11.7	4.11
Ross, Joe	Was	29	16	16	87	89	12	30	83	7	5	5	.500	0	13.0	4.34
Rucker, Michael	ChC	28	37	0	53	56	10	18	59	4	2	4	.333	0	13.2	4.59
Ruiz, Jose	CWS	27	64	0	68	65	9	28	66	1	4	4	.500	0	12.4	4.18
Ryan, Joe	Min	26	24	24	136	95	26	28	174	4	10	5	.667	0	8.4	3.09
Ryu, Hyun-Jin	Tor	35	30	30	164	167	21	34	140	3	10	8	.556	0	11.2	3.93
Sadler, Casey	Sea	31	59	0	58	49	7	18	53	3	3	3	.500	0	10.9	3.76
Sale, Chris	Bos	33	29	29	160	136	18	42	217	14	11	7	.611	0	10.8	3.27
Sampson, Adrian	ChC	30	19	9	70	79	15	23	53	6	2	5	.286	0	13.9	5.27
Sanchez, Sixto	Mia	23	26	26	146	148	13	38	131	6	7	9	.438	0	11.8	3.85
Sandoval, Patrick	LAA	25	22	22	128	121	17	53	137	4	7	7	.500	0	12.5	4.08
Sanmartin, Reiver	Cin	26	9	9	43	42	4	13	45	1	3	2	.600	0	11.7	3.64
Santana, Dennis	Tex	26	67	0	66	68	9	36	65	5	3	5	.375	0	14.9	4.91
Santana, Edgar	Atl	30	37	0	38	36	6	10	30	1	2	2	.500	0	11.1	4.08
Santana, Ervin	KC	39	44	0	71	83	15	25	51	3	3	5	.375	0	14.1	5.33
Santillan, Tony	Cin	25	38	4	80	72	11	37	95	6	5	4	.556	0	12.9	4.05
Sawamura, Hirokazu	Bos	34	54	0	52	43	8	30	58	2	3	3	.500	0	13.0	4.24
Sborz, Josh	Tex	28	63	0	63	62	6	30	72	0	3	4	.429	0	13.1	3.93
Scherzer, Max	LAD	37	30	30	192	147	25	43	245	9	16	6	.727	0	9.3	3.06
Schmidt, Clarke	NYY	26	15	15	75	75	11	29	80	6	4	4	.500	0	13.2	4.32
Scott, Tanner	Bal	27	57	0	53	47	5	31	67	4	3	3	.500	0	13.9	4.00
Senzatela, Antonio	Col	27	29	29	171	202	22	46	112	8	8	11	.421	0	13.5	4.79
Severino, Luis	NYY	28	25	25	148	117	14	35	181	5	11	6	.647	0	9.5	3.03
Sewald, Paul	Sea	32	71	0	79	68	12	27	112	2	5	4	.556	5	11.1	3.44
Shaw, Bryan	Cle	34	74	0	73	75	12	35	64	2	3	5	.375	0	13.8	4.87
Sheffield, Jordan	Col	27	34	0	33	25	4	19	26	2	2	2	.500	0	12.5	4.29
Sheffield, Justus	Sea	26	22	22	108	116	13	54	98	5	5	7	.417	0	14.6	4.79
Shreve, Chasen	Pit	31	54	0	54	46	8	27	49	2	3	3	.500	0	12.5	4.27
Sims, Lucas	Cin	28	50	0	51	40	8	23	71	4	3	2	.600	12	11.8	3.68
Singer, Brady	KC	25	30	30	157	166	19	60	155	12	8	10	.444	0	13.6	4.45
Skubal, Tarik	Det	25	30	30	148	144	32	49	168	6	7	9	.438	0	12.1	4.32
Smith, Caleb	Ari	30	44	9	101	87	21	52	109	5	5	6	.455	0	12.8	4.55
Smith, Joe	Sea	38	54	0	44	44	6	9	38	2	2	3	.400	0	11.3	4.03
Smith, Riley	Ari	27	20	0	44	55	7	11	28	2	2	3	.400	0	13.9	5.12
Smith, Will	Atl	32	70	0	72	55	12	27	90	3	5	3	.625	34	10.6	3.55
Smyly, Drew	Atl	33	29	13	96	106	22	35	92	2	5	6	.455	0	13.4	5.02
Snell, Blake	SD	29	26	26	138	110	17	65	176	2	9	6	.600	0	11.5	3.59

2022 Pitcher Projections

Pitcher	Team	Age	G	GS	IP	H	HR	BB	SO	HB	W	L	Pct	Sv	BR/9	ERA
Soria, Joakim	Tor	38	34	0	30	29	4	9	31	1	2	1	.667	0	11.7	3.80
Soto, Gregory	Det	27	56	0	63	58	9	37	71	2	3	4	.429	14	13.9	4.50
Springs, Jeffrey	TB	29	44	0	45	42	6	17	61	1	3	2	.600	0	12.0	3.63
Stammen, Craig	SD	38	64	0	86	84	10	15	77	3	5	4	.556	0	10.7	3.71
Stanek, Ryne	Hou	30	71	0	70	52	11	36	82	3	4	4	.500	0	11.7	3.92
Staumont, Josh	KC	28	70	0	71	56	7	38	81	3	4	4	.500	11	12.3	3.82
Steckenrider, Drew	Sea	31	67	0	75	63	9	22	65	4	4	4	.500	5	10.7	3.79
Steele, Justin	ChC	26	25	25	126	112	17	63	130	8	6	8	.429	0	13.1	4.29
Stephan, Trevor	Cle	26	40	0	59	60	9	29	69	5	3	4	.429	6	14.3	4.65
Stephenson, Robert	Col	29	55	0	56	54	9	25	62	2	3	3	.500	0	13.0	4.26
Strahm, Matt	SD	30	28	0	35	35	6	8	34	3	2	2	.500	0	11.8	4.24
Strasburg, Stephen	Was	33	27	27	149	131	19	53	163	8	9	7	.563	0	11.6	3.79
Stratton, Chris	Pit	31	69	0	76	76	11	32	77	1	4	5	.444	10	12.9	4.26
Strickland, Hunter	Mil	33	57	0	60	51	10	23	57	3	3	3	.500	0	11.6	4.10
Stripling, Ross	Tor	32	22	16	87	92	16	24	78	2	5	5	.500	0	12.2	4.45
Stroman, Marcus	NYM	31	31	31	183	173	18	52	157	5	10	10	.500	0	11.3	3.83
Suarez, Jose	LAA	24	25	23	135	140	18	51	121	8	7	8	.467	0	13.3	4.47
Suarez, Ranger	Phi	26	31	31	186	168	16	60	177	9	12	9	.571	0	11.5	3.73
Suero, Wander	Was	30	34	0	36	37	4	13	38	3	2	2	.500	0	13.3	4.13
Sulser, Cole	Bal	32	60	0	67	61	6	27	75	1	4	3	.571	13	12.0	3.64
Suter, Brent	Mil	32	59	0	71	68	10	19	67	2	4	4	.500	0	11.3	3.92
Swanson, Erik	Sea	28	42	0	41	39	8	12	41	1	2	2	.500	0	11.4	4.18
Syndergaard, Noah	NYM	29	26	26	158	152	16	40	157	6	9	8	.529	0	11.3	3.68
Taillon, Jameson	NYY	30	27	27	137	126	20	39	128	5	8	7	.533	0	11.2	3.94
Tapia, Domingo	KC	30	58	0	59	57	7	30	48	2	3	4	.429	0	13.6	4.50
Tate, Dillon	Bal	28	66	0	69	68	9	23	52	7	3	4	.429	5	12.8	4.44
Taylor, Blake	Hou	26	55	0	44	38	5	21	42	1	3	2	.600	0	12.3	4.03
Taylor, Josh	Bos	29	47	0	40	39	3	19	48	3	2	2	.500	0	13.7	3.94
Tepera, Ryan	CWS	34	60	0	56	42	7	20	64	3	4	3	.571	0	10.4	3.46
Thielbar, Caleb	Min	35	61	0	69	64	7	19	78	2	5	3	.625	0	11.1	3.50
Thompson, Keegan	ChC	27	35	12	67	58	7	34	68	3	3	4	.429	0	12.8	4.06
Thompson, Ryan	TB	30	36	0	37	34	4	12	39	1	2	2	.500	0	11.4	3.73
Thompson, Zach	Mia	28	42	0	93	94	15	33	90	4	4	6	.400	0	12.7	4.35
Thornton, Trent	Tor	28	30	0	39	41	6	13	38	2	2	2	.500	0	12.9	4.38
Toussaint, Touki	Atl	26	15	15	76	71	10	42	83	9	4	4	.500	0	14.4	4.62
Treinen, Blake	LAD	33	73	0	77	60	7	29	84	3	6	3	.667	9	10.8	3.44
Trivino, Lou	Oak	30	69	0	72	61	7	33	67	3	4	4	.500	22	12.1	3.96
Underwood Jr., Duane	Pit	27	35	0	62	69	8	25	59	3	3	4	.429	0	14.1	4.65
Urena, Jose	Det	30	25	10	81	91	12	31	54	4	3	6	.333	0	14.0	5.00
Urias, Julio	LAD	25	31	31	184	149	21	45	189	7	14	6	.700	0	9.8	3.38
Urquidy, Jose	Hou	27	22	22	135	117	22	26	121	2	8	7	.533	0	9.7	3.70
Valdez, Framber	Hou	28	25	25	161	145	15	65	156	12	10	8	.556	0	12.4	3.97
Velasquez, Vince	SD	30	17	17	66	62	12	32	74	4	3	4	.429	0	13.4	4.50
Voth, Austin	Was	30	46	0	50	51	8	20	49	2	3	3	.500	0	13.1	4.50
Wacha, Michael	TB	30	29	25	142	149	28	43	133	5	7	9	.438	0	12.5	4.57
Wainwright, Adam	StL	40	30	30	184	172	23	52	150	8	11	10	.524	0	11.3	3.99
Walker, Taijuan	NYM	29	28	28	162	140	26	58	147	6	9	9	.500	0	11.3	4.09
Warren, Austin	LAA	26	45	0	44	44	3	19	49	2	3	2	.600	0	13.3	3.91
Watson, Tony	SF	37	63	0	61	53	7	17	47	2	4	3	.571	0	10.6	3.82
Weathers, Ryan	SD	22	30	16	95	104	19	29	77	3	5	6	.455	0	12.9	4.84
Weaver, Luke	Ari	28	18	18	100	100	16	33	100	3	5	6	.455	0	12.2	4.19
Webb, Jacob	Atl	28	39	0	40	34	5	17	43	1	3	2	.600	4	11.7	3.80
Webb, Logan	SF	25	31	31	188	179	16	55	193	11	11	10	.524	0	11.7	3.70
Wells, Alexander	Bal	25	13	13	62	69	9	15	47	2	3	4	.429	0	12.5	4.43
Wells, Tyler	Bal	27	48	0	62	50	9	15	70	1	4	3	.571	20	9.6	3.35
Wendelken, J.B.	Ari	29	54	0	52	49	6	24	52	1	3	3	.500	17	12.8	4.16
Wheeler, Zack	Phi	32	31	31	210	189	20	52	220	9	14	9	.609	0	10.7	3.48
White, Mitch	LAD	27	20	0	50	47	7	18	52	1	3	2	.600	0	11.9	3.99
Whitley, Forrest	Hou	24	13	13	65	65	12	39	89	4	3	4	.429	0	15.0	4.85
Whitlock, Garrett	Bos	26	44	0	70	69	6	19	73	3	4	3	.571	1	11.7	3.67
Wick, Rowan	ChC	29	51	0	53	43	4	27	64	2	3	3	.500	10	12.2	3.58
Widener, Taylor	Ari	27	22	22	105	105	19	47	112	7	5	7	.417	0	13.6	4.68
Williams, Devin	Mil	27	55	0	55	35	6	28	86	2	4	2	.667	5	10.6	3.04
Williams, Trevor	NYM	30	25	11	94	92	14	31	84	4	5	6	.455	0	12.2	4.21
Wilson, Bryse	Pit	24	19	19	97	115	15	32	75	3	4	7	.364	0	13.9	4.97
Wilson, Justin	Cin	34	49	0	39	36	5	20	37	1	2	2	.500	0	13.2	4.39
Wisler, Matt	TB	29	46	0	46	40	6	12	56	1	3	2	.600	0	10.4	3.36
Wittgren, Nick	Cle	31	63	0	70	71	14	20	69	4	3	5	.375	0	12.2	4.44
Wood, Alex	SF	31	26	26	139	138	18	41	143	14	8	8	.500	0	12.5	4.08
Woodford, Jake	StL	25	21	11	76	73	11	31	58	5	4	5	.444	0	12.9	4.56
Woodruff, Brandon	Mil	29	27	27	161	132	19	44	184	7	10	7	.588	0	10.2	3.37
Yarbrough, Ryan	TB	30	29	19	150	151	19	30	117	10	8	9	.471	0	11.5	4.04
Ynoa, Huascar	Atl	24	29	29	147	144	25	52	160	8	8	8	.500	0	12.5	4.23
Young, Alex	Cle	28	33	0	41	46	8	16	35	2	2	3	.400	0	14.0	5.16
Zimmer, Kyle	KC	30	42	0	46	41	5	26	42	0	2	3	.400	0	13.1	4.22
Zimmermann, Bruce	Bal	27	20	20	95	107	16	38	86	3	4	6	.400	0	14.0	4.93

The Favorite Toy

Sarah Thompson

Bill James devised a system, dubbed "The Favorite Toy," that determines the likelihood of a player achieving a certain milestone.

Since most of these milestones are counting stats, the shortened 2020 season did a number on most people's chances of hitting milestones already difficult to reach. But not all.

Our most likely milestone to be achieved is 3,000 hits by Miguel Cabrera, clocking in at 98%. This number makes sense—he only needs 13. He began the 2021 season 134 hits short of the mark and did a good job to cover some ground. He has a non-trivial chance (28%) at reaching 2,000 RBI, though with 1804 to the day, that's much less guaranteed. What's interesting is that this season, he had his most RBIs collected (75) since 2016 (108), a year in which he slashed .316/.393/.563.

The next-most-likely milestone is Nelson Cruz's chance to hit 500 home runs. Having hit 32 homers in his age-40 season, it's certainly not out of the question that he collects 51 more before he hangs up the cleats.

A name you'll see around a lot is Fernando Tatis Jr. The combination of his youth and demonstrated power gives him non-trivial odds to hit a lot of these milestones. They're long shots—I don't know if we'll ever see 762 home runs surpassed—but it's still exciting to have these possibilities in the back of your head every time you see Tatis hit one out of the park.

We also calculate likelihoods of a pitcher throwing a no-hitter. It's not a hard sell to present Jacob deGrom as the most likely guy to throw a no-no with a 44% chance. You might be surprised to see Dylan Cease not too far behind him at 37%, though. He had two one-hitters this year, but both were through 6 innings and with pitch counts of 103 and 98. While he can keep the hits down, whether or not he can be efficient enough to finish a no-hitter remains to be seen.

Career Targets

762 Home Runs
% chance to break record

Tatis Jr., Fernando	4%
Guerrero Jr., Vladimir	< 1%

2,298 RBI
% chance to break record

Devers, Rafael	3%
Pujols, Albert	< 1%

2,296 Runs Scored
% chance to break record

Soto, Juan	5%
Freeman, Freddie	< 1%

4,257 Hits
% chance to break record

900 Home Runs
% chance to reach milestone

2,000 RBI
% chance to reach milestone

Pujols, Albert	done
Cabrera, Miguel	28%
Devers, Rafael	10%
Machado, Manny	10%
Soto, Juan	6%
Guerrero Jr., Vladimir	5%
Freeman, Freddie	4%
Arenado, Nolan	3%
Tatis Jr., Fernando	2%
Harper, Bryce	1%

6,857 Total Bases
% chance to break record

Guerrero Jr., Vladimir	< 1%
Devers, Rafael	< 1%

4,000 Hits
% chance to reach milestone

800 Home Runs
% chance to reach milestone

Tatis Jr., Fernando	1%

600 Home Runs
% chance to reach milestone

Pujols, Albert	done
Harper, Bryce	18%
Alonso, Pete	13%
Tatis Jr., Fernando	11%
Devers, Rafael	10%
Machado, Manny	10%
Guerrero Jr., Vladimir	9%
Olson, Matt	8%
Soto, Juan	7%
Acuna Jr., Ronald	5%

793 Doubles
% chance to break record

Devers, Rafael	8%
Castellanos, Nick	< 1%

3,000 Hits
% chance to reach milestone

Pujols, Albert	done
Cabrera, Miguel	98%
Freeman, Freddie	28%
Machado, Manny	20%
Altuve, Jose	18%
Bogaerts, Xander	15%
Turner, Trea	12%
Devers, Rafael	10%
Harper, Bryce	10%
Guerrero Jr., Vladimir	8%

700 Home Runs
% chance to reach milestone

Pujols, Albert	53%
Tatis Jr., Fernando	8%
Guerrero Jr., Vladimir	5%
Harper, Bryce	3%
Alonso, Pete	2%
Devers, Rafael	< 1%

500 Home Runs
% chance to reach milestone

Pujols, Albert	done
Cabrera, Miguel	done
Cruz, Nelson	56%
Stanton, Giancarlo	36%
Harper, Bryce	34%
Machado, Manny	28%
Arenado, Nolan	28%
Trout, Mike	24%
Freeman, Freddie	23%
Olson, Matt	22%

1,000 Stolen Bases
% chance to reach milestone

Most Likely No-Hitter
% chance to reach milestone

deGrom, Jacob	44%
Burnes, Corbin	40%
Peralta, Freddy	39%
Cease, Dylan	37%
Rodon, Carlos	33%
Cole, Gerrit	30%
Snell, Blake	30%
Ray, Robbie	29%
Scherzer, Max	25%
Glasnow, Tyler	22%

The 300-Win Candidates

Mark Simon

The 300-win pitcher looks like it's going to go the way of the dinosaur. Bill James acknowledged this in the 2015 edition of the Handbook. But we still hold onto a speck of hope each year by publishing this essay.

Barring MLB changing the criteria by which a pitcher earns a win, this year's list might be the last speck.

We list only two pitchers with a greater than 5% chance of reaching that milestone.

Max Scherzer held steady at an 11% chance to reach 300 wins by winning 15 games in 2021. The problem is, Scherzer could win 15 games the next seven seasons (at which point he'll be entering his age 44 season) and not reach 300.

Zack Greinke's listed at 6%, down from 16% a year ago, though I would put a caveat in here. Greinke could admittedly decide to retire at any time, but given his intelligence and creativity as a pitcher, couldn't you see a scenario in which he chose to reinvent himself as a knuckleballer so that he could pitch until he was 45? We're grasping here, I know.

Entering the 2015 season, Clayton Kershaw had a 31% chance at reaching 300 wins. Now he's at 1%. Kershaw won 16 games as recently as 2019. But even if he averaged 16 wins in his age 34-40 seasons, he'd still be short.

Adam Wainwright and Jon Lester probably don't have more than a year left, so there's not much to say there.

One pitcher not on our list should also be noted. Justin Verlander's virtually two-season absence from the sport almost certainly robbed him of the opportunity. Even if Verlander won 17 games in each year from 2022 to 2025, he'd be heading into his age-43 season still short of 300 wins.

Pitchers on Course For 300 Wins

Name	2021 Age	R/L	W	L	EWL	Momentum	Chance
Scherzer, Max	36	R	190	97	13.8	.762	11%
Greinke, Zack	37	R	219	132	9.9	.705	6%
Wainwright, Adam	39	R	184	105	13.0	.670	3%
Kershaw, Clayton	33	L	185	84	9.8	.659	1%
Lester, Jon	37	L	200	117	7.2	.598	<1%

EWL: Established Win Level

Minor League Abbreviation Key

Abbreviation	Team	Level	League	MLB Affiliate	First Year	Last Year
Abrdn	Aberdeen IronBirds	A-	New York-Penn League	Baltimore Orioles	2019	2019
Abrdn	Aberdeen IronBirds	A+	High-A East	Baltimore Orioles	2021	2021
Akron	Akron RubberDucks	AA	Double-A Northeast	Cleveland Indians	2021	2021
Albq	Albuquerque Isotopes	AAA	Triple-A West	Colorado Rockies	2021	2021
Altna	Altoona Curve	AA	Double-A Northeast	Pittsburgh Pirates	2018	2021
Amrllo	Amarillo Sod Poodles	AA	Texas League	San Diego Padres	2019	2019
Amrllo	Amarillo Sod Poodles	AA	Double-A Central	Arizona Diamondbacks	2021	2021
Angels	AZL Angels	R	Arizona League	Los Angeles Angels	2021	2021
Ark	Arkansas Travelers	AA	Double-A Central	Seattle Mariners	2019	2021
AsGold	AZL Athletics Gold	R	Arizona League	Oakland Athletics	2021	2021
Ashvll	Asheville Tourists	A+	High-A East	Houston Astros	2021	2021
Astros	GCL Astros	R	Gulf Coast League	Houston Astros	2021	2021
Augsta	Augusta GreenJackets	A	South Atlantic League	San Francisco Giants	2019	2019
Augsta	Augusta GreenJackets	A	Low-A East	Atlanta Braves	2021	2021
B Jays	GCL Blue Jays	R	Gulf Coast League	Toronto Blue Jays	2017	2017
B Jays	GCL Blue Jays	R	Gulf Coast League	Toronto Blue Jays	2021	2021
Batvia	Batavia Muckdogs	A-	New York-Penn League	Miami Marlins	2017	2017
Beloit	Beloit Snappers	A+	High-A Central	Miami Marlins	2021	2021
BG	Bowling Green Hot Rods	A	Midwest League	Tampa Bay Rays	2017	2019
BG	Bowling Green Hot Rods	A+	High-A East	Tampa Bay Rays	2021	2021
Biloxi	Biloxi Shuckers	AA	Double-A South	Milwaukee Brewers	2021	2021
Bklyn	Brooklyn Cyclones	A-	New York-Penn League	New York Mets	2019	2019
Bklyn	Brooklyn Cyclones	A+	High-A East	New York Mets	2021	2021
Bnghtn	Binghamton Rumble Ponies	AA	Double-A Northeast	New York Mets	2021	2021
Bowie	Bowie Baysox	AA	Double-A Northeast	Baltimore Orioles	2017	2021
Bradtn	Bradenton Marauders	A+	Florida State League	Pittsburgh Pirates	2017	2019
Bradtn	Bradenton Marauders	A	Low-A Southeast	Pittsburgh Pirates	2021	2021
Braves	GCL Braves	R	Gulf Coast League	Atlanta Braves	2021	2021
BrewersB	AZL Brewers Blue	R	Arizona League	Milwaukee Brewers	2021	2021
BrewrsGold	AZL Brewers Gold	R	Arizona League	Milwaukee Brewers	2021	2021
Brham	Birmingham Barons	AA	Double-A South	Chicago White Sox	2017	2021
Brstol	Bristol Pirates	R+	Appalachian League	Pittsburgh Pirates	2018	2018
Buffalo	Buffalo Bisons	AAA	Triple-A East	Toronto Blue Jays	2019	2021
Cards	GCL Cardinals	R	Gulf Coast League	St Louis Cardinals	2021	2021
Carlina	Carolina Mudcats	A+	Carolina League	Milwaukee Brewers	2019	2019
Carlina	Carolina Mudcats	A	Low-A East	Milwaukee Brewers	2021	2021
Charllt	Charlotte NC Knights	AAA	Triple-A East	Chicago White Sox	2017	2021
Charltt	Charlotte FL Stone Crabs	A+	Florida State League	Tampa Bay Rays	2018	2019
Chatt	Chattanooga Lookouts	AA	Double-A South	Cincinnati Reds	2021	2021
Clmbs	Columbus Clippers	AAA	Triple-A East	Cleveland Indians	2021	2021
Clrwtr	Clearwater Threshers	A+	Florida State League	Philadelphia Phillies	2017	2019
Clrwtr	Clearwater Threshers	A	Low-A Southeast	Philadelphia Phillies	2021	2021
Columb	Columbia Fireflies	A	South Atlantic League	New York Mets	2019	2019
Columb	Columbia Fireflies	A	Low-A East	Kansas City Royals	2021	2021
Conn	Connecticut Tigers	A-	New York-Penn League	Detroit Tigers	2017	2019
CpChr	Corpus Christi Hooks	AA	Double-A Central	Houston Astros	2021	2021
Crpds	Cedar Rapids Kernels	A	Midwest League	Minnesota Twins	2017	2018
Crpds	Cedar Rapids Kernels	A+	High-A Central	Minnesota Twins	2021	2021
CtnSC	Charleston RiverDogs	A	South Atlantic League	New York Yankees	2018	2018
CtnSC	Charleston RiverDogs	A	Low-A East	Tampa Bay Rays	2021	2021
Cubs Blue	AZL Cubs Blue	R	Arizona League	Chicago Cubs	2021	2021
Cubs2	AZL Cubs2	R	Arizona League	Chicago Cubs	2018	2018
Dayton	Dayton Dragons	A	Midwest League	Cincinnati Reds	2018	2018
Dayton	Dayton Dragons	A+	High-A Central	Cincinnati Reds	2021	2021
Dbcks	AZL D-backs	R	Arizona League	Arizona Diamondbacks	2018	2021
Ddgrs	AZL Dodgers 1	R	Arizona League	Los Angeles Dodgers	2021	2021
Dlmrva	Delmarva Shorebirds	A	South Atlantic League	Baltimore Orioles	2018	2019
Dlmrva	Delmarva Shorebirds	A	Low-A East	Baltimore Orioles	2021	2021
Dnedin	Dunedin Blue Jays	A+	Florida State League	Toronto Blue Jays	2018	2019
Dnedin	Dunedin Blue Jays	A	Low-A Southeast	Toronto Blue Jays	2021	2021
Drham	Durham Bulls	AAA	Triple-A East	Tampa Bay Rays	2021	2021
DwnEast	Down East Wood Ducks	A	Low-A East	Texas Rangers	2021	2021

Minor League Abbreviation Key

Abbreviation	Team	Level	League	MLB Affiliate	First Year	Last Year
Dytona	Daytona Tortugas	A+	Florida State League	Cincinnati Reds	2019	2019
Dytona	Daytona Tortugas	A	Low-A Southeast	Cincinnati Reds	2021	2021
ElPaso	El Paso Chihuahuas	AAA	Triple-A West	San Diego Padres	2021	2021
Erie	Erie SeaWolves	AA	Double-A Northeast	Detroit Tigers	2018	2021
Eugene	Eugene Emeralds	A+	High-A West	San Francisco Giants	2021	2021
Everett	Everett AquaSox	A+	High-A West	Seattle Mariners	2021	2021
Faytvll	Fayetteville Woodpeckers	A	Low-A East	Houston Astros	2021	2021
Florida	Florida Fire Frogs	A+	Florida State League	Atlanta Braves	2018	2018
Frdrck	Frederick Keys	A+	Carolina League	Baltimore Orioles	2017	2019
Fred	Fredericksburg Nationals	A	Low-A East	Washington Nationals	2021	2021
Fresno	Fresno Grizzlies	A	Low-A West	Colorado Rockies	2021	2021
Frisco	Frisco RoughRiders	AA	Double-A Central	Texas Rangers	2021	2021
FtMyrs	Fort Myers Miracle	A+	Florida State League	Minnesota Twins	2018	2019
FtMyrs	Fort Myers Mighty Mussels	A	Low-A Southeast	Minnesota Twins	2021	2021
FtWyn	Fort Wayne TinCaps	A	Midwest League	San Diego Padres	2018	2019
FtWyn	Fort Wayne TinCaps	A+	High-A Central	San Diego Padres	2021	2021
Giants Blk	AZL Giants Black	R	Arizona League	San Francisco Giants	2021	2021
Giants Orng	AZL Giants Orange	R	Arizona League	San Francisco Giants	2018	2021
Grnsbr	Greensboro Grasshoppers	A	South Atlantic League	Miami Marlins	2018	2018
Grnsbr	Greensboro Grasshoppers	A+	High-A East	Pittsburgh Pirates	2021	2021
Grnvlle	Greenville Drive	A	South Atlantic League	Boston Red Sox	2019	2019
Grnvlle	Greenville Drive	A+	High-A East	Boston Red Sox	2021	2021
Gt Lks	Great Lakes Loons	A	Midwest League	Los Angeles Dodgers	2017	2017
Gt Lks	Great Lakes Loons	A+	High-A Central	Los Angeles Dodgers	2021	2021
Gwnntt	Gwinnett Stripers	AAA	Triple-A East	Atlanta Braves	2019	2021
Helena	Helena Brewers	R+	Pioneer League	Milwaukee Brewers	2018	2018
Hkry	Hickory Crawdads	A+	High-A East	Texas Rangers	2021	2021
Hlsbro	Hillsboro Hops	A-	Northwest League	Arizona Diamondbacks	2018	2019
Hlsbro	Hillsboro Hops	A+	High-A West	Arizona Diamondbacks	2021	2021
Hrsbrg	Harrisburg Senators	AA	Double-A Northeast	Washington Nationals	2021	2021
Hrtfrd	Hartford Yard Goats	AA	Double-A Northeast	Colorado Rockies	2021	2021
HudVal	Hudson Valley Renegades	A-	New York-Penn League	Tampa Bay Rays	2017	2017
HudVal	Hudson Valley Renegades	A+	High-A East	New York Yankees	2021	2021
Indians	AZL Indians Blue	R	Arizona League	Cleveland Indians	2021	2021
Indy	Indianapolis Indians	AAA	Triple-A East	Pittsburgh Pirates	2019	2021
InldEm	Inland Empire 66ers	A	Low-A West	Los Angeles Angels	2021	2021
Iowa	Iowa Cubs	AAA	Triple-A East	Chicago Cubs	2021	2021
Jacksn	Jackson Generals	AA	Southern League	Arizona Diamondbacks	2019	2019
Jaxnvl	Jacksonville Jumbo Shrimp	AA	Southern League	Miami Marlins	2019	2019
Jaxnvl	Jacksonville Jumbo Shrimp	AAA	Triple-A East	Miami Marlins	2021	2021
Jhscty	Johnson City Cardinals	R+	Appalachian League	St Louis Cardinals	2018	2018
JrsyShr	Jersey Shore BlueClaws	A+	High-A East	Philadelphia Phillies	2021	2021
Jupiter	Jupiter Hammerheads	A+	Florida State League	Miami Marlins	2019	2019
Jupiter	Jupiter Hammerheads	A	Low-A Southeast	Miami Marlins	2021	2021
Kane	Kane County Cougars	A	Midwest League	Arizona Diamondbacks	2017	2019
Knapol	Kannapolis Intimidators	A	South Atlantic League	Chicago White Sox	2018	2019
Knapol	Kannapolis Cannon Ballers	A	Low-A East	Chicago White Sox	2021	2021
Kngspt	Kingsport Mets	R+	Appalachian League	New York Mets	2018	2018
Lakwd	Lakewood BlueClaws	A	South Atlantic League	Philadelphia Phillies	2017	2018
Lk Cty	Lake County Captains	A+	High-A Central	Cleveland Indians	2021	2021
Lk Els	Lake Elsinore Storm	A+	California League	San Diego Padres	2019	2019
Lk Els	Lake Elsinore Storm	A	Low-A West	San Diego Padres	2021	2021
Lkland	Lakeland Flying Tigers	A+	Florida State League	Detroit Tigers	2018	2019
Lkland	Lakeland Flying Tigers	A	Low-A Southeast	Detroit Tigers	2021	2021
Lnsng	Lansing Lugnuts	A+	High-A Central	Oakland Athletics	2021	2021
LsVgs	Las Vegas Aviators	AAA	Triple-A West	Oakland Athletics	2021	2021
Lsvlle	Louisville Bats	AAA	Triple-A East	Cincinnati Reds	2021	2021
LV	Lehigh Valley IronPigs	AAA	Triple-A East	Philadelphia Phillies	2021	2021
Lynbrg	Lynchburg Hillcats	A	Low-A East	Cleveland Indians	2021	2021
Mdest	Modesto Nuts	A+	California League	Seattle Mariners	2019	2019
Mdest	Modesto Nuts	A	Low-A West	Seattle Mariners	2021	2021
Mdlnd	Midland RockHounds	AA	Double-A Central	Oakland Athletics	2021	2021
Memp	Memphis Redbirds	AAA	Pacific Coast League	St Louis Cardinals	2019	2019
Memp	Memphis Redbirds	AAA	Triple-A East	St Louis Cardinals	2021	2021

Minor League Abbreviation Key

Abbreviation	Team	Level	League	MLB Affiliate	First Year	Last Year
Mets	GCL Mets	R	Gulf Coast League	New York Mets	2018	2021
Missi	Mississippi Braves	AA	Double-A South	Atlanta Braves	2018	2021
Mont	Montgomery Biscuits	AA	Southern League	Tampa Bay Rays	2019	2019
Mont	Montgomery Biscuits	AA	Double-A South	Tampa Bay Rays	2021	2021
Mrlns	GCL Marlins	R	Gulf Coast League	Miami Marlins	2021	2021
MrtlBh	Myrtle Beach Pelicans	A	Low-A East	Chicago Cubs	2021	2021
Ms	AZL Mariners	R	Arizona League	Seattle Mariners	2021	2021
Msoula	Missoula Osprey	R+	Pioneer League	Arizona Diamondbacks	2018	2018
Nashv	Nashville Sounds	AAA	Triple-A East	Milwaukee Brewers	2021	2021
Nats	GCL Nationals	R	Gulf Coast League	Washington Nationals	2021	2021
Nham	New Hampshire Fisher Cats	AA	Double-A Northeast	Toronto Blue Jays	2019	2021
Norfolk	Norfolk Tides	AAA	Triple-A East	Baltimore Orioles	2019	2021
NWArk	NW Arkansas Naturals	AA	Double-A Central	Kansas City Royals	2021	2021
OkCity	Oklahoma City Dodgers	AAA	Pacific Coast League	Los Angeles Dodgers	2019	2019
OkCity	Oklahoma City Dodgers	AAA	Triple-A West	Los Angeles Dodgers	2021	2021
Omha	Omaha Storm Chasers	AAA	Triple-A East	Kansas City Royals	2021	2021
Orioles	GCL Orioles	R	Gulf Coast League	Baltimore Orioles	2017	2021
Padres	AZL Padres	R	Arizona League	San Diego Padres	2017	2021
Padres2	AZL Padres2	R	Arizona League	San Diego Padres	2017	2017
Peoria	Peoria Chiefs	A	Midwest League	St Louis Cardinals	2017	2019
Peoria	Peoria Chiefs	A+	High-A Central	St Louis Cardinals	2021	2021
Phillies	GCL Phillies	R	Gulf Coast League	Philadelphia Phillies	2019	2021
PhilliesW	GCL Phillies West	R	Gulf Coast League	Philadelphia Phillies	2019	2019
Pirates	GCL Pirates	R	Gulf Coast League	Pittsburgh Pirates	2017	2017
Pirates	GCL Pirates	R	Gulf Coast League	Pittsburgh Pirates	2019	2021
PlmBh	Palm Beach Cardinals	A+	Florida State League	St Louis Cardinals	2018	2019
PlmBh	Palm Beach Cardinals	A	Low-A Southeast	St Louis Cardinals	2021	2021
Pnscla	Pensacola Blue Wahoos	AA	Southern League	Minnesota Twins	2019	2019
Pnscla	Pensacola Blue Wahoos	AA	Double-A South	Miami Marlins	2021	2021
Portlnd	Portland ME Sea Dogs	AA	Double-A Northeast	Boston Red Sox	2021	2021
Prnctn	Princeton Rays	R+	Appalachian League	Tampa Bay Rays	2018	2018
Pulski	Pulaski Yankees	R+	Appalachian League	New York Yankees	2017	2017
QuadC	Quad Cities River Bandits	A+	High-A Central	Kansas City Royals	2021	2021
Rays	GCL Rays	R	Gulf Coast League	Tampa Bay Rays	2021	2021
Rchmd	Richmond Flying Squirrels	AA	Double-A Northeast	San Francisco Giants	2019	2021
Rcuca	Rancho Cucamonga Quakes	A+	California League	Los Angeles Dodgers	2017	2017
Rcuca	Rancho Cucamonga Quakes	A	Low-A West	Los Angeles Dodgers	2021	2021
Rdng	Reading Fightin Phils	AA	Double-A Northeast	Philadelphia Phillies	2019	2021
RdRck	Round Rock Express	AAA	Triple-A West	Texas Rangers	2021	2021
Reds	AZL Reds	R	Arizona League	Cincinnati Reds	2021	2021
RedSx	GCL Red Sox	R	Gulf Coast League	Boston Red Sox	2018	2021
Reno	Reno Aces	AAA	Triple-A West	Arizona Diamondbacks	2021	2021
Rngrs	AZL Rangers	R	Arizona League	Texas Rangers	2021	2021
Roch	Rochester Red Wings	AAA	Triple-A East	Washington Nationals	2021	2021
Rock	Rocket City Trash Pandas	AA	Double-A South	Los Angeles Angels	2021	2021
Rome	Rome Braves	A	South Atlantic League	Atlanta Braves	2017	2017
Rome	Rome Braves	A+	High-A East	Atlanta Braves	2021	2021
Royals	AZL Royals	R	Arizona League	Kansas City Royals	2019	2021
Salem	Salem Red Sox	A+	Carolina League	Boston Red Sox	2019	2019
Salem	Salem Red Sox	A	Low-A East	Boston Red Sox	2021	2021
Salt Lk	Salt Lake City Bees	AAA	Triple-A West	Los Angeles Angels	2021	2021
Sbend	South Bend Cubs	A	Midwest League	Chicago Cubs	2019	2019
Sbend	South Bend Cubs	A+	High-A Central	Chicago Cubs	2021	2021
Scrmto	Sacramento River Cats	AAA	Triple-A West	San Francisco Giants	2021	2021
SgrLnd	Sugar Land Skeeters	AAA	Triple-A West	Houston Astros	2021	2021
SlKzr	Salem-Keizer Volcanoes	A-	Northwest League	San Francisco Giants	2018	2019
Smrst	Somerset Patriots	AA	Double-A Northeast	New York Yankees	2021	2021
SnAnt	San Antonio Missions	AA	Double-A Central	San Diego Padres	2021	2021
SnJos	San Jose Giants	A+	California League	San Francisco Giants	2019	2019
SnJos	San Jose Giants	A	Low-A West	San Francisco Giants	2021	2021
Spkane	Spokane Indians	A+	High-A West	Colorado Rockies	2021	2021
Sprgfld	Springfield Cardinals	AA	Double-A Central	St Louis Cardinals	2019	2021
Stcktn	Stockton Ports	A	Low-A West	Oakland Athletics	2021	2021
Stluci	St. Lucie Mets	A	Low-A Southeast	New York Mets	2021	2021

Minor League Abbreviation Key

Abbreviation	Team	Level	League	MLB Affiliate	First Year	Last Year
StPaul	St. Paul Saints	AAA	Triple-A East	Minnesota Twins	2021	2021
S-WB	Scranton WB RailRiders	AAA	Triple-A East	New York Yankees	2019	2021
Syrcse	Syracuse Mets	AAA	Triple-A East	New York Mets	2021	2021
Tacom	Tacoma Rainiers	AAA	Triple-A West	Seattle Mariners	2021	2021
Tampa	Tampa Tarpons	A+	Florida State League	New York Yankees	2018	2019
Tampa	Tampa Tarpons	A	Low-A Southeast	New York Yankees	2021	2021
Tenn	Tennessee Smokies	AA	Double-A South	Chicago Cubs	2021	2021
Tigers	GCL Tigers	R	Gulf Coast League	Detroit Tigers	2021	2021
TigersW	GCL Tigers West	R	Gulf Coast League	Detroit Tigers	2018	2018
TigersW	GCL Tigers West	R	Gulf Coast League	Detroit Tigers	2019	2021
Toledo	Toledo Mud Hens	AAA	Triple-A East	Detroit Tigers	2021	2021
TriCity	Tri-City Dust Devils	A+	High-A West	Los Angeles Angels	2021	2021
Trntn	Trenton Thunder	AA	Eastern League	New York Yankees	2018	2019
Tulsa	Tulsa Drillers	AA	Double-A Central	Los Angeles Dodgers	2018	2021
Twins	GCL Twins	R	Gulf Coast League	Minnesota Twins	2017	2021
Vancvr	Vancouver Canadians	A-	Northwest League	Toronto Blue Jays	2017	2017
Vancvr	Vancouver Canadians	A+	High-A West	Toronto Blue Jays	2021	2021
Visalia	Visalia Rawhide	A+	California League	Arizona Diamondbacks	2018	2019
Visalia	Visalia Rawhide	A	Low-A West	Arizona Diamondbacks	2021	2021
Wich	Wichita Wind Surge	AA	Double-A Central	Minnesota Twins	2021	2021
Wilmg	Wilmington Blue Rocks	A+	High-A East	Washington Nationals	2021	2021
WinSa	Winston-Salem Dash	A+	Carolina League	Chicago White Sox	2018	2019
WinSa	Winston-Salem Dash	A+	High-A East	Chicago White Sox	2021	2021
Wisc	Wisconsin Timber Rattlers	A	Midwest League	Milwaukee Brewers	2018	2019
Wisc	Wisconsin Timber Rattlers	A+	High-A Central	Milwaukee Brewers	2021	2021
Wmich	West Michigan Whitecaps	A	Midwest League	Detroit Tigers	2017	2019
Wmich	West Michigan Whitecaps	A+	High-A Central	Detroit Tigers	2021	2021
Wmspt	Williamsport Crosscutters	A-	New York-Penn League	Philadelphia Phillies	2017	2017
Wrcstr	Worcester Red Sox	AAA	Triple-A East	Boston Red Sox	2021	2021
Wsox	AZL White Sox	R	Arizona League	Chicago White Sox	2018	2021
WV	West Virginia Power	A	South Atlantic League	Pittsburgh Pirates	2017	2018
WV	West Virginia Black Bears	A-	New York-Penn League	Pittsburgh Pirates	2019	2019
WV	West Virginia Power	A	South Atlantic League	Seattle Mariners	2019	2019
Yanks1	GCL Yankees	R	Gulf Coast League	New York Yankees	2021	2021
Yanks2	GCL Yankees2	R	Gulf Coast League	New York Yankees	2017	2017

Baseball Glossary

% Inherited Scored
The percentage of inherited baserunners a relief pitcher allows to score.

% Pitches Taken
The percentage of pitches that a batter does not swing at out of the total number of pitches thrown to him.

1st Batter Average
The Batting Average that a relief pitcher allows to the first batter he faces when he enters a game.

1st Batter OBP
The On-Base Percentage that a relief pitcher allows to the first batter he faces when he enters a game.

1st to 3rd (Baserunning)
"Moved" is the number of times a runner goes from 1st base to 3rd base on a SINGLE. "Chances" are the number of times a runner is on 1st base and a batter is credited with a SINGLE.

1st to Home (Baserunning)
"Moved" is the number of times a runner goes from 1st base to home on a DOUBLE. "Chances" are the number of times a runner is on 1st base and a batter is credited with a DOUBLE.

2nd to Home (Baserunning)
"Moved" is the number of times a runner goes from 2nd base to home on a SINGLE. "Chances" are the number of times a runner is on 2nd base and a batter is credited with a SINGLE.

Active Career Batting Leaders
A list of batting leaders among active (appearing in the most recent season) players. An active player is eligible when he meets the minimum requirements for the following categories:

> 1,000 At Bats—Batting Average, On-Base Percentage, Slugging Average, At
> Bats Per HR, At Bats Per GDP, At Bats Per RBI, Strikeout-to-Walk Ratio
> 100 Stolen Base Attempts—Stolen Base Success Percentage

Active Career Pitching Leaders
A list of pitching leaders among active (appearing in the most recent season) players. An active player is eligible when he meets the minimum requirements for the following categories:

> 750 Innings Pitched—Earned Run Average, Opponent Batting Average, all "Per
> 9 Innings" categories, Strikeout-to-Walk Ratio
> 250 Games Started—Complete Game Frequency
> 100 Decisions—Win-Loss Percentage

ART
See PART System

BA w/ RISP
The Batting Average allowed by a pitcher while pitching with runners in scoring position.

Base Taken
A player is credited with a Base Taken whenever he moves up a base on a Wild Pitch, Passed Ball, Balk, Sacrifice Fly, or Defensive Indifference.

Batting Average
Hits divided by at bats.

Batting Average on Balls in Play (BABIP)
Hits in play divided by balls in play. Home runs are not counted as balls in play.

Batting Average Plus Slugging (BPS)
Batting Average plus Slugging Average. Used in Leaderboards on out-of-zone pitches (OutZ).

Blown Save
When a relief pitcher enters a game in a Save Situation (see definition for Save Situation) and allows the other team to score the tying or go-ahead run.

Bomb (Intentional Walk)
An Intentional Walk is counted as a "Bomb" if
1. The next batter, after the IBB, does not ground into a double play, and
2. Multiple runs are scored in the inning, after the intentional walk.

BR Gain (Baserunning)
BR Gain (or Loss if a negative number) is the total of all the types of extra baserunning advances minus the (triple) penalty for all the BR Outs compared with what would be expected based on the MLB averages.

BR Outs (Baserunning)
BR Outs include the sum of Outs Advancing, Doubled Offs, and when a runner is tagged out on the bases when another runner moves up on a Wild Pitch, Passed Ball, or scores on a Sacrifice Fly.

BS Win
A Blown Save Win is a "win" credited to a reliever who has blown a save opportunity.

Career Targets
This method, also called the Favorite Toy, is a way to estimate the probability that a player will achieve a specific career goal. In this example, 3,000 hits will be used. The four components of the formula are:

1. Needed Hits. This is the number of Hits (or any statistic) that a player needs to reach a desired goal.

2. Years Remaining. This is the estimated number of years remaining in the player's career. It is determined using the player's age (on June 30th of the previous year; after a given season ends, use the season when making the calculation). The formula is (42 - age) divided by two. This means a player who is 20 years old will have 11 remaining seasons, a player who is 25 years old will have 8.5 remaining seasons and a player who is 35 years old will have 3.5 remaining seasons. If the player is a catcher, then multiply his remaining seasons by .7. The only stipulation is that years remaining must always be greater than or equal to 1.5.

3. Established Hit Level. The Established Hit Level is a weighted average of the player's hits over the past three seasons. To calculate the Established Hit Level after a given season is complete, add (Hits from two years ago), (Hits from last year multiplied by two), and (Hits from this year multiplied by three), then divide by six. If the Established Hit Level is less than 75% of the most recent performance, then the Established Hit Level is equal to .75 times the most recent performance.

4. Projected Remaining Hits. This is calculated by multiplying Years Remaining by the Established Hit Level.

The probability of achieving the specified goal is found by dividing Projected Remaining Hits by Needed Hits, then subtracting .5. The maximum that any player has of achieving a goal is .85 raised to the power of (Need Hits / Established Hit Level). This prevents the possibility of a player reaching a goal from being higher than 100 percent, which is impossible.

Catcher Pickoffs (CPO, CPkof)
The number of baserunners thrown out when a catcher throws to a base with a leading baserunner, and the runner is tagged out attempting to return to the base. Catcher pickoffs are not an official statistic and are not counted toward Caught Stealing totals.

Catcher's ERA
The ERA for a catcher is equal to the ERA of pitchers pitching while the catcher is playing behind the plate. It is calculated exactly like ERA for pitchers. Take the number of earned runs allowed while the catcher is playing, multiply it by 9 and then divide it by the total number of defensive innings that the catcher was behind the plate.

Cheap Win
A starting pitcher who wins the game with a game score under 50 gets credit for a cheap win. See Game Score.

Clean Outing
A Clean Outing is a game in which the reliever is not charged with a run (earned or otherwise) AND does not allow an inherited runner to score.

Cleanup Slugging Average
The Slugging Average of a batter when he bats in the cleanup spot, or fourth, in the batting order.

Close and Late
A situation in a game that is very similar to a Save Situation. The following requirements are necessary for a Close and Late game:
1. The game is in the seventh inning or later AND
2. The batting team is either leading by one run or tied OR
3. The tying run is on base, at bat, or on deck.

Component ERA (ERC)
A statistic that estimates what a pitcher's ERA should have been, based on his pitching performance. The ERC formula is calculated as follows:

1. Subtract the pitcher's Home Runs Allowed from his Hits Allowed.

2. Multiply Step 1 by 1.255.
3. Multiply his Home Runs Allowed by four.
4. Add Steps 2 and 3 together.
5. Multiply Step 4 by .89.
6. Add his Walks and Hit Batsmen.
7. Multiply Step 6 by .475.
8. Add Steps 5 and 7 together.

This yields the pitcher's total base estimate (PTB), which is:

$$\text{PTB} = 0.89 \times (1.255 \times (\text{H} - \text{HR}) + 4 \times \text{HR}) + 0.475 \times (\text{BB} + \text{HB})$$

For those pitchers for whom there is intentional walk data, use this formula instead:

$$\text{PTB} = 0.89 \times (1.255 \times (\text{H} - \text{HR}) + 4 \times \text{HR}) + 0.56 \times (\text{BB} + \text{HB} - \text{IBB})$$

9. Add Hits and Walks and Hit Batsmen.
10. Multiply Step 9 by PTB.
11. Divide Step 10 by Batters Facing Pitcher. If BFP data is unavailable, approximate it by multiplying Innings Pitched by 2.9, then adding Step 9.
12. Multiply Step 11 by 9.
13. Divide Step 12 by Innings Pitched.
14. Subtract .56 from Step 13.

This is the pitcher's ERC, which is:

$$\frac{(\text{H} + \text{BB} + \text{HB}) \times \text{PTB}}{\text{BFP} \times \text{IP}} \times 9 - 0.56$$

If the result after Step 13 is less than 2.24, adjust the formula as follows:

$$\frac{(\text{H} + \text{BB} + \text{HB}) \times \text{PTB}}{\text{BFP} \times \text{IP}} \times 9 \times 0.75$$

Consecutive Days
A count of how many times the pitcher was used after having pitched on the previous day or (in a few cases) in an earlier game on the same day.

Defensive Misplay
Any play which is not an error (or a passed ball) on which the fielder surrenders a base advance or the opportunity to make an out when a better play or a different play would have or might have gotten the out or prevented the advancement.

Defensive Runs Saved
Defensive Runs Saved (Runs Saved, for short) is the innovative metric introduced by John Dewan in *The Fielding Bible—Volume II* and modified in each subsequent volume. The Runs Saved value indicates how many runs a player saved or cost his team in the field compared to the average player at his position. A player of zero Runs Saved is about average; a positive number of runs saved indicates above-average

616

defense, below-average fielders post negative Runs Saved totals. There are eight components of Runs Saved:

PART Runs Saved (all positions; outfielders or players prior to 2013 use the Range and Positioning System)
Range and Positioning Runs Saved (non-catchers prior to 2013 and outfielders from 2013 forward.)
Adjusted Earned Runs Saved (Catchers)
Strike Zone Runs Saved (Catchers)
Stolen Base Runs Saved (Catchers, Pitchers)
Bunt Runs Saved (Corner Infielders, Pitchers, Catchers)
Double Play Runs Saved (Infielders)
Outfield Arm Runs Saved (Outfielders)
Good Play/Misplay Runs Saved (All Positions)

Double Play %
Successful Double Plays divided by the number of Double Play opportunities. This statistic includes both the fielder who started the play and the pivot man.

Double Play Opportunity
A fielder is considered to have a double play opportunity when a ground ball is hit with a runner on first base and less than 2 outs and that fielder is involved in the play. This is used to calculate Double Play % and Pivot %.

Doubled Off
A runner is Doubled Off when he is out for failing to get back to his base before he, or the base, is tagged after a ball hit in the air is caught.

Early Entry
A count of the number of times the reliever entered the game in the sixth inning or earlier.

Earned Run Average
The number of earned runs that a pitcher surrenders per nine innings that he pitches. It is calculated by multiplying the total earned runs allowed by nine and dividing by the total number of innings pitched.

Easy Save
This label is used to separate Saves by difficulty level (Easy or Tough). A Save is considered Easy if the relief pitcher enters the game, pitches one inning or less, and the first batter he faces does not at least represent the tying run.

Fielding Percentage
The percentage of plays a player makes in the field without making an error out of his total opportunities. Calculated by dividing (Putouts plus Assists) by (Putouts plus Assists plus Errors).

Games Finished
The relief pitcher who is in the game for each team when the game ends is credited with a Game Finished.

Game Score (Hitters)

To determine a hitter's Game Score:

Start with 15.

Add 10 times his Runs Created in the game (Runs Created for a single game is described in this Glossary).

Add 5 times his Runs Scored.

Add 5 times his RBI.

Game Score (Pitchers)

To determine the starting pitcher's Game Score:

Start with 50.

Add 1 point for each out recorded by the starting pitcher.

Add 2 points for each inning the pitcher completes after the fourth inning.

Add 1 point for each strikeout.

Subtract 2 points for each hit allowed.

Subtract 4 points for each earned run allowed.

Subtract 2 points for an unearned run.

Subtract 1 point for each walk.

GDP

Grounded into Double Play.

GDP Opportunity

This is a situation where the batter has a chance to ground into a double play. It occurs with at least a runner on first base and less than two outs.

Good Fielding Play

A Good Fielding Play is a play that is made when it is not clear whether or not the play can be made. It is a play that is made when, had the play not been made, no one would have faulted the fielder for not making it.

Ground / Fly Ratio (Grd/Fly, GB/FB)

Calculated for both batters and pitchers. For batters, it is the number of groundballs hit divided by the number of flyballs hit. For pitchers, it is exactly the same but uses the number of groundballs and flyballs allowed. Every fair batted ball is included except for bunts and line drives.

Hold

A relief pitcher is given a Hold anytime he enters the game in a Save Situation (see definition for Save Situation), records one out or more, and exits the game without giving up the lead. If the pitcher finishes the game, then he will only earn credit for a Save. He cannot receive credit for both a Hold and a Save.

Holds Adjusted Save Percentage (same as Save/Hold Percentage)

Holds plus Saves divided by Holds plus Saves Opportunities.

Inherited Runner

Any runner who was on base at the time a relief pitcher enters the game.

Isolated Power

Slugging Average minus Batting Average.

K/BB Ratio
Strikeouts divided by Walks.

Leadoff On-Base Percentage
The On-Base Percentage of a batter when he bats leadoff, or first, in the batting order.

Leverage Index
Leverage is the amount of swing in the possible change in win probability, compared to the average swing in all situations. The average swing value, by definition, is indexed to 1.00.

If the score of the game is 12-0 or 14-1 the possible changes in win probability will be very close to negligible. Whether the pitcher gives up a home run or gets a double play ball doesn't really change the outcome of the game. There won't be much swing in either direction for the probability of the win. But in the late innings of a close game, the change in win probability among the various events will have rather wild swings. With a runner on first, two outs, down by one, and in the bottom of the ninth, the game can hinge on one swing of the bat. A home run and an out will both end the game, but with different outcomes for the teams involved. The Leverage Index we use (LI) was developed at the website Tangotiger.net, and compiled at the website FanGraphs.com.

Long Outing
A Long Outing is one in which the starting pitcher throws more than 110 pitches. Prior to 2002, we used 120 pitches as the cutoff in the Manager's Record section.

Long Save
A Long Save is when the pitcher credited with a save pitches more than one inning.

Manufactured Runs
1. A run that scores without a hit, or a run on which the only hit(s) is/are infield hits, is always scored as a Manufactured Run.
2. A run which is driven in by a home run is never scored a Manufactured Run, under any circumstance.
3. A run which is driven in by a double or a triple is scored as a Manufactured Run only if *two* of the four bases result from advancing on one of these four acts: a sacrifice bunt, a stolen base, a hit and run, or a bunt single.
4. Otherwise, a run is considered to be a Manufactured Run if two of the four bases do not result from the runner being forced along by a walk, a hit batsman, or a safe hit reaching the outfield.
5. A forceout or fielder's choice which does not improve the position of the base runners should not be counted as contributing toward a Manufactured Run. Advancing on a forceout or a fielder's choice DOES count toward a manufactured run, if the play is one which improves the position of the baserunners.
6. A base "gained" on a double play does not count as a contribution to a Manufactured Run. A run scored on a double play is a Manufactured Run only if two of the OTHER bases are not attributable to forced advancement.

Net Gain
Net Gain is a statistic that measures baserunning production that includes all baserunning advancements on both hits and outs (BR Gain) and stolen bases (SB Gain).

Not Good Outcome (Intentional Walk)

A Not Good Outcome (NG) for an Intentional Walk occurs when one run scored in the inning after the intentional walk (and the next batter after the intentional walk did not ground into a double play).

Offensive Winning Percentage (OWP)

A player's Offensive Winning Percentage is the winning percentage of a hypothetical team which has an offense consisting of nine of that player, and pitching and defense which is average for the player's league. It is calculated by taking the square of RC/27 (see the definition for Runs Created per 27 Outs), dividing it by the sum of the square of RC/27 and the square of the average runs scored per game in the league.

On-Base Percentage

(Hits plus Walks plus Hit by Pitcher) divided by (At Bats plus Walks plus Hit by Pitcher plus Sacrifice Flies).

$$\frac{H + BB + HBP}{AB + BB + HBP + SF}$$

On-Base Plus Slugging (OPS)

On-Base Percentage plus Slugging Average

$$\frac{H + BB + HBP}{AB + BB + HBP + SF} + \frac{TB}{AB}$$

Opponent Batting Average

Hits Allowed divided by at-bats against a pitcher.

Opposition OPS

The OPS of the hitters facing the pitcher.

Out Advancing

A runner is out advancing when he is tagged out attempting to score from 2nd base on a single or from 1st base on a double, or attempting to go from 1st base to 3rd base on a single.

OutZ

Pitches outside the strike zone

Park Index

To calculate the park index for home runs in a given ballpark, we take the total home runs of both the home team and its opponents at the ballpark and compare it to the total home runs of the home team and its opponents in other games. We then divide each of those totals by the at-bats in the equivalent situations, so that if there are more at-bats in either situation, the index is not skewed. The result is then multiplied by 100 to yield the familiar form.

The park indices for doubles, triples, walks, strikeouts and home runs by lefties and righties are determined like home runs above—relative to at-bats. Indices of at-bats, runs, hits, errors and infield fielding errors (E-Infield) are calculated relative to games. The three batting average indices are calculated as is, since these are already relative to at-bats.

PART System (Positioning, Airballs, Range, and Throwing)

The PART System, introduced in *The Bill James Handbook 2020* and formalized in *The Fielding Bible–Volume V*, is a method for evaluating defensive play on batted balls, and is used in Defensive Runs Saved for infielders from 2013 forward.

The core of the system is similar to the Range and Positioning System, which is still used for DRS prior to 2013 and for outfielders from 2013 forward, in that it evaluates players through a system of credits and debits compared to the average fielder against similar batted balls.

The PART System evaluates players' positioning, range, and throwing based on how frequently they make plays compared to the average player as measured from different points in the play: before considering positioning, after considering positioning, and after the ball was fielded. Positioning Runs Saved, while measured in PART Runs Saved, is considered to be the team's responsibility, and is only included for the purposes of team totals. Individual infielder DRS consists of Air, Range and Throwing Runs Saved, along with the other components of DRS.

PCS (Pitchers' Caught Stealing)

The number of runners officially scored as Caught Stealing where the pitcher initiated the play. PCS plays are often referred to as pickoffs, but differ when the runner breaks towards the next base instead of returning to the base he was on. Pickoffs, which aren't an official statistic, involve the pitcher throwing to the base the runner was leading from, and the runner is out trying to return there.

Pitcher Pickoffs (PPO, PPkof)

The number of baserunners thrown out when a pitcher throws to a base with a leading baserunner, and the runner is tagged out attempting to return to the base. PPO is not an official statistic and does not count toward Caught Stealing totals.

Pivot %

Successful Double Plays turned by pivot man divided by the number of Double Play opportunities with that pivot man involved.

Plate Appearances

At Bats plus Total Walks plus Hit By Pitches plus Sacrifice Hits plus Sacrifice Flies plus Times Reached on Defensive Interference.

Platoon Advantage %

Platoon Advantage % is the percentage of players in the starting lineup who have the platoon advantage (i.e. bats right against a left-handed pitcher or bats left against a right-hander) against the starting pitcher; e.g. if the opposing starting pitcher is right handed and the batting team has six left-handed batters in its lineup, the platoon advantage for that game would be 67%.

Power/Speed Number

A single number that reflects a combination of power and speed. To calculate the Power/Speed Number, multiply Home Runs by Stolen Bases by two, and divide by the sum of Home Runs and Stolen Bases.

$$\frac{2 \times HR \times SB}{HR + SB}$$

Productive Out

An out made by the batter which advances at least one runner. See also Unproductive Out.

Quality Start

A game where the starting pitcher pitches for at least six innings and allows no more than three earned runs.

Quality Start Percentage

Quality Starts divided by Games Started (see the definition for Quality Start).

Quick Hooks

Used in the Manager's Record. For Quick Hooks and Slow Hooks a score is calculated for each game that is the sum of the number of Pitches plus 10 times the number of Runs Allowed. The bottom 25% of scores in the league are considered to be Quick Hooks.

Range and Positioning System

Formerly called the Plus/Minus System, the Range and Positioning System is a method for evaluating defensive play on batted balls, and is used in Defensive Runs Saved for non-catchers prior to 2013 and outfielders from 2013 forward.

It is made possible by a game scoring system in which each batted ball is rated for type (line drive, grounder, etc.), velocity within its type (based on hang time for flyballs and time to the infielder or through the infield on groundballs), and location on the field.

A player gets credit (a "plus" number) if he makes a play that at least one other player at his position missed during the season and he loses credit (a "minus" number") if he misses a play that at least one player made. The size of the credits are proportional to the percentage of times all players make the play.

All plays for each player at his position are summed to get his total Plays Saved for the season. A total of zero would be average and any other number would approximate how many plays more or less the player made than the average player at the position for the number of chances the player had to field batted balls.

Range Factor

The number of Successful Chances (Putouts plus Assists) times nine divided by the number of Defensive Innings Played.

RBI %

The percentage of all potential runs driven in by a certain hitter. Simply put, it's RBIs divided by RBI Opportunities. RBI Opportunities are defined as RBI plus a weighted total of baserunners who the hitter failed to drive in. Any plays where the batter reached safely and no outs were recorded aren't counted as missed opportunities. They are defined like so:

> 1.00 for each runner on third base with less than 2 outs, plus
> .70 for each runner on third base with 2 outs, plus
> .70 for each runner on second base, plus
> .40 for each runner on first base, plus
> .10 for each bases-empty plate appearance.

Regular Saves

Any save which does not meet the definition either of an Easy Save or a Tough Save is a "Regular" Save.

R/P
See Range and Positioning System

Run Support Per 9 IP
The total number of runs scored by a pitcher's team while he is in the game multiplied by nine and divided by total Innings Pitched.

Runs Created
"Runs Created" is an estimate of the number of a team's runs which are created by each individual hitter. There are many different formulas for estimating runs created. . .did you want the one that involves swinging a dead cat in the cemetery under a full moon? Yeah, I don't blame you. . .worm-eaten persimmons are so hard to find in the modern world.

This is the one we use now; it is complicated enough. First, there is an "A" Factor in the formula, a "B" Factor, and a "C" factor. The "A" Factor, which represents the number of times the hitter is on base, is Hits, Plus Walks, Plus Hit Batsmen, Minus Caught Stealing, Minus Grounded Into Double Play. The "B" Factor, which represents the hitter's ability to advance other runners, is 1.125 times the player's Singles, plus 1.69 times his Doubles, plus 3.02 times his Triples, plus 3.73 times his Home Runs, plus .29 times his Walks and Hit Batsmen, not counting intentional walks, plus .492 times Sacrifice Hits, Sacrifice Flies and Stolen Bases, minus .04 times Strikeouts. The "C" Factor, which represents opportunities, is At Bats, Plus Walks, Plus Hit By Pitch, Plus Sacrifice Hits, Plus Sacrifice Flies.

Having made these initial calculations of the A, B and C factors, we then change the "A" factor to "A plus 2.4 times C".

We change the "B" factor to "B plus 3 times C".

We change the "C" factor to "9 times C".

Multiply A times B, divide by the new C ("9 times C"), and subtract .90 times by the original C.

This is our first, temporary estimate of the player's runs created. What we have done here is to ask these questions:

1. How many runs would a team probably score that consisted of eight "ordinary" type of hitters, plus this particular hitter?
2. How many of those runs would be created by the eight ordinary type of hitters?
3. What is the difference and thus, how many runs did our player create?

To estimate this, we have placed our player in the context of eight hitters with a .300 on base percentage (2.4 divided by 8) and a .375 advancement percentage (3 divided by 8). For each trip through the batting order, the eight ordinary-type hitters would produce 9/10 of a run (2.4 times 3, divided by 8). The "9" in the denominator is eight ordinary hitters plus our man. The "-.9" being subtracted at the end is the runs created by the "ordinary" hitters. In essence, we have placed the hitter in a neutral solution, measured the neutral solution without our hitter, measured it with our hitter, and then estimated the contribution of this hitter as being the difference between the two.

We're not quite done. After that, we adjust the player's runs created estimate for his performance in two "run-sensitive" situations. Suppose that a player whose overall batting average is .250, has batted 100 times with runners in scoring position, and has gone 30-for-100. That's five hits better than expected, 30 hits where we would have expected 25. His team will score an extra five runs because he has done that, and so we increase the player's runs created estimate by five runs. If the player has hit poorly with runners in scoring position, we decrease it by the shortfall in the same way.

Suppose that a player has batted 250 times with runners on base, 250 times with the bases empty, and that he has hit 20 home runs overall. We would expect him to have hit 10 with men on base, 10 with the bases empty, right?

Suppose that he didn't. Suppose that he hit 12 with the bases empty, 8 with men on base. His team would score two runs less than expected because he did this, and we would thus penalize him two runs for the shortfall.

This is our second runs created estimate: the player's runs created, adjusted for his batting performance in run sensitive situations.

Suppose, however, that we figure the runs created for all of the individuals on a team, and we add them up, and it doesn't match the runs actually scored by the team? What if the formulas say that the team should have scored 800 runs, but they actually scored 820?

Then obviously, the formulas missed. We're trying to measure the runs ACTUALLY created by each hitter as best we can, in the real world, not the theoretical impact of some combination of singles, doubles, triples and walks. If the actual number is different than the estimates, we have to adjust the estimates to fit the facts. In this case—820 runs scored with only 800 runs created— we would multiply each runs created estimate by 820/800, or 1.025. Then we round it off to an integer, and that's the player's estimated runs created.

Let go of that cat, Arthur. Heck, the moon isn't full for three weeks, anyway.

Runs Created (Single Game)
The single-game Runs Created Formula, like all Runs Created formulas, has an A Factor, a B Factor, and a C Factor.

The A factor, which is basically "Times On Base", is
H + BB + HBP - (IBB/3) - GDP - CS

In other words, intentional walks count as times on base, but they only count as 2/3 of a time on base, because the intentional walk generally occurs late in the inning. Nobody intentionally walks the leadoff hitter.

The B Factor, which is basically "Potential advancement of other runners", is:
TB + (BB + HBP - IBB) * .3 + (SH + SF + 1.6 * SB) * .4 - SO * .07

And the C factor, which is basically "Context", is just plate appearances:
AB + BB + HBP + SH + SF

But these are not put together simply as A * B / C, as some runs created formulas are, but rather are placed in a neutral context before they are evaluated. The formula is:

(11.035 + A Factor) * (13 + B Factor) / (36 + C Factor) - 4 + (.0015 * (C Factor = 0))

So let us say that a player goes 1 for 4 with the one hit being a single, but also has a strikeout in the game. Then his A factor would be 1.00, his B factor would be .93, and his C Factor would be 4. So his Runs Created in the game would be

(12.035 * 13.93) / 40 - 4 + (0)

Which is .191. Basically, we expect his team to score 4 runs in every game, PLUS however many he creates. The +.0015 if the C factor is zero is just a little nuisance thing. .0015 is 1 over 667; for some reason the formula is just that much off of zero if a player has no plate appearance (and no stolen base or caught stealing), which you don't need to worry about unless he has no plate appearances, in which case it looks weird to say that he created .0015 runs.

Or, to take a complicated one, let us suppose that a player in a game goes two-for-four, both singles, but let us suppose that in that game he also has two walks, one of them intentional and the other not, and that in that game he also has a stolen base, a caught stealing, and grounds into a double play. (That would be Paul Molitor on June 8, 1985). Then in runs created for the game would be:
A Factor = 1.67 (2 + 2 - .333 - 1 - 1)
B Factor = 2.94 (2 + .3 + (.16 * .4))
C Factor = 6
Runs Created = (12.705 * 15.94) / 42 - 4
Which works out to .821.

Add up the Runs Created in each game and it should match a player's season-level Runs Created as nearly as possible.

Runs Created per 27 Outs (RC/27)
This statistic estimates the number of runs per game that a team made up of nine of the same player would score. To calculate RC/27, multiply Runs Created by league outs per team game, divide the result by outs made by the player (the sum of at bats plus sacrifice hits plus sacrifice flies plus caught stealing plus grounded into double plays, minus hits). The formula written out is:

$$\frac{\frac{RC \times 3 \times LgIP}{2 \times LgG}}{AB - H + SH + SF + CS + GDP}$$

Runs Saved
See Defensive Runs Saved.

Save Opportunities
The sum of Saves and Blown Saves (see Save Situation).

Save/Hold Percentage (same as Holds Adjusted Saves Percentage)
The sum of Saves and Holds, divided by the sum of Saves, Holds, and Blown Saves.

For several years we figured "Save Percentage", which is simply Saves divided by Save Opportunities, and this stat had some currency in the game. But the Save Percentage severely discriminates against middle relievers, who have no real chance to be credited with the Save, since they will be taken out of the game and replaced by the Closer even if they throw 110 miles an hour and strike out everybody they see. Middle relievers typically have Save Percentages of zero, even if they pitch well. The Save/Hold Percentage is a much more realistic evaluation of a pitcher's success in Save situations.

Save Percentage
A pitcher's Saves divided by the total number of Save Situations he faces (see definition for Save Situation).

Save Situation
A relief pitcher is in a Save Situation when he enters the game with his team in the lead, has the opportunity to finish the game, is not the winning pitcher of record at the time, and meets any one of the three following conditions:

1. The pitcher's team is leading by no more than three runs and the pitcher has the chance to pitch for at least one inning,

OR

2. The pitcher enters the game with the potential tying run on base, at bat, or on deck,

OR

3. The pitcher pitches three or more effective innings regardless of the lead. The determination of a save in this situation is made by the official scorer.

It is not possible to have more than one save credited to a single team in a game.

SB Gain (Baserunning)
Stolen Base attempts must be successful greater than about two thirds of the time to have a positive result on the number of runs scored. SB gain is therefore the number of bases stolen minus two times the number of caught stealing (SB Gain = SB - 2CS). For example, a runner steals 30 bases and is caught stealing 7 times. His SB Gain would be 30 - 2 * 7 = +16. Another runner steals 10 bases and is caught stealing 6 times. His SB Gain (actually a loss) would be 10 - 2 * 6 = -2.

SB Success Percentage
Stolen Bases divided by the number of Stolen Base attempts (Stolen Bases plus Caught Stealing).

$$\frac{SB}{SB + CS}$$

Secondary Average
A number meant to reflect everything else except for batting average. A player will have a high Secondary Average if he hits for power, takes walks and steals bases. It is calculated with the following formula:

$$\frac{TB - H + BB + SB}{AB}$$

Similarity Score
A number which reflects the similarity between two different statistical lines, either for a player or for a team. A score of 1,000 means that the statistical lines are identical.

Slow Hooks
Used in the Manager's Record. For Quick Hooks and Slow Hooks a score is calculated for each game that is the sum of the number of Pitches plus 10 times the number of Runs Allowed. The top 25% of scores in the league are considered to be Slow Hooks.

Slugging Average
Total Bases divided by At Bats.

Slugging Average on Balls in Play (SlgBIP)
Total bases gained on balls in play divided by balls in play. Home runs are not counted as balls in play.

Speed Score
Speed score is an estimate of a player's running speed, based on six indicators of running speed found in his batting and fielding records. Those six indicators are stolen base success rate, the frequency of stolen base attempts, triples, grounding into double plays, runs scored as a percentage of times on base, and defensive position and range.

The full process of estimating Speed Scores is long and complex, and can be found on Bill James Online or by contacting Sports Info Solutions.

Total Bases (TB)
Hits plus Doubles plus (2 times Triples) plus (3 times Home Runs).

$$H + 2B + (2 \times 3B) + (3 \times HR)$$

Tough Loss
A starting pitcher who loses the game with a game score (see definition for Game Score) over 50 gets credit for a tough loss.

Tough Save
This label is used to separate Saves by difficulty level (Easy or Tough). A Save is considered Tough if the relief pitcher enters the game with the tying run on base.

Total Chances (TC)
The number of plays in which a defensive player participated, determined as Assists + Putouts + Errors.

Unproductive Out
An out made by the batter with runners on base that fails to advance any baserunner or results in a weaker baserunner configuration than before. Excludes the third out of an inning. See also Productive Out.

Win Probability
The probability of a team winning the game determined at any time during the game based on the score, inning, outs and base situation.

Win Shares

Win Shares are a system devised by Bill James for valuing a player's overall contribution to his team over a season. This allows us to more effectively compare players across positions, even between pitchers and position players. The use of the word "shares" is important, because they are split up among players based on how many wins a team actually earns. For each win, a team has three Win Shares to allocate among its players. Those shares are then allocated according to how much each player contributed to the team's run scoring and prevention.

Winning Percentage

Wins divided by (Wins plus Losses).

Sports Info Solutions

Since the company's founding, analytics' place in sports has changed a lot, but Sports Info Solutions (SIS) has remained true to its objective. The company's mission is to provide the most accurate, in-depth, and timely professional baseball, football, basketball and gaming data, including cutting-edge research and analysis, striving to educate professional teams and the public about sports analytics. SIS is thrilled to work with the majority of Major League Baseball teams as a part of that goal. The company originally operated as Baseball Info Solutions, before expanding its industry footprint delivering NFL and NCAA FBS advanced data to broadcasters, NFL teams and directly to the public, as well as advanced NBA event data and draft prospect data to NBA teams. The data is also instrumental in the sports betting and fantasy arenas, providing unique insights and a competitive edge to subscribers.

It all begins with the data collection operation. Specifically, SIS's staff of baseball operations analysts does excellent work in organizing the ever-expanding crew of highly trained video scouts, and together they record data from every Major League Baseball, Nippon Professional Baseball, and Korean Baseball Organization game, as well as many minor league games. That data covers everything from basic box score data to pitch locations, types, and velocities to batted ball hang times, defensive shifts, and much more. SIS collects many data points that cannot be found any place else. SIS video scouts log 10-12 hours on every game capturing the most in-depth information possible.

The data itself is valuable to many clients, but SIS's research and development department creates analytics and undertakes research projects with the data to help it reach its full potential utility. Their most well-known endeavor is the Defensive Runs Saved statistic, which estimates how many runs fielders save their teams because of a variety of skills such as range, throwing, prevention of stolen bases, pitch framing, and many other factors.

John Dewan co-founded SIS in 2002, having already spent a couple of decades in the industry at the forefront of the sabermetric movement. He got his start in the field as the Executive Director of Project Scoresheet, which was a Bill James–led effort to comprehensively collect baseball data. This led to the incorporation and development of STATS Inc. from a bedroom office to its sale to News Corp in 2000. Without those efforts, many of the statistics and analytics that we all take for granted may not even be available at all.

If you would like to contact Sports Info Solutions for data inquiries, potential job openings, or additional information, you can reach us at:

Sports Info Solutions
41 S. 2nd Street
Coplay, PA 18037
610-261-2370
www.sportsinfosolutions.com
www.sportsinfosolutionsblog.com

Acknowledgments

Although this is the 33rd edition of *The Bill James Handbook*, it is the 1st edition officially under the Sports Info Solutions (SIS) name after 18 consecutive seasons of Baseball Info Solutions' perfect deliveries. Same great company, amazing new ventures to keep the growing audience satiated. And that means that the number of people who contribute to this publication continue to grow as well, and an extra special thank you goes out to each one of them.

As always, at the top of the list of people to thank is Bill James, without whom none of what we all get to do for a living would be possible. He has inspired all of us, and we are grateful for the opportunity to work with him and to continue to be enriched by his insight.

John and Sue Dewan have worked very closely with Bill for many years now and started the company in 2002 along with Steve Moyer, who has since passed but whose contributions live on. As Chairman of the Board, John provides his extensive expertise in business, sports, and analytics, and is final approver of everything that goes into the *Handbook*. Sue leads our Human Resources department and is on the SIS Board of Directors.

As great as it is to celebrate the longevity and consistency of the *Handbook*, it is also great to celebrate the new developments. Dan Hannigan Daley is the new CEO of the company and leads the charge blazing our new strategic vision.

The President of Sports Info Solutions, Rob Dougherty, carefully orchestrates the day-to-day activities and operations of the company as it continues to grow. In terms of the book process, Rob oversees things from an executive level and works with our publisher to handle the business of the book.

Joe Rosales continues to do a truly extraordinary job as the point person for the production of *The Bill James Handbook*. If there were a statistic for book production that could take into account context akin to the way that DRS adjusts for play difficulty, it would show that Joe had an October that would make Reggie Jackson blush. Mark Simon is an annual All-Star in our production line-up with his engaging and prolific writing skills, and plays a prominent role in the company's social and public outreach.

Along with Joe and Mark, there are a few individuals who went above-and-beyond to make this book possible. Jon Vrecsics leads the quality control process on every statistic in the book, a massive undertaking. On the technical side, Will Creager has the unenviable task of coordinating the technical aspects of the book's production. It would be more efficient to list the aspects of the book that Brian Reiff isn't involved in than to list his contributions. Sarah Thompson and Allen Ho were constantly fulfilling R&D requests to keep the book on course.

Our Operations department is responsible for gathering the data that is at the very core of what we do. They deserve great thanks for both their incredible attention to detail and their ability to continually readjust to all the challenges placed in front of us. Vrecsics is our Director of Operations, leading a team that includes Dan Casey, Todd Radcliffe, Nathan Phares, Michael Churchward, Josh Hofer, John Verros, Ted Baarda, Justin Stine, Evan Butler, Nick Rabasco, Ken Gaffney, Ben Hrkach, Stephen Marciello, Christian Beyer, David Salway, and Jason Paff.

Operations Assistants are full-time employees who contribute to multiple operations within the company. They include Jordan Edwards, Theo Fornaciari, Jacob Halleen, Trey Lake, Joey Mahon, Alec Mallon, Glen Mueller, Jeremy Percy, Chad Tedder, and Dan Wallie.

Matt Manocherian has been instrumental in the success of the expansion as Vice President of Football and Research. Dan Foehrenbach quarterbacks the football operations group. They are joined by Nate Cooper, John Todd, Segev Golderg, and Jeff Dean.

Vice President of Basketball and New Initiatives Jake Loos applies his ground-breaking vision in NBA Draft and game analytics for our basketball department. Their team is led by Stephen Pelkofer on the research side and Spencer Pearlman on the operations side.

Lead Research Analyst Joe Rosales leads all baseball-related research initiatives, while Manocherian oversees the Research and Development Department. Their team includes the key staff responsible for the bulk of the content and analytics that you find in the book. Lindsay Zeck, Alex Vigderman, Mark Simon, John Shirley, Bryce Rossler, Sarah Thompson and Allen Ho round out the current R&D team, and we'd also like to thank Sam Linker and Cam Harrigan for their contributions over the past year. Check out SportsInfoSolutionsBlog.com for more baseball, football, and basketball research all year long!

Highly-touted newcomer, VP Product and Engineering Will Hester, has a dedicated team of engineers that include Joe Baranoski, Carmen Fortino, Tim Paul, Zach Smith, Ruben Agosto, and Ronan Potts. They work tirelessly to develop new applications for internal and external use. On the product side are Cassie Sosnovich, Barbara Jewell, and Noah Gatsik.

The Information and Security Operations Department is the silent engine that enables all of this data collection and research to make it to our team clients and the public. Director of ISO Patrick Coyle leads an incredibly talented team featuring Will Creager, Brian Reiff, Brandyn Bechtel, Ryne Rogers, Daniel Stonehouse and Stephen Polacheck. They service the myriad needs of our clients in all sports.

Another new addition to the company family is Michael Montpetit. As Director of Sales and Business Development, Michael spearheads our sales processes and interactions. Corey March, now leading Customer Success, continues to excel at making our customers happy with the assistance of Kyle Rodemann. Tanya Bentz leads our marketing initiatives.

Jason Trifilo, our Director of Accounting, makes sure that the finances are in order and that those last-minute *Handbook* invoices for photos or graphics get handled quickly for our vendors. Lauren Backsa is also there to provide the assist. On the Human Resources side, in addition to Sue Dewan, we have Richard Lively assisting us in various areas and Carol Olsen, our office manager, who ensures that everyone has what they need to get onboarded at the company and coordinates the various social events that help us to share great memories amongst our coworkers.

We are especially grateful to our outstanding team of scouts. Their dedication and attention to detail provide the foundation of our business. Our Video Scout Associates have spent multiple seasons with us, and they include: Brendon Baker, Christian Chavez, Patrick Deken, Brett Downey, Corey Eiferman, Louis Goedeker, Noah Hole, Luke Iorio, Jeff Israel, Ben Jaffy, Johnny Kraft, Adam Lan, Cullen Mersch, Spencer Moyer, Kyle Price, Dominick Ricotta, Brandon Tew, and Daniel Worth.

Our Video Scouts are made up of: Stephen Adams, Gregory Allen, Trusten Annin, Alberto Aranda, Alexander Arcidiacono, Shay Bahner, Brett Barnes, Spencer Bayes, Maddisen Bieber, Ryan Blake, Quinton Bonnell, Mark Bricker, RJ Burson, Matthew Carr, Jason Carroll, Christian Chase, Nicholas Chiappetta, Patrick

Commers, Joseph Curtis, Brian Duffley, Cody Elliott, Matthew Evans, Charlie Fletcher, Fernando Gil, Lucas Grennan, Douglas Heron Jr., Hung-Pin Hsu, Wally Huron, Connor Johnson, Gabriel Kaufman, John Keuler, Matthew Lehman, Austin Leonard, Matt Martin, Nihar Maskara, Shayla Medows, David Michaylira, Ryan Moralejo, John Michael Morris, Brad Moylan, Ryan Murray, Joaquin Murrieta, Sam Nalli, Gregory Nevins, Jake Pennel, Lang Perdue, Lucas Reimink, Dagin Renck, Charles Robinson, Christopher Russo, Anthony Sagrestano, William Schiff, Benjamin Shufelto, Avery Slack, Stephen Souden, Bennett Spector, Delionte West II, and Teddy Zaphiris.

We also thank our Video Editors: Garrett Bentley, Amar Chowdhury, Justin Goldberg, Matthew Grone, Wesley King, Benjamin Remelius, Dylan Rudolph, Christopher Turrisi, Brian Uhler, and Douglas Ziefel.

Our partners at ACTA Publications include publisher Greg Pierce, cover designer Tom Wright, Fielding Bible logo designer Patricia Lynch, and customer service and fulfillment team Mary Rickey, Kathy Pierce, and Isz.

Thank you to our friends in the baseball industry who have helped us over the years. They include: Andy Andres, David Appelman, Emma Baccellieri, Scott Bush, Jim Callis, Dave Cameron, Benjie Cherniak, Chris Dial, Rylan Edwards, Tony Farwell, Bob Forman, Sean Forman, Fred Fosnacht, Peter Gammons, Vince Genarro, Jason Grey, Ben Jedlovec, Christina Kahrl, Brian Kenny, Zach Kram, Peter Kreutzer, Michael Lehrer, Ben Lindbergh, Rob Mains, Moses Massena, Rob MacKay, Gene McCaffrey, Tim McSweeney, Jared Melillo, Bob Meyerhoff, Mike Murphy, Rob Neyer, Alex Patton, Eduardo Pérez, Mike Phillips, David Pinto, Joe Posnanski, Pat Quinn, Adam Richman, Hal Richman, Meg Rowley, Travis Sawchik, Brett Sayre, Peter Schoenke, Ron Shandler, Joe Sheehan, John Sickels, Chris Singleton, Dave Studenmund, Tom Tango, Rick Wilton, Don Zminda and Pete Zundel. We would also like to thank Steve Ruskowski for his assistance in stat-checking.

There are too many people to thank for making this book possible to fit them all in this section, but you know who you are, and we extend our sincerest gratitude for your help.

Most importantly, thank you to all of our readers. You inspire us and empower us to continue to dive deeper, and we're thrilled that you keep coming back to learn more about the game that we all love. Thank you for your continued support, and we're already excited to share what we learn with you next year.